this
BIBLE
belongs to

THEREFORE
Go and Make
disciples of ALL
NATIONS, baptizing them
in the NAME of the FATHER
and the SON and the HOLY SPIRIT,
teaching them to obey
everything I have commanded
you. AND REMEMBER
I AM with you ALWAYS
to the end
of the age

Letter from the Editors

A simple declaration became a daily word of encouragement. That encouragement turned into the battle cry of thousands of women across the globe: Love God Greatly.

This is our heart. We desire to be people who love God with our whole selves and our whole lives, every day. We've found the best way to love Him greatly is to study His Word and know His character.

There are a lot of Bibles available today, especially for those of us who speak English. We have many options when it comes to translation, style, color, content, and size. Many Christians around the world do not have these same options. They aren't able to read God's Word in their own language, let alone access a Bible study that helps them understand God's Word and apply it to their lives.

At Love God Greatly, we create Bible study materials for women and kids. Then, we translate those Bible studies into over twenty different languages and give them to women and children all over the world. Can you imagine being handed a Bible study in your own language for the first time?

Our heart is to love God with our lives, to know and study His Word, and to break down barriers that keep women from knowing and loving God. Whether it be language barriers or financial barriers, we do our best to eliminate obstacles keeping women from deepening their relationships with God.

We created this Bible with this goal in mind. We hope you'll join us, not only in studying God's Word and seeking to love Him greatly, but also in helping women all over the world gain access to quality Bible study materials. We hope this Bible encourages you in your personal walk with God, helps you increase your faith, and challenges you daily to love God greatly. We also hope you'll join us in our mission of making disciples of all nations, as we seek to bring the truth of the gospel to every tribe and tongue.

Angela Perritt

Melissa Fuller

Table of Contents

The Old Testament

The New Testament

God loves you.

God's Word says, "For this is the way God loved the world: He gave his one and only Son, so that everyone who believes in him will not perish but have eternal life" (John 3:16).

Our sin separates us from God.

We are all sinners by nature and by choice, and because of this we are separated from God, who is holy. God's Word says, "for all have sinned and fall short of the glory of God" (Rom 3:23).

Jesus died so you might have life.

The consequence of sin is death, but God's free gift of salvation is available to us. Jesus took the penalty for our sin when He died on the cross.

God's Word says, "For the payoff of sin is death, but the gift of God is eternal life in Christ Jesus our Lord" (Rom 6:23); "But God demonstrates his own love for us, in that while we were still sinners, Christ died for us" (Rom 5:8).

Jesus lives!

Death could not hold Him, and three days after His body was placed in the tomb Jesus rose again, defeating sin and death forever. He lives today in heaven and is preparing a place in eternity for all who believe in Him.

Jesus says, "There are many dwelling places in my Father's house. Otherwise, I would have told you, because I am going away to make ready a place for you. And if I go and make ready a place for you, I will come again and take you to be with me, so that where I am you may be too" (John 14:2–3).

You can know that you are forgiven.

Accepting Jesus as your Savior is not about what you can do, but rather about having faith in what Jesus has already done. It takes recognizing you are a sinner, believing Jesus died for your sins, and asking for forgiveness by placing your full trust in Jesus' work on the cross.

God's Word says, "if you confess with your mouth that Jesus is Lord and believe in your heart that God raised him from the dead, you will be saved. For with the heart one believes and thus has righteousness and with the mouth one confesses and thus has salvation" (Rom 10:9–10).

Soap Bible Study Method

At Love God Greatly, we are convinced that the Word of God is living and active. We believe the words of Scripture are powerful and effective and relevant for life in all times and all cultures. We also know the Bible was written to specific audiences in specific cultures at specific times. We believe in order to interpret the Bible correctly, we need an understanding of the context and culture of the original writings.

As we study the Bible, we use the SOAP Bible Study Method. The acronym stands for Scripture, Observation, Application, and Prayer. It's one thing to simply read Scripture. When you interact with it, intentionally slowing down to reflect, truths start jumping off the page. The SOAP Method allows us to dig deeper into Scripture and see more than we would if we simply read the verses. We're better equipped to live out the message God's Word carries and not merely listen to it (Jas 1:22).

In all of our reading plans, we read a passage of Scripture and then apply the SOAP Method to a few verses from that passage or a related passage. We believe using this method allows us to glean a greater understanding of Scripture, which allows us to apply it effectively to our lives.

The SOAP Method includes four steps:

1. Scripture. Write out the verses at least one time. Slow down and copy the passage from the text, focusing on what you are writing. Writing it more than one time is always helpful.

2. Observation. Take time to carefully observe the passage. What do you see in the verses you're reading? Who is the intended audience? To whom is the writer speaking? What cultural factors are at play? Are any words or themes repeated? What literary devices are being used?

3. Application. After carefully observing what is happening in the passage, determine the main message or truth of the passage. How can you apply this truth to your life?

4. Prayer. Pray God's Word back to Him. If He has revealed something to you during this time, pray about it. Confess any sin God has revealed. Pray through the truth of the passage.

The most important ingredients in the SOAP Method are your interaction with God's Word and your application of it to your life. God's Word is powerful and effective. You will never waste time in God's Word. Take time to study it carefully, discovering the truth of God's character and His heart for the world.

Features

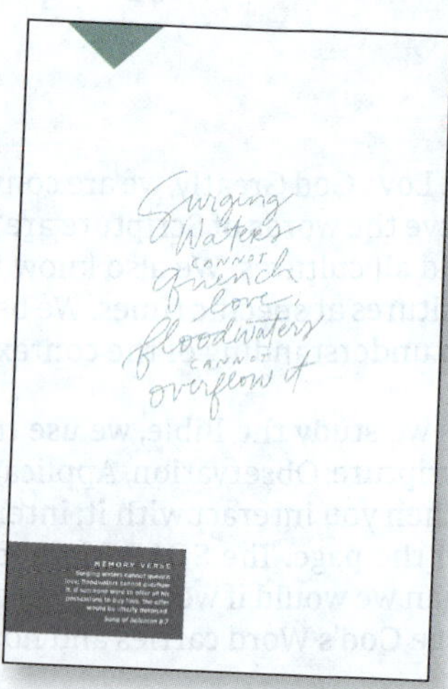

Memory Verses. A memory verse has been chosen for each book of the Bible. These verses are beautifully designed to aid in memorization. Together, these verses show God's heart for His people throughout the story of Scripture.

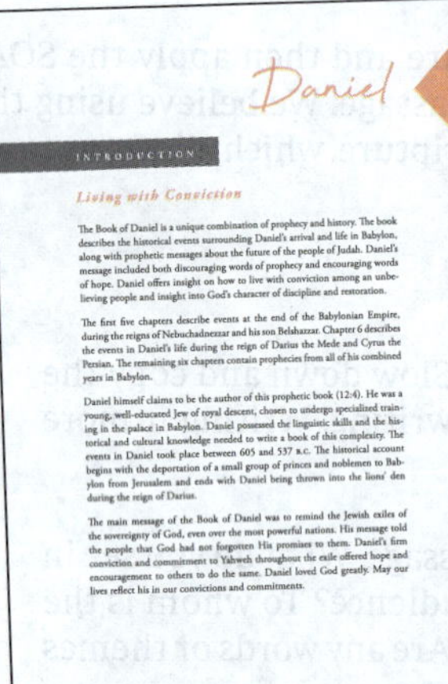

Daniel

INTRODUCTION

Living with Conviction

The Book of Daniel is a unique combination of prophecy and history. The book describes the historical events surrounding Daniel's arrival and life in Babylon, along with prophetic messages about the future of the people of Judah. Daniel's message included both discouraging words of prophecy and encouraging words of hope. Daniel offers insight on how to live with conviction among an unbelieving people and insight into God's character of discipline and restoration.

The first five chapters describe events at the end of the Babylonian Empire, during the reigns of Nebuchadnezzar and his son Belshazzar. Chapter 6 describes the events in Daniel's life during the reign of Darius the Mede and Cyrus the Persian. The remaining six chapters contain prophecies from all of his combined years in Babylon.

Daniel himself claims to be the author of this prophetic book (12:4). He was a young, well-educated Jew of royal descent, chosen to undergo specialized training in the palace in Babylon. Daniel possessed the linguistic skills and the historical and cultural knowledge needed to write a book of this complexity. The events in Daniel took place between 605 and 537 B.C. The historical account begins with the deportation of a small group of princes and noblemen to Babylon from Jerusalem and ends with Daniel being thrown into the lions' den during the reign of Darius.

The main message of the Book of Daniel was to remind the Jewish exiles of the sovereignty of God, even over the most powerful nations. His message told the people that God had not forgotten His promises to them. Daniel's firm conviction and commitment to Yahweh throughout the exile offered hope and encouragement to others to do the same. Daniel loved God greatly. May our lives reflect his in our convictions and commitments.

Book Introductions. For each book of the Bible you will find a brief introduction including cultural context, historical information, a brief explanation of themes, author and date information, and how each particular book encourages us to love God greatly.

Country Profiles. Accompanying each woman's testimony are brief facts about her home country, ways to pray, and brief historical information about the spread of the gospel, church history, and Bible translation.

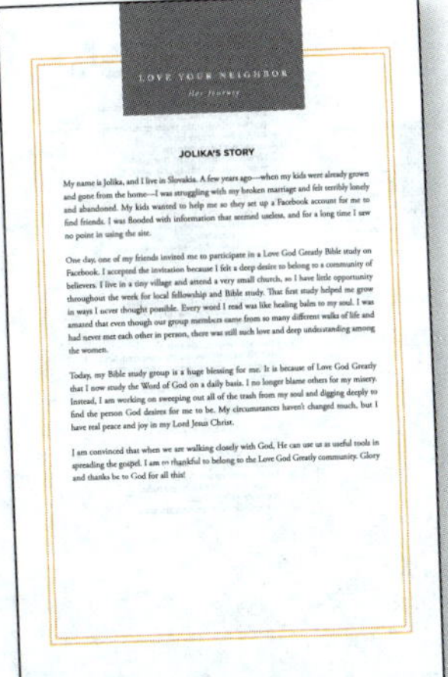

LOVE YOUR NEIGHBOR

Her Journey

JOLIKA'S STORY

My name is Jolika, and I live in Slovakia. A few years ago—when my kids were already grown and gone from the home—I was struggling with my broken marriage and felt terribly lonely and abandoned. My kids wanted to help me so they set up a Facebook account for me to find friends. I was flooded with information that seemed useless, and for a long time I saw no point in using the site.

One day, one of my friends invited me to participate in a Love God Greatly Bible study on Facebook. I accepted the invitation because I felt a deep desire to belong to a community of believers. I live in a tiny village and attend a very small church, so I have little opportunity throughout the week for local fellowship and Bible study. That first study helped me grow in ways I never thought possible. Every word I read was like healing balm to my soul. I was amazed that even though our group members came from so many different walks of life and had never met each other in person, there was still such love and deep understanding among the women.

Today, my Bible study group is a huge blessing for me. It is because of Love God Greatly that I now study the Word of God on a daily basis. I no longer blame others for my misery. Instead, I am working on sweeping out all of the trash from my soul and digging deeply to find the person God desires for me to be. My circumstances haven't changed much, but I have real peace and joy in my Lord Jesus Christ.

I am convinced that when we are walking closely with God, He can use us as useful tools in spreading the gospel. I am so thankful to belong to the Love God Greatly community. Glory and thanks be to God for all this!

Testimonies. Women from forty-five countries have shared personal testimonies and insights about their personal faith and Christianity in their home countries. You can find their unique and powerful stories in each book introduction.

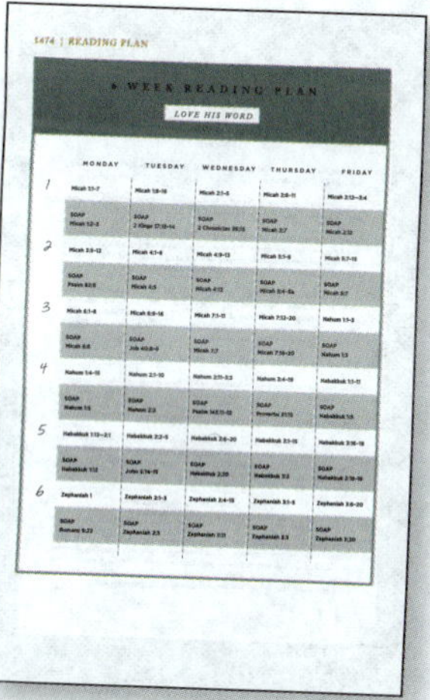

1474 | READING PLAN

6 WEEK READING PLAN

LOVE HIS WORD

	MONDAY	TUESDAY	WEDNESDAY	THURSDAY	FRIDAY
1	Micah 1:1-7	Micah 1:8-16	Micah 2:1-5	Micah 2:6-11	Micah 2:12–3:4
	SOAP Micah 1:2-3	SOAP 2 Kings 17:13-14	SOAP 2 Chronicles 36:15	SOAP Micah 2:7	SOAP Micah 2:12
2	Micah 3:5-12	Micah 4:1-8	Micah 4:9-13	Micah 5:1-6	Micah 5:7-15
	SOAP Psalm 82:8	SOAP Micah 4:5	SOAP Micah 4:12	SOAP Micah 5:4-5a	SOAP Micah 5:7
3	Micah 6:1-8	Micah 6:9-16	Micah 7:1-11	Micah 7:12-20	Nahum 1:1-3
	SOAP Micah 6:8	SOAP Job 40:8-9	SOAP Micah 7:7	SOAP Micah 7:18-20	SOAP Nahum 1:3
4	Nahum 1:4-15	Nahum 2:1-10	Nahum 2:11–3:3	Nahum 3:4-19	Habakkuk 1:1-11
	SOAP Nahum 1:5	SOAP Nahum 2:2	SOAP Psalm 145:11-12	SOAP Proverbs 21:15	SOAP Habakkuk 1:5
5	Habakkuk 1:12–2:1	Habakkuk 2:2-5	Habakkuk 2:6-20	Habakkuk 3:1-15	Habakkuk 3:16-19
	SOAP Habakkuk 1:12	SOAP John 3:14-15	SOAP Habakkuk 2:20	SOAP Habakkuk 3:2	SOAP Habakkuk 3:18-19
6	Zephaniah 1	Zephaniah 2:1-3	Zephaniah 2:4-15	Zephaniah 3:1-8	Zephaniah 3:8-20
	SOAP Romans 5:22	SOAP Zephaniah 2:3	SOAP Zephaniah 3:11	SOAP Zephaniah 3:3	SOAP Zephaniah 3:20

Reading Plans. Fifty reading plans have been carefully crafted for reading through Scripture. Each plan includes daily reading and SOAP passages for greater understanding.

EZRA 10:14 | 705

from one end to the other with their filthiness. 12 Therefore do not
give your daughters in marriage to their sons, and do not take their
daughters in marriage for your sons. Do not ever seek their peace
or welfare, so that you may be strong and may eat the good of the
land and may leave it as an inheritance for your children forever.'
13 "Everything that has happened to us has come about because of
our wicked actions and our great guilt. Even so, our God, you have
exercised restraint toward our iniquities and have given us a remnant such as this. 14 Shall we once again break your commandments
and intermarry with these abominable peoples? Would you not
be so angered by us that you would wipe us out, with no survivor
or remnant? 15 O LORD God of Israel, you are righteous, for we are
left as a remnant this day. Indeed, we stand before you in our guilt.
However, because of this guilt no one can really stand before you."

THE PEOPLE CONFESS THEIR SINS

10 While Ezra was praying and confessing, weeping and throwing himself to the ground before the temple of God, a very
large crowd of Israelites—men, women, and children alike—gathered around him. The people wept loudly. 2 Then Shecaniah son
of Jehiel, from the descendants of Elam, addressed Ezra:
"We have been unfaithful to our God by marrying foreign wom-
en from the local peoples. Nonetheless, there is still hope for Israel in this regard. 3 Therefore let us enact a covenant with our
God to send away all these women and their offspring, in keeping with your counsel, my lord, and that of those who respect
the commandments of our God. And let it be done according to
the law. 4 Get up, for this matter concerns you. We are with you,
so be strong and act decisively!"
5 So Ezra got up and made the leading priests and Levites and
all Israel take an oath to carry out this plan. And they all took a
solemn oath. 6 Then Ezra got up from in front of the temple of
God and went to the room of Jehohanan son of Eliashib. While
he stayed there, he did not eat food or drink water, for he was
in mourning over the infidelity of the exiles.
7 A proclamation was circulated throughout Judah and Jerusalem that all the exiles were to be assembled in Jerusalem. 8 Everyone who did not come within three days would thereby forfeit
all his property, in keeping with the counsel of the officials and
the elders. Furthermore, he himself would be excluded from the
assembly of the exiles.
9 All the men of Judah and Benjamin were gathered in Jerusalem
within the three days. (It was in the ninth month, on the twentieth
day of that month.) All the people sat in the square at the temple
of God, trembling because of this matter and because of the rains.
10 Then Ezra the priest stood up and said to them, "You have
behaved in an unfaithful manner by taking foreign wives! This
has contributed to the guilt of Israel. 11 Now give praise to the
LORD God of your fathers, and do his will. Separate yourselves
from the local residents and from these foreign wives."
12 All the assembly replied in a loud voice: "We will do just as
you have said! 13 However, the people are numerous and it is
the rainy season. We are unable to stand here outside. Furthermore, this business cannot be resolved in a day or two, for we

REFLECT

Is there something God has asked you to break away from or eliminate from your life that is causing you to stray from Him? What might be keeping you from letting go of these things?

Reflection Questions. You will find questions throughout the margins of each book of the Bible to aid your reflection and understanding of God's Word.

Challenges. Throughout each book of the Bible you will find challenges to encourage further study and references to additional passages of Scripture.

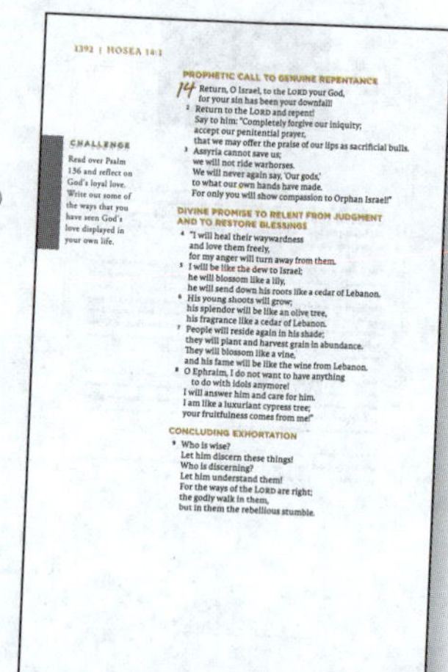

1392 | HOSEA 14:1

PROPHETIC CALL TO GENUINE REPENTANCE

14 Return, O Israel, to the LORD your God,
for your sin has been your downfall!
2 Return to the LORD and repent!
Say to him: "Completely forgive our iniquity;
accept our penitential prayer,
that we may offer the praise of our lips as sacrificial bulls.
3 Assyria cannot save us;
we will not ride warhorses.
We will never again say, 'Our gods,'
to what our own hands have made.
For only you will show compassion to Orphan Israel!"

CHALLENGE

Read over Psalm 136 and reflect on God's loyal love. Write out some of the ways that you have seen God's love displayed in your own life.

DIVINE PROMISE TO RELENT FROM JUDGMENT AND TO RESTORE BLESSINGS

4 "I will heal their waywardness
and love them freely,
for my anger will turn away from them.
5 I will be like the dew to Israel;
he will blossom like a lily,
he will send down his roots like a cedar of Lebanon.
6 His young shoots will grow;
his splendor will be like an olive tree,
his fragrance like a cedar of Lebanon.
7 People will reside again in his shade;
they will plant and harvest grain in abundance.
They will blossom like a vine,
and his fame will be like the wine from Lebanon.
8 O Ephraim, I do not want to have anything
to do with idols anymore!
I will answer him and care for him.
I am like a luxuriant cypress tree;
your fruitfulness comes from me!"

CONCLUDING EXHORTATION

9 Who is wise?
Let him discern these things!
Who is discerning?
Let him understand them!
For the ways of the LORD are right;
the godly walk in them,
but in them the rebellious stumble.

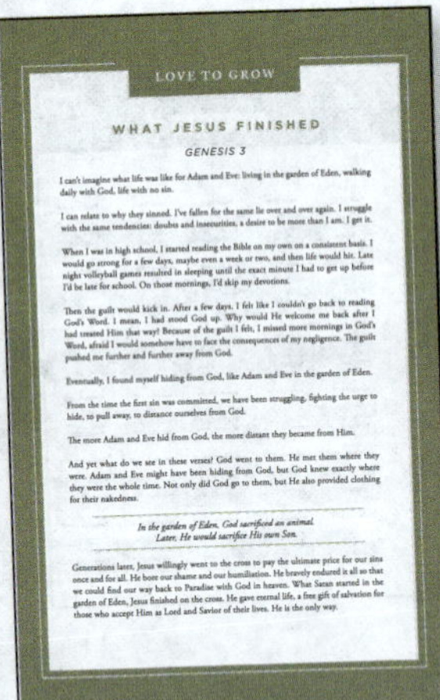

LOVE TO GROW

WHAT JESUS FINISHED

GENESIS 3

I can't imagine what life was like for Adam and Eve: living in the garden of Eden, walking daily with God, life with no sin.

I can relate to why they sinned. I've fallen for the same lie over and over again. I struggle with the same tendencies: doubts and insecurities, a desire to be more than I am. I get it.

When I was in high school, I started reading the Bible on my own on a consistent basis. I would go strong for a few days, maybe even a week or two, and then life would hit. Late night volleyball games resulted in sleeping until the exact minute I had to get up before I'd be late for school. On those mornings, I'd skip my devotions.

Then the guilt would kick in. After a few days, I felt like I couldn't go back to reading God's Word. I mean, I had stood God up. Why would He welcome me back after I had treated Him that way? Because of the guilt I felt, I missed more mornings in God's Word, afraid I would somehow have to face the consequences of my negligence. The guilt pushed me further and further away from God.

Eventually, I found myself hiding from God, like Adam and Eve in the garden of Eden.

From the time the first sin was committed, we have been struggling, fighting the urge to hide, to pull away, to distance ourselves from God.

The more Adam and Eve hid from God, the more distant they became from Him.

And yet what do we see in these verses? God went to them. He met them where they were. Adam and Eve might have been hiding from God, but God knew exactly where they were the whole time. Not only did God go to them, but He also provided clothing for their nakedness.

In the garden of Eden, God sacrificed an animal.
Later, He would sacrifice His own Son.

Generations later, Jesus willingly went to the cross to pay the ultimate price for our sins once and for all. He bore our shame and our humiliation. He bravely endured it all so that we could find our way back to Paradise with God in heaven. What Satan started in the garden of Eden, Jesus finished on the cross. He gave eternal life, a free gift of salvation for those who accept Him as Lord and Savior of their lives. He is the only way.

Devotionals. Throughout the Bible, 163 devotionals offer deeper insight into God's Word. Read encouragement and instruction from our Love God Greatly team as you study Scripture along with us.

Maps. Eight full-color maps paint a visual picture of the geography of the world of the patriarchs, the kingdom of Israel, Jerusalem in the time of Jesus, and the missionary journeys of the apostles.

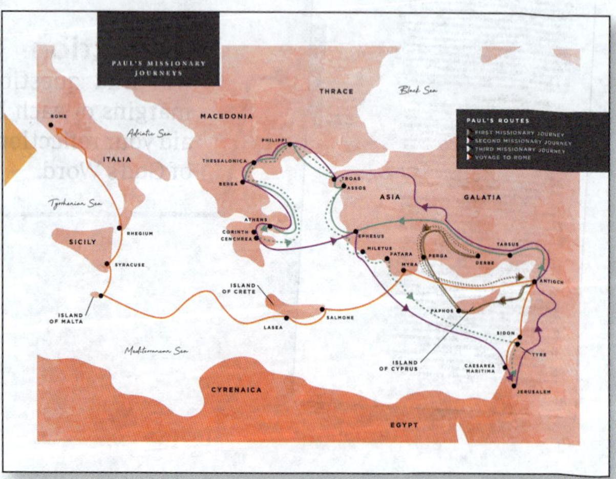

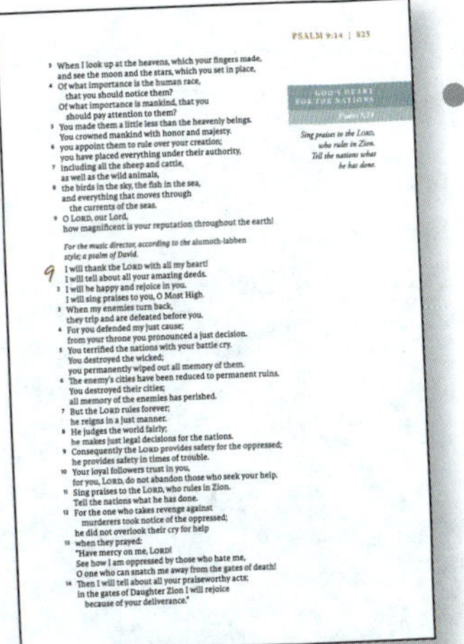

PSALM 9:14 | 825

3 When I look up at the heavens, which your fingers made,
and see the moon and the stars, which you set in place,
4 Of what importance is the human race,
that you should notice them?
Of what importance is mankind, that you
should pay attention to them?
5 You made them a little less than the heavenly beings.
You crowned mankind with honor and majesty.
6 you appoint them to rule over your creation;
you have placed everything under their authority,
7 including all the sheep and cattle,
as well as the wild animals,
8 the birds in the sky, the fish in the sea,
and everything that moves through
the currents of the seas.
9 O LORD, our Lord,
how magnificent is your reputation throughout the earth!

For the music director, according to the alumoth-labben *style; a psalm of David.*

9 I will thank the LORD with all my heart!
I will tell about all your amazing deeds.
2 I will be happy and rejoice in you.
I will sing praises to you, O Most High.
3 When my enemies turn back,
they trip and are defeated before you.
4 For you defended my just cause;
from your throne you pronounced a just decision.
5 You terrified the nations with your battle cry.
You destroyed the wicked;
you permanently wiped out all memory of them.
6 The enemy's cities have been reduced to permanent ruins.
You destroyed their cities;
all memory of the enemies has perished.
7 But the LORD rules forever;
he reigns in a just manner.
8 He judges the world fairly;
he makes just legal decisions for the nations.
9 Consequently the LORD provides safety for the oppressed;
he provides safety in times of trouble.
10 Your loyal followers trust in you,
for you, LORD, do not abandon those who seek your help.
11 Sing praises to the LORD, who rules in Zion.
Tell the nations what he has done.
12 For the one who takes revenge against
murderers took notice of the oppressed;
he did not overlook their cry for help
13 when they prayed:
"Have mercy on me, LORD!
See how I am oppressed by those who hate me,
O one who can snatch me away from the gates of death!
14 Then I will tell about all your praiseworthy acts;
in the gates of Daughter Zion I will rejoice
because of your deliverance."

GOD'S HEART FOR THE NATIONS

Sing praises to the LORD,
who rules in Zion.
Tell the nations what
he has done.

For the Nations Verses. You will find thirty-two verses throughout the margins that display God's heart for the nations.

Genre Divisions. The colors included in the introductory pages and devotionals in each book of the Bible indicate the genre of the book. For more information on the different genres of Scripture, see page 2089.

To the Reader

An Introduction to the New English Translation

"You have been born anew . . . through the living
and enduring word of God."

1 PETER 1:23

The New English Translation (NET) is the newest complete translation of the original biblical languages into English. In 1995 a multi-denominational team of more than twenty-five of the world's foremost biblical scholars gathered around the shared vision of creating an English Bible translation that could overcome old challenges and boldly open the door for new possibilities. The translators completed the first edition in 2001 and incorporated revisions based on scholarly and user feedback in 2003 and 2005. In 2019 a major update reached its final stages. The NET's unique translation process has yielded a beautiful, faithful English Bible for the worldwide church today.

What sets the NET Bible apart from other translations? We encourage you to read the full story of the NET's development and additional details about its translation philosophy at netbible.com/net-bible-preface. But we would like to draw your attention to a few features that commend the NET to all readers of the Word.

Transparent and Accountable

Have you ever wished you could look over a Bible translator's shoulder as he or she worked?

Bible translation usually happens behind closed doors—few outside the translation committee see the complex decisions underlying the words that appear in their English Bibles. Fewer still have the opportunity to review and speak into the translators' decisions.

Throughout the NET's translation process, every working draft was made publicly available on the Internet. Bible scholars, ministers, and laypersons from around the world logged millions of review sessions. No other translation is so openly accountable to the worldwide church or has been so thoroughly vetted.

And yet, the ultimate accountability was to the biblical text itself. The NET Bible is neither crowdsourced nor a "translation by consensus." Rather, the NET translators filtered every question and suggestion through the very best insights from biblical linguistics, textual criticism, and their unswerving commitment to following the text wherever it leads. Thus, the NET remains supremely accurate and trustworthy, while also benefiting from extensive review by those who would be reading, studying, and teaching from its pages.

Beyond the "Readable vs. Accurate" Divide

The uniquely transparent and accountable translation process of the NET has been crystalized in the most extensive set of Bible translators' notes ever created. More than 60,000 notes highlight every major decision, outline alternative views, and explain difficult or nontraditional renderings. Freely available at netbible.org and in print in the *NET Bible, Full Notes Edition,* these notes help the NET overcome one of the biggest challenges facing any Bible translation: the tension between *accuracy* and *readability*.

If you have spent more than a few minutes researching English versions of the Bible, you have probably encountered a "translation spectrum"—a simple chart with the most wooden-but-precise translations on the far left (representing a "word-for-word" translation approach) and the loosest-but-easiest-to-read translations and paraphrases on the far right (representing a "thought-for-thought" philosophy of translation). Some translations intentionally lean toward one end of the spectrum or the other, embracing the strengths and weaknesses of their chosen approach. Most try to strike a balance between the extremes, weighing accuracy against readability—striving to reflect the grammar of the underlying biblical languages while still achieving acceptable English style.

But the NET moves beyond that old dichotomy. Because of the extensive translators' notes, the NET never has to compromise. Whenever faced with a difficult translation choice, the translators were free to put the strongest option in the main text while documenting the challenge, their thought process, and the solution in the notes.

The benefit to you, the reader? You can be sure that the NET is a translation you can trust—nothing has been lost in translation or obscured by a translator's dilemma. Instead, you are invited to see for yourself, and gain the kind of transparent access to the biblical languages previously only available to scholars.

Ministry First

One more reason to love the NET: Modern Bible translations are typically copyrighted, posing a challenge for ministries hoping to quote more than a few passages in their Bible study resources, curriculum, or other programming. But the NET is for everyone, with "ministry first" copyright innovations that encourage ministries to quote and share the life-changing message of Scripture as freely as possible. In fact, one of the major motivations behind the creation of the NET was the desire to ensure that ministries had unfettered access to a top-quality modern Bible translation, without needing to embark on a complicated process of securing permissions.

Visit netbible.com/net-bible-copyright to learn more.

Take Up and Read

With its balanced, easy-to-understand English text and a transparent translation process that invites you to see for yourself the richness of the biblical languages, the NET is a Bible you can embrace as your own. Clear, readable, elegant, and accurate, the NET presents Scripture as meaningfully and powerfully today as when these words were first communicated to the people of God.

Our prayer is that the NET will be a fresh and exciting invitation to you—and Bible readers everywhere—to "let the word of Christ dwell in you richly" (Col 3:16).

THE PUBLISHERS

Explanatory Notes

***1 Samuel 13:1** MT *a son of a year*; a few Greek manuscripts read *thirty*.

†**1 Samuel 13:1** MT *two years*; Acts 13:21 has *forty*; some English translations add these two, resulting in *forty-two*.

‡**Ezra 4:7** Since it makes no sense to say the letter was first written in Aramaic and then translated into Aramaic, the second mention of Aramaic is probably a scribal notation that what follows is in Aramaic.

§**Matthew 17:20** Many significant manuscripts omit **17:21** *But this kind does not go out except by prayer and fasting.*

||**Matthew 18:10** The most significant manuscripts do not include **18:11** *For the Son of Man came to seek the lost.*

¶**Matthew 23:13** The most important manuscripts omit **23:14** *Woe to you experts in the law and you Pharisees, hypocrites! You devour widows' houses and for show you pray long prayers! Therefore you will receive the greater condemnation.*

***Mark 7:15** The best manuscripts omit **7:16** *Let anyone with ears to hear, listen.*

†**Mark 9:43** The best manuscripts omit **9:44** *where their worm never dies and the fire is never quenched.* (identical to v. 48)

‡**Mark 9:45** The best manuscripts omit **9:46** *where their worm never dies and the fire is never quenched.* (identical to v. 48)

§**Mark 11:25** The best manuscripts omit **11:26** *But if you do not forgive, neither will your Father in heaven forgive your sins.*

||**Mark 15:27** The best manuscripts omit **15:28** *And the scripture was fulfilled that says, "He was counted with the lawless ones."*

¶**Mark 16:8** Mark ends at this point in some manuscripts, including two of the most respected ones. Other manuscripts supply a shorter ending: "They reported briefly to those around Peter all that they had been commanded. After these things Jesus himself sent out through them, from the east to the west, the holy and imperishable preaching of eternal salvation. Amen." Some manuscripts supply both endings. Because of questions about the authenticity of these alternative endings, 16:8 is usually regarded as the last verse of the Gospel of Mark.

***Luke 17:35** The best manuscripts do not include **17:36** *There will be two in the field; one will be taken and other left.*

†**Luke 22:44** Some important manuscripts lack **22:43–44**.

‡**Luke 23:16** Many of the best manuscripts do not include **23:17** *(Now he was obligated to release one individual for them at the feast.)*

§**Luke 23:34** Many significant manuscripts omit v. 34a; because of uncertainty of its authenticity it has been placed in brackets in the translation.

||**John 5:3** Some manuscripts add *waiting for the moving of the water.* **5:4** *For an angel of the Lord went down and stirred up the water at certain times. Whoever first stepped in after the stirring of the water was healed from whatever disease which he suffered.*

¶John 7:53–8:11 is not contained in the earliest and best manuscripts and was almost certainly not an original part of the Gospel of John; one group of manuscripts places it after Luke 21:38.

***John 9:39** Some significant manuscripts lack v. 38 and the first part of v. 39; because of uncertainty over the authenticity of this material it has been placed in brackets in the translation.

†**Acts 8:36** A few later manuscripts add **8:37** *He said to him, "If you believe with your whole heart, you may." He replied, "I believe that Jesus Christ is the Son of God."*

‡**Acts 15:33** A few later manuscripts add **15:34** *But Silas decided to stay there.*

§**Acts 24:6** Some later manuscripts include 24:7 and parts of vv. 6 and 8: *and we wanted to judge him according to our law.* **24:7** *But Lysias the commanding officer came and took him out of our hands with a great deal of violence,* **24:8** *ordering those who accused him to come before you.*

||**Acts 28:28** Some later manuscripts include **28:29** *When he had said these things, the Jews departed, having a great dispute among themselves.*

¶**Romans 16:23** Some later manuscripts add **16:24** *The grace of our Lord Jesus Christ be with all of you. Amen.*

***Ephesians 1:1** The earliest and most significant manuscripts omit *in Ephesus* (for further discussion of this complex problem see the note in the full-notes edition of the NET or online at netbible.org).

The Old Testament

TRAVELS OF THE PATRIARCHS

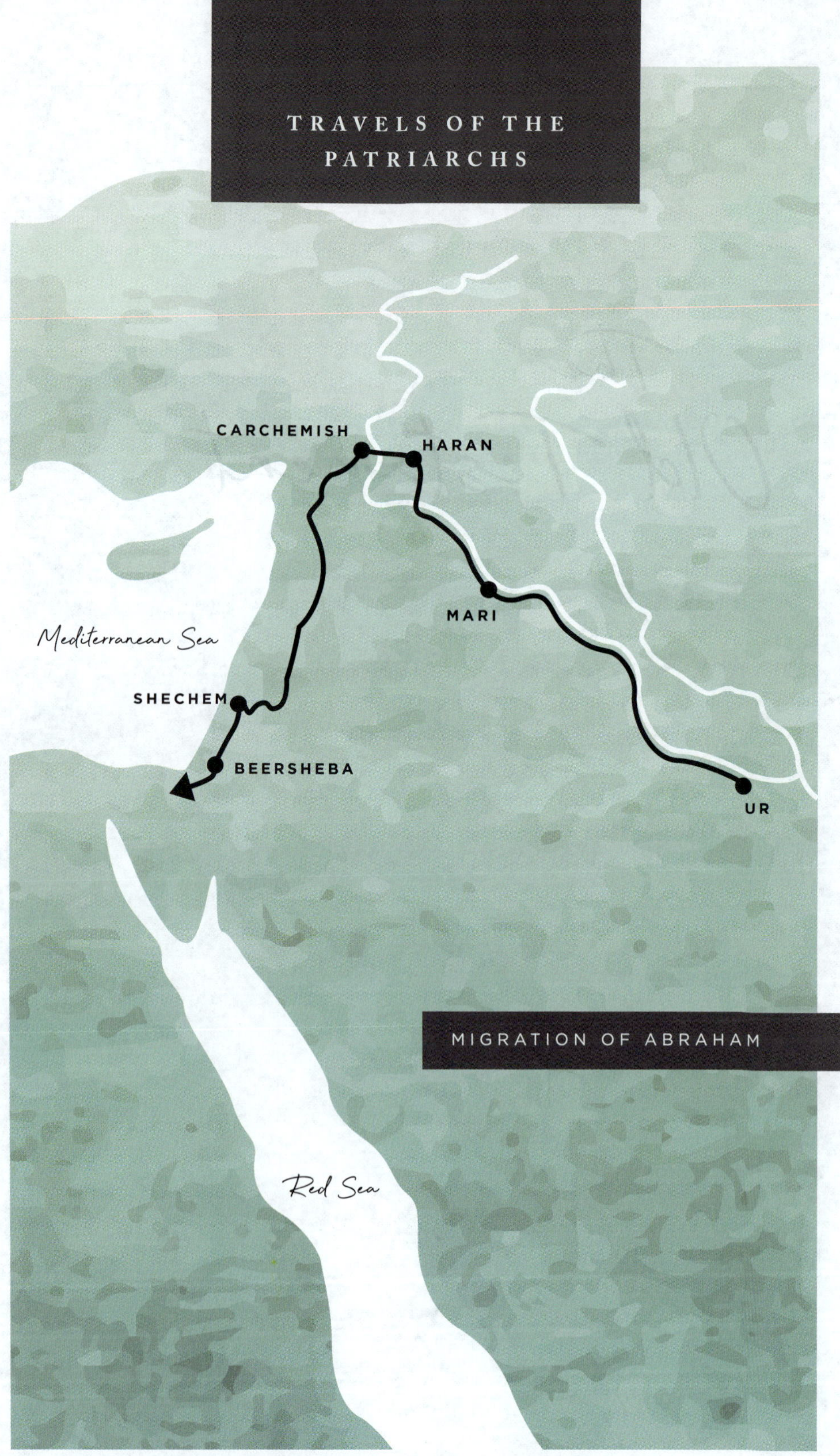

MIGRATION OF ABRAHAM

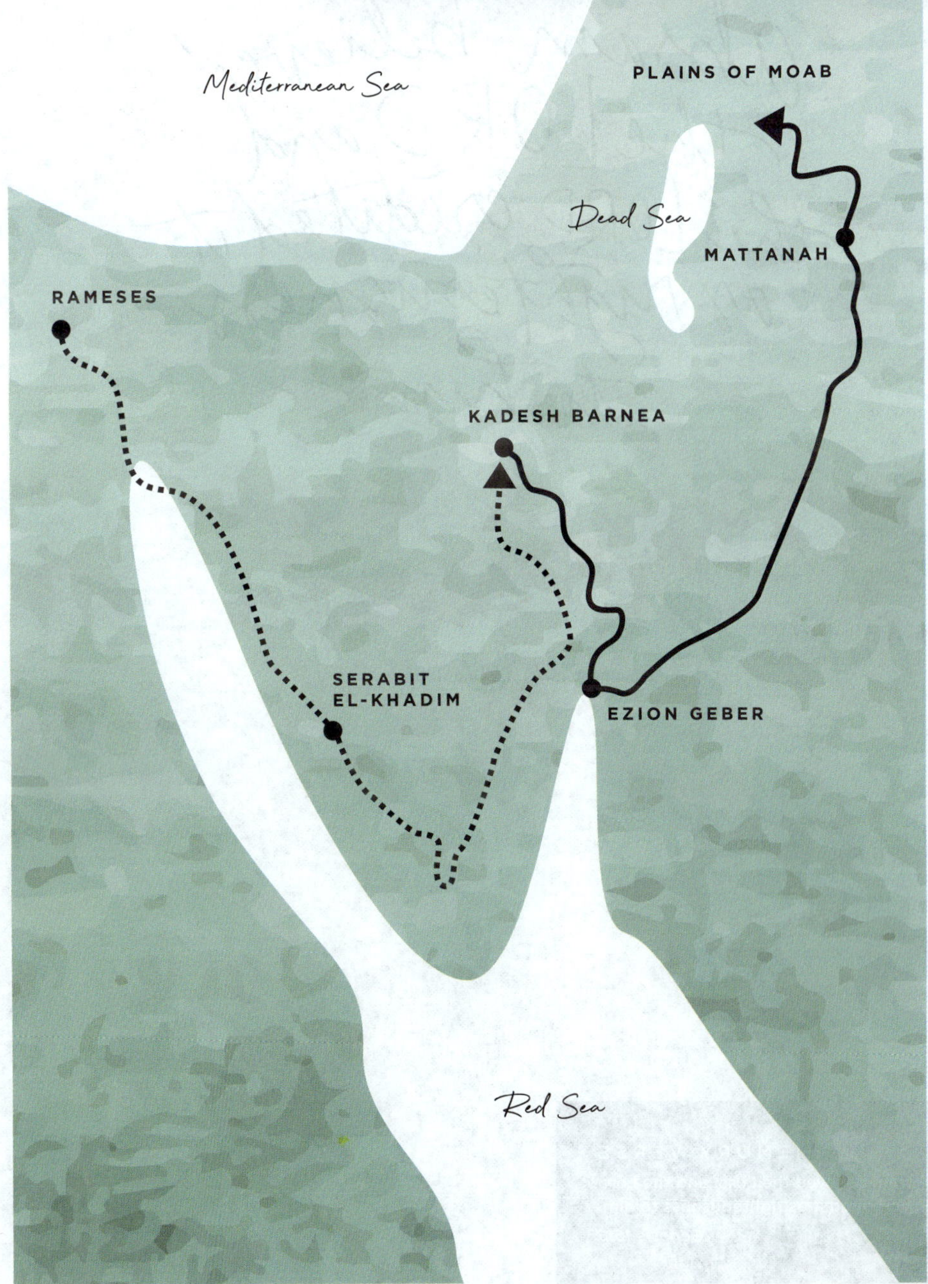

POSSIBLE ROUTE OF THE EXODUS
JOURNEY INTO CANAAN
Mediterranean Sea
PLAINS OF MOAB
Dead Sea
MATTANAH
RAMESES
KADESH BARNEA
SERABIT
EL-KHADIM
EZION GEBER
Red Sea

Abram believed
the LORD, and
the LORD credited it
as righteousness
to him

MEMORY VERSE

Abram believed the LORD, and the LORD credited it as righteousness to him.

Genesis 15:6

Genesis

INTRODUCTION

Faith in the Promise

The Book of Genesis displays the nature and character of God. These fifty chapters exemplify the kindness, goodness, creativity, holiness, justice, wrath, power, majesty, and awesomeness of Yahweh.

Genesis is divided into two sections: chapters 1–11 and chapters 12–50. The first eleven chapters describe the way God created the world. These chapters were written to illuminate the holiness of God and show that humankind carries His image. They show God's faithfulness to those who followed Him and the way He dealt with those who, in rebellion, turned from His ways. In Genesis 12–50, the promises God made in Genesis 3 take shape. God chose a man named Abram and promised to make him a great nation; his descendant would redeem the world from sin. These remaining chapters of Genesis follow Abram and his family and the formation of the nation of Israel.

Most evangelical scholars agree that Genesis was written by Moses during the time the Israelites wandered in the wilderness of Zin, around 1440 B.C. Written to the generation of Israelites preparing to enter and live in the promised land of Canaan, the words of Genesis reminded them who their God is, and what it looked like to walk with Him.

Genesis helps us love God greatly by showing us who God is and how He interacts with humanity. It encourages as it shows, over and over again, God's faithfulness to His people, His promises, and His covenant. His creativity is on display, reminding us of the vastness of His ability. God's heart for His children overflows as He displays His love, care, and provision.

Ireland

OFFICIAL LANGUAGE
English and Irish (Gaelic)
POPULATION
4,830,000
UNREACHED POPULATION
46,000
PROFESSING CHRISTIANS
91.4%

Suzie's Home

Say a Prayer Today

Pray for the Irish people, that they would find freedom in Christ. Pray they would find the grace that Christ offers, grace that is not tied to ritual or ceremony, but faith alone.

HISTORY BIT

In 1602 the first translation of the New Testament in Irish was printed. The Old Testament in Irish was printed in 1680.*

Source Information:
https://joshuaproject.net/countries/EI
*John Bowden, A Chronology of World Christianity (New York, NY: Continuum, 2007), 299, 320.

LOVE GOD GREATLY BIBLE

Angela Perritt, General Editor
Melissa Fuller, ThM, General Editor
Philip Nation, DMin, Publisher
Victoria Green, Managing Editor

www.ThomasNelson.com

Love God Greatly Bible

Published in Nashville, Tennessee, by HarperCollins Christian Publishing, Inc.

For free access to the NET Bible, the complete set of more than 60,000 translators' notes, and Bible study resources, visit:

bible.org
netbible.org
netbible.com

Library of Congress Control Number: 2020932849

This Bible was set in the Thomas Nelson NET Typeface, created at the 2K/DENMARK A/S type foundry.

www.thomasnelson.com/bibles/

Printed in South Korea

20 21 22 23 24 25 26 27 /SWK/ 15 14 13 12 11 10 9 8 7 6 5 4 3 2 1

LOVE YOUR NEIGHBOR

Her Journey

SUZIE'S STORY

Once known as "the Land of Saints and Scholars," the attitude toward church and religion in Ireland has changed in the last thirty years. When I was growing up, Ireland was a highly religious country. However, many Irish people, both in the past and today, have been confused about how to attain righteousness before God.

Nobody would have blamed Abraham if he had felt the same. After all, he'd had a personal calling from God, he acted in obedience, he set aside time to worship God, he showed kindness to his family and neighbors, and he gave a tenth of his possessions to God. Anyone seeing Abraham's life would have assumed that these things are what made him righteous before God.

The truth is, none of these things made Abraham righteous. It was Abraham's faith that made him righteous.

Coming from a tradition of ritual righteousness, I've often struggled to believe that faith alone can save me. I've believed God's promises over my life, acted in obedience, repented from my sin, worshiped God, been charitable to others, and given back to God. Yet none of these things have earned me righteous standing before God. None of these things earn me a place in heaven or restore my righteousness. Righteousness comes through faith in God alone.

God desires our faith, not our works. He wants our hearts to be aligned with Him, and after that, our actions will follow.

6 WEEK READING PLAN

LOVE HIS WORD

	MONDAY	TUESDAY	WEDNESDAY	THURSDAY	FRIDAY
1	Genesis 1-2	Genesis 3	Genesis 4-5	Genesis 6-7	Genesis 8-9
	SOAP Genesis 1:27	SOAP Psalm 139:1-3	SOAP Genesis 5:1-2	SOAP Psalm 37:38-40	SOAP Genesis 9:13-15
2	Genesis 10:1—11:26	Genesis 11:27—13:18	Genesis 14-15	Genesis 16-17	Genesis 18-19
	SOAP Acts 17:26	SOAP Genesis 12:1-2	SOAP Genesis 15:6	SOAP Genesis 16:13	SOAP Genesis 18:13-15
3	Genesis 20	Genesis 21	Genesis 22-23	Genesis 24	Genesis 25:1—26:33
	SOAP Philippians 4:6-7	SOAP Genesis 21:1-2	SOAP Genesis 22:13-14	SOAP Matthew 6:6-8	SOAP Genesis 25:21
4	Genesis 26:34—28:22	Genesis 29-30	Genesis 31	Genesis 32-33	Genesis 34-35
	SOAP Genesis 28:15	SOAP Genesis 30:22-23	SOAP Romans 12:16-18	SOAP Genesis 32:26-28	SOAP Psalm 77:11-12
5	Genesis 36	Genesis 37	Genesis 38	Genesis 39-40	Genesis 41
	SOAP Obadiah 15	SOAP Psalm 77:2	SOAP Matthew 1:1, 3	SOAP Genesis 39:2-3	SOAP 2 Corinthians 9:8
6	Genesis 42	Genesis 43-44	Genesis 45:1—47:12	Genesis 47:13—48:22	Genesis 49-50
	SOAP Proverbs 12:23	SOAP Proverbs 16:4	SOAP Genesis 47:11-12	SOAP Isaiah 63:9	SOAP Genesis 50:19-20

THE CREATION OF THE WORLD

1 In the beginning God created the heavens and the earth.
2 Now the earth was without shape and empty, and darkness
was over the surface of the watery deep, but the Spirit of God
was moving over the surface of the water. 3 God said, "Let there
be light." And there was light! 4 God saw that the light was good,
so God separated the light from the darkness. 5 God called the
light "day" and the darkness "night." There was evening, and there
was morning, marking the first day.
6 God said, "Let there be an expanse in the midst of the waters
and let it separate water from water." 7 So God made the expanse
and separated the water under the expanse from the water above
it. It was so. 8 God called the expanse "sky." There was evening,
and there was morning, a second day.
9 God said, "Let the water under the sky be gathered to one
place and let dry ground appear." It was so. 10 God called the dry
ground "land" and the gathered waters he called "seas." God saw
that it was good.
11 God said, "Let the land produce vegetation: plants yielding
seeds and trees on the land bearing fruit with seed in it, according to their kinds." It was so. 12 The land produced vegetation—plants yielding seeds according to their kinds, and trees
bearing fruit with seed in it according to their kinds. God saw
that it was good. 13 There was evening, and there was morning,
a third day.
14 God said, "Let there be lights in the expanse of the sky to
separate the day from the night, and let them be signs to indicate seasons and days and years, 15 and let them serve as lights
in the expanse of the sky to give light on the earth." It was so.
16 God made two great lights—the greater light to rule over the
day and the lesser light to rule over the night. He made the
stars also. 17 God placed the lights in the expanse of the sky to
shine on the earth, 18 to preside over the day and the night, and
to separate the light from the darkness. God saw that it was
good. 19 There was evening, and there was morning, a fourth day.
20 God said, "Let the water swarm with swarms of living creatures and let birds fly above the earth across the expanse of
the sky." 21 God created the great sea creatures and every living
and moving thing with which the water swarmed, according to
their kinds, and every winged bird according to its kind. God
saw that it was good. 22 God blessed them and said, "Be fruitful
and multiply and fill the water in the seas, and let the birds multiply on the earth." 23 There was evening, and there was morning, a fifth day.
24 God said, "Let the land produce living creatures according
to their kinds: cattle, creeping things, and wild animals, each
according to its kind." It was so. 25 God made the wild animals
according to their kinds, the cattle according to their kinds, and
all the creatures that creep along the ground according to their
kinds. God saw that it was good.
26 Then God said, "Let us make humankind in our image, after
our likeness, so they may rule over the fish of the sea and the
birds of the air, over the cattle, and over all the earth, and over
all the creatures that move on the earth."

REFLECT

What does it mean
to be created in
the image of God?

27 God created humankind in his own image,
in the image of God he created them,
male and female he created them.

28 God blessed them and said to them, “Be fruitful and multiply!
Fill the earth and subdue it! Rule over the fish of the sea and the
birds of the air and every creature that moves on the ground.”
29 Then God said, “I now give you every seed-bearing plant on the
face of the entire earth and every tree that has fruit with seed
in it. They will be yours for food. 30 And to all the animals of the
earth, and to every bird of the air, and to all the creatures that
move on the ground—everything that has living breath in it—I
give every green plant for food.” It was so.
31 God saw all that he had made—and it was very good! There
was evening, and there was morning, the sixth day.
2 The heavens and the earth were completed with everything
that was in them. 2 By the seventh day God finished the work
that he had been doing, and he ceased on the seventh day all the
work that he had been doing. 3 God blessed the seventh day and
made it holy because on it he ceased all the work that he had
been doing in creation.

THE CREATION OF MAN AND WOMAN

4 This is the account of the heavens and the earth when they
were created—when the LORD God made the earth and heavens.
5 Now no shrub of the field had yet grown on the earth, and no
plant of the field had yet sprouted, for the LORD God had not
caused it to rain on the earth, and there was no man to cultivate
the ground. 6 Springs would well up from the earth and water the
whole surface of the ground. 7 The LORD God formed the man
from the soil of the ground and breathed into his nostrils the
breath of life, and the man became a living being.
8 The LORD God planted an orchard in the east, in Eden; and
there he placed the man he had formed. 9 The LORD God made all
kinds of trees grow from the soil, every tree that was pleasing to
look at and good for food. (Now the tree of life and the tree of the
knowledge of good and evil were in the middle of the orchard.)
10 Now a river flows from Eden to water the orchard, and from
there it divides into four headstreams. 11 The name of the first is
Pishon; it runs through the entire land of Havilah, where there
is gold. 12 (The gold of that land is pure; pearls and lapis lazuli
are also there.) 13 The name of the second river is Gihon; it runs
through the entire land of Cush. 14 The name of the third river
is Tigris; it runs along the east side of Assyria. The fourth river
is the Euphrates.
15 The LORD God took the man and placed him in the orchard in
Eden to care for it and to maintain it. 16 Then the LORD God commanded the man, “You may freely eat fruit from every tree of the
orchard, 17 but you must not eat from the tree of the knowledge
of good and evil, for when you eat from it you will surely die.”
18 The LORD God said, “It is not good for the man to be alone. I
will make a companion for him who corresponds to him.” 19 The
LORD God formed out of the ground every living animal of the
field and every bird of the air. He brought them to the man to

see what he would name them, and whatever the man called
each living creature, that was its name. 20 So the man named
all the animals, the birds of the air, and the living creatures of
the field, but for Adam no companion who corresponded to
him was found. 21 So the LORD God caused the man to fall into
a deep sleep, and while he was asleep, he took part of the man's
side and closed up the place with flesh. 22 Then the LORD God
made a woman from the part he had taken out of the man, and
he brought her to the man. 23 Then the man said,

"This one at last is bone of my bones
and flesh of my flesh;
this one will be called 'woman,'
for she was taken out of man."

24 That is why a man leaves his father and mother and unites
with his wife, and they become one family. 25 The man and his
wife were both naked, but they were not ashamed.

THE TEMPTATION AND THE FALL

3 Now the serpent was shrewder than any of the wild animals
that the LORD God had made. He said to the woman, "Is it
really true that God said, 'You must not eat from any tree of the
orchard'?" 2 The woman said to the serpent, "We may eat of the
fruit from the trees of the orchard; 3 but concerning the fruit of
the tree that is in the middle of the orchard God said, 'You must
not eat from it, and you must not touch it, or else you will die.'"
4 The serpent said to the woman, "Surely you will not die, 5 for
God knows that when you eat from it your eyes will open and
you will be like God, knowing good and evil."
6 When the woman saw that the tree produced fruit that was
good for food, was attractive to the eye, and was desirable for
making one wise, she took some of its fruit and ate it. She also
gave some of it to her husband who was with her, and he ate
it. 7 Then the eyes of both of them opened, and they knew they
were naked; so they sewed fig leaves together and made coverings for themselves.

THE JUDGMENT ORACLES OF GOD AT THE FALL

8 Then the man and his wife heard the sound of the LORD God
moving about in the orchard at the breezy time of the day, and
they hid from the LORD God among the trees of the orchard.
9 But the LORD God called to the man and said to him, "Where
are you?" 10 The man replied, "I heard you moving about in the
orchard, and I was afraid because I was naked, so I hid." 11 And
the LORD God said, "Who told you that you were naked? Did you
eat from the tree that I commanded you not to eat from?" 12 The
man said, "The woman whom you gave me, she gave me some
fruit from the tree and I ate it." 13 So the LORD God said to the
woman, "What is this you have done?" And the woman replied,
"The serpent tricked me, and I ate."
14 The LORD God said to the serpent,

"Because you have done this,
cursed are you above all the cattle
and all the living creatures of the field!

LOVE TO GROW

WHAT JESUS FINISHED

GENESIS 3

I can't imagine what life was like for Adam and Eve: living in the garden of Eden, walking daily with God, life with no sin.

I can relate to why they sinned. I've fallen for the same lie over and over again. I struggle with the same tendencies: doubts and insecurities, a desire to be more than I am. I get it.

When I was in high school, I started reading the Bible on my own on a consistent basis. I would go strong for a few days, maybe even a week or two, and then life would hit. Late night volleyball games resulted in sleeping until the exact minute I had to get up before I'd be late for school. On those mornings, I'd skip my devotions.

Then the guilt would kick in. After a few days, I felt like I couldn't go back to reading God's Word. I mean, I had stood God up. Why would He welcome me back after I had treated Him that way? Because of the guilt I felt, I missed more mornings in God's Word, afraid I would somehow have to face the consequences of my negligence. The guilt pushed me further and further away from God.

Eventually, I found myself hiding from God, like Adam and Eve in the garden of Eden.

From the time the first sin was committed, we have been struggling, fighting the urge to hide, to pull away, to distance ourselves from God.

The more Adam and Eve hid from God, the more distant they became to Him.

And yet what do we see in these verses? God went to them. He met them where they were. Adam and Eve might have been hiding from God, but God knew exactly where they were the whole time. Not only did God go to them, but He also provided clothing for their nakedness.

In the garden of Eden, God sacrificed an animal.
Later, He would sacrifice His own Son.

Generations later, Jesus willingly went to the cross to pay the ultimate price for our sins once and for all. He bore our shame and our humiliation. He bravely endured it all so that we could find our way back to Paradise with God in heaven. What Satan started in the garden of Eden, Jesus finished on the cross. He gave eternal life, a free gift of salvation for those who accept Him as Lord and Savior of their lives. Jesus is the only way.

On your belly you will crawl
and dust you will eat all the days of your life.
15 And I will put hostility between you and the woman
and between your offspring and her offspring;
he will strike your head,
and you will strike his heel."

16 To the woman he said,
"I will greatly increase your labor pains;
with pain you will give birth to children.
You will want to control your husband,
but he will dominate you."

17 But to Adam he said,
"Because you obeyed your wife
and ate from the tree about which I commanded you,
'You must not eat from it,'
the ground is cursed because of you;
in painful toil you will eat of it all the days of your life.
18 It will produce thorns and thistles for you,
but you will eat the grain of the field.
19 By the sweat of your brow you will eat food
until you return to the ground,
for out of it you were taken;
for you are dust, and to dust you will return."

20 The man named his wife Eve, because she was the mother of
all the living. 21 The LORD God made garments from skin for Adam
and his wife, and clothed them. 22 And the LORD God said, "Now
that the man has become like one of us, knowing good and evil, he
must not be allowed to stretch out his hand and take also from the
tree of life and eat, and live forever." 23 So the LORD God expelled
him from the orchard in Eden to cultivate the ground from which
he had been taken. 24 When he drove the man out, he placed on
the eastern side of the orchard in Eden angelic sentries who used
the flame of a whirling sword to guard the way to the tree of life.

THE STORY OF CAIN AND ABEL

4 Now the man was intimate with his wife Eve, and she became pregnant and gave birth to Cain. Then she said, "I have
created a man just as the LORD did!" 2 Then she gave birth to
his brother Abel. Abel took care of the flocks, while Cain cultivated the ground.

3 At the designated time Cain brought some of the fruit of the
ground for an offering to the LORD. 4 But Abel brought some of
the firstborn of his flock—even the fattest of them. And the LORD
was pleased with Abel and his offering, 5 but with Cain and his
offering he was not pleased. So Cain became very angry, and his
expression was downcast.

6 Then the LORD said to Cain, "Why are you angry, and why is
your expression downcast? 7 Is it not true that if you do what
is right, you will be fine? But if you do not do what is right, sin
is crouching at the door. It desires to dominate you, but you
must subdue it."

CHALLENGE

What promise does God make in Genesis 3:15? How is this promise fulfilled throughout the rest of Scripture?

8 Cain said to his brother Abel, "Let's go out to the field." While
they were in the field, Cain attacked his brother Abel and killed
him.
9 Then the LORD said to Cain, "Where is your brother Abel?"
And he replied, "I don't know! Am I my brother's guardian?" 10 But
the LORD said, "What have you done? The voice of your brother's blood is crying out to me from the ground! 11 So now you are
banished from the ground, which has opened its mouth to receive your brother's blood from your hand. 12 When you try to
cultivate the ground it will no longer yield its best for you. You
will be a homeless wanderer on the earth."
13 Then Cain said to the LORD, "My punishment is too great
to endure! 14 Look, you are driving me off the land today, and I
must hide from your presence. I will be a homeless wanderer on
the earth; whoever finds me will kill me!" 15 But the LORD said
to him, "All right then, if anyone kills Cain, Cain will be avenged
seven times as much." Then the LORD put a special mark on Cain
so that no one who found him would strike him down. 16 So Cain
went out from the presence of the LORD and lived in the land
of Nod, east of Eden.

THE BEGINNING OF CIVILIZATION

17 Cain was intimate with his wife, and she became pregnant and
gave birth to Enoch. Cain was building a city, and he named the
city after his son Enoch. 18 To Enoch was born Irad, and Irad was
the father of Mehujael. Mehujael was the father of Methushael,
and Methushael was the father of Lamech.
19 Lamech took two wives for himself; the name of the first
was Adah, and the name of the second was Zillah. 20 Adah gave
birth to Jabal; he was the first of those who live in tents and
keep livestock. 21 The name of his brother was Jubal; he was
the first of all who play the harp and the flute. 22 Now Zillah
also gave birth to Tubal-Cain, who heated metal and shaped
all kinds of tools made of bronze and iron. The sister of Tubal-
Cain was Naamah.
23 Lamech said to his wives,
"Adah and Zillah, listen to me!
You wives of Lamech, hear my words!
I have killed a man for wounding me,
a young man for hurting me.
24 If Cain is to be avenged seven times as much,
then Lamech seventy-seven times!"

25 And Adam was intimate with his wife again, and she gave
birth to a son. She named him Seth, saying, "God has given me
another child in place of Abel because Cain killed him." 26 And a
son was also born to Seth, whom he named Enosh. At that time
people began to worship the LORD.

FROM ADAM TO NOAH

5 This is the record of the family line of Adam.
When God created humankind, he made them in the likeness of God. 2 He created them male and female; when they were
created, he blessed them and named them "humankind."

[3]When Adam had lived 130 years he fathered a son in his own
likeness, according to his image, and he named him Seth. [4]The
length of time Adam lived after he became the father of Seth
was 800 years; during this time he had other sons and daughters.
[5]The entire lifetime of Adam was 930 years, and then he died.
[6]When Seth had lived 105 years, he became the father of Enosh.
[7]Seth lived 807 years after he became the father of Enosh, and
he had other sons and daughters. [8]The entire lifetime of Seth
was 912 years, and then he died.
[9]When Enosh had lived 90 years, he became the father of Kenan. [10]Enosh lived 815 years after he became the father of Kenan, and he had other sons and daughters. [11]The entire lifetime
of Enosh was 905 years, and then he died.
[12]When Kenan had lived 70 years, he became the father of
Mahalalel. [13]Kenan lived 840 years after he became the father
of Mahalalel, and he had other sons and daughters. [14]The entire
lifetime of Kenan was 910 years, and then he died.
[15]When Mahalalel had lived 65 years, he became the father of
Jared. [16]Mahalalel lived 830 years after he became the father of
Jared, and he had other sons and daughters. [17]The entire lifetime
of Mahalalel was 895 years, and then he died.
[18]When Jared had lived 162 years, he became the father of
Enoch. [19]Jared lived 800 years after he became the father of
Enoch, and he had other sons and daughters. [20]The entire lifetime of Jared was 962 years, and then he died.
[21]When Enoch had lived 65 years, he became the father of Methuselah. [22]After he became the father of Methuselah, Enoch
walked with God for 300 years, and he had other sons and daughters. [23]The entire lifetime of Enoch was 365 years. [24]Enoch walked
with God, and then he disappeared because God took him away.
[25]When Methuselah had lived 187 years, he became the father
of Lamech. [26]Methuselah lived 782 years after he became the
father of Lamech, and he had other sons and daughters. [27]The
entire lifetime of Methuselah was 969 years, and then he died.
[28]When Lamech had lived 182 years, he had a son. [29]He named
him Noah, saying, "This one will bring us comfort from our labor and from the painful toil of our hands because of the ground
that the LORD has cursed." [30]Lamech lived 595 years after he became the father of Noah, and he had other sons and daughters.
[31]The entire lifetime of Lamech was 777 years, and then he died.
[32]After Noah was 500 years old, he became the father of Shem,
Ham, and Japheth.

GOD'S GRIEF OVER HUMANKIND'S WICKEDNESS

6 When humankind began to multiply on the face of the earth,
and daughters were born to them, [2]the sons of God saw that
the daughters of humankind were beautiful. Thus they took
wives for themselves from any they chose. [3]So the LORD said,
"My Spirit will not remain in humankind indefinitely, since they
are mortal. They will remain for 120 more years."
[4]The Nephilim were on the earth in those days (and also after this) when the sons of God would sleep with the daughters
of humankind, who gave birth to their children. They were the
mighty heroes of old, the famous men.

5 But the LORD saw that the wickedness of humankind had
become great on the earth. Every inclination of the thoughts
of their minds was only evil all the time. 6 The LORD regretted
that he had made humankind on the earth, and he was highly offended. 7 So the LORD said, "I will wipe humankind, whom I have
created, from the face of the earth—everything from humankind
to animals, including creatures that move on the ground and
birds of the air, for I regret that I have made them."
8 But Noah found favor in the sight of the LORD.

THE JUDGMENT OF THE FLOOD

9 This is the account of Noah.
Noah was a godly man; he was blameless among his contemporaries. He walked with God. 10 Noah had three sons: Shem,
Ham, and Japheth.
11 The earth was ruined in the sight of God; the earth was filled
with violence. 12 God saw the earth, and indeed it was ruined,
for all living creatures on the earth were sinful. 13 So God said to
Noah, "I have decided that all living creatures must die, for the
earth is filled with violence because of them. Now I am about
to destroy them and the earth. 14 Make for yourself an ark of cypress wood. Make rooms in the ark, and cover it with pitch inside and out. 15 This is how you should make it: The ark is to be
450 feet long, 75 feet wide, and 45 feet high. 16 Make a roof for
the ark and finish it, leaving 18 inches from the top. Put a door
in the side of the ark, and make lower, middle, and upper decks.
17 I am about to bring floodwaters on the earth to destroy from
under the sky all the living creatures that have the breath of
life in them. Everything that is on the earth will die, 18 but I will
confirm my covenant with you. You will enter the ark—you, your
sons, your wife, and your sons' wives with you. 19 You must bring
into the ark two of every kind of living creature from all flesh,
male and female, to keep them alive with you. 20 Of the birds after their kinds, and of the cattle after their kinds, and of every
creeping thing of the ground after its kind, two of every kind will
come to you so you can keep them alive. 21 And you must take for
yourself every kind of food that is eaten, and gather it together.
It will be food for you and for them."
22 And Noah did all that God commanded him—he did indeed.
7 The LORD said to Noah, "Come into the ark, you and all your
household, for I consider you godly among this generation.
2 You must take with you seven pairs of every kind of clean animal, the male and its mate, two of every kind of unclean animal, the male and its mate, 3 and also seven pairs of every kind of
bird in the sky, male and female, to preserve their offspring on
the face of the entire earth. 4 For in seven days I will cause it to
rain on the earth for forty days and forty nights, and I will wipe
from the face of the ground every living thing that I have made."
5 And Noah did all that the LORD commanded him.
6 Noah was 600 years old when the floodwaters engulfed the
earth. 7 Noah entered the ark along with his sons, his wife, and
his sons' wives because of the floodwaters. 8 Pairs of clean animals, of unclean animals, of birds, and of everything that creeps
along the ground, 9 male and female, came into the ark to Noah,

just as God had commanded him. 10 And after seven days the floodwaters engulfed the earth.

11 In the six hundredth year of Noah's life, in the second month, on the seventeenth day of the month—on that day all the fountains of the great deep burst open and the floodgates of the heavens were opened. 12 And the rain fell on the earth forty days and forty nights.

13 On that very day Noah entered the ark, accompanied by his sons Shem, Ham, and Japheth, along with his wife and his sons' three wives. 14 They entered, along with every living creature after its kind, every animal after its kind, every creeping thing that creeps on the earth after its kind, and every bird after its kind, everything with wings. 15 Pairs of all creatures that have the breath of life came into the ark to Noah. 16 Those that entered were male and female, just as God commanded him. Then the LORD shut him in.

17 The flood engulfed the earth for forty days. As the waters increased, they lifted the ark and raised it above the earth. 18 The waters completely overwhelmed the earth, and the ark floated on the surface of the waters. 19 The waters completely inundated the earth so that even all the high mountains under the entire sky were covered. 20 The waters rose more than 20 feet above the mountains. 21 And all living things that moved on the earth died, including the birds, domestic animals, wild animals, all the creatures that swarm over the earth, and all humankind. 22 Everything on dry land that had the breath of life in its nostrils died. 23 So the LORD destroyed every living thing that was on the surface of the ground, including people, animals, creatures that creep along the ground, and birds of the sky. They were wiped off the earth. Only Noah and those who were with him in the ark survived. 24 The waters prevailed over the earth for 150 days.

8 But God remembered Noah and all the wild animals and domestic animals that were with him in the ark. God caused a wind to blow over the earth and the waters receded. 2 The fountains of the deep and the floodgates of heaven were closed, and the rain stopped falling from the sky. 3 The waters kept receding steadily from the earth, so that they had gone down by the end of the 150 days. 4 On the seventeenth day of the seventh month, the ark came to rest on one of the mountains of Ararat. 5 The waters kept on receding until the tenth month. On the first day of the tenth month, the tops of the mountains became visible.

6 At the end of forty days, Noah opened the window he had made in the ark 7 and sent out a raven; it kept flying back and forth until the waters had dried up on the earth.

8 Then Noah sent out a dove to see if the waters had receded from the surface of the ground. 9 The dove could not find a resting place for its feet because water still covered the surface of the entire earth, and so it returned to Noah in the ark. He stretched out his hand, took the dove, and brought it back into the ark. 10 He waited seven more days and then sent out the dove again from the ark. 11 When the dove returned to him in the evening, there was a freshly plucked olive leaf in its beak! Noah knew that the waters had receded from the earth. 12 He waited another

seven days and sent the dove out again, but it did not return to
him this time.
13 In Noah's six hundred and first year, in the first day of the
first month, the waters had dried up from the earth, and Noah
removed the covering from the ark and saw that the surface of
the ground was dry. 14 And by the twenty-seventh day of the second month the earth was dry.
15 Then God spoke to Noah and said, 16 "Come out of the ark,
you, your wife, your sons, and your sons' wives with you. 17 Bring
out with you all the living creatures that are with you. Bring
out every living thing, including the birds, animals, and every
creeping thing that creeps on the earth. Let them increase and
be fruitful and multiply on the earth!"
18 Noah went out along with his sons, his wife, and his sons'
wives. 19 Every living creature, every creeping thing, every bird,
and everything that moves on the earth went out of the ark in
their groups.
20 Noah built an altar to the LORD. He then took some of every
kind of clean animal and clean bird and offered burnt offerings
on the altar. 21 And the LORD smelled the soothing aroma and
said to himself, "I will never again curse the ground because of
humankind, even though the inclination of their minds is evil
from childhood on. I will never again destroy everything that
lives, as I have just done.

22 "While the earth continues to exist,
planting time and harvest,
cold and heat,
summer and winter,
and day and night will not cease."

GOD'S COVENANT WITH HUMANKIND THROUGH NOAH

9 Then God blessed Noah and his sons and said to them, "Be
fruitful and multiply and fill the earth. 2 Every living creature
of the earth and every bird of the sky will be terrified of you. Everything that creeps on the ground and all the fish of the sea
are under your authority. 3 You may eat any moving thing that
lives. As I gave you the green plants, I now give you everything.
4 "But you must not eat meat with its life (that is, its blood) in
it. 5 For your lifeblood I will surely exact punishment, from every living creature I will exact punishment. From each person
I will exact punishment for the life of the individual since the
man was his relative.

6 "Whoever sheds human blood,
by other humans
must his blood be shed;
for in God's image
God has made humankind.

7 "But as for you, be fruitful and multiply; increase abundantly
on the earth and multiply on it."
8 God said to Noah and his sons, 9 "Look. I now confirm my
covenant with you and your descendants after you 10 and with
every living creature that is with you, including the birds, the

domestic animals, and every living creature of the earth with
you, all those that came out of the ark with you—every living
creature of the earth. 11 I confirm my covenant with you: Never
again will all living things be wiped out by the waters of a flood;
never again will a flood destroy the earth."
12 And God said, "This is the guarantee of the covenant I am
making with you and every living creature with you, a covenant
for all subsequent generations: 13 I will place my rainbow in the
clouds, and it will become a guarantee of the covenant between
me and the earth. 14 Whenever I bring clouds over the earth and
the rainbow appears in the clouds, 15 then I will remember my
covenant with you and with all living creatures of all kinds. Never
again will the waters become a flood and destroy all living things.
16 When the rainbow is in the clouds, I will notice it and remember the perpetual covenant between God and all living creatures
of all kinds that are on the earth."
17 So God said to Noah, "This is the guarantee of the covenant
that I am confirming between me and all living things that are
on the earth."

THE CURSE ON CANAAN

18 The sons of Noah who came out of the ark were Shem, Ham,
and Japheth. (Now Ham was the father of Canaan.) 19 These were
the three sons of Noah, and from them the whole earth was
populated.
20 Noah, a man of the soil, began to plant a vineyard. 21 When
he drank some of the wine, he got drunk and uncovered himself inside his tent. 22 Ham, the father of Canaan, saw his father's
nakedness and told his two brothers who were outside. 23 Shem
and Japheth took the garment and placed it on their shoulders.
Then they walked in backwards and covered up their father's nakedness. Their faces were turned the other way so they did not
see their father's nakedness.
24 When Noah awoke from his drunken stupor he learned what
his youngest son had done to him. 25 So he said,
"Cursed be Canaan!
The lowest of slaves
he will be to his brothers."

26 He also said,
"Worthy of praise is the LORD, the God of Shem!
May Canaan be the slave of Shem!
27 May God enlarge Japheth's territory and numbers!
May he live in the tents of Shem
and may Canaan be the slave of Japheth!"

28 After the flood Noah lived 350 years. 29 The entire lifetime
of Noah was 950 years, and then he died.

THE TABLE OF NATIONS

10 This is the account of Noah's sons: Shem, Ham, and Japheth.
Sons were born to them after the flood.
2 The sons of Japheth were Gomer, Magog, Madai, Javan, Tubal,
Meshech, and Tiras. 3 The sons of Gomer were Ashkenaz, Riphath,

and Togarmah. 4The sons of Javan were Elishah, Tarshish, the
Kittim, and the Dodanim. 5From these the coastlands of the nations were separated into their lands, every one according to its
language, according to their families, by their nations.
6The sons of Ham were Cush, Mizraim, Put, and Canaan. 7The
sons of Cush were Seba, Havilah, Sabtah, Raamah, and Sabteca.
The sons of Raamah were Sheba and Dedan.
8Cush was the father of Nimrod; he began to be a valiant warrior on the earth. 9He was a mighty hunter before the LORD.
(That is why it is said, "Like Nimrod, a mighty hunter before
the LORD.") 10The primary regions of his kingdom were Babel,
Erech, Akkad, and Calneh in the land of Shinar. 11From that land
he went to Assyria, where he built Nineveh, Rehoboth Ir, Calah,
12and Resen, which is between Nineveh and the great city Calah.
13Mizraim was the father of the Ludites, Anamites, Lehabites,
Naphtuhites, 14Pathrusites, Casluhites (from whom the Philistines came), and Caphtorites.
15Canaan was the father of Sidon his firstborn, Heth, 16the
Jebusites, Amorites, Girgashites, 17Hivites, Arkites, Sinites, 18Ar-
vadites, Zemarites, and Hamathites. Eventually the families of
the Canaanites were scattered 19and the borders of Canaan extended from Sidon all the way to Gerar as far as Gaza, and all
the way to Sodom, Gomorrah, Admah, and Zeboyim, as far as
Lasha. 20These are the sons of Ham, according to their families,
according to their languages, by their lands, and by their nations.
21And sons were also born to Shem (the older brother of Japheth), the father of all the sons of Eber.
22The sons of Shem were Elam, Asshur, Arphaxad, Lud, and
Aram. 23The sons of Aram were Uz, Hul, Gether, and Mash. 24Ar-
phaxad was the father of Shelah, and Shelah was the father of
Eber. 25Two sons were born to Eber: One was named Peleg because in his days the earth was divided, and his brother's name
was Joktan. 26Joktan was the father of Almodad, Sheleph, Hazarmaveth, Jerah, 27Hadoram, Uzal, Diklah, 28Obal, Abimael,
Sheba, 29Ophir, Havilah, and Jobab. All these were sons of Joktan. 30Their dwelling place was from Mesha all the way to Sephar
in the eastern hills. 31These are the sons of Shem according to
their families, according to their languages, by their lands, and
according to their nations.
32These are the families of the sons of Noah, according to their
genealogies, by their nations, and from these the nations spread
over the earth after the flood.

THE DISPERSION OF THE NATIONS AT BABEL

11 The whole earth had a common language and a common vo-
cabulary. 2When the people moved eastward, they found a
plain in Shinar and settled there. 3Then they said to one another,
"Come, let's make bricks and bake them thoroughly." (They had
brick instead of stone and tar instead of mortar.) 4Then they
said, "Come, let's build ourselves a city and a tower with its top
in the heavens so that we may make a name for ourselves. Otherwise we will be scattered across the face of the entire earth."
5But the LORD came down to see the city and the tower that
the people had started building. 6And the LORD said, "If as one

people all sharing a common language they have begun to do this, then nothing they plan to do will be beyond them. 7 Come, let's go down and confuse their language so they won't be able to understand each other."

8 So the LORD scattered them from there across the face of the entire earth, and they stopped building the city. 9 That is why its name was called Babel—because there the LORD confused the language of the entire world, and from there the LORD scattered them across the face of the entire earth.

THE GENEALOGY OF SHEM

10 This is the account of Shem.

Shem was 100 years old when he became the father of Arphaxad, two years after the flood. 11 And after becoming the father of Arphaxad, Shem lived 500 years and had other sons and daughters.

12 When Arphaxad had lived 35 years, he became the father of Shelah. 13 And after he became the father of Shelah, Arphaxad lived 403 years and had other sons and daughters.

14 When Shelah had lived 30 years, he became the father of Eber. 15 And after he became the father of Eber, Shelah lived 403 years and had other sons and daughters.

16 When Eber had lived 34 years, he became the father of Peleg. 17 And after he became the father of Peleg, Eber lived 430 years and had other sons and daughters.

18 When Peleg had lived 30 years, he became the father of Reu. 19 And after he became the father of Reu, Peleg lived 209 years and had other sons and daughters.

20 When Reu had lived 32 years, he became the father of Serug. 21 And after he became the father of Serug, Reu lived 207 years and had other sons and daughters.

22 When Serug had lived 30 years, he became the father of Nahor. 23 And after he became the father of Nahor, Serug lived 200 years and had other sons and daughters.

24 When Nahor had lived 29 years, he became the father of Terah. 25 And after he became the father of Terah, Nahor lived 119 years and had other sons and daughters.

26 When Terah had lived 70 years, he became the father of Abram, Nahor, and Haran.

THE RECORD OF TERAH

27 This is the account of Terah.

Terah became the father of Abram, Nahor, and Haran. And Haran became the father of Lot. 28 Haran died in the land of his birth, in Ur of the Chaldeans, while his father Terah was still alive. 29 And Abram and Nahor took wives for themselves. The name of Abram's wife was Sarai. And the name of Nahor's wife was Milcah; she was the daughter of Haran, who was the father of both Milcah and Iscah. 30 But Sarai was barren; she had no children.

31 Terah took his son Abram, his grandson Lot (the son of Haran), and his daughter-in-law Sarai, his son Abram's wife, and with them he set out from Ur of the Chaldeans to go to Canaan. When they came to Haran, they settled there. 32 The lifetime of Terah was 205 years, and he died in Haran.

THE OBEDIENCE OF ABRAM

12 Now the LORD said to Abram,
"Go out from your country, your relatives,
and your father's household
to the land that I will show you.
2 Then I will make you into a great
nation, and I will bless you,
and I will make your name great,
so that you will exemplify divine blessing.
3 I will bless those who bless you,
but the one who treats you lightly I must curse,
so that all the families of the earth may
receive blessing through you."

4 So Abram left, just as the LORD had told him to do, and Lot went with him. (Now Abram was 75 years old when he departed from Haran.) 5 And Abram took his wife Sarai, his nephew Lot, and all the possessions they had accumulated and the people they had acquired in Haran, and they left for the land of Canaan. They entered the land of Canaan.

6 Abram traveled through the land as far as the oak tree of Moreh at Shechem. (At that time the Canaanites were in the land.) 7 The LORD appeared to Abram and said, "To your descendants I will give this land." So Abram built an altar there to the LORD, who had appeared to him.

8 Then he moved from there to the hill country east of Bethel and pitched his tent, with Bethel on the west and Ai on the east. There he built an altar to the LORD and worshiped the LORD. 9 Abram continually journeyed by stages down to the Negev.

THE PROMISED BLESSING JEOPARDIZED

10 There was a famine in the land, so Abram went down to Egypt to stay for a while because the famine was severe. 11 As he approached Egypt, he said to his wife Sarai, "Look, I know that you are a beautiful woman. 12 When the Egyptians see you they will say, 'This is his wife.' Then they will kill me but will keep you alive. 13 So tell them you are my sister so that it may go well for me because of you and my life will be spared on account of you."

14 When Abram entered Egypt, the Egyptians saw that the woman was very beautiful. 15 When Pharaoh's officials saw her, they praised her to Pharaoh. So Abram's wife was taken into the household of Pharaoh, 16 and he did treat Abram well on account of her. Abram received sheep and cattle, male donkeys, male servants, female servants, female donkeys, and camels.

17 But the LORD struck Pharaoh and his household with severe diseases because of Sarai, Abram's wife. 18 So Pharaoh summoned Abram and said, "What is this you have done to me? Why didn't you tell me that she was your wife? 19 Why did you say, 'She is my sister,' so that I took her to be my wife? Now, here is your wife. Take her and go!" 20 Pharaoh gave his men orders about Abram, and so they expelled him, along with his wife and all his possessions.

ABRAM'S SOLUTION TO THE STRIFE

13 So Abram went up from Egypt into the Negev. He took his wife and all his possessions with him, as well as Lot. 2 (Now Abram was very wealthy in livestock, silver, and gold.)

3 And he journeyed from place to place from the Negev as far as Bethel. He returned to the place where he had pitched his tent at the beginning, between Bethel and Ai. 4 This was the place where he had first built the altar, and there Abram worshiped the LORD.

5 Now Lot, who was traveling with Abram, also had flocks, herds, and tents. 6 But the land could not support them while they were living side by side. Because their possessions were so great, they were not able to live alongside one another. 7 So there were quarrels between Abram's herdsmen and Lot's herdsmen. (Now the Canaanites and the Perizzites were living in the land at that time.)

8 Abram said to Lot, "Let there be no quarreling between me and you, and between my herdsmen and your herdsmen, for we are close relatives. 9 Is not the whole land before you? Separate yourself now from me. If you go to the left, then I'll go to the right, but if you go to the right, then I'll go to the left."

10 Lot looked up and saw the whole region of the Jordan. He noticed that all of it was well watered (this was before the LORD obliterated Sodom and Gomorrah) like the garden of the LORD, like the land of Egypt, all the way to Zoar. 11 Lot chose for himself the whole region of the Jordan and traveled toward the east.

So the relatives separated from each other. 12 Abram settled in the land of Canaan, but Lot settled among the cities of the Jordan plain and pitched his tents next to Sodom. 13 (Now the people of Sodom were extremely wicked rebels against the LORD.)

14 After Lot had departed, the LORD said to Abram, "Look from the place where you stand to the north, south, east, and west. 15 I will give all the land that you see to you and your descendants forever. 16 And I will make your descendants like the dust of the earth, so that if anyone is able to count the dust of the earth, then your descendants also can be counted. 17 Get up and walk throughout the land, for I will give it to you."

18 So Abram moved his tents and went to live by the oaks of Mamre in Hebron, and he built an altar to the LORD there.

THE BLESSING OF VICTORY FOR GOD'S PEOPLE

14 At that time Amraphel king of Shinar, Arioch king of Ellasar, Kedorlaomer king of Elam, and Tidal king of nations 2 went to war against Bera king of Sodom, Birsha king of Gomorrah, Shinab king of Admah, Shemeber king of Zeboyim, and the king of Bela (that is, Zoar). 3 These last five kings joined forces in the Valley of Siddim (that is, the Salt Sea). 4 For twelve years they had served Kedorlaomer, but in the thirteenth year they rebelled. 5 In the fourteenth year, Kedorlaomer and the kings who were his allies came and defeated the Rephaites in Ashteroth Karnaim, the Zuzites in Ham, the Emites in Shaveh Kiriathaim, 6 and the Horites in their hill country of Seir, as far as El Paran, which is near the desert. 7 Then they attacked En Mishpat (that is, Kadesh) again, and they conquered all the territory of the Amalekites, as well as the Amorites who were living in Hazezon Tamar.

8 Then the king of Sodom, the king of Gomorrah, the king of
Admah, the king of Zeboyim, and the king of Bela (that is, Zoar)
went out and prepared for battle. In the Valley of Siddim they
met 9 Kedorlaomer king of Elam, Tidal king of nations, Amraphel king of Shinar, and Arioch king of Ellasar. Four kings fought
against five. 10 Now the Valley of Siddim was full of tar pits. When
the kings of Sodom and Gomorrah fled, they fell into them, but
some survivors fled to the hills. 11 The four victorious kings took
all the possessions and food of Sodom and Gomorrah and left.
12 They also took Abram's nephew Lot and his possessions when
they left, for Lot was living in Sodom.

13 A fugitive came and told Abram the Hebrew. Now Abram was
living by the oaks of Mamre the Amorite, the brother of Eshcol
and Aner. (All these were allied by treaty with Abram.) 14 When
Abram heard that his nephew had been taken captive, he mo-
bilized his 318 trained men who had been born in his household, and he pursued the invaders as far as Dan. 15 Then, during
the night, Abram divided his forces against them and defeated
them. He chased them as far as Hobah, which is north of Damascus. 16 He retrieved all the stolen property. He also brought
back his nephew Lot and his possessions, as well as the women
and the rest of the people.

17 After Abram returned from defeating Kedorlaomer and
the kings who were with him, the king of Sodom went out to
meet Abram in the Valley of Shaveh (known as the King's Valley). 18 Melchizedek king of Salem brought out bread and wine.
(Now he was the priest of the Most High God.) 19 He blessed
Abram, saying,

"Blessed be Abram by the Most High God,
Creator of heaven and earth.
20 Worthy of praise is the Most High God,
who delivered your enemies into your hand."

Abram gave Melchizedek a tenth of everything.

21 Then the king of Sodom said to Abram, "Give me the people
and take the possessions for yourself." 22 But Abram replied to
the king of Sodom, "I raise my hand to the LORD, the Most High
God, Creator of heaven and earth, and vow 23 that I will take nothing belonging to you, not even a thread or the strap of a sandal.
That way you can never say, 'It is I who made Abram rich.' 24 I will
take nothing except compensation for what the young men have
eaten. As for the share of the men who went with me—Aner, Eshcol, and Mamre—let them take their share."

THE CUTTING OF THE COVENANT

15 After these things the LORD's message came to Abram in a
vision: "Fear not, Abram! I am your shield and the one who
will reward you in great abundance."

2 But Abram said, "O Sovereign LORD, what will you give me
since I continue to be childless, and my heir is Eliezer of Damascus?" 3 Abram added, "Since you have not given me a descendant,
then look, one born in my house will be my heir!"

4 But look, the LORD's message came to him: "This man will not
be your heir, but instead a son who comes from your own body

will be your heir.” 5 The LORD took him outside and said, “Gaze
into the sky and count the stars—if you are able to count them!”
Then he said to him, “So will your descendants be.”
6 Abram believed the LORD, and the LORD credited it as righteousness to him.
7 The LORD said to him, “I am the LORD who brought you out
from Ur of the Chaldeans to give you this land to possess.” 8 But
Abram said, “O Sovereign LORD, by what can I know that I am
to possess it?”
9 The LORD said to him, “Take for me a heifer, a goat, and a ram,
each three years old, along with a dove and a young pigeon.”
10 So Abram took all these for him and then cut them in two
and placed each half opposite the other, but he did not cut the
birds in half. 11 When birds of prey came down on the carcasses,
Abram drove them away.
12 When the sun went down, Abram fell sound asleep, and great
terror overwhelmed him. 13 Then the LORD said to Abram, “Know
for certain that your descendants will be strangers in a foreign
country. They will be enslaved and oppressed for 400 years. 14 But
I will execute judgment on the nation that they will serve. Afterward they will come out with many possessions. 15 But as for you,
you will go to your ancestors in peace and be buried at a good
old age. 16 In the fourth generation your descendants will return
here, for the sin of the Amorites has not yet reached its limit.”
17 When the sun had gone down and it was dark, a smoking
firepot with a flaming torch passed between the animal parts.
18 That day the LORD made a covenant with Abram: “To your descendants I give this land, from the river of Egypt to the great
river, the Euphrates River—19 the land of the Kenites, Kenizzites,
Kadmonites, 20 Hittites, Perizzites, Rephaites, 21 Amorites, Canaanites, Girgashites, and Jebusites.”

THE BIRTH OF ISHMAEL

16 Now Sarai, Abram’s wife, had not given birth to any children, but she had an Egyptian servant named Hagar. 2 So
Sarai said to Abram, “Since the LORD has prevented me from
having children, please sleep with my servant. Perhaps I can
have a family by her.” Abram did what Sarai told him.
3 So after Abram had lived in Canaan for ten years, Sarai,
Abram’s wife, gave Hagar, her Egyptian servant, to her husband
to be his wife. 4 He slept with Hagar, and she became pregnant.
Once Hagar realized she was pregnant, she despised Sarai. 5 Then
Sarai said to Abram, “You have brought this wrong on me! I gave
my servant into your embrace, but when she realized that she
was pregnant, she despised me. May the LORD judge between
you and me!”
6 Abram said to Sarai, “Since your servant is under your authority, do to her whatever you think best.” Then Sarai treated
Hagar harshly, so she ran away from Sarai.
7 The angel of the LORD found Hagar near a spring of water in
the wilderness—the spring that is along the road to Shur. 8 He
said, “Hagar, servant of Sarai, where have you come from, and
where are you going?” She replied, “I’m running away from my
mistress, Sarai.”

9 Then the angel of the LORD said to her, "Return to your mistress and submit to her authority. 10 I will greatly multiply your descendants," the angel of the LORD added, "so that they will be too numerous to count." 11 Then the angel of the LORD said to her,

"You are now pregnant
and are about to give birth to a son.
You are to name him Ishmael,
for the LORD has heard your painful groans.
12 He will be a wild donkey of a man.
He will be hostile to everyone,
and everyone will be hostile to him.
He will live away from his brothers."

REFLECT

What did it mean to Hagar to know that God saw her? Do you believe that God also sees you? Why or why not?

13 So Hagar named the LORD who spoke to her, "You are the God who sees me," for she said, "Here I have seen one who sees me!" 14 That is why the well was called Beer Lahai Roi. (It is located between Kadesh and Bered.)

15 So Hagar gave birth to Abram's son, whom Abram named Ishmael. 16 (Now Abram was 86 years old when Hagar gave birth to Ishmael.)

THE SIGN OF THE COVENANT

17 When Abram was 99 years old, the LORD appeared to him and said, "I am the Sovereign God. Walk before me and be blameless. 2 Then I will confirm my covenant between me and you, and I will give you a multitude of descendants."

3 Abram bowed down with his face to the ground, and God said to him, 4 "As for me, this is my covenant with you: You will be the father of a multitude of nations. 5 No longer will your name be Abram. Instead, your name will be Abraham because I will make you the father of a multitude of nations. 6 I will make you extremely fruitful. I will make nations of you, and kings will descend from you. 7 I will confirm my covenant as a perpetual covenant between me and you. It will extend to your descendants after you throughout their generations. I will be your God and the God of your descendants after you. 8 I will give the whole land of Canaan—the land where you are now residing—to you and your descendants after you as a permanent possession. I will be their God."

9 Then God said to Abraham, "As for you, you must keep the covenantal requirement I am imposing on you and your descendants after you throughout their generations. 10 This is my requirement that you and your descendants after you must keep: Every male among you must be circumcised. 11 You must circumcise the flesh of your foreskins. This will be a reminder of the covenant between me and you. 12 Throughout your generations every male among you who is eight days old must be circumcised, whether born in your house or bought with money from any foreigner who is not one of your descendants. 13 They must indeed be circumcised, whether born in your house or bought with money. The sign of my covenant will be visible in your flesh as a permanent reminder. 14 Any uncircumcised male who has not been circumcised in the flesh of his foreskin will be cut off from his people—he has failed to carry out my requirement."

15 Then God said to Abraham, "As for your wife, you must no

longer call her Sarai; Sarah will be her name. 16 I will bless her and
will give you a son through her. I will bless her and she will become a mother of nations. Kings of countries will come from her!"
17 Then Abraham bowed down with his face to the ground and
laughed as he said to himself, "Can a son be born to a man who is
a hundred years old? Can Sarah bear a child at the age of ninety?"
18 Abraham said to God, "O that Ishmael might live before you!"
19 God said, "No, Sarah your wife is going to bear you a son, and
you will name him Isaac. I will confirm my covenant with him as
a perpetual covenant for his descendants after him. 20 As for Ishmael, I have heard you. I will indeed bless him, make him fruitful,
and give him a multitude of descendants. He will become the father of twelve princes; I will make him into a great nation. 21 But
I will establish my covenant with Isaac, whom Sarah will bear
to you at this set time next year." 22 When he finished speaking
with Abraham, God went up from him.
23 Abraham took his son Ishmael and every male in his household (whether born in his house or bought with money) and
circumcised them on that very same day, just as God had told
him to do. 24 Now Abraham was 99 years old when he was circumcised; 25 his son Ishmael was thirteen years old when he was
circumcised. 26 Abraham and his son Ishmael were circumcised
on the very same day. 27 All the men of his household, whether
born in his household or bought with money from a foreigner,
were circumcised with him.

THREE SPECIAL VISITORS

18 The LORD appeared to Abraham by the oaks of Mamre while
he was sitting at the entrance to his tent during the hottest
time of the day. 2 Abraham looked up and saw three men standing across from him. When he saw them he ran from the entrance of the tent to meet them and bowed low to the ground.
3 He said, "My lord, if I have found favor in your sight, do not
pass by and leave your servant. 4 Let a little water be brought so
that you may all wash your feet and rest under the tree. 5 And
let me get a bit of food so that you may refresh yourselves since
you have passed by your servant's home. After that you may be
on your way." "All right," they replied, "you may do as you say."
6 So Abraham hurried into the tent and said to Sarah, "Quick!
Take three measures of fine flour, knead it, and make bread."
7 Then Abraham ran to the herd and chose a fine, tender calf,
and gave it to a servant, who quickly prepared it. 8 Abraham then
took some curds and milk, along with the calf that had been prepared, and placed the food before them. They ate while he was
standing near them under a tree.
9 Then they asked him, "Where is Sarah your wife?" He replied,
"There, in the tent." 10 One of them said, "I will surely return to
you when the season comes round again, and your wife Sarah
will have a son!" (Now Sarah was listening at the entrance to the
tent, not far behind him. 11 Abraham and Sarah were old and advancing in years; Sarah had long since passed menopause.) 12 So
Sarah laughed to herself, thinking, "After I am worn out will I
have pleasure, especially when my husband is old too?"
13 The LORD said to Abraham, "Why did Sarah laugh and say,

LOVE TO GROW

IS ANYTHING IMPOSSIBLE?

GENESIS 18:9–15

Infertility.

It is painful, emotionally draining, and all-consuming. Many women wait all their lives to have children, only to be met with the bitter disappointment of infertility. A number of women in the Bible experienced infertility: Sarah (Gen 18), Rachel (Gen 30), Manoah's wife (Judg 13), Hannah (1 Sam 1), and Michel (2 Sam 6).

Sarah was ninety years old before she had a child. Perhaps by then, she had resigned herself to the fact that she was never going to be a mother. In her impatience and desperation, she gave her maidservant to her husband to try to conceive a child. Still, the promise for her own child from her own womb remained.

"Is anything impossible for the LORD?" (Gen 18:14).

Sarah was faced with this question. She may have believed it in her head, but she doubted it in her heart. Maybe she didn't think anything was impossible for God. Maybe she thought the unchangeable God had decided not to give her a child.

"Is anything impossible for the LORD?" (Gen 18:14).

The answer is, "Of course not!" The Lord can do anything according to His will. He can heal bodies in ways that baffle doctors. He can give children to couples who never thought it was possible. He can give us the one thing we long for in a package that far exceeds our expectations.

God can give real joy and contentment in the midst of great disappointment. A barren womb conceiving a baby can seem like an impossibility, but, with God, nothing is impossible. His power is stronger than any suffering. He heals the sick, raises the dead, and changes the hearts of sinners. He creates something out of nothing. He can bring contentment and joy to the brokenhearted.

Draw close to Him. Trust the promises in His Word. Go to Him with your hurts and frustrations in prayer and praise Him through the tears. He is faithful. He is worthy.

When we put our hope in Him, we can expect what we may have thought was impossible. Wait confidently for God to work in your life. He will bring you joy deep in your heart and contentment that rests on the assurance of His goodness.

'Will I really have a child when I am old?' [14]Is anything impossible for the LORD? I will return to you when the season comes
round again and Sarah will have a son." [15]Then Sarah lied, saying, "I did not laugh," because she was afraid. But the LORD said,
"No! You did laugh."

ABRAHAM PLEADS FOR SODOM

[16]When the men got up to leave, they looked out over Sodom.
(Now Abraham was walking with them to see them on their way.)
[17]Then the LORD said, "Should I hide from Abraham what I am
about to do? [18]After all, Abraham will surely become a great and
powerful nation, and all the nations on the earth may receive
blessing through him. [19]I have chosen him so that he may command his children and his household after him to keep the way
of the LORD by doing what is right and just. Then the LORD will
give to Abraham what he promised him."

[20]So the LORD said, "The outcry against Sodom and Gomorrah is so great and their sin so blatant [21]that I must go down
and see if they are as wicked as the outcry suggests. If not, I
want to know."

[22]The two men turned and headed toward Sodom, but Abraham was still standing before the LORD. [23]Abraham approached
and said, "Will you really sweep away the godly along with the
wicked? [24]What if there are fifty godly people in the city? Will
you really wipe it out and not spare the place for the sake of the
fifty godly people who are in it? [25]Far be it from you to do such
a thing—to kill the godly with the wicked, treating the godly and
the wicked alike! Far be it from you! Will not the judge of the
whole earth do what is right?"

[26]So the LORD replied, "If I find in the city of Sodom fifty godly
people, I will spare the whole place for their sake."

[27]Then Abraham asked, "Since I have undertaken to speak to
the Lord (although I am but dust and ashes), [28]what if there are
five less than the fifty godly people? Will you destroy the whole
city because five are lacking?" He replied, "I will not destroy it
if I find forty-five there."

[29]Abraham spoke to him again, "What if forty are found there?"
He replied, "I will not do it for the sake of the forty."

[30]Then Abraham said, "May the Lord not be angry so that I
may speak! What if thirty are found there?" He replied, "I will
not do it if I find thirty there."

[31]Abraham said, "Since I have undertaken to speak to the Lord,
what if only twenty are found there?" He replied, "I will not destroy it for the sake of the twenty."

[32]Finally Abraham said, "May the Lord not be angry so that I
may speak just once more. What if ten are found there?" He replied, "I will not destroy it for the sake of the ten."

[33]The LORD went on his way when he had finished speaking
to Abraham. Then Abraham returned home.

THE DESTRUCTION OF SODOM AND GOMORRAH

19 The two angels came to Sodom in the evening while Lot was
sitting in the city's gateway. When Lot saw them, he got up
to meet them and bowed down with his face toward the ground.

GOD'S HEART FOR THE NATIONS

Genesis 18:18

"After all, Abraham will surely become a great and powerful nation, and all the nations on the earth may receive blessing through him."

2 He said, "Here, my lords, please turn aside to your servant's
house. Stay the night and wash your feet. Then you can be on
your way early in the morning." "No," they replied, "we'll spend
the night in the town square."
3 But he urged them persistently, so they turned aside with
him and entered his house. He prepared a feast for them, including bread baked without yeast, and they ate. 4 Before they
could lie down to sleep, all the men—both young and old, from
every part of the city of Sodom—surrounded the house. 5 They
shouted to Lot, "Where are the men who came to you tonight?
Bring them out to us so we can take carnal knowledge of them!"
6 Lot went outside to them, shutting the door behind him.
7 He said, "No, my brothers! Don't act so wickedly! 8 Look, I have
two daughters who have never been intimate with a man. Let
me bring them out to you, and you can do to them whatever
you please. Only don't do anything to these men, for they have
come under the protection of my roof."
9 "Out of our way!" they cried, "This man came to live here as a
foreigner, and now he dares to judge us! We'll do more harm to
you than to them!" They kept pressing in on Lot until they were
close enough to break down the door.
10 So the men inside reached out and pulled Lot back into the
house as they shut the door. 11 Then they struck the men who
were at the door of the house, from the youngest to the oldest,
with blindness. The men outside wore themselves out trying to
find the door. 12 Then the two visitors said to Lot, "Who else do
you have here? Do you have any sons-in-law, sons, daughters, or
other relatives in the city? Get them out of this place 13 because
we are about to destroy it. The outcry against this place is so great
before the LORD that he has sent us to destroy it."
14 Then Lot went out and spoke to his sons-in-law who were going to marry his daughters. He said, "Quick, get out of this place
because the LORD is about to destroy the city!" But his sons-in-
law thought he was ridiculing them.
15 At dawn the angels hurried Lot along, saying, "Get going! Take
your wife and your two daughters who are here, or else you will
be destroyed when the city is judged!" 16 When Lot hesitated, the
men grabbed his hand and the hands of his wife and two daughters because the LORD had compassion on them. They led them
away and placed them outside the city. 17 When they had brought
them outside, they said, "Run for your lives! Don't look behind
you or stop anywhere in the valley! Escape to the mountains or
you will be destroyed!"
18 But Lot said to them, "No, please, Lord! 19 Your servant has
found favor with you, and you have shown me great kindness
by sparing my life. But I am not able to escape to the mountains because this disaster will overtake me and I'll die. 20 Look,
this town over here is close enough to escape to, and it's just a
little one. Let me go there. It's just a little place, isn't it? Then
I'll survive."
21 "Very well," he replied, "I will grant this request too and will
not overthrow the town you mentioned. 22 Run there quickly,
for I cannot do anything until you arrive there." (This incident
explains why the town was called Zoar.)

23 The sun had just risen over the land as Lot reached Zoar.
24 Then the LORD rained down sulfur and fire on Sodom and
Gomorrah. It was sent down from the sky by the LORD. 25 So he
overthrew those cities and all that region, including all the inhabitants of the cities and the vegetation that grew from the
ground. 26 But Lot's wife looked back longingly and was turned
into a pillar of salt.

27 Abraham got up early in the morning and went to the place
where he had stood before the LORD. 28 He looked out toward
Sodom and Gomorrah and all the land of that region. As he did
so, he saw the smoke rising up from the land like smoke from
a furnace.

29 So when God destroyed the cities of the region, God honored Abraham's request. He removed Lot from the midst of the
destruction when he destroyed the cities Lot had lived in.

30 Lot went up from Zoar with his two daughters and settled
in the mountains because he was afraid to live in Zoar. So he
lived in a cave with his two daughters. 31 Later the older daughter said to the younger, "Our father is old, and there is no man
in the country to sleep with us, the way everyone does. 32 Come,
let's make our father drunk with wine so we can go to bed with
him and preserve our family line through our father."

33 So that night they made their father drunk with wine, and
the older daughter came in and went to bed with her father. But
he was not aware of when she lay down with him or when she got
up. 34 So in the morning the older daughter said to the younger,
"Since I went to bed with my father last night, let's make him
drunk again tonight. Then you go in and go to bed with him so
we can preserve our family line through our father." 35 So they
made their father drunk that night as well, and the younger one
came and went to bed with him. But he was not aware of when
she lay down with him or when she got up.

36 In this way both of Lot's daughters became pregnant by their
father. 37 The older daughter gave birth to a son and named him
Moab. He is the ancestor of the Moabites of today. 38 The younger daughter also gave birth to a son and named him Ben Ammi.
He is the ancestor of the Ammonites of today.

ABRAHAM AND ABIMELECH

20 Abraham journeyed from there to the Negev region and
settled between Kadesh and Shur. While he lived as a temporary resident in Gerar, 2 Abraham said about his wife Sarah,
"She is my sister." So Abimelech, king of Gerar, sent for Sarah
and took her.

3 But God appeared to Abimelech in a dream at night and said
to him, "You are as good as dead because of the woman you have
taken, for she is someone else's wife."

4 Now Abimelech had not gone near her. He said, "Lord, would
you really slaughter an innocent nation? 5 Did Abraham not say
to me, 'She is my sister'? And she herself said, 'He is my brother.' I
have done this with a clear conscience and with innocent hands!"

6 Then in the dream God replied to him, "Yes, I know that you
have done this with a clear conscience. That is why I have kept
you from sinning against me and why I did not allow you to

touch her. 7 But now give back the man's wife. Indeed he is a
prophet and he will pray for you; thus you will live. But if you
don't give her back, know that you will surely die along with all
who belong to you."

8 Early in the morning Abimelech summoned all his servants.
When he told them about all these things, they were terrified.
9 Abimelech summoned Abraham and said to him, "What have
you done to us? What sin did I commit against you that would
cause you to bring such great guilt on me and my kingdom? You
have done things to me that should not be done!" 10 Then Abimelech asked Abraham, "What prompted you to do this thing?"

11 Abraham replied, "Because I thought, 'Surely no one fears
God in this place. They will kill me because of my wife.' 12 What's
more, she is indeed my sister, my father's daughter, but not my
mother's daughter. She became my wife. 13 When God made me
wander from my father's house, I told her, 'This is what you can
do to show your loyalty to me: Every place we go, say about me,
"He is my brother."'"

14 So Abimelech gave sheep, cattle, and male and female servants to Abraham. He also gave his wife Sarah back to him. 15 Then
Abimelech said, "Look, my land is before you; live wherever you
please."

16 To Sarah he said, "Look, I have given 1,000 pieces of silver
to your 'brother.' This is compensation for you so that you will
stand vindicated before all who are with you."

17 Abraham prayed to God, and God healed Abimelech, as well
as his wife and female slaves so that they were able to have
children. 18 For the LORD had caused infertility to strike every
woman in the household of Abimelech because he took Sarah,
Abraham's wife.

THE BIRTH OF ISAAC

21 The LORD visited Sarah just as he had said he would and did
for Sarah what he had promised. 2 So Sarah became pregnant and bore Abraham a son in his old age at the appointed
time that God had told him. 3 Abraham named his son—whom
Sarah bore to him—Isaac. 4 When his son Isaac was eight days
old, Abraham circumcised him just as God had commanded him
to do. 5 (Now Abraham was 100 years old when his son Isaac was
born to him.)

6 Sarah said, "God has made me laugh. Everyone who hears
about this will laugh with me." 7 She went on to say, "Who would
have said to Abraham that Sarah would nurse children? Yet I
have given birth to a son for him in his old age!"

8 The child grew and was weaned. Abraham prepared a great
feast on the day that Isaac was weaned. 9 But Sarah noticed the
son of Hagar the Egyptian—the son whom Hagar had borne to
Abraham—mocking. 10 So she said to Abraham, "Banish that slave
woman and her son, for the son of that slave woman will not be
an heir along with my son Isaac!"

11 Sarah's demand displeased Abraham greatly because Ishmael was his son. 12 But God said to Abraham, "Do not be upset
about the boy or your slave wife. Do all that Sarah is telling you
because through Isaac your descendants will be counted. 13 But

I will also make the son of the slave wife into a great nation, for
he is your descendant too."
14 Early in the morning Abraham took some food and a skin of
water and gave them to Hagar. He put them on her shoulders,
gave her the child, and sent her away. So she went wandering
aimlessly through the wilderness of Beer Sheba. 15 When the water in the skin was gone, she shoved the child under one of the
shrubs. 16 Then she went and sat down by herself across from
him at quite a distance, about a bowshot, away; for she thought,
"I refuse to watch the child die." So she sat across from him and
wept uncontrollably.
17 But God heard the boy's voice. The angel of God called to
Hagar from heaven and asked her, "What is the matter, Hagar?
Don't be afraid, for God has heard the boy's voice right where he
is crying. 18 Get up! Help the boy up and hold him by the hand,
for I will make him into a great nation." 19 Then God enabled Hagar to see a well of water. She went over and filled the skin with
water, and then gave the boy a drink.
20 God was with the boy as he grew. He lived in the wilderness
and became an archer. 21 He lived in the wilderness of Paran. His
mother found a wife for him from the land of Egypt.
22 At that time Abimelech and Phicol, the commander of
his army, said to Abraham, "God is with you in all that you do.
23 Now swear to me right here in God's name that you will not
deceive me, my children, or my descendants. Show me, and
the land where you are staying, the same loyalty that I have
shown you."
24 Abraham said, "I swear to do this." 25 But Abraham lodged
a complaint against Abimelech concerning a well that Abimelech's servants had seized. 26 "I do not know who has done this
thing," Abimelech replied. "Moreover, you did not tell me. I did
not hear about it until today."
27 Abraham took some sheep and cattle and gave them to
Abimelech. The two of them made a treaty. 28 Then Abraham
set seven ewe lambs apart from the flock by themselves. 29 Abimelech asked Abraham, "What is the meaning of these seven ewe
lambs that you have set apart?" 30 He replied, "You must take
these seven ewe lambs from my hand as legal proof that I dug
this well." 31 That is why he named that place Beer Sheba, because
the two of them swore an oath there.
32 So they made a treaty at Beer Sheba; then Abimelech and
Phicol, the commander of his army, returned to the land of the
Philistines. 33 Abraham planted a tamarisk tree in Beer Sheba.
There he worshiped the LORD, the eternal God. 34 So Abraham
stayed in the land of the Philistines for quite some time.

THE SACRIFICE OF ISAAC

22 Some time after these things God tested Abraham.
He said to him, "Abraham!" "Here I am!" Abraham replied. 2 God said, "Take your son—your only son, whom you love,
Isaac—and go to the land of Moriah! Offer him up there as a burnt
offering on one of the mountains which I will indicate to you."
3 Early in the morning Abraham got up and saddled his donkey. He took two of his young servants with him, along with his

son Isaac. When he had cut the wood for the burnt offering, he
started out for the place God had spoken to him about.
4 On the third day Abraham caught sight of the place in the
distance. 5 So he said to his servants, "You two stay here with
the donkey while the boy and I go up there. We will worship and
then return to you."
6 Abraham took the wood for the burnt offering and put it on
his son Isaac. Then he took the fire and the knife in his hand,
and the two of them walked on together. 7 Isaac said to his father
Abraham, "My father?" "What is it, my son?" he replied. "Here
is the fire and the wood," Isaac said, "but where is the lamb for
the burnt offering?" 8 "God will provide for himself the lamb for
the burnt offering, my son," Abraham replied. The two of them
continued on together.
9 When they came to the place God had told him about, Abraham built the altar there and arranged the wood on it. Next he
tied up his son Isaac and placed him on the altar on top of the
wood. 10 Then Abraham reached out his hand, took the knife,
and prepared to slaughter his son. 11 But the angel of the LORD
called to him from heaven, "Abraham! Abraham!" "Here I am!"
he answered. 12 "Do not harm the boy!" the angel said. "Do not do
anything to him, for now I know that you fear God because you
did not withhold your son, your only son, from me."
13 Abraham looked up and saw behind him a ram caught in
the bushes by its horns. So he went over and got the ram and offered it up as a burnt offering instead of his son. 14 And Abraham
called the name of that place "The LORD provides." It is said to
this day, "In the mountain of the LORD provision will be made."
15 The angel of the LORD called to Abraham a second time from
heaven 16 and said, "I solemnly swear by my own name, decrees
the LORD, that because you have done this and have not withheld your son, your only son, 17 I will indeed bless you, and I will
greatly multiply your descendants so that they will be as countless as the stars in the sky or the grains of sand on the seashore.
Your descendants will take possession of the strongholds of their
enemies. 18 Because you have obeyed me, all the nations of the
earth will pronounce blessings on one another using the name
of your descendants."
19 Then Abraham returned to his servants, and they set out together for Beer Sheba where Abraham stayed.
20 After these things Abraham was told, "Milcah also has borne
children to your brother Nahor—21 Uz the firstborn, his brother
Buz, Kemuel (the father of Aram), 22 Kesed, Hazo, Pildash, Jidlaph,
and Bethuel." 23 (Now Bethuel became the father of Rebekah.)
These were the eight sons Milcah bore to Abraham's brother Nahor. 24 His concubine, whose name was Reumah, also bore him
children—Tebah, Gaham, Tahash, and Maacah.

THE DEATH OF SARAH

23 Sarah lived 127 years. 2 Then she died in Kiriath Arba
(that is, Hebron) in the land of Canaan. Abraham went
to mourn for Sarah and to weep for her.
3 Then Abraham got up from mourning his dead wife and said
to the sons of Heth, 4 "I am a foreign resident, a temporary settler,

LOVE TO GROW

JEHOVAH JIREH

GENESIS 22:1–19

God's name is Jehovah-Jireh: The Lord Provides.

There are some stories in the Bible that make me a little uneasy. This story is one of them. I struggle with the idea of Abraham willingly sacrificing Isaac. The thought makes my stomach turn and my mind spin. It's unnatural. It's cruel. Even though it is central to the gospel message, we don't like to talk about sacrifice, much less make it personal. Yet personal is right where God goes.

Abraham treasured Isaac. He was the son of promise. He was the one whom God had promised would become a great nation. He was the offspring of Abraham and Sarah, the sign of God's covenant with Abraham.

God said, "Take your son—your only son, whom you love, Isaac—and go to the land of Moriah! Offer him up there as a burnt offering on one of the mountains which I will indicate to you" (Gen 22:2).

God told Abraham to sacrifice Isaac. He calls us to do the same. Whatever the "Isaac" is in our lives, nothing and no one should take the place of God in our hearts. Our earthly things are poor substitutes. Only God can fill our needs. We have all fallen for the lie that we know what's better for us than God does. We struggle because, at the heart of the matter, we don't trust God to provide.

We fear He's not as faithful or as trustworthy as He claims to be. We fear He won't provide for our needs. We fear He won't come through for us. We fear the sacrifice required by our obedience.

Abraham trusted God would live up to His name: Jehovah Jireh, The Lord Provides. He told his servants: "We will worship and then return to you" (Gen 22:5).

Abraham, like all of us, was a work in progress. There were plenty of times he didn't trust God (see Gen 12:10–20; 16:1–16; 20:1–18). Yet even in Abraham's disobedience, God was faithful and used those experiences to grow and refine his faith. Through both obedience and disobedience, Abraham learned to trust God.

Jehovah Jireh. The Lord Provides. No matter the circumstance, He provides. We can trust Him.

among you. Grant me ownership of a burial site among you so that I may bury my dead."

5 The sons of Heth answered Abraham, 6 "Listen, sir, you are a mighty prince among us! You may bury your dead in the choicest of our tombs. None of us will refuse you his tomb to prevent you from burying your dead."

7 Abraham got up and bowed down to the local people, the sons of Heth. 8 Then he said to them, "If you agree that I may bury my dead, then hear me out. Ask Ephron the son of Zohar 9 if he will sell me the cave of Machpelah that belongs to him; it is at the end of his field. Let him sell it to me publicly for the full price, so that I may own it as a burial site."

10 (Now Ephron was sitting among the sons of Heth.) Ephron the Hittite replied to Abraham in the hearing of the sons of Heth—before all who entered the gate of his city—11 "No, my lord! Hear me out. I sell you both the field and the cave that is in it. In the presence of my people I sell it to you. Bury your dead."

12 Abraham bowed before the local people 13 and said to Ephron in their hearing, "Hear me, if you will. I pay to you the price of the field. Take it from me so that I may bury my dead there."

14 Ephron answered Abraham, saying to him, 15 "Hear me, my lord. The land is worth 400 pieces of silver, but what is that between me and you? So bury your dead."

16 So Abraham agreed to Ephron's price and weighed out for him the price that Ephron had quoted in the hearing of the sons of Heth—400 pieces of silver, according to the standard measurement at the time.

17 So Abraham secured Ephron's field in Machpelah, next to Mamre, including the field, the cave that was in it, and all the trees that were in the field and all around its border, 18 as his property in the presence of the sons of Heth before all who entered the gate of Ephron's city.

19 After this Abraham buried his wife Sarah in the cave in the field of Machpelah next to Mamre (that is, Hebron) in the land of Canaan. 20 So Abraham secured the field and the cave that was in it as a burial site from the sons of Heth.

THE WIFE FOR ISAAC

24 Now Abraham was old, well advanced in years, and the LORD had blessed him in everything. 2 Abraham said to his servant, the senior one in his household who was in charge of everything he had, "Put your hand under my thigh 3 so that I may make you solemnly promise by the LORD, the God of heaven and the God of the earth: You must not acquire a wife for my son from the daughters of the Canaanites, among whom I am living. 4 You must go instead to my country and to my relatives to find a wife for my son Isaac."

5 The servant asked him, "What if the woman is not willing to come back with me to this land? Must I then take your son back to the land from which you came?"

6 "Be careful never to take my son back there!" Abraham told him. 7 "The LORD, the God of heaven, who took me from my father's house and the land of my relatives, promised me with a solemn oath, 'To your descendants I will give this land.' He will

send his angel before you so that you may find a wife for my son
from there. 8 But if the woman is not willing to come back with
you, you will be free from this oath of mine. But you must not
take my son back there!" 9 So the servant placed his hand under
the thigh of his master Abraham and gave his solemn promise
he would carry out his wishes.

10 Then the servant took ten of his master's camels and departed
with all kinds of gifts from his master at his disposal. He journeyed to the region of Aram Naharaim and the city of Nahor. 11 He
made the camels kneel down by the well outside the city. It was
evening, the time when the women would go out to draw water.
12 He prayed, "O LORD, God of my master Abraham, guide me today.
Be faithful to my master Abraham. 13 Here I am, standing by the
spring, and the daughters of the people who live in the town are
coming out to draw water. 14 I will say to a young woman, 'Please
lower your jar so I may drink.' May the one you have chosen for
your servant Isaac reply, 'Drink, and I'll give your camels water too.'
In this way I will know that you have been faithful to my master."

15 Before he had finished praying, there came Rebekah with
her water jug on her shoulder. She was the daughter of Bethuel
son of Milcah (Milcah was the wife of Abraham's brother Nahor).
16 Now the young woman was very beautiful. She was a virgin;
no man had ever been physically intimate with her. She went
down to the spring, filled her jug, and came back up. 17 Abraham's
servant ran to meet her and said, "Please give me a sip of water
from your jug." 18 "Drink, my lord," she replied, and quickly lowering her jug to her hands, she gave him a drink. 19 When she had
done so, she said, "I'll draw water for your camels too, until they
have drunk as much as they want." 20 She quickly emptied her
jug into the watering trough and ran back to the well to draw
more water until she had drawn enough for all his camels. 21 Silently the man watched her with interest to determine if the
LORD had made his journey successful or not.

22 After the camels had finished drinking, the man took out
a gold nose ring weighing a beka and two gold wrist bracelets
weighing ten shekels and gave them to her. 23 "Whose daughter
are you?" he asked. "Tell me, is there room in your father's house
for us to spend the night?"

24 She said to him, "I am the daughter of Bethuel the son of
Milcah, whom Milcah bore to Nahor. 25 We have plenty of straw
and feed," she added, "and room for you to spend the night."

26 The man bowed his head and worshiped the LORD, 27 saying,
"Praised be the LORD, the God of my master Abraham, who has
not abandoned his faithful love for my master! The LORD has
led me to the house of my master's relatives!"

28 The young woman ran and told her mother's household all
about these things. 29 (Now Rebekah had a brother named Laban.) Laban rushed out to meet the man at the spring. 30 When
he saw the bracelets on his sister's wrists and the nose ring and
heard his sister Rebekah say, "This is what the man said to me,"
he went out to meet the man. There he was, standing by the
camels near the spring. 31 Laban said to him, "Come, you who
are blessed by the LORD! Why are you standing out here when I
have prepared the house and a place for the camels?"

32 So Abraham's servant went to the house and unloaded the
camels. Straw and feed were given to the camels, and water was
provided so that he and the men who were with him could wash
their feet. 33 When food was served, he said, "I will not eat until I
have said what I want to say." "Tell us," Laban said.
34 "I am the servant of Abraham," he began. 35 "The LORD has
richly blessed my master and he has become very wealthy. The
LORD has given him sheep and cattle, silver and gold, male and
female servants, and camels and donkeys. 36 My master's wife
Sarah bore a son to him when she was old, and my master has
given him everything he owns. 37 My master made me swear an
oath. He said, 'You must not acquire a wife for my son from the
daughters of the Canaanites, among whom I am living, 38 but you
must go to the family of my father and to my relatives to find a
wife for my son.' 39 But I said to my master, 'What if the woman
does not want to go with me?' 40 He answered, 'The LORD, before
whom I have walked, will send his angel with you. He will make
your journey a success and you will find a wife for my son from
among my relatives, from my father's family. 41 You will be free
from your oath if you go to my relatives and they will not give her
to you. Then you will be free from your oath.' 42 When I came to
the spring today, I prayed, 'O LORD, God of my master Abraham,
if you have decided to make my journey successful, may events
unfold as follows: 43 Here I am, standing by the spring. When the
young woman goes out to draw water, I'll say, "Please give me a
little water to drink from your jug." 44 Then she will reply to me,
"Drink, and I'll draw water for your camels too." May that woman be the one whom the LORD has chosen for my master's son.'
45 "Before I finished praying in my heart, along came Rebekah
with her water jug on her shoulder! She went down to the spring
and drew water. So I said to her, 'Please give me a drink.' 46 She
quickly lowered her jug from her shoulder and said, 'Drink, and
I'll give your camels water too.' So I drank, and she also gave the
camels water. 47 Then I asked her, 'Whose daughter are you?' She
replied, 'The daughter of Bethuel the son of Nahor, whom Milcah
bore to Nahor.' I put the ring in her nose and the bracelets on her
wrists. 48 Then I bowed down and worshiped the LORD. I praised
the LORD, the God of my master Abraham, who had led me on
the right path to find the granddaughter of my master's brother for his son. 49 Now, if you will show faithful love to my master,
tell me. But if not, tell me as well, so that I may go on my way."
50 Then Laban and Bethuel replied, "This is the LORD's doing.
Our wishes are of no concern. 51 Rebekah stands here before you.
Take her and go so that she may become the wife of your master's son, just as the LORD has decided."
52 When Abraham's servant heard their words, he bowed down
to the ground before the LORD. 53 Then he brought out gold, silver jewelry, and clothing and gave them to Rebekah. He also
gave valuable gifts to her brother and to her mother. 54 After
this, he and the men who were with him ate a meal and stayed
there overnight.

When they got up in the morning, he said, "Let me leave now
so I can return to my master." 55 But Rebekah's brother and
her mother replied, "Let the girl stay with us a few more days,

perhaps ten. Then she can go." 56 But he said to them, "Don't de-
tain me—the LORD has granted me success on my journey. Let
me leave now so I may return to my master." 57 Then they said,
"We'll call the girl and find out what she wants to do." 58 So they
called Rebekah and asked her, "Do you want to go with this man?"
She replied, "I want to go."
59 So they sent their sister Rebekah on her way, accompanied
by her female attendant, with Abraham's servant and his men.
60 They blessed Rebekah with these words:

"Our sister, may you become the mother
of thousands of ten thousands!
May your descendants possess the
strongholds of their enemies."

61 Then Rebekah and her female servants mounted the camels and rode away with the man. So Abraham's servant took Rebekah and left.
62 Now Isaac came from Beer Lahai Roi, for he was living in the
Negev. 63 He went out to relax in the field in the early evening.
Then he looked up and saw that there were camels approaching. 64 Rebekah looked up and saw Isaac. She got down from her
camel 65 and asked Abraham's servant, "Who is that man walking in the field toward us?" "That is my master," the servant replied. So she took her veil and covered herself.
66 The servant told Isaac everything that had happened. 67 Then
Isaac brought Rebekah into his mother Sarah's tent. He took
her as his wife and loved her. So Isaac was comforted after his
mother's death.

THE DEATH OF ABRAHAM

25 Abraham had taken another wife, named Keturah. 2 She
bore him Zimran, Jokshan, Medan, Midian, Ishbak, and
Shuah. 3 Jokshan became the father of Sheba and Dedan. The descendants of Dedan were the Asshurites, Letushites, and Leum-
mites. 4 The sons of Midian were Ephah, Epher, Hanoch, Abida,
and Eldaah. All these were descendants of Keturah.
5 Everything he owned Abraham left to his son Isaac. 6 But
while he was still alive, Abraham gave gifts to the sons of his concubines and sent them off to the east, away from his son Isaac.
7 Abraham lived a total of 175 years. 8 Then Abraham breathed
his last and died at a good old age, an old man who had lived a
full life. He joined his ancestors. 9 His sons Isaac and Ishmael
buried him in the cave of Machpelah near Mamre, in the field
of Ephron the son of Zohar, the Hittite. 10 This was the field Abraham had purchased from the sons of Heth. There Abraham was
buried with his wife Sarah. 11 After Abraham's death, God blessed
his son Isaac. Isaac lived near Beer Lahai Roi.

THE SONS OF ISHMAEL

12 This is the account of Abraham's son Ishmael, whom Hagar the
Egyptian, Sarah's servant, bore to Abraham.
13 These are the names of Ishmael's sons, by their names according to their records: Nebaioth (Ishmael's firstborn), Kedar,
Adbeel, Mibsam, 14 Mishma, Dumah, Massa, 15 Hadad, Tema,

Jetur, Naphish, and Kedemah. 16 These are the sons of Ishmael, and these are their names by their settlements and their camps—twelve princes according to their clans.

17 Ishmael lived a total of 137 years. He breathed his last and died; then he joined his ancestors. 18 His descendants settled from Havilah to Shur, which runs next to Egypt all the way to Asshur. They settled away from all their relatives.

JACOB AND ESAU

19 This is the account of Isaac, the son of Abraham.

Abraham became the father of Isaac. 20 When Isaac was forty years old, he married Rebekah, the daughter of Bethuel the Aramean from Paddan Aram and sister of Laban the Aramean.

21 Isaac prayed to the LORD on behalf of his wife because she was childless. The LORD answered his prayer, and his wife Rebekah became pregnant. 22 But the children struggled inside her, and she said, "Why is this happening to me?" So she asked the LORD, 23 and the LORD said to her,

"Two nations are in your womb,
and two peoples will be separated from within you.
One people will be stronger than the other,
and the older will serve the younger."

24 When the time came for Rebekah to give birth, there were twins in her womb. 25 The first came out reddish all over, like a hairy garment, so they named him Esau. 26 When his brother came out with his hand clutching Esau's heel, they named him Jacob. Isaac was sixty years old when they were born.

27 When the boys grew up, Esau became a skilled hunter, a man of the open fields, but Jacob was an even-tempered man, living in tents. 28 Isaac loved Esau because he had a taste for fresh game, but Rebekah loved Jacob.

29 Now Jacob cooked some stew, and when Esau came in from the open fields, he was famished. 30 So Esau said to Jacob, "Feed me some of the red stuff—yes, this red stuff—because I'm starving!" (That is why he was also called Edom.)

31 But Jacob replied, "First sell me your birthright." 32 "Look," said Esau, "I'm about to die! What use is the birthright to me?" 33 But Jacob said, "Swear an oath to me now." So Esau swore an oath to him and sold his birthright to Jacob.

34 Then Jacob gave Esau some bread and lentil stew; Esau ate and drank, then got up and went out. So Esau despised his birthright.

ISAAC AND ABIMELECH

26 There was a famine in the land, subsequent to the earlier famine that occurred in the days of Abraham. Isaac went to Abimelech king of the Philistines at Gerar. 2 The LORD appeared to Isaac and said, "Do not go down to Egypt; settle down in the land that I will point out to you. 3 Stay in this land. Then I will be with you and will bless you, for I will give all these lands to you and to your descendants, and I will fulfill the solemn promise I made to your father Abraham. 4 I will multiply your descendants so they will be as numerous as the stars in the

sky, and I will give them all these lands. All the nations of the
earth will pronounce blessings on one another using the name
of your descendants. [5]All this will come to pass because Abraham obeyed me and kept my charge, my commandments, my
statutes, and my laws." [6]So Isaac settled in Gerar.

[7]When the men of that place asked him about his wife, he replied, "She is my sister." He was afraid to say, "She is my wife,"
for he thought to himself, "The men of this place will kill me to
get Rebekah because she is very beautiful."

[8]After Isaac had been there a long time, Abimelech king of
the Philistines happened to look out a window and observed
Isaac caressing his wife Rebekah. [9]So Abimelech summoned
Isaac and said, "She is really your wife! Why did you say, 'She is
my sister'?" Isaac replied, "Because I thought someone might
kill me to get her."

[10]Then Abimelech exclaimed, "What in the world have you
done to us? One of the men nearly took your wife to bed, and you
would have brought guilt on us!" [11]So Abimelech commanded all
the people, "Whoever touches this man or his wife will surely
be put to death."

[12]When Isaac planted in that land, he reaped in the same year
a hundred times what he had sown, because the LORD blessed
him. [13]The man became wealthy. His influence continued to
grow until he became very prominent. [14]He had so many sheep
and cattle and such a great household of servants that the Philistines became jealous of him. [15]So the Philistines took dirt and
filled up all the wells that his father's servants had dug back in
the days of his father Abraham.

[16]Then Abimelech said to Isaac, "Leave us and go elsewhere, for
you have become much more powerful than we are." [17]So Isaac
left there and settled in the Gerar Valley. [18]Isaac reopened the
wells that had been dug back in the days of his father Abraham,
for the Philistines had stopped them up after Abraham died.
Isaac gave these wells the same names his father had given them.

[19]When Isaac's servants dug in the valley and discovered a well
with fresh flowing water there, [20]the herdsmen of Gerar quarreled with Isaac's herdsmen, saying, "The water belongs to us!" So
Isaac named the well Esek because they argued with him about
it. [21]His servants dug another well, but they quarreled over it too,
so Isaac named it Sitnah. [22]Then he moved away from there and
dug another well. They did not quarrel over it, so Isaac named
it Rehoboth, saying, "For now the LORD has made room for us,
and we will prosper in the land."

[23]From there Isaac went up to Beer Sheba. [24]The LORD appeared to him that night and said, "I am the God of your father
Abraham. Do not be afraid, for I am with you. I will bless you and
multiply your descendants for the sake of my servant Abraham."
[25]Then Isaac built an altar there and worshiped the LORD. He
pitched his tent there, and his servants dug a well.

[26]Now Abimelech had come to him from Gerar along with
Ahuzzah his friend and Phicol the commander of his army.
[27]Isaac asked them, "Why have you come to me? You hate me
and sent me away from you." [28]They replied, "We could plainly
see that the LORD is with you. So we decided there should be a

pact between us—between us and you. Allow us to make a treaty
with you 29 so that you will not do us any harm, just as we have
not harmed you, but have always treated you well before sending you away in peace. Now you are blessed by the LORD."
30 So Isaac held a feast for them and they celebrated. 31 Early in
the morning the men made a treaty with each other. Isaac sent
them off; they separated on good terms.
32 That day Isaac's servants came and told him about the well
they had dug. "We've found water," they reported. 33 So he named
it Shibah; that is why the name of the city has been Beer Sheba
to this day.
34 When Esau was forty years old, he married Judith the daughter of Beeri the Hittite, as well as Basemath the daughter of
Elon the Hittite. 35 They caused Isaac and Rebekah great anxiety.

JACOB CHEATS ESAU OUT OF THE BLESSING

27 When Isaac was old and his eyes were so weak that he was
almost blind, he called his older son Esau and said to him,
"My son!" "Here I am!" Esau replied. 2 Isaac said, "Since I am so
old, I could die at any time. 3 Therefore, take your weapons—your
quiver and your bow—and go out into the open fields and hunt
down some wild game for me. 4 Then prepare for me some tasty
food, the kind I love, and bring it to me. Then I will eat it so that
I may bless you before I die."
5 Now Rebekah had been listening while Isaac spoke to his son
Esau. When Esau went out to the open fields to hunt down some
wild game and bring it back, 6 Rebekah said to her son Jacob,
"Look, I overheard your father tell your brother Esau, 7 'Bring me
some wild game and prepare for me some tasty food. Then I will
eat it and bless you in the presence of the LORD before I die.' 8 Now
then, my son, do exactly what I tell you! 9 Go to the flock and get
me two of the best young goats. I'll prepare them in a tasty way
for your father, just the way he loves them. 10 Then you will take
it to your father. Thus he will eat it and bless you before he dies."
11 "But Esau my brother is a hairy man," Jacob protested to his
mother Rebekah, "and I have smooth skin! 12 My father may touch
me! Then he'll think I'm mocking him and I'll bring a curse on
myself instead of a blessing." 13 So his mother told him, "Any
curse against you will fall on me, my son! Just obey me! Go and
get them for me!"
14 So he went and got the goats and brought them to his mother. She prepared some tasty food, just the way his father loved
it. 15 Then Rebekah took her older son Esau's best clothes, which
she had with her in the house, and put them on her younger son
Jacob. 16 She put the skins of the young goats on his hands and
the smooth part of his neck. 17 Then she handed the tasty food
and the bread she had made to her son Jacob.
18 He went to his father and said, "My father!" Isaac replied,
"Here I am. Which are you, my son?" 19 Jacob said to his father,
"I am Esau, your firstborn. I've done as you told me. Now sit up
and eat some of my wild game so that you can bless me." 20 But
Isaac asked his son, "How in the world did you find it so quickly,
my son?" "Because the LORD your God brought it to me," he replied. 21 Then Isaac said to Jacob, "Come closer so I can touch you,

my son, and know for certain if you really are my son Esau." 22 So
Jacob went over to his father Isaac, who felt him and said, "The
voice is Jacob's, but the hands are Esau's." 23 He did not recognize him because his hands were hairy, like his brother Esau's
hands. So Isaac blessed Jacob. 24 Then he asked, "Are you really
my son Esau?" "I am," Jacob replied. 25 Isaac said, "Bring some of
the wild game for me to eat, my son. Then I will bless you." So Jacob brought it to him, and he ate it. He also brought him wine,
and Isaac drank. 26 Then his father Isaac said to him, "Come here
and kiss me, my son." 27 So Jacob went over and kissed him. When
Isaac caught the scent of his clothing, he blessed him, saying,

"Yes, my son smells
like the scent of an open field
which the LORD has blessed.
28 May God give you
the dew of the sky
and the richness of the earth,
and plenty of grain and new wine.
29 May peoples serve you
and nations bow down to you.
You will be lord over your brothers,
and the sons of your mother will bow down to you.
May those who curse you be cursed,
and those who bless you be blessed."

30 Isaac had just finished blessing Jacob, and Jacob had scarcely
left his father's presence, when his brother Esau returned from
the hunt. 31 He also prepared some tasty food and brought it
to his father. Esau said to him, "My father, get up and eat some
of your son's wild game. Then you can bless me." 32 His father
Isaac asked, "Who are you?" "I am your firstborn son," he replied,
"Esau!" 33 Isaac began to shake violently and asked, "Then who
else hunted game and brought it to me? I ate all of it just before you arrived, and I blessed him. He will indeed be blessed!"
34 When Esau heard his father's words, he wailed loudly and
bitterly. He said to his father, "Bless me too, my father!" 35 But
Isaac replied, "Your brother came in here deceitfully and took
away your blessing." 36 Esau exclaimed, "Jacob is the right name
for him! He has tripped me up two times! He took away my birthright, and now, look, he has taken away my blessing!" Then he
asked, "Have you not kept back a blessing for me?"
37 Isaac replied to Esau, "Look! I have made him lord over you.
I have made all his relatives his servants and provided him with
grain and new wine. What is left that I can do for you, my son?"
38 Esau said to his father, "Do you have only that one blessing,
my father? Bless me too!" Then Esau wept loudly.
39 So his father Isaac said to him,

"See here, your home will be by the richness of the earth,
and by the dew of the sky above.
40 You will live by your sword
but you will serve your brother.
When you grow restless,
you will tear off his yoke
from your neck."

41 So Esau hated Jacob because of the blessing his father had
given to his brother. Esau said privately, "The time of mourning
for my father is near; then I will kill my brother Jacob!"
42 When Rebekah heard what her older son Esau had said,
she quickly summoned her younger son Jacob and told him,
"Look, your brother Esau is planning to get revenge by killing
you. 43 Now then, my son, do what I say. Run away immediately
to my brother Laban in Haran. 44 Live with him for a little while
until your brother's rage subsides. 45 Stay there until your brother's anger against you subsides and he forgets what you did to
him. Then I'll send someone to bring you back from there. Why
should I lose both of you in one day?"
46 Then Rebekah said to Isaac, "I am deeply depressed because
of the daughters of Heth. If Jacob were to marry one of these
daughters of Heth who live in this land, I would want to die!"

28 So Isaac called for Jacob and blessed him. Then he commanded him, "You must not marry a Canaanite woman!
2 Leave immediately for Paddan Aram! Go to the house of Bethuel, your mother's father, and find yourself a wife there, among
the daughters of Laban, your mother's brother. 3 May the Sovereign God bless you! May he make you fruitful and give you a
multitude of descendants! Then you will become a large nation.
4 May he give you and your descendants the blessing he gave to
Abraham so that you may possess the land God gave to Abraham,
the land where you have been living as a temporary resident."
5 So Isaac sent Jacob on his way, and he went to Paddan Aram,
to Laban son of Bethuel the Aramean and brother of Rebekah,
the mother of Jacob and Esau.
6 Esau saw that Isaac had blessed Jacob and sent him off to
Paddan Aram to find a wife there. As he blessed him, Isaac commanded him, "You must not marry a Canaanite woman." 7 Jacob
obeyed his father and mother and left for Paddan Aram. 8 Then
Esau realized that the Canaanite women were displeasing to his
father Isaac. 9 So Esau went to Ishmael and married Mahalath,
the sister of Nebaioth and daughter of Abraham's son Ishmael,
along with the wives he already had.

JACOB'S DREAM AT BETHEL

10 Meanwhile Jacob left Beer Sheba and set out for Haran. 11 He
reached a certain place where he decided to camp because
the sun had gone down. He took one of the stones and placed
it near his head. Then he fell asleep in that place 12 and had a
dream. He saw a stairway erected on the earth with its top
reaching to the heavens. The angels of God were going up and
coming down it 13 and the LORD stood at its top. He said, "I am
the LORD, the God of your grandfather Abraham and the God
of your father Isaac. I will give you and your descendants the
ground you are lying on. 14 Your descendants will be like the
dust of the earth, and you will spread out to the west, east,
north, and south. And so all the families of the earth may receive blessings through you and through your descendants.
15 I am with you! I will protect you wherever you go and will
bring you back to this land. I will not leave you until I have
done what I promised you!"

16 Then Jacob woke up and thought, "Surely the LORD is in this
place, but I did not realize it!" 17 He was afraid and said, "What
an awesome place this is! This is nothing else than the house of
God! This is the gate of heaven!"
18 Early in the morning Jacob took the stone he had placed
near his head and set it up as a sacred stone. Then he poured oil
on top of it. 19 He called that place Bethel, although the former
name of the town was Luz. 20 Then Jacob made a vow, saying,
"If God is with me and protects me on this journey I am taking
and gives me food to eat and clothing to wear, 21 and I return
safely to my father's home, then the LORD will become my God.
22 Then this stone that I have set up as a sacred stone will be the
house of God, and I will surely give you back a tenth of everything you give me."

THE MARRIAGES OF JACOB

29 So Jacob moved on and came to the land of the eastern
people. 2 He saw in the field a well with three flocks of
sheep lying beside it, because the flocks were watered from that
well. Now a large stone covered the mouth of the well. 3 When
all the flocks were gathered there, the shepherds would roll the
stone off the mouth of the well and water the sheep. Then they
would put the stone back in its place over the well's mouth.
4 Jacob asked them, "My brothers, where are you from?" They
replied, "We're from Haran." 5 So he said to them, "Do you know
Laban, the grandson of Nahor?" "We know him," they said. 6 "Is
he well?" Jacob asked. They replied, "He is well. Now look, here
comes his daughter Rachel with the sheep." 7 Then Jacob said,
"Since it is still the middle of the day, it is not time for the flocks
to be gathered. You should water the sheep and then go and
let them graze some more." 8 "We can't," they said, "until all the
flocks are gathered and the stone is rolled off the mouth of the
well. Then we water the sheep."
9 While he was still speaking with them, Rachel arrived with
her father's sheep, for she was tending them. 10 When Jacob saw
Rachel, the daughter of his uncle Laban, and the sheep of his
uncle Laban, he went over and rolled the stone off the mouth
of the well and watered the sheep of his uncle Laban. 11 Then Jacob kissed Rachel and began to weep loudly. 12 When Jacob explained to Rachel that he was a relative of her father and the son
of Rebekah, she ran and told her father. 13 When Laban heard this
news about Jacob, his sister's son, he rushed out to meet him. He
embraced him and kissed him and brought him to his house. Jacob told Laban how he was related to him. 14 Then Laban said to
him, "You are indeed my own flesh and blood." So Jacob stayed
with him for a month.
15 Then Laban said to Jacob, "Should you work for me for nothing because you are my relative? Tell me what your wages should
be." 16 (Now Laban had two daughters; the older one was named
Leah, and the younger one Rachel. 17 Leah's eyes were tender, but
Rachel had a lovely figure and beautiful appearance.) 18 Since Jacob had fallen in love with Rachel, he said, "I'll serve you seven
years in exchange for your younger daughter Rachel." 19 Laban
replied, "I'd rather give her to you than to another man. Stay

with me." 20 So Jacob worked for seven years to acquire Rachel. But they seemed like only a few days to him because his love for her was so great.

21 Finally Jacob said to Laban, "Give me my wife, for my time of service is up. And I want to sleep with her." 22 So Laban invited all the people of that place and prepared a feast. 23 In the evening he brought his daughter Leah to Jacob, and he slept with her. 24 (Laban gave his female servant Zilpah to his daughter Leah to be her servant.)

25 In the morning Jacob discovered it was Leah! So Jacob said to Laban, "What in the world have you done to me? Didn't I work for you in exchange for Rachel? Why have you tricked me?" 26 "It is not our custom here," Laban replied, "to give the younger daughter in marriage before the firstborn. 27 Complete my older daughter's bridal week. Then we will give you the younger one too, in exchange for seven more years of work."

28 Jacob did as Laban said. When Jacob completed Leah's bridal week, Laban gave him his daughter Rachel to be his wife. 29 (Laban gave his female servant Bilhah to his daughter Rachel to be her servant.) 30 Jacob slept with Rachel as well. He also loved Rachel more than Leah. Then he worked for Laban for seven more years.

THE FAMILY OF JACOB

31 When the LORD saw that Leah was unloved, he enabled her to become pregnant while Rachel remained childless. 32 So Leah became pregnant and gave birth to a son. She named him Reuben, for she said, "The LORD has looked with pity on my oppressed condition. Surely my husband will love me now."

33 She became pregnant again and had another son. She said, "Because the LORD heard that I was unloved, he gave me this one too." So she named him Simeon.

34 She became pregnant again and had another son. She said, "Now this time my husband will show me affection, because I have given birth to three sons for him." That is why he was named Levi.

35 She became pregnant again and had another son. She said, "This time I will praise the LORD." That is why she named him Judah. Then she stopped having children.

30 When Rachel saw that she could not give Jacob children, she became jealous of her sister. She said to Jacob, "Give me children or I'll die!" 2 Jacob became furious with Rachel and exclaimed, "Am I in the place of God, who has kept you from having children?" 3 She replied, "Here is my servant Bilhah! Sleep with her so that she can bear children for me and I can have a family through her."

4 So Rachel gave him her servant Bilhah as a wife, and Jacob slept with her. 5 Bilhah became pregnant and gave Jacob a son. 6 Then Rachel said, "God has vindicated me. He has responded to my prayer and given me a son." That is why she named him Dan. 7 Bilhah, Rachel's servant, became pregnant again and gave Jacob another son. 8 Then Rachel said, "I have fought a desperate struggle with my sister, but I have won." So she named him Naphtali.

9 When Leah saw that she had stopped having children, she
gave her servant Zilpah to Jacob as a wife. 10 Soon Leah's servant Zilpah gave Jacob a son. 11 Leah said, "How fortunate!" So
she named him Gad.
12 Then Leah's servant Zilpah gave Jacob another son. 13 Leah
said, "How happy I am, for women will call me happy!" So she
named him Asher.
14 At the time of the wheat harvest Reuben went out and found
some mandrake plants in a field and brought them to his mother Leah. Rachel said to Leah, "Give me some of your son's mandrakes." 15 But Leah replied, "Wasn't it enough that you've taken
away my husband? Would you take away my son's mandrakes
too?" "All right," Rachel said, "he may go to bed with you tonight
in exchange for your son's mandrakes." 16 When Jacob came in
from the fields that evening, Leah went out to meet him and
said, "You must sleep with me because I have paid for your services with my son's mandrakes." So he went to bed with her that
night. 17 God paid attention to Leah; she became pregnant and
gave Jacob a son for the fifth time. 18 Then Leah said, "God has
granted me a reward because I gave my servant to my husband
as a wife." So she named him Issachar.
19 Leah became pregnant again and gave Jacob a son for the
sixth time. 20 Then Leah said, "God has given me a good gift. Now
my husband will honor me because I have given him six sons."
So she named him Zebulun.
21 After that she gave birth to a daughter and named her Dinah.
22 Then God took note of Rachel. He paid attention to her
and enabled her to become pregnant. 23 She became pregnant
and gave birth to a son. Then she said, "God has taken away my
shame." 24 She named him Joseph, saying, "May the LORD give
me yet another son."

THE FLOCKS OF JACOB

25 After Rachel had given birth to Joseph, Jacob said to Laban,
"Send me on my way so that I can go home to my own country.
26 Let me take my wives and my children whom I have acquired
by working for you. Then I'll depart, because you know how hard
I've worked for you."
27 But Laban said to him, "If I have found favor in your sight,
please stay here, for I have learned by divination that the LORD
has blessed me on account of you." 28 He added, "Just name your
wages—I'll pay whatever you want."
29 "You know how I have worked for you," Jacob replied, "and
how well your livestock have fared under my care. 30 Indeed,
you had little before I arrived, but now your possessions have
increased many times over. The LORD has blessed you wherever
I worked. But now, how long must it be before I do something
for my own family too?"
31 So Laban asked, "What should I give you?" "You don't need
to give me a thing," Jacob replied, "but if you agree to this one
condition, I will continue to care for your flocks and protect
them: 32 Let me walk among all your flocks today and remove
from them every speckled or spotted sheep, every dark-colored
lamb, and the spotted or speckled goats. These animals will be

REFLECT

What does it mean that God paid attention to Rachel? How does this give you hope, knowing that God pays attention to you, even in the midst of difficult circumstances?

my wages. 33 My integrity will testify for me later on. When you
come to verify that I've taken only the wages we agreed on, if I
have in my possession any goat that is not speckled or spotted
or any sheep that is not dark-colored, it will be considered stolen." 34 "Agreed!" said Laban, "It will be as you say."
35 So that day Laban removed the male goats that were streaked
or spotted, all the female goats that were speckled or spotted
(all that had any white on them), and all the dark-colored lambs,
and put them in the care of his sons. 36 Then he separated them
from Jacob by a three-day journey, while Jacob was taking care
of the rest of Laban's flocks.
37 But Jacob took fresh-cut branches from poplar, almond, and
plane trees. He made white streaks by peeling them, making the
white inner wood in the branches visible. 38 Then he set up the
peeled branches in all the watering troughs where the flocks
came to drink. He set up the branches in front of the flocks
when they were in heat and came to drink. 39 When the sheep
mated in front of the branches, they gave birth to young that
were streaked or speckled or spotted. 40 Jacob removed these
lambs, but he made the rest of the flock face the streaked and
completely dark-colored animals in Laban's flock. So he made
separate flocks for himself and did not mix them with Laban's
flocks. 41 When the stronger females were in heat, Jacob would
set up the branches in the troughs in front of the flock, so they
would mate near the branches. 42 But if the animals were weaker,
he did not set the branches there. So the weaker animals ended
up belonging to Laban and the stronger animals to Jacob. 43 In
this way Jacob became extremely prosperous. He owned large
flocks, male and female servants, camels, and donkeys.

JACOB'S FLIGHT FROM LABAN

31 Jacob heard that Laban's sons were complaining, "Jacob has
taken everything that belonged to our father! He has gotten rich at our father's expense!" 2 When Jacob saw the look on
Laban's face, he could tell his attitude toward him had changed.
3 The LORD said to Jacob, "Return to the land of your fathers
and to your relatives. I will be with you." 4 So Jacob sent a message for Rachel and Leah to come to the field where his flocks
were. 5 There he said to them, "I can tell that your father's attitude toward me has changed, but the God of my father has been
with me. 6 You know that I've worked for your father as hard as
I could, 7 but your father has humiliated me and changed my
wages ten times. But God has not permitted him to do me any
harm. 8 If he said, 'The speckled animals will be your wage,' then
the entire flock gave birth to speckled offspring. But if he said,
'The streaked animals will be your wage,' then the entire flock
gave birth to streaked offspring. 9 In this way God has snatched
away your father's livestock and given them to me.
10 "Once during breeding season I saw in a dream that the male
goats mating with the flock were streaked, speckled, and spotted.
11 In the dream the angel of God said to me, 'Jacob!' 'Here I am!' I
replied. 12 Then he said, 'Observe that all the male goats mating
with the flock are streaked, speckled, or spotted, for I have observed all that Laban has done to you. 13 I am the God of Bethel,

where you anointed the sacred stone and made a vow to me. Now
leave this land immediately and return to your native land.'"
14 Then Rachel and Leah replied to him, "Do we still have any
portion or inheritance in our father's house? 15 Hasn't he treated
us like foreigners? He not only sold us, but completely wasted
the money paid for us! 16 Surely all the wealth that God snatched
away from our father belongs to us and to our children. So now
do everything God has told you."
17 So Jacob immediately put his children and his wives on the
camels. 18 He took away all the livestock he had acquired in Paddan
Aram and all his moveable property that he had accumulated. Then
he set out toward the land of Canaan to return to his father Isaac.
19 While Laban had gone to shear his sheep, Rachel stole the
household idols that belonged to her father. 20 Jacob also deceived Laban the Aramean by not telling him that he was leaving. 21 He left with all he owned. He quickly crossed the Euphrates
River and headed for the hill country of Gilead.
22 Three days later Laban discovered Jacob had left. 23 So he
took his relatives with him and pursued Jacob for seven days.
He caught up with him in the hill country of Gilead. 24 But God
came to Laban the Aramean in a dream at night and warned him,
"Be careful that you neither bless nor curse Jacob."
25 Laban overtook Jacob, and when Jacob pitched his tent in
the hill country of Gilead, Laban and his relatives set up camp
there too. 26 "What have you done?" Laban demanded of Jacob.
"You've deceived me and carried away my daughters as if they
were captives of war! 27 Why did you run away secretly and deceive me? Why didn't you tell me so I could send you off with
a celebration complete with singing, tambourines, and harps?
28 You didn't even allow me to kiss my daughters and my grandchildren goodbye. You have acted foolishly! 29 I have the power
to do you harm, but the God of your father told me last night,
'Be careful that you neither bless nor curse Jacob.' 30 Now I understand that you have gone away because you longed desperately for your father's house. Yet why did you steal my gods?"
31 "I left secretly because I was afraid!" Jacob replied to Laban. "I
thought you might take your daughters away from me by force.
32 Whoever has taken your gods will be put to death! In the presence of our relatives identify whatever is yours and take it." (Now
Jacob did not know that Rachel had stolen them.)
33 So Laban entered Jacob's tent, and Leah's tent, and the tent of
the two female servants, but he did not find the idols. Then he left
Leah's tent and entered Rachel's. 34 (Now Rachel had taken the
idols and put them inside her camel's saddle and sat on them.)
Laban searched the whole tent, but did not find them. 35 Rachel
said to her father, "Don't be angry, my lord. I cannot stand up in
your presence because I am having my period." So he searched
thoroughly, but did not find the idols.
36 Jacob became angry and argued with Laban. "What did I do
wrong?" he demanded of Laban. "What sin of mine prompted you
to chase after me in hot pursuit? 37 When you searched through
all my goods, did you find anything that belonged to you? Set it
here before my relatives and yours, and let them settle the dispute between the two of us!

38 “I have been with you for the past twenty years. Your ewes
and female goats have not miscarried, nor have I eaten rams
from your flocks. 39 Animals torn by wild beasts I never brought
to you; I always absorbed the loss myself. You always made me
pay for every missing animal, whether it was taken by day or at
night. 40 I was consumed by scorching heat during the day and
by piercing cold at night, and I went without sleep. 41 This was
my lot for twenty years in your house: I worked like a slave for
you—fourteen years for your two daughters and six years for
your flocks—but you changed my wages ten times! 42 If the God of
my father—the God of Abraham, the one whom Isaac fears—had
not been with me, you would certainly have sent me away empty-handed! But God saw how I was oppressed and how hard I
worked, and he rebuked you last night.”

43 Laban replied to Jacob, “These women are my daughters,
these children are my grandchildren, and these flocks are my
flocks. All that you see belongs to me. But how can I harm these
daughters of mine today or the children to whom they have given
birth? 44 So now, come, let’s make a formal agreement, you and
I, and it will be proof that we have made peace.”

45 So Jacob took a stone and set it up as a memorial pillar.
46 Then he said to his relatives, “Gather stones.” So they brought
stones and put them in a pile. They ate there by the pile of stones.
47 Laban called it Jegar Sahadutha, but Jacob called it Galeed.

48 Laban said, “This pile of stones is a witness of our agreement
today.” That is why it was called Galeed. 49 It was also called Mizpah because he said, “May the LORD watch between us when we
are out of sight of one another. 50 If you mistreat my daughters
or if you take wives besides my daughters, although no one else
is with us, realize that God is witness to your actions.”

51 “Here is this pile of stones and this pillar I have set up between me and you,” Laban said to Jacob. 52 “This pile of stones
and the pillar are reminders that I will not pass beyond this pile
to come to harm you and that you will not pass beyond this pile
and this pillar to come to harm me. 53 May the God of Abraham
and the god of Nahor, the gods of their father, judge between
us.” Jacob took an oath by the God whom his father Isaac feared.
54 Then Jacob offered a sacrifice on the mountain and invited his
relatives to eat the meal. They ate the meal and spent the night
on the mountain.

55 Early in the morning Laban kissed his grandchildren and
his daughters goodbye and blessed them. Then Laban left and
returned home.

JACOB WRESTLES AT PENIEL

32 So Jacob went on his way and the angels of God met him.
2 When Jacob saw them, he exclaimed, “This is the camp
of God!” So he named that place Mahanaim.

3 Jacob sent messengers on ahead to his brother Esau in the
land of Seir, the region of Edom. 4 He commanded them, “This is
what you must say to my lord Esau: ‘This is what your servant Jacob says: I have been staying with Laban until now. 5 I have oxen,
donkeys, sheep, and male and female servants. I have sent this
message to inform my lord, so that I may find favor in your sight.’”

6 The messengers returned to Jacob and said, "We went to your
brother Esau. He is coming to meet you and has 400 men with
him." 7 Jacob was very afraid and upset. So he divided the people
who were with him into two camps, as well as the flocks, herds,
and camels. 8 "If Esau attacks one camp," he thought, "then the
other camp will be able to escape."

9 Then Jacob prayed, "O God of my father Abraham, God of my
father Isaac, O LORD, you said to me, 'Return to your land and to
your relatives and I will make you prosper.' 10 I am not worthy of
all the faithful love you have shown your servant. With only my
walking stick I crossed the Jordan, but now I have become two
camps. 11 Rescue me, I pray, from the hand of my brother Esau,
for I am afraid he will come and attack me, as well as the mothers with their children. 12 But you said, 'I will certainly make you
prosper and will make your descendants like the sand on the
seashore, too numerous to count.'"

13 Jacob stayed there that night. Then he sent as a gift to his
brother Esau 14 200 female goats and 20 male goats, 200 ewes
and 20 rams, 15 30 female camels with their young, 40 cows and
10 bulls, and 20 female donkeys and 10 male donkeys. 16 He entrusted them to his servants, who divided them into herds. He
told his servants, "Pass over before me, and keep some distance
between one herd and the next." 17 He instructed the servant
leading the first herd, "When my brother Esau meets you and
asks, 'To whom do you belong? Where are you going? Whose
herds are you driving?' 18 then you must say, 'They belong to your
servant Jacob. They have been sent as a gift to my lord Esau. In
fact Jacob himself is behind us.'"

19 He also gave these instructions to the second and third servants, as well as all those who were following the herds, saying, "You must say the same thing to Esau when you meet him.
20 You must also say, 'In fact your servant Jacob is behind us.'" Jacob thought, "I will first appease him by sending a gift ahead of
me. After that I will meet him. Perhaps he will accept me." 21 So
the gifts were sent on ahead of him while he spent that night
in the camp.

22 During the night Jacob quickly took his two wives, his two
female servants, and his eleven sons and crossed the ford of
the Jabbok. 23 He took them and sent them across the stream
along with all his possessions. 24 So Jacob was left alone. Then
a man wrestled with him until daybreak. 25 When the man
saw that he could not defeat Jacob, he struck the socket of his
hip so the socket of Jacob's hip was dislocated while he wrestled with him.

26 Then the man said, "Let me go, for the dawn is breaking." "I
will not let you go," Jacob replied, "unless you bless me." 27 The
man asked him, "What is your name?" He answered, "Jacob."
28 "No longer will your name be Jacob," the man told him, "but
Israel, because you have fought with God and with men and
have prevailed."

29 Then Jacob asked, "Please tell me your name." "Why do you
ask my name?" the man replied. Then he blessed Jacob there.
30 So Jacob named the place Peniel, explaining, "Certainly I have
seen God face to face and have survived."

LOVE TO GROW

WHAT IS YOUR NAME?

GENESIS 32:22-32

In Hebrew, Jacob's name is pronounced Ya'aqob. It sounds like the word 'aqab, which means "to grasp the heel" or "to deceive." 'Aqab literally means "to grasp the heel" but it was used figuratively to describe deception, or metaphorically to suggest tripping someone up by their heels. Jacob literally seized his twin brother's heel at his birth, and he figuratively seized heels his whole life (Gen 25:19–26).

Jacob was known as a deceiver. He deceived his brother (Gen 25:27–34), his father (Gen 27:1–36), and his uncle (Gen 31:20). Being a deceiver was Jacob's identity. It was even his name, until God met him one night at Penuel.

Jacob wrestled with a man that night. Before the sun rose, the man told Jacob to let him go. When Jacob asked for a blessing, the man said, "What is your name?" He answered, "Jacob." Jacob introduced himself by his name, which carried with it his reputation and identity as a deceiver. He was reminded in that moment, and so are we, that he was still a mess.

"No longer will your name be Jacob," the man told him, "but Israel, because you have fought with God and with men and have prevailed" (Gen 32:28).

In that this moment, God gave Jacob a new identity. Jacob had not asked for a new identity, but he needed one. God marked Jacob for who he would become, not who he had been. God gave him a new identity as a promise of who he would one day become.

The point of Jacob's story is not that he figured his life out and then God used him. He did nothing to earn a blessing. We see no evidence that Jacob changed or that he felt remorse or conviction for all his deception. Even his children showed signs of practicing deception (Gen 34; 38; 44–45), a trait they likely learned from their father.

God took a broken man and blessed him and his descendants with a new identity. God was faithful, even when Jacob wasn't.

God chooses us despite our sin. We did nothing to deserve the cross, nothing to earn it. We are saved by His grace alone. He gives us a new identity when we place our faith in Him. He calls us His children. Our identity is in Him, not our past, or even our future. We take on His identity and His righteousness before God. Our names may not change, but the identity that comes with our name surely does.

[31]The sun rose over him as he crossed over Penuel, but he was
limping because of his hip. [32]That is why to this day the Israelites do not eat the sinew which is attached to the socket of
the hip, because he struck the socket of Jacob's hip near the attached sinew.

JACOB MEETS ESAU

33 Jacob looked up and saw that Esau was coming along with
400 men. So he divided the children among Leah, Rachel,
and the two female servants. [2]He put the servants and their children in front, with Leah and her children behind them, and Rachel and Joseph behind them. [3]But Jacob himself went on ahead
of them, and he bowed toward the ground seven times as he approached his brother. [4]But Esau ran to meet him, embraced him,
hugged his neck, and kissed him. Then they both wept. [5]When
Esau looked up and saw the women and the children, he asked,
"Who are these people with you?" Jacob replied, "The children
whom God has graciously given your servant." [6]The female servants came forward with their children and bowed down. [7]Then
Leah came forward with her children and they bowed down. Finally Joseph and Rachel came forward and bowed down.
[8]Esau then asked, "What did you intend by sending all these
herds to meet me?" Jacob replied, "To find favor in your sight,
my lord." [9]But Esau said, "I have plenty, my brother. Keep what
belongs to you." [10]"No, please take them," Jacob said. "If I have
found favor in your sight, accept my gift from my hand. Now that
I have seen your face and you have accepted me, it is as if I have
seen the face of God. [11]Please take my present that was brought
to you, for God has been generous to me and I have all I need."
When Jacob urged him, he took it.
[12]Then Esau said, "Let's be on our way! I will go in front of you."
[13]But Jacob said to him, "My lord knows that the children are
young, and that I have to look after the sheep and cattle that are
nursing their young. If they are driven too hard for even a single day, all the animals will die. [14]Let my lord go on ahead of his
servant. I will travel more slowly, at the pace of the herds and
the children, until I come to my lord at Seir."
[15]So Esau said, "Let me leave some of my men with you." "Why do
that?" Jacob replied. "My lord has already been kind enough to me."
[16]So that same day Esau made his way back to Seir. [17]But Jacob traveled to Sukkoth where he built himself a house and
made shelters for his livestock. That is why the place was called
Sukkoth.
[18]After he left Paddan Aram, Jacob came safely to the city of
Shechem in the land of Canaan, and he camped near the city.
[19]Then he purchased the portion of the field where he had
pitched his tent; he bought it from the sons of Hamor, Shechem's
father, for 100 pieces of money. [20]There he set up an altar and
called it "The God of Israel is God."

DINAH AND THE SHECHEMITES

34 Now Dinah, Leah's daughter whom she bore to Jacob,
went to meet the young women of the land. [2]When Shechem son of Hamor the Hivite, who ruled that area, saw her, he

grabbed her, forced himself on her, and sexually assaulted her.
[3]Then he became very attached to Dinah, Jacob's daughter. He
fell in love with the young woman and spoke romantically to
her. [4]Shechem said to his father Hamor, "Acquire this young girl
as my wife." [5]When Jacob heard that Shechem had violated his
daughter Dinah, his sons were with the livestock in the field. So
Jacob remained silent until they came in.

[6]Then Shechem's father Hamor went to speak with Jacob about
Dinah. [7]Now Jacob's sons had come in from the field when they
heard the news. They were offended and very angry because Shechem had disgraced Israel by sexually assaulting Jacob's daughter, a crime that should not be committed.

[8]But Hamor made this appeal to them: "My son Shechem is
in love with your daughter. Please give her to him as his wife.
[9]Intermarry with us. Let us marry your daughters, and take our
daughters as wives for yourselves. [10]You may live among us, and
the land will be open to you. Live in it, travel freely in it, and acquire property in it."

[11]Then Shechem said to Dinah's father and brothers, "Let me
find favor in your sight, and whatever you require of me I'll give.
[12]You can make the bride price and the gift I must bring very
expensive, and I'll give whatever you ask of me. Just give me the
young woman as my wife!"

[13]Jacob's sons answered Shechem and his father Hamor deceitfully when they spoke because Shechem had violated their
sister Dinah. [14]They said to them, "We cannot give our sister to
a man who is not circumcised, for it would be a disgrace to us.
[15]We will give you our consent on this one condition: You must
become like us by circumcising all your males. [16]Then we will give
you our daughters to marry, and we will take your daughters as
wives for ourselves, and we will live among you and become one
people. [17]But if you do not agree to our terms by being circumcised, then we will take our sister and depart."

[18]Their offer pleased Hamor and his son Shechem. [19]The young
man did not delay in doing what they asked because he wanted
Jacob's daughter Dinah badly. (Now he was more important than
anyone in his father's household.) [20]So Hamor and his son Shechem went to the gate of their city and spoke to the men of their
city, [21]"These men are at peace with us. So let them live in the
land and travel freely in it, for the land is wide enough for them.
We will take their daughters for wives, and we will give them
our daughters to marry. [22]Only on this one condition will these
men consent to live with us and become one people: They demand that every male among us be circumcised just as they are
circumcised. [23]If we do so, won't their livestock, their property,
and all their animals become ours? So let's consent to their demand, so they will live among us."

[24]All the men who assembled at the city gate agreed with
Hamor and his son Shechem. Every male who assembled at the
city gate was circumcised. [25]In three days, when they were still
in pain, two of Jacob's sons, Simeon and Levi, Dinah's brothers, each took his sword and went to the unsuspecting city
and slaughtered every male. [26]They killed Hamor and his son
Shechem with the sword, took Dinah from Shechem's house,

and left. 27 Jacob's sons killed them and looted the city because
their sister had been violated. 28 They took their flocks, herds,
and donkeys, as well as everything in the city and in the surrounding fields. 29 They captured as plunder all their wealth,
all their little ones, and their wives, including everything in
the houses.

30 Then Jacob said to Simeon and Levi, "You have brought ruin
on me by making me a foul odor among the inhabitants of the
land—among the Canaanites and the Perizzites. I am few in number; they will join forces against me and attack me, and both I
and my family will be destroyed!" 31 But Simeon and Levi replied,
"Should he treat our sister like a common prostitute?"

THE RETURN TO BETHEL

35 Then God said to Jacob, "Go up at once to Bethel and live
there. Make an altar there to God, who appeared to you
when you fled from your brother Esau." 2 So Jacob told his household and all who were with him, "Get rid of the foreign gods you
have among you. Purify yourselves and change your clothes. 3 Let
us go up at once to Bethel. Then I will make an altar there to God,
who responded to me in my time of distress and has been with
me wherever I went."

4 So they gave Jacob all the foreign gods that were in their possession and the rings that were in their ears. Jacob buried them
under the oak near Shechem 5 and they started on their journey. The surrounding cities were afraid of God, and they did not
pursue the sons of Jacob.

6 Jacob and all those who were with him arrived at Luz (that is,
Bethel) in the land of Canaan. 7 He built an altar there and named
the place El Bethel because there God had revealed himself to
him when he was fleeing from his brother. 8 (Deborah, Rebekah's
nurse, died and was buried under the oak below Bethel; thus it
was named Oak of Weeping.)

9 God appeared to Jacob again after he returned from Paddan Aram and blessed him. 10 God said to him, "Your name is Jacob, but your name will no longer be called Jacob; Israel will be
your name." So God named him Israel. 11 Then God said to him,
"I am the Sovereign God. Be fruitful and multiply! A nation—
even a company of nations—will descend from you; kings will
be among your descendants! 12 The land I gave to Abraham and
Isaac I will give to you. To your descendants I will also give this
land." 13 Then God went up from the place where he spoke with
him. 14 So Jacob set up a sacred stone pillar in the place where
God spoke with him. He poured out a drink offering on it, and
then he poured oil on it. 15 Jacob named the place where God
spoke with him Bethel.

16 They traveled on from Bethel, and when Ephrath was still
some distance away, Rachel went into labor—and her labor was
hard. 17 When her labor was at its hardest, the midwife said to
her, "Don't be afraid, for you are having another son." 18 With her
dying breath, she named him Ben Oni. But his father called him
Benjamin instead. 19 So Rachel died and was buried on the way to
Ephrath (that is, Bethlehem). 20 Jacob set up a marker over her
grave; it is the Marker of Rachel's Grave to this day.

[21]Then Israel traveled on and pitched his tent beyond Migdal
Eder. [22]While Israel was living in that land, Reuben went to bed
with Bilhah, his father's concubine, and Israel heard about it.
Jacob had twelve sons:

[23] The sons of Leah were Reuben, Jacob's firstborn, as
well as Simeon, Levi, Judah, Issachar, and Zebulun.
[24] The sons of Rachel were Joseph and Benjamin.
[25] The sons of Bilhah, Rachel's servant,
were Dan and Naphtali.
[26] The sons of Zilpah, Leah's servant, were Gad and Asher.

These were the sons of Jacob who were born to him in Paddan Aram.

[27]So Jacob came back to his father Isaac in Mamre, to Kiriath
Arba (that is, Hebron), where Abraham and Isaac had stayed.
[28]Isaac lived to be 180 years old. [29]Then Isaac breathed his last
and joined his ancestors. He died an old man who had lived a
full life. His sons Esau and Jacob buried him.

THE DESCENDANTS OF ESAU

36 What follows is the account of Esau (also known as Edom).
[2]Esau took his wives from the Canaanites: Adah the
daughter of Elon the Hittite, and Oholibamah the daughter of
Anah and granddaughter of Zibeon the Hivite, [3]in addition to
Basemath the daughter of Ishmael and sister of Nebaioth.

[4]Adah bore Eliphaz to Esau, Basemath bore Reuel, [5]and Oholibamah bore Jeush, Jalam, and Korah. These were the sons of Esau
who were born to him in the land of Canaan.

[6]Esau took his wives, his sons, his daughters, all the people
in his household, his livestock, his animals, and all his possessions that he had acquired in the land of Canaan, and he went
to a land some distance away from Jacob his brother [7]because
they had too many possessions to be able to stay together, and
the land where they had settled was not able to support them
because of their livestock. [8]So Esau (also known as Edom) lived
in the hill country of Seir.

[9]This is the account of Esau, the father of the Edomites, in the
hill country of Seir.

[10]These were the names of Esau's sons: Eliphaz, the son of
Esau's wife Adah, and Reuel, the son of Esau's wife Basemath.

[11]These were the sons of Eliphaz: Teman, Omar, Zepho, Gatam,
and Kenaz.

[12]Timna, a concubine of Esau's son Eliphaz, bore Amalek to
Eliphaz. These were the sons of Esau's wife Adah.

[13]These were the sons of Reuel: Nahath, Zerah, Shammah, and
Mizzah. These were the sons of Esau's wife Basemath.

[14]These were the sons of Esau's wife Oholibamah the daughter
of Anah and granddaughter of Zibeon: She bore Jeush, Jalam, and
Korah to Esau.

[15]These were the chiefs among the descendants of Esau, the
sons of Eliphaz, Esau's firstborn: chief Teman, chief Omar, chief
Zepho, chief Kenaz, [16]chief Korah, chief Gatam, chief Amalek.
These were the chiefs descended from Eliphaz in the land of
Edom; these were the sons of Adah.

17 These were the sons of Esau's son Reuel: chief Nahath, chief
Zerah, chief Shammah, chief Mizzah. These were the chiefs descended from Reuel in the land of Edom; these were the sons
of Esau's wife Basemath.
18 These were the sons of Esau's wife Oholibamah: chief Jeush,
chief Jalam, chief Korah. These were the chiefs descended from
Esau's wife Oholibamah, the daughter of Anah.
19 These were the sons of Esau (also known as Edom), and these
were their chiefs.
20 These were the sons of Seir the Horite, who were living in the land:
Lotan, Shobal, Zibeon, Anah, 21 Dishon, Ezer, and Dishan. These were
the chiefs of the Horites, the descendants of Seir in the land of Edom.
22 The sons of Lotan were Hori and Homam; Lotan's sister was
Timna.
23 These were the sons of Shobal: Alvan, Manahath, Ebal, She-
pho, and Onam.
24 These were the sons of Zibeon: Aiah and Anah (who discovered the hot springs in the wilderness as he pastured the donkeys of his father Zibeon).
25 These were the children of Anah: Dishon and Oholibamah,
the daughter of Anah.
26 These were the sons of Dishon: Hemdan, Eshban, Ithran,
and Keran.
27 These were the sons of Ezer: Bilhan, Zaavan, and Akan.
28 These were the sons of Dishan: Uz and Aran.
29 These were the chiefs of the Horites: chief Lotan, chief Shobal, chief Zibeon, chief Anah, 30 chief Dishon, chief Ezer, chief
Dishan. These were the chiefs of the Horites, according to their
chief lists in the land of Seir.
31 These were the kings who reigned in the land of Edom before any king ruled over the Israelites:
32 Bela the son of Beor reigned in Edom; the name of his city
was Dinhabah.
33 When Bela died, Jobab the son of Zerah from Bozrah reigned
in his place.
34 When Jobab died, Husham from the land of the Temanites
reigned in his place.
35 When Husham died, Hadad the son of Bedad, who defeated
the Midianites in the land of Moab, reigned in his place; the
name of his city was Avith.
36 When Hadad died, Samlah from Masrekah reigned in his place.
37 When Samlah died, Shaul from Rehoboth on the River
reigned in his place.
38 When Shaul died, Baal Hanan the son of Achbor reigned
in his place.
39 When Baal Hanan the son of Achbor died, Hadad reigned
in his place; the name of his city was Pau. His wife's name was
Mehetabel, the daughter of Matred, the daughter of Me-Zahab.
40 These were the names of the chiefs of Esau, according to their
families, according to their places, by their names: chief Timna,
chief Alvah, chief Jetheth, 41 chief Oholibamah, chief Elah, chief Pinon, 42 chief Kenaz, chief Teman, chief Mibzar, 43 chief Magdiel, chief
Iram. These were the chiefs of Edom, according to their settlements
in the land they possessed. This was Esau, the father of the Edomites.

JOSEPH'S DREAMS

37 But Jacob lived in the land where his father had stayed,
in the land of Canaan.
2 This is the account of Jacob.
Joseph, his seventeen-year-old son, was taking care of the
flocks with his brothers. Now he was a youngster working with
the sons of Bilhah and Zilpah, his father's wives. Joseph brought
back a bad report about them to their father.
3 Now Israel loved Joseph more than all his sons because he
was a son born to him late in life, and he made a special tunic for
him. 4 When Joseph's brothers saw that their father loved him
more than any of them, they hated Joseph and were not able to
speak to him kindly.
5 Joseph had a dream, and when he told his brothers about
it they hated him even more. 6 He said to them, "Listen to this
dream I had: 7 There we were, binding sheaves of grain in the middle of the field. Suddenly my sheaf rose up and stood upright
and your sheaves surrounded my sheaf and bowed down to it!"
8 Then his brothers asked him, "Do you really think you will rule
over us or have dominion over us?" They hated him even more
because of his dream and because of what he said.
9 Then he had another dream, and told it to his brothers. "Look,"
he said. "I had another dream. The sun, the moon, and eleven
stars were bowing down to me." 10 When he told his father and
his brothers, his father rebuked him, saying, "What is this dream
that you had? Will I, your mother, and your brothers really come
and bow down to you?" 11 His brothers were jealous of him, but
his father kept in mind what Joseph said.
12 When his brothers had gone to graze their father's flocks near
Shechem, 13 Israel said to Joseph, "Your brothers are grazing the
flocks near Shechem. Come, I will send you to them." "I'm ready,"
Joseph replied. 14 So Jacob said to him, "Go now and check on the
welfare of your brothers and of the flocks, and bring me word."
So Jacob sent him from the valley of Hebron.
15 When Joseph reached Shechem, a man found him wandering in the field, so the man asked him, "What are you looking
for?" 16 He replied, "I'm looking for my brothers. Please tell me
where they are grazing their flocks." 17 The man said, "They left
this area, for I heard them say, 'Let's go to Dothan.'" So Joseph
went after his brothers and found them at Dothan.
18 Now Joseph's brothers saw him from a distance, and before
he reached them, they plotted to kill him. 19 They said to one
another, "Here comes this master of dreams! 20 Come now, let's
kill him, throw him into one of the cisterns, and then say that
a wild animal ate him. Then we'll see how his dreams turn out!"
21 When Reuben heard this, he rescued Joseph from their
hands, saying, "Let's not take his life!" 22 Reuben continued, "Don't
shed blood! Throw him into this cistern that is here in the wilderness, but don't lay a hand on him." (Reuben said this so he
could rescue Joseph from them and take him back to his father.)
23 When Joseph reached his brothers, they stripped him of his
tunic, the special tunic that he wore. 24 Then they took him and
threw him into the cistern. (Now the cistern was empty; there
was no water in it.)

THE GOD OF DREAMS

GENESIS 37:18–19

Years ago, I picked up the pieces of a shattered dream and tried to move forward in faith. I knew God had more for me, but I felt empty inside after experiencing rejection and opposition at every turn. I was frustrated because I thought I had failed. Maybe if I had prayed more or worked harder, my story would have had a happier ending. I had pictured my life full of confetti and multi-colored sprinkles, but somehow I ended up with coal and sooty ashes instead. I wished I could start again and get a dream do-over.

What I didn't realize at the time was that God specializes in spectacular turns of events. He had big plans for my future. His plan was much more beautiful and fulfilling than I could have ever imagined.

Joseph's beautiful coat was torn into pieces, and those closest to him turned into enemies. Alone in an empty, waterless pit, he must have wondered why. Each stage of Joseph's story prepared him for the grander plan God would unfold. The shackles Joseph wore could not stop him from freely seeking God's favor and protection. No matter where he landed, the dreamer always looked to God and determined to persevere. Never once did he compromise his integrity or choose to go his own way.

We may never land in prison like Joseph did, but we often feel imprisoned by less than favorable circumstances. Seeing God's providence at work in Joseph's story can encourage us to trust that God is sovereignly ordering our steps to see us through to a desired end. Even when our dreams get ripped asunder, we can hold on to hope:

God's redemptive plan is always at work in our lives.

No earthly obstacle can deter the plans God has for His children. Even if we are standing in ashes today, one day we'll look back and see how His hand created order from chaos. Like the Psalmist, we will declare, "When the Lord restored the well-being of Zion, we thought we were dreaming. At that time we laughed loudly and shouted for joy. At that time the nations said, 'The Lord has accomplished great things for these people.' The Lord did indeed accomplish great things for us. We were happy" (Ps 126:1–3).

Get your confetti and sprinkles ready. A celebration is on the way.

[25]When they sat down to eat their food, they looked up and saw
a caravan of Ishmaelites coming from Gilead. Their camels were
carrying spices, balm, and myrrh down to Egypt. [26]Then Judah
said to his brothers, "What profit is there if we kill our brother
and cover up his blood? [27]Come, let's sell him to the Ishmaelites,
but let's not lay a hand on him, for after all, he is our brother, our
own flesh." His brothers agreed. [28]So when the Midianite merchants passed by, Joseph's brothers pulled him out of the cistern
and sold him to the Ishmaelites for twenty pieces of silver. The
Ishmaelites then took Joseph to Egypt.

[29]Later Reuben returned to the cistern to find that Joseph
was not in it! He tore his clothes, [30]returned to his brothers,
and said, "The boy isn't there! And I, where can I go?" [31]So they
took Joseph's tunic, killed a young goat, and dipped the tunic
in the blood. [32]Then they brought the special tunic to their father and said, "We found this. Determine now whether it is your
son's tunic or not."

[33]He recognized it and exclaimed, "It is my son's tunic! A wild
animal has eaten him! Joseph has surely been torn to pieces!"
[34]Then Jacob tore his clothes, put on sackcloth, and mourned for
his son many days. [35]All his sons and daughters stood by him to
console him, but he refused to be consoled. "No," he said, "I will go
to the grave mourning my son." So Joseph's father wept for him.
[36]Now in Egypt the Midianites sold Joseph to Potiphar, one
of Pharaoh's officials, the captain of the guard.

JUDAH AND TAMAR

38 At that time Judah left his brothers and stayed with an
Adullamite man named Hirah. [2]There Judah saw the
daughter of a Canaanite man named Shua. Judah acquired her
as a wife and slept with her. [3]She became pregnant and had a
son. Judah named him Er. [4]She became pregnant again and had
another son, whom she named Onan. [5]Then she had yet another
son, whom she named Shelah. She gave birth to him in Kezib.

[6]Judah acquired a wife for Er his firstborn; her name was Tamar. [7]But Er, Judah's firstborn, was evil in the LORD's sight, so
the LORD killed him.

[8]Then Judah said to Onan, "Sleep with your brother's wife and
fulfill the duty of a brother-in-law to her so that you may raise
up a descendant for your brother." [9]But Onan knew that the
child would not be considered his. So whenever he slept with
his brother's wife, he wasted his emission on the ground so as
not to give his brother a descendant. [10]What he did was evil in
the LORD's sight, so the LORD killed him too.

[11]Then Judah said to his daughter-in-law Tamar, "Live as a
widow in your father's house until Shelah my son grows up."
For he thought, "I don't want him to die like his brothers." So
Tamar went and lived in her father's house.

[12]After some time Judah's wife, the daughter of Shua, died.
After Judah was consoled, he left for Timnah to visit his sheepshearers, along with his friend Hirah the Adullamite. [13]Tamar
was told, "Look, your father-in-law is going up to Timnah to shear
his sheep." [14]So she removed her widow's clothes and covered
herself with a veil. She wrapped herself and sat at the entrance

to Enaim which is on the way to Timnah. (She did this because
she saw that she had not been given to Shelah as a wife, even
though he had now grown up.)
15 When Judah saw her, he thought she was a prostitute because she had covered her face. 16 He turned aside to her along
the road and said, "Come, please, I want to sleep with you." (He
did not realize it was his daughter-in-law.) She asked, "What will
you give me so that you may sleep with me?" 17 He replied, "I'll
send you a young goat from the flock." She asked, "Will you give
me a pledge until you send it?" 18 He said, "What pledge should I
give you?" She replied, "Your seal, your cord, and the staff that's
in your hand." So he gave them to her, then slept with her, and
she became pregnant by him. 19 She left immediately, removed
her veil, and put on her widow's clothes.
20 Then Judah had his friend Hirah the Adullamite take a
young goat to get back from the woman the items he had given
in pledge, but Hirah could not find her. 21 He asked the men who
were there, "Where is the cult prostitute who was at Enaim by
the road?" But they replied, "There has been no cult prostitute
here." 22 So he returned to Judah and said, "I couldn't find her.
Moreover, the men of the place said, 'There has been no cult
prostitute here.'" 23 Judah said, "Let her keep the things for herself. Otherwise we will appear to be dishonest. I did indeed send
this young goat, but you couldn't find her."
24 After three months Judah was told, "Your daughter-in-law
Tamar has turned to prostitution, and as a result she has become
pregnant." Judah said, "Bring her out and let her be burned!"
25 While they were bringing her out, she sent word to her father-
in-law: "I am pregnant by the man to whom these belong." Then
she said, "Identify the one to whom the seal, cord, and staff belong." 26 Judah recognized them and said, "She is more upright
than I am, because I wouldn't give her to Shelah my son." He was
not physically intimate with her again.
27 When it was time for her to give birth, there were twins in her
womb. 28 While she was giving birth, one child put out his hand,
and the midwife took a scarlet thread and tied it on his hand,
saying, "This one came out first." 29 But then he drew back his
hand, and his brother came out before him. She said, "How you
have broken out of the womb!" So he was named Perez. 30 Afterward his brother came out—the one who had the scarlet thread
on his hand—and he was named Zerah.

JOSEPH AND POTIPHAR'S WIFE

39 Now Joseph had been brought down to Egypt. An Egyptian
named Potiphar, an official of Pharaoh and the captain of
the guard, purchased him from the Ishmaelites who had brought
him there. 2 The LORD was with Joseph. He was successful and
lived in the household of his Egyptian master. 3 His master observed that the LORD was with him and that the LORD made everything he was doing successful. 4 So Joseph found favor in his
sight and became his personal attendant. Potiphar appointed
Joseph overseer of his household and put him in charge of everything he owned. 5 From the time Potiphar appointed him over
his household and over all that he owned, the LORD blessed the

Egyptian's household for Joseph's sake. The blessing of the LORD was on everything that he had, both in his house and in his fields. 6 So Potiphar left everything he had in Joseph's care; he gave no thought to anything except the food he ate.

Now Joseph was well built and good-looking. 7 Soon after these things, his master's wife took notice of Joseph and said, "Come to bed with me." 8 But he refused, saying to his master's wife, "Look, my master does not give any thought to his household with me here, and everything that he owns he has put into my care. 9 There is no one greater in this household than I am. He has withheld nothing from me except you because you are his wife. So how could I do such a great evil and sin against God?" 10 Even though she continued to speak to Joseph day after day, he did not respond to her invitation to go to bed with her.

11 One day he went into the house to do his work when none of the household servants were there in the house. 12 She grabbed him by his outer garment, saying, "Come to bed with me!" But he left his outer garment in her hand and ran outside. 13 When she saw that he had left his outer garment in her hand and had run outside, 14 she called for her household servants and said to them, "See, my husband brought in a Hebrew man to us to humiliate us. He tried to go to bed with me, but I screamed loudly. 15 When he heard me raise my voice and scream, he left his outer garment beside me and ran outside."

16 So she laid his outer garment beside her until his master came home. 17 This is what she said to him: "That Hebrew slave you brought to us tried to humiliate me, 18 but when I raised my voice and screamed, he left his outer garment and ran outside."

19 When his master heard his wife say, "This is the way your slave treated me," he became furious. 20 Joseph's master took him and threw him into the prison, the place where the king's prisoners were confined. So he was there in the prison.

21 But the LORD was with Joseph and showed him kindness. He granted him favor in the sight of the prison warden. 22 The warden put all the prisoners under Joseph's care. He was in charge of whatever they were doing. 23 The warden did not concern himself with anything that was in Joseph's care because the LORD was with him and whatever he was doing the LORD was making successful.

REFLECT

How is God's kindness shown to Joseph in prison? How have you seen God show His kindness to you when you least expected it?

THE CUPBEARER AND THE BAKER

40 After these things happened, the cupbearer to the king of Egypt and the royal baker offended their master, the king of Egypt. 2 Pharaoh was enraged with his two officials, the cupbearer and the baker, 3 so he imprisoned them in the house of the captain of the guard in the same facility where Joseph was confined. 4 The captain of the guard appointed Joseph to be their attendant, and he served them.

They spent some time in custody. 5 Both of them, the cupbearer and the baker of the king of Egypt, who were confined in the prison, had a dream the same night. Each man's dream had its own meaning. 6 When Joseph came to them in the morning, he saw that they were looking depressed. 7 So he asked Pharaoh's officials, who were with him in custody in his master's house, "Why

do you look so sad today?" 8 They told him, "We both had dreams,
but there is no one to interpret them." Joseph responded, "Don't
interpretations belong to God? Tell them to me."
9 So the chief cupbearer told his dream to Joseph: "In my
dream, there was a vine in front of me. 10 On the vine there were
three branches. As it budded, its blossoms opened and its clusters ripened into grapes. 11 Now Pharaoh's cup was in my hand,
so I took the grapes, squeezed them into his cup, and put the
cup in Pharaoh's hand."
12 "This is its meaning," Joseph said to him. "The three branches
represent three days. 13 In three more days Pharaoh will reinstate
you and restore you to your office. You will put Pharaoh's cup in
his hand, just as you did before when you were cupbearer. 14 But
remember me when it goes well for you, and show me kindness.
Make mention of me to Pharaoh and bring me out of this prison,
15 for I really was kidnapped from the land of the Hebrews and
I have done nothing wrong here for which they should put me
in a dungeon."
16 When the chief baker saw that the interpretation of the
first dream was favorable, he said to Joseph, "I also appeared in
my dream and there were three baskets of white bread on my
head. 17 In the top basket there were baked goods of every kind
for Pharaoh, but the birds were eating them from the basket
that was on my head."
18 Joseph replied, "This is its meaning: The three baskets represent three days. 19 In three more days Pharaoh will decapi-
tate you and impale you on a pole. Then the birds will eat your
flesh from you."
20 On the third day it was Pharaoh's birthday, so he gave a feast
for all his servants. He "lifted up" the head of the chief cupbearer
and the head of the chief baker in the midst of his servants. 21 He
restored the chief cupbearer to his former position so that he
placed the cup in Pharaoh's hand, 22 but the chief baker he impaled, just as Joseph had predicted. 23 But the chief cupbearer
did not remember Joseph—he forgot him.

JOSEPH'S RISE TO POWER

41 At the end of two full years Pharaoh had a dream. As he was
standing by the Nile, 2 seven fine-looking, fat cows were
coming up out of the Nile, and they grazed in the reeds. 3 Then
seven bad-looking, thin cows were coming up after them from
the Nile, and they stood beside the other cows at the edge of the
river. 4 The bad-looking, thin cows ate the seven fine-looking, fat
cows. Then Pharaoh woke up.
5 Then he fell asleep again and had a second dream: There were
seven heads of grain growing on one stalk, healthy and good.
6 Then seven heads of grain, thin and burned by the east wind,
were sprouting up after them. 7 The thin heads swallowed up the
seven healthy and full heads. Then Pharaoh woke up and realized it was a dream.
8 In the morning he was troubled, so he called for all the diviner-priests of Egypt and all its wise men. Pharaoh told them his
dreams, but no one could interpret them for him. 9 Then the chief
cupbearer said to Pharaoh, "Today I recall my failures. 10 Pharaoh

was enraged with his servants, and he put me in prison in the house of the captain of the guards—me and the chief baker. 11 We each had a dream one night; each of us had a dream with its own meaning. 12 Now a young man, a Hebrew, a servant of the captain of the guards, was with us there. We told him our dreams, and he interpreted the meaning of each of our respective dreams for us. 13 It happened just as he had said to us—Pharaoh restored me to my office, but he impaled the baker."

14 Then Pharaoh summoned Joseph. So they brought him quickly out of the dungeon; he shaved himself, changed his clothes, and came before Pharaoh. 15 Pharaoh said to Joseph, "I had a dream, and there is no one who can interpret it. But I have heard about you, that you can interpret dreams." 16 Joseph replied to Pharaoh, "It is not within my power, but God will speak concerning the welfare of Pharaoh."

17 Then Pharaoh said to Joseph, "In my dream I was standing by the edge of the Nile. 18 Then seven fat and fine-looking cows were coming up out of the Nile, and they grazed in the reeds. 19 Then seven other cows came up after them; they were scrawny, very bad looking, and lean. I had never seen such bad-looking cows as these in all the land of Egypt! 20 The lean, bad-looking cows ate up the seven fat cows. 21 When they had eaten them, no one would have known that they had done so, for they were just as bad-looking as before. Then I woke up. 22 I also saw in my dream seven heads of grain growing on one stalk, full and good. 23 Then seven heads of grain, withered and thin and burned with the east wind, were sprouting up after them. 24 The thin heads of grain swallowed up the seven good heads of grain. So I told all this to the diviner-priests, but no one could tell me its meaning."

25 Then Joseph said to Pharaoh, "Both dreams of Pharaoh have the same meaning. God has revealed to Pharaoh what he is about to do. 26 The seven good cows represent seven years, and the seven good heads of grain represent seven years. Both dreams have the same meaning. 27 The seven lean, bad-looking cows that came up after them represent seven years, as do the seven empty heads of grain burned with the east wind. They represent seven years of famine. 28 This is just what I told Pharaoh: God has shown Pharaoh what he is about to do. 29 Seven years of great abundance are coming throughout the whole land of Egypt. 30 But seven years of famine will occur after them, and all the abundance will be forgotten in the land of Egypt. The famine will devastate the land. 31 The previous abundance of the land will not be remembered because of the famine that follows, for the famine will be very severe. 32 The dream was repeated to Pharaoh because the matter has been decreed by God, and God will make it happen soon.

33 "So now Pharaoh should look for a wise and discerning man and give him authority over all the land of Egypt. 34 Pharaoh should do this—he should appoint officials throughout the land to collect one-fifth of the produce of the land of Egypt during the seven years of abundance. 35 They should gather all the excess food during these good years that are coming. By Pharaoh's authority they should store up grain so the cities will have food, and they should preserve it. 36 This food should be held in storage for the land in preparation for the seven years of famine that

will occur throughout the land of Egypt. In this way the land will
survive the famine."
37 This advice made sense to Pharaoh and all his officials. 38 So
Pharaoh asked his officials, "Can we find a man like Joseph, one
in whom the Spirit of God is present?" 39 So Pharaoh said to Joseph, "Because God has enabled you to know all this, there is
no one as wise and discerning as you are! 40 You will oversee my
household, and all my people will submit to your commands.
Only I, the king, will be greater than you.
41 "See here," Pharaoh said to Joseph, "I place you in authority
over all the land of Egypt." 42 Then Pharaoh took his signet ring
from his own hand and put it on Joseph's. He clothed him with
fine linen clothes and put a gold chain around his neck. 43 Pharaoh had him ride in the chariot used by his second-in-command,
and they cried out before him, "Kneel down!" So he placed him
over all the land of Egypt. 44 Pharaoh also said to Joseph, "I am
Pharaoh, but without your permission no one will move his hand
or his foot in all the land of Egypt." 45 Pharaoh gave Joseph the
name Zaphenath-Paneah. He also gave him Asenath daughter
of Potiphera, priest of On, to be his wife. So Joseph took charge
of all the land of Egypt.
46 Now Joseph was 30 years old when he began serving Pharaoh king of Egypt. Joseph was commissioned by Pharaoh and
was in charge of all the land of Egypt. 47 During the seven years
of abundance the land produced large, bountiful harvests. 48 Joseph collected all the excess food in the land of Egypt during
the seven years and stored it in the cities. In every city he put
the food gathered from the fields around it. 49 Joseph stored up
a vast amount of grain, like the sand of the sea, until he stopped
measuring it because it was impossible to measure.
50 Two sons were born to Joseph before the famine came. Asenath daughter of Potiphera, priest of On, was their mother. 51 Joseph named the firstborn Manasseh, saying, "Certainly God has
made me forget all my trouble and all my father's house." 52 He
named the second child Ephraim, saying, "Certainly God has
made me fruitful in the land of my suffering."
53 The seven years of abundance in the land of Egypt came to an
end. 54 Then the seven years of famine began, just as Joseph had
predicted. There was famine in all the other lands, but throughout the land of Egypt there was food. 55 When all the land of
Egypt experienced the famine, the people cried out to Pharaoh
for food. Pharaoh said to all the people of Egypt, "Go to Joseph
and do whatever he tells you."
56 While the famine was over all the earth, Joseph opened the
storehouses and sold grain to the Egyptians. The famine was severe throughout the land of Egypt. 57 People from every country
came to Joseph in Egypt to buy grain because the famine was
severe throughout the earth.

JOSEPH'S BROTHERS IN EGYPT

42 When Jacob heard there was grain in Egypt, he said to his
sons, "Why are you looking at each other?" 2 He then said,
"Look, I hear that there is grain in Egypt. Go down there and buy
grain for us so that we may live and not die."

3 So ten of Joseph's brothers went down to buy grain from Egypt. 4 But Jacob did not send Joseph's brother Benjamin with his brothers, for he said, "What if some accident happens to him?" 5 So Israel's sons came to buy grain among the other travelers, for the famine was severe in the land of Canaan.

6 Now Joseph was the ruler of the country, the one who sold grain to all the people of the country. Joseph's brothers came and bowed down before him with their faces to the ground. 7 When Joseph saw his brothers, he recognized them, but he pretended to be a stranger to them and spoke to them harshly. He asked, "Where do you come from?" They answered, "From the land of Canaan, to buy grain for food."

8 Joseph recognized his brothers, but they did not recognize him. 9 Then Joseph remembered the dreams he had dreamed about them, and he said to them, "You are spies; you have come to see if our land is vulnerable!"

10 But they exclaimed, "No, my lord! Your servants have come to buy grain for food! 11 We are all the sons of one man; we are honest men! Your servants are not spies."

12 "No," he insisted, "but you have come to see if our land is vulnerable." 13 They replied, "Your servants are from a family of twelve brothers. We are the sons of one man in the land of Canaan. The youngest is with our father at this time, and one is no longer alive."

14 But Joseph told them, "It is just as I said to you: You are spies! 15 You will be tested in this way: As surely as Pharaoh lives, you will not depart from this place unless your youngest brother comes here. 16 One of you must go and get your brother, while the rest of you remain in prison. In this way your words may be tested to see if you are telling the truth. If not, then, as surely as Pharaoh lives, you are spies!" 17 He imprisoned them all for three days. 18 On the third day Joseph said to them, "Do as I say and you will live, for I fear God. 19 If you are honest men, leave one of your brothers confined here in prison while the rest of you go and take grain back for your hungry families. 20 But you must bring your youngest brother to me. Then your words will be verified and you will not die." They did as he said.

21 They said to one another, "Surely we're being punished because of our brother, because we saw how distressed he was when he cried to us for mercy, but we refused to listen. That is why this distress has come on us!" 22 Reuben said to them, "Didn't I say to you, 'Don't sin against the boy,' but you wouldn't listen? So now we must pay for shedding his blood!" 23 (Now they did not know that Joseph could understand them, for he was speaking through an interpreter.) 24 He turned away from them and wept. When he turned around and spoke to them again, he had Simeon taken from them and tied up before their eyes.

25 Then Joseph gave orders to fill their bags with grain, to return each man's money to his sack, and to give them provisions for the journey. His orders were carried out. 26 So they loaded their grain on their donkeys and left.

27 When one of them opened his sack to get feed for his donkey at their resting place, he saw his money in the mouth of his sack. 28 He said to his brothers, "My money was returned! Here

it is in my sack!" They were dismayed; they turned trembling to
one another and said, "What in the world has God done to us?"
29 They returned to their father Jacob in the land of Canaan and
told him all the things that had happened to them, saying, 30 "The
man, the lord of the land, spoke harshly to us and treated us as if
we were spying on the land. 31 But we said to him, 'We are honest
men; we are not spies! 32 We are from a family of twelve brothers; we are the sons of one father. One is no longer alive, and the
youngest is with our father at this time in the land of Canaan.'
33 "Then the man, the lord of the land, said to us, 'This is how I
will find out if you are honest men. Leave one of your brothers
with me, and take grain for your hungry households and go. 34 But
bring your youngest brother back to me so I will know that you
are honest men and not spies. Then I will give your brother back
to you and you may move about freely in the land.'"
35 When they were emptying their sacks, there was each man's
bag of money in his sack! When they and their father saw the bags
of money, they were afraid. 36 Their father Jacob said to them,
"You are making me childless! Joseph is gone. Simeon is gone.
And now you want to take Benjamin! Everything is against me."
37 Then Reuben said to his father, "You may put my two sons
to death if I do not bring him back to you. Put him in my care
and I will bring him back to you." 38 But Jacob replied, "My son
will not go down there with you, for his brother is dead and he
alone is left. If an accident happens to him on the journey you
have to make, then you will bring down my gray hair in sorrow
to the grave."

THE SECOND JOURNEY TO EGYPT

43 Now the famine was severe in the land. 2 When they finished eating the grain they had brought from Egypt, their
father said to them, "Return, buy us a little more food."
3 But Judah said to him, "The man solemnly warned us, 'You will
not see my face unless your brother is with you.' 4 If you send our
brother with us, we'll go down and buy food for you. 5 But if you
will not send him, we won't go down there because the man said
to us, 'You will not see my face unless your brother is with you.'"
6 Israel said, "Why did you bring this trouble on me by telling
the man you had one more brother?"
7 They replied, "The man questioned us thoroughly about ourselves and our family, saying, 'Is your father still alive? Do you have
another brother?' So we answered him in this way. How could
we possibly know that he would say, 'Bring your brother down'?"
8 Then Judah said to his father Israel, "Send the boy with me and
we will go immediately. Then we will live and not die—we and you
and our little ones. 9 I myself pledge security for him; you may hold
me liable. If I do not bring him back to you and place him here before you, I will bear the blame before you all my life. 10 But if we had
not delayed, we could have traveled there and back twice by now!"
11 Then their father Israel said to them, "If it must be so, then
do this: Take some of the best products of the land in your
bags, and take a gift down to the man—a little balm and a little
honey, spices and myrrh, pistachios and almonds. 12 Take double the money with you; you must take back the money that was

returned in the mouths of your sacks—perhaps it was an oversight. [13] Take your brother too, and go right away to the man.
[14] May the Sovereign God grant you mercy before the man so
that he may release your other brother and Benjamin! As for
me, if I lose my children I lose them."

[15] So the men took these gifts, and they took double the money
with them, along with Benjamin. Then they hurried down to
Egypt and stood before Joseph. [16] When Joseph saw Benjamin
with them, he said to the servant who was over his household,
"Bring the men to the house. Slaughter an animal and prepare
it, for the men will eat with me at noon." [17] The man did just as
Joseph said; he brought the men into Joseph's house.

[18] But the men were afraid when they were brought to Joseph's
house. They said, "We are being brought in because of the money
that was returned in our sacks last time. He wants to capture
us, make us slaves, and take our donkeys!" [19] So they approached
the man who was in charge of Joseph's household and spoke to
him at the entrance to the house. [20] They said, "My lord, we did
indeed come down the first time to buy food. [21] But when we
came to the place where we spent the night, we opened our
sacks and each of us found his money—the full amount—in the
mouth of his sack. So we have returned it. [22] We have brought
additional money with us to buy food. We do not know who put
the money in our sacks!"

[23] "Everything is fine," the man in charge of Joseph's household
told them. "Don't be afraid. Your God and the God of your father
has given you treasure in your sacks. I had your money." Then he
brought Simeon out to them.

[24] The servant in charge brought the men into Joseph's house.
He gave them water, and they washed their feet. Then he gave food
to their donkeys. [25] They got their gifts ready for Joseph's arrival
at noon, for they had heard that they were to have a meal there.
[26] When Joseph came home, they presented him with the gifts
they had brought inside, and they bowed down to the ground
before him. [27] He asked them how they were doing. Then he said,
"Is your aging father well, the one you spoke about? Is he still
alive?" [28] "Your servant our father is well," they replied. "He is
still alive." They bowed down in humility.

[29] When Joseph looked up and saw his brother Benjamin, his
mother's son, he said, "Is this your youngest brother, whom you
told me about?" Then he said, "May God be gracious to you, my
son." [30] Joseph hurried out, for he was overcome by affection
for his brother and was at the point of tears. So he went to his
room and wept there.

[31] Then he washed his face and came out. With composure he
said, "Set out the food." [32] They set a place for him, a separate place
for his brothers, and another for the Egyptians who were eating
with him. (The Egyptians are not able to eat with Hebrews, for the
Egyptians think it is disgusting to do so.) [33] They sat before him, arranged by order of birth, beginning with the firstborn and ending
with the youngest. The men looked at each other in astonishment.
[34] He gave them portions of the food set before him, but the portion for Benjamin was five times greater than the portions for any
of the others. They drank with Joseph until they all became drunk.

THE FINAL TEST

44 He instructed the servant who was over his household,
"Fill the sacks of the men with as much food as they can
carry and put each man's money in the mouth of his sack. 2 Then
put my cup—the silver cup—in the mouth of the youngest one's
sack, along with the money for his grain." He did as Joseph instructed.
3 When morning came, the men and their donkeys were sent
off. 4 They had not gone very far from the city when Joseph said
to the servant who was over his household, "Pursue the men at
once! When you overtake them, say to them, 'Why have you repaid good with evil? 5 Doesn't my master drink from this cup and
use it for divination? You have done wrong!'"
6 When the man overtook them, he spoke these words to them.
7 They answered him, "Why does my lord say such things? Far
be it from your servants to do such a thing! 8 Look, the money
that we found in the mouths of our sacks we brought back to
you from the land of Canaan. Why then would we steal silver or
gold from your master's house? 9 If one of us has it, he will die,
and the rest of us will become my lord's slaves!"
10 He replied, "You have suggested your own punishment! The
one who has it will become my slave, but the rest of you will go
free." 11 So each man quickly lowered his sack to the ground and
opened it. 12 Then the man searched. He began with the oldest
and finished with the youngest. The cup was found in Benjamin's sack! 13 They all tore their clothes! Then each man loaded
his donkey, and they returned to the city.
14 So Judah and his brothers came back to Joseph's house. He
was still there, and they threw themselves to the ground before
him. 15 Joseph said to them, "What did you think you were doing? Don't you know that a man like me can find out things like
this by divination?"
16 Judah replied, "What can we say to my lord? What can we
speak? How can we clear ourselves? God has exposed the sin of
your servants! We are now my lord's slaves, we and the one in
whose possession the cup was found."
17 But Joseph said, "Far be it from me to do this! The man in
whose hand the cup was found will become my slave, but the
rest of you may go back to your father in peace."
18 Then Judah approached him and said, "My lord, please allow
your servant to speak a word with you. Please do not get angry
with your servant, for you are just like Pharaoh. 19 My lord asked
his servants, 'Do you have a father or a brother?' 20 We said to my
lord, 'We have an aged father, and there is a young boy who was
born when our father was old. The boy's brother is dead. He is
the only one of his mother's sons left, and his father loves him.'
21 "Then you told your servants, 'Bring him down to me so I can
see him.' 22 We said to my lord, 'The boy cannot leave his father.
If he leaves his father, his father will die.' 23 But you said to your
servants, 'If your youngest brother does not come down with
you, you will not see my face again.' 24 When we returned to your
servant my father, we told him the words of my lord.
25 "Then our father said, 'Go back and buy us a little food.' 26 But
we replied, 'We cannot go down there. If our youngest brother

is with us, then we will go, for we won't be permitted to see the man's face if our youngest brother is not with us.'

27 "Then your servant my father said to us, 'You know that my wife gave me two sons. 28 The first disappeared and I said, "He has surely been torn to pieces." I have not seen him since. 29 If you take this one from me too and an accident happens to him, then you will bring down my gray hair in tragedy to the grave.'

30 "So now, when I return to your servant my father, and the boy is not with us—his very life is bound up in his son's life. 31 When he sees the boy is not with us, he will die, and your servants will bring down the gray hair of your servant our father in sorrow to the grave. 32 Indeed, your servant pledged security for the boy with my father, saying, 'If I do not bring him back to you, then I will bear the blame before my father all my life.'

33 "So now, please let your servant remain as my lord's slave instead of the boy. As for the boy, let him go back with his brothers. 34 For how can I go back to my father if the boy is not with me? I couldn't bear to see my father's pain."

THE RECONCILIATION OF THE BROTHERS

45 Joseph was no longer able to control himself before all his attendants, so he cried out, "Make everyone go out from my presence!" No one remained with Joseph when he made himself known to his brothers. 2 He wept loudly; the Egyptians heard it and Pharaoh's household heard about it.

3 Joseph said to his brothers, "I am Joseph! Is my father still alive?" His brothers could not answer him because they were dumbfounded before him. 4 Joseph said to his brothers, "Come closer to me," so they came near. Then he said, "I am Joseph your brother, whom you sold into Egypt. 5 Now, do not be upset and do not be angry with yourselves because you sold me here, for God sent me ahead of you to preserve life! 6 For these past two years there has been famine in the land and for five more years there will be neither plowing nor harvesting. 7 God sent me ahead of you to preserve you on the earth and to save your lives by a great deliverance. 8 So now, it is not you who sent me here, but God. He has made me an adviser to Pharaoh, lord over all his household, and ruler over all the land of Egypt. 9 Now go up to my father quickly and tell him, 'This is what your son Joseph says: "God has made me lord of all Egypt. Come down to me; do not delay! 10 You will live in the land of Goshen, and you will be near me—you, your children, your grandchildren, your flocks, your herds, and everything you have. 11 I will provide you with food there because there will be five more years of famine. Otherwise you would become poor—you, your household, and everyone who belongs to you."' 12 You and my brother Benjamin can certainly see with your own eyes that I really am the one who speaks to you. 13 So tell my father about all my honor in Egypt and about everything you have seen. But bring my father down here quickly!"

14 Then he threw himself on the neck of his brother Benjamin and wept, and Benjamin wept on his neck. 15 He kissed all his brothers and wept over them. After this his brothers talked with him.

LOVE TO GROW

BETTER THAN OUR OWN

GENESIS 45

Joseph's story is an encouraging example of how God's plans are better than our own, even when we don't understand what is going on.

Joseph had dreams, literally, about what God had promised to do in his life. He dreamed He would be a leader and that even his brothers would bow down to him. It's no surprise that his family didn't love the idea. The path to get there looked nothing like Joseph had hoped: dropped in a well, sold into slavery, imprisoned, and falsely accused. Because of Joseph's love for God, he served and worked humbly, honoring God with his actions. In the end, Joseph saw God keep His promise.

Along the way, Joseph connected with people, used his talents, and grew into a godly man. When we rush to make our plans and dreams happen in our own time, we often miss the opportunities God gives us to learn, grow, and connect.

None of my own dreams have happened the way that I thought they would. God has taken me on a winding journey that, like Joseph's, has been for God's glory but not always for my comfort. In Genesis 45:5–8 Joseph told his brothers,

"Now, do not be upset and do not be angry with yourselves because you sold me here, for God sent me ahead of you to preserve life! . . . God sent me ahead of you to preserve you on the earth and to save your lives by a great deliverance. So now, it is not you who sent me here, but God."

When our dreams feel derailed, it's easy to strive to make things happen on our own. We hide from our responsibilities out of disappointment. We read a passage of Scripture like this and think, "How nice for Joseph, it all worked out for him." God not only provided a way for Joseph; He sent Jesus to be our great deliverance. God isn't done paving a way, a path, or a detour that takes us to the place He has planned for us.

When we take time to look back on what God has done in our lives, we can find hope and peace in seeing what God can do with a detour. It's more than we could ever imagine!

16 Now it was reported in the household of Pharaoh, "Joseph's brothers have arrived." It pleased Pharaoh and his servants. 17 Pharaoh said to Joseph, "Say to your brothers, 'Do this: Load your animals and go to the land of Canaan! 18 Get your father and your households and come to me! Then I will give you the best land in Egypt and you will eat the best of the land.' 19 You are also commanded to say, 'Do this: Take for yourselves wagons from the land of Egypt for your little ones and for your wives. Bring your father and come. 20 Don't worry about your belongings, for the best of all the land of Egypt will be yours.'"

21 So the sons of Israel did as he said. Joseph gave them wagons as Pharaoh had instructed, and he gave them provisions for the journey. 22 He gave sets of clothes to each one of them, but to Benjamin he gave 300 pieces of silver and five sets of clothes. 23 To his father he sent the following: ten donkeys loaded with the best products of Egypt and ten female donkeys loaded with grain, food, and provisions for his father's journey. 24 Then he sent his brothers on their way and they left. He said to them, "As you travel don't be overcome with fear."

25 So they went up from Egypt and came to their father Jacob in the land of Canaan. 26 They told him, "Joseph is still alive and he is ruler over all the land of Egypt!" Jacob was stunned, for he did not believe them. 27 But when they related to him everything Joseph had said to them, and when he saw the wagons that Joseph had sent to transport him, their father Jacob's spirit revived. 28 Then Israel said, "Enough! My son Joseph is still alive! I will go and see him before I die."

THE FAMILY OF JACOB GOES TO EGYPT

46 So Israel began his journey, taking with him all that he had. When he came to Beer Sheba he offered sacrifices to the God of his father Isaac. 2 God spoke to Israel in a vision during the night and said, "Jacob, Jacob!" He replied, "Here I am!" 3 He said, "I am God, the God of your father. Do not be afraid to go down to Egypt, for I will make you into a great nation there. 4 I will go down with you to Egypt and I myself will certainly bring you back from there. Joseph will close your eyes."

5 Then Jacob started out from Beer Sheba, and the sons of Israel carried their father Jacob, their little children, and their wives in the wagons that Pharaoh had sent along to transport him. 6 Jacob and all his descendants took their livestock and the possessions they had acquired in the land of Canaan, and they went to Egypt. 7 He brought with him to Egypt his sons and grandsons, his daughters and granddaughters—all his descendants.

8 These are the names of the sons of Israel who went to Egypt—Jacob and his sons: Reuben, the firstborn of Jacob.

9 The sons of Reuben: Hanoch, Pallu, Hezron, and Carmi.
10 The sons of Simeon: Jemuel, Jamin, Ohad, Jakin, Zohar, and Shaul (the son of a Canaanite woman).
11 The sons of Levi: Gershon, Kohath, and Merari.
12 The sons of Judah: Er, Onan, Shelah, Perez, and Zerah (but Er and Onan died in the land of Canaan).
The sons of Perez were Hezron and Hamul.
13 The sons of Issachar: Tola, Puah, Jashub, and Shimron.

14 The sons of Zebulun: Sered, Elon, and Jahleel.
15 These were the sons of Leah, whom she bore to Jacob
in Paddan Aram, along with Dinah his daughter. His
sons and daughters numbered thirty-three in all.
16 The sons of Gad: Zephon, Haggi, Shuni,
Ezbon, Eri, Arodi, and Areli.
17 The sons of Asher: Imnah, Ishvah, Ishvi,
Beriah, and Serah their sister.
The sons of Beriah were Heber and Malkiel.
18 These were the sons of Zilpah, whom Laban gave to Leah
his daughter. She bore these to Jacob, sixteen in all.
19 The sons of Rachel the wife of Jacob: Joseph and Benjamin.
20 Manasseh and Ephraim were born to Joseph
in the land of Egypt. Asenath daughter of
Potiphera, priest of On, bore them to him.
21 The sons of Benjamin: Bela, Beker, Ashbel, Gera,
Naaman, Ehi, Rosh, Muppim, Huppim and Ard.
22 These were the sons of Rachel who were
born to Jacob, fourteen in all.
23 The son of Dan: Hushim.
24 The sons of Naphtali: Jahziel, Guni, Jezer, and Shillem.
25 These were the sons of Bilhah, whom Laban gave to Rachel
his daughter. She bore these to Jacob, seven in all.

26 All the direct descendants of Jacob who went to Egypt with
him were sixty-six in number. (This number does not include
the wives of Jacob's sons.) 27 Counting the two sons of Joseph
who were born to him in Egypt, all the people of the household
of Jacob who were in Egypt numbered seventy.

28 Jacob sent Judah before him to Joseph to accompany him
to Goshen. So they came to the land of Goshen. 29 Joseph harnessed his chariot and went up to meet his father Israel in Goshen. When he met him, he hugged his neck and wept on his
neck for quite some time.

30 Israel said to Joseph, "Now let me die since I have seen your
face and know that you are still alive." 31 Then Joseph said to his
brothers and his father's household, "I will go up and tell Pharaoh, 'My brothers and my father's household who were in the
land of Canaan have come to me. 32 The men are shepherds; they
take care of livestock. They have brought their flocks and their
herds and all that they have.' 33 Pharaoh will summon you and
say, 'What is your occupation?' 34 Tell him, 'Your servants have
taken care of cattle from our youth until now, both we and our
fathers,' so that you may live in the land of Goshen, for everyone
who takes care of sheep is disgusting to the Egyptians."

JOSEPH'S WISE ADMINISTRATION

47 Joseph went and told Pharaoh, "My father, my brothers,
their flocks and herds, and all that they own have arrived
from the land of Canaan. They are now in the land of Goshen."
2 He took five of his brothers and introduced them to Pharaoh.

3 Pharaoh said to Joseph's brothers, "What is your occupation?"
They said to Pharaoh, "Your servants take care of flocks, just as
our ancestors did." 4 Then they said to Pharaoh, "We have come

to live as temporary residents in the land. There is no pasture
for your servants' flocks because the famine is severe in the land
of Canaan. So now, please let your servants live in the land of
Goshen."

5 Pharaoh said to Joseph, "Your father and your brothers have
come to you. 6 The land of Egypt is before you; settle your father
and your brothers in the best region of the land. They may live
in the land of Goshen. If you know of any highly capable men
among them, put them in charge of my livestock."

7 Then Joseph brought in his father Jacob and presented him before Pharaoh. Jacob blessed Pharaoh. 8 Pharaoh said to Jacob, "How
long have you lived?" 9 Jacob said to Pharaoh, "All the years of my
travels are 130. All the years of my life have been few and painful;
the years of my travels are not as long as those of my ancestors."
10 Then Jacob blessed Pharaoh and went out from his presence.

11 So Joseph settled his father and his brothers. He gave them
territory in the land of Egypt, in the best region of the land, the
land of Rameses, just as Pharaoh had commanded. 12 Joseph also
provided food for his father, his brothers, and all his father's
household, according to the number of their little children.

13 But there was no food in all the land because the famine was
very severe; the land of Egypt and the land of Canaan wasted
away because of the famine. 14 Joseph collected all the money that
could be found in the land of Egypt and in the land of Canaan as
payment for the grain they were buying. Then Joseph brought
the money into Pharaoh's palace. 15 When the money from the
lands of Egypt and Canaan was used up, all the Egyptians came
to Joseph and said, "Give us food! Why should we die before your
very eyes because our money has run out?"

16 Then Joseph said, "If your money is gone, bring your livestock,
and I will give you food in exchange for your livestock." 17 So they
brought their livestock to Joseph, and Joseph gave them food in
exchange for their horses, the livestock of their flocks and herds,
and their donkeys. He got them through that year by giving them
food in exchange for all their livestock.

18 When that year was over, they came to him the next year
and said to him, "We cannot hide from our lord that the money
is used up and the livestock and the animals belong to our lord.
Nothing remains before our lord except our bodies and our land.
19 Why should we die before your very eyes, both we and our land?
Buy us and our land in exchange for food, and we, with our land,
will become Pharaoh's slaves. Give us seed that we may live and
not die. Then the land will not become desolate."

20 So Joseph bought all the land of Egypt for Pharaoh. Each
of the Egyptians sold his field, for the famine was severe. So
the land became Pharaoh's. 21 Joseph made all the people slaves
from one end of Egypt's border to the other end of it. 22 But he
did not purchase the land of the priests because the priests had
an allotment from Pharaoh and they ate from their allotment
that Pharaoh gave them. That is why they did not sell their land.

23 Joseph said to the people, "Since I have bought you and your
land today for Pharaoh, here is seed for you. Cultivate the land.
24 When the crop comes in, give one-fifth of it to Pharaoh. The
remaining four-fifths will be yours for seed for the fields and

for you to eat, including those in your households and your little children." 25 They replied, "You have saved our lives! You are showing us favor, and we will be Pharaoh's slaves."

26 So Joseph made it a statute, which is in effect to this day throughout the land of Egypt: One-fifth belongs to Pharaoh. Only the land of the priests did not become Pharaoh's.

27 Israel settled in the land of Egypt, in the land of Goshen, and they owned land there. They were fruitful and increased rapidly in number.

28 Jacob lived in the land of Egypt seventeen years; the years of Jacob's life were 147 in all. 29 The time for Israel to die approached, so he called for his son Joseph and said to him, "If now I have found favor in your sight, put your hand under my thigh and show me kindness and faithfulness. Do not bury me in Egypt, 30 but when I rest with my fathers, carry me out of Egypt and bury me in their burial place." Joseph said, "I will do as you say."

31 Jacob said, "Swear to me that you will do so." So Joseph gave him his word. Then Israel bowed down at the head of his bed.

MANASSEH AND EPHRAIM

48 After these things Joseph was told, "Your father is weakening." So he took his two sons Manasseh and Ephraim with him. 2 When Jacob was told, "Your son Joseph has just come to you," Israel regained strength and sat up on his bed. 3 Jacob said to Joseph, "The Sovereign God appeared to me at Luz in the land of Canaan and blessed me. 4 He said to me, 'I am going to make you fruitful and will multiply you. I will make you into a group of nations, and I will give this land to your descendants as an everlasting possession.'

5 "Now, as for your two sons, who were born to you in the land of Egypt before I came to you in Egypt, they will be mine. Ephraim and Manasseh will be mine just as Reuben and Simeon are. 6 Any children that you father after them will be yours; they will be listed under the names of their brothers in their inheritance. 7 But as for me, when I was returning from Paddan, Rachel died—to my sorrow—in the land of Canaan. It happened along the way, some distance from Ephrath. So I buried her there on the way to Ephrath" (that is, Bethlehem).

8 When Israel saw Joseph's sons, he asked, "Who are these?" 9 Joseph said to his father, "They are the sons God has given me in this place." His father said, "Bring them to me so I may bless them." 10 Now Israel's eyes were failing because of his age; he was not able to see well. So Joseph brought his sons near to him, and his father kissed them and embraced them. 11 Israel said to Joseph, "I never expected to see you again, but now God has allowed me to see your children too."

12 So Joseph moved them from Israel's knees and bowed down with his face to the ground. 13 Joseph positioned them; he put Ephraim on his right hand across from Israel's left hand, and Manasseh on his left hand across from Israel's right hand. Then Joseph brought them closer to his father. 14 Israel stretched out his right hand and placed it on Ephraim's head, although he was the younger. Crossing his hands, he put his left hand on Manasseh's head, for Manasseh was the firstborn.

15 Then he blessed Joseph and said,
"May the God before whom my fathers
Abraham and Isaac walked—
the God who has been my shepherd
all my life long to this day,
16 the angel who has protected me
from all harm—
bless these boys.
May my name be named in them,
and the name of my fathers Abraham and Isaac.
May they grow into a multitude on the earth."

17 When Joseph saw that his father placed his right hand on
Ephraim's head, it displeased him. So he took his father's hand
to move it from Ephraim's head to Manasseh's head. 18 Joseph
said to his father, "Not so, my father, for this is the firstborn. Put
your right hand on his head."
19 But his father refused and said, "I know, my son, I know. He
too will become a nation and he too will become great. In spite
of this, his younger brother will be even greater and his descendants will become a multitude of nations." 20 So he blessed them
that day, saying,
"By you will Israel bless, saying,
'May God make you like Ephraim and Manasseh.'"
Thus he put Ephraim before Manasseh.

21 Then Israel said to Joseph, "I am about to die, but God will
be with you and will bring you back to the land of your fathers.
22 As one who is above your brothers, I give to you the mountain slope, which I took from the Amorites with my sword and
my bow."

THE BLESSING OF JACOB

49 Jacob called for his sons and said, "Gather together so I can
tell you what will happen to you in future days.
2 "Assemble and listen, you sons of Jacob;
listen to Israel, your father.
3 Reuben, you are my firstborn,
my might and the beginning of my strength,
outstanding in dignity, outstanding in power.
4 You are destructive like water and will not excel,
for you got on your father's bed,
then you defiled it—he got on my couch!
5 Simeon and Levi are brothers,
weapons of violence are their knives!
6 O my soul, do not come into their council,
do not be united to their assembly, my heart,
for in their anger they have killed men,
and for pleasure they have hamstrung oxen.
7 Cursed be their anger, for it was fierce,
and their fury, for it was cruel.
I will divide them in Jacob,
and scatter them in Israel!
8 Judah, your brothers will praise you.

Your hand will be on the neck of your enemies,
your father's sons will bow down before you.
9 You are a lion's cub, Judah,
from the prey, my son, you have gone up.
He crouches and lies down like a lion;
like a lioness—who will rouse him?
10 The scepter will not depart from Judah,
nor the ruler's staff from between his feet,
until he comes to whom it belongs;
the nations will obey him.
11 Binding his foal to the vine,
and his colt to the choicest vine,
he will wash his garments in wine,
his robes in the blood of grapes.
12 His eyes will be red from wine,
and his teeth white from milk.
13 Zebulun will live by the haven of the sea
and become a haven for ships;
his border will extend to Sidon.
14 Issachar is a strong-boned donkey
lying down between two saddlebags.
15 When he sees a good resting place,
and the pleasant land,
he will bend his shoulder to the burden
and become a slave laborer.
16 Dan will judge his people
as one of the tribes of Israel.
17 May Dan be a snake beside the road,
a viper by the path,
that bites the heels of the horse
so that its rider falls backward.
18 I wait for your deliverance, O LORD.
19 Gad will be raided by marauding bands,
but he will attack them at their heels.
20 Asher's food will be rich,
and he will provide delicacies to royalty.
21 Naphtali is a free running doe,
he speaks delightful words.
22 Joseph is a fruitful bough,
a fruitful bough near a spring
whose branches climb over the wall.
23 The archers will attack him,
they will shoot at him and oppose him.
24 But his bow will remain steady,
and his hands will be skillful;
because of the hands of the Powerful One of Jacob,
because of the Shepherd, the Rock of Israel,
25 because of the God of your father,
who will help you,
because of the Sovereign God,
who will bless you
with blessings from the sky above,
blessings from the deep that lies below,
and blessings of the breasts and womb.

26 The blessings of your father are greater
than the blessings of the eternal mountains
or the desirable things of the age-old hills.
They will be on the head of Joseph
and on the brow of the prince of his brothers.
27 Benjamin is a ravenous wolf;
in the morning devouring the prey,
and in the evening dividing the plunder."

28 These are the twelve tribes of Israel. This is what their father said to them when he blessed them. He gave each of them
an appropriate blessing.
29 Then he instructed them, "I am about to go to my people.
Bury me with my fathers in the cave in the field of Ephron the
Hittite. 30 It is the cave in the field of Machpelah, near Mamre
in the land of Canaan, which Abraham bought for a burial plot
from Ephron the Hittite. 31 There they buried Abraham and his
wife Sarah; there they buried Isaac and his wife Rebekah; and
there I buried Leah. 32 The field and the cave in it were acquired
from the sons of Heth."
33 When Jacob finished giving these instructions to his sons,
he pulled his feet up onto the bed, breathed his last breath, and
went to his people.

THE BURIALS OF JACOB AND JOSEPH

50 Then Joseph hugged his father's face. He wept over him
and kissed him. 2 Joseph instructed the physicians in his
service to embalm his father, so the physicians embalmed Israel.
3 They took forty days, for that is the full time needed for em-
balming. The Egyptians mourned for him seventy days.
4 When the days of mourning had passed, Joseph said to Pharaoh's royal court, "If I have found favor in your sight, please say
to Pharaoh, 5 'My father made me swear an oath. He said, "I am
about to die. Bury me in my tomb that I dug for myself there in
the land of Canaan." Now let me go and bury my father; then I
will return.'" 6 So Pharaoh said, "Go and bury your father, just as
he made you swear to do."
7 So Joseph went up to bury his father; all Pharaoh's officials
went with him—the senior courtiers of his household, all the
senior officials of the land of Egypt, 8 all Joseph's household, his
brothers, and his father's household. But they left their little
children and their flocks and herds in the land of Goshen. 9 Chariots and horsemen also went up with him, so it was a very large
entourage.
10 When they came to the threshing floor of Atad on the other
side of the Jordan, they mourned there with very great and bitter
sorrow. There Joseph observed a seven-day period of mourning
for his father. 11 When the Canaanites who lived in the land saw
them mourning at the threshing floor of Atad, they said, "This is
a very sad occasion for the Egyptians." That is why its name was
called Abel Mizraim, which is beyond the Jordan.
12 So the sons of Jacob did for him just as he had instructed
them. 13 His sons carried him to the land of Canaan and buried
him in the cave of the field of Machpelah, near Mamre. This is

REFLECT

Which aspects of God's character are displayed through Joseph's story?

the field Abraham purchased as a burial plot from Ephron the
Hittite. 14 After he buried his father, Joseph returned to Egypt,
along with his brothers and all who had accompanied him to
bury his father.

15 When Joseph's brothers saw that their father was dead, they
said, "What if Joseph bears a grudge and wants to repay us in full
for all the harm we did to him?" 16 So they sent word to Joseph,
saying, "Your father gave these instructions before he died: 17 'Tell
Joseph this: Please forgive the sin of your brothers and the wrong
they did when they treated you so badly.' Now please forgive the
sin of the servants of the God of your father." When this message was reported to him, Joseph wept. 18 Then his brothers also
came and threw themselves down before him; they said, "Here
we are; we are your slaves." 19 But Joseph answered them, "Don't
be afraid. Am I in the place of God? 20 As for you, you meant to
harm me, but God intended it for a good purpose, so he could
preserve the lives of many people, as you can see this day. 21 So
now, don't be afraid. I will provide for you and your little children." Then he consoled them and spoke kindly to them.

22 Joseph lived in Egypt, along with his father's family. Joseph
lived 110 years. 23 Joseph saw the descendants of Ephraim to the
third generation. He also saw the children of Makir the son of
Manasseh; they were given special inheritance rights by Joseph.

24 Then Joseph said to his brothers, "I am about to die. But God
will surely come to you and lead you up from this land to the land
he swore on oath to give to Abraham, Isaac, and Jacob." 25 Joseph
made the sons of Israel swear an oath. He said, "God will surely
come to you. Then you must carry my bones up from this place."
26 So Joseph died at the age of 110. After they embalmed him, his
body was placed in a coffin in Egypt.

BY your Loyal Love you WILL lead the people whom you have redeemed

MEMORY VERSE

"By your loyal love you will lead the people whom you have redeemed; you will guide them by your strength to your holy dwelling place." *Exodus 15:13*

Exodus

INTRODUCTION

God's Power

The Book of Exodus displays the wondrous works of God. Despite the unfaithfulness of the Israelites, God demonstrated faithfulness to both His covenant and His people. This book records the first account of God giving the written law to humanity. The Ten Commandments, also known as the Decalogue, lay out God's standards for His people as they walk with Him.

Exodus is divided into two main sections. Chapters 1–19 display God's saving work and His miraculous hand. It describes how God delivered His people, Israel, from the Egyptians. Chapters 20–40 contain a series of laws and instructions that God gave to the Israelites. Many of these laws provided instructions on how to build the tabernacle, the place where God's Spirit would dwell, but the Decalogue remains the most recognized section of all the laws.

Moses is most commonly believed to be the author of Exodus, as well as the other four books that comprise the Pentateuch, the first five books of the Old Testament. Moses wrote these words as the Israelites wandered in the wilderness of Zin before they were permitted to enter the promised land of Canaan. The events occurred a few decades before Moses recorded them, around 1440 B.C. Along with the other writings in the Pentateuch, Moses wrote Exodus to the generation of Israelites preparing to enter the promised land of Canaan. Moses wrote down the wonders and miracles God performed in Egypt and in the wilderness to remind the people of God's guidance and His commitment to His promises. His deliverance of Israel out of Egypt and through the desert was a testament to His covenant love and faithfulness as He prepared them to enter Canaan.

When we read the Book of Exodus, we can be encouraged to love God greatly. God's hand is firmly on the lives and stories of His people, even when they disobey and turn from Him. God's care for His people is evident, and His character as Savior and Provider, as well as Lawgiver and Holy One, are on display on every page.

Jordan

OFFICIAL LANGUAGE
Arabic
POPULATION
10,021,000
UNREACHED POPULATION
9,339,000
PROFESSING CHRISTIANS
2.3%

Majd's Home

Say a Prayer Today

Pray for Majd and her ministry to Arab women. Pray that God will use her life and testimony to bring many to Himself.

HISTORY BIT

The country of Jordan lies where the two and a half Transjordan tribes of Israel settled after the conquest of Canaan. The people living in these areas in the first century were some of the first to hear the news of the gospel of Jesus. While it is a Muslim nation today, there are still many influential Christians in all classes of society.*

Source Information:
https://joshuaproject.net/countries/JO
*David B. Barrett, World Christian Encyclopedia, Jordan (New York, NY: Oxford University Press, 1982), 428.

MAJD'S STORY

The people of Israel crossed the Red Sea and were rescued from their Egyptian enemies. The victorious redemption of God led Moses and the people to sing the first song recorded in the Bible. God led the people of Israel out of slavery by His loyal love and strength. God chose the people of Israel, and because of His faithfulness and loyal love, He led them out of slavery and into the promised land.

When I read about God's loyal love as displayed in the Book of Exodus I remember when I moved to the United States. I was a single woman moving from my home in Jordan, away from my family and comfort zone, to serve as a missionary for Arab women. Serving as a missionary is a very uncommon thing for a woman to do in my culture, especially as a single woman.

I was far from my family and on my own for the first time. I did not have adequate financial resources, causing me to often question God's calling. However, even in the difficulty, I experienced God's loyal love. I experienced what it truly means to have the Lord guide me by His loyal love alone. I praise Him now for those difficult times because of the way I experienced His strength, faithfulness, and loyal love.

God is faithful, and He continues, in His loyal love, to lead and guide us through life. God's love is life-transforming. It is a source of strength and peace in my life, and it is by His loyal love alone that I can confidently walk through hardship and difficulty. His love is overwhelming, whether it manifests in the splitting of a sea or comfort in loneliness and worry.

6 WEEK READING PLAN

LOVE HIS WORD

Week	MONDAY	TUESDAY	WEDNESDAY	THURSDAY	FRIDAY
1	Exodus 1	Exodus 2:1-22	Exodus 2:23—3:22	Exodus 4	Exodus 5:1-21
	SOAP Exodus 1:20-21	SOAP Genesis 15:13-14	SOAP Exodus 3:14-15	SOAP Exodus 4:30-31	SOAP Psalm 10:17-18
2	Exodus 5:22—7:13	Exodus 7:14—8:15	Exodus 8:16—9:7	Exodus 9:8-35	Exodus 10-11
	SOAP Exodus 7:3-5	SOAP Psalm 95:3-5	SOAP Exodus 8:30-32	SOAP Job 38:22-23	SOAP Exodus 11:9-10
3	Exodus 12	Exodus 13	Exodus 14-15	Exodus 16-17	Exodus 18-19
	SOAP Exodus 12:14	SOAP Exodus 13:3	SOAP Exodus 15:13	SOAP Philippians 4:19	SOAP Exodus 19:5-6
4	Exodus 20	Exodus 21-22	Exodus 23-24	Exodus 25	Exodus 26
	SOAP Exodus 20:1-2	SOAP Psalm 19:7	SOAP Exodus 23:6-7	SOAP Hebrews 9:23	SOAP Matthew 27:50-51
5	Exodus 27-28	Exodus 29	Exodus 30	Exodus 31	Exodus 32-33
	SOAP Hebrews 7:20-22	SOAP Exodus 29:45-46	SOAP 1 Peter 1:15-16	SOAP Exodus 31:12-13	SOAP Exodus 32:13-14
6	Exodus 34	Exodus 35:1—36:7	Exodus 36:8—37:29	Exodus 38-39	Exodus 40
	SOAP Exodus 34:6-7	SOAP Exodus 35:21-22	SOAP 1 Corinthians 10:31	SOAP Hebrews 9:11-12	SOAP Exodus 40:38

BLESSING DURING BONDAGE IN EGYPT

1 These are the names of the sons of Israel who entered
Egypt—each man with his household entered with Jacob: 2 Reuben, Simeon, Levi, and Judah, 3 Issachar, Zebulun, and Benjamin,
4 Dan and Naphtali, Gad and Asher. 5 All the people who were
directly descended from Jacob numbered seventy. But Joseph
was already in Egypt, 6 and in time Joseph and his brothers and
all that generation died. 7 The Israelites, however, were fruitful,
increased greatly, multiplied, and became extremely strong, so
that the land was filled with them.

8 Then a new king, who did not know about Joseph, came to
power over Egypt. 9 He said to his people, "Look at the Israelite
people, more numerous and stronger than we are! 10 Come, let's
deal wisely with them. Otherwise they will continue to multiply, and if a war breaks out, they will ally themselves with our
enemies and fight against us and leave the country."

11 So they put foremen over the Israelites to oppress them with
hard labor. As a result they built Pithom and Rameses as store
cities for Pharaoh. 12 But the more the Egyptians oppressed them,
the more they multiplied and spread. As a result the Egyptians
loathed the Israelites, 13 and they made the Israelites serve rigor-
ously. 14 They made their lives bitter by hard service with mortar
and bricks and by all kinds of service in the fields. Every kind of
service the Israelites were required to give was rigorous.

15 The king of Egypt said to the Hebrew midwives, one of whom
was named Shiphrah and the other Puah, 16 "When you assist
the Hebrew women in childbirth, observe at the delivery: If it
is a son, kill him, but if it is a daughter, she may live." 17 But the
midwives feared God and did not do what the king of Egypt had
told them; they let the boys live.

18 Then the king of Egypt summoned the midwives and said
to them, "Why have you done this and let the boys live?" 19 The
midwives said to Pharaoh, "Because the Hebrew women are
not like the Egyptian women—for the Hebrew women are vigorous; they give birth before the midwife gets to them!" 20 So
God treated the midwives well, and the people multiplied and
became very strong. 21 And because the midwives feared God, he
made households for them.

22 Then Pharaoh commanded all his people, "All sons that are
born you must throw into the river, but all daughters you may
let live."

CHALLENGE

As you read through the Book of Exodus, keep a running tally of the miracles God performed. What do these miracles reveal about God's character?

REFLECT

Examine the ethical dilemma of the two midwives. Were they right to lie to the king to save the Israelite babies? Why or why not?

THE BIRTH OF THE DELIVERER

2 A man from the household of Levi married a woman who
was a descendant of Levi. 2 The woman became pregnant and
gave birth to a son. When she saw that he was a healthy child, she
hid him for three months. 3 But when she was no longer able to
hide him, she took a papyrus basket for him and sealed it with
bitumen and pitch. She put the child in it and set it among the
reeds along the edge of the Nile. 4 His sister stationed herself at
a distance to find out what would happen to him.

5 Then the daughter of Pharaoh came down to wash herself
by the Nile, while her attendants were walking alongside the
river, and she saw the basket among the reeds. She sent one of

her attendants, took it, 6 opened it, and saw the child—a boy, crying!—and she felt compassion for him and said, "This is one of the Hebrews' children."

7 Then his sister said to Pharaoh's daughter, "Shall I go and get a nursing woman for you from the Hebrews, so that she may nurse the child for you?" 8 Pharaoh's daughter said to her, "Yes, do so." So the young girl went and got the child's mother. 9 Pharaoh's daughter said to her, "Take this child and nurse him for me, and I will pay your wages." So the woman took the child and nursed him.

10 When the child grew older she brought him to Pharaoh's daughter, and he became her son. She named him Moses, saying, "Because I drew him from the water."

THE PRESUMPTION OF THE DELIVERER

11 In those days, when Moses had grown up, he went out to his people and observed their hard labor, and he saw an Egyptian man attacking a Hebrew man, one of his own people. 12 He looked this way and that and saw that no one was there, and then he attacked the Egyptian and concealed the body in the sand. 13 When he went out the next day, there were two Hebrew men fighting. So he said to the one who was in the wrong, "Why are you attacking your fellow Hebrew?"

14 The man replied, "Who made you a ruler and a judge over us? Are you planning to kill me like you killed that Egyptian?" Then Moses was afraid, thinking, "Surely what I did has become known." 15 When Pharaoh heard about this event, he sought to kill Moses. So Moses fled from Pharaoh and settled in the land of Midian, and he settled by a certain well.

16 Now a priest of Midian had seven daughters, and they came and began to draw water and fill the troughs in order to water their father's flock. 17 When some shepherds came and drove them away, Moses came up and defended them and then watered their flock. 18 So when they came home to their father Reuel, he asked, "Why have you come home so early today?" 19 They said, "An Egyptian man rescued us from the shepherds, and he actually drew water for us and watered the flock!" 20 He said to his daughters, "So where is he? Why in the world did you leave the man? Call him, so that he may eat a meal with us."

21 Moses agreed to stay with the man, and he gave his daughter Zipporah to Moses in marriage. 22 When she bore a son, Moses named him Gershom, for he said, "I have become a resident foreigner in a foreign land."

THE CALL OF THE DELIVERER

23 During that long period of time the king of Egypt died, and the Israelites groaned because of the slave labor. They cried out, and their desperate cry because of their slave labor went up to God. 24 God heard their groaning; God remembered his covenant with Abraham, with Isaac, and with Jacob. 25 God saw the Israelites, and God understood.

3 Now Moses was shepherding the flock of his father-in-law Jethro, the priest of Midian, and he led the flock to the far side of the desert and came to the mountain of God, to Horeb.

2 The angel of the LORD appeared to him in a flame of fire from
within a bush. He looked, and the bush was ablaze with fire, but it
was not being consumed! 3 So Moses thought, "I will turn aside to
see this amazing sight. Why does the bush not burn up?" 4 When
the LORD saw that he had turned aside to look, God called to
him from within the bush and said, "Moses, Moses!" And Moses
said, "Here I am." 5 God said, "Do not approach any closer! Take
your sandals off your feet, for the place where you are standing
is holy ground." 6 He added, "I am the God of your father, the God
of Abraham, the God of Isaac, and the God of Jacob." Then Moses
hid his face, because he was afraid to look at God.

7 The LORD said, "I have surely seen the affliction of my people
who are in Egypt. I have heard their cry because of their task-
masters, for I know their sorrows. 8 I have come down to deliver them from the hand of the Egyptians and to bring them
up from that land to a land that is both good and spacious, to a
land flowing with milk and honey, to the region of the Canaanites, Hittites, Amorites, Perizzites, Hivites, and Jebusites. 9 And
now indeed the cry of the Israelites has come to me, and I have
also seen how severely the Egyptians oppress them. 10 So now
go, and I will send you to Pharaoh to bring my people, the Israelites, out of Egypt."

11 Moses said to God, "Who am I that I should go to Pharaoh,
or that I should bring the Israelites out of Egypt?" 12 He replied,
"Surely I will be with you, and this will be the sign to you that I
have sent you: When you bring the people out of Egypt, you and
they will serve God at this mountain."

13 Moses said to God, "If I go to the Israelites and tell them, 'The
God of your fathers has sent me to you,' and they ask me, 'What
is his name?'—what should I say to them?"

14 God said to Moses, "I AM that I AM." And he said, "You must
say this to the Israelites, 'I AM has sent me to you.'" 15 God also
said to Moses, "You must say this to the Israelites, 'The LORD—the
God of your fathers, the God of Abraham, the God of Isaac, and
the God of Jacob—has sent me to you. This is my name forever,
and this is my memorial from generation to generation.'

16 "Go and bring together the elders of Israel and tell them, 'The
LORD, the God of your fathers, appeared to me—the God of Abraham, Isaac, and Jacob—saying, "I have attended carefully to you
and to what has been done to you in Egypt, 17 and I have promised that I will bring you up out of the affliction of Egypt to the
land of the Canaanites, Hittites, Amorites, Perizzites, Hivites,
and Jebusites, to a land flowing with milk and honey."'

18 "The elders will listen to you, and then you and the elders
of Israel must go to the king of Egypt and tell him, 'The LORD,
the God of the Hebrews, has met with us. So now, let us go three
days' journey into the wilderness, so that we may sacrifice to
the LORD our God.' 19 But I know that the king of Egypt will not
let you go, not even under force. 20 So I will extend my hand and
strike Egypt with all my wonders that I will do among them, and
after that he will release you.

21 "I will grant this people favor with the Egyptians, so that
when you depart you will not leave empty-handed. 22 Every woman will ask her neighbor and the one who happens to be staying

in her house for items of silver and gold and for clothing. You
will put these articles on your sons and daughters—thus you
will plunder Egypt!"

THE SOURCE OF SUFFICIENCY

4 Moses answered again, "And if they do not believe me or pay
attention to me, but say, 'The LORD has not appeared to you'?"
2 The LORD said to him, "What is that in your hand?" He said, "A
staff." 3 The LORD said, "Throw it to the ground." So he threw it to
the ground, and it became a snake, and Moses ran from it. 4 But
the LORD said to Moses, "Put out your hand and grab it by the
tail"—so he put out his hand and caught it, and it became a staff
in his hand—5 "that they may believe that the LORD, the God of
their fathers, the God of Abraham, the God of Isaac, and the God
of Jacob, has appeared to you."

6 The LORD also said to him, "Put your hand into your robe." So
he put his hand into his robe, and when he brought it out—there
was his hand, leprous like snow! 7 He said, "Put your hand back
into your robe." So he put his hand back into his robe, and when
he brought it out from his robe—there it was, restored like the
rest of his skin! 8 "If they do not believe you or pay attention to
the former sign, then they may believe the latter sign. 9 And if
they do not believe even these two signs or listen to you, then
take some water from the Nile and pour it out on the dry ground.
The water you take out of the Nile will become blood on the dry
ground."

10 Then Moses said to the LORD, "O my Lord, I am not an eloquent man, neither in the past nor since you have spoken to your
servant, for I am slow of speech and slow of tongue."

11 The LORD said to him, "Who gave a mouth to man, or who
makes a person mute or deaf or seeing or blind? Is it not I, the
LORD? 12 So now go, and I will be with your mouth and will teach
you what you must say."

13 But Moses said, "O my Lord, please send anyone else whom
you wish to send!"

14 Then the LORD became angry with Moses, and he said, "What
about your brother Aaron the Levite? I know that he can speak
very well. Moreover, he is coming to meet you, and when he sees
you he will be glad in his heart.

15 "So you are to speak to him and put the words in his mouth.
And as for me, I will be with your mouth and with his mouth,
and I will teach you both what you must do. 16 He will speak for
you to the people, and it will be as if he were your mouth and as
if you were his God. 17 You will also take in your hand this staff,
with which you will do the signs."

THE RETURN OF MOSES

18 So Moses went back to his father-in-law Jethro and said to him,
"Let me go, so that I may return to my relatives in Egypt and see
if they are still alive." Jethro said to Moses, "Go in peace." 19 The
LORD said to Moses in Midian, "Go back to Egypt, because all the
men who were seeking your life are dead." 20 Then Moses took
his wife and sons and put them on a donkey and headed back to
the land of Egypt, and Moses took the staff of God in his hand.

LOVE TO GROW

YOU ARE NOT ENOUGH

EXODUS 4:1–12

"You are not enough."

That lie has taken on many variations, nuances, and forms throughout time. It's the lie whispered to us by the enemy since the beginning of creation. It's a lie meant to keep us from stepping forward in faith to the things God has called us to do.

Sometimes the lie comes coupled with shame, fear, or comparison. We feel unqualified, unprepared, and unfit to fulfill the purpose God has for us. Whatever the form, it tricks us into thinking that somehow, at our very core, we aren't enough.

God created us with a purpose in mind. He does not view us as "not enough." There is no limitation that exists in us that God isn't ready to equip, fill, and empower. He prepared us in advance with everything we would need to do what He called us to do.

In Exodus 4:1–12 God told Moses what to do to rescue the Israelites from slavery in Egypt, but Moses wouldn't stop bringing up his limitations. He felt afraid, unqualified, and inadequate. He offered up every possible excuse to get out of the assignment God had given him.

I can relate to Moses. A few years ago, I was invited to be interviewed on a podcast to share part of my testimony. I had never done anything like that before, and public speaking was not on my list of things I aspired to do. When the interview began, I sensed the Holy Spirit giving me the right words to say. He helped me articulate my thoughts in a way that didn't come from my own public speaking ability. I didn't magically become a polished, well-trained speaker on the spot.

His grace allowed me to do what He had asked me to do.

That's why I know God meant it when He spoke to Moses in Exodus 4:11–12: "Who gave a mouth to man, or who makes a person mute or deaf or seeing or blind? Is it not I, the Lord? So now go, and I will be with your mouth and will teach you what you must say."

I learned after that interview that if God calls us to do something, He has already put the tools in our hands, the words in our mouths, and the resources in our lives. It's not because of who we are or what we are capable of on our own. It's because of the living and active Spirit of God in us. We are enough because Jesus is enough.

21 The LORD said to Moses, "When you go back to Egypt, see that
you do before Pharaoh all the wonders I have put under your
control. But I will harden his heart and he will not let the people
go. 22 You must say to Pharaoh, 'This is what the LORD has said,
"Israel is my son, my firstborn, 23 and I said to you, 'Let my son
go that he may serve me,' but since you have refused to let him
go, I will surely kill your son, your firstborn!'"'"

24 Now on the way, at a place where they stopped for the night,
the LORD met Moses and sought to kill him. 25 But Zipporah
took a flint knife, cut off the foreskin of her son and touched it
to Moses' feet, and said, "Surely you are a bridegroom of blood
to me." 26 So the LORD let him alone. (At that time she said, "A
bridegroom of blood," referring to the circumcision.)

27 The LORD said to Aaron, "Go to the wilderness to meet Moses. So he went and met him at the mountain of God and greeted
him with a kiss. 28 Moses told Aaron all the words of the LORD
who had sent him and all the signs that he had commanded him.
29 Then Moses and Aaron went and brought together all the Israelite elders. 30 Aaron spoke all the words that the LORD had
spoken to Moses and did the signs in the sight of the people,
31 and the people believed. When they heard that the LORD had
attended to the Israelites and that he had seen their affliction,
they bowed down close to the ground.

OPPOSITION TO THE PLAN OF GOD

5 Afterward Moses and Aaron went to Pharaoh and said, "This
is what the LORD, the God of Israel, has said, 'Release my people so that they may hold a pilgrim feast to me in the wilderness.'"
2 But Pharaoh said, "Who is the LORD that I should obey him by
releasing Israel? I do not know the LORD, and I will not release
Israel!" 3 And they said, "The God of the Hebrews has met with
us. Let us go a three-day journey into the wilderness so that we
may sacrifice to the LORD our God, so that he does not strike
us with plague or the sword." 4 The king of Egypt said to them,
"Moses and Aaron, why do you cause the people to refrain from
their work? Return to your labor!" 5 Pharaoh was thinking, "The
people of the land are now many, and you are giving them rest
from their labor."

6 That same day Pharaoh commanded the slave masters and
foremen who were over the people: 7 "You must no longer give
straw to the people for making bricks as before. Let them go and
collect straw for themselves. 8 But you must require of them the
same quota of bricks that they were making before. Do not reduce it, for they are slackers. That is why they are crying, 'Let us
go sacrifice to our God.' 9 Make the work harder for the men so
they will keep at it and pay no attention to lying words!"

10 So the slave masters of the people and their foremen went
to the Israelites and said, "Thus says Pharaoh: 'I am not giving
you straw. 11 You go get straw for yourselves wherever you can
find it, because there will be no reduction at all in your work-
load.'" 12 So the people spread out through all the land of Egypt
to collect stubble for straw. 13 The slave masters were pressuring
them, saying, "Complete your work for each day, just like when
there was straw!" 14 The Israelite foremen whom Pharaoh's slave

masters had set over them were beaten and were asked, "Why
did you not complete your requirement for brickmaking as in
the past—both yesterday and today?"
15 The Israelite foremen went and cried out to Pharaoh, "Why
are you treating your servants this way? 16 No straw is given to
your servants, but we are told, 'Make bricks!' Your servants are
even being beaten, but the fault is with your people."
17 But Pharaoh replied, "You are slackers! Slackers! That is why
you are saying, 'Let us go sacrifice to the LORD.'" 18 So now, get
back to work! You will not be given straw, but you must still produce your quota of bricks!" 19 The Israelite foremen saw that they
were in trouble when they were told, "You must not reduce the
daily quota of your bricks."
20 When they went out from Pharaoh, they encountered Moses and Aaron standing there to meet them, 21 and they said to
them, "May the LORD look on you and judge, because you have
made us stink in the opinion of Pharaoh and his servants, so
that you have given them an excuse to kill us!"

THE ASSURANCE OF DELIVERANCE

22 Moses returned to the LORD, and said, "Lord, why have you
caused trouble for this people? Why did you ever send me?
23 From the time I went to speak to Pharaoh in your name, he
has caused trouble for this people, and you have certainly not
rescued them!"
6 Then the LORD said to Moses, "Now you will see what I will
do to Pharaoh, for compelled by my strong hand he will release them, and by my strong hand he will drive them out of
his land."
2 God spoke to Moses and said to him, "I am the LORD. 3 I appeared to Abraham, to Isaac, and to Jacob as God Almighty, but
by my name 'the LORD' I was not known to them. 4 I also established my covenant with them to give them the land of Canaan,
where they were living as resident foreigners. 5 I have also heard
the groaning of the Israelites, whom the Egyptians are enslaving,
and I have remembered my covenant. 6 Therefore, tell the Israelites, 'I am the LORD. I will bring you out from your enslavement
to the Egyptians, I will rescue you from the hard labor they impose, and I will redeem you with an outstretched arm and with
great judgments. 7 I will take you to myself for a people, and I
will be your God. Then you will know that I am the LORD your
God, who brought you out from your enslavement to the Egyptians. 8 I will bring you to the land I swore to give to Abraham,
to Isaac, and to Jacob—and I will give it to you as a possession.
I am the LORD.'"
9 Moses told this to the Israelites, but they did not listen to
him because of their discouragement and hard labor. 10 Then
the LORD said to Moses, 11 "Go, tell Pharaoh king of Egypt that he
must release the Israelites from his land." 12 But Moses replied
to the LORD, "If the Israelites did not listen to me, then how will
Pharaoh listen to me, since I speak with difficulty?"
13 The LORD spoke to Moses and Aaron and gave them a charge
for the Israelites and Pharaoh king of Egypt to bring the Israelites out of the land of Egypt.

THE ANCESTRY OF MOSES AND AARON

14 These were the heads of their fathers' households:

The sons of Reuben, the firstborn son of Israel, were Hanoch and Pallu, Hezron and Carmi. These were the clans of Reuben. 15 The sons of Simeon were Jemuel, Jamin, Ohad, Jakin, Zohar, and Shaul, the son of a Canaanite woman. These were the clans of Simeon.

16 Now these were the names of the sons of Levi, according to their records: Gershon, Kohath, and Merari. (The length of Levi's life was 137 years.)

17 The sons of Gershon, by their families, were Libni and Shimei. 18 The sons of Kohath were Amram, Izhar, Hebron, and Uzziel. (The length of Kohath's life was 133 years.)

19 The sons of Merari were Mahli and Mushi. These were the clans of Levi, according to their records.

20 Amram married his father's sister Jochebed, and she bore him Aaron and Moses. (The length of Amram's life was 137 years.)

21 The sons of Izhar were Korah, Nepheg, and Zikri.

22 The sons of Uzziel were Mishael, Elzaphan, and Sithri.

23 Aaron married Elisheba, the daughter of Amminadab and sister of Nahshon, and she bore him Nadab and Abihu, Eleazar and Ithamar.

24 The sons of Korah were Assir, Elkanah, and Abiasaph. These were the Korahite clans.

25 Now Eleazar son of Aaron married one of the daughters of Putiel and she bore him Phinehas.

These were the heads of the fathers' households of Levi according to their clans.

26 It was the same Aaron and Moses to whom the LORD said, "Bring the Israelites out of the land of Egypt by their regiments." 27 They were the men who were speaking to Pharaoh king of Egypt, in order to bring the Israelites out of Egypt. It was the same Moses and Aaron.

THE AUTHENTICATION OF THE WORD

28 When the LORD spoke to Moses in the land of Egypt, 29 he said to him, "I am the LORD. Tell Pharaoh king of Egypt all that I am telling you." 30 But Moses said before the LORD, "Since I speak with difficulty, why should Pharaoh listen to me?"

7 So the LORD said to Moses, "See, I have made you like God to Pharaoh, and your brother Aaron will be your prophet. 2 You are to speak everything I command you, and your brother Aaron is to tell Pharaoh that he must release the Israelites from his land. 3 But I will harden Pharaoh's heart, and although I will multiply my signs and my wonders in the land of Egypt, 4 Pharaoh will not listen to you. I will reach into Egypt and bring out my regiments, my people the Israelites, from the land of Egypt with great acts of judgment. 5 Then the Egyptians will know that I am the LORD when I extend my hand over Egypt and bring the Israelites out from among them."

6 And Moses and Aaron did so; they did just as the LORD commanded them. 7 Now Moses was eighty years old and Aaron was eighty-three years old when they spoke to Pharaoh.

8 The LORD said to Moses and Aaron, 9 "When Pharaoh says

to you, 'Do a miracle,' and you say to Aaron, 'Take your staff and
throw it down before Pharaoh,' it will become a snake." 10 When
Moses and Aaron went to Pharaoh, they did so, just as the LORD
had commanded them—Aaron threw down his staff before Pharaoh and his servants and it became a snake. 11 Then Pharaoh also
summoned wise men and sorcerers, and the magicians of Egypt
by their secret arts did the same thing. 12 Each man threw down
his staff, and the staffs became snakes. But Aaron's staff swallowed up their staffs. 13 Yet Pharaoh's heart became hard, and he
did not listen to them, just as the LORD had predicted.

PLAGUE ONE: WATER TO BLOOD

14 The LORD said to Moses, "Pharaoh's heart is hard; he refuses
to release the people. 15 Go to Pharaoh in the morning when he
goes out to the water. Position yourself to meet him by the edge
of the Nile, and take in your hand the staff that was turned into
a snake. 16 Tell him, 'The LORD, the God of the Hebrews, has sent
me to you to say, "Release my people, that they may serve me
in the wilderness!" But until now you have not listened. 17 This
is what the LORD has said: "By this you will know that I am the
LORD: I am going to strike the water of the Nile with the staff
that is in my hand, and it will be turned into blood. 18 Fish in
the Nile will die, the Nile will stink, and the Egyptians will be
unable to drink water from the Nile."'" 19 Then the LORD said to
Moses, "Tell Aaron, 'Take your staff and stretch out your hand
over Egypt's waters—over their rivers, over their canals, over
their ponds, and over all their reservoirs—so that it becomes
blood.' There will be blood everywhere in the land of Egypt,
even in wooden and stone containers." 20 Moses and Aaron did
so, just as the LORD had commanded. He raised the staff and
struck the water that was in the Nile right before the eyes of
Pharaoh and his servants, and all the water that was in the Nile
was turned to blood. 21 When the fish that were in the Nile died,
the Nile began to stink, so that the Egyptians could not drink
water from the Nile. There was blood everywhere in the land
of Egypt! 22 But the magicians of Egypt did the same by their
secret arts, and so Pharaoh's heart remained hard, and he refused to listen to Moses and Aaron—just as the LORD had predicted. 23 And Pharaoh turned and went into his house. He did
not pay any attention to this. 24 All the Egyptians dug around
the Nile for water to drink, because they could not drink the
water of the Nile.

PLAGUE TWO: FROGS

8 25 Seven full days passed after the LORD struck the Nile. 1 Then
the LORD said to Moses, "Go to Pharaoh and tell him, 'This is
what the LORD has said: "Release my people in order that they
may serve me! 2 But if you refuse to release them, then I am going to plague all your territory with frogs. 3 The Nile will swarm
with frogs, and they will come up and go into your house, in
your bedroom, and on your bed, and into the houses of your
servants and your people, and into your ovens and your kneading troughs. 4 Frogs will come up against you, your people, and
all your servants."'"

5 The LORD spoke to Moses, "Tell Aaron, 'Extend your hand with
your staff over the rivers, over the canals, and over the ponds,
and bring the frogs up over the land of Egypt.'" 6 So Aaron extended his hand over the waters of Egypt, and frogs came up and
covered the land of Egypt.
7 The magicians did the same with their secret arts and brought
up frogs on the land of Egypt too.
8 Then Pharaoh summoned Moses and Aaron and said, "Pray
to the LORD that he may take the frogs away from me and my
people, and I will release the people that they may sacrifice to
the LORD." 9 Moses said to Pharaoh, "You may have the honor
over me—when shall I pray for you, your servants, and your people, for the frogs to be removed from you and your houses, so
that they will be left only in the Nile?" 10 He said, "Tomorrow."
And Moses said, "It will be as you say, so that you may know that
there is no one like the LORD our God. 11 The frogs will depart
from you, your houses, your servants, and your people; they will
be left only in the Nile."
12 Then Moses and Aaron went out from Pharaoh, and Moses
cried to the LORD because of the frogs that he had brought on
Pharaoh. 13 The LORD did as Moses asked—the frogs died in the
houses, the villages, and the fields. 14 The Egyptians piled them
in countless heaps, and the land stank. 15 But when Pharaoh saw
that there was relief, he hardened his heart and did not listen
to them, just as the LORD had predicted.

PLAGUE THREE: GNATS

16 The LORD said to Moses, "Tell Aaron, 'Extend your staff and
strike the dust of the ground, and it will become gnats throughout all the land of Egypt.'" 17 They did so; Aaron extended his hand
with his staff, he struck the dust of the ground, and it became
gnats on people and on animals. All the dust of the ground became gnats throughout all the land of Egypt. 18 When the magicians attempted to bring forth gnats by their secret arts, they
could not. So there were gnats on people and on animals. 19 The
magicians said to Pharaoh, "It is the finger of God!" But Pharaoh's
heart remained hard, and he did not listen to them, just as the
LORD had predicted.

PLAGUE FOUR: FLIES

20 The LORD said to Moses, "Get up early in the morning and position yourself before Pharaoh as he goes out to the water, and tell
him, 'This is what the LORD has said, "Release my people that they
may serve me! 21 If you do not release my people, then I am going
to send swarms of flies on you and on your servants and on your
people and in your houses. The houses of the Egyptians will be full
of flies, and even the ground they stand on. 22 But on that day I will
mark off the land of Goshen, where my people are staying, so that
no swarms of flies will be there, that you may know that I am the
LORD in the midst of this land. 23 I will put a division between my
people and your people. This sign will take place tomorrow."'" 24 The
LORD did so; a thick swarm of flies came into Pharaoh's house and
into the houses of his servants, and throughout the whole land of
Egypt the land was ruined because of the swarms of flies.

25Then Pharaoh summoned Moses and Aaron and said, "Go,
sacrifice to your God within the land." 26But Moses said, "That
would not be the right thing to do, for the sacrifices we make to
the LORD our God would be an abomination to the Egyptians.
If we make sacrifices that are an abomination to the Egyptians
right before their eyes, will they not stone us? 27We must go on a
three-day journey into the wilderness and sacrifice to the LORD
our God, just as he is telling us."

28Pharaoh said, "I will release you so that you may sacrifice
to the LORD your God in the wilderness. Only you must not go
very far. Do pray for me."

29Moses said, "I am going to go out from you and pray to the
LORD, and the swarms of flies will go away from Pharaoh, from
his servants, and from his people tomorrow. Only do not let Pharaoh deal falsely again by not releasing the people to sacrifice to
the LORD." 30So Moses went out from Pharaoh and prayed to
the LORD, 31and the LORD did as Moses asked—he removed the
swarms of flies from Pharaoh, from his servants, and from his
people. Not one remained! 32But Pharaoh hardened his heart
this time also and did not release the people.

PLAGUE FIVE: DISEASE

9 Then the LORD said to Moses, "Go to Pharaoh and tell him,
'This is what the LORD, the God of the Hebrews, has said, "Release my people that they may serve me! 2For if you refuse to
release them and continue holding them, 3then the hand of the
LORD will surely bring a very terrible plague on your livestock
in the field, on the horses, the donkeys, the camels, the herds,
and the flocks. 4But the LORD will distinguish between the livestock of Israel and the livestock of Egypt, and nothing will die
of all that the Israelites have."'"

5The LORD set an appointed time, saying, "Tomorrow the LORD
will do this in the land." 6And the LORD did this on the next day;
all the livestock of the Egyptians died, but of the Israelites' livestock not one died. 7Pharaoh sent representatives to investigate,
and indeed, not even one of the livestock of Israel had died. But
Pharaoh's heart remained hard, and he did not release the people.

PLAGUE SIX: BOILS

8Then the LORD said to Moses and Aaron, "Take handfuls of soot
from a furnace, and have Moses throw it into the air while Pharaoh is watching. 9It will become fine dust over the whole land of
Egypt and will cause boils to break out and fester on both people
and animals in all the land of Egypt." 10So they took soot from a
furnace and stood before Pharaoh, Moses threw it into the air, and
it caused festering boils to break out on both people and animals.

11The magicians could not stand before Moses because of the
boils, for boils were on the magicians and on all the Egyptians.
12But the LORD hardened Pharaoh's heart, and he did not listen
to them, just as the LORD had predicted to Moses.

PLAGUE SEVEN: HAIL

13The LORD said to Moses, "Get up early in the morning, stand
before Pharaoh, and tell him, 'This is what the LORD, the God

of the Hebrews, has said: "Release my people so that they may
serve me! 14 For this time I will send all my plagues on your
very self and on your servants and your people, so that you
may know that there is no one like me in all the earth. 15 For
by now I could have stretched out my hand and struck you
and your people with plague, and you would have been destroyed from the earth. 16 But for this purpose I have caused
you to stand: to show you my strength, and so that my name
may be declared in all the earth. 17 You are still exalting yourself against my people by not releasing them. 18 I am going to
cause very severe hail to rain down about this time tomorrow, such hail as has never occurred in Egypt from the day it
was founded until now. 19 So now, send instructions to gather your livestock and all your possessions in the fields to a
safe place. Every person or animal caught in the field and not
brought into the house—the hail will come down on them,
and they will die!"'"

20 Those of Pharaoh's servants who feared the LORD's message
hurried to bring their servants and livestock into the houses,
21 but those who did not take the LORD's message seriously left
their servants and their cattle in the field.

22 Then the LORD said to Moses, "Extend your hand toward
the sky that there may be hail in all the land of Egypt, on people
and on animals, and on everything that grows in the field in the
land of Egypt." 23 When Moses extended his staff toward the sky,
the LORD sent thunder and hail, and fire fell to the earth; so the
LORD caused hail to rain down on the land of Egypt. 24 Hail fell
and fire mingled with the hail; the hail was so severe that there
had not been any like it in all the land of Egypt since it had become a nation. 25 The hail struck everything in the open fields,
both people and animals, throughout all the land of Egypt. The
hail struck everything that grows in the field, and it broke all the
trees of the field to pieces. 26 Only in the land of Goshen, where
the Israelites lived, was there no hail.

27 So Pharaoh sent and summoned Moses and Aaron and said
to them, "I have sinned this time! The LORD is righteous, and I
and my people are guilty. 28 Pray to the LORD, for the mighty
thunderings and hail are too much! I will release you and you
will stay no longer."

29 Moses said to him, "When I leave the city I will spread my
hands to the LORD, the thunder will cease, and there will be no
more hail, so that you may know that the earth belongs to the
LORD. 30 But as for you and your servants, I know that you do not
yet fear the LORD God."

31 (Now the flax and the barley were struck by the hail, for the
barley had ripened and the flax was in bud. 32 But the wheat and
the spelt were not struck, for they are later crops.)

33 So Moses left Pharaoh, went out of the city, and spread out
his hands to the LORD, and the thunder and the hail ceased, and
the rain stopped pouring on the earth. 34 When Pharaoh saw that
the rain and hail and thunder ceased, he sinned again: both he
and his servants hardened their hearts. 35 So Pharaoh's heart remained hard, and he did not release the Israelites, as the LORD
had predicted through Moses.

PLAGUE EIGHT: LOCUSTS

10 The LORD said to Moses, "Go to Pharaoh, for I have hardened
his heart and the heart of his servants, in order to display
these signs of mine before him, 2 and in order that in the hearing
of your son and your grandson you may tell how I made fools of
the Egyptians and about my signs that I displayed among them,
so that you may know that I am the LORD."

3 So Moses and Aaron came to Pharaoh and told him, "This is
what the LORD, the God of the Hebrews, has said: 'How long do
you refuse to humble yourself before me? Release my people so
that they may serve me! 4 But if you refuse to release my people,
I am going to bring locusts into your territory tomorrow. 5 They
will cover the surface of the earth, so that you will be unable to
see the ground. They will eat the remainder of what escaped—
what is left over for you—from the hail, and they will eat every
tree that grows for you from the field. 6 They will fill your houses,
the houses of your servants, and all the houses of Egypt, such
as neither your fathers nor your grandfathers have seen since
they have been in the land until this day!'" Then Moses turned
and went out from Pharaoh.

7 Pharaoh's servants said to him, "How long will this man be
a menace to us? Release the people so that they may serve the
LORD their God. Do you not know that Egypt is destroyed?"

8 So Moses and Aaron were brought back to Pharaoh, and he
said to them, "Go, serve the LORD your God. Exactly who is going
with you?" 9 Moses said, "We will go with our young and our old,
with our sons and our daughters, and with our sheep and our cattle we will go, because we are to hold a pilgrim feast for the LORD."

10 He said to them, "The LORD will need to be with you if I release you and your dependents! Watch out! Trouble is right in
front of you. 11 No! Go, you men only, and serve the LORD, for
that is what you want." Then Moses and Aaron were driven out
of Pharaoh's presence.

12 The LORD said to Moses, "Extend your hand over the land
of Egypt for the locusts, that they may come up over the land of
Egypt and eat everything that grows in the ground, everything
that the hail has left." 13 So Moses extended his staff over the
land of Egypt, and then the LORD brought an east wind on the
land all that day and all night. The morning came, and the east
wind had brought up the locusts! 14 The locusts went up over all
the land of Egypt and settled down in all the territory of Egypt.
It was very severe; there had been no locusts like them before,
nor will there be such ever again. 15 They covered the surface
of all the ground so that the ground became dark with them,
and they ate all the vegetation of the ground and all the fruit
of the trees that the hail had left. Nothing green remained on
the trees or on anything that grew in the fields throughout the
whole land of Egypt.

16 Then Pharaoh quickly summoned Moses and Aaron and said,
"I have sinned against the LORD your God and against you! 17 So
now, forgive my sin this time only, and pray to the LORD your
God that he would only take this death away from me." 18 Moses
went out from Pharaoh and prayed to the LORD, 19 and the LORD
turned a very strong west wind, and it picked up the locusts and

blew them into the Red Sea. Not one locust remained in all the
territory of Egypt. 20 But the LORD hardened Pharaoh's heart,
and he did not release the Israelites.

PLAGUE NINE: DARKNESS

21 The LORD said to Moses, "Extend your hand toward heaven so
that there may be darkness over the land of Egypt, a darkness
so thick it can be felt."
22 So Moses extended his hand toward heaven, and there was
absolute darkness throughout the land of Egypt for three days.
23 No one could see another person, and no one could rise from
his place for three days. But the Israelites had light in the places
where they lived.
24 Then Pharaoh summoned Moses and said, "Go, serve the
LORD—only your flocks and herds will be detained. Even your
families may go with you."
25 But Moses said, "Will you also provide us with sacrifices and
burnt offerings that we may present them to the LORD our God?
26 Our livestock must also go with us! Not a hoof is to be left behind! For we must take these animals to serve the LORD our
God. Until we arrive there, we do not know what we must use
to serve the LORD."
27 But the LORD hardened Pharaoh's heart, and he was not willing to release them. 28 Pharaoh said to him, "Go from me! Watch
out for yourself! Do not appear before me again, for when you
see my face you will die!" 29 Moses said, "As you wish! I will not
see your face again."

PLAGUE TEN: DEATH

11 The LORD said to Moses, "I will bring one more plague on Pharaoh and on Egypt; after that he will release you from this place.
When he releases you, he will drive you out completely from this
place. 2 Instruct the people that each man and each woman is to
request from his or her neighbor items of silver and gold."
3 (Now the LORD granted the people favor with the Egyptians.
Moreover, the man Moses was very great in the land of Egypt,
respected by Pharaoh's servants and by the Egyptian people.)
4 Moses said, "This is what the LORD has said: 'About midnight
I will go throughout Egypt, 5 and all the firstborn in the land of
Egypt will die, from the firstborn son of Pharaoh who sits on his
throne, to the firstborn son of the slave girl who is at her hand
mill, and all the firstborn of the cattle. 6 There will be a great cry
throughout the whole land of Egypt, such as there has never been,
nor ever will be again. 7 But against any of the Israelites not even
a dog will bark against either people or animals, so that you may
know that the LORD distinguishes between Egypt and Israel.' 8 All
these your servants will come down to me and bow down to me,
saying, 'Go, you and all the people who follow you,' and after that
I will go out." Then Moses went out from Pharaoh in great anger.
9 The LORD said to Moses, "Pharaoh will not listen to you, so
that my wonders may be multiplied in the land of Egypt."
10 So Moses and Aaron did all these wonders before Pharaoh,
but the LORD hardened Pharaoh's heart, and he did not release
the Israelites from his land.

REFLECT

What does it mean that God hardened Pharaoh's heart? Why is this significant?

THE INSTITUTION OF THE PASSOVER

12 The LORD said to Moses and Aaron in the land of Egypt, 2 "This month is to be your beginning of months; it will be your first month of the year. 3 Tell the whole community of Israel, 'On the tenth day of this month they each must take a lamb for themselves according to their families—a lamb for each household. 4 If any household is too small for a lamb, the man and his next-door neighbor are to take a lamb according to the number of people—you will make your count for the lamb according to how much each one can eat. 5 Your lamb must be perfect, a male, one year old; you may take it from the sheep or from the goats. 6 You must care for it until the fourteenth day of this month, and then the whole community of Israel will kill it around sundown. 7 They will take some of the blood and put it on the two side posts and top of the doorframe of the houses where they will eat it. 8 They will eat the meat the same night; they will eat it roasted over the fire with bread made without yeast and with bitter herbs. 9 Do not eat it raw or boiled in water, but roast it over the fire with its head, its legs, and its entrails. 10 You must leave nothing until morning, but you must burn with fire whatever remains of it until morning. 11 This is how you are to eat it—dressed to travel, your sandals on your feet, and your staff in your hand. You are to eat it in haste. It is the LORD's Passover.

12 'I will pass through the land of Egypt in the same night, and I will attack all the firstborn in the land of Egypt, both of humans and of animals, and on all the gods of Egypt I will execute judgment. I am the LORD. 13 The blood will be a sign for you on the houses where you are, so that when I see the blood I will pass over you, and this plague will not fall on you to destroy you when I attack the land of Egypt.

14 'This day will become a memorial for you, and you will celebrate it as a festival to the LORD—you will celebrate it perpetually as a lasting ordinance. 15 For seven days you must eat bread made without yeast. Surely on the first day you must put away yeast from your houses because anyone who eats bread made with yeast from the first day to the seventh day will be cut off from Israel.

16 'On the first day there will be a holy convocation, and on the seventh day there will be a holy convocation for you. You must do no work of any kind on them, only what every person will eat—that alone may be prepared for you. 17 So you will keep the Feast of Unleavened Bread, because on this very day I brought your regiments out from the land of Egypt, and so you must keep this day perpetually as a lasting ordinance. 18 In the first month, from the fourteenth day of the month, in the evening, you will eat bread made without yeast until the twenty-first day of the month in the evening. 19 For seven days yeast must not be found in your houses, for whoever eats what is made with yeast—that person will be cut off from the community of Israel, whether a resident foreigner or one born in the land. 20 You will not eat anything made with yeast; in all the places where you live you must eat bread made without yeast.'"

21 Then Moses summoned all the elders of Israel, and told them, "Go and select for yourselves a lamb or young goat for

your families, and kill the Passover animals. 22 Take a branch of
hyssop, dip it in the blood that is in the basin, and apply to the
top of the doorframe and the two side posts some of the blood
that is in the basin. Not one of you is to go out the door of his
house until morning. 23 For the LORD will pass through to strike
Egypt, and when he sees the blood on the top of the doorframe
and the two side posts, then the LORD will pass over the door,
and he will not permit the destroyer to enter your houses to
strike you. 24 You must observe this event as an ordinance for
you and for your children forever. 25 When you enter the land
that the LORD will give to you, just as he said, you must observe
this ceremony. 26 When your children ask you, 'What does this
ceremony mean to you?'—27 then you will say, 'It is the sacrifice of the LORD's Passover, when he passed over the houses of
the Israelites in Egypt, when he struck Egypt and delivered our
households.'" The people bowed down low to the ground, 28 and
the Israelites went away and did exactly as the LORD had commanded Moses and Aaron.

THE DELIVERANCE FROM EGYPT

29 It happened at midnight—the LORD attacked all the firstborn
in the land of Egypt, from the firstborn of Pharaoh who sat on
his throne to the firstborn of the captive who was in the prison,
and all the firstborn of the cattle. 30 Pharaoh got up in the night,
along with all his servants and all Egypt, and there was a great cry
in Egypt, for there was no house in which there was not someone dead. 31 Pharaoh summoned Moses and Aaron in the night
and said, "Get up, get out from among my people, both you and
the Israelites! Go, serve the LORD as you have requested! 32 Also,
take your flocks and your herds, just as you have requested, and
leave. But bless me also."

33 The Egyptians were urging the people on, in order to send
them out of the land quickly, for they were saying, "We are all
dead!" 34 So the people took their dough before the yeast was
added, with their kneading troughs bound up in their clothing on their shoulders. 35 Now the Israelites had done as Moses
told them—they had requested from the Egyptians silver and
gold items and clothing. 36 The LORD gave the people favor in
the sight of the Egyptians, and they gave them whatever they
wanted, and so they plundered Egypt.

37 The Israelites journeyed from Rameses to Sukkoth. There
were about 600,000 men on foot, plus their dependents. 38 A
mixed multitude also went up with them, and flocks and herds—a
very large number of cattle. 39 They baked cakes of bread without yeast using the dough they had brought from Egypt, for it
was made without yeast. Because they were thrust out of Egypt
and were not able to delay, they could not prepare food for themselves either.

40 Now the length of time the Israelites lived in Egypt was
430 years. 41 At the end of the 430 years, on the very day, all the
regiments of the LORD went out of the land of Egypt. 42 It was a
night of vigil for the LORD to bring them out from the land of
Egypt, and so on this night all Israel is to keep the vigil to the
LORD for generations to come.

PARTICIPATION IN THE PASSOVER

43 The LORD said to Moses and Aaron, "This is the ordinance of
the Passover. No foreigner may share in eating it. 44 But everyone's servant who is bought for money, after you have circumcised him, may eat it. 45 A foreigner and a hired worker must not
eat it. 46 It must be eaten in one house; you must not bring any
of the meat outside the house, and you must not break a bone
of it. 47 The whole community of Israel must observe it.

48 "When a resident foreigner lives with you and wants to observe the Passover to the LORD, all his males must be circumcised, and then he may approach and observe it, and he will be
like one who is born in the land—but no uncircumcised person
may eat of it. 49 The same law will apply to the person who is native-born and to the resident foreigner who lives among you."

50 So all the Israelites did exactly as the LORD commanded
Moses and Aaron. 51 And on this very day the LORD brought the
Israelites out of the land of Egypt by their regiments.

THE LAW OF THE FIRSTBORN

13 The LORD spoke to Moses, 2 "Set apart to me every firstborn
male—the first offspring of every womb among the Israelites, whether human or animal; it is mine."

3 Moses said to the people, "Remember this day on which you
came out from Egypt, from the place where you were enslaved,
for the LORD brought you out of there with a mighty hand—and
no bread made with yeast may be eaten. 4 On this day, in the
month of Abib, you are going out.

5 "When the LORD brings you to the land of the Canaanites,
Hittites, Amorites, Hivites, and Jebusites, which he swore to
your fathers to give you, a land flowing with milk and honey,
then you will keep this ceremony in this month. 6 For seven days
you must eat bread made without yeast, and on the seventh day
there is to be a festival to the LORD. 7 Bread made without yeast
must be eaten for seven days; no bread made with yeast shall be
seen among you, and you must have no yeast among you within
any of your borders.

8 "You are to tell your son on that day, 'It is because of what the
LORD did for me when I came out of Egypt.' 9 It will be a sign for
you on your hand and a memorial on your forehead, so that the
law of the LORD may be in your mouth, for with a mighty hand
the LORD brought you out of Egypt. 10 So you must keep this ordinance at its appointed time from year to year.

11 "When the LORD brings you into the land of the Canaanites,
as he swore to you and to your fathers, and gives it to you, 12 then
you must give over to the LORD the first offspring of every womb.
Every firstling of a beast that you have—the males will be the
LORD's. 13 Every firstling of a donkey you must redeem with a
lamb, and if you do not redeem it, then you must break its neck.
Every firstborn of your sons you must redeem.

14 "In the future, when your son asks you 'What is this?' you are
to tell him, 'With a mighty hand the LORD brought us out from
Egypt, from the land of slavery. 15 When Pharaoh stubbornly refused to release us, the LORD killed all the firstborn in the land
of Egypt, from the firstborn of people to the firstborn of animals.

That is why I am sacrificing to the LORD the first male offspring of every womb, but all my firstborn sons I redeem.' 16 It will be for a sign on your hand and for frontlets on your forehead, for with a mighty hand the LORD brought us out of Egypt."

THE LEADING OF GOD

17 When Pharaoh released the people, God did not lead them by the way to the land of the Philistines, although that was nearby, for God said, "Lest the people change their minds and return to Egypt when they experience war." 18 So God brought the people around by the way of the wilderness to the Red Sea, and the Israelites went up from the land of Egypt prepared for battle.

19 Moses took the bones of Joseph with him, for Joseph had made the Israelites solemnly swear, "God will surely attend to you, and you will carry my bones up from this place with you."

20 They journeyed from Sukkoth and camped in Etham, on the edge of the desert. 21 Now the LORD was going before them by day in a pillar of cloud to lead them in the way, and by night in a pillar of fire to give them light, so that they could travel day or night. 22 He did not remove the pillar of cloud by day nor the pillar of fire by night from before the people.

THE VICTORY AT THE RED SEA

14 The LORD spoke to Moses, 2 "Tell the Israelites that they must turn and camp before Pi Hahiroth, between Migdol and the sea; you are to camp by the sea before Baal Zephon opposite it. 3 Pharaoh will think regarding the Israelites, 'They are wandering around confused in the land—the desert has closed in on them.' 4 I will harden Pharaoh's heart, and he will chase after them. I will gain honor because of Pharaoh and because of all his army, and the Egyptians will know that I am the LORD." So this is what they did.

5 When it was reported to the king of Egypt that the people had fled, the heart of Pharaoh and his servants was turned against the people, and the king and his servants said, "What in the world have we done? For we have released the people of Israel from serving us!" 6 Then he prepared his chariots and took his army with him. 7 He took 600 select chariots, and all the rest of the chariots of Egypt, and officers on all of them.

8 But the LORD hardened the heart of Pharaoh king of Egypt, and he chased after the Israelites. Now the Israelites were going out defiantly. 9 The Egyptians chased after them, and all the horses and chariots of Pharaoh and his horsemen and his army overtook them camping by the sea, beside Pi Hahiroth, before Baal Zephon. 10 When Pharaoh got closer, the Israelites looked up, and there were the Egyptians marching after them, and they were terrified. The Israelites cried out to the LORD, 11 and they said to Moses, "Is it because there are no graves in Egypt that you have taken us away to die in the desert? What in the world have you done to us by bringing us out of Egypt? 12 Isn't this what we told you in Egypt, 'Leave us alone so that we can serve the Egyptians, because it is better for us to serve the Egyptians than to die in the desert!'"

13 Moses said to the people, "Do not fear! Stand firm and see
the salvation of the LORD that he will provide for you today; for
the Egyptians that you see today you will never, ever see again.
14 The LORD will fight for you, and you can be still."
15 The LORD said to Moses, "Why do you cry out to me? Tell the
Israelites to move on. 16 And as for you, lift up your staff and extend your hand toward the sea and divide it, so that the Israelites may go through the middle of the sea on dry ground. 17 And
as for me, I am going to harden the hearts of the Egyptians so
that they will come after them, that I may be honored because of
Pharaoh and his army and his chariots and his horsemen. 18 And
the Egyptians will know that I am the LORD when I have gained
my honor because of Pharaoh, his chariots, and his horsemen."
19 The angel of God, who was going before the camp of Israel,
moved and went behind them, and the pillar of cloud moved
from before them and stood behind them. 20 It came between
the Egyptian camp and the Israelite camp; it was a dark cloud
and it lit up the night so that one camp did not come near the
other the whole night. 21 Moses stretched out his hand toward
the sea, and the LORD drove the sea apart by a strong east wind
all that night, and he made the sea into dry land, and the water
was divided. 22 So the Israelites went through the middle of the
sea on dry ground, the water forming a wall for them on their
right and on their left.
23 The Egyptians chased them and followed them into the middle of the sea—all the horses of Pharaoh, his chariots, and his
horsemen. 24 In the morning watch the LORD looked down on
the Egyptian army through the pillar of fire and cloud, and he
threw the Egyptian army into a panic. 25 He jammed the wheels
of their chariots so that they had difficulty driving, and the Egyptians said, "Let's flee from Israel, for the LORD fights for them
against Egypt!"
26 The LORD said to Moses, "Extend your hand toward the sea,
so that the waters may flow back on the Egyptians, on their chariots, and on their horsemen!" 27 So Moses extended his hand toward the sea, and the sea returned to its normal state when the
sun began to rise. Now the Egyptians were fleeing before it, but
the LORD overthrew the Egyptians in the middle of the sea. 28 The
water returned and covered the chariots and the horsemen and
all the army of Pharaoh that was coming after the Israelites into
the sea—not so much as one of them survived! 29 But the Israelites walked on dry ground in the middle of the sea, the water
forming a wall for them on their right and on their left. 30 So
the LORD saved Israel on that day from the power of the Egyptians, and Israel saw the Egyptians dead on the shore of the sea.
31 When Israel saw the great power that the LORD had exercised
over the Egyptians, they feared the LORD, and they believed in
the LORD and in his servant Moses.

THE SONG OF TRIUMPH

15 Then Moses and the Israelites sang this song to the LORD.
They said,

"I will sing to the LORD, for he has triumphed gloriously,
the horse and its rider he has thrown into the sea.

DON'T BE AFRAID

EXODUS 14:13–14

They were ready to go back into slavery, to the life they once knew.

Was their former life painful? Sure. Was it oppressive? You bet. But life in Egypt as slaves was all the Israelites knew. They found themselves free people, in a dry desert, with a sea in front of them, and an army of angry Egyptians behind them.

They did not sign up for this. They cried and groaned to the Lord, wishing they had never left their land of familiar slavery in the first place. Fear had overtaken them. All they wanted was to return to Egypt, to the land of slavery. They were convinced that leaving their slavery was a mistake.

They had forgotten.

In their moment of fear, they forgot all that God had miraculously done on their behalf to rescue them from their bondage. They had forgotten, in a moment of fear, that God was with them and was leading them out of captivity. All they had to do was continue to walk forward in faith with their eyes on God. Whether it was day or night, God's presence was always with them on their journey out of slavery and into freedom.

Yet they feared.

Sometimes fear poisons our memory. It makes us want to return to captivity because it is what we know, instead of facing the uncertainty that comes with freedom. Regardless of the fear, God calls us onward. He proves to us time and time again that He is trustworthy. He lovingly calls us to step forward in faith and to trust Him.

Instead of allowing fear to poison our hearts and minds, we are to stand firm in the direction God is leading us to go. We are not called to fight these battles, but rather to trust God, stand firm in His calling, and be still. We are called to wait on the Lord as He fights on our behalf.

Take heart, sweet friend, you were not made for a land of slavery. Trust Him in the direction He is leading you to travel. Keep your eyes on Him, walk forward in faith, and do not let your heart be fearful. God is with you!

2 The LORD is my strength and my song,
and he has become my salvation.
This is my God, and I will praise him,
my father's God, and I will exalt him.
3 The LORD is a warrior—
the LORD is his name.
4 The chariots of Pharaoh and his army
he has thrown into the sea,
and his chosen officers were drowned in the Red Sea.
5 The depths have covered them;
they went down to the bottom like a stone.
6 Your right hand, O LORD, was majestic in power;
your right hand, O LORD, shattered the enemy.
7 In the abundance of your majesty you have overthrown
those who rise up against you.
You sent forth your wrath;
it consumed them like stubble.
8 By the blast of your nostrils the waters were piled up,
the flowing water stood upright like a heap,
and the deep waters were solidified in the heart of the sea.
9 The enemy said, 'I will chase, I will overtake,
I will divide the spoil;
my desire will be satisfied on them.
I will draw my sword, my hand will destroy them.'
10 But you blew with your breath, and the sea covered them.
They sank like lead in the mighty waters.
11 Who is like you, O LORD, among the gods?
Who is like you—majestic in holiness, fearful
in praises, working wonders?
12 You stretched out your right hand,
the earth swallowed them.
13 By your loyal love you will lead the people
whom you have redeemed;
you will guide them by your strength
to your holy dwelling place.
14 The nations will hear and tremble;
anguish will seize the inhabitants of Philistia.
15 Then the chiefs of Edom will be terrified,
trembling will seize the leaders of Moab,
and the inhabitants of Canaan will shake.
16 Fear and dread will fall on them;
by the greatness of your arm they will be as still as stone
until your people pass by, O LORD,
until the people whom you have bought pass by.
17 You will bring them in and plant them in
the mountain of your inheritance,
in the place you made for your residence, O LORD,
the sanctuary, O Lord, that your hands have established.
18 The LORD will reign forever and ever!
19 For the horses of Pharaoh came with his
chariots and his footmen into the sea,
and the LORD brought back the waters of the sea on them,
but the Israelites walked on dry land
in the middle of the sea."

REFLECT

Exodus 15 is the first recorded song in the Bible. Take a few minutes to read through this song to praise God for His deliverance in your life, looking forward to what He will do in your future.

20 Miriam the prophetess, the sister of Aaron, took a hand
drum in her hand, and all the women went out after her with
hand drums and with dances. 21 Miriam sang in response to them,
"Sing to the LORD, for he has triumphed gloriously;
the horse and its rider he has thrown into the sea."

THE BITTER WATER

22 Then Moses led Israel to journey away from the Red Sea. They
went out to the wilderness of Shur, walked for three days into
the wilderness, and found no water. 23 Then they came to Marah,
but they were not able to drink the waters of Marah, because
they were bitter. (That is why its name was Marah.)
24 So the people murmured against Moses, saying, "What can
we drink?" 25 He cried out to the LORD, and the LORD showed
him a tree. When Moses threw it into the water, the water became safe to drink. There the LORD made for them a binding
ordinance, and there he tested them. 26 He said, "If you will diligently obey the LORD your God, and do what is right in his sight,
and pay attention to his commandments, and keep all his statutes, then all the diseases that I brought on the Egyptians I will
not bring on you, for I, the LORD, am your healer."
27 Then they came to Elim, where there were twelve wells of water and seventy palm trees, and they camped there by the water.

THE PROVISION OF MANNA

16 When they journeyed from Elim, the entire company of
Israelites came to the wilderness of Sin, which is between
Elim and Sinai, on the fifteenth day of the second month after
their exodus from the land of Egypt. 2 The entire company of Israelites murmured against Moses and Aaron in the wilderness.
3 The Israelites said to them, "If only we had died by the hand of
the LORD in the land of Egypt, when we sat by the pots of meat,
when we ate bread to the full, for you have brought us out into
this wilderness to kill this whole assembly with hunger!"
4 Then the LORD said to Moses, "I am going to rain bread from
heaven for you, and the people will go out and gather the amount
for each day, so that I may test them. Will they walk in my law or
not? 5 On the sixth day they will prepare what they bring in, and
it will be twice as much as they gather every other day."
6 Moses and Aaron said to all the Israelites, "In the evening
you will know that the LORD has brought you out of the land of
Egypt, 7 and in the morning you will see the glory of the LORD,
because he has heard your murmurings against the LORD. As for
us, what are we, that you should murmur against us?"
8 Moses said, "You will know this when the LORD gives you
meat to eat in the evening and bread in the morning to satisfy
you, because the LORD has heard your murmurings that you are
murmuring against him. As for us, what are we? Your murmurings are not against us, but against the LORD."
9 Then Moses said to Aaron, "Tell the whole community of the
Israelites, 'Come before the LORD, because he has heard your
murmurings.'"
10 As Aaron spoke to the whole community of the Israelites
and they looked toward the wilderness, there the glory of the

LORD appeared in the cloud, 11 and the LORD spoke to Moses, 12 "I
have heard the murmurings of the Israelites. Tell them, 'During
the evening you will eat meat, and in the morning you will be
satisfied with bread, so that you may know that I am the LORD
your God.'"

13 In the evening the quail came up and covered the camp, and
in the morning a layer of dew was all around the camp. 14 When
the layer of dew had evaporated, there on the surface of the wilderness was a thin flaky substance, thin like frost on the earth.
15 When the Israelites saw it, they said to one another, "What is
it?" because they did not know what it was. Moses said to them,
"It is the bread that the LORD has given you for food.

16 "This is what the LORD has commanded: 'Each person is to
gather from it what he can eat, an omer per person according
to the number of your people; each one will pick it up for whoever lives in his tent.'" 17 The Israelites did so, and they gathered—
some more, some less. 18 When they measured with an omer, the
one who gathered much had nothing left over, and the one who
gathered little lacked nothing; each one had gathered what he
could eat.

19 Moses said to them, "No one is to keep any of it until morning." 20 But they did not listen to Moses; some kept part of it
until morning, and it was full of worms and began to stink, and
Moses was angry with them. 21 So they gathered it each morning, each person according to what he could eat, and when the
sun got hot, it would melt. 22 And on the sixth day they gathered
twice as much food, two omers per person; and all the leaders of
the community came and told Moses. 23 He said to them, "This is
what the LORD has said: 'Tomorrow is a time of cessation from
work, a holy Sabbath to the LORD. Whatever you want to bake,
bake today; whatever you want to boil, boil today; whatever is
left put aside for yourselves to be kept until morning.'"

24 So they put it aside until the morning, just as Moses had
commanded, and it did not stink, nor were there any worms in
it. 25 Moses said, "Eat it today, for today is a Sabbath to the LORD;
today you will not find it in the area. 26 Six days you will gather
it, but on the seventh day, the Sabbath, there will not be any."

27 On the seventh day some of the people went out to gather
it, but they found nothing. 28 So the LORD said to Moses, "How
long do you refuse to obey my commandments and my instructions? 29 See, because the LORD has given you the Sabbath, that
is why he is giving you food for two days on the sixth day. Each
of you stay where you are; let no one go out of his place on the
seventh day." 30 So the people rested on the seventh day.

31 The house of Israel called its name "manna." It was like coriander seed and was white, and it tasted like wafers with honey.

32 Moses said, "This is what the LORD has commanded: 'Fill an
omer with it to be kept for generations to come, so that they
may see the food I fed you in the wilderness when I brought
you out from the land of Egypt.'" 33 Moses said to Aaron, "Take a
jar and put in it an omer full of manna, and place it before the
LORD to be kept for generations to come." 34 Just as the LORD
commanded Moses, so Aaron placed it before the ark of the testimony for safekeeping.

35 Now the Israelites ate manna forty years, until they came
to a land that was inhabited; they ate manna until they came to
the border of the land of Canaan. 36 (Now an omer is one-tenth
of an ephah.)

WATER AT MASSAH AND MERIBAH

17 The whole community of the Israelites traveled on their
journey from the wilderness of Sin according to the LORD's
instruction, and they pitched camp in Rephidim. Now there was
no water for the people to drink. 2 So the people contended with
Moses, and they said, "Give us water to drink!" Moses said to them,
"Why do you contend with me? Why do you test the LORD?" 3 But
the people were very thirsty there for water, and they murmured
against Moses and said, "Why in the world did you bring us up
from Egypt—to kill us and our children and our cattle with thirst?"
4 Then Moses cried out to the LORD, "What will I do with this
people?—a little more and they will stone me!" 5 The LORD said
to Moses, "Go over before the people; take with you some of the
elders of Israel and take in your hand your staff with which you
struck the Nile and go. 6 I will be standing before you there on
the rock in Horeb, and you will strike the rock, and water will
come out of it so that the people may drink." And Moses did so
in plain view of the elders of Israel.
7 He called the name of the place Massah and Meribah, because
of the contending of the Israelites and because of their testing
the LORD, saying, "Is the LORD among us or not?"

VICTORY OVER THE AMALEKITES

8 Amalek came and attacked Israel in Rephidim. 9 So Moses said
to Joshua, "Choose some of our men and go out, fight against
Amalek. Tomorrow I will stand on top of the hill with the staff
of God in my hand."
10 So Joshua fought against Amalek just as Moses had instructed him, and Moses and Aaron and Hur went up to the top
of the hill. 11 Whenever Moses would raise his hands, then Israel
prevailed, but whenever he would rest his hands, then Amalek
prevailed. 12 When the hands of Moses became heavy, they took
a stone and put it under him, and Aaron and Hur held up his
hands, one on one side and one on the other, and so his hands
were steady until the sun went down. 13 So Joshua destroyed Amalek and his army with the sword.
14 The LORD said to Moses, "Write this as a memorial in the
book, and rehearse it in Joshua's hearing; for I will surely wipe out
the remembrance of Amalek from under heaven." 15 Moses built
an altar, and he called it "The LORD is my Banner," 16 for he said,
"For a hand was lifted up to the throne of the LORD—that the
LORD will have war with Amalek from generation to generation."

THE ADVICE OF JETHRO

18 Jethro, the priest of Midian, Moses' father-in-law, heard
about all that God had done for Moses and for his people
Israel, that the LORD had brought Israel out of Egypt.
2 Jethro, Moses' father-in-law, took Moses' wife Zipporah after he had sent her back, 3 and her two sons, one of whom was

named Gershom (for Moses had said, "I have been a foreigner
in a foreign land") 4 and the other Eliezer (for Moses had said,
"The God of my father has been my help and delivered me from
the sword of Pharaoh").

5 Jethro, Moses' father-in-law, together with Moses' sons and
his wife, came to Moses in the wilderness where he was camping
by the mountain of God. 6 He said to Moses, "I, your father-in-law
Jethro, am coming to you, along with your wife and her two sons
with her." 7 Moses went out to meet his father-in-law and bowed
down and kissed him; they each asked about the other's welfare,
and then they went into the tent. 8 Moses told his father-in-law
all that the LORD had done to Pharaoh and to Egypt for Israel's
sake, and all the hardship that had come on them along the way,
and how the LORD had delivered them.

9 Jethro rejoiced because of all the good that the LORD had
done for Israel, whom he had delivered from the hand of Egypt.
10 Jethro said, "Blessed be the LORD who has delivered you from
the hand of Egypt, and from the hand of Pharaoh, who has delivered the people from the Egyptians' control! 11 Now I know that
the LORD is greater than all the gods, for in the thing in which
they dealt proudly against them he has destroyed them." 12 Then
Jethro, Moses' father-in-law, brought a burnt offering and sacrifices for God, and Aaron and all the elders of Israel came to eat
food with the father-in-law of Moses before God.

13 On the next day Moses sat to judge the people, and the people stood around Moses from morning until evening. 14 When
Moses' father-in-law saw all that he was doing for the people,
he said, "What is this that you are doing for the people? Why
are you sitting by yourself, and all the people stand around you
from morning until evening?"

15 Moses said to his father-in-law, "Because the people come
to me to inquire of God. 16 When they have a dispute, it comes
to me and I decide between a man and his neighbor, and I make
known the decrees of God and his laws."

17 Moses' father-in-law said to him, "What you are doing is not
good! 18 You will surely wear out, both you and these people who
are with you, for this is too heavy a burden for you; you are not
able to do it by yourself. 19 Now listen to me, I will give you advice,
and may God be with you. You be a representative for the people
to God, and you bring their disputes to God; 20 warn them of the
statutes and the laws, and make known to them the way in which
they must walk and the work they must do. 21 But you choose
from the people capable men, God-fearing men, men of truth,
those who hate bribes, and put them over the people as rulers
of thousands, rulers of hundreds, rulers of fifties, and rulers of
tens. 22 They will judge the people under normal circumstances,
and every difficult case they will bring to you, but every small
case they themselves will judge, so that you may make it easier
for yourself, and they will bear the burden with you. 23 If you do
this thing, and God so commands you, then you will be able to
endure, and all these people will be able to go home satisfied."

24 Moses listened to his father-in-law and did everything he had
said. 25 Moses chose capable men from all Israel, and he made them
heads over the people, rulers of thousands, rulers of hundreds,

rulers of fifties, and rulers of tens. 26 They judged the people under normal circumstances; the difficult cases they would bring to Moses, but every small case they would judge themselves.

27 Then Moses sent his father-in-law on his way, and so Jethro went to his own land.

ISRAEL AT SINAI

19 In the third month after the Israelites went out from the land of Egypt, on the very day, they came to the desert of Sinai. 2 After they journeyed from Rephidim, they came to the desert of Sinai, and they camped in the desert; Israel camped there in front of the mountain.

3 Moses went up to God, and the LORD called to him from the mountain, "Thus you will tell the house of Jacob, and declare to the people of Israel: 4 'You yourselves have seen what I did to Egypt and how I lifted you on eagles' wings and brought you to myself. 5 And now, if you will diligently listen to me and keep my covenant, then you will be my special possession out of all the nations, for all the earth is mine, 6 and you will be to me a kingdom of priests and a holy nation.' These are the words that you will speak to the Israelites."

7 So Moses came and summoned the elders of Israel. He set before them all these words that the LORD had commanded him, 8 and all the people answered together, "All that the LORD has commanded we will do!" So Moses brought the words of the people back to the LORD.

9 The LORD said to Moses, "I am going to come to you in a dense cloud, so that the people may hear when I speak with you and so that they will always believe in you." And Moses told the words of the people to the LORD.

10 The LORD said to Moses, "Go to the people and sanctify them today and tomorrow, and make them wash their clothes 11 and be ready for the third day, for on the third day the LORD will come down on Mount Sinai in the sight of all the people. 12 You must set boundaries for the people all around, saying, 'Take heed to yourselves not to go up on the mountain nor touch its edge. Whoever touches the mountain will surely be put to death! 13 No hand will touch him—but he will surely be stoned or shot through, whether a beast or a human being; he must not live.' When the ram's horn sounds a long blast they may go up on the mountain."

14 Then Moses went down from the mountain to the people and sanctified the people, and they washed their clothes. 15 He said to the people, "Be ready for the third day. Do not approach your wives for marital relations."

16 On the third day in the morning there was thunder and lightning and a dense cloud on the mountain, and the sound of a very loud horn; all the people who were in the camp trembled. 17 Moses brought the people out of the camp to meet God, and they took their place at the foot of the mountain. 18 Now Mount Sinai was completely covered with smoke because the LORD had descended on it in fire, and its smoke went up like the smoke of a great furnace, and the whole mountain shook violently. 19 When the sound of the horn grew louder and louder, Moses was speaking and God was answering him with a voice.

20 The LORD came down on Mount Sinai, on the top of the mountain, and the LORD summoned Moses to the top of the mountain, and Moses went up. 21 The LORD said to Moses, "Go down and solemnly warn the people, lest they force their way through to the LORD to look, and many of them perish. 22 Let the priests also, who approach the LORD, sanctify themselves, lest the LORD break through against them."

23 Moses said to the LORD, "The people are not able to come up to Mount Sinai, because you solemnly warned us, 'Set boundaries for the mountain and set it apart.'" 24 The LORD said to him, "Go, get down, and then come up, and Aaron with you, but do not let the priests and the people force their way through to come up to the LORD, lest he break through against them." 25 So Moses went down to the people and spoke to them.

THE DECALOGUE

20 God spoke all these words:
2 "I, the LORD, am your God, who brought you from the land of Egypt, from the house of slavery.

3 "You shall have no other gods before me.

4 "You shall not make for yourself a carved image or any likeness of anything that is in heaven above or that is on the earth beneath or that is in the water below. 5 You shall not bow down to them or serve them, for I, the LORD, your God, am a jealous God, responding to the transgression of fathers by dealing with children to the third and fourth generations of those who reject me, 6 and showing covenant faithfulness to a thousand generations of those who love me and keep my commandments.

7 "You shall not take the name of the LORD your God in vain, for the LORD will not hold guiltless anyone who takes his name in vain.

8 "Remember the Sabbath day to set it apart as holy. 9 For six days you may labor and do all your work, 10 but the seventh day is a Sabbath to the LORD your God; on it you shall not do any work, you, or your son, or your daughter, or your male servant, or your female servant, or your cattle, or the resident foreigner who is in your gates. 11 For in six days the LORD made the heavens and the earth and the sea and all that is in them, and he rested on the seventh day; therefore the LORD blessed the Sabbath day and set it apart as holy.

12 "Honor your father and your mother, that you may live a long time in the land the LORD your God is giving to you.

13 "You shall not murder.

14 "You shall not commit adultery.

15 "You shall not steal.

16 "You shall not give false testimony against your neighbor.

17 "You shall not covet your neighbor's house. You shall not covet your neighbor's wife, nor his male servant, nor his female servant, nor his ox, nor his donkey, nor anything that belongs to your neighbor."

18 All the people were seeing the thundering and the lightning, and heard the sound of the horn, and saw the mountain smoking—and when the people saw it they trembled with fear and kept their distance. 19 They said to Moses, "You speak to us

and we will listen, but do not let God speak with us, lest we die."
20 Moses said to the people, "Do not fear, for God has come to
test you, that the fear of him may be before you so that you do
not sin." 21 The people kept their distance, but Moses drew near
the thick darkness where God was.

THE ALTAR

22 The LORD said to Moses, "Thus you will tell the Israelites: 'You
yourselves have seen that I have spoken with you from heaven.
23 You must not make gods of silver alongside me, nor make gods
of gold for yourselves.
24 "'You must make for me an altar made of earth, and you
will sacrifice on it your burnt offerings and your peace offerings, your sheep and your cattle. In every place where I cause my
name to be honored I will come to you and I will bless you. 25 If
you make me an altar of stone, you must not build it of stones
shaped with tools, for if you use your tool on it you have defiled
it. 26 And you must not go up by steps to my altar, so that your
nakedness is not exposed.'

THE ORDINANCES

21 "These are the ordinances that you will set before them:

HEBREW SERVANTS

2 "If you buy a Hebrew servant, he is to serve you for six years,
but in the seventh year he will go out free without paying anything. 3 If he came in by himself he will go out by himself; if he
had a wife when he came in, then his wife will go out with him.
4 If his master gave him a wife, and she bore sons or daughters,
the wife and the children will belong to her master, and he will
go out by himself. 5 But if the servant should declare, 'I love my
master, my wife, and my children; I will not go out free,' 6 then
his master must bring him to the judges, and he will bring him
to the door or the doorpost, and his master will pierce his ear
with an awl, and he shall serve him forever.
7 "If a man sells his daughter as a female servant, she will not
go out as the male servants do. 8 If she does not please her master, who has designated her for himself, then he must let her
be redeemed. He has no right to sell her to a foreign nation, because he has dealt deceitfully with her. 9 If he designated her for
his son, then he will deal with her according to the customary
rights of daughters. 10 If he takes another wife, he must not diminish the first one's food, her clothing, or her marital rights.
11 If he does not provide her with these three things, then she
will go out free, without paying money.

PERSONAL INJURIES

12 "Whoever strikes someone so that he dies must surely be
put to death. 13 But if he does not do it with premeditation,
but it happens by accident, then I will appoint for you a place
where he may flee. 14 But if a man willfully attacks his neighbor to kill him cunningly, you will take him even from my altar that he may die.

15 "Whoever strikes his father or his mother must surely be
put to death.
16 "Whoever kidnaps someone and sells him, or is caught still
holding him, must surely be put to death.
17 "Whoever treats his father or his mother disgracefully must
surely be put to death.
18 "If men fight, and one strikes his neighbor with a stone or
with his fist and he does not die, but must remain in bed, 19 and
then if he gets up and walks about outside on his staff, then the
one who struck him is innocent, except he must pay for the injured person's loss of time and see to it that he is fully healed.
20 "If a man strikes his male servant or his female servant with a
staff so that he or she dies as a result of the blow, he will surely be
punished. 21 However, if the injured servant survives one or two
days, the owner will not be punished, for he has suffered the loss.
22 "If men fight and hit a pregnant woman and her child is born
prematurely, but there is no serious injury, the one who hit her
will surely be punished in accordance with what the woman's
husband demands of him, and he will pay what the court decides. 23 But if there is serious injury, then you will give a life for
a life, 24 eye for eye, tooth for tooth, hand for hand, foot for foot,
25 burn for burn, wound for wound, bruise for bruise.
26 "If a man strikes the eye of his male servant or his female
servant so that he destroys it, he will let the servant go free as
compensation for the eye. 27 If he knocks out the tooth of his
male servant or his female servant, he will let the servant go
free as compensation for the tooth.

LAWS ABOUT ANIMALS

28 "If an ox gores a man or a woman so that either dies, then the
ox must surely be stoned and its flesh must not be eaten, but the
owner of the ox will be acquitted. 29 But if the ox had the habit
of goring, and its owner was warned but he did not take the necessary precautions, and then it killed a man or a woman, the ox
must be stoned and the man must be put to death. 30 If a ransom
is set for him, then he must pay the redemption for his life according to whatever amount was set for him. 31 If the ox gores a son or
a daughter, the owner will be dealt with according to this rule. 32 If
the ox gores a male servant or a female servant, the owner must
pay thirty shekels of silver, and the ox must be stoned.
33 "If a man opens a pit or if a man digs a pit and does not cover
it and an ox or a donkey falls into it, 34 the owner of the pit must
repay the loss. He must give money to its owner, and the dead
animal will become his. 35 If the ox of one man injures the ox of
his neighbor so that it dies, then they will sell the live ox and
divide its proceeds, and they will also divide the dead ox. 36 Or
if it is known that the ox had the habit of goring, and its owner
did not take the necessary precautions, he must surely pay ox
for ox, and the dead animal will become his.

LAWS ABOUT PROPERTY

22 "If a man steals an ox or a sheep and kills it or sells it,
he must pay back five head of cattle for the ox, and four
sheep for the one sheep.

2 "If a thief is caught breaking in and is struck so that he dies,
there will be no blood guilt for him. 3 If the sun has risen on him,
then there is blood guilt for him. A thief must surely make full
restitution; if he has nothing, then he will be sold for his theft.
4 If the stolen item should in fact be found alive in his possession, whether it be an ox or a donkey or a sheep, he must pay
back double.

5 "If a man grazes his livestock in a field or a vineyard and he
lets the livestock loose and they graze in the field of another
man, he must make restitution from the best of his own field
and the best of his own vineyard.

6 "If a fire breaks out and spreads to thorn bushes, so that
stacked grain or standing grain or the whole field is consumed,
the one who started the fire must surely make restitution.

7 "If a man gives his neighbor money or articles for safekeeping and it is stolen from the man's house, if the thief is caught,
he must repay double. 8 If the thief is not caught, then the owner
of the house will be brought before the judges to see whether he
has laid his hand on his neighbor's goods. 9 In all cases of illegal
possessions, whether for an ox, a donkey, a sheep, a garment, or
any kind of lost item, about which someone says 'This belongs to
me,' the matter of the two of them will come before the judges,
and the one whom the judges declare guilty must repay double
to his neighbor. 10 If a man gives his neighbor a donkey or an ox
or a sheep or any beast to keep, and it dies or is injured or is carried away without anyone seeing it, 11 then there will be an oath
to the LORD between the two of them, that he has not laid his
hand on his neighbor's goods, and its owner will accept this, and
he will not have to pay. 12 But if it was stolen from him, he will
pay its owner. 13 If it is torn in pieces, then he will bring it for evidence, and he will not have to pay for what was torn.

14 "If a man borrows an animal from his neighbor and it is hurt
or dies when its owner was not with it, the man who borrowed it
will surely pay. 15 If its owner was with it, he will not have to pay;
if it was hired, what was paid for the hire covers it.

MORAL AND CEREMONIAL LAWS

16 "If a man seduces a virgin who is not engaged and goes to bed
with her, he must surely pay the marriage price for her to be
his wife. 17 If her father refuses to give her to him, he must pay
money for the bride price of virgins.

18 "You must not allow a sorceress to live.

19 "Whoever has sexual relations with a beast must surely be
put to death.

20 "Whoever sacrifices to a god other than the LORD alone must
be utterly destroyed.

21 "You must not wrong a resident foreigner nor oppress him,
for you were foreigners in the land of Egypt.

22 "You must not afflict any widow or orphan. 23 If you afflict
them in any way and they cry to me, I will surely hear their cry,
24 and my anger will burn and I will kill you with the sword, and
your wives will be widows and your children will be fatherless.

25 "If you lend money to any of my people who are needy among
you, do not be like a moneylender to him; do not charge him

interest. 26 If you do take the garment of your neighbor in pledge,
you must return it to him by the time the sun goes down, 27 for it is
his only covering—it is his garment for his body. What else can he
sleep in? And when he cries out to me, I will hear, for I am gracious.
28 "You must not blaspheme God or curse the ruler of your
people.
29 "Do not hold back offerings from your granaries or your vats.
You must give me the firstborn of your sons. 30 You must also do
this for your oxen and for your sheep; seven days they may remain with their mothers, but give them to me on the eighth day.
31 "You will be holy people to me; you must not eat any meat
torn by animals in the field. You must throw it to the dogs.

JUSTICE

23 "You must not give a false report. Do not make common
cause with the wicked to be a malicious witness.
2 "You must not follow a crowd in doing evil things; in a lawsuit you must not offer testimony that agrees with a crowd so as
to pervert justice, 3 and you must not show partiality to a poor
man in his lawsuit.
4 "If you encounter your enemy's ox or donkey wandering off,
you must by all means return it to him. 5 If you see the donkey
of someone who hates you fallen under its load, you must not
ignore him, but be sure to help him with it.
6 "You must not turn away justice for your poor people in their
lawsuits. 7 Keep your distance from a false charge—do not kill
the innocent and the righteous, for I will not justify the wicked.
8 "You must not accept a bribe, for a bribe blinds those who
see and subverts the words of the righteous.
9 "You must not oppress a resident foreigner, since you know
the life of a foreigner, for you were foreigners in the land of Egypt.

SABBATHS AND FEASTS

10 "For six years you are to sow your land and gather in its produce. 11 But in the seventh year you must let it lie fallow and
leave it alone so that the poor of your people may eat, and what
they leave any animal in the field may eat; you must do likewise
with your vineyard and your olive grove. 12 For six days you are to
do your work, but on the seventh day you must cease, in order
that your ox and your donkey may rest and that your female servant's son and the resident foreigner may refresh themselves.
13 "Pay attention to do everything I have told you, and do not
even mention the names of other gods—do not let them be heard
on your lips.
14 "Three times in the year you must make a pilgrim feast to me.
15 You are to observe the Feast of Unleavened Bread; seven days
you must eat bread made without yeast, as I commanded you,
at the appointed time of the month of Abib, for at that time you
came out of Egypt. No one may appear before me empty-handed.
16 "You are also to observe the Feast of Harvest, the firstfruits
of your labors that you have sown in the field, and the Feast of
Ingathering at the end of the year when you have gathered in
your harvest out of the field. 17 At three times in the year all your
males will appear before the Sovereign LORD.

[18]"You must not offer the blood of my sacrifice with bread containing yeast; the fat of my festal sacrifice must not remain until morning. [19]The first of the firstfruits of your soil you must bring to the house of the LORD your God.

"You must not cook a young goat in its mother's milk.

THE ANGEL OF THE PRESENCE

[20]"I am going to send an angel before you to protect you as you journey and to bring you into the place that I have prepared. [21]Take heed because of him, and obey his voice; do not rebel against him, for he will not pardon your transgressions, for my Name is in him. [22]But if you diligently obey him and do all that I command, then I will be an enemy to your enemies, and I will be an adversary to your adversaries. [23]For my angel will go before you and bring you to the Amorites, the Hittites, the Perizzites, the Canaanites, the Hivites, and the Jebusites, and I will destroy them completely.

[24]"You must not bow down to their gods; you must not serve them or do according to their practices. Instead you must completely overthrow them and smash their standing stones to pieces. [25]You must serve the LORD your God, and he will bless your bread and your water, and I will remove sickness from your midst. [26]No woman will miscarry her young or be barren in your land. I will fulfill the number of your days.

[27]"I will send my terror before you, and I will alarm all the people whom you encounter; I will make all your enemies turn their backs to you. [28]I will send hornets before you that will drive out the Hivite, the Canaanite, and the Hittite before you. [29]I will not drive them out before you in one year, lest the land become desolate and the wild animals multiply against you. [30]Little by little I will drive them out before you, until you become fruitful and inherit the land. [31]I will set your boundaries from the Red Sea to the Sea of the Philistines, and from the desert to the River, for I will deliver the inhabitants of the land into your hand, and you will drive them out before you.

[32]"You must make no covenant with them or with their gods. [33]They must not live in your land, lest they make you sin against me, for if you serve their gods, it will surely be a snare to you."

THE LORD RATIFIES THE COVENANT

24 But to Moses the LORD said, "Come up to the LORD, you and Aaron, Nadab and Abihu, and seventy of the elders of Israel, and worship from a distance. [2]Moses alone may come near the LORD, but the others must not come near, nor may the people go up with him."

[3]Moses came and told the people all the LORD's words and all the decisions. All the people answered together, "We are willing to do all the words that the LORD has said," [4]and Moses wrote down all the words of the LORD. Early in the morning he built an altar at the foot of the mountain and arranged twelve standing stones—according to the twelve tribes of Israel. [5]He sent young Israelite men, and they offered burnt offerings and sacrificed young bulls for peace offerings to the LORD. [6]Moses took half of the blood and put it in bowls, and half of the blood he

splashed on the altar. 7 He took the Book of the Covenant and
read it aloud to the people, and they said, "We are willing to do
and obey all that the LORD has spoken." 8 So Moses took the
blood and splashed it on the people and said, "This is the blood
of the covenant that the LORD has made with you in accordance
with all these words."

9 Moses and Aaron, Nadab and Abihu, and the seventy elders of Israel went up, 10 and they saw the God of Israel. Under his feet there was something like a pavement made of
sapphire, clear like the sky itself. 11 But he did not lay a hand
on the leaders of the Israelites, so they saw God, and they ate
and they drank.

12 The LORD said to Moses, "Come up to me on the mountain
and remain there, and I will give you the stone tablets with the
law and the commandments that I have written, so that you
may teach them." 13 So Moses set out with Joshua his attendant,
and Moses went up the mountain of God. 14 He told the elders,
"Wait for us in this place until we return to you. Here are Aaron
and Hur with you. Whoever has any matters of dispute can approach them."

15 Moses went up the mountain, and the cloud covered the
mountain. 16 The glory of the LORD resided on Mount Sinai, and
the cloud covered it for six days. On the seventh day he called to
Moses from within the cloud. 17 Now the appearance of the glory
of the LORD was like a devouring fire on the top of the mountain
in plain view of the people. 18 Moses went into the cloud when
he went up the mountain, and Moses was on the mountain forty
days and forty nights.

THE MATERIALS FOR THE TABERNACLE

25 The LORD spoke to Moses, 2 "Tell the Israelites to take an
offering for me; from every person motivated by a willing heart you are to receive my offering. 3 This is the offering you
are to accept from them: gold, silver, bronze, 4 blue, purple, scarlet, fine linen, goats' hair, 5 ram skins dyed red, fine leather, acacia wood, 6 oil for the light, spices for the anointing oil and for
fragrant incense, 7 onyx stones, and other gems to be set in the
ephod and in the breastpiece. 8 Let them make for me a sanctuary, so that I may live among them. 9 According to all that I am
showing you—the pattern of the tabernacle and the pattern of
all its furnishings—you must make it exactly so.

THE ARK OF THE TESTIMONY

10 "They are to make an ark of acacia wood—its length is to be 45
inches, its width 27 inches, and its height 27 inches. 11 You are to
overlay it with pure gold—both inside and outside you must overlay it, and you are to make a surrounding border of gold over it.
12 You are to cast four gold rings for it and put them on its four
feet, with two rings on one side and two rings on the other side.
13 You are to make poles of acacia wood, overlay them with gold,
14 and put the poles into the rings at the sides of the ark in order to carry the ark with them. 15 The poles must remain in the
rings of the ark; they must not be removed from it. 16 You are to
put into the ark the testimony that I will give to you.

17 "You are to make an atonement lid of pure gold; its length
is to be 45 inches, and its width is to be 27 inches. 18 You are to
make two cherubim of gold; you are to make them of hammered
metal on the two ends of the atonement lid. 19 Make one cherub
on one end and one cherub on the other end; from the atonement lid you are to make the cherubim on the two ends. 20 The
cherubim are to be spreading their wings upward, overshadowing the atonement lid with their wings, and the cherubim are
to face each other, looking toward the atonement lid. 21 You are
to put the atonement lid on top of the ark, and in the ark you
are to put the testimony I am giving you. 22 I will meet with you
there, and from above the atonement lid, from between the two
cherubim that are over the ark of the testimony, I will speak
with you about all that I will command you for the Israelites.

THE TABLE FOR THE BREAD OF THE PRESENCE

23 "You are to make a table of acacia wood; its length is to be 36
inches, its width 18 inches, and its height 27 inches. 24 You are
to overlay it with pure gold, and you are to make a surrounding
border of gold for it. 25 You are to make a surrounding frame for
it about three inches broad, and you are to make a surrounding
border of gold for its frame. 26 You are to make four rings of gold
for it and attach the rings at the four corners where its four legs
are. 27 The rings are to be close to the frame to provide places
for the poles to carry the table. 28 You are to make the poles of
acacia wood and overlay them with gold, so that the table may
be carried with them. 29 You are to make its plates, its ladles, its
pitchers, and its bowls, to be used in pouring out offerings; you
are to make them of pure gold. 30 You are to set the Bread of the
Presence on the table before me continually.

THE LAMPSTAND

31 "You are to make a lampstand of pure gold. The lampstand is
to be made of hammered metal; its base and its shaft, its cups,
its buds, and its blossoms are to be from the same piece. 32 Six
branches are to extend from the sides of the lampstand, three
branches of the lampstand from one side of it and three branches
of the lampstand from the other side of it. 33 Three cups shaped
like almond flowers with buds and blossoms are to be on one
branch, and three cups shaped like almond flowers with buds
and blossoms are to be on the next branch, and the same for the
six branches extending from the lampstand. 34 On the lampstand
there are to be four cups shaped like almond flowers with buds
and blossoms, 35 with a bud under the first two branches from it,
and a bud under the next two branches from it, and a bud under
the third two branches from it, according to the six branches that
extend from the lampstand. 36 Their buds and their branches will
be one piece, all of it one hammered piece of pure gold.

37 "You are to make its seven lamps and then set its lamps up
on it, so that it will give light to the area in front of it. 38 Its trimmers and its trays are to be of pure gold. 39 About seventy-five
pounds of pure gold is to be used for it and for all these utensils.
40 Now be sure to make them according to the pattern you were
shown on the mountain.

THE TABERNACLE

26 "The tabernacle itself you are to make with ten curtains
of fine twisted linen and blue and purple and scarlet; you
are to make them with cherubim that are the work of an artistic designer. 2 The length of each curtain is to be 42 feet, and the
width of each curtain is to be 6 feet—the same size for each of
the curtains. 3 Five curtains are to be joined, one to another, and
the other five curtains are to be joined, one to another. 4 You are
to make loops of blue material along the edge of the end curtain in one set, and in the same way you are to make loops in
the outer edge of the end curtain in the second set. 5 You are to
make fifty loops on the one curtain, and you are to make fifty
loops on the end curtain which is on the second set, so that the
loops are opposite one to another. 6 You are to make fifty gold
clasps and join the curtains together with the clasps, so that the
tabernacle is a unit.

7 "You are to make curtains of goats' hair for a tent over the
tabernacle; you are to make eleven curtains. 8 The length of
each curtain is to be 45 feet, and the width of each curtain is
to be 6 feet—the same size for the eleven curtains. 9 You are
to join five curtains by themselves and six curtains by themselves. You are to double over the sixth curtain at the front
of the tent. 10 You are to make fifty loops along the edge of
the end curtain in one set and fifty loops along the edge of
the curtain that joins the second set. 11 You are to make fifty
bronze clasps and put the clasps into the loops and join the
tent together so that it is a unit. 12 Now the part that remains
of the curtains of the tent—the half curtain that remains will
hang over at the back of the tabernacle. 13 The foot and a half
on the one side and the foot and a half on the other side of
what remains in the length of the curtains of the tent will
hang over the sides of the tabernacle, on one side and the
other side, to cover it.

14 "You are to make a covering for the tent out of ram skins
dyed red and over that a covering of fine leather.

15 "You are to make the frames for the tabernacle out of acacia
wood as uprights. 16 Each frame is to be 15 feet long, and each
frame is to be 27 inches wide, 17 with two projections per frame
parallel one to another. You are to make all the frames of the
tabernacle in this way. 18 So you are to make the frames for the
tabernacle: twenty frames for the south side, 19 and you are to
make forty silver bases to go under the twenty frames—two
bases under the first frame for its two projections, and likewise
two bases under the next frame for its two projections; 20 and
for the second side of the tabernacle, the north side, twenty
frames, 21 and their forty silver bases, two bases under the first
frame, and two bases under the next frame. 22 And for the back
of the tabernacle on the west you will make six frames. 23 You
are to make two frames for the corners of the tabernacle on the
back. 24 At the two corners they must be doubled at the lower
end and finished together at the top in one ring. So it will be for
both. 25 So there are to be eight frames and their silver bases,
sixteen bases, two bases under the first frame, and two bases
under the next frame.

26 “You are to make bars of acacia wood, five for the frames on one side of the tabernacle, 27 and five bars for the frames on the second side of the tabernacle, and five bars for the frames on the back of the tabernacle on the west. 28 The middle bar in the center of the frames will reach from end to end. 29 You are to overlay the frames with gold and make their rings of gold to provide places for the bars, and you are to overlay the bars with gold. 30 You are to set up the tabernacle according to the plan that you were shown on the mountain.

31 “You are to make a special curtain of blue, purple, and scarlet yarn and fine twisted linen; it is to be made with cherubim, the work of an artistic designer. 32 You are to hang it with gold hooks on four posts of acacia wood overlaid with gold, set in four silver bases. 33 You are to hang this curtain under the clasps and bring the ark of the testimony in there behind the curtain. The curtain will make a division for you between the Holy Place and the Most Holy Place. 34 You are to put the atonement lid on the ark of the testimony in the Most Holy Place. 35 You are to put the table outside the curtain and the lampstand on the south side of the tabernacle, opposite the table, and you are to place the table on the north side.

36 “You are to make a hanging for the entrance of the tent of blue, purple, and scarlet yarn and fine twisted linen, the work of an embroiderer. 37 You are to make for the hanging five posts of acacia wood and overlay them with gold, and their hooks will be gold, and you are to cast five bronze bases for them.

THE ALTAR

27 “You are to make the altar of acacia wood, 7½ feet long, and 7½ feet wide; the altar is to be square, and its height is to be 4½ feet . 2 You are to make its four horns on its four corners; its horns will be part of it, and you are to overlay it with bronze. 3 You are to make its pots for the ashes, its shovels, its tossing bowls, its meat hooks, and its fire pans—you are to make all its utensils of bronze. 4 You are to make a grating for it, a network of bronze, and you are to make on the network four bronze rings on its four corners. 5 You are to put it under the ledge of the altar below, so that the network will come halfway up the altar. 6 You are to make poles for the altar, poles of acacia wood, and you are to overlay them with bronze. 7 The poles are to be put into the rings so that the poles will be on two sides of the altar when carrying it. 8 You are to make the altar hollow, out of boards. Just as it was shown you on the mountain, so they must make it.

THE COURTYARD

9 “You are to make the courtyard of the tabernacle. For the south side there are to be hangings for the courtyard of fine twisted linen, 150 feet long for one side, 10 with twenty posts and their twenty bronze bases, with the hooks of the posts and their bands of silver. 11 Likewise for its length on the north side, there are to be hangings for 150 feet, with twenty posts and their twenty bronze bases, with silver hooks and bands on the posts. 12 The width of the court on the west side is to be 75 feet with hangings, with their ten posts and their ten bases. 13 The width of the

court on the east side, toward the sunrise, is to be 75 feet. 14 The
hangings on one side of the gate are to be 22½ feet long, with
their three posts and their three bases. 15 On the second side
there are to be hangings 22½ feet long, with their three posts
and their three bases. 16 For the gate of the courtyard there is to
be a curtain of 30 feet, of blue, purple, and scarlet yarn and fine
twisted linen, the work of an embroiderer, with four posts and
their four bases. 17 All the posts around the courtyard are to have
silver bands; their hooks are to be silver, and their bases bronze.
18 The length of the courtyard is to be 150 feet and the width 75
feet, and the height of the fine twisted linen hangings is to be
7½ feet, with their bronze bases. 19 All the utensils of the tabernacle used in all its service, all its tent pegs, and all the tent pegs
of the courtyard are to be made of bronze.

OFFERING THE OIL

20 "You are to command the Israelites that they bring to you pure
oil of pressed olives for the light, so that the lamps will burn regularly. 21 In the tent of meeting outside the curtain that is before
the testimony, Aaron and his sons are to arrange it from evening
to morning before the LORD. This is to be a lasting ordinance
among the Israelites for generations to come.

THE CLOTHING OF THE PRIESTS

28 "And you, bring near to you your brother Aaron and his
sons with him from among the Israelites, so that they may
minister as my priests—Aaron, Nadab and Abihu, Eleazar and
Ithamar, Aaron's sons. 2 You must make holy garments for your
brother Aaron, for glory and for beauty. 3 You are to speak to all
who are specially skilled, whom I have filled with the spirit of wisdom, so that they may make Aaron's garments to set him apart
to minister as my priest. 4 Now these are the garments that they
are to make: a breastpiece, an ephod, a robe, a fitted tunic, a turban, and a sash. They are to make holy garments for your brother
Aaron and for his sons, that they may minister as my priests. 5 The
artisans are to use the gold, blue, purple, scarlet, and fine linen.

6 "They are to make the ephod of gold, blue, purple, scarlet, and
fine twisted linen, the work of an artistic designer. 7 It is to have
two shoulder pieces attached to two of its corners, so it can be
joined together. 8 The artistically woven waistband of the ephod
that is on it is to be like it, of one piece with the ephod, of gold,
blue, purple, scarlet, and fine twisted linen.

9 "You are to take two onyx stones and engrave on them the
names of the sons of Israel, 10 six of their names on one stone,
and the six remaining names on the second stone, according to
the order of their birth. 11 You are to engrave the two stones with
the names of the sons of Israel with the work of an engraver in
stone, like the engravings of a seal; you are to have them set
in gold filigree settings. 12 You are to put the two stones on the
shoulders of the ephod, stones of memorial for the sons of Israel, and Aaron will bear their names before the LORD on his
two shoulders for a memorial. 13 You are to make filigree settings
of gold 14 and two braided chains of pure gold, like a cord, and attach the chains to the settings.

15 “You are to make a breastpiece for use in making decisions, the work of an artistic designer; you are to make it in the same fashion as the ephod; you are to make it of gold, blue, purple, scarlet, and fine twisted linen. 16 It is to be square when doubled, nine inches long and nine inches wide. 17 You are to set in it a setting for stones, four rows of stones, a row with a ruby, a topaz, and a beryl—the first row; 18 and the second row, a turquoise, a sapphire, and an emerald; 19 and the third row, a jacinth, an agate, and an amethyst; 20 and the fourth row, a chrysolite, an onyx, and a jasper. They are to be enclosed in gold in their filigree settings. 21 The stones are to be for the names of the sons of Israel, twelve, according to the number of their names. Each name according to the twelve tribes is to be like the engravings of a seal.

22 “You are to make for the breastpiece braided chains like cords of pure gold, 23 and you are to make for the breastpiece two gold rings and attach the two rings to the upper two ends of the breastpiece. 24 You are to attach the two gold chains to the two rings at the ends of the breastpiece; 25 the other two ends of the two chains you will attach to the two settings and then attach them to the shoulder pieces of the ephod at the front of it. 26 You are to make two rings of gold and put them on the other two ends of the breastpiece, on its edge that is on the inner side of the ephod. 27 You are to make two more gold rings and attach them to the bottom of the two shoulder pieces on the front of the ephod, close to the juncture above the waistband of the ephod. 28 They are to tie the breastpiece by its rings to the rings of the ephod by blue cord, so that it may be above the waistband of the ephod, and so that the breastpiece will not be loose from the ephod. 29 Aaron will bear the names of the sons of Israel in the breastpiece of decision over his heart when he goes into the Holy Place, for a memorial before the LORD continually.

30 “You are to put the Urim and the Thummim into the breastpiece of decision; and they are to be over Aaron’s heart when he goes in before the LORD. Aaron is to bear the decisions of the Israelites over his heart before the LORD continually.

31 “You are to make the robe of the ephod completely blue. 32 There is to be an opening in its top in the center of it, with an edge all around the opening, the work of a weaver, like the opening of a collar, so that it cannot be torn. 33 You are to make pomegranates of blue, purple, and scarlet all around its hem and bells of gold between them all around. 34 The pattern is to be a gold bell and a pomegranate, a gold bell and a pomegranate, all around the hem of the robe. 35 The robe is to be on Aaron as he ministers, and his sound will be heard when he enters the Holy Place before the LORD and when he leaves, so that he does not die.

36 “You are to make a plate of pure gold and engrave on it the way a seal is engraved: ‘Holiness to the LORD.’ 37 You are to attach to it a blue cord so that it will be on the turban; it is to be on the front of the turban. 38 It will be on Aaron’s forehead, and Aaron will bear the iniquity of the holy things, which the Israelites are to sanctify by all their holy gifts; it will always be on his forehead, for their acceptance before the LORD. 39 You are to weave the tunic of fine linen and make the turban of fine linen, and make the sash the work of an embroiderer.

40 "For Aaron's sons you are to make tunics, sashes, and headbands for glory and for beauty.
41 "You are to clothe them—your brother Aaron and his sons
with him—and anoint them and ordain them and set them apart
as holy, so that they may minister as my priests. 42 Make for them
linen undergarments to cover their naked bodies; they must
cover from the waist to the thighs. 43 These must be on Aaron
and his sons when they enter the tent of meeting, or when they
approach the altar to minister in the Holy Place, so that they
bear no iniquity and die. It is to be a perpetual ordinance for
him and for his descendants after him.

THE CONSECRATION OF AARON AND HIS SONS

29 "Now this is what you are to do for them to consecrate
them so that they may minister as my priests. Take a
young bull and two rams without blemish; 2 and bread made
without yeast, and perforated cakes without yeast mixed with
oil, and wafers without yeast spread with oil—you are to make
them using fine wheat flour. 3 You are to put them in one basket and present them in the basket, along with the bull and the
two rams.
4 "You are to present Aaron and his sons at the entrance of the
tent of meeting. You are to wash them with water 5 and take the
garments and clothe Aaron with the tunic, the robe of the ephod,
the ephod, and the breastpiece; you are to fasten the ephod on
him by using the skillfully woven waistband. 6 You are to put the
turban on his head and put the holy diadem on the turban. 7 You
are to take the anointing oil and pour it on his head and anoint
him. 8 You are to present his sons and clothe them with tunics
9 and wrap the sashes around Aaron and his sons and put headbands on them, and so the ministry of priesthood will belong
to them by a perpetual ordinance. Thus you are to consecrate
Aaron and his sons.
10 "You are to present the bull at the front of the tent of meeting, and Aaron and his sons are to put their hands on the head
of the bull. 11 You are to kill the bull before the LORD at the entrance to the tent of meeting 12 and take some of the blood of
the bull and put it on the horns of the altar with your finger; all
the rest of the blood you are to pour out at the base of the altar.
13 You are to take all the fat that covers the entrails, and the lobe
that is above the liver, and the two kidneys and the fat that is on
them, and burn them on the altar. 14 But the meat of the bull, its
skin, and its dung you are to burn up outside the camp. It is the
purification offering.
15 "You are to take one ram, and Aaron and his sons are to lay
their hands on the ram's head, 16 and you are to kill the ram and
take its blood and splash it all around on the altar. 17 Then you
are to cut the ram into pieces and wash the entrails and its legs
and put them on its pieces and on its head 18 and burn the whole
ram on the altar. It is a burnt offering to the LORD, a soothing
aroma; it is an offering made by fire to the LORD.
19 "You are to take the second ram, and Aaron and his sons are
to lay their hands on the ram's head, 20 and you are to kill the ram
and take some of its blood and put it on the tip of the right ear

of Aaron, on the tip of the right ear of his sons, on the thumb of
their right hand, and on the big toe of their right foot, and then
splash the blood all around on the altar. 21 You are to take some
of the blood that is on the altar and some of the anointing oil
and sprinkle it on Aaron, on his garments, on his sons, and on
his sons' garments with him, so that he may be holy, he and his
garments along with his sons and his sons' garments.

22 "You are to take from the ram the fat, the fat tail, the fat
that covers the entrails, the lobe of the liver, the two kidneys
and the fat that is on them, and the right thigh—for it is the ram
for consecration—23 and one round flat cake of bread, one perforated cake of oiled bread, and one wafer from the basket of bread
made without yeast that is before the LORD. 24 You are to put
all these in Aaron's hands and in his sons' hands, and you are to
wave them as a wave offering before the LORD. 25 Then you are
to take them from their hands and burn them on the altar for
a burnt offering, for a soothing aroma before the LORD. It is an
offering made by fire to the LORD. 26 You are to take the breast
of the ram of Aaron's consecration; you are to wave it as a wave
offering before the LORD, and it is to be your share. 27 You are
to sanctify the breast of the wave offering and the thigh of the
contribution, which were waved and lifted up as a contribution
from the ram of consecration, from what belongs to Aaron and
to his sons. 28 It is to belong to Aaron and to his sons from the
Israelites, by a perpetual ordinance, for it is a contribution. It is
to be a contribution from the Israelites from their peace offerings, their contribution to the LORD.

29 "The holy garments that belong to Aaron are to belong to
his sons after him, so that they may be anointed in them and
consecrated in them. 30 The priest who succeeds him from his
sons, when he first comes to the tent of meeting to minister in
the Holy Place, is to wear them for seven days.

31 "You are to take the ram of the consecration and cook its
meat in a holy place. 32 Aaron and his sons are to eat the meat
of the ram and the bread that was in the basket at the entrance
of the tent of meeting. 33 They are to eat those things by which
atonement was made to consecrate and to set them apart, but
no one else may eat them, for they are holy. 34 If any of the meat
from the consecration offerings or any of the bread is left over
until morning, then you are to burn up what is left over. It must
not be eaten, because it is holy.

35 "Thus you are to do for Aaron and for his sons according to
all that I have commanded you; you are to consecrate them for
seven days. 36 Every day you are to prepare a bull for a purification offering for atonement. You are to purify the altar by making atonement for it, and you are to anoint it to set it apart as
holy. 37 For seven days you are to make atonement for the altar
and set it apart as holy. Then the altar will be most holy. Anything that touches the altar will be holy.

38 "Now this is what you are to prepare on the altar every day
continually: two lambs a year old. 39 The first lamb you are to prepare in the morning, and the second lamb you are to prepare
around sundown. 40 With the first lamb offer a tenth of an ephah
of fine flour mixed with a fourth of a hin of oil from pressed olives,

and a fourth of a hin of wine as a drink offering. 41 The second lamb
you are to offer around sundown; you are to prepare for it the
same meal offering as for the morning and the same drink offering, for a soothing aroma, an offering made by fire to the LORD.
42 "This will be a regular burnt offering throughout your generations at the entrance of the tent of meeting before the LORD,
where I will meet with you to speak to you there. 43 There I will
meet with the Israelites, and it will be set apart as holy by my glory.
44 "So I will set apart as holy the tent of meeting and the altar, and I will set apart as holy Aaron and his sons that they may
minister as priests to me. 45 I will reside among the Israelites,
and I will be their God, 46 and they will know that I am the LORD
their God, who brought them out from the land of Egypt, so that
I may reside among them. I am the LORD their God.

THE ALTAR OF INCENSE

30 "You are to make an altar for burning incense; you are to
make it of acacia wood. 2 Its length is to be 18 inches and
its width 18 inches; it will be square. Its height is to be 36 inches,
with its horns of one piece with it. 3 You are to overlay it with pure
gold—its top, its four walls, and its horns—and make a surrounding border of gold for it. 4 You are to make two gold rings for it
under its border, on its two flanks; you are to make them on its
two sides. The rings will be places for poles to carry it with. 5 You
are to make the poles of acacia wood and overlay them with gold.
6 "You are to put it in front of the curtain that is before the ark
of the testimony (before the atonement lid that is over the testimony), where I will meet you. 7 Aaron is to burn sweet incense on
it morning by morning; when he attends to the lamps he is to burn
incense. 8 When Aaron sets up the lamps around sundown he is to
burn incense on it; it is to be a regular incense offering before the
LORD throughout your generations. 9 You must not offer strange
incense on it, nor burnt offering, nor meal offering, and you must
not pour out a drink offering on it. 10 Aaron is to make atonement
on its horns once in the year with some of the blood of the sin offering for atonement; once in the year he is to make atonement
on it throughout your generations. It is most holy to the LORD."

THE RANSOM MONEY

11 The LORD spoke to Moses, 12 "When you take a census of the
Israelites according to their number, then each man is to pay a
ransom for his life to the LORD when you number them, so that
there will be no plague among them when you number them.
13 Everyone who crosses over to those who are numbered is to
pay this: a half shekel according to the shekel of the sanctuary
(a shekel weighs twenty gerahs). The half shekel is to be an offering to the LORD. 14 Everyone who crosses over to those numbered, from twenty years old and up, is to pay an offering to the
LORD. 15 The rich are not to pay more and the poor are not to pay
less than the half shekel when giving the offering of the LORD, to
make atonement for your lives. 16 You are to receive the atonement money from the Israelites and give it for the service of the
tent of meeting. It will be a memorial for the Israelites before
the LORD, to make atonement for your lives."

THE BRONZE LAVER

17 The LORD spoke to Moses, 18 "You are also to make a large bronze basin with a bronze stand for washing. You are to put it between the tent of meeting and the altar and put water in it, 19 and Aaron and his sons must wash their hands and their feet from it. 20 When they enter the tent of meeting, they must wash with water so that they do not die. Also, when they approach the altar to minister by burning incense as an offering made by fire to the LORD, 21 they must wash their hands and their feet so that they do not die. And this will be a perpetual ordinance for them and for their descendants throughout their generations."

OIL AND INCENSE

22 The LORD spoke to Moses, 23 "Take choice spices: 12½ pounds of free-flowing myrrh, half that—about 6¼ pounds—of sweet-smelling cinnamon, 6¼ pounds of sweet-smelling cane, 24 and 12½ pounds of cassia, all weighed according to the sanctuary shekel, and four quarts of olive oil. 25 You are to make this into a sacred anointing oil, a perfumed compound, the work of a perfumer. It will be sacred anointing oil.

26 "With it you are to anoint the tent of meeting, the ark of the testimony, 27 the table and all its utensils, the lampstand and its utensils, the altar of incense, 28 the altar for the burnt offering and all its utensils, and the laver and its base. 29 So you are to sanctify them, and they will be most holy; anything that touches them will be holy.

30 "You are to anoint Aaron and his sons and sanctify them so that they may minister as my priests. 31 And you are to tell the Israelites: 'This is to be my sacred anointing oil throughout your generations. 32 It must not be applied to people's bodies, and you must not make any like it with the same recipe. It is holy, and it must be holy to you. 33 Whoever makes perfume like it and whoever puts any of it on someone not a priest will be cut off from his people.'"

34 The LORD said to Moses, "Take spices, gum resin, onycha, galbanum, and pure frankincense of equal amounts 35 and make it into an incense, a perfume, the work of a perfumer. It is to be finely ground, and pure and sacred. 36 You are to beat some of it very fine and put some of it before the ark of the testimony in the tent of meeting where I will meet with you; it is to be most holy to you. 37 And the incense that you are to make, you must not make for yourselves using the same recipe; it is to be most holy to you, belonging to the LORD. 38 Whoever makes anything like it, to use as perfume, will be cut off from his people."

WILLING ARTISANS

31 The LORD spoke to Moses, 2 "See, I have chosen Bezalel son of Uri, the son of Hur, of the tribe of Judah, 3 and I have filled him with the Spirit of God in skill, in understanding, in knowledge, and in all kinds of craftsmanship, 4 to make artistic designs for work with gold, with silver, and with bronze, 5 and with cutting and setting stone, and with cutting wood, to work in all kinds of craftsmanship. 6 Moreover, I have also given him Oholiab son of Ahisamach, of the tribe of Dan, and I have given

ability to all the specially skilled, that they may make everything
I have commanded you: 7 the tent of meeting, the ark of the testimony, the atonement lid that is on it, all the furnishings of the
tent, 8 the table with its utensils, the pure lampstand with all its
utensils, the altar of incense, 9 the altar for the burnt offering
with all its utensils, the large basin with its base, 10 the woven
garments, the holy garments for Aaron the priest and the garments for his sons, to minister as priests, 11 the anointing oil, and
sweet incense for the Holy Place. They will make all these things
just as I have commanded you."

SABBATH OBSERVANCE

12 The LORD said to Moses, 13 "Tell the Israelites, 'Surely you must
keep my Sabbaths, for it is a sign between me and you throughout your generations, that you may know that I am the LORD
who sanctifies you. 14 So you must keep the Sabbath, for it is holy
for you. Everyone who defiles it must surely be put to death; indeed, if anyone does any work on it, then that person will be cut
off from among his people. 15 Six days work may be done, but on
the seventh day is a Sabbath of complete rest, holy to the LORD;
anyone who does work on the Sabbath day must surely be put
to death. 16 The Israelites must keep the Sabbath by observing
the Sabbath throughout their generations as a perpetual covenant. 17 It is a sign between me and the Israelites forever; for in
six days the LORD made the heavens and the earth, and on the
seventh day he rested and was refreshed.'"

18 He gave Moses two tablets of testimony when he had finished speaking with him on Mount Sinai, tablets of stone written by the finger of God.

THE SIN OF THE GOLDEN CALF

32 When the people saw that Moses delayed in coming down
from the mountain, they gathered around Aaron and
said to him, "Get up, make us gods that will go before us. As for
this fellow Moses, the man who brought us up from the land of
Egypt, we do not know what has become of him!"
2 So Aaron said to them, "Break off the gold earrings that are on
the ears of your wives, your sons, and your daughters, and bring
them to me." 3 So all the people broke off the gold earrings that
were on their ears and brought them to Aaron. 4 He accepted the
gold from them, fashioned it with an engraving tool, and made a
molten calf. Then they said, "These are your gods, O Israel, who
brought you up out of Egypt."
5 When Aaron saw this, he built an altar before it, and Aaron
made a proclamation and said, "Tomorrow will be a feast to the
LORD." 6 So they got up early on the next day and offered up burnt
offerings and brought peace offerings, and the people sat down
to eat and drink, and they rose up to play.
7 The LORD spoke to Moses, "Go quickly, descend, because your
people, whom you brought up from the land of Egypt, have acted
corruptly. 8 They have quickly turned aside from the way that I
commanded them—they have made for themselves a molten calf
and have bowed down to it and sacrificed to it and said, 'These are
your gods, O Israel, which brought you up from the land of Egypt.'"

REFLECT

What does God's provision of skilled workers reveal about His character? How have you seen God's provision in similar ways in your own life?

9 Then the LORD said to Moses, "I have seen this people. Look what a stiff-necked people they are! 10 So now, leave me alone so that my anger can burn against them and I can destroy them, and I will make from you a great nation."

11 But Moses sought the favor of the LORD his God and said, "O LORD, why does your anger burn against your people, whom you have brought out from the land of Egypt with great power and with a mighty hand? 12 Why should the Egyptians say, 'For evil he led them out to kill them in the mountains and to destroy them from the face of the earth'? Turn from your burning anger, and relent of this evil against your people. 13 Remember Abraham, Isaac, and Israel your servants, to whom you swore by yourself and told them, 'I will multiply your descendants like the stars of heaven, and all this land that I have spoken about I will give to your descendants, and they will inherit it forever.'" 14 Then the LORD relented over the evil that he had said he would do to his people.

15 Moses turned and went down from the mountain with the two tablets of the testimony in his hands. The tablets were written on both sides—they were written on the front and on the back. 16 Now the tablets were the work of God, and the writing was the writing of God, engraved on the tablets. 17 When Joshua heard the noise of the people as they shouted, he said to Moses, "It is the sound of war in the camp!" 18 Moses said, "It is not the sound of those who shout for victory, nor is it the sound of those who cry because they are overcome, but the sound of singing I hear."

19 When he approached the camp and saw the calf and the dancing, Moses became extremely angry. He threw the tablets from his hands and broke them to pieces at the bottom of the mountain. 20 He took the calf they had made and burned it in the fire, ground it to powder, poured it out on the water, and made the Israelites drink it.

21 Moses said to Aaron, "What did this people do to you, that you have brought on them so great a sin?" 22 Aaron said, "Do not let your anger burn hot, my lord; you know these people, that they tend to evil. 23 They said to me, 'Make us gods that will go before us, for as for this fellow Moses, the man who brought us up out of the land of Egypt, we do not know what has happened to him.' 24 So I said to them, 'Whoever has gold, break it off.' So they gave it to me, and I threw it into the fire, and this calf came out."

25 Moses saw that the people were running wild, for Aaron had let them get completely out of control, causing derision from their enemies. 26 So Moses stood at the entrance of the camp and said, "Whoever is for the LORD, come to me." All the Levites gathered around him, 27 and he said to them, "This is what the LORD, the God of Israel, has said 'Each man fasten his sword on his side, and go back and forth from entrance to entrance throughout the camp, and each one kill his brother, his friend, and his neighbor.'"

28 The Levites did what Moses ordered, and that day about 3,000 men of the people died. 29 Moses said, "You have been consecrated today for the LORD, for each of you was against his son or against his brother, so he has given a blessing to you today."

LOVE TO GROW

THE POWER OF PRAYER

EXODUS 32:7–14

Sometimes people consider prayer a less-effective form of action, saying, "All we can do is pray." Not so. Prayer is our greatest weapon! Evil is real in this world, and prayer is the best tool we have for protecting our marriages, guiding our kids, and discerning life's trials.

Exodus should give us great confidence in the power of prayer and in the availability and intimacy of God. The Bible tells us to pray for one another. Exodus 32–33 records the power of Moses' intercessory prayers on behalf of the Israelite people. Moses' pleadings convinced God not to destroy the rebellious Israelites and not to remove His presence from them as they traveled to the promised land. What if Moses hadn't uttered those prayers? What if he had hesitated because he felt unworthy, exhausted, or unsure? If Moses had not interceded in prayer, it likely would have meant disaster for the wayward Israelites and changed the course of history.

Sometimes praying can feel intimidating. Praying out loud in front of others can rouse our anxiety. Take heart, it's not meant to be rigid or a production. Sometimes we don't feel worthy or capable of praying the "right" prayers. Our prayers should be reverent, but they can also be simple and conversational. God hears and honors our cry, whether we are on our knees in a sanctuary, circled around a table, or driving down a highway. You can say it, sing it, or think it.

Romans 8:26 assures us that, "the Spirit helps us in our weakness, for we do not know how we should pray, but the Spirit himself intercedes for us with inexpressible groanings" (see also Heb 4:16). What an overwhelming privilege to be able to speak directly to our God, to confidently approach the throne of grace and mercy.

God hears our prayers. He is not annoyed or surprised with the shortcomings of our flesh. He didn't care that Moses stuttered, and He doesn't mind if you do either.

Friends, let's pray often and with boldness. Let's pray for the things in our own lives, but let's also remember the privilege and honor of praying for one another.

30 The next day Moses said to the people, "You have committed a very serious sin, but now I will go up to the LORD—perhaps I can make atonement on behalf of your sin."

31 So Moses returned to the LORD and said, "Alas, this people has committed a very serious sin, and they have made for themselves gods of gold. 32 But now, if you will forgive their sin..., but if not, wipe me out from your book that you have written." 33 The LORD said to Moses, "Whoever has sinned against me—that person I will wipe out of my book. 34 So now go, lead the people to the place I have spoken to you about. See, my angel will go before you. But on the day that I punish, I will indeed punish them for their sin."

35 And the LORD sent a plague on the people because they had made the calf—the one Aaron made.

33 The LORD said to Moses, "Go up from here, you and the people whom you brought up out of the land of Egypt, to the land I promised on oath to Abraham, to Isaac, and to Jacob, saying, 'I will give it to your descendants.' 2 I will send an angel before you, and I will drive out the Canaanite, the Amorite, the Hittite, the Perizzite, the Hivite, and the Jebusite. 3 Go up to a land flowing with milk and honey. But I will not go up among you, for you are a stiff-necked people, and I might destroy you on the way."

4 When the people heard this troubling word they mourned; no one put on his ornaments. 5 For the LORD had said to Moses, "Tell the Israelites, 'You are a stiff-necked people. If I went up among you for a moment, I might destroy you. Now take off your ornaments that I may know what I should do to you.'" 6 So the Israelites stripped off their ornaments by Mount Horeb.

THE PRESENCE OF THE LORD

7 Moses took the tent and pitched it outside the camp, at a good distance from the camp, and he called it the tent of meeting. Anyone seeking the LORD would go out to the tent of meeting that was outside the camp.

8 And when Moses went out to the tent, all the people would get up and stand at the entrance to their tents and watch Moses until he entered the tent. 9 And whenever Moses entered the tent, the pillar of cloud would descend and stand at the entrance of the tent, and the LORD would speak with Moses. 10 When all the people would see the pillar of cloud standing at the entrance of the tent, all the people, each one at the entrance of his own tent, would rise and worship. 11 The LORD would speak to Moses face to face, the way a person speaks to a friend. Then Moses would return to the camp, but his servant, Joshua son of Nun, a young man, did not leave the tent.

12 Moses said to the LORD, "See, you have been saying to me, 'Bring this people up,' but you have not let me know whom you will send with me. But you said, 'I know you by name, and also you have found favor in my sight.' 13 Now if I have found favor in your sight, show me your way, that I may know you, that I may continue to find favor in your sight. And see that this nation is your people."

14 And the LORD said, "My presence will go with you, and I will give you rest."

15 And Moses said to him, "If your presence does not go with
us, do not take us up from here. 16 For how will it be known then
that I have found favor in your sight, I and your people? Is it not
by your going with us, so that we will be distinguished, I and your
people, from all the people who are on the face of the earth?"
17 The LORD said to Moses, "I will do this thing also that you
have requested, for you have found favor in my sight, and I know
you by name."
18 And Moses said, "Show me your glory."
19 And the LORD said, "I will make all my goodness pass before
your face, and I will proclaim the LORD by name before you; I
will be gracious to whom I will be gracious; I will show mercy to
whom I will show mercy." 20 But he added, "You cannot see my
face, for no one can see me and live." 21 The LORD said, "Here is a
place by me; you will station yourself on a rock. 22 When my glory
passes by, I will put you in a cleft in the rock and will cover you
with my hand while I pass by. 23 Then I will take away my hand,
and you will see my back, but my face must not be seen."

THE NEW TABLETS OF THE COVENANT

34 The LORD said to Moses, "Cut out two tablets of stone
like the first, and I will write on the tablets the words
that were on the first tablets, which you smashed. 2 Be prepared
in the morning, and go up in the morning to Mount Sinai, and
station yourself for me there on the top of the mountain. 3 No
one is to come up with you; do not let anyone be seen anywhere
on the mountain; not even the flocks or the herds may graze in
front of that mountain." 4 So Moses cut out two tablets of stone
like the first; early in the morning he went up to Mount Sinai,
just as the LORD had commanded him, and he took in his hand
the two tablets of stone.
5 The LORD descended in the cloud and stood with him there
and proclaimed the LORD by name. 6 The LORD passed by before
him and proclaimed: "The LORD, the LORD, the compassionate
and gracious God, slow to anger, and abounding in loyal love and
faithfulness, 7 keeping loyal love for thousands, forgiving iniquity and transgression and sin. But he by no means leaves the
guilty unpunished, responding to the transgression of fathers
by dealing with children and children's children, to the third
and fourth generation."
8 Moses quickly bowed to the ground and worshiped 9 and said,
"If now I have found favor in your sight, O Lord, let my Lord go
among us, for we are a stiff-necked people; pardon our iniquity
and our sin, and take us for your inheritance."
10 He said, "See, I am going to make a covenant before all your
people. I will do wonders such as have not been done in all the
earth, nor in any nation. All the people among whom you live
will see the work of the LORD, for it is a fearful thing that I am
doing with you.
11 "Obey what I am commanding you this day. I am going to
drive out before you the Amorite, the Canaanite, the Hittite, the
Perizzite, the Hivite, and the Jebusite. 12 Be careful not to make a
covenant with the inhabitants of the land where you are going,
lest it become a snare among you. 13 Rather you must destroy

GOD'S HEART FOR THE NATIONS

Exodus 34:10

He said, "See, I am going to make a covenant before all your people. I will do wonders such as have not been done in all the earth, nor in any nation. All the people among whom you live will see the work of the LORD, for it is a fearful thing that I am doing with you."

REFLECT

What are the first words God used to describe Himself in Exodus 34:6? Why was it significant that He began His description in this way?

their altars, smash their images, and cut down their Asherah
poles. 14 For you must not worship any other god, for the LORD,
whose name is Jealous, is a jealous God. 15 Be careful not to make
a covenant with the inhabitants of the land, for when they prostitute themselves to their gods and sacrifice to their gods, and
someone invites you, you will eat from his sacrifice; 16 and you
then take his daughters for your sons, and when his daughters
prostitute themselves to their gods, they will make your sons
prostitute themselves to their gods as well. 17 You must not make
yourselves molten gods.

18 "You must keep the Feast of Unleavened Bread. For seven
days you must eat bread made without yeast, as I commanded
you; do this at the appointed time of the month Abib, for in the
month Abib you came out of Egypt.

19 "Every firstborn of the womb belongs to me, even every firstborn of your cattle that is a male, whether ox or sheep. 20 Now
the firstling of a donkey you may redeem with a lamb, but if you
do not redeem it, then break its neck. You must redeem all the
firstborn of your sons.

"No one will appear before me empty-handed.

21 "On six days you may labor, but on the seventh day you must
rest; even at the time of plowing and of harvest you are to rest.

22 "You must observe the Feast of Weeks—the firstfruits of the
harvest of wheat—and the Feast of Ingathering at the end of the
year. 23 At three times in the year all your men must appear before the Sovereign LORD, the God of Israel. 24 For I will drive out
the nations before you and enlarge your borders; no one will
covet your land when you go up to appear before the LORD your
God three times in the year.

25 "You must not offer the blood of my sacrifice with yeast; the
sacrifice from the Feast of Passover must not remain until the
following morning.

26 "The first of the firstfruits of your soil you must bring to the
house of the LORD your God.

"You must not cook a young goat in its mother's milk."

27 The LORD said to Moses, "Write down these words, for in
accordance with these words I have made a covenant with you
and with Israel." 28 So he was there with the LORD forty days
and forty nights; he did not eat bread, and he did not drink water. He wrote on the tablets the words of the covenant, the Ten
Commandments.

THE RADIANT FACE OF MOSES

29 Now when Moses came down from Mount Sinai with the two
tablets of the testimony in his hand—when he came down from
the mountain, Moses did not know that the skin of his face shone
while he talked with him. 30 When Aaron and all the Israelites
saw Moses, the skin of his face shone, and they were afraid to
approach him. 31 But Moses called to them, so Aaron and all the
leaders of the community came back to him, and Moses spoke
to them. 32 After this all the Israelites approached, and he commanded them all that the LORD had spoken to him on Mount
Sinai. 33 When Moses finished speaking with them, he would put
a veil on his face. 34 But when Moses went in before the LORD

to speak with him, he would remove the veil until he came out.
Then he would come out and tell the Israelites what he had been
commanded. 35 When the Israelites would see the face of Moses,
that the skin of Moses' face shone, Moses would put the veil on
his face again, until he went in to speak with the LORD.

SABBATH REGULATIONS

35 Moses assembled the whole community of the Israelites
and said to them, "These are the things that the LORD has
commanded you to do. 2 In six days work may be done, but on
the seventh day there must be a holy day for you, a Sabbath of
complete rest to the LORD. Anyone who does work on it will be
put to death. 3 You must not kindle a fire in any of your homes
on the Sabbath day."

WILLING WORKERS

4 Moses spoke to the whole community of the Israelites, "This
is the word that the LORD has commanded: 5 'Take an offering
for the LORD. Let everyone who has a willing heart bring an offering to the LORD: gold, silver, bronze; 6 blue, purple, and scarlet yarn; fine linen; goats' hair; 7 ram skins dyed red; fine leather;
acacia wood; 8 olive oil for the light; spices for the anointing oil
and for the fragrant incense; 9 onyx stones, and other gems for
mounting on the ephod and the breastpiece. 10 Every skilled person among you is to come and make all that the LORD has commanded: 11 the tabernacle with its tent, its covering, its clasps, its
frames, its crossbars, its posts, and its bases; 12 the ark, with its
poles, the atonement lid, and the special curtain that conceals
it; 13 the table with its poles and all its vessels, and the Bread of
the Presence; 14 the lampstand for the light and its accessories,
its lamps, and oil for the light; 15 and the altar of incense with its
poles, the anointing oil, and the fragrant incense; the hanging
for the door at the entrance of the tabernacle; 16 the altar for the
burnt offering with its bronze grating that is on it, its poles, and
all its utensils; the large basin and its pedestal; 17 the hangings
of the courtyard, its posts and its bases, and the curtain for the
gateway to the courtyard; 18 tent pegs for the tabernacle and tent
pegs for the courtyard and their ropes; 19 the woven garments
for serving in the Holy Place, the holy garments for Aaron the
priest, and the garments for his sons to minister as priests.'"

20 So the whole community of the Israelites went out from
the presence of Moses. 21 Everyone whose heart stirred him to
action and everyone whose spirit was willing came and brought
the offering for the LORD for the work of the tent of meeting, for
all its service, and for the holy garments. 22 They came, men and
women alike, all who had willing hearts. They brought brooches,
earrings, rings and ornaments, all kinds of gold jewelry, and everyone came who waved a wave offering of gold to the LORD.

23 Everyone who had blue, purple, or scarlet yarn, fine linen,
goats' hair, ram skins dyed red, or fine leather brought them.
24 Everyone making an offering of silver or bronze brought it
as an offering to the LORD, and everyone who had acacia wood
for any work of the service brought it. 25 Every woman who was
skilled spun with her hands and brought what she had spun,

blue, purple, or scarlet yarn, or fine linen, 26 and all the women
whose heart stirred them to action and who were skilled spun
goats' hair.
27 The leaders brought onyx stones and other gems to be
mounted for the ephod and the breastpiece, 28 and spices and olive
oil for the light, for the anointing oil, and for the fragrant incense.
29 The Israelites brought a freewill offering to the LORD, every man and woman whose heart was willing to bring materials
for all the work that the LORD through Moses had commanded
them to do.
30 Moses said to the Israelites, "See, the LORD has chosen Bezalel son of Uri, the son of Hur, of the tribe of Judah. 31 He has filled
him with the Spirit of God—with skill, with understanding, with
knowledge, and in all kinds of work—32 to design artistic designs,
to work in gold, in silver, and in bronze, 33 and in cutting stones
for their setting, and in cutting wood, to do work in every artistic craft. 34 And he has put it in his heart to teach, he and Oholiab son of Ahisamach, of the tribe of Dan. 35 He has filled them
with skill to do all kinds of work as craftsmen, as designers, as
embroiderers in blue, purple, and scarlet yarn and in fine linen,
and as weavers. They are craftsmen in all the work and artistic
36 designers. 1 So Bezalel and Oholiab and every skilled person in whom the LORD has put skill and ability to know
how to do all the work for the service of the sanctuary are to do
the work according to all that the LORD has commanded."
2 Moses summoned Bezalel and Oholiab and every skilled person in whom the LORD had put skill—everyone whose heart
stirred him to volunteer to do the work. 3 They received from
Moses all the offerings the Israelites had brought to do the work
for the service of the sanctuary, and they still continued to bring
him a freewill offering each morning. 4 So all the skilled people
who were doing all the work on the sanctuary came from the
work they were doing 5 and told Moses, "The people are bringing much more than is needed for the completion of the work
which the LORD commanded us to do!"
6 Moses instructed them to take his message throughout the
camp, saying, "Let no man or woman do anymore work for the
offering for the sanctuary." So the people were restrained from
bringing any more. 7 Now the materials were more than enough
for them to do all the work.

THE BUILDING OF THE TABERNACLE

8 All the skilled among those who were doing the work made the
tabernacle with ten curtains of fine twisted linen and blue and
purple and scarlet yarn; they were made with cherubim that
were the work of an artistic designer. 9 The length of one curtain
was 42 feet, and the width of one curtain was 6 feet—the same
size for each of the curtains. 10 He joined five of the curtains to
one another, and the other five curtains he joined to one another. 11 He made loops of blue material along the edge of the
end curtain in the first set; he did the same along the edge of the
end curtain in the second set. 12 He made fifty loops on the first
curtain, and he made fifty loops on the end curtain that was in
the second set, with the loops opposite one another. 13 He made

fifty gold clasps and joined the curtains together to one another with the clasps, so that the tabernacle was a unit.

14 He made curtains of goats' hair for a tent over the tabernacle; he made eleven curtains. 15 The length of one curtain was 45 feet, and the width of one curtain was 6 feet—one size for all eleven curtains. 16 He joined five curtains by themselves and six curtains by themselves. 17 He made fifty loops along the edge of the end curtain in the first set and fifty loops along the edge of the curtain that joined the second set. 18 He made fifty bronze clasps to join the tent together so that it might be a unit. 19 He made a covering for the tent out of ram skins dyed red and over that a covering of fine leather.

20 He made the frames for the tabernacle of acacia wood as uprights. 21 The length of each frame was 15 feet, the width of each frame was 2¼ feet, 22 with two projections per frame parallel one to another. He made all the frames of the tabernacle in this way. 23 So he made frames for the tabernacle: twenty frames for the south side. 24 He made forty silver bases under the twenty frames—two bases under the first frame for its two projections, and likewise two bases under the next frame for its two projections, 25 and for the second side of the tabernacle, the north side, he made twenty frames 26 and their forty silver bases, two bases under the first frame and two bases under the next frame. 27 And for the back of the tabernacle on the west he made six frames. 28 He made two frames for the corners of the tabernacle on the back. 29 At the two corners they were doubled at the lower end and finished together at the top in one ring. So he did for both. 30 So there were eight frames and their silver bases, sixteen bases, two bases under each frame.

31 He made bars of acacia wood, five for the frames on one side of the tabernacle 32 and five bars for the frames on the second side of the tabernacle, and five bars for the frames of the tabernacle for the back side on the west. 33 He made the middle bar to reach from end to end in the center of the frames. 34 He overlaid the frames with gold and made their rings of gold to provide places for the bars, and he overlaid the bars with gold.

35 He made the special curtain of blue, purple, and scarlet yarn and fine twisted linen; he made it with cherubim, the work of an artistic designer. 36 He made for it four posts of acacia wood and overlaid them with gold, with gold hooks, and he cast for them four silver bases.

37 He made a hanging for the entrance of the tent of blue, purple, and scarlet yarn and fine twisted linen, the work of an embroiderer, 38 and its five posts and their hooks. He overlaid their tops and their bands with gold, but their five bases were bronze.

THE MAKING OF THE ARK

37 Bezalel made the ark of acacia wood; its length was 45 inches, its width 27 inches, and its height 27 inches. 2 He overlaid it with pure gold, inside and out, and he made a surrounding border of gold for it. 3 He cast four gold rings for it that he put on its four feet, with two rings on one side and two rings on the other side. 4 He made poles of acacia wood, overlaid them with gold, 5 and put the poles into the rings on the sides of the ark in order to carry the ark.

[6] He made an atonement lid of pure gold; its length was 45
inches, and its width was 27 inches. [7] He made two cherubim
of gold; he made them of hammered metal on the two ends of
the atonement lid, [8] one cherub on one end and one cherub on
the other end. He made the cherubim from the atonement lid
on its two ends. [9] The cherubim were spreading their wings upward, overshadowing the atonement lid with their wings. The
cherubim faced each other, looking toward the atonement lid.

THE MAKING OF THE TABLE

[10] Bezalel made the table of acacia wood; its length was 36 inches,
its width 18 inches, and its height 27 inches. [11] He overlaid it with
pure gold, and he made a surrounding border of gold for it. [12] He
made a surrounding frame for it about three inches wide, and
he made a surrounding border of gold for its frame. [13] He cast
four gold rings for it and attached the rings at the four corners
where its four legs were. [14] The rings were close to the frame to
provide places for the poles to carry the table. [15] He made the
poles of acacia wood and overlaid them with gold, to carry the
table. [16] He made the vessels which were on the table out of pure
gold, its plates, its ladles, its pitchers, and its bowls, to be used
in pouring out offerings.

THE MAKING OF THE LAMPSTAND

[17] Bezalel made the lampstand of pure gold. He made the lampstand of hammered metal; its base and its shaft, its cups, its buds,
and its blossoms were from the same piece. [18] Six branches were
extending from its sides, three branches of the lampstand from
one side of it, and three branches of the lampstand from the other side of it. [19] Three cups shaped like almond flowers with buds
and blossoms were on the first branch, and three cups shaped
like almond flowers with buds and blossoms were on the next
branch, and the same for the six branches that were extending
from the lampstand. [20] On the lampstand there were four cups
shaped like almond flowers with buds and blossoms, [21] with a bud
under the first two branches from it, and a bud under the next
two branches from it, and a bud under the third two branches
from it; according to the six branches that extended from it.
[22] Their buds and their branches were of one piece; all of it was
one hammered piece of pure gold. [23] He made its seven lamps, its
trimmers, and its trays of pure gold. [24] He made the lampstand
and all its accessories with seventy-five pounds of pure gold.

THE MAKING OF THE ALTAR OF INCENSE

[25] Bezalel made the incense altar of acacia wood. Its length was
18 inches and its width 18 inches—a square—and its height was
36 inches. Its horns were of one piece with it. [26] He overlaid it
with pure gold—its top, its four walls, and its horns—and he made
a surrounding border of gold for it. [27] He also made two gold
rings for it under its border, on its two sides, on opposite sides,
as places for poles to carry it with. [28] He made the poles of acacia wood and overlaid them with gold.

[29] He made the sacred anointing oil and the pure fragrant incense, the work of a perfumer.

THE MAKING OF THE ALTAR FOR THE BURNT OFFERING

38 Bezalel made the altar for the burnt offering of acacia
wood 7½ feet long and 7½ feet wide—it was square—and
its height was 4½ feet. 2 He made its horns on its four corners; its
horns were part of it, and he overlaid it with bronze. 3 He made
all the utensils of the altar—the pots, the shovels, the tossing
bowls, the meat hooks, and the fire pans—he made all its utensils of bronze. 4 He made a grating for the altar, a network of
bronze under its ledge, halfway up from the bottom. 5 He cast
four rings for the four corners of the bronze grating, to provide
places for the poles. 6 He made the poles of acacia wood and
overlaid them with bronze. 7 He put the poles into the rings on
the sides of the altar, with which to carry it. He made the altar
hollow, out of boards.
8 He made the large basin of bronze and its pedestal of bronze
from the mirrors of the women who served at the entrance of
the tent of meeting.

THE CONSTRUCTION OF THE COURTYARD

9 Bezalel made the courtyard. For the south side the hangings
of the courtyard were of fine twisted linen, 150 feet long, 10 with
their twenty posts and their twenty bronze bases, with the hooks
of the posts and their bands of silver. 11 For the north side the
hangings were 150 feet, with their twenty posts and their twenty
bronze bases, with the hooks of the posts and their bands of silver. 12 For the west side there were hangings 75 feet long, with
their ten posts and their ten bases, with the hooks of the posts
and their bands of silver. 13 For the east side, toward the sunrise,
it was 75 feet wide, 14 with hangings on one side of the gate that
were 22½ feet long, with their three posts and their three bases,
15 and for the second side of the gate of the courtyard, just like the
other, the hangings were 22½ feet long, with their three posts
and their three bases. 16 All the hangings around the courtyard
were of fine twisted linen. 17 The bases for the posts were bronze.
The hooks of the posts and their bands were silver, their tops
were overlaid with silver, and all the posts of the courtyard had
silver bands. 18 The curtain for the gate of the courtyard was of
blue, purple, and scarlet yarn and fine twisted linen, the work of
an embroiderer. It was 30 feet long and, like the hangings in the
courtyard, it was 7½ feet high, 19 with four posts and their four
bronze bases. Their hooks and their bands were silver, and their
tops were overlaid with silver. 20 All the tent pegs of the tabernacle and of the courtyard all around were bronze.

THE MATERIALS OF THE CONSTRUCTION

21 This is the inventory of the tabernacle, the tabernacle of the
testimony, which was counted by the order of Moses, being the
work of the Levites under the direction of Ithamar, son of Aaron
the priest. 22 Now Bezalel son of Uri, the son of Hur, of the tribe
of Judah, made everything that the LORD had commanded Moses; 23 and with him was Oholiab son of Ahisamach, of the tribe
of Dan, an artisan, a designer, and an embroiderer in blue, purple, and scarlet yarn and fine linen.

24 All the gold that was used for the work, in all the work of the sanctuary (namely, the gold of the wave offering) was 29 talents and 730 shekels, according to the sanctuary shekel.

25 The silver of those who were numbered of the community was 100 talents and 1,775 shekels, according to the sanctuary shekel, 26 one beka per person, that is, a half shekel, according to the sanctuary shekel, for everyone who crossed over to those numbered, from twenty years old or older, 603,550 in all. 27 The 100 talents of silver were used for casting the bases of the sanctuary and the bases of the special curtain—100 bases for 100 talents, one talent per base. 28 From the remaining 1,775 shekels he made hooks for the posts, overlaid their tops, and made bands for them.

29 The bronze of the wave offering was seventy talents and 2,400 shekels. 30 With it he made the bases for the door of the tent of meeting, the bronze altar, the bronze grating for it, and all the utensils of the altar, 31 the bases for the courtyard all around, the bases for the gate of the courtyard, all the tent pegs of the tabernacle, and all the tent pegs of the courtyard all around.

THE MAKING OF THE PRIESTLY GARMENTS

39 From the blue, purple, and scarlet yarn they made woven garments for serving in the sanctuary; they made holy garments that were for Aaron, just as the LORD had commanded Moses.

THE EPHOD

2 He made the ephod of gold, blue, purple, scarlet yarn, and fine twisted linen. 3 They hammered the gold into thin sheets and cut it into narrow strips to weave them into the blue, purple, and scarlet yarn, and into the fine linen, the work of an artistic designer. 4 They made shoulder pieces for it, attached to two of its corners, so it could be joined together. 5 The artistically woven waistband of the ephod that was on it was like it, of one piece with it, of gold, blue, purple, and scarlet yarn and fine twisted linen, just as the LORD had commanded Moses.

6 They set the onyx stones in gold filigree settings, engraved as with the engravings of a seal with the names of the sons of Israel. 7 He put them on the shoulder pieces of the ephod as stones of memorial for the Israelites, just as the LORD had commanded Moses.

THE BREASTPIECE OF DECISION

8 He made the breastpiece, the work of an artistic designer, in the same fashion as the ephod, of gold, blue, purple, and scarlet yarn, and fine twisted linen. 9 It was square—they made the breastpiece doubled, nine inches long and nine inches wide when doubled. 10 They set on it four rows of stones: a row with a ruby, a topaz, and a beryl—the first row; 11 and the second row, a turquoise, a sapphire, and an emerald; 12 and the third row, a jacinth, an agate, and an amethyst; 13 and the fourth row, a chrysolite, an onyx, and a jasper. They were enclosed in gold filigree settings. 14 The stones were for the names of the sons of Israel, twelve, corresponding to the number of their names. Each name corresponding to one of the twelve tribes was like the engravings of a seal.

15 They made for the breastpiece braided chains like cords of
pure gold, 16 and they made two gold filigree settings and two
gold rings, and they attached the two rings to the upper two
ends of the breastpiece. 17 They attached the two gold chains
to the two rings at the ends of the breastpiece; 18 the other two
ends of the two chains they attached to the two settings, and
they attached them to the shoulder pieces of the ephod at
the front of it. 19 They made two rings of gold and put them on
the other two ends of the breastpiece on its edge, which is on the
inner side of the ephod. 20 They made two more gold rings and
attached them to the bottom of the two shoulder pieces on the
front of the ephod, close to the juncture above the waistband of
the ephod. 21 They tied the breastpiece by its rings to the rings
of the ephod by blue cord, so that it was above the waistband of
the ephod, so that the breastpiece would not be loose from the
ephod, just as the LORD had commanded Moses.

THE OTHER GARMENTS

22 He made the robe of the ephod completely blue, the work of
a weaver. 23 There was an opening in the center of the robe, like
the opening of a collar, with an edge all around the opening so
that it could not be torn. 24 They made pomegranates of blue,
purple, and scarlet yarn and twisted linen around the hem of
the robe. 25 They made bells of pure gold and attached the bells
between the pomegranates around the hem of the robe between
the pomegranates. 26 There was a bell and a pomegranate, a bell
and a pomegranate, all around the hem of the robe, to be used
in ministering, just as the LORD had commanded Moses.

27 They made tunics of fine linen—the work of a weaver, for
Aaron and for his sons—28 and the turban of fine linen, the headbands of fine linen, and the undergarments of fine twisted linen.
29 The sash was of fine twisted linen and blue, purple, and scarlet yarn, the work of an embroiderer, just as the LORD had commanded Moses. 30 They made a plate, the holy diadem, of pure
gold and wrote on it an inscription, as on the engravings of a seal,
"Holiness to the LORD." 31 They attached to it a blue cord to attach
it to the turban above, just as the LORD had commanded Moses.

MOSES INSPECTS THE TABERNACLE

32 So all the work of the tabernacle, the tent of meeting, was
completed, and the Israelites did according to all that the LORD
had commanded Moses—they did it exactly so. 33 They brought
the tabernacle to Moses, the tent and all its furnishings, clasps,
frames, bars, posts, and bases; 34 and the coverings of ram skins
dyed red, the covering of fine leather, and the protecting curtain;
35 the ark of the testimony and its poles, and the atonement lid;
36 the table, all its utensils, and the Bread of the Presence; 37 the
pure lampstand, its lamps, with the lamps set in order, and all
its accessories, and oil for the light; 38 and the gold altar, and the
anointing oil, and the fragrant incense; and the curtain for the
entrance to the tent; 39 the bronze altar and its bronze grating,
its poles, and all its utensils; the large basin with its pedestal;
40 the hangings of the courtyard, its posts and its bases, and the
curtain for the gateway of the courtyard, its ropes and its tent

pegs, and all the furnishings for the service of the tabernacle, for the tent of meeting; 41 the woven garments for serving in the sanctuary, the holy garments for Aaron the priest, and the garments for his sons to minister as priests.

42 The Israelites did all the work according to all that the LORD had commanded Moses. 43 Moses inspected all the work, and they had done it just as the LORD had commanded—they had done it exactly—and Moses blessed them.

SETTING UP THE SANCTUARY

40 Then the LORD spoke to Moses: 2 "On the first day of the first month you are to set up the tabernacle, the tent of meeting. 3 You are to place the ark of the testimony in it and shield the ark with the special curtain. 4 You are to bring in the table and set out the things that belong on it; then you are to bring in the lampstand and set up its lamps. 5 You are to put the gold altar for incense in front of the ark of the testimony and put the curtain at the entrance to the tabernacle. 6 You are to put the altar for the burnt offering in front of the entrance to the tabernacle, the tent of meeting. 7 You are to put the large basin between the tent of meeting and the altar and put water in it. 8 You are to set up the courtyard around it and put the curtain at the gate of the courtyard. 9 And take the anointing oil, and anoint the tabernacle and all that is in it, and sanctify it and all its furnishings, and it will be holy. 10 Then you are to anoint the altar for the burnt offering with all its utensils; you are to sanctify the altar, and it will be the most holy altar. 11 You must also anoint the large basin and its pedestal, and you are to sanctify it.

12 "You are to bring Aaron and his sons to the entrance of the tent of meeting and wash them with water. 13 Then you are to clothe Aaron with the holy garments and anoint him and sanctify him so that he may minister as my priest. 14 You are to bring his sons and clothe them with tunics 15 and anoint them just as you anointed their father, so that they may minister as my priests; their anointing will make them a priesthood that will continue throughout their generations." 16 This is what Moses did, according to all the LORD had commanded him—so he did.

17 So the tabernacle was set up on the first day of the first month, in the second year. 18 When Moses set up the tabernacle and put its bases in place, he set up its frames, attached its bars, and set up its posts. 19 Then he spread the tent over the tabernacle and put the covering of the tent over it, as the LORD had commanded him. 20 He took the testimony and put it in the ark, attached the poles to the ark, and then put the atonement lid on the ark. 21 And he brought the ark into the tabernacle, hung the protecting curtain, and shielded the ark of the testimony from view, just as the LORD had commanded him.

22 And Moses put the table in the tent of meeting, on the north side of the tabernacle, outside the curtain. 23 And he set the bread in order on it before the LORD, just as the LORD had commanded him.

24 And he put the lampstand in the tent of meeting opposite the table, on the south side of the tabernacle. 25 Then he set up the lamps before the LORD, just as the LORD had commanded him.

26 And he put the gold altar in the tent of meeting in front of
the curtain, 27 and he burned fragrant incense on it, just as the
LORD had commanded him.
28 Then Moses put the curtain at the entrance to the tabernacle. 29 He also put the altar for the burnt offering by the entrance to the tabernacle, the tent of meeting, and offered on it
the burnt offering and the meal offering, just as the LORD had
commanded him.
30 Then he put the large basin between the tent of meeting and the altar and put water in it for washing. 31 Moses and
Aaron and his sons would wash their hands and their feet from
it. 32 Whenever they entered the tent of meeting, and whenever
they approached the altar, they would wash, just as the LORD
had commanded Moses.
33 And he set up the courtyard around the tabernacle and the
altar, and put the curtain at the gate of the courtyard. So Moses finished the work.
34 Then the cloud covered the tent of meeting, and the glory
of the LORD filled the tabernacle. 35 Moses was not able to enter the tent of meeting because the cloud settled on it and the
glory of the LORD filled the tabernacle. 36 But when the cloud
was lifted up from the tabernacle, the Israelites would set out
on all their journeys; 37 but if the cloud was not lifted up, then
they would not journey farther until the day it was lifted up.
38 For the cloud of the LORD was on the tabernacle by day, but
fire would be on it at night, in plain view of all the house of Israel throughout all their journeys.

You must
be holy
to me
because
I, the LORD,
am holy

MEMORY VERSE

"You must be holy to me, because I, the LORD, am holy, and I have set you apart from the other peoples to be mine."

Leviticus 20:26

Leviticus

INTRODUCTION

Honoring God Through Obedience

The Book of Leviticus amplifies the holiness of God. Its 613 case laws were more than a list of rules. They provided practical application of the decalogue (the Ten Commandments) to everyday life in order for the Israelites to maintain their relationship with the God who redeemed them. Together the laws form a manual for living in holy relationship with a holy God.

Leviticus also prescribes the offerings and sacrifices that were required by God's covenant people. These offerings and sacrifices restored a person to righteousness and demonstrated God's long-suffering through forgiveness of sins. God was not only honored by their sacrifice, but also by their worship. The rituals of worship and sacrifice continued until the destruction of the temple in Jerusalem in 586 B.C. In the sixth century B.C., the exiles returning from Babylon rebuilt the temple under the leadership of Ezra, and the rituals of worship and sacrifice resumed. They continued until the destruction of the temple in Jerusalem by the Romans in A.D. 70.

Most evangelical scholars believe Leviticus was written by Moses, as were the other books of the Pentateuch (the first five books of the Bible). The instructions in Leviticus were given to the Israelites as they wandered through the wilderness. Moses recorded these instructions for the future generations who would live in the land of Canaan.

Even though Leviticus can be a difficult book to read, we are encouraged to love God greatly as we study this book. God's character is on display throughout its chapters. His provision is evident in the methods of sacrifice; His long-suffering is shown as the people sin and He forgives them; and His holiness is made evident as we learn more about our sinful condition. The law was not given to trap God's people in their sin, but to reveal His holiness and the great wonder of being called His people.

China

OFFICIAL LANGUAGE
Mandarin Chinese/Standard Chinese
POPULATION
1,419,883,000
UNREACHED POPULATION
148,152,000
PROFESSING CHRISTIANS
9.2%

Bi's Home

Say a Prayer Today

Pray today for Bi and the Love God Greatly Chinese translation team. Pray these women will be energized and equipped to continue in the work God has given them.

HISTORY BIT

While there have been efforts to evangelize the people of China since A.D. 578, the China Inland Mission was established in 1865. With over 1,000 missionaries in China in 1914, it grew to be the largest mission in China and became a model for the faith missions approach.*

Source Information:
https://joshuaproject.net/countries/CH
David B. Barrett, World *Christian Encyclopedia*, China (New York, NY: Oxford University Press, 1982), 232–233.

BI'S STORY

My name is Bi, and I am a translator for the Love God Greatly Chinese branch. I currently live in the United States, but my home is in Shanghai, China.

Growing up in the biggest city in China, Shanghai, I deeply feel the need for the truth of God's Word for women in China. Like women everywhere else, they experience the fallen nature of the world on a daily basis and fight to find their own place. Many are driven by the motivation to excel, to achieve an identity by what they do, how they look, or what they possess. Yet access to the Bible, Christian books, and study materials is still relatively scarce in China. As I translate, I pray that these materials will be used by God in ways that I cannot fathom.

Though it is still humanly impossible to reach women in mainland China on a large scale, I trust the mighty hand of God. God is faithful. I continue to translate Bible study materials for women into Chinese so women can grow in God's Word. Along with the rest of the Chinese team, I continue in obedience even when I cannot see any fruit from our labor. We are called to be faithful and persevere, and we are thankful for the opportunity to serve in this way.

A few years ago God graciously allowed me to see the fruit of this labor. Another translator for Love God Greatly contacted me with incredible news. She informed me that a group of Chinese women were using the Chinese Love God Greatly studies in Budapest, Hungary. Budapest! The moment she told me I was in shock and awe and immediately praised God. When we were discouraged that God was not using our work in one area, He was using it in incredible ways elsewhere.

Praise God that He does incredible work like this. In our obedience, He is faithful. He does not stop working!

4 WEEK READING PLAN

LOVE HIS WORD

	MONDAY	TUESDAY	WEDNESDAY	THURSDAY	FRIDAY
1	Leviticus 1-2	Leviticus 3	Leviticus 4-5	Leviticus 6	Leviticus 7
	SOAP Hebrews 9:11-12	SOAP Hebrews 9:13-14	SOAP Hebrews 10:1-3	SOAP Hebrews 10:4-7	SOAP Hebrews 10:8-9
2	Leviticus 8	Leviticus 9	Leviticus 10	Leviticus 11	Leviticus 12-13
	SOAP Hebrews 10:10-11	SOAP Hebrews 10:12-13	SOAP Hebrews 10:14	SOAP Hebrews 10:15-16	SOAP Hebrews 10:17-18
3	Leviticus 14-15	Leviticus 16	Leviticus 17	Leviticus 18-19	Leviticus 20
	SOAP Hebrews 10:19-22	SOAP Hebrews 10:23	SOAP Hebrews 10: 24-25	SOAP Hebrews 10:26-27	SOAP Leviticus 20:26
4	Leviticus 21	Leviticus 22	Leviticus 23-24	Leviticus 25	Leviticus 26-27
	SOAP Hebrews 10:28-29	SOAP Hebrews 10:30-31	SOAP Hebrews 10:32-34	SOAP Hebrews 10:35-36	SOAP Hebrews 10:37-39

INTRODUCTION TO THE SACRIFICIAL REGULATIONS

1 Then the LORD called to Moses and spoke to him from the
Meeting Tent: 2“Speak to the Israelites and tell them, ‘When
someone among you presents an offering to the LORD, you must
present your offering from the domesticated animals, either
from the herd or from the flock.

BURNT-OFFERING REGULATIONS: ANIMAL FROM THE HERD

3“‘If his offering is a burnt offering from the herd he must present it as a flawless male; he must present it at the entrance
of the Meeting Tent for its acceptance before the LORD. 4He
must lay his hand on the head of the burnt offering, and it will
be accepted for him to make atonement on his behalf. 5Then
the one presenting the offering must slaughter the bull before the LORD, and the sons of Aaron, the priests, must present the blood and splash the blood against the sides of the
altar, which is at the entrance of the Meeting Tent. 6Next, the
one presenting the offering must skin the burnt offering and
cut it into parts, 7and the sons of Aaron, the priest, must put
fire on the altar and arrange wood on the fire. 8Then the sons
of Aaron, the priests, must arrange the parts with the head
and the suet on the wood that is in the fire on the altar. 9Fi-
nally, the one presenting the offering must wash its entrails
and its legs in water and the priest must offer all of it up in
smoke on the altar—it is a burnt offering, a gift of a soothing
aroma to the LORD.

REFLECT

Why were sacrifices and offerings such a crucial part of the system of worship God designed for His people?

ANIMAL FROM THE FLOCK

10“‘If his offering is from the flock for a burnt offering—from the
sheep or the goats—he must present a flawless male, 11and must
slaughter it on the north side of the altar before the LORD, and
the sons of Aaron, the priests, will splash its blood against the
altar’s sides. 12Next, the one presenting the offering must cut
it into parts, with its head and its suet, and the priest must arrange them on the wood that is in the fire on the altar. 13Then
the one presenting the offering must wash the entrails and the
legs in water, and the priest must present all of it and offer it
up in smoke on the altar—it is a burnt offering, a gift of a soothing aroma to the LORD.

OFFERING OF BIRDS

14“‘If his offering to the LORD is a burnt offering of birds, he must
present his offering from the turtledoves or from the young pigeons. 15The priest must present it at the altar, pinch off its head
and offer the head up in smoke on the altar, and its blood must
be drained out against the side of the altar. 16Then the priest
must remove its entrails by cutting off its tail feathers, and throw
them to the east side of the altar into the place of fatty ashes,
17and tear it open by its wings without dividing it into two parts.
Finally, the priest must offer it up in smoke on the altar on the
wood which is in the fire—it is a burnt offering, a gift of a soothing aroma to the LORD.

GRAIN-OFFERING REGULATIONS: OFFERING OF RAW FLOUR

2 "'When a person presents a grain offering to the LORD, his offering must consist of choice wheat flour, and he must pour
olive oil on it and put frankincense on it. 2 Then he must bring it to
the sons of Aaron, the priests, and the priest must scoop out from
there a handful of its choice wheat flour and some of its olive oil
in addition to all of its frankincense, and the priest must offer its
memorial portion up in smoke on the altar—it is a gift of a soothing
aroma to the LORD. 3 The remainder of the grain offering belongs
to Aaron and to his sons—it is most holy from the gifts of the LORD.

PROCESSED GRAIN OFFERINGS

4 "'When you present an offering of grain baked in an oven, it
must be made of choice wheat flour baked into unleavened
loaves mixed with olive oil or unleavened wafers smeared with
olive oil. 5 If your offering is a grain offering made on the griddle,
it must be choice wheat flour mixed with olive oil, unleavened.
6 Crumble it in pieces and pour olive oil on it—it is a grain offering. 7 If your offering is a grain offering made in a pan, it must be
made of choice wheat flour deep fried in olive oil.

8 "'You must bring the grain offering that must be made from
these to the LORD. Present it to the priest, and he will bring it to
the altar. 9 Then the priest must take up from the grain offering
its memorial portion and offer it up in smoke on the altar—it is
a gift of a soothing aroma to the LORD. 10 The remainder of the
grain offering belongs to Aaron and to his sons—it is most holy
from the gifts of the LORD.

ADDITIONAL GRAIN-OFFERING REGULATIONS

11 "'No grain offering which you present to the LORD can be made
with yeast, for you must not offer up in smoke any yeast or honey
as a gift to the LORD. 12 You can present them to the LORD as an
offering of firstfruit, but they must not go up to the altar for a
soothing aroma. 13 Moreover, you must season every one of your
grain offerings with salt; you must not allow the salt of the covenant of your God to be missing from your grain offering—on
every one of your grain offerings you must present salt.

14 "'If you present a grain offering of first ripe grain to the LORD,
you must present your grain offering of first ripe grain as soft
kernels roasted in fire—crushed bits of fresh grain. 15 And you
must put olive oil on it and set frankincense on it—it is a grain
offering. 16 Then the priest must offer its memorial portion up
in smoke—some of its crushed bits, some of its olive oil, in addition to all of its frankincense—it is a gift to the LORD.

PEACE-OFFERING REGULATIONS: ANIMAL FROM THE HERD

3 "'Now if his offering is a peace-offering sacrifice, if he presents
an offering from the herd, he must present before the LORD
a flawless male or a female. 2 He must lay his hand on the head
of his offering and slaughter it at the entrance of the Meeting
Tent, and the sons of Aaron, the priests, must splash the blood
against the altar's sides. 3 Then the one presenting the offering

must present a gift to the LORD from the peace-offering sacrifice: He must remove the fat that covers the entrails and all the fat that surrounds the entrails, 4 the two kidneys with the fat on their sinews, and the protruding lobe on the liver (which he is to remove along with the kidneys). 5 Then the sons of Aaron must offer it up in smoke on the altar atop the burnt offering that is on the wood in the fire as a gift of a soothing aroma to the LORD.

ANIMAL FROM THE FLOCK

6 “‘If his offering for a peace-offering sacrifice to the LORD is from the flock, he must present a flawless male or female. 7 If he presents a sheep as his offering, he must present it before the LORD. 8 He must lay his hand on the head of his offering and slaughter it before the Meeting Tent, and the sons of Aaron must splash its blood against the altar's sides. 9 Then he must present a gift to the LORD from the peace-offering sacrifice: He must remove all the fatty tail up to the end of the spine, the fat covering the entrails, and all the fat on the entrails, 10 the two kidneys with the fat on their sinews, and the protruding lobe on the liver (which he is to remove along with the kidneys). 11 Then the priest must offer it up in smoke on the altar as a food gift to the LORD.

12 “‘If his offering is a goat he must present it before the LORD, 13 lay his hand on its head, and slaughter it before the Meeting Tent, and the sons of Aaron must splash its blood against the altar's sides. 14 Then he must present from it his offering as a gift to the LORD: the fat which covers the entrails and all the fat on the entrails, 15 the two kidneys with the fat on their sinews, and the protruding lobe on the liver (which he is to remove along with the kidneys). 16 Then the priest must offer them up in smoke on the altar as a food gift for a soothing aroma—all the fat belongs to the LORD. 17 This is a perpetual statute throughout your generations in all the places where you live: You must never eat any fat or any blood.’”

SIN-OFFERING REGULATIONS

4 Then the LORD spoke to Moses: 2 “Tell the Israelites, ‘When a person sins by straying unintentionally from any of the LORD's commandments which must not be violated, and violates any one of them—

FOR THE PRIEST

3 “‘If the high priest sins so that the people are guilty, on account of the sin he has committed he must present a flawless young bull to the LORD for a sin offering. 4 He must bring the bull to the entrance of the Meeting Tent before the LORD, lay his hand on the head of the bull, and slaughter the bull before the LORD. 5 Then that high priest must take some of the blood of the bull and bring it to the Meeting Tent. 6 The priest must dip his finger in the blood and sprinkle some of it seven times before the LORD toward the front of the special curtain of the sanctuary. 7 The priest must put some of the blood on the horns of the altar of fragrant incense that is before the LORD in the Meeting Tent, and all the rest of the bull's blood he must pour out at the base of the altar of burnt offering that is at the entrance of the Meeting Tent.

8 "'Then he must take up all the fat from the sin offering bull: the fat covering the entrails and all the fat surrounding the entrails, 9 the two kidneys with the fat on their sinews, and the protruding lobe on the liver (which he is to remove along with the kidneys) 10 —just as it is taken from the ox of the peace-offering sacrifice—and the priest must offer them up in smoke on the altar of burnt offering. 11 But the hide of the bull, all its flesh along with its head and its legs, its entrails, and its dung—12 all the rest of the bull—he must bring outside the camp to a ceremonially clean place, to the fatty-ash pile, and he must burn it on a wood fire; it must be burned on the fatty-ash pile.

FOR THE WHOLE CONGREGATION

13 "'If the whole congregation of Israel strays unintentionally and the matter is not noticed by the assembly, and they violate one of the LORD's commandments, which must not be violated, so they become guilty, 14 the assembly must present a young bull for a sin offering when the sin they have committed becomes known. They must bring it before the Meeting Tent, 15 the elders of the congregation must lay their hands on the head of the bull before the LORD, and someone must slaughter the bull before the LORD. 16 Then the high priest must bring some of the blood of the bull to the Meeting Tent, 17 and that priest must dip his finger in the blood and sprinkle some of the blood seven times before the LORD toward the front of the curtain. 18 He must put some of the blood on the horns of the altar which is before the LORD in the Meeting Tent, and all the rest of the blood he must pour out at the base of the altar of burnt offering that is at the entrance of the Meeting Tent.

19 "'Then the priest must take all its fat and offer the fat up in smoke on the altar. 20 He must do with the rest of the bull just as he did with the bull of the sin offering; this is what he must do with it. So the priest will make atonement on their behalf and they will be forgiven. 21 He must bring the rest of the bull outside the camp and burn it just as he burned the first bull—it is the sin offering of the assembly.

FOR THE LEADER

22 "'Whenever a leader, by straying unintentionally, sins and violates one of the commandments of the LORD his God which must not be violated, and he pleads guilty, 23 or his sin that he committed is made known to him, he must bring a flawless male goat as his offering. 24 He must lay his hand on the head of the male goat and slaughter it in the place where the burnt offering is slaughtered before the LORD—it is a sin offering. 25 Then the priest must take some of the blood of the sin offering with his finger and put it on the horns of the altar of burnt offering, and he must pour out the rest of its blood at the base of the altar of burnt offering. 26 Then the priest must offer all of its fat up in smoke on the altar like the fat of the peace-offering sacrifice. So the priest will make atonement on his behalf for his sin and he will be forgiven.

FOR THE COMMON PERSON

27 "'If an ordinary individual sins by straying unintentionally when he violates one of the LORD's commandments which must not be violated, and he pleads guilty, 28 or his sin that he committed is made known to him, he must bring a flawless female goat as his offering for the sin that he committed. 29 He must lay his hand on the head of the sin offering and slaughter the sin offering in the place where the burnt offering is slaughtered. 30 Then the priest must take some of its blood with his finger and put it on the horns of the altar of burnt offering, and he must pour out all the rest of its blood at the base of the altar. 31 Then he must remove all of its fat (just as fat was removed from the peace-offering sacrifice) and the priest must offer it up in smoke on the altar for a soothing aroma to the LORD. So the priest will make atonement on his behalf and he will be forgiven.

32 "'But if he brings a sheep as his offering, for a sin offering, he must bring a flawless female. 33 He must lay his hand on the head of the sin offering and slaughter it for a sin offering in the place where the burnt offering is slaughtered. 34 Then the priest must take some of the blood of the sin offering with his finger and put it on the horns of the altar of burnt offering, and he must pour out all the rest of its blood at the base of the altar. 35 Then the one who brought the offering must remove all its fat (just as the fat of the sheep is removed from the peace-offering sacrifice) and the priest must offer them up in smoke on the altar on top of the other gifts for the LORD. So the priest will make atonement on his behalf for his sin which he has committed and he will be forgiven.

ADDITIONAL SIN-OFFERING REGULATIONS

5 "'When a person sins in that he hears a public curse against one who fails to testify and he is a witness (he either saw or knew what had happened) and he does not make it known, then he will bear his punishment for iniquity. 2 Or when there is a person who touches anything ceremonially unclean, whether the carcass of an unclean wild animal, or the carcass of an unclean domesticated animal, or the carcass of an unclean creeping thing, even if he did not realize it, he has become unclean and is guilty; 3 or when he touches human uncleanness with regard to anything by which he can become unclean, even if he did not realize it, but he has later come to know it and is guilty; 4 or when a person swears an oath, speaking thoughtlessly with his lips, whether to do evil or to do good, with regard to anything which the individual might speak thoughtlessly in an oath, even if he did not realize it, but he has later come to know it and is guilty with regard to one of these oaths—5 when an individual becomes guilty with regard to one of these things he must confess how he has sinned, 6 and he must bring his penalty for guilt to the LORD for his sin that he has committed—a female from the flock, whether a female sheep or a female goat, for a sin offering. So the priest will make atonement on his behalf for his sin.

7 "'If he cannot afford an animal from the flock, he must bring his penalty for guilt for his sin that he has committed, two turtledoves or two young pigeons, to the LORD, one for a sin offering

CHALLENGE

How is the sin offering different from the guilt offering? In what way did Christ fulfill the requirements for both the sin and the guilt offering for believers today?

LOVE TO GROW

EQUAL OPPORTUNITY RESTORATION

LEVITICUS 5:1–13

A few years ago, I did a project on the Book of Leviticus for a seminary class. That project turned out to be one of my favorite assignments of all time. As I read, I saw an aspect of God's character I never would have noticed had I not read it so thoroughly.

Leviticus opens with God giving Moses the commands for each type of sacrifice and the rituals that belong with each. There are five main sacrifices: the burnt offering, the grain offering, the peace offering, the sin offering, and the guilt offering. The burnt offering, grain offering, and peace offering were regular sacrifices that the Israelites made to the Lord. They were "voluntary requirements," as my professor would say, and were expected to be made based on what an individual or family could afford.

The only required sacrifice for an individual was the sin offering. In certain circumstances, a person could go their whole life without needing to offer a guilt sacrifice, but no Israelite was free from sin. An individual paid for their sin with the blood of their own animal. They felt both the loss and cost of their sin as they regularly made trips to the temple to offer sacrifices from their own flocks and herds.

Not everyone in Israel had an abundance of flocks and herds. What were they to do? If they couldn't produce a sheep or a goat, would God refuse to forgive their sin? Leviticus 5 shows God's heart for His people. Not only did He provide them with a way to atone for their sin, but He allowed everyone the opportunity to offer what they could afford.

If an Israelite didn't have a sheep or a goat, they could bring a small bird. If they didn't own a bird, they could bring a handful of grain. If they couldn't afford grain, they could catch a pigeon on the street and present it to God.

God provides. He always provides.

God provides for His people, even in the depth of their sin. The sin offering was only required when someone had sinned against God, therefore separating them from Him. Even in this situation, and even if they couldn't afford an animal, God provided a way for His people to restore their relationship with Him.

When we find ourselves far from God, He still provides a way to bring us back to Him. No matter the circumstance, God provides for His people.

and one for a burnt offering. 8 He must bring them to the priest
and present first the one that is for a sin offering. The priest must
pinch its head at the nape of its neck, but must not sever the
head from the body. 9 Then he must sprinkle some of the blood
of the sin offering on the wall of the altar, and the remainder of
the blood must be squeezed out at the base of the altar—it is a
sin offering. 10 The second bird he must make a burnt offering
according to the standard regulation. So the priest will make
atonement on behalf of this person for his sin which he has
committed, and he will be forgiven.

11 "'If he cannot afford two turtledoves or two young pigeons,
he must bring as his offering for his sin which he has committed
a tenth of an ephah of choice wheat flour for a sin offering. He
must not place olive oil on it, and he must not put frankincense
on it, because it is a sin offering. 12 He must bring it to the priest,
and the priest must scoop out from it a handful as its memorial
portion and offer it up in smoke on the altar on top of the other
gifts of the LORD—it is a sin offering. 13 So the priest will make
atonement on his behalf for his sin which he has committed by
doing one of these things, and he will be forgiven. The remainder
of the offering will belong to the priest like the grain offering.'"

GUILT-OFFERING REGULATIONS: KNOWN TRESPASS

14 Then the LORD spoke to Moses: 15 "When a person commits
a trespass and sins by straying unintentionally from the regulations about the LORD's holy things, then he must bring his
penalty for guilt to the LORD, a flawless ram from the flock, convertible into silver shekels according to the standard of the sanctuary shekel, for a guilt offering. 16 And whatever holy thing he
violated he must restore and must add one-fifth to it and give
it to the priest. So the priest will make atonement on his behalf
with the guilt-offering ram and he will be forgiven.

UNKNOWN TRESPASS

17 "If a person sins and violates any of the LORD's commandments
that must not be violated (although he did not know it at the
time, but later realizes he is guilty), then he will bear his punishment for iniquity 18 and must bring a flawless ram from the
flock, convertible into silver shekels, for a guilt offering to the
priest. So the priest will make atonement on his behalf for his
error that he committed (although he himself had not known
it) and he will be forgiven. 19 It is a guilt offering; he was surely
guilty before the LORD."

TRESPASS BY DECEPTION AND FALSE OATH

6 Then the LORD spoke to Moses: 2 "When a person sins and
commits a trespass against the LORD by deceiving his fellow citizen in regard to something held in trust, or a pledge, or
something stolen, or by extorting something from his fellow
citizen, 3 or has found something lost and denies it and swears
falsely concerning any one of the things that someone might
do to sin—4 when it happens that he sins and he is found guilty
then he must return whatever he had stolen, or whatever he had
extorted, or the thing that he had held in trust, or the lost thing

that he had found, 5 or anything about which he swears falsely. He must restore it in full and add one-fifth to it; he must give it to its owner when he is found guilty. 6 Then he must bring his guilt offering to the LORD, a flawless ram from the flock, convertible into silver shekels, for a guilt offering to the priest. 7 So the priest will make atonement on his behalf before the LORD and he will be forgiven for whatever he has done to become guilty."

SACRIFICIAL INSTRUCTIONS FOR THE PRIESTS: THE BURNT OFFERING

8 Then the LORD spoke to Moses: 9 "Command Aaron and his sons, 'This is the law of the burnt offering. The burnt offering is to remain on the hearth on the altar all night until morning, and the fire of the altar must be kept burning on it. 10 Then the priest must put on his linen robe and must put linen leggings over his bare flesh, and he must take up the fatty ashes of the burnt offering that the fire consumed on the altar, and he must place them beside the altar. 11 Then he must take off his clothes and put on other clothes, and he must bring the fatty ashes outside the camp to a ceremonially clean place, 12 but the fire which is on the altar must be kept burning on it. It must not be extinguished. So the priest must kindle wood on it morning by morning, and he must arrange the burnt offering on it and offer the fat of the peace offering up in smoke on it. 13 A continual fire must be kept burning on the altar. It must not be extinguished.

THE GRAIN OFFERING OF THE COMMON PERSON

14 "'This is the law of the grain offering. The sons of Aaron are to present it before the LORD in front of the altar, 15 and the priest must take up with his hand some of the choice wheat flour of the grain offering and some of its olive oil, and all of the frankincense that is on the grain offering, and he must offer its memorial portion up in smoke on the altar as a soothing aroma to the LORD. 16 Aaron and his sons are to eat what is left over from it. It must be eaten unleavened in a holy place; they are to eat it in the courtyard of the Meeting Tent. 17 It must not be baked with yeast. I have given it as their portion from my gifts. It is most holy, like the sin offering and the guilt offering. 18 Every male among the sons of Aaron may eat it. It is a perpetual allotted portion throughout your generations from the gifts of the LORD. Anyone who touches these gifts must be holy.'"

THE GRAIN OFFERING OF THE PRIESTS

19 Then the LORD spoke to Moses: 20 "This is the offering of Aaron and his sons which they must present to the LORD on the day when he is anointed: a tenth of an ephah of choice wheat flour as a continual grain offering, half of it in the morning and half of it in the evening. 21 It must be made with olive oil on a griddle and you must bring it well soaked, so you must present a grain offering of broken pieces as a soothing aroma to the LORD. 22 The high priest who succeeds him from among his sons must do it. It is a perpetual statute; it must be offered up in smoke as a whole offering to the LORD. 23 Every grain offering of a priest must be a whole offering; it must not be eaten."

THE SIN OFFERING

24 Then the LORD spoke to Moses: 25 "Tell Aaron and his sons,
'This is the law of the sin offering. In the place where the burnt
offering is slaughtered the sin offering must be slaughtered before the LORD. It is most holy. 26 The priest who offers it for sin
is to eat it. It must be eaten in a holy place, in the courtyard of
the Meeting Tent. 27 Anyone who touches its meat must be holy,
and whoever spatters some of its blood on a garment must wash
whatever he spatters it on in a holy place. 28 Any clay vessel it is
boiled in must be broken, and if it was boiled in a bronze vessel,
then that vessel must be rubbed out and rinsed in water. 29 Any
male among the priests may eat it. It is most holy. 30 But any sin
offering from which some of its blood is brought into the Meeting Tent to make atonement in the sanctuary must not be eaten.
It must be burned up in the fire.

THE GUILT OFFERING

7 "'This is the law of the guilt offering. It is most holy. 2 In the
place where they slaughter the burnt offering they must
slaughter the guilt offering, and the officiating priest must
splash the blood against the altar's sides. 3 Then the one making the offering must present all its fat: the fatty tail, the fat covering the entrails, 4 the two kidneys and the fat on their sinews,
and the protruding lobe on the liver (which he must remove
along with the kidneys). 5 Then the priest must offer them up
in smoke on the altar as a gift to the LORD. It is a guilt offering.
6 Any male among the priests may eat it. It must be eaten in a
holy place. It is most holy. 7 The law is the same for the sin offering and the guilt offering; it belongs to the priest who makes
atonement with it.

PRIESTLY PORTIONS OF BURNT AND GRAIN OFFERINGS

8 "'As for the priest who presents someone's burnt offering, the
hide of that burnt offering which he presented belongs to him.
9 Every grain offering which is baked in the oven or made in the
pan or on the griddle belongs to the priest who presented it.
10 Every grain offering, whether mixed with olive oil or dry, belongs to all the sons of Aaron, each one alike.

THE PEACE OFFERING

11 "'This is the law of the peace-offering sacrifice which he is to
present to the LORD. 12 If he presents it on account of thanksgiving, along with the thank-offering sacrifice he must present unleavened loaves mixed with olive oil, unleavened wafers smeared
with olive oil, and well-soaked, ring-shaped loaves made of choice
wheat flour mixed with olive oil. 13 He must present this grain offering in addition to ring-shaped loaves of leavened bread which
regularly accompany the sacrifice of his thanksgiving peace offering. 14 He must present one of each kind of grain offering as
a contribution offering to the LORD; it belongs to the priest
who splashes the blood of the peace offering. 15 The meat of his
thanksgiving peace offering must be eaten on the day of his offering; he must not set any of it aside until morning.

16 "'If his offering is a votive or freewill sacrifice, it may be eaten on the day he presents his sacrifice, and also the leftovers from it may be eaten on the next day, 17 but the leftovers from the meat of the sacrifice must be burned up in the fire on the third day. 18 If some of the meat of his peace-offering sacrifice is ever eaten on the third day it will not be accepted; it will not be accounted to the one who presented it since it is spoiled, and the person who eats from it will bear his punishment for iniquity. 19 The meat which touches anything ceremonially unclean must not be eaten; it must be burned up in the fire. As for ceremonially clean meat, everyone who is ceremonially clean may eat the meat. 20 The person who eats meat from the peace-offering sacrifice which belongs to the LORD while that person's uncleanness persists will be cut off from his people. 21 When a person touches anything unclean (whether human uncleanness, or an unclean animal, or an unclean detestable creature) and eats some of the meat of the peace-offering sacrifice which belongs to the LORD, that person will be cut off from his people.'"

SACRIFICIAL INSTRUCTIONS FOR THE COMMON PEOPLE: FAT AND BLOOD

22 Then the LORD spoke to Moses: 23 "Tell the Israelites, 'You must not eat any fat of an ox, sheep, or goat. 24 Moreover, the fat of an animal that has died of natural causes and the fat of an animal torn by beasts may be used for any other purpose, but you must certainly never eat it. 25 If anyone eats fat from the animal from which he presents a gift to the LORD, that person will be cut off from his people. 26 And you must not eat any blood of the birds or of the domesticated land animals in any of the places where you live. 27 Any person who eats any blood—that person will be cut off from his people.'"

PRIESTLY PORTIONS OF PEACE OFFERINGS

28 Then the LORD spoke to Moses: 29 "Tell the Israelites, 'The one who presents his peace-offering sacrifice to the LORD must bring part of his offering to the LORD as his sacrifice. 30 With his own hands he must bring the LORD's gifts. He must bring the fat with the breast to wave the breast as a wave offering before the LORD, 31 and the priest must offer the fat up in smoke on the altar, but the breast will belong to Aaron and his sons. 32 The right thigh you must give as a contribution offering to the priest from your peace-offering sacrifice. 33 The one from Aaron's sons who presents the blood of the peace offering and fat will have the right thigh as his share, 34 for the breast of the wave offering and the thigh of the contribution offering I have taken from the Israelites out of their peace-offering sacrifices and have given them to Aaron the priest and to his sons from the people of Israel as a perpetual allotted portion.'"

35 This is the allotment of Aaron and the allotment of his sons from the LORD's gifts on the day Moses presented them to serve as priests to the LORD. 36 This is what the LORD commanded to give to them from the Israelites on the day Moses anointed them—a perpetual allotted portion throughout their generations.

SUMMARY OF SACRIFICIAL REGULATIONS IN LEVITICUS 6:8–7:36

37 This is the law for the burnt offering, the grain offering, the
sin offering, the guilt offering, the ordination offering, and the
peace-offering sacrifice, 38 which the LORD commanded Moses
on Mount Sinai on the day he commanded the Israelites to present their offerings to the LORD in the desert of Sinai.

ORDINATION OF THE PRIESTS

8 Then the LORD spoke to Moses: 2 "Take Aaron and his sons
with him, and the garments, the anointing oil, the sin offering bull, the two rams, and the basket of unleavened bread, 3 and
assemble the whole congregation at the entrance of the Meeting
Tent." 4 So Moses did just as the LORD commanded him, and the
congregation assembled at the entrance of the Meeting Tent.
5 Then Moses said to the congregation: "This is what the LORD
has commanded to be done."

CLOTHING AARON

6 So Moses brought Aaron and his sons forward and washed
them with water. 7 Then he put the tunic on Aaron, wrapped
the sash around him, and clothed him with the robe. Next
he put the ephod on him and placed on him the decorated
band of the ephod, and fastened the ephod closely to him
with the band. 8 He then set the breastpiece on him and put
the Urim and Thummim into the breastpiece. 9 Finally, he
set the turban on his head and attached the gold plate, the
holy diadem, to the front of the turban just as the LORD had
commanded Moses.

ANOINTING THE TABERNACLE AND AARON, AND CLOTHING AARON'S SONS

10 Then Moses took the anointing oil and anointed the tabernacle and everything in it, and so consecrated them. 11 Next he
sprinkled some of it on the altar seven times and so anointed
the altar, all its vessels, and the washbasin and its stand to consecrate them. 12 He then poured some of the anointing oil on
the head of Aaron and anointed him to consecrate him. 13 Moses also brought forward Aaron's sons, clothed them with tunics,
wrapped sashes around them, and wrapped headbands on them
just as the LORD had commanded Moses.

CONSECRATION OFFERINGS

14 Then he brought near the sin offering bull and Aaron and his
sons laid their hands on the head of the sin offering bull, 15 and he
slaughtered it. Moses then took the blood and put it all around
on the horns of the altar with his finger and purified the altar,
and he poured out the rest of the blood at the base of the altar and so consecrated it to make atonement on it. 16 Then he
took all the fat on the entrails, the protruding lobe of the liver,
and the two kidneys and their fat, and Moses offered it all up in
smoke on the altar, 17 but the rest of the bull—its hide, its flesh,
and its dung—he completely burned up outside the camp just
as the LORD had commanded Moses.

18 Then he presented the burnt offering ram and Aaron and his sons laid their hands on the head of the ram, 19 and he slaughtered it. Moses then splashed the blood against the altar's sides. 20 Then he cut the ram into parts, and Moses offered the head, the parts, and the suet up in smoke, 21 but the entrails and the legs he washed with water, and Moses offered the whole ram up in smoke on the altar—it was a burnt offering for a soothing aroma, a gift to the LORD, just as the LORD had commanded Moses.

22 Then he presented the second ram, the ram of ordination, and Aaron and his sons laid their hands on the head of the ram 23 and he slaughtered it. Moses then took some of its blood and put it on Aaron's right earlobe, on the thumb of his right hand, and on the big toe of his right foot. 24 Next he brought Aaron's sons forward, and Moses put some of the blood on their right earlobes, on their right thumbs, and on the big toes of their right feet, and Moses splashed the rest of the blood against the altar's sides.

25 Then he took the fat (the fatty tail, all the fat on the entrails, the protruding lobe of the liver, and the two kidneys and their fat) and the right thigh, 26 and from the basket of unleavened bread that was before the LORD he took one unleavened loaf, one loaf of bread mixed with olive oil, and one wafer, and placed them on the fat parts and on the right thigh. 27 He then put all of them on the palms of Aaron and his sons, who waved them as a wave offering before the LORD. 28 Moses then took them from their palms and offered them up in smoke on the altar on top of the burnt offering—they were an ordination offering for a soothing aroma; it was a gift to the LORD. 29 Finally, Moses took the breast and waved it as a wave offering before the LORD from the ram of ordination. It was Moses' share just as the LORD had commanded Moses.

ANOINTING AARON, HIS SONS, AND THEIR GARMENTS

30 Then Moses took some of the anointing oil and some of the blood which was on the altar and sprinkled it on Aaron and his garments, and on his sons and his sons' garments. So he consecrated Aaron, his garments, and his sons and his sons' garments. 31 Then Moses said to Aaron and his sons, "Boil the meat at the entrance of the Meeting Tent, and there you are to eat it and the bread which is in the ordination offering basket, just as I have commanded, saying, 'Aaron and his sons are to eat it,' 32 but the remainder of the meat and the bread you must burn with fire. 33 And you must not go out from the entrance of the Meeting Tent for seven days, until the day when your days of ordination are completed, because you must be ordained over a seven-day period. 34 What has been done on this day the LORD has commanded to be done to make atonement for you. 35 You must reside at the entrance of the Meeting Tent day and night for seven days and keep the charge of the LORD so that you will not die, for this is what I have been commanded." 36 So Aaron and his sons did all the things the LORD had commanded through Moses.

INAUGURATION OF TABERNACLE WORSHIP

9 On the eighth day Moses summoned Aaron and his sons and
the elders of Israel, 2 and said to Aaron, "Take for yourself a
bull calf for a sin offering and a ram for a burnt offering, both
flawless, and present them before the LORD. 3 Then tell the Israelites: 'Take a male goat for a sin offering and a calf and a lamb,
both a year old and flawless, for a burnt offering, 4 and an ox
and a ram for peace offerings to sacrifice before the LORD, and
a grain offering mixed with olive oil, for today the LORD is going
to appear to you.'" 5 So they took what Moses had commanded
to the front of the Meeting Tent and the whole congregation
presented them and stood before the LORD. 6 Then Moses said,
"This is what the LORD has commanded you to do so that the
glory of the LORD may appear to you." 7 Moses then said to Aaron,
"Approach the altar and make your sin offering and your burnt
offering, and make atonement on behalf of yourself and on behalf of the people; and also make the people's offering and make
atonement on behalf of them just as the LORD has commanded."

THE SIN OFFERING FOR THE PRIESTS

8 So Aaron approached the altar and slaughtered the sin offering calf which was for himself. 9 Then Aaron's sons presented the
blood to him and he dipped his finger in the blood and put it on
the horns of the altar, and the rest of the blood he poured out at
the base of the altar. 10 The fat and the kidneys and the protruding lobe of the liver from the sin offering he offered up in smoke
on the altar just as the LORD had commanded Moses, 11 but the
flesh and the hide he completely burned up outside the camp.

THE BURNT OFFERING FOR THE PRIESTS

12 He then slaughtered the burnt offering, and his sons handed
the blood to him and he splashed it against the altar's sides. 13 The
burnt offering itself they handed to him by its parts, including
the head, and he offered them up in smoke on the altar, 14 and he
washed the entrails and the legs and offered them up in smoke
on top of the burnt offering on the altar.

THE OFFERINGS FOR THE PEOPLE

15 Then he presented the people's offering. He took the sin offering male goat which was for the people, slaughtered it, and
performed a purification rite with it like the first one. 16 He then
presented the burnt offering, and did it according to the standard regulation. 17 Next he presented the grain offering, filled
his hand with some of it, and offered it up in smoke on the altar in addition to the morning burnt offering. 18 Then he slaughtered the ox and the ram—the peace-offering sacrifices which
were for the people—and Aaron's sons handed the blood to him
and he splashed it against the altar's sides. 19 As for the fat parts
from the ox and from the ram (the fatty tail, the fat covering
the entrails, the kidneys, and the protruding lobe of the liver),
20 they set those on the breasts and he offered the fat parts up
in smoke on the altar. 21 Finally Aaron waved the breasts and
the right thigh as a wave offering before the LORD just as Moses had commanded.

22 Then Aaron lifted up his hands toward the people and blessed them and descended from making the sin offering, the burnt offering, and the peace offering. 23 Moses and Aaron then entered into the Meeting Tent. When they came out, they blessed the people, and the glory of the LORD appeared to all the people. 24 Then fire went out from the presence of the LORD and consumed the burnt offering and the fat parts on the altar, and all the people saw it, so they shouted loudly and fell down with their faces to the ground.

REFLECT

What did Nadab and Abihu do that angered God? Why was God justified in His response?

NADAB AND ABIHU

10 Then Aaron's sons, Nadab and Abihu, each took his fire pan and put fire in it, set incense on it, and presented strange fire before the LORD, which he had not commanded them to do. 2 So fire went out from the presence of the LORD and consumed them so that they died before the LORD. 3 Moses then said to Aaron, "This is what the LORD spoke: 'Among the ones close to me I will show myself holy, and in the presence of all the people I will be honored.'" So Aaron kept silent. 4 Moses then called to Mishael and Elzaphan, the sons of Uzziel, Aaron's uncle, and said to them, "Come near, carry your brothers from the front of the sanctuary to a place outside the camp." 5 So they came near and carried them away in their tunics to a place outside the camp just as Moses had spoken. 6 Then Moses said to Aaron and to Eleazar and Ithamar his other two sons, "Do not dishevel the hair of your heads and do not tear your garments, so that you do not die and so that wrath does not come on the whole congregation. Your brothers, all the house of Israel, are to mourn the burning that the LORD has caused, 7 but you must not go out from the entrance of the Meeting Tent lest you die, for the LORD's anointing oil is on you." So they acted according to the word of Moses.

PERPETUAL STATUTES THE LORD SPOKE TO AARON

8 Then the LORD spoke to Aaron, 9 "Do not drink wine or strong drink, you and your sons with you, when you enter into the Meeting Tent, so that you do not die. This is a perpetual statute throughout your generations, 10 as well as to distinguish between the holy and the common, and between the unclean and the clean, 11 and to teach the Israelites all the statutes that the LORD has spoken to them through Moses."

PERPETUAL STATUTES MOSES SPOKE TO AARON

12 Then Moses spoke to Aaron and to Eleazar and Ithamar, his remaining sons, "Take the grain offering which remains from the gifts of the LORD and eat it unleavened beside the altar, for it is most holy. 13 You must eat it in a holy place because it is your allotted portion and the allotted portion of your sons from the gifts of the LORD, for this is what I have been commanded. 14 Also, the breast of the wave offering and the thigh of the contribution offering you must eat in a ceremonially clean place, you and your sons and daughters with you, for the foods have been given as your allotted portion and the allotted portion of your sons from the peace-offering sacrifices of the Israelites. 15 The thigh of the contribution offering and the breast of the wave offering they must

bring in addition to the gifts of the fat parts to wave them as a wave offering before the LORD, and it will belong to you and your sons with you for a perpetual statute just as the LORD has commanded."

THE PROBLEM WITH THE INAUGURAL SIN OFFERING

16 Later Moses sought diligently for the sin offering male goat, but it had actually been burnt. So he became angry at Eleazar and Ithamar, Aaron's remaining sons, saying, 17 "Why did you not eat the sin offering in the sanctuary? For it is most holy and he gave it to you to bear the iniquity of the congregation, to make atonement on their behalf before the LORD. 18 See here! Its blood was not brought into the Holy Place within! You should certainly have eaten it in the sanctuary just as I commanded!" 19 But Aaron spoke to Moses, "See here! Just today they presented their sin offering and their burnt offering before the LORD and such things as these have happened to me! If I had eaten a sin offering today would the LORD have been pleased?" 20 When Moses heard this explanation, he was satisfied.

CLEAN AND UNCLEAN LAND CREATURES

11 The LORD spoke to Moses and Aaron, saying to them, 2 "Tell the Israelites: 'This is the kind of creature you may eat from among all the animals that are on the land. 3 You may eat any among the animals that has a divided hoof (the hooves are completely split in two) and that also chews the cud. 4 However, you must not eat these from among those that chew the cud and have divided hooves: The camel is unclean to you because it chews the cud even though its hoof is not divided. 5 The rock badger is unclean to you because it chews the cud even though its hoof is not divided. 6 The hare is unclean to you because it chews the cud even though its hoof is not divided. 7 The pig is unclean to you because its hoof is divided (the hoof is completely split in two) , even though it does not chew the cud. 8 You must not eat from their meat and you must not touch their carcasses; they are unclean to you.

CLEAN AND UNCLEAN WATER CREATURES

9 "'These you can eat from all creatures that are in the water: Any creatures in the water that have both fins and scales, whether in the seas or in the streams, you may eat. 10 But any creatures that do not have both fins and scales, whether in the seas or in the streams, from all the swarming things of the water and from all the living creatures that are in the water, are detestable to you. 11 Since they are detestable to you, you must not eat their meat and their carcass you must detest. 12 Any creature in the water that does not have both fins and scales is detestable to you.

CLEAN AND UNCLEAN BIRDS

13 "'These you are to detest from among the birds—they must not be eaten, because they are detestable: the griffon vulture, the bearded vulture, the black vulture, 14 the kite, the buzzard of any kind, 15 every kind of crow, 16 the eagle owl, the short-eared owl, the long-eared owl, the hawk of any kind, 17 the little owl, the cormorant, the screech owl, 18 the white owl, the scops owl, the osprey, 19 the stork, the heron of any kind, the hoopoe, and the bat.

CLEAN AND UNCLEAN INSECTS

20 "'Every winged swarming thing that walks on all fours is detestable to you. 21 However, this you may eat from all the winged
swarming things that walk on all fours, which have jointed legs to
hop with on the land. 22 These you may eat from them: the locust
of any kind, the bald locust of any kind, the cricket of any kind,
the grasshopper of any kind. 23 But any other winged swarming
thing that has four legs is detestable to you.

CARCASS UNCLEANNESS

24 "'By these you defile yourselves—anyone who touches their
carcass will be unclean until the evening, 25 and anyone who
carries their carcass must wash his clothes and will be unclean
until the evening.

INEDIBLE LAND QUADRUPEDS

26 "'All animals that divide the hoof, but it is not completely split
in two, and do not chew the cud are unclean to you; anyone
who touches them becomes unclean. 27 All that walk on their
paws among all the creatures that walk on all fours are unclean
to you. Anyone who touches their carcass will be unclean until the evening, 28 and the one who carries their carcass must
wash his clothes and be unclean until the evening; they are unclean to you.

CREATURES THAT SWARM ON THE LAND

29 "'Now this is what is unclean to you among the swarming things
that swarm on the land: the rat, the mouse, the large lizard of
any kind, 30 the Mediterranean gecko, the spotted lizard, the
wall gecko, the skink, and the chameleon. 31 These are the ones
that are unclean to you among all the swarming things. Anyone
who touches these creatures when they die will be unclean until evening. 32 Also, anything they fall on when they die will become unclean—any wood vessel or garment or article of leather
or sackcloth. Any such vessel with which work is done must be
immersed in water and will be unclean until the evening. Then
it will become clean. 33 As for any clay vessel they fall into, everything in it will become unclean and you must break it. 34 Any food
that may be eaten which becomes soaked with water will become
unclean. Anything drinkable in any such vessel will become unclean. 35 Anything their carcass may fall on will become unclean.
An oven or small stove must be smashed to pieces; they are unclean, and they will stay unclean to you. 36 However, a spring or a
cistern which collects water will be clean, but one who touches
the creature's carcass will be unclean. 37 Now, if such a carcass falls
on any sowing seed which is to be sown, it is clean, 38 but if water is
put on the seed and such a carcass falls on it, it is unclean to you.

EDIBLE LAND ANIMALS

39 "'Now if an animal that you may eat dies, whoever touches its
carcass will be unclean until the evening. 40 One who eats from its
carcass must wash his clothes and be unclean until the evening,
and whoever carries its carcass must wash his clothes and be unclean until the evening. 41 Every swarming thing that swarms on

the land is detestable; it must not be eaten. 42 You must not eat
anything that crawls on its belly or anything that walks on all fours
or on any number of legs of all the swarming things that swarm on
the land, because they are detestable. 43 Do not make yourselves
detestable by any of the swarming things. You must not defile
yourselves by them and become unclean by them, 44 for I am the
LORD your God and you are to sanctify yourselves and be holy
because I am holy. You must not defile yourselves by any of the
swarming things that creep on the ground, 45 for I am the LORD
who brought you up from the land of Egypt to be your God, and
you are to be holy because I am holy. 46 This is the law of the land
animals, the birds, all the living creatures that move in the water,
and all the creatures that swarm on the land, 47 to distinguish between the unclean and the clean, between the living creatures that
may be eaten and the living creatures that must not be eaten.'"

PURIFICATION OF A WOMAN AFTER CHILDBIRTH

12 The LORD spoke to Moses: 2 "Tell the Israelites, 'When a
woman produces offspring and bears a male child, she will
be unclean seven days, as she is unclean during the days of her
menstruation. 3 On the eighth day the flesh of his foreskin must
be circumcised. 4 Then she will remain thirty-three days in blood
purity. She must not touch anything holy and she must not enter the sanctuary until the days of her purification are fulfilled.
5 If she bears a female child, she will be impure fourteen days as
during her menstrual flow, and she will remain sixty-six days
in blood purity.

6 "'When the days of her purification are completed for a son
or for a daughter, she must bring a one-year-old lamb for a burnt
offering and a young pigeon or turtledove for a sin offering to
the entrance of the Meeting Tent, to the priest. 7 The priest is to
present it before the LORD and make atonement on her behalf,
and she will be clean from her flow of blood. This is the law of
the one who bears a child, for the male or the female child. 8 If
she cannot afford a sheep, then she must take two turtledoves
or two young pigeons, one for a burnt offering and one for a sin
offering, and the priest is to make atonement on her behalf, and
she will be clean.'"

INFECTIONS ON THE SKIN

13 The LORD spoke to Moses and Aaron: 2 "When someone
has a swelling or a scab or a bright spot on the skin of his
body that may become a diseased infection, he must be brought
to Aaron the priest or one of his sons, the priests. 3 The priest
must then examine the infection on the skin of the body, and
if the hair in the infection has turned white and the infection
appears to be deeper than the skin of the body, then it is a diseased infection, so when the priest examines it he must pronounce the person unclean.

A BRIGHT SPOT ON THE SKIN

4 "If it is a white bright spot on the skin of his body, but it does
not appear to be deeper than the skin, and the hair has not
turned white, then the priest is to quarantine the person with

the infection for seven days. 5 The priest must then examine it
on the seventh day, and if, as far as he can see, the infection has
stayed the same and has not spread on the skin, then the priest
is to quarantine the person for another seven days. 6 The priest
must then examine it again on the seventh day, and if the infection has faded and has not spread on the skin, then the priest
is to pronounce the person clean. It is a scab, so he must wash
his clothes and be clean. 7 If, however, the scab is spreading further on the skin after he has shown himself to the priest for
his purification, then he must show himself to the priest a second time. 8 The priest must then examine it, and if the scab has
spread on the skin, then the priest is to pronounce the person
unclean. It is a disease.

A SWELLING ON THE SKIN

9 "When someone has a diseased infection, he must be brought to
the priest. 10 The priest will then examine it, and if a white swelling is on the skin, it has turned the hair white, and there is raw
flesh in the swelling, 11 it is a chronic disease on the skin of his
body, so the priest is to pronounce him unclean. The priest must
not merely quarantine him, for he is unclean. 12 If, however, the
disease breaks out on the skin so that the disease covers all the
skin of the person with the infection from his head to his feet,
as far as the priest can see, 13 the priest must then examine it,
and if the disease covers his whole body, he is to pronounce the
person with the infection clean. He has turned all white, so he is
clean. 14 But whenever raw flesh appears in it he will be unclean,
15 so the priest is to examine the raw flesh and pronounce him
unclean—it is diseased. 16 If, however, the raw flesh once again
turns white, then he must come to the priest. 17 The priest will
then examine it, and if the infection has turned white, the priest
is to pronounce the person with the infection clean—he is clean.

A BOIL ON THE SKIN

18 "When someone's body has a boil on its skin and it heals, 19 and
in the place of the boil there is a white swelling or a reddish
white bright spot, he must show himself to the priest. 20 The
priest will then examine it, and if it appears to be deeper than
the skin and its hair has turned white, then the priest is to pronounce the person unclean. It is a diseased infection that has
broken out in the boil. 21 If, however, the priest examines it, and
there is no white hair in it, it is not deeper than the skin, and it
has faded, then the priest is to quarantine him for seven days.
22 If it is spreading farther on the skin, then the priest is to pronounce him unclean. It is an infection. 23 But if the bright spot
stays in its place and has not spread, it is the scar of the boil, so
the priest is to pronounce him clean.

A BURN ON THE SKIN

24 "When a body has a burn on its skin and the raw area of the
burn becomes a reddish white or white bright spot, 25 the priest
must examine it, and if the hair has turned white in the bright
spot and it appears to be deeper than the skin, it is a disease
that has broken out in the burn. The priest is to pronounce the

person unclean. It is a diseased infection. 26 If, however, the priest
examines it and there is no white hair in the bright spot, it is
not deeper than the skin, and it has faded, then the priest is to
quarantine him for seven days. 27 The priest must then examine it on the seventh day, and if it is spreading further on the
skin, then the priest is to pronounce him unclean. It is a diseased infection. 28 But if the bright spot stays in its place, has
not spread on the skin, and it has faded, then it is the swelling
of the burn, so the priest is to pronounce him clean, because it
is the scar of the burn.

SCALL ON THE HEAD OR IN THE BEARD

29 "When a man or a woman has an infection on the head or in
the beard, 30 the priest is to examine the infection, and if it appears to be deeper than the skin and the hair in it is reddish
yellow and thin, then the priest is to pronounce the person unclean. It is scall, a disease of the head or the beard. 31 But if the
priest examines the scall infection and it does not appear to be
deeper than the skin, and there is no black hair in it, then the
priest is to quarantine the person with the scall infection for
seven days. 32 The priest must then examine the infection on
the seventh day, and if the scall has not spread, there is no reddish yellow hair in it, and the scall does not appear to be deeper
than the skin, 33 then the individual is to shave himself, but he
must not shave the area affected by the scall, and the priest is
to quarantine the person with the scall for another seven days.
34 The priest must then examine the scall on the seventh day,
and if the scall has not spread on the skin and it does not appear to be deeper than the skin, then the priest is to pronounce
him clean. So he is to wash his clothes and be clean. 35 If, however, the scall spreads further on the skin after his purification,
36 then the priest is to examine it, and if the scall has spread on
the skin the priest is not to search further for reddish yellow
hair. The person is unclean. 37 If, as far as the priest can see, the
scall has stayed the same and black hair has sprouted in it, the
scall has been healed; the person is clean. So the priest is to pronounce him clean.

BRIGHT WHITE SPOTS ON THE SKIN

38 "When a man or a woman has bright spots—white bright
spots—on the skin of their body, 39 the priest is to examine them,
and if the bright spots on the skin of their body are faded white, it is
a harmless rash that has broken out on the skin. The person is clean.

BALDNESS ON THE HEAD

40 "When a man's head is bare so that he is balding in back, he is
clean. 41 If his head is bare on the forehead so that he is balding
in front, he is clean. 42 But if there is a reddish white infection
in the back or front bald area, it is a disease breaking out in his
back or front bald area. 43 The priest is to examine it, and if the
swelling of the infection is reddish white in the back or the front
bald area like the appearance of a disease on the skin of the body,
44 he is a diseased man. He is unclean. The priest must surely
pronounce him unclean because of his infection on his head.

THE LIFE OF THE PERSON WITH SKIN DISEASE

45 "As for the diseased person who has the infection, his clothes must be torn, the hair of his head must be unbound, he must cover his mustache, and he must call out 'Unclean! Unclean!' 46 The whole time he has the infection he will be continually unclean. He must live in isolation, and his place of residence must be outside the camp.

INFECTIONS IN GARMENTS, CLOTH, OR LEATHER

47 "When a garment has a diseased infection in it, whether a wool or linen garment, 48 or in the warp or woof of the linen or the wool, or in leather or anything made of leather, 49 if the infection in the garment or leather or warp or woof or any article of leather is yellowish green or reddish, it is a diseased infection and it must be shown to the priest. 50 The priest is to examine and then quarantine the article with the infection for seven days. 51 He must then examine the infection on the seventh day. If the infection has spread in the garment, or in the warp, or in the woof, or in the leather—whatever the article into which the leather was made—the infection is a malignant disease. It is unclean. 52 He must burn the garment or the warp or the woof, whether wool or linen, or any article of leather which has the infection in it. Because it is a malignant disease it must be burned up in the fire. 53 But if the priest examines it and the infection has not spread in the garment or in the warp or in the woof or in any article of leather, 54 the priest is to command that they wash whatever has the infection and quarantine it for another seven days. 55 The priest must then examine it after the infection has been washed out, and if the infection has not changed its appearance even though the infection has not spread, it is unclean. You must burn it up in the fire. It is a fungus, whether on the back side or front side of the article. 56 But if the priest has examined it and the infection has faded after it has been washed, he is to tear it out of the garment or the leather or the warp or the woof. 57 Then if it still appears again in the garment or the warp or the woof, or in any article of leather, it is an outbreak. Whatever has the infection in it you must burn up in the fire. 58 But the garment or the warp or the woof or any article of leather which you wash and infection disappears from it is to be washed a second time and it will be clean."

SUMMARY OF INFECTION REGULATIONS

59 This is the law of the diseased infection in the garment of wool or linen, or the warp or woof, or any article of leather, for pronouncing it clean or unclean.

PURIFICATION OF DISEASED SKIN INFECTIONS

14 The LORD spoke to Moses: 2 "This is the law of the diseased person on the day of his purification, when he is brought to the priest. 3 The priest is to go outside the camp and examine the infection. If the infection of the diseased person has been healed, 4 then the priest will command that two live clean birds, a piece of cedar wood, a scrap of crimson fabric, and some twigs of hyssop be taken up for the one being cleansed. 5 The priest will

then command that one bird be slaughtered into a clay vessel
over fresh water. 6 Then he is to take the live bird along with the
piece of cedar wood, the scrap of crimson fabric, and the twigs
of hyssop, and he is to dip them and the live bird in the blood of
the bird slaughtered over the fresh water, 7 and sprinkle it seven
times on the one being cleansed from the disease, pronounce
him clean, and send the live bird away over the open countryside.

THE SEVEN DAYS OF PURIFICATION

8 "The one being cleansed must then wash his clothes, shave
off all his hair, and bathe in water, and so be clean. Then afterward he may enter the camp, but he must live outside his tent
seven days. 9 When the seventh day comes he must shave all
his hair—his head, his beard, his eyebrows, all his hair—and he
must wash his clothes, bathe his body in water, and so be clean.

THE EIGHTH-DAY ATONEMENT RITUALS

10 "On the eighth day he must take two flawless male lambs, one
flawless yearling female lamb, three-tenths of an ephah of choice
wheat flour as a grain offering mixed with olive oil, and one log
of olive oil, 11 and the priest who pronounces him clean will have
the man who is being cleansed stand along with these offerings
before the LORD at the entrance of the Meeting Tent.

12 "The priest is to take one male lamb and present it for a guilt
offering along with the log of olive oil and present them as a
wave offering before the LORD. 13 He must then slaughter the
male lamb in the place where the sin offering and the burnt offering are slaughtered, in the sanctuary, because, like the sin
offering, the guilt offering belongs to the priest; it is most holy.
14 Then the priest is to take some of the blood of the guilt offering and put it on the right earlobe of the one being cleansed, on
the thumb of his right hand, and on the big toe of his right foot.
15 The priest will then take some of the log of olive oil and pour
it into his own left hand. 16 Then the priest is to dip his right
forefinger into the olive oil that is in his left hand, and sprinkle some of the olive oil with his finger seven times before the
LORD. 17 The priest will then put some of the rest of the olive oil
that is in his hand on the right earlobe of the one being cleansed,
on the thumb of his right hand, and on the big toe of his right
foot, on the blood of the guilt offering, 18 and the remainder of
the olive oil that is in his hand the priest is to put on the head
of the one being cleansed. So the priest is to make atonement
for him before the LORD.

19 "The priest must then perform the sin offering and make
atonement for the one being cleansed from his impurity. After
that he is to slaughter the burnt offering, 20 and the priest is to
offer the burnt offering and the grain offering on the altar. So
the priest is to make atonement for him and he will be clean.

THE EIGHTH-DAY ATONEMENT RITUALS FOR THE POOR PERSON

21 "If the person is poor and does not have sufficient means, he
must take one male lamb as a guilt offering for a wave offering to make atonement for himself, one-tenth of an ephah of

choice wheat flour mixed with olive oil for a grain offering, a log of olive oil, 22 and two turtledoves or two young pigeons, which are within his means. One will be a sin offering and the other a burnt offering.

23 "On the eighth day he must bring them for his purification to the priest at the entrance of the Meeting Tent before the LORD, 24 and the priest is to take the male lamb of the guilt offering and the log of olive oil and wave them as a wave offering before the LORD. 25 Then he is to slaughter the male lamb of the guilt offering, and the priest is to take some of the blood of the guilt offering and put it on the right earlobe of the one being cleansed, on the thumb of his right hand, and on the big toe of his right foot. 26 The priest will then pour some of the olive oil into his own left hand, 27 and sprinkle some of the olive oil that is in his left hand with his right forefinger seven times before the LORD. 28 Then the priest is to put some of the olive oil that is in his hand on the right earlobe of the one being cleansed, on the thumb of his right hand, and on the big toe of his right foot, on the place of the blood of the guilt offering, 29 and the remainder of the olive oil that is in the hand of the priest he is to put on the head of the one being cleansed to make atonement for him before the LORD.

30 "He will then make one of the turtledoves or young pigeons, which are within his means, 31 a sin offering and the other a burnt offering along with the grain offering. So the priest is to make atonement for the one being cleansed before the LORD. 32 This is the law of the one in whom there is a diseased infection, who does not have sufficient means for his purification."

PURIFICATION OF DISEASE-INFECTED HOUSES

33 The Lord spoke to Moses and Aaron: 34 "When you enter the land of Canaan which I am about to give to you for a possession, and I put a diseased infection in a house in the land you are to possess, 35 then whoever owns the house must come and declare to the priest, 'Something like an infection is visible to me in the house.' 36 Then the priest will command that the house be cleared before the priest enters to examine the infection so that everything in the house does not become unclean, and afterward the priest will enter to examine the house. 37 He is to examine the infection, and if the infection in the walls of the house consists of yellowish green or reddish eruptions, and it appears to be deeper than the surface of the wall, 38 then the priest is to go out of the house to the doorway of the house and quarantine the house for seven days. 39 The priest must return on the seventh day and examine it, and if the infection has spread in the walls of the house, 40 then the priest is to command that the stones that had the infection in them be pulled and thrown outside the city into an unclean place. 41 Then they shall scrape the house all around on the inside, and the plaster which they have scraped off must be dumped outside the city into an unclean place. 42 They are then to take other stones and replace those stones, and he is to take other plaster and replaster the house.

43 "If the infection returns and breaks out in the house after he has pulled out the stones, scraped the house, and it is

replastered, 44 the priest is to come and examine it, and if the
infection has spread in the house, it is a malignant disease in the
house. It is unclean. 45 He must tear down the house, its stones,
its wood, and all the plaster of the house, and bring all of it outside the city to an unclean place. 46 Anyone who enters the house
all the days the priest has quarantined it will be unclean until
evening. 47 Anyone who lies down in the house must wash his
clothes. Anyone who eats in the house must wash his clothes.
48 "If, however, the priest enters and examines it, and the infection has not spread in the house after the house has been
replastered, then the priest is to pronounce the house clean
because the infection has been healed. 49 Then he is to take two
birds, a piece of cedar wood, a scrap of crimson fabric, and some
twigs of hyssop to purify the house, 50 and he is to slaughter one
bird into a clay vessel over fresh water. 51 He must then take the
piece of cedar wood, the twigs of hyssop, the scrap of crimson
fabric, and the live bird, and dip them in the blood of the slaughtered bird and in the fresh water, and sprinkle the house seven
times. 52 So he is to purify the house with the blood of the bird,
the fresh water, the live bird, the piece of cedar wood, the twigs
of hyssop, and the scrap of crimson fabric, 53 and he is to send
the live bird away outside the city into the open countryside.
So he is to make atonement for the house and it will be clean.

SUMMARY OF PURIFICATION REGULATIONS FOR INFECTIONS

54 "This is the law for all diseased infections, for scall, 55 for the
diseased garment, for the house, 56 for the swelling, for the scab,
and for the bright spot, 57 to teach when something is unclean
and when it is clean. This is the law for dealing with infectious
disease."

MALE BODILY DISCHARGES

15 The LORD spoke to Moses and Aaron: 2 "Speak to the Israelites and tell them, 'When any man has a discharge from
his body, his discharge is unclean. 3 Now this is his uncleanness
in regard to his discharge—whether his body secretes his discharge or blocks his discharge, he is unclean. All the days that
his body has a discharge or his body blocks his discharge, this
is his uncleanness.
4 "'Any bed the man with a discharge lies on will be unclean, and
any furniture he sits on will be unclean. 5 Anyone who touches
his bed must wash his clothes, bathe in water, and be unclean
until evening. 6 The one who sits on the furniture the man with
a discharge sits on must wash his clothes, bathe in water, and
be unclean until evening. 7 The one who touches the body of
the man with a discharge must wash his clothes, bathe in water, and be unclean until evening. 8 If the man with a discharge
spits on a person who is ceremonially clean, that person must
wash his clothes, bathe in water, and be unclean until evening.
9 Any means of riding that the man with a discharge rides on
will be unclean. 10 Anyone who touches anything that was under him will be unclean until evening, and the one who carries those items must wash his clothes, bathe in water, and be

unclean until evening. 11 Anyone whom the man with the discharge touches without having rinsed his hands in water must wash his clothes, bathe in water, and be unclean until evening. 12 A clay vessel which the man with the discharge touches must be broken, and any wooden utensil must be rinsed in water.

PURITY REGULATIONS FOR MALE BODILY DISCHARGES

13 "'When the man with the discharge becomes clean from his discharge he is to count off for himself seven days for his purification, and he must wash his clothes, bathe in fresh water, and be clean. 14 Then on the eighth day he is to take for himself two turtledoves or two young pigeons, and he is to present himself before the LORD at the entrance of the Meeting Tent and give them to the priest, 15 and the priest is to make one of them a sin offering and the other a burnt offering. So the priest is to make atonement for him before the LORD for his discharge.

16 "'When a man has a seminal emission, he must bathe his whole body in water and be unclean until evening, 17 and he must wash in water any clothing or leather that has semen on it, and it will be unclean until evening. 18 As for a woman whom a man goes to bed with, then has a seminal emission, they must bathe in water and be unclean until evening.

FEMALE BODILY DISCHARGES

19 "'When a woman has a discharge and her discharge is blood from her body, she is to be in her menstruation seven days, and anyone who touches her will be unclean until evening. 20 Anything she lies on during her menstruation will be unclean, and anything she sits on will be unclean. 21 Anyone who touches her bed must wash his clothes, bathe in water, and be unclean until evening. 22 Anyone who touches any furniture she sits on must wash his clothes, bathe in water, and be unclean until evening. 23 If there is something on the bed or on the furniture she sits on, when he touches it he will be unclean until evening, 24 and if a man actually goes to bed with her so that her menstrual impurity touches him, then he will be unclean seven days and any bed he lies on will be unclean.

25 "'When a woman's discharge of blood flows many days not at the time of her menstruation, or if it flows beyond the time of her menstruation, all the days of her discharge of impurity will be like the days of her menstruation—she is unclean. 26 Any bed she lies on all the days of her discharge will be to her like the bed of her menstruation, any furniture she sits on will be unclean like the impurity of her menstruation, 27 and anyone who touches them will be unclean, and he must wash his clothes, bathe in water, and be unclean until evening.

PURITY REGULATIONS FOR FEMALE BODILY DISCHARGES

28 "'If she becomes clean from her discharge, then she is to count off for herself seven days, and afterward she will be clean. 29 Then on the eighth day she must take for herself two turtledoves or two young pigeons and she must bring them to the priest at the

entrance of the Meeting Tent, 30 and the priest is to make one
a sin offering and the other a burnt offering. So the priest is to
make atonement for her before the LORD from her discharge
of impurity.

SUMMARY OF PURIFICATION REGULATIONS FOR BODILY DISCHARGES

31 "'Thus you are to set the Israelites apart from their impurity
so that they do not die in their impurity by defiling my tabernacle which is in their midst. 32 This is the law for the one with a
discharge: for the one who has a seminal emission and becomes
unclean by it, 33 for the one who is sick in her menstruation, for
the one with a discharge, whether male or female, and for a man
who goes to bed with an unclean woman.'"

THE DAY OF ATONEMENT

16 The LORD spoke to Moses after the death of Aaron's two
sons when they approached the presence of the LORD and
died, 2 and the LORD said to Moses: "Tell Aaron your brother
that he must not enter at any time into the Holy Place inside
the special curtain in front of the atonement lid that is on the
ark so that he may not die, for I will appear in the cloud over
the atonement lid.

DAY OF ATONEMENT OFFERINGS

3 "In this way Aaron is to enter into the sanctuary—with a young
bull for a sin offering and a ram for a burnt offering. 4 He must
put on a holy linen tunic, linen leggings are to cover his body, and
he is to wrap himself with a linen sash and wrap his head with a
linen turban. They are holy garments, so he must bathe his body
in water and put them on. 5 He must also take two male goats
from the congregation of the Israelites for a sin offering and one
ram for a burnt offering. 6 Then Aaron is to present the sin offering bull which is for himself and is to make atonement on behalf
of himself and his household. 7 Next he must take the two goats
and stand them before the LORD at the entrance of the Meeting
Tent, 8 and Aaron is to cast lots over the two goats, one lot for
the LORD and one lot for Azazel. 9 Aaron must then present the
goat which has been designated by lot for the LORD, and he is to
make it a sin offering, 10 but the goat which has been designated
by lot for Azazel is to be stood alive before the LORD to make
atonement on it by sending it away into the desert to Azazel.

THE SIN-OFFERING SACRIFICIAL PROCEDURES

11 "Aaron is to present the sin-offering bull which is for himself,
and he is to make atonement on behalf of himself and his household. He is to slaughter the sin-offering bull which is for himself,
12 and take a censer full of coals of fire from the altar before the
LORD and a full double handful of finely ground fragrant incense,
and bring them inside the curtain. 13 He must then put the incense on the fire before the LORD, and the cloud of incense will
cover the atonement lid which is above the ark of the testimony,
so that he will not die. 14 Then he is to take some of the blood of
the bull and sprinkle it with his finger on the eastern face of the

atonement lid, and in front of the atonement lid he is to sprinkle some of the blood seven times with his finger.

[15] "Aaron must then slaughter the sin-offering goat which is for the people. He is to bring its blood inside the curtain, and he is to do with its blood just as he did to the blood of the bull: He is to sprinkle it on the atonement lid and in front of the atonement lid. [16] So he is to make atonement for the Holy Place from the impurities of the Israelites and from their transgressions with regard to all their sins, and thus he is to do for the Meeting Tent which resides with them in the midst of their impurities. [17] Nobody is to be in the Meeting Tent when he enters to make atonement in the Holy Place until he goes out, and he has made atonement on his behalf, on behalf of his household, and on behalf of the whole assembly of Israel.

[18] "Then Aaron is to go out to the altar which is before the LORD and make atonement for it. He is to take some of the blood of the bull and some of the blood of the goat, and put it all around on the horns of the altar. [19] Then he is to sprinkle on it some of the blood with his finger seven times, and cleanse and consecrate it from the impurities of the Israelites.

THE LIVE GOAT RITUAL PROCEDURES

[20] "When Aaron has finished purifying the Holy Place, the Meeting Tent, and the altar, he is to present the live goat. [21] Aaron is to lay his two hands on the head of the live goat and confess over it all the iniquities of the Israelites and all their transgressions in regard to all their sins, and thus he is to put them on the head of the goat and send it away into the desert by the hand of a man standing ready. [22] The goat is to bear on itself all their iniquities into an inaccessible land, so he is to send the goat away into the desert.

THE CONCLUDING RITUALS

[23] "Aaron must then enter the Meeting Tent and take off the linen garments which he had put on when he entered the sanctuary, and leave them there. [24] Then he must bathe his body in water in the Holy Place, put on his clothes, and go out and make his burnt offering and the people's burnt offering. So he is to make atonement on behalf of himself and the people.

[25] "Then he is to offer up the fat of the sin offering in smoke on the altar, [26] and the one who sent the goat away to Azazel must wash his clothes, bathe his body in water, and afterward he may reenter the camp. [27] The bull of the sin offering and the goat of the sin offering, whose blood was brought to make atonement in the Holy Place, must be brought outside the camp and their hide, their flesh, and their dung must be burned up, [28] and the one who burns them must wash his clothes and bathe his body in water, and afterward he may reenter the camp.

REFLECT

Why did the priest send the live goat into the wilderness? What did this signify to the people about their sin?

REVIEW OF THE DAY OF ATONEMENT

[29] "This is to be a perpetual statute for you. In the seventh month, on the tenth day of the month, you must humble yourselves and do no work of any kind, both the native citizen and the resident foreigner who lives in your midst, [30] for on this day atonement is

to be made for you to cleanse you from all your sins; you must be
clean before the LORD. 31 It is to be a Sabbath of complete rest for
you, and you must humble yourselves. It is a perpetual statute.
32 "The priest who is anointed and ordained to act as high priest
in place of his father is to make atonement. He is to put on the
linen garments, the holy garments, 33 and he is to purify the Most
Holy Place, he is to purify the Meeting Tent and the altar, and
he is to make atonement for the priests and for all the people of
the assembly. 34 This is to be a perpetual statute for you to make
atonement for the Israelites for all their sins once a year." So he
did just as the LORD had commanded Moses.

THE SLAUGHTER OF ANIMALS

17 The LORD spoke to Moses, 2 "Speak to Aaron, his sons, and
all the Israelites, and tell them, 'This is the word that the
LORD has commanded, 3 "Blood guilt will be accounted to any
man from the house of Israel who slaughters an ox or a lamb
or a goat inside the camp or outside the camp, 4 but has not
brought it to the entrance of the Meeting Tent to present it as
an offering to the LORD before the tabernacle of the LORD. He
has shed blood, so that man will be cut off from the midst of his
people. 5 This is so that the Israelites will bring their sacrifices
that they are sacrificing in the open field to the LORD at the entrance of the Meeting Tent—to the priest—and sacrifice them
there as peace-offering sacrifices to the LORD. 6 The priest is
to splash the blood on the altar of the LORD at the entrance of
the Meeting Tent, and offer the fat up in smoke for a soothing
aroma to the LORD. 7 So the people must no longer offer their
sacrifices to the goat demons, acting like prostitutes by going
after them. This is to be a perpetual statute for them throughout their generations."'
8 "You are to say to them: 'Any man from the house of Israel or
from the resident foreigners who live in their midst, who offers
a burnt offering or a sacrifice 9 but does not bring it to the entrance of the Meeting Tent to offer it to the LORD—that person
will be cut off from his people.

PROHIBITION AGAINST EATING BLOOD

10 "'Any man from the house of Israel or from the resident foreigners who live in their midst who eats any blood, I will set my
face against that person who eats the blood, and I will cut him
off from the midst of his people, 11 for the life of every living thing
is in the blood. So I myself have assigned it to you on the altar to
make atonement for your lives, for the blood makes atonement
by means of the life. 12 Therefore, I have said to the Israelites: No
person among you is to eat blood, and no resident foreigner who
lives among you is to eat blood.
13 "'Any man from the Israelites or from the resident foreigners who live in their midst who hunts a wild animal or a bird
that may be eaten must pour out its blood and cover it with
soil, 14 for the life of all flesh is its blood. So I have said to the
Israelites: You must not eat the blood of any living thing because the life of every living thing is its blood—all who eat it
will be cut off.

REGULATIONS FOR EATING CARCASSES

15 "'Any person who eats an animal that has died of natural causes or an animal torn by beasts, whether a native citizen or a resident foreigner, must wash his clothes, bathe in water, and be unclean until evening; then he will be clean. 16 But if he does not wash his clothes and does not bathe his body, he will bear his punishment for his iniquity.'"

EXHORTATION TO OBEDIENCE AND LIFE

18 The LORD spoke to Moses: 2 "Speak to the Israelites and tell them, 'I am the LORD your God! 3 You must not do as they do in the land of Egypt where you have been living, and you must not do as they do in the land of Canaan into which I am about to bring you; you must not walk in their statutes. 4 You must observe my regulations and you must be sure to walk in my statutes. I am the LORD your God. 5 So you must keep my statutes and my regulations; anyone who does so will live by keeping them. I am the LORD.

LAWS OF SEXUAL RELATIONS

6 "'No man is to approach any close relative to have sexual relations with her. I am the LORD. 7 You must not expose your father's nakedness by having sexual relations with your mother. She is your mother; you must not have sexual relations with her. 8 You must not have sexual relations with your father's wife; she is your father's nakedness. 9 You must not have sexual relations with your sister, whether she is your father's daughter or your mother's daughter, whether she is born in the same household or born outside it; you must not have sexual relations with either of them. 10 You must not expose the nakedness of your son's daughter or your daughter's daughter by having sexual relations with them, because they are your own nakedness. 11 You must not have sexual relations with the daughter of your father's wife born of your father; she is your sister. You must not have sexual relations with her. 12 You must not have sexual relations with your father's sister; she is your father's flesh. 13 You must not have sexual relations with your mother's sister, because she is your mother's flesh. 14 You must not expose the nakedness of your father's brother; you must not approach his wife to have marital relations with her. She is your aunt. 15 You must not have sexual relations with your daughter-in-law; she is your son's wife. You must not have sexual relations with her. 16 You must not have sexual relations with your brother's wife; she is your brother's nakedness. 17 You must not have sexual relations with both a woman and her daughter; you must not take as wife either her son's daughter or her daughter's daughter to have sexual relations with them. They are closely related to her—it is lewdness. 18 You must not take a woman in marriage and then marry her sister as a rival wife while she is still alive, to have sexual relations with her.

19 "'You must not approach a woman in her menstrual impurity to have sexual relations with her. 20 You must not have sexual relations with the wife of your fellow citizen to become unclean with her. 21 You must not give any of your children as

an offering to Molech, so that you do not profane the name of your God. I am the LORD! 22 You must not have sexual relations with a male as one has sexual relations with a woman; it is a detestable act. 23 You must not have sexual relations with any animal to become defiled with it, and a woman must not stand before an animal to have sexual relations with it; it is a perversion.

WARNING AGAINST THE ABOMINATIONS OF THE NATIONS

24 "'Do not defile yourselves with any of these things, for the nations that I am about to drive out before you have been defiled with all these things. 25 Therefore the land has become unclean and I have brought the punishment for its iniquity upon it, so that the land has vomited out its inhabitants. 26 You yourselves must obey my statutes and my regulations and must not do any of these abominations, both the native citizen and the resident foreigner in your midst, 27 for the people who were in the land before you have done all these abominations, and the land has become unclean. 28 So do not make the land vomit you out because you defile it just as it has vomited out the nations that were before you. 29 For if anyone does any of these abominations, that person who does them will be cut off from the midst of the people. 30 You must obey my charge not to practice any of the abominable statutes that have been done before you, so that you do not defile yourselves by them. I am the LORD your God.'"

RELIGIOUS AND SOCIAL REGULATIONS

19 The LORD spoke to Moses: 2 "Speak to the whole congregation of the Israelites and tell them, 'You must be holy because I, the LORD your God, am holy. 3 Each of you must respect his mother and his father, and you must keep my Sabbaths. I am the LORD your God. 4 Do not turn to idols, and you must not make for yourselves gods of cast metal. I am the LORD your God.

EATING THE PEACE OFFERING

5 "'When you sacrifice a peace-offering sacrifice to the LORD, you must sacrifice it so that it is accepted for you. 6 It must be eaten on the day of your sacrifice and on the following day, but what is left over until the third day must be burned up. 7 If, however, it is eaten on the third day, it is spoiled; it will not be accepted, 8 and the one who eats it will bear his punishment for iniquity because he has profaned what is holy to the LORD. That person will be cut off from his people.

LEAVING THE GLEANINGS

9 "'When you gather in the harvest of your land, you must not completely harvest the corner of your field, and you must not gather up the gleanings of your harvest. 10 You must not pick your vineyard bare, and you must not gather up the fallen grapes of your vineyard. You must leave them for the poor and the resident foreigner. I am the LORD your God.

DEALING HONESTLY

11 "'You must not steal, you must not tell lies, and you must not
deal falsely with your fellow citizen. 12 You must not swear falsely
in my name, so that you do not profane the name of your God.
I am the LORD. 13 You must not oppress your neighbor or commit robbery against your neighbor. You must not withhold the
wages of the hired laborer overnight until morning. 14 You must
not curse a deaf person or put a stumbling block in front of a
blind person. You must fear your God; I am the LORD.

JUSTICE, LOVE, AND PROPRIETY

15 "'You must not deal unjustly in judgment: You must neither
show partiality to the poor nor honor the rich. You must judge
your fellow citizen fairly. 16 You must not go about as a slanderer
among your people. You must not stand idly by when your neighbor's life is at stake. I am the LORD. 17 You must not hate your
brother in your heart. You must surely reprove your fellow citizen so that you do not incur sin on account of him. 18 You must
not take vengeance or bear a grudge against any of your people,
but you must love your neighbor as yourself. I am the LORD.
19 You must keep my statutes. You must not allow two different
kinds of your animals to breed together, you must not sow your
field with two different kinds of seed, and you must not wear a
garment made of two different kinds of material.

LYING WITH A SLAVE WOMAN

20 "'When a man goes to bed with a woman for intercourse, although she is a slave woman designated for another man and she
has not yet been ransomed, or freedom has not been granted to
her, there will be an obligation to pay compensation. They must
not be put to death, because she was not free. 21 He must bring
his guilt offering to the LORD at the entrance of the Meeting
Tent, a guilt offering ram, 22 and the priest is to make atonement
for him with the ram of the guilt offering before the LORD for
his sin that he has committed, and he will be forgiven of his sin
that he has committed.

THE PRODUCE OF FRUIT TREES

23 "'When you enter the land and plant any fruit tree, you must
consider its fruit to be forbidden. Three years it will be forbidden to you; it must not be eaten. 24 In the fourth year all its fruit
will be holy, praise offerings to the LORD. 25 Then in the fifth year
you may eat its fruit to add its produce to your harvest. I am the
LORD your God.

BLOOD, HAIR, BODY, AND PROSTITUTION

26 "'You must not eat anything with the blood still in it. You
must not practice either divination or soothsaying. 27 You must
not round off the corners of the hair on your head or ruin the
corners of your beard. 28 You must not slash your body for a
dead person or incise a tattoo on yourself. I am the LORD. 29 Do
not profane your daughter by making her a prostitute, so that
the land does not practice prostitution and become full of
lewdness.

GET TO KNOW THE LAWGIVER

LEVITICUS 19:1–18

Leviticus is a beautiful book that reveals extraordinary truth about God, yet it's the place where many of my Bible reading plans died.

At first glance, Leviticus appears to be a book of rules given to a foreign people group. The commands can seem abstract, and its rules can feel inapplicable to our world. Thankfully, I discovered this could not be further from the truth.

Leviticus 19:1–18 is a laundry list of laws. Each one concludes with the phrase, "I am the LORD your God."

Leave grapes in the vineyard for the poor: I am the Lord your God.

Do not lie to one another: I am the Lord your God.

Love one another: I am the Lord your God.

Every law tells us about God's character. Every law reveals what God cares about. These commands are not the purposeless whims of a demanding God, but rather, an extension of His grace. Each law is not pointless, but instead points us to the Lawgiver. This understanding drastically changed the way I read Leviticus. No longer is it a rulebook, but now it is a stunning depiction of God and His heart for those He desperately loves.

Each rule in Leviticus 19 expresses the truth that God is holy, completely and utterly set apart from all we know or see. Yet, despite being holy, God deeply longs to dwell with His people. In Exodus 19:5–6 God told Israel,

> *"And now, if you will diligently listen to me and keep my covenant, then you will be my special possession out of all the nations, for all the earth is mine, and you will be to me a kingdom of priests and a holy nation."*

Through Israel's laws, God provided for those who could not provide for themselves and loved those that others might overlook. The incredible thing is Jesus embodied, and ultimately fulfilled, God's law (Matt 5:17–18). He is holy. Jesus cared for the poor. He noticed those who were hidden by the crowd. He sought out the hurting. He gave His life for the lost. He fulfilled all the law and removed the requirement from us.

Don't skip over the laws in Leviticus. Soak them in deeply. Always ask, "What does this law teach me about the Lawgiver?" He'll reveal Himself to you in deep and significant ways.

SABBATHS, PURITY, HONOR, RESPECT, AND HONESTY

30 "'You must keep my Sabbaths and fear my sanctuary. I am
the LORD. 31 Do not turn to the spirits of the dead and do not
seek familiar spirits to become unclean by them. I am the
LORD your God. 32 You must stand up in the presence of the
aged, honor the presence of an elder, and fear your God. I am
the LORD. 33 When a resident foreigner lives with you in your
land, you must not oppress him. 34 The resident foreigner who
lives with you must be to you as a native citizen among you;
so you must love the foreigner as yourself, because you were
foreigners in the land of Egypt. I am the LORD your God. 35 You
must not do injustice in the regulation of measures, whether of length, weight, or volume. 36 You must have honest balances, honest weights, an honest ephah, and an honest hin. I
am the LORD your God who brought you out from the land of
Egypt. 37 You must be sure to obey all my statutes and regulations. I am the LORD.'"

PROHIBITIONS AGAINST ILLEGITIMATE FAMILY WORSHIP

20 The LORD spoke to Moses: 2 "You are to say to the Israelites, 'Any man from the Israelites (or any of the resident
foreigners who live in Israel) who gives any of his children to
Molech must be put to death; the people of the land must pelt
him with stones. 3 I myself will set my face against that man and
cut him off from the midst of his people, because he has given
some of his children to Molech and thereby defiled my sanctuary and profaned my holy name. 4 If, however, the people of
the land shut their eyes to that man when he gives some of his
children to Molech so that they do not put him to death, 5 I myself will set my face against that man and his clan. I will cut off
from the midst of the people both him and all who follow after
him in spiritual prostitution, committing prostitution by worshiping Molech.

PROHIBITION AGAINST SPIRITISTS AND MEDIUMS

6 "'The person who turns to the spirits of the dead and familiar
spirits to commit prostitution by going after them, I will set
my face against that person and cut him off from the midst of
his people.

EXHORTATION TO HOLINESS AND OBEDIENCE

7 "'You must sanctify yourselves and be holy, because I am the
LORD your God. 8 You must be sure to obey my statutes. I am the
LORD who sanctifies you.

FAMILY LIFE AND SEXUAL PROHIBITIONS

9 "'If anyone curses his father or mother he must be put to
death. He has cursed his father or mother; his blood guilt is
on himself. 10 If a man commits adultery with his neighbor's
wife, both the adulterer and the adulteress must be put to
death. 11 If a man goes to bed with his father's wife, he has exposed his father's nakedness. Both of them must be put to

death; their blood guilt is on themselves. 12 If a man goes to
bed with his daughter-in-law, both of them must be put to
death. They have committed perversion; their blood guilt is
on themselves. 13 If a man goes to bed with a male as one goes
to bed with a woman, the two of them have committed an
abomination. They must be put to death; their blood guilt is
on themselves. 14 If a man has marital relations with both a
woman and her mother, it is lewdness. Both he and they must
be burned to death, so there is no lewdness in your midst. 15 If
a man has sexual relations with any animal, he must be put to
death, and you must kill the animal. 16 If a woman approaches
any animal to copulate with it, you must kill the woman,
and the animal must be put to death; their blood guilt is
on themselves.

17 "'If a man has marital relations with his sister, whether the
daughter of his father or of his mother, so that he sees her nakedness and she sees his nakedness, it is a disgrace. They must
be cut off in the sight of the children of their people. He has
exposed his sister's nakedness; he will bear his punishment for
iniquity. 18 If a man goes to bed with a menstruating woman
and uncovers her nakedness, he has laid bare her fountain of
blood and she has exposed the fountain of her blood, so both
of them must be cut off from the midst of their people. 19 You
must not expose the nakedness of your mother's sister or your
father's sister, for such a person has exposed his own close relative. They must bear their punishment for iniquity. 20 If a man
goes to bed with his aunt, he has exposed his uncle's nakedness; they must bear responsibility for their sin, they will die
childless. 21 If a man has marital relations with his brother's
wife, it is indecency. He has exposed his brother's nakedness;
they will be childless.

EXHORTATION TO HOLINESS AND OBEDIENCE

22 "'You must be sure to obey all my statutes and regulations, so
that the land to which I am about to bring you to take up residence does not vomit you out. 23 You must not walk in the statutes of the nations which I am about to drive out before you,
because they have done all these things and I am filled with disgust against them. 24 So I have said to you: You yourselves will
possess their land and I myself will give it to you for a possession, a land flowing with milk and honey. I am the LORD your
God who has set you apart from the other peoples. 25 Therefore
you must distinguish between the clean animal and the unclean,
and between the unclean bird and the clean, and you must not
make yourselves detestable by means of an animal or bird or
anything that creeps on the ground—creatures I have distinguished for you as unclean. 26 You must be holy to me because
I, the LORD, am holy, and I have set you apart from the other
peoples to be mine.

PROHIBITION AGAINST SPIRITISTS AND MEDIUMS

27 "'A man or woman who has in them a spirit of the dead or a
familiar spirit must be put to death. They must pelt them with
stones; their blood guilt is on themselves.'"

REFLECT

Why was it so important that the Israelites be holy and imitate the holiness of God? Though we are no longer under the law, why is it important for believers in Christ to be holy?

RULES FOR THE PRIESTS

21 The LORD said to Moses, "Say to the priests, the sons of Aaron—say to them: 'For a dead person no priest is to defile himself among his people, 2 except for his close relative who is near
to him—his mother, his father, his son, his daughter, his brother,
3 and his virgin sister who is near to him, who has no husband—he
may defile himself for her. 4 He must not defile himself as a husband among his people so as to profane himself. 5 Priests must not
have a bald spot shaved on their head, they must not shave the
corner of their beard, and they must not cut slashes in their body.
6 "'They must be holy to their God, and they must not profane
the name of their God, because they are the ones who present
the LORD's gifts, the food of their God. Therefore they must be
holy. 7 They must not take a wife defiled by prostitution, nor are
they to take a wife divorced from her husband, for the priest is
holy to his God. 8 You must sanctify him because he presents the
food of your God. He must be holy to you because I, the LORD
who sanctifies you all, am holy. 9 If a daughter of a priest profanes
herself by engaging in prostitution, she is profaning her father.
She must be burned to death.

RULES FOR THE HIGH PRIEST

10 "'The high priest—who is greater than his brothers, and on
whose head the anointing oil is poured, and who has been ordained to wear the priestly garments—must neither dishevel the
hair of his head nor tear his garments. 11 He must not go where
there is any dead person; he must not defile himself even for his
father or for his mother. 12 He must not go out from the sanctuary and must not profane the sanctuary of his God, because
the dedication of the anointing oil of his God is on him. I am
the LORD. 13 He must take a wife who is a virgin. 14 He must not
marry a widow, a divorced woman, or one profaned by prostitution; he may only take a virgin from his people as a wife, 15 so
that he does not profane his children among his people, for I am
the LORD who sanctifies him.'"

RULES FOR THE PRIESTHOOD

16 The LORD spoke to Moses: 17 "Tell Aaron, 'No man from your
descendants throughout their generations who has a physical
flaw is to approach to present the food of his God. 18 Certainly no
man who has a physical flaw is to approach: a blind man, or one
who is lame, or one with a slit nose, or who has a limb too long,
19 or a man who has had a broken leg or arm, 20 or a hunchback,
or a dwarf, or one with a spot in his eye, or a festering eruption,
or a feverish rash, or a crushed testicle. 21 No man from the descendants of Aaron the priest who has a physical flaw may step
forward to present the LORD's gifts; he has a physical flaw, so he
must not step forward to present the food of his God. 22 He may
eat both the most holy and the holy food of his God, 23 but he
must not go near the special curtain or step forward to the altar because he has a physical flaw. Thus he must not profane my
holy places, for I am the LORD who sanctifies them.'"
24 So Moses spoke these things to Aaron, his sons, and all the
Israelites.

REGULATIONS FOR THE EATING OF PRIESTLY STIPENDS

22 The LORD spoke to Moses: 2 "Tell Aaron and his sons that
they must deal respectfully with the holy offerings of
the Israelites, which they consecrate to me, so that they do not
profane my holy name. I am the LORD. 3 Say to them, 'Throughout your generations, if any man from all your descendants approaches the holy offerings, which the Israelites consecrate to
the LORD, while he is impure, that person must be cut off from
before me. I am the LORD. 4 No man from the descendants of
Aaron who is diseased or has a discharge may eat the holy offerings until he becomes clean. The one who touches anything
made unclean by contact with a dead person, or with a man who
has a seminal emission, 5 or with a man who touches a swarming
thing by which he becomes unclean, or who touches a person
by which he becomes unclean, whatever that person's impurity—6 the person who touches any of these will be unclean until evening and must not eat from the holy offerings unless he
has bathed his body in water. 7 When the sun goes down he will
be clean, and afterward he may eat from the holy offerings, because they are his food. 8 He must not eat an animal that has
died of natural causes or an animal torn by beasts and thus become unclean by it. I am the LORD. 9 They must keep my charge
so that they do not incur sin on account of it and therefore die
because they profane it. I am the LORD who sanctifies them.

10 "'No lay person may eat anything holy. Neither a priest's
lodger nor a hired laborer may eat anything holy, 11 but if a priest
buys a person with his own money, that person may eat the holy
offerings, and those born in the priest's own house may eat his
food. 12 If a priest's daughter marries a lay person, she may not
eat the holy contribution offerings, 13 but if a priest's daughter
is a widow or divorced, and she has no children so that she returns to live in her father's house as in her youth, she may eat
from her father's food, but no lay person may eat it.

14 "'If a man eats a holy offering by mistake, he must add one-
fifth to it and give the holy offering to the priest. 15 They must
not profane the holy offerings which the Israelites contribute
to the LORD, 16 and so cause them to incur a penalty for guilt
when they eat their holy offerings, for I am the LORD who sanctifies them.'"

REGULATIONS FOR OFFERING VOTIVE AND FREEWILL OFFERINGS

17 The LORD spoke to Moses: 18 "Speak to Aaron, his sons, and all
the Israelites and tell them, 'When any man from the house of
Israel or from the resident foreigners in Israel presents his offering for any of the votive or freewill offerings, which they present to the LORD as a burnt offering, 19 if it is to be acceptable for
your benefit it must be a flawless male from the cattle, sheep, or
goats. 20 You must not present anything that has a flaw, because
it will not be acceptable for your benefit. 21 If a man presents a
peace-offering sacrifice to the LORD for a special votive offering or for a freewill offering from the herd or the flock, it must
be flawless to be acceptable; it must have no flaw.

22 “‘You must not present to the LORD something blind, or with
a broken bone, or mutilated, or with a running sore, or with a
festering eruption, or with a feverish rash. You must not give
any of these as a gift on the altar to the LORD. 23 As for an ox or
a sheep with a limb too long or stunted, you may present it as a
freewill offering, but it will not be acceptable for a votive offering. 24 You must not present to the LORD something with testi-
cles that are bruised, crushed, torn, or cut off; you must not do
this in your land. 25 Even from a foreigner you must not present
the food of your God from such animals as these, for they are
ruined and flawed; they will not be acceptable for your benefit.’”

26 The LORD spoke to Moses: 27 “When an ox, lamb, or goat is
born, it must be under the care of its mother seven days, but
from the eighth day onward it will be acceptable as an offering
gift to the LORD. 28 You must not slaughter an ox or a sheep and
its young on the same day. 29 When you sacrifice a thanksgiving
offering to the LORD, you must sacrifice it so that it is acceptable for your benefit. 30 On that very day it must be eaten; you
must not leave any part of it over until morning. I am the LORD.

31 “You must be sure to do my commandments. I am the LORD.
32 You must not profane my holy name, and I will be sanctified
in the midst of the Israelites. I am the LORD who sanctifies you,
33 the one who brought you out from the land of Egypt to be your
God. I am the LORD.”

REGULATIONS FOR ISRAEL’S APPOINTED TIMES

23 The LORD spoke to Moses: 2 “Speak to the Israelites and
tell them, ‘These are the LORD’s appointed times which
you must proclaim as holy assemblies—my appointed times.

THE WEEKLY SABBATH

3 “‘Six days work may be done, but on the seventh day there must be
a Sabbath of complete rest, a holy assembly. You must not do any
work; it is a Sabbath to the LORD in all the places where you live.

THE PASSOVER AND FEAST OF UNLEAVENED BREAD

4 “‘These are the LORD’s appointed times, holy assemblies, which
you must proclaim at their appointed time. 5 In the first month,
on the fourteenth day of the month, at twilight, is a Passover offering to the LORD. 6 Then on the fifteenth day of the same month
will be the Feast of Unleavened Bread to the LORD; seven days
you must eat unleavened bread. 7 On the first day there will be a
holy assembly for you; you must not do any regular work. 8 You
must present a gift to the LORD for seven days, and the seventh
day is a holy assembly; you must not do any regular work.’”

THE PRESENTATION OF FIRSTFRUITS

9 The LORD spoke to Moses: 10 “Speak to the Israelites and tell them,
‘When you enter the land that I am about to give to you and you
gather in its harvest, then you must bring the sheaf of the first portion of your harvest to the priest, 11 and he must wave the sheaf before the LORD to be accepted for your benefit—on the day after the
Sabbath the priest is to wave it. 12 On the day you wave the sheaf
you must also offer a flawless yearling lamb for a burnt offering to

the LORD, 13 along with its grain offering, two-tenths of an ephah
of choice wheat flour mixed with olive oil, as a gift to the LORD, a
soothing aroma, and its drink offering, one-fourth of a hin of wine.
14 You must not eat bread, roasted grain, or fresh grain until this very
day, until you bring the offering to your God. This is a perpetual statute throughout your generations in all the places where you live.

THE FEAST OF WEEKS

15 "'You must count for yourselves seven weeks from the day after the Sabbath, from the day you bring the wave offering sheaf;
they must be complete weeks. 16 You must count fifty days—until the day after the seventh Sabbath—and then you must present a new grain offering to the LORD. 17 From the places where
you live you must bring two loaves of bread for a wave offering;
they must be made from two-tenths of an ephah of fine wheat
flour, baked with yeast, as firstfruits to the LORD. 18 Along with
the loaves of bread, you must also present seven flawless yearling lambs, one young bull, and two rams. They are to be a burnt
offering to the LORD along with their grain offering and drink
offerings, a gift of a soothing aroma to the LORD. 19 You must also
offer one male goat for a sin offering and two yearling lambs for
a peace-offering sacrifice, 20 and the priest is to wave them—the
two lambs—along with the bread of the firstfruits, as a wave offering before the LORD; they will be holy to the LORD for the priest.
21 "'On this very day you must proclaim an assembly; it is to be a
holy assembly for you. You must not do any regular work. This is a
perpetual statute in all the places where you live throughout your
generations. 22 When you gather in the harvest of your land, you
must not completely harvest the corner of your field, and you must
not gather up the gleanings of your harvest. You must leave them
for the poor and the resident foreigner. I am the LORD your God.'"

THE FEAST OF HORN BLASTS

23 The LORD spoke to Moses: 24 "Tell the Israelites, 'In the seventh
month, on the first day of the month, you must have a complete
rest, a memorial announced by loud horn blasts, a holy assembly. 25 You must not do any regular work, but you must present
a gift to the LORD.'"

THE DAY OF ATONEMENT

26 The LORD spoke to Moses: 27 "The tenth day of this seventh
month is the Day of Atonement. It is to be a holy assembly for
you, and you must humble yourselves and present a gift to the
LORD. 28 You must not do any work on this particular day, because it is a day of atonement to make atonement for yourselves
before the LORD your God. 29 Indeed, any person who does not
behave with humility on this particular day will be cut off from
his people. 30 As for any person who does any work on this particular day, I will exterminate that person from the midst of his
people—31 you must not do any work! This is a perpetual statute
throughout your generations in all the places where you live.
32 It is a Sabbath of complete rest for you, and you must humble
yourselves on the ninth day of the month in the evening, from
evening until evening you must observe your Sabbath."

THE FEAST OF TEMPORARY SHELTERS

33 The LORD spoke to Moses: 34 "Tell the Israelites, 'On the fifteenth day of this seventh month is the Feast of Shelters for seven days to the LORD. 35 On the first day is a holy assembly; you must do no regular work. 36 For seven days you must present a gift to the LORD. On the eighth day there is to be a holy assembly for you, and you must present a gift to the LORD. It is a solemn assembly day; you must not do any regular work.

37 "'These are the appointed times of the LORD that you must proclaim as holy assemblies to present a gift to the LORD—burnt offering, grain offering, sacrifice, and drink offerings, each day according to its regulation, 38 besides the Sabbaths of the LORD and all your gifts, votive offerings, and freewill offerings which you must give to the LORD.

39 "'On the fifteenth day of the seventh month, when you gather in the produce of the land, you must celebrate a pilgrim festival of the LORD for seven days. On the first day is a complete rest and on the eighth day is complete rest. 40 On the first day you must take for yourselves branches from majestic trees—palm branches, branches of leafy trees, and willows of the brook—and you must rejoice before the LORD your God for seven days. 41 You must celebrate it as a pilgrim festival to the LORD for seven days in the year. This is a perpetual statute throughout your generations; you must celebrate it in the seventh month. 42 You must live in temporary shelters for seven days; every native citizen in Israel must live in shelters, 43 so that your future generations may know that I made the Israelites live in shelters when I brought them out from the land of Egypt. I am the LORD your God.'"

44 So Moses spoke to the Israelites about the appointed times of the LORD.

REGULATIONS FOR THE LAMPSTAND AND THE TABLE OF BREAD

24 The LORD spoke to Moses: 2 "Command the Israelites to bring to you pure oil of beaten olives for the light, to make a lamp burn continually. 3 Outside the special curtain of the congregation in the Meeting Tent, Aaron must arrange it from evening until morning before the LORD continually. This is a perpetual statute throughout your generations. 4 On the ceremonially pure lampstand he must arrange the lamps before the LORD continually.

5 "You must take choice wheat flour and bake twelve loaves; there must be two-tenths of an ephah of flour in each loaf, 6 and you must set them in two rows, six in a row, on the ceremonially pure table before the LORD. 7 You must put pure frankincense on each row, and it will become a memorial portion for the bread, a gift to the LORD. 8 Each Sabbath day Aaron must arrange it before the LORD continually; this portion is from the Israelites as a perpetual covenant. 9 It will belong to Aaron and his sons, and they must eat it in a holy place because it is most holy to him, a perpetually-allotted portion from the gifts of the LORD."

A CASE OF BLASPHEMING THE NAME

10 Now an Israelite woman's son whose father was an Egyptian
went out among the Israelites, and the Israelite woman's son and
an Israelite man had a fight in the camp. 11 The Israelite woman's
son misused the Name and cursed, so they brought him to Moses. (Now his mother's name was Shelomith, daughter of Dibri,
of the tribe of Dan.) 12 So they placed him in custody until they
were able to make a clear legal decision for themselves based
on words from the mouth of the LORD.
13 Then the LORD spoke to Moses: 14 "Bring the one who cursed
outside the camp, and all who heard him are to lay their hands
on his head, and the whole congregation is to stone him to death.
15 Moreover, you are to tell the Israelites, 'If any man curses his
God he will bear responsibility for his sin, 16 and one who misuses the name of the LORD must surely be put to death. The
whole congregation must surely stone him, whether he is a resident foreigner or a native citizen; when he misuses the Name
he must be put to death.
17 "'If a man beats any person to death, he must be put to death.
18 One who beats an animal to death must make restitution for
it, life for life. 19 If a man inflicts an injury on his fellow citizen,
just as he has done it must be done to him—20 fracture for fracture, eye for eye, tooth for tooth—just as he inflicts an injury on
another person that same injury must be inflicted on him. 21 One
who beats an animal to death must make restitution for it, but
one who beats a person to death must be put to death. 22 There
will be one regulation for you, whether a resident foreigner or
a native citizen, for I am the LORD your God.'"
23 Then Moses spoke to the Israelites and they brought the
one who cursed outside the camp and stoned him with stones.
So the Israelites did just as the LORD had commanded Moses.

REGULATIONS FOR THE SABBATICAL YEAR

25 The LORD spoke to Moses at Mount Sinai: 2 "Speak to the
Israelites and tell them, 'When you enter the land that
I am giving you, the land must observe a Sabbath to the LORD.
3 Six years you may sow your field, and six years you may prune
your vineyard and gather the produce, 4 but in the seventh year
the land must have a Sabbath of complete rest—a Sabbath to
the LORD. You must not sow your field or prune your vineyard.
5 You must not gather in the aftergrowth of your harvest and
you must not pick the grapes of your unpruned vines; the land
must have a year of complete rest. 6 You may have the Sabbath
produce of the land to eat—you, your male servant, your female
servant, your hired worker, the resident foreigner who stays with
you, 7 your cattle, and the wild animals that are in your land—all
its produce will be for you to eat.

REFLECT

What did Sabbath days and years provide the people other than a time of rest? Why was keeping the Sabbath so important to God?

REGULATIONS FOR THE JUBILEE YEAR OF RELEASE

8 "'You must count off seven weeks of years, seven times seven
years, and the days of the seven weeks of years will amount to
forty-nine years. 9 You must sound loud horn blasts—in the seventh month, on the tenth day of the month, on the Day of Atonement—you must sound the horn in your entire land. 10 So you

must consecrate the fiftieth year, and you must proclaim a release in the land for all its inhabitants. That year will be your Jubilee; each one of you must return to his property and each one
of you must return to his clan. 11 That fiftieth year will be your Jubilee; you must not sow the land, harvest its aftergrowth, or pick
the grapes of its unpruned vines. 12 Because that year is a Jubilee,
it will be holy to you—you may eat its produce from the field.

RELEASE OF LANDED PROPERTY

13 "'In this Year of Jubilee you must each return to your property. 14 If you make a sale to your fellow citizen or buy from your
fellow citizen, no one is to wrong his brother. 15 You may buy it
from your fellow citizen according to the number of years since
the last Jubilee; he may sell it to you according to the years of
produce that are left. 16 The more years there are, the more you
may make its purchase price, and the fewer years there are, the
less you must make its purchase price, because he is only selling to you a number of years of produce. 17 No one is to oppress
his fellow citizen, but you must fear your God, because I am the
LORD your God. 18 You must obey my statutes and my regulations; you must be sure to keep them so that you may live securely in the land.
19 "'The land will give its fruit and you may eat until you are satisfied, and you may live securely in the land. 20 If you say, "What
will we eat in the seventh year if we do not sow and gather our
produce?" 21 I will command my blessing for you in the sixth year
so that it may yield the produce for three years, 22 and you may
sow the eighth year and eat from that sixth year's produce—old
produce. Until you bring in the ninth year's produce, you may
eat old produce. 23 The land must not be sold without reclaim
because the land belongs to me, for you are foreign residents,
temporary settlers, with me. 24 In all your landed property you
must provide for the right of redemption of the land.
25 "'If your brother becomes impoverished and sells some of
his property, his near redeemer is to come to you and redeem
what his brother sold. 26 If a man has no redeemer, but he prospers and gains enough for its redemption, 27 he is to calculate
the value of the years it was sold, refund the balance to the man
to whom he had sold it, and return to his property. 28 If he has
not prospered enough to refund a balance to him, then what he
sold will belong to the one who bought it until the Jubilee year,
but it must revert in the Jubilee and the original owner may return to his property.

RELEASE OF HOUSES

29 "'If a man sells a residential house in a walled city, its right
of redemption must extend until one full year from its sale; its
right of redemption must extend to a full calendar year. 30 If it is
not redeemed before the full calendar year is ended, the house
in the walled city will belong without reclaim to the one who
bought it throughout his generations; it will not revert in the
Jubilee. 31 The houses of villages, however, which have no wall
surrounding them must be considered as the field of the land;
they will have the right of redemption and must revert in the

Jubilee. 32 As for the cities of the Levites, the houses in the cities which they possess, the Levites must have a perpetual right
of redemption. 33 Whatever someone among the Levites might
redeem—the sale of a house which is his property in a city—must
revert in the Jubilee, because the houses of the cities of the Levites are their property in the midst of the Israelites. 34 Moreover, the open field areas of their cities must not be sold, because
that is their perpetual possession.

DEBT AND SLAVE REGULATIONS

35 "'If your brother becomes impoverished and is indebted to
you, you must support him; he must live with you like a foreign resident. 36 Do not take interest or profit from him, but
you must fear your God and your brother must live with you.
37 You must not lend him your money at interest and you must
not sell him food for profit. 38 I am the LORD your God who
brought you out from the land of Egypt to give you the land of
Canaan—to be your God.

39 "'If your brother becomes impoverished with regard to you
so that he sells himself to you, you must not subject him to slave
service. 40 He must be with you as a hired worker, as a resident
foreigner; he must serve with you until the Year of Jubilee, 41 but
then he may go free, he and his children with him, and may return to his family and to the property of his ancestors. 42 Since
the Israelites are my servants whom I brought out from the land
of Egypt, they must not be sold in a slave sale. 43 You must not
rule over them harshly, but you must fear your God.

44 "'As for your male and female slaves who may belong to
you—you may buy male and female slaves from the nations all
around you. 45 Also, you may buy slaves from the children of the
foreigners who reside with you, and from their families that are
with you, whom they have fathered in your land; they may become your property. 46 You may give them as an inheritance to
your children after you to possess as property. You may enslave
them perpetually. However, as for your brothers the Israelites,
no man may rule over his brother harshly.

47 "'If a resident foreigner who is with you prospers and your
brother becomes impoverished with regard to him so that he
sells himself to a resident foreigner who is with you or to a member of a foreigner's family, 48 after he has sold himself he retains
a right of redemption. One of his brothers may redeem him,
49 or his uncle or his cousin may redeem him, or any one of the
rest of his blood relatives—his family—may redeem him, or if
he prospers he may redeem himself. 50 He must calculate with
the one who bought him the number of years from the year he
sold himself to him until the Jubilee year, and the cost of his
sale must correspond to the number of years, according to the
rate of wages a hired worker would have earned while with him.
51 If there are still many years, in keeping with them he must refund most of the cost of his purchase for his redemption, 52 but
if only a few years remain until the Jubilee, he must calculate
for himself in keeping with the remaining years and refund it
for his redemption. 53 He must be with the one who bought him
like a yearly hired worker. The one who bought him must not

rule over him harshly in your sight. 54 If, however, he is not redeemed in these ways, he must go free in the Jubilee year, he and his children with him, 55 because the Israelites are my own servants; they are my servants whom I brought out from the land of Egypt. I am the LORD your God.

EXHORTATION TO OBEDIENCE

26 "'You must not make for yourselves idols, so you must not set up for yourselves a carved image or a pillar, and you must not place a sculpted stone in your land to bow down before it, for I am the LORD your God. 2 You must keep my Sabbaths and reverence my sanctuary. I am the LORD.

THE BENEFITS OF OBEDIENCE

3 "'If you walk in my statutes and are sure to obey my commandments, 4 I will give you your rains in their time so that the land will give its yield and the trees of the field will produce their fruit. 5 Threshing season will extend for you until the season for harvesting grapes, and the season for harvesting grapes will extend until sowing season, so you will eat your bread until you are satisfied, and you will live securely in your land. 6 I will grant peace in the land so that you will lie down to sleep without anyone terrifying you. I will remove harmful animals from the land, and no sword of war will pass through your land. 7 You will pursue your enemies and they will fall before you by the sword. 8 Five of you will pursue a hundred, and a hundred of you will pursue ten thousand, and your enemies will fall before you by the sword. 9 I will turn to you, make you fruitful, multiply you, and maintain my covenant with you. 10 You will still be eating stored produce from the previous year and will have to clean out what is stored from the previous year to make room for new.

11 "'I will put my tabernacle in your midst and I will not abhor you. 12 I will walk among you, and I will be your God and you will be my people. 13 I am the LORD your God who brought you out from the land of Egypt, from being their slaves, and I broke the bars of your yoke and caused you to walk upright.

THE CONSEQUENCES OF DISOBEDIENCE

14 "'If, however, you do not obey me and keep all these commandments—15 if you reject my statutes and abhor my regulations so that you do not keep all my commandments and you break my covenant—16 I for my part will do this to you: I will inflict horror on you, consumption and fever, which diminish eyesight and drain away the vitality of life. You will sow your seed in vain because your enemies will eat it. 17 I will set my face against you. You will be struck down before your enemies, those who hate you will rule over you, and you will flee when there is no one pursuing you.

18 "'If, in spite of all these things, you do not obey me, I will discipline you seven times more on account of your sins. 19 I will break your strong pride and make your sky like iron and your land like bronze. 20 Your strength will be used up in vain, your land will not give its yield, and the trees of the land will not produce their fruit.

21 "'If you walk in hostility against me and are not willing to
obey me, I will increase your affliction seven times according
to your sins. 22 I will send the wild animals against you and
they will bereave you of your children, annihilate your cattle,
and diminish your population so that your roads will become
deserted.

23 "'If in spite of these things you do not allow yourselves to be
disciplined and you walk in hostility against me, 24 then I myself will also walk in hostility against you and strike you seven
times on account of your sins. 25 I will bring on you an avenging sword, a covenant vengeance. Although you will gather together into your cities, I will send pestilence among you and
you will be given into enemy hands. 26 When I break off your
supply of bread, ten women will bake your bread in one oven;
they will ration your bread by weight, and you will eat and not
be satisfied.

27 "'If in spite of this you do not obey me but walk in hostility against me, 28 I will walk in hostile rage against you and I
myself will also discipline you seven times on account of your
sins. 29 You will eat the flesh of your sons and the flesh of your
daughters. 30 I will destroy your high places and cut down
your incense altars, and I will stack your dead bodies on top of
the lifeless bodies of your idols. I will abhor you. 31 I will lay your
cities waste and make your sanctuaries desolate, and I will refuse to smell your soothing aromas. 32 I myself will make the
land desolate and your enemies who live in it will be appalled.
33 I will scatter you among the nations and unsheathe the sword
after you, so your land will become desolate and your cities will
become a waste.

34 "'Then the land will make up for its Sabbaths all the days
it lies desolate while you are in the land of your enemies; then
the land will rest and make up its Sabbaths. 35 All the days of the
desolation it will have the rest it did not have on your Sabbaths
when you lived on it.

36 "'As for the ones who remain among you, I will bring despair
into their hearts in the lands of their enemies. The sound of a
blowing leaf will pursue them, and they will flee as one who flees
the sword and will fall down even though there is no pursuer.
37 They will stumble over each other as those who flee before
a sword, though there is no pursuer, and there will be no one
to take a stand for you before your enemies. 38 You will perish
among the nations; the land of your enemies will consume you.

RESTORATION THROUGH CONFESSION AND REPENTANCE

39 "'As for the ones who remain among you, they will rot away
because of their iniquity in the lands of your enemies, and they
will also rot away because of their ancestors' iniquities which
are with them. 40 However, when they confess their iniquity and
their ancestors' iniquities which they committed by trespassing
against me, by which they also walked in hostility against me
41 (and I myself will walk in hostility against them and bring them
into the land of their enemies), and then their uncircumcised
hearts become humbled and they make up for their iniquities,

42 I will remember my covenant with Jacob and also my covenant with Isaac and also my covenant with Abraham, and I will remember the land. 43 The land will be abandoned by them in order that it may make up for its Sabbaths while it is made desolate without them, and they will make up for their iniquity because they have rejected my regulations and have abhorred my statutes. 44 In spite of this, however, when they are in the land of their enemies I will not reject them and abhor them to make a complete end of them, to break my covenant with them, for I am the LORD their God. 45 I will remember for them the covenant with their ancestors whom I brought out from the land of Egypt in the sight of the nations to be their God. I am the LORD.'"

SUMMARY COLOPHON

46 These are the statutes, regulations, and instructions which the LORD established between himself and the Israelites at Mount Sinai through Moses.

REDEMPTION OF PERSONS GIVEN AS VOTIVE OFFERINGS

27 The LORD spoke to Moses: 2 "Speak to the Israelites and tell them, 'When a man makes a special votive offering based on the conversion value of a person to the LORD, 3 the conversion value of the male from twenty years old up to sixty years old is fifty shekels by the standard of the sanctuary shekel. 4 If the person is a female, the conversion value is thirty shekels. 5 If the person is from five years old up to twenty years old, the conversion value of the male is twenty shekels, and for the female ten shekels. 6 If the person is one month old up to five years old, the conversion value of the male is five shekels of silver, and for the female the conversion value is three shekels of silver. 7 If the person is from sixty years old and older, if he is a male the conversion value is fifteen shekels, and for the female ten shekels. 8 If the person making the votive offering is too poor to pay the conversion value, he must stand the person before the priest and the priest will establish his conversion value; according to what the man who made the votive offering can afford, the priest will establish his conversion value.

REDEMPTION OF ANIMALS GIVEN AS VOTIVE OFFERINGS

9 "'If what is vowed is a kind of animal from which an offering may be presented to the LORD, anything which he gives to the LORD from this kind of animal will be holy. 10 He must not replace or exchange it, good for bad or bad for good, and if he does indeed exchange one animal for another animal, then both the original animal and its substitute will be holy. 11 If what is vowed is an unclean animal from which an offering must not be presented to the LORD, then he must stand the animal before the priest, 12 and the priest will establish its conversion value, whether good or bad. According to the conversion value assessed by the priest, thus it will be. 13 If, however, the person who made the vow redeems the animal, he must add one-fifth to its conversion value.

REDEMPTION OF HOUSES GIVEN AS VOTIVE OFFERINGS

14 "'If a man consecrates his house as holy to the LORD, the priest will establish its conversion value, whether good or bad. Just as the priest establishes its conversion value, thus it will stand. 15 If the one who consecrates it redeems his house, he must add to it one-fifth of its conversion value in silver, and it will belong to him.

REDEMPTION OF FIELDS GIVEN AS VOTIVE OFFERINGS

16 "'If a man consecrates to the LORD some of his own landed property, the conversion value must be calculated in accordance with the amount of seed needed to sow it, a homer of barley seed being priced at fifty shekels of silver. 17 If he consecrates his field in the Jubilee year, the conversion value will stand, 18 but if he consecrates his field after the Jubilee, the priest will calculate the price for him according to the years that are left until the next Jubilee year, and it will be deducted from the conversion value. 19 If, however, the one who consecrated the field redeems it, he must add to it one-fifth of the conversion price and it will belong to him. 20 If he does not redeem the field, but sells the field to someone else, he may never redeem it. 21 When it reverts in the Jubilee, the field will be holy to the LORD like a permanently dedicated field; it will become the priest's property.

22 "'If he consecrates to the LORD a field he has purchased, which is not part of his own landed property, 23 the priest will calculate for him the amount of its conversion value until the Jubilee year, and he must pay the conversion value on that Jubilee day as something that is holy to the LORD. 24 In the Jubilee year the field will return to the one from whom he bought it, the one to whom it belongs as landed property. 25 Every conversion value must be calculated by the standard of the sanctuary shekel; twenty gerahs to the shekel.

REDEMPTION OF THE FIRSTBORN

26 "'Surely no man may consecrate a firstborn that already belongs to the LORD as a firstborn among the animals; whether it is an ox or a sheep, it belongs to the LORD. 27 If, however, it is among the unclean animals, he may ransom it according to its conversion value and must add one-fifth to it, but if it is not redeemed it must be sold according to its conversion value.

THINGS PERMANENTLY DEDICATED TO THE LORD

28 "'Surely anything that a man permanently dedicates to the LORD from all that belongs to him, whether from people, animals, or his landed property, must be neither sold nor redeemed; anything permanently dedicated is most holy to the LORD. 29 Any human being who is permanently dedicated to the LORD must not be ransomed; such a person must be put to death.

REDEMPTION OF THE TITHE

[30] "'Any tithe of the land, from the grain of the land or from the fruit of the trees, belongs to the LORD; it is holy to the LORD. [31] If a man redeems part of his tithe, however, he must add one-fifth to it. [32] All the tithe of herds or flocks, everything which passes under the rod, the tenth one will be holy to the LORD. [33] The owner must not examine the animals to distinguish between good and bad, and he must not exchange it. If, however, he does exchange it, both the original animal and its substitute will be holy and must not be redeemed.'"

FINAL COLOPHON

[34] These are the commandments which the LORD commanded Moses to tell the Israelites at Mount Sinai.

THE *Lord* IS slow to anger & ABOUNDING in loyal love

MEMORY VERSE

"The LORD is slow to anger and abounding in loyal love, forgiving iniquity and transgression, but by no means clearing the guilty, visiting the iniquity of the fathers on the children until the third and fourth generations."

Numbers 14:18

Numbers

INTRODUCTION

God's Justice

Numbers is a message of both great tragedy and great hope. This book continues the narrative of God's people as it describes their great failure to believe His promises. Tragedy struck early as God's people rebelled. However, hope was born out of God's promise to remain faithful to His people, even though that meant the current generation would not experience the promised land.

This book of the Bible is named for the two censuses taken of the Israelite fighting men. Moses conducted the first census and sent the spies into the land of Canaan. When the spies came back with a negative report, the people rebelled. They were sure that God could not deliver them if they tried to conquer the land of Canaan—so God disciplined them. Numbers chronicles the wanderings of the Israelites in the wilderness for over forty years. The second census, taken forty years later, as the Israelites prepared to enter the promised land, was a reminder to the Israelites of what had happened with their parents' generation and the consequences of their disobedience. God would finally allow His people to enter the land promised to them.

Numbers is part of the Pentateuch, the first five books of the Bible whose authorship are commonly attributed to Moses by evangelical scholars. Like the other books in the Pentateuch, Numbers was written to the generation of Israelites headed into the promised land. It was written shortly before the Israelites entered the land of Canaan, around 1400 B.C.

Numbers reminds us of God's faithfulness. While the first generation of Israelites rebelled and needed discipline, God did not forget nor abandon His promise. He remained faithful to His covenant and allowed the next generation to enter into and live in the promised land. We can be encouraged to love God greatly, confident in the truth that, regardless of our unfaithfulness, grumbling, and complaining, God remains faithful.

South Africa

TOP SPOKEN LANGUAGES
Afrikaans and English
POPULATION
58,425,000
UNREACHED POPULATION
971,000
PROFESSING CHRISTIANS
77.0%

Marissa's Home

Say a Prayer Today

Pray for Marissa and those like her who have moved their lives to new countries. Pray for them as they transition and build new lives. Pray God will give them peace and hope in uncertain circumstances.

HISTORY BIT

In 1665 Johann van Arkel arrived at the Cape of Good Hope. It was originally a trading outpost for sailors traveling to the East Indies, and it had grown into a small farming community. Arkel was the first Dutch Reformed Church minister in South Africa.*

Source Information:
https://joshuaproject.net/countries/SF
*John Bowden, A Chronology of World Christianity (New York, NY: Continuum, 2007), 314.

MARISSA'S STORY

Four months after my second child was born, my husband and I decided, rather suddenly, to move from our home in South Africa to Canada. Initially, things happen slowly as we waited for the house to sell and completed paperwork and visa applications, things happened slowly. Then, what seemed like overnight, we sold our house and furniture, purchased our plane tickets, and packed up our lives. Finally everything was in place for our big move, and that's when it all came loose.

My oldest child came down with a cold, tonsillitis, kidney problems, a high fever, and a rash that left both my pediatrician and me confused and concerned. I found myself sitting in a hospital bed with my sick four-year-old who was scheduled for surgery the next day, realizing that he might not be well enough to fly in five days. In desperation I started praying as he lay sleeping in my arms.

I discerned that I never cleared this huge step with my heavenly Father. Instead of seeking His wisdom, I used my own wisdom, logic, and discernment to make these plans. It was a busy time, full of the thirty seconds of prayer about everything, without any deliberate prayer about one of the biggest decisions of our lives.

I was overcome with guilt. As I sat in that hospital, I surrendered to Him. If He had a purpose for us there, we would stay in that scary, uncertain place. As I came undone, I could feel the Holy Spirit moving in me, comforting me. I perceived that the Lord was not against us moving but that He was against us doing it on our own. In that hospital bed I committed our family's comings and goings to the Creator. As peace settled in my heart, my son's fever broke, and the third course of antibiotics started working.

That night forever changed my way of making decisions. Praise be to the Lord who is slow to anger, who is abounding in love, and who forgives my sin and rebellion.

4 WEEK READING PLAN

LOVE HIS WORD

MONDAY	TUESDAY	WEDNESDAY	THURSDAY	FRIDAY
Numbers 1	Numbers 2-3	Numbers 4-5	Numbers 6-7	Numbers 8-9
SOAP Hebrews 11:1-3	SOAP Hebrews 11:4	SOAP Hebrews 11:5-6	SOAP Hebrews 11:7	SOAP Hebrews 11:8-10
Numbers 10-11	Numbers 12	Numbers 13-14	Numbers 15-16	Numbers 17-18
SOAP Hebrews 11:11-12	SOAP Hebrews 11:13-14	SOAP Numbers 14:18	SOAP Hebrews 11:15-16	SOAP Hebrews 11:17-19
Numbers 19-20	Numbers 21	Numbers 22-23	Numbers 24-25	Numbers 26-27
SOAP Hebrews 11:20-22	SOAP Hebrews 11:23-25	SOAP Hebrews 11:26	SOAP Hebrews 11:27-29	SOAP Hebrews 11:30-31
Numbers 28-29	Numbers 30-31	Numbers 32	Numbers 33-34	Numbers 35-36
SOAP Hebrews 11:32-34	SOAP Hebrews 11:35-36	SOAP Hebrews 11:37-38	SOAP Hebrews 11:39-40	SOAP Hebrews 12:1-2

ORGANIZING THE CENSUS OF THE ISRAELITES

1 Now the LORD spoke to Moses in the tent of meeting in the
desert of Sinai on the first day of the second month of the second year after the Israelites departed from the land of Egypt.
He said: 2“Take a census of the entire Israelite community by
their clans and families, counting the name of every individual
male. 3You and Aaron are to number all in Israel who can serve
in the army, those who are twenty years old or older, by their divisions. 4And to help you there is to be a man from each tribe,
each man the head of his family. 5Now these are the names of
the men who are to help you:
from Reuben, Elizur son of Shedeur;
6 from Simeon, Shelumiel son of Zurishaddai;
7 from Judah, Nahshon son of Amminadab;
8 from Issachar, Nethanel son of Zuar;
9 from Zebulun, Eliab son of Helon;
10 from the sons of Joseph:
from Ephraim, Elishama son of Ammihud;
from Manasseh, Gamaliel son of Pedahzur;
11 from Benjamin, Abidan son of Gideoni;
12 from Dan, Ahiezer son of Ammishaddai;
13 from Asher, Pagiel son of Ocran;
14 from Gad, Eliasaph son of Deuel;
15 from Naphtali, Ahira son of Enan.”

THE CENSUS OF THE TRIBES

16These were the ones chosen from the community, leaders of their
ancestral tribes. They were the heads of the thousands of Israel.
17So Moses and Aaron took these men who had been mentioned specifically by name, 18and they assembled the entire
community together on the first day of the second month. Then
the people recorded their ancestry by their clans and families,
and the men who were twenty years old or older were listed by
name individually, 19just as the LORD had commanded Moses.
And so he numbered them in the desert of Sinai.
20And they were as follows:
The descendants of Reuben, the firstborn son of Israel: According to the records of their clans and families, all the males
twenty years old or older who could serve in the army were listed
by name individually. 21Those of them who were numbered from
the tribe of Reuben were 46,500.
22From the descendants of Simeon: According to the records of
their clans and families, all the males numbered of them twenty
years old or older who could serve in the army were listed by
name individually. 23Those of them who were numbered from
the tribe of Simeon were 59,300.
24From the descendants of Gad: According to the records of
their clans and families, all the males twenty years old or older who could serve in the army were listed by name. 25Those of
them who were numbered from the tribe of Gad were 45,650.
26From the descendants of Judah: According to the records of
their clans and families, all the males twenty years old or older who could serve in the army were listed by name. 27Those of
them who were numbered from the tribe of Judah were 74,600.

[28]From the descendants of Issachar: According to the records
of their clans and families, all the males twenty years old or older who could serve in the army were listed by name. [29]Those
of them who were numbered from the tribe of Issachar were
54,400.
[30]From the descendants of Zebulun: According to the records
of their clans and families, all the males twenty years old or older
who could serve in the army were listed by name. [31]Those of them
who were numbered from the tribe of Zebulun were 57,400.
[32]From the sons of Joseph:

From the descendants of Ephraim: According to the records
of their clans and families, all the males twenty years old or
older who could serve in the army were listed by name. [33]Those
of them who were numbered from the tribe of Ephraim were
40,500. [34]From the descendants of Manasseh: According to the
records of their clans and families, all the males twenty years
old or older who could serve in the army were listed by name.
[35]Those of them who were numbered from the tribe of Manasseh were 32,200.

[36]From the descendants of Benjamin: According to the records of their clans and families, all the males twenty years old or
older who could serve in the army were listed by name. [37]Those
of them who were numbered from the tribe of Benjamin were
35,400.

[38]From the descendants of Dan: According to the records of
their clans and families, all the males twenty years old or older who could serve in the army were listed by name. [39]Those of
them who were numbered from the tribe of Dan were 62,700.
[40]From the descendants of Asher: According to the records of
their clans and families, all the males twenty years old or older who could serve in the army were listed by name. [41]Those of
them who were numbered from the tribe of Asher were 41,500.
[42]From the descendants of Naphtali: According to the records of their clans and families, all the males twenty years old or
older who could serve in the army were listed by name. [43]Those
of them who were numbered from the tribe of Naphtali were
53,400.
[44]These were the men whom Moses and Aaron numbered
along with the twelve leaders of Israel, each of whom was from
his own family. [45]All the Israelites who were twenty years old or
older, who could serve in Israel's army, were numbered according to their families. [46]And all those numbered totaled 603,550.

THE EXEMPTION OF THE LEVITES

[47]But the Levites, according to the tribe of their fathers, were not
numbered among them. [48]The LORD had said to Moses, [49]"Only
the tribe of Levi you must not number or count with the other
Israelites. [50]But appoint the Levites over the tabernacle of the
testimony, over all its furnishings and over everything in it. They
must carry the tabernacle and all its furnishings; and they must
attend to it and camp around it. [51]Whenever the tabernacle is
to move, the Levites must take it down, and whenever the tabernacle is to be reassembled, the Levites must set it up. Any unauthorized person who approaches it must be killed.

52 "The Israelites will camp according to their divisions, each
man in his camp, and each man by his standard. 53 But the Levites
must camp around the tabernacle of the testimony, so that the
LORD's anger will not fall on the Israelite community. The Levites
are responsible for the care of the tabernacle of the testimony."
54 The Israelites did according to all that the LORD commanded
Moses—that is what they did.

THE ARRANGEMENT OF THE TRIBES

2 The LORD spoke to Moses and to Aaron: 2 "Every one of the
Israelites must camp under his standard with the emblems
of his family; they must camp at some distance around the tent
of meeting.

THE TRIBES ON THE EAST

3 "Now those who will be camping on the east, toward the sunrise, are the divisions of the camp of Judah under their standard.
The leader of the people of Judah is Nahshon son of Amminadab.
4 Those numbered in his division are 74,600. 5 Those who will be
camping next to them are the tribe of Issachar. The leader of the
people of Issachar is Nethanel son of Zuar. 6 Those numbered in his
division are 54,400. 7 Next will be the tribe of Zebulun. The leader of
the people of Zebulun is Eliab son of Helon. 8 Those numbered in his
division are 57,400. 9 All those numbered of the camp of Judah, according to their divisions, are 186,400. They will travel at the front.

THE TRIBES ON THE SOUTH

10 "On the south will be the divisions of the camp of Reuben under their standard. The leader of the people of Reuben is Elizur
son of Shedeur. 11 Those numbered in his division are 46,500.
12 Those who will be camping next to them are the tribe of Simeon. The leader of the people of Simeon is Shelumiel son of Zurishaddai. 13 Those numbered in his division are 59,300. 14 Next
will be the tribe of Gad. The leader of the people of Gad is Eliasaph son of Deuel. 15 Those numbered in his division are 45,650.
16 All those numbered of the camp of Reuben, according to their
divisions, are 151,450. They will travel second.

THE TRIBE IN THE CENTER

17 "Then the tent of meeting with the camp of the Levites will
travel in the middle of the camps. They will travel in the same
order as they camped, each in his own place under his standard.

THE TRIBES ON THE WEST

18 "On the west will be the divisions of the camp of Ephraim
under their standard. The leader of the people of Ephraim is
Elishama son of Ammihud. 19 Those numbered in his division are
40,500. 20 Next to them will be the tribe of Manasseh. The leader
of the people of Manasseh is Gamaliel son of Pedahzur. 21 Those
numbered in his division are 32,200. 22 Next will be the tribe of
Benjamin. The leader of the people of Benjamin is Abidan son
of Gideoni. 23 Those numbered in his division are 35,400. 24 All
those numbered of the camp of Ephraim, according to their divisions, are 108,100. They will travel third.

THE TRIBES ON THE NORTH

25 "On the north will be the divisions of the camp of Dan, under
their standards. The leader of the people of Dan is Ahiezer son
of Ammishaddai. 26 Those numbered in his division are 62,700.
27 Those who will be camping next to them are the tribe of Asher.
The leader of the people of Asher is Pagiel son of Ocran. 28 Those
numbered in his division are 41,500. 29 Next will be the tribe of
Naphtali. The leader of the people of Naphtali is Ahira son of
Enan. 30 Those numbered in his division are 53,400. 31 All those
numbered of the camp of Dan are 157,600. They will travel last,
under their standards."

SUMMARY

32 These are the Israelites, numbered according to their families.
All those numbered in the camps, by their divisions, are 603,550.
33 But the Levites were not numbered among the other Israelites, as the LORD commanded Moses.
34 So the Israelites did according to all that the LORD commanded Moses; that is the way they camped under their standards, and that is the way they traveled, each with his clan and
family.

THE SONS OF AARON

3 Now these are the records of Aaron and Moses when the
LORD spoke with Moses on Mount Sinai. 2 These are the
names of the sons of Aaron: Nadab the firstborn, Abihu, Eleazar, and Ithamar. 3 These are the names of the sons of Aaron,
the anointed priests, whom he consecrated to minister as
priests.
4 Nadab and Abihu died before the LORD when they offered
strange fire before the LORD in the desert of Sinai, and they had
no children. So Eleazar and Ithamar ministered as priests in the
presence of Aaron their father.

THE ASSIGNMENT OF THE LEVITES

5 The LORD spoke to Moses: 6 "Bring the tribe of Levi near, and
present them before Aaron the priest, that they may serve
him. 7 They are responsible for his needs and the needs of the
whole community before the tent of meeting, by attending to
the service of the tabernacle. 8 And they are responsible for
all the furnishings of the tent of meeting, and for the needs of
the Israelites, as they serve in the tabernacle. 9 You are to assign the Levites to Aaron and his sons; they will be assigned
exclusively to him out of all the Israelites. 10 So you are to appoint Aaron and his sons, and they will be responsible for their
priesthood, but the unauthorized person who comes near must
be put to death."
11 Then the LORD spoke to Moses: 12 "Look, I myself have taken
the Levites from among the Israelites instead of every firstborn who opens the womb among the Israelites. So the Levites
belong to me, 13 because all the firstborn are mine. When I destroyed all the firstborn in the land of Egypt, I set apart for myself all the firstborn in Israel, both man and beast. They belong
to me. I am the LORD."

THE NUMBERING OF THE LEVITES

14 Then the LORD spoke to Moses in the desert of Sinai: 15 "Number the Levites by their clans and their families; every male from a month old and upward you are to number." 16 So Moses numbered them according to the word of the LORD, just as he had been commanded.

THE SUMMARY OF FAMILIES

17 These were the sons of Levi by their names: Gershon, Kohath, and Merari.

18 These are the names of the sons of Gershon by their families: Libni and Shimei. 19 The sons of Kohath by their families were: Amram, Izhar, Hebron, and Uzziel. 20 The sons of Merari by their families were Mahli and Mushi. These are the families of the Levites by their clans.

THE NUMBERING OF THE GERSHONITES

21 From Gershon came the family of the Libnites and the family of the Shimeites; these were the families of the Gershonites. 22 Those of them who were numbered, counting every male from a month old and upward, were 7,500. 23 The families of the Gershonites were to camp behind the tabernacle toward the west. 24 Now the leader of the clan of the Gershonites was Eliasaph son of Lael.

25 And the responsibilities of the Gershonites in the tent of meeting included the tabernacle, the tent with its covering, the curtain at the entrance of the tent of meeting, 26 the hangings of the courtyard, the curtain at the entrance to the courtyard that surrounded the tabernacle and the altar, and their ropes, plus all the service connected with these things.

THE NUMBERING OF THE KOHATHITES

27 From Kohath came the family of the Amramites, the family of the Izharites, the family of the Hebronites, and the family of the Uzzielites; these were the families of the Kohathites. 28 Counting every male from a month old and upward, there were 8,600. They were responsible for the care of the sanctuary. 29 The families of the Kohathites were to camp on the south side of the tabernacle. 30 Now the leader of the clan of the families of the Kohathites was Elizaphan son of Uzziel.

31 Their responsibilities included the ark, the table, the lampstand, the altars, and the utensils of the sanctuary with which they ministered, the curtain, and all their service. 32 Now the head of all the Levitical leaders was Eleazar son of Aaron the priest. He was appointed over those who were responsible for the sanctuary.

THE NUMBERING OF MERARI

33 From Merari came the family of the Mahlites and the family of the Mushites; these were the families of Merari. 34 Those of them who were numbered, counting every male from a month old and upward, were 6,200. 35 Now the leader of the clan of the families of Merari was Zuriel son of Abihail. These were to camp on the north side of the tabernacle.

36 The appointed responsibilities of the Merarites included the frames of the tabernacle, its crossbars, its posts, its sockets, its utensils, plus all the service connected with these things, 37 and the pillars of the courtyard all around, with their sockets, their pegs, and their ropes.

38 But those who were to camp in front of the tabernacle on the east, in front of the tent of meeting, were Moses, Aaron, and his sons. They were responsible for the needs of the sanctuary and for the needs of the Israelites, but the unauthorized person who approached was to be put to death. 39 All who were numbered of the Levites, whom Moses and Aaron numbered by the word of the LORD, according to their families, every male from a month old and upward, were 22,000.

THE SUBSTITUTION FOR THE FIRSTBORN

40 Then the LORD said to Moses, "Number all the firstborn males of the Israelites from a month old and upward, and take the number of their names. 41 And take the Levites for me—I am the LORD—instead of all the firstborn males among the Israelites, and the livestock of the Levites instead of all the firstborn of the livestock of the Israelites." 42 So Moses numbered all the firstborn males among the Israelites, as the LORD had commanded him. 43 And all the firstborn males, by the number of the names from a month old and upward, totaled 22,273.

44 Then the LORD spoke to Moses: 45 "Take the Levites instead of all the firstborn males among the Israelites, and the livestock of the Levites instead of their livestock. And the Levites will be mine. I am the LORD. 46 And for the redemption of the 273 firstborn males of the Israelites who exceed the number of the Levites, 47 collect five shekels for each one individually; you are to collect this amount in the currency of the sanctuary shekel (this shekel is twenty gerahs). 48 And give the money for the redemption of the excess number of them to Aaron and his sons."

49 So Moses took the redemption money from those who were in excess of those redeemed by the Levites. 50 From the firstborn males of the Israelites he collected the money, 1,365 shekels, according to the sanctuary shekel. 51 Moses gave the redemption money to Aaron and his sons, according to the word of the LORD, as the LORD had commanded Moses.

REFLECT

Why was it so significant to God that the firstborn males and the firstborn of all of the flocks and herds be set apart for Him? What does this communicate to us, today, about sacrifice and dedication to God?

THE SERVICE OF THE KOHATHITES

4 Then the LORD spoke to Moses and Aaron: 2 "Take a census of the Kohathites from among the Levites, by their families and by their clans, 3 from thirty years old and upward to fifty years old, all who enter the company to do the work in the tent of meeting. 4 This is the service of the Kohathites in the tent of meeting, relating to the most holy things. 5 When it is time for the camp to journey, Aaron and his sons must come and take down the screening curtain and cover the ark of the testimony with it. 6 Then they must put over it a covering of fine leather and spread over that a cloth entirely of blue, and then they must insert its poles.

7 "On the table of the presence they must spread a blue cloth, and put on it the dishes, the pans, the bowls, and the pitchers for pouring, and the Bread of the Presence must be on it continually.

[8]They must spread over them a scarlet cloth, and cover the same
with a covering of fine leather; and they must insert its poles.
[9]"They must take a blue cloth and cover the lampstand of the
light, with its lamps, its wick-trimmers, its trays, and all its oil
vessels, with which they service it. [10]Then they must put it with
all its utensils in a covering of fine leather, and put it on a carrying beam.
[11]"They must spread a blue cloth on the gold altar, and cover
it with a covering of fine leather; and they must insert its poles.
[12]Then they must take all the utensils of the service, with which
they serve in the sanctuary, put them in a blue cloth, cover them
with a covering of fine leather, and put them on a carrying beam.
[13]Also, they must take away the ashes from the altar and spread
a purple cloth over it. [14]Then they must place on it all its implements with which they serve there—the trays, the meat forks, the
shovels, the basins, and all the utensils of the altar—and they must
spread on it a covering of fine leather, and then insert its poles.
[15]"When Aaron and his sons have finished covering the sanctuary and all the furnishings of the sanctuary, when the camp is
ready to journey, then the Kohathites will come to carry them;
but they must not touch any holy thing, or they will die. These are
the responsibilities of the Kohathites with the tent of meeting.
[16]"The appointed responsibility of Eleazar son of Aaron the
priest is for the oil for the light, and the spiced incense, and the
daily grain offering, and the anointing oil; he also has the appointed responsibility over all the tabernacle with all that is in
it, over the sanctuary and over all its furnishings."
[17]Then the LORD spoke to Moses and Aaron: [18]"Do not allow the
tribe of the families of the Kohathites to be cut off from among
the Levites; [19]but in order that they will live and not die when
they approach the most holy things, do this for them: Aaron and
his sons will go in and appoint each man to his service and his
responsibility. [20]But the Kohathites are not to go in to watch
while the holy things are being covered, or they will die."

THE SERVICE OF THE GERSHONITES

[21]Then the LORD spoke to Moses: [22]"Also take a census of the Gershonites also, by their clans and by their families. [23]You must
number them from thirty years old and upward to fifty years old,
all who enter the company to do the work of the tent of meeting.
[24]This is the service of the families of Gershonites, as they serve
and carry it. [25]They must carry the curtains for the tabernacle and
the tent of meeting with its covering, the covering of fine leather
that is over it, the curtains for the entrance of the tent of meeting, [26]the hangings for the courtyard, the curtain for the entrance
of the gate of the court, which is around the tabernacle and the
altar, and their ropes, along with all the furnishings for their service and everything that is made for them. So they are to serve.
[27]"All the service of the Gershonites, whether carrying loads
or for any of their work, will be at the direction of Aaron and his
sons. You will assign them all their tasks as their responsibility.
[28]This is the service of the families of the Gershonites concerning the tent of meeting. Their responsibilities will be under the
authority of Ithamar son of Aaron the priest.

THE SERVICE OF THE MERARITES

29 "As for the sons of Merari, you are to number them by their families and by their clans. 30 You must number them from thirty years old and upward to fifty years old, all who enter the company to do the work of the tent of meeting. 31 This is what they are responsible to carry as their entire service in the tent of meeting: the frames of the tabernacle, its crossbars, its posts, its sockets, 32 and the posts of the surrounding courtyard with their sockets, tent pegs, and ropes, along with all their furnishings and everything for their service. You are to assign by name the items that each man is responsible to carry. 33 This is the service of the families of the Merarites, their entire service concerning the tent of meeting, under the authority of Ithamar son of Aaron the priest."

SUMMARY

34 So Moses and Aaron and the leaders of the community numbered the Kohathites by their families and by clans, 35 from thirty years old and upward to fifty years old, everyone who entered the company for the work in the tent of meeting; 36 and those of them numbered by their families were 2,750. 37 These were those numbered from the families of the Kohathites, everyone who served in the tent of meeting, whom Moses and Aaron numbered according to the word of the LORD by the authority of Moses.

38 Those numbered from the Gershonites, by their families and by their clans, 39 from thirty years old and upward to fifty years old, everyone who entered the company for the work in the tent of meeting—40 those of them numbered by their families, by their clans, were 2,630. 41 These were those numbered from the families of the Gershonites, everyone who served in the tent of meeting, whom Moses and Aaron numbered according to the word of the LORD.

42 Those numbered from the families of the Merarites, by their families, by their clans, 43 from thirty years old and upward to fifty years old, everyone who entered the company for the work in the tent of meeting—44 those of them numbered by their families were 3,200. 45 These are those numbered from the families of the Merarites, whom Moses and Aaron numbered according to the word of the LORD by the authority of Moses.

46 All who were numbered of the Levites, whom Moses, Aaron, and the leaders of Israel numbered by their families and by their clans, 47 from thirty years old and upward to fifty years old, everyone who entered to do the work of service and the work of carrying relating to the tent of meeting—48 those of them numbered were 8,580. 49 According to the word of the LORD they were numbered, by the authority of Moses, each according to his service and according to what he was to carry. Thus were they numbered by him, as the LORD had commanded Moses.

SEPARATION OF THE UNCLEAN

5 Then the LORD spoke to Moses: 2 "Command the Israelites to expel from the camp every leper, everyone who has a discharge, and whoever becomes defiled by a corpse. 3 You must expel both men and women; you must put them outside the camp,

so that they will not defile their camps, among which I live." 4 So
the Israelites did so, and expelled them outside the camp. As the
LORD had spoken to Moses, so the Israelites did.

RESTITUTION FOR SIN

5 Then the LORD spoke to Moses: 6 "Tell the Israelites, 'When a
man or a woman commits any sin that people commit, thereby
breaking faith with the LORD, and that person is found guilty,
7 then he must confess his sin that he has committed and must
make full reparation, add one-fifth to it, and give it to whomever he wronged. 8 But if the individual has no close relative to
whom reparation can be made for the wrong, the reparation for
the wrong must be paid to the LORD for the priest, in addition
to the ram of atonement by which atonement is made for him.
9 Every offering of all the Israelites' holy things that they bring
to the priest will be his. 10 Every man's holy things will be his;
whatever any man gives the priest will be his.'"

THE JEALOUSY ORDEAL

11 The LORD spoke to Moses: 12 "Speak to the Israelites and tell
them, 'If any man's wife goes astray and behaves unfaithfully toward him, 13 and a man goes to bed with her for sexual relations
without her husband knowing it, and it is undetected that she
has defiled herself since there was no witness against her, nor
was she caught in the act—14 and if jealous feelings come over
him and he becomes suspicious of his wife when she is defiled,
or if jealous feelings come over him and he becomes suspicious
of his wife, when she is not defiled—15 then the man must bring
his wife to the priest, and he must bring the offering required
for her, one-tenth of an ephah of barley meal; he must not pour
olive oil on it or put frankincense on it because it is a grain offering of suspicion, a grain offering for remembering, for bringing iniquity to remembrance.

16 "'Then the priest will bring her near and have her stand before the LORD. 17 The priest will then take holy water in a pottery
jar, and take some of the dust that is on the floor of the tabernacle, and put it into the water. 18 Then the priest will have the
woman stand before the LORD, and he will uncover the woman's
head and put the grain offering for remembering in her hands,
which is the grain offering of suspicion. The priest will hold in
his hand the bitter water that brings a curse. 19 Then the priest
will put the woman under oath and say to her, "If no other man
has gone to bed with you, and if you have not gone astray and
become defiled while under your husband's authority, may you
be free from this bitter water that brings a curse. 20 But if you
have gone astray while under your husband's authority, and if
you have defiled yourself and some man other than your husband has had sexual relations with you—" 21 (then the priest will
put the woman under the oath of the curse and will say to her)
"the LORD make you an attested curse among your people if the
LORD makes your thigh fall away and your abdomen swell, 22 and
this water that causes the curse will go into your stomach and
make your abdomen swell and your thigh rot." Then the woman
must say, "Amen, amen."

23 "'Then the priest will write these curses on a scroll and then scrape them off into the bitter water. 24 He will make the woman drink the bitter water that brings a curse, and the water that brings a curse will enter her to produce bitterness. 25 The priest will take the grain offering of suspicion from the woman's hand, wave the grain offering before the LORD, and bring it to the altar. 26 Then the priest will take a handful of the grain offering as its memorial portion, burn it on the altar, and afterward make the woman drink the water. 27 When he has made her drink the water, then if she has defiled herself and behaved unfaithfully toward her husband, the water that brings a curse will enter her to produce bitterness—her abdomen will swell, her thigh will fall away, and the woman will become a curse among her people. 28 But if the woman has not defiled herself, and is clean, then she will be free of ill effects and will be able to bear children.

29 "'This is the law for cases of jealousy, when a wife, while under her husband's authority, goes astray and defiles herself, 30 or when jealous feelings come over a man and he becomes suspicious of his wife; then he must have the woman stand before the LORD, and the priest will carry out all this law upon her. 31 Then the man will be free from iniquity, but that woman will bear the consequences of her iniquity.'"

THE NAZIRITE VOW

6 Then the LORD spoke to Moses: 2 "Speak to the Israelites, and tell them, 'When someone—either a man or a woman—takes a special vow, to take a vow as a Nazirite, to separate himself to the LORD, 3 he must separate himself from wine and strong drink; he must drink neither vinegar made from wine nor vinegar made from strong drink, nor may he drink any juice of grapes, nor eat fresh grapes or raisins. 4 All the days of his separation he must not eat anything that is produced by the grapevine, from seed to skin.

5 "'All the days of the vow of his separation no razor may be used on his head until the time is fulfilled for which he separated himself to the LORD. He will be holy, and he must let the locks of hair on his head grow long.

6 "'All the days that he separates himself to the LORD he must not contact a dead body. 7 He must not defile himself even for his father or his mother or his brother or his sister if they die, because the separation for his God is on his head. 8 All the days of his separation he must be holy to the LORD.

CONTINGENCIES FOR DEFILEMENT

9 "'If anyone dies very suddenly beside him and he defiles his consecrated head, then he must shave his head on the day of his purification—on the seventh day he must shave it. 10 On the eighth day he is to bring two turtledoves or two young pigeons to the priest, to the entrance to the tent of meeting. 11 Then the priest will offer one for a purification offering and the other as a burnt offering, and make atonement for him, because of his transgression in regard to the corpse. So he must reconsecrate his head on that day. 12 He must rededicate to the LORD the days of his separation and bring a male lamb in its first year as a reparation offering, but the former days will not be counted because his separation was defiled.

FULFILLING THE VOWS

13 "'Now this is the law of the Nazirite: When the days of his
separation are fulfilled, he must be brought to the entrance
of the tent of meeting, 14 and he must present his offering to
the LORD: one male lamb in its first year without blemish for
a burnt offering, one ewe lamb in its first year without blemish for a purification offering, one ram without blemish for a
peace offering, 15 and a basket of bread made without yeast,
cakes of fine flour mixed with olive oil, wafers made without
yeast and smeared with olive oil, and their grain offering and
their drink offerings.

16 "'Then the priest must present all these before the LORD and
offer his purification offering and his burnt offering. 17 Then he
must offer the ram as a peace offering to the LORD along with
the basket of bread made without yeast; the priest must also offer his grain offering and his drink offering.

18 "'Then the Nazirite must shave his consecrated head at the
entrance to the tent of meeting and must take the hair from his
consecrated head and put it on the fire where the peace offering is burning. 19 And the priest must take the boiled shoulder
of the ram, one cake made without yeast from the basket, and
one wafer made without yeast, and put them on the hands of
the Nazirite after he has shaved his consecrated head; 20 then
the priest must wave them as a wave offering before the LORD;
it is a holy portion for the priest, together with the breast of the
wave offering and the thigh of the raised offering. After this the
Nazirite may drink wine.

21 "'This is the law of the Nazirite who vows to the LORD his offering according to his separation, as well as whatever else he
can provide. Thus he must fulfill his vow that he makes, according to the law of his separation.'"

THE PRIESTLY BENEDICTION

22 The LORD spoke to Moses: 23 "Tell Aaron and his sons, 'This is
the way you are to bless the Israelites. Say to them:

24 "The LORD bless you and protect you;
25 The LORD make his face to shine upon you,
and be gracious to you;
26 The LORD lift up his countenance upon you
and give you peace."'

27 "So they will put my name on the Israelites, and I will bless
them."

THE LEADER'S OFFERINGS

7 When Moses had completed setting up the tabernacle, he
anointed it and consecrated it and all its furnishings, and he
anointed and consecrated the altar and all its utensils. 2 Then
the leaders of Israel, the heads of their clans, made an offering.
They were the leaders of the tribes; they were the ones who had
been supervising the numbering. 3 They brought their offerings
before the LORD, six covered carts and twelve oxen—one cart for
every two of the leaders, and an ox for each one; and they presented them in front of the tabernacle.

THE DISTRIBUTION OF THE GIFTS

[4]Then the LORD spoke to Moses: [5]"Receive these gifts from them,
that they may be used in doing the work of the tent of meeting;
and you must give them to the Levites, to every man as his service requires."

[6]So Moses accepted the carts and the oxen and gave them to
the Levites. [7]He gave two carts and four oxen to the Gershonites, as their service required; [8]and he gave four carts and eight
oxen to the Merarites, as their service required, under the authority of Ithamar son of Aaron the priest. [9]But to the Kohathites he gave none, because the service of the holy things, which
they carried on their shoulders, was their responsibility.

THE TIME OF PRESENTATION

[10]The leaders offered gifts for the dedication of the altar when
it was anointed. And the leaders presented their offering before the altar. [11]For the LORD said to Moses, "They must present their offering, one leader for each day, for the dedication
of the altar."

THE TRIBAL OFFERINGS

[12]The one who presented his offering on the first day was Nahshon son of Amminadab, from the tribe of Judah. [13]His offering
was one silver platter weighing 130 shekels, and one silver sprinkling bowl weighing 70 shekels, both according to the sanctuary shekel, each of them full of fine flour mixed with olive oil as
a grain offering; [14]one gold pan weighing 10 shekels, full of incense; [15]one young bull, one ram, and one male lamb in its first
year, for a burnt offering; [16]one male goat for a purification offering; [17]and for the sacrifice of peace offerings: two bulls, five
rams, five male goats, and five male lambs in their first year. This
was the offering of Nahshon son of Amminadab.

[18]On the second day Nethanel son of Zuar, leader of Issachar,
presented an offering. [19]He offered for his offering one silver
platter weighing 130 shekels and one silver sprinkling bowl
weighing 70 shekels, both according to the sanctuary shekel,
each of them full of fine flour mixed with olive oil as a grain offering; [20]one gold pan weighing 10 shekels, full of incense; [21]one
young bull, one ram, and one male lamb in its first year, for a
burnt offering; [22]one male goat for a purification offering; [23]and
for the sacrifice of peace offerings: two bulls, five rams, five male
goats, and five male lambs in their first year. This was the offering of Nethanel son of Zuar.

[24]On the third day Eliab son of Helon, leader of the Zebulunites, presented an offering. [25]His offering was one silver platter
weighing 130 shekels and one silver sprinkling bowl weighing
70 shekels, both according to the sanctuary shekel, each of them
full of fine flour mixed with olive oil as a grain offering; [26]one
gold pan weighing 10 shekels, full of incense; [27]one young bull,
one ram, and one male lamb in its first year, for a burnt offering; [28]one male goat for a purification offering; [29]and for the
sacrifice of peace offerings: two bulls, five rams, five male goats,
and five male lambs in their first year. This was the offering of
Eliab son of Helon.

30 On the fourth day Elizur son of Shedeur, leader of the Reubenites, presented an offering. 31 His offering was one silver platter weighing 130 shekels and one silver sprinkling bowl weighing
70 shekels, both according to the sanctuary shekel, each of them
full of fine flour mixed with olive oil as a grain offering; 32 one
gold pan weighing 10 shekels, full of incense; 33 one young bull,
one ram, and one male lamb in its first year, for a burnt offering; 34 one male goat for a purification offering; 35 and for the
sacrifice of peace offerings: two bulls, five rams, five male goats,
and five lambs in their first year. This was the offering of Elizur
son of Shedeur.
36 On the fifth day Shelumiel son of Zurishaddai, leader of the
Simeonites, presented an offering. 37 His offering was one silver platter weighing 130 shekels and one silver sprinkling bowl
weighing 70 shekels, both according to the sanctuary shekel,
each of them full of fine flour mixed with olive oil as a grain offering; 38 one gold pan weighing 10 shekels, full of incense; 39 one
young bull, one ram, and one male lamb in its first year, for a
burnt offering; 40 one male goat for a purification offering; 41 and
for the sacrifice of peace offerings: two bulls, five rams, five male
goats, and five lambs in their first year. This was the offering of
Shelumiel son of Zurishaddai.
42 On the sixth day Eliasaph son of Deuel, leader of the Gadites,
presented an offering. 43 His offering was one silver platter weighing 130 shekels and one silver sprinkling bowl weighing 70 shekels, both according to the sanctuary shekel, each of them full of
fine flour mixed with olive oil as a grain offering; 44 one gold pan
weighing 10 shekels, full of incense; 45 one young bull, one ram,
and one male lamb in its first year, for a burnt offering; 46 one male
goat for a purification offering; 47 and for the sacrifice of peace
offerings: two bulls, five rams, five male goats, and five lambs in
their first year. This was the offering of Eliasaph son of Deuel.
48 On the seventh day Elishama son of Ammihud, leader of the
Ephraimites, presented an offering. 49 His offering was one silver platter weighing 130 shekels and one silver sprinkling bowl
weighing 70 shekels, both according to the sanctuary shekel,
each of them full of fine flour mixed with olive oil as a grain offering; 50 one gold pan weighing 10 shekels, full of incense; 51 one
young bull, one ram, and one male lamb in its first year, for a
burnt offering; 52 one male goat for a purification offering; 53 and
for the sacrifice of peace offerings: two bulls, five rams, five male
goats, and five lambs in their first year. This was the offering of
Elishama son of Ammihud.
54 On the eighth day Gamaliel son of Pedahzur, leader of the
Manassehites, presented an offering. 55 His offering was one silver platter weighing 130 shekels and one silver sprinkling bowl
weighing 70 shekels, both according to the sanctuary shekel,
each of them full of fine flour mixed with olive oil as a grain offering; 56 one gold pan weighing 10 shekels, full of incense; 57 one
young bull, one ram, and one male lamb in its first year, for a
burnt offering; 58 one male goat for a purification offering; 59 and
for the sacrifice of peace offerings: two bulls, five rams, five male
goats, and five lambs in their first year. This was the offering of
Gamaliel son of Pedahzur.

60 On the ninth day Abidan son of Gideoni, leader of the Benjaminites, presented an offering. 61 His offering was one silver platter weighing 130 shekels and one silver sprinkling bowl weighing
70 shekels, both according to the sanctuary shekel, each of them
full of fine flour mixed with olive oil as a grain offering; 62 one
gold pan weighing 10 shekels, full of incense; 63 one young bull,
one ram, and one male lamb in its first year, for a burnt offering; 64 one male goat for a purification offering; 65 and for the
sacrifice of peace offerings: two bulls, five rams, five male goats,
and five lambs in their first year. This was the offering of Abidan son of Gideoni.

66 On the tenth day Ahiezer son of Ammishaddai, leader of the
Danites, presented an offering. 67 His offering was one silver platter weighing 130 shekels and one silver sprinkling bowl weighing 70 shekels, both according to the sanctuary shekel, each of
them full of fine flour mixed with olive oil as a grain offering;
68 one gold pan weighing 10 shekels, full of incense; 69 one young
bull, one ram, and one male lamb in its first year, for a burnt offering; 70 one male goat for a purification offering; 71 and for the
sacrifice of peace offerings: two bulls, five rams, five male goats,
and five lambs in their first year. This was the offering of Ahiezer son of Ammishaddai.

72 On the eleventh day Pagiel son of Ocran, leader of the Asherites, presented an offering. 73 His offering was one silver platter
weighing 130 shekels and one silver sprinkling bowl weighing
70 shekels, both according to the sanctuary shekel, each of them
full of fine flour mixed with olive oil as a grain offering; 74 one
gold pan weighing 10 shekels, full of incense; 75 one young bull,
one ram, and one male lamb in its first year, for a burnt offering; 76 one male goat for a purification offering; 77 and for the
sacrifice of peace offerings: two bulls, five rams, five male goats,
and five lambs in their first year. This was the offering of Pagiel
son of Ocran.

78 On the twelfth day Ahira son of Enan, leader of the Naphtalites, presented an offering. 79 His offering was one silver platter
weighing 130 shekels and one silver sprinkling bowl weighing 70
shekels, both according to the sanctuary shekel, each of them
full of fine flour mixed with olive oil as a grain offering; 80 one
gold pan weighing 10 shekels, full of incense; 81 one young bull,
one ram, and one male lamb in its first year, for a burnt offering; 82 one male goat for a purification offering; 83 and for the
sacrifice of peace offerings: two bulls, five rams, five male goats,
and five lambs in their first year. This was the offering of Ahira
son of Enan.

SUMMARY

84 This was the dedication for the altar from the leaders of Israel,
when it was anointed: twelve silver platters, twelve silver sprinkling bowls, and twelve gold pans. 85 Each silver platter weighed
130 shekels, and each silver sprinkling bowl weighed 70 shekels.
All the silver of the vessels weighed 2,400 shekels, according
to the sanctuary shekel. 86 The twelve gold pans full of incense
weighed 10 shekels each, according to the sanctuary shekel; all
the gold of the pans weighed 120 shekels. 87 All the animals for

the burnt offering were 12 young bulls, 12 rams, 12 male lambs in
their first year, with their grain offering, and 12 male goats for a
purification offering. 88 All the animals for the sacrifice for the
peace offering were 24 young bulls, 60 rams, 60 male goats, and
60 lambs in their first year. These were the dedication offerings
for the altar after it was anointed.

89 Now when Moses went into the tent of meeting to speak
with the LORD, he heard the voice speaking to him from above
the atonement lid that was on the ark of the testimony, from
between the two cherubim. Thus he spoke to him.

LIGHTING THE LAMPS

8 The LORD spoke to Moses: 2 "Speak to Aaron and tell him,
'When you set up the lamps, the seven lamps are to give light
in front of the lampstand.'"

3 And Aaron did so; he set up the lamps to face toward the front
of the lampstand, as the LORD commanded Moses. 4 This is how
the lampstand was made: It was beaten work in gold; from its
shaft to its flowers it was beaten work. According to the pattern
that the LORD had shown Moses, so he made the lampstand.

THE SEPARATION OF THE LEVITES

5 Then the LORD spoke to Moses: 6 "Take the Levites from among
the Israelites and purify them. 7 And do this to them to purify
them: Sprinkle water of purification on them; then have them
shave all their body and wash their clothes, and so purify themselves. 8 Then they are to take a young bull with its grain offering of
fine flour mixed with olive oil; and you are to take a second young
bull for a purification offering. 9 You are to bring the Levites before
the tent of meeting and assemble the entire community of the Israelites. 10 Then you are to bring the Levites before the LORD, and
the Israelites are to lay their hands on the Levites; 11 and Aaron is
to offer the Levites before the LORD as a wave offering from the
Israelites, that they may do the work of the LORD. 12 When the Levites lay their hands on the heads of the bulls, offer the one for a
purification offering and the other for a whole burnt offering to
the LORD, to make atonement for the Levites. 13 You are to have
the Levites stand before Aaron and his sons, and then offer them
as a wave offering to the LORD. 14 And so you are to separate the
Levites from among the Israelites, and the Levites will be mine.

15 "After this, the Levites will go in to do the work of the tent of
meeting. So you must cleanse them and offer them like a wave
offering. 16 For they are entirely given to me from among the Israelites. I have taken them for myself instead of all who open the
womb, the firstborn sons of all the Israelites. 17 For all the firstborn males among the Israelites are mine, both humans and animals; when I destroyed all the firstborn in the land of Egypt I set
them apart for myself. 18 So I have taken the Levites instead of all
the firstborn sons among the Israelites. 19 I have given the Levites
as a gift to Aaron and his sons from among the Israelites, to do
the work for the Israelites in the tent of meeting, and to make
atonement for the Israelites, so there will be no plague among
the Israelites when the Israelites come near the sanctuary."

20 So Moses and Aaron and the entire community of the

Israelites did this with the Levites. According to all that the LORD
commanded Moses concerning the Levites, this is what the Israelites did with them. 21 The Levites purified themselves and
washed their clothing; then Aaron presented them like a wave
offering before the LORD, and Aaron made atonement for them
to purify them. 22 After this, the Levites went in to do their work
in the tent of meeting before Aaron and before his sons. As the
LORD had commanded Moses concerning the Levites, so they did.

THE WORK OF THE LEVITES

23 Then the LORD spoke to Moses: 24 "This is what pertains to the
Levites: At the age of twenty-five years and upward one may begin
to join the company in the work of the tent of meeting, 25 and at
the age of fifty years they must retire from performing the work
and may no longer work. 26 They may assist their colleagues in the
tent of meeting to attend to needs, but they must do no work. This
is the way you must establish the Levites regarding their duties."

PASSOVER REGULATIONS

9 The LORD spoke to Moses in the desert of Sinai, in the first
month of the second year after they had come out of the land
of Egypt:

2 "The Israelites are to observe the Passover at its appointed
time. 3 In the fourteenth day of this month, at twilight, you are to
observe it at its appointed time; you must keep it in accordance
with all its statutes and all its customs." 4 So Moses instructed
the Israelites to observe the Passover. 5 And they observed the
Passover on the fourteenth day of the first month at twilight
in the desert of Sinai; in accordance with all that the LORD had
commanded Moses, so the Israelites did.

6 It happened that some men who were ceremonially defiled
by the dead body of a man could not keep the Passover on that
day, so they came before Moses and before Aaron on that day.
7 And those men said to Moses, "We are ceremonially defiled by
the dead body of a man; why are we kept back from offering the
LORD's offering at its appointed time among the Israelites?" 8 So
Moses said to them, "Remain here and I will hear what the LORD
will command concerning you."

9 The LORD spoke to Moses: 10 "Tell the Israelites, 'If any of you
or of your posterity become ceremonially defiled by touching a
dead body, or are on a journey far away, then he may observe the
Passover to the LORD. 11 They may observe it on the fourteenth
day of the second month at twilight; they are to eat it with bread
made without yeast and with bitter herbs. 12 They must not leave
any of it until morning, nor break any of its bones; they must observe it in accordance with every statute of the Passover.

13 "'But the man who is ceremonially clean, and was not on a
journey, and fails to keep the Passover, that person must be cut
off from his people. Because he did not bring the LORD's offering
at its appointed time, that man must bear his sin. 14 If a resident
foreigner lives among you and wants to keep the Passover to the
LORD, he must do so according to the statute of the Passover, and
according to its custom. You must have the same statute for the
resident foreigner and for the one who was born in the land.'"

THE LORD LEADS THE ISRAELITES BY THE CLOUD

15 On the day that the tabernacle was set up, the cloud covered
the tabernacle—the tent of the testimony—and from evening
until morning there was a fiery appearance over the tabernacle.
16 This is the way it used to be continually: The cloud would cover
it by day, and there was a fiery appearance by night. 17 Whenever the cloud was taken up from the tabernacle, then after
that the Israelites would begin their journey; and in whatever
place the cloud settled, there the Israelites would make camp.
18 At the commandment of the LORD the Israelites would begin their journey, and at the commandment of the LORD they
would make camp; as long as the cloud remained settled over
the tabernacle they would camp. 19 When the cloud remained
over the tabernacle many days, then the Israelites obeyed the
instructions of the LORD and did not journey.
20 When the cloud remained over the tabernacle a number of
days, they remained camped according to the LORD's commandment, and according to the LORD's commandment they would
journey. 21 And when the cloud remained only from evening until
morning, when the cloud was taken up the following morning,
then they traveled on. Whether by day or by night, when the cloud
was taken up they traveled. 22 Whether it was for two days, or a
month, or a year that the cloud prolonged its stay over the tabernacle, the Israelites remained camped without traveling; but
when it was taken up, they traveled on. 23 At the commandment
of the LORD they camped, and at the commandment of the LORD
they traveled on; they kept the instructions of the LORD according to the commandment of the LORD, by the authority of Moses.

THE BLOWING OF TRUMPETS

10 The LORD spoke to Moses: 2 "Make two trumpets of silver;
you are to make them from a single hammered piece. You
will use them for assembling the community and for directing the traveling of the camps. 3 When they blow them both, all
the community must come to you to the entrance of the tent
of meeting.
4 "But if they blow with one trumpet, then the leaders, the heads
of the thousands of Israel, must come to you. 5 When you blow
an alarm, then the camps that are located on the east side must
begin to travel. 6 And when you blow an alarm the second time,
then the camps that are located on the south side must begin to
travel. An alarm must be sounded for their journeys. 7 But when
you assemble the community, you must blow the trumpets, but
you must not sound an alarm. 8 The sons of Aaron, the priests,
must blow the trumpets, and they will be to you for an eternal
ordinance throughout your generations. 9 If you go to war in your
land against an adversary who opposes you, then you must sound
an alarm with the trumpets, and you will be remembered before
the LORD your God, and you will be saved from your enemies.
10 "Also, in the time when you rejoice, such as on your appointed festivals or at the beginnings of your months, you must
blow with your trumpets over your burnt offerings and over
the sacrifices of your peace offerings, so that they may become
a memorial for you before your God: I am the LORD your God."

THE JOURNEY FROM SINAI TO KADESH

[11]On the twentieth day of the second month, in the second year,
the cloud was taken up from the tabernacle of the testimony.
[12]So the Israelites set out on their journeys from the desert of
Sinai; and the cloud settled in the wilderness of Paran.

JUDAH BEGINS THE JOURNEY

[13]This was the first time they set out on their journey according
to the commandment of the LORD, by the authority of Moses.

[14]The standard of the camp of the Judahites set out first according to their companies, and over his company was Nahshon son of Amminadab.

[15]Over the company of the tribe of Issacharites was Nathanel
son of Zuar, [16]and over the company of the tribe of the Zebulunites was Eliab son of Helon. [17]Then the tabernacle was dismantled, and the sons of Gershon and the sons of Merari set out,
carrying the tabernacle.

JOURNEY ARRANGEMENTS FOR THE TRIBES

[18]The standard of the camp of Reuben set out according to their
companies; over his company was Elizur son of Shedeur. [19]Over
the company of the tribe of the Simeonites was Shelumiel son
of Zurishaddai, [20]and over the company of the tribe of the Gadites was Eliasaph son of Deuel. [21]And the Kohathites set out,
carrying the articles for the sanctuary; the tabernacle was to be
set up before they arrived. [22]And the standard of the camp of
the Ephraimites set out according to their companies; over his
company was Elishama son of Ammihud. [23]Over the company
of the tribe of the Manassehites was Gamaliel son of Pedahzur,
[24]and over the company of the tribe of Benjaminites was Abidan son of Gideoni.

[25]The standard of the camp of the Danites set out, which
was the rear guard of all the camps by their companies; over
his company was Ahiezer son of Ammishaddai. [26]Over the
company of the tribe of the Asherites was Pagiel son of Ocran, [27]and over the company of the tribe of the Naphtalites
was Ahira son of Enan. [28]These were the traveling arrangements of the Israelites according to their companies when
they traveled.

THE APPEAL TO HOBAB

[29]Moses said to Hobab son of Reuel, the Midianite, Moses' father-in-law, "We are journeying to the place about which the
LORD said, 'I will give it to you.' Come with us and we will treat
you well, for the LORD has promised good things for Israel." [30]But
Hobab said to him, "I will not go, but I will go instead to my own
land and to my kindred." [31]Moses said, "Do not leave us, because
you know places for us to camp in the wilderness, and you could
be our guide. [32]And if you come with us, it is certain that whatever good things the LORD will favor us with, we will share with
you as well."

[33]So they traveled from the mountain of the LORD three days'
journey; and the ark of the covenant of the LORD was traveling
before them during the three days' journey, to find a resting

place for them. 34 And the cloud of the LORD was over them by day, when they traveled from the camp. 35 And when the ark traveled, Moses would say, "Rise up, O LORD! May your enemies be scattered, and may those who hate you flee before you!" 36 And when it came to rest he would say, "Return, O LORD, to the many thousands of Israel!"

THE ISRAELITES COMPLAIN

11 When the people complained, it displeased the LORD. When the LORD heard it, his anger burned, and so the fire of the LORD burned among them and consumed some of the outer parts of the camp. 2 When the people cried to Moses, he prayed to the LORD, and the fire died out. 3 So he called the name of that place Taberah because there the fire of the LORD burned among them.

COMPLAINTS ABOUT FOOD

4 Now the mixed multitude who were among them craved more desirable foods, and so the Israelites wept again and said, "If only we had meat to eat! 5 We remember the fish we used to eat freely in Egypt, the cucumbers, the melons, the leeks, the onions, and the garlic. 6 But now we are dried up, and there is nothing at all before us except this manna!" 7 (Now the manna was like coriander seed, and its color like the color of bdellium. 8 And the people went about and gathered it, and ground it with mills or pounded it in mortars; they baked it in pans and made cakes of it. It tasted like fresh olive oil. 9 And when the dew came down on the camp in the night, the manna fell with it.)

MOSES' COMPLAINT TO THE LORD

10 Moses heard the people weeping throughout their families, everyone at the door of his tent; and when the anger of the LORD was kindled greatly, Moses was also displeased. 11 And Moses said to the LORD, "Why have you afflicted your servant? Why have I not found favor in your sight, that you lay the burden of this entire people on me? 12 Did I conceive this entire people? Did I give birth to them, that you should say to me, 'Carry them in your arms, as a foster father bears a nursing child,' to the land that you swore to their fathers? 13 From where shall I get meat to give to this entire people, for they cry to me, 'Give us meat, that we may eat!' 14 I am not able to bear this entire people alone, because it is too heavy for me! 15 But if you are going to deal with me like this, then kill me immediately. If I have found favor in your sight then do not let me see my trouble."

THE RESPONSE OF GOD

16 The LORD said to Moses, "Gather to me seventy men of the elders of Israel, whom you know are elders of the people and officials over them, and bring them to the tent of meeting; let them take their position there with you. 17 Then I will come down and speak with you there, and I will take part of the Spirit that is on you, and will put it on them, and they will bear some of the

burden of the people with you, so that you do not bear it all by
yourself.
[18]"And say to the people, 'Sanctify yourselves for tomorrow, and
you will eat meat, for you have wept in the hearing of the LORD,
saying, "Who will give us meat to eat, for life was good for us in
Egypt?" Therefore the LORD will give you meat, and you will eat.
[19]You will eat, not just one day, nor two days, nor five days, nor
ten days, nor twenty days, [20]but a whole month, until it comes
out your nostrils and makes you sick, because you have despised
the LORD who is among you and have wept before him, saying,
"Why did we ever come out of Egypt?"'"
[21]Moses said, "The people around me are 600,000 on foot; but
you say, 'I will give them meat, that they may eat for a whole
month.' [22]Would they have enough if the flocks and herds were
slaughtered for them? If all the fish of the sea were caught for
them, would they have enough?" [23]And the LORD said to Moses,
"Is the LORD's hand shortened? Now you will see whether my
word to you will come true or not!"
[24]So Moses went out and told the people the words of the
LORD. He then gathered seventy men of the elders of the people and had them stand around the tabernacle. [25]And the LORD
came down in the cloud and spoke to them, and he took some
of the Spirit that was on Moses and put it on the seventy elders. When the Spirit rested on them, they prophesied, but did
not do so again.

ELDAD AND MEDAD

[26]But two men remained in the camp; one's name was Eldad, and
the other's name was Medad. And the Spirit rested on them. (Now
they were among those in the registration, but had not gone to
the tabernacle.) So they prophesied in the camp. [27]And a young
man ran and told Moses, "Eldad and Medad are prophesying in
the camp!" [28]Joshua son of Nun, the servant of Moses, one of his
choice young men, said, "My lord Moses, stop them!" [29]Moses said
to him, "Are you jealous for me? I wish that all the LORD's people were prophets, that the LORD would put his Spirit on them!"
[30]Then Moses returned to the camp along with the elders of Israel.

PROVISION OF QUAIL

[31]Now a wind went out from the LORD and brought quail from
the sea, and let them fall near the camp, about a day's journey on
this side, and about a day's journey on the other side, all around
the camp, and about three feet high on the surface of the ground.
[32]And the people stayed up all that day, all that night, and all
the next day, and gathered the quail. The one who gathered the
least gathered ten homers, and they spread them out for themselves all around the camp. [33]But while the meat was still between their teeth, before they chewed it, the anger of the LORD
burned against the people, and the LORD struck the people with
a very great plague.
[34]So the name of that place was called Kibroth Hattaavah, because there they buried the people that craved different food.
[35]The people traveled from Kibroth Hattaavah to Hazeroth, and
they stayed at Hazeroth.

LOVE TO GROW

GRATITUDE THROUGH TRIALS

NUMBERS 11

As a family engaged as caregivers in the foster care system, we've experienced plenty of highs and lows. The lows have felt excruciating, unique, and distinct from anything I've previously encountered. The journey through them has been long and hard. At moments, I've felt utterly defeated.

One day, in the wake of yet another destructive episode from one of our foster children, I sobbed and honestly asked, "God, where are you? I feel like you've deserted me here."

In the past as I've read through Numbers, the complaining Israelites irked me at times. They wandered the wilderness led by a pillar of fire and replenished each morning with food from heaven. Couldn't they be thankful? They saw God create a walking path through the middle of the sea. He supernaturally released them from slavery. How hard can it be to trust Him?

With time and trial, I too complained. I've seen God part seas for me. I've witnessed unexplainable things. For example, a complete stranger told me that God had angels surrounding our home following a physical threat against us relating to foster care. I've been floored by His reassurance of love and protection.

Nevertheless, I sobbed in my pitiful heap. "Where are you, God?" Then it came to me again, as real as a tray of manna:

Remember all He has done. Remember who He is. Thank Him.

Thank Him? That felt like the last thing I could do living in survival mode. Didn't I need to feel slightly more stable to contemplate gratitude? Despite my doubt, I knew it was my ladder out of the pit. I wrote in my journal: "Here's my battle plan. I will give thanks, even though I don't feel thankful at the moment. I will remember what the Lord has done, who He is, and what He promises."

Gratitude brings clarity, so I list aloud or with my pen all the Lord has done. More importantly, gratitude is obedience. God knew it was true for the Israelites, and He knows it is true for me. Gratitude is for our good and for our blessing. If the complaining buries us deeper into a pit, gratitude builds a strong ladder out.

MIRIAM AND AARON OPPOSE MOSES

12 Then Miriam and Aaron spoke against Moses because of
the Cushite woman he had married (for he had married
an Ethiopian woman). 2 They said, "Has the LORD spoken only
through Moses? Has he not also spoken through us?" And the
LORD heard it.

3 (Now the man Moses was very humble, more so than any man
on the face of the earth.)

THE RESPONSE OF THE LORD

4 The LORD spoke immediately to Moses, Aaron, and Miriam:
"The three of you come to the tent of meeting." So the three of
them went. 5 And the LORD came down in a pillar of cloud and
stood at the entrance of the tent; he then called Aaron and Miriam, and they both came forward.

6 The LORD said, "Hear now my words: If there is a prophet
among you, I the LORD will make myself known to him in a vision; I will speak with him in a dream. 7 My servant Moses is not
like this; he is faithful in all my house. 8 With him I will speak
face to face, openly and not in riddles, and he will see the form
of the LORD. Why then were you not afraid to speak against my
servant Moses?" 9 The anger of the LORD burned against them,
and he departed. 10 After the cloud had departed from above the
tent, there was Miriam, leprous like snow. Then Aaron turned
toward Miriam, and realized that she was leprous.

THE INTERCESSION OF MOSES

11 So Aaron said to Moses, "O my lord, please do not hold this sin
against us, in which we have acted foolishly and have sinned!
12 Do not let her be like a baby born dead, whose flesh is half consumed when it comes out of its mother's womb!"

13 Then Moses cried to the LORD, "Heal her now, O God." 14 The
LORD said to Moses, "If her father had only spit in her face, would
she not have been disgraced for seven days? Shut her out from
the camp seven days, and afterward she can be brought back
in again."

15 So Miriam was shut outside of the camp for seven days, and
the people did not journey on until Miriam was brought back
in. 16 After that the people moved from Hazeroth and camped
in the wilderness of Paran.

SPIES SENT OUT

13 The LORD spoke to Moses: 2 "Send out men to investigate
the land of Canaan, which I am giving to the Israelites. You
are to send one man from each ancestral tribe, each one a leader
among them." 3 So Moses sent them from the wilderness of Paran at the command of the LORD. All of them were leaders of
the Israelites.

4 Now these were their names: from the tribe of Reuben, Sham-
mua son of Zaccur; 5 from the tribe of Simeon, Shaphat son of
Hori; 6 from the tribe of Judah, Caleb son of Jephunneh; 7 from the
tribe of Issachar, Igal son of Joseph; 8 from the tribe of Ephraim,
Hoshea son of Nun; 9 from the tribe of Benjamin, Palti son of
Raphu; 10 from the tribe of Zebulun, Gaddiel son of Sodi; 11 from

the tribe of Joseph, namely, the tribe of Manasseh, Gaddi son of
Susi; 12 from the tribe of Dan, Ammiel son of Gemalli; 13 from the
tribe of Asher, Sethur son of Michael; 14 from the tribe of Naphtali, Nahbi son of Vopshi; 15 from the tribe of Gad, Geuel son of
Maki. 16 These are the names of the men whom Moses sent to
investigate the land. And Moses gave Hoshea son of Nun the
name Joshua.

THE SPIES' INSTRUCTIONS

17 When Moses sent them to investigate the land of Canaan, he
told them, "Go up through the Negev, and then go up into the
hill country 18 and see what the land is like, and whether the people who live in it are strong or weak, few or many, 19 and whether
the land they live in is good or bad, and whether the cities they
inhabit are like camps or fortified cities, 20 and whether the land
is rich or poor, and whether or not there are forests in it. And be
brave, and bring back some of the fruit of the land." Now it was
the time of year for the first ripe grapes.

THE SPIES' ACTIVITIES

21 So they went up and investigated the land from the wilderness of Zin to Rehob, at Lebo Hamath. 22 When they went up
through the Negev, they came to Hebron where Ahiman, Sheshai, and Talmai, descendants of Anak, were living. (Now Hebron had been built seven years before Zoan in Egypt.) 23 When
they came to the valley of Eshcol, they cut down from there a
branch with one cluster of grapes, and they carried it on a staff
between two men, as well as some of the pomegranates and the
figs. 24 That place was called the Eshcol Valley, because of the cluster of grapes that the Israelites cut from there. 25 They returned
from investigating the land after forty days.

THE SPIES' REPORTS

26 They came back to Moses and Aaron and to the whole community of the Israelites in the wilderness of Paran at Kadesh.
They reported to the whole community and showed the fruit
of the land. 27 They told Moses, "We went to the land where you
sent us. It is indeed flowing with milk and honey, and this is its
fruit. 28 But the inhabitants are strong, and the cities are fortified and very large. Moreover we saw the descendants of Anak
there. 29 The Amalekites live in the land of the Negev; the Hittites, Jebusites, and Amorites live in the hill country; and the
Canaanites live by the sea and along the banks of the Jordan."

30 Then Caleb silenced the people before Moses, saying, "Let
us go up and occupy it, for we are well able to conquer it." 31 But
the men who had gone up with him said, "We are not able to
go up against these people, because they are stronger than we
are!" 32 Then they presented the Israelites with a discouraging
report of the land they had investigated, saying, "The land that
we passed through to investigate is a land that devours its inhabitants. All the people we saw there are of great stature. 33 We
even saw the Nephilim there (the descendants of Anak came
from the Nephilim), and we seemed like grasshoppers both to
ourselves and to them."

THE ISRAELITES RESPOND IN UNBELIEF

14 Then all the community raised a loud cry, and the people
wept that night. 2 And all the Israelites murmured against
Moses and Aaron, and the whole congregation said to them, "If
only we had died in the land of Egypt, or if only we had perished
in this wilderness! 3 Why has the LORD brought us into this land
only to be killed by the sword, that our wives and our children
should become plunder? Wouldn't it be better for us to return
to Egypt?" 4 So they said to one another, "Let's appoint a leader
and return to Egypt."

5 Then Moses and Aaron fell down with their faces to the
ground before the whole assembled community of the Israelites. 6 And Joshua son of Nun and Caleb son of Jephunneh, two
of those who had investigated the land, tore their garments.
7 They said to the whole community of the Israelites, "The land
we passed through to investigate is an exceedingly good land. 8 If
the LORD delights in us, then he will bring us into this land and
give it to us—a land that is flowing with milk and honey. 9 Only
do not rebel against the LORD, and do not fear the people of the
land, for they are bread for us. Their protection has turned aside
from them, but the LORD is with us. Do not fear them!"

10 However, the whole community threatened to stone them.
But the glory of the LORD appeared to all the Israelites at the
tent of meeting.

THE PUNISHMENT FROM GOD

11 The LORD said to Moses, "How long will this people despise me,
and how long will they not believe in me, in spite of the signs
that I have done among them? 12 I will strike them with the pestilence, and I will disinherit them—I will make you into a nation
that is greater and mightier than they!"

13 Moses said to the LORD, "When the Egyptians hear it—for you
brought up this people by your power from among them—14 then
they will tell it to the inhabitants of this land. They have heard that
you, LORD, are among this people, that you, LORD, are seen face
to face, that your cloud stands over them, and that you go before
them by day in a pillar of cloud and in a pillar of fire by night. 15 If
you kill this entire people at once, then the nations that have heard
of your fame will say, 16 'Because the LORD was not able to bring
this people into the land that he swore to them, he killed them in
the wilderness.' 17 So now, let the power of my Lord be great, just as
you have said, 18 'The LORD is slow to anger and abounding in loyal
love, forgiving iniquity and transgression, but by no means clearing the guilty, visiting the iniquity of the fathers on the children
until the third and fourth generations.' 19 Please forgive the iniquity of this people according to your great loyal love, just as you
have forgiven this people from Egypt even until now."

20 Then the LORD said, "I have forgiven them as you asked.
21 But truly, as I live, all the earth will be filled with the glory of
the LORD. 22 For all the people have seen my glory and my signs
that I did in Egypt and in the wilderness, and yet have tempted
me now these ten times, and have not obeyed me—23 they will
by no means see the land that I promised on oath to their fathers, nor will any of them who despised me see it—24 Only my

servant Caleb, because he had a different spirit and has followed
me fully—I will bring him into the land where he had gone, and
his descendants will possess it. 25 (Now the Amalekites and the
Canaanites were living in the valleys.) Tomorrow, turn and journey into the wilderness by the way of the Red Sea."
26 The LORD spoke to Moses and Aaron: 27 "How long must I
bear with this evil congregation that murmurs against me? I
have heard the complaints of the Israelites that they murmured
against me. 28 Say to them, 'As I live, says the LORD, I will surely
do to you just what you have spoken in my hearing. 29 Your dead
bodies will fall in this wilderness—all those of you who were numbered, according to your full number, from twenty years old and
upward, who have murmured against me. 30 You will by no means
enter into the land where I swore to settle you. The only exceptions are Caleb son of Jephunneh and Joshua son of Nun. 31 But I
will bring in your little ones, whom you said would become victims of war, and they will enjoy the land that you have despised.
32 But as for you, your dead bodies will fall in this wilderness, 33 and
your children will wander in the wilderness forty years and suffer
for your unfaithfulness, until your dead bodies lie finished in the
wilderness. 34 According to the number of the days you have investigated this land, forty days—one day for a year—you will suffer
for your iniquities, forty years, and you will know what it means
to thwart me. 35 I, the LORD, have said, "I will surely do so to all
this evil congregation that has gathered together against me. In
this wilderness they will be finished, and there they will die!"'"
36 The men whom Moses sent to investigate the land, who returned and made the whole community murmur against him
by producing an evil report about the land, 37 those men who
produced the evil report about the land, died by the plague before the LORD. 38 But Joshua son of Nun and Caleb son of Jephunneh, who were among the men who went to investigate the land,
lived. 39 When Moses told these things to all the Israelites, the
people mourned greatly.
40 And early in the morning they went up to the crest of the
hill country, saying, "Here we are, and we will go up to the place
that the LORD commanded, for we have sinned." 41 But Moses
said, "Why are you now transgressing the commandment of
the LORD? It will not succeed! 42 Do not go up, for the LORD is
not among you, and you will be defeated before your enemies.
43 For the Amalekites and the Canaanites are there before you,
and you will fall by the sword. Because you have turned away
from the LORD, the LORD will not be with you."
44 But they dared to go up to the crest of the hill, although neither the ark of the covenant of the LORD nor Moses departed
from the camp. 45 So the Amalekites and the Canaanites who
lived in that hill country swooped down and attacked them as
far as Hormah.

REFLECT

Why was the rebellion of the Israelites and their refusal to enter the land of Canaan so significant? Do you believe God was justified in His reaction?

SACRIFICIAL RULINGS

15 The LORD spoke to Moses: 2 "Speak to the Israelites and tell
them, 'When you enter the land where you are to live, which
I am giving you, 3 and you make an offering by fire to the LORD
from the herd or from the flock (whether a burnt offering or a

sacrifice for discharging a vow or as a freewill offering or in your
solemn feasts) to create a pleasing aroma to the LORD, [4] then the
one who presents his offering to the LORD must bring a grain
offering of one-tenth of an ephah of finely ground flour mixed
with one-fourth of a hin of olive oil. [5] You must also prepare one-
fourth of a hin of wine for a drink offering with the burnt offering
or the sacrifice for each lamb. [6] Or for a ram, you must prepare
as a grain offering two-tenths of an ephah of finely ground flour
mixed with one-third of a hin of olive oil, [7] and for a drink offering you must offer one-third of a hin of wine as a pleasing aroma
to the LORD. [8] And when you prepare a young bull as a burnt offering or a sacrifice for discharging a vow or as a peace offering
to the LORD, [9] then a grain offering of three-tenths of an ephah
of finely ground flour mixed with half a hin of olive oil must be
presented with the young bull, [10] and you must present as the
drink offering half a hin of wine with the fire offering as a pleasing aroma to the LORD. [11] This is what is to be done for each ox,
or each ram, or each of the male lambs or the goats. [12] You must
do so for each one according to the number that you prepare.
[13] "'Every native-born person must do these things in this way
to present an offering made by fire as a pleasing aroma to the
LORD. [14] If a resident foreigner is living with you—or whoever
is among you in future generations—and prepares an offering
made by fire as a pleasing aroma to the LORD, he must do it the
same way you are to do it. [15] One statute must apply to you who
belong to the congregation and to the resident foreigner who
is living among you, as a permanent statute for your future generations. You and the resident foreigner will be alike before the
LORD. [16] One law and one custom must apply to you and to the
resident foreigner who lives alongside you.'"

RULES FOR FIRSTFRUITS

[17] The LORD spoke to Moses: [18] "Speak to the Israelites and tell
them, 'When you enter the land to which I am bringing you
[19] and you eat some of the food of the land, you must offer up a
raised offering to the LORD. [20] You must offer up a cake of the
first of your finely ground flour as a raised offering; as you offer
the raised offering of the threshing floor, so you must offer it
up. [21] You must give to the LORD some of the first of your finely
ground flour as a raised offering in your future generations.

RULES FOR UNINTENTIONAL OFFENSES

[22] "'If you sin unintentionally and do not observe all these commandments that the LORD has spoken to Moses—[23] all that the
LORD has commanded you by the authority of Moses, from the
day that the LORD commanded Moses and continuing through
your future generations—[24] then if anything is done unintentionally without the knowledge of the community, the whole community must prepare one young bull for a burnt offering—for a
pleasing aroma to the LORD—along with its grain offering and its
customary drink offering, and one male goat for a purification
offering. [25] And the priest is to make atonement for the whole
community of the Israelites, and they will be forgiven, because
it was unintentional and they have brought their offering, an

offering made by fire to the LORD, and their purification offering before the LORD, for their unintentional offense. 26 And the
whole community of the Israelites and the resident foreigner
who lives among them will be forgiven, since all the people were
involved in the unintentional offense.

27 "'If any person sins unintentionally, then he must bring a
yearling female goat for a purification offering. 28 And the priest
must make atonement for the person who sins unintentionally—when he sins unintentionally before the LORD—to make
atonement for him, and he will be forgiven. 29 You must have
one law for the person who sins unintentionally, both for the
native-born among the Israelites and for the resident foreigner
who lives among them.

DELIBERATE SIN

30 "'But the person who acts defiantly, whether native-born or
a resident foreigner, insults the LORD. That person must be cut
off from among his people. 31 Because he has despised the LORD's
message and has broken his commandment, that person must
be completely cut off. His iniquity will be on him.'"

32 When the Israelites were in the wilderness they found a
man gathering wood on the Sabbath day. 33 Those who found
him gathering wood brought him to Moses and Aaron and to the
whole community. 34 They put him in custody, because there was
no clear instruction about what should be done to him. 35 Then
the LORD said to Moses, "The man must surely be put to death;
the whole community must stone him with stones outside the
camp." 36 So the whole community took him outside the camp
and stoned him to death, just as the LORD commanded Moses.

RULES FOR TASSELS

37 The LORD spoke to Moses: 38 "Speak to the Israelites and tell
them to make tassels for themselves on the corners of their
garments throughout their generations, and put a blue thread
on the tassel of the corners. 39 You must have this tassel so that
you may look at it and remember all the commandments of
the LORD and obey them and so that you do not follow after
your own heart and your own eyes that lead you to unfaithfulness. 40 Thus you will remember and obey all my commandments and be holy to your God. 41 I am the LORD your God, who
brought you out of the land of Egypt to be your God. I am the
LORD your God."

THE REBELLION OF KORAH

16 Now Korah son of Izhar, the son of Kohath, the son of
Levi, and Dathan and Abiram, the sons of Eliab, and On
son of Peleth, who were Reubenites, took men 2 and rebelled
against Moses, along with some of the Israelites, 250 leaders
of the community, chosen from the assembly, famous men.
3 And they assembled against Moses and Aaron, saying to them,
"You take too much upon yourselves, seeing that the whole
community is holy, every one of them, and the LORD is among
them. Why then do you exalt yourselves above the community of the LORD?"

4 When Moses heard it he fell down with his face to the ground. 5 Then he said to Korah and to all his company, "In the morning the LORD will make known who are his, and who is holy. He will cause that person to approach him; the person he has chosen he will cause to approach him. 6 Do this, Korah, you and all your company: Take censers, 7 put fire in them, and set incense on them before the LORD tomorrow, and the man whom the LORD chooses will be holy. You take too much upon yourselves, you sons of Levi!" 8 Moses said to Korah, "Listen now, you sons of Levi! 9 Does it seem too small a thing to you that the God of Israel has separated you from the community of Israel to bring you near to himself, to perform the service of the tabernacle of the LORD, and to stand before the community to minister to them? 10 He has brought you near and all your brothers, the sons of Levi, with you. Do you now seek the priesthood also? 11 Therefore you and all your company have assembled together against the LORD! And Aaron—what is he that you murmur against him?" 12 Then Moses summoned Dathan and Abiram, the sons of Eliab, but they said, "We will not come up. 13 Is it a small thing that you have brought us up out of the land that flows with milk and honey, to kill us in the wilderness? Now do you want to make yourself a prince over us? 14 Moreover, you have not brought us into a land that flows with milk and honey, nor given us an inheritance of fields and vineyards. Do you think you can blind these men? We will not come up."

CHALLENGE

Why does God take Korah's rebellion so seriously? Look up other instances of rebellion and defiance against God and note how God responds. How is His reaction different or similar in each situation? What do God's responses reveal about His character and whom and what He cares about?

15 Moses was very angry, and he said to the LORD, "Have no respect for their offering! I have not taken so much as one donkey from them, nor have I harmed any one of them!"

16 Then Moses said to Korah, "You and all your company present yourselves before the LORD—you and they, and Aaron—tomorrow. 17 And each of you take his censer, put incense in it, and then each of you present his censer before the LORD: 250 censers, along with you, and Aaron—each of you with his censer." 18 So everyone took his censer, put fire in it, and set incense on it, and stood at the entrance of the tent of meeting, with Moses and Aaron. 19 When Korah assembled the whole community against them at the entrance of the tent of meeting, then the glory of the LORD appeared to the whole community.

THE JUDGMENT ON THE REBELS

20 The LORD spoke to Moses and Aaron: 21 "Separate yourselves from among this community, that I may consume them in an instant." 22 Then they threw themselves down with their faces to the ground and said, "O God, the God of the spirits of all people, will you be angry with the whole community when only one man sins?"

23 So the LORD spoke to Moses: 24 "Tell the community: 'Get away from around the homes of Korah, Dathan, and Abiram.'" 25 Then Moses got up and went to Dathan and Abiram; and the elders of Israel went after him. 26 And he said to the community, "Move away from the tents of these wicked men, and do not touch anything they have, lest you be destroyed because of all their sins." 27 So they got away from the homes of Korah, Dathan, and Abiram on every side, and Dathan and Abiram came

out and stationed themselves in the entrances of their tents
with their wives, their children, and their toddlers. 28 Then Moses said, "This is how you will know that the LORD has sent me
to do all these works, for I have not done them of my own will.
29 If these men die a natural death, or if they share the fate of
all men, then the LORD has not sent me. 30 But if the LORD does
something entirely new, and the earth opens its mouth and swallows them up along with all that they have, and they go down
alive to the grave, then you will know that these men have despised the LORD!"

31 When he had finished speaking all these words, the ground
that was under them split open, 32 and the earth opened its
mouth and swallowed them, along with their households, and
all Korah's men, and all their goods. 33 They and all that they had
went down alive into the pit, and the earth closed over them. So
they perished from among the community. 34 All the Israelites
who were around them fled at their cry, for they said, "What if
the earth swallows us too?" 35 Then a fire went out from the LORD
and devoured the 250 men who offered incense.

THE ATONEMENT FOR THE REBELLION

36 The LORD spoke to Moses: 37 "Tell Eleazar son of Aaron the
priest to pick up the censers out of the flame, for they are holy,
and then scatter the coals of fire at a distance. 38 As for the censers of these men who sinned at the cost of their lives, they must
be made into hammered sheets for covering the altar, because
they presented them before the LORD and sanctified them. They
will become a sign to the Israelites." 39 So Eleazar the priest took
the bronze censers presented by those who had been burned up,
and they were hammered out as a covering for the altar. 40 It was
a memorial for the Israelites, that no outsider who is not a descendant of Aaron should approach to burn incense before the
LORD, that he might not become like Korah and his company—
just as the LORD had spoken by the authority of Moses. 41 But
on the next day the whole community of Israelites murmured
against Moses and Aaron, saying, "You have killed the LORD's
people!" 42 When the community assembled against Moses and
Aaron, they turned toward the tent of meeting—and the cloud
covered it, and the glory of the LORD appeared. 43 Then Moses
and Aaron stood before the tent of meeting.

44 The LORD spoke to Moses: 45 "Get away from this community,
so that I can consume them in an instant!" But they threw themselves down with their faces to the ground. 46 Then Moses said to
Aaron, "Take the censer, put burning coals from the altar in it,
place incense on it, and go quickly into the assembly and make
atonement for them, for wrath has gone out from the LORD—the
plague has begun!" 47 So Aaron did as Moses commanded and
ran into the middle of the assembly, where the plague was just
beginning among the people. So he placed incense on the coals
and made atonement for the people. 48 He stood between the
dead and the living, and the plague was stopped. 49 Now 14,700
people died in the plague, in addition to those who died in the
event with Korah. 50 Then Aaron returned to Moses at the entrance of the tent of meeting, and the plague was stopped.

THE BUDDING OF AARON'S STAFF

17 The LORD spoke to Moses: 2 "Speak to the Israelites, and
receive from them a staff from each tribe, one from every
tribal leader, twelve staffs; you must write each man's name on
his staff. 3 You must write Aaron's name on the staff of Levi; for
one staff is for the head of every tribe. 4 You must place them
in the tent of meeting before the ark of the covenant where I
meet with you. 5 And the staff of the man whom I choose will
blossom; so I will rid myself of the complaints of the Israelites,
which they murmur against you."
6 So Moses spoke to the Israelites, and each of their leaders gave
him a staff, one for each leader, according to their tribes—twelve
staffs; the staff of Aaron was among their staffs. 7 Then Moses
placed the staffs before the LORD in the tent of the testimony.
8 On the next day Moses went into the tent of the testimony—and the staff of Aaron for the house of Levi had sprouted,
and brought forth buds, and produced blossoms, and yielded
almonds! 9 So Moses brought out all the staffs from before the
LORD to all the Israelites. They looked at them, and each man
took his staff.

THE MEMORIAL

10 The LORD said to Moses, "Bring Aaron's staff back before the
testimony to be preserved for a sign to the rebels, so that you
may bring their murmurings to an end before me, that they will
not die." 11 So Moses did as the LORD commanded him—this is
what he did.
12 The Israelites said to Moses, "We are bound to die! We perish, we all perish! 13 Anyone who even comes close to the tabernacle of the LORD will die! Are we all to die?"

RESPONSIBILITIES OF THE PRIESTS

18 The LORD said to Aaron, "You and your sons and your tribe
with you must bear the iniquity of the sanctuary, and you
and your sons with you must bear the iniquity of your priesthood.
2 "Bring with you your brothers, the tribe of Levi, the tribe of
your father, so that they may join with you and minister to you
while you and your sons with you are before the tent of the testimony. 3 They must be responsible to care for you and to care
for the entire tabernacle. However, they must not come near
the furnishings of the sanctuary and the altar, or both they and
you will die. 4 They must join with you, and they will be responsible for the care of the tent of meeting, for all the service of the
tent, but no unauthorized person may approach you. 5 You will
be responsible for the care of the sanctuary and the care of the
altar, so that there will be no more wrath on the Israelites. 6 I
myself have chosen your brothers the Levites from among the
Israelites. They are given to you as a gift from the LORD, to perform the duties of the tent of meeting. 7 But you and your sons
with you are responsible for your priestly duties, for everything
at the altar and within the curtain. And you must serve. I give
you the priesthood as a gift for service, but the unauthorized
person who approaches must be put to death."

THE PORTION OF THE PRIESTS

8 The LORD spoke to Aaron, "See, I have given you the responsibility for my raised offerings; I have given all the holy things of
the Israelites to you as your priestly portion and to your sons
as a perpetual ordinance. 9 Of all the most holy offerings reserved from the fire this will be yours: Every offering of theirs,
whether from every grain offering or from every purification
offering or from every reparation offering which they bring
to me, will be most holy for you and for your sons. 10 You are
to eat it as a most holy offering; every male may eat it. It will
be holy to you.

11 "And this is yours: the raised offering of their gift, along with
all the wave offerings of the Israelites. I have given them to you
and to your sons and daughters with you as a perpetual ordinance. Everyone who is ceremonially clean in your household
may eat of it.

12 "All the best of the olive oil and all the best of the wine and
of the wheat, the firstfruits of these things that they give to the
LORD, I have given to you. 13 And whatever first ripe fruit in their
land they bring to the LORD will be yours; everyone who is ceremonially clean in your household may eat of it.

14 "Everything devoted in Israel will be yours. 15 The firstborn
of every womb which they present to the LORD, whether human or animal, will be yours. Nevertheless, the firstborn sons
you must redeem, and the firstborn males of unclean animals
you must redeem. 16 And those that must be redeemed you are
to redeem when they are a month old, according to your estimation, for five shekels of silver according to the sanctuary shekel
(which is twenty gerahs). 17 But you must not redeem the firstborn of a cow or a sheep or a goat; they are holy. You must splash
their blood on the altar and burn their fat for an offering made
by fire for a pleasing aroma to the LORD. 18 And their meat will
be yours, just as the breast and the right hip of the raised offering is yours. 19 All the raised offerings of the holy things that
the Israelites offer to the LORD, I have given to you, and to your
sons and daughters with you, as a perpetual ordinance. It is a
covenant of salt forever before the LORD for you and for your
descendants with you."

DUTIES OF THE LEVITES

20 The LORD spoke to Aaron, "You will have no inheritance in
their land, nor will you have any portion of property among
them—I am your portion and your inheritance among the Israelites. 21 See, I have given the Levites all the tithes in Israel for
an inheritance, for their service that they perform—the service
of the tent of meeting. 22 No longer may the Israelites approach
the tent of meeting, or else they will bear their sin and die. 23 But
the Levites must perform the service of the tent of meeting, and
they must bear their iniquity. It will be a perpetual ordinance
throughout your generations that among the Israelites the Levites have no inheritance. 24 But I have given to the Levites for
an inheritance the tithes of the Israelites that are offered to the
LORD as a raised offering. That is why I said to them that among
the Israelites they are to have no inheritance."

INSTRUCTIONS FOR THE LEVITES

25 The LORD spoke to Moses: 26 "You are to speak to the Levites, and you must tell them, 'When you receive from the Israelites the tithe that I have given you from them as your inheritance, then you are to offer up from it as a raised offering to the LORD a tenth of the tithe. 27 And your raised offering will be credited to you as though it were grain from the threshing floor or as new wine from the winepress. 28 Thus you are to offer up a raised offering to the LORD of all your tithes that you receive from the Israelites; and you must give the LORD's raised offering from it to Aaron the priest. 29 From all your gifts you must offer up every raised offering due the LORD, from all the best of it, and the holiest part of it.'

30 "Therefore you will say to them, 'When you offer up the best of it, then it will be credited to the Levites as the product of the threshing floor and as the product of the winepress. 31 And you may eat it in any place, you and your household, because it is your wages for your service in the tent of meeting. 32 And you will bear no sin concerning it when you offer up the best of it. And you must not profane the holy things of the Israelites, or else you will die.'"

THE RED HEIFER RITUAL

19 The LORD spoke to Moses and Aaron: 2 "This is the ordinance of the law that the LORD has commanded: 'Instruct the Israelites to bring you a red heifer without blemish, which has no defect and has never carried a yoke. 3 You must give it to Eleazar the priest so that he can take it outside the camp, and it must be slaughtered before him. 4 Eleazar the priest is to take some of its blood with his finger, and sprinkle some of the blood seven times in the direction of the front of the tent of meeting. 5 Then the heifer must be burned in his sight—its skin, its flesh, its blood, and its offal is to be burned. 6 And the priest must take cedar wood, hyssop, and scarlet wool and throw them into the midst of the fire where the heifer is burning. 7 Then the priest must wash his clothes and bathe himself in water, and afterward he may come into the camp, but the priest will be ceremonially unclean until evening. 8 The one who burns it must wash his clothes in water and bathe himself in water. He will be ceremonially unclean until evening.

9 "'Then a man who is ceremonially clean must gather up the ashes of the red heifer and put them in a ceremonially clean place outside the camp. They must be kept for the community of the Israelites for use in the water of purification—it is a purification for sin. 10 The one who gathers the ashes of the heifer must wash his clothes and be ceremonially unclean until evening. This will be a permanent ordinance both for the Israelites and the resident foreigner who lives among them.

PURIFICATION FROM UNCLEANNESS

11 "'Whoever touches the corpse of any person will be ceremonially unclean seven days. 12 He must purify himself with water on the third day and on the seventh day, and so will be clean. But if he does not purify himself on the third day and the seventh day, then he will not be clean. 13 Anyone who touches the corpse of

any dead person and does not purify himself defiles the tabernacle of the LORD. And that person must be cut off from Israel,
because the water of purification was not sprinkled on him. He
will be unclean; his uncleanness remains on him.
14 "'This is the law: When a man dies in a tent, anyone who
comes into the tent and all who are in the tent will be ceremonially unclean seven days. 15 And every open container that has
no covering fastened on it is unclean. 16 And whoever touches
the body of someone killed with a sword in the open fields, or
the body of someone who died of natural causes, or a human
bone, or a grave, will be unclean seven days.
17 "'For a ceremonially unclean person you must take some of
the ashes of the heifer burnt for purification from sin and pour
fresh running water over them in a vessel. 18 Then a ceremonially
clean person must take hyssop, dip it in the water, and sprinkle
it on the tent, on all its furnishings, and on the people who were
there, or on the one who touched a bone, or one who was killed,
or one who died, or a grave. 19 And the clean person must sprinkle the unclean on the third day and on the seventh day; and on
the seventh day he must purify him, and then he must wash his
clothes, and bathe in water, and he will be clean in the evening.
20 But the man who is unclean and does not purify himself, that
person must be cut off from among the community, because he
has polluted the sanctuary of the LORD; the water of purification was not sprinkled on him, so he is unclean.
21 "'So this will be a perpetual ordinance for them: The one who
sprinkles the water of purification must wash his clothes, and
the one who touches the water of purification will be unclean
until evening. 22 And whatever the unclean person touches will
be unclean, and the person who touches it will be unclean until evening.'"

THE ISRAELITES COMPLAIN AGAIN

20 Then the entire community of Israel entered the wilderness of Zin in the first month, and the people stayed in
Kadesh. Miriam died and was buried there.
2 And there was no water for the community, and so they gathered themselves together against Moses and Aaron. 3 The people contended with Moses, saying, "If only we had died when our
brothers died before the LORD! 4 Why have you brought up the
LORD's community into this wilderness? So that we and our cattle should die here? 5 Why have you brought us up from Egypt
only to bring us to this dreadful place? It is no place for grain, or
figs, or vines, or pomegranates; nor is there any water to drink!"

MOSES RESPONDS

6 So Moses and Aaron went from the presence of the assembly to
the entrance to the tent of meeting. They then threw themselves
down with their faces to the ground, and the glory of the LORD
appeared to them. 7 Then the LORD spoke to Moses: 8 "Take the
staff and assemble the community, you and Aaron your brother,
and then speak to the rock before their eyes. It will pour forth
its water, and you will bring water out of the rock for them, and
so you will give the community and their beasts water to drink."

REFLECT

How did Moses' actions display a lack of faith? Why was this incident so significant that God would discipline Moses by keeping him from entering the promised land?

LOVE TO GROW

THE RESPONSIBILITY OF AUTHORITY

NUMBERS 20

Anyone who has ever served in a children's Sunday school class knows what real chaos can look like: twenty wild toddlers, baby dolls, and toy trucks strewn across a room, and two frazzled leaders trying simultaneously to sweep up crushed Cheerios and operate a felt board. They try to keep everyone happy, but supplies are limited, and they realize their authority only goes so far.

This might be how Moses and Aaron felt in Numbers 20. They juggled a lot of concerns and complaints from God's forgetful people. They tried to keep morale up when resources were low and the future looked different than God had promised. All the while, they tried to maintain their fragile measure of authority.

At first glance, Moses seemed to fulfill God's command: He took his staff, gathered the people, struck a rock, and water came forth. But Moses' actions and words portray a lack of trust in God. Ultimately, his disobedience failed to show God as holy before the Israelites (Num 20:12), and he did not get to live in the promised land.

Moses' frustration with the Israelites had stirred his personal weakness, the exact place where God's strength is perfected (2 Cor 12:9). When God called Moses to lead the Israelites out of Egypt as God performed miracles for their deliverance, Moses asked Him, "And if they don't believe me or pay attention to me (Exod 4:1)?" He even went so far as to ask God to send someone else (Exod 4:12).

Moses and Aaron displayed characteristics typical of human leaders: We fear failure to the point of doubting God, and we lash out when our authority is questioned.

Christians today may never lead God's people through the wilderness, but all of us have spheres of authority given to us by God: in our families, with our friends, in our church, and in our communities.

The responsibility of representing God's universal authority over creation is a great and weighty task that comes with its own temptations and pitfalls. Yet as the end of this story demonstrates, God is gracious with unfaithful communities and their fearful leaders, even as He points us back to the real purpose of all of our work: glorifying Him.

[9] So Moses took the staff from before the LORD, just as he commanded him. [10] Then Moses and Aaron gathered the community together in front of the rock, and he said to them, "Listen,
you rebels, must we bring water out of this rock for you?" [11] Then
Moses raised his hand, and struck the rock twice with his staff.
And water came out abundantly. So the community drank, and
their beasts drank too.

THE LORD'S JUDGMENT

[12] Then the LORD spoke to Moses and Aaron, "Because you did
not trust me enough to show me as holy before the Israelites,
therefore you will not bring this community into the land I have
given them."

[13] These are the waters of Meribah, because the Israelites contended with the LORD, and his holiness was maintained among
them.

REJECTION BY THE EDOMITES

[14] Moses sent messengers from Kadesh to the king of Edom:
"Thus says your brother Israel: 'You know all the hardships we
have experienced, [15] how our ancestors went down into Egypt,
and we lived in Egypt a long time, and the Egyptians treated
us and our ancestors badly. [16] So when we cried to the LORD, he
heard our voice and sent a messenger, and has brought us up
out of Egypt. Now we are here in Kadesh, a town on the edge of
your country. [17] Please let us pass through your country. We will
not pass through the fields or through the vineyards, nor will
we drink water from any well. We will go by the King's Highway;
we will not turn to the right or the left until we have passed
through your region.'"

[18] But Edom said to him, "You will not pass through me, or I
will come out against you with the sword." [19] Then the Israelites
said to him, "We will go along the highway, and if we or our cattle drink any of your water, we will pay for it. We will only pass
through on our feet, without doing anything else."

[20] But he said, "You may not pass through." Then Edom came
out against them with a large and powerful force. [21] So Edom refused to give Israel passage through his border; therefore Israel
turned away from him.

AARON'S DEATH

[22] So the entire company of Israelites traveled from Kadesh
and came to Mount Hor. [23] And the LORD spoke to Moses and
Aaron at Mount Hor, by the border of the land of Edom. He said:
[24] "Aaron will be gathered to his ancestors, for he will not enter
into the land I have given to the Israelites because both of you
rebelled against my word at the waters of Meribah. [25] Take Aaron
and Eleazar his son, and bring them up on Mount Hor. [26] Remove
Aaron's priestly garments and put them on Eleazar his son, and
Aaron will be gathered to his ancestors and will die there."

[27] So Moses did as the LORD commanded; and they went up
Mount Hor in the sight of the whole community. [28] And Moses
removed Aaron's garments and put them on his son Eleazar. So
Aaron died there on the top of the mountain. And Moses and

Eleazar came down from the mountain. 29 When all the community saw that Aaron was dead, the whole house of Israel mourned for Aaron thirty days.

VICTORY AT HORMAH

21 When the Canaanite king of Arad who lived in the Negev heard that Israel was approaching along the road to Atharim, he fought against Israel and took some of them prisoner.

2 So Israel made a vow to the LORD and said, "If you will indeed deliver this people into our hand, then we will utterly destroy their cities." 3 The LORD listened to the voice of Israel and delivered up the Canaanites, and they utterly destroyed them and their cities. So the name of the place was called Hormah.

REFLECT

How does the incident with the bronze snake show God's faithfulness despite Israel's rebellion? How has God responded to you in your seasons of rebellion?

FIERY SERPENTS

4 Then they traveled from Mount Hor by the road to the Red Sea, to go around the land of Edom, but the people became impatient along the way. 5 And the people spoke against God and against Moses, "Why have you brought us up from Egypt to die in the wilderness, for there is no bread or water, and we detest this worthless food."

6 So the LORD sent venomous snakes among the people, and they bit the people; many people of Israel died. 7 Then the people came to Moses and said, "We have sinned, for we have spoken against the LORD and against you. Pray to the LORD that he would take away the snakes from us." So Moses prayed for the people.

8 The LORD said to Moses, "Make a poisonous snake and set it on a pole. When anyone who is bitten looks at it, he will live." 9 So Moses made a bronze snake and put it on a pole, so that if a snake had bitten someone, when he looked at the bronze snake he lived.

THE APPROACH TO MOAB

10 The Israelites traveled on and camped in Oboth. 11 Then they traveled on from Oboth and camped at Iye Abarim, in the wilderness that is before Moab on the eastern side. 12 From there they moved on and camped in the valley of Zered. 13 From there they moved on and camped on the other side of the Arnon, in the wilderness that extends from the regions of the Amorites, for Arnon is the border of Moab, between Moab and the Amorites. 14 This is why it is said in the Book of the Wars of the LORD,

"Waheb in Suphah and the wadis,
the Arnon 15 and the slope of the valleys
that extends to the dwelling of Ar,
and falls off at the border of Moab."

16 And from there they traveled to Beer; that is the well where the LORD spoke to Moses, "Gather the people and I will give them water." 17 Then Israel sang this song:

"Spring up, O well, sing to it!
18 The well which the princes dug,
which the leaders of the people opened
with their scepters and their staffs."

And from the wilderness they traveled to Mattanah; 19 and
from Mattanah to Nahaliel; and from Nahaliel to Bamoth; 20 and
from Bamoth to the valley that is in the country of Moab, near
the top of Pisgah, which overlooks the wastelands.

THE VICTORY OVER SIHON AND OG

21 Then Israel sent messengers to King Sihon of the Amorites,
saying,
22 "Let us pass through your land; we will not turn aside into the
fields or into the vineyards, nor will we drink water from any well,
but we will go along the King's Highway until we pass your borders." 23 But Sihon did not permit Israel to pass through his border;
he gathered all his forces together and went out against Israel into
the wilderness. When he came to Jahaz, he fought against Israel.
24 But the Israelites defeated him in battle and took possession of
his land from the Arnon to the Jabbok, as far as the Ammonites, for
the border of the Ammonites was strongly defended. 25 So Israel
took all these cities; and Israel settled in all the cities of the Amorites, in Heshbon, and in all its villages. 26 For Heshbon was the
city of King Sihon of the Amorites. Now he had fought against the
former king of Moab and had taken all his land from his control,
as far as the Arnon. 27 That is why those who speak in proverbs say,

"Come to Heshbon, let it be built.
Let the city of Sihon be established!
28 For fire went out from Heshbon,
a flame from the city of Sihon.
It has consumed Ar of Moab
and the lords of the high places of Arnon.
29 Woe to you, Moab.
You are ruined, O people of Chemosh!
He has made his sons fugitives,
and his daughters the prisoners of
King Sihon of the Amorites.
30 We have overpowered them;
Heshbon has perished as far as Dibon.
We have shattered them as far as Nophah,
which reaches to Medeba."

31 So the Israelites lived in the land of the Amorites. 32 Moses
sent spies to reconnoiter Jazer, and they captured its villages
and dispossessed the Amorites who were there.
33 Then they turned and went up by the road to Bashan. And King
Og of Bashan and all his forces marched out against them to do battle at Edrei. 34 And the LORD said to Moses, "Do not fear him, for I
have delivered him and all his people and his land into your hand.
You will do to him what you did to King Sihon of the Amorites,
who lived in Heshbon." 35 So they defeated Og, his sons, and all his
people, until there were no survivors, and they possessed his land.

BALAAM REFUSES TO CURSE ISRAEL

22 The Israelites traveled on and camped in the rift valley
plains of Moab on the side of the Jordan River across from
Jericho. 2 Balak son of Zippor saw all that the Israelites had done
to the Amorites. 3 And the Moabites were greatly afraid of the

people, because they were so numerous. The Moabites were sick
with fear because of the Israelites.
4 So the Moabites said to the elders of Midian, "Now this mass
of people will lick up everything around us, as the bull devours
the grass of the field." Now Balak son of Zippor was king of the
Moabites at this time. 5 And he sent messengers to Balaam son
of Beor at Pethor, which is by the Euphrates River in the land of
Amaw, to summon him, saying, "Look, a nation has come out of
Egypt. They cover the face of the earth, and they are settling next
to me. 6 So now, please come and curse this nation for me, for they
are too powerful for me. Perhaps I will prevail so that we may
conquer them and drive them out of the land. For I know that
whoever you bless is blessed, and whoever you curse is cursed."
7 So the elders of Moab and the elders of Midian departed with
the fee for divination in their hands. They came to Balaam and reported to him the words of Balak. 8 He replied to them, "Stay here
tonight, and I will bring back to you whatever word the LORD
may speak to me." So the princes of Moab stayed with Balaam.
9 And God came to Balaam and said, "Who are these men with
you?" 10 Balaam said to God, "Balak son of Zippor, king of Moab,
has sent a message to me, saying, 11 'Look, a nation has come out
of Egypt, and it covers the face of the earth. Come now and put
a curse on them for me; perhaps I will be able to defeat them
and drive them out.'" 12 But God said to Balaam, "You must not go
with them; you must not curse the people, for they are blessed."
13 So Balaam got up in the morning, and said to the princes of
Balak, "Go to your land, for the LORD has refused to permit me to
go with you." 14 So the princes of Moab departed and went back
to Balak and said, "Balaam refused to come with us."

BALAAM ACCOMPANIES THE MOABITE PRINCES

15 Balak again sent princes, more numerous and more distinguished than the first. 16 And they came to Balaam and said to him,
"Thus says Balak son of Zippor: 'Please do not let anything hinder
you from coming to me. 17 For I will honor you greatly, and whatever
you tell me I will do. So come, put a curse on this nation for me.'"
18 Balaam replied to the servants of Balak, "Even if Balak would
give me his palace full of silver and gold, I could not transgress
the commandment of the LORD my God to do less or more.
19 Now therefore, please stay the night here also, that I may know
what more the LORD might say to me." 20 God came to Balaam
that night, and said to him, "If the men have come to call you,
get up and go with them, but the word that I will say to you, that
you must do." 21 So Balaam got up in the morning, saddled his
donkey, and went with the princes of Moab.

GOD OPPOSES BALAAM

22 Then God's anger was kindled because he went, and the angel
of the LORD stood in the road to oppose him. Now he was riding
on his donkey and his two servants were with him. 23 And the
donkey saw the angel of the LORD standing in the road with his
sword drawn in his hand, so the donkey turned aside from the
road and went into the field. But Balaam beat the donkey, to
make her turn back to the road.

24 Then the angel of the LORD stood in a path among the vineyards, where there was a wall on either side. 25 And when the donkey saw the angel of the LORD, she pressed herself into the wall, and crushed Balaam's foot against the wall. So he beat her again.

26 Then the angel of the LORD went farther, and stood in a narrow place, where there was no way to turn either to the right or to the left. 27 When the donkey saw the angel of the LORD, she crouched down under Balaam. Then Balaam was angry, and he beat his donkey with a staff.

28 Then the LORD opened the mouth of the donkey, and she said to Balaam, "What have I done to you that you have beaten me these three times?" 29 And Balaam said to the donkey, "You have made me look stupid; I wish there were a sword in my hand, for I would kill you right now." 30 The donkey said to Balaam, "Am I not your donkey that you have ridden ever since I was yours until this day? Have I ever attempted to treat you this way?" And he said, "No." 31 Then the LORD opened Balaam's eyes, and he saw the angel of the LORD standing in the way with his sword drawn in his hand; so he bowed his head and threw himself down with his face to the ground. 32 The angel of the LORD said to him, "Why have you beaten your donkey these three times? Look, I came out to oppose you because what you are doing is perverse before me. 33 The donkey saw me and turned from me these three times. If she had not turned from me, I would have killed you but saved her alive." 34 Balaam said to the angel of the LORD, "I have sinned, for I did not know that you stood against me in the road. So now, if it is evil in your sight, I will go back home." 35 But the angel of the LORD said to Balaam, "Go with the men, but you may only speak the word that I will speak to you." So Balaam went with the princes of Balak.

BALAAM MEETS BALAK

36 When Balak heard that Balaam was coming, he went out to meet him at a city of Moab that was on the border of the Arnon at the boundary of his territory. 37 Balak said to Balaam, "Did I not send again and again to you to summon you? Why did you not come to me? Am I not able to honor you?" 38 Balaam said to Balak, "Look, I have come to you. Now, am I able to speak just anything? I must speak only the word that God puts in my mouth." 39 So Balaam went with Balak, and they came to Kiriath Huzoth. 40 And Balak sacrificed bulls and sheep, and sent some to Balaam, and to the princes who were with him. 41 Then on the next morning Balak took Balaam, and brought him up to Bamoth Baal. From there he saw the extent of the nation.

BALAAM BLESSES ISRAEL

23 Balaam said to Balak, "Build me seven altars here, and prepare for me here seven bulls and seven rams." 2 So Balak did just as Balaam had said. Balak and Balaam then offered on each altar a bull and a ram. 3 Balaam said to Balak, "Station yourself by your burnt offering, and I will go off; perhaps the LORD will come to meet me, and whatever he reveals to me I will tell you." Then he went to a deserted height.

4 Then God met Balaam, who said to him, "I have prepared

seven altars, and I have offered on each altar a bull and a ram."
5 Then the LORD put a message in Balaam's mouth and said, "Return to Balak, and speak what I tell you."
6 So he returned to him, and he was still standing by his burnt
offering, he and all the princes of Moab. 7 Then Balaam uttered
his oracle, saying,

"Balak, the king of Moab, brought me from Aram,
out of the mountains of the east, saying,
'Come, pronounce a curse on Jacob for me;
come, denounce Israel.'
8 How can I curse one whom God has not cursed,
or how can I denounce one whom the
LORD has not denounced?
9 For from the top of the rocks I see them;
from the hills I watch them.
Indeed, a nation that lives alone,
and it will not be reckoned among the nations.
10 Who can count the dust of Jacob,
or number the fourth part of Israel?
Let me die the death of the upright,
and let the end of my life be like theirs."

BALAAM RELOCATES

11 Then Balak said to Balaam, "What have you done to me? I
brought you to curse my enemies, but on the contrary you have
only blessed them!" 12 Balaam replied, "Must I not be careful to
speak what the LORD has put in my mouth?" 13 Balak said to him,
"Please come with me to another place from which you can observe them. You will see only a part of them, but you will not see
all of them. Curse them for me from there."
14 So Balak brought Balaam to the field of Zophim, to the top
of Pisgah, where he built seven altars and offered a bull and a
ram on each altar. 15 And Balaam said to Balak, "Station yourself here by your burnt offering, while I meet the LORD there."
16 Then the LORD met Balaam and put a message in his mouth
and said, "Return to Balak, and speak what I tell you." 17 When
Balaam came to him, he was still standing by his burnt offering,
along with the princes of Moab. And Balak said to him, "What
has the LORD spoken?"

BALAAM PROPHESIES AGAIN

18 Balaam uttered his oracle, and said,

"Rise up, Balak, and hear;
Listen to me, son of Zippor:
19 God is not a man, that he should lie,
nor a human being, that he should change his mind.
Has he said, and will he not do it?
Or has he spoken, and will he not make it happen?
20 Indeed, I have received a command to bless;
he has blessed, and I cannot reverse it.
21 He has not looked on iniquity in Jacob,
nor has he seen trouble in Israel.
The LORD their God is with them;
his acclamation as king is among them.

22 God brought them out of Egypt.
They have, as it were, the strength of a wild bull.
23 For there is no spell against Jacob,
nor is there any divination against Israel.
At this time it must be said of Jacob
and of Israel, 'Look at what God has done!'
24 Indeed, the people will rise up like a lioness,
and like a lion raises himself up;
they will not lie down until they eat their prey,
and drink the blood of the slain."

BALAAM RELOCATES YET AGAIN

25 Balak said to Balaam, "Neither curse them at all nor bless them
at all!" 26 But Balaam replied to Balak, "Did I not tell you, 'All that
the LORD speaks, I must do'?"

27 Balak said to Balaam, "Come, please; I will take you to another place. Perhaps it will please God to let you curse them
for me from there." 28 So Balak took Balaam to the top of Peor,
that looks toward the wastelands. 29 Then Balaam said to Balak,
"Build seven altars here for me, and prepare seven bulls and
seven rams." 30 So Balak did as Balaam had said, and offered a
bull and a ram on each altar.

BALAAM PROPHESIES YET AGAIN

24 When Balaam saw that it pleased the LORD to bless
Israel, he did not go as at the other times to seek for
omens, but he set his face toward the wilderness. 2 When Balaam lifted up his eyes, he saw Israel camped tribe by tribe;
and the Spirit of God came upon him. 3 Then he uttered
this oracle:

"The oracle of Balaam son of Beor,
the oracle of the man whose eyes are open,
4 the oracle of the one who hears the words of God,
who sees a vision from the Almighty,
although falling flat on the ground with eyes open:
5 'How beautiful are your tents, O Jacob,
and your dwelling places, O Israel!
6 They are like valleys stretched forth,
like gardens by the river's side,
like aloes that the LORD has planted,
and like cedar trees beside the waters.
7 He will pour the water out of his buckets,
and their descendants will be like abundant water;
their king will be greater than Agag,
and their kingdom will be exalted.
8 God brought them out of Egypt.
They have, as it were, the strength of a young bull;
they will devour hostile people,
and will break their bones,
and will pierce them through with arrows.
9 They crouch and lie down like a lion,
and as a lioness, who can stir him?
Blessed is the one who blesses you,
and cursed is the one who curses you!'"

10 Then Balak became very angry at Balaam, and he struck his
hands together. Balak said to Balaam, "I called you to curse my
enemies, and look, you have done nothing but bless them these
three times! 11 So now, go back where you came from! I said that
I would greatly honor you, but now the LORD has stood in the
way of your honor."
12 Balaam said to Balak, "Did I not also tell your messengers whom you sent to me, 13 'If Balak would give me his
palace full of silver and gold, I cannot go beyond the commandment of the LORD to do either good or evil of my own will,
but whatever the LORD tells me I must speak'? 14 And now, I
am about to go back to my own people. Come now, and I will
advise you as to what this people will do to your people in
future days."

BALAAM PROPHESIES A FOURTH TIME

15 Then he uttered this oracle:
"The oracle of Balaam son of Beor,
the oracle of the man whose eyes are open,
16 the oracle of the one who hears the words of God,
and who knows the knowledge of the Most High,
who sees a vision from the Almighty,
although falling flat on the ground with eyes open:
17 'I see him, but not now;
I behold him, but not close at hand.
A star will march forth out of Jacob,
and a scepter will rise out of Israel.
He will crush the skulls of Moab,
and the heads of all the sons of Sheth.
18 Edom will be a possession,
Seir, his enemy, will also be a possession;
but Israel will act valiantly.
19 A ruler will be established from Jacob;
he will destroy the remains of the city.'"

BALAAM'S FINAL PROPHECIES

20 Then Balaam looked on Amalek and delivered this oracle:
"Amalek was the first of the nations,
but his end will be that he will perish."

21 Then he looked on the Kenites and uttered this oracle:
"Your dwelling place seems strong,
and your nest is set on a rocky cliff.
22 Nevertheless the Kenite will be consumed.
How long will Asshur take you away captive?"

23 Then he uttered this oracle:
"O, who will survive when God does this!
24 Ships will come from the coast of Kittim,
and will afflict Asshur, and will afflict Eber,
and he will also perish forever."

25 Balaam got up and departed and returned to his home, and
Balak also went his way.

ISRAEL'S SIN WITH THE MOABITE WOMEN

25 When Israel lived in Shittim, the people began to commit
sexual immorality with the daughters of Moab. 2 These wom-
en invited the people to the sacrifices of their gods; then the people
ate and bowed down to their gods. 3 When Israel joined themselves
to Baal Peor, the anger of the LORD flared up against Israel.

GOD'S PUNISHMENT

4 The LORD said to Moses, "Arrest all the leaders of the people,
and hang them up before the LORD in broad daylight, so that
the fierce anger of the LORD may be turned away from Israel."
5 So Moses said to the judges of Israel, "Each of you must execute
those of his men who were joined to Baal Peor."

6 Just then one of the Israelites came and brought to his brothers a Midianite woman in the plain view of Moses and of the
whole community of the Israelites, while they were weeping at
the entrance of the tent of meeting. 7 When Phinehas son of Eleazar, the son of Aaron the priest, saw it, he got up from among
the assembly, took a javelin in his hand, 8 and went after the Israelite man into the tent and thrust through the Israelite man
and into the woman's abdomen. So the plague was stopped from
the Israelites. 9 Those that died in the plague were 24,000.

THE AFTERMATH

10 The LORD spoke to Moses: 11 "Phinehas son of Eleazar, the son
of Aaron the priest, has turned my anger away from the Israelites, when he manifested such zeal for my sake among them,
so that I did not consume the Israelites in my zeal. 12 Therefore,
announce: 'I am going to give to him my covenant of peace. 13 So
it will be to him and his descendants after him a covenant of a
permanent priesthood, because he has been zealous for his God,
and has made atonement for the Israelites.'"

14 Now the name of the Israelite who was stabbed—the one who
was stabbed with the Midianite woman—was Zimri son of Salu,
a leader of a clan of the Simeonites. 15 The name of the Midianite woman who was killed was Cozbi daughter of Zur. He was a
leader over the people of a clan of Midian.

16 Then the LORD spoke to Moses: 17 "Bring trouble to the Midianites, and destroy them, 18 because they bring trouble to you by
their treachery with which they have deceived you in the matter of Peor, and in the matter of Cozbi, the daughter of a prince
of Midian, their sister, who was killed on the day of the plague
that happened as a result of Peor."

A SECOND CENSUS REQUIRED

26 After the plague the LORD said to Moses and to Eleazar
son of Aaron the priest, 2 "Take a census of the whole community of Israelites, from twenty years old and upward, by their
clans, everyone who can serve in the army of Israel." 3 So Moses
and Eleazar the priest spoke with them in the rift valley plains
of Moab, along the Jordan River across from Jericho. They said,
4 "Number the people from twenty years old and upward, just as
the LORD commanded Moses and the Israelites who went out
from the land of Egypt."

REUBEN

[5]Reuben was the firstborn of Israel. The Reubenites: from Hanoch, the family of the Hanochites; from Pallu, the family of
the Palluites; [6]from Hezron, the family of the Hezronites; from
Carmi, the family of the Carmites. [7]These were the families of
the Reubenites; and those numbered of them were 43,730. [8]Pal-
lu's descendant was Eliab. [9]Eliab's descendants were Nemuel,
Dathan, and Abiram. It was Dathan and Abiram who as leaders of the community rebelled against Moses and Aaron with
the followers of Korah when they rebelled against the LORD.
[10]The earth opened its mouth and swallowed them and Korah
at the time that company died, when the fire consumed 250
men. So they became a warning. [11]But the descendants of Korah did not die.

SIMEON

[12]The Simeonites by their families: from Nemuel, the family of
the Nemuelites; from Jamin, the family of the Jaminites; from
Jakin, the family of the Jakinites; [13]from Zerah, the family of the
Zerahites; and from Shaul, the family of the Shaulites. [14]These
were the families of the Simeonites, 22,200.

GAD

[15]The Gadites by their families: from Zephon, the family of the
Zephonites; from Haggi, the family of the Haggites; from Shuni,
the family of the Shunites; [16]from Ozni, the family of the Oznites;
from Eri, the family of the Erites; [17]from Arod, the family of the
Arodites; and from Areli, the family of the Arelites. [18]These were
the families of the Gadites according to those numbered of them,
40,500.

JUDAH

[19]The descendants of Judah were Er and Onan, but Er and Onan
died in the land of Canaan. [20]And the Judahites by their families were: from Shelah, the family of the Shelahites; from Perez, the family of the Perezites; and from Zerah, the family of
the Zerahites. [21]And the Perezites were: from Hezron, the family of the Hezronites; from Hamul, the family of the Hamulites.
[22]These were the families of Judah according to those numbered
of them, 76,500.

ISSACHAR

[23]The Issacharites by their families: from Tola, the family of the
Tolaites; from Puah, the family of the Puites; [24]from Jashub,
the family of the Jashubites; and from Shimron, the family of
the Shimronites. [25]These were the families of Issachar, according to those numbered of them, 64,300.

ZEBULUN

[26]The Zebulunites by their families: from Sered, the family of
the Sardites; from Elon, the family of the Elonites; from Jahleel, the family of the Jahleelites. [27]These were the families
of the Zebulunites, according to those numbered of them,
60,500.

MANASSEH

28 The descendants of Joseph by their families: Manasseh and
Ephraim. 29 The Manassehites: from Machir, the family of the
Machirites (now Machir became the father of Gilead); from Gilead, the family of the Gileadites. 30 These were the Gileadites:
from Iezer, the family of the Iezerites; from Helek, the family
of the Helekites; 31 from Asriel, the family of the Asrielites; from
Shechem, the family of the Shechemites; 32 from Shemida, the
family of the Shemidaites; from Hepher, the family of the He-
pherites. 33 Now Zelophehad son of Hepher had no sons, but
only daughters; and the names of the daughters of Zelophehad
were Mahlah, Noah, Hoglah, Milcah, and Tirzah. 34 These were
the families of Manasseh; those numbered of them were 52,700.

EPHRAIM

35 These are the Ephraimites by their families: from Shuthelah,
the family of the Shuthelahites; from Beker, the family of the
Bekerites; from Tahan, the family of the Tahanites. 36 Now these
were the Shuthelahites: from Eran, the family of the Eranites.
37 These were the families of the Ephraimites, according to those
numbered of them, 32,500. These were the descendants of Joseph by their families.

BENJAMIN

38 The Benjaminites by their families: from Bela, the family of
the Belaites; from Ashbel, the family of the Ashbelites; from Ahi-
ram, the family of the Ahiramites; 39 from Shupham, the family of
the Shuphamites; from Hupham, the family of the Huphamites.
40 The descendants of Bela were Ard and Naaman. From Ard, the
family of the Ardites; from Naaman, the family of the Naama-
nites. 41 These are the Benjaminites, according to their families,
and according to those numbered of them, 45,600.

DAN

42 These are the Danites by their families: from Shuham, the family of the Shuhamites. These were the families of Dan, according
to their families. 43 All the families of the Shuhamites according
to those numbered of them were 64,400.

ASHER

44 The Asherites by their families: from Imnah, the family of the
Imnahites; from Ishvi, the family of the Ishvites; from Beriah,
the family of the Beriahites. 45 From the Beriahites: from Heber, the family of the Heberites; from Malkiel, the family of the
Malkielites. 46 Now the name of the daughter of Asher was Serah. 47 These are the families of the Asherites, according to those
numbered of them, 53,400.

NAPHTALI

48 The Naphtalites by their families: from Jahzeel, the family of
the Jahzeelites; from Guni, the family of the Gunites; 49 from Jezer, the family of the Jezerites; from Shillem, the family of the
Shillemites. 50 These were the families of Naphtali according to
their families; and those numbered of them were 45,400.

TOTAL NUMBER AND DIVISION OF THE LAND

51 These were those numbered of the Israelites, 601,730.

52 Then the LORD spoke to Moses: 53 "To these the land must be divided as an inheritance according to the number of the names. 54 To a larger group you will give a larger inheritance, and to a smaller group you will give a smaller inheritance. To each one its inheritance must be given according to the number of people in it. 55 The land must be divided by lot; and they will inherit in accordance with the names of their ancestral tribes. 56 Their inheritance must be apportioned by lot among the larger and smaller groups."

57 And these are the Levites who were numbered according to their families: from Gershon, the family of the Gershonites; of Kohath, the family of the Kohathites; from Merari, the family of the Merarites. 58 These are the families of the Levites: the family of the Libnites, the family of the Hebronites, the family of the Mahlites, the family of the Mushites, the family of the Korahites. Kohath became the father of Amram. 59 Now the name of Amram's wife was Jochebed, daughter of Levi, who was born to Levi in Egypt. And to Amram she bore Aaron, Moses, and Miriam their sister. 60 And to Aaron were born Nadab and Abihu, Eleazar and Ithamar. 61 But Nadab and Abihu died when they offered strange fire before the LORD. 62 Those of the Levites who were numbered were 23,000, all males from a month old and upward, for they were not numbered among the Israelites; no inheritance was given to them among the Israelites.

63 These are those who were numbered by Moses and Eleazar the priest, who numbered the Israelites in the rift valley plains of Moab along the Jordan River opposite Jericho. 64 But there was not a man among these who had been among those numbered by Moses and Aaron the priest when they numbered the Israelites in the desert of Sinai. 65 For the LORD had said of them, "They will surely die in the wilderness." And there was not left a single man of them, except Caleb son of Jephunneh and Joshua son of Nun.

SPECIAL INHERITANCE LAWS

27 Then the daughters of Zelophehad son of Hepher, the son of Gilead, the son of Machir, the son of Manasseh of the families of Manasseh, the son of Joseph came forward. Now these are the names of his daughters: Mahlah, Noah, Hoglah, Milcah, and Tirzah. 2 And they stood before Moses and Eleazar the priest and the leaders of the whole assembly at the entrance to the tent of meeting and said, 3 "Our father died in the wilderness, although he was not part of the company of those that gathered themselves together against the LORD in the company of Korah, but he died for his own sin, and he had no sons. 4 Why should the name of our father be lost from among his family because he had no son? Give us a possession among the relatives of our father."

5 So Moses brought their case before the LORD. 6 The LORD said to Moses: 7 "The daughters of Zelophehad have a valid claim. You must indeed give them possession of an inheritance among their father's relatives, and you must transfer the inheritance of their father to them. 8 And you must tell the Israelites, 'If a man

dies and has no son, then you must transfer his inheritance to
his daughter; 9 and if he has no daughter, then you are to give
his inheritance to his brothers; 10 and if he has no brothers, then
you are to give his inheritance to his father's brothers; 11 and if
his father has no brothers, then you are to give his inheritance
to his relative nearest to him from his family, and he will possess it. This will be for the Israelites a legal requirement, as the
LORD commanded Moses.'"

LEADERSHIP CHANGE

12 Then the LORD said to Moses, "Go up this mountain of the
Abarim range, and see the land I have given to the Israelites.
13 When you have seen it, you will be gathered to your ancestors, as Aaron your brother was gathered to his ancestors. 14 For
in the wilderness of Zin when the community rebelled against
me, you rebelled against my command to show me as holy before their eyes over the water—the water of Meribah in Kadesh
in the wilderness of Zin."

15 Then Moses spoke to the LORD: 16 "Let the LORD, the God of
the spirits of all humankind, appoint a man over the community, 17 who will go out before them, and who will come in before
them, and who will lead them out, and who will bring them in,
so that the community of the LORD may not be like sheep that
have no shepherd."

18 The LORD replied to Moses, "Take Joshua son of Nun, a man
in whom is the Spirit, and lay your hand on him; 19 set him before Eleazar the priest and before the whole community, and
commission him publicly. 20 Then you must delegate some of
your authority to him, so that the whole community of the Israelites will be obedient. 21 And he will stand before Eleazar the
priest, who will seek counsel for him before the LORD by the decision of the Urim. At his command they will go out, and at his
command they will come in, he and all the Israelites with him,
the whole community."

22 So Moses did as the LORD commanded him; he took Joshua
and set him before Eleazar the priest and before the whole community. 23 He laid his hands on him and commissioned him, just
as the LORD commanded, by the authority of Moses.

REFLECT

Why was it significant that the daughters of Zelophehad received an inheritance? What does this tell us about the culture and treatment of women in this period?

DAILY OFFERINGS

28 The LORD spoke to Moses: 2 "Command the Israelites:
'With regard to my offering, be sure to offer my food for
my offering made by fire, as a pleasing aroma to me at its appointed time.' 3 You will say to them, 'This is the offering made
by fire that you must offer to the LORD: two unblemished lambs
one year old each day for a continual burnt offering. 4 The first
lamb you must offer in the morning, and the second lamb you
must offer in the late afternoon, 5 with one-tenth of an ephah
of finely ground flour as a grain offering mixed with one-quarter of a hin of pressed olive oil. 6 It is a continual burnt offering
that was instituted on Mount Sinai as a pleasing aroma, an offering made by fire to the LORD.

7 "'And its drink offering must be one-quarter of a hin for each
lamb. You must pour out the strong drink as a drink offering to

the LORD in the Holy Place. 8 And the second lamb you must offer in the late afternoon; just as you offered the grain offering and drink offering in the morning, you must offer it as an offering made by fire, as a pleasing aroma to the LORD.

WEEKLY OFFERINGS

9 "'On the Sabbath day, you must offer two unblemished lambs a year old, and two-tenths of an ephah of finely ground flour as a grain offering, mixed with olive oil, along with its drink offering. 10 This is the burnt offering for every Sabbath, besides the continual burnt offering and its drink offering.

MONTHLY OFFERINGS

11 "'On the first day of each month you must offer as a burnt offering to the LORD two young bulls, one ram, and seven unblemished lambs a year old, 12 with three-tenths of an ephah of finely ground flour mixed with olive oil as a grain offering for each bull, and two-tenths of an ephah of finely ground flour mixed with olive oil as a grain offering for the ram, 13 and one-tenth of an ephah of finely ground flour mixed with olive oil as a grain offering for each lamb, as a burnt offering for a pleasing aroma, an offering made by fire to the LORD. 14 For their drink offerings, include half a hin of wine with each bull, one-third of a hin for the ram, and one-fourth of a hin for each lamb. This is the burnt offering for each month throughout the months of the year. 15 And one male goat must be offered to the LORD as a purification offering, in addition to the continual burnt offering and its drink offering.

THE PASSOVER

16 "'On the fourteenth day of the first month is the LORD's Passover. 17 And on the fifteenth day of this month is the festival. For seven days bread made without yeast must be eaten. 18 And on the first day there is to be a holy assembly; you must do no ordinary work on it.

19 "'But you must offer to the LORD an offering made by fire, a burnt offering of two young bulls, one ram, and seven lambs one year old; they must all be unblemished. 20 And their grain offering is to be of finely ground flour mixed with olive oil. For each bull you must offer three-tenths of an ephah, and two-tenths for the ram. 21 For each of the seven lambs you are to offer one-tenth of an ephah, 22 as well as one goat for a purification offering, to make atonement for you. 23 You must offer these in addition to the burnt offering in the morning that is for a continual burnt offering. 24 In this manner you must offer daily throughout the seven days the food of the sacrifice made by fire as a sweet aroma to the LORD. It is to be offered in addition to the continual burnt offering and its drink offering. 25 On the seventh day you are to have a holy assembly, you must do no regular work.

FIRSTFRUITS

26 "'Also, on the day of the firstfruits, when you bring a new grain offering to the LORD during your Feast of Weeks, you are to have a holy assembly. You must do no ordinary work. 27 But you must offer as the burnt offering, as a sweet aroma to the LORD, two

young bulls, one ram, seven lambs one year old, 28 with their grain
offering of finely ground flour mixed with olive oil: three-tenths
of an ephah for each bull, two-tenths for the one ram, 29 with one-
tenth for each of the seven lambs, 30 as well as one male goat to
make an atonement for you. 31 You are to offer them with their
drink offerings in addition to the continual burnt offering and
its grain offering—they must be unblemished.

BLOWING TRUMPETS

29 "'On the first day of the seventh month, you are to hold a
holy assembly. You must not do your ordinary work, for
it is a day of blowing trumpets for you. 2 You must offer a burnt
offering as a sweet aroma to the LORD: one young bull, one ram,
and seven lambs one year old without blemish.
3 "'Their grain offering is to be of finely ground flour mixed
with olive oil, three-tenths of an ephah for the bull, two-tenths
of an ephah for the ram, 4 and one-tenth for each of the seven
lambs, 5 with one male goat for a purification offering to make
an atonement for you; 6 this is in addition to the monthly burnt
offering and its grain offering, and the daily burnt offering with
its grain offering and their drink offerings as prescribed, as a
sweet aroma, a sacrifice made by fire to the LORD.

THE DAY OF ATONEMENT

7 "'On the tenth day of this seventh month you are to have a holy
assembly. You must humble yourselves; you must not do any
work on it. 8 But you must offer a burnt offering as a pleasing
aroma to the LORD, one young bull, one ram, and seven lambs
one year old, all of them without blemish. 9 Their grain offerings
must be of finely ground flour mixed with olive oil, three-tenths
of an ephah for the bull, two-tenths for the ram, 10 and one-tenth
for each of the seven lambs, 11 along with one male goat for a purification offering, in addition to the purification offering for
atonement and the continual burnt offering with its grain offering and their drink offerings.

THE FEAST OF TEMPORARY SHELTERS

12 "'On the fifteenth day of the seventh month you are to have
a holy assembly; you must do no ordinary work, and you must
keep a festival to the LORD for seven days. 13 You must offer a
burnt offering, an offering made by fire as a pleasing aroma to
the LORD: thirteen young bulls, two rams, and fourteen lambs
each one year old, all of them without blemish. 14 Their grain offerings must be of finely ground flour mixed with olive oil, three-
tenths of an ephah for each of the thirteen bulls, two-tenths of
an ephah for each of the two rams, 15 and one-tenth for each of
the fourteen lambs, 16 along with one male goat for a purification offering, in addition to the continual burnt offering with
its grain offering and its drink offering.
17 "'On the second day you must offer twelve young bulls, two
rams, fourteen lambs one year old, all without blemish, 18 and
their grain offerings and their drink offerings for the bulls, for
the rams, and for the lambs, according to their number as prescribed, 19 along with one male goat for a purification offering,

in addition to the continual burnt offering with its grain offering and their drink offerings.
20 "'On the third day you must offer eleven bulls, two rams, fourteen lambs one year old, all without blemish, 21 and their grain offerings and their drink offerings for the bulls, for the rams, and for
the lambs, according to their number as prescribed, 22 along with
one male goat for a purification offering, in addition to the continual burnt offering with its grain offering and its drink offering.
23 "'On the fourth day you must offer ten bulls, two rams, and fourteen lambs one year old, all without blemish, 24 and their grain offerings and their drink offerings for the bulls, for the rams, and for
the lambs, according to their number as prescribed, 25 along with
one male goat for a purification offering, in addition to the continual burnt offering with its grain offering and its drink offering.
26 "'On the fifth day you must offer nine bulls, two rams, and fourteen lambs one year old, all without blemish, 27 and their grain offerings and their drink offerings for the bulls, for the rams, and for
the lambs, according to their number as prescribed, 28 along with
one male goat for a purification offering, in addition to the continual burnt offering with its grain offering and its drink offering.
29 "'On the sixth day you must offer eight bulls, two rams,
and fourteen lambs one year old, all without blemish, 30 and
their grain offering and their drink offerings for the bulls, for
the rams, and for the lambs, according to their number as prescribed, 31 along with one male goat for a purification offering,
in addition to the continual burnt offering with its grain offering and its drink offering.
32 "'On the seventh day you must offer seven bulls, two rams, and
fourteen lambs one year old, all without blemish, 33 and their grain
offerings and their drink offerings for the bulls, for the rams, and for
the lambs, according to their number as prescribed, 34 along with
one male goat for a purification offering, in addition to the continual burnt offering with its grain offering and its drink offering.
35 "'On the eighth day you are to have a holy assembly; you must
do no ordinary work on it. 36 But you must offer a burnt offering, an offering made by fire, as a pleasing aroma to the LORD,
one bull, one ram, seven lambs one year old, all of them without blemish, 37 and with their grain offerings and their drink
offerings for the bull, for the ram, and for the lambs, according
to their number as prescribed, 38 along with one male goat for a
purification offering, in addition to the continual burnt offering with its grain offering and its drink offering.
39 "'These things you must present to the LORD at your appointed times, in addition to your vows and your freewill offerings, as your burnt offerings, your grain offerings, your drink
offerings, and your peace offerings.'" 40 So Moses told the Israelites everything, just as the LORD had commanded him.

VOWS MADE BY MEN

30 Moses told the leaders of the tribes concerning the Israelites, "This is what the LORD has commanded: 2 If a man
makes a vow to the LORD or takes an oath of binding obligation
on himself, he must not break his word, but must do whatever
he has promised.

VOWS MADE BY SINGLE WOMEN

3“If a young woman who is still living in her father’s house makes a vow to the LORD or places herself under an obligation, 4and her father hears of her vow or the obligation to which she has pledged herself, and her father remains silent about her, then all her vows will stand, and every obligation to which she has pledged herself will stand. 5But if her father overrules her when he hears about it, then none of her vows or her obligations that she has pledged for herself will stand. And the LORD will release her from it, because her father overruled her.

VOWS MADE BY MARRIED WOMEN

6“And if she marries a husband while under a vow, or she uttered anything impulsively by which she has pledged herself, 7and her husband hears about it but remains silent about her when he hears about it, then her vows will stand and her obligations that she has pledged for herself will stand. 8But if when her husband hears it he overrules her, then he will nullify the vow she has taken, and whatever she uttered impulsively that she has pledged for herself. And the LORD will release her from it.

VOWS MADE BY WIDOWS

9“But every vow of a widow or of a divorced woman which she has pledged for herself will remain intact. 10If she made the vow in her husband’s house or put herself under obligation with an oath, 11and her husband heard about it, but remained silent about her, and did not overrule her, then all her vows will stand, and every obligation which she pledged for herself will stand. 12But if her husband clearly nullifies them when he hears them, then whatever she says by way of vows or obligations will not stand. Her husband has made them void, and the LORD will release her from them.

13“Any vow or sworn obligation that would bring affliction to her, her husband can confirm or nullify. 14But if her husband remains completely silent about her from day to day, he thus confirms all her vows or all her obligations which she is under; he confirms them because he remained silent about her when he heard them. 15But if he should nullify them after he has heard them, then he will bear her iniquity.”

16These are the statutes that the LORD commanded Moses, relating to a man and his wife, and a father and his young daughter who is still living in her father’s house.

THE MIDIANITE WAR

31 The LORD spoke to Moses: 2“Exact vengeance for the Israelites from the Midianites—after that you will be gathered to your people.”

3So Moses spoke to the people: “Arm men from among you for the war, to attack the Midianites and to execute the LORD’s vengeance on Midian. 4You must send to the battle 1,000 men from every tribe throughout all the tribes of Israel.” 5So 1,000 from every tribe, 12,000 armed for battle in all, were provided out of the thousands of Israel.

CAMPAIGN AGAINST THE MIDIANITES

6 So Moses sent them to the war, 1,000 from every tribe, with Phinehas son of Eleazar the priest, who was in charge of the holy articles and the signal trumpets. 7 They fought against the Midianites, as the LORD commanded Moses, and they killed every male. 8 They killed the kings of Midian in addition to those slain—Evi, Rekem, Zur, Hur, and Reba—five Midianite kings. They also killed Balaam son of Beor with the sword.

9 The Israelites took the women of Midian captive along with their little ones, and took all their herds, all their flocks, and all their goods as plunder. 10 They burned all their towns where they lived and all their encampments. 11 They took all the plunder and all the spoils, both people and animals. 12 They brought the captives and the spoils and the plunder to Moses, to Eleazar the priest, and to the Israelite community, to the camp on the rift valley plains of Moab, along the Jordan River across from Jericho. 13 Moses, Eleazar the priest, and all the leaders of the community went out to meet them outside the camp.

THE DEATH OF THE MIDIANITE WOMEN

14 But Moses was furious with the officers of the army, the commanders over thousands and commanders over hundreds, who had come from service in the war. 15 Moses said to them, "Have you allowed all the women to live? 16 Look, these people through the counsel of Balaam caused the Israelites to act treacherously against the LORD in the matter of Peor—which resulted in the plague among the community of the LORD! 17 Now therefore kill every boy, and kill every woman who has been intimate with a man in bed. 18 But all the young women who have not experienced a man's bed will be yours.

PURIFICATION AFTER BATTLE

19 "Any of you who has killed anyone or touched any of the dead, remain outside the camp for seven days; purify yourselves and your captives on the third day, and on the seventh day. 20 You must purify each garment and everything that is made of skin, everything made of goats' hair, and everything made of wood."

21 Then Eleazar the priest said to the men of war who had gone into the battle, "This is the ordinance of the law that the LORD commanded Moses: 22 'Only the gold, the silver, the bronze, the iron, the tin, and the lead, 23 everything that may stand the fire, you are to pass through the fire, and it will be ceremonially clean, but it must still be purified with the water of purification. Anything that cannot withstand the fire you must pass through the water. 24 You must wash your clothes on the seventh day, and you will be ceremonially clean, and afterward you may enter the camp.'"

THE DISTRIBUTION OF SPOILS

25 Then the LORD spoke to Moses: 26 "You and Eleazar the priest, and all the family leaders of the community, take the sum of the plunder that was captured, both people and animals. 27 Divide the plunder into two parts, one for those who took part in the war—who went out to battle—and the other for all the community.

28“You must exact a tribute for the LORD from the fighting
men who went out to battle: one life out of 500, from the people, the cattle, and from the donkeys and the sheep. 29You are to
take it from their half share and give it to Eleazar the priest for
a raised offering to the LORD. 30From the Israelites' half share
you are to take one portion out of fifty of the people, the cattle,
the donkeys, and the sheep—from every kind of animal—and you
are to give them to the Levites, who are responsible for the care
of the LORD's tabernacle.”

31So Moses and Eleazar the priest did as the LORD commanded
Moses. 32The spoil that remained of the plunder that the fighting
men had gathered was 675,000 sheep, 3372,000 cattle, 3461,000
donkeys, 35and 32,000 young women who had not experienced
a man's bed.

36The half portion of those who went to war numbered 337,500
sheep; 37the LORD's tribute from the sheep was 675. 38The cattle numbered 36,000; the LORD's tribute was 72. 39The donkeys
were 30,500, of which the LORD's tribute was 61. 40The people
were 16,000, of which the LORD's tribute was 32 people.

41So Moses gave the tribute, which was the LORD's raised offering, to Eleazar the priest, as the LORD commanded Moses.

42From the Israelites' half share that Moses had separated
from the fighting men, 43there were 337,500 sheep from the
portion belonging to the community, 4436,000 cattle, 4530,500
donkeys, 46and 16,000 people.

47From the Israelites' share Moses took one of every fifty
people and animals and gave them to the Levites who were responsible for the care of the LORD's tabernacle, just as the LORD
commanded Moses.

48Then the officers who were over the thousands of the army,
the commanders over thousands and the commanders over hundreds, approached Moses 49and said to him, “Your servants have
taken a count of the men who were in the battle, who were under
our authority, and not one is missing. 50So we have brought as
an offering for the LORD what each man found: gold ornaments,
armlets, bracelets, signet rings, earrings, and necklaces, to make
atonement for ourselves before the LORD.” 51Moses and Eleazar the priest took the gold from them, all of it in the form of
ornaments. 52All the gold of the offering they offered up to the
LORD from the commanders of thousands and the commanders of hundreds weighed 16,750 shekels. 53Each soldier had taken
plunder for himself. 54So Moses and Eleazar the priest received
the gold from the commanders of thousands and commanders
of hundreds and brought it into the tent of meeting as a memorial for the Israelites before the LORD.

THE PETITION OF THE REUBENITES AND GADITES

32 Now the Reubenites and the Gadites possessed a very
large number of cattle. When they saw that the lands of
Jazer and Gilead were ideal for cattle, 2the Gadites and the Reubenites came and addressed Moses, Eleazar the priest, and the
leaders of the community. They said, 3“Ataroth, Dibon, Jazer,
Nimrah, Heshbon, Elealeh, Sebam, Nebo, and Beon, 4the land
that the LORD subdued before the community of Israel, is ideal

for cattle, and your servants have cattle." 5 So they said, "If we
have found favor in your sight, let this land be given to your servants for our inheritance. Do not have us cross the Jordan River."

MOSES' RESPONSE

6 Moses said to the Gadites and the Reubenites, "Must your brothers go to war while you remain here? 7 Why do you frustrate the
intent of the Israelites to cross over into the land that the LORD
has given them? 8 Your fathers did the same thing when I sent
them from Kadesh Barnea to see the land. 9 When they went up
to the Eshcol Valley and saw the land, they frustrated the intent
of the Israelites so that they did not enter the land that the LORD
had given them. 10 So the anger of the LORD was kindled that day,
and he swore, 11 'Because they have not followed me wholeheartedly, not one of the men twenty years old and upward who came
from Egypt will see the land that I swore to give to Abraham,
Isaac, and Jacob, 12 except Caleb son of Jephunneh the Kenizzite,
and Joshua son of Nun, for they followed the LORD wholeheartedly.' 13 So the LORD's anger was kindled against the Israelites,
and he made them wander in the wilderness for forty years, until all that generation that had done wickedly before the LORD
was finished. 14 Now look, you are standing in your fathers' place,
a brood of sinners, to increase still further the fierce wrath of the
LORD against the Israelites. 15 For if you turn away from following him, he will once again abandon them in the wilderness, and
you will be the reason for their destruction."

THE OFFER OF THE REUBENITES AND GADITES

16 Then they came very close to him and said, "We will build sheep
folds here for our flocks and cities for our families, 17 but we will
maintain ourselves in armed readiness and go before the Israelites until whenever we have brought them to their place.
Our descendants will be living in fortified towns as a protection against the inhabitants of the land. 18 We will not return
to our homes until every Israelite has his inheritance. 19 For we
will not accept any inheritance on the other side of the Jordan
River and beyond, because our inheritance has come to us on
this eastern side of the Jordan."

20 Then Moses replied, "If you will do this thing, and if you
will arm yourselves for battle before the LORD, 21 and if all your
armed men cross the Jordan before the LORD until he drives
out his enemies from his presence 22 and the land is subdued
before the LORD, then afterward you may return and be free of
your obligation to the LORD and to Israel. This land will then be
your possession in the LORD's sight.

23 "But if you do not do this, then look, you will have sinned
against the LORD. And know that your sin will find you out. 24 So
build cities for your descendants and pens for your sheep, but
do what you have said you would do."

25 So the Gadites and the Reubenites replied to Moses, "Your
servants will do as my lord commands. 26 Our children, our wives,
our flocks, and all our livestock will be there in the cities of Gilead, 27 but your servants will cross over, every man armed for
war, to do battle in the LORD's presence, just as my lord says."

28 So Moses gave orders about them to Eleazar the priest, to
Joshua son of Nun, and to the heads of the families of the Israelite tribes. 29 Moses said to them: "If the Gadites and the Reubenites cross the Jordan with you, each one equipped for battle in
the LORD's presence, and you conquer the land, then you must
allot them the territory of Gilead as their possession. 30 But if
they do not cross over with you armed, they must receive possessions among you in Canaan." 31 Then the Gadites and the Reubenites answered, "Your servants will do what the LORD has spoken.
32 We will cross armed in the LORD's presence into the land of
Canaan, and then the possession of our inheritance that we inherit will be ours on this side of the Jordan River."

LAND ASSIGNMENT

33 So Moses gave to the Gadites, the Reubenites, and to half the
tribe of Manasseh son of Joseph the realm of King Sihon of the
Amorites, and the realm of King Og of Bashan, the entire land
with its cities and the territory surrounding them. 34 The Gadites
rebuilt Dibon, Ataroth, Aroer, 35 Atroth Shophan, Jazer, Jogbehah, 36 Beth Nimrah, and Beth Haran as fortified cities, and constructed pens for their flocks. 37 The Reubenites rebuilt Heshbon,
Elealeh, Kiriathaim, 38 Nebo, Baal Meon (with a change of name),
and Sibmah. They renamed the cities they built.

39 The descendants of Machir son of Manasseh went to Gilead,
took it, and dispossessed the Amorites who were in it. 40 So Moses gave Gilead to Machir, son of Manasseh, and he lived there.
41 Now Jair son of Manasseh went and captured their small towns
and named them Havvoth Jair. 42 Then Nobah went and captured
Kenath and its villages and called it Nobah after his own name.

WANDERINGS FROM EGYPT TO SINAI

33 These are the journeys of the Israelites, who went out of
the land of Egypt by their divisions under the authority
of Moses and Aaron. 2 Moses recorded their departures according to their journeys, by the commandment of the LORD; now
these are their journeys according to their departures. 3 They departed from Rameses in the first month, on the fifteenth day of
the first month; on the day after the Passover the Israelites went
out defiantly in plain sight of all the Egyptians. 4 Now the Egyptians were burying all their firstborn, whom the LORD had killed
among them; the LORD also executed judgments on their gods.

5 The Israelites traveled from Rameses and camped in Sukkoth.

6 They traveled from Sukkoth, and camped in Etham, which is on
the edge of the desert. 7 They traveled from Etham, and turned again
to Pi Hahiroth, which is before Baal Zephon; and they camped before Migdal. 8 They traveled from Pi Hahiroth, and passed through
the middle of the sea into the wilderness, and went three days'
journey in the wilderness of Etham, and camped in Marah. 9 They
traveled from Marah and came to Elim; in Elim there are twelve
fountains of water and seventy palm trees, so they camped there.

10 They traveled from Elim, and camped by the Red Sea. 11 They
traveled from the Red Sea and camped in the wilderness of Sin.
12 They traveled from the wilderness of Sin and camped in Dophkah. 13 And they traveled from Dophkah, and camped in Alush.

14 They traveled from Alush and camped at Rephidim, where
there was no water for the people to drink. 15 They traveled from
Rephidim and camped in the desert of Sinai.

WANDERINGS IN THE WILDERNESS

16 They traveled from the desert of Sinai and camped at Kibroth
Hattaavah. 17 They traveled from Kibroth Hattaavah and camped
at Hazeroth. 18 They traveled from Hazeroth and camped in Rithmah. 19 They traveled from Rithmah and camped at Rimmon Perez. 20 They traveled from Rimmon Perez and camped in Libnah.
21 They traveled from Libnah and camped at Rissah. 22 They traveled from Rissah and camped in Kehelathah. 23 They traveled
from Kehelathah and camped at Mount Shepher. 24 They traveled from Mount Shepher and camped in Haradah. 25 They traveled from Haradah and camped in Makheloth. 26 They traveled
from Makheloth and camped at Tahath. 27 They traveled from
Tahath and camped at Terah. 28 They traveled from Terah and
camped in Mithcah. 29 They traveled from Mithcah and camped
in Hashmonah. 30 They traveled from Hashmonah and camped in
Moseroth. 31 They traveled from Moseroth and camped in Bene
Jaakan. 32 They traveled from Bene Jaakan and camped at Hor
Haggidgad. 33 They traveled from Hor Haggidgad and camped in
Jotbathah. 34 They traveled from Jotbathah and camped in Abronah. 35 They traveled from Abronah and camped at Ezion Geber.
36 They traveled from Ezion Geber and camped in the wilderness
of Zin, that is, Kadesh.

WANDERINGS FROM KADESH TO MOAB

37 They traveled from Kadesh and camped at Mount Hor at the
edge of the land of Edom. 38 Aaron the priest ascended Mount
Hor at the command of the LORD, and he died there in the fortieth year after the Israelites had come out of the land of Egypt
on the first day of the fifth month. 39 Now Aaron was 123 years old
when he died on Mount Hor. 40 The king of Arad, the Canaanite
king who lived in the south of the land of Canaan, heard about
the approach of the Israelites.

41 They traveled from Mount Hor and camped in Zalmonah.
42 They traveled from Zalmonah and camped in Punon. 43 They
traveled from Punon and camped in Oboth. 44 They traveled from
Oboth and camped in Iye Abarim, on the border of Moab. 45 They
traveled from Iim and camped in Dibon Gad. 46 They traveled
from Dibon Gad and camped in Almon Diblathaim. 47 They traveled from Almon Diblathaim and camped in the mountains of
Abarim before Nebo. 48 They traveled from the mountains of
Abarim and camped in the rift valley plains by Moab along the
Jordan River across from Jericho. 49 They camped by the Jordan,
from Beth Jeshimoth as far as Abel Shittim in the rift valley
plains of Moab.

AT THE BORDER OF CANAAN

50 The LORD spoke to Moses in the rift valley plains of Moab along
the Jordan, across from Jericho. He said: 51 "Speak to the Israelites and tell them, 'When you have crossed the Jordan into the
land of Canaan, 52 you must drive out all the inhabitants of the

land before you. Destroy all their carved images, all their molten images, and demolish their high places. 53 You must dispossess the inhabitants of the land and live in it, for I have given
you the land to possess it. 54 You must divide the land by lot for
an inheritance among your families. To a larger group you must
give a larger inheritance, and to a smaller group you must give
a smaller inheritance. Everyone's inheritance must be in the
place where his lot falls. You must inherit according to your ancestral tribes. 55 But if you do not drive out the inhabitants of
the land before you, then those whom you allow to remain will
be irritants in your eyes and thorns in your side, and will cause
you trouble in the land where you will be living. 56 And what I
intended to do to them I will do to you.'"

THE SOUTHERN BORDER OF THE LAND

34 Then the LORD spoke to Moses: 2 "Give these instructions
to the Israelites, and tell them: 'When you enter Canaan,
the land that has been assigned to you as an inheritance, the
land of Canaan with its borders, 3 your southern border will extend from the wilderness of Zin along the Edomite border, and
your southern border will run eastward to the extremity of the
Salt Sea, 4 and then the border will turn from the south to the
Scorpion Ascent, continue to Zin, and then its direction will be
from the south to Kadesh Barnea. Then it will go to Hazar Addar
and pass over to Azmon. 5 There the border will turn from Azmon to the Stream of Egypt, and then its direction is to the sea.

THE WESTERN BORDER OF THE LAND

6 "'And for a western border you will have the Great Sea. This will
be your western border.

THE NORTHERN BORDER OF THE LAND

7 "'And this will be your northern border: From the Great Sea you
will draw a line to Mount Hor; 8 from Mount Hor you will draw
a line to Lebo Hamath, and the direction of the border will be
to Zedad. 9 The border will continue to Ziphron, and its direction will be to Hazar Enan. This will be your northern border.

THE EASTERN BORDER OF THE LAND

10 "'For your eastern border you will draw a line from Hazar
Enan to Shepham. 11 The border will run down from Shepham
to Riblah, on the east side of Ain, and the border will descend
and reach the eastern side of the Sea of Kinnereth. 12 Then the
border will continue down the Jordan River and its direction
will be to the Salt Sea. This will be your land by its borders that
surround it.'"

13 Then Moses commanded the Israelites: "This is the land that
you will inherit by lot, which the LORD has commanded to be
given to the nine-and-a-half tribes, 14 because the tribe of the
Reubenites by their families, the tribe of the Gadites by their
families, and the half-tribe of Manasseh have received their inheritance. 15 The two-and-a-half tribes have received their inheritance on this side of the Jordan, east of Jericho, toward the
sunrise."

APPOINTED OFFICIALS

16 The LORD said to Moses: 17 "These are the names of the men who are to allocate the land to you as an inheritance: Eleazar the priest and Joshua son of Nun. 18 You must take one leader from every tribe to assist in allocating the land as an inheritance. 19 These are the names of the men: from the tribe of Judah, Caleb son of Jephunneh; 20 from the tribe of the Simeonites, Shemuel son of Ammihud; 21 from the tribe of Benjamin, Elidad son of Kislon; 22 and from the tribe of the Danites, a leader, Bukki son of Jogli. 23 From the Josephites, Hanniel son of Ephod, a leader from the tribe of Manasseh; 24 from the tribe of the Ephraimites, a leader, Kemuel son of Shiphtan; 25 from the tribe of the Zebulunites, a leader, Elizaphan son of Parnach; 26 from the tribe of the Issacharites, a leader, Paltiel son of Azzan; 27 from the tribe of the Asherites, a leader, Ahihud son of Shelomi; 28 and from the tribe of the Naphtalites, a leader, Pedahel son of Ammihud." 29 These are the ones whom the LORD commanded to divide up the inheritance among the Israelites in the land of Canaan.

THE LEVITICAL CITIES

35 Then the LORD spoke to Moses in the rift valley plains of Moab along the Jordan near Jericho. He said: 2 "Instruct the Israelites to give the Levites towns to live in from the inheritance the Israelites will possess. You must also give the Levites grazing land around the towns. 3 Thus they will have towns in which to live, and their grazing lands will be for their cattle, for their possessions, and for all their animals. 4 The grazing lands around the towns that you will give to the Levites must extend to a distance of 500 yards from the town wall.

5 "You must measure from outside the wall of the town on the east 1,000 yards, and on the south side 1,000 yards, and on the west side 1,000 yards, and on the north side 1,000 yards, with the town in the middle. This territory must belong to them as grazing land for the towns. 6 Now from these towns that you will give to the Levites you must select six towns of refuge to which a person who has killed someone may flee. And you must give them forty-two other towns.

7 "So the total of the towns you will give the Levites is forty-eight. You must give these together with their grazing lands. 8 The towns you will give must be from the possession of the Israelites. From the larger tribes you must give more; and from the smaller tribes fewer. Each must contribute some of its own towns to the Levites in proportion to the inheritance allocated to each.

THE CITIES OF REFUGE

9 Then the LORD spoke to Moses: 10 "Speak to the Israelites and tell them, 'When you cross over the Jordan River into the land of Canaan, 11 you must then designate some towns as towns of refuge for you, to which a person who has killed someone unintentionally may flee. 12 And they must stand as your towns of refuge from the avenger in order that the killer may not die until

he has stood trial before the community. 13 These towns that you
must give shall be your six towns for refuge.
14 "'You must give three towns on this side of the Jordan, and
you must give three towns in the land of Canaan; they must be
towns of refuge. 15 These six towns will be places of refuge for
the Israelites, and for the resident foreigner, and for the settler
among them, so that anyone who kills any person accidentally
may flee there.
16 "'But if he hits someone with an iron tool so that he dies, he
is a murderer. The murderer must surely be put to death. 17 If he
strikes him by throwing a stone large enough that he could die,
and he dies, he is a murderer. The murderer must surely be put
to death. 18 Or if he strikes him with a wooden hand weapon so
that he could die, and he dies, he is a murderer. The murderer
must surely be put to death. 19 The avenger of blood himself must
kill the murderer; when he meets him, he must kill him.
20 "'But if he strikes him out of hatred or throws something at
him intentionally so that he dies, 21 or with enmity he strikes him
with his hand and he dies, the one who struck him must surely
be put to death, for he is a murderer. The avenger of blood must
kill the murderer when he meets him.
22 "But if he strikes him suddenly, without enmity, or throws
anything at him unintentionally, 23 or with any stone large
enough that a man could die, without seeing him, and throws
it at him, and he dies, even though he was not his enemy nor
sought his harm, 24 then the community must judge between
the slayer and the avenger of blood according to these decisions. 25 The community must deliver the slayer out of the
hand of the avenger of blood, and the community must restore him to the town of refuge to which he fled, and he must
live there until the death of the high priest, who was anointed
with the consecrated oil. 26 But if the slayer at any time goes
outside the boundary of the town to which he had fled, 27 and
the avenger of blood finds him outside the borders of the
town of refuge, and the avenger of blood kills the slayer, he
will not be guilty of blood, 28 because the slayer should have
stayed in his town of refuge until the death of the high priest.
But after the death of the high priest, the slayer may return
to the land of his possessions. 29 So these things must be a
statutory ordinance for you throughout your generations, in
all the places where you live.
30 "Whoever kills any person, the murderer must be put to
death by the testimony of witnesses, but one witness cannot testify against any person to cause him to be put to death. 31 Moreover, you must not accept a ransom for the life of a murderer
who is guilty of death; he must surely be put to death. 32 And you
must not accept a ransom for anyone who has fled to a town of
refuge, to allow him to return home and live on his own land
before the death of the high priest.
33 "'You must not pollute the land where you live, for blood
defiles the land, and the land cannot be cleansed of the blood
that is shed there, except by the blood of the person who shed it.
34 Therefore do not defile the land that you will inhabit, in which
I live, for I the LORD live among the Israelites.'"

WOMEN AND LAND INHERITANCE

36 Then the heads of the family groups of the Gileadites, the descendant of Machir, the descendant of Manasseh, who were from the Josephite families, approached and spoke before Moses and the leaders who were the heads of the Israelite families. 2 They said, "The LORD commanded my lord to give the land as an inheritance by lot to the Israelites; and my lord was commanded by the LORD to give the inheritance of our brother Zelophehad to his daughters. 3 Now if they should be married to one of the men from another Israelite tribe, their inheritance would be taken from the inheritance of our fathers and added to the inheritance of the tribe into which they marry. As a result, it will be taken from the lot of our inheritance. 4 And when the Jubilee of the Israelites is to take place, their inheritance will be added to the inheritance of the tribe into which they marry. So their inheritance will be taken away from the inheritance of our ancestral tribe."

MOSES' DECISION

5 Then Moses gave a ruling to the Israelites by the word of the LORD: "What the tribe of the Josephites is saying is right. 6 This is what the LORD has commanded for Zelophehad's daughters: 'Let them marry whomever they think best, only they must marry within the family of their father's tribe. 7 In this way the inheritance of the Israelites will not be transferred from tribe to tribe. But every one of the Israelites must retain the ancestral heritage. 8 And every daughter who possesses an inheritance from any of the tribes of the Israelites must become the wife of a man from any family in her father's tribe, so that every Israelite may retain the inheritance of his fathers. 9 No inheritance may pass from tribe to tribe. But every one of the tribes of the Israelites must retain its inheritance.'"

10 As the LORD had commanded Moses, so the daughters of Zelophehad did. 11 For the daughters of Zelophehad—Mahlah, Tirzah, Hoglah, Milcah, and Noah—were married to the sons of their uncles. 12 They were married into the families of the Manassehites, the descendants of Joseph, and their inheritance remained in the tribe of their father's family.

13 These are the commandments and the decisions that the LORD commanded the Israelites through the authority of Moses, in the rift valley plains by Moab along the Jordan River opposite Jericho.

WHAT I AM COMMANDING you today is to love THE LORD your GOD, TO WALK IN His ways, and to OBEY His COMMANDMENTS, His statutes, and His ordinances

MEMORY VERSE

"What I am commanding you today is to love the LORD your God, to walk in his ways, and to obey his commandments, his statutes, and his ordinances. Then you will live and become numerous and the LORD your God will bless you in the land that you are about to possess."

Deuteronomy 30:16

Deuteronomy

INTRODUCTION

Covenant Faithfulness

God's covenant faithfulness is on display throughout every page of the Book of Deuteronomy. Deuteronomy reestablished God's covenant with the nation of Israel as they prepared to enter the land God promised to give them. God's faithfulness is evident to both the people of Israel and the surrounding nations.

As the Israelites prepared to enter the land of Canaan, God reminded them of the law He gave them forty years earlier on Mount Sinai. The pattern and language of Deuteronomy are the same as many other ancient Middle Eastern treaties between a lord and a servant. In Deuteronomy, Israel is reestablished as Yahweh's people, and Yahweh as their Lord. By renewing His covenant with them, God reminded Israel of His faithfulness. He would lead them into the land if they would follow Him and keep His commands.

Like the rest of the Pentateuch (Genesis, Exodus, Leviticus, and Numbers), Deuteronomy was written for the generation of Israelites entering the land of Canaan. These writings reminded them of God's faithfulness from their exodus from Egypt to their wanderings in the desert. Once they were established in the promised land, the Book of Deuteronomy served as a reminder of God's covenant and His covenant faithfulness.

Deuteronomy offers encouragement in many ways. It shows the people of God how far God will go to keep His covenant promises. Even though their rebellion cost them greatly in the desert, God's covenant faithfulness was greater than their sin. Deuteronomy encourages us to love God greatly as we see the steadfastness of His character and His constant pursuit of His people.

The Netherlands

OFFICIAL LANGUAGE
Dutch
POPULATION
16,994,000
UNREACHED POPULATION
887,000
PROFESSING CHRISTIANS
47.2%

Willemin's Home

Say a Prayer Today

Please pray for Willemin and her ministry to the Dutch people. Pray that the people of the Netherlands will remember their legacy and turn their hearts back to God.

HISTORY BIT

The Bible was first translated into Dutch from the original Hebrew and Greek manuscripts in 1637. Called the Statenvertaling, this translation remained the generally accepted translation into the twentieth century.*

Source Information:
https://joshuaproject.net/countries/NL
*John Bowden, A Chronology of World Christianity (New York, NY: Continuum, 2007), 309.

WILLEMIN'S STORY

Every year on May 4 the people of the Netherlands observe two minutes of silence at eight o'clock in the evening.

Together, we commemorate Dutch victims of the Second World War. People stop whatever they are doing, even travelers park their cars on the side of the road. Through the television, the radio, or in person, the people experience a common silence throughout Amsterdam or on the field at Waalsdorpervlakte, a battlefield where many Dutch soldiers were killed.

During those two minutes I think of my grandfather who served as a medic during a foreign mission. For those two minutes I think of the weight that was on his shoulders. And in those two minutes I think of his shoulders on which I symbolically stand. He didn't speak much, my grandfather, but he never failed to mention how he and my grandma always prayed for me. I know I can stand on the legacy they built for the future of our country and on our family's faith in Jesus Christ.

Would the Israelites have remembered the prayers of their ancestors when they were allowed to enter the promised land? Moses told them to remember what happened in Egypt and in the desert. He wanted the people to remember how God had redeemed them and how God provided everything that was needed. So often the people forgot what God had done for them and how special the covenant was that He made with them.

That's what my people are doing. Less than half of the population of the Netherlands believes in Jesus Christ. Over seventy-five percent of my people rarely or never attend a church service. And yet, on May 4 we sing our national anthem together, which says: "You are my shield and You are faithful O God my Lord, so I will build on You. You never leave me." That is my prayer for my people, that they will remember God and build on Him. My hope is to be a light to my people, by standing on the legacy of the past and bringing our hearts back to God.

6 WEEK READING PLAN

LOVE HIS WORD

	MONDAY	TUESDAY	WEDNESDAY	THURSDAY	FRIDAY
1	Deuteronomy 1	Deuteronomy 2	Deuteronomy 3	Deuteronomy 4	Deuteronomy 5
	SOAP Deuteronomy 1:6-8	SOAP Deuteronomy 2:24-25	SOAP Psalm 95:7	SOAP Deuteronomy 4:1-2	SOAP Deuteronomy 5:32-33
2	Deuteronomy 6-7	Deuteronomy 8	Deuteronomy 9	Deuteronomy 10	Deuteronomy 11
	SOAP Deuteronomy 7:9-11	SOAP Deuteronomy 8:5-6	SOAP Deuteronomy 9:5	SOAP Deuteronomy 10:17-20	SOAP Deuteronomy 11:1-2, 11
3	Deuteronomy 12-13	Deuteronomy 14	Deuteronomy 15	Deuteronomy 16-17	Deuteronomy 18
	SOAP Deuteronomy 13:4	SOAP Deuteronomy 14:2	SOAP Deuteronomy 15:6	SOAP Deuteronomy 16:19-20	SOAP Deuteronomy 18:18
4	Deuteronomy 19	Deuteronomy 20	Deuteronomy 21	Deuteronomy 22	Deuteronomy 23:1—24:7
	SOAP Romans 12:17-19	SOAP Deuteronomy 20:3-4	SOAP Psalm 77:13	SOAP Galatians 6:2	SOAP Deuteronomy 23:21-23
5	Deuteronomy 24:8—25:19	Deuteronomy 26	Deuteronomy 27	Deuteronomy 28	Deuteronomy 29
	SOAP Proverbs 11:1	SOAP Deuteronomy 26:17-19	SOAP Deuteronomy 27:1-3	SOAP Deuteronomy 28:1-2	SOAP Deuteronomy 29:13-15
6	Deuteronomy 30	Deuteronomy 31	Deuteronomy 32	Deuteronomy 33	Deuteronomy 34
	SOAP Deuteronomy 30:16	SOAP Deuteronomy 31:6	SOAP Deuteronomy 32:3-4	SOAP Deuteronomy 33:26-29	SOAP Deuteronomy 34:10-12

THE COVENANT SETTING

1 This is what Moses said to all of Israel in the Transjordanian wilderness, the arid rift valley opposite Suph, between Paran and Tophel, Laban, Hazeroth, and Di Zahab. 2 Now it is ordinarily an eleven-day journey from Horeb to Kadesh Barnea by way of Mount Seir. 3 However, it was not until the first day of the eleventh month of the fortieth year that Moses addressed the Israelites just as the LORD had instructed him to do. 4 This took place after the defeat of King Sihon of the Amorites, whose capital was in Heshbon, and King Og of Bashan, whose capital was in Ashtaroth, specifically in Edrei. 5 So it was in the Transjordan, in Moab, that Moses began to deliver these words:

REFLECT

What do you think the Israelites experienced when they realized it was time for God to fulfill His promise?

EVENTS AT HOREB

6 The LORD our God spoke to us at Horeb and said, "You have stayed in the area of this mountain long enough. 7 Head out and resume your journey. Enter the Amorite hill country, and all its neighboring areas, including the rift valley, the hill country, the foothills, the Negev, and the coastal plain—all of Canaan and Lebanon as far as the Great River, that is, the Euphrates. 8 Look! I have already given the land to you. Go, occupy the territory that I, the LORD, promised to give to your ancestors Abraham, Isaac, and Jacob, and to their descendants." 9 I also said to you at that time, "I am no longer able to sustain you by myself. 10 The LORD your God has increased your population to the point that you are now as numerous as the very stars of the sky. 11 Indeed, may the LORD, the God of your ancestors, make you a thousand times more numerous than you are now, blessing you just as he said he would! 12 But how can I alone bear up under the burden of your hardship and strife? 13 Select wise and practical men, those known among your tribes, whom I may appoint as your leaders." 14 You replied to me that what I had said to you was good. 15 So I chose as your tribal leaders wise and well-known men, placing them over you as administrators of groups of thousands, hundreds, fifties, and tens, and also as other tribal officials. 16 I furthermore admonished your judges at that time that they should pay attention to issues among your fellow citizens and judge fairly, whether between one person and a native Israelite or a resident foreigner. 17 They must not discriminate in judgment, but hear the lowly and the great alike. Nor should they be intimidated by human beings, for judgment belongs to God. If the matter being adjudicated is too difficult for them, they should bring it before me for a hearing.

INSTRUCTIONS AT KADESH BARNEA

18 So I instructed you at that time regarding everything you should do. 19 Then we left Horeb and passed through all that immense, forbidding wilderness that you saw on the way to the Amorite hill country as the LORD our God had commanded us to do, finally arriving at Kadesh Barnea. 20 Then I said to you, "You have come to the Amorite hill country, which the LORD our God is about to give us. 21 Look, he has placed the land in front of you! Go up, take possession of it, just as the LORD, the God of your ancestors, said to do. Do not be afraid or discouraged!" 22 So all of

you approached me and said, "Let's send some men ahead of us
to scout out the land and bring us back word as to how we should
attack it and what the cities are like there." 23 I thought this was
a good idea, so I sent twelve men from among you, one from each
tribe. 24 They left and went up to the hill country, coming to the
Eshcol Valley, which they scouted out. 25 Then they took some
of the produce of the land and carried it back down to us. They
also brought a report to us, saying, "The land that the LORD our
God is about to give us is good."

DISOBEDIENCE AT KADESH BARNEA

26 You were not willing to go up, however, but instead rebelled
against the LORD your God. 27 You complained among yourselves
privately and said, "Because the LORD hates us he brought us
from Egypt to deliver us over to the Amorites so they could destroy us! 28 What is going to happen to us? Our brothers have
drained away our courage by describing people who are more
numerous and taller than we are, and great cities whose defenses
appear to be as high as heaven itself! Moreover, they said they
saw Anakites there." 29 So I responded to you, "Do not be terrified of them! 30 The LORD your God is about to go ahead of you;
he will fight for you, just as you saw him do in Egypt 31 and in the
wilderness, where you saw him carrying you along like a man
carries his son. This he did everywhere you went until you came
to this very place." 32 However, through all this you did not have
confidence in the LORD your God, 33 who would go before you
on the way to find places for you to camp, appearing in a fire at
night and in a cloud by day to show you the way you ought to go.

JUDGMENT AT KADESH BARNEA

34 When the LORD heard you, he became angry and made this
vow: 35 "Not a single person of this evil generation will see the
good land that I promised to give to your ancestors! 36 The exception is Caleb son of Jephunneh; he will see it and I will give
him and his descendants the territory on which he has walked,
because he has wholeheartedly followed me." 37 As for me, the
LORD was also angry with me on your account. He said, "You also
will not be able to go there. 38 However, Joshua son of Nun, your
assistant, will go. Encourage him, because he will enable Israel
to inherit the land. 39 Also, your infants, who you thought would
die on the way, and your children, who as yet do not know good
from bad, will go there; I will give them the land and they will
possess it. 40 But as for you, turn back and head for the wilderness by the way to the Red Sea."

UNSUCCESSFUL CONQUEST OF CANAAN

41 Then you responded to me and admitted, "We have sinned
against the LORD. We will now go up and fight as the LORD our
God has told us to do." So you each put on your battle gear and
prepared to go up to the hill country. 42 But the LORD told me:
"Tell them this: 'Do not go up and fight, because I will not be
with you and you will be defeated by your enemies.'" 43 I spoke
to you, but you did not listen. Instead you rebelled against the
LORD and recklessly went up to the hill country. 44 The Amorite

inhabitants of that area confronted you and chased you like a
swarm of bees, striking you down from Seir as far as Hormah.
45 Then you came back and wept before the LORD, but he paid
no attention to you whatsoever. 46 Therefore, you remained at
Kadesh for a long time—indeed, for the full time.

THE JOURNEY FROM KADESH BARNEA TO MOAB

2 Then we turned and set out toward the wilderness on the
way to the Red Sea just as the LORD told me to do, detouring
around Mount Seir for a long time. 2 At this point the LORD said
to me, 3 "You have circled around this mountain long enough;
now turn north. 4 Instruct these people as follows: 'You are about
to cross the border of your relatives the descendants of Esau,
who inhabit Seir. They will be afraid of you, so watch yourselves
carefully. 5 Do not be hostile toward them, because I am not giving you any of their land, not even a footprint, for I have given
Mount Seir as an inheritance for Esau. 6 You may purchase food
to eat and water to drink from them. 7 All along the way I, the
LORD your God, have blessed your every effort. I have been attentive to your travels through this great wilderness. These forty
years I have been with you; you have lacked nothing.'"

8 So we turned away from our relatives the descendants of
Esau, the inhabitants of Seir, turning from the route of the rift
valley which comes up from Elat and Ezion Geber, and traveling the way of the wilderness of Moab. 9 Then the LORD said to
me, "Do not harass Moab and provoke them to war, for I will not
give you any of their land as your territory. This is because I have
given Ar to the descendants of Lot as their possession. 10 (The
Emites used to live there, a people as powerful, numerous, and
tall as the Anakites. 11 These people, as well as the Anakites, are
also considered Rephaites; the Moabites call them Emites. 12 Previously the Horites lived in Seir, but the descendants of Esau dispossessed and destroyed them and settled in their place, just as
Israel did to the land it came to possess, the land the LORD gave
them.) 13 Now, get up and cross the Wadi Zered." So we did so.
14 Now the length of time it took for us to go from Kadesh Barnea
to the crossing of Wadi Zered was thirty-eight years, time for all
the military men of that generation to die, just as the LORD had
vowed to them. 15 Indeed, it was the very hand of the LORD that
eliminated them from within the camp until they were all gone.

INSTRUCTIONS CONCERNING AMMON

16 So it was that after all the military men had been eliminated
from the community, 17 the LORD said to me, 18 "Today you are
going to cross the border of Moab, that is, of Ar. 19 But when you
come close to the Ammonites, do not harass or provoke them
because I am not giving you any of the Ammonites' land as your
possession; I have already given it to Lot's descendants as their
possession."

20 (That also is considered to be a land of the Rephaites. The
Rephaites lived there originally; the Ammonites call them Zam-
zummites. 21 They are a people as powerful, numerous, and tall as
the Anakites. But the LORD destroyed the Rephaites in advance
of the Ammonites, so they dispossessed them and settled down

in their place. 22 This is exactly what he did for the descendants of Esau who lived in Seir when he destroyed the Horites before them so that they could dispossess them and settle in their area to this very day. 23 As for the Avvites who lived in settlements as far west as Gaza, Caphtorites who came from Crete destroyed them and settled down in their place.)

24 "Get up, make your way across Wadi Arnon. Look, I have already delivered over to you Sihon the Amorite, king of Heshbon, and his land. Go ahead—take it! Engage him in war! 25 This very day I will begin to fill all the people of the earth with dread and to terrify them when they hear about you. They will shiver and shake in anticipation of your approach."

DEFEAT OF SIHON, KING OF HESHBON

26 Then I sent messengers from the Kedemoth wilderness to King Sihon of Heshbon with an offer of peace: 27 "Let me pass through your land; I will keep strictly to the roadway. I will not turn aside to the right or the left. 28 Sell me food for cash so that I can eat and sell me water to drink. Just allow me to go through on foot, 29 just as the descendants of Esau who live at Seir and the Moabites who live in Ar did for me, until I cross the Jordan to the land the LORD our God is giving us." 30 But King Sihon of Heshbon was unwilling to allow us to pass near him because the LORD our God had made him obstinate and stubborn so that he might deliver him over to you this very day. 31 The LORD said to me, "Look! I have already begun to give over Sihon and his land to you. Start right now to take his land as your possession." 32 When Sihon and all his troops emerged to encounter us in battle at Jahaz, 33 the LORD our God delivered him over to us and we struck him down, along with his sons and everyone else. 34 At that time we seized all his cities and put every one of them under divine judgment, including even the women and children; we left no survivors. 35 We kept only the livestock and plunder from the cities for ourselves. 36 From Aroer, which is at the edge of Wadi Arnon (it is the city in the wadi), all the way to Gilead there was not a town able to resist us—the LORD our God gave them all to us. 37 However, you did not approach the land of the Ammonites, the Wadi Jabbok, the cities of the hill country, or any place else forbidden by the LORD our God.

DEFEAT OF KING OG OF BASHAN

3 Next we set out on the route to Bashan, but King Og of Bashan and his whole army came out to meet us in battle at Edrei. 2 The LORD, however, said to me, "Don't be afraid of him because I have already given him, his whole army, and his land to you. You will do to him exactly what you did to King Sihon of the Amorites who lived in Heshbon." 3 So the LORD our God did indeed give over to us King Og of Bashan and his whole army, and we struck them down until not a single survivor was left. 4 We captured all his cities at that time—there was not a town we did not take from them—sixty cities, all the region of Argob, the dominion of Og in Bashan. 5 All of these cities were fortified by high walls, gates, and locking bars; in addition there were a great many open villages. 6 We put all of these under divine judgment

just as we had done to King Sihon of Heshbon—every occupied city, including women and children. 7 But all the livestock and plunder from the cities we kept for ourselves. 8 So at that time we took the land of the two Amorite kings in the Transjordan from Wadi Arnon to Mount Hermon 9 (the Sidonians call Hermon Sirion and the Amorites call it Senir), 10 all the cities of the plateau, all of Gilead and Bashan as far as Salecah and Edrei, cities of the kingdom of Og in Bashan. 11 Only King Og of Bashan was left of the remaining Rephaites. (It is noteworthy that his sarcophagus was made of iron. Does it not, indeed, still remain in Rabbath of the Ammonites? It is 13½ feet long and 6 feet wide according to standard measure.)

DISTRIBUTION OF THE TRANSJORDANIAN ALLOTMENTS

12 This is the land we brought under our control at that time: The territory extending from Aroer by the Wadi Arnon and half the Gilead hill country with its cities I gave to the Reubenites and Gadites. 13 The rest of Gilead and all of Bashan, the kingdom of Og, I gave to half the tribe of Manasseh. (All the region of Argob, that is, all Bashan, is called the land of Rephaim. 14 Jair, son of Manasseh, took all the Argob region as far as the border with the Geshurites and Maacathites—namely Bashan—and called it by his name, Havvoth Jair, which it retains to this very day.) 15 I gave Gilead to Machir. 16 To the Reubenites and Gadites I allocated the territory extending from Gilead as far as Wadi Arnon (the exact middle of the wadi was a boundary) all the way to the Wadi Jabbok, the Ammonite border. 17 The rift valley and the Jordan River were also a border, from the Sea of Kinnereth to the sea of the rift valley (that is, the Salt Sea), beneath the slopes of Pisgah to the east.

INSTRUCTIONS TO THE TRANSJORDANIAN TRIBES

18 At that time I instructed you as follows: "The LORD your God has given you this land for your possession. You warriors are to cross over equipped for battle before your fellow Israelites. 19 But your wives, children, and livestock (of which I know you have many) may remain in the cities I have given you. 20 You must fight until the LORD gives your countrymen victory as he did you and they take possession of the land that the LORD your God is giving them on the other side of the Jordan River. Then each of you may return to his own territory that I have given you." 21 I also commanded Joshua at the same time, "You have seen everything the LORD your God did to these two kings; he will do the same to all the kingdoms where you are going. 22 Do not be afraid of them, for the LORD your God will personally fight for you."

DENIAL TO MOSES OF THE PROMISED LAND

23 Moreover, at that time I pleaded with the LORD, 24 "O, Sovereign LORD, you have begun to show me your greatness and strength. (What god in heaven or earth can rival your works and mighty deeds?) 25 Let me please cross over to see the good land on the other side of the Jordan River—this good hill country and the Lebanon!" 26 But the LORD was angry at me because of you

and would not listen to me. Instead, he said to me, "Enough of that! Do not speak to me anymore about this matter. 27 Go up to the top of Pisgah and take a good look to the west, north, south, and east, for you will not be allowed to cross the Jordan. 28 Commission Joshua, and encourage and strengthen him, because he will lead these people over and will enable them to inherit the land you will see." 29 So we settled down in the valley opposite Beth Peor.

THE PRIVILEGES OF THE COVENANT

4 Now, Israel, pay attention to the statutes and ordinances I am about to teach you, so that you might live and go on to enter and take possession of the land that the LORD, the God of your ancestors, is giving you. 2 Do not add a thing to what I command you nor subtract from it, so that you may keep the commandments of the LORD your God that I am delivering to you. 3 You have witnessed what the LORD did at Baal Peor, how he eradicated from your midst everyone who followed Baal Peor. 4 But you who remained faithful to the LORD your God are still alive to this very day, every one of you. 5 Look! I have taught you statutes and ordinances just as the LORD my God told me to do, so that you might carry them out in the land you are about to enter and possess. 6 So be sure to do them, because this will testify of your wise understanding to the people who will learn of all these statutes and say, "Indeed, this great nation is a very wise people." 7 In fact, what other great nation has a god so near to them like the LORD our God whenever we call on him? 8 And what other great nation has statutes and ordinances as just as this whole law that I am about to share with you today?

REMINDER OF THE HOREB COVENANT

9 Again, however, pay very careful attention, lest you forget the things you have seen and disregard them for the rest of your life; instead teach them to your children and grandchildren. 10 You stood before the LORD your God at Horeb and he said to me, "Assemble the people before me so that I can tell them my commands. Then they will learn to revere me all the days they live in the land, and they will instruct their children." 11 You approached and stood at the foot of the mountain, a mountain ablaze to the sky above it and yet dark with a thick cloud. 12 Then the LORD spoke to you from the middle of the fire; you heard speech but you could not see anything—only a voice was heard. 13 And he revealed to you the covenant he has commanded you to keep, the Ten Commandments, writing them on two stone tablets. 14 Moreover, at that same time the LORD commanded me to teach you statutes and ordinances for you to keep in the land that you are about to enter and possess.

THE NATURE OF ISRAEL'S GOD

15 Be very careful, then, because you saw no form at the time the LORD spoke to you at Horeb from the middle of the fire. 16 I say this so you will not corrupt yourselves by making an image in the form of any kind of figure. This includes the likeness of a human male or female, 17 any kind of land animal, any bird that

flies in the sky, 18 anything that crawls on the ground, or any fish in the deep waters under the earth. 19 When you look up to the sky and see the sun, moon, and stars—the whole heavenly creation—you must not be seduced to worship and serve them, for the LORD your God has assigned them to all the people of the world. 20 You, however, the LORD has selected and brought from Egypt, that iron-smelting furnace, to be his special people as you are today. 21 But the LORD became angry with me because of you and vowed that I would never cross the Jordan nor enter the good land that he is about to give you. 22 So I must die here in this land; I will not cross the Jordan. But you are going over and will possess that good land. 23 Be on guard so that you do not forget the covenant of the LORD your God that he has made with you, and that you do not make an image of any kind, just as he has forbidden you. 24 For the LORD your God is a consuming fire; he is a jealous God.

THREAT AND BLESSING FOLLOWING COVENANT DISOBEDIENCE

25 After you have produced children and grandchildren and have been in the land a long time, if you become corrupt and make an image of any kind and do other evil things before the LORD your God that enrage him, 26 I invoke heaven and earth as witnesses against you today that you will surely and swiftly be removed from the very land you are about to cross the Jordan to possess. You will not last long there because you will surely be annihilated. 27 Then the LORD will scatter you among the peoples and there will be very few of you among the nations where the LORD will drive you. 28 There you will worship gods made by human hands—wood and stone that can neither see, hear, eat, nor smell. 29 But if you seek the LORD your God from there, you will find him, if, indeed, you seek him with all your heart and soul. 30 In your distress when all these things happen to you in future days, if you return to the LORD your God and obey him 31 (for he is a merciful God), he will not let you down or destroy you, for he cannot forget the covenant with your ancestors that he confirmed by oath to them.

THE UNIQUENESS OF ISRAEL'S GOD

32 Indeed, ask about the distant past, starting from the day God created humankind on the earth, and ask from one end of heaven to the other, whether there has ever been such a great thing as this, or even a rumor of it. 33 Have a people ever heard the voice of God speaking from the middle of fire, as you yourselves have, and lived to tell about it? 34 Or has God ever before tried to deliver a nation from the middle of another nation, accompanied by judgments, signs, wonders, war, strength, power, and other very terrifying things like the LORD your God did for you in Egypt before your very eyes? 35 You have been taught that the LORD alone is God—there is no other besides him. 36 From heaven he spoke to you in order to teach you, and on earth he showed you his great fire from which you also heard his words. 37 Moreover, because he loved your ancestors, he chose their descendants who followed them and personally brought you out of Egypt with his

REFLECT

Which unique attributes or actions of God have you experienced in your own life that give you the assurance that He exists and is for you?

great power [38]to dispossess nations greater and stronger than
you and brought you here this day to give you their land as your
property. [39]Today realize and carefully consider that the LORD
is God in heaven above and on earth below—there is no other!
[40]Keep his statutes and commandments that I am setting forth
today so that it may go well with you and your descendants and
that you may enjoy longevity in the land that the LORD your God
is about to give you as a permanent possession."

THE NARRATIVE CONCERNING CITIES OF REFUGE

[41]Then Moses selected three cities in the Transjordan, toward
the east. [42]Anyone who accidentally killed someone without
hating him at the time of the accident could flee to one of those
cities and be safe. [43]These cities are Bezer, in the wilderness plateau, for the Reubenites; Ramoth in Gilead for the Gadites; and
Golan in Bashan for the Manassehites.

THE SETTING AND INTRODUCTION OF THE COVENANT

[44]This is the law that Moses set before the Israelites. [45]These
are the stipulations, statutes, and ordinances that Moses spoke
to the Israelites after he had brought them out of Egypt, [46]in
the Transjordan, in the valley opposite Beth Peor, in the land
of King Sihon of the Amorites, who lived in Heshbon. (It is he
whom Moses and the Israelites attacked after they came out
of Egypt. [47]They possessed his land and that of King Og of Bashan—both of whom were Amorite kings in the Transjordan, to
the east. [48]Their territory extended from Aroer at the edge of
the Arnon valley as far as Mount Siyon—that is, Hermon—[49]in-
cluding all the rift valley of the Transjordan in the east to the
sea of the rift valley, beneath the slopes of Pisgah.)

THE OPENING EXHORTATION

5 Then Moses called all the people of Israel together and said
to them: "Listen, Israel, to the statutes and ordinances that
I am about to deliver to you today; learn them and be careful
to keep them! [2]The LORD our God made a covenant with us at
Horeb. [3]He did not make this covenant with our ancestors but
with us, we who are here today, all of us living now. [4]The LORD
spoke face to face with you at the mountain, from the middle of
the fire. [5](I was standing between the LORD and you at that time
to reveal the LORD's message to you, because you were afraid of
the fire and would not go up the mountain.) He said:

THE TEN COMMANDMENTS

[6]"I am the LORD your God—he who brought you from the land
of Egypt, from the place of slavery.

[7]"You must not have any other gods besides me.

[8]"You must not make for yourself an image of anything in
heaven above, on earth below, or in the waters beneath. [9]You must
not worship or serve them, for I, the LORD your God, am a jealous
God. I punish the sons, grandsons, and great-grandsons for the sin
of the fathers who reject me, [10]but I show covenant faithfulness
to the thousands who choose me and keep my commandments.

11 "You must not make use of the name of the LORD your God
for worthless purposes, for the LORD will not exonerate anyone
who abuses his name that way.

12 "Be careful to observe the Sabbath day just as the LORD your
God has commanded you. 13 You are to work and do all your tasks
in six days, 14 but the seventh day is the Sabbath of the LORD your
God. On that day you must not do any work, you, your son, your
daughter, your male slave, your female slave, your ox, your donkey, any other animal, or the resident foreigner who lives with
you, so that your male and female slaves, like yourself, may have
rest. 15 Recall that you were slaves in the land of Egypt and that
the LORD your God brought you out of there by strength and
power. That is why the LORD your God has commanded you to
observe the Sabbath day.

16 "Honor your father and your mother just as the LORD your
God has commanded you to do, so that your days may be extended and that it may go well with you in the land that he is
about to give you.

17 "You must not murder.

18 "You must not commit adultery.

19 "You must not steal.

20 "You must not offer false testimony against another. 21 You
must not desire another man's wife, nor should you crave his
house, his field, his male and female servants, his ox, his donkey, or anything else he owns."

THE NARRATIVE OF THE SINAI REVELATION AND ISRAEL'S RESPONSE

22 The LORD said these things to your entire assembly at the
mountain from the middle of the fire, the cloud, and the darkness with a loud voice, and that was all he said. Then he inscribed
the words on two stone tablets and gave them to me. 23 Then,
when you heard the voice from the midst of the darkness while
the mountain was ablaze, all your tribal leaders and elders approached me. 24 You said, "The LORD our God has shown us his
great glory, and we have heard him speak from the middle of
the fire. It is now clear to us that God can speak to human beings and they can keep on living. 25 But now, why should we die,
because this intense fire will consume us? If we keep hearing
the voice of the LORD our God we will die! 26 Who is there from
the entire human race who has heard the voice of the living God
speaking from the middle of the fire as we have, and has lived?
27 You go near so that you can hear everything the LORD our God
is saying and then you can tell us whatever he says to you; then
we will pay attention and do it." 28 When the LORD heard you
speaking to me, he said to me, "I have heard what these people
have said to you—they have spoken well. 29 If only it would really
be their desire to fear me and obey all my commandments in
the future, so that it may go well with them and their descendants forever. 30 Go and tell them, 'Return to your tents!' 31 But
as for you, remain here with me so I can declare to you all the
commandments, statutes, and ordinances that you are to teach
them, so that they can carry them out in the land I am about to
give them." 32 Be careful, therefore, to do exactly what the LORD

your God has commanded you; do not turn right or left! 33 Walk
just as he has commanded you so that you may live, that it may
go well with you, and that you may live long in the land you are
going to possess.

EXHORTATION TO KEEP THE COVENANT PRINCIPLES

6 Now these are the commandments, statutes, and ordinances
that the LORD your God instructed me to teach you so that
you may carry them out in the land where you are headed 2 and
that you may so revere the LORD your God that you will keep all
his statutes and commandments that I am giving you—you, your
children, and your grandchildren—all your lives, to prolong your
days. 3 Pay attention, Israel, and be careful to do this so that it
may go well with you and that you may increase greatly in number—as the LORD, the God of your ancestors, said to you, you will
have a land flowing with milk and honey.

THE ESSENCE OF THE COVENANT PRINCIPLES

4 Hear, O Israel: The LORD is our God, the LORD is one! 5 You must
love the LORD your God with your whole mind, your whole being, and all your strength.

EXHORTATION TO TEACH THE COVENANT PRINCIPLES

6 These words I am commanding you today must be kept in
mind, 7 and you must teach them to your children and speak
of them as you sit in your house, as you walk along the road, as
you lie down, and as you get up. 8 You should tie them as a reminder on your forearm and fasten them as symbols on your
forehead. 9 Inscribe them on the doorframes of your houses
and gates.

EXHORTATION TO WORSHIP THE LORD EXCLUSIVELY

10 Then when the LORD your God brings you to the land he promised your ancestors Abraham, Isaac, and Jacob to give you—a land
with large, fine cities you did not build, 11 houses filled with choice
things you did not accumulate, hewn-out cisterns you did not
dig, and vineyards and olive groves you did not plant—and you
eat your fill, 12 be careful not to forget the LORD who brought
you out of Egypt, that place of slavery. 13 You must revere the
LORD your God, serve him, and take oaths using only his name.
14 You must not go after other gods, those of the surrounding
peoples, 15 for the LORD your God, who is present among you, is
a jealous God—his anger will erupt against you and remove you
from the land.

EXHORTATION TO OBEY THE LORD EXCLUSIVELY

16 You must not put the LORD your God to the test as you did at
Massah. 17 Keep his commandments very carefully, as well as the
stipulations and statutes he commanded you to observe. 18 Do
whatever is proper and good before the LORD so that it may go
well with you and that you may enter and occupy the good land
that he promised your ancestors, 19 and that you may drive out
all your enemies just as the LORD said.

CHEERIOS AND HAND MOTIONS

DEUTERONOMY 6:1–9

Deuteronomy 6:5 was the first verse I ever taught my children. I remember sitting with them at the kitchen table, breakfast Cheerios still all over the table and floor, fighting the urge to clean up. Instead, I chose to capture the small window of time I had to teach them this important Bible lesson before their attention span expired. Basically, less than three minutes.

We read in Deuteronomy 6:7 the importance of teaching our children about God in the common, everyday activities of life: eating around the kitchen table, driving to and from school, cooking dinner, or playing outside.

Equipped with hand movements to go with it I would recite Deuteronomy 6:5 over and over again as we memorized it together. I prayed the wisdom would stay with them the rest of their lives. I prayed the importance of this verse would be remembered long after the season of messy Cheerio breakfasts and hand motion memory verses faded.

There in the bright morning light that spilled into my messy kitchen we would say, "Love God with all our heart," as they gently place their little hands over their hearts, "all our soul," as they hugged themselves and giggled, "and all our strength," as they lifted up their preschool arms and flexed their muscles.

As the years have gone by, I haven't stopped reciting this verse over them. Now it's not as much during morning breakfasts but more at night as I pray with them at their beds. I want my girls to daily be reminded to love God with everything He has generously given to them.

It's a daily surrender, an intentional choice to love God, to dwell on truth, and to trust His wisdom over the wisdom the world gives.

Time and time again, I remind my girls of the importance to obey God, not out of obligation, but out of love. Our obedience flows out of our love for Him like His obedience on the cross flowed out of His love for us.

When love is the motivation, obedience flows out of it. This is what I hope my girls will remember: not all the Cheerios I left on the floor, but how to surrender their hearts and lives to the God who made them, loves them, and is always working for their good.

EXHORTATION TO REMEMBER THE PAST

20 When your children ask you later on, "What are the stipulations, statutes, and ordinances that the LORD our God commanded you?" 21 you must say to them, "We were Pharaoh's slaves in Egypt, but the LORD brought us out of Egypt in a powerful way. 22 And he brought signs and great, devastating wonders on Egypt, on Pharaoh, and on his whole family before our very eyes. 23 He delivered us from there so that he could give us the land he had promised our ancestors. 24 The LORD commanded us to obey all these statutes and to revere him so that it may always go well for us and he may preserve us, as he has to this day. 25 We will be innocent if we carefully keep all these commandments before the LORD our God, just as he demands."

THE DISPOSSESSION OF NONVASSALS

7 When the LORD your God brings you to the land that you are going to occupy and forces out many nations before you—Hittites, Girgashites, Amorites, Canaanites, Perizzites, Hivites, and Jebusites, seven nations more numerous and powerful than you— 2 and he delivers them over to you and you attack them, you must utterly annihilate them. Make no treaty with them and show them no mercy! 3 You must not intermarry with them. Do not give your daughters to their sons or take their daughters for your sons, 4 for they will turn your sons away from me to worship other gods. Then the anger of the LORD will erupt against you and he will quickly destroy you. 5 Instead, this is what you must do to them: You must tear down their altars, shatter their sacred pillars, cut down their sacred Asherah poles, and burn up their idols. 6 For you are a people holy to the LORD your God. He has chosen you to be his people, prized above all others on the face of the earth.

THE BASIS OF ISRAEL'S ELECTION

7 It is not because you were more numerous than all the other peoples that the LORD favored and chose you—for in fact you were the least numerous of all peoples. 8 Rather it is because of his love for you and his faithfulness to the promise he solemnly vowed to your ancestors that the LORD brought you out with great power, redeeming you from the place of slavery, from the power of Pharaoh king of Egypt. 9 So realize that the LORD your God is the true God, the faithful God who keeps covenant faithfully with those who love him and keep his commandments, to a thousand generations, 10 but who pays back those who hate him as they deserve and destroys them. He will not ignore those who hate him but will repay them as they deserve! 11 So keep the commandments, statutes, and ordinances that I today am commanding you to do.

PROMISES OF GOOD FOR COVENANT OBEDIENCE

12 If you obey these ordinances and are careful to do them, the LORD your God will faithfully keep covenant with you as he promised your ancestors. 13 He will love and bless you, and make you numerous. He will bless you with many children, with the produce of your soil, your grain, your new wine, your olive oil, the offspring of your oxen, and the young of your flocks in the land that he promised your ancestors to give you. 14 You will be blessed

beyond all peoples; there will be no barrenness among you or
your livestock. 15 The LORD will protect you from all sickness, and
you will not experience any of the terrible diseases that you knew
in Egypt; instead he will inflict them on all those who hate you.

EXHORTATION TO DESTROY CANAANITE PAGANISM

16 You must destroy all the people whom the LORD your God is
about to deliver over to you; you must not pity them or worship
their gods, for that will be a snare to you. 17 If you think, "These
nations are more numerous than I—how can I dispossess them?"
18 you must not fear them. You must carefully recall what the
LORD your God did to Pharaoh and all Egypt, 19 the great judgments you saw, the signs and wonders, the strength and power
by which he brought you out—thus the LORD your God will do
to all the people you fear. 20 Furthermore, the LORD your God
will release hornets among them until the very last ones who
hide from you perish. 21 You must not tremble in their presence,
for the LORD your God, who is present among you, is a great and
awesome God. 22 He, the God who leads you, will expel the nations little by little. You will not be allowed to destroy them all
at once lest the wild animals overrun you. 23 The LORD your God
will give them over to you; he will throw them into a great panic
until they are destroyed. 24 He will hand over their kings to you,
and you will erase their very names from memory. Nobody will
be able to resist you until you destroy them. 25 You must burn
the images of their gods, but do not covet the silver and gold that
covers them so much that you take it for yourself and thus become ensnared by it; for it is abhorrent to the LORD your God.
26 You must not bring any abhorrent thing into your house and
thereby become an object of divine wrath along with it. You must
absolutely detest and abhor it, for it is an object of divine wrath.

THE LORD'S PROVISION IN THE DESERT

8 You must keep carefully all these commandments I am giving you today so that you may live, increase in number, and
go in and occupy the land that the LORD promised to your ancestors. 2 Remember the whole way by which he has brought you
these forty years through the wilderness so that he might, by
humbling you, test you to see if you have it within you to keep
his commandments or not. 3 So he humbled you by making you
hungry and then feeding you with unfamiliar manna. He did this
to teach you that humankind cannot live by bread alone, but also
by everything that comes from the LORD's mouth. 4 Your clothing did not wear out nor did your feet swell all these forty years.
5 Be keenly aware that just as a parent disciplines his child, so the
LORD your God disciplines you. 6 So you must keep his commandments, live according to his standards, and revere him. 7 For the
LORD your God is bringing you to a good land, a land of brooks,
springs, and fountains flowing forth in valleys and hills, 8 a land
of wheat, barley, vines, fig trees, and pomegranates, of olive trees
and honey, 9 a land where you may eat food in plenty and find no
lack of anything, a land whose stones are iron and from whose
hills you can mine copper. 10 You will eat your fill and then praise
the LORD your God because of the good land he has given you.

EXHORTATION TO REMEMBER THAT BLESSING COMES FROM GOD

11 Be sure you do not forget the LORD your God by not keeping
his commandments, ordinances, and statutes that I am giving
you today. 12 When you eat your fill, when you build and occupy
good houses, 13 when your cattle and flocks increase, when you
have plenty of silver and gold, and when you have abundance
of everything, 14 be sure you do not feel self-important and forget the LORD your God who brought you from the land of Egypt,
the place of slavery, 15 and who brought you through the great,
fearful wilderness of venomous serpents and scorpions, an arid
place with no water. He made water flow from a flint rock and
16 fed you in the wilderness with manna (which your ancestors
had never before known) so that he might by humbling you test
you and eventually bring good to you. 17 Be careful not to say, "My
own ability and skill have gotten me this wealth." 18 You must remember the LORD your God, for he is the one who gives ability
to get wealth; if you do this he will confirm his covenant that
he made by oath to your ancestors, even as he has to this day.
19 Now if you forget the LORD your God at all and follow other
gods, worshiping and prostrating yourselves before them, I testify to you today that you will surely be annihilated. 20 Just like
the nations the LORD is about to destroy from your sight, so he
will do to you because you would not obey him.

THEOLOGICAL JUSTIFICATION OF THE CONQUEST

9 Listen, Israel: Today you are about to cross the Jordan so you
can dispossess the nations there, people greater and stronger
than you who live in large cities with extremely high fortifications. 2 They include the Anakites, a numerous and tall people
whom you know about and of whom it is said, "Who is able to
resist the Anakites?" 3 Understand today that the LORD your
God who goes before you is a devouring fire; he will defeat and
subdue them before you. You will dispossess and destroy them
quickly just as he has told you. 4 Do not think to yourself after
the LORD your God has driven them out before you, "Because
of my own righteousness the LORD has brought me here to possess this land." It is because of the wickedness of these nations
that the LORD is driving them out ahead of you. 5 It is not because of your righteousness, or even your inner uprightness,
that you have come here to possess their land. Instead, because
of the wickedness of these nations, the LORD your God is driving them out ahead of you in order to confirm the promise he
made on oath to your ancestors, to Abraham, Isaac, and Jacob.
6 Understand, therefore, that it is not because of your righteousness that the LORD your God is about to give you this good land
as a possession, for you are a stubborn people!

THE HISTORY OF ISRAEL'S STUBBORNNESS

7 Remember—don't ever forget—how you provoked the LORD
your God in the wilderness; from the time you left the land of
Egypt until you came to this place you were constantly rebelling against him. 8 At Horeb you provoked him and he was angry

enough with you to destroy you. 9 When I went up the mountain
to receive the stone tablets, the tablets of the covenant that the
LORD made with you, I remained there forty days and nights,
eating and drinking nothing. 10 The LORD gave me the two stone
tablets, written by the very finger of God, and on them was everything he said to you at the mountain from the midst of the
fire at the time of that assembly. 11 Now at the end of the forty
days and nights the LORD presented me with the two stone tablets, the tablets of the covenant. 12 And he said to me, "Get up, go
down at once from here because your people whom you brought
out of Egypt have sinned! They have quickly turned from the
way I commanded them and have made for themselves a cast
metal image." 13 Moreover, he said to me, "I have taken note of
these people; they are a stubborn lot! 14 Stand aside and I will
destroy them, obliterating their very name from memory, and I
will make you into a stronger and more numerous nation than
they are."
15 So I turned and went down the mountain while it was blazing with fire; the two tablets of the covenant were in my hands.
16 When I looked, you had indeed sinned against the LORD your
God and had cast for yourselves a metal calf; you had quickly
turned aside from the way he had commanded you! 17 I grabbed
the two tablets, threw them down, and shattered them before
your very eyes. 18 Then I again fell down before the LORD for forty
days and nights; I ate and drank nothing because of all the sin
you had committed, doing such evil before the LORD as to enrage him. 19 For I was terrified at the LORD's intense anger that
threatened to destroy you. But he listened to me this time as
well. 20 The LORD was also angry enough at Aaron to kill him, but
at that time I prayed for him too. 21 As for your sinful thing that
you had made, the calf, I took it, melted it down, ground it up
until it was as fine as dust, and tossed the dust into the stream
that flows down the mountain. 22 Moreover, you continued to
provoke the LORD at Taberah, Massah, and Kibroth Hattaavah.
23 And when he sent you from Kadesh Barnea and told you, "Go
up and possess the land I have given you," you rebelled against
the LORD your God and would neither believe nor obey him.
24 You have been rebelling against him from the very first day
I knew you!

MOSES' PLEA ON BEHALF OF GOD'S REPUTATION

25 I lay flat on the ground before the LORD for forty days and
nights, for he had said he would destroy you. 26 I prayed to him:
O, Sovereign LORD, do not destroy your people, your valued property that you have powerfully redeemed, whom you brought out
of Egypt by your strength. 27 Remember your servants Abraham,
Isaac, and Jacob; ignore the stubbornness, wickedness, and sin
of these people. 28 Otherwise the people of the land from which
you brought us will say, "The LORD was unable to bring them to
the land he promised them, and because of his hatred for them
he has brought them out to kill them in the wilderness." 29 They
are your people, your valued property, whom you brought out
with great strength and power.

THE OPPORTUNITY TO BEGIN AGAIN

10 At that same time the LORD said to me, "Carve out for yourself two stone tablets like the first ones and come up the
mountain to me; also make for yourself a wooden ark. 2 I will
write on the tablets the same words that were on the first tablets you broke, and you must put them into the ark." 3 So I made
an ark of acacia wood and carved out two stone tablets just like
the first ones. Then I went up the mountain with the two tablets in my hands. 4 The LORD then wrote on the tablets the same
words, the Ten Commandments, which he had spoken to you at
the mountain from the middle of the fire at the time of that assembly, and he gave them to me. 5 Then I turned, went down the
mountain, and placed the tablets into the ark I had made—they
are still there, just as the LORD commanded me.

CONCLUSION OF THE HISTORICAL RÉSUMÉ

6 During those days the Israelites traveled from Beeroth Bene
Jaakan to Moserah. There Aaron died and was buried, and his
son Eleazar became priest in his place. 7 From there they traveled to Gudgodah, and from Gudgodah to Jotbathah, a place
of flowing streams. 8 At that time the LORD set apart the tribe
of Levi to carry the ark of the LORD's covenant, to stand before the LORD to serve him, and to formulate blessings in his
name, as they do to this very day. 9 Therefore Levi has no allotment or inheritance among his brothers; the LORD is his inheritance just as the LORD your God told him. 10 As for me, I
stayed at the mountain as I did the first time, forty days and
nights. The LORD listened to me that time as well and decided
not to destroy you. 11 Then he said to me, "Get up, set out leading the people so they may go and possess the land I promised
to give to their ancestors."

AN EXHORTATION TO LOVE BOTH GOD AND PEOPLE

12 Now, Israel, what does the LORD your God require of you except to revere him, to obey all his commandments, to love him,
to serve him with all your mind and being, 13 and to keep the
LORD's commandments and statutes that I am giving you today
for your own good? 14 The heavens—indeed the highest heavens—
belong to the LORD your God, as does the earth and everything
in it. 15 However, only to your ancestors did he show his loving
favor, and he chose you, their descendants, from all peoples—as
is apparent today. 16 Therefore, cleanse your hearts and stop being so stubborn! 17 For the LORD your God is God of gods and
Lord of lords, the great, mighty, and awesome God who is unbiased and takes no bribe, 18 who justly treats the orphan and
widow, and who loves resident foreigners, giving them food and
clothing. 19 So you must love the resident foreigner because you
were foreigners in the land of Egypt. 20 Revere the LORD your
God, serve him, be loyal to him, and take oaths only in his name.
21 He is the one you should praise; he is your God, the one who
has done these great and awesome things for you that you have
seen. 22 When your ancestors went down to Egypt, they numbered only seventy, but now the LORD your God has made you
as numerous as the stars of the sky.

REITERATION OF THE CALL TO OBEDIENCE

11 You must love the LORD your God and do what he requires;
keep his statutes, ordinances, and commandments at all
times. 2 Bear in mind today that I am not speaking to your children who have not personally experienced the judgments of
the LORD your God, which revealed his greatness, strength, and
power. 3 They did not see the awesome deeds he performed in the
midst of Egypt against Pharaoh king of Egypt and his whole land,
4 or what he did to the army of Egypt, including their horses and
chariots, when he made the waters of the Red Sea overwhelm
them while they were pursuing you and he annihilated them.
5 They did not see what he did to you in the wilderness before
you reached this place, 6 or what he did to Dathan and Abiram,
sons of Eliab the Reubenite, when the earth opened its mouth in
the middle of the Israelite camp and swallowed them, their families, their tents, and all the property they brought with them.
7 I am speaking to you because you are the ones who saw with
your own eyes all the great deeds of the LORD.

THE ABUNDANCE OF THE LAND OF PROMISE

8 Now pay attention to all the commandments I am giving you
today, so that you may be strong enough to enter and possess the
land where you are headed, 9 and that you may enjoy long life in
the land the LORD promised to give to your ancestors and their
descendants, a land flowing with milk and honey. 10 For the land
where you are headed is not like the land of Egypt from which
you came, a land where you planted seed and which you irri-
gated by hand like a vegetable garden. 11 Instead, the land you are
crossing the Jordan to occupy is one of hills and valleys, a land
that drinks in water from the rains, 12 a land the LORD your God
looks after. He is constantly attentive to it from the beginning
to the end of the year. 13 Now, if you pay close attention to my
commandments that I am giving you today and love the LORD
your God and serve him with all your mind and being, 14 then
he promises, "I will send rain for your land in its season, the autumn and the spring rains, so that you may gather in your grain,
new wine, and olive oil. 15 I will provide pasture for your livestock
and you will eat your fill."

EXHORTATION TO INSTRUCTION AND OBEDIENCE

16 Make sure you do not turn away to serve and worship other
gods! 17 Then the anger of the LORD will erupt against you, and
he will close up the sky so that it does not rain. The land will not
yield its produce, and you will soon be removed from the good
land that the LORD is about to give you. 18 Fix these words of mine
into your mind and being, tie them as a reminder on your hands,
and let them be symbols on your forehead. 19 Teach them to your
children and speak of them as you sit in your house, as you walk
along the road, as you lie down, and as you get up. 20 Inscribe them
on the doorframes of your houses and on your gates 21 so that your
days and those of your descendants may be extended in the land
that the LORD promised to give to your ancestors, like the days
of heaven itself. 22 For if you carefully observe all of these commandments I am giving you and love the LORD your God, live

according to his standards, and remain loyal to him, 23 then he
will drive out all these nations ahead of you, and you will dispossess nations greater and stronger than you. 24 Every place you set
your foot will be yours; your border will extend from the desert
to Lebanon and from the River (that is, the Euphrates) as far as
the Mediterranean Sea. 25 Nobody will be able to resist you; the
LORD your God will spread the fear and terror of you over the
whole land on which you walk, just as he promised you.

ANTICIPATION OF A BLESSING AND CURSING CEREMONY

26 Take note—I am setting before you today a blessing and a curse:
27 the blessing if you take to heart the commandments of the LORD
your God that I am giving you today, 28 and the curse if you pay no
attention to his commandments and turn from the way I am setting before you today to pursue other gods you have not known.
29 When the LORD your God brings you into the land you are to
possess, you must pronounce the blessing on Mount Gerizim and
the curse on Mount Ebal. 30 Are they not across the Jordan River,
toward the west, in the land of the Canaanites who live in the rift
valley opposite Gilgal near the oak of Moreh? 31 For you are about
to cross the Jordan to possess the land the LORD your God is giving you, and you will possess and inhabit it. 32 Be certain to keep
all the statutes and ordinances that I am presenting to you today.

THE CENTRAL SANCTUARY

12 These are the statutes and ordinances you must be careful
to obey as long as you live in the land the LORD, the God of
your ancestors, has given you to possess. 2 You must by all means
destroy all the places where the nations you are about to dispossess worship their gods—on the high mountains and hills and under every leafy tree. 3 You must tear down their altars, shatter their
sacred pillars, burn up their sacred Asherah poles, and cut down
the images of their gods; you must eliminate their very memory
from that place. 4 You must not worship the LORD your God the way
they worship. 5 But you must seek only the place he chooses from
all your tribes to establish his name as his place of residence, and
you must go there. 6 And there you must take your burnt offerings,
your sacrifices, your tithes, the personal offerings you have prepared, your votive offerings, your freewill offerings, and the firstborn of your herds and flocks. 7 Both you and your families must
feast there before the LORD your God and rejoice in all the output
of your labor with which he has blessed you. 8 You must not do as
we are doing here today, with everyone doing what seems best to
him, 9 for you have not yet come to the final stop and inheritance
the LORD your God is giving you. 10 When you do go across the Jordan River and settle in the land he is granting you as an inheritance and you find relief from all the enemies who surround you,
you will live in safety. 11 Then you must come to the place the LORD
your God chooses for his name to reside, bringing everything I am
commanding you—your burnt offerings, sacrifices, tithes, the personal offerings you have prepared, and all your choice votive offerings that you devote to him. 12 You shall rejoice in the presence
of the LORD your God, along with your sons, daughters, male and

female servants, and the Levites in your villages (since they have
no allotment or inheritance with you). 13 Make sure you do not offer burnt offerings in any place you wish, 14 for you may do so only
in the place the LORD chooses in one of your tribal areas—there
you may do everything I am commanding you.

REGULATIONS FOR EATING SACRIFICIAL AND NON-SACRIFICIAL FOODS

15 On the other hand, you may slaughter and eat meat as you
please when the LORD your God blesses you in all your villages.
Both the ritually pure and impure may eat it, whether it is a gazelle or an ibex. 16 However, you must not eat blood—pour it out on
the ground like water. 17 You will not be allowed to eat in your villages your tithe of grain, new wine, olive oil, the firstborn of your
herd and flock, any votive offerings you have vowed, or your freewill and personal offerings. 18 Only in the presence of the LORD
your God may you eat these, in the place he chooses. This applies
to you, your son, your daughter, your male and female servants,
and the Levites in your villages. In that place you will rejoice before the LORD your God in all the output of your labor. 19 Be careful not to overlook the Levites as long as you live in the land.

THE SANCTITY OF BLOOD

20 When the LORD your God extends your borders as he said he
would do and you say, "I want to eat meat just as I please," you
may do so as you wish. 21 If the place he chooses to locate his name
is too far for you, you may slaughter any of your herd and flock
he has given you just as I have stipulated; you may eat them in
your villages just as you wish. 22 As you eat the gazelle or ibex, so
you may eat these; the ritually impure and pure alike may eat
them. 23 However, by no means eat the blood, for the blood is life
itself—you must not eat the life with the meat. 24 You must not
eat it! You must pour it out on the ground like water. 25 You must
not eat it so that it may go well with you and your children after
you; you will be doing what is right in the LORD's sight. 26 But the
holy things and votive offerings that belong to you, you must
pick up and take to the place the LORD will choose. 27 You must
offer your burnt offerings, both meat and blood, on the altar of
the LORD your God; the blood of your other sacrifices you must
pour out on his altar while you eat the meat. 28 Pay careful attention to all these things I am commanding you so that it may
always go well with you and your children after you when you
do what is good and right in the sight of the LORD your God.

THE ABOMINATION OF PAGAN GODS

29 When the LORD your God eliminates the nations from the
place where you are headed and you dispossess them, you will
settle down in their land. 30 After they have been destroyed from
your presence, be careful not to be ensnared like they are; do not
pursue their gods and say, "How do these nations serve their
gods? I will do the same." 31 You must not worship the LORD your
God the way they do! For everything that is abhorrent to him, everything he hates, they have done when worshiping their gods.
They even burn up their sons and daughters before their gods!

IDOLATRY AND FALSE PROPHETS

32 You must be careful to do everything I am commanding you.
13 Do not add to it or subtract from it! 1 Suppose a prophet or
one who foretells by dreams should appear among you and
show you a sign or wonder, 2 and the sign or wonder should come
to pass concerning what he said to you, namely, "Let us follow
other gods"—gods whom you have not previously known—"and
let us serve them." 3 You must not listen to the words of that
prophet or dreamer, for the LORD your God will be testing you
to see if you love him with all your mind and being. 4 You must
follow the LORD your God and revere only him; and you must
observe his commandments, obey him, serve him, and remain
loyal to him. 5 As for that prophet or dreamer, he must be executed because he encouraged rebellion against the LORD your
God who brought you from the land of Egypt, redeeming you
from that place of slavery, and because he has tried to entice you
from the way the LORD your God has commanded you to go. In
this way you must purge evil from among you.

FALSE PROPHETS IN THE FAMILY

6 Suppose your own full brother, your son, your daughter, your
beloved wife, or your closest friend should seduce you secretly
and encourage you to go and serve other gods that neither you
nor your ancestors have previously known, 7 the gods of the surrounding people (whether near you or far from you, from one
end of the earth to the other). 8 You must not give in to him or
even listen to him; do not feel sympathy for him or spare him or
cover up for him. 9 Instead, you must kill him without fail! Your
own hand must be the first to strike him, and then the hands of
the whole community. 10 You must stone him to death because
he tried to entice you away from the LORD your God, who delivered you from the land of Egypt, that place of slavery. 11 Thus
all Israel will hear and be afraid; no longer will they continue to
do evil like this among you.

PUNISHMENT OF COMMUNITY IDOLATRY

12 Suppose you should hear in one of your cities, which the LORD
your God is giving you as a place to live, that 13 some evil people
have departed from among you to entice the inhabitants of their
cities, saying, "Let's go and serve other gods" (whom you have not
known before). 14 You must investigate thoroughly and inquire
carefully. If it is indeed true that such a disgraceful thing is being done among you, 15 you must by all means slaughter the inhabitants of that city with the sword; annihilate with the sword
everyone in it, as well as the livestock. 16 You must gather all of
its plunder into the middle of the plaza and burn the city and
all its plunder as a whole burnt offering to the LORD your God.
It will be an abandoned ruin forever—it must never be rebuilt
again. 17 You must not take for yourself anything that has been
placed under judgment. Then the LORD will relent from his intense anger, show you compassion, have mercy on you, and multiply you as he promised your ancestors. 18 Thus you must obey
the LORD your God, keeping all his commandments that I am
giving you today and doing what is right before him.

THE HOLY AND THE PROFANE

14 You are children of the LORD your God. Do not cut yourselves
or shave your forehead bald for the sake of the dead. 2 For
you are a people holy to the LORD your God. He has chosen you
to be his people, prized above all others on the face of the earth.
3 You must not eat any forbidden thing. 4 These are the animals
you may eat: the ox, the sheep, the goat, 5 the ibex, the gazelle, the
deer, the wild goat, the antelope, the wild oryx, and the mountain sheep. 6 You may eat any animal that has hooves divided into
two parts and that chews the cud. 7 However, you may not eat the
following animals among those that chew the cud or those that
have divided hooves: the camel, the hare, and the rock badger.
(Although they chew the cud, they do not have divided hooves
and are therefore ritually impure to you.) 8 Also, the pig is ritually
impure to you; though it has divided hooves, it does not chew
the cud. You may not eat their meat or even touch their remains.
9 These you may eat from among water creatures: anything
with fins and scales you may eat, 10 but whatever does not have
fins and scales you may not eat; it is ritually impure to you.
11 All ritually clean birds you may eat. 12 These are the ones you
may not eat: the eagle, the vulture, the black vulture, 13 the kite,
the black kite, the dayyah after its species, 14 every raven after
its species, 15 the ostrich, the owl, the seagull, the falcon after its
species, 16 the little owl, the long-eared owl, the white owl, 17 the
jackdaw, the carrion vulture, the cormorant, 18 the stork, the
heron after its species, the hoopoe, and the bat.
19 And any swarming winged thing is impure to you—they may
not be eaten. 20 You may eat any winged creature that is clean.
21 You may not eat any corpse, though you may give it to the resident foreigner who is living in your villages and he may eat it,
or you may sell it to a foreigner. You are a people holy to the
LORD your God. Do not boil a young goat in its mother's milk.

THE OFFERING OF TITHES

22 You must be certain to tithe all the produce of your seed that
comes from the field year after year. 23 In the presence of the
LORD your God, in the place he chooses to locate his name, you
must eat from the tithe of your grain, your new wine, your olive
oil, and the firstborn of your herds and flocks, so that you may
learn to revere the LORD your God always. 24 When he blesses you,
if the place where he chooses to locate his name is distant, 25 you
may convert the tithe into money, secure the money, and travel
to the place the LORD your God chooses for himself. 26 Then you
may spend the money however you wish for cattle, sheep, wine,
beer, or whatever you desire. You and your household may eat
there in the presence of the LORD your God and enjoy it. 27 As
for the Levites in your villages, you must not ignore them, for
they have no allotment or inheritance along with you. 28 At the
end of every three years you must bring all the tithe of your produce, in that very year, and you must store it up in your villages.
29 Then the Levites (because they have no allotment or inheritance with you), the resident foreigners, the orphans, and the
widows of your villages may come and eat their fill so that the
LORD your God may bless you in all the work you do.

THE YEAR OF DEBT RELEASE

15 At the end of every seven years you must declare a cancellation of debts. 2 This is the nature of the cancellation: Every
creditor must remit what he has loaned to another person; he
must not force payment from his fellow Israelite, for it is to be
recognized as "the LORD's cancellation of debts." 3 You may exact payment from a foreigner, but whatever your fellow Israelite
owes you, you must remit. 4 However, there should not be any
poor among you, for the LORD will surely bless you in the land
that he is giving you as an inheritance, 5 if you carefully obey him
by keeping all these commandments that I am giving you today.
6 For the LORD your God will bless you just as he has promised;
you will lend to many nations but will not borrow from any, and
you will rule over many nations but they will not rule over you.

THE SPIRIT OF LIBERALITY

7 If a fellow Israelite from one of your villages in the land that
the LORD your God is giving you should be poor, you must not
harden your heart or be insensitive to his impoverished condition. 8 Instead, you must be sure to open your hand to him and
generously lend him whatever he needs. 9 Be careful lest you
entertain the wicked thought that the seventh year, the year
of cancellation of debts, has almost arrived, and your attitude
be wrong toward your impoverished fellow Israelite and you
do not lend him anything; he will cry out to the LORD against
you, and you will be regarded as having sinned. 10 You must by
all means lend to him and not be upset by doing it, for because
of this the LORD your God will bless you in all your work and
in everything you attempt. 11 There will never cease to be some
poor people in the land; therefore, I am commanding you to
make sure you open your hand to your fellow Israelites who are
needy and poor in your land.

RELEASE OF DEBT SLAVES

12 If your fellow Hebrew—whether male or female—is sold to you
and serves you for six years, then in the seventh year you must
let that servant go free. 13 If you set them free, you must not send
them away empty-handed. 14 You must supply them generously
from your flock, your threshing floor, and your winepress—as
the LORD your God has blessed you, you must give to them. 15 Remember that you were a slave in the land of Egypt and the LORD
your God redeemed you; therefore, I am commanding you to do
this thing today. 16 However, if the servant says to you, "I do not
want to leave you," because he loves you and your household,
since he is well off with you, 17 you shall take an awl and pierce a
hole through his ear to the door. Then he will become your servant permanently (this applies to your female servant as well).
18 You should not consider it difficult to let him go free, for he will
have served you for six years, twice the time of a hired worker;
the LORD your God will bless you in everything you do.

GIVING GOD THE BEST

19 You must set apart for the LORD your God every firstborn
male born to your herds and flocks. You must not work the

firstborn of your bulls or shear the firstborn of your flocks.
20 You and your household must eat them annually before
the LORD your God in the place he chooses. 21 If one of them
has any kind of blemish—lameness, blindness, or anything
else—you may not offer it as a sacrifice to the LORD your God.
22 You may eat it in your villages, whether you are ritually impure or clean, just as you would eat a gazelle or an ibex. 23 However, you must not eat its blood; you must pour it out on the
ground like water.

THE PASSOVER

16 Observe the month Abib and keep the Passover to the LORD
your God, for in that month he brought you out of Egypt by
night. 2 You must sacrifice the Passover animal (from the flock or
the herd) to the LORD your God in the place where he chooses to
locate his name. 3 You must not eat any yeast with it; for seven
days you must eat bread made without yeast, as symbolic of affliction, for you came out of Egypt hurriedly. You must do this so
you will remember for the rest of your lives the day you came out
of the land of Egypt. 4 There must not be a scrap of yeast within
your land for seven days, nor can any of the meat you sacrifice
on the evening of the first day remain until the next morning.
5 You may not sacrifice the Passover in just any of your villages
that the LORD your God is giving you, 6 but you must sacrifice
it in the evening in the place where he chooses to locate his
name, at sunset, the time of day you came out of Egypt. 7 You
must cook and eat it in the place the LORD your God chooses;
you may return the next morning to your tents. 8 You must eat
bread made without yeast for six days. The seventh day you are
to hold an assembly for the LORD your God; you must not do
any work on that day.

THE FEAST OF WEEKS

9 You must count seven weeks; you must begin to count them
from the time you begin to harvest the standing grain. 10 Then
you are to celebrate the Feast of Weeks before the LORD your God
with the voluntary offering that you will bring, in proportion to
how he has blessed you. 11 You shall rejoice before him—you, your
son, your daughter, your male and female slaves, the Levites in
your villages, the resident foreigners, the orphans, and the widows among you—in the place where the LORD chooses to locate
his name. 12 Furthermore, remember that you were a slave in
Egypt, and so be careful to observe these statutes.

THE FEAST OF TEMPORARY SHELTERS

13 You must celebrate the Feast of Shelters for seven days, at
the time of the grain and grape harvest. 14 You are to rejoice in
your festival, you, your son, your daughter, your male and female slaves, the Levites, the resident foreigners, the orphans,
and the widows who are in your villages. 15 You are to celebrate
the festival seven days before the LORD your God in the place
he chooses, for he will bless you in all your productivity and in
whatever you do; so you will indeed rejoice! 16 Three times a year
all your males must appear before the LORD your God in the

REFLECT

Why was it essential for the Israelites to give God their best? Is this still important to us today? How do we do this in our everyday lives?

place he chooses for the Feast of Unleavened Bread, the Feast
of Weeks, and the Feast of Shelters; and they must not appear
before him empty-handed. 17 Every one of you must give as you
are able, according to the blessing of the LORD your God that
he has given you.

PROVISION FOR JUSTICE

18 You must appoint judges and civil servants for each tribe in
all your villages that the LORD your God is giving you, and they
must judge the people fairly. 19 You must not pervert justice or
show favor. Do not take a bribe, for bribes blind the eyes of the
wise and distort the words of the righteous. 20 You must pursue
justice alone so that you may live and inherit the land the LORD
your God is giving you.

EXAMPLES OF LEGAL CASES

21 You must not plant any kind of tree as a sacred Asherah pole
near the altar of the LORD your God which you build for yourself. 22 You must not erect a sacred pillar, a thing the LORD your
God detests.

17 You must not sacrifice to him a bull or sheep that has a
blemish or any other defect, because that is considered
offensive to the LORD your God. 2 Suppose a man or woman is
discovered among you in one of your villages that the LORD
your God is giving you who sins before the LORD your God
and breaks his covenant 3 by serving other gods and worshiping them—the sun, moon, or any other heavenly bodies that
I have not permitted you to worship. 4 When it is reported to
you and you hear about it, you must investigate carefully. If it
is indeed true that such a disgraceful thing is being done in
Israel, 5 you must bring to your city gates that man or woman
who has done this wicked thing—that very man or woman—and
you must stone that person to death. 6 At the testimony of two
or three witnesses the person must be executed. They cannot
be put to death on the testimony of only one witness. 7 The witnesses must be first to begin the execution, and then all the
people are to join in afterward. In this way you will purge the
evil from among you.

APPEAL TO A HIGHER COURT

8 If a matter is too difficult for you to judge—bloodshed, legal
claim, or assault—matters of controversy in your villages—you
must leave there and go up to the place the LORD your God
chooses. 9 You will go to the Levitical priests and the judge in
office in those days and seek a solution; they will render a verdict. 10 You must then do as they have determined at that place
the LORD chooses. Be careful to do just as you are taught. 11 You
must do what you are instructed, and the verdict they pronounce to you, without fail. Do not deviate right or left from
what they tell you. 12 The person who pays no attention to the
priest currently serving the LORD your God there, or to the
judge—that person must die, so that you may purge evil from
Israel. 13 Then all the people will hear and be afraid, and not be
so presumptuous again.

PROVISION FOR KINGSHIP

14 When you come to the land the LORD your God is giving you
and take it over and live in it and then say, "I will select a king
like all the nations surrounding me," 15 you must select without
fail a king whom the LORD your God chooses. From among your
fellow citizens you must appoint a king—you may not designate
a foreigner who is not one of your fellow Israelites. 16 Moreover,
he must not accumulate horses for himself or allow the people
to return to Egypt to do so, for the LORD has said you must never
again return that way. 17 Furthermore, he must not marry many
wives lest his affections turn aside, and he must not accumulate
much silver and gold. 18 When he sits on his royal throne he must
make a copy of this law on a scroll given to him by the Levitical
priests. 19 It must be with him constantly, and he must read it
as long as he lives, so that he may learn to revere the LORD his
God and observe all the words of this law and these statutes and
carry them out. 20 Then he will not exalt himself above his fellow
citizens or turn from the commandments to the right or left,
and he and his descendants will enjoy many years ruling over
his kingdom in Israel.

PROVISION FOR PRIESTS AND LEVITES

18 The Levitical priests—indeed, the entire tribe of Levi—will
have no allotment or inheritance with Israel; they may eat
the burnt offerings of the LORD and of his inheritance. 2 They
will have no inheritance in the midst of their fellow Israelites;
the LORD alone is their inheritance, just as he had told them.
3 This shall be the priests' fair allotment from the people who
offer sacrifices, whether bull or sheep—they must give to the
priest the shoulder, the jowls, and the stomach. 4 You must give
them the best of your grain, new wine, and olive oil, as well as
the best of your wool when you shear your flocks. 5 For the LORD
your God has chosen them and their sons from all your tribes
to stand and serve in his name permanently. 6 Suppose a Levite
comes by his own free will from one of your villages, from any
part of Israel where he is living, to the place the LORD chooses
7 and serves in the name of the LORD his God like his fellow Levites who stand there before the LORD. 8 He must eat the same
share they do, despite any profits he may gain from the sale of
his family's inheritance.

PROHIBITED OCCULT PRACTICES

9 When you enter the land the LORD your God is giving you, you
must not learn the abhorrent practices of those nations. 10 There
must never be found among you anyone who sacrifices his son or
daughter in the fire, anyone who practices divination, an omen
reader, a soothsayer, a sorcerer, 11 one who casts spells, one who
conjures up spirits, a practitioner of the occult, or a necromancer. 12 Whoever does these things is abhorrent to the LORD, and
because of these detestable things the LORD your God is about
to drive them out from before you. 13 You must be blameless before the LORD your God. 14 Those nations that you are about to
dispossess listen to omen readers and diviners, but the LORD
your God has not given you permission to do such things.

WRITING THE WORD OF GOD

DEUTERONOMY 17:14–20

In the early days of Israel, the nation was not ruled by human kings, like other nations. As God's chosen people, God was their King. Initially, Israel was ruled by judges. These judges were helped by the Levites, who instituted the law of God and maintained the sacrificial system in Israel.

God knew Israel would ask for a human king to be like the rest of nations (Deut 17:14; 1 Sam 8:5). He knows our hearts better than we do. That's why He left qualifications for this eventual king in Deuteronomy 17.

The first qualification for a king was that he had to be chosen by God. This king had to be "from among your fellow citizens," not a foreigner (Deut 17:15). He was not to depend on the strength of horses (Deut 17:16). He was not to have many wives or much silver or gold (Deut 17:17).

The most important qualification for the king of Israel was to know the law of God. In order to be wise, the king had to write for himself a copy of the law (Deut 17:18). Psalm 119:97–98 says,

---

"O how I love your law! All day long I meditate on it. Your commandments make me wiser than my enemies, for I am always aware of them."

Why was the king instructed to write God's Word? Why is it valuable for us to write out God's Word today? We find the answer to this question in Deuteronomy 17:19–20. Writing the law of God and reading it every day would make the king familiar with it. He would know the law, would keep it, and, most importantly, he would live it. It enabled him to rule according to the law.

Writing out God's Word helps us to see it in a different way. By slowing down and writing out the words of Scripture we can meditate on truth, gaining a deeper understanding of God's character and heart for the world. Understanding His heart will help us to live it out, a powerful reality that makes all the difference in our lives.

15 The LORD your God will raise up for you a prophet like me
from among you—from your fellow Israelites; you must listen
to him. 16 This accords with what happened at Horeb in the
day of the assembly. You asked the LORD your God: "Please do
not make us hear the voice of the LORD our God anymore or
see this great fire anymore lest we die." 17 The LORD then said
to me, "What they have said is good. 18 I will raise up a prophet
like you for them from among their fellow Israelites. I will
put my words in his mouth and he will speak to them whatever I command. 19 I will personally hold responsible anyone
who then pays no attention to the words that prophet speaks
in my name.
20 "But if any prophet presumes to speak anything in my name
that I have not authorized him to speak, or speaks in the name of
other gods, that prophet must die. 21 Now if you say to yourselves,
'How can we tell that a message is not from the LORD?'—22 whenever a prophet speaks in my name and the prediction is not fulfilled, then I have not spoken it; the prophet has presumed to
speak it, so you need not fear him."

CHALLENGE

God established Moses as a type of Christ, promising to raise up another prophet like him from among Israel. In what other ways was Moses a precursor to Christ (see Exod 32:30-35; Deut 18:16–19; 33:4–5; 34:10–12; Acts 7:37)?

LAWS CONCERNING MANSLAUGHTER

19 When the LORD your God destroys the nations whose land
he is about to give you and you dispossess them and settle
in their cities and houses, 2 you must set apart for yourselves
three cities in the middle of your land that the LORD your God
is giving you as a possession. 3 You shall build a roadway and divide into thirds the whole extent of your land that the LORD
your God is providing as your inheritance; anyone who kills
another person should flee to the closest of these cities. 4 Now
this is the law pertaining to one who flees there in order to
live, if he has accidentally killed another without hating him at
the time of the accident. 5 Suppose he goes with someone else
to the forest to cut wood and when he raises the ax to cut the
tree, the ax head flies loose from the handle and strikes his fellow worker so hard that he dies. The person responsible may
then flee to one of these cities to save himself. 6 Otherwise the
blood avenger will chase after the killer in the heat of his anger,
eventually overtake him, and kill him, though this is not a capital case since he did not hate him at the time of the accident.
7 Therefore, I am commanding you to set apart for yourselves
three cities. 8 If the LORD your God enlarges your borders as he
promised your ancestors and gives you all the land he pledged
to them, 9 and then you are careful to observe all these commandments I am giving you today (namely, to love the LORD
your God and to always walk in his ways), then you must add
three more cities to these three. 10 You must not shed innocent
blood in your land that the LORD your God is giving you as an
inheritance, for that would make you guilty. 11 However, suppose
a person hates someone else and stalks him, attacks him, kills
him, and then flees to one of these cities. 12 The elders of his own
city must send for him and remove him from there to deliver
him over to the blood avenger to die. 13 You must not pity him,
but purge from Israel the guilt of shedding innocent blood, so
that it may go well with you.

LAWS CONCERNING WITNESSES

14 You must not encroach on your neighbor's property, which will have been defined in the inheritance you will obtain in the land the LORD your God is giving you.

15 A single witness may not testify against another person for any trespass or sin that he commits. A matter may be legally established only on the testimony of two or three witnesses. 16 If a false witness testifies against another person and accuses him of a crime, 17 then both parties to the controversy must stand before the LORD, that is, before the priests and judges who will be in office in those days. 18 The judges will thoroughly investigate the matter, and if the witness should prove to be false and to have given false testimony against the accused, 19 you must do to him what he had intended to do to the accused. In this way you will purge the evil from among you. 20 The rest of the people will hear and become afraid to keep doing such evil among you. 21 You must not show pity; the principle will be a life for a life, an eye for an eye, a tooth for a tooth, a hand for a hand, and a foot for a foot.

LAWS CONCERNING WAR WITH DISTANT ENEMIES

20 When you go to war against your enemies and see chariotry and troops who outnumber you, do not be afraid of them, for the LORD your God, who brought you up out of the land of Egypt, is with you. 2 As you move forward for battle, the priest will approach and say to the soldiers, 3 "Listen, Israel! Today you are moving forward to do battle with your enemies. Do not be fainthearted. Do not fear and tremble or be terrified because of them, 4 for the LORD your God goes with you to fight on your behalf against your enemies to give you victory." 5 Moreover, the officers are to say to the troops, "Who among you has built a new house and not dedicated it? He may go home, lest he die in battle and someone else dedicate it. 6 Or who among you has planted a vineyard and not benefited from it? He may go home, lest he die in battle and someone else benefit from it. 7 Or who among you has become engaged to a woman but has not married her? He may go home, lest he die in battle and someone else marry her." 8 In addition, the officers are to say to the troops, "Who among you is afraid and fainthearted? He may go home so that he will not make his fellow soldier's heart as fearful as his own." 9 Then, when the officers have finished speaking, they must appoint unit commanders to lead the troops.

10 When you approach a city to wage war against it, offer it terms of peace. 11 If it accepts your terms and submits to you, all the people found in it will become your slaves. 12 If it does not accept terms of peace but makes war with you, then you are to lay siege to it. 13 The LORD your God will deliver it over to you, and you must kill every single male by the sword. 14 However, the women, little children, cattle, and anything else in the city—all its plunder—you may take for yourselves as spoil. You may take from your enemies the plunder that the LORD your God has given you. 15 This is how you are to deal with all those cities located far from you, those that do not belong to these nearby nations.

LAWS CONCERNING WAR WITH CANAANITE NATIONS

16 As for the cities of these peoples that the LORD your God is going to give you as an inheritance, you must not allow a single living
thing to survive. 17 Instead you must utterly annihilate them—the
Hittites, Amorites, Canaanites, Perizzites, Hivites, and Jebusites—
just as the LORD your God has commanded you, 18 so that they
cannot teach you all the abhorrent ways they worship their gods,
causing you to sin against the LORD your God. 19 If you besiege a city
for a long time while attempting to capture it, you must not chop
down its trees, for you may eat fruit from them and should not cut
them down. A tree in the field is not human that you should besiege it! 20 However, you may chop down any tree you know is not
suitable for food, and you may use it to build siege works against
the city that is making war with you until that city falls.

LAWS CONCERNING UNSOLVED MURDER

21 If a homicide victim should be found lying in a field in the
land the LORD your God is giving you, and no one knows
who killed him, 2 your elders and judges must go out and measure how far it is to the cities in the vicinity of the corpse. 3 Then
the elders of the city nearest to the corpse must take from the
herd a heifer that has not been worked—that has never pulled
with the yoke—4 and bring the heifer down to a wadi with flowing water, to a valley that is neither plowed nor sown. There at
the wadi they are to break the heifer's neck. 5 Then the Levitical
priests will approach (for the LORD your God has chosen them
to serve him and to pronounce blessings in his name, and to decide every judicial verdict), 6 and all the elders of that city nearest the corpse must wash their hands over the heifer whose neck
was broken in the valley. 7 Then they must proclaim, "Our hands
have not spilled this blood, nor have we witnessed the crime. 8 Do
not blame your people Israel whom you redeemed, O LORD, and
do not hold them accountable for the bloodshed of an innocent
person." Then atonement will be made for the bloodshed. 9 In this
manner you will purge the guilt of innocent blood from among
you, for you must do what is right before the LORD.

LAWS CONCERNING FEMALE CAPTIVES

10 When you go out to do battle with your enemies and the LORD
your God allows you to prevail and you take prisoners, 11 if you
should see among them an attractive woman whom you wish
to take as a wife, 12 you may bring her back to your house. She
must shave her head, trim her nails, 13 discard the clothing she
was wearing when captured, and stay in your house, lamenting
for her father and mother for a full month. After that you may
sleep with her and become her husband and she your wife. 14 If
you are not pleased with her, then you must let her go where
she pleases. You cannot in any case sell her; you must not take
advantage of her, since you have already humiliated her.

LAWS CONCERNING CHILDREN

15 Suppose a man has two wives, one whom he loves more than
the other, and they both bear him sons, with the firstborn being the child of the less-loved wife. 16 In the day he divides his

inheritance he must not appoint as firstborn the son of the favorite wife in place of the other wife's son who is actually the
firstborn. 17 Rather, he must acknowledge the son of the less-
loved wife as firstborn and give him the double portion of all
he has, for that son is the beginning of his father's procreative
power—to him should go the right of the firstborn.

18 If a person has a stubborn, rebellious son who pays no attention to his father or mother, and they discipline him to no avail,
19 his father and mother must seize him and bring him to the elders at the gate of his city. 20 They must declare to the elders of his
city, "Our son is stubborn and rebellious and pays no attention to
what we say—he is a glutton and drunkard." 21 Then all the men of
his city must stone him to death. In this way you will purge wickedness from among you, and all Israel will hear about it and be afraid.

DISPOSITION OF A CRIMINAL'S REMAINS

22 If a person commits a sin punishable by death and is executed,
and you hang the corpse on a tree, 23 his body must not remain
all night on the tree; instead you must make certain you bury
him that same day, for the one who is left exposed on a tree is
cursed by God. You must not defile your land that the LORD your
God is giving you as an inheritance.

LAWS CONCERNING PRESERVATION OF LIFE

22 When you see your neighbor's ox or sheep going astray, do
not ignore it; you must return it without fail to your neighbor. 2 If the owner does not live near you or you do not know who
the owner is, then you must corral the animal at your house and
let it stay with you until the owner looks for it; then you must return it to him. 3 You shall do the same to his donkey, his clothes,
or anything else your neighbor has lost and you have found; you
must not refuse to get involved. 4 When you see your neighbor's
donkey or ox fallen along the road, do not ignore it; instead, you
must be sure to help him get the animal on its feet again.

5 A woman must not wear men's clothing, nor should a man
dress up in women's clothing, for anyone who does this is offensive to the LORD your God.

6 If you happen to notice a bird's nest along the road, whether in a tree or on the ground, and there are chicks or eggs with
the mother bird sitting on them, you must not take the mother from the young. 7 You must be sure to let the mother go, but
you may take the young for yourself. Do this so that it may go
well with you and you may have a long life.

8 If you build a new house, you must construct a guardrail
around your roof to avoid being culpable in the event someone
should fall from it.

ILLUSTRATIONS OF THE PRINCIPLE OF PURITY

9 You must not plant your vineyard with two kinds of seed; otherwise the entire yield, both of the seed you plant and the produce
of the vineyard, will be defiled. 10 You must not plow with an ox
and a donkey harnessed together. 11 You must not wear clothing
made with wool and linen meshed together. 12 You shall make
yourselves tassels for the four corners of the clothing you wear.

PURITY IN THE MARRIAGE RELATIONSHIP

13 Suppose a man marries a woman, sleeps with her, and then rejects her, 14 accusing her of impropriety and defaming her reputation by saying, "I married this woman but when I approached
her for marital relations I discovered she was not a virgin!" 15 Then
the father and mother of the young woman must produce the
evidence of virginity for the elders of the city at the gate. 16 The
young woman's father must say to the elders, "I gave my daughter to this man and he has rejected her. 17 Moreover, he has raised
accusations of impropriety by saying, 'I discovered your daughter was not a virgin,' but this is the evidence of my daughter's
virginity!" The cloth must then be spread out before the city's elders. 18 The elders of that city must then seize the man and punish him. 19 They will fine him 100 shekels of silver and give them
to the young woman's father, for the man who made the accusation ruined the reputation of an Israelite virgin. She will then
become his wife, and he may never divorce her as long as he lives.

20 But if the accusation is true and the young woman was not
a virgin, 21 the men of her city must bring the young woman to
the door of her father's house and stone her to death, for she has
done a disgraceful thing in Israel by behaving like a prostitute
while living in her father's house. In this way you will purge the
evil from among you.

22 If a man is discovered in bed with a married woman, both the
man lying in bed with the woman and the woman herself must
die; in this way you will purge the evil from Israel.

23 If a virgin is engaged to a man and another man meets her
in the city and goes to bed with her, 24 you must bring the two of
them to the gate of that city and stone them to death, the young
woman because she did not cry out though in the city and the
man because he violated his neighbor's fiancée; in this way you
will purge evil from among you. 25 But if the man came across
the engaged woman in the field and overpowered her and raped
her, then only the rapist must die. 26 You must not do anything
to the young woman—she has done nothing deserving of death.
This case is the same as when someone attacks another person
and murders him, 27 for the man met her in the field and the
engaged woman cried out, but there was no one to rescue her.

28 Suppose a man comes across a virgin who is not engaged
and takes hold of her and sleeps with her and they are discovered. 29 The man who has slept with her must pay her father fifty
shekels of silver and she must become his wife. Because he has
humiliated her, he may never divorce her as long as he lives.

30 A man may not marry his father's former wife and in this
way dishonor his father.

PURITY IN PUBLIC WORSHIP

23 A man with crushed or severed genitals may not enter
the assembly of the LORD. 2 A person of illegitimate birth
may not enter the assembly of the LORD; to the tenth generation no one related to him may do so.

3 No Ammonite or Moabite may enter the assembly of the
LORD; to the tenth generation none of their descendants shall
ever do so, 4 for they did not meet you with food and water on

the way as you came from Egypt, and furthermore, they hired Balaam son of Beor of Pethor in Aram Naharaim to curse you. 5 But the LORD your God refused to listen to Balaam and changed the curse to a blessing, for the LORD your God loves you. 6 You must not seek peace and prosperity for them through all the ages to come. 7 You must not hate an Edomite, for he is your relative; you must not hate an Egyptian, for you lived as a foreigner in his land. 8 Children of the third generation born to them may enter the assembly of the LORD.

PURITY IN PERSONAL HYGIENE

9 When you go out as an army against your enemies, guard yourselves against anything impure. 10 If there is someone among you who is impure because of some nocturnal emission, he must leave the camp; he may not reenter it immediately. 11 When evening arrives he must wash himself with water, and then at sunset he may reenter the camp.

12 You are to have a place outside the camp to serve as a latrine. 13 You must have a spade among your other equipment, and when you relieve yourself outside you must dig a hole with the spade and then turn and cover your excrement. 14 For the LORD your God walks about in the middle of your camp to deliver you and defeat your enemies for you. Therefore your camp should be holy, so that he does not see anything indecent among you and turn away from you.

PURITY IN THE TREATMENT OF THE UNPRIVILEGED

15 You must not return an escaped slave to his master when he has run away to you. 16 Indeed, he may live among you in any place he chooses, in whichever of your villages he prefers; you must not oppress him.

CULTIC PROSTITUTION BANNED

17 There must never be a sacred prostitute among the young women of Israel nor a sacred male prostitute among the young men of Israel. 18 You must never bring the pay of a female prostitute or the wage of a male prostitute into the temple of the LORD your God in fulfillment of any vow, for both of these are abhorrent to the LORD your God.

RESPECT FOR OTHERS' PROPERTY

19 You must not charge interest on a loan to your fellow Israelite, whether on money, food, or anything else that has been loaned with interest. 20 You may lend with interest to a foreigner, but not to your fellow Israelite; if you keep this command the LORD your God will bless you in all you undertake in the land you are about to enter to possess. 21 When you make a vow to the LORD your God you must not delay in fulfilling it, for otherwise he will surely hold you accountable as a sinner. 22 If you refrain from making a vow, it will not be sinful. 23 Whatever you vow, you must be careful to do what you have promised, such as what you have vowed to the LORD your God as a freewill offering. 24 When you enter the vineyard of your neighbor you may eat as many grapes as you please, but you must not take away any in a container.

25 When you go into the ripe grain fields of your neighbor you may pluck off the kernels with your hand, but you must not use a sickle on your neighbor's ripe grain.

24 If a man marries a woman and she does not please him because he has found something indecent in her, then he may draw up a divorce document, give it to her, and evict her from his house. 2 When she has left him she may go and become someone else's wife. 3 If the second husband rejects her and then divorces her, gives her the papers, and evicts her from his house, or if the second husband who married her dies, 4 her first husband who divorced her is not permitted to remarry her after she has become ritually impure, for that is offensive to the LORD. You must not bring guilt on the land that the LORD your God is giving you as an inheritance.

5 When a man is newly married, he need not go into the army nor be obligated in any way; he must be free to stay at home for a full year and bring joy to the wife he has married.

6 One must not take either lower or upper millstones as security on a loan, for that is like taking a life itself as security.

7 If a man is found kidnapping a person from among his fellow Israelites, and regards him as mere property and sells him, that kidnapper must die. In this way you will purge the evil from among you.

RESPECT FOR HUMAN DIGNITY

8 Be careful during an outbreak of leprosy to follow precisely all that the Levitical priests instruct you; as I have commanded them, so you should do. 9 Remember what the LORD your God did to Miriam along the way after you left Egypt.

10 When you make any kind of loan to your neighbor, you may not go into his house to claim what he is offering as security. 11 You must stand outside and the person to whom you are making the loan will bring out to you what he is offering as security. 12 If the person is poor you may not use what he gives you as security for a covering. 13 You must by all means return to him at sunset the item he gave you as security so that he may sleep in his outer garment and bless you for it; it will be considered a just deed by the LORD your God.

14 You must not oppress a lowly and poor servant, whether one from among your fellow Israelites or from the resident foreigners who are living in your land and villages. 15 You must pay his wage that very day before the sun sets, for he is poor and his life depends on it. Otherwise he will cry out to the LORD against you, and you will be guilty of sin.

16 Fathers must not be put to death for what their children do, nor children for what their fathers do; each must be put to death for his own sin.

17 You must not pervert justice due a resident foreigner or an orphan, or take a widow's garment as security for a loan. 18 Remember that you were slaves in Egypt and that the LORD your God redeemed you from there; therefore I am commanding you to do all this. 19 Whenever you reap your harvest in your field and leave some unraked grain there, you must not return to get it; it should go to the resident foreigner, orphan, and widow so that the LORD your God may bless all the work you do. 20 When

you beat your olive tree you must not repeat the procedure; the remaining olives belong to the resident foreigner, orphan, and widow. 21 When you gather the grapes of your vineyard you must not do so a second time; they should go to the resident foreigner, orphan, and widow. 22 Remember that you were slaves in the land of Egypt; therefore, I am commanding you to do all this.

25 If controversy arises between people, they should go to court for judgment. When the judges hear the case, they shall exonerate the innocent but condemn the guilty. 2 Then, if the guilty person is sentenced to a beating, the judge shall force him to lie down and be beaten in his presence with the number of blows his wicked behavior deserves. 3 The judge may sentence him to forty blows, but no more. If he is struck with more than these, you might view your fellow Israelite with contempt.

4 You must not muzzle your ox when it is treading grain.

RESPECT FOR THE SANCTITY OF OTHERS

5 If brothers live together and one of them dies without having a son, the dead man's wife must not remarry someone outside the family. Instead, her late husband's brother must go to her, marry her, and perform the duty of a brother-in-law. 6 Then the first son she bears will continue the name of the dead brother, thus preventing his name from being blotted out of Israel. 7 But if the man does not want to marry his brother's widow, then she must go to the elders at the town gate and say, "My husband's brother refuses to preserve his brother's name in Israel; he is unwilling to perform the duty of a brother-in-law to me!" 8 Then the elders of his city must summon him and speak to him. If he persists, saying, "I don't want to marry her," 9 then his sister-in-law must approach him in view of the elders, remove his sandal from his foot, and spit in his face. She will then respond, "Thus may it be done to any man who does not maintain his brother's family line!" 10 His family name will be referred to in Israel as "the family of the one whose sandal was removed."

11 If two men get into a hand-to-hand fight, and the wife of one of them gets involved to help her husband against his attacker, and she reaches out her hand and grabs his private parts, 12 then you must cut off her hand—do not pity her.

13 You must not have in your bag different stone weights, a heavy and a light one. 14 You must not have in your house different measuring containers, a large and a small one. 15 You must have an accurate and correct stone weight and an accurate and correct measuring container, so that your life may be extended in the land the LORD your God is about to give you. 16 For anyone who acts dishonestly in these ways is abhorrent to the LORD your God.

TREATMENT OF THE AMALEKITES

17 Remember what the Amalekites did to you on your way from Egypt, 18 how they met you along the way and cut off all your stragglers in the rear of the march when you were exhausted and tired; they were unafraid of God. 19 So when the LORD your God gives you relief from all the enemies who surround you in the land he is giving you as an inheritance, you must wipe out the memory of the Amalekites from under heaven—do not forget!

PRESENTATION OF THE FIRSTFRUITS

26 When you enter the land that the LORD your God is giving you as an inheritance, and you occupy it and live in it,
2 you must take the first of all the ground's produce you harvest
from the land the LORD your God is giving you, place it in a basket, and go to the place where he chooses to locate his name. 3 You
must go to the priest in office at that time and say to him, "I declare today to the LORD your God that I have come into the land
that the LORD promised to our ancestors to give us." 4 The priest
will then take the basket from you and set it before the altar of
the LORD your God. 5 Then you must affirm before the LORD your
God, "A wandering Aramean was my ancestor, and he went down
to Egypt and lived there as a foreigner with a household few in
number, but there he became a great, powerful, and numerous
people. 6 But the Egyptians mistreated and oppressed us, forcing
us to do burdensome labor. 7 So we cried out to the LORD, the God
of our ancestors, and he heard us and saw our humiliation, toil,
and oppression. 8 Therefore the LORD brought us out of Egypt with
tremendous strength and power, as well as with great awe-inspiring signs and wonders. 9 Then he brought us to this place and gave
us this land, a land flowing with milk and honey. 10 So now, look!
I have brought the first of the ground's produce that you, LORD,
have given me." Then you must set it down before the LORD your
God and worship before him. 11 You will celebrate all the good
things that the LORD your God has given you and your family,
along with the Levites and the resident foreigners among you.

PRESENTATION OF THE THIRD-YEAR TITHE

12 When you finish tithing all your income in the third year (the
year of tithing), you must give it to the Levites, the resident foreigners, the orphans, and the widows so that they may eat to their
satisfaction in your villages. 13 Then you shall say before the LORD
your God, "I have removed the sacred offering from my house and
given it to the Levites, the resident foreigners, the orphans, and
the widows just as you have commanded me. I have not violated
or forgotten your commandments. 14 I have not eaten anything
when I was in mourning, or removed any of it while ceremonially
unclean, or offered any of it to the dead; I have obeyed you and
have done everything you have commanded me. 15 Look down
from your holy dwelling place in heaven and bless your people
Israel and the land you have given us, just as you promised our
ancestors—a land flowing with milk and honey."

NARRATIVE INTERLUDE

16 Today the LORD your God is commanding you to keep these
statutes and ordinances, something you must do with all your
heart and soul. 17 Today you have declared the LORD to be your
God, and that you will walk in his ways, keep his statutes, commandments, and ordinances, and obey him. 18 And today the
LORD has declared you to be his special people (as he already
promised you) so you may keep all his commandments. 19 Then
he will elevate you above all the nations he has made and you
will receive praise, fame, and honor. You will be a people holy to
the LORD your God, as he has said.

REFLECT

Did God choose the people of Israel because of their obedience to the law, or because of His faithfulness? How do you know?

THE ASSEMBLY AT SHECHEM

27 Then Moses and the elders of Israel commanded the people: "Pay attention to all the commandments I am giving you today. 2 When you cross the Jordan River to the land the LORD your God is giving you, you must erect great stones and cover them with plaster. 3 Then you must inscribe on them all the words of this law when you cross over, so that you may enter the land the LORD your God is giving you, a land flowing with milk and honey just as the LORD, the God of your ancestors, said to you. 4 So when you cross the Jordan you must erect on Mount Ebal these stones about which I am commanding you today, and you must cover them with plaster. 5 Then you must build an altar there to the LORD your God, an altar of stones—do not use an iron tool on them. 6 You must build the altar of the LORD your God with whole stones and offer burnt offerings on it to the LORD your God. 7 Also you must offer fellowship offerings and eat them there, rejoicing before the LORD your God. 8 You must inscribe on the stones all the words of this law, making them clear."

9 Then Moses and the Levitical priests spoke to all Israel: "Be quiet and pay attention, Israel. Today you have become the people of the LORD your God. 10 You must obey him and keep his commandments and statutes that I am giving you today." 11 Moreover, Moses commanded the people that day: 12 "The following tribes must stand to bless the people on Mount Gerizim when you cross the Jordan: Simeon, Levi, Judah, Issachar, Joseph, and Benjamin. 13 And these other tribes must stand for the curse on Mount Ebal: Reuben, Gad, Asher, Zebulun, Dan, and Naphtali.

THE COVENANT CURSES

14 "The Levites will call out to every Israelite with a loud voice: 15 'Cursed is the one who makes a carved or metal image—something abhorrent to the LORD, the work of the craftsman—and sets it up in a secret place.' Then all the people will say, 'Amen!' 16 'Cursed is the one who disrespects his father and mother.' Then all the people will say, 'Amen!' 17 'Cursed is the one who moves his neighbor's boundary marker.' Then all the people will say, 'Amen!' 18 'Cursed is the one who misleads a blind person on the road.' Then all the people will say, 'Amen!' 19 'Cursed is the one who perverts justice for the resident foreigner, the orphan, and the widow.' Then all the people will say, 'Amen!' 20 'Cursed is the one who goes to bed with his father's former wife, for he dishonors his father.' Then all the people will say, 'Amen!' 21 'Cursed is the one who commits bestiality.' Then all the people will say, 'Amen!' 22 'Cursed is the one who goes to bed with his sister, the daughter of either his father or mother.' Then all the people will say, 'Amen!' 23 'Cursed is the one who goes to bed with his mother-in-law.' Then all the people will say, 'Amen!' 24 'Cursed is the one who kills his neighbor in private.' Then all the people will say, 'Amen!' 25 'Cursed is the one who takes a bribe to kill an innocent person.' Then all the people will say, 'Amen!' 26 'Cursed is the one who refuses to keep the words of this law.' Then all the people will say, 'Amen!'

THE COVENANT BLESSINGS

28 "If you indeed obey the LORD your God and are careful to observe all his commandments I am giving you today, the LORD your God will elevate you above all the nations of the earth. 2 All these blessings will come to you in abundance if you obey the LORD your God: 3 You will be blessed in the city and blessed in the field. 4 Your children will be blessed, as well as the produce of your soil, the offspring of your livestock, the calves of your herds, and the lambs of your flocks. 5 Your basket and your mixing bowl will be blessed. 6 You will be blessed when you come in and blessed when you go out. 7 The LORD will cause your enemies who attack you to be struck down before you; they will attack you from one direction but flee from you in seven different directions. 8 The LORD will decree blessing for you with respect to your barns and in everything you do—yes, he will bless you in the land he is giving you. 9 The LORD will designate you as his holy people just as he promised you, if you keep his commandments and obey him. 10 Then all the peoples of the earth will see that you belong to the LORD, and they will respect you. 11 The LORD will greatly multiply your children, the offspring of your livestock, and the produce of your soil in the land that he promised your ancestors he would give you. 12 The LORD will open for you his good treasure house, the heavens, to give you rain for the land in its season and to bless all you do; you will lend to many nations but you will not borrow from any. 13 The LORD will make you the head and not the tail, and you will always end up at the top and not at the bottom, if you obey his commandments that I am urging you today to be careful to do. 14 But you must not turn away from all the commandments I am giving you today, to either the right or left, nor pursue other gods and worship them.

CURSES AS REVERSAL OF BLESSINGS

15 "But if you ignore the LORD your God and are not careful to keep all his commandments and statutes I am giving you today, then all these curses will come upon you in full force: 16 You will be cursed in the city and cursed in the field. 17 Your basket and your mixing bowl will be cursed. 18 Your children will be cursed, as well as the produce of your soil, the calves of your herds, and the lambs of your flocks. 19 You will be cursed when you come in and cursed when you go out.

CURSES BY DISEASE AND DROUGHT

20 "The LORD will send on you a curse, confusing you and opposing you in everything you undertake until you are destroyed and quickly perish because of the evil of your deeds, in that you have forsaken me. 21 The LORD will plague you with deadly diseases until he has completely removed you from the land you are about to possess. 22 He will afflict you with weakness, fever, inflammation, infection, sword, blight, and mildew; these will attack you until you perish. 23 The sky above your heads will be bronze and the earth beneath you iron. 24 The LORD will make the rain of your land powder and dust; it will come down on you from the sky until you are destroyed.

CURSES BY DEFEAT AND DEPORTATION

25 "The LORD will allow you to be struck down before your enemies; you will attack them from one direction but flee from them in seven directions and will become an object of terror to all the kingdoms of the earth. 26 Your carcasses will be food for every bird of the sky and wild animal of the earth, and there will be no one to chase them off. 27 The LORD will afflict you with the boils of Egypt and with tumors, eczema, and scabies, all of which cannot be healed. 28 The LORD will also subject you to madness, blindness, and confusion of mind. 29 You will feel your way along at noon like the blind person does in darkness and you will not succeed in anything you do; you will be constantly oppressed and continually robbed, with no one to save you. 30 You will be engaged to a woman, and another man will rape her. You will build a house but not live in it. You will plant a vineyard but not even begin to use it. 31 Your ox will be slaughtered before your very eyes, but you will not eat of it. Your donkey will be stolen from you as you watch and will not be returned to you. Your flock of sheep will be given to your enemies, and there will be no one to save you. 32 Your sons and daughters will be given to another people while you look on in vain all day, and you will be powerless to do anything about it. 33 As for the produce of your land and all your labor, a people you do not know will consume it, and you will be nothing but oppressed and crushed for the rest of your lives. 34 You will go insane from seeing all this. 35 The LORD will afflict you in your knees and on your legs with painful, incurable boils—from the soles of your feet to the top of your head. 36 The LORD will force you and your king whom you will appoint over you to go away to a people whom you and your ancestors have not known, and you will serve other gods of wood and stone there. 37 You will become an occasion of horror, a proverb, and an object of ridicule to all the peoples to whom the LORD will drive you.

THE CURSE OF REVERSED STATUS

38 "You will take much seed to the field but gather little harvest, because locusts will consume it. 39 You will plant vineyards and cultivate them, but you will not drink wine or gather in grapes, because worms will eat them. 40 You will have olive trees throughout your territory, but you will not anoint yourself with olive oil, because the olives will drop off the trees while still unripe. 41 You will bear sons and daughters but not keep them, because they will be taken into captivity. 42 Whirring locusts will take over every tree and all the produce of your soil. 43 The resident foreigners who reside among you will become higher and higher over you, and you will become lower and lower. 44 They will lend to you, but you will not lend to them; they will become the head, and you will become the tail!

45 "All these curses will fall on you, pursuing and overtaking you until you are destroyed, because you would not obey the LORD your God by keeping his commandments and statutes that he has given you. 46 These curses will be a perpetual sign and wonder with reference to you and your descendants.

THE CURSE OF MILITARY SIEGE

47 "Because you have not served the LORD your God joyfully and
wholeheartedly with the abundance of everything you have, 48 instead in hunger, thirst, nakedness, and poverty you will serve
your enemies whom the LORD will send against you. They will
place an iron yoke on your neck until they have destroyed you.
49 The LORD will raise up a distant nation against you, one from
the other side of the earth as the eagle flies, a nation whose language you will not understand, 50 a nation of stern appearance
that will have no regard for the elderly or pity for the young.
51 They will devour the offspring of your livestock and the produce of your soil until you are destroyed. They will not leave you
with any grain, new wine, olive oil, calves of your herds, or lambs
of your flocks until they have destroyed you. 52 They will besiege
all of your villages until all of your high and fortified walls collapse—those in which you put your confidence throughout the
land. They will besiege all your villages throughout the land the
LORD your God has given you. 53 You will then eat your own offspring, the flesh of the sons and daughters the LORD your God
has given you, because of the severity of the siege by which your
enemies will constrict you. 54 The man among you who is by nature tender and sensitive will turn against his brother, his beloved wife, and his remaining children. 55 He will withhold from
all of them his children's flesh that he is eating (since there is
nothing else left), because of the severity of the siege by which
your enemy will constrict you in your villages. 56 Likewise, the
most tender and delicate of your women, who would never think
of putting even the sole of her foot on the ground because of her
daintiness, will turn against her beloved husband, her sons and
daughters, 57 and will secretly eat her afterbirth and her newborn
children (since she has nothing else), because of the severity of
the siege by which your enemy will constrict you in your villages.

THE CURSE OF COVENANT TERMINATION

58 "If you refuse to obey all the words of this law, the things
written in this scroll, and refuse to fear this glorious and awesome name, the LORD your God, 59 then the LORD will increase
your punishments and those of your descendants—great and
long-lasting afflictions and severe, enduring illnesses. 60 He will
infect you with all the diseases of Egypt that you dreaded, and
they will persistently afflict you. 61 Moreover, the LORD will bring
upon you every kind of sickness and plague not mentioned in
this scroll of commandments, until you have perished. 62 There
will be very few of you left, though at one time you were as numerous as the stars in the sky, because you will have disobeyed
the LORD your God. 63 This is what will happen: Just as the LORD
delighted to do good for you and make you numerous, so he will
also take delight in destroying and decimating you. You will be
uprooted from the land you are about to possess. 64 The LORD
will scatter you among all nations, from one end of the earth to
the other. There you will worship other gods that neither you nor
your ancestors have known, gods of wood and stone. 65 Among
those nations you will have no rest, nor will there be a place of
peaceful rest for the soles of your feet, for there the LORD will

give you an anxious heart, failing eyesight, and a spirit of despair.
66 Your life will hang in doubt before you; you will be terrified by
night and day and will have no certainty of surviving from one
day to the next. 67 In the morning you will say, 'If only it were
evening!' And in the evening you will say, 'I wish it were morning!' because of the things you will fear and the things you will
see. 68 Then the LORD will make you return to Egypt by ship, over
a route I said to you that you would never see again. There you
will sell yourselves to your enemies as male and female slaves,
but no one will buy you."

NARRATIVE INTERLUDE

29 These are the words of the covenant that the LORD commanded Moses to make with the people of Israel in the
land of Moab, in addition to the covenant he had made with
them at Horeb.

THE EXODUS, WANDERING, AND CONQUEST REVIEWED

2 Moses proclaimed to all Israel as follows: "You have seen all that
the LORD did in the land of Egypt to Pharaoh, all his servants,
and his land. 3 Your eyes have seen the great judgments, those
signs and mighty wonders. 4 But to this very day the LORD has not
given you an understanding mind, perceptive eyes, or discerning ears! 5 I have led you through the wilderness for forty years.
Your clothing has not worn out nor have your sandals deterio-
rated. 6 You have eaten no bread and drunk no wine or beer—all
so that you might know that I am the LORD your God! 7 When
you came to this place King Sihon of Heshbon and King Og of
Bashan came out to make war and we defeated them. 8 Then we
took their land and gave it as an inheritance to Reuben, Gad, and
half the tribe of Manasseh.

THE PRESENT COVENANT SETTING

9 "Therefore, keep the terms of this covenant and obey them
so that you may be successful in everything you do. 10 You are
standing today, all of you, before the LORD your God—the heads
of your tribes, your elders, your officials, every Israelite man,
11 your infants, your wives, and the resident foreigners living in
your encampment, those who chop wood and those who carry
water—12 so that you may enter by oath into the covenant the
LORD your God is making with you today. 13 Today he will affirm
that you are his people and that he is your God, just as he promised you and as he swore by oath to your ancestors Abraham,
Isaac, and Jacob. 14 It is not with you alone that I am making this
covenant by oath, 15 but with whoever stands with us here today
before the LORD our God as well as those not with us here today.

THE RESULTS OF DISOBEDIENCE

16 "(For you know how we lived in the land of Egypt and how we
crossed through the nations as we traveled. 17 You have seen their
detestable things and idols of wood, stone, silver, and gold.) 18 Beware that the heart of no man, woman, clan, or tribe among you
turns away from the LORD our God today to pursue and serve

the gods of those nations; beware that there is among you no
root producing poisonous and bitter fruit. 19 When such a person hears the words of this oath he secretly blesses himself and
says, ‘I will have peace though I continue to walk with a stubborn
spirit.’ This will destroy the watered ground with the parched.
20 The LORD will be unwilling to forgive him, and his intense anger will rage against that man; all the curses written in this scroll
will fall upon him, and the LORD will obliterate his name from
memory. 21 The LORD will single him out for judgment from all
the tribes of Israel according to all the curses of the covenant
written in this scroll of the law. 22 The generation to come—your
descendants who will rise up after you, as well as the foreigner
who will come from distant places—will see the afflictions of that
land and the illnesses that the LORD has brought on it. 23 The
whole land will be covered with brimstone, salt, and burning
debris; it will not be planted nor will it sprout or produce grass.
It will resemble the destruction of Sodom and Gomorrah, Admah and Zeboyim, which the LORD destroyed in his intense
anger. 24 Then all the nations will ask, ‘Why has the LORD done
all this to this land? What is this fierce, heated display of anger all about?’ 25 Then people will say, ‘Because they abandoned
the covenant of the LORD, the God of their ancestors, which he
made with them when he brought them out of the land of Egypt.
26 They went and served other gods and worshiped them, gods
they did not know and that he did not permit them to worship.
27 That is why the LORD’s anger erupted against this land, bringing on it all the curses written in this scroll. 28 So the LORD has
uprooted them from their land in anger, wrath, and great rage
and has deported them to another land, as is clear today.’ 29 The
secret things belong to the LORD our God, but those that are
revealed belong to us and our descendants forever, so that we
might obey all the words of this law.

THE RESULTS OF COVENANT REAFFIRMATION

30 “When you have experienced all these things, both the
blessings and the curses I have set before you, you will
reflect upon them in all the nations where the LORD your God
has banished you. 2 Then if you and your descendants turn to the
LORD your God and obey him with your whole mind and being
just as I am commanding you today, 3 the LORD your God will
reverse your captivity and have pity on you. He will turn and
gather you from all the peoples among whom he has scattered
you. 4 Even if your exiles are in the most distant land, from there
the LORD your God will gather you and bring you back. 5 Then
he will bring you to the land your ancestors possessed and you
also will possess it; he will do better for you and multiply you
more than he did your ancestors. 6 The LORD your God will also
cleanse your heart, and the hearts of your descendants so that
you may love him with all your mind and being and so that you
may live. 7 Then the LORD your God will put all these curses on
your enemies, on those who hate you and persecute you. 8 You
will return and obey the LORD, keeping all his commandments
I am giving you today. 9 The LORD your God will make the labor
of your hands abundantly successful and multiply your children,

the offspring of your cattle, and the produce of your soil. For the LORD will once more rejoice over you to make you prosperous just as he rejoiced over your ancestors, 10 if you obey the LORD your God and keep his commandments and statutes that are written in this scroll of the law. But you must turn to him with your whole mind and being.

EXHORTATION TO COVENANT OBEDIENCE

11 "This commandment I am giving you today is not too difficult for you, nor is it too remote. 12 It is not in heaven, as though one must say, 'Who will go up to heaven to get it for us and proclaim it to us so we may obey it?' 13 And it is not across the sea, as though one must say, 'Who will cross over to the other side of the sea and get it for us and proclaim it to us so we may obey it?' 14 For the thing is very near you—it is in your mouth and in your mind so that you can do it.

15 "Look! I have set before you today life and prosperity on the one hand, and death and disaster on the other. 16 What I am commanding you today is to love the LORD your God, to walk in his ways, and to obey his commandments, his statutes, and his ordinances. Then you will live and become numerous and the LORD your God will bless you in the land that you are about to possess. 17 However, if you turn aside and do not obey, but are lured away to worship and serve other gods, 18 I declare to you this very day that you will certainly perish! You will not extend your time in the land you are crossing the Jordan to possess. 19 Today I invoke heaven and earth as witnesses against you that I have set life and death, blessing and curse, before you. Therefore choose life so that you and your descendants may live! 20 I also call on you to love the LORD your God, to obey him and be loyal to him, for he gives you life and enables you to live continually in the land the LORD promised to give to your ancestors Abraham, Isaac, and Jacob."

SUCCESSION OF MOSES BY JOSHUA

31 Then Moses went and spoke these words to all Israel. 2 He said to them, "Today I am 120 years old. I am no longer able to get about, and the LORD has said to me, 'You will not cross the Jordan.' 3 As for the LORD your God, he is about to cross over before you; he will destroy these nations before you, and you will dispossess them. As for Joshua, he is about to cross before you just as the LORD has said. 4 The LORD will do to them just what he did to Sihon and Og, the Amorite kings, and to their land, which he destroyed. 5 The LORD will deliver them over to you, and you will do to them according to the whole commandment I have given you. 6 Be strong and courageous! Do not fear or tremble before them, for the LORD your God is the one who is going with you. He will not fail you or abandon you!" 7 Then Moses called out to Joshua in the presence of all Israel, "Be strong and courageous, for you will accompany these people to the land that the LORD promised to give their ancestors, and you will enable them to inherit it. 8 The LORD is indeed going before you—he will be with you; he will not fail you or abandon you. Do not be afraid or discouraged!"

LOVE TO GROW

STRONG AND COURAGEOUS

DEUTERONOMY 31:7–8

Moses is one of my favorite Bible characters. He was a man who made many mistakes, had his shortcomings and flaws out on display, felt weak and insecure, and wasn't up to the task God gave him.

I can relate. I've messed up more times than I'd like to admit. I've allowed fear to cripple me, hold me back, and cause more sleepless nights than a newborn baby.

I'm always praying, asking God to place an "Aaron" in my life. Someone who can speak on my behalf. Someone who is eloquent and confident. I often don't feel like I have what it takes to lead a ministry. Moses may have stuttered his words, but I mess mine up more times than I care to share.

In spite of my weaknesses and brokenness, God chose to use me anyway. He chooses to use you too.

Because of Moses' personal relationship with God, he was able to encourage the people of Israel. He challenged them to be strong and courageous. Moses learned how to be strong and courageous by trusting God and watching Him work in his life time and time again. Moses challenged the Israelites to do the same.

Because of God's faithfulness in Moses' life, Moses was able to speak into the lives of the next generation and say, "Be strong and courageous! Don't be afraid! Your God goes before you like He did for me!"

That's what we need these days. We need women in the older generations to give hope to those in the younger generations, saying "Be strong and courageous!"

I ask you today: Will you be a "Moses" for the next generation? Will you be brave and courageous by sharing your personal testimonies of God's faithfulness? Will you declare to the "Joshuas" of today that His words are true?

Moses' story encourages us to be strong and courageous in whatever battle we face. To whatever land God is sending us, we are not to be afraid. Our God is with us. Let's be strong and courageous together!

THE DEPOSIT OF THE COVENANT TEXT

9 Then Moses wrote down this law and gave it to the Levitical priests, who carry the ark of the LORD's covenant, and to all Israel's elders. 10 He commanded them: "At the end of seven years, at the appointed time of the cancellation of debts, at the Feast of Shelters, 11 when all Israel comes to appear before the LORD your God in the place he chooses, you must read this law before them within their hearing. 12 Gather the people—men, women, and children, as well as the resident foreigners in your villages—so they may hear and thus learn about and fear the LORD your God and carefully obey all the words of this law. 13 Then their children, who have not known this law, will also hear about and learn to fear the LORD your God for as long as you live in the land you are crossing the Jordan to possess."

THE COMMISSIONING OF JOSHUA

14 Then the LORD said to Moses, "The day of your death is near. Summon Joshua and present yourselves in the tent of meeting so that I can commission him." So Moses and Joshua presented themselves in the tent of meeting. 15 The LORD appeared in the tent in a pillar of cloud that stood above the door of the tent.

16 Then the LORD said to Moses, "You are about to die, and then these people will begin to prostitute themselves with the foreign gods of the land into which they are going. They will reject me and break my covenant that I have made with them. 17 At that time my anger will erupt against them, and I will abandon them and hide my face from them until they are devoured. Many disasters and distresses will overcome them so that they will say at that time, 'Have not these disasters overcome us because our God is not among us ?' 18 But I will certainly hide myself at that time because of all the wickedness they will have done by turning to other gods. 19 Now write down for yourselves the following song and teach it to the Israelites. Put it into their very mouths so that this song may serve as my witness against the Israelites! 20 For after I have brought them to the land I promised to their ancestors—one flowing with milk and honey—and they eat their fill and become fat, then they will turn to other gods and worship them; they will reject me and break my covenant. 21 Then when many disasters and distresses overcome them this song will testify against them, for their descendants will not forget it. I know the intentions they have in mind today, even before I bring them to the land I have promised." 22 So on that day Moses wrote down this song and taught it to the Israelites, 23 and the LORD commissioned Joshua son of Nun, "Be strong and courageous, for you will take the Israelites to the land I have promised them, and I will be with you."

ANTICIPATION OF DISOBEDIENCE

24 When Moses finished writing on a scroll the words of this law in their entirety, 25 he commanded the Levites who carried the ark of the LORD's covenant, 26 "Take this scroll of the law and place it beside the ark of the covenant of the LORD your God. It will remain there as a witness against you, 27 for

I know about your rebellion and stubbornness. Indeed, even while I have been living among you to this very day, you have rebelled against the LORD; you will be even more rebellious after my death! 28 Gather to me all your tribal elders and officials so I can speak to them directly about these things and call the heavens and the earth to witness against them. 29 For I know that after I die you will totally corrupt yourselves and turn away from the path I have commanded you to walk. Disaster will confront you in future days because you will act wickedly before the LORD, inciting him to anger because of your actions." 30 Then Moses recited the words of this song from start to finish in the hearing of the whole assembly of Israel:

INVOCATION OF WITNESSES

32 Listen, O heavens, and I will speak;
hear, O earth, the words of my mouth.
2 My teaching will drop like the rain,
my sayings will drip like the dew,
as rain drops upon the grass,
and showers upon new growth.
3 For I will proclaim the name of the LORD;
you must acknowledge the greatness of our God.
4 As for the Rock, his work is perfect,
for all his ways are just.
He is a reliable God who is never unjust,
he is fair and upright.
5 His people have been unfaithful to him;
they have not acted like his children—this is their sin.
They are a perverse and deceitful generation.
6 Is this how you repay the LORD,
you foolish, unwise people?
Is he not your father, your Creator?
He has made you and established you.
7 Remember the ancient days;
bear in mind the years of past generations.
Ask your father and he will inform you,
your elders, and they will tell you.
8 When the Most High gave the nations their inheritance,
when he divided up humankind,
he set the boundaries of the peoples,
according to the number of the heavenly assembly.
9 For the LORD's allotment is his people,
Jacob is his special possession.
10 The LORD found him in a desolate land,
in an empty wasteland where animals howl.
He continually guarded him and taught him;
he continually protected him like the pupil of his eye.
11 Like an eagle that stirs up its nest,
that hovers over its young,
so the LORD spread out his wings and took him,
he lifted him up on his pinions.
12 The LORD alone was guiding him,
no foreign god was with him.

13 He enabled him to travel over the
high terrain of the land,
and he ate of the produce of the fields.
He provided honey for him from the cliffs,
and olive oil from the hardest of rocks,
14 butter from the herd
and milk from the flock,
along with the fat of lambs,
rams and goats of Bashan,
along with the best of the kernels of wheat;
and from the juice of grapes you drank wine.

ISRAEL'S REBELLION

15 But Jeshurun became fat and kicked;
you got fat, thick, and stuffed!
Then he deserted the God who made him,
and treated the Rock who saved
him with contempt.
16 They made him jealous with other gods,
they enraged him with abhorrent idols.
17 They sacrificed to demons, not God,
to gods they had not known;
to new gods who had recently come along,
gods your ancestors had not known about.
18 You forgot the Rock who fathered you,
and put out of mind the God who gave you birth.

A WORD OF JUDGMENT

19 But the LORD took note and despised them
because his sons and daughters enraged him.
20 He said, "I will reject them.
I will see what will happen to them;
for they are a perverse generation,
children who show no loyalty.
21 They have made me jealous with false gods,
enraging me with their worthless gods;
so I will make them jealous with a
people they do not recognize,
with a nation slow to learn I will enrage them.
22 For a fire has been kindled by my anger,
and it burns to lowest Sheol;
it consumes the earth and its produce,
and ignites the foundations of the mountains.
23 I will increase their disasters;
I will use up my arrows on them.
24 They will be starved by famine,
eaten by plague, and bitterly stung;
I will send the teeth of wild animals against them,
along with the poison of creatures
that crawl in the dust.
25 The sword will make people childless outside,
and terror will do so inside;
they will destroy both the young man and the virgin,
the infant and the gray-haired man.

THE WEAKNESS OF OTHER GODS

26 "I said, 'I want to cut them in pieces.
I want to make people forget they ever existed.
27 But I fear the reaction of their enemies,
for their adversaries would misunderstand
and say, "Our power is great,
and the LORD has not done all this!"'
28 They are a nation devoid of wisdom,
and there is no understanding among them.
29 I wish that they were wise and could understand this,
and that they could comprehend
what will happen to them."
30 How can one man chase a thousand of them,
and two pursue ten thousand,
unless their Rock had delivered them up—
and the LORD had handed them over?
31 For our enemies' rock is not like our Rock,
as even our enemies concede.
32 For their vine is from the stock of Sodom,
and from the fields of Gomorrah.
Their grapes contain venom;
their clusters of grapes are bitter.
33 Their wine is snakes' poison,
the deadly venom of cobras.
34 "Is this not stored up with me?" says the LORD,
"Is it not sealed up in my storehouses?
35 I will get revenge and pay them back
at the time their foot slips;
for the day of their disaster is near,
and the impending judgment is rushing upon them!"
36 The LORD will judge his people,
and will change his plans concerning his servants;
when he sees that their power has disappeared,
and that no one is left, whether confined or set free.
37 He will say, "Where are their gods,
the rock in whom they sought security,
38 who ate the best of their sacrifices,
and drank the wine of their drink offerings?
Let them rise and help you;
let them be your refuge!

THE VINDICATION OF THE LORD

39 "See now that I, indeed I, am he!" says the LORD,
"and there is no other god besides me.
I kill and give life,
I smash and I heal,
and none can resist my power.
40 For I raise up my hand to heaven,
and say, 'As surely as I live forever,
41 I will sharpen my lightning-like sword,
and my hand will grasp hold of the
weapon of judgment;
I will execute vengeance on my foes,
and repay those who hate me!

42 I will make my arrows drunk with blood,
and my sword will devour flesh—
the blood of the slaughtered and captured,
the chief of the enemy's leaders.'"
43 Cry out, O nations, with his people,
for he will avenge his servants' blood;
he will take vengeance against his enemies,
and make atonement for his land and people.

NARRATIVE INTERLUDE

44 Then Moses went with Joshua son of Nun and recited all the
words of this song to the people. 45 When Moses finished reciting
all these words to all Israel 46 he said to them, "Keep in mind all the
words I am solemnly proclaiming to you today; you must command
your children to observe carefully all the words of this law. 47 For
this is no idle word for you—it is your life! By this word you will live
a long time in the land you are about to cross the Jordan to possess."

INSTRUCTIONS ABOUT MOSES' DEATH

48 Then the LORD said to Moses that same day, 49 "Go up to this
Abarim hill country, to Mount Nebo (which is in the land of
Moab opposite Jericho), and look at the land of Canaan that I
am giving to the Israelites as a possession. 50 You will die on the
mountain that you ascend and join your deceased ancestors,
just as Aaron your brother died on Mount Hor and joined his
deceased ancestors, 51 for both of you rebelled against me among
the Israelites at the waters of Meribah Kadesh in the wilderness
of Zin when you did not show me proper respect among the Israelites. 52 You will see the land before you, but you will not enter the land that I am giving to the Israelites."

INTRODUCTION TO THE BLESSING OF MOSES

33 This is the blessing Moses the man of God pronounced
upon the Israelites before his death. 2 He said:

A HISTORICAL REVIEW

"The LORD came from Sinai
and revealed himself to Israel from Seir.
He appeared in splendor from Mount Paran,
and came forth with ten thousand holy ones.
With his right hand he gave a fiery law to them.
3 Surely he loves the people;
all your holy ones are in your power.
And they sit at your feet,
each receiving your words.
4 Moses delivered to us a law,
an inheritance for the assembly of Jacob.
5 The LORD was king over Jeshurun,
when the leaders of the people assembled,
the tribes of Israel together.

BLESSING ON REUBEN

6 "May Reuben live and not die,
and may his people multiply."

BLESSING ON JUDAH

7 And this is the blessing to Judah. He said,
"Listen, O LORD, to Judah's voice,
and bring him to his people.
May his power be great,
and may you help him against his foes."

BLESSING ON LEVI

8 Of Levi he said:
"Your Thummim and Urim belong to your godly one,
whose authority you challenged at Massah,
and with whom you argued at the waters of Meribah.
9 He said to his father and mother,
'I have not seen him,'
and he did not acknowledge his own brothers
or know his own children,
for they kept your word,
and guarded your covenant.
10 They will teach Jacob your ordinances
and Israel your law;
they will offer incense as a pleasant odor,
and a whole offering on your altar.
11 Bless, O LORD, his goods,
and be pleased with his efforts;
undercut the legs of any who attack him,
and of those who hate him, so that they cannot stand."

BLESSING ON BENJAMIN

12 Of Benjamin he said:
"The beloved of the LORD will live safely by him;
he protects him all the time,
and the LORD places him on his chest."

BLESSING ON JOSEPH

13 Of Joseph he said:
"May the LORD bless his land
with the harvest produced by the sky, by the dew,
and by the depths crouching beneath;
14 with the harvest produced by the daylight
and by the moonlight;
15 with the best of the ancient mountains
and the harvest produced by the age-old hills;
16 with the harvest of the earth and its fullness
and the pleasure of him who resided
in the burning bush.
May blessing rest on Joseph's head,
and on the top of the head of the one
set apart from his brothers.
17 May the firstborn of his bull bring him honor,
and may his horns be those of a wild ox;
with them may he gore all peoples,
all the far reaches of the earth.
They are the ten thousands of Ephraim,
and they are the thousands of Manasseh."

BLESSING ON ZEBULUN AND ISSACHAR

18 Of Zebulun he said:
"Rejoice, Zebulun, when you go outside,
and Issachar, when you are in your tents.
19 They will summon peoples to the mountain,
there they will sacrifice proper sacrifices;
for they will enjoy the abundance of the seas,
and the hidden treasures of the shores."

BLESSING ON GAD

20 Of Gad he said:
"Blessed be the one who enlarges Gad.
Like a lioness he will dwell;
he will tear at an arm—indeed, a scalp.
21 He has selected the best part for himself,
for the portion of the ruler is set aside there;
he came with the leaders of the people,
he obeyed the righteous laws of the LORD
and his ordinances with Israel."

BLESSING ON DAN

22 Of Dan he said:
"Dan is a lion's cub;
he will leap forth from Bashan."

BLESSING ON NAPHTALI

23 Of Naphtali he said:
"O Naphtali, overflowing with favor,
and full of the LORD's blessing,
possess the west and south."

BLESSING ON ASHER

24 Of Asher he said:
"Asher is blessed with children;
may he be favored by his brothers,
and may he dip his foot in olive oil.
25 The bars of your gates will be made
of iron and bronze,
and may you have lifelong strength."

GENERAL PRAISE AND BLESSING

26 "There is no one like God, O Jeshurun,
who rides through the sky to help you,
on the clouds in majesty.
27 The everlasting God is a refuge,
and underneath you are his eternal arms;
he has driven out enemies before you,
and has said, "Destroy!"
28 Israel lives in safety,
the fountain of Jacob is quite secure,
in a land of grain and new wine;
indeed, its heavens rain down dew.
29 You have joy, Israel! Who is like you?
You are a people delivered by the LORD,

your protective shield
and your exalted sword.
May your enemies cringe before you;
may you trample on their backs."

THE DEATH OF MOSES

34 Then Moses ascended from the rift valley plains of Moab
to Mount Nebo, to the summit of Pisgah, which is opposite Jericho. The LORD showed him the whole land—Gilead to
Dan, 2 and all of Naphtali, the land of Ephraim and Manasseh,
all the land of Judah as far as the distant sea, 3 the Negev, and the
plain of the Valley of Jericho, the city of date palm trees, as far as
Zoar. 4 Then the LORD said to him, "This is the land I promised to
Abraham, Isaac, and Jacob when I said, 'I will give it to your descendants.' I have let you see it, but you will not cross over there."
5 So Moses, the servant of the LORD, died there in the land of
Moab as the LORD had said. 6 He buried him in the valley in the
land of Moab near Beth Peor, but no one knows his exact burial
place to this very day. 7 Moses was 120 years old when he died,
but his eye was not dull nor had his vitality departed. 8 The Israelites mourned for Moses in the rift valley plains of Moab for
thirty days; then the days of mourning for Moses ended.

AN EPITAPH FOR MOSES

9 Now Joshua son of Nun was full of the spirit of wisdom, for Moses had placed his hands on him; and the Israelites listened to
him and did just what the LORD had commanded Moses. 10 No
prophet ever again arose in Israel like Moses, who knew the
LORD face to face. 11 He did all the signs and wonders the LORD
had sent him to do in the land of Egypt, to Pharaoh, all his servants, and the whole land, 12 and he displayed great power and
awesome might in view of all Israel.

REFLECT

Many who deny the authority of Scripture claim Moses could not have written Deuteronomy since it records his death. How do we reconcile or explain this confusion without undermining the authority of God's Word?

ISRAEL IN THE TRIBAL PERIOD

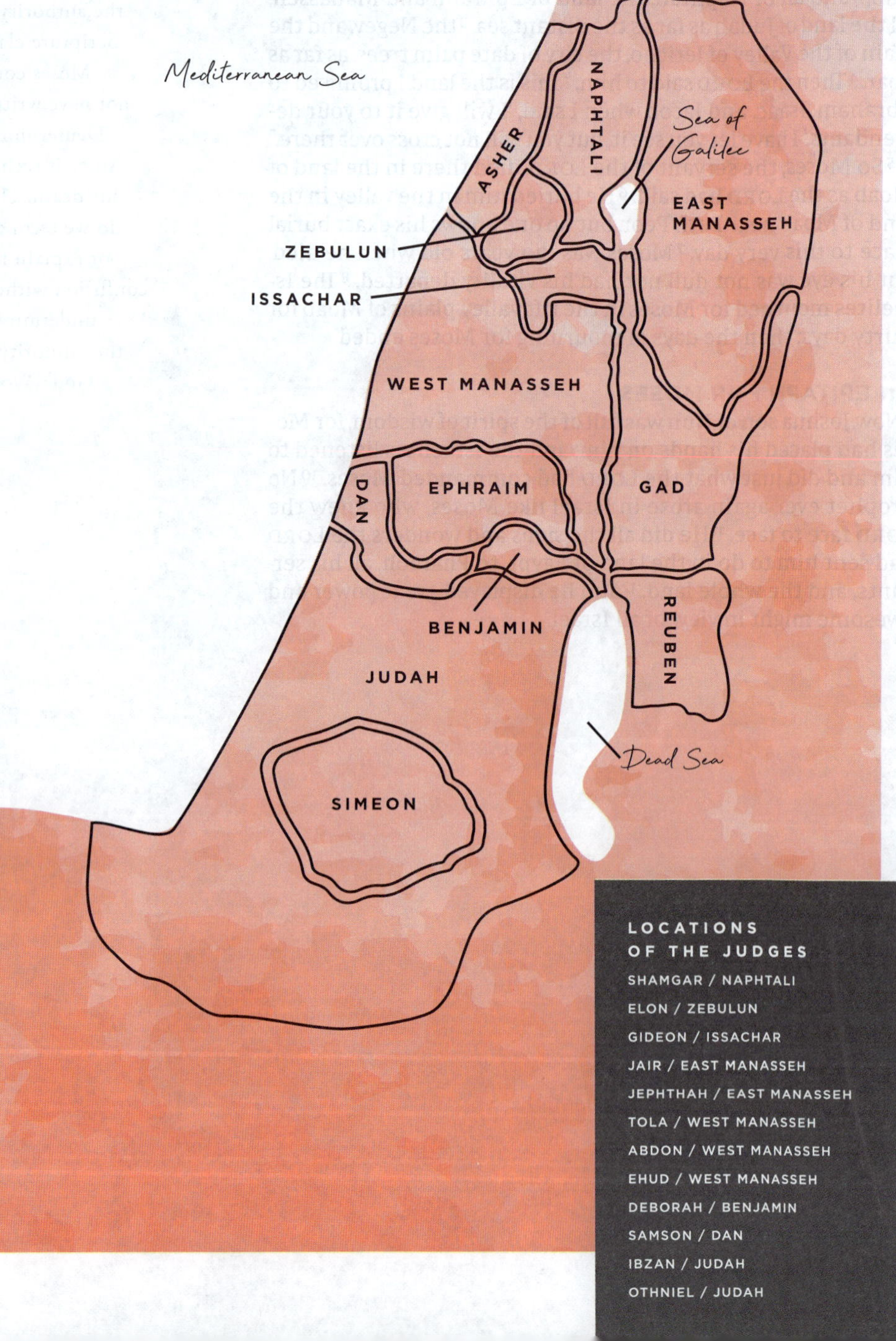

LOCATIONS OF THE JUDGES

SHAMGAR / NAPHTALI
ELON / ZEBULUN
GIDEON / ISSACHAR
JAIR / EAST MANASSEH
JEPHTHAH / EAST MANASSEH
TOLA / WEST MANASSEH
ABDON / WEST MANASSEH
EHUD / WEST MANASSEH
DEBORAH / BENJAMIN
SAMSON / DAN
IBZAN / JUDAH
OTHNIEL / JUDAH

THE KINGDOMS OF ISRAEL AND JUDAH

Not one of the LORD's faithful promises to the family of ISRAEL was left unfulfilled; every one was realized

MEMORY VERSE

Not one of the LORD's faithful promises to the family of Israel was left unfulfilled; every one was realized.

Joshua 21:45

Joshua

INTRODUCTION

Promises Fulfilled

God's power is on display in the Book of Joshua. He fulfills His promises through magnificent works of His strength and creativity. He leads His people and brings them into the land He promised. His heart for justice and righteousness is shown through His defeat of the enemies of His people.

The Book of Joshua details the conquest of the land of Canaan by God's chosen people, the nation of Israel. This military-style history book shows how Yahweh was faithful to fulfill the promises He made to Abraham, Isaac, and Jacob. Joshua also shows how God fought for His people by performing wonders from city walls falling to the sun standing still. The details of the conquest show God's faithfulness and power. God provided a place for His people to dwell, granting them rest and the inheritance they were promised.

While both the author and date of writing of the Book of Joshua are unknown, there is evidence that Joshua wrote portions of it. There are also indications that the book was written shortly after the conquest of Canaan, while many of the Israelites who participated in these events were still living. The primary purpose was to provide a record of the allotment of land and to serve as a reminder of all God had done for His people.

Joshua is a fascinating book that displays God's character in unique ways. God makes huge gestures for His chosen people, fulfilling the promises He made to even the smallest detail. God cared for His people, not allowing them to overtake the land too quickly or in ways that would cause them more harm. Joshua opens our eyes to the power and thoughtfulness of God. We can love Him greatly, confident that He knows our lives and needs from the smallest details to the most extravagant gestures. As He was with Joshua, God will be with us as He leads us into our promised lands.

Kenya

OFFICIAL LANGUAGE
Swahili
POPULATION
52,470,000
UNREACHED POPULATION
5,663,000
PROFESSING CHRISTIANS
78.0%

Setty's Home

Say a Prayer Today

Pray for Setty and her people in Kenya. Pray for the people of Kenya that they would trust God's faithfulness and believe His promises.

HISTORY BIT

Johann Ludwig Kraph, a German missionary, was the first to translate the New Testament into Swahili. His translation was completed in 1844.*

Source Information:
https://joshuaproject.net/countries/KE
*John Bowden, A Chronology of World Christianity (New York, NY: Continuum, 2007), 369.

SETTY'S STORY

I've always had a passion for the hospitality industry, but, somehow, I ended up working in the market research industry.

This was not what I had hoped for. I woke up every morning feeling like I was battling myself. I was unhappy. Every day was a fight to get out of bed and go into the office, and I knew it was time to make a change.

I applied for several jobs in the hospitality industry. I'd been sending applications for months, but I'd never received any responses. I knew God could and would fulfill His plans for my life, but I wondered if this was actually His plan. I decided to apply for one more job. I sent the application to the restaurant and tried not to think about it.

A few weeks later, I came home from work to find I'd received a call from the restaurant where I truly wanted to work. They wanted me to come in for an interview! I was elated. I jumped up and down around my house with my sister. I fell to my knees and started praying, praising God and thanking Him for answering my prayer. As I did, I began singing the lyrics to one of my favorite songs:

God is not an idol; He is no man; He doesn't lie.
His promises are yes and amen.
I have seen Him.
If He says *yes* no one can go against.
If He promises He will fulfill in His own time.

Let's not lose hope! What He has promised, He will fulfill. We can trust Him. You can trust Him.

6 WEEK READING PLAN

LOVE HIS WORD

	MONDAY	TUESDAY	WEDNESDAY	THURSDAY	FRIDAY
1	Joshua 1	Joshua 2	Joshua 3	Joshua 4:1—5:1	Joshua 5:2-12
	SOAP Joshua 1:8	SOAP Hebrews 11:31	SOAP Joshua 3:5	SOAP Joshua 4:6-7	SOAP Psalm 105:8
2	Joshua 5:13—6:27	Joshua 7	Joshua 8:1-29	Joshua 8:30-35	Joshua 9
	SOAP Romans 8:31	SOAP Joshua 7:11	SOAP 1 Samuel 15:22	SOAP Deuteronomy 28:1-2	SOAP Psalm 33:10-11
3	Joshua 10:1-27	Joshua 10:28-43	Joshua 11:1-15	Joshua 11:16-23	Joshua 12
	SOAP Joshua 10:14	SOAP Jeremiah 1:19	SOAP 2 Kings 6:16	SOAP Joshua 11:23	SOAP Psalm 103:19
4	Joshua 13	Joshua 14	Joshua 15	Joshua 16	Joshua 17
	SOAP Isaiah 66:3-4	SOAP Joshua 14:12	SOAP 1 Peter 1:3-5	SOAP Genesis 12:1-3	SOAP 1 Corinthians 5:6-8
5	Joshua 18:1-10	Joshua 18:11-28	Joshua 19:1-31	Joshua 19:32-51	Joshua 20
	SOAP Proverbs 10:4	SOAP Deuteronomy 1:8	SOAP Joshua 34:4	SOAP Joshua 19:49-50	SOAP Psalm 94:22
6	Joshua 21	Joshua 22:1-9	Joshua 22:10-34	Joshua 23	Joshua 24
	SOAP Joshua 21:45	SOAP Joshua 14:15	SOAP Joshua 22:26-27	SOAP Joshua 23:8	SOAP Joshua 24:15

THE LORD COMMISSIONS JOSHUA

1 After Moses the LORD's servant died, the LORD said to Joshua son of Nun, Moses' assistant: 2 "Moses my servant is dead. Get ready! Cross the Jordan River. Lead these people into the land that I am ready to hand over to them. 3 I am handing over to you every place you set foot, as I promised Moses. 4 Your territory will extend from the desert in the south to Lebanon in the north. It will extend all the way to the great River Euphrates in the east (including all Syria) and all the way to the Mediterranean Sea in the west. 5 No one will be able to resist you all the days of your life. As I was with Moses, so I will be with you. I will not abandon you or leave you alone. 6 Be strong and brave! You must lead these people in the conquest of this land that I solemnly promised their ancestors I would hand over to them. 7 Make sure you are very strong and brave! Carefully obey all the law my servant Moses charged you to keep. Do not swerve from it to the right or to the left, so that you may be successful in all you do. 8 This law scroll must not leave your lips. You must memorize it day and night so you can carefully obey all that is written in it. Then you will prosper and be successful. 9 I repeat, be strong and brave! Don't be afraid and don't panic, for I, the LORD your God, am with you in all you do."

JOSHUA PREPARES FOR THE INVASION

10 Joshua instructed the leaders of the people: 11 "Go through the camp and command the people, 'Prepare your supplies, for within three days you will cross the Jordan River and begin the conquest of the land the LORD your God is ready to hand over to you.'"

12 Joshua told the Reubenites, the Gadites, and the half-tribe of Manasseh: 13 "Remember what Moses the LORD's servant commanded you. The LORD your God is giving you a place to settle and is handing this land over to you. 14 Your wives, children, and cattle may stay in the land that Moses assigned to you east of the Jordan River. But all of you warriors must cross over armed for battle ahead of your brothers. You must help them 15 until the LORD gives your brothers a place like yours to settle and they conquer the land the LORD your God is ready to hand over to them. Then you may go back to your allotted land and occupy the land Moses the LORD's servant assigned you east of the Jordan."

16 They told Joshua, "We will do everything you say. We will go wherever you send us. 17 Just as we obeyed Moses, so we will obey you. But may the LORD your God be with you as he was with Moses. 18 Any man who rebels against what you say and does not obey all your commands will be executed. But be strong and brave!"

JOSHUA SENDS SPIES INTO THE LAND

2 Joshua son of Nun sent two spies out from Shittim secretly and instructed them: "Find out what you can about the land, especially Jericho." They stopped at the house of a prostitute named Rahab and spent the night there. 2 The king of Jericho received this report: "Note well! Israelite men have come here

LOVE TO GROW

STRONG AND BRAVE

JOSHUA 2

It was the middle of the night in Jericho. Two of the king's men came to Rahab's house and questioned her about the two Israelite spies. Rahab had a secret: She was hiding them in the stalks of flax on her rooftop.

If the spies were discovered, she would find herself in grave danger. If she turned them over to the king's men, she would provoke the all-powerful God of Israel, whom she had heard parted the Red Sea to bring the Israelites out of Egypt (Josh 2:9–11).

This was a defining moment in Rahab's life: Would she fear the king's men in front of her, or would she courageously choose faith in the unseen God of Israel?

Despite her nationality, she recognized in reverent awe the authority of the God of Israel who worked mighty acts through His people. She told the king's men that the Israelite spies were no longer at her house. Then she exclaimed, "Chase after them quickly, for you have time to catch them!" (Josh 2:5).

No one would have expected such action from a Canaanite prostitute. Yet this woman with a sordid past, who had almost certainly worshiped the false gods of her people, feared the God of Israel and, in faith, protected the Israelite spies. Make no mistake, Rahab is the heroine of this story. She certainly is strong and brave.

After the king's men left, Rahab declared to the spies that she believed in God—their God, the God of Israel. She asked the spies to save her and her family when the Israelites laid siege to Jericho, because she knew the God of Israel would grant them victory. She protected the Israelite spies, and the spies promised to spare her life and the lives of her family members.

In this defining moment, Rahab boldly and courageously chose to trust in the God of Israel.

My friend, what courageous step do you need to take today? I commend to you the same command that Joshua issued to the leaders of Israel: "Be strong and brave!" (Josh 1:18). Go forward with the same courage as Rahab. Walk forward in your life confident that God is with you and will grant you victory.

tonight to spy on the land." 3 So the king of Jericho sent this order to Rahab: "Turn over the men who came to you—the ones
who came to your house—for they have come to spy on the whole
land!" 4 But the woman hid the two men and replied, "Yes, these
men were clients of mine, but I didn't know where they came
from. 5 When it was time to shut the city gate for the night, the
men left. I don't know where they were heading. Chase after
them quickly, for you have time to catch them!" 6 (Now she had
taken them up to the roof and had hidden them in the stalks
of flax she had spread out on the roof.) 7 Meanwhile, the king's
men tried to find them on the road to the Jordan River near
the fords. The city gate was shut as soon as they set out in pursuit of them.

8 Now before the spies went to sleep, Rahab went up to the roof.
9 She said to the men, "I know the LORD is handing this land over
to you. We are absolutely terrified of you, and all who live in the
land are cringing before you. 10 For we heard how the LORD dried
up the water of the Red Sea before you when you left Egypt and
how you annihilated the two Amorite kings, Sihon and Og, on
the other side of the Jordan. 11 When we heard the news we lost
our courage and no one could even breathe for fear of you. For
the LORD your God is God in heaven above and on earth below!
12 So now, promise me this with an oath sworn in the LORD's
name. Because I have shown allegiance to you, show allegiance
to my family. Give me a solemn pledge 13 that you will spare the
lives of my father, mother, brothers, sisters, and all who belong
to them, and will rescue us from death." 14 The men said to her,
"If you die, may we die too! If you do not report what we've been
up to, then we will show unswerving allegiance to you when the
LORD hands the land over to us."

15 Then Rahab let them down by a rope through the window.
(Her house was built as part of the city wall; she lived in the
wall.) 16 She told them, "Head to the hill country, so the ones
chasing you don't find you. Hide from them there for three days,
long enough for those chasing you to return. Then you can be
on your way." 17 The men said to her, "We are not bound by this
oath you made us swear unless the following conditions are
met: 18 When we invade the land, tie this red rope in the window through which you let us down, and gather together in
your house your father, mother, brothers, and all who live in
your father's house. 19 Anyone who leaves your house will be responsible for his own death—we are innocent in that case! But if
anyone with you in the house is harmed, we will be responsible.
20 If you should report what we've been up to, we are not bound
by this oath you made us swear." 21 She said, "I agree to these
conditions." She sent them on their way and then tied the red
rope in the window. 22 They went to the hill country and stayed
there for three days, long enough for those chasing them to return. Their pursuers looked all along the way but did not find
them. 23 Then the two men returned—they came down from the
hills, crossed the river, came to Joshua son of Nun, and reported
to him all they had discovered. 24 They told Joshua, "Surely the
LORD is handing over all the land to us! All who live in the land
are cringing before us!"

CHALLENGE

Joshua sent spies into the land of Canaan as Moses did in Numbers 13. How do the two reports differ? What changed for the Israelites that made their response different this time?

ISRAEL CROSSES THE JORDAN

3 Bright and early the next morning Joshua and the Israelites left Shittim and came to the Jordan. They camped there before crossing the river. 2 After three days the leaders went through the camp 3 and commanded the people: "When you see the ark of the covenant of the LORD your God being carried by the Levitical priests, you must leave here and walk behind it. 4 But stay about 3,000 feet behind it. Keep your distance so you can see which way you should go, for you have not traveled this way before."

5 Joshua told the people, "Ritually consecrate yourselves, for tomorrow the LORD will perform miraculous deeds among you." 6 Joshua told the priests, "Pick up the ark of the covenant and pass on ahead of the people." So they picked up the ark of the covenant and went ahead of the people.

7 The LORD told Joshua, "This very day I will begin to honor you before all Israel, so they will know that I am with you just as I was with Moses. 8 Instruct the priests carrying the ark of the covenant, 'When you reach the bank of the Jordan River, wade into the water.'"

9 Joshua told the Israelites, "Come here and listen to the words of the LORD your God!" 10 Joshua continued, "This is how you will know the living God is among you and that he will truly drive out before you the Canaanites, Hittites, Hivites, Perizzites, Girgashites, Amorites, and Jebusites. 11 Look! The ark of the covenant of the Lord of the whole earth is ready to enter the Jordan ahead of you. 12 Now select for yourselves twelve men from the tribes of Israel, one per tribe. 13 When the feet of the priests carrying the ark of the LORD, the Lord of the whole earth, touch the water of the Jordan, the water coming downstream toward you will stop flowing and pile up."

14 So when the people left their tents to cross the Jordan, the priests carrying the ark of the covenant went ahead of them. 15 When the ones carrying the ark reached the Jordan, and the feet of the priests carrying the ark touched the surface of the water–(the Jordan is at flood stage all during harvest time)–16 the water coming downstream toward them stopped flowing. It piled up far upstream at Adam (the city near Zarethan); there was no water at all flowing to the sea of the rift valley (the Salt Sea). The people crossed the river opposite Jericho. 17 The priests carrying the ark of the covenant of the LORD stood firmly on dry ground in the middle of the Jordan. All Israel crossed over on dry ground until the entire nation was on the other side.

REFLECT

Why was it necessary for the Israelites to commemorate the crossing of the Jordan River? How can you celebrate the faithfulness of God in your life?

ISRAEL COMMEMORATES THE CROSSING

4 When the entire nation was on the other side, the LORD told Joshua, 2 "Select for yourselves twelve men from the people, one per tribe. 3 Instruct them, 'Pick up twelve stones from the middle of the Jordan, from the very place where the priests stand firmly, and carry them over with you and put them in the place where you camp tonight.'"

4 Joshua summoned the twelve men he had appointed from the Israelites, one per tribe. 5 Joshua told them, "Go in front of the ark of the LORD your God to the middle of the Jordan. Each of

you is to put a stone on his shoulder, according to the number of
the Israelite tribes. 6 The stones will be a reminder to you. When
your children ask someday, 'Why are these stones important to
you?' 7 tell them how the water of the Jordan stopped flowing
before the ark of the covenant of the LORD. When it crossed the
Jordan, the water of the Jordan stopped flowing. These stones
will be a lasting memorial for the Israelites."
8 The Israelites did just as Joshua commanded. They picked up
twelve stones, according to the number of the Israelite tribes,
from the middle of the Jordan as the LORD had instructed Joshua.
They carried them over with them to the camp and put them
there. 9 Joshua also set up twelve stones in the middle of the Jordan in the very place where the priests carrying the ark of the
covenant stood. They remain there to this very day.
10 Now the priests carrying the ark of the covenant were standing in the middle of the Jordan until everything the Lord had commanded Joshua to tell the people was accomplished, in accordance
with all that Moses had commanded Joshua. The people went
across quickly, 11 and when all the people had finished crossing,
the ark of the LORD and the priests crossed as the people looked
on. 12 The Reubenites, the Gadites, and the half-tribe of Manasseh crossed over armed for battle ahead of the Israelites, just as
Moses had instructed them. 13 About 40,000 battle-ready troops
marched past the LORD to fight on the rift valley plains of Jericho. 14 That day the LORD brought honor to Joshua before all Israel.
They respected him all his life, just as they had respected Moses.
15 The LORD told Joshua, 16 "Instruct the priests carrying the ark
of the covenantal laws to come up from the Jordan." 17 So Joshua
instructed the priests, "Come up from the Jordan!" 18 The priests
carrying the ark of the covenant of the LORD came up from the
middle of the Jordan, and as soon as they set foot on dry land,
the water of the Jordan flowed again and returned to flood stage.
19 The people went up from the Jordan on the tenth day of the
first month and camped in Gilgal on the eastern border of Jericho. 20 Now Joshua set up in Gilgal the twelve stones they had
taken from the Jordan. 21 He told the Israelites, "When your children someday ask their fathers, 'What do these stones represent?'
22 explain to your children, 'Israel crossed the Jordan River on dry
ground.' 23 For the LORD your God dried up the water of the Jordan
before you while you crossed over. It was just like when the LORD
your God dried up the Red Sea before us while we crossed it. 24 He
has done this so all the nations of the earth might recognize the
LORD's power and so you might always obey the LORD your God."
5 When all the Amorite kings on the west side of the Jordan
and all the Canaanite kings along the seacoast heard how the
LORD had dried up the water of the Jordan before the Israelites
while they crossed, they lost their courage and could not even
breathe for fear of the Israelites.

A NEW GENERATION IS CIRCUMCISED

2 At that time the LORD told Joshua, "Make flint knives and circumcise the Israelites once again." 3 So Joshua made flint knives
and circumcised the Israelites at the Hill of the Foreskins. 4 This
is why Joshua had to circumcise them: All the men old enough

GOD'S HEART FOR THE NATIONS

Joshua 4:24

"He has done this so all the nations of the earth might recognize the LORD's power and so you might always obey the LORD your God."

to fight when they left Egypt died on the journey through the wilderness after they left Egypt. 5 Now all the men who left were circumcised, but all the sons born on the journey through the wilderness after they left Egypt were uncircumcised. 6 Indeed, for forty years the Israelites traveled through the wilderness until all the men old enough to fight when they left Egypt, the ones who had disobeyed the LORD, died off. For the LORD had sworn a solemn oath to them that he would not let them see the land he had sworn by oath to their ancestors to give them, a land rich in milk and honey. 7 He replaced them with their sons, whom Joshua circumcised. They were uncircumcised; their fathers had not circumcised them along the way. 8 When all the men had been circumcised, they stayed there in the camp until they had healed. 9 The LORD said to Joshua, "Today I have taken away the disgrace of Egypt from you." So that place is called Gilgal even to this day.

10 So the Israelites camped in Gilgal and celebrated the Passover in the evening of the fourteenth day of the month in the rift valley plains of Jericho. 11 They ate some of the produce of the land the day after the Passover, including unleavened bread and roasted grain. 12 The manna stopped appearing the day they ate some of the produce of the land; the Israelites never ate manna again. They ate from the produce of the land of Canaan that year.

ISRAEL CONQUERS JERICHO

13 When Joshua was near Jericho, he looked up and saw a man standing in front of him holding a drawn sword. Joshua approached him and asked him, "Are you on our side or allied with our enemies?" 14 He answered, "Truly I am the commander of the LORD's army. Now I have arrived!" Joshua bowed down with his face to the ground and asked, "What does my master want to say to his servant?" 15 The commander of the LORD's army answered Joshua, "Remove your sandals from your feet, because the place where you stand is holy." Joshua did so.

6 Now Jericho was shut tightly because of the Israelites. No one was allowed to leave or enter. 2 The LORD told Joshua, "See, I am about to defeat Jericho for you, along with its king and its warriors. 3 Have all the warriors march around the city one time; do this for six days. 4 Have seven priests carry seven rams' horns in front of the ark. On the seventh day march around the city seven times, while the priests blow the horns. 5 When you hear the signal from the ram's horn, have the whole army give a loud battle cry. Then the city wall will collapse, and the warriors should charge straight ahead."

6 So Joshua son of Nun summoned the priests and instructed them, "Pick up the ark of the covenant, and seven priests must carry seven rams' horns in front of the ark of the LORD." 7 And he told the army, "Move ahead and march around the city, with armed troops going ahead of the ark of the LORD."

8 When Joshua gave the army its orders, the seven priests carrying the seven rams' horns before the LORD moved ahead and blew the horns as the ark of the covenant of the LORD followed behind. 9 Armed troops marched ahead of the priests blowing the horns, while the rear guard followed along behind the ark

blowing rams' horns. 10 Now Joshua had instructed the army,
"Do not give a battle cry or raise your voices; say nothing until
the day I tell you, 'Give the battle cry.' Then give the battle cry!"
11 So Joshua made sure they marched the ark of the LORD around
the city one time. Then they went back to the camp and spent
the night there.

12 Bright and early the next morning Joshua had the priests
pick up the ark of the LORD. 13 The seven priests carrying the
seven rams' horns before the ark of the LORD marched along
blowing their horns. Armed troops marched ahead of them,
while the rear guard followed along behind the ark of the LORD
blowing rams' horns. 14 They marched around the city one time
on the second day, then returned to the camp. They did this six
days in all.

15 On the seventh day they were up at the crack of dawn and
marched around the city as before—only this time they marched
around it seven times. 16 The seventh time around, the priests
blew the rams' horns, and Joshua told the army, "Give the battle
cry, for the LORD is handing the city over to you! 17 The city and
all that is in it must be set apart for the LORD; only Rahab the
prostitute and all who are with her in her house will live, because
she hid the spies we sent. 18 But be careful when you are setting
apart the riches for God. If you take any of it, then you will make
the Israelite camp subject to annihilation and cause a disaster.
19 All the silver and gold, as well as bronze and iron items, belong
to the LORD. They must go into the LORD's treasury."

20 The rams' horns sounded, and when the army heard the
signal, they gave a loud battle cry. The wall collapsed, and the
warriors charged straight ahead into the city and captured it.
21 They annihilated with the sword everything that breathed
in the city, including men and women, young and old, as well
as cattle, sheep, and donkeys. 22 Joshua told the two men who
had spied on the land, "Enter the prostitute's house and bring
out the woman and all who belong to her as you promised her."
23 So the young spies went and brought out Rahab, her father,
mother, brothers, and all who belonged to her. They brought
out her whole family and took them to a place outside the Israelite camp. 24 But they burned the city and all that was in it, except for the silver, gold, and bronze and iron items they put in
the treasury of the LORD's house. 25 Yet Joshua spared Rahab the
prostitute, her father's family, and all who belonged to her. She
lives in Israel to this very day because she hid the messengers
Joshua sent to spy on Jericho. 26 At that time Joshua made this
solemn declaration: "The man who attempts to rebuild this city
of Jericho will stand condemned before the LORD. He will lose
his firstborn son when he lays its foundations and his youngest
son when he erects its gates!" 27 The LORD was with Joshua and
he became famous throughout the land.

ACHAN SINS AND IS PUNISHED

7 But the Israelites disobeyed the command about the city's
riches. Achan son of Carmi, son of Zabdi, son of Zerah, from
the tribe of Judah, stole some of the riches. The LORD was furious with the Israelites.

REFLECT

Why was Achan's sin so destructive to the community? What does this tell us about the way God deals with our sin?

2 Joshua sent men from Jericho to Ai (which is located near
Beth Aven, east of Bethel) and instructed them, "Go up and spy
on the land." So the men went up and spied on Ai. 3 They returned
and reported to Joshua, "Don't send the whole army. About two
or three thousand men are adequate to defeat Ai. Don't tire out
the whole army, for Ai is small."

4 So about 3,000 men went up, but they fled from the men of
Ai. 5 The men of Ai killed about thirty-six of them and chased
them from in front of the city gate all the way to the fissures and
defeated them on the steep slope. The people's courage melted
away like water.

6 Joshua tore his clothes; he and the leaders of Israel lay face
down on the ground before the ark of the LORD until evening and
threw dirt on their heads. 7 Joshua prayed, "O, Sovereign LORD!
Why did you bring these people across the Jordan to hand us over
to the Amorites so they could destroy us? If only we had been satisfied to live on the other side of the Jordan! 8 O Lord, what can
I say now that Israel has retreated before its enemies? 9 When
the Canaanites and all who live in the land hear about this, they
will turn against us and destroy the very memory of us from
the earth. What will you do to protect your great reputation?"

10 The LORD responded to Joshua, "Get up! Why are you lying
there face down? 11 Israel has sinned; they have violated my covenantal commandment! They have taken some of the riches;
they have stolen them and deceitfully put them among their
own possessions. 12 The Israelites are unable to stand before
their enemies; they retreat because they have become subject
to annihilation. I will no longer be with you, unless you destroy
what has contaminated you. 13 Get up! Ritually consecrate the
people and tell them this: 'Ritually consecrate yourselves for
tomorrow, because this is what the LORD God of Israel has said,
"You are contaminated, O Israel! You will not be able to stand
before your enemies until you remove what is contaminating
you." 14 In the morning you must approach in tribal order. The
tribe the LORD selects must approach by clans. The clan the
LORD selects must approach by families. The family the LORD
selects must approach man by man. 15 The one caught with the
riches must be burned up along with all who belong to him, because he violated the LORD's covenant and did such a disgraceful
thing in Israel.'"

16 Bright and early the next morning Joshua made Israel approach in tribal order, and the tribe of Judah was selected. 17 He
then made the clans of Judah approach, and the clan of the Zerahites was selected. He made the clan of the Zerahites approach,
and Zabdi was selected. 18 He then made Zabdi's family approach
man by man and Achan son of Carmi, son of Zabdi, son of Zerah,
from the tribe of Judah, was selected. 19 So Joshua said to Achan,
"My son, honor the LORD God of Israel and give him praise! Tell
me what you did; don't hide anything from me." 20 Achan told
Joshua, "It is true. I have sinned against the LORD God of Israel
in this way: 21 I saw among the goods we seized a nice robe from
Babylon, 200 silver pieces, and a bar of gold weighing 50 shekels.
I wanted them, so I took them. They are hidden in the ground
right in the middle of my tent, with the silver underneath."

22 Joshua sent messengers who ran to the tent. The things were
hidden right in his tent, with the silver underneath. 23 They took
it all from the middle of the tent, brought it to Joshua and all the
Israelites, and placed it before the LORD. 24 Then Joshua and all
Israel took Achan, son of Zerah, along with the silver, the robe,
the bar of gold, his sons, daughters, oxen, donkeys, sheep, tent,
and all that belonged to him and brought them up to the Valley of Disaster. 25 Joshua said, "Why have you brought disaster on
us? The LORD will bring disaster on you today!" All Israel stoned
him to death. (They also stoned and burned the others.) 26 Then
they erected over him a large pile of stones (it remains to this
very day) and the LORD's anger subsided. So that place is called
the Valley of Disaster to this very day.

ISRAEL CONQUERS AI

8 The LORD told Joshua, "Don't be afraid and don't panic! Take
the whole army with you and march against Ai! See, I am
handing over to you the king of Ai, along with his people, city,
and land. 2 Do to Ai and its king what you did to Jericho and its
king, except you may plunder its goods and cattle. Set an ambush behind the city."

3 Joshua and the whole army marched against Ai. Joshua selected
30,000 brave warriors and sent them out at night. 4 He ordered
them, "Look, set an ambush behind the city. Don't go very far from
the city; all of you be ready! 5 I and all the troops who are with me
will approach the city. When they come out to fight us like before,
we will retreat from them. 6 They will attack us until we have lured
them from the city, for they will say, 'They are retreating from us
like before.' We will retreat from them. 7 Then you rise up from
your hiding place and seize the city. The LORD your God will hand
it over to you. 8 When you capture the city, set it on fire in keeping
with the Lord's message. See, I have given you orders." 9 Joshua sent
them away and they went to their hiding place west of Ai, between
Bethel and Ai. Joshua spent that night with the army.

10 Bright and early the next morning Joshua gathered the army,
and he and the leaders of Israel marched at the head of it to Ai.
11 All the troops that were with him marched up and drew near
the city. They camped north of Ai on the other side of the valley. 12 He took 5,000 men and set an ambush west of the city between Bethel and Ai. 13 The army was in position—the main army
north of the city and the rear guard west of the city. That night
Joshua went into the middle of the valley.

14 When the king of Ai and all his people saw Israel, they rushed
to get up early. Then the king and the men of the city went out to
meet Israel in battle, at the meeting place near the rift valley. But
he did not realize an ambush was waiting for him behind the city.
15 Joshua and all Israel pretended to be defeated by them, and they
retreated along the way to the wilderness. 16 All the reinforcements
in Ai were ordered to chase them; they chased Joshua and were
lured away from the city. 17 No men were left in Ai or Bethel; they all
went out after Israel. They left the city wide open and chased Israel.

18 The LORD told Joshua, "Hold out toward Ai the curved sword
in your hand, for I am handing the city over to you." So Joshua
held out toward Ai the curved sword in his hand. 19 When he

held out his hand, the men waiting in ambush rose up quickly from their place and attacked. They entered the city, captured it, and immediately set it on fire. 20 When the men of Ai turned around, they saw the smoke from the city ascending into the sky and were so shocked they were unable to flee in any direction. In the meantime the men who were retreating to the wilderness turned against their pursuers. 21 When Joshua and all Israel saw that the men in ambush had captured the city and that the city was going up in smoke, they turned around and struck down the men of Ai. 22 At the same time the men who had taken the city came out to fight, and the men of Ai were trapped in the middle. The Israelites struck them down, leaving no survivors or refugees. 23 But they captured the king of Ai alive and brought him to Joshua.

24 When Israel had finished killing all the men of Ai who had chased them toward the wilderness (they all fell by the sword), all Israel returned to Ai and put the sword to it. 25 12,000 men and women died that day, including all the men of Ai. 26 Joshua kept holding out his curved sword until Israel had annihilated all who lived in Ai. 27 But Israel did plunder the cattle and the goods of the city, in keeping with the LORD's orders to Joshua. 28 Joshua burned Ai and made it a permanently uninhabited mound (it remains that way to this very day). 29 He hung the king of Ai on a tree, leaving him exposed until evening. At sunset Joshua ordered that his corpse be taken down from the tree. They threw it down at the entrance of the city gate and erected over it a large pile of stones (it remains to this very day).

COVENANT RENEWAL

30 Then Joshua built an altar for the LORD God of Israel on Mount Ebal, 31 just as Moses the LORD's servant had commanded the Israelites. As described in the law scroll of Moses, it was made with uncut stones untouched by an iron tool. On it they offered burnt sacrifices to the LORD and sacrificed tokens of peace. 32 There, in the presence of the Israelites, Joshua inscribed on the stones a duplicate of the law written by Moses. 33 All the people, rulers, leaders, and judges were standing on either side of the ark, in front of the Levitical priests who carried the ark of the covenant of the LORD. Both resident foreigners and native Israelites were there. Half the people stood in front of Mount Gerizim and the other half in front of Mount Ebal, as Moses the LORD's servant had previously instructed them to do for the formal blessing ceremony. 34 Then Joshua read aloud all the words of the law, including the blessings and the curses, just as they are written in the law scroll. 35 Joshua read aloud every commandment Moses had given before the whole assembly of Israel, including the women, children, and resident foreigners who lived among them.

THE GIBEONITES DECEIVE ISRAEL

9 When the news reached all the kings on the west side of the Jordan—in the hill country, the foothills, and all along the Mediterranean coast as far as Lebanon (including the Hittites, Amorites, Canaanites, Perizzites, Hivites, and Jebusites)—2 they formed an alliance to fight against Joshua and Israel.

3 When the residents of Gibeon heard what Joshua did to Jericho and Ai, 4 they did something clever. They collected some
provisions and put worn-out sacks on their donkeys, along with
worn-out wineskins that were ripped and patched. 5 They had
worn-out, patched sandals on their feet and dressed in worn-out
clothes. All their bread was dry and hard. 6 They came to Joshua
at the camp in Gilgal and said to him and the men of Israel, "We
have come from a distant land. Make a treaty with us." 7 The men
of Israel said to the Hivites, "Perhaps you live near us. So how
can we make a treaty with you?" 8 But they said to Joshua, "We
are willing to be your subjects." So Joshua said to them, "Who
are you and where do you come from?" 9 They told him, "Your
subjects have come from a very distant land because of the reputation of the LORD your God, for we have heard the news about
all he did in Egypt 10 and all he did to the two Amorite kings on
the other side of the Jordan—King Sihon of Heshbon and King
Og of Bashan in Ashtaroth. 11 Our leaders and all who live in our
land told us, 'Take provisions for your journey and go meet them.
Tell them, "We are willing to be your subjects. Make a treaty
with us."' 12 This bread of ours was warm when we packed it in
our homes the day we started out to meet you, but now it is dry
and hard. 13 These wineskins we filled were brand new, but look
how they have ripped. Our clothes and sandals have worn out
because it has been a very long journey." 14 The men examined
some of their provisions, but they failed to ask the LORD's advice. 15 Joshua made a peace treaty with them and agreed to let
them live. The leaders of the community sealed it with an oath.

16 Three days after they made the treaty with them, the Israelites found out they were from the local area and lived nearby.
17 So the Israelites set out and on the third day arrived at their
cities—Gibeon, Kephirah, Beeroth, and Kiriath Jearim. 18 The Israelites did not attack them because the leaders of the community had sworn an oath to them in the name of the LORD God of
Israel. The whole community criticized the leaders, 19 but all the
leaders told the whole community, "We swore an oath to them in
the name of the LORD God of Israel! So now we can't hurt them.
20 We must let them live so we can escape the curse attached
to the oath we swore to them." 21 The leaders then added, "Let
them live." So they became woodcutters and water carriers for
the whole community, as the leaders had decided.

22 Joshua summoned the Gibeonites and said to them, "Why
did you trick us by saying, 'We live far away from you,' when you
really live nearby? 23 Now you are condemned to perpetual servitude as woodcutters and water carriers for the house of my God."
24 They said to Joshua, "It was carefully reported to your subjects
how the LORD your God commanded Moses his servant to assign you the whole land and to destroy all who live in the land
from before you. Because of you we were terrified we would lose
our lives, so we did this thing. 25 So now we are in your power. Do
to us what you think is good and appropriate." 26 Joshua did as
they said; he kept the Israelites from killing them 27 and that day
made them woodcutters and water carriers for the community
and for the altar of the LORD at the divinely chosen site. (They
continue in that capacity to this very day.)

ISRAEL DEFEATS AN AMORITE COALITION

10 Adoni-Zedek, king of Jerusalem, heard how Joshua captured Ai and annihilated it and its king as he did Jericho and its king. He also heard how the people of Gibeon made peace with Israel and lived among them. 2 All Jerusalem was terrified because Gibeon was a large city, like one of the royal cities. It was larger than Ai and all its men were warriors. 3 So King Adoni-Zedek of Jerusalem sent this message to King Hoham of Hebron, King Piram of Jarmuth, King Japhia of Lachish, and King Debir of Eglon: 4 "Come to my aid so we can attack Gibeon, for it has made peace with Joshua and the Israelites." 5 So the five Amorite kings (the kings of Jerusalem, Hebron, Jarmuth, Lachish, and Eglon) and all their troops gathered together and advanced. They deployed their troops and fought against Gibeon.

6 The men of Gibeon sent this message to Joshua at the camp in Gilgal, "Do not abandon your subjects! Come up here quickly and rescue us! Help us! For all the Amorite kings living in the hill country are attacking us." 7 So Joshua and his whole army, including the bravest warriors, marched up from Gilgal. 8 The LORD told Joshua, "Don't be afraid of them, for I am handing them over to you. Not one of them can resist you." 9 Joshua attacked them by surprise after marching all night from Gilgal. 10 The LORD routed them before Israel. Israel thoroughly defeated them at Gibeon. They chased them up the road to the pass of Beth Horon and struck them down all the way to Azekah and Makkedah. 11 As they fled from Israel on the slope leading down from Beth Horon, the LORD threw down on them large hailstones from the sky, all the way to Azekah. They died—in fact, more died from the hailstones than the Israelites killed with the sword.

12 The day the LORD delivered the Amorites over to the Israelites, Joshua prayed to the LORD before Israel:

"O sun, stand still over Gibeon;
O moon, over the Valley of Aijalon!"

13 The sun stood still and the moon stood motionless while the nation took vengeance on its enemies. The event is recorded in the Scroll of the Upright One. The sun stood motionless in the middle of the sky and did not set for about a full day. 14 There has not been a day like it before or since. The LORD listened to a human being, for the LORD fought for Israel! 15 Then Joshua and all Israel returned to the camp at Gilgal.

16 The five Amorite kings ran away and hid in the cave at Makkedah. 17 Joshua was told, "The five kings have been found hiding in the cave at Makkedah." 18 Joshua said, "Roll large stones over the mouth of the cave and post guards in front of it. 19 But don't you delay! Chase your enemies and catch them. Don't allow them to retreat to their cities, for the LORD your God is handing them over to you." 20 Joshua and the Israelites almost totally wiped them out, but some survivors did escape to the fortified cities. 21 Then the whole army safely returned to Joshua at the camp in Makkedah. No one dared threaten the Israelites. 22 Joshua said, "Open the cave's mouth and bring the five kings out of the cave to me." 23 They did as ordered; they brought the five kings out of

REFLECT

What does this incredible moment display about the power of God? If He can control the sun and the moon, what does that mean He can do in your life?

LOVE TO GROW

ONLY HIS POWER

JOSHUA 10

Sometimes we wonder why God shares certain events with us, like all the names and battles in the Book of Joshua. We know they are important because God included them in Scripture. Every part of God's Word reveals something about God and humanity's relationship to Him.

In Joshua 10, five Amorite kings joined forces to attack Gibeon, a large, impressive city that had made peace with the Israelites. The city was located on high ground. When its watchmen realized the city was under attack, they called on Joshua for help. The Lord encouraged Joshua not to be afraid, for the Lord assured him that Israel would win the battle.

God did amazing things for Israel that day. He routed the five Amorite armies before them, and He pummeled their enemy with a serious hailstorm. More Amorites died from hailstones than the Israelites killed with the sword.

Then God caused the sun and moon to stand still, allowing Joshua to defeat his enemies.

This account showcases the omnipotence of God. He displayed His infinite power and total control over what He had created and demonstrated faithfulness to His name and His chosen people. He showed that His hand is involved in history and everyday life. He is intimately involved in the lives of His people.

Do you sing loudly the songs that display the power and works of our amazing God? Do you praise Him regularly for all He has done, is doing, and will do in your life? Does seeing the power of God grow your faith? Is anything too hard for the God who can stop the sun in its tracks? Do you trust that the almighty, omnipotent God loves you beyond words and cares for you?

Believe it, dear friend. He is powerful and mighty. The God who caused the sun to stand still is the same God who raised Jesus from the grave. This same faithful God brings resurrected life to those who believe. Even though you may not be able to see it in this moment, He is using His power for your good. Stand and be still; God will fight for you!

the cave to him—the kings of Jerusalem, Hebron, Jarmuth, Lachish, and Eglon. 24 When they brought the kings out to Joshua,
he summoned all the men of Israel and said to the commanders of the troops who accompanied him, "Come here and put
your feet on the necks of these kings." So they came up and put
their feet on their necks. 25 Then Joshua said to them, "Don't be
afraid and don't panic! Be strong and brave, for the LORD will do
the same thing to all your enemies you fight." 26 Then Joshua executed them and hung them on five trees. They were left hanging on the trees until evening. 27 At sunset Joshua ordered his
men to take them down from the trees. They threw them into
the cave where they had hidden and piled large stones over the
mouth of the cave. (They remain to this very day.)

JOSHUA LAUNCHES A SOUTHERN CAMPAIGN

28 That day Joshua captured Makkedah and put the sword to it
and its king. He annihilated everyone who lived in it; he left
no survivors. He did to its king what he had done to the king
of Jericho.

29 Joshua and all Israel marched from Makkedah to Libnah
and fought against it. 30 The LORD handed it and its king over
to Israel, and Israel put the sword to all who lived there; they
left no survivors. They did to its king what they had done to the
king of Jericho.

31 Joshua and all Israel marched from Libnah to Lachish. He
deployed his troops and fought against it. 32 The LORD handed
Lachish over to Israel, and they captured it on the second day.
They put the sword to all who lived there, just as they had done
to Libnah. 33 Then King Horam of Gezer came up to help Lachish,
but Joshua struck him down, as well as his army, until no survivors remained.

34 Joshua and all Israel marched from Lachish to Eglon. They
deployed troops and fought against it. 35 That day they captured
it and put the sword to all who lived there. That day they annihilated it just as they had done to Lachish.

36 Joshua and all Israel marched up from Eglon to Hebron and
fought against it. 37 They captured it and put the sword to its
king, all its surrounding cities, and all who lived in it; they left
no survivors. As they had done at Eglon, they annihilated it and
all who lived there.

38 Joshua and all Israel turned to Debir and fought against it.
39 They captured it, its king, and all its surrounding cities and put
the sword to them. They annihilated everyone who lived there;
they left no survivors. They did to Debir and its king what they
had done to Libnah and its king and to Hebron.

40 Joshua defeated the whole land, including the hill country,
the Negev, the foothills, the slopes, and all their kings. He left
no survivors. He annihilated everything that breathed, just as
the LORD God of Israel had commanded. 41 Joshua conquered
the area between Kadesh Barnea and Gaza and the whole region of Goshen, all the way to Gibeon. 42 Joshua captured in one
campaign all these kings and their lands, for the LORD God of
Israel fought for Israel. 43 Then Joshua and all Israel returned to
the camp at Gilgal.

ISRAEL DEFEATS A NORTHERN COALITION

11 When King Jabin of Hazor heard the news about Israel's victories, he organized a coalition, including King Jobab of Madon, the king of Shimron, the king of Acshaph, 2 and the northern kings who ruled in the hill country, in the rift valley south of Kinnereth, in the foothills, and on the heights of Dor to the west. 3 Canaanites came from the east and west; Amorites, Hittites, Perizzites, and Jebusites from the hill country; and Hivites from below Hermon in the area of Mizpah. 4 These kings came out with their armies; they were as numerous as the sand on the seashore and had a large number of horses and chariots. 5 All these kings gathered and joined forces at the Waters of Merom to fight Israel.

6 The LORD told Joshua, "Don't be afraid of them, for about this time tomorrow I will cause all of them to lie dead before Israel. You must hamstring their horses and burn their chariots." 7 Joshua and his whole army caught them by surprise at the Waters of Merom and attacked them. 8 The LORD handed them over to Israel, and they struck them down and chased them all the way to Greater Sidon, Misrephoth Maim, and the Mizpah Valley to the east. They struck them down until no survivors remained. 9 Joshua did to them as the LORD had commanded him; he hamstrung their horses and burned their chariots.

10 At that time Joshua turned, captured Hazor, and struck down its king with the sword, for Hazor was at that time the leader of all these kingdoms. 11 They annihilated everyone who lived there with the sword—no one who breathed remained—and burned Hazor.

12 Joshua captured all these royal cities and all their kings and annihilated them with the sword, as Moses the LORD's servant had commanded. 13 But Israel did not burn any of the cities located on mounds except for Hazor; it was the only one Joshua burned. 14 The Israelites plundered all the goods of these cities and the cattle, but they totally destroyed all the people and allowed no one who breathed to live. 15 Moses the LORD's servant passed on the LORD's commands to Joshua, and Joshua did as he was told. He did not ignore any of the commands the LORD had given Moses.

A SUMMARY OF ISRAEL'S VICTORIES

16 Joshua conquered the whole land, including the hill country, all the Negev, all the land of Goshen, the foothills, the rift valley, the hill country of Israel and its foothills, 17 from Mount Halak up to Seir, as far as Baal Gad in the Lebanon Valley below Mount Hermon. He captured all their kings and executed them. 18 Joshua campaigned against these kings for quite some time. 19 No city made peace with the Israelites (except the Hivites living in Gibeon); they had to conquer all of them, 20 for the LORD determined to make them obstinate so they would attack Israel. He wanted Israel to annihilate them without mercy, as he had instructed Moses.

21 At that time Joshua attacked and eliminated the Anakites from the hill country—from Hebron, Debir, Anab, and all the hill country of Judah and Israel. Joshua annihilated them and

their cities. 22 No Anakites were left in Israelite territory, though
some remained in Gaza, Gath, and Ashdod. 23 Joshua conquered
the whole land, just as the LORD had promised Moses, and he assigned Israel their tribal portions. Then the land was free of war.

12 Now these are the kings of the land whom the Israelites
defeated and drove from their land on the east side of the
Jordan, from the Arnon Valley to Mount Hermon, including all
the eastern rift valley:

2 King Sihon of the Amorites who lived in Heshbon and ruled
from Aroer (on the edge of the Arnon Valley)—including the city
in the middle of the valley and half of Gilead—all the way to the
Jabbok Valley bordering Ammonite territory. 3 His kingdom included the eastern rift valley from the Sea of Kinnereth to the
sea of the rift valley (the Salt Sea), including the route to Beth
Jeshimoth and the area southward below the slopes of Pisgah.

4 The territory of King Og of Bashan, one of the few remaining Rephaites, who lived in Ashtaroth and Edrei 5 and ruled over
Mount Hermon, Salecah, all Bashan to the border of the Geshurites and Maacathites, and half of Gilead as far as the border
of King Sihon of Heshbon.

6 Moses the LORD's servant and the Israelites defeated them
and Moses the LORD's servant assigned their land to Reuben,
Gad, and the half-tribe of Manasseh.

7 These are the kings of the land whom Joshua and the Israelites defeated on the west side of the Jordan, from Baal Gad in the
Lebanon Valley to Mount Halak up to Seir. Joshua assigned this
territory to the Israelite tribes, 8 including the hill country, the
foothills, the rift valley, the slopes, the wilderness, and the Negev—the land of the Hittites, Amorites, Canaanites, Perizzites,
Hivites, and Jebusites:

9 the king of Jericho (one),
the king of Ai—located near Bethel—(one),
10 the king of Jerusalem (one),
the king of Hebron (one),
11 the king of Jarmuth (one),
the king of Lachish (one),
12 the king of Eglon (one),
the king of Gezer (one),
13 the king of Debir (one),
the king of Geder (one),
14 the king of Hormah (one),
the king of Arad (one),
15 the king of Libnah (one),
the king of Adullam (one),
16 the king of Makkedah (one),
the king of Bethel (one),
17 the king of Tappuah (one),
the king of Hepher (one),
18 the king of Aphek (one),
the king of Lasharon (one),
19 the king of Madon (one),
the king of Hazor (one),
20 the king of Shimron Meron (one),
the king of Acshaph (one),

21 the king of Taanach (one),
the king of Megiddo (one),
22 the king of Kedesh (one),
the king of Jokneam near Carmel (one),
23 the king of Dor—near Naphath Dor—(one),
the king of Goyim—near Gilgal—(one),
24 the king of Tirzah (one),
a total of thirty-one kings.

THE LORD SPEAKS TO JOSHUA

13 When Joshua was very old, the LORD told him, "You are very
old, and a great deal of land remains to be conquered. 2 This
is the land that remains: all the territory of the Philistines and
all the Geshurites, 3 from the Shihor River east of Egypt northward to the territory of Ekron (it is regarded as Canaanite territory), including the area belonging to the five Philistine lords
who ruled in Gaza, Ashdod, Ashkelon, Gath, and Ekron, as well as
Avvite land 4 to the south; all the Canaanite territory, from Arah
in the region of Sidon to Aphek, as far as Amorite territory; 5 the
territory of Byblos and all Lebanon to the east, from Baal Gad
below Mount Hermon to Lebo Hamath. 6 I will drive out before
the Israelites all who live in the hill country from Lebanon to
Misrephoth Maim, all the Sidonians; you be sure to parcel it out
to Israel as I instructed you. 7 Now, divide up this land among
the nine tribes and the half-tribe of Manasseh."

TRIBAL LANDS EAST OF THE JORDAN

8 The other half of Manasseh, Reuben, and Gad received their allotted tribal lands on east side of the Jordan, just as Moses, the
LORD's servant, had assigned them. 9 Their territory started from
Aroer (on the edge of the Arnon Valley), included the city in the
middle of the valley, the whole plain of Medeba as far as Dibon,
10 and all the cities of King Sihon of the Amorites who ruled in
Heshbon, and ended at the Ammonite border. 11 Their territory
also included Gilead, Geshurite and Maacathite territory, all
Mount Hermon, and all Bashan to Salecah—12 the whole kingdom of Og in Bashan, who ruled in Ashtaroth and Edrei. (He was
one of the few remaining Rephaites.) Moses defeated them and
took their lands. 13 But the Israelites did not conquer the Geshurites and Maacathites; Geshur and Maacah live among Israel
to this very day. 14 However, Moses did not assign land as an inheritance to the Levites; their inheritance is the sacrificial offerings made to the LORD God of Israel, as he instructed them.
15 Moses assigned land to the tribe of Reuben by its clans.
16 Their territory started at Aroer (on the edge of the Arnon Valley) and included the city in the middle of the valley, the whole
plain of Medeba, 17 Heshbon and all its surrounding cities on the
plain, including Dibon, Bamoth Baal, Beth Baal Meon, 18 Jahaz,
Kedemoth, Mephaath, 19 Kiriathaim, Sibmah, Zereth Shahar on
the hill in the valley, 20 Beth Peor, the slopes of Pisgah, and Beth
Jeshimoth. 21 It encompassed all the cities of the plain and the
whole realm of King Sihon of the Amorites who ruled in Heshbon. Moses defeated him and the Midianite leaders Evi, Rekem,
Zur, Hur, and Reba (they were subjects of Sihon and lived in his

territory). 22 The Israelites killed Balaam son of Beor, the omen reader, along with the others. 23 The border of the tribe of Reuben was the Jordan. The land allotted to the tribe of Reuben by its clans included these cities and their towns.

24 Moses assigned land to the tribe of Gad by its clans. 25 Their territory included Jazer, all the cities of Gilead, and half the Ammonite territory as far as Aroer near Rabbah. 26 Their territory ran from Heshbon to Ramath Mizpah and Betonim, and from Mahanaim to the territory of Debir. 27 It included the valley of Beth Haram, Beth Nimrah, Sukkoth, and Zaphon, and the rest of the realm of King Sihon of Heshbon, the area east of the Jordan to the end of the Sea of Kinnereth. 28 The land allotted to the tribe of Gad by its clans included these cities and their towns.

29 Moses assigned land to the half-tribe of Manasseh by its clans. 30 Their territory started at Mahanaim and encompassed all Bashan, the whole realm of King Og of Bashan, including all sixty cities in Havvoth Jair in Bashan. 31 Half of Gilead, Ashtaroth, and Edrei, cities in the kingdom of Og in Bashan, were assigned to the descendants of Makir son of Manasseh, to half the descendants of Makir by their clans.

32 These are the land assignments made by Moses in the rift valley plains of Moab east of the Jordan River opposite Jericho. 33 However, Moses did not assign land as an inheritance to the Levites; their inheritance is the LORD God of Israel, as he instructed them.

JUDAH'S TRIBAL LANDS

14 The following is a record of the territory assigned to the Israelites in the land of Canaan by Eleazar the priest, Joshua son of Nun, and the Israelite tribal leaders. 2 The land assignments to the nine-and-a-half tribes were made by drawing lots, as the LORD had instructed Moses. 3 Now Moses had assigned land to the two-and-a-half tribes east of the Jordan, but he assigned no land to the Levites. 4 The descendants of Joseph were considered as two tribes, Manasseh and Ephraim. The Levites were allotted no territory, though they were assigned cities in which to live, along with the grazing areas for their cattle and possessions. 5 The Israelites followed the LORD's instructions to Moses and divided up the land.

6 The men of Judah approached Joshua in Gilgal, and Caleb son of Jephunneh the Kenizzite said to him, "You know what the LORD said about you and me to Moses, the man of God, at Kadesh Barnea. 7 I was forty years old when Moses, the LORD's servant, sent me from Kadesh Barnea to spy on the land and I brought back to him an honest report. 8 My countrymen who accompanied me frightened the people, but I remained loyal to the LORD my God. 9 That day Moses made this solemn promise: 'Surely the land on which you walked will belong to you and your descendants permanently, for you remained loyal to the LORD your God.' 10 So now, look, the LORD has preserved my life, just as he promised, these past forty-five years since the LORD spoke these words to Moses, while Israel traveled through the wilderness. See here, I am today eighty-five years old! 11 Today I am still as strong as when Moses sent me out. I can fight and go about my daily activities with the same energy I had then. 12 Now,

assign me this hill country that the LORD promised me at that
time! No doubt you heard then that the Anakites live there in
large, fortified cities. But assuming the LORD is with me, I will
conquer them, as the LORD promised." 13 Joshua asked God to
empower Caleb son of Jephunneh and assigned him Hebron.
14 So Hebron remains the assigned land of Caleb son of Jephunneh the Kenizzite to this very day because he remained loyal
to the LORD God of Israel. 15 (Hebron used to be called Kiriath
Arba. Arba was a famous Anakite.) Then the land was free of war.

15 The land allotted to the tribe of Judah by its clans reached
to the border of Edom, to the wilderness of Zin in the Negev far to the south. 2 Their southern border started at the southern tip of the Salt Sea, 3 extended south of the Scorpion Ascent,
crossed to Zin, went up from the south to Kadesh Barnea, crossed
to Hezron, went up to Addar, and turned toward Karka. 4 It then
crossed to Azmon, extended to the Stream of Egypt, and ended
at the Mediterranean Sea. This was their southern border.

5 The eastern border was the Salt Sea to the mouth of the Jordan River.

The northern border started north of the Salt Sea at the mouth
of the Jordan, 6 went up to Beth Hoglah, crossed north of Beth
Arabah, and went up to the Stone of Bohan son of Reuben. 7 It
then went up to Debir from the Valley of Achor, turning northward to Gilgal (which is opposite the Pass of Adummim south of
the valley), crossed to the waters of En Shemesh and extended
to En Rogel. 8 It then went up the Valley of Ben Hinnom to the
slope of the Jebusites on the south (that is, Jerusalem), going
up to the top of the hill opposite the Valley of Ben Hinnom to
the west, which is at the end of the Valley of the Rephaites to the
north. 9 It then went from the top of the hill to the spring of the
waters of Nephtoah, extended to the cities of Mount Ephron, and
went to Baalah (that is, Kiriath Jearim). 10 It then turned from
Baalah westward to Mount Seir, crossed to the slope of Mount
Jearim on the north (that is Kesalon), descended to Beth Shemesh, and crossed to Timnah. 11 It then extended to the slope of
Ekron to the north, went toward Shikkeron, crossed to Mount
Baalah, extended to Jabneel, and ended at the sea.

12 The western border was the Mediterranean Sea. These were
the borders of the tribe of Judah and its clans.

13 Caleb son of Jephunneh was assigned Kiriath Arba (that is
Hebron) within the tribe of Judah, according to the LORD's instructions to Joshua. (Arba was the father of Anak.) 14 Caleb drove
out from there three Anakites—Sheshai, Ahiman, and Talmai, descendants of Anak. 15 From there he attacked the people of Debir.
(Debir used to be called Kiriath Sepher.) 16 Caleb said, "To the man
who attacks and captures Kiriath Sepher I will give my daughter
Achsah as a wife." 17 When Othniel son of Kenaz, Caleb's brother, captured it, Caleb gave Achsah his daughter to him as a wife.

18 One time Achsah came and charmed her father so that she
could ask him for some land. When she got down from her donkey, Caleb said to her, "What would you like?" 19 She answered,
"Please give me a special present. Since you have given me land
in the Negev, now give me springs of water." So he gave her both
the upper and lower springs.

20 This is the land assigned to the tribe of Judah by its clans: 21 These cities were located at the southern extremity of Judah's tribal land near the border of Edom: Kabzeel, Eder, Jagur, 22 Kinah, Dimonah, Adadah, 23 Kedesh, Hazor, Ithnan, 24 Ziph, Telem, Bealoth, 25 Hazor Hadattah, Kerioth Hezron (that is, Hazor), 26 Amam, Shema, Moladah, 27 Hazar Gaddah, Heshbon, Beth Pelet, 28 Hazar Shual, Beer Sheba, Biziothiah, 29 Baalah, Iim, Ezem, 30 Eltolad, Kesil, Hormah, 31 Ziklag, Madmannah, Sansannah, 32 Lebaoth, Shilhim, Ain, and Rimmon—a total of twenty-nine cities and their towns.

33 These cities were in the foothills: Eshtaol, Zorah, Ashnah, 34 Zanoah, En Gannim, Tappuah, Enam, 35 Jarmuth, Adullam, Socoh, Azekah, 36 Shaaraim, Adithaim, and Gederah (or Gederothaim)—a total of fourteen cities and their towns.

37 Zenan, Hadashah, Migdal Gad, 38 Dilean, Mizpah, Joktheel, 39 Lachish, Bozkath, Eglon, 40 Cabbon, Lahmas, Kitlish, 41 Gederoth, Beth Dagon, Naamah, and Makkedah—a total of sixteen cities and their towns.

42 Libnah, Ether, Ashan, 43 Iphtah, Ashnah, Nezib, 44 Keilah, Achzib, and Mareshah—a total of nine cities and their towns.

45 Ekron and its surrounding towns and settlements; 46 from Ekron westward, all those in the vicinity of Ashdod and their towns; 47 Ashdod with its surrounding towns and settlements, and Gaza with its surrounding towns and settlements, as far as the Stream of Egypt and the border at the Mediterranean Sea.

48 These cities were in the hill country: Shamir, Jattir, Socoh, 49 Dannah, Kiriath Sannah (that is, Debir), 50 Anab, Eshtemoh, Anim, 51 Goshen, Holon, and Giloh—a total of eleven cities and their towns.

52 Arab, Dumah, Eshan, 53 Janim, Beth Tappuah, Aphekah, 54 Humtah, Kiriath Arba (that is, Hebron), and Zior—a total of nine cities and their towns.

55 Maon, Carmel, Ziph, Juttah, 56 Jezreel, Jokdeam, Zanoah, 57 Kain, Gibeah, and Timnah—a total of ten cities and their towns.

58 Halhul, Beth Zur, Gedor, 59 Maarath, Beth Anoth, and Eltekon—a total of six cities and their towns.

60 Kiriath Baal (that is, Kiriath Jearim) and Rabbah—a total of two cities and their towns.

61 These cities were in the wilderness: Beth Arabah, Middin, Secacah, 62 Nibshan, the City of Salt, and En Gedi—a total of six cities and their towns.

63 The men of Judah were unable to conquer the Jebusites living in Jerusalem. The Jebusites live with the people of Judah in Jerusalem to this very day.

JOSEPH'S TRIBAL LANDS

16 The land allotted to Joseph's descendants extended from the Jordan at Jericho to the waters of Jericho to the east, through the desert and on up from Jericho into the hill country of Bethel. 2 The southern border extended from Bethel to Luz, and crossed to Arkite territory at Ataroth. 3 It then descended westward to Japhletite territory, as far as the territory of lower Beth Horon and Gezer, and ended at the sea.

4 Joseph's descendants, Manasseh and Ephraim, were assigned their land. 5 The territory of the tribe of Ephraim by its clans

included the following: The border of their assigned land to the
east was Ataroth Addar as far as upper Beth Horon. 6 It then extended on to the sea, with Micmethath on the north. It turned
eastward to Taanath Shiloh and crossed it on the east to Janoah. 7 It then descended from Janoah to Ataroth and Naarah,
touched Jericho, and extended to the Jordan River. 8 From Tappuah it went westward to the Valley of Kanah and ended at the
sea. This is the land assigned to the tribe of Ephraim by its clans.
9 Also included were the cities set apart for the tribe of Ephraim
within Manasseh's territory, along with their towns.

10 The Ephraimites did not conquer the Canaanites living in
Gezer. The Canaanites live among the Ephraimites to this very
day and do hard labor as their servants.

17 The tribe of Manasseh, Joseph's firstborn son, was also allotted
land. The descendants of Makir, Manasseh's firstborn and the
father of Gilead, received land, for they were warriors. They were
assigned Gilead and Bashan. 2 The rest of Manasseh's descendants
were also assigned land by their clans, including the descendants
of Abiezer, Helek, Asriel, Shechem, Hepher, and Shemida. These
are the male descendants of Manasseh son of Joseph by their clans.
3 Now Zelophehad son of Hepher, son of Gilead, son of Makir, son
of Manasseh, had no sons, only daughters. These are the names of
his daughters: Mahlah, Noah, Hoglah, Milcah, and Tirzah. 4 They
went before Eleazar the priest, Joshua son of Nun, and the leaders
and said, "The LORD told Moses to assign us land among our relatives." So Joshua assigned them land among their uncles, as the
LORD had commanded. 5 Manasseh was allotted ten shares of land,
in addition to the land of Gilead and Bashan east of the Jordan, 6 for
the daughters of Manasseh were assigned land among his sons. The
land of Gilead belonged to the rest of the descendants of Manasseh.

7 The border of Manasseh went from Asher to Micmethath,
which is near Shechem. It then went south toward those who live
by En Tappuah. 8 (The land of Tappuah belonged to Manasseh, but
Tappuah, located on the border of Manasseh, belonged to the tribe
of Ephraim.) 9 The border then descended southward to the Valley of Kanah. Ephraim was assigned cities there among the cities
of Manasseh, but the border of Manasseh was north of the valley
and ended at the sea. 10 Ephraim's territory was to the south, and
Manasseh's to the north. The sea was Manasseh's western border
and their territory touched Asher on the north and Issachar on
the east. 11 Within Issachar's and Asher's territories Manasseh was
assigned Beth Shean, Ibleam, the residents of Dor, the residents
of Endor, the residents of Taanach, the residents of Megiddo, the
three of Napheth, and the towns surrounding all these cities. 12 But
the men of Manasseh were unable to conquer these cities; the Canaanites managed to remain in those areas. 13 Whenever the Israelites were strong militarily, they forced the Canaanites to do hard
labor, but they never totally conquered them.

14 The descendants of Joseph said to Joshua, "Why have you
assigned us only one tribal allotment? After all, we have many
people, for until now the LORD has enabled us to increase in
number." 15 Joshua replied to them, "Since you have so many people, go up into the forest and clear out a place to live in the land
of the Perizzites and Rephaites, if the hill country of Ephraim is

too small for you." 16 The descendants of Joseph said, "The whole hill country is inadequate for us, and the Canaanites living down in the valley in Beth Shean and its surrounding towns and in the Valley of Jezreel have chariots with iron-rimmed wheels." 17 Joshua said to the family of Joseph—to both Ephraim and Manasseh: "You have many people and great military strength. You will not have just one tribal allotment. 18 The whole hill country will be yours; though it is a forest, you can clear it, and it will be entirely yours. You can conquer the Canaanites, though they have chariots with iron-rimmed wheels and are strong."

THE TRIBES MEET AT SHILOH

18 The entire Israelite community assembled at Shiloh and there they set up the tent of meeting. Though they had subdued the land, 2 seven Israelite tribes had not been assigned their allotted land. 3 So Joshua said to the Israelites: "How long do you intend to put off occupying the land the LORD God of your ancestors has given you? 4 Pick three men from each tribe. I will send them out to walk through the land and make a map of it for me. 5 Divide it into seven regions. Judah will stay in its territory in the south, and the family of Joseph in its territory in the north. 6 But as for you, map out the land into seven regions and bring it to me. I will draw lots for you here before the LORD our God. 7 But the Levites will not have an allotted portion among you, for their inheritance is to serve the LORD. Gad, Reuben, and the half-tribe of Manasseh have already received their allotted land east of the Jordan, which Moses the LORD's servant assigned them."

8 When the men started out, Joshua told those going to map out the land, "Go, walk through the land, map it out, and return to me. Then I will draw lots for you before the LORD here in Shiloh." 9 The men journeyed through the land and mapped it and its cities out into seven regions on a scroll. Then they came to Joshua at the camp in Shiloh. 10 Joshua drew lots for them in Shiloh before the LORD and divided the land among the Israelites according to their allotted portions.

BENJAMIN'S TRIBAL LANDS

11 The first lot belonged to the tribe of Benjamin by its clans. Their allotted territory was between Judah and Joseph. 12 Their northern border started at the Jordan, went up to the slope of Jericho on the north, ascended westward to the hill country, and extended to the wilderness of Beth Aven. 13 It then crossed from there to Luz, to the slope of Luz to the south (that is, Bethel), and descended to Ataroth Addar located on the hill that is south of lower Beth Horon. 14 It then turned on the west side southward from the hill near Beth Horon on the south and extended to Kiriath Baal (that is, Kiriath Jearim), a city belonging to the tribe of Judah. This is the western border. 15 The southern side started on the edge of Kiriath Jearim and extended westward to the spring of the waters of Nephtoah. 16 The border then descended to the edge of the hill country near the Valley of Ben Hinnom located in the Valley of the Rephaites to the north. It descended through the Valley of Hinnom to the slope of the Jebusites to the south and then down to En Rogel. 17 It went northward, extending to

En Shemesh and Geliloth opposite the Pass of Adummim, and descended to the Stone of Bohan son of Reuben. 18 It crossed to the slope in front of the rift valley to the north and descended into the rift valley. 19 It then crossed to the slope of Beth Hoglah to the north and ended at the northern tip of the Salt Sea at the mouth of the Jordan River. This was the southern border. 20 The Jordan River bordered it on the east. These were the borders of the land assigned to the tribe of Benjamin by its clans.

21 These cities belonged to the tribe of Benjamin by its clans: Jericho, Beth Hoglah, Emek Keziz, 22 Beth Arabah, Zemaraim, Bethel, 23 Avvim, Parah, Ophrah, 24 Kephar Ammoni, Ophni, and Geba—a total of twelve cities and their towns.

25 Gibeon, Ramah, Beeroth, 26 Mizpah, Kephirah, Mozah, 27 Rekem, Irpeel, Taralah, 28 Zelah, Haeleph, the Jebusite city (that is, Jerusalem), Gibeah, and Kiriath—a total of fourteen cities and their towns. This was the land assigned to the tribe of Benjamin by its clans.

SIMEON'S TRIBAL LANDS

19 The second lot belonged to the tribe of Simeon by its clans. Their assigned land was in the middle of Judah's assigned land. 2 Their assigned land included Beer Sheba, Moladah, 3 Hazar Shual, Balah, Ezem, 4 Eltolad, Bethul, Hormah, 5 Ziklag, Beth Marcaboth, Hazar Susah, 6 Beth Lebaoth, and Sharuhen—a total of thirteen cities and their towns, 7 Ain, Rimmon, Ether, and Ashan—a total of four cities and their towns, 8 as well as all the towns around these cities as far as Baalath Beer (Ramah of the Negev). This was the land assigned to the tribe of Simeon by its clans. 9 Simeon's assigned land was taken from Judah's allotted portion, for Judah's territory was too large for them; so Simeon was assigned land within Judah.

ZEBULUN'S TRIBAL LANDS

10 The third lot belonged to the tribe of Zebulun by its clans. The border of their territory extended to Sarid. 11 Their border went up westward to Maralah and touched Dabbesheth and the valley near Jokneam. 12 From Sarid it turned eastward to the territory of Kisloth Tabor, extended to Daberath, and went up to Japhia. 13 From there it crossed eastward to Gath Hepher and Eth Kazin and extended to Rimmon, turning toward Neah. 14 It then turned on the north to Hannathon and ended at the Valley of Iphtah El. 15 Their territory included Kattah, Nahalal, Shimron, Idalah, and Bethlehem; in all they had twelve cities and their towns. 16 This was the land assigned to the tribe of Zebulun by its clans, including these cities and their towns.

ISSACHAR'S TRIBAL LANDS

17 The fourth lot belonged to the tribe of Issachar by its clans. 18 Their assigned land included Jezreel, Kesulloth, Shunem, 19 Hapharaim, Shion, Anaharath, 20 Rabbith, Kishion, Ebez, 21 Remeth, En Gannim, En Haddah and Beth Pazzez. 22 Their border touched Tabor, Shahazumah, and Beth Shemesh, and ended at the Jordan. They had sixteen cities and their towns. 23 This was the land assigned to the tribe of Issachar by its clans, including these cities and their towns.

ASHER'S TRIBAL LANDS

24 The fifth lot belonged to the tribe of Asher by its clans. 25 Their
territory included Helkath, Hali, Beten, Acshaph, 26 Alammelech,
Amad, and Mishal. Their border touched Carmel to the west
and Shihor Libnath. 27 It turned eastward toward Beth Dagon,
touched Zebulun and the Valley of Iphtah El to the north, as well
as Beth Emek and Neiel, and extended to Cabul on the north
28 and on to Ebron, Rehob, Hammon, and Kanah, as far as Greater
Sidon. 29 It then turned toward Ramah as far as the fortified
city of Tyre, turned to Hosah, and ended at the sea near Hebel,
Achzib, 30 Umah, Aphek, and Rehob. In all they had twenty-
two cities and their towns. 31 This was the land assigned to the
tribe of Asher by its clans, including these cities and their towns.

NAPHTALI'S TRIBAL LANDS

32 The sixth lot belonged to the tribe of Naphtali by its clans.
33 Their border started at Heleph and the oak of Zaanannim, went
to Adami Nekeb, Jabneel and on to Lakkum, and ended at the
Jordan River. 34 It turned westward to Aznoth Tabor, extended
from there to Hukok, touched Zebulun on the south, Asher on
the west, and the Jordan on the east. 35 The fortified cities included Ziddim, Zer, Hammath, Rakkath, Kinnereth, 36 Adamah,
Ramah, Hazor, 37 Kedesh, Edrei, En Hazor, 38 Yiron, Migdal El, Ho-
rem, Beth Anath, and Beth Shemesh. In all they had nineteen
cities and their towns. 39 This was the land assigned to the tribe
of Naphtali by its clans, including these cities and their towns.

DAN'S TRIBAL LANDS

40 The seventh lot belonged to the tribe of Dan by its clans. 41 Their
assigned land included Zorah, Eshtaol, Ir Shemesh, 42 Shaalab-
bin, Aijalon, Ithlah, 43 Elon, Timnah, Ekron, 44 Eltekeh, Gibbethon,
Baalath, 45 Jehud, Bene Berak, Gath Rimmon, 46 the waters of Jar-
kon, and Rakkon, including the territory in front of Joppa. 47 (The
Danites failed to conquer their territory, so they went up and
fought with Leshem and captured it. They put the sword to it,
took possession of it, and lived in it. They renamed it Dan after
their ancestor.) 48 This was the land assigned to the tribe of Dan
by its clans, including these cities and their towns.

JOSHUA RECEIVES LAND

49 When they finished dividing the land into its regions, the Israelites gave Joshua son of Nun some land. 50 As the LORD had
instructed, they gave him the city he requested—Timnath Serah
in the Ephraimite hill country. He built up the city and lived in it.

51 These are the land assignments that Eleazar the priest,
Joshua son of Nun, and the Israelite tribal leaders made by drawing lots in Shiloh before the LORD at the entrance of the tent of
meeting. So they finished dividing up the land.

ISRAEL DESIGNATES CITIES OF REFUGE

20 The LORD instructed Joshua: 2 "Have the Israelites select
the cities of refuge that I told you about through Moses.
3 Anyone who accidentally kills someone can escape there; these
cities will be a place of asylum from the avenger of blood. 4 The

LOVE TO GROW

CITIES OF REFUGE

JOSHUA 20

In these final chapters of Joshua, the Israelites divided up the promised land by tribe. They decided where each tribe would settle and how much land each would receive. There were lots of logistics involved. Sometimes a tribe came back and said, "Oops, we need a little more room," or "Actually, this land has a big hole in it—we'd like to exchange it." We all know the logistics of moving—it gets complicated.

In the hustle and bustle of divvying up the land, God gave Joshua some guidelines, and one of them was this: He wanted Joshua to make sure there were six cities set aside for asylum. Anyone, Israelite or foreigner, who accidentally killed a person could flee to one of these cities and find safety.

This kind of treatment of the accused was not normal at the time; innocent until proven guilty was not the standard. In fact, treating accused persons with dignity was unheard of.

The cities of refuge show us that God cares about true justice: He wants the accused to be treated fairly and cared for until they have been heard out.

This passage shows me God cares about the intentions and motivations of the heart. He is not preoccupied with outward appearances; He cares about the consequences of our actions.

For me, this means two things. First, God wants me to treat others with the same radical justice and grace I see in this passage. He wants me to listen with an open heart and care enough about people to get into the gritty details of their lives and stories. He wants me to give everyone a fair shot. And you know what else? He wants me to extend that same radical justice and grace He asks me to extend to others to myself.

God cares about what is in our hearts. He was willing to set aside six parts of the precious promised land for the safety of the accused. This passage says everyone, both Israelite and foreigner, was welcome in these cities of refuge. Everyone's side of the story deserves to be heard in God's kingdom.

My heart responds to this passage with gratitude and praise. God wants to hear my side of the story; God wants to know the whole truth. I do not have to worry about my voice being dismissed because my God bends His ear to listen closely to me and to each one of us, no matter how small. Hallelujah.

one who committed manslaughter should escape to one of these
cities, stand at the entrance of the city gate, and present his case
to the leaders of that city. They should then bring him into the
city, give him a place to stay, and let him live there. 5 When the
avenger of blood comes after him, they must not hand over to
him the one who committed manslaughter, for he accidentally
killed his fellow man without premeditation. 6 He must remain
in that city until his case is decided by the assembly, and the high
priest dies. Then the one who committed manslaughter may return home to the city from which he escaped."

7 So they selected Kedesh in Galilee in the hill country of Naphtali, Shechem in the hill country of Ephraim, and Kiriath Arba
(that is, Hebron) in the hill country of Judah. 8 Beyond the Jordan
east of Jericho they selected Bezer in the wilderness on the plain
belonging to the tribe of Reuben, Ramoth in Gilead belonging
to the tribe of Gad, and Golan in Bashan belonging to the tribe
of Manasseh. 9 These were the cities of refuge appointed for all
the Israelites and for resident foreigners living among them.
Anyone who accidentally killed someone could escape there
and not be executed by the avenger of blood, at least until his
case was reviewed by the assembly.

LEVITICAL CITIES

21 The tribal leaders of the Levites went before Eleazar the
priest and Joshua son of Nun and the Israelite tribal leaders 2 in Shiloh in the land of Canaan and said, "The LORD told
Moses to assign us cities in which to live along with the grazing
areas for our cattle." 3 So the Israelites assigned these cities and
their grazing areas to the Levites from their own holdings, as
the LORD had instructed.

4 The first lot belonged to the Kohathite clans. The Levites who
were descendants of Aaron the priest were allotted thirteen cities from the tribes of Judah, Simeon, and Benjamin. 5 The rest
of Kohath's descendants were allotted ten cities from the clans
of the tribe of Ephraim, and from the tribe of Dan and the half-
tribe of Manasseh. 6 Gershon's descendants were allotted thirteen cities from the clans of the tribe of Issachar, and from the
tribes of Asher and Naphtali and the half-tribe of Manasseh
in Bashan. 7 Merari's descendants by their clans were allotted
twelve cities from the tribes of Reuben, Gad, and Zebulun. 8 So
the Israelites assigned to the Levites by lot these cities and their
grazing areas, as the LORD had instructed Moses.

9 They assigned from the tribes of Judah and Simeon the cities
listed below. 10 (They were assigned to the Kohathite clans of the
Levites who were descendants of Aaron, for the first lot fell to
them.) 11 They assigned them Kiriath Arba (Arba was the father
of Anak), that is, Hebron, in the hill country of Judah, along with
its surrounding grazing areas. 12 (Now the city's fields and surrounding towns they had assigned to Caleb son of Jephunneh as
his property.) 13 So to the descendants of Aaron the priest they
assigned Hebron (a city of refuge for one who committed manslaughter), Libnah, 14 Jattir, Eshtemoa, 15 Holon, Debir, 16 Ain, Juttah, and Beth Shemesh, along with the grazing areas of each—a
total of nine cities taken from these two tribes. 17 From the tribe

of Benjamin they assigned Gibeon, Geba, [18] Anathoth, and Almon, along with the grazing areas of each—a total of four cities. [19] The priests descended from Aaron received thirteen cities and their grazing areas.

[20] The rest of the Kohathite clans of the Levites were allotted cities from the tribe of Ephraim. [21] They assigned them Shechem (a city of refuge for one who committed manslaughter) in the hill country of Ephraim, Gezer, [22] Kibzaim, and Beth Horon, along with the grazing areas of each—a total of four cities. [23] From the tribe of Dan they assigned Eltekeh, Gibbethon, [24] Aijalon, and Gath Rimmon, along with the grazing areas of each—a total of four cities. [25] From the half-tribe of Manasseh they assigned Taanach and Gath Rimmon, along with the grazing areas of each—a total of two cities. [26] The rest of the Kohathite clans received ten cities and their grazing areas.

[27] They assigned to the Gershonite clans of the Levites the following cities: from the half-tribe of Manasseh: Golan in Bashan (a city of refuge for one who committed manslaughter) and Beeshtarah, along with the grazing areas of each—a total of two cities; [28] from the tribe of Issachar: Kishon, Daberath, [29] Jarmuth, and En Gannim, along with the grazing areas of each—a total of four cities; [30] from the tribe of Asher: Mishal, Abdon, [31] Helkath, and Rehob, along with the grazing areas of each—a total of four cities; [32] from the tribe of Naphtali: Kedesh in Galilee (a city of refuge for one who committed manslaughter), Hammoth Dor, and Kartan, along with the grazing areas of each—a total of three cities. [33] The Gershonite clans received thirteen cities and their grazing areas.

[34] They assigned to the Merarite clans (the remaining Levites) the following cities: from the tribe of Zebulun: Jokneam, Kartah, [35] Dimnah, and Nahalal, along with the grazing areas of each—a total of four cities; [36] from the tribe of Reuben: Bezer, Jahaz, [37] Kedemoth, and Mephaath, along with the grazing areas of each—a total of four cities; [38] from the tribe of Gad: Ramoth in Gilead (a city of refuge for one who committed manslaughter), Mahanaim, [39] Heshbon, and Jazer, along with the grazing areas of each—a total of four cities. [40] The Merarite clans (the remaining Levites) were allotted twelve cities.

[41] The Levites received within the land owned by the Israelites forty-eight cities in all and their grazing areas. [42] Each of these cities had grazing areas around it; they were alike in this regard.

[43] So the LORD gave Israel all the land he had solemnly promised to their ancestors, and they conquered it and lived in it. [44] The LORD made them secure, in fulfillment of all he had solemnly promised their ancestors. None of their enemies could resist them. The LORD handed all their enemies over to them. [45] Not one of the LORD's faithful promises to the family of Israel was left unfulfilled; every one was realized.

REFLECT

What does this verse tell us about the character of God? How sure can you be that He will keep His promises and be faithful in your life? What gives you that assurance?

JOSHUA SENDS HOME THE EASTERN TRIBES

22 Then Joshua summoned the Reubenites, the Gadites, and the half-tribe of Manasseh [2] and told them: "You have carried out all the instructions of Moses the LORD's servant, and you have obeyed all I have told you. [3] You have not abandoned your

fellow Israelites this entire time, right up to this very day. You
have completed the task given you by the LORD your God. 4 Now
the LORD your God has made your fellow Israelites secure, just as
he promised them. So now you may turn around and go to your
homes in your own land that Moses the LORD's servant assigned
to you east of the Jordan. 5 But carefully obey the commands
and instructions Moses the LORD's servant gave you. Love the
LORD your God, follow all his instructions, obey his commands,
be loyal to him, and serve him with all your heart and being!"

6 Joshua rewarded them and sent them on their way; they
returned to their homes. 7 (Now to one half-tribe of Manasseh, Moses had assigned land in Bashan; and to the other half
Joshua had assigned land on the west side of the Jordan with
their fellow Israelites.) When Joshua sent them home, he rewarded them, 8 saying, "Take home great wealth, a lot of cattle,
silver, gold, bronze, iron, and a lot of clothing. Divide up the
goods captured from your enemies with your brothers." 9 So
the Reubenites, the Gadites, and the half-tribe of Manasseh
left the Israelites in Shiloh in the land of Canaan and headed
home to their own land in Gilead, which they acquired by the
LORD's command through Moses.

CIVIL WAR IS AVERTED

10 The Reubenites, the Gadites, and the half-tribe of Manasseh
came to Geliloth near the Jordan in the land of Canaan and
built there, near the Jordan, an impressive altar. 11 The Israelites received this report: "Look, the Reubenites, the Gadites,
and the half-tribe of Manasseh have built an altar at the entrance to the land of Canaan, at Geliloth near the Jordan on
the Israelite side." 12 When the Israelites heard this, the entire Israelite community assembled at Shiloh to launch an
attack against them.

13 The Israelites sent Phinehas son of Eleazar, the priest, to the
land of Gilead to the Reubenites, the Gadites, and the half-tribe
of Manasseh. 14 He was accompanied by ten leaders, one from
each of the Israelite tribes, each one a family leader among the
Israelite clans. 15 They went to the land of Gilead to the Reubenites, the Gadites, and the half-tribe of Manasseh, and said
to them: 16 "The entire community of the LORD says, 'Why have
you disobeyed the God of Israel by turning back today from following the LORD? You built an altar for yourselves and have rebelled today against the LORD. 17 The sin we committed at Peor
was bad enough. To this very day we have not purified ourselves;
it even brought a plague on the community of the LORD. 18 Now
today you dare to turn back from following the LORD! You are
rebelling today against the LORD; tomorrow he may break out
in anger against the entire community of Israel. 19 But if your
own land is impure, cross over to the LORD's own land, where the
LORD himself lives, and settle down among us. But don't rebel
against the LORD or us by building for yourselves an altar other
than the altar of the LORD our God. 20 When Achan son of Zerah
disobeyed the command about the city's riches, the entire Israelite community was judged, though only one man had sinned.
He most certainly died for his sin!'"

21 The Reubenites, the Gadites, and the half-tribe of Manasseh answered the leaders of the Israelite clans: 22 "El, God, the LORD! El, God, the LORD! He knows the truth! Israel must also know! If we have rebelled or disobeyed the LORD, don't spare us today! 23 If we have built an altar for ourselves to turn back from following the LORD by making burnt sacrifices and grain offerings on it, or by offering tokens of peace on it, the LORD himself will punish us. 24 We swear we have done this because we were worried that in the future your descendants would say to our descendants, 'What relationship do you have with the LORD God of Israel? 25 The LORD made the Jordan a boundary between us and you Reubenites and Gadites. You have no right to worship the LORD.' In this way your descendants might cause our descendants to stop obeying the LORD. 26 So we decided to build this altar, not for burnt offerings and sacrifices, 27 but as a reminder to us and you and our descendants who follow us, that we will honor the LORD in his very presence with burnt offerings, sacrifices, and tokens of peace. Then in the future your descendants will not be able to say to our descendants, 'You have no right to worship the LORD.' 28 We said, 'If in the future they say such a thing to us or to our descendants, we will reply, "See the model of the LORD's altar that our ancestors made, not for burnt offerings or sacrifices, but as a reminder to us and you."' 29 Far be it from us to rebel against the LORD by turning back today from following after the LORD by building an altar for burnt offerings, sacrifices, and tokens of peace aside from the altar of the LORD our God located in front of his dwelling place!"

30 When Phinehas the priest and the community leaders and Israel's clan leaders who accompanied him heard the defense of the Reubenites, the Gadites, and the Manassehites, they were satisfied. 31 Phinehas son of Eleazar, the priest, said to the Reubenites, the Gadites, and the Manassehites, "Today we know that the LORD is among us, because you have not disobeyed the LORD in this. Now you have rescued the Israelites from the LORD's judgment."

32 Phinehas son of Eleazar, the priest, and the leaders left the Reubenites and Gadites in the land of Gilead and reported back to the Israelites in the land of Canaan. 33 The Israelites were satisfied with their report and gave thanks to God. They said nothing more about launching an attack to destroy the land in which the Reubenites and Gadites lived. 34 The Reubenites and Gadites named the altar, "Surely it is a Reminder to us that the LORD is God."

JOSHUA CHALLENGES ISRAEL TO BE FAITHFUL

23 A long time passed after the LORD made Israel secure from all their enemies, and Joshua was very old. 2 So Joshua summoned all Israel, including the elders, rulers, judges, and leaders, and told them: "I am very old. 3 You saw everything the LORD your God did to all these nations on your behalf, for the LORD your God fights for you. 4 See, I have parceled out to your tribes these remaining nations, from the Jordan to the Mediterranean Sea in the west, including all the nations I defeated.

5 The LORD your God will drive them out from before you and remove them, so you can occupy their land as the LORD your God promised you. 6 Be very strong! Carefully obey all that is written in the law scroll of Moses so you won't swerve from it to the right or the left, 7 or associate with these nations that remain near you. You must not invoke or make solemn declarations by the names of their gods! You must not worship or bow down to them! 8 But you must be loyal to the LORD your God, as you have been to this very day.

9 "The LORD drove out from before you great and mighty nations; no one has been able to resist you to this very day. 10 One of you makes a thousand run away, for the LORD your God fights for you, as he promised you he would. 11 Watch yourselves carefully! Love the LORD your God! 12 But if you ever turn away and make alliances with these nations that remain near you, and intermarry with them and establish friendly relations with them, 13 know for certain that the LORD your God will no longer drive out these nations from before you. They will trap and ensnare you; they will be a whip that tears your sides and thorns that blind your eyes until you disappear from this good land the LORD your God gave you.

14 "Look, today I am about to die. You know with all your heart and being that not even one of all the faithful promises the LORD your God made to you is left unfulfilled; every one was realized—not one promise is unfulfilled! 15 But in the same way every faithful promise the LORD your God made to you has been realized, it is just as certain that if you disobey, then the LORD will bring on you every judgment until he destroys you from this good land that the LORD your God gave you. 16 If you violate the covenantal laws of the LORD your God which he commanded you to keep, and follow, worship, and bow down to other gods, then the LORD will be very angry with you and you will disappear quickly from the good land that he gave to you."

ISRAEL RENEWS ITS COMMITMENT TO THE LORD

24 Joshua assembled all the Israelite tribes at Shechem. He summoned Israel's elders, rulers, judges, and leaders, and they appeared before God. 2 Joshua told all the people, "This is what the LORD God of Israel has said: 'In the distant past your ancestors lived beyond the Euphrates River, including Terah the father of Abraham and Nahor. They worshiped other gods, 3 but I took your father Abraham from beyond the Euphrates and brought him into the entire land of Canaan. I made his descendants numerous; I gave him Isaac, 4 and to Isaac I gave Jacob and Esau. To Esau I assigned Mount Seir, while Jacob and his sons went down to Egypt. 5 I sent Moses and Aaron, and I struck Egypt down when I intervened in their land. Then I brought you out. 6 When I brought your fathers out of Egypt, you arrived at the sea. The Egyptians chased your fathers with chariots and horsemen to the Red Sea. 7 Your fathers cried out for help to the LORD; he made the area between you and the Egyptians dark, and then he drowned them in the sea. You witnessed with your very own eyes what I did in Egypt. You lived in the wilderness for

a long time. 8 Then I brought you to the land of the Amorites who
lived east of the Jordan. They fought with you, but I handed them
over to you; you conquered their land, and I destroyed them
from before you. 9 Balak son of Zippor, king of Moab, launched
an attack against Israel. He summoned Balaam son of Beor to
call down judgment on you. 10 I refused to respond to Balaam;
he kept prophesying good things about you, and I rescued you
from his power. 11 You crossed the Jordan and came to Jericho. The
leaders of Jericho, as well as the Amorites, Perizzites, Canaanites, Hittites, Girgashites, Hivites, and Jebusites, fought with
you, but I handed them over to you. 12 I sent terror ahead of you
to drive out before you the two Amorite kings. I gave you the
victory; it was not by your swords or bows. 13 I gave you a land in
which you had not worked hard; you took up residence in cities
you did not build, and you are eating the produce of vineyards
and olive groves you did not plant.'

14 "Now obey the LORD and worship him with integrity and
loyalty. Put aside the gods your ancestors worshiped beyond the
Euphrates and in Egypt, and worship the LORD. 15 If you have no
desire to worship the LORD, then choose today whom you will
worship, whether it be the gods whom your ancestors worshiped
beyond the Euphrates, or the gods of the Amorites in whose
land you are living. But I and my family will worship the LORD."

16 The people responded, "Far be it from us to abandon the
LORD so we can worship other gods! 17 For the LORD our God
took us and our fathers out of slavery in the land of Egypt and
performed these awesome miracles before our very eyes. He
continually protected us as we traveled and when we passed
through nations. 18 The LORD drove out from before us all the
nations, including the Amorites who lived in the land. So we too
will worship the LORD, for he is our God!"

19 Joshua warned the people, "You will not keep worshiping
the LORD, for he is a holy God. He is a jealous God who will
not forgive your rebellion or your sins. 20 If you abandon the
LORD and worship foreign gods, he will turn against you; he
will bring disaster on you and destroy you, though he once
treated you well."

21 The people said to Joshua, "No! We really will worship the
LORD." 22 Joshua said to the people, "Do you agree to be witnesses
against yourselves that you have chosen to worship the LORD?"
They replied, "We are witnesses!" 23 Joshua said, "Now put aside
the foreign gods that are among you and submit to the LORD
God of Israel."

24 The people said to Joshua, "We will worship the LORD our
God and obey him."

25 That day Joshua drew up an agreement for the people, and he
established rules and regulations for them in Shechem. 26 Joshua
wrote these words in the Law Scroll of God. He then took a large
stone and set it up there under the oak tree near the LORD's
sanctuary. 27 Joshua said to all the people, "Look, this stone will
be a witness against us, for it has heard everything the LORD
said to us. It will be a witness against you if you deny your God."
28 When Joshua dismissed the people, they went to their allotted portions of land.

AN ERA ENDS

29 After all this Joshua son of Nun, the LORD's servant, died at
the age of 110. 30 They buried him in his allotted territory in Timnath Serah in the hill country of Ephraim, north of Mount Gaash. 31 Israel worshiped the LORD throughout Joshua's lifetime
and as long as the elderly men who outlived him remained alive.
These men had experienced firsthand everything the LORD had
done for Israel.
32 The bones of Joseph, which the Israelites had brought up
from Egypt, were buried at Shechem in the part of the field that
Jacob bought from the sons of Hamor, the father of Shechem,
for 100 pieces of money. So it became the inheritance of the
tribe of Joseph.
33 Eleazar son of Aaron died, and they buried him in Gibeah in
the hill country of Ephraim, where his son Phinehas had been
assigned land.

REFLECT

Why did the Israelites fall away from God after this generation passed away? How are you communicating and displaying the power, love, and faithfulness of God to the younger generation?

IN THOSE DAYS Israel HAD NO KING. EACH MAN DID WHAT he CONSIDERED TO BE RIGHT.

MEMORY VERSE

In those days Israel had no king. Each man did what he considered to be right.

Judges 21:25

Judges

INTRODUCTION

God Disciplines His People

The Book of Judges is not merely a historical record of the nation of Israel. This book shows the patience and faithfulness of God despite the apostasy of the Israelites. Even though they continually turned against Him, God continued to deliver them. He kept the covenant He made with Abraham, Isaac, and Jacob by disciplining His people, yet He always displayed His love and faithfulness to them.

The Book of Judges is written as a historical narrative. While there is some evidence that portions of the book may not be recorded in a linear timeline, the pattern of the narrative is consistent throughout the book. Fourteen times Israel disobeyed and was unfaithful to God. Fourteen times another nation or people group oppressed the people of Israel. Fourteen times the people cried out to God for deliverance and salvation. Fourteen times God provided different judges as a type of savior for the people to rule them, to provide them with spiritual direction, and to bring about their physical deliverance. And fourteen times, the people of Israel once again fell into disobedience.

The events recorded in the Book of Judges take place after the conquest of the land of Canaan, specifically after the death of Joshua, the successor of Moses. After Joshua and the other leaders died, the people began to do whatever seemed right to them. This behavior continued until the period of the monarchy, which began shortly after the events recorded in Judges. The author of the Book of Judges is largely unknown, while some scholars believe Samuel to be the author.

Each new outbreak of disobedience and idolatry took Israel further away from God and deeper into sin and misery. By the end of the book, it is clear the Israelites had violated their covenant with God in almost every imaginable way. Even in their disobedience and rebellion, God demonstrated His compassion. He didn't punish them with no regard for their restoration, but He disciplined them with the intent of bringing His wayward people back to Himself. God is the hero of the Book of Judges. His discipline is evidence of His love and faithfulness. Let's continue to love Him greatly as we reflect on how He alone remains faithful despite the failings of His people.

United States of America

OFFICIAL LANGUAGE
English
POPULATION
326,302,000
UNREACHED POPULATION
4,827,000
PROFESSING CHRISTIANS
77.5%

Casey's Home

Say a Prayer Today

Pray for the many student ministries that exist on college and university campuses across the United States. Pray for those who minister to college students and for college students as they make serious decisions about their faith in their college years.

HISTORY BIT

In 1807 the first graduate school was founded in North America. Andover Newton Theological Seminary was founded for the education of congregational ministers.*

Source Information:
https://joshuaproject.net/countries/US
*https://andovernewton.yale.edu/about/history

CASEY'S STORY

I grew up in the United States. I was raised going to church and believed in Jesus Christ as my Lord and Savior at a very young age. I believed Jesus was who He said He was, I believed the Bible, I memorized verses, and I prayed regularly. Into my early teen years I even attended my youth group, brought non-believing friends, and went on several short-term mission trips.

Even in all of my activity, I always felt there was something missing. I stopped praying regularly, and I was no longer reading God's Word. I identify with how the Israelites behaved in the Book of Judges when they only did what was right in their own eyes. I felt that without guidance, I was simply doing what I thought was best and hoped it was enough to please God.

When I entered college I met some Christians who prayed out loud and were on fire for the Lord. Their love for Jesus and wholehearted devotion to Him caught my attention. I knew at that moment I wanted to have a deeper relationship with Jesus, and I made Him Lord of my life.

I finally understood what it meant to be saved by His grace. I am not saved through my actions, my Christian activities, or how many days a week I read my Bible. Salvation is a gift from God, not something that is attainable by works. I am so thankful to the Lord for not only saving me from my sins but for continually pursuing my heart and always bringing me closer to Him.

6 WEEK READING PLAN

LOVE HIS WORD

MONDAY	TUESDAY	WEDNESDAY	THURSDAY	FRIDAY
Judges 1:1-21	Judges 1:22-36	Judges 2:1-19	Judges 2:20—3:11	Judges 3:12-31
SOAP Judges 1:19	SOAP Judges 1:27-28	SOAP Judges 2:18-19	SOAP Judges 3:8-9	SOAP Judges 3:15
Judges 4	Judges 5	Judges 6:1-24	Judges 6:25-40	Judges 7:1—8:3
SOAP Judges 4:4-5	SOAP Judges 5:31	SOAP Judges 6:14	SOAP Judges 6:39-40	SOAP Judges 7:9-10
Judges 8:4-21	Judges 8:22-35	Judges 9:1-21	Judges 9:22-57	Judges 10:1-16
SOAP Psalm 20:6-8	SOAP Judges 8:33-34	SOAP Psalm 104:16-17	SOAP Judges 9:56-57	SOAP Judges 10:14-16
Judges 10:17—11:11	Judges 11:12-40	Judges 12:1-7	Judges 12:8-15	Judges 13
SOAP Hosea 8:4	SOAP Judges 11:39-40	SOAP Psalm 64:3-4	SOAP Proverbs 28:2	SOAP Judges 13:2-3
Judges 14	Judges 15	Judges 16:1-22	Judges 16:23-31	Judges 17
SOAP Judges 14:4	SOAP Judges 15:18-19	SOAP Proverbs 7:25-27	SOAP Hebrews 2:14-15	SOAP Judges 17:6
Judges 18	Judges 19	Judges 20:1-28	Judges 20:29-48	Judges 21
SOAP Psalm 81:11-12	SOAP Romans 1:28	SOAP Judges 20:12-13	SOAP Deuteronomy 20:3-4	SOAP Judges 21:25

JUDAH TAKES THE LEAD

1 After Joshua died, the Israelites asked the LORD, "Who should lead the invasion against the Canaanites and launch the attack?" 2 The LORD said, "The men of Judah should take the lead. Be sure of this! I am handing the land over to them." 3 The men of Judah said to their relatives, the men of Simeon, "Invade our allotted land with us and help us attack the Canaanites. Then we will go with you into your allotted land." So the men of Simeon went with them.

4 The men of Judah attacked, and the LORD handed the Canaanites and Perizzites over to them. They killed 10,000 men at Bezek. 5 They met Adoni-Bezek at Bezek and fought him. They defeated the Canaanites and Perizzites. 6 When Adoni-Bezek ran away, they chased him and captured him. Then they cut off his thumbs and big toes. 7 Adoni-Bezek said, "Seventy kings, with thumbs and big toes cut off, used to lick up food scraps under my table. God has repaid me for what I did to them." They brought him to Jerusalem, where he died. 8 The men of Judah attacked Jerusalem and captured it. They put the sword to it and set the city on fire.

9 Later the men of Judah went down to attack the Canaanites living in the hill country, the Negev, and the foothills. 10 The men of Judah attacked the Canaanites living in Hebron. (Hebron used to be called Kiriath Arba.) They killed Sheshai, Ahiman, and Talmai. 11 From there they attacked the people of Debir. (Debir used to be called Kiriath Sepher.) 12 Caleb said, "To the man who attacks and captures Kiriath Sepher I will give my daughter Achsah as a wife." 13 When Othniel son of Kenaz, Caleb's younger brother, captured it, Caleb gave him his daughter Achsah as a wife.

14 One time Achsah came and charmed her father so she could ask him for some land. When she got down from her donkey, Caleb said to her, "What would you like?" 15 She answered, "Please give me a special present. Since you have given me land in the Negev, now give me springs of water." So Caleb gave her both the upper and lower springs.

16 Now the descendants of the Kenite, Moses' father-in-law, went up with the people of Judah from the city of date palm trees to Arad in the wilderness of Judah, located in the Negev. They went and lived with the people of Judah.

17 The men of Judah went with their brothers the men of Simeon and defeated the Canaanites living in Zephath. They wiped out Zephath. So people now call the city Hormah. 18 The men of Judah captured Gaza, Ashkelon, Ekron, and the territory surrounding each of these cities.

19 The LORD was with the men of Judah. They conquered the hill country, but they could not conquer the people living in the coastal plain, because they had chariots with iron-rimmed wheels. 20 Caleb received Hebron, just as Moses had promised. He drove out the three Anakites. 21 The men of Benjamin, however, did not conquer the Jebusites living in Jerusalem. The Jebusites live with the people of Benjamin in Jerusalem to this very day.

PARTIAL SUCCESS

22 When the men of Joseph attacked Bethel, the LORD was with them. 23 When the men of Joseph spied out Bethel (it used to be called Luz), 24 the spies spotted a man leaving the city. They

said to him, "If you show us a secret entrance into the city, we
will reward you." [25] He showed them a secret entrance into the
city, and they put the city to the sword. But they let the man and
his extended family leave safely. [26] He moved to Hittite country and built a city. He named it Luz, and it has kept that name
to this very day.
[27] The men of Manasseh did not conquer Beth Shean, Taanach,
or their surrounding towns. Nor did they conquer the people
living in Dor, Ibleam, Megiddo or their surrounding towns. The
Canaanites managed to remain in those areas. [28] Whenever Israel was strong militarily, they forced the Canaanites to do hard
labor, but they never totally conquered them.
[29] The men of Ephraim did not conquer the Canaanites living
in Gezer. The Canaanites lived among them in Gezer.
[30] The men of Zebulun did not conquer the people living in
Kitron and Nahalol. The Canaanites lived among them and were
forced to do hard labor.
[31] The men of Asher did not conquer the people living in Acco
or Sidon, nor did they conquer Ahlab, Achzib, Helbah, Aphek, or
Rehob. [32] The people of Asher live among the Canaanites residing in the land because they did not conquer them.
[33] The men of Naphtali did not conquer the people living in
Beth Shemesh or Beth Anath. They live among the Canaanites
residing in the land. The Canaanites living in Beth Shemesh and
Beth Anath were forced to do hard labor for them.
[34] The Amorites forced the people of Dan to live in the hill
country. They did not allow them to live in the coastal plain.
[35] The Amorites managed to remain in Har Heres, Aijalon, and
Shaalbim. Whenever the tribe of Joseph was strong militarily,
the Amorites were forced to do hard labor. [36] The border of Amorite territory ran from the Scorpion Ascent to Sela and on up.

CONFRONTATION AND REPENTANCE AT BOKIM

2 The angel of the LORD went up from Gilgal to Bokim. He said,
"I brought you up from Egypt and led you into the land I had
solemnly promised to give to your ancestors. I said, 'I will never
break my covenant with you, [2] but you must not make an agreement with the people who live in this land. You should tear down
the altars where they worship.' But you have disobeyed me. Why
would you do such a thing? [3] At that time I also warned you, 'If
you disobey, I will not drive out the Canaanites before you. They
will ensnare you and their gods will lure you away.'"
[4] When the angel of the LORD finished speaking these words
to all the Israelites, the people wept loudly. [5] They named that
place Bokim and offered sacrifices to the LORD there.

THE END OF AN ERA

[6] When Joshua dismissed the people, the Israelites went to their
allotted portions of territory, intending to take possession of the
land. [7] The people worshiped the LORD throughout Joshua's lifetime and as long as the elderly men who outlived him remained
alive. These men had witnessed all the great things the LORD
had done for Israel. [8] Joshua son of Nun, the LORD's servant, died
at the age of 110. [9] The people buried him in his allotted land in

LOVE TO GROW

THE ONE TRUE GOD

JUDGES 2:1–4

We are surrounded by many "gods" fighting for our affection: the god of comfort, the god of popularity, the god of success, the god of health. Does it matter which one we follow? Can we follow these gods and still follow the one true God?

At the end of the Book of Joshua, Joshua called the people to choose whom they would serve: idols or the one true God. As they moved in to take possession of the promised land, God told them not to make a covenant with other nations but to tear down the altars of their false gods.

They only partly obeyed. Because they did not totally rid their land of idols, those who worshiped them became a snare to the Israelites. This began the downward spiral of the sin of the people of Israel as recorded in the Book of Judges.

God displayed His mercy by raising up judges to deliver the people from their enemies. Still, they soon fell back into the same problems. Why? Because the Israelites did not take seriously God's command to actively deal with the idolatry around them. As they tolerated the worship of false gods, they were pulled away from relationship with the one true God.

We are susceptible to the same fate when we don't take our relationship with God seriously. We look at a friend who seems to be worshiping the god of comfort with positive results, and we daydream of having a life like theirs. We split our affections and are in danger of being ensnared by false worship that leads to our destruction.

Beware of believing the lie that anything or anyone other than the God of the Bible can satisfy our deepest needs. We would be wise to remember what God said to the Israelites in this passage: for better or worse, He will not break His covenant promises to His people. Only He can meet our deepest needs for security, acceptance, and significance. He is faithful to that promise, even when we are faithless. Remembering God's faithfulness in our past helps us battle the lies that the gods around us are worth following.

Because of His great faithfulness, we remain faithful to Him.
Because of His great love for us, we love Him greatly.

Timnath Heres in the hill country of Ephraim, north of Mount Gaash. 10 That entire generation passed away; a new generation grew up that had not personally experienced the LORD's presence or seen what he had done for Israel.

A MONOTONOUS CYCLE

11 The Israelites did evil before the LORD by worshiping the Baals. 12 They abandoned the LORD God of their ancestors who brought them out of the land of Egypt. They followed other gods—the gods of the nations who lived around them. They worshiped them and made the LORD angry. 13 They abandoned the LORD and worshiped Baal and the Ashtoreths.

14 The LORD was furious with Israel and handed them over to robbers who plundered them. He turned them over to their enemies who lived around them. They could no longer withstand their enemies' attacks. 15 Whenever they went out to fight, the LORD did them harm, just as he had warned and solemnly vowed he would do. They suffered greatly.

16 The LORD raised up leaders who delivered them from these robbers. 17 But they did not obey their leaders. Instead they prostituted themselves to other gods and worshiped them. They quickly turned aside from the path their ancestors had walked. Their ancestors had obeyed the LORD's commands, but they did not. 18 When the LORD raised up leaders for them, the LORD was with each leader and delivered the people from their enemies while the leader remained alive. The LORD felt sorry for them when they cried out in agony because of what their harsh oppressors did to them. 19 When a leader died, the next generation would again act more wickedly than the previous one. They would follow after other gods, worshiping them and bowing down to them. They did not give up their practices or their stubborn ways.

A DIVINE DECISION

20 The LORD was furious with Israel. He said, "This nation has violated the terms of the covenant I made with their ancestors by disobeying me. 21 So I will no longer remove before them any of the nations that Joshua left unconquered when he died, 22 in order to test Israel. I want to see whether or not the people will carefully walk in the path marked out by the LORD, as their ancestors were careful to do." 23 This is why the LORD permitted these nations to remain and did not conquer them immediately; he did not hand them over to Joshua.

3 These were the nations the LORD permitted to remain so he could use them to test Israel—he wanted to test all those who had not experienced battle against the Canaanites. 2 He left those nations simply because he wanted to teach the subsequent generations of Israelites, who had not experienced the earlier battles, how to conduct holy war. 3 These were the nations: the five lords of the Philistines, all the Canaanites, the Sidonians, and the Hivites living in Mount Lebanon, from Mount Baal Hermon to Lebo Hamath. 4 They were left to test Israel, so the LORD would know if his people would obey the commands he gave their ancestors through Moses.

5 The Israelites lived among the Canaanites, Hittites, Amorites,
Perizzites, Hivites, and Jebusites. 6 They took the Canaanites'
daughters as wives and gave their daughters to the Canaanites;
they worshiped their gods as well.

OTHNIEL: A MODEL LEADER

7 The Israelites did evil in the LORD's sight. They forgot the LORD
their God and worshiped the Baals and the Asherahs. 8 The LORD
was furious with Israel and turned them over to King Cushan
Rishathaim of Armon Haraim. They were Cushan Rishathaim's
subjects for eight years. 9 When the Israelites cried out for help
to the LORD, he raised up a deliverer for the Israelites who rescued them. His name was Othniel son of Kenaz, Caleb's younger
brother. 10 The LORD's Spirit empowered him and he led Israel.
When he went to do battle, the LORD handed over to him King
Cushan Rishathaim of Armon and he overpowered him. 11 The
land had rest for forty years; then Othniel son of Kenaz died.

DECEIT, ASSASSINATION, AND DELIVERANCE

12 The Israelites again did evil in the LORD's sight. The LORD gave
King Eglon of Moab control over Israel because they had done
evil in the LORD's sight. 13 Eglon formed alliances with the Ammonites and Amalekites. He came and defeated Israel, and they
seized the city of date palm trees. 14 The Israelites were subject
to King Eglon of Moab for eighteen years.

15 When the Israelites cried out for help to the LORD, he raised
up a deliverer for them. His name was Ehud son of Gera the Benjaminite, a left-handed man. The Israelites sent him to King Eglon of Moab with their tribute payment. 16 Ehud made himself a
sword—it had two edges and was 18 inches long. He strapped it
under his coat on his right thigh. 17 He brought the tribute payment to King Eglon of Moab. (Now Eglon was a very fat man.)
18 After Ehud brought the tribute payment, he dismissed the
people who had carried it. 19 But he went back once he reached
the carved images at Gilgal. He said to Eglon, "I have a secret
message for you, O king." Eglon said, "Be quiet!" All his attendants left. 20 When Ehud approached him, he was sitting in his
well-ventilated upper room all by himself. Ehud said, "I have a
message from God for you." When Eglon rose up from his seat,
21 Ehud reached with his left hand, pulled the sword from his
right thigh, and drove it into Eglon's belly. 22 The handle went
in after the blade, and the fat closed around the blade, for Ehud
did not pull the sword out of his belly. 23 As Ehud went out into
the vestibule, he closed the doors of the upper room behind
him and locked them.

24 When Ehud had left, Eglon's servants came and saw the
locked doors of the upper room. They said, "He must be reliev-
ing himself in the well-ventilated inner room." 25 They waited
so long they were embarrassed, but he still did not open the
doors of the upper room. Finally they took the key and opened
the doors. Right before their eyes was their master, sprawled
out dead on the floor! 26 Now Ehud had escaped while they
were delaying. When he passed the carved images, he escaped
to Seirah.

27 When he reached Seirah, he blew a trumpet in the Ephraimite hill country. The Israelites went down with him from the hill country, with Ehud in the lead. 28 He said to them, "Follow me, for the LORD is about to defeat your enemies, the Moabites!" They followed him, captured the fords of the Jordan River opposite Moab, and did not let anyone cross. 29 That day they killed about 10,000 Moabites—all strong, capable warriors; not one escaped. 30 Israel humiliated Moab that day, and the land had rest for eighty years.

31 After Ehud came Shamgar son of Anath. He killed 600 Philistines with an oxgoad. So he also delivered Israel.

CHALLENGE

Note how women are treated in Israel from the beginning of the Book of Judges through the end. What differences occur? How are women viewed at the beginning of the book versus the end? How is the decline of the treatment of women similar to the spiritual decline of the nation of Israel? Do you think there is a connection?

DEBORAH SUMMONS BARAK

4 The Israelites again did evil in the LORD's sight after Ehud's death. 2 The LORD turned them over to King Jabin of Canaan, who ruled in Hazor. The general of his army was Sisera, who lived in Harosheth Haggoyim. 3 The Israelites cried out for help to the LORD, because Sisera had 900 chariots with iron-rimmed wheels, and he cruelly oppressed the Israelites for twenty years.

4 Now Deborah, a prophetess, wife of Lappidoth, was leading Israel at that time. 5 She would sit under the Date Palm Tree of Deborah between Ramah and Bethel in the Ephraimite hill country. The Israelites would come up to her to have their disputes settled.

6 She summoned Barak son of Abinoam from Kedesh in Naphtali. She said to him, "Is it not true that the LORD God of Israel is commanding you? Go, march to Mount Tabor! Take with you 10,000 men from Naphtali and Zebulun. 7 I will bring Sisera, the general of Jabin's army, to you at the Kishon River, along with his chariots and huge army. I will hand him over to you." 8 Barak said to her, "If you go with me, I will go. But if you do not go with me, I will not go." 9 She said, "I will indeed go with you. But you will not gain fame on the expedition you are undertaking, for the LORD will turn Sisera over to a woman." Deborah got up and went with Barak to Kedesh. 10 Barak summoned men from Zebulun and Naphtali to Kedesh, and 10,000 men followed him; Deborah went up with him as well. 11 Now Heber the Kenite had moved away from the Kenites, the descendants of Hobab, Moses' father-in-law. He lived near the great tree in Zaanannim near Kedesh.

12 When Sisera heard that Barak son of Abinoam had gone up to Mount Tabor, 13 he ordered all his chariotry—900 chariots with iron-rimmed wheels—and all the troops he had with him to go from Harosheth Haggoyim to the Kishon River. 14 Deborah said to Barak, "Spring into action, for this is the day the LORD is handing Sisera over to you! Has the LORD not taken the lead?" So Barak went down from Mount Tabor with 10,000 men following him. 15 The LORD routed Sisera, all his chariotry, and all his army with the edge of the sword. Sisera jumped out of his chariot and ran away on foot. 16 Now Barak chased the chariots and the army all the way to Harosheth Haggoyim. Sisera's whole army died by the edge of the sword; not even one survived!

17 Now Sisera ran away on foot to the tent of Jael, wife of Heber

the Kenite, for King Jabin of Hazor and the family of Heber the
Kenite had made a peace treaty. 18 Jael came out to welcome
Sisera. She said to him, "Stop and rest, my lord. Stop and rest
with me. Don't be afraid." So Sisera stopped to rest in her tent,
and she put a blanket over him. 19 He said to her, "Give me a little water to drink, because I'm thirsty." She opened a goatskin
container of milk and gave him some milk to drink. Then she
covered him up again. 20 He said to her, "Stand watch at the entrance to the tent. If anyone comes along and asks you, 'Is there
a man here?' say, 'No.'" 21 Then Jael wife of Heber took a tent peg
in one hand and a hammer in the other. She crept up on him,
drove the tent peg through his temple into the ground while
he was asleep from exhaustion, and he died. 22 Now Barak was
chasing Sisera. Jael went out to welcome him. She said to him,
"Come here and I will show you the man you are searching for."
He went with her into the tent, and there he saw Sisera sprawled
out dead with the tent peg through his temple.

23 That day God humiliated King Jabin of Canaan before the
Israelites. 24 Israel's power continued to overwhelm King Jabin
of Canaan until they did away with him.

CELEBRATING THE VICTORY IN SONG

5 On that day Deborah and Barak son of Abinoam sang this
victory song:

2 "When the leaders took the lead in Israel,
When the people answered the call to war—
Praise the LORD!
3 Hear, O kings!
Pay attention, O rulers!
I will sing to the LORD!
I will sing to the LORD God of Israel!

4 O LORD, when you departed from Seir,
when you marched from Edom's plains,
the earth shook, the heavens poured down,
the clouds poured down rain.
5 The mountains trembled before the
LORD, the God of Sinai;
before the LORD God of Israel.

6 In the days of Shamgar son of Anath,
in the days of Jael caravans disappeared;
travelers had to go on winding side roads.
7 Warriors were scarce;
they were scarce in Israel,
until you arose, Deborah,
until you arose as a motherly protector in Israel.
8 God chose new leaders,
then fighters appeared in the city gates;
but, I swear, not a shield or spear could be found
among forty military units in Israel.
9 My heart went out to Israel's leaders,
to the people who answered the call to war.
Praise the LORD!

10 You who ride on light-colored female donkeys,
who sit on saddle blankets,
you who walk on the road, pay attention!
11 Hear the sound of those who divide the
sheep among the watering places;
there they tell of the LORD's victorious deeds,
the victorious deeds of his warriors in Israel.
Then the LORD's people went down to the city gates—

12 Wake up, wake up, Deborah!
Wake up, wake up, sing a song!
Get up, Barak!
Capture your prisoners of war, son of Abinoam!
13 Then the survivors came down to the mighty ones;
the LORD's people came down to me as warriors.
14 They came from Ephraim, who uprooted Amalek;
they follow after you, Benjamin, with your soldiers.
From Makir leaders came down,
from Zebulun came the ones who march
carrying an officer's staff.
15 Issachar's leaders were with Deborah;
the men of Issachar supported Barak;
into the valley they were sent under Barak's command.
Among the clans of Reuben there was
intense heart searching.
16 Why do you remain among the sheepfolds,
listening to the shepherds playing their pipes for their flocks?
As for the clans of Reuben—there was
intense searching of heart.
17 Gilead stayed put beyond the Jordan River.
As for Dan—why did he seek temporary
employment in the shipyards?
Asher remained on the seacoast;
he stayed by his harbors.
18 The men of Zebulun were not concerned about their lives;
Naphtali charged onto the battlefields.

19 Kings came, they fought;
the kings of Canaan fought
at Taanach by the waters of Megiddo,
but they took no silver as plunder.
20 From the sky the stars fought,
from their paths in the heavens they fought against Sisera.
21 The Kishon River carried them off;
the river confronted them—the Kishon River.
Step on the necks of the strong!

22 The horses' hooves pounded the ground;
the stallions galloped madly.
23 'Call judgment down on Meroz,' says the angel of the LORD;
'Be sure to call judgment down on those who live there,
because they did not come to help in the LORD's battle,
to help in the LORD's battle against the warriors.'

24 The most rewarded of women should be Jael,
the wife of Heber the Kenite!
She should be the most rewarded of
women who live in tents.
25 He asked for water,
and she gave him milk;
in a bowl fit for a king,
she served him curds.
26 Her left hand reached for the tent peg,
her right hand for the workmen's hammer.
She "hammered" Sisera,
she shattered his skull,
she smashed his head,
she drove the tent peg through his temple.
27 Between her feet he collapsed,
he fell limp and was lifeless;
between her feet he collapsed and fell,
in the spot where he collapsed,
there he fell—violently killed!
28 Through the window she looked;
Sisera's mother cried out through the lattice:
'Why is his chariot so slow to return?
Why are the hoofbeats of his chariot horses delayed?'
29 The wisest of her ladies answer;
indeed she even thinks to herself,
30 'No doubt they are gathering and dividing the plunder—
a girl or two for each man to rape!
Sisera is grabbing up colorful cloth,
he is grabbing up colorful embroidered cloth,
two pieces of colorful embroidered cloth,
for the neck of the plunderer!'

31 May all your enemies perish like this, O LORD!
But may those who love you shine
like the rising sun at its brightest."

And the land had rest for forty years.

OPPRESSION AND CONFRONTATION

6 The Israelites did evil in the LORD's sight, so the LORD turned
them over to Midian for seven years. 2 The Midianites overwhelmed Israel. Because of Midian the Israelites made shelters
for themselves in the hills, caves, and strongholds. 3 Whenever
the Israelites planted their crops, the Midianites, Amalekites,
and the people from the east would attack them. 4 They invaded
the land and devoured its crops all the way to Gaza. They left
nothing for the Israelites to eat, and they took away the sheep,
oxen, and donkeys. 5 When they invaded with their cattle and
tents, they were as thick as locusts. Neither they nor their camels could be counted. They came to devour the land. 6 Israel was
so severely weakened by Midian that the Israelites cried out to
the LORD for help.

REFLECT

God faithfully answered Gideon's request to give him a clear sign with the fleece. From what you know about the character of God, do you believe God was upset or irritated with Gideon for doing this? What do Gideon's requests say about His faith?

[7]When the Israelites cried out to the LORD for help because of Midian, [8]the LORD sent a prophet to the Israelites. He said to them, "This is what the LORD God of Israel has said: 'I brought you up from Egypt and took you out of that place of slavery. [9]I rescued you from Egypt's power and from the power of all who oppressed you. I drove them out before you and gave their land to you. [10]I said to you, "I am the LORD your God! Do not worship the gods of the Amorites, in whose land you are now living." But you have disobeyed me.'"

GIDEON MEETS SOME VISITORS

[11]The angel of the LORD came and sat down under the oak tree in Ophrah owned by Joash the Abiezrite. He arrived while Joash's son Gideon was threshing wheat in a winepress so he could hide it from the Midianites. [12]The angel of the LORD appeared and said to him, "The LORD is with you, courageous warrior!" [13]Gideon said to him, "Pardon me, but if the LORD is with us, why has such disaster overtaken us? Where are all his miraculous deeds our ancestors told us about? They said, 'Did the LORD not bring us up from Egypt?' But now the LORD has abandoned us and handed us over to Midian." [14]Then the LORD himself turned to him and said, "You have the strength. Deliver Israel from the power of the Midianites! Have I not sent you?" [15]Gideon said to him, "But Lord, how can I deliver Israel? Just look! My clan is the weakest in Manasseh, and I am the youngest in my family." [16]The LORD said to him, "Ah, but I will be with you! You will strike down the whole Midianite army." [17]Gideon said to him, "If you really are pleased with me, then give me a sign as proof that it is really you speaking with me. [18]Do not leave this place until I come back with a gift and present it to you." The LORD said, "I will stay here until you come back."

[19]Gideon went and prepared a young goat, along with unleavened bread made from an ephah of flour. He put the meat in a basket and the broth in a pot. He brought the food to him under the oak tree and presented it to him. [20]God's angel said to him, "Put the meat and unleavened bread on this rock, and pour out the broth." Gideon did as instructed. [21]The angel of the LORD touched the meat and the unleavened bread with the tip of his staff. Fire flared up from the rock and consumed the meat and unleavened bread. The angel of the LORD then disappeared.

[22]When Gideon realized that it was the angel of the LORD, he said, "Oh no! Sovereign LORD! I have seen the angel of the LORD face-to-face!" [23]The LORD said to him, "You are safe! Do not be afraid. You are not going to die!" [24]Gideon built an altar for the LORD there, and named it "The LORD is on friendly terms with me." To this day it is still there in Ophrah of the Abiezrites.

GIDEON DESTROYS THE ALTAR

[25]That night the LORD said to him, "Take the bull from your father's herd, as well as a second bull, one that is seven years old. Pull down your father's Baal altar and cut down the nearby Asherah pole. [26]Then build an altar for the LORD your God on the top of this stronghold according to the proper pattern. Take the second bull and offer it as a burnt sacrifice on the wood from

the Asherah pole that you cut down." 27 So Gideon took ten of his servants and did just as the LORD had told him. He was too afraid of his father's family and the men of the city to do it in broad daylight, so he waited until nighttime.

28 When the men of the city got up the next morning, they saw the Baal altar pulled down, the nearby Asherah pole cut down, and the second bull sacrificed on the newly built altar. 29 They said to one another, "Who did this?" They investigated the matter thoroughly and concluded that Gideon son of Joash had done it. 30 The men of the city said to Joash, "Bring out your son, so we can execute him! He pulled down the Baal altar and cut down the nearby Asherah pole." 31 But Joash said to all those who confronted him, "Must you fight Baal's battles? Must you rescue him? Whoever takes up his cause will die by morning! If he really is a god, let him fight his own battles! After all, it was his altar that was pulled down." 32 That very day Gideon's father named him Jerub Baal, because he had said, "Let Baal fight with him, for it was his altar that was pulled down."

GIDEON SUMMONS AN ARMY AND SEEKS CONFIRMATION

33 All the Midianites, Amalekites, and the people from the east assembled. They crossed the Jordan River and camped in the Jezreel Valley. 34 The LORD's Spirit took control of Gideon. He blew a trumpet, summoning the Abiezrites to follow him. 35 He sent messengers throughout Manasseh and summoned them to follow him as well. He also sent messengers throughout Asher, Zebulun, and Naphtali, and they came up to meet him.

36 Gideon said to God, "If you really intend to use me to deliver Israel, as you promised, then give me a sign as proof. 37 Look, I am putting a wool fleece on the threshing floor. If there is dew only on the fleece, and the ground around it is dry, then I will be sure that you will use me to deliver Israel, as you promised." 38 The LORD did as he asked. When he got up the next morning, he squeezed the fleece, and enough dew dripped from it to fill a bowl. 39 Gideon said to God, "Please do not get angry at me, when I ask for just one more sign. Please allow me one more test with the fleece. This time make only the fleece dry, while the ground around it is covered with dew." 40 That night God did as he asked. Only the fleece was dry and the ground around it was covered with dew.

GIDEON REDUCES THE RANKS

7 Jerub Baal (that is, Gideon) and his men got up the next morning and camped near the spring of Harod. The Midianites were camped north of them near the hill of Moreh in the valley. 2 The LORD said to Gideon, "You have too many men for me to hand Midian over to you. Israel might brag, 'Our own strength has delivered us.' 3 Now, announce to the men, 'Whoever is shaking with fear may turn around and leave Mount Gilead.'" 22,000 men went home; 10,000 remained. 4 The LORD spoke to Gideon again, "There are still too many men. Bring them down to the water and I will thin the ranks some more. When I say, 'This one should go with you,' pick him to go; when I say, 'This one should not go with

you,' do not take him." 5 So he brought the men down to the water. Then the LORD said to Gideon, "Separate those who lap the
water as a dog laps from those who kneel to drink." 6 Only 300
men lapped with their hands to their mouths; the rest of the
men kneeled to drink water. 7 The LORD said to Gideon, "With
the 300 men who lapped I will deliver the whole army and I will
hand Midian over to you. The rest of the men should go home."
8 The men who were chosen took supplies and their trumpets.
Gideon sent all the men of Israel back to their homes; he kept
only 300 men. Now the Midianites were camped down below
in the valley.

GIDEON REASSURED OF VICTORY

9 That night the LORD said to Gideon, "Get up! Attack the camp,
for I am handing it over to you. 10 But if you are afraid to attack,
go down to the camp with Purah your servant 11 and listen to what
they are saying. Then you will be brave and attack the camp." So
he went down with Purah his servant to where the sentries were
guarding the camp. 12 Now the Midianites, Amalekites, and the
people from the east covered the valley like a swarm of locusts.
Their camels could not be counted; they were as innumerable
as the sand on the seashore. 13 When Gideon arrived, he heard a
man telling another man about a dream he had. The man said,
"Look! I had a dream. I saw a stale cake of barley bread rolling
into the Midianite camp. It hit a tent so hard it knocked it over
and turned it upside down. The tent just collapsed." 14 The other
man said, "Without a doubt this symbolizes the sword of Gideon son of Joash, the Israelite. God is handing Midian and all
the army over to him."

GIDEON ROUTS THE ENEMY

15 When Gideon heard the report of the dream and its interpretation, he praised God. Then he went back to the Israelite camp
and said, "Get up, for the LORD is handing the Midianite army
over to you!" 16 He divided the 300 men into three units. He gave
them all trumpets and empty jars with torches inside them.
17 He said to them, "Watch me and do as I do. Watch closely! I am
going to the edge of the camp. Do as I do! 18 When I and all who
are with me blow our trumpets, you also blow your trumpets
all around the camp. Then say, 'For the LORD and for Gideon!'"

19 Gideon took 100 men to the edge of the camp at the beginning of the middle watch, just after they had changed the
guards. They blew their trumpets and broke the jars they were
carrying. 20 All three units blew their trumpets and broke their
jars. They held the torches in their left hand and the trumpets
in their right. Then they yelled, "A sword for the LORD and for
Gideon!" 21 They stood in order all around the camp. The whole
Midianite army ran away; they shouted as they scrambled away.
22 When the 300 men blew their trumpets, the LORD caused the
Midianites to attack one another with their swords throughout
the camp. The army fled to Beth Shittah on the way to Zererah.
They went to the border of Abel Meholah near Tabbath. 23 Israelites from Naphtali, Asher, and Manasseh answered the call
and chased the Midianites.

GIDEON APPEASES THE EPHRAIMITES

24 Now Gideon sent messengers throughout the Ephraimite hill country who announced, "Go down and head off the Midianites. Take control of the fords of the streams all the way to Beth Barah and the Jordan River." When all the Ephraimites had assembled, they took control of the fords all the way to Beth Barah and the Jordan River. 25 They captured the two Midianite generals, Oreb and Zeeb. They executed Oreb on the rock of Oreb and Zeeb in the winepress of Zeeb. They chased the Midianites and brought the heads of Oreb and Zeeb to Gideon, who was now on the other side of the Jordan River.

8 The Ephraimites said to him, "Why have you done such a thing to us? You did not summon us when you went to fight the Midianites!" They argued vehemently with him. 2 He said to them, "Now what have I accomplished compared to you? Even Ephraim's leftover grapes are better quality than Abiezer's harvest! 3 It was to you that God handed over the Midianite generals, Oreb and Zeeb! What did I accomplish to rival that?" When he said this, they calmed down.

GIDEON TRACKS DOWN THE MIDIANITE KINGS

4 Now Gideon and his 300 men had crossed over the Jordan River, and even though they were exhausted, they were still chasing the Midianites. 5 He said to the men of Sukkoth, "Give some loaves of bread to the men who are following me, because they are exhausted. I am chasing Zebah and Zalmunna, the kings of Midian." 6 The officials of Sukkoth said, "You have not yet overpowered Zebah and Zalmunna. So why should we give bread to your army?" 7 Gideon said, "Since you will not help, after the LORD hands Zebah and Zalmunna over to me, I will thresh your skin with desert thorns and briers." 8 He went up from there to Penuel and made the same request. The men of Penuel responded the same way the men of Sukkoth had. 9 He also threatened the men of Penuel, warning, "When I return victoriously, I will tear down this tower."

10 Now Zebah and Zalmunna were in Karkor with their armies. There were about 15,000 survivors from the army of the eastern peoples; 120,000 sword-wielding soldiers had been killed. 11 Gideon went up the road of the nomads east of Nobah and Jogbehah and ambushed the surprised army. 12 When Zebah and Zalmunna ran away, Gideon chased them and captured the two Midianite kings, Zebah and Zalmunna. He had surprised their entire army.

13 Gideon son of Joash returned from the battle by the pass of Heres. 14 He captured a young man from Sukkoth and interrogated him. The young man wrote down for him the names of Sukkoth's officials and city leaders—seventy-seven men in all. 15 He approached the men of Sukkoth and said, "Look what I have! Zebah and Zalmunna! You insulted me, saying, 'You have not yet overpowered Zebah and Zalmunna. So why should we give bread to your exhausted men?'" 16 He seized the leaders of the city, along with some desert thorns and briers; he then "threshed" the men of Sukkoth with them. 17 He also tore down the tower of Penuel and executed the city's men.

18 He said to Zebah and Zalmunna, "Describe for me the men
you killed at Tabor." They said, "They were like you. Each one
looked like a king's son." 19 He said, "They were my brothers, the
sons of my mother. I swear, as surely as the LORD is alive, if you
had let them live, I would not kill you." 20 He ordered Jether his
firstborn son, "Come on! Kill them!" But Jether was too afraid
to draw his sword, because he was still young. 21 Zebah and Zalmunna said to Gideon, "Come on, you strike us, for a man is
judged by his strength." So Gideon killed Zebah and Zalmunna,
and he took the crescent-shaped ornaments that were on the
necks of their camels.

GIDEON REJECTS A CROWN BUT MAKES AN EPHOD

22 The men of Israel said to Gideon, "Rule over us—you, your son,
and your grandson. For you have delivered us from Midian's
power." 23 Gideon said to them, "I will not rule over you, nor will
my son rule over you. The LORD will rule over you." 24 Gideon
continued, "I would like to make one request. Each of you give
me an earring from the plunder you have taken." (The Midianites had gold earrings because they were Ishmaelites.) 25 They
said, "We are happy to give you earrings." So they spread out a
garment, and each one threw an earring from his plunder onto
it. 26 The total weight of the gold earrings he requested came to
1,700 gold shekels. This was in addition to the crescent-shaped
ornaments, jewelry, purple clothing worn by the Midianite kings,
and the necklaces on the camels. 27 Gideon used all this to make
an ephod, which he put in his hometown of Ophrah. All the Israelites prostituted themselves to it by worshiping it there. It
became a snare to Gideon and his family.

GIDEON'S STORY ENDS

28 The Israelites humiliated Midian; the Midianites' fighting
spirit was broken. The land had rest for forty years during Gideon's time. 29 Then Jerub Baal son of Joash went home and settled down. 30 Gideon fathered seventy sons through his many
wives. 31 His concubine, who lived in Shechem, also gave him a
son, whom he named Abimelech. 32 Gideon son of Joash died at
a very old age and was buried in the tomb of his father Joash located in Ophrah of the Abiezrites.

ISRAEL RETURNS TO BAAL WORSHIP

33 After Gideon died, the Israelites again prostituted themselves
to the Baals. They made Baal Berith their god. 34 The Israelites
did not remain true to the LORD their God, who had delivered
them from all the enemies who lived around them. 35 They did
not treat the family of Jerub Baal (that is, Gideon) fairly in return for all the good he had done for Israel.

ABIMELECH MURDERS HIS BROTHERS

9 Now Abimelech son of Jerub Baal went to Shechem to see his
mother's relatives. He said to them and to his mother's entire extended family, 2 "Tell all the leaders of Shechem this: 'Why
would you want to have seventy men, all Jerub Baal's sons, ruling over you, when you can have just one ruler? Recall that I am

your own flesh and blood.'" 3 His mother's relatives spoke on his
behalf to all the leaders of Shechem and reported his proposal.
The leaders were drawn to Abimelech; they said, "He is our close
relative." 4 They paid him seventy silver shekels out of the temple of Baal Berith. Abimelech then used the silver to hire some
lawless, dangerous men as his followers. 5 He went to his father's
home in Ophrah and murdered his half brothers, the seventy
legitimate sons of Jerub Baal, on one stone. Only Jotham, Jerub
Baal's youngest son, escaped, because he hid. 6 All the leaders of
Shechem and Beth Millo assembled and then went and made
Abimelech king by the oak near the pillar in Shechem.

JOTHAM'S PARABLE

7 When Jotham heard the news, he went and stood on the top of
Mount Gerizim. He spoke loudly to the people below, "Listen to
me, leaders of Shechem, so that God may listen to you!

8 "The trees were determined to go out and choose a king for
themselves. They said to the olive tree, 'Be our king!' 9 But the olive
tree said to them, 'I am not going to stop producing my oil, which
is used to honor gods and men, just to sway above the other trees!'

10 "So the trees said to the fig tree, 'You come and be our king!'
11 But the fig tree said to them, 'I am not going to stop producing my
sweet figs, my excellent fruit, just to sway above the other trees!'

12 "So the trees said to the grapevine, 'You come and be our
king!' 13 But the grapevine said to them, 'I am not going to stop
producing my wine, which makes gods and men so happy, just
to sway above the other trees!'

14 "So all the trees said to the thornbush, 'You come and be
our king!' 15 The thornbush said to the trees, 'If you really want
to choose me as your king, then come along, find safety under
my branches. Otherwise may fire blaze from the thornbush and
consume the cedars of Lebanon!'

16 "Now, if you have shown loyalty and integrity when you made
Abimelech king, if you have done right to Jerub Baal and his family, if you have properly repaid him—17 my father fought for you; he
risked his life and delivered you from Midian's power. 18 But you
have attacked my father's family today. You murdered his seventy
legitimate sons on one stone and made Abimelech, the son of his
female slave, king over the leaders of Shechem, just because he is
your close relative. 19 So if you have shown loyalty and integrity to
Jerub Baal and his family today, then may Abimelech bring you
happiness and may you bring him happiness! 20 But if not, may fire
blaze from Abimelech and consume the leaders of Shechem and
Beth Millo! May fire also blaze from the leaders of Shechem and
Beth Millo and consume Abimelech!" 21 Then Jotham ran away to
Beer and lived there to escape from Abimelech his half-brother.

GOD FULFILLS JOTHAM'S CURSE

22 Abimelech commanded Israel for three years. 23 God sent a
spirit to stir up hostility between Abimelech and the leaders of
Shechem. He made the leaders of Shechem disloyal to Abimelech. 24 He did this so the violent deaths of Jerub Baal's seventy
sons might be avenged and Abimelech, their half-brother who
murdered them, might have to pay for their spilled blood, along

with the leaders of Shechem who helped him murder them.
25 The leaders of Shechem rebelled against Abimelech by putting bandits in the hills, who robbed everyone who traveled by
on the road. But Abimelech found out about it.
26 Gaal son of Ebed came through Shechem with his brothers.
The leaders of Shechem transferred their loyalty to him. 27 They
went out to the field, harvested their grapes, squeezed out the
juice, and celebrated. They came to the temple of their god and
ate, drank, and cursed Abimelech. 28 Gaal son of Ebed said, "Who
is Abimelech and who is Shechem, that we should serve him? Is
he not the son of Jerub Baal, and is not Zebul the deputy he appointed? Serve the sons of Hamor, the father of Shechem! But
why should we serve Abimelech? 29 If only these men were under my command, I would get rid of Abimelech!" He challenged
Abimelech, "Muster your army and come out for battle!"
30 When Zebul, the city commissioner, heard the words of Gaal
son of Ebed, he was furious. 31 He sent messengers to Abimelech,
who was in Arumah, reporting, "Beware! Gaal son of Ebed and his
brothers are coming to Shechem and inciting the city to rebel
against you. 32 Now, come up at night with your men and set an
ambush in the field outside the city. 33 In the morning at sunrise quickly attack the city. When he and his men come out to
fight you, do what you can to him."
34 So Abimelech and all his men came up at night and set an
ambush outside Shechem; they divided into four units. 35 When
Gaal son of Ebed came out and stood at the entrance to the city's
gate, Abimelech and his men got up from their hiding places.
36 Gaal saw the men and said to Zebul, "Look, men are coming
down from the tops of the hills." But Zebul said to him, "You are
seeing the shadows on the hills—it just looks like men." 37 Gaal
again said, "Look, men are coming down from the very center of
the land. A unit is coming by way of the Oak Tree of the Diviners." 38 Zebul said to him, "Where now are your bragging words,
'Who is Abimelech that we should serve him?' Are these not
the men you insulted? Go out now and fight them!" 39 So Gaal
led the leaders of Shechem out and fought Abimelech. 40 Abimelech chased him, and Gaal ran from him. Many Shechemites
fell wounded at the entrance of the gate. 41 Abimelech went back
to Arumah; Zebul drove Gaal and his brothers out of Shechem.
42 The next day the Shechemites came out to the field. When
Abimelech heard about it, 43 he took his men and divided them
into three units and set an ambush in the field. When he saw
the people coming out of the city, he attacked and struck them
down. 44 Abimelech and his units attacked and blocked the entrance to the city's gate. Two units then attacked all the people
in the field and struck them down. 45 Abimelech fought against
the city all that day. He captured the city and killed all the people in it. Then he leveled the city and spread salt over it.
46 When all the leaders of the Tower of Shechem heard the
news, they went to the stronghold of the temple of El Berith.
47 Abimelech heard that all the leaders of the Tower of Shechem
were in one place. 48 He and all his men went up on Mount Zalmon. He took an ax in his hand and cut off a tree branch. He put
it on his shoulder and said to his men, "Quickly, do what you have

just seen me do!" 49 So each of his men also cut off a branch and followed Abimelech. They put the branches against the stronghold and set fire to it. All the people of the Tower of Shechem died—about 1,000 men and women.

50 Abimelech moved on to Thebez; he besieged and captured it. 51 There was a fortified tower in the center of the city, so all the men and women, as well as the city's leaders, ran into it and locked the entrance. Then they went up to the roof of the tower. 52 Abimelech came and attacked the tower. When he approached the entrance of the tower to set it on fire, 53 a woman threw an upper millstone down on his head and shattered his skull. 54 He quickly called to the young man who carried his weapons, "Draw your sword and kill me, so they will not say, 'A woman killed him.'" So the young man stabbed him and he died. 55 When the Israelites saw that Abimelech was dead, they went home.

56 God repaid Abimelech for the evil he did to his father by murdering his seventy half brothers. 57 God also repaid the men of Shechem for their evil deeds. The curse spoken by Jotham son of Jerub Baal fell on them.

STABILITY RESTORED

10 After Abimelech's death, Tola son of Puah, grandson of Dodo, from the tribe of Issachar, rose up to deliver Israel. He lived in Shamir in the Ephraimite hill country. 2 He led Israel for twenty-three years, then died and was buried in Shamir.

3 Jair the Gileadite rose up after him; he led Israel for twenty-two years. 4 He had thirty sons who rode on thirty donkeys and possessed thirty cities. To this day these towns are called Havvoth Jair—they are in the land of Gilead. 5 Jair died and was buried in Kamon.

THE LORD'S PATIENCE RUNS SHORT

6 The Israelites again did evil in the LORD's sight. They worshiped the Baals and the Ashtoreths, as well as the gods of Syria, Sidon, Moab, the Ammonites, and the Philistines. They abandoned the LORD and did not worship him. 7 The LORD was furious with Israel and turned them over to the Philistines and Ammonites. 8 They ruthlessly oppressed the Israelites that eighteenth year—that is, all the Israelites living east of the Jordan in Amorite country in Gilead. 9 The Ammonites crossed the Jordan to fight with Judah, Benjamin, and Ephraim. Israel suffered greatly.

10 The Israelites cried out for help to the LORD: "We have sinned against you. We abandoned our God and worshiped the Baals." 11 The LORD said to the Israelites, "Did I not deliver you from Egypt, the Amorites, the Ammonites, the Philistines, 12 the Sidonians, Amalek, and Midian when they oppressed you? You cried out for help to me, and I delivered you from their power. 13 But since you abandoned me and worshiped other gods, I will not deliver you again. 14 Go and cry for help to the gods you have chosen! Let them deliver you from trouble!" 15 But the Israelites said to the LORD, "We have sinned. You do to us as you see fit, but deliver us today!" 16 They threw away the foreign gods they owned and worshiped the LORD. Finally the LORD grew tired of seeing Israel suffer so much.

AN OUTCAST BECOMES A GENERAL

17 The Ammonites assembled and camped in Gilead; the Israelites gathered together and camped in Mizpah. 18 The leaders of Gilead said to one another, "Who is willing to lead the charge against the Ammonites? He will become the leader of all who live in Gilead!"

REFLECT

Why was Jephthah's vow so foolish? Have you ever made a deal like this with God? What does God desire from us more than our vows or promises?

11 Now Jephthah the Gileadite was a brave warrior. His mother was a prostitute, but Gilead was his father. 2 Gilead's wife also gave him sons. When his wife's sons grew up, they made Jephthah leave and said to him, "You are not going to inherit any of our father's wealth, because you are another woman's son." 3 So Jephthah left his half brothers and lived in the land of Tob. Lawless men joined Jephthah's gang and traveled with him.

4 It was some time after this when the Ammonites fought with Israel. 5 When the Ammonites attacked, the leaders of Gilead asked Jephthah to come back from the land of Tob. 6 They said, "Come, be our commander, so we can fight with the Ammonites." 7 Jephthah said to the leaders of Gilead, "But you hated me and made me leave my father's house. Why do you come to me now, when you are in trouble?" 8 The leaders of Gilead said to Jephthah, "That may be true, but now we pledge to you our loyalty. Come with us and fight with the Ammonites. Then you will become the leader of all who live in Gilead." 9 Jephthah said to the leaders of Gilead, "All right. If you take me back to fight with the Ammonites and the LORD gives them to me, I will be your leader." 10 The leaders of Gilead said to Jephthah, "The LORD will judge any grievance you have against us, if we do not do as you say." 11 So Jephthah went with the leaders of Gilead. The people made him their leader and commander. Jephthah repeated the terms of the agreement before the LORD in Mizpah.

JEPHTHAH GIVES A HISTORY LESSON

12 Jephthah sent messengers to the Ammonite king, saying, "Why have you come against me to attack my land?" 13 The Ammonite king said to Jephthah's messengers, "Because Israel stole my land when they came up from Egypt—from the Arnon River in the south to the Jabbok River in the north, and as far west as the Jordan. Now return it peaceably!"

14 Jephthah sent messengers back to the Ammonite king 15 and said to him, "This is what Jephthah says, 'Israel did not steal the land of Moab and the land of the Ammonites. 16 When they left Egypt, Israel traveled through the desert as far as the Red Sea and then came to Kadesh. 17 Israel sent messengers to the king of Edom, saying, "Please allow us to pass through your land." But the king of Edom rejected the request. Israel sent the same request to the king of Moab, but he was unwilling to cooperate. So Israel stayed at Kadesh. 18 Then Israel went through the wilderness and bypassed the land of Edom and the land of Moab. They traveled east of the land of Moab and camped on the other side of the Arnon River; they did not go through Moabite territory (the Arnon was Moab's border). 19 Israel sent messengers to King Sihon, the Amorite king who ruled in Heshbon, and said to him, "Please allow us to

LOVE TO GROW

AN UNLIKELY HERO

JUDGES 11

Kids are fantastically gifted at negotiating. Tell them to go to bed or eat their vegetables and you're guaranteed to get a glimpse of their great powers. Parents or caretakers are in a position of great authority, and kids know that if they want to get their own way, they'll have to persuade or bargain. If mom or dad has already promised a child a special treat, it would be foolish for them to start bargaining for it—their treat is already guaranteed!

Jephthah made a foolish bargain with God. He led God's people into battle against the Ammonites, a people who wrongly attacked Israel (Judg 11:12–28). Jephthah was empowered by the Lord's Spirit (Judg 11:29). He had every reason to trust a coming victory over the Ammonites as well as the plans God intended for him as judge over Israel. But Jephthah was a negotiator.

Instead of trusting God's sovereign plan after Gilead's repentance, Jephthah tried to force God's hand to ensure his leadership. His plea showed a lack of fear of God's authority over his circumstances, and he tested the Lord: "If you really do hand the Ammonites over . . ." (Judg 11:30).

Scripture attests to God's faithfulness in unexpected places and to unexpected people. Though Jephthah was denied his family's inheritance and driven away because he was the son of a prostitute, God raised him up as a judge and great military leader. His vow displayed evidence of syncretistic religion involving human sacrifice and personal power mongering. His foolish decision resulted in the death of his only offspring, a daughter. She, however, displayed unwavering confidence and respect of God's authority, even though her own father had not.

God will always recognize those who recognize His sovereignty.

The Bible records that each year the young women of Israel went out and commemorated the daughter of Jephthah, who honored both God's commands and her father's vow to God (Judg 11:40). God does not bow to the desires of the powerful or to the skilled negotiator. Instead, He desires, and rewards, our faithfulness in difficult circumstances.

The hero in this story does not end up with God's reward or favor, but the unexpected faith of a young woman inspired admiration and celebration from her wayward people.

pass through your land to our land." 20 But Sihon did not trust
Israel to pass through his territory. He assembled his whole
army, camped in Jahaz, and fought with Israel. 21 The LORD God
of Israel handed Sihon and his whole army over to Israel and
they defeated them. Israel took all the land of the Amorites
who lived in that land. 22 They took all the Amorite territory
from the Arnon River on the south to the Jabbok River on the
north, from the desert in the east to the Jordan in the west.
23 Since the LORD God of Israel has driven out the Amorites
before his people Israel, do you think you can just take it from
them? 24 You have the right to take what Chemosh your god
gives you, but we will take the land of all whom the LORD our
God has driven out before us. 25 Are you really better than Balak son of Zippor, king of Moab? Did he dare to quarrel with
Israel? Did he dare to fight with them? 26 Israel has been living in Heshbon and its nearby towns, in Aroer and its nearby
towns, and in all the cities along the Arnon for 300 years! Why
did you not reclaim them during that time? 27 I have not done
you wrong, but you are doing wrong by attacking me. May the
LORD, the Judge, judge this day between the Israelites and the
Ammonites!'" 28 But the Ammonite king disregarded the message sent by Jephthah.

A FOOLISH VOW SPELLS DEATH FOR A DAUGHTER

29 The LORD's Spirit empowered Jephthah. He passed through
Gilead and Manasseh and went to Mizpah in Gilead. From there
he approached the Ammonites. 30 Jephthah made a vow to the
LORD, saying, "If you really do hand the Ammonites over to me,
31 then whoever is the first to come through the doors of my
house to meet me when I return safely from fighting the Ammonites—he will belong to the LORD and I will offer him up as
a burnt sacrifice." 32 Jephthah approached the Ammonites to
fight with them, and the LORD handed them over to him. 33 He
defeated them from Aroer all the way to Minnith—twenty cities in all, even as far as Abel Keramim. He wiped them out! The
Israelites humiliated the Ammonites.

34 When Jephthah came home to Mizpah, there was his daughter hurrying out to meet him, dancing to the rhythm of tambourines. She was his only child; except for her he had no son
or daughter. 35 When he saw her, he ripped his clothes and said,
"Oh no! My daughter! You have completely ruined me! You have
brought me disaster! I made an oath to the LORD, and I cannot
break it." 36 She said to him, "My father, since you made an oath
to the LORD, do to me as you promised. After all, the LORD vindicated you before your enemies, the Ammonites." 37 She then
said to her father, "Please grant me this one wish. For two months
allow me to walk through the hills with my friends and mourn
my virginity." 38 He said, "You may go." He permitted her to leave
for two months. She went with her friends and mourned her virginity as she walked through the hills. 39 After two months she
returned to her father, and he did to her as he had vowed. She
died a virgin. Her tragic death gave rise to a custom in Israel.
40 Every year Israelite women commemorate the daughter of
Jephthah the Gileadite for four days.

CIVIL STRIFE MARS THE VICTORY

12 The Ephraimites assembled and crossed over to Zaphon.
They said to Jephthah, "Why did you go and fight with the
Ammonites without asking us to go with you? We will burn your
house down right over you!"
2 Jephthah said to them, "My people and I were in a struggle
and the Ammonites were oppressing me greatly. I asked for your
help, but you did not deliver me from their power. 3 When I saw
that you were not going to help, I risked my life and advanced
against the Ammonites, and the LORD handed them over to me.
Why have you come up to fight with me today?" 4 Jephthah assembled all the men of Gilead and they fought with Ephraim.
The men of Gilead defeated Ephraim, because the Ephraimites
insulted them, saying, "You Gileadites are refugees in Ephraim,
living within Ephraim's and Manasseh's territory." 5 The Gileadites captured the fords of the Jordan River opposite Ephraim.
Whenever an Ephraimite fugitive said, "Let me cross over," the
men of Gilead asked him, "Are you an Ephraimite?" If he said,
"No," 6 then they said to him, "Say 'Shibboleth!'" If he said, "Sibbo-
leth" (and could not pronounce the word correctly), they grabbed
him and executed him right there at the fords of the Jordan. On
that day 42,000 Ephraimites fell dead.
7 Jephthah led Israel for six years; then he died and was buried in his town in Gilead.

ORDER RESTORED

8 After him Ibzan of Bethlehem led Israel. 9 He had thirty sons.
He arranged for thirty of his daughters to be married outside
his extended family, and he arranged for thirty young women
to be brought from outside as wives for his sons. Ibzan led Israel
for seven years; 10 then he died and was buried in Bethlehem.
11 After him Elon the Zebulunite led Israel for ten years. 12 Then
Elon the Zebulunite died and was buried in Aijalon in the land
of Zebulun.
13 After him Abdon son of Hillel the Pirathonite led Israel.
14 He had forty sons and thirty grandsons who rode on seventy
donkeys. He led Israel for eight years. 15 Then Abdon son of Hillel the Pirathonite died and was buried in Pirathon in the land
of Ephraim, in the hill country of the Amalekites.

SAMSON'S BIRTH

13 The Israelites again did evil in the LORD's sight, so the LORD
handed them over to the Philistines for forty years.
2 There was a man named Manoah from Zorah, from the Danite
tribe. His wife was infertile and childless. 3 The angel of the LORD
appeared to the woman and said to her, "You are infertile and childless, but you will conceive and have a son. 4 Now be careful! Do not
drink wine or beer, and do not eat any food that will make you ritually unclean. 5 Look, you will conceive and have a son. You must
never cut his hair, for the child will be dedicated to God from birth.
He will begin to deliver Israel from the power of the Philistines."
6 The woman went and said to her husband, "A man sent from
God came to me! He looked like God's angel—he was very awesome. I did not ask him where he came from, and he did not tell

me his name. 7 He said to me, 'Look, you will conceive and have a son. So now, do not drink wine or beer and do not eat any food that will make you ritually unclean. For the child will be dedicated to God from birth till the day he dies.'"

8 Manoah prayed to the LORD, "Please, Lord, allow the man sent from God to visit us again, so he can teach us how we should raise the child who will be born." 9 God answered Manoah's prayer. God's angel visited the woman again while she was sitting in the field. But her husband Manoah was not with her. 10 The woman ran at once and told her husband, "Come quickly, the man who visited me the other day has appeared to me!" 11 So Manoah got up and followed his wife. When he met the man, he said to him, "Are you the man who spoke to my wife?" He said, "Yes." 12 Manoah said, "Now, when your announcement comes true, how should the child be raised and what should he do?" 13 The angel of the LORD told Manoah, "Your wife should pay attention to everything I told her. 14 She should not drink anything that the grapevine produces. She must not drink wine or beer, and she must not eat any food that will make her ritually unclean. She should obey everything I commanded her to do." 15 Manoah said to the angel of the LORD, "Please stay here awhile, so we can prepare a young goat for you to eat." 16 The angel of the LORD said to Manoah, "If I stay, I will not eat your food. But if you want to make a burnt sacrifice to the LORD, you should offer it." (He said this because Manoah did not know that he was the angel of the LORD.) 17 Manoah said to the angel of the LORD, "Tell us your name, so we can honor you when your announcement comes true." 18 The angel of the LORD said to him, "You should not ask me my name, because you cannot comprehend it." 19 Manoah took a young goat and a grain offering and offered them on a rock to the LORD. The LORD's messenger did an amazing thing as Manoah and his wife watched. 20 As the flame went up from the altar toward the sky, the angel of the LORD went up in it while Manoah and his wife watched. They fell facedown to the ground.

21 The angel of the LORD did not appear again to Manoah and his wife. After all this happened Manoah realized that the visitor had been the angel of the LORD. 22 Manoah said to his wife, "We will certainly die, because we have seen a supernatural being!" 23 But his wife said to him, "If the LORD wanted to kill us, he would not have accepted the burnt offering and the grain offering from us. He would not have shown us all these things, or have spoken to us like this just now."

24 Manoah's wife gave birth to a son and named him Samson. The child grew and the LORD empowered him. 25 The LORD's Spirit began to control him in Mahaneh Dan between Zorah and Eshtaol.

SAMSON'S UNCONSUMMATED MARRIAGE

14 Samson went down to Timnah, where a Philistine girl caught his eye. 2 When he got home, he told his father and mother, "A Philistine girl in Timnah has caught my eye. Now get her for my wife." 3 But his father and mother said to him, "Certainly you can find a wife among your relatives or among all

our people! You should not have to go and get a wife from the
uncircumcised Philistines." But Samson said to his father, "Get
her for me, because she is the right one for me." 4 Now his father
and mother did not realize this was the LORD's doing, because
he was looking for an opportunity to stir up trouble with the
Philistines (for at that time the Philistines were ruling Israel).
5 Samson went down to Timnah. When he approached the
vineyards of Timnah, he saw a roaring young lion attacking him.
6 The LORD's Spirit empowered him, and he tore the lion in two
with his bare hands as easily as one would tear a young goat. But
he did not tell his father or mother what he had done.
7 Samson continued on down to Timnah and spoke to the girl.
In his opinion, she was just the right one. 8 Some time later,
when he went back to marry her, he turned aside to see the
lion's remains. He saw a swarm of bees in the lion's carcass, as
well as some honey. 9 He scooped it up with his hands and ate it
as he walked along. When he returned to his father and mother,
he offered them some and they ate it. But he did not tell them
he had scooped the honey out of the lion's carcass.
10 Then Samson's father accompanied him to Timnah for the
marriage. Samson hosted a party there, for this was customary
for bridegrooms to do. 11 When the Philistines saw he had no attendants, they gave him thirty groomsmen who kept him company. 12 Samson said to them, "I will give you a riddle. If you really
can solve it during the seven days the party lasts, I will give you
thirty linen robes and thirty sets of clothes. 13 But if you cannot solve it, you will give me thirty linen robes and thirty sets
of clothes." They said to him, "Let us hear your riddle." 14 He said
to them,

"Out of the one who eats came something to eat;
out of the strong one came something sweet."

They could not solve the riddle for three days.
15 On the fourth day they said to Samson's bride, "Trick your
husband into giving the solution to the riddle. If you refuse, we
will burn up you and your father's family. Did you invite us here
to make us poor?" 16 So Samson's bride cried on his shoulder and
said, "You must hate me; you do not love me! You told the young
men a riddle, but you have not told me the solution." He said
to her, "Look, I have not even told my father or mother. Do you
really expect me to tell you?" 17 She cried on his shoulder until
the party was almost over. Finally, on the seventh day, he told her
because she had nagged him so much. Then she told the young
men the solution to the riddle. 18 On the seventh day, before the
sun set, the men of the city said to him,

"What is sweeter than honey?
What is stronger than a lion?"

He said to them,

"If you had not plowed with my heifer,
you would not have solved my riddle!"

19 The LORD's Spirit empowered him. He went down to Ashkelon and killed thirty men. He took their clothes and gave them
to the men who had solved the riddle. He was furious as he went
back home. 20 Samson's bride was then given to his best man.

REFLECT

Even though Samson's capture by the Philistines happened a few chapters later, what happened in chapter 14 that began Samson's tragic story, leading him down a path of destruction?

SAMSON VERSUS THE PHILISTINES

15 Sometime later, during the wheat harvest, Samson took a young goat as a gift and went to visit his bride. He said to her father, "I want to sleep with my bride in her bedroom!" But her father would not let him enter. 2 Her father said, "I really thought you absolutely despised her, so I gave her to your best man. Her younger sister is more attractive than she is. Take her instead!" 3 Samson said to them, "This time I am justified in doing the Philistines harm!" 4 Samson went and captured 300 jackals and got some torches. He tied the jackals in pairs by their tails and then tied a torch to each pair. 5 He lit the torches and set the jackals loose in the Philistines' standing grain. He burned up the grain heaps and the standing grain, as well as the vineyards and olive groves. 6 The Philistines asked, "Who did this?" They were told, "Samson, the Timnite's son-in-law, because the Timnite took Samson's bride and gave her to his best man." So the Philistines went up and burned her and her father. 7 Samson said to them, "Because you did this, I will get revenge against you before I quit fighting." 8 He struck them down and defeated them. Then he went down and lived for a time in the cave in the cliff of Etam.

9 The Philistines went up and invaded Judah. They arrayed themselves for battle in Lehi. 10 The men of Judah said, "Why are you attacking us?" The Philistines said, "We have come up to take Samson prisoner so we can do to him what he has done to us." 11 So 3,000 men of Judah went down to the cave in the cliff of Etam and said to Samson, "Do you not know that the Philistines rule over us? Why have you done this to us?" He said to them, "I have only done to them what they have done to me." 12 They said to him, "We have come down to take you prisoner so we can hand you over to the Philistines." Samson said to them, "Promise me you will not kill me." 13 They said to him, "We promise! We will only take you prisoner and hand you over to them. We promise not to kill you." They tied him up with two brand new ropes and led him up from the cliff. 14 When he arrived in Lehi, the Philistines shouted as they approached him. But the LORD's Spirit empowered him. The ropes around his arms were like flax dissolving in fire, and they melted away from his hands. 15 He happened to see a solid jawbone of a donkey. He grabbed it and struck down 1,000 men. 16 Samson then said,

"With the jawbone of a donkey
I have left them in heaps;
with the jawbone of a donkey
I have struck down a thousand men!"

17 When he finished speaking, he threw the jawbone down and named that place Ramath Lehi.

18 He was very thirsty, so he cried out to the LORD and said, "You have given your servant this great victory. But now must I die of thirst and fall into the hands of these uncircumcised Philistines?" 19 So God split open the basin at Lehi and water flowed out from it. When he took a drink, his strength was restored and he revived. For this reason he named the spring En Hakkore. It remains in Lehi to this very day. 20 Samson led Israel for twenty years during the days of Philistine prominence.

SAMSON'S DOWNFALL

16 Samson went to Gaza. There he saw a prostitute and slept with her. 2 The Gazites were told, "Samson has come here!" So they surrounded the town and hid all night at the city gate, waiting for him to leave. They relaxed all night, thinking, "He will not leave until morning comes; then we will kill him!" 3 Samson spent half the night with the prostitute; then he got up in the middle of the night and left. He grabbed the doors of the city gate, as well as the two posts, and pulled them right off, bar and all. He put them on his shoulders and carried them up to the top of a hill east of Hebron.

4 After this Samson fell in love with a woman named Delilah, who lived in the Sorek Valley. 5 The rulers of the Philistines went up to visit her and said to her, "Trick him! Find out what makes him so strong and how we can subdue him and humiliate him. Each one of us will give you 1,100 silver pieces."

6 So Delilah said to Samson, "Tell me what makes you so strong and how you can be subdued and humiliated." 7 Samson said to her, "If they tie me up with seven fresh bowstrings that have not been dried, I will become weak and be just like any other man." 8 So the rulers of the Philistines brought her seven fresh bowstrings that had not been dried, and she tied him up with them. 9 They hid in the bedroom and then she said to him, "The Philistines are here, Samson!" He snapped the bowstrings as easily as a thread of yarn snaps when it is put close to fire. The secret of his strength was not discovered.

10 Delilah said to Samson, "Look, you deceived me and told me lies! Now tell me how you can be subdued." 11 He said to her, "If they tie me tightly with brand new ropes that have never been used, I will become weak and be just like any other man." 12 So Delilah took new ropes and tied him with them and said to him, "The Philistines are here, Samson!" (The Philistines were hiding in the bedroom.) But he tore the ropes from his arms as if they were a piece of thread.

13 Delilah said to Samson, "Up to now you have deceived me and told me lies. Tell me how you can be subdued." He said to her, "If you weave the seven braids of my hair into the fabric on the loom and secure it with the pin, I will become weak and be like any other man." 14 So she made him go to sleep, wove the seven braids of his hair into the fabric on the loom, fastened it with the pin, and said to him, "The Philistines are here, Samson!" He woke up and tore away the pin of the loom and the fabric.

15 She said to him, "How can you say, 'I love you,' when you will not share your secret with me? Three times you have deceived me and have not told me what makes you so strong." 16 She nagged him every day and pressured him until he was sick to death of it. 17 Finally he told her his secret. He said to her, "My hair has never been cut, for I have been dedicated to God from the time I was conceived. If my head were shaved, my strength would leave me; I would become weak and be just like all other men." 18 When Delilah saw that he had told her his secret, she sent for the rulers of the Philistines, saying, "Come up here again, for he has told me his secret." So the rulers of the Philistines went up to visit her, bringing the silver in their hands.

19 She made him go to sleep on her lap and then called a man in to shave off the seven braids of his hair. She made him vulnerable and his strength left him. 20 She said, "The Philistines are here, Samson!" He woke up and thought, "I will do as I did before and shake myself free." But he did not realize that the LORD had left him. 21 The Philistines captured him and gouged out his eyes. They brought him down to Gaza and bound him in bronze chains. He became a grinder in the prison. 22 His hair began to grow back after it had been shaved off.

SAMSON'S DEATH AND BURIAL

23 The rulers of the Philistines gathered to offer a great sacrifice to Dagon their god and to celebrate. They said, "Our god has handed Samson, our enemy, over to us." 24 When the people saw him, they praised their god, saying, "Our god has handed our enemy over to us, the one who ruined our land and killed so many of us!"

25 When they really started celebrating, they said, "Call for Samson so he can entertain us!" So they summoned Samson from the prison and he entertained them. They made him stand between two pillars. 26 Samson said to the young man who held his hand, "Position me so I can touch the pillars that support the temple. Then I can lean on them." 27 Now the temple was filled with men and women, and all the rulers of the Philistines were there. There were 3,000 men and women on the roof watching Samson entertain. 28 Samson called to the LORD, "O Sovereign LORD, remember me! Strengthen me just one more time, O God, so I can get swift revenge against the Philistines for my two eyes!" 29 Samson took hold of the two middle pillars that supported the temple and he leaned against them, with his right hand on one and his left hand on the other. 30 Samson said, "Let me die with the Philistines!" He pushed hard, and the temple collapsed on the rulers and all the people in it. He killed many more people in his death than he had killed during his life. 31 His brothers and all his family went down and brought him back. They buried him between Zorah and Eshtaol in the tomb of Manoah his father. He had led Israel for twenty years.

MICAH MAKES HIS OWN RELIGION

17 There was a man named Micah from the Ephraimite hill country. 2 He said to his mother, "You know the 1,100 pieces of silver which were stolen from you, about which I heard you pronounce a curse? Look here, I have the silver. I stole it, but now I am giving it back to you." His mother said, "May the LORD reward you, my son!" 3 When he gave back to his mother the 1,100 pieces of silver, his mother said, "I solemnly dedicate this silver to the LORD. It will be for my son's benefit. We will use it to make a carved image and a metal image." 4 When he gave the silver back to his mother, she took 200 pieces of silver to a silversmith, who made them into a carved image and a metal image. She then put them in Micah's house. 5 Now this man Micah owned a shrine. He made an ephod and some personal idols and hired one of his sons to serve as a priest. 6 In those days Israel had no king. Each man did what he considered to be right.

LIFELONG FAITHFULNESS

JUDGES 16

We know the stories all too well: the pastor who embezzled funds, the speaker caught in an affair, or the author accused of plagiarism. Most of us have experienced the disappointment and betrayal of a discredited Christian leader on a personal level.

We wonder at the disgrace of it and reaffirm it could never, would never, happen to us. If we're honest, we must admit that any of these things could happen to any one of us. No one sets out to be an adulterer, a thief, or a liar. Our life's goal is never to throw away the ministry to which we give our lives. We often fail to recognize the seemingly inconsequential choices that move us closer or further away from the heart of Jesus.

Small compromises can lead to significant disobedience.

Before he was born, Samson was set apart for God's purposes. Judges 13 says that God would use Samson to "begin to deliver Israel from the power of the Philistines" (Judg 16:5). Talk about a powerful calling.

As we read through Samson's life, we see a giant chasm between his remarkable physical strength and his devastating moral weakness. I wonder how many people stood in awe of Samson, applauding him for his physical power while completely overlooking his corrupt character.

We do the same thing. We often assume that being busy for Christ means we are privately connected to Christ. We assume results affirm favor or that great talent verifies great character. We cannot measure success only by outward actions. When we do, we begin to neglect the inner commitment to faithfully knowing and obeying God. We begin to depend on our own talents rather than the power of the Holy Spirit.

Samson's life reminds us that it's not what's on the outside that matters. God's call for us is not what we do or how we start, but who we are and how we continue. We must pay attention to the inner life and continue to invite Jesus to transform us on the inside and the outside.

Lifelong faithfulness is a fight. He will be faithful even when you are not, and He will hold on to you as you seek to hold on to Him. As we seek to love God greatly, we must remember the inner life—a yielded will, faithful obedience, and commitment to the Word and ways of God.

MICAH HIRES A PROFESSIONAL

7 There was a young man from Bethlehem in Judah. He was a
Levite who had been temporarily residing among the tribe of
Judah. 8 This man left the town of Bethlehem in Judah to find
another place to live. He came to the Ephraimite hill country
and made his way to Micah's house. 9 Micah said to him, "Where
do you come from?" He replied, "I am a Levite from Bethlehem
in Judah. I am looking for a new place to live." 10 Micah said to
him, "Stay with me. Become my adviser and priest. I will give you
ten pieces of silver per year, plus clothes and food." 11 So the Levite agreed to stay with the man; the young man was like a son
to Micah. 12 Micah paid the Levite; the young man became his
priest and lived in Micah's house. 13 Micah said, "Now I know the
LORD will make me rich, because I have this Levite as my priest."

THE TRIBE OF DAN FINDS AN INHERITANCE

18 In those days Israel had no king. And in those days the Danite tribe was looking for a place to settle, because at that
time they did not yet have a place to call their own among the
tribes of Israel. 2 The Danites sent out from their whole tribe
five representatives, capable men from Zorah and Eshtaol, to
spy out the land and explore it. They said to them, "Go, explore
the land." They came to the Ephraimite hill country and spent
the night at Micah's house. 3 As they approached Micah's house,
they recognized the accent of the young Levite. So they stopped
there and said to him, "Who brought you here? What are you doing in this place? What is your business here?" 4 He told them
what Micah had done for him, saying, "He hired me, and I became his priest." 5 They said to him, "Seek a divine oracle for us,
so we can know if we will be successful on our mission." 6 The
priest said to them, "Go with confidence. The LORD will be with
you on your mission."

7 So the five men journeyed on and arrived in Laish. They noticed that the people there were living securely, like the Sidonians do, undisturbed and unsuspecting. No conqueror was
troubling them in any way. They lived far from the Sidonians
and had no dealings with anyone. 8 When the Danites returned
to their tribe in Zorah and Eshtaol, their kinsmen asked them,
"How did it go?" 9 They said, "Come on, let's attack them, for we
saw their land and it is very good. You seem lethargic, but don't
hesitate to invade and conquer the land. 10 When you invade,
you will encounter unsuspecting people. The land is wide! God
is handing it over to you—a place that lacks nothing on earth!"

11 So 600 Danites, fully armed, set out from Zorah and Eshtaol.
12 They went up and camped in Kiriath Jearim in Judah. (To this
day that place is called Camp of Dan. It is west of Kiriath Jearim.) 13 From there they traveled through the Ephraimite hill
country and arrived at Micah's house. 14 The five men who had
gone to spy out the land of Laish said to their kinsmen, "Do you
realize that inside these houses are an ephod, some personal
idols, a carved image, and a metal image? Decide now what you
want to do." 15 They stopped there, went inside the young Levite's house (which belonged to Micah), and asked him how he
was doing. 16 Meanwhile the 600 Danites, fully armed, stood at

the entrance to the gate. 17 The five men who had gone to spy
out the land broke in and stole the carved image, the ephod,
the personal idols, and the metal image, while the priest was
standing at the entrance to the gate with the 600 fully armed
men. 18 When these men broke into Micah's house and stole the
carved image, the ephod, the personal idols, and the metal image, the priest said to them, "What are you doing?" 19 They said
to him, "Shut up! Put your hand over your mouth and come with
us! You can be our adviser and priest. Wouldn't it be better to be
a priest for a whole Israelite tribe than for just one man's family?" 20 The priest was happy. He took the ephod, the personal
idols, and the carved image and joined the group.

21 They turned and went on their way, but they walked behind
the children, the cattle, and their possessions. 22 After they had
gone a good distance from Micah's house, Micah's neighbors
gathered together and caught up with the Danites. 23 When they
called out to the Danites, the Danites turned around and said to
Micah, "Why have you gathered together?" 24 He said, "You stole
my gods that I made, as well as this priest, and then went away.
What do I have left? How can you have the audacity to say to me,
'What do you want?'" 25 The Danites said to him, "Don't say another word to us, or some very angry men will attack you, and
you and your family will die." 26 The Danites went on their way;
when Micah realized they were too strong to resist, he turned
around and went home.

27 Now the Danites took what Micah had made, as well as his
priest, and came to Laish, where the people were undisturbed
and unsuspecting. They struck them down with the sword and
burned the city. 28 No one came to the rescue because the city
was far from Sidon and they had no dealings with anyone. The
city was in a valley near Beth Rehob. The Danites rebuilt the city
and occupied it. 29 They named it Dan after their ancestor, who
was one of Israel's sons. But the city's name used to be Laish.
30 The Danites worshiped the carved image. Jonathan, descendant of Gershom, son of Moses, and his descendants served as
priests for the tribe of Dan until the time of the exile. 31 They
worshiped Micah's carved image the whole time God's authorized shrine was in Shiloh.

SODOM AND GOMORRAH REVISITED

19 In those days Israel had no king. There was a Levite living
temporarily in the remote region of the Ephraimite hill
country. He acquired a concubine from Bethlehem in Judah.
2 However, she got angry at him and went home to her father's
house in Bethlehem in Judah. When she had been there four
months, 3 her husband came after her, hoping he could convince
her to return. He brought with him his servant and a pair of
donkeys. When she brought him into her father's house and
the girl's father saw him, he greeted him warmly. 4 His father-in-
law, the girl's father, persuaded him to stay with him for three
days, and they ate and drank together, and spent the night there.
5 On the fourth day they woke up early and the Levite got ready
to leave. But the girl's father said to his son-in-law, "Have a bite
to eat for some energy, then you can go." 6 So the two of them

REFLECT

How do the horrifying events surrounding the concubine's death show the spiritual climate of Israel?

sat down and had a meal together. Then the girl's father said to the man, "Why not stay another night and have a good time?" 7 When the man got ready to leave, his father-in-law convinced him to stay another night. 8 He woke up early in the morning on the fifth day so he could leave, but the girl's father said, "Get some energy! Wait until later in the day to leave." So they ate a meal together. 9 When the man got ready to leave with his concubine and his servant, his father-in-law, the girl's father, said to him, "Look! The day is almost over. Stay another night! Since the day is over, stay another night here and have a good time. You can get up early tomorrow and start your trip home." 10 But the man did not want to stay another night. He left and traveled as far as Jebus (that is, Jerusalem). He had with him a pair of saddled donkeys and his concubine.

11 When they got near Jebus, it was getting quite late and the servant said to his master, "Come on, let's stop at this Jebusite city and spend the night in it." 12 But his master said to him, "We should not stop at a foreign city where non-Israelites live. We will travel on to Gibeah." 13 He said to his servant, "Come on, we will go into one of the other towns and spend the night in Gibeah or Ramah." 14 So they traveled on, and the sun went down when they were near Gibeah in the territory of Benjamin. 15 They stopped there and decided to spend the night in Gibeah. They came into the city and sat down in the town square, but no one invited them to spend the night.

16 But then an old man passed by, returning at the end of the day from his work in the field. The man was from the Ephraimite hill country; he was living temporarily in Gibeah. (The residents of the town were Benjaminites.) 17 When he looked up and saw the traveler in the town square, the old man said, "Where are you heading? Where do you come from?" 18 The Levite said to him, "We are traveling from Bethlehem in Judah to the remote region of the Ephraimite hill country. That's where I'm from. I had business in Bethlehem in Judah, but now I'm heading home. But no one has invited me into their home. 19 We have enough straw and grain for our donkeys, and there is enough food and wine for me, your female servant, and the young man who is with your servants. We lack nothing." 20 The old man said, "Everything is just fine. I will take care of all your needs. But don't spend the night in the town square." 21 So he brought him to his house and fed the donkeys. They washed their feet and had a meal.

22 They were having a good time, when suddenly some men of the city, some good-for-nothings, surrounded the house and kept beating on the door. They said to the old man who owned the house, "Send out the man who came to visit you so we can take carnal knowledge of him." 23 The man who owned the house went outside and said to them, "No, my brothers! Don't do this wicked thing! After all, this man is a guest in my house. Don't do such a disgraceful thing! 24 Here are my virgin daughter and my guest's concubine. I will send them out and you can abuse them and do to them whatever you like. But don't do such a disgraceful thing to this man!" 25 The men refused to listen to him, so the Levite grabbed his concubine and made her go outside. They raped her and abused her all night long until morning.

They let her go at dawn. 26 The woman arrived back at daybreak and was sprawled out on the doorstep of the house where her master was staying until it became light. 27 When her master got up in the morning, opened the doors of the house, and went outside to start on his journey, there was the woman, his concubine, sprawled out on the doorstep of the house with her hands on the threshold. 28 He said to her, "Get up, let's leave." But there was no response. He put her on the donkey and went home. 29 When he got home, he took a knife, grasped his concubine, and carved her up into twelve pieces. Then he sent the pieces throughout Israel. 30 Everyone who saw the sight said, "Nothing like this has happened or been witnessed during the entire time since the Israelites left the land of Egypt! Take careful note of it! Discuss it and speak!"

CIVIL WAR BREAKS OUT

20 All the Israelites from Dan to Beer Sheba and from the land of Gilead left their homes and assembled together before the LORD at Mizpah. 2 The leaders of all the people from all the tribes of Israel took their places in the assembly of God's people, which numbered 400,000 sword-wielding foot soldiers. 3 The Benjaminites heard that the Israelites had gone up to Mizpah. Then the Israelites said, "Explain how this wicked thing happened!" 4 The Levite, the husband of the murdered woman, spoke up, "I and my concubine stopped in Gibeah in the territory of Benjamin to spend the night. 5 The leaders of Gibeah attacked me and at night surrounded the house where I was staying. They wanted to kill me; instead they abused my concubine so badly that she died. 6 I took hold of my concubine and carved her up and sent the pieces throughout the territory occupied by Israel, because they committed such an unthinkable atrocity in Israel. 7 All you Israelites, make a decision here!"

8 All Israel rose up in unison and said, "Not one of us will go home! Not one of us will return to his house! 9 Now this is what we will do to Gibeah: We will attack the city as the lot dictates. 10 We will take ten of every group of a hundred men from all the tribes of Israel (and a hundred of every group of a thousand, and a thousand of every group of ten thousand) to get supplies for the army. When they arrive in Gibeah of Benjamin, they will punish them for the atrocity that they committed in Israel." 11 So all the men of Israel gathered together at the city as allies.

12 The tribes of Israel sent men throughout the tribe of Benjamin, saying, "How could such a wicked thing take place? 13 Now, hand over the good-for-nothings in Gibeah so we can execute them and purge Israel of wickedness." But the Benjaminites refused to listen to their Israelite brothers. 14 The Benjaminites came from their cities and assembled at Gibeah to make war against the Israelites. 15 That day the Benjaminites mustered from their cities 26,000 sword-wielding soldiers, besides 700 well-trained soldiers from Gibeah. 16 Among this army were 700 specially trained left-handed soldiers. Each one could sling a stone and hit even the smallest target. 17 The men of Israel (not counting Benjamin) had mustered 400,000 sword-wielding soldiers, every one an experienced warrior.

18 The Israelites went up to Bethel and asked God, "Who should lead the charge against the Benjaminites?" The LORD said, "Judah should lead." 19 The Israelites got up the next morning and moved against Gibeah. 20 The men of Israel marched out to fight Benjamin; they arranged their battle lines against Gibeah. 21 The Benjaminites attacked from Gibeah and struck down 22,000 Israelites that day.

22 The Israelite army took heart and once more arranged their battle lines, in the same place where they had taken their positions the day before. 23 The Israelites went up and wept before the LORD until evening. They asked the LORD, "Should we again march out to fight the Benjaminites, our brothers?" The LORD said, "Attack them." 24 So the Israelites marched toward the Benjaminites the next day. 25 The Benjaminites again attacked them from Gibeah and struck down 18,000 sword-wielding Israelite soldiers.

26 So all the Israelites, the whole army, went up to Bethel. They wept and sat there before the LORD; they did not eat anything that day until evening. They offered up burnt sacrifices and tokens of peace to the LORD. 27 The Israelites asked the LORD (for the ark of God's covenant was there in those days; 28 Phinehas son of Eleazar, son of Aaron, was serving the LORD in those days), "Should we once more march out to fight the Benjaminites our brothers, or should we quit?" The LORD said, "Attack, for tomorrow I will hand them over to you."

29 So Israel hid men in ambush outside Gibeah. 30 The Israelites attacked the Benjaminites the next day; they took their positions against Gibeah just as they had done before. 31 The Benjaminites attacked the army, leaving the city unguarded. They began to strike down their enemy just as they had done before. On the main roads (one leads to Bethel, the other to Gibeah) and in the field, they struck down about thirty Israelites. 32 Then the Benjaminites said, "They are defeated just as before." But the Israelites said, "Let's retreat and lure them away from the city into the main roads." 33 All the men of Israel got up from their places and took their positions at Baal Tamar, while the Israelites hiding in ambush jumped out of their places west of Gibeah. 34 Then 10,000 men, well-trained soldiers from all Israel, made a frontal assault against Gibeah; the battle was fierce. But the Benjaminites did not realize that disaster was at their doorstep. 35 The LORD annihilated Benjamin before Israel; the Israelites struck down that day 25,100 sword-wielding Benjaminites. 36 Then the Benjaminites saw they were defeated.

The Israelites retreated before Benjamin, because they had confidence in the men they had hidden in ambush outside Gibeah. 37 The men hiding in ambush made a mad dash to Gibeah. They attacked and put the sword to the entire city. 38 The Israelites and the men hiding in ambush had arranged a signal. When the men hiding in ambush sent up a smoke signal from the city, 39 the Israelites counterattacked. Benjamin had begun to strike down the Israelites; they struck down about thirty men. They said, "There's no doubt about it! They are totally defeated as in the earlier battle." 40 But when the signal, a pillar of smoke, began to rise up from the city, the Benjaminites

turned around and saw the whole city going up in a cloud of
smoke that rose high into the sky. 41 When the Israelites turned
around, the Benjaminites panicked because they could see
that disaster was on their doorstep. 42 They retreated before
the Israelites, taking the road to the wilderness. But the battle overtook them as men from the surrounding cities struck
them down. 43 They surrounded the Benjaminites, chased them
from Nohah, and annihilated them all the way to a spot east
of Geba. 44 So 18,000 Benjaminites, all of them capable warriors, fell dead. 45 The rest turned and ran toward the wilderness, heading toward the cliff of Rimmon. But the Israelites
caught 5,000 of them on the main roads. They stayed right on
their heels all the way to Gidom and struck down 2,000 more.
46 That day 25,000 sword-wielding Benjaminites fell in battle,
all of them capable warriors. 47 But 600 survivors turned and
ran away to the wilderness, to the cliff of Rimmon. They stayed
there four months. 48 The Israelites returned to the Benjaminite towns and put the sword to them. They wiped out the cities, the animals, and everything they could find. They set fire
to every city in their path.

SIX HUNDRED BRIDES FOR SIX HUNDRED BROTHERS

21 The Israelites had taken an oath in Mizpah, saying, "Not
one of us will allow his daughter to marry a Benjaminite."
2 So the people came to Bethel and sat there before God until
evening, weeping loudly and uncontrollably. 3 They said, "Why, O
LORD God of Israel, has this happened in Israel? An entire tribe
has disappeared from Israel today!"

4 The next morning the people got up early and built an altar
there. They offered up burnt sacrifices and tokens of peace. 5 The
Israelites asked, "Who from all the Israelite tribes has not assembled before the LORD?" They had made a solemn oath that
whoever did not assemble before the LORD at Mizpah must certainly be executed. 6 The Israelites regretted what had happened
to their brother Benjamin. They said, "Today we cut off an entire tribe from Israel! 7 How can we find wives for those who are
left? After all, we took an oath in the LORD's name not to give
them our daughters as wives." 8 So they asked, "Who from all the
Israelite tribes did not assemble before the LORD at Mizpah?"
Now it just so happened no one from Jabesh Gilead had come
to the gathering. 9 When they took roll call, they noticed none of
the inhabitants of Jabesh Gilead were there. 10 So the assembly
sent 12,000 capable warriors against Jabesh Gilead. They commanded them, "Go and kill with your swords the inhabitants
of Jabesh Gilead, including the women and little children. 11 Do
this: Exterminate every male, as well as every woman who has
experienced a man's bed. But spare the lives of any virgins." So
they did as instructed. 12 They found among the inhabitants of
Jabesh Gilead 400 young girls who were virgins who had never
been intimate with a man in bed. They brought them back to
the camp at Shiloh in the land of Canaan.

13 The entire assembly sent messengers to the Benjaminites at
the cliff of Rimmon and assured them they would not be harmed.
14 The Benjaminites returned at that time, and the Israelites

gave to them the women they had spared from Jabesh Gilead.
But there were not enough to go around.
15 The people regretted what had happened to Benjamin because the LORD had weakened the Israelite tribes. 16 The leaders of the assembly said, "How can we find wives for those who
are left? After all, the Benjaminite women have been wiped out.
17 The remnant of Benjamin must be preserved. An entire Israelite tribe should not be wiped out. 18 But we can't allow our
daughters to marry them, for the Israelites took an oath, saying, 'Whoever gives a woman to a Benjaminite will be destroyed.'
19 However, there is an annual festival to the LORD in Shiloh,
which is north of Bethel (east of the main road that goes up
from Bethel to Shechem) and south of Lebonah." 20 So they commanded the Benjaminites, "Go hide in the vineyards, 21 and keep
your eyes open. When you see the daughters of Shiloh coming out to dance in the celebration, jump out from the vineyards. Each one of you, catch yourself a wife from among the
daughters of Shiloh and then go home to the land of Benjamin.
22 When their fathers or brothers come and protest to us, we'll
say to them, 'Do us a favor and let them be, for we could not
get each one a wife through battle. Don't worry about breaking
your oath! You would only be guilty if you had voluntarily given
them wives.'"
23 The Benjaminites did as instructed. They abducted 200 of the
dancing girls to be their wives. They went home to their own territory, rebuilt their cities, and settled down. 24 Then the Israelites
dispersed from there to their respective tribal and clan territories. Each went from there to his own property. 25 In those days
Israel had no king. Each man did what he considered to be right.

REFLECT

In the time of the judges, everyone in Israel did whatever he or she thought was right. Why is following one's own "truth" so dangerous? What truth should we follow?

May the LORD be praised because He has not left you without a guardian today

MEMORY VERSE

The village women said to Naomi, "May the LORD be praised because he has not left you without a guardian today! May he become famous in Israel!"

Ruth 4:14

INTRODUCTION

God's Goodness

"God is good, but is He good to me?" The Book of Ruth poses this question through the story of a widow and her widowed daughter-in-law. God used this unlikely pair, in a seemingly impossible circumstance, to continue bringing about His covenant promises. They may not have always been able to perceive it, but God overwhelmed Naomi and Ruth with His goodness and faithfulness. His lovingkindness and covenant faithfulness are woven throughout the story of Ruth.

Ruth is a historical narrative told as a personal story. The author included all kinds of literary devices throughout the narrative, including foil characters, foreshadowing, symbolism, and irony. Ruth follows a classic literary structure, complete with an opening exposition, conflict, rising action, climax, falling action, resolution, and conclusion. Its construction also follows a loose chiastic structure in which early sections are mirrored in later chapters.

While the author and date of its writing are uncertain, the text in Ruth clearly states that the events took place during the time of judges. There is evidence that Ruth was written during Solomon's reign, sometimes regarded as the Golden Age of Hebrew writing. The genealogy of David included at the end of Ruth indicates that the book was probably written sometime after David became king of Israel.

There are many ways that Ruth encourages us to love God greatly. It displays God's goodness to Naomi, even in the depths of her bitterness and unbelief. It shows God's creative work and His sovereign hand in the story of Boaz and Ruth. Ruth is an overwhelming example of God's redemptive work. While He may allow suffering and pain for a time, God is ever-present, visiting His people, meeting their needs, and redeeming their circumstances to the fullest extent.

South Africa

TOP SPOKEN LANGUAGES
Afrikaans and English
POPULATION
58,425,000
UNREACHED POPULATION
971,000
PROFESSING CHRISTIANS
77.0%

Velia's Home

Say a Prayer Today

Please pray for Velia and Jessica and their relationship to grow closer to one another and to be an encouragement to others.

HISTORY BIT

The first missionary to South Africa, a man named Georg Schmidt, arrived in Table Bay in July 1737. He established a mission station for the Hottentot people and shared the gospel, marking the beginnings of Protestant missionary activity in South Africa.*

Source Information:
https://joshuaproject.net/countries/SF
*David B. Barrett, *World Christian Encyclopedia*, South Africa (New York, NY: Oxford University Press, 1982), 622.

VELIA'S STORY

I love the story of Ruth and Naomi. I've always been encouraged by the love Ruth had for Naomi and by her commitment not to leave her mother-in-law. I would have loved to be a Ruth to someone in my life. Unfortunately, I did not have a good relationship with my mother or my mother-in-law. Thankfully, God, in His goodness, gave me another opportunity for this special type of relationship.

After Jessica married my son, our relationship was rocky at best. We never got along. I was heartbroken because as much as I wanted to get to know her, our relationship was strained. After losing her first child at only twenty-five days old, Jessica became pregnant again. Things started to change, and we began to put aside our differences and grow closer.

When my grandson was four months old, Jessica came to me for encouragement in a difficult season. We spent a lot of time talking, and I kept encouraging her to turn to the Lord and ask Him for help. One Sunday afternoon, Jessica phoned and asked if my husband and I would go to church with her, our son, and our grandson. Though my husband and I had not been to church in years, we joined them.

Jessica changed our lives that day. My husband gave his life to the Lord, and both he and I were baptized that next Easter Sunday.

While I was not able to be a Ruth to my own mother-in-law, Jessica is a Ruth to me. God's goodness is evident throughout our relationship as He continues to draw us closer and unite us through His love. The story of Ruth is such an inspiration and encouragement to our family, constantly reminding us of the wonderful message of God's goodness.

4 WEEK READING PLAN

LOVE HIS WORD

MONDAY	TUESDAY	WEDNESDAY	THURSDAY	FRIDAY
Ruth 1:1-3	Ruth 1:4-5	Ruth 1:6-14	Ruth 1:15-18	Ruth 1:19-22
SOAP Ruth 1:1-3	SOAP Ruth 1:4-5	SOAP Ruth 1:8	SOAP Ruth 1:16-17	SOAP Ruth 1:20-21
Ruth 2:1-3	Ruth 2:4-7	Ruth 2:8-13	Ruth 2:14-17	Ruth 2:18-23
SOAP Ruth 2:3	SOAP Ruth 2:7	SOAP Ruth 2:11-12	SOAP Ruth 2:17	SOAP Ruth 2:20
Ruth 3:1-5	Ruth 3:6-9	Ruth 3:10-11	Ruth 3:12-13	Ruth 3:14-18
SOAP Ruth 3:3-4	SOAP Ruth 3:8-9	SOAP Ruth 3:11	SOAP Ruth 3:12-13	SOAP Ruth 3:14-15
Ruth 4:1-6	Ruth 4:7-10	Ruth 4:11-12	Ruth 4:13-16	Ruth 4:17-22
SOAP Ruth 4:5-6	SOAP Ruth 4:9-10	SOAP Ruth 4:11-12	SOAP Ruth 4:14	SOAP Ruth 4:17

A FAMILY TRAGEDY: FAMINE AND DEATH

1 During the time of the judges, there was a famine in the land of
Judah. So a man from Bethlehem in Judah went to live as a resident foreigner in the region of Moab, along with his wife and two
sons. 2 (Now the man's name was Elimelech, his wife was Naomi,
and his two sons were Mahlon and Kilion. They were of the clan
of Ephrath from Bethlehem in Judah.) They entered the region of
Moab and settled there. 3 Sometime later Naomi's husband Elimelech died, so she and her two sons were left alone. 4 Both her sons
married Moabite women. (One was named Orpah and the other
Ruth.) And they continued to live there about ten years. 5 Then
Naomi's two sons, Mahlon and Kilion, also died. So the woman
was left all alone—bereaved of her two children as well as her husband! 6 So she decided to return home from the region of Moab,
accompanied by her daughters-in-law, because while she was living in Moab she had heard that the LORD had shown concern for
his people, reversing the famine by providing abundant crops.

REFLECT

What do the first few verses tell us about the setting of the Book of Ruth? How are these aspects significant to the rest of the story?

RUTH RETURNS WITH NAOMI

7 Now as she and her two daughters-in-law began to leave the
place where she had been living to return to the land of Judah,
8 Naomi said to her two daughters-in-law, "Listen to me! Each of
you should return to your mother's home. May the LORD show
you the same kind of devotion that you have shown to your deceased husbands and to me. 9 May the LORD enable each of you
to find security in the home of a new husband." Then she kissed
them goodbye, and they wept loudly. 10 But they said to her, "No!
We will return with you to your people."

11 But Naomi replied, "Go back home, my daughters! There is no
reason for you to return to Judah with me. I am no longer capable
of giving birth to sons who might become your husbands! 12 Go
back home, my daughters! For I am too old to get married again.
Even if I thought that there was hope that I could get married
tonight and conceive sons, 13 surely you would not want to wait
until they were old enough to marry. Surely you would not remain unmarried all that time! No, my daughters, you must not
return with me. For my intense suffering is too much for you to
bear. For the LORD is afflicting me!"

14 Again they wept loudly. Then Orpah kissed her mother-in-law
goodbye, but Ruth clung tightly to her. 15 So Naomi said, "Look,
your sister-in-law is returning to her people and to her god. Follow your sister-in-law back home!" 16 But Ruth replied,

"Stop urging me to abandon you!
For wherever you go, I will go.
Wherever you live, I will live.
Your people will become my people,
and your God will become my God.
17 Wherever you die, I will die—and there I will be buried.
May the LORD punish me severely if I do not keep my promise!
Only death will be able to separate me from you!"

18 When Naomi realized that Ruth was determined to go with
her, she stopped trying to dissuade her. 19 So the two of them
journeyed together until they arrived in Bethlehem.

LOVE TO GROW

IS HE GOOD TO ME?

RUTH 1

Naomi knew God was sovereign; she returned to Bethlehem because the Lord had provided food for His people (Ruth 1:6). She knew God was good; she believed He would provide husbands for her daughters-in-law (Ruth 1:9). But she didn't believe He was good to her; all she saw and felt was God's affliction on her (Ruth 1:13).

Naomi, whose name means "my delight," told the women of the city to call her Mara, meaning "bitter." Her statement shows the disconnect between her knowledge of God's character and her disillusionment at how her life was turning out.

The names Naomi used for God in verses 20–21 show us how convinced she was of God's sovereignty. It's as if Naomi is saying, "Call me Bitter because the One who is sovereign over all has treated me harshly. I left full, but Yahweh has not been with me and has ignored my need. Why do you call me Naomi, seeing that the God who is all powerful has caused me to suffer?"

There is little more difficult than believing that the God who you know is for you seems to be acting for your destruction. Naomi knew God was for her, but she felt His actions communicated He was leading her toward destruction. Have you ever felt this way? I certainly have.

Verse 22 reveals there was more to the story: "Now they arrived in Bethlehem at the beginning of the barley harvest." Though things seemed bleak for Naomi, the timing of her return to Bethlehem was not a coincidence. It reminded the Israelite, as it does for us today, that God is always with us, working for our good and answering our prayers, even though we may not see Him.

He is sovereign. He is good. He is good to you.

Maybe today His goodness is unnoticeable. Maybe today God's goodness is in a work that you won't see or recognize for years.

Even when we can't see the end of the story, we can trust in His goodness. Look for signs of it in the lives of those who, like Naomi, are suffering a time of doubt and pain. Naomi's story shows us that God is always working for our good and for His glory, whether or not we see it today.

He is good. We can believe in His goodness. We can trust His character.

NAOMI AND RUTH ARRIVE IN BETHLEHEM

When they entered Bethlehem, the whole village was excited
about their arrival. The women of the village said, "Can this be
Naomi?" 20 But she replied to them, "Don't call me 'Naomi'! Call
me 'Mara' because the Sovereign One has treated me very harshly.
21 I left here full, but the LORD has caused me to return empty-handed. Why do you call me 'Naomi,' seeing that the LORD has
opposed me, and the Sovereign One has caused me to suffer?"
22 So Naomi returned, accompanied by her Moabite daughter-in-
law Ruth, who came back with her from the region of Moab. (Now
they arrived in Bethlehem at the beginning of the barley harvest.)

RUTH WORKS IN THE FIELD OF BOAZ

2 Now Naomi had a relative on her husband's side of the family named Boaz. He was a wealthy, prominent man from the
clan of Elimelech. 2 One day Ruth the Moabite said to Naomi,
"Let me go to the fields so I can gather grain behind whoever
permits me to do so." Naomi replied, "You may go, my daughter." 3 So Ruth went and gathered grain in the fields behind the
harvesters. Now she just happened to end up in the portion of
the field belonging to Boaz, who was from the clan of Elimelech.

BOAZ AND RUTH MEET

4 Now at that very moment, Boaz arrived from Bethlehem and
greeted the harvesters, "May the LORD be with you!" They replied,
"May the LORD bless you!" 5 Boaz asked his servant in charge of the
harvesters, "To whom does this young woman belong?" 6 The servant in charge of the harvesters replied, "She's the young Moabite
woman who came back with Naomi from the region of Moab. 7 She
asked, 'May I follow the harvesters and gather grain among the bundles?' Since she arrived she has been working hard from this morning until now—except for sitting in the resting hut a short time."
8 So Boaz said to Ruth, "Listen carefully, my dear! Do not leave
to gather grain in another field. You need not go beyond the
limits of this field. You may go along beside my female workers.
9 Take note of the field where the men are harvesting and follow behind with the female workers. I will tell the men to leave
you alone. When you are thirsty, you may go to the water jars
and drink some of the water the servants draw."
10 Ruth knelt before him with her forehead to the ground and
said to him, "Why are you so kind and so attentive to me, even
though I am a foreigner?" 11 Boaz replied to her, "I have been
given a full report of all that you have done for your mother-in-
law following the death of your husband—how you left your father and your mother, as well as your homeland, and came to
live among people you did not know previously. 12 May the LORD
reward your efforts! May your acts of kindness be repaid fully
by the LORD God of Israel, from whom you have sought protection." 13 She said, "You really are being kind to me, sir, for you
have reassured and encouraged me, your servant, even though
I will never be like one of your servants."
14 Later during the mealtime Boaz said to her, "Come here and
have some food! Dip your bread in the vinegar." So she sat down
beside the harvesters. Then he handed her some roasted grain.

REFLECT

In what ways do Naomi's words not line up? When have you experienced a time when what you knew to be true about God did not line up with what it appeared He was doing?

REFLECT

The author says Ruth "just happened to end up" (2:3) in Boaz's field. Did Ruth really "happen" to end up in this field? How do you see God's sovereignty playing a part in the story so far?

She ate until she was full and saved the rest. 15 When she got up
to gather grain, Boaz told his male servants, "Let her gather grain
even among the bundles. Don't chase her off! 16 Make sure you
pull out ears of grain for her and drop them so she can gather
them up. Don't tell her not to!" 17 So she gathered grain in the
field until evening. When she threshed what she had gathered,
it came to about thirty pounds of barley.

RUTH RETURNS TO NAOMI

18 She carried it back to town, and her mother-in-law saw how
much grain she had gathered. Then Ruth gave her the roasted
grain she had saved from mealtime. 19 Her mother-in-law asked
her, "Where did you gather grain today? Where did you work?
May the one who took notice of you be rewarded!" So Ruth told
her mother-in-law with whom she had worked. She said, "The
name of the man with whom I worked today is Boaz." 20 Naomi
said to her daughter-in-law, "May he be rewarded by the LORD
because he has shown loyalty to the living on behalf of the dead!"
Then Naomi said to her, "This man is a close relative of ours; he
is our guardian." 21 Ruth the Moabite replied, "He even told me,
'You may go along beside my servants until they have finished
gathering all my harvest!'" 22 Naomi then said to her daughter-
in-law Ruth, "It is good, my daughter, that you should go out to
work with his female servants. That way you will not be harmed,
which could happen in another field." 23 So Ruth worked beside
Boaz's female servants, gathering grain until the end of the barley harvest as well as the wheat harvest. After that she stayed
home with her mother-in-law.

NAOMI INSTRUCTS RUTH

3 At that time, Naomi, her mother-in-law, said to her, "My
daughter, I must find a home for you so you will be secure.
2 Now Boaz, with whose female servants you worked, is our close
relative. Look, tonight he is winnowing barley at the threshing
floor. 3 So bathe yourself, rub on some perfumed oil, and get
dressed up. Then go down to the threshing floor. But don't let
the man know you're there until he finishes his meal. 4 When he
gets ready to go to sleep, take careful notice of the place where
he lies down. Then go, uncover his legs, and lie down beside him.
He will tell you what you should do." 5 Ruth replied to Naomi, "I
will do everything you have told me to do."

RUTH VISITS BOAZ

6 So she went down to the threshing floor and did everything
her mother-in-law had instructed her to do. 7 When Boaz had
finished his meal and was feeling satisfied, he lay down to sleep
at the far end of the grain heap. Then Ruth crept up quietly, uncovered his legs, and lay down beside him. 8 In the middle of the
night he was startled and turned over. Now he saw a woman lying beside him! 9 He said, "Who are you?" She replied, "I am Ruth,
your servant. Marry your servant, for you are a guardian of the
family interests." 10 He said, "May you be rewarded by the LORD,
my dear! This act of devotion is greater than what you did before.
For you have not sought to marry one of the young men, whether

REFLECT

How do Boaz's actions the night Ruth visited him prove that he was a man of noble character?

rich or poor. 11 Now, my dear, don't worry! I intend to do for you
everything you propose, for everyone in the village knows that
you are a worthy woman. 12 Now yes, it is true that I am a guardian, but there is another guardian who is a closer relative than
I am. 13 Remain here tonight. Then in the morning, if he agrees
to marry you, fine, let him do so. But if he does not want to do
so, I promise, as surely as the LORD lives, to marry you. Sleep
here until morning." 14 So she slept beside him until morning.
She woke up while it was still dark. Boaz thought, "No one must
know that a woman visited the threshing floor." 15 Then he said,
"Hold out the shawl you are wearing and grip it tightly." As she
held it tightly, he measured out about sixty pounds of barley
into the shawl and put it on her shoulders. Then he went into
town, 16 and she returned to her mother-in-law.

RUTH RETURNS TO NAOMI

When Ruth returned to her mother-in-law, Naomi asked, "How
did things turn out for you, my daughter?" Ruth told her about
all the man had done for her. 17 She said, "He gave me these sixty
pounds of barley, for he said to me, 'Do not go to your mother-in-
law empty-handed.'" 18 Then Naomi said, "Stay put, my daughter,
until you know how the matter turns out. For the man will not
rest until he has taken care of the matter today."

BOAZ SETTLES THE MATTER

4 Now Boaz went up to the village gate and sat there. Then along
came the guardian whom Boaz had mentioned to Ruth. Boaz
said, "Come here, what's-your-name, and sit down." So he came
and sat down. 2 Boaz chose ten of the village leaders and said, "Sit
down here!" So they sat down. 3 Then Boaz said to the guardian,
"Naomi, who has returned from the region of Moab, is selling
the portion of land that belongs to our relative Elimelech. 4 So
I am legally informing you: Acquire it before those sitting here
and before the leaders of my people. If you want to exercise your
right to redeem it, then do so. But if not, then tell me so I will
know. For you possess the first option to redeem it; I am next
in line after you." He replied, "I will redeem it." 5 Then Boaz said,
"When you acquire the field from Naomi, you must also acquire
Ruth the Moabite, the wife of our deceased relative, in order to
preserve his family name by raising up a descendant who will
inherit his property." 6 The guardian said, "Then I am unable to
redeem it, for I would ruin my own inheritance in that case. You
may exercise my redemption option, for I am unable to redeem
it." 7 (Now this used to be the customary way to finalize a transaction involving redemption in Israel: A man would remove his
sandal and give it to the other party. This was a legally binding
act in Israel.) 8 So the guardian said to Boaz, "You may acquire
it," and he removed his sandal. 9 Then Boaz said to the leaders
and all the people, "You are witnesses today that I have acquired
from Naomi all that belonged to Elimelech, Kilion, and Mahlon.
10 I have also acquired Ruth the Moabite, the wife of Mahlon, as
my wife to raise up a descendant who will inherit his property
so the name of the deceased might not disappear from among
his relatives and from his village. You are witnesses today." 11 All

CHALLENGE

Boaz goes to great lengths to redeem Ruth and Naomi. He is wise and discerning as he interacts with their other relative. How is Boaz a type of Christ in this story?

LOVE TO GROW

HAPPILY EVER AFTER

RUTH 4

The Book of Ruth has a unique ending. The story of Ruth ends with Ruth living happily ever after with Boaz, but the book itself ends with a genealogy.

Most of us don't like reading biblical genealogies. We often skim over them or skip them all together. They are usually filled with names difficult to pronounce and people we have never heard of. Genealogies are important. If they weren't, God would not have included so many of them in Scripture.

Genealogies show us how God used ordinary people for His extraordinary work. Naomi, Ruth, and Boaz are part of a much larger story, one guided by the hand of God to bring about the coming of the Savior. We see Him accomplish this by using people like Ruth, with a common life, and like Boaz, a field owner who lived in a small, insignificant town like Bethlehem.

God used what we might deem as insignificant and humble to bring about the extraordinary.

What is more extraordinary than the true Kinsman-Redeemer being born to the undistinguished descendants of Ruth and Boaz?

Genealogies show that we belong. When you study your own genealogy, you will quickly find out that you belong to a family with a heritage and to a certain culture and ethnicity. When we trust in Jesus, we gain the unearned privilege of entry into the family of God with all its rights, privileges, and inheritance. We receive a heritage rich in grace, mercy, forgiveness, and love.

The Bible's genealogies make it a point to reveal the grace and mercy of God. They show how God uses imperfect people for His perfect plan. In Matthew 1 the genealogy of Jesus includes a list of people who made mistakes: Jacob, a liar and a thief; Rahab, a former prostitute; and David, an adulterer and murderer. God brought the Messiah through this line of misfits. There are no perfect people, yet God uses us and our ordinary lives to bring about His kingdom work.

Continue in your faithfulness to the calling God has for you no matter how ordinary you may feel it is. You are part of a much larger story: the story of the kingdom of God.

the people who were at the gate and the elders replied, "We are
witnesses. May the LORD make the woman who is entering your
home like Rachel and Leah, both of whom built up the house
of Israel! May you prosper in Ephrathah and become famous
in Bethlehem. 12 May your family become like the family of Perez—whom Tamar bore to Judah—through the descendants the
LORD gives you by this young woman."

REFLECT

While the book is named after Ruth, how do these final verses express that the story was really about Naomi?

A GRANDSON IS BORN TO NAOMI

13 So Boaz married Ruth and slept with her. The LORD enabled
her to conceive and she gave birth to a son. 14 The village wom-
en said to Naomi, "May the LORD be praised because he has not
left you without a guardian today! May he become famous in
Israel! 15 He will encourage you and provide for you when you
are old, for your daughter-in-law, who loves you, has given him
birth. She is better to you than seven sons!" 16 Naomi took the
child and placed him on her lap; she became his caregiver. 17 The
neighbor women gave him a name, saying, "A son has been born
to Naomi." They named him Obed. Now he became the father
of Jesse—David's father.

EPILOGUE: OBED IN THE GENEALOGY OF DAVID

18 These are the descendants of Perez: Perez was the father of
Hezron, 19 Hezron was the father of Ram, Ram was the father
of Amminadab, 20 Amminadab was the father of Nachshon,
Nachshon was the father of Salmah, 21 Salmon was the father
of Boaz, Boaz was the father of Obed, 22 Obed was the father of
Jesse, and Jesse was the father of David.

He watches over
His holy ones,
but the wicked are
made speechless in
the darkness
for it is not by
one's own
strength
that one prevails.

MEMORY VERSE

"He watches over his holy ones, but the wicked are made speechless in the darkness, for it is not by one's own strength that one prevails."

1 Samuel 2:9

1 Samuel

INTRODUCTION

God's Providence

From answering the prayer of a barren woman to raising up a king after His own heart, God displays His providence for His people throughout the books of 1 and 2 Samuel. Despite the rebellious nature of the nation of Israel, God provided for them.

First Samuel is a historical narrative that chronicles the lives of three main characters: Samuel, Saul, and David. Samuel is the last judge of Israel, Saul is the first king, and David is the king after God's own heart. The Israelites pleaded for a king and God gave them Saul, a ruthless, wicked king who did not follow God. However, God provided exactly what the people needed through David, a young man with a rural upbringing from a family with little influence. David was a shepherd who would guide the people back to their true King.

First and 2 Samuel were originally one book called, "The Book of Samuel" in the Hebrew Bible. Around 150 B.C. these books were translated from the original Hebrew into Greek and combined with 1 and 2 Kings. These writings made up the history of the Israelite monarchy. They were later divided into the four books we have today. There is evidence that Samuel wrote the first sections of the book while the prophet Nathan and the seer Gad wrote the remaining portions. Later editors might also account for the additions regarding the events, which occurred after the deaths of these three authors. The authors of 1 and 2 Samuel recorded their events as they experienced them firsthand. It is believed that the events in 1 Samuel occurred between 1100 and 1000 B.C.

First Samuel is a book of history that gives a faithful record of the events that occurred in Israel at the establishment of the monarchy. However, this book provides a great deal of insight into the character of God. God provided for His people by meeting their most significant needs. He established a kingdom and a family line which would ultimately usher in the life of His Son, Jesus Christ, the eternal King, who would meet the most significant need of the world: salvation. We can love God greatly, resting in the truth that He meets our needs, no matter how small, urgent, or unexpected.

Slovakia

OFFICIAL LANGUAGE
Slovak
POPULATION
5,400,000
UNREACHED POPULATION
2,600
PROFESSING CHRISTIANS
92.8%

Jolika's Home

Say a Prayer Today

Pray for Jolika, that she would be a comfort to others in the same way she was comforted. Pray for her Love God Greatly group, that they would be a light for the gospel and would continue to build one another up in truth.

HISTORY BIT

Slovakia is a small country in eastern Europe. Though it has a rich heritage and a long history, the Republic of Slovakia has only been an independent state since 1993.*

Source Information:
https://joshuaproject.net/countries/LO
*Jason Mandryk, Operation World, 7th edition (Colorado Springs, CO: Biblica Publishing, 2010), 747.

LOVE YOUR NEIGHBOR

Her Journey

JOLIKA'S STORY

My name is Jolika, and I live in Slovakia. A few years ago—when my kids were already grown and gone from the home—I was struggling with my broken marriage and felt terribly lonely and abandoned. My kids wanted to help me so they set up a Facebook account for me to find friends. I was flooded with information that seemed useless, and for a long time I saw no point in using the site.

One day, one of my friends invited me to participate in a Love God Greatly Bible study on Facebook. I accepted the invitation because I felt a deep desire to belong to a community of believers. I live in a tiny village and attend a very small church, so I have little opportunity throughout the week for local fellowship and Bible study. That first study helped me grow in ways I never thought possible. Every word I read was like healing balm to my soul. I was amazed that even though our group members came from so many different walks of life and had never met each other in person, there was still such love and deep understanding among the women.

Today, my Bible study group is a huge blessing for me. It is because of Love God Greatly that I now study the Word of God on a daily basis. I no longer blame others for my misery. Instead, I am working on sweeping out all of the trash from my soul and digging deeply to find the person God desires for me to be. My circumstances haven't changed much, but I have real peace and joy in my Lord Jesus Christ.

I am convinced that when we are walking closely with God, He can use us as useful tools in spreading the gospel. I am so thankful to belong to the Love God Greatly community. Glory and thanks be to God for all this!

6 WEEK READING PLAN

LOVE HIS WORD

	MONDAY	TUESDAY	WEDNESDAY	THURSDAY	FRIDAY
1	1 Samuel 1	1 Samuel 2	1 Samuel 3	1 Samuel 4	1 Samuel 5
	SOAP 1 Samuel 1:15-17	SOAP 1 Samuel 2:9-10	SOAP 1 Samuel 3:19-21	SOAP 1 Samuel 4:22	SOAP 1 Samuel 5:11
2	1 Samuel 6:1—7:1	1 Samuel 7:2-17	1 Samuel 8	1 Samuel 9	1 Samuel 10
	SOAP 1 Samuel 6:20	SOAP 1 Samuel 7:3-4	SOAP 1 Samuel 8:6-7	SOAP 1 Samuel 9:17	SOAP 1 Samuel 10:24-25
3	1 Samuel 11:1-11	1 Samuel 11:12—12:25	1 Samuel 13:1-22	1 Samuel 13:23—14:52	1 Samuel 15
	SOAP Psalm 18:2	SOAP 1 Samuel 12:23-25	SOAP 1 Samuel 13:13-14	SOAP 1 Samuel 14:22-23a	SOAP 1 Samuel 15:22-23
4	1 Samuel 16	1 Samuel 17	1 Samuel 18	1 Samuel 19	1 Samuel 20
	SOAP 1 Samuel 16:7	SOAP 1 Samuel 17:36-37	SOAP 1 Samuel 18:28-29	SOAP Psalm 59:4-5	SOAP Psalm 11:4-5
5	1 Samuel 21	1 Samuel 22	1 Samuel 23	1 Samuel 24	1 Samuel 25
	SOAP Psalm 56:9-11	SOAP Psalm 142:1-2	SOAP Psalm 54:4-7	SOAP Psalm 63:7-9	SOAP Psalm 109:26-28
6	1 Samuel 26	1 Samuel 27	1 Samuel 28	1 Samuel 29	1 Samuel 30-31
	SOAP Psalm 35:17-18	SOAP Psalm 141:8-10	SOAP Psalm 57:1-2	SOAP Psalm 64:10	SOAP Psalm 31:7-8

HANNAH IS CHILDLESS

1 There was a man from Ramathaim Zophim, from the hill country of Ephraim. His name was Elkanah. He was the son of Jeroham, the son of Elihu, the son of Tohu, the son of Zuph, an
Ephraimite. 2 He had two wives; the name of the first was Hannah and the name of the second was Peninnah. Peninnah had
children, but Hannah had no children. 3 This man would go up
from his city year after year to worship and to sacrifice to the
LORD of Heaven's Armies at Shiloh. (It was there that the two
sons of Eli, Hophni and Phinehas, served as the LORD's priests.)
4 The day came, and Elkanah sacrificed.

(Now he used to give meat portions to his wife Peninnah and
to all her sons and daughters. 5 But to Hannah he would give a
double portion because he loved Hannah, although the LORD
had not enabled her to have children. 6 Her rival used to aggra-
vate her to the point of exasperation, just to irritate her, since
the LORD had not enabled her to have children. 7 This is how it
would go year after year. As often as she went up to the LORD's
house, Peninnah would offend her in that way.)

So she cried and refused to eat. 8 Then her husband Elkanah
said to her, "Hannah, why are you crying and why won't you eat?
Why are you so upset? Am I not better to you than ten sons?"
9 So Hannah got up after they had finished eating and drinking in Shiloh.

At the time Eli the priest was sitting in his chair by the doorpost of the LORD's sanctuary. 10 As for Hannah, she was very distressed. She prayed to the LORD and was, in fact, weeping. 11 She
made a vow saying, "O LORD of Heaven's Armies, if you would
truly look on the suffering of your servant, and would keep me
in mind and not neglect your servant, and give your servant a
male child, then I will dedicate him to the LORD all the days of
his life. His hair will never be cut."

12 It turned out that she did a great deal of praying before the
LORD. Meanwhile Eli was watching her mouth. 13 As for Hannah, she was speaking in her mind. Only her lips were moving;
her voice could not be heard. So Eli thought she was a drunkard.
14 Then he said to her, "How much longer do you intend to get
drunk? Put away your wine!" 15 But Hannah replied, "Not so, my
lord! I am a woman under a great deal of stress. I haven't drunk
wine or beer. But I have poured out my soul before the LORD.
16 Don't consider your servant a wicked woman. It's just that, to
this point, I have spoken from my deep pain and anguish."

17 Eli replied, "Go in peace, and may the God of Israel grant the
request that you have asked of him." 18 She said, "May I, your servant, find favor in your sight." So the woman went her way and
got something to eat. Her face no longer looked sad.

19 They got up early the next morning. Then they worshiped
the LORD and returned to their home at Ramathaim. Elkanah
was intimate with his wife Hannah, and the LORD called her to
mind. 20 Then Hannah became pregnant.

HANNAH DEDICATES SAMUEL TO THE LORD

In the course of time she gave birth to a son. And she named
him Samuel, thinking, "I asked the LORD for him." 21 Then the

WEEPING WITH BITTERNESS

1 SAMUEL 1:1–20

First Samuel opens, and we meet Elkanah and his two wives, Hannah and Peninnah. God had closed Hannah's womb. If this were not hard enough to bear, the odds continued to stack against her.

Peninnah, Elkanah's second wife, incessantly tormented Hannah for her inability to conceive. Year after year, Peninnah's provocation continued while Hannah's grief increased.

Hannah was married to a man who was devoted to God and who loved her especially. Yet even with this security, Hannah was deeply hurt because of her infertility. Every year at the annual festivals, Hannah found herself overwhelmed with sorrow and would weep in the presence of God.

Have you ever suffered this type of distress? Perhaps you lost a family member or, like Hannah, are experiencing infertility. Maybe it seems God is not answering your prayers for a husband, a new job, or financial provision. It may feel like God is ignoring you or, even worse, that He is being cruel to you. In times like these, where do you turn?

Hannah turned to the Lord in her pain.

Verse 10 says, "She was very distressed. She prayed to the LORD, and was, in fact, weeping."

Hannah chose vulnerability with God in her distress rather than attacking her rival. She cried out to God rather than crying to the world for help. She believed God wanted to hear her despair and be with her in the intensity of her pain and tears. She shared her deepest sorrow and most unbearable wounds with the one true Comforter, the One who is ever present and intimately personal.

Hannah was vulnerable with God because she lived by faith. In 1 Samuel 2, we learn that Hannah believed God was a rock on which to stand (v. 2), the giver of life (v. 6), the One who exalts (v. 7), ruler over the earth (v. 8), and the One who guards the faithful (v. 9).

Do you feel this level of comfort with God? Do you turn to Him in your pain? Our belief about God's character will determine where we run in times of turmoil. Do we think He cares intimately about our pain? Scriptures like these remind us that He does. Turn to Him today. He is waiting to comfort you.

man Elkanah and all his family went up to make the yearly
sacrifice to the LORD and to keep his vow. 22 But Hannah did
not go up with them, because she had told her husband, "Not
until the boy is weaned. Then I will bring him so that he
may appear before the LORD. And he will remain there from
then on."

23 Then her husband Elkanah said to her, "Do what you think
best. Stay until you have weaned him. Only may the LORD fulfill his promise."

So the woman stayed and nursed her son until she had
weaned him. 24 Then she took him up with her as soon as she
had weaned him, along with three bulls, an ephah of flour, and
a container of wine. She came to the LORD's house at Shiloh,
and the boy was with them. 25 They slaughtered the bull, then
brought the boy to Eli. 26 She said, "My lord. Just as surely as
you are alive, my lord, I am the woman who previously stood
here with you in order to pray to the LORD. 27 For this boy I
prayed, and the LORD has given me the request that I asked
of him. 28 So I also dedicate him to the LORD. For all the days
of his life he is dedicated to the LORD." Then he bowed down
there in worship to the LORD.

HANNAH EXALTS THE LORD IN PRAYER

2 Hannah prayed,
"My heart has rejoiced in the LORD;
my horn has been raised high because of the LORD.
I have loudly denounced my enemies.
Indeed I rejoice in your deliverance.
2 No one is holy like the LORD!
There is no one other than you!
There is no rock like our God!
3 Don't keep speaking so arrogantly.
Proud talk should not come out of your mouth,
for the LORD is a God who knows;
he evaluates what people do.
4 The bows of warriors are shattered,
but those who stumbled have taken on strength.
5 The well fed hire themselves out to earn food,
but the hungry no longer lack.
Even the barren woman has given birth to seven,
but the one with many children has declined.
6 The LORD both kills and gives life;
he brings down to the grave and raises up.
7 The LORD impoverishes and makes wealthy;
he humbles and he exalts.
8 He lifts the weak from the dust;
he raises the poor from the ash heap
to seat them with princes—
he bestows on them an honored position.
The foundations of the earth belong to the LORD—
he placed the world on them.
9 He watches over his holy ones,
but the wicked are made speechless in the darkness,
for it is not by one's own strength that one prevails.

CHALLENGE

Hannah's prayer in 1 Samuel inspires later writers of Scripture. One psalmist reflects her words in Psalm 113 and Mary, the mother of Jesus, uses both of these passages in her hymn of praise in Luke 1. Read all three of these passages. What similarities and differences do you see? On what truths do all three writers focus? What do these truths tell you about God?

10 The LORD shatters his adversaries;
he thunders against them from the heavens.
The LORD executes judgment to the ends of the earth.
He will strengthen his king
and exalt the power of his anointed one."

11 Then Elkanah went back home to Ramah.

ELI'S SONS MISUSE THEIR SACRED OFFICE

The boy Samuel was serving the LORD with the favor of Eli the priest. 12 But the sons of Eli were wicked men. They did not acknowledge the LORD's authority. 13 This was the priests' routine with the people. Whenever anyone was making a sacrifice, the priest's attendant would come with a three-pronged fork in his hand, just as the meat was boiling. 14 He would jab it into the basin, kettle, cauldron, or pot. Everything that the fork would bring up the priest would take for himself. This is how they used to treat all the Israelites who came there to Shiloh.

15 Also, before they burned the fat the priest's attendant would come and say to the person who was making the sacrifice, "Give some meat for the priest to roast! He won't accept boiled meat from you, but only raw." 16 If the individual said to him, "They should certainly burn the fat away first, then take for yourself whatever you wish," then he would say, "No! Give it now! If not, I'll take it by force!" 17 The sin of these young men was very great in the LORD's sight, for they treated the LORD's offering with contempt.

18 Now Samuel was ministering with the favor of the LORD. The boy was dressed in a linen ephod. 19 His mother used to make him a small robe and bring it to him from time to time when she would go up with her husband to make the annual sacrifice. 20 Eli would bless Elkanah and his wife saying, "May the LORD establish descendants for you from this woman in place of the one that she dedicated to the LORD." Then they would go to their home. 21 And indeed the LORD attended to Hannah. She got pregnant and gave birth to three sons and two daughters. But the boy Samuel grew up before the LORD.

22 Eli was very old. And he would hear about everything that his sons used to do to all the people of Israel and how they used to go to bed with the women who were stationed at the entrance to the tent of meeting. 23 So he said to them, "Why do you do these things, these evil things that I hear about from all these people? 24 No, my sons! For the report that I hear circulating among the LORD's people is not good. 25 If a man sins against a man, one may appeal to God on his behalf. But if a man sins against the LORD, who can intercede for him?" But Eli's sons would not listen to their father. Indeed the LORD had decided to kill them. 26 However, the boy Samuel was growing up and finding favor both with the LORD and with people.

THE LORD JUDGES THE HOUSE OF ELI

27 Then a man of God came to Eli and said to him, "This is what the LORD has said: 'I plainly revealed myself to your ancestor's house when they were slaves to the house of Pharaoh in Egypt. 28 I chose your ancestor from all the tribes of Israel to be my

priest, to offer sacrifice on my altar, to burn incense, and to bear the ephod before me. I gave to your ancestor's house all the fire offerings made by the Israelites. 29 Why are you scorning my sacrifice and my offering that I commanded for my dwelling place? You have honored your sons more than you have me by having made yourselves fat from the best parts of all the offerings of my people Israel.'

30 "Therefore the LORD, the God of Israel, says, 'I really did say that your house and your ancestor's house would serve me forever.' But now the LORD says, 'May it never be! For I will honor those who honor me, but those who despise me will be cursed! 31 In fact, days are coming when I will remove your strength and the strength of your father's house. There will not be an old man in your house! 32 You will see trouble in my dwelling place! Israel will experience blessings, but there will not be an old man in your house for all time. 33 Any man of yours that I do not cut off from my altar, I will cause his eyes to fail and will cause him grief. All those born to your family will die by the sword of man. 34 This will be a confirming sign for you that will be fulfilled through your two sons, Hophni and Phinehas: in a single day they both will die! 35 Then I will raise up for myself a faithful priest. He will do what is in my heart and soul. I will build for him a lasting dynasty, and he will serve my chosen one for all time. 36 Everyone who remains in your house will come to bow before him for a little money and for a scrap of bread. Each will say, "Assign me to a priestly task so I can eat a scrap of bread."'"

THE CALL OF SAMUEL

3 Now the boy Samuel continued serving the LORD under Eli's supervision. Receiving a message from the LORD was rare in those days; revelatory visions were infrequent.

2 Eli's eyes had begun to fail, so that he was unable to see well. At that time he was lying down in his place, 3 and the lamp of God had not yet been extinguished. Samuel was lying down in the temple of the LORD as well; the ark of God was also there. 4 The LORD called to Samuel, and he replied, "Here I am!" 5 Then he ran to Eli and said, "Here I am, for you called me." But Eli said, "I didn't call you. Go back and lie down." So he went back and lay down. 6 The LORD again called, "Samuel!" So Samuel got up and went to Eli and said, "Here I am, for you called me." But Eli said, "I didn't call you, my son. Go back and lie down."

7 Now Samuel did not yet know the LORD; the LORD's messages had not yet been revealed to him. 8 Then the LORD called Samuel a third time. So he got up and went to Eli and said, "Here I am, for you called me!" Eli then realized that it was the LORD who was calling the boy. 9 So Eli said to Samuel, "Go back and lie down. When he calls you, say, 'Speak, LORD, for your servant is listening.'" So Samuel went back and lay down in his place.

10 Then the LORD came and stood nearby, calling as he had previously done, "Samuel! Samuel!" Samuel replied, "Speak, for your servant is listening!" 11 The LORD said to Samuel, "Look! I am about to do something in Israel; when anyone hears about it, both of his ears will tingle. 12 On that day I will carry out against

Eli everything that I spoke about his house—from start to finish!
13 You should tell him that I am about to judge his house forever
because of the sin that he knew about. For his sons were cursing
God, and he did not rebuke them. 14 Therefore I swore an oath
to the house of Eli, 'The sin of the house of Eli can never be forgiven by sacrifice or by grain offering.'"
15 So Samuel lay down until morning. Then he opened the doors
of the LORD's house. But Samuel was afraid to tell Eli about the
vision. 16 However, Eli called Samuel and said, "Samuel, my son!"
He replied, "Here I am." 17 Eli said, "What message did he speak
to you? Don't conceal it from me. God will judge you severely if
you conceal from me anything that he said to you!"
18 So Samuel told him everything. He did not hold back anything from him. Eli said, "The LORD will do what he pleases."
19 Samuel continued to grow, and the LORD was with him. None
of his prophecies fell to the ground unfulfilled. 20 All Israel
from Dan to Beer Sheba realized that Samuel was confirmed as
a prophet of the LORD. 21 Then the LORD again appeared in Shiloh, for it was in Shiloh that the LORD had revealed himself to
4 Samuel through a message from the LORD. 1 Samuel revealed
the word of the LORD to all Israel.

THE ARK OF THE COVENANT IS LOST TO THE PHILISTINES

Then the Israelites went out to fight the Philistines. They camped
at Ebenezer, and the Philistines camped at Aphek. 2 The Philistines arranged their forces to fight Israel. As the battle spread
out, Israel was defeated by the Philistines, who killed about
4,000 men in the battle line in the field.
3 When the army came back to the camp, the elders of Israel
said, "Why did the LORD let us be defeated today by the Philistines? Let's take with us the ark of the covenant of the LORD
from Shiloh. When it is with us, it will save us from the hand of
our enemies."
4 So the army sent to Shiloh, and they took from there the ark
of the covenant of the LORD of Heaven's Armies, who sits between the cherubim. Now the two sons of Eli, Hophni and Phinehas, were there with the ark of the covenant of God. 5 When the
ark of the covenant of the LORD arrived at the camp, all Israel
shouted so loudly that the ground shook.
6 When the Philistines heard the sound of the shout, they said,
"What is this loud shout in the camp of the Hebrews?" Then
they realized that the ark of the LORD had arrived at the camp.
7 The Philistines were scared because they thought that gods had
come to the camp. They said, "Woe to us! We've never seen anything like this! 8 Woe to us! Who can deliver us from the hand
of these mighty gods? These are the gods who struck the Egyptians with all sorts of plagues in the desert! 9 Be strong and act
like men, you Philistines, or else you will wind up serving the
Hebrews the way they have served you! Act like men and fight!"
10 So the Philistines fought. Israel was defeated; they all ran
home. The slaughter was very great; 30,000 foot soldiers from
Israel fell in battle. 11 The ark of God was taken, and the two sons
of Eli, Hophni and Phinehas, were killed.

ELI DIES

12 On that day a Benjaminite ran from the battle lines and came
to Shiloh. His clothes were torn, and dirt was on his head. 13 When
he arrived in Shiloh, Eli was sitting in his chair on the lookout
by the side of the road, for he was very worried about the ark of
God. As the man entered the city to give his report, the whole
city cried out.
14 When Eli heard the outcry, he said, "What's this commotion?" The man quickly came and told Eli. 15 Now Eli was ninety-
eight years old and his eyes looked straight ahead; he was unable
to see.
16 The man said to Eli, "I am the one who came from the battle lines! Just today I fled from the battle lines!" Eli asked, "How
did things go, my son?" 17 The messenger replied, "Israel has fled
from the Philistines! The army has suffered a great defeat! Your
two sons, Hophni and Phinehas, are dead! The ark of God has
been captured!"
18 When he mentioned the ark of God, Eli fell backward from
his chair beside the gate. He broke his neck and died, for he was
old and heavy. He had judged Israel for forty years.
19 His daughter-in-law, the wife of Phinehas, was pregnant and
close to giving birth. When she heard that the ark of God was
captured and that her father-in-law and her husband were dead,
she doubled over and gave birth. But her labor pains were too
much for her. 20 As she was dying, the women who were there
with her said, "Don't be afraid! You have given birth to a son!"
But she did not reply or pay any attention.
21 She named the boy Ichabod, saying, "The glory has departed
from Israel," referring to the capture of the ark of God and the
deaths of her father-in-law and her husband. 22 She said, "The
glory has departed from Israel, because the ark of God has been
captured."

GOD SENDS TROUBLE FOR THE PHILISTINES WHO HAVE THE ARK

5 Now the Philistines had captured the ark of God and
brought it from Ebenezer to Ashdod. 2 The Philistines took
the ark of God and brought it into the temple of Dagon, where
they positioned it beside Dagon. 3 When the residents of Ashdod got up early the next day, Dagon was lying on the ground
before the ark of the LORD. So they took Dagon and set him
back in his place. 4 But when they got up early the following
day, Dagon was again lying on the ground before the ark of the
LORD. The head of Dagon and his two hands were sheared off
and were lying at the threshold. Only Dagon's body was left intact. 5 (For this reason, to this very day, neither Dagon's priests
nor anyone else who enters Dagon's temple steps on Dagon's
threshold in Ashdod.)
6 The LORD attacked the residents of Ashdod severely, bringing devastation on them. He struck the people of both Ashdod
and the surrounding area with sores. 7 When the people of Ashdod saw what was happening, they said, "The ark of the God of
Israel should not remain with us, for he has attacked both us
and our god Dagon!"

8 So they assembled all the leaders of the Philistines and asked,
"What should we do with the ark of the God of Israel?" They replied, "The ark of the God of Israel should be moved to Gath." So
they moved the ark of the God of Israel.
9 But after it had been moved the LORD attacked that city as
well, causing a great deal of panic. He struck all the people of that
city with sores. 10 So they sent the ark of God to Ekron.
But when the ark of God arrived at Ekron, the residents of Ekron cried out saying, "They have brought the ark of the God of
Israel here to kill our people!" 11 So they assembled all the leaders of the Philistines and said, "Get the ark of the God of Israel
out of here! Let it go back to its own place so that it won't kill us
and our people!" The terror of death was throughout the entire
city; God was attacking them very severely there. 12 The people
who did not die were struck with sores; the city's cry for help
went all the way up to heaven.

THE PHILISTINES RETURN THE ARK

6 When the ark of the LORD had been in the land of the Philistines for seven months, 2 the Philistines called the priests
and the omen readers, saying, "What should we do with the ark of
the LORD? Advise us as to how we should send it back to its place."
3 They replied, "If you are going to send the ark of the God of
Israel back, don't send it away empty. Be sure to return it with a
guilt offering. Then you will be healed, and you will understand
why his hand has not been removed from you." 4 They inquired,
"What is the guilt offering that we should send to him?"
They replied, "The Philistine leaders number five. So send five
gold sores and five gold mice, for it is the same plague that has
afflicted both you and your leaders. 5 You should make images
of the sores and images of the mice that are destroying the land.
You should honor the God of Israel. Perhaps he will release his
grip on you, your gods, and your land. 6 Why harden your hearts
like the Egyptians and Pharaoh did? When God treated them
harshly, didn't the Egyptians send the Israelites on their way?
7 So now go and make a new cart. Get two cows that have calves
and that have never had a yoke placed on them. Harness the
cows to the cart, and take their calves from them back to their
stalls. 8 Then take the ark of the LORD and place it on the cart,
and put in a chest beside it the gold objects you are sending to
him as a guilt offering. You should then send it on its way. 9 But
keep an eye on it. If it should go up by the way of its own border
to Beth Shemesh, then he has brought this great calamity on us.
But if that is not the case, then we will know that it was not his
hand that struck us; rather, it just happened to us by accident."
10 So the men did as instructed. They took two cows that had
calves and harnessed the cows to a cart; they also removed their
calves to their stalls. 11 They put the ark of the LORD on the cart,
along with the chest, the gold mice, and the images of the sores.
12 Then the cows went directly on the road to Beth Shemesh. They
went along that route, bellowing more and more; they turned
neither to the right nor to the left. The leaders of the Philistines were walking along behind them all the way to the border of Beth Shemesh.

13 Now the residents of Beth Shemesh were harvesting wheat in the valley. When they looked up and saw the ark, they were pleased at the sight. 14 The cart was coming to the field of Joshua, who was from Beth Shemesh. It paused there near a big stone. Then they cut up the wood of the cart and offered the cows as a burnt offering to the LORD. 15 The Levites took down the ark of the LORD and the chest that was with it, which contained the gold objects. They placed them near the big stone. At that time the people of Beth Shemesh offered burnt offerings and made sacrifices to the LORD. 16 The five leaders of the Philistines watched what was happening and then returned to Ekron on the same day.

17 These are the gold sores that the Philistines brought as a guilt offering to the LORD—one for each of the following cities: Ashdod, Gaza, Ashkelon, Gath, and Ekron. 18 The gold mice corresponded in number to all the Philistine cities of the five leaders, from the fortified cities to hamlet villages, to greater Abel. They positioned the ark of the LORD on a rock until this very day in the field of Joshua who was from Beth Shemesh.

19 But the LORD struck down some of the people of Beth Shemesh because they had looked into the ark of the LORD; he struck down 50,070 of the men. The people grieved because the LORD had struck the people with a hard blow. 20 The residents of Beth Shemesh asked, "Who is able to stand before the LORD, this holy God? To whom will the ark go up from here?"

21 So they sent messengers to the residents of Kiriath Jearim, saying, "The Philistines have returned the ark of the LORD. Come down here and take it back home with you."

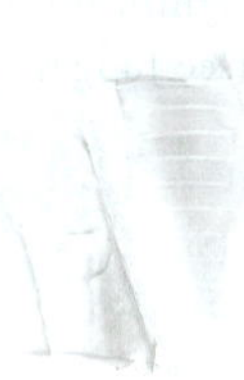

7 Then the people of Kiriath Jearim came and took the ark of the LORD; they brought it to the house of Abinadab located on the hill. They consecrated Eleazar his son to guard the ark of the LORD.

FURTHER CONFLICT WITH THE PHILISTINES

2 It was quite a long time—some twenty years in all—that the ark stayed at Kiriath Jearim. All the people of Israel longed for the LORD. 3 Samuel said to all the people of Israel, "If you are really turning to the LORD with all your hearts, remove from among you the foreign gods and the images of Ashtoreth. Give your hearts to the LORD and serve only him. Then he will deliver you from the hand of the Philistines." 4 So the Israelites removed the Baals and images of Ashtoreth. They served only the LORD.

5 Then Samuel said, "Gather all Israel to Mizpah, and I will pray to the LORD on your behalf." 6 After they had assembled at Mizpah, they drew water and poured it out before the LORD. They fasted on that day, and they confessed there, "We have sinned against the LORD." So Samuel led the people of Israel at Mizpah.

7 When the Philistines heard that the Israelites had gathered at Mizpah, the leaders of the Philistines went up against Israel. When the Israelites heard about this, they were afraid of the Philistines. 8 The Israelites said to Samuel, "Keep crying out to the LORD our God so that he may save us from the hand of the Philistines!" 9 So Samuel took a nursing lamb and offered it as a whole burnt offering to the LORD. Samuel cried out to the LORD on Israel's behalf, and the LORD answered him.

10 As Samuel was offering burnt offerings, the Philistines approached to do battle with Israel. But on that day the LORD thundered loudly against the Philistines. He caused them to panic, and they were defeated by Israel. 11 Then the men of Israel left Mizpah and chased the Philistines, striking them down all the way to an area below Beth Car.

12 Samuel took a stone and placed it between Mizpah and Shen. He named it Ebenezer, saying, "Up to here the LORD has helped us." 13 So the Philistines were defeated; they did not invade Israel again. The hand of the LORD was against the Philistines all the days of Samuel.

REFLECT

How does Israel's request for a king display the spiritual climate of the nation? What was the spiritual climate of the nation, and why was this so significant to God (see Judges 21:25)?

14 The cities that the Philistines had captured from Israel were returned to Israel, from Ekron to Gath. Israel also delivered their territory from the control of the Philistines. There was also peace between Israel and the Amorites. 15 So Samuel led Israel all the days of his life. 16 Year after year he used to travel the circuit of Bethel, Gilgal, and Mizpah; he used to judge Israel in all these places. 17 Then he would return to Ramah, because his home was there. He also judged Israel there and built an altar to the LORD there.

ISRAEL SEEKS A KING

8 In his old age Samuel appointed his sons as judges over Israel. 2 The name of his firstborn son was Joel, and the name of his second son was Abijah. They were judges in Beer Sheba. 3 But his sons did not follow his ways. Instead, they made money dishonestly, accepted bribes, and perverted justice.

4 So all the elders of Israel gathered together and approached Samuel at Ramah. 5 They said to him, "Look, you are old, and your sons don't follow your ways. So now appoint over us a king to lead us, just like all the other nations have."

6 But this request displeased Samuel, for they said, "Give us a king to lead us." So Samuel prayed to the LORD. 7 The LORD said to Samuel, "Do everything the people request of you. For it is not you that they have rejected, but it is me that they have rejected as their king. 8 Just as they have done from the day that I brought them up from Egypt until this very day, they have rejected me and have served other gods. This is what they are also doing to you. 9 So now do as they say. But you must warn them and make them aware of the policies of the king who will rule over them."

10 So Samuel spoke all the LORD's words to the people who were asking him for a king. 11 He said, "Here are the policies of the king who will rule over you: He will conscript your sons and put them in his chariot forces and in his cavalry; they will run in front of his chariot. 12 He will appoint for himself leaders of thousands and leaders of fifties, as well as those who plow his ground, reap his harvest, and make his weapons of war and his chariot equipment. 13 He will take your daughters to be ointment makers, cooks, and bakers. 14 He will take your best fields, vineyards, and olive groves, and give them to his own servants. 15 He will demand a tenth of your seed and of the produce of your vineyards and give it to his administrators and his servants. 16 He will take your male and female servants, as well as your best

cattle and your donkeys, and assign them for his own use. 17 He
will demand a tenth of your flocks, and you yourselves will be
his servants. 18 In that day you will cry out because of your king
whom you have chosen for yourselves, but the LORD won't answer you in that day."

19 But the people refused to heed Samuel's warning. Instead
they said, "No! There will be a king over us! 20 We will be like all
the other nations. Our king will judge us and lead us and fight
our battles."

21 So Samuel listened to everything the people said and then
reported it to the LORD. 22 The LORD said to Samuel, "Do as they
say and install a king over them." Then Samuel said to the men
of Israel, "Each of you go back to his own city."

SAMUEL MEETS WITH SAUL

9 There was a Benjaminite man named Kish son of Abiel, the
son of Zeror, the son of Becorath, the son of Aphiah of Benjamin. Kish was a prominent person. 2 He had a son named Saul,
a handsome young man. There was no one among the Israelites more handsome than he was; he stood head and shoulders
above all the people.

3 The donkeys of Saul's father Kish wandered off, so Kish said
to his son Saul, "Take one of the servants with you and go look
for the donkeys." 4 So Saul crossed through the hill country of
Ephraim, passing through the land of Shalisha, but they did not
find them. So they crossed through the land of Shaalim, but they
were not there. Then he crossed through the land of Benjamin,
and still they did not find them.

5 When they came to the land of Zuph, Saul said to his servant
who was with him, "Come on, let's head back before my father
quits worrying about the donkeys and becomes anxious about
us!" 6 But the servant said to him, "Look, there is a man of God
in this town. He is highly respected. Everything that he says
really happens. Now let's go there. Perhaps he will tell us where
we should go from here." 7 So Saul said to his servant, "All right,
we can go. But what can we bring the man, since the food in our
bags is used up? We have no gift to take to the man of God. What
do we have?" 8 The servant went on to answer Saul, "Look, I happen to have in my hand a quarter shekel of silver. I will give it to
the man of God and he will tell us where we should go." 9 (Now
it used to be in Israel that whenever someone went to inquire
of God he would say, "Come on, let's go to the seer." For today's
prophet used to be called a seer.) 10 So Saul said to his servant,
"That's a good idea! Come on. Let's go." So they went to the town
where the man of God was.

11 As they were going up the ascent to the town, they met some
girls coming out to draw water. They said to them, "Is this where
the seer is?" 12 They replied, "Yes, straight ahead! But hurry now,
for he came to the town today, and the people are making a
sacrifice at the high place. 13 When you enter the town, you can
find him before he goes up to the high place to eat. The people
won't eat until he arrives, for he must bless the sacrifice. Once
that happens, those who have been invited will eat. Now go on
up, for this is the time when you can find him."

[14] So they went up to the town. As they were heading for the
middle of the town, Samuel was coming in their direction to
go up to the high place. [15] Now the day before Saul arrived, the
LORD had told Samuel: [16] "At this time tomorrow I will send to
you a man from the land of Benjamin. You must consecrate him
as a leader over my people Israel. He will save my people from
the hand of the Philistines. For I have looked with favor on my
people. Their cry has reached me."
[17] When Samuel saw Saul, the LORD said, "Here is the man
that I told you about. He will rule over my people." [18] As Saul approached Samuel in the middle of the gate, he said, "Please tell
me where the seer's house is."
[19] Samuel replied to Saul, "I am the seer! Go up in front of me
to the high place! Today you will eat with me and in the morning I will send you away. I will tell you everything that you are
thinking. [20] Don't be concerned about the donkeys that you lost
three days ago, for they have been found. Whom does all Israel
desire? Is it not you, and all your father's family?"
[21] Saul replied, "Am I not a Benjaminite, from the smallest of Israel's tribes, and is not my family clan the smallest of all the clans
in the tribe of Benjamin? Why do you speak to me in this way?"
[22] Then Samuel brought Saul and his servant into the room
and gave them a place at the head of those who had been invited. There were about thirty people present. [23] Samuel said to
the cook, "Give me the portion of meat that I gave to you—the
one I asked you to keep with you."
[24] So the cook picked up the leg and brought it and set it in front
of Saul. Samuel said, "What was kept is now set before you! Eat,
for it has been kept for you for this meeting time, from the time I
said, 'I have invited the people.'" So Saul ate with Samuel that day.
[25] When they came down from the high place to the town,
Samuel spoke with Saul on the roof. [26] They got up at dawn and
Samuel called to Saul on the roof, "Get up, so I can send you on
your way." So Saul got up and the two of them—he and Samuel—
went outside. [27] While they were going down to the edge of town,
Samuel said to Saul, "Tell the servant to go on ahead of us." So
he did. Samuel then said, "You remain here awhile, so I can inform you of God's message."

SAMUEL ANOINTS SAUL

10 Then Samuel took a small container of olive oil and poured
it on Saul's head. Samuel kissed him and said, "The LORD has
chosen you to lead his people Israel! You will rule over the LORD's
people and you will deliver them from the power of the enemies who surround them. This will be your sign that the LORD
has chosen you as leader over his inheritance. [2] When you leave
me today, you will find two men near Rachel's tomb at Zelzah on
Benjamin's border. They will say to you, 'The donkeys you have
gone looking for have been found. Your father is no longer concerned about the donkeys but has become anxious about you
two! He is asking, "What should I do about my son?"'
[3] "As you continue on from there, you will come to the tall tree of
Tabor. At that point three men who are going up to God at Bethel
will meet you. One of them will be carrying three young goats, one

of them will be carrying three round loaves of bread, and one of them will be carrying a container of wine. 4 They will ask you how you're doing and will give you two loaves of bread. You will accept them. 5 Afterward you will go to Gibeah of God, where there are Philistine officials. When you enter the town, you will meet a company of prophets coming down from the high place. They will have harps, tambourines, flutes, and lyres, and they will be prophesying. 6 Then the Spirit of the LORD will rush upon you and you will prophesy with them. You will be changed into a different person.

7 "When these signs have taken place, do whatever your hand finds to do, for God will be with you. 8 You will go down to Gilgal before me. I am going to join you there to offer burnt offerings and to make peace offerings. You should wait for seven days until I arrive and tell you what to do."

SAUL BECOMES KING

9 As Saul turned to leave Samuel, God changed his inmost person. All these signs happened on that very day. 10 When Saul and his servant arrived at Gibeah, a company of prophets was coming out to meet him. Then the Spirit of God rushed upon Saul and he prophesied among them. 11 When everyone who had known him previously saw him prophesying with the prophets, the people asked one another, "What on earth has happened to the son of Kish? Does even Saul belong with the prophets?"

12 A man who was from there replied, "And who is their father?" Therefore this became a proverb: "Is even Saul among the prophets?" 13 When Saul had finished prophesying, he went to the high place.

14 Saul's uncle asked him and his servant, "Where did you go?" Saul replied, "To look for the donkeys. But when we realized they were lost, we went to Samuel." 15 Saul's uncle said, "Tell me what Samuel said to you." 16 Saul said to his uncle, "He assured us that the donkeys had been found." But Saul did not tell him what Samuel had said about the matter of kingship.

17 Then Samuel called the people together before the LORD at Mizpah. 18 He said to the Israelites, "This is what the LORD God of Israel has said, 'I brought Israel up from Egypt and I delivered you from the power of the Egyptians and from the power of all the kingdoms that oppressed you. 19 But today you have rejected your God who saves you from all your trouble and distress. You have said, "No! Appoint a king over us." Now take your positions before the LORD by your tribes and by your clans.'"

20 Then Samuel brought all the tribes of Israel near, and the tribe of Benjamin was chosen by lot. 21 Then he brought the tribe of Benjamin near by its families, and the family of Matri was chosen by lot. At last Saul son of Kish was chosen by lot. But when they looked for him, he was nowhere to be found. 22 So they inquired again of the LORD, "Has the man arrived here yet?" The LORD said, "He has hidden himself among the equipment."

23 So they ran and brought him from there. When he took his position among the people, he stood head and shoulders above them all. 24 Then Samuel said to all the people, "Do you see the one whom the LORD has chosen? Indeed, there is no one like him among all the people." All the people shouted out, "Long live the king!"

25 Then Samuel talked to the people about how the kingship would work. He wrote it all down on a scroll and set it before the LORD. Then Samuel sent all the people away to their homes. 26 Even Saul went to his home in Gibeah. With him went some brave men whose hearts God had touched. 27 But some wicked men said, "How can this man save us?" They despised him and did not even bring him a gift. But Saul said nothing about it.

SAUL COMES TO THE AID OF JABESH

11 Nahash the Ammonite marched against Jabesh Gilead. All the men of Jabesh Gilead said to Nahash, "Make a treaty with us and we will serve you."

2 But Nahash the Ammonite said to them, "The only way I will make a treaty with you is if you let me gouge out the right eye of every one of you and in so doing humiliate all Israel!"

3 The elders of Jabesh said to him, "Leave us alone for seven days so that we can send messengers throughout the territory of Israel. If there is no one who can deliver us, we will come out voluntarily to you."

4 When the messengers went to Gibeah (where Saul lived) and informed the people of these matters, all the people wept loudly. 5 Now Saul was walking behind the oxen as he came from the field. Saul asked, "What has happened to the people? Why are they weeping?" So they told him about the men of Jabesh.

6 The Spirit of God rushed upon Saul when he heard these words, and he became very angry. 7 He took a pair of oxen and cut them up. Then he sent the pieces throughout the territory of Israel by the hand of messengers, who said, "Whoever does not go out after Saul and after Samuel should expect this to be done to his oxen!" Then the terror of the LORD fell on the people, and they went out as one army. 8 When Saul counted them at Bezek, the Israelites were 300,000 strong and the men of Judah numbered 30,000.

9 They said to the messengers who had come, "Here's what you should say to the men of Jabesh Gilead: 'Tomorrow deliverance will come to you when the sun is fully up.'" When the messengers went and told the men of Jabesh Gilead, they were happy. 10 The men of Jabesh said, "Tomorrow we will come out to you and you can do with us whatever you wish."

11 The next day Saul placed the people in three groups. They went to the Ammonite camp during the morning watch and struck them down until the hottest part of the day. The survivors scattered; no two of them remained together.

SAUL IS ESTABLISHED AS KING

12 Then the people said to Samuel, "Who were the ones asking, 'Will Saul reign over us?' Hand over those men so we may execute them!" 13 But Saul said, "No one will be killed on this day. For today the LORD has given Israel a victory!" 14 Samuel said to the people, "Come on! Let's go to Gilgal and renew the kingship there." 15 So all the people went to Gilgal, where they established Saul as king in the LORD's presence. They offered up peace offerings there in the LORD's presence. Saul and all the Israelites were very happy.

12 Samuel said to all Israel, "I have done everything you requested. I have given you a king. 2 Now look! This king walks
before you. As for me, I am old and gray, and my sons are here
with you. I have walked before you from the time of my youth
till the present day. 3 Here I am. Bring a charge against me before
the LORD and before his chosen king. Whose ox have I taken?
Whose donkey have I taken? Whom have I wronged? Whom have
I oppressed? From whose hand have I taken a bribe so that I
would overlook something? Tell me, and I will return it to you!"
4 They replied, "You have not wronged us or oppressed us. You
have not taken anything from the hand of anyone." 5 He said to
them, "The LORD is witness against you, and his chosen king is
witness this day, that you have not found any reason to accuse
me." They said, "He is witness!"
6 Samuel said to the people, "The LORD is the one who chose
Moses and Aaron and who brought your ancestors up from the
land of Egypt. 7 Now take your positions, so I may confront you
before the LORD regarding all the LORD's just actions toward you
and your ancestors. 8 When Jacob entered Egypt, your ancestors
cried out to the LORD. The LORD sent Moses and Aaron, and they
led your ancestors out of Egypt and settled them in this place.
9 "But they forgot the LORD their God, so he gave them into
the hand of Sisera, the general in command of Hazor's army,
and into the hands of the Philistines and the king of Moab, and
they fought against them. 10 Then they cried out to the LORD
and admitted, 'We have sinned, for we have forsaken the LORD
and have served the Baals and the images of Ashtoreth. Now
deliver us from the hands of our enemies so that we may serve
you.' 11 So the LORD sent Jerub Baal, Barak, Jephthah, and Samuel,
and he delivered you from the hands of the enemies all around
you, and you were able to live securely.
12 "When you saw that King Nahash of the Ammonites was advancing against you, you said to me, 'No! A king will rule over
us'—even though the LORD your God is your king. 13 Now look!
Here is the king you have chosen—the one that you asked for!
Look, the LORD has given you a king. 14 If you fear the LORD, serving him and obeying him and not rebelling against what he says,
and if both you and the king who rules over you follow the LORD
your God, all will be well. 15 But if you don't obey the LORD and
rebel against what the LORD says, the hand of the LORD will be
against both you and your king.
16 "So now, take your positions and watch this great thing that
the LORD is about to do in your sight. 17 Is this not the time of the
wheat harvest? I will call on the LORD so that he makes it thunder and rain. Realize and see what a great sin you have committed before the LORD by asking for a king for yourselves."
18 So Samuel called to the LORD, and the LORD made it thunder and rain that day. All the people were very afraid of both the
LORD and Samuel. 19 All the people said to Samuel, "Pray to the
LORD your God on behalf of us—your servants—so we won't die,
for we have added to all our sins by asking for a king."
20 Then Samuel said to the people, "Don't be afraid. You have
indeed sinned. However, don't turn aside from the LORD. Serve
the LORD with all your heart. 21 You should not turn aside after

empty things that can't profit and can't deliver, since they are empty. 22 The LORD will not abandon his people because he wants to uphold his great reputation. The LORD was pleased to make you his own people. 23 As far as I am concerned, far be it from me to sin against the LORD by ceasing to pray for you! I will instruct you in the way that is good and upright. 24 However, fear the LORD and serve him faithfully with all your heart. Just look at the great things he has done for you! 25 But if you continue to do evil, both you and your king will be swept away."

SAUL FAILS THE LORD

13 Saul was [thirty]* years old when he began to reign; he ruled over Israel for [forty]† years. 2 Saul selected for himself 3,000 men from Israel. Of these 2,000 were with Saul at Micmash and in the hill country of Bethel; the remaining 1,000 were with Jonathan at Gibeah in the territory of Benjamin. He sent all the rest of the people back home.

3 Jonathan attacked the Philistine outpost that was at Geba and the Philistines heard about it. Then Saul alerted all the land saying, "Let the Hebrews pay attention!" 4 All Israel heard this message, "Saul has attacked the Philistine outpost, and now Israel is repulsive to the Philistines!" So the people were summoned to join Saul at Gilgal.

5 Meanwhile the Philistines gathered to battle with Israel. Then they went up against Israel with 3,000 chariots, 6,000 horsemen, and an army as numerous as the sand on the seashore. They went up and camped at Micmash, east of Beth Aven. 6 The men of Israel realized they had a problem because their army was hard pressed. So the army hid in caves, thickets, cliffs, strongholds, and cisterns. 7 Some of the Hebrews crossed over the Jordan River to the land of Gad and Gilead. But Saul stayed at Gilgal; the entire army that was with him was terrified. 8 He waited for seven days, the time period indicated by Samuel. But Samuel did not come to Gilgal, and the army began to abandon Saul.

9 So Saul said, "Bring me the burnt offering and the peace offerings." Then he offered a burnt offering. 10 Just when he had finished offering the burnt offering, Samuel appeared on the scene. Saul went out to meet him and to greet him.

11 But Samuel said, "What have you done?" Saul replied, "When I saw that the army had started to abandon me, and that you didn't come at the appointed time, and that the Philistines had assembled at Micmash, 12 I thought, 'Now the Philistines will come down on me at Gilgal and I have not sought the LORD's favor.' So I felt obligated to offer the burnt offering."

13 Then Samuel said to Saul, "You have made a foolish choice! You have not obeyed the commandment that the LORD your God gave you. Had you done that, the LORD would have established your kingdom over Israel forever. 14 But now your kingdom will not continue. The LORD has sought out for himself a man who is loyal to him, and the LORD has appointed him to be leader over his people, for you have not obeyed what the LORD commanded you."

15 Then Samuel set out and went up from Gilgal to Gibeah in the territory of Benjamin. Saul mustered the army that remained

with him; there were about 600 men. 16 Saul, his son Jonathan,
and the army that remained with them stayed in Gibeah in the
territory of Benjamin, while the Philistines camped in Micmash.
17 Raiding bands went out from the camp of the Philistines in
three groups. One band turned toward the road leading to Ophrah by the land of Shual; 18 another band turned toward the road
leading to Beth Horon; and yet another band turned toward the
road leading to the border that overlooks the valley of Zeboyim
in the direction of the desert.

19 A blacksmith could not be found in all the land of Israel, for
the Philistines had said, "This will prevent the Hebrews from
making swords and spears." 20 So all Israel had to go down to
the Philistines in order to get their plowshares, cutting instruments, axes, and sickles sharpened. 21 They charged two-thirds
of a shekel to sharpen plowshares and cutting instruments, and
one-third of a shekel to sharpen picks and axes, and to set ox
goads. 22 So on the day of the battle no sword or spear was to
be found in the hand of anyone in the army that was with Saul
and Jonathan. No one but Saul and his son Jonathan had them.

JONATHAN IGNITES A BATTLE

23 A garrison of the Philistines had gone out to the pass at Micmash.

14 Then one day Jonathan son of Saul said to his armor-bearer,
"Come on, let's go over to the Philistine garrison that is opposite us." But he did not let his father know.

2 Now Saul was sitting under a pomegranate tree in Migron, on
the outskirts of Gibeah. The army that was with him numbered
about 600 men. 3 Now Ahijah was carrying an ephod. He was
the son of Ahitub, who was the brother of Ichabod and a son of
Phinehas, son of Eli, the priest of the LORD in Shiloh. The army
was unaware that Jonathan had left.

4 Now there was a steep cliff on each side of the pass through
which Jonathan intended to go to reach the Philistine garrison.
One cliff was named Bozez, the other Seneh. 5 The cliff to the
north was closer to Micmash, the one to the south closer to Geba.

6 Jonathan said to his armor-bearer, "Come on, let's go over to
the garrison of these uncircumcised men. Perhaps the LORD
will intervene for us. Nothing can prevent the LORD from delivering, whether by many or by a few." 7 His armor-bearer said to
him, "Do everything that is on your mind. Do as you're inclined.
I'm with you all the way!"

8 Jonathan replied, "All right. We'll go over to these men and
fight them. 9 If they say to us, 'Stay put until we approach you,'
we will stay right there and not go up to them. 10 But if they say,
'Come up against us,' we will go up. For in that case the LORD has
given them into our hand—it will be a sign to us."

11 When they made themselves known to the Philistine garrison, the Philistines said, "Look! The Hebrews are coming out of
the holes in which they hid themselves." 12 Then the men of the
garrison said to Jonathan and his armor-bearer, "Come on up
to us so we can teach you a thing or two!" Then Jonathan said to
his armor-bearer, "Come up behind me, for the LORD has given
them into the hand of Israel!"

[13]Jonathan crawled up on his hands and feet, with his armor-
bearer following behind him. Jonathan struck down the Philistines, while his armor-bearer came along behind him and killed
them. [14]In this initial skirmish Jonathan and his armor-bearer
struck down about twenty men in an area that measured half
an acre.
[15]Then fear overwhelmed those who were in the camp, those who
were in the field, all the army in the garrison, and the raiding bands.
They trembled and the ground shook. This fear was caused by God.
[16]Saul's watchmen at Gibeah in the territory of Benjamin
looked on as the crowd of soldiers seemed to melt away first in
one direction and then in another. [17]So Saul said to the army that
was with him, "Muster the troops and see who is no longer with
us." When they mustered the troops, Jonathan and his armor-
bearer were not there. [18]So Saul said to Ahijah, "Bring near the
ephod," for he was at that time wearing the ephod in front of the
Israelites. [19]While Saul spoke to the priest, the panic in the Philistines' camp was becoming greater and greater. So Saul said to
the priest, "Withdraw your hand."
[20]Saul and all the army assembled and marched into battle,
where they found the Philistines in total panic killing one another with their swords. [21]The Hebrews who had earlier gone
over to the Philistine side joined the Israelites who were with
Saul and Jonathan. [22]When all the Israelites who had hidden
themselves in the hill country of Ephraim heard that the Philistines had fled, they too pursued them in battle. [23]So the LORD delivered Israel that day, and the battle shifted over to Beth Aven.

JONATHAN VIOLATES SAUL'S OATH

[24]Now the men of Israel were hard pressed that day, for Saul had
made the army agree to this oath: "Cursed be the man who eats
food before evening. I will get my vengeance on my enemies!"
So no one in the army ate anything.
[25]Now the whole army entered the forest, and there was honey
on the ground. [26]When the army entered the forest, they saw the
honey flowing, but no one ate any of it, for the army was afraid
of the oath. [27]But Jonathan had not heard about the oath his father had made the army take. He extended the end of his staff
that was in his hand and dipped it in the honeycomb. When
he ate it, his eyes gleamed. [28]Then someone from the army informed him, "Your father put the army under a strict oath saying,
'Cursed be the man who eats food today.' That is why the army
is tired." [29]Then Jonathan said, "My father has caused trouble
for the land. See how my eyes gleamed when I tasted just a little of this honey. [30]Certainly if the army had eaten some of the
enemies' provisions that they came across today, would not the
slaughter of the Philistines have been even greater?"
[31]On that day the army struck down the Philistines from
Micmash to Aijalon, and they became very tired. [32]So the army
rushed greedily on the plunder, confiscating sheep, cattle, and
calves. They slaughtered them right on the ground, and the army
ate them, blood and all.
[33]Now it was reported to Saul, "Look, the army is sinning
against the LORD by eating even the blood." He said, "All of you

have broken the covenant! Roll a large stone over here to me."
34 Then Saul said, "Scatter out among the army and say to them,
'Each of you bring to me your ox and sheep and slaughter them
in this spot and eat. But don't sin against the LORD by eating the
blood.'" So that night each one brought his ox and slaughtered
it there. 35 Then Saul built an altar for the LORD; it was the first
time he had built an altar for the LORD.

36 Saul said, "Let's go down after the Philistines at night; we
will rout them until the break of day. We won't leave any of
them alive!" They replied, "Do whatever seems best to you." But
the priest said, "Let's approach God here." 37 So Saul asked God,
"Should I go down after the Philistines? Will you deliver them
into the hand of Israel?" But he did not answer him that day.

38 Then Saul said, "All you leaders of the army come here. Find
out how this sin occurred today. 39 For as surely as the LORD, the
deliverer of Israel, lives, even if it turns out to be my own son Jonathan, he will certainly die!" But no one from the army said anything.

40 Then he said to all Israel, "You will be on one side, and I and
my son Jonathan will be on the other side." The army replied to
Saul, "Do whatever you think is best."

41 Then Saul said, "O LORD God of Israel! If this sin has been
committed by me or by my son Jonathan, then, O LORD God of
Israel, respond with Urim. But if this sin has been committed
by your people Israel, respond with Thummim." Then Jonathan
and Saul were indicated by lot, while the army was exonerated.
42 Then Saul said, "Cast the lot between me and my son Jonathan!" Jonathan was indicated by lot.

43 So Saul said to Jonathan, "Tell me what you have done." Jonathan told him, "I used the end of the staff that was in my hand
to taste a little honey. I must die!" 44 Saul said, "God will punish
me severely if Jonathan doesn't die!"

45 But the army said to Saul, "Should Jonathan, who won this
great victory in Israel, die? May it never be! As surely as the LORD
lives, not a single hair of his head will fall to the ground, for it is
with the help of God that he has acted today." So the army rescued Jonathan from death.

46 Then Saul stopped chasing the Philistines, and the Philistines went back home. 47 After Saul had secured his royal position over Israel, he fought against all their enemies on all
sides—the Moabites, Ammonites, Edomites, the kings of Zobah, and the Philistines. In every direction that he turned, he
was victorious. 48 He fought bravely, striking down the Amalekites and delivering Israel from the hand of its enemies.

MEMBERS OF SAUL'S FAMILY

49 The sons of Saul were Jonathan, Ishvi, and Malki-Shua. He had
two daughters; the older one was named Merab and the younger
Michal. 50 The name of Saul's wife was Ahinoam, the daughter of
Ahimaaz. The name of the general in command of his army was
Abner son of Ner, Saul's uncle. 51 Kish was the father of Saul, and
Ner the father of Abner was the son of Abiel.

52 There was fierce war with the Philistines all the days of Saul.
So whenever Saul saw anyone who was a warrior or a brave individual, he would conscript him.

SAUL IS REJECTED AS KING

15 Then Samuel said to Saul, "I was the one the LORD sent to
anoint you as king over his people Israel. Now listen to what
the LORD says. 2 Here is what the LORD of Heaven's Armies has
said: 'I carefully observed how the Amalekites opposed Israel
along the way when Israel came up from Egypt. 3 So go now and
strike down the Amalekites. Destroy everything they have. Don't
spare them. Put them to death—man, woman, child, infant, ox,
sheep, camel, and donkey alike.'"
4 So Saul assembled the army and mustered them at Telaim.
There were 200,000 foot soldiers and 10,000 men of Judah. 5 Saul
proceeded to the city of Amalek, where he set an ambush in the
wadi. 6 Saul said to the Kenites, "Go on and leave! Go down from
among the Amalekites. Otherwise I will sweep you away with
them. After all, you were kind to all the Israelites when they
came up from Egypt." So the Kenites withdrew from among the
Amalekites.
7 Then Saul struck down the Amalekites all the way from Havilah to Shur, which is next to Egypt. 8 He captured King Agag of
the Amalekites alive, but he executed all Agag's people with the
sword. 9 However, Saul and the army spared Agag, along with
the best of the flock, the cattle, the fatlings, and the lambs, as
well as everything else that was of value. They were not willing
to slaughter them. But they did slaughter everything that was
despised and worthless.
10 Then the LORD's message came to Samuel: 11 "I regret that I
have made Saul king, for he has turned away from me and has
not done what I told him to do." Samuel became angry and he
cried out to the LORD all that night.
12 Then Samuel got up early to meet Saul the next morning.
But Samuel was informed, "Saul has gone to Carmel where he
is setting up a monument for himself." Then Samuel left and
went down to Gilgal. 13 When Samuel came to Saul, Saul said to
him, "May the LORD bless you! I have fulfilled the LORD's orders."
14 Samuel replied, "If that is the case, then what is this sound
of sheep in my ears and the sound of cattle that I hear?" 15 Saul
said, "They were brought from the Amalekites; the army spared
the best of the flocks and cattle to sacrifice to the LORD our God.
But everything else we slaughtered."
16 Then Samuel said to Saul, "Wait a minute! Let me tell you
what the LORD said to me last night." Saul said to him, "Tell me."
17 Samuel said, "Is it not true that when you were insignificant
in your own eyes, you became head of the tribes of Israel? The
LORD chose you as king over Israel. 18 The LORD sent you on a campaign saying, 'Go and exterminate those sinful Amalekites! Fight
against them until you have destroyed them.' 19 Why haven't you
obeyed the LORD? Instead you have greedily rushed upon the
plunder! You have done what is wrong in the LORD's estimation."
20 Then Saul said to Samuel, "But I have obeyed the LORD! I
went on the campaign the LORD sent me on. I brought back
King Agag of the Amalekites after exterminating the Amalekites. 21 But the army took from the plunder some of the sheep
and cattle—the best of what was to be slaughtered—to sacrifice
to the LORD your God in Gilgal."

REFLECT

What was so significant about Saul's actions that caused God to reject him as king? Was God justified in His actions toward Saul?

[22]Then Samuel said,
"Does the LORD take pleasure in burnt
offerings and sacrifices
as much as he does in obedience?
Certainly, obedience is better than sacrifice;
paying attention is better than the fat of rams.
23 For rebellion is like the sin of divination,
and presumption is like the evil of idolatry.
Because you have rejected the LORD's orders,
he has rejected you from being king."

[24]Then Saul said to Samuel, "I have sinned, for I have disobeyed
what the LORD commanded and your words as well. For I was
afraid of the army, and I obeyed their voice. [25]Now please forgive
my sin. Go back with me so I can worship the LORD."
[26]Samuel said to Saul, "I will not go back with you, for you have
rejected the LORD's orders, and the LORD has rejected you from
being king over Israel!"
[27]When Samuel turned to leave, Saul grabbed the edge of his
robe and it tore. [28]Samuel said to him, "The LORD has torn the
kingdom of Israel from you this day and has given it to one of
your colleagues who is better than you! [29]The Preeminent One
of Israel does not go back on his word or change his mind, for
he is not a human being who changes his mind." [30]Saul again
replied, "I have sinned. But please honor me before the elders
of my people and before Israel. Go back with me so I may worship the LORD your God." [31]So Samuel followed Saul back, and
Saul worshiped the LORD.

SAMUEL PUTS AGAG TO DEATH

[32]Then Samuel said, "Bring me King Agag of the Amalekites." So
Agag came to him trembling, thinking to himself, "Surely death
is bitter!" [33]Samuel said, "Just as your sword left women childless,
so your mother will be the most bereaved among women." Then
Samuel hacked Agag to pieces there in Gilgal before the LORD.
[34]Then Samuel went to Ramah, while Saul went up to his home
in Gibeah of Saul. [35]Until the day he died, Samuel did not see
Saul again. Samuel did, however, mourn for Saul, but the LORD
regretted that he had made Saul king over Israel.

SAMUEL ANOINTS DAVID AS KING

16 The LORD said to Samuel, "How long do you intend to
mourn for Saul? I have rejected him as king over Israel.
Fill your horn with olive oil and go. I am sending you to Jesse
in Bethlehem, for I have selected a king for myself from among
his sons."
[2]Samuel replied, "How can I go? Saul will hear about it and kill
me!" But the LORD said, "Take a heifer with you and say, 'I have
come to sacrifice to the LORD.' [3]Then invite Jesse to the sacrifice,
and I will show you what you should do. You will anoint for me
the one I point out to you."
[4]Samuel did what the LORD told him. When he arrived in Bethlehem, the elders of the city were afraid to meet him. They said,
"Do you come in peace?" [5]He replied, "Yes, in peace. I have come

REFLECT

Why is it significant that David was anointed king before he defeated Goliath? How do you think this affected his encounter with Goliath?

to sacrifice to the LORD. Consecrate yourselves and come with me to the sacrifice." So he consecrated Jesse and his sons and invited them to the sacrifice.

6 When they arrived, Samuel noticed Eliab and said to himself, "Surely, here before the LORD stands his chosen king." 7 But the LORD said to Samuel, "Don't be impressed by his appearance or his height, for I have rejected him. God does not view things the way people do. People look on the outward appearance, but the LORD looks at the heart."

8 Then Jesse called Abinadab and presented him to Samuel. But Samuel said, "The LORD has not chosen this one either." 9 Then Jesse presented Shammah. But Samuel said, "The LORD has not chosen this one either." 10 Jesse presented seven of his sons to Samuel. But Samuel said to Jesse, "The LORD has not chosen any of these." 11 Then Samuel asked Jesse, "Is that all the young men?" Jesse replied, "There is still the youngest one, but he's taking care of the flock." Samuel said to Jesse, "Send and get him, for we cannot turn our attention to other things until he comes here." 12 So Jesse had him brought in. Now he was ruddy, with attractive eyes and a handsome appearance. The LORD said, "Go and anoint him. This is the one." 13 So Samuel took the horn full of olive oil and anointed him in the presence of his brothers. The Spirit of the LORD rushed upon David from that day onward. Then Samuel got up and went to Ramah.

DAVID APPEARS BEFORE SAUL

14 Now the Spirit of the LORD had turned away from Saul, and an evil spirit from the LORD tormented him. 15 Then Saul's servants said to him, "Look, an evil spirit from God is tormenting you. 16 Let our lord instruct his servants who are here before you to look for a man who knows how to play the lyre. Then whenever the evil spirit from God comes upon you, he can play the lyre and you will feel better." 17 So Saul said to his servants, "Find me a man who plays well and bring him to me." 18 One of his attendants replied, "I have seen a son of Jesse in Bethlehem who knows how to play the lyre. He is a brave warrior and is articulate and handsome, for the LORD is with him."

19 So Saul sent messengers to Jesse and said, "Send me your son David, who is out with the sheep." 20 So Jesse took a donkey loaded with bread, a container of wine, and a young goat and sent them to Saul with his son David. 21 David came to Saul and stood before him. Saul liked him a great deal, and he became his armor-bearer. 22 Then Saul sent word to Jesse saying, "Let David be my servant, for I am very pleased with him."

23 So whenever the spirit from God would come upon Saul, David would take his lyre and play it. This would bring relief to Saul and make him feel better. Then the evil spirit would leave him alone.

DAVID KILLS GOLIATH

17 The Philistines gathered their troops for battle. They assembled at Socoh in Judah. They camped in Ephes Dammim, between Socoh and Azekah. 2 Saul and the Israelite army assembled and camped in the valley of Elah, where they arranged their

battle lines to fight against the Philistines. [3]The Philistines were
standing on one hill, and the Israelites on another hill, with the
valley between them.

[4]Then a champion came out from the camp of the Philistines.
His name was Goliath; he was from Gath. He was close to seven
feet tall. [5]He had a bronze helmet on his head and was wearing
scale body armor. The weight of his bronze body armor was 5,000
shekels. [6]He had bronze shin guards on his legs, and a bronze
javelin was slung over his shoulders. [7]The shaft of his spear was
like a weaver's beam, and the iron point of his spear weighed 600
shekels. His shield bearer was walking before him.

[8]Goliath stood and called to Israel's troops, "Why do you come
out to prepare for battle? Am I not the Philistine, and are you
not the servants of Saul? Choose for yourselves a man so he
may come down to me! [9]If he is able to fight with me and strike
me down, we will become your servants. But if I prevail against
him and strike him down, you will become our servants and will
serve us." [10]Then the Philistine said, "I defy Israel's troops this
day! Give me a man so we can fight each other!" [11]When Saul and
all the Israelites heard these words of the Philistine, they were
upset and very afraid.

[12]Now David was the son of an Ephrathite named Jesse from
Bethlehem in Judah. He had eight sons, and in Saul's days he was
old and well advanced in years. [13]Jesse's three oldest sons had followed Saul to war. The names of the three sons who went to war
were Eliab, his firstborn, Abinadab, the second oldest; and Shammah, the third oldest. [14]Now David was the youngest. While the
three oldest sons followed Saul, [15]David was going back and forth
from Saul in order to care for his father's sheep in Bethlehem.

[16]Meanwhile for forty days the Philistine approached every
morning and evening and took his position. [17]Jesse said to his
son David, "Take your brothers this ephah of roasted grain and
these ten loaves of bread; go quickly to the camp to your brothers. [18]Also take these ten portions of cheese to their commanding officer. Find out how your brothers are doing and bring back
their pledge that they received the goods. [19]They are with Saul
and the whole Israelite army in the valley of Elah, fighting with
the Philistines."

[20]So David got up early in the morning and entrusted the flock
to someone else who would watch over it. After loading up, he
went just as Jesse had instructed him. He arrived at the camp
as the army was going out to the battle lines shouting its battle
cry. [21]Israel and the Philistines drew up their battle lines opposite one another. [22]After David had entrusted his cargo to the
care of the supply officer, he ran to the battlefront. When he arrived, he asked his brothers how they were doing. [23]As he was
speaking with them, the champion named Goliath, the Philistine from Gath, was coming up from the battle lines of the Philistines. He spoke the way he usually did, and David heard it.
[24]When all the men of Israel saw this man, they retreated from
his presence and were very afraid.

[25]The men of Israel said, "Have you seen this man who is coming up? He does so to defy Israel. But the king will make the
man who can strike him down very wealthy! He will give him

his daughter in marriage, and he will make his father's house
exempt from tax obligations in Israel."
26 David asked the men who were standing near him, "What
will be done for the man who strikes down this Philistine and
frees Israel from this humiliation? For who is this uncircumcised
Philistine, that he defies the armies of the living God?" 27 The soldiers told him what had been promised, saying, "This is what will
be done for the man who can strike him down."
28 When David's oldest brother Eliab heard him speaking to
the men, he became angry with David and said, "Why have you
come down here? To whom did you entrust those few sheep in
the wilderness? I am familiar with your pride and deceit! You
have come down here to watch the battle."
29 David replied, "What have I done now? Can't I say anything?"
30 Then he turned from those who were nearby to someone else
and asked the same question, but they gave him the same answer
as before. 31 When David's words were overheard and reported
to Saul, he called for him.
32 David said to Saul, "Don't let anyone be discouraged. Your
servant will go and fight this Philistine!" 33 But Saul replied to
David, "You aren't able to go against this Philistine and fight
him. You're just a boy! He has been a warrior from his youth."
34 David replied to Saul, "Your servant has been a shepherd
for his father's flock. Whenever a lion or bear would come and
carry off a sheep from the flock, 35 I would go out after it, strike it
down, and rescue the sheep from its mouth. If it rose up against
me, I would grab it by its jaw, strike it, and kill it. 36 Your servant
has struck down both the lion and the bear. This uncircumcised
Philistine will be just like one of them, for he has defied the armies of the living God." 37 David went on to say, "The LORD who
delivered me from the lion and the bear will also deliver me
from the hand of this Philistine." Then Saul said to David, "Go!
The LORD will be with you."
38 Then Saul clothed David with his own fighting attire and put a
bronze helmet on his head. He also put body armor on him. 39 David strapped on his sword over his fighting attire and tried to walk
around, but he was not used to them. David said to Saul, "I can't
walk in these things, for I'm not used to them." So David removed
them. 40 He took his staff in his hand, picked out five smooth
stones from the stream, placed them in the pouch of his shepherd's bag, took his sling in hand, and approached the Philistine.
41 The Philistine, with his shield bearer walking in front of him,
kept coming closer to David. 42 When the Philistine looked carefully at David, he despised him, for he was only a ruddy and handsome boy. 43 The Philistine said to David, "Am I a dog, that you
are coming after me with sticks?" Then the Philistine cursed
David by his gods. 44 The Philistine said to David, "Come here to
me, so I can give your flesh to the birds of the sky and the wild
animals of the field!"
45 But David replied to the Philistine, "You are coming against
me with sword and spear and javelin. But I am coming against
you in the name of the LORD of Heaven's Armies, the God of Israel's armies, whom you have defied! 46 This very day the LORD
will deliver you into my hand. I will strike you down and cut off

your head. This day I will give the corpses of the Philistine army
to the birds of the sky and the wild animals of the land. Then all
the land will realize that Israel has a God, 47 and all this assembly
will know that it is not by sword or spear that the LORD saves! For
the battle is the LORD's, and he will deliver you into our hand."
48 The Philistine drew steadily closer to David to attack him,
while David quickly ran toward the battle line to attack the Philistine. 49 David reached his hand into the bag and took out a
stone. He slung it, striking the Philistine on the forehead. The
stone sank deeply into his forehead, and he fell down with his
face to the ground.
50 David prevailed over the Philistine with just the sling and
the stone. He struck down the Philistine and killed him. David
did not even have a sword in his hand. 51 David ran and stood
over the Philistine. He grabbed Goliath's sword, drew it from its
sheath, and after killing him, he cut off his head with it. When
the Philistines saw their champion was dead, they ran away.
52 Then the men of Israel and Judah charged forward, shouting a battle cry. They chased the Philistines to the valley and to
the very gates of Ekron. The Philistine corpses lay fallen along
the Shaaraim road to Gath and Ekron. 53 When the Israelites returned from their hot pursuit of the Philistines, they looted their
camp. 54 David took the head of the Philistine and brought it to
Jerusalem, and he put Goliath's weapons in his tent.
55 Now as Saul watched David going out to fight the Philistine,
he asked Abner, the general in command of the army, "Whose
son is that young man, Abner?" Abner replied, "As surely as you
live, O king, I don't know." 56 The king said, "Find out whose son
this boy is."
57 So when David returned from striking down the Philistine,
Abner took him and brought him before Saul. He still had the
head of the Philistine in his hand. 58 Saul said to him, "Whose
son are you, young man?" David replied, "I am the son of your
servant Jesse in Bethlehem."

SAUL COMES TO FEAR DAVID

18 When David had finished talking with Saul, Jonathan and
David became bound together in close friendship. Jonathan
loved David as much as he did his own life. 2 Saul retained David on that day and did not allow him to return to his father's
house. 3 Jonathan made a covenant with David, for he loved him
as much as he did his own life. 4 Jonathan took off the robe he
was wearing and gave it to David, along with the rest of his gear
including his sword, his bow, and even his belt.
5 On every mission on which Saul sent him, David achieved success. So Saul appointed him over the men of war. This pleased
not only all the army, but also Saul's servants.
6 When the men arrived after David returned from striking
down the Philistine, the women from all the cities of Israel came
out singing and dancing to meet King Saul. They were happy as
they played their tambourines and three-stringed instruments.
7 The women who were playing the music sang,

"Saul has struck down his thousands,
but David his tens of thousands!"

8 This made Saul very angry. The statement displeased him and he thought, "They have attributed to David tens of thousands, but to me they have attributed only thousands. What does he lack, except the kingdom?" 9 So Saul was keeping an eye on David from that day onward.

10 The next day an evil spirit from God rushed upon Saul and he prophesied within his house. Now David was playing the lyre as usual. There was a spear in Saul's hand, 11 and Saul threw the spear, thinking, "I'll nail David to the wall!" But David escaped from him on two different occasions.

12 So Saul feared David, because the LORD was with David but had departed from Saul. 13 Saul removed David from his presence and made him a commanding officer. David led the army out to battle and back. 14 Now David achieved success in all he did, for the LORD was with him. 15 When Saul saw how very successful he was, he was afraid of him. 16 But all Israel and Judah loved David, for he was the one leading them out to battle and back.

17 Then Saul said to David, "Here's my oldest daughter, Merab. I want to give her to you in marriage. Only be a brave warrior for me and fight the battles of the LORD." For Saul thought, "There's no need for me to raise my hand against him. Let it be the hand of the Philistines!"

18 David said to Saul, "Who am I? Who are my relatives or the clan of my father in Israel that I should become the king's son-in-law?" 19 When the time came for Merab, Saul's daughter, to be given to David, she instead was given in marriage to Adriel, who was from Meholah.

20 Now Michal, Saul's daughter, loved David. When they told Saul about this, it pleased him. 21 Saul said, "I will give her to him so that she may become a snare to him and so the hand of the Philistines may be against him." So Saul said to David, "Today is the second time for you to become my son-in-law."

22 Then Saul instructed his servants, "Tell David secretly, 'The king is pleased with you, and all his servants like you. So now become the king's son-in-law.'" 23 So Saul's servants spoke these words privately to David. David replied, "Is becoming the king's son-in-law something insignificant to you? I'm just a poor and lightly esteemed man!"

24 When Saul's servants reported what David had said, 25 Saul replied, "Here is what you should say to David: 'There is nothing that the king wants as a price for the bride except 100 Philistine foreskins, so that he can be avenged of his enemies.'" (Now Saul was thinking that he could kill David by the hand of the Philistines.)

26 So his servants told David these things and David agreed to become the king's son-in-law. Now the specified time had not yet expired 27 when David, along with his men, went out and struck down 200 Philistine men. David brought their foreskins and presented all of them to the king so that he could become the king's son-in-law. Saul then gave him his daughter Michal in marriage.

28 When Saul realized that the LORD was with David and that his daughter Michal loved David, 29 Saul became even more afraid of him. Saul continued to be at odds with David from then on. 30 The leaders of the Philistines would march out, and as often as they did so, David achieved more success than all of Saul's servants. His name was held in high esteem.

LOVE TO GROW

DAVID THE WARRIOR

1 SAMUEL 18:1–16

David is often viewed as a mighty warrior. He fought Goliath, conquered armies, and led with boldness.

But David was not fearless. There are many instances in Psalms where David admitted his fears. In fact, sometimes he was so fearful that he was almost debilitated. Despite his fear, God used David's boldness to grow him into a mighty warrior.

David became so successful in his military campaigns that poets wrote songs for him. First Samuel 18:7 recounts that the people celebrated his victory over the Philistines while the women sang, "Saul has struck down his thousands, but David his tens of thousands!"

Saul's mood soured quickly and jealousy overtook him. In an attempt to kill David, Saul hurled his spear at him—twice!

In another attempt to get rid of David, Saul made him a commanding officer. Again, God gave David great victory in this role. Saul continued in his jealousy, but he began to fear when he realized God was with David.

David was a great man, but we must realize it was God who made him great. David was not a mighty warrior because of his own strength and power but because of the strength God had given him. Instead of thinking, "Oh, I wish I were bold and brave like David," let's encourage ourselves to think, "I want to know and trust God the way David knew and trusted God."

May we earnestly desire for God to use us for the advancement of His kingdom in whatever way He sees fit. For some of us, this may mean being bold and brave in the midst of persecution. For others, this may mean being bold and brave in the treacheries of everyday life. Living a countercultural life, no matter the specifics, takes boldness and bravery.

David was a mighty warrior, but there is One even mightier whose power works through the weak and whose battle cry is one of victory and glory. Look to Him!

SAUL REPEATEDLY ATTEMPTS TO TAKE DAVID'S LIFE

19 Then Saul told his son Jonathan and all his servants to kill
David. But Saul's son Jonathan liked David very much. 2 So
Jonathan told David, "My father Saul is trying to kill you. So be
careful tomorrow morning. Find a hiding place and stay in seclusion. 3 I will go out and stand beside my father in the field
where you are. I will speak to my father about you. When I find
out what the problem is, I will let you know."

4 So Jonathan spoke on David's behalf to his father Saul. He
said to him, "The king should not sin against his servant David,
for he has not sinned against you. On the contrary, his actions
have been very beneficial for you. 5 He risked his life when he
struck down the Philistine, and the LORD gave all Israel a great
victory. When you saw it, you were happy. So why would you sin
against innocent blood by putting David to death for no reason?"
6 Saul accepted Jonathan's advice and took an oath, "As surely
as the LORD lives, he will not be put to death." 7 Then Jonathan
called David and told him all these things. Jonathan brought David to Saul, and he served him as he had done formerly.

8 Now once again there was war. So David went out to fight the
Philistines. He defeated them thoroughly, and they ran away
from him. 9 Then an evil spirit from the LORD came upon Saul.
He was sitting in his house with his spear in his hand, while David was playing the lyre. 10 Saul tried to nail David to the wall with
the spear, but he escaped from Saul's presence, and the spear
drove into the wall. David escaped quickly that night.

11 Saul sent messengers to David's house to guard it and to kill
him in the morning. Then David's wife Michal told him, "If you
do not save yourself tonight, tomorrow you will be dead!" 12 So
Michal lowered David through the window, and he ran away
and escaped.

13 Then Michal took a household idol and put it on the bed.
She put a quilt made of goats' hair over its head and then covered the idol with a garment. 14 When Saul sent messengers to
arrest David, she said, "He's sick."

15 Then Saul sent the messengers back to see David, saying,
"Bring him up to me on his bed so I can kill him." 16 When the
messengers came, they found only the idol on the bed and the
quilt made of goats' hair at its head.

17 Saul said to Michal, "Why have you deceived me this way by
sending my enemy away? Now he has escaped!" Michal replied
to Saul, "He said to me, 'Help me get away or else I will kill you!'"

18 Now David had run away and escaped. He went to Samuel in
Ramah and told him everything that Saul had done to him. Then
he and Samuel went and stayed at Naioth. 19 It was reported to
Saul saying, "David is at Naioth in Ramah." 20 So Saul sent messengers to capture David. When they saw a company of prophets prophesying with Samuel standing there as their leader, the
Spirit of God came upon Saul's messengers, and they also prophesied. 21 When it was reported to Saul, he sent more messengers,
but they prophesied too. So Saul sent messengers a third time,
but they also prophesied. 22 Finally Saul himself went to Ramah.
When he arrived at the large cistern that is in Secu, he asked,
"Where are Samuel and David?" They said, "At Naioth in Ramah."

23 So Saul went to Naioth in Ramah. The Spirit of God came
upon him as well, and he walked along prophesying until he came
to Naioth in Ramah. 24 He even stripped off his clothes and prophesied before Samuel. He lay there naked all that day and night.
(For that reason it is asked, "Is Saul also among the prophets?")

JONATHAN SEEKS TO PROTECT DAVID

20 David fled from Naioth in Ramah. He came to Jonathan
and asked, "What have I done? What is my offense? How
have I sinned before your father, that he is seeking my life?"
2 Jonathan said to him, "By no means are you going to die! My
father does nothing large or small without making me aware
of it. Why would my father hide this matter from me? It just
won't happen!"
3 Taking an oath, David again said, "Your father is very much
aware of the fact that I have found favor with you, and he has
thought, 'Don't let Jonathan know about this, or he will be upset.' But as surely as the LORD lives and you live, there is about
one step between me and death!" 4 Jonathan replied to David,
"Tell me what I can do for you."
5 David said to Jonathan, "Tomorrow is the new moon, and I
am certainly expected to join the king for a meal. You must send
me away so I can hide in the field until the third evening from
now. 6 If your father happens to miss me, you should say, 'David
urgently requested me to let him go to his town Bethlehem,
for there is an annual sacrifice there for his entire family.' 7 If
he should then say, 'That's fine,' then your servant is safe. But if
he becomes very angry, be assured that he has decided to harm
me. 8 You must be loyal to your servant, for you have made a covenant with your servant in the LORD's name. If I am guilty, you
yourself kill me! Why bother taking me to your father?"
9 Jonathan said, "Far be it from you to suggest this! If I were
at all aware that my father had decided to harm you, wouldn't
I tell you about it?" 10 David said to Jonathan, "Who will tell me
if your father answers you harshly?" 11 Jonathan said to David,
"Come on. Let's go out to the field."
When the two of them had gone out into the field, 12 Jonathan
said to David, "The LORD God of Israel is my witness! I will feel
out my father about this time the day after tomorrow. If he is favorably inclined toward David, will I not then send word to you
and let you know? 13 But if my father intends to do you harm,
may the LORD do all this and more to Jonathan, if I don't let you
know and send word to you, so you can go safely on your way.
May the LORD be with you, as he was with my father. 14 While I
am still alive, extend to me the loyalty of the LORD, or else I will
die. 15 Don't ever cut off your loyalty to my family, not even when
the LORD has cut off every one of David's enemies from the face
of the earth 16 and called David's enemies to account." So Jonathan made a covenant with the house of David. 17 Jonathan once
again took an oath with David, because he loved him. In fact Jonathan loved him as much as he did his own life. 18 Jonathan said
to him, "Tomorrow is the new moon, and you will be missed, for
your seat will be empty. 19 On the third day you should go down
quickly and come to the place where you hid yourself the day this

REFLECT

What does Jonathan's desire to protect David show about his faith in God? (Jonathan's father was king, but he was loyal to the one whom God had anointed.)

all started. Stay near the stone Ezel. 20 I will shoot three arrows
near it, as though I were shooting at a target. 21 When I send a boy
after them, I will say, 'Go and find the arrows.' If I say to the boy,
'Look, the arrows are on this side of you; get them,' then come
back. For as surely as the LORD lives, you will be safe and there
will be no problem. 22 But if I say to the boy, 'Look, the arrows
are on the other side of you,' then get away. For in that case the
LORD has sent you away. 23 With regard to the matter that you
and I discussed, the LORD is the witness between us forever."

24 So David hid in the field. When the new moon came, the king
sat down to eat his meal. 25 The king sat down in his usual place
by the wall, with Jonathan opposite him and Abner at his side.
But David's place was vacant. 26 However, Saul said nothing about
it that day, for he thought, "Something has happened to make
him ceremonially unclean. Yes, he must be unclean." 27 But the
next morning, the second day of the new moon, David's place
was still vacant. So Saul said to his son Jonathan, "Why has Jesse's son not come to the meal yesterday or today?"

28 Jonathan replied to Saul, "David urgently requested that he
be allowed to go to Bethlehem. 29 He said, 'Permit me to go, for we
are having a family sacrifice in the town, and my brother urged me
to be there. So now, if I have found favor with you, let me go to see
my brothers.' For that reason he has not come to the king's table."

30 Saul became angry with Jonathan and said to him, "You stupid traitor! Don't I realize that to your own disgrace and to the
disgrace of your mother's nakedness you have chosen this son
of Jesse? 31 For as long as this son of Jesse is alive on the earth,
you and your kingdom will not be established. Now, send some
men and bring him to me. For he is as good as dead!"

32 Jonathan responded to his father Saul, "Why should he be put
to death? What has he done?" 33 Then Saul threw his spear at Jonathan in order to strike him down. So Jonathan was convinced that
his father had decided to kill David. 34 Jonathan got up from the
table enraged. He did not eat any food on that second day of the
new moon, for he was upset that his father had humiliated David.

35 The next morning Jonathan, along with a young servant, went
out to the field to meet David. 36 He said to his servant, "Run,
find the arrows that I am about to shoot." As the servant ran,
Jonathan shot the arrow beyond him. 37 When the servant came
to the place where Jonathan had shot the arrow, Jonathan called
out to the servant, "Isn't the arrow farther beyond you?" 38 Jonathan called out to the servant, "Hurry! Go faster! Don't delay!"
Jonathan's servant retrieved the arrow and came back to his
master. 39 (Now the servant did not understand any of this. Only
Jonathan and David knew what was going on.) 40 Then Jonathan
gave his equipment to the servant who was with him. He said to
him, "Go, take these things back to the town."

41 When the servant had left, David got up from beside the
mound, knelt with his face to the ground, and bowed three times.
Then they kissed each other and they both wept, especially David. 42 Jonathan said to David, "Go in peace, for the two of us have
sworn together in the name of the LORD saying, 'The LORD will
be between me and you and between my descendants and your
descendants forever.'"

DAVID GOES TO NOB

Then David got up and left, while Jonathan went back to the
21 town of Naioth. 1 David went to Ahimelech the priest in
Nob. Ahimelech was shaking with fear when he met David, and said to him, "Why are you by yourself with no one accompanying you?" 2 David replied to Ahimelech the priest, "The
king instructed me to do something, but he said to me, 'Don't let
anyone know the reason I am sending you or the instructions I
have given you.' I have told my soldiers to wait at a certain place.
3 Now what do you have at your disposal? Give me five loaves of
bread, or whatever can be found."
4 The priest replied to David, "I don't have any ordinary bread
at my disposal. Only holy bread is available, and then only if your
soldiers have abstained from relations with women." 5 David said
to the priest, "Certainly women have been kept away from us,
just as on previous occasions when I have set out. The soldiers'
equipment is holy, even on an ordinary journey. How much more
so will they be holy today, along with their equipment!"
6 So the priest gave him holy bread, for there was no bread
there other than the Bread of the Presence. It had been removed
from before the LORD in order to replace it with hot bread on
the day it had been taken away. 7 (One of Saul's servants was
there that day, detained before the LORD. His name was Doeg
the Edomite, who was in charge of Saul's shepherds.) 8 David
said to Ahimelech, "Is there no sword or spear here at your disposal? I don't have my own sword or equipment in hand due to
the urgency of the king's instructions."

DAVID GOES TO GATH

9 The priest replied, "The sword of Goliath the Philistine, whom
you struck down in the valley of Elah, is wrapped in a garment
behind the ephod. If you wish, take it for yourself. Other than
that one, there's no sword here." David said, "There's nothing like
it. Give it to me." 10 So on that day David arose and fled from Saul.
He went to King Achish of Gath. 11 The servants of Achish said to
him, "Isn't this David, the king of the land? Isn't he the one that
they sing about when they dance, saying,
'Saul struck down his thousands,
but David his tens of thousands'?"

12 David thought about what they said and was very afraid of
King Achish of Gath. 13 He altered his behavior in their presence. Since he was in their power, he pretended to be insane,
making marks on the doors of the gate and letting his saliva
run down his beard.
14 Achish said to his servants, "Look at this madman! Why did
you bring him to me? 15 Do I have a shortage of fools so that you
have brought me this man to display his insanity in front of me?
Should this man enter my house?"

DAVID GOES TO ADULLAM AND MIZPAH

22 So David left there and escaped to the cave of Adullam.
When his brothers and the rest of his father's family
learned about it, they went down there to him. 2 All those who

LOVE TO GROW

WHEN FEAR GRIPS OUR HEARTS

1 SAMUEL 21:9–14

What an amazing God we have! How gracious He is to record testimonies of His faithfulness throughout the Bible. When we read about David's life, we see the difference between living for God and living for ourselves and the consequences that result from both.

David knew that God chose him and God was with him, and his confidence rested in God alone. It seemed everything he did was a huge success, so much so that it made King Saul very jealous. So jealous, in fact, that the king wanted to kill David. That's when David allowed fear to determine his actions instead of putting his faith in God.

David literally ran for his life. Though God had worked through him powerfully before, David took his eyes off God and took matters into his own hands.

Sadly, David turned to everyone but God. One by one, the titles and relationships David ran to for comfort were removed.

David was desperate. He had nowhere to turn, so he entered the land of his enemies, the Philistines, to find refuge. Sounds crazy, doesn't it? David had previously defeated their armies and their giant, Goliath, yet he turned to them for refuge from King Saul.

Fear caused David to run from relationship to relationship, from comfort to comfort, instead of turning to God. He allowed fear to chase him and exhaust him. Fear caused him to sacrifice his dignity in front of the very people to whom he had demonstrated God's power as a young man (1 Sam 17:45–47).

God allowed David to go through this season so he would learn to fully rely on God for safety and provision.

How many of us have done the very same thing, running back to things from our past in moments of weakness? It's a hard lesson to learn. It's much easier to trust in friendship, titles, status, and success for our security instead of turning to God. It's in God alone where we find the safety we seek.

If you've taken your eyes off of your Savior to find love or safety, be encouraged. If a person who authored so many psalms that show his love for God can fall into the fear trap, you're in good company. Let's not stay there. Commit to leaning on God and His Word, and find your strength and rest in Him.

were in trouble or owed someone money or were discontented
gathered around him, and he became their leader. He had about
400 men with him.
3 Then David went from there to Mizpah in Moab, where he
said to the king of Moab, "Please let my father and mother stay
with you until I know what God is going to do for me." 4 So he
had them stay with the king of Moab; they stayed with him
the whole time that David was in the stronghold. 5 Then Gad the
prophet said to David, "Don't stay in the stronghold. Go to the
land of Judah." So David left and went to the forest of Hereth.

SAUL EXECUTES THE PRIESTS

6 But Saul found out the whereabouts of David and the men who
were with him. Now Saul was sitting at Gibeah under the tamarisk tree at an elevated location with his spear in hand and all
his servants stationed around him. 7 Saul said to his servants,
"Listen up, you Benjaminites! Is Jesse's son giving fields and vineyards to all of you? Or is he making all of you commanders and
officers? 8 For all of you have conspired against me! No one informs me when my own son makes an agreement with the son
of Jesse. Not one of you feels sorry for me or informs me that my
own son has commissioned my own servant to hide in ambush
against me, as is the case today!"
9 But Doeg the Edomite, who had stationed himself with the
servants of Saul, replied, "I saw this son of Jesse come to Ahimelech son of Ahitub at Nob. 10 He inquired of the LORD for him
and gave him provisions. He also gave him the sword of Goliath
the Philistine."
11 Then the king arranged for a meeting with the priest Ahimelech son of Ahitub and all the priests of his father's house who
were at Nob. They all came to the king. 12 Then Saul said, "Listen, son of Ahitub." He replied, "Here I am, my lord." 13 Saul said
to him, "Why have you conspired against me, you and this son
of Jesse? You gave him bread and a sword and inquired of God
on his behalf, so that he opposes me and waits in ambush, as is
the case today!"
14 Ahimelech replied to the king, "Who among all your servants
is faithful like David? He is the king's son-in-law, the leader of your
bodyguard, and honored in your house. 15 Was it just today that
I began to inquire of God on his behalf? Far be it from me! The
king should not accuse his servant or any of my father's house,
for your servant is not aware of all this—not in whole or in part!"
16 But the king said, "You will surely die, Ahimelech, you and
all your father's house!" 17 Then the king said to the messengers
who were stationed beside him, "Turn and kill the priests of the
LORD, for they too have sided with David. They knew he was fleeing, but they did not inform me." But the king's servants refused
to harm the priests of the LORD.
18 Then the king said to Doeg, "You turn and strike down
the priests!" So Doeg the Edomite turned and struck down
the priests. He killed on that day eighty-five men who wore the
linen ephod. 19 As for Nob, the city of the priests, Doeg struck
down men and women, children and infants, oxen, donkeys, and
sheep—all with the sword.

20 But one of the sons of Ahimelech son of Ahitub escaped and fled to David. His name was Abiathar. 21 Abiathar told David that Saul had killed the priests of the LORD. 22 Then David said to Abiathar, "I knew that day when Doeg the Edomite was there that he would certainly tell Saul! I am guilty of all the deaths in your father's house. 23 Stay with me. Don't be afraid. Whoever seeks my life is seeking your life as well. You are secure with me."

DAVID DELIVERS THE CITY OF KEILAH

23 They told David, "The Philistines are fighting in Keilah and are looting the threshing floors." 2 So David asked the LORD, "Should I go and strike down these Philistines?" The LORD said to David, "Go, strike down the Philistines and deliver Keilah."

3 But David's men said to him, "We are afraid while we are still here in Judah. What will it be like if we go to Keilah against the armies of the Philistines?" 4 So David asked the LORD once again. But again the LORD replied, "Arise, go down to Keilah, for I will give the Philistines into your hand."

5 So David and his men went to Keilah and fought the Philistines. He took away their cattle and thoroughly defeated them. David delivered the inhabitants of Keilah.

DAVID ELUDES SAUL AGAIN

6 Now when Abiathar son of Ahimelech had fled to David at Keilah, he had brought with him an ephod. 7 When Saul was told that David had come to Keilah, Saul said, "God has delivered him into my hand, for he has boxed himself into a corner by entering a city with two barred gates." 8 So Saul mustered all his army to go down to Keilah and besiege David and his men.

9 When David realized that Saul was planning to harm him, he told Abiathar the priest, "Bring the ephod." 10 Then David said, "O LORD God of Israel, your servant has clearly heard that Saul is planning to come to Keilah to destroy the city because of me. 11 Will the leaders of Keilah deliver me into his hand? Will Saul come down as your servant has heard? O LORD God of Israel, please inform your servant."

Then the LORD said, "He will come down." 12 David asked, "Will the leaders of Keilah deliver me and my men into Saul's hand?" The LORD said, "They will deliver you over."

13 So David and his men, who numbered about 600, set out and left Keilah; they moved around from one place to another. When told that David had escaped from Keilah, Saul called a halt to his expedition. 14 David stayed in the strongholds that were in the desert and in the hill country of the wilderness of Ziph. Saul looked for him all the time, but God did not deliver David into his hands. 15 David realized that Saul had come out to seek his life; at that time David was in Horesh in the wilderness of Ziph.

16 Then Jonathan son of Saul left and went to David at Horesh. He encouraged him through God. 17 He said to him, "Don't be afraid! For the hand of my father Saul cannot find you. You will rule over Israel, and I will be your second in command. Even my father Saul realizes this." 18 When the two of them had made a covenant before the LORD, David stayed at Horesh, but Jonathan went to his house.

19 Then the Ziphites went up to Saul at Gibeah and said, "Isn't
David hiding among us in the strongholds at Horesh on the hill
of Hakilah, south of Jeshimon? 20 Now at your own discretion,
O king, come down. Delivering him into the king's hand will be
our responsibility."
21 Saul replied, "May you be blessed by the LORD, for you have
had compassion on me. 22 Go and make further arrangements.
Determine precisely where he is and who has seen him there,
for I am told that he is extremely cunning. 23 Locate precisely all
the places where he hides and return to me with dependable information. Then I will go with you. If he is in the land, I will find
him among all the thousands of Judah."
24 So they left and went to Ziph ahead of Saul. Now David and
his men were in the wilderness of Maon, in the rift valley to the
south of Jeshimon. 25 Saul and his men went to look for him. But
David was informed and went down to the rock and stayed in
the wilderness of Maon. When Saul heard about it, he pursued
David in the wilderness of Maon. 26 Saul went on one side of the
mountain, while David and his men went on the other side of the
mountain. David was hurrying to get away from Saul, but Saul
and his men were surrounding David and his men to capture
them. 27 But a messenger came to Saul saying, "Come quickly,
for the Philistines have raided the land!"
28 So Saul stopped pursuing David and went to confront the
Philistines. Therefore that place is called Sela Hammahlekoth.
29 Then David went up from there and stayed in the strongholds
of En Gedi.

DAVID SPARES SAUL'S LIFE

24 When Saul returned from pursuing the Philistines, he
was told, "Look, David is in the desert of En Gedi." 2 So
Saul took 3,000 select men from all Israel and went to find David and his men in the region of the rocks of the mountain goats.
3 He came to the sheepfolds by the road, where there was a cave.
Saul went into it to relieve himself.
Now David and his men were sitting in the recesses of the cave.
4 David's men said to him, "This is the day about which the LORD
said to you, 'I will give your enemy into your hand, and you can
do to him whatever seems appropriate to you.'" So David got up
and quietly cut off an edge of Saul's robe. 5 Afterward David's conscience bothered him because he had cut off an edge of Saul's
robe. 6 He said to his men, "May the LORD keep me far away from
doing such a thing to my lord, who is the LORD's chosen one, by
extending my hand against him. After all, he is the LORD's chosen one." 7 David restrained his men with these words and did
not allow them to rise up against Saul. Then Saul left the cave
and started down the road.
8 Afterward David got up and went out of the cave. He called
out to Saul, "My lord, O king!" When Saul looked behind him, David kneeled down and bowed with his face to the ground. 9 David
said to Saul, "Why do you pay attention when men say, 'David
is seeking to do you harm'? 10 Today your own eyes see how the
LORD delivered you—this very day—into my hands in the cave.
Some told me to kill you, but I had pity on you and said, 'I will

not extend my hand against my lord, for he is the LORD's chosen one.' 11 Look, my father, and see the edge of your robe in my
hand! When I cut off the edge of your robe, I didn't kill you. So
realize and understand that I am not planning evil or rebellion.
Even though I have not sinned against you, you are waiting in
ambush to take my life. 12 May the LORD judge between the two
of us, and may the LORD vindicate me over you, but my hand
will not be against you. 13 It's like the old proverb says: 'From
evil people evil proceeds.' But my hand will not be against you.
14 Who has the king of Israel come out after? Who is it that you
are pursuing? A dead dog? A single flea? 15 May the LORD be our
judge and arbiter. May he see and arbitrate my case and deliver
me from your hands."

16 When David finished speaking these words to Saul, Saul said,
"Is that your voice, my son David?" Then Saul wept loudly. 17 He
said to David, "You are more innocent than I, for you have treated
me well, even though I have tried to harm you. 18 You have explained today how you have treated me well. The LORD delivered
me into your hand, but you did not kill me. 19 Now if a man finds
his enemy, does he send him on his way in good shape? May the
LORD repay you with good this day for what you have done to
me. 20 Now look, I realize that you will in fact be king and that
the kingdom of Israel will be established in your hands. 21 So now
swear to me in the LORD's name that you will not kill my descendants after me or destroy my name from the house of my father."

22 David promised Saul this on oath. Then Saul went to his
house, and David and his men went up to the stronghold.

THE DEATH OF SAMUEL

25 Samuel died, and all Israel assembled and mourned him.
They buried him at his home in Ramah. Then David left
and went down to the wilderness of Paran.

DAVID MARRIES ABIGAIL THE WIDOW OF NABAL

2 There was a man in Maon whose business was in Carmel. This
man was very wealthy; he owned 3,000 sheep and 1,000 goats.
At that time he was shearing his sheep in Carmel. 3 The man's
name was Nabal, and his wife's name was Abigail. She was both
wise and beautiful, but the man was harsh and his deeds were
evil. He was a Calebite.

4 When David heard in the wilderness that Nabal was shearing
his sheep, 5 he sent ten servants, saying to them, "Go up to Carmel to see Nabal and give him greetings in my name. 6 Then you
will say to my brother, 'Peace to you and your house! Peace to all
that is yours! 7 Now I hear that they are shearing sheep for you.
When your shepherds were with us, we neither insulted them
nor harmed them the whole time they were in Carmel. 8 Ask
your own servants; they can tell you! May my servants find favor
in your sight, for we have come at the time of a holiday. Please
provide us—your servants and your son David—with whatever
you can spare.'"

9 So David's servants went and spoke all these words to Nabal in David's name. Then they paused. 10 But Nabal responded
to David's servants, "Who is David, and who is this son of Jesse?

This is a time when many servants are breaking away from their
masters! 11 Should I take my bread and my water and my meat
that I have slaughtered for my shearers and give them to these
men? I don't even know where they came from!"
12 So David's servants went on their way. When they had returned, they came and told David all these things. 13 Then David instructed his men, "Each of you strap on your sword!" So
each one strapped on his sword, and David also strapped on his
sword. About 400 men followed David, while 200 stayed behind
with the equipment.
14 But one of the servants told Nabal's wife Abigail, "David
sent messengers from the wilderness to greet our lord, but he
screamed at them. 15 These men were very good to us. They did
not insult us, nor did we sustain any loss during the entire time
we were together in the field. 16 Both night and day they were a
protective wall for us the entire time we were with them, while
we were tending our flocks. 17 Now be aware of this, and see what
you can do. For disaster has been planned for our lord and his
entire household. He is such a wicked person that no one tells
him anything!"
18 So Abigail quickly took 200 loaves of bread, two containers of wine, five prepared sheep, five seahs of roasted grain, 100
bunches of raisins, and 200 lumps of pressed figs. She loaded
them on donkeys 19 and said to her servants, "Go on ahead of me.
I will come after you." But she did not tell her husband Nabal.
20 Riding on her donkey, she went down under cover of the
mountain. David and his men were coming down to meet her,
and she encountered them. 21 Now David had been thinking, "In
vain I guarded everything that belonged to this man in the wilderness. I didn't take anything from him. But he has repaid my
good with evil. 22 God will severely punish David, if I leave alive
until morning even one male from all those who belong to him!"
23 When Abigail saw David, she got down quickly from the donkey, threw herself facedown before David, and bowed to the
ground. 24 Falling at his feet, she said, "My lord, I accept all the
guilt! But please let your female servant speak to you! Please listen to the words of your servant! 25 My lord should not pay attention to this wicked man Nabal. He simply lives up to his name!
His name means 'fool,' and he is indeed foolish! But I, your servant, did not see the servants my lord sent.
26 "Now, my lord, as surely as the LORD lives and as surely as
you live, it is the LORD who has kept you from shedding blood
and taking matters into your own hands. Now may your enemies
and those who seek to harm my lord be like Nabal. 27 Now let this
present that your servant has brought to my lord be given to the
servants who follow my lord. 28 Please forgive the sin of your servant, for the LORD will certainly establish a lasting dynasty for my
lord, because my lord fights the battles of the LORD. May no evil
be found in you all your days! 29 When someone sets out to chase
you and to take your life, the life of my lord will be wrapped securely in the bag of the living by the LORD your God. But he will
sling away the lives of your enemies from the sling's pocket! 30 The
LORD will do for my lord everything that he promised you, and he
will make you a leader over Israel. 31 Your conscience will not be

overwhelmed with guilt for having poured out innocent blood and for having taken matters into your own hands. When the LORD has granted my lord success, please remember your servant."

32 Then David said to Abigail, "Praised be the LORD, the God of Israel, who has sent you this day to meet me! 33 Praised be your good judgment! May you yourself be rewarded for having prevented me this day from shedding blood and taking matters into my own hands! 34 Otherwise, as surely as the LORD, the God of Israel, lives—he who has prevented me from harming you—if you had not come so quickly to meet me, by morning's light not even one male belonging to Nabal would have remained alive!" 35 Then David took from her hand what she had brought to him. He said to her, "Go back to your home in peace. Be assured that I have listened to you and responded favorably."

36 When Abigail went back to Nabal, he was holding a banquet in his house like that of the king. Nabal was having a good time and was very intoxicated. She told him absolutely nothing until morning's light. 37 In the morning, when Nabal was sober, his wife told him about these matters. He had a stroke and was paralyzed. 38 After about ten days the LORD struck Nabal down and he died.

39 When David heard that Nabal had died, he said, "Praised be the LORD who has vindicated me and avenged the insult that I suffered from Nabal! The LORD has kept his servant from doing evil, and he has repaid Nabal for his evil deeds." Then David sent word to Abigail and asked her to become his wife.

40 So the servants of David went to Abigail at Carmel and said to her, "David has sent us to you to bring you back to be his wife." 41 She arose, bowed her face toward the ground, and said, "Your female servant, like a lowly servant, will wash the feet of the servants of my lord." 42 Then Abigail quickly went and mounted her donkey, with five of her female servants accompanying her. She followed David's messengers and became his wife.

43 David had also married Ahinoam from Jezreel; the two of them became his wives. 44 (Now Saul had given his daughter Michal, David's wife, to Paltiel son of Laish, who was from Gallim.)

DAVID SPARES SAUL'S LIFE AGAIN

26 The Ziphites came to Saul at Gibeah and said, "Isn't David hiding on the hill of Hakilah near Jeshimon?" 2 So Saul arose and went down to the wilderness of Ziph, accompanied by 3,000 select men of Israel, to look for David in the wilderness of Ziph. 3 Saul camped by the road on the hill of Hakilah near Jeshimon, but David was staying in the wilderness. When he realized that Saul had come to the wilderness to find him, 4 David sent scouts and verified that Saul had indeed arrived.

5 So David set out and went to the place where Saul was camped. David saw the place where Saul and Abner son of Ner, the general in command of his army, were sleeping. Now Saul was lying in the entrenchment, and the army was camped all around him. 6 David said to Ahimelech the Hittite and Abishai son of Zeruiah, Joab's brother, "Who will go down with me to Saul in the camp?" Abishai replied, "I will go down with you."

7 So David and Abishai approached the army at night and found
Saul lying asleep in the entrenchment with his spear stuck in the
ground by his head. Abner and the army were lying all around
him. 8 Abishai said to David, "Today God has delivered your enemy into your hands. Now let me drive the spear right through
him into the ground with one swift jab! A second jab won't be
necessary!"

9 But David said to Abishai, "Don't kill him! Who can extend
his hand against the LORD's chosen one and remain guiltless?"
10 David went on to say, "As the LORD lives, the LORD himself will
strike him down. Either his day will come and he will die, or he
will go down into battle and be swept away. 11 But may the LORD
prevent me from extending my hand against the LORD's chosen
one! Now take the spear by Saul's head and the jug of water, and
let's get out of here!" 12 So David took the spear and the jug of water by Saul's head, and they got out of there. No one saw them or
was aware of their presence or woke up. All of them were asleep,
for the LORD had caused a deep sleep to fall on them.

13 Then David crossed to the other side and stood on the top of
the hill some distance away; there was a considerable distance
between them. 14 David called to the army and to Abner son of
Ner, "Won't you answer, Abner?" Abner replied, "Who are you,
that you have called to the king?" 15 David said to Abner, "Aren't
you a man? After all, who is like you in Israel? Why then haven't
you protected your lord the king? One of the soldiers came to
kill your lord the king. 16 This failure on your part isn't good! As
surely as the LORD lives, you people who have not protected your
lord, the LORD's chosen one, are as good as dead! Now look where
the king's spear and the jug of water that was by his head are!"

17 When Saul recognized David's voice, he said, "Is that your
voice, my son David?" David replied, "Yes, it's my voice, my lord
the king." 18 He went on to say, "Why is my lord chasing his servant? What have I done? What wrong have I done? 19 So let my
lord the king now listen to the words of his servant. If the LORD
has incited you against me, may he take delight in an offering.
But if men have instigated this, may they be cursed before the
LORD! For they have driven me away this day from being united
with the LORD's inheritance, saying, 'Go on, serve other gods!'
20 Now don't let my blood fall to the ground away from the LORD's
presence, for the king of Israel has gone out to look for a flea the
way one looks for a partridge in the hill country."

21 Saul replied, "I have sinned. Come back, my son David. I won't
harm you anymore, for you treated my life with value this day. I
have behaved foolishly and have made a very terrible mistake!"
22 David replied, "Here is the king's spear! Let one of your servants cross over and get it. 23 The LORD rewards each man for his
integrity and loyalty. Even though today the LORD delivered you
into my hand, I was not willing to extend my hand against the
LORD's chosen one. 24 In the same way that I valued your life this
day, may the LORD value my life and deliver me from all danger."
25 Saul replied to David, "May you be rewarded, my son David!
You will without question be successful!" So David went on his
way, and Saul returned to his place.

REFLECT

Why did David spare Saul's life (for the second time)? What does this say about David's character? How does David's character compare to Saul's?

DAVID ALIGNS HIMSELF WITH THE PHILISTINES

27 David thought to himself, "One of these days I'm going to
be swept away by the hand of Saul! There is nothing better
for me than to escape to the land of the Philistines. Then Saul
will despair of searching for me through all the territory of Israel and I will escape from his hand."
2 So David left and crossed over to King Achish son of Maoch of
Gath accompanied by his 600 men. 3 David settled with Achish
in Gath, along with his men and their families. David had with
him his two wives, Ahinoam the Jezreelite and Abigail the Carmelite, Nabal's widow. 4 When Saul learned that David had fled
to Gath, he did not mount a new search for him.
5 David said to Achish, "If I have found favor with you, let me be
given a place in one of the country towns so that I can live there.
Why should your servant settle in the royal city with you?" 6 So
Achish gave him Ziklag on that day. (For that reason Ziklag has
belonged to the kings of Judah until this very day.) 7 The length
of time that David lived in the Philistine countryside was a year
and four months.
8 Then David and his men went up and raided the Geshurites,
the Girzites, and the Amalekites. (They had been living in that
land for a long time, from the approach to Shur as far as the land
of Egypt.) 9 When David would attack a district, he would leave
neither man nor woman alive. He would take sheep, cattle, donkeys, camels, and clothing and would then go back to Achish.
10 When Achish would ask, "Where did you raid today?" David
would say, "The Negev of Judah" or "The Negev of Jerahmeel" or
"The Negev of the Kenites." 11 Neither man nor woman would David leave alive so as to bring them back to Gath. He was thinking, "This way they can't tell on us, saying, 'This is what David
did.'" Such was his practice the entire time that he lived in the
country of the Philistines. 12 So Achish trusted David, thinking
to himself, "He is really hated among his own people in Israel!
From now on he will be my servant."

THE WITCH OF ENDOR

28 In those days the Philistines gathered their troops for war
in order to fight Israel. Achish said to David, "You should
fully understand that you and your men must go with me into
the battle." 2 David replied to Achish, "That being the case, you
will come to know what your servant can do!" Achish said to David, "Then I will make you my bodyguard from now on."
3 Now Samuel had died, and all Israel had lamented over him
and had buried him in Ramah, his hometown. In the meantime
Saul had removed the mediums and magicians from the land.
4 The Philistines assembled; they came and camped at Shunem.
Saul mustered all Israel and camped at Gilboa. 5 When Saul saw
the camp of the Philistines, he was absolutely terrified. 6 So Saul
inquired of the LORD, but the LORD did not answer him—not by
dreams nor by Urim nor by the prophets. 7 So Saul instructed his
servants, "Find me a woman who is a medium, so that I may go
to her and inquire of her." His servants replied to him, "There is
a woman who is a medium in Endor."
8 So Saul disguised himself and put on other clothing and left,

accompanied by two of his men. They came to the woman at
night and said, "Use your ritual pit to conjure up for me the
one I tell you."
9 But the woman said to him, "Look, you are aware of what
Saul has done; he has removed the mediums and magicians
from the land! Why are you trapping me so you can put me to
death?" 10 But Saul swore an oath to her by the LORD, "As surely
as the LORD lives, you will not incur guilt in this matter!" 11 The
woman replied, "Who is it that I should bring up for you?" He
said, "Bring up for me Samuel."
12 When the woman saw Samuel, she cried out loudly. The woman said to Saul, "Why have you deceived me? You are Saul!" 13 The
king said to her, "Don't be afraid! But what have you seen?" The
woman replied to Saul, "I have seen a divine being coming up
from the ground!" 14 He said to her, "What about his appearance?"
She said, "An old man is coming up! He is wrapped in a robe!"
Then Saul realized it was Samuel, and he bowed his face toward
the ground and kneeled down. 15 Samuel said to Saul, "Why have
you disturbed me by bringing me up?" Saul replied, "I am terribly troubled! The Philistines are fighting against me and God
has turned away from me. He does not answer me anymore—
not by the prophets nor by dreams. So I have called on you to
tell me what I should do."
16 Samuel said, "Why are you asking me, now that the LORD has
turned away from you and has become your enemy? 17 The LORD
has done exactly as I prophesied! The LORD has torn the kingdom from your hand and has given it to your neighbor David!
18 Since you did not obey the LORD and did not carry out his fierce
anger against the Amalekites, the LORD has done this thing to
you today. 19 The LORD will hand you and Israel over to the Philistines! Tomorrow both you and your sons will be with me. The
LORD will also hand the army of Israel over to the Philistines!"
20 Saul quickly fell full length on the ground and was very afraid
because of Samuel's words. He was completely drained of energy,
having not eaten anything all that day and night. 21 When the woman came to Saul and saw how terrified he was, she said to him,
"Your servant has done what you asked. I took my life into my
own hands and did what you told me. 22 Now it's your turn to listen
to your servant! Let me set before you a bit of bread so that you
can eat. When you regain your strength, you can go on your way."
23 But he refused, saying, "I won't eat!" Both his servants and
the woman urged him to eat, so he gave in. He got up from the
ground and sat down on the bed. 24 Now the woman had a well-
fed calf at her home that she quickly slaughtered. Taking some
flour, she kneaded it and baked bread without leaven. 25 She
brought it to Saul and his servants, and they ate. Then they arose
and left that same night.

DAVID IS REJECTED BY THE PHILISTINE LEADERS

29 The Philistines assembled all their troops at Aphek, while
Israel camped at the spring that is in Jezreel. 2 When the
leaders of the Philistines were passing in review at the head of
their units of hundreds and thousands, David and his men were
passing in review in the rear with Achish.

3 The leaders of the Philistines asked, "What about these Hebrews?" Achish said to the leaders of the Philistines, "Isn't this
David, the servant of King Saul of Israel, who has been with me
for quite some time? I have found no fault with him from the
day of his defection until the present time!"
4 But the leaders of the Philistines became angry with him and
said to him, "Send the man back! Let him return to the place that
you assigned him! Don't let him go down with us into the battle,
for he might become our adversary in the battle. What better
way to please his lord than with the heads of these men? 5 Isn't
this David, of whom they sang as they danced,

'Saul has struck down his thousands,
but David his tens of thousands'?"

6 So Achish summoned David and said to him, "As surely as
the LORD lives, you are an honest man, and I am glad to have
you serving with me in the army. I have found no fault with you
from the day that you first came to me until the present time.
But in the opinion of the leaders, you are not reliable. 7 So turn
and leave in peace. You must not do anything that the leaders
of the Philistines consider improper!"
8 But David said to Achish, "What have I done? What have you
found in your servant from the day that I first came into your
presence until the present time, that I shouldn't go and fight the
enemies of my lord the king?" 9 Achish replied to David, "I am
convinced that you are as reliable as the angel of God! However,
the leaders of the Philistines have said, 'He must not go up with
us in the battle.' 10 So get up early in the morning along with the
servants of your lord who have come with you. When you get up
early in the morning, as soon as it is light enough to see, leave."
11 So David and his men got up early in the morning to return to
the land of the Philistines, but the Philistines went up to Jezreel.

DAVID DEFEATS THE AMALEKITES

30 On the third day David and his men came to Ziklag. Now
the Amalekites had raided the Negev and Ziklag. They
attacked Ziklag and burned it. 2 They took captive the women
and all who were in it, from the youngest to the oldest, but they
did not kill anyone. They simply carried them off and went on
their way.
3 When David and his men came to the city, they found it
burned. Their wives, sons, and daughters had been taken captive.
4 Then David and the men who were with him wept loudly until they could weep no more. 5 David's two wives had been taken
captive—Ahinoam the Jezreelite and Abigail the Carmelite, Nabal's widow. 6 David was very upset, for the men were thinking of
stoning him; each man grieved bitterly over his sons and daughters. But David drew strength from the LORD his God.
7 Then David said to the priest Abiathar son of Ahimelech,
"Bring me the ephod." So Abiathar brought the ephod to David.
8 David inquired of the LORD, saying, "Should I pursue this raiding band? Will I overtake them?" He said to him, "Pursue, for you
will certainly overtake them and carry out a rescue!"
9 So David went, accompanied by his 600 men. When he came

to the Wadi Besor, those who were in the rear stayed there. [10] David and 400 men continued the pursuit, but 200 men who were
too exhausted to cross the Wadi Besor stayed there.

[11] Then they found an Egyptian in the field and brought him to
David. They gave him bread to eat and water to drink. [12] They gave
him a slice of pressed figs and two bunches of raisins to eat. This
greatly refreshed him, for he had not eaten food or drunk water
for three days and three nights. [13] David said to him, "To whom
do you belong, and where are you from?" The young man said,
"I am an Egyptian, the servant of an Amalekite man. My master
abandoned me when I was ill for three days. [14] We conducted a
raid on the Negev of the Kerethites, on the area of Judah, and
on the Negev of Caleb. We burned Ziklag." [15] David said to him,
"Can you take us down to this raiding party?" He said, "Swear to
me by God that you will not kill me or hand me over to my master, and I will take you down to this raiding party."

[16] So he took David down, and they found them spread out
over the land. They were eating and drinking and enjoying themselves because of all the loot they had taken from the land of
the Philistines and from the land of Judah. [17] But David struck
them down from twilight until the following evening. None of
them escaped, with the exception of 400 young men who got
away on camels. [18] David retrieved everything the Amalekites
had taken; he also rescued his two wives. [19] There was nothing
missing, whether small or great. He retrieved sons and daughters, the plunder, and everything else they had taken. David
brought everything back. [20] David took all the flocks and herds
and drove them in front of the rest of the animals. People were
saying, "This is David's plunder!"

[21] Then David approached the 200 men who had been too exhausted to go with him, those whom they had left at the Wadi
Besor. They went out to meet David and the people who were
with him. When David approached the people, he asked how they
were doing. [22] But all the evil and worthless men among those
who had gone with David said, "Since they didn't go with us, we
won't give them any of the loot we retrieved! They may take only
their wives and children. Let them lead them away and be gone!"

[23] But David said, "No! You shouldn't do this, my brothers. Look
at what the LORD has given us! He has protected us and has delivered into our hands the raiding party that came against us.
[24] Who will listen to you in this matter? The portion of the one
who went down into the battle will be the same as the portion
of the one who remained with the equipment! Let their portions be the same!"

[25] From that time onward it was a binding ordinance for Israel,
right up to the present time.

[26] When David came to Ziklag, he sent some of the plunder to
the elders of Judah who were his friends, saying, "Here's a gift for
you from the looting of the LORD's enemies!" [27] The gift was for
those in the following locations: for those in Bethel, Ramoth Negev, and Jattir; [28] for those in Aroer, Siphmoth, Eshtemoa, [29] and
Racal; for those in the cities of the Jerahmeelites and Kenites;
[30] for those in Hormah, Bor Ashan, Athach, [31] and Hebron; and for
those in whatever other places David and his men had traveled.

THE DEATH OF SAUL

31 Now the Philistines were fighting against Israel. The men of Israel fled from the Philistines and many of them fell dead on Mount Gilboa. 2 The Philistines stayed right on the heels of Saul and his sons. They struck down Saul's sons Jonathan, Abinadab, and Malki-Shua. 3 Saul himself was in the thick of the battle; the archers spotted him and wounded him severely.

4 Saul said to his armor-bearer, "Draw your sword and stab me with it! Otherwise these uncircumcised people will come, stab me, and torture me." But his armor-bearer refused to do it, because he was very afraid. So Saul took his sword and fell on it. 5 When his armor-bearer saw that Saul was dead, he also fell on his own sword and died with him. 6 So Saul, his three sons, his armor-bearer, and all his men died together that day.

7 When the men of Israel who were in the valley and across the Jordan saw that the men of Israel had fled and that Saul and his sons were dead, they abandoned the cities and fled. The Philistines came and occupied them.

8 The next day, when the Philistines came to strip loot from the corpses, they discovered Saul and his three sons lying dead on Mount Gilboa. 9 They cut off Saul's head and stripped him of his armor. They sent messengers to announce the news in the temple of their idols and among their people throughout the surrounding land of the Philistines. 10 They placed Saul's armor in the temple of the Ashtoreths and hung his corpse on the city wall of Beth Shan.

11 When the residents of Jabesh Gilead heard what the Philistines had done to Saul, 12 all their warriors set out and traveled throughout the night. They took Saul's corpse and the corpses of his sons from the city wall of Beth Shan and went to Jabesh, where they burned them. 13 They took the bones and buried them under the tamarisk tree at Jabesh; then they fasted for seven days.

HE is faithful to David and to his descendants FOREVER

MEMORY VERSE

"He gives his king magnificent victories; he is faithful to his chosen ruler, to David and to his descendants forever!"

2 Samuel 22:51

2 Samuel

INTRODUCTION

God's Providence

From answering the prayer of a barren woman to raising up a king after His own heart, God displays His providence for His people throughout the books of 1 and 2 Samuel. Despite the rebellious nature of the nation of Israel, God provided for them.

Second Samuel is a historical narrative that chronicles the life and reign of King David, the only king of Israel of whom God said, "a man after my heart, who will accomplish everything I want him to do" (Acts 13:22). After a period of rebellion and sin, David's reign was a time of restoration in Israel, turning the hearts of the people back to their true King. The first ten chapters of 2 Samuel show the triumphs of David while chapters 11–20 describe his troubles and failures. Even though David was not a perfect king, he was still God's chosen person to lead Israel back to Him.

First and 2 Samuel were originally one book called, "The Book of Samuel." Around 150 B.C. these books were translated from the original Hebrew into Greek and combined with 1 and 2 Kings. These writings made up the history of the Israelite monarchy. They were later divided into the four books we have today. There is evidence that Samuel wrote the first sections of the book while the prophet Nathan and the seer Gad wrote the remaining portions. Later editors might also account for the additions regarding the events which occurred after the deaths of these three authors. The authors of 1 and 2 Samuel recorded their events as they experienced them first hand. It is believed that the events in 2 Samuel occurred between 1000 and 970 B.C.

Second Samuel is a book of history that gives a faithful record of the events of David's reign. This book also provides a great deal of insight into the character of God. God provided for His people by meeting their most significant needs. He established a kingdom and a family line that would ultimately usher in the life of His Son, Jesus Christ, the eternal King who would meet the most significant need of the world: salvation. We can love God greatly, resting in the truth that He meets our needs, no matter how small, urgent, or unexpected.

Switzerland

OFFICIAL LANGUAGES
French, German, Italian, and Romansh

POPULATION
8,526,000

UNREACHED POPULATION
231,000

PROFESSING CHRISTIANS
76.5%

Thirza's Home

Say a Prayer Today

Pray for Thirza and her ministry. Pray God would continue to provide for her, meeting each one of her needs in the perfect way that only He can.

HISTORY BIT

Built in 1380, the organ in Sion Church, located in Switzerland, is the world's oldest functioning organ.*

Source Information:
https://joshuaproject.net/countries/SZ
*John Bowden, A Chronology of World Christianity (New York, NY: Continuum, 2007), 232.

LOVE YOUR NEIGHBOR

Her Journey

THIRZA'S STORY

I held the bill in my hand, and I'm sure my heart skipped a beat. How on earth would I be able to pay that kind of money? I was a missionary, after all, supported by friends and relatives, with no regular income. I had just returned to Switzerland, my home country, for a furlough and had received a letter from the pension insurance, stating that I had to fill a gap of $2,000. I didn't own $2,000. How was I supposed to pay this?

Several years earlier I had given my life to the Lord and followed His call to go abroad and work with homeless children. My lifelong school of learning that God is enough had just started. I was without regular income, completely dependent on what the Lord wanted to give me week after week. I was slowly learning that my hope is truly in Him alone. He is my provider, and He knows what I need when I need it. Again and again, He provided and supplied, and I never lacked a single thing.

Until this day. This bill. This amount. My faith wavered. It's one thing to trust Him in daily matters. It's something else with a huge mountain like this. I decided not to tell anyone about this mountain but to truly put my hope in the Lord alone, to wait for Him. I decided to grow my faith and trust Him. Surely He would do something.

A few days later I went to church. After the service, an elderly gentleman came up to me with an envelope. "This is for you," he said. "I felt the Lord tell me to give it to you." I thanked him and my heart soared. Could it possibly be? I knew the answer when I opened the envelope at home. I didn't even need to count the money that was in it. He had provided for me once again. He is enough. He is all I need. The $2,000 in the envelope proved it, once again.

4 WEEK READING PLAN

LOVE HIS WORD

MONDAY	TUESDAY	WEDNESDAY	THURSDAY	FRIDAY
2 Samuel 1	2 Samuel 2:1—3:5	2 Samuel 3:6-39	2 Samuel 4-5	2 Samuel 6
SOAP 2 Samuel 1:11-12	SOAP 2 Samuel 2:5-7	SOAP Psalm 144:1-2	SOAP Psalm 45:5-6	SOAP 2 Samuel 6:17-19
2 Samuel 7	2 Samuel 8	2 Samuel 9-10	2 Samuel 11	2 Samuel 12
SOAP 2 Samuel 7:18-21	SOAP 2 Samuel 8:13-14	SOAP Psalm 20:3-5	SOAP Psalm 103:8-10	SOAP Psalm 51:1-4
2 Samuel 13	2 Samuel 14	2 Samuel 15	2 Samuel 16-17	2 Samuel 18:1—19:8
SOAP Psalm 72:3-4	SOAP Psalm 143:10	SOAP Psalm 3:7-8	SOAP Psalm 4:1	SOAP Psalm 71:19-21
2 Samuel 19:9-43	2 Samuel 20-21	2 Samuel 22	2 Samuel 23	2 Samuel 24
SOAP Psalm 43:4-5	SOAP Psalm 143:1-2	SOAP 2 Samuel 22:51	SOAP 2 Samuel 23:2-4	SOAP 2 Samuel 24:25

DAVID LEARNS OF THE DEATHS OF SAUL AND JONATHAN

1 After the death of Saul, when David had returned from defeating the Amalekites, he stayed at Ziklag for two days. 2 On the
third day a man arrived from the camp of Saul with his clothes
torn and dirt on his head. When he approached David, the man
threw himself to the ground.
3 David asked him, "Where are you coming from?" He replied,
"I have escaped from the camp of Israel." 4 David inquired, "How
were things going? Tell me!" He replied, "The people fled from
the battle and many of them fell dead. Even Saul and his son Jonathan are dead!" 5 David said to the young man who was telling
him this, "How do you know that Saul and his son Jonathan are
dead?" 6 The young man said, "I just happened to be on Mount
Gilboa and came across Saul leaning on his spear for support.
The chariots and leaders of the horsemen were in hot pursuit of
him. 7 When he turned around and saw me, he called out to me. I
answered, 'Here I am!' 8 He asked me, 'Who are you?' I told him,
'I'm an Amalekite.' 9 He said to me, 'Stand over me and finish me
off! I'm very dizzy, even though I'm still alive.' 10 So I stood over
him and put him to death, since I knew that he couldn't live in
such a condition. Then I took the crown which was on his head
and the bracelet which was on his arm. I have brought them
here to my lord."
11 David then grabbed his own clothes and tore them, as did
all the men who were with him. 12 They lamented and wept and
fasted until evening because Saul, his son Jonathan, the LORD's
army, and the house of Israel had fallen by the sword.
13 David said to the young man who told this to him, "Where are
you from?" He replied, "I am an Amalekite, the son of a resident
foreigner." 14 David replied to him, "How is it that you were not
afraid to reach out your hand to destroy the LORD's anointed?"
15 Then David called one of the soldiers and said, "Come here and
strike him down!" So he struck him down, and he died. 16 David
said to him, "Your blood be on your own head! Your own mouth
has testified against you, saying 'I have put the LORD's anointed
to death.'"

DAVID'S TRIBUTE TO SAUL AND JONATHAN

17 Then David chanted this lament over Saul and his son Jonathan. 18 (He gave instructions that the people of Judah should
be taught "The Bow." Indeed, it is written down in the Scroll of
the Upright One.)

19 "The beauty of Israel lies slain on your high places!
How the mighty have fallen!
20 Don't report it in Gath,
don't spread the news in the streets of Ashkelon,
or the daughters of the Philistines will rejoice,
the daughters of the uncircumcised will celebrate!
21 O mountains of Gilboa,
may there be no dew or rain on you,
nor fields of grain offerings!
For it was there that the shield of warriors was defiled;
the shield of Saul lies neglected without oil.

22 From the blood of the slain, from the fat of warriors,
the bow of Jonathan was not turned away.
The sword of Saul never returned empty.
23 Saul and Jonathan were greatly loved during their lives,
and not even in their deaths were they separated.
They were swifter than eagles, stronger than lions.
24 O daughters of Israel, weep over Saul,
who clothed you in scarlet as well as jewelry,
who put gold jewelry on your clothes.
25 How the warriors have fallen
in the midst of battle!
Jonathan lies slain on your high places!
26 I grieve over you, my brother Jonathan.
You were very dear to me.
Your love was more special to me
than the love of women.
27 How the warriors have fallen!
The weapons of war are destroyed!

DAVID IS ANOINTED KING

2 Afterward David inquired of the LORD, "Should I go up to
one of the cities of Judah?" The LORD told him, "Go up." David asked, "Where should I go?" The LORD replied, "To Hebron."
2 So David went up, along with his two wives, Ahinoam the Jezreelite and Abigail, formerly the wife of Nabal the Carmelite.
3 David also brought along the men who were with him, each
with his family. They settled in the cities of Hebron. 4 The men
of Judah came and there they anointed David as king over the
people of Judah.

David was told, "The people of Jabesh Gilead are the ones who
buried Saul." 5 So David sent messengers to the people of Jabesh
Gilead and told them, "May you be blessed by the LORD because
you have shown this kindness to your lord Saul by burying him.
6 Now may the LORD show you true kindness! I also will reward
you, because you have done this deed. 7 Now be courageous and
prove to be valiant warriors, for your lord Saul is dead. The people of Judah have anointed me as king over them."

DAVID'S ARMY CLASHES WITH THE ARMY OF SAUL

8 Now Abner son of Ner, the general in command of Saul's army,
had taken Saul's son Ish Bosheth and had brought him to Mahanaim. 9 He appointed him king over Gilead, the Geshurites,
Jezreel, Ephraim, Benjamin, and all Israel. 10 Ish Bosheth son of
Saul was forty years old when he began to rule over Israel. He
ruled two years. However, the people of Judah followed David.
11 David was king in Hebron over the people of Judah for seven-
and-a-half years.

12 Then Abner son of Ner and the servants of Ish Bosheth son of
Saul went out from Mahanaim to Gibeon. 13 Joab son of Zeruiah
and the servants of David also went out and confronted them
at the pool of Gibeon. One group stationed themselves on one
side of the pool, and the other group on the other side of the
pool. 14 Abner said to Joab, "Let the soldiers get up and fight before us." Joab said, "So be it!"

15 So they got up and crossed over by number: twelve belonging to Benjamin and to Ish Bosheth son of Saul, and twelve from
the servants of David. 16 As they grappled with one another, each
one stabbed his opponent with his sword and they fell dead together. So that place is called the Field of Flints; it is in Gibeon.
17 Now the battle was very severe that day; Abner and the men of
Israel were overcome by David's soldiers. 18 The three sons of Zeruiah were there—Joab, Abishai, and Asahel. (Now Asahel was as quick
on his feet as one of the gazelles in the field.) 19 Asahel chased Abner, without turning to the right or to the left as he followed Abner.
20 Then Abner turned and asked, "Is that you, Asahel?" He replied, "Yes it is!" 21 Abner said to him, "Turn aside to your right or
to your left. Capture one of the soldiers and take his equipment
for yourself!" But Asahel was not willing to turn aside from following him. 22 So Abner spoke again to Asahel, "Turn aside from
following me! I do not want to strike you to the ground. How then
could I show my face in the presence of Joab your brother?" 23 But
Asahel refused to turn aside. So Abner struck him in the abdomen
with the back end of his spear. The spear came out his back; Asahel
collapsed on the spot and died there right before Abner. Everyone
who came to the place where Asahel fell dead paused in respect.
24 So Joab and Abishai chased Abner. At sunset they came to
the hill of Ammah near Giah on the way to the wilderness of
Gibeon. 25 The Benjaminites formed their ranks behind Abner
and were like a single army, standing at the top of a certain hill.
26 Then Abner called out to Joab, "Must the sword devour forever? Don't you realize that this will turn bitter in the end? When
will you tell the people to turn aside from pursuing their brothers?" 27 Joab replied, "As surely as God lives, if you had not said
this, it would have been morning before the people would have
abandoned pursuit of their brothers." 28 Then Joab blew the ram's
horn and all the people stopped in their tracks. They stopped
chasing Israel and ceased fighting. 29 Abner and his men went
through the rift valley all that night. They crossed the Jordan
River and went through the whole region of Bitron and came
to Mahanaim.
30 Now Joab returned from chasing Abner and assembled all
the people. Nineteen of David's soldiers were missing, in addition to Asahel. 31 But David's soldiers had slaughtered the Benjaminites and Abner's men—in all, 360 men had died! 32 They took
Asahel's body and buried him in his father's tomb at Bethlehem. Joab and his men then traveled all that night and reached
3 Hebron by dawn. 1 However, the war was prolonged between
the house of Saul and the house of David. David was becoming steadily stronger, while the house of Saul was becoming increasingly weaker.
2 Now sons were born to David in Hebron. His firstborn was
Amnon, born to Ahinoam the Jezreelite. 3 His second son was Kil-
eab, born to Abigail the widow of Nabal the Carmelite. His third
son was Absalom, the son of Maacah daughter of King Talmai of
Geshur. 4 His fourth son was Adonijah, the son of Haggith. His
fifth son was Shephatiah, the son of Abital. 5 His sixth son was
Ithream, born to David's wife Eglah. These sons were all born to
David in Hebron.

ABNER DEFECTS TO DAVID'S CAMP

[6]As the war continued between the house of Saul and the house
of David, Abner was becoming more influential in the house of
Saul. [7]Now Saul had a concubine named Rizpah daughter of
Aiah. Ish Bosheth said to Abner, "Why did you sleep with my father's concubine?"
[8]These words of Ish Bosheth really angered Abner and he
said, "Am I the head of a dog that belongs to Judah? This very
day I am demonstrating loyalty to the house of Saul your father and to his relatives and his friends! I have not betrayed
you into the hand of David. Yet you have accused me of sinning with this woman today! [9]God will severely judge Abner
if I do not do for David exactly what the LORD has promised
him, [10]namely, to transfer the kingdom from the house of Saul
and to establish the throne of David over Israel and over Judah all the way from Dan to Beer Sheba!" [11]Ish Bosheth was
unable to answer Abner with even a single word because he
was afraid of him.
[12]Then Abner sent messengers to David saying, "To whom
does the land belong? Make an agreement with me, and I will
do whatever I can to cause all Israel to turn to you." [13]So David
said, "Good! I will make an agreement with you. I ask only one
thing from you. You will not see my face unless you bring Saul's
daughter Michal when you come to visit me."
[14]David sent messengers to Ish Bosheth son of Saul with this
demand: "Give me my wife Michal whom I acquired for 100 Philistine foreskins." [15]So Ish Bosheth took her from her husband
Paltiel son of Laish. [16]Her husband went along behind her, weeping all the way to Bahurim. Finally Abner said to him, "Go back!"
So he returned home.
[17]Abner advised the elders of Israel, "Previously you were wanting David to be your king. [18]Act now! For the LORD has said to
David, 'By the hand of my servant David I will save my people
Israel from the Philistines and from all their enemies.'"
[19]Then Abner spoke privately with the Benjaminites. Abner
also went to Hebron to inform David privately of all that Israel
and the entire house of Benjamin had agreed to. [20]When Abner,
accompanied by twenty men, came to David in Hebron, David
prepared a banquet for Abner and the men who were with him.
[21]Abner said to David, "Let me leave so that I may go and gather
all Israel to my lord the king so that they may make an agreement with you. Then you will rule over all that you desire." So
David sent Abner away, and he left in peace.

ABNER IS KILLED

[22]Now David's soldiers and Joab were coming back from a raid,
bringing a great deal of plunder with them. Abner was no longer
with David in Hebron, for David had sent him away and he had
left in peace. [23]When Joab and all the army that was with him
arrived, Joab was told: "Abner the son of Ner came to the king;
he sent him away, and he left in peace!"
[24]So Joab went to the king and said, "What have you done? Abner has come to you. Why would you send him away? Now he's
gone on his way! [25]You know Abner the son of Ner. Surely he

came here to spy on you and to determine when you leave and
when you return and to discover everything that you are doing!"
26 Then Joab left David and sent messengers after Abner. They
brought him back from the well of Sirah. (But David was not
aware of it.) 27 When Abner returned to Hebron, Joab took him
aside at the gate as if to speak privately with him. Joab then
stabbed him in the abdomen and killed him, avenging the shed
blood of his brother Asahel.
28 When David later heard about this, he said, "I and my kingdom are forever innocent before the LORD of the shed blood of
Abner son of Ner. 29 May his blood whirl over the head of Joab
and the entire house of his father! May the males of Joab's house
never cease to have someone with a running sore or a skin disease or one who works at the spindle or one who falls by the
sword or one who lacks food!"
30 So Joab and his brother Abishai killed Abner, because he had
killed their brother Asahel in Gibeon during the battle.
31 David instructed Joab and all the people who were with him,
"Tear your clothes. Put on sackcloth. Lament before Abner!" Now
King David followed behind the funeral pallet. 32 So they buried Abner in Hebron. The king cried loudly over Abner's grave,
and all the people wept too. 33 The king chanted the following
lament for Abner:

"Should Abner have died like a fool?
34 Your hands were not bound,
and your feet were not put into irons.
You fell the way one falls before criminals."

All the people wept over him again. 35 Then all the people came
and encouraged David to eat food while it was still day. But David took an oath saying, "God will punish me severely if I taste
bread or anything whatsoever before the sun sets!"
36 All the people noticed this and it pleased them. In fact, everything the king did pleased all the people. 37 All the people
and all Israel realized on that day that the killing of Abner son
of Ner was not done at the king's instigation.
38 Then the king said to his servants, "Do you not realize that
a great leader has fallen this day in Israel? 39 Today I am weak,
even though I am anointed as king. These men, the sons of Zeruiah, are too much for me to bear! May the LORD punish appropriately the one who has done this evil thing!"

ISH BOSHETH IS KILLED

4 When Ish Bosheth the son of Saul heard that Abner had died
in Hebron, he was very disheartened, and all Israel was afraid.
2 Now Saul's son had two men who were in charge of raiding
units; one was named Baanah and the other Recab. They were
sons of Rimmon the Beerothite, who was a Benjaminite. (Beeroth is regarded as belonging to Benjamin, 3 for the Beerothites
fled to Gittaim and have remained there as resident foreigners
until the present time.)
4 Now Saul's son Jonathan had a son who was crippled in both
feet. He was five years old when the news about Saul and Jonathan arrived from Jezreel. His nurse picked him up and fled,

but in her haste to get away, he fell and was injured. Mephibosheth was his name.

5 Now the sons of Rimmon the Beerothite—Recab and Baanah—went at the hottest part of the day to the home of Ish Bosheth, as he was enjoying his midday rest. 6 They entered the house under the pretense of getting wheat and mortally wounded him in the stomach. Then Recab and his brother Baanah escaped.

7 They had entered the house while Ish Bosheth was resting on his bed in his bedroom. They mortally wounded him and then cut off his head. Taking his head, they traveled on the way of the rift valley all that night. 8 They brought the head of Ish Bosheth to David in Hebron, saying to the king, "Look! The head of Ish Bosheth son of Saul, your enemy who sought your life! The LORD has granted vengeance to my lord the king this day against Saul and his descendants!"

9 David replied to Recab and his brother Baanah, the sons of Rimmon the Beerothite, "As surely as the LORD lives, who has delivered my life from all adversity, 10 when someone told me that Saul was dead—even though he thought he was bringing good news—I seized him and killed him in Ziklag. That was the good news I gave to him! 11 Surely when wicked men have killed an innocent man as he slept in his own house, should I not now require his blood from your hands and remove you from the earth?"

12 So David issued orders to the soldiers and they put them to death. Then they cut off their hands and feet and hung them near the pool in Hebron. But they took the head of Ish Bosheth and buried it in the tomb of Abner in Hebron.

DAVID IS ANOINTED KING OVER ISRAEL

5 All the tribes of Israel came to David at Hebron saying, "Look, we are your very flesh and blood! 2 In the past, when Saul was our king, you were the real leader in Israel. The LORD said to you, 'You will shepherd my people Israel; you will rule over Israel.'"

3 When all the leaders of Israel came to the king at Hebron, King David made an agreement with them in Hebron before the LORD. They designated David as king over Israel. 4 David was thirty years old when he began to reign and he reigned for forty years. 5 In Hebron he reigned over Judah for seven years and six months, and in Jerusalem he reigned for thirty-three years over all Israel and Judah.

DAVID OCCUPIES JERUSALEM

6 Then the king and his men advanced to Jerusalem against the Jebusites who lived in the land. The Jebusites said to David, "You cannot invade this place! Even the blind and the lame will turn you back, saying, 'David cannot invade this place!'"

7 But David captured the fortress of Zion (that is, the City of David). 8 David said on that day, "Whoever attacks the Jebusites must approach the 'lame' and the 'blind' who are David's enemies by going through the water tunnel." For this reason it is said, "The blind and the lame cannot enter the palace."

9 So David lived in the fortress and called it the City of David. David built all around it, from the terrace inwards. 10 David's power grew steadily, for the LORD God of Heaven's Armies was with him.

LOVE TO GROW

THE PROMISE OF A BETTER KING

2 SAMUEL 5:10

From the time we are young, life is full of promises. If we live long enough we soon find that always and forever often ends in sometimes and never. In this world, hope is often deferred: Dreams die, possessions break, and relationships end without warning.

In 2 Samuel 5:10 we read about God's relationship with David. From the very beginning, God had a great purpose for David's life. From a young shepherd boy to king of Israel, God took the unlikely and placed him in the most prominent position in the kingdom. Ultimately, David's lineage led to the Messiah and Savior of the world.

"Your house and your kingdom will stand before me permanently; your dynasty will be permanent" (2 Sam 7:16).

David didn't live forever, but this promise extended far beyond the imperfect kings who followed him. When "forever" was in jeopardy, God made a way. A child was born who fulfilled the need for a righteous son of David to take the throne. His name was Jesus, and His kingdom will never end.

God provided a forever inheritance. Through the line of David, a king was born for a great purpose: to establish a kingdom not of this world. This King is for you. This King is mighty to save, and He's worthy of your trust and confidence in the here and now.

When was the last time you thought about the fact that as a child of God, you are an heir to a forever inheritance, one that is imperishable, undefiled, and unfading (1 Pet 1:4)? Whatever we strive to achieve on earth cannot touch what is ours in Christ. In this world we will have trouble, but let's take courage, our King has conquered the world!

11 King Hiram of Tyre sent messengers to David, along with cedar logs, carpenters, and stonemasons. They built a palace for David. 12 David realized that the LORD had established him as king over Israel and that he had elevated his kingdom for the sake of his people Israel. 13 David married more concubines and wives from Jerusalem after he arrived from Hebron. Even more sons and daughters were born to David. 14 These are the names of children born to him in Jerusalem: Shammua, Shobab, Nathan, Solomon, 15 Ibhar, Elishua, Nepheg, Japhia, 16 Elishama, Eliada, and Eliphelet.

CONFLICT WITH THE PHILISTINES

17 When the Philistines heard that David had been designated king over Israel, they all went up to search for David. When David heard about it, he went down to the fortress. 18 Now the Philistines had arrived and spread out in the valley of Rephaim. 19 So David asked the LORD, "Should I march up against the Philistines? Will you hand them over to me?" The LORD said to David, "March up, for I will indeed hand the Philistines over to you."

20 So David marched against Baal Perazim and defeated them there. Then he said, "The LORD has burst out against my enemies like water bursts out." So he called the name of that place Baal Perazim. 21 The Philistines abandoned their idols there, and David and his men picked them up.

22 The Philistines again came up and spread out in the valley of Rephaim. 23 So David asked the LORD what he should do. This time the LORD said to him, "Don't march straight up. Instead, circle around behind them and come against them opposite the trees. 24 When you hear the sound of marching in the tops of the trees, act decisively. For at that moment the LORD is going before you to strike down the army of the Philistines." 25 David did just as the LORD commanded him, and he struck down the Philistines from Gibeon all the way to Gezer.

DAVID BRINGS THE ARK TO JERUSALEM

6 David again assembled all the best men in Israel, 30,000 in number. 2 David and all the men who were with him traveled to Baalah in Judah to bring up from there the ark of God which is called by the name of the LORD of Heaven's Armies, who sits enthroned between the cherubim that are on it. 3 They loaded the ark of God on a new cart and carried it from the house of Abinadab, which was on the hill. Uzzah and Ahio, the sons of Abinadab, were guiding the new cart. 4 They brought it with the ark of God from the house of Abinadab on the hill. Ahio was walking in front of the ark, 5 while David and all Israel were energetically celebrating before the LORD, singing and playing various stringed instruments, tambourines, rattles, and cymbals.

REFLECT

God allowed David to bring the ark back to Jerusalem. How does this display God's provision?

6 When they arrived at the threshing floor of Nacon, Uzzah reached out and grabbed hold of the ark of God, because the oxen stumbled. 7 The LORD was so furious with Uzzah, he killed him on the spot for his negligence. He died right there beside the ark of God.

8 David was angry because the LORD attacked Uzzah; so he called that place Perez Uzzah, which remains its name to this

very day. 9 David was afraid of the LORD that day and said, "How will the ark of the LORD ever come to me?" 10 So David was no longer willing to bring the ark of the LORD to be with him in the City of David. David left it in the house of Obed-Edom the Gittite. 11 The ark of the LORD remained in the house of Obed-Edom the Gittite for three months. The LORD blessed Obed-Edom and all his family. 12 King David was told, "The LORD has blessed the family of Obed-Edom and everything he owns because of the ark of God." So David went and joyfully brought the ark of God from the house of Obed-Edom to the City of David. 13 Those who carried the ark of the LORD took six steps and then David sacrificed an ox and a fatling calf. 14 Now David, wearing a linen ephod, was dancing with all his strength before the LORD. 15 David and all Israel were bringing up the ark of the LORD, shouting and blowing trumpets.

16 As the ark of the LORD entered the City of David, Saul's daughter Michal looked out the window. When she saw King David leaping and dancing before the LORD, she despised him. 17 They brought the ark of the LORD and put it in its place in the middle of the tent that David had pitched for it. Then David offered burnt sacrifices and peace offerings before the LORD. 18 When David finished offering the burnt sacrifices and peace offerings, he pronounced a blessing over the people in the name of the LORD of Heaven's Armies. 19 He then handed out to each member of the entire assembly of Israel, both men and women, a portion of bread, a date cake, and a raisin cake. Then all the people went home. 20 When David went home to pronounce a blessing on his own house, Michal, Saul's daughter, came out to meet him. She said, "How the king of Israel has distinguished himself this day! He has exposed himself today before his servants' slave girls the way a vulgar fool might do!"

21 David replied to Michal, "It was before the LORD! I was celebrating before the LORD, who chose me over your father and his entire family and appointed me as leader over the LORD's people Israel. 22 I am willing to shame and humiliate myself even more than this. But with the slave girls whom you mentioned, let me be distinguished." 23 Now Michal, Saul's daughter, had no children to the day of her death.

THE LORD ESTABLISHES A COVENANT WITH DAVID

7 The king settled into his palace, for the LORD gave him relief from all his enemies on all sides. 2 The king said to Nathan the prophet, "Look! I am living in a palace made from cedar, while the ark of God sits in the middle of a tent." 3 Nathan replied to the king, "You should go and do whatever you have in mind, for the LORD is with you." 4 That night the LORD's message came to Nathan, 5 "Go, tell my servant David, 'This is what the LORD has said: Do you really intend to build a house for me to live in? 6 I have not lived in a house from the time I brought the Israelites up from Egypt to the present day. Instead, I was traveling with them and living in a tent. 7 Wherever I moved among all the Israelites, I did not say to any of their leaders whom I appointed to care for my people Israel, "Why have you not built me a house made from cedar?"'

8 "So now, say this to my servant David, 'This is what the LORD of Heaven's Armies has said: I took you from the pasture and from your work as a shepherd to make you leader of my people Israel. 9 I was with you wherever you went, and I defeated all your enemies before you. Now I will make you as famous as the great men of the earth. 10 I will establish a place for my people Israel and settle them there; they will live there and not be disturbed anymore. Violent men will not oppress them again, as they did in the beginning 11 and during the time when I appointed judges to lead my people Israel. Instead, I will give you relief from all your enemies. The LORD declares to you that he himself will build a dynastic house for you. 12 When the time comes for you to die, I will raise up your descendant, one of your own sons, to succeed you, and I will establish his kingdom. 13 He will build a house for my name, and I will make his dynasty permanent. 14 I will become his father and he will become my son. When he sins, I will correct him with the rod of men and with wounds inflicted by human beings. 15 But my loyal love will not be removed from him as I removed it from Saul, whom I removed from before you. 16 Your house and your kingdom will stand before me permanently; your dynasty will be permanent.'" 17 Nathan told David all these words that were revealed to him.

CHALLENGE

God established a covenant with David in which He promised to make his name great and to establish David's kingdom forever. How does the genealogy recorded in Matthew 1 show that God fulfilled this promise?

DAVID OFFERS A PRAYER TO GOD

18 King David went in, sat before the LORD, and said, "Who am I, O Sovereign LORD, and what is my family, that you should have brought me to this point? 19 And you didn't stop there, O LORD God! You have also spoken about the future of your servant's family. Is this your usual way of dealing with men, O Sovereign LORD? 20 What more can David say to you? You have given your servant special recognition, O Sovereign LORD! 21 For the sake of your promise and according to your purpose you have done this great thing in order to reveal it to your servant. 22 Therefore you are great, O Sovereign LORD, for there is none like you. There is no God besides you! What we have heard is true. 23 Who is like your people, Israel, a unique nation on the earth? Their God went to claim a nation for himself and to make a name for himself! You did great and awesome acts for your land, before your people whom you delivered for yourself from the Egyptian empire and its gods. 24 You made Israel your very own people for all time. You, O LORD, became their God. 25 So now, O LORD God, make this promise you have made about your servant and his family a permanent reality. Do as you promised, 26 so you may gain lasting fame, as people say, 'The LORD of Heaven's Armies is God over Israel!' The dynasty of your servant David will be established before you, 27 for you, O LORD of Heaven's Armies, the God of Israel, have told your servant, 'I will build you a dynastic house.' That is why your servant has had the courage to pray this prayer to you. 28 Now, O Sovereign LORD, you are the true God. May your words prove to be true! You have made this good promise to your servant. 29 Now be willing to bless your servant's dynasty so that it may stand permanently before you, for you, O Sovereign LORD, have spoken. By your blessing may your servant's dynasty be blessed from now on into the future!"

DAVID SUBJUGATES NEARBY NATIONS

8 Later David defeated the Philistines and subdued them. David took Metheg Ammah from the Philistines. 2 He defeated
the Moabites. He made them lie on the ground and then used a
rope to measure them off. He put two-thirds of them to death
and spared the other third. The Moabites became David's subjects and brought tribute. 3 David defeated King Hadadezer son
of Rehob of Zobah when he came to reestablish his authority
over the Euphrates River. 4 David seized from him 1,700 charioteers and 20,000 infantrymen. David cut the hamstrings of
all but 100 of the chariot horses. 5 The Arameans of Damascus
came to help King Hadadezer of Zobah, but David killed 22,000
of the Arameans. 6 David placed garrisons in the territory of the
Arameans of Damascus; the Arameans became David's subjects
and brought tribute. The LORD protected David wherever he
campaigned. 7 David took the golden shields that belonged to
Hadadezer's servants and brought them to Jerusalem. 8 From
Tebah and Berothai, Hadadezer's cities, King David took a great
deal of bronze.

9 When King Toi of Hamath heard that David had defeated the
entire army of Hadadezer, 10 he sent his son Joram to King David
to extend his best wishes and to pronounce a blessing on him for
his victory over Hadadezer, for Toi had been at war with Hadadezer. He brought with him various items made of silver, gold, and
bronze. 11 King David dedicated these things to the LORD, along
with the dedicated silver and gold that he had taken from all the
nations that he had subdued, 12 including Edom, Moab, the Ammonites, the Philistines, and Amalek. This also included some of
the plunder taken from King Hadadezer son of Rehob of Zobah.

13 David became famous when he returned from defeating the
Edomites in the Valley of Salt; he defeated 18,000 in all. 14 He
placed garrisons throughout Edom, and all the Edomites became David's subjects. The LORD protected David wherever he
campaigned. 15 David reigned over all Israel; he guaranteed justice for all his people.

DAVID'S CABINET

16 Joab son of Zeruiah was general in command of the army; Jehoshaphat son of Ahilud was secretary; 17 Zadok son of Ahitub
and Ahimelech son of Abiathar were priests; Seraiah was scribe;
18 Benaiah son of Jehoiada supervised the Kerethites and Pelethites; and David's sons were priests.

DAVID FINDS MEPHIBOSHETH

9 Then David asked, "Is anyone still left from the family of Saul,
so that I may extend kindness to him for the sake of Jonathan?"

2 Now there was a servant from Saul's house named Ziba, so he
was summoned to David. The king asked him, "Are you Ziba?" He
replied, "At your service." 3 The king asked, "Is there not someone
left from Saul's family that I may extend God's kindness to him?"
Ziba said to the king, "One of Jonathan's sons is left; both of his
feet are crippled." 4 The king asked him, "Where is he?" Ziba told
the king, "He is at the house of Makir son of Ammiel in Lo Debar."

5 So King David had him brought from the house of Makir son of Ammiel in Lo Debar. 6 When Mephibosheth son of Jonathan, the son of Saul, came to David, he bowed low with his face toward the ground. David said, "Mephibosheth?" He replied, "Yes, at your service."

7 David said to him, "Don't be afraid, because I will certainly extend kindness to you for the sake of Jonathan your father. I will give back to you all the land that belonged to your grandfather Saul, and you will be a regular guest at my table." 8 Then Mephibosheth bowed and said, "Of what importance am I, your servant, that you show regard for a dead dog like me?"

REFLECT

How do David's actions with Mephibosheth reflect God's heart for the oppressed and marginalized?

9 Then the king summoned Ziba, Saul's attendant, and said to him, "Everything that belonged to Saul and to his entire house I hereby give to your master's grandson. 10 You will cultivate the land for him—you and your sons and your servants. You will bring its produce and it will be food for your master's grandson to eat. But Mephibosheth, your master's grandson, will be a regular guest at my table." (Now Ziba had fifteen sons and twenty servants.)

11 Ziba said to the king, "Your servant will do everything that my lord the king has instructed his servant to do." So Mephibosheth was a regular guest at David's table, just as though he were one of the king's sons.

12 Now Mephibosheth had a young son whose name was Mica. All the members of Ziba's household were Mephibosheth's servants. 13 Mephibosheth was living in Jerusalem, for he was a regular guest at the king's table. But both his feet were crippled.

DAVID AND THE AMMONITES

10 Later the king of the Ammonites died and his son Hanun succeeded him. 2 David said, "I will express my loyalty to Hanun son of Nahash just as his father was loyal to me." So David sent his servants with a message expressing sympathy over his father's death. When David's servants entered the land of the Ammonites, 3 the Ammonite officials said to their lord Hanun, "Do you really think David is trying to honor your father by sending these messengers to express his sympathy? No, David has sent his servants to you to get information about the city and spy on it so they can overthrow it!"

4 So Hanun seized David's servants and shaved off half of each one's beard. He cut the lower part of their robes off so that their buttocks were exposed, and then sent them away. 5 Messengers told David what had happened, so he sent them to the men who were thoroughly humiliated. The king said, "Stay in Jericho until your beards have grown again; then you may come back."

6 When the Ammonites realized that David was disgusted with them, they sent and hired 20,000 foot soldiers from Aram Beth Rehob and Aram Zobah, in addition to 1,000 men from the king of Maacah and 12,000 men from Ish Tob.

7 When David heard the news, he sent Joab and the entire army to meet them. 8 The Ammonites marched out and were deployed for battle at the entrance of the city gate, while the men from Aram Zobah, Rehob, Ish Tob, and Maacah were by themselves in the field.

9 When Joab saw that the battle would be fought on two fronts, he chose some of Israel's best men and deployed them against the Arameans. 10 He put his brother Abishai in charge of the rest of the army and they were deployed against the Ammonites. 11 Joab said, "If the Arameans start to overpower me, you come to my rescue. If the Ammonites start to overpower you, I will come to your rescue. 12 Be strong! Let's fight bravely for the sake of our people and the cities of our God! The LORD will do what he decides is best!"

13 So Joab and his men marched out to do battle with the Arameans, and they fled before him. 14 When the Ammonites saw the Arameans flee, they fled before his brother Abishai and went into the city. Joab withdrew from fighting the Ammonites and returned to Jerusalem.

15 When the Arameans realized that they had been defeated by Israel, they consolidated their forces. 16 Then Hadadezer sent for Arameans from beyond the Euphrates River, and they came to Helam. Shobach, the general in command of Hadadezer's army, led them.

17 When David was informed, he gathered all Israel, crossed the Jordan River, and came to Helam. The Arameans deployed their forces against David and fought with him. 18 The Arameans fled before Israel. David killed 700 Aramean charioteers and 40,000 foot soldiers. He also struck down Shobach, the general in command of the army, who died there. 19 When all the kings who were subject to Hadadezer saw they were defeated by Israel, they made peace with Israel and became subjects of Israel. The Arameans were no longer willing to help the Ammonites.

DAVID COMMITS ADULTERY WITH BATHSHEBA

11 In the spring of the year, at the time when kings normally conduct wars, David sent out Joab with his officers and the entire Israelite army. They defeated the Ammonites and besieged Rabbah. But David stayed behind in Jerusalem. 2 One evening David got up from his bed and walked around on the roof of his palace. From the roof he saw a woman bathing. Now this woman was very attractive. 3 So David sent someone to inquire about the woman. The messenger said, "Isn't this Bathsheba, the daughter of Eliam, the wife of Uriah the Hittite?"

4 David sent some messengers to get her. She came to him and he went to bed with her. (Now at that time she was in the process of purifying herself from her menstrual uncleanness.) Then she returned to her home. 5 The woman conceived and then sent word to David saying, "I'm pregnant."

6 So David sent a message to Joab that said, "Send me Uriah the *Hittite." So Joab sent Uriah to David.* 7 When Uriah came to him, David asked about how Joab and the army were doing and how the campaign was going. 8 Then David said to Uriah, "Go down to your home and relax." When Uriah left the palace, the king sent a gift to him. 9 But Uriah stayed at the door of the palace with all the servants of his lord. He did not go down to his house.

10 So they informed David, "Uriah has not gone down to his house." So David said to Uriah, "Haven't you just arrived from a journey? Why haven't you gone down to your house?" 11 Uriah

replied to David, "The ark and Israel and Judah reside in temporary shelters, and my lord Joab and my lord's soldiers are camping in the open field. Should I go to my house to eat and drink
and go to bed with my wife? As surely as you are alive, I will not
do this thing!" 12 So David said to Uriah, "Stay here another day.
Tomorrow I will send you back." So Uriah stayed in Jerusalem
both that day and the following one. 13 Then David summoned
him. He ate and drank with him, and got him drunk. But in the
evening he went out to sleep on his bed with the servants of his
lord; he did not go down to his own house.

14 In the morning David wrote a letter to Joab and sent it with
Uriah. 15 In the letter he wrote: "Station Uriah at the front in
the thick of the battle and then withdraw from him so he will
be cut down and killed."

16 So as Joab kept watch on the city, he stationed Uriah at the
place where he knew the best enemy soldiers were. 17 When the
men of the city came out and fought with Joab, some of David's
soldiers fell in battle. Uriah the Hittite also died.

18 Then Joab sent a full battle report to David. 19 He instructed
the messenger as follows: "When you finish giving the battle report to the king, 20 if the king becomes angry and asks you, 'Why
did you go so close to the city to fight? Didn't you realize they
would shoot from the wall? 21 Who struck down Abimelech the
son of Jerub-Besheth? Didn't a woman throw an upper millstone
down on him from the wall so that he died in Thebez? Why did
you go so close to the wall?' just say to him, 'Your servant Uriah
the Hittite is also dead.'"

22 So the messenger departed. When he arrived, he informed
David of all the news that Joab had sent with him. 23 The messenger said to David, "The men overpowered us and attacked
us in the field. But we forced them to retreat all the way to the
door of the city gate. 24 Then the archers shot at your servants
from the wall and some of the king's soldiers died. Your servant
Uriah the Hittite is also dead." 25 David said to the messenger,
"Tell Joab, 'Don't let this thing upset you. There is no way to anticipate whom the sword will cut down. Press the battle against
the city and conquer it.' Encourage him with these words."

26 When Uriah's wife heard that her husband Uriah was dead,
she mourned for him. 27 When the time of mourning passed,
David had her brought to his palace. She became his wife and
she bore him a son. But what David had done upset the LORD.

NATHAN THE PROPHET CONFRONTS DAVID

12 So the LORD sent Nathan to David. When he came to David,
Nathan said, "There were two men in a certain city, one rich
and the other poor. 2 The rich man had a great many flocks and
herds. 3 But the poor man had nothing except for a little lamb he
had acquired. He raised it, and it grew up alongside him and his
children. It used to eat his food, drink from his cup, and sleep in
his arms. It was just like a daughter to him.

4 "When a traveler arrived at the rich man's home, he did not
want to use one of his own sheep or cattle to feed the traveler
who had come to visit him. Instead, he took the poor man's lamb
and cooked it for the man who had come to visit him."

5 Then David became very angry at this man. He said to Nathan,
"As surely as the LORD lives, the man who did this deserves to
die! 6 Because he committed this cold-hearted crime, he must
pay for the lamb four times over!"
7 Nathan said to David, "You are that man! This is what the
LORD God of Israel has said: 'I chose you to be king over Israel and I rescued you from the hand of Saul. 8 I gave you
your master's house, and put your master's wives into your
arms. I also gave you the house of Israel and Judah. And if all
that somehow seems insignificant, I would have given you
so much more as well! 9 Why have you shown contempt for
the LORD's decrees by doing evil in my sight? You have struck
down Uriah the Hittite with the sword and you have taken
his wife to be your own wife! You have killed him with the
sword of the Ammonites. 10 So now the sword will never depart from your house. For you have despised me by taking
the wife of Uriah the Hittite as your own!' 11 This is what the
LORD has said: 'I am about to bring disaster on you from inside your own household! Right before your eyes I will take
your wives and hand them over to your companion. He will
go to bed with your wives in broad daylight! 12 Although you
have acted in secret, I will do this thing before all Israel, and
in broad daylight.'"
13 Then David exclaimed to Nathan, "I have sinned against the
LORD!" Nathan replied to David, "Yes, and the LORD has forgiven
your sin. You are not going to die. 14 Nonetheless, because you
have treated the LORD with such contempt in this matter, the
son who has been born to you will certainly die."
15 Then Nathan went to his home. The LORD struck the child
that Uriah's wife had borne to David, and the child became
very ill. 16 Then David prayed to God for the child and fasted.
He would even go and spend the night lying on the ground.
17 The elders of his house stood over him and tried to lift him
from the ground, but he was unwilling, and refused to eat food
with them.
18 On the seventh day the child died. But the servants of David
were afraid to inform him that the child had died, for they said,
"While the child was still alive he would not listen to us when
we spoke to him. How can we tell him that the child is dead? He
will do himself harm!"
19 When David saw that his servants were whispering to one
another, he realized that the child was dead. So David asked his
servants, "Is the child dead?" They replied, "Yes, he's dead." 20 So
David got up from the ground, bathed, put on oil, and changed
his clothes. He went to the house of the LORD and worshiped.
Then, when he entered his palace, he requested that food be
brought to him, and he ate.
21 His servants said to him, "What is this that you have done?
While the child was still alive, you fasted and wept. Once the
child was dead you got up and ate food!" 22 He replied, "While the
child was still alive, I fasted and wept because I thought, 'Perhaps the LORD will show pity and the child will live.' 23 But now
he is dead. Why should I fast? Am I able to bring him back at this
point? I will go to him, but he cannot return to me!"

REFLECT

Why was the way that Nathan confronted David so effective in getting his message across? What type of emotions did Nathan's story bring up in David? Did this help David see his sin?

DAVID THE SINNER

2 SAMUEL 12:7–14

It would be easy to read about David the Sinner and respond with a hearty, "Not me. Lord, I've never acted like David did. Lord, I've never conspired the death of another. Lord, I've never . . ."

We're pros at it, you and me. We're quick to recognize sin in others. What about our own sin? We'd much rather refer to ourselves as The Faithful Friend, The Brave Warrior in the Faith, A Woman After God's Own Heart.

We conceal our sin, praying that with enough distraction and cover-up, no one will ever notice. We compare our sin, pointing out the speck in another's eye instead of recognizing the log in our own. We contribute good works to "outweigh" our sin, working harder and doing more in hopes of finding favor with God and with others.

As Nathan said to David, "You are that man!" (2 Sam 12:7), so it can be said of each of us. We are all sinners.

As much as we want to escape our sin, it's ever before us. No amount of concealing, comparing, or contributing will ever resolve our sin issue. We can learn from David. Instead of denying or continuing to run from his sin, David responded to Nathan's convicting words in repentance that began with his confession, "I have sinned against the LORD!" (2 Sam 12:13).

True repentance brings about a significant change of heart. This cannot happen without first acknowledging our sin for what it is and recognizing our need for repentance. We cannot experience this complete change if we are trying to cover up our sin with self-righteousness. When we acknowledge our need for forgiveness, God changes our hearts.

David was honest with God about his sin. He had to accept the consequences of his actions, even though he was fully forgiven. When David stopped trying to cover his sin, God was able to then correct him, redeem him, and restore him.

Let's determine to be honest before the Lord about the sin in our lives. The process won't be easy. In fact, it's likely to be downright painful. But David's story doesn't end with his sin, and our story doesn't have to either. There is something better: His name is Jesus, the Hope of Sinners, and His gift of forgiveness is for all who believe.

24 So David comforted his wife Bathsheba. He came to her and
went to bed with her. Later she gave birth to a son, and David
named him Solomon. Now the LORD loved the child 25 and sent
word through Nathan the prophet that he should be named Jed-
idiah for the LORD's sake.

DAVID'S FORCES DEFEAT THE AMMONITES

26 So Joab fought against Rabbah of the Ammonites and captured the royal city. 27 Joab then sent messengers to David, saying, "I have fought against Rabbah and have captured the water
supply of the city. 28 So now assemble the rest of the army and
besiege the city and capture it. Otherwise I will capture the city
and it will be named for me."

29 So David assembled all the army and went to Rabbah and
fought against it and captured it. 30 He took the crown of their
king from his head—it was gold, weighed about seventy-five
pounds, and held a precious stone—and it was placed on David's head. He also took from the city a great deal of plunder.
31 He removed the people who were in it and made them labor
with saws, iron picks, and iron axes, putting them to work at the
brick kiln. This was his policy with all the Ammonite cities. Then
David and all the army returned to Jerusalem.

THE RAPE OF TAMAR

13 Now David's son Absalom had a beautiful sister named Tamar. In the course of time David's son Amnon fell madly
in love with her. 2 But Amnon became frustrated because he
was so lovesick over his sister Tamar. For she was a virgin, and
to Amnon it seemed out of the question to do anything to her.

3 Now Amnon had a friend named Jonadab, the son of David's
brother Shimeah. Jonadab was a very crafty man. 4 He asked
Amnon, "Why are you, the king's son, so depressed every morning? Can't you tell me?" So Amnon said to him, "I'm in love with
Tamar the sister of my brother Absalom." 5 Jonadab replied to
him, "Lie down on your bed and pretend to be sick. When your
father comes in to see you, say to him, 'Please let my sister Tamar come in so she can fix some food for me. Let her prepare the
food in my sight so I can watch. Then I will eat from her hand.'"

6 So Amnon lay down and pretended to be sick. When the king
came in to see him, Amnon said to the king, "Please let my sister
Tamar come in so she can make a couple of cakes in my sight.
Then I will eat from her hand."

7 So David sent Tamar to the house saying, "Please go to the
house of Amnon your brother and prepare some food for him."
8 So Tamar went to the house of Amnon her brother, who was
lying down. She took the dough, kneaded it, made some cakes
while he watched, and baked them. 9 But when she took the pan
and set it before him, he refused to eat. Instead Amnon said, "Get
everyone out of here!" So everyone left.

10 Then Amnon said to Tamar, "Bring the cakes into the bedroom; then I will eat from your hand." So Tamar took the cakes
that she had prepared and brought them to her brother Amnon
in the bedroom. 11 As she brought them to him to eat, he grabbed
her and said to her, "Come on! Get in bed with me, my sister!"

12 But she said to him, "No, my brother! Don't humiliate me! This
just isn't done in Israel! Don't do this foolish thing! 13 How could I
ever be rid of my humiliation? And you would be considered one
of the fools in Israel! Just speak to the king, for he will not withhold me from you." 14 But he refused to listen to her. He overpowered her and humiliated her by raping her. 15 Then Amnon greatly
despised her. His disdain toward her surpassed the love he had
previously felt toward her. Amnon said to her, "Get up and leave!"

16 But she said to him, "No I won't, for sending me away now
would be worse than what you did to me earlier!" But he refused
to listen to her. 17 He called his personal attendant and said to him,
"Take this woman out of my sight and lock the door behind her!"
18 (Now she was wearing a long robe, for this is what the king's virgin daughters used to wear.) So Amnon's attendant removed her
and bolted the door behind her. 19 Then Tamar put ashes on her
head and tore the long robe she was wearing. She put her hands
on her head and went on her way, wailing as she went.

20 Her brother Absalom said to her, "Was Amnon your brother with you? Now be quiet, my sister. He is your brother. Don't
take it so seriously!" Tamar, devastated, lived in the house of
her brother Absalom.

21 Now King David heard about all these things and was very
angry. 22 But Absalom said nothing to Amnon, either bad or good,
yet Absalom hated Amnon because he had humiliated his sister Tamar.

ABSALOM HAS AMNON PUT TO DEATH

23 Two years later Absalom's sheepshearers were in Baal Hazor,
near Ephraim. Absalom invited all the king's sons. 24 Then Absalom went to the king and said, "My shearers have begun their
work. Let the king and his servants go with me."

25 But the king said to Absalom, "No, my son. We shouldn't all go.
We shouldn't burden you in that way." Though Absalom pressed
him, the king was not willing to go. Instead, David blessed him.

26 Then Absalom said, "If you will not go, then let my brother
Amnon go with us." The king replied to him, "Why should he go
with you?" 27 But when Absalom pressed him, he sent Amnon
and all the king's sons along with him.

28 Absalom instructed his servants, "Look! When Amnon is
drunk and I say to you, 'Strike Amnon down,' kill him then and
there. Don't fear! Is it not I who have given you these instructions? Be strong and courageous!" 29 So Absalom's servants did to
Amnon exactly what Absalom had instructed. Then all the king's
sons got up; each one rode away on his mule and fled.

30 While they were still on their way, the following report
reached David: "Absalom has killed all the king's sons; not one
of them is left!" 31 Then the king stood up and tore his garments
and lay down on the ground. All his servants were standing there
with torn garments as well.

32 Jonadab, the son of David's brother Shimeah, said, "My lord
should not say, 'They have killed all the young men who are the
king's sons.' For only Amnon is dead. This is what Absalom has
talked about from the day that Amnon humiliated his sister Tamar. 33 Now don't let my lord the king be concerned about the

report that has come saying, 'All the king's sons are dead.' It is
only Amnon who is dead."
34 In the meantime Absalom fled. When the servant who was
the watchman looked up, he saw many people coming from the
west on a road beside the hill. 35 Jonadab said to the king, "Look!
The king's sons have come! It's just as I said."
36 Just as he finished speaking, the king's sons arrived, wailing
and weeping. The king and all his servants wept loudly as well.
37 But Absalom fled and went to King Talmai son of Ammihud
of Geshur. And David grieved over his son every day.
38 After Absalom fled and went to Geshur, he remained there
for three years. 39 The king longed to go to Absalom, for he had
since been consoled over the death of Amnon.

DAVID PERMITS ABSALOM TO RETURN TO JERUSALEM

14 Now Joab son of Zeruiah realized that the king longed to see
Absalom. 2 So Joab sent to Tekoa and brought from there a
wise woman. He told her, "Pretend to be in mourning and put on
garments for mourning. Don't anoint yourself with oil. Instead,
act like a woman who has been mourning for the dead for some
time. 3 Go to the king and speak to him in the following fashion."
Then Joab told her what to say.
4 So the Tekoan woman went to the king. She bowed down with
her face to the ground in deference to him and said, "Please help
me, O king!" 5 The king replied to her, "What do you want?" She
answered, "I am a widow; my husband is dead. 6 Your servant has
two sons. When the two of them got into a fight in the field, there
was no one present who could intervene. One of them struck
the other and killed him. 7 Now the entire family has risen up
against your servant, saying, 'Turn over the one who struck down
his brother, so that we can execute him and avenge the death of
his brother whom he killed. In so doing we will also destroy the
heir.' They want to extinguish my remaining coal, leaving no one
on the face of the earth to carry on the name of my husband."
8 Then the king told the woman, "Go to your home. I will give instructions concerning your situation." 9 The Tekoan woman said
to the king, "My lord the king, let any blame fall on me and on the
house of my father. But let the king and his throne be innocent!"
10 The king said, "Bring to me whoever speaks to you, and he
won't bother you again!" 11 She replied, "In that case, let the king
invoke the name of the LORD your God so that the avenger of
blood may not add to the killing! Then they will not destroy my
son!" He replied, "As surely as the LORD lives, not a single hair
of your son's head will fall to the ground."
12 Then the woman said, "Please permit your servant to speak to
my lord the king about another matter." He replied, "Tell me." 13 The
woman said, "Why have you devised something like this against
God's people? When the king speaks in this fashion, he makes himself guilty, for the king has not brought back the one he has banished. 14 Certainly we must die, and are like water spilled on the
ground that cannot be gathered up again. But God does not take
away life; instead he devises ways for the banished to be restored.
15 I have now come to speak with my lord the king about this matter,

because the people have made me fearful. But your servant said,
'I will speak to the king! Perhaps the king will do what his female
servant asks. 16 Yes! The king may listen and deliver his female servant from the hand of the man who seeks to remove both me and
my son from the inheritance God has given us!' 17 So your servant
said, 'May the word of my lord the king be my security, for my lord
the king is like the angel of God when it comes to deciding between
right and wrong! May the LORD your God be with you!'"

18 Then the king replied to the woman, "Don't hide any information from me when I question you." The woman said, "Let
my lord the king speak." 19 The king said, "Did Joab put you up to
all of this?" The woman answered, "As surely as you live, my lord
the king, there is no deviation to the right or to the left from all
that my lord the king has said. For your servant Joab gave me instructions. He has put all these words in your servant's mouth.
20 Your servant Joab did this so as to change this situation. But
my lord has wisdom like that of the angel of God, and knows everything that is happening in the land."

21 Then the king said to Joab, "All right! I will do this thing. Go
and bring back the young man Absalom!" 22 Then Joab bowed
down with his face toward the ground and thanked the king.
Joab said, "Today your servant knows that I have found favor in
your sight, my lord the king, because the king has granted the
request of your servant!"

23 So Joab got up and went to Geshur and brought Absalom
back to Jerusalem. 24 But the king said, "Let him go over to his
own house. He may not see my face." So Absalom went over to
his own house; he did not see the king's face.

25 Now in all Israel everyone acknowledged that there was
no man as handsome as Absalom. From the soles of his feet to
the top of his head he was perfect in appearance. 26 When he
would shave his head—at the end of every year he used to shave
his head, for it grew too long and he would shave it—he used to
weigh the hair of his head at three pounds according to the king's
weight. 27 Absalom had three sons and one daughter, whose name
was Tamar. She was a very attractive woman.

28 Absalom lived in Jerusalem for two years without seeing the
king's face. 29 Then Absalom sent a message to Joab asking him to
send him to the king, but Joab was not willing to come to him. So
he sent a second message to him, but he still was not willing to
come. 30 So he said to his servants, "Look, Joab has a portion of field
adjacent to mine and he has some barley there. Go and set it on
fire." So Absalom's servants set Joab's portion of the field on fire.

31 Then Joab got up and came to Absalom's house. He said to
him, "Why did your servants set my portion of field on fire?"
32 Absalom said to Joab, "Look, I sent a message to you saying,
'Come here so that I can send you to the king with this message:
"Why have I come from Geshur? It would be better for me if I
were still there."' Let me now see the face of the king. If I am at
fault, let him put me to death!"

33 So Joab went to the king and informed him. The king summoned Absalom, and he came to the king. Absalom bowed down
before the king with his face toward the ground and the king
kissed him.

ABSALOM LEADS AN INSURRECTION AGAINST DAVID

15 Some time later Absalom managed to acquire a chariot and
horses, as well as fifty men to serve as his royal guard. 2 Now
Absalom used to get up early and stand beside the road that led to
the city gate. Whenever anyone came by who had a complaint to
bring to the king for arbitration, Absalom would call out to him,
"What city are you from?" The person would answer, "I, your servant, am from one of the tribes of Israel." 3 Absalom would then
say to him, "Look, your claims are legitimate and appropriate.
But there is no representative of the king who will listen to you."
4 Absalom would then say, "If only they would make me a judge
in the land! Then everyone who had a judicial complaint could
come to me and I would make sure he receives a just settlement."
5 When someone approached to bow before him, Absalom would
extend his hand and embrace him and kiss him. 6 Absalom acted
this way toward everyone in Israel who came to the king for justice. In this way Absalom won the loyalty of the citizens of Israel.
7 After four years Absalom said to the king, "Let me go and
repay my vow that I made to the LORD while I was in Hebron.
8 For I made this vow when I was living in Geshur in Aram: 'If the
LORD really does allow me to return to Jerusalem, I will serve
the LORD.'" 9 The king replied to him, "Go in peace." So Absalom
got up and went to Hebron.
10 Then Absalom sent spies through all the tribes of Israel who
said, "When you hear the sound of the horn, you may assume
that Absalom rules in Hebron." 11 Now 200 men had gone with
Absalom from Jerusalem. Since they were invited, they went na-
ively and were unaware of what Absalom was planning. 12 While
he was offering sacrifices, Absalom sent for Ahithophel the Gilonite, David's adviser, to come from his city, Giloh. The conspiracy was gaining momentum, and the people were starting
to side with Absalom.

DAVID FLEES FROM JERUSALEM

13 Then a messenger came to David and reported, "The men of
Israel are loyal to Absalom!" 14 So David said to all his servants
who were with him in Jerusalem, "Come on! Let's escape! Otherwise no one will be delivered from Absalom! Go immediately,
or else he will quickly overtake us and bring disaster on us and
kill the city's residents with the sword." 15 The king's servants replied to the king, "We will do whatever our lord the king decides."
16 So the king and all the members of his royal court set out on
foot, though the king left behind ten concubines to attend to the
palace. 17 The king and all the people set out on foot, pausing at
a spot some distance away. 18 All his servants were leaving with
him, along with all the Kerethites, all the Pelethites, and all the
Gittites—some 600 men who had come on foot from Gath. They
were leaving with the king.
19 Then the king said to Ittai the Gittite, "Why should you come
with us? Go back and stay with the new king, for you are a foreigner and an exile from your own country. 20 It seems as if you
arrived just yesterday. Today should I make you wander around
by going with us? I go where I must go. But as for you, go back and
take your men with you. May genuine loyal love protect you!"

21 But Ittai replied to the king, "As surely as the LORD lives and
as my lord the king lives, wherever my lord the king is, whether
it means death or life, there I will be as well!" 22 So David said to
Ittai, "Come along then." So Ittai the Gittite went along, accompanied by all his men and all the dependents who were with him.
23 All the land was weeping loudly as all these people were
leaving. As the king was crossing over the Kidron Valley, all the
people were leaving on the road that leads to the desert. 24 Zadok and all the Levites who were with him were carrying the
ark of the covenant of God. When they positioned the ark of
God, Abiathar offered sacrifices until all the people had finished
leaving the city.
25 Then the king said to Zadok, "Take the ark of God back to the
city. If I find favor in the LORD's sight he will bring me back and
enable me to see both it and his dwelling place again. 26 However, if he should say, 'I do not take pleasure in you,' then he will
deal with me in a way that he considers appropriate."
27 The king said to Zadok the priest, "Are you a seer? Go back to
the city in peace! Your son Ahimaaz and Abiathar's son Jonathan
may go with you and Abiathar. 28 Look, I will be waiting at the fords
of the desert until word from you reaches me." 29 So Zadok and Abiathar took the ark of God back to Jerusalem and remained there.
30 As David was going up the Mount of Olives, he was weeping
as he went; his head was covered and his feet were bare. All the
people who were with him also had their heads covered and were
weeping as they went up. 31 Now David had been told, "Ahithophel has sided with the conspirators who are with Absalom." So
David prayed, "Make the advice of Ahithophel foolish, O LORD."
32 When David reached the summit, where he used to worship
God, Hushai the Arkite met him with his clothes torn and dirt
on his head. 33 David said to him, "If you leave with me you will
be a burden to me. 34 But you will be able to counter the advice
of Ahithophel if you go back to the city and say to Absalom, 'I
will be your servant, O king! Previously I was your father's servant, and now I will be your servant.' 35 Zadok and Abiathar the
priests will be there with you. Everything you hear in the king's
palace you must tell Zadok and Abiathar the priests. 36 Furthermore, their two sons are there with them, Zadok's son Ahimaaz
and Abiathar's son Jonathan. You must send them to me with
any information you hear."
37 So David's friend Hushai arrived in the city, just as Absalom
was entering Jerusalem.

DAVID RECEIVES GIFTS FROM ZIBA

16 When David had gone a short way beyond the summit, Ziba
the servant of Mephibosheth was there to meet him. He
had a couple of donkeys that were saddled, and on them were
200 loaves of bread, 100 raisin cakes, 100 baskets of summer
fruit, and a container of wine.
2 The king asked Ziba, "Why did you bring these things?" Ziba
replied, "The donkeys are for the king's family to ride on, the
loaves of bread and the summer fruit are for the attendants to
eat, and the wine is for those who get exhausted in the desert."
3 The king asked, "Where is your master's grandson?" Ziba replied

to the king, "He remains in Jerusalem, for he said, 'Today the
house of Israel will give back to me my grandfather's kingdom.'"
4 The king said to Ziba, "Everything that was Mephibosheth's now
belongs to you." Ziba replied, "I bow before you. May I find favor
in your sight, my lord the king."

SHIMEI CURSES DAVID AND HIS MEN

5 Then King David reached Bahurim. There a man from Saul's
extended family named Shimei son of Gera came out, yelling
curses as he approached. 6 He threw stones at David and all of
King David's servants, as well as all the people and the soldiers
who were on his right and on his left. 7 As he yelled curses, Shimei
said, "Leave! Leave! You man of bloodshed, you wicked man! 8 The
LORD has punished you for all the spilled blood of the house of
Saul, in whose place you rule. Now the LORD has given the kingdom into the hand of your son Absalom. Disaster has overtaken
you, for you are a man of bloodshed!"

9 Then Abishai son of Zeruiah said to the king, "Why should
this dead dog curse my lord the king? Let me go over and cut off
his head!" 10 But the king said, "What do we have in common, you
sons of Zeruiah? If he curses because the LORD has said to him,
'Curse David!,' who can say to him, 'Why have you done this?'"
11 Then David said to Abishai and to all his servants, "My own
son, my very own flesh and blood, is trying to take my life. So
also now this Benjaminite! Leave him alone so that he can curse,
for the LORD has spoken to him. 12 Perhaps the LORD will notice
my affliction and this day grant me good in place of his curse."

13 So David and his men went on their way. But Shimei kept
going along the side of the hill opposite him, yelling curses as
he threw stones and dirt at them. 14 The king and all the people who were with him arrived exhausted at their destination,
where David refreshed himself.

THE ADVICE OF AHITHOPHEL

15 Now when Absalom and all the men of Israel arrived in Jerusalem, Ahithophel was with him. 16 When David's friend Hushai
the Arkite came to Absalom, Hushai said to him, "Long live the
king! Long live the king!"

17 Absalom said to Hushai, "Do you call this loyalty to your
friend? Why didn't you go with your friend?" 18 Hushai replied
to Absalom, "No, I will be loyal to the one whom the LORD, these
people, and all the men of Israel have chosen. 19 Moreover, whom
should I serve? Should it not be his son? Just as I served your father, so I will serve you."

20 Then Absalom said to Ahithophel, "Give us your advice. What
should we do?" 21 Ahithophel replied to Absalom, "Sleep with
your father's concubines whom he left to care for the palace. All
Israel will hear that you have made yourself repulsive to your father. Then your followers will be motivated to support you." 22 So
they pitched a tent for Absalom on the roof, and Absalom slept
with his father's concubines in the sight of all Israel.

23 In those days Ahithophel's advice was considered as valuable as a prophetic revelation. Both David and Absalom highly
regarded the advice of Ahithophel.

THE DEATH OF AHITHOPHEL

17 Ahithophel said to Absalom, "Let me pick out 12,000 men.
Then I will go and pursue David this very night. 2 When I
catch up with him he will be exhausted and worn out. I will rout
him, and the entire army that is with him will flee. I will kill only
the king 3 and will bring the entire army back to you. In exchange
for the life of the man you are seeking, you will get back everyone. The entire army will return unharmed."
4 This seemed like a good idea to Absalom and to all the leaders
of Israel. 5 But Absalom said, "Call for Hushai the Arkite, and let's
hear what he has to say." 6 So Hushai came to Absalom. Absalom
said to him, "Here is what Ahithophel has advised. Should we
follow his advice? If not, what would you recommend?"
7 Hushai replied to Absalom, "Ahithophel's advice is not sound
this time." 8 Hushai went on to say, "You know your father and
his men—they are soldiers and are as dangerous as a bear out
in the wild that has been robbed of her cubs. Your father is an
experienced soldier; he will not stay overnight with the army.
9 At this very moment he is hiding out in one of the caves or in
some other similar place. If it should turn out that he attacks
our troops first, whoever hears about it will say, 'Absalom's army
has been slaughtered!' 10 If that happens even the bravest soldier—one who is lion-hearted—will virtually melt away. For all
Israel knows that your father is a warrior and that those who
are with him are brave. 11 My advice therefore is this: Let all Israel from Dan to Beer Sheba—in number like the sand by the
sea—be mustered to you, and you lead them personally into
battle. 12 We will come against him wherever he happens to be
found. We will descend on him like the dew falls on the ground.
Neither he nor any of the men who are with him will be spared
alive—not one of them! 13 If he regroups in a city, all Israel will
take up ropes to that city and drag it down to the valley, so that
not a single pebble will be left there!"
14 Then Absalom and all the men of Israel said, "The advice
of Hushai the Arkite sounds better than the advice of Ahithophel." Now the LORD had decided to frustrate the sound advice
of Ahithophel, so that the LORD could bring disaster on Absalom.
15 Then Hushai reported to Zadok and Abiathar the priests,
"Here is what Ahithophel has advised Absalom and the leaders of Israel to do, and here is what I have advised. 16 Now send
word quickly to David and warn him, "Don't spend the night at
the fords of the wilderness tonight. Instead, be sure you cross
over, or else the king and everyone who is with him may be overwhelmed."
17 Now Jonathan and Ahimaaz were staying in En Rogel. A female servant would go and inform them, and they would then
go and inform King David. It was not advisable for them to be
seen going into the city. 18 But a young man saw them on one
occasion and informed Absalom. So the two of them quickly
departed and went to the house of a man in Bahurim. There
was a well in his courtyard, and they got down in it. 19 His wife
then took the covering and spread it over the top of the well
and scattered some grain over it. No one was aware of what
she had done.

20 When the servants of Absalom approached the woman at her
home, they asked, "Where are Ahimaaz and Jonathan?" The woman replied to them, "They crossed over the stream." Absalom's men
searched but did not find them, so they returned to Jerusalem.
21 After the men had left, Ahimaaz and Jonathan climbed out of
the well. Then they left and informed King David. They advised
David, "Get up and cross the stream quickly, for Ahithophel has
devised a plan to catch you." 22 So David and all the people who
were with him got up and crossed the Jordan River. By dawn
there was not one person left who had not crossed the Jordan.
23 When Ahithophel realized that his advice had not been followed, he saddled his donkey and returned to his house in his
hometown. After setting his household in order, he hanged himself. So he died and was buried in the grave of his father.
24 Meanwhile David had gone to Mahanaim, while Absalom
and all the men of Israel had crossed the Jordan River. 25 Absalom had made Amasa general in command of the army in place
of Joab. (Now Amasa was the son of an Israelite man named Jether, who had married Abigail the daughter of Nahash and sister of Zeruiah, Joab's mother.) 26 The army of Israel and Absalom
camped in the land of Gilead.
27 When David came to Mahanaim, Shobi the son of Nahash
from Rabbah of the Ammonites, Makir the son of Ammiel from
Lo Debar, and Barzillai the Gileadite from Rogelim 28 brought
bedding, basins, and pottery utensils. They also brought food for
David and all who were with him, including wheat, barley, flour,
roasted grain, beans, lentils, 29 honey, curds, flocks, and cheese.
For they said, "The people are no doubt hungry, tired, and thirsty
there in the desert."

THE DEATH OF ABSALOM

18 David assembled the army that was with him. He appointed
leaders of thousands and leaders of hundreds. 2 David then
sent out the army—a third under the leadership of Joab, a third
under the leadership of Joab's brother Abishai son of Zeruiah,
and a third under the leadership of Ittai the Gittite. The king said
to the troops, "I too will indeed march out with you."
3 But the soldiers replied, "You should not do this! For if we
should have to make a rapid retreat, they won't be concerned
about us. Even if half of us should die, they won't be concerned.
But you are like 10,000 of us! So it is better if you remain in the
city for support." 4 Then the king said to them, "I will do whatever seems best to you."

So the king stayed beside the city gate, while all the army
marched out by hundreds and by thousands. 5 The king gave this
order to Joab, Abishai, and Ittai: "For my sake deal gently with the
young man Absalom." Now the entire army was listening when
the king gave all the leaders this order concerning Absalom.
6 Then the army marched out to the field to fight against Israel. The battle took place in the forest of Ephraim. 7 The army
of Israel was defeated there by David's men. The slaughter there
was great that day—20,000 soldiers were killed. 8 The battle there
was spread out over the whole area, and the forest consumed
more soldiers than the sword devoured that day.

9 Then Absalom happened to come across David's men. Now as
Absalom was riding on his mule, it went under the branches of
a large oak tree. His head got caught in the oak and he was suspended in midair, while the mule he had been riding kept going.
10 When one of the men saw this, he reported it to Joab saying,
"I saw Absalom hanging in an oak tree." 11 Joab replied to the man
who was telling him this, "What! You saw this? Why didn't you
strike him down right on the spot? I would have given you ten
pieces of silver and a commemorative belt!"
12 The man replied to Joab, "Even if I were receiving 1,000 pieces
of silver, I would not strike the king's son! In our very presence the
king gave this order to you and Abishai and Ittai, 'Protect the young
man Absalom for my sake.' 13 If I had acted at risk of my own life—and
nothing is hidden from the king—you would have abandoned me."
14 Joab replied, "I will not wait around like this for you!" He
took three spears in his hand and thrust them into the middle
of Absalom while he was still alive in the middle of the oak tree.
15 Then ten soldiers who were Joab's armor-bearers struck Absalom and finished him off.
16 Then Joab blew the trumpet and the army turned back from
chasing Israel, for Joab had called for the army to halt. 17 They took
Absalom, threw him into a large pit in the forest, and stacked a
huge pile of stones over him. In the meantime all the Israelite
soldiers fled to their homes.
18 Before this Absalom had set up a monument and dedicated
it to himself in the King's Valley, reasoning, "I have no son who
will carry on my name." He named the monument after himself,
and to this day it is known as Absalom's Memorial.

DAVID LEARNS OF ABSALOM'S DEATH

19 Then Ahimaaz the son of Zadok said, "Let me run and give the
king the good news that the LORD has vindicated him before
his enemies." 20 But Joab said to him, "You will not be a bearer
of good news today. You will bear good news some other day, but
not today, for the king's son is dead."
21 Then Joab said to the Cushite, "Go and tell the king what you
have seen." After bowing to Joab, the Cushite ran off. 22 Ahimaaz
the son of Zadok again spoke to Joab, "Whatever happens, let me
go after the Cushite." But Joab said, "Why is it that you want to
go, my son? You have no good news that will bring you a reward."
23 But he said, "Whatever happens, I want to go!" So Joab said to
him, "Then go!" So Ahimaaz ran by the way of the Jordan plain,
and he passed the Cushite.
24 Now David was sitting between the inner and outer gates,
and the watchman went up to the roof over the gate at the wall.
When he looked, he saw a man running by himself. 25 So the
watchman called out and informed the king. The king said, "If he
is by himself, he brings good news." The runner came ever closer.
26 Then the watchman saw another man running. The watchman called out to the gatekeeper, "There is another man running
by himself." The king said, "This one also is bringing good news."
27 The watchman said, "It appears to me that the first runner is
Ahimaaz son of Zadok." The king said, "He is a good man, and he
comes with good news."

28 Then Ahimaaz called out and said to the king, "Greetings!"
He bowed down before the king with his face toward the ground
and said, "May the LORD your God be praised because he has defeated the men who opposed my lord the king!"
29 The king replied, "How is the young man Absalom?" Ahimaaz
replied, "I saw a great deal of confusion when Joab was sending
the king's servant and me, your servant, but I don't know what
it was all about." 30 The king said, "Turn aside and take your place
here." So he turned aside and waited.
31 Then the Cushite arrived and said, "May my lord the king
now receive the good news! The LORD has vindicated you today and delivered you from the hand of all who have rebelled
against you!" 32 The king asked the Cushite, "How is the young
man Absalom?" The Cushite replied, "May the enemies of my
lord the king and all who have plotted against you be like that
young man!"
33 The king then became very upset. He went up to the upper
room over the gate and wept. As he went he said, "My son, Absalom! My son, my son, Absalom! If only I could have died in your
place! Absalom, my son, my son!"
19 Joab was told, "The king is weeping and mourning over Absalom." 2 So the victory of that day was turned to mourning
as far as all the people were concerned. For the people heard
on that day, "The king is grieved over his son." 3 That day the
people stole away to go to the city the way people who are embarrassed steal away in fleeing from battle. 4 The king covered
his face and cried out loudly, "My son, Absalom! Absalom, my
son, my son!"
5 So Joab visited the king at his home. He said, "Today you have
embarrassed all your servants who have saved your life this day,
as well as the lives of your sons, your daughters, your wives, and
your concubines. 6 You seem to love your enemies and hate your
friends! For you have as much as declared today that leaders and
servants don't matter to you. I realize now that if Absalom were
alive and all of us were dead today, it would be all right with you.
7 So get up now and go out and give some encouragement to your
servants. For I swear by the LORD that if you don't go out there,
not a single man will stay here with you tonight! This disaster
will be worse for you than any disaster that has overtaken you
from your youth right to the present time!"
8 So the king got up and sat at the city gate. When all the people were informed that the king was sitting at the city gate, they
all came before him.

DAVID GOES BACK TO JERUSALEM

But the Israelite soldiers had all fled to their own homes. 9 All the
people throughout all the tribes of Israel were arguing among
themselves saying, "The king delivered us from the hand of our
enemies. He rescued us from the hand of the Philistines, but
now he has fled from the land because of Absalom. 10 But Absalom, whom we anointed as our king, has died in battle. So now
why do you hesitate to bring the king back?"
11 Then King David sent a message to Zadok and Abiathar the
priests saying, "Tell the elders of Judah, 'Why should you delay

any further in bringing the king back to his palace, when everything Israel is saying has come to the king's attention. 12 You are
my brothers—my very own flesh and blood! Why should you delay
any further in bringing the king back?' 13 Say to Amasa, 'Are you
not my flesh and blood? God will punish me severely, if from this
time on you are not the commander of my army in place of Joab!'"

14 He won over the hearts of all the men of Judah as though
they were one man. Then they sent word to the king saying, "Return, you and all your servants as well." 15 So the king returned
and came to the Jordan River.

Now the people of Judah had come to Gilgal to meet the king
and to help him cross the Jordan. 16 Shimei son of Gera the Benjaminite from Bahurim came down quickly with the men of Judah to meet King David. 17 There were 1,000 men from Benjamin
with him, along with Ziba the servant of Saul's household, and
with him his fifteen sons and twenty servants. They hurriedly
crossed the Jordan within sight of the king. 18 They crossed at
the ford in order to help the king's household cross and to do
whatever he thought appropriate.

Now after he had crossed the Jordan, Shimei son of Gera threw
himself down before the king. 19 He said to the king, "Don't think
badly of me, my lord, and don't recall the sin of your servant on
the day when you, my lord the king, left Jerusalem! Please don't
call it to mind! 20 For I, your servant, know that I sinned, and I
have come today as the first of all the house of Joseph to come
down to meet my lord the king."

21 Abishai son of Zeruiah replied, "For this should not Shimei
be put to death? After all, he cursed the LORD's anointed!" 22 But
David said, "What do we have in common, you sons of Zeruiah?
You are like my enemy today! Should anyone be put to death
in Israel today? Don't I know that today I am king over Israel?"
23 The king said to Shimei, "You won't die." The king vowed an
oath concerning this.

24 Now Mephibosheth, Saul's grandson, came down to meet
the king. From the day the king had left until the day he safely
returned, Mephibosheth had not cared for his feet nor trimmed
his mustache nor washed his clothes.

25 When he came from Jerusalem to meet the king, the king
asked him, "Why didn't you go with me, Mephibosheth?" 26 He
replied, "My lord the king, my servant deceived me! I said, 'Let
me get my donkey saddled so that I can ride on it and go with
the king,' for I am lame. 27 But my servant has slandered me to
my lord the king. But my lord the king is like an angel of God.
Do whatever seems appropriate to you. 28 After all, there was no
one in the entire house of my grandfather who did not deserve
death from my lord the king. But instead you allowed me to eat
at your own table! What further claim do I have to ask the king
for anything?"

29 Then the king replied to him, "Why should you continue
speaking like this? You and Ziba will inherit the field together."
30 Mephibosheth said to the king, "Let him have the whole thing!
My lord the king has returned safely to his house!"

31 Now when Barzillai the Gileadite had come down from Rogelim, he crossed the Jordan with the king so he could send him

on his way from there. [32] But Barzillai was very old—eighty years
old, in fact—and he had taken care of the king when he stayed
in Mahanaim, for he was a very rich man. [33] So the king said to
Barzillai, "Cross over with me, and I will take care of you while
you are with me in Jerusalem."
[34] Barzillai replied to the king, "How many days do I have left
to my life, that I should go up with the king to Jerusalem? [35] I am
now eighty years old. Am I able to discern good and bad? Can I
taste what I eat and drink? Am I still able to hear the voices of
male and female singers? Why should I continue to be a burden to my lord the king? [36] I will cross the Jordan with the king
and go a short distance. Why should the king reward me in this
way? [37] Let me return so that I may die in my own town near the
grave of my father and my mother. But look, here is your servant
Kimham. Let him cross over with my lord the king. Do for him
whatever seems appropriate to you."
[38] The king replied, "Kimham will cross over with me, and I
will do for him whatever I deem appropriate. And whatever you
choose, I will do for you."
[39] So all the people crossed the Jordan, as did the king. After the
king had kissed him and blessed him, Barzillai returned to his
home. [40] When the king crossed over to Gilgal, Kimham crossed
over with him. Now all the soldiers of Judah along with half the
soldiers of Israel had helped the king cross over.
[41] Then all the men of Israel began coming to the king. They
asked the king, "Why did our brothers, the men of Judah, sneak
the king away and help the king and his household cross the
Jordan—and not only him but all of David's men as well?" [42] All
the men of Judah replied to the men of Israel, "Because the king
is our close relative! Why are you so upset about this? Have we
eaten at the king's expense? Or have we misappropriated anything for our own use?" [43] The men of Israel replied to the men
of Judah, "We have ten shares in the king, and we have a greater
claim on David than you do! Why do you want to curse us?
Weren't we the first to suggest bringing back our king?" But the
comments of the men of Judah were more severe than those of
the men of Israel.

SHEBA'S REBELLION

20 Now a wicked man named Sheba son of Bikri, a Benjaminite, happened to be there. He blew the trumpet and said,

"We have no share in David;
we have no inheritance in this son of Jesse!
Every man go home, O Israel!"

[2] So all the men of Israel deserted David and followed Sheba
son of Bikri. But the men of Judah stuck by their king all the way
from the Jordan River to Jerusalem.
[3] Then David went to his palace in Jerusalem. The king took
the ten concubines he had left to care for the palace and placed
them under confinement. Though he provided for their needs,
he did not sleep with them. They remained under restriction until the day they died, living out the rest of their lives
as widows.

4 Then the king said to Amasa, "Call the men of Judah together
for me in three days, and you be present here with them too." 5 So
Amasa went out to call Judah together. But in doing so he took
longer than the time that the king had allotted him.

6 Then David said to Abishai, "Now Sheba son of Bikri will cause
greater disaster for us than Absalom did! Take your lord's servants and pursue him. Otherwise he will secure fortified cities
for himself and get away from us." 7 So Joab's men, accompanied
by the Kerethites, the Pelethites, and all the warriors, left Jerusalem to pursue Sheba son of Bikri.

8 When they were near the big rock that is in Gibeon, Amasa
came to them. Now Joab was dressed in military attire and had
a dagger in its sheath belted to his waist. When he advanced,
it fell out.

9 Joab said to Amasa, "How are you, my brother?" With his right
hand Joab took hold of Amasa's beard as if to greet him with a
kiss. 10 Amasa did not protect himself from the knife in Joab's
other hand, and Joab stabbed him in the abdomen, causing Amasa's intestines to spill out on the ground. There was no need to
stab him again; the first blow was fatal. Then Joab and his brother Abishai pursued Sheba son of Bikri.

11 One of Joab's soldiers who stood over Amasa said, "Whoever
is for Joab and whoever is for David, follow Joab!" 12 Amasa was
squirming in his own blood in the middle of the path, and this
man had noticed that all the soldiers stopped. Having noticed
that everyone who came across Amasa stopped, the man pulled
him away from the path and into the field and threw a garment
over him. 13 Once he had removed Amasa from the path, everyone followed Joab to pursue Sheba son of Bikri.

14 Sheba traveled through all the tribes of Israel to Abel of Beth
Maacah and all the Berite region. When they had assembled,
they too joined him. 15 So Joab's men came and laid siege against
him in Abel of Beth Maacah. They prepared a siege ramp outside
the city that stood against its outer rampart. As all of Joab's soldiers were trying to break through the wall so that it would collapse, 16 a wise woman called out from the city, "Listen up! Listen
up! Tell Joab, 'Come near so that I may speak to you.'"

17 When he approached her, the woman asked, "Are you Joab?"
He replied, "I am." She said to him, "Listen to the words of your
servant." He said, "Go ahead. I'm listening." 18 She said, "In the
past they would always say, 'Let them inquire in Abel,' and that is
how they settled things. 19 I represent the peaceful and the faithful in Israel. You are attempting to destroy an important city
in Israel. Why should you swallow up the LORD's inheritance?"

20 Joab answered, "Not at all! I don't intend to swallow up or
destroy anything! 21 That's not the way things are. There is a man
from the hill country of Ephraim named Sheba son of Bikri. He
has rebelled against King David. Give me just this one man, and
I will leave the city." The woman said to Joab, "This very minute
his head will be thrown over the wall to you!"

22 Then the woman went to all the people with her wise advice
and they cut off Sheba's head and threw it out to Joab. Joab blew
the trumpet, and his men dispersed from the city, each going to
his own home. Joab returned to the king in Jerusalem.

23 Now Joab was the general in command of all the army of Israel. Benaiah the son of Jehoiada was over the Kerethites and the Perethites. 24 Adoniram was supervisor of the work crews. Jehoshaphat son of Ahilud was the secretary. 25 Sheva was the scribe, and Zadok and Abiathar were the priests. 26 Ira the Jairite was David's personal priest.

THE GIBEONITES DEMAND REVENGE

21 During David's reign there was a famine for three consecutive years. So David inquired of the LORD. The LORD said, "It is because of Saul and his bloodstained family, because he murdered the Gibeonites."

2 So the king summoned the Gibeonites and spoke with them. (Now the Gibeonites were not descendants of Israel; they were a remnant of the Amorites. The Israelites had made a promise to them, but Saul tried to kill them because of his zeal for the people of Israel and Judah.) 3 David said to the Gibeonites, "What can I do for you, and how can I make amends so that you will bless the LORD's inheritance?"

4 The Gibeonites said to him, "We have no claim to silver or gold from Saul or from his family, nor would we be justified in putting to death anyone in Israel." David asked, "What then are you asking me to do for you?" 5 They replied to the king, "As for this man who exterminated us and who schemed against us so that we were destroyed and left without status throughout all the borders of Israel—6 let seven of his male descendants be turned over to us, and we will execute them before the LORD in Gibeah of Saul, who was the LORD's chosen one." The king replied, "I will turn them over."

7 The king had mercy on Mephibosheth son of Jonathan, the son of Saul, in light of the LORD's oath that had been taken between David and Jonathan son of Saul. 8 So the king took Armoni and Mephibosheth, the two sons of Aiah's daughter Rizpah whom she had born to Saul, and the five sons of Saul's daughter Merab whom she had born to Adriel the son of Barzillai the Meholathite. 9 He turned them over to the Gibeonites, and they executed them on a hill before the LORD. The seven of them died together; they were put to death during harvest time—during the first days of the beginning of the barley harvest.

10 Rizpah the daughter of Aiah took sackcloth and spread it out for herself on a rock. From the beginning of the harvest until the rain fell on them, she did not allow the birds of the air to feed on them by day, nor the wild animals by night. 11 When David was told what Rizpah daughter of Aiah, Saul's concubine, had done, 12 he went and took the bones of Saul and of his son Jonathan from the leaders of Jabesh Gilead. (They had secretly taken them from the plaza at Beth Shan. It was there that Philistines publicly exposed their corpses after they had killed Saul at Gilboa.) 13 David brought the bones of Saul and of Jonathan his son from there; they also gathered up the bones of those who had been executed.

14 They buried the bones of Saul and his son Jonathan in the land of Benjamin at Zela in the grave of his father Kish. After they had done everything that the king had commanded, God responded to their prayers for the land.

ISRAEL ENGAGES IN VARIOUS BATTLES WITH THE PHILISTINES

15 Another battle was fought between the Philistines and Israel.
So David went down with his soldiers and fought the Philistines.
David became exhausted. 16 Now Ishbi-Benob, one of the descendants of Rapha, had a spear that weighed 300 bronze shekels,
and he was armed with a new weapon. He had said that he would
kill David. 17 But Abishai the son of Zeruiah came to David's aid,
striking the Philistine down and killing him. Then David's men
took an oath saying, "You will not go out to battle with us again!
You must not extinguish the lamp of Israel!"

18 Later there was another battle with the Philistines, this time
in Gob. On that occasion Sibbekai the Hushathite killed Saph,
who was one of the descendants of Rapha. 19 Yet another battle
occurred with the Philistines in Gob. On that occasion Elhanan
the son of Jair the Bethlehemite killed the brother of Goliath
the Gittite, the shaft of whose spear was like a weaver's beam.
20 Yet another battle occurred in Gath. On that occasion there
was a large man who had six fingers on each hand and six toes on
each foot, twenty-four in all! He too was a descendant of Rapha.
21 When he taunted Israel, Jonathan, the son of David's brother
Shimeah, killed him. 22 These four were the descendants of Rapha who lived in Gath; they were killed by David and his soldiers.

DAVID SINGS TO THE LORD

22 David sang to the LORD the words of this song when the
LORD rescued him from the power of all his enemies, including Saul. 2 He said:

"The LORD is my high ridge, my stronghold, my deliverer.
3 My God is my rocky summit where I take shelter,
my shield, the horn that saves me, my stronghold,
my refuge, my savior. You save me from violence!
4 I called to the LORD, who is worthy of praise,
and I was delivered from my enemies.
5 The waves of death engulfed me;
the currents of chaos overwhelmed me.
6 The ropes of Sheol tightened around me;
the snares of death trapped me.
7 In my distress I called to the LORD;
I called to my God.
From his heavenly temple he heard my voice;
he listened to my cry for help.
8 The earth heaved and shook;
the foundations of the sky trembled.
They heaved because he was angry.
9 Smoke ascended from his nose;
fire devoured as it came from his mouth;
he hurled down fiery coals.
10 He made the sky sink as he descended;
a thick cloud was under his feet.
11 He mounted a winged angel and flew;
he glided on the wings of the wind.
12 He shrouded himself in darkness,
in thick rain clouds.

REFLECT

On which attributes of God's character does David focus his praise? How had David seen these attributes displayed in his life?

13 From the brightness in front of him
came coals of fire.
14 The LORD thundered from the sky;
the Most High shouted loudly.
15 He shot arrows and scattered them,
lightning and routed them.
16 The depths of the sea were exposed;
the inner regions of the world were uncovered
by the LORD's battle cry,
by the powerful breath from his nose.
17 He reached down from above and grabbed me;
he pulled me from the surging water.
18 He rescued me from my strong enemy,
from those who hate me,
for they were too strong for me.
19 They confronted me in my day of calamity,
but the LORD helped me.
20 He brought me out into a wide open place;
he delivered me because he was pleased with me.
21 The LORD repaid me for my godly deeds;
he rewarded my blameless behavior.
22 For I have obeyed the LORD's commands;
I have not rebelled against my God.
23 For I am aware of all his regulations,
and I do not reject his rules.
24 I was blameless before him;
I kept myself from sinning.
25 The LORD rewarded me for my godly deeds;
he took notice of my blameless behavior.
26 You prove to be loyal to one who is faithful;
you prove to be trustworthy to one who is innocent.
27 You prove to be reliable to one who is blameless,
but you prove to be deceptive to one who is perverse.
28 You deliver oppressed people,
but you watch the proud and bring them down.
29 Indeed, you are my lamp, LORD.
The LORD illumines the darkness around me.
30 Indeed, with your help I can charge against an army;
by my God's power I can jump over a wall.
31 The one true God acts in a faithful manner;
the LORD's promise is reliable;
he is a shield to all who take shelter in him.
32 Indeed, who is God besides the LORD?
Who is a protector besides our God?
33 The one true God is my mighty refuge;
he removes the obstacles in my way.
34 He gives me the agility of a deer;
he enables me to negotiate the rugged terrain.
35 He trains my hands for battle;
my arms can bend even the strongest bow.
36 You give me your protective shield;
your willingness to help enables me to prevail.
37 You widen my path;
my feet do not slip.

GOD'S HEART FOR THE NATIONS

2 Samuel 22:50

"So I will give you thanks, O LORD, before the nations! I will sing praises to you."

38 I chase my enemies and destroy them;
I do not turn back until I wipe them out.
39 I wipe them out and beat them to death;
they cannot get up;
they fall at my feet.
40 You give me strength for battle;
you make my foes kneel before me.
41 You make my enemies retreat;
I destroy those who hate me.
42 They cry out, but there is no one to help them;
they cry out to the LORD, but he does not answer them.
43 I grind them as fine as the dust of the ground;
I crush them and stomp them like clay in the streets.
44 You rescue me from a hostile army;
you preserve me as a leader of nations;
people over whom I had no authority
are now my subjects.
45 Foreigners are powerless before me;
when they hear of my exploits, they submit to me.
46 Foreigners lose their courage;
they shake with fear as they leave their strongholds.
47 The LORD is alive!
My Protector is praiseworthy!
The God who delivers me is exalted as king!
48 The one true God completely vindicates me;
he makes nations submit to me.
49 He delivers me from my enemies;
you snatch me away from those who attack me;
you rescue me from violent men.
50 So I will give you thanks, O LORD, before the nations!
I will sing praises to you.
51 He gives his king magnificent victories;
he is faithful to his chosen ruler,
to David and to his descendants forever!"

DAVID'S FINAL WORDS

23 These are the final words of David:
"The oracle of David son of Jesse,
the oracle of the man raised up as
the ruler chosen by the God of Jacob,
Israel's beloved singer of songs:
2 The LORD's Spirit spoke through me;
his word was on my tongue.
3 The God of Israel spoke,
the Protector of Israel spoke to me.
The one who rules fairly among men,
the one who rules in the fear of God,
4 is like the light of morning when the sun comes up,
a morning in which there are no clouds.
He is like the brightness after rain
that produces grass from the earth.
5 My dynasty is approved by God,
for he has made a perpetual covenant with me,
arranged in all its particulars and secured.

He always delivers me,
and brings all I desire to fruition.
6 But evil people are like thorns—
all of them are tossed away,
for they cannot be held in the hand.
7 The one who touches them
must use an iron instrument
or the wooden shaft of a spear.
They are completely burned up right where they lie!"

DAVID'S WARRIORS

8 These are the names of David's warriors:
Josheb Basshebeth, a Tahkemonite, was head of the officers. He
killed 800 men with his spear in one battle. 9 Next in command
was Eleazar son of Dodo, the son of Ahohi. He was one of the three
warriors who were with David when they defied the Philistines
who were assembled there for battle. When the men of Israel retreated, 10 he stood his ground and fought the Philistines until his
hand grew so tired that it seemed stuck to his sword. The LORD
gave a great victory on that day. When the army returned to him,
the only thing left to do was to plunder the corpses.
11 Next in command was Shammah son of Agee the Hararite.
When the Philistines assembled at Lehi, where there happened
to be an area of a field that was full of lentils, the army retreated
before the Philistines. 12 But he made a stand in the middle of
that area. He defended it and defeated the Philistines; the LORD
gave them a great victory.
13 At the time of the harvest three of the thirty leaders went
down to David at the cave of Adullam. A band of Philistines was
camped in the valley of Rephaim. 14 David was in the stronghold
at the time, while a Philistine garrison was in Bethlehem. 15 David was thirsty and said, "How I wish someone would give me
some water to drink from the cistern in Bethlehem near the
gate!" 16 So the three elite warriors broke through the Philistine
forces and drew some water from the cistern in Bethlehem near
the gate. They carried it back to David, but he refused to drink it.
He poured it out as a drink offering to the LORD 17 and said, "O
LORD, I will not do this! It is equivalent to the blood of the men
who risked their lives by going." So he refused to drink it. Such
were the exploits of the three elite warriors.
18 Abishai son of Zeruiah, the brother of Joab, was head of the
three. He killed 300 men with his spear and gained fame among
the three. 19 From the three he was given honor and he became
their officer, even though he was not one of the three.
20 Benaiah son of Jehoiada was a brave warrior from Kabzeel
who performed great exploits. He struck down the two sons of
Ariel of Moab. He also went down and killed a lion in a cistern on
a snowy day. 21 He also killed an impressive-looking Egyptian. The
Egyptian wielded a spear, while Benaiah attacked him with a club.
He grabbed the spear out of the Egyptian's hand and killed him
with his own spear. 22 Such were the exploits of Benaiah son of Jehoiada, who gained fame among the three elite warriors. 23 He received honor from the thirty warriors, though he was not one of
the three elite warriors. David put him in charge of his bodyguard.

24 Included with the thirty were the following: Asahel the brother of Joab, Elhanan son of Dodo from Bethlehem, 25 Shammah the Harodite, Elika the Harodite, 26 Helez the Paltite, Ira son of Ikkesh from Tekoa, 27 Abiezer the Anathothite, Mebunnai the Hushathite, 28 Zalmon the Ahohite, Maharai the Netophathite, 29 Heled son of Baanah the Netophathite, Ittai son of Ribai from Gibeah in Benjamin, 30 Benaiah the Pirathonite, Hiddai from the wadis of Gaash, 31 Abi-Albon the Arbathite, Azmaveth the Barhumite, 32 Eliahba the Shaalbonite, the sons of Jashen, Jonathan 33 son of Shammah the Hararite, Ahiam son of Sharar the Hararite, 34 Eliphelet son of Ahasbai the Maacathite, Eliam son of Ahithophel the Gilonite, 35 Hezrai the Carmelite, Paarai the Arbite, 36 Igal son of Nathan from Zobah, Bani the Gadite, 37 Zelek the Ammonite, Naharai the Beerothite (the armor-bearer of Joab son of Zeruiah), 38 Ira the Ithrite, Gareb the Ithrite, 39 and Uriah the Hittite. Altogether there were thirty-seven.

DAVID DISPLEASES THE LORD BY TAKING A CENSUS

24 The LORD's anger again raged against Israel, and he incited David against them, saying, "Go count Israel and Judah." 2 The king told Joab, the general in command of his army, "Go through all the tribes of Israel from Dan to Beer Sheba and muster the army, so I may know the size of the army."

3 Joab replied to the king, "May the LORD your God make the army a hundred times larger right before the eyes of my lord the king! But why does my master the king want to do this?"

4 But the king's edict stood, despite the objections of Joab and the leaders of the army. So Joab and the leaders of the army left the king's presence in order to muster the Israelite army.

5 They crossed the Jordan and camped at Aroer, on the south side of the city, at the wadi of Gad, near Jazer. 6 Then they went on to Gilead and to the region of Tahtim Hodshi, coming to Dan Jaan and on around to Sidon. 7 Then they went to the fortress of Tyre and all the cities of the Hivites and the Canaanites. Then they went on to the Negev of Judah, to Beer Sheba. 8 They went through all the land and after nine months and twenty days came back to Jerusalem.

9 Joab reported the number of warriors to the king. In Israel there were 800,000 sword-wielding warriors, and in Judah there were 500,000 soldiers.

10 David felt guilty after he had numbered the army. David said to the LORD, "I have sinned greatly by doing this! Now, O LORD, please remove the guilt of your servant, for I have acted very foolishly."

11 When David got up the next morning, the LORD's message had already come to the prophet Gad, David's seer: 12 "Go, tell David, 'This is what the LORD has said: I am offering you three forms of judgment. Pick one of them and I will carry it out against you.'"

13 Gad went to David and told him, "Shall seven years of famine come upon your land? Or shall you flee for three months from your enemies with them in hot pursuit? Or shall there be three days of plague in your land? Now decide what I should tell the one who sent me." 14 David said to Gad, "I am very upset! I prefer that we be attacked by the LORD, for his mercy is great; I do not want to be attacked by human hands!"

REFLECT

What does God's response to David's sin reveal about God's character?

15 So the LORD sent a plague through Israel from the morning
until the completion of the appointed time, and 70,000 people
died from Dan to Beer Sheba. 16 When the angel extended his
hand to destroy Jerusalem, the LORD relented from his judgment. He told the angel who was killing the people, "That's
enough! Stop now!" (Now the angel of the LORD was near the
threshing floor of Araunah the Jebusite.)

17 When he saw the angel who was destroying the people, David said to the LORD, "Look, it is I who have sinned and done this
evil thing! As for these sheep—what have they done? Attack me
and my family."

DAVID ACQUIRES A THRESHING FLOOR AND CONSTRUCTS AN ALTAR THERE

18 So Gad went to David that day and told him, "Go up and build
an altar for the LORD on the threshing floor of Araunah the Jebusite." 19 So David went up as Gad instructed him to do, according to the LORD's instructions.

20 When Araunah looked out and saw the king and his servants
approaching him, he went out and bowed to the king with his
face to the ground. 21 Araunah said, "Why has my lord the king
come to his servant?" David replied, "To buy from you the threshing floor so I can build an altar for the LORD, so that the plague
may be removed from the people." 22 Araunah told David, "My
lord the king may take whatever he wishes and offer it. Look!
Here are oxen for burnt offerings, and threshing sledges and
harnesses for wood. 23 I, the servant of my lord the king, give it
all to the king!" Araunah also told the king, "May the LORD your
God show you favor!" 24 But the king said to Araunah, "No, I insist on buying it from you! I will not offer to the LORD my God
burnt sacrifices that cost me nothing."

So David bought the threshing floor and the oxen for fifty
pieces of silver. 25 Then David built an altar for the LORD there
and offered burnt sacrifices and peace offerings. And the LORD
accepted prayers for the land, and the plague was removed from
Israel.

Forgive all the rebellious acts of your sinful people and cause their captors to have mercy on them

MEMORY VERSE

"Forgive all the rebellious acts of your *sinful people and cause their captors* to have mercy on them."

1 Kings 8:50

1 Kings

INTRODUCTION

God's Patience

God displays His great patience in the successes and failures, victories and defeats, and loyalty and disobedience recorded in the Book of 1 Kings. While focusing on the spiritual successes and failures in Israel and Judah, 1 Kings displays a picture of the patience and long-suffering of God.

First Kings chronicles the lives and reigns of many kings and prophets in the kingdoms of Israel and Judah. The split of the united kingdom of Israel into the divided kingdoms of Israel and Judah is detailed in this book. First Kings explores Israel's spiritual odyssey and the results. While some kings were devoted to God, many rejected the covenant He made with them and suffered the consequences. However, God's patience is on display as He gave His people many opportunities to return to Him.

First Kings takes place in the ninth and tenth centuries B.C. The writings of 1 and 2 Kings were originally one combined writing, later divided by the translators of the Septuagint, the Greek Old Testament. Traditionally, Jeremiah is identified as the author of 1 and 2 Kings. However, later scholarship suggests that these books were a result of a compilation process that began with the initial composition of the books in the late seventh century B.C. and concluded in the middle of the sixth century B.C.

First Kings encourages us to love God greatly as we see His great patience in the midst of His people's persistent sin. Despite their failures, God was patient and longed for His people to return to Him. God did not destroy His people but rather disciplined them with warnings and, eventually, exile. Although they were removed from their land, God kept a remnant of His people to preserve their name, and His, on the earth.

Canada

OFFICIAL LANGUAGE
English
POPULATION
37,315,000
UNREACHED POPULATION
1,954,000
PROFESSING CHRISTIANS
73.0%

Meg's Home

Say a Prayer Today

Pray for the people of Canada and the social reconciliation that is taking place. Pray that God, who is the author of peace, would bring peace, healing, and restoration to a difficult situation.

HISTORY BIT

In 1676 Chrestien Le Clercq arrived in Mi'kmaq, present day Nova Scotia and New Brunswick, to share the gospel with the native people. Finding that the Mi'kmaq people already had a hieroglyphic language tradition, Le Clercq created a set of images and pictures to communicate the gospel. These were handed down in the community for two hundred years.*

Source Information:
https://joshuaproject.net/countries/CA
*Linford D Fisher, Indigenous Language Tradition in The Oxford Handbook of the Bible in America, Paul C. Gutjahr, ed. (New York, NY: Oxford University Press, 2017), 46–47.

MEG'S STORY

First Kings 8:50 reveals the truth of God's character. God not only wants us to understand we are forgiven, but He also wants us to extend forgiveness to others, especially those who oppose us. God instructs us to forgive others to the same measure that Christ forgave us.

I am often convicted about my willingness to forgive others. I hold others to a higher standard than I set for myself and am often unwilling to forgive those who have hurt me. But when I am living out of the forgiveness and grace that Christ has given me, I am more inclined to have compassion for my coworkers and friends when they hurt me. It is a daily refining experience to forgive others and to extend the same compassion, humility, and kindness that Christ extends to me.

Canada has a Christian heritage, but it has long been moving away from the principles on which it was founded. As a society, Canadians are more and more focused on social reconciliation, especially regarding the colonization of indigenous people by church leaders.

Canada stands at a critical time in history in which the believers of Christ must demonstrate the true depth of forgiveness. It is our time to actively live out 1 Kings 8:50. Locally, I see more churches moving away from self-focused ministry to a tangible ministry of feeding the hungry, clothing the poor, advocating for the oppressed, and truly being the hands and feet of Christ. More believers are involved in political activism at all levels of government to address the reconciliation issues. I'm excited to see how the body of Christ is moving and how the Lord will restore our nation.

4 WEEK READING PLAN

LOVE HIS WORD

	MONDAY	TUESDAY	WEDNESDAY	THURSDAY	FRIDAY
1	1 Kings 1	1 Kings 2	1 Kings 3-4	1 Kings 5	1 Kings 6
	SOAP Psalm 95:1-2	SOAP Psalm 95:3-5	SOAP Psalm 95:6-7	SOAP Psalm 95:8-9	SOAP Psalm 95:10-11
2	1 Kings 7	1 Kings 8	1 Kings 9	1 Kings 10	1 Kings 11
	SOAP Psalm 96:1-3	SOAP 1 Kings 8:50	SOAP Psalm 96:4-6	SOAP Psalm 96:7-9	SOAP Psalm 96:10-13
3	1 Kings 12:1-32	1 Kings 12:33—13:32	1 Kings 13:33—14:31	1 Kings 15:1-32	1 Kings 15:33—16:34
	SOAP Psalm 97:1	SOAP Psalm 97:2-6	SOAP Psalm 97:7-8	SOAP Psalm 97:9-10	SOAP Psalm 97:11-12
4	1 Kings 17-18	1 Kings 19	1 Kings 20	1 Kings 21	1 Kings 22
	SOAP Psalm 98:1	SOAP Psalm 98:2-3	SOAP Psalm 98:4-5	SOAP Psalm 98:6-7	SOAP Psalm 98:8-9

ADONIJAH TRIES TO SEIZE THE THRONE

1 King David was very old; even when they covered him with blankets, he could not get warm. 2 His servants advised him, "A young virgin must be found for our master, the king, to take care of the king's needs and serve as his nurse. She can also sleep with you and keep our master, the king, warm." 3 So they looked through all Israel for a beautiful young woman and found Abishag, a Shunammite, and brought her to the king. 4 The young woman was very beautiful; she became the king's nurse and served him, but the king was not intimate with her.

5 Now Adonijah, son of David and Haggith, was promoting himself, boasting, "I will be king!" He managed to acquire chariots and horsemen, as well as fifty men to serve as his royal guard. 6 (Now his father had never corrected him by saying, "Why do you do such things?" He was also very handsome and had been born right after Absalom.) 7 He collaborated with Joab son of Zeruiah and with Abiathar the priest, and they supported him. 8 But Zadok the priest, Benaiah son of Jehoiada, Nathan the prophet, Shimei, Rei, and David's elite warriors did not ally themselves with Adonijah. 9 Adonijah sacrificed sheep, cattle, and fattened steers at the Stone of Zoheleth near En Rogel. He invited all his brothers, the king's sons, as well as all the men of Judah, the king's servants. 10 But he did not invite Nathan the prophet, Benaiah, the elite warriors, or his brother Solomon.

11 Nathan said to Bathsheba, Solomon's mother, "Has it been reported to you that Haggith's son Adonijah has become king behind our master David's back? 12 Now let me give you some advice as to how you can save your life and your son Solomon's life. 13 Visit King David and say to him, 'My master, O king, did you not solemnly promise your servant, "Surely your son Solomon will be king after me; he will sit on my throne"? So why has Adonijah become king?' 14 While you are still there speaking to the king, I will arrive and verify your report."

15 So Bathsheba visited the king in his private quarters. (The king was very old, and Abishag the Shunammite was serving the king.) 16 Bathsheba bowed down on the floor before the king. The king said, "What do you want?" 17 She replied to him, "My master, you swore an oath to your servant by the LORD your God, 'Solomon your son will be king after me and he will sit on my throne.' 18 But now, look, Adonijah has become king! But you, my master the king, are not even aware of it! 19 He has sacrificed many cattle, steers, and sheep and has invited all the king's sons, Abiathar the priest, and Joab, the commander of the army, but he has not invited your servant Solomon. 20 Now, my master, O king, all Israel is watching anxiously to see who is named to succeed my master the king on the throne. 21 If a decision is not made, when my master the king is buried with his ancestors, my son Solomon and I will be considered state criminals."

22 Just then, while she was still speaking to the king, Nathan the prophet arrived. 23 The king was told, "Nathan the prophet is here." Nathan entered and bowed before the king with his face to the floor. 24 Nathan said, "My master, O king, did you announce, 'Adonijah will be king after me; he will sit on my

throne'? 25 For today he has gone down and sacrificed many
cattle, steers, and sheep and has invited all the king's sons, the
army commanders, and Abiathar the priest. At this moment
they are having a feast in his presence, and they have declared,
'Long live King Adonijah!' 26 But he did not invite me—your servant—or Zadok the priest, or Benaiah son of Jehoiada, or your
servant Solomon. 27 Has my master the king authorized this
without informing your servants who should succeed my master the king on his throne?"

DAVID PICKS SOLOMON AS HIS SUCCESSOR

28 King David responded, "Summon Bathsheba!" She came and
stood before the king. 29 The king swore an oath: "As certainly
as the LORD lives (he who has rescued me from every danger),
30 I will keep today the oath I swore to you by the LORD God of
Israel: 'Surely Solomon your son will be king after me; he will
sit in my place on my throne.'" 31 Bathsheba bowed down to the
king with her face to the floor and said, "May my master, King
David, live forever!"

32 King David said, "Summon Zadok the priest, Nathan the
prophet, and Benaiah son of Jehoiada." They came before the
king, 33 and he told them, "Take your master's servants with you,
put my son Solomon on my mule, and lead him down to Gihon.
34 There Zadok the priest and Nathan the prophet will anoint
him king over Israel; then blow the trumpet and declare, 'Long
live King Solomon!' 35 Then follow him up as he comes and sits
on my throne. He will be king in my place; I have decreed that
he will be ruler over Israel and Judah." 36 Benaiah son of Jehoiada responded to the king: "So be it! May the LORD God of my
master the king confirm it! 37 As the LORD is with my master the
king, so may he be with Solomon, and may he make him an even
greater king than my master King David!"

38 So Zadok the priest, Nathan the prophet, Benaiah son of
Jehoiada, the Kerethites, and the Pelethites went down, put
Solomon on King David's mule, and led him to Gihon. 39 Zadok the priest took a horn filled with olive oil from the tent
and poured it on Solomon; the trumpet was blown and all the
people declared, "Long live King Solomon!" 40 All the people
followed him up, playing flutes and celebrating so loudly they
made the ground shake.

41 Now Adonijah and all his guests heard the commotion just
as they had finished eating. When Joab heard the sound of the
trumpet, he asked, "Why is there such a noisy commotion in
the city?" 42 As he was still speaking, Jonathan son of Abiathar
the priest arrived. Adonijah said, "Come in, for an important
man like you must be bringing good news." 43 Jonathan replied to
Adonijah: "No! Our master King David has made Solomon king.
44 The king sent with him Zadok the priest, Nathan the prophet,
Benaiah son of Jehoiada, the Kerethites, and the Pelethites and
they put him on the king's mule. 45 Then Zadok the priest and
Nathan the prophet anointed him king in Gihon. They went
up from there rejoicing, and the city is in an uproar. That is the
sound you hear. 46 Furthermore, Solomon has assumed the royal
throne. 47 The king's servants have even come to congratulate our

master King David, saying, 'May your God make Solomon more
famous than you and make him an even greater king than you!'
Then the king leaned on the bed 48 and said this: 'The LORD God
of Israel is worthy of praise because today he has placed a successor on my throne and allowed me to see it.'"
49 All of Adonijah's guests panicked; they jumped up and
rushed off their separate ways. 50 Adonijah feared Solomon, so
he got up and went and grabbed hold of the horns of the altar.
51 Solomon was told, "Look, Adonijah fears you; see, he has taken
hold of the horns of the altar, saying, 'May King Solomon solemnly promise me today that he will not kill his servant with
the sword.'" 52 Solomon said, "If he is a loyal subject, not a hair
of his head will be harmed, but if he is found to be a traitor, he
will die." 53 King Solomon sent men to bring him down from the
altar. He came and bowed down to King Solomon, and Solomon
told him, "Go home."

DAVID'S FINAL WORDS TO SOLOMON

2 When David was close to death, he told Solomon his son: 2 "I
am about to die. Be strong and become a man! 3 Do the job the
LORD your God has assigned you by following his instructions
and obeying his rules, commandments, regulations, and laws as
written in the law of Moses. Then you will succeed in all you do
and seek to accomplish, 4 and the LORD will fulfill his promise
to me, 'If your descendants watch their step and live faithfully
in my presence with all their heart and being, then,' he promised, 'you will not fail to have a successor on the throne of Israel.'
5 "You know what Joab son of Zeruiah did to me—how he murdered two commanders of the Israelite armies, Abner son of Ner
and Amasa son of Jether. During peacetime he struck them down
as if in battle; when he shed their blood, he stained the belt on his
waist and the sandals on his feet. 6 Do to him what you think is
appropriate, but don't let him live long and die a peaceful death.
7 "Treat fairly the sons of Barzillai of Gilead and provide for
their needs, because they helped me when I had to flee from
your brother Absalom.
8 "Note well, you still have to contend with Shimei son of Gera,
the Benjaminite from Bahurim, who tried to call down upon
me a horrible judgment when I went to Mahanaim. He came
down and met me at the Jordan, and I solemnly promised him by
the LORD, 'I will not strike you down with the sword.' 9 But now
don't treat him as if he were innocent. You are a wise man and
you know how to handle him; make sure he has a bloody death."
10 Then David passed away and was buried in the City of David. 11 David reigned over Israel forty years; he reigned in Hebron
seven years, and in Jerusalem thirty-three years.

SOLOMON SECURES THE THRONE

12 Solomon sat on his father David's throne, and his royal authority was firmly solidified.
13 Haggith's son Adonijah visited Bathsheba, Solomon's mother. She asked, "Do you come in peace?" He answered, "Yes." 14 He
added, "I have something to say to you." She replied, "Speak."
15 He said, "You know that the kingdom was mine and all Israel

REFLECT

What can we learn from the way David handed his throne to his son Solomon? In what ways did he prepare Solomon for what he would face as king? How can we do this for the next generation in our sphere of influence?

considered me king. But then the kingdom was given to my brother, for the LORD decided it should be his. 16 Now I'd like to ask you
for just one thing. Please don't refuse me." She said, "Go ahead and
ask." 17 He said, "Please ask King Solomon if he would give me Abishag the Shunammite as a wife, for he won't refuse you." 18 Bathsheba replied, "That's fine; I'll speak to the king on your behalf."
19 So Bathsheba visited King Solomon to speak to him on Adonijah's behalf. The king got up to greet her, bowed to her, and
then sat on his throne. He ordered a throne to be brought for the
king's mother, and she sat at his right hand. 20 She said, "I would
like to ask you for just one small favor. Please don't refuse me."
He said, "Go ahead and ask, my mother, for I would not refuse
you." 21 She said, "Allow Abishag the Shunammite to be given to
your brother Adonijah as a wife." 22 King Solomon answered his
mother, "Why just request Abishag the Shunammite for him?
Since he is my older brother, you should also request the kingdom for him, for Abiathar the priest, and for Joab son of Zeruiah!"
23 King Solomon then swore an oath by the LORD, "May God
judge me severely, if Adonijah does not pay for this request with
his life! 24 Now, as certainly as the LORD lives (he who made me
secure, allowed me to sit on my father David's throne, and established a dynasty for me as he promised), Adonijah will be
executed today!" 25 King Solomon then sent Benaiah son of Jehoiada, and he killed Adonijah.
26 The king then told Abiathar the priest, "Go back to your
property in Anathoth. You deserve to die, but today I will not
kill you because you did carry the ark of the Sovereign LORD before my father David and you suffered with my father through
all his difficult times." 27 Solomon removed Abiathar from being
a priest for the LORD, fulfilling the LORD's message that he had
pronounced against the family of Eli in Shiloh.
28 When the news reached Joab (for Joab had supported Adonijah, although he had not supported Absalom), he ran to the tent
of the LORD and grabbed hold of the horns of the altar. 29 When
King Solomon heard that Joab had run to the tent of the LORD
and was right there beside the altar, he ordered Benaiah son of
Jehoiada, "Go, strike him down." 30 When Benaiah arrived at the
tent of the LORD, he said to him, "The king says, 'Come out!'" But
he replied, "No, I will die here!" So Benaiah sent word to the king
and reported Joab's reply. 31 The king told him, "Do as he said!
Strike him down and bury him. Take away from me and from
my father's family the guilt of Joab's murderous, bloody deeds.
32 May the LORD punish him for the blood he shed; behind my father David's back he struck down and murdered with the sword
two men who were more innocent and morally upright than
he—Abner son of Ner, commander of Israel's army, and Amasa
son of Jether, commander of Judah's army. 33 May Joab and his
descendants be perpetually guilty of their shed blood, but may
the LORD give perpetual peace to David, his descendants, his
family, and his dynasty." 34 So Benaiah son of Jehoiada went up
and executed Joab; he was buried at his home in the wilderness.
35 The king appointed Benaiah son of Jehoiada to take his place
at the head of the army, and the king appointed Zadok the priest
to take Abiathar's place.

36 Next the king summoned Shimei and told him, "Build yourself a house in Jerusalem and live there, but you may not leave there to go anywhere. 37 If you ever do leave and cross the Kidron Valley, know for sure that you will certainly die. You will be responsible for your own death." 38 Shimei said to the king, "My master the king's proposal is acceptable. Your servant will do as you say." So Shimei lived in Jerusalem for a long time.

39 Three years later two of Shimei's servants ran away to King Achish son of Maacah of Gath. Shimei was told, "Look, your servants are in Gath." 40 So Shimei got up, saddled his donkey, and went to Achish at Gath to find his servants; Shimei went and brought back his servants from Gath. 41 When Solomon was told that Shimei had gone from Jerusalem to Gath and had then returned, 42 the king summoned Shimei and said to him, "You will recall that I made you take an oath by the LORD, and I solemnly warned you, 'If you ever leave and go anywhere, know for sure that you will certainly die.' You said to me, 'The proposal is acceptable; I agree to it.' 43 Why then have you broken the oath you made before the LORD and disobeyed the order I gave you?" 44 Then the king said to Shimei, "You are well aware of the way you mistreated my father David. The LORD will punish you for what you did. 45 But King Solomon will be empowered, and David's dynasty will endure permanently before the LORD." 46 The king then gave the order to Benaiah son of Jehoiada who went and executed Shimei.

So Solomon took firm control of the kingdom.

THE LORD GIVES SOLOMON WISDOM

3 Solomon made an alliance by marriage with Pharaoh, king of Egypt; he married Pharaoh's daughter. He brought her to the City of David until he could finish building his residence and the temple of the LORD and the wall around Jerusalem. 2 Now the people were offering sacrifices at the high places, because in those days a temple had not yet been built to honor the LORD. 3 Solomon demonstrated his loyalty to the LORD by following the practices of his father David, except that he offered sacrifices and burned incense on the high places.

4 The king went to Gibeon to offer sacrifices, for it had the most prominent of the high places. Solomon would offer up 1,000 burnt sacrifices on the altar there. 5 One night in Gibeon the LORD appeared to Solomon in a dream. God said, "Tell me what I should give you." 6 Solomon replied, "You demonstrated great loyalty to your servant, my father David, as he served you faithfully, properly, and sincerely. You have maintained this great loyalty to this day by allowing his son to sit on his throne. 7 Now, O LORD my God, you have made your servant king in my father David's place, even though I am only a young man and am inexperienced. 8 Your servant stands among your chosen people; they are a great nation that is too numerous to count or number. 9 So give your servant a discerning mind so he can make judicial decisions for your people and distinguish right from wrong. Otherwise no one is able to make judicial decisions for this great nation of yours." 10 The Lord was pleased that Solomon made this request. 11 God said to him, "Because you asked for the ability to make wise judicial decisions, and not for long life, or riches, or

vengeance on your enemies, 12 I grant your request and give you
a wise and discerning mind superior to that of anyone who has
preceded or will succeed you. 13 Furthermore, I am giving you
what you did not request—riches and honor so that you will be
the greatest king of your generation. 14 If you follow my instructions by obeying my rules and regulations, just as your father
David did, then I will grant you long life." 15 Solomon then woke
up and realized it was a dream. He went to Jerusalem, stood before the ark of the Lord's covenant, offered up burnt sacrifices,
presented peace offerings, and held a feast for all his servants.

SOLOMON DEMONSTRATES HIS WISDOM

16 Then two prostitutes came to the king and stood before him.
17 One of the women said, "My master, this woman and I live
in the same house. I had a baby while she was with me in the
house. 18 Then three days after I had my baby, this woman also
had a baby. We were alone; there was no one else in the house
except the two of us. 19 This woman's child suffocated during the
night when she rolled on top of him. 20 She got up in the middle
of the night and took my son from my side, while your servant
was sleeping. She put him in her arms, and put her dead son in
my arms. 21 I got up in the morning to nurse my son, and there
he was, dead! But when I examined him carefully in the morning, I realized it was not my baby." 22 The other woman said, "No!
My son is alive; your son is dead!" But the first woman replied,
"No, your son is dead; my son is alive." Each presented her case
before the king.

23 The king said, "One says, 'My son is alive; your son is dead,'
while the other says, 'No, your son is dead; my son is alive.'" 24 The
king ordered, "Get me a sword." So they placed a sword before
the king. 25 The king then said, "Cut the living child in two, and
give half to one and half to the other!" 26 The real mother spoke
up to the king, for her motherly instincts were awakened. She
said, "My master, give her the living child! Whatever you do, don't
kill him!" But the other woman said, "Neither one of us will have
him. Let them cut him in two!" 27 The king responded, "Give the
first woman the living child; don't kill him. She is the mother."
28 When all Israel heard about the judicial decision which the
king had rendered, they respected the king, for they realized
that he possessed divine wisdom to make judicial decisions.

SOLOMON'S ROYAL COURT AND ADMINISTRATORS

4 King Solomon ruled over all Israel. 2 These were his officials:
Azariah son of Zadok was the priest.
3 Elihoreph and Ahijah, the sons of Shisha, wrote down what
happened.
Jehoshaphat son of Ahilud was in charge of the records.
4 Benaiah son of Jehoiada was commander of the army.
Zadok and Abiathar were priests.
5 Azariah son of Nathan was supervisor of the district governors.
Zabud son of Nathan was a priest and adviser to the king.
6 Ahishar was supervisor of the palace.
Adoniram son of Abda was supervisor of the work crews.

7 Solomon had twelve district governors appointed throughout
Israel who acquired supplies for the king and his palace. Each was
responsible for one month in the year. 8 These were their names:
Ben Hur was in charge of the hill country of Ephraim.
9 Ben Deker was in charge of Makaz, Shaalbim, Beth Shemesh,
and Elon Beth Hanan.
10 Ben Hesed was in charge of Arubboth; he controlled Socoh
and all the territory of Hepher.
11 Ben Abinadab was in charge of Naphath Dor. (He was married to Solomon's daughter Taphath.)
12 Baana son of Ahilud was in charge of Taanach and Megiddo,
as well as all of Beth Shean next to Zarethan below Jezreel, from
Beth Shean to Abel Meholah and on past Jokmeam.
13 Ben Geber was in charge of Ramoth Gilead; he controlled
the villages of Jair son of Manasseh in Gilead, as well as the region of Argob in Bashan, including sixty large walled cities with
bronze bars locking their gates.
14 Ahinadab son of Iddo was in charge of Mahanaim.
15 Ahimaaz was in charge of Naphtali. (He married Solomon's
daughter Basemath.)
16 Baana son of Hushai was in charge of Asher and Aloth.
17 Jehoshaphat son of Paruah was in charge of Issachar.
18 Shimei son of Ela was in charge of Benjamin.
19 Geber son of Uri was in charge of the land of Gilead (the territory which had once belonged to King Sihon of the Amorites
and to King Og of Bashan). He was sole governor of the area.

SOLOMON'S WEALTH AND FAME

20 The people of Judah and Israel were as innumerable as the
sand on the seashore; they had plenty to eat and drink and
were happy. 21 Solomon ruled all the kingdoms from the Euphrates River to the land of the Philistines, as far as the border
of Egypt. These kingdoms paid tribute as Solomon's subjects
throughout his lifetime. 22 Each day Solomon's royal court consumed thirty cors of finely milled flour, sixty cors of cereal,
23 ten calves fattened in the stall, 20 calves from the pasture,
and 100 sheep, not to mention rams, gazelles, deer, and well-
fed birds. 24 His royal court was so large because he ruled over
all the kingdoms west of the Euphrates River from Tiphsah
to Gaza; he was at peace with all his neighbors. 25 All the people of Judah and Israel had security; everyone from Dan to
Beer Sheba enjoyed the produce of their vines and fig trees
throughout Solomon's lifetime. 26 Solomon had 4,000 stalls
for his chariot horses and 12,000 horses. 27 The district governors acquired supplies for King Solomon and all who ate in his
royal palace. Each was responsible for one month in the year;
they made sure nothing was lacking. 28 Each one also brought
to the assigned location his quota of barley and straw for the
various horses.
29 God gave Solomon wisdom and very great discernment; the
breadth of his understanding was as infinite as the sand on the
seashore. 30 Solomon was wiser than all the men of the east and
all the sages of Egypt. 31 He was wiser than any man, including
Ethan the Ezrahite or Heman, Calcol, and Darda, the sons of

Mahol. He was famous in all the neighboring nations. 32 He composed 3,000 proverbs and 1,005 songs. 33 He produced manuals on botany, describing every kind of plant, from the cedars of Lebanon to the hyssop that grows on walls. He also produced manuals on biology, describing animals, birds, insects, and fish. 34 People from all nations came to hear Solomon's display of wisdom; they came from all the kings of the earth who heard about his wisdom.

SOLOMON GATHERS BUILDING MATERIALS FOR THE TEMPLE

5 King Hiram of Tyre sent messengers to Solomon when he heard that he had been anointed king in his father's place. (Hiram had always been an ally of David.) 2 Solomon then sent this message to Hiram: 3 "You know that my father David was unable to build a temple to honor the LORD his God, for he was busy fighting battles on all fronts while the LORD subdued his enemies. 4 But now the LORD my God has made me secure on all fronts; there is no adversary or dangerous threat. 5 So I have decided to build a temple to honor the LORD my God, as the LORD instructed my father David, 'Your son, whom I will put on your throne in your place, is the one who will build a temple to honor me.' 6 So now order some cedars of Lebanon to be cut for me. My servants will work with your servants. I will pay your servants whatever you say is appropriate, for you know that we have no one among us who knows how to cut down trees like the Sidonians."

7 When Hiram heard Solomon's message, he was very happy. He said, "The LORD is worthy of praise today because he has given David a wise son to rule over this great nation." 8 Hiram then sent this message to Solomon: "I received the message you sent to me. I will give you all the cedars and evergreens you need. 9 My servants will bring the timber down from Lebanon to the sea. I will send it by sea in raft-like bundles to the place you designate. There I will separate the logs and you can carry them away. In exchange you will supply the food I need for my royal court."

10 So Hiram supplied the cedars and evergreens Solomon needed, 11 and Solomon supplied Hiram annually with 20,000 cors of wheat as provision for his royal court, as well as 120,000 gallons of pure olive oil. 12 So the LORD gave Solomon wisdom, as he had promised him. And Hiram and Solomon were at peace and made a treaty.

13 King Solomon conscripted work crews from throughout Israel, 30,000 men in all. 14 He sent them to Lebanon in shifts of 10,000 men per month. They worked in Lebanon for one month, and then spent two months at home. Adoniram was supervisor of the work crews. 15 Solomon also had 70,000 common laborers and 80,000 stonecutters in the hills, 16 besides 3,300 officials who supervised the workers. 17 By royal order they supplied large valuable stones in order to build the temple's foundation with chiseled stone. 18 Solomon's and Hiram's construction workers, along with men from Byblos, did the chiseling and prepared the wood and stones for the building of the temple.

THE BUILDING OF THE TEMPLE

6 In the four hundred and eightieth year after the Israelites
left Egypt, in the fourth year of Solomon's reign over Israel,
during the month Ziv (the second month), he began building the
LORD's temple. 2 The temple King Solomon built for the LORD was
90 feet long, 30 feet wide, and 45 feet high. 3 The porch in front of
the main hall of the temple was 30 feet long, corresponding to the
width of the temple. It was 15 feet wide, extending out from the
front of the temple. 4 He made framed windows for the temple.
5 He built an extension all around the walls of the temple's main
hall and Holy Place and constructed side rooms in it. 6 The bottom
floor of the extension was 7½ feet wide, the middle floor 9 feet
wide, and the third floor 10½ feet wide. He made ledges on the
temple's outer walls so the beams would not have to be inserted
into the walls. 7 As the temple was being built, only stones shaped
at the quarry were used; the sound of hammers, pickaxes, or any
other iron tool was not heard at the temple while it was being
built. 8 The entrance to the bottom level of side rooms was on the
south side of the temple; stairs went up to the middle floor and
then on up to the third floor. 9 He finished building the temple
and covered it with rafters and boards made of cedar. 10 He built
an extension all around the temple; it was 7½ feet high and it
was attached to the temple by cedar beams.

11 The LORD's message came to Solomon: 12 "As for this temple
you are building, if you follow my rules, observe my regulations,
and obey all my commandments, I will fulfill through you the
promise I made to your father David. 13 I will live among the Israelites and will not abandon my people Israel."

14 So Solomon finished building the temple. 15 He constructed
the walls inside the temple with cedar planks; he paneled the
inside with wood from the floor of the temple to the rafters of
the ceiling. He covered the temple floor with boards made from
the wood of evergreens. 16 He built a wall 30 feet in from the rear
of the temple as a partition for an inner sanctuary that would
be the Most Holy Place. He paneled the wall with cedar planks
from the floor to the rafters. 17 The main hall in front of the inner
sanctuary was 60 feet long. 18 The inside of the temple was all cedar and was adorned with carvings of round ornaments and of
flowers in bloom. Everything was cedar; no stones were visible.

19 He prepared the inner sanctuary inside the temple so that
the ark of the covenant of the LORD could be placed there. 20 The
inner sanctuary was 30 feet long, 30 feet wide, and 30 feet high.
He plated it with gold, as well as the cedar altar. 21 Solomon plated
the inside of the temple with gold. He hung golden chains in
front of the inner sanctuary and plated the inner sanctuary with
gold. 22 He plated the entire inside of the temple with gold, as
well as the altar inside the inner sanctuary.

23 In the inner sanctuary he made two cherubim of olive wood;
each stood 15 feet high. 24 Each of the first cherub's wings was 7½
feet long; its entire wingspan was 15 feet. 25 The second cherub
also had a wingspan of 15 feet; it was identical to the first in measurements and shape. 26 Each cherub stood 15 feet high. 27 He
put the cherubim in the inner sanctuary of the temple. Their
wings were spread out. One of the first cherub's wings touched

one wall and one of the other cherub's wings touched the opposite wall. The first cherub's other wing touched the second
cherub's other wing in the middle of the room. 28 He plated the
cherubim with gold.
29 On all the walls around the temple, inside and out, he carved
cherubim, palm trees, and flowers in bloom. 30 He plated the floor
of the temple with gold, inside and out. 31 He made doors of olive wood at the entrance to the inner sanctuary; the pillar on
each doorpost was five-sided. 32 On the two doors made of olive
wood he carved cherubim, palm trees, and flowers in bloom, and
he plated them with gold. He plated the cherubim and the palm
trees with hammered gold. 33 In the same way he made doorposts of olive wood for the entrance to the main hall, only with
four-sided pillars. 34 He also made two doors out of wood from
evergreens; each door had two folding leaves. 35 He carved cherubim, palm trees, and flowers in bloom and plated them with
gold, leveled out over the carvings. 36 He built the inner courtyard with three rows of chiseled stones and a row of cedar beams.
37 In the month of Ziv in the fourth year of Solomon's reign
the foundation was laid for the LORD's temple. 38 In the eleventh year, in the month of Bul (the eighth month) the temple
was completed in accordance with all its specifications and blueprints. It took seven years to build.

THE BUILDING OF THE ROYAL PALACE

7 Solomon took thirteen years to build his palace. 2 He named
it "The Palace of the Lebanon Forest"; it was 150 feet long, 75
feet wide, and 45 feet high. It had four rows of cedar pillars and
cedar beams above the pillars. 3 The roof above the beams supported by the pillars was also made of cedar; there were forty-five
beams, fifteen per row. 4 There were three rows of windows arranged in sets of three. 5 All the entrances were rectangular in
shape and they were arranged in sets of three. 6 He made a col-
onnade 75 feet long and 45 feet wide. There was a porch in front
of this and pillars and a roof in front of the porch. 7 He also made
a throne room, called "The Hall of Judgment," where he made judicial decisions. It was paneled with cedar from the floor to the
rafters. 8 The palace where he lived was constructed in a similar way. He also constructed a palace like this hall for Pharaoh's
daughter, whom he had married. 9 All these were built with the
best stones, chiseled to the right size and cut with a saw on all
sides, from the foundation to the edge of the roof and from the
outside to the great courtyard. 10 The foundation was made of
large valuable stones, measuring either 15 feet or 12 feet. 11 Above
the foundation the best stones, chiseled to the right size, were
used along with cedar. 12 Around the great courtyard were three
rows of chiseled stones and one row of cedar beams, like the inner courtyard of the LORD's temple and the hall of the palace.

SOLOMON COMMISSIONS HIRAM TO SUPPLY THE TEMPLE

13 King Solomon sent for Hiram of Tyre. 14 He was the son of a
widow from the tribe of Naphtali, and his father was a craftsman
in bronze from Tyre. He had the skill and knowledge to make

all kinds of works of bronze. He reported to King Solomon and did all the work he was assigned.

15 He fashioned two bronze pillars; each pillar was 27 feet high and 18 feet in circumference. 16 He made two bronze tops for the pillars; each was 7½ feet high. 17 The latticework on the tops of the pillars was adorned with ornamental wreaths and chains; the top of each pillar had seven groupings of ornaments. 18 When he made the pillars, there were two rows of pomegranate-shaped ornaments around the latticework covering the top of each pillar. 19 The tops of the two pillars in the porch were shaped like lilies and were six feet high. 20 On the top of each pillar, right above the bulge beside the latticework, there were 200 pomegranate-shaped ornaments arranged in rows all the way around. 21 He set up the pillars on the porch in front of the main hall. He erected one pillar on the right side and called it Yakin; he erected the other pillar on the left side and called it Boaz. 22 The tops of the pillars were shaped like lilies. So the construction of the pillars was completed.

23 He also made the large bronze basin called "The Sea." It measured 15 feet from rim to rim, was circular in shape, and stood 7½ feet high. Its circumference was 45 feet. 24 Under the rim all the way around it were round ornaments arranged in settings 15 feet long. The ornaments were in two rows and had been cast with "The Sea." 25 "The Sea" stood on top of twelve bulls. Three faced northward, three westward, three southward, and three eastward. "The Sea" was placed on top of them, and they all faced outward. 26 It was four fingers thick and its rim was like that of a cup shaped like a lily blossom. It could hold about 12,000 gallons.

27 He also made ten bronze movable stands. Each stand was 6 feet long, 6 feet wide, and 4½ feet high. 28 The stands were constructed with frames between the joints. 29 On these frames and joints were ornamental lions, bulls, and cherubim. Under the lions and bulls were decorative wreaths. 30 Each stand had four bronze wheels with bronze axles and four supports. Under the basin the supports were fashioned on each side with wreaths. 31 Inside the stand was a round opening that was 18 inches deep; it had a support that was 27 inches long. On the edge of the opening were carvings in square frames. 32 The four wheels were under the frames, and the crossbars of the axles were connected to the stand. Each wheel was 27 inches high. 33 The wheels were constructed like chariot wheels; their crossbars, rims, spokes, and hubs were made of cast metal. 34 Each stand had four supports, one per side projecting out from the stand. 35 On top of each stand was a round opening three-quarters of a foot deep; there were also supports and frames on top of the stands. 36 He engraved ornamental cherubim, lions, and palm trees on the plates of the supports and frames wherever there was room, with wreaths all around. 37 He made the ten stands in this way. All of them were cast in one mold and were identical in measurements and shape.

38 He also made ten bronze basins, each of which could hold about 240 gallons. Each basin was 6 feet in diameter; there was one basin for each stand. 39 He put five basins on the south side of the temple and five on the north side. He put "The Sea" on the south side, in the southeast corner.

40 Hiram also made basins, shovels, and bowls. He finished all the work on the LORD's temple he had been assigned by King Solomon. 41 He made the two pillars, the two bowl-shaped tops of the pillars, the latticework for the bowl-shaped tops of the two pillars, 42 the 400 pomegranate-shaped ornaments for the latticework of the two pillars (each latticework had two rows of these ornaments at the bowl-shaped top of the pillar), 43 the ten movable stands with their ten basins, 44 the big bronze basin called "The Sea" with its twelve bulls underneath, 45 and the pots, shovels, and bowls. All these items King Solomon assigned Hiram to make for the LORD's temple were made from polished bronze. 46 The king had them cast in earth foundries in the region of the Jordan between Sukkoth and Zarethan. 47 Solomon left all these items unweighed; there were so many of them they did not weigh the bronze.

48 Solomon also made all these items for the LORD's temple: the gold altar, the gold table on which was kept the Bread of the Presence, 49 the pure gold lampstands at the entrance to the inner sanctuary (five on the right and five on the left), the gold flower-shaped ornaments, lamps, and tongs, 50 the pure gold bowls, trimming shears, basins, pans, and censers, and the gold door sockets for the inner sanctuary (the Most Holy Place) and for the doors of the main hall of the temple. 51 When King Solomon finished constructing the LORD's temple, he put the holy items that belonged to his father David (the silver, gold, and other articles) in the treasuries of the LORD's temple.

SOLOMON MOVES THE ARK INTO THE TEMPLE

8 Then Solomon convened in Jerusalem Israel's elders, all the leaders of the Israelite tribes and families, so they could witness the transferal of the ark of the LORD's covenant from the City of David (that is, Zion). 2 All the men of Israel assembled before King Solomon during the festival in the month of Ethanim (the seventh month). 3 When all Israel's elders had arrived, the priests lifted the ark. 4 The priests and Levites carried the ark of the LORD, the tent of meeting, and all the holy items in the tent. 5 Now King Solomon and all the Israelites who had assembled with him went on ahead of the ark and sacrificed more sheep and cattle than could be counted or numbered.

6 The priests brought the ark of the LORD's covenant to its assigned place in the inner sanctuary of the temple, in the Most Holy Place, under the wings of the cherubim. 7 The cherubim's wings extended over the place where the ark sat; the cherubim overshadowed the ark and its poles. 8 The poles were so long their ends were visible from the Holy Place in front of the inner sanctuary, but they could not be seen from beyond that point. They have remained there to this very day. 9 There was nothing in the ark except the two stone tablets Moses had placed there in Horeb. It was there that the LORD made a covenant with the Israelites after he brought them out of the land of Egypt. 10 Once the priests left the Holy Place, a cloud filled the LORD's temple. 11 The priests could not carry out their duties because of the cloud; the LORD's glory filled his temple.

12 Then Solomon said, "The LORD has said that he lives in thick
darkness. 13 O LORD, truly I have built a lofty temple for you, a
place where you can live permanently." 14 Then the king turned
around and pronounced a blessing over the whole Israelite assembly as they stood there. 15 He said, "The LORD God of Israel
is worthy of praise because he has fulfilled what he promised
my father David. 16 He told David, 'Since the day I brought my
people Israel out of Egypt, I have not chosen a city from all the
tribes of Israel to build a temple in which to live. But I have chosen David to lead my people Israel.' 17 Now my father David had
a strong desire to build a temple to honor the LORD God of Israel. 18 The LORD told my father David, 'It is right for you to have
a strong desire to build a temple to honor me. 19 But you will not
build the temple; your very own son will build the temple for my
honor.' 20 The LORD has kept the promise he made. I have taken
my father David's place and have occupied the throne of Israel,
as the LORD promised. I have built this temple for the honor of
the LORD God of Israel 21 and set up in it a place for the ark containing the covenant the LORD made with our ancestors when
he brought them out of the land of Egypt."

SOLOMON PRAYS FOR ISRAEL

22 Solomon stood before the altar of the LORD in front of the entire assembly of Israel and spread out his hands toward the sky.
23 He prayed: "O LORD, God of Israel, there is no god like you in
heaven above or on earth below! You maintain covenantal loyalty to your servants who obey you with sincerity. 24 You have
kept your word to your servant, my father David; this very day
you have fulfilled what you promised. 25 Now, O LORD, God of Israel, keep the promise you made to your servant, my father David, when you said, 'You will never fail to have a successor ruling
before me on the throne of Israel, provided that your descendants watch their step and serve me as you have done.' 26 Now,
O God of Israel, may the promise you made to your servant, my
father David, be realized.

27 "God does not really live on the earth! Look, if the sky and
the highest heaven cannot contain you, how much less this temple I have built! 28 But respond favorably to your servant's prayer
and his request for help, O LORD my God. Answer the desperate
prayer your servant is presenting to you today. 29 Night and day
may you watch over this temple, the place where you promised
you would live. May you answer your servant's prayer for this
place. 30 Respond to the request of your servant and your people Israel for this place. Hear from inside your heavenly dwelling place and respond favorably.

31 "When someone is accused of sinning against his neighbor
and the latter pronounces a curse on the alleged offender before
your altar in this temple, be willing to forgive the accused if the
accusation is false. 32 Listen from heaven and make a just decision
about your servants' claims. Condemn the guilty party, declare
the other innocent, and give both of them what they deserve.

33 "The time will come when your people Israel are defeated
by an enemy because they sinned against you. If they come back
to you, renew their allegiance to you, and pray for your help in

REFLECT

What does Solomon's prayer reveal about the character of God?

GOD'S HEART FOR THE NATIONS

1 Kings 8:41–43

"Foreigners, who do not belong to your people Israel, will come from a distant land because of your reputation. When they hear about your great reputation and your ability to accomplish mighty deeds, they will come and direct their prayers toward this temple. Then listen from your heavenly dwelling place and answer all the prayers of the foreigners. Then all the nations of the earth will acknowledge your reputation, obey you as your people Israel do, and recognize that this temple I built belongs to you."

this temple, 34 then listen from heaven, forgive the sin of your
people Israel, and bring them back to the land you gave to their
ancestors.

35 "The time will come when the skies are shut up tightly and
no rain falls because your people sinned against you. When they
direct their prayers toward this place, renew their allegiance
to you, and turn away from their sin because you punish them,
36 then listen from heaven and forgive the sin of your servants,
your people Israel. Certainly you will then teach them the right
way to live and send rain on your land that you have given your
people to possess.

37 "The time will come when the land suffers from a famine, a
plague, blight and disease, or a locust invasion, or when their enemy lays siege to the cities of the land, or when some other type
of plague or epidemic occurs. 38 When all your people Israel pray
and ask for help, as they acknowledge their pain and spread out
their hands toward this temple, 39 then listen from your heavenly dwelling place, forgive their sin, and act favorably toward
each one based on your evaluation of his motives. (Indeed you
are the only one who can correctly evaluate the motives of all
people.) 40 Then they will obey you throughout their lifetimes
as they live on the land you gave to our ancestors.

41 "Foreigners, who do not belong to your people Israel, will come
from a distant land because of your reputation. 42 When they hear
about your great reputation and your ability to accomplish mighty
deeds, they will come and direct their prayers toward this temple. 43 Then listen from your heavenly dwelling place and answer
all the prayers of the foreigners. Then all the nations of the earth
will acknowledge your reputation, obey you as your people Israel
do, and recognize that this temple I built belongs to you.

44 "When you direct your people to march out and fight their
enemies, and they direct their prayers to the LORD toward his
chosen city and this temple I built for your honor, 45 then listen from heaven to their prayers for help and vindicate them.

46 "The time will come when your people will sin against you
(for there is no one who is sinless!) and you will be angry with
them and deliver them over to their enemies, who will take
them as prisoners to their own land, whether far away or close
by. 47 When your people come to their senses in the land where
they are held prisoner, they will repent and beg for your mercy
in the land of their imprisonment, admitting, 'We have sinned
and gone astray; we have done evil.' 48 When they return to you
with all their heart and being in the land where they are held
prisoner, and direct their prayers to you toward the land you
gave to their ancestors, your chosen city, and the temple I built
for your honor, 49 then listen from your heavenly dwelling place
to their prayers for help and vindicate them. 50 Forgive all the
rebellious acts of your sinful people and cause their captors to
have mercy on them. 51 After all, they are your people and your
special possession whom you brought out of Egypt, from the
middle of the iron-smelting furnace.

52 "May you be attentive to your servant's and your people Israel's requests for help and may you respond to all their prayers
to you. 53 After all, you picked them out of all the nations of

the earth to be your special possession, just as you, O Sovereign LORD, announced through your servant Moses when you
brought our ancestors out of Egypt."
54 When Solomon finished presenting all these prayers and requests to the LORD, he got up from before the altar of the LORD
where he had kneeled and spread out his hands toward the sky.
55 When he stood up, he pronounced a blessing over the entire
assembly of Israel, saying in a loud voice: 56 "The LORD is worthy
of praise because he has made Israel his people secure just as he
promised! Not one of all the faithful promises he made through
his servant Moses is left unfulfilled! 57 May the LORD our God be
with us, as he was with our ancestors. May he not abandon us or
leave us. 58 May he make us submissive, so we can follow all his instructions and obey the commandments, rules, and regulations
he commanded our ancestors. 59 May the LORD our God be constantly aware of these requests of mine I have presented to him,
so that he might vindicate his servant and his people Israel as
the need arises. 60 Then all the nations of the earth will recognize
that the LORD is the only genuine God. 61 May you demonstrate
wholehearted devotion to the LORD our God by following his
rules and obeying his commandments, as you are now doing."

SOLOMON DEDICATES THE TEMPLE

62 The king and all Israel with him were presenting sacrifices
to the LORD. 63 Solomon offered as peace offerings to the LORD
22,000 cattle and 120,000 sheep. Then the king and all the Israelites dedicated the LORD's temple. 64 That day the king consecrated the middle of the courtyard that is in front of the LORD's
temple. He offered there burnt sacrifices, grain offerings, and
the fat from the peace offerings, because the bronze altar that
stood before the LORD was too small to hold all these offerings.
65 At that time Solomon and all Israel with him celebrated a festival before the LORD our God for two entire weeks. This great
assembly included people from all over the land, from Lebo Hamath in the north to the Stream of Egypt in the south. 66 On the
fifteenth day after the festival started, he dismissed the people.
They asked God to empower the king and then went to their
homes, happy and content because of all the good the LORD had
done for his servant David and his people Israel.

THE LORD GIVES SOLOMON A PROMISE AND A WARNING

9 After Solomon finished building the LORD's temple, the
royal palace, and all the other construction projects he had
planned, 2 the LORD appeared to Solomon a second time, in the
same way he had appeared to him at Gibeon. 3 The LORD said
to him, "I have answered your prayer and your request for help
that you made to me. I have consecrated this temple you built
by making it my permanent home; I will be constantly present
there. 4 You must serve me with integrity and sincerity, just as
your father David did. Do everything I commanded and obey my
rules and regulations. 5 Then I will allow your dynasty to rule over
Israel permanently, just as I promised your father David, 'You
will not fail to have a successor on the throne of Israel.'

6 "But if you or your sons ever turn away from me, fail to obey the regulations and rules I instructed you to keep, and decide to serve and worship other gods, 7 then I will remove Israel from the land I have given them, I will abandon this temple I have consecrated with my presence, and Israel will be mocked and ridiculed among all the nations. 8 This temple will become a heap of ruins; everyone who passes by it will be shocked and will hiss out their scorn, saying, 'Why did the LORD do this to this land and this temple?' 9 Others will then answer, 'Because they abandoned the LORD their God, who led their ancestors out of Egypt. They embraced other gods whom they worshiped and served. That is why the LORD has brought all this disaster down on them.'"

FOREIGN AFFAIRS AND BUILDING PROJECTS

10 After twenty years, during which Solomon built the LORD's temple and the royal palace, 11 King Solomon gave King Hiram of Tyre twenty towns in the region of Galilee, because Hiram had supplied Solomon with cedars, evergreens, and all the gold he wanted. 12 When Hiram went out from Tyre to inspect the towns Solomon had given him, he was not pleased with them. 13 Hiram asked, "Why did you give me these towns, my friend?" He called that area the region of Cabul, a name which it has retained to this day. 14 Hiram had sent to the king 120 talents of gold.

15 Here are the details concerning the work crews King Solomon conscripted to build the LORD's temple, his palace, the terrace, the wall of Jerusalem, and the cities of Hazor, Megiddo, and Gezer. 16 (Pharaoh, king of Egypt, had attacked and captured Gezer. He burned it and killed the Canaanites who lived in the city. He gave it as a wedding present to his daughter, who had married Solomon.) 17 Solomon built up Gezer, lower Beth Horon, 18 Baalath, Tadmor in the wilderness, 19 all the storage cities that belonged to him, and the cities where chariots and horses were kept. He built whatever he wanted in Jerusalem, Lebanon, and throughout his entire kingdom. 20 Now several non-Israelite peoples were left in the land after the conquest of Joshua, including the Amorites, Hittites, Perizzites, Hivites, and Jebusites. 21 Their descendants remained in the land (the Israelites were unable to wipe them out completely). Solomon conscripted them for his work crews, and they continue in that role to this very day. 22 Solomon did not assign Israelites to these work crews; the Israelites served as his soldiers, attendants, officers, charioteers, and commanders of his chariot forces. 23 These men were also in charge of Solomon's work projects; there were a total of 550 men who supervised the workers. 24 Solomon built the terrace as soon as Pharaoh's daughter moved up from the City of David to the palace Solomon built for her.

25 Three times a year Solomon offered burnt offerings and peace offerings on the altar he had built for the LORD, burning incense along with them before the LORD. He made the temple his official worship place.

26 King Solomon also built ships in Ezion Geber, which is located near Elat in the land of Edom, on the shore of the Red Sea.

27 Hiram sent his fleet and some of his sailors, who were well
acquainted with the sea, to serve with Solomon's men. 28 They
sailed to Ophir, took from there 420 talents of gold, and then
brought them to King Solomon.

SOLOMON ENTERTAINS A QUEEN

10 When the queen of Sheba heard about Solomon, she came
to challenge him with difficult questions. 2 She arrived in Jerusalem with a great display of pomp, bringing with her camels
carrying spices, a very large quantity of gold, and precious gems.
She visited Solomon and discussed with him everything that
was on her mind. 3 Solomon answered all her questions; there
was no question too complex for the king. 4 When the queen of
Sheba saw for herself Solomon's extensive wisdom, the palace
he had built, 5 the food in his banquet hall, his servants and attendants, their robes, his cupbearers, and his burnt offerings
which he presented in the LORD's temple, she was amazed. 6 She
said to the king, "The report I heard in my own country about
your wise sayings and insight was true! 7 I did not believe these
things until I came and saw them with my own eyes. Indeed, I
didn't hear even half the story! Your wisdom and wealth surpass what was reported to me. 8 Your attendants, who stand before you at all times and hear your wise sayings, are truly happy!
9 May the LORD your God be praised because he favored you by
placing you on the throne of Israel! Because of the LORD's eternal love for Israel, he made you king so you could make just
and right decisions." 10 She gave the king 120 talents of gold,
a very large quantity of spices, and precious gems. The quantity of spices the queen of Sheba gave King Solomon has never
been matched. 11 (Hiram's fleet, which carried gold from Ophir,
also brought from Ophir a very large quantity of fine timber
and precious gems. 12 With the timber the king made supports
for the LORD's temple and for the royal palace and stringed instruments for the musicians. No one has seen so much of this
fine timber to this very day.) 13 King Solomon gave the queen
of Sheba everything she requested, besides what he had freely
offered her. Then she left and returned to her homeland with
her attendants.

SOLOMON'S WEALTH

14 Solomon received 666 talents of gold per year, 15 besides what
he collected from the merchants, traders, Arabian kings, and
governors of the land. 16 King Solomon made 200 large shields of
hammered gold; 600 measures of gold were used for each shield.
17 He also made 300 small shields of hammered gold; three minas
of gold were used for each of these shields. The king placed them
in the Palace of the Lebanon Forest.

18 The king made a large throne decorated with ivory and
overlaid it with pure gold. 19 There were six steps leading up to
the throne, and the back of it was rounded on top. The throne
had two armrests with a statue of a lion standing on each side.
20 There were twelve statues of lions on the six steps, one lion
at each end of each step. There was nothing like it in any other kingdom.

21 All of King Solomon's cups were made of gold, and all the household items in the Palace of the Lebanon Forest were made of pure gold. There were no silver items, for silver was not considered very valuable in Solomon's time. 22 Along with Hiram's fleet, the king had a fleet of large merchant ships that sailed the sea. Once every three years the fleet came into port with cargoes of gold, silver, ivory, apes, and peacocks.

23 King Solomon was wealthier and wiser than any of the kings of the earth. 24 Everyone in the world wanted to visit Solomon to see him display his God-given wisdom. 25 Year after year visitors brought their gifts, which included items of silver, items of gold, clothes, perfume, spices, horses, and mules.

26 Solomon accumulated chariots and horses. He had 1,400 chariots and 12,000 horses. He kept them in assigned cities and in Jerusalem. 27 The king made silver as plentiful in Jerusalem as stones; cedar was as plentiful as sycamore fig trees are in the foothills. 28 Solomon acquired his horses from Egypt and from Que; the king's traders purchased them from Que. 29 They paid 600 silver pieces for each chariot from Egypt and 150 silver pieces for each horse. They also sold chariots and horses to all the kings of the Hittites and to the kings of Syria.

THE LORD PUNISHES SOLOMON FOR IDOLATRY

11 King Solomon fell in love with many foreign women (besides Pharaoh's daughter), including Moabites, Ammonites, Edomites, Sidonians, and Hittites. 2 They came from nations about which the LORD had warned the Israelites, "You must not establish friendly relations with them! If you do, they will surely shift your allegiance to their gods." But Solomon was irresistibly attracted to them.

3 He had 700 royal wives and 300 concubines; his wives had a powerful influence over him. 4 When Solomon became old, his wives shifted his allegiance to other gods; he was not wholeheartedly devoted to the LORD his God, as his father David had been. 5 Solomon worshiped the Sidonian goddess Astarte and the detestable Ammonite god Milcom. 6 Solomon did evil in the LORD's sight; he did not remain loyal to the LORD, as his father David had. 7 Furthermore, on the hill east of Jerusalem Solomon built a high place for the detestable Moabite god Chemosh and for the detestable Ammonite god Milcom. 8 He built high places for all his foreign wives so they could burn incense and make sacrifices to their gods.

9 The LORD was angry with Solomon because he had shifted his allegiance away from the LORD, the God of Israel, who had appeared to him on two occasions 10 and had warned him about this very thing, so that he would not follow other gods. But he did not obey the LORD's command. 11 So the LORD said to Solomon, "Because you insist on doing these things and have not kept the covenantal rules I gave you, I will surely tear the kingdom away from you and give it to your servant. 12 However, for your father David's sake I will not do this while you are alive. I will tear it away from your son's hand instead. 13 But I will not tear away the entire kingdom; I will leave your son one tribe for my servant David's sake and for the sake of my chosen city Jerusalem."

LOVE TO GROW

NOT-SO-WISE KING

1 KINGS 11:1–13

Solomon had everything he could ever want. He was rich. He was wise. He had a spotless reputation. Despite all these things, his wealth and riches were not enough. Solomon wanted more. He married a lot (and I do mean a lot) of foreign women. These women worshiped many false gods. The presence of these foreign women and their false gods negatively influenced Solomon. He went from worshiping the one true God to worshiping false gods. Not only did he worship these gods, but he also built places of worship for them in Jerusalem.

Solomon's story serves as a warning. God became angry with Solomon. He had twice appeared to Solomon, and He had twice warned him. God disciplined Solomon by removing his kingdom, except for the tribes of Judah and Benjamin, out from under his son because of his unfaithfulness.

Solomon's downfall can be traced to two actions: He "did evil in the LORD's sight; he did not remain loyal to the LORD," and he "shifted his allegiance away from the LORD" (1 Kgs 11:6, 9).

Solomon allowed himself to be influenced by the people around him. Instead of remaining faithful to God, he allowed the pagan faiths of his wives to impact him. He became distracted with pleasing his wives and ended up turning from God. Solomon shifted his priorities and his allegiance away from God.

We are all prone to distraction. Many things vie for our attention and affection. Even though we may not worship stone idols like Solomon and his wives, we make idols out of other things. Idols can be possessions, people, success, pleasure, status, and even food. Whatever they are, they can easily shift our priorities and loyalty from the Lord.

God disciplined Solomon because God desired Solomon's heart. God was jealous for Solomon's affections the same way He is jealous for ours.

Rather than allowing ourselves to be distracted, let's remember today who we love and serve. May we fight the distractions in our lives that easily turn to idols and pull us away from our heavenly Father. Nothing is as precious as Jesus. He is our true treasure. May our hearts always be turned toward Him.

[14]The LORD brought against Solomon an enemy, Hadad the
Edomite, a descendant of the Edomite king. [15]During David's
campaign against Edom, Joab, the commander of the army, while
on a mission to bury the dead, killed every male in Edom. [16]For
Joab and the entire Israelite army stayed there six months until
they had exterminated every male in Edom. [17]Hadad, who was
only a small boy at the time, escaped with some of his father's
Edomite servants and headed for Egypt. [18]They went from Midian to Paran; they took some men from Paran and went to Egypt.
Pharaoh, king of Egypt, gave him a house and some land and supplied him with food. [19]Pharaoh liked Hadad so well he gave him
his sister-in-law (Queen Tahpenes' sister) as a wife. [20]Tahpenes'
sister gave birth to his son, named Genubath. Tahpenes raised
him in Pharaoh's palace; Genubath grew up in Pharaoh's palace
among Pharaoh's sons. [21]While in Egypt Hadad heard that David
had passed away and that Joab, the commander of the army, was
dead. So Hadad asked Pharaoh, "Give me permission to leave so
I can return to my homeland." [22]Pharaoh said to him, "What do
you lack here that makes you want to go to your homeland?" Hadad replied, "Nothing, but please give me permission to leave."
[23]God also brought against Solomon another enemy, Rezon
son of Eliada who had run away from his master, King Hadadezer of Zobah. [24]He gathered some men and organized a raiding
band. When David tried to kill them, they went to Damascus,
where they settled down and gained control of the city. [25]He
was Israel's enemy throughout Solomon's reign and, like Hadad,
caused trouble. He loathed Israel and ruled over Syria.

[26]Jeroboam son of Nebat, one of Solomon's servants, rebelled
against the king. He was an Ephraimite from Zeredah whose
mother was a widow named Zeruah. [27]This is what prompted
him to rebel against the king: Solomon built a terrace, and he
closed up a gap in the wall of the city of his father David. [28]Jer-
oboam was a talented man; when Solomon saw that the young
man was an accomplished worker, he made him the leader of
the work crew from the tribe of Joseph. [29]At that time, when
Jeroboam had left Jerusalem, the prophet Ahijah the Shilonite
met him on the road; the two of them were alone in the open
country. Ahijah was wearing a brand new robe, [30]and he grabbed
the robe and tore it into twelve pieces. [31]Then he told Jeroboam,
"Take ten pieces, for this is what the LORD God of Israel has said:
'Look, I am about to tear the kingdom from Solomon's hand and
I will give ten tribes to you. [32]He will retain one tribe, for my servant David's sake and for the sake of Jerusalem, the city I have
chosen out of all the tribes of Israel. [33]I am taking the kingdom
from him because they have abandoned me and worshiped the
Sidonian goddess Astarte, the Moabite god Chemosh, and the
Ammonite god Milcom. They have not followed my instructions
by doing what I approve and obeying my rules and regulations,
as Solomon's father David did. [34]I will not take the whole kingdom from his hand. I will allow him to be ruler for the rest of
his life for the sake of my chosen servant David who kept my
commandments and rules. [35]I will take the kingdom from the
hand of his son and give ten tribes to you. [36]I will leave his son
one tribe so my servant David's dynasty may continue to serve

CHALLENGE

How did Solomon's unfaithfulness lead to the loss of the kingdom for his son Rehoboam? Was God justified in removing the kingdom from Rehoboam? Why or why not?

me in Jerusalem, the city I have chosen as my home. 37 I will select you; you will rule over all you desire to have and you will be
king over Israel. 38 You must obey all I command you to do, follow my instructions, do what I approve, and keep my rules and
commandments, as my servant David did. Then I will be with you
and establish for you a lasting dynasty, as I did for David; I will
give you Israel. 39 I will humiliate David's descendants because
of this, but not forever.'" 40 Solomon tried to kill Jeroboam, but
Jeroboam escaped to Egypt and found refuge with King Shishak
of Egypt. He stayed in Egypt until Solomon died.

SOLOMON'S REIGN ENDS

41 The rest of the events of Solomon's reign, including all his accomplishments and his wise decisions, are recorded in the scroll
called the Annals of Solomon. 42 Solomon ruled over all Israel
from Jerusalem for forty years. 43 Then Solomon passed away and
was buried in the city of his father David. His son Rehoboam replaced him as king.

REHOBOAM LOSES HIS KINGDOM

12 Rehoboam traveled to Shechem, for all Israel had gathered
in Shechem to make Rehoboam king. 2 When Jeroboam son
of Nebat heard the news, he was still in Egypt, where he had fled
from King Solomon and had been living ever since. 3 They sent
for him, and Jeroboam and the whole Israelite assembly came
and spoke to Rehoboam, saying, 4 "Your father made us work too
hard. Now if you lighten the demands he made and don't make
us work as hard, we will serve you." 5 He said to them, "Go away
for three days, then return to me." So the people went away.

6 King Rehoboam consulted with the older advisers who had
served his father Solomon when he had been alive. He asked
them, "How do you advise me to answer these people?" 7 They
said to him, "Today if you will be a servant to these people and
grant their request, speaking kind words to them, they will be
your servants from this time forward." 8 But Rehoboam rejected
their advice and consulted the young advisers who served him,
with whom he had grown up. 9 He asked them, "How do you advise me to respond to these people who said to me, 'Lessen the
demands your father placed on us'?" 10 The young advisers with
whom Rehoboam had grown up said to him, "Say this to these
people who have said to you, 'Your father made us work hard, but
now lighten our burden.' Say this to them: 'I am a lot harsher than
my father! 11 My father imposed heavy demands on you; I will
make them even heavier. My father punished you with ordinary
whips; I will punish you with whips that really sting your flesh.'"

12 Jeroboam and all the people reported to Rehoboam on the
third day, just as the king had ordered when he said, "Return to
me on the third day." 13 The king responded to the people harshly.
He rejected the advice of the older men 14 and followed the advice of the younger ones. He said, "My father imposed heavy
demands on you; I will make them even heavier. My father punished you with ordinary whips; I will punish you with whips that
really sting your flesh." 15 The king refused to listen to the people,
because the LORD was instigating this turn of events so that he

might bring to pass the prophetic announcement he had made
through Ahijah the Shilonite to Jeroboam son of Nebat.
16 When all Israel saw that the king refused to listen to them,
the people answered the king, "We have no portion in David, no
share in the son of Jesse! Return to your homes, O Israel! Now,
look after your own dynasty, O David!" So Israel returned to their
homes. 17 (Rehoboam continued to rule over the Israelites who
lived in the cities of Judah.) 18 King Rehoboam sent Adoniram,
the supervisor of the work crews, out after them, but all Israel
stoned him to death. King Rehoboam managed to jump into
his chariot and escape to Jerusalem. 19 So Israel has been in rebellion against the Davidic dynasty to this very day. 20 When all
Israel heard that Jeroboam had returned, they summoned him
to the assembly and made him king over all Israel. No one except the tribe of Judah remained loyal to the Davidic dynasty.
21 When Rehoboam arrived in Jerusalem, he summoned
180,000 skilled warriors from all Judah and the tribe of Benjamin to attack Israel and restore the kingdom to Rehoboam son
of Solomon. 22 But God told Shemaiah the prophet, 23 "Say this
to King Rehoboam son of Solomon of Judah, and to all Judah and
Benjamin, as well as the rest of the people, 24 'This is what the
LORD has said: "Do not attack and make war with your brothers, the Israelites. Each of you go home. Indeed this thing has
happened because of me."'" So they obeyed the LORD's message.
They went home in keeping with the LORD's message.

JEROBOAM MAKES GOLDEN CALVES

25 Jeroboam built up Shechem in the Ephraimite hill country and
lived there. From there he went out and built up Penuel. 26 Jeroboam then thought to himself: "Now the Davidic dynasty could regain the kingdom. 27 If these people go up to offer sacrifices in the
LORD's temple in Jerusalem, their loyalty could shift to their former
master, King Rehoboam of Judah. They might kill me and return to
King Rehoboam of Judah." 28 After the king had consulted with his
advisers, he made two golden calves. Then he said to the people,
"It is too much trouble for you to go up to Jerusalem. Look, Israel,
here are your gods who brought you up from the land of Egypt."
29 He put one in Bethel and the other in Dan. 30 This caused Israel
to sin; the people went to Bethel and Dan to worship the calves.
31 He built temples on the high places and appointed as priests
common people who were not Levites. 32 Jeroboam inaugurated
a festival on the fifteenth day of the eighth month, like the festival celebrated in Judah. On the altar in Bethel he offered sacrifices to the calves he had made. In Bethel he also appointed
priests for the high places he had made.

A PROPHET FROM JUDAH VISITS BETHEL

33 On the fifteenth day of the eighth month (a date he had arbi-
trarily chosen) Jeroboam offered sacrifices on the altar he had
made in Bethel. He inaugurated a festival for the Israelites and
13 went up to the altar to offer sacrifices. 1 Just then a prophet
arrived from Judah with the LORD's message for Bethel, as
Jeroboam was standing near the altar ready to offer a sacrifice.
2 He cried out against the altar with the LORD's message, "O altar,

altar! This is what the LORD has said, 'Look, a son named Josiah
will be born to the Davidic dynasty. He will sacrifice on you the
priests of the high places who offer sacrifices on you. Human
bones will be burned on you.'" 3 That day he had also given a
sign, saying, "This is the sign that the LORD has declared: The altar will split open and the ashes on it will pour out." 4 When the
king heard the prophet's message that he had cried out against
the altar in Bethel, Jeroboam took his hand from the altar and
pointed it saying, "Seize him!" Then the hand that he had pointed
at him stiffened up, and he could not pull it back. 5 Meanwhile
the altar split open, and the ashes poured from the altar in fulfillment of the sign the prophet had given with the LORD's message. 6 The king responded to the prophet, "Seek the favor of
the LORD your God and pray for me, so that my hand may be restored." So the prophet sought the LORD's favor and the king's
hand was restored as it was at first. 7 The king then said to the
prophet, "Come home with me and have something to eat, so
that I may give you a gift." 8 But the prophet said to the king,
"Even if you were to give me half your possessions, I would not
go with you. I am not allowed to eat food or drink water in this
place. 9 For this is how I was commanded in the LORD's message,
'Eat no food. Drink no water. And do not return by the way you
came.'" 10 So he started back on another road; he did not travel
back on the same road he had taken to Bethel.

11 Now there was an old prophet living in Bethel. When his sons
came home, they told him everything the prophet had done in
Bethel that day. And they told their father all the words that he
had spoken to the king. 12 Their father asked them, "Which road
did he take?" His sons showed him the road the prophet from
Judah had taken. 13 He then told his sons, "Saddle the donkey for
me." When they had saddled the donkey for him, he mounted it
14 and took off after the prophet, whom he found sitting under
an oak tree. He asked him, "Are you the prophet from Judah?" He
answered, "Yes, I am." 15 He then said to him, "Come home with
me and eat something." 16 But he replied, "I can't go back with
you. I am not allowed to eat food or to drink water with you in
this place. 17 For an order came to me in the LORD's message, 'Eat
no food. Drink no water there. And do not return by the way you
came.'" 18 Then the old prophet said, "I too am a prophet like you.
And an angel has told me in a message from the LORD, 'Bring
him back with you to your house so he can eat food and drink
water.'" But he had lied to him. 19 So the prophet went back with
him. He ate food in his house and he drank water.

20 While they were sitting at the table, the LORD's message
came to the old prophet who had brought him back. 21 So he
cried out to the prophet who had come from Judah, "This is
what the LORD has said, 'You have rebelled against the LORD's
instruction and have not obeyed the command the LORD your
God gave you. 22 You went back. You ate food. And you drank water in the place of which he had said to you, "Eat no food. Drink
no water." Therefore your corpse will not be buried in your ancestral tomb.'"

23 So this is what happened after he had eaten food and drunk
water. The old prophet saddled the donkey for the prophet whom

he had brought back. 24 So the prophet from Judah travelled on.
Then a lion attacked him on the road and killed him.

There was his body lying on the road, with the donkey standing next to it, and the lion just standing there by the body.
25 Then some men came passing by and saw the body lying in
the road with the lion standing next to the body. They went and
reported what they had seen in the city where the old prophet
lived. 26 When the old prophet who had invited him to his house
heard the news, he said, "It is the prophet who rebelled against
the LORD. The LORD delivered him over to the lion and it tore
him up and killed him, in keeping with the LORD's message that
he had spoken to him." 27 He told his sons, "Saddle my donkey." So
they saddled it. 28 He went and found the body lying in the road
with the donkey and the lion standing beside it; the lion had neither eaten the body nor attacked the donkey. 29 The old prophet
picked up the prophet's body, put it on the donkey, and brought
it back. The old prophet then entered the city to mourn him
and to bury him. 30 He put the body into his own tomb, and they
mourned over him, saying, "Ah, my brother!" 31 After he buried
him, he said to his sons, "When I die, bury me in the tomb where
the prophet is buried; put my bones right beside his bones, 32 because the message that he announced as the LORD's message
against the altar in Bethel and against all the temples on the
high places in the cities of the north will certainly be fulfilled."

A PROPHET ANNOUNCES THE END OF JEROBOAM'S DYNASTY

33 After this happened, Jeroboam still did not change his evil
ways; he continued to appoint common people as priests at the
high places. Anyone who wanted the job he consecrated as a
priest. 34 This sin caused Jeroboam's dynasty to come to an end
and to be destroyed from the face of the earth.

14 At that time Jeroboam's son Abijah became sick. 2 Jeroboam
told his wife, "Disguise yourself so that people cannot recognize you are Jeroboam's wife. Then go to Shiloh; Ahijah the
prophet, who told me I would rule over this nation, lives there.
3 Take ten loaves of bread, some small cakes, and a container of
honey and visit him. He will tell you what will happen to the boy."

4 Jeroboam's wife did as she was told. She went to Shiloh and
visited Ahijah. Now Ahijah could not see; he had lost his eyesight in his old age. 5 But the LORD had told Ahijah, "Look, Jeroboam's wife is coming to find out from you what will happen to
her son, for he is sick. Tell her such and such. When she comes,
she will be in a disguise." 6 When Ahijah heard the sound of her
footsteps as she came through the door, he said, "Come on in,
wife of Jeroboam! Why are you pretending to be someone else?
I have been commissioned to give you bad news. 7 Go, tell Jeroboam, 'This is what the LORD God of Israel has said: "I raised you
up from among the people and made you ruler over my people
Israel. 8 I tore the kingdom away from the Davidic dynasty and
gave it to you. But you are not like my servant David, who kept
my commandments and followed me wholeheartedly by doing
only what I approve. 9 You have sinned more than all who came
before you. You went and angered me by making other gods,

formed out of metal; you have completely disregarded me. 10 So I am ready to bring disaster on the dynasty of Jeroboam. I will cut off every last male belonging to Jeroboam in Israel, including even the weak and incapacitated. I will burn up the dynasty of Jeroboam, just as one burns manure until it is completely consumed. 11 Dogs will eat the members of your family who die in the city, and the birds of the sky will eat the ones who die in the country.'" Indeed, the LORD has announced it!

12 "As for you, get up and go home. When you set foot in the city, the boy will die. 13 All Israel will mourn him and bury him. He is the only one in Jeroboam's family who will receive a decent burial, for he is the only one in whom the LORD God of Israel found anything good. 14 The LORD will raise up a king over Israel who will cut off Jeroboam's dynasty. It is ready to happen! 15 The LORD will attack Israel, making it like a reed that sways in the water. He will remove Israel from this good land he gave to their ancestors and scatter them beyond the Euphrates River, because they angered the LORD by making Asherah poles. 16 He will hand Israel over to their enemies because of the sins which Jeroboam committed and which he made Israel commit."

17 So Jeroboam's wife got up and went back to Tirzah. As she crossed the threshold of the house, the boy died. 18 All Israel buried him and mourned for him, in keeping with the LORD's message that he had spoken through his servant, the prophet Ahijah.

JEROBOAM'S REIGN ENDS

19 The rest of the events of Jeroboam's reign, including the details of his battles and rule, are recorded in the scroll called the Annals of the Kings of Israel. 20 Jeroboam ruled for twenty-two years; then he passed away. His son Nadab replaced him as king.

REHOBOAM'S REIGN OVER JUDAH

21 Now Rehoboam son of Solomon ruled in Judah. He was forty-one years old when he became king and he ruled for seventeen years in Jerusalem, the city the LORD chose from all the tribes of Israel to be his home. His mother was an Ammonite woman named Naamah.

22 Judah did evil in the sight of the LORD. They made him more jealous by their sins than their ancestors had done. 23 They even built for themselves high places, sacred pillars, and Asherah poles on every high hill and under every green tree. 24 There were also male cultic prostitutes in the land. They committed the same horrible sins as the nations that the LORD had driven out from before the Israelites.

25 In King Rehoboam's fifth year, King Shishak of Egypt attacked Jerusalem. 26 He took away the treasures of the LORD's temple and of the royal palace; he took everything, including all the golden shields that Solomon had made. 27 King Rehoboam made bronze shields to replace them and assigned them to the officers of the royal guard who protected the entrance to the royal palace. 28 Whenever the king visited the LORD's temple, the royal guard carried them and then brought them back to the guardroom.

29 The rest of the events of Rehoboam's reign, including his accomplishments, are recorded in the scroll called the Annals of
the Kings of Judah. 30 Rehoboam and Jeroboam were continually
at war with each other. 31 Rehoboam passed away and was buried
with his ancestors in the City of David. His mother was an Ammonite named Naamah. His son Abijah replaced him as king.

ABIJAH'S REIGN OVER JUDAH

15 In the eighteenth year of the reign of Jeroboam son of Nebat, Abijah became king over Judah. 2 He ruled for three
years in Jerusalem. His mother was Maacah, the daughter of
Abishalom. 3 He followed all the sinful practices of his father before him. He was not wholeheartedly devoted to the LORD his
God, as his ancestor David had been. 4 Nevertheless for David's
sake the LORD his God maintained his dynasty in Jerusalem by
giving him a son to succeed him and by protecting Jerusalem.
5 He did this because David had done what he approved and had
not disregarded any of his commandments his entire lifetime,
except for the incident involving Uriah the Hittite. 6 Rehoboam
and Jeroboam were continually at war with each other throughout Abijah's lifetime. 7 The rest of the events of Abijah's reign, including all his accomplishments, are recorded in the scroll called
the Annals of the Kings of Judah. Abijah and Jeroboam had been
at war with each other. 8 Abijah passed away and was buried in
the City of David. His son Asa replaced him as king.

ASA'S REIGN OVER JUDAH

9 In the twentieth year of Jeroboam's reign over Israel, Asa became the king of Judah. 10 He ruled for forty-one years in Jerusalem. His grandmother was Maacah daughter of Abishalom. 11 Asa
did what the LORD approved as his ancestor David had done.
12 He removed the male cultic prostitutes from the land and got
rid of all the disgusting idols his ancestors had made. 13 He also
removed Maacah his grandmother from her position as queen
mother because she had made a loathsome Asherah pole. Asa
cut down her loathsome pole and burned it in the Kidron Valley.
14 The high places were not eliminated, yet Asa was wholeheartedly devoted to the LORD throughout his lifetime. 15 He brought
the holy items that he and his father had made into the LORD's
temple, including the silver, gold, and other articles.

16 Now Asa and King Baasha of Israel were continually at war
with each other. 17 King Baasha of Israel attacked Judah and established Ramah as a military outpost to prevent anyone from leaving
or entering the land of King Asa of Judah. 18 Asa took all the silver
and gold that was left in the treasuries of the LORD's temple and of
the royal palace and handed it to his servants. He then told them
to deliver it to Ben Hadad son of Tabrimmon, the son of Hezion,
king of Syria, ruler in Damascus, along with this message: 19 "I want
to make a treaty with you, like the one our fathers made. See, I
have sent you silver and gold as a present. Break your treaty with
King Baasha of Israel, so he will retreat from my land." 20 Ben Hadad accepted King Asa's offer and ordered his army commanders
to attack the cities of Israel. They conquered Ijon, Dan, Abel Beth
Maacah, and all the territory of Naphtali, including the region

of Kinnereth. 21 When Baasha heard the news, he stopped fortifying Ramah and settled down in Tirzah. 22 King Asa ordered all
the men of Judah (no exemptions were granted) to carry away the
stones and wood that Baasha had used to build Ramah. King Asa
used the materials to build up Geba (in Benjamin) and Mizpah.
23 The rest of the events of Asa's reign, including all his successes and accomplishments, as well as a record of the cities he
built, are recorded in the scroll called the Annals of the Kings
of Judah. Yet when he was very old he developed a foot disease.
24 Asa passed away and was buried with his ancestors in the city
of his ancestor David. His son Jehoshaphat replaced him as king.

NADAB'S REIGN OVER ISRAEL

25 In the second year of Asa's reign over Judah, Jeroboam's son
Nadab became the king of Israel; he ruled Israel for two years.
26 He did evil in the sight of the LORD. He followed in his father's
footsteps and encouraged Israel to sin.
27 Baasha son of Ahijah, from the tribe of Issachar, conspired
against Nadab and assassinated him in Gibbethon, which was in
Philistine territory. This happened while Nadab and all the Israelite
army were besieging Gibbethon. 28 Baasha killed him in the third
year of Asa's reign over Judah and replaced him as king. 29 When he
became king, he executed Jeroboam's entire family. He wiped out
everyone who breathed, in keeping with the LORD's message that
he had spoken through his servant Ahijah the Shilonite. 30 This happened because of the sins which Jeroboam committed and which
he made Israel commit. These sins angered the LORD God of Israel.
31 The rest of the events of Nadab's reign, including all his accomplishments, are recorded in the scroll called the Annals of
the Kings of Israel. 32 Asa and King Baasha of Israel were continually at war with each other.

BAASHA'S REIGN OVER ISRAEL

33 In the third year of Asa's reign over Judah, Baasha son of Ahijah
became king over all Israel in Tirzah; he ruled for twenty-four
years. 34 He did evil in the sight of the LORD; he followed in Jeroboam's footsteps and encouraged Israel to sin.
16 The LORD's message against Baasha came to Jehu son of Hanani: 2 "I raised you up from the dust and made you ruler
over my people Israel. Yet you followed in Jeroboam's footsteps
and encouraged my people Israel to sin; their sins have made
me angry. 3 So I am ready to burn up Baasha and his family, and
make your family like the family of Jeroboam son of Nebat. 4 Dogs
will eat the members of Baasha's family who die in the city, and
the birds of the sky will eat the ones who die in the country."
5 The rest of the events of Baasha's reign, including his accomplishments and successes, are recorded in the scroll called the
Annals of the Kings of Israel. 6 Baasha passed away and was buried in Tirzah. His son Elah replaced him as king. 7 And so it was
the LORD's message came through the prophet Jehu son of Hanani against Baasha and his family. This was because of all the
evil he had done in the LORD's view, by angering him with his
deeds and becoming like Jeroboam's dynasty, and because of
how he had destroyed Jeroboam's dynasty.

ELAH'S REIGN OVER ISRAEL

8 In the twenty-sixth year of Asa's reign over Judah, Baasha's son
Elah became king over Israel; he ruled in Tirzah for two years.
9 His servant Zimri, a commander of half of his chariot force, conspired against him. While Elah was in Tirzah drinking heavily at
the house of Arza, who supervised the palace in Tirzah, 10 Zimri
came in and struck him dead. (This happened in the twenty-seventh year of Asa's reign over Judah.) Zimri replaced Elah as king.
11 When he became king and occupied the throne, he killed Baasha's entire family. He did not spare any male belonging to him;
he killed his relatives and his friends. 12 Zimri destroyed Baasha's entire family, in keeping with the LORD's message which
he had spoken against Baasha through Jehu the prophet. 13 This
happened because of all the sins which Baasha and his son Elah
committed and which they made Israel commit. They angered
the LORD God of Israel with their worthless idols.

14 The rest of the events of Elah's reign, including all his accomplishments, are recorded in the scroll called the Annals of
the Kings of Israel.

ZIMRI'S REIGN OVER ISRAEL

15 In the twenty-seventh year of Asa's reign over Judah, Zimri
became king over Israel; he ruled for seven days in Tirzah. Zimri's revolt took place while the army was deployed in Gibbethon, which was in Philistine territory. 16 While deployed there,
the army received this report: "Zimri has conspired against
the king and assassinated him." So all Israel made Omri, the
commander of the army, king over Israel that very day in the
camp. 17 Omri and all Israel went up from Gibbethon and besieged Tirzah. 18 When Zimri saw that the city was captured,
he went into the fortified area of the royal palace. He set the
palace on fire and died in the flames. 19 This happened because
of the sins he committed. He did evil in the sight of the LORD
and followed in Jeroboam's footsteps and encouraged Israel
to continue sinning.

20 The rest of the events of Zimri's reign, including the details
of his revolt, are recorded in the scroll called the Annals of the
Kings of Israel.

OMRI'S REIGN OVER ISRAEL

21 At that time the people of Israel were divided in their loyalties. Half the people supported Tibni son of Ginath and wanted
to make him king; the other half supported Omri. 22 Omri's supporters were stronger than those who supported Tibni son of
Ginath. Tibni died; Omri became king.

23 In the thirty-first year of Asa's reign over Judah, Omri became king over Israel. He ruled for twelve years, six of them in
Tirzah. 24 He purchased the hill of Samaria from Shemer for two
talents of silver. He launched a construction project there and
named the city he built after Shemer, the former owner of the
hill of Samaria. 25 Omri did more evil in the sight of the LORD
than all who were before him. 26 He followed in the footsteps of
Jeroboam son of Nebat and encouraged Israel to sin; they angered the LORD God of Israel with their worthless idols.

27 The rest of the events of Omri's reign, including his accomplishments and successes, are recorded in the scroll called the
Annals of the Kings of Israel. 28 Omri passed away and was buried in Samaria. His son Ahab replaced him as king.

AHAB PROMOTES IDOLATRY

29 In the thirty-eighth year of Asa's reign over Judah, Omri's son
Ahab became king over Israel. Ahab son of Omri ruled over Israel for twenty-two years in Samaria. 30 Ahab son of Omri did
more evil in the sight of the LORD than all who were before him.
31 As if following in the sinful footsteps of Jeroboam son of Nebat
were not bad enough, he married Jezebel the daughter of King
Ethbaal of the Sidonians. Then he worshiped and bowed to Baal.
32 He set up an altar for Baal in the temple of Baal he had built
in Samaria. 33 Ahab also made an Asherah pole; he did more to
anger the LORD God of Israel than all the kings of Israel who
were before him.

34 During Ahab's reign, Hiel the Bethelite rebuilt Jericho. Abiram, his firstborn son, died when he laid the foundation; Segub,
his youngest son, died when he erected its gates, in keeping
with the LORD's message that he had spoken through Joshua
son of Nun.

ELIJAH VISITS A WIDOW IN SIDONIAN TERRITORY

17 Elijah the Tishbite, from Tishbe in Gilead, said to Ahab, "As
certainly as the LORD God of Israel lives (whom I serve),
there will be no dew or rain in the years ahead unless I give the
command." 2 The LORD's message came to him: 3 "Leave here and
travel eastward. Hide out in the Kerith Valley near the Jordan.
4 Drink from the stream; I have already told the ravens to bring
you food there." 5 So he carried out the LORD's message; he went
and lived in the Kerith Valley near the Jordan. 6 The ravens would
bring him bread and meat each morning and evening, and he
would drink from the stream.

7 After a while, the stream dried up because there had been no
rain in the land. 8 The LORD's message came to him, 9 "Get up, go
to Zarephath in Sidonian territory, and live there. I have already
told a widow who lives there to provide for you." 10 So he got up
and went to Zarephath. When he went through the city gate,
there was a widow gathering wood. He called out to her, "Please
give me a little water in a cup, so I can take a drink." 11 As she went
to get it, he called out to her, "Please bring me a piece of bread."
12 She said, "As certainly as the LORD your God lives, I have no food,
except for a handful of flour in a jar and a little olive oil in a jug.
Right now I am gathering a couple of sticks for a fire. Then I'm
going home to make one final meal for my son and myself. After
we have eaten that, we will die of starvation." 13 Elijah said to her,
"Don't be afraid. Go and do as you planned. But first make me a
small cake and bring it to me; then make something for yourself
and your son. 14 For this is what the LORD God of Israel has said:
'The jar of flour will not be empty and the jug of oil will not run
out until the day the LORD makes it rain on the surface of the
ground.'" 15 She went and did as Elijah told her; there was always
enough food for Elijah and for her and her family. 16 The jar of

REFLECT

What can be said about the faith of the widow and the faith of Elijah in these verses? How did Elijah's plea to save the widow's son display his faith?

flour was never empty and the jug of oil never ran out, in keeping with the LORD's message that he had spoken through Elijah.
17 After this the son of the woman who owned the house got
sick. His illness was so severe he could no longer breathe. 18 She
asked Elijah, "Why, prophet, have you come to me to confront
me with my sin and kill my son?" 19 He said to her, "Hand me your
son." He took him from her arms, carried him to the upper room
where he was staying, and laid him down on his bed. 20 Then he
called out to the LORD, "O LORD, my God, are you also bringing
disaster on this widow I am staying with by killing her son?"
21 He stretched out over the boy three times and called out to
the LORD, "O LORD, my God, please let this boy's breath return
to him." 22 The LORD answered Elijah's prayer; the boy's breath
returned to him and he lived. 23 Elijah took the boy, brought him
down from the upper room to the house, and handed him to his
mother. Elijah then said, "See, your son is alive!" 24 The woman
said to Elijah, "Now I know that you are a prophet and that the
LORD's message really does come through you."

ELIJAH MEETS THE KING'S SERVANT

18 Some time later, in the third year of the famine, the LORD's
message came to Elijah, "Go, make an appearance before
Ahab, so I may send rain on the surface of the ground." 2 So Elijah went to make an appearance before Ahab.
Now the famine was severe in Samaria. 3 So Ahab summoned
Obadiah, who supervised the palace. (Now Obadiah was a very
loyal follower of the LORD. 4 When Jezebel was killing the LORD's
prophets, Obadiah took 100 prophets and hid them in two caves
in two groups of fifty. He also brought them food and water.)
5 Ahab told Obadiah, "Go through the land to all the springs and
valleys. Maybe we can find some grazing areas so we can keep the
horses and mules alive and not have to kill some of the animals."
6 They divided up the land between them to search it; Ahab went
one way by himself and Obadiah went the other way by himself.
7 As Obadiah was traveling along, Elijah met him. When he
recognized him, he fell facedown to the ground and said, "Is
it really you, my master, Elijah?" 8 He replied, "Yes, go and say
to your master, 'Elijah is back.'" 9 Obadiah said, "What sin have
I committed that you are ready to hand your servant over to
Ahab for execution? 10 As certainly as the LORD your God lives,
my master has sent to every nation and kingdom in an effort to
find you. When they say, 'He's not here,' he makes them swear an
oath that they could not find you. 11 Now you say, 'Go and say to
your master, "Elijah is back."' 12 But when I leave you, the LORD's
Spirit will carry you away so I can't find you. If I go tell Ahab I've
seen you, he won't be able to find you and he will kill me. That
would not be fair, because your servant has been a loyal follower
of the LORD from my youth. 13 Certainly my master is aware of
what I did when Jezebel was killing the LORD's prophets. I hid
100 of the LORD's prophets in two caves in two groups of fifty
and I brought them food and water. 14 Now you say, 'Go and say
to your master, "Elijah is back,"' but he will kill me." 15 But Elijah
said, "As certainly as the LORD of Heaven's Armies lives (whom
I serve), I will make an appearance before him today."

NOTHING LEFT TO QUESTION

1 KINGS 18

From the world's perspective, the odds weren't in Elijah's favor. The nation of Israel was divided. King Ahab had turned his back on God and had sided with Baal and its false prophets. Drought and famine ruled the land, and everyone blamed Elijah (1 Kgs 17:1).

The people of Israel wavered in their faith and had a choice to make: Would they choose to follow God or Baal? Soon enough, a showdown at Mount Carmel ensued (1 Kgs 18:20–24). Elijah, prophet of God, stood against 450 prophets of Baal.

Each side had a bull and a stack of wood, but their motivations couldn't have been more different. The prophets of Baal wanted to prove to the people—and likely to themselves—that Baal was a god who heard their cries. Elijah had no doubt that his God, Yahweh, the maker of heaven and earth, was the only true God. He always heard the cries of His people. Elijah's aim was to turn the hearts of the Israelites back to their Creator.

"Then you will invoke the name of your god, and I will invoke the name of the LORD. The god who responds with fire will demonstrate that he is the true God" (1 Kgs 18:24).

All day the prophets of Baal cried out to their god. All that resulted was silence: no fanfare, no fire—only exhausted prophets, weary from their self-mutilation and ecstatic entreaties.

Though Elijah was outnumbered four-hundred fifty to one, the odds are never stacked against you when the one true God is on your side.

Elijah built a trench around his altar and doused everything with water, not once, but three times. Elijah wasn't intimidated or silenced. Nothing in the natural was an obstacle for the God who is supernatural.

"Then fire from the LORD fell from the sky. It consumed the offering, the wood, the stones, and the dirt, and licked up the water in the trench" (1 Kgs 18:38).

In that moment, there was nothing left to question. The people fell on their faces and proclaimed, "The LORD is the true God! The LORD is the true God!" (1 Kgs 18:39). The Israelites required a miracle in order to return their hearts to God. May we be people who believe Him and His promises regardless of His actions. He alone is worthy.

ELIJAH CONFRONTS BAAL'S PROPHETS

16 When Obadiah went and informed Ahab, the king went to
meet Elijah. 17 When Ahab saw Elijah, he said to him, "Is it really
you, the one who brings disaster on Israel?" 18 Elijah replied, "I
have not brought disaster on Israel. But you and your father's
dynasty have, by abandoning the LORD's commandments and
following the Baals. 19 Now send out messengers and assemble
all Israel before me at Mount Carmel, as well as the 450 prophets
of Baal and 400 prophets of Asherah whom Jezebel supports."

20 Ahab sent messengers to all the Israelites and had the
prophets assemble at Mount Carmel. 21 Elijah approached all
the people and said, "How long are you going to be paralyzed by
indecision? If the LORD is the true God, then follow him, but if
Baal is, follow him!" But the people did not say a word. 22 Elijah
said to them: "I am the only prophet of the LORD who is left, but
there are 450 prophets of Baal. 23 Let them bring us two bulls.
Let them choose one of the bulls for themselves, cut it up into
pieces, and place it on the wood. But they must not set it on fire.
I will do the same to the other bull and place it on the wood.
But I will not set it on fire. 24 Then you will invoke the name of
your god, and I will invoke the name of the LORD. The god who
responds with fire will demonstrate that he is the true God." All
the people responded, "This will be a fair test."

25 Elijah told the prophets of Baal, "Choose one of the bulls for
yourselves and go first, for you are the majority. Invoke the name
of your god, but do not light a fire." 26 So they took a bull, as he
had suggested, and prepared it. They invoked the name of Baal
from morning until noon, saying, "Baal, answer us." But there was
no sound and no answer. They jumped around on the altar they
had made. 27 At noon Elijah mocked them, "Yell louder! After all,
he is a god; he may be deep in thought, or perhaps he stepped
out for a moment or has taken a trip. Perhaps he is sleeping and
needs to be awakened." 28 So they yelled louder and, in accordance with their prescribed ritual, mutilated themselves with
swords and spears until their bodies were covered with blood.
29 Throughout the afternoon they were in an ecstatic frenzy, but
there was no sound, no answer, and no response.

30 Elijah then told all the people, "Approach me." So all the people approached him. He repaired the altar of the LORD that had
been torn down. 31 Then Elijah took twelve stones, corresponding
to the number of tribes that descended from Jacob, to whom the
LORD's message had come, "Israel will be your name." 32 With the
stones he constructed an altar for the LORD. Around the altar he
made a trench large enough to contain two seahs of seed. 33 He
arranged the wood, cut up the bull, and placed it on the wood.
Then he said, "Fill four water jars and pour the water on the offering and the wood." 34 When they had done so, he said, "Do it
again." So they did it again. Then he said, "Do it a third time." So
they did it a third time. 35 The water flowed down all sides of the
altar and filled the trench. 36 When it was time for the evening
offering, Elijah the prophet approached the altar and prayed: "O
LORD God of Abraham, Isaac, and Israel, prove today that you
are God in Israel and that I am your servant and have done all
these things at your command. 37 Answer me, O LORD, answer

me, so these people will know that you, O LORD, are the true
God and that you are winning back their allegiance." 38 Then fire
from the LORD fell from the sky. It consumed the offering, the
wood, the stones, and the dirt, and licked up the water in the
trench. 39 When all the people saw this, they threw themselves
down with their faces to the ground and said, "The LORD is the
true God! The LORD is the true God!" 40 Elijah told them, "Seize
the prophets of Baal! Don't let even one of them escape!" So they
seized them, and Elijah led them down to the Kishon Valley and
executed them there.
41 Then Elijah told Ahab, "Go on up and eat and drink, for the
sound of a heavy rainstorm can be heard." 42 So Ahab went on
up to eat and drink, while Elijah climbed to the top of Carmel.
He bent down toward the ground and put his face between his
knees. 43 He told his servant, "Go on up and look in the direction of the sea." So he went on up, looked, and reported, "There
is nothing." Seven times Elijah sent him to look. 44 The seventh
time the servant said, "Look, a small cloud, the size of the palm
of a man's hand, is rising up from the sea." Elijah then said, "Go
and tell Ahab, 'Hitch up the chariots and go down, so that the
rain won't overtake you.'" 45 Meanwhile the sky was covered with
dark clouds, the wind blew, and there was a heavy rainstorm.
Ahab rode toward Jezreel. 46 Now the LORD energized Elijah with
power; he tucked his robe into his belt and ran ahead of Ahab
all the way to Jezreel.

ELIJAH RUNS FOR HIS LIFE

19 Ahab told Jezebel all that Elijah had done, including a detailed account of how he killed all the prophets with the
sword. 2 Jezebel sent a messenger to Elijah with this warning,
"May the gods judge me severely if by this time tomorrow I do
not take your life as you did theirs!"
3 Elijah was afraid, so he got up and fled for his life to Beer
Sheba in Judah. He left his servant there, 4 while he went a day's
journey into the wilderness. He went and sat down under a shrub
and asked the LORD to take his life: "I've had enough! Now, O
LORD, take my life. After all, I'm no better than my ancestors."
5 He stretched out and fell asleep under the shrub. Suddenly an
angelic messenger touched him and said, "Get up and eat." 6 He
looked and right there by his head was a cake baking on hot
coals and a jug of water. He ate and drank and then slept some
more. 7 The angel of the LORD came back again, touched him, and
said, "Get up and eat, for otherwise you won't be able to make
the journey." 8 So he got up and ate and drank. That meal gave
him the strength to travel forty days and forty nights until he
reached Horeb, the mountain of God.
9 He went into a cave there and spent the night. Suddenly the
LORD's message came to him, "Why are you here, Elijah?" 10 He
answered, "I have been absolutely loyal to the LORD God of Heav-
en's Armies, even though the Israelites have abandoned the covenant they made with you, torn down your altars, and killed your
prophets with the sword. I alone am left and now they want to
take my life." 11 The LORD said, "Go out and stand on the mountain before the LORD. Look, the LORD is ready to pass by."

REFLECT

Which aspect of God's character is displayed in His care for Elijah when he ran in fear for his life? Rather than rebuking Elijah for his lack of faith, what did God do instead? How did He meet Elijah's need?

A very powerful wind went before the LORD, digging into
the mountain and causing landslides, but the LORD was not in
the wind. After the windstorm there was an earthquake, but the
LORD was not in the earthquake. 12 After the earthquake, there
was a fire, but the LORD was not in the fire. After the fire, there
was a soft whisper. 13 When Elijah heard it, he covered his face
with his robe and went out and stood at the entrance to the
cave. Suddenly a voice asked him, "Why are you here, Elijah?"
14 He answered, "I have been absolutely loyal to the LORD God
of Heaven's Armies, even though the Israelites have abandoned
the covenant they made with you, torn down your altars, and
killed your prophets with the sword. I alone am left and now
they want to take my life." 15 The LORD said to him, "Go back the
way you came and then head for the wilderness of Damascus. Go
and anoint Hazael king over Syria. 16 You must anoint Jehu son
of Nimshi king over Israel, and Elisha son of Shaphat from Abel
Meholah to take your place as prophet. 17 Jehu will kill anyone
who escapes Hazael's sword, and Elisha will kill anyone who escapes Jehu's sword. 18 I still have left in Israel 7,000 followers who
have not bowed their knees to Baal or kissed the images of him."
19 Elijah went from there and found Elisha son of Shaphat. He
was plowing with twelve pairs of oxen; he was near the twelfth
pair. Elijah passed by him and threw his robe over him. 20 He left
the oxen, ran after Elijah, and said, "Please let me kiss my father
and mother goodbye, then I will follow you." Elijah said to him,
"Go back! Indeed, what have I done to you?" 21 Elisha went back
and took his pair of oxen and slaughtered them. He cooked the
meat over a fire that he made by burning the harness and yoke.
He gave the people meat and they ate. Then he got up and followed Elijah and became his assistant.

BEN HADAD INVADES ISRAEL

20 Now King Ben Hadad of Syria assembled all his army, along
with thirty-two other kings with their horses and chariots.
He marched against Samaria and besieged and attacked it. 2 He
sent messengers to King Ahab of Israel, who was in the city. He
said to him, "This is what Ben Hadad says: 3 'Your silver and your
gold are mine, as well as the best of your wives and sons.'" 4 The
king of Israel replied, "It is just as you say, my master, O king. I
and all I own belong to you."
5 The messengers came again and said, "This is what Ben Hadad says: 'I sent this message to you, "You must give me your
silver, gold, wives, and sons." 6 But now at this time tomorrow I
will send my servants to you and they will search through your
palace and your servants' houses. They will carry away all your
valuables.'" 7 The king of Israel summoned all the leaders of the
land and said, "Notice how this man is looking for trouble. Indeed, he demanded my wives, sons, silver, and gold, and I did
not resist him." 8 All the leaders and people said to him, "Do not
give in or agree to his demands." 9 So he said to the messengers
of Ben Hadad, "Say this to my master, the king: 'I will give you
everything you demanded at first from your servant, but I am
unable to agree to this latest demand.'" So the messengers went
back and gave their report.

10 Ben Hadad sent another message to him, "May the gods
judge me severely if there is enough dirt left in Samaria for all
my soldiers to scoop up in their hands." 11 The king of Israel replied, "Tell him the one who puts on his battle gear should not
boast like one who is taking it off." 12 When Ben Hadad received
this reply, he and the other kings were drinking in their quarters. He ordered his servants, "Get ready to attack!" So they got
ready to attack the city.

THE LORD DELIVERS ISRAEL

13 Now a prophet visited King Ahab of Israel and said, "This is
what the LORD has said: 'Do you see this huge army? Look, I am
going to hand it over to you this very day. Then you will know
that I am the LORD.'" 14 Ahab asked, "By whom will this be accomplished?" He answered, "This is what the LORD has said, 'By
the servants of the district governors.'" Ahab asked, "Who will
launch the attack?" He answered, "You will."

15 So Ahab assembled the 232 servants of the district governors. After that he assembled all the Israelite army, numbering
7,000. 16 They marched out at noon, while Ben Hadad and the 32
kings allied with him were drinking heavily in their quarters.
17 The servants of the district governors led the march. When
Ben Hadad sent messengers, they reported back to him, "Men
are marching out of Samaria." 18 He ordered, "Whether they come
in peace or to do battle, take them alive." 19 They marched out of
the city with the servants of the district governors in the lead
and the army behind them. 20 Each one struck down an enemy
soldier; the Syrians fled and Israel chased them. King Ben Hadad of Syria escaped on horseback with some horsemen. 21 Then
the king of Israel marched out and struck down the horses and
chariots; he thoroughly defeated Syria.

THE LORD GIVES ISRAEL ANOTHER VICTORY

22 The prophet visited the king of Israel and instructed him, "Go,
fortify your defenses. Determine what you must do, for in the
spring the king of Syria will attack you." 23 Now the advisers of
the king of Syria said to him: "Their God is a god of the mountains. That's why they overpowered us. But if we fight them in the
plains, we will certainly overpower them. 24 So do this: Dismiss
the kings from their command, and replace them with military
commanders. 25 Muster an army like the one you lost, with the
same number of horses and chariots. Then we will fight them
in the plains; we will certainly overpower them." He approved
their plan and did as they advised.

26 In the spring Ben Hadad mustered the Syrian army and
marched to Aphek to fight Israel. 27 When the Israelites had
mustered and received their supplies, they marched out to face
them in battle. When the Israelites deployed opposite them,
they were like two small flocks of goats, but the Syrians filled
the land. 28 The prophet visited the king of Israel and said, "This
is what the LORD has said: 'Because the Syrians said, "The LORD
is a god of the mountains and not a god of the valleys," I will deliver this entire huge army into to your control. Then you will
know that I am the LORD.'

29 The armies were deployed opposite each other for seven
days. On the seventh day the battle began, and the Israelites
killed 100,000 Syrian foot soldiers in one day. 30 The remaining
27,000 ran to Aphek and went into the city, but the wall fell on
them. Now Ben Hadad ran into the city and hid in an inner room.
31 His advisers said to him, "Look, we have heard that the kings of
the Israelite dynasty are kind. Allow us to put sackcloth around
our waists and ropes on our heads and surrender to the king of
Israel. Maybe he will spare our lives." 32 So they put sackcloth
around their waists and ropes on their heads and went to the
king of Israel. They said, "Your servant Ben Hadad says, 'Please
let me live!'" Ahab replied, "Is he still alive? He is my brother."
33 The men took this as a good omen and quickly accepted his
offer, saying, "Ben Hadad is your brother." Ahab then said, "Go,
get him." So Ben Hadad came out to him, and Ahab pulled him
up into his chariot. 34 Ben Hadad said, "I will return the cities my
father took from your father. You may set up markets in Damascus, just as my father did in Samaria." Ahab then said, "I want
to make a treaty with you before I dismiss you." So he made a
treaty with him and then dismissed him.

A PROPHET DENOUNCES AHAB'S ACTIONS

35 One of the members of the prophetic guild told his companion
a message from the LORD, "Please wound me!" But the man refused to wound him. 36 So the prophet said to him, "Because you
have disobeyed the LORD, as soon as you leave me a lion will kill
you." When he left him, a lion attacked and killed him. 37 He found
another man and said, "Wound me!" So the man wounded him
severely. 38 The prophet then went and stood by the road, waiting for the king. He also disguised himself by putting a bandage
down over his eyes. 39 When the king passed by, he called out to
the king, "Your servant went out into the heat of the battle, and
then a man turned aside and brought me a prisoner. He told me,
'Guard this prisoner. If he ends up missing for any reason, you
will pay with your life or with a talent of silver.' 40 Well, it just so
happened that while your servant was doing this and that, he
disappeared." The king of Israel said to him, "Your punishment
is already determined by your own testimony." 41 The prophet
quickly removed the bandage from his eyes, and the king of Israel recognized he was one of the prophets. 42 The prophet then
said to him, "This is what the LORD has said: 'Because you released
a man I had determined should die, you will pay with your life,
and your people will suffer instead of his people.'" 43 The king of
Israel went home to Samaria bitter and angry.

AHAB MURDERS NABOTH

21 After this the following episode took place. Naboth the Jezreelite owned a vineyard in Jezreel adjacent to the palace
of King Ahab of Samaria. 2 Ahab said to Naboth, "Give me your
vineyard so I can make a vegetable garden out of it, for it is adjacent to my palace. I will give you an even better vineyard in its
place, or if you prefer, I will pay you silver for it." 3 But Naboth
replied to Ahab, "The LORD forbid that I should sell you my ancestral inheritance."

4 So Ahab went into his palace, bitter and angry that Naboth
the Jezreelite had said, "I will not sell to you my ancestral inheritance." He lay down on his bed, pouted, and would not eat.
5 Then his wife Jezebel came in and said to him, "Why do you have
a bitter attitude and refuse to eat?" 6 He answered her, "While I
was talking to Naboth the Jezreelite, I said to him, 'Sell me your
vineyard for silver, or if you prefer, I will give you another vineyard in its place.' But he said, 'I will not sell you my vineyard.'"
7 His wife Jezebel said to him, "You are the king of Israel! Get up,
eat some food, and have a good time. I will get the vineyard of
Naboth the Jezreelite for you."

8 She wrote out orders, signed Ahab's name to them, and sealed
them with his seal. She then sent the orders to the leaders and
to the nobles who lived in Naboth's city. 9 This is what she wrote:
"Observe a time of fasting and seat Naboth in front of the people. 10 Also seat two villains opposite him and have them testify, 'You cursed God and the king.' Then take him out and stone
him to death."

11 The men of the city, the leaders, and the nobles who lived
there followed the written orders Jezebel had sent them. 12 They
observed a time of fasting and put Naboth in front of the people.
13 The two villains arrived and sat opposite him. Then the villains
testified against Naboth right before the people, saying, "Naboth
cursed God and the king." So they dragged him outside the city
and stoned him to death. 14 Then they reported to Jezebel, "Naboth has been stoned to death."

15 When Jezebel heard that Naboth had been stoned to death,
she said to Ahab, "Get up, take possession of the vineyard Naboth the Jezreelite refused to sell you for silver, for Naboth is
no longer alive; he's dead." 16 When Ahab heard that Naboth was
dead, he got up and went down to take possession of the vineyard of Naboth the Jezreelite.

17 The LORD's message came to Elijah the Tishbite: 18 "Get up, go
down and meet King Ahab of Israel who lives in Samaria. He is at
the vineyard of Naboth; he has gone down there to take possession of it. 19 Say to him, 'This is what the LORD has said: "Haven't
you committed murder and taken possession of the property
of the deceased?"' Then say to him, 'This is what the LORD has
said: "In the spot where dogs licked up Naboth's blood they will
also lick up your blood—yes, yours!"'"

20 When Elijah arrived, Ahab said to him, "So, you have found
me, my enemy!" Elijah replied, "I have found you, because you
are committed to doing evil in the sight of the LORD. 21 The LORD
says, 'Look, I am ready to bring disaster on you. I will destroy you
and cut off every last male belonging to Ahab in Israel, including even the weak and incapacitated. 22 I will make your dynasty
like those of Jeroboam son of Nebat and Baasha son of Ahijah
because you angered me and made Israel sin.' 23 The LORD says
this about Jezebel, 'Dogs will devour Jezebel by the outer wall
of Jezreel.' 24 As for Ahab's family, dogs will eat the ones who die
in the city, and the birds of the sky will eat the ones who die in
the country." 25 (There had never been anyone like Ahab, who
was firmly committed to doing evil in the sight of the LORD,
urged on by his wife Jezebel. 26 He was so wicked he worshiped

the disgusting idols, just as the Amorites whom the LORD had
driven out from before the Israelites.)
27 When Ahab heard these words, he tore his clothes, put on
sackcloth, and fasted. He slept in sackcloth and walked around
dejected. 28 The LORD's message came to Elijah the Tishbite,
29 "Have you noticed how Ahab shows remorse before me? Because he shows remorse before me, I will not bring disaster on
his dynasty during his lifetime, but during the reign of his son."

REFLECT

Even though Ahab was the most wicked king in Israel, God had compassion on him. What does this say about God's character, even to those who reject Him?

AHAB DIES IN BATTLE

22 There was no war between Syria and Israel for three years.
2 In the third year King Jehoshaphat of Judah came down
to visit the king of Israel. 3 The king of Israel said to his servants,
"Surely you recognize that Ramoth Gilead belongs to us, though
we are hesitant to reclaim it from the king of Syria." 4 Then he
said to Jehoshaphat, "Will you go with me to attack Ramoth
Gilead?" Jehoshaphat replied to the king of Israel, "I will support you; my army and horses are at your disposal." 5 But then
Jehoshaphat said to Israel's king, "Please seek a message from
the LORD this very day." 6 So the king of Israel assembled about
400 prophets and asked them, "Should I attack Ramoth Gilead
or not?" They said, "Attack! The Sovereign One will hand it over
to the king." 7 But Jehoshaphat asked, "Is there not a prophet of
the LORD still here, that we may ask him?" 8 The king of Israel
answered Jehoshaphat, "There is still one man through whom
we can seek the LORD's will. But I despise him because he does
not prophesy prosperity for me, but disaster. His name is Micaiah son of Imlah." Jehoshaphat said, "The king should not say
such things." 9 The king of Israel summoned an official and said,
"Quickly bring Micaiah son of Imlah."
10 Now the king of Israel and King Jehoshaphat of Judah were
sitting on their respective thrones, dressed in their robes, at the
threshing floor at the entrance of the gate of Samaria. All the
prophets were prophesying before them. 11 Zedekiah son of Kenaanah made iron horns and said, "This is what the LORD has
said, 'With these you will gore Syria until they are destroyed.'"
12 All the prophets were prophesying the same, saying, "Attack
Ramoth Gilead! You will succeed; the LORD will hand it over to
the king." 13 Now the messenger who went to summon Micaiah
said to him, "Look, the prophets are in complete agreement that
the king will succeed. Your words must agree with theirs; you
must predict success." 14 But Micaiah said, "As certainly as the
LORD lives, I will say what the LORD tells me to say."
15 When he came before the king, the king asked him, "Micaiah, should we attack Ramoth Gilead or not?" He answered
him, "Attack! You will succeed; the LORD will hand it over to the
king." 16 The king said to him, "How many times must I make you
solemnly promise in the name of the LORD to tell me only the
truth?" 17 Micaiah said, "I saw all Israel scattered on the mountains like sheep that have no shepherd. Then the LORD said, 'They
have no master. They should go home in peace.'" 18 The king of
Israel said to Jehoshaphat, "Didn't I tell you he does not prophesy prosperity for me, but disaster?" 19 Micaiah said, "That being
the case, listen to the LORD's message. I saw the LORD sitting

on his throne, with all the heavenly assembly standing beside
him on his right and on his left. 20 The LORD said, 'Who will deceive Ahab, so he will attack Ramoth Gilead and die there?' One
said this and another that. 21 Then a spirit stepped forward and
stood before the LORD. He said, 'I will deceive him.' 22 The LORD
asked him, 'How?' He replied, 'I will go out and be a lying spirit
in the mouths of all his prophets.' The LORD said, 'Deceive and
overpower him. Go out and do as you have proposed.' 23 So now,
look, the LORD has placed a lying spirit in the mouths of all
these prophets of yours, but the LORD has decreed disaster for
you." 24 Zedekiah son of Kenaanah approached, hit Micaiah on
the jaw, and said, "Which way did the LORD's Spirit go when he
went from me to speak to you?" 25 Micaiah replied, "Look, you will
see in the day when you go into an inner room to hide." 26 Then
the king of Israel said, "Take Micaiah and return him to Amon
the city official and Joash the king's son. 27 Say, 'This is what the
king says, "Put this man in prison. Give him only a little bread
and water until I safely return."'" 28 Micaiah said, "If you really
do safely return, then the LORD has not spoken through me."
Then he added, "Take note, all you people."

29 The king of Israel and King Jehoshaphat of Judah attacked
Ramoth Gilead. 30 The king of Israel said to Jehoshaphat, "I will
disguise myself and then enter into the battle, but you wear your
royal robes." So the king of Israel disguised himself and then
entered into the battle. 31 Now the king of Syria had ordered his
thirty-two chariot commanders, "Do not fight common soldiers
or high-ranking officers; fight only the king of Israel." 32 When
the chariot commanders saw Jehoshaphat, they said, "He must
be the king of Israel." So they turned and attacked him, but Jehoshaphat cried out. 33 When the chariot commanders realized
he was not the king of Israel, they turned away from him. 34 Now
an archer shot an arrow at random, and it struck the king of Israel between the plates of his armor. The king ordered his charioteer, "Turn around and take me from the battle line, because
I'm wounded." 35 While the battle raged throughout the day, the
king stood propped up in his chariot opposite the Syrians. He
died in the evening; the blood from the wound ran down into
the bottom of the chariot. 36 As the sun was setting, a cry went
through the camp, "Each one should return to his city and to his
homeland." 37 So the king died and was taken to Samaria, where
they buried him. 38 They washed off the chariot at the pool of
Samaria. Then the dogs licked his blood, while the prostitutes
bathed, in keeping with the LORD's message that he had spoken.

39 The rest of the events of Ahab's reign, including a record of
his accomplishments and how he built a luxurious palace and
various cities, are recorded in the scroll called the Annals of the
Kings of Israel. 40 Ahab passed away. His son Ahaziah replaced
him as king.

JEHOSHAPHAT'S REIGN OVER JUDAH

41 In the fourth year of Ahab's reign over Israel, Asa's son Jehoshaphat became king over Judah. 42 Jehoshaphat was thirty-five
years old when he became king and he reigned for twenty-five
years in Jerusalem. His mother was Azubah, the daughter of

Shilhi. 43 He followed in his father Asa's footsteps and was careful to do what the LORD approved. However, the high places
were not eliminated; the people continued to offer sacrifices
and burn incense on the high places. 44 Jehoshaphat was also at
peace with the king of Israel.

45 The rest of the events of Jehoshaphat's reign, including his
successes and military exploits, are recorded in the scroll called
the Annals of the Kings of Judah. 46 He removed from the land
any male cultic prostitutes who had managed to survive the
reign of his father Asa. 47 There was no king in Edom at this time;
a governor ruled. 48 Jehoshaphat built a fleet of large merchant
ships to travel to Ophir for gold, but they never made the voyage because they were shipwrecked in Ezion Geber. 49 Then Ahaziah son of Ahab said to Jehoshaphat, "Let my sailors join yours
in the fleet," but Jehoshaphat refused.

50 Jehoshaphat passed away and was buried with his ancestors in the city of his ancestor David. His son Jehoram replaced
him as king.

AHAZIAH'S REIGN OVER ISRAEL

51 In the seventeenth year of Jehoshaphat's reign over Judah,
Ahab's son Ahaziah became king over Israel in Samaria. He ruled
for two years over Israel. 52 He did evil in the sight of the LORD
and followed in the footsteps of his father and mother; like Jeroboam son of Nebat, he encouraged Israel to sin. 53 He worshiped
and bowed down to Baal, angering the LORD God of Israel just
as his father had done.

TURN BACK from your evil ways; OBEY MY COMMANDMENTS

MEMORY VERSE

The LORD solemnly warned Israel and Judah through all his prophets and all the seers, "Turn back from your evil ways; obey my commandments and rules that are recorded in the law. I ordered your ancestors to keep this law and sent my servants the prophets to remind you of its demands."

2 Kings 17:13

2 Kings

INTRODUCTION

God's Patience

God displayed His great patience in the successes and failures, victories and defeats, and loyalty and disobedience recorded in the Book of 2 Kings. While focusing on the spiritual successes and failures in Israel and Judah, 2 Kings displays a picture of the patience and long-suffering of God.

Second Kings chronicles the lives and reigns of many kings and prophets in the kingdoms of Israel and Judah. The split of the united kingdom of Israel into the divided kingdoms of Israel and Judah is detailed. Second Kings explores Israel's spiritual odyssey and the results. While some kings were devoted to God, many rejected the covenant He made with them and suffered the consequences. However, God's patience is on display as He gave His people many opportunities to return to Him.

Second Kings takes place in the ninth through sixth centuries B.C. The writings of 1 and 2 Kings were originally one combined writing, later divided by the translators of the Septuagint, the Greek Old Testament. Traditionally, Jeremiah is identified as the author of 1 and 2 Kings. However, later scholarship suggests that these books were a result of a compilation process that began with the initial composition of the books in the late seventh century B.C. and concluded in the middle of the sixth century B.C.

Second Kings encourages us to love God greatly as we see His great patience in the midst of His people's persistent sin. Despite their failures, God was patient and longed for His people to return to Him. God did not destroy His people but rather disciplined them with warnings and, eventually, exile. Although they were removed from their land, God kept a remnant of His people to preserve their name, and His, on the earth.

North Macedonia

OFFICIAL LANGUAGES
Macedonian and Albanian
POPULATION
2,073,000
UNREACHED POPULATION
638,000
PROFESSING CHRISTIANS
62.1%

Tanja's Home

Say a Prayer Today

Pray for the Christians in North Macedonia facing opposition to the faith. Pray the tactics of the government to hold back the church from growing would be stopped and that the church would grow without hindrance.

HISTORY BIT

Acts 16 records Paul's travels to Macedonia. While the borders of the country are slightly different today, Christianity has a long, rich history in this region. Macedonia contained the cities of Philippi, Thessalonica, and Berea, all which had a significant impact on the spread of the gospel in the first century.*

Source Information:
https://joshuaproject.net/countries/MK
*Acts 16

LOVE YOUR NEIGHBOR

Her Journey

TANJA'S STORY

I grew up in Macedonia in a non-Christian family. Growing up, I would often cry out to God in prayer. Even though I was not sure who God was, I always felt comfort when I would pray to Him. I was involved in religious behavior, but I did not have a real, intimate relationship with Him. I was unaware of His character, unaware of His kindness, and unaware of the depth of the goodness He longed to pour over me.

God grabbed hold of my life on a long train ride. Alone in a compartment with one other passenger, I experienced God's goodness for the first time. I felt as though God Himself had come to speak to me. For three hours, I talked with my fellow passenger, and I can only describe the events as supernatural. I felt like Thomas, needing proof from God. After this incredible experience, I fell deeply in love with God, convinced that He was for me and was always pursuing me.

My entire life turned upside down after that day. Words cannot describe the loving-kindness and goodness God has for each one of us. As I continue to walk in faith with the Lord, I am confident that He continues to guide my life in a special way. I am confident in His presence, His character, His goodness, and His everlasting love.

Even though I had lived a life of ritualistic religion, God was patient with me. He continued to pursue me and turned my heart to Him. He does the same for all of us. He reaches out to us and guides us through life, softening our hearts and making us more and more like Him.

4 WEEK READING PLAN

LOVE HIS WORD

	MONDAY	TUESDAY	WEDNESDAY	THURSDAY	FRIDAY
1	2 Kings 1	2 Kings 2	2 Kings 3	2 Kings 4	2 Kings 5:1—6:23
	SOAP Psalm 81:1-2	SOAP Psalm 81:3-4	SOAP Psalm 81:5-6	SOAP Psalm 81:7	SOAP Psalm 81:8-10
2	2 Kings 6:24—7:20	2 Kings 8	2 Kings 9	2 Kings 10	2 Kings 11-12
	SOAP Psalm 81:11-12	SOAP Psalm 81:13-14	SOAP Psalm 81:15-16	SOAP Psalm 82:1-2	SOAP Psalm 82:3-4
3	2 Kings 13-14	2 Kings 15	2 Kings 16	2 Kings 17	2 Kings 18-19
	SOAP Psalm 82:5-7	SOAP Psalm 82:8	SOAP Psalm 83:1-4	SOAP 2 Kings 17:13	SOAP Psalm 83:5-8
4	2 Kings 20	2 Kings 21	2 Kings 22	2 Kings 23:1—24:7	2 Kings 24:8—25:30
	SOAP Psalm 83:9-10	SOAP Psalm 83:11-12	SOAP Psalm 83:13-15	SOAP Psalm 83:16-17	SOAP Psalm 83:18

ELIJAH CONFRONTS THE KING AND HIS COMMANDERS

1 After Ahab died, Moab rebelled against Israel. 2 Ahaziah fell
through a window lattice in his upper chamber in Samaria and
was injured. He sent messengers with these orders, "Go, ask Baal
Zebub, the god of Ekron, if I will survive this injury."
3 But the angel of the LORD told Elijah the Tishbite, "Get up; go to
meet the messengers from the king of Samaria. Say this to them:
'You must think there is no God in Israel! That explains why you are
on your way to seek an oracle from Baal Zebub the god of Ekron.
4 Therefore this is what the LORD has said, "You will not leave the
bed you lie on, for you will certainly die!"'" So Elijah went on his way.
5 When the messengers returned to the king, he asked them,
"Why have you returned?" 6 They replied, "A man came up to
meet us. He told us, 'Go back to the king who sent you and tell
him, "This is what the LORD has said: 'You must think there is
no God in Israel! That explains why you are sending for an oracle from Baal Zebub, the god of Ekron. Therefore you will not
leave the bed you lie on, for you will certainly die.'"'" 7 The king
asked them, "Describe the appearance of this man who came up
to meet you and told you these things." 8 They replied, "He was
a hairy man and had a leather belt tied around his waist." The
king said, "He is Elijah the Tishbite."
9 The king sent a captain and his fifty soldiers to retrieve Elijah.
The captain went up to him while he was sitting on the top of a
hill. He told him, "Prophet, the king says, 'Come down!'" 10 Elijah replied to the captain, "If I am indeed a prophet, may fire come down
from the sky and consume you and your fifty soldiers!" Fire then
came down from the sky and consumed him and his fifty soldiers.
11 The king sent another captain and his fifty soldiers to retrieve
Elijah. He went up and told him, "Prophet, this is what the king
says, 'Come down at once!'" 12 Elijah replied to them, "If I am indeed a prophet, may fire come down from the sky and consume
you and your fifty soldiers!" Fire from God came down from the
sky and consumed him and his fifty soldiers.
13 The king sent a third captain and his fifty soldiers. This third
captain went up and fell on his knees before Elijah. He begged for
mercy, "Prophet, please have respect for my life and for the lives
of these fifty servants of yours. 14 Indeed, fire came down from the
sky and consumed the two captains who came before me, along
with their men. So now, please have respect for my life." 15 The angel of the LORD said to Elijah, "Go down with him. Don't be afraid
of him." So he got up and went down with him to the king.
16 Elijah said to the king, "This is what the LORD has said, 'You
sent messengers to seek an oracle from Baal Zebub, the god of
Ekron. Is it because there is no God in Israel from whom you can
seek a message? Therefore you will not leave the bed you lie on,
for you will certainly die.'"
17 And he did die in keeping with the LORD's message that he had
spoken through Elijah. In the second year of the reign of King Jehoram son of Jehoshaphat over Judah, Ahaziah's brother Jehoram
replaced him as king of Israel, because he had no son. 18 The rest
of the events of Ahaziah's reign, including his accomplishments,
are recorded in the scroll called the Annals of the Kings of Israel.

ELIJAH MAKES A SWIFT DEPARTURE

2 Just before the LORD took Elijah up to heaven in a windstorm, Elijah and Elisha were traveling from Gilgal. 2 Elijah told Elisha, "Stay here, for the LORD has sent me to Bethel." But Elisha said, "As certainly as the LORD lives and as you live, I will not leave you." So they went down to Bethel. 3 Some members of the prophetic guild in Bethel came out to Elisha and said, "Do you know that today the LORD is going to take your master from you?" He answered, "Yes, I know. Be quiet."

4 Elijah said to him, "Elisha, stay here, for the LORD has sent me to Jericho." But he replied, "As certainly as the LORD lives and as you live, I will not leave you." So they went to Jericho. 5 Some members of the prophetic guild in Jericho approached Elisha and said, "Do you know that today the LORD is going to take your master from you?" He answered, "Yes, I know. Be quiet."

6 Elijah said to him, "Stay here, for the LORD has sent me to the Jordan." But he replied, "As certainly as the LORD lives and as you live, I will not leave you." So they traveled on together. 7 The fifty members of the prophetic guild went and stood opposite them at a distance, while Elijah and Elisha stood by the Jordan. 8 Elijah took his cloak, folded it up, and hit the water with it. The water divided, and the two of them crossed over on dry ground.

9 When they had crossed over, Elijah said to Elisha, "What can I do for you, before I am taken away from you?" Elisha answered, "May I receive a double portion of the prophetic spirit that energizes you?" 10 Elijah replied, "That's a difficult request! If you see me taken from you, may it be so, but if you don't, it will not happen."

11 As they were walking along and talking, suddenly a fiery chariot pulled by fiery horses appeared. They went between Elijah and Elisha, and Elijah went up to heaven in a windstorm. 12 While Elisha was watching, he was crying out, "My father, my father! The chariot and horsemen of Israel!" Then he could no longer see him. He grabbed his clothes and tore them in two. 13 He picked up Elijah's cloak, which had fallen off him, and went back and stood on the shore of the Jordan. 14 He took the cloak that had fallen off Elijah, hit the water with it, and said, "Where is the LORD, the God of Elijah?" When he hit the water, it divided and Elisha crossed over.

15 When the members of the prophetic guild in Jericho, who were standing at a distance, saw him do this, they said, "The spirit that energized Elijah rests upon Elisha." They went to meet him and bowed down to the ground before him. 16 They said to him, "Look, there are fifty capable men with your servants. Let them go and look for your master, for the wind sent from the LORD may have carried him away and dropped him on one of the hills or in one of the valleys." But Elisha replied, "Don't send them out." 17 But they were so insistent that he became embarrassed. So he said, "Send them out." They sent the fifty men out, and they looked for three days, but could not find Elijah. 18 When they came back, Elisha was staying in Jericho. He said to them, "Didn't I tell you, 'Don't go'?"

ELISHA DEMONSTRATES HIS AUTHORITY

19 The men of the city said to Elisha, "Look, the city has a good location, as our master can see. But the water is bad and the land doesn't produce crops." 20 Elisha said, "Get me a new jar and put some salt in it." So they got it. 21 He went out to the spring and threw the salt in. Then he said, "This is what the LORD has said, 'I have purified this water. It will no longer cause death or fail to produce crops.'" 22 The water has been pure to this very day, just as Elisha prophesied.

23 He went up from there to Bethel. As he was traveling up the road, some young boys came out of the city and made fun of him, saying, "Go on up, baldy! Go on up, baldy!" 24 When he turned around and saw them, he called God's judgment down on them. Two female bears came out of the woods and ripped forty-two of the boys to pieces. 25 From there he traveled to Mount Carmel and then back to Samaria.

MOAB FIGHTS WITH ISRAEL

3 In the eighteenth year of King Jehoshaphat's reign over Judah, Ahab's son Jehoram became king over Israel in Samaria; he ruled for twelve years. 2 He did evil in the sight of the LORD, but not to the same degree as his father and mother. He did remove the sacred pillar of Baal that his father had made. 3 Yet he persisted in the sins of Jeroboam son of Nebat, who encouraged Israel to sin; he did not turn from them.

4 Now King Mesha of Moab was a sheep breeder. He would send as tribute to the king of Israel 100,000 male lambs and the wool of 100,000 rams. 5 When Ahab died, the king of Moab rebelled against the king of Israel. 6 At that time King Jehoram left Samaria and assembled all Israel for war. 7 He sent this message to King Jehoshaphat of Judah: "The king of Moab has rebelled against me. Will you fight with me against Moab?" Jehoshaphat replied, "I will join you in the campaign; my army and horses are at your disposal." 8 He then asked, "Which invasion route are we going to take?" Jehoram answered, "By the road through the wilderness of Edom." 9 So the kings of Israel, Judah, and Edom set out together. They wandered around on the road for seven days and finally ran out of water for the men and animals they had with them. 10 The king of Israel said, "Oh no! Certainly the LORD has summoned these three kings so that he can hand them over to the king of Moab!" 11 Jehoshaphat asked, "Is there no prophet of the LORD here that we might seek the LORD's direction?" One of the servants of the king of Israel answered, "Elisha son of Shapat is here; he used to be Elijah's servant." 12 Jehoshaphat said, "Yes, he receives the LORD's messages." So the king of Israel and Jehoshaphat and the king of Edom went down to visit him.

13 Elisha said to the king of Israel, "Why are you here? Go to your father's prophets or your mother's prophets!" The king of Israel replied to him, "No, for the LORD is the one who summoned these three kings so that he can hand them over to Moab." 14 Elisha said, "As certainly as the LORD of Heaven's Armies lives (whom I serve), if I did not respect King Jehoshaphat of Judah, I would not pay attention to you or acknowledge you.

15 But now, get me a musician." When the musician played, the
LORD energized him, 16 and he said, "This is what the LORD has
said, 'Make many cisterns in this valley,' 17 for this is what the
LORD has said, 'You will not feel any wind or see any rain, but
this valley will be full of water, and you and your cattle and animals will drink.' 18 This is an easy task for the LORD; he will also
hand Moab over to you. 19 You will defeat every fortified city
and every important city. You must chop down every productive tree, stop up all the springs, and cover all the cultivated
land with stones."

20 Sure enough, the next morning, at the time of the morning
sacrifice, water came flowing down from Edom and filled the
land. 21 Now all Moab had heard that the kings were attacking,
so everyone old enough to fight was mustered and placed at the
border. 22 When they got up early the next morning, the sun was
shining on the water. To the Moabites, who were some distance
away, the water looked red like blood. 23 The Moabites said, "It's
blood! The kings must have fought one another! The soldiers
have struck one another down! Now, Moab, seize the plunder!"
24 When they approached the Israelite camp, the Israelites rose
up and struck down the Moabites, who then ran from them. The
Israelites thoroughly defeated Moab. 25 They tore down the cities, and each man threw a stone into every cultivated field until
they were covered. They stopped up every spring and chopped
down every productive tree.

Only Kir Hareseth was left intact, but the soldiers armed with
slings surrounded it and attacked it. 26 When the king of Moab
realized he was losing the battle, he and 700 swordsmen tried
to break through and attack the king of Edom, but they failed.
27 So he took his firstborn son, who was to succeed him as king,
and offered him up as a burnt sacrifice on the wall. There was
an outburst of divine anger against Israel, so they broke off the
attack and returned to their homeland.

ELISHA HELPS A WIDOW AND HER SONS

4 Now a wife of one of the prophets appealed to Elisha for help,
saying, "Your servant, my husband is dead. You know that
your servant was a loyal follower of the LORD. Now the creditor
is coming to take away my two boys to be his servants." 2 Elisha
said to her, "What can I do for you? Tell me, what do you have
in the house?" She answered, "Your servant has nothing in the
house except a small jar of olive oil." 3 He said, "Go and ask all
your neighbors for empty containers. Get as many as you can.
4 Go and close the door behind you and your sons. Pour the olive oil into all the containers; set aside each one when you have
filled it." 5 So she left him and closed the door behind her and
her sons. As they were bringing the containers to her, she was
pouring the olive oil. 6 When the containers were full, she said
to one of her sons, "Bring me another container." But he answered her, "There are no more." Then the olive oil stopped flowing. 7 She went and told the prophet. He said, "Go, sell the olive
oil. Repay your creditor, and then you and your sons can live off
the rest of the profit."

REFLECT

How did the Shunammite woman display faith in these events?

ELISHA GIVES LIFE TO A BOY

[8] One day Elisha traveled to Shunem, where a prominent woman
lived. She insisted that he stop for a meal. So whenever he was
passing through, he would stop in there for a meal. [9] She said to
her husband, "Look, I'm sure that the man who regularly passes
through here is a very special prophet. [10] Let's make a small, private upper room and furnish it with a bed, table, chair, and lamp.
When he visits us, he can stay there."

[11] One day Elisha came for a visit; he went into the upper room
and rested. [12] He told his servant Gehazi, "Ask the Shunammite
woman to come here." So he did so and she came to him. [13] Elisha
said to Gehazi, "Tell her, 'Look, you have treated us with such great
respect. What can I do for you? Can I put in a good word for you
with the king or the commander of the army?'" She replied, "I'm
quite secure." [14] So he asked Gehazi, "What can I do for her?" Gehazi replied, "She has no son, and her husband is old." [15] Elisha told
him, "Ask her to come here." So he did so and she came and stood
in the doorway. [16] He said, "About this time next year you will be
holding a son." She said, "No, my master! O prophet, do not lie to
your servant!" [17] The woman did conceive, and at the specified time
the next year she gave birth to a son, just as Elisha had told her.

[18] The boy grew and one day he went out to see his father who
was with the harvest workers. [19] He said to his father, "My head!
My head!" His father told a servant, "Carry him to his mother."
[20] So he picked him up and took him to his mother. He sat on
her lap until noon and then died. [21] She went up and laid him
down on the prophet's bed. She shut the door behind her and
left. [22] She called to her husband, "Send me one of the servants
and one of the donkeys, so I can go see the prophet quickly and
then return." [23] He said, "Why do you want to go see him today?
It is not the new moon or the Sabbath." She said, "Everything's
fine." [24] She saddled the donkey and told her servant, "Lead on.
Do not stop unless I say so."

[25] So she went to visit the prophet at Mount Carmel. When he
saw her at a distance, he said to his servant Gehazi, "Look, it's
the Shunammite woman. [26] Now, run to meet her and ask her,
'Are you well? Are your husband and the boy well?'" She told Gehazi, "Everything's fine." [27] But when she reached the prophet on
the mountain, she grabbed hold of his feet. Gehazi came near to
push her away, but the prophet said, "Leave her alone, for she is
very upset. The LORD has kept the matter hidden from me; he
didn't tell me about it." [28] She said, "Did I ask my master for a son?
Didn't I say, 'Don't mislead me?'" [29] Elisha told Gehazi, "Tuck your
robes into your belt, take my staff, and go! Don't stop to exchange
greetings with anyone! Place my staff on the child's face." [30] The
mother of the child said, "As certainly as the LORD lives and as you
live, I will not leave you." So Elisha got up and followed her back.

[31] Now Gehazi went on ahead of them. He placed the staff on
the child's face, but there was no sound or response. When he
came back to Elisha he told him, "The child did not wake up."
[32] When Elisha arrived at the house, there was the child lying
dead on his bed. [33] He went in by himself and closed the door.
Then he prayed to the LORD. [34] He got up on the bed and spread
his body out over the boy; he put his mouth on the boy's mouth,

his eyes over the boy's eyes, and the palms of his hands against
the boy's palms. As he bent down across him, the boy's skin grew
warm. 35 Elisha went back and walked around in the house. Then
he got up on the bed again and bent down over him. The child
sneezed seven times and opened his eyes. 36 Elisha called to Gehazi and said, "Get the Shunammite woman." So he did so and she
came to him. He said to her, "Take your son." 37 She came in, fell
at his feet, and bowed down. Then she picked up her son and left.

ELISHA MAKES A MEAL EDIBLE

38 Now Elisha went back to Gilgal, while there was a famine in
the land. Some of the prophets were visiting him and he told his
servant, "Put the big pot on the fire and boil some stew for the
prophets." 39 Someone went out to the field to gather some herbs
and found a wild vine. He picked some of its fruit, enough to fill
up the fold of his robe. He came back, cut it up, and threw the
slices into the stew pot, not knowing they were harmful. 40 The
stew was poured out for the men to eat. When they ate some of
the stew, they cried out, "Death is in the pot, O prophet!" They
could not eat it. 41 He said, "Get some flour." Then he threw it into
the pot and said, "Now pour some out for the men so they may
eat." There was no longer anything harmful in the pot.

ELISHA MIRACULOUSLY FEEDS A HUNDRED PEOPLE

42 Now a man from Baal Shalisha brought some food for the
prophet—twenty loaves of bread made from the firstfruits of
the barley harvest, as well as fresh ears of grain. Elisha said, "Set
it before the people so they may eat." 43 But his attendant said,
"How can I feed a hundred men with this?" He replied, "Set it before the people so they may eat, for this is what the LORD has said,
'They will eat and have some left over.'" 44 So he set it before them;
they ate and had some left over, just as in the LORD's message.

ELISHA HEALS A SYRIAN GENERAL

5 Now Naaman, the commander of the king of Syria's army,
was esteemed and respected by his master, for through him
the LORD had given Syria military victories. But this great warrior had a skin disease. 2 Raiding parties went out from Syria and
took captive from the land of Israel a young girl, who became
a servant to Naaman's wife. 3 She told her mistress, "If only my
master were in the presence of the prophet who is in Samaria!
Then he would cure him of his skin disease."

4 Naaman went and told his master what the girl from the land
of Israel had said. 5 The king of Syria said, "Go! I will send a letter
to the king of Israel." So Naaman went, taking with him 10 talents of silver, 6,000 shekels of gold, and 10 suits of clothes. 6 He
brought the letter to the king of Israel. It read: "This is a letter
of introduction for my servant Naaman, whom I have sent to be
cured of his skin disease." 7 When the king of Israel read the letter, he tore his clothes and said, "Am I God? Can I kill or restore
life? Why does he ask me to cure a man of his skin disease? Certainly you must see that he is looking for an excuse to fight me!"

8 When Elisha the prophet heard that the king of Israel had
torn his clothes, he sent this message to the king, "Why did you

LOVE TO GROW

CARE FOR GOD'S PEOPLE

2 KINGS 4:42–44

Second Kings introduces us to Elisha, a prophet trying to teach Israel, who was deeply saturated in Baal worship, about Yahweh again. Elisha's prophetic ministry centered on communicating God's judgment and displaying God's provision for His people—especially in mundane, material ways.

When a man brought loaves of bread to Elisha, he was not offering the prophet a snack. These loaves were made from the firstfruits of the barley harvest, an agricultural provision intended to be given to Israel's priests as an offering (Num 18:13; Deut 18:4–5). In a syncretistic nation corrupted by idol worship, this man's action was a way of aligning himself with Elisha as the true representative for Yahweh. This offering was an act of faith in God's future provision, and Elisha used it as an immediate display of God's faithfulness and provision.

Even Elisha's attendant, a man who had already witnessed the God-enabled miracles that Elisha performed, was doubtful this offering was sufficient to meet their needs. An offering of twenty loaves of bread was sufficient for a hundred men. In the midst of the large-scale military and religious crises in Israel, God was attentive to even the most down-to-earth, practical needs of His people.

God is not distant from the needs of His children.

This miracle is similar to the miraculous feedings Jesus performed. Disconnected from God's grand story of cosmic redemption, these stories of provision from Jesus or Elisha are little more than party tricks—they satisfy an immediate physical need but don't do very much to address larger issues like poverty, famine, or the spiritual condition of the crowds. When viewed in the context of God's ultimate provision and protection of His people, these miracles become signs of the shape of the coming kingdom of God.

Elisha's prophetic ministry, and the future ministry of Jesus to which it points, would not be complete without these instances of caring for people's physical and material needs. Elisha came to proclaim the truth of God's power and the desperate need for the people of Israel to repent and live rightly in the context of their covenant with God. His message of judgment and repentance complemented his compassion and care for the needs of God's people. Elisha acted as a representative of God's character—a loving father who cares deeply about the needs of His children.

tear your clothes? Send him to me so he may know there is a
prophet in Israel." 9 So Naaman came with his horses and chariots and stood in the doorway of Elisha's house. 10 Elisha sent
out a messenger who told him, "Go and wash seven times in the
Jordan; your skin will be restored and you will be healed." 11 Naaman went away angry. He said, "Look, I thought for sure he would
come out, stand there, invoke the name of the LORD his God,
wave his hand over the area, and cure the skin disease. 12 The rivers of Damascus, the Abana and Pharpar, are better than any of
the waters of Israel! Could I not wash in them and be healed?"
So he turned around and went away angry. 13 His servants approached and said to him, "O master, if the prophet had told
you to do some difficult task, you would have been willing to do
it. It seems you should be happy that he simply said, 'Wash and
you will be healed.' 14 So he went down and dipped in the Jordan
seven times, as the prophet had instructed. His skin became as
smooth as a young child's and he was healed.

15 He and his entire entourage returned to the prophet. Naaman came and stood before him. He said, "For sure I know that
there is no God in all the earth except in Israel! Now, please accept a gift from your servant." 16 But Elisha replied, "As certainly
as the LORD lives (whom I serve), I will take nothing from you."
Naaman insisted that he take it, but he refused. 17 Naaman said,
"If not, then please give your servant a load of dirt, enough for
a pair of mules to carry, for your servant will never again offer a
burnt offering or sacrifice to a god other than the LORD. 18 May
the LORD forgive your servant for this one thing: When my master enters the temple of Rimmon to worship, and he leans on my
arm and I bow down in the temple of Rimmon, may the LORD
forgive your servant for this." 19 Elisha said to him, "Go in peace."

When he had gone a short distance, 20 Gehazi, the prophet Elisha's servant, thought, "Look, my master did not accept what this
Syrian Naaman offered him. As certainly as the LORD lives, I will
run after him and accept something from him." 21 So Gehazi ran
after Naaman. When Naaman saw someone running after him,
he got down from his chariot to meet him and asked, "Is everything all right?" 22 He answered, "Everything is fine. My master
sent me with this message, 'Look, two servants of the prophets
just arrived from the Ephraimite hill country. Please give them a
talent of silver and two suits of clothes.'" 23 Naaman said, "Please
accept two talents of silver." He insisted, and tied up two talents
of silver in two bags, along with two suits of clothes. He gave
them to two of his servants and they carried them for Gehazi.
24 When he arrived at the hill, he took them from the servants
and put them in the house. Then he sent the men on their way.
25 When he came and stood before his master, Elisha asked
him, "Where have you been, Gehazi?" He answered, "Your servant hasn't been anywhere." 26 Elisha replied, "I was there in spirit
when a man turned and got down from his chariot to meet you.
This is not the proper time to accept silver or to accept clothes,
olive groves, vineyards, sheep, cattle, and male and female servants. 27 Therefore Naaman's skin disease will afflict you and your
descendants forever!" When Gehazi went out from his presence,
his skin was as white as snow.

ELISHA MAKES AN AX HEAD FLOAT

6 Some of the prophets said to Elisha, "Look, the place where
we meet with you is too cramped for us. 2 Let's go to the
Jordan. Each of us will get a log from there, and we will build a
meeting place for ourselves there." He said, "Go." 3 One of them
said, "Please come along with your servants." He replied, "All
right, I'll come." 4 So he went with them. When they arrived at
the Jordan, they started cutting down trees. 5 As one of them
was felling a tree, the ax head dropped into the water. He
shouted, "Oh no, my master! It was borrowed!" 6 The prophet
asked, "Where did it drop in?" When he showed him the spot,
Elisha cut off a branch, threw it in at that spot, and made the
ax head float. 7 He said, "Lift it out." So he reached out his hand
and grabbed it.

ELISHA DEFEATS AN ARMY

8 Now the king of Syria was at war with Israel. He consulted his
advisers, who said, "Invade at such and such a place." 9 But the
prophet sent this message to the king of Israel, "Make sure you
don't pass through this place because Syria is invading there."
10 So the king of Israel sent a message to the place the prophet
had pointed out, warning it to be on its guard. This happened on
several occasions. 11 This made the king of Syria upset. So he summoned his advisers and said to them, "One of us must be helping the king of Israel." 12 One of his advisers said, "No, my master,
O king. The prophet Elisha who lives in Israel keeps telling the
king of Israel the things you say in your bedroom." 13 The king
ordered, "Go, find out where he is, so I can send some men to
capture him." The king was told, "He is in Dothan." 14 So he sent
horses and chariots there, along with a good-sized army. They
arrived during the night and surrounded the city.

15 The prophet's attendant got up early in the morning. When
he went outside there was an army surrounding the city, along
with horses and chariots. He said to Elisha, "Oh no, my master!
What will we do?" 16 He replied, "Don't be afraid, for our side out-
numbers them." 17 Then Elisha prayed, "O LORD, open his eyes
so he can see." The LORD opened the servant's eyes, and he saw
that the hill was full of horses and chariots of fire all around Elisha. 18 As the army approached him, Elisha prayed to the LORD,
"Strike these people with blindness." The LORD struck them with
blindness as Elisha requested. 19 Then Elisha said to them, "This
is not the right road or city. Follow me, and I will lead you to the
man you're looking for." He led them to Samaria.

20 When they had entered Samaria, Elisha said, "O LORD, open
their eyes, so they can see." The LORD opened their eyes, and
they saw that they were in the middle of Samaria. 21 When the
king of Israel saw them, he asked Elisha, "Should I strike them
down, my master?" 22 He replied, "Do not strike them down! You
did not capture them with your sword or bow, so what gives you
the right to strike them down? Give them some food and water,
so they can eat and drink and then go back to their master." 23 So
he threw a big banquet for them and they ate and drank. Then
he sent them back to their master. After that no Syrian raiding
parties again invaded the land of Israel.

THE LORD SAVES SAMARIA

24 Later King Ben Hadad of Syria assembled his entire army and
attacked and besieged Samaria. 25 Samaria's food supply ran out.
They laid siege to it so long that a donkey's head was selling for
eighty shekels of silver and a quarter of a kab of dove's droppings
for five shekels of silver.
26 While the king of Israel was passing by on the city wall, a woman shouted to him, "Help us, my master, O king!" 27 He replied, "No,
let the LORD help you. How can I help you? The threshing floor
and winepress are empty." 28 Then the king asked her, "What's your
problem?" She answered, "This woman said to me, 'Hand over your
son; we'll eat him today and then eat my son tomorrow.' 29 So we
boiled my son and ate him. Then I said to her the next day, 'Hand
over your son and we'll eat him.' But she hid her son!" 30 When the
king heard what the woman said, he tore his clothes. As he was
passing by on the wall, the people could see he was wearing sackcloth under his clothes. 31 Then he said, "May God judge me severely
if Elisha son of Shaphat still has his head by the end of the day!"
32 Now Elisha was sitting in his house with the community
leaders. The king sent a messenger on ahead, but before he arrived, Elisha said to the leaders, "Do you realize this assassin intends to cut off my head? Look, when the messenger arrives, shut
the door and lean against it. His master will certainly be right
behind him." 33 He was still talking to them when the messenger approached and said, "Look, the LORD is responsible for this
disaster! Why should I continue to wait for the LORD to help?"
7 1 Elisha replied, "Listen to the LORD's message. This is what
the LORD has said, 'About this time tomorrow a seah of finely
milled flour will sell for a shekel and two seahs of barley for a
shekel at the gate of Samaria.'" 2 An officer who was the king's
right-hand man responded to the prophet, "Look, even if the
LORD made it rain by opening holes in the sky, could this happen so soon?" Elisha said, "Look, you will see it happen with your
own eyes, but you will not eat any of the food!"
3 Now four men with a skin disease were sitting at the entrance
of the city gate. They said to one another, "Why are we just sitting
here waiting to die? 4 If we go into the city, we'll die of starvation,
and if we stay here we'll die! So come on, let's defect to the Syrian camp! If they spare us, we'll live; if they kill us—well, we were
going to die anyway." 5 So they started toward the Syrian camp at
dusk. When they reached the edge of the Syrian camp, there was
no one there. 6 The Lord had caused the Syrian camp to hear the
sound of chariots and horses and a large army. Then they said to
one another, "Look, the king of Israel has paid the kings of the
Hittites and Egyptians to attack us!" 7 So they got up and fled at
dusk, leaving behind their tents, horses, and donkeys. They left
the camp as it was and ran for their lives. 8 When the men with
a skin disease reached the edge of the camp, they entered a tent
and had a meal. They also took some silver, gold, and clothes and
went and hid it all. Then they went back and entered another
tent. They looted it and went and hid what they had taken. 9 Then
they said to one another, "It's not right what we're doing! This is
a day to celebrate, but we haven't told anyone. If we wait until
dawn, we'll be punished. So come on, let's go and inform the royal

palace." 10 So they went and called out to the gatekeepers of the
city. They told them, "We entered the Syrian camp and there was
no one there. We didn't even hear a man's voice. But the horses
and donkeys are still tied up, and the tents remain up." 11 The gatekeepers relayed the news to the royal palace.
12 The king got up in the night and said to his advisers, "I will tell
you what the Syrians have done to us. They know we are starving, so they left the camp and hid in the field, thinking, 'When
they come out of the city, we will capture them alive and enter
the city.'" 13 One of his advisers replied, "Pick some men and have
them take five of the horses that are left in the city. (Even if they
are killed, their fate will be no different than that of all the Israelite people—we're all going to die!) Let's send them out so we can
know for sure what's going on." 14 So they picked two horsemen
and the king sent them out to track the Syrian army. He ordered
them, "Go and find out what's going on." 15 So they tracked them as
far as the Jordan. The road was filled with clothes and equipment
that the Syrians had discarded in their haste. The scouts went
back and told the king. 16 Then the people went out and looted
the Syrian camp. A seah of finely milled flour sold for a shekel,
and two seahs of barley for a shekel, just as in the LORD's message.
17 Now the king had placed the officer who was his right-hand
man at the city gate. When the people rushed out, they trampled
him to death in the gate. This fulfilled the prophet's word which
he had spoken when the king tried to arrest him. 18 The prophet
had told the king, "Two seahs of barley will sell for a shekel, and
a seah of finely milled flour for a shekel; this will happen about
this time tomorrow in the gate of Samaria." 19 But the officer had
replied to the prophet, "Look, even if the LORD made it rain by
opening holes in the sky, could this happen so soon?" Elisha had
said, "Look, you will see it happen with your own eyes, but you
will not eat any of the food!" 20 This is exactly what happened to
him. The people trampled him to death in the city gate.

ELISHA AGAIN HELPS THE SHUNAMMITE WOMAN

8 Now Elisha advised the woman whose son he had brought
back to life, "You and your family should go and live somewhere else for a while, for the LORD has decreed that a famine
will overtake the land for seven years." 2 So the woman did as the
prophet said. She and her family went and lived in the land of
the Philistines for seven years. 3 After seven years the woman
returned from the land of the Philistines and went to ask the
king to give her back her house and field. 4 Now the king was
talking to Gehazi, the prophet's servant, and said, "Tell me all
the great things that Elisha has done." 5 While Gehazi was telling the king how Elisha had brought the dead back to life, the
woman whose son he had brought back to life came to ask the
king for her house and field. Gehazi said, "My master, O king,
this is the very woman, and this is her son whom Elisha brought
back to life!" 6 The king asked the woman about it, and she gave
him the details. The king assigned a eunuch to take care of her
request and ordered him, "Give her back everything she owns,
as well as the amount of crops her field produced from the day
she left the land until now."

ELISHA MEETS WITH HAZAEL

7 Elisha traveled to Damascus while King Ben Hadad of Syria was
sick. The king was told, "The prophet has come here." 8 So the king
told Hazael, "Take a gift and go visit the prophet. Request from
him an oracle from the LORD. Ask him, 'Will I recover from this
sickness?'" 9 So Hazael went to visit Elisha. He took along a gift,
as well as forty camel-loads of all the fine things of Damascus.
When he arrived, he stood before him and said, "Your son, King
Ben Hadad of Syria, has sent me to you with this question, 'Will
I recover from this sickness?'" 10 Elisha said to him, "Go and tell
him, 'You will surely recover,' but the LORD has revealed to me
that he will surely die." 11 Elisha just stared at him until Hazael
became uncomfortable. Then the prophet started crying. 12 Hazael asked, "Why are you crying, my master?" He replied, "Because I know the trouble you will cause the Israelites. You will
set fire to their fortresses, kill their young men with the sword,
smash their children to bits, and rip open their pregnant wom-
en." 13 Hazael said, "How could your servant, who is as insignificant as a dog, accomplish this great military victory?" Elisha
answered, "The LORD has revealed to me that you will be the
king of Syria." 14 He left Elisha and went to his master. Ben Hadad asked him, "What did Elisha tell you?" Hazael replied, "He
told me you would surely recover." 15 The next day Hazael took a
piece of cloth, dipped it in water, and spread it over Ben Hadad's
face until he died. Then Hazael replaced him as king.

JEHORAM'S REIGN OVER JUDAH

16 In the fifth year of the reign of Israel's King Joram, son of Ahab,
Jehoshaphat's son Jehoram became king over Judah. 17 He was thirty-two years old when he became king and he reigned for eight
years in Jerusalem. 18 He followed in the footsteps of the kings
of Israel, just as Ahab's dynasty had done, for he married Ahab's
daughter. He did evil in the sight of the LORD. 19 But the LORD was
unwilling to destroy Judah. He preserved Judah for the sake of
his servant David to whom he had promised a perpetual dynasty.

20 During his reign Edom freed themselves from Judah's control and set up their own king. 21 Jehoram crossed over to Zair
with all his chariots. The Edomites, who had surrounded him,
attacked at night and defeated him and his chariot officers. The
Israelite army retreated to their homeland. 22 So Edom has remained free from Judah's control to this very day. At that same
time Libnah also rebelled.

23 The rest of the events of Jehoram's reign, including a record
of his accomplishments, are recorded in the scroll called the
Annals of the Kings of Judah. 24 Jehoram passed away and was
buried with his ancestors in the City of David. His son Ahaziah
replaced him as king.

AHAZIAH TAKES THE THRONE OF JUDAH

25 In the twelfth year of the reign of Israel's King Joram, son of
Ahab, Jehoram's son Ahaziah became king over Judah. 26 Ahaziah
was twenty-two years old when he became king and he reigned
for one year in Jerusalem. His mother was Athaliah, the granddaughter of King Omri of Israel. 27 He followed in the footsteps

of Ahab's dynasty and did evil in the sight of the LORD, as Ahab's
dynasty had done, for he was related to Ahab's family.
28 He joined Ahab's son Joram in a battle against King Hazael
of Syria at Ramoth Gilead in which the Syrians defeated Joram.
29 King Joram returned to Jezreel to recover from the wounds
he received from the Syrians in Ramah when he fought against
King Hazael of Syria. King Ahaziah son of Jehoram of Judah went
down to visit Joram son of Ahab in Jezreel, for he was ill.

JEHU BECOMES KING

9 Now Elisha the prophet summoned a member of the prophetic guild and told him, "Tuck your robes into your belt,
take this container of olive oil in your hand, and go to Ramoth
Gilead. 2 When you arrive there, look for Jehu son of Jehoshaphat
son of Nimshi and take him aside into an inner room. 3 Take the
container of olive oil, pour it over his head, and say, 'This is what
the LORD has said, "I have designated you as king over Israel."'
Then open the door and run away quickly!"
4 So the young prophet went to Ramoth Gilead. 5 When he arrived, the officers of the army were sitting there. So he said, "I
have a message for you, O officer." Jehu asked, "For which one of
us?" He replied, "For you, O officer." 6 So Jehu got up and went inside. Then the prophet poured the olive oil on his head and said
to him, "This is what the LORD God of Israel has said, 'I have designated you as king over the LORD's people Israel. 7 You will destroy the family of your master Ahab. I will get revenge against
Jezebel for the shed blood of my servants the prophets and for
the shed blood of all the LORD's servants. 8 Ahab's entire family
will die. I will cut off every last male belonging to Ahab in Israel,
including even the weak and incapacitated. 9 I will make Ahab's
dynasty like those of Jeroboam son of Nebat and Baasha son of
Ahijah. 10 Dogs will devour Jezebel on the plot of ground in Jezreel;
she will not be buried.'" Then he opened the door and ran away.
11 When Jehu rejoined his master's servants, they asked him,
"Is everything all right? Why did this madman visit you?" He replied, "Ah, it's not important. You know what kind of man he is
and the kinds of things he says." 12 But they said, "You're lying!
Tell us what he said." So he told them what he had said. He also
related how he had said, "This is what the LORD has said, 'I have
designated you as king over Israel.'" 13 Each of them quickly took
off his cloak, and they spread them out at Jehu's feet on the steps.
The trumpet was blown and they shouted, "Jehu is king!" 14 Then
Jehu son of Jehoshaphat son of Nimshi conspired against Joram.

JEHU THE ASSASSIN

Now Joram had been in Ramoth Gilead with the whole Israelite
army, guarding against an invasion by King Hazael of Syria. 15 But
King Joram had returned to Jezreel to recover from the wounds
he received from the Syrians when he fought against King Hazael
of Syria. Jehu told his supporters, "If you really want me to be king,
then don't let anyone escape from the city to go and warn Jezreel."
16 Jehu drove his chariot to Jezreel, for Joram was recuperating
there. (Now King Ahaziah of Judah had come down to visit Joram.)
17 Now the watchman was standing on the tower in Jezreel and

REFLECT

How do Jehu's actions, though gruesome, display the heart of God for His people?

saw Jehu's troops approaching. He said, "I see troops!" Joram ordered, "Send a rider out to meet them and have him ask, 'Is everything all right?'" 18 So the horseman went to meet him and said,
"This is what the king says, 'Is everything all right?'" Jehu replied,
"None of your business! Follow me." The watchman reported, "The
messenger reached them, but hasn't started back." 19 So he sent a
second horseman out to them and he said, "This is what the king
says, 'Is everything all right?'" Jehu replied, "None of your business! Follow me." 20 The watchman reported, "He reached them,
but hasn't started back. The one who drives the lead chariot drives
like Jehu son of Nimshi; he drives recklessly." 21 Joram ordered,
"Hitch up my chariot." When his chariot had been hitched up,
King Joram of Israel and King Ahaziah of Judah went out in their
respective chariots to meet Jehu. They met up with him in the
plot of land that had once belonged to Naboth of Jezreel.

22 When Joram saw Jehu, he asked, "Is everything all right,
Jehu?" He replied, "How can everything be all right as long as
your mother Jezebel promotes idolatry and pagan practices?"
23 Joram turned his chariot around and took off. He said to Ahaziah, "It's a trap, Ahaziah!" 24 Jehu aimed his bow and shot an arrow right between Joram's shoulders. The arrow went through
his heart and he fell to his knees in his chariot. 25 Jehu ordered
his officer Bidkar, "Pick him up and throw him into the part of
the field that once belonged to Naboth of Jezreel. Remember,
you and I were riding together behind his father, Ahab, when the
LORD pronounced this oracle against him, 26 '"Know for sure that
I saw the shed blood of Naboth and his sons yesterday," says the
LORD, "and that I will give you what you deserve right here in
this plot of land," says the LORD.' So now pick him up and throw
him into this plot of land, just as in the LORD's message."

27 When King Ahaziah of Judah saw what happened, he took off
up the road to Beth Haggan. Jehu chased him and ordered, "Shoot
him too." They shot him while he was driving his chariot up the ascent of Gur near Ibleam. He fled to Megiddo and died there. 28 His
servants took his body back to Jerusalem and buried him in his
tomb with his ancestors in the City of David. 29 Ahaziah had become king over Judah in the eleventh year of Joram son of Ahab.

30 Jehu approached Jezreel. When Jezebel heard the news, she
put on some eye liner, fixed up her hair, and leaned out the window. 31 When Jehu came through the gate, she said, "Is everything
all right, Zimri, murderer of his master?" 32 He looked up at the window and said, "Who is on my side? Who?" Two or three eunuchs
looked down at him. 33 He said, "Throw her down!" So they threw her
down, and when she hit the ground, her blood splattered against
the wall and the horses, and Jehu drove his chariot over her. 34 He
went inside and had a meal. Then he said, "Dispose of this accursed
woman's corpse. Bury her, for after all, she was a king's daughter."
35 But when they went to bury her, they found nothing left but the
skull, feet, and palms of the hands. 36 So they went back and told
him. Then he said, "It is the fulfillment of the LORD's message that
he had spoken through his servant, Elijah the Tishbite, 'In the plot
of land at Jezreel, dogs will devour Jezebel's flesh. 37 Jezebel's corpse
will be like manure on the surface of the ground in the plot of land
at Jezreel. People will not be able to even recognize her.'"

JEHU WIPES OUT AHAB'S FAMILY

10 Ahab had seventy sons living in Samaria. So Jehu wrote
letters and sent them to Samaria to the leading officials of
Jezreel and to the guardians of Ahab's dynasty. This is what the
letters said, 2 "You have with you the sons of your master, chariots
and horses, a fortified city, and weapons. So when this letter arrives, 3 pick the best and most capable of your master's sons, place
him on his father's throne, and defend your master's dynasty."
4 They were absolutely terrified and said, "Look, two kings could
not stop him! How can we?" 5 So the palace supervisor, the city
commissioner, the leaders, and the guardians sent this message
to Jehu, "We are your subjects! Whatever you say, we will do. We
will not make anyone king. Do what you consider proper."
6 He wrote them a second letter, saying, "If you are really on my
side and are willing to obey me, then take the heads of your master's sons and come to me in Jezreel at this time tomorrow." Now
the king had seventy sons, and the prominent men of the city were
raising them. 7 When they received the letter, they seized the king's
sons and executed all seventy of them. They put their heads in baskets and sent them to him in Jezreel. 8 The messenger came and
told Jehu, "They have brought the heads of the king's sons." Jehu
said, "Stack them in two piles at the entrance of the city gate until morning." 9 In the morning he went out and stood there. Then
he said to all the people, "You are innocent. I conspired against
my master and killed him. But who struck down all of these men?
10 Therefore take note that not one of the LORD's words which he
pronounced against Ahab's dynasty will fail to materialize. The
LORD has done what he announced through his servant Elijah."
11 Then Jehu killed all who were left of Ahab's family in Jezreel, and
all his nobles, close friends, and priests. He left no survivors.
12 Jehu then left there and set out for Samaria. While he was
traveling through Beth Eked of the Shepherds, 13 Jehu encountered the relatives of King Ahaziah of Judah. He asked, "Who are
you?" They replied, "We are Ahaziah's relatives. We have come
down to see how the king's sons and the queen mother's sons are
doing." 14 He said, "Capture them alive!" So they captured them
alive and then executed all forty-two of them by the cistern at
Beth Eked. He left no survivors.
15 When he left there, he met Jehonadab son of Rekab who had
been looking for him. Jehu greeted him and asked, "Are you as
committed to me as I am to you?" Jehonadab answered, "I am!"
Jehu replied, "If so, give me your hand." So he offered his hand
and Jehu pulled him up into the chariot. 16 Jehu said, "Come with
me and see how zealous I am for the LORD's cause." So he took
him along in his chariot. 17 He went to Samaria and killed each
of Ahab's remaining family members who were in Samaria until
he destroyed them, in keeping with the LORD's message which
he had announced to Elijah.

JEHU EXECUTES THE PROPHETS AND PRIESTS OF BAAL

18 Jehu assembled all the people and said to them, "Ahab worshiped Baal a little; Jehu will worship him with great devotion.
19 So now, bring to me all the prophets of Baal, as well as all his

servants and priests. None of them must be absent, for I am offering a great sacrifice to Baal. Any of them who fails to appear will lose his life." But Jehu was tricking them so he could destroy the servants of Baal. [20]Then Jehu ordered, "Make arrangements for a celebration for Baal." So they announced it. [21]Jehu sent invitations throughout Israel, and all the servants of Baal came; not one was absent. They arrived at the temple of Baal and filled it up from end to end. [22]Jehu ordered the one who was in charge of the wardrobe, "Bring out robes for all the servants of Baal." So he brought out robes for them. [23]Then Jehu and Jehonadab son of Rekab went to the temple of Baal. Jehu said to the servants of Baal, "Make sure there are no servants of the LORD here with you; there must be only servants of Baal." [24]They went inside to offer sacrifices and burnt offerings. Now Jehu had stationed eighty men outside. He had told them, "If any of the men inside gets away, you will pay with your lives!"

[25]When he finished offering the burnt sacrifice, Jehu ordered the royal guard and officers, "Come in and strike them down! Don't let any escape!" So the royal guard and officers struck them down with the sword and left their bodies lying there. Then they entered the inner sanctuary of the temple of Baal. [26]They hauled out the sacred pillar of the temple of Baal and burned it. [27]They demolished the sacred pillar of Baal and the temple of Baal; it is used as a latrine to this very day. [28]So Jehu eradicated Baal worship from Israel.

A SUMMARY OF JEHU'S REIGN

[29]However, Jehu did not repudiate the sins that Jeroboam son of Nebat had encouraged Israel to commit; the golden calves remained in Bethel and Dan. [30]The LORD said to Jehu, "You have done well. You have accomplished my will and carried out my wishes with regard to Ahab's dynasty. Therefore four generations of your descendants will rule over Israel." [31]But Jehu did not carefully and wholeheartedly obey the law of the LORD God of Israel. He did not repudiate the sins which Jeroboam had encouraged Israel to commit.

[32]In those days the LORD began to reduce the size of Israel's territory. Hazael attacked their eastern border. [33]He conquered all the land of Gilead, including the territory of Gad, Reuben, and Manasseh, extending all the way from the Aroer in the Arnon Valley through Gilead to Bashan.

[34]The rest of the events of Jehu's reign, including all his accomplishments and successes, are recorded in the scroll called the Annals of the Kings of Israel. [35]Jehu passed away and was buried in Samaria. His son Jehoahaz replaced him as king. [36]Jehu reigned over Israel for twenty-eight years in Samaria.

ATHALIAH IS ELIMINATED

11 When Athaliah, the mother of Ahaziah, saw that her son was dead, she was determined to destroy the entire royal line. [2]So Jehosheba, the daughter of King Jehoram and sister of Ahaziah, took Ahaziah's son Joash and stole him away from the rest of the royal descendants who were to be executed. She hid him and his nurse in the room where the bed covers were stored. So he was

hidden from Athaliah and escaped execution. 3 He hid out with
his nurse in the LORD's temple for six years, while Athaliah was
ruling over the land.
4 In the seventh year Jehoiada summoned the officers of the
units of hundreds of the Carians and the royal bodyguard. He
met with them in the LORD's temple. He made an agreement
with them and made them swear an oath of allegiance in the
LORD's temple. Then he showed them the king's son. 5 He ordered
them, "This is what you must do. One third of the unit that is on
duty during the Sabbath will guard the royal palace. 6 Another
third of you will be stationed at the Foundation Gate. Still another third of you will be stationed at the gate behind the royal
guard. You will take turns guarding the palace. 7 The two units
who are off duty on the Sabbath will guard the LORD's temple and
protect the king. 8 You must surround the king. Each of you must
hold his weapon in his hand. Whoever approaches your ranks
must be killed. You must accompany the king wherever he goes."
9 The officers of the units of hundreds did just as Jehoiada the
priest ordered. Each of them took his men, those who were on
duty during the Sabbath as well as those who were off duty on
the Sabbath, and reported to Jehoiada the priest. 10 The priest
gave to the officers of the units of hundreds King David's spears
and the shields that were kept in the LORD's temple. 11 The royal
bodyguard took their stations, each holding his weapon in his
hand. They lined up from the south side of the temple to the
north side and stood near the altar and the temple, surrounding the king. 12 Jehoiada led out the king's son and placed on him
the crown and the royal insignia. They proclaimed him king and
poured olive oil on his head. They clapped their hands and cried
out, "Long live the king!"
13 When Athaliah heard the royal guard shout, she joined the
crowd at the LORD's temple. 14 Then she saw the king standing
by the pillar, according to custom. The officers stood beside the
king with their trumpets, and all the people of the land were celebrating and blowing trumpets. Athaliah tore her clothes and
screamed, "Treason, treason!" 15 Jehoiada the priest ordered the
officers of the units of hundreds, who were in charge of the army,
"Bring her outside the temple to the guards. Put to death by the
sword anyone who follows her." The priest gave this order because
he had decided she should not be executed in the LORD's temple. 16 They seized her and took her into the precincts of the royal
palace through the horses' entrance. There she was executed.
17 Jehoiada then drew up a covenant between the LORD and
the king and people, stipulating that they should be loyal to the
LORD. 18 All the people of the land went and demolished the temple of Baal. They smashed its altars and idols to bits. They killed
Mattan the priest of Baal in front of the altar. Jehoiada the priest
then placed guards at the LORD's temple. 19 He took the officers of
the units of hundreds, the Carians, the royal bodyguard, and all the
people of the land, and together they led the king down from the
LORD's temple. They entered the royal palace through the Gate of
the Royal Bodyguard, and the king sat down on the royal throne.
20 All the people of the land celebrated, for the city had rest now
that they had killed Athaliah with the sword in the royal palace.

JOASH'S REIGN OVER JUDAH

12 21 Jehoash was seven years old when he began to reign. 1 In
Jehu's seventh year Jehoash became king; he reigned for
forty years in Jerusalem. His mother was Zibiah, who was from
Beer Sheba. 2 Jehoash did what the LORD approved all his days
when Jehoiada the priest taught him. 3 But the high places were
not eliminated; the people continued to offer sacrifices and burn
incense on the high places.
4 Jehoash said to the priests, "I place at your disposal all the
consecrated silver that has been brought to the LORD's temple,
including the silver collected from the census tax, the silver received from those who have made vows, and all the silver that
people have voluntarily contributed to the LORD's temple. 5 The
priests should receive the silver they need from the treasurers
and repair any damage to the temple they discover."
6 By the twenty-third year of King Jehoash's reign the priests
had still not repaired the damage to the temple. 7 So King Jehoash summoned Jehoiada the priest along with the other priests,
and said to them, "Why have you not repaired the damage to the
temple? Now, take no more silver from your treasurers unless
you intend to use it to repair the damage." 8 The priests agreed
not to collect silver from the people and relieved themselves of
personal responsibility for the temple repairs.
9 Jehoiada the priest took a chest and drilled a hole in its lid. He
placed it on the right side of the altar near the entrance of the
LORD's temple. The priests who guarded the entrance would put
into it all the silver brought to the LORD's temple. 10 When they
saw the chest was full of silver, the royal secretary and the high
priest counted the silver that had been brought to the LORD's
temple and bagged it up. 11 They would then hand over the silver
that had been weighed to the construction foremen assigned to
the LORD's temple. They hired carpenters and builders to work
on the LORD's temple, 12 as well as masons and stonecutters. They
bought wood and chiseled stone to repair the damage to the
LORD's temple and also paid for all the other expenses. 13 The silver brought to the LORD's temple was not used for silver bowls,
trimming shears, basins, trumpets, or any kind of gold or silver
implements. 14 It was handed over to the foremen who used it
to repair the LORD's temple. 15 They did not audit the treasurers
who disbursed the funds to the foremen, for they were honest.
16 (The silver collected in conjunction with reparation offerings
and sin offerings was not brought to the LORD's temple; it belonged to the priests.)
17 At that time King Hazael of Syria attacked Gath and captured
it. Hazael then decided to attack Jerusalem. 18 King Jehoash of
Judah collected all the sacred items that his ancestors Jehoshaphat, Jehoram, and Ahaziah, kings of Judah, had consecrated,
as well as his own sacred items and all the gold that could be
found in the treasuries of the LORD's temple and the royal palace. He sent it all to King Hazael of Syria, who then withdrew
from Jerusalem.
19 The rest of the events of Joash's reign, including all his accomplishments, are recorded in the scroll called the Annals of
the Kings of Judah. 20 His servants conspired against him and

REFLECT

Why was it significant that the high places were not taken away? Are there any areas of your life where you are holding onto sin instead of completely removing it?

murdered Joash at Beth Millo, on the road that goes down to Silla. 21 His servants Jozabad son of Shimeath and Jehozabad son of Shomer murdered him. He was buried with his ancestors in the City of David. His son Amaziah replaced him as king.

JEHOAHAZ'S REIGN OVER ISRAEL

13 In the twenty-third year of the reign of Judah's King Joash son of Ahaziah, Jehu's son Jehoahaz became king over Israel. He reigned in Samaria for seventeen years. 2 He did evil in the sight of the LORD. He continued in the sinful ways of Jeroboam son of Nebat who had encouraged Israel to sin; he did not repudiate those sins. 3 The LORD was furious with Israel and handed them over to King Hazael of Syria and to Hazael's son Ben Hadad for many years.

4 Jehoahaz asked for the LORD's mercy, and the LORD responded favorably, for he saw that Israel was oppressed by the king of Syria. 5 The LORD provided a deliverer for Israel, and they were freed from Syria's power. The Israelites once more lived in security. 6 But they did not repudiate the sinful ways of the family of Jeroboam, who encouraged Israel to sin; they continued in those sins. There was even an Asherah pole standing in Samaria. 7 Jehoahaz had no army left except for 50 horsemen, 10 chariots, and 10,000 foot soldiers. The king of Syria had destroyed his troops and trampled on them as dust.

8 The rest of the events of Jehoahaz's reign, including all his accomplishments and successes, are recorded in the scroll called the Annals of the Kings of Israel. 9 Jehoahaz passed away and was buried in Samaria. His son Jehoash replaced him as king.

JEHOASH'S REIGN OVER ISRAEL

10 In the thirty-seventh year of King Jehoash's reign over Judah, Jehoahaz's son Jehoash became king over Israel. He reigned in Samaria for sixteen years. 11 He did evil in the sight of the LORD. He did not repudiate the sinful ways of Jeroboam son of Nebat who encouraged Israel to sin; he continued in those sins. 12 The rest of the events of Jehoash's reign, including all his accomplishments and his successful war with King Amaziah of Judah, are recorded in the scroll called the Annals of the Kings of Israel. 13 Jehoash passed away and Jeroboam succeeded him on the throne. Jehoash was buried in Samaria with the kings of Israel.

ELISHA MAKES ONE FINAL PROPHECY

14 Now Elisha had a terminal illness. King Jehoash of Israel went down to visit him. He wept before him and said, "My father, my father! The chariot and horsemen of Israel!" 15 Elisha told him, "Take a bow and some arrows," and he did so. 16 Then Elisha told the king of Israel, "Aim the bow." He did so, and Elisha placed his hands on the king's hands. 17 Elisha said, "Open the east window," and he did so. Elisha said, "Shoot!" and he did so. Elisha said, "This arrow symbolizes the victory the LORD will give you over Syria. You will annihilate Syria in Aphek!" 18 Then Elisha said, "Take the arrows," and he did so. He told the king of Israel, "Strike the ground!" He struck the ground three times and stopped. 19 The prophet got angry at him and said, "If you had struck the ground

five or six times, you would have annihilated Syria! But now, you
will defeat Syria only three times."
20 Elisha died and was buried. Moabite raiding parties invaded the land at the beginning of the year. 21 One day some
men were burying a man when they spotted a raiding party. So
they threw the dead man into Elisha's tomb. When the body
touched Elisha's bones, the dead man came to life and stood
on his feet.
22 Now King Hazael of Syria oppressed Israel throughout Jehoahaz's reign. 23 But the LORD had mercy on them and felt pity
for them. He extended his favor to them because of the promise
he had made to Abraham, Isaac, and Jacob. He has been unwilling to destroy them or remove them from his presence to this
very day. 24 When King Hazael of Syria died, his son Ben Hadad
replaced him as king. 25 Jehoahaz's son Jehoash took back from
Ben Hadad son of Hazael the cities that he had taken from his
father Jehoahaz in war. Jehoash defeated him three times and
recovered the Israelite cities.

AMAZIAH'S REIGN OVER JUDAH

14 In the second year of the reign of Israel's King Joash son
of Joahaz, Joash's son Amaziah became king over Judah.
2 He was twenty-five years old when he began to reign, and he
reigned for twenty-nine years in Jerusalem. His mother was Jehoaddan, who was from Jerusalem. 3 He did what the LORD approved, but not like David his ancestor had done. He followed
the example of his father Joash. 4 But the high places were not
eliminated; the people continued to offer sacrifices and burn
incense on the high places.
5 When he had secured control of the kingdom, he executed
the servants who had assassinated his father. 6 But he did not
execute the sons of the assassins. He obeyed the LORD's commandment as recorded in the scroll of the law of Moses, "Fathers must not be put to death for what their sons do, and sons
must not be put to death for what their fathers do. A man must
be put to death only for his own sin."
7 He defeated 10,000 Edomites in the Salt Valley; he captured
Sela in battle and renamed it Joktheel, a name it has retained
to this very day. 8 Then Amaziah sent messengers to Jehoash
son of Jehoahaz son of Jehu, king of Israel. He said, "Come, let's
meet face to face." 9 King Jehoash of Israel sent this message back
to King Amaziah of Judah, "A thornbush in Lebanon sent this
message to a cedar in Lebanon, 'Give your daughter to my son
as a wife.' Then a wild animal of Lebanon came by and trampled
down the thorn. 10 You thoroughly defeated Edom, and it has
gone to your head! Gloat over your success, but stay in your palace. Why bring calamity on yourself? Why bring down yourself
and Judah along with you?" 11 But Amaziah would not heed the
warning, so King Jehoash of Israel attacked. He and King Amaziah of Judah met face to face in Beth Shemesh of Judah. 12 Judah
was defeated by Israel, and each man ran back home. 13 King Jehoash of Israel captured King Amaziah of Judah, son of Jehoash
son of Ahaziah, in Beth Shemesh. He attacked Jerusalem and
broke down the wall of Jerusalem from the Gate of Ephraim to

the Corner Gate—a distance of about 600 feet. 14 He took away all the gold and silver, all the items found in the LORD's temple and in the treasuries of the royal palace, and some hostages. Then he went back to Samaria.

15 The rest of the events of Jehoash's reign, including all his accomplishments and his successful war with King Amaziah of Judah, are recorded in the scroll called the Annals of the Kings of Israel. 16 Jehoash passed away and was buried in Samaria with the kings of Israel. His son Jeroboam replaced him as king.

17 King Amaziah son of Joash of Judah lived for fifteen years after the death of King Jehoash son of Jehoahaz of Israel. 18 The rest of the events of Amaziah's reign are recorded in the scroll called the Annals of the Kings of Judah. 19 Conspirators plotted against him in Jerusalem, so he fled to Lachish. But they sent assassins after him, and they killed him there. 20 His body was carried back by horses, and he was buried in Jerusalem with his ancestors in the City of David. 21 All the people of Judah took Azariah, who was sixteen years old, and made him king in his father Amaziah's place. 22 Azariah built up Elat and restored it to Judah after the king had passed away.

JEROBOAM II'S REIGN OVER ISRAEL

23 In the fifteenth year of the reign of Judah's King Amaziah son of Joash, Jeroboam son of Joash became king over Israel. He reigned for forty-one years in Samaria. 24 He did evil in the sight of the LORD; he did not repudiate the sinful ways of Jeroboam son of Nebat who encouraged Israel to sin. 25 He restored the border of Israel from Lebo Hamath in the north to the sea of the rift valley in the south, just as in the message from the LORD God of Israel that he had announced through his servant Jonah son of Amittai, the prophet from Gath Hepher. 26 The LORD saw Israel's intense suffering; everyone was weak and incapacitated and Israel had no deliverer. 27 The LORD had not decreed that he would blot out Israel's memory from under heaven, so he delivered them through Jeroboam son of Joash.

28 The rest of the events of Jeroboam's reign, including all his accomplishments, his military success in restoring Israelite control over Damascus and Hamath, are recorded in the scroll called the Annals of the Kings of Israel. 29 Jeroboam passed away and was buried in Samaria with the kings of Israel. His son Zechariah replaced him as king.

AZARIAH'S REIGN OVER JUDAH

15 In the twenty-seventh year of King Jeroboam's reign over Israel, Amaziah's son Azariah became king over Judah. 2 He was sixteen years old when he began to reign, and he reigned for fifty-two years in Jerusalem. His mother's name was Jecholiah, who was from Jerusalem. 3 He did what the LORD approved, just as his father Amaziah had done. 4 But the high places were not eliminated; the people continued to offer sacrifices and burn incense on the high places. 5 The LORD afflicted the king with an illness; he suffered from a skin disease until the day he died. He lived in separate quarters, while his son Jotham was in charge of the palace and ruled over the people of the land.

6 The rest of the events of Azariah's reign, including all his accomplishments, are recorded in the scroll called the Annals of the Kings of Judah. 7 Azariah passed away and was buried with his ancestors in the City of David. His son Jotham replaced him as king.

ZECHARIAH'S REIGN OVER ISRAEL

8 In the thirty-eighth year of King Azariah's reign over Judah, Jeroboam's son Zechariah became king over Israel. He reigned in Samaria for six months. 9 He did evil in the sight of the LORD, as his ancestors had done. He did not repudiate the sinful ways of Jeroboam son of Nebat who encouraged Israel to sin. 10 Shallum son of Jabesh conspired against him; he assassinated him in Ibleam and took his place as king. 11 The rest of the events of Zechariah's reign are recorded in the scroll called the Annals of the Kings of Israel. 12 His assassination fulfilled the LORD's message to Jehu, "Four generations of your descendants will rule on Israel's throne." And that is how it happened.

13 Shallum son of Jabesh became king in the thirty-ninth year of King Uzziah's reign over Judah. He reigned for one month in Samaria. 14 Menahem son of Gadi went up from Tirzah to Samaria and attacked Shallum son of Jabesh. He killed him and took his place as king. 15 The rest of the events of Shallum's reign, including the conspiracy he organized, are recorded in the scroll called the Annals of the Kings of Israel. 16 At that time Menahem came from Tirzah and attacked Tiphsah. He struck down all who lived in the city and the surrounding territory, because they would not surrender. He even ripped open the pregnant women.

MENAHEM'S REIGN OVER ISRAEL

17 In the thirty-ninth year of King Azariah's reign over Judah, Menahem son of Gadi became king over Israel. He reigned for ten years in Samaria. 18 He did evil in the sight of the LORD; he did not repudiate the sinful ways of Jeroboam son of Nebat, who encouraged Israel to sin.

During his reign, 19 Pul king of Assyria invaded the land, and Menahem paid him 1,000 talents of silver to gain his support and to solidify his control of the kingdom. 20 Menahem got this silver by taxing all the wealthy men in Israel; he took fifty shekels of silver from each one of them and paid it to the king of Assyria. Then the king of Assyria left; he did not stay there in the land.

21 The rest of the events of Menahem's reign, including all his accomplishments, are recorded in the scroll called the Annals of the Kings of Israel. 22 Menahem passed away and his son Pekahiah replaced him as king.

PEKAHIAH'S REIGN OVER ISRAEL

23 In the fiftieth year of King Azariah's reign over Judah, Menahem's son Pekahiah became king over Israel. He reigned in Samaria for two years. 24 He did evil in the sight of the LORD; he did not repudiate the sinful ways of Jeroboam son of Nebat who encouraged Israel to sin. 25 His officer Pekah son of Remaliah conspired against him. He and fifty Gileadites assassinated

Pekahiah, as well as Argob and Arieh, in Samaria in the fortress of the royal palace. Pekah then took his place as king.

26 The rest of the events of Pekahiah's reign, including all his accomplishments, are recorded in the scroll called the Annals of the Kings of Israel.

PEKAH'S REIGN OVER ISRAEL

27 In the fifty-second year of King Azariah's reign over Judah, Pekah son of Remaliah became king over Israel. He reigned in Samaria for twenty years. 28 He did evil in the sight of the LORD; he did not repudiate the sinful ways of Jeroboam son of Nebat who encouraged Israel to sin. 29 During Pekah's reign over Israel, King Tiglath-Pileser of Assyria came and captured Ijon, Abel Beth Maacah, Janoah, Kedesh, Hazor, Gilead, and Galilee, including all the territory of Naphtali. He deported the people to Assyria. 30 Hoshea son of Elah conspired against Pekah son of Remaliah. He assassinated him and took his place as king, in the twentieth year of the reign of Jotham son of Uzziah.

31 The rest of the events of Pekah's reign, including all his accomplishments, are recorded in the scroll called the Annals of the Kings of Israel.

JOTHAM'S REIGN OVER JUDAH

32 In the second year of the reign of Israel's King Pekah son of Remaliah, Uzziah's son Jotham became king over Judah. 33 He was twenty-five years old when he began to reign, and he reigned for sixteen years in Jerusalem. His mother was Jerusha the daughter of Zadok. 34 He did what the LORD approved, just as his father Uzziah had done. 35 But the high places were not eliminated; the people continued to offer sacrifices and burn incense on the high places. He built the Upper Gate to the LORD's temple.

36 The rest of the events of Jotham's reign, including his accomplishments, are recorded in the scroll called the Annals of the Kings of Judah. 37 In those days the LORD prompted King Rezin of Syria and Pekah son of Remaliah to attack Judah. 38 Jotham passed away and was buried with his ancestors in the city of his ancestor David. His son Ahaz replaced him as king.

AHAZ'S REIGN OVER JUDAH

16 In the seventeenth year of the reign of Pekah son of Remaliah, Jotham's son Ahaz became king over Judah. 2 Ahaz was twenty years old when he began to reign, and he reigned for sixteen years in Jerusalem. He did not do what pleased the LORD his God, in contrast to his ancestor David. 3 He followed in the footsteps of the kings of Israel. He passed his son through the fire, a horrible sin practiced by the nations whom the LORD drove out from before the Israelites. 4 He offered sacrifices and burned incense on the high places, on the hills, and under every green tree.

5 At that time King Rezin of Syria and King Pekah son of Remaliah of Israel attacked Jerusalem. They besieged Ahaz, but were unable to conquer him. 6 (At that time King Rezin of Syria recovered Elat for Syria; he drove the Judahites from there. Syrians arrived in Elat and live there to this very day.) 7 Ahaz sent

messengers to King Tiglath-Pileser of Assyria, saying, "I am your servant and your dependent. March up and rescue me from the power of the king of Syria and the king of Israel, who have attacked me." [8]Then Ahaz took the silver and gold that were in the LORD's temple and in the treasuries of the royal palace and sent it as tribute to the king of Assyria. [9]The king of Assyria responded favorably to his request; he attacked Damascus and captured it. He deported the people to Kir and executed Rezin.

[10]When King Ahaz went to meet with King Tiglath-Pileser of Assyria in Damascus, he saw the altar there. King Ahaz sent to Uriah the priest a drawing of the altar and a blueprint for its design. [11]Uriah the priest built an altar in conformity to the plans King Ahaz had sent from Damascus. Uriah the priest finished it before King Ahaz arrived back from Damascus. [12]When the king arrived back from Damascus and saw the altar, he approached it and offered a sacrifice on it. [13]He offered his burnt sacrifice and his grain offering. He poured out his libation and sprinkled the blood from his peace offerings on the altar. [14]He moved the bronze altar that stood in the LORD's presence from the front of the temple (between the altar and the LORD's temple) and put it on the north side of the new altar. [15]King Ahaz ordered Uriah the priest, "On the large altar offer the morning burnt sacrifice, the evening grain offering, the royal burnt sacrifices and grain offering, the burnt sacrifice for all the people of the land, their grain offering, and their libations. Sprinkle all the blood of the burnt sacrifice and other sacrifices on it. The bronze altar will be for my personal use." [16]So Uriah the priest did exactly as King Ahaz ordered.

[17]King Ahaz took off the frames of the movable stands, and removed the basins from them. He took "The Sea" down from the bronze bulls that supported it and put it on the stone pavement. [18]He also removed the Sabbath awning that had been built in the temple and the king's outer entranceway to the LORD's temple, on account of the king of Assyria.

[19]The rest of the events of Ahaz's reign, including his accomplishments, are recorded in the scroll called the Annals of the Kings of Judah. [20]Ahaz passed away and was buried with his ancestors in the City of David. His son Hezekiah replaced him as king.

HOSHEA'S REIGN OVER ISRAEL

17 In the twelfth year of King Ahaz's reign over Judah, Hoshea son of Elah became king over Israel. He reigned in Samaria for nine years. [2]He did evil in the sight of the LORD, but not to the same degree as the Israelite kings who preceded him. [3]King Shalmaneser of Assyria marched up to attack him; so Hoshea became his subject and paid him tribute. [4]The king of Assyria discovered that Hoshea was planning a revolt. Hoshea had sent messengers to King So of Egypt and had not sent his annual tribute to the king of Assyria. So the king of Assyria arrested him and imprisoned him. [5]The king of Assyria marched through the whole land. He attacked Samaria and besieged it for three years. [6]In the ninth year of Hoshea's reign, the king of Assyria captured Samaria and deported the people of Israel to Assyria. He settled them in Halah, along the Habor (the river of Gozan), and in the cities of the Medes.

LOVE TO GROW

NEVER ABANDONED

2 KINGS 17:1–23

In the beginning, God created the heavens and the earth. Soon after, humanity disobeyed God and sin entered the world. God chose one man, Abraham, to bring about His plan for the redemption of humanity. In Genesis 12:2–3, God said to Abraham, "I will make you into a great nation, and I will bless you, and I will make your name great, so that you will exemplify divine blessing." Here, God promised Abraham the land of Israel, many descendants, and His blessing. This is where Israel's story began.

The Old Testament traces Israel's relationship with God. Chapter after chapter, the people of Israel fell in and out of favor with the One they claimed to love. Second Kings 17 details the fall of Israel to the nation of Assyria. Israel is left utterly hopeless.

Looking at Scripture, we know two things:

First, God disciplines those He loves (Heb 12:1–13). Though God had warned Israel against idolatry, the people served foreign gods, worshiped their idols, and did such evil that He had to intervene. Like a loving father disciplining his children, God allowed a foreign nation to overcome His people, and Israel was taken into exile. God's hope? The Israelites would see the error in their ways and return to Yahweh.

Second, Scripture promises that God never abandons His people. Despite their blatant disobedience, God was consistently present. Though His people rejected Him, God never rejected His people. He wants us. He constantly pursues us through our mess, our pain, and our rebellion. Nothing we do or say can change this.

God disciplines us because He loves us. He is always faithful, even when we choose to be faithless.

While the Israelites' fall is one of the lowest points in their history, there is much more to the story. God not only rescued the people of Israel by returning them to the promised land, but He also rescued humanity by sending His Son to die for them on a cross. God may discipline, but He never abandons those He loves.

All of Scripture is a story of rescue. From creation to the new heavens and earth, God set a plan in motion to save us. Let us follow God's way, not because this earns His approval, but because it brings us life. Let us not believe the lie that God leaves when things get hard, but instead remember God's promise to always be with us (Matt 28:19–20).

A SUMMARY OF ISRAEL'S SINFUL HISTORY

7 This happened because the Israelites sinned against the LORD their God, who brought them up from the land of Egypt and freed them from the power of Pharaoh king of Egypt. They worshiped other gods; 8 they observed the practices of the nations whom the LORD had driven out from before them, and followed the example of the kings of Israel. 9 The Israelites said things about the LORD their God that were not right. They built high places in all their towns, from watchtower to fortified city. 10 They set up sacred pillars and Asherah poles on every high hill and under every green tree. 11 They burned incense on all the high places just like the nations whom the LORD had driven away before them did. Their evil practices made the LORD angry. 12 They worshiped the disgusting idols in blatant disregard of the LORD's command.

13 The LORD solemnly warned Israel and Judah through all his prophets and all the seers, "Turn back from your evil ways; obey my commandments and rules that are recorded in the law. I ordered your ancestors to keep this law and sent my servants the prophets to remind you of its demands." 14 But they did not pay attention and were as stubborn as their ancestors, who had not trusted the LORD their God. 15 They rejected his rules, the covenant he had made with their ancestors, and the laws he had commanded them to obey. They paid allegiance to worthless idols, and so became worthless to the LORD. They copied the practices of the surrounding nations in blatant disregard of the LORD's command. 16 They abandoned all the commandments of the LORD their God; they made two metal calves and an Asherah pole, bowed down to all the stars in the sky, and worshiped Baal. 17 They passed their sons and daughters through the fire, and practiced divination and omen reading. They committed themselves to doing evil in the sight of the LORD and made him angry.

18 So the LORD was furious with Israel and rejected them; only the tribe of Judah was left. 19 Judah also failed to keep the commandments of the LORD their God; they followed Israel's example. 20 So the LORD rejected all of Israel's descendants; he humiliated them and handed them over to robbers, until he had thrown them from his presence. 21 He tore Israel away from David's dynasty, and Jeroboam son of Nebat became their king. Jeroboam drove Israel away from the LORD and encouraged them to commit a serious sin. 22 The Israelites followed in the sinful ways of Jeroboam and did not repudiate them. 23 Finally the LORD rejected Israel just as he had warned he would do through all his servants the prophets. Israel was deported from its land to Assyria and remains there to this very day.

CHALLENGE

How does the destruction of Israel display the promise-keeping nature of God? How did God fulfill the promises He made in Deuteronomy 28 through the exile of Israel?

THE KING OF ASSYRIA POPULATES ISRAEL WITH FOREIGNERS

24 The king of Assyria brought foreigners from Babylon, Cuthah, Avva, Hamath, and Sepharvaim and settled them in the cities of Samaria in place of the Israelites. They took possession of Samaria and lived in its cities. 25 When they first moved in, they did not worship the LORD. So the LORD sent lions among them and the lions were killing them. 26 The king of Assyria was told, "The nations whom you deported and settled in the

cities of Samaria do not know the requirements of the God of
the land, so he has sent lions among them. They are killing the
people because they do not know the requirements of the God
of the land." 27 So the king of Assyria ordered, "Take back one
of the priests whom you deported from there. He must settle there and teach them the requirements of the God of the
land." 28 So one of the priests whom they had deported from
Samaria went back and settled in Bethel. He taught them how
to worship the LORD.

29 But each of these nations made its own gods and put them
in the shrines on the high places that the people of Samaria had
made. Each nation did this in the cities where they lived. 30 The
people from Babylon made Sukkoth Benoth, the people from
Cuth made Nergal, the people from Hamath made Ashima, 31 the
Avvites made Nibhaz and Tartak, and the Sepharvites burned
their sons in the fire as an offering to Adrammelech and Anam-
melech, the gods of Sepharvaim. 32 At the same time they worshiped the LORD. They appointed some of their own people to
serve as priests in the shrines on the high places. 33 They were
worshiping the LORD and at the same time serving their own
gods in accordance with the practices of the nations from which
they had been deported.

34 To this very day they observe their earlier practices. They
do not worship the LORD; they do not obey the rules, regulations, law, and commandments that the LORD gave the descendants of Jacob, whom he renamed Israel. 35 The LORD made a
covenant with them and instructed them, "You must not worship other gods. Do not bow down to them, serve them, or offer
sacrifices to them. 36 Instead you must worship the LORD, who
brought you up from the land of Egypt by his great power and
military ability; bow down to him and offer sacrifices to him.
37 You must carefully obey at all times the rules, regulations, law,
and commandments he wrote down for you. You must not worship other gods. 38 You must never forget the covenant I made
with you, and you must not worship other gods. 39 Instead you
must worship the LORD your God; then he will rescue you from
the power of all your enemies." 40 But they paid no attention;
instead they observed their earlier practices. 41 These nations
were worshiping the LORD and at the same time serving their
idols; their sons and grandsons are doing just as their fathers
have done, to this very day.

HEZEKIAH BECOMES KING OF JUDAH

18 In the third year of the reign of Israel's King Hoshea son
of Elah, Ahaz's son Hezekiah became king over Judah. 2 He
was twenty-five years old when he began to reign, and he reigned
twenty-nine years in Jerusalem. His mother was Abi, the daughter of Zechariah. 3 He did what the LORD approved, just as his ancestor David had done. 4 He eliminated the high places, smashed
the sacred pillars to bits, and cut down the Asherah pole. He also
demolished the bronze serpent that Moses had made, for up to
that time the Israelites had been offering incense to it; it was
called Nehushtan. 5 He trusted in the LORD God of Israel; in this
regard there was none like him among the kings of Judah either

before or after. 6 He was loyal to the LORD and did not abandon him. He obeyed the commandments that the LORD had given to Moses. 7 The LORD was with him; he succeeded in all his endeavors. He rebelled against the king of Assyria and refused to submit to him. 8 He defeated the Philistines as far as Gaza and its territory, from watchtower to fortified city.

9 In the fourth year of King Hezekiah's reign (it was the seventh year of the reign of Israel's King Hoshea, son of Elah), King Shalmaneser of Assyria marched up against Samaria and besieged it. 10 After three years he captured it (in the sixth year of Hezekiah's reign); in the ninth year of King Hoshea's reign over Israel, Samaria was captured. 11 The king of Assyria deported the people of Israel to Assyria. He settled them in Halah, along the Habor (the river of Gozan), and in the cities of the Medes. 12 This happened because they did not obey the LORD their God and broke his covenant with them. They did not pay attention to and obey all that Moses, the LORD's servant, had commanded.

SENNACHERIB INVADES JUDAH

13 In the fourteenth year of King Hezekiah's reign, King Sennacherib of Assyria marched up against all the fortified cities of Judah and captured them. 14 King Hezekiah of Judah sent this message to the king of Assyria, who was at Lachish, "I have violated our treaty. If you leave, I will do whatever you demand." So the king of Assyria demanded that King Hezekiah of Judah pay 300 talents of silver and thirty talents of gold. 15 Hezekiah gave him all the silver in the LORD's temple and in the treasuries of the royal palace. 16 At that time King Hezekiah of Judah stripped the metal overlays from the doors of the LORD's temple and from the posts that he had plated and gave them to the king of Assyria.

17 The king of Assyria sent his commanding general, the chief eunuch, and the chief adviser from Lachish to King Hezekiah in Jerusalem, along with a large army. They went up and arrived at Jerusalem. They went and stood at the conduit of the upper pool which is located on the road to the field where they wash and dry cloth. 18 They summoned the king, so Eliakim son of Hilkiah, the palace supervisor, accompanied by Shebna, the scribe, and Joah son of Asaph, the secretary, went out to meet them.

19 The chief adviser said to them, "Tell Hezekiah: 'This is what the great king, the king of Assyria, says: "What is your source of confidence? 20 Your claim to have a strategy and military strength is just empty talk. In whom are you trusting that you would dare to rebel against me? 21 Now look, you must be trusting in Egypt, that splintered reed staff. If a man leans for support on it, it punctures his hand and wounds him. That is what Pharaoh king of Egypt does to all who trust in him. 22 Perhaps you will tell me, 'We are trusting in the LORD our God.' But Hezekiah is the one who eliminated his high places and altars and then told the people of Judah and Jerusalem, 'You must worship at this altar in Jerusalem.' 23 Now make a deal with my master the king of Assyria, and I will give you 2,000 horses, provided you can find enough riders for them. 24 Certainly you will not refuse one of my master's minor officials and trust in Egypt for chariots and horsemen. 25 Furthermore it was by the command

of the LORD that I marched up against this place to destroy it.
The LORD told me, 'March up against this land and destroy it.'""
26 Eliakim son of Hilkiah, Shebna, and Joah said to the chief
adviser, "Speak to your servants in Aramaic, for we understand
it. Don't speak with us in the Judahite dialect in the hearing of
the people who are on the wall." 27 But the chief adviser said to
them, "My master did not send me to speak these words only
to your master and to you. His message is also for the men who
sit on the wall, for they will eat their own excrement and drink
their own urine along with you."

28 The chief adviser then stood there and called out loudly in
the Judahite dialect, "Listen to the message of the great king,
the king of Assyria. 29 This is what the king says: 'Don't let Hezekiah mislead you, for he is not able to rescue you from my hand!
30 Don't let Hezekiah talk you into trusting in the LORD when
he says, "The LORD will certainly rescue us; this city will not be
handed over to the king of Assyria." 31 Don't listen to Hezekiah!'
For this is what the king of Assyria says, 'Send me a token of your
submission and surrender to me. Then each of you may eat from
his own vine and fig tree and drink water from his own cistern,
32 until I come and take you to a land just like your own—a land
of grain and new wine, a land of bread and vineyards, a land of
olive oil and honey. Then you will live and not die. Don't listen to
Hezekiah, for he is misleading you when he says, "The LORD will
rescue us." 33 Have any of the gods of the nations actually rescued
his land from the power of the king of Assyria? 34 Where are the
gods of Hamath and Arpad? Where are the gods of Sepharvaim,
Hena, and Ivvah? Indeed, did any gods rescue Samaria from my
power? 35 Who among all the gods of the lands has rescued their
lands from my power? So how can the LORD rescue Jerusalem
from my power?'" 36 The people were silent and did not respond,
for the king had ordered, "Don't respond to him."

37 Eliakim son of Hilkiah, the palace supervisor, accompanied
by Shebna the scribe and Joah son of Asaph, the secretary, went
to Hezekiah with their clothes torn and reported to him what
19 the chief adviser had said. 1 When King Hezekiah heard
this, he tore his clothes, put on sackcloth, and went to the
LORD's temple. 2 He sent Eliakim the palace supervisor, Shebna
the scribe, and the leading priests, clothed in sackcloth, to the
prophet Isaiah son of Amoz. 3 They told him, "This is what Hezekiah says: 'This is a day of distress, insults, and humiliation, as
when a baby is ready to leave the birth canal, but the mother
lacks the strength to push it through. 4 Perhaps the LORD your
God will hear all these things the chief adviser has spoken on
behalf of his master, the king of Assyria, who sent him to taunt
the living God. When the LORD your God hears, perhaps he will
punish him for the things he has said. So pray for this remnant
that remains.'"

5 When King Hezekiah's servants came to Isaiah, 6 Isaiah said
to them, "Tell your master this: 'This is what the LORD has said:
"Don't be afraid because of the things you have heard, because
the Assyrian king's officers have insulted me. 7 Look, I will take
control of his mind; he will receive a report and return to his
own land. I will cut him down with a sword in his own land."'"

8 When the chief adviser heard the king of Assyria had departed from Lachish, he left and went to Libnah, where the king
was campaigning. 9 The king heard that King Tirhakah of Ethiopia was marching out to fight him. He again sent messengers to
Hezekiah, ordering them: 10 “Tell King Hezekiah of Judah this:
‘Don’t let your God in whom you trust mislead you when he says,
“Jerusalem will not be handed over to the king of Assyria.” 11 Certainly you have heard how the kings of Assyria have annihilated
all lands. Do you really think you will be rescued? 12 Were the
nations whom my ancestors destroyed—the nations of Gozan,
Haran, Rezeph, and the people of Eden in Telassar—rescued by
their gods? 13 Where are the king of Hamath, the king of Arpad,
and the kings of Lair, Sepharvaim, Hena, and Ivvah?’”
14 Hezekiah took the letter from the messengers and read it.
Then Hezekiah went up to the LORD’s temple and spread it out
before the LORD. 15 Hezekiah prayed before the LORD: “LORD
God of Israel, who is enthroned above the cherubim! You alone
are God over all the kingdoms of the earth. You made the sky
and the earth. 16 Pay attention, LORD, and hear! Open your eyes,
LORD, and observe! Listen to the message Sennacherib sent and
how he taunts the living God! 17 It is true, LORD, that the kings of
Assyria have destroyed the nations and their lands. 18 They have
burned the gods of the nations, for they are not really gods, but
only the product of human hands manufactured from wood and
stone. That is why the Assyrians could destroy them. 19 Now, O
LORD our God, rescue us from his power, so that all the kingdoms of the earth will know that you, LORD, are the only God.”
20 Isaiah son of Amoz sent this message to Hezekiah: “This is
what the LORD God of Israel has said: ‘I have heard your prayer
concerning King Sennacherib of Assyria. 21 This is what the LORD
says about him:

“‘“The virgin daughter Zion
despises you, she makes fun of you;
Daughter Jerusalem
shakes her head after you.
22 Whom have you taunted and hurled insults at?
At whom have you shouted,
and looked so arrogantly?
At the Holy One of Israel!
23 Through your messengers you taunted
the Sovereign Master,
‘With my many chariots
I climbed up the high mountains,
the slopes of Lebanon.
I cut down its tall cedars
and its best evergreens.
I invaded its most remote regions,
its thickest woods.
24 I dug wells and drank
water in foreign lands.
With the soles of my feet I dried up
all the rivers of Egypt.’
25 Certainly you must have heard!
Long ago I worked it out.

DON'T DIG UP IN DOUBT

2 KINGS 19

Hezekiah had been king of Judah for fourteen years. King Sennacherib of Assyria came against Judah and captured some of her fortified cities. He then began to taunt King Hezekiah, challenging him and mocking him for putting his faith in God.

Hezekiah was steadfast in his faith. Even though the Assyrians had a vast and powerful army, he was confident God would rescue them. Their army was powerful, but so was his God. God had spoken through the prophet Isaiah and promised to cut down Sennacherib and the Assyrians.

Sennacherib sent a message to Hezekiah saying, "Don't let your God in whom you trust mislead you when he says, 'Jerusalem will not be handed over to the king of Assyria.' Certainly you have heard how the kings of Assyria have annihilated all lands. Do you really think you will be rescued?" (2 Kgs 19:10–11).

The easiest way to make us lose our faith, falter in obedience, and go our own way is to make us question what God has said. In the garden of Eden, the serpent made Eve question what God had commanded her: "Is it really true that God said . . . ?" (Gen 3:1). Eve doubted God's words; she trusted herself instead of her God.

When Hezekiah's enemy wanted to gain a foothold, he did the same thing. He undermined what God had said, forcing Hezekiah to make a decision. Would he hold fast to his faith and believe in the power and sovereignty of his God, or would he cower in fear to an enemy who had defeated much stronger nations?

Elisabeth Elliot gives us a great reminder:

"Don't dig up in doubt what you planted in faith."

What God has said, we can believe. When our enemy tempts us with doubt and fear, we must remember what God has planted in our hearts in faith. We can place our trust in Him because He is trustworthy. Human promises, temporary securities, and self-sufficiency will always fail. The one thing that remains secure is the promise of God. He's given us an entire Bible full of promises. Let's plant them deep in our hearts.

In ancient times I planned it;
and now I am bringing it to pass.
The plan is this:
Fortified cities will crash
into heaps of ruins.
26 Their residents are powerless,
they are terrified and ashamed.
They are as short-lived as plants in the field,
or green vegetation.
They are as short-lived as grass on the rooftops
when it is scorched by the east wind.
27 I know where you live
and everything you do.
28 Because you rage against me,
and the uproar you create has reached my ears,
I will put my hook in your nose,
and my bridle between your lips,
and I will lead you back the way
you came."

29 "'This will be your confirmation that I have spoken the truth:
This year you will eat what grows wild, and next year what grows
on its own from that. But in the third year you will plant seed
and harvest crops; you will plant vines and consume their produce. 30 Those who remain in Judah will take root in the ground
and bear fruit.
31 "'For a remnant will leave Jerusalem;
survivors will come out of Mount Zion.
The zeal of the LORD of Heaven's
Armies will accomplish this.
32 So this is what the LORD has said
about the king of Assyria:
"He will not enter this city,
nor will he shoot an arrow here.
He will not attack it with his shield-carrying warriors,
nor will he build siege works against it.
33 He will go back the way he came.
He will not enter this city," says the LORD.

34 "'I will shield this city and rescue it for the sake of my reputation and because of my promise to David my servant.'"
35 That very night the angel of the LORD went out and killed
185,000 in the Assyrian camp. When they got up early the next
morning, there were all the corpses. 36 So King Sennacherib of
Assyria broke camp and went on his way. He went home and
stayed in Nineveh. 37 One day, as he was worshiping in the temple
of his god Nisroch, his sons Adrammelech and Sharezer struck
him down with the sword. They escaped to the land of Ararat;
his son Esarhaddon replaced him as king.

HEZEKIAH IS HEALED

20 In those days Hezekiah was stricken with a terminal illness. The prophet Isaiah son of Amoz visited him and
told him, "This is what the LORD has said, 'Give your household

instructions, for you are about to die; you will not get well.'" 2 He turned his face to the wall and prayed to the LORD, 3 "Please, LORD. Remember how I have served you faithfully and with wholehearted devotion, and how I have carried out your will." Then Hezekiah wept bitterly.

4 Isaiah had not yet left the middle courtyard when the LORD's message came to him, 5 "Go back and tell Hezekiah, the leader of my people: 'This is what the LORD God of your ancestor David has said: "I have heard your prayer; I have seen your tears. Look, I will heal you. The day after tomorrow you will go up to the LORD's temple. 6 I will add fifteen years to your life and rescue you and this city from the king of Assyria. I will shield this city for the sake of my reputation and because of my promise to David my servant."'" 7 Isaiah ordered, "Get a fig cake." So they did as he ordered and placed it on the ulcerated sore, and he recovered.

8 Hezekiah had said to Isaiah, "What is the confirming sign that the LORD will heal me and that I will go up to the LORD's temple the day after tomorrow?" 9 Isaiah replied, "This is your sign from the LORD confirming that the LORD will do what he has said. Do you want the shadow to move ahead ten steps or to go back ten steps?" 10 Hezekiah answered, "It is easy for the shadow to lengthen ten steps, but not for it to go back ten steps." 11 Isaiah the prophet called out to the LORD, and the LORD made the shadow go back ten steps on the stairs of Ahaz.

MESSENGERS FROM BABYLON VISIT HEZEKIAH

12 At that time Merodach Baladan son of Baladan, king of Babylon, sent messengers with letters and a gift to Hezekiah, for he had heard that Hezekiah was ill. 13 Hezekiah welcomed them and showed them his whole storehouse, with its silver, gold, spices, and high quality olive oil, as well as his armory and everything in his treasuries. Hezekiah showed them everything in his palace and in his whole kingdom. 14 Isaiah the prophet visited King Hezekiah and asked him, "What did these men say? Where do they come from?" Hezekiah replied, "They come from the distant land of Babylon." 15 Isaiah asked, "What have they seen in your palace?" Hezekiah replied, "They have seen everything in my palace. I showed them everything in my treasuries." 16 Isaiah said to Hezekiah, "Listen to the LORD's message, 17 'Look, a time is coming when everything in your palace and the things your ancestors have accumulated to this day will be carried away to Babylon; nothing will be left,' says the LORD. 18 'Some of your very own descendants whom you father will be taken away and will be made eunuchs in the palace of the king of Babylon.'" 19 Hezekiah said to Isaiah, "The LORD's message which you have announced is appropriate." Then he added, "At least there will be peace and stability during my lifetime."

20 The rest of the events of Hezekiah's reign and all his accomplishments, including how he built a pool and conduit to bring water into the city, are recorded in the scroll called the Annals of the Kings of Judah. 21 Hezekiah passed away and his son Manasseh replaced him as king.

MANASSEH'S REIGN OVER JUDAH

21 Manasseh was twelve years old when he became king, and he reigned for fifty-five years in Jerusalem. His mother was Hephzibah. 2 He did evil in the sight of the LORD and committed the same horrible sins practiced by the nations whom the LORD drove out before the Israelites. 3 He rebuilt the high places that his father Hezekiah had destroyed; he set up altars for Baal and made an Asherah pole just as King Ahab of Israel had done. He bowed down to all the stars in the sky and worshiped them. 4 He built altars in the LORD's temple, about which the LORD had said, "Jerusalem will be my home." 5 In the two courtyards of the LORD's temple he built altars for all the stars in the sky. 6 He passed his son through the fire and practiced divination and omen reading. He set up a ritual pit to conjure up underworld spirits and appointed magicians to supervise it. He did a great amount of evil in the sight of the LORD, provoking him to anger. 7 He put an idol of Asherah he had made in the temple, about which the LORD had said to David and to his son Solomon, "This temple in Jerusalem, which I have chosen out of all the tribes of Israel, will be my permanent home. 8 I will not make Israel again leave the land I gave to their ancestors, provided that they carefully obey all I commanded them, the whole law my servant Moses ordered them to obey." 9 But they did not obey, and Manasseh misled them so that they sinned more than the nations whom the LORD had destroyed from before the Israelites.

10 So the LORD announced through his servants the prophets: 11 "King Manasseh of Judah has committed horrible sins. He has sinned more than the Amorites before him and has encouraged Judah to sin by worshiping his disgusting idols. 12 So this is what the LORD God of Israel has said, 'I am about to bring disaster on Jerusalem and Judah. The news will reverberate in the ears of those who hear about it. 13 I will destroy Jerusalem the same way I did Samaria and the dynasty of Ahab. I will wipe Jerusalem clean, just as one wipes a plate on both sides. 14 I will abandon this last remaining tribe among my people and hand them over to their enemies; they will be plundered and robbed by all their enemies, 15 because they have done evil in my sight and have angered me from the time their ancestors left Egypt right up to this very day!'"

16 Furthermore Manasseh killed so many innocent people, he stained Jerusalem with their blood from end to end, in addition to encouraging Judah to sin by doing evil in the sight of the LORD.

17 The rest of the events of Manasseh's reign and all his accomplishments, as well as the sinful acts he committed, are recorded in the scroll called the Annals of the Kings of Judah. 18 Manasseh passed away and was buried in his palace garden, the garden of Uzzah, and his son Amon replaced him as king.

AMON'S REIGN OVER JUDAH

19 Amon was twenty-two years old when he became king, and he reigned for two years in Jerusalem. His mother was Meshullemeth, the daughter of Haruz, from Jotbah. 20 He did evil in the sight of the LORD, just as his father Manasseh had done. 21 He followed in the footsteps of his father and worshiped and bowed

down to the disgusting idols that his father had worshiped. 22 He abandoned the LORD, God of his ancestors, and did not follow the LORD's instructions. 23 Amon's servants conspired against him and killed the king in his palace. 24 The people of the land executed all those who had conspired against King Amon, and they made his son Josiah king in his place.

25 The rest of Amon's accomplishments are recorded in the scroll called the Annals of the Kings of Judah. 26 He was buried in his tomb in the garden of Uzzah, and his son Josiah replaced him as king.

JOSIAH REPENTS

22 Josiah was eight years old when he became king, and he reigned for thirty-one years in Jerusalem. His mother was Jedidah, daughter of Adaiah, from Bozkath. 2 He did what the LORD approved and followed in his ancestor David's footsteps; he did not deviate to the right or the left.

3 In the eighteenth year of King Josiah's reign, the king sent the scribe Shaphan son of Azaliah, son of Meshullam, to the LORD's temple with these orders: 4 "Go up to Hilkiah the high priest and have him melt down the silver that has been brought by the people to the LORD's temple and has been collected by the guards at the door. 5 Have them hand it over to the construction foremen assigned to the LORD's temple. They in turn should pay the temple workers to repair it, 6 including craftsmen, builders, and masons, and should buy wood and chiseled stone for the repair work. 7 Do not audit the foremen who disburse the silver, for they are honest."

8 Hilkiah the high priest informed Shaphan the scribe, "I found the scroll of the law in the LORD's temple." Hilkiah gave the scroll to Shaphan and he read it. 9 Shaphan the scribe went to the king and reported, "Your servants melted down the silver in the temple and handed it over to the construction foremen assigned to the LORD's temple." 10 Then Shaphan the scribe told the king, "Hilkiah the priest has given me a scroll." Shaphan read it out loud before the king. 11 When the king heard the words of the law scroll, he tore his clothes. 12 The king ordered Hilkiah the priest, Ahikam son of Shaphan, Achbor son of Micaiah, Shaphan the scribe, and Asaiah the king's servant, 13 "Go, seek an oracle from the LORD for me and the people—for all Judah. Find out about the words of this scroll that has been discovered. For the LORD's great fury has been ignited against us, because our ancestors have not obeyed the words of this scroll by doing all that it instructs us to do."

14 So Hilkiah the priest, Ahikam, Achbor, Shaphan, and Asaiah *went to Huldah the* prophetess, the wife of Shullam son of Tikvah, the son of Harhas, the supervisor of the wardrobe. (She lived in Jerusalem in the Mishneh district.) They stated their business, 15 and she said to them: "This is what the LORD God of Israel has said: 'Say this to the man who sent you to me: 16 "This is what the LORD has said: 'I am about to bring disaster on this place and its residents, all the things in the scroll that the king of Judah has read. 17 This will happen because they have abandoned me and offered sacrifices to other gods, angering me with

all the idols they have made. My anger will ignite against this
place and will not be extinguished!'" 18 Say this to the king of Judah, who sent you to seek an oracle from the LORD: "This is what
the LORD God of Israel has said concerning the words you have
heard: 19 'You displayed a sensitive spirit and humbled yourself
before the LORD when you heard how I intended to make this
place and its residents into an appalling example of an accursed
people. You tore your clothes and wept before me, and I have
heard you,' says the LORD. 20 'Therefore I will allow you to die and
be buried in peace. You will not have to witness all the disaster I
will bring on this place.'"'" Then they reported back to the king.

THE KING INSTITUTES RELIGIOUS REFORM

23 The king summoned all the leaders of Judah and Jerusalem. 2 The king went up to the LORD's temple, accompanied by all the people of Judah, all the residents of Jerusalem,
the priests, and the prophets. All the people were there, from
the youngest to the oldest. He read aloud all the words of the
scroll of the covenant that had been discovered in the LORD's
temple. 3 The king stood by the pillar and renewed the covenant
before the LORD, agreeing to follow the LORD and to obey his
commandments, laws, and rules with all his heart and being, by
carrying out the terms of this covenant recorded on this scroll.
All the people agreed to keep the covenant.

4 The king ordered Hilkiah the high priest, the high-ranking
priests, and the guards to bring out of the LORD's temple all
the items that were used in the worship of Baal, Asherah, and
all the stars of the sky. The king burned them outside of Jerusalem in the terraces of Kidron, and carried their ashes to Bethel.
5 He eliminated the pagan priests whom the kings of Judah had
appointed to offer sacrifices on the high places in the cities of
Judah and in the area right around Jerusalem. (They offered sacrifices to Baal, the sun god, the moon god, the constellations, and
all the stars in the sky.) 6 He removed the Asherah pole from the
LORD's temple and took it outside Jerusalem to the Kidron Valley, where he burned it. He smashed it to dust and then threw
the dust in the public graveyard. 7 He tore down the quarters of
the male cultic prostitutes in the LORD's temple, where women
were weaving shrines for Asherah.

8 He brought all the priests from the cities of Judah and ruined the high places where the priests had offered sacrifices,
from Geba to Beer Sheba. He tore down the high place of the
goat idols situated at the entrance of the gate of Joshua, the city
official, on the left side of the city gate. 9 (Now the priests of the
high places did not go up to the altar of the LORD in Jerusalem,
but they did eat unleavened cakes among their fellow priests.)
10 The king ruined Topheth in the Valley of Ben Hinnom so that
no one could pass his son or his daughter through the fire to
Molech. 11 He removed from the entrance to the LORD's temple
the statues of horses that the kings of Judah had placed there in
honor of the sun god. (They were kept near the room of Nathan
Melech the eunuch, which was situated among the courtyards.)
He burned up the chariots devoted to the sun god. 12 The king
tore down the altars the kings of Judah had set up on the roof

of Ahaz's upper room, as well as the altars Manasseh had set up
in the two courtyards of the LORD's temple. He crushed them
and threw the dust in the Kidron Valley. 13 The king ruined the
high places east of Jerusalem, south of the Mount of Destruction, that King Solomon of Israel had built for the detestable
Sidonian goddess Astarte, the detestable Moabite god Chemosh,
and the horrible Ammonite god Milcom. 14 He smashed the sacred pillars to bits, cut down the Asherah poles, and filled those
shrines with human bones.

15 He also tore down the altar in Bethel at the high place made
by Jeroboam son of Nebat, who encouraged Israel to sin. He
burned all the combustible items at that high place and crushed
them to dust, including the Asherah pole. 16 When Josiah turned
around, he saw the tombs there on the hill. So he ordered the
bones from the tombs to be brought; he burned them on the
altar and defiled it, just as in the LORD's message that was announced by the prophet while Jeroboam stood by the altar during a festival. Then the king turned and saw the grave of the
prophet who had foretold this. 17 He asked, "What is this grave
marker I see?" The men from the city replied, "It's the grave of
the prophet who came from Judah and foretold these very things
you have done to the altar of Bethel." 18 The king said, "Leave it
alone! No one must touch his bones." So they left his bones undisturbed, as well as the bones of the Israelite prophet buried
beside him.

19 Josiah also removed all the shrines on the high places in the
cities of Samaria. The kings of Israel had made them and angered
the LORD. He did to them what he had done to the high place in
Bethel. 20 He sacrificed all the priests of the high places on the
altars located there, and burned human bones on them. Then
he returned to Jerusalem.

21 The king ordered all the people, "Observe the Passover of
the LORD your God, as prescribed in this scroll of the covenant."
22 He issued this edict because a Passover like this had not been
observed since the days of the judges who led Israel; it was neglected for the entire period of the kings of Israel and Judah.
23 But in the eighteenth year of King Josiah's reign, such a Passover of the LORD was observed in Jerusalem.

24 Josiah also got rid of the ritual pits used to conjure up spirits, the magicians, personal idols, disgusting images, and all the
detestable idols that had appeared in the land of Judah and in
Jerusalem. In this way he carried out the terms of the law recorded on the scroll that Hilkiah the priest had discovered in
the LORD's temple. 25 No king before or after repented before
the LORD as he did, with his whole heart, soul, and being in accordance with the whole law of Moses.

26 Yet the LORD's great anger against Judah did not subside; he
was still infuriated by all the things Manasseh had done. 27 The
LORD announced, "I will also spurn Judah, just as I spurned Israel. I will reject this city that I chose—both Jerusalem and the
temple, about which I said, 'I will live there.'

28 The rest of the events of Josiah's reign and all his accomplishments are recorded in the scroll called the Annals of the
Kings of Judah. 29 During Josiah's reign Pharaoh Necho king of

REFLECT

Why was the faithfulness of King Josiah so significant? How did it change the course of the nation of Judah?

Egypt marched toward the Euphrates River to help the king of
Assyria. King Josiah marched out to fight him, but Necho killed
him at Megiddo when he saw him. [30] His servants transported
his dead body from Megiddo in a chariot and brought it to Jerusalem, where they buried him in his tomb. The people of the
land took Josiah's son Jehoahaz, poured olive oil on his head, and
made him king in his father's place.

JEHOAHAZ'S REIGN OVER JUDAH

[31] Jehoahaz was twenty-three years old when he became king,
and he reigned three months in Jerusalem. His mother was
Hamutal the daughter of Jeremiah, from Libnah. [32] He did evil
in the sight of the LORD as his ancestors had done. [33] Pharaoh
Necho imprisoned him in Riblah in the land of Hamath and
prevented him from ruling in Jerusalem. He imposed on the
land a special tax of 100 talents of silver and a talent of gold.
[34] Pharaoh Necho made Josiah's son Eliakim king in Josiah's
place, and changed his name to Jehoiakim. He took Jehoahaz to
Egypt, where he died. [35] Jehoiakim paid Pharaoh the required
amount of silver and gold, but to meet Pharaoh's demands Jehoiakim had to tax the land. He collected an assessed amount
from each man among the people of the land in order to pay
Pharaoh Necho.

JEHOIAKIM'S REIGN OVER JUDAH

[36] Jehoiakim was twenty-five years old when he became king,
and he reigned for eleven years in Jerusalem. His mother was
Zebidah the daughter of Pedaiah, from Rumah. [37] He did evil in
the sight of the LORD as his ancestors had done.

24 During Jehoiakim's reign, King Nebuchadnezzar of Babylon attacked. Jehoiakim was his subject for three years,
but then he rebelled against him. [2] The LORD sent against him
Babylonian, Syrian, Moabite, and Ammonite raiding bands; he
sent them to destroy Judah, just as in the LORD's message that
he had announced through his servants the prophets. [3] Just as
the LORD had announced, he rejected Judah because of all the
sins that Manasseh had committed. [4] Because he killed innocent people and stained Jerusalem with their blood, the LORD
was unwilling to forgive them.

[5] The rest of the events of Jehoiakim's reign and all his accomplishments, are recorded in the scroll called the Annals of the
Kings of Judah. [6] He passed away and his son Jehoiachin replaced
him as king. [7] The king of Egypt did not march out from his land
again, for the king of Babylon conquered all the territory that
the king of Egypt had formerly controlled between the Stream
of Egypt and the Euphrates River.

JEHOIACHIN'S REIGN OVER JUDAH

[8] Jehoiachin was eighteen years old when he became king, and he
reigned three months in Jerusalem. His mother was Nehushta
the daughter of Elnathan, from Jerusalem. [9] He did evil in the
sight of the LORD as his ancestors had done.

[10] At that time the generals of King Nebuchadnezzar of
Babylon marched to Jerusalem and besieged the city. [11] King

Nebuchadnezzar of Babylon came to the city while his generals were besieging it. 12 King Jehoiachin of Judah, along with
his mother, his servants, his officials, and his eunuchs surrendered to the king of Babylon. The king of Babylon, in the
eighth year of his reign, took Jehoiachin prisoner. 13 Nebuchadnezzar took from there all the riches in the treasuries
of the LORD's temple and of the royal palace. He removed all
the gold items that King Solomon of Israel had made for the
LORD's temple, just as the LORD had warned. 14 He deported
all the residents of Jerusalem, including all the officials and
all the soldiers (10,000 people in all). This included all the
craftsmen and those who worked with metal. No one was left
except for the poorest among the people of the land. 15 He deported Jehoiachin from Jerusalem to Babylon, along with the
king's mother and wives, his eunuchs, and the high-ranking
officials of the land. 16 The king of Babylon deported to Babylon
all the soldiers (there were 7,000), as well as 1,000 craftsmen
and metal workers. This included all the best warriors. 17 The
king of Babylon made Mattaniah, Jehoiachin's uncle, king in
Jehoiachin's place. He renamed him Zedekiah.

ZEDEKIAH'S REIGN OVER JUDAH

18 Zedekiah was twenty-one years old when he became king, and
he ruled for eleven years in Jerusalem. His mother was Hamutal, the daughter of Jeremiah, from Libnah. 19 He did evil in the
sight of the LORD, as Jehoiakim had done.

20 What follows is a record of what happened to Jerusalem and
Judah because of the LORD's anger; he finally threw them out
of his presence. Zedekiah rebelled against the king of Babylon.

25 1 So King Nebuchadnezzar of Babylon came against Jerusalem with his whole army and set up camp outside
it. They built siege ramps all around it. He arrived on the tenth
day of the tenth month in the ninth year of Zedekiah's reign.
2 The city remained under siege until King Zedekiah's eleventh
year. 3 By the ninth day of the fourth month the famine in the
city was so severe the residents had no food. 4 The enemy broke
through the city walls, and all the soldiers tried to escape. They
left the city during the night. They went through the gate between the two walls, which is near the king's garden. (The Babylonians were all around the city.) Then they headed for the rift
valley. 5 But the Babylonian army chased after the king. They
caught up with him in the rift valley plains of Jericho, and his
entire army deserted him. 6 They captured the king and brought
him up to the king of Babylon at Riblah, where he passed sentence on him. 7 Zedekiah's sons were executed while Zedekiah
was forced to watch. The king of Babylon then had Zedekiah's
eyes put out, bound him in bronze chains, and carried him off
to Babylon.

NEBUCHADNEZZAR DESTROYS JERUSALEM

8 On the seventh day of the fifth month, in the nineteenth year
of King Nebuchadnezzar of Babylon, Nebuzaradan, the captain
of the royal guard, who served the king of Babylon, arrived in Jerusalem. 9 He burned down the LORD's temple, the royal palace,

and all the houses in Jerusalem, including every large house. 10 The whole Babylonian army that came with the captain of the royal guard tore down the walls that surrounded Jerusalem. 11 Nebuzaradan, the captain of the royal guard, deported the rest of the people who were left in the city, those who had deserted to the king of Babylon, and the rest of the craftsmen. 12 But he left behind some of the poor of the land and gave them fields and vineyards.

REFLECT

How does the destruction of Judah display God's patience with His people?

13 The Babylonians broke the two bronze pillars in the LORD's temple, as well as the movable stands and the big bronze basin called "The Sea." They took the bronze to Babylon. 14 They also took the pots, shovels, trimming shears, pans, and all the bronze utensils used by the priests. 15 The captain of the royal guard took the golden and silver censers and basins. 16 The bronze of the items that King Solomon made for the LORD's temple—including the two pillars, the big bronze basin called "The Sea," the twelve bronze bulls under "The Sea," and the movable stands—was too heavy to be weighed. 17 Each of the pillars was about twenty-seven feet high. The bronze top of one pillar was about 4½ feet high and had bronze latticework and pomegranate-shaped ornaments all around it. The second pillar with its latticework was like it.

18 The captain of the royal guard took Seraiah, the chief priest, and Zephaniah, the priest who was second in rank, and the three doorkeepers. 19 From the city he took a eunuch who was in charge of the soldiers, five of the king's advisers who were discovered in the city, an official army secretary who drafted citizens for military service, and sixty citizens from the people of the land who were discovered in the city. 20 Nebuzaradan, captain of the royal guard, took them and brought them to the king of Babylon at Riblah. 21 The king of Babylon ordered them to be executed at Riblah in the territory of Hamath. So Judah was deported from its land.

GEDALIAH APPOINTED GOVERNOR

22 Now King Nebuchadnezzar of Babylon appointed Gedaliah son of Ahikam, son of Shaphan, as governor over the people whom he allowed to remain in the land of Judah. 23 All the officers of the Judahite army and their troops heard that the king of Babylon had appointed Gedaliah to govern. So they came to Gedaliah at Mizpah. The officers who came were Ishmael son of Nethaniah, Johanan son of Kareah, Seraiah son of Tanhumeth the Netophathite, and Jaazaniah son of the Maacathite. 24 Gedaliah took an oath so as to give them and their troops some assurance of safety. He said, "You don't need to be afraid to submit to the Babylonian officials. Settle down in the land and submit to the king of Babylon. Then things will go well for you." 25 But in the seventh month Ishmael son of Nethaniah, son of Elishama, who was a member of the royal family, came with ten of his men and murdered Gedaliah, as well as the Judeans and Babylonians who were with him at Mizpah. 26 Then all the people, from the youngest to the oldest, as well as the army officers, left for Egypt, because they were afraid of what the Babylonians might do.

JEHOIACHIN IN BABYLON

27 In the thirty-seventh year of the exile of King Jehoiachin of Judah, on the twenty-seventh day of the twelfth month, King Evil
Merodach of Babylon, in the first year of his reign, pardoned
King Jehoiachin of Judah and released him from prison. 28 He
spoke kindly to him and gave him a more prestigious position
than the other kings who were with him in Babylon. 29 Jehoiachin took off his prison clothes and ate daily in the king's presence for the rest of his life. 30 He was given daily provisions by
the king for the rest of his life until the day he died.

O Lord,
there is
NONE like you;
There IS No GOD
besides you!
What we
have heard
is TRUE!

MEMORY VERSE

"O Lord, for the sake of your servant and according to your will, you have done this great thing in order to reveal your greatness. O Lord, there is none like you; there is no God besides you! What we heard is true!"

1 Chronicles 17:19–20

1 Chronicles

INTRODUCTION

A Covenant-Keeping God

First Chronicles was originally written as a message to the Jews who had returned to Jerusalem from exile in Babylon. The covenant faithfulness of God is the main focus, as it displays the ways God saved and restored Judah. First Chronicles focuses on the life of David, reminding the Jews of their rich spiritual heritage and encouraging them to establish the worship of God as the center of their life.

The Book of 1 Chronicles begins with a record of the nation of Israel. The chronicler emphasized the Israelites' continuity with their past as the remnant returned to Jerusalem to rebuild the temple. The remainder of 1 Chronicles recounts the life of David, to whom God had promised that He would always keep one of his descendants on the throne. The chronicler reminds the people of God's faithfulness to His promises and His covenant by retelling David's life and legacy.

The events in 1 Chronicles take place during the reign of David, about 1010 to 970 B.C. The book was likely written around 425 B.C. by Ezra, as Jewish tradition identifies. First and 2 Chronicles were originally one book, and the overall consistency of style indicates that although several contributors may have worked on it, one editor shaped the final product. Jewish tradition holds that the book was compiled by Ezra, who used several sources and documents to reconstruct Israel's history.

The Book of 1 Chronicles displays the covenant-keeping character of God. Written to inspire the remnant of Judah to follow in the spiritual footsteps of David, this book reveals the way God's kingdom and people prevail because of His faithfulness. By understanding that our God today is the same God who established, protected, and redeemed Judah, we can more clearly see the covenant faithfulness He displays in our own lives and love Him greatly.

Myanmar

OFFICIAL LANGUAGE
Burmese
POPULATION
53,973,000
UNREACHED POPULATION
45,093,000
PROFESSING CHRISTIANS
8.1%

Moo's Home

Say a Prayer Today

Pray for the church in Myanmar, as it faces much opposition from the government and political leaders. Pray that believers in Christ will be able to practice their faith and that God would bless their faithfulness in persecution.

HISTORY BIT

Adoniram Judson translated the complete Bible from the original Greek and Hebrew into Burmese in 1834. He also wrote what is now a standard Burmese dictionary, published in 1826.*

Source Information:
https://joshuaproject.net/countries/BM
*https://www.britannica.com/biography/Adoniram-Judson

MOO'S STORY

My family has a strong traditional culture. From the Karen family in Myanmar (formerly Burma), we have a rich history of tradition tied to the Karen people. For a long time, even though I was a Christian, I still participated in traditional religious practices, like many who live in Myanmar.

My family has a long history of pagan religious practices. My grandfather was a healer of sorts who worked with a bad spirit. He often engaged in magic and miraculous healings. Sick people often came to him to be healed. My grandfather called himself a Christian, even though he still practiced magic.

My parents suffered a great deal as well. They were very poor, despite working incredibly hard. During the Second World War, my mother's house was burned down and all their land was taken away by the government. Bitterness entered my heart as I watched my parents suffer.

I began to recognize the generational sin that existed in our family. I asked God for forgiveness and began to seek Him with my whole life and heart. I asked Him to make my generation and the generation of my children new and that we would no longer continue in the sinful ways of our ancestors. He is faithful. I have seen God renew my life and my family. He forgave my sins and made me new. He has a blessing for me every day, and I thank Him for showing me the truth and for pursuing my heart every day.

4 WEEK READING PLAN

LOVE HIS WORD

	MONDAY	TUESDAY	WEDNESDAY	THURSDAY	FRIDAY
1	1 Chronicles 1-2	1 Chronicles 3-4	1 Chronicles 5-6	1 Chronicles 7:1—9:1a	1 Chronicles 9:1b-44
	SOAP Genesis 29:31-35	SOAP Genesis 30:4-8	SOAP Genesis 30:9-13	SOAP Genesis 30:17-21	SOAP Genesis 30:22-24
2	1 Chronicles 10	1 Chronicles 11	1 Chronicles 12	1 Chronicles 13-14	1 Chronicles 15
	SOAP Psalm 139:1-5	SOAP Psalm 139:6-10	SOAP Psalm 139:11-13	SOAP Psalm 139:14-16	SOAP Psalm 139:17-18
3	1 Chronicles 16	1 Chronicles 17-18	1 Chronicles 19-20	1 Chronicles 21:1—22:1	1 Chronicles 22:2-19
	SOAP Psalm 96:1-4	SOAP 1 Chronicles 17:19-20	SOAP Psalm 46:1-3	SOAP Psalm 30:3-5	SOAP Psalm 30:10-12
4	1 Chronicles 23	1 Chronicles 24	1 Chronicles 25-26	1 Chronicles 27-28	1 Chronicles 29
	SOAP Psalm 72:1-3	SOAP Psalm 72:7-9	SOAP Psalm 72:11-14	SOAP Psalm 72:16-17	SOAP Psalm 72:18-20

ADAM'S DESCENDANTS

1 Adam, Seth, Enosh, 2 Kenan, Mahalalel, Jered, 3 Enoch, Methuselah, Lamech, 4 Noah, Shem, Ham, and Japheth.

JAPHETH'S DESCENDANTS

5 The sons of Japheth: Gomer, Magog, Madai, Javan, Tubal, Meshech, and Tiras.
6 The sons of Gomer: Ashkenaz, Riphath, and Togarmah.
7 The sons of Javan: Elishah, Tarshish, the Kittites, and the
Rodanites.

HAM'S DESCENDANTS

8 The sons of Ham: Cush, Mizraim, Put, and Canaan.
9 The sons of Cush: Seba, Havilah, Sabta, Raamah, and Sabteca.
The sons of Raamah: Sheba and Dedan.
10 Cush was the father of Nimrod, who established himself as
a mighty warrior on earth.
11 Mizraim was the father of the Ludites, Anamites, Lehabites,
Naphtuhites, 12 Pathrusites, Casluhites (from whom the Philistines descended), and the Caphtorites.
13 Canaan was the father of Sidon—his firstborn—and Heth, 14 as
well as the Jebusites, Amorites, Girgashites, 15 Hivites, Arkites,
Sinites, 16 Arvadites, Zemarites, and Hamathites.

SHEM'S DESCENDANTS

17 The sons of Shem: Elam, Asshur, Arphaxad, Lud, and Aram.
The sons of Aram: Uz, Hul, Gether, and Meshech.
18 Arphaxad was the father of Shelah, and Shelah was the father of Eber. 19 Two sons were born to Eber: the first was named
Peleg, for during his lifetime the earth was divided; his brother's name was Joktan.
20 Joktan was the father of Almodad, Sheleph, Hazarmaveth,
Jerah, 21 Hadoram, Uzal, Diklah, 22 Ebal, Abimael, Sheba, 23 Ophir,
Havilah, and Jobab. All these were the sons of Joktan.
24 Shem, Arphaxad, Shelah, 25 Eber, Peleg, Reu, 26 Serug, Nahor,
Terah, 27 Abram (that is, Abraham).
28 The sons of Abraham: Isaac and Ishmael.
29 These were their descendants:

ISHMAEL'S DESCENDANTS

Ishmael's firstborn son was Nebaioth; the others were Kedar,
Adbeel, Mibsam, 30 Mishma, Dumah, Massa, Hadad, Tema, 31 Jetur, Naphish, and Kedemah. These were the sons of Ishmael.

KETURAH'S DESCENDANTS

32 The sons to whom Keturah, Abraham's concubine, gave birth:
Zimran, Jokshan, Medan, Midian, Ishbak, Shuah.
The sons of Jokshan: Sheba and Dedan.
33 The sons of Midian: Ephah, Epher, Hanoch, Abida, and Eldaah. All these were the sons of Keturah.

ISAAC'S DESCENDANTS

34 Abraham was the father of Isaac. The sons of Isaac: Esau and
Israel.

ESAU'S DESCENDANTS

35 The sons of Esau: Eliphaz, Reuel, Jeush, Jalam, and Korah.

36 The sons of Eliphaz: Teman, Omar, Zephi, Gatam, Kenaz, and (by Timna) Amalek.

37 The sons of Reuel: Nahath, Zerah, Shammah, and Mizzah.

THE DESCENDANTS OF SEIR

38 The sons of Seir: Lotan, Shobal, Zibeon, Anah, Dishon, Ezer, and Dishan.

39 The sons of Lotan: Hori and Homam. (Timna was Lotan's sister.)

40 The sons of Shobal: Alyan, Manahath, Ebal, Shephi, and Onam.

The sons of Zibeon: Aiah and Anah.

41 The son of Anah: Dishon.

The sons of Dishon: Hamran, Eshban, Ithran, and Keran.

42 The sons of Ezer: Bilhan, Zaavan, Jaakan.

The sons of Dishan: Uz and Aran.

KINGS OF EDOM

43 These were the kings who reigned in the land of Edom before any king ruled over the Israelites: Bela son of Beor; the name of his city was Dinhabah.

44 When Bela died, Jobab son of Zerah from Bozrah, succeeded him.

45 When Jobab died, Husham from the land of the Temanites succeeded him.

46 When Husham died, Hadad son of Bedad succeeded him. He struck down the Midianites in the plains of Moab; the name of his city was Avith.

47 When Hadad died, Samlah from Masrekah succeeded him.

48 When Samlah died, Shaul from Rehoboth on the River succeeded him.

49 When Shaul died, Baal Hanan son of Achbor succeeded him.

50 When Baal Hanan died, Hadad succeeded him; the name of his city was Pai. His wife was Mehetabel, daughter of Matred, daughter of Me-Zahab.

51 Hadad died.

TRIBAL CHIEFS OF EDOM

The tribal chiefs of Edom were: Timna, Alvah, Jetheth, 52 Oholibamah, Elah, Pinon, 53 Kenaz, Teman, Mibzar, 54 Magdiel, and
Iram. These were the tribal chiefs of Edom.

ISRAEL'S DESCENDANTS

2 These were the sons of Israel: Reuben, Simeon, Levi, and Judah; Issachar and Zebulun;

2 Dan, Joseph, and Benjamin;

Naphtali, Gad, and Asher.

JUDAH'S DESCENDANTS

3 The sons of Judah: Er, Onan, and Shelah. These three were born to him by Bathshua, a Canaanite woman. Er, Judah's firstborn, displeased the LORD, so the LORD killed him.

4 Tamar, Judah's daughter-in-law, bore to him Perez and Zerah.
Judah had five sons in all.

5 The sons of Perez: Hezron and Hamul.

6 The sons of Zerah: Zimri, Ethan, Heman, Kalkol, Dara—five
in all.

7 The son of Carmi: Achan, who brought the disaster on Israel
when he stole what was devoted to God.

8 The son of Ethan: Azariah.

9 The sons born to Hezron: Jerahmeel, Ram, and Caleb.

RAM'S DESCENDANTS

10 Ram was the father of Amminadab, and Amminadab was the
father of Nahshon, the tribal chief of Judah. 11 Nahshon was the
father of Salma, and Salma was the father of Boaz. 12 Boaz was
the father of Obed, and Obed was the father of Jesse.

13 Jesse was the father of Eliab, his firstborn; Abinadab was born
second, Shimea third, 14 Nethanel fourth, Raddai fifth, 15 Ozem
sixth, and David seventh. 16 Their sisters were Zeruiah and Abigail. Zeruiah's three sons were Abshai, Joab, and Asahel. 17 Abigail
bore Amasa, whose father was Jether the Ishmaelite.

CALEB'S DESCENDANTS

18 Caleb son of Hezron fathered sons by his wife Azubah (also
known as Jerioth). Her sons were Jesher, Shobab, and Ardon.
19 When Azubah died, Caleb married Ephrath, who bore him Hur.
20 Hur was the father of Uri, and Uri was the father of Bezalel.

21 Later Hezron slept with the daughter of Makir, the father
of Gilead. (He had married her when he was sixty years old.)
She bore him Segub. 22 Segub was the father of Jair, who owned
twenty-three cities in the land of Gilead. 23 (Geshur and Aram
captured the towns of Jair, along with Kenath and its sixty surrounding towns.) All these were descendants of Makir, the father of Gilead.

24 After Hezron's death, Caleb slept with Ephrath, his father
Hezron's widow, and she bore to him Ashhur the father of Tekoa.

JERAHMEEL'S DESCENDANTS

25 The sons of Jerahmeel, Hezron's firstborn, were Ram, the firstborn, Bunah, Oren, Ozem, and Ahijah. 26 Jerahmeel had another
wife named Atarah; she was Onam's mother.

27 The sons of Ram, Jerahmeel's firstborn, were Maaz, Jamin,
and Eker.

28 The sons of Onam were Shammai and Jada.

The sons of Shammai: Nadab and Abishur.

29 Abishur's wife was Abihail, who bore him Ahban and Mo-
lid. 30 The sons of Nadab: Seled and Appaim. (Seled died without having sons.)

31 The son of Appaim: Ishi.

The son of Ishi: Sheshan.

The son of Sheshan: Ahlai.

32 The sons of Jada, Shammai's brother: Jether and Jonathan.
(Jether died without having sons.)

33 The sons of Jonathan: Peleth and Zaza.

These were the descendants of Jerahmeel.

34 Sheshan had no sons, only daughters. Sheshan had an Egyptian servant named Jarha. 35 Sheshan gave his daughter to his
servant Jarha as a wife; she bore him Attai.
36 Attai was the father of Nathan, and Nathan was the father
of Zabad. 37 Zabad was the father of Ephlal, and Ephlal was the
father of Obed. 38 Obed was the father of Jehu, and Jehu was the
father of Azariah. 39 Azariah was the father of Helez, and Helez
was the father of Eleasah. 40 Eleasah was the father of Sismai,
and Sismai was the father of Shallum. 41 Shallum was the father
of Jekamiah, and Jekamiah was the father of Elishama.

MORE OF CALEB'S DESCENDANTS

42 The sons of Caleb, Jerahmeel's brother: His firstborn Mesha,
the father of Ziph, and his second son Mareshah, the father of
Hebron.
43 The sons of Hebron: Korah, Tappuah, Rekem, and Shema.
44 Shema was the father of Raham, the father of Jorkeam. Rekem was the father of Shammai. 45 Shammai's son was Maon,
who was the father of Beth Zur.
46 Caleb's concubine Ephah bore Haran, Moza, and Gazez. Haran was the father of Gazez.
47 The sons of Jahdai: Regem, Jotham, Geshan, Pelet, Ephah,
and Shaaph.
48 Caleb's concubine Maacah bore Sheber and Tirhanah. 49 She
also bore Shaaph the father of Madmannah and Sheva the father of Machbenah and Gibea. Caleb's daughter was Achsah.
50 These were the descendants of Caleb.
The sons of Hur, the firstborn of Ephrath: Shobal, the father of
Kiriath Jearim, 51 Salma, the father of Bethlehem, and Hareph,
the father of Beth Gader.
52 The sons of Shobal, the father of Kiriath Jearim, were Ha-
roeh, half the Manahathites, 53 the clans of Kiriath Jearim—the
Ithrites, Puthites, Shumathites, and Mishraites. (The Zorathites
and Eshtaolites descended from these groups.)
54 The sons of Salma: Bethlehem, the Netophathites, Atroth
Beth Joab, half the Manahathites, the Zorites, 55 and the clans
of the scribes who lived in Jabez: the Tirathites, Shimeathites,
and Sucathites. These are the Kenites who descended from Hammath, the father of Beth Rechab.

DAVID'S DESCENDANTS

3 These were the sons of David who were born to him in Hebron:
The firstborn was Amnon, whose mother was Ahinoam
from Jezreel;
the second was Daniel, whose mother was Abigail from Carmel;
2 the third was Absalom whose mother was Maacah, daughter
of King Talmai of Geshur;
the fourth was Adonijah, whose mother was Haggith;
3 the fifth was Shephatiah, whose mother was Abital;
the sixth was Ithream, whose mother was Eglah, David's wife.
4 These six were born to David in Hebron, where he ruled for
seven years and six months.
He ruled thirty-three years in Jerusalem. 5 These were the sons
born to him in Jerusalem:

Shimea, Shobab, Nathan, and Solomon—the mother of these
four was Bathsheba the daughter of Ammiel.
6 The other nine were Ibhar, Elishua, Elpelet, 7 Nogah, Nepheg,
Japhia, 8 Elishama, Eliada, and Eliphelet.
9 These were all the sons of David, not counting the sons of his
concubines. Tamar was their sister.

SOLOMON'S DESCENDANTS

10 Solomon's son was Rehoboam,
followed by Abijah his son,
Asa his son,
Jehoshaphat his son,
11 Joram his son,
Ahaziah his son,
Joash his son,
12 Amaziah his son,
Azariah his son,
Jotham his son,
13 Ahaz his son,
Hezekiah his son,
Manasseh his son,
14 Amon his son,
Josiah his son.
15 The sons of Josiah: Johanan was the firstborn; Jehoiakim was
born second; Zedekiah third; and Shallum fourth.
16 The sons of Jehoiakim: his son Jehoiachin and his son Zedekiah.
17 The sons of Jehoiachin the exile: Shealtiel his son, 18 Malki-
ram, Pedaiah, Shenazzar, Jekamiah, Hoshama, and Nedabiah.
19 The sons of Pedaiah: Zerubbabel and Shimei.
The sons of Zerubbabel: Meshullam and Hananiah. Shelomith
was their sister.
20 The five others were Hashubah, Ohel, Berechiah, Hasadiah,
and Jushab Hesed.
21 The descendants of Hananiah: Pelatiah, Jeshaiah, the sons of
Rephaiah, of Arnan, of Obadiah, and of Shecaniah.
22 The descendants of Shecaniah: Shemaiah and his sons: Hattush, Igal, Bariah, Neariah, and Shaphat—six in all.
23 The sons of Neariah: Elioenai, Hizkiah, and Azrikam—three
in all.
24 The sons of Elioenai: Hodaviah, Eliashib, Pelaiah, Akkub, Johanan, Delaiah, and Anani—seven in all.

JUDAH'S DESCENDANTS

4 The descendants of Judah: Perez, Hezron, Carmi, Hur, and
Shobal.
2 Reaiah the son of Shobal was the father of Jahath, and Jahath was the father of Ahumai and Lahad. These were the clans
of the Zorathites.
3 These were the sons of Etam: Jezreel, Ishma, and Idbash. Their
sister was Hazzelelponi.
4 Penuel was the father of Gedor, and Ezer was the father of
Hushah. These were the descendants of Hur, the firstborn of
Ephrathah and the father of Bethlehem.

CHALLENGE

How do the genealogies of David's descendants show the fulfillment of the covenant given in 1 Chronicles 17? How does the genealogy in Matthew 1 provide even more insight into the fulfillment of this covenant?

5 Ashhur the father of Tekoa had two wives, Helah and Naarah. 6 Naarah bore him Ahuzzam, Hepher, Temeni, and Haahashtari. These were the sons of Naarah. 7 The sons of Helah: Zereth, Zohar, Ethnan, 8 and Koz, who was the father of Anub, Hazzobebah, and the clans of Aharhel the son of Harum.

9 Jabez was more respected than his brothers. His mother had named him Jabez, for she said, "I experienced pain when I gave birth to him." 10 Jabez called out to the God of Israel, "If only you would greatly bless me and expand my territory. May your hand be with me! Keep me from harm so I might not endure pain." God answered his prayer.

11 Kelub, the brother of Shuhah, was the father of Mehir, who was the father of Eshton. 12 Eshton was the father of Beth Rapha, Paseah, and Tehinnah, the father of Ir Nahash. These were the men of Recah.

13 The sons of Kenaz: Othniel and Seraiah.

The sons of Othniel: Hathath and Meonothai. 14 Meonothai was the father of Ophrah.

Seraiah was the father of Joab, the father of those who live in the Valley of the Craftsmen, for they were craftsmen.

15 The sons of Caleb son of Jephunneh: Iru, Elah, and Naam.

The son of Elah: Kenaz.

16 The sons of Jehallelel: Ziph, Ziphah, Tiria, and Asarel.

17 The sons of Ezrah: Jether, Mered, Epher, and Jalon.

Mered's wife Bithiah gave birth to Miriam, Shammai, and Ishbah, the father of Eshtemoa. 18 (His Judahite wife gave birth to Jered the father of Gedor, Heber the father of Soco, and Jekuthiel the father of Zanoah.) These were the sons of Pharaoh's daughter Bithiah, whom Mered married.

19 The sons of Hodiah's wife, the sister of Naham: the father of Keilah the Garmite, and Eshtemoa the Maacathite.

20 The sons of Shimon: Amnon, Rinnah, Ben Hanan, and Tilon.

The descendants of Ishi: Zoheth and Ben Zoheth.

21 The sons of Shelah son of Judah: Er the father of Lecah, Laadah the father of Mareshah, the clans of the linen workers at Beth Ashbea, 22 Jokim, the men of Cozeba, and Joash and Saraph, both of whom ruled in Moab and Jashubi Lehem. (This information is from ancient records.) 23 They were the potters who lived in Netaim and Gederah; they lived there and worked for the king.

SIMEON'S DESCENDANTS

24 The descendants of Simeon: Nemuel, Jamin, Jarib, Zerah, Shaul, 25 his son Shallum, his son Mibsam, and his son Mishma.

26 The descendants of Mishma: his son Hammuel, his son Zaccur, and his son Shimei.

27 Shimei had sixteen sons and six daughters. But his brothers did not have many sons, so their whole clan was not as numerous as the sons of Judah. 28 They lived in Beer Sheba, Moladah, Hazar Shual, 29 Bilhah, Ezem, Tolad, 30 Bethuel, Hormah, Ziklag, 31 Beth Marcaboth, Hazar Susim, Beth Biri, and Shaaraim. These were their towns until the reign of David. 32 Their settlements also included Etam, Ain, Rimmon, Tochen, and Ashan—five towns, 33 along with all their settlements that surrounded these towns as far as Baal. These were the places where they lived; they kept genealogical records.

34 Their clan leaders were: Meshobab, Jamlech, Joshah son of
Amaziah, 35 Joel, Jehu son of Joshibiah (son of Seraiah, son of
Asiel), 36 Eleoenai, Jaakobah, Jeshohaiah, Asaiah, Adiel, Jesimiel,
Benaiah, 37 Ziza son of Shipi (son of Allon, son of Jedaiah, son of
Shimri, son of Shemaiah). 38 These who are named above were
the leaders of their clans.
Their extended families increased greatly in numbers. 39 They
went to the entrance of Gedor, to the east of the valley, looking
for pasture for their sheep. 40 They found fertile and rich pasture;
the land was very broad, undisturbed and peaceful. Indeed some
Hamites had been living there before that. 41 The men whose
names are listed came during the time of King Hezekiah of Judah and attacked the Hamites' settlements, as well as the Meunites they discovered there, and they wiped them out, as can
be seen to this very day. They dispossessed them, for they found
pasture for their sheep there. 42 Five hundred men of Simeon,
led by Pelatiah, Neariah, Rephaiah, and Uzziel, the sons of Ishi,
went to the hill country of Seir 43 and defeated the rest of the
Amalekite refugees; they live there to this very day.

REUBEN'S DESCENDANTS

5 The sons of Reuben, Israel's firstborn—
(Now he was the firstborn, but when he defiled his father's
bed, his rights as firstborn were given to the sons of Joseph, Israel's son. So Reuben is not listed as firstborn in the genealogical
records. 2 Though Judah was the strongest among his brothers
and a leader descended from him, the right of the firstborn belonged to Joseph.)
3 The sons of Reuben, Israel's firstborn: Hanoch, Pallu, Hezron, and Carmi.
4 The descendants of Joel: his son Shemaiah, his son Gog, his
son Shimei, 5 his son Micah, his son Reaiah, his son Baal, 6 and
his son Beerah, whom King Tiglath-Pileser of Assyria carried
into exile. Beerah was the tribal leader of Reuben.
7 His brothers by their clans, as listed in their genealogical
records:
The leader Jeiel, Zechariah, 8 and Bela son of Azaz, son of
Shema, son of Joel.
They lived in Aroer as far as Nebo and Baal Meon. 9 In the
east they settled as far as the entrance to the wilderness that
stretches to the Euphrates River, for their cattle had increased
in numbers in the land of Gilead. 10 During the time of Saul they
attacked the Hagrites and defeated them. They took over their
territory in the entire eastern region of Gilead.

GAD'S DESCENDANTS

11 The descendants of Gad lived near them in the land of Bashan,
as far as Salecah.
12 They included Joel the leader, Shapham the second in command, Janai, and Shaphat in Bashan. 13 Their relatives, listed according to their families, included Michael, Meshullam, Sheba,
Jorai, Jacan, Zia, and Eber—seven in all.
14 These were the sons of Abihail son of Huri, son of Jaroah, son
of Gilead, son of Michael, son of Jeshishai, son of Jahdo, son of

Buz. 15 Ahi son of Abdiel, son of Guni, was the leader of the family. 16 They lived in Gilead, in Bashan and its surrounding settlements, and in the pasturelands of Sharon to their very borders.
17 All of them were listed in the genealogical records in the time of
King Jotham of Judah and in the time of King Jeroboam of Israel.
18 The Reubenites, Gadites, and the half-tribe of Manasseh
had 44,760 men in their combined armies, warriors who carried
shields and swords, were equipped with bows, and were trained
for war. 19 They attacked the Hagrites, Jetur, Naphish, and Nodab.
20 They received divine help in fighting them, and the Hagrites
and all their allies were handed over to them. They cried out to
God during the battle; he responded to their prayers because
they trusted in him. 21 They seized the Hagrites' animals, including 50,000 camels, 250,000 sheep, and 2,000 donkeys. They also
took captive 100,000 people. 22 Because God fought for them,
they killed many of the enemy. They dispossessed the Hagrites
and lived in their land until the exile.

THE HALF-TRIBE OF MANASSEH

23 The half-tribe of Manasseh settled in the land from Bashan
as far as Baal Hermon, Senir, and Mount Hermon. They grew
in number.
24 These were the leaders of their families:
Epher, Ishi, Eliel, Azriel, Jeremiah, Hodaviah, and Jahdiel. They
were skilled warriors, men of reputation, and leaders of their
families. 25 But they were unfaithful to the God of their ancestors and worshiped instead the gods of the native peoples whom
God had destroyed before them. 26 So the God of Israel stirred
up King Pul of Assyria (that is, King Tiglath-Pileser of Assyria),
and he carried away the Reubenites, Gadites, and half-tribe of
Manasseh and took them to Halah, Habor, Hara, and the river
of Gozan, where they remain to this very day.

LEVI'S DESCENDANTS

6 The sons of Levi: Gershon, Kohath, and Merari.
2 The sons of Kohath: Amram, Izhar, Hebron, and Uzziel.
3 The children of Amram: Aaron, Moses, and Miriam.
The sons of Aaron: Nadab, Abihu, Eleazar, and Ithamar.
4 Eleazar was the father of Phinehas, and Phinehas was the
father of Abishua. 5 Abishua was the father of Bukki, and Bukki
was the father of Uzzi. 6 Uzzi was the father of Zerahiah, and Zerahiah was the father of Meraioth. 7 Meraioth was the father of
Amariah, and Amariah was the father of Ahitub. 8 Ahitub was the
father of Zadok, and Zadok was the father of Ahimaaz. 9 Ahimaaz was the father of Azariah, and Azariah was the father of Johanan. 10 Johanan was the father of Azariah, who served as a
priest in the temple Solomon built in Jerusalem. 11 Azariah was
the father of Amariah, and Amariah was the father of Ahitub.
12 Ahitub was the father of Zadok, and Zadok was the father of
Shallum. 13 Shallum was the father of Hilkiah, and Hilkiah was
the father of Azariah. 14 Azariah was the father of Seraiah, and
Seraiah was the father of Jehozadak. 15 Jehozadak went into exile when the LORD sent the people of Judah and Jerusalem into
exile by the hand of Nebuchadnezzar.

[16]The sons of Levi: Gershom, Kohath, and Merari.
[17]These are the names of the sons Gershom: Libni and Shimei.
[18]The sons of Kohath: Amram, Izhar, Hebron, and Uzziel.
[19]The sons of Merari: Mahli and Mushi.
These are the clans of the Levites by their families.
[20]To Gershom: his son Libni, his son Jahath, his son Zimmah,
[21]his son Joah, his son Iddo, his son Zerah, and his son Jeatherai.
[22]The sons of Kohath: his son Amminadab, his son Korah,
his son Assir, [23]his son Elkanah, his son Ebiasaph, his son
Assir, [24]his son Tahath, his son Uriel, his son Uzziah, and his
son Shaul.
[25]The sons of Elkanah: Amasai, Ahimoth, [26]his son Elkanah,
his son Zophai, his son Nahath, [27]his son Eliab, his son Jeroham,
and his son Elkanah.
[28]The sons of Samuel: Joel the firstborn and Abijah the second oldest.
[29]The descendants of Merari: Mahli, his son Libni, his son
Shimei, his son Uzzah, [30]his son Shimea, his son Haggiah, and
his son Asaiah.

PROFESSIONAL MUSICIANS

[31]These are the men David put in charge of music in the LORD's sanctuary, after the ark was placed there. [32]They performed music before the sanctuary of the meeting tent until Solomon built the LORD's temple in Jerusalem. They carried out their tasks according to regulations.
[33]These are the ones who served along with their sons:
From the Kohathites: Heman the musician, son of Joel, son
of Samuel, [34]son of Elkanah, son of Jeroham, son of Eliel, son
of Toah, [35]son of Zuph, son of Elkanah, son of Mahath, son of
Amasai, [36]son of Elkanah, son of Joel, son of Azariah, son of Zephaniah, [37]son of Tahath, son of Assir, son of Ebiasaph, son of Korah,
[38]son of Izhar, son of Kohath, son of Levi, son of Israel.
[39]Serving beside him was his fellow Levite Asaph, son of Berechiah, son of Shimea, [40]son of Michael, son of Baaseiah, son
of Malkijah, [41]son of Ethni, son of Zerah, son of Adaiah, [42]son
of Ethan, son of Zimmah, son of Shimei, [43]son of Jahath, son of
Gershom, son of Levi.
[44]Serving beside them were their fellow Levites, the descendants of Merari, led by Ethan, son of Kishi, son of Abdi, son of
Malluch, [45]son of Hashabiah, son of Amaziah, son of Hilkiah,
[46]son of Amzi, son of Bani, son of Shemer, [47]son of Mahli, son
of Mushi, son of Merari, son of Levi.
[48]The rest of their fellow Levites were assigned to perform
the remaining tasks at God's sanctuary. [49]But Aaron and his descendants offered sacrifices on the altar for burnt offerings and on the altar for incense as they had been assigned to do in the Most Holy Sanctuary. They made atonement for Israel, just as God's servant Moses had ordered.
[50]These were the descendants of Aaron:
His son Eleazar, his son Phinehas, his son Abishua, [51]his
son Bukki, his son Uzzi, his son Zerahiah, [52]his son Meraioth,
his son Amariah, his son Ahitub, [53]his son Zadok, and his son
Ahimaaz.

54 These were the areas where Aaron's descendants lived:
The following belonged to the Kohathite clan, for they received
the first allotment:
55 They were allotted Hebron in the territory of Judah, as well
as its surrounding pasturelands. 56 (But the city's land and nearby
towns were allotted to Caleb son of Jephunneh.) 57 The descendants of Aaron were also allotted as cities of refuge Hebron, Libnah and its pasturelands, Jattir, Eshtemoa and its pasturelands,
58 Hilez and its pasturelands, Debir and its pasturelands, 59 Ashan
and its pasturelands, and Beth Shemesh and its pasturelands.
60 Within the territory of the tribe of Benjamin they were allotted Geba and its pasturelands, Alemeth and its pasturelands,
and Anathoth and its pasturelands. Their clans were allotted
thirteen cities in all. 61 The rest of Kohath's descendants were
allotted ten cities in the territory of the half-tribe of Manasseh.
62 The clans of Gershom's descendants received thirteen cities within the territory of the tribes of Issachar, Asher, Naphtali,
and Manasseh (in Bashan).
63 The clans of Merari's descendants were allotted twelve cities
within the territory of the tribes of Reuben, Gad, and Zebulun.
64 So the Israelites gave to the Levites these cities and their
pasturelands. 65 They allotted these previously named cities from
the territory of the tribes of Judah, Simeon, and Benjamin.
66 The clans of Kohath's descendants also received cities as
their territory within the tribe of Ephraim. 67 They were allotted as cities of refuge Shechem and its pasturelands (in the hill
country of Ephraim), Gezer and its pasturelands, 68 Jokmeam
and its pasturelands, Beth Horon and its pasturelands, 69 Aijalon
and its pasturelands, and Gath Rimmon and its pasturelands.
70 Within the territory of the half-tribe of Manasseh, the rest
of Kohath's descendants received Aner and its pasturelands and
Bileam and its pasturelands.
71 The following belonged to Gershom's descendants:
Within the territory of the half-tribe of Manasseh: Golan in
Bashan and its pasturelands and Ashtaroth and its pasturelands.
72 Within the territory of the tribe of Issachar: Kedesh and its
pasturelands, Daberath and its pasturelands, 73 Ramoth and its
pasturelands, and Anem and its pasturelands.
74 Within the territory of the tribe of Asher: Mashal and its
pasturelands, Abdon and its pasturelands, 75 Hukok and its pasturelands, and Rehob and its pasturelands.
76 Within the territory of the tribe of Naphtali: Kedesh in Galilee and its pasturelands, Hammon and its pasturelands, and
Kiriathaim and its pasturelands.
77 The following belonged to the rest of Merari's descendants:
Within the territory of the tribe of Zebulun: Rimmono and its
pasturelands, and Tabor and its pasturelands.
78 Within the territory of the tribe of Reuben across the Jordan
River east of Jericho: Bezer in the wilderness and its pasturelands, Jahzah and its pasturelands, 79 Kedemoth and its pasturelands, and Mephaath and its pasturelands.
80 Within the territory of the tribe of Gad: Ramoth in Gilead
and its pasturelands, Mahanaim and its pasturelands, 81 Heshbon and its pasturelands, and Jazer and its pasturelands.

REFLECT

Even though the Levites weren't given territory like the other tribes, God still provided for them by giving them land and provision through the temple sacrifices. How have you seen God provide for you in unexpected or nontraditional ways?

ISSACHAR'S DESCENDANTS

7 The sons of Issachar: Tola, Puah, Jashub, and Shimron—four
in all.
2 The sons of Tola: Uzzi, Rephaiah, Jeriel, Jahmai, Jibsam, and
Samuel. They were leaders of their families. In the time of David
there were 22,600 warriors listed in Tola's genealogical records.
3 The son of Uzzi: Izrahiah.
The sons of Izrahiah: Michael, Obadiah, Joel, and Isshiah. All
five were leaders.
4 According to the genealogical records of their families, they
had 36,000 warriors available for battle, for they had numerous
wives and sons. 5 Altogether the genealogical records of the clans
of Issachar listed 87,000 warriors.

BENJAMIN'S DESCENDANTS

6 The sons of Benjamin: Bela, Beker, and Jediael—three in all.
7 The sons of Bela: Ezbon, Uzzi, Uzziel, Jerimoth, and Iri. The
five of them were leaders of their families. There were 22,034
warriors listed in their genealogical records.
8 The sons of Beker: Zemirah, Joash, Eliezer, Elioenai, Omri, Jeremoth, Abijah, Anathoth, and Alemeth. All these were the sons
of Beker. 9 There were 20,200 family leaders and warriors listed
in their genealogical records.
10 The son of Jediael: Bilhan.
The sons of Bilhan: Jeush, Benjamin, Ehud, Kenaanah, Zethan,
Tarshish, and Ahishahar. 11 All these were the sons of Jediael.
There were 17,200 family leaders and warriors who were capable of marching out to battle.
12 The Shuppites and Huppites were descendants of Ir; the Hu-
shites were descendants of Aher.

NAPHTALI'S DESCENDANTS

13 The sons of Naphtali: Jahziel, Guni, Jezer, and Shallum—sons
of Bilhah.

MANASSEH'S DESCENDANTS

14 The sons of Manasseh: Asriel, who was born to Manasseh's
Aramean concubine. She also gave birth to Makir the father
of Gilead. 15 Now Makir married a wife from the Huppites and
Shuppites. (His sister's name was Maacah.)
Zelophehad was Manasseh's second son; he had only daughters.
16 Maacah, Makir's wife, gave birth to a son, whom she named
Peresh. His brother was Sheresh, and his sons were Ulam and
Rekem.
17 The son of Ulam: Bedan.
These were the sons of Gilead, son of Makir, son of Manasseh. 18 His sister Hammoleketh gave birth to Ishhod, Abiezer,
and Mahlah.
19 The sons of Shemida were Ahian, Shechem, Likhi, and Aniam.

EPHRAIM'S DESCENDANTS

20 The descendants of Ephraim: Shuthelah, his son Bered, his son
Tahath, his son Eleadah, his son Tahath, 21 his son Zabad, his son
Shuthelah (Ezer and Elead were killed by the men of Gath, who

were natives of the land, when they went down to steal their cattle. 22 Their father Ephraim mourned for them many days and his brothers came to console him. 23 He slept with his wife; she became pregnant and gave birth to a son. Ephraim named him Beriah because tragedy had come to his family. 24 His daughter was Sheerah, who built Lower and Upper Beth Horon, as well as Uzzen Sheerah),

25 his son Rephah, his son Resheph, his son Telah, his son Tahan, 26 his son Ladan, his son Ammihud, his son Elishama, 27 his son Nun, and his son Joshua.

28 Their property and settlements included Bethel and its surrounding towns, Naaran to the east, Gezer and its surrounding towns to the west, and Shechem and its surrounding towns as far as Ayyah and its surrounding towns. 29 On the border of Manasseh's territory were Beth Shean and its surrounding towns, Taanach and its surrounding towns, Megiddo and its surrounding towns, and Dor and its surrounding towns. The descendants of Joseph, Israel's son, lived here.

ASHER'S DESCENDANTS

30 The sons of Asher: Imnah, Ishvah, Ishvi, and Beriah. Serah was their sister.

31 The sons of Beriah: Heber and Malkiel, who was the father of Birzaith.

32 Heber was the father of Japhlet, Shomer, Hotham, and Shua their sister.

33 The sons of Japhlet: Pasach, Bimhal, and Ashvath. These were Japhlet's sons.

34 The sons of his brother Shemer: Rohgah, Hubbah, and Aram.

35 The sons of his brother Helem: Zophah, Imna, Shelesh, and Amal.

36 The sons of Zophah: Suah, Harnepher, Shual, Beri, Imrah, 37 Bezer, Hod, Shamma, Shilshah, Ithran, and Beera.

38 The sons of Jether: Jephunneh, Pispah, and Ara.

39 The sons of Ulla: Arah, Hanniel, and Rizia.

40 All these were the descendants of Asher. They were the leaders of their families, the most capable men, who were warriors and served as head chiefs. There were 26,000 warriors listed in their genealogical records as capable of doing battle.

BENJAMIN'S DESCENDANTS (CONTINUED)

8 Benjamin was the father of Bela, his firstborn; Ashbel was born second, Aharah third, 2 Nohah fourth, and Rapha fifth.

3 Bela's sons were Addar, Gera, Abihud, 4 Abishua, Naaman, Ahoah, 5 Gera, Shephuphan, and Huram.

6 These were the descendants of Ehud who were leaders of the families living in Geba who were forced to move to Manahath: 7 Naaman, Ahijah, and Gera, who moved them. Gera was the father of Uzzah and Ahihud.

8 Shaharaim fathered sons in Moab after he divorced his wives Hushim and Baara. 9 By his wife Hodesh he fathered Jobab, Zibia, Mesha, Malkam, 10 Jeuz, Sakia, and Mirmah. These were his sons; they were family leaders. 11 By Hushim he fathered Abitub and Elpaal.

12 The sons of Elpaal: Eber, Misham, Shemed (who built Ono
and Lod, as well as its surrounding towns), 13 Beriah, and Shema.
They were leaders of the families living in Aijalon and chased
out the inhabitants of Gath.

14 Ahio, Shashak, Jeremoth, 15 Zebadiah, Arad, Eder, 16 Michael,
Ishpah, and Joha were the sons of Beriah.

17 Zebadiah, Meshullam, Hizki, Heber, 18 Ishmerai, Izliah, and
Jobab were the sons of Elpaal.

19 Jakim, Zikri, Zabdi, 20 Elienai, Zillethai, Eliel, 21 Adaiah, Ber-
aiah, and Shimrath were the sons of Shimei.

22 Ishpan, Eber, Eliel, 23 Abdon, Zikri, Hanan, 24 Hananiah, Elam,
Anthothijah, 25 Iphdeiah, and Penuel were the sons of Shashak.

26 Shamsherai, Shechariah, Athaliah, 27 Jaareshiah, Elijah, and
Zikri were the sons of Jeroham. 28 These were the family leaders listed in the genealogical records; they lived in Jerusalem.

29 The father of Gibeon lived in Gibeon; his wife's name was
Maacah. 30 His firstborn son was Abdon, followed by Zur, Kish,
Baal, Nadab, 31 Gedor, Ahio, Zeker, and Mikloth.

32 Mikloth was the father of Shimeah. They also lived near their
relatives in Jerusalem.

33 Ner was the father of Kish, and Kish was the father of Saul.
Saul was the father of Jonathan, Malki-Shua, Abinadab, and Eshbaal.

34 The son of Jonathan: Meribbaal.

Meribbaal was the father of Micah.

35 The sons of Micah: Pithon, Melech, Tarea, and Ahaz.

36 Ahaz was the father of Jehoaddah, and Jehoaddah was the
father of Alemeth, Azmaveth, and Zimri. Zimri was the father of
Moza, 37 and Moza was the father of Binea. His son was Raphah,
whose son was Eleasah, whose son was Azel.

38 Azel had six sons: Azrikam his firstborn, followed by Ishmael,
Sheariah, Obadiah, and Hanan. All these were the sons of Azel.

39 The sons of his brother Eshek:

Ulam was his firstborn, Jeush second, and Eliphelet third.

40 The sons of Ulam were warriors who were adept archers. They
had many sons and grandsons, a total of 150.

All these were the descendants of Benjamin.

9 Genealogical records were kept for all Israel; they are recorded
in the Scroll of the Kings of Israel.

EXILES WHO RESETTLED IN JERUSALEM

The people of Judah were carried away to Babylon because of
their unfaithfulness. 2 The first to resettle on their property and
in their cities were some Israelites, priests, Levites, and temple servants. 3 Some from the tribes of Judah, Benjamin, and
Ephraim and Manasseh settled in Jerusalem.

4 The settlers included: Uthai son of Ammihud, son of Omri,
son of Imri, son of Bani, who was a descendant of Perez son of
Judah.

5 From the Shilonites: Asaiah the firstborn and his sons.

6 From the descendants of Zerah: Jeuel.

Their relatives numbered 690.

7 From the descendants of Benjamin:

Sallu son of Meshullam, son of Hodaviah, son of Hassenuah;

8 Ibneiah son of Jeroham; Elah son of Uzzi, son of Mikri; and Meshullam son of Shephatiah, son of Reuel, son of Ibnijah.

9 Their relatives, listed in their genealogical records, numbered 956. All these men were leaders of their families.

10 From the priests:

Jedaiah; Jehoiarib; Jakin; 11 Azariah son of Hilkiah, son of Meshullam, son of Zadok, son of Meraioth, son of Ahitub the leader in God's temple; 12 Adaiah son of Jeroham, son of Pashhur, son of Malkijah; and Maasai son of Adiel, son of Jahzerah, son of Meshullam, son of Meshillemith, son of Immer.

13 Their relatives, who were leaders of their families, numbered 1,760. They were capable men who were assigned to carry out the various tasks of service in God's temple.

14 From the Levites:

Shemaiah son of Hasshub, son of Azrikam, son of Hashabiah a descendant of Merari; 15 Bakbakkar; Heresh; Galal; Mattaniah son of Mika, son of Zikri, son of Asaph; 16 Obadiah son of Shemaiah, son of Galal, son of Jeduthun; and Berechiah son of Asa, son of Elkanah, who lived among the settlements of the Netophathites.

17 The gatekeepers were:

Shallum, Akkub, Talmon, Ahiman, and their brothers. Shallum was the leader; 18 he serves to this day at the King's Gate on the east. These were the gatekeepers from the camp of the descendants of Levi.

19 Shallum son of Kore, son of Ebiasaph, son of Korah, and his relatives from his family (the Korahites) were assigned to guard the entrance to the sanctuary. Their ancestors had guarded the entrance to the LORD's dwelling place. 20 Phinehas son of Eleazar had been their leader in earlier times, and the LORD was with him. 21 Zechariah son of Meshelemiah was the guard at the entrance to the meeting tent.

22 All those selected to be gatekeepers at the entrances numbered 212. Their names were recorded in the genealogical records of their settlements. David and Samuel the prophet had appointed them to their positions. 23 They and their descendants were assigned to guard the gates of the LORD's sanctuary (that is, the tabernacle). 24 The gatekeepers were posted on all four sides—east, west, north, and south. 25 Their relatives, who lived in their settlements, came from time to time and served with them for seven-day periods. 26 The four head gatekeepers, who were Levites, were assigned to guard the storerooms and treasuries in God's sanctuary. 27 They would spend the night in their posts all around God's sanctuary, for they were assigned to guard it and would open it with the key every morning. 28 Some of them were in charge of the articles used by those who served; they counted them when they brought them in and when they brought them out. 29 Some of them were in charge of the equipment and articles of the sanctuary, as well as the flour, wine, olive oil, incense, and spices. 30 (But some of the priests mixed the spices.) 31 Mattithiah, a Levite, the firstborn son of Shallum the Korahite, was in charge of baking the bread for offerings. 32 Some of the Kohathites, their relatives, were in charge of preparing the bread that is displayed each Sabbath.

33 The musicians and Levite family leaders stayed in rooms at the sanctuary and were exempt from other duties, for day and night they had to carry out their assigned tasks. 34 These were the family leaders of the Levites, as listed in their genealogical records. They lived in Jerusalem.

JEIEL'S DESCENDANTS

35 Jeiel (the father of Gibeon) lived in Gibeon. His wife was Maacah. 36 His firstborn son was Abdon, followed by Zur, Kish, Baal, Ner, Nadab, 37 Gedor, Ahio, Zechariah, and Mikloth. 38 Mikloth was the father of Shimeam. They also lived near their relatives in Jerusalem.

39 Ner was the father of Kish, and Kish was the father of Saul. Saul was the father of Jonathan, Malki-Shua, Abinadab, and Eshbaal.

40 The son of Jonathan:
Meribbaal, who was the father of Micah.

41 The sons of Micah:
Pithon, Melech, Tahrea, and Ahaz.

42 Ahaz was the father of Jarah, and Jarah was the father of Alemeth, Azmaveth, and Zimri. Zimri was the father of Moza, 43 and Moza was the father of Binea. His son was Rephaiah, whose son was Eleasah, whose son was Azel.

44 Azel had six sons: Azrikam his firstborn, followed by Ishmael, Sheariah, Obadiah, and Hanan. These were the sons of Azel.

SAUL'S DEATH

10 Now the Philistines fought against Israel. The Israelites fled before the Philistines and many of them fell dead on Mount Gilboa. 2 The Philistines stayed right on the heels of Saul and his sons. They struck down Saul's sons Jonathan, Abinadab, and Malki-Shua. 3 The battle was thick around Saul; the archers spotted him and wounded him. 4 Saul told his armor-bearer, "Draw your sword and stab me with it. Otherwise these uncircumcised people will come and torture me." But his armor-bearer refused to do it, because he was very afraid. So Saul took the sword and fell on it. 5 When his armor-bearer saw that Saul was dead, he also fell on his sword and died. 6 So Saul and his three sons died; his whole household died together. 7 When all the Israelites who were in the valley saw that the army had fled and that Saul and his sons were dead, they abandoned their cities and fled. The Philistines came and occupied them.

8 The next day, when the Philistines came to strip loot from the corpses, they discovered Saul and his sons lying dead on Mount Gilboa. 9 They stripped his corpse, and then carried off his head and his armor. They sent messengers throughout the land of the Philistines proclaiming the news to their idols and their people. 10 They placed his armor in the temple of their gods and hung his head in the temple of Dagon. 11 When all the residents of Jabesh Gilead heard about everything the Philistines had done to Saul, 12 all the warriors went and recovered the bodies of Saul and his sons and brought them to Jabesh. They buried their remains under the oak tree in Jabesh and fasted for seven days.

13 So Saul died because he was unfaithful to the LORD and did not obey the LORD's instructions; he even tried to conjure up underworld spirits. 14 He did not seek the LORD's guidance, so the LORD killed him and transferred the kingdom to David son of Jesse.

DAVID BECOMES KING

11 All Israel joined David at Hebron and said, "Look, we are your very flesh and blood! 2 In the past, even when Saul was king, you were Israel's commanding general. The LORD your God said to you, 'You will shepherd my people Israel; you will rule over my people Israel.'" 3 When all the leaders of Israel came to the king at Hebron, David made a covenant with them in Hebron before the LORD. They anointed David king over Israel, in keeping with the LORD's message that came through Samuel.

DAVID CONQUERS JERUSALEM

4 David and the whole Israelite army advanced to Jerusalem (that is, Jebus). (The Jebusites, the land's original inhabitants, lived there.) 5 The residents of Jebus said to David, "You cannot invade this place!" But David captured the fortress of Zion (that is, the City of David). 6 David said, "Whoever attacks the Jebusites first will become commanding general!" So Joab son of Zeruiah attacked first and became commander. 7 David lived in the fortress; for this reason it is called the City of David. 8 He built up the city around it, from the terrace to the surrounding walls; Joab restored the rest of the city. 9 David's power steadily grew, for the LORD of Heaven's Armies was with him.

DAVID'S WARRIORS

10 These were the leaders of David's warriors who, together with all Israel, stood courageously with him in his kingdom by installing him as king, in keeping with the LORD's message concerning Israel. 11 This is the list of David's warriors:

Jashobeam, a Hacmonite, was head of the officers. He killed 300 men with his spear in a single battle.

12 Next in command was Eleazar son of Dodo the Ahohite. He was one of the three elite warriors. 13 He was with David in Pas Dammim when the Philistines assembled there for battle. In an area of the field that was full of barley, the army retreated before the Philistines, 14 but then they made a stand in the middle of that area. They defended it and defeated the Philistines; the LORD gave them a great victory.

15 Three of the thirty leaders went down to David at the rocky cliff at the cave of Adullam, while a Philistine force was camped in the Valley of Rephaim. 16 David was in the stronghold at the time, while a Philistine garrison was in Bethlehem. 17 David was thirsty and said, "How I wish someone would give me some water to drink from the cistern in Bethlehem near the city gate!" 18 So the three elite warriors broke through the Philistine forces and drew some water from the cistern in Bethlehem near the city gate. They carried it back to David, but David refused to drink it. He poured it out as a drink offering to the LORD 19 and said, "God forbid that I should do this! Should I drink the blood of these men who risked their lives?" Because they risked their lives to bring it to him, he refused to drink it. Such were the exploits of the three elite warriors.

20 Abishai the brother of Joab was head of the three elite warriors. He killed 300 men with his spear and gained fame along with the three elite warriors. 21 From the three he was given

LOVE TO GROW

DAVID'S MIGHTY MEN

1 CHRONICLES 11:10–47

When I read about David's life and legacy in Scripture, I am often overwhelmed at how his mighty men blessed his life. These thirty or so men personified loyalty to both God and David.

Even before David was king, these men showed unyielding support. While Saul pursued David in the wilderness, six hundred faithful men were with him in Keilah (1 Sam 23). Abishai was the one who offered to take Saul's life in the wilderness of Ziph for David (1 Sam 26). First Chronicles 11:10 tells us that the leaders of the warriors, along with all Israel, "stood courageously with [David] in his kingdom."

David's men respected him, and David had mutual respect for his men. When the king thirsted for a glass of water, three of the mighty men risked their lives to quench David's thirst. The king poured out the water to the Lord out of respect for those who risked their lives for him.

David and his mighty men are an example of how God uses others to fulfill His Word and His promises in our lives. God promised to establish David's kingdom. He used David's mighty men to help accomplish His plan. The Lord gave these men victory over their enemies and the ability to accomplish amazing feats. David honored these men by chronicling their accomplishments and their loyalty.

God created us for community. Jesus commanded us to love one another. It is by this love that the world will know that we are His disciples (John 13:34–35).

I am grateful to have had several mighty women in my own life. These women support me, encourage me, and speak truth to me in all kinds of situations. I know that I can call on them to pray for me and come to my aid in times of need. We have laughed together, cried together, prayed together, and played together. Our moments together enable us to do immeasurably more than we would ever do on our own.

Who are your mighty warriors? Who are the people God has given you to propel you further to accomplish all the Lord has in store for you? If we desire to love God greatly, let's challenge ourselves to be vulnerable. By doing so we allow God to use others to make a difference in our lives. None of us can do this alone. Let's surround ourselves with mighty women and men to help us reach the goal.

double honor and he became their officer, even though he was
not one of them.
22 Benaiah son of Jehoiada was a brave warrior from Kabzeel
who performed great exploits. He struck down the two sons of
Ariel of Moab; he also went down and killed a lion inside a cistern
on a snowy day. 23 He even killed an Egyptian who was 7½ feet
tall. The Egyptian had a spear in his hand as big as the crossbeam
of a weaver's loom; Benaiah attacked him with a club. He grabbed
the spear out of the Egyptian's hand and killed him with his own
spear. 24 Such were the exploits of Benaiah son of Jehoiada, who
gained fame along with the three elite warriors. 25 He received
honor from the thirty warriors, though he was not one of the
three elite warriors. David put him in charge of his bodyguard.

26 The mighty warriors were:
Asahel the brother of Joab,
Elhanan son of Dodo, from Bethlehem,
27 Shammoth the Harorite,
Helez the Pelonite,
28 Ira son of Ikkesh the Tekoite,
Abiezer the Anathothite,
29 Sibbekai the Hushathite,
Ilai the Ahohite,
30 Maharai the Netophathite,
Heled son of Baanah the Netophathite,
31 Ithai son of Ribai from Gibeah in Benjaminite territory,
Benaiah the Pirathonite,
32 Hurai from the valleys of Gaash,
Abiel the Arbathite,
33 Azmaveth the Baharumite,
Eliahba the Shaalbonite,
34 the sons of Hashem the Gizonite,
Jonathan son of Shageh the Hararite,
35 Ahiam son of Sakar the Hararite,
Eliphal son of Ur,
36 Hepher the Mekerathite,
Ahijah the Pelonite,
37 Hezro the Carmelite,
Naarai son of Ezbai,
38 Joel the brother of Nathan,
Mibhar son of Hagri,
39 Zelek the Ammonite,
Naharai the Beerothite, the armor-bearer of Joab son of Zeruiah,
40 Ira the Ithrite,
Gareb the Ithrite,
41 Uriah the Hittite,
Zabad son of Achli,
42 Adina son of Shiza the Reubenite, leader of the Reubenites
and the thirty warriors with him,
43 Hanan son of Maacah,
Joshaphat the Mithnite,
44 Uzzia the Ashterathite,
Shama and Jeiel, the sons of Hotham the Aroerite,
45 Jediael son of Shimri,
and Joha his brother, the Tizite,

46 Eliel the Mahavite,
and Jeribai and Joshaviah, the sons of Elnaam,
and Ithmah the Moabite,
47 Eliel,
and Obed,
and Jaasiel the Mezobaite.

WARRIORS WHO JOINED DAVID AT ZIKLAG

12 These were the men who joined David in Ziklag, when he
was banished from the presence of Saul son of Kish. (They
were among the warriors who assisted him in battle. 2 They were
armed with bows and could shoot arrows or sling stones right
or left-handed. They were fellow tribesmen of Saul from Benjamin.) These were:
3 Ahiezer, the leader, and Joash, the sons of Shemaah the
Gibeathite; Jeziel and Pelet, the sons of Azmaveth; Berachah,
Jehu the Anathothite,
4 Ishmaiah the Gibeonite, one of the thirty warriors and their
leader, Jeremiah, Jahaziel, Johanan, Jozabad the Gederathite,
5 Eluzai, Jerimoth, Bealiah, Shemariah, Shephatiah the Haruphite,
6 Elkanah, Isshiah, Azarel, Joezer, and Jashobeam, who were
Korahites,
7 and Joelah and Zebadiah, the sons of Jeroham from Gedor.
8 Some of the Gadites joined David at the stronghold in the
wilderness. They were warriors who were trained for battle; they
carried shields and spears. They were as fierce as lions and could
run as quickly as gazelles across the hills. 9 Ezer was the leader,
Obadiah the second in command, Eliab the third, 10 Mishmannah
the fourth, Jeremiah the fifth, 11 Attai the sixth, Eliel the seventh,
12 Johanan the eighth, Elzabad the ninth, 13 Jeremiah the tenth,
and Machbannai the eleventh. 14 These Gadites were military
leaders; the least led a hundred men, the greatest a thousand.
15 They crossed the Jordan River in the first month, when it was
overflowing its banks, and routed those living in all the valleys
to the east and west.
16 Some from Benjamin and Judah also came to David's stronghold. 17 David went out to meet them and said, "If you come to
me in peace and want to help me, then I will make an alliance
with you. But if you come to betray me to my enemies when I
have not harmed you, may the God of our ancestors take notice
and judge!" 18 But a spirit empowered Amasai, the leader of the
group of warriors known as the Thirty, and he said:

"We are yours, O David!
We support you, O son of Jesse!
May you greatly prosper.
May those who help you prosper.
Indeed your God helps you!"

So David accepted them and made them leaders of raiding bands.
19 Some men from Manasseh joined David when he went with
the Philistines to fight against Saul. (But in the end they did not
help the Philistines because, after taking counsel, the Philistine
lords sent David away, saying, "It would be disastrous for us if he
deserts to his master Saul.") 20 When David went to Ziklag, the
men of Manasseh who joined him were Adnach, Jozabad, Jediael,

Michael, Jozabad, Elihu, and Zillethai, leaders of 1,000 soldiers each
in the tribe of Manasseh. 21 They helped David fight against raiding
bands, for all of them were warriors and leaders in the army. 22 Each
day men came to help David until his army became very large.

SUPPORT FOR DAVID IN HEBRON

23 The following is a record of the armed warriors who came with
their leaders and joined David in Hebron in order to make David king in Saul's place, in accordance with the LORD's decree:
24 From Judah came 6,800 trained warriors carrying shields
and spears.
25 From Simeon there were 7,100 warriors.
26 From Levi there were 4,600. 27 Jehoiada, the leader of Aaron's
descendants, brought 3,700 men with him, 28 along with Zadok,
a young warrior, and 22 leaders from his family.
29 From Benjamin, Saul's tribe, there were 3,000, most of whom,
up to that time, had been loyal to Saul.
30 From Ephraim there were 20,800 warriors, who had brought
fame to their families.
31 From the half-tribe of Manasseh there were 18,000 who had
been designated by name to come and make David king.
32 From Issachar there were 200 leaders and all their relatives
at their command—they understood the times and knew what
Israel should do.
33 From Zebulun there were 50,000 warriors who were prepared for battle, equipped with all kinds of weapons, and ready
to give their undivided loyalty.
34 From Naphtali there were 1,000 officers, along with 37,000
men carrying shields and spears.
35 From Dan there were 28,600 men prepared for battle.
36 From Asher there were 40,000 warriors prepared for battle.
37 From the other side of the Jordan, from Reuben, Gad, and
the half-tribe of Manasseh, there were 120,000 men armed with
all kinds of weapons.
38 All these men were warriors who were ready to march. They
came to Hebron to make David king over all Israel by acclamation; all the rest of the Israelites also were in agreement that
David should become king. 39 They spent three days feasting
there with David, for their relatives had given them provisions.
40 Also their neighbors, from as far away as Issachar, Zebulun,
and Naphtali, were bringing food on donkeys, camels, mules, and
oxen. There were large supplies of flour, fig cakes, raisins, wine,
olive oil, beef, and lamb, for Israel was celebrating.

UZZAH MEETS DISASTER

13 David consulted with his military officers, including those
who led groups of a thousand and those who led groups of a
hundred. 2 David said to the whole Israelite assembly, "If you so
desire and the LORD our God approves, let's spread the word to
our brothers who remain in all the regions of Israel, and to the
priests and Levites in their cities, so they may join us. 3 Let's move
the ark of our God back here, for we did not seek his will throughout Saul's reign." 4 The whole assembly agreed to do this, for the
proposal seemed right to all the people. 5 So David assembled all

Israel from the Shihor River in Egypt to Lebo Hamath, to bring the ark of God from Kiriath Jearim. 6 David and all Israel went up to Baalah (that is, Kiriath Jearim) in Judah to bring up from there the ark of God the LORD, who sits enthroned between the cherubim—the ark that is called by his Name.

7 They transported the ark of God on a new cart from the house of Abinadab; Uzzah and Ahio were guiding the cart, 8 while David and all Israel were energetically celebrating before God, singing and playing various stringed instruments, tambourines, cymbals, and trumpets. 9 When they arrived at the threshing floor of Kidon, Uzzah reached out his hand to take hold of the ark, because the oxen stumbled. 10 The LORD was so furious with Uzzah, he killed him, because he reached out his hand and touched the ark. He died right there before God.

11 David was angry because the LORD attacked Uzzah; so he called that place Perez Uzzah, which remains its name to this very day. 12 David was afraid of God that day and said, "How will I ever be able to bring the ark of God up here?" 13 So David did not move the ark to the City of David; he left it in the house of Obed-Edom the Gittite. 14 The ark of God remained in Obed-Edom's house for three months; the LORD blessed Obed-Edom's family and everything that belonged to him.

DAVID'S PRESTIGE GROWS

14 King Hiram of Tyre sent messengers to David, along with cedar logs, stonemasons, and carpenters to build a palace for him. 2 David realized that the LORD had established him as king over Israel and that he had elevated his kingdom for the sake of his people Israel.

3 In Jerusalem David married more wives and fathered more sons and daughters. 4 These are the names of children born to him in Jerusalem: Shammua, Shobab, Nathan, Solomon, 5 Ibhar, Elishua, Elpelet, 6 Nogah, Nepheg, Japhia, 7 Elishama, Beeliada, and Eliphelet.

8 When the Philistines heard that David had been anointed king of all Israel, all the Philistines marched up to confront him. When David heard about it, he marched out against them. 9 Now the Philistines had come and raided the Valley of Rephaim. 10 David asked God, "Should I march up against the Philistines? Will you hand them over to me?" The LORD said to him, "March up! I will hand them over to you!" 11 So they marched against Baal Perazim and David defeated them there. David said, "Using me as his instrument, God has burst out against my enemies like water bursts out." So that place is called Baal Perazim. 12 The Philistines left their idols there, so David ordered that they be burned.

13 The Philistines again raided the valley. 14 So David again asked God what he should do. This time God told him, "Don't march up after them; circle around them and come against them in front of the trees. 15 When you hear the sound of marching in the tops of the trees, then attack. For at that moment God is going before you to strike down the army of the Philistines." 16 David did just as God commanded him, and they struck down the Philistine army from Gibeon to Gezer.

17 So David became famous in all the lands; the LORD caused all the nations to fear him.

DAVID BRINGS THE ARK TO JERUSALEM

15 David constructed buildings in the City of David; he then
prepared a place for the ark of God and pitched a tent for
it. 2 Then David said, "Only the Levites may carry the ark of God,
for the LORD chose them to carry the ark of the LORD and to
serve before him perpetually." 3 David assembled all Israel at
Jerusalem to bring the ark of the LORD up to the place he had
prepared for it. 4 David gathered together the descendants of
Aaron and the Levites:

5 From the descendants of Kohath: Uriel the leader and 120
of his relatives.

6 From the descendants of Merari: Asaiah the leader and 220
of his relatives.

7 From the descendants of Gershom: Joel the leader and 130
of his relatives.

8 From the descendants of Elizaphan: Shemaiah the leader
and 200 of his relatives.

9 From the descendants of Hebron: Eliel the leader and 80 of
his relatives.

10 From the descendants of Uzziel: Amminadab the leader and
112 of his relatives.

11 David summoned the priests Zadok and Abiathar, along with
the Levites Uriel, Asaiah, Joel, Shemaiah, Eliel, and Amminadab.
12 He told them: "You are the leaders of the Levites' families. You
and your relatives must consecrate yourselves and bring the ark
of the LORD God of Israel up to the place I have prepared for it.
13 The first time you did not carry it; that is why the LORD God
attacked us, because we did not ask him about the proper way
to carry it." 14 The priests and Levites consecrated themselves
so they could bring up the ark of the LORD God of Israel. 15 The
descendants of Levi carried the ark of God on their shoulders
with poles, just as Moses had commanded in keeping with the
LORD's instruction.

16 David told the leaders of the Levites to appoint some of their
relatives as musicians; they were to play various instruments,
including stringed instruments and cymbals, and to sing loudly
and joyfully. 17 So the Levites appointed Heman son of Joel; one of
his relatives, Asaph son of Berechiah; one of the descendants of
Merari, Ethan son of Kushaiah; 18 along with some of their relatives who were second in rank, including Zechariah, Jaaziel, Shemiramoth, Jehiel, Unni, Eliab, Benaiah, Maaseiah, Mattithiah,
Eliphelehu, Mikneiah, Obed-Edom, and Jeiel, the gatekeepers.

19 The musicians Heman, Asaph, and Ethan were to sound the
bronze cymbals; 20 Zechariah, Aziel, Shemiramoth, Jehiel, Unni,
Eliab, Maaseiah, and Benaiah were to play the harps according to the *alamoth* style; 21 Mattithiah, Eliphelehu, Mikneiah,
Obed-Edom, Jeiel, and Azaziah were to play the lyres according to the *sheminith* style, as led by the director; 22 Kenaniah,
the leader of the Levites, was in charge of transport, for he was
well-informed on this matter; 23 Berechiah and Elkanah were
guardians of the ark; 24 Shebaniah, Joshaphat, Nethanel, Amasai,
Zechariah, Benaiah, and Eliezer the priests were to blow the
trumpets before the ark of God; Obed-Edom and Jehiel were
also guardians of the ark.

25 So David, the leaders of Israel, and the commanders of units
of a thousand went to bring up the ark of the LORD's covenant
from the house of Obed-Edom with celebration. 26 When God
helped the Levites who were carrying the ark of the LORD's covenant, they sacrificed seven bulls and seven rams. 27 David was
wrapped in a linen robe, as were all the Levites carrying the ark,
the musicians, and Kenaniah the supervisor of transport and the
musicians; David also wore a linen ephod. 28 All Israel brought
up the ark of the LORD's covenant; they were shouting, blowing
trumpets, sounding cymbals, and playing stringed instruments.
29 As the ark of the LORD's covenant entered the City of David,
Michal, Saul's daughter, looked out the window. When she saw
King David jumping and celebrating, she despised him.

GOD'S HEART FOR THE NATIONS

1 Chronicles 16:8

"Give thanks to the LORD! Call on his name! Make known his accomplishments among the nations!"

DAVID LEADS IN WORSHIP

16 They brought the ark of God and put it in the middle of the
tent David had pitched for it. Then they offered burnt sacrifices and peace offerings before God. 2 When David finished
offering burnt sacrifices and peace offerings, he pronounced a
blessing over the people in the LORD's name. 3 He then handed
out to each Israelite man and woman a loaf of bread, a date cake,
and a raisin cake. 4 He appointed some of the Levites to serve
before the ark of the LORD, to offer prayers, songs of thanks,
and hymns to the LORD God of Israel. 5 Asaph was the leader
and Zechariah second-in-command, followed by Jeiel, Shemiramoth, Jehiel, Mattithiah, Eliab, Benaiah, Obed-Edom, and Jeiel. They were to play stringed instruments, Asaph was to sound
the cymbals, 6 and the priests Benaiah and Jahaziel were to blow
trumpets regularly before the ark of God's covenant.

DAVID THANKS GOD

7 That day David first gave to Asaph and his colleagues this song
of thanks to the LORD.

8 Give thanks to the LORD!
Call on his name!
Make known his accomplishments among the nations.
9 Sing to him! Make music to him!
Tell about all his miraculous deeds.
10 Boast about his holy name.
Let the hearts of those who seek the LORD rejoice.
11 Seek the LORD and the strength he gives.
Seek his presence continually!
12 Recall the miraculous deeds he performed,
his mighty acts and the judgments he decreed,
13 O children of Israel, God's servant,
you descendants of Jacob, God's chosen ones!
14 He is the LORD our God;
he carries out judgment throughout the earth.
15 Remember continually his covenantal decree,
the promise he made to a thousand generations—
16 the promise he made to Abraham,
the promise he made by oath to Isaac!
17 He gave it to Jacob as a decree,
to Israel as a lasting promise,

REFLECT

How does David's psalm of thanksgiving encourage you to offer praise and thanksgiving to God when He moves in your life?

GOD'S HEART FOR THE NATIONS

1 Chronicles 16:31

*"Let the heavens rejoice,
and the earth be happy!
Let the nations say,
'The LORD reigns!'"*

18 saying, "To you I will give the land of Canaan
as the portion of your inheritance."
19 When they were few in number,
just a very few, and foreign residents within it,
20 they wandered from nation to nation,
and from one kingdom to another.
21 He let no one oppress them;
he disciplined kings for their sake,
22 saying, "Don't touch my anointed ones!
Don't harm my prophets!"
23 Sing to the LORD, all the earth!
Announce every day how he delivers.
24 Tell the nations about his splendor,
tell all the nations about his miraculous deeds.
25 For the LORD is great and certainly worthy of praise,
he is more awesome than all gods.
26 For all the gods of the nations are worthless,
but the LORD made the heavens.
27 Majestic splendor emanates from him,
he is the source of strength and joy.
28 Ascribe to the LORD, O families of the nations,
ascribe to the LORD splendor and strength!
29 Ascribe to the LORD the splendor he deserves!
Bring an offering and enter his presence!
Worship the LORD in holy attire!
30 Tremble before him, all the earth!
The world is established, it cannot be moved.
31 Let the heavens rejoice, and the earth be happy!
Let the nations say, "The LORD reigns!"
32 Let the sea and everything in it shout!
Let the fields and everything in them celebrate!
33 Then let the trees of the forest shout
with joy before the LORD,
for he comes to judge the earth!
34 Give thanks to the LORD, for he is good
and his loyal love endures.
35 Say this prayer: "Deliver us, O God who delivers us!
Gather us! Rescue us from the nations!
Then we will give thanks to your holy name,
and boast about your praiseworthy deeds."
36 May the LORD God of Israel be praised,
in the future and forevermore.
Then all the people said, "We agree! Praise the LORD."

DAVID APPOINTS WORSHIP LEADERS

37 David left Asaph and his colleagues there before the ark of the
LORD's covenant to serve before the ark regularly and fulfill each
day's requirements, 38 including Obed-Edom and sixty-eight colleagues. Obed-Edom son of Jeduthun and Hosah were gatekeepers. 39 Zadok the priest and his fellow priests served before the
LORD's tabernacle at the worship center in Gibeon, 40 regularly
offering burnt sacrifices to the LORD on the altar for burnt sacrifice, morning and evening, according to what is prescribed in
the law of the LORD which he charged Israel to observe. 41 Joining

PROCLAIMING HIS GOODNESS

1 CHRONICLES 16:8–36

When something I'm passionate about comes up in conversation, my entire demeanor changes. The more excited I get, the louder my voice becomes.

This happens to many of us when we talk about our favorite things. For some it's a favorite restaurant, a clothing store, or a brand of shoes. Maybe it's a television series or a new book. Whatever it may be, we talk about these things because we have experienced something good, and we want others to experience the same goodness.

What about God? What do we know to be true about Him that motivates us to get loud about His goodness? Whenever He has His rightful place in our lives, it's inevitable that thankfulness and gratitude will flow from our mouths.

It is believed that the Books of 1 and 2 Chronicles were written by Ezra, a scribe and serious student of God's Word. Ezra recorded the Chronicles from a perspective of pain and silence that had come during Israel's exile.

However, here, in chapter 16, Ezra recorded a story of celebration. David brought the ark of God to the City of David and threw a celebration for its arrival. Then David gave thanks to the Lord in front of all the people. David praised God for what He had done in the past and what he was certain He would do in the future. Ezra's record of David's thanksgiving reminded his audience of the faithfulness and power of God.

The key to a thankful heart is to remember in the present what God has done in the past. His faithfulness in the past is a reminder of what He will do in the future.

After walking out my greatest nightmare of disappointments and betrayals, I have clung tightly to what I know to be the goodness and faithfulness of the Lord: He rescued me once, and He will do it again. As I consume God's truth through Scripture, worship music, and time with His church, thankfulness and faith flow from my heart. May we always give thanks, remembering who God is. He is the ultimate encounter that we want others to experience. God is good all the time, and we always have something to celebrate. He is our Lord, Redeemer, and Friend.

them were Heman, Jeduthun, and the rest of those chosen and
designated by name to give thanks to the LORD. (For his loyal
love endures!) 42 Heman and Jeduthun were in charge of the music, including the trumpets, cymbals, and the other musical instruments used in praising God. The sons of Jeduthun guarded
the entrance.
43 Then all the people returned to their homes, and David went
to pronounce a blessing on his family.

GOD MAKES A PROMISE TO DAVID

17 When David had settled into his palace, he said to Nathan
the prophet, "Look, I am living in a palace made from cedar, while the ark of the LORD's covenant is under a tent." 2 Nathan said to David, "You should do whatever you have in mind,
for God is with you."
3 That night God told Nathan, 4 "Go, tell my servant David: 'This
is what the LORD says: "You must not build me a house in which
to live. 5 For I have not lived in a house from the time I brought
Israel up from Egypt to the present day. I have lived in a tent
that has been in various places. 6 Wherever I moved throughout Israel, I did not say to any of the leaders whom I appointed
to care for my people Israel, 'Why have you not built me a house
made from cedar?'""
7 "So now, say this to my servant David: 'This is what the LORD
of Heaven's Armies says: "I took you from the pasture and from
your work as a shepherd to make you a leader of my people Israel. 8 I was with you wherever you went and I defeated all your
enemies before you. Now I will make you as famous as the great
men of the earth. 9 I will establish a place for my people Israel
and settle them there; they will live there and not be disturbed
anymore. Violent men will not oppress them again, as they did
in the beginning 10 and during the time when I appointed judges
to lead my people Israel. I will subdue all your enemies.
"""I declare to you that the LORD will build a dynastic house for
you! 11 When the time comes for you to die, I will raise up your
descendant, one of your own sons, to succeed you, and I will establish his kingdom. 12 He will build me a house, and I will make
his dynasty permanent. 13 I will become his father and he will
become my son. I will never withhold my loyal love from him,
as I withheld it from the one who ruled before you. 14 I will put
him in permanent charge of my house and my kingdom; his dynasty will be permanent."'" 15 Nathan told David all these words
that were revealed to him.

DAVID PRAISES GOD

16 King David went in, sat before the LORD, and said: "Who am
I, O LORD God, and what is my family, that you should have
brought me to this point? 17 And you did not stop there, O God!
You have also spoken about the future of your servant's family. You have revealed to me what men long to know, O LORD
God. 18 What more can David say to you? You have honored your
servant; you have given your servant special recognition. 19 O
LORD, for the sake of your servant and according to your will,
you have done this great thing in order to reveal your greatness.

20 O LORD, there is none like you; there is no God besides you!
What we heard is true! 21 And who is like your people, Israel, a
unique nation in the earth? Their God went to claim a nation
for himself! You made a name for yourself by doing great and
awesome deeds when you drove out nations before your people whom you had delivered from the Egyptian empire and its
gods. 22 You made Israel your very own nation for all time. You,
O LORD, became their God. 23 So now, O LORD, may the promise
you made about your servant and his family become a permanent reality! Do as you promised, 24 so it may become a reality and you may gain lasting fame, as people say, 'The LORD of
Heaven's Armies is the God of Israel.' The dynasty of your servant David will be established before you, 25 for you, my God,
have revealed to your servant that you will build a dynasty for
him. That is why your servant has had the courage to pray to
you. 26 Now, O LORD, you are the true God; you have made this
good promise to your servant. 27 Now you are willing to bless
your servant's dynasty so that it may stand permanently before
you, for you, O LORD, have blessed it and it will be blessed from
now on into the future."

DAVID CONQUERS THE NEIGHBORING NATIONS

18 Later David defeated the Philistines and subdued them.
He took Gath and its surrounding towns away from the
Philistines.
2 He defeated the Moabites; the Moabites became David's subjects and brought tribute.
3 David defeated King Hadadezer of Zobah as far as Hamath,
when he went to extend his authority to the Euphrates River.
4 David seized from him 1,000 chariots, 7,000 charioteers, and
20,000 infantrymen. David cut the hamstrings of all but 100 of
Hadadezer's chariot horses. 5 The Arameans of Damascus came
to help King Hadadezer of Zobah, but David killed 22,000 of
the Arameans. 6 David placed garrisons in the territory of the
Arameans of Damascus; the Arameans became David's subjects
and brought tribute. The LORD protected David wherever he
campaigned. 7 David took the golden shields which Hadadezer's
servants had carried and brought them to Jerusalem. 8 From
Tibhath and Kun, Hadadezer's cities, David took a great deal of
bronze. (Solomon used it to make the big bronze basin called
"The Sea," the pillars, and other bronze items.)
9 When King Tou of Hamath heard that David had defeated the
entire army of King Hadadezer of Zobah, 10 he sent his son Hadoram to King David to extend his best wishes and to pronounce
a blessing on him for his victory over Hadadezer, for Tou had
been at war with Hadadezer. He also sent various items made
of gold, silver, and bronze. 11 King David dedicated these things
to the LORD, along with the silver and gold which he had carried
off from all the nations, including Edom, Moab, the Ammonites,
the Philistines, and Amalek.
12 Abishai son of Zeruiah killed 18,000 Edomites in the Valley
of Salt. 13 He placed garrisons in Edom, and all the Edomites became David's subjects. The LORD protected David wherever he
campaigned.

DAVID'S OFFICIALS

14 David reigned over all Israel; he guaranteed justice for all his people. 15 Joab son of Zeruiah was commanding general of the army; Jehoshaphat son of Ahilud was secretary; 16 Zadok son of Ahitub and Abimelech son of Abiathar were priests; Shavsha was scribe; 17 Benaiah son of Jehoiada supervised the Kerethites and Pelethites; and David's sons were the king's leading officials.

DAVID'S CAMPAIGN AGAINST THE AMMONITES

19 Later King Nahash of the Ammonites died and his son succeeded him. 2 David said, "I will express my loyalty to Hanun son of Nahash, for his father was loyal to me." So David sent messengers to express his sympathy over his father's death. When David's servants entered Ammonite territory to visit Hanun and express the king's sympathy, 3 the Ammonite officials said to Hanun, "Do you really think David is trying to honor your father by sending these messengers to express his sympathy? No, his servants have come to you so they can get information and spy out the land!" 4 So Hanun seized David's servants and shaved their beards off. He cut off the lower part of their robes so that their buttocks were exposed and then sent them away. 5 People came and told David what had happened to the men, so he sent messengers to meet them, for the men were thoroughly humiliated. The king said, "Stay in Jericho until your beards grow again; then you may come back."

6 When the Ammonites realized that David was disgusted with them, Hanun and the Ammonites sent 1,000 talents of silver to hire chariots and charioteers from Aram Naharaim, Aram Maacah, and Zobah. 7 They hired 32,000 chariots, along with the king of Maacah and his army, who came and camped in front of Medeba. The Ammonites also assembled from their cities and marched out to do battle.

8 When David heard the news, he sent Joab and the entire army to meet them. 9 The Ammonites marched out and were deployed for battle at the entrance to the city, while the kings who had come were by themselves in the field. 10 When Joab saw that the battle would be fought on two fronts, he chose some of Israel's best men and deployed them against the Arameans. 11 He put his brother Abishai in charge of the rest of the army and they were deployed against the Ammonites. 12 Joab said, "If the Arameans start to overpower me, you come to my rescue. If the Ammonites start to overpower you, I will come to your rescue. 13 Be strong! Let's fight bravely for the sake of our people and the cities of our God! The LORD will do what he decides is best!" 14 So Joab and his men marched toward the Arameans to do battle, and they fled before him. 15 When the Ammonites saw the Arameans flee, they fled before Joab's brother Abishai and withdrew into the city. Joab went back to Jerusalem.

16 When the Arameans realized they had been defeated by Israel, they sent for reinforcements from beyond the Euphrates River, led by Shophach the commanding general of Hadadezer's army. 17 When David was informed, he gathered all Israel, crossed the Jordan River, and marched against them. David deployed his army against the Arameans for battle and they fought against

him. [18] The Arameans fled before Israel. David killed 7,000 Aramean charioteers and 40,000 infantrymen; he also killed Shophach the commanding general. [19] When Hadadezer's subjects
saw they were defeated by Israel, they made peace with David
and became his subjects. The Arameans were no longer willing
to help the Ammonites.
20 In the spring, at the time when kings normally conduct
wars, Joab led the army into battle and devastated the land
of the Ammonites. He went and besieged Rabbah, while David
stayed in Jerusalem. Joab defeated Rabbah and tore it down. [2] David took the crown from the head of their king and wore it (its
weight was a talent of gold and it was set with precious stones).
He took a large amount of plunder from the city. [3] He removed
the city's residents and made them labor with saws, iron picks,
and axes. This was his policy with all the Ammonite cities. Then
David and all the army returned to Jerusalem.

BATTLES WITH THE PHILISTINES

[4] Later there was a battle with the Philistines in Gezer. At that
time Sibbekai the Hushathite killed Sippai, one of the descendants of the Rephaim, and the Philistines were subdued.
[5] There was another battle with the Philistines in which Elhanan son of Jair the Bethlehemite killed the brother of Goliath
the Gittite, whose spear had a shaft as big as the crossbeam of
a weaver's loom.
[6] In a battle in Gath there was a large man who had six fingers
on each hand and six toes on each foot—twenty-four in all! He
too was a descendant of Rapha. [7] When he taunted Israel, Jonathan son of Shimea, David's brother, killed him.
[8] These were the descendants of Rapha who lived in Gath; they
were killed by the hand of David and his soldiers.

THE LORD SENDS A PLAGUE AGAINST ISRAEL

21 An adversary opposed Israel, inciting David to count how
many warriors Israel had. [2] David told Joab and the leaders
of the army, "Go, count the number of warriors from Beer Sheba
to Dan. Then bring back a report to me so I may know how many
we have." [3] Joab replied, "May the LORD make his army a hundred times larger! My master, O king, do not all of them serve
my master? Why does my master want to do this? Why bring
judgment on Israel?"
[4] But the king's edict stood, despite Joab's objections. So Joab
left and traveled throughout Israel before returning to Jerusalem. [5] Joab reported to David the number of warriors. In all Israel there were 1,100,000 sword-wielding soldiers; Judah alone
had 470,000 sword-wielding soldiers. [6] Now Joab did not number Levi and Benjamin, for the king's edict disgusted him. [7] God
was also offended by it, so he attacked Israel.
[8] David said to God, "I have sinned greatly by doing this! Now,
please remove the guilt of your servant, for I have acted very
foolishly." [9] The LORD told Gad, David's prophet, [10] "Go, tell David, 'This is what the LORD says: "I am offering you three forms of
judgment from which to choose. Pick one of them."'" [11] Gad went
to David and told him, "This is what the LORD says: 'Pick one of

REFLECT

God faithfully gave the Israelites victory over the Philistines. What has God consistently given you victory over in your life? Do you believe He will continue to give you victory in the future?

REFLECT

How did God bring about His greater purpose as a result of David's sin? How have you seen God use your mistakes for His glory and purpose?

these: 12 three years of famine, or three months being chased by
your enemies and struck down by their swords, or three days being struck down by the LORD, during which a plague will invade
the land and the angel of the LORD will destroy throughout Israel's territory.' Now, decide what I should tell the one who sent
me." 13 David said to Gad, "I am very upset! I prefer to be attacked
by the LORD, for his mercy is very great; I do not want to be attacked by men!" 14 So the LORD sent a plague through Israel, and
70,000 Israelite men died.
15 God sent an angel to ravage Jerusalem. As he was doing so,
the LORD watched and relented from his judgment. He told the
angel who was destroying, "That's enough! Stop now!"
Now the angel of the LORD was standing near the threshing
floor of Ornan the Jebusite. 16 David looked up and saw the angel
of the LORD standing between the earth and sky with his sword
drawn and in his hand, stretched out over Jerusalem. David and
the leaders, covered with sackcloth, threw themselves down with
their faces to the ground. 17 David said to God, "Was I not the one
who decided to number the army? I am the one who sinned and
committed this awful deed! As for these sheep—what have they
done? O LORD my God, attack me and my family, but remove the
plague from your people!"
18 So the angel of the LORD told Gad to instruct David to go
up and build an altar for the LORD on the threshing floor of
Ornan the Jebusite. 19 So David went up as Gad instructed him
to do in the name of the LORD. 20 While Ornan was threshing wheat, he turned and saw the messenger, and he and his
four sons hid themselves. 21 When David came to Ornan, Ornan looked and saw David; he came out from the threshing
floor and bowed to David with his face to the ground. 22 David
said to Ornan, "Sell me the threshing floor so I can build on
it an altar for the LORD—I'll pay top price—so that the plague
may be removed from the people." 23 Ornan told David, "You
can have it! My master, the king, may do what he wants. Look,
I am giving you the oxen for burnt sacrifices, the threshing
sledges for wood, and the wheat for an offering. I give it all to
you." 24 King David replied to Ornan, "No, I insist on buying
it for top price. I will not offer to the LORD what belongs to
you or offer a burnt sacrifice that cost me nothing. 25 So David
bought the place from Ornan for 600 pieces of gold. 26 David
built there an altar to the LORD and offered burnt sacrifices
and peace offerings. He called out to the LORD, and the LORD
responded by sending fire from the sky and consuming the
burnt sacrifice on the altar. 27 The LORD ordered the messenger to put his sword back into its sheath.
28 At that time, when David saw that the LORD responded to
him at the threshing floor of Ornan the Jebusite, he sacrificed
there. 29 Now the LORD's tabernacle (which Moses had made in
the wilderness) and the altar for burnt sacrifices were at that
time at the worship center in Gibeon. 30 But David could not
go before it to seek God's will, for he was afraid of the sword of
22 the angel of the LORD. 1 David then said, "This is the place
where the temple of the LORD God will be, along with the
altar for burnt sacrifices for Israel."

DAVID ORDERS A TEMPLE TO BE BUILT

2 David ordered the resident foreigners in the land of Israel to be
called together. He appointed some of them to be stonecutters
to chisel stones for the building of God's temple. 3 David supplied
a large amount of iron for the nails of the doors of the gates and
for braces, more bronze than could be weighed, 4 and more cedar logs than could be counted. (The Sidonians and Tyrians had
brought a large amount of cedar logs to David.)

5 David said, "My son Solomon is just an inexperienced young
man, and the temple to be built for the LORD must be especially
magnificent so it will become famous and be considered splendid
by all the nations. Therefore I will make preparations for its construction." So David made extensive preparations before he died.

6 He summoned his son Solomon and charged him to build a
temple for the LORD God of Israel. 7 David said to Solomon: "My
son, I really wanted to build a temple to honor the LORD my
God. 8 But this was the LORD's message to me: 'You have spilled
a great deal of blood and fought many battles. You must not
build a temple to honor me, for you have spilled a great deal of
blood on the ground before me. 9 Look, you will have a son, who
will be a peaceful man. I will give him rest from all his enemies
on every side. Indeed, Solomon will be his name; I will give Israel peace and quiet during his reign. 10 He will build a temple to
honor me; he will become my son, and I will become his father.
I will grant to his dynasty permanent rule over Israel.'

11 "Now, my son, may the LORD be with you! May you succeed
and build a temple for the LORD your God, just as he announced
you would. 12 Only may the LORD give you insight and understanding when he places you in charge of Israel, so you may obey
the law of the LORD your God. 13 Then you will succeed, if you
carefully obey the rules and regulations which the LORD ordered
Moses to give to Israel. Be strong and brave! Don't be afraid and
don't panic! 14 Now, look, I have made every effort to supply what
is needed to build the LORD's temple. I have stored up 100,000
talents of gold, 1,000,000 talents of silver, and so much bronze
and iron it cannot be weighed, as well as wood and stones. Feel
free to add more! 15 You also have available many workers, including stonecutters, masons, carpenters, and an innumerable
array of workers who are skilled 16 in using gold, silver, bronze,
and iron. Get up and begin the work! May the LORD be with you!"

17 David ordered all the officials of Israel to support his son
Solomon. 18 He told them, "The LORD your God is with you! He
has made you secure on every side, for he handed over to me
the inhabitants of the region and the region is subdued before
the LORD and his people. 19 Now seek the LORD your God wholeheartedly and with your entire being! Get up and build the sanctuary of the LORD God! Then you can bring the ark of the LORD's
covenant and the holy items dedicated to God's service into the
temple that is built to honor the LORD."

DAVID ORGANIZES THE LEVITES

23 When David was old and approaching the end of his life,
he made his son Solomon king over Israel.

2 David assembled all the leaders of Israel, along with the

priests and the Levites. 3 The Levites who were thirty years old and up were counted; there were 38,000 men. 4 David said, "Of these, 24,000 are to direct the work of the LORD's temple; 6,000 are to be officials and judges; 5 4,000 are to be gatekeepers; and 4,000 are to praise the LORD with the instruments I supplied for worship." 6 David divided them into groups corresponding to the sons of Levi: Gershon, Kohath, and Merari.

7 The Gershonites included Ladan and Shimei.

8 The sons of Ladan: Jehiel the oldest, Zetham, and Joel—three in all.

9 The sons of Shimei: Shelomoth, Haziel, and Haran—three in all.

These were the leaders of the family of Ladan.

10 The sons of Shimei: Jahath, Zina, Jeush, and Beriah. These were Shimei's sons—four in all. 11 Jahath was the oldest and Zizah the second oldest. Jeush and Beriah did not have many sons, so they were considered one family with one responsibility.

12 The sons of Kohath: Amram, Izhar, Hebron, and Uzziel—four in all.

13 The sons of Amram: Aaron and Moses.

Aaron and his descendants were chosen on a permanent basis to consecrate the most holy items, to offer sacrifices before the LORD, to serve him, and to praise his name. 14 The descendants of Moses the man of God were considered Levites.

15 The sons of Moses: Gershom and Eliezer.

16 The son of Gershom: Shebuel the oldest.

17 The son of Eliezer was Rehabiah, the oldest. Eliezer had no other sons, but Rehabiah had many descendants.

18 The son of Izhar: Shelomith the oldest.

19 The sons of Hebron: Jeriah the oldest, Amariah the second, Jahaziel the third, and Jekameam the fourth.

20 The sons of Uzziel: Micah the oldest, and Isshiah the second.

21 The sons of Merari: Mahli and Mushi.

The sons of Mahli: Eleazar and Kish.

22 Eleazar died without having sons; he had only daughters. The sons of Kish, their cousins, married them.

23 The sons of Mushi: Mahli, Eder, and Jeremoth—three in all.

24 These were the descendants of Levi according to their families, that is, the leaders of families as counted and individually listed who carried out assigned tasks in the LORD's temple and were twenty years old and up. 25 For David said, "The LORD God of Israel has given his people rest and has permanently settled in Jerusalem. 26 So the Levites no longer need to carry the tabernacle or any of the items used in its service." 27 According to David's final instructions, the Levites twenty years old or older were counted.

28 Their job was to help Aaron's descendants in the service of the LORD's temple. They were to take care of the courtyards, the rooms, ceremonial purification of all holy items, and other jobs related to the service of God's temple. 29 They also took care of the bread that is displayed, the flour for offerings, the unleavened wafers, the round cakes, the mixing, and all the measuring. 30 They also stood in a designated place every morning and offered thanks and praise to the LORD. They also did

this in the evening 31 and whenever burnt sacrifices were offered to the LORD on the Sabbath and at new moon festivals
and assemblies. A designated number were to serve before the
LORD regularly in accordance with regulations. 32 They were
in charge of the meeting tent and the Holy Place, and helped
their relatives, the descendants of Aaron, in the service of the
LORD's temple.

DAVID ORGANIZES THE PRIESTS

24 The divisions of Aaron's descendants were as follows:
The sons of Aaron: Nadab, Abihu, Eleazar, and Ithamar.
2 Nadab and Abihu died before their father did; they had no
sons. Eleazar and Ithamar served as priests.
3 David, Zadok (a descendant of Eleazar), and Ahimelech (a descendant of Ithamar) divided them into groups to carry out their
assigned responsibilities. 4 The descendants of Eleazar had more
leaders than the descendants of Ithamar, so they divided them
up accordingly; the descendants of Eleazar had sixteen leaders,
while the descendants of Ithamar had eight. 5 They divided them
by lots, for there were officials of the Holy Place and officials
designated by God among the descendants of both Eleazar and
Ithamar. 6 The scribe Shemaiah son of Nethanel, a Levite, wrote
down their names before the king, the officials, Zadok the priest,
Ahimelech son of Abiathar, and the leaders of the priestly and
Levite families. One family was drawn by lot from Eleazar, and
then the next from Ithamar.

7 The first lot went to Jehoiarib,
the second to Jedaiah,
8 the third to Harim,
the fourth to Seorim,
9 the fifth to Malkijah,
the sixth to Mijamin,
10 the seventh to Hakkoz,
the eighth to Abijah,
11 the ninth to Jeshua,
the tenth to Shecaniah,
12 the eleventh to Eliashib,
the twelfth to Jakim,
13 the thirteenth to Huppah,
the fourteenth to Jeshebeab,
14 the fifteenth to Bilgah,
the sixteenth to Immer,
15 the seventeenth to Hezir,
the eighteenth to Happizzez,
16 the nineteenth to Pethahiah,
the twentieth to Jehezkel,
17 the twenty-first to Jakin,
the twenty-second to Gamul,
18 the twenty-third to Delaiah,
the twenty-fourth to Maaziah.

19 This was the order in which they carried out their assigned
responsibilities when they entered the LORD's temple, according to the regulations given them by their ancestor Aaron, just
as the LORD God of Israel had instructed him.

REMAINING LEVITES

20 The rest of the Levites included:
Shubael from the sons of Amram,
Jehdeiah from the sons of Shubael,
21 the firstborn Isshiah from Rehabiah and the sons of Rehabiah,
22 Shelomoth from the Izharites,
Jahath from the sons of Shelomoth.
23 The sons of Hebron: Jeriah, Amariah the second, Jahaziel the
third, and Jekameam the fourth.
24 The son of Uzziel: Micah;
Shamir from the sons of Micah.
25 The brother of Micah: Isshiah.
Zechariah from the sons of Isshiah.
26 The sons of Merari: Mahli and Mushi.
The son of Jaaziah: Beno.
27 The sons of Merari, from Jaaziah: Beno, Shoham, Zaccur, and
Ibri.
28 From Mahli: Eleazar, who had no sons.
29 From Kish: Jerahmeel.
30 The sons of Mushi: Mahli, Eder, and Jerimoth.
These were the Levites, listed by their families.
31 Like their relatives, the descendants of Aaron, they also cast
lots before King David, Zadok, Ahimelech, the leaders of families, the priests, and the Levites. The families of the oldest son cast lots along with those of the youngest.

DAVID ORGANIZES THE MUSICIANS

25 David and the army officers selected some of the sons of Asaph, Heman, and Jeduthun to prophesy as they played stringed instruments and cymbals. The following men were assigned this responsibility:
2 From the sons of Asaph: Zaccur, Joseph, Nethaniah, and Asarelah. The sons of Asaph were supervised by Asaph, who prophesied under the king's supervision.
3 From the sons of Jeduthun: Gedaliah, Zeri, Jeshaiah, Hashabiah, and Mattithiah—six in all, under supervision of their father Jeduthun, who prophesied as he played a harp, giving thanks and praise to the LORD.
4 From the sons of Heman: Bukkiah, Mattaniah, Uzziel, Shebuel, Jerimoth, Hananiah, Hanani, Eliathah, Giddalti, Romamti-Ezer, Joshbekashah, Mallothi, Hothir, and Mahazioth.
5 All these were the sons of Heman, the king's prophet. God had promised him these sons in order to make him prestigious. God gave Heman fourteen sons and three daughters.
6 All these were under the supervision of their fathers; they were musicians in the LORD's temple, playing cymbals and stringed instruments as they served in God's temple. Asaph, Jeduthun, and Heman were under the supervision of the king.
7 They and their relatives, all of them skilled and trained to make music to the LORD, numbered 288.
8 They cast lots to determine their responsibilities—oldest as well as youngest, teacher as well as student.
9 The first lot went to Asaph's son Joseph and his relatives and sons—twelve in all,

the second to Gedaliah and his relatives and sons—twelve in all,
10 the third to Zaccur and his sons and relatives—twelve in all,
11 the fourth to Izri and his sons and relatives—twelve in all,
12 the fifth to Nethaniah and his sons and relatives—twelve
in all,
13 the sixth to Bukkiah and his sons and relatives—twelve in all,
14 the seventh to Jesharelah and his sons and relatives—twelve
in all,
15 the eighth to Jeshaiah and his sons and relatives—twelve in all,
16 the ninth to Mattaniah and his sons and relatives—twelve
in all,
17 the tenth to Shimei and his sons and relatives—twelve in all,
18 the eleventh to Azarel and his sons and relatives—twelve
in all,
19 the twelfth to Hashabiah and his sons and relatives—twelve
in all,
20 the thirteenth to Shubael and his sons and relatives—twelve
in all,
21 the fourteenth to Mattithiah and his sons and relatives—
twelve in all,
22 the fifteenth to Jerimoth and his sons and relatives—twelve
in all,
23 the sixteenth to Hananiah and his sons and relatives—twelve
in all,
24 the seventeenth to Joshbekashah and his sons and relatives—
twelve in all,
25 the eighteenth to Hanani and his sons and relatives—twelve
in all,
26 the nineteenth to Mallothi and his sons and relatives—
twelve in all,
27 the twentieth to Eliathah and his sons and relatives—twelve
in all,
28 the twenty-first to Hothir and his sons and relatives—twelve
in all,
29 the twenty-second to Giddalti and his sons and relatives—
twelve in all,
30 the twenty-third to Mahazioth and his sons and relatives—
twelve in all,
31 the twenty-fourth to Romamti-Ezer and his sons and relatives—twelve in all.

DIVISIONS OF GATEKEEPERS

26 The divisions of the gatekeepers:
From the Korahites: Meshelemiah, son of Kore, one of
the sons of Asaph.
2 Meshelemiah's sons:
The firstborn Zechariah, the second Jediael, the third Zebadiah, the fourth Jathniel, 3 the fifth Elam, the sixth Jehohanan,
and the seventh Elihoenai.
4 Obed-Edom's sons:
The firstborn Shemaiah, the second Jehozabad, the third Joah,
the fourth Sakar, the fifth Nethanel, 5 the sixth Ammiel, the seventh Issachar, and the eighth Peullethai. (Indeed, God blessed
Obed-Edom.)

6 His son Shemaiah also had sons, who were leaders of their families, for they were highly respected. 7 The sons of Shemaiah:

Othni, Rephael, Obed, and Elzabad. His relatives Elihu and Semakiah were also respected.

8 All these were the descendants of Obed-Edom. They and their sons and relatives were respected men, capable of doing their responsibilities. There were sixty-two of them related to Obed-Edom.

9 Meshelemiah had sons and relatives who were respected—eighteen in all.

10 Hosah, one of the descendants of Merari, had sons:

The firstborn Shimri (he was not actually the firstborn, but his father gave him that status), 11 the second Hilkiah, the third Tebaliah, and the fourth Zechariah. All Hosah's sons and relatives numbered thirteen.

12 These divisions of the gatekeepers, corresponding to their leaders, had assigned responsibilities, like their relatives, as they served in the LORD's temple.

13 They cast lots, both young and old, according to their families, to determine which gate they would be responsible for. 14 The lot for the east gate went to Shelemiah. They then cast lots for his son Zechariah, a wise adviser, and the lot for the north gate went to him. 15 Obed-Edom was assigned the south gate, and his sons were assigned the storehouses. 16 Shuppim and Hosah were assigned the west gate, along with the Shalleketh gate on the upper road. One guard was adjacent to another. 17 Each day there were six Levites posted on the east, four on the north, and four on the south. At the storehouses they were posted in pairs. 18 At the court on the west there were four posted on the road and two at the court. 19 These were the divisions of the gatekeepers who were descendants of Korah and Merari.

SUPERVISORS OF THE STOREHOUSES

20 Their fellow Levites were in charge of the storehouses in God's temple and the storehouses containing consecrated items. 21 The descendants of Ladan, who were descended from Gershon through Ladan and were leaders of the families of Ladan the Gershonite, included Jehieli 22 and the sons of Jehieli, Zetham and his brother Joel. They were in charge of the storehouses in the LORD's temple.

23 As for the Amramites, Izharites, Hebronites, and Uzzielites:

24 Shebuel son of Gershom, the son of Moses, was the supervisor of the storehouses. 25 His relatives through Eliezer included: Rehabiah his son, Jeshaiah his son, Joram his son, Zikri his son, and Shelomith his son. 26 Shelomith and his relatives were in charge of all the storehouses containing the consecrated items dedicated by King David, the family leaders who led units of a thousand and a hundred, and the army officers. 27 They had dedicated some of the plunder taken in battles to be used for repairs on the LORD's temple. 28 They were also in charge of everything dedicated by Samuel the prophet, Saul son of Kish, Abner son of Ner, and Joab son of Zeruiah; Shelomith and his relatives were in charge of everything that had been dedicated.

29 As for the Izharites: Kenaniah and his sons were given responsibilities outside the temple as officers and judges over Israel.

30 As for the Hebronites: Hashabiah and his relatives, 1,700 respected men, were assigned responsibilities in Israel west of the
Jordan; they did the LORD's work and the king's service.
31 As for the Hebronites: Jeriah was the leader of the Hebronites
according to the genealogical records. In the fortieth year of David's reign, they examined the records and discovered there were
highly respected men in Jazer in Gilead. 32 Jeriah had 2,700 relatives
who were respected family leaders. King David placed them in
charge of the Reubenites, the Gadites, and the half-tribe of Manasseh; they took care of all matters pertaining to God and the king.

LEADERS OF THE ARMY

27 What follows is a list of Israelite family leaders and commanders of units of a thousand and a hundred, as well as
their officers who served the king in various matters. Each division was assigned to serve for one month during the year; each
consisted of 24,000 troops.
2 Jashobeam son of Zabdiel was in charge of the first division,
which was assigned the first month. His division consisted of
24,000 troops. 3 He was a descendant of Perez; he was in charge
of all the army officers for the first month.
4 Dodai the Ahohite was in charge of the division assigned the
second month; Mikloth was the next in rank. His division consisted of 24,000 troops.
5 The third army commander, assigned the third month, was
Benaiah son of Jehoiada the priest. He was the leader of his division, which consisted of 24,000 troops. 6 Benaiah was the leader
of the thirty warriors and his division; his son was Ammizabad.
7 The fourth, assigned the fourth month, was Asahel, brother
of Joab; his son Zebadiah succeeded him. His division consisted
of 24,000 troops.
8 The fifth, assigned the fifth month, was the commander
Shamhuth the Izrahite. His division consisted of 24,000 troops.
9 The sixth, assigned the sixth month, was Ira son of Ikkesh the
Tekoite. His division consisted of 24,000 troops.
10 The seventh, assigned the seventh month, was Helez the Pelonite, an Ephraimite. His division consisted of 24,000 troops.
11 The eighth, assigned the eighth month, was Sibbekai the
Hushathite, a Zerahite. His division consisted of 24,000 troops.
12 The ninth, assigned the ninth month, was Abiezer the Anathothite, a Benjaminite. His division consisted of 24,000 troops.
13 The tenth, assigned the tenth month, was Maharai the Netophathite, a Zerahite. His division consisted of 24,000 troops.
14 The eleventh, assigned the eleventh month, was Benaiah the
Pirathonite, an Ephraimite. His division consisted of 24,000
troops.
15 The twelfth, assigned the twelfth month, was Heldai the Netophathite, a descendant of Othniel. His division consisted of
24,000 troops.
16 The officers of the Israelite tribes:
Eliezer son of Zikri was the leader of the Reubenites,
Shephatiah son of Maacah led the Simeonites,
17 Hashabiah son of Kemuel led the Levites,
Zadok led the descendants of Aaron,

18 Elihu, a brother of David, led Judah,
Omri son of Michael led Issachar,
19 Ishmaiah son of Obadiah led Zebulun,
Jerimoth son of Azriel led Naphtali,
20 Hoshea son of Azaziah led the Ephraimites,
Joel son of Pedaiah led the half-tribe of Manasseh,
21 Iddo son of Zechariah led the half-tribe of Manasseh in Gilead,
Jaasiel son of Abner led Benjamin,
22 Azarel son of Jeroham led Dan.
These were the commanders of the Israelite tribes.

23 David did not count the males twenty years old and under,
for the LORD had promised to make Israel as numerous as the
stars in the sky. 24 Joab son of Zeruiah started to count the men
but did not finish. God was angry with Israel because of this, so
the number was not recorded in the scroll called The Annals of
King David.

ROYAL OFFICIALS

25 Azmaveth son of Adiel was in charge of the king's storehouses;
Jonathan son of Uzziah was in charge of the storehouses in the field, in the cities, in the towns, and in the towers.
26 Ezri son of Kelub was in charge of the field workers who farmed the land.
27 Shimei the Ramathite was in charge of the vineyards;
Zabdi the Shiphmite was in charge of the wine stored in the vineyards.
28 Baal Hanan the Gederite was in charge of the olive and sycamore trees in the foothills;
Joash was in charge of the storehouses of olive oil.
29 Shitrai the Sharonite was in charge of the cattle grazing in Sharon;
Shaphat son of Adlai was in charge of the cattle in the valleys.
30 Obil the Ishmaelite was in charge of the camels;
Jehdeiah the Meronothite was in charge of the donkeys.
31 Jaziz the Hagrite was in charge of the sheep.
All these were the officials in charge of King David's property.
32 Jonathan, David's uncle, was a wise adviser and scribe;
Jehiel son of Hacmoni cared for the king's sons.
33 Ahithophel was the king's adviser;
Hushai the Arkite was the king's confidant.
34 Ahithophel was succeeded by Jehoiada son of Benaiah and by Abiathar.
Joab was the commanding general of the king's army.

DAVID COMMISSIONS SOLOMON TO BUILD THE TEMPLE

28 David assembled in Jerusalem all the officials of Israel, including the commanders of the tribes, the commanders of the army divisions that served the king, the commanders of units of a thousand and a hundred, the officials who were in charge of all the property and livestock of the king and his sons, the eunuchs, and the warriors, including the most skilled of them.

2 King David rose to his feet and said: "Listen to me, my brothers and my people. I wanted to build a temple where the ark of
the LORD's covenant could be placed as a footstool for our God. I
have made the preparations for building it. 3 But God said to me,
'You must not build a temple to honor me, for you are a warrior
and have spilled blood.' 4 The LORD God of Israel chose me out
of my father's entire family to become king over Israel and have
a permanent dynasty. Indeed, he chose Judah as leader, and my
father's family within Judah, and then he picked me out from
among my father's sons and made me king over all Israel. 5 From
all the many sons the LORD has given me, he chose Solomon my
son to rule on his behalf over Israel. 6 He said to me, 'Solomon
your son is the one who will build my temple and my courts, for
I have chosen him to become my son and I will become his father. 7 I will establish his kingdom permanently, if he remains
committed to obeying my commands and regulations, as you
are doing this day.' 8 So now, in the sight of all Israel, the LORD's
assembly, and in the hearing of our God, I say this: Carefully observe all the commands of the LORD your God, so that you may
possess this good land and may leave it as a permanent inheritance for your children after you.

9 "And you, Solomon my son, obey the God of your father and
serve him with a submissive attitude and a willing spirit, for
the LORD examines all minds and understands every motive of
one's thoughts. If you seek him, he will let you find him, but if
you abandon him, he will reject you permanently. 10 Realize now
that the LORD has chosen you to build a temple as his sanctuary. Be strong and do it!"

11 David gave to his son Solomon the blueprints for the temple porch, its buildings, its treasuries, its upper areas, its inner
rooms, and the room for atonement. 12 He gave him the blueprints of all he envisioned for the courts of the LORD's temple,
all the surrounding rooms, the storehouses of God's temple, and
the storehouses for the holy items.

13 He gave him the regulations for the divisions of priests and
Levites, for all the assigned responsibilities within the LORD's
temple, and for all the items used in the service of the LORD's
temple.

14 He gave him the prescribed weight for all the gold items to
be used in various types of service in the LORD's temple, for all
the silver items to be used in various types of service, 15 for the
gold lampstands and their gold lamps, including the weight of
each lampstand and its lamps, for the silver lampstands, including the weight of each lampstand and its lamps, according
to the prescribed use of each lampstand, 16 for the gold used in
the display tables, including the amount to be used in each table, for the silver to be used in the silver tables, 17 for the pure
gold used for the meat forks, bowls, and jars, for the small gold
bowls, including the weight for each bowl, for the small silver
bowls, including the weight for each bowl, 18 and for the refined
gold of the incense altar.

He gave him the blueprint for the seat of the gold cherubim that spread their wings and provide shelter for the ark of the LORD's covenant.

19 David said, "All this I put in writing as the LORD directed
me and gave me insight regarding the details of the blueprints."
20 David said to his son Solomon: "Be strong and brave! Do it!
Don't be afraid and don't panic! For the LORD God, my God, is
with you. He will not leave you or abandon you before all the
work for the service of the LORD's temple is finished. 21 Here are
the divisions of the priests and Levites who will perform all the
service of God's temple. All the willing and skilled men are ready
to assist you in all the work and perform their service. The officials and all the people are ready to follow your instructions."

REFLECT

How can you be faithful in the work God has given you to do? How can you find peace in the truth that He will not abandon you as you do His kingdom work?

THE PEOPLE CONTRIBUTE TO THE PROJECT

29 King David said to the entire assembly: "My son Solomon,
the one whom God has chosen, is just an inexperienced
young man, and the task is great, for this palace is not for man,
but for the LORD God. 2 So I have made every effort to provide
what is needed for the temple of my God, including the gold, silver, bronze, iron, wood, as well as a large amount of onyx, settings
of antimony and other stones, all kinds of precious stones, and
alabaster. 3 Now, to show my commitment to the temple of my
God, I donate my personal treasure of gold and silver to the temple of my God, in addition to all that I have already supplied for
this holy temple. 4 This includes 3,000 talents of gold from Ophir
and 7,000 talents of refined silver for overlaying the walls of the
buildings, 5 for gold and silver items, and for all the work of the
craftsmen. Who else wants to contribute to the LORD today?"
6 The leaders of the families, the leaders of the Israelite tribes,
the commanders of units of a thousand and a hundred, and the
supervisors of the king's work contributed willingly. 7 They donated for the service of God's temple 5,000 talents and 10,000
darics of gold, 10,000 talents of silver, 18,000 talents of bronze,
and 100,000 talents of iron. 8 All who possessed precious stones
donated them to the treasury of the LORD's temple, which was
under the supervision of Jehiel the Gershonite. 9 The people
were delighted with their donations, for they contributed to the
LORD with a willing attitude; King David was also very happy.

DAVID PRAISES THE LORD

10 David praised the LORD before the entire assembly:
"O LORD God of our father Israel, you deserve praise forevermore! 11 O LORD, you are great, mighty, majestic, magnificent,
glorious, and sovereign over all the sky and earth! You, LORD,
have dominion and exalt yourself as the ruler of all. 12 You are
the source of wealth and honor; you rule over all. You possess
strength and might to magnify and give strength to all. 13 Now,
our God, we give thanks to you and praise your majestic name!
14 "But who am I and who are my people, that we should be in
a position to contribute this much? Indeed, everything comes
from you, and we have simply given back to you what is yours.
15 For we are resident foreigners and temporary settlers in your
presence, as all our ancestors were; our days are like a shadow
on the earth, without security. 16 O LORD our God, all this wealth,
which we have collected to build a temple for you to honor your
holy name, comes from you; it all belongs to you. 17 I know, my

God, that you examine thoughts and are pleased with integrity.
With pure motives I contribute all this; and now I look with joy
as your people who have gathered here contribute to you. [18]O
LORD God of our ancestors Abraham, Isaac, and Israel, always
maintain these motives of your people and keep them devoted
to you. [19]Make my son Solomon willing to obey your commands,
rules, and regulations, and to complete building the palace for
which I have made preparations."

[20]David told the entire assembly: "Praise the LORD your God!"
So the entire assembly praised the LORD God of their ancestors;
they bowed down and stretched out flat on the ground before
the LORD and the king.

DAVID DESIGNATES SOLOMON KING

[21]The next day they made sacrifices and offered burnt sacrifices
to the LORD (1,000 bulls, 1,000 rams, 1,000 lambs), along with
their accompanying drink offerings and many other sacrifices
for all Israel. [22]They held a feast before the LORD that day and
celebrated.

Then they designated Solomon, David's son, as king a second
time; before the LORD they anointed him as ruler and Zadok
as priest. [23]Solomon sat on the LORD's throne as king in place
of his father David; he was successful and all Israel was loyal
to him. [24]All the officers and warriors, as well as all of King David's sons, pledged their allegiance to King Solomon. [25]The LORD
greatly magnified Solomon before all Israel and bestowed on
him greater majesty than any king of Israel before him.

DAVID'S REIGN COMES TO AN END

[26]David son of Jesse reigned over all Israel. [27]He reigned over
Israel forty years; he reigned in Hebron seven years and in Jerusalem thirty-three years. [28]He died at a good old age, having enjoyed long life, wealth, and honor. His son Solomon succeeded
him. [29]King David's accomplishments, from start to finish, are
recorded in the Annals of Samuel the prophet, the Annals of Nathan the prophet, and the Annals of Gad the prophet. [30]Recorded
there are all the facts about his reign and accomplishments, and
an account of the events that involved him, Israel, and all the
neighboring kingdoms.

HE felt COMPASSION for HIS PEOPLE

MEMORY VERSE

The Lord God of their ancestors continually warned them through his messengers, for he felt compassion for his people and his dwelling place.

2 Chronicles 36:15

2 Chronicles

INTRODUCTION

A Covenant-Keeping God

Second Chronicles was originally written as a message to the Jews who returned to Jerusalem from exile in Babylon. The covenant faithfulness of God is the main focus, as it displays the ways God saved and restored Judah. Second Chronicles focuses on the covenant promises of God, despite Israel's disobedience, as it recounts the reigns of the many kings of the nations of Israel and Judah.

The Book of 2 Chronicles begins with the reign of Solomon and ends with the deportation of the people of Judah from Jerusalem by the Babylonians. Second Chronicles focuses on the covenant God made with David and the continuation of that line through the nation of Judah, the inheritors of God's promise to David. It follows a similar pattern as the books of 1 and 2 Kings, but with a strong focus on the kings of Judah and their successes and failures that led to the eventual destruction of Jerusalem and exile by the Babylonians.

The events in 2 Chronicles take place during the monarchy period, about 970 to 586 B.C. The book was likely written around 425 B.C. by Ezra, as Jewish tradition identifies. First and Second Chronicles were originally one book, and the overall consistency of style indicates that although several contributors might have worked on it, one editor shaped the final product. Jewish tradition holds that the book was compiled by Ezra, who used several sources and documents to reconstruct Israel's history.

The Book of 2 Chronicles displays the covenant-keeping character of God. Written to inspire the remnant of Judah to follow in the spiritual footsteps of David, this book reveals the way God's kingdom and people prevail because of His faithfulness. By understanding that our God today is the same God who established, protected, and redeemed Judah, we can more clearly see the covenant faithfulness He displays in our own lives and love Him greatly.

France

OFFICIAL LANGUAGE
French
POPULATION
64,920,000
UNREACHED POPULATION
4,231,000
PROFESSING CHRISTIANS
62.3%

Jessica's Ministry

Say a Prayer Today

Pray for Jessica and her ministry working with the Love God Greatly French branch. Pray God would continue to work in and transform the lives of women who study God's Word through these resources.

HISTORY BIT

The Bible was first translated into French in 1530 by Jacques Lefèvre d'Étaples. At this time, translations of the Bible in languages other than Latin were believed to be heretical and were burned, and the people who translated and distributed them were persecuted.*

Source Information:
https://joshuaproject.net/countries/FR
*John Bowden, A Chronology of World Christianity (New York, NY: Continuum, 2007), 270.

JESSICA'S STORY

I thought I was too busy. With a full time job, an active teenager, a preschooler, and a husband working six days a week, there was no way I could add something else to my plate. I knew I wanted and needed to be involved in a Bible study, but I couldn't seem to find a time that worked. I came across the Love God Greatly community and decided to try one of the Bible studies.

One thing led to another, and I found myself working closely with the French translation branch, creating graphics for their ministry. I only spoke a little French, but God took the small skill I had and multiplied it.

What I have seen most in the years I've worked with Love God Greatly is the way God fulfills His promise to send messengers to the ends of the earth. Women all over the world are desperate for Bible studies in their native language, especially Bible studies created for women. I've seen God answer prayers and impact lives through the faithful ministry of others.

In my own life there have been hard times, but having the Lord as my Savior and godly women in my life has made all the difference. We can count on Him. He has always been faithful to His people, even when they have turned from Him. When we turn back to God, no matter how far we've strayed, He answers us. He will never leave us nor forsake us. He is the covenant-keeping God.

4 WEEK READING PLAN

LOVE HIS WORD

	MONDAY	TUESDAY	WEDNESDAY	THURSDAY	FRIDAY
1	2 Chronicles 1-2	2 Chronicles 3:1—5:1	2 Chronicles 5:2—6:42	2 Chronicles 7-8	2 Chronicles 9:1—11:4
	SOAP Psalm 73:1-3	SOAP Psalm 73:4-6	SOAP Psalm 73:7-9	SOAP Psalm 73:10-12	SOAP Psalm 73:13-15
2	2 Chronicles 11:5—12:16	2 Chronicles 13:1—14:1	2 Chronicles 14:2—15:18	2 Chronicles 15:19—17:19	2 Chronicles 18:1—19:3
	SOAP Psalm 73:16-17	SOAP Psalm 73:18-20	SOAP Psalm 73:21-23	SOAP Psalm 73:24-35	SOAP Psalm 73:26-28
3	2 Chronicles 19:4—21:1	2 Chronicles 21:2—22:9	2 Chronicles 22:10—23:21	2 Chronicles 24-25	2 Chronicles 26-27
	SOAP Psalm 74:1-2	SOAP Psalm 74:3-5	SOAP Psalm 74:6-8	SOAP Psalm 74:9-10	SOAP Psalm 74:11-13
4	2 Chronicles 28-29	2 Chronicles 30:1—31:1	2 Chronicles 31:2—32:33	2 Chronicles 33-34	2 Chronicles 35-36
	SOAP Psalm 74:14-16	SOAP Psalm 74:17-18	SOAP Psalm 74:19-21	SOAP Psalm 74:22-23	SOAP 2 Chronicles 36:15

THE LORD GIVES SOLOMON WISDOM

1 Solomon son of David solidified his royal authority, for the
LORD his God was with him and magnified him greatly.
2 Solomon addressed all Israel, including those who commanded units of a thousand and a hundred, the judges, and all
the leaders of all Israel who were heads of families. 3 Solomon
and the entire assembly went to the worship center in Gibeon,
for the tent where they met God was located there, which Moses the LORD's servant had made in the wilderness. 4 (Now David had brought up the ark of God from Kiriath Jearim to the
place he had prepared for it, for he had pitched a tent for it in
Jerusalem. 5 But the bronze altar made by Bezalel son of Uri, son
of Hur, was in front of the LORD's tabernacle. Solomon and the
entire assembly prayed to him there.) 6 Solomon went up to the
bronze altar before the LORD which was at the meeting tent, and
he offered up 1,000 burnt sacrifices.
7 That night God appeared to Solomon and said to him, "Tell me
what I should give you." 8 Solomon replied to God, "You demonstrated great loyalty to my father David and have made me king in
his place. 9 Now, LORD God, may your promise to my father David
be realized, for you have made me king over a great nation as numerous as the dust of the earth. 10 Now give me wisdom and discernment so I can effectively lead this nation. Otherwise no one
is able to make judicial decisions for this great nation of yours."
11 God said to Solomon, "Because you desire this, and did not ask
for riches, wealth, and honor, or for vengeance on your enemies,
and because you did not ask for long life, but requested wisdom
and discernment so you can make judicial decisions for my people over whom I have made you king, 12 you are granted wisdom
and discernment. Furthermore I am giving you riches, wealth,
and honor surpassing that of any king before or after you."
13 Solomon left the meeting tent at the worship center in Gibeon and went to Jerusalem, where he reigned over Israel.

SOLOMON'S WEALTH

14 Solomon accumulated chariots and horses. He had 1,400 chariots and 12,000 horses . He kept them in assigned cities and in
Jerusalem. 15 The king made silver and gold as plentiful in Jerusalem as stones; cedar was as plentiful as sycamore fig trees are
in the foothills. 16 Solomon acquired his horses from Egypt and
from Que; the king's traders purchased them from Que. 17 They
paid 600 silver pieces for each chariot from Egypt, and 150 silver pieces for each horse. They also sold chariots and horses to
all the kings of the Hittites and to the kings of Syria.

SOLOMON GATHERS BUILDING MATERIALS FOR THE TEMPLE

2 Solomon ordered a temple to be built to honor the LORD,
as well as a royal palace for himself. 2 Solomon had 70,000
common laborers and 80,000 stonecutters in the hills, in addition to 3,600 supervisors.
3 Solomon sent a message to King Huram of Tyre: "Help me as
you did my father David, when you sent him cedar logs for the
construction of his palace. 4 Look, I am ready to build a temple

to honor the LORD my God and to dedicate it to him in order to
burn fragrant incense before him, to set out the bread that is
regularly displayed, and to offer burnt sacrifices each morning
and evening, and on Sabbaths, new moon festivals, and at other
times appointed by the LORD our God. This is something Israel
must do on a permanent basis. 5 I will build a great temple, for
our God is greater than all gods. 6 Of course, who can really build
a temple for him, since the sky and the highest heavens cannot
contain him? Who am I that I should build him a temple! It will
really be only a place to offer sacrifices before him.

7 "Now send me a man who is skilled in working with gold,
silver, bronze, and iron, as well as purple-, crimson-, and blue-
colored fabrics, and who knows how to engrave. He will work with
my skilled craftsmen here in Jerusalem and Judah, whom my father David provided. 8 Send me cedars, evergreens, and algum
trees from Lebanon, for I know your servants are adept at cutting
down trees in Lebanon. My servants will work with your servants
9 to supply me with large quantities of timber, for I am building a great, magnificent temple. 10 Look, I will pay your servants
who cut the timber 20,000 cors of ground wheat, 20,000 cors of
barley, 120,000 gallons of wine, and 120,000 gallons of olive oil."

11 King Huram of Tyre sent this letter to Solomon: "Because
the LORD loves his people, he has made you their king." 12 Huram also said, "Worthy of praise is the LORD God of Israel, who
made the sky and the earth! He has given King David a wise son
who has discernment and insight and will build a temple for
the LORD, as well as a royal palace for himself. 13 Now I am sending you Huram Abi, a skilled and capable man, 14 whose mother
is a Danite and whose father is a Tyrian. He knows how to work
with gold, silver, bronze, iron, stones, and wood, as well as purple, blue, white, and crimson fabrics. He knows how to do all
kinds of engraving and understands any design given to him.
He will work with your skilled craftsmen and the skilled craftsmen of my lord David your father. 15 Now let my lord send to his
servants the wheat, barley, olive oil, and wine he has promised;
16 we will get all the timber you need from Lebanon and bring
it in raft-like bundles by sea to Joppa. You can then haul it on
up to Jerusalem."

17 Solomon took a census of all the male resident foreigners in
the land of Israel, after the census his father David had taken.
There were 153,600 in all. 18 He designated 70,000 as common
laborers, 80,000 as stonecutters in the hills, and 3,600 as supervisors to make sure the people completed the work.

THE BUILDING OF THE TEMPLE

3 Solomon began building the LORD's temple in Jerusalem on
Mount Moriah, where the LORD had appeared to his father
David. This was the place that David prepared at the threshing
floor of Ornan the Jebusite. 2 He began building on the second
day of the second month of the fourth year of his reign.

3 Solomon laid the foundation for God's temple; its length (determined according to the old standard of measure) was 90 feet,
and its width 30 feet. 4 The porch in front of the main hall was 30
feet long, corresponding to the width of the temple, and its height

was 30 feet. He plated the inside with pure gold. 5 He paneled the
main hall with boards made from evergreen trees and plated it
with fine gold, decorated with palm trees and chains. 6 He decorated the temple with precious stones; the gold he used came
from Parvaim. 7 He overlaid the temple's rafters, thresholds, walls
and doors with gold; he carved decorative cherubim on the walls.
8 He made the Most Holy Place; its length was 30 feet, corresponding to the width of the temple, and its width 30 feet. He
plated it with 600 talents of fine gold. 9 The gold nails weighed 50
shekels; he also plated the upper areas with gold. 10 In the Most
Holy Place he made two images of cherubim and plated them
with gold. 11 The combined wing span of the cherubim was 30 feet.
One of the first cherub's wings was 7½ long and touched one
wall of the temple; its other wing was also 7½ long and touched
one of the second cherub's wings. 12 Likewise one of the second
cherub's wings was 7½ long and touched the other wall of the
temple; its other wing was also 7½ long and touched one of the
first cherub's wings. 13 The combined wingspan of these cherubim was 30 feet. They stood upright, facing inward. 14 He made
the curtain out of blue, purple, crimson, and white fabrics, and
embroidered on it decorative cherubim.
15 In front of the temple he made two pillars which had a combined length of 52½ feet, with each having a plated capital 7½
high. 16 He made ornamental chains and put them on top of the
pillars. He also made 100 pomegranate-shaped ornaments and
arranged them within the chains. 17 He set up the pillars in front
of the temple, one on the right side and the other on the left. He
named the one on the right Yakin, and the one on the left Boaz.
4 He made a bronze altar, 30 feet long, 30 feet wide, and 15 feet
high. 2 He also made the big bronze basin called "The Sea."
It measured 15 feet from rim to rim, was circular in shape, and
stood 7½ high. Its circumference was 45 feet. 3 Images of bulls
were under it all the way around, ten every 18 inches all the way
around. The bulls were in two rows and had been cast with "The
Sea." 4 "The Sea" stood on top of twelve bulls. Three faced northward, three westward, three southward, and three eastward. "The
Sea" was placed on top of them, and they all faced outward. 5 It
was four fingers thick, and its rim was like that of a cup shaped
like a lily blossom. It could hold 18,000 gallons. 6 He made ten
washing basins; he put five on the south side and five on the
north side. In them they rinsed the items used for burnt sacrifices; the priests washed in "The Sea."
7 He made ten gold lampstands according to specifications
and put them in the temple, five on the right and five on the
left. 8 He made ten tables and set them in the temple, five on
the right and five on the left. He also made 100 gold bowls. 9 He
made the courtyard of the priests and the large enclosure and
its doors; he plated their doors with bronze. 10 He put "The Sea"
on the south side, in the southeast corner.
11 Huram Abi made the pots, shovels, and bowls. He finished all
the work on God's temple he had been assigned by King Solomon.
12 He made the two pillars, the two bowl-shaped tops of the pillars, the latticework for the bowl-shaped tops of the two pillars,
13 the 400 pomegranate-shaped ornaments for the latticework

of the two pillars (each latticework had two rows of these ornaments at the bowl-shaped top of the pillar), 14 the ten movable
stands with their ten basins, 15 the big bronze basin called "The
Sea" with its twelve bulls underneath, 16 and the pots, shovels,
and meat forks. All the items King Solomon assigned Huram
Abi to make for the LORD's temple were made from polished
bronze. 17 The king had them cast in earth foundries in the region of the Jordan between Sukkoth and Zarethan. 18 Solomon
made so many of these items they did not weigh the bronze.

19 Solomon also made these items for God's temple: the gold
altar, the tables on which the Bread of the Presence was kept,
20 the pure gold lampstands and their lamps which burned as
specified at the entrance to the inner sanctuary, 21 the pure gold
flower-shaped ornaments, lamps, and tongs, 22 the pure gold
trimming shears, basins, pans, and censers, and the gold door
sockets for the inner sanctuary (the Most Holy Place) and for
5 the doors of the main hall of the temple. 1 When Solomon
had finished constructing the LORD's temple, he put the holy
items that belonged to his father David (the silver, gold, and all
the other articles) in the treasuries of God's temple.

SOLOMON MOVES THE ARK INTO THE TEMPLE

2 Then Solomon convened Israel's elders—all the leaders of the
Israelite tribes and families—in Jerusalem, so they could witness
the transferal of the ark of the covenant of the LORD from the
City of David (that is, Zion). 3 All the men of Israel assembled before the king during the festival in the seventh month. 4 When
all Israel's elders had arrived, the Levites lifted the ark. 5 The
priests and Levites carried the ark, the tent where God appeared
to his people, and all the holy items in the tent. 6 Now King Solomon and all the Israelites who had assembled with him went
on ahead of the ark and sacrificed more sheep and cattle than
could be counted or numbered.

7 The priests brought the ark of the covenant of the LORD to
its assigned place in the inner sanctuary of the temple, in the
Most Holy Place under the wings of the cherubim. 8 The cherubim's wings extended over the place where the ark sat; the cherubim overshadowed the ark and its poles. 9 The poles were so long
their ends extending out from the ark were visible from in front
of the inner sanctuary, but they could not be seen from beyond
that point. They have remained there to this very day. 10 There
was nothing in the ark except the two tablets Moses had placed
there in Horeb. (It was there that the LORD made a covenant with
the Israelites after he brought them out of the land of Egypt.)

11 The priests left the Holy Place. All the priests who participated had consecrated themselves, no matter which division
they represented. 12 All the Levites who were musicians, including Asaph, Heman, Jeduthun, and their sons and relatives, wore
linen. They played cymbals and stringed instruments as they
stood east of the altar. They were accompanied by 120 priests
who blew trumpets. 13 The trumpeters and musicians played together, praising and giving thanks to the LORD. Accompanied by
trumpets, cymbals, and other instruments, they loudly praised
the LORD, singing: "Certainly he is good; certainly his loyal love

endures!" Then a cloud filled the LORD's temple. 14 The priests
could not carry out their duties because of the cloud; the LORD's
splendor filled God's temple.

6 Then Solomon said, "The LORD has said that he lives in thick
darkness. 2 O LORD, I have built a lofty temple for you, a place
where you can live permanently." 3 Then the king turned around
and pronounced a blessing over the whole Israelite assembly as
they stood there. 4 He said, "The LORD God of Israel is worthy of
praise because he has fulfilled what he promised my father David. 5 He told David, 'Since the day I brought my people out of the
land of Egypt, I have not chosen a city from all the tribes of Israel
to build a temple in which to live. Nor did I choose a man as leader
of my people Israel. 6 But now I have chosen Jerusalem as a place to
live, and I have chosen David to lead my people Israel.' 7 Now my father David had a strong desire to build a temple to honor the LORD
God of Israel. 8 The LORD told my father David, 'It is right for you to
have a strong desire to build a temple to honor me. 9 But you will
not build the temple; your very own son will build the temple for
my honor.' 10 The LORD has kept the promise he made. I have taken
my father David's place and have occupied the throne of Israel, as
the LORD promised. I have built this temple for the honor of the
LORD God of Israel 11 and set up in it a place for the ark containing
the covenant the LORD made with the Israelites."

12 He stood before the altar of the LORD in front of the entire
assembly of Israel and spread out his hands. 13 Solomon had made
a bronze platform and had placed it in the middle of the enclosure. It was 7½ long, 7½ wide, and 4½ feet high. He stood on it
and then got down on his knees in front of the entire assembly
of Israel. He spread out his hands toward the sky, 14 and prayed:
"O LORD God of Israel, there is no god like you in heaven or on
earth! You maintain covenantal loyalty to your servants who
obey you with sincerity. 15 You have kept your word to your servant, my father David; this very day you have fulfilled what you
promised. 16 Now, O LORD God of Israel, keep the promise you
made to your servant, my father David, when you said, 'You will
never fail to have a successor ruling before me on the throne of
Israel, provided that your descendants watch their step and obey
my law as you have done.' 17 Now, O LORD God of Israel, may the
promise you made to your servant David be realized.

18 "God does not really live with humankind on the earth! Look,
if the sky and the highest heaven cannot contain you, how much
less this temple I have built! 19 But respond favorably to your servant's prayer and his request for help, O LORD my God. Answer
the desperate prayer your servant is presenting to you. 20 Night
and day may you watch over this temple, the place where you
promised you would live. May you answer your servant's prayer
for this place. 21 Respond to the requests of your servant and your
people Israel for this place. Hear from your heavenly dwelling
place and respond favorably and forgive.

22 "When someone is accused of sinning against his neighbor
and the latter pronounces a curse on the alleged offender before
your altar in this temple, 23 listen from heaven and make a just decision about your servants' claims. Condemn the guilty party, declare the other innocent, and give both of them what they deserve.

REFLECT

In what ways have you seen God fulfill the promises made in His Word in your life? Praise Him for His faithfulness.

24 "If your people Israel are defeated by an enemy because they sinned against you, then if they come back to you, renew their allegiance to you, and pray for your help before you in this temple, 25 then listen from heaven, forgive the sin of your people Israel, and bring them back to the land you gave to them and their ancestors.

26 "The time will come when the skies are shut up tightly and no rain falls because your people sinned against you. When they direct their prayers toward this place, renew their allegiance to you, and turn away from their sin because you punish them, 27 then listen from heaven and forgive the sin of your servants, your people Israel. Certainly you will then teach them the right way to live and send rain on your land that you have given your people to possess.

28 "The time will come when the land suffers from a famine, a plague, blight, and disease, or a locust invasion, or when their enemy lays siege to the cities of the land, or when some other type of plague or epidemic occurs. 29 When all your people Israel pray and ask for help, as they acknowledge their intense pain and spread out their hands toward this temple, 30 then listen from your heavenly dwelling place, forgive their sin, and act favorably toward each one based on your evaluation of their motives. (Indeed you are the only one who can correctly evaluate the motives of all people.) 31 Then they will honor you by obeying you throughout their lifetimes as they live on the land you gave to our ancestors.

32 "Foreigners who do not belong to your people Israel will come from a distant land because of your great reputation and your ability to accomplish mighty deeds; they will come and direct their prayers toward this temple. 33 Then listen from your heavenly dwelling place and answer all the prayers of the foreigners. Then all the nations of the earth will acknowledge your reputation, obey you as your people Israel do, and recognize that this temple I built belongs to you.

34 "When you direct your people to march out and fight their enemies, and they direct their prayers to you toward this chosen city and this temple I built for your honor, 35 then listen from heaven to their prayers for help and vindicate them.

36 "The time will come when your people will sin against you (for there is no one who is sinless!) and you will be angry at them and deliver them over to their enemies, who will take them as prisoners to their land, whether far away or close by. 37 When your people come to their senses in the land where they are held prisoner, they will repent and beg for your mercy in the land of their imprisonment, admitting, 'We have sinned and gone astray, we have done evil!' 38 When they return to you with all their heart and being in the land where they are held prisoner and direct their prayers toward the land you gave to their ancestors, your chosen city, and the temple I built for your honor, 39 then listen from your heavenly dwelling place to their prayers for help, vindicate them, and forgive your sinful people.

40 "Now, my God, may you be attentive and responsive to the prayers offered in this place. 41 Now ascend, O LORD God, to your resting place, you and the ark of your strength! May your priests, O LORD God, experience your deliverance. May your loyal followers rejoice in the prosperity you give. 42 O LORD God, do not reject your chosen ones! Remember the faithful promises you made to your servant David!"

SOLOMON DEDICATES THE TEMPLE

7 When Solomon finished praying, fire came down from heaven
and consumed the burnt offering and the sacrifices, and the
LORD's splendor filled the temple. 2 The priests were unable to
enter the LORD's temple because the LORD's splendor filled
the LORD's temple. 3 When all the Israelites saw the fire come
down and the LORD's splendor over the temple, they got on their
knees with their faces downward toward the pavement. They
worshiped and gave thanks to the LORD, saying, "Certainly he
is good; certainly his loyal love endures!"
4 The king and all the people were presenting sacrifices to
the LORD. 5 King Solomon sacrificed 22,000 cattle and 120,000
sheep. Then the king and all the people dedicated God's temple. 6 The priests stood in their assigned spots, along with the
Levites who had the musical instruments used for praising
the LORD. (These were the ones King David made for giving
thanks to the LORD and which were used by David when he
offered praise, saying, "Certainly his loyal love endures.") Opposite the Levites, the priests were blowing the trumpets,
while all Israel stood there. 7 Solomon consecrated the middle of the courtyard that is in front of the LORD's temple. He
offered burnt sacrifices, grain offerings, and the fat from the
peace offerings there, because the bronze altar that Solomon
had made was too small to hold all these offerings. 8 At that
time Solomon and all Israel with him celebrated a festival for
seven days. This great assembly included people from Lebo Hamath in the north to the Stream of Egypt in the south. 9 On
the eighth day they held an assembly, for they had dedicated
the altar for seven days and celebrated the festival for seven
more days. 10 On the twenty-third day of the seventh month,
Solomon sent the people home. They left happy and contented
because of the good the LORD had done for David, Solomon,
and his people Israel.

THE LORD GIVES SOLOMON A PROMISE AND A WARNING

11 After Solomon finished building the LORD's temple and the
royal palace and accomplished all his plans for the LORD's temple and his royal palace, 12 the LORD appeared to Solomon at
night and said to him: "I have answered your prayer and chosen this place to be my temple where sacrifices are to be made.
13 When I close up the sky so that it doesn't rain, or command
locusts to devour the land's vegetation, or send a plague among
my people, 14 if my people, who belong to me, humble themselves, pray, seek to please me, and repudiate their sinful practices, then I will respond from heaven, forgive their sin, and
heal their land. 15 Now I will be attentive and responsive to the
prayers offered in this place. 16 Now I have chosen and consecrated this temple by making it my permanent home; I will be
constantly present there. 17 You must serve me as your father
David did. Do everything I commanded and obey my rules and
regulations. 18 Then I will establish your dynasty, just as I promised your father David, 'You will not fail to have a successor ruling over Israel.'

LOVE TO GROW

IF MY PEOPLE . . .

2 CHRONICLES 7:14

Reading 2 Chronicles 7:14 reminds me of how amazing our God is! Like a loving Father, He always makes a way to forgiveness. He reminds us that we are His, called by His name. There is no mistake to whom we belong. Even in our mistakes, even in our rebellion, even in our sin, we are still His.

I've prayed 2 Chronicles 7:14 over and over in the past few years: "Father, forgive us. Heal our land, heal our homes, heal our hearts. We've turned from You." Oh sisters, we are the modern-day Israelites. God has done amazing things in our lives, in our families, and in our countries, and we have forgotten. We have turned to fake gods to find our answers, our worth, our hope, and our future. We have grieved the heart of the One who laid His life down for ours.

God, in His great mercy, once again extends forgiveness. Second Chronicles 7:14 reminds us of His heart for His children. He gave the Israelites four commands that we can follow today.

> Humble yourselves: Acknowledge we aren't God and we don't know it all. Confess we've sinned and gone our own way instead of His.
>
> Pray: Confess our shortcomings and ask God for forgiveness. Admit where we've gone wrong and own up to it.
>
> Seek to please Me: Instead of turning away from God due to our sin, we must turn to God and seek Him, His help, His mercy, and His will instead of our own. A heart that seeks to please God is a heart that pleases God.
>
> Turn from sin: We must put our words into action and change. Words are meaningless if a changed behavior doesn't follow.

God promises that when His people do these things He will "respond from heaven, forgive their sin, and heal their land" (2 Chr 7:14).

Hear, forgive, and heal. We must never forget we serve a holy and grace-filled God. Now is the time to humble ourselves, admit where we have strayed, and seek the One who first sought us. With His power we turn from our sins, embrace His forgiveness, and live as daughters of the King of kings!

19 “But if you people ever turn away from me, fail to obey the
regulations and rules I instructed you to keep, and decide to
serve and worship other gods, 20 then I will remove you from
my land I have given you, I will abandon this temple I have consecrated with my presence, and I will make you an object of
mockery and ridicule among all the nations. 21 As for this temple, which was once majestic, everyone who passes by it will be
shocked and say, ‘Why did the LORD do this to this land and this
temple?’ 22 Others will then answer, ‘Because they abandoned the
LORD God of their ancestors, who led them out of Egypt. They
embraced other gods whom they worshiped and served. That is
why he brought all this disaster down on them.’”

BUILDING PROJECTS AND COMMERCIAL EFFORTS

8 After twenty years, during which Solomon built the LORD’s
temple and his royal palace, 2 Solomon rebuilt the cities that
Huram had given him and settled Israelites there. 3 Solomon
went to Hamath Zobah and seized it. 4 He built up Tadmor in the
wilderness and all the storage cities he had built in Hamath. 5 He
made upper Beth Horon and lower Beth Horon fortified cities
with walls and barred gates, 6 and built up Baalath, all the storage cities that belonged to him, and all the cities where chariots
and horses were kept. He built whatever he wanted in Jerusalem, Lebanon, and throughout his entire kingdom.

7 Now several non-Israelite peoples were left in the land after
the conquest of Joshua, including the Hittites, Amorites, Perizzites, Hivites, and Jebusites. 8 Their descendants remained in the
land (the Israelites were unable to wipe them out). Solomon conscripted them for his work crews, and they continue in that role
to this very day. 9 Solomon did not assign Israelites to these work
crews; the Israelites served as his soldiers, officers, charioteers,
and commanders of his chariot forces. 10 These men worked for
King Solomon as supervisors; there were a total of 250 of them
who were in charge of the people.

11 Solomon moved Pharaoh’s daughter up from the City of David to the palace he had built for her, for he said, “My wife must
not live in the palace of King David of Israel, for the places where
the ark of the LORD has entered are holy.”

12 Then Solomon offered burnt sacrifices to the LORD on the
altar of the LORD which he had built in front of the temple’s
porch. 13 He observed the daily requirements for sacrifices that
Moses had specified for Sabbaths, new moon festivals, and the
three annual celebrations—the Feast of Unleavened Bread, the
Feast of Weeks, and the Feast of Shelters. 14 As his father David
had decreed, Solomon appointed the divisions of the priests
to do their assigned tasks, the Levitical orders to lead worship
and help the priests with their daily tasks, and the divisions of
the gatekeepers to serve at their assigned gates. This was what
David the man of God had ordered. 15 They did not neglect any
detail of the king’s orders pertaining to the priests, Levites, and
treasuries.

16 All the work ordered by Solomon was completed, from the
day the foundation of the LORD’s temple was laid until it was
finished; the LORD’s temple was completed.

17 Then Solomon went to Ezion Geber and to Elat on the coast in the land of Edom. 18 Huram sent him ships and some of his sailors, men who were well acquainted with the sea. They sailed with Solomon's men to Ophir and took from there 450 talents of gold, which they brought back to King Solomon.

SOLOMON ENTERTAINS A QUEEN

9

When the queen of Sheba heard about Solomon, she came to challenge him with difficult questions. She arrived in Jerusalem with a great display of pomp, bringing with her camels carrying spices, a very large quantity of gold, and precious gems. She visited Solomon and discussed with him everything that was on her mind. 2 Solomon answered all her questions; there was no question too complex for the king. 3 When the queen of Sheba saw for herself Solomon's wisdom, the palace he had built, 4 the food in his banquet hall, his servants and attendants in their robes, his cupbearers in their robes, and his burnt sacrifices which he presented in the LORD's temple, she was amazed. 5 She said to the king, "The report I heard in my own country about your wise sayings and insight was true! 6 I did not believe these things until I came and saw them with my own eyes. Indeed, I didn't hear even half the story! Your wisdom surpasses what was reported to me. 7 Your attendants, who stand before you at all times and hear your wise sayings, are truly happy! 8 May the LORD your God be praised because he favored you by placing you on his throne as the one ruling on his behalf. Because of your God's love for Israel and his lasting commitment to them, he made you king over them so you could make just and right decisions." 9 She gave the king 120 talents of gold and a very large quantity of spices and precious gems. The quantity of spices the queen of Sheba gave King Solomon has never been matched. 10 (Huram's servants, aided by Solomon's servants, brought gold from Ophir, as well as fine timber and precious gems. 11 With the timber the king made steps for the LORD's temple and royal palace as well as stringed instruments for the musicians. No one had seen anything like them in the land of Judah before that.) 12 King Solomon gave the queen of Sheba everything she requested, more than what she had brought him. Then she left and returned to her homeland with her attendants.

SOLOMON'S WEALTH

13 Solomon received 666 talents of gold per year, 14 besides what he collected from the merchants and traders. All the Arabian kings and the governors of the land also brought gold and silver to Solomon. 15 King Solomon made 200 large shields of hammered gold; 600 measures of hammered gold were used for each shield. 16 He also made 300 small shields of hammered gold; 300 measures of gold were used for each of those shields. The king placed them in the Palace of the Lebanon Forest.

17 The king made a large throne decorated with ivory and overlaid it with pure gold. 18 There were six steps leading up to the throne, and a gold footstool was attached to the throne. The throne had two armrests with a statue of a lion standing on each side. 19 There were twelve statues of lions on the six steps, one lion at each end of each step. There was nothing like it in any other kingdom.

20 All of King Solomon's cups were made of gold, and all the household items in the Palace of the Lebanon Forest were made of pure gold. There were no silver items, for silver was not considered very valuable in Solomon's time. 21 The king had a fleet of large merchant ships manned by Huram's men that sailed the sea. Once every three years the fleet came into port with cargoes of gold, silver, ivory, apes, and peacocks.

22 King Solomon was wealthier and wiser than any of the kings of the earth. 23 All the kings of the earth wanted to visit Solomon to see him display his God-given wisdom. 24 Year after year visitors brought their gifts, which included items of silver, items of gold, clothes, perfume, spices, horses, and mules.

25 Solomon had 4,000 stalls for his chariot horses and 12,000 horses. He kept them in assigned cities and also with him in Jerusalem. 26 He ruled all the kingdoms from the Euphrates River to the land of the Philistines as far as the border of Egypt. 27 The king made silver as plentiful in Jerusalem as stones; cedar was as plentiful as sycamore fig trees are in the foothills. 28 Solomon acquired horses from Egypt and from all the lands.

SOLOMON'S REIGN ENDS

29 The rest of the events of Solomon's reign, from start to finish, are recorded in the Annals of Nathan the Prophet, the Prophecy of Ahijah the Shilonite, and the Vision of Iddo the Seer pertaining to Jeroboam son of Nebat. 30 Solomon ruled over all Israel from Jerusalem for forty years. 31 Then Solomon passed away and was buried in the city of his father David. His son Rehoboam replaced him as king.

THE NORTHERN TRIBES REBEL

10 Rehoboam traveled to Shechem, for all Israel had gathered in Shechem to make Rehoboam king. 2 When Jeroboam son of Nebat heard the news, he was still in Egypt, where he had fled from King Solomon. Jeroboam returned from Egypt. 3 They sent for him, and Jeroboam and all Israel came and spoke to Rehoboam, saying, 4 "Your father made us work too hard! Now if you lighten the demands he made and don't make us work as hard, we will serve you." 5 He said to them, "Go away for three days, then return to me." So the people went away.

6 King Rehoboam consulted with the older advisers who had served his father Solomon when he had been alive. He asked them, "How do you advise me to answer these people?" 7 They said to him, "If you are fair to these people, grant their request, and are cordial to them, they will be your servants from this time forward." 8 But Rehoboam rejected their advice and consulted the young advisers who served him, with whom he had grown up. 9 He asked them, "How do you advise me to respond to these people who said to me, 'Lessen the demands your father placed on us'?" 10 The young advisers with whom Rehoboam had grown up said to him, "Say this to these people who have said to you, 'Your father made us work hard, but now lighten our burden'—say this to them: 'I am a lot harsher than my father! 11 My father imposed heavy demands on you; I will make them even heavier. My father punished you with ordinary whips; I will punish you with whips that really sting your flesh.'"

REFLECT

When have you rejected wise counsel? How did it turn out? What can we learn from Rehoboam's mistake?

12 Jeroboam and all the people reported to Rehoboam on the
third day, just as the king had ordered when he said, "Return
to me on the third day." 13 The king responded to the people
harshly. He rejected the advice of the older men 14 and followed
the advice of the younger ones. He said, "My father imposed
heavy demands on you; I will make them even heavier. My father punished you with ordinary whips; I will punish you with
whips that really sting your flesh." 15 The king refused to listen
to the people, because God was instigating this turn of events
so that he might bring to pass the prophetic announcement
he had made through Ahijah the Shilonite to Jeroboam son
of Nebat.

16 When all Israel saw that the king refused to listen to them,
the people answered the king, "We have no portion in David—no
share in the son of Jesse! Return to your homes, O Israel! Now,
look after your own dynasty, O David!" So all Israel returned to
their homes. 17 (Rehoboam continued to rule over the Israelites
who lived in the cities of Judah.) 18 King Rehoboam sent Hadoram, the supervisor of the work crews, out after them, but the
Israelites stoned him to death. King Rehoboam managed to
jump into his chariot and escape to Jerusalem. 19 So Israel has
been in rebellion against the Davidic dynasty to this very day.

11 When Rehoboam arrived in Jerusalem, he summoned 180,000
skilled warriors from Judah and Benjamin to attack Israel
and restore the kingdom to Rehoboam. 2 But the LORD's message came to the prophet Shemaiah, 3 "Say this to King Rehoboam son of Solomon of Judah and to all the Israelites in Judah
and Benjamin, 4 'The LORD says this: "Do not attack and make
war with your brothers. Each of you go home, for I have caused
this to happen."'" They obeyed the LORD and called off the attack against Jeroboam.

REHOBOAM'S REIGN

5 Rehoboam lived in Jerusalem; he built up these fortified cities
throughout Judah: 6 Bethlehem, Etam, Tekoa, 7 Beth Zur, Soco,
Adullam, 8 Gath, Mareshah, Ziph, 9 Adoraim, Lachish, Azekah,
10 Zorah, Aijalon, and Hebron. These were the fortified cities in
Judah and Benjamin. 11 He fortified these cities and placed officers in them, as well as storehouses of food, olive oil, and wine.
12 In each city there were shields and spears; he strongly fortified them. Judah and Benjamin belonged to him.

13 The priests and Levites who lived throughout Israel supported him, no matter where they resided. 14 The Levites even
left their pasturelands and their property behind and came to
Judah and Jerusalem, for Jeroboam and his sons prohibited them
from serving as the LORD's priests. 15 Jeroboam appointed his
own priests to serve at the worship centers and to lead in the
worship of the goat idols and calf idols he had made. 16 Those
among all the Israelite tribes who were determined to worship
the LORD God of Israel followed them to Jerusalem to sacrifice
to the LORD God of their ancestors. 17 They supported the kingdom of Judah and were loyal to Rehoboam son of Solomon for
three years; they followed the edicts of David and Solomon for
three years.

18 Rehoboam married Mahalath the daughter of David's son
Jerimoth and of Abihail, the daughter of Jesse's son Eliab. 19 She
bore him sons named Jeush, Shemariah, and Zaham. 20 He later
married Maacah the daughter of Absalom. She bore to him
Abijah, Attai, Ziza, and Shelomith. 21 Rehoboam loved Maacah
daughter of Absalom more than his other wives and concubines.
He had eighteen wives and sixty concubines; he fathered twenty-
eight sons and sixty daughters.

22 Rehoboam appointed Abijah son of Maacah as the leader over
his brothers, for he intended to name him his successor. 23 He
wisely placed some of his many sons throughout the regions of Judah and Benjamin in the various fortified cities. He supplied them
with abundant provisions and acquired many wives for them.

12 After Rehoboam's rule was established and solidified, he
and all Israel rejected the law of the LORD. 2 Because they
were unfaithful to the LORD, in King Rehoboam's fifth year, King
Shishak of Egypt attacked Jerusalem. 3 He had 1,200 chariots,
60,000 horsemen, and an innumerable number of soldiers who
accompanied him from Egypt, including Libyans, Sukkites, and
Cushites. 4 He captured the fortified cities of Judah and marched
against Jerusalem.

5 Shemaiah the prophet visited Rehoboam and the leaders of
Judah who were assembled in Jerusalem because of Shishak. He
said to them, "This is what the LORD says: 'You have rejected me,
so I have rejected you and will hand you over to Shishak.'" 6 The
leaders of Israel and the king humbled themselves and said, "The
LORD is just." 7 When the LORD saw that they humbled themselves, the LORD's message came to Shemaiah: "They have humbled themselves, so I will not destroy them. I will deliver them
soon. My anger will not be unleashed against Jerusalem through
Shishak. 8 Yet they will become his subjects, so they can experience
how serving me differs from serving the surrounding nations."

9 King Shishak of Egypt attacked Jerusalem and took away the
treasures of the LORD's temple and of the royal palace; he took
everything, including the gold shields that Solomon had made.
10 King Rehoboam made bronze shields to replace them and assigned them to the officers of the royal guard who protected the
entrance to the royal palace. 11 Whenever the king visited the
LORD's temple, the royal guards carried them and then brought
them back to the guardroom.

12 So when Rehoboam humbled himself, the LORD relented
from his anger and did not annihilate him; Judah experienced
some good things. 13 King Rehoboam solidified his rule in Jerusalem; he was forty-one years old when he became king, and he
ruled for seventeen years in Jerusalem, the city the LORD chose
from all the tribes of Israel to be his home. Rehoboam's mother
was an Ammonite named Naamah. 14 He did evil because he was
not determined to follow the LORD.

15 The events of Rehoboam's reign, from start to finish, are recorded in the Annals of Shemaiah the Prophet and of Iddo the
Seer that include genealogical records. There were wars between
Rehoboam and Jeroboam continually. 16 Then Rehoboam passed
away and was buried in the City of David. His son Abijah replaced him as king.

ABIJAH'S REIGN

13 In the eighteenth year of the reign of King Jeroboam, Abijah became king over Judah. 2 He ruled for three years in Jerusalem. His mother was Michaiah, the daughter of Uriel from Gibeah.

There was war between Abijah and Jeroboam. 3 Abijah launched the attack with 400,000 well-trained warriors, while Jeroboam deployed against him 800,000 well-trained warriors.

4 Abijah ascended Mount Zemaraim, in the Ephraimite hill country, and said: "Listen to me, Jeroboam and all Israel! 5 Don't you realize that the LORD God of Israel has given David and his dynasty lasting dominion over Israel by a formal covenant? 6 Jeroboam son of Nebat, a servant of Solomon son of David, rose up and rebelled against his master. 7 Lawless good-for-nothing men gathered around him and conspired against Rehoboam son of Solomon, when Rehoboam was an inexperienced young man and could not resist them. 8 Now you are declaring that you will resist the LORD's rule through the Davidic dynasty. You have a huge army, and bring with you the gold calves that Jeroboam made for you as gods. 9 But you banished the LORD's priests, Aaron's descendants, and the Levites, and appointed your own priests just as the surrounding nations do! Anyone who comes to consecrate himself with a young bull or seven rams becomes a priest of these fake gods! 10 But as for us, the LORD is our God and we have not rejected him. Aaron's descendants serve as the LORD's priests, and the Levites assist them with the work. 11 They offer burnt sacrifices to the LORD every morning and every evening, along with fragrant incense. They arrange the Bread of the Presence on a ritually clean table and light the lamps on the gold lampstand every evening. Certainly we are observing the LORD our God's regulations, but you have rejected him. 12 Now look, God is with us as our leader. His priests are ready to blow the trumpets to signal the attack against you. You Israelites, don't fight against the LORD God of your ancestors, for you will not win!"

13 Now Jeroboam had sent some men to ambush the Judahite army from behind. The main army was in front of the Judahite army; the ambushers were behind it. 14 The men of Judah turned around and realized they were being attacked from the front and the rear. So they cried out to the LORD for help. The priests blew their trumpets, 15 and the men of Judah gave the battle cry. As the men of Judah gave the battle cry, God struck down Jeroboam and all Israel before Abijah and Judah. 16 The Israelites fled from before the Judahite army, and God handed them over to the men of Judah. 17 Abijah and his army thoroughly defeated them; 500,000 well-trained Israelite men fell dead. 18 That day the Israelites were defeated; the men of Judah prevailed because they relied on the LORD God of their ancestors.

19 Abijah chased Jeroboam; he seized from him these cities: Bethel and its surrounding towns, Jeshanah and its surrounding towns, and Ephron and its surrounding towns. 20 Jeroboam did not regain power during the reign of Abijah. The LORD struck him down and he died. 21 Abijah's power grew; he had fourteen wives and fathered twenty-two sons and sixteen daughters.

22 The rest of the events of Abijah's reign, including his deeds
and sayings, are recorded in the writings of the prophet Iddo.
14 Abijah passed away and was buried in the City of David. His
son Asa replaced him as king. During his reign the land had
rest for ten years.

ASA'S RELIGIOUS AND MILITARY ACCOMPLISHMENTS

2 Asa did what the LORD his God desired and approved. 3 He removed the pagan altars and the high places, smashed the sacred
pillars, and cut down the Asherah poles. 4 He ordered Judah to
seek the LORD God of their ancestors and to observe his law and
commands. 5 He removed the high places and the incense altars
from all the towns of Judah. The kingdom had rest under his rule.
6 He built fortified cities throughout Judah, for the land was
at rest and there was no war during those years; the LORD gave
him peace. 7 He said to the people of Judah: "Let's build these
cities and fortify them with walls, towers, and barred gates. The
land remains ours because we have followed the LORD our God;
we have followed him, and he has made us secure on all sides."
So they built the cities and prospered.
8 Asa had an army of 300,000 men from Judah, equipped with
large shields and spears. He also had 280,000 men from Benjamin who carried small shields and were adept archers; they were
all skilled warriors. 9 Zerah the Cushite marched against them
with an army of 1,000,000 men and 300 chariots . He arrived at
Mareshah, 10 and Asa went out to oppose him. They deployed for
battle in the Valley of Zephathah near Mareshah.
11 Asa prayed to the LORD his God: "O LORD, there is no one but
you who can help the weak when they are vastly outnumbered.
Help us, O LORD our God, for we rely on you and have marched
on your behalf against this huge army. O LORD, you are our God;
don't let men prevail against you!" 12 The LORD struck down the
Cushites before Asa and Judah. The Cushites fled, 13 and Asa and
his army chased them as far as Gerar. The Cushites were wiped
out; they were shattered before the LORD and his army. The men
of Judah carried off a huge amount of plunder. 14 They defeated
all the towns surrounding Gerar, for the LORD caused them to
panic. The men of Judah looted all the towns, for they contained
a huge amount of goods. 15 They also attacked the tents of the
herdsmen in charge of the livestock. They carried off many sheep
and camels and then returned to Jerusalem.
15 God's Spirit came upon Azariah son of Oded. 2 He met Asa
and told him, "Listen to me, Asa and all Judah and Benjamin! The LORD is with you when you are loyal to him. If you seek
him, he will respond to you, but if you reject him, he will reject
you. 3 For a long time Israel had not sought the one true God, or
a priest to instruct them, or the law. 4 Because of their distress,
they turned back to the LORD God of Israel. They sought him
and he responded to them. 5 In those days no one could travel
safely, for total chaos had overtaken all the people of the surrounding lands. 6 One nation was crushed by another, and one
city by another, for God caused them to be in great turmoil. 7 But
as for you, be strong and don't get discouraged, for your work
will be rewarded."

CHALLENGE

While it appears that God is keeping score of Judah's right and wrong actions, He is displaying His faithfulness to His covenant and to His people. How do Deuteronomy 27 and 28 and James 4:8 also display the covenant-keeping character of God?

8 When Asa heard these words and the prophecy of Oded the
prophet, he was encouraged. He removed the detestable idols
from the entire land of Judah and Benjamin and from the cities he had seized in the Ephraimite hill country. He repaired
the altar of the LORD in front of the porch of the LORD's temple.
9 He assembled all Judah and Benjamin, as well as the settlers
from Ephraim, Manasseh, and Simeon who had come to live
with them. Many people from Israel had come there to live when
they saw that the LORD his God was with him. 10 They assembled in Jerusalem in the third month of the fifteenth year of
Asa's reign. 11 At that time they sacrificed to the LORD some of
the plunder they had brought back, including 700 head of cattle
and 7,000 sheep. 12 They solemnly agreed to seek the LORD God
of their ancestors with their whole heart and being. 13 Anyone
who would not seek the LORD God of Israel would be executed,
whether they were young or old, male or female. 14 They swore
their allegiance to the LORD, shouting their approval loudly and
sounding trumpets and horns. 15 All Judah was happy about the
oath, because they made the vow with their whole heart. They
willingly sought the LORD and he responded to them. He made
them secure on every side.
16 King Asa also removed Maacah his grandmother from her
position as queen mother because she had made a loathsome
Asherah pole. Asa cut down her loathsome pole and crushed
and burned it in the Kidron Valley. 17 The high places were not
eliminated from Israel, yet Asa was wholeheartedly devoted to
the LORD throughout his lifetime. 18 He brought the holy items
that his father and he had made into God's temple, including
the silver, gold, and other articles.

ASA'S FAILURES

19 There was no more war until the thirty-fifth year of Asa's reign.
16 1 In the thirty-sixth year of Asa's reign, King Baasha of Israel attacked Judah, and he established Ramah as a military
outpost to prevent anyone from leaving or entering the land of
King Asa of Judah. 2 Asa took all the silver and gold that was left
in the treasuries of the LORD's temple and of the royal palace
and sent it to King Ben Hadad of Syria, ruler in Damascus, along
with this message: 3 "I want to make a treaty with you, like the
one our fathers made. See, I have sent you silver and gold. Break
your treaty with King Baasha of Israel, so he will retreat from my
land." 4 Ben Hadad accepted King Asa's offer and ordered his army
commanders to attack the cities of Israel. They conquered Ijon,
Dan, Abel Maim, and all the storage cities of Naphtali. 5 When
Baasha heard the news, he stopped fortifying Ramah and abandoned the project. 6 King Asa ordered all the men of Judah to
carry away the stones and wood that Baasha had used to build
Ramah. He used the materials to build up Geba and Mizpah.
7 At that time Hanani the prophet visited King Asa of Judah
and said to him: "Because you relied on the king of Syria and
did not rely on the LORD your God, the army of the king of Syria
has escaped from your hand. 8 Did not the Cushites and Libyans
have a huge army with chariots and a very large number of horsemen? But when you relied on the LORD, he handed them over

to you! 9 Certainly the LORD watches the whole earth carefully
and is ready to strengthen those who are devoted to him. You
have acted foolishly in this matter; from now on you will have
war." 10 Asa was so angry at the prophet, he put him in jail. Asa
also oppressed some of the people at that time.

ASA'S REIGN ENDS

11 The events of Asa's reign, from start to finish, are recorded in the
Scroll of the Kings of Judah and Israel. 12 In the thirty-ninth year of
his reign, Asa developed a foot disease and his disease became severe. Yet even in his disease, he did not seek the LORD, but only the
doctors. 13 Asa passed away in the forty-first year of his reign. 14 He
was buried in the tomb he had carved out in the City of David. They
laid him to rest on a platform covered with spices and assorted
mixtures of ointments. They made a huge bonfire to honor him.

JEHOSHAPHAT BECOMES KING

17 His son Jehoshaphat replaced him as king and solidified his
rule over Israel. 2 He placed troops in all Judah's fortified cities and posted garrisons throughout the land of Judah and in
the cities of Ephraim that his father Asa had seized.
3 The LORD was with Jehoshaphat because he followed in his
ancestor David's footsteps at the beginning of his reign. He did
not seek the Baals, 4 but instead sought the God of his ancestors and obeyed his commands, unlike the Israelites. 5 The LORD
made his kingdom secure; all Judah brought tribute to Jehoshaphat, and he became very wealthy and greatly respected. 6 He
was committed to following the LORD; he even removed the
high places and Asherah poles from Judah.
7 In the third year of his reign he sent his officials Ben Hail,
Obadiah, Zechariah, Nethanel, and Micaiah to teach in the cities of Judah. 8 They were accompanied by the Levites Shemaiah,
Nethaniah, Zebadiah, Asahel, Shemiramoth, Jehonathan, Adonijah, Tobijah, and Tob-Adonijah, and by the priests Elishama
and Jehoram. 9 They taught throughout Judah, taking with them
the scroll of the law of the LORD. They traveled to all the cities
of Judah and taught the people.
10 The LORD put fear into all the kingdoms surrounding Judah;
they did not make war with Jehoshaphat. 11 Some of the Philistines brought Jehoshaphat tribute, including a load of silver. The
Arabs brought him 7,700 rams and 7,700 goats from their flocks.
12 Jehoshaphat's power kept increasing. He built fortresses and
storage cities throughout Judah. 13 He had many supplies stored
in the cities of Judah and an army of skilled warriors stationed
in Jerusalem. 14 These were their divisions by families:
There were 1,000 officers from Judah. Adnah the commander
led 300,000 skilled warriors, 15 Jehochanan the commander led
280,000, 16 and Amasiah son of Zikri, who volunteered to serve
the LORD, led 200,000 skilled warriors.
17 From Benjamin, Eliada, a skilled warrior, led 200,000 men
who were equipped with bows and shields, 18 and Jehozabad led
180,000 trained warriors.
19 These were the ones who served the king, besides those
whom the king placed in the fortified cities throughout Judah.

JEHOSHAPHAT ALLIES WITH AHAB

18 Jehoshaphat was very wealthy and greatly respected. He
made an alliance by marriage with Ahab, 2 and after several years went down to visit Ahab in Samaria. Ahab slaughtered
many sheep and cattle to honor Jehoshaphat and those who
came with him. He persuaded him to join in an attack against Ramoth Gilead. 3 King Ahab of Israel said to King Jehoshaphat of Judah, "Will you go with me to attack Ramoth Gilead?" He replied,
"I will support you; my army is at your disposal and will support you in battle." 4 Then Jehoshaphat said further to the king
of Israel, "First, please seek an oracle from the LORD." 5 So the
king of Israel assembled 400 prophets and asked them, "Should
we attack Ramoth Gilead or not?" They said, "Attack! God will
hand it over to the king." 6 But Jehoshaphat asked, "Is there not a
prophet of the LORD still here, that we may ask him?" 7 The king
of Israel answered Jehoshaphat, "There is still one man through
whom we can seek the LORD's will, but I despise him because he
does not prophesy prosperity for me, but always disaster—Micaiah son of Imlah." Jehoshaphat said, "The king should not say
such things!" 8 The king of Israel summoned an officer and said,
"Quickly bring Micaiah son of Imlah."

9 Now the king of Israel and King Jehoshaphat of Judah were
sitting on their respective thrones, dressed in their royal robes,
at the threshing floor at the entrance of the gate of Samaria. All
the prophets were prophesying before them. 10 Zedekiah son
of Kenaanah made iron horns and said, "This is what the LORD
says, 'With these you will gore Syria until they are destroyed.'"
11 All the prophets were prophesying the same, saying, "Attack
Ramoth Gilead! You will succeed; the LORD will hand it over to
the king." 12 Now the messenger who went to summon Micaiah
said to him, "Look, the prophets are in complete agreement that
the king will succeed. Your words must agree with theirs; you
must predict success!" 13 But Micaiah said, "As certainly as the
LORD lives, I will say what my God tells me to say!"

14 Micaiah came before the king and the king asked him, "Micaiah, should we attack Ramoth Gilead or not?" He answered him,
"Attack! You will succeed; they will be handed over to you." 15 The
king said to him, "How many times must I make you solemnly
promise in the name of the LORD to tell me only the truth?" 16 Micaiah replied, "I saw all Israel scattered on the mountains like
sheep that have no shepherd. Then the LORD said, 'They have no
master. They should go home in peace.'" 17 The king of Israel said
to Jehoshaphat, "Didn't I tell you he does not prophesy prosperity for me, but disaster?" 18 Micaiah said, "That being the case, listen to the LORD's message. I saw the LORD sitting on his throne,
with all the heavenly assembly standing on his right and on his
left. 19 The LORD said, 'Who will deceive King Ahab of Israel, so he
will attack Ramoth Gilead and die there?' One said this and another that. 20 Then a spirit stepped forward and stood before the
LORD. He said, 'I will deceive him.' The LORD asked him, 'How?'
21 He replied, 'I will go out and be a lying spirit in the mouths of
all his prophets.' The LORD said, 'Deceive and overpower him.
Go out and do as you have proposed.' 22 So now, look, the LORD
has placed a lying spirit in the mouths of all these prophets of

yours, but the LORD has decreed disaster for you." 23 Zedekiah
son of Kenaanah approached, hit Micaiah on the jaw, and said,
"Which way did the LORD's Spirit go when he went from me to
speak to you?" 24 Micaiah replied, "Look, you will see in the day
when you go into an inner room to hide." 25 Then the king of Israel said, "Take Micaiah and return him to Amon the city official
and Joash the king's son. 26 Say, 'This is what the king says: "Put
this man in prison. Give him only a little bread and water until
I return safely."'" 27 Micaiah said, "If you really do return safely,
then the LORD has not spoken through me!" Then he added,
"Take note, all you people."

28 The king of Israel and King Jehoshaphat of Judah attacked
Ramoth Gilead. 29 The king of Israel said to Jehoshaphat, "I will
disguise myself and then enter the battle, but you wear your
royal attire." So the king of Israel disguised himself and they
entered the battle. 30 Now the king of Syria had ordered his
chariot commanders, "Do not fight common soldiers or high
ranking officers; fight only the king of Israel!" 31 When the chariot commanders saw Jehoshaphat, they said, "He must be the
king of Israel!" So they turned and attacked him, but Jehoshaphat cried out. The LORD helped him; God lured them away from
him. 32 When the chariot commanders realized he was not the
king of Israel, they turned away from him. 33 Now an archer shot
an arrow at random, and it struck the king of Israel between
the plates of his armor. The king ordered his charioteer, "Turn
around and take me from the battle line, for I am wounded."
34 While the battle raged throughout the day, the king of Israel
stood propped up in his chariot opposite the Syrians. He died
in the evening as the sun was setting.

19 When King Jehoshaphat of Judah returned home safely to
Jerusalem, 2 the prophet Jehu son of Hanani confronted
him; he said to King Jehoshaphat, "Is it right to help the wicked
and be an ally of those who oppose the LORD? Because you have
done this, the LORD is angry with you! 3 Nevertheless you have
done some good things; you removed the Asherah poles from
the land and you were determined to follow God."

JEHOSHAPHAT APPOINTS JUDGES

4 Jehoshaphat lived in Jerusalem. He went out among the people
from Beer Sheba to the hill country of Ephraim and encouraged
them to follow the LORD God of their ancestors. 5 He appointed
judges throughout the land and in each of the fortified cities
of Judah. 6 He told the judges, "Be careful what you do, for you
are not judging for men, but for the LORD, who will be with you
when you make judicial decisions. 7 Respect the LORD and make
careful decisions, for the LORD our God disapproves of injustice,
partiality, and bribery."

8 In Jerusalem Jehoshaphat appointed some Levites, priests,
and Israelite family leaders to judge on behalf of the LORD and
to settle disputes among the residents of Jerusalem. 9 He commanded them: "Carry out your duties with respect for the LORD,
with honesty, and with pure motives. 10 Whenever your countrymen who live in the cities bring a case before you (whether
it involves a violent crime or other matters related to the law,

commandments, rules, and regulations), warn them that they
must not sin against the LORD. If you fail to do so, God will be
angry with you and your colleagues, but if you obey, you will be
free of guilt. 11 Take note, Amariah the chief priest will oversee
you in every matter pertaining to the LORD and Zebadiah son of
Ishmael, the leader of the family of Judah, in every matter pertaining to the king. The Levites will serve as officials before you.
Act courageously, and may the LORD be with those who do well!"

THE LORD GIVES JEHOSHAPHAT MILITARY SUCCESS

20 Later the Moabites and Ammonites, along with some
of the Meunites, attacked Jehoshaphat. 2 Messengers arrived and reported to Jehoshaphat, "A huge army is attacking
you from the other side of the Dead Sea, from the direction of
Edom. Look, they are in Hazazon Tamar (that is, En Gedi)." 3 Jehoshaphat was afraid, so he decided to seek the LORD's advice.
He decreed that all Judah should observe a fast. 4 The people of
Judah assembled to ask for the LORD's help; they came from all
the cities of Judah to ask for the LORD's help.

5 Jehoshaphat stood before the assembly of Judah and Jerusalem at the LORD's temple, in front of the new courtyard. 6 He
prayed: "O LORD God of our ancestors, you are the God who
lives in heaven and rules over all the kingdoms of the nations.
You possess strength and power; no one can stand against you.
7 Our God, you drove out the inhabitants of this land before
your people Israel and gave it as a permanent possession to
the descendants of your friend Abraham. 8 They settled down
in it and built in it a temple to honor you, saying, 9 'If disaster
comes on us in the form of military attack, judgment, plague,
or famine, we will stand in front of this temple before you, for
you are present in this temple. We will cry out to you for help
in our distress, so that you will hear and deliver us.' 10 Now the
Ammonites, Moabites, and men from Mount Seir are coming!
When Israel came from the land of Egypt, you did not allow
them to invade these lands. They bypassed them and did not
destroy them. 11 Look how they are repaying us! They come to
drive us out of our allotted land which you assigned to us! 12 Our
God, will you not judge them? For we are powerless against this
huge army that attacks us. We don't know what we should do;
we look to you for help."

13 All the men of Judah were standing before the LORD, along
with their infants, wives, and children. 14 Then in the midst of the
assembly, the LORD's Spirit came upon Jachaziel son of Zechariah, son of Benaiah, son of Jeiel, son of Mattaniah, a Levite and
descendant of Asaph. 15 He said: "Pay attention, all you people
of Judah, residents of Jerusalem, and King Jehoshaphat! This is
what the LORD says to you: 'Don't be afraid and don't panic because of this huge army! For the battle is not yours, but God's.
16 Tomorrow march down against them as they come up the Ascent of Ziz. You will find them at the end of the ravine in front of
the wilderness of Jeruel. 17 You will not fight in this battle. Take
your positions, stand, and watch the LORD deliver you, O Judah
and Jerusalem. Don't be afraid and don't panic! Tomorrow march
out toward them; the LORD is with you!'"

GOD REIGNS SUPREME

2 CHRONICLES 20

Second Chronicles details the history of the divided nations of Israel and Judah, leading up to the fall of these nations into captivity. It chronicles the reigns of the royal line of kings descended from King David in the southern kingdom of Judah. Some kings were godly, leading Judah to worship God. Other kings were greedy and selfish, leading Judah far from God.

One of the most notable kings of Judah was King Jehoshaphat. He began his reign walking in obedience to God's commandments. He delighted in the Lord and sent priests throughout Judah to teach everyone God's law. He stood firm against sin, bringing religious reform to the nation.

In 2 Chronicles 20, when Judah faced attack from all sides, King Jehoshaphat gathered the kingdom together to fast and pray before the Lord. God gave them victory over all their enemies, and the surrounding nations feared the Lord. As a result, there was peace during Jehoshaphat's reign. Although King Jehoshaphat made some ungodly choices in his political alliances, God remained faithful to him from the beginning of his reign until the end.

In verse 12, King Jehoshaphat prayed, "For we are powerless against this huge army that attacks us. We don't know what we should do; we look to you for help."

Perhaps you are in the midst of a battle facing a terrifying enemy. You are not alone or forgotten: God sees you.

God's response to Jehoshaphat was His immediate presence and faithful assurance. For those who are His, God promises refuge. He will never leave or abandon His children. God is at work in our lives even when we don't see it, feel it, or believe it. We need only look to God. He is with us!

It is tempting to be discouraged by the culture's rejection of God, His ways, and the subsequent advancement of wickedness we see in the world. God remains sovereign. He has demonstrated that He is able to use any person or circumstance, good or bad, to carry out His divine plan.

God reigns supreme. He holds our lives in His hand. As we love God greatly, we cling confidently to God's promises, trusting and believing that nothing can stand against us or against God's plans and purposes for our lives.

18 Jehoshaphat bowed down with his face toward the ground, and all the people of Judah and the residents of Jerusalem fell down before the LORD and worshiped him. 19 Then some Levites, from the Kohathites and Korahites, got up and loudly praised the LORD God of Israel.

20 Early the next morning they marched out to the wilderness of Tekoa. When they were ready to march, Jehoshaphat stood up and said: "Listen to me, you people of Judah and residents of Jerusalem! Trust in the LORD your God and you will be safe! Trust in the message of his prophets and you will win." 21 He met with the people and appointed musicians to play before the LORD and praise his majestic splendor. As they marched ahead of the warriors they said: "Give thanks to the LORD, for his loyal love endures."

22 When they began to shout and praise, the LORD suddenly attacked the Ammonites, Moabites, and men from Mount Seir who were invading Judah, and they were defeated. 23 The Ammonites and Moabites attacked the men from Mount Seir and annihilated them. When they had finished off the men of Seir, they attacked and destroyed one another. 24 When the men of Judah arrived at the observation post overlooking the wilderness and looked at the huge army, they saw dead bodies on the ground; there were no survivors. 25 Jehoshaphat and his men went to gather the plunder; they found a huge amount of supplies, clothing, and valuable items. They carried away everything they could. There was so much plunder, it took them three days to haul it off.

26 On the fourth day they assembled in the Valley of Berachah, where they praised the LORD. So that place is called the Valley of Berachah to this very day. 27 Then all the men of Judah and Jerusalem returned joyfully to Jerusalem with Jehoshaphat leading them; the LORD had given them reason to rejoice over their enemies. 28 They entered Jerusalem to the sound of stringed instruments and trumpets and proceeded to the temple of the LORD. 29 All the kingdoms of the surrounding lands were afraid of God when they heard how the LORD had fought against Israel's enemies. 30 Jehoshaphat's kingdom enjoyed peace; his God made him secure on every side.

JEHOSHAPHAT'S REIGN ENDS

31 Jehoshaphat reigned over Judah. He was thirty-five years old when he became king and he reigned for twenty-five years in Jerusalem. His mother was Azubah, the daughter of Shilhi. 32 He followed in his father Asa's footsteps and was careful to do what the LORD approved. 33 However, the high places were not eliminated; the people were still not devoted to the God of their ancestors.

34 The rest of the events of Jehoshaphat's reign, from start to finish, are recorded in the Annals of Jehu son of Hanani, which are included in the Scroll of the Kings of Israel.

35 Later King Jehoshaphat of Judah made an alliance with King Ahaziah of Israel, who did evil. 36 They agreed to make large seagoing merchant ships; they built the ships in Ezion Geber. 37 Eliezer son of Dodavahu from Mareshah prophesied against

Jehoshaphat, "Because you made an alliance with Ahaziah, the
LORD will shatter what you have made." The ships were wrecked
and unable to go to sea.
21 Jehoshaphat passed away and was buried with his ancestors
in the City of David. His son Jehoram replaced him as king.

JEHORAM'S REIGN

2 His brothers, Jehoshaphat's sons, were Azariah, Jechiel, Zechariah, Azariahu, Michael, and Shephatiah. All these were sons
of King Jehoshaphat of Israel. 3 Their father gave them many
presents, including silver, gold, and other precious items, along
with fortified cities in Judah. But he gave the kingdom to Jehoram because he was the firstborn.
4 Jehoram took control of his father's kingdom and became powerful. Then he killed all his brothers, as well as some of the officials
of Israel. 5 Jehoram was thirty-two years old when he became king,
and he reigned for eight years in Jerusalem. 6 He followed in the
footsteps of the kings of Israel, just as Ahab's dynasty had done, for
he married Ahab's daughter. He did evil in the sight of the LORD.
7 But the LORD was unwilling to destroy David's dynasty because
of the promise he had made to give David a perpetual dynasty.
8 During Jehoram's reign Edom freed themselves from Judah's control and set up their own king. 9 Jehoram crossed over
with his officers and all his chariots. The Edomites, who had surrounded him, attacked at night and defeated him and his chariot
officers. 10 So Edom has remained free from Judah's control to
this very day. At that same time Libnah also rebelled and freed
themselves from Judah's control because Jehoram rejected the
LORD God of his ancestors. 11 He also built high places on the hills
of Judah; he encouraged the residents of Jerusalem to be unfaithful to the LORD and led Judah away from the LORD.
12 Jehoram received this letter from Elijah the prophet: "This
is what the LORD God of your ancestor David says: 'You have
not followed in the footsteps of your father Jehoshaphat and of
King Asa of Judah, 13 but have instead followed in the footsteps
of the kings of Israel. You encouraged the people of Judah and
the residents of Jerusalem to be unfaithful to the LORD, just as
the family of Ahab does in Israel. You also killed your brothers,
members of your father's family, who were better than you. 14 So
look, the LORD is about to severely afflict your people, your sons,
your wives, and all you own. 15 And you will get a serious, chronic
intestinal disease which will cause your intestines to come out.'"
16 The LORD stirred up against Jehoram the Philistines and the
Arabs who lived beside the Cushites. 17 They attacked Judah and
swept through it. They carried off everything they found in the
royal palace, including his sons and wives. None of his sons was
left, except for his youngest, Ahaziah. 18 After all this happened,
the LORD afflicted him with an incurable intestinal disease. 19 After about two years his intestines came out because of the disease, so that he died a very painful death. His people did not
make a bonfire to honor him, as they had done for his ancestors.
20 Jehoram was thirty-two years old when he became king and
he reigned eight years in Jerusalem. No one regretted his death;
he was buried in the City of David, but not in the royal tombs.

AHAZIAH'S REIGN

22 The residents of Jerusalem made his youngest son Ahaziah king in his place, for the raiding party that invaded the camp with the Arabs had killed all the older sons. So Ahaziah son of Jehoram became king of Judah. 2 Ahaziah was twenty-two years old when he became king, and he reigned for one year in Jerusalem. His mother was Athaliah, the granddaughter of Omri. 3 He followed in the footsteps of Ahab's dynasty, for his mother gave him evil advice. 4 He did evil in the sight of the LORD like Ahab's dynasty because, after his father's death, they gave him advice that led to his destruction. 5 He followed their advice and joined Ahab's son King Joram of Israel in a battle against King Hazael of Syria at Ramoth Gilead in which the Syrians defeated Joram. 6 Joram returned to Jezreel to recover from the wounds he received from the Syrians in Ramah when he fought against King Hazael of Syria. Ahaziah son of King Jehoram of Judah went down to visit Joram son of Ahab in Jezreel, because he had been wounded.

7 God brought about Ahaziah's downfall through his visit to Joram. When Ahaziah arrived, he went out with Joram to meet Jehu son of Nimshi, whom the LORD had commissioned to wipe out Ahab's family. 8 While Jehu was dishing out punishment to Ahab's family, he discovered the officials of Judah and the sons of Ahaziah's relatives who were serving Ahaziah and killed them. 9 He looked for Ahaziah, who was captured while hiding in Samaria. They brought him to Jehu and then executed him. They did give him a burial, for they reasoned, "He is the son of Jehoshaphat, who sought the LORD with his whole heart." There was no one in Ahaziah's family strong enough to rule in his place.

ATHALIAH IS ELIMINATED

10 When Athaliah the mother of Ahaziah saw that her son was dead, she was determined to destroy the entire royal line of Judah. 11 So Jehoshabeath, the daughter of King Jehoram, took Ahaziah's son Joash and stole him away from the rest of the royal descendants who were to be executed. She hid him and his nurse in the room where the bed covers were stored. So Jehoshabeath the daughter of King Jehoram, wife of Jehoiada the priest and sister of Ahaziah, hid him from Athaliah so she could not execute him. 12 He remained in hiding in God's temple for six years while Athaliah was ruling over the land.

23 In the seventh year Jehoiada made a bold move. He made a pact with the officers of the units of hundreds: Azariah son of Jehoram, Ishmael son of Jehochanan, Azariah son of Obed, Maaseiah son of Adaiah, and Elishaphat son of Zikri. 2 They traveled throughout Judah and assembled the Levites from all the cities of Judah, as well as the Israelite family leaders.

They came to Jerusalem, 3 and the whole assembly made a covenant with the king in the temple of God. Jehoiada said to them, "The king's son will rule, just as the LORD promised David's descendants. 4 This is what you must do. One-third of you priests and Levites who are on duty during the Sabbath will guard the doors. 5 Another third of you will be stationed at the

REFLECT

How is God's faithfulness displayed through Jehoshabeath's courage?

royal palace and still another third at the Foundation Gate. All
the others will stand in the courtyards of the LORD's temple.
6 No one must enter the LORD's temple except the priests and
Levites who are on duty. They may enter because they are ceremonially pure. All the others should carry out their assigned
service to the LORD. 7 The Levites must surround the king. Each
of you must hold his weapon in his hand. Whoever tries to enter the temple must be killed. You must accompany the king
wherever he goes."

8 The Levites and all the men of Judah did just as Jehoiada
the priest ordered. Each of them took his men, those who
were on duty during the Sabbath as well as those who were
off duty on the Sabbath. Jehoiada the priest did not release
his divisions from their duties. 9 Jehoiada the priest gave to
the officers of the units of hundreds King David's spears and
shields that were kept in God's temple. 10 He placed the men
at their posts, each holding his weapon in his hand. They lined
up from the south side of the temple to the north side and
stood near the altar and the temple, surrounding the king.
11 Jehoiada and his sons led out the king's son and placed on
him the crown and the royal insignia. They proclaimed him
king and poured olive oil on his head. They declared, "Long
live the king!"

12 When Athaliah heard the royal guard shouting and praising the king, she joined the crowd at the LORD's temple. 13 Then
she saw the king standing by his pillar at the entrance. The officers and trumpeters stood beside the king and all the people of
the land were celebrating and blowing trumpets, and the musicians with various instruments were leading the celebration.
Athaliah tore her clothes and yelled, "Treason! Treason!" 14 Jehoiada the priest sent out the officers of the units of hundreds,
who were in charge of the army, and ordered them, "Bring her
outside the temple to the guards. Put the sword to anyone who
follows her." The priest gave this order because he had decided
she should not be executed in the LORD's temple. 15 They seized
her and took her into the precincts of the royal palace through
the horses' entrance. There they executed her.

16 Jehoiada then drew up a covenant stipulating that he, all the
people, and the king should be loyal to the LORD. 17 All the people went and demolished the temple of Baal. They smashed its
altars and idols. They killed Mattan the priest of Baal in front
of the altars. 18 Jehoiada then assigned the duties of the LORD's
temple to the priests, the Levites whom David had assigned to
the LORD's temple. They were responsible for offering burnt sacrifices to the LORD with joy and music, according to the law of
Moses and the edict of David. 19 He posted guards at the gates of
the LORD's temple, so no one who was ceremonially unclean in
any way could enter. 20 He summoned the officers of the units of
hundreds, the nobles, the rulers of the people, and all the people of the land, and he then led the king down from the LORD's
temple. They entered the royal palace through the Upper Gate
and seated the king on the royal throne. 21 All the people of the
land celebrated, for the city had rest now that they had killed
Athaliah.

JOASH'S REIGN

24 Joash was seven years old when he began to reign. He
reigned for forty years in Jerusalem. His mother was Zibiah, who was from Beer Sheba. 2 Joash did what the LORD approved throughout the lifetime of Jehoiada the priest. 3 Jehoiada
chose two wives for him who gave him sons and daughters.

4 Later, Joash was determined to repair the LORD's temple. 5 He
assembled the priests and Levites and ordered them, "Go out to
the cities of Judah and collect the annual quota of silver from
all Israel for repairs on the temple of your God. Be quick about
it!" But the Levites delayed.

6 So the king summoned Jehoiada the chief priest, and said to
him, "Why have you not made the Levites collect from Judah and
Jerusalem the tax authorized by Moses the LORD's servant and
by the assembly of Israel at the tent containing the tablets of
the law?" 7 (Wicked Athaliah and her sons had broken into God's
temple and used all the holy items of the LORD's temple in their
worship of the Baals.) 8 The king ordered a chest to be made and
placed outside the gate of the LORD's temple. 9 An edict was sent
throughout Judah and Jerusalem requiring the people to bring
to the LORD the tax that Moses, God's servant, imposed on Israel in the wilderness. 10 All the officials and all the people gladly
brought their silver and threw it into the chest until it was full.
11 Whenever the Levites brought the chest to the royal accountant and they saw there was a lot of silver, the royal scribe and
the accountant of the high priest emptied the chest and then
took it back to its place. They went through this routine every
day and collected a large amount of silver.

12 The king and Jehoiada gave it to the construction foremen
assigned to the LORD's temple. They hired carpenters and craftsmen to repair the LORD's temple, as well as those skilled in working with iron and bronze to restore the LORD's temple. 13 They
worked hard and made the repairs. They followed the measurements specified for God's temple and restored it. 14 When they
were finished, they brought the rest of the silver to the king
and Jehoiada. They used it to make items for the LORD's temple,
including items used in the temple service and for burnt sacrifices, pans, and various other gold and silver items. Throughout Jehoiada's lifetime, burnt sacrifices were offered regularly
in the LORD's temple.

15 Jehoiada grew old and died at the age of 130. 16 He was buried in the City of David with the kings, because he had accomplished good in Israel and for God and his temple.

17 After Jehoiada died, the officials of Judah visited the king
and declared their loyalty to him. The king listened to their advice. 18 They abandoned the temple of the LORD God of their
ancestors and worshiped the Asherah poles and idols. Because
of this sinful activity, God was angry with Judah and Jerusalem.
19 The LORD sent prophets among them to lead them back to
him. They warned the people, but they would not pay attention.
20 God's Spirit energized Zechariah son of Jehoiada the priest. He
stood up before the people and said to them, "This is what God
says: 'Why are you violating the commands of the LORD? You
will not be prosperous. Because you have rejected the LORD, he

has rejected you!'" 21 They plotted against him and by royal decree stoned him to death in the courtyard of the LORD's temple.
22 King Joash disregarded the loyalty Zechariah's father Jehoiada
had shown him and killed Jehoiada's son. As Zechariah was dying, he said, "May the LORD take notice and seek vengeance!"
23 At the beginning of the year the Syrian army attacked Joash and invaded Judah and Jerusalem. They wiped out all the
leaders of the people and sent all the plunder they gathered
to the king of Damascus. 24 Even though the invading Syrian
army was relatively weak, the LORD handed over to them Judah's very large army, for the people of Judah had abandoned the
LORD God of their ancestors. The Syrians gave Joash what he deserved. 25 When they withdrew, they left Joash badly wounded.
His servants plotted against him because of what he had done
to the son of Jehoiada the priest. They murdered him on his bed.
Thus he died and was buried in the City of David, but not in the
tombs of the kings. 26 The conspirators were Zabad son of Shimeath (an Ammonite woman) and Jehozabad son of Shimrith (a
Moabite woman).
27 The list of Joash's sons, the many prophetic oracles about
him, and the account of his building project on God's temple are
included in the record of the Scroll of the Kings. His son Amaziah replaced him as king.

AMAZIAH'S REIGN

25 Amaziah was twenty-five years old when he began to
reign, and he reigned for twenty-nine years in Jerusalem.
His mother was Jehoaddan, who was from Jerusalem. 2 He did
what the LORD approved, but not with wholehearted devotion.
3 When he had secured control of the kingdom, he executed
the servants who had assassinated his father the king. 4 However,
he did not execute their sons. He obeyed the LORD's commandment as recorded in the law scroll of Moses, "Fathers must not
be executed for what their sons do, and sons must not be executed for what their fathers do. A man must be executed only
for his own sin."
5 Amaziah assembled the people of Judah and assigned them by
families to the commanders of units of 1,000 and the commanders of units of 100 for all Judah and Benjamin. He counted those
twenty years old and up and discovered there were 300,000
young men of fighting age equipped with spears and shields.
6 He hired 100,000 Israelite warriors for 100 talents of silver.
7 But a prophet visited him and said: "O king, the Israelite
troops must not go with you, for the LORD is not with Israel or
any of the Ephraimites. 8 Even if you go and fight bravely in battle, God will defeat you before the enemy. God is capable of helping or defeating." 9 Amaziah asked the prophet: "But what should
I do about the 100 talents of silver I paid the Israelite troops?"
The prophet replied, "The LORD is capable of giving you more
than that." 10 So Amaziah dismissed the troops that had come to
him from Ephraim and sent them home. They were very angry
at Judah and returned home incensed. 11 Amaziah boldly led his
army to the Valley of Salt, where he defeated 10,000 Edomites.
12 The men of Judah captured 10,000 men alive. They took them

to the top of a cliff and threw them over. All the captives fell to
their death. 13 Now the troops Amaziah had dismissed and had
not allowed to fight in the battle raided the cities of Judah from
Samaria to Beth Horon. They killed 3,000 people and carried off
a large amount of plunder.
14 When Amaziah returned from defeating the Edomites, he
brought back the gods of the people of Seir and made them his
personal gods. He bowed down before them and offered them
sacrifices. 15 The LORD was angry at Amaziah and sent a prophet
to him, who said, "Why are you following these gods that could
not deliver their own people from your power?" 16 While he was
speaking, Amaziah said to him, "Did we appoint you to be a royal
counselor? Stop prophesying or else you will be killed!" So the
prophet stopped, but added, "I know that God has decided to
destroy you, because you have done this thing and refused to
listen to my advice."
17 After King Amaziah of Judah consulted with his advisers, he
sent this message to the king of Israel, Joash son of Jehoahaz, the
son of Jehu, "Come, face me on the battlefield." 18 King Joash of
Israel sent this message back to King Amaziah of Judah, "A thorn
bush in Lebanon sent this message to a cedar in Lebanon, 'Give
your daughter to my son as a wife.' Then a wild animal of Lebanon came by and trampled down the thorn bush. 19 You defeated
Edom and it has gone to your head. Gloat over your success, but
stay in your palace. Why bring calamity on yourself? Why bring
down yourself and Judah along with you?"
20 But Amaziah did not heed the warning, for God wanted to
hand them over to Joash because they followed the gods of Edom.
21 So King Joash of Israel attacked. He and King Amaziah of Judah
faced each other on the battlefield in Beth Shemesh of Judah.
22 Judah was defeated by Israel, and each man ran back home.
23 King Joash of Israel captured King Amaziah of Judah, son of
Joash son of Jehoahaz, in Beth Shemesh and brought him to Jerusalem. He broke down the wall of Jerusalem from the Gate of
Ephraim to the Corner Gate—a distance of about 600 feet. 24 He
took away all the gold and silver, all the items found in God's
temple that were in the care of Obed-Edom, the riches in the
royal palace, and some hostages. Then he went back to Samaria.
25 King Amaziah son of Joash of Judah lived for fifteen years after the death of King Joash son of Jehoahaz of Israel. 26 The rest of
the events of Amaziah's reign, from start to finish, are recorded in
the Scroll of the Kings of Judah and Israel. 27 From the time Amaziah turned from following the LORD, conspirators plotted against
him in Jerusalem, so he fled to Lachish. But they sent assassins after him and they killed him there. 28 His body was carried back by
horses, and he was buried with his ancestors in the City of David.

UZZIAH'S REIGN

26 All the people of Judah took Uzziah, who was sixteen
years old, and made him king in his father Amaziah's
place. 2 Uzziah built up Elat and restored it to Judah after King
Amaziah had passed away.
3 Uzziah was sixteen years old when he began to reign, and
he reigned for fifty-two years in Jerusalem. His mother's name

was Jecholiah, who was from Jerusalem. 4 He did what the LORD
approved, just as his father Amaziah had done. 5 He followed
God during the lifetime of Zechariah, who taught him how to
honor God. As long as he followed the LORD, God caused him
to succeed.

6 Uzziah attacked the Philistines and broke down the walls
of Gath, Jabneh, and Ashdod. He built cities in the region of
Ashdod and throughout Philistine territory. 7 God helped him
in his campaigns against the Philistines, the Arabs living in
Gur Baal, and the Meunites. 8 The Ammonites paid tribute to
Uzziah and his fame reached the border of Egypt, for he grew
in power.

9 Uzziah built and fortified towers in Jerusalem at the Corner Gate, Valley Gate, and at the Angle. 10 He built towers in the
wilderness and dug many cisterns, for he owned many herds in
the foothills and on the plain. He had workers in the fields and
vineyards in the hills and in Carmel, for he loved agriculture.

11 Uzziah had an army of skilled warriors trained for battle. They
were organized by divisions according to the muster rolls made
by Jeiel the scribe and Maaseiah the officer under the authority
of Hananiah, a royal official. 12 The total number of family leaders who led warriors was 2,600. 13 They commanded an army of
307,500 skilled and able warriors who were ready to defend the
king against his enemies. 14 Uzziah supplied shields, spears, helmets, breastplates, bows, and slingstones for the entire army. 15 In
Jerusalem he made war machines carefully designed to shoot arrows and large stones from the towers and corners of the walls.
He became very famous, for he received tremendous support
and became powerful.

16 But once he became powerful, his pride destroyed him. He
disobeyed the LORD his God. He entered the LORD's temple
to offer incense on the incense altar. 17 Azariah the priest and
eighty other brave priests of the LORD followed him in. 18 They
confronted King Uzziah and said to him, "It is not proper for you,
Uzziah, to offer incense to the LORD. That is the responsibility
of the priests, the descendants of Aaron, who are consecrated
to offer incense. Leave the sanctuary, for you have disobeyed
and the LORD God will not honor you!" 19 Uzziah, who had an incense censer in his hand, became angry. While he was ranting
and raving at the priests, a skin disease appeared on his forehead
right there in front of the priests in the LORD's temple near the
incense altar. 20 When Azariah the high priest and the other
priests looked at him, there was a skin disease on his forehead.
They hurried him out of there; even the king himself wanted to
leave quickly because the LORD had afflicted him. 21 King Uzziah
suffered from a skin disease until the day he died. He lived in
separate quarters, afflicted by a skin disease and banned from
the LORD's temple. His son Jotham was in charge of the palace
and ruled over the people of the land.

22 The rest of the events of Uzziah's reign, from start to finish, were recorded by the prophet Isaiah son of Amoz. 23 Uzziah
passed away and was buried near his ancestors in a cemetery
belonging to the kings. (This was because he had a skin disease.)
His son Jotham replaced him as king.

LOVE TO GROW

PRIDE AND POWER

2 CHRONICLES 26:16

In 2 Chronicles, we encounter several kings who were almost great but fell short. They started out with the Lord's favor, but over time failed to faithfully adhere to God's commands. Their unfaithfulness came at a great cost to them, and they often paid for their disobedience with their lives.

As I read these chapters, I can't help but think about the beast we call pride: how it ushers us into darkness and separates us from the One who gave us our talent, position, means, and success in the first place.

> *"But once he became powerful, his pride destroyed him. He disobeyed the LORD his God. He entered the LORD's temple to offer incense on the incense altar"* (2 Chr 26:16).

When the Lord gives us success at His hand, it can be easy to take the credit. If we believe our own hand brought us greatness, pride can sway us to assert ourselves over God. When Uzziah burned the incense, he performed an act God prescribed only to the priests. God afflicted King Uzziah with a skin disease from which he never recovered. For the rest of his days, he lived in separate quarters and was banned from the Lord's temple.

We live in a loud world that tells us to "Make it happen!" and "Crush your goals!" Yet the Bible teaches: "If the LORD does not build a house, then those who build it work in vain" (Ps 127:1). We absolutely have the choice to build, but we must always ask ourselves which kingdom we are building. Are we building God's kingdom or our own?

All these failing kings point us to our need for one unfailing King, a great King who doesn't almost save us, almost live faithfully, or almost carry out God's will.

Jesus is the great King, and His motives were perfect. Jesus came to save us from our pride and usher us into friendship with God forever. In gratitude, we can joyfully repent of our arrogance and the ways we have tried to save ourselves. Let's turn away from our pride and realize His ways and His kingdom are always better. What a wonderful King we serve!

JOTHAM'S REIGN

27 Jotham was twenty-five years old when he began to reign, and he reigned for sixteen years in Jerusalem. His mother was Jerusha the daughter of Zadok. 2 He did what the LORD approved, just as his father Uzziah had done. (He did not, however, have the audacity to enter the temple.) Yet the people were still sinning.

3 He built the Upper Gate to the LORD's temple and did a lot of work on the wall in the area known as Ophel. 4 He built cities in the hill country of Judah and fortresses and towers in the forests. 5 He launched a military campaign against the king of the Ammonites and defeated them. That year the Ammonites paid him 100 talents of silver, 10,000 cors of wheat, and 10,000 cors of barley. The Ammonites also paid this same amount of annual tribute the next two years.

6 Jotham grew powerful because he was determined to please the LORD his God. 7 The rest of the events of Jotham's reign, including all his military campaigns and his accomplishments, are recorded in the Scroll of the Kings of Israel and Judah. 8 He was twenty-five years old when he began to reign, and he reigned for sixteen years in Jerusalem. 9 Jotham passed away and was buried in the City of David. His son Ahaz replaced him as king.

AHAZ'S REIGN

28 Ahaz was twenty years old when he began to reign, and he reigned for sixteen years in Jerusalem. He did not do what pleased the LORD, in contrast to his ancestor David. 2 He followed in the footsteps of the kings of Israel; he also made images of the Baals. 3 He offered sacrifices in the Valley of Ben Hinnom and passed his sons through the fire, a horrible sin practiced by the nations whom the LORD drove out before the Israelites. 4 He offered sacrifices and burned incense on the high places, on the hills, and under every green tree.

5 The LORD his God handed him over to the king of Syria. The Syrians defeated him and deported many captives to Damascus. He was also handed over to the king of Israel, who thoroughly defeated him. 6 In one day Pekah son of Remaliah killed 120,000 warriors in Judah, because they had abandoned the LORD God of their ancestors. 7 Zikri, an Ephraimite warrior, killed the king's son Maaseiah, Azrikam, the supervisor of the palace, and Elkanah, the king's second-in-command. 8 The Israelites seized from their brothers 200,000 wives, sons, and daughters. They also carried off a huge amount of plunder and took it back to Samaria.

9 Oded, a prophet of the LORD, was there. He went to meet the army as they arrived in Samaria and said to them: "Look, because the LORD God of your ancestors was angry with Judah he handed them over to you. You have killed them so mercilessly that God has taken notice. 10 And now you are planning to enslave the people of Judah and Jerusalem. Yet are you not also guilty before the LORD your God? 11 Now listen to me! Send back those you have seized from your brothers, for the LORD is very angry at you!" 12 So some of the Ephraimite family leaders, Azariah son of Jehochanan, Berechiah son of Meshillemoth, Jechizkiah son of Shallum, and Amasa son of Hadlai confronted those

REFLECT

Was God just in His actions toward wicked kings? Why would He treat some kings so harshly and show more mercy to others?

returning from the battle. 13 They said to them, "Don't bring those
captives here! Are you planning on making us even more sinful
and guilty before the LORD? Our guilt is already great, and the
LORD is very angry at Israel." 14 So the soldiers released the captives and the plunder before the officials and the entire assembly. 15 Men were assigned to take the prisoners and find clothes
among the plunder for those who were naked. So they clothed
them, supplied them with sandals, gave them food and drink,
and provided them with oil to rub on their skin. They put the
ones who couldn't walk on donkeys. They brought them back to
their brothers at Jericho, the city of date palm trees, and then
returned to Samaria.

16 At that time King Ahaz asked the king of Assyria for help.
17 The Edomites had again invaded and defeated Judah and carried off captives. 18 The Philistines had raided the cities of Judah in the foothills and the Negev. They captured and settled
in Beth Shemesh, Aijalon, Gederoth, Soco and its surrounding
villages, Timnah and its surrounding villages, and Gimzo and its
surrounding villages. 19 The LORD humiliated Judah because of
King Ahaz of Israel, for he encouraged Judah to sin and was very
unfaithful to the LORD. 20 King Tiglath-Pileser of Assyria came,
but he gave him more trouble than support. 21 Ahaz gathered
riches from the LORD's temple, the royal palace, and the officials and gave them to the king of Assyria, but that did not help.

22 During his time of trouble King Ahaz was even more unfaithful to the LORD. 23 He offered sacrifices to the gods of Damascus
whom he thought had defeated him. He reasoned, "Since the
gods of the kings of Syria helped them, I will sacrifice to them so
they will help me." But they caused him and all Israel to stumble.
24 Ahaz gathered the items in God's temple and removed them.
He shut the doors of the LORD's temple and erected altars on
every street corner in Jerusalem. 25 In every city throughout Judah he set up high places to offer sacrifices to other gods. He
angered the LORD God of his ancestors.

26 The rest of the events of Ahaz's reign, including his accomplishments from start to finish, are recorded in the Scroll of the
Kings of Judah and Israel. 27 Ahaz passed away and was buried in
the city of Jerusalem; they did not bring him to the tombs of the
kings of Israel. His son Hezekiah replaced him as king.

HEZEKIAH CONSECRATES THE TEMPLE

29 Hezekiah was twenty-five years old when he began to
reign, and he reigned twenty-nine years in Jerusalem. His
mother was Abijah, the daughter of Zechariah. 2 He did what the
LORD approved, just as his ancestor David had done.

3 In the first month of the first year of his reign, he opened the
doors of the LORD's temple and repaired them. 4 He brought in
the priests and Levites and assembled them in the square on
the east side. 5 He said to them: "Listen to me, you Levites! Now
consecrate yourselves, so you can consecrate the temple of the
LORD God of your ancestors. Remove from the sanctuary what is
ceremonially unclean. 6 For our fathers were unfaithful; they did
what is evil in the sight of the LORD our God and abandoned him.
They turned away from the LORD's dwelling place and rejected

him. 7 They closed the doors of the temple porch and put out the
lamps; they did not offer incense or burnt sacrifices in the sanctuary of the God of Israel. 8 The LORD was angry at Judah and Jerusalem and made them an appalling object of horror at which
people hiss out their scorn, as you can see with your own eyes.
9 Look, our fathers died violently and our sons, daughters, and
wives were carried off because of this. 10 Now I intend to make
a covenant with the LORD God of Israel, so that he may relent
from his raging anger. 11 My sons, do not be negligent now, for
the LORD has chosen you to stand in his presence, to minister
to him, to be his ministers, and offer sacrifices."

12 The following Levites prepared to carry out the king's orders:

From the Kohathites: Mahath son of Amasai and Joel son of Azariah;

from the Merarites: Kish son of Abdi and Azariah son of Jehallelel;

from the Gershonites: Joah son of Zimmah and Eden son of Joah;

13 from the descendants of Elizaphan: Shimri and Jeiel;

from the descendants of Asaph: Zechariah and Mattaniah;

14 from the descendants of Heman: Jehiel and Shimei;

from the descendants of Jeduthun: Shemaiah and Uzziel.

15 They assembled their brothers and consecrated themselves.
Then they went in to purify the LORD's temple, just as the king
had ordered, in accordance with the word of the LORD. 16 The
priests then entered the LORD's temple to purify it; they brought
out to the courtyard of the LORD's temple every ceremonially
unclean thing they discovered inside. The Levites took them out
to the Kidron Valley. 17 On the first day of the first month they began consecrating; by the eighth day of the month they reached
the porch of the LORD's temple. For eight more days they consecrated the LORD's temple. On the sixteenth day of the first
month they were finished. 18 They went to King Hezekiah and
said: "We have purified the entire temple of the LORD, including
the altar of burnt sacrifice and all its equipment, and the table
for the Bread of the Presence and all its equipment. 19 We have
prepared and consecrated all the items that King Ahaz removed
during his reign when he acted unfaithfully. They are in front of
the altar of the LORD."

20 Early the next morning King Hezekiah assembled the city
officials and went up to the LORD's temple. 21 They brought seven
bulls, seven rams, seven lambs, and seven goats as a sin offering for the kingdom, the sanctuary, and Judah. The king told
the priests, the descendants of Aaron, to offer burnt sacrifices
on the altar of the LORD. 22 They slaughtered the bulls, and the
priests took the blood and splashed it on the altar. Then they
slaughtered the rams and splashed the blood on the altar; next
they slaughtered the lambs and splashed the blood on the altar.
23 Finally they brought the goats for the sin offering before the
king and the assembly, and they placed their hands on them.
24 Then the priests slaughtered them. They offered their blood
as a sin offering on the altar to make atonement for all Israel,
because the king had decreed that the burnt sacrifice and sin
offering were for all Israel.

25 Hezekiah stationed the Levites in the LORD's temple with cymbals and stringed instruments just as David, Gad the king's prophet, and Nathan the prophet had ordered. (The LORD had actually given these orders through his prophets.) 26 The Levites had David's musical instruments and the priests had trumpets. 27 Hezekiah ordered the burnt sacrifice to be offered on the altar. As they began to offer the sacrifice, they also began to sing to the LORD, accompanied by the trumpets and the musical instruments of King David of Israel. 28 The entire assembly worshiped, as the singers sang and the trumpeters played. They continued until the burnt sacrifice was completed.

29 When the sacrifices were completed, the king and all who were with him bowed down and worshiped. 30 King Hezekiah and the officials told the Levites to praise the LORD, using the psalms of David and Asaph the prophet. So they joyfully offered praise and bowed down and worshiped. 31 Hezekiah said, "Now you have consecrated yourselves to the LORD. Come and bring sacrifices and thank offerings to the LORD's temple." So the assembly brought sacrifices and thank offerings, and whoever desired to do so brought burnt sacrifices.

32 The assembly brought a total of 70 bulls, 100 rams, and 200 lambs as burnt sacrifices to the LORD, 33 and 600 bulls and 3,000 sheep were consecrated. 34 But there were not enough priests to skin all the animals, so their brothers, the Levites, helped them until the work was finished and the priests could consecrate themselves. (The Levites had been more conscientious about consecrating themselves than the priests.) 35 There was a large number of burnt sacrifices, as well as fat from the peace offerings and drink offerings that accompanied the burnt sacrifices. So the service of the LORD's temple was reinstituted. 36 Hezekiah and all the people were happy about what God had done for them, for it had been done quickly.

HEZEKIAH OBSERVES THE PASSOVER

30 Hezekiah sent messages throughout Israel and Judah; he even wrote letters to Ephraim and Manasseh, summoning them to come to the LORD's temple in Jerusalem and observe a Passover celebration for the LORD God of Israel. 2 The king, his officials, and the entire assembly in Jerusalem decided to observe the Passover in the second month. 3 They were unable to observe it at the regular time because not enough priests had consecrated themselves and the people had not assembled in Jerusalem. 4 The proposal seemed appropriate to the king and the entire assembly. 5 So they sent an edict throughout Israel from Beer Sheba to Dan, summoning the people to come and observe a Passover for the LORD God of Israel in Jerusalem, for they had not observed it on a nationwide scale as prescribed in the law. 6 Messengers delivered the letters from the king and his officials throughout Israel and Judah.

This royal edict read: "O Israelites, return to the LORD God of Abraham, Isaac, and Israel, so he may return to you who have been spared from the kings of Assyria. 7 Don't be like your fathers and brothers who were unfaithful to the LORD God of their ancestors, provoking him to destroy them, as you can see. 8 Now,

don't be stubborn like your fathers. Submit to the LORD and
come to his sanctuary which he has permanently consecrated.
Serve the LORD your God so that he might relent from his raging anger. 9 For if you return to the LORD, your brothers and sons
will be shown mercy by their captors and return to this land.
The LORD your God is merciful and compassionate; he will not
reject you if you return to him."

10 The messengers journeyed from city to city through the land
of Ephraim and Manasseh as far as Zebulun, but people mocked
and ridiculed them. 11 But some men from Asher, Manasseh, and
Zebulun humbled themselves and came to Jerusalem. 12 In Judah God moved the people to unite and carry out the edict of
the king and the officers in keeping with the LORD's message.
13 A huge crowd assembled in Jerusalem to observe the Feast of
Unleavened Bread in the second month. 14 They removed the altars in Jerusalem; they also removed all the incense altars and
threw them into the Kidron Valley.

15 They slaughtered the Passover lamb on the fourteenth day
of the second month. The priests and Levites were ashamed,
so they consecrated themselves and brought burnt sacrifices
to the LORD's temple. 16 They stood at their posts according to
the regulations outlined in the law of Moses, the man of God.
The priests were splashing the blood as the Levites handed it
to them. 17 Because many in the assembly had not consecrated
themselves, the Levites slaughtered the Passover lambs of all
who were ceremonially unclean and could not consecrate their
sacrifice to the LORD. 18 The majority of the many people from
Ephraim, Manasseh, Issachar, and Zebulun were ceremonially
unclean, yet they ate the Passover in violation of what is prescribed in the law. For Hezekiah prayed for them, saying: "May
the LORD, who is good, forgive 19 everyone who has determined
to follow God, the LORD God of his ancestors, even if he is not
ceremonially clean according to the standards of the temple."
20 The LORD responded favorably to Hezekiah and forgave the
people.

21 The Israelites who were in Jerusalem observed the Feast of
Unleavened Bread for seven days with great joy. The Levites and
priests were praising the LORD every day with all their might.
22 Hezekiah expressed his appreciation to all the Levites, who
demonstrated great skill in serving the LORD. They feasted for
the seven days of the festival, and were making peace offerings
and giving thanks to the LORD God of their ancestors.

23 The entire assembly then decided to celebrate for seven
more days; so they joyfully celebrated for seven more days.
24 King Hezekiah of Judah supplied 1,000 bulls and 7,000 sheep
for the assembly, while the officials supplied them with 1,000
bulls and 10,000 sheep. Many priests consecrated themselves.
25 The celebration included the entire assembly of Judah, the
priests, the Levites, the entire assembly of those who came
from Israel, the resident foreigners who came from the land
of Israel, and those who were residents of Judah. 26 There
was a great celebration in Jerusalem, unlike anything that
had occurred in Jerusalem since the time of King Solomon
son of David of Israel. 27 The priests and Levites got up and

pronounced blessings on the people. The LORD responded
favorably to them as their prayers reached his holy dwelling
place in heaven.

31 When all this was over, the Israelites who were in the cities
of Judah went out and smashed the sacred pillars, cut down
the Asherah poles, and demolished all the high places and altars
throughout Judah, Benjamin, Ephraim, and Manasseh. Then all
the Israelites returned to their own homes in their cities.

THE PEOPLE CONTRIBUTE TO THE TEMPLE

2 Hezekiah appointed the divisions of the priests and Levites to
do their assigned tasks—to offer burnt sacrifices and present offerings and to serve, give thanks, and offer praise in the gates of
the LORD's sanctuary.

3 The king contributed some of what he owned for burnt sacrifices, including the morning and evening burnt sacrifices and
the burnt sacrifices made on Sabbaths, new moon festivals, and
at other appointed times prescribed in the law of the LORD. 4 He
ordered the people living in Jerusalem to contribute the portion
prescribed for the priests and Levites so they might be obedient
to the law of the LORD. 5 When the edict was issued, the Israelites freely contributed the initial portion of their grain, wine,
olive oil, honey, and all the produce of their fields. They brought
a tenth of everything, which added up to a huge amount. 6 The
Israelites and people of Judah who lived in the cities of Judah
also contributed a tenth of their cattle and sheep, as well as a
tenth of the holy items consecrated to the LORD their God. They
brought them and placed them in many heaps. 7 In the third
month they began piling their contributions in heaps and finished in the seventh month. 8 When Hezekiah and the officials
came and saw the heaps, they praised the LORD and pronounced
blessings on his people Israel.

9 When Hezekiah asked the priests and Levites about the
heaps, 10 Azariah, the head priest from the family of Zadok, said
to him, "Since the contributions began arriving in the LORD's
temple, we have had plenty to eat and have a large quantity left
over. For the LORD has blessed his people, and this large amount
remains." 11 Hezekiah ordered that storerooms be prepared in
the LORD's temple. When this was done, 12 they brought in the
contributions, tithes, and consecrated items that had been offered. Konaniah, a Levite, was in charge of all this, assisted by
his brother Shimei. 13 Jehiel, Azaziah, Nahath, Asahel, Jerimoth,
Jozabad, Eliel, Ismakiah, Mahath, and Benaiah worked under
the supervision of Konaniah and his brother Shimei, as directed
by King Hezekiah and Azariah, the supervisor of God's temple.

14 Kore son of Imnah, a Levite and the guard on the east side,
was in charge of the voluntary offerings made to God and disbursed the contributions made to the LORD and the consecrated
items. 15 In the cities of the priests, Eden, Miniamin, Jeshua, Shemaiah, Amariah, and Shecaniah faithfully assisted him in making disbursements to their fellow priests according to their
divisions, regardless of age. 16 They made disbursements to all
the males three years old and up who were listed in the genealogical records—to all who would enter the LORD's temple to

serve on a daily basis and fulfill their duties as assigned to their
divisions. 17 They made disbursements to the priests listed in the
genealogical records by their families, and to the Levites twenty
years old and up, according to their duties as assigned to their
divisions, 18 and to all the infants, wives, sons, and daughters of
the entire assembly listed in the genealogical records, for they
faithfully consecrated themselves. 19 As for the descendants of
Aaron, the priests who lived in the outskirts of all their cities,
men were assigned to disburse portions to every male among
the priests and to every Levite listed in the genealogical records.

20 This is what Hezekiah did throughout Judah. He did what
the LORD his God considered good and right and faithful. 21 He
wholeheartedly and successfully reinstituted service in God's
temple and obedience to the law, in order to follow his God.

SENNACHERIB INVADES JUDAH

32 After these faithful deeds were accomplished, King Sennacherib of Assyria invaded Judah. He besieged the fortified cities, intending to seize them. 2 When Hezekiah saw that
Sennacherib had invaded and intended to attack Jerusalem, 3 he
consulted with his advisers and military officers about stopping up the springs outside the city, and they supported him.
4 A large number of people gathered together and stopped up
all the springs and the stream that flowed through the district.
They reasoned, "Why should the kings of Assyria come and find
plenty of water?" 5 Hezekiah energetically rebuilt every broken
wall. He erected towers and an outer wall and fortified the terrace of the City of David. He made many weapons and shields.

6 He appointed military officers over the army and assembled
them in the square at the city gate. He encouraged them, saying,
7 "Be strong and brave! Don't be afraid and don't panic because
of the king of Assyria and this huge army that is with him. We
have with us one who is stronger than those who are with him.
8 He has with him mere human strength, but the LORD our God
is with us to help us and fight our battles!" The army was encouraged by the words of King Hezekiah of Judah.

9 Afterward King Sennacherib of Assyria, while attacking Lachish with all his military might, sent his messengers to Jerusalem. The message was for King Hezekiah of Judah and all the
people of Judah who were in Jerusalem. It read: 10 "This is what
King Sennacherib of Assyria says: 'Why are you so confident that
you remain in Jerusalem while it is under siege? 11 Hezekiah says,
"The LORD our God will rescue us from the power of the king
of Assyria." But he is misleading you, and you will die of hunger
and thirst! 12 Hezekiah is the one who eliminated the LORD's high
places and altars and then told Judah and Jerusalem, "At one altar you must worship and offer sacrifices." 13 Are you not aware
of what I and my predecessors have done to all the nations of
the surrounding lands? Have the gods of the surrounding lands
actually been able to rescue their lands from my power? 14 Who
among all the gods of these nations whom my predecessors annihilated was able to rescue his people from my power, that your
God would be able to rescue you from my power? 15 Now don't
let Hezekiah deceive you or mislead you like this. Don't believe

him, for no god of any nation or kingdom has been able to rescue his people from my power or the power of my predecessors. So how can your gods rescue you from my power?'"

[16] Sennacherib's servants further insulted the LORD God and
his servant Hezekiah. [17] He wrote letters mocking the LORD God
of Israel and insulting him with these words: "The gods of the surrounding nations could not rescue their people from my power. Neither can Hezekiah's god rescue his people from my
power." [18] They called out loudly in the Judahite dialect to the
people of Jerusalem who were on the wall, trying to scare and
terrify them so they could seize the city. [19] They talked about the
God of Jerusalem as if he were one of the man-made gods of the nations of the earth.

[20] King Hezekiah and the prophet Isaiah son of Amoz prayed
about this and cried out to heaven. [21] The LORD sent a messen-
ger and he wiped out all the soldiers, princes, and officers in the army of the king of Assyria. So Sennacherib returned home humiliated. When he entered the temple of his god, some of his
own sons struck him down with the sword. [22] The LORD deliv-
ered Hezekiah and the residents of Jerusalem from the power of King Sennacherib of Assyria and from all the other nations. He
made them secure on every side. [23] Many were bringing presents
to the LORD in Jerusalem and precious gifts to King Hezekiah of Judah. From that time on he was respected by all the nations.

HEZEKIAH'S SHORTCOMINGS AND ACCOMPLISHMENTS

[24] In those days Hezekiah was stricken with a terminal illness. He prayed to the LORD, who answered him and gave him a sign confirming that he would be healed. [25] But Hezekiah was ungrateful;
he had a proud attitude, provoking God to be angry at him, as well
as Judah and Jerusalem. [26] But then Hezekiah and the residents of
Jerusalem humbled themselves and abandoned their pride, and the LORD was not angry with them for the rest of Hezekiah's reign.

[27] Hezekiah was very wealthy and greatly respected. He made storehouses for his silver, gold, precious stones, spices, shields,
and all his other valuable possessions. [28] He made storerooms
for the harvest of grain, wine, and olive oil, and stalls for all his
various kinds of livestock and his flocks. [29] He built royal cities
and owned a large number of sheep and cattle, for God gave him a huge amount of possessions.

[30] Hezekiah dammed up the source of the waters of the Upper Gihon and directed them down to the west side of the City
of David. Hezekiah succeeded in all that he did. [31] So when the
envoys arrived from the Babylonian officials to visit him and inquire about the sign that occurred in the land, God left him alone to test him, in order to know his true motives.

[32] The rest of the events of Hezekiah's reign, including his faith-
ful deeds, are recorded in the vision of the prophet Isaiah son of Amoz, included in the Scroll of the Kings of Judah and Israel.
[33] Hezekiah passed away and was buried on the ascent of the
tombs of the descendants of David. All the people of Judah and the residents of Jerusalem buried him with great honor. His son Manasseh replaced him as king.

MANASSEH'S REIGN

33 Manasseh was twelve years old when he became king,
and he reigned for fifty-five years in Jerusalem. 2 He did
evil in the sight of the LORD and committed the same horrible
sins practiced by the nations whom the LORD drove out ahead
of the Israelites. 3 He rebuilt the high places that his father Hezekiah had destroyed; he set up altars for the Baals and made
Asherah poles. He bowed down to all the stars in the sky and
worshiped them. 4 He built altars in the LORD's temple, about
which the LORD had said, "Jerusalem will be my permanent
home." 5 In the two courtyards of the LORD's temple he built
altars for all the stars in the sky. 6 He passed his sons through
the fire in the Valley of Ben Hinnom and practiced divination,
omen reading, and sorcery. He set up a ritual pit to conjure up
underworld spirits and appointed magicians to supervise it. He
did a great amount of evil in the sight of the LORD and angered
him. 7 He put an idolatrous image he had made in God's temple, about which God had said to David and to his son Solomon,
"This temple in Jerusalem, which I have chosen out of all the
tribes of Israel, will be my permanent home. 8 I will not make
Israel again leave the land I gave to their ancestors, provided
that they carefully obey all I commanded them, the whole law,
the rules and regulations given through Moses." 9 But Manasseh misled the people of Judah and the residents of Jerusalem
so that they sinned more than the nations whom the LORD had
destroyed ahead of the Israelites.

10 The LORD confronted Manasseh and his people, but they
paid no attention. 11 So the LORD brought against them the commanders of the army of the king of Assyria. They seized Manasseh, put hooks in his nose, bound him with bronze chains, and
carried him away to Babylon. 12 In his pain Manasseh asked the
LORD his God for mercy and truly humbled himself before the
God of his ancestors. 13 When he prayed to the LORD, the LORD
responded to him and answered favorably his cry for mercy. The
LORD brought him back to Jerusalem to his kingdom. Then Manasseh realized that the LORD is the true God.

14 After this Manasseh built up the outer wall of the City of
David on the west side of the Gihon in the valley to the entrance of the Fish Gate and all around the terrace; he made it
much higher. He placed army officers in all the fortified cities in Judah.

15 He removed the foreign gods and images from the LORD's
temple and all the altars he had built on the hill of the LORD's
temple and in Jerusalem; he threw them outside the city. 16 He
erected the altar of the LORD and offered on it peace offerings
and thank offerings. He told the people of Judah to serve the
LORD God of Israel. 17 However, the people continued to offer
sacrifices at the high places, but only to the LORD their God.

18 The rest of the events of Manasseh's reign, including his
prayer to his God and the words the prophets spoke to him in
the name of the LORD God of Israel, are recorded in the Annals
of the Kings of Israel. 19 The Annals of the Prophets include his
prayer, give an account of how the LORD responded to it, record
all his sins and unfaithful acts, and identify the sites where he

built high places and erected Asherah poles and idols before he
humbled himself. 20 Manasseh passed away and was buried in
his palace. His son Amon replaced him as king.

AMON'S REIGN

21 Amon was twenty-two years old when he became king, and
he reigned for two years in Jerusalem. 22 He did evil in the sight
of the LORD, just as his father Manasseh had done. Amon offered sacrifices to all the idols his father Manasseh had made,
and worshiped them. 23 He did not humble himself before the
LORD as his father Manasseh had done. Amon was guilty of
great sin. 24 His servants conspired against him and killed him
in his palace. 25 The people of the land executed all who had conspired against King Amon, and they made his son Josiah king in
his place.

JOSIAH INSTITUTES RELIGIOUS REFORMS

34 Josiah was eight years old when he became king, and he
reigned for thirty-one years in Jerusalem. 2 He did what
the LORD approved and followed in his ancestor David's footsteps; he did not deviate to the right or the left.

3 In the eighth year of his reign, while he was still young, he
began to seek the God of his ancestor David. In his twelfth year
he began ridding Judah and Jerusalem of the high places, Asherah poles, idols, and images. 4 He ordered the altars of the Baals
to be torn down, and broke the incense altars that were above
them. He smashed the Asherah poles, idols, and images, crushed
them, and sprinkled the dust over the tombs of those who had
sacrificed to them. 5 He burned the bones of the pagan priests
on their altars; he purified Judah and Jerusalem. 6 In the cities
of Manasseh, Ephraim, and Simeon, as far as Naphtali, and in
the ruins around them, 7 he tore down the altars and Asherah
poles, demolished the idols, and smashed all the incense altars
throughout the land of Israel. Then he returned to Jerusalem.

8 In the eighteenth year of his reign, he continued his policy
of purifying the land and the temple. He sent Shaphan son of
Azaliah, Maaseiah the city official, and Joah son of Joahaz the
secretary to repair the temple of the LORD his God. 9 They went
to Hilkiah the high priest and gave him the silver that had been
brought to God's temple. The Levites who guarded the door had
collected it from the people of Manasseh and Ephraim and from
all who were left in Israel, as well as from all the people of Judah
and Benjamin and the residents of Jerusalem. 10 They handed it
over to the construction foremen assigned to the LORD's temple. They in turn paid the temple workers to restore and repair
it. 11 They gave money to the craftsmen and builders to buy chiseled stone and wood for the braces and rafters of the buildings
that the kings of Judah had allowed to fall into disrepair. 12 The
men worked faithfully. Their supervisors were Jahath and Obadiah (Levites descended from Merari), as well as Zechariah and
Meshullam (descendants of Kohath). The Levites, all of whom
were skilled musicians, 13 supervised the laborers and all the
foremen on their various jobs. Some of the Levites were scribes,
officials, and guards.

14 When they took out the silver that had been brought to the
LORD's temple, Hilkiah the priest found the law scroll the LORD
had given to Moses. 15 Hilkiah informed Shaphan the scribe,
"I found the law scroll in the LORD's temple." Hilkiah gave the
scroll to Shaphan. 16 Shaphan brought the scroll to the king and
reported, "Your servants are doing everything assigned to them.
17 They melted down the silver in the LORD's temple and handed
it over to the supervisors and the construction foremen." 18 Then
Shaphan the scribe told the king, "Hilkiah the priest has given
me a scroll." Shaphan read it out loud before the king. 19 When
the king heard the words of the law, he tore his clothes. 20 The
king ordered Hilkiah, Ahikam son of Shaphan, Abdon son of Micah, Shaphan the scribe, and Asaiah the king's servant, 21 "Go, ask
the LORD for me and for those who remain in Israel and Judah
about the words of this scroll that has been discovered. For the
LORD's great fury has been ignited against us, because our ancestors did not obey the word of the LORD by living according
to all that is written in this scroll."

22 So Hilkiah and the others sent by the king went to Huldah the
prophetess, the wife of Shallum son of Tokhath, the son of Hasrah,
the supervisor of the wardrobe. (She lived in Jerusalem in the Mishneh district.) They stated their business, 23 and she said to them:
"This is what the LORD God of Israel says: 'Say this to the man who
sent you to me: 24 "This is what the LORD says: 'I am about to bring
disaster on this place and its residents, all the curses that are recorded in the scroll which they read before the king of Judah. 25 This
will happen because they have abandoned me and offered sacrifices
to other gods, angering me with all the idols they have made. My
anger will ignite against this place and will not be extinguished!'"
26 Say this to the king of Judah, who sent you to seek an oracle from
the LORD: "This is what the LORD God of Israel says concerning the
words you have heard: 27 'You displayed a sensitive spirit and humbled yourself before God when you heard his words concerning this
place and its residents. You humbled yourself before me, tore your
clothes and wept before me, and I have heard you,' says the LORD.
28 'Therefore I will allow you to die and be buried in peace. You will
not have to witness all the disaster I will bring on this place and its
residents.'"'" Then they reported back to the king.

29 The king summoned all the leaders of Judah and Jerusalem.
30 The king went up to the LORD's temple, accompanied by all the
people of Judah, the residents of Jerusalem, the priests, and the
Levites. All the people were there, from the oldest to the youngest.
He read aloud all the words of the scroll of the covenant that had
been discovered in the LORD's temple. 31 The king stood by his pillar and renewed the covenant before the LORD, agreeing to follow
the LORD and to obey his commandments, laws, and rules with
all his heart and being, by carrying out the terms of this covenant
recorded on this scroll. 32 He made all who were in Jerusalem and
Benjamin agree to it. The residents of Jerusalem acted in accordance with the covenant of God, the God of their ancestors. 33 Josiah removed all the detestable idols from all the areas belonging
to the Israelites and encouraged all who were in Israel to worship
the LORD their God. Throughout the rest of his reign they did not
turn aside from following the LORD God of their ancestors.

JOSIAH OBSERVES THE PASSOVER

35 Josiah observed a Passover festival for the LORD in Jerusalem. They slaughtered the Passover lambs on the fourteenth day of the first month. 2 He appointed the priests to fulfill their duties and encouraged them to carry out their service in the LORD's temple. 3 He told the Levites, who instructed all Israel about things consecrated to the LORD, "Place the holy ark in the temple which King Solomon son of David of Israel built. Don't carry it on your shoulders. Now serve the LORD your God and his people Israel! 4 Prepare yourselves by your families according to your divisions, as instructed in writing by King David of Israel and his son Solomon. 5 Stand in the sanctuary and, together with the Levites, represent the family divisions of your countrymen. 6 Slaughter the Passover lambs, consecrate yourselves, and make preparations for your countrymen to celebrate according to the LORD's message which came through Moses."

7 From his own royal flocks and herds, Josiah supplied the people with 30,000 lambs and goats for the Passover sacrifice, as well as 3,000 cattle. 8 His officials also willingly contributed to the people, priests, and Levites. Hilkiah, Zechariah, and Jehiel, the leaders of God's temple, gave the priests 2,600 Passover sacrifices and 300 cattle. 9 Konaniah and his brothers Shemaiah and Nethanel, along with Hashabiah, Jeiel, and Jozabad, the officials of the Levites, supplied the Levites with 5,000 Passover sacrifices and 500 cattle. 10 Preparations were made, and the priests stood at their posts and the Levites in their divisions as prescribed by the king. 11 They slaughtered the Passover lambs and the priests splashed the blood, while the Levites skinned the animals. 12 They reserved the burnt offerings and the cattle for the family divisions of the people to present to the LORD, as prescribed in the scroll of Moses. 13 They cooked the Passover sacrifices over the open fire as prescribed and cooked the consecrated offerings in pots, kettles, and pans. They quickly served them to all the people. 14 Afterward they made preparations for themselves and for the priests, because the priests, the descendants of Aaron, were offering burnt sacrifices and fat portions until evening. The Levites made preparations for themselves and for the priests, the descendants of Aaron. 15 The musicians, the descendants of Asaph, manned their posts, as prescribed by David, Asaph, Heman, and Jeduthun the king's prophet. The guards at the various gates did not need to leave their posts, for their fellow Levites made preparations for them. 16 So all the preparations for the LORD's service were made that day, as the Passover was observed and the burnt sacrifices were offered on the altar of the LORD, as prescribed by King Josiah. 17 So the Israelites who were present observed the Passover at that time, as well as the Feast of Unleavened Bread for seven days. 18 A Passover like this had not been observed in Israel since the days of Samuel the prophet. None of the kings of Israel had observed a Passover like the one celebrated by Josiah, the priests, the Levites, all the people of Judah and Israel who were there, and the residents of Jerusalem. 19 This Passover was observed in the eighteenth year of Josiah's reign.

JOSIAH'S REIGN ENDS

20 After Josiah had done all this for the temple, King Necho of Egypt
marched up to do battle at Carchemish on the Euphrates River.
Josiah marched out to oppose him. 21 Necho sent messengers to
him, saying, "Why are you opposing me, O king of Judah? I am
not attacking you today, but the kingdom with which I am at war.
God told me to hurry. Stop opposing God, who is with me, or else
he will destroy you." 22 But Josiah did not turn back from him; he
disguised himself for battle. He did not take seriously the words
of Necho which he had received from God; he went to fight him
in the Plain of Megiddo. 23 Archers shot King Josiah; the king ordered his servants, "Take me out of this chariot, for I am seriously
wounded." 24 So his servants took him out of the chariot, put him
in another chariot that he owned, and brought him to Jerusalem,
where he died. He was buried in the tombs of his ancestors; all
the people of Judah and Jerusalem mourned Josiah. 25 Jeremiah
composed laments for Josiah which all the male and female singers use to mourn Josiah to this very day. It has become customary
in Israel to sing these; they are recorded in the Book of Laments.

26 The rest of the events of Josiah's reign, including the faithful acts he did in obedience to what is written in the law of the
LORD 27 and his accomplishments, from start to finish, are recorded in the Scroll of the Kings of Israel and Judah.

JEHOAHAZ'S REIGN

36 The people of the land took Jehoahaz son of Josiah and
made him king in his father's place in Jerusalem. 2 Jehoahaz was twenty-three years old when he became king, and he
reigned three months in Jerusalem. 3 The king of Egypt prevented
him from ruling in Jerusalem and imposed on the land a special tax of 100 talents of silver and a talent of gold. 4 The king of
Egypt made Jehoahaz's brother Eliakim king over Judah and Jerusalem, and changed his name to Jehoiakim. Necho seized his
brother Jehoahaz and took him to Egypt.

JEHOIAKIM'S REIGN

5 Jehoiakim was twenty-five years old when he became king, and
he reigned for eleven years in Jerusalem. He did evil in the sight
of the LORD his God. 6 King Nebuchadnezzar of Babylon attacked
him, bound him with bronze chains, and carried him away to
Babylon. 7 Nebuchadnezzar took some of the items in the LORD's
temple to Babylon and put them in his palace there.

8 The rest of the events of Jehoiakim's reign, including the horrible sins he committed and his shortcomings, are recorded in
the Scroll of the Kings of Israel and Judah. His son Jehoiachin
replaced him as king.

JEHOIACHIN'S REIGN

9 Jehoiachin was eighteen years old when he became king, and he
reigned three months and ten days in Jerusalem. He did evil in
the sight of the LORD. 10 At the beginning of the year King Nebuchadnezzar ordered him to be brought to Babylon, along with the
valuable items in the LORD's temple. In his place Nebuchadnezzar
made Jehoiachin's relative Zedekiah king over Judah and Jerusalem.

REFLECT

How do the actions of the final three kings of Judah lead to the destruction of Jerusalem and the exile of the people?

ZEDEKIAH'S REIGN

11 Zedekiah was twenty-one years old when he became king, and
he ruled for eleven years in Jerusalem. 12 He did evil in the sight
of the LORD his God. He did not humble himself before Jeremiah
the prophet, the LORD's spokesman. 13 He also rebelled against
King Nebuchadnezzar, who had made him vow allegiance in the
name of God. He was stubborn and obstinate, and refused to return to the LORD God of Israel. 14 All the leaders of the priests
and people became more unfaithful and committed the same
horrible sins practiced by the nations. They defiled the LORD's
temple which he had consecrated in Jerusalem.

THE BABYLONIANS DESTROY JERUSALEM

15 The LORD God of their ancestors continually warned them
through his messengers, for he felt compassion for his people
and his dwelling place. 16 But they mocked God's messengers,
despised his warnings, and ridiculed his prophets. Finally the
LORD got very angry at his people and there was no one who
could prevent his judgment. 17 He brought against them the king
of the Babylonians, who slaughtered their young men in their
temple. He did not spare young men or women, or even the
old and aging. God handed everyone over to him. 18 He carried
away to Babylon all the items in God's temple, whether large or
small, as well as what was in the treasuries of the LORD's temple
and in the treasuries of the king and his officials. 19 They burned
down God's temple and tore down the wall of Jerusalem. They
burned all its fortified buildings and destroyed all its valuable
items. 20 He deported to Babylon all who escaped the sword.
They served him and his sons until the Persian kingdom rose
to power. 21 This took place to fulfill the LORD's message spoken
through Jeremiah and lasted until the land experienced its sab-
batical years. All the time of its desolation the land rested in order to fulfill the seventy years.

CYRUS ALLOWS THE EXILES TO GO HOME

22 In the first year of King Cyrus of Persia, in fulfillment of the
LORD's message spoken through Jeremiah, the LORD motivated
King Cyrus of Persia to issue a proclamation throughout his kingdom and also to put it in writing. It read:
23 "This is what King Cyrus of Persia says:
'The LORD God of heaven has given me all the kingdoms of the
earth. He has appointed me to build a temple for him in Jerusalem, which is in Judah. Anyone of his people among you may go
up there, and may the LORD his God be with him.'"

He has left us a remnant and has given us a secure position in His holy place

MEMORY VERSE

"But now briefly we have received mercy from the LORD our God, in that he has left us a remnant and has given us a secure position in his holy place. Thus our God has enlightened our eyes and has given us a little relief in our time of servitude."

Ezra 9:8

Ezra

INTRODUCTION

Promises Restored

The Book of Ezra displays the incredible faithfulness of God to His covenant people. Through kings, leaders, prophets, and priests, God restored the people of Judah to their home in Jerusalem, and the people rebuilt the temple. The restoration God promised to bring to His people is finally brought about in the events in the Book of Ezra. His faithfulness is on display as He continued to fulfill the promises He made to Abraham, Isaac, Jacob, and David.

The Books of Ezra and Nehemiah are one work in the Hebrew Bible; together they offer a full account of the return of the Babylonian exiles to Jerusalem. The combined narrative presents the story of the exiles' return in two periods, each marked by two prominent leaders. Ezra, the first account, records the rebuilding of the temple under Zerubbabel and Joshua the priest. Nehemiah, the second account, details the restoration of the worship of God and rebuilding of Jerusalem's walls under Ezra and Nehemiah.

The events in Ezra and Nehemiah take place between 600 and 400 B.C. They include the time of the deportation of the people of Judah to Babylon to the return journey of Nehemiah and his work rebuilding the wall of Jerusalem. Ezra is traditionally believed to be the author of both books, although he likely compiled the books using various documents and sources, as it is believed he did when writing 1 and 2 Chronicles. The Book of Ezra was written in two languages, Aramaic, the international language of the Persian world, and Hebrew.

As He promised, God restored His people. Ezra is the record of their restoration. God returned the remnant of His people to Jerusalem with hope of rebuilding the nation. Ezra guided the people's return to wholehearted worship and devotion to God, helping them to remain steadfast and committed to Him. God not only rebuilt the city and the temple, but He rebuilt the hearts of His people so they would truly worship Him. As we seek to love God greatly, we can rest in the truth that our God is always faithful to His promise.

South Africa

TOP SPOKEN LANGUAGES
Afrikaans and English
POPULATION
58,425,000
UNREACHED POPULATION
971,000
PROFESSING CHRISTIANS
77.0%

Eloise's Home

Say a Prayer Today

Pray for the Bible Society of South Africa, that they would be able to continue their mission of providing affordable Bibles for everyone in their own language.

HISTORY BIT

The South African Bible Society, now the Bible Society of South Africa, was established in 1820.* The first translation of the Bible in Afrikaans was completed in 1933.**

Source Information:
https://joshuaproject.net/countries/SF
*https://www.biblesociety.co.za/index.php/about-us/our-story/2-our-story
**John Bowden, *A Chronology of World Christianity* (New York, NY: Continuum, 2007), 411.

ELOISE'S STORY

For my first twenty-nine years, I had a pretty good life. I lived in South Africa, working in townships and rural villages. I also worked in Zambia and Zimbabwe and never experienced any major hardships. I moved to Canada when I was twenty-nine. After marrying my Canadian-born husband four years later, I settled into what I thought would be a pleasant new season.

Within the first year of our marriage I significantly injured my back and my husband tore his Achilles tendon. We were both out of work for several months. Soon after, my husband came down with a serious illness, was hospitalized for six weeks, and had to relearn how to walk. And then the worst happened.

I suffered two miscarriages, one at five months and one at four. My mental health suffered, and I attempted to take my own life. I was lost in a deep darkness and an enormous emptiness filled my heart. Finally, I began attending a grief support group. As I shared my story and my journey with others God began to heal my brokenness.

A year after my second miscarriage, I gave birth to a beautiful, healthy baby boy. Through a season of deep suffering, I learned to sit in the sanctuary of God. Now, I can clearly see Jesus carrying me through those dark years. He showed me His provision and love through the people that came around us and supported us. God walked with me and was there with me every step of the way. He is good and gracious. Even when we walk through the valley of death, He will be there.

6 WEEK READING PLAN

LOVE HIS WORD

	MONDAY	TUESDAY	WEDNESDAY	THURSDAY	FRIDAY
1	Ezra 1	Ezra 2:1-42	Ezra 2:43-70	Ezra 3	Ezra 4
	SOAP Psalm 121:1-2	SOAP Psalm 121:3	SOAP Psalm 121:4-5	SOAP Psalm 121:6-7	SOAP Psalm 121:8
2	Ezra 5	Ezra 6	Ezra 7	Ezra 8:1-14	Ezra 8:15-36
	SOAP Psalm 123:1-2	SOAP Psalm 123:3-4	SOAP Psalm 124:1-3	SOAP Psalm 124:4-5	SOAP Psalm 124:6-8
3	Ezra 9	Ezra 10:1-17	Ezra 10:18-44	Nehemiah 1	Nehemiah 2:1-10
	SOAP Ezra 9:8	SOAP Psalm 125:1-2	SOAP Psalm 125:3	SOAP Psalm 125:4-5	SOAP Psalm 126:1-2
4	Nehemiah 2:11-20	Nehemiah 3	Nehemiah 4	Nehemiah 5	Nehemiah 6:1-14
	SOAP Psalm 126:3	SOAP Psalm 126:4-6	SOAP Psalm 128:1-2	SOAP Psalm 128:3-4	SOAP Nehemiah 6:3
5	Nehemiah 6:15—7:7	Nehemiah 7:8-44	Nehemiah 7:45-73a	Nehemiah 7:73b—8:18	Nehemiah 9:1-37
	SOAP Psalm 128:5-6	SOAP Psalm 129:1-2	SOAP Psalm 129:3-4	SOAP Psalm 129:5-7	SOAP Psalm 129:8
6	Nehemiah 9:38—10:39	Nehemiah 11	Nehemiah 12:1-26	Nehemiah 12:27-47	Nehemiah 13
	SOAP Psalm 130:1-2	SOAP Psalm 130:3-4	SOAP Psalm 130:5	SOAP Psalm 130:6	SOAP Psalm 103:7-8

THE DECREE OF CYRUS

1 In the first year of King Cyrus of Persia, in fulfillment of the
LORD's message spoken through Jeremiah, the LORD motivated King Cyrus of Persia to issue a proclamation throughout
his kingdom and also to put it in writing. It read:
2 "This is what King Cyrus of Persia says:
"'The LORD God of heaven has given me all the kingdoms of the
earth. He has appointed me to build a temple for him in Jerusalem, which is in Judah. 3 Anyone of his people among you (may
his God be with him!) may go up to Jerusalem, which is in Judah,
and may build the temple of the LORD God of Israel—he is the
God who is in Jerusalem. 4 Anyone who survives in any of those
places where he is a resident foreigner must be helped by his
neighbors with silver, gold, equipment, and animals, along with
voluntary offerings for the temple of God which is in Jerusalem.'"

CHALLENGE

How is the truth of Proverbs 21:1 displayed in the Book of Ezra?

THE EXILES PREPARE TO RETURN TO JERUSALEM

5 Then the leaders of Judah and Benjamin, along with the priests
and the Levites—all those whose mind God had stirred—got
ready to go up in order to build the temple of the LORD in Jerusalem. 6 All their neighbors assisted them with silver utensils,
gold, equipment, animals, and expensive gifts, not to mention
all the voluntary offerings.
7 Then King Cyrus brought out the vessels of the LORD's temple which Nebuchadnezzar had brought from Jerusalem and
had displayed in the temple of his gods. 8 King Cyrus of Persia
entrusted them to Mithredath the treasurer, who counted them
out to Sheshbazzar the leader of the Judahite exiles.
9 The inventory of these items was as follows:
30 gold basins,
1,000 silver basins,
29 silver utensils,
10 30 gold bowls,
410 other silver bowls,
and 1,000 other vessels.

11 All these gold and silver vessels totaled 5,400. Sheshbazzar
brought them all along when the captives were brought up from
Babylon to Jerusalem.

THE NAMES OF THE RETURNING EXILES

2 These are the people of the province who were going up,
from the captives of the exile whom King Nebuchadnezzar
of Babylon had forced into exile in Babylon. They returned to
Jerusalem and Judah, each to his own city. 2 They came with Zerubbabel, Jeshua, Nehemiah, Seraiah, Reelaiah, Mordecai, Bilshan, Mispar, Bigvai, Rehum, and Baanah.
The number of Israelites was as follows:
3 the descendants of Parosh: 2,172;
4 the descendants of Shephatiah: 372;
5 the descendants of Arah: 775;
6 the descendants of Pahath Moab (from the line of Jeshua
and Joab): 2,812;
7 the descendants of Elam: 1,254;

8 the descendants of Zattu: 945;
9 the descendants of Zaccai: 760;
10 the descendants of Bani: 642;
11 the descendants of Bebai: 623;
12 the descendants of Azgad: 1,222;
13 the descendants of Adonikam: 666;
14 the descendants of Bigvai: 2,056;
15 the descendants of Adin: 454;
16 the descendants of Ater (through Hezekiah): 98;
17 the descendants of Bezai: 323;
18 the descendants of Jorah: 112;
19 the descendants of Hashum: 223;
20 the descendants of Gibbar: 95.
21 The men of Bethlehem: 123;
22 the men of Netophah: 56;
23 the men of Anathoth: 128;
24 the men of the family of Azmaveth: 42;
25 the men of Kiriath Jearim, Kephirah and Beeroth: 743;
26 the men of Ramah and Geba: 621;
27 the men of Micmash: 122;
28 the men of Bethel and Ai: 223;
29 the descendants of Nebo: 52;
30 the descendants of Magbish: 156;
31 the descendants of the other Elam: 1,254;
32 the descendants of Harim: 320;
33 the men of Lod, Hadid, and Ono: 725;
34 the men of Jericho: 345;
35 the descendants of Senaah: 3,630.
36 The priests: the descendants of Jedaiah (through the family
of Jeshua): 973;
37 the descendants of Immer: 1,052;
38 the descendants of Pashhur: 1,247;
39 the descendants of Harim: 1,017.
40 The Levites: the descendants of Jeshua and Kadmiel (through
the line of Hodaviah): 74.
41 The singers: the descendants of Asaph: 128.
42 The gatekeepers: the descendants of Shallum, the descendants of Ater, the descendants of Talmon, the descendants of Akkub, the descendants of Hatita, and the descendants of Shobai: 139.
43 The temple servants: the descendants of Ziha, the descendants of Hasupha, the descendants of Tabbaoth, 44 the descendants of Keros, the descendants of Siaha, the descendants of
Padon, 45 the descendants of Lebanah, the descendants of Hagabah, the descendants of Akkub, 46 the descendants of Hagab,
the descendants of Shalmai, the descendants of Hanan, 47 the
descendants of Giddel, the descendants of Gahar, the descendants of Reaiah, 48 the descendants of Rezin, the descendants
of Nekoda, the descendants of Gazzam, 49 the descendants of
Uzzah, the descendants of Paseah, the descendants of Besai,
50 the descendants of Asnah, the descendants of Meunim, the
descendants of Nephussim, 51 the descendants of Bakbuk, the
descendants of Hakupha, the descendants of Harhur, 52 the de-
scendants of Bazluth, the descendants of Mehida, the descen-
dants of Harsha, 53 the descendants of Barkos, the descendants

of Sisera, the descendants of Temah, [54]the descendants of Neziah, and the descendants of Hatipha.
[55]The descendants of the servants of Solomon: the descendants of Sotai, the descendants of Hassophereth, the descendants of Peruda, [56]the descendants of Jaala, the descendants of
Darkon, the descendants of Giddel, [57]the descendants of Shephatiah, the descendants of Hattil, the descendants of Pokereth
Hazzebaim, and the descendants of Ami.
[58]All the temple servants and the descendants of the servants
of Solomon: 392.
[59]These are the ones that came up from Tel Melah, Tel Harsha, Kerub, Addon, and Immer (although they were unable to
certify their family connection or their ancestry, as to whether
they really were from Israel):
[60]the descendants of Delaiah, the descendants of Tobiah, and
the descendants of Nekoda: 652.
[61]And from among the priests: the descendants of Hobaiah,
the descendants of Hakkoz, and the descendants of Barzillai
(who had taken a wife from the daughters of Barzillai the Gileadite and was called by that name). [62]They searched for their
records in the genealogical materials, but did not find them.
They were therefore excluded from the priesthood. [63]The governor instructed them not to eat any of the sacred food until
there was a priest who could consult the Urim and Thummim.
[64]The entire group numbered 42,360, [65]not counting their
male and female servants, who numbered 7,337. They also had 200
male and female singers [66]and 736 horses, 245 mules, [67]435 camels, and 6,720 donkeys. [68]When they came to the LORD's temple
in Jerusalem, some of the family leaders offered voluntary offerings for the temple of God in order to rebuild it on its site. [69]As
they were able, they gave to the treasury for this work 61,000
drachmas of gold, 5,000 minas of silver, and 100 priestly robes.
[70]The priests, the Levites, some of the people, the singers, the
gatekeepers, and the temple servants lived in their towns, and
all the rest of Israel lived in their towns.

THE ALTAR IS REBUILT

3 When the seventh month arrived and the Israelites were
living in their towns, the people assembled in Jerusalem.
[2]Then Jeshua the son of Jozadak and his priestly colleagues and
Zerubbabel son of Shealtiel and his colleagues started to build
the altar of the God of Israel so they could offer burnt offerings
on it as required by the law of Moses the man of God. [3]They established the altar on its foundations, even though they were
in terror of the local peoples, and they offered burnt offerings
on it to the LORD, both the morning and the evening offerings.
[4]They observed the Feast of Shelters as required and offered
the proper number of daily burnt offerings according to the requirement for each day. [5]Afterward they offered the continual
burnt offerings and those for the new moons and those for all
the holy assemblies of the LORD and all those that were being
voluntarily offered to the LORD. [6]From the first day of the seventh month they began to offer burnt offerings to the LORD.
However, the LORD's temple was not at that time established.

REFLECT

How do your actions, especially in worship, affect or influence the state of your heart toward God?

PREPARATIONS FOR REBUILDING THE TEMPLE

7 So they provided money for the masons and carpenters, and food, beverages, and olive oil for the people of Sidon and Tyre, so that they would bring cedar timber from Lebanon to the seaport at Joppa, in accord with the edict of King Cyrus of Persia. 8 In the second year after they had come to the temple of God in Jerusalem, in the second month, Zerubbabel the son of Shealtiel and Jeshua the son of Jozadak initiated the work, along with the rest of their associates, the priests and the Levites, and all those who were coming to Jerusalem from the exile. They appointed the Levites who were at least twenty years old to take charge of the work on the LORD's temple. 9 So Jeshua appointed both his sons and his relatives, Kadmiel and his sons (the sons of Yehudah), to take charge of the workers in the temple of God, along with the sons of Henadad, their sons, and their relatives the Levites. 10 When the builders established the LORD's temple, the priests, ceremonially attired and with their clarions, and the Levites (the sons of Asaph) with their cymbals, stood to praise the LORD according to the instructions left by King David of Israel. 11 With antiphonal response they sang, praising and glorifying the LORD:

"For he is good;
his loyal love toward Israel is forever."

All the people gave a loud shout as they praised the LORD when the temple of the LORD was established. 12 Many of the priests, the Levites, and the leaders—older people who had seen with their own eyes the former temple while it was still established—were weeping loudly, and many others raised their voice in a joyous shout. 13 People were unable to tell the difference between the sound of joyous shouting and the sound of the people's weeping, for the people were shouting so loudly that the sound was heard a long way off.

OPPOSITION TO THE BUILDING EFFORTS

4 When the enemies of Judah and Benjamin learned that the former exiles were building a temple for the LORD God of Israel, 2 they came to Zerubbabel and the leaders and said to them, "Let us help you build, for like you we seek your God and we have been sacrificing to him from the time of King Esarhaddon of Assyria, who brought us here." 3 But Zerubbabel, Jeshua, and the rest of the leaders of Israel said to them, "You have no right to help us build the temple of our God. We will build it by ourselves for the LORD God of Israel, just as King Cyrus, the king of Persia, has commanded us." 4 Then the local people began to discourage the people of Judah and to dishearten them from building. 5 They were hiring advisers to oppose them, so as to frustrate their plans, throughout the time of King Cyrus of Persia until the reign of King Darius of Persia.

REFLECT

How do you respond when you face opposition when doing what God has called you to do?

OFFICIAL COMPLAINTS ARE LODGED AGAINST THE JEWS

6 At the beginning of the reign of Ahasuerus they filed an accusation against the inhabitants of Judah and Jerusalem. 7 And during the reign of Artaxerxes, Bishlam, Mithredath, Tabeel,

LOVE TO GROW

THE HARD WORK OF REBUILDING

EZRA 3

The Book of Ezra recounts the rebuilding of the temple in Jerusalem. Fifty-thousand Jewish exiles in Babylon returned to Jerusalem to undertake this important work.

Ezra 3 is a beautiful reminder of three things: Everyone has a role to play in the kingdom of God; we should take time to celebrate the work being done; and joy and sorrow are often two sides of the same coin.

A rebuilding project of this magnitude called for a group of people dedicated to the same goal and ready and willing to honor God using whatever resources and skills He had given them. From those who contributed financially, to supervisors, builders, gatekeepers, priests, and temple servants, everyone worked together to accomplish the goal of rebuilding.

I love Ezra 3:11, "They sang, praising and glorifying the LORD: 'For he is good; his loyal love toward Israel is forever.'" The people weren't singing at the ribbon cutting of the new temple. They sang when the foundation was finished. This was only step one, but it was a moment to honor and celebrate because it was a solid, physical reminder that God keeps His promises.

Not all who were there were filled with joy. Some who had seen the temple in its original state wept loudly. They mourned what they had lost. A bare foundation could never compare to the glorious temple they had known. God is here for it all. He is here when we praise Him and sing joyful songs, and He is here for us when we weep loudly.

I've gone through seasons like this in my life. I've experienced the joy of discovering I was pregnant while simultaneously weeping over the pregnancy I had previously lost. I have praised God for new ministry opportunities while my heart was heavy with sorrow over the people and work I would be leaving behind.

Jesus came so we might know that the solid rock upon which we stand isn't the temporary foundation of a physical temple, but the strong, firm, permanent love of God.

When others try to discourage us, distract us, or destroy our plans, like the Israelites experienced, we continue the work, knowing that nothing can stop what God has set in motion.

and the rest of their colleagues wrote to King Artaxerxes of Persia. This letter was first written in Aramaic but then translated.
[What follows is in Aramaic]‡
8 Rehum the commander and Shimshai the scribe wrote a letter
concerning Jerusalem to King Artaxerxes as follows: 9 From Rehum
the commander, Shimshai the scribe, and the rest of their colleagues—the judges, the rulers, the officials, the secretaries, the Ere-
chites, the Babylonians, the people of Susa (that is, the Elamites),
10 and the rest of the nations whom the great and noble Ashurba-
nipal deported and settled in the cities of Samaria and other places
in Trans-Euphrates. 11 (This is a copy of the letter they sent to him.)
"To King Artaxerxes, from your servants in Trans-Euphrates:
12 Now let the king be aware that the Jews who came up to us from
you have gone to Jerusalem. They are rebuilding that rebellious
and odious city. They are completing its walls and repairing its
foundations. 13 Let the king also be aware that if this city is built
and its walls are completed, no more tax, custom, or toll will be
paid, and the royal treasury will suffer loss. 14 In light of the fact
that we are loyal to the king, and since it does not seem appropriate to us that the king should sustain damage, we are sending the king this information 15 so that he may initiate a search
of the records of his predecessors and discover in those records
that this city is rebellious and injurious to both kings and provinces, producing internal revolts from long ago. It is for this very
reason that this city was destroyed. 16 We therefore are informing
the king that if this city is rebuilt and its walls are completed,
you will not retain control of this portion of Trans-Euphrates."
17 The king sent the following response:
"To Rehum the commander, Shimshai the scribe, and the
rest of their colleagues who live in Samaria and other parts of
Trans-Euphrates: Greetings! 18 The letter you sent to us has been
translated and read in my presence. 19 So I gave orders, and it was
determined that this city from long ago has been engaging in
insurrection against kings. It has continually engaged in rebellion and revolt. 20 Powerful kings have been over Jerusalem who
ruled throughout the entire Trans-Euphrates and who were the
beneficiaries of tribute, custom, and toll. 21 Now give orders that
these men cease their work and that this city not be rebuilt until such time as I so instruct. 22 Exercise appropriate caution so
that there is no negligence in this matter. Why should danger
increase to the point that the king sustains damage?"
23 Then, as soon as the copy of the letter from King Artaxerxes
was read in the presence of Rehum, Shimshai the scribe, and
their colleagues, they proceeded promptly to the Jews in Jerusalem and stopped them with threat of armed force.
24 So the work on the temple of God in Jerusalem came to a
halt. It remained halted until the second year of the reign of
King Darius of Persia.

TATTENAI APPEALS TO DARIUS

5 Then the prophets Haggai and Zechariah son of Iddo prophesied concerning the Jews who were in Judah and Jerusalem in
the name of the God of Israel who was over them. 2 Then Zerubbabel the son of Shealtiel and Jeshua the son of Jozadak began

to rebuild the temple of God in Jerusalem. The prophets of God
were with them, supporting them.
3 At that time Tattenai governor of Trans-Euphrates, Shethar-
Bozenai, and their colleagues came to them and asked, "Who gave
you authority to rebuild this temple and to complete this structure?" 4 They also asked them, "What are the names of the men who
are building this edifice?" 5 But God was watching over the elders
of Judah, and they were not stopped until a report could be dis-
patched to Darius and a letter could be sent back concerning this.
6 This is a copy of the letter that Tattenai governor of Trans-Euphrates, Shethar-Bozenai, and his colleagues (who were the officials of Trans-Euphrates) sent to King Darius. 7 The report they
sent to him was written as follows:
"To King Darius: All greetings! 8 Let it be known to the king that
we have gone to the province of Judah, to the temple of the great
God. It is being built with large stones, and timbers are being
placed in the walls. This work is being done with all diligence and
is prospering in their hands. 9 We inquired of those elders, asking
them, 'Who gave you the authority to rebuild this temple and to
complete this structure?' 10 We also inquired of their names in order to inform you, so that we might write the names of the men
who were their leaders. 11 They responded to us in the following
way: 'We are servants of the God of heaven and earth. We are rebuilding the temple which was previously built many years ago.
A great king of Israel built it and completed it. 12 But after our ancestors angered the God of heaven, he delivered them into the
hands of King Nebuchadnezzar of Babylon, the Chaldean, who destroyed this temple and exiled the people to Babylon. 13 But in the
first year of King Cyrus of Babylon, King Cyrus enacted a decree
to rebuild this temple of God. 14 Even the gold and silver vessels
of the temple of God that Nebuchadnezzar had taken from the
temple in Jerusalem and had brought to the palace of Babylon—
even those things King Cyrus brought from the palace of Babylon
and presented to a man by the name of Sheshbazzar whom he
had appointed as governor. 15 He said to him, "Take these vessels
and go deposit them in the temple in Jerusalem, and let the house
of God be rebuilt in its proper location." 16 Then this Sheshbazzar
went and laid the foundations of the temple of God in Jerusalem.
From that time to the present moment it has been in the process
of being rebuilt, although it is not yet finished.'
17 "Now if the king is so inclined, let a search be conducted in
the royal archives there in Babylon in order to determine whether King Cyrus did in fact issue orders for this temple of God to
be rebuilt in Jerusalem. Then let the king send us a decision concerning this matter."

DARIUS ISSUES A DECREE

6 So Darius the king issued orders, and they searched in the
archives of the treasury which were deposited there in Babylon. 2 A scroll was found in the citadel of Ecbatana which is in
the province of Media, and it was inscribed as follows:
"Memorandum: 3 In the first year of his reign, King Cyrus gave
orders concerning the temple of God in Jerusalem: 'Let the temple
be rebuilt as a place where sacrifices are offered. Let its foundations

be set in place. Its height is to be 90 feet and its width 90 feet, [4]with
three layers of large stones and one layer of timber. The expense is
to be subsidized by the royal treasury. [5]Furthermore, let the gold
and silver vessels of the temple of God, which Nebuchadnezzar
brought from the temple in Jerusalem and carried to Babylon, be
returned and brought to their proper place in the temple in Jerusalem. Let them be deposited in the temple of God.'

[6]"Now Tattenai governor of Trans-Euphrates, Shethar-Bozenai, and their colleagues, the officials of Trans-Euphrates—all
of you stay far away from there. [7]Leave the work on this temple
of God alone. Let the governor of the Jews and the elders of the
Jews rebuild this temple of God in its proper place.

[8]"I also hereby issue orders as to what you are to do with those
elders of the Jews in order to rebuild this temple of God. From
the royal treasury, from the taxes of Trans-Euphrates, the complete costs are to be given to these men so that there may be no
interruption of the work. [9]Whatever is needed—whether oxen
or rams or lambs for burnt offerings for the God of heaven or
wheat or salt or wine or oil, as required by the priests who are
in Jerusalem—must be given to them daily without any neglect,
[10]so that they may be offering incense to the God of heaven and
may be praying for the good fortune of the king and his family.

[11]"I hereby give orders that if anyone changes this directive a
beam is to be pulled out from his house and he is to be raised up
and impaled on it, and his house is to be reduced to a rubbish
heap for this indiscretion. [12]May God who makes his name to reside there overthrow any king or nation who reaches out to cause
such change so as to destroy this temple of God in Jerusalem. I,
Darius, have given orders. Let them be carried out with precision!"

THE TEMPLE IS FINALLY DEDICATED

[13]Then Tattenai governor of Trans-Euphrates, Shethar-Bozenai,
and their colleagues acted accordingly—with precision, just as
Darius the king had given instructions. [14]The elders of the Jews
continued building and prospering, while at the same time Haggai the prophet and Zechariah the son of Iddo continued prophesying. They built and brought it to completion by the command
of the God of Israel and by the command of Cyrus and Darius
and Artaxerxes king of Persia. [15]They finished this temple on
the third day of the month Adar, which is the sixth year of the
reign of King Darius.

[16]The people of Israel—the priests, the Levites, and the rest of
the exiles—observed the dedication of this temple of God with
joy. [17]For the dedication of this temple of God they offered 100
bulls, 200 rams, 400 lambs, and 12 male goats for the sin of all
Israel, according to the number of the tribes of Israel. [18]They appointed the priests by their divisions and the Levites by their
divisions over the worship of God at Jerusalem, in accord with
the book of Moses. [19]The exiles observed the Passover on the
fourteenth day of the first month. [20]The priests and the Levites
had purified themselves, every last one, and they all were ceremonially pure. They sacrificed the Passover lamb for all the exiles, for their colleagues the priests, and for themselves. [21]The
Israelites who were returning from the exile ate it, along with all

REFLECT

How do you feel when you complete a big task for the Lord? How do you think the completion of the temple affected the morale of the Jews?

those who had joined them in separating themselves from the
uncleanness of the nations of the land to seek the LORD God of
Israel. 22 They observed the Feast of Unleavened Bread for seven
days with joy, for the LORD had given them joy and had changed
the opinion of the king of Assyria toward them so that he assisted them in the work on the temple of God, the God of Israel.

THE ARRIVAL OF EZRA

7 Now after these things had happened, during the reign of King
Artaxerxes of Persia, Ezra came up from Babylon. Ezra was the
son of Seraiah, who was the son of Azariah, who was the son of Hilkiah, 2 who was the son of Shallum, who was the son of Zadok, who
was the son of Ahitub, 3 who was the son of Amariah, who was the
son of Azariah, who was the son of Meraioth, 4 who was the son
of Zerahiah, who was the son of Uzzi, who was the son of Bukki,
5 who was the son of Abishua, who was the son of Phinehas, who
was the son of Eleazar, who was the son of Aaron the chief priest.
6 This Ezra is the one who came up from Babylon. He was a scribe
who was skilled in the law of Moses which the LORD God of Israel
had given. The king supplied him with everything he requested,
for the hand of the LORD his God was on him. 7 In the seventh year
of King Artaxerxes, Ezra brought up to Jerusalem some of the Israelites and some of the priests, the Levites, the attendants, the
gatekeepers, and the temple servants. 8 He entered Jerusalem in
the fifth month of the seventh year of the king. 9 On the first day
of the first month he had determined to make the ascent from
Babylon, and on the first day of the fifth month he arrived at Jerusalem, for the good hand of his God was on him. 10 Now Ezra
had dedicated himself to the study of the law of the LORD, to its
observance, and to teaching its statutes and judgments in Israel.

REFLECT

In what ways, like Ezra, has God equipped, prepared, and gone ahead of you to accomplish the work He has given you?

ARTAXERXES GIVES OFFICIAL ENDORSEMENT TO EZRA'S MISSION

11 What follows is a copy of the letter that King Artaxerxes gave to
Ezra the priestly scribe. Ezra was a scribe in matters pertaining
to the commandments of the LORD and his statutes over Israel:
12 "Artaxerxes, king of kings, to Ezra the priest, a scribe of the
law of the God of heaven: 13 I have now issued a decree that anyone in my kingdom from the people of Israel—even the priests
and Levites—who wishes to do so may go up with you to Jerusalem. 14 You are authorized by the king and his seven advisers to
inquire concerning Judah and Jerusalem, according to the law of
your God which is in your possession, 15 and to bring silver and
gold which the king and his advisers have freely contributed to
the God of Israel, who resides in Jerusalem, 16 along with all the
silver and gold that you may collect throughout all the province
of Babylon and the contributions of the people and the priests for
the temple of their God which is in Jerusalem. 17 With this money
you should be sure to purchase bulls, rams, and lambs, along
with the appropriate meal offerings and libations. You should
bring them to the altar of the temple of your God which is in Jerusalem. 18 You may do whatever seems appropriate to you and
your colleagues with the rest of the silver and the gold, in keeping with the will of your God. 19 Deliver to the God of Jerusalem

the vessels that are given to you for the service of the temple of
your God. 20 The rest of the needs for the temple of your God that
you may have to supply, you may do so from the royal treasury.
21 "I, King Artaxerxes, hereby issue orders to all the treasurers
of Trans-Euphrates, that you precisely execute all that Ezra the
priestly scribe of the law of the God of heaven may request of
you—22 up to 100 talents of silver, 100 cors of wheat, 100 baths of
wine, 100 baths of olive oil, and unlimited salt. 23 Everything that
the God of heaven has required should be precisely done for the
temple of the God of heaven. Why should there be wrath against
the empire of the king and his sons? 24 Furthermore, be aware of
the fact that you have no authority to impose tax, tribute, or toll
on any of the priests, the Levites, the musicians, the doorkeepers,
the temple servants, or the attendants at the temple of this God.
25 "Now you, Ezra, in keeping with the wisdom of your God
which you possess, appoint judges and court officials who can
arbitrate cases on behalf of all the people who are in Trans-Euphrates who know the laws of your God. Those who do not know
this law should be taught. 26 Everyone who does not observe both
the law of your God and the law of the king will be completely
liable to the appropriate penalty, whether it is death or ban-
ishment or confiscation of property or detainment in prison."
27 Blessed be the LORD God of our fathers, who so moved in
the heart of the king to so honor the temple of the LORD which
is in Jerusalem! 28 He has also conferred his favor on me before
the king, his advisers, and all the influential leaders of the king.
I gained strength as the hand of the LORD my God was on me,
and I gathered leaders from Israel to go up with me.

THE LEADERS WHO RETURNED WITH EZRA

8 These are the leaders and those enrolled with them by genealogy who were coming up with me from Babylon during
the reign of King Artaxerxes:
2 from the descendants of Phinehas, Gershom;
from the descendants of Ithamar, Daniel;
from the descendants of David, Hattush 3 the son of Shecaniah;
from the descendants of Parosh, Zechariah, and with him were
enrolled by genealogy 150 men;
4 from the descendants of Pahath Moab, Eliehoenai son of Zerahiah, and with him 200 men;
5 from the descendants of Zattu, Shecaniah son of Jahaziel,
and with him 300 men;
6 from the descendants of Adin, Ebed son of Jonathan, and
with him 50 men;
7 from the descendants of Elam, Jeshaiah son of Athaliah, and
with him 70 men;
8 from the descendants of Shephatiah, Zebadiah son of Michael, and with him 80 men;
9 from the descendants of Joab, Obadiah son of Jehiel, and with
him 218 men;
10 from the descendants of Bani, Shelomith son of Josiphiah,
and with him 160 men;
11 from the descendants of Bebai, Zechariah son of Bebai, and
with him 28 men;

12 from the descendants of Azgad, Johanan son of Hakkatan,
and with him 110 men;
13 from the descendants of Adonikam there were the latter
ones. Their names were Eliphelet, Jeuel, and Shemaiah, and with
them 60 men;
14 from the descendants of Bigvai, Uthai, and Zaccur, and with
them 70 men.

THE EXILES TRAVEL TO JERUSALEM

15 I had them assemble at the canal that flows toward Ahava, and
we camped there for three days. I observed that the people and
the priests were present, but I found no Levites there. 16 So I sent
for Eliezer, Ariel, Shemaiah, Elnathan, Jarib, Elnathan, Nathan,
Zechariah, and Meshullam, who were leaders, and Joiarib and
Elnathan, who were teachers. 17 I sent them to Iddo, who was the
leader in the place called Casiphia. I told them what to say to
Iddo and his relatives, who were the temple servants in Casiphia,
so they would bring us attendants for the temple of our God.
18 Due to the fact that the good hand of our God was on us,
they brought us a skilled man, from the descendants of Mahli
the son of Levi son of Israel. This man was Sherebiah, who was
accompanied by his sons and brothers, 18 men; 19 and Hashabiah,
along with Jeshaiah from the descendants of Merari, with his
brothers and their sons, 20 men; 20 and some of the temple servants that David and his officials had established for the work
of the Levites—220 of them. They were all designated by name.
21 I called for a fast there by the Ahava Canal, so that we might
humble ourselves before our God and seek from him a safe journey for us, our children, and all our property. 22 I was embarrassed
to request soldiers and horsemen from the king to protect us
from the enemy along the way, because we had said to the king,
"The good hand of our God is on everyone who is seeking him,
but his great anger is against everyone who forsakes him." 23 So
we fasted and prayed to our God about this, and he answered us.
24 Then I set apart twelve of the leading priests, together with
Sherebiah, Hashabiah, and ten of their brothers, 25 and I weighed out
to them the silver, the gold, and the vessels intended for the temple of our God—items that the king, his advisers, his officials, and all
Israel who were present had contributed. 26 I weighed out to them:
650 talents of silver, silver vessels worth 100 talents, 100 talents of
gold, 27 20 gold bowls worth 1,000 darics, and 2 exquisite vessels of
gleaming bronze, as valuable as gold. 28 Then I said to them, "You are
holy to the LORD, just as these vessels are holy. The silver and the
gold are a voluntary offering to the LORD, the God of your fathers.
29 Be careful with them and protect them, until you weigh them out
before the leading priests and the Levites and the family leaders of
Israel in Jerusalem, in the storerooms of the temple of the LORD."
30 Then the priests and the Levites took charge of the silver,
the gold, and the vessels that had been weighed out, to transport them to Jerusalem to the temple of our God.
31 On the twelfth day of the first month we began traveling from
the Ahava Canal to go to Jerusalem. The hand of our God was on
us, and he delivered us from our enemies and from bandits along
the way. 32 So we came to Jerusalem, and we stayed there for three

days. 33 On the fourth day we weighed out the silver, the gold, and
the vessels in the house of our God into the care of Meremoth
son of Uriah, the priest, and Eleazar son of Phinehas, who were
accompanied by Jozabad son of Jeshua and Noadiah son of Binnui, who were Levites. 34 Everything was verified by number and
by weight, and the total weight was written down at that time.
35 The exiles who were returning from the captivity offered
burnt offerings to the God of Israel—twelve bulls for all Israel,
ninety-six rams, seventy-seven male lambs, along with twelve
male goats as a sin offering. All this was a burnt offering to the
LORD. 36 Then they presented the decrees of the king to the king's
satraps and to the governors of Trans-Euphrates, who assisted
the people and the temple of God.

A PRAYER OF EZRA

9 Now when these things had been completed, the leaders approached me and said, "The people of Israel, the priests, and
the Levites have not separated themselves from the local residents who practice detestable things similar to those of the
Canaanites, the Hittites, the Perizzites, the Jebusites, the Ammonites, the Moabites, the Egyptians, and the Amorites. 2 Indeed,
they have taken some of their daughters as wives for themselves
and for their sons, so that the holy race has become intermingled
with the local residents. Worse still, the leaders and the officials
have been at the forefront of all this unfaithfulness!"
3 When I heard this report, I tore my tunic and my robe and
ripped out some of the hair from my head and beard. Then I sat
down, quite devastated. 4 Everyone who held the words of the
God of Israel in awe gathered around me because of the unfaithful acts of the people of the exile. Devastated, I continued to sit
there until the evening offering.
5 At the time of the evening offering I got up from my self-abase-
ment, with my tunic and robe torn, and then dropped to my
knees and spread my hands to the LORD my God. 6 I prayed:
"O my God, I am ashamed and embarrassed to lift my face to
you, my God! For our iniquities have climbed higher than our
heads, and our guilt extends to the heavens. 7 From the days of
our fathers until this very day our guilt has been great. Because
of our iniquities we, along with our kings and priests, have been
delivered over by the local kings to sword, captivity, plunder, and
embarrassment—right up to the present time.
8 "But now briefly we have received mercy from the LORD our
God, in that he has left us a remnant and has given us a secure position in his holy place. Thus our God has enlightened our eyes and
has given us a little relief in our time of servitude. 9 Although we
are slaves, our God has not abandoned us in our servitude. He has
extended kindness to us in the sight of the kings of Persia, in that
he has revived us to restore the temple of our God and to raise up
its ruins and to give us a protective wall in Judah and Jerusalem.
10 "And now what are we able to say after this, our God? For we
have forsaken your commandments 11 which you commanded us
through your servants the prophets with these words: 'The land
that you are entering to possess is a land defiled by the impurities
of the local residents! With their abominations they have filled it

from one end to the other with their filthiness. 12 Therefore do not
give your daughters in marriage to their sons, and do not take their
daughters in marriage for your sons. Do not ever seek their peace
or welfare, so that you may be strong and may eat the good of the
land and may leave it as an inheritance for your children forever.'
13 "Everything that has happened to us has come about because of
our wicked actions and our great guilt. Even so, our God, you have
exercised restraint toward our iniquities and have given us a remnant such as this. 14 Shall we once again break your commandments
and intermarry with these abominable peoples? Would you not
be so angered by us that you would wipe us out, with no survivor
or remnant? 15 O LORD God of Israel, you are righteous, for we are
left as a remnant this day. Indeed, we stand before you in our guilt.
However, because of this guilt no one can really stand before you."

THE PEOPLE CONFESS THEIR SINS

10 While Ezra was praying and confessing, weeping and throwing himself to the ground before the temple of God, a very
large crowd of Israelites—men, women, and children alike—gathered around him. The people wept loudly. 2 Then Shecaniah son
of Jehiel, from the descendants of Elam, addressed Ezra:
"We have been unfaithful to our God by marrying foreign wom-
en from the local peoples. Nonetheless, there is still hope for Israel in this regard. 3 Therefore let us enact a covenant with our
God to send away all these women and their offspring, in keeping with your counsel, my lord, and that of those who respect
the commandments of our God. And let it be done according to
the law. 4 Get up, for this matter concerns you. We are with you,
so be strong and act decisively!"
5 So Ezra got up and made the leading priests and Levites and
all Israel take an oath to carry out this plan. And they all took a
solemn oath. 6 Then Ezra got up from in front of the temple of
God and went to the room of Jehohanan son of Eliashib. While
he stayed there, he did not eat food or drink water, for he was
in mourning over the infidelity of the exiles.
7 A proclamation was circulated throughout Judah and Jerusalem that all the exiles were to be assembled in Jerusalem. 8 Everyone who did not come within three days would thereby forfeit
all his property, in keeping with the counsel of the officials and
the elders. Furthermore, he himself would be excluded from the
assembly of the exiles.
9 All the men of Judah and Benjamin were gathered in Jerusalem
within the three days. (It was in the ninth month, on the twentieth
day of that month.) All the people sat in the square at the temple
of God, trembling because of this matter and because of the rains.
10 Then Ezra the priest stood up and said to them, "You have
behaved in an unfaithful manner by taking foreign wives! This
has contributed to the guilt of Israel. 11 Now give praise to the
LORD God of your fathers, and do his will. Separate yourselves
from the local residents and from these foreign wives."
12 All the assembly replied in a loud voice: "We will do just as
you have said! 13 However, the people are numerous and it is
the rainy season. We are unable to stand here outside. Furthermore, this business cannot be resolved in a day or two, for we

REFLECT

Is there something God has asked you to break away from or eliminate from your life that is causing you to stray from Him? What might be keeping you from letting go of these things?

LOVE TO GROW

CONFESS AND REPENT

EZRA 10:1–4

Every time I read Ezra 10 I think about the confession services of the Curripaco tribe in the jungles of Venezuela. My family and I are missionaries to this people group who live near the Orinoco and Atabapo rivers.

Small, indigenous villages scatter the riversides. Those that have a physical church building gather together there to take the Lord's Supper, attend special services, and hold conferences. When a Curripaco church is in charge of organizing an event involving other villages, they hold a special confession service the night before the event begins. Everyone in the congregation stands up and confesses their sin and prays together for forgiveness. This is their way of preparing for the event with a clean heart.

When Ezra began to mourn the people's sins, many others gathered around him, recognized their own sins, and wept bitterly (Ezra 10:1). God had repeatedly commanded Israel not to intermarry with other nations. He knew the Israelites' hearts would be turned away from wholehearted devotion (Deut 7:1–4). Still, the men of Israel had disobeyed God by marrying foreign women.

This passage sets a biblical principle for us today: We need to confess our sins, but we also have to do something about them. Confession washes us before God, but we must also repent by changing our behavior. In Ezra 10:3, the people made a covenant with the Lord to send away their foreign wives and children and to live according to His laws.

Repentance is essential for a healthy spiritual relationship with God. It aligns our hearts with God's heart.

When we repent, we see sin the same way God sees it. This prompts us to correct our behavior and leave our sin behind.

Repentance follows an awareness of the depth of our sin, recognizing the pain and destruction it has caused. When we pray, we must look deeply inside our hearts and ask God to help us see our sins (Ps 139:23–24), repent, and change our behavior. We need to make confession a part of our daily time with God. The more we see our sin, the better we will be able to live out His perfect will.

have sinned greatly in this matter. 14 Let our leaders take steps
on behalf of all the assembly. Let all those in our towns who have
married foreign women come at an appointed time, and with
them the elders of each town and its judges, until the hot anger
of our God is turned away from us in this matter."

15 Only Jonathan son of Asahel and Jahzeiah son of Tikvah were
against this, assisted by Meshullam and Shabbethai the Levite.
16 So the exiles proceeded accordingly. Ezra the priest separated
out by name men who were leaders in their family groups. They
sat down to consider this matter on the first day of the tenth
month, 17 and on the first day of the first month they finished
considering all the men who had married foreign wives.

THOSE WHO HAD TAKEN FOREIGN WIVES

18 It was determined that from the descendants of the priests,
the following had taken foreign wives: from the descendants of
Jeshua son of Jozadak, and his brothers: Maaseiah, Eliezer, Jarib,
and Gedaliah. 19 (They gave their word to send away their wives;
their guilt offering was a ram from the flock for their guilt.)

20 From the descendants of Immer: Hanani and Zebadiah.

21 From the descendants of Harim: Maaseiah, Elijah, Shemaiah, Jehiel, and Uzziah.

22 From the descendants of Pashhur: Elioenai, Maaseiah, Ishmael, Nethanel, Jozabad, and Elasah.

23 From the Levites: Jozabad, Shimei, Kelaiah (also known as Kelita), Pethahiah, Judah, and Eliezer.

24 From the singers: Eliashib. From the gatekeepers: Shallum, Telem, and Uri.

25 From the Israelites: from the descendants of Parosh: Ramiah, Izziah, Malkijah, Mijamin, Eleazar, Malkijah, and Benaiah.

26 From the descendants of Elam: Mattaniah, Zechariah, Jehiel, Abdi, Jeremoth, and Elijah.

27 From the descendants of Zattu: Elioenai, Eliashib, Mattaniah, Jeremoth, Zabad, and Aziza.

28 From the descendants of Bebai: Jehohanan, Hananiah, Zabbai, and Athlai.

29 From the descendants of Bani: Meshullam, Malluch, Adaiah, Jashub, Sheal, and Jeremoth.

30 From the descendants of Pahath Moab: Adna, Kelal, Benaiah, Maaseiah, Mattaniah, Bezalel, Binnui, and Manasseh.

31 From the descendants of Harim: Eliezer, Ishijah, Malkijah,
Shemaiah, Shimeon, 32 Benjamin, Malluch, and Shemariah.

33 From the descendants of Hashum: Mattenai, Mattattah, Zabad, Eliphelet, Jeremai, Manasseh, and Shimei.

34 From the descendants of Bani: Maadai, Amram, Uel, 35 Benaiah, Bedeiah, Keluhi, 36 Vaniah, Meremoth, Eliashib, 37 Mattaniah, Mattenai, and Jaasu.

38 From the descendants of Binnui: Shimei, 39 Shelemiah, Nathan, Adaiah, 40 Machnadebai, Shashai, Sharai, 41 Azarel, Shelemiah, Shemariah, 42 Shallum, Amariah, and Joseph.

43 From the descendants of Nebo: Jeiel, Mattithiah, Zabad, Zebina, Jaddai, Joel, and Benaiah.

44 All these had taken foreign wives, and some of them also had children by these women.

I AM ENGAGED in an IMPORTANT WORK

MEMORY VERSE

So I sent messengers to them saying, "I am engaged in an important work, and I am unable to come down. Why *should the work come to a halt when I* leave it to come down to you?"

Nehemiah 6:3

Nehemiah

INTRODUCTION

Faithful Leadership

The Book of Nehemiah displays the incredible faithfulness of God to His covenant people. God used His loyal servant Nehemiah to lead His people back to Jerusalem and to rebuild the wall of the city. Nehemiah not only led the building efforts, he encouraged and urged the people to work hard and to return to proper worship of Yahweh. Nehemiah is the faithful leader the people needed so that they could remember the faithfulness of their God during a time of transition and confusion.

The Books of Ezra and Nehemiah are one work in the Hebrew Bible; together they offer a full account of the return of the Babylonian exiles to Jerusalem. The combined narrative presents the story of the exiles' return over two periods, each marked by two prominent leaders. Ezra, the first account, records the rebuilding of the temple under Zerubbabel and Joshua the priest. Nehemiah, the second account, details the restoration of the worship of God and rebuilding of Jerusalem's walls under Ezra and Nehemiah.

The events in Ezra and Nehemiah take place between 600 and 400 B.C., from the time of the deportation of the people of Judah to Babylon to the return journey of Nehemiah and his work rebuilding the wall of Jerusalem. Ezra is traditionally considered the author of both books, although he likely compiled the books using various documents and sources, as it is believed he did when writing 1 and 2 Chronicles.

The Book of Nehemiah makes it clear that God did not restore His people only once. Instead, He repeatedly, consistently, and continually restored His people. Nehemiah was the final leader God used to encourage and exhort the people to return to proper worship of God. Nehemiah's faithful leadership reflects the faithful leadership of Yahweh. God not only led His people back to the land He promised them, but remained with them to accomplish His will, in spite of their unfaithfulness. As we seek to love Him greatly, we can rest in the confidence that He always has our best interests in mind and He is the faithful leader we can always trust.

Spain

OFFICIAL LANGUAGE
Spanish
POPULATION
46,657,000
UNREACHED POPULATION
1,008,000
PROFESSING CHRISTIANS
77.5%

Esther's Home

Say a Prayer Today

Pray for Esther and others who are dealing with wounds from the church. Pray God would heal their wounds and that they would be welcomed back into the body of Christ in healthy fellowship and community.

HISTORY BIT

Spanish is the official language in twenty countries across the world today. The first translations of Scripture into Spanish were widely discouraged by the Catholic Church and many lost their lives in the efforts. The first complete translation of the Bible was printed in 1569 in Basil, Switzerland.*

Source Information:
https://joshuaproject.net/countries/SP
*http://www.rrb3.com/mypub/books/brief_history_spn_bible.htm
https://www.biblestudytools.com/rvr/

ESTHER'S STORY

My name is Esther, and I am from Spain. My story begins in a difficult season, one that God faithfully brought me through. It is also one I see reflected in the story of Nehemiah, as he faithfully led God's people through a difficult time.

My soul and emotions felt like a desert. I felt empty, broken, and without hope. I had lost trust in Christian leadership after years of being spiritually abused. Not only did this affect my ability to be involved in Christian community, but it also greatly affected my relationship with God. I couldn't worship and felt discouraged and frustrated every time I tried to open my Bible or pray.

I came across a Love God Greatly study and decided to give community one more try. The study was on the Book of Ruth. The Lord surprised me on the very first day of the study when my group facilitator explained that she was there to learn alongside all of us. At first I was shocked, but I was also refreshed. She led faithfully by sharing what she was learning and experiencing along with us.

It was beautiful how we were all learning from each other. As the study went on and I started to hear what my sisters shared, the wall of protection I had built around myself began to fall down. I felt that God was rescuing me from the bottom of the sea where I was drowning. I felt like I was breathing again and God was telling me, "There are people who love Me and crave to fill up with My Word." That day I started to cry as God began to heal my broken heart.

Now I want to read my Bible again, I want to pray, and I want to worship like never before. I crave to know God more and to live a new life. Thank you, Jesus.

6 WEEK READING PLAN

LOVE HIS WORD

	MONDAY	TUESDAY	WEDNESDAY	THURSDAY	FRIDAY
1	Ezra 1	Ezra 2:1-42	Ezra 2:43-70	Ezra 3	Ezra 4
	SOAP Psalm 121:1-2	SOAP Psalm 121:3	SOAP Psalm 121:4-5	SOAP Psalm 121:6-7	SOAP Psalm 121:8
2	Ezra 5	Ezra 6	Ezra 7	Ezra 8:1-14	Ezra 8:15-36
	SOAP Psalm 123:1-2	SOAP Psalm 123:3-4	SOAP Psalm 124:1-3	SOAP Psalm 124:4-5	SOAP Psalm 124:6-8
3	Ezra 9	Ezra 10:1-17	Ezra 10:18-44	Nehemiah 1	Nehemiah 2:1-10
	SOAP Ezra 9:8	SOAP Psalm 125:1-2	SOAP Psalm 125:3	SOAP Psalm 125:4-5	SOAP Psalm 126:1-2
4	Nehemiah 2:11-20	Nehemiah 3	Nehemiah 4	Nehemiah 5	Nehemiah 6:1-14
	SOAP Psalm 126:3	SOAP Psalm 126:4-6	SOAP Psalm 128:1-2	SOAP Psalm 128:3-4	SOAP Nehemiah 6:3
5	Nehemiah 6:15—7:7	Nehemiah 7:8-44	Nehemiah 7:45-73a	Nehemiah 7:73b—8:18	Nehemiah 9:1-37
	SOAP Psalm 128:5-6	SOAP Psalm 129:1-2	SOAP Psalm 129:3-4	SOAP Psalm 129:5-7	SOAP Psalm 129:8
6	Nehemiah 9:38—10:39	Nehemiah 11	Nehemiah 12:1-26	Nehemiah 12:27-47	Nehemiah 13
	SOAP Psalm 130:1-2	SOAP Psalm 130:3-4	SOAP Psalm 130:5	SOAP Psalm 130:6	SOAP Psalm 103:7-8

A PRAYER OF NEHEMIAH

1 These are the words of Nehemiah son of Hacaliah:
It so happened that in the month of Kislev, in the twentieth
year, I was in Susa the citadel. 2 Hanani, who was one of my relatives, along with some of the men from Judah, came to me, and
I asked them about the Jews who had escaped and had survived
the exile, and about Jerusalem.
3 They said to me, "The remnant that remains from the exile
there in the province are experiencing considerable adversity
and reproach. The wall of Jerusalem lies breached, and its gates
have been burned down!"
4 When I heard these things I sat down abruptly, crying and
mourning for several days. I continued fasting and praying before the God of heaven. 5 Then I said, "Please, O LORD God of
heaven, great and awesome God, who keeps his loving covenant
with those who love him and obey his commandments, 6 may
your ear be attentive and your eyes be open to hear the prayer
of your servant that I am praying to you today throughout both
day and night on behalf of your servants the Israelites. I am confessing the sins of the Israelites that we have committed against
you—both I myself and my family have sinned. 7 We have behaved corruptly against you, not obeying the commandments,
the statutes, and the judgments that you commanded your servant Moses. 8 Please recall the word you commanded your servant Moses: 'If you act unfaithfully, I will scatter you among the
nations. 9 But if you repent and obey my commandments and
do them, then even if your dispersed people are in the most remote location, I will gather them from there and bring them to
the place I have chosen for my name to reside.' 10 They are your
servants and your people, whom you have redeemed by your
mighty strength and by your powerful hand. 11 Please, Lord, listen attentively to the prayer of your servant and to the prayer
of your servants who take pleasure in showing respect to your
name. Grant your servant success today and show compassion
to me in the presence of this man."
Now I was cupbearer for the king.

REFLECT

What causes you to mourn and weep for God's people the way Nehemiah did over the destruction of Jerusalem? How does Nehemiah's prayer encourage you to pray and seek God's favor over this issue?

NEHEMIAH IS PERMITTED TO GO TO JERUSALEM

2 Then in the month of Nisan, in the twentieth year of King
Artaxerxes, when wine was brought to me, I took the wine
and gave it to the king. Previously I had not been depressed in
the king's presence. 2 So the king said to me, "Why do you appear
to be depressed when you aren't sick? What can this be other
than sadness of heart?" This made me very fearful.
3 I replied to the king, "O king, live forever! Why would I not appear dejected when the city with the graves of my ancestors lies
desolate and its gates destroyed by fire?" 4 The king responded,
"What is it you are seeking?" Then I quickly prayed to the God
of heaven 5 and said to the king, "If the king is so inclined and if
your servant has found favor in your sight, dispatch me to Judah,
to the city with the graves of my ancestors, so that I can rebuild
it." 6 Then the king, with his consort sitting beside him, replied,
"How long would your trip take, and when would you return?"
Since the king was pleased to send me, I gave him a time. 7 I said

to the king, "If the king is so inclined, let him give me letters for the governors of Trans-Euphrates that will enable me to travel safely until I reach Judah, 8 and a letter for Asaph the keeper of the king's nature preserve, so that he will give me timber for beams for the gates of the fortress adjacent to the temple and for the city wall and for the house to which I go." So the king granted me these requests, for the good hand of my God was on me. 9 Then I went to the governors of Trans-Euphrates, and I presented to them the letters from the king. The king had sent with me officers of the army and horsemen. 10 When Sanballat the Horonite and Tobiah the Ammonite official heard all this, they were very displeased that someone had come to seek benefit for the Israelites.

NEHEMIAH ARRIVES IN JERUSALEM

11 So I came to Jerusalem. When I had been there for three days, 12 I got up during the night, along with a few men who were with me. But I did not tell anyone what my God was putting on my heart to do for Jerusalem. There were no animals with me, except for the one I was riding. 13 I proceeded through the Valley Gate by night, in the direction of the Well of the Dragons and the Dung Gate, inspecting the walls of Jerusalem that had been breached and its gates that had been destroyed by fire. 14 I passed on to the Gate of the Well and the King's Pool, where there was not enough room for my animal to pass with me. 15 I continued up the valley during the night, inspecting the wall. Then I turned back and came to the Valley Gate, and so returned. 16 The officials did not know where I had gone or what I had been doing, for up to this point I had not told any of the Jews or the priests or the nobles or the officials or the rest of the workers. 17 Then I said to them, "You see the problem that we have—Jerusalem is desolate and its gates are burned. Come on! Let's rebuild the wall of Jerusalem so that this reproach will not continue." 18 Then I related to them how the good hand of my God was on me and what the king had said to me. Then they replied, "Let's begin rebuilding right away!" So they readied themselves for this good project. 19 But when Sanballat the Horonite, Tobiah the Ammonite official, and Geshem the Arab heard all this, they derided us and expressed contempt toward us. They said, "What is this you are doing? Are you rebelling against the king?" 20 I responded to them by saying, "The God of heaven will prosper us. We his servants will start the rebuilding. But you have no just or ancient right in Jerusalem."

THE NAMES OF THE BUILDERS

3 Then Eliashib the high priest and his priestly colleagues arose and built the Sheep Gate. They dedicated it and erected its doors, working as far as the Tower of the Hundred and the Tower of Hananel. 2 The men of Jericho built adjacent to it, and Zaccur son of Imri built adjacent to them.

3 The sons of Hassenaah rebuilt the Fish Gate. They laid its beams and positioned its doors, its bolts, and its bars. 4 Meremoth son of Uriah, the son of Hakoz, worked on the section adjacent to them. Meshullam son of Berechiah the son of Meshezabel worked

on the section next to them. And Zadok son of Baana worked on
the section adjacent to them. 5 The men of Tekoa worked on the
section adjacent to them, but their town leaders would not assist with the work of their master.
6 Joiada son of Paseah and Meshullam son of Besodeiah worked
on the Jeshanah Gate. They laid its beams and positioned its
doors, its bolts, and its bars. 7 Adjacent to them worked Mela-
tiah the Gibeonite and Jadon the Meronothite, who were men
of Gibeon and Mizpah. These towns were under the jurisdiction of the governor of Trans-Euphrates. 8 Uzziel son of Harha-
iah, a member of the goldsmiths' guild, worked on the section
adjacent to him. Hananiah, a member of the perfumers' guild,
worked on the section adjacent to him. They plastered the city
wall of Jerusalem as far as the Broad Wall. 9 Rephaiah son of Hur,
head of a half-district of Jerusalem, worked on the section adjacent to them. 10 Jedaiah son of Harumaph worked on the section adjacent to them opposite his house, and Hattush son of
Hashabneiah worked on the section adjacent to him. 11 Malkijah son of Harim and Hasshub son of Pahath Moab worked on
another section and the Tower of the Ovens. 12 Shallum son of
Hallohesh, head of a half-district of Jerusalem, worked on the
section adjacent to him, assisted by his daughters.
13 Hanun and the residents of Zanoah worked on the Valley
Gate. They rebuilt it and positioned its doors, its bolts, and its
bars, in addition to working on 1,500 feet of the wall as far as
the Dung Gate.
14 Malkijah son of Recab, head of the district of Beth Hakkerem, worked on the Dung Gate. He rebuilt it and positioned its
doors, its bolts, and its bars.
15 Shallun son of Col-Hozeh, head of the district of Mizpah,
worked on the Fountain Gate. He rebuilt it, put on its roof, and
positioned its doors, its bolts, and its bars. In addition, he rebuilt the wall of the Pool of Siloam, by the royal garden, as far
as the steps that go down from the City of David. 16 Nehemiah
son of Azbuk, head of a half-district of Beth Zur, worked after
him as far as the tombs of David and the artificial pool and the
House of the Warriors.
17 After him the Levites worked—Rehum son of Bani and after
him Hashabiah, head of half the district of Keilah, for his district.
18 After him their relatives worked—Binnui son of Henadad, head
of a half-district of Keilah. 19 Adjacent to him Ezer son of Jeshua,
head of Mizpah, worked on another section, opposite the ascent
to the armory at the buttress. 20 After him Baruch son of Zabbai
worked on another section, from the buttress to the door of the
house of Eliashib the high priest. 21 After him Meremoth son of
Uriah, the son of Hakkoz, worked on another section from the
door of Eliashib's house to the end of it.
22 After him the priests worked, men of the nearby district. 23 After them Benjamin and Hasshub worked opposite their house.
After them Azariah son of Maaseiah, the son of Ananiah, worked
near his house. 24 After him Binnui son of Henadad worked on
another section, from the house of Azariah to the buttress and
the corner. 25 After him Palal son of Uzai worked opposite the
buttress and the tower that protrudes from the upper palace of

REFLECT

What does the record of the reconstruction teach us about teamwork and unity? How can we apply these principles in the church today?

the court of the guard. After him Pedaiah son of Parosh 26 and
the temple servants who were living on Ophel worked up to the
area opposite the Water Gate toward the east and the protruding
tower. 27 After them the men of Tekoa worked on another section,
from opposite the great protruding tower to the wall of Ophel.
28 Above the Horse Gate the priests worked, each in front of his
house. 29 After them Zadok son of Immer worked opposite his
house, and after him Shemaiah son of Shecaniah, guard at the East
Gate, worked. 30 After him Hananiah son of Shelemiah, and Hanun,
the sixth son of Zalaph, worked on another section. After them Meshullam son of Berechiah worked opposite his quarters. 31 After him
Malkijah, one of the goldsmiths, worked as far as the house of the
temple servants and the traders, opposite the Inspection Gate, and
up to the room above the corner. 32 And between the room above
the corner and the Sheep Gate the goldsmiths and traders worked.

OPPOSITION TO THE WORK CONTINUES

4 Now when Sanballat heard that we were rebuilding the wall he
became angry and was quite upset. He derided the Jews, 2 and
in the presence of his colleagues and the army of Samaria he said,
"What are these feeble Jews doing? Will they be left to themselves?
Will they again offer sacrifice? Will they finish this in a day? Can
they bring these burnt stones to life again from piles of dust?"
3 Then Tobiah the Ammonite, who was close by, said, "If even
a fox were to climb up on what they are building, it would break
down their wall of stones!"
4 Hear, O our God, for we are despised. Return their reproach
on their own head. Reduce them to plunder in a land of exile!
5 Do not cover their iniquity, and do not wipe out their sin from
your sight, for they have bitterly offended the builders.
6 So we rebuilt the wall, and the entire wall was joined together
up to half its height. The people were enthusiastic in their work.
7 When Sanballat, Tobiah, the Arabs, the Ammonites, and the
people of Ashdod heard that the restoration of the walls of Jerusalem had moved ahead and that the breaches had begun to
be closed, they were very angry. 8 All of them conspired together
to move with armed forces against Jerusalem and to create a disturbance in it. 9 So we prayed to our God and stationed a guard
to protect against them both day and night. 10 Then those in Judah said, "The strength of the laborers has failed! The debris is
so great that we are unable to rebuild the wall."
11 Our adversaries also boasted, "Before they are aware or anticipate anything, we will come in among them and kill them,
and we will bring this work to a halt!"
12 So it happened that the Jews who were living near them
came and warned us repeatedly about all the schemes they were
plotting against us.
13 So I stationed people at the lower places behind the wall in
the exposed places. I stationed the people by families, with their
swords, spears, and bows. 14 When I had made an inspection, I
stood up and said to the nobles, the officials, and the rest of the
people, "Don't be afraid of them. Remember the great and awesome Lord, and fight on behalf of your brothers, your sons, your
daughters, your wives, and your families!"

LOVE TO GROW

THE POWER OF WORDS

NEHEMIAH 4:1–6

Make no mistake, whenever you set out to rebuild something—whether it is a wall (like in Nehemiah's case), a broken relationship, or a crumbling life—opposition always occurs. Satan hates restoration.

First, you may be hit with discouraging words. These words can be from friends, family, or as in Nehemiah's case, an enemy. You may hear doubts and accusations in your mind and assume they are from God.

Despite what we learned as children, that "sticks and stones may break my bones, but words will never hurt me," words do hurt. They pierce our hearts, steal our courage, and tempt us to lose faith. That's exactly what Satan wants. He wants to discourage us, make us feel too weak for the task, and lose hope.

How did Nehemiah respond when he was attacked? He prayed an honest prayer asking God for help. Then he went to work. He didn't entertain the enemy's insults. He didn't allow their words to define him, his people, or his mission. He went to work, and so did those who were with him.

We learn a very valuable lesson in a few short verses: Just because someone says something about you doesn't make it true.

Don't entertain words that are spoken to you from someone who doesn't want the best for you. Keep focused on the purpose God has for your life.

There will be people who don't want to see you rebuild. Do it anyway. They will mock you, threaten you, and tempt you to fear. Like Nehemiah, don't give in to their intimidation. Instead, get to work. Be aware of their attacks and be prepared, but don't let them discourage you for a second from the calling God has on your life. Keep your eyes focused on Jesus and your hands busy rebuilding, restoring, and reimagining. God can build something even better through you this time. Powerful things happen when we dismiss the distractions and get to work.

Like Nehemiah and the Israelites rebuilding the wall, do the work God has called you to do with all your heart. Realize there is a greater purpose than what you can see at this time. And remember, you are never working alone. God is with you. He will help you rebuild what has been torn down, stone by stone.

15 It so happened that when our adversaries heard that we were aware of these matters, God frustrated their intentions. Then all of us returned to the wall, each to his own work. 16 From that day forward, half my men were doing the work and half were taking up spears, shields, bows, and body armor. Now the officers were behind all the people of Judah 17 who were rebuilding the wall. Those who were carrying loads did so by keeping one hand on the work and the other on their weapon. 18 The builders, to a man, had their swords strapped to their sides while they were building. But the trumpeter remained with me.

19 I said to the nobles, the officials, and the rest of the people, "The work is demanding and extensive, and we are spread out on the wall, far removed from one another. 20 Wherever you hear the sound of the trumpet, gather there with us. Our God will fight for us!"

21 So we worked on, with half holding spears, from dawn till dusk. 22 At that time I instructed the people, "Let every man and his coworker spend the night in Jerusalem and let them be guards for us by night and workers by day." 23 We did not change clothes—not I, nor my relatives, nor my workers, nor the watchmen who were with me. Each had his weapon, even when getting a drink of water.

NEHEMIAH INTERVENES ON BEHALF OF THE OPPRESSED

5 Then there was a great outcry from the people and their wives against their fellow Jews. 2 There were those who said, "With our sons and daughters, we are many. We must obtain grain in order to eat and stay alive." 3 There were others who said, "We are putting up our fields, our vineyards, and our houses as collateral in order to obtain grain during the famine." 4 Then there were those who said, "We have borrowed money to pay our taxes to the king on our fields and our vineyards. 5 And now, though we share the same flesh and blood as our fellow countrymen and our children are just like their children, still we have found it necessary to subject our sons and daughters to slavery. Some of our daughters have been subjected to slavery, while we are powerless to help, since our fields and vineyards now belong to other people."

6 I was very angry when I heard their outcry and these complaints. 7 I considered these things carefully and then registered a complaint with the wealthy and the officials. I said to them, "Each one of you is seizing the collateral from your own countrymen!" Because of them I called for a great public assembly. 8 I said to them, "To the extent possible we have bought back our fellow Jews who had been sold to the Gentiles. But now you yourselves want to sell your own countrymen, so that we can then buy them back!" They were utterly silent, and could find nothing to say.

9 Then I said, "The thing that you are doing is wrong! Should you not conduct yourselves in the fear of our God in order to avoid the reproach of the Gentiles who are our enemies? 10 Even I and my relatives and my associates are lending them money and grain. But let us abandon this practice of seizing collateral! 11 This very day return to them their fields, their vineyards, their

REFLECT

How do you respond when you see injustice? How do Nehemiah's actions encourage you to speak out against injustice?

olive trees, and their houses, along with the interest that you are exacting from them on the money, the grain, the new wine, and the olive oil."

12 They replied, "We will return these things, and we will no longer demand anything from them. We will do just as you say." Then I called the priests and made the wealthy and the officials swear to do what had been promised.
13 I also shook out my garment, and I said, "In this way may God shake out from his house and his property every person who does not carry out this matter. In this way may he be shaken out and emptied!" All the assembly replied, "So be it!" and they praised the LORD. Then the people did as they had promised.

14 From the day that I was appointed governor in the land of Judah, that is, from the twentieth year until the thirty-second year of King Artaxerxes—twelve years in all—neither I nor my relatives ate the food allotted to the governor.
15 But the former governors who preceded me had burdened the people and had taken food and wine from them, in addition to forty shekels of silver. Their associates were also domineering over the people. But I did not behave in this way, due to my fear of God.
16 I gave myself to the work on this wall, without even purchasing a field. All my associates were gathered there for the work.

17 There were 150 Jews and officials who dined with me routinely, in addition to those who came to us from the nations all around us.
18 Every day one ox, six select sheep, and some birds were prepared for me, and every ten days all kinds of wine in abundance. Despite all this I did not require the food allotted to the governor, for the work was demanding on this people.

19 Please remember me for good, O my God, for all that I have done for this people.

OPPOSITION TO THE REBUILDING EFFORTS CONTINUES

6 When Sanballat, Tobiah, Geshem the Arab, and the rest of our enemies heard that I had rebuilt the wall and no breach remained in it (even though up to that time I had not positioned doors in the gates),
2 Sanballat and Geshem sent word to me saying, "Come on! Let's set up a time to meet together at Kephirim in the plain of Ono." Now they intended to do me harm.

3 So I sent messengers to them saying, "I am engaged in an important work, and I am unable to come down. Why should the work come to a halt when I leave it to come down to you?"
4 They contacted me four times in this way, and I responded the same way each time.

5 The fifth time that Sanballat sent his assistant to me in this way, he had an open letter in his hand.
6 Written in it were the following words:

"Among the nations it is rumored (and Geshem has substantiated this) that you and the Jews have intentions of revolting, and for this reason you are building the wall. Furthermore, according to these rumors you are going to become their king.
7 You have also established prophets to announce in Jerusalem on your behalf, 'We have a king in Judah!' Now the king is going to hear about these rumors. So come on, let's talk about this."

REFLECT

What kind of focus and determination was required of Nehemiah to respond this way to his enemies? How can you have the same focus in your work for the kingdom?

8 I sent word back to him, "We are not engaged in these activities
you are describing. All of this is a figment of your imagination."
9 All of them were wanting to scare us, supposing, "Their hands
will grow slack from the work, and it won't get done."
So now, strengthen my hands!
10 Then I went to the house of Shemaiah son of Delaiah, the son
of Mehetabel. He was confined to his home. He said, "Let's set
up a time to meet in the house of God, within the temple. Let's
close the doors of the temple, for they are coming to kill you. It
will surely be at night that they will come to kill you."
11 But I replied, "Should a man like me run away? Would someone like me flee to the temple in order to save his life? I will not
go!" 12 I recognized the fact that God had not sent him, for he
had spoken the prophecy against me as a hired agent of Tobiah
and Sanballat. 13 He had been hired to scare me so that I would
do this and thereby sin. They would thus bring reproach on me
and I would be discredited.
14 Remember, O my God, Tobiah and Sanballat in light of these
actions of theirs—also Noadiah the prophetess and the other
prophets who have been trying to scare me!

THE REBUILDING OF THE WALL IS FINALLY COMPLETED

15 So the wall was completed on the twenty-fifth day of Elul, in
just fifty-two days. 16 When all our enemies heard and all the nations who were around us saw this, they were greatly disheartened. They knew that this work had been accomplished with
the help of our God.
17 In those days the aristocrats of Judah repeatedly sent letters
to Tobiah, and responses from Tobiah were repeatedly coming
to them. 18 For many in Judah had sworn allegiance to him, because he was the son-in-law of Shecaniah son of Arah. His son
Jonathan had married the daughter of Meshullam son of Berechiah. 19 They were telling me about his good deeds and then
taking back to him the things I said. Tobiah, on the other hand,
sent letters in order to scare me.

7 When the wall had been rebuilt and I had positioned the
doors, and the gatekeepers, the singers, and the Levites had
been appointed, 2 I then put in charge over Jerusalem my brother Hanani and Hananiah the chief of the citadel, for he was a
faithful man and feared God more than many do. 3 I said to them,
"The gates of Jerusalem must not be opened in the early morning, until those who are standing guard close the doors and lock
them. Position residents of Jerusalem as guards, some at their
guard stations and some near their homes." 4 Now the city was
spread out and large, and there were not a lot of people in it. At
that time houses had not been rebuilt. 5 My God placed it on my
heart to gather the leaders, the officials, and the ordinary people so they could be enrolled on the basis of genealogy. I found
the genealogical records of those who had formerly returned.
Here is what I found written in that record:
6 These are the people of the province who returned from the
captivity of the exiles, whom King Nebuchadnezzar of Babylon
had forced into exile. They returned to Jerusalem and to Judah,

each to his own city. 7 They came with Zerubbabel, Jeshua, Nehemiah, Azariah, Raamiah, Nahamani, Mordecai, Bilshan, Mis-
pereth, Bigvai, Nehum, and Baanah.
The number of Israelite men was as follows:
8 the descendants of Parosh: 2,172;
9 the descendants of Shephatiah: 372;
10 the descendants of Arah: 652;
11 the descendants of Pahath Moab (from the line of Jeshua
and Joab): 2,818;
12 the descendants of Elam: 1,254;
13 the descendants of Zattu: 845;
14 the descendants of Zaccai: 760;
15 the descendants of Binnui: 648;
16 the descendants of Bebai: 628;
17 the descendants of Azgad: 2,322;
18 the descendants of Adonikam: 667;
19 the descendants of Bigvai: 2,067;
20 the descendants of Adin: 655;
21 the descendants of Ater (through Hezekiah): 98;
22 the descendants of Hashum: 328;
23 the descendants of Bezai: 324;
24 the descendants of Harif: 112;
25 the descendants of Gibeon: 95;
26 The men of Bethlehem and Netophah: 188;
27 the men of Anathoth: 128;
28 the men of the family of Azmaveth: 42;
29 the men of Kiriath Jearim, Kephirah, and Beeroth: 743;
30 the men of Ramah and Geba: 621;
31 the men of Micmash: 122;
32 the men of Bethel and Ai: 123;
33 the men of the other Nebo: 52;
34 the descendants of the other Elam: 1,254;
35 the descendants of Harim: 320;
36 the descendants of Jericho: 345;
37 the descendants of Lod, Hadid, and Ono: 721;
38 the descendants of Senaah: 3,930;
39 The priests: the descendants of Jedaiah (through the family of Jeshua): 973;
40 the descendants of Immer: 1,052;
41 the descendants of Pashhur: 1,247;
42 the descendants of Harim: 1,017.
43 The Levites: the descendants of Jeshua (through Kadmiel,
through the line of Hodaviah): 74.
44 The singers: the descendants of Asaph: 148.
45 The gatekeepers: the descendants of Shallum, the descendants of Ater, the descendants of Talmon, the descendants of Akkub, the descendants of Hatita, and the descendants of Shobai: 138.
46 The temple servants: the descendants of Ziha, the descendants of Hasupha, the descendants of Tabbaoth, 47 the descendants of Keros, the descendants of Sia, the descendants of Padon,
48 the descendants of Lebanah, the descendants of Hagabah, the
descendants of Shalmai, 49 the descendants of Hanan, the de-
scendants of Giddel, the descendants of Gahar, 50 the descen-
dants of Reaiah, the descendants of Rezin, the descendants of

Nekoda, 51 the descendants of Gazzam, the descendants of Uzzah, the descendants of Paseah, 52 the descendants of Besai, the
descendants of Meunim, the descendants of Nephussim, 53 the
descendants of Bakbuk, the descendants of Hakupha, the descendants of Harhur, 54 the descendants of Bazluth, the descendants
of Mehida, the descendants of Harsha, 55 the descendants of Barkos, the descendants of Sisera, the descendants of Temah, 56 the
descendants of Neziah, the descendants of Hatipha.

57 The descendants of the servants of Solomon: the descendants of Sotai, the descendants of Sophereth, the descendants
of Perida, 58 the descendants of Jaala, the descendants of Darkon,
the descendants of Giddel, 59 the descendants of Shephatiah, the
descendants of Hattil, the descendants of Pokereth Hazzebaim,
and the descendants of Amon.

60 All the temple servants and the descendants of the servants
of Solomon, 392.

61 These are the ones who came up from Tel Melah, Tel Harsha, Kerub, Addon, and Immer (although they were unable to
certify their family connection or their ancestry, as to whether
they were really from Israel):

62 the descendants of Delaiah, the descendants of Tobiah, and
the descendants of Nekoda, 642.

63 And from among the priests: the descendants of Hobaiah,
the descendants of Hakkoz, and the descendants of Barzillai
(who had married a woman from the daughters of Barzillai the
Gileadite and was called by that name). 64 They searched for their
records in the genealogical materials, but none were found. They
were therefore excluded from the priesthood. 65 The governor instructed them not to eat any of the sacred food until there was
a priest who could consult the Urim and Thummim.

66 The entire group numbered 42,360—67 not counting their
7,337 male and female servants. They also had 245 male and female singers. 68 They had 736 horses, 245 mules, 69 435 camels,
and 6,720 donkeys. 70 Some of the family leaders contributed to
the work. The governor contributed to the treasury 1,000 gold
drachmas, 50 bowls, and 530 priestly garments. 71 Some of the
family leaders gave to the project treasury 20,000 gold drachmas and 2,200 silver minas. 72 What the rest of the people gave
amounted to 20,000 gold drachmas, 2,000 silver minas, and 67
priestly garments.

73 The priests, the Levites, the gatekeepers, the singers, some
of the people, the temple servants, and all the rest of Israel lived
in their cities.

THE PEOPLE RESPOND TO THE READING OF THE LAW

When the seventh month arrived and the Israelites were settled
8 in their towns, 1 all the people gathered together in the plaza
which was in front of the Water Gate. They asked Ezra the
scribe to bring the book of the law of Moses which the LORD had
commanded Israel. 2 So Ezra the priest brought the law before
the assembly which included men and women and all those able
to understand what they heard. (This happened on the first day
of the seventh month.) 3 So he read it before the plaza in front of
the Water Gate from dawn till noon before the men and women

and those children who could understand. All the people were
eager to hear the book of the law.
4 Ezra the scribe stood on a towering wooden platform constructed for this purpose. Standing near him on his right were
Mattithiah, Shema, Anaiah, Uriah, Hilkiah, and Masseiah. On
his left were Pedaiah, Mishael, Malkijah, Hashum, Hashbad-
danah, Zechariah, and Meshullam. 5 Ezra opened the book
in plain view of all the people, for he was elevated above all
the people. When he opened the book, all the people stood
up. 6 Ezra blessed the LORD, the great God, and all the people
replied "Amen! Amen!" as they lifted their hands. Then they
bowed down and worshiped the LORD with their faces to the
ground.
7 Jeshua, Bani, Sherebiah, Jamin, Akkub, Shabbethai, Hodiah,
Maaseiah, Kelita, Azariah, Jozabad, Hanan, and Pelaiah—all of
whom were Levites—were teaching the people the law, as the
people remained standing. 8 They read from the book of God's
law, explaining it and imparting insight. Thus the people gained
understanding from what was read.
9 Then Nehemiah the governor, Ezra the priestly scribe, and
the Levites who were imparting understanding to the people
said to all of them, "This day is holy to the LORD your God. Do
not mourn or weep." For all the people had been weeping when
they heard the words of the law. 10 He said to them, "Go and eat
delicacies and drink sweet drinks and send portions to those for
whom nothing is prepared. For this day is holy to our Lord. Do
not grieve, for the joy of the LORD is your strength."
11 Then the Levites quieted all the people saying, "Be quiet, for
this day is holy. Do not grieve." 12 So all the people departed to
eat and drink and to share their food with others and to enjoy
tremendous joy, for they had gained insight in the matters that
had been made known to them.
13 On the second day of the month the family leaders met with
Ezra the scribe, together with all the people, the priests, and
the Levites, to consider the words of the law. 14 They discovered
written in the law that the LORD had commanded through Moses that the Israelites should live in temporary shelters during
the festival of the seventh month, 15 and that they should make
a proclamation and disseminate this message in all their cities
and in Jerusalem: "Go to the hill country and bring back olive
branches and branches of wild olive trees, myrtle trees, date
palms, and other leafy trees to construct temporary shelters,
as it is written."
16 So the people went out and brought these things back and
constructed temporary shelters for themselves, each on his roof
and in his courtyard and in the courtyards of the temple of God
and in the plaza of the Water Gate and the plaza of the Ephraim
Gate. 17 So all the assembly which had returned from the exile
constructed temporary shelters and lived in them. The Israelites had not done so from the days of Joshua son of Nun until
that day. Everyone experienced very great joy. 18 Ezra read in the
book of the law of God day by day, from the first day to the last.
They observed the festival for seven days, and on the eighth day
they held an assembly as was required.

THE PEOPLE ACKNOWLEDGE THEIR SIN BEFORE GOD

9 On the twenty-fourth day of this same month the Israelites assembled; they were fasting and wearing sackcloth, their heads covered with dust. 2 Those truly of Israelite descent separated from all the foreigners, standing and confessing their sins and the iniquities of their ancestors. 3 For one-fourth of the day they stood in their place and read from the book of the law of the LORD their God, and for another fourth they were confessing their sins and worshiping the LORD their God. 4 Then the Levites—Jeshua, Binnui, Kadmiel, Shebaniah, Bunni, Sherebiah, Bani, and Kenani—stood on the steps and called out loudly to the LORD their God. 5 The Levites—Jeshua, Kadmiel, Bani, Hashabneiah, Sherebiah, Hodiah, Shebaniah, and Pethahiah—said, "Stand up and bless the LORD your God!"

REFLECT

Was the people's repentance genuine? How does genuine repentance differ from ritual repentance? Which one honors God more?

"May you be blessed, O LORD our God, from age to age. May your glorious name be blessed; may it be lifted up above all blessing and praise. 6 You alone are the LORD. You made the heavens, even the highest heavens, along with all their multitude of stars, the earth and all that is on it, the seas and all that is in them. You impart life to them all, and the multitudes of heaven worship you.

7 "You are the LORD God who chose Abram and brought him forth from Ur of the Chaldeans. You changed his name to Abraham. 8 When you perceived that his heart was faithful toward you, you established a covenant with him to give his descendants the land of the Canaanites, the Hittites, the Amorites, the Perizzites, the Jebusites, and the Girgashites. You have fulfilled your promise, for you are righteous.

9 "You saw the affliction of our ancestors in Egypt, and you heard their cry at the Red Sea. 10 You performed awesome signs against Pharaoh, against his servants, and against all the people of his land, for you knew that the Egyptians had acted presumptuously against them. You made for yourself a name that is celebrated to this day. 11 You split the sea before them, and they crossed through the sea on dry ground. But you threw their pursuers into the depths, like a stone into surging waters. 12 You guided them with a pillar of cloud by day and with a pillar of fire by night to illumine for them the path they were to travel.

13 "You came down on Mount Sinai and spoke with them from heaven. You provided them with just judgments, true laws, and good statutes and commandments. 14 You made known to them your holy Sabbath; you issued commandments, statutes, and laws to them through Moses your servant. 15 You provided bread from heaven for them in their time of hunger, and you brought forth water from the rock for them in their time of thirst. You told them to enter in order to possess the land that you had sworn to give them.

16 "But they—our ancestors—behaved presumptuously; they rebelled and did not obey your commandments. 17 They refused to obey and did not recall your miracles that you had performed among them. Instead, they rebelled and appointed a leader to return to their bondage in Egypt. But you are a God of forgiveness, merciful and compassionate, slow to get angry and unfailing in

LOVE TO GROW

WHEN WE'RE CONVICTED

NEHEMIAH 9

When was the last time that you were so convicted by the Holy Spirit that it led you to worship? As the Spirit works, He humbles us to our knees because He sees our desperate need for the one true Savior.

The Book of Nehemiah shows us what this looks like. It testifies to God's protection of His people, the need for true devotion and faithful worship, the keeping of the Torah, and the rebuilding of Jerusalem. Though Nehemiah struggled and faced opposition as he sought to lead the people to rebuild the wall, God faithfully delivered him. After a time, the walls were securely fastened and reconstructed. However, God's plan was not only for a physical reconstruction but also for a spiritual reconstruction of His people.

In chapter 9, we see the Jews' response to their recommitment to God's law, which was given to them by God to make them holy and to distinguish them from other nations. Their heartfelt return to obedience to the Torah displayed their love, devotion, and trust in the Lord to rule over them again, to be their God, and to provide for them.

In their posture of prayer, the Israelites responded to the reading of the Word with praise and adoration. They said, "May your glorious name be blessed; may it be lifted up above all blessing and praise. You alone are the LORD" (Neh 9:5–6). When they began praising God, they reoriented their hearts to Yahweh, positioning themselves as His people. They recounted all of Israel's history and God's faithfulness to their ancestors through His mighty deliverance of them from their enemies.

"But you are a God of forgiveness, merciful and compassionate, slow to get angry and unfailing in your loyal love. You did not abandon them" (Neh 9:17).

May the raw worship and celebration of God's character in the life of the Israelites compel us to meditate on the goodness of the Lord, to stand on the Rock of our salvation in the midst of our struggles, and to recount the many blessings and grace He has given us. We must allow the conviction of the Holy Spirit to compel us to repentance, worship, and adoration of who He is. May we dwell on the beauty of His nature. May we be a people who humbly confess our sins to the Sovereign One and respond with a growing love and devotion for Him.

your loyal love. You did not abandon them, 18 even when they
made a cast image of a calf for themselves and said, 'This is your
God who brought you up from Egypt,' or when they committed
atrocious blasphemies.
19 "Due to your great compassion you did not abandon them
in the wilderness. The pillar of cloud did not stop guiding them
in the path by day, nor did the pillar of fire stop illuminating for
them by night the path on which they should travel. 20 You imparted your good Spirit to instruct them. You did not withhold
your manna from their mouths; you provided water for their
thirst. 21 For forty years you sustained them. Even in the wilderness they never lacked anything. Their clothes did not wear out
and their feet did not swell.
22 "You gave them kingdoms and peoples, and you allocated them to every corner of the land. They inherited the
land of King Sihon of Heshbon and the land of King Og of
Bashan. 23 You multiplied their descendants like the stars of
the sky. You brought them to the land you had told their ancestors to enter in order to possess. 24 Their descendants entered and possessed the land. You subdued before them the
Canaanites who were the inhabitants of the land. You delivered them into their hand, together with their kings and the
peoples of the land, to deal with as they pleased. 25 They captured fortified cities and fertile land. They took possession of
houses full of all sorts of good things—wells previously dug,
vineyards, olive trees, and fruit trees in abundance. They ate
until they were full and grew fat. They enjoyed to the full your
great goodness.
26 "Nonetheless they grew disobedient and rebelled against
you; they disregarded your law. They killed your prophets who
had solemnly admonished them in order to cause them to return to you. They committed atrocious blasphemies. 27 Therefore you delivered them into the hand of their adversaries, who
oppressed them. But in the time of their distress they called to
you, and you heard from heaven. In your abundant compassion
you provided them with deliverers to rescue them from their
adversaries.
28 "Then, when they were at rest again, they went back to
doing evil before you. Then you abandoned them to their
enemies, and they gained dominion over them. When they
again cried out to you, in your compassion you heard from
heaven and rescued them time and again. 29 And you solemnly
admonished them in order to return them to your law, but
they behaved presumptuously and did not obey your commandments. They sinned against your ordinances—those by
which an individual, if he obeys them, will live. They boldly
turned from you; they rebelled and did not obey. 30 You prolonged your kindness with them for many years, and you
solemnly admonished them by your Spirit through your
prophets. Still they paid no attention, so you delivered them
into the hands of the neighboring peoples. 31 However, due
to your abundant mercy you did not do away with them altogether; you did not abandon them. For you are a merciful and
compassionate God.

32"So now, our God—the great, powerful, and awesome God,
who keeps covenant fidelity—do not regard as inconsequential
all the hardship that has befallen us—our kings, our leaders,
our priests, our prophets, our ancestors, and all your people—
from the days of the kings of Assyria until this very day. 33You
are righteous with regard to all that has happened to us, for you
have acted faithfully. It is we who have been in the wrong! 34Our
kings, our leaders, our priests, and our ancestors have not kept
your law. They have not paid attention to your commandments
or your testimonies by which you have solemnly admonished
them. 35Even when they were in their kingdom and benefiting
from your incredible goodness that you had lavished on them
in the spacious and fertile land you had set before them, they
did not serve you, nor did they turn from their evil practices.

36"So today we are slaves! In the very land you gave to our ancestors to eat its fruit and to enjoy its good things—we are slaves.
37Its abundant produce goes to the kings you have placed over
us due to our sins. They rule over our bodies and our livestock
as they see fit, and we are in great distress!

THE PEOPLE PLEDGE TO BE FAITHFUL

38"Because of all this we are entering into a binding covenant
in written form; our leaders, our Levites, and our priests have
affixed their names on the sealed document."

10 On the sealed documents were the following names:
Nehemiah the governor, son of Hacaliah, along with
Zedekiah,
2Seraiah, Azariah, Jeremiah,
3Pashhur, Amariah, Malkijah,
4Hattush, Shebaniah, Malluch,
5Harim, Meremoth, Obadiah,
6Daniel, Ginnethon, Baruch,
7Meshullam, Abijah, Mijamin,
8Maaziah, Bilgai, and Shemaiah. These were the priests.
9The Levites were as follows:
Jeshua son of Azaniah, Binnui of the sons of Henadad, Kadmiel.
10Their colleagues were as follows:
Shebaniah, Hodiah, Kelita, Pelaiah, Hanan,
11Mica, Rehob, Hashabiah,
12Zaccur, Sherebiah, Shebaniah,
13Hodiah, Bani, and Beninu.
14The leaders of the people were as follows:
Parosh, Pahath Moab, Elam, Zattu, Bani,
15Bunni, Azgad, Bebai,
16Adonijah, Bigvai, Adin,
17Ater, *Hezekiah*, Azzur,
18Hodiah, Hashum, Bezai,
19Hariph, Anathoth, Nebai,
20Magpiash, Meshullam, Hezir,
21Meshezabel, Zadok, Jaddua,
22Pelatiah, Hanan, Anaiah,
23Hoshea, Hananiah, Hasshub,
24Hallohesh, Pilha, Shobek,
25Rehum, Hashabnah, Maaseiah,

26 Ahiah, Hanan, Anan,
27 Malluch, Harim, and Baanah.

28 "Now the rest of the people—the priests, the Levites, the gatekeepers, the singers, the temple attendants, and all those who have separated themselves from the neighboring peoples because of the law of God, along with their wives, their sons, and their daughters, all of whom are able to understand—29 hereby participate with their colleagues the town leaders and enter into a curse and an oath to adhere to the law of God which was given through Moses the servant of God, and to obey carefully all the commandments of the LORD our Lord, along with his ordinances and his statutes.

30 "We will not give our daughters in marriage to the neighboring peoples, and we will not take their daughters in marriage for our sons. 31 We will not buy on the Sabbath or on a holy day from the neighboring peoples who bring their wares and all kinds of grain to sell on the Sabbath day. We will let the fields lie fallow every seventh year, and we will cancel every loan. 32 We accept responsibility for fulfilling the commands to give one third of a shekel each year for the work of the temple of our God, 33 for the loaves of presentation and for the regular grain offerings and regular burnt offerings, for the Sabbaths, for the new moons, for the appointed meetings, for the holy offerings, for the sin offerings to make atonement for Israel, and for all the work of the temple of our God.

34 "We—the priests, the Levites, and the people—have cast lots concerning the wood offerings, to bring them to the temple of our God according to our families at the designated times year by year to burn on the altar of the LORD our God, as is written in the law. 35 We also accept responsibility for bringing the firstfruits of our land and the firstfruits of every fruit tree year by year to the temple of the LORD. 36 We also accept responsibility, as is written in the law, for bringing the firstborn of our sons and our cattle and the firstborn of our herds and of our flocks to the temple of our God, to the priests who are ministering in the temple of our God. 37 We will also bring the first of our coarse meal, of our contributions, of the fruit of every tree, of new wine, and of olive oil to the priests at the storerooms of the temple of our God, along with a tenth of the produce of our land to the Levites, for the Levites are the ones who collect the tithes in all the cities where we work. 38 A priest of Aaron's line will be with the Levites when the Levites collect the tithes, and the Levites will bring up a tenth of the tithes to the temple of our God, to the storerooms of the treasury. 39 The Israelites and the Levites will bring the contribution of the grain, the new wine, and the olive oil to the storerooms where the utensils of the sanctuary are kept, and where the priests who minister stay, along with the gatekeepers and the singers. We will not neglect the temple of our God."

THE POPULATION OF JERUSALEM

11 So the leaders of the people settled in Jerusalem, while the rest of the people cast lots to bring one out of every ten to settle in Jerusalem, the holy city, while the other nine remained

in other cities. [2]The people gave their blessing on all the men
who volunteered to settle in Jerusalem.

[3]These are the provincial leaders who settled in Jerusalem.
(While other Israelites, the priests, the Levites, the temple attendants, and the sons of the servants of Solomon settled in the
cities of Judah, each on his own property in their cities, [4]some of
the descendants of Judah and some of the descendants of Benjamin settled in Jerusalem.)

Of the descendants of Judah:

Athaiah son of Uzziah, the son of Zechariah, the son of Amariah, the son of Shephatiah, the son of Mahalalel, from the descendants of Perez; [5]and Maaseiah son of Baruch, the son of
Col-Hozeh, the son of Hazaiah, the son of Adaiah, the son of
Joiarib, the son of Zechariah, from the descendants of Shelah.
[6]The sum total of the descendants of Perez who were settling
in Jerusalem was 468 exceptional men.

[7]These are the descendants of Benjamin:

Sallu son of Meshullam, the son of Joed, the son of Pedaiah, the
son of Kolaiah, the son of Maaseiah, the son of Ithiel, the son of
Jeshaiah, [8]and his followers, Gabbai and Sallai—928 in all. [9]Joel
son of Zicri was the officer in charge of them, and Judah son of
Hassenuah was second-in-command over the city.

[10]From the priests:

Jedaiah son of Joiarib, Jakin, [11]Seraiah son of Hilkiah, the son
of Meshullam, the son of Zadok, the son of Meraioth, the son of
Ahitub, supervisor in the temple of God, [12]and their colleagues
who were carrying out work for the temple—822; and Adaiah
son of Jeroham, the son of Pelaliah, the son of Amzi, the son of
Zechariah, the son of Pashhur, the son of Malkijah, [13]and his
colleagues who were heads of families—242; and Amashsai son
of Azarel, the son of Ahzai, the son of Meshillemoth, the son of
Immer, [14]and his colleagues who were exceptional men—128. The
officer over them was Zabdiel the son of Haggedolim.

[15]From the Levites:

Shemaiah son of Hasshub, the son of Azrikam, the son of Hashabiah, the son of Bunni; [16]Shabbethai and Jozabad, leaders of the
Levites, were in charge of the external work for the temple of
God; [17]Mattaniah son of Mica, the son of Zabdi, the son of Asaph,
the praise leader who led in thanksgiving and prayer; Bakbukiah, second among his colleagues; and Abda son of Shammua,
the son of Galal, the son of Jeduthun. [18]The sum total of the Levites in the holy city was 284.

[19]And the gatekeepers:

Akkub, Talmon and their colleagues who were guarding the
gates—172.

[20]And the rest of the Israelites, with the priests and the Levites, were in all the cities of Judah, each on his own property.

[21]The temple attendants were living on Ophel, and Ziha and
Gishpa were over them.

[22]The overseer of the Levites in Jerusalem was Uzzi son of Bani,
the son of Hashabiah, the son of Mattaniah, the son of Mica. He
was one of Asaph's descendants, who were the singers responsible for the service of the temple of God. [23]For they were under
royal orders which determined their activity day by day.

24 Pethahiah son of Meshezabel, one of the descendants of Zerah son of Judah, was an adviser to the king in every matter pertaining to the people.

25 As for the settlements with their fields, some of the people of Judah settled in Kiriath Arba and its neighboring villages, in Dibon and its villages, in Jekabzeel and its settlements, 26 in Jeshua, in Moladah, in Beth Pelet, 27 in Hazar Shual, in Beer Sheba and its villages, 28 in Ziklag, in Meconah and its villages, 29 in En Rimmon, in Zorah, in Jarmuth, 30 Zanoah, Adullam and their settlements, in Lachish and its fields, and in Azekah and its villages. So they were encamped from Beer Sheba to the Valley of Hinnom.

31 Some of the descendants of Benjamin settled in Geba, Micmash, Aija, Bethel and its villages, 32 in Anathoth, Nob, and Ananiah, 33 in Hazor, Ramah, and Gittaim, 34 in Hadid, Zeboyim, and Neballat, 35 in Lod, Ono, and the Valley of the Craftsmen. 36 Some of the Judean divisions of the Levites settled in Benjamin.

THE PRIESTS AND THE LEVITES WHO RETURNED TO JERUSALEM

12 These are the priests and Levites who returned with Zerubbabel son of Shealtiel and Jeshua: Seraiah, Jeremiah, Ezra, 2 Amariah, Malluch, Hattush, 3 Shecaniah, Rehum, Meremoth, 4 Iddo, Ginnethon, Abijah, 5 Mijamin, Moadiah, Bilgah, 6 Shemaiah, Joiarib, Jedaiah, 7 Sallu, Amok, Hilkiah, and Jedaiah. These were the leaders of the priests and their colleagues in the days of Jeshua.

8 And the Levites: Jeshua, Binnui, Kadmiel, Sherebiah, Judah, and Mattaniah, who together with his colleagues was in charge of the songs of thanksgiving. 9 Bakbukiah and Unni, their colleagues, stood opposite them in the services.

10 Jeshua was the father of Joiakim, Joiakim was the father of Eliashib, Eliashib was the father of Joiada, 11 Joiada was the father of Jonathan, and Jonathan was the father of Jaddua.

12 In the days of Joiakim, these were the priests who were leaders of the families: of Seraiah, Meraiah; of Jeremiah, Hananiah; 13 of Ezra, Meshullam; of Amariah, Jehohanan; 14 of Malluch, Jonathan; of Shecaniah, Joseph; 15 of Harim, Adna; of Meremoth, Helkai; 16 of Iddo, Zechariah; of Ginnethon, Meshullam; 17 of Abijah, Zicri; of Miniamin and of Moadiah, Piltai; 18 of Bilgah, Shammua; of Shemaiah, Jehonathan; 19 of Joiarib, Mattenai; of Jedaiah, Uzzi; 20 of Sallu, Kallai; of Amok, Eber; 21 of Hilkiah, Hashabiah; of Jedaiah, Nethanel.

22 As for the Levites, in the days of Eliashib, Joiada, Johanan and Jaddua the heads of families were recorded, as were the priests during the reign of Darius the Persian. 23 The descendants of Levi were recorded in the Book of the Chronicles as heads of families up to the days of Johanan son of Eliashib. 24 And the leaders of the Levites were Hashabiah, Sherebiah, Jeshua son of Kadmiel, and their colleagues, who stood opposite them to offer praise and thanks, one contingent corresponding to the other, as specified by David the man of God.

25 Mattaniah, Bakbukiah, Obadiah, Meshullam, Talmon, and Akkub were gatekeepers who were guarding the storerooms at the gates. 26 These all served in the days of Joiakim son of Jeshua, the son of Jozadak, and in the days of Nehemiah the governor and of Ezra the priestly scribe.

THE WALL OF JERUSALEM IS DEDICATED

27 At the dedication of the wall of Jerusalem, they sought out the
Levites from all the places they lived to bring them to Jerusalem
to celebrate the dedication joyfully with songs of thanksgiving
and songs accompanied by cymbals, harps, and lyres. 28 The singers were also assembled from the district around Jerusalem and
from the settlements of the Netophathites 29 and from Beth Gilgal and from the fields of Geba and Azmaveth, for the singers
had built settlements for themselves around Jerusalem. 30 When
the priests and Levites had purified themselves, they purified
the people, the gates, and the wall.

31 I brought the leaders of Judah up on top of the wall, and I
appointed two large choirs to give thanks. One was to proceed
on the top of the wall southward toward the Dung Gate. 32 Going after them were Hoshaiah, half the leaders of Judah, 33 Azariah, Ezra, Meshullam, 34 Judah, Benjamin, Shemaiah, Jeremiah,
35 some of the priests with trumpets, Zechariah son of Jonathan,
the son of Shemaiah, the son of Mattaniah, the son of Micaiah,
the son of Zaccur, the son of Asaph, 36 and his colleagues—Shemaiah, Azarel, Milalai, Gilalai, Maai, Nethanel, Judah, and Hanani—with musical instruments of David the man of God. (Ezra
the scribe led them.) 37 They went over the Fountain Gate and
continued directly up the steps of the City of David on the ascent to the wall. They passed the house of David and continued
on to the Water Gate toward the east.

38 The second choir was proceeding in the opposite direction. I
followed them, along with half the people, on top of the wall, past
the Tower of the Ovens to the Broad Wall, 39 over the Ephraim
Gate, the Jeshanah Gate, the Fish Gate, the Tower of Hananel,
and the Tower of the Hundred, to the Sheep Gate. They stopped
at the Gate of the Guard.

40 Then the two choirs that gave thanks took their stations in
the temple of God. I did also, along with half the officials with me,
41 and the priests—Eliakim, Maaseiah, Miniamin, Micaiah, Elioenai, Zechariah, and Hananiah, with their trumpets—42 and also
Maaseiah, Shemaiah, Eleazar, Uzzi, Jehohanan, Malkijah, Elam,
and Ezer. The choirs sang loudly under the direction of Jezrahiah.
43 And on that day they offered great sacrifices and rejoiced, for
God had given them great joy. The women and children also rejoiced. The rejoicing in Jerusalem could be heard from far away.

44 On that day men were appointed over the storerooms for the
contributions, firstfruits, and tithes, to gather into them from
the fields of the cities the portions prescribed by the law for the
priests and the Levites, for the people of Judah took delight in
the priests and Levites who were ministering. 45 They performed
the service of their God and the service of purification, along
with the singers and gatekeepers, according to the commandment of David and his son Solomon. 46 For long ago, in the days
of David and Asaph, there had been directors for the singers and
for the songs of praise and thanks to God. 47 So in the days of Zerubbabel and in the days of Nehemiah, all Israel was contributing
the portions for the singers and gatekeepers, according to the
daily need. They also set aside the portion for the Levites, and
the Levites set aside the portion for the descendants of Aaron.

LOVE TO GROW

THE ART OF CELEBRATION

NEHEMIAH 12:43

Rebuilding the wall of Jerusalem was no small feat for Nehemiah and his men. They faced much opposition from their enemies on top of the grueling work of rebuilding. Finally, after much hard work, the wall was rebuilt.

The reconstruction of the wall meant a great deal to the people of Israel. It meant protection from foreign invaders and God's favor on Israel. After the wall was rebuilt, it was time for the people of Israel to enjoy the fruits of their labor.

As part of this celebration, many Israelites gathered in Jerusalem. They dedicated the wall to God and praised Him for the completion of the wall. God had done something great for his people, and the Israelites did not miss an opportunity to commemorate His work in their lives.

"And on that day they offered great sacrifices and rejoiced, for God had given them great joy. The women and children also rejoiced. The rejoicing in Jerusalem could be heard from far away" (Neh 12:43).

This celebration in Nehemiah is so great that echoes of the celebration could be heard from far away. Even from a distance, people heard the celebration of God's goodness. How often do we stop to celebrate when we see evidence of God working in our lives? When a prayer is answered or when God clearly performs a miracle in my life, many times I continue on with my life without celebrating. As a result, I quickly forget.

Nehemiah shows us how to celebrate. When God works and moves in our lives, we have the opportunity to give God all the glory and praise Him for what He has done. Celebration tells others about God's goodness in our lives, and it builds our faith during difficult times.

Let's celebrate our God today. No matter our circumstances, let's stop and praise Him for the way He has worked in our past, expectant that He will work the same way in our future. He is faithful and He is working. Let's celebrate His work and goodness like the people in Nehemiah, rejoicing so fervently that it can be heard from far away!

FURTHER REFORMS BY NEHEMIAH

13 On that day the book of Moses was read aloud in the hearing of the people. They found written in it that no Ammonite or Moabite may ever enter the assembly of God, 2 for they had
not met the Israelites with food and water, but instead had hired
Balaam to curse them. (Our God, however, turned the curse into
blessing.) 3 When they heard the law, they removed from Israel
all who were of mixed ancestry.
4 But before this time, Eliashib the priest, a relative of Tobiah,
had been appointed over the storerooms of the temple of our
God. 5 He made for himself a large storeroom where previously
they had been keeping the grain offering, the incense, and the
vessels, along with the tithes of the grain, the new wine, and the
olive oil as commanded for the Levites, the singers, the gatekeepers, and the offering for the priests.
6 During all this time I was not in Jerusalem, for in the thirty-second year of King Artaxerxes of Babylon, I had gone back to
the king. After some time I had requested leave of the king, 7 and
I returned to Jerusalem. Then I discovered the evil that Eliashib
had done for Tobiah by supplying him with a storeroom in the
courts of the temple of God. 8 I was very upset, and I threw all
of Tobiah's household possessions out of the storeroom. 9 Then
I gave instructions that the storerooms should be purified, and
I brought back the equipment of the temple of God, along with
the grain offering and the incense.
10 I also discovered that the portions for the Levites had not
been provided, and that as a result the Levites and the singers
who performed this work had all gone off to their fields. 11 So
I registered a complaint with the leaders, asking, "Why is the
temple of God neglected?" Then I gathered them and reassigned
them to their positions.
12 Then all of Judah brought the tithe of the grain, the new
wine, and the olive oil to the storerooms. 13 I gave instructions
that Shelemiah the priest, Zadok the scribe, and a certain Levite
named Pedaiah be put in charge of the storerooms, and that Hanan son of Zaccur, the son of Mattaniah, be their assistant, for
they were regarded as trustworthy. It was then their responsibility to oversee the distribution to their colleagues.
14 Please remember me for this, O my God, and do not wipe
out the kindness that I have done for the temple of my God and
for its services!
15 In those days I saw people in Judah treading winepresses on
the Sabbath, bringing in heaps of grain and loading them onto
donkeys, along with wine, grapes, figs, and all kinds of loads, and
bringing them to Jerusalem on the Sabbath day. So I warned
them on the day that they sold these provisions. 16 The people
from Tyre who lived there were bringing fish and all kinds of
merchandise and were selling it on the Sabbath to the people
of Judah—and in Jerusalem, of all places! 17 So I registered a complaint with the nobles of Judah, saying to them, "What is this evil
thing that you are doing, profaning the Sabbath day? 18 Isn't this
the way your ancestors acted, causing our God to bring on them
and on this city all this misfortune? And now you are causing
even more wrath on Israel, profaning the Sabbath like this!"

LOVE TO GROW

THE KEY TO RESTORATION

NEHEMIAH 13:4–9

After the Jews had returned to Israel from their captivity in Babylon, they began to restore the temple of God. However, there were many complications along the way. One in particular occurred when Eliashib the priest took over the storerooms of the temple, allowing Tobiah to use one of them for his personal belongings instead of the appointed uses for temple worship. When Nehemiah found out, he was livid.

> *"I was very upset, and I threw all of Tobiah's household possessions out of the storeroom. Then I gave instructions that the storerooms should be purified, and I brought back the equipment of the temple of God, along with the grain offering and the incense"* (Neh 13:8–9).

C. S. Lewis said it best when he encouraged us to imagine ourselves as a living house, a house that God comes to abide and live in. Each room, each pipe, each door of the home, He examines, walks through, and repairs.

This is a beautiful parallel to our hearts. The heart is the house that Christ Himself comes to indwell. The Master Builder walks with us and rebuilds our lives. Over time, certain spaces can become run down. Boards crack, foundations shake, and ordinary things we never intended to occupy these previously well-tended places appear.

Christ cannot fill rooms that we choose to crowd with other things; our calling is to make room for Him. Each and every day, we make more and more room. Our surrender and willingness to remove worldly ways is a key in the restoration process. In these surrendered spaces, deep down in each crevice and crack, He does His beautiful, cleansing work. Rooms of insecurity, abandonment, or loss He replaces and restores with security, belonging, and knowledge of Him. This is a wholeness no person can ever give to or take from us.

My journey is one from brokenness to wholeness, to beauty from ashes. I've learned that through the Holy Spirit's power, I can walk in freedom. Through Christ, our sure foundation, and the indwelling of God's Spirit, we daily renew our minds and make sure each room is open and ready for Him to come live and abide in.

In Jesus, wholeness and life are given to us. Renewal and restoration are His promises. We can be sure of that.

19 When the evening shadows began to fall on the gates of Jerusalem before the Sabbath, I ordered the doors to be closed.
I further directed that they were not to be opened until after
the Sabbath. I positioned some of my young men at the gates
so that no load could enter on the Sabbath day. 20 The traders
and sellers of all kinds of merchandise spent the night outside
Jerusalem once or twice. 21 But I warned them and said, "Why do
you spend the night by the wall? If you repeat this, I will forcibly
remove you!" From that time on they did not show up on the
Sabbath. 22 Then I directed the Levites to purify themselves and
come and guard the gates in order to keep the Sabbath day holy.

For this please remember me, O my God, and have pity on me in keeping with your great love.

23 Also in those days I saw the men of Judah who had married
women from Ashdod, Ammon, and Moab. 24 Half their children
spoke the language of Ashdod (or the language of one of the other peoples mentioned) and were unable to speak the language
of Judah. 25 So I entered a complaint with them. I called down
a curse on them, and I struck some of the men and pulled out
their hair. I had them swear by God saying, "You will not marry
off your daughters to their sons, and you will not take any of
their daughters as wives for your sons or for yourselves. 26 Was
it not because of things like these that King Solomon of Israel
sinned? Among the many nations there was no king like him.
He was loved by his God, and God made him king over all Israel.
But the foreign wives made even him sin! 27 Should we then in
your case hear that you do all this great evil, thereby being unfaithful to our God by marrying foreign wives?"

28 Now one of the sons of Joiada son of Eliashib the high priest
was a son-in-law of Sanballat the Horonite. So I banished him
from my sight.

29 Please remember them, O my God, because they have defiled
the priesthood, the covenant of the priesthood, and the Levites.

30 So I purified them of everything foreign, and I assigned specific duties to the priests and the Levites. 31 I also provided for the
wood offering at the appointed times and also for the firstfruits.

Please remember me for good, O my God.

CHALLENGE

How does Nehemiah display faithful leadership throughout the rebuilding efforts? What other leaders of Israel led Israel with the same steadfast leadership and devotion to God?

IT MAY
very well
be that
you have
ACHIEVED
Royal Status
for SUCH a TIME
as THIS

MEMORY VERSE

"It may very well be that you have achieved royal status for such a time as this!"

Esther 4:14

Esther

INTRODUCTION

God's Sovereignty

Through the twists and turns of the Book of Esther, an underlying theme of God's character remains clear: the covenant-keeping God of Israel is always sovereign and will forever faithfully preserve His people. Even in a seemingly hopeless situation, God was still working. The Book of Esther contains more than a message about God's sovereignty, and is, in fact, a thrilling story complete with villains, heroes, romance, intrigue, and humor.

The Book of Esther describes the events surrounding the reign of King Ahasuerus of Persia and an attempt by one of his advisers to annihilate the Jewish people. The book begins with the search for a new queen and ends with the establishment of the Jewish feast of Purim. However, how God brought about these events was nothing short of a miracle, one that God carefully orchestrated through His sovereign hand in the lives of many people.

The events in the Book of Esther span a decade during the height of the Persian Empire from about 483 to 473 B.C. Ahasuerus was the ruler of the Empire during this time. While unknown, the author of the Book of Esther was likely a Jew living in Persia shortly after this time. The book was probably written after the reign of Ahasuerus, around 465 B.C. The events took place around the same time the Jews were returning to Jerusalem to rebuild the city wall and the temple as described in the Books of Ezra and Nehemiah.

Despite the fact that God's name is not explicitly mentioned, the Book of Esther is an incredible testament to how we can love God greatly. He was at work through His people who upheld His laws and revered His name. No matter the circumstance, we can be confident that God is always present with us and sees our situations. He is sovereign over all, even the situations that seem utterly hopeless.

Nigeria

OFFICIAL LANGUAGE
English
POPULATION
200,771,000
UNREACHED POPULATION
62,889,000
PROFESSING CHRISTIANS
51.8%

Ebos' Home

Say a Prayer Today

Please pray for Ebos and her ministry to the Nigerian people. Pray the Christians of Nigeria find courage to continue in their faith and find hope in a difficult circumstance.

HISTORY BIT

Since 1966, the Bible Society of Nigeria has translated the Bible into twenty-six Nigerian languages, including Hausa.* Hausa is spoken by an estimated sixty-three million people and is considered the lingua franca (common language or trade language) throughout much of Western Africa.**

Source Information:
https://joshuaproject.net/countries/NI
*http://biblesociety-nigeria.org/new/about-us/our-history/
**https://www.britannica.com/topic/Hausa-language

LOVE YOUR NEIGHBOR

Her Journey

EBOS' STORY

On February 18, 2006, soon after I turned fifteen, religious extremists broke into my home and destroyed almost everything we owned. They knew we were Christians and that my parents were influential leaders in our church. My comfortable, peaceful life was ripped from under my feet. My family plunged into a time of immense pain, lack, and uncertainty.

Since that painful day I have seen God's hands in everything. Those days prepared me for my current work as a translator for Love God Greatly, translating Bible studies for the people of Nigeria in the Hausa language. Even though I did not know God personally until six years after that tragic day, those events sowed seeds of a life dedicated and surrendered to God. If they could destroy my life for their god, why can't I build others and lead them to God with mine?

God is sovereign over every situation in my life. All I am and have must be used for His glory, no matter what it takes or where it takes me. There were times I questioned Him and why He allowed such evil to happen. Instead, He showed me the good He does and the good I can do by pointing others to Him.

There is a lot of corruption, pain, lack, and evil happening in my country, Nigeria. Professionals are fleeing the country and moving to other nations to seek peace and a better life. But when it looks like all will be lost and Satan and his cohorts will have the upper hand, God miraculously intervenes and thwarts the plans of evil.

A lot of people call Nigeria a hopeless case, but I see God working. I see His hands even in the bad. Like the Jews during Esther's time, God will destroy His enemies. He is God both in the good and bad times, in the tough circumstances and easy moments, in plenty and in famine. He is God and He always knows what He is doing. He never leads us into darkness.

6 WEEK READING PLAN

LOVE HIS WORD

	MONDAY	TUESDAY	WEDNESDAY	THURSDAY	FRIDAY
1	Esther 1:1–9	Esther 1:10–12	Esther 1:13–18	Esther 1:19–22	Esther 2:1–4
	SOAP Matthew 6:19–21	SOAP Proverbs 12:16	SOAP Proverbs 14:8	SOAP Ephesians 5:33	SOAP Ephesians 5:15
2	Esther 2:5–11	Esther 2:12–18	Esther 2:19–23	Esther 3:1–4	Esther 3:5–11
	SOAP Psalm 112:1	SOAP Esther 2:15	SOAP Proverbs 19:20	SOAP Psalm 95:6	SOAP Psalm 52:2
3	Esther 3:12–15	Esther 4:1–7	Esther 4:8–11	Esther 4:12–14	Esther 4:15–17
	SOAP Proverbs 25:19	SOAP Psalm 51:17	SOAP Proverbs 20:28	SOAP Esther 4:14	SOAP Psalm 32:8
4	Esther 5:1–5	Esther 5:6–11	Esther 5:12–14	Esther 6:1–5	Esther 6:6–9
	SOAP Psalm 34:7	SOAP Proverbs 25:11	SOAP Proverbs 14:22	SOAP Proverbs 16:13	SOAP Romans 12:3
5	Esther 6:10–11	Esther 6:12–14	Esther 7:1–4	Esther 7:5–6	Esther 7:7–8
	SOAP Proverbs 25:6–7	SOAP Genesis 12:3	SOAP Philippians 4:6	SOAP Psalm 37:28	SOAP Proverbs 16:4
6	Esther 7:9–10	Esther 8:1–17	Esther 9:1–10	Esther 9:11–22	Esther 9:23—10:3
	SOAP Proverbs 26:27	SOAP Proverbs 28:20	SOAP Psalm 71:13	SOAP Psalm 71:24	SOAP Esther 10:3

THE KING THROWS A LAVISH PARTY

1 The following events happened in the days of Ahasuerus. (I am
referring to that Ahasuerus who used to rule over 127 provinces extending all the way from India to Ethiopia.) 2 In those
days, as King Ahasuerus sat on his royal throne in Susa the citadel, 3 in the third year of his reign he provided a banquet for all
his officials and his servants. The army of Persia and Media was
present, as well as the nobles and the officials of the provinces.
4 He displayed the riches of his royal glory and the splendor of
his majestic greatness for a lengthy period of time—180 days, to
be exact! 5 When those days were completed, the king then provided a seven-day banquet for all the people who were present in
Susa the citadel, for those of highest standing to the most lowly.
It was held in the court located in the garden of the royal palace.
6 The furnishings included white linen and blue curtains hung by
cords of the finest linen and purple wool on silver rings, alabaster columns, gold and silver couches displayed on a floor made of
valuable stones of alabaster, mother-of-pearl, and mineral stone.
7 Drinks were served in golden containers, all of which differed
from one another. Royal wine was available in abundance at the
king's expense. 8 There were no restrictions on the drinking, for
the king had instructed all his supervisors that they should do
as everyone so desired. 9 Queen Vashti also gave a banquet for
the women in King Ahasuerus' royal palace.

QUEEN VASHTI IS REMOVED FROM HER ROYAL POSITION

10 On the seventh day, as King Ahasuerus was feeling the effects of
the wine, he ordered Mehuman, Biztha, Harbona, Bigtha, Abag-
tha, Zethar, and Carcas, the seven eunuchs who attended him, 11 to
bring Queen Vashti into the king's presence wearing her royal
high turban. He wanted to show the people and the officials her
beauty, for she was very attractive. 12 But Queen Vashti refused to
come at the king's bidding conveyed through the eunuchs. Then
the king became extremely angry, and his rage consumed him.
13 The king then inquired of the wise men who were discern-
ers of the times—for it was the royal custom to confer with all
those who were proficient in laws and legalities. 14 Those who
were closest to him were Carshena, Shethar, Admatha, Tarshish,
Meres, Marsena, and Memucan. These men were the seven officials of Persia and Media who saw the king on a regular basis
and had the most prominent offices in the kingdom. 15 The king
asked, "By law, what should be done to Queen Vashti in light of
the fact that she has not obeyed the instructions of King Ahasuerus conveyed through the eunuchs?"
16 Memucan then replied to the king and the officials, "The
wrong of Queen Vashti is not against the king alone, but against
all the officials and all the people who are throughout all the provinces of King Ahasuerus. 17 For the matter concerning the queen
will spread to all the women, leading them to treat their husbands
with contempt, saying, 'When King Ahasuerus gave orders to bring
Queen Vashti into his presence, she would not come.' 18 And this
very day the noble ladies of Persia and Media who have heard
the matter concerning the queen will respond in the same way

LOVE TO GROW

VASHTI: A STORY OF GREAT BRAVERY

ESTHER 1

It was the seventh day of the king's banquet. The king had been drinking wine for seven days, then he sent seven of his men to retrieve his wife, Vashti. He wanted everyone to see how absolutely beautiful she was.

Vasht had to disobey the king or subject herself to mistreatment. Many scholars believe the king's request was disrespectful to Vashti because it devalued her as a human being. At the same time, Vashti would put herself in danger if she disobeyed the king.

Vashti demonstrated remarkable boldness in an unthinkable situation. She refused the king's request. Her boldness not only affected her life, but the lives of all the women in the Persian Empire.

Vashti's defiance to Ahasuerus shocked an entire empire. The king's advisers warned him that if he didn't do something about Vashti's actions, women all over the empire would "treat their husbands with contempt" (Esth 1:17). In a society and culture that did not value women and viewed them as less than a person, Vashti's actions were jaw-dropping. Her boldness to stand up to the king of Persia had a significant impact, one the leaders of the empire tried to repress.

Vashti's actions, her boldness and courage to stand up for herself in an oppressive situation, were heard throughout the empire.

Some time later, another young girl faced a deadly situation. Esther was faced with a decision to spare her own life or to stand up for her people and make her request known to the king—the same one who disposed of Vashti after she disobeyed him.

Esther had to approach the king without being asked or witness the annihilation of her people, the Jews. She approached King Ahasuerus with boldness and presented her request. Ultimately, her bravery led to the salvation of her people.

Is there an area of your life where you are fearful? Where do you need to act with boldness? My friend, with the wise courage of Vashti and Esther, choose boldness over fear. God is fighting with and for you. You may be surprised, but your boldness may inspire someone else to be brave as well.

to all the royal officials, and there will be more than enough contempt and anger. 19 If the king is so inclined, let a royal edict go
forth from him, and let it be written in the laws of Persia and Media that cannot be repealed, that Vashti may not come into the
presence of King Ahasuerus, and let the king convey her royalty
to another who is more deserving than she. 20 And let the king's
decision that he will enact be disseminated throughout all his
kingdom, vast though it is. Then all the women will give honor to
their husbands, from the most prominent to the lowly."
21 The matter seemed appropriate to the king and the officials.
So the king acted on the advice of Memucan. 22 He sent letters
throughout all the royal provinces, to each province according
to its own script and to each people according to their own language, that every man should be ruling his family and should
be speaking the language of his own people.

ESTHER BECOMES QUEEN IN VASHTI'S PLACE

2 When these things had been accomplished and the rage of
King Ahasuerus had diminished, he remembered Vashti and
what she had done and what had been decided against her. 2 The
king's servants who attended him said, "Let a search be conducted on the king's behalf for attractive young women. 3 And
let the king appoint officers throughout all the provinces of his
kingdom to gather all the attractive young women to Susa the
citadel, to the harem under the authority of Hegai, the king's
eunuch who oversees the women, and let him provide whatever cosmetics they desire. 4 Let the young woman whom the
king finds most attractive become queen in place of Vashti."
This seemed like a good idea to the king, so he acted accordingly.
5 Now there happened to be a Jewish man in Susa the citadel
whose name was Mordecai. He was the son of Jair, the son of
Shimei, the son of Kish, a Benjaminite, 6 who had been taken
into exile from Jerusalem with the captives who had been carried
into exile with Jeconiah king of Judah, whom Nebuchadnezzar
king of Babylon had taken into exile. 7 Now he was acting as the
guardian of Hadassah (that is, Esther), the daughter of his uncle, for neither her father nor her mother was alive. This young
woman was very attractive and had a beautiful figure. When her
father and mother died, Mordecai had raised her as if she were
his own daughter.
8 It so happened that when the king's edict and his law became
known many young women were taken to Susa the citadel to be
placed under the authority of Hegai. Esther also was taken to the
royal palace to be under the authority of Hegai, who was overseeing the women. 9 This young woman pleased him, and she found
favor with him. He quickly provided her with her cosmetics and
her rations; he also provided her with the seven specially chosen
young women who were from the palace. He then transferred
her and her young women to the best quarters in the harem.
10 Now Esther had not disclosed her people or her lineage,
for Mordecai had instructed her not to do so. 11 And day after
day Mordecai used to walk back and forth in front of the court
of the harem in order to learn how Esther was doing and what
might happen to her.

CHALLENGE

How does Mordecai's seemingly small act of faithfulness have significant implications later in the story? How does this show the sovereignty and work of God, even in situations where He seems absent? (Hint: see chs. 6, 10.)

12 At the end of the twelve months that were required for the
women, when the turn of each young woman arrived to go to King
Ahasuerus—for in this way they had to fulfill their time of cos-
metic treatment: six months with oil of myrrh, and six months
with perfume and various ointments used by women—13 the woman would go to the king in the following way: Whatever she asked
for would be provided for her to take with her from the harem to
the royal palace. 14 In the evening she went, and in the morning
she returned to a separate part of the harem, to the authority of
Shaashgaz, the king's eunuch who was overseeing the concubines.
She would not go back to the king unless the king was pleased
with her and she was requested by name.
15 When it became the turn of Esther daughter of Abihail the
uncle of Mordecai (who had raised her as if she were his own
daughter) to go to the king, she did not request anything except
what Hegai the king's eunuch, who was overseer of the women,
had recommended. Yet Esther met with the approval of all who
saw her. 16 Then Esther was taken to King Ahasuerus at his royal
residence in the tenth month (that is, the month of Tebeth) in
the seventh year of his reign. 17 And the king loved Esther more
than all the other women, and she met with his loving approval
more than all the other young women. So he placed the royal
high turban on her head and appointed her queen in place of
Vashti. 18 Then the king prepared a large banquet for all his officials and his servants—it was actually Esther's banquet. He also
set aside a holiday for the provinces, and he provided for offerings at the king's expense.

MORDECAI LEARNS OF A PLOT AGAINST THE KING

19 Now when the young women were being gathered again, Mordecai was sitting at the king's gate. 20 Esther was still not divulg-
ing her lineage or her people, just as Mordecai had instructed
her. Esther continued to do whatever Mordecai said, just as she
had done when he was raising her.
21 In those days while Mordecai was sitting at the king's gate,
Bigthan and Teresh, two of the king's eunuchs who protected the
entrance, became angry and plotted to assassinate King Ahasuerus. 22 When Mordecai learned of the conspiracy, he informed
Queen Esther, and Esther told the king in Mordecai's name. 23 The
king then had the matter investigated and, finding it to be so,
had the two conspirators hanged on a gallows. It was then recorded in the daily chronicles in the king's presence.

HAMAN CONSPIRES TO DESTROY THE JEWS

3 Some time later King Ahasuerus promoted Haman the son of
Hammedatha, the Agagite, exalting him and setting his position above that of all the officials who were with him. 2 As a result,
all the king's servants who were at the king's gate were bowing
and paying homage to Haman, for the king had so commanded.
However, Mordecai did not bow, nor did he pay him homage.
3 Then the servants of the king who were at the king's gate
asked Mordecai, "Why are you violating the king's commandment?" 4 And after they had spoken to him day after day without his paying any attention to them, they informed Haman to

see whether this attitude on Mordecai's part would be permitted. Furthermore, he had disclosed to them that he was a Jew.
5 When Haman saw that Mordecai was not bowing or paying
homage to him, he was filled with rage. 6 But the thought of striking out against Mordecai alone was repugnant to him, for he had
been informed of the identity of Mordecai's people. So Haman
sought to destroy all the Jews (that is, the people of Mordecai)
who were in all the kingdom of Ahasuerus.
7 In the first month (that is, the month of Nisan), in the twelfth
year of King Ahasuerus' reign, *pur* (that is, the lot) was cast before Haman in order to determine a day and a month. It turned
out to be the twelfth month (that is, the month of Adar).
8 Then Haman said to King Ahasuerus, "There is a particular people that is dispersed and spread among the inhabitants
throughout all the provinces of your kingdom whose laws differ
from those of all other peoples. Furthermore, they do not observe
the king's laws. It is not appropriate for the king to provide a haven for them. 9 If the king is so inclined, let an edict be issued to
destroy them. I will pay 10,000 talents of silver to be conveyed to
the king's treasuries for the officials who carry out this business."
10 So the king removed his signet ring from his hand and gave
it to Haman the son of Hammedatha, the Agagite, who was hostile toward the Jews. 11 The king replied to Haman, "Keep your
money, and do with those people whatever you wish."
12 So the royal scribes were summoned in the first month, on
the thirteenth day of the month. Everything Haman commanded
was written to the king's satraps and governors who were in every province and to the officials of every people, province by
province according to its script and people by people according
to their language. In the name of King Ahasuerus it was written
and sealed with the king's signet ring. 13 Letters were sent by the
runners to all the king's provinces stating that they should destroy, kill, and annihilate all the Jews, from youth to elderly, both
women and children, on a particular day, namely the thirteenth
day of the twelfth month (that is, the month of Adar), and to loot
and plunder their possessions. 14 A copy of this edict was to be
presented as law throughout every province; it was to be made
known to all the inhabitants, so that they would be prepared for
this day. 15 The messengers scurried forth with the king's order.
The edict was issued in Susa the citadel. While the king and Haman sat down to drink, the city of Susa was in an uproar.

ESTHER DECIDES TO RISK EVERYTHING IN ORDER TO HELP HER PEOPLE

4 Now when Mordecai became aware of all that had been done,
he tore his garments and put on sackcloth and ashes. He went
out into the city, crying out in a loud and bitter voice. 2 But he
went no farther than the king's gate, for no one was permitted to
enter the king's gate clothed in sackcloth. 3 Throughout each and
every province where the king's edict and law were announced
there was considerable mourning among the Jews, along with
fasting, weeping, and sorrow. Sackcloth and ashes were characteristic of many. 4 When Esther's female attendants and her eunuchs came and informed her about Mordecai's behavior, the

LOVE TO GROW

GOD'S PROVIDENTIAL POWER

ESTHER 4:14

In the Book of Esther we are whisked away to a kingdom filled with intrigue, romance, courage, and faith. From the fall of Queen Vashti to the rise of Esther, the young Jewish girl who took her place, God takes our breath away as we watch Him work through the faithfulness of Esther's family line to thwart Haman's plot to annihilate the Jews.

Mordecai challenged Esther to step up on behalf of her people when he said, "If you keep quiet at this time, liberation and protection for the Jews will appear from another source, while you and your father's household perish. It may very well be that you have achieved royal status for such a time as this!" (Esth 4:14).

Esther's position gave her access to the ear of the king. Through her boldness and courage an entire people group was saved.

Throughout the Old Testament God sovereignly led and protected His people. He chose Abraham and through him birthed Israel to carry His name and exemplify divine blessing (see Gen 12:2.). God raised up Moses to free His people from slavery. He used Esther as an instrument to deliver His people from death. Through the preservation of God's people came the Messiah: The Redeemer who paid the ransom for believers from every nation, absorbing God's wrath on their behalf on the cross.

The question we should ask ourselves is, "So what?" How should this affect the way we think and act?

As inheritors of the same promises God made to Abraham, Romans 8:28 promises that "all things work together for good for those who love God, who are called according to his purpose."

God's providential power extends to us as well. Not only has He placed us here to glorify Him in our various callings, but His hand is also working in all our circumstances. Whether our days are hard or easy, He is working through them to bring us closer to Himself and to bring glory to His name. We may not always understand all that God is doing, but we can live with the confidence that He is always at work.

Practice seeing God's providence not only in history but also in your own life. Why has He placed you here? What has He called you to do? Whom has He placed in your life to influence? How can you glorify God? Like Esther, you are here for such a time as this.

queen was overcome with anguish. Although she sent garments
for Mordecai to put on so that he could remove his sackcloth,
he would not accept them. 5 So Esther called for Hathach, one
of the king's eunuchs who had been placed at her service, and
instructed him to find out the cause and reason for Mordecai's
behavior. 6 So Hathach went to Mordecai at the plaza of the city
in front of the king's gate. 7 Then Mordecai related to him everything that had happened to him, even the specific amount of
money that Haman had offered to pay to the king's treasuries
for the Jews to be destroyed. 8 He also gave him a written copy of
the law that had been disseminated in Susa for their destruction
so that he could show it to Esther and talk to her about it. He
also gave instructions that she should go to the king to implore
him and petition him on behalf of her people. 9 So Hathach returned and related Mordecai's instructions to Esther.
10 Then Esther replied to Hathach with instructions for Mordecai: 11 "All the servants of the king and the people of the king's
provinces know that there is only one law applicable to any
man or woman who comes uninvited to the king in the inner
court—that person will be put to death, unless the king extends
to him the gold scepter, permitting him to be spared. Now I
have not been invited to come to the king for some thirty days."
12 When Esther's reply was conveyed to Mordecai, 13 he said to
take back this answer to Esther: "Don't imagine that because
you are part of the king's household you will be the one Jew who
will escape. 14 If you keep quiet at this time, liberation and protection for the Jews will appear from another source, while you
and your father's household perish. It may very well be that you
have achieved royal status for such a time as this!"
15 Then Esther sent this reply to Mordecai: 16 "Go, assemble all
the Jews who are found in Susa, and fast on my behalf. Don't
eat and don't drink for three days, night or day. My female attendants and I will also fast in the same way. Afterward I will go
to the king, even though it violates the law. If I perish, I perish."
17 So Mordecai set out to do everything that Esther had instructed him.

ESTHER APPEALS TO THE KING FOR HELP

5 It so happened that on the third day Esther put on her royal
attire and stood in the inner court of the palace, opposite the
king's quarters. The king was sitting on his royal throne in the
palace, opposite the entrance. 2 When the king saw Queen Esther standing in the court, she met with his approval. The king
extended to Esther the gold scepter that was in his hand, and
Esther approached and touched the end of the scepter.
3 The king said to her, "What is on your mind, Queen Esther?
What is your request? Even as much as half the kingdom will
be given to you."
4 Esther replied, "If the king is so inclined, let the king and
Haman come today to the banquet that I have prepared for the
king." 5 The king replied, "Find Haman quickly so that we can do
as Esther requests."
So the king and Haman went to the banquet that Esther had
prepared. 6 While at the banquet of wine, the king said to Esther,

REFLECT

How did Esther display her faith in an uncertain situation? How do her actions encourage you to do the same?

"What is your request? It shall be given to you. What is your petition? Ask for as much as half the kingdom, and it shall be done." 7 Esther responded, "My request and my petition is this: 8 If I have found favor in the king's sight and if the king is inclined to grant my request and approve my petition, let the king and Haman come tomorrow to the banquet that I will prepare for them. At that time I will do as the king wishes."

REFLECT

Why did Esther ask the king to a banquet instead of presenting her real request? Was this a wise decision?

HAMAN EXPRESSES HIS HATRED OF MORDECAI

9 Now Haman went forth that day pleased and very much encouraged. But when Haman saw Mordecai at the king's gate, and he did not rise or tremble in his presence, Haman was filled with rage toward Mordecai. 10 But Haman restrained himself and went on to his home.

He then sent for his friends to join him, along with his wife Zeresh. 11 Haman then recounted to them his fabulous wealth, his many sons, and how the king had magnified him and exalted him over the king's other officials and servants. 12 Haman said, "Furthermore, Queen Esther invited only me to accompany the king to the banquet that she prepared. And also tomorrow I am invited along with the king. 13 Yet all this fails to satisfy me so long as I have to see Mordecai the Jew sitting at the king's gate." 14 Haman's wife Zeresh and all his friends said to him, "Have a gallows 75 feet high built, and in the morning tell the king that Mordecai should be hanged on it. Then go with the king to the banquet contented."

It seemed like a good idea to Haman, so he had the gallows built.

THE TURNING POINT: THE KING HONORS MORDECAI

6 Throughout that night the king was unable to sleep, so he asked for the book containing the historical records to be brought. As the records were being read in the king's presence, 2 it was found written that Mordecai had disclosed that Bigthana and Teresh, two of the king's eunuchs who guarded the entrance, had plotted to assassinate King Ahasuerus.

3 The king asked, "What great honor was bestowed on Mordecai because of this?" The king's attendants who served him responded, "Not a thing was done for him."

4 Then the king said, "Who is that in the courtyard?" Now Haman had come to the outer courtyard of the palace to suggest that the king hang Mordecai on the gallows that he had constructed for him. 5 The king's attendants said to him, "It is Haman who is standing in the courtyard." The king said, "Let him enter."

6 So Haman came in, and the king said to him, "What should be done for the man whom the king wishes to honor?" Haman thought to himself, "Who is it that the king would want to honor more than me?" 7 So Haman said to the king, "For the man whom the king wishes to honor, 8 let them bring royal attire which the king himself has worn and a horse on which the king himself has ridden—one bearing the royal insignia. 9 Then let this clothing and this horse be given to one of the king's noble officials. Let him then clothe the man whom the king wishes to honor, and let him lead him about through the plaza of the city on the

horse, calling before him, 'So shall it be done to the man whom
the king wishes to honor!'"
10 The king then said to Haman, "Go quickly! Take the clothing and the horse, just as you have described, and do as you just
indicated to Mordecai the Jew, who sits at the king's gate. Don't
neglect a single thing of all that you have said."
11 So Haman took the clothing and the horse, and he clothed
Mordecai. He led him about on the horse throughout the plaza
of the city, calling before him, "So shall it be done to the man
whom the king wishes to honor!"
12 Then Mordecai again sat at the king's gate, while Haman hurried away to his home, mournful and with a veil over his head.
13 Haman then related to his wife Zeresh and to all his friends
everything that had happened to him. These wise men, along
with his wife Zeresh, said to him, "If indeed this Mordecai before whom you have begun to fall is Jewish, you will not prevail
against him. No, you will surely fall before him!"
14 While they were still speaking with him, the king's eunuchs
arrived. They quickly brought Haman to the banquet that Esther had prepared.

REFLECT

How is God's sovereignty displayed in the king's insomnia? What situations or difficulties in your life could God be using to bring about a higher purpose or result?

THE KING HAS HAMAN EXECUTED

7 So the king and Haman came to dine with Queen Esther. 2 On
the second day of the banquet of wine the king asked Esther,
"What is your request, Queen Esther? It shall be granted to you.
And what is your petition? Ask for up to half the kingdom, and
it shall be done."
3 Queen Esther replied, "If I have met with your approval, O
king, and if the king is so inclined, grant me my life as my request,
and my people as my petition. 4 For we have been sold—both I
and my people—to destruction and to slaughter and to annihilation. If we had simply been sold as male and female slaves, I
would have remained silent, for such distress would not have
been sufficient for troubling the king."
5 Then King Ahasuerus responded to Queen Esther, "Who is
this individual? Where is this person to be found who is presumptuous enough to act in this way?"
6 Esther replied, "The oppressor and enemy is this evil Haman!"
Then Haman became terrified in the presence of the king and
queen. 7 In rage the king arose from the banquet of wine and
withdrew to the palace garden. Meanwhile, Haman stood to beg
Queen Esther for his life, for he realized that the king had now
determined a catastrophic end for him.
8 When the king returned from the palace garden to the banquet of wine, Haman was throwing himself down on the couch
where Esther was lying. The king exclaimed, "Will he also attempt
to rape the queen while I am still in the building?"
As these words left the king's mouth, they covered Haman's
face. 9 Harbona, one of the king's eunuchs, said, "Indeed, there is
the gallows that Haman made for Mordecai, who spoke out on the
king's behalf. It stands near Haman's home and is 75 feet high."
The king said, "Hang him on it!" 10 So they hanged Haman on
the very gallows that he had prepared for Mordecai. The king's
rage then abated.

REFLECT

How does the plot of the story of Esther change in this chapter? How was God's hand active in this story since the beginning? Is He active in your story in the same way?

THEN QUEEN ESTHER REPLIED

ESTHER 7

Esther was a smart, beautiful, and kind biblical heroine. My favorite quality about Esther is her keen sense of timing. Esther was not manipulative, but she was discerning and weighed her choices carefully. She was strategic in her plan to speak up on behalf of the Jews, and she waited for the right moment to act. When that moment arrived, she made her request directly to the king, even though it could have meant her life.

Queen Esther replied, "If I have met with your approval, O king, and if the king is so inclined, grant me my life as my request, and my people as my petition" (Esth 7:3).

Esther demonstrated immeasurable courage by making this request. King Ahasuerus was a volatile and narcissistic leader, and he would not hesitate to destroy anyone who threatened his ego. Esther was careful to show respect, but she did not cower before the king. She not only requested that the Jews be saved, but she also revealed herself to be one of those in danger of execution. She did this in front of Haman, the very man who ordered the death of the Jews. This was bold—and very risky.

The king believed her words and granted her request without reservation. Everything changed in an instant: The king ordered Haman be hanged on the very gallows he had prepared for Mordecai, and the Jewish people were allowed to defend themselves from their attackers.

It is often said that God does not appear in the Book of Esther, but I think God shines through in the book's protagonist. Esther shows us God is bold and heroic and His powerful voice can change things on a dime. Esther shows us God's timing is perfect, that He can make a way in an impossible situation, and that His plans for His people often come in unexpected ways.

I have watched God choose key strategic moments, like the one in this passage, to make a change that ripples through my life. In what seems like a single instant, He has brought redemption when I was sure there was none.

The story of Esther swells my heart with love for God and fills my spirit with trust in Him. Esther's decision reminds me of my favorite verse in Acts: "But Peter . . . raised his voice" (Acts 2:14). Peter began to preach, God's church began to spread, and many people were saved and began to follow Jesus. I thank God for Esther, one of Peter's predecessors of faith—who lifted up her voice many years before. Her courage has blessed us all.

My prayer is that God will raise up more women, like Esther, around the world for such a time as this.

THE KING ACTS TO PROTECT THE JEWS

8 On that same day King Ahasuerus gave the estate of Haman,
that adversary of the Jews, to Queen Esther. Now Mordecai
had come before the king, for Esther had revealed how he was
related to her. 2 The king then removed his signet ring (the very
one he had taken back from Haman) and gave it to Mordecai. And
Esther designated Mordecai to be in charge of Haman's estate.
3 Then Esther again spoke with the king, falling at his feet. She
wept and begged him for mercy, that he might nullify the evil of
Haman the Agagite and the plot that he had intended against
the Jews. 4 When the king extended to Esther the gold scepter,
she arose and stood before the king.
5 She said, "If the king is so inclined, and if I have met with
his approval, and if the matter is agreeable to the king, and if I
am attractive to him, let an edict be written rescinding those
recorded intentions of Haman the son of Hammedatha, the
Agagite, which he wrote in order to destroy the Jews who are
throughout all the king's provinces. 6 For how can I watch the
calamity that will befall my people, and how can I watch the destruction of my relatives?"
7 King Ahasuerus replied to Queen Esther and to Mordecai the
Jew, "Look, I have already given Haman's estate to Esther, and
he has been hanged on the gallows because he took hostile action against the Jews. 8 Now write in the king's name whatever
in your opinion is appropriate concerning the Jews and seal it
with the king's signet ring. Any decree that is written in the king's
name and sealed with the king's signet ring cannot be rescinded."
9 The king's scribes were quickly summoned—in the third
month (that is, the month of Sivan), on the twenty-third day.
They wrote out everything that Mordecai instructed to the Jews,
and to the satraps, and the governors, and the officials of the
provinces all the way from India to Ethiopia—a 127 provinces
in all—to each province in its own script and to each people in
their own language, and to the Jews according to their own script
and their own language. 10 Mordecai wrote in the name of King
Ahasuerus and sealed it with the king's signet ring. He then sent
letters by couriers, who rode royal horses that were very swift.
11 The king thereby allowed the Jews who were in every city
to assemble and to stand up for themselves—to destroy, to kill,
and to annihilate any army of whatever people or province that
should become their adversaries, including their women and
children, and to confiscate their property. 12 This was to take place
on a certain day throughout all the provinces of King Ahasuerus—namely, on the thirteenth day of the twelfth month (that
is, the month of Adar). 13 A copy of the edict was to be presented
as law throughout each and every province and made known to
all peoples, so that the Jews might be prepared on that day to
avenge themselves on their enemies.
14 The couriers who were riding the royal horses went forth
with the king's edict without delay. And the law was presented
in Susa the citadel as well.
15 Now Mordecai went out from the king's presence in blue and
white royal attire, with a large golden crown and a purple linen
mantle. The city of Susa shouted with joy. 16 For the Jews there

was radiant happiness and joyous honor. 17 Throughout every
province and throughout every city where the king's edict and
his law arrived, the Jews experienced happiness and joy, banquets and holidays. Many of the resident peoples pretended to
be Jews, because the fear of the Jews had overcome them.

THE JEWS PREVAIL OVER THEIR ENEMIES

9 In the twelfth month (that is, the month of Adar), on its
thirteenth day, the edict of the king and his law were to be
executed. It was on this day that the enemies of the Jews had
supposed that they would gain power over them. But contrary
to expectations, the Jews gained power over their enemies. 2 The
Jews assembled themselves in their cities throughout all the
provinces of King Ahasuerus to strike out against those who were
seeking their harm. No one was able to stand before them, for
dread of them fell on all the peoples. 3 All the officials of the provinces, the satraps, the governors, and those who performed the
king's business were assisting the Jews, for the dread of Mordecai
had fallen on them. 4 Mordecai was of high rank in the king's palace, and word about him was spreading throughout all the provinces. His influence continued to become greater and greater.
5 The Jews struck all their enemies with the sword, bringing
death and destruction, and they did as they pleased with their
enemies. 6 In Susa the citadel the Jews killed and destroyed 500
men. 7 In addition, they also killed Parshandatha, Dalphon, As-
patha, 8 Poratha, Adalia, Aridatha, 9 Parmashta, Arisai, Aridai,
and Vaizatha, 10 the ten sons of Haman son of Hammedatha, the
enemy of the Jews. But they did not confiscate their property.

11 On that same day the number of those killed in Susa the citadel was brought to the king's attention. 12 Then the king said to
Queen Esther, "In Susa the citadel the Jews have killed and destroyed 500 men and the ten sons of Haman. What then have
they done in the rest of the king's provinces? What is your request? It shall be given to you. What other petition do you have?
It shall be done."

13 Esther replied, "If the king is so inclined, let the Jews who are
in Susa be permitted to act tomorrow also according to today's
law, and let them hang the ten sons of Haman on the gallows."
14 So the king issued orders for this to be done. A law was passed
in Susa, and the ten sons of Haman were hanged. 15 The Jews who
were in Susa then assembled on the fourteenth day of the month
of Adar, and they killed 300 men in Susa. But they did not confiscate their property.

16 The rest of the Jews who were throughout the provinces of
the king assembled in order to stand up for themselves and to
have rest from their enemies. They killed 75,000 of their adversaries, but they did not confiscate their property. 17 All this happened on the thirteenth day of the month of Adar. They then
rested on the fourteenth day and made it a day for banqueting
and happiness.

THE ORIGINS OF THE FEAST OF PURIM

18 But the Jews who were in Susa assembled on the thirteenth
and fourteenth days, and rested on the fifteenth, making it a day

for banqueting and happiness. 19 This is why the Jews who are in
the rural country—those who live in rural villages—set aside the
fourteenth day of the month of Adar for happiness, banqueting,
a holiday, and sending gifts to one another.
20 Mordecai wrote these matters down and sent letters to all
the Jews who were throughout all the provinces of King Ahasuerus, both near and far, 21 to have them observe the fourteenth
and the fifteenth days of the month of Adar each year 22 as the
time when the Jews gave themselves rest from their enemies—
the month when their trouble was turned to happiness and their
mourning to a holiday. These were to be days of banqueting, happiness, sending gifts to one another, and providing for the poor.
23 So the Jews committed themselves to continuing what they
had begun to do and to what Mordecai had written to them.
24 For Haman the son of Hammedatha, the Agagite, the enemy of
all the Jews, had devised plans against the Jews to destroy them.
He had cast *pur* (that is, the lot) in order to afflict and destroy
them. 25 But when the matter came to the king's attention, the
king gave written orders that Haman's evil intentions that he
had devised against the Jews should fall on his own head. He and
his sons were hanged on the gallows. 26 For this reason these days
are known as *Purim*, after the name of *pur*. Therefore, because
of the account found in this letter and what they had faced in
this regard and what had happened to them, 27 the Jews established as binding on themselves, their descendants, and all who
joined their company that they should observe these two days
without fail, just as written and at the appropriate time on an
annual basis. 28 These days were to be remembered and to be celebrated in every generation and in every family, every province,
and every city. The Jews were not to fail to observe these days
of Purim; the remembrance of them was not to cease among
their descendants.
29 So Queen Esther, the daughter of Abihail, and Mordecai the
Jew wrote with full authority to confirm this second letter about
Purim. 30 Letters were sent to all the Jews in the 127 provinces
of the empire of Ahasuerus—words of true peace—31 to establish
these days of Purim in their proper times, just as Mordecai the
Jew and Queen Esther had established, and just as they had established both for themselves and their descendants, matters
pertaining to fasting and lamentation. 32 Esther's command established these matters of Purim, and the matter was officially
recorded.

REFLECT

Why is it important to commemorate the great things God has done in our lives? What has He done for you that you need to celebrate?

MORDECAI'S FAME INCREASES

10 King Ahasuerus then imposed forced labor on the land
and on the coastlands of the sea. 2 Now all the actions carried out under his authority and his great achievements, along
with an exact statement concerning the greatness of Mordecai,
whom the king promoted, are they not written in the Book of the
Chronicles of the Kings of Media and Persia? 3 Mordecai the Jew
was second only to King Ahasuerus. He was the highest-ranking
Jew, and he was admired by his numerous relatives. He worked
enthusiastically for the good of his people and was an advocate
for the welfare of all his descendants.

THE *Lord* *gives,* AND THE LORD *takes away.* *May* THE NAME OF THE *Lord* BE *blessed*

MEMORY VERSE

"The Lord gives, and the Lord takes away. May the name of the Lord be blessed!" In all this Job did not sin, nor did he charge God with moral impropriety.

Job 1:21–22

Job

INTRODUCTION

Faith in Suffering

Suffering is a reality of life. The Book of Job offers a theology of suffering that is contrary to the world's: even through heartache and deep pain, God is present and sees our suffering. While He does not always reveal His motivations, we can believe God is present in our suffering, and, no matter the cause, we can rest in the truth that He will be glorified.

The Book of Job describes a righteous man suffering great loss and the events that followed. At the beginning of the book, the author provides a rare glimpse into a conversation between God and Satan, one where Satan wanted to discredit God's servant Job. After Satan inflicted terrible losses upon Job, Job's friends offered him their best guesses as to why it had happened. Finally, after all of Job's questions, God answered Job. Without revealing His reasons, God displayed His love, sovereignty, grace, and patience.

The Book of Job is classified as Hebrew poetry. Most evangelical scholars agree the events likely occurred during the patriarchal period, around the time of Abraham. While the author is unknown, there is historical evidence that suggests it was written during the reign of Solomon when wisdom literature was flourishing.

Job addresses big questions we all face: Why do the righteous suffer? Where is God in the midst of pain? Is God sovereign, even in loss and heartache? The answers are not explicitly answered in the text, but what is revealed is the faithfulness of God and His presence with us when we suffer. God loves us greatly and is with us, even in the depths of our pain. We can love Him greatly, resting in the confidence that no matter the circumstance, He remains sovereign and faithful.

United States of America

OFFICIAL LANGUAGE
English
POPULATION
326,302,000
UNREACHED POPULATION
4,827,000
PROFESSING CHRISTIANS
77.5%

Vicky's Home

Say a Prayer Today

Please pray for the missionaries from the United States serving in other countries. Pray for Vicky and her family that God would continue to use them for His glory as they share the gospel with the world.

HISTORY BIT

Of the estimated 400,000 missionaries worldwide in 2010, 127,000 of them were from the United States.* The first missionaries from the United States were Adoniram and Ann Hasseltine Judson. They were missionaries to Burma, now known as Myanmar.**

Source Information:
https://joshuaproject.net/countries/US
*https://www.reuters.com/article/us-missionary-massachusetts/in-200-year-tradition-most-christian-missionaries-are-american-idUSTRE81J0ZD20120221
**Mark A. Noll, A History of Christianity in the United States and Canada (Grand Rapids, MI: William B. Eerdman's Publishing Company, 1992), 187.

VICKY'S STORY

Job's life has always been an encouragement to me in times of trial. Job's story reminds me that no matter how bad things can get, or seem to get, I can trust God. Whether I understand the situation or not, I can keep my eyes on Jesus. Believing God created me and has a plan for me gives me the comfort I need to continue to trust in Him and His promises.

In Matthew 16:24–25 Jesus asked His disciples to deny themselves and follow Him. He asks us to do the same as we trust in His will. When God called my family to serve on the other side of the world, to leave the comforts of America and our loved ones, I knew I needed and wanted to follow Him. I was convinced that no matter the cost, we would trust and follow God.

In our first two years of living abroad, my family experienced a whirlwind of trials. Within the first year, my family was in the hospital with strange illnesses every couple of weeks. While lying in a hospital bed reflecting on my life, thinking I was going to die, I asked God, "Why? What more do you want of me?" Would God call us away from home only to have us suffer?

He reminded me with His soft voice, "deny yourself and follow me." Moving from a country where much of the suffering is internal to a country where the suffering is external has increased my desire to pray for all countries. I count the suffering I experienced as a blessing because it showed me the significance of each day. How precious our loving Jesus is that He suffered more than we could ever imagine.

Blessed be the name of the Lord. May He be glorified through my life.

6 WEEK READING PLAN

LOVE HIS WORD

	MONDAY	TUESDAY	WEDNESDAY	THURSDAY	FRIDAY
1	Job 1	Job 2	Job 3	Job 4-5	Job 6-7
	SOAP Job 1:21-22	SOAP Job 2:10	SOAP Job 3:25-26	SOAP Job 5:8-9	SOAP Job 6:34-35
2	Job 8-9	Job 10	Job 11-12	Job 13	Job 14
	SOAP Job 9:1-3	SOAP Job 10:8-9	SOAP Job 11:13-14	SOAP Job 13:21-24	SOAP Job 14:16-19
3	Job 15-17	Job 18	Job 19	Job 20	Job 21
	SOAP Job 17:1-3	SOAP Job 18:5-7	SOAP Job 19:15	SOAP Job 20:27-29	SOAP Job 21:22
4	Job 22	Job 23-24	Job 25-26	Job 27	Job 28
	SOAP Job 22:26-28	SOAP Job 23:8-10	SOAP Job 25:2-3	SOAP Job 27:2-4	SOAP Job 28:20-21
5	Job 29	Job 30	Job 31	Job 32-33	Job 34-35
	SOAP Job 29:2-3	SOAP Job 20:16-17	SOAP Job 31:15-16	SOAP Job 33:27-28	SOAP Job 34:29-30
6	Job 36-37	Job 38-39	Job 40	Job 41	Job 42
	SOAP Job 36:5-6	SOAP Job 38:4-5	SOAP Job 40:1-4	SOAP Job 41:1-2	SOAP Job 42:2-3

I. THE PROLOGUE (1:1—2:13)

JOB'S GOOD LIFE

1 There was a man in the land of Uz whose name was Job. And
that man was blameless and upright, one who feared God and
turned away from evil. 2 Seven sons and three daughters were
born to him. 3 His possessions included 7,000 sheep, 3,000 camels, 500 yoke of oxen, and 500 female donkeys; in addition he
had a very great household. Thus he was the greatest of all the
people in the east.

4 Now his sons used to go and hold a feast in the house of each
one in turn, and they would send and invite their three sisters
to eat and to drink with them. 5 When the days of their feasting
were finished, Job would send for them and sanctify them; he
would get up early in the morning and offer burnt offerings according to the number of them all. For Job thought, "Perhaps
my children have sinned and cursed God in their hearts." This
was Job's customary practice.

SATAN'S ACCUSATION OF JOB

6 Now the day came when the sons of God came to present themselves before the LORD—and Satan also arrived among them.
7 The LORD said to Satan, "Where have you come from?" And Satan answered the LORD, "From roving about on the earth, and
from walking back and forth across it." 8 So the LORD said to Satan, "Have you considered my servant Job? There is no one like
him on the earth, a blameless and upright man, one who fears
God and turns away from evil."

9 Then Satan answered the LORD, "Is it for nothing that Job
fears God? 10 Have you not made a hedge around him and his
household and all that he has on every side? You have blessed
the work of his hands, and his livestock have increased in the
land. 11 But extend your hand and strike everything he has, and
he will no doubt curse you to your face!"

12 So the LORD said to Satan, "All right then, everything he has
is in your power. Only do not extend your hand against the man
himself!" So Satan went out from the presence of the LORD.

JOB'S INTEGRITY IN ADVERSITY

13 Now the day came when Job's sons and daughters were eating and drinking wine in their oldest brother's house, 14 and
a messenger came to Job, saying, "The oxen were plowing and
the donkeys were grazing beside them, 15 and the Sabeans
swooped down and carried them all away, and they killed the
servants with the sword! And I—only I alone—escaped to tell
you!"

16 While this one was still speaking, another messenger arrived and said, "The fire of God has fallen from heaven and has
burned up the sheep and the servants—it has consumed them!
And I—only I alone—escaped to tell you!"

17 While this one was still speaking another messenger arrived and said, "The Chaldeans formed three bands and made
a raid on the camels and carried them all away, and they killed
the servants with the sword! And I—only I alone—escaped to
tell you!"

LOVE TO GROW

MY SERVANT

JOB 1:8

I don't know about you, but Job has always been a confusing book for me. What's the point of this story? Why would God let a righteous man suffer like this? Does God ever explain to Job that he didn't do anything wrong?

Thankfully, we get an anchoring detail at the beginning of the story. In Job 1:8, God told Satan, "There is no one like [Job] on earth, a blameless and upright man, one who fears God and turns away from evil." Through the twists and turns of Job's suffering, his friends' bad advice, and his cries to God, we can remind ourselves of this crucial detail over and over—God said Job was a righteous man.

This is certainly the truth Job held tightly to as he suffered. He knew that he loved and followed God, and he remained unwavering in this belief no matter what his wife said, what his friends said, or how he suffered. He cried out in anguish and confusion, but he never conceded that he deserved the suffering he faced. Instead, he held tight to the one thing he did know—he loved God and followed Him.

Sometimes, life can hand us a similar tidal wave of suffering and confusion. It can be difficult to make sense of life's struggles, causing us to question things we have always believed.

We see in Job's example that staying rooted in our relationship with God gives us grounding wisdom.

Job had the spiritual strength to dismiss the bad advice of his wife and friends. He stayed steadfast in his assertion that he was blameless before God. We know (from v. 8) that he was right. He is the only one in the entire book who agreed with God.

No matter how confusing life can get, God wants us to stay grounded in the truth of what He said about us—that He loves us and cares for us. If we love Him and shun evil, we will have strong minds and hearts to endure confusing and painful struggles, even when those around us cannot offer comfort. We see in Job what results for a righteous person who knows she is loved: the strength to endure. May we grow in God's love and wisdom in the same way.

18 While this one was still speaking another messenger arrived
and said, "Your sons and your daughters were eating and drinking wine in their oldest brother's house, 19 and suddenly a great
wind swept across the wilderness and struck the four corners
of the house, and it fell on the young people, and they died! And
I—only I alone—escaped to tell you!"
20 Then Job got up and tore his robe. He shaved his head, and
then he threw himself down with his face to the ground. 21 He
said, "Naked I came from my mother's womb, and naked I will
return there. The LORD gives, and the LORD takes away. May the
name of the LORD be blessed!" 22 In all this Job did not sin, nor
did he charge God with moral impropriety.

REFLECT
How was Job's perspective consistent with his faith? How did this give him comfort in the midst of all he had lost?

SATAN'S ADDITIONAL CHARGE

2 Again the day came when the sons of God came to present
themselves before the LORD, and Satan also arrived among
them to present himself before the LORD. 2 And the LORD said to
Satan, "Where have you come from?" Satan answered the LORD,
"From roving about on the earth, and from walking back and
forth across it." 3 Then the LORD said to Satan, "Have you considered my servant Job? For there is no one like him on the earth, a
pure and upright man, one who fears God and turns away from
evil. And he still holds firmly to his integrity, so that you stirred
me up to destroy him without reason."
4 But Satan answered the LORD, "Skin for skin! Indeed, a man
will give up all that he has to save his life. 5 But extend your hand
and strike his bone and his flesh, and he will no doubt curse you
to your face!"
6 So the LORD said to Satan, "All right, he is in your power; only
preserve his life."

JOB'S INTEGRITY IN SUFFERING

7 So Satan went out from the presence of the LORD, and he afflicted Job with a malignant ulcer from the soles of his feet to
the top of his head. 8 Job took a shard of broken pottery to scrape
himself with while he was sitting among the ashes.
9 Then his wife said to him, "Are you still holding firmly to your
integrity? Curse God, and die!" 10 But he replied, "You're talking
like one of the godless women would do! Should we receive what
is good from God, and not also receive what is evil?" In all this
Job did not sin by what he said.

THE VISIT OF JOB'S FRIENDS

11 When Job's three friends heard about all this calamity that had
happened to him, each of them came from his own country—Eliphaz the Temanite, Bildad the Shuhite, and Zophar the Naamathite. They met together to come to show sympathy for him and
to console him. 12 But when they gazed intently from a distance
but did not recognize him, they began to weep loudly. Each of
them tore his robes, and they threw dust into the air over their
heads. 13 Then they sat down with him on the ground for seven
days and seven nights, yet no one spoke a word to him, for they
saw that his pain was very great.

II. JOB'S DIALOGUE WITH HIS FRIENDS (3:1–27:23)

JOB REGRETS HIS BIRTH

3 After this Job opened his mouth and cursed the day he was
born. 2 Job spoke up and said:

3 "Let the day on which I was born perish,
and the night that said,
'A man has been conceived!'
4 That day—let it be darkness;
let not God on high regard it,
nor let light shine on it!
5 Let darkness and the deepest
shadow claim it;
let a cloud settle on it;
let whatever blackens the day terrify it.
6 That night—let darkness seize it;
let it not be included among
the days of the year;
let it not enter among the
number of the months!
7 Indeed, let that night be barren;
let no shout of joy penetrate it!
8 Let those who curse the day curse it—
those who are prepared to rouse Leviathan.
9 Let its morning stars be darkened;
let it wait for daylight but find none,
nor let it see the first rays of dawn,
10 because it did not shut the doors of
my mother's womb on me,
nor did it hide trouble from my eyes.

JOB WISHES HE HAD DIED AT BIRTH

11 "Why did I not die at birth,
and why did I not expire
as I came out of the womb?
12 Why did the knees welcome me,
and why were there two breasts
that I might nurse at them?
13 For now I would be lying down
and would be quiet,
I would be asleep and then at peace
14 with kings and counselors of the earth
who built for themselves places now desolate,
15 or with princes who possessed gold,
who filled their palaces with silver.
16 Or why was I not buried
like a stillborn infant,
like infants who have never seen the light?
17 There the wicked cease from turmoil,
and there the weary are at rest.
18 There the prisoners relax together;
they do not hear the voice of the oppressor.
19 Small and great are there,
and the slave is free from his master.

LONGING FOR DEATH

20 "Why does God give light to one who is in misery,
and life to those whose soul is bitter,
21 to those who wait for death that does not come,
and search for it
more than for hidden treasures,
22 who rejoice even to jubilation,
and are exultant when they find the grave?
23 Why is light given to a man
whose way is hidden,
and whom God has hedged in?
24 For my sighing comes in place of my food,
and my groanings flow forth like water.
25 For the very thing I dreaded has happened to me,
and what I feared has come upon me.
26 I have no ease, I have no quietness;
I cannot rest; turmoil has come upon me."

ELIPHAZ BEGINS TO SPEAK

4 Then Eliphaz the Temanite answered:
2 "If someone should attempt a word with you,
will you be impatient?
But who can refrain from speaking?
3 Look, you have instructed many;
you have strengthened feeble hands.
4 Your words have supported those
who stumbled,
and you have strengthened the knees
that gave way.
5 But now the same thing comes to you,
and you are discouraged;
it strikes you,
and you are terrified.
6 Is not your piety your confidence,
and your blameless ways your hope?
7 Call to mind now:
Who, being innocent, ever perished?
And where were upright people ever destroyed?
8 Even as I have seen, those who plow iniquity
and those who sow trouble reap the same.
9 By the breath of God they perish,
and by the blast of his anger they are consumed.
10 There is the roaring of the lion
and the growling of the young lion,
but the teeth of the young lions are broken.
11 The mighty lion perishes for lack of prey,
and the cubs of the lioness are scattered.

UNGODLY COMPLAINERS PROVOKE GOD'S WRATH

12 "Now a word was stealthily brought to me,
and my ear caught a whisper of it.
13 In the troubling thoughts of
the dreams in the night
when a deep sleep falls on men,

14 dread gripped me and trembling,
which made all my bones shake.
15 Then a breath of air passes by my face;
it makes the hair of my flesh stand up.
16 It stands still,
but I cannot recognize its appearance;
an image is before my eyes,
and I hear a murmuring voice:
17 'Is a mortal man righteous before God?
Or a man pure before his Creator?
18 If God puts no trust in his servants
and attributes folly to his angels,
19 how much more to those who live in houses of clay,
whose foundation is in the dust,
who are crushed like a moth?
20 They are destroyed between morning and evening;
they perish forever without anyone regarding it.
21 Is not their excess wealth taken away from them?
They die, yet without attaining wisdom.'

5 "Call now! Is there anyone who will answer you?
To which of the holy ones will you turn?
2 For wrath kills the foolish person,
and anger slays the silly one.
3 I myself have seen the fool taking root,
but suddenly I cursed his place of residence.
4 His children are far from safety,
and they are crushed at the place
where judgment is rendered,
nor is there anyone to deliver them.
5 The hungry eat up his harvest,
and take it even from behind the thorns,
and the thirsty pant for their wealth.
6 For evil does not come up from the dust,
nor does trouble spring up from the ground,
7 but people are born to trouble,
as surely as the sparks fly upward.

BLESSINGS FOR THE ONE WHO SEEKS GOD

8 "But as for me, I would seek God,
and to God I would set forth my case.
9 He does great and unsearchable things,
marvelous things without number;
10 he gives rain on the earth,
and sends water on the fields;
11 he sets the lowly on high,
that those who mourn are raised to safety.
12 He frustrates the plans of the crafty
so that their hands cannot accomplish
what they had planned.
13 He catches the wise in their own craftiness,
and the counsel of the cunning is brought to a quick end.
14 They meet with darkness in the daytime,
and grope about in the noontime as if it were night.

15 So he saves from the sword that comes
from their mouth,
even the poor from the hand of the powerful.
16 Thus the poor have hope,
and iniquity shuts its mouth.

17 "Therefore, blessed is the man whom God corrects,
so do not despise the discipline of the Almighty.
18 For he wounds, but he also bandages;
he strikes, but his hands also heal.
19 He will deliver you from six calamities;
yes, in seven no evil will touch you.
20 In time of famine he will redeem you from death,
and in time of war from the power of the sword.
21 You will be protected from malicious gossip,
and will not be afraid of the destruction when it comes.
22 You will laugh at destruction and famine
and need not be afraid of the beasts of the earth.
23 For you will have a pact with the stones of the field,
and the wild animals will be at peace with you.
24 And you will know that your home will be secure,
and when you inspect your domains,
you will not be missing anything.
25 You will also know that your children will be numerous,
and your descendants like the grass of the earth.
26 You will come to your grave in a full age,
As stacks of grain are harvested in their season.
27 Look, we have investigated this, so it is true.
Hear it, and apply it for your own good."

JOB REPLIES TO ELIPHAZ

6 Then Job responded:
2 "Oh, if only my grief could be weighed,
and my misfortune laid on the scales too!
3 But because it is heavier than the sand of the sea,
that is why my words have been wild.
4 For the arrows of the Almighty are within me;
my spirit drinks their poison;
God's sudden terrors are arrayed against me.

COMPLAINTS REFLECT SUFFERING

5 "Does the wild donkey bray when it is near grass?
Or does the ox bellow over its fodder?
6 Can food that is tasteless be eaten without salt?
Or is there any taste in the white of an egg?
7 I have refused to touch such things;
they are like loathsome food to me.

A CRY FOR DEATH

8 "Oh that my request would be realized,
and that God would grant me what I long for!
9 And that God would be willing to crush me,
that he would let loose his hand
and kill me.

10 Then I would yet have my comfort,
then I would rejoice,
in spite of pitiless pain,
for I have not concealed the words of the Holy One.
11 What is my strength, that I should wait?
And what is my end,
that I should prolong my life?
12 Is my strength like that of stones?
Or is my flesh made of bronze?
13 Is not my power to help myself nothing,
and has not every resource
been driven from me?

DISAPPOINTING FRIENDS

14 "To the one in despair, kindness should
come from his friend
even if he forsakes the fear of the Almighty.
15 My brothers have been as treacherous
as a seasonal stream,
and as the riverbeds of the intermittent streams
that flow away.
16 They are dark because of ice;
snow is piled up over them.
17 When they are scorched, they dry up,
when it is hot, they vanish from their place.
18 Caravans turn aside from their routes;
they go into the wasteland and perish.
19 The caravans of Tema looked intently
for these streams;
the traveling merchants of Sheba hoped for them.
20 They were distressed,
because each one had been so confident;
they arrived there, but were disappointed.
21 For now you have become like these
streams that are no help;
you see a terror, and are afraid.

FRIENDS' FEARS

22 "Have I ever said, 'Give me something,
and from your fortune make
gifts in my favor'?
23 Or, 'Deliver me from the enemy's power,
and from the hand of tyrants ransom me'?

NO SIN DISCOVERED

24 "Teach me and I, for my part, will be silent;
explain to me how I have been mistaken.
25 How painful are honest words!
But what does your reproof prove?
26 Do you intend to criticize mere words,
and treat the words of a
despairing man as wind?
27 Yes, you would gamble for the fatherless,
and auction off your friend.

OTHER EXPLANATION

28 "Now then, be good enough to look at me;
and I will not lie to your face!
29 Relent, let there be no falsehood;
reconsider, for my righteousness is intact!
30 Is there any falsehood on my lips?
Can my mouth not discern evil things?

THE BREVITY OF LIFE

7 "Does not humanity have hard service on earth?
Are not their days also like the days
of a hired man?
2 Like a servant longing for the evening shadow,
and like a hired man looking for his wages,
3 thus I have been made to inherit
months of futility,
and nights of sorrow
have been appointed to me.
4 If I lie down, I say, 'When will I arise?'
And the night stretches on
and I toss and turn restlessly
until the day dawns.
5 My body is clothed with worms
and dirty scabs;
my skin is broken and festering.
6 My days are swifter than a weaver's shuttle
and they come to an end without hope.
7 Remember that my life is but a breath,
that my eyes will never again see happiness.
8 The eye of him who sees me now
will see me no more;
your eyes will look for me,
but I will be gone.
9 As a cloud is dispersed and then disappears,
so the one who goes down to the grave
does not come up again.
10 He returns no more to his house,
nor does his place of residence
know him anymore.

JOB REMONSTRATES WITH GOD

11 "Therefore, I will not refrain my mouth;
I will speak in the anguish of my spirit;
I will complain in the bitterness of my soul.
12 Am I the sea, or the creature of the deep,
that you must put me under guard?
13 If I say, 'My bed will comfort me,
my couch will ease my complaint,'
14 then you scare me with dreams
and terrify me with visions,
15 so that I would prefer strangling,
and death more than life.
16 I loathe it; I do not want to live forever;
leave me alone, for my days are a vapor!

INSIGNIFICANCE OF HUMANS

17 "What is mankind that you make so much of them,
and that you pay attention to them?
18 And that you visit them every morning,
and try them every moment?
19 Will you never look away from me,
will you not let me alone
long enough to swallow my spittle?
20 If I have sinned—what have I done to you,
O watcher of men?
Why have you set me as your target?
Have I become a burden to you?
21 And why do you not pardon my transgression,
and take away my iniquity?
For now I will lie down in the dust,
and you will seek me diligently,
but I will be gone."

BILDAD'S FIRST SPEECH TO JOB

8 Then Bildad the Shuhite spoke up and said:
2 "How long will you speak these things,
seeing that the words of your mouth
are like a great wind?
3 Does God pervert justice?
Or does the Almighty pervert what is right?
4 If your children sinned against him,
he gave them over to the penalty of their sin.
5 But if you will look to God,
and make your supplication to the Almighty,
6 if you become pure and upright,
even now he will rouse himself for you,
and will restore your righteous home.
7 Your beginning will seem so small,
since your future will flourish.

8 "For inquire now of the former generation,
and pay attention to the findings
of their ancestors;
9 For we were born yesterday and do not have knowledge,
since our days on earth are but a shadow.
10 Will they not instruct you and speak to you,
and bring forth words
from their understanding?
11 Can the papyrus plant grow tall
where there is no marsh?
Can reeds flourish without water?
12 While they are still beginning to flower
and not ripe for cutting,
they can wither away
faster than any grass.
13 Such is the destiny of all who forget God;
the hope of the godless perishes,
14 whose trust is in something futile,
whose security is a spider's web.

LOVE TO GROW

NO SMOKE WITHOUT FIRE

JOB 8

Have you ever avoided helping a friend who was suffering because you didn't know what to do or say? I know I have. In those situations it is easy to find ourselves avoiding the topic, possibly causing more pain with our silence.

After reading the interactions between Job and his friends, we might think we have a good reason for this approach. Rather than giving up too soon, we would do well to learn from their stories and glean some principles for how to mourn with those who mourn.

Job's suffering threatened to unravel Bildad's understanding of God. His counsel revealed his belief that the righteous would prosper and the wicked would suffer. He believed there must have been sin in Job's life causing his suffering. There is no smoke without fire.

If Job's suffering wasn't a result of his sin, what does this mean for Bildad? What does this mean for us? We want to be able to guarantee God's blessing in our lives if we do good things. As Job's story proves, there is often more to our situations than meets the eye.

It's easier to squeeze the reasons for God's interactions with us into our preconceived molds instead of broadening our understanding of His infinite character.

God's ways are not always black and white, but rather reflect His multifaceted wisdom. To admit that Job might have suffered even though he was a righteous man gives us a glimpse into the fact there is more to our God and His purposes than we often allow.

We may prefer to face someone who is hurting only if we have an answer to their pain. Having all the answers means we can offer a quick fix and get back to what's comfortable. We have to fight the instinct to give an answer that will make it all make sense. Instead, let's do the hard work of climbing down into the pit with a suffering friend and mourning with them. God will meet both of us there and work out the rest for His glory.

We rarely know the full story or have all the answers. Knowing God is in control, that He is good and just and gracious, is sometimes all we can cling to during times of suffering. The joy that comes through suffering is not because of a change in circumstances, but in the experience of knowing God more intimately through it.

15 He leans against his house but it does not hold up,
he takes hold of it but it does not stand.
16 He is a well-watered plant in the sun,
its shoots spread over its garden.
17 It wraps its roots around a heap of stones
and it looks for a place among stones.

18 If he is uprooted from his place,
then that place will disown him, saying,
'I have never seen you!'
19 Indeed, this is the joy of his way,
and out of the earth others spring up.

20 "Surely, God does not reject a blameless man,
nor does he grasp the hand
of the evildoers.
21 He will yet fill your mouth with laughter,
and your lips with gladness.
22 Those who hate you will be clothed with shame,
and the tent of the wicked will be no more."

JOB'S REPLY TO BILDAD

9 Then Job answered:
2 "Truly, I know that this is so.
But how can a human be just before God?
3 If someone wishes to contend with him,
he cannot answer him one time in a thousand.
4 He is wise in heart and mighty in strength—
who has resisted him and remained safe?
5 He who removes mountains suddenly,
who overturns them in his anger,
6 he who shakes the earth out of its place
so that its pillars tremble,
7 he who commands the sun, and it does not shine
and seals up the stars,
8 he alone spreads out the heavens,
and treads on the waves of the sea.
9 He makes the Bear, Orion, and the Pleiades,
and the constellations of the southern sky;
10 he does great and unsearchable things,
and wonderful things without number.
11 If he passes by me, I cannot see him,
if he goes by, I cannot perceive him.
12 If he snatches away, who can turn him back?
Who dares to say to him, 'What are you doing?'
13 God does not restrain his anger;
under him the helpers of Rahab lie crushed.

THE IMPOSSIBILITY OF FACING GOD IN COURT

14 "How much less, then, can I answer him
and choose my words to argue with him.
15 Although I am innocent,
I could not answer him;
I could only plead with my judge for mercy.

16 If I summoned him, and he answered me,
I would not believe
that he would be listening to my voice—
17 he who crushes me with a tempest,
and multiplies my wounds for no reason.
18 He does not allow me to recover my breath,
for he fills me with bitterness.
19 If it is a matter of strength,
most certainly he is the strong one!
And if it is a matter of justice,
he will say, 'Who will summon me?'
20 Although I am innocent,
my mouth would condemn me,
although I am blameless,
it would declare me perverse.
21 I am blameless. I do not know myself.
I despise my life.

ACCUSATION OF GOD'S JUSTICE

22 "It is all one! That is why I say,
'He destroys the blameless and the guilty.'
23 If a scourge brings sudden death,
he mocks at the despair of the innocent.
24 If a land has been given
into the hand of a wicked man,
he covers the faces of its judges;
if it is not he, then who is it?

RENEWED COMPLAINT

25 "My days are swifter than a runner,
they speed by without seeing happiness.
26 They glide by like reed boats,
like an eagle that swoops down on its prey.
27 If I say, 'I will forget my complaint,
I will change my expression and be cheerful,'
28 I dread all my sufferings,
for I know that you do not hold me blameless.
29 If I am guilty,
why then weary myself in vain?
30 If I wash myself with snow-melt water,
and make my hands clean with lye,
31 then you plunge me into a slimy pit
and my own clothes abhor me.
32 For he is not a human being like I am,
that I might answer him,
that we might come together
in judgment.
33 Nor is there an arbiter between us,
who might lay his hand on us both,
34 who would take his rod away from me
so that his terror would not
make me afraid.
35 Then would I speak and not fear him,
but it is not so with me.

AN APPEAL FOR REVELATION

10 "I am weary of my life;
I will complain freely without restraint;
I will speak in the bitterness of my soul.
2 I will say to God, 'Do not condemn me;
tell me why you are contending with me.'
3 Is it good for you to oppress,
to despise the work of your hands,
while you smile
on the schemes of the wicked?

MOTIVATIONS OF GOD

4 "Do you have eyes of flesh,
or do you see as a human being sees?
5 Are your days like the days of a mortal,
or your years like the years of a mortal,
6 that you must search out my iniquity,
and inquire about my sin,
7 although you know that I am not guilty,
and that there is no one who can deliver
out of your hand?

CONTRADICTIONS IN GOD'S DEALINGS

8 "Your hands have shaped me and made me,
but now you destroy me completely.
9 Remember that you have made me
as with the clay;
will you return me to dust?
10 Did you not pour me out like milk,
and curdle me like cheese?
11 You clothed me with skin and flesh
and knit me together with bones and sinews.
12 You gave me life and favor,
and your intervention watched over my spirit.

13 "But these things you have concealed in your heart;
I know that this is with you:
14 If I sinned, then you would watch me
and you would not acquit me of my iniquity.
15 If I am guilty, woe to me,
and if I am innocent, I cannot lift my head;
I am full of shame,
and satiated with my affliction.
16 If I lift myself up,
you hunt me as a fierce lion,
and again you display your power against me.
17 You bring new witnesses against me,
and increase your anger against me;
relief troops come against me.

AN APPEAL FOR RELIEF

18 "Why then did you bring me out from the womb?
I should have died
and no eye would have seen me!

19 I should have been as though I had never existed;
I should have been carried
right from the womb to the grave!
20 Are not my days few?
Cease, then, and leave me alone
that I may find a little comfort,
21 before I depart, never to return,
to the land of darkness
and the deepest shadow,
22 to the land of utter darkness,
like the deepest darkness,
and the deepest shadow and disorder,
where even the light is like darkness."

ZOPHAR'S FIRST SPEECH TO JOB

11 Then Zophar the Naamathite spoke up and said:
2 "Should not this abundance of words be answered,
or should this talkative man
be vindicated?
3 Should people remain silent at your idle talk,
and should no one rebuke you when you mock?
4 For you have said, 'My teaching is flawless,
and I am pure in your sight.'
5 But if only God would speak,
if only he would open his lips against you,
6 and reveal to you the secrets of wisdom—
for true wisdom has two sides—
so that you would know
that God has forgiven some of your sins.

7 "Can you discover the essence of God?
Can you find out the perfection
of the Almighty?
8 It is higher than the heavens—what can you do?
It is deeper than Sheol—what can you know?
9 Its measure is longer than the earth,
and broader than the sea.
10 If he comes by and confines you
and convenes a court,
then who can prevent him?
11 For he knows deceitful men;
when he sees evil, will he not consider it?
12 But an empty man will become wise,
when a wild donkey's colt is born
a human being.

13 "As for you, if you prove faithful,
and if you stretch out your hands toward him,
14 if iniquity is in your hand—put it far away,
and do not let evil reside in your tents.
15 For then you will lift up your face
without blemish;
you will be securely established
and will not fear.

16 For you will forget your trouble;
you will remember it
like water that has flowed away.
17 And life will be brighter than the noonday;
though there be darkness,
it will be like the morning.
18 And you will be secure, because there is hope;
you will be protected
and will take your rest in safety.
19 You will lie down with no one
to make you afraid,
and many will seek your favor.
20 But the eyes of the wicked fail,
and escape eludes them;
their one hope is to breathe their last."

JOB'S REPLY TO ZOPHAR

12 Then Job answered:
2 "Without a doubt you are the people,
and wisdom will die with you.
3 I also have understanding as well as you;
I am not inferior to you.
Who does not know such things as these?
4 I am a laughingstock to my friends,
I, who called on God and whom he answered—
a righteous and blameless man
is a laughingstock!
5 For calamity, there is derision
(according to the ideas of the fortunate)—
a fate for those whose feet slip.
6 But the tents of robbers are peaceful,
and those who provoke God are confident—
who carry their god in their hands.

KNOWLEDGE OF GOD'S WISDOM

7 "But now, ask the animals
and they will teach you,
or the birds of the sky and they will tell you.
8 Or speak to the earth and it will teach you,
or let the fish of the sea declare to you.
9 Which of all these does not know
that the hand of the LORD has done this?
10 In his hand is the life of every creature
and the breath of all the human race.
11 Does not the ear test words,
as the tongue tastes food?
12 Is not wisdom found among the aged?
Does not long life bring understanding?
13 "With God are wisdom and power;
counsel and understanding are his.
14 If he tears down, it cannot be rebuilt;
if he imprisons a person, there is no escape.
15 If he holds back the waters, then they dry up;
if he releases them, they destroy the land.

16 With him are strength and prudence;
both the one who goes astray
and the one who misleads are his.
17 He leads counselors away stripped
and makes judges into fools.
18 He loosens the bonds of kings
and binds a loincloth around their waist.
19 He leads priests away stripped
and overthrows the potentates.
20 He deprives the trusted advisers of speech
and takes away the discernment of elders.
21 He pours contempt on noblemen
and disarms the powerful.
22 He reveals the deep things of darkness,
and brings deep shadows into the light.
23 He makes nations great,
and destroys them;
he extends the boundaries of nations
and disperses them.
24 He deprives the leaders of the earth
of their understanding;
he makes them wander
in a trackless desert waste.
25 They grope about in darkness
without light;
he makes them stagger like drunkards.

JOB PLEADS HIS CAUSE TO GOD

13 "Indeed, my eyes have seen all this,
my ears have heard and understood it.
2 What you know, I know also;
I am not inferior to you!
3 But I wish to speak to the Almighty,
and I desire to argue my case with God.
4 But you, however, are inventors of lies;
all of you are worthless physicians!
5 If only you would keep completely silent!
For you, that would be wisdom.
6 "Listen now to my argument,
and be attentive to my lips' contentions.
7 Will you speak wickedly on God's behalf?
Will you speak deceitfully for him?
8 Will you show him partiality?
Will you argue the case for God?
9 Would it turn out well if he would
examine you?
Or as one deceives a man would
you deceive him?
10 He would certainly rebuke you
if you secretly showed partiality.
11 Would not his splendor terrify you
and the fear he inspires fall on you?
12 Your maxims are proverbs of ashes;
your defenses are defenses of clay.

CHALLENGE

How does Job's speech in chapter 12 align with God's questions of Job in chapters 38 and 39? Do Job's words reflect the faith he has in the sovereignty of God?

13 "Refrain from talking with me
so that I may speak;
then let come to me what may.
14 Why do I put myself in peril,
and take my life in my hands?
15 Even if he slays me, I will hope in him;
I will surely defend my ways to his face.
16 Moreover, this will become my deliverance,
for no godless person would come before him.
17 Listen carefully to my words;
let your ears be attentive to my explanation.
18 See now, I have prepared my case;
I know that I am right.
19 Who will contend with me?
If anyone can, I will be silent and die.
20 Only in two things spare me, O God,
and then I will not hide from your face:
21 Remove your hand far from me
and stop making me afraid with your terror.
22 Then call, and I will answer,
or I will speak, and you respond to me.
23 How many are my iniquities and sins?
Show me my transgression and my sin.
24 Why do you hide your face
and regard me as your enemy?
25 Do you wish to torment a windblown leaf
and chase after dry chaff?
26 For you write down bitter things against me
and cause me to inherit the sins of my youth.
27 And you put my feet in the stocks
and you watch all my movements;
you put marks on the soles of my feet.
28 So I waste away like something rotten,
like a garment eaten by moths.

THE BREVITY OF LIFE

14 "Man, born of woman,
lives but a few days, and they are full of trouble.
2 He grows up like a flower and then withers away;
he flees like a shadow, and does not remain.
3 Do you fix your eye on such a one?
And do you bring me before you for judgment?
4 Who can make a clean thing come from an unclean?
No one!
5 Since man's days are determined,
the number of his months is under your control;
you have set his limit and he cannot pass it.
6 Look away from him and let him desist,
until he fulfills his time like a hired man.

THE INEVITABILITY OF DEATH

7 "But there is hope for a tree:
If it is cut down, it will sprout again,
and its new shoots will not fail.

8 Although its roots may grow old in the ground
and its stump begins to die in the soil,
9 at the scent of water it will flourish
and put forth shoots like a new plant.
10 But man dies and is powerless;
he expires—and where is he?
11 As water disappears from the sea,
or a river drains away and dries up,
12 so man lies down and does not rise;
until the heavens are no more,
they will not awake
nor arise from their sleep.

THE POSSIBILITY OF ANOTHER LIFE

13 "O that you would hide me in Sheol,
and conceal me till your anger has passed!
O that you would set me a time
and then remember me!
14 If a man dies, will he live again?
All the days of my hard service I will wait
until my release comes.
15 You will call and I—I will answer you;
you will long for the creature you have made.

THE PRESENT CONDITION

16 "Surely now you count my steps;
then you would not mark my sin.
17 My offenses would be sealed up in a bag;
you would cover over my sin.
18 But as a mountain falls away and crumbles,
and as a rock will be removed from its place,
19 as water wears away stones,
and torrents wash away the soil,
so you destroy man's hope.
20 You overpower him once for all,
and he departs;
you change his appearance
and send him away.
21 If his sons are honored,
he does not know it;
if they are brought low,
he does not see it.
22 His flesh only has pain for him,
and he mourns for himself."

ELIPHAZ'S SECOND SPEECH

15 Then Eliphaz the Temanite answered:
2 "Does a wise man answer with
blustery knowledge,
or fill his belly with the east wind?
3 Does he argue with useless talk,
with words that have no value in them?
4 But you even break off piety,
and hinder meditation before God.

5 Your sin inspires your mouth;
you choose the language of the crafty.
6 Your own mouth condemns you, not I;
your own lips testify against you.

7 "Were you the first man ever born?
Were you brought forth before the hills?
8 Do you listen in on God's secret council?
Do you limit wisdom to yourself?
9 What do you know that we don't know?
What do you understand that we don't understand?
10 The gray-haired and the aged are on our side,
men far older than your father.
11 Are God's consolations too trivial for you,
or a word spoken in gentleness to you?
12 Why has your heart carried you away,
and why do your eyes flash,
13 when you turn your rage against God
and allow such words to escape from your mouth?
14 What is man that he should be pure,
or one born of woman, that he should be righteous?
15 If God places no trust in his holy ones,
if even the heavens are not pure in his eyes,
16 how much less man, who is abominable and corrupt,
who drinks in evil like water!
17 "I will explain to you;
listen to me,
and what I have seen, I will declare,
18 what wise men declare,
hiding nothing,
from the tradition of their ancestors,
19 to whom alone the land was given
when no foreigner passed among them.
20 All his days the wicked man suffers torment,
throughout the number of the years
that are stored up for the tyrant.
21 Terrifying sounds fill his ears;
in a time of peace marauders attack him.
22 He does not expect to escape from darkness;
he is marked for the sword;
23 he wanders about—food for vultures—
he knows that the day of darkness is at hand.
24 Distress and anguish terrify him;
they prevail against him
like a king ready to launch an attack,
25 for he stretches out his hand against God,
and vaunts himself against the Almighty,
26 defiantly charging against him
with a thick, strong shield!
27 Because he covered his face with fat,
and made his hips bulge with fat,
28 he lived in ruined towns
and in houses where no one lives,
where they are ready to crumble into heaps.

29 He will not grow rich,
and his wealth will not endure,
nor will his possessions spread over the land.
30 He will not escape the darkness;
a flame will wither his shoots
and he will depart
by the breath of God's mouth.
31 Let him not trust in what is worthless,
deceiving himself;
for worthlessness will be his reward.
32 Before his time he will be paid in full,
and his branches will not flourish.
33 Like a vine he will let his sour grapes fall,
and like an olive tree
he will shed his blossoms.
34 For the company of the godless is barren,
and fire consumes the tents of those
who accept bribes.
35 They conceive trouble and bring forth evil;
their belly prepares deception."

JOB'S REPLY TO ELIPHAZ

16 Then Job replied:
2 "I have heard many things like these before.
What miserable comforters are you all!
3 Will there be an end to your windy words?
Or what provokes you that you answer?
4 I also could speak like you,
if you were in my place;
I could pile up words against you
and I could shake my head at you.
5 But I would strengthen you with my words;
comfort from my lips would bring you relief.

ABANDONMENT BY GOD AND MAN

6 "But if I speak, my pain is not relieved,
and if I refrain from speaking,
how much of it goes away?
7 Surely now he has worn me out,
you have devastated my entire household.
8 You have seized me,
and it has become a witness;
my leanness has risen up against me
and testifies against me.
9 His anger has torn me and persecuted me;
he has gnashed at me with his teeth;
my adversary locks his eyes on me.
10 People have opened their mouths against me,
they have struck my cheek in scorn;
they unite together against me.
11 God abandons me to evil men,
and throws me into the hands of wicked men.
12 I was in peace, and he has shattered me.
He has seized me by the neck and crushed me.

He has made me his target;
13 his archers surround me.
Without pity he pierces my kidneys
and pours out my gall on the ground.
14 He breaks through against me,
time and time again;
he rushes against me like a warrior.
15 I have sewed sackcloth on my skin,
and buried my horn in the dust;
16 my face is reddened because of weeping,
and on my eyelids there is a deep darkness,
17 although there is no violence in my hands
and my prayer is pure.

AN APPEAL TO GOD AS WITNESS

18 "O earth, do not cover my blood,
nor let there be a secret place for my cry.
19 Even now my witness is in heaven;
my advocate is on high.
20 My intercessor is my friend
as my eyes pour out tears to God;
21 and he contends with God on behalf of man
as a man pleads for his friend.
22 For the years that lie ahead are few,
and then I will go on the way of no return.

17 My spirit is broken,
my days have faded out,
the grave awaits me.
2 Surely mockery is with me;
my eyes must dwell on their hostility.
3 Set my pledge beside you.
Who else will put up security for me?
4 Because you have closed their minds
to understanding,
therefore you will not exalt them.
5 If a man denounces his friends for personal gain,
the eyes of his children will fail.
6 He has made me a byword to people,
I am the one in whose face they spit.
7 My eyes have grown dim with grief;
my whole frame is but a shadow.
8 Upright men are appalled at this;
the innocent man is troubled with the godless.
9 But the righteous man holds to his way,
and the one with clean hands grows stronger.

ANTICIPATION OF DEATH

10 "But turn, all of you, and come now!
I will not find a wise man among you.
11 My days have passed, my plans are shattered,
even the desires of my heart.
12 These men change night into day;
they say, 'The light is near
in the face of darkness.'

13 If I hope for the grave to be my home,
if I spread out my bed in darkness,
14 if I cry out to corruption, 'You are my father,'
and to the worm, 'My mother,' or 'My sister,'
15 where then is my hope?
And my hope, who sees it?
16 Will it go down to the barred gates of death?
Will we descend together into the dust?"

BILDAD'S SECOND SPEECH

18 Then Bildad the Shuhite answered:
2 "How long until you make an end of words?
You must consider, and then we can talk.
3 Why should we be regarded as beasts,
and considered stupid in your sight?
4 You who tear yourself to pieces in your anger,
will the earth be abandoned for your sake?
Or will a rock be moved from its place?

5 "Yes, the lamp of the wicked is extinguished;
his flame of fire does not shine.
6 The light in his tent grows dark;
his lamp above him is extinguished.
7 His vigorous steps are restricted,
and his own counsel throws him down.
8 For he has been thrown into a net by his feet
and he wanders into a mesh.
9 A trap seizes him by the heel;
a snare grips him.
10 A rope is hidden for him on the ground
and a trap for him lies on the path.
11 Terrors frighten him on all sides
and dog his every step.
12 Calamity is hungry for him,
and misfortune is ready at his side.
13 It eats away parts of his skin;
the most terrible death devours his limbs.
14 He is dragged from the security of his tent,
and marched off to the king of terrors.
15 Fire resides in his tent;
over his residence burning sulfur is scattered.
16 Below his roots dry up,
and his branches wither above.
17 His memory perishes from the earth,
he has no name in the land.
18 He is driven from light into darkness
and is banished from the world.
19 He has neither children nor descendants
among his people,
no survivor in those places he once stayed.
20 People of the west are appalled at his fate;
people of the east are seized with horror, saying,
21 'Surely such is the residence of an evil man;
and this is the place of one who has not known God.'"

JOB'S REPLY TO BILDAD

19 Then Job answered:
2 "How long will you torment me
and crush me with your words?
3 These ten times you have been reproaching me;
you are not ashamed to attack me.
4 But even if it were true that I have erred,
my error remains solely my concern!
5 If indeed you would exalt yourselves above me
and plead my disgrace against me,
6 know then that God has wronged me
and encircled me with his net.

REFLECT

Job's friends caused him great pain in their accusations of his sin. How can we learn from their actions about what not to do when supporting others in their grief?

JOB'S ABANDONMENT AND AFFLICTION

7 "If I cry out, 'Violence!'
I receive no answer;
I cry for help,
but there is no justice.
8 He has blocked my way so I cannot pass,
and has set darkness over my paths.
9 He has stripped me of my honor
and has taken the crown off my head.
10 He tears me down on every side until I perish;
he uproots my hope like an uprooted tree.
11 Thus his anger burns against me,
and he considers me among his enemies.
12 His troops advance together;
they throw up a siege ramp against me,
and they camp around my tent.

JOB'S FORSAKEN STATE

13 "He has put my relatives far from me;
my acquaintances only turn away from me.
14 My kinsmen have failed me;
my friends have forgotten me.
15 My guests and my servant girls
consider me a stranger;
I am a foreigner in their eyes.
16 I summon my servant, but he does not respond,
even though I implore him with my own mouth.
17 My breath is repulsive to my wife;
I am loathsome to my brothers.
18 Even youngsters have scorned me;
when I get up, they scoff at me.
19 All my closest friends detest me;
and those whom I love have turned against me.
20 My bones stick to my skin and my flesh;
I have escaped alive with only
the skin of my teeth.
21 Have pity on me, my friends,
have pity on me,
for the hand of God has struck me.
22 Why do you pursue me like God does?
Will you never be satiated with my flesh?

JOB'S ASSURANCE OF VINDICATION

23 "O that my words were written down!
O that they were written on a scroll!
24 O that with an iron chisel and with lead
they were engraved in a rock forever!
25 As for me, I know that my Redeemer lives,
and that as the last
he will stand upon the earth.
26 And after my skin has been destroyed,
yet in my flesh I will see God,
27 whom I will see for myself,
and whom my own eyes will behold,
and not another.
My heart grows faint within me.
28 If you say, 'How we will pursue him,
since the root of the trouble is found in him!'
29 Fear the sword yourselves,
for wrath brings the punishment by the sword,
so that you may know
that there is judgment."

ZOPHAR'S SECOND SPEECH

20 Then Zophar the Naamathite answered:
2 "This is why my troubled thoughts
bring me back—
because of my feelings within me.
3 When I hear a reproof that dishonors me,
then my understanding prompts me to answer.

4 "Surely you know that it has been from old,
ever since humankind was placed on the earth,
5 that the elation of the wicked is brief,
the joy of the godless lasts but a moment.
6 Even though his stature reaches to the heavens
and his head touches the clouds,
7 he will perish forever, like his own excrement;
those who used to see him will say, 'Where is he?'
8 Like a dream he flies away, never again to be found,
and like a vision of the night he is put to flight.
9 People who had seen him will not see him again,
and the place where he was
will recognize him no longer.
10 His sons must recompense the poor;
his own hands must return his wealth.
11 His bones were full of his youthful vigor,
but that vigor will lie down with him in the dust.

12 "If evil is sweet in his mouth
and he hides it under his tongue,
13 if he retains it for himself
and does not let it go,
and holds it fast in his mouth,
14 his food is turned sour in his stomach;
it becomes the venom of serpents within him.

15 The wealth that he consumed he vomits up,
God will make him throw it out of his stomach.
16 He sucks the poison of serpents;
the fangs of a viper kill him.
17 He will not look on the streams,
the rivers that are the torrents
of honey and butter.
18 He gives back the ill-gotten gain
without assimilating it;
he will not enjoy the wealth from his commerce.
19 For he has oppressed the poor and abandoned them;
he has seized a house which he did not build.
20 For he knows no satisfaction in his appetite;
he does not let anything he desires escape.
21 "Nothing is left for him to devour;
that is why his prosperity does not last.
22 In the fullness of his sufficiency,
distress overtakes him.
The full force of misery will come upon him.
23 "While he is filling his belly,
God sends his burning anger against him,
and rains down his blows upon him.
24 If he flees from an iron weapon,
then an arrow from a bronze bow pierces him.
25 When he pulls it out and it comes out of his back,
the gleaming point out of his liver,
terrors come over him.
26 Total darkness waits to receive his treasures;
a fire that has not been kindled
will consume him and devour what is left in his tent.
27 The heavens reveal his iniquity;
the earth rises up against him.
28 A flood will carry off his house,
rushing waters on the day of God's wrath.
29 Such is the lot God allots the wicked,
and the heritage of his appointment from God."

JOB'S REPLY TO ZOPHAR

21 Then Job answered:
2 "Listen carefully to my words;
let this be the consolation you offer me.
3 Bear with me and I will speak,
and after I have spoken you may mock.
4 Is my complaint against a man?
If so, why should I not be impatient?
5 Look at me and be appalled;
put your hands over your mouths.
6 For, when I think about this, I am terrified
and my body feels a shudder.

THE WICKED PROSPER

7 "Why do the wicked go on living,
grow old, even increase in power?
8 Their children are firmly established in their presence,

their offspring before their eyes.
9 Their houses are safe and without fear;
and no rod of punishment from God is upon them.
10 Their bulls breed without fail;
their cows calve and do not miscarry.
11 They allow their children to run like a flock;
their little ones dance about.
12 They sing to the accompaniment of tambourine and harp,
and make merry to the sound of the flute.
13 They live out their years in prosperity
and go down to the grave in peace.
14 So they say to God, 'Turn away from us!
We do not want to know your ways.
15 Who is the Almighty, that we should serve him?
What would we gain
if we were to pray to him?'
16 But their prosperity is not their own doing.
The counsel of the wicked is far from me!

HOW OFTEN DO THE WICKED SUFFER?

17 "How often is the lamp of the wicked extinguished?
How often does their misfortune come upon them?
How often does God apportion pain to them in his anger?
18 How often are they like straw before the wind,
and like chaff swept away by a whirlwind?
19 You may say, 'God stores up a man's
punishment for his children!'
Instead let him repay the man himself
so that he may be humbled!
20 Let his own eyes see his destruction;
let him drink of the anger of the Almighty.
21 For what is his interest in his home
after his death,
when the number of his months
has been broken off?
22 Can anyone teach God knowledge,
since he judges those that are on high?

DEATH LEVELS EVERYTHING

23 "One man dies in his full vigor,
completely secure and prosperous,
24 his body well nourished,
and the marrow of his bones moist.
25 And another man dies in bitterness of soul,
never having tasted anything good.
26 Together they lie down in the dust,
and worms cover over them both.

FUTILE WORDS, DECEPTIVE ANSWERS

27 "Yes, I know what you are thinking,
the schemes by which you would wrong me.
28 For you say,
'Where now is the nobleman's house,
and where are the tents in which the wicked lived?'

REFLECT

Where is God when the wicked prosper? Does He turn away from the needs of the righteous and allow the wicked to succeed? How is He just in His actions, even when the wicked seem to thrive in their wickedness?

29 Have you never questioned those who travel the roads?
Do you not recognize their accounts—
30 that the evil man is spared
from the day of his misfortune,
that he is delivered
from the day of God's wrath?
31 No one denounces his conduct to his face;
no one repays him for what he has done.
32 And when he is carried to the tombs,
and watch is kept over the funeral mound,
33 The clods of the torrent valley are sweet to him;
behind him everybody follows in procession,
and before him goes a countless throng.
34 So how can you console me with your futile words?
Nothing is left of your answers but deception!"

ELIPHAZ'S THIRD SPEECH

22 Then Eliphaz the Temanite answered:
2 "Is it to God that a strong man is of benefit?
Is it to him that even a wise man is profitable?
3 Is it of any special benefit to the Almighty
that you should be righteous,
or is it any gain to him
that you make your ways blameless?
4 Is it because of your piety that he rebukes you
and goes to judgment with you?
5 Is not your wickedness great
and is there no end to your iniquity?

6 "For you took pledges from your brothers
for no reason,
and you stripped the clothing from the naked.
7 You gave the weary no water to drink
and from the hungry you withheld food.
8 Although you were a powerful man,
owning land,
an honored man living on it,
9 you sent widows away empty-handed,
and the arms of the orphans you crushed.
10 That is why snares surround you,
and why sudden fear terrifies you,
11 why it is so dark you cannot see,
and why a flood of water covers you.

12 "Is not God on high in heaven?
And see the lofty stars, how high they are!
13 But you have said, 'What does God know?
Does he judge through such deep darkness?
14 Thick clouds are a veil for him, so he does not see us,
as he goes back and forth
in the vault of heaven.'
15 Will you keep to the old path
that evil men have walked—
16 men who were carried off before their time,

when the flood was poured out
on their foundations?
17 They were saying to God, 'Turn away from us,'
and, 'What can the Almighty do to us?'
18 But it was he who filled their houses
with good things—
yet the counsel of the wicked
was far from me.
19 The righteous see their destruction and rejoice;
the innocent mock them scornfully, saying,
20 'Surely our enemies are destroyed,
and fire consumes their wealth.'

21 "Reconcile yourself with God,
and be at peace with him;
in this way your prosperity will be good.
22 Accept instruction from his mouth
and store up his words in your heart.
23 If you return to the Almighty, you will be built up;
if you remove wicked behavior far from your tent,
24 and throw your gold in the dust—
your gold of Ophir
among the rocks in the ravines—
25 then the Almighty himself will be your gold,
and the choicest silver for you.
26 Surely then you will delight yourself
in the Almighty,
and will lift up your face toward God.
27 You will pray to him and he will hear you,
and you will fulfill your vows to him.
28 Whatever you decide on a matter,
it will be established for you,
and light will shine on your ways.
29 When people are brought low and you say,
'Lift them up!'
then he will save the downcast;
30 he will deliver even someone who is not innocent,
who will escape through the cleanness of your hands."

JOB'S REPLY TO ELIPHAZ

23 Then Job answered:
2 "Even today my complaint is still bitter;
his hand is heavy despite my groaning.
3 O that I knew where I might find him,
that I could come to his place of residence!
4 I would lay out my case before him
and fill my mouth with arguments.
5 I would know with what words he would answer me,
and understand what he would say to me.
6 Would he contend with me with great power?
No, he would only pay attention to me.
7 There an upright person
could present his case before him,
and I would be delivered forever from my judge.

THE INACCESSIBILITY AND POWER OF GOD

8 "If I go to the east, he is not there,
and to the west, yet I do not perceive him.
9 In the north when he is at work,
I do not see him;
when he turns to the south,
I see no trace of him.
10 But he knows the pathway that I take;
if he tested me, I would come forth like gold.
11 My feet have followed his steps closely;
I have kept to his way and have not turned aside.
12 I have not departed from the commands of his lips;
I have treasured the words of his mouth
more than my allotted portion.
13 But he is unchangeable, and who can change him?
Whatever he has desired, he does.
14 For he fulfills his decree against me,
and many such things are his plans.
15 That is why I am terrified in his presence;
when I consider, I am afraid because of him.
16 Indeed, God has made my heart faint;
the Almighty has terrified me.
17 Yet I have not been silent because of the darkness,
because of the thick darkness
that covered my face.

THE APPARENT INDIFFERENCE OF GOD

24 "Why are times not appointed by the Almighty?
Why do those who know him not see his days?
2 Men move boundary stones;
they seize the flock and pasture them.
3 They drive away the orphan's donkey;
they take the widow's ox as a pledge.
4 They turn the needy from the pathway,
and the poor of the land hide themselves together.
5 Like wild donkeys in the wilderness,
they go out to their labor seeking diligently for food;
the arid rift valley provides food for
them and for their children.
6 They reap fodder in the field,
and glean in the vineyard of the wicked.
7 They spend the night naked because they lack clothing;
they have no covering against the cold.
8 They are soaked by mountain rains
and huddle in the rocks because they lack shelter.
9 The fatherless child is snatched from the breast,
the infant of the poor is taken as a pledge.
10 They go about naked, without clothing,
and go hungry while they carry the sheaves.
11 They press out the olive oil between the rows of olive trees;
they tread the winepresses while they are thirsty.
12 From the city the dying groan,
and the wounded cry out for help,
but God charges no one with wrongdoing.

13 There are those who rebel against the light;
they do not know its ways
and they do not stay on its paths.
14 Before daybreak the murderer rises up;
he kills the poor and the needy;
in the night he is like a thief.
15 And the eye of the adulterer watches
for the twilight,
thinking, 'No eye can see me,'
and covers his face with a mask.
16 In the dark the robber breaks into houses,
but by day they shut themselves in;
they do not know the light.
17 For all of them, the morning is to them
like deep darkness;
they are friends with the terrors of darkness.

18 "You say, 'He is foam on the face of the waters;
their portion of the land is cursed
so that no one goes to their vineyard.
19 The drought as well as the heat
snatch up the melted snow;
so the grave snatches up the sinner.
20 The womb forgets him,
the worm feasts on him,
no longer will he be remembered.
Like a tree, wickedness will be broken down.
21 He preys on the barren and childless woman,
and does not treat the widow well.
22 But God drags off the mighty by his power;
when God rises up against him,
he has no faith in his life.
23 God may let them rest in a feeling of security,
but he is constantly watching all their ways.
24 They are exalted for a little while,
and then they are gone,
they are brought low like all others, and gathered in,
and like a head of grain they are cut off.'

25 "If this is not so, who can prove me a liar
and reduce my words to nothing?"

BILDAD'S THIRD SPEECH

25 Then Bildad the Shuhite answered:
2 "Dominion and awesome might belong to God;
he establishes peace in his heights.
3 Can his armies be numbered?
On whom does his light not rise?
4 How then can a human being be righteous before God?
How can one born of a woman be pure?
5 If even the moon is not bright,
and the stars are not pure as far as he is concerned,
6 how much less a mortal man, who is but a maggot—
a son of man, who is only a worm!"

JOB'S REPLY TO BILDAD

26 Then Job replied:
2 "How you have helped the powerless!
How you have saved the person who has no strength!
3 How you have advised the one without wisdom,
and abundantly revealed your insight!
4 To whom did you utter these words?
And whose spirit has come forth from your mouth?

A BETTER DESCRIPTION OF GOD'S GREATNESS

5 "The dead tremble—
those beneath the waters
and all that live in them.
6 The underworld is naked before God;
the place of destruction lies uncovered.
7 He spreads out the northern skies over empty space;
he suspends the earth on nothing.
8 He locks the waters in his clouds,
and the clouds do not burst with the weight of them.
9 He conceals the face of the full moon,
shrouding it with his clouds.
10 He marks out the horizon on the surface of the waters
as a boundary between light and darkness.
11 The pillars of the heavens tremble
and are amazed at his rebuke.
12 By his power he stills the sea;
by his wisdom he cut Rahab the great
sea monster to pieces.
13 By his breath the skies became fair;
his hand pierced the fleeing serpent.
14 Indeed, these are but the outer fringes of his ways!
How faint is the whisper we hear of him!
But who can understand the thunder of his power?"

A PROTEST OF INNOCENCE

27 And Job took up his discourse again:
2 "As surely as God lives, who has denied me justice,
the Almighty, who has made my life bitter—
3 for while my spirit is still in me,
and the breath from God is in my nostrils,
4 my lips will not speak wickedness,
and my tongue will whisper no deceit.
5 I will never declare that you three are in the right;
until I die, I will not set aside my integrity!
6 I will maintain my righteousness
and never let it go;
my conscience will not reproach me
for as long as I live.

THE CONDITION OF THE WICKED

7 "May my enemy be like the wicked,
my adversary like the unrighteous.
8 For what hope does the godless have when he is cut off,
when God takes away his life?

9 Does God listen to his cry
when distress overtakes him?
10 Will he find delight in the Almighty?
Will he call out to God at all times?
11 I will teach you about the power of God;
what is on the Almighty's mind
I will not conceal.
12 If you yourselves have all seen this,
Why in the world do you continue
this meaningless talk?
13 This is the portion of the wicked man
allotted by God,
the inheritance that evildoers receive
from the Almighty.
14 If his children increase—it is for the sword!
His offspring never have enough to eat.
15 Those who survive him are buried by the plague,
and their widows do not mourn for them.
16 If he piles up silver like dust
and stores up clothing like mounds of clay,
17 what he stores up a righteous man will wear,
and an innocent man will inherit his silver.
18 The house he builds is as fragile
as a moth's cocoon,
like a hut that a watchman has made.
19 He goes to bed wealthy,
but will do so no more.
When he opens his eyes, it is all gone.
20 Terrors overwhelm him like a flood;
at night a whirlwind carries him off.
21 The east wind carries him away, and he is gone;
it sweeps him out of his place.
22 It hurls itself against him without pity
as he flees headlong from its power.
23 It claps its hands at him in derision
and hisses him away from his place.

III. JOB'S SEARCH FOR WISDOM (28:1–28)

NO KNOWN ROAD TO WISDOM

28 "Surely there is a mine for silver,
and a place where gold is refined.
2 Iron is taken from the ground,
and rock is poured out as copper.
3 Man puts an end to the darkness;
he searches the farthest recesses
for the ore in the deepest darkness.
4 Far from where people live he sinks a shaft,
in places travelers have long forgotten,
far from other people he dangles and sways.
5 The earth, from which food comes,
is overturned below as though by fire;
6 a place whose stones are sapphires
that contain dust of gold;

7 a hidden path no bird of prey knows—
no falcon's eye has spotted it.
8 Proud beasts have not set foot on it,
and no lion has passed along it.
9 On the flinty rock man has set to work
with his hand;
he has overturned mountains at their bases.
10 He has cut out channels through the rocks;
his eyes have spotted every precious thing.
11 He has searched the sources of the rivers
and what was hidden he has brought into the light.

NO PRICE CAN BUY WISDOM

12 "But wisdom—where can it be found?
Where is the place of understanding?
13 Mankind does not know its place;
it cannot be found in the land of the living.
14 The deep says, 'It is not with me.'
And the sea says, 'It is not with me.'
15 Fine gold cannot be given in exchange for it,
nor can its price be weighed out in silver.
16 It cannot be measured out for purchase
with the gold of Ophir,
with precious onyx or sapphires.
17 Neither gold nor crystal can be compared with it,
nor can a vase of gold match its worth.
18 Of coral and jasper no mention will be made;
the price of wisdom is more than pearls.
19 The topaz of Cush cannot be compared with it;
it cannot be purchased with pure gold.

GOD ALONE HAS WISDOM

20 "But wisdom—where does it come from?
Where is the place of understanding?
21 For it has been hidden
from the eyes of every living creature,
and from the birds of the sky it
has been concealed.
22 Destruction and Death say,
'With our ears we have heard a rumor
about where it can be found.'
23 God understands the way to it,
and he alone knows its place.
24 For he looks to the ends of the earth
and observes everything under the heavens.
25 When he made the force of the wind
and measured the waters with a gauge,
26 when he imposed a limit for the rain,
and a path for the thunderstorm,
27 then he looked at wisdom and assessed its value;
he established it and examined it closely.
28 And he said to mankind,
'The fear of the Lord—that is wisdom,
and to turn away from evil is understanding.'"

IV. JOB'S CONCLUDING SOLILOQUY (29:1–31:40)

JOB RECALLS HIS FORMER CONDITION

29 Then Job continued his speech:
2 "O that I could be as I was
in the months now gone,
in the days when God watched over me,
3 when he caused his lamp
to shine upon my head,
and by his light
I walked through darkness;
4 just as I was in my most productive time,
when God's intimate friendship was
experienced in my tent,
5 when the Almighty was still with me
and my children were around me;
6 when my steps were bathed with butter
and the rock poured out for me streams of olive oil!
7 When I went out to the city gate
and secured my seat in the public square,
8 the young men would see me and step aside,
and the old men would get up
and remain standing;
9 the chief men refrained from talking
and covered their mouths with their hands;
10 the voices of the nobles fell silent,
and their tongues stuck to the roof
of their mouths.

JOB'S BENEVOLENCE

11 "As soon as the ear heard these things,
it blessed me,
and when the eye saw them, it bore witness to me,
12 for I rescued the poor who cried out for help,
and the orphan who had no one to assist him;
13 the blessing of the dying man descended on me,
and I made the widow's heart rejoice;
14 I put on righteousness and it clothed me,
my just dealing was like a robe and a turban;
15 I was eyes for the blind
and feet for the lame;
16 I was a father to the needy,
and I investigated the case of the person
I did not know;
17 I broke the fangs of the wicked,
and made him drop his prey from his teeth.

JOB'S CONFIDENCE

18 "Then I thought, 'I will die in my own home,
my days as numerous as the grains of sand.
19 My roots reach the water,
and the dew lies on my branches all night long.
20 My glory will always be fresh in me,
and my bow ever new in my hand.'

JOB'S REPUTATION

21 "People listened to me and waited silently;
they kept silent for my advice.
22 After I had spoken, they did not respond;
my words fell on them drop by drop.
23 They waited for me as people wait for the rain,
and they opened their mouths as for the spring rains.
24 If I smiled at them, they hardly believed it;
and they did not cause the light of my face to darken.
25 I chose the way for them
and sat as their chief;
I lived like a king among his troops;
I was like one who comforts mourners.

JOB'S PRESENT MISERY

30 "But now they mock me, those who are younger than I,
whose fathers I disdained too much
to put with my sheep dogs.
2 Moreover, the strength of their hands—
what use was it to me?
Those whose strength had perished,
3 gaunt with want and hunger,
they would roam the parched land,
by night a desolate waste.
4 By the brush they would gather herbs
from the salt marshes,
and the root of the broom tree was their food.
5 They were banished from the community—
people shouted at them
as they would shout at thieves—
6 so that they had to live
in the dry stream beds,
in the holes of the ground, and among the rocks.
7 They brayed like animals among the bushes
and were huddled together under the nettles.
8 Sons of senseless and nameless people,
they were driven out of the land with whips.

JOB'S INDIGNITIES

9 "And now I have become their taunt song;
I have become a byword among them.
10 They detest me and maintain their distance;
they do not hesitate to spit in my face.
11 Because God has untied my tent cord
and afflicted me,
people throw off all restraint in my presence.
12 On my right the young rabble rise up;
they drive me from place to place,
and build up siege ramps against me.
13 They destroy my path;
they succeed in destroying me
without anyone assisting them.
14 They come in as through a wide breach;
amid the crash they come rolling in.

15 Terrors are turned loose on me;
they drive away my honor like the wind,
and as a cloud my deliverance has passed away.

JOB'S DESPONDENCY

16 "And now my soul pours itself out within me;
days of suffering take hold of me.
17 Night pierces my bones;
my gnawing pains never cease.
18 With great power God grasps my clothing;
he binds me like the collar of my tunic.
19 He has flung me into the mud,
and I have come to resemble dust and ashes.
20 I cry out to you, but you do not answer me;
I stand up, and you only look at me.
21 You have become cruel to me;
with the strength of your hand you attack me.
22 You pick me up on the wind and make me ride on it;
you toss me about in the storm.
23 I know that you are bringing me to death,
to the meeting place for all the living.

THE CONTRAST WITH THE PAST

24 "Surely one does not stretch out his hand
against a broken man
when he cries for help in his distress.
25 Have I not wept for the unfortunate?
Was not my soul grieved for the poor?
26 But when I hoped for good, trouble came;
when I expected light, then darkness came.
27 My heart is in turmoil unceasingly;
the days of my affliction confront me.
28 I go about blackened, but not by the sun;
in the assembly I stand up and cry for help.
29 I have become a brother to jackals
and a companion of ostriches.
30 My skin has turned dark on me;
my body is hot with fever.
31 My harp is used for mourning
and my flute for the sound of weeping.

JOB VINDICATES HIMSELF

31 "I made a covenant with my eyes;
how then could I entertain thoughts against a virgin?
2 What then would be one's lot from God above,
one's heritage from the Almighty on high?
3 Is it not misfortune for the unjust,
and disaster for those who work iniquity?
4 Does he not see my ways
and count all my steps?
5 If I have walked in falsehood,
and if my foot has hastened to deceit—
6 let him weigh me with honest scales;
then God will discover my integrity.

7 If my footsteps have strayed from the way,
if my heart has gone after my eyes,
or if anything has defiled my hands,
8 then let me sow and let another eat,
and let my crops be uprooted.
9 If my heart has been enticed by a woman,
and I have lain in wait at my neighbor's door,
10 then let my wife turn the millstone for another man,
and may other men commit adultery with her.
11 For I would have committed a shameful act,
an iniquity to be judged.
12 For it is a fire that devours even to Destruction,
and it would uproot all my harvest.

13 "If I have disregarded the right of my male servants
or my female servants
when they disputed with me,
14 then what will I do when God confronts me in judgment;
when he intervenes,
how will I respond to him?
15 Did not the one who made me in the womb make them?
Did not the same one form us in the womb?
16 If I have refused to give the poor what they desired,
or caused the eyes of the widow to fail,
17 If I ate my morsel of bread myself,
and did not share any of it with orphans—
18 but from my youth I raised the orphan like a father,
and from my mother's womb I guided the widow—
19 If I have seen anyone about to perish for lack of clothing,
or a poor man without a coat,
20 whose heart did not bless me
as he warmed himself with the fleece of my sheep,
21 if I have raised my hand to vote against the orphan,
when I saw my support in the court,
22 then let my arm fall from the shoulder,
let my arm be broken off at the socket.
23 For the calamity from God was a terror to me,
and by reason of his majesty I was powerless.

24 "If I have put my confidence in gold
or said to pure gold,
'You are my security!'
25 if I have rejoiced because of the extent of my wealth,
or because of the great wealth my hand had gained,
26 if I looked at the sun when it was shining,
and the moon advancing as a precious thing,
27 so that my heart was secretly enticed,
and my hand threw them a kiss from my mouth,
28 then this also would be iniquity to be judged,
for I would have been false to God above.
29 If I have rejoiced over the misfortune of my enemy
or exulted because calamity found him—
30 I have not even permitted my mouth to sin
by asking for his life through a curse—

31 if the members of my household have never said,
'If only there were someone
who has not been satisfied from Job's meat!'—
32 But no stranger had to spend the night outside,
for I opened my doors to the traveler—
33 if I have covered my transgressions as men do,
by hiding iniquity in my heart,
34 because I was terrified of the great multitude,
and the contempt of families terrified me,
so that I remained silent
and would not go outdoors—

JOB'S APPEAL

35 "If only I had someone to hear me!
Here is my signature—
let the Almighty answer me!
If only I had an indictment
that my accuser had written.
36 Surely I would wear it proudly on my shoulder,
I would bind it on me like a crown;
37 I would give him an accounting of my steps;
like a prince I would draw near to him.

JOB'S FINAL SOLEMN OATH

38 "If my land cried out against me
and all its furrows wept together,
39 if I have eaten its produce without paying,
or caused the death of its owners,
40 then let thorns sprout up in place of wheat,
and in place of barley, noxious weeds."

The words of Job are ended.

V. THE SPEECHES OF ELIHU (32:1—37:24)

ELIHU'S FIRST SPEECH

32 So these three men refused to answer Job further, because he was righteous in his own eyes. 2 Then Elihu son
of Barakel the Buzite, of the family of Ram, became very angry.
He was angry with Job for justifying himself rather than God.
3 With Job's three friends he was also angry, because they could
not find an answer, and so declared Job guilty. 4 Now Elihu had
waited before speaking to Job, because the others were older
than he was. 5 But when Elihu saw that the three men had no
further reply, he became very angry.

ELIHU CLAIMS WISDOM

6 So Elihu son of Barakel the Buzite spoke up:
"I am young, but you are elderly;
that is why I was fearful,
and afraid to explain to you what I know.
7 I said to myself, 'Age should speak,
and length of years should make
wisdom known.'

8 But it is a spirit in people,
the breath of the Almighty,
that makes them understand.
9 It is not the aged who are wise,
nor old men who understand what is right.
10 Therefore I say, 'Listen to me.
I, even I, will explain what I know.'
11 Look, I waited for you to speak;
I listened closely to your wise thoughts,
while you were searching for words.
12 Now I was paying you close attention,
yet there was no one proving Job wrong,
not one of you was answering his statements.
13 So do not say, 'We have found wisdom.
God will refute him, not man.'
14 Job has not directed his words to me,
and so I will not reply to him with your arguments.

JOB'S FRIENDS FAILED TO ANSWER

15 "They are dismayed and cannot answer anymore;
they have nothing left to say.
16 And I have waited. But because they do not speak,
because they stand there and answer no more,
17 I too will answer my part,
I too will explain what I know.
18 For I am full of words,
and the spirit within me constrains me.
19 Inside I am like wine that has no outlet,
like new wineskins ready to burst!
20 I will speak, so that I may find relief;
I will open my lips, so that I may answer.
21 I will not show partiality to any person,
nor will I confer a title on anyone.
22 For I do not know how to give honorary titles,
if I did, my Creator would quickly
do away with me.

ELIHU INVITES JOB'S ATTENTION

33 "But now, O Job, listen to my words,
and hear everything I have to say.
2 See now, I have opened my mouth;
my tongue in my mouth has spoken.
3 My words come from the uprightness
of my heart,
and my lips will utter knowledge sincerely.
4 The Spirit of God has made me,
and the breath of the Almighty gives me life.
5 Reply to me, if you can;
set your arguments in order before me
and take your stand.
6 Look, I am just like you in relation to God;
I too have been molded from clay.
7 Therefore no fear of me should terrify you,
nor should my pressure be heavy on you.

ELIHU REJECTS JOB'S PLEA OF INNOCENCE

8 "Indeed, you have said in my hearing
(I heard the sound of the words!):
9 'I am pure, without transgression;
I am clean and have no iniquity.
10 Yet God finds occasions with me;
he regards me as his enemy.
11 He puts my feet in shackles;
he watches closely all my paths.'
12 Now in this, you are not right—I answer you,
for God is greater than a human being.
13 Why do you contend against him,
that he does not answer all a person's words?

ELIHU DISAGREES WITH JOB'S VIEW OF GOD

14 "For God speaks, the first time in one way,
the second time in another,
though a person does not perceive it.
15 In a dream, a night vision,
when deep sleep falls on people
as they sleep in their beds.
16 Then he gives a revelation to people,
and terrifies them with warnings,
17 to turn a person from his sin,
and to cover a person's pride.
18 He spares a person's life from corruption,
his very life from crossing over the river.
19 Or a person is chastened by pain on his bed,
and with the continual strife of his bones,
20 so that his life loathes food,
and his soul rejects appetizing fare.
21 His flesh wastes away from sight,
and his bones, which were not seen,
are easily visible.
22 He draws near to the place of corruption,
and his life to the messengers of death.
23 If there is an angel beside him,
one mediator out of a thousand,
to tell a person what constitutes his uprightness;
24 and if God is gracious to him and says,
'Spare him from going down
to the place of corruption,
I have found a ransom for him,'
25 then his flesh is restored like a youth's;
he returns to the days of his youthful vigor.
26 He entreats God, and God delights in him,
he sees God's face with rejoicing,
and God restores to him his righteousness.
27 That person sings to others, saying:
'I have sinned and falsified what is right,
but I was not punished according to what I deserved.
28 He redeemed my life
from going down to the place of corruption,
and my life sees the light!'

REFLECT

When Job and Elihu disagree on their view of God, who is right? How do we reconcile with other believers when we have a different understanding of God's sovereignty or His actions?

ELIHU'S APPEAL TO JOB

29 "Indeed, God does all these things,
twice, three times, in his dealings with a person,
30 to turn back his life from the place of corruption,
that he may be enlightened with the light of life.
31 Pay attention, Job—listen to me;
be silent, and I will speak.
32 If you have any words, reply to me;
speak, for I want to justify you.
33 If not, you listen to me;
be silent, and I will teach you wisdom."

ELIHU'S SECOND SPEECH

34 Elihu answered:
2 "Listen to my words, you wise men;
hear me, you learned men.
3 For the ear assesses words
as the mouth tastes food.
4 Let us evaluate for ourselves what is right;
let us come to know among ourselves what is good.
5 For Job says, 'I am innocent,
but God turns away my right.
6 Concerning my right, should I lie?
My wound is incurable,
although I am without transgression.'
7 Who is there like Job,
who drinks derision like water?
8 He goes about in company with evildoers,
he goes along with wicked men.
9 For he says, 'It does not profit a man
when he makes his delight with God.'

GOD IS NOT UNJUST

10 "Therefore, listen to me, you men
of understanding.
Far be it from God to do wickedness,
from the Almighty to do evil.
11 For he repays a person for his work,
and according to the conduct of a person,
he causes the consequences to find him.
12 Indeed, in truth, God does not act wickedly,
and the Almighty does not pervert justice.
13 Who entrusted to him the earth?
And who put him over the whole world?
14 If God were to set his heart on it,
and gather in his spirit and his breath,
15 all flesh would perish together
and human beings would return to dust.

GOD IS IMPARTIAL AND OMNISCIENT

16 "If you have understanding, listen to this,
hear what I have to say.
17 Do you really think
that one who hates justice can govern?

And will you declare guilty
the supremely Righteous One,
18 who says to a king, 'Worthless man,'
and to nobles, 'Wicked men,'
19 who shows no partiality to princes,
and does not take note of the rich
more than the poor,
because all of them are the work of his hands?
20 In a moment they die, in the middle of the night,
people are shaken and they pass away.
The mighty are removed effortlessly.
21 For his eyes are on the ways of an individual,
he observes all a person's steps.
22 There is no darkness, and no deep darkness,
where evildoers can hide themselves.
23 For he does not still consider a person,
that he should come before God in judgment.
24 He shatters the great without inquiry,
and sets up others in their place.
25 Therefore, he knows their deeds,
he overthrows them in the night
and they are crushed.
26 He strikes them for their wickedness,
in a place where people can see,
27 because they have turned away from following him,
and have not understood any of his ways,
28 so that they caused the cry of the poor
to come before him,
so that he hears the cry of the needy.
29 But if God is quiet, who can condemn him?
If he hides his face, then who can see him?
Yet he is over the individual and the nation alike,
30 so that the godless man should not rule,
and not lay snares for the people.

JOB IS FOOLISH TO REBEL

31 "Has anyone said to God,
'I have endured chastisement,
but I will not act wrongly any more;
32 teach me what I cannot see;
if I have done evil, I will do so no more'?
33 Is it your opinion that God should recompense it,
because you reject this?
But you must choose, and not I,
so tell us what you know.
34 Men of understanding say to me—
any wise man listening to me says—
35 that Job speaks without knowledge
and his words are without understanding.
36 But Job will be tested to the end,
because his answers are like those of wicked men.
37 For he adds transgression to his sin;
in our midst he claps his hands,
and multiplies his words against God."

ELIHU'S THIRD SPEECH

35 Then Elihu answered:
2 "Do you think this to be just
when you say, 'My right before God'?
3 But you say, 'What will it profit you,'
and, 'What do I gain by not sinning?'
4 I will reply to you,
and to your friends with you.
5 Gaze at the heavens and see;
consider the clouds, which are higher than you.
6 If you sin, how does it affect God?
If your transgressions are many,
what does it do to him?
7 If you are righteous, what do you give to God,
or what does he receive from your hand?
8 Your wickedness affects only a person like yourself,
and your righteousness only other people.

9 "People cry out
because of the excess of oppression;
they cry out for help
because of the power of the mighty.
10 But no one says, 'Where is God, my Creator,
who gives songs in the night,
11 who teaches us more than the wild animals of the earth,
and makes us wiser than the birds of the sky?'
12 Then they cry out—but he does not answer—
because of the arrogance of the wicked.
13 Surely it is an empty cry—God does not hear it;
the Almighty does not take notice of it.
14 How much less, then,
when you say that you do not perceive him,
that the case is before him
and you are waiting for him!
15 And further, when you say
that his anger does not punish,
and that he does not know transgression!
16 So Job opens his mouth to no purpose;
without knowledge he multiplies words."

ELIHU'S FOURTH SPEECH

36 Elihu said further:
2 "Be patient with me a little longer
and I will instruct you,
for I still have words to speak on God's behalf.
3 With my knowledge I will speak comprehensively,
and to my Creator I will ascribe righteousness.
4 For in truth, my words are not false;
it is one complete in knowledge
who is with you.
5 Indeed, God is mighty; and he does not despise people,
he is mighty, and firm in his intent.
6 He does not allow the wicked to live,
but he gives justice to the poor.

7 He does not take his eyes off the righteous;
but with kings on the throne
he seats the righteous and exalts them forever.
8 But if they are bound in chains,
and held captive by the cords of affliction,
9 then he reveals to them what they have done,
and their transgressions,
that they were behaving proudly.
10 And he reveals this for correction,
and says that they must turn from evil.
11 If they obey and serve him,
they live out their days in prosperity
and their years in pleasantness.
12 But if they refuse to listen,
they pass over the river of death,
and expire without knowledge.
13 The godless at heart nourish anger,
they do not cry out even when he binds them.
14 They die in their youth,
and their life ends among the male cultic prostitutes.
15 He delivers the afflicted by their afflictions,
he reveals himself to them by their suffering.
16 And surely, he drew you from the mouth of distress,
to a wide place, unrestricted,
and to the comfort of your table
filled with rich food.
17 But now you are preoccupied with the
judgment due the wicked,
judgment and justice take hold of you.
18 Be careful that no one entices you with riches;
do not let a large bribe turn you aside.
19 Would your wealth sustain you,
so that you would not be in distress,
even all your mighty efforts?
20 Do not long for the cover of night
to drag people away from their homes.
21 Take heed, do not turn to evil,
for because of this you have been tested by affliction.
22 Indeed, God is exalted in his power;
who is a teacher like him?
23 Who has prescribed his ways for him?
Or said to him, 'You have done what is wicked'?
24 Remember to extol his work,
which people have praised in song.
25 All humanity has seen it;
people gaze on it from afar.

THE WORK AND WISDOM OF GOD

26 "Yes, God is great—beyond our knowledge!
The number of his years is unsearchable.
27 He draws up drops of water;
they distill the rain into its mist,
28 which the clouds pour down
and shower on humankind abundantly.

29 Who can understand the spreading of the clouds,
the thunderings of his pavilion?
30 See how he scattered his lightning about him;
he has covered the depths of the sea.
31 It is by these that he judges the nations
and supplies food in abundance.
32 With his hands he covers the lightning,
and directs it against its target.
33 His thunder announces the coming storm,
the cattle also, concerning the storm's approach.

37 At this also my heart pounds
and leaps from its place.
2 Listen carefully to the thunder of his voice,
to the rumbling that proceeds from his mouth.
3 Under the whole heaven he lets it go,
even his lightning to the far corners of the earth.
4 After that a voice roars;
he thunders with an exalted voice,
and he does not hold back his lightning bolts
when his voice is heard.
5 God thunders with his voice in marvelous ways;
he does great things beyond our understanding.
6 For to the snow he says, 'Fall to earth,'
and to the torrential rains, 'Pour down.'
7 He causes everyone to stop working,
so that all people may know his work.
8 The wild animals go to their lairs,
and in their dens they remain.
9 A tempest blows out from its chamber,
icy cold from the driving winds.
10 The breath of God produces ice,
and the breadth of the waters freeze solid.
11 He loads the clouds with moisture;
he scatters his lightning through the clouds.
12 The clouds go round in circles,
wheeling about according to his plans,
to carry out all that he commands them
over the face of the whole inhabited world.
13 Whether it is for punishment,
or for his land,
or for mercy,
he causes it to find its mark.

14 "Pay attention to this, Job!
Stand still and consider the wonders God works.
15 Do you know how God commands them,
how he makes lightning flash in his storm cloud?
16 Do you know about the balancing of the clouds,
that wondrous activity of him who
is perfect in knowledge?
17 You, whose garments are hot
when the earth is still because of the south wind,
18 will you, with him, spread out the clouds,
solid as a mirror of molten metal?

19 Tell us what we should say to him.
We cannot prepare a case
because of the darkness.
20 Should he be informed that I want to speak?
If a man speaks, surely he will be swallowed up!
21 But now, the sun cannot be looked at—
it is bright in the skies—
after a wind passed and swept the clouds away.
22 From the north he comes in golden splendor;
around God is awesome majesty.
23 As for the Almighty, we cannot attain to him!
He is great in power,
but justice and abundant righteousness
he does not oppress.
24 Therefore people fear him,
for he does not regard all the wise in heart."

VI. THE DIVINE SPEECHES (38:1—42:6)

THE LORD'S FIRST SPEECH

38 Then the LORD answered Job out of the whirlwind:
2 "Who is this who darkens counsel
with words without knowledge?
3 Get ready for a difficult task like a man;
I will question you
and you will inform me.

GOD'S QUESTIONS TO JOB

4 "Where were you
when I laid the foundation of the earth?
Tell me, if you possess understanding.
5 Who set its measurements—if you know—
or who stretched a measuring line across it?
6 On what were its bases set,
or who laid its cornerstone—
7 when the morning stars sang in chorus,
and all the sons of God shouted for joy?

8 "Who shut up the sea with doors
when it burst forth, coming out of the womb,
9 when I made the storm clouds its garment,
and thick darkness its swaddling band,
10 when I prescribed its limits,
and set in place its bolts and doors,
11 when I said, 'To here you may come
and no farther,
here your proud waves will be confined'?
12 Have you ever in your life commanded
the morning,
or made the dawn know its place,
13 that it might seize the corners of the earth,
and shake the wicked out of it?
14 The earth takes shape like clay under a seal;
its features are dyed like a garment.

WHERE WERE YOU?

JOB 38

"Where were You, Lord?" I have asked God this question many times. I want to know where He was when tragedy struck. Why didn't He prevent it? Wasn't He supposed to be on my side? Where was He?

Job suffered tremendous loss. He did not curse God, but he came to God with questions. He was broken, confused, and overwhelmed. He wanted to know why God had allowed him to suffer. He was a righteous man, and by allowing this affliction, it seemed God was against him.

Finally, God answered Job. However, God didn't directly answer Job's questions. God didn't tell Job why He allowed his suffering. He didn't explain the significance of Job's suffering for God's eternal glory. Instead, He turned the tables and asked Job questions that revealed His character:

"Where were you when I laid the foundation of the earth?" (Job 38:4).

God wanted Job to remember His sovereignty and power. God is the Creator, the one who establishes and maintains life and order in the world. He alone allows the newness of the morning. He is powerful enough to move and affect stars, constellations, solar systems, and galaxies. He is so detailed and caring that He guides each animal, showing it the path to care for its young. Surely He understood how to help Job.

After all God's questions, Job answered Him. He said, "I have declared without understanding things too wonderful for me to know" (Job 42:3). Job recognized the sovereignty of God and his own frailty. He remembered God, and that changed his entire perspective. Instead of being angry and questioning God for his suffering, Job remembered the character of the One who made him, redeemed him, and loved him.

God presented these questions to Job not to punish him, but to remind him of who He was. Without knowing the character of God, it is impossible to trust Him. He is for us. His actions are for us. Though the world and our circumstances may tell us otherwise, He is sovereign and good.

If God can be trusted to create and sustain the universe, with all its details and intricacies, how much more can He be trusted to sustain us in our moment of need? We can trust His character.

15 Then from the wicked the light is withheld,
and the arm raised in violence is broken.
16 Have you gone to the springs that fill the sea,
or walked about in the recesses of the deep?
17 Have the gates of death been revealed to you?
Have you seen the gates of deepest darkness?
18 Have you considered the vast
expanses of the earth?
Tell me, if you know it all.

19 "In what direction does light reside,
and darkness, where is its place,
20 that you may take them to their borders
and perceive the pathways to their homes?
21 You know, for you were born before them;
and the number of your days is great!
22 Have you entered the storehouse of the snow,
or seen the armory of the hail,
23 which I reserve for the time of trouble,
for the day of war and battle?
24 In what direction is lightning dispersed,
or the east winds scattered over the earth?
25 Who carves out a channel for the heavy rains,
and a path for the rumble of thunder,
26 to cause it to rain on an uninhabited land,
a wilderness where there are no human beings,
27 to satisfy a devastated and desolate land,
and to cause it to sprout with vegetation?
28 Does the rain have a father,
or who has fathered the drops of the dew?
29 From whose womb does the ice emerge,
and the frost from the sky,
who gives birth to it,
30 when the waters become hard like stone,
when the surface of the deep is frozen solid?
31 Can you tie the bands of the Pleiades,
or release the cords of Orion?
32 Can you lead out
the constellations in their seasons,
or guide the Bear with its cubs?
33 Do you know the laws of the heavens,
or can you set up their rule over the earth?
34 Can you raise your voice to the clouds
so that a flood of water covers you?
35 Can you send out lightning bolts,
and they go?
Will they say to you, 'Here we are'?
36 Who has put wisdom in the heart,
or has imparted understanding to the mind?
37 Who by wisdom can count the clouds,
and who can tip over the water jars of heaven,
38 when the dust hardens into a mass,
and the clumps of earth stick together?

39 "Do you hunt prey for the lioness,
and satisfy the appetite of the lions
40 when they crouch in their dens,
when they wait in ambush in the thicket?
41 Who prepares prey for the raven,
when its young cry out to God
and wander about for lack of food?

39 "Are you acquainted with the way
the mountain goats give birth?
Do you watch as the wild deer give
birth to their young?
2 Do you count the months they must fulfill,
and do you know the time they give birth?
3 They crouch, they bear their young,
they bring forth the offspring they have carried.
4 Their young grow strong, and grow up in the open;
they go off, and do not return to them.
5 Who let the wild donkey go free?
Who released the bonds of the donkey,
6 to whom I appointed the arid rift valley for its home,
the salt wastes as its dwelling place?
7 It scorns the tumult in the town;
it does not hear the shouts of a driver.
8 It ranges the hills as its pasture,
and searches after every green plant.
9 Is the wild ox willing to be your servant?
Will it spend the night at your feeding trough?
10 Can you bind the wild ox to a furrow with its rope,
will it till the valleys, following after you?
11 Will you rely on it because its strength is great?
Will you commit your labor to it?
12 Can you count on it to bring in your grain,
and gather the grain to your threshing floor?

13 "The wings of the ostrich flap with joy,
but are they the pinions and plumage of a stork?
14 For she leaves her eggs on the ground,
and lets them be warmed on the soil.
15 She forgets that a foot might crush them,
or that a wild animal might trample them.
16 She is harsh with her young,
as if they were not hers;
she is unconcerned about the
uselessness of her labor.
17 For God deprived her of wisdom,
and did not impart understanding to her.
18 But as soon as she springs up,
she laughs at the horse and its rider.

19 "Do you give the horse its strength?
Do you clothe its neck with a mane?
20 Do you make it leap like a locust?
Its proud neighing is terrifying!

21 It paws the ground in the valley,
exulting mightily,
it goes out to meet the weapons.
22 It laughs at fear and is not dismayed;
it does not shy away from the sword.
23 On it the quiver rattles;
the lance and javelin flash.
24 In excitement and impatience it consumes the ground;
it cannot stand still when the trumpet is blown.
25 At the sound of the trumpet, it says, 'Aha!'
And from a distance it catches the scent of battle,
the thunderous shouting of commanders,
and the battle cries.

26 "Is it by your understanding that the hawk soars,
and spreads its wings toward the south?
27 Is it at your command that the eagle soars,
and builds its nest on high?
28 It lives on a rock and spends the night there,
on a rocky crag and a fortress.
29 From there it spots its prey,
its eyes gaze intently from a distance.
30 And its young ones devour the blood,
and where the dead carcasses are,
there it is."

JOB'S REPLY TO GOD'S CHALLENGE

40 Then the LORD answered Job:
2 "Will the one who contends with
the Almighty correct him?
Let the person who accuses God
give him an answer!"

3 Then Job answered the LORD:
4 "Indeed, I am completely unworthy—
how could I reply to you?
I put my hand over my mouth to silence myself.
5 I have spoken once, but I cannot answer;
twice, but I will say no more."

THE LORD'S SECOND SPEECH

6 Then the LORD answered Job from the whirlwind:
7 "Get ready for a difficult task like a man.
I will question you and you will inform me.
8 Would you indeed annul my justice?
Would you declare me guilty so that
you might be right?
9 Do you have an arm as powerful as God's,
and can you thunder with a voice like his?
10 Adorn yourself, then, with
majesty and excellency,
and clothe yourself with glory and honor.
11 Scatter abroad the abundance of your anger.
Look at every proud man and bring him low;

12 Look at every proud man and abase him;
crush the wicked on the spot.
13 Hide them in the dust together,
imprison them in the grave.
14 Then I myself will acknowledge to you
that your own right hand can save you.

THE DESCRIPTION OF BEHEMOTH

15 "Look now at Behemoth, which
I made as I made you;
it eats grass like the ox.
16 Look at its strength in its loins,
and its power in the muscles of its belly.
17 It makes its tail stiff like a cedar,
the sinews of its thighs are tightly wound.
18 Its bones are tubes of bronze,
its limbs like bars of iron.
19 It ranks first among the works of God,
the One who made it
has furnished it with a sword.
20 For the hills bring it food,
where all the wild animals play.
21 Under the lotus trees it lies,
in the secrecy of the reeds and the marsh.
22 The lotus trees conceal it in their shadow;
the poplars by the stream conceal it.
23 If the river rages, it is not disturbed,
it is secure, though the Jordan
should surge up to its mouth.
24 Can anyone catch it by its eyes,
or pierce its nose with a snare?

THE DESCRIPTION OF LEVIATHAN

41 "Can you pull in Leviathan with a hook,
and tie down its tongue with a rope?
2 Can you put a cord through its nose,
or pierce its jaw with a hook?
3 Will it make numerous supplications to you,
will it speak to you with tender words?
4 Will it make a pact with you,
so you could take it as your slave for life?
5 Can you play with it, like a bird,
or tie it on a leash for your girls?
6 Will partners bargain for it?
Will they divide it up among the merchants?
7 Can you fill its hide with harpoons
or its head with fishing spears?
8 If you lay your hand on it,
you will remember the fight.
Do not do it again!
9 See, his expectation is wrong,
he is laid low even at the sight of it.
10 Is it not fierce when it is awakened?
Who is he, then, who can stand before it?

11 Who has confronted me that I should repay?
Everything under heaven belongs to me!
12 I will not keep silent about its limbs,
and the extent of its might,
and the grace of its arrangement.
13 Who can uncover its outer covering?
Who can penetrate to the inside of its armor?
14 Who can open the doors of its mouth?
Its teeth all around are fearsome.
15 Its back has rows of shields,
shut up closely together as with a seal;
16 each one is so close to the next
that no air can come between them.
17 They lock tightly together, one to the next;
they cling together and cannot be separated.
18 Its snorting throws out flashes of light;
its eyes are like the red glow of dawn.
19 Out of its mouth go flames,
sparks of fire shoot forth!
20 Smoke streams from its nostrils
as from a boiling pot over burning rushes.
21 Its breath sets coals ablaze
and a flame shoots from its mouth.
22 Strength lodges in its neck,
and despair runs before it.
23 The folds of its flesh are tightly joined;
they are firm on it, immovable.
24 Its heart is hard as rock,
hard as a lower millstone.
25 When it rises up, the mighty are terrified,
at its thrashing about they withdraw.
26 Whoever strikes it with a sword
will have no effect,
nor with the spear, arrow, or dart.
27 It regards iron as straw
and bronze as rotten wood.
28 Arrows do not make it flee;
slingstones become like chaff to it.
29 A club is counted as a piece of straw;
it laughs at the rattling of the lance.
30 Its underparts are the sharp
points of potsherds,
it leaves its mark in the mud
like a threshing sledge.
31 It makes the deep boil like a cauldron
and stirs up the sea like
a pot of ointment,
32 It leaves a glistening wake behind it;
one would think the deep had
a head of white hair.
33 The likes of it is not on earth,
a creature without fear.
34 It looks on every haughty being;
it is king over all that are proud."

JOB'S CONFESSION

42 Then Job answered the LORD:
2 "I know that you can do all things;
no purpose of yours can be thwarted;
3 you asked, 'Who is this who darkens
counsel without knowledge?'
But I have declared without understanding
things too wonderful for me to know.
4 You said, 'Pay attention, and I will speak;
I will question you, and you will answer me.'
5 I had heard of you by the hearing of the ear,
but now my eye has seen you.
6 Therefore I despise myself,
and I repent in dust and ashes!"

REFLECT

God restored all that Job had lost, but He doesn't always work this way. How do we reconcile our losses with our confidence in God's sovereignty when He doesn't give us what we ask?

VII. THE EPILOGUE (42:7–17)

JOB'S RESTORATION

7 After the LORD had spoken these things to Job, he said to Eliphaz the Temanite, "My anger is stirred up against you and
your two friends, because you have not spoken about me what
is right, as my servant Job has. 8 So now take seven bulls and
seven rams and go to my servant Job and offer a burnt offering
for yourselves. And my servant Job will intercede for you, and
I will respect him, so that I do not deal with you according to
your folly, because you have not spoken about me what is right,
as my servant Job has."
9 So they went, Eliphaz the Temanite, Bildad the Shuhite, and
Zophar the Naamathite, and did just as the LORD had told them;
and the LORD had respect for Job.
10 So the LORD restored what Job had lost after he prayed for
his friends, and the LORD doubled all that had belonged to Job.
11 So they came to him, all his brothers and sisters and all who
had known him before, and they dined with him in his house.
They comforted him and consoled him for all the trouble the
LORD had brought on him, and each one gave him a piece of silver and a gold ring.
12 So the LORD blessed the second part of Job's life more than
the first. He had 14,000 sheep, 6,000 camels, 1,000 yoke of oxen,
and 1,000 female donkeys. 13 And he also had seven sons and
three daughters. 14 The first daughter he named Jemimah, the
second Keziah, and the third Keren-Happuch. 15 Nowhere in all
the land could women be found who were as beautiful as Job's
daughters, and their father granted them an inheritance alongside their brothers.
16 After this Job lived 140 years; he saw his children and their
children to the fourth generation. 17 And so Job died, old and
full of days.

GIVE *thanks* to the LORD, FOR HE IS *good*, FOR HIS *Loyal Love* ENDURES

MEMORY VERSE

Give thanks to the LORD, for he is good,
for his loyal love endures.

Psalm 136:1

Psalms

INTRODUCTION

His Loyal Love Endures

The loyal love of Yahweh overflows from every page in the Book of Psalms. From saving His people when they are in distress to destroying the wicked, from providing abundantly for His people to granting wisdom and guidance, God's loyal love endures. The psalms offer hope for the broken, encouragement for the weary, and abundant mercy for the sinner. This beautiful collection of songs, prayers, and poetry expresses the deepest passions of humanity and exuberant praise of God.

The Book of Psalms is divided into five sections. Book I contains Psalms 1–41; Book II, Psalms 42–72; Book III, Psalms 73–89; Book IV, Psalms 90–106; and Book V, Psalms 107–150. These divisions were likely made based on the use of the psalms in temple worship. The psalms were composed individually for vastly different purposes. Some are psalms of worship, some are of lament. Some were for public worship, and others were private, personal cries of the soul. No matter their purpose, each psalm leads the worshiper back to the loyal love of God.

There were many composers of the psalms, including Moses, Ethan, Heman, and Asaph. David was the most frequent composer of the psalms, and over seventy are attributed to him. The psalms were written over a period spanning thousands of years, beginning with the time of Moses and ending around the time of Ezra. The collection and arrangement of the psalms also occurred over many centuries.

The Book of Psalms provides clear evidence that God is always with His people, no matter their circumstances. He is faithful to pour out His *hesed*, His loyal love, to His people. The psalms encourage us to love God greatly because they show us the vast ways we can worship Him, pour out our hearts to Him, trust Him, rely on Him, and offer praise to Him. His loyal love endures forever. Hallelujah.

Germany

OFFICIAL LANGUAGE
German
POPULATION
83,265,000
UNREACHED POPULATION
3,398,000
PROFESSING CHRISTIANS
65.4%

Emily's Home

Say a Prayer Today

Pray for the German people and their hearts for God. Pray they would see their need for God and turn to Him and praise Him for the abundant blessings He has given them.

HISTORY BIT

The most influential Bible translated into German is known as Luther's Bible, translated in 1534 by Martin Luther.* Luther was a leading figure in the German Protestant Revolution, seeking to make the Bible accessible to ordinary Christians.**

Source Information:
https://joshuaproject.net/countries/GM
*John Bowden, A Chronology of World Christianity (New York, NY: Continuum, 2007), 272.
**John D. Hannah, Invitation to Church *History; World* (Grand Rapids, MI: Kregel Publications, 2018), 281.

EMILY'S STORY

I will never forget the day doctors told me and my husband we would not be able to have children.

That devastating message left me questioning God's goodness and His endless love. Looking back, I am deeply moved by what I was able to learn about God's unfailing love. Once I could see beyond my pain and grief, I was able to see His perfect plan. His love is a love that never runs dry. Today, three precious children I was told I'd never have dance around my feet. I can give thanks to the Lord, confident that His loyal love endures forever.

Germany, the country I call home, has overcome the devastating effects of two world wars in the past century. Today, Germany has great influence as the world's fourth-largest economy with a very high standard of living. Often these blessings are taken for granted, the past hardship and suffering quickly forgotten. Times of peace are attributed to chance or to one's own achievements.

Due to an abundance of wealth, status, and luxury, this small country is failing to see its desire and need for God's goodness and enduring love.

Everyone has a story to tell about God's goodness. For some, the experience may be dramatic or intense, like the writer of Psalm 136 who recounted how God delivered His people from captivity and conquered His enemies. Others, like me, experience God's endless love in their personal lives again and again. Remembering who God is and what He has done brings out praise and thanksgiving that glorifies Him.

God's goodness is the very first and most important reason to be thankful. Give thanks to the Lord, not only because He does good, but because He is good. Not only because He is merciful, but because His mercy endures forever.

16 WEEK READING PLAN

LOVE HIS WORD

	MONDAY	TUESDAY	WEDNESDAY	THURSDAY	FRIDAY
1	Psalms 1-2	Psalms 3-4	Psalms 5-6	Psalms 7-8	Psalms 9-10
	SOAP Psalm 1:6	SOAP Psalm 4:1	SOAP Psalm 5:2-3	SOAP Psalm 8:3-4	SOAP Psalm 9:10
2	Psalms 11-12	Psalms 13-14	Psalms 15-16	Psalms 17-18	Psalms 19-20
	SOAP Psalm 11:4-5	SOAP Psalm 13:5-6	SOAP Psalm 16:5-6	SOAP Psalm 18:30-31	SOAP Psalm 20:4-5
3	Psalms 21-22	Psalms 23-24	Psalms 25-26	Psalms 27-28	Psalms 29-30
	SOAP Psalm 22:21-24	SOAP Psalm 23:6	SOAP Psalm 25:6-7	SOAP Psalm 28:8-9	SOAP Psalm 29:10-11
4	Psalms 31-32	Psalms 33-34	Psalms 35-36	Psalms 37-38	Psalms 39-40
	SOAP Psalm 31:1-2	SOAP Psalm 33:4-5	SOAP Psalm 35:17-19	SOAP Psalm 37:7	SOAP Psalm 40:1-3
5	Psalms 41-42	Psalms 43-44	Psalms 45-46	Psalms 47-48	Psalms 49-50
	SOAP Psalm 41:11-12	SOAP Psalm 43:5	SOAP Psalm 45:6-7	SOAP Psalm 48:14	SOAP Psalm 50:15
6	Psalms 51-52	Psalms 53-54	Psalms 55-56	Psalms 57-58	Psalms 59-60
	SOAP Psalm 52:8-9	SOAP Psalm 54:4-5	SOAP Psalm 55:22	SOAP Psalm 57:1-3	SOAP Psalm 59:16-17
7	Psalms 61-62	Psalms 63-64	Psalms 65-66	Psalms 67-68	Psalms 69-70
	SOAP Psalm 61:1-2	SOAP Psalm 63:3-5	SOAP Psalm 66:19-20	SOAP Psalm 68:5-6	SOAP Psalm 69:13-14

8	Psalms 71–72	Psalms 73–74	Psalms 75–76	Psalms 77–78	Psalms 79–80
	SOAP Psalm 71:20–21	SOAP Psalm 73:26	SOAP Psalm 76:11–12	SOAP Psalm 77:11–12	SOAP Psalm 79:8
9	Psalms 81–82	Psalms 83–84	Psalms 85–86	Psalms 87–88	Psalms 89–90
	SOAP Psalm 81:10	SOAP Psalm 84:11–12	SOAP Psalm 86:17	SOAP Psalm 88:13–14	SOAP Psalm 89:32
10	Psalms 91–92	Psalms 93–94	Psalms 95–96	Psalms 97–98	Psalms 99–100
	SOAP Psalm 91:15	SOAP Psalm 94:12–15	SOAP Psalm 96:1–3	SOAP Psalm 98:7–9	SOAP Psalm 100:5
11	Psalms 101–102	Psalms 103–104	Psalms 105–106	Psalms 107–108	Psalms 109–110
	SOAP Psalm 102:1–2	SOAP Psalm 103:17–19	SOAP Psalm 106:44–45	SOAP Psalm 107:1–3	SOAP Psalm 110:5–7
12	Psalms 111–112	Psalms 113–114	Psalms 115–116	Psalms 117–118	Psalm 119:1–40
	SOAP Psalm 111:9	SOAP Psalm 113:4–6	SOAP Psalm 116:12	SOAP Psalm 118:13–14	SOAP Psalm 119:15–16
13	Psalm 119:41–72	Psalm 119:73–96	Psalm 119:97–128	Psalm 119:129–152	Psalm 119:153–176
	SOAP Psalm 119:41–42	SOAP Psalm 119:73–74	SOAP Psalm 119:116	SOAP Psalm 119:151–152	SOAP Psalm 119:160
14	Psalms 120–122	Psalms 123–124	Psalms 125–126	Psalms 127–128	Psalms 129–130
	SOAP Psalm 121:3–4	SOAP Psalm 124:1–5	SOAP Psalm 125:1–2	SOAP Psalm 127:1–2	SOAP Psalm 130:1–2
15	Psalms 131–132	Psalms 133–134	Psalms 135–136	Psalms 137–138	Psalms 139–140
	SOAP Psalm 132:11–12	SOAP Psalm 133:1–2	SOAP Psalm 136:1	SOAP Psalm 138:7–8	SOAP Psalm 139:23–24
16	Psalms 141–142	Psalms 143–144	Psalms 145–146	Psalms 147–148	Psalms 149–150
	SOAP Psalm 141:3–4	SOAP Psalm 144:1–2	SOAP Psalm 145:17–21	SOAP Psalm 147:11	SOAP Psalm 149:4–5

BOOK 1 (PSALMS 1–41)

1 How blessed is the one who does not
follow the advice of the wicked,
or stand in the pathway with sinners,
or sit in the assembly of scoffers.
2 Instead he finds pleasure in obeying
the LORD's commands;
he meditates on his commands day and night.
3 He is like a tree planted by flowing streams;
it yields its fruit at the proper time,
and its leaves never fall off.
He succeeds in everything he attempts.
4 Not so with the wicked!
Instead they are like wind-driven chaff.
5 For this reason the wicked cannot
withstand judgment,
nor can sinners join the assembly of the godly.
6 Certainly the LORD guards the way of the godly,
but the way of the wicked ends in destruction.

2 Why do the nations rebel?
Why are the countries devising plots that will fail?
2 The kings of the earth form a united front;
the rulers collaborate
against the LORD and his anointed king.
3 They say, "Let's tear off the shackles
they've put on us.
Let's free ourselves from their ropes."
4 The one enthroned in heaven laughs in disgust;
the Lord taunts them.
5 Then he angrily speaks to them
and terrifies them in his rage, saying,
6 "I myself have installed my king
on Zion, my holy hill."
7 The king says, "I will announce the
LORD's decree. He said to me:
'You are my son. This very day I have
become your father.
8 Ask me,
and I will give you the nations
as your inheritance,
the ends of the earth as your personal property.
9 You will break them with an iron scepter;
you will smash them like a potter's jar.'"
10 So now, you kings, do what is wise;
you rulers of the earth, submit to correction.
11 Serve the LORD in fear.
Repent in terror.
12 Give sincere homage.
Otherwise he will be angry,
and you will die because of your behavior,
when his anger quickly ignites.
How blessed are all who take shelter in him!

A psalm of David, written when he fled from his son Absalom.

3 LORD, how numerous are my enemies!
Many attack me.
2 Many say about me,
"God will not deliver him." *Selah*
3 But you, LORD, are a shield that protects me;
you are my glory and the one who restores me.
4 To the LORD I cried out,
and he answered me from his holy hill. *Selah*
5 I rested and slept;
I awoke, for the LORD protects me.
6 I am not afraid of the multitude of people
who attack me from all directions.
7 Rise up, LORD!
Deliver me, my God!
Yes, you will strike all my enemies on the jaw;
you will break the teeth of the wicked.
8 The LORD delivers;
you show favor to your people. *Selah*

For the music director, to be accompanied by stringed instruments; a psalm of David.

4 When I call out, answer me,
O God who vindicates me.
Though I am hemmed in, you will lead
me into a wide, open place.
Have mercy on me and respond to my prayer.
2 You men, how long will you try to
turn my honor into shame?
How long will you love what is worthless
and search for what is deceptive? *Selah*
3 Realize that the LORD shows the godly special favor;
the LORD responds when I cry out to him.
4 Tremble with fear and do not sin.
Meditate as you lie in bed, and repent of your ways. *Selah*
5 Offer the prescribed sacrifices
and trust in the LORD.
6 Many say, "Who can show us anything good?"
Smile upon us, LORD!
7 You make me happier
than those who have abundant grain and wine.
8 I will lie down and sleep peacefully,
for you, LORD, make me safe and secure.

For the music director, to be accompanied by wind instruments; a psalm of David.

5 Listen to what I say, LORD!
Carefully consider my complaint!
2 Pay attention to my cry for help,
my King and my God,
for I am praying to you!
3 LORD, in the morning you will hear me;
in the morning I will present my case to you
and then wait expectantly for an answer.

LOVE TO GROW

HOLY CONFIDENCE

PSALM 3

When I read Psalm 3, I envision a person with strong, unshakable faith offering this prayer with assurance. But when King David wrote Psalm 3, that was not the case. The psalm begins, "Many attack me. Many say about me, 'God will not deliver him'"(v. 2). David was distressed, surrounded by enemies, abandoned, and alone. He did not know where to go or what to do. Have you ever felt that way? I know I have.

David remembered God's faithfulness. David was desperate and down, yet confident in God. David's prayer was, in essence, "Yes, I'm under attack, but God is my shield." He knew his God, and his God was his confidence. David did not pray what he saw or felt, he prayed what he knew was true about God.

It takes a holy confidence to pray believing the truth of God's promises despite our current circumstances.

When we feel distressed, abandoned or alone, let us remember God's goodness. Let us take hold of the promises of His faithfulness to be our shield, our deliverer, our provider, and our protector. God is always with us and is always for us. Let that truth sink deep into your heart so you can recall it anytime you face troubles and trials.

Despite the enemies surrounding me, God is my shield. Despite my brokenness, God restores me. Despite my loneliness, God answers me. Despite my fear, God protects me. Despite the attacks, God is with me: I am not afraid.

How beautiful it is to serve a God who hears our cries and delivers us from our troubles. Like David, when we confide in God in our time of need, we display our great love for Him. We might not know where to go or what to do, but we can have faith God is on our side. We can proclaim God's promises and put our trust in Him. We can rest peacefully and walk fearlessly. We can live with a holy confidence with God as our shield.

4 Certainly you are not a God who approves of evil;
evil people cannot dwell with you.
5 Arrogant people cannot stand in your presence;
you hate all who behave wickedly.
6 You destroy liars;
the LORD despises violent and deceitful people.
7 But as for me, because of your great
faithfulness I will enter your house;
I will bow down toward your holy temple as I worship you.
8 LORD, lead me in your righteousness
because of those who wait to ambush me,
remove the obstacles in the way in
which you are guiding me.
9 For they do not speak the truth;
their stomachs are like the place of destruction,
their throats like an open grave,
their tongues like a steep slope leading into it.
10 Condemn them, O God!
May their own schemes be their downfall.
Drive them away because of their
many acts of insurrection,
for they have rebelled against you.
11 But may all who take shelter in you be happy.
May they continually shout for joy.
Shelter them so that those who are
loyal to you may rejoice.
12 Certainly you reward the godly, LORD.
Like a shield you protect them in your good favor.

For the music director, to be accompanied by stringed instruments, according to the sheminith *style; a psalm of David.*

6 LORD, do not rebuke me in your anger.
Do not discipline me in your raging fury.
2 Have mercy on me, LORD, for I am frail.
Heal me, LORD, for my bones are shaking.
3 I am absolutely terrified,
and you, LORD—how long will this continue?
4 Relent, LORD, rescue me!
Deliver me because of your faithfulness.
5 For no one remembers you in the realm of death.
In Sheol who gives you thanks?
6 I am exhausted as I groan.
All night long I drench my bed in tears;
my tears saturate the cushion beneath me.
7 My eyes grow dim from suffering;
they grow weak because of all my enemies.
8 Turn back from me, all you who behave wickedly,
for the LORD has heard the sound of my weeping.
9 The LORD has heard my appeal for mercy;
the LORD has accepted my prayer.
10 They will be humiliated and absolutely terrified.
All my enemies will turn back
and be suddenly humiliated.

A musical composition by David, which he sang to the
LORD concerning a Benjaminite named Cush.

7 O LORD my God, in you I have taken shelter.
Deliver me from all who chase me. Rescue me!
2 Otherwise they will rip me to shreds like a lion;
they will tear me to bits and no one
will be able to rescue me.
3 O LORD my God, if I have done what they say,
or am guilty of unjust actions,
4 or have wronged my ally,
or helped his lawless enemy,
5 may an enemy relentlessly chase me and catch me;
may he trample me to death
and leave me lying dishonored in the dust. *Selah*
6 Stand up angrily, LORD.
Rise up with raging fury against my enemies.
Wake up for my sake, and execute the
judgment you have decreed for them.
7 The countries are assembled all around you;
take once more your rightful place over them.
8 The LORD judges the nations.
Vindicate me, LORD, because I am innocent,
because I am blameless, O Exalted One.
9 May the evil deeds of the wicked come to an end.
But make the innocent secure,
O righteous God,
you who examine inner thoughts and motives.
10 The Exalted God is my shield,
the one who delivers the morally upright.
11 God is a just judge;
he is angry throughout the day.
12 If a person does not repent, God will wield his sword.
He has prepared to shoot his bow.
13 He has prepared deadly weapons to use against him;
he gets ready to shoot flaming arrows.
14 See the one who is pregnant with wickedness,
who conceives destructive plans,
and gives birth to harmful lies—
15 he digs a pit
and then falls into the hole he has made.
16 He becomes the victim of his own destructive plans—
and the violence he intended for
others falls on his own head.
17 I will thank the LORD for his justice;
I will sing praises to the LORD Most High!

For the music director, according to the
gittith *style; a psalm of David.*

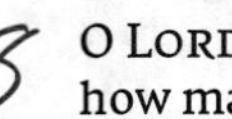
O LORD, our Lord,
how magnificent is your reputation throughout the earth!
You reveal your majesty in the heavens above.
2 From the mouths of children and nursing babies
you have ordained praise on account of your adversaries,
so that you might put an end to the vindictive enemy.

GOD'S HEART FOR THE NATIONS

Psalm 8:1

O LORD, our Lord,
how magnificent
is your reputation
throughout the earth!
You reveal your majesty
in the heavens above.

3 When I look up at the heavens, which your fingers made,
and see the moon and the stars, which you set in place,
4 Of what importance is the human race,
that you should notice them?
Of what importance is mankind, that you
should pay attention to them?
5 You made them a little less than the heavenly beings.
You crowned mankind with honor and majesty.
6 you appoint them to rule over your creation;
you have placed everything under their authority,
7 including all the sheep and cattle,
as well as the wild animals,
8 the birds in the sky, the fish in the sea,
and everything that moves through
the currents of the seas.
9 O LORD, our Lord,
how magnificent is your reputation throughout the earth!

For the music director, according to the alumoth-labben *style; a psalm of David.*

9 I will thank the LORD with all my heart!
I will tell about all your amazing deeds.
2 I will be happy and rejoice in you.
I will sing praises to you, O Most High.
3 When my enemies turn back,
they trip and are defeated before you.
4 For you defended my just cause;
from your throne you pronounced a just decision.
5 You terrified the nations with your battle cry.
You destroyed the wicked;
you permanently wiped out all memory of them.
6 The enemy's cities have been reduced to permanent ruins.
You destroyed their cities;
all memory of the enemies has perished.
7 But the LORD rules forever;
he reigns in a just manner.
8 He judges the world fairly;
he makes just legal decisions for the nations.
9 Consequently the LORD provides safety for the oppressed;
he provides safety in times of trouble.
10 Your loyal followers trust in you,
for you, LORD, do not abandon those who seek your help.
11 Sing praises to the LORD, who rules in Zion.
Tell the nations what he has done.
12 For the one who takes revenge against
murderers took notice of the oppressed;
he did not overlook their cry for help
13 when they prayed:
"Have mercy on me, LORD!
See how I am oppressed by those who hate me,
O one who can snatch me away from the gates of death!
14 Then I will tell about all your praiseworthy acts;
in the gates of Daughter Zion I will rejoice
because of your deliverance."

GOD'S HEART FOR THE NATIONS

Psalm 9:11

Sing praises to the LORD,
who rules in Zion.
Tell the nations what
he has done.

15 The nations fell into the pit they had made;
their feet were caught in the net they had hidden.
16 The LORD revealed himself;
he accomplished justice.
The wicked were ensnared by
their own actions. *Higgaion. Selah*
17 The wicked are turned back and sent to Sheol;
this is the destiny of all the nations that ignore God,
18 for the needy are not permanently ignored,
the hopes of the oppressed are not forever dashed.
19 Rise up, LORD!
Don't let men be defiant.
May the nations be judged in your presence.
20 Terrify them, LORD.
Let the nations know they are mere mortals. *Selah*

10 Why, LORD, do you stand far off?
Why do you pay no attention during times of trouble?
2 The wicked arrogantly chase the oppressed;
the oppressed are trapped by the schemes
the wicked have dreamed up.
3 Yes, the wicked man boasts because he gets what he wants;
the one who robs others curses and rejects the LORD.
4 The wicked man is so arrogant he always thinks,
"God won't hold me accountable; he doesn't care."
5 He is secure at all times.
He has no regard for your commands;
he disdains all his enemies.
6 He says to himself,
"I will never be shaken,
because I experience no calamity."
7 His mouth is full of curses and deceptive, harmful words;
his tongue injures and destroys.
8 He waits in ambush near the villages;
in hidden places he kills the innocent.
His eyes look for some unfortunate victim.
9 He lies in ambush in a hidden place, like a lion in a thicket.
He lies in ambush, waiting to catch the oppressed;
he catches the oppressed by pulling in his net.
10 His victims are crushed and beaten down;
they are trapped in his sturdy nets.
11 He says to himself,
"God overlooks it;
he does not pay attention;
he never notices."
12 Rise up, LORD!
O God, strike him down.
Do not forget the oppressed.
13 Why does the wicked man reject God?
He says to himself, "You will not hold me accountable."
14 You have taken notice,
for you always see one who inflicts pain and suffering.
The unfortunate victim entrusts his cause to you;
you deliver the fatherless.

15 Break the arm of the wicked and evil man.
Hold him accountable for his wicked deeds,
which he thought you would not discover.
16 The LORD rules forever!
The nations are driven out of his land.
17 LORD, you have heard the request of the oppressed;
you make them feel secure because
you listen to their prayer.
18 You defend the fatherless and oppressed,
so that mere mortals may no longer terrorize them.

For the music director, by David.

11 In the LORD I have taken shelter.
How can you say to me,
"Flee to a mountain like a bird.
2 For look, the wicked prepare their bows,
they put their arrows on the strings,
to shoot in the darkness at the morally upright.
3 When the foundations are destroyed,
what can the godly accomplish?"
4 The LORD is in his holy temple;
the LORD's throne is in heaven.
His eyes watch;
his eyes examine all people.
5 The LORD approves of the godly,
but he hates the wicked and those
who love to do violence.
6 May he rain down burning coals and
brimstone on the wicked!
A whirlwind is what they deserve.
7 Certainly the LORD is just;
he rewards godly deeds.
The upright will experience his favor.

For the music director, according to the
sheminith *style; a psalm of David.*

12 Deliver, LORD!
For the godly have disappeared;
people of integrity have vanished.
2 People lie to one another;
they flatter and deceive.
3 May the LORD cut off all flattering lips,
and the tongue that boasts!
4 They say, "We speak persuasively;
we know how to flatter and boast.
Who is our master?"
5 "Because of the violence done to the oppressed,
because of the painful cries of the needy,
I will spring into action," says the LORD.
"I will provide the safety they so desperately desire."
6 The LORD's words are absolutely reliable.
They are as untainted as silver purified
in a furnace on the ground,
where it is thoroughly refined.

7 You, LORD, will protect them;
you will continually shelter each one
from these evil people,
8 for the wicked seem to be everywhere,
when people promote evil.

For the music director, a psalm of David.

13 How long, LORD, will you continue to ignore me?
How long will you pay no attention to me?
2 How long must I worry,
and suffer in broad daylight?
How long will my enemy gloat over me?
3 Look at me! Answer me, O LORD my God!
Revive me, or else I will die.
4 Then my enemy will say, "I have defeated him."
Then my foes will rejoice because I am shaken.
5 But I trust in your faithfulness.
May I rejoice because of your deliverance.
6 I will sing praises to the LORD
when he vindicates me.

REFLECT

Have you ever felt like God was ignoring you? How did the psalmist respond to God when he felt this way? Do you think this is an appropriate way to talk to God?

For the music director, by David.

14 Fools say to themselves, "There is no God."
They sin and commit evil deeds;
none of them does what is right.
2 The LORD looks down from heaven at the human race,
to see if there is anyone who is wise and seeks God.
3 Everyone rejects God;
they are all morally corrupt.
None of them does what is right,
not even one.
4 All those who behave wickedly do not understand—
those who devour my people as if they were eating bread,
and do not call out to the LORD.
5 They are absolutely terrified,
for God defends the godly.
6 You want to humiliate the oppressed,
even though the LORD is their shelter.
7 I wish the deliverance of Israel would come from Zion!
When the LORD restores the well-being of his people,
may Jacob rejoice,
may Israel be happy!

A psalm of David.

15 LORD, who may be a guest in your home?
Who may live on your holy hill?
2 Whoever lives a blameless life,
does what is right,
and speaks honestly.
3 He does not slander,
or do harm to others,
or insult his neighbor.
4 He despises a reprobate,
but honors the LORD's loyal followers.

He makes firm commitments and does
not renege on his promise.
5 He does not charge interest when he lends his money.
He does not take bribes to testify against the innocent.
The one who lives like this will never be shaken.

A prayer of David.

16 Protect me, O God, for I have taken shelter in you.
2 I say to the LORD, "You are the Lord,
my only source of well-being."
3 As for God's chosen people who are in the land,
and the leading officials I admired so much—
4 their troubles multiply;
they desire other gods.
I will not pour out drink offerings
of blood to their gods,
nor will I make vows in the name of their gods.
5 LORD, you give me stability and prosperity;
you make my future secure.
6 It is as if I have been given fertile fields
or received a beautiful tract of land.
7 I will praise the LORD who guides me;
yes, during the night I reflect and learn.
8 I constantly trust in the LORD;
because he is at my right hand, I will not be shaken.
9 So my heart rejoices
and I am happy;
my life is safe.
10 You will not abandon me to Sheol;
you will not allow your faithful follower to see the Pit.
11 You lead me in the path of life.
I experience absolute joy in your presence;
you always give me sheer delight.

A prayer of David.

17 LORD, consider my just cause.
Pay attention to my cry for help.
Listen to the prayer
I sincerely offer.
2 Make a just decision on my behalf.
Decide what is right.
3 You have scrutinized my inner motives;
you have examined me during the night.
You have carefully evaluated me,
but you find no sin.
I am determined I will say nothing sinful.
4 As for the actions of people—
just as you have commanded,
I have not followed in the footsteps of violent men.
5 I carefully obey your commands;
I do not deviate from them.
6 I call to you because you will answer me, O God.
Listen to me!
Hear what I say!

7 Accomplish awesome, faithful deeds,
you who powerfully deliver those who look to
you for protection from their enemies.
8 Protect me as you would protect the pupil of your eye.
Hide me in the shadow of your wings.
9 Protect me from the wicked men who attack me,
my enemies who crowd around me for the kill.
10 They are calloused;
they speak arrogantly.
11 They attack me, now they surround me;
they intend to throw me to the ground.
12 He is like a lion that wants to tear its prey to bits,
like a young lion crouching in hidden places.
13 Rise up, LORD!
Confront him. Knock him down.
Use your sword to rescue me from the wicked man.
14 LORD, use your power to deliver me
from these murderers,
from the murderers of this world.
They enjoy prosperity;
you overwhelm them with the riches they desire.
They have many children,
and leave their wealth to their offspring.
15 As for me, because I am innocent I will see your face;
when I awake you will reveal yourself to me.

For the music director, by the LORD's servant David, who sang to the LORD the words of this song when the LORD rescued him from the power of all his enemies, including Saul.

18 He said:
"I love you, LORD, my source of strength!
2 The LORD is my high ridge, my stronghold, my deliverer.
My God is my rocky summit where I take shelter,
my shield, the horn that saves me, and my refuge.
3 I called to the LORD, who is worthy of praise,
and I was delivered from my enemies.
4 The waves of death engulfed me,
the currents of chaos overwhelmed me.
5 The ropes of Sheol tightened around me,
the snares of death trapped me.
6 In my distress I called to the LORD;
I cried out to my God.
From his heavenly temple he heard my voice;
he listened to my cry for help.
7 The earth heaved and shook.
The roots of the mountains trembled;
they heaved because he was angry.
8 Smoke ascended from his nose;
fire devoured as it came from his mouth.
He hurled down fiery coals.
9 He made the sky sink as he descended;
a thick cloud was under his feet.
10 He mounted a winged angel and flew;
he glided on the wings of the wind.

11 He shrouded himself in darkness,
in thick rain clouds.
12 From the brightness in front of him came
hail and fiery coals.
13 The LORD thundered in the sky;
the Most High shouted.
14 He shot his arrows and scattered them,
many lightning bolts and routed them.
15 The depths of the sea were exposed;
the inner regions of the world were uncovered
by your battle cry, LORD,
by the powerful breath from your nose.
16 He reached down from above and took hold of me;
he pulled me from the surging water.
17 He rescued me from my strong enemy,
from those who hate me,
for they were too strong for me.
18 They confronted me in my day of calamity,
but the LORD helped me.
19 He brought me out into a wide open place;
he delivered me because he was pleased with me.
20 The LORD repaid me for my godly deeds;
he rewarded my blameless behavior.
21 For I have obeyed the LORD's commands;
I have not rebelled against my God.
22 For I am aware of all his regulations,
and I do not reject his rules.
23 I was innocent before him,
and kept myself from sinning.
24 The LORD rewarded me for my godly deeds;
he took notice of my blameless behavior.
25 You prove to be loyal to one who is faithful;
you prove to be trustworthy to one who is innocent.
26 You prove to be reliable to one who is blameless,
but you prove to be deceptive to one who is perverse.
27 For you deliver oppressed people,
but you bring down those who have a proud look.
28 Indeed, you light my lamp, LORD.
My God illuminates the darkness around me.
29 Indeed, with your help I can charge against an army;
by my God's power I can jump over a wall.
30 The one true God acts in a faithful manner;
the LORD's promise is reliable.
He is a shield to all who take shelter in him.
31 Indeed, who is God besides the LORD?
Who is a protector besides our God?
32 The one true God gives me strength;
he removes the obstacles in my way.
33 He gives me the agility of a deer;
he enables me to negotiate the rugged terrain.
34 He trains my hands for battle;
my arms can bend even the strongest bow.
35 You give me your protective shield;
your right hand supports me.

Your willingness to help enables me to prevail.
36 You widen my path;
my feet do not slip.
37 I chase my enemies and catch them;
I do not turn back until I wipe them out.
38 I beat them to death;
they fall at my feet.
39 You give me strength for battle;
you make my foes kneel before me.
40 You make my enemies retreat;
I destroy those who hate me.
41 They cry out, but there is no one to help them;
they cry out to the LORD, but he does not answer them.
42 I grind them as fine windblown dust;
I beat them underfoot like clay in the streets.
43 You rescue me from a hostile army.
You make me a leader of nations;
people over whom I had no authority
are now my subjects.
44 When they hear of my exploits, they submit to me.
Foreigners are powerless before me.
45 Foreigners lose their courage;
they shake with fear as they leave their strongholds.
46 The LORD is alive!
My Protector is praiseworthy.
The God who delivers me is exalted as king.
47 The one true God completely vindicates me;
he makes nations submit to me.
48 He delivers me from my enemies.
You snatch me away from those who attack me;
you rescue me from violent men.
49 So I will give you thanks before the nations, O LORD.
I will sing praises to you.
50 He gives his king magnificent victories;
he is faithful to his chosen ruler,
to David and his descendants forever."

For the music director, a psalm of David.

19 The heavens declare the glory of God;
the sky displays his handiwork.
2 Day after day it speaks out;
night after night it reveals his greatness.
3 There is no actual speech or word,
nor is its voice literally heard.
4 Yet its voice echoes throughout the earth;
its words carry to the distant horizon.
In the sky he has pitched a tent for the sun.
5 Like a bridegroom it emerges from its chamber;
like a strong man it enjoys running its course.
6 It emerges from the distant horizon,
and goes from one end of the sky to the other;
nothing can escape its heat.
7 The law of the LORD is perfect
and preserves one's life.

The rules set down by the LORD are reliable
and impart wisdom to the inexperienced.
8 The LORD's precepts are fair
and make one joyful.
The LORD's commands are pure
and give insight for life.
9 The commands to fear the LORD are right
and endure forever.
The judgments given by the LORD are trustworthy
and absolutely just.
10 They are of greater value than gold,
than even a great amount of pure gold;
they bring greater delight than honey,
than even the sweetest honey from a honeycomb.
11 Yes, your servant finds moral guidance there;
those who obey them receive a rich reward.
12 Who can know all his errors?
Please do not punish me for sins I am unaware of.
13 Moreover, keep me from committing flagrant sins;
do not allow such sins to control me.
Then I will be blameless,
and innocent of blatant rebellion.
14 May my words and my thoughts
be acceptable in your sight,
O LORD, my sheltering rock and my redeemer.

For the music director, a psalm of David.

20 May the LORD answer you when you are in trouble;
may the God of Jacob make you secure.
2 May he send you help from his temple;
from Zion may he give you support.
3 May he take notice of all your offerings;
may he accept your burnt sacrifice. *Selah*
4 May he grant your heart's desire;
may he bring all your plans to pass.
5 Then we will shout for joy over your victory;
we will rejoice in the name of our God.
May the LORD grant all your requests.
6 Now I am sure that the LORD will deliver his chosen king;
he will intervene for him from his holy,
heavenly temple,
and display his mighty ability to deliver.
7 Some trust in chariots and others in horses,
but we depend on the LORD our God.
8 They will fall down,
but we will stand firm.
9 The LORD will deliver the king;
he will answer us when we call to him for help!

For the music director, a psalm of David.

21 O LORD, the king rejoices in the strength you give;
he takes great delight in the deliverance you provide.
2 You grant him his heart's desire;
you do not refuse his request. *Selah*

3 For you bring him rich blessings;
you place a golden crown on his head.
4 He asked you to sustain his life,
and you have granted him long life
and an enduring dynasty.
5 Your deliverance brings him great honor;
you give him majestic splendor.
6 For you grant him lasting blessings;
you give him great joy by allowing him into your presence.
7 For the king trusts in the LORD,
and because of the Most High's
faithfulness he is not shaken.
8 You prevail over all your enemies;
your power is too great for those who hate you.
9 You burn them up like a fiery furnace when you appear.
The LORD angrily devours them;
the fire consumes them.
10 You destroy their offspring from the earth,
their descendants from among the human race.
11 Yes, they intend to do you harm;
they dream up a scheme, but they do not succeed.
12 For you make them retreat
when you aim your arrows at them.
13 Rise up, O LORD, in strength!
We will sing and praise your power.

For the music director, according to the tune "Morning Doe"; a psalm of David.

22 My God, my God, why have you abandoned me?
I groan in prayer, but help seems far away.
2 My God, I cry out during the day,
but you do not answer,
and during the night my prayers do not let up.
3 You are holy;
you sit as king receiving the praises of Israel.
4 In you our ancestors trusted;
they trusted in you and you rescued them.
5 To you they cried out, and they were saved;
in you they trusted and they were not disappointed.
6 But I am a worm, not a man;
people insult me and despise me.
7 All who see me taunt me;
they mock me and shake their heads.
8 They say,
"Commit yourself to the LORD!
Let the LORD rescue him!
Let the LORD deliver him, for he delights in him."
9 Yes, you are the one who brought me out from the womb
and made me feel secure on my mother's breasts.
10 I have been dependent on you since birth;
from the time I came out of my mother's
womb you have been my God.
11 Do not remain far away from me,
for trouble is near and I have no one to help me.

12 Many bulls surround me;
powerful bulls of Bashan hem me in.
13 They open their mouths to devour me
like a roaring lion that rips its prey.
14 My strength drains away like water;
all my bones are dislocated.
My heart is like wax;
it melts away inside me.
15 The roof of my mouth is as dry as a piece of pottery;
my tongue sticks to my gums.
You set me in the dust of death.
16 Yes, wild dogs surround me—
a gang of evil men crowd around me;
like a lion they pin my hands and feet.
17 I can count all my bones;
my enemies are gloating over me in triumph.
18 They are dividing up my clothes among themselves;
they are rolling dice for my garments.
19 But you, O LORD, do not remain far away.
You are my source of strength. Hurry and help me!
20 Deliver me from the sword.
Save my life from the claws of the wild dogs.
21 Rescue me from the mouth of the lion,
and from the horns of the wild oxen.
You have answered me.
22 I will declare your name to my countrymen.
In the middle of the assembly I will praise you.
23 You loyal followers of the LORD, praise him.
All you descendants of Jacob, honor him.
All you descendants of Israel, stand in awe of him.
24 For he did not despise or detest the
suffering of the oppressed.
He did not ignore him;
when he cried out to him, he responded.
25 You are the reason I offer praise in the great assembly;
I will fulfill my promises before the LORD's loyal followers.
26 Let the oppressed eat and be filled.
Let those who seek his help praise the LORD.
May you live forever!
27 Let all the people of the earth acknowledge
the LORD and turn to him.
Let all the nations worship you.
28 For the LORD is king
and rules over the nations.
29 All the thriving people of the earth will
join the celebration and worship;
all those who are descending into the
grave will bow before him,
including those who cannot preserve their lives.
30 A whole generation will serve him;
they will tell the next generation about the Lord.
31 They will come and tell about his saving deeds;
they will tell a future generation
what he has accomplished.

GOD'S HEART FOR THE NATIONS

Psalm 22:27–28

Let all the people of the earth acknowledge the LORD and turn to him. Let all the nations worship you. For the LORD is king and rules over the nations.

A psalm of David.

23 The LORD is my shepherd,
I lack nothing.
2 He takes me to lush pastures,
he leads me to refreshing water.
3 He restores my strength.
He leads me down the right paths
for the sake of his reputation.
4 Even when I must walk through the darkest valley,
I fear no danger,
for you are with me;
your rod and your staff reassure me.
5 You prepare a feast before me
in plain sight of my enemies.
You refresh my head with oil;
my cup is completely full.
6 Surely your goodness and faithfulness
will pursue me all my days,
and I will live in the LORD's house for the rest of my life.

A psalm of David.

24 The LORD owns the earth and all it contains,
the world and all who live in it.
2 For he set its foundation upon the seas,
and established it upon the ocean currents.
3 Who is allowed to ascend the mountain of the LORD?
Who may go up to his holy dwelling place?
4 The one whose deeds are blameless
and whose motives are pure,
who does not lie,
or make promises with no intention of keeping them.
5 Such godly people are rewarded by the LORD,
and vindicated by the God who delivers them.
6 Such purity characterizes the people who seek his favor,
Jacob's descendants, who pray to him. *Selah*
7 Look up, you gates.
Rise up, you eternal doors.
Then the majestic king will enter.
8 Who is this majestic king?
The LORD who is strong and mighty.
The LORD who is mighty in battle.
9 Look up, you gates.
Rise up, you eternal doors.
Then the majestic king will enter.
10 Who is this majestic king?
The LORD of Heaven's Armies.
He is the majestic king. *Selah*

By David.

25 O LORD, I come before you in prayer.
2 My God, I trust in you.
Please do not let me be humiliated;
do not let my enemies triumphantly rejoice over me.
3 Certainly none who rely on you will be humiliated.

Those who deal in treachery will be
thwarted and humiliated.
4 Make me understand your ways, O LORD.
Teach me your paths.
5 Guide me into your truth and teach me.
For you are the God who delivers me;
on you I rely all day long.
6 Remember your compassionate and
faithful deeds, O LORD,
for you have always acted in this manner.
7 Do not hold against me the sins of my
youth or my rebellious acts.
Because you are faithful to me, extend
to me your favor, O LORD.
8 The LORD is both kind and fair;
that is why he teaches sinners the right way to live.
9 May he show the humble what is right.
May he teach the humble his way.
10 The LORD always proves faithful and reliable
to those who follow the demands of his covenant.
11 For the sake of your reputation, O LORD,
forgive my sin, because it is great.
12 The LORD shows his faithful followers
the way they should live.
13 They experience his favor;
their descendants inherit the land.
14 The LORD's loyal followers receive his guidance,
and he reveals his covenantal demands to them.
15 I continually look to the LORD for help,
for he will free my feet from the enemy's net.
16 Turn toward me and have mercy on me,
for I am alone and oppressed.
17 Deliver me from my distress;
rescue me from my suffering.
18 See my pain and suffering.
Forgive all my sins.
19 Watch my enemies, for they outnumber me;
they hate me and want to harm me.
20 Protect me and deliver me!
Please do not let me be humiliated,
for I have taken shelter in you.
21 May integrity and godliness protect me,
for I rely on you.
22 O God, rescue Israel
from all their distress!

By David.

26 Vindicate me, O LORD,
for I have integrity,
and I trust in the LORD without wavering.
2 Examine me, O LORD, and test me.
Evaluate my inner thoughts and motives.
3 For I am ever aware of your faithfulness,
and your loyalty continually motivates me.

4 I do not associate with deceitful men,
or consort with those who are dishonest.
5 I hate the mob of evil men,
and do not associate with the wicked.
6 I maintain a pure lifestyle,
so I can appear before your altar, O LORD,
7 to give you thanks,
and to tell about all your amazing deeds.
8 O LORD, I love the temple where you live,
the place where your splendor is revealed.
9 Do not sweep me away with sinners,
or execute me along with violent people,
10 who are always ready to do wrong
or offer a bribe.
11 But I have integrity.
Rescue me and have mercy on me!
12 I am safe,
and among the worshipers I will praise the LORD.

By David.

27 The LORD is my light and my salvation.
I fear no one.
The LORD protects my life.
I am afraid of no one.
2 When evil men attack me
to devour my flesh,
when my adversaries and enemies attack me,
they stumble and fall.
3 Even when an army is deployed against me,
I do not fear.
Even when war is imminent,
I remain confident.
4 I have asked the LORD for one thing—
this is what I desire!
I want to live in the LORD's house all the days of my life,
so I can gaze at the splendor of the LORD
and contemplate in his temple.
5 He will surely give me shelter in the day of danger;
he will hide me in his home.
He will place me on an inaccessible rocky summit.
6 Now I will triumph
over my enemies who surround me.
I will offer sacrifices in his dwelling place
and shout for joy.
I will sing praises to the LORD.
7 Hear me, O LORD, when I cry out.
Have mercy on me and answer me.
8 My heart tells me to pray to you,
and I do pray to you, O LORD.
9 Do not reject me.
Do not push your servant away in anger.
You are my deliverer.
Do not forsake or abandon me,
O God who vindicates me.

10 Even if my father and mother abandoned me,
the LORD would take me in.
11 Teach me how you want me to live, LORD;
lead me along a level path because of
those who wait to ambush me.
12 Do not turn me over to my enemies,
for false witnesses who want to destroy
me testify against me.
13 Where would I be if I did not believe I would experience
the LORD's favor in the land of the living?
14 Rely on the LORD!
Be strong and confident!
Rely on the LORD!

By David.

28 To you, O LORD, I cry out!
My Protector, do not ignore me.
If you do not respond to me,
I will join those who are descending into the grave.
2 Hear my plea for mercy when I cry out to you for help,
when I lift my hands toward your holy temple.
3 Do not drag me away with evil men,
with those who behave wickedly,
who talk so friendly to their neighbors,
while they plan to harm them.
4 Pay them back for their evil deeds.
Pay them back for what they do.
Punish them.
5 For they do not understand the LORD's actions,
or the way he carries out justice.
The LORD will permanently demolish them.
6 The LORD deserves praise,
for he has heard my plea for mercy.
7 The LORD strengthens and protects me;
I trust in him with all my heart.
I am rescued and my heart is full of joy;
I will sing to him in gratitude.
8 The LORD strengthens his people;
he protects and delivers his chosen king.
9 Deliver your people.
Empower the nation that belongs to you.
Care for them like a shepherd and carry
them in your arms at all times!

A psalm of David.

29 Acknowledge the LORD, you heavenly beings,
acknowledge the LORD's majesty and power.
2 Acknowledge the majesty of the LORD's reputation.
Worship the LORD in holy attire.
3 The LORD's shout is heard over the water;
the majestic God thunders,
the LORD appears over the surging water.
4 The LORD's shout is powerful,
the LORD's shout is majestic.

ENTHRONED

PSALM 29

I couldn't escape.

Before I knew it, my mind was overwhelmed with emotions. The sadness came in like a flood. I wanted to cry, but I was stuck in a meeting, trying to maintain my composure and remain professional. I was caught in the engulfing waters of depression.

Emotions can overtake us like a physical flood. Depression can capture the mind in a way that feels impossible to overcome. But whether it is a mental illness, physical pain, sudden loss, crippling fear, or relational distress, when the engulfing waters come they can overwhelm us unexpectedly.

They say when you come to a flooded roadway, you shouldn't try to drive through it. Instead, you should turn around and take another road. You never know how deep the water is or if the road has been washed away. Flooding water can quickly fill a car, potentially leaving you trapped or drowned.

I would never attempt to navigate floodwater, but when I'm engulfed by depression, I often try to navigate its flood alone.

When the waters come, I remember Psalm 29. This psalm of praise acknowledges God's power. The imagery throughout the psalm describes the ways in which God is sovereign over all He has made, including the water when it surges.

The word used in Hebrew for engulfing waters is the same word used in Psalm 29 and in Genesis to describe the flood of Noah. If God is King of that flood, the one that destroyed all life on earth, then He is certainly King of your flood. He is certainly enthroned over the engulfing waters of your emotions, your loneliness, your disaster, your fear, and your pain. When the floods come, remember His voice. He thunders and appears over the waters as they threaten to overcome (v. 3).

The LORD sits enthroned over the engulfing waters, the LORD sits enthroned as the eternal king (Ps 29:10).

No matter the strength or volume of the waters, He is King. He is enthroned over them. He is enthroned over all.

5 The LORD's shout breaks the cedars,
the LORD shatters the cedars of Lebanon.
6 He makes them skip like a calf,
Lebanon and Sirion like a young ox.
7 The LORD's shout strikes with flaming fire.
8 The LORD's shout shakes the wilderness,
the LORD shakes the wilderness of Kadesh.
9 The LORD's shout bends the large trees
and strips the leaves from the forests.
Everyone in his temple says, "Majestic!"
10 The LORD sits enthroned over the engulfing waters,
the LORD sits enthroned as the eternal king.
11 The LORD gives his people strength;
the LORD grants his people security.

A psalm, a song used at the dedication of the temple; by David.

30 I will praise you, O LORD, for you lifted me up,
and did not allow my enemies to gloat over me.
2 O LORD my God,
I cried out to you and you healed me.
3 O LORD, you pulled me up from Sheol;
you rescued me from among those
descending into the grave.
4 Sing to the LORD, you faithful followers of his;
give thanks to his holy name.
5 For his anger lasts only a brief moment,
and his good favor restores one's life.
One may experience sorrow during the night,
but joy arrives in the morning.
6 In my self-confidence I said,
"I will never be shaken."
7 O LORD, in your good favor you made me secure.
Then you rejected me and I was terrified.
8 To you, O LORD, I cried out;
I begged the Lord for mercy:
9 "What profit is there in taking my life,
in my descending into the Pit?
Can the dust of the grave praise you?
Can it declare your loyalty?
10 Hear, O LORD, and have mercy on me.
O LORD, deliver me."
11 Then you turned my lament into dancing;
you removed my sackcloth and covered me with joy.
12 So now my heart will sing to you and not be silent;
O LORD my God, I will always give thanks to you.

For the music director, a psalm of David.

31 In you, O LORD, I have taken shelter.
Never let me be humiliated.
Vindicate me by rescuing me.
2 Listen to me.
Quickly deliver me.
Be my protector and refuge,
a stronghold where I can be safe.

3 For you are my high ridge and my stronghold;
for the sake of your own reputation
you lead me and guide me.
4 You will free me from the net they hid for me,
for you are my place of refuge.
5 Into your hand I entrust my life;
you will rescue me, O LORD, the faithful God.
6 I hate those who serve worthless idols,
but I trust in the LORD.
7 I will be happy and rejoice in your faithfulness,
because you notice my pain
and you are aware of how distressed I am.
8 You do not deliver me over to the power
of the enemy;
you enable me to stand in a wide open place.
9 Have mercy on me, LORD, for I am in distress!
My eyes grow dim from suffering.
I have lost my strength.
10 For my life nears its end in pain;
my years draw to a close as I groan.
My strength fails me because of my sin,
and my bones become brittle.
11 Because of all my enemies, people disdain me;
my neighbors are appalled by my suffering—
those who know me are horrified by my condition;
those who see me in the street run away from me.
12 I am forgotten, like a dead man no one thinks about;
I am regarded as worthless, like a broken jar.
13 For I hear what so many are saying,
the terrifying news that comes from every direction.
When they plot together against me,
they figure out how they can take my life.
14 But I trust in you, O LORD!
I declare, "You are my God!"
15 You determine my destiny.
Rescue me from the power of my enemies
and those who chase me.
16 Smile on your servant.
Deliver me because of your faithfulness.
17 O LORD, do not let me be humiliated,
for I call out to you.
May evil men be humiliated.
May they go wailing to the grave.
18 May lying lips be silenced—
lips that speak defiantly against the innocent
with arrogance and contempt.
19 How great is your favor,
which you store up for your loyal followers.
In plain sight of everyone you bestow it
on those who take shelter in you.
20 You hide them with you, where they are
safe from the attacks of men;
you conceal them in a shelter, where they
are safe from slanderous attacks.

21 The LORD deserves praise
for he demonstrated his amazing faithfulness
to me when I was besieged by enemies.
22 I jumped to conclusions and said,
"I am cut off from your presence!"
But you heard my plea for mercy when
I cried out to you for help.
23 Love the LORD, all you faithful followers of his!
The LORD protects those who have integrity,
but he pays back in full the one who acts arrogantly.
24 Be strong and confident,
all you who wait on the LORD.

By David; a well-written song.

32 How blessed is the one whose
rebellious acts are forgiven,
whose sin is pardoned.
2 How blessed is the one whose wrongdoing
the LORD does not punish,
in whose spirit there is no deceit.
3 When I refused to confess my sin,
my whole body wasted away,
while I groaned in pain all day long.
4 For day and night you tormented me;
you tried to destroy me in the intense heat
of summer. *Selah*
5 Then I confessed my sin;
I no longer covered up my wrongdoing.
I said, "I will confess my rebellious acts to the LORD."
And then you forgave my sins. *Selah*
6 For this reason every one of your faithful
followers should pray to you
while there is a window of opportunity.
Certainly when the surging water rises,
it will not reach them.
7 You are my hiding place;
you protect me from distress.
You surround me with shouts of joy from those
celebrating deliverance. *Selah*
8 I will instruct and teach you about how
you should live.
I will advise you as I look you in the eye.
9 Do not be like an unintelligent horse or mule,
which will not obey you
unless they are controlled by a bridle and bit.
10 An evil person suffers much pain,
but the LORD's faithfulness overwhelms
the one who trusts in him.
11 Rejoice in the LORD and be happy, you who are godly!
Shout for joy, all you who are morally upright!

33 You godly ones, shout for joy because of the LORD!
It is appropriate for the morally
upright to offer him praise.

2 Give thanks to the LORD with the harp.
Sing to him to the accompaniment of
a ten-stringed instrument.
3 Sing to him a new song.
Play skillfully as you shout out your praises to him.
4 For the LORD's decrees are just,
and everything he does is fair.
5 He promotes equity and justice;
the LORD's faithfulness extends throughout the earth.
6 By the LORD's decree the heavens were made,
and by the breath of his mouth all the starry hosts.
7 He piles up the water of the sea;
he puts the oceans in storehouses.
8 Let the whole earth fear the LORD.
Let all who live in the world stand in awe of him.
9 For he spoke, and it came into existence.
He issued the decree, and it stood firm.
10 The LORD frustrates the decisions of the nations;
he nullifies the plans of the peoples.
11 The LORD's decisions stand forever;
his plans abide throughout the ages.
12 How blessed is the nation whose God is the LORD,
the people whom he has chosen to
be his special possession.
13 The LORD watches from heaven;
he sees all people.
14 From the place where he lives he looks carefully
at all the earth's inhabitants.
15 He is the one who forms every human heart,
and takes note of all their actions.
16 No king is delivered by his vast army;
a warrior is not saved by his great might.
17 A horse disappoints those who trust in it for victory;
despite its great strength, it cannot deliver.
18 Look, the LORD takes notice of his loyal followers,
those who wait for him to demonstrate
his faithfulness
19 by saving their lives from death
and sustaining them during times of famine.
20 We wait for the LORD;
he is our deliverer and shield.
21 For our hearts rejoice in him,
for we trust in his holy name.
22 May we experience your faithfulness, O LORD,
for we wait for you.

By David, when he pretended to be insane before Abimelech, causing the king to send him away.

34 I will praise the LORD at all times;
my mouth will continually praise him.
2 I will boast in the LORD;
let the oppressed hear and rejoice.
3 Magnify the LORD with me.
Let us praise his name together.

4 I sought the LORD's help and he answered me;
he delivered me from all my fears.
5 Look to him and be radiant;
do not let your faces be ashamed.
6 This oppressed man cried out and the LORD heard;
he saved him from all his troubles.
7 The angel of the LORD camps around
the LORD's loyal followers and delivers them.
8 Taste and see that the LORD is good.
How blessed is the one who takes shelter in him.
9 Fear the LORD, you chosen people of his,
for those who fear him lack nothing.
10 Even young lions sometimes lack food and are hungry,
but those who seek the LORD lack no good thing.
11 Come children. Listen to me.
I will teach you what it means to fear the LORD.
12 Do you want to really live?
Would you love to live a long, happy life?
13 Then make sure you don't speak evil words
or use deceptive speech.
14 Turn away from evil and do what is right.
Strive for peace and promote it.
15 The LORD pays attention to the godly
and hears their cry for help.
16 But the LORD opposes evildoers
and wipes out all memory of them from the earth.
17 The godly cry out and the LORD hears;
he saves them from all their troubles.
18 The LORD is near the brokenhearted;
he delivers those who are discouraged.
19 The godly face many dangers,
but the LORD saves them from each one of them.
20 He protects all his bones;
not one of them is broken.
21 Evil people self-destruct;
those who hate the godly are punished.
22 The LORD rescues his servants;
all who take shelter in him escape punishment.

By David.

35 O LORD, fight those who fight with me.
Attack those who attack me.
2 Grab your small shield and large shield,
and rise up to help me.
3 Use your spear and lance against those who chase me.
Assure me with these words: "I am your deliverer."
4 May those who seek my life be
embarrassed and humiliated.
May those who plan to harm me be
turned back and ashamed.
5 May they be like wind-driven chaff,
as the angel of the LORD attacks them.
6 May their path be dark and slippery,
as the angel of the LORD chases them.

LOVE TO GROW

TO REALLY LIVE

PSALM 34:12–15

If someone asked me if I wanted to really live, I would wonder if it was a trick question. To "really live," I believe, is to live life to the fullest. Yes, of course I want to really live!

In Psalm 34, King David asked, "Would you love to live a long, happy life?" (v. 12), and it was not a trick question. David had seen and experienced enough to offer wisdom that the key to living a long, happy life lies in doing the right thing, turning away from evil, and striving for peace.

Do you want to really live? Would you love to live a long, happy life? Then make sure you don't speak evil words or use deceptive speech. Turn away from evil and do what is right. Strive for peace and promote it. The LORD pays attention to the godly and hears their cry for help (Ps 34:12–15).

We need this reminder every day, don't we? We want to live a long, happy life. We want to really live. We want God's blessing on our lives.

All too often, we look for happiness in the wrong places. We fill our calendars with activities and our homes with things. We sacrifice our relationships chasing achievement, glorifying success, and prioritizing accolades and advancement. We compare and compete, all for the sake of seeking happiness.

It is an exhausting and never-ending pursuit, because happiness is not found in anything apart from God.

The way to a long, happy life is not to strive for more things, more money, more success, more fame, or even more happiness but instead to strive for peace. David knew the Israelites would receive his counsel on how to live a long, happy life. David had been through enough to know the only way to experience God's blessing is to live according to His will.

His advice was as relevant to the ancient Israelites as it is for us today: Don't speak evil words or use deceptive speech; turn away from evil and do what is right; strive for peace and promote it!

The psalms teach us many things, and the lesson found in Psalm 34:12–15 is that a life turned away from evil, doing what is right, striving for peace, and speaking God's truth is a happy life. Living aligned with God's Word is really living.

7 I did not harm them, but they hid a net to catch me
and dug a pit to trap me.
8 Let destruction take them by surprise.
Let the net they hid catch them.
Let them fall into destruction.
9 Then I will rejoice in the LORD
and be happy because of his deliverance.
10 With all my strength I will say,
"O LORD, who can compare to you?
You rescue the oppressed from those
who try to overpower them,
the oppressed and needy from those who try to rob them."
11 Violent men perjure themselves,
and falsely accuse me.
12 They repay me evil for the good I have done;
I am overwhelmed with sorrow.
13 When they were sick, I wore sackcloth,
and refrained from eating food.
(If I am lying, may my prayers go unanswered.)
14 I mourned for them as I would for a friend or my brother.
I bowed down in sorrow as if I were
mourning for my mother.
15 But when I stumbled, they rejoiced and gathered together;
they gathered together to ambush me.
They tore at me without stopping to rest.
16 When I tripped, they taunted me relentlessly,
and tried to bite me.
17 O Lord, how long are you going to watch this?
Rescue me from their destructive attacks;
guard my life from the young lions.
18 Then I will give you thanks in the great assembly;
I will praise you before a large crowd of people.
19 Do not let those who are my enemies
for no reason gloat over me.
Do not let those who hate me without cause
carry out their wicked schemes.
20 For they do not try to make peace with others,
but plan ways to deceive those who
live peacefully in the land.
21 They are ready to devour me;
they say, "Aha! Aha! We've got you!"
22 But you take notice, LORD; do not be silent!
O Lord, do not remain far away from me.
23 Rouse yourself, wake up and vindicate me.
My God and Lord, defend my just cause.
24 Vindicate me by your justice, O LORD my God.
Do not let them gloat over me.
25 Do not let them say to themselves, "Aha!
We have what we wanted!"
Do not let them say, "We have devoured him."
26 May those who rejoice in my troubles be
totally embarrassed and ashamed.
May those who arrogantly taunt me be
covered with shame and humiliation.

27 May those who desire my vindication
shout for joy and rejoice.
May they continually say, "May the LORD be
praised, for he wants his servant to be secure."
28 Then I will tell others about your justice,
and praise you all day long.

For the music director, an oracle, written
by the LORD's servant David.

36 An evil man is rebellious to the core.
He does not fear God,
2 for he is too proud
to recognize and give up his sin.
3 The words he speaks are sinful and deceitful;
he does not care about doing what is wise and right.
4 While he lies in bed he plans ways to sin.
He is committed to a sinful lifestyle;
he does not reject what is evil.
5 O LORD, your loyal love reaches to the sky,
your faithfulness to the clouds.
6 Your justice is like the highest mountains,
your fairness like the deepest sea;
you, LORD, preserve mankind and the animal kingdom.
7 How precious is your loyal love, O God!
The human race finds shelter under your wings.
8 They are filled with food from your house,
and you allow them to drink from the
river of your delicacies.
9 For with you is the fountain of life;
in your light we see light.
10 Extend your loyal love to your faithful followers,
and vindicate the morally upright.
11 Do not let arrogant men overtake me,
or let evil men make me homeless.
12 I can see the evildoers! They have fallen.
They have been knocked down and are unable to get up.

By David.

37 Do not fret when wicked men seem to succeed.
Do not envy evildoers.
2 For they will quickly dry up like grass,
and wither away like plants.
3 Trust in the LORD and do what is right.
Settle in the land and maintain your integrity.
4 Then you will take delight in the LORD,
and he will answer your prayers.
5 Commit your future to the LORD.
Trust in him, and he will act on your behalf.
6 He will vindicate you in broad daylight,
and publicly defend your just cause.
7 Wait patiently for the LORD!
Wait confidently for him!
Do not fret over the apparent success of a sinner,
a man who carries out wicked schemes.

8 Do not be angry and frustrated.
Do not fret. That only leads to trouble.
9 Wicked men will be wiped out,
but those who rely on the LORD are the
ones who will possess the land.
10 Evil men will soon disappear;
you will stare at the spot where they once
were, but they will be gone.
11 But the oppressed will possess the land
and enjoy great prosperity.
12 Evil men plot against the godly
and viciously attack them.
13 The Lord laughs in disgust at them,
for he knows that their day is coming.
14 Evil men draw their swords
and prepare their bows,
to bring down the oppressed and needy,
and to slaughter those who are godly.
15 Their swords will pierce their own hearts,
and their bows will be broken.
16 The little bit that a godly man owns is better than
the wealth of many evil men,
17 for evil men will lose their power,
but the LORD sustains the godly.
18 The LORD watches over the innocent day by day,
and they possess a permanent inheritance.
19 They will not be ashamed when hard times come;
when famine comes they will have enough to eat.
20 But evil men will die;
the LORD's enemies will be incinerated—
they will go up in smoke.
21 Evil men borrow, but do not repay their debt,
but the godly show compassion and are generous.
22 Surely those favored by the LORD will possess the land,
but those rejected by him will be wiped out.
23 The LORD grants success to the one
whose behavior he finds commendable.
24 Even if he trips, he will not fall headlong,
for the LORD holds his hand.
25 I was once young, now I am old.
I have never seen the godly abandoned,
or their children forced to search for food.
26 All day long they show compassion and lend to others,
and their children are blessed.
27 Turn away from evil. Do what is right.
Then you will enjoy lasting security.
28 For the LORD promotes justice,
and never abandons his faithful followers.
They are permanently secure,
but the children of the wicked are wiped out.
29 The godly will possess the land
and will dwell in it permanently.
30 The godly speak wise words
and promote justice.

31 The law of their God controls their thinking;
their feet do not slip.
32 The wicked set an ambush for the godly
and try to kill them.
33 But the LORD does not surrender the godly,
or allow them to be condemned in a court of law.
34 Rely on the LORD. Obey his commands.
Then he will permit you to possess the land;
you will see the demise of the wicked.
35 I have seen ruthless, wicked people
growing in influence, like a green tree
grows in its native soil.
36 But then one passes by, and suddenly
they have disappeared.
I looked for them, but they could not be found.
37 Take note of the one who has integrity.
Observe the upright.
For the one who promotes peace has a future.
38 Sinful rebels are totally destroyed;
the wicked have no future.
39 But the LORD delivers the godly;
he protects them in times of trouble.
40 The LORD helps them and rescues them;
he rescues them from the wicked and delivers them,
for they seek his protection.

A psalm of David, written to get God's attention.

38 O LORD, do not continue to rebuke me in your anger.
Do not continue to punish me in your raging fury.
2 For your arrows pierce me,
and your hand presses me down.
3 My whole body is sick because of your judgment;
I am deprived of health because of my sin.
4 For my sins overwhelm me;
like a heavy load, they are too much for me to bear.
5 My wounds are infected and starting to smell,
because of my foolish sins.
6 I am dazed and completely humiliated;
all day long I walk around mourning.
7 For I am overcome with shame,
and my whole body is sick.
8 I am numb with pain and severely battered;
I groan loudly because of the anxiety I feel.
9 O Lord, you understand my heart's desire;
my groaning is not hidden from you.
10 My heart beats quickly;
my strength leaves me.
I can hardly see.
11 Because of my condition, even my friends and
acquaintances keep their distance;
my neighbors stand far away.
12 Those who seek my life try to entrap me;
those who want to harm me speak destructive words.
All day long they say deceitful things.

13 But I am like a deaf man—I hear nothing;
I am like a mute who cannot speak.
14 I am like a man who cannot hear
and is incapable of arguing his defense.
15 Yet I wait for you, O LORD!
You will respond, O Lord, my God!
16 I have prayed for deliverance, because
otherwise they will gloat over me;
when my foot slips they will arrogantly taunt me.
17 For I am about to stumble,
and I am in constant pain.
18 Yes, I confess my wrongdoing,
and I am concerned about my sins.
19 But those who are my enemies for
no reason are numerous;
those who hate me without cause outnumber me.
20 They repay me evil for the good I have done;
though I have tried to do good to them,
they hurl accusations at me.
21 Do not abandon me, O LORD.
My God, do not remain far away from me.
22 Hurry and help me, O Lord, my deliverer.

For the music director, Jeduthun; a psalm of David.

39 I decided, "I will watch what I say
and make sure I do not sin with my tongue.
I will put a muzzle over my mouth
while in the presence of an evil person."
2 I was stone silent;
I held back the urge to speak.
My frustration grew;
3 my anxiety intensified.
As I thought about it, I became impatient.
Finally I spoke these words:
4 "O LORD, help me understand my mortality
and the brevity of life.
Let me realize how quickly my life will pass.
5 Look, you make my days short-lived,
and my life span is nothing from your perspective.
Surely all people, even those who seem secure,
are nothing but vapor. *Selah*
6 Surely people go through life as mere ghosts.
Surely they accumulate worthless wealth
without knowing who will eventually haul it away."
7 But now, O Lord, upon what am I relying?
You are my only hope!
8 Deliver me from all my sins of rebellion.
Do not make me the object of fools' insults.
9 I am silent and cannot open my mouth
because of what you have done.
10 Please stop wounding me.
You have almost beaten me to death.
11 You severely discipline people for their sins;
like a moth you slowly devour their strength.

Surely all people are a mere vapor. *Selah*
12 Hear my prayer, O LORD.
Listen to my cry for help.
Do not ignore my sobbing.
For I am a resident foreigner with you,
a temporary settler, just as all my ancestors were.
13 Turn your angry gaze away from me, so I can be happy
before I pass away.

For the music director, a psalm of David.

40 I relied completely on the LORD,
and he turned toward me
and heard my cry for help.
2 He lifted me out of the watery pit,
out of the slimy mud.
He placed my feet on a rock
and gave me secure footing.
3 He gave me reason to sing a new song,
praising our God.
May many see what God has done,
so that they might swear allegiance to
him and trust in the LORD.
4 How blessed is the one who trusts in the LORD
and does not seek help from the proud or from liars.
5 O LORD, my God, you have accomplished many things;
you have done amazing things and
carried out your purposes for us.
No one can thwart you.
I want to declare your deeds and talk about them,
but they are too numerous to recount.
6 Receiving sacrifices and offerings are
not your primary concern.
You make that quite clear to me.
You do not ask for burnt sacrifices and sin offerings.
7 Then I say,
"Look, I come!
What is written in the scroll pertains to me.
8 I want to do what pleases you, my God.
Your law dominates my thoughts."
9 I have told the great assembly about your justice.
Look, I spare no words.
O LORD, you know this is true.
10 I have not failed to tell about your justice;
I spoke about your reliability and deliverance.
I have not neglected to tell the great assembly
about your loyal love and faithfulness.
11 O LORD, you do not withhold your compassion from me.
May your loyal love and faithfulness
continually protect me!
12 For innumerable dangers surround me.
My sins overtake me
so I am unable to see;
they outnumber the hairs of my head
so my strength fails me.

REFLECT

When has God lifted you out of the pit? How can you praise Him today for His faithfulness to you?

13 Please be willing, O LORD, to rescue me!
O LORD, hurry and help me!
14 May those who are trying to snatch away my life
be totally embarrassed and ashamed.
May those who want to harm me
be turned back and ashamed.
15 May those who say to me, "Aha! Aha!"
be humiliated and disgraced.
16 May all those who seek you be happy
and rejoice in you.
May those who love to experience your
deliverance say continually,
"May the LORD be praised!"
17 I am oppressed and needy.
May the Lord pay attention to me.
You are my helper and my deliverer.
O my God, do not delay.

For the music director, a psalm of David.

41 How blessed is the one who treats the poor properly.
When trouble comes, may the LORD deliver him.
2 May the LORD protect him and save his life.
May he be blessed in the land.
Do not turn him over to his enemies.
3 The LORD supports him on his sickbed;
you have healed him from his illness.
4 As for me, I said:
"O LORD, have mercy on me!
Heal me, for I have sinned against you.
5 My enemies ask this cruel question about me,
'When will he finally die and be forgotten?'
6 When someone comes to visit,
he pretends to be friendly;
he thinks of ways to defame me,
and when he leaves he slanders me.
7 All who hate me whisper insults
about me to one another;
they plan ways to harm me.
8 They say,
'An awful disease overwhelms him,
and now that he is bedridden he will never recover.'
9 Even my close friend whom I trusted,
he who shared meals with me,
has turned against me.
10 As for you, O LORD, have mercy on me
and raise me up,
so I can pay them back!"
11 By this I know that you are pleased with me,
for my enemy does not triumph over me.
12 As for me, you uphold me because of my integrity;
you allow me permanent access to your presence.
13 The LORD God of Israel deserves praise
in the future and forevermore.
We agree! We agree!

BOOK 2 (PSALMS 42–72)

For the music director, a well-written song by the Korahites.

42 As a deer longs for streams of water,
so I long for you, O God!
2 I thirst for God,
for the living God.
I say, "When will I be able to go and
appear in God's presence?"
3 I cannot eat; I weep day and night.
All day long they say to me, "Where is your God?"
4 I will remember and weep.
For I was once walking along with the
great throng to the temple of God,
shouting and giving thanks along with the
crowd as we celebrated the holy festival.
5 Why are you depressed, O my soul?
Why are you upset?
Wait for God!
For I will again give thanks
to my God for his saving intervention.
6 I am depressed,
so I will pray to you while in the
region of the upper Jordan,
from Hermon, from Mount Mizar.
7 One deep stream calls out to another at
the sound of your waterfalls;
all your billows and waves overwhelm me.
8 By day the LORD decrees his loyal love,
and by night he gives me a song,
a prayer to the God of my life.
9 I will pray to God, my high ridge:
"Why do you ignore me?
Why must I walk around mourning
because my enemies oppress me?"
10 My enemies' taunts cut me to the bone,
as they say to me all day long, "Where is your God?"
11 Why are you depressed, O my soul?
Why are you upset?
Wait for God!
For I will again give thanks
to my God for his saving intervention.

43 Vindicate me, O God!
Fight for me against an ungodly nation.
Deliver me from deceitful and evil men.
2 For you are the God who shelters me.
Why do you reject me?
Why must I walk around mourning
because my enemies oppress me?
3 Reveal your light and your faithfulness.
They will lead me;
they will escort me back to your holy hill,
and to the place where you live.

4 Then I will go to the altar of God,
to the God who gives me ecstatic joy,
so that I may express my thanks to you,
O God, my God, with a harp.
5 Why are you depressed, O my soul?
Why are you upset?
Wait for God!
For I will again give thanks
to my God for his saving intervention.

For the music director, by the Korahites; a well-written song.

44 O God, we have clearly heard;
our ancestors have told us
what you did in their days,
in ancient times.
2 You, by your power, defeated nations and
settled our fathers on their land;
you crushed the people living there and
enabled our ancestors to occupy it.
3 For they did not conquer the land by their swords,
and they did not prevail by their strength,
but rather by your power, strength, and good favor,
for you were partial to them.
4 You are my king, O God.
Decree Jacob's deliverance.
5 By your power we will drive back our enemies;
by your strength we will trample down our foes.
6 For I do not trust in my bow,
and I do not prevail by my sword.
7 For you deliver us from our enemies;
you humiliate those who hate us.
8 In God we boast all day long,
and we will continually give thanks to your name. *Selah*
9 But you rejected and embarrassed us.
You did not go into battle with our armies.
10 You made us retreat from the enemy.
Those who hate us take whatever they want from us.
11 You handed us over like sheep to be eaten;
you scattered us among the nations.
12 You sold your people for a pittance;
you did not ask a high price for them.
13 You made us an object of disdain to our neighbors;
those who live on our borders taunt and insult us.
14 You made us an object of ridicule among the nations;
foreigners treat us with contempt.
15 All day long I feel humiliated
and am overwhelmed with shame,
16 before the vindictive enemy
who ridicules and insults me.
17 All this has happened to us, even though
we have not rejected you
or violated your covenant with us.
18 We have not been unfaithful,
nor have we disobeyed your commands.

19 Yet you have battered us, leaving us a heap
of ruins overrun by wild dogs;
you have covered us with darkness.
20 If we had rejected our God,
and spread out our hands in prayer to another god,
21 would not God discover it,
for he knows a person's secret thoughts?
22 Yet because of you we are killed all day long;
we are treated like sheep at the slaughtering block.
23 Rouse yourself! Why do you sleep, O Lord?
Wake up! Do not reject us forever.
24 Why do you look the other way,
and ignore the way we are oppressed and mistreated?
25 For we lie in the dirt,
with our bellies pressed to the ground.
26 Rise up and help us.
Rescue us because of your loyal love.

For the music director, according to the tune of "Lilies";
by the Korahites, a well-written poem, a love song.

45 My heart is stirred by a beautiful song.
I say, "I have composed this special song for the king;
my tongue is as skilled as the stylus
of an experienced scribe."
2 You are the most handsome of all men.
You speak in an impressive and fitting manner.
For this reason God grants you continual blessings.
3 Strap your sword to your thigh, O warrior.
Appear in your majestic splendor.
4 Appear in your majesty and be victorious.
Ride forth for the sake of what is right,
on behalf of justice.
Then your right hand will accomplish mighty acts.
5 Your arrows are sharp
and penetrate the hearts of the king's enemies.
Nations fall at your feet.
6 Your throne, O God, is permanent.
The scepter of your kingdom is a scepter of justice.
7 You love justice and hate evil.
For this reason God, your God, has anointed you
with the oil of joy, elevating you above
your companions.
8 All your garments are perfumed with
myrrh, aloes, and cassia.
From the luxurious palaces comes the music of
stringed instruments that makes you happy.
9 Princesses are among your honored women.
Your bride stands at your right hand, wearing
jewelry made with gold from Ophir.
10 Listen, O princess.
Observe and pay attention!
Forget your homeland and your family.
11 Then the king will be attracted by your beauty.
After all, he is your master. Submit to him.

12 Rich people from Tyre
will seek your favor by bringing a gift.
13 The princess looks absolutely magnificent,
decked out in pearls and clothed in a
brocade trimmed with gold.
14 In embroidered robes she is escorted to the king.
Her attendants, the maidens of honor who follow her,
are led before you.
15 They are bubbling with joy as they walk in procession
and enter the royal palace.
16 Your sons will carry on the dynasty of your ancestors;
you will make them princes throughout the land.
17 I will proclaim your greatness through the coming years,
then the nations will praise you forever.

GOD'S HEART FOR THE NATIONS

Psalm 45:17

I will proclaim your greatness through the coming years, then the nations will praise you forever.

For the music director, by the Korahites; according to the alamoth *style; a song.*

46 God is our strong refuge;
he is truly our helper in times of trouble.
2 For this reason we do not fear when the earth shakes,
and the mountains tumble into the depths of the sea,
3 when its waves crash and foam,
and the mountains shake before the surging sea. *Selah*
4 The river's channels bring joy to the city of God,
the special, holy dwelling place of the Most High.
5 God lives within it, it cannot be moved.
God rescues it at the break of dawn.
6 Nations are in uproar, kingdoms are overthrown.
God gives a shout, the earth dissolves.
7 The LORD of Heaven's Armies is on our side.
The God of Jacob is our stronghold. *Selah*
8 Come, Witness the exploits of the LORD,
who brings devastation to the earth.
9 He brings an end to wars throughout the earth.
He shatters the bow and breaks the spear;
he burns the shields with fire.
10 He says, "Stop your striving and recognize that I am God.
I will be exalted over the nations! I will
be exalted over the earth!"
11 The LORD of Heaven's Armies is on our side!
The God of Jacob is our stronghold! *Selah*

For the music director, by the Korahites; a psalm.

47 All you nations, clap your hands.
Shout out to God in celebration.
2 For the LORD Most High is awe-inspiring;
he is the great king who rules the whole earth!
3 He subdued nations beneath us
and countries under our feet.
4 He picked out for us a special land
to be a source of pride for Jacob, whom he loves. *Selah*
5 God has ascended his throne amid loud shouts;
the LORD has ascended amid
the blaring of ram's horns.

6 Sing to God! Sing!
Sing to our king! Sing!
7 For God is king of the whole earth.
Sing a well-written song.
8 God reigns over the nations.
God sits on his holy throne.
9 The nobles of the nations assemble,
along with the people of the God of Abraham,
for God has authority over the rulers of the earth.
He is highly exalted.

A song, a psalm by the Korahites.

48 The LORD is great and certainly worthy of praise
in the city of our God, his holy hill.
2 It is lofty and pleasing to look at,
a source of joy to the whole earth.
Mount Zion resembles the peaks of Zaphon;
it is the city of the great king.
3 God is in its fortresses;
he reveals himself as its defender.
4 For look, the kings assemble;
they advance together.
5 As soon as they see, they are shocked;
they are terrified, they quickly retreat.
6 Look at them shake uncontrollably,
like a woman writhing in childbirth.
7 With an east wind
you shatter the large ships.
8 We heard about God's mighty deeds;
now we have seen them,
in the city of the LORD of Heaven's Armies,
in the city of our God.
God makes it permanently secure. *Selah*
9 Within your temple
we reflect on your loyal love, O God.
10 The praise you receive as far away as the ends of the earth
is worthy of your reputation, O God.
You execute justice.
11 Mount Zion rejoices;
the towns of Judah are happy,
because of your acts of judgment.
12 Walk around Zion. Encircle it.
Count its towers.
13 Consider its defenses.
Walk through its fortresses,
so you can tell the next generation about it.
14 For God, our God, is our defender forever.
He guides us.

For the music director, a psalm by the Korahites.

49 Listen to this, all you nations.
Pay attention, all you inhabitants of the world.
2 Pay attention, all you people,
both rich and poor.

3 I will declare a wise saying;
I will share my profound thoughts.
4 I will learn a song that imparts wisdom;
I will then sing my insightful song to
the accompaniment of a harp.
5 Why should I be afraid in times of trouble,
when the sinful deeds of deceptive men
threaten to overwhelm me?
6 They trust in their wealth
and boast in their great riches.
7 Certainly a man cannot rescue his brother;
he cannot pay God an adequate ransom price
8 (the ransom price for a human life is too high,
and people go to their final destiny),
9 so that he might continue to live forever
and not experience death.
10 Surely one sees that even wise people die;
fools and spiritually insensitive people all pass away
and leave their wealth to others.
11 Their grave becomes their permanent residence,
their eternal dwelling place.
They name their lands after themselves,
12 but, despite their wealth, people do not last.
They are like animals that perish.
13 This is the destiny of fools,
and of those who approve of their philosophy. *Selah*
14 They will travel to Sheol like sheep,
with death as their shepherd.
The godly will rule over them when the
day of vindication dawns.
Sheol will consume their bodies, and they will
no longer live in impressive houses.
15 But God will rescue my life from the power of Sheol;
certainly he will pull me to safety. *Selah*
16 Do not be afraid when a man becomes rich
and his wealth multiplies.
17 For he will take nothing with him when he dies;
his wealth will not follow him down into the grave.
18 He pronounces this blessing on himself
while he is alive:
"May men praise you, for you have done well."
19 But he will join his ancestors;
they will never again see the light of day.
20 Wealthy people do not understand;
they are like animals that perish.

A psalm by Asaph.

50 El, God, the LORD has spoken,
and summoned the earth to come
from the east and west.
2 From Zion, the most beautiful of all places,
God has come in splendor.
3 "May our God come
and not be silent."

Consuming fire goes ahead of him,
and all around him a storm rages.
4 He summons the heavens above,
as well as the earth, so that he might judge his people.
5 He says:
"Assemble my covenant people before me,
those who ratified a covenant with me by sacrifice."
6 The heavens declare his fairness,
for God is judge. *Selah*
7 He says:
"Listen, my people. I am speaking!
Listen, Israel. I am accusing you.
I am God, your God!
8 I am not condemning you because
of your sacrifices,
or because of your burnt sacrifices that
you continually offer me.
9 I do not need to take a bull from your household
or goats from your sheepfolds.
10 For every wild animal in the forest belongs to me,
as well as the cattle that graze on a
thousand hills.
11 I keep track of every bird in the hills,
and the insects of the field are mine.
12 Even if I were hungry, I would not tell you,
for the world and all it contains belong to me.
13 Do I eat the flesh of bulls?
Do I drink the blood of goats?
14 Present to God a thank offering.
Repay your vows to the Most High.
15 Pray to me when you are in trouble.
I will deliver you, and you will honor me."
16 God says this to the evildoer:
"How can you declare my commands,
and talk about my covenant?
17 For you hate instruction
and reject my words.
18 When you see a thief, you join him;
you associate with men who are unfaithful
to their wives.
19 You do damage with words,
and use your tongue to deceive.
20 You plot against your brother;
you slander your own brother.
21 When you did these things, I was silent,
so you thought I was exactly like you.
But now I will condemn you
and state my case against you.
22 Carefully consider this, you who reject God.
Otherwise I will rip you to shreds
and no one will be able to rescue you.
23 Whoever presents a thank offering honors me.
To whoever obeys my commands, I will
reveal my power to deliver."

For the music director, a psalm of David, written when Nathan the prophet confronted him after David's affair with Bathsheba.

51 Have mercy on me, O God, because of your loyal love.
Because of your great compassion,
wipe away my rebellious acts.
2 Wash away my wrongdoing.
Cleanse me of my sin.
3 For I am aware of my rebellious acts;
I am forever conscious of my sin.
4 Against you—you above all—I have sinned;
I have done what is evil in your sight.
So you are just when you confront me;
you are right when you condemn me.
5 Look, I was guilty of sin from birth,
a sinner the moment my mother conceived me.
6 Look, you desire integrity in the inner man;
you want me to possess wisdom.
7 Cleanse me with hyssop and I will be pure;
wash me and I will be whiter than snow.
8 Grant me the ultimate joy of being forgiven.
May the bones you crushed rejoice.
9 Hide your face from my sins.
Wipe away all my guilt.
10 Create for me a pure heart, O God.
Renew a resolute spirit within me.
11 Do not reject me.
Do not take your holy Spirit away from me.
12 Let me again experience the joy of your deliverance.
Sustain me by giving me the desire to obey.
13 Then I will teach rebels your merciful ways,
and sinners will turn to you.
14 Rescue me from the guilt of murder,
O God, the God who delivers me.
Then my tongue will shout for joy
because of your righteousness.
15 O Lord, give me the words.
Then my mouth will praise you.
16 Certainly you do not want a sacrifice,
or else I would offer it;
you do not desire a burnt sacrifice.
17 The sacrifice God desires is a humble spirit—
O God, a humble and repentant heart you will not reject.
18 Because you favor Zion, do what is good for her.
Fortify the walls of Jerusalem.
19 Then you will accept the proper sacrifices,
burnt sacrifices and whole offerings;
then bulls will be sacrificed on your altar.

For the music director, a well-written song by David. It was written when Doeg the Edomite went and informed Saul: "David has arrived at the home of Ahimelech."

52 Why do you boast about your evil
plans, O powerful man?
God's loyal love protects me all day long.

2 Your tongue carries out your destructive plans;
it is as effective as a sharp razor, O deceiver.
3 You love evil more than good,
lies more than speaking the truth. *Selah*
4 You love to use all the words that destroy,
and the tongue that deceives.
5 Yet God will make you a permanent heap of ruins.
He will scoop you up and remove you from your home;
he will uproot you from the land of the living. *Selah*
6 When the godly see this, they will be filled with awe,
and will mock the evildoer, saying:
7 "Look, here is the man who would not
make God his protector.
He trusted in his great wealth
and was confident about his plans to destroy others."
8 But I am like a flourishing olive tree in the house of God;
I continually trust in God's loyal love.
9 I will continually thank you when you execute judgment;
I will rely on you, for your loyal
followers know you are good.

For the music director, according to the machalath *style; a well-written song by David.*

53 Fools say to themselves, "There is no God."
They sin and commit evil deeds;
none of them does what is right.
2 God looks down from heaven at the human race,
to see if there is anyone who is wise and seeks God.
3 Everyone rejects God;
they are all morally corrupt.
None of them does what is right,
not even one!
4 All those who behave wickedly do not understand—
those who devour my people as if they were eating bread,
and do not call out to God.
5 They are absolutely terrified,
even by things that do not normally cause fear.
For God annihilates those who attack you.
You are able to humiliate them because
God has rejected them.
6 I wish the deliverance of Israel would come from Zion!
When God restores the well-being of his people,
may Jacob rejoice,
may Israel be happy!

For the music director, to be accompanied by stringed instruments; a well-written song by David. It was written when the Ziphites came and informed Saul: "David is hiding with us."

54 O God, deliver me by your name.
Vindicate me by your power.
2 O God, listen to my prayer.
Pay attention to what I say.
3 For foreigners attack me;
ruthless men, who do not respect God, seek my life. *Selah*

4 Look, God is my deliverer.
The Lord is among those who support me.
5 May those who wait to ambush me be repaid for their evil.
As a demonstration of your faithfulness, destroy them.
6 With a freewill offering I will sacrifice to you.
I will give thanks to your name, O LORD, for it is good.
7 Surely he rescues me from all trouble,
and I triumph over my enemies.

For the music director, to be accompanied by stringed instruments; a well-written song by David.

55 Listen, O God, to my prayer.
Do not ignore my appeal for mercy.
2 Pay attention to me and answer me.
I am so upset and distressed, I am beside myself,
3 because of what the enemy says,
and because of how the wicked pressure me,
for they hurl trouble down upon me
and angrily attack me.
4 My heart beats violently within me;
the horrors of death overcome me.
5 Fear and panic overpower me;
terror overwhelms me.
6 I say, "I wish I had wings like a dove.
I would fly away and settle in a safe place.
7 Look, I will escape to a distant place;
I will stay in the wilderness. *Selah*
8 I will hurry off to a place that is safe
from the strong wind and the gale."
9 Confuse them, O Lord.
Frustrate their plans.
For I see violence and conflict in the city.
10 Day and night they walk around on its walls,
while wickedness and destruction are within it.
11 Disaster is within it;
violence and deceit do not depart
from its public square.
12 Indeed, it is not an enemy who insults me,
or else I could bear it;
it is not one who hates me who arrogantly taunts me,
or else I could hide from him.
13 But it is you, a man like me,
my close friend in whom I confided.
14 We would share personal thoughts with each other;
in God's temple we would walk together
among the crowd.
15 May death destroy them.
May they go down alive into Sheol.
For evil is in their dwelling place and in their midst.
16 As for me, I will call out to God,
and the LORD will deliver me.
17 During the evening, morning, and noontime
I will lament and moan,
and he will hear me.

18 He will rescue me and protect me
from those who attack me,
even though they greatly outnumber me.
19 God, the one who has reigned as king from long ago,
will hear and humiliate them. *Selah*
They refuse to change,
and do not fear God.
20 He attacks his friends;
he breaks his solemn promises to them.
21 His words are as smooth as butter,
but he harbors animosity in his heart.
His words seem softer than oil,
but they are really like sharp swords.
22 Throw your burden upon the LORD,
and he will sustain you.
He will never allow the godly to be shaken.
23 But you, O God, will bring them down to the deep Pit.
Violent and deceitful people will not live
even half a normal lifespan.
But as for me, I trust in you.

For the music director, according to the yonath-elem-rekhoqim *style; a prayer of David, written when the Philistines captured him in Gath.*

56 Have mercy on me, O God, for men are attacking me.
All day long hostile enemies are tormenting me.
2 Those who anticipate my defeat attack me all day long.
Indeed, many are fighting against me, O Exalted One.
3 When I am afraid,
I trust in you.
4 In God—I boast in his promise—
in God I trust; I am not afraid.
What can mere men do to me?
5 All day long they cause me trouble;
they make a habit of plotting my demise.
6 They stalk and lurk;
they watch my every step,
as they prepare to take my life.
7 Because they are bent on violence, do not let them escape.
In your anger bring down the nations, O God.
8 You keep track of my misery.
Put my tears in your leather container.
Are they not recorded in your scroll?
9 My enemies will turn back when I cry out to you for help;
I know that God is on my side.
10 In God—I boast in his promise—
in the LORD—I boast in his promise—
11 in God I trust; I am not afraid.
What can mere men do to me?
12 I am obligated to fulfill the vows I made to you, O God;
I will give you the thank offerings you deserve,
13 when you deliver my life from death.
You keep my feet from stumbling,
so that I might serve God as I enjoy life.

LOVE TO GROW

TAKING SIDES

PSALM 56

I read the three-sentence email, and then I had a good cry. The hateful words on the computer screen stabbed my sensitive heart and reopened wounds I thought had healed long ago. My attacker had twisted my words and misjudged my motives, and we stood on opposite sides of a sea of misunderstanding. I wanted to delete the emotionally explosive message, but instead I stared blankly at the screen and prayed for God to help me figure out what to say in response.

Sadly, we live in a world where bullies hide behind computer screens and hit us with verbal bombs. They type words on a page they would never speak to a stranger in person, and we are left speechless. Like the psalmist, we look to heaven and cry out, "Have mercy on me, O God, for men are attacking me" (Ps 56:1).

David faced harassment when he penned the words of this psalm. As an exile living in enemy territory, he was continually tormented by his adversaries. Taking his words to heart can help us find hope as we work through our own hurts.

Three times David boasted in the promises of God (Ps 56:4, 10). When we plant our feet firmly on the truth, fear loses its grip on our hearts. Victory comes when we place our trust in the faithful promise of God's Word and do not fear what man may do to us. God's overcoming power will fill our hearts with peace and override all opposition.

David looked forward in hope and lifted his battered heart to God in praise. When we use our words to exercise our faith instead of engaging in foolish arguments, God is glorified by our sacrificial offering of thanks. We can worship and wait for sure deliverance as we joyfully serve God.

In God I trust; I am not afraid. What can mere men do to me? (Ps 56:11).

Whenever we are under attack, we can trust that God sees our suffering. He is keeping track of every heartbreak and collecting our tears. Our Helper hears our every cry and covers us in His compassion. When the angry words of foolish men overwhelm us, our Deliverer fights for us. He picks us up when we fall and gives us a firm place to stand.

Friend, fix your thoughts on this one truth: "I know that God is on my side" (Ps 56:9). Your faithful Father always stands beside you, and He speaks life and peace over you.

For the music director, according to the al-tashcheth *style; a prayer of David, written when he fled from Saul into the cave.*

57 Have mercy on me, O God. Have mercy on me.
For in you I have taken shelter.
In the shadow of your wings I take shelter
until trouble passes.
2 I cry out for help to God Most High,
to the God who vindicates me.
3 May he send help from heaven and deliver me
from my enemies who hurl insults. *Selah*
May God send his loyal love and faithfulness.
4 I am surrounded by lions;
I lie down among those who want to devour me,
men whose teeth are spears and arrows,
whose tongues are sharp swords.
5 Rise up above the sky, O God.
May your splendor cover the whole earth.
6 They have prepared a net to trap me;
I am discouraged.
They have dug a pit for me.
They will fall into it. *Selah*
7 I am determined, O God. I am determined.
I will sing and praise you.
8 Awake, my soul!
Awake, O stringed instrument and harp!
I will wake up at dawn.
9 I will give you thanks before the nations, O Lord.
I will sing praises to you before foreigners.
10 For your loyal love extends beyond the sky,
and your faithfulness reaches the clouds.
11 Rise up above the sky, O God.
May your splendor cover the whole earth.

For the music director, according to the al-tashcheth *style; a prayer of David.*

58 Do you rulers really pronounce just decisions?
Do you judge people fairly?
2 No! You plan how to do what is unjust;
you deal out violence in the earth.
3 The wicked turn aside from birth;
liars go astray as soon as they are born.
4 Their venom is like that of a snake,
like a deaf serpent that does not hear,
5 that does not respond to the magicians,
or to a skilled snake charmer.
6 O God, break the teeth in their mouths!
Smash the jawbones of the lions, O LORD.
7 Let them disappear like water that flows away.
Let them wither like grass.
8 Let them be like a snail that melts away as it moves along.
Let them be like stillborn babies that never see the sun.
9 Before the kindling is even placed under your pots,
he will sweep it away along with both
the raw and cooked meat.

10 The godly will rejoice when they see
vengeance carried out;
they will bathe their feet in the blood of the wicked.
11 Then observers will say,
"Yes indeed, the godly are rewarded.
Yes indeed, there is a God who judges in the earth."

For the music director, according to the al-tashcheth
style; a prayer of David, written when Saul sent
men to surround his house and murder him.

59 Deliver me from my enemies, my God.
Protect me from those who attack me.
2 Deliver me from evildoers.
Rescue me from violent men.
3 For look, they wait to ambush me;
powerful men stalk me,
but not because I have rebelled or sinned, O Lord.
4 Though I have done nothing wrong,
they are anxious to attack.
Spring into action and help me. Take notice of me.
5 You, O Lord God of Heaven's Armies, the God of Israel,
rouse yourself and punish all the nations.
Have no mercy on any treacherous evildoers. *Selah*
6 They return in the evening;
they growl like dogs
and prowl around outside the city.
7 Look, they hurl insults at me
and openly threaten to kill me,
for they say,
"Who hears?"
8 But you, O Lord, laugh in disgust at them;
you taunt all the nations.
9 You are my source of strength. I will wait for you.
For God is my refuge.
10 The God who loves me will help me;
God will enable me to triumph over my enemies.
11 Do not strike them dead suddenly,
because then my people might forget the lesson.
Use your power to make them homeless
vagabonds and then bring them down,
O Lord who shields us.
12 They speak sinful words.
So let them be trapped by their own pride
and by the curses and lies they speak.
13 Angrily wipe them out. Wipe them out so they vanish.
Let them know that God rules
over Jacob and to the ends of the earth. *Selah*
14 They return in the evening;
they growl like dogs
and prowl around outside the city.
15 They wander around looking for something to eat;
they refuse to sleep until they are full.
16 As for me, I will sing about your strength;
I will praise your loyal love in the morning.

For you are my refuge
and my place of shelter when I face trouble.
17 You are my source of strength. I will sing praises to you.
For God is my refuge, the God who loves me.

For the music director, according to the shushan-eduth *style; a prayer of David written to instruct others. It was written when he fought against Aram Naharaim and Aram Zobah. That was when Joab turned back and struck down 12,000 Edomites in the Valley of Salt.*

60 O God, you have rejected us.
You suddenly turned on us in your anger.
Please restore us!
2 You made the earth quake; you split it open.
Repair its breaches, for it is ready to fall.
3 You have made your people experience hard times;
you have made us drink intoxicating wine.
4 You have given your loyal followers a rallying flag,
so that they might seek safety from the bow. *Selah*
5 Deliver by your power and answer me,
so that the ones you love may be safe.
6 God has spoken in his sanctuary:
"I will triumph. I will parcel out Shechem;
the Valley of Sukkoth I will measure off.
7 Gilead belongs to me,
as does Manasseh.
Ephraim is my helmet,
Judah my royal scepter.
8 Moab is my washbasin.
I will make Edom serve me.
I will shout in triumph over Philistia."
9 Who will lead me into the fortified city?
Who will bring me to Edom?
10 Have you not rejected us, O God?
O God, you do not go into battle with our armies.
11 Give us help against the enemy,
for any help men might offer is futile.
12 By God's power we will conquer;
he will trample down our enemies.

For the music director, to be played on a stringed instrument; written by David.

61 O God, hear my cry for help.
Pay attention to my prayer.
2 From the remotest place on earth
I call out to you in my despair.
Lead me up to a rocky summit where I can be safe.
3 Indeed, you are my shelter,
a strong tower that protects me from the enemy.
4 I will be a permanent guest in your home;
I will find shelter in the protection of your wings. *Selah*
5 For you, O God, hear my vows;
you grant me the reward that belongs
to your loyal followers.

6 Give the king long life.
Make his lifetime span several generations.
7 May he reign forever before God.
Decree that your loyal love and
faithfulness should protect him.
8 Then I will sing praises to your name continually,
as I fulfill my vows day after day.

For the music director, Jeduthun; a psalm of David.

62 For God alone I patiently wait;
he is the one who delivers me.
2 He alone is my protector and deliverer.
He is my refuge; I will not be upended.
3 How long will you threaten a man like me?
All of you are murderers,
as dangerous as a leaning wall or an unstable fence.
4 They spend all their time planning how
to bring their victim down.
They love to use deceit;
they pronounce blessings with their mouths,
but inwardly they utter curses. *Selah*
5 Patiently wait for God alone, my soul!
For he is the one who gives me hope.
6 He alone is my protector and deliverer.
He is my refuge; I will not be shaken.
7 God delivers me and exalts me;
God is my strong protector and my shelter.
8 Trust in him at all times, you people!
Pour out your hearts before him.
God is our shelter. *Selah*
9 Men are nothing but a mere breath;
human beings are unreliable.
When they are weighed in the scales,
all of them together are lighter than air.
10 Do not trust in what you can gain by oppression.
Do not put false confidence in what
you can gain by robbery.
If wealth increases, do not become attached to it.
11 God has declared one principle;
two principles I have heard:
God is strong,
12 and you, O Lord, demonstrate loyal love.
For you repay men for what they do.

A psalm of David, written when he was in the Judean wilderness.

63 O God, you are my God. I long for you.
My soul thirsts for you,
my flesh yearns for you,
in a dry and parched land where there is no water.
2 Yes, in the sanctuary I have seen you,
and witnessed your power and splendor.
3 Because experiencing your loyal love
is better than life itself,
my lips will praise you.

4 For this reason I will praise you while I live;
in your name I will lift up my hands.
5 As with choice meat you satisfy my soul.
My mouth joyfully praises you,
6 whenever I remember you on my bed,
and think about you during the nighttime hours.
7 For you are my deliverer;
under your wings I rejoice.
8 My soul pursues you;
your right hand upholds me.
9 Enemies seek to destroy my life,
but they will descend into the depths of the earth.
10 Each one will be handed over to the sword;
their corpses will be eaten by jackals.
11 But the king will rejoice in God;
everyone who takes oaths in his name will boast,
for the mouths of those who speak lies will be shut up.

For the music director, a psalm of David.

64 Listen to me, O God, as I offer my lament!
Protect my life from the enemy's terrifying attacks.
2 Hide me from the plots of evil men,
from the crowd of evildoers.
3 They sharpen their tongues like swords;
they aim their arrows, a slanderous charge,
4 in order to shoot down the innocent in secluded places.
They shoot at him suddenly and are
unafraid of retaliation.
5 They encourage one another to carry out their evil deed.
They plan how to hide snares,
and boast, "Who will see them?"
6 They devise unjust schemes;
they disguise a well-conceived plot.
Man's inner thoughts cannot be discovered.
7 But God will shoot at them;
suddenly they will be wounded by an arrow.
8 Their slander will bring about their demise.
All who see them will shudder,
9 and all people will fear.
They will proclaim what God has done,
and reflect on his deeds.
10 The godly will rejoice in the LORD
and take shelter in him.
All the morally upright will boast.

For the music director, a psalm of David, a song.

65 Praise awaits you, O God, in Zion.
Vows made to you are fulfilled.
2 You hear prayers;
all people approach you.
3 Our record of sins overwhelms me,
but you forgive our acts of rebellion.
4 How blessed is the one whom you choose,
and allow to live in your palace courts.

May we be satisfied with the good things of your house—
your holy palace.
5 You answer our prayers by performing
awesome acts of deliverance,
O God, our savior.
All the ends of the earth trust in you,
as well as those living across the wide seas.
6 You created the mountains by your power,
and demonstrated your strength.
7 You calmed the raging seas
and their roaring waves,
as well as the commotion made by the nations.
8 Even those living in the remotest areas
are awestruck by your acts;
you cause those living in the east
and west to praise you.
9 You visit the earth and give it rain;
you make it rich and fertile.
God's streams are full of water;
you provide grain for the people of the earth,
for you have prepared the earth in this way.
10 You saturate its furrows,
and soak its plowed ground.
With rain showers you soften its soil,
and make its crops grow.
11 You crown the year with your good blessings,
and you leave abundance in your wake.
12 The pastures in the wilderness glisten with moisture,
and the hills are clothed with joy.
13 The meadows are clothed with sheep,
and the valleys are covered with grain.
They shout joyfully, yes, they sing.

For the music director, a song, a psalm.

66 Shout out praise to God, all the earth!
2 Sing praises about the majesty of his reputation.
Give him the honor he deserves!
3 Say to God:
"How awesome are your deeds!
Because of your great power your enemies
cower in fear before you.
4 All the earth worships you
and sings praises to you.
They sing praises to your name." *Selah*
5 Come and witness God's exploits!
His acts on behalf of people are awesome.
6 He turned the sea into dry land;
they passed through the river on foot.
Let us rejoice in him there.
7 He rules by his power forever;
he watches the nations.
Stubborn rebels should not exalt themselves. *Selah*
8 Praise our God, you nations.
Loudly proclaim his praise.

GOD'S HEART FOR THE NATIONS

Psalm 65:5

You answer our prayers by performing awesome acts of deliverance,
O God, our savior.
All the ends of the earth trust in you,
as well as those living across the wide seas.

9 He preserves our lives
and does not allow our feet to slip.
10 For you, O God, tested us;
you purified us like refined silver.
11 You led us into a trap;
you caused us to suffer.
12 You allowed men to ride over our heads;
we passed through fire and water,
but you brought us out into a wide open place.
13 I will enter your temple with burnt sacrifices;
I will fulfill the vows I made to you,
14 which my lips uttered
and my mouth spoke when I was in trouble.
15 I will offer up to you fattened animals
as burnt sacrifices,
along with the smell of sacrificial rams.
I will offer cattle and goats. *Selah*
16 Come! Listen, all you who are loyal to God.
I will declare what he has done for me.
17 I cried out to him for help
and praised him with my tongue.
18 If I had harbored sin in my heart,
the Lord would not have listened.
19 However, God heard;
he listened to my prayer.
20 God deserves praise,
for he did not reject my prayer
or abandon his love for me.

For the music director, to be accompanied by stringed instruments; a psalm, a song.

67 May God show us his favor and bless us.
May he smile on us. *Selah*
2 Then those living on earth will know what you are like;
all nations will know how you deliver your people.
3 Let the nations thank you, O God.
Let all the nations thank you.
4 Let foreigners rejoice and celebrate.
For you execute justice among the nations,
and govern the people living on earth. *Selah*
5 Let the nations thank you, O God.
Let all the nations thank you.
6 The earth yields its crops.
May God, our God, bless us.
7 May God bless us.
Then all the ends of the earth will give
him the honor he deserves.

For the music director, by David, a psalm, a song.

68 God springs into action.
His enemies scatter;
his adversaries run from him.
2 As smoke is driven away by the wind,
so you drive them away.

LOVE TO GROW

ALL NATIONS, ALL PEOPLE

PSALM 67

Too often the world feels divided. It feels polarized and extreme. We are segregated by lines of culture, nationality, color, lifestyle, and politics. Hatred makes one difference in opinion enough to exile us. Our cultural biases and prejudices are deeply rooted and strongly influence the lens through which we view the world.

Psalm 67 is a message we need to hear today. It reminds us that God came to deliver all people. "Then those living on earth will know what you are like; all nations will know how you deliver your people. Let the nations thank you, O God. Let all the nations thank you" (vv. 2–3).

All the nations. All the people.

This is not a new struggle. The early church wrestled with this because it understood the Jews to be God's chosen people, but it gradually realized and accepted that Gentiles could also be grafted into the family of God.

Jesus was straightforward about being inclusive when He said in John 10:16, "I have other sheep that do not come from this sheepfold. I must bring them too, and they will listen to my voice, so that there will be one flock and one shepherd." He also said in Matthew 28:19, "Therefore go and make disciples of all nations."

When you look at people, remind yourself that they, too, are made in the image of God. They, too, are His handiwork. There is nothing about a person or a group of people that could ever make them unloved by their Creator or should ever make them unwelcome in the church. He pursues all lost sheep. He even pursues the hearts of those who are hostile to Christians, like Paul.

If the church does not welcome sinners, then the pews will be empty. No person except Jesus is, or ever has been, sinless.

If the church does not welcome all nationalities across all cultures, we will be shortchanging the family of God.

Let's get busy sharing the good news.

As wax melts before fire,
so the wicked are destroyed before God.
3 But the godly are happy;
they rejoice before God
and are overcome with joy.
4 Sing to God! Sing praises to his name.
Exalt the one who rides on the clouds.
For the LORD is his name.
Rejoice before him.
5 He is a father to the fatherless
and an advocate for widows.
God rules from his holy dwelling place.
6 God settles in their own homes those
who have been deserted;
he frees prisoners and grants them prosperity.
But sinful rebels live in the desert.
7 O God, when you lead your people into battle,
when you march through the wastelands, *Selah*
8 the earth shakes.
Yes, the heavens pour down rain
before God, the God of Sinai,
before God, the God of Israel.
9 O God, you cause abundant showers to
fall on your chosen people.
When they are tired, you sustain them,
10 for you live among them.
You sustain the oppressed with your
good blessings, O God.
11 The Lord speaks;
many, many women spread the good news.
12 Kings leading armies run away—they run away!
The lovely lady of the house divides up the loot.
13 When you lie down among the sheepfolds,
the wings of the dove are covered with silver
and with glittering gold.
14 When the Sovereign One scatters kings,
let it snow on Zalmon.
15 The mountain of Bashan is a towering mountain;
the mountain of Bashan is a mountain with many peaks.
16 Why do you look with envy,
O mountains with many peaks,
at the mountain where God has decided to live?
Indeed the LORD will live there permanently.
17 God has countless chariots;
they number in the thousands.
The Lord comes from Sinai in holy splendor.
18 You ascend on high;
you have taken many captives.
You receive tribute from men,
including even sinful rebels.
Indeed, the LORD God lives there.
19 The Lord deserves praise.
Day after day he carries our burden,
the God who delivers us. *Selah*

20 Our God is a God who delivers;
the LORD, the Sovereign Lord, can rescue from death.
21 Indeed, God strikes the heads of his enemies,
the hairy foreheads of those who persist in rebellion.
22 The Lord says,
"I will retrieve them from Bashan.
I will bring them back from the depths of the sea,
23 so that your feet may stomp in their blood,
and your dogs may eat their portion
of the enemies' corpses."
24 They see your processions, O God—
the processions of my God, my king, who
marches along in holy splendor.
25 Singers walk in front;
musicians follow playing their stringed instruments,
in the midst of young women playing tambourines.
26 In your large assemblies praise God,
the LORD, in the assemblies of Israel.
27 There is little Benjamin, their ruler,
and the princes of Judah in their robes,
along with the princes of Zebulun and
the princes of Naphtali.
28 God has decreed that you will be powerful.
O God, you who have acted on our behalf,
demonstrate your power.
29 Because of your temple in Jerusalem,
kings bring tribute to you.
30 Sound your battle cry against the
wild beast of the reeds,
and the nations that assemble like a
herd of calves led by bulls.
They humble themselves and offer
gold and silver as tribute.
God scatters the nations that like to do battle.
31 They come with red cloth from Egypt.
Ethiopia voluntarily offers tribute to God.
32 O kingdoms of the earth, sing to God.
Sing praises to the Lord, *Selah*
33 to the one who rides through the sky from ancient times.
Look! He thunders loudly.
34 Acknowledge God's power,
his sovereignty over Israel,
and the power he reveals in the skies.
35 You are awe-inspiring, O God, as you
emerge from your holy temple.
It is the God of Israel who gives the
people power and strength.
God deserves praise!

For the music director, according to the tune of "Lilies"; by David.

69 Deliver me, O God,
for the water has reached my neck.
2 I sink into the deep mire
where there is no solid ground;

I am in deep water,
and the current overpowers me.
3 I am exhausted from shouting for help.
My throat is sore;
my eyes grow tired from looking for my God.
4 Those who hate me without cause
are more numerous than the hairs of my head.
Those who want to destroy me,
my enemies for no reason,
outnumber me.
They make me repay what I did not steal.
5 O God, you are aware of my foolish sins;
my guilt is not hidden from you.
6 Let none who rely on you be disgraced because of me,
O Sovereign LORD of Heaven's Armies.
Let none who seek you be ashamed because of me,
O God of Israel.
7 For I suffer humiliation for your sake
and am thoroughly disgraced.
8 My own brothers treat me like a stranger;
they act as if I were a foreigner.
9 Certainly zeal for your house consumes me;
I endure the insults of those who insult you.
10 I weep and refrain from eating food,
which causes others to insult me.
11 I wear sackcloth
and they ridicule me.
12 Those who sit at the city gate gossip about me;
drunkards mock me in their songs.
13 O LORD, may you hear my prayer and
be favorably disposed to me.
O God, because of your great loyal love,
answer me with your faithful deliverance.
14 Rescue me from the mud. Don't let me sink.
Deliver me from those who hate me,
from the deep water.
15 Don't let the current overpower me.
Don't let the deep swallow me up.
Don't let the Pit devour me.
16 Answer me, O LORD, for your loyal love is good.
Because of your great compassion, turn toward me.
17 Do not ignore your servant,
for I am in trouble. Answer me right away.
18 Come near me and redeem me.
Because of my enemies, rescue me.
19 You know how I am insulted, humiliated, and disgraced;
you can see all my enemies.
20 Their insults are painful and make me lose heart;
I look for sympathy, but receive none,
for comforters, but find none.
21 They put bitter poison into my food,
and to quench my thirst they give me vinegar to drink.
22 May their dining table become a trap before them.
May it be a snare for that group of friends.

23 May their eyes be blinded.
Make them shake violently.
24 Pour out your judgment on them.
May your raging anger overtake them.
25 May their camp become desolate,
their tents uninhabited.
26 For they harass the one whom you discipline;
they spread the news about the suffering
of those whom you punish.
27 Hold them accountable for all their sins.
Do not vindicate them.
28 May their names be deleted from the scroll of the living.
Do not let their names be listed with the godly.
29 I am oppressed and suffering.
O God, deliver and protect me.
30 I will sing praises to God's name.
I will magnify him as I give him thanks.
31 That will please the LORD more than an ox or a bull
with horns and hooves.
32 The oppressed look on—let them rejoice.
You who seek God, may you be encouraged.
33 For the LORD listens to the needy;
he does not despise his captive people.
34 Let the heavens and the earth praise him,
along with the seas and everything that swims in them.
35 For God will deliver Zion
and rebuild the cities of Judah,
and his people will again live in them and possess Zion.
36 The descendants of his servants will inherit it,
and those who are loyal to him will live in it.

For the music director, by David; written to get God's attention.

70 O God, please be willing to rescue me.
O LORD, hurry and help me.
2 May those who are trying to take my life
be embarrassed and ashamed.
May those who want to harm me
be turned back and ashamed.
3 May those who say, "Aha! Aha!"
be driven back and disgraced.
4 May all those who seek you be happy
and rejoice in you.
May those who love to experience your
deliverance say continually,
"May God be praised!"
5 I am oppressed and needy.
O God, hurry to me.
You are my helper and my deliverer.
O LORD, do not delay.

71 In you, O LORD, I have taken shelter.
Never let me be humiliated.
2 Vindicate me by rescuing me.
Listen to me. Deliver me.

3 Be my protector and refuge,
a stronghold where I can be safe.
For you are my high ridge and my stronghold.
4 My God, rescue me from the power of the wicked,
from the hand of the cruel oppressor.
5 For you are my hope;
O Sovereign LORD, I have trusted in you since I was young.
6 I have leaned on you since birth;
you pulled me from my mother's womb.
I praise you continually.
7 Many are appalled when they see me,
but you are my secure shelter.
8 I praise you constantly
and speak of your splendor all day long.
9 Do not reject me in my old age.
When my strength fails, do not abandon me.
10 For my enemies talk about me;
those waiting for a chance to kill me plot my demise.
11 They say, "God has abandoned him.
Run and seize him, for there is no one who will rescue him."
12 O God, do not remain far away from me.
My God, hurry and help me.
13 May my accusers be humiliated and defeated.
May those who want to harm me be
covered with scorn and disgrace.
14 As for me, I will wait continually,
and will continue to praise you.
15 I will tell about your justice,
and all day long proclaim your salvation,
though I cannot fathom its full extent.
16 I will come and tell about the mighty
acts of the Sovereign LORD.
I will proclaim your justice—yours alone.
17 O God, you have taught me since I was young,
and I am still declaring your amazing deeds.
18 Even when I am old and gray,
O God, do not abandon me,
until I tell the next generation about your strength,
and those coming after me about your power.
19 Your justice, O God, extends to the skies above;
you have done great things.
O God, who can compare to you?
20 Though you have allowed me to experience
much trouble and distress,
revive me once again.
Bring me up once again from the depths of the earth.
21 Raise me to a position of great honor.
Turn and comfort me.
22 I will express my thanks to you with a stringed instrument,
praising your faithfulness, O my God.
I will sing praises to you accompanied by a harp,
O Holy One of Israel.
23 My lips will shout for joy. Yes, I will sing your praises.
I will praise you when you rescue me.

24 All day long my tongue will also tell about your justice,
for those who want to harm me will be
embarrassed and ashamed.

For Solomon.

72 O God, grant the king the ability to make just decisions.
Grant the king's son the ability to make fair decisions.
2 Then he will judge your people fairly,
and your oppressed ones equitably.
3 The mountains will bring news of peace to the people,
and the hills will announce justice.
4 He will defend the oppressed among the people;
he will deliver the children of the poor
and crush the oppressor.
5 People will fear you as long as the sun
and moon remain in the sky,
for generation after generation.
6 He will descend like rain on the mown grass,
like showers that drench the earth.
7 During his days the godly will flourish;
peace will prevail as long as the moon remains in the sky.
8 May he rule from sea to sea,
and from the Euphrates River to the ends of the earth.
9 Before him the coastlands will bow down,
and his enemies will lick the dust.
10 The kings of Tarshish and the coastlands will offer gifts;
the kings of Sheba and Seba will bring tribute.
11 All kings will bow down to him;
all nations will serve him.
12 For he will rescue the needy when they cry out for help,
and the oppressed who have no defender.
13 He will take pity on the poor and needy;
the lives of the needy he will save.
14 From harm and violence he will defend them;
he will value their lives.
15 May he live! May they offer him gold from Sheba.
May they continually pray for him.
May they pronounce blessings on him all day long.
16 May there be an abundance of grain in the earth;
on the tops of the mountains may it sway.
May its fruit trees flourish like the forests of Lebanon.
May its crops be as abundant as the grass of the earth.
17 May his fame endure.
May his dynasty last as long as the sun remains in the sky.
May they use his name when they
formulate their blessings.
May all nations consider him to be favored by God.
18 The LORD God, the God of Israel, deserves praise.
He alone accomplishes amazing things.
19 His glorious name deserves praise forevermore.
May his majestic splendor fill the whole earth.
We agree! We agree!
20 This collection of the prayers of David
son of Jesse ends here.

BOOK 3 (PSALMS 73–89)

A psalm by Asaph.

73 Certainly God is good to Israel,
and to those whose motives are pure.
2 But as for me, my feet almost slipped;
my feet almost slid out from under me.
3 For I envied those who are proud,
as I observed the prosperity of the wicked.
4 For they suffer no pain;
their bodies are strong and well fed.
5 They are immune to the trouble common to men;
they do not suffer as other men do.
6 Arrogance is their necklace,
and violence covers them like clothing.
7 Their prosperity causes them to do wrong;
their thoughts are sinful.
8 They mock and say evil things;
they proudly threaten violence.
9 They speak as if they rule in heaven,
and lay claim to the earth.
10 Therefore they have more than enough food to eat,
and even suck up the water of the sea.
11 They say, "How does God know what we do?
Is the Most High aware of what goes on?"
12 Take a good look. This is what the wicked are like,
those who always have it so easy
and get richer and richer.
13 I concluded, "Surely in vain I have kept my motives pure
and maintained a pure lifestyle.
14 I suffer all day long,
and am punished every morning."
15 If I had publicized these thoughts,
I would have betrayed your people.
16 When I tried to make sense of this,
it was troubling to me.
17 Then I entered the precincts of God's temple,
and understood the destiny of the wicked.
18 Surely you put them in slippery places;
you bring them down to ruin.
19 How desolate they become in a mere moment.
Terrifying judgments make their demise complete.
20 They are like a dream after one wakes up.
O Lord, when you awake you will despise them.
21 Yes, my spirit was bitter,
and my insides felt sharp pain.
22 I was ignorant and lacked insight;
I was as senseless as an animal before you.
23 But I am continually with you;
you hold my right hand.
24 You guide me by your wise advice,
and then you will lead me to a position of honor.
25 Whom do I have in heaven but you?
On earth there is no one I desire but you.

26 My flesh and my heart may grow weak,
but God always protects my heart and gives me stability.
27 Yes, look! Those far from you die;
you destroy everyone who is unfaithful to you.
28 But as for me, God's presence is all I need.
I have made the Sovereign LORD my shelter,
as I declare all the things you have done.

A well-written song by Asaph.

74 Why, O God, have you permanently rejected us?
Why does your anger burn against
the sheep of your pasture?
2 Remember your people whom you
acquired in ancient times,
whom you rescued so they could be
your very own nation,
as well as Mount Zion, where you dwell.
3 Hurry to the permanent ruins,
and to all the damage the enemy has done to the temple.
4 Your enemies roar in the middle of your sanctuary;
they set up their battle flags.
5 They invade like lumberjacks
swinging their axes in a thick forest.
6 And now they are tearing down all its engravings
with axes and crowbars.
7 They set your sanctuary on fire;
they desecrate your dwelling place by
knocking it to the ground.
8 They say to themselves,
"We will oppress all of them."
They burn down all the places in the land
where people worship God.
9 We do not see any signs of God's presence;
there are no longer any prophets,
and we have no one to tell us how long this will last.
10 How long, O God, will the adversary hurl insults?
Will the enemy blaspheme your name forever?
11 Why do you remain inactive?
Intervene and destroy him.
12 But God has been my king from ancient times,
performing acts of deliverance on the earth.
13 You destroyed the sea by your strength;
you shattered the heads of the sea monster in the water.
14 You crushed the heads of Leviathan;
you fed him to the people who live along the coast.
15 You broke open the spring and the stream;
you dried up perpetually flowing rivers.
16 You established the cycle of day and night;
you put the moon and sun in place.
17 You set up all the boundaries of the earth;
you created the cycle of summer and winter.
18 Remember how the enemy hurls insults, O LORD,
and how a foolish nation blasphemes your name.
19 Do not hand the life of your dove over to a wild animal.

Do not continue to disregard the lives
of your oppressed people.
20 Remember your covenant promises,
for the dark regions of the earth are full
of places where violence rules.
21 Do not let the afflicted be turned back in shame.
Let the oppressed and poor praise your name.
22 Rise up, O God. Defend your honor.
Remember how fools insult you all day long.
23 Do not disregard what your enemies say,
or the unceasing shouts of those who defy you.

For the music director, according to the al-tashcheth *style; a psalm of Asaph, a song.*

75 We give thanks to you, O God. We give thanks.
You reveal your presence;
people tell about your amazing deeds.
2 God says,
"At the appointed times,
I judge fairly.
3 When the earth and all its inhabitants dissolve in fear,
I make its pillars secure." *Selah*
4 I say to the proud, "Do not be proud,"
and to the wicked, "Do not be so confident of victory.
5 Do not be so certain you have won.
Do not speak with your head held so high.
6 For victory does not come from the east or west,
or from the wilderness.
7 For God is the judge.
He brings one down and exalts another.
8 For the LORD holds in his hand a cup
full of foaming wine mixed with spices,
and pours it out.
Surely all the wicked of the earth
will slurp it up and drink it to its very last drop."
9 As for me, I will continually tell what you have done;
I will sing praises to the God of Jacob.
10 God says,
"I will bring down all the power of the wicked;
the godly will be victorious."

For the music director, to be accompanied by stringed instruments; a psalm of Asaph, a song.

76 God has revealed himself in Judah;
in Israel his reputation is great.
2 He lives in Salem;
he dwells in Zion.
3 There he shattered the arrows,
the shield, the sword, and the rest
of the weapons of war. *Selah*
4 You shine brightly and reveal your majesty,
as you descend from the hills where you killed your prey.
5 The bravehearted were plundered;
they "fell asleep."

All the warriors were helpless.
6 At the sound of your battle cry, O God of Jacob,
both rider and horse "fell asleep."
7 You are awesome! Yes, you!
Who can withstand your intense anger?
8 From heaven you announced what
their punishment would be.
The earth was afraid and silent
9 when God arose to execute judgment,
and to deliver all the oppressed of the earth. *Selah*
10 Certainly your angry judgment upon
men will bring you praise;
you reveal your anger in full measure.
11 Make vows to the LORD your God and repay them.
Let all those who surround him bring
tribute to the awesome one.
12 He humbles princes;
the kings of the earth regard him as awesome.

For the music director, Jeduthun; a psalm of Asaph.

77 I will cry out to God and call for help.
I will cry out to God and he will pay attention to me.
2 In my time of trouble I sought the Lord.
I kept my hand raised in prayer throughout the night.
I refused to be comforted.
3 I said, "I will remember God while I groan;
I will think about him while my strength leaves me." *Selah*
4 You held my eyelids open;
I was troubled and could not speak.
5 I thought about the days of old,
about ancient times.
6 I said, "During the night I will remember
the song I once sang;
I will think very carefully."
I tried to make sense of what was happening.
7 I asked, "Will the Lord reject me forever?
Will he never again show me his favor?
8 Has his loyal love disappeared forever?
Has his promise failed forever?
9 Has God forgotten to be merciful?
Has his anger stifled his compassion?" *Selah*
10 Then I said, "I am sickened by the thought
that the Most High might become inactive.
11 I will remember the works of the LORD.
Yes, I will remember the amazing
things you did long ago.
12 I will think about all you have done;
I will reflect upon your deeds."
13 O God, your deeds are extraordinary.
What god can compare to our great God?
14 You are the God who does amazing things;
you have revealed your strength among the nations.
15 You delivered your people by your strength—
the children of Jacob and Joseph. *Selah*

REFLECT

Does God ever remove His loyal love from His people? Do His promises ever fail? What about the times when it seems like God is far away? How can He be present with His people when they are experiencing trouble?

16 The waters saw you, O God,
the waters saw you and trembled.
Yes, the depths of the sea shook with fear.
17 The clouds poured down rain;
the skies thundered.
Yes, your arrows flashed about.
18 Your thunderous voice was heard in the wind;
the lightning bolts lit up the world.
The earth trembled and shook.
19 You walked through the sea;
you passed through the surging waters,
but left no footprints.
20 You led your people like a flock of sheep,
by the hand of Moses and Aaron.

A well-written song by Asaph.

78 Pay attention, my people, to my instruction.
Listen to the words I speak.
2 I will sing a song that imparts wisdom;
I will make insightful observations about the past.
3 What we have heard and learned—
that which our ancestors have told us—
4 we will not hide from their descendants.
We will tell the next generation
about the LORD's praiseworthy acts,
about his strength and the amazing things he has done.
5 He established a rule in Jacob;
he set up a law in Israel.
He commanded our ancestors
to make his deeds known to their descendants,
6 so that the next generation, children yet to be born,
might know about them.
They will grow up and tell their descendants about them.
7 Then they will place their confidence in God.
They will not forget the works of God,
and they will obey his commands.
8 Then they will not be like their ancestors,
who were a stubborn and rebellious generation,
a generation that was not committed
and faithful to God.
9 The Ephraimites were armed with bows,
but they retreated in the day of battle.
10 They did not keep their covenant with God,
and they refused to obey his law.
11 They forgot what he had done,
the amazing things he had shown them.
12 He did amazing things in the sight of their ancestors,
in the land of Egypt, in the region of Zoan.
13 He divided the sea and led them across it;
he made the water stand in a heap.
14 He led them with a cloud by day,
and with the light of a fire all night long.
15 He broke open rocks in the wilderness,
and gave them enough water to fill the depths of the sea.

16 He caused streams to flow from the rock,
and made the water flow like rivers.
17 Yet they continued to sin against him,
and rebelled against the Most High in the desert.
18 They willfully challenged God
by asking for food to satisfy their appetite.
19 They insulted God, saying,
"Is God really able to give us food in the wilderness?
20 Yes, he struck a rock and water flowed out;
streams gushed forth.
But can he also give us food?
Will he provide meat for his people?"
21 When the LORD heard this, he was furious.
A fire broke out against Jacob,
and his anger flared up against Israel,
22 because they did not have faith in God,
and did not trust his ability to deliver them.
23 He gave a command to the clouds above,
and opened the doors in the sky.
24 He rained down manna for them to eat;
he gave them the grain of heaven.
25 Man ate the food of the mighty ones.
He sent them more than enough to eat.
26 He brought the east wind through the sky,
and by his strength led forth the south wind.
27 He rained down meat on them like dust,
birds as numerous as the sand on the seashores.
28 He caused them to fall right in the middle of their camp,
all around their homes.
29 They ate until they were beyond full;
he gave them what they desired.
30 They were not yet filled up;
their food was still in their mouths,
31 when the anger of God flared up against them.
He killed some of the strongest of them;
he brought the young men of Israel to their knees.
32 Despite all this, they continued to sin,
and did not trust him to do amazing things.
33 So he caused them to die unsatisfied
and filled with terror.
34 When he struck them down, they sought his favor;
they turned back and longed for God.
35 They remembered that God was their protector,
and that God Most High was their deliverer.
36 But they deceived him with their words,
and lied to him.
37 They were not really committed to him,
and they were unfaithful to his covenant.
38 Yet he is compassionate.
He forgives sin and does not destroy.
He often holds back his anger,
and does not stir up his fury.
39 He remembered that they were made of flesh,
and were like a wind that blows past and does not return.

40 How often they rebelled against him in the wilderness,
and insulted him in the wastelands.
41 They again challenged God,
and offended the Holy One of Israel.
42 They did not remember what he had done,
how he delivered them from the enemy,
43 when he performed his awesome deeds in Egypt,
and his acts of judgment in the region of Zoan.
44 He turned their rivers into blood,
and they could not drink from their streams.
45 He sent swarms of biting insects against them,
as well as frogs that overran their land.
46 He gave their crops to the grasshopper,
the fruit of their labor to the locust.
47 He destroyed their vines with hail,
and their sycamore-fig trees with driving rain.
48 He rained hail down on their cattle,
and hurled lightning bolts down on their livestock.
49 His raging anger lashed out against them.
He sent fury, rage, and trouble
as messengers who bring disaster.
50 He sent his anger in full force.
He did not spare them from death;
he handed their lives over to destruction.
51 He struck down all the firstborn in Egypt,
the firstfruits of their reproductive
power in the tents of Ham.
52 Yet he brought out his people like sheep;
he led them through the wilderness like a flock.
53 He guided them safely along,
and they were not afraid;
but the sea covered their enemies.
54 He brought them to the border of his holy land,
to this mountainous land that his right hand acquired.
55 He drove the nations out from before them;
he assigned them their tribal allotments
and allowed the tribes of Israel to settle down.
56 Yet they challenged and defied God Most High,
and did not obey his commands.
57 They were unfaithful and acted as
treacherously as their ancestors;
they were as unreliable as a malfunctioning bow.
58 They made him angry with their pagan shrines,
and made him jealous with their idols.
59 God heard and was angry;
he completely rejected Israel.
60 He abandoned the sanctuary at Shiloh,
the tent where he lived among men.
61 He allowed the symbol of his strong
presence to be captured;
he gave the symbol of his splendor
into the hand of the enemy.
62 He delivered his people over to the sword,
and was angry with his chosen nation.

63 Fire consumed their young men,
and their virgins remained unmarried.
64 Their priests fell by the sword,
but their widows did not weep.
65 But then the Lord awoke from his sleep;
he was like a warrior in a drunken rage.
66 He drove his enemies back;
he made them a permanent target for insults.
67 He rejected the tent of Joseph;
he did not choose the tribe of Ephraim.
68 He chose the tribe of Judah
and Mount Zion, which he loves.
69 He made his sanctuary as enduring
as the heavens above,
as secure as the earth, which he established permanently.
70 He chose David, his servant,
and took him from the sheepfolds.
71 He took him away from following the mother sheep,
and made him the shepherd of Jacob, his people,
and of Israel, his chosen nation.
72 David cared for them with pure motives;
he led them with skill.

A psalm of Asaph.

79 O God, foreigners have invaded your chosen land;
they have polluted your holy temple
and turned Jerusalem into a heap of ruins.
2 They have given the corpses of your servants
to the birds of the sky,
the flesh of your loyal followers
to the beasts of the earth.
3 They have made their blood flow like water
all around Jerusalem, and there is no one to bury them.
4 We have become an object of disdain to our neighbors;
those who live on our borders taunt and insult us.
5 How long will this go on, O LORD?
Will you stay angry forever?
How long will your rage burn like fire?
6 Pour out your anger on the nations
that do not acknowledge you,
on the kingdoms that do not pray to you.
7 For they have devoured Jacob
and destroyed his home.
8 Do not hold us accountable for the
sins of earlier generations.
Quickly send your compassion our way,
for we are in serious trouble.
9 Help us, O God, our deliverer!
For the sake of your glorious reputation, rescue us.
Forgive our sins for the sake of your reputation.
10 Why should the nations say, "Where is their God?"
Before our very eyes may the shed
blood of your servants
be avenged among the nations.

11 Listen to the painful cries of the prisoners.
Use your great strength to set free
those condemned to die.
12 Pay back our neighbors in full.
May they be insulted the same way
they insulted you, O Lord.
13 Then we, your people, the sheep of your pasture,
will continually thank you.
We will tell coming generations
of your praiseworthy acts.

For the music director, according to the shushan-eduth *style; a psalm of Asaph.*

80 O Shepherd of Israel, pay attention,
you who lead Joseph like a flock of sheep.
You who sit enthroned above the
cherubim, reveal your splendor.
2 In the sight of Ephraim, Benjamin, and
Manasseh reveal your power.
Come and deliver us.
3 O God, restore us.
Smile on us. Then we will be delivered.
4 O LORD God of Heaven's Armies,
how long will you remain angry at your
people while they pray to you?
5 You have given them tears as food;
you have made them drink tears by the measure.
6 You have made our neighbors dislike us,
and our enemies insult us.
7 O God of Heaven's Armies, restore us.
Smile on us. Then we will be delivered.
8 You uprooted a vine from Egypt;
you drove out nations and transplanted it.
9 You cleared the ground for it;
it took root,
and filled the land.
10 The mountains were covered by its shadow,
the highest cedars by its branches.
11 Its branches reached the Mediterranean Sea,
and its shoots the Euphrates River.
12 Why did you break down its walls,
so that all who pass by pluck its fruit?
13 The wild boars of the forest ruin it;
the insects of the field feed on it.
14 O God of Heaven's Armies, come back.
Look down from heaven and take notice.
Take care of this vine,
15 the root your right hand planted,
the shoot you made to grow.
16 It is burned and cut down.
May those who did this die because you
are displeased with them.
17 May you give support to the one you have chosen,
to the one whom you raised up for yourself.

18 Then we will not turn away from you.
Revive us and we will pray to you.
19 O LORD God of Heaven's Armies, restore us.
Smile on us. Then we will be delivered.

For the music director, according to the gittith *style; by Asaph.*

81 Shout for joy to God, our source of strength!
Shout out to the God of Jacob!
2 Sing a song and play the tambourine,
the pleasant-sounding harp, and the
ten-stringed instrument.
3 Sound the ram's horn on the day of the new moon,
and on the day of the full moon when our festival begins.
4 For observing the festival is a requirement for Israel;
it is an ordinance given by the God of Jacob.
5 He decreed it as a regulation in Joseph,
when he attacked the land of Egypt.
I heard a voice I did not recognize.
6 It said: "I removed the burden from his shoulder;
his hands were released from holding the basket.
7 In your distress you called out and I rescued you.
I answered you from a dark thundercloud.
I tested you at the waters of Meribah. *Selah*
8 I said, 'Listen, my people!
I will warn you.
O Israel, if only you would obey me!
9 There must be no other god among you.
You must not worship a foreign god.
10 I am the LORD, your God,
the one who brought you out of the land of Egypt.
Open your mouth wide and I will fill it.'
11 But my people did not obey me;
Israel did not submit to me.
12 I gave them over to their stubborn desires;
they did what seemed right to them.
13 If only my people would obey me!
If only Israel would keep my commands!
14 Then I would quickly subdue their enemies,
and attack their adversaries."
15 (May those who hate the LORD cower in fear before him.
May they be permanently humiliated.)
16 "I would feed Israel the best wheat,
and would satisfy your appetite with
honey from the rocky cliffs."

A psalm of Asaph.

82 God stands in the assembly of El;
in the midst of the gods he renders judgment.
2 He says, "How long will you make unjust legal decisions
and show favoritism to the wicked? *Selah*
3 Defend the cause of the poor and the fatherless.
Vindicate the oppressed and suffering.
4 Rescue the poor and needy.
Deliver them from the power of the wicked.

5 They neither know nor understand.
They stumble around in the dark,
while all the foundations of the earth crumble.
6 I thought, 'You are gods;
all of you are sons of the Most High.'
7 Yet you will die like mortals;
you will fall like all the other rulers."
8 Rise up, O God, and execute judgment on the earth!
For you own all the nations.

A song, a psalm of Asaph.

83 O God, do not be silent.
Do not ignore us. Do not be inactive, O God.
2 For look, your enemies are making a commotion;
those who hate you are hostile.
3 They carefully plot against your people,
and make plans to harm the ones you cherish.
4 They say, "Come on, let's annihilate them
so they are no longer a nation.
Then the name of Israel will be remembered no more."
5 Yes, they devise a unified strategy;
they form an alliance against you.
6 It includes the tents of Edom and the Ishmaelites,
Moab and the Hagrites,
7 Gebal, Ammon, and Amalek,
Philistia and the inhabitants of Tyre.
8 Even Assyria has allied with them,
lending its strength to the descendants of Lot. *Selah*
9 Do to them as you did to Midian—
as you did to Sisera and Jabin at the Kishon River.
10 They were destroyed at Endor;
their corpses were like manure on the ground.
11 Make their nobles like Oreb and Zeeb,
and all their rulers like Zebah and Zalmunna,
12 who said, "Let's take over the pastures of God."
13 O my God, make them like dead thistles,
like dead weeds blown away by the wind.
14 Like the fire that burns down the forest,
or the flames that consume the mountainsides,
15 chase them with your gale winds,
and terrify them with your windstorm.
16 Cover their faces with shame,
so they might seek you, O LORD.
17 May they be humiliated and continually terrified.
May they die in shame.
18 Then they will know that you alone are the LORD,
the Most High over all the earth.

For the music director, according to the gittith
style; written by the Korahites, a psalm.

84 How lovely is the place where you live,
O LORD of Heaven's Armies!
2 I desperately want to be
in the courts of the LORD's temple.

My heart and my entire being shout for joy
to the living God.
3 Even the birds find a home there,
and the swallow builds a nest,
where she can protect her young
near your altars, O LORD of Heaven's Armies,
my King and my God.
4 How blessed are those who live in your temple
and praise you continually. *Selah*
5 How blessed are those who find their strength in you,
and long to travel the roads that lead to your temple.
6 As they pass through the Baca Valley,
he provides a spring for them.
The rain even covers it with pools of water.
7 They are sustained as they travel along;
each one appears before God in Zion.
8 O LORD God of Heaven's Armies,
hear my prayer.
Listen, O God of Jacob. *Selah*
9 O God, take notice of our shield.
Show concern for your chosen king.
10 Certainly spending just one day in
your temple courts is better
than spending a thousand elsewhere.
I would rather stand at the entrance
to the temple of my God
than live in the tents of the wicked.
11 For the LORD God is our sovereign protector.
The LORD bestows favor and honor;
he withholds no good thing from
those who have integrity.
12 O LORD of Heaven's Armies,
how blessed are those who trust in you.

For the music director, written by the Korahites, a psalm.

85 O LORD, you showed favor to your land;
you restored the well-being of Jacob.
2 You pardoned the wrongdoing of your people;
you forgave all their sin. *Selah*
3 You withdrew all your fury;
you turned back from your raging anger.
4 Restore us, O God our deliverer.
Do not be displeased with us.
5 Will you stay mad at us forever?
Will you remain angry throughout
future generations?
6 Will you not revive us once more?
Then your people will rejoice in you.
7 O LORD, show us your loyal love.
Bestow on us your deliverance.
8 I will listen to what God the LORD says.
For he will make peace with his people,
his faithful followers.
Yet they must not return to their foolish ways.

9 Certainly his loyal followers will soon
experience his deliverance;
then his splendor will again appear in our land.
10 Loyal love and faithfulness meet;
deliverance and peace greet each other with a kiss.
11 Faithfulness grows from the ground,
and deliverance looks down from the sky.
12 Yes, the LORD will bestow his good blessings,
and our land will yield its crops.
13 Deliverance goes before him,
and prepares a pathway for him.

A prayer of David.

86 Listen, O LORD. Answer me.
For I am oppressed and needy.
2 Protect me, for I am loyal.
You are my God; deliver your servant who trusts in you.
3 Have mercy on me, O Lord,
for I cry out to you all day long.
4 Make your servant glad,
for to you, O Lord, I pray.
5 Certainly, O Lord, you are kind and forgiving,
and show great faithfulness to all who cry out to you.
6 O LORD, hear my prayer.
Pay attention to my plea for mercy.
7 In my time of trouble I cry out to you,
for you will answer me.
8 None can compare to you among the gods, O Lord.
Your exploits are incomparable.
9 All the nations, whom you created,
will come and worship you, O Lord.
They will honor your name.
10 For you are great and do amazing things.
You alone are God.
11 O LORD, teach me how you want me to live.
Then I will obey your commands.
Make me wholeheartedly committed to you.
12 O Lord, my God, I will give you thanks
with my whole heart.
I will honor your name continually.
13 For you will extend your great loyal love to me,
and will deliver my life from the depths of Sheol.
14 O God, arrogant men attack me;
a gang of ruthless men, who do not
respect you, seek my life.
15 But you, O Lord, are a compassionate and merciful God.
You are patient and demonstrate great
loyal love and faithfulness.
16 Turn toward me and have mercy on me.
Give your servant your strength.
Deliver this son of your female servant.
17 Show me evidence of your favor.
Then those who hate me will see it and be ashamed,
for you, O LORD, will help me and comfort me.

Written by the Korahites; a psalm, a song.

87 The LORD's city is in the holy hills.
2 The LORD loves the gates of Zion
more than all the dwelling places of Jacob.
3 People say wonderful things about you,
O city of God. *Selah*
4 I mention Rahab and Babylon to my followers.
Here are Philistia and Tyre, along with Ethiopia.
It is said of them, "This one was born there."
5 But it is said of Zion's residents,
"Each one of these was born in her,
and the Most High makes her secure."
6 The LORD writes in the census book of the nations,
"This one was born there." *Selah*
7 As for the singers, as well as the pipers—
all of them sing within your walls.

A song, a psalm written by the Korahites, for the music director, according to the machalath-leannoth *style; a well-written song by Heman the Ezrahite.*

88 O LORD God who delivers me,
by day I cry out
and at night I pray before you.
2 Listen to my prayer.
Pay attention to my cry for help.
3 For my life is filled with troubles,
and I am ready to enter Sheol.
4 They treat me like those who descend
into the grave.
I am like a helpless man,
5 adrift among the dead,
like corpses lying in the grave,
whom you remember no more,
and who are cut off from your power.
6 You place me in the lowest regions of the Pit,
in the dark places, in the watery depths.
7 Your anger bears down on me,
and you overwhelm me with all your waves. *Selah*
8 You cause those who know me to keep their distance;
you make me an appalling sight to them.
I am trapped and cannot get free.
9 My eyes grow weak because of oppression.
I call out to you, O LORD, all day long;
I spread out my hands in prayer to you.
10 Do you accomplish amazing things for the dead?
Do the departed spirits rise up and give you thanks? *Selah*
11 Is your loyal love proclaimed in the grave,
or your faithfulness in the place of the dead?
12 Are your amazing deeds experienced in the dark region,
or your deliverance in the land of oblivion?
13 As for me, I cry out to you, O LORD;
in the morning my prayer confronts you.
14 O LORD, why do you reject me,
and pay no attention to me?

15 I am oppressed and have been on the
verge of death since my youth.
I have been subjected to your horrors
and am numb with pain.
16 Your anger overwhelms me;
your terrors destroy me.
17 They surround me like water all day long;
they join forces and encircle me.
18 You cause my friends and neighbors
to keep their distance;
those who know me leave me alone in the darkness.

A well-written song by Ethan the Ezrahite.

89 I will sing continually about the LORD's faithful deeds;
to future generations I will proclaim your faithfulness.
2 For I say, "Loyal love is permanently established;
in the skies you set up your faithfulness."
3 The LORD said,
"I have made a covenant with my chosen one;
I have made a promise on oath to David, my servant:
4 'I will give you an eternal dynasty
and establish your throne throughout future
generations.'" *Selah*
5 O LORD, the heavens praise your amazing deeds,
as well as your faithfulness in the angelic assembly.
6 For who in the skies can compare to the LORD?
Who is like the LORD among the heavenly beings,
7 a God who is honored in the great angelic assembly,
and more awesome than all who surround him?
8 O LORD God of Heaven's Armies!
Who is strong like you, O LORD?
Your faithfulness surrounds you.
9 You rule over the proud sea.
When its waves surge, you calm them.
10 You crushed the Proud One and killed it;
with your strong arm you scattered your enemies.
11 The heavens belong to you, as does the earth.
You made the world and all it contains.
12 You created the north and the south.
Tabor and Hermon rejoice in your name.
13 Your arm is powerful,
your hand strong,
your right hand victorious.
14 Equity and justice are the foundation
of your throne.
Loyal love and faithfulness characterize your rule.
15 How blessed are the people who worship you!
O LORD, they experience your favor.
16 They rejoice in your name all day long,
and are vindicated by your justice.
17 For you give them splendor and strength.
By your favor we are victorious.
18 For our shield belongs to the LORD,
our king to the Holy One of Israel.

19 Then you spoke through a vision to your
faithful followers and said:
"I have placed a young hero over a warrior;
I have raised up a young man from the people.
20 I have discovered David, my servant.
With my holy oil I have anointed him as king.
21 My hand will support him,
and my arm will strengthen him.
22 No enemy will be able to exact tribute from him;
a violent oppressor will not be able to humiliate him.
23 I will crush his enemies before him;
I will strike down those who hate him.
24 He will experience my faithfulness and loyal love,
and by my name he will win victories.
25 I will place his hand over the sea,
his right hand over the rivers.
26 He will call out to me,
'You are my father, my God, and the
protector who delivers me.'
27 I will appoint him to be my firstborn son,
the most exalted of the earth's kings.
28 I will always extend my loyal love to him,
and my covenant with him is secure.
29 I will give him an eternal dynasty,
and make his throne as enduring as the skies above.
30 If his sons reject my law
and disobey my regulations,
31 if they break my rules
and do not keep my commandments,
32 I will punish their rebellion by beating
them with a club,
their sin by inflicting them with bruises.
33 But I will not remove my loyal love from him,
nor be unfaithful to my promise.
34 I will not break my covenant
or go back on what I promised.
35 Once and for all I have vowed by my own holiness,
I will never deceive David.
36 His dynasty will last forever.
His throne will endure before me, like the sun;
37 it will remain stable, like the moon.
His throne will endure like the skies." *Selah*
38 But you have spurned and rejected him;
you are angry with your chosen king.
39 You have repudiated your covenant with your servant;
you have thrown his crown to the ground.
40 You have broken down all his walls;
you have made his strongholds a heap of ruins.
41 All who pass by have robbed him;
he has become an object of disdain to his neighbors.
42 You have allowed his adversaries to be victorious,
and all his enemies to rejoice.
43 You turn back his sword from the adversary,
and have not sustained him in battle.

44 You have brought to an end his splendor,
and have knocked his throne to the ground.
45 You have cut short his youth,
and have covered him with shame. *Selah*
46 How long, O LORD, will this last?
Will you remain hidden forever?
Will your anger continue to burn like fire?
47 Take note of my brief lifespan.
Why do you make all people so mortal?
48 No man can live on without experiencing death,
or deliver his life from the power of Sheol. *Selah*
49 Where are your earlier faithful deeds, O Lord,
the ones performed in accordance with
your reliable oath to David?
50 Take note, O Lord, of the way your servants are taunted,
and of how I must bear so many insults from people.
51 Your enemies, O LORD, hurl insults;
they insult your chosen king as they dog his footsteps.
52 The LORD deserves praise forevermore!
We agree! We agree!

BOOK 4 (PSALMS 90–106)

A prayer of Moses, the man of God.

90 O Lord, you have been our protector
through all generations.
2 Even before the mountains came into existence,
or you brought the world into being,
you were the eternal God.
3 You make mankind return to the dust,
and say, "Return, O people."
4 Yes, in your eyes a thousand years
are like yesterday that quickly passes,
or like one of the divisions of the nighttime.
5 You bring their lives to an end and they "fall asleep."
In the morning they are like the grass
that sprouts up:
6 In the morning it glistens and sprouts up;
at evening time it withers and dries up.
7 Yes, we are consumed by your anger;
we are terrified by your wrath.
8 You are aware of our sins;
you even know about our hidden sins.
9 Yes, throughout all our days we
experience your raging fury;
the years of our lives pass quickly, like a sigh.
10 The days of our lives add up to seventy years,
or eighty, if one is especially strong.
But even one's best years are marred
by trouble and oppression.
Yes, they pass quickly and we fly away.
11 Who can really fathom the intensity of your anger?
Your raging fury causes people to fear you.

LOVE TO GROW

13,001

PSALM 90

In Psalm 90, Moses asked God for a proper understanding of mortality. Why did Moses ask this? So he and God's people might live this breath of a life wisely, unfettered by fear, and victorious because they revered and exalted a holy God.

Moses and the Israelites, who escaped a life of slavery in Egypt, witnessed God's holiness. They saw Him as they wandered the wilderness day after day, year after year. His power was majestic and stunning, demonstrated in both His wrath and His mercy. They knew God's fury and they knew His love.

Like the Israelites, we resort to fear in the face of uncertainty. In an instant, we can forget all God's miraculous kindnesses. Fear has many faces: fear of man, fear of failure, and fear of suffering to name a few. We forget God's perfect love and His goodwill toward us, so we fear. But do we really want to waste even a moment living in unnecessary bondage?

Satisfy us in the morning with your loyal love (Ps 90:14).

Satisfaction in God's love will bring rejoicing and gladness no matter the details of the day, no matter the trials that assail us. Moses asked to understand the brevity of life so he and those wilderness wanderers wouldn't waste their one life; He wanted them to learn to be satisfied and full in God's love.

It feels a bit morbid, but as I contemplate the idea of numbering my days, I want to know my number. An online calculator displays the days I've been alive. Today is day 13,001. It's fleeting and brief, yet so significant. I surrender day 13,001 to God. He already knows about tomorrow, day 13,002, and—should He grant it—day 17,999. With faith, when that day arrives, I will surrender it to Him as well.

Psalm 90 ends with a request that Moses extended to God: "May your servants see your work. May their sons see your majesty. May our Sovereign God extend his favor to us. Make our endeavors successful. Yes, make them successful" (vv. 16–17). Moses knew his life was fleeting, but he knew that for his days to truly be measured with success, the majesty of God must be present in them.

12 So teach us to consider our mortality,
so that we might live wisely.
13 Turn back toward us, O LORD.
How long must this suffering last?
Have pity on your servants.
14 Satisfy us in the morning with your loyal love.
Then we will shout for joy and be happy all our days.
15 Make us happy in proportion to the
days you have afflicted us,
in proportion to the years we have experienced trouble.
16 May your servants see your work.
May their sons see your majesty.
17 May our Sovereign God extend his favor to us.
Make our endeavors successful.
Yes, make them successful.

91 As for you, the one who lives in the
shelter of the Most High,
and resides in the protective shadow
of the Sovereign One—
2 I say this about the LORD, my shelter and my stronghold,
my God in whom I trust—
3 he will certainly rescue you from the snare of the hunter
and from the destructive plague.
4 He will shelter you with his wings;
you will find safety under his wings.
His faithfulness is like a shield or a protective wall.
5 You need not fear the terrors of the night,
the arrow that flies by day,
6 the plague that stalks in the darkness,
or the disease that ravages at noon.
7 Though a thousand may fall beside you,
and a multitude on your right side,
it will not reach you.
8 Certainly you will see it with your very own eyes—
you will see the wicked paid back.
9 For you have taken refuge in the LORD,
my shelter, the Most High.
10 No harm will overtake you;
no illness will come near your home.
11 For he will order his angels
to protect you in all you do.
12 They will lift you up in their hands,
so you will not slip and fall on a stone.
13 You will subdue a lion and a snake;
you will trample underfoot a young lion and a serpent.
14 The LORD says,
"Because he is devoted to me, I will deliver him;
I will protect him because he is loyal to me.
15 When he calls out to me, I will answer him.
I will be with him when he is in trouble;
I will rescue him and bring him honor.
16 I will satisfy him with long life,
and will let him see my salvation."

A psalm; a song for the Sabbath day.

92 It is fitting to thank the LORD,
and to sing praises to your name, O Most High.
2 It is fitting to proclaim your loyal love in the morning,
and your faithfulness during the night,
3 to the accompaniment of a ten-stringed
instrument and a lyre,
to the accompaniment of the meditative tone of the harp.
4 For you, O LORD, have made me happy by your work.
I will sing for joy because of what you have done.
5 How great are your works, O LORD!
Your plans are very intricate!
6 The spiritually insensitive do not recognize this;
the fool does not understand this.
7 When the wicked sprout up like grass,
and all the evildoers glisten,
it is so that they may be annihilated.
8 But you, O LORD, reign forever.
9 Indeed, look at your enemies, O LORD.
Indeed, look at how your enemies perish.
All the evildoers are scattered.
10 You exalt my horn like that of a wild ox.
I am covered with fresh oil.
11 I gloat in triumph over those who tried to ambush me;
I hear the defeated cries of the evil foes who attacked me.
12 The godly grow like a palm tree;
they grow high like a cedar in Lebanon.
13 Planted in the LORD's house,
they grow in the courts of our God.
14 They bear fruit even when they are old;
they are filled with vitality and have many leaves.
15 So they proclaim that the LORD, my Protector,
is just and never unfair.

93 The LORD reigns.
He is robed in majesty.
The LORD is robed;
he wears strength around his waist.
Indeed, the world is established; it cannot be moved.
2 Your throne has been secure from ancient times;
you have always been king.
3 The waves roar, O LORD,
the waves roar,
the waves roar and crash.
4 Above the sound of the surging water,
and the mighty waves of the sea,
the LORD sits enthroned in majesty.
5 The rules you set down are completely reliable.
Holiness aptly adorns your house, O LORD, forever.

94 O LORD, the God who avenges!
O God who avenges, reveal your splendor.
2 Rise up, O judge of the earth.
Pay back the proud.

3 O LORD, how long will the wicked,
how long will the wicked celebrate?
4 They spew out threats and speak defiantly;
all the evildoers boast.
5 O LORD, they crush your people;
they oppress the nation that belongs to you.
6 They kill the widow and the resident foreigner,
and they murder the fatherless.
7 Then they say, "The LORD does not see this;
the God of Jacob does not take notice of it."
8 Take notice of this, you ignorant people.
You fools, when will you ever understand?
9 Does the one who makes the human ear not hear?
Does the one who forms the human eye not see?
10 Does the one who disciplines the nations not punish?
He is the one who imparts
knowledge to human beings!
11 The LORD knows that peoples' thoughts
are morally bankrupt.
12 How blessed is the one whom you instruct, O LORD,
the one whom you teach from your law,
13 in order to protect him from times of trouble,
until the wicked are destroyed.
14 Certainly the LORD does not forsake his people;
he does not abandon the nation that belongs to him.
15 For justice will prevail,
and all the morally upright will be vindicated.
16 Who will rise up to defend me against the wicked?
Who will stand up for me against the evildoers?
17 If the LORD had not helped me,
I would soon have dwelt in the silence of death.
18 If I say, "My foot is slipping,"
your loyal love, O LORD, supports me.
19 When worries threaten to overwhelm me,
your soothing touch makes me happy.
20 Cruel rulers are not your allies,
those who make oppressive laws.
21 They conspire against the blameless,
and condemn to death the innocent.
22 But the LORD will protect me,
and my God will shelter me.
23 He will pay them back for their sin.
He will destroy them because of their evil;
the LORD our God will destroy them.

95 Come, let us sing for joy to the LORD.
Let us shout out praises to our
Protector who delivers us.
2 Let us enter his presence with thanksgiving.
Let us shout out to him in celebration.
3 For the LORD is a great God,
a great king who is superior to all gods.
4 The depths of the earth are in his hand,
and the mountain peaks belong to him.

5 The sea is his, for he made it.
His hands formed the dry land.
6 Come, let us bow down and worship.
Let us kneel before the LORD, our Creator.
7 For he is our God;
we are the people of his pasture,
the sheep he owns.
Today, if only you would obey him.
8 He says, "Do not be stubborn like they were at Meribah,
like they were that day at Massah in the wilderness,
9 where your ancestors challenged my authority,
and tried my patience, even though
they had seen my work.
10 For forty years I was continually
disgusted with that generation,
and I said, 'These people desire to go astray;
they do not obey my commands.'
11 So I made a vow in my anger,
'They will never enter into the resting
place I had set aside for them.'"

96 Sing to the LORD a new song.
Sing to the LORD, all the earth.
2 Sing to the LORD. Praise his name.
Announce every day how he delivers.
3 Tell the nations about his splendor.
Tell all the nations about his amazing deeds.
4 For the LORD is great and certainly worthy of praise;
he is more awesome than all gods.
5 For all the gods of the nations are worthless,
but the LORD made the sky.
6 Majestic splendor emanates from him;
his sanctuary is firmly established and beautiful.
7 Ascribe to the LORD, O families of the nations,
ascribe to the LORD splendor and strength.
8 Ascribe to the LORD the splendor he deserves.
Bring an offering and enter his courts.
9 Worship the LORD in holy attire.
Tremble before him, all the earth.
10 Say among the nations, "The LORD reigns!
The world is established; it cannot be moved.
He judges the nations fairly."
11 Let the sky rejoice, and the earth be happy.
Let the sea and everything in it shout.
12 Let the fields and everything in them celebrate.
Then let the trees of the forest shout with joy
13 before the LORD, for he comes.
For he comes to judge the earth.
He judges the world fairly,
and the nations in accordance with his justice.

97 The LORD reigns.
Let the earth be happy.
Let the many coastlands rejoice.

GOD'S HEART FOR THE NATIONS

Psalm 96:10

Say among the nations, "The LORD reigns! The world is established; it cannot be moved. He judges the nations fairly."

2 Dark clouds surround him;
equity and justice are the foundation of his throne.
3 Fire goes before him;
on every side it burns up his enemies.
4 His lightning bolts light up the world;
the earth sees and trembles.
5 The mountains melt like wax before the LORD,
before the Lord of the whole earth.
6 The sky declares his justice,
and all the nations see his splendor.
7 All who worship idols are ashamed,
those who boast about worthless idols.
All the gods bow down before him.
8 Zion hears and rejoices,
the towns of Judah are happy,
because of your judgments, O LORD.
9 For you, O LORD, are the Most High over the whole earth;
you are elevated high above all gods.
10 You who love the LORD, hate evil!
He protects the lives of his faithful followers;
he delivers them from the power of the wicked.
11 The godly bask in the light;
the morally upright experience joy.
12 You godly ones, rejoice in the LORD.
Give thanks to his holy name.

A psalm.

98 Sing to the LORD a new song,
for he performs amazing deeds.
His right hand and his mighty arm
accomplish deliverance.
2 The LORD demonstrates his power to deliver;
in the sight of the nations he reveals his justice.
3 He remains loyal and faithful to the family of Israel.
All the ends of the earth see our God deliver us.
4 Shout out praises to the LORD, all the earth.
Break out in a joyful shout and sing!
5 Sing to the LORD accompanied by a harp,
accompanied by a harp and the sound of music.
6 With trumpets and the blaring of the ram's horn,
shout out praises before the king, the LORD.
7 Let the sea and everything in it shout,
along with the world and those who live in it.
8 Let the rivers clap their hands!
Let the mountains sing in unison
9 before the LORD.
For he comes to judge the earth.
He judges the world fairly,
and the nations in a just manner.

99 The LORD reigns!
The nations tremble.
He sits enthroned above the cherubim;
the earth shakes.

2 The LORD is elevated in Zion;
he is exalted over all the nations.
3 Let them praise your great and awesome name.
He is holy!
4 The king is strong;
he loves justice.
You ensure that legal decisions will be made fairly;
you promote justice and equity in Jacob.
5 Praise the LORD our God.
Worship before his footstool.
He is holy!
6 Moses and Aaron were among his priests;
Samuel was one of those who prayed to him.
They prayed to the LORD and he answered them.
7 He spoke to them from a pillar of cloud;
they obeyed his regulations and the
ordinance he gave them.
8 O LORD our God, you answered them.
They found you to be a forgiving God,
but also one who punished their sinful deeds.
9 Praise the LORD our God!
Worship on his holy hill,
for the LORD our God is holy.

A thanksgiving psalm.

100 Shout out praises to the LORD, all the earth!
2 Worship the LORD with joy.
Enter his presence with joyful singing.
3 Acknowledge that the LORD is God.
He made us and we belong to him,
we are his people, the sheep of his pasture.
4 Enter his gates with thanksgiving,
and his courts with praise.
Give him thanks.
Praise his name.
5 For the LORD is good.
His loyal love endures,
and he is faithful through all generations.

A psalm of David.

101 I will sing about loyalty and justice.
To you, O LORD, I will sing praises.
2 I will walk in the way of integrity.
When will you come to me?
I will conduct my business with integrity
in the midst of my palace.
3 I will not even consider doing what is dishonest.
I hate doing evil;
I will have no part of it.
4 I will have nothing to do with a perverse person;
I will not permit evil.
5 I will destroy anyone who slanders his neighbor in secret.
I will not tolerate anyone who has a haughty
demeanor and an arrogant attitude.

6 I will favor the honest people of the land,
and allow them to live with me.
Those who walk in the way of integrity will attend me.
7 Deceitful people will not live in my palace.
Liars will not be welcome in my presence.
8 Each morning I will destroy all the
wicked people in the land,
and remove all evildoers from the city of the LORD.

GOD'S HEART FOR THE NATIONS

Psalm 102:15

The nations will respect the reputation of the LORD, and all the kings of the earth will respect his splendor.

The prayer of an oppressed man, as he grows faint and pours out his lament before the LORD.

102 O LORD, hear my prayer.
Pay attention to my cry for help.
2 Do not ignore me in my time of trouble.
Listen to me.
When I call out to you, quickly answer me.
3 For my days go up in smoke,
and my bones are charred as in a fireplace.
4 My heart is parched and withered like grass,
for I am unable to eat food.
5 Because of the anxiety that makes me groan,
my bones protrude from my skin.
6 I am like an owl in the wilderness;
I am like a screech owl among the ruins.
7 I stay awake;
I am like a solitary bird on a roof.
8 All day long my enemies taunt me;
those who mock me use my name in their curses.
9 For I eat ashes as if they were bread,
and mix my drink with my tears,
10 because of your anger and raging fury.
Indeed, you pick me up and throw me away.
11 My days are coming to an end,
and I am withered like grass.
12 But you, O LORD, rule forever,
and your reputation endures.
13 You will rise up and have compassion on Zion.
For it is time to have mercy on her,
for the appointed time has come.
14 Indeed, your servants take delight in her stones,
and feel compassion for the dust of her ruins.
15 The nations will respect the reputation of the LORD,
and all the kings of the earth will respect his splendor,
16 when the LORD rebuilds Zion,
and reveals his splendor,
17 when he responds to the prayer of the destitute,
and does not reject their request.
18 The account of his intervention will be
recorded for future generations;
people yet to be born will praise the LORD.
19 For he will look down from his sanctuary above;
from heaven the LORD will look toward earth,
20 in order to hear the painful cries of the prisoners,
and to set free those condemned to die,

21 so they may proclaim the name of the LORD in Zion,
and praise him in Jerusalem,
22 when the nations gather together,
and the kingdoms pay tribute to the LORD.
23 He has taken away my strength in the middle of life;
he has cut short my days.
24 I say, "O my God, please do not take me
away in the middle of my life.
You endure through all generations.
25 In earlier times you established the earth;
the skies are your handiwork.
26 They will perish,
but you will endure.
They will wear out like a garment;
like clothes you will remove them and they will disappear.
27 But you remain;
your years do not come to an end.
28 The children of your servants will settle down here,
and their descendants will live securely in your presence."

By David.

103 Praise the LORD, O my soul.
With all that is within me, praise his holy name.
2 Praise the LORD, O my soul.
Do not forget all his kind deeds.
3 He is the one who forgives all your sins,
who heals all your diseases,
4 who delivers your life from the Pit,
who crowns you with his loyal love and compassion,
5 who satisfies your life with good things,
so your youth is renewed like an eagle's.
6 The LORD does what is fair,
and executes justice for all the oppressed.
7 The LORD revealed his faithful acts to Moses,
his deeds to the Israelites.
8 The LORD is compassionate and merciful;
he is patient and demonstrates great loyal love.
9 He does not always accuse,
and does not stay angry.
10 He does not deal with us as our sins deserve;
he does not repay us as our misdeeds deserve.
11 For as the skies are high above the earth,
so his loyal love towers over his faithful followers.
12 As far as the eastern horizon is from the west,
so he removes the guilt of our rebellious actions from us.
13 As a father has compassion on his children,
so the LORD has compassion on his faithful followers.
14 For he knows what we are made of;
he realizes we are made of clay.
15 A person's life is like grass.
Like a flower in the field it flourishes,
16 but when the hot wind blows, it disappears,
and one can no longer even spot the
place where it once grew.

PRAISE THE LORD

PSALM 103

I found myself pouting on my bed again.

I had every right to feel sorry for myself. Things hadn't turned out the way I thought they should on my last big project. On top of this, the kids were arguing, and my husband was out of town. I was disappointed again.

I consider myself to be a fairly optimistic person. I can almost always see the silver lining or imagine a way God can use any situation for good, but this time I had succumbed to discouragement.

I was so caught up in what was going wrong, I missed all that was right. How easy it is to forget our purpose and our place when we're focused on our pain.

Many of us are familiar with the apostle Paul's words to the Thessalonians to give thanks in all circumstances, but we can struggle to do it. How do we give thanks when the circumstances are marked by disappointment, heartbreak, or frustration?

Psalm 103 speaks to some of life's most pressing issues: wrongdoing, forgiveness, sickness, healing, failure, redemption, oppression, justice, honor, contentment, purpose, and love. The psalmist refers to the very things we struggle with on a daily basis and concludes over and over again that deliverance, forgiveness, and freedom are only found in the Lord.

Praise is the weapon to defeat doubt, discouragement, disillusionment, and despair. We remember what God has done in the past, and we remember His promise for the future.

Praise the Lord, O my soul. Do not forget all his kind deeds (Ps 103:2).

Keep track of the blessings God brings about on your behalf. When you see answered prayer, when God works in your church and community, in your family and among friends, write the blessings down and remember!

17 But the LORD continually shows loyal
love to his faithful followers,
and is faithful to their descendants,
18 to those who keep his covenant,
who are careful to obey his commands.
19 The LORD has established his throne in heaven;
his kingdom extends over everything.
20 Praise the LORD, you angels of his,
you powerful warriors who carry out his decrees
and obey his orders.
21 Praise the LORD, all you warriors of his,
you servants of his who carry out his desires.
22 Praise the LORD, all that he has made,
in all the regions of his kingdom.
Praise the LORD, O my soul.

104 Praise the LORD, O my soul!
O LORD my God, you are magnificent.
You are robed in splendor and majesty.
2 He covers himself with light as if it were a garment.
He stretches out the skies like a tent curtain,
3 and lays the beams of the upper rooms
of his palace on the rain clouds.
He makes the clouds his chariot,
and travels on the wings of the wind.
4 He makes the winds his messengers,
and the flaming fire his attendant.
5 He established the earth on its foundations;
it will never be moved.
6 The watery deep covered it like a garment;
the waters reached above the mountains.
7 Your shout made the waters retreat;
at the sound of your thunderous voice they hurried off—
8 as the mountains rose up,
and the valleys went down—
to the place you appointed for them.
9 You set up a boundary for them
that they could not cross,
so that they would not cover the earth again.
10 He turns springs into streams;
they flow between the mountains.
11 They provide water for all the animals in the field;
the wild donkeys quench their thirst.
12 The birds of the sky live beside them;
they chirp among the bushes.
13 He waters the mountains from the
upper rooms of his palace;
the earth is full of the fruit you cause to grow.
14 He provides grass for the cattle,
and crops for people to cultivate,
so they can produce food from the ground,
15 as well as wine that makes people glad,
and olive oil to make their faces shine,
as well as bread that sustains them.

16 The trees of the LORD receive all the rain they need,
the cedars of Lebanon that he planted,
17 where the birds make nests,
near the evergreens in which the herons live.
18 The wild goats live in the high mountains;
the rock badgers find safety in the cliffs.
19 He made the moon to mark the months,
and the sun sets according to a regular schedule.
20 You make it dark and night comes,
during which all the beasts of the forest prowl around.
21 The lions roar for prey,
seeking their food from God.
22 When the sun rises, they withdraw
and sleep in their dens.
23 People then go out to do their work,
and they labor until evening.
24 How many living things you have made, O LORD!
You have exhibited great skill in making all of them;
the earth is full of the living things you have made.
25 Over here is the deep, wide sea,
which teems with innumerable swimming creatures,
living things both small and large.
26 The ships travel there,
and over here swims the whale you made to play in it.
27 All your creatures wait for you
to provide them with food on a regular basis.
28 You give food to them and they receive it;
you open your hand and they are filled with food.
29 When you ignore them, they panic.
When you take away their life's breath,
they die and return to dust.
30 When you send your life-giving breath,
they are created,
and you replenish the surface of the ground.
31 May the splendor of the LORD endure.
May the LORD find pleasure in the
living things he has made.
32 He looks down on the earth and it shakes;
he touches the mountains and they start to smolder.
33 I will sing to the LORD as long as I live;
I will sing praise to my God as long as I exist.
34 May my thoughts be pleasing to him.
I will rejoice in the LORD.
35 May sinners disappear from the earth,
and the wicked vanish.
Praise the LORD, O my soul.
Praise the LORD.

105 Give thanks to the LORD.
Call on his name.
Make known his accomplishments among the nations.
2 Sing to him.
Make music to him.
Tell about all his miraculous deeds.

3 Boast about his holy name.
Let the hearts of those who seek the LORD rejoice.
4 Seek the LORD and the strength he gives.
Seek his presence continually.
5 Recall the miraculous deeds he performed,
his mighty acts and the judgments he decreed,
6 O children of Abraham, God's servant,
you descendants of Jacob, God's chosen ones.
7 He is the LORD our God;
he carries out judgment throughout the earth.
8 He always remembers his covenantal decree,
the promise he made to a thousand generations—
9 the promise he made to Abraham,
the promise he made by oath to Isaac.
10 He gave it to Jacob as a decree,
to Israel as a lasting promise,
11 saying, "To you I will give the land of Canaan
as the portion of your inheritance."
12 When they were few in number,
just a very few, and resident foreigners within it,
13 they wandered from nation to nation,
and from one kingdom to another.
14 He let no one oppress them;
he disciplined kings for their sake,
15 saying, "Don't touch my chosen ones.
Don't harm my prophets."
16 He called down a famine upon the earth;
he cut off all the food supply.
17 He sent a man ahead of them—
Joseph was sold as a servant.
18 The shackles hurt his feet;
his neck was placed in an iron collar,
19 until the time when his prediction came true.
The LORD's word proved him right.
20 The king authorized his release;
the ruler of nations set him free.
21 He put him in charge of his palace,
and made him manager of all his property,
22 giving him authority to imprison his officials
and to teach his advisers.
23 Israel moved to Egypt;
Jacob lived for a time in the land of Ham.
24 The LORD made his people very fruitful,
and made them more numerous than their enemies.
25 He caused the Egyptians to hate his people,
and to mistreat his servants.
26 He sent his servant Moses,
and Aaron, whom he had chosen.
27 They executed his miraculous signs among them,
and his amazing deeds in the land of Ham.
28 He made it dark;
Moses and Aaron did not disobey his orders.
29 He turned the Egyptians' water into blood,
and killed their fish.

30 Their land was overrun by frogs,
which even got into the rooms of their kings.
31 He ordered flies to come;
gnats invaded their whole territory.
32 He sent hail along with the rain;
there was lightning in their land.
33 He destroyed their vines and fig trees,
and broke the trees throughout their territory.
34 He ordered locusts to come,
innumerable grasshoppers.
35 They ate all the vegetation in their land,
and devoured the crops of their fields.
36 He struck down all the firstborn in their land,
the firstfruits of their reproductive power.
37 He brought his people out enriched with silver and gold;
none of his tribes stumbled.
38 Egypt was happy when they left,
for they were afraid of them.
39 He spread out a cloud for a cover,
and provided a fire to light up the night.
40 They asked for food, and he sent quail;
he satisfied them with food from the sky.
41 He opened up a rock and water flowed out;
a river ran through dry regions.
42 Yes, he remembered the sacred promise
he made to Abraham his servant.
43 When he led his people out, they rejoiced;
his chosen ones shouted with joy.
44 He handed the territory of nations over to them,
and they took possession of what
other peoples had produced,
45 so that they might keep his commands
and obey his laws.
Praise the LORD.

106 Praise the LORD.
Give thanks to the LORD, for he is good,
and his loyal love endures.
2 Who can adequately recount the LORD's mighty acts,
or relate all his praiseworthy deeds?
3 How blessed are those who promote justice,
and do what is right all the time.
4 Remember me, O LORD, when you
show favor to your people.
Pay attention to me, when you deliver,
5 so I may see the prosperity of your chosen ones,
rejoice along with your nation,
and boast along with the people who belong to you.
6 We have sinned like our ancestors;
we have done wrong, we have done evil.
7 Our ancestors in Egypt failed to appreciate
your miraculous deeds.
They failed to remember your many acts of loyal love,
and they rebelled at the sea, by the Red Sea.

8 Yet he delivered them for the sake of his reputation,
that he might reveal his power.
9 He shouted at the Red Sea and it dried up;
he led them through the deep water as if it were a desert.
10 He delivered them from the power of
the one who hated them,
and rescued them from the power of the enemy.
11 The water covered their enemies;
not even one of them survived.
12 They believed his promises;
they sang praises to him.
13 They quickly forgot what he had done;
they did not wait for his instructions.
14 In the wilderness they had an insatiable craving for meat;
they challenged God in the wastelands.
15 He granted their request,
then struck them with a disease.
16 In the camp they resented Moses,
and Aaron, the LORD's holy priest.
17 The earth opened up and swallowed Dathan;
it engulfed the group led by Abiram.
18 Fire burned their group;
the flames scorched the wicked.
19 They made an image of a calf at Horeb,
and worshiped a metal idol.
20 They traded their majestic God
for the image of an ox that eats grass.
21 They rejected the God who delivered them,
the one who performed great deeds in Egypt,
22 amazing feats in the land of Ham,
mighty acts by the Red Sea.
23 He threatened to destroy them,
but Moses, his chosen one, interceded with him
and turned back his destructive anger.
24 They rejected the fruitful land;
they did not believe his promise.
25 They grumbled in their tents;
they did not obey the LORD.
26 So he made a solemn vow
that he would make them die in the wilderness,
27 make their descendants die among the nations,
and scatter them among foreign lands.
28 They worshiped Baal of Peor,
and ate sacrifices offered to the dead.
29 They made the LORD angry by their actions,
and a plague broke out among them.
30 Phinehas took a stand and intervened,
and the plague subsided.
31 This was credited to Phinehas as a righteous act
for all generations to come.
32 They made him angry by the waters of Meribah,
and Moses suffered because of them,
33 for they aroused his temper,
and he spoke rashly.

34 They did not destroy the nations,
as the LORD had commanded them to do.
35 They mixed in with the nations
and learned their ways.
36 They worshiped their idols,
which became a snare to them.
37 They sacrificed their sons and daughters to demons.
38 They shed innocent blood—
the blood of their sons and daughters,
whom they sacrificed to the idols of Canaan.
The land was polluted by bloodshed.
39 They were defiled by their deeds,
and unfaithful in their actions.
40 So the LORD was angry with his people
and despised the people who belonged to him.
41 He handed them over to the nations,
and those who hated them ruled over them.
42 Their enemies oppressed them;
they were subject to their authority.
43 Many times he delivered them,
but they had a rebellious attitude,
and degraded themselves by their sin.
44 Yet he took notice of their distress,
when he heard their cry for help.
45 He remembered his covenant with them,
and relented because of his great loyal love.
46 He caused all their conquerors
to have pity on them.
47 Deliver us, O LORD, our God.
Gather us from among the nations.
Then we will give thanks to your holy name,
and boast about your praiseworthy deeds.
48 The LORD God of Israel deserves praise,
in the future and forevermore.
Let all the people say, "We agree! Praise the LORD!"

BOOK 5 (PSALMS 107–150)

107 Give thanks to the LORD, for he is good,
and his loyal love endures.
2 Let those delivered by the LORD speak out,
those whom he delivered from the power of the enemy,
3 and gathered from foreign lands,
from east and west,
from north and south.
4 They wandered through the wilderness, in a wasteland;
they found no road to a city in which to live.
5 They were hungry and thirsty;
they fainted from exhaustion.
6 They cried out to the LORD in their distress;
he delivered them from their troubles.
7 He led them on a level road,
that they might find a city in which to live.

8 Let them give thanks to the LORD for his loyal love,
and for the amazing things he has done for people.
9 For he has satisfied those who thirst,
and those who hunger he has filled with food.
10 They sat in utter darkness,
bound in painful iron chains,
11 because they had rebelled against God's commands,
and rejected the instructions of the Most High.
12 So he used suffering to humble them;
they stumbled and no one helped them up.
13 They cried out to the LORD in their distress;
he delivered them from their troubles.
14 He brought them out of the utter darkness,
and tore off their shackles.
15 Let them give thanks to the LORD for his loyal love,
and for the amazing things he has done for people.
16 For he shattered the bronze gates,
and hacked through the iron bars.
17 They acted like fools in their rebellious ways,
and suffered because of their sins.
18 They lost their appetite for all food,
and they drew near the gates of death.
19 They cried out to the LORD in their distress;
he delivered them from their troubles.
20 He sent them an assuring word and healed them;
he rescued them from the pits where they were trapped.
21 Let them give thanks to the LORD for his loyal love,
and for the amazing things he has done for people.
22 Let them present thank offerings,
and loudly proclaim what he has done.
23 Some traveled on the sea in ships,
and carried cargo over the vast waters.
24 They witnessed the acts of the LORD,
his amazing feats on the deep water.
25 He gave the order for a windstorm,
and it stirred up the waves of the sea.
26 They reached up to the sky,
then dropped into the depths.
The sailors' strength left them because
the danger was so great.
27 They swayed and staggered like drunks,
and all their skill proved ineffective.
28 They cried out to the LORD in their distress;
he delivered them from their troubles.
29 He calmed the storm,
and the waves grew silent.
30 The sailors rejoiced because the waves grew quiet,
and he led them to the harbor they desired.
31 Let them give thanks to the LORD for his loyal love,
and for the amazing things he has done for people.
32 Let them exalt him in the assembly of the people.
Let them praise him in the place where the leaders preside.
33 He turned streams into a desert,
springs of water into arid land,

34 and a fruitful land into a barren place,
because of the sin of its inhabitants.
35 As for his people, he turned a desert into a pool of water,
and a dry land into springs of water.
36 He allowed the hungry to settle there,
and they established a city in which to live.
37 They cultivated fields,
and planted vineyards,
which yielded a harvest of fruit.
38 He blessed them so that they became very numerous.
He would not allow their cattle to decrease in number.
39 As for their enemies, they decreased in
number and were beaten down,
because of painful distress and suffering.
40 He would pour contempt upon princes,
and he made them wander in a wasteland with no road.
41 Yet he protected the needy from oppression,
and cared for his families like a flock of sheep.
42 When the godly see this, they rejoice,
and every sinner shuts his mouth.
43 Whoever is wise, let him take note of these things.
Let them consider the LORD's acts of loyal love.

A song, a psalm of David.

108 I am determined, O God.
I will sing and praise you with my whole heart.
2 Awake, O stringed instrument and harp.
I will wake up at dawn.
3 I will give you thanks before the nations, O LORD.
I will sing praises to you before foreigners.
4 For your loyal love extends beyond the sky,
and your faithfulness reaches the clouds.
5 Rise up above the sky, O God.
May your splendor cover the whole earth.
6 Deliver by your power and answer me,
so that the ones you love may be safe.
7 God has spoken in his sanctuary:
"I will triumph! I will parcel out Shechem;
the Valley of Sukkoth I will measure off.
8 Gilead belongs to me,
as does Manasseh.
Ephraim is my helmet,
Judah my royal scepter.
9 Moab is my washbasin.
I will make Edom serve me.
I will shout in triumph over Philistia."
10 Who will lead me into the fortified city?
Who will bring me to Edom?
11 Have you not rejected us, O God?
O God, you do not go into battle with our armies.
12 Give us help against the enemy,
for any help men might offer is futile.
13 By God's power we will conquer;
he will trample down our enemies.

For the music director, a psalm of David.

109 O God whom I praise, do not ignore me.
2 For they say cruel and deceptive things to me;
they lie to me.
3 They surround me and say hateful things;
they attack me for no reason.
4 They repay my love with accusations,
but I continue to pray.
5 They repay me evil for good,
and hate for love.
6 Appoint an evil man to testify against him.
May an accuser stand at his right side.
7 When he is judged, he will be found guilty.
Then his prayer will be regarded as sinful.
8 May his days be few.
May another take his job.
9 May his children be fatherless,
and his wife a widow.
10 May his children roam around begging,
asking for handouts as they leave their ruined home.
11 May the creditor seize all he owns.
May strangers loot his property.
12 May no one show him kindness.
May no one have compassion on
his fatherless children.
13 May his descendants be cut off.
May the memory of them be wiped out by
the time the next generation arrives.
14 May his ancestors' sins be remembered by the LORD.
May his mother's sin not be forgotten.
15 May the LORD be constantly aware of them,
and cut off the memory of his children from the earth.
16 For he never bothered to show kindness;
he harassed the oppressed and needy,
and killed the disheartened.
17 He loved to curse others, so those
curses have come upon him.
He had no desire to bless anyone, so he
has experienced no blessings.
18 He made cursing a way of life,
so curses poured into his stomach like water
and seeped into his bones like oil.
19 May a curse attach itself to him, like
a garment one puts on,
or a belt one wears continually.
20 May the LORD repay my accusers in this way,
those who say evil things about me.
21 O Sovereign LORD,
intervene on my behalf for the sake of your reputation.
Because your loyal love is good, deliver me.
22 For I am oppressed and needy,
and my heart beats violently within me.
23 I am fading away like a shadow at the end of the day;
I am shaken off like a locust.

24 I am so starved my knees shake;
I have turned into skin and bones.
25 I am disdained by them.
When they see me, they shake their heads.
26 Help me, O LORD my God.
Because you are faithful to me, deliver me.
27 Then they will realize this is your work,
and that you, LORD, have accomplished it.
28 They curse, but you will bless.
When they attack, they will be humiliated,
but your servant will rejoice.
29 My accusers will be covered with shame,
and draped in humiliation as if it were a robe.
30 I will thank the LORD profusely.
In the middle of a crowd I will praise him,
31 because he stands at the right hand of the needy,
to deliver him from those who threaten his life.

A psalm of David.

110 Here is the LORD's proclamation to my lord:
"Sit down at my right hand until I make
your enemies your footstool."
2 The LORD extends your dominion from Zion.
Rule in the midst of your enemies.
3 Your people willingly follow you when you go into battle.
On the holy hills at sunrise the dew of
your youth belongs to you.
4 The LORD makes this promise on
oath and will not revoke it:
"You are an eternal priest after the
pattern of Melchizedek."
5 O Lord, at your right hand
he strikes down kings in the day he unleashes his anger.
6 He executes judgment against the nations.
He fills the valleys with corpses;
he shatters their heads over the vast battlefield.
7 From the stream along the road he drinks;
then he lifts up his head.

111 Praise the LORD!
I will give thanks to the LORD with my whole heart,
in the assembly of the godly and the congregation.
2 The LORD's deeds are great,
eagerly awaited by all who desire them.
3 His work is majestic and glorious,
and his faithfulness endures forever.
4 He does amazing things that will be remembered;
the LORD is merciful and compassionate.
5 He gives food to his faithful followers;
he always remembers his covenant.
6 He announced that he would do mighty deeds for his people,
giving them a land that belonged to other nations.
7 His acts are characterized by faithfulness and justice;
all his precepts are reliable.

LOVE TO GROW

IN THE STORM

PSALM 109:30–31

Have you ever had moments, days, maybe even years in your life when you could identify with the nearness of death and the pursuit of your enemies, like David in the Psalms?

If not in the literal sense, maybe you've mourned the death of a dream or endured a load too heavy to bear. Maybe you're reaping the consequences of sin, experiencing the death of a relationship, or grieving the loss of hope and security for your future.

Are you longing to feel alive again?

Oh friend, run to your compassionate Father. Fix your eyes on the One who came not only as sacrificial Lamb, but also as Savior who would reign victorious over sin and death! Like David, you can praise Him in the midst of the storm because His sovereignty and goodness can be trusted. His love endures forever, and He stands ready to save those who trust in Him.

I will thank the LORD profusely. In the middle of a crowd I will praise him, because he stands at the right hand of the needy, to deliver him from those who threaten his life (Ps 109:30–31).

God pours out His love, grace, and compassion on us, and He changes us. His presence and peace transform us and bring hope and security that is not of this world. His forgiveness cleanses us, gifts us with a new start, and makes us alive in Him. He turns our mourning into dancing. We can tell of His goodness and can encourage those in the trenches with us, not because life is easy or because we have it all figured out. Rather, it's because the hope that Jesus gives is far beyond what this world can offer.

God pursues you in the valley to bring His love and compassion to your situation. Once you've experienced them, you shouldn't be able to keep the news of the experience to yourself. You'll be able to say that you more than lived through your trial! You'll bear witness to His redemptive work in it as Savior. Nothing is too hard for Him. He doesn't waste a thing. He specializes in making beauty from ashes.

Even in the storm, will you take time to praise Him for who He is today?

8 They are forever firm,
and should be faithfully and properly carried out.
9 He delivered his people;
he ordained that his covenant be observed forever.
His name is holy and awesome.
10 To obey the LORD is the fundamental
principle for wise living;
all who carry out his precepts acquire good moral insight.
He will receive praise forever.

112 Praise the LORD!
How blessed is the one who obeys the LORD,
who takes great delight in keeping his commands.
2 His descendants will be powerful on the earth;
the godly will be blessed.
3 His house contains wealth and riches;
his integrity endures.
4 In the darkness a light shines for the godly,
for each one who is merciful, compassionate, and just.
5 It goes well for the one who generously lends money,
and conducts his business honestly.
6 For he will never be shaken;
others will always remember one who is just.
7 He does not fear bad news.
He is confident; he trusts in the LORD.
8 His resolve is firm; he will not succumb to fear
before he looks in triumph on his enemies.
9 He generously gives to the needy;
his integrity endures.
He will be vindicated and honored.
10 When the wicked see this, they will worry;
they will grind their teeth in frustration and melt away.
The desire of the wicked will perish.

CHALLENGE

Psalm 113 was inspired by Hannah's song in 1 Samuel 2, and both inspired Mary's song in Luke 1. How are these three passages similar? What truth about God's character do they express?

113 Praise the LORD.
Praise, you servants of the LORD,
praise the name of the LORD.
2 May the LORD's name be praised
now and forevermore.
3 From east to west
the LORD's name is deserving of praise.
4 The LORD is exalted over all the nations;
his splendor reaches beyond the sky.
5 Who can compare to the LORD our God,
who sits on a high throne?
6 He bends down to look
at the sky and the earth.
7 He raises the poor from the dirt,
and lifts up the needy from the garbage pile,
8 that he might seat him with princes,
with the princes of his people.
9 He makes the barren woman of the family
a happy mother of children.
Praise the LORD.

114 When Israel left Egypt,
when the family of Jacob left a foreign nation behind,
2 Judah became his sanctuary,
Israel his kingdom.
3 The sea looked and fled;
the Jordan River turned back.
4 The mountains skipped like rams,
the hills like lambs.
5 Why do you flee, O sea?
Why do you turn back, O Jordan River?
6 Why do you skip like rams, O mountains,
like lambs, O hills?
7 Tremble, O earth, before the Lord—
before the God of Jacob,
8 who turned a rock into a pool of water,
a hard rock into springs of water.

115 Not to us, O LORD, not to us,
but to your name bring honor,
for the sake of your loyal love
and faithfulness.
2 Why should the nations say,
"Where is their God?"
3 Our God is in heaven.
He does whatever he pleases.
4 Their idols are made of silver and gold—
they are man-made.
5 They have mouths, but cannot speak,
eyes, but cannot see,
6 ears, but cannot hear,
noses, but cannot smell,
7 hands, but cannot touch,
feet, but cannot walk.
They cannot even clear their throats.
8 Those who make them will end up like them,
as will everyone who trusts in them.
9 O Israel, trust in the LORD.
He is their deliverer and protector.
10 O family of Aaron, trust in the LORD.
He is their deliverer and protector.
11 You loyal followers of the LORD,
trust in the LORD.
He is their deliverer and protector.
12 The LORD takes notice of us; he will bless—
he will bless the family of Israel,
he will bless the family of Aaron.
13 He will bless his loyal followers,
both young and old.
14 May he increase your numbers,
yours and your children's.
15 May you be blessed by the LORD,
the Creator of heaven and earth.
16 The heavens belong to the LORD,
but the earth he has given to mankind.

17 The dead do not praise the LORD,
nor do any of those who descend into the silence of death.
18 But we will praise the LORD
now and forevermore.
Praise the LORD!

116 I love the LORD
because he heard my plea for mercy,
2 and listened to me.
As long as I live, I will call to him when I need help.
3 The ropes of death tightened around me,
the snares of Sheol confronted me.
I was confronted with trouble and sorrow.
4 I called on the name of the LORD,
"Please, LORD, rescue my life!"
5 The LORD is merciful and fair;
our God is compassionate.
6 The LORD protects the untrained;
I was in serious trouble and he delivered me.
7 Rest once more, my soul,
for the LORD has vindicated you.
8 Yes, LORD, you rescued my life from death,
kept my eyes from tears
and my feet from stumbling.
9 I will serve the LORD
in the land of the living.
10 I had faith when I said,
"I am severely oppressed."
11 I rashly declared,
"All men are liars."
12 How can I repay the LORD
for all his acts of kindness to me?
13 I will celebrate my deliverance,
and call on the name of the LORD.
14 I will fulfill my vows to the LORD
before all his people.
15 The LORD values
the lives of his faithful followers.
16 Yes, LORD! I am indeed your servant;
I am your servant, the son of your female servant.
You saved me from death.
17 I will present a thank offering to you,
and call on the name of the LORD.
18 I will fulfill my vows to the LORD
before all his people,
19 in the courts of the LORD's temple,
in your midst, O Jerusalem.
Praise the LORD!

117 Praise the LORD, all you nations.
Applaud him, all you foreigners.
2 For his loyal love towers over us,
and the LORD's faithfulness endures.
Praise the LORD.

118 Give thanks to the LORD, for he is good,
and his loyal love endures.
2 Let Israel say,
"Yes, his loyal love endures."
3 Let the family of Aaron say,
"Yes, his loyal love endures."
4 Let the loyal followers of the LORD say,
"Yes, his loyal love endures."
5 In my distress I cried out to the LORD.
The LORD answered me and put me in a wide open place.
6 The LORD is on my side; I am not afraid.
What can people do to me?
7 The LORD is on my side as my helper.
I look in triumph on those who hate me.
8 It is better to take shelter in the LORD
than to trust in people.
9 It is better to take shelter in the LORD
than to trust in princes.
10 All the nations surrounded me.
Indeed, in the name of the LORD I pushed them away.
11 They surrounded me, yes, they surrounded me.
Indeed, in the name of the LORD I pushed them away.
12 They surrounded me like bees.
But they disappeared as quickly as a fire among thorns.
Indeed, in the name of the LORD I pushed them away.
13 "You aggressively attacked me and
tried to knock me down,
but the LORD helped me.
14 The LORD gives me strength and protects me;
he has become my deliverer."
15 They celebrate deliverance in the tents of the godly.
The LORD's right hand conquers.
16 The LORD's right hand gives victory;
the LORD's right hand conquers.
17 I will not die, but live,
and I will proclaim what the LORD has done.
18 The LORD severely punished me,
but he did not hand me over to death.
19 Open for me the gates of the just king's temple.
I will enter through them and give thanks to the LORD.
20 This is the LORD's gate—
the godly enter through it.
21 I will give you thanks, for you answered me,
and have become my deliverer.
22 The stone that the builders discarded
has become the cornerstone.
23 This is the LORD's work.
We consider it amazing!
24 This is the day the LORD has brought about.
We will be happy and rejoice in it.
25 Please, LORD, deliver!
Please, LORD, grant us success!
26 May the one who comes in the name
of the LORD be blessed.

We will pronounce blessings on you in the LORD's temple.
27 The LORD is God, and he has delivered us.
Tie the offering with ropes
to the horns of the altar.
28 You are my God, and I will give you thanks.
You are my God and I will praise you.
29 Give thanks to the LORD, for he is good
and his loyal love endures."

א (ALEF)

119 How blessed are those whose actions are blameless,
who obey the law of the LORD.
2 How blessed are those who observe his rules,
and seek him with all their heart,
3 who, moreover, do no wrong,
but follow in his footsteps.
4 You demand that your precepts
be carefully kept.
5 If only I were predisposed
to keep your statutes.
6 Then I would not be ashamed,
if I were focused on all your commands.
7 I will give you sincere thanks,
when I learn your just regulations.
8 I will keep your statutes.
Do not completely abandon me.

ב (BET)

9 How can a young person maintain a pure life?
By guarding it according to your instructions.
10 With all my heart I seek you.
Do not allow me to stray from your commands.
11 In my heart I store up your words,
so I might not sin against you.
12 You deserve praise, O LORD.
Teach me your statutes.
13 With my lips I proclaim
all the regulations you have revealed.
14 I rejoice in the lifestyle prescribed by your rules
as if they were riches of all kinds.
15 I will meditate on your precepts
and focus on your behavior.
16 I find delight in your statutes;
I do not forget your instructions.

ג (GIMEL)

17 Be kind to your servant.
Then I will live and keep your instructions.
18 Open my eyes so I can truly see
the marvelous things in your law.
19 I am a resident foreigner in this land.
Do not hide your commands from me.
20 I desperately long to know
your regulations at all times.

21 You reprimand arrogant people.
Those who stray from your commands are doomed.
22 Spare me shame and humiliation,
for I observe your rules.
23 Though rulers plot and slander me,
your servant meditates on your statutes.
24 Yes, I find delight in your rules;
they give me guidance.

ד (DALET)

25 I collapse in the dirt.
Revive me with your word.
26 I told you about my ways and you answered me.
Teach me your statutes.
27 Help me to understand what your precepts mean.
Then I can meditate on your marvelous teachings.
28 I collapse from grief.
Sustain me by your word.
29 Remove me from the path of deceit.
Graciously give me your law.
30 I choose the path of faithfulness;
I am committed to your regulations.
31 I hold fast to your rules.
O LORD, do not let me be ashamed.
32 I run along the path of your commands,
for you enable me to do so.

ה (HE)

33 Teach me, O LORD, the lifestyle
prescribed by your statutes,
so that I might observe it continually.
34 Give me understanding so that
I might observe your law,
and keep it with all my heart.
35 Guide me in the path of your commands,
for I delight to walk in it.
36 Give me a desire for your rules,
rather than for wealth gained unjustly.
37 Turn my eyes away from what is worthless.
Revive me with your word.
38 Confirm to your servant your promise,
which you made to the one who honors you.
39 Take away the insults that I dread.
Indeed, your regulations are good.
40 Look, I long for your precepts.
Revive me with your deliverance.

ו (VAV)

41 May I experience your loyal love, O LORD,
and your deliverance, as you promised.
42 Then I will have a reply for the one who insults me,
for I trust in your word.
43 Do not completely deprive me of a truthful testimony,
for I await your justice.

44 Then I will keep your law continually
now and for all time.
45 I will be secure,
for I seek your precepts.
46 I will speak about your regulations before kings
and not be ashamed.
47 I will find delight in your commands,
which I love.
48 I will lift my hands to your commands,
which I love,
and I will meditate on your statutes.

ז (ZAYIN)
49 Remember your word to your servant,
for you have given me hope.
50 This is what comforts me in my trouble,
for your promise revives me.
51 Arrogant people do nothing but scoff at me.
Yet I do not turn aside from your law.
52 I remember your ancient regulations,
O LORD, and console myself.
53 Rage takes hold of me because of the wicked,
those who reject your law.
54 Your statutes have been my songs
in the house where I live.
55 I remember your name during the night,
O LORD,
and I will keep your law.
56 This has been my practice,
for I observe your precepts.

ח (KHET)
57 The LORD is my source of security.
I have determined to follow your instructions.
58 I seek your favor with all my heart.
Have mercy on me as you promised.
59 I consider my actions
and follow your rules.
60 I keep your commands eagerly
and without delay.
61 The ropes of the wicked tighten around me,
but I do not forget your law.
62 In the middle of the night I arise to thank you
for your just regulations.
63 I am a friend to all your loyal followers,
and to those who keep your precepts.
64 O LORD, your loyal love fills the earth.
Teach me your statutes!

ט (TET)
65 You are good to your servant,
O LORD, just as you promised.
66 Teach me proper discernment and understanding.
For I consider your commands to be reliable.

67 Before I was afflicted I used to stray off,
but now I keep your instructions.
68 You are good and you do good.
Teach me your statutes.
69 Arrogant people smear my reputation with lies,
but I observe your precepts with all my heart.
70 Their hearts are calloused,
but I find delight in your law.
71 It was good for me to suffer,
so that I might learn your statutes.
72 The law you have revealed is more important to me
than thousands of pieces of gold and silver.

י (YOD)

73 Your hands made me and formed me.
Give me understanding so that I might
learn your commands.
74 Your loyal followers will be glad
when they see me,
for I find hope in your word.
75 I know, LORD, that your regulations are just.
You disciplined me because of your
faithful devotion to me.
76 May your loyal love console me,
as you promised your servant.
77 May I experience your compassion,
so I might live.
For I find delight in your law.
78 May the arrogant be humiliated, for
they have slandered me.
But I meditate on your precepts.
79 May your loyal followers turn to me,
those who know your rules.
80 May I be fully committed to your statutes,
so that I might not be ashamed.

כ (KAF)

81 I desperately long for your deliverance.
I find hope in your word.
82 My eyes grow tired as I wait for your
promise to be fulfilled.
I say, "When will you comfort me?"
83 For I am like a wineskin dried up in smoke.
I do not forget your statutes.
84 How long must your servant endure this?
When will you judge those who pursue me?
85 The arrogant dig pits to trap me,
which violates your law.
86 All your commands are reliable.
I am pursued without reason. Help me!
87 They have almost destroyed me here on the earth,
but I do not reject your precepts.
88 Revive me with your loyal love,
that I might keep the rules you have revealed.

ל (LAMED)

89 O LORD, your instructions endure;
they stand secure in heaven.
90 You demonstrate your faithfulness to all generations.
You established the earth and it stood firm.
91 Today they stand firm by your decrees,
for all things are your servants.
92 If I had not found encouragement in your law,
I would have died in my sorrow.
93 I will never forget your precepts,
for by them you have revived me.
94 I belong to you. Deliver me!
For I seek your precepts.
95 The wicked prepare to kill me,
yet I concentrate on your rules.
96 I realize that everything has its limits,
but your commands are beyond full comprehension.

מ (MEM)

97 O how I love your law!
All day long I meditate on it.
98 Your commandments make me wiser than my enemies,
for I am always aware of them.
99 I have more insight than all my teachers,
for I meditate on your rules.
100 I am more discerning than those older than I,
for I observe your precepts.
101 I stay away from every evil path,
so that I might keep your instructions.
102 I do not turn aside from your regulations,
for you teach me.
103 Your words are sweeter
in my mouth than honey!
104 Your precepts give me discernment.
Therefore I hate all deceitful actions.

נ (NUN)

105 Your word is a lamp to walk by,
and a light to illumine my path.
106 I have vowed and solemnly sworn
to keep your just regulations.
107 I am suffering terribly.
O LORD, revive me with your word.
108 O LORD, please accept the freewill offerings
of my praise.
Teach me your regulations.
109 My life is in continual danger,
but I do not forget your law.
110 The wicked lay a trap for me,
but I do not wander from your precepts.
111 I claim your rules as my permanent possession,
for they give me joy.
112 I am determined to obey your statutes
at all times, to the very end.

ס (SAMEK)

113 I hate people with divided loyalties,
but I love your law.
114 You are my hiding place and my shield.
I find hope in your word.
115 Turn away from me, you evil men,
so that I can observe the commands of my God.
116 Sustain me as you promised, so that I will live.
Do not disappoint me.
117 Support me, so that I will be delivered.
Then I will focus on your statutes continually.
118 You despise all who stray from your statutes,
for such people are deceptive and unreliable.
119 You remove all the wicked of the earth like slag.
Therefore I love your rules.
120 My body trembles because I fear you;
I am afraid of your judgments.

ע (AYIN)

121 I do what is fair and right.
Do not abandon me to my oppressors.
122 Guarantee the welfare of your servant.
Do not let the arrogant oppress me.
123 My eyes grow tired as I wait for your deliverance,
for your reliable promise to be fulfilled.
124 Show your servant your loyal love.
Teach me your statutes.
125 I am your servant. Give me insight,
so that I can understand your rules.
126 It is time for the LORD to act—
they break your law.
127 For this reason I love your commands
more than gold, even purest gold.
128 For this reason I carefully follow all your precepts.
I hate all deceitful actions.

פ (PE)

129 Your rules are marvelous.
Therefore I observe them.
130 Your instructions are a doorway
through which light shines.
They give insight to the untrained.
131 I open my mouth and pant,
because I long for your commands.
132 Turn toward me and extend mercy to me,
as you typically do to your loyal followers.
133 Direct my steps by your word.
Do not let any sin dominate me.
134 Deliver me from oppressive men,
so that I can keep your precepts.
135 Smile on your servant.
Teach me your statutes!
136 Tears stream down from my eyes,
because people do not keep your law.

צ (TSADE)

137 You are just, O LORD,
and your judgments are fair.
138 The rules you impose are just,
and absolutely reliable.
139 My zeal consumes me,
for my enemies forget your instructions.
140 Your word is absolutely pure,
and your servant loves it.
141 I am insignificant and despised,
yet I do not forget your precepts.
142 Your justice endures,
and your law is reliable.
143 Distress and hardship confront me,
yet I find delight in your commands.
144 Your rules remain just.
Give me insight so that I can live.

ק (QOF)

145 I cried out with all my heart,
"Answer me, O LORD!
I will observe your statutes."
146 I cried out to you, "Deliver me,
so that I can keep your rules."
147 I am up before dawn crying for help.
I find hope in your word.
148 My eyes anticipate the nighttime hours,
so that I can meditate on your word.
149 Listen to me because of your loyal love.
O LORD, revive me, as you typically do.
150 Those who are eager to do wrong draw near;
they are far from your law.
151 You are near, O LORD,
and all your commands are reliable.
152 I learned long ago that
you ordained your rules to last.

ר (RESH)

153 See my pain and rescue me.
For I do not forget your law.
154 Fight for me and defend me.
Revive me with your word.
155 The wicked have no chance for deliverance,
for they do not seek your statutes.
156 Your compassion is great, O LORD.
Revive me, as you typically do.
157 The enemies who chase me are numerous.
Yet I do not turn aside from your rules.
158 I take note of the treacherous and despise them,
because they do not keep your instructions.
159 See how I love your precepts.
O LORD, revive me with your loyal love.
160 Your instructions are totally reliable;
all your just regulations endure.

שׂ/שׁ (SIN/SHIN)

161 Rulers pursue me for no reason,
yet I am more afraid of disobeying your instructions.
162 I rejoice in your instructions,
like one who finds much plunder.
163 I hate and despise deceit;
I love your law.
164 Seven times a day I praise you
because of your just regulations.
165 Those who love your law are completely secure;
nothing causes them to stumble.
166 I hope for your deliverance, O LORD,
and I obey your commands.
167 I keep your rules;
I love them greatly.
168 I keep your precepts and rules,
for you are aware of everything I do.

ת (TAV)

169 Listen to my cry for help, O LORD.
Give me insight by your word.
170 Listen to my appeal for mercy.
Deliver me, as you promised.
171 May praise flow freely from my lips,
for you teach me your statutes.
172 May my tongue sing about your instructions,
for all your commands are just.
173 May your hand help me,
for I choose to obey your precepts.
174 I long for your deliverance, O LORD;
I find delight in your law.
175 May I live and praise you.
May your regulations help me.
176 I have wandered off like a lost sheep.
Come looking for your servant,
for I do not forget your commands.

A song of ascents.

120 In my distress I cried out
to the LORD and he answered me.
2 I said, "O LORD, rescue me
from those who lie with their lips
and those who deceive with their tongues.
3 How will he severely punish you,
you deceptive talker?
4 Here's how! With the sharp arrows of warriors,
with arrowheads forged over the hot coals.
5 How miserable I am.
For I have lived temporarily in Meshech;
I have resided among the tents of Kedar.
6 For too long I have had to reside
with those who hate peace.
7 I am committed to peace,
but when I speak, they want to make war.

A song of ascents.

121 I look up toward the hills.
From where does my help come?
2 My help comes from the LORD,
the Creator of heaven and earth.
3 May he not allow your foot to slip.
May your Protector not sleep.
4 Look! Israel's Protector
does not sleep or slumber.
5 The LORD is your protector;
the LORD is the shade at your right hand.
6 The sun will not harm you by day,
or the moon by night.
7 The LORD will protect you from all harm;
he will protect your life.
8 The LORD will protect you in all you do,
now and forevermore.

A song of ascents; by David.

122 I was glad because they said to me,
"We will go to the LORD's temple."
2 Our feet are standing
inside your gates, O Jerusalem.
3 Jerusalem is a city designed
to accommodate an assembly.
4 The tribes go up there,
the tribes of the LORD,
where it is required that Israel
give thanks to the name of the LORD.
5 Indeed, the leaders sit there on thrones
and make legal decisions,
on the thrones of the house of David.
6 Pray for the peace of Jerusalem.
May those who love her prosper.
7 May there be peace inside your defenses,
and prosperity inside your fortresses.
8 For the sake of my brothers and my neighbors
I will say, "May there be peace in you."
9 For the sake of the temple of the LORD our God
I will pray for you to prosper.

A song of ascents.

123 I look up toward you,
the one enthroned in heaven.
2 Look, as the eyes of servants look to the hand of their master,
as the eyes of a female servant look to
the hand of her mistress,
so our eyes will look to the LORD, our
God, until he shows us favor.
3 Show us favor, O LORD, show us favor!
For we have had our fill of humiliation, and then some.
4 We have had our fill
of the taunts of the self-assured,
of the contempt of the proud.

A song of ascents; by David.

124 "If the LORD had not been on our side"–
let Israel say this.–
2 if the LORD had not been on our side,
when men attacked us,
3 they would have swallowed us alive,
when their anger raged against us.
4 The water would have overpowered us;
the current would have overwhelmed us.
5 The raging water
would have overwhelmed us.
6 The LORD deserves praise,
for he did not hand us over as prey to their teeth.
7 We escaped with our lives, like a bird
from a hunter's snare.
The snare broke, and we escaped.
8 Our deliverer is the LORD,
the Creator of heaven and earth.

A song of ascents.

125 Those who trust in the LORD are like Mount Zion,
which cannot be moved and will endure forever.
2 As the mountains surround Jerusalem,
so the LORD surrounds his people,
now and forevermore.
3 Indeed, the scepter of a wicked king will not settle
upon the allotted land of the godly.
Otherwise the godly
might do what is wrong.
4 Do good, O LORD, to those who are good,
to the morally upright.
5 As for those who are bent on traveling a sinful path,
may the LORD remove them, along with
those who behave wickedly.
May Israel experience peace.

A song of ascents.

126 When the LORD restored the well-being of Zion,
we thought we were dreaming.
2 At that time we laughed loudly
and shouted for joy.
At that time the nations said,
"The LORD has accomplished great
things for these people."
3 The LORD did indeed accomplish great things for us.
We were happy.
4 O LORD, restore our well-being,
just as the streams in the arid south are replenished.
5 Those who shed tears as they plant
will shout for joy when they reap the harvest.
6 The one who weeps as he walks along,
carrying his bag of seed,
will certainly come in with a shout of joy,
carrying his sheaves of grain.

LOVE TO GROW

UNTIL THE HARVEST

PSALM 126

Psalm 126:5 has been a lifeline to me in recent seasons. There's so much hope and promise packed into it. I love that it acknowledges our tears and that God's Word doesn't stifle emotions.

Those who shed tears as they plant will shout for joy when they reap the harvest (Ps 126:5).

The eyes of the exiles in this psalm were blurred by their tears, still they continued planting. They knew a harvest was coming. Even when life isn't going as planned, we plant as we trust God through our disappointment. We cling to His kindness and compassion, which are fresh every morning.

I don't know what your story entails, but we all have one. I never dreamed that my story would include losing my mom, dad, and sister over a period of only five years. And I wish it didn't include the heartbreaking loss of my thirteen-year marriage.

No matter our circumstances, God is faithful. Any seed we sow in love and faithful obedience to Him eventually yields a harvest of righteousness. He always draws near to the brokenhearted.

My seasons of pain and darkness have been a gift. I felt Christ's presence in the midst of the suffering. He brought me comfort, sustaining me and providing for me in numerous ways. As a mother, I would do anything to console my children and wipe away their tears. Our heavenly Father loves us with a perfect love. How much more will He do for us?

Verse 1 says, "When the Lord restored the well-being of Zion, we thought we were dreaming." The exiles in Psalm 126 were so overwhelmed by God's restoration they could hardly believe it was true. As He restored the Israelites, God desires to restore you too. When darkness threatens to overcome, cling to His Word and hope in His promises. He will glorify Himself through you and your circumstances.

Keep planting in the midst of your tears. A harvest is coming.

A song of ascents; by Solomon.

127 If the LORD does not build a house,
then those who build it work in vain.
If the LORD does not guard a city,
then the watchman stands guard in vain.
2 It is vain for you to rise early, come home late,
and work so hard for your food.
Yes, he provides for those whom he
loves even when they sleep.
3 Yes, sons are a gift from the LORD;
the fruit of the womb is a reward.
4 Sons born during one's youth
are like arrows in a warrior's hand.
5 How blessed is the man who fills his quiver with them.
They will not be put to shame when they
confront enemies at the city gate.

A song of ascents.

128 How blessed is every one of the LORD's loyal followers,
each one who keeps his commands.
2 You will eat what you worked so hard to grow.
You will be blessed and secure.
3 Your wife will be like a fruitful vine
in the inner rooms of your house;
your children will be like olive branches,
as they sit all around your table.
4 Yes indeed, the man who fears the LORD
will be blessed in this way.
5 May the LORD bless you from Zion,
that you might see Jerusalem prosper
all the days of your life,
6 and that you might see your grandchildren.
May Israel experience peace.

A song of ascents.

129 "Since my youth they have often attacked me,"
let Israel say.
2 "Since my youth they have often attacked me,
but they have not defeated me.
3 The plowers plowed my back;
they made their furrows long.
4 The LORD is just;
he cut the ropes of the wicked."
5 May all who hate Zion
be humiliated and turned back.
6 May they be like the grass on the rooftops,
which withers before one can even pull it up,
7 which cannot fill the reaper's hand,
or the lap of the one who gathers the grain.
8 Those who pass by will not say,
"May you experience the LORD's blessing!
We pronounce a blessing on you
in the name of the LORD."

LOVE TO GROW

WHITE FLAG

PSALM 127:2

Driving seventy-five miles per hour felt too slow for a Texas highway. I decided to go eighty instead. The police officer who pulled me over wasn't too fond of my decision.

Like that speed limit, there are many other limits I push. I find limits restricting and unfair. However, this overexertion results in pain when I jog the extra mile, exhaustion when I delay bedtime, and strain when I overbook my schedule.

When examining Psalm 127, a strange principle emerges: Life is found in the surrender of self-sufficiency. Limits provide freedom when they promote dependence on the Lord.

Yes, he can provide for those whom he loves
even when they sleep (Ps 127:2).

This verse paints a picture of God's freedom for us. Our Father is busy taking care of our needs, even when we sleep, but we often feel the self-inflicted burden of being the sole provider for ourselves.

The psalmist emphasizes the foolish lengths humans will go to provide for ourselves when we leave the whole matter to our own hands. If God provides for our needs even in our sleep, why do we deprive ourselves of rest and work anxiously?

God wants His children to experience the joy and freedom of reliance on their Father. When we choose to raise the white flag bearing the words "I can't do it all," we honor our Father.

We were not designed to live without rest. This psalm invites His calming presence into our frantic pace. When we work ourselves into exhaustion, are we working to honor Him, or for the illusion of perfection or control?

In a vain effort I diligently tried to be the builder and provider of my security and peace. Only my heavenly Father can do that. He alone offers joy and peace in surrender. He calls us His beloved, regardless of how much we work.

Let's embrace the peace and stability offered us in the truth that today's needs are not solely dependent on the amount of effort we exert. He is providing for you, His beloved, even as you sleep. Rest well.

A song of ascents.

130 From the deep water I cry out to you, O LORD.
2 O Lord, listen to me.
Pay attention to my plea for mercy.
3 If you, O LORD, were to keep track of sins,
O Lord, who could stand before you?
4 But you are willing to forgive,
so that you might be honored.
5 I rely on the LORD.
I rely on him with my whole being;
I wait for his assuring word.
6 I yearn for the Lord,
more than watchmen do for the morning,
yes, more than watchmen do for the morning.
7 O Israel, hope in the LORD,
for the LORD exhibits loyal love,
and is more than willing to deliver.
8 He will deliver Israel
from all their sins.

A song of ascents, by David.

131 O LORD, my heart is not proud,
nor do I have a haughty look.
I do not have great aspirations,
or concern myself with things that are beyond me.
2 Indeed, I have calmed and quieted myself
like a weaned child with its mother;
I am content like a young child.
3 O Israel, hope in the LORD
now and forevermore!

A song of ascents.

132 O LORD, for David's sake remember
all his strenuous effort,
2 and how he made a vow to the LORD,
and swore an oath to the Powerful One of Jacob.
3 He said, "I will not enter my own home,
or get into my bed.
4 I will not allow my eyes to sleep,
or my eyelids to slumber,
5 until I find a place for the LORD,
a fine dwelling place for the Powerful One of Jacob."
6 Look, we heard about it in Ephrathah;
we found it in the territory of Jaar.
7 Let us go to his dwelling place.
Let us worship before his footstool.
8 Ascend, O LORD, to your resting place,
you and the ark of your strength.
9 May your priests be clothed with integrity.
May your loyal followers shout for joy.
10 For the sake of David, your servant,
do not reject your chosen king.
11 The LORD made a reliable promise to David;
he will not go back on his word.

He said, "I will place one of your
descendants on your throne.
12 If your sons keep my covenant
and the rules I teach them,
their sons will also sit on your throne forever."
13 Certainly the LORD has chosen Zion;
he decided to make it his home.
14 He said, "This will be my resting place forever;
I will live here, for I have chosen it.
15 I will abundantly supply what she needs;
I will give her poor all the food they need.
16 I will protect her priests,
and her godly people will shout exuberantly.
17 There I will make David strong;
I have determined that my chosen
king's dynasty will continue.
18 I will humiliate his enemies,
and his crown will shine."

A song of ascents; by David.

133 Look! How good and how pleasant it is
when brothers truly live in unity.
2 It is like fine oil poured on the head,
which flows down the beard—
Aaron's beard,
and then flows down his garments.
3 It is like the dew of Hermon,
which flows down upon the hills of Zion.
Indeed, that is where the LORD has decreed
a blessing will be available—eternal life.

A song of ascents.

134 Attention! Praise the LORD,
all you servants of the LORD,
who serve in the LORD's temple during the night.
2 Lift your hands toward the sanctuary
and praise the LORD.
3 May the LORD, the Creator of heaven and earth,
bless you from Zion.

135 Praise the LORD.
Praise the name of the LORD.
Offer praise, you servants of the LORD,
2 who serve in the LORD's temple,
in the courts of the temple of our God.
3 Praise the LORD, for the LORD is good.
Sing praises to his name, for it is pleasant.
4 Indeed, the LORD has chosen Jacob for himself,
Israel to be his special possession.
5 Yes, I know the LORD is great,
and our Lord is superior to all gods.
6 He does whatever he pleases
in heaven and on earth,
in the seas and all the ocean depths.

7 He causes the clouds to arise from the end of the earth,
makes lightning bolts accompany the rain,
and brings the wind out of his storehouses.
8 He struck down the firstborn of Egypt,
including both men and animals.
9 He performed awesome deeds and acts of judgment
in your midst, O Egypt,
against Pharaoh and all his servants.
10 He defeated many nations,
and killed mighty kings—
11 Sihon, king of the Amorites,
and Og, king of Bashan,
and all the kingdoms of Canaan.
12 He gave their land as an inheritance,
as an inheritance to Israel his people.
13 O LORD, your name endures,
your reputation, O LORD, lasts.
14 For the LORD vindicates his people,
and has compassion on his servants.
15 The nations' idols are made of silver and gold;
they are man-made.
16 They have mouths, but cannot speak,
eyes, but cannot see,
17 and ears, but cannot hear.
Indeed, they cannot breathe.
18 Those who make them will end up like them,
as will everyone who trusts in them.
19 O family of Israel, praise the LORD.
O family of Aaron, praise the LORD.
20 O family of Levi, praise the LORD.
You loyal followers of the LORD, praise the LORD.
21 The LORD deserves praise in Zion—
he who dwells in Jerusalem.
Praise the LORD.

136 Give thanks to the LORD, for he is good,
for his loyal love endures.
2 Give thanks to the God of gods,
for his loyal love endures.
3 Give thanks to the Lord of lords,
for his loyal love endures,
4 to the one who performs magnificent,
amazing deeds all by himself,
for his loyal love endures,
5 to the one who used wisdom to make the heavens,
for his loyal love endures,
6 to the one who spread out the earth over the water,
for his loyal love endures,
7 to the one who made the great lights,
for his loyal love endures,
8 the sun to rule by day,
for his loyal love endures,
9 the moon and stars to rule by night,
for his loyal love endures,

REFLECT

What are the ways you have seen God's loyal love endure in your life? Write out a few lines of a psalm like Psalm 136, praising God for all the ways His love endures.

10 to the one who struck down the firstborn of Egypt,
for his loyal love endures,
11 and led Israel out from their midst,
for his loyal love endures,
12 with a strong hand and an outstretched arm,
for his loyal love endures,
13 to the one who divided the Red Sea in two,
for his loyal love endures,
14 and led Israel through its midst,
for his loyal love endures,
15 and tossed Pharaoh and his army into the Red Sea,
for his loyal love endures,
16 to the one who led his people
through the wilderness,
for his loyal love endures,
17 to the one who struck down great kings,
for his loyal love endures,
18 and killed powerful kings,
for his loyal love endures,
19 Sihon, king of the Amorites,
for his loyal love endures,
20 Og, king of Bashan,
for his loyal love endures,
21 and gave their land as an inheritance,
for his loyal love endures,
22 as an inheritance to Israel his servant,
for his loyal love endures,
23 to the one who remembered us when we were down,
for his loyal love endures,
24 and snatched us away from our enemies,
for his loyal love endures,
25 to the one who gives food to all living things,
for his loyal love endures.
26 Give thanks to the God of heaven,
for his loyal love endures!

137 By the rivers of Babylon
we sit down and weep
when we remember Zion.
2 On the poplars in her midst
we hang our harps,
3 for there our captors ask us to compose songs;
those who mock us demand that we be happy, saying:
"Sing for us a song about Zion!"
4 How can we sing a song to the LORD
in a foreign land?
5 If I forget you, O Jerusalem,
may my right hand be crippled.
6 May my tongue stick to the roof of my mouth,
if I do not remember you,
and do not give Jerusalem priority
over whatever gives me the most joy.
7 Remember, O LORD, what the Edomites did
on the day Jerusalem fell.

They said, "Tear it down, tear it down,
right to its very foundation!"
8 O daughter Babylon, soon to be devastated,
how blessed will be the one who repays you
for what you dished out to us.
9 How blessed will be the one who grabs your babies
and smashes them on a rock.

By David.

138 I will give you thanks with all my heart;
before the heavenly assembly I
will sing praises to you.
2 I will bow down toward your holy temple,
and give thanks to your name,
because of your loyal love and faithfulness,
for you have exalted your promise
above the entire sky.
3 When I cried out for help, you answered me.
You made me bold and energized me.
4 Let all the kings of the earth give thanks to you, O LORD,
when they hear the words you speak.
5 Let them sing about the LORD's deeds,
for the LORD's splendor is magnificent.
6 Though the LORD is exalted, he looks after the lowly,
and from far away humbles the proud.
7 Even when I must walk in the midst
of danger, you revive me.
You oppose my angry enemies,
and your right hand delivers me.
8 The LORD avenges me.
O LORD, your loyal love endures.
Do not abandon those whom you have made.

For the music director, a psalm of David.

139 O LORD, you examine me and know me.
2 You know when I sit down and when I get up;
even from far away you understand my motives.
3 You carefully observe me when I travel
or when I lie down to rest;
you are aware of everything I do.
4 Certainly my tongue does not frame a word
without you, O LORD, being thoroughly aware of it.
5 You squeeze me in from behind and in front;
you place your hand on me.
6 Your knowledge is beyond my comprehension;
it is so far beyond me, I am unable to fathom it.
7 Where can I go to escape your Spirit?
Where can I flee to escape your presence?
8 If I were to ascend to heaven, you would be there.
If I were to sprawl out in Sheol, there you would be.
9 If I were to fly away on the wings of the dawn,
and settle down on the other side of the sea,
10 even there your hand would guide me,
your right hand would grab hold of me.

11 If I were to say, "Certainly the darkness will cover me,
and the light will turn to night all around me,"
12 even the darkness is not too dark for you to see,
and the night is as bright as day;
darkness and light are the same to you.
13 Certainly you made my mind and heart;
you wove me together in my mother's womb.
14 I will give you thanks because your deeds
are awesome and amazing.
You knew me thoroughly;
15 my bones were not hidden from you,
when I was made in secret
and sewed together in the depths of the earth.
16 Your eyes saw me when I was inside the womb.
All the days ordained for me
were recorded in your scroll
before one of them came into existence.
17 How difficult it is for me to fathom your
thoughts about me, O God!
How vast is their sum total.
18 If I tried to count them,
they would outnumber the grains of sand.
Even if I finished counting them,
I would still have to contend with you.
19 If only you would kill the wicked, O God!
Get away from me, you violent men!
20 They rebel against you and act deceitfully;
your enemies lie.
21 O LORD, do I not hate those who hate you,
and despise those who oppose you?
22 I absolutely hate them;
they have become my enemies.
23 Examine me, O God, and probe my thoughts.
Test me, and know my concerns.
24 See if there is any idolatrous way in me,
and lead me in the everlasting way.

For the music director, a psalm of David.

140 O LORD, rescue me from wicked men.
Protect me from violent men,
2 who plan ways to harm me.
All day long they stir up conflict.
3 Their tongues wound like a serpent;
a viper's venom is behind their lips. *Selah*
4 O LORD, shelter me from the power of the wicked.
Protect me from violent men,
who plan to knock me over.
5 Proud men hide a snare for me;
evil men spread a net by the path.
They set traps for me. *Selah*
6 I say to the LORD, "You are my God."
O LORD, pay attention to my plea for mercy.
7 O Sovereign LORD, my strong deliverer,
you shield my head in the day of battle.

8 O Lord, do not let the wicked have their way.
Do not allow their plan to succeed when they attack. *Selah*
9 As for the heads of those who surround me—
may the harm done by their lips overwhelm them.
10 May he rain down fiery coals upon them.
May he throw them into the fire.
From bottomless pits they will not escape.
11 A slanderer will not endure on the earth;
calamity will hunt down a violent
man and strike him down.
12 I know that the Lord defends the cause of the oppressed
and vindicates the poor.
13 Certainly the godly will give thanks to your name;
the morally upright will live in your presence.

A psalm of David.

141 O Lord, I cry out to you. Come quickly to me.
Pay attention to me when I cry out to you.
2 May you accept my prayer like incense,
my uplifted hands like the evening offering.
3 O Lord, place a guard on my mouth.
Protect the opening of my lips.
4 Do not let me have evil desires,
or participate in sinful activities
with men who behave wickedly.
I will not eat their delicacies.
5 May the godly strike me in love and correct me.
May my head not refuse choice oil.
Indeed, my prayer is a witness against their evil deeds.
6 They will be thrown over the side of a cliff by their judges.
They will listen to my words, for they are pleasant.
7 As when one plows and breaks up the soil,
so our bones are scattered at the mouth of Sheol.
8 Surely I am looking to you, O Sovereign Lord.
In you I take shelter.
Do not expose me to danger.
9 Protect me from the snare they have laid for me,
and the traps the evildoers have set.
10 Let the wicked fall into their own nets,
while I escape.

A well-written song by David, when he was in the cave; a prayer.

142 To the Lord I cry out;
to the Lord I plead for mercy.
2 I pour out my lament before him;
I tell him about my troubles.
3 Even when my strength leaves me,
you watch my footsteps.
In the path where I walk
they have hidden a trap for me.
4 Look to the right and see.
No one cares about me.
I have nowhere to run;
no one is concerned about my life.

5 I cry out to you, O LORD;
I say, "You are my shelter,
my security in the land of the living."
6 Listen to my cry for help,
for I am in serious trouble.
Rescue me from those who chase me,
for they are stronger than I am.
7 Free me from prison,
that I may give thanks to your name.
Because of me the godly will assemble,
for you will vindicate me.

A psalm of David.

143 O LORD, hear my prayer.
Pay attention to my plea for help.
Because of your faithfulness
and justice, answer me.
2 Do not sit in judgment on your servant,
for no one alive is innocent before you.
3 Certainly my enemies chase me.
They smash me into the ground.
They force me to live in dark regions,
like those who have been dead for ages.
4 My strength leaves me;
I am absolutely shocked.
5 I recall the old days.
I meditate on all you have done;
I reflect on your accomplishments.
6 I spread my hands out to you in prayer;
my soul thirsts for you in a parched land. *Selah*
7 Answer me quickly, LORD.
My strength is fading.
Do not reject me,
or I will join those descending
into the grave.
8 May I hear about your loyal love
in the morning,
for I trust in you.
Show me the way I should go,
because I long for you.
9 Rescue me from my enemies, O LORD.
I run to you for protection.
10 Teach me to do what pleases you,
for you are my God.
May your kind presence
lead me into a level land.
11 O LORD, for the sake of your
reputation, revive me.
Because of your justice,
rescue me from trouble.
12 As a demonstration of your loyal love,
destroy my enemies.
Annihilate all who threaten my life,
for I am your servant.

By David.

144 The LORD, my Protector, deserves praise—
the one who trains my hands for battle,
and my fingers for war,
2 who loves me and is my stronghold,
my refuge and my deliverer,
my shield and the one in whom I take shelter,
who makes nations submit to me.
3 O LORD, of what importance is the human
race, that you should notice them?
Of what importance is mankind, that you
should be concerned about them?
4 People are like a vapor,
their days like a shadow that disappears.
5 O LORD, make the sky sink and come down.
Touch the mountains and make them smolder.
6 Hurl lightning bolts and scatter the enemy.
Shoot your arrows and rout them.
7 Reach down from above.
Grab me and rescue me from the surging water,
from the power of foreigners,
8 who speak lies,
and make false promises.
9 O God, I will sing a new song to you.
Accompanied by a ten-stringed instrument,
I will sing praises to you,
10 the one who delivers kings,
and rescued David his servant from a deadly sword.
11 Grab me and rescue me from the power of foreigners,
who speak lies,
and make false promises.
12 Then our sons will be like plants,
that quickly grow to full size.
Our daughters will be like corner pillars,
carved like those in a palace.
13 Our storehouses will be full,
providing all kinds of food.
Our sheep will multiply by the thousands
and fill our pastures.
14 Our cattle will be weighted down with produce.
No one will break through our walls,
no one will be taken captive,
and there will be no terrified cries in our city squares.
15 How blessed are the people who
experience these things.
How blessed are the people whose God is the LORD.

A psalm of praise; by David.

145 I will extol you, my God, O King.
I will praise your name continually.
2 Every day I will praise you.
I will praise your name continually.
3 The LORD is great and certainly worthy of praise.
No one can fathom his greatness.

4 One generation will praise your deeds to another,
and tell about your mighty acts.
5 I will focus on your honor and majestic splendor,
and your amazing deeds.
6 They will proclaim the power of your awesome acts.
I will declare your great deeds.
7 They will talk about the fame of your great kindness,
and sing about your justice.
8 The LORD is merciful and compassionate;
he is patient and demonstrates great loyal love.
9 The LORD is good to all,
and has compassion on all he has made.
10 All your works will give thanks to you, LORD.
Your loyal followers will praise you.
11 They will proclaim the splendor of your kingdom;
they will tell about your power,
12 so that mankind might acknowledge your mighty acts,
and the majestic splendor of your kingdom.
13 Your kingdom is an eternal kingdom,
and your dominion endures through all generations.
14 The LORD supports all who fall,
and lifts up all who are bent over.
15 Everything looks to you in anticipation,
and you provide them with food on a regular basis.
16 You open your hand,
and fill every living thing with the food it desires.
17 The LORD is just in all his actions,
and exhibits love in all he does.
18 The LORD is near all who cry out to him,
all who cry out to him sincerely.
19 He satisfies the desire of his loyal followers;
he hears their cry for help and delivers them.
20 The LORD protects all those who love him,
but he destroys all the wicked.
21 My mouth will praise the LORD.
Let all who live praise his holy name forever.

146 Praise the LORD.
Praise the LORD, O my soul.
2 I will praise the LORD as long as I live.
I will sing praises to my God as long as I exist.
3 Do not trust in princes,
or in human beings, who cannot deliver.
4 Their life's breath departs, they return to the ground.
On that day their plans die.
5 How blessed is the one whose helper
is the God of Jacob,
whose hope is in the LORD his God,
6 the one who made heaven and earth,
the sea, and all that is in them,
who remains forever faithful,
7 vindicates the oppressed,
and gives food to the hungry.
The LORD releases the imprisoned.

8 The LORD gives sight to the blind.
The LORD lifts up all who are bent over.
The LORD loves the godly.
9 The LORD protects the resident foreigner.
He lifts up the fatherless and the widow,
but he opposes the wicked.
10 The LORD rules forever,
your God, O Zion, throughout the generations to come.
Praise the LORD!

147 Praise the LORD,
for it is good to sing praises to our God.
Yes, praise is pleasant and appropriate.
2 The LORD rebuilds Jerusalem,
and gathers the exiles of Israel.
3 He heals the brokenhearted,
and bandages their wounds.
4 He counts the number of the stars;
he names all of them.
5 Our Lord is great and has awesome power;
there is no limit to his wisdom.
6 The LORD lifts up the oppressed,
but knocks the wicked to the ground.
7 Offer to the LORD a song of thanks.
Sing praises to our God to the
accompaniment of a harp.
8 He covers the sky with clouds,
provides the earth with rain,
and causes grass to grow on the hillsides.
9 He gives food to the animals,
and to the young ravens when they chirp.
10 He is not enamored with the strength of a horse,
nor is he impressed by the warrior's strong legs.
11 The LORD takes delight in his faithful followers,
and in those who wait for his loyal love.
12 Extol the LORD, O Jerusalem.
Praise your God, O Zion.
13 For he makes the bars of your gates strong.
He blesses your children within you.
14 He brings peace to your territory.
He abundantly provides for you the best grain.
15 He sends his command through the earth;
swiftly his order reaches its destination.
16 He sends the snow that is white like wool;
he spreads the frost that is white like ashes.
17 He throws his hailstones like crumbs.
Who can withstand the cold wind he sends?
18 He then orders it all to melt;
he breathes on it, and the water flows.
19 He proclaims his word to Jacob,
his statutes and regulations to Israel.
20 He has not done so with any other nation;
they are not aware of his regulations.
Praise the LORD!

148 Praise the LORD.
Praise the LORD from the sky.
Praise him in the heavens.
2 Praise him, all his angels.
Praise him, all his heavenly assembly.
3 Praise him, O sun and moon.
Praise him, all you shiny stars.
4 Praise him, O highest heaven,
and you waters above the sky.
5 Let them praise the name of the LORD,
for he gave the command and
they came into existence.
6 He established them so they would endure;
he issued a decree that will not be revoked.
7 Praise the LORD from the earth,
you sea creatures and all you ocean depths,
8 O fire and hail, snow and clouds,
O stormy wind that carries out his orders,
9 you mountains and all you hills,
you fruit trees and all you cedars,
10 you animals and all you cattle,
you creeping things and birds,
11 you kings of the earth and all you nations,
you princes and all you leaders on the earth,
12 you young men and young women,
you elderly, along with you children.
13 Let them praise the name of the LORD,
for his name alone is exalted;
his majesty extends over the earth and sky.
14 He has made his people victorious,
and given all his loyal followers reason to praise—
the Israelites, the people
who are close to him.
Praise the LORD!

149 Praise the LORD.
Sing to the LORD a new song.
Praise him in the assembly of the godly.
2 Let Israel rejoice in their Creator.
Let the people of Zion delight in their King.
3 Let them praise his name with dancing.
Let them sing praises to him to the accompaniment
of the tambourine and harp.
4 For the LORD takes delight in his people;
he exalts the oppressed by delivering them.
5 Let the godly rejoice because
of their vindication.
Let them shout for joy upon their beds.
6 May the praises of God be in their mouths
and a two-edged sword in their hands,
7 in order to take revenge on the nations,
and punish foreigners.
8 The godly bind their enemies' kings in chains,
and their nobles in iron shackles,

9 and execute the judgment to which their
enemies have been sentenced.
All his loyal followers will be vindicated.
Praise the LORD.

150 Praise the LORD!
Praise God in his sanctuary;
praise him in the sky, which testifies to his strength!
2 Praise him for his mighty acts;
praise him for his surpassing greatness!
3 Praise him with the blast of the horn;
praise him with the lyre and the harp!
4 Praise him with the tambourine and with dancing;
praise him with stringed instruments and the flute!
5 Praise him with loud cymbals;
praise him with clanging cymbals!
6 Let everything that has breath praise the LORD!
Praise the LORD!

REFLECT

Why is it important to offer praise to the Lord? How can you make praise a daily habit in your life?

for the LORD gives WISDOM, and from His mouth comes KNOWLEDGE and understanding

MEMORY VERSE

For the LORD gives wisdom, and from his mouth comes knowledge and understanding.

Proverbs 2:6

Proverbs

INTRODUCTION

The Way of Wisdom

The Book of Proverbs informs us that only by fearing the Lord will we be motivated to obey God's commands and walk in wisdom. This book offers timeless wisdom to any who read it. If we desire to live successful, God-honoring lives, we can find much wisdom and guidance within its chapters. Proverbs offers advice over many areas of life, including finances, relationships, parenting, discipline, faith, and work.

The Book of Proverbs is divided into four main sections: the instruction of wisdom (1:1—9:18), the proverbs of Solomon (10:1—22:16), further sayings of the wise (22:17—24:34), and assorted proverbs (25:1—31:31). These proverbs include metaphors and allegories, simple sayings, poems, and stories all with the same goal: to remind readers that the fear of God brings wisdom.

Much of the authorship of the Book of Proverbs is attributed to Solomon, and his writings take up the most extensive section of the book. The remainder of Proverbs was written by others, including Agur, Lemuel, and Solomon's men who recorded more of his sayings. The book is believed to have been compiled by a group of assistants to King Hezekiah. There is no certainty as to when the book was completed, but we know that it was written primarily in the time of Solomon (around 950 B.C.) and compiled in the time of Hezekiah (about 700 B.C.).

While Solomon may have recorded these incredible sayings, God alone is the author of wisdom. It was God who made Solomon wise, and it is God who grants any of us wisdom. True wisdom is only found in Him. As we grow to love God more and more, we learn to fear Him and follow His commands. In doing this, we find the wisdom to love our neighbor, honor our commitments, work hard at our jobs, and honor our God in all things.

Kazakhstan

OFFICIAL LANGUAGES
Russian and Kazakh
POPULATION
18,425,000
UNREACHED POPULATION
13,480,000
PROFESSING CHRISTIANS
14.8%

Karina's Home

Say a Prayer Today

Pray for the people of Kazakhstan and the persecuted church there. Pray for boldness and open doors, that the church would be strengthened even amidst difficulties.

HISTORY BIT

The Christian church in Kazakhstan is relatively young but is indeed growing. With increasing government control, many Christian gatherings are regulated by the state. There are also many Christians from Muslim backgrounds who face persecution from *their own families and communities.*

Source Information:
https://joshuaproject.net/countries/KZ

LOVE YOUR NEIGHBOR

Her Journey

KARINA'S STORY

I was born in Kazakhstan to a nominal Muslim family, where we did not talk about faith or how God works in our lives. I learned that the source of wisdom and guidance is a legacy of our past, handed down from generation to generation. I eventually left my home country to study in Poland at the age of twenty-two. The only guiding principle in my life was "use your common sense," something that was neither rooted in anything real nor provided a source of peace.

As I began my young adulthood in a new country of many churches, I asked myself, "What do people learn in these churches? What do they believe?" These simple questions led me to attend a Sunday service at one of them. That Sunday was a turning point in my life.

Through the community of believers I got to know and the Bible studies I attended, I came to understand the character of God: holy, righteous, and forever faithful. I also learned who I am: a sinner who needs the Lord Jesus Christ, the only way to eternal life.

The more I studied the Word with the church group, the clearer I could see that wisdom, knowledge, love, patience, and faith come from God. I saw and was grateful for the Giver, not only the gifts. I could not be more grateful for the way He found me and turned my beliefs upside down.

I attended a conference in Northern Ireland a few months later, not knowing it was a Love God Greatly event. When I arrived, I learned more about their ministry and how God has been working all over the world. I met one of the women on the Polish team and asked if there was a Russian translation. She said, "No, but you could start one!" God has allowed me to get involved with Love God Greatly, and I am so grateful for this incredible community of women. I am now starting the Russian translation branch and am excited to see the ways God will continue to spread His Word and His truth in Russian.

Although I live far from my home country, this was part of His plan. I pray that God would reach more people in Kazakhstan with the truth of the gospel and that the Church there will grow in God's wisdom.

6 WEEK READING PLAN

LOVE HIS WORD

	MONDAY	TUESDAY	WEDNESDAY	THURSDAY	FRIDAY
1	Proverbs 1	Proverbs 2	Proverbs 3	Proverbs 4	Proverbs 5
	SOAP Proverbs 1:7	SOAP Proverbs 2:6	SOAP Proverbs 3:5-6	SOAP Proverbs 4:23	SOAP Proverbs 5:1
2	Proverbs 6	Proverbs 7	Proverbs 8	Proverbs 9	Proverbs 10
	SOAP Proverbs 6:20-21	SOAP Proverbs 7:1-2	SOAP Proverbs 8:11	SOAP Proverbs 9:9	SOAP Proverbs 10:19-20
3	Proverbs 11	Proverbs 12	Proverbs 13	Proverbs 14	Proverbs 15
	SOAP Proverbs 11:18	SOAP Proverbs 12:1	SOAP Proverbs 13:5-6	SOAP Proverbs 14:1	SOAP Proverbs 15:1-2
4	Proverbs 16	Proverbs 17	Proverbs 18	Proverbs 19	Proverbs 20
	SOAP Proverbs 16:9	SOAP Proverbs 17:22	SOAP Proverbs 18:10	SOAP Proverbs 19:20-21	SOAP Proverbs 20:28
5	Proverbs 21	Proverbs 22	Proverbs 23	Proverbs 24	Proverbs 25
	SOAP Proverbs 21:1-2	SOAP Proverbs 22:6	SOAP Proverbs 23:17-19	SOAP Proverbs 24:16	SOAP Proverbs 25:28
6	Proverbs 26	Proverbs 27	Proverbs 28	Proverbs 29	Proverbs 30-31
	SOAP Proverbs 26:20	SOAP Proverbs 27:1	SOAP Proverbs 28:13	SOAP Proverbs 29:27	SOAP Proverbs 30:4

INTRODUCTION TO THE BOOK

1 The proverbs of Solomon, son of David, king of Israel:
2 To learn wisdom and moral instruction,
to discern wise counsel.
3 To receive moral instruction in skillful living,
with righteousness, justice, and equity.
4 To impart shrewdness to the morally naive,
a discerning plan to the young person.
5 (Let the wise also hear and gain instruction,
and let the discerning acquire guidance!)
6 To discern the meaning
of a proverb and a parable,
the sayings of the wise and their riddles.

INTRODUCTION TO THE THEME OF THE BOOK

7 Fearing the LORD is the beginning of discernment,
but fools have despised wisdom and moral instruction.
8 Listen, my child, to the instruction from your father,
and do not forsake the teaching from your mother.
9 For they will be like an elegant garland on your head,
and like pendants around your neck.

ADMONITION TO AVOID EASY BUT UNJUST RICHES

10 My child, if sinners try to entice you,
do not consent!
11 If they say, "Come with us!
We will lie in wait to shed blood;
we will ambush an innocent person capriciously.
12 We will swallow them alive like Sheol,
those full of vigor like those going down to the Pit.
13 We will seize all kinds of precious wealth;
we will fill our houses with plunder.
14 Join with us!
We will all share equally in what we steal."
15 My child, do not go down their way,
withhold yourself from their path;
16 for they are eager to inflict harm,
and they hasten to shed blood.
17 Surely it is futile to spread a net
in plain sight of any bird,
18 but these men lie in wait for their own blood,
they ambush their own lives!
19 Such are the ways of all who gain profit unjustly;
it takes away the life of those who obtain it!

WARNING AGAINST DISREGARDING WISDOM

20 Wisdom calls out in the street,
she shouts loudly in the plazas;
21 at the head of the noisy streets she calls,
in the entrances of the gates in the
city she utters her words:
22 "How long will you simpletons love naiveté?
How long have mockers delighted in mockery?
And how long will fools hate knowledge?

23 You should respond to my rebuke.
Then I would pour out my thoughts to you;
I would make my words known to you.
24 However, because I called but you refused to listen,
because I stretched out my hand but
no one was paying attention,
25 and you neglected all my advice,
and did not comply with my rebuke,
26 so I myself will laugh when disaster strikes you,
I will mock when what you dread comes,
27 when what you dread comes like a whirlwind,
and disaster strikes you like a devastating storm,
when distressing trouble comes on you.
28 Then they will call to me, but I will not answer;
they will diligently seek me, but they will not find me.
29 Because they hated moral knowledge,
and did not choose to fear the LORD,
30 they did not comply with my advice,
they spurned all my rebuke.
31 Therefore they will eat from the fruit of their way,
and they will be stuffed full of their own counsel.
32 For the waywardness of the
simpletons will kill them,
and the careless ease of fools will destroy them.
33 But the one who listens to me will live in security,
and will be at ease from the dread of harm."

BENEFITS OF SEEKING WISDOM

2 My child, if you receive my words,
and store up my commands inside yourself,
2 by making your ear attentive to wisdom,
and by turning your heart to understanding,
3 indeed, if you call out for discernment—
shout loudly for understanding—
4 if you seek it like silver,
and search for it like hidden treasure,
5 then you will understand how to fear the LORD,
and you will discover knowledge about God.
6 For the LORD gives wisdom,
and from his mouth comes knowledge and understanding.
7 He stores up effective counsel for the upright,
and is like a shield for those who live with integrity,
8 to guard the paths of the righteous
and to protect the way of his pious ones.
9 Then you will understand righteousness and justice
and equity—every good way.
10 For wisdom will enter your heart,
and moral knowledge will be attractive to you.
11 Discretion will protect you,
understanding will guard you,
12 to deliver you from the way of the wicked,
from those speaking perversity,
13 who leave the upright paths
to walk on the dark ways,

TREASURE HUNT

PROVERBS 2:1–5

I grew up thinking that because I was a Christian, I would have all the answers. I thought God's wisdom would magically fall on me because I'd accepted Christ into my heart as a young child. Proverbs 2:1–5 shows us that acceptance is only the beginning of our journey in acquiring the precious jewels of wisdom.

If you seek it like silver, and search for it like hidden treasure, then you will understand how to fear the LORD and you will discover knowledge about God (Prov 2:4–5).

Have you ever gone to the store before a snowstorm to get provisions to ride out the bad weather? We often forget that while we may not use what we memorize or read from God's Word on the day we receive it, we need to fill the storehouses of our hearts. Storing up God's Word guards our hearts and minds with truth and makes us attentive and responsive to wisdom.

Gain without use adds no real value to our lives. We don't store up the tools we need to stare at them and say, "Look at how many snow shovels I've accumulated!"

Luke 6:49 says, "But the person who hears and does not put my words into practice is like a man who built a house on the ground without a foundation. When the river burst against that house, it collapsed immediately, and was utterly destroyed!" Without putting God's Word into practice, we become fools who are easily destroyed.

We should ask God for wisdom. James 1:5 says God gives wisdom generously to those who are deficient. When we seek God's help, we acknowledge our need for a savior. Praise Him that Jesus Christ is that Savior! He has made a way for us to the Father who, in His kindness, is ready and willing to impart His wisdom to us without reprimand.

God wants us to commit ourselves to finding wisdom as one would commit to finding hidden treasure. When we seek it this way, we understand how to fear the LORD, and we discover knowledge about God.

Seeking God's Word for wisdom is a treasure hunt worthy of our efforts. What a sweet promise to know our God grants us wisdom whenever we ask!

14 who delight in doing evil,
they rejoice in perverse evil;
15 whose paths are morally crooked,
and who are devious in their ways;
16 to deliver you from the adulterous woman,
from the loose woman who has
flattered you with her words;
17 who leaves the husband from her younger days,
and has ignored her marriage covenant made before God.
18 For she has set her house by death,
and her paths by the place of the departed spirits.
19 None who go in to her will return,
nor will they reach the paths of life.
20 So you will walk in the way of good people,
and will keep on the paths of the righteous.
21 For the upright will reside in the land,
and those with integrity will remain in it,
22 but the wicked will be removed from the land,
and the treacherous will be torn away from it.

EXHORTATIONS TO SEEK WISDOM AND WALK WITH THE LORD

3 My child, do not forget my teaching,
but let your heart keep my commandments,
2 for they will provide a long and full life,
and well-being for you.
3 Do not let mercy and truth leave you;
bind them around your neck,
write them on the tablet of your heart.
4 Then you will find favor and good understanding,
in the sight of God and people.
5 Trust in the LORD with all your heart,
and do not rely on your own understanding.
6 Acknowledge him in all your ways,
and he will make your paths straight.
7 Do not be wise in your own estimation;
fear the LORD and turn away from evil.
8 This will bring healing to your body,
and refreshment to your inner self.
9 Honor the LORD from your wealth
and from the firstfruits of all your crops;
10 then your barns will be filled completely,
and your vats will overflow with new wine.
11 My child, do not despise discipline from the LORD,
and do not loathe his rebuke.
12 For the LORD disciplines those he loves,
just as a father disciplines the son
in whom he delights.

CHALLENGE

How does the truth of Proverbs 3:12 resonate with the whole story of Scripture? In what ways does Scripture testify that God disciplines those He loves?

BLESSINGS OF OBTAINING WISDOM

13 Blessed is the one who has found wisdom,
and the one who obtains understanding.
14 For her benefit is more profitable than silver,
and her gain is better than gold.

15 She is more precious than rubies,
and none of the things you desire can compare with her.
16 Long life is in her right hand;
in her left hand are riches and honor.
17 Her ways are very pleasant,
and all her paths are peaceful.
18 She is like a tree of life to those who grasp onto her,
and everyone who takes hold of her will be blessed.
19 By wisdom the LORD laid the foundation of the earth;
he established the heavens by understanding.
20 By his knowledge the primordial sea was broken open,
so that the clouds drip down dew.
21 My child, do not let them escape from your sight;
safeguard sound wisdom and discretion.
22 So they will become life for your soul,
and grace around your neck.
23 Then you will walk on your way with security,
and you will not stumble.
24 When you lie down you will not be filled with fear;
when you lie down your sleep will be pleasant.
25 Do not be afraid of sudden disaster,
or when destruction overtakes the wicked;
26 for the LORD will be the source of your confidence,
and he will guard your foot from being caught in a trap.

WISDOM DEMONSTRATED IN RELATIONSHIPS WITH PEOPLE

27 Do not withhold good from those who need it,
when you have the ability to help.
28 Do not say to your neighbor, "Go! Return tomorrow
and I will give it," when you have it
with you at the time.
29 Do not plot evil against your neighbor
when he dwells by you unsuspectingly.
30 Do not accuse anyone without legitimate cause,
if he has not treated you wrongly.
31 Do not envy a violent man,
and do not choose any of his ways;
32 for one who goes astray is an
abomination to the LORD,
but he reveals his intimate counsel to the upright.
33 The LORD's curse is on the household of the wicked,
but he blesses the home of the righteous.
34 With arrogant scoffers he is scornful,
yet he shows favor to the humble.
35 The wise inherit honor,
but he holds fools up to public contempt.

ADMONITION TO FOLLOW RIGHTEOUSNESS AND AVOID WICKEDNESS

4 Listen, children, to a father's instruction,
and pay attention so that you may gain discernment.
2 Because I hereby give you good instruction,
do not forsake my teaching.

3 When I was a son to my father,
a tender, only child before my mother,
4 he taught me, and he said to me:
"Let your heart lay hold of my words;
keep my commands so that you will live.
5 Acquire wisdom, acquire understanding;
do not forget and do not turn aside from the words I speak.
6 Do not forsake wisdom, and she will protect you;
love her, and she will guard you.
7 Wisdom is supreme—so acquire wisdom,
and whatever you acquire, acquire understanding!
8 Esteem her highly and she will exalt you;
she will honor you if you embrace her.
9 She will place a fair garland on your head;
she will bestow a beautiful crown on you."
10 Listen, my child, and accept my words,
so that the years of your life will be many.
11 I hereby guide you in the way of wisdom
and I lead you in upright paths.
12 When you walk, your steps will not be hampered,
and when you run, you will not stumble.
13 Hold on to instruction, do not let it go;
protect it, because it is your life.
14 Do not enter the path of the wicked
or walk in the way of those who are evil.
15 Avoid it, do not go on it;
turn away from it, and go on.
16 For they cannot sleep unless they cause harm;
they are robbed of sleep until they
make someone stumble.
17 Indeed they have eaten bread gained from wickedness
and drink wine obtained from violence.
18 But the path of the righteous is like
the bright morning light,
growing brighter and brighter until full day.
19 The way of the wicked is like gloomy darkness;
they do not know what they stumble over.

20 My child, pay attention to my words;
listen attentively to my sayings.
21 Do not let them depart from your sight,
guard them within your heart;
22 for they are life to those who find them
and healing to one's entire body.
23 Guard your heart with all vigilance,
for from it are the sources of life.
24 Remove perverse speech from your mouth;
keep devious talk far from your lips.
25 Let your eyes look directly in front of you
and let your gaze look straight before you.
26 Make the path for your feet level,
so that all your ways may be established.
27 Do not turn to the right or to the left;
turn yourself away from evil.

ADMONITION TO AVOID SEDUCTION TO EVIL

5 My child, be attentive to my wisdom,
pay close attention to my understanding,
2 in order to safeguard discretion,
and that your lips may guard knowledge.
3 For the lips of the adulterous woman drip honey,
and her seductive words are smoother
than olive oil,
4 but in the end she is bitter as wormwood,
sharp as a two-edged sword.
5 Her feet go down to death;
her steps lead straight to the grave.
6 Lest she should make level
the path leading to life,
her paths have wandered, but she
is not able to discern it.
7 So now, children, listen to me;
do not turn aside from the words I speak.
8 Keep yourself far from her,
and do not go near the door of her house,
9 lest you give your vigor to others
and your years to a cruel person,
10 lest strangers devour your strength,
and your labor benefit another man's house.
11 And at the end of your life you will groan
when your flesh and your body are wasted away.
12 And you will say, "How I hated discipline!
My heart spurned reproof!
13 For I did not obey my teachers
and I did not heed my instructors.
14 I almost came to complete ruin
in the midst of the whole congregation!"
15 Drink water from your own cistern
and running water from your own well.
16 Should your springs be dispersed outside,
your streams of water in the wide plazas?
17 Let them be for yourself alone,
and not for strangers with you.
18 May your fountain be blessed,
and may you rejoice in the wife you
married in your youth—
19 a loving doe, a graceful deer;
may her breasts satisfy you at all times,
may you be captivated by her love always.
20 But why should you be captivated,
my son, by an adulteress,
and embrace the bosom of a different woman?
21 For the ways of a person are in front
of the LORD's eyes,
and the LORD weighs all that person's paths.
22 The wicked will be captured by his own iniquities,
and he will be held by the cords of his own sin.
23 He will die because there was no discipline;
because of the greatness of his folly he will reel.

ADMONITIONS AND WARNINGS AGAINST DANGEROUS AND DESTRUCTIVE ACTS

6 My child, if you have made a pledge for your neighbor,
if you have become a guarantor for a stranger,
2 if you have been ensnared by the words you have uttered,
and have been caught by the words you have spoken,
3 then, my child, do this in order to deliver yourself,
because you have fallen into your neighbor's power:
Go, humble yourself,
and appeal firmly to your neighbor.
4 Permit no sleep to your eyes
or slumber to your eyelids.
5 Deliver yourself like a gazelle from a snare,
and like a bird from the trap of the fowler.
6 Go to the ant, you sluggard;
observe her ways and be wise!
7 It has no commander,
overseer, or ruler,
8 yet it would prepare its food in the summer;
it gathered at the harvest what it will eat.
9 How long, you sluggard, will you lie there?
When will you rise from your sleep?
10 A little sleep, a little slumber,
a little folding of the hands to relax,
11 and your poverty will come like a robber,
and your need like an armed man.
12 A worthless and wicked person
walks around saying perverse things;
13 he winks with his eyes,
signals with his feet,
and points with his fingers;
14 he plots evil with perverse thoughts in his heart,
he spreads contention at all times.
15 Therefore, his disaster will come suddenly;
in an instant he will be broken, and
there will be no remedy.
16 There are six things that the LORD hates,
even seven things that are an abomination to him:
17 haughty eyes, a lying tongue,
and hands that shed innocent blood,
18 a heart that devises wicked plans,
feet that are swift to run to evil,
19 a false witness who pours out lies,
and a person who spreads discord among family members.
20 My child, guard the commands of your father
and do not forsake the instruction of your mother.
21 Bind them on your heart continually;
fasten them around your neck.
22 When you walk about, they will guide you;
when you lie down, they will watch over you;
when you wake up, they will talk to you.
23 For the commandments are like a lamp,
instruction is like a light,
and rebukes of discipline are like the road leading to life,

24 by keeping you from the evil woman,
from the smooth tongue of the loose woman.
25 Do not lust in your heart for her beauty,
and do not let her captivate you with her alluring eyes;
26 for on account of a prostitute one is
brought down to a loaf of bread,
but the wife of another man preys on your precious life.
27 Can a man hold fire against his chest
without burning his clothes?
28 Can a man walk on hot coals
without scorching his feet?
29 So it is with the one who sleeps with his neighbor's wife;
no one who touches her will escape punishment.
30 People do not despise a thief when he steals
to fulfill his need when he is hungry.
31 Yet if he is caught he must repay seven times over,
he might even have to give all the wealth of his house.
32 A man who commits adultery with a woman lacks sense,
whoever does it destroys his own life.
33 He will be beaten and despised,
and his reproach will not be wiped away;
34 for jealousy kindles a husband's rage,
and he will not show mercy when he takes revenge.
35 He will not consider any compensation;
he will not be willing, even if you multiply the compensation.

REFLECT

How does this imagery encourage you to flee from sin?

ADMONITION TO AVOID THE WILES OF THE ADULTERESS

7 My child, devote yourself to my words
and store up my commands inside yourself.
2 Keep my commands so that you may live,
and obey my instruction as your most prized possession.
3 Bind them on your forearm;
write them on the tablet of your heart.
4 Say to wisdom, "You are my sister,"
and call understanding a close relative,
5 so that they may keep you from the adulterous woman,
from the loose woman who has
flattered you with her words.
6 For at the window of my house
through my window lattice I looked out
7 and I saw among the naive—
I discerned among the youths—
a young man who lacked sense.
8 He was passing by the street near her corner,
making his way along the road to her house
9 in the twilight, the evening,
in the dark of the night.
10 Suddenly a woman came out to meet him!
She was dressed like a prostitute and with secret intent.
11 (She is loud and rebellious,
she does not remain at home—
12 at one time outside, at another in the wide plazas,
and by every corner she lies in wait.)

13 So she grabbed him and kissed him,
and with a bold expression she said to him,
14 "I have meat from my peace offerings at home;
today I have fulfilled my vows!
15 That is why I came out to meet you,
to look for you, and I found you!
16 I have spread my bed with elegant coverings,
with richly colored fabric from Egypt.
17 I have perfumed my bed
with myrrh, aloes, and cinnamon.
18 Come, let's drink deeply of lovemaking until morning,
let's delight ourselves with love's pleasures.
19 For my husband is not at home;
he has gone on a journey of some distance.
20 He has taken a bag of money with him;
he will not return until the end of the month."
21 She turned him aside with her persuasions;
with her smooth talk she was enticing him along.
22 Suddenly he was going after her
like an ox that goes to the slaughter,
like a stag prancing into a trapper's snare
23 till an arrow pierces his liver—
like a bird hurrying into a trap,
and he does not know that it will cost him his life.
24 So now, sons, listen to me,
and pay attention to the words I speak.
25 Do not let your heart turn aside to her ways—
do not wander into her pathways;
26 for she has brought down many fatally wounded,
and all those she has slain are many.
27 Her house is the way to the grave,
going down to the chambers of death.

THE APPEAL OF WISDOM

8 Does not wisdom call out?
Does not understanding raise her voice?
2 At the top of the prominent places along the way,
at the intersection of the paths she has taken her stand;
3 beside the gates opening into the city,
at the entrance of the doorways she cries out:
4 "To you, O people, I call out,
and my voice calls to all mankind.
5 You who are naive, discern wisdom!
And you fools, understand discernment!
6 Listen, for I will speak excellent things,
and my lips will utter what is right.
7 For my mouth speaks truth,
and my lips hate wickedness.
8 All the words of my mouth are righteous;
there is nothing in them twisted or crooked.
9 All of them are clear to the discerning
and upright to those who find knowledge.
10 Receive my instruction rather than silver,
and knowledge rather than choice gold.

11 For wisdom is better than rubies,
and desirable things cannot be compared to her.
12 "I, wisdom, have dwelt with prudence,
and I find knowledge and discretion.
13 The fear of the LORD is to hate evil;
I hate arrogant pride and the evil way
and perverse utterances.
14 Counsel and sound wisdom belong to me;
I possess understanding and might.
15 By me kings reign,
and by me potentates decree righteousness;
16 by me princes rule,
as well as nobles and all righteous judges.
17 I will love those who love me,
and those who seek me diligently will find me.
18 Riches and honor are with me,
long-lasting wealth and righteousness.
19 My fruit is better than the purest gold,
and my harvest is better than choice silver.
20 I walk in the path of righteousness,
in the pathway of justice,
21 that I may cause those who love me to inherit wealth,
and that I may fill their treasuries.
22 The LORD created me as the beginning of his works,
before his deeds of long ago.
23 From eternity I have been fashioned,
from the beginning, from before the world existed.
24 When there were no deep oceans I was born,
when there were no springs overflowing with water;
25 before the mountains were set in place—
before the hills—I was born,
26 before he made the earth and its fields,
or the top soil of the world.
27 When he established the heavens, I was there;
when he marked out the horizon over
the face of the deep,
28 when he established the clouds above,
when he secured the fountains of the deep,
29 when he gave the sea his decree
that the waters should not pass over his command,
when he marked out the foundations of the earth,
30 then I was beside him as a master craftsman,
and I was his delight day by day,
rejoicing before him at all times,
31 rejoicing in the habitable part of his earth,
and delighting in its people.

32 "So now, children, listen to me;
blessed are those who keep my ways.
33 Listen to my instruction so that you may be wise,
and do not neglect it.
34 Blessed is the one who listens to me,
watching at my doors day by day,
waiting beside my doorway.

REFLECT

How is wisdom a blessing? How does it enrich one's life?

35 For the one who finds me has found life
and received favor from the LORD.
36 But the one who misses me brings harm to himself;
all who hate me love death."

THE CONSEQUENCES OF ACCEPTING WISDOM OR FOLLY

9 Wisdom has built her house;
she has carved out its seven pillars.
2 She has prepared her meat, she has mixed her wine;
she also has arranged her table.
3 She has sent out her female servants;
she calls out on the highest places of the city.
4 "Whoever is naive, let him turn in here."
To those who lack understanding, she has said,
5 "Come, eat some of my food,
and drink some of the wine I have mixed.
6 Abandon your foolish ways so that you may live,
and proceed in the way of understanding."
7 Whoever corrects a mocker is asking for insult;
whoever reproves a wicked person receives abuse.
8 Do not reprove a mocker or he will hate you;
reprove a wise person and he will love you.
9 Give instruction to a wise person, and
he will become wiser still;
teach a righteous person and he will add to his learning.
10 The beginning of wisdom is to fear the LORD,
and acknowledging the Holy One is understanding.
11 For because of me your days will be many,
and years will be added to your life.
12 If you are wise, you are wise to your own advantage,
but if you have mocked, you alone must bear it.
13 The woman called Folly is brash,
she is naive and does not know anything.
14 And she has sat down at the door of her house,
on a seat at the highest point of the city,
15 calling out to those who are passing by her in the way,
who go straight on their way.
16 "Whoever is naive, let him turn in here,"
To those who lack understanding she has said,
17 "Stolen waters are sweet,
and food obtained in secret is pleasant!"
18 But they do not realize that the dead are there,
that her guests are in the depths of the grave.

THE FIRST COLLECTION OF SOLOMONIC PROVERBS

10 The proverbs of Solomon:

A wise child makes a father rejoice,
but a foolish child is a grief to his mother.
2 Treasures gained by wickedness do not profit,
but righteousness delivers from death.
3 The LORD satisfies the appetite of the righteous,
but he thwarts the craving of the wicked.

4 The one who is lazy becomes poor,
but the one who works diligently becomes wealthy.
5 The one who gathers crops in the summer is a wise son,
but the one who sleeps during harvest is a shameful son.
6 Blessings are on the head of the righteous,
but the speech of the wicked conceals violence.
7 The memory of the righteous is a blessing,
but the reputation of the wicked will rot.
8 The wise person accepts instructions,
but the one who speaks foolishness will come to ruin.
9 The one who conducts himself in
integrity will live securely,
but the one who behaves perversely will be found out.
10 The one who winks his eye causes trouble,
and the one who speaks foolishness will come to ruin.
11 The speech of the righteous is a fountain of life,
but the speech of the wicked conceals violence.
12 Hatred stirs up dissension,
but love covers all transgressions.
13 Wisdom is found in the words of the discerning person,
but the one who lacks sense will be disciplined.
14 Those who are wise store up knowledge,
but foolish speech leads to imminent destruction.
15 The wealth of a rich person is like a fortified city,
but the poor are brought to ruin by their poverty.
16 The reward that the righteous receive is life;
the recompense that the wicked receive is judgment.
17 The one who heeds instruction is on the way to life,
but the one who rejects rebuke goes astray.
18 The one who conceals hatred utters lies,
and the one who spreads slander is certainly a fool.
19 When words abound, transgression is inevitable,
but the one who restrains his words is wise.
20 What the righteous say is like the best silver,
but what the wicked think is of little value.
21 The teaching of the righteous feeds many,
but fools die for lack of sense.
22 The blessing from the LORD makes a person rich,
and he adds no sorrow to it.
23 Carrying out a wicked scheme is enjoyable to a fool,
and so is wisdom for the one who has discernment.
24 What the wicked fears will come on him;
what the righteous desire will be granted.
25 When the storm passes through, the
wicked are swept away,
but the righteous are an everlasting foundation.
26 Like vinegar to the teeth and like smoke to the eyes,
so is the sluggard to those who send him.
27 Fearing the LORD prolongs life,
but the life span of the wicked will be shortened.
28 The hope of the righteous is joy,
but the expectation of the wicked perishes.
29 The way of the LORD is like a stronghold for the upright,
but it is destruction to evildoers.

30 The righteous will never be moved,
but the wicked will not inhabit the land.
31 The speech of the righteous bears the fruit of wisdom,
but the one who speaks perversion will be destroyed.
32 The lips of the righteous know what is pleasing,
but the speech of the wicked is perverse.

11 The LORD abhors dishonest scales,
but an accurate weight is his delight.
2 After pride came, disgrace followed;
but wisdom came with humility.
3 The integrity of the upright guides them,
but the crookedness of the treacherous destroys them.
4 Wealth does not profit in the day of wrath,
but righteousness delivers from death.
5 The righteousness of the blameless
will make their way smooth,
but the wicked will fall through their own wickedness.
6 The righteousness of the upright will deliver them,
but the treacherous will be ensnared
by their own desires.
7 When a wicked person dies, his expectation perishes,
and hope based on power has perished.
8 A righteous person was delivered out of trouble,
then a wicked person took his place.
9 With his speech the godless person
destroys his neighbor,
but by knowledge the righteous will be delivered.
10 When the righteous do well, the city rejoices;
when the wicked perish, there is joy.
11 A city is exalted by the blessing
provided from the upright,
but it is destroyed by the counsel of the wicked.
12 The one who denounces his neighbor lacks sense,
but a discerning person keeps silent.
13 The one who goes about slandering others reveals secrets,
but the one who is trustworthy conceals a matter.
14 When there is no guidance a nation falls,
but there is success in the abundance of counselors.
15 The one who has put up security for a
stranger will surely have trouble,
but whoever avoids shaking hands is secure.
16 A generous woman gains honor,
and ruthless men seize wealth.
17 A kind person benefits himself,
but a cruel person brings himself trouble.
18 The wicked person earns deceitful wages,
but the one who sows righteousness
reaps a genuine reward.
19 True righteousness leads to life,
but the one who pursues evil pursues it to his own death.
20 The LORD abhors those who are perverse in heart,
but those who are blameless in their ways are his delight.
21 Be assured that the evil person will not be unpunished,
but the descendants of the righteous have escaped harm.

22 Like a gold ring in a pig's snout
is a beautiful woman who rejects discretion.
23 The desire of the righteous is only good,
but the expectation of the wicked is wrath.
24 One person is generous and yet grows more wealthy,
but another withholds more than he
should and comes to poverty.
25 A generous person will be enriched,
and the one who provides water for
others will himself be satisfied.
26 People will curse the one who withholds grain,
but they will praise the one who sells it.
27 The one who diligently seeks good seeks favor,
but the one who searches for evil—it will come to him.
28 The one who trusts in his riches will fall,
but the righteous will flourish like a green leaf.
29 The one who troubles his family will inherit nothing,
and the fool will be a servant to the wise person.
30 The fruit of the righteous is like a tree producing life,
and the one who wins souls is wise.
31 If the righteous are recompensed on earth,
how much more the wicked sinner!

12 The one who loves discipline loves knowledge,
but the one who hates reproof is stupid.
2 A good person obtains favor from the LORD,
but the LORD condemns a person with wicked schemes.
3 No one can be established through wickedness,
but a righteous root cannot be moved.
4 A noble wife is the crown of her husband,
but the wife who acts shamefully is
like rottenness in his bones.
5 The plans of the righteous are just;
the counsels of the wicked are deceitful.
6 The words of the wicked lie in wait to shed innocent blood,
but the words of the upright will deliver them.
7 The wicked are overthrown and perish,
but the righteous household will stand.
8 A person will be praised in accordance with his wisdom,
but the one with a bewildered mind will be despised.
9 Better is a person of humble standing
who works for himself,
than one who pretends to be somebody
important yet has no food.
10 A righteous person cares for the life of his animal,
but even the most compassionate
acts of the wicked are cruel.
11 The one who works his field will have plenty of food,
but whoever chases daydreams lacks sense.
12 The wicked person has desired the
stronghold of the wicked,
but the root of the righteous will yield fruit.
13 The evil person is ensnared by the
transgression of his speech,
but the righteous person escapes out of trouble.

14 A person will be satisfied with good
from the fruit of his words,
and the work of his hands will be rendered to him.
15 The way of a fool is right in his own opinion,
but the one who listens to advice is wise.
16 A fool's annoyance is known at once,
but the prudent conceals dishonor.
17 The faithful witness tells what is right,
but a false witness speaks deceit.
18 Speaking recklessly is like the thrusts of a sword,
but the words of the wise bring healing.
19 The one who tells the truth will endure forever,
but the one who lies will last only for a moment.
20 Deceit is in the heart of those who plot evil,
but those who promote peace have joy.
21 No harm will be directed at the righteous,
but the wicked are filled with calamity.
22 The LORD abhors a person who lies,
but those who deal truthfully are his delight.
23 The shrewd person conceals knowledge,
but foolish people proclaim folly.
24 The diligent person will rule,
but the slothful will be put to forced labor.
25 Anxiety in a person's heart weighs him down,
but an encouraging word brings him joy.
26 The righteous person is cautious in his friendship,
but the way of the wicked leads them astray.
27 The lazy person does not roast his prey,
but personal possessions are precious to the diligent.
28 In the path of righteousness there is life,
but another path leads to death.

13 A wise son accepts his father's discipline,
but a scoffer has never listened to rebuke.
2 From the fruit of his speech a person eats good things,
but the treacherous desire the fruit of violence.
3 The one who guards his words guards his life;
whoever is talkative will come to ruin.
4 The appetite of the sluggard craves but gets nothing,
but the desire of the diligent will be abundantly satisfied.
5 The righteous person will reject anything false,
but the wicked person will act in shameful disgrace.
6 Righteousness guards the one who lives with integrity,
but wickedness overthrows the sinner.
7 There is one who pretends to be rich and yet has nothing;
another pretends to be poor and yet
possesses great wealth.
8 The ransom of a person's life is his wealth,
thus the poor person has never heard a threat.
9 The light of the righteous shines brightly,
but the lamp of the wicked goes out.
10 With pride comes only contention,
but wisdom is with the well-advised.
11 Wealth gained quickly will dwindle away,
but the one who gathers it little by little will become rich.

12 Hope deferred makes the heart sick,
but a longing fulfilled is like a tree of life.
13 The one who despises instruction will pay the penalty,
but whoever esteems direction will be rewarded.
14 Instruction from the wise is like a life-giving fountain,
to turn a person from deadly snares.
15 Keen insight wins favor,
but the conduct of the treacherous ends in destruction.
16 Every shrewd person acts with knowledge,
but a fool displays his folly.
17 An unreliable messenger falls into trouble,
but a faithful envoy brings healing.
18 The one who neglects discipline ends
up in poverty and shame,
but the one who accepts reproof is honored.
19 A desire fulfilled will be sweet to the soul,
but fools abhor turning away from evil.
20 The one who associates with the wise grows wise,
but a companion of fools suffers harm.
21 Calamity pursues sinners,
but prosperity rewards the righteous.
22 A good person leaves an inheritance for his grandchildren,
but the wealth of a sinner is stored up for the righteous.
23 Abundant food may come from the field of the poor,
but it is swept away by injustice.
24 The one who spares his rod hates his child,
but the one who loves his child is
diligent in disciplining him.
25 The righteous has enough food to satisfy his appetite,
but the belly of the wicked will be empty.

14 Every wise woman has built her household,
but a foolish woman tears it down with her own hands.
2 The one who walks in his uprightness fears the LORD,
but the one who is perverted in his ways despises him.
3 In the speech of a fool is a rod for his back,
but the words of the wise protect them.
4 Where there are no oxen, the feeding trough is clean,
but an abundant harvest is produced by strong oxen.
5 A truthful witness does not lie,
but a false witness breathes out lies.
6 The scorner sought wisdom—there was none,
but understanding was easy for a discerning person.
7 Walk abreast with a foolish person,
and you do not understand wise counsel.
8 The wisdom of the shrewd person is to discern his way,
but the folly of fools is deception.
9 Fools mock at reparation,
but among the upright there is favor.
10 The heart knows its own bitterness,
and with its joy no one else can share.
11 The household of the wicked will be destroyed,
but the tent of the upright will flourish.
12 There is a way that seems right to a person,
but its end is the way that leads to death.

REFLECT

Have you ever experienced the way deferred hope makes your heart sick? What truths can you cling to in situations like those?

LOVE TO GROW

WITH HER OWN HANDS

PROVERBS 14:1

I've been a runner since I started racing around the track as a fourteen-year-old. A few years ago, I signed up (and paid) to run the Chicago Marathon. It was a long-time goal I was excited to accomplish.

As I started the necessary long training runs, I developed migraines that increased in both frequency and severity. I suffered at least two a week and would often force myself to push through the pain and run through them. When I accepted that there might be a connection between the increased migraines and increased mileage, I sought medical advice.

I was told that if I wanted my migraines to get better, I needed to stop running.

I was devastated and wrestled with what to do. I loved running. It was such a huge part of my life; I couldn't imagine living without it.

Every wise woman has built her household, but a foolish woman tears it down with her own hands (Prov 14:1).

Wisdom builds a house. Foolishness destroys what wisdom has built. This proverb does not condemn but instead offers a reminder. We are always either building or destroying. We cannot both build our house and destroy it at the same time. It's one or the other. I wanted to be someone who was building. I definitely didn't want to be someone who was destroying what I had built myself.

I stopped running for several months in order to let my body heal. I had been unknowingly hurting myself by continuing to run. Instead of tearing down my house with my own hands, thankfully, I listened to wisdom and was able to build it up instead. The building in that season was in the healing.

After a few months, I began to run again. A year later, I ran a full marathon. In that season, the building was in running again. Building will not look the same in every season of our lives. With discernment, let's seek the wisdom found in God's Word and look to Jesus as our guide.

The important thing is to keep building. No matter the cost, keep building. God is doing something. Let's listen to wisdom to find out where He is at work so we can build with Him.

13 Even in laughter the heart may ache,
and the end of joy may be grief.
14 The backslider will be paid back from his own ways,
but a good person will be rewarded for his.
15 A naive person will believe anything,
but the shrewd person discerns his steps.
16 A wise person is cautious and turns from evil,
but a fool throws off restraint and is overconfident.
17 A person who has a quick temper will do foolish things,
and a person with crafty schemes will be hated.
18 The naive have inherited folly,
but the shrewd will be crowned with knowledge.
19 Bad people have bowed before good people,
and wicked people have bowed at the
gates of someone righteous.
20 A poor person will be disliked even by his neighbors,
but those who love the rich are many.
21 The one who despises his neighbor sins,
but whoever is kind to the needy is blessed.
22 Do not those who devise evil go astray?
But those who plan good exhibit faithful covenant love.
23 In all hard work there is profit,
but merely talking about it only brings poverty.
24 The crown of the wise is their riches,
but the folly of fools is folly.
25 A truthful witness rescues lives,
but one who testifies falsely betrays them.
26 In the fear of the LORD one has strong confidence,
and it will be a refuge for his children.
27 The fear of the LORD is like a life-giving fountain,
to turn people from deadly snares.
28 A king's glory is the abundance of people,
but the lack of subjects is the ruin of a ruler.
29 Someone with great understanding is slow to anger,
but the one who has a quick temper exalts folly.
30 A tranquil spirit revives the body,
but envy is rottenness to the bones.
31 The one who oppresses the poor has insulted his Creator,
but whoever honors him shows favor to the needy.
32 An evil person will be thrown down through his wickedness,
but a righteous person takes refuge in his integrity.
33 Wisdom rests in the heart of the discerning;
it is not known in the inner parts of fools.
34 Righteousness exalts a nation,
but sin is a disgrace to any people.
35 The king shows favor to a wise servant,
but his wrath falls on one who acts shamefully.

15 A gentle response turns away anger,
but a harsh word stirs up wrath.
2 The tongue of the wise treats knowledge correctly,
but the mouth of the fool spouts out folly.
3 The eyes of the LORD are in every place,
keeping watch on those who are evil
and those who are good.

4 Speech that heals is like a life-giving tree,
but a perverse speech breaks the spirit.
5 A fool rejects his father's discipline,
but whoever heeds reproof shows good sense.
6 In the house of the righteous is abundant wealth,
but the income of the wicked will be ruined.
7 The lips of the wise spread knowledge,
but not so the heart of fools.
8 The LORD abhors the sacrifice of the wicked,
but the prayer of the upright pleases him.
9 The LORD abhors the way of the wicked,
but he will love those who pursue righteousness.
10 Severe discipline is for the one who abandons the way;
the one who hates reproof will die.
11 Death and Destruction are before the LORD—
how much more the hearts of humans!
12 The scorner will not love one who corrects him;
he will not go to the wise.
13 A joyful heart makes the face cheerful,
but by a painful heart the spirit is broken.
14 The discerning mind seeks knowledge,
but the mouth of fools feeds on folly.
15 All the days of the afflicted are bad,
but one with a cheerful heart has a continual feast.
16 Better is little with the fear of the LORD
than great wealth and turmoil with it.
17 Better a meal of vegetables where there is love
than a fattened ox where there is hatred.
18 A quick-tempered person stirs up dissension,
but one who is slow to anger calms a quarrel.
19 The way of the sluggard is like a hedge of thorns,
but the path of the upright is like a highway.
20 A wise child brings joy to his father,
but a foolish person despises his mother.
21 Folly is a joy to one who lacks sense,
but one who has understanding follows an upright course.
22 Plans fail when there is no counsel,
but with abundant advisers they are established.
23 A person has joy in giving an appropriate answer,
and a word at the right time—how good it is!
24 The path of life is upward for the wise person,
to keep him from going downward to Sheol.
25 The LORD tears down the house of the proud,
but he maintains the boundaries of the widow.
26 The LORD abhors the plans of the wicked,
but pleasant words are pure.
27 The one who is greedy for gain troubles his household,
but whoever hates bribes will live.
28 The heart of the righteous considers how to answer,
but the mouth of the wicked pours out evil things.
29 The LORD is far from the wicked,
but he hears the prayer of the righteous.
30 A bright look brings joy to the heart,
and good news gives health to the body.

31 The person who hears the reproof that leads to life
is at home among the wise.
32 The one who refuses correction despises himself,
but whoever listens to reproof acquires understanding.
33 The fear of the LORD provides wise instruction,
and before honor comes humility.

16 The intentions of the heart belong to a man,
but the answer of the tongue comes from the LORD.
2 All a person's ways seem right in his own opinion,
but the LORD evaluates the motives.
3 Commit your works to the LORD,
and your plans will be established.
4 The LORD has worked everything for his own ends—
even the wicked for the day of disaster.
5 The LORD abhors every arrogant person;
rest assured that they will not go unpunished.
6 Through loyal love and truth iniquity is appeased;
through fearing the LORD one avoids evil.
7 When a person's ways are pleasing to the LORD,
he even reconciles his enemies to himself.
8 Better to have a little with righteousness
than to have abundant income without justice.
9 A person plans his course,
but the LORD directs his steps.
10 The divine verdict is in the words of the king,
his pronouncements must not act
treacherously against justice.
11 Honest scales and balances are from the LORD;
all the weights in the bag are his handiwork.
12 Doing wickedness is an abomination to kings,
because a throne is established in righteousness.
13 The delight of a king is righteous counsel,
and he will love the one who speaks uprightly.
14 A king's wrath is like a messenger of death,
but a wise person appeases it.
15 In the light of the king's face there is life,
and his favor is like the clouds of the spring rain.
16 How much better it is to acquire wisdom than gold;
to acquire understanding is more desirable than silver.
17 The highway of the upright is to turn away from evil;
the one who guards his way safeguards his life.
18 Pride goes before destruction,
and a haughty spirit before a fall.
19 It is better to be lowly in spirit with the afflicted
than to share the spoils with the proud.
20 The one who deals wisely in a matter will find success,
and blessed is the one who trusts in the LORD.
21 The one who is wise in heart is called discerning,
and kind speech increases persuasiveness.
22 Insight is like a life-giving fountain to
the one who possesses it,
but folly leads to the discipline of fools.
23 A wise person's heart makes his speech wise
and it adds persuasiveness to his words.

24 Pleasant words are like a honeycomb,
sweet to the soul and healing to the bones.
25 There is a way that seems right to a person,
but its end is the way that leads to death.
26 A laborer's appetite has labored for him,
for his hunger has pressed him to work.
27 A wicked scoundrel digs up evil,
and his slander is like a scorching fire.
28 A perverse person spreads dissension,
and a gossip separates the closest friends.
29 A violent person entices his neighbor,
and then leads him down a path that is terrible.
30 The one who winks his eyes devises perverse things,
and one who compresses his lips has accomplished evil.
31 Gray hair is like a crown of glory;
it is attained in the path of righteousness.
32 Better to be slow to anger than to be a mighty warrior,
and one who controls his temper is better
than one who captures a city.
33 The dice are thrown into the lap,
but their every decision is from the LORD.

17 Better is a dry crust of bread where there is quietness
than a house full of feasting with strife.
2 A servant who acts wisely will rule
over an heir who behaves shamefully,
and will share the inheritance along with the relatives.
3 The crucible is for refining silver and the furnace is for gold,
likewise the LORD tests hearts.
4 One who acts wickedly pays attention to evil counsel;
a liar listens to a malicious tongue.
5 The one who mocks the poor has insulted his Creator;
whoever rejoices over disaster will not go unpunished.
6 Grandchildren are like a crown to the elderly,
and the glory of children is their parents.
7 Excessive speech is not becoming for a fool;
how much less are lies for a ruler!
8 A bribe works like a charm for the one who offers it;
in whatever he does he succeeds.
9 The one who forgives an offense seeks love,
but whoever repeats a matter separates close friends.
10 A rebuke makes a greater impression on a discerning person
than a hundred blows on a fool.
11 An evil person seeks only rebellion,
and so a cruel messenger will be sent against him.
12 It is better for a person to meet a mother
bear being robbed of her cubs,
than to encounter a fool in his folly.
13 As for the one who repays evil for good,
evil will not leave his house.
14 Starting a quarrel is like letting out water;
abandon strife before it breaks out!
15 The one who acquits the guilty and the one
who condemns the innocent—
both of them are an abomination to the LORD.

16 What's the point of a fool having money in hand
to buy wisdom, when his head is empty?
17 A friend loves at all times,
and a relative is born to help in adversity.
18 The one who lacks sense strikes hands in pledge,
and puts up financial security for his neighbor.
19 The one who loves a quarrel loves transgression;
whoever builds his gate high seeks destruction.
20 The one who has a perverse heart does not find good,
and the one who is deceitful in speech falls into trouble.
21 Whoever brings a fool into the world does so to his grief,
and the father of a fool has no joy.
22 A cheerful heart brings good healing,
but a crushed spirit dries up the bones.
23 A wicked person receives a bribe secretly
to pervert the ways of justice.
24 Wisdom is directly in front of the discerning person,
but the eyes of a fool run to the ends of the earth.
25 A foolish child is a grief to his father,
and bitterness to the mother who bore him.
26 It is terrible to punish a righteous person,
and to flog honorable men is wrong.
27 The truly wise person restrains his words,
and the one who stays calm is discerning.
28 Even a fool who remains silent is considered wise,
and the one who holds his tongue is deemed discerning.

18 One who has isolated himself seeks his own desires;
he rejects all sound judgment.
2 A fool takes no pleasure in understanding
but only in disclosing what is on his mind.
3 When a wicked person arrives,
contempt shows up with him,
and with shame comes a reproach.
4 The words of a person's mouth are like deep waters,
and the fountain of wisdom is like a flowing brook.
5 It is terrible to show partiality to the wicked,
by depriving a righteous man of justice.
6 The lips of a fool enter into strife,
and his mouth invites a flogging.
7 The mouth of a fool is his ruin,
and his lips are a snare for his life.
8 The words of a gossip are like choice morsels;
and they have gone down into the
person's innermost being.
9 The one who is slack in his work
is a brother to one who destroys.
10 The name of the LORD is like a strong tower;
the righteous person runs to it and is set safely on high.
11 The wealth of a rich person is like a strong city,
and it is like a high wall in his imagination.
12 Before destruction the heart of a person is proud,
but humility comes before honor.
13 The one who gives an answer before he listens—
that is his folly and his shame.

14 A person's spirit sustains him through sickness—
but who can bear a crushed spirit?
15 The discerning person acquires knowledge,
and the wise person seeks knowledge.
16 A person's gift makes room for him,
and leads him before important people.
17 The first to state his case seems right,
until his opponent begins to cross-examine him.
18 A toss of a coin ends disputes,
and settles the issue between strong opponents.
19 A relative offended is harder to reach than a strong city,
and disputes are like the barred gates of a fortified citadel.
20 From the fruit of a person's mouth his
stomach will be satisfied,
with the product of his lips he will be satisfied.
21 Death and life are in the power of the tongue,
and those who love its use will eat its fruit.
22 The one who has found a good wife
has found what goodness is,
and obtained a delightful gift from the LORD.
23 A poor person makes supplications,
but a rich man answers harshly.
24 There are companions who harm one another,
but there is a friend who sticks closer than a brother.

19 Better is a poor person who walks in his integrity
than one who is perverse in his speech and is a fool.
2 It is dangerous to have zeal without knowledge,
and the one who acts hastily makes poor choices.
3 A person's folly subverts his way,
and his heart rages against the LORD.
4 Wealth adds many friends,
but a poor person is separated from his friend.
5 A false witness will not go unpunished,
and the one who spouts out lies will
not escape punishment.
6 Many people entreat the favor of a generous person,
and everyone is the friend of the person who gives gifts.
7 All the relatives of a poor person hate him;
how much more do his friends avoid him—
one who chases words, which are nothing.
8 The one who acquires understanding loves himself;
the one who preserves understanding will prosper.
9 A false witness will not go unpunished,
and the one who spouts out lies will perish.
10 Luxury is not appropriate for a fool;
how much less for a servant to rule over princes!
11 A person's wisdom has made him slow to anger,
and it is his glory to overlook an offense.
12 A king's wrath is like the roar of a lion,
but his favor is like dew on the grass.
13 A foolish child is the ruin of his father,
and a contentious wife is like a constant dripping.
14 A house and wealth are inherited from parents,
but a prudent wife is from the LORD.

15 Laziness brings on a deep sleep,
and the idle person will go hungry.
16 The one who obeys commandments guards his life;
the one who despises his ways will die.
17 The one who is gracious to the poor lends to the LORD,
and the LORD will repay him for his good deed.
18 Discipline your child, for there is hope,
but do not set your heart on causing his death.
19 A person with great anger bears the penalty,
but if you deliver him from it once,
you will have to do it again.
20 Listen to advice and receive discipline,
that you may become wise by the end of your life.
21 There are many plans in a person's mind,
but it is the counsel of the LORD that will stand.
22 What is desirable for a person is to show loyal love,
and a poor person is better than a liar.
23 Fearing the LORD leads to life,
and one who does so will live satisfied; he
will not be afflicted by calamity.
24 The sluggard has plunged his hand into the dish,
and he will not even bring it back to his mouth!
25 Flog a scorner, and as a result the
simpleton will learn prudence;
correct a discerning person, and as a result
he will understand knowledge.
26 The one who robs his father and chases away his mother
is a son who brings shame and disgrace.
27 If you stop listening to instruction, my child,
you will stray from the words of knowledge.
28 A crooked witness scorns justice,
and the mouth of the wicked devours iniquity.
29 Penalties have been prepared for scorners,
and floggings for the backs of fools.
20 Wine is a mocker and strong drink is a brawler;
whoever goes astray by them is not wise.
2 The king's terrifying anger is like the roar of a lion;
whoever provokes him sins against himself.
3 It is an honor for a person to cease from strife,
but every fool quarrels.
4 The sluggard will not plow during the planting season,
so at harvest time he asks for grain but has nothing.
5 Counsel in a person's heart is like deep water,
but an understanding person draws it out.
6 Many people profess their loyalty,
but a faithful person—who can find?
7 The righteous person behaves in integrity;
blessed are his children after him.
8 A king sitting on the throne to judge
separates out all evil with his eyes.
9 Who can say, "I have kept my heart clean;
I am pure from my sin"?
10 Diverse weights and diverse measures—
the LORD abhors both of them.

11 Even a young man is known by his actions,
whether his activity is pure and whether it is right.
12 The ear that hears and the eye that sees—
the LORD has made them both.
13 Do not love sleep, lest you become impoverished;
open your eyes so that you might
be satisfied with food.
14 "It's worthless! It's worthless!" says the buyer,
but when he goes on his way, he boasts.
15 There is gold, and an abundance of rubies,
but words of knowledge are like a precious jewel.
16 Take a man's garment when he has
given security for a stranger,
and hold him in pledge on behalf of strangers.
17 Bread gained by deceit tastes sweet to a person,
but afterward his mouth will be filled with gravel.
18 Plans are established by counsel,
so make war with guidance.
19 The one who goes about gossiping reveals secrets;
therefore do not associate with someone
who is always opening his mouth.
20 The one who curses his father and his mother,
his lamp will be extinguished in the blackest darkness.
21 An inheritance gained easily in the beginning
will not be blessed in the end.
22 Do not say, "I will pay back evil!"
Wait for the LORD, so that he may vindicate you.
23 The LORD abhors differing weights,
and dishonest scales are wicked.
24 The steps of a person are ordained by the LORD—
so how can anyone understand his own way?
25 It is a snare for a person to rashly cry, "Holy!"
and only afterward to consider what he has vowed.
26 A wise king separates out the wicked;
he turns the threshing wheel over them.
27 The human spirit is like the lamp of the LORD,
searching all his innermost parts.
28 Loyal love and truth preserve a king,
and his throne is upheld by loyal love.
29 The glory of young men is their strength,
and the splendor of old men is gray hair.
30 Beatings and wounds cleanse away evil,
and floggings cleanse the innermost being.

21 The king's heart is in the hand of the
LORD like channels of water;
he turns it wherever he wants.
2 All a person's ways seem right in his own opinion,
but the LORD evaluates his thoughts.
3 To do righteousness and justice
is more acceptable to the LORD than sacrifice.
4 Haughty eyes and a proud heart—
what the wicked cultivate is sin.
5 The plans of the diligent lead only to plenty,
but everyone who is hasty comes only to poverty.

REFLECT

How can you be sure that your ways align with God's? Where can you find the wisdom to know whether or not your ways are right?

6 Making a fortune by a lying tongue is like
a vapor driven back and forth;
they seek death.
7 The violence done by the wicked will drag them away
because they have refused to do what is right.
8 The way of the guilty person is devious,
but as for the pure, his way is upright.
9 It is better to live on a corner of the housetop
than to share a house with a quarrelsome wife.
10 The appetite of the wicked has desired evil;
his neighbor is shown no favor in his eyes.
11 When a scorner is punished, the naive becomes wise;
when a wise person is instructed, he gains knowledge.
12 The Righteous One considers the house of the wicked;
he overthrows the wicked to their ruin.
13 The one who shuts his ears to the cry of the poor,
he too will cry out and will not be answered.
14 A gift given in secret subdues anger,
and a bribe given secretly subdues strong wrath.
15 Doing justice brings joy to the righteous
and terror to those who do evil.
16 The one who wanders from the way of wisdom
will end up in the company of the departed.
17 The one who loves pleasure will be a poor person;
whoever loves wine and anointing oil will not be rich.
18 The wicked become a ransom for the righteous,
and the treacherous are taken in the place of the upright.
19 It is better to live in the wilderness
than with a quarrelsome and easily provoked woman.
20 There is desirable treasure and olive oil
in the dwelling of the wise,
but a foolish person devours all he has.
21 The one who pursues righteousness and love
finds life, bounty, and honor.
22 A wise man went up against the city of the mighty
and brought down the stronghold in which they trust.
23 The one who guards his mouth and his tongue
keeps his life from troubles.
24 A proud and arrogant person, whose name is "Scoffer,"
acts with overbearing pride.
25 What the sluggard desires will kill him,
for his hands have refused to work.
26 All day long he has craved greedily,
but the righteous person gives and does not hold back.
27 The wicked person's sacrifice is an abomination;
how much more when he brings it with evil intent!
28 A lying witness will perish,
but the one who reports accurately speaks forever.
29 A wicked person has put on a bold face,
but as for the upright, he establishes his ways.
30 There is no wisdom and there is no understanding,
and there is no counsel against the LORD.
31 A horse is prepared for the day of battle,
but the victory is from the LORD.

22 A good name is to be chosen rather than great wealth,
good favor more than silver or gold.
2 The rich and the poor are met together;
the LORD is the Creator of them both.
3 A shrewd person saw danger and hid himself,
but the naive passed on by and paid for it.
4 The reward for humility and fearing the LORD
is riches and honor and life.
5 Thorns and snares are in the path of the perverse,
but the one who guards himself keeps far from them.
6 Train a child in the way that he should go,
and when he is old he will not turn from it.
7 The rich rule over the poor,
and the borrower is servant to the lender.
8 The one who sows iniquity will reap trouble,
and the rod of his fury will end.
9 A generous person will be blessed,
for he has given some of his food to the poor.
10 Drive out the scorner and contention will leave;
strife and insults will cease.
11 The one who loves a pure heart
and whose speech is gracious—the king will be his friend.
12 The eyes of the LORD watched over a cause,
and subverted the words of the treacherous person.
13 The sluggard has said, "There is a lion outside!
I will be killed in the middle of the streets!"
14 The mouth of an adulteress is like a deep pit;
the one against whom the LORD is angry will fall into it.
15 Folly is bound up in the heart of a child,
but the rod of discipline will drive it far from him.
16 The one who oppresses the poor to increase his own gain
and the one who gives to the rich—
both end up only in poverty.

THE SAYINGS OF THE WISE

17 Incline your ear and listen to the words of the wise,
and apply your mind to my instruction.
18 For it is pleasing if you keep these sayings within you,
and they are ready on your lips.
19 So that your confidence may be in the LORD,
I hereby make them known to you today—even you.
20 Have I not written thirty sayings for you,
sayings of counsel and knowledge,
21 to show you true and reliable words,
so that you may give accurate answers
to those who sent you?
22 Do not exploit a poor person because he is poor
and do not crush the needy in court,
23 for the LORD will plead their case
and will rob the life of those who are robbing them.
24 Do not make friends with an angry person,
and do not associate with a wrathful person,
25 lest you learn his ways
and entangle yourself in a snare.

26 Do not be one who strikes hands in pledge
or who puts up security for debts.
27 If you do not have enough to pay,
your bed will be taken right out from under you!
28 Do not move an ancient boundary stone
that was put in place by your ancestors.
29 You have seen a person skilled in his work—
he will take his position before kings;
he will not take his position before obscure people.

23 When you sit down to eat with a ruler,
consider carefully what is before you,
2 and put a knife to your throat
if you possess a large appetite.
3 Do not crave that ruler's delicacies,
for that food is deceptive.
4 Do not wear yourself out to become rich;
be wise enough to restrain yourself.
5 When you gaze upon riches, they are gone,
for they surely make wings for themselves,
and fly off into the sky like an eagle!
6 Do not eat the food of a stingy person,
do not crave his delicacies;
7 for he is like someone who has calculated
the cost in his mind.
"Eat and drink," he says to you,
but his heart is not with you;
8 you will vomit up the little bit you have eaten,
and will have wasted your pleasant words.
9 Do not speak in the ears of a fool,
for he will despise the wisdom of your words.
10 Do not move an ancient boundary stone,
or take over the fields of the fatherless,
11 for their Protector is strong;
he will plead their case against you.
12 Apply your heart to instruction
and your ears to the words of knowledge.
13 Do not withhold discipline from a child;
even if you strike him with the rod, he will not die.
14 If you strike him with the rod,
you will deliver him from death.
15 My child, if your heart is wise,
then my heart also will be glad;
16 my soul will rejoice
when your lips speak what is right.
17 Do not let your heart envy sinners,
but rather be zealous in fearing the LORD all the time.
18 For surely there is a future,
and your hope will not be cut off.
19 Listen, my child, and be wise,
and guide your heart on the right way.
20 Do not spend time among drunkards,
among those who eat too much meat,
21 because drunkards and gluttons become impoverished,
and drowsiness clothes them with rags.

22 Listen to your father who gave you life,
and do not despise your mother when she is old.
23 Acquire truth and do not sell it—
wisdom, and discipline, and understanding.
24 The father of a righteous person will rejoice greatly;
whoever fathers a wise child will have joy in him.
25 May your father and your mother have joy;
may she who bore you rejoice.
26 Give me your heart, my son,
and let your eyes observe my ways;
27 for a prostitute is like a deep pit;
a harlot is like a narrow well.
28 Indeed, she lies in wait like a robber,
and increases the unfaithful among men.
29 Who has woe? Who has sorrow?
Who has contentions? Who has complaints?
Who has wounds without cause? Who
has dullness of the eyes?
30 Those who linger over wine,
those who go looking for mixed wine.
31 Do not look on the wine when it is red,
when it sparkles in the cup,
when it goes down smoothly.
32 Afterward it bites like a snake,
and stings like a viper.
33 Your eyes will see strange things,
and your mind will speak perverse things.
34 And you will be like one who lies down
in the midst of the sea,
and like one who lies down on the top of the rigging.
35 You will say, "They have struck me,
but I am not harmed!
They beat me, but I did not know it!
When will I awake? I will look for another drink."

24 Do not envy evil people,
do not desire to be with them;
2 for their hearts contemplate violence,
and their lips speak harm.
3 By wisdom a house is built,
and through understanding it is established;
4 by knowledge its rooms are filled
with all kinds of precious and pleasing treasures.
5 A wise warrior is strong,
and a man of knowledge makes his strength stronger;
6 for with guidance you wage your war,
and with numerous advisers there is victory.
7 Wisdom is unattainable for a fool;
in court he does not open his mouth.
8 The one who plans to do evil
will be called a scheming person.
9 A foolish scheme is sin,
and the scorner is an abomination to people.
10 You have slacked off in the day of trouble—
your strength is small!

11 Deliver those being taken away to death,
and hold back those slipping to the slaughter.
12 If you say, "But we did not know about this,"
won't the one who evaluates hearts discern it?
Won't the one who guards your life realize
and repay each person according to his deeds?
13 Eat honey, my child, for it is good,
and honey from the honeycomb
is sweet to your taste.
14 Likewise, know that wisdom is sweet to your soul;
if you have found it, you have a future,
and your hope will not be cut off.
15 Do not lie in wait like the wicked against
the place where the righteous live;
do not assault his home.
16 Indeed a righteous person will fall seven
times, and then get up again,
but the guilty will collapse in calamity.
17 Do not rejoice when your enemy falls,
and when he stumbles do not let your heart rejoice,
18 lest the LORD see it, and be displeased,
and turn his wrath away from him.
19 Do not fret because of evil people
or be envious of wicked people,
20 for the evil person has no future,
and the lamp of the wicked will be extinguished.
21 Fear the LORD, my child, as well as the king,
and do not associate with rebels,
22 for suddenly their destruction will overtake them,
and who knows the ruinous judgment both
the LORD and the king can bring?

FURTHER SAYINGS OF THE WISE

23 These sayings also are from the wise:
To show partiality in judgment is terrible:
24 The one who says to the guilty, "You are innocent,"
peoples will curse him, and nations will denounce him.
25 But there will be delight for those who convict the guilty,
and a pleasing blessing will come on them.
26 Like a kiss on the lips
is the one who gives an honest answer.
27 Establish your work outside and get your fields ready;
afterward build your house.
28 Do not be a witness against your neighbor without cause,
and do not deceive with your words.
29 Do not say, "I will do to him just as he has done to me;
I will pay him back according to what he has done."
30 I passed by the field of a sluggard,
by the vineyard of one who lacks sense.
31 I saw that thorns had grown up all over it,
the ground was covered with weeds,
and its stone wall was broken down.
32 Then I scrutinized it. I was putting my mind to it—
I saw; I took in a lesson:

33 "A little sleep, a little slumber,
a little folding of the hands to relax,
34 and your poverty will come like a bandit,
and your need like an armed robber."

PROVERBS OF SOLOMON COLLECTED BY HEZEKIAH

25 These also are proverbs of Solomon, which the men of
King Hezekiah of Judah copied:

2 It is the glory of God to conceal a matter,
and it is the glory of a king to search out a matter.
3 As the heaven is high and the earth is deep
so the hearts of kings are unsearchable.
4 Remove the dross from the silver,
and material for the silversmith will emerge;
5 remove the wicked from before the king,
and his throne will be established in righteousness.
6 Do not honor yourself before the king,
and do not stand in the place of great men;
7 for it is better for him to say to you, "Come up here,"
than to put you lower before a prince,
whom your eyes have seen.
8 Do not go out hastily to litigation,
or what will you do afterward
when your neighbor puts you to shame?
9 When you argue a case with your neighbor,
do not reveal the secret of another person,
10 lest the one who hears it put you to shame
and your infamy will never go away.
11 Like apples of gold in settings of silver,
so is a word skillfully spoken.
12 Like an earring of gold and an ornament of fine gold,
so is a wise reprover to the ear of the one who listens.
13 Like the cold of snow in the time of harvest,
so is a faithful messenger to those who send him,
for he refreshes the heart of his masters.
14 Like cloudy skies and wind that produce no rain,
so is the one who boasts of a gift not given.
15 Through patience a ruler can be persuaded,
and a soft tongue can break a bone.
16 You have found honey—eat only what
is sufficient for you,
lest you become stuffed with it and vomit it up.
17 Don't set foot too frequently in your neighbor's house,
lest he become weary of you and hate you.
18 Like a club or a sword or a sharp arrow,
so is the one who testifies against his
neighbor as a false witness.
19 Like a bad tooth or a foot out of joint,
so is confidence in an unfaithful person
at the time of trouble.
20 Like one who takes off a garment on a cold day,
or like vinegar poured on soda,
so is one who sings songs to a heavy heart.

21 If your enemy is hungry, give him food to eat,
and if he is thirsty, give him water to drink,
22 for you will heap coals of fire on his head,
and the LORD will reward you.
23 The north wind brings forth rain,
and a gossiping tongue brings forth an angry look.
24 It is better to live on a corner of the housetop
than in a house in company with a quarrelsome wife.
25 Like cold water to a weary person,
so is good news from a distant land.
26 Like a muddied spring and a polluted well,
so is a righteous person who
gives way before the wicked.
27 It is not good to eat too much honey,
nor is it honorable for people to seek their own glory.
28 Like a city that is broken down and without a wall,
so is a person who cannot control his temper.

26 Like snow in summer or rain in harvest,
so honor is not fitting for a fool.
2 Like a fluttering bird or like a flying swallow,
so a curse without cause does not come to rest.
3 A whip for the horse and a bridle for the donkey,
and a rod for the backs of fools!
4 Do not answer a fool according to his folly,
lest you yourself also be like him.
5 Answer a fool according to his folly,
lest he be wise in his own opinion.
6 Like cutting off the feet or drinking violence,
so is sending a message by the hand of a fool.
7 Like legs dangle uselessly from the lame,
so a proverb dangles in the mouth of fools.
8 Like tying a stone in a sling,
so is giving honor to a fool.
9 Like a thorn has gone up into the hand of a drunkard,
so a proverb has gone up into the mouth of a fool.
10 Like an archer who wounds at random,
so is the one who hires a fool or hires any passerby.
11 Like a dog that returns to its vomit,
so a fool repeats his folly.
12 You have seen a man wise in his own opinion—
there is more hope for a fool than for him.
13 The sluggard has said, "There is a lion in the road!
A lion in the streets!"
14 Like a door that turns on its hinges,
so a sluggard turns on his bed.
15 The sluggard has plunged his hand in the dish;
he is too lazy to bring it back to his mouth.
16 The sluggard is wiser in his own opinion
than seven people who respond with good sense.
17 Like one who grabs a wild dog by the ears,
so is the person passing by who becomes
furious over a quarrel not his own.
18 Like a madman who shoots
firebrands and deadly arrows,

19 so is a person who has deceived his neighbor,
and said, "Was I not only joking?"
20 Where there is no wood, a fire goes out,
and where there is no gossip, contention ceases.
21 Like charcoal is to burning coals, and wood to fire,
so is a contentious person to kindle strife.
22 The words of a gossip are like choice morsels;
and they have gone down into a person's innermost being.
23 Like a coating of glaze over earthenware
are fervent lips with an evil heart.
24 The one who hates others disguises it with his lips,
but he stores up deceit within him.
25 When he speaks graciously, do not believe him,
for there are seven abominations within him.
26 Though his hatred may be concealed by deceit,
his evil will be uncovered in the assembly.
27 The one who digs a pit will fall into it;
the one who rolls a stone—it will come back on him.
28 A lying tongue hates those crushed by it,
and a flattering mouth works ruin.

27 Do not boast about tomorrow;
for you do not know what a day may bring forth.
2 Let another praise you, and not your own mouth;
someone else, and not your own lips.
3 A stone is heavy and sand is weighty,
but vexation by a fool is more burdensome
than the two of them.
4 Wrath is cruel and anger is overwhelming,
but who can stand before jealousy?
5 Better is open rebuke
than hidden love.
6 Faithful are the wounds of a friend,
but the kisses of an enemy are excessive.
7 The one whose appetite is satisfied loathes honey,
but to the hungry mouth every bitter thing is sweet.
8 Like a bird that wanders from its nest,
so is a person who wanders from his home.
9 Ointment and incense make the heart rejoice,
likewise the sweetness of one's friend
from sincere counsel.
10 Do not forsake your friend and your father's friend,
and do not enter your brother's house
in the day of your disaster;
a neighbor nearby is better than a brother far away.
11 Be wise, my son, and make my heart glad,
so that I may answer anyone who taunts me.
12 A shrewd person saw danger—he hid himself;
the naive passed right on by—they had to pay for it.
13 Take a man's garment when he has
given security for a stranger,
and hold him in pledge on behalf of a stranger.
14 If someone blesses his neighbor with a
loud voice early in the morning,
it will be counted as a curse to him.

15 A continual dripping on a rainy day—
a contentious wife makes herself like that.
16 Whoever contains her has contained the wind
or can grasp oil with his right hand.
17 As iron sharpens iron,
so a person sharpens his friend.
18 The one who tends a fig tree will eat its fruit,
and whoever takes care of his master will be honored.
19 As in water the face is reflected as a face,
so a person's heart reflects the person.
20 As Death and Destruction are never satisfied,
so the eyes of a person are never satisfied.
21 As the crucible is for silver and the furnace is for gold,
so a person must put his praise to the test.
22 If you should pound the fool in the mortar
among the grain with the pestle,
his foolishness would not depart from him.
23 Pay careful attention to the condition of your flocks,
set your mind on your herds,
24 for riches do not last forever,
nor does a crown last from generation to generation.
25 When the hay is removed and new grass appears,
and the grass from the hills is gathered in,
26 the lambs will be for your clothing,
and the goats will be for the price of a field.
27 And there will be enough goat's milk for your food,
for the food of your household,
and for the sustenance of your servant girls.

28 The wicked person fled, though no one was pursuing,
but the righteous person can be as confident as a lion.
2 When a country is rebellious it has many princes,
but by someone who is discerning and
knowledgeable order is maintained.
3 A poor person who oppresses the weak
is like a driving rain without food.
4 Those who forsake the law praise the wicked,
but those who keep the law contend with them.
5 Evil people do not understand justice,
but those who seek the LORD understand it all.
6 A poor person who walks in his integrity is better
than one who is perverse in his ways
even though he is rich.
7 The one who keeps the law is a discerning child,
but a companion of gluttons brings
shame to his parents.
8 The one who increases his wealth by increasing interest
gathers it for someone who is gracious to the needy.
9 The one who turns away his ear from hearing the law,
even his prayer is an abomination.
10 The one who leads the upright astray in an evil way
will himself fall into his own pit,
but the blameless will inherit what is good.
11 A rich person is wise in his own opinion,
but a discerning poor person can evaluate him properly.

REFLECT

In which areas of your walk with Christ do you need to be sharpened? Who in your life can be iron for you? How can you encourage others?

12 When the righteous rejoice, great is the glory,
but when the wicked rise to power, people are sought out.
13 The one who covers his transgressions will not prosper,
but whoever confesses them and
forsakes them will find mercy.
14 Blessed is the one who is always cautious,
but whoever hardens his heart will fall into evil.
15 Like a roaring lion or a roving bear,
so is a wicked ruler over a poor people.
16 The prince who is a great oppressor lacks wisdom,
but the one who hates unjust gain will prolong his days.
17 The one who is tormented by the murder
of another will flee to the pit;
let no one support him.
18 The one who walks blamelessly will be delivered,
but whoever is perverse in his ways will fall at once.
19 The one who works his land will be satisfied with food,
but whoever chases daydreams will have his fill of poverty.
20 A faithful person will have an abundance of blessings,
but the one who hastens to gain riches
will not go unpunished.
21 To show partiality is terrible,
for a person will transgress over the
smallest piece of bread.
22 The stingy person hastens after riches
and does not know that poverty will overtake him.
23 The one who reproves another will
in the end find more favor
than the one who flatters with the tongue.
24 The one who robs his father and mother and
says, "There is no transgression,"
is a companion to the one who destroys.
25 The greedy person stirs up dissension,
but the one who trusts in the LORD will prosper.
26 The one who trusts in his own heart is a fool,
but the one who walks in wisdom will escape.
27 The one who gives to the poor will not lack,
but whoever shuts his eyes to them
will receive many curses.
28 When the wicked gain control, people hide themselves,
but when they perish, the righteous increase.

29 The one who stiffens his neck after numerous rebukes
will suddenly be destroyed without remedy.
2 When the righteous become numerous, the people rejoice;
when the wicked rule, the people groan.
3 The man who loves wisdom brings joy to his father,
but whoever associates with prostitutes
wastes his wealth.
4 A king brings stability to a land by justice,
but one who exacts tribute tears it down.
5 The one who flatters his neighbor
spreads a net for his steps.
6 In the transgression of an evil person there is a snare,
but a righteous person can sing and rejoice.

7 The righteous person cares for the legal rights of the poor;
the wicked person does not understand such knowledge.
8 Scornful people inflame a city,
but those who are wise turn away wrath.
9 When a wise person goes to court with a foolish person,
there is no peace whether he is angry or laughs.
10 Bloodthirsty people hate someone with integrity;
as for the upright, they seek his life.
11 A fool lets fly with all his temper,
but a wise person keeps it back.
12 If a ruler listens to lies,
all his ministers will be wicked.
13 The poor person and the oppressor have this in common:
the LORD gives light to the eyes of them both.
14 If a king judges the poor in truth,
his throne will be established forever.
15 A rod and reproof impart wisdom,
but a child who is unrestrained brings
shame to his mother.
16 When the wicked increase, transgression increases,
but the righteous will see their downfall.
17 Discipline your child, and he will give you rest;
he will bring you happiness.
18 When there is no prophetic vision the
people cast off restraint,
but the one who keeps the law, blessed is he!
19 A servant cannot be corrected by words,
for although he understands, there is no answer.
20 You have seen someone who is hasty in his words—
there is more hope for a fool than for him.
21 If someone pampers his servant from youth,
he will be a weakling in the end.
22 An angry person stirs up dissension,
and a wrathful person is abounding in transgression.
23 A person's pride will bring him low,
but one who has a lowly spirit will gain honor.
24 Whoever shares with a thief is his own enemy;
he hears the oath to testify, but does not talk.
25 The fear of people becomes a snare,
but whoever trusts in the LORD will be set on high.
26 Many people seek the face of a ruler,
but it is from the LORD that one receives justice.
27 An unjust person is an abomination to the righteous,
and the one who lives an upright life is
an abomination to the wicked.

THE WORDS OF AGUR

30 The words of Agur, the son of Jakeh; an oracle:
This man says to Ithiel, to Ithiel and to Ukal:
2 Surely I am more brutish than any other human being,
and I do not have human understanding;
3 I have not learned wisdom,
nor can I have knowledge of the Holy One.
4 Who has ascended into heaven, and then descended?

Who has gathered up the winds in his fists?
Who has bound up the waters in his cloak?
Who has established all the ends of the earth?
What is his name, and what is his son's
name? Surely you can know!
5 Every word of God is purified;
he is like a shield for those who take refuge in him.
6 Do not add to his words,
lest he reprove you, and prove you to be a liar.
7 Two things I have asked from you;
do not refuse me before I die:
8 Remove falsehood and lies far from me;
do not give me poverty or riches,
feed me with my allotted portion of bread,
9 lest I become satisfied and act deceptively
and say, "Who is the LORD?"
Or lest I become poor and steal
and demean the name of my God.
10 Do not slander a servant to his master,
lest he curse you, and you are found guilty.
11 There is a generation who curse their fathers
and do not bless their mothers.
12 There is a generation who are pure in their own opinion
and yet are not washed from their filthiness.
13 There is a generation whose eyes are so lofty,
and whose eyelids are lifted up disdainfully.
14 There is a generation whose teeth are like swords
and whose molars are like knives
to devour the poor from the earth
and the needy from among the human race.
15 The leech has two daughters:
"Give! Give!"
There are three things that will never be satisfied,
four that have never said, "Enough"—
16 the grave, the barren womb;
earth has not been satisfied with water;
and fire has never said, "Enough!"
17 The eye that mocks at a father
and despises obeying a mother—
the ravens of the valley will peck it out
and the young vultures will eat it.
18 There are three things that are too wonderful for me,
four that I do not understand:
19 the way of an eagle in the sky,
the way of a snake on a rock,
the way of a ship in the sea,
and the way of a man with a woman.
20 This is the way of an adulterous woman:
she has eaten and wiped her mouth
and has said, "I have not done wrong."
21 Under three things the earth has trembled,
and under four things it cannot bear up:
22 under a servant who becomes king,
under a fool who becomes stuffed with food,

23 under an unloved woman who becomes married,
and under a female servant who dispossesses her mistress.
24 There are four things on earth that are small,
but they are exceedingly wise:
25 ants are creatures with little strength,
but they prepare their food in the summer;
26 rock badgers are creatures with little power,
but they make their homes in the crags;
27 locusts have no king,
but they all go forward by ranks;
28 a lizard you can catch with the hand,
but it gets into the palaces of the king.
29 There are three things that are
magnificent in their step,
four things that move about magnificently:
30 a lion, mightiest of the beasts,
who does not retreat from anything;
31 a strutting rooster, a male goat,
and a king with his army around him.
32 If you have done foolishly by exalting yourself
or if you have planned evil,
put your hand over your mouth!
33 For as the churning of milk produces butter
and as punching the nose produces blood,
so stirring up anger produces strife.

THE WORDS OF LEMUEL

31 The words of King Lemuel, an oracle that his mother taught
him:
2 O my son, O son of my womb,
O son of my vows,
3 do not give your strength to women,
nor your ways to that which ruins kings.
4 It is not for kings, O Lemuel,
it is not for kings to drink wine,
or for rulers to crave strong drink,
5 lest they drink and forget what is decreed,
and remove from all the poor their legal rights.
6 Give strong drink to the one who is perishing,
and wine to those who are bitterly distressed;
7 let them drink and forget their poverty,
and remember their misery no more.
8 Open your mouth on behalf of those unable to speak,
for the legal rights of all the dying.
9 Open your mouth, judge in righteousness,
and plead the cause of the poor and needy.

THE WIFE OF NOBLE CHARACTER

10 Who can find a wife of noble character?
For her value is far more than rubies.
11 Her husband's heart has trusted her,
and he does not lack the dividends.
12 She has rewarded him with good and not harm
all the days of her life.

LOVE TO GROW

WISDOM AND THE FEAR OF THE LORD

PROVERBS 31:10–31

I used to have a love-hate relationship with the elusive Proverbs 31 woman. In my ignorance, she was the woman I aspired to become in order to be "worthy" of a husband. Early in my marriage, she was the woman I could never live up to. As I have grown in my relationship with the Lord, my understanding of Proverbs 31:10–31 has matured.

This Hebrew acrostic poem is not a historical description of any particular woman but rather a literary example of what it means to fear the Lord. It's a look at the practical incarnation of wisdom. The poem is the culmination of all the preceding proverbs.

The poem begins by telling us the value of wisdom: It is worth more than jewels. We then see wisdom characterized as a married (covenanted) woman: The wife of noble character is prudent, hardworking, industrious, and charitable. Her husband has full confidence in her. She provides for her family and fulfills her responsibilities. She is profitable because of her diligence. Her words are filled with wisdom, and she is not anxious about the future. The end of the poem concludes with praises of wisdom. The one who acts wisely gets the attention of others.

Where charm and beauty fade, someone who fears the Lord deserves praise.

When I look at this passage as a description of someone who fears the Lord, I am both encouraged and challenged in my faith. Proverbs 31:10–31 inspires us to walk in wisdom, not so we can be a better wife or become a wife someday, but so we can walk in wisdom and in the fear of the Lord.

When our goal is to draw closer to God, to seek Him first, and to love Him more, our priorities change. We begin to seek to honor God above all else. I have found that when I start my days with Him in mind, I am more loving, productive, wise, helpful, and honorable.

This world values charm and beauty. How much do you value the external over the internal? Have you been spending more time on the things that will fade rather than the things that will last for eternity? If we desire to love God greatly and live for Him in all things, we must strive to walk in wisdom daily. As a result, we will live a life of value and purpose.

13 She sought out wool and flax,
then worked happily with her hands.
14 She was like the merchant ships;
she would bring in her food from afar.
15 Then she rose while it was still night,
and provided food for her household and
a portion to her female servants.
16 She considered a field and bought it;
from her own income she planted a vineyard.
17 She clothed herself in might,
and she strengthened her arms.
18 She perceived that her merchandise was good.
Her lamp would not go out in the night.
19 She extended her hands to the spool,
and her hands grasped the spindle.
20 She opened her hand to the poor,
and extended her hands to the needy.
21 She would not fear for her household in winter,
because all her household were clothed with scarlet,
22 because she had made coverings for herself;
and because her clothing was fine linen and purple.
23 Her husband is well-known in the city gate
when he sits with the elders of the land.
24 She made linen garments then sold them,
and traded belts to the merchants;
25 her clothing was strong and splendid;
and she laughed at the time to come.
26 She has opened her mouth with wisdom,
with loving instruction on her tongue.
27 Watching over the ways of her household,
she would not eat the bread of idleness.
28 Her children have risen and called her blessed;
her husband also has praised her:
29 "Many daughters have done valiantly,
but you have surpassed them all!"
30 Charm is deceitful and beauty is fleeting.
A woman who fears the LORD—she
makes herself praiseworthy.
31 Give her credit for what she has accomplished,
and let her works praise her in the city gates.

God has made everything fit Beautifully in its appropriate time

MEMORY VERSE

God has made everything fit beautifully in its appropriate time, but he has also placed ignorance in the human heart so that people cannot discover what God has ordained, from the beginning to the end of their lives.

Ecclesiastes 3:11

Ecclesiastes

INTRODUCTION

Finding Fulfillment in God

Humans have been asking questions about the meaning of life since the beginning of time. The Book of Ecclesiastes asks these questions and offers the answer: the purpose of human life is to fear and obey God. Even though there are challenges, joy is found in the fear and worship of God. The author of Ecclesiastes presents difficult questions that lead readers to search their hearts to determine where their value and motivation are found.

God has placed eternity in the hearts of humans, and the author attempts to understand how the present world influences eternity. Ultimately, the author determines that riches and pleasures are futile, leading humans to live a vain existence. However, joy and satisfaction are found in a relationship with God.

Many scholars agree Solomon was most likely the author of this book. It is believed he wrote the Book of Ecclesiastes toward the end of his life, around 930 B.C. Ecclesiastes does not describe any historical events. However, based on the tone and content, Solomon likely wrote this after he had repented of idolatry and his pursuit of foreign wives. This book is offered as a guide for others as they navigate the pitfalls and perils of life.

Ecclesiastes is a challenging book to read as the author presents many questions and uncertainties about the meaning and purpose of life. However, one theme is clear: the purpose of life is to fear God and keep His commands. As we seek to love God greatly, we can revere, worship, and serve Him, turning from evil and honoring Him with our lives. We can be confident in our eternity because we have a relationship with the One who created us to live with Him forever.

Vietnam

OFFICIAL LANGUAGE
Vietnamese
POPULATION
96,380,000
UNREACHED POPULATION
8,612,000
PROFESSING CHRISTIANS
10.1%

Ly's Home

Say a Prayer Today

Pray for the church in Vietnam to be strengthened. Pray for believers to have boldness to share their faith with those around them, even in a society where faith in Christ is a foreign concept.

HISTORY BIT

The first missionaries to Vietnam were Franciscan (a religious order of the Roman Catholic Church founded in the thirteenth century by St. Francis of Assisi*) missionaries from the Philippines. They arrived in Cochin China (Vietnam) in 1581.**

Source Information:
https://joshuaproject.net/countries/VM
*https://www.britannica.com/topic/Franciscans
**John Bowden, *A Chronology of World Christianity* (New York, NY: Continuum, 2007), 291.

LY'S STORY

Growing up in Vietnam, my family practiced Buddhism and ancestor worship. My childhood was a nightmare. I suffered physically and emotionally because of an alcoholic father. I grew up angry and confused. After such difficulty, I felt that my life had no meaning and I contemplated committing suicide.

Then God intervened. I came to believe in Christ through the love of born-again believers. Since then God has restored me. He has given me hope. I am confident that what Ecclesiastes 3:11 says is true: God makes everything beautiful in its appointed time. God heard my cries and saw my tears. He knew I was suffering, but in His perfect timing, He drew me close. I cling tightly to the faith and hope I have in Him.

As I look back, my past is filled with ugliness and shamefulness. God did not rewrite my story, nor did He allow me to forget it. Instead, He redeemed my past through the power of Christ's blood. He did not abandon me in my past; He was there with me. As this truth sank into my heart I stopped complaining and being ashamed of my past. I have peace to accept what happened to me, knowing God had a greater purpose through it all.

God has transformed my life from hopelessness to hopefulness, from confusion to peace, from hatred to love, and from chaos to order. He is in control over everything from beginning to end. He is the Almighty! I am currently studying the Word of God at a seminary in America, proof that He can transform my life in ways I never imagined. Even though I do not know exactly what my future holds, I know the one who holds my future.

4 WEEK READING PLAN

LOVE HIS WORD

	MONDAY	TUESDAY	WEDNESDAY	THURSDAY	FRIDAY
1	Ecclesiastes 1	Ecclesiastes 2	Ecclesiastes 3	Ecclesiastes 4	Ecclesiastes 5
	SOAP Ecclesiastes 1:17-18	SOAP Ecclesiastes 2:11	SOAP Ecclesiastes 3:11	SOAP Ecclesiastes 4:9-10	SOAP Ecclesiastes 5:10
2	Ecclesiastes 6	Ecclesiastes 7	Ecclesiastes 8	Ecclesiastes 9:1—10:1	Ecclesiastes 10:2-20
	SOAP Ecclesiastes 6:12	SOAP Ecclesiastes 7:11-12	SOAP Ecclesiastes 8:15	SOAP Ecclesiastes 9:11	SOAP Ecclesiastes 10:12
3	Ecclesiastes 11	Ecclesiastes 12	Song of Solomon 1	Song of Solomon 2	Song of Solomon 3
	SOAP Ecclesiastes 11:7-8	SOAP Ecclesiastes 12:13-14	SOAP Song of Solomon 1:15	SOAP Song of Solomon 2:10-11	SOAP Song of Solomon 3:5
4	Song of Solomon 4:1—5:1	Song of Solomon 5:2-16	Song of Solomon 6:1-12	Song of Solomon 6:13—7:13	Song of Solomon 8
	SOAP Song of Solomon 4:9	SOAP Song of Solomon 5:9	SOAP Song of Solomon 6:3	SOAP Song of Solomon 7:6	SOAP Song of Solomon 8:7

TITLE

1 The words of the Teacher, the son of David, king in Jerusalem:

INTRODUCTION: UTTER FUTILITY

2 "Futile! Futile!" laments the Teacher.
"Absolutely futile! Everything is futile!"

FUTILITY ILLUSTRATED FROM NATURE

3 What benefit do people get from all the effort
which they expend on earth?
4 A generation comes and a generation goes,
but the earth remains the same through the ages.
5 The sun rises and the sun sets;
it hurries away to a place from which it rises again.
6 The wind goes to the south and circles around to the north;
round and round the wind goes and
on its rounds it returns.
7 All the streams flow into the sea, but the sea is not full,
and to the place where the streams flow,
there they will flow again.
8 All this monotony is tiresome; no
one can bear to describe it.
The eye is never satisfied with seeing, nor is
the ear ever content with hearing.
9 What exists now is what will be,
and what has been done is what will be done;
there is nothing truly new on earth.
10 Is there anything about which someone
can say, "Look at this! It is new"?
It was already done long ago, before our time.
11 No one remembers the former events,
nor will anyone remember the events
that are yet to happen;
they will not be remembered by the future generations.

FUTILITY OF SECULAR ACCOMPLISHMENT

12 I, the Teacher, have been king over Israel in Jerusalem.
13 I decided to carefully and thoroughly examine
all that has been accomplished on earth.
I concluded: God has given people a burdensome task
that keeps them occupied.
14 I reflected on everything that is
accomplished by man on earth,
and I concluded: Everything he has accomplished
is futile—like chasing the wind!
15 What is bent cannot be straightened,
and what is missing cannot be supplied.

FUTILITY OF SECULAR WISDOM

16 I thought to myself,
"I have become much wiser than any of my
predecessors who ruled over Jerusalem;
I have acquired much wisdom and knowledge."

REFLECT

Have you ever felt like your life was futile? What does God say about the significance of our lives?

17 So I decided to discern the benefit of wisdom and
knowledge over foolish behavior and ideas;
however, I concluded that even this endeavor
is like trying to chase the wind.
18 For with great wisdom comes great frustration;
whoever increases his knowledge merely
increases his heartache.

FUTILITY OF SELF-INDULGENT PLEASURE

2 I thought to myself,
"Come now, I will try self-indulgent
pleasure to see if it is worthwhile."
But I found that it also is futile.
2 I said of partying, "It is folly,"
and of self-indulgent pleasure, "It accomplishes nothing!"
3 I thought deeply about the effects of
indulging myself with wine
(all the while my mind was guiding me with wisdom)
and the effects of behaving foolishly,
so that I might discover what is profitable
for people to do on earth during the few days of their lives.

FUTILITY OF MATERIALISM

4 I increased my possessions:
I built houses for myself;
I planted vineyards for myself.
5 I designed royal gardens and parks for myself,
and I planted all kinds of fruit trees in them.
6 I constructed pools of water for myself,
to irrigate my grove of flourishing trees.
7 I purchased male and female slaves,
and I owned slaves who were born in my house;
I also possessed more livestock—both herds and flocks—
than any of my predecessors in Jerusalem.
8 I also amassed silver and gold for myself,
as well as valuable treasures taken from
kingdoms and provinces.
I acquired male singers and female singers for myself,
and what gives a man sensual delight—a
harem of beautiful concubines.
9 So I was far wealthier than all my
predecessors in Jerusalem,
yet I maintained my objectivity.
10 I did not restrain myself from getting whatever I wanted;
I did not deny myself anything that
would bring me pleasure.
So all my accomplishments gave me joy;
this was my reward for all my effort.
11 Yet when I reflected on everything I had accomplished
and on all the effort that I had expended to accomplish it,
I concluded: "All these achievements and
possessions are ultimately profitless—
like chasing the wind!
There is nothing gained from them on earth."

WISDOM IS BETTER THAN FOLLY

12 Next, I decided to consider wisdom, as
well as foolish behavior and ideas.
For what more can the king's successor do
than what the king has already done?
13 I realized that wisdom is preferable to folly,
just as light is preferable to darkness:
14 The wise man can see where he is going,
but the fool walks in darkness.
Yet I also realized that the same fate happens to them both.
15 So I thought to myself, "The fate of the
fool will happen even to me!
Then what did I gain by becoming so excessively wise?"
So I lamented to myself,
"The benefits of wisdom are ultimately meaningless!"
16 For the wise man, like the fool, will not
be remembered for very long,
because in the days to come, both will
already have been forgotten.
Alas, the wise man dies—just like the fool!
17 So I loathed life because what
happens on earth seems awful to me;
for all the benefits of wisdom are futile—
like chasing the wind.

FUTILITY OF BEING A WORKAHOLIC

18 So I loathed all the fruit of my effort,
for which I worked so hard on earth,
because I must leave it behind in the hands of my successor.
19 Who knows if he will be a wise man or a fool?
Yet he will be master over all the fruit of my labor
for which I worked so wisely on earth.
This also is futile!
20 So I began to despair about all the fruit of my labor
for which I worked so hard on earth.
21 For a man may do his work with
wisdom, knowledge, and skill;
however, he must hand over the fruit
of his labor as an inheritance
to someone else who did not work for it.
This also is futile, and an awful injustice!

PAINFUL DAYS AND RESTLESS NIGHTS

22 What does a man acquire from all his labor
and from the anxiety that accompanies his toil on earth?
23 For all day long his work produces pain and frustration,
and even at night his mind cannot relax.
This also is futile!

ENJOY WORK AND ITS BENEFITS

24 There is nothing better for people than to eat and drink,
and to find enjoyment in their work.
I also perceived that this ability to find
enjoyment comes from God.

25 For no one can eat and drink
or experience joy apart from him.
26 For to the one who pleases him, God gives
wisdom, knowledge, and joy,
but to the sinner, he gives the task of amassing wealth—
only to give it to the one who pleases God.
This task of the wicked is futile—like chasing the wind!

REFLECT

Why is real joy impossible apart from God? How can we find joy in our lives in God?

A TIME FOR ALL EVENTS IN LIFE

3 For everything there is an appointed time,
and an appropriate time for every activity on earth:
2 A time to be born, and a time to die;
a time to plant, and a time to uproot what was planted;
3 a time to kill, and a time to heal;
a time to break down, and a time to build up;
4 a time to weep, and a time to laugh;
a time to mourn, and a time to dance.
5 A time to throw away stones, and a time to gather stones;
a time to embrace, and a time to refrain from embracing;
6 a time to search, and a time to give something up as lost;
a time to keep, and a time to throw away;
7 a time to rip, and a time to sew;
a time to keep silent, and a time to speak.
8 A time to love, and a time to hate;
a time for war, and a time for peace.

MAN IS IGNORANT OF GOD'S TIMING

9 What benefit can a worker gain from his toil?
10 I have observed the burden
that God has given to people to keep them occupied.
11 God has made everything fit beautifully
in its appropriate time,
but he has also placed ignorance in the human heart
so that people cannot discover what God has ordained,
from the beginning to the end of their lives.

ENJOY LIFE IN THE PRESENT

12 I have concluded that there is nothing better for people
than to be happy and to enjoy
themselves as long as they live,
13 and also that everyone should eat and drink,
and find enjoyment in all his toil,
for these things are a gift from God.

GOD'S SOVEREIGNTY

14 I also know that whatever God does
will endure forever;
nothing can be added to it, and
nothing taken away from it.
God has made it this way, so that men will fear him.
15 Whatever exists now has already been, and
whatever will be has already been;
for God will seek to do again what
has occurred in the past.

LOVE TO GROW

BEAUTY IN EVERY SEASON

ECCLESIASTES 3:11

Waiting is hard. It's one of my least favorite things. In fact, I often read the ending of a book soon after I start reading it because I cannot wait to find out the ending. Maybe you do not read the end of books like me, but do you, in general, have a hard time waiting? Do you, like me, want to know the ending of the difficult parts of your story?

Take heart, my friends. Ecclesiastes 3:11 has something to say about waiting:

God has made everything fit beautifully in its appropriate time (Eccl 3:11).

Beauty: That's the ending of our stories. No, we do not know exactly how our stories will end, but we know God will make them beautiful in their time. This verse does not say some things, or even most things, will be made beautiful. Everything, it says, will be made beautiful.

God, in His wisdom, does not reveal the future. The end of Ecclesiastes 3:11 tells us that our minds were created so we do not know the future. The matter at hand is trust. If we trust God, then we believe He can and will make everything beautiful. Even though we do not know the future, we know that the One who holds our future can be trusted.

When I'm reading a book by a new author, I'm not yet sure I can trust the author, and I like to read the ending of that book. I don't want to invest time or energy in the story only to find that the ending leaves me heartbroken or with more questions than answers. But when I read a book by an author I've read before, I do not read the ending. I already trust the author to write a compelling story with a beautiful ending.

If I can trust a human author to deliver a trustworthy story, how much more can I trust the God who created me to make every chapter of my story beautiful in its time? Hasn't God proven Himself trustworthy to make something beautiful in every difficult chapter of my life thus far?

If He has done it before, then He will do it again. We can trust Him.

What are you waiting on today? I cannot tell you how this chapter of your story will end, but I can promise that God will make it beautiful in its time. Will you trust Him?

THE PROBLEM OF INJUSTICE AND OPPRESSION

16 I saw something else on earth:
In the place of justice, there was wickedness,
and in the place of fairness, there was wickedness.
17 I thought to myself, "God will judge both
the righteous and the wicked;
for there is an appropriate time for every activity,
and there is a time of judgment for every deed."
18 I also thought to myself, "It is for the sake of people,
so God can clearly show them that they are like animals.
19 For the fate of humans and the fate of animals are the same:
As one dies, so dies the other; both have the same breath.
There is no advantage for humans over animals,
for both are fleeting.
20 Both go to the same place,
both come from the dust,
and to dust both return.
21 Who really knows if the human spirit ascends upward,
and the animal's spirit descends into the earth?"
22 So I perceived there is nothing better than
for people to enjoy their work,
because that is their reward;
for who can show them what the future holds?

EVIL OPPRESSION ON EARTH

4 So I again considered all the oppression
that continually occurs on earth.
This is what I saw:
The oppressed were in tears, but no one was comforting them;
no one delivers them from the power of their oppressors.
2 So I considered those who are dead and gone
more fortunate than those who are still alive.
3 But better than both is the one who has not been born
and has not seen the evil things that are done on earth.

LABOR MOTIVATED BY ENVY

4 Then I considered all the skillful work that is done:
Surely it is nothing more than competition
between one person and another.
This also is profitless—like chasing the wind.
5 The fool folds his hands and does no work,
so he has nothing to eat but his own flesh.
6 Better is one handful with some rest
than two hands full of toil and chasing the wind.

LABOR MOTIVATED BY GREED

7 So I again considered another futile thing on earth:
8 A man who is all alone with no companion,
he has no children nor siblings;
yet there is no end to all his toil,
and he is never satisfied with riches.
He laments, "For whom am I toiling and
depriving myself of pleasure?"
This also is futile and a burdensome task!

LABOR IS BENEFICIAL WHEN ITS REWARDS ARE SHARED

9 Two people are better than one,
because they can reap more benefit from their labor.
10 For if they fall, one will help his companion up,
but pity the person who falls down and
has no one to help him up.
11 Furthermore, if two lie down together,
they can keep each other warm,
but how can one person keep warm by himself?
12 Although an assailant may overpower one person,
two can withstand him.
Moreover, a three-stranded cord
is not quickly broken.

LABOR MOTIVATED BY PRESTIGE SEEKING

13 A poor but wise youth is better than
an old and foolish king
who no longer knows how to receive advice.
14 For he came out of prison to become king,
even though he had been born poor in
what would become his kingdom.
15 I considered all the living who walk on earth,
as well as the successor who would arise in his place.
16 There is no end to all the people nor
to the past generations,
yet future generations will not rejoice in him.
This also is profitless and like chasing the wind.

RASH VOWS

5 Be careful what you do when you go to the temple of God;
draw near to listen rather than to
offer a sacrifice like fools,
for they do not realize that they are doing wrong.
2 Do not be rash with your mouth or hasty in your
heart to bring up a matter before God,
for God is in heaven and you are on earth!
Therefore, let your words be few.
3 Just as dreams come when there are many cares,
so the rash vow of a fool occurs when
there are many words.
4 When you make a vow to God,
do not delay in paying it.
For God takes no pleasure in fools:
Pay what you vow!
5 It is better for you not to vow
than to vow and not pay it.
6 Do not let your mouth cause you to sin,
and do not tell the priest, "It was a mistake!"
Why make God angry at you
so that he would destroy the work of your hands?
7 Just as there is futility in many dreams,
so also in many words.
Therefore, fear God.

REFLECT

Though it is often hard to work with or depend on others, why is community such a crucial aspect of our lives?

GOVERNMENT CORRUPTION

8 If you see the extortion of the poor,
or the perversion of justice and
fairness in the government,
do not be astonished by the matter.
For the high official is watched by a higher official,
and there are higher ones over them!
9 The produce of the land is seized by all of them,
even the king is served by the fields.

COVETOUSNESS

10 The one who loves money will never
be satisfied with money,
he who loves wealth will never be satisfied with his income.
This also is futile.
11 When someone's prosperity increases, those
who consume it also increase;
so what does its owner gain, except that
he gets to see it with his eyes?
12 The sleep of the laborer is pleasant—
whether he eats little or much—
but the wealth of the rich will not allow him to sleep.

MATERIALISM THWARTS ENJOYMENT OF LIFE

13 Here is a misfortune on earth that I have seen:
Wealth hoarded by its owner to his own misery.
14 Then that wealth was lost through bad luck;
although he fathered a son, he has nothing left to give him.
15 Just as he came forth from his mother's womb,
naked will he return as he came,
and he will take nothing in his hand that
he may carry away from his toil.
16 This is another misfortune:
Just as he came, so will he go.
What did he gain from toiling for the wind?
17 Surely, he ate in darkness every day of his life,
and he suffered greatly with sickness and anger.

ENJOY THE FRUIT OF YOUR LABOR

18 I have seen personally what is the only beneficial
and appropriate course of action for people:
to eat and drink, and find enjoyment in
all their hard work on earth
during the few days of their life that God has given them,
for this is their reward.
19 To every man whom God has given wealth and possessions,
he has also given him the ability
to eat from them, to receive his reward,
and to find enjoyment in his toil;
these things are the gift of God.
20 For he does not think much about
the fleeting days of his life
because God keeps him preoccupied with
the joy he derives from his activity.

NOT EVERYONE ENJOYS LIFE

6 Here is another misfortune that I have seen on earth,
and it weighs heavily on people:
2 God gives a man riches, property, and wealth
so that he lacks nothing that his heart desires,
yet God does not enable him to enjoy
the fruit of his labor—
instead, someone else enjoys it!
This is fruitless and a grave misfortune.
3 Even if a man fathers a hundred
children and lives many years,
even if he lives a long, long time, but
cannot enjoy his prosperity—
even if he were to live forever—
I would say, "A stillborn child is better off than he is."
4 Though the stillborn child came into the world
for no reason and departed into darkness,
though its name is shrouded in darkness,
5 though it never saw the light of day nor knew anything,
yet it has more rest than that man—
6 if he should live a thousand years twice,
yet does not enjoy his prosperity.
For both of them die!
7 All man's labor is for nothing more
than to fill his stomach—
yet his appetite is never satisfied!
8 So what advantage does a wise man have over a fool?
And what advantage does a pauper gain
by knowing how to survive?
9 It is better to be content with what the eyes can see
than for one's heart always to crave more.
This continual longing is futile—like chasing the wind.

THE FUTILE WAY LIFE WORKS

10 Whatever has happened was foreordained,
and what happens to a person was also foreknown.
It is useless for him to argue with God about his fate
because God is more powerful than he is.
11 The more one argues with words, the less he accomplishes.
How does that benefit him?
12 For no one knows what is best for a person during his life—
during the few days of his fleeting life—
for they pass away like a shadow.
Nor can anyone tell him what the future
will hold for him on earth.

LIFE IS BRIEF AND DEATH IS CERTAIN

7 A good reputation is better than precious perfume;
likewise, the day of one's death is better
than the day of one's birth.
2 It is better to go to a funeral
than a feast.
For death is the destiny of every person,
and the living should take this to heart.

3 Sorrow is better than laughter,
because sober reflection is good for the heart.
4 The heart of the wise is in the house of mourning,
but the heart of fools is in the house of merrymaking.

FRIVOLOUS LIVING VERSUS WISDOM

5 It is better for a person to receive a
rebuke from those who are wise
than to listen to the song of fools.
6 For like the crackling of quick-burning
thorns under a cooking pot,
so is the laughter of the fool.
This kind of folly also is useless.

HUMAN WISDOM OVERTURNED BY ADVERSITY

7 Surely oppression can turn a wise person into a fool;
likewise, a bribe corrupts the heart.
8 The end of a matter is better than its beginning;
likewise, patience is better than pride.
9 Do not let yourself be quickly provoked,
for anger resides in the lap of fools.
10 Do not say, "Why were the old days
better than these days?"
for it is not wise to ask that.

WISDOM CAN LENGTHEN ONE'S LIFE

11 Wisdom, like an inheritance, is a good thing;
it benefits those who see the light of day.
12 For wisdom provides protection,
just as money provides protection.
But the advantage of knowledge is this:
Wisdom preserves the life of its owner.

WISDOM ACKNOWLEDGES GOD'S ORCHESTRATION OF LIFE

13 Consider the work of God:
For who can make straight what he has bent?
14 In times of prosperity be joyful,
but in times of adversity consider this:
God has made one as well as the other,
so that no one can discover what the future holds.

REFLECT

How does the sovereignty of God keep our lives together? Are we able to change God's mind?

EXCEPTIONS TO THE LAW OF RETRIBUTION

15 During the days of my fleeting life I have
seen both of these things:
Sometimes a righteous person dies prematurely
in spite of his righteousness,
and sometimes a wicked person lives
long in spite of his evil deeds.
16 So do not be excessively righteous
or excessively wise;
otherwise you might be disappointed.
17 Do not be excessively wicked and do not be a fool;
otherwise you might die before your time.

18 It is best to take hold of one warning without
letting go of the other warning;
for the one who fears God will follow both warnings.

WISDOM NEEDED BECAUSE NO ONE IS TRULY RIGHTEOUS

19 Wisdom gives a wise person more protection
than ten rulers in a city.
20 For there is not one truly righteous person on the earth
who continually does good and never sins.
21 Also, do not pay attention to everything that people say;
otherwise, you might even hear your servant cursing you.
22 For you know in your own heart
that you also have cursed others many times.

HUMAN WISDOM IS LIMITED

23 I have examined all this by wisdom;
I said, "I am determined to comprehend
this"—but it was beyond my grasp.
24 Whatever has happened is beyond human understanding;
it is far deeper than anyone can fathom.

TRUE RIGHTEOUSNESS AND WISDOM ARE VIRTUALLY NONEXISTENT

25 I tried to understand, examine, and comprehend
the role of wisdom in the scheme of things,
and to understand the stupidity of
wickedness and the insanity of folly.
26 I discovered this:
More bitter than death is the kind of
woman who is like a hunter's snare;
her heart is like a hunter's net and her
hands are like prison chains.
The man who pleases God escapes her,
but the sinner is captured by her.
27 The Teacher says:
I discovered this while trying to discover
the scheme of things, item by item.
28 What I have continually sought, I have not found;
I have found only one upright man among a thousand,
but I have not found one upright
woman among all of them.
29 This alone have I discovered: God
made humankind upright,
but they have sought many evil schemes.

HUMAN GOVERNMENT DEMONSTRATES LIMITATIONS OF WISDOM

8 Who is a wise person? Who knows
the solution to a problem?
A person's wisdom brightens his appearance,
and softens his harsh countenance.
2 Obey the king's command,
because you took an oath before God to be loyal to him.

3 Do not rush out of the king's presence in haste—
do not delay when the matter is unpleasant,
for he can do whatever he pleases.
4 Surely the king's authority is absolute;
no one can say to him, "What are you doing?"
5 Whoever obeys his command will not experience harm,
and a wise person knows the proper time and procedure.
6 For there is a proper time and procedure for every matter,
for the oppression of the king is severe upon his victim.
7 Surely no one knows the future,
and no one can tell another person what will happen.
8 Just as no one has power over the wind to restrain it,
so no one has power over the day of his death.
Just as no one can be discharged during the battle,
so wickedness cannot rescue the wicked.
9 While applying my mind to everything that
happens in this world, I have seen all this:
Sometimes one person dominates
other people to their harm.

CONTRADICTIONS TO THE LAW OF RETRIBUTION

10 Not only that, but I have seen the wicked
approaching and entering the temple,
and as they left the holy temple, they
boasted in the city that they had done so.
This also is an enigma.
11 When a sentence is not executed at once against a crime,
the human heart is encouraged to do evil.
12 Even though a sinner might commit a hundred
crimes and still live a long time,
yet I know that it will go well with God-fearing
people—for they stand in fear before him.
13 But it will not go well with the wicked,
nor will they prolong their days like a shadow,
because they do not stand in fear before God.
14 Here is another enigma that occurs on earth:
Sometimes there are righteous people
who get what the wicked deserve,
and sometimes there are wicked people
who get what the righteous deserve.
I said, "This also is an enigma."

ENJOY LIFE IN SPITE OF ITS INJUSTICES

15 So I recommend the enjoyment of life,
for there is nothing better on earth for a person
to do except to eat, drink, and enjoy life.
So joy will accompany him in his toil
during the days of his life that God gives him on earth.

LIMITATIONS OF HUMAN WISDOM

16 When I tried to gain wisdom
and to observe the activity on earth—
even though it prevents anyone from sleeping day or night—
17 then I discerned all that God has done:

No one really comprehends what happens on earth.
Despite all human efforts to discover
it, no one can ever grasp it.
Even if a wise person claimed that he understood,
he would not really comprehend it.

EVERYONE WILL DIE

9 So I reflected on all this, attempting to clear it all up.
I concluded that the righteous and the wise, as
well as their works, are in the hand of God;
whether a person will be loved or hated—
no one knows what lies ahead.
2 Everyone shares the same fate—
the righteous and the wicked,
the good and the bad,
the ceremonially clean and unclean,
those who offer sacrifices and those who do not.
What happens to the good person,
also happens to the sinner;
what happens to those who make vows, also
happens to those who are afraid to make vows.
3 This is the unfortunate fact about
everything that happens on earth:
the same fate awaits everyone.
In addition to this, the hearts
of all people are full of evil,
and there is folly in their hearts during
their lives—then they die.

BETTER TO BE POOR BUT ALIVE THAN RICH BUT DEAD

4 But whoever is among the living has hope;
a live dog is better than a dead lion.
5 For the living know that they will die, but
the dead do not know anything;
they have no further reward—and even
the memory of them disappears.
6 What they loved, as well as what they hated
and envied, perished long ago,
and they no longer have a part in
anything that happens on earth.

LIFE IS BRIEF, SO CHERISH ITS JOYS

7 Go, eat your food with joy,
and drink your wine with a happy heart,
because God has already approved your works.
8 Let your clothes always be white,
and do not spare precious ointment on your head.
9 Enjoy life with your beloved wife during
all the days of your fleeting life
that God has given you on earth during
all your fleeting days;
for that is your reward in life and in your
burdensome work on earth.

CHALLENGE

Ecclesiastes realistically depicts the struggles and frustrations of life, and it commends taking joy in God's gifts (food, drink, relationships, and work). How does rejoicing in these small things help us with the things we don't understand, like death and suffering?

10 Whatever you find to do with your hands,
do it with all your might,
because there is neither work nor planning
nor knowledge nor wisdom in the grave,
the place where you will eventually go.

WISDOM CANNOT PROTECT AGAINST SEEMINGLY CHANCE EVENTS

11 Again, I observed this on the earth:
the race is not always won by the swiftest,
the battle is not always won by the strongest;
prosperity does not always belong to
those who are the wisest,
wealth does not always belong to those
who are the most discerning,
nor does success always come to those
with the most knowledge—
for time and chance may overcome them all.
12 Surely, no one knows his appointed time.
Like fish that are caught in a deadly net, and
like birds that are caught in a snare—
just like them, all people are ensnared at an
unfortunate time that falls upon them suddenly.

MOST PEOPLE ARE NOT RECEPTIVE TO WISE COUNSEL

13 This is what I also observed about wisdom on earth,
and it is a great burden to me:
14 There was once a small city with a few men in it,
and a mighty king attacked it, besieging it and
building strong siege works against it.
15 However, a poor but wise man lived in the city,
and he could have delivered the city by his wisdom,
but no one listened to that poor man.
16 So I concluded that wisdom is better than might,
but a poor man's wisdom is despised; no
one ever listens to his advice.

WISDOM VERSUS FOOLS, SIN, AND FOLLY

17 The words of the wise are heard in quiet,
more than the shouting of a ruler
is heard among fools.
18 Wisdom is better than weapons of war,
but one sinner can destroy much that is good.

10 One dead fly makes the perfumer's
ointment give off a rancid stench,
so a little folly can outweigh much wisdom.

WISDOM CAN BE NULLIFIED BY THE CAPRICE OF RULERS

2 A wise person's good sense protects him,
but a fool's lack of sense leaves him vulnerable.
3 Even when a fool walks along the road he lacks sense,
and shows everyone what a fool he is.

4 If the anger of the ruler flares up against you,
do not resign from your position,
for a calm response can undo great offenses.
5 I have seen another misfortune on the earth:
It is an error a ruler makes.
6 Fools are placed in many positions of authority,
while wealthy men sit in lowly positions.
7 I have seen slaves on horseback
and princes walking on foot like slaves.

WISDOM IS NEEDED TO AVERT DANGERS IN EVERYDAY LIFE

8 One who digs a pit may fall into it,
and one who breaks through a wall
may be bitten by a snake.
9 One who quarries stones may
be injured by them;
one who splits logs may be endangered by them.
10 If an iron axhead is blunt and a workman
does not sharpen its edge,
he must exert a great deal of effort;
so wisdom has the advantage
of giving success.
11 If the snake should bite before it is charmed,
the snake charmer is in trouble.

WORDS AND WORKS OF WISE MEN AND FOOLS

12 The words of a wise person win him favor,
but the words of a fool are self-destructive.
13 At the beginning his words are foolish
and at the end his talk is wicked madness,
14 yet a fool keeps on babbling.
No one knows what will happen;
who can tell him what will happen in the future?
15 The toil of a stupid fool wears him out,
because he does not even know the way to the city.

THE PROBLEM WITH FOOLISH RULERS

16 Woe to you, O land, when your king is childish,
and your princes feast in the morning.
17 Blessed are you, O land, when your
king is the son of nobility,
and your princes feast at the proper time—
with self-control and not in drunkenness.
18 Because of laziness the roof caves in,
and because of idle hands the house leaks.
19 Feasts are made for laughter,
and wine makes life merry,
but money is the answer for everything.
20 Do not curse a king even in your thoughts,
and do not curse the rich while in your bedroom;
for a bird might report what you are thinking,
or some winged creature might
repeat your words.

IGNORANCE OF THE FUTURE DEMANDS DILIGENCE IN THE PRESENT

11 Send your grain overseas,
for after many days you will get a return.
2 Divide your merchandise among seven
or even eight investments,
for you do not know what calamity may happen on earth.
3 If the clouds are full of rain, they will
empty themselves on the earth,
and whether a tree falls to the south or to the
north, the tree will lie wherever it falls.
4 He who watches the wind will not sow,
and he who observes the clouds will not reap.
5 Just as you do not know the path of the wind,
or how the bones form in the womb of a pregnant woman,
so you do not know the work of God
who makes everything.
6 Sow your seed in the morning,
and do not stop working until the evening;
for you do not know which activity will succeed—
whether this one or that one, or whether
both will prosper equally.

LIFE SHOULD BE ENJOYED BECAUSE DEATH IS INEVITABLE

7 Light is sweet,
and it is pleasant for a person to see the sun.
8 So, if a man lives many years, let him rejoice in them all,
but let him remember that the days of darkness will
be many—all that is about to come is obscure.

ENJOY LIFE TO THE FULLEST UNDER THE FEAR OF GOD

9 Rejoice, young man, while you are young,
and let your heart cheer you in the days of your youth.
Follow the impulses of your heart and
the desires of your eyes,
but know that God will judge your motives and actions.
10 Banish emotional stress from your mind.
and put away pain from your body;
for youth and the prime of life are fleeting.

FEAR GOD NOW BECAUSE OLD AGE AND DEATH COME QUICKLY

12 So remember your Creator in the days of your youth—
before the difficult days come,
and the years draw near when you will
say, "I have no pleasure in them";
2 before the sun and the light of the
moon and the stars grow dark,
and the clouds disappear after the rain;
3 when those who keep watch over the
house begin to tremble,
and the virile men begin to stoop over,

and the grinders begin to cease because they grow few,
and those who look through the windows grow dim,
4 and the doors along the street are shut;
when the sound of the grinding mill grows low,
and one is awakened by the sound of a bird,
and all their songs grow faint,
5 and they are afraid of heights and
the dangers in the street;
the almond blossoms grow white,
and the grasshopper drags itself along,
and the caper berry shrivels up—
because man goes to his eternal home,
and the mourners go about in the streets—
6 before the silver cord is removed,
or the golden bowl is broken,
or the pitcher is shattered at the well,
or the water wheel is broken at the cistern—
7 and the dust returns to the earth as it was,
and the life's breath returns to God who gave it.

REFLECT

Do you agree with the author's outlook on life? Do you think it is wise to live this way? Why or why not?

CONCLUDING REFRAIN: THE TEACHER RESTATES HIS THESIS

8 "Absolutely futile!" laments the Teacher,
"All these things are futile!"

CONCLUDING EPILOGUE: THE TEACHER'S ADVICE IS WISE

9 Not only was the Teacher wise,
but he also taught knowledge to the people;
he carefully evaluated and arranged many proverbs.
10 The Teacher sought to find delightful words,
and to write accurately truthful sayings.
11 The words of the sages are like prods,
and the collected sayings are like firmly fixed nails;
they are given by one shepherd.

CONCLUDING EXHORTATION: FEAR GOD AND OBEY HIS COMMANDS

12 Be warned, my son, of anything in addition to them.
There is no end to the making of many books,
and much study is exhausting to the body.
13 Having heard everything, I have reached this conclusion:
Fear God and keep his commandments,
because this is the whole duty of man.
14 For God will evaluate every deed,
including every secret thing, whether good or evil.

Surging Waters CANNOT quench love; floodwaters CANNOT overflow it

MEMORY VERSE

Surging waters cannot quench love; floodwaters cannot overflow it. If someone were to offer all his possessions to buy love, the offer would be utterly despised.

Song of Solomon 8:7

Song of Solomon

INTRODUCTION

The Power of Love

Song of Solomon is a stunning work of poetry describing the beauty and intimacy of married love. Song of Solomon exemplifies a way to express love in a healthy, sexual relationship within the context of marriage. While the book has been interpreted in many different ways, it communicates a central truth: God approves and encourages sexual pleasure in marriage.

Song of Solomon is classified as a poetic book, but its uniqueness lies in its lyric idyll form. The two main characteristics of this type of poetry include events that do not occur in chronological order and the use of a chorus. Some of the events and speeches are not written in the order they occur, and the storyline is often suspended. The chorus provides transitions between scenes and adds emphasis to relevant themes.

King Solomon is the author of the Book of Song of Solomon. He is named several times in the book (1:1; 3:7, 9, 11; 8:11, 12). Solomon was known for his great wisdom, but he was not known for his commitment to one wife. Scholars suggest that this was written near the end of Solomon's life when he had seen the error in his ways and the futility of his many relationships.

Song of Solomon is a unique book that provides insight into what God desires for His people. While marriage does not complete our humanity or make us holy (Jesus was the only perfect human, and He was both celibate and unmarried), it does provide a safe place for the sexual expression God designed. Song of Solomon encourages us to love God greatly by showing us how God provides for us and protects us and by giving us a clear context in which to express sexual love. It also offers us a glimpse into the unconditional, powerful love of our Creator, who loves us infinitely more than a spouse ever could.

Spain

OFFICIAL LANGUAGE
Spanish
POPULATION
46,657,000
UNREACHED POPULATION
1,008,000
PROFESSING CHRISTIANS
77.5%

Angela's Home

Say a Prayer Today

Pray for Angela as she shares the gospel with others in Spain. Pray that her ministry would be effective and clear and that many would come to know the love of Christ through her life.

HISTORY BIT

It is believed that Paul traveled to Spain on one of his later missionary journeys. In A.D. 409 the Arians invaded the peninsula and converted the area to Catholicism, which was declared the state religion in A.D. 589.*

Source Information:
https://joshuaproject.net/countries/SP
*David B. Barrett, *World Christian Encyclopedia*, Spain (New York, NY: Oxford University Press, 1982), 628.

LOVE YOUR NEIGHBOR

Her Journey

ANGELA'S STORY

When thinking about relationships that have suffered one too many setbacks, disappointments, or extremely hurt feelings seemingly beyond repair, I am often reminded that God's truth and the world's truth are not one and the same.

When the world would have you abruptly turn your back on someone, God's heart chooses love instead. Even if there is a need to part ways, I have learned firsthand, that when we act in God's love, it ultimately brings about His better plan for everyone involved. His supernatural love brings us together and allows the Holy Spirit to restore what has been broken.

On the mission field in Europe, we see how popular wisdom has blurred the reality of God's perfect love and will for His children. Our hearts yearn for the secular world to understand the power of God's love. What seems impossible, humanly speaking, God views as an opportunity to show His amazing restorative power to reconcile us to one another, and most importantly, to Himself.

As we share God's truth in Spain, our desire is that people would see this power in the midst of our own struggling relationships. God desires to show a broken world that only He is able to keep love's flame alive. Even when this love is not reciprocated, the Holy Spirit enables us to become a reflection of God's faithful love.

Song of Solomon is like opening a box of love notes stored in a corner of the attic, filled with old pictures of young, almost naive love. And still, we are overwhelmed by the bigger picture these passages depict: Christ's profound supernatural love for His bride, the Church. His plan for us is magnificent: through Christ in us, we love others regardless of the many waters that may arise.

4 WEEK READING PLAN

LOVE HIS WORD

	MONDAY	TUESDAY	WEDNESDAY	THURSDAY	FRIDAY
1	Ecclesiastes 1	Ecclesiastes 2	Ecclesiastes 3	Ecclesiastes 4	Ecclesiastes 5
	SOAP Ecclesiastes 1:17–18	SOAP Ecclesiastes 2:11	SOAP Ecclesiastes 3:11	SOAP Ecclesiastes 4:9–10	SOAP Ecclesiastes 5:10
2	Ecclesiastes 6	Ecclesiastes 7	Ecclesiastes 8	Ecclesiastes 9:1—10:1	Ecclesiastes 10:2–20
	SOAP Ecclesiastes 6:12	SOAP Ecclesiastes 7:11–12	SOAP Ecclesiastes 8:15	SOAP Ecclesiastes 9:11	SOAP Ecclesiastes 10:12
3	Ecclesiastes 11	Ecclesiastes 12	Song of Solomon 1	Song of Solomon 2	Song of Solomon 3
	SOAP Ecclesiastes 11:7–8	SOAP Ecclesiastes 12:13–14	SOAP Song of Solomon 1:15	SOAP Song of Solomon 2:10–11	SOAP Song of Solomon 3:5
4	Song of Solomon 4:1—5:1	Song of Solomon 5:2–16	Song of Solomon 6:1–12	Song of Solomon 6:13—7:13	Song of Solomon 8
	SOAP Song of Solomon 4:9	SOAP Song of Solomon 5:9	SOAP Song of Solomon 6:3	SOAP Song of Solomon 7:6	SOAP Song of Solomon 8:7

TITLE/SUPERSCRIPTION

1 Solomon's Most Excellent Love Song.

THE DESIRE FOR LOVE

The Beloved to Her Lover:

2 Oh, how I wish you would kiss me passionately!
For your lovemaking is more delightful than wine.
3 The fragrance of your colognes is delightful;
your name is like the finest perfume.
No wonder the young women adore you!
4 Draw me after you; let us hurry!
May the king bring me into
his bedroom chambers!

The Maidens to the Lover:

We will rejoice and delight in you;
we will praise your love more than wine.

The Beloved to Her Lover:

How rightly the young women adore you!

THE COUNTRY MAIDEN AND THE DAUGHTERS OF JERUSALEM

The Beloved to the Maidens:

5 I am dark but lovely, O maidens of Jerusalem,
dark like the tents of Qedar,
lovely like the tent curtains of Salmah.
6 Do not stare at me because I am dark,
for the sun has burned my skin.
My brothers were angry with me;
they made me the keeper of the vineyards.
Alas, my own vineyard I could not keep!

THE SHEPHERD AND THE SHEPHERDESS

The Beloved to Her Lover:

7 Tell me, O you whom my heart loves,
where do you pasture your sheep?
Where do you rest your sheep
during the midday heat?
Tell me lest I wander around
beside the flocks of your companions!

The Lover to His Beloved:

8 If you do not know, O most beautiful of women,
simply follow the tracks of my flock,
and pasture your little lambs
beside the tents of the shepherds.

THE BEAUTIFUL MARE AND THE FRAGRANT MYRRH

The Lover to His Beloved:

9 O my beloved, you are like a mare
among Pharaoh's stallions.

10 Your cheeks are beautiful with ornaments;
your neck is lovely with strings of jewels.
11 We will make for you gold ornaments
studded with silver.

The Beloved about Her Lover:

12 While the king was at his banqueting table,
my nard gave forth its fragrance.
13 My beloved is like a fragrant pouch of myrrh
spending the night between my breasts.
14 My beloved is like a cluster of henna blossoms
in the vineyards of En Gedi.

REFLECT

The Lover and the Beloved continually tell each other what they love and admire about one another. How important are words of affirmation within a marriage relationship?

MUTUAL PRAISE AND ADMIRATION

The Lover to His Beloved:

15 Oh, how beautiful you are, my beloved!
Oh, how beautiful you are!
Your eyes are like doves!

The Beloved to Her Lover:

16 Oh, how handsome you are, my lover!
Oh, how delightful you are!
The lush foliage is our canopied bed;
17 the cedars are the beams of our bedroom chamber;
the pines are the rafters of our bedroom.

THE LILY AMONG THE THORNS AND THE APPLE TREE IN THE FOREST

The Beloved to Her Lover:

I am a meadow flower from Sharon,
a lily from the valleys.

The Lover to His Beloved:

2 Like a lily among the thorns,
so is my darling among the maidens.

The Beloved about Her Lover:

3 Like an apple tree among the trees of the forest,
so is my beloved among the young men.
I delight to sit in his shade,
and his fruit is sweet to my taste.

THE BANQUET HALL FOR THE LOVESICK

The Beloved about Her Lover:

4 He brought me into the banquet hall,
and he looked at me lovingly.
5 Sustain me with raisin cakes,
refresh me with apples,
for I am faint with love.

THE DOUBLE REFRAIN: EMBRACING AND ADJURATION

6 His left hand is under my head,
and his right hand embraces me.

The Beloved to the Maidens:

7 I admonish you, O maidens of Jerusalem,
by the gazelles and by the young does
of the open fields:
Do not awaken or arouse love until it pleases!

THE ARRIVAL OF THE LOVER

The Beloved about Her Lover:

8 Listen! My lover is approaching!
Look! Here he comes,
leaping over the mountains,
bounding over the hills!
9 My lover is like a gazelle or a young stag.
Look! There he stands behind our wall,
gazing through the window,
peering through the lattice.

REFLECT

How does the Lover pursue his Beloved? Why is it essential to pursue one another in marriage?

THE SEASON OF LOVE AND THE SONG OF THE TURTLEDOVE

The Lover to His Beloved:

10 My lover spoke to me, saying:
"Arise, my darling;
My beautiful one, come away with me!
11 Look! The winter has passed,
the winter rains are over and gone.
12 Blossoms have appeared in the land,
the time for pruning and singing has come;
the voice of the turtledove is heard in our land.
13 The fig tree has ripened its figs,
the vines have blossomed and
give off their fragrance.
Arise, come away my darling;
my beautiful one, come away with me!"

THE DOVE IN THE CLEFTS OF EN GEDI

The Lover to His Beloved:

14 O my dove, in the clefts of the rock,
in the hiding places of the mountain crags,
let me see your face,
let me hear your voice;
for your voice is sweet,
and your face is lovely.

THE FOXES IN THE VINEYARD

The Beloved to Her Lover:

15 Catch the foxes for us,
the little foxes,
that ruin the vineyards—
for our vineyard is in bloom.

POETIC REFRAIN: MUTUAL POSSESSION

The Beloved about Her Lover:

16 My lover is mine and I am his;
he grazes among the lilies.

LOVE TO GROW

THE LITTLE FOXES

SONG OF SOLOMON 2:15

Even in the greatest of love stories, there will be challenges, opposition, and conflict. Often times, it is the little things that threaten an intimate relationship. In Song of Solomon 2, the beloved bride speaks to her bridegroom. After describing the intense love she has for him, she urges him in verse 15, "Catch the foxes for us, the little foxes, that ruin the vineyards——for our vineyard is in bloom."

Jesus describes Himself in John 15:5 saying,

"I am the vine; you are the branches. The one who remains in me—and I in him—bears much fruit."

The fruit of the Spirit is love, joy, peace, patience, kindness, goodness, faithfulness, gentleness, and self-control (see Gal 5:22–23). Our relationships have the potential to grow into a fruitful vineyard. However, the development of this fruit requires Christ-centered commitment, obedience, discipline, and intentional effort.

The little foxes described in Song of Solomon 2:15 represent the sins, obstacles, and distractions that threaten to destroy our relationships and devour our fruit. What are the little foxes in our lives that decrease our love, steal our joy, disrupt our peace, and test our patience? We must be diligent in our relationships to ruthlessly capture and remove these potential threats before they grow larger and consume our blossoming fruit.

God calls us to an intimate, loving relationship with Him. He helps us center our relationships with others around His unfailing love. True love is a gift from God. Therefore, our relationships must be submitted to Him in order to thrive and persevere. The fruit that results from a Christ-centered marriage will feed and bless those God places around it.

Of course, no marriage is perfect. When two imperfect people become one, there will be conflict and disagreement. However, love is perfected wherever God dwells. As we diligently seek Him, He guides the way to forgiveness, reconciliation, and peace.

As we love God greatly, we embed Him confidently at the center of our marriages, our families, and our friendships. We protect our vineyards by catching little foxes quickly and nurturing our fruit so it will thrive and bloom.

THE GAZELLE AND THE RUGGED MOUNTAINS

The Beloved to Her Lover:

17 Until the dawn arrives and the shadows flee,
turn, my beloved—
be like a gazelle or a young stag
on the mountain gorges.

THE LOST LOVER IS FOUND

The Beloved about Her Lover:

3 All night long on my bed
I longed for my lover.
I longed for him but he never appeared.
2 "I will arise and look all around throughout the town,
and throughout the streets and squares;
I will search for my beloved."
I searched for him but I did not find him.
3 The night watchmen found me—the
ones who guard the city walls.
"Have you seen my beloved?"
4 Scarcely had I passed them by
when I found my beloved!
I held onto him tightly and would not let him go
until I brought him to my mother's house,
to the bedroom chamber of the one who conceived me.

THE ADJURATION REFRAIN

The Beloved to the Maidens:

5 I admonish you, O maidens of Jerusalem,
by the gazelles and by the young does of the open fields:
"Do not awaken or arouse love until it pleases!"

THE ROYAL WEDDING PROCESSION

The Speaker:

6 Who is this coming up from the wilderness
like a column of smoke,
like a fragrant billow of myrrh and frankincense,
every kind of fragrant powder
of the traveling merchants?
7 Look! It is Solomon's portable couch!
It is surrounded by sixty warriors,
some of Israel's mightiest warriors.
8 All of them are skilled with a sword,
well trained in the art of warfare.
Each has his sword at his side,
to guard against the terrors of the night.
9 King Solomon made a sedan chair for himself
of wood imported from Lebanon.
10 Its posts were made of silver;
its back was made of gold.
Its seat was upholstered with purple wool;
its interior was inlaid with leather by
the maidens of Jerusalem.
11 Come out, O maidens of Zion,
and gaze upon King Solomon!

REFLECT

When is it appropriate to awaken love? Why is it so important to be careful not to awaken love until the proper time?

He is wearing the crown with which
his mother crowned him
on his wedding day,
on the most joyous day of his life!

THE WEDDING NIGHT: PRAISE OF THE BRIDE

The Lover to His Beloved:

4 Oh, you are beautiful, my darling!
Oh, you are beautiful!
Your eyes behind your veil are like doves.
Your hair is like a flock of female goats
descending from Mount Gilead.
2 Your teeth are like a flock of newly shorn sheep
coming up from the washing place;
each of them has a twin,
and not one of them is missing.
3 Your lips are like a scarlet thread;
your mouth is lovely.
Your forehead behind your veil
is like a slice of pomegranate.
4 Your neck is like the tower of David
built with courses of stones;
one thousand shields are hung on it—
all shields of valiant warriors.
5 Your two breasts are like two fawns,
twins of the gazelle
grazing among the lilies.
6 Until the dawn arrives
and the shadows flee,
I will go up to the mountain of myrrh,
and to the hill of frankincense.
7 You are altogether beautiful, my darling!
There is no blemish in you!

THE WEDDING NIGHT: BEAUTIFUL AS LEBANON

8 Come with me from Lebanon, my bride,
come with me from Lebanon.
Descend from the crest of Amana,
from the top of Senir, the summit of Hermon,
from the lions' dens
and the mountain haunts of the leopards.
9 You have stolen my heart, my sister, my bride!
You have stolen my heart with one
glance of your eyes,
with one jewel of your necklace.
10 How delightful is your love, my sister, my bride!
How much better is your love than wine;
the fragrance of your perfume
is better than any spice!
11 Your lips drip sweetness like
the honeycomb, my bride,
honey and milk are under your tongue.
The fragrance of your garments is like
the fragrance of Lebanon.

THE WEDDING NIGHT: THE DELIGHTFUL GARDEN

The Lover to His Beloved:

12 You are a locked garden, my sister, my bride;
you are an enclosed spring, a sealed-up fountain.
13 Your shoots are a royal garden full of pomegranates
with choice fruits:
henna with nard,
14 nard and saffron,
calamus and cinnamon with every kind of spice,
myrrh and aloes with all the finest spices.
15 You are a garden spring,
a well of fresh water flowing down from Lebanon.

The Beloved to Her Lover:

16 Awake, O north wind; come, O south wind!
Blow on my garden so that its fragrant spices
  may send out their sweet smell.
May my beloved come into his garden
and eat its delightful fruit!

The Lover to His Beloved:

I have entered my garden, O my sister, my bride;
I have gathered my myrrh with my balsam spice.
I have eaten my honeycomb and my honey;
I have drunk my wine and my milk!

The Poet to the Couple:

Eat, friends, and drink!
Drink freely, O lovers!

THE TRIALS OF LOVE: THE BELOVED'S DREAM OF LOSING HER LOVER

The Beloved about Her Lover:

2 I was asleep, but my mind was dreaming.
Listen! My lover is knocking at the door!

The Lover to His Beloved:

"Open for me, my sister, my darling,
my dove, my flawless one!
My head is drenched with dew,
my hair with the dampness of the night."

The Beloved to Her Lover:

3 "I have already taken off my robe—must I put it on again?
I have already washed my feet—must I soil them again?"
4 My lover thrust his hand through the hole,
and my feelings were stirred for him.
5 I arose to open for my beloved;
my hands dripped with myrrh—
my fingers flowed with myrrh
on the handles of the lock.
6 I opened for my beloved,
but my lover had already turned and gone away.
I fell into despair when he departed.

I looked for him but did not find him;
I called him but he did not answer me.
7 The watchmen found me as they made
their rounds in the city.
They beat me, they bruised me;
they took away my cloak, those watchmen on the walls!

REFLECT

How does the way the Beloved described her Lover encourage us to speak about a spouse?

THE TRIUMPH OF LOVE: THE BELOVED PRAISES HER LOVER

The Beloved to the Maidens:

8 I admonish you, O maidens of Jerusalem—
If you find my beloved, what will you tell him?
Tell him that I am lovesick!

The Maidens to The Beloved:

9 Why is your beloved better than others,
O most beautiful of women?
Why is your beloved better than others,
that you would admonish us in this manner?

The Beloved to the Maidens:

10 My beloved is dazzling and ruddy;
he stands out in comparison to all other men.
11 His head is like the purest gold.
His hair is curly—black like a raven.
12 His eyes are like doves by streams of water,
washed in milk, mounted like jewels.
13 His cheeks are like garden beds full of
balsam trees yielding perfume.
His lips are like lilies dripping with drops of myrrh.
14 His arms are like rods of gold set with chrysolite.
His abdomen is like polished ivory
inlaid with sapphires.
15 His legs are like pillars of marble
set on bases of pure gold.
His appearance is like Lebanon, choice as its cedars.
16 His mouth is very sweet;
he is totally desirable.
This is my beloved!
This is my companion, O maidens of Jerusalem!

THE LOST LOVER FOUND

The Maidens to the Beloved:

Where has your beloved gone,
O most beautiful among women?
Where has your beloved turned?
Tell us, that we may seek him with you.

The Beloved to the Maidens:

2 My beloved has gone down to his garden,
to the flowerbeds of balsam spices,
to graze in the gardens,
and to gather lilies.

POETIC REFRAIN: MUTUAL POSSESSION

The Beloved about Her Lover:

3 I am my lover's and my lover is mine;
he grazes among the lilies.

THE RENEWAL OF LOVE

The Lover to His Beloved:

4 My darling, you are as beautiful as Tirzah,
as lovely as Jerusalem,
as awe-inspiring as bannered armies.
5 Turn your eyes away from me—
they overwhelm me!
Your hair is like a flock of goats
descending from Mount Gilead.
6 Your teeth are like a flock of sheep
coming up from the washing;
each has its twin;
not one of them is missing.
7 Like a slice of pomegranate
is your forehead behind your veil.
8 There may be sixty queens,
and eighty concubines,
and young women without number.
9 But she is unique,
my dove, my perfect one!
She is the special daughter of her mother;
she is the favorite of the one who bore her.
The maidens saw her and
complimented her;
the queens and concubines praised her:
10 "Who is this who appears like the dawn?
Beautiful as the moon, bright as the sun,
awe-inspiring as the stars in procession?"

THE RETURN TO THE VINEYARDS

The Lover to His Beloved:

11 I went down to the orchard
of walnut trees,
to look for the blossoms of the valley,
to see if the vines had budded
or if the pomegranates were in bloom.
12 I was beside myself with joy!
There please give me your myrrh,
O daughter of my princely people.

THE LOVE SONG AND DANCE

The Lover to His Beloved:

13 Turn, turn, O Perfect One!
Turn, turn, that I may stare at you!

The Beloved to Her Lover:

Why do you gaze upon the Perfect One
like the dance of the Mahanaim?

The Lover to His Beloved:

7 How beautiful are your sandaled feet,
O nobleman's daughter!
The curves of your thighs are like jewels,
the work of the hands of a master craftsman.
2 Your navel is a round mixing bowl—
may it never lack mixed wine!
Your belly is a mound of wheat,
encircled by lilies.
3 Your two breasts are like two fawns,
twins of a gazelle.
4 Your neck is like a tower made of ivory.
Your eyes are the pools in Heshbon
by the gate of Bath Rabbim.
Your nose is like the tower of Lebanon
overlooking Damascus.
5 Your head crowns you like Mount Carmel.
The locks of your hair are like
royal tapestries—
the king is held captive in its tresses!
6 How beautiful you are! How lovely,
O love, with your delights!

THE PALM TREE AND THE PALM TREE CLIMBER

The Lover to His Beloved:

7 Your stature is like a palm tree,
and your breasts are like clusters of grapes.
8 I want to climb the palm tree,
and take hold of its fruit stalks.
May your breasts be like the clusters of grapes,
and may the fragrance of your breath
be like apples!
9 May your mouth be like the best wine,
flowing smoothly for my beloved,
gliding gently over our lips as we sleep together.

POETIC REFRAIN: MUTUAL POSSESSION

The Beloved about Her Lover:

10 I am my beloved's,
and he desires me!

THE JOURNEY TO THE COUNTRYSIDE

The Beloved to Her Lover:

11 Come, my beloved, let us go to the countryside;
let us spend the night in the villages.
12 Let us rise early to go to the vineyards,
to see if the vines have budded,
to see if their blossoms have opened,
if the pomegranates are in bloom—
there I will give you my love.
13 The mandrakes send out their fragrance;
over our door is every delicacy,
both new and old, which I have
stored up for you, my lover.

REFLECT

Why is sexual intimacy important in a marriage relationship? How does this strengthen the bond between husband and wife?

THE BELOVED'S WISH SONG

The Beloved to Her Lover:

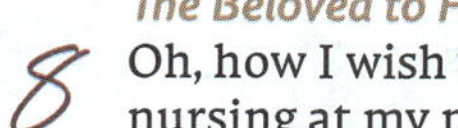
Oh, how I wish you were my little brother,
nursing at my mother's breasts;
if I saw you outside, I could kiss you—
surely no one would despise me!
2 I would lead you and bring you
to my mother's house,
the one who taught me.
I would give you spiced wine to drink,
the nectar of my pomegranates.

DOUBLE REFRAIN: EMBRACING AND ADJURATION

The Beloved about Her Lover:

3 His left hand is under my head,
and his right hand embraces me.

The Beloved to the Maidens:

4 I admonish you, O maidens of Jerusalem:
"Do not arouse or awaken love until it pleases!"

THE AWAKENING OF LOVE

The Maidens about His Beloved:

5 Who is this coming up from the wilderness,
leaning on her beloved?

The Beloved to Her Lover:

Under the apple tree I aroused you;
there your mother conceived you,
there she who bore you was in labor of childbirth.

THE NATURE OF TRUE LOVE

The Beloved to Her Lover:

6 Set me like a cylinder seal over your heart,
like a signet on your arm.
For love is as strong as death,
passion is as unrelenting as Sheol.
Its flames burst forth,
it is a blazing flame.
7 Surging waters cannot quench love;
floodwaters cannot overflow it.
If someone were to offer all his possessions to buy love,
the offer would be utterly despised.

CHALLENGE

What does this verse tell you about the importance of love? How does God display His powerful love to His people throughout Scripture?

THE BROTHER'S PLAN AND THE SISTER'S REWARD

The Beloved's Brothers:

8 We have a little sister,
and as yet she has no breasts.
What shall we do for our sister
on the day when she is spoken for?
9 If she is a wall,
we will build on her a battlement of silver;
but if she is a door,
we will barricade her with boards of cedar.

The Beloved:

10 I was a wall,
and my breasts were like fortress towers.
Then I found favor in his eyes.

SOLOMON'S VINEYARD AND THE BELOVED'S VINEYARD

The Beloved to Her Lover:

11 Solomon had a vineyard at Baal Hamon;
he leased out the vineyard to those who maintained it.
Each was to bring 1,000 shekels of silver for its fruit.
12 My vineyard, which belongs to me, is at my disposal alone.
The thousand shekels belong to you, O Solomon,
and 200 shekels belong to those who
maintain it for its fruit.

EPILOGUE: THE LOVER'S REQUEST AND HIS BELOVED'S INVITATION

The Lover to His Beloved:

13 O you who stay in the gardens,
my companions are listening attentively for your voice;
let me be the one to hear it!

The Beloved to Her Lover:

14 Make haste, my beloved!
Be like a gazelle or a young stag
on the mountains of spices.

PROPHECY
FOR THE NATIONS

PHOENICIA
♥

Mediterranean Sea

BASHAN
✚♠

♥●☗▲■✚
ISRAEL

GILEAD
♥✚

AMMON
♥●■

PHILISTIA
♥●▲■

MOAB
♥●▲■

EDOM
♥●■☾

EGYPT
●▲■

Red Sea

ABOUT THE PROPHETS

Throughout the history of Israel and Judah, God spoke through prophets. Some of these prophetic messages warned of coming judgment upon a nation. Others were messages for Israel about the judgment God would bring upon other nations. This map shows the connection between the prophets and the nations to whom or about whom they prophesied.

PROPHETS AND KEY LOCATIONS

- ♥ AMOS
- ★ DANIEL
- ● EZEKIEL
- ☗ HOSEA
- ▲ ISAIAH
- ■ JEREMIAH
- ◆ JONAH
- ✚ MICAH
- ♠ NAHUM
- ☾ OBADIAH

FOR I, THE LORD,
love justice AND
hate robbery AND SIN.
I WILL repay them
because of my
FAITHFULNESS;
I WILL MAKE A
permanent
COVENANT
with them

MEMORY VERSE

"For I, the LORD, love justice and hate robbery and sin. I will repay them because of my faithfulness; I will make a permanent covenant with them."

Isaiah 61:8

Isaiah

INTRODUCTION

Promise in the Midst of Judgment

The Book of Isaiah includes prophecies of destruction and judgment, but also beautiful promises of the coming Messiah. God called Isaiah to speak to the people concerning pending judgment, but also of their future restoration and hope. While Isaiah's words exhorted and warned the people, God also gave him a message to remind the people that He was a God who would always keep His promises.

Isaiah has sixty-six chapters, much like the canon of Scripture has sixty-six books. Chapters 1–39 carried a message of condemnation to the Israelites in the eighth century, warning them of their coming destruction by the nation of Assyria. Chapters 40–55 offered comfort to the future generation of exiles. It holds a message of hope and promise to the Jews in Babylon who thought God had abandoned His commitment. In chapters 56–66, Isaiah exhorted the people who had returned to Jerusalem with a message of promise of the coming Messiah and the new heaven and new earth.

The prophecies in Isaiah cover approximately three hundred years. Since prophecy is often a message from God about future events, it is reasonable to believe that God gave Isaiah this message for a future generation. Much of Isaiah's style and tone is consistent from beginning to end, offering strong evidence for one author, the prophet Isaiah himself. Isaiah began his prophetic ministry to the people of Judah around 755 B.C., thirty years before the Assyrian invasion of Israel.

Isaiah provides some of the most detailed depictions of the character of the coming Messiah. This book of prophecy encourages us to love God greatly as we read of His incredible heart to redeem His people. By sending His servant to become a sacrifice for His people, God displays His everlasting covenant and faithful love toward His children.

Czech Republic

OFFICIAL LANGUAGE
Czech
POPULATION
10,646,000
UNREACHED POPULATION
12,000
PROFESSING CHRISTIANS
26.9%

Petra's Home

Say a Prayer Today

Pray for the church in the Czech Republic. Pray it would continue to grow as more and more people see their need for Christ.

HISTORY BIT

The Bible was first translated into Czech around 1360 from the Latin Vulgate, the first Latin version of the Old and New Testaments.* The Bible was translated into Czech from the original Greek and Hebrew languages in 1613.**

Source Information:
https://joshuaproject.net/countries/EZ
*John Bowden, A Chronology of World Christianity (New York, NY: Continuum, 2007), 228.
**https://www.biblesociety.org.uk/products/filters/Czech%20(Český)/

LOVE YOUR NEIGHBOR

Her Journey

PETRA'S STORY

I grew up in a post-communist country in the middle of Europe. No one in my family, including myself, knew Christ. I didn't hear the gospel until I was in my late teens. Later, I decided to accept Jesus as my Lord and Savior.

Growing up, I struggled with questions too big for me, and I struggled to make sense of the world. The questions in my head grew louder, and I started coping the only way I knew how, by controlling what I could. Eventually, I developed a serious eating disorder. I praise God that His story for me did not end there. He has—in His grace and mercy—redeemed me and given me a purpose, renewed my heart, and bound up my broken soul. My eating disorder, however, has left a mark on my mental health. The mark is a daily reminder that I am in desperate need of the great I Am.

My country and my people have also gone through some dark times. We are a small country in the middle of Europe that spent most of the twentieth century under oppression.

During that time, Czechs fought for an independent country they could call their own. Not only were they robbed of the majority of their land before the Second World War, they were threatened and forced to surrender to greater powers over and over. The movement toward freedom and democracy began slowly with students protesting in the streets. These peaceful demonstrations eventually lead to the collapse of the Communist Party and is known as the Velvet Revolution.

In 1989, Czechoslovakia became a sovereign state. The Church bloomed inside of its newly-found freedom. Missionaries began entering the country, bringing the good news of Jesus Christ to a long-oppressed people.

Friends, it is not the circumstances around us but the fire within us that matters. Let's keep running after what we know is true. The Lord our God equips us with the incomparable greatness of his power toward us who believe (Eph 1:19). Let's join in His mission! He will faithfully give us recompense for all the injustices and dark moments we go through. His covenant with us is everlasting and His mighty arms hold us securely.

6 WEEK READING PLAN

LOVE HIS WORD

	MONDAY	TUESDAY	WEDNESDAY	THURSDAY	FRIDAY
1	Isaiah 1-2	Isaiah 3-5	Isaiah 6-7	Isaiah 8:1—10:4	Isaiah 10:5—12:6
	SOAP Isaiah 1:18-20	SOAP Isaiah 5:7	SOAP Isaiah 6:7	SOAP Isaiah 8:17-18	SOAP Isaiah 12:1-2
2	Isaiah 13-14	Isaiah 15-16	Isaiah 17-18	Isaiah 19-20	Isaiah 21-22
	SOAP Isaiah 14:1-2	SOAP Isaiah 16:13-14	SOAP Isaiah 17:7-8	SOAP Isaiah 19:21-22	SOAP Isaiah 22:5
3	Isaiah 23-25	Isaiah 26-27	Isaiah 28-29	Isaiah 30-31	Isaiah 32-33
	SOAP Isaiah 25:1	SOAP Isaiah 26:5-6	SOAP Isaiah 28:16-17	SOAP Isaiah 30:18	SOAP Isaiah 33:2
4	Isaiah 34-35	Isaiah 36-37	Isaiah 38-40	Isaiah 41-42	Isaiah 43:1—45:8
	SOAP Isaiah 35:1-2	SOAP Isaiah 37:33-35	SOAP Isaiah 40:29-31	SOAP Isaiah 41:8-10	SOAP Isaiah 44:21-22
5	Isaiah 45:9—46:13	Isaiah 47-48	Isaiah 49-50	Isaiah 51-53	Isaiah 54-55
	SOAP Isaiah 46:13	SOAP Isaiah 48:10-11	SOAP Isaiah 49:14-15	SOAP Isaiah 51:6	SOAP Isaiah 55:6
6	Isaiah 56-57	Isaiah 58-59	Isaiah 60-62	Isaiah 63-64	Isaiah 65-66
	SOAP Isaiah 57:18-19	SOAP Isaiah 59:1-2	SOAP Isaiah 61:8	SOAP Isaiah 63:7	SOAP Isaiah 65:18-19

HEADING

1 Here is the message about Judah and Jerusalem that was revealed to Isaiah son of Amoz during the time when Uzziah, Jotham, Ahaz, and Hezekiah reigned over Judah.

OBEDIENCE, NOT SACRIFICE

2 Listen, O heavens,
pay attention, O earth!
For the LORD speaks:
"I raised children, I brought them up,
but they have rebelled against me!
3 An ox recognizes its owner,
a donkey recognizes where its owner puts its food;
but Israel does not recognize me,
my people do not understand."
4 Beware sinful nation,
the people weighed down by evil deeds.
They are offspring who do wrong,
children who do wicked things.
They have abandoned the LORD,
and rejected the Holy One of Israel.
They are alienated from him.
5 Why do you insist on being battered?
Why do you continue to rebel?
Your head has a massive wound,
your whole heart is sick.
6 From the soles of your feet to your head,
there is no spot that is unharmed.
There are only bruises, cuts,
and open wounds.
They have not been cleansed or bandaged,
nor have they been treated with olive oil.
7 Your land is devastated,
your cities burned with fire.
Right before your eyes your crops
are being destroyed by foreign invaders.
They leave behind devastation and destruction.
8 Daughter Zion is left isolated,
like a hut in a vineyard,
or a shelter in a cucumber field;
she is a besieged city.
9 If the LORD of Heaven's Armies had not left us a few survivors,
we would have quickly been like Sodom,
we would have become like Gomorrah.
10 Listen to the LORD's message,
you leaders of Sodom!
Pay attention to our God's rebuke,
people of Gomorrah!
11 "Of what importance to me are your many sacrifices?"
says the LORD.
"I have had my fill of burnt sacrifices,
of rams and the fat from steers.
The blood of bulls, lambs, and goats
I do not want.

12 When you enter my presence,
do you actually think I want this—
animals trampling on my courtyards?
13 Do not bring any more meaningless offerings;
I consider your incense detestable!
You observe new moon festivals,
Sabbaths, and convocations,
but I cannot tolerate sin-stained celebrations!
14 I hate your new moon festivals and assemblies;
they are a burden
that I am tired of carrying.
15 When you spread out your hands in prayer,
I look the other way;
when you offer your many prayers,
I do not listen,
because your hands are covered with blood.
16 Wash! Cleanse yourselves!
Remove your sinful deeds
from my sight.
Stop sinning.
17 Learn to do what is right.
Promote justice.
Give the oppressed reason to celebrate.
Take up the cause of the orphan.
Defend the rights of the widow.

18 Come, let's consider your options," says the LORD.
"Though your sins have stained you like the color red,
you can become white like snow;
though they are as easy to see as the color scarlet,
you can become white like wool.
19 If you have a willing attitude and obey,
then you will again eat the good crops of the land.
20 But if you refuse and rebel,
you will be devoured by the sword."
Know for certain that the LORD has spoken.

PURIFYING JUDGMENT

21 How tragic that the once-faithful city
has become a prostitute!
She was once a center of justice;
fairness resided in her—
but now only murderers!
22 Your silver has become scum,
your beer is diluted with water.
23 Your officials are rebels,
they associate with thieves.
All of them love bribery,
and look for payoffs.
They do not take up the cause of the orphan,
or defend the rights of the widow.
24 Therefore, the Sovereign LORD of Heaven's Armies,
the Powerful One of Israel, says this:
"Ah, I will seek vengeance against my adversaries,

I will take revenge against my enemies.
25 I will attack you;
I will purify your metal with flux.
I will remove all your slag.
26 I will reestablish honest judges as in former times,
wise advisers as in earlier days.
Then you will be called, 'The Just City,
Faithful Town.'"
27 Zion will be freed by justice,
and her returnees by righteousness.
28 All rebellious sinners will be shattered,
those who abandon the LORD will perish.
29 Indeed, they will be ashamed of the sacred trees
you find so desirable;
you will be embarrassed because of the sacred orchards
where you choose to worship.
30 For you will be like a tree whose leaves wither,
like an orchard that is unwatered.
31 The powerful will be like a thread of yarn,
their deeds like a spark;
both will burn together,
and no one will put out the fire.

THE FUTURE GLORY OF JERUSALEM

2 Here is the message about Judah and Jerusalem that was revealed to Isaiah son of Amoz.
2 In future days
the mountain of the LORD's temple will endure
as the most important of mountains,
and will be the most prominent of hills.
All the nations will stream to it;
3 many peoples will come and say,
"Come, let us go up to the LORD's mountain,
to the temple of the God of Jacob,
so he can teach us his requirements,
and we can follow his standards."
For Zion will be the center for moral instruction;
the LORD's message will issue from Jerusalem.
4 He will judge disputes between nations;
he will settle cases for many peoples.
They will beat their swords into plowshares,
and their spears into pruning hooks.
Nations will not take up the sword
against other nations,
and they will no longer train for war.
5 O descendants of Jacob,
come, let us walk in the LORD's guiding light.

THE LORD'S DAY OF JUDGMENT

6 Indeed, O LORD, you have abandoned your people,
the descendants of Jacob.
For diviners from the east are everywhere;
they consult omen readers like the Philistines do.
Plenty of foreigners are around.

REFLECT

Amid woes of judgment God offered a glimpse into the future glory of Jerusalem. What does this reveal about His character?

7 Their land is full of gold and silver;
there is no end to their wealth.
Their land is full of horses;
there is no end to their chariots.
8 Their land is full of worthless idols;
they worship the product of their own hands,
what their own fingers have fashioned.
9 Men bow down to them in homage,
they lie flat on the ground in worship.
Don't spare them!
10 Go up into the rocky cliffs,
hide in the ground.
Get away from the dreadful judgment of the LORD,
from his royal splendor!
11 Proud men will be brought low,
arrogant men will be humiliated;
the LORD alone will be exalted
in that day.
12 Indeed, the LORD of Heaven's Armies
has planned a day of judgment,
for all the high and mighty,
for all who are proud—they will be humiliated;
13 for all the cedars of Lebanon,
that are so high and mighty,
for all the oaks of Bashan;
14 for all the tall mountains,
for all the high hills,
15 for every high tower,
for every fortified wall,
16 for all the large ships,
for all the impressive ships.
17 Proud men will be humiliated,
arrogant men will be brought low;
the LORD alone will be exalted
in that day.
18 The worthless idols will be completely eliminated.
19 They will go into caves in the rocky cliffs
and into holes in the ground,
trying to escape the dreadful judgment of the LORD
and his royal splendor,
when he rises up to terrify the earth.
20 At that time men will throw
their silver and gold idols,
which they made for themselves to worship,
into the caves where rodents and bats live,
21 so they themselves can go into the
crevices of the rocky cliffs
and the openings under the rocky overhangs,
trying to escape the dreadful judgment of the LORD
and his royal splendor,
when he rises up to terrify the earth.
22 Stop trusting in human beings,
whose life's breath is in their nostrils.
For why should they be given special consideration?

A COMING LEADERSHIP CRISIS

3 Look, the Sovereign LORD of Heaven's Armies
is about to remove from Jerusalem and Judah
every source of security, including
all the food and water,
2 the mighty men and warriors,
judges and prophets,
omen readers and leaders,
3 captains of groups of fifty,
the respected citizens,
advisers and those skilled in magical arts,
and those who know incantations.
4 The LORD says, "I will make youths their officials;
malicious young men will rule over them.
5 The people will treat each other harshly;
men will oppose each other;
neighbors will fight.
Youths will proudly defy the elderly
and riffraff will challenge those who were once respected.
6 Indeed, a man will grab his brother
right in his father's house and say,
'You own a coat—
you be our leader!
This heap of ruins will be under your control.'
7 At that time the brother will shout,
'I am no doctor,
I have no food or coat in my house;
don't make me a leader of the people!'"
8 Jerusalem certainly stumbles,
Judah falls,
for their words and their actions offend the LORD;
they rebel against his royal authority.
9 The look on their faces testifies to their guilt;
like the people of Sodom they openly boast of their sin.
Woe to them!
For they bring disaster on themselves.
10 Tell the innocent it will go well with them,
for they will be rewarded for what they have done.
11 Woe to the wicked sinners!
For they will get exactly what they deserve.
12 Oppressors treat my people cruelly;
creditors rule over them.
My people, your leaders mislead you;
they give you confusing directions.
13 The LORD takes his position to judge;
he stands up to pass sentence on his people.
14 The LORD comes to pronounce judgment
on the leaders of his people and their officials.
He says, "It is you who have ruined the vineyard!
You have stashed in your houses what
you have stolen from the poor.
15 Why do you crush my people
and grind the faces of the poor?"
The Sovereign LORD of Heaven's Armies has spoken.

WASHING AWAY IMPURITY

16 The LORD says,
"The women of Zion are proud.
They walk with their heads high
and flirt with their eyes.
They skip along
and the jewelry on their ankles jingles.
17 So the Lord will afflict the foreheads of
Zion's women with skin diseases;
the LORD will make the front of their heads bald."

18 At that time the Lord will remove their beautiful ankle jewelry, neck ornaments, crescent-shaped ornaments, 19 earrings,
bracelets, veils, 20 headdresses, ankle ornaments, sashes, sa-
chets, amulets, 21 rings, nose rings, 22 festive dresses, robes, shawls,
purses, 23 garments, vests, head coverings, and gowns.

24 A putrid stench will replace the smell of spices,
a rope will replace a belt,
baldness will replace braided locks of hair,
a sackcloth garment will replace a fine robe,
and a prisoner's brand will replace beauty.
25 Your men will fall by the sword,
your strong men will die in battle.
26 Her gates will mourn and lament;
deprived of her people, she will sit on the ground.

4 Seven women will grab hold of
one man at that time.
They will say, "We will provide our own food,
we will provide our own clothes;
but let us belong to you—
take away our shame!"

THE BRANCH OF THE LORD

2 At that time
the crops given by the LORD will bring admiration and honor;
the produce of the land will be a source of pride and delight
to those who remain in Israel.
3 Those remaining in Zion, those left in Jerusalem,
will be called "holy,"
all in Jerusalem who are destined to live.
4 At that time the Lord will wash the
excrement from Zion's women,
he will rinse the bloodstains from Jerusalem's midst,
as he comes to judge
and to bring devastation.
5 Then the LORD will create
over all Mount Zion
and over its convocations
a cloud and smoke by day
and a bright flame of fire by night;
indeed a canopy will accompany the
LORD's glorious presence.
6 By day it will be a shelter to provide shade from the heat,
as well as safety and protection from the heavy downpour.

A LOVE SONG GONE SOUR

5 I will sing to my love—
a song to my lover about his vineyard.
My love had a vineyard
on a fertile hill.
2 He built a hedge around it, removed its stones,
and planted a vine.
He built a tower in the middle of it,
and constructed a winepress.
He waited for it to produce edible grapes,
but it produced sour ones instead.
3 So now, residents of Jerusalem,
people of Judah,
you decide between me and my vineyard!
4 What more can I do for my vineyard
beyond what I have already done?
When I waited for it to produce edible grapes,
why did it produce sour ones instead?
5 Now I will inform you
what I am about to do to my vineyard:
I will remove its hedge and turn it into pasture,
I will break its wall and allow animals to graze there.
6 I will make it a wasteland;
no one will prune its vines or hoe its ground,
and thorns and briers will grow there.
I will order the clouds
not to drop any rain on it.
7 Indeed, Israel is the vineyard of the
LORD of Heaven's Armies,
the people of Judah are the cultivated
place in which he took delight.
He waited for justice, but look what he got—disobedience!
He waited for fairness, but look what he got—cries for help!

DISASTER IS COMING

8 Beware, those who accumulate houses,
who also accumulate field after field
until there is no land left,
and you are the only landowners
remaining within the land.
9 The LORD of Heaven's Armies told me this:
"Many houses will certainly become desolate,
large, impressive houses will have
no one living in them.
10 Indeed, a large vineyard will produce just a few gallons,
and enough seed to yield several bushels
will produce less than a bushel."
11 Beware, those who get up early to drink beer,
those who keep drinking long after dark
until they are intoxicated with wine.
12 They have stringed instruments, tambourines, flutes,
and wine at their parties.
So they do not recognize what the LORD is doing,
they do not perceive what he is bringing about.

13 Therefore my people will be deported
because of their lack of understanding.
Their leaders will have nothing to eat,
their masses will have nothing to drink.
14 So Death will open up its throat,
and open wide its mouth;
Zion's dignitaries and masses will descend into it,
including those who revel and celebrate within her.
15 Men will be humiliated,
they will be brought low;
the proud will be brought low.
16 The LORD of Heaven's Armies will be
exalted when he punishes,
the holy God's authority will be recognized when he judges.
17 Lambs will graze as if in their pastures,
amid the ruins the rich sojourners will graze.
18 Beware, those who pull evil along using cords
of emptiness are as good as dead,
who pull sin as with cart ropes.
19 They say, "Let him hurry, let him act quickly,
so we can see;
let the plan of the Holy One of Israel
take shape and come to pass,
then we will know it!"
20 Beware, those who call evil good and good evil,
who turn darkness into light and light into darkness,
who turn bitter into sweet and sweet into bitter.
21 Beware, those who think they are wise,
those who think they possess understanding.
22 Beware, those who are champions at drinking,
who display great courage when mixing strong drinks.
23 They pronounce the guilty innocent for a payoff,
they ignore the just cause of the innocent.
24 Therefore, as flaming fire devours straw,
and dry grass disintegrates in the flames,
so their root will rot,
and their flower will blow away like dust.
For they have rejected the law of the
LORD of Heaven's Armies,
they have spurned the commands
of the Holy One of Israel.
25 So the LORD is furious with his people;
he lifts his hand and strikes them.
The mountains shake,
and corpses lie like manure in the middle of the streets.
Despite all this, his anger does not subside,
and his hand is ready to strike again.
26 He lifts a signal flag for a distant nation,
he whistles for it to come from the far regions of the earth.
Look, they come quickly and swiftly.
27 None tire or stumble,
they don't stop to nap or sleep.
They don't loosen their belts,
or unstrap their sandals to rest.

28 Their arrows are sharpened,
and all their bows are prepared.
The hooves of their horses are hard as flint,
and their chariot wheels are like a windstorm.
29 Their roar is like a lion's;
they roar like young lions.
They growl and seize their prey;
they drag it away and no one can come to the rescue.
30 At that time they will growl over their prey,
it will sound like sea waves crashing against rocks.
One will look out over the land and
see the darkness of disaster,
clouds will turn the light into darkness.

ISAIAH'S COMMISSION

6 In the year of King Uzziah's death, I saw the Lord seated on
a high, elevated throne. The hem of his robe filled the temple. 2 Seraphs stood over him; each one had six wings. With two
wings they covered their faces, with two they covered their feet,
and they used the remaining two to fly. 3 They called out to one
another, "Holy, holy, holy is the LORD of Heaven's Armies! His
majestic splendor fills the entire earth!" 4 The sound of their
voices shook the door frames, and the temple was filled with
smoke.
5 I said, "Woe to me! I am destroyed, for my lips are contaminated by sin, and I live among people whose lips are contaminated by sin. My eyes have seen the king, the LORD of Heaven's
Armies." 6 But then one of the seraphs flew toward me. In his
hand was a hot coal he had taken from the altar with tongs.
7 He touched my mouth with it and said, "Look, this coal has
touched your lips. Your evil is removed; your sin is forgiven." 8 I
heard the voice of the Lord say, "Whom will I send? Who will go
on our behalf?" I answered, "Here I am, send me!" 9 He said, "Go
and tell these people:
"'Listen continually, but don't understand.
Look continually, but don't perceive.'
10 Make the hearts of these people calloused;
make their ears deaf and their eyes blind.
Otherwise they might see with their
eyes and hear with their ears,
their hearts might understand and they
might repent and be healed."
11 I replied, "How long, Lord?" He said,
"Until cities are in ruins and unpopulated,
and houses are uninhabited,
and the land is ruined and devastated,
12 and the LORD has sent the people off to a distant place,
and the very heart of the land is completely abandoned.
13 Even if only a tenth of the people remain in the land,
it will again be destroyed,
like one of the large sacred trees or an Asherah pole,
when a sacred pillar on a high place is thrown down.
That sacred pillar symbolizes the
special chosen family."

AHAZ RECEIVES A SIGN

7 During the reign of Ahaz son of Jotham, son of Uzziah, king of
Judah, King Rezin of Syria and King Pekah son of Remaliah of
Israel marched up to Jerusalem to do battle, but they were un-
able to prevail against it.

2 It was reported to the family of David, "Syria has allied with
Ephraim." They and their people were emotionally shaken, just
as the trees of the forest shake before the wind. 3 So the LORD
told Isaiah, "Go out with your son Shear Jashub and meet Ahaz
at the end of the conduit of the upper pool that is located on
the road to the field where they wash and dry cloth. 4 Tell him,
'Make sure you stay calm! Don't be afraid. Don't be intimidated
by these two stubs of smoking logs, or by the raging anger of
Rezin, Syria, and the son of Remaliah. 5 Syria has plotted with
Ephraim and the son of Remaliah to bring about your demise.
6 They say, "Let's attack Judah, terrorize it, and conquer it. Then
we'll set up the son of Tabeel as its king." 7 For this reason the
Sovereign LORD says:

"'It will not take place;
it will not happen.
8 For Syria's leader is Damascus,
and the leader of Damascus is Rezin.
Within sixty-five years Ephraim will
no longer exist as a nation.
9 Ephraim's leader is Samaria,
and Samaria's leader is the son of Remaliah.
If your faith does not remain firm,
then you will not remain secure.'"

10 The LORD again spoke to Ahaz: 11 "Ask for a confirming sign
from the LORD your God. You can even ask for something miraculous." 12 But Ahaz responded, "I don't want to ask; I don't want to
put the LORD to a test." 13 So Isaiah replied, "Pay attention, family
of David. Do you consider it too insignificant to try the patience
of men? Is that why you are also trying the patience of my God?
14 For this reason the Lord himself will give you a confirming sign.
Look, this young woman is about to conceive and will give birth
to a son. You, young woman, will name him Immanuel. 15 He will
eat sour milk and honey, which will help him know how to reject
evil and choose what is right. 16 Here is why this will be so: Before
the child knows how to reject evil and choose what is right, the
land whose two kings you fear will be desolate. 17 The LORD will
bring on you, your people, and your father's family a time unlike
any since Ephraim departed from Judah—the king of Assyria!"

18 At that time the LORD will whistle for flies from the distant
streams of Egypt and for bees from the land of Assyria. 19 All of
them will come and make their home in the ravines between the
cliffs and in the crevices of the cliffs, in all the thorn bushes, and
in all the watering holes. 20 At that time the Lord will use a razor
hired from the banks of the Euphrates River, the king of Assyria,
to shave the hair off the head and private parts; it will also shave
off the beard. 21 At that time a man will keep alive a young cow
from the herd and a couple of goats. 22 From the abundance of
milk they produce, he will have sour milk for his meals. Indeed,

everyone left in the heart of the land will eat sour milk and honey.
23 At that time every place where there had been 1,000 vines
worth 1,000 silver shekels will be overrun with thorns and briers. 24 With bow and arrow people will hunt there, for the whole
land will be covered with thorns and briers. 25 They will stay away
from all the hills that were cultivated for fear of the thorns and
briers. Cattle will graze there, and sheep will trample on them.

A CHILD IS BORN FOR A SIGN

8 The LORD told me, "Take a large tablet and inscribe these
words on it with an ordinary stylus: 'Maher Shalal Hash Baz.'
2 Then I will summon as my reliable witnesses Uriah the priest
and Zechariah son of Jeberekiah." 3 I then approached the prophetess for marital relations; she conceived and gave birth to a son.
The LORD told me, "Name him Maher Shalal Hash Baz, 4 for before the child knows how to cry out 'My father' or 'My mother,'
the wealth of Damascus and the plunder of Samaria will be carried off by the king of Assyria."
5 The LORD spoke to me again: 6 "These people have rejected
the gently flowing waters of Shiloah and melt in fear over Rezin and the son of Remaliah. 7 So look, the Lord is bringing up
against them the turbulent and mighty waters of the Euphrates River—the king of Assyria and all his majestic power. It will
reach flood stage and overflow its banks. 8 It will spill into Judah,
flooding and engulfing, as it reaches to the necks of its victims.
He will spread his wings out over your entire land, O Immanuel."

9 You will be broken, O nations;
you will be shattered!
Pay attention, all you distant lands of the earth.
Get ready for battle, and you will be shattered!
Get ready for battle, and you will be shattered!
10 Devise your strategy, but it will be thwarted.
Issue your orders, but they will not be executed!
For God is with us!

THE LORD ENCOURAGES ISAIAH

11 Indeed this is what the LORD told me quite forcefully. He
warned me not to act like these people:

12 "Do not say, 'Conspiracy,' every time
these people say the word.
Don't be afraid of what scares them; don't be terrified.
13 You must recognize the authority of
the LORD of Heaven's Armies.
He is the one you must respect;
he is the one you must fear.
14 He will become a sanctuary,
but a stone that makes a person trip,
and a rock that makes one stumble—
to the two houses of Israel.
He will become a trap and a snare
to the residents of Jerusalem.
15 Many will stumble over the stone and the rock,
and will fall and be seriously injured,
and will be ensnared and captured."

16 Tie up the scroll as legal evidence,
seal the official record of God's instructions
and give it to my followers.
17 I will wait patiently for the LORD,
who has rejected the family of Jacob;
I will wait for him.

18 Look, I and the sons whom the LORD has given me are
reminders and object lessons in Israel, sent from the
LORD of Heaven's Armies, who lives on Mount Zion.

DARKNESS TURNS TO LIGHT AS AN IDEAL KING ARRIVES

19 They will say to you, "Seek oracles at the pits used to conjure
up underworld spirits, from the magicians who chirp and mut-
ter incantations. Should people not seek oracles from their gods,
by asking the dead about the destiny of the living?" 20 Then you
must recall the LORD's instructions and the prophetic testimony
of what would happen. Certainly they say such things because
their minds are spiritually darkened. 21 They will pass through
the land destitute and starving. Their hunger will make them
angry, and they will curse their king and their God as they look
upward. 22 When one looks out over the land, he sees distress
and darkness, gloom and anxiety, darkness and people forced
9 from the land. 1 The gloom will be dispelled for those who
were anxious.

In earlier times he humiliated
the land of Zebulun,
and the land of Naphtali;
but now he brings honor
to the way of the sea,
the region beyond the Jordan,
and Galilee of the nations.
2 The people walking in darkness
see a bright light;
light shines
on those who live in a land of deep darkness.
3 You have enlarged the nation;
you give them great joy.
They rejoice in your presence
as harvesters rejoice;
as warriors celebrate when they divide up the plunder.
4 For their oppressive yoke
and the club that strikes their shoulders,
the cudgel the oppressor uses on them,
you have shattered, as in the day of Midian's defeat.
5 Indeed every boot that marches and shakes the earth
and every garment dragged through blood
is used as fuel for the fire.
6 For a child has been born to us,
a son has been given to us.
He shoulders responsibility
and is called
Wonderful Adviser,

HIS NAME SHALL BE CALLED . . .

ISAIAH 9:6

When my husband and I began to consider a name for our first daughter, we wanted a name that was sweet yet strong, friendly yet smart, a name that would describe who we hoped she'd become with God's help.

God intentionally named His Son. He entered our world as a baby, and the Father placed our sinless Lord in the hands of the sinful people He came to save.

Unlike us, when God named His Son, He knew who He was.

Wonderful Adviser: He would guide His people as they put their trust in Him. He is the creator of wisdom and the giver of knowledge. Our precious Lord is not a stingy giver of wisdom. Oh no, He gives generously to all who ask (see Jas 1:5).

Mighty God: He is mighty to save. Powerful in every way possible. He is God. That problem you are facing? It's no match for the All-Powerful One (see Rev 1:8)!

Everlasting Father: Christ made a bridge for us to the Father and now lives to intercede with Him on our behalf. God is the Father to the fatherless and the Father of all fathers. He is the dad who stays, the dad who cares, and the dad who deeply loves us. He is everlasting, and He will never fail us or abandon us (see Deut 31:6). Like the Good Shepherd He is, He looks over us, tends to us, and helps us to grow in our faith and knowledge of Him.

Prince of Peace: He is the ruler of peace, the giver of peace, and true peace can only be found in Him.

Our God is mighty to handle anything that comes your way. Turn to Him and seek His involvement in your life. He is mighty to help, save, and redeem!

He is holy, yet He came to us completely vulnerable: "For a child has been born to us" (Isa 9:6).

Thank you, Jesus, for being exactly who You said You are.

Mighty God,
Everlasting Father,
Prince of Peace.
7 His dominion will be vast,
and he will bring immeasurable prosperity.
He will rule on David's throne
and over David's kingdom,
establishing it and strengthening it
by promoting justice and fairness,
from this time forward and forevermore.
The zeal of the LORD of Heaven's
Armies will accomplish this.

GOD'S JUDGMENT INTENSIFIES

8 The Lord decreed judgment on Jacob,
and it fell on Israel.
9 All the people were aware of it,
the people of Ephraim and those living in Samaria.
Yet with pride and an arrogant attitude, they said,
10 "The bricks have fallen,
but we will rebuild with chiseled stone;
the sycamore fig trees have been cut down,
but we will replace them with cedars."
11 Then the LORD provoked their
adversaries to attack them,
he stirred up their enemies—
12 Syria from the east,
and the Philistines from the west;
they gobbled up Israelite territory.
Despite all this, his anger does not subside,
and his hand is ready to strike again.
13 The people did not return to the one who struck them,
they did not seek reconciliation with
the LORD of Heaven's Armies.
14 So the LORD cut off Israel's head and tail,
both the shoots and stalk in one day.
15 The leaders and the highly respected people are the head,
the prophets who teach lies are the tail.
16 The leaders of this nation were misleading people,
and the people being led were destroyed.
17 So the Lord was not pleased with their young men,
he took no pity on their orphans and widows;
for the whole nation was godless and did wicked things,
every mouth was speaking disgraceful words.
Despite all this, his anger does not subside,
and his hand is ready to strike again.
18 For evil burned like a fire,
it consumed thorns and briers;
it burned up the thickets of the forest,
and they went up in smoke.
19 Because of the anger of the LORD of Heaven's
Armies, the land was scorched,
and the people became fuel for the fire.
People had no compassion on one another.

20 They devoured on the right, but were still hungry;
they ate on the left, but were not satisfied.
People even ate the flesh of their own arm!
21 Manasseh fought against Ephraim,
and Ephraim against Manasseh;
together they fought against Judah.
Despite all this, his anger does not subside,
and his hand is ready to strike again.
10 Beware, those who enact unjust policies;
those who are always instituting unfair regulations,
2 to keep the poor from getting fair treatment,
and to deprive the oppressed among my people of justice,
so they can steal what widows own,
and loot what belongs to orphans.
3 What will you do on judgment day,
when destruction arrives from a distant place?
To whom will you run for help?
Where will you leave your wealth?
4 You will have no place to go, except to
kneel with the prisoners,
or to fall among those who have been killed.
Despite all this, his anger does not subside,
and his hand is ready to strike again.

THE LORD TURNS ON ARROGANT ASSYRIA

5 "Beware, Assyria, the club I use to vent my anger,
a cudgel with which I angrily punish.
6 I sent him against a godless nation,
I ordered him to attack the people with whom I was angry,
to take plunder and to carry away loot,
to trample them down like dirt in the streets.
7 But he does not agree with this;
his mind does not reason this way,
for his goal is to destroy,
and to eliminate many nations.
8 Indeed, he says:
'Are not my officials all kings?
9 Is not Calneh like Carchemish?
Hamath like Arpad?
Samaria like Damascus?
10 I overpowered kingdoms ruled by idols,
whose carved images were more impressive
than Jerusalem's or Samaria's.
11 As I have done to Samaria and its idols,
so I will do to Jerusalem and its idols."

12 But when the Lord finishes judging Mount Zion and Jerusalem,
then he will punish the king of Assyria for what he has proudly
planned and for the arrogant attitude he displays. 13 For he says:
"By my strong hand I have accomplished this,
by my strategy that I devised.
I invaded the territory of nations,
and looted their storehouses.
Like a mighty conqueror, I brought down rulers.

14 My hand discovered the wealth of the
nations, as if it were in a nest,
as one gathers up abandoned eggs,
I gathered up the whole earth.
There was no wing flapping,
or open mouth chirping."
15 Does an ax exalt itself over the one who wields it,
or a saw magnify itself over the one who cuts with it?
As if a scepter should brandish the one who raises it,
or a staff should lift up what is not made of wood!
16 For this reason the Sovereign LORD of Heaven's Armies
will make his healthy ones emaciated.
His majestic glory will go up in smoke.
17 The Light of Israel will become a fire,
their Holy One will become a flame;
it will burn and consume the Assyrian king's briers
and his thorns in one day.
18 The splendor of his forest and his orchard
will be completely destroyed,
as when a sick man's life ebbs away.
19 There will be so few trees left in his forest,
a child will be able to count them.

20 At that time those left in Israel, those who remain of the
family of Jacob, will no longer rely on a foreign leader that
abuses them. Instead they will truly rely on the LORD, the Holy
One of Israel. 21 A remnant will come back, a remnant of Jacob, to the mighty God. 22 For though your people, Israel, are
as numerous as the sand on the seashore, only a remnant will
come back. Destruction has been decreed; just punishment
is about to engulf you. 23 The Sovereign LORD of Heaven's Armies is certainly ready to carry out the decreed destruction
throughout the land.

24 So here is what the Sovereign LORD of Heaven's Armies
says: "My people who live in Zion, do not be afraid of Assyria,
even though they beat you with a club and lift their cudgel
against you as Egypt did. 25 For very soon my fury will subside,
and my anger will be directed toward their destruction." 26 The
LORD of Heaven's Armies is about to beat them with a whip,
similar to the way he struck down Midian at the rock of Oreb.
He will use his staff against the sea, lifting it up as he did in
Egypt.

27 At that time
the LORD will remove their burden from your shoulders,
and their yoke from your neck;
the yoke will be taken off because
your neck will be too large.
28 They attacked Aiath,
moved through Migron,
depositing their supplies at Micmash.
29 They went through the pass,
spent the night at Geba.
Ramah trembled,
Gibeah of Saul ran away.

30 Shout out, daughter of Gallim!
Pay attention, Laishah!
Answer her, Anathoth!
31 Madmenah flees,
the residents of Gebim have hidden.
32 This very day, standing in Nob,
they shake their fist at Daughter Zion's mountain—
at the hill of Jerusalem.
33 Look, the Sovereign LORD of Heaven's Armies
is ready to cut off the branches with terrifying power.
The tallest trees will be cut down,
the loftiest ones will be brought low.
34 The thickets of the forest will be chopped down with an ax,
and mighty Lebanon will fall.

AN IDEAL KING ESTABLISHES A KINGDOM OF PEACE

11 A shoot will grow out of Jesse's root stock,
a bud will sprout from his roots.
2 The LORD's Spirit will rest on him—
a Spirit that gives extraordinary wisdom,
a Spirit that provides the ability to execute plans,
a Spirit that produces absolute loyalty to the LORD.
3 He will take delight in obeying the LORD.
He will not judge by mere appearances,
or make decisions on the basis of hearsay.
4 He will treat the poor fairly,
and make right decisions for the downtrodden of the earth.
He will strike the earth with the rod of his mouth,
and order the wicked to be executed.
5 Justice will be like a belt around his waist,
integrity will be like a belt around his hips.
6 A wolf will reside with a lamb,
and a leopard will lie down with a young goat;
an ox and a young lion will graze together,
as a small child leads them along.
7 A cow and a bear will graze together,
their young will lie down together.
A lion, like an ox, will eat straw.
8 A baby will play
over the hole of a snake;
over the nest of a serpent
an infant will put his hand.
9 They will no longer injure or destroy
on my entire royal mountain.
For there will be universal submission
to the LORD's sovereignty,
just as the waters completely cover the sea.

ISRAEL IS RECLAIMED AND REUNITED

10 At that time a root from Jesse will stand like a signal flag for
the nations. Nations will look to him for guidance, and his residence will be majestic. 11 At that time the Lord will again lift his
hand to reclaim the remnant of his people from Assyria, Egypt,
Pathros, Cush, Elam, Shinar, Hamath, and the seacoasts.

12 He will lift a signal flag for the nations;
he will gather Israel's dispersed people
and assemble Judah's scattered people
from the four corners of the earth.
13 Ephraim's jealousy will end,
and Judah's hostility will be eliminated.
Ephraim will no longer be jealous of Judah,
and Judah will no longer be hostile toward Ephraim.
14 They will swoop down on the Philistine hills to the west;
together they will loot the people of the east.
They will take over Edom and Moab,
and the Ammonites will be their subjects.
15 The LORD will divide the gulf of the Egyptian Sea;
he will wave his hand over the Euphrates
River and send a strong wind;
he will turn it into seven dried-up streams,
and enable them to walk across in their sandals.
16 There will be a highway leading out of Assyria
for the remnant of his people,
just as there was for Israel,
when they went up from the land of Egypt.

12 At that time you will say:
"I praise you, O LORD,
for even though you were angry with me,
your anger subsided, and you consoled me.
2 Look, God is my deliverer!
I will trust in him and not fear.
For the LORD gives me strength and protects me;
he has become my deliverer."
3 Joyfully you will draw water
from the springs of deliverance.
4 At that time you will say:
"Praise the LORD!
Ask him for help!
Publicize his mighty acts among the nations.
Make it known that he is unique.
5 Sing to the LORD, for he has done magnificent things;
let this be known throughout the earth.
6 Cry out and shout for joy, O citizens of Zion,
for the Holy One of Israel acts mightily among you!"

THE LORD WILL JUDGE BABYLON

13 This is an oracle about Babylon that
Isaiah son of Amoz saw:
2 On a bare hill raise a signal flag;
shout to them,
wave your hand,
so they might enter the gates of the princes!
3 I have given orders to my chosen soldiers;
I have summoned the warriors through
whom I will vent my anger—
my boasting, arrogant ones.
4 There is a loud noise on the mountains—
it sounds like a large army!

There is great commotion among the kingdoms—
nations are being assembled!
The LORD of Heaven's Armies is mustering
forces for battle.
5 They come from a distant land,
from the horizon.
It is the LORD with his instruments of judgment,
coming to destroy the whole earth.
6 Wail, for the LORD's day of judgment is near;
it comes with all the destructive
power of the Sovereign One.
7 For this reason all hands hang limp,
every human heart loses its courage.
8 They panic—
cramps and pain seize hold of them
like those of a woman who is straining to give birth.
They look at one another in astonishment;
their faces are flushed red.
9 Look, the LORD's day of judgment is coming;
it is a day of cruelty and savage, raging anger,
destroying the earth
and annihilating its sinners.
10 Indeed the stars in the sky and their constellations
no longer give out their light;
the sun is darkened as soon as it rises,
and the moon does not shine.
11 I will punish the world for its evil,
and wicked people for their sin.
I will put an end to the pride of the insolent,
I will bring down the arrogance of tyrants.
12 I will make human beings more
scarce than pure gold,
and people more scarce than gold from Ophir.
13 So I will shake the heavens,
and the earth will shake loose from its foundation,
because of the fury of the LORD of Heaven's Armies,
in the day he vents his raging anger.
14 Like a frightened gazelle
or a sheep with no shepherd,
each will turn toward home,
each will run to his homeland.
15 Everyone who is caught will be stabbed;
everyone who is seized will die by the sword.
16 Their children will be smashed to
pieces before their very eyes;
their houses will be looted
and their wives raped.
17 Look, I am stirring up the Medes to attack them;
they are not concerned about silver,
nor are they interested in gold.
18 Their arrows will cut young men to ribbons;
they have no compassion on a person's offspring;
they will not look with pity on children.
19 Babylon, the most admired of kingdoms,

the Chaldeans' source of honor and pride,
will be destroyed by God
just as Sodom and Gomorrah were.
20 No one will live there again;
no one will ever reside there again.
No bedouin will camp there,
no shepherds will rest their flocks there.
21 Wild animals will rest there,
the ruined houses will be full of hyenas.
Ostriches will live there,
wild goats will skip among the ruins.
22 Wild dogs will yip in her ruined fortresses,
jackals will yelp in the once-splendid palaces.
Her time is almost up,
her days will not be prolonged.

14 The LORD will certainly have compassion on Jacob; he will
again choose Israel as his special people and restore them
to their land. Resident foreigners will join them and unite with
the family of Jacob. 2 Nations will take them and bring them back
to their own place. Then the family of Israel will make foreigners
their servants as they settle in the LORD's land. They will make
their captors captives and rule over the ones who oppressed
them. 3 When the LORD gives you relief from your suffering and
anxiety and from the hard labor that you were made to perform,
4 you will taunt the king of Babylon with these words:

"Look how the oppressor has met his end!
Hostility has ceased!
5 The LORD has broken the club of the wicked,
the scepter of rulers.
6 It furiously struck down nations
with unceasing blows.
It angrily ruled over nations,
oppressing them without restraint.
7 The whole earth rests and is quiet;
they break into song.
8 The evergreens also rejoice over your demise,
as do the cedars of Lebanon, singing,
'Since you fell asleep,
no woodsman comes up to chop us down!'
9 Sheol below is stirred up about you,
ready to meet you when you arrive.
It rouses the spirits of the dead for you,
all the former leaders of the earth;
it makes all the former kings of the nations
rise from their thrones.
10 All of them respond to you, saying:
'You too have become weak like us!
You have become just like us!
11 Your splendor has been brought down to Sheol,
as well as the sound of your stringed instruments.
You lie on a bed of maggots,
with a blanket of worms over you.

REFLECT

God disciplined the people of Israel for their sin, but He also promised to give them relief from their enemies. What is the difference between discipline and judgment?

12 Look how you have fallen from the sky,
O shining one, son of the dawn!
You have been cut down to the ground,
O conqueror of the nations!
13 You said to yourself,
'I will climb up to the sky.
Above the stars of El
I will set up my throne.
I will rule on the mountain of assembly
on the remote slopes of Zaphon.
14 I will climb up to the tops of the clouds;
I will make myself like the Most High!'
15 But you were brought down to Sheol,
to the remote slopes of the Pit.
16 Those who see you stare at you,
they look at you carefully, thinking:
'Is this the man who shook the earth,
the one who made kingdoms tremble?
17 Is this the one who made the world like a wilderness,
who ruined its cities,
and refused to free his prisoners so
they could return home?'
18 As for all the kings of the nations,
all of them lie down in splendor,
each in his own tomb.
19 But you have been thrown out of your grave
like a shoot that is thrown away.
You lie among the slain,
among those who have been slashed by the sword,
among those headed for the stones of the Pit,
as if you were a mangled corpse.
20 You will not be buried with them,
because you destroyed your land
and killed your people.

The offspring of the wicked
will never be mentioned again.
21 Prepare to execute his sons
for the sins their ancestors have committed.
They must not rise up and take possession of the earth,
or fill the surface of the world with cities.

22 "I will rise up against them,"
says the LORD of Heaven's Armies.
"I will blot out all remembrance of Babylon
and destroy all her people,
including the offspring she produces,"
says the LORD.
23 "I will turn her into a place that is
overrun with wild animals
and covered with pools of stagnant water.
I will get rid of her, just as one sweeps
away dirt with a broom,"
says the LORD of Heaven's Armies.

24 The LORD of Heaven's Armies makes this solemn vow:
"Be sure of this:
Just as I have intended, so it will be;
just as I have planned, it will happen.
25 I will break Assyria in my land,
I will trample them underfoot on my hills.
Their yoke will be removed from my people,
the burden will be lifted from their shoulders.
26 This is the plan I have devised for the whole earth;
my hand is ready to strike all the nations."
27 Indeed, the LORD of Heaven's Armies has a plan,
and who can possibly frustrate it?
His hand is ready to strike,
and who can possibly stop it?

THE LORD WILL JUDGE THE PHILISTINES

28 This oracle came in the year that King Ahaz died:
29 Don't be so happy, all you Philistines,
just because the club that beat you has been broken!
For a viper will grow out of the serpent's root,
and its fruit will be a darting adder.
30 The poor will graze in my pastures;
the needy will rest securely.
But I will kill your root by famine;
it will put to death all your survivors.
31 Wail, O city gate!
Cry out, O city!
Melt with fear, all you Philistines!
For out of the north comes a cloud of smoke,
and there are no stragglers in its ranks.
32 How will they respond to the messengers of this nation?
Indeed, the LORD has made Zion secure;
the oppressed among his people will find safety in her.

THE LORD WILL JUDGE MOAB

15 This is an oracle about Moab:
Indeed, in a night it is devastated,
Ar of Moab is destroyed!
Indeed, in a night it is devastated,
Kir of Moab is destroyed!
2 They went up to the temple;
the people of Dibon went up to the high places to lament.
Because of what happened to Nebo
and Medeba, Moab wails.
Every head is shaved bare,
every beard is trimmed off.
3 In their streets they wear sackcloth;
on their roofs and in their town squares
all of them wail;
they fall down weeping.
4 The people of Heshbon and Elealeh cry out;
their voices are heard as far away as Jahaz.
For this reason Moab's soldiers shout in distress;
their courage wavers.

5 My heart cries out because of Moab's plight,
and for the fugitives stretched out as far
as Zoar and Eglath Shelishiyah.
For they weep as they make their way
up the ascent of Luhith;
they loudly lament their demise on
the road to Horonaim.
6 For the waters of Nimrim are gone;
the grass is dried up,
the vegetation has disappeared,
and there are no plants.
7 For this reason what they have made and stored up,
they carry over the Stream of the Poplars.
8 Indeed, the cries of distress echo
throughout Moabite territory;
their wailing can be heard in Eglaim and Beer Elim.
9 Indeed, the waters of Dimon are full of blood!
Indeed, I will heap even more trouble on Dimon.
A lion will attack the Moabite fugitives
and the people left in the land.
16 Send rams as tribute to the ruler of the land,
from Sela in the wilderness
to the hill of Daughter Zion.
2 At the fords of the Arnon
the Moabite women are like a bird
that flies about when forced from its nest.
3 "Bring a plan, make a decision.
Provide some shade in the middle of the day.
Hide the fugitives! Do not betray the
one who tries to escape.
4 Please let the Moabite fugitives live among you.
Hide them from the destroyer!"
Certainly the one who applies pressure will cease;
the destroyer will come to an end;
those who trample will disappear from the earth.
5 Then a trustworthy king will be established;
he will rule in a reliable manner,
this one from David's family.
He will be sure to make just decisions
and will be experienced in executing justice.
6 We have heard about Moab's pride—
their great arrogance—
their boasting, pride, and excess.
But their boastful claims are empty.
7 So Moab wails over its demise—
they all wail!
Completely devastated, they moan
about what has happened to the raisin
cakes of Kir Hareseth.
8 For the fields of Heshbon are dried up,
as well as the vines of Sibmah.
The rulers of the nations trample all over its vines,
which reach Jazer and spread to the wilderness;
their shoots spread out and cross the sea.

9 So I weep along with Jazer
over the vines of Sibmah.
I will saturate you with my tears, Heshbon and Elealeh,
for the conquering invaders shout triumphantly
over your fruit and crops.
10 Joy and happiness disappear from the orchards,
and in the vineyards no one rejoices or shouts;
no one treads out juice in the wine vats—
I have brought the joyful shouts to an end.
11 So my heart constantly sighs for Moab,
like the strumming of a harp,
my inner being sighs for Kir Hareseth.
12 When the Moabites plead with all their
might at their high places,
and enter their temples to pray, their
prayers will be ineffective.

13 This is the message the LORD previously announced about
Moab. 14 Now the LORD makes this announcement: "Within exactly three years Moab's splendor will disappear, along with all
her many people; there will be only a few insignificant survivors left."

THE LORD WILL JUDGE DAMASCUS

17 This is an oracle about Damascus:
"Look, Damascus is no longer a city,
it is a heap of ruins!
2 The cities of Aroer are abandoned.
They will be used for herds,
which will lie down there in peace.
3 Fortified cities will disappear from Ephraim,
and Damascus will lose its kingdom.
The survivors in Syria
will end up like the splendor of the Israelites,"
says the LORD of Heaven's Armies.
4 "At that time
Jacob's splendor will be greatly diminished,
and he will become skin and bones.
5 It will be as when one gathers the grain harvest,
and his hand gleans the ear of grain.
It will be like one gathering the ears of grain
in the Valley of Rephaim.
6 There will be some left behind,
as when an olive tree is beaten—
two or three ripe olives remain
toward the very top,
four or five on its fruitful branches,"
says the LORD God of Israel.
7 At that time men will trust in their Creator;
they will depend on the Holy One of Israel.
8 They will no longer trust in the
altars their hands made,
or depend on the Asherah poles and
incense altars their fingers made.

9 At that time their fortified cities will be
like the abandoned summits of the Amorites,
which they abandoned because of the Israelites;
there will be desolation.
10 For you ignore the God who rescues you;
you pay no attention to your strong protector.
So this is what happens:
You cultivate beautiful plants
and plant exotic vines.
11 The day you begin cultivating, you do
what you can to make it grow;
the morning you begin planting, you do
what you can to make it sprout.
Yet the harvest will disappear in the day of disease
and incurable pain.
12 Beware, you many nations massing together,
those who make a commotion as loud as
the roaring of the sea's waves.
Beware, you people making such an uproar,
those who make an uproar as loud as
the roaring of powerful waves.
13 Though these people make an uproar as loud
as the roaring of powerful waves,
when he shouts at them, they will flee to a distant land,
driven before the wind like dead weeds on the hills,
or like dead thistles before a strong gale.
14 In the evening there is sudden terror;
by morning they vanish.
This is the fate of those who try to plunder us,
the destiny of those who try to loot us!

THE LORD WILL JUDGE A DISTANT LAND IN THE SOUTH

18 Beware, land of buzzing wings,
the one beyond the rivers of Cush,
2 that sends messengers by sea,
who glide over the water's surface in boats made of papyrus.
Go, you swift messengers,
to a nation of tall, smooth-skinned people,
to a people that are feared far and wide,
to a nation strong and victorious,
whose land rivers divide.
3 All you who live in the world,
who reside on the earth,
you will see a signal flag raised on the mountains;
you will hear a trumpet being blown.
4 For this is what the LORD has told me:
"I will wait and watch from my place,
like scorching heat produced by the sunlight,
like a cloud of mist in the heat of harvest."
5 For before the harvest, when the bud has sprouted,
and the ripening fruit appears,
he will cut off the unproductive shoots with pruning knives;
he will prune the tendrils.

6 They will all be left for the birds of the hills
and the wild animals;
the birds will eat them during the summer,
and all the wild animals will eat them during the winter.
7 At that time
tribute will be brought to the LORD of Heaven's Armies,
by a people that are tall and smooth-skinned,
a people that are feared far and wide,
a nation strong and victorious,
whose land rivers divide.
The tribute will be brought to the place where the LORD of
Heaven's Armies has chosen to reside, on Mount Zion.

THE LORD WILL JUDGE EGYPT

19 This is an oracle about Egypt:
Look, the LORD rides on a swift-moving cloud
and approaches Egypt.
The idols of Egypt tremble before him;
the Egyptians lose their courage.
2 "I will provoke civil strife in Egypt:
brothers will fight with one another,
as will neighbors,
cities, and kingdoms.
3 The Egyptians will panic,
and I will confuse their strategy.
They will seek guidance from the idols
and from the spirits of the dead,
from the pits used to conjure up underworld
spirits, and from the magicians.
4 I will hand Egypt over to a harsh master;
a powerful king will rule over them,"
says the Sovereign LORD of Heaven's Armies.
5 The water of the sea will be dried up,
and the river will dry up and be empty.
6 The canals will stink;
the streams of Egypt will trickle and then dry up;
the bulrushes and reeds will decay,
7 along with the plants by the mouth of the river.
All the cultivated land near the river
will turn to dust and be blown away.
8 The fishermen will mourn and lament;
all those who cast a fishhook into the river,
and those who spread out a net on the
water's surface will grieve.
9 Those who make clothes from combed
flax will be embarrassed;
those who weave will turn pale.
10 Those who make cloth will be demoralized;
all the hired workers will be depressed.
11 The officials of Zoan are nothing but fools;
Pharaoh's wise advisers give stupid advice.
How dare you say to Pharaoh,
"I am one of the sages,
one well-versed in the writings of the ancient kings?"

12 But where, oh where, are your wise men?
Let them tell you, let them find out
what the LORD of Heaven's Armies has planned for Egypt.
13 The officials of Zoan are fools,
the officials of Memphis are misled;
the rulers of her tribes lead Egypt astray.
14 The LORD has made them undiscerning;
they lead Egypt astray in all she does,
so that she is like a drunk sliding around in his own vomit.
15 Egypt will not be able to do a thing,
head or tail, shoots or stalk.

16 At that time the Egyptians will be like women. They will
tremble and fear because the LORD of Heaven's Armies bran-
dishes his fist against them. 17 The land of Judah will humiliate Egypt. Everyone who hears about Judah will be afraid
because of what the LORD of Heaven's Armies is planning to
do to them.

18 At that time five cities in the land of Egypt will speak the
language of Canaan and swear allegiance to the LORD of Heav-
en's Armies. One will be called the City of the Sun. 19 At that
time there will be an altar for the LORD in the middle of the
land of Egypt, as well as a sacred pillar dedicated to the LORD
at its border. 20 It will become a visual reminder in the land
of Egypt of the LORD of Heaven's Armies. When they cry out
to the LORD because of oppressors, he will send them a deliverer and defender who will rescue them. 21 The LORD will reveal himself to the Egyptians, and they will acknowledge the
LORD's authority at that time. They will present sacrifices and
offerings; they will make vows to the LORD and fulfill them.
22 The LORD will strike Egypt, striking and then healing them.
They will turn to the LORD, and he will listen to their prayers
and heal them.

23 At that time there will be a highway from Egypt to Assyria. The Assyrians will visit Egypt, and the Egyptians will
visit Assyria. The Egyptians and Assyrians will worship together. 24 At that time Israel will be the third member of the
group, along with Egypt and Assyria, and will be a recipient
of blessing in the earth. 25 The LORD of Heaven's Armies will
pronounce a blessing over the earth, saying, "Blessed be my
people, Egypt, and the work of my hands, Assyria, and my special possession, Israel!"

20 The LORD revealed the following message during the
year in which King Sargon of Assyria sent his commanding general to Ashdod, and he fought against it and captured
it. 2 At that time the LORD announced through Isaiah son of
Amoz: "Go, remove the sackcloth from your waist and take
your sandals off your feet." He did as instructed and walked
around in undergarments and barefoot. 3 Later the LORD explained, "In the same way that my servant Isaiah has walked
around in undergarments and barefoot for the past three
years, as an object lesson and omen pertaining to Egypt and
Cush, 4 so the king of Assyria will lead away the captives of
Egypt and the exiles of Cush, both young and old. They will be

in undergarments and barefoot, with the buttocks exposed;
the Egyptians will be publicly humiliated. 5 Those who put
their hope in Cush and took pride in Egypt will be afraid and
embarrassed. 6 At that time those who live on this coast will
say, 'Look what has happened to our source of hope to whom
we fled for help, expecting to be rescued from the king of Assyria! How can we escape now?'"

THE LORD WILL JUDGE BABYLON

21 This is an oracle about the wilderness by the Sea:
Like strong winds blowing in the south,
one invades from the wilderness,
from a land that is feared.
2 I have received a distressing message:
"The deceiver deceives,
the destroyer destroys.
Attack, you Elamites!
Lay siege, you Medes!
I will put an end to all the groaning."
3 For this reason my stomach churns;
cramps overwhelm me
like the contractions of a woman in labor.
I am disturbed by what I hear,
horrified by what I see.
4 My heart palpitates,
I shake in fear;
the twilight I desired
has brought me terror.
5 Arrange the table,
lay out the carpet,
eat and drink!
Get up, you officers,
smear oil on the shields!

6 For this is what the Lord has told me:
"Go, post a guard!
He must report what he sees.
7 When he sees chariots,
teams of horses,
riders on donkeys,
riders on camels,
he must be alert,
very alert."
8 Then the guard cries out:
"On the watchtower, O Lord,
I stand all day long;
at my post
I am stationed every night.
9 Look what's coming!
A charioteer,
a team of horses."
When questioned, he replies,
"Babylon has fallen, fallen!
All the idols of her gods lie shattered on the ground!"

10 O my downtrodden people, crushed like
stalks on the threshing floor,
what I have heard
from the LORD of Heaven's Armies,
the God of Israel,
I have reported to you.

BAD NEWS FOR SEIR

11 This is an oracle about Dumah:
Someone calls to me from Seir,
"Watchman, what is left of the night?
Watchman, what is left of the night?"
12 The watchman replies,
"Morning is coming, but then night.
If you want to ask, ask;
come back again."

THE LORD WILL JUDGE ARABIA

13 This is an oracle about Arabia:
In the thicket of Arabia you spend the night,
you Dedanite caravans.
14 Bring out some water for the thirsty.
You who live in the land of Tema,
bring some food for the fugitives.
15 For they flee from the swords—
from the drawn sword,
and from the battle-ready bow,
and from the severity of the battle.

16 For this is what the Lord has told me: "Within exactly one
year all the splendor of Kedar will come to an end. 17 Just a handful of archers, the warriors of Kedar, will be left." Indeed, the
LORD God of Israel has spoken.

THE LORD WILL JUDGE JERUSALEM

22 This is an oracle about the Valley of Vision:
What is the reason
that all of you go up to the rooftops?
2 The noisy city is full of raucous sounds;
the town is filled with revelry.
Your slain were not cut down by the sword;
they did not die in battle.
3 All your leaders ran away together—
they fled to a distant place;
all your refugees were captured together—
they were captured without a single arrow being shot.
4 So I say:
"Don't look at me!
I am weeping bitterly.
Don't try to console me
concerning the destruction
of my defenseless people."
5 For the Sovereign LORD of Heaven's Armies,
has planned a day of panic, defeat, and confusion.

In the Valley of Vision people shout
and cry out to the hill.
6 The Elamites picked up the quiver,
and came with chariots and horsemen;
the men of Kir prepared the shield.
7 Your very best valleys were full of chariots;
horsemen confidently took their positions at the gate.
8 They removed the defenses of Judah.
At that time you looked
for the weapons in the House of the Forest.
9 You saw the many breaks
in the walls of the City of David;
you stored up water in the lower pool.
10 You counted the houses in Jerusalem,
and demolished houses so you could have
material to reinforce the wall.
11 You made a reservoir between the two walls
for the water of the old pool—
but you did not trust in the one who made it;
you did not depend on the one who formed it long ago.
12 At that time the Sovereign LORD of Heaven's
Armies called for weeping and mourning,
for shaved heads and sackcloth.
13 But look, there is outright celebration!
You say, "Kill the ox and slaughter the sheep,
eat meat and drink wine.
Eat and drink, for tomorrow we die!"

14 The LORD of Heaven's Armies told me this: "Certainly this
sin will not be forgiven as long as you live," says the Sovereign
LORD of Heaven's Armies.

15 This is what the Sovereign LORD of Heaven's Armies says:
"Go visit this administrator, Shebna, who
supervises the palace, and tell him:
16 'What right do you have to be here? What
relatives do you have buried here?
Why do you chisel out a tomb for yourself here?
He chisels out his burial site in an elevated place,
he carves out his tomb on a cliff.
17 Look, the LORD will throw you far away, you mere man!
He will wrap you up tightly.
18 He will wind you up tightly into a ball
and throw you into a wide, open land.
There you will die,
and there with you will be your impressive chariots,
which bring disgrace to the house of your master.
19 I will remove you from your office;
you will be thrown down from your position.

20 "'At that time I will summon my servant Eliakim, son of
Hilkiah. 21 I will put your robe on him, tie your belt around him,
and transfer your authority to him. He will become a protector of the residents of Jerusalem and of the people of Judah.
22 I will place the key to the house of David on his shoulder.

When he opens the door, no one can close it; when he closes
the door, no one can open it. 23 I will fasten him like a peg into
a solid place; he will bring honor and respect to his father's
family. 24 His father's family will gain increasing prominence
because of him, including the offspring and the offshoots. All
the small containers, including the bowls and all the jars, will
hang from this peg.'

25 "At that time," says the LORD of Heaven's Armies, "the peg
fastened into a solid place will come loose. It will be cut off and
fall, and the load hanging on it will be cut off." Indeed, the LORD
has spoken.

THE LORD WILL JUDGE TYRE

23 This is an oracle about Tyre:
Wail, you large ships,
for the port is too devastated to enter!
From the land of Cyprus this news is announced to them.
2 Lament, you residents of the coast,
you merchants of Sidon who travel over the sea,
whose agents sail over 3 the deep waters.
Grain from the Shihor region,
crops grown near the Nile she receives;
she is the trade center of the nations.
4 Be ashamed, O Sidon,
for the sea says this, O fortress of the sea:
"I have not gone into labor
or given birth;
I have not raised young men
or brought up young women."
5 When the news reaches Egypt,
they will be shaken by what has happened to Tyre.
6 Travel to Tarshish!
Wail, you residents of the coast!
7 Is this really your boisterous city
whose origins are in the distant past,
and whose feet led her to a distant land to reside?
8 Who planned this for royal Tyre,
whose merchants are princes,
whose traders are the dignitaries of the earth?
9 The LORD of Heaven's Armies planned it—
to dishonor the pride that comes from all her beauty,
to humiliate all the dignitaries of the earth.
10 Daughter Tarshish, travel back to your
land, as one crosses the Nile;
there is no longer any marketplace in Tyre.
11 The LORD stretched out his hand over the sea,
he shook kingdoms;
he gave the order
to destroy Canaan's fortresses.
12 He said,
"You will no longer celebrate,
oppressed virgin daughter Sidon!
Get up, travel to Cyprus,
but you will find no relief there."

13 Look at the land of the Chaldeans,
these people who have lost their identity!
The Assyrians have made it a home for wild animals.
They erected their siege towers,
demolished its fortresses,
and turned it into a heap of ruins.
14 Wail, you large ships,
for your fortress is destroyed!

15 At that time Tyre will be forgotten for seventy years, the typical life span of a king. At the end of seventy years Tyre will try to
attract attention again, like the prostitute in the popular song:
16 "Take the harp,
go through the city,
forgotten prostitute!
Play it well,
play lots of songs,
so you'll be noticed."

17 At the end of seventy years the LORD will revive Tyre. She will
start making money again by selling her services to all the earth's
kingdoms. 18 Her profits and earnings will be set apart for the
LORD. They will not be stored up or accumulated, for her profits
will be given to those who live in the LORD's presence and will be
used to purchase large quantities of food and beautiful clothes.

THE LORD WILL JUDGE THE EARTH

24 Look, the LORD is ready to devastate the earth
and leave it in ruins;
he will mar its surface
and scatter its inhabitants.
2 Everyone will suffer—the priest as well as the people,
the master as well as the servant,
the elegant lady as well as the female attendant,
the seller as well as the buyer,
the borrower as well as the lender,
the creditor as well as the debtor.
3 The earth will be completely devastated
and thoroughly ransacked.
For the LORD has decreed this judgment.
4 The earth dries up and withers,
the world shrivels up and withers;
the prominent people of the earth fade away.
5 The earth is defiled by its inhabitants,
for they have violated laws,
disregarded the regulation,
and broken the permanent treaty.
6 So a treaty curse devours the earth;
its inhabitants pay for their guilt.
This is why the inhabitants of the earth disappear,
and are reduced to just a handful of people.
7 The new wine dries up,
the vines shrivel up,
all those who like to celebrate groan.

8 The happy sound of the tambourines stops,
the revelry of those who celebrate comes to a halt,
the happy sound of the harp ceases.
9 They no longer sing and drink wine;
the beer tastes bitter to those who drink it.
10 The ruined town is shattered;
all the houses are shut up tight.
11 They howl in the streets because of
what happened to the wine;
all joy turns to sorrow;
celebrations disappear from the earth.
12 The city is left in ruins;
the gate is reduced to rubble.
13 This is what will happen throughout the earth,
among the nations.
It will be like when they beat an olive tree,
and just a few olives are left at the end of the harvest.
14 They lift their voices and shout joyfully;
they praise the majesty of the LORD in the west.
15 So in the east extol the LORD,
along the seacoasts extol the fame of the LORD God of Israel.
16 From the ends of the earth we hear songs—
the Just One is majestic.
But I say, "I'm wasting away! I'm wasting away! I'm doomed!
Deceivers deceive, deceivers thoroughly deceive!"
17 Terror, pit, and snare
are ready to overtake, you inhabitants of the earth!
18 The one who runs away from the sound of the terror
will fall into the pit;
the one who climbs out of the pit
will be trapped by the snare.
For the floodgates of the heavens are opened up
and the foundations of the earth shake.
19 The earth is broken in pieces,
the earth is ripped to shreds,
the earth shakes violently.
20 The earth will stagger around like a drunk;
it will sway back and forth like a hut in a windstorm.
Its sin will weigh it down,
and it will fall and never get up again.

THE LORD WILL BECOME KING

21 At that time the LORD will punish
the heavenly forces in the heavens
and the earthly kings on the earth.
22 They will be imprisoned in a pit,
locked up in a prison,
and after staying there for a long time,
they will be punished.
23 The full moon will be covered up,
the bright sun will be darkened;
for the LORD of Heaven's Armies will rule
on Mount Zion in Jerusalem
in the presence of his assembly, in majestic splendor.

25 O LORD, you are my God!
I will exalt you in praise, I will extol your fame.
For you have done extraordinary things,
and executed plans made long ago exactly as you decreed.
2 Indeed, you have made the city into a heap of rubble,
the fortified town into a heap of ruins;
the fortress of foreigners is no longer a city,
it will never be rebuilt.
3 So a strong nation will extol you;
the towns of powerful nations will fear you.
4 For you are a protector for the poor,
a protector for the needy in their distress,
a shelter from the rainstorm,
a shade from the heat.
Though the breath of tyrants is like a winter rainstorm,
5 like heat in a dry land,
you humble the boasting foreigners.
Just as the shadow of a cloud causes the heat to subside,
so he causes the song of tyrants to cease.
6 The LORD of Heaven's Armies will hold a banquet
for all the nations on this mountain.
At this banquet there will be plenty
of meat and aged wine—
tender meat and choicest wine.
7 On this mountain he will swallow up
the shroud that is over all the peoples,
the woven covering that is over all the nations;
8 he will swallow up death permanently.
The Sovereign LORD will wipe away
the tears from every face,
and remove his people's disgrace from all the earth.
Indeed, the LORD has announced it!
9 At that time they will say,
"Look, here is our God!
We waited for him, and he delivered us.
Here is the LORD! We waited for him.
Let's rejoice and celebrate his deliverance!"
10 For the LORD's power will make this mountain secure.
Moab will be trampled down where it stands,
as a heap of straw is trampled down in a manure pile.
11 Moab will spread out its hands in the middle of it,
just as a swimmer spreads his hands to swim;
the LORD will bring down Moab's
pride as it spreads its hands.
12 The fortified city (along with the very tops
of your walls) he will knock down,
he will bring it down, he will throw it
down to the dusty ground.

JUDAH WILL CELEBRATE

26 At that time this song will be sung in the land of Judah:
"We have a strong city!
The LORD's deliverance, like walls and
a rampart, makes it secure.

2 Open the gates so a righteous nation can enter—
one that remains trustworthy.
3 You keep completely safe the people
who maintain their faith,
for they trust in you.
4 Trust in the LORD from this time forward,
even in YAH, the LORD, an enduring protector!
5 Indeed, the LORD knocks down those
who live in a high place,
he brings down an elevated town;
he brings it down to the ground,
he throws it down to the dust.
6 It is trampled underfoot
by the feet of the oppressed,
by the soles of the poor."

GOD'S PEOPLE ANTICIPATE VINDICATION

7 The way of the righteous is level,
the path of the righteous that you prepare is straight.
8 Yes, as your judgments unfold,
O LORD, we wait for you.
We desire your fame and reputation to grow.
9 I look for you during the night;
my spirit within me seeks you at dawn,
for when your judgments come upon the earth,
those who live in the world learn about justice.
10 If the wicked are shown mercy,
they do not learn about justice.
Even in a land where right is rewarded, they act unjustly;
they do not see the LORD's majesty revealed.
11 O LORD, you are ready to act,
but they don't even notice.
They will see and be put to shame by your
angry judgment against humankind;
yes, fire will consume your enemies.
12 O LORD, you make us secure,
for even all we have accomplished, you have done for us.
13 O LORD, our God,
masters other than you have ruled us,
but we praise your name alone.
14 The dead do not come back to life,
the spirits of the dead do not rise.
That is because you came in judgment
and destroyed them,
you wiped out all memory of them.
15 You have made the nation larger, O LORD;
you have made the nation larger and
revealed your splendor;
you have extended all the borders of the land.
16 O LORD, in distress they looked for you;
they uttered incantations because of your discipline.
17 As when a pregnant woman gets ready to deliver
and strains and cries out because of her labor pains,
so were we because of you, O LORD.

18 We were pregnant, we strained,
we gave birth, as it were, to wind.
We cannot produce deliverance on the earth;
no people are born to populate the world.
19 Your dead will come back to life;
your corpses will rise up.
Wake up and shout joyfully,
you who live in the ground!
For you will grow like plants drenched
with the morning dew,
and the earth will bring forth its dead spirits.
20 Go, my people! Enter your inner rooms!
Close your doors behind you!
Hide for a little while,
until his angry judgment is over.
21 For look, the LORD is coming out of
the place where he lives,
to punish the sin of those who live on the earth.
The earth will display the blood shed on it;
it will no longer cover up its slain.

27 At that time the LORD will punish
with his destructive, great, and powerful sword
Leviathan the fast-moving serpent,
Leviathan the squirming serpent;
he will kill the sea monster.
2 When that time comes,
sing about a delightful vineyard!
3 "I, the LORD, protect it;
I water it regularly.
I guard it night and day,
so no one can harm it.
4 I am not angry.
I wish I could confront some thorns and briers!
Then I would march against them for battle;
I would set them all on fire,
5 unless they became my subjects
and made peace with me;
let them make peace with me."

6 The time is coming when Jacob will take root;
Israel will blossom and grow branches.
The produce will fill the surface of the world.
7 Has the LORD struck down Israel as
he did their oppressors?
Has Israel been killed like their enemies?
8 When you summon her for divorce, you prosecute her;
he drives her away with his strong wind
in the day of the east wind.
9 So in this way Jacob's sin will be forgiven,
and this is how they will show they are finished sinning:
They will make all the stones of the altars
like crushed limestone,
and the Asherah poles and the incense
altars will no longer stand.

10 For the fortified city is left alone;
it is a deserted settlement
and abandoned like the wilderness.
Calves graze there;
they lie down there
and eat its branches bare.
11 When its branches get brittle, they break;
women come and use them for kindling.
For these people lack understanding,
therefore the one who made them has
no compassion on them;
the one who formed them has no mercy on them.

12 At that time the LORD will shake the tree, from the Euphrates River to the Stream of Egypt. Then you will be gathered up
one by one, O Israelites. 13 At that time a large trumpet will be
blown, and the ones lost in the land of Assyria will come, as well
as the refugees in the land of Egypt. They will worship the LORD
on the holy mountain in Jerusalem.

REFLECT

Why was it important for the people of Israel to worship the Lord after they were gathered back to Him? What does this reveal about the importance of worship?

THE LORD WILL JUDGE EPHRAIM

28 The splendid crown of Ephraim's drunkards is doomed,
the withering flower, its beautiful splendor,
situated at the head of a rich valley,
the crown of those overcome with wine.
2 Look, the Lord sends a strong, powerful one.
With the force of a hailstorm or
a destructive windstorm,
with the might of a driving, torrential rainstorm,
he will knock that crown to the ground with his hand.
3 The splendid crown of Ephraim's drunkards
will be trampled underfoot.
4 The withering flower, its beautiful splendor,
situated at the head of a rich valley,
will be like an early fig before harvest—
as soon as someone notices it,
he grabs it and swallows it.
5 At that time the LORD of Heaven's Armies
will become a beautiful crown
and a splendid diadem for the remnant of his people.
6 He will give discernment to the one
who makes judicial decisions,
and strength to those who defend
the city from attackers.
7 Even these men stagger because of wine;
they stumble around because of beer—
priests and prophets stagger because of beer,
they are confused because of wine,
they stumble around because of beer;
they stagger while seeing prophetic visions,
they totter while making legal decisions.
8 Indeed, all the tables
are covered with vomit,
with filth, leaving no clean place.

9 Who is the LORD trying to teach?
To whom is he explaining a message?
To those just weaned from milk!
To those just taken from their mother's breast!
10 Indeed, they will hear meaningless gibberish,
senseless babbling,
a syllable here, a syllable there.
11 For with mocking lips and a foreign tongue
he will speak to these people.
12 In the past he said to them,
"This is where security can be found.
Provide security for the one who is exhausted.
This is where rest can be found."
But they refused to listen.
13 So the LORD's message to them will sound like
meaningless gibberish,
senseless babbling,
a syllable here, a syllable there.
As a result, they will fall on their
backsides when they try to walk,
and be injured, ensnared, and captured.

THE LORD WILL JUDGE JERUSALEM

14 Therefore, listen to the LORD's message,
you who mock,
you rulers of these people
who reside in Jerusalem.
15 For you say,
"We have made a treaty with death,
with Sheol we have made an agreement.
When the overwhelming judgment sweeps by
it will not reach us.
For we have made a lie our refuge,
we have hidden ourselves in a deceitful word."

16 Therefore, this is what the Sovereign LORD, says:
"Look, I am laying a stone in Zion,
an approved stone,
set in place as a precious cornerstone for
the foundation.
The one who maintains his faith will not panic.
17 I will make justice the measuring line,
fairness the plumb line;
hail will sweep away the unreliable refuge,
the floodwaters will overwhelm the hiding place.
18 Your treaty with death will be dissolved;
your agreement with Sheol will not last.
When the overwhelming judgment sweeps by,
you will be overrun by it.
19 Whenever it sweeps by, it will overtake you;
indeed, every morning it will sweep by,
it will come through during the day and the night."
When this announcement is understood,
it will cause nothing but terror.

20 For the bed is too short to stretch out on,
and the blanket is too narrow to wrap around oneself.
21 For the LORD will rise up, as he did at Mount Perazim;
he will rouse himself, as he did in the Valley of Gibeon,
to accomplish his work,
his peculiar work,
to perform his task,
his strange task.
22 So now, do not mock,
or your chains will become heavier!
For I have heard a message about decreed destruction,
from the Sovereign LORD of Heaven's
Armies against the entire land.
23 Pay attention and listen to my message.
Be attentive and listen to what I have to say!
24 Does a farmer just keep on plowing at planting time?
Does he keep breaking up and harrowing his ground?
25 Once he has leveled its surface,
does he not scatter the seed of the caraway plant,
sow the seed of the cumin plant,
and plant the wheat, barley, and grain
in their designated places?
26 His God instructs him;
he teaches him the principles of agriculture.
27 Certainly caraway seed is not threshed with a sledge,
nor is the wheel of a cart rolled over cumin seed.
Certainly caraway seed is beaten with a stick,
and cumin seed with a flail.
28 Grain is crushed,
though one certainly does not thresh it forever.
The wheel of one's wagon rolls over it,
but his horses do not crush it.
29 This also comes from the LORD of Heaven's Armies,
who gives supernatural guidance and
imparts great wisdom.

ARIEL IS BESIEGED

29 Ariel is as good as dead—
Ariel, the town David besieged!
Keep observing your annual rituals;
celebrate your festivals on schedule.
2 I will threaten Ariel,
and she will mourn intensely
and become like an altar hearth before me.
3 I will lay siege to you on all sides;
I will besiege you with troops;
I will raise siege works against you.
4 You will fall;
while lying on the ground you will speak;
from the dust where you lie, your words will be heard.
Your voice will sound like a spirit
speaking from the underworld;
from the dust you will chirp as if
muttering an incantation.

5 But the horde of invaders will be like fine dust,
the horde of tyrants like chaff that is blown away.
It will happen suddenly, in a flash.
6 Judgment will come from the LORD of Heaven's Armies,
accompanied by thunder, earthquake, and a loud noise,
by a strong gale, a windstorm, and a consuming flame of fire.
7 It will be like a dream, a night vision.
There will be a horde from all the nations
that fight against Ariel,
those who attack her and her stronghold and besiege her.
8 It will be like a hungry man dreaming that he is eating,
only to awaken and find that his stomach is empty.
It will be like a thirsty man dreaming that he is drinking,
only to awaken and find that he is still
weak and his thirst unquenched.
So it will be for the horde from all the nations
that fight against Mount Zion.

GOD'S PEOPLE ARE SPIRITUALLY INSENSITIVE

9 You will be shocked and amazed!
You are totally blind!
They are drunk, but not because of wine;
they stagger, but not because of beer.
10 For the LORD has poured out on you
a strong urge to sleep deeply.
He has shut your eyes (you prophets),
and covered your heads (you seers).

11 To you this entire prophetic revelation is like words in a
sealed scroll. When they hand it to one who can read and say,
"Read this," he responds, "I can't, because it is sealed." 12 Or when
they hand the scroll to one who can't read and say, "Read this,"
he says, "I can't read."

13 The Lord says,
"These people say they are loyal to me;
they say wonderful things about me,
but they are not really loyal to me.
Their worship consists of
nothing but man-made ritual.
14 Therefore I will again do an amazing
thing for these people—
an absolutely extraordinary deed.
Wise men will have nothing to say,
the sages will have no explanations."
15 Those who try to hide their plans from
the LORD are as good as dead,
who do their work in secret and boast,
"Who sees us? Who knows what we're doing?"
16 Your thinking is perverse!
Should the potter be regarded as clay?
Should the thing made say about its
maker, "He didn't make me"?
Or should the pottery say about the
potter, "He doesn't understand"?

CHANGES ARE COMING

17 In just a very short time
Lebanon will turn into an orchard,
and the orchard will be considered a forest.
18 At that time the deaf will be able to
hear words read from a scroll,
and the eyes of the blind will be able to
see through deep darkness.
19 The downtrodden will again rejoice in the LORD;
the poor among humankind will take
delight in the Holy One of Israel.
20 For tyrants will disappear,
those who taunt will vanish,
and all those who love to do wrong will be eliminated—
21 those who bear false testimony against a person,
who entrap the one who arbitrates at the city gate
and deprive the innocent of justice
by making false charges.
22 So this is what the LORD, the one who delivered
Abraham, has said to the family of Jacob:
"Jacob will no longer be ashamed;
their faces will no longer show their embarrassment.
23 For when they see their children,
whom I will produce among them,
they will honor my name.
They will honor the Holy One of Jacob;
they will respect the God of Israel.
24 Those who stray morally will gain understanding;
those who complain will acquire insight.

EGYPT WILL PROVE UNRELIABLE

30 "The rebellious children are as good
as dead," says the LORD,
"those who make plans without consulting me,
who form alliances without consulting my Spirit,
and thereby compound their sin.
2 They travel down to Egypt
without seeking my will,
seeking Pharaoh's protection,
and looking for safety in Egypt's protective shade.
3 But Pharaoh's protection will bring
you nothing but shame,
and the safety of Egypt's protective
shade nothing but humiliation.
4 Though his officials are in Zoan
and his messengers arrive at Hanes,
5 all will be put to shame
because of a nation that cannot help them,
who cannot give them aid or help,
but only shame and disgrace."
6 This is an oracle about the animals in the Negev:
Through a land of distress and danger,
inhabited by lionesses and roaring lions,
by snakes and darting adders,

they transport their wealth on the backs of donkeys,
their riches on the humps of camels,
to a nation that cannot help them.
7 Egypt is totally incapable of helping.
For this reason I call her
"Proud one who is silenced."
8 Now go, write it down on a tablet in their presence,
inscribe it on a scroll,
so that it might be preserved for a future time
as an enduring witness.
9 For these are rebellious people—
they are lying children,
children unwilling to obey the LORD's law.
10 They say to the visionaries, "See no more visions!"
and to the seers, "Don't relate messages
to us about what is right!
Tell us nice things;
relate deceptive messages.
11 Turn aside from the way;
stray off the path.
Remove from our presence the Holy One of Israel."

12 For this reason this is what the Holy One of Israel says:
"You have rejected this message;
you trust instead in your ability to oppress and trick,
and rely on that kind of behavior.
13 So this sin will become your downfall.
You will be like a high wall
that bulges and cracks and is ready to collapse;
it crumbles suddenly, in a flash.
14 It shatters in pieces like a clay jar,
so shattered to bits that none of it can be salvaged.
Among its fragments one cannot
find a shard large enough
to scoop a hot coal from a fire
or to skim off water from a cistern."

15 For this is what the Sovereign LORD, the Holy One of Israel says:
"If you repented and patiently waited
for me, you would be delivered;
if you calmly trusted in me, you would find strength,
but you are unwilling.
16 You say, 'No, we will flee on horses,'
so you will indeed flee.
You say, 'We will ride on fast horses,'
so your pursuers will be fast.
17 One thousand will scurry at the battle
cry of one enemy soldier;
at the battle cry of five enemy soldiers
you will all run away,
until the remaining few are as isolated
as a flagpole on a mountaintop
or a signal flag on a hill."

THE LORD WILL NOT ABANDON HIS PEOPLE

18 For this reason the LORD is ready to show you mercy;
he sits on his throne, ready to have compassion on you.
Indeed, the LORD is a just God;
all who wait for him in faith will be blessed.
19 For people will live in Zion;
in Jerusalem you will weep no more.
When he hears your cry of despair, he
will indeed show you mercy;
when he hears it, he will respond to you.
20 The Lord will give you distress to eat
and suffering to drink;
but your teachers will no longer be hidden;
your eyes will see them.
21 You will hear a word spoken behind you, saying,
"This is the correct way, walk in it,"
whether you are heading to the right or the left.
22 You will desecrate your silver-plated idols
and your gold-plated images.
You will throw them away as if they were a menstrual rag,
saying to them, "Get out!"
23 He will water the seed you plant in the ground,
and the ground will produce crops in abundance.
At that time your cattle will graze in wide pastures.
24 The oxen and donkeys used in plowing
will eat seasoned feed winnowed with a shovel and pitchfork.
25 On every high mountain
and every high hill
there will be streams flowing with water,
at the time of great slaughter when
the fortified towers collapse.
26 The light of the full moon will be like the sun's glare,
and the sun's glare will be seven times brighter,
like the light of seven days,
when the LORD binds up his people's fractured bones
and heals their severe wound.
27 Look, the name of the LORD comes from a distant place
in raging anger and awesome splendor.
He speaks angrily,
and his word is like destructive fire.
28 His battle cry overwhelms like a flooding river
that reaches one's neck.
He shakes the nations in a sieve that isolates the chaff;
he puts a bit into the mouth of the nations
and leads them to destruction.
29 You will sing
as you do in the evening when you are celebrating a festival.
You will be happy like one who plays a flute
as he goes to the mountain of the LORD,
the Rock who shelters Israel.
30 The LORD will give a mighty shout
and intervene in power,
with furious anger and flaming, destructive fire,
with a driving rainstorm and hailstones.

31 Indeed, the LORD's shout will shatter Assyria;
he will beat them with a club.
32 Every blow from his punishing cudgel
with which the LORD will beat them
will be accompanied by music from
the tambourine and harp,
and he will attack them with his weapons.
33 For the burial place is already prepared;
it has been made deep and wide for the king.
The firewood is piled high on it.
The LORD's breath, like a stream
flowing with brimstone,
will ignite it.

EGYPT WILL DISAPPOINT

31 Those who go down to Egypt for help are as good as dead;
those who rely on war horses,
and trust in Egypt's many chariots
and in their many, many horsemen.
But they do not rely on the Holy One of Israel
and do not seek help from the LORD.
2 Yet he too is wise and he will bring disaster;
he does not retract his decree.
He will attack the wicked nation,
and the nation that helps those who commit sin.
3 The Egyptians are mere humans, not God;
their horses are made of flesh, not spirit.
The LORD will strike with his hand;
the one who helps will stumble
and the one being helped will fall.
Together they will perish.

THE LORD WILL DEFEND ZION

4 Indeed, this is what the LORD has said to me:
"The LORD will be like a growling lion,
like a young lion growling over its prey.
Though a whole group of shepherds gathers against it,
it is not afraid of their shouts
or intimidated by their yelling.
In this same way the LORD of Heaven's
Armies will descend
to do battle on Mount Zion and on its hill.
5 Just as birds hover over a nest,
so the LORD of Heaven's Armies will protect Jerusalem.
He will protect and deliver it;
as he passes over he will rescue it."

6 You Israelites! Return to the one you have so blatantly rebelled against! 7 For at that time every one will get rid of the silver and gold idols your hands sinfully made.
8 "Assyria will fall by a sword, but not one human-made;
a sword not made by humankind will destroy them.
They will run away from this sword
and their young men will be forced to do hard labor.

9 They will surrender their stronghold because of fear;
their officers will be afraid of the LORD's battle flag."
This is what the LORD says—
the one whose fire is in Zion,
whose firepot is in Jerusalem.

JUSTICE AND WISDOM WILL PREVAIL

32 Look, a king will promote fairness;
officials will promote justice.
2 Each of them will be like a shelter from the wind
and a refuge from a rainstorm;
like streams of water in a dry region
and like the shade of a large cliff in a parched land.
3 Eyes will no longer be blind
and ears will be attentive.
4 The mind that acts rashly will possess discernment,
and the tongue that stutters will
speak with ease and clarity.
5 A fool will no longer be called honorable;
a deceiver will no longer be called principled.
6 For a fool speaks disgraceful things;
his mind plans out sinful deeds.
He commits godless deeds
and says misleading things about the LORD;
he gives the hungry nothing
to satisfy their appetite
and gives the thirsty nothing to drink.
7 A deceiver's methods are evil;
he dreams up evil plans
to ruin the poor with lies,
even when the needy are in the right.
8 An honorable man makes honorable plans;
his honorable character gives him security.

THE LORD WILL GIVE TRUE SECURITY

9 You complacent women,
get up and listen to me!
You carefree daughters,
pay attention to what I say!
10 In a year's time
you carefree ones will shake with fear,
for the grape harvest will fail,
and the fruit harvest will not arrive.
11 Tremble, you complacent ones!
Shake with fear, you carefree ones!
Strip off your clothes and expose yourselves—
put sackcloth around your waists.
12 Mourn over the field,
over the delightful fields
and the fruitful vine.
13 Mourn over the land of my people,
which is overgrown with thorns and briers,
and over all the once-happy houses
in the city filled with revelry.

14 For the fortress is neglected;
the once-crowded city is abandoned.
Hill and watchtower
are permanently uninhabited.
Wild donkeys love to go there,
and flocks graze there.
15 This desolation will continue until new life
is poured out on us from heaven.
Then the wilderness will become an orchard
and the orchard will be considered a forest.
16 Justice will settle down in the wilderness
and fairness will live in the orchard.
17 Fairness will produce peace
and result in lasting security.
18 My people will live in peaceful settlements,
in secure homes,
and in safe, quiet places.
19 Even if the forest is destroyed
and the city is annihilated,
20 you will be blessed,
you who plant seed by all the banks of the streams,
you who let your ox and donkey graze.

THE LORD WILL RESTORE ZION

33 The destroyer is as good as dead,
you who have not been destroyed!
The deceitful one is as good as dead,
the one whom others have not deceived!
When you are through destroying,
you will be destroyed;
when you finish deceiving,
others will deceive you!
2 LORD, be merciful to us! We wait for you.
Give us strength each morning.
Deliver us when distress comes.
3 The nations run away when they
hear a loud noise;
the nations scatter when you spring into action!
4 Your plunder disappears as
if locusts were eating it;
they swarm over it like locusts.
5 The LORD is exalted,
indeed, he lives in heaven;
he fills Zion with justice and fairness.
6 He is your constant source of stability;
he abundantly provides safety and great wisdom;
he gives all this to those who fear him.
7 Look, ambassadors cry out in the streets;
messengers sent to make peace weep bitterly.
8 Highways are empty,
there are no travelers.
Treaties are broken,
witnesses are despised,
human life is treated with disrespect.

9 The land dries up and withers away;
the forest of Lebanon shrivels up and decays.
Sharon is like the arid rift valley;
Bashan and Carmel are parched.
10 "Now I will rise up," says the LORD.
"Now I will exalt myself;
now I will magnify myself.
11 You conceive straw,
you give birth to chaff;
your breath is a fire that destroys you.
12 The nations will be burned to ashes;
like thorn bushes that have been cut
down, they will be set on fire.
13 You who are far away, listen to what I have done!
You who are close by, recognize my strength."
14 Sinners are afraid in Zion;
panic grips the godless.
They say, "Who among us can
coexist with destructive fire?
Who among us can coexist with unquenchable fire?"
15 The one who lives uprightly
and speaks honestly;
the one who refuses to profit from oppressive measures
and rejects a bribe;
the one who does not plot violent crimes
and does not seek to harm others—
16 this is the person who will live in a secure place;
he will find safety in the rocky, mountain strongholds;
he will have food
and a constant supply of water.
17 You will see a king in his splendor;
you will see a wide land.
18 Your mind will recall the terror you experienced,
and you will ask yourselves, "Where is the scribe?
Where is the one who weighs the money?
Where is the one who counts the towers?"
19 You will no longer see a defiant people
whose language you do not comprehend,
whose derisive speech you do not understand.
20 Look at Zion, the city where
we hold religious festivals!
You will see Jerusalem,
a peaceful settlement,
a tent that stays put;
its stakes will never be pulled up;
none of its ropes will snap in two.
21 Instead the LORD will rule there as our mighty king.
Rivers and wide streams will flow through it;
no war galley will enter;
no large ships will sail through.
22 For the LORD, our ruler,
the LORD, our commander,
the LORD, our king—
he will deliver us.

23 Though at this time your ropes are slack,
the mast is not secured,
and the sail is not unfurled,
at that time you will divide up a great quantity of loot;
even the lame will drag off plunder.
24 No resident of Zion will say, "I am ill";
the people who live there will have their sin forgiven.

THE LORD WILL JUDGE EDOM

34 Come near, you nations, and listen!
Pay attention, you people!
The earth and everything it contains must listen,
the world and everything that lives in it.
2 For the LORD is angry at all the nations
and furious with all their armies.
He will annihilate them and slaughter them.
3 Their slain will be left unburied,
their corpses will stink;
the hills will soak up their blood.
4 All the stars in the sky will fade away,
the sky will roll up like a scroll;
all its stars will wither,
like a leaf withers and falls from a vine
or a fig withers and falls from a tree.
5 He says, "Indeed, my sword has
slaughtered heavenly powers.
Look, it now descends on Edom,
on the people I will annihilate in judgment."
6 The LORD's sword is dripping with blood,
it is covered with fat;
it drips with the blood of young rams and goats
and is covered with the fat of rams' kidneys.
For the LORD is holding a sacrifice in Bozrah,
a bloody slaughter in the land of Edom.
7 Wild oxen will be slaughtered along with them,
as well as strong bulls.
Their land is drenched with blood,
their soil is covered with fat.
8 For the LORD has planned a day of revenge,
a time when he will repay Edom for
her hostility toward Zion.
9 Edom's streams will be turned into pitch
and her soil into brimstone;
her land will become burning pitch.
10 Night and day it will burn;
its smoke will ascend continually.
Generation after generation it
will be a wasteland,
and no one will ever pass through it again.
11 Owls and wild animals will live there,
all kinds of wild birds will settle in it.
The LORD will stretch out over her
the measuring line of ruin
and the plumb line of destruction.

12 Her nobles will have nothing left to call a kingdom,
and all her officials will disappear.
13 Her fortresses will be overgrown with thorns;
thickets and weeds will grow in her fortified cities.
Jackals will settle there;
ostriches will live there.
14 Wild animals and wild dogs will congregate there;
wild goats will bleat to one another.
Yes, nocturnal animals will rest there
and make for themselves a nest.
15 Owls will make nests and lay eggs there;
they will hatch them and protect them.
Yes, hawks will gather there,
each with its mate.
16 Carefully read the scroll of the LORD!
Not one of these creatures will be missing,
none will lack a mate.
For the LORD has issued the decree,
and his own spirit gathers them.
17 He assigns them their allotment;
he measures out their assigned place.
They will live there permanently;
they will settle in it through successive generations.

THE LAND AND ITS PEOPLE ARE TRANSFORMED

35 Let the wilderness and desert be happy;
let the arid rift valley rejoice and bloom like a lily!
2 Let it richly bloom;
let it rejoice and shout with delight!
It is given the grandeur of Lebanon,
the splendor of Carmel and Sharon.
They will see the grandeur of the LORD,
the splendor of our God.
3 Strengthen the hands that have gone limp,
steady the knees that shake.
4 Tell those who panic,
"Be strong! Do not fear!
Look, your God comes to avenge;
with divine retribution he comes to deliver you."
5 Then blind eyes will open,
deaf ears will hear.
6 Then the lame will leap like a deer,
the mute tongue will shout for joy;
for water will burst forth in the wilderness,
streams in the arid rift valley.
7 The dry soil will become a pool of water,
the parched ground springs of water.
Where jackals once lived and sprawled out,
grass, reeds, and papyrus will grow.
8 A thoroughfare will be there—
it will be called the Way of Holiness.
The unclean will not travel on it;
it is reserved for those authorized to use it—
fools will not stray into it.

9 No lions will be there,
no ferocious wild animals will be on it—
they will not be found there.
Those delivered from bondage will travel on it,
10 those whom the LORD has ransomed will return that way.
They will enter Zion with a happy shout.
Unending joy will crown them,
happiness and joy will overwhelm them;
grief and suffering will disappear.

SENNACHERIB INVADES JUDAH

36 In the fourteenth year of King Hezekiah's reign, King Sennacherib of Assyria marched up against all the fortified
cities of Judah and captured them. 2 The king of Assyria sent his
chief adviser from Lachish to King Hezekiah in Jerusalem, along
with a large army. The chief adviser stood at the conduit of the
upper pool that is located on the road to the field where they
wash and dry cloth. 3 Eliakim son of Hilkiah, the palace supervisor, accompanied by Shebna the scribe and Joah son of Asaph,
the secretary, went out to meet him.

4 The chief adviser said to them, "Tell Hezekiah: 'This is what
the great king, the king of Assyria, says: "What is your source of
confidence? 5 Your claim to have a strategy and military strength
is just empty talk. In whom are you trusting, that you would dare
to rebel against me? 6 Look, you must be trusting in Egypt, that
splintered reed staff. If someone leans on it for support, it punctures his hand and wounds him. That is what Pharaoh king of
Egypt does to all who trust in him! 7 Perhaps you will tell me, 'We
are trusting in the LORD our God.' But Hezekiah is the one who
eliminated his high places and altars and then told the people
of Judah and Jerusalem, 'You must worship at this altar.' 8 Now
make a deal with my master the king of Assyria, and I will give
you 2,000 horses, provided you can find enough riders for them.
9 Certainly you will not refuse one of my master's minor officials
and trust in Egypt for chariots and horsemen. 10 Furthermore
it was by the command of the LORD that I marched up against
this land to destroy it. The LORD told me, 'March up against this
land and destroy it!'"'"

11 Eliakim, Shebna, and Joah said to the chief adviser, "Speak
to your servants in Aramaic, for we understand it. Don't speak
with us in the Judahite dialect in the hearing of the people who
are on the wall." 12 But the chief adviser said, "My master did not
send me to speak these words only to your master and to you. His
message is also for the men who sit on the wall, for they will eat
their own excrement and drink their own urine along with you!"

13 The chief adviser then stood there and called out loudly in
the Judahite dialect, "Listen to the message of the great king, the
king of Assyria. 14 This is what the king says: 'Don't let Hezekiah
mislead you, for he is not able to rescue you! 15 Don't let Hezekiah
talk you into trusting in the LORD by saying, "The LORD will certainly rescue us; this city will not be handed over to the king of
Assyria." 16 Don't listen to Hezekiah!' For this is what the king of
Assyria says, 'Send me a token of your submission and surrender
to me. Then each of you may eat from his own vine and fig tree

and drink water from his own cistern, 17 until I come and take
you to a land just like your own—a land of grain and new wine, a
land of bread and vineyards. 18 Hezekiah is misleading you when
he says, "The LORD will rescue us." Have any of the gods of the nations rescued their lands from the power of the king of Assyria?
19 Where are the gods of Hamath and Arpad? Where are the gods
of Sepharvaim? Indeed, did any gods rescue Samaria from my
power? 20 Who among all the gods of these lands have rescued
their lands from my power? So how can the LORD rescue Jerusalem from my power?'" 21 They were silent and did not respond,
for the king had ordered, "Don't respond to him."

22 Eliakim son of Hilkiah, the palace supervisor, accompanied
by Shebna the scribe and Joah son of Asaph, the secretary, went
to Hezekiah with their clothes torn and reported to him what
the chief adviser had said.

37 When King Hezekiah heard this, he tore his clothes, put
on sackcloth, and went to the LORD's temple. 2 Eliakim the
palace supervisor, Shebna the scribe, and the leading priests,
clothed in sackcloth, sent this message to the prophet Isaiah
son of Amoz: 3 "This is what Hezekiah says: 'This is a day of distress, insults, and humiliation, as when a baby is ready to leave
the birth canal, but the mother lacks the strength to push it
through. 4 Perhaps the LORD your God will hear all these things
the chief adviser has spoken on behalf of his master, the king of
Assyria, who sent him to taunt the living God. When the LORD
your God hears, perhaps he will punish him for the things he
has said. So pray for this remnant that remains.'"

5 When King Hezekiah's servants came to Isaiah, 6 Isaiah said
to them, "Tell your master this: 'This is what the LORD has said:
"Don't be afraid because of the things you have heard—these insults the king of Assyria's servants have hurled against me. 7 Look,
I will take control of his mind; he will receive a report and return
to his own land. I will cut him down with a sword in his own land."'"

8 When the chief adviser heard the king of Assyria had departed from Lachish, he left and went to Libnah, where the king
was campaigning. 9 The king heard that King Tirhakah of Ethiopia was marching out to fight him. He again sent messengers to
Hezekiah, ordering them: 10 "Tell King Hezekiah of Judah this:
'Don't let your God in whom you trust mislead you when he says,
"Jerusalem will not be handed over to the king of Assyria." 11 Certainly you have heard how the kings of Assyria have annihilated
all lands. Do you really think you will be rescued? 12 Were the nations whom my predecessors destroyed—the nations of Gozan,
Haran, Rezeph, and the people of Eden in Telassar—rescued by
their gods? 13 Where is the king of Hamath or the king of Arpad
or the kings of Lair, Sepharvaim, Hena, and Ivvah?'"

14 Hezekiah took the letter from the messengers and read it. Then
Hezekiah went up to the LORD's temple and spread it out before
the LORD. 15 Hezekiah prayed before the LORD: 16 "O LORD of Heav-
en's Armies, O God of Israel, who is enthroned on the cherubim!
You alone are God over all the kingdoms of the earth. You made the
sky and the earth. 17 Pay attention, LORD, and hear! Open your eyes,
LORD, and observe! Listen to this entire message Sennacherib sent
and how he taunts the living God! 18 It is true, LORD, that the kings

of Assyria have destroyed all the nations and their lands. 19 They
have burned the gods of the nations, for they are not really gods,
but only the product of human hands manufactured from wood
and stone. That is why the Assyrians could destroy them. 20 Now,
O LORD our God, rescue us from his power, so all the kingdoms of
the earth may know that you alone are the LORD."

21 Isaiah son of Amoz sent this message to Hezekiah: "This is
what the LORD God of Israel has said: 'As to what you have prayed
to me concerning King Sennacherib of Assyria, 22 this is what the
LORD says about him:

"'The virgin daughter Zion
despises you—she makes fun of you;
daughter Jerusalem
shakes her head after you.

23 Whom have you taunted and hurled insults at?
At whom have you shouted
and looked so arrogantly?
At the Holy One of Israel!
24 Through your messengers you taunted the Lord,
"With my many chariots I climbed up
the high mountains,
the slopes of Lebanon.
I cut down its tall cedars
and its best evergreens.
I invaded its remotest regions,
its thickest woods.
25 I dug wells
and drank water.
With the soles of my feet I dried up
all the rivers of Egypt."'

26 Certainly you must have heard!
Long ago I worked it out,
in ancient times I planned it,
and now I am bringing it to pass.
The plan is this:
Fortified cities will crash
into heaps of ruins.
27 Their residents are powerless;
they are terrified and ashamed.
They are as short-lived as plants in the field
or green vegetation.
They are as short-lived as grass on the rooftops
when it is scorched by the east wind.
28 I know where you live
and everything you do
and how you rage against me.
29 Because you rage against me
and the uproar you create has reached my ears,
I will put my hook in your nose,
and my bit between your lips,
and I will lead you back
the way you came.'

30 "This will be your reminder that I have spoken the truth:
This year you will eat what grows wild, and next year what grows
on its own. But the year after that you will plant seed and harvest crops; you will plant vines and consume their produce.
31 Those who remain in Judah will take root in the ground and
bear fruit.

32 "For a remnant will leave Jerusalem;
survivors will come out of Mount Zion.
The zeal of the LORD of Heaven's
Armies will accomplish this.

33 So this is what the LORD says about the king
of Assyria:
"'He will not enter this city,
nor will he shoot an arrow here.
He will not attack it with his shielded warriors,
nor will he build siege works against it.
34 He will go back the way he came—
he will not enter this city,' says the LORD.
35 I will shield this city and rescue it
for the sake of my reputation and because
of my promise to David my servant."

36 The angel of the LORD went out and killed 185,000 troops
in the Assyrian camp. When they got up early the next morning, there were all the corpses! 37 So King Sennacherib of Assyria
broke camp and went on his way. He went home and stayed in
Nineveh. 38 One day, as he was worshiping in the temple of his
god Nisroch, his sons Adrammelech and Sharezer struck him
down with the sword. They ran away to the land of Ararat; his
son Esarhaddon replaced him as king.

THE LORD HEARS HEZEKIAH'S PRAYER

38 In those days Hezekiah was stricken with a terminal illness. The prophet Isaiah son of Amoz visited him and
told him, "This is what the LORD says, 'Give instructions to
your household, for you are about to die; you will not get well.'"
2 Hezekiah turned his face to the wall and prayed to the LORD,
3 "Please, LORD. Remember how I have served you faithfully and
with wholehearted devotion, and how I have carried out your
will." Then Hezekiah wept bitterly.
4 The LORD's message came to Isaiah, 5 "Go and tell Hezekiah: 'This is what the LORD God of your ancestor David says:
"I have heard your prayer; I have seen your tears. Look, I will
add fifteen years to your life. 6 I will also rescue you and this
city from the king of Assyria. I will shield this city."'" 7 Isaiah
replied, "This is your sign from the LORD confirming that the
LORD will do what he has said: 8 Look, I will make the shadow
go back ten steps on the stairs of Ahaz." And then the shadow
went back ten steps.

HEZEKIAH'S SONG OF THANKS

9 This is the prayer of King Hezekiah of Judah when he was sick
and then recovered from his illness:

10 "I thought,
'In the middle of my life I must walk
through the gates of Sheol,
I am deprived of the rest of my years.'

11 "I thought,
'I will no longer see the LORD in the land of the living,
I will no longer look on humankind with
the inhabitants of the world.
12 My dwelling place is removed and taken away from me
as a shepherd's tent.
I rolled up my life like a weaver rolls cloth;
from the loom he cuts me off.
You turn day into night and end my life.
13 I cry out until morning;
like a lion he shatters all my bones;
you turn day into night and end my life.
14 Like a swallow or a thrush I chirp,
I coo like a dove;
my eyes grow tired from looking up to the sky.
O Lord, I am oppressed;
help me!
15 What can I say?
He has decreed and acted.
I will walk slowly all my years because
I am overcome with grief.
16 O Lord, your decrees can give men life;
may years of life be restored to me.
Restore my health and preserve my life.'

17 "Look, the grief I experienced was for my benefit.
You delivered me from the Pit of oblivion.
For you removed all my sins from your sight.
18 Indeed Sheol does not give you thanks;
death does not praise you.
Those who descend into the Pit do not
anticipate your faithfulness.
19 The living person, the living person, he gives you thanks,
as I do today.
A father tells his sons about your faithfulness.
20 The LORD is about to deliver me,
and we will celebrate with music
for the rest of our lives in the LORD's temple."

21 (Isaiah ordered, "Let them take a fig cake and
apply it to the ulcerated sore and he will get
well." 22 Hezekiah said, "What is the confirming
sign that I will go up to the LORD's temple?")

MESSENGERS FROM BABYLON VISIT HEZEKIAH

39 At that time Merodach Baladan son of Baladan, king of
Babylon, sent letters and a gift to Hezekiah, for he heard
that Hezekiah had been ill and had recovered. 2 Hezekiah welcomed them and showed them his storehouse with its silver,

gold, spices, and high-quality olive oil, as well as his whole armory and everything in his treasuries. Hezekiah showed them
everything in his palace and in his whole kingdom. 3 Isaiah the
prophet visited King Hezekiah and asked him, "What did these
men say? Where do they come from?" Hezekiah replied, "They
come from the distant land of Babylon." 4 Isaiah asked, "What
have they seen in your palace?" Hezekiah replied, "They have
seen everything in my palace. I showed them everything in my
treasuries." 5 Isaiah said to Hezekiah, "Listen to the message of
the LORD of Heaven's Armies: 6 'Look, a time is coming when everything in your palace and the things your ancestors have accumulated to this day will be carried away to Babylon; nothing
will be left,' says the LORD. 7 'Some of your very own descendants
whom you father will be taken away and will be made eunuchs
in the palace of the king of Babylon.'" 8 Hezekiah said to Isaiah,
"The LORD's message that you have announced is appropriate."
Then he thought, "For there will be peace and stability during
my lifetime."

THE LORD RETURNS TO JERUSALEM

40 "Comfort, comfort my people,"
says your God.
2 "Speak kindly to Jerusalem and tell her
that her time of warfare is over,
that her punishment is completed.
For the LORD has made her pay double for all her sins."
3 A voice cries out,
"In the wilderness clear a way for the LORD;
build a level road through the rift valley for our God.
4 Every valley must be elevated,
and every mountain and hill leveled.
The rough terrain will become a level plain,
the rugged landscape a wide valley.
5 The splendor of the LORD will be revealed,
and all people will see it at the same time.
For the LORD has decreed it."
6 A voice says, "Cry out!"
Another asks, "What should I cry out?"
The first voice responds: "All people are like grass,
and all their promises are like the flowers in the field.
7 The grass dries up,
the flowers wither,
when the wind sent by the LORD blows on them.
Surely humanity is like grass.
8 The grass dries up,
the flowers wither,
but the decree of our God is forever reliable."
9 Go up on a high mountain, O herald Zion.
Shout out loudly, O herald Jerusalem!
Shout, don't be afraid!
Say to the towns of Judah,
"Here is your God!"
10 Look, the Sovereign LORD comes as a victorious warrior;
his military power establishes his rule.

LOVE TO GROW

GOD'S ENDURING WORD

ISAIAH 40:8

When I first devoted my life to the Lord, I had no idea of the immense significance of the Bible. At that time, I only knew a handful of the Ten Commandments. I attended a church that emphasized praise and worship over Bible teaching. Both are important, but for a long time, I thought the Bible was only a rule book.

As God continued to reveal Himself to me, He stirred up an unquenchable thirst and insatiable hunger to know Him. Church attendance alone wasn't enough to satisfy me.

Who was this God Almighty who knew me perfectly and loved me unconditionally? What did He desire from me? Why was life still so hard? When I needed answers, the Holy Spirit drew me to God's Word.

The Bible is much more than a rule book, a self-help manual, or an encyclopedia of facts about God and His people. It is God's living, breathing, divine revelation of Himself to human beings. In sixty-six books, it tells of His grand plan of redemption for humankind through His Son, Jesus Christ.

What I didn't know at the beginning of my spiritual walk with God was that in order to truly know God, I needed to know His Word. The Bible holds the answers to our deepest needs and most difficult questions.

It amazes me to hear that the Bible has remained the best-selling book of all time, year after year, for centuries. The Bible was written over a span of 1500 years by more than forty divinely-inspired authors from different time periods, occupations, ethnicities, and backgrounds.

No matter the time, culture, political environment, social norms, spiritual diversity, or philosophical theories, God's Word endures. It is always true, inerrant, relevant, unchanging, and uncompromising. In a world that is constantly changing, believers will always have the unchanging Word of God.

We read the Bible because it is our light in this dark, broken world. It brings peace and hope when everything around us is chaotic and bleak. And it makes our paths clear when we are unsure how to proceed.

God's Word will never fail us because God never fails us. His Word endures forever.

Look, his reward is with him;
his prize goes before him.
11 Like a shepherd he tends his flock;
he gathers up the lambs with his arm;
he carries them close to his heart;
he leads the ewes along.

THE LORD IS INCOMPARABLE

12 Who has measured out the waters
in the hollow of his hand,
or carefully measured the sky,
or carefully weighed the soil of the earth,
or weighed the mountains in a balance,
or the hills on scales?
13 Who comprehends the mind of the LORD,
or gives him instruction as his counselor?
14 From whom does he receive directions?
Who teaches him the correct way to do things,
or imparts knowledge to him,
or instructs him in skillful design?
15 Look, the nations are like a drop in a bucket;
they are regarded as dust on the scales.
He lifts the coastlands as if they were dust.
16 Not even Lebanon could supply enough
firewood for a sacrifice;
its wild animals would not provide enough burnt offerings.
17 All the nations are insignificant before him;
they are regarded as absolutely nothing.
18 To whom can you compare God?
To what image can you liken him?
19 A craftsman casts an idol;
a metalsmith overlays it with gold
and forges silver chains for it.
20 To make a contribution one selects wood that will not rot;
he then seeks a skilled craftsman
to make an idol that will not fall over.
21 Do you not know?
Do you not hear?
Has it not been told to you since the very beginning?
Have you not understood from the time
the earth's foundations were made?
22 He is the one who sits on the earth's horizon;
its inhabitants are like grasshoppers before him.
He is the one who stretches out the sky like a thin curtain,
and spreads it out like a pitched tent.
23 He is the one who reduces rulers to nothing;
he makes the earth's leaders insignificant.
24 Indeed, they are barely planted;
yes, they are barely sown;
yes, they barely take root in the earth,
and then he blows on them, causing them to dry up,
and the wind carries them away like straw.
25 "To whom can you compare me? Whom do I resemble?"
says the Holy One.

REFLECT

What are some of the characteristics of God that are most significant to you? Take time today to worship God for His unique qualities.

26 Look up at the sky!
Who created all these heavenly lights?
He is the one who leads out their ranks;
he calls them all by name.
Because of his absolute power and awesome strength,
not one of them is missing.
27 Why do you say, Jacob,
Why do you say, Israel,
"The LORD is not aware of what is happening to me;
My God is not concerned with my vindication"?
28 Do you not know?
Have you not heard?
The LORD is an eternal God,
the Creator of the whole earth.
He does not get tired or weary;
there is no limit to his wisdom.
29 He gives strength to those who are tired;
to the ones who lack power, he gives renewed energy.
30 Even youths get tired and weary;
even strong young men clumsily stumble.
31 But those who wait for the LORD's
help find renewed strength;
they rise up as if they had eagles' wings,
they run without growing weary,
they walk without getting tired.

THE LORD CHALLENGES THE NATIONS

41 "Listen to me in silence, you coastlands!
Let the nations find renewed strength!
Let them approach and then speak;
let us come together for debate.
2 Who stirs up this one from the east?
Who officially commissions him for service?
He hands nations over to him,
and enables him to subdue kings.
He makes them like dust with his sword,
like windblown straw with his bow.
3 He pursues them and passes by unharmed;
he advances with great speed.
4 Who acts and carries out decrees?
Who summons the successive generations
from the beginning?
I, the LORD, am present at the very beginning,
and at the very end—I am the one.
5 The coastlands see and are afraid;
the whole earth trembles;
they approach and come.
6 They help one another;
one says to the other, 'Be strong!'
7 The craftsman encourages the metalsmith,
the one who wields the hammer encourages
the one who pounds on the anvil.
He approves the quality of the welding,
and nails it down so it won't fall over.

THE LORD ENCOURAGES HIS PEOPLE

8 "You, my servant Israel,
Jacob, whom I have chosen,
offspring of Abraham my friend,
9 you whom I am bringing back from
the earth's extremities,
and have summoned from the remote regions—
I told you, 'You are my servant.'
I have chosen you and not rejected you.
10 Don't be afraid, for I am with you!
Don't be frightened, for I am your God!
I strengthen you—
yes, I help you—
yes, I uphold you with my victorious right hand!
11 Look, all who were angry at you will be
ashamed and humiliated;
your adversaries will be reduced to nothing and perish.
12 When you will look for your opponents,
you will not find them;
your enemies will be reduced to absolutely nothing.
13 For I am the LORD your God,
the one who takes hold of your right hand,
who says to you, 'Don't be afraid, I am helping you.'
14 Don't be afraid, despised insignificant Jacob,
men of Israel.
I am helping you," says the LORD,
your Protector, the Holy One of Israel.
15 "Look, I am making you like a sharp threshing sledge,
new and double-edged.
You will thresh the mountains and crush them;
you will make the hills like straw.
16 You will winnow them and the wind
will blow them away;
the wind will scatter them.
You will rejoice in the LORD;
you will boast in the Holy One of Israel.
17 The oppressed and the poor look for
water, but there is none;
their tongues are parched from thirst.
I, the LORD, will respond to their prayers;
I, the God of Israel, will not abandon them.
18 I will make streams flow down the slopes
and produce springs in the middle of the valleys.
I will turn the wilderness into a pool of water
and the arid land into springs.
19 I will make cedars, acacias, myrtles, and
olive trees grow in the wilderness;
I will make evergreens, firs, and cypresses
grow together in the arid rift valley.
20 I will do this so people will observe and recognize,
so they will pay attention and understand
that the LORD's power has accomplished this,
and that the Holy One of Israel
has brought it into being.

THE LORD CHALLENGES THE PAGAN GODS

21 "Present your argument," says the LORD.
"Produce your evidence," says Jacob's king.
22 "Let them produce evidence! Let them
tell us what will happen!
Tell us about your earlier predictive oracles,
so we may examine them and see how they were fulfilled.
Or decree for us some future events!
23 Predict how future events will turn out,
so we might know you are gods.
Yes, do something good or something bad,
so we might be frightened and in awe.
24 Look, you are nothing, and your
accomplishments are nonexistent;
the one who chooses to worship you is disgusting.
25 I have stirred up one out of the north and he advances,
one from the eastern horizon who prays in my name.
He steps on rulers as if they were clay,
like a potter treading the clay.
26 Who decreed this from the beginning,
so we could know?
Who announced it ahead of time, so
we could say, 'He's correct'?
Indeed, none of them decreed it.
Indeed, none of them announced it.
Indeed, no one heard you say anything!
27 I first decreed to Zion, 'Look, here's what will happen!'
I sent a herald to Jerusalem.
28 I look, but there is no one,
among them there is no one who serves as an adviser,
that I might ask questions and receive answers.
29 Look, all of them are nothing,
their accomplishments are nonexistent;
their metal images lack any real substance.

THE LORD COMMISSIONS HIS SPECIAL SERVANT

42 "Here is my servant whom I support,
my chosen one in whom I take pleasure.
I have placed my Spirit on him;
he will make just decrees for the nations.
2 He will not cry out or shout;
he will not publicize himself in the streets.
3 A crushed reed he will not break,
a dim wick he will not extinguish;
he will faithfully make just decrees.
4 He will not grow dim or be crushed
before establishing justice on the earth;
the coastlands will wait in anticipation for his decrees."
5 This is what the true God, the LORD, says—
the one who created the sky and stretched it out,
the one who fashioned the earth and
everything that lives on it,
the one who gives breath to the people on it,
and life to those who live on it:

6 "I, the LORD, officially commission you;
I take hold of your hand.
I protect you and make you a covenant
mediator for people,
and a light to the nations,
7 to open blind eyes,
to release prisoners from dungeons,
those who live in darkness from prisons.

THE LORD INTERVENES

8 "I am the LORD! That is my name!
I will not share my glory with anyone else,
or the praise due me with idols.
9 Look, my earlier predictive oracles
have come to pass;
now I announce new events.
Before they begin to occur,
I reveal them to you."

10 Sing to the LORD a brand new song!
Praise him from the horizon of the earth,
you who go down to the sea,
and everything that lives in it,
you coastlands and those who live there.
11 Let the wilderness and its cities shout out,
the towns where the nomads of Kedar live.
Let the residents of Sela shout joyfully;
let them shout loudly from the mountaintops.
12 Let them give the LORD the honor he deserves;
let them praise his deeds in the coastlands.
13 The LORD emerges like a hero,
like a warrior he inspires himself for battle;
he shouts, yes, he yells,
he shows his enemies his power.
14 "I have been inactive for a long time;
I kept quiet and held back.
Like a woman in labor I groan;
I pant and gasp.
15 I will make the trees on the mountains
and hills wither up;
I will dry up all their vegetation.
I will turn streams into islands,
and dry up pools of water.
16 I will lead the blind along an unfamiliar way;
I will guide them down paths they
have never traveled.
I will turn the darkness in front
of them into light,
and level out the rough ground.
This is what I will do for them.
I will not abandon them.
17 Those who trust in idols
will turn back and be utterly humiliated,
those who say to metal images, 'You are our gods.'

THE LORD REASONS WITH HIS PEOPLE

18 "Listen, you deaf ones!
Take notice, you blind ones!
19 My servant is truly blind,
my messenger is truly deaf.
My covenant partner, the servant of the LORD, is truly blind.
20 You see many things, but don't comprehend;
their ears are open, but do not hear."
21 The LORD wanted to exhibit his justice
by magnifying his law and displaying it.
22 But these people are looted and plundered;
all of them are trapped in pits
and held captive in prisons.
They were carried away as loot with no one to rescue them;
they were carried away as plunder, and
no one says, "Bring that back!"
23 Who among you will pay attention to this?
Who will listen attentively in the future?
24 Who handed Jacob over to the robber?
Who handed Israel over to the looters?
Was it not the LORD, against whom we sinned?
They refused to follow his commands;
they disobeyed his law.
25 So he poured out his fierce anger on them,
along with the devastation of war.
Its flames encircled them, but they did not realize it;
it burned against them, but they did not take it to heart.

THE LORD WILL RESCUE HIS PEOPLE

43 Now, this is what the LORD says,
the one who created you, O Jacob,
and formed you, O Israel:
"Don't be afraid, for I will protect you.
I call you by name, you are mine.
2 When you pass through the waters, I am with you;
when you pass through the streams,
they will not overwhelm you.
When you walk through the fire, you will not be burned;
the flames will not harm you.
3 For I am the LORD your God,
the Holy One of Israel, your deliverer.
I have handed over Egypt as a ransom price,
Ethiopia and Seba in place of you.
4 Since you are precious and special in my sight,
and I love you,
I will hand over people in place of you,
nations in place of your life.
5 Don't be afraid, for I am with you.
From the east I will bring your descendants;
from the west I will gather you.
6 I will say to the north, 'Hand them over!'
and to the south, 'Don't hold any back!'
Bring my sons from distant lands,
and my daughters from the remote regions of the earth,

7 everyone who belongs to me,
whom I created for my glory,
whom I formed—yes, whom I made.

THE LORD DECLARES HIS SOVEREIGNTY

8 Bring out the people who are blind,
even though they have eyes,
those who are deaf, even though they have ears!
9 All nations gather together,
the peoples assemble.
Who among them announced this?
Who predicted earlier events for us?
Let them produce their witnesses
to testify they were right;
let them listen and affirm, "It is true."
10 You are my witnesses," says the LORD,
"my servant whom I have chosen,
so that you may consider and believe in me,
and understand that I am he.
No god was formed before me,
and none will outlive me.
11 I, I am the LORD,
and there is no deliverer besides me.
12 I decreed and delivered and proclaimed,
and there was no other god among you.
You are my witnesses," says the LORD, "that I am God.
13 From this day forward I am he;
no one can deliver from my power;
I will act, and who can prevent it?"

THE LORD WILL DO SOMETHING NEW

14 This is what the LORD says,
your Protector, the Holy One of Israel:
"For your sake I send to Babylon
and make them all fugitives,
turning the Babylonians' joyful shouts
into mourning songs.
15 I am the LORD, your Holy One,
the one who created Israel, your king."
16 This is what the LORD says,
the one who made a road through the sea,
a pathway through the surging waters,
17 the one who led chariots and
horses to destruction,
together with a mighty army.
They fell down, never to rise again;
they were extinguished, put out like a burning wick:
18 "Don't remember these earlier events;
don't recall these former events.

19 Look, I am about to do something new.
Now it begins to happen! Do you not recognize it?
Yes, I will make a road in the wilderness
and paths in the wastelands.

20 The wild animals honor me,
the jackals and ostriches,
because I put water in the wilderness
and streams in the wastelands,
to quench the thirst of my chosen people,
21 the people whom I formed for myself,
so they might praise me.

THE LORD REBUKES HIS PEOPLE

22 "But you did not call for me, O Jacob;
you did not long for me, O Israel.
23 You did not bring me lambs for
your burnt offerings;
you did not honor me with your sacrifices.
I did not burden you with offerings;
I did not make you weary by demanding incense.
24 You did not buy me aromatic reeds;
you did not present to me the fat of your sacrifices.
Yet you burdened me with your sins;
you made me weary with your evil deeds.
25 I, I am the one who blots out your
rebellious deeds for my sake;
your sins I do not remember.
26 Remind me of what happened. Let's debate!
You, prove to me that you are right!
27 The father of your nation sinned;
your spokesmen rebelled against me.
28 So I defiled your holy princes,
and handed Jacob over to destruction,
and subjected Israel to humiliating abuse.

THE LORD WILL RENEW ISRAEL

44 "Now, listen, Jacob my servant,
Israel whom I have chosen!"
2 This is what the LORD, the one who made you, says—
the one who formed you in the womb and helps you:
"Don't be afraid, my servant Jacob,
Jeshurun, whom I have chosen.
3 For I will pour water on the parched ground
and cause streams to flow on the dry land.
I will pour my Spirit on your offspring
and my blessing on your children.
4 They will sprout up like a tree in the grass,
like poplars beside channels of water.
5 One will say, 'I belong to the LORD,'
and another will use the name 'Jacob.'
One will write on his hand, 'The LORD's,'
and use the name 'Israel.'"

THE ABSURDITY OF IDOLATRY

6 This is what the LORD, Israel's king, says,
their Protector, the LORD of Heaven's Armies:
"I am the first and I am the last,
there is no God but me.

7 Who is like me? Let him make his claim!
Let him announce it and explain it to me—
since I established an ancient people—
let them announce future events.
8 Don't panic! Don't be afraid!
Did I not tell you beforehand and decree it?
You are my witnesses! Is there any God but me?
There is no other sheltering rock;
I know of none.
9 All who form idols are nothing;
the things in which they delight are worthless.
Their witnesses cannot see;
they recognize nothing, so they
are put to shame.
10 Who forms a god and casts an idol
that will prove worthless?
11 Look, all his associates will be put to shame;
the craftsmen are mere humans.
Let them all assemble and take their stand.
They will panic and be put to shame.
12 A blacksmith works with his tool
and forges metal over the coals.
He forms it with hammers;
he makes it with his strong arm.
He gets hungry and loses his energy;
he drinks no water and gets tired.
13 A carpenter takes measurements;
he marks out an outline of its form;
he scrapes it with chisels,
and marks it with a compass.
He patterns it after the human form,
like a well-built human being,
and puts it in a shrine.
14 He cuts down cedars
and acquires a cypress or an oak.
He gets trees from the forest;
he plants a cedar and the rain makes it grow.
15 A man uses it to make a fire;
he takes some of it and warms himself.
Yes, he kindles a fire and bakes bread.
Then he makes a god and worships it;
he makes an idol and bows down to it.
16 Half of it he burns in the fire—
over that half he cooks meat;
he roasts a meal and fills himself.
Yes, he warms himself and says,
'Ah! I am warm as I look at the fire.'
17 With the rest of it he makes a god, his idol;
he bows down to it and worships it.
He prays to it, saying,
'Rescue me, for you are my god!'
18 They do not comprehend or understand,
for their eyes are blind and cannot see;
their minds do not discern.

19 No one thinks to himself,
nor do they comprehend or understand
and say to themselves:
'I burned half of it in the fire—
yes, I baked bread over the coals;
I roasted meat and ate it.
With the rest of it should I make a disgusting idol?
Should I bow down to dry wood?'
20 He feeds on ashes;
his deceived mind misleads him.
He cannot rescue himself,
nor does he say, 'Is this not a false god
I hold in my right hand?'
21 Remember these things, O Jacob,
O Israel, for you are my servant.
I formed you to be my servant;
O Israel, I will not forget you!
22 I remove the guilt of your rebellious
deeds as if they were a cloud,
the guilt of your sins as if they were a cloud.
Come back to me, for I protect you."
23 Shout for joy, O sky, for the LORD intervenes;
shout out, you subterranean regions of the earth.
O mountains, give a joyful shout;
you too, O forest and all your trees!
For the LORD protects Jacob;
he reveals his splendor through Israel.

THE LORD EMPOWERS CYRUS

24 This is what the LORD, your Protector, says,
the one who formed you in the womb:
"I am the LORD, who made everything,
who alone stretched out the sky,
who fashioned the earth all by myself,
25 who frustrates the omens of the empty talkers
and humiliates the omen readers,
who overturns the counsel of the wise men
and makes their advice seem foolish,
26 who fulfills the oracles of his prophetic servants
and brings to pass the announcements
of his messengers,
who says about Jerusalem, 'She will be inhabited,'
and about the towns of Judah, 'They will be rebuilt,
her ruins I will raise up,'
27 who says to the deep sea, 'Be dry!
I will dry up your sea currents,'
28 who commissions Cyrus, the one I appointed as shepherd
to carry out all my wishes
and to decree concerning Jerusalem, 'She will be rebuilt,'
and concerning the temple, 'It will be reconstructed.'

45 "This is what the LORD says to his chosen one,
to Cyrus, whose right hand I hold
in order to subdue nations before him,

and disarm kings,
to open doors before him,
so gates remain unclosed:

2 'I will go before you
and level mountains.
Bronze doors I will shatter
and iron bars I will hack through.
3 I will give you hidden treasures,
riches stashed away in secret places,
so you may recognize that I am the LORD,
the one who calls you by name, the God of Israel.
4 For the sake of my servant Jacob,
Israel, my chosen one,
I call you by name
and give you a title of respect, even
though you do not submit to me.
5 I am the LORD, I have no peer,
there is no God but me.
I arm you for battle, even though you do not recognize me.
6 I do this so people will recognize from east to west
that there is no God but me;
I am the LORD, I have no peer.
7 I am the one who forms light
and creates darkness;
the one who brings about peace
and creates calamity.
I am the LORD, who accomplishes all these things.
8 O sky, rain down from above!
Let the clouds send down showers of deliverance!
Let the earth absorb it so salvation may grow,
and deliverance may sprout up along with it.
I, the LORD, create it.'"

THE LORD GIVES A WARNING

9 One who argues with his Creator is in grave danger,
one who is like a mere shard among the
other shards on the ground!
The clay should not say to the potter,
"What in the world are you doing?
Your work lacks skill!"
10 Danger awaits one who says to his father,
"What in the world are you fathering?"
and to his mother,
"What in the world are you bringing forth?"
11 This is what the LORD says,
the Holy One of Israel, the one who formed him,
concerning things to come:
"How dare you question me about my children!
How dare you tell me what to do with
the work of my own hands!
12 I made the earth;
I created the people who live on it.
It was me—my hands stretched out the sky.

I give orders to all the heavenly lights.
13 It is me—I stir him up and commission him;
I will make all his ways level.
He will rebuild my city;
he will send my exiled people home,
but not for a price or a bribe,"
says the LORD of Heaven's Armies.

THE LORD IS THE NATIONS' ONLY HOPE

14 This is what the LORD says:
"The profit of Egypt and the revenue of Ethiopia,
along with the Sabeans, those tall men,
will be brought to you and become yours.
They will walk behind you, coming along in chains.
They will bow down to you
and pray to you:
'Truly God is with you; he has no peer;
there is no other God!'"
15 Yes, you are a God who keeps hidden,
O God of Israel, deliverer!
16 They will all be ashamed and embarrassed;
those who fashion idols will all be humiliated.
17 Israel will be delivered once and for all by the LORD;
you will never again be ashamed or humiliated.
18 For this is what the LORD says,
the one who created the sky—
he is the true God,
the one who formed the earth and made it;
he established it,
he did not create it without order,
he formed it to be inhabited:
"I am the LORD, I have no peer.
19 I have not spoken in secret,
in some hidden place.
I did not tell Jacob's descendants,
'Seek me in vain!'
I am the LORD,
the one who speaks honestly,
who makes reliable announcements.
20 Gather together and come!
Approach together, you refugees from the nations.
Those who carry wooden idols know nothing,
those who pray to a god that cannot deliver.
21 Tell me! Present the evidence!
Let them consult with one another.
Who predicted this in the past?
Who announced it beforehand?
Was it not I, the LORD?
I have no peer, there is no God but me,
a God who vindicates and delivers;
there is none but me.
22 Turn to me so you can be delivered,
all you who live in the earth's remote regions!
For I am God, and I have no peer.

23 I solemnly make this oath—
what I say is true and reliable:
'Surely every knee will bow to me,
every tongue will solemnly affirm;
24 they will say about me,
"Yes, the LORD is a powerful deliverer."'"
All who are angry at him will cower before him.
25 All the descendants of Israel will be
vindicated by the LORD
and will boast in him.

THE LORD CARRIES HIS PEOPLE

46 Bel kneels down,
Nebo bends low.
Their images weigh down animals and beasts.
Your heavy images are burdensome to tired animals.
2 Together they bend low and kneel down;
they are unable to rescue the images;
they themselves head off into captivity.
3 "Listen to me, O family of Jacob,
all you who are left from the family of Israel,
you who have been carried from birth,
you who have been supported from
the time you left the womb.
4 Even when you are old, I will take care of you,
even when you have gray hair, I will carry you.
I made you and I will support you;
I will carry you and rescue you.
5 To whom can you compare and liken me?
Tell me whom you think I resemble,
so we can be compared!
6 Those who empty out gold from a purse
and weigh out silver on the scale
hire a metalsmith, who makes it into a god.
They then bow down and worship it.
7 They put it on their shoulder and carry it;
they put it in its place and it just stands there;
it does not move from its place.
Even when someone cries out to it,
it does not reply;
it does not deliver him from his distress.
8 Remember this, so you can be brave.
Think about it, you rebels!
9 Remember what I accomplished in antiquity.
Truly I am God, I have no peer;
I am God, and there is none like me,
10 who announces the end from the beginning
and reveals beforehand what has not yet occurred;
who says, 'My plan will be realized,
I will accomplish what I desire;'
11 who summons an eagle from the east,
from a distant land, one who carries out my plan.
Yes, I have decreed,
yes, I will bring it to pass;

I have formulated a plan,
yes, I will carry it out.
12 Listen to me, you stubborn people,
you who distance yourselves from doing what is right.
13 I am bringing my deliverance near, it is not far away;
I am bringing my salvation near, it does not wait.
I will save Zion;
I will adorn Israel with my splendor.

BABYLON WILL FALL

47 "Fall down! Sit in the dirt,
O virgin daughter Babylon!
Sit on the ground, not on a throne,
O daughter of the Babylonians!
Indeed, you will no longer be called
delicate and pampered.
2 Pick up millstones and grind flour.
Remove your veil,
strip off your skirt,
expose your legs,
cross the streams.
3 Let your naked body be exposed.
Your shame will be on display!
I will get revenge;
I will not have pity on anyone,"
4 says our Protector—
the LORD of Heaven's Armies is his name,
the Holy One of Israel.
5 "Sit silently! Go to a hiding place,
O daughter of the Babylonians!
Indeed, you will no longer be called
'Queen of kingdoms.'
6 I was angry at my people;
I defiled my special possession
and handed them over to you.
You showed them no mercy;
you even placed a very heavy burden on old people.
7 You said,
'I will rule forever as permanent queen!'
You did not think about these things;
you did not consider how it would turn out.
8 So now, listen to this,
O one who lives so lavishly,
who lives securely,
who says to herself,
'I am unique! No one can compare to me!
I will never have to live as a widow;
I will never lose my children.'
9 Both of these will come upon you
suddenly, in one day!
You will lose your children and be widowed.
You will be overwhelmed by these tragedies,
despite your many incantations
and your numerous amulets.

10 You were complacent in your evil deeds;
you thought, 'No one sees me.'
Your self-professed wisdom and knowledge lead you astray,
when you say, 'I am unique! No one can compare to me!'
11 Disaster will overtake you;
you will not know how to charm it away.
Destruction will fall on you;
you will not be able to appease it.
Calamity will strike you suddenly,
before you recognize it.
12 Persist in trusting your amulets
and your many incantations,
which you have faithfully recited since your youth!
Maybe you will be successful—
maybe you will scare away disaster.
13 You are tired out from listening to so much advice.
Let them take their stand—
the ones who see omens in the sky,
who gaze at the stars,
who make monthly predictions—
let them rescue you from the disaster
that is about to overtake you!
14 Look, they are like straw,
that the fire burns up;
they cannot rescue themselves
from the heat of the flames.
There are no coals to warm them,
no firelight to enjoy.
15 They will disappoint you,
those you have so faithfully dealt with since your youth.
Each strays off in his own direction,
leaving no one to rescue you."

THE LORD APPEALS TO THE EXILES

48 Listen to this, O family of Jacob,
you who are called by the name 'Israel,'
and are descended from Judah,
who take oaths in the name of the LORD,
and invoke the God of Israel—
but not in an honest and just manner.
2 Indeed, they live in the holy city;
they trust in the God of Israel,
whose name is the LORD of Heaven's Armies.
3 "I announced events beforehand,
I issued the decrees and made the predictions;
suddenly I acted and they came to pass.
4 I did this because I know how stubborn you are.
Your neck muscles are like iron
and your forehead like bronze.
5 I announced them to you beforehand;
before they happened, I predicted them for you,
so you could never say,
'My image did these things,
my idol, my cast image, decreed them.'

6 You have heard; now look at all the evidence!
Will you not admit that what I say is true?
From this point on I am announcing to you new events
that are previously unrevealed and you do not know about.
7 Now they come into being, not in the past;
before today you did not hear about them,
so you could not say,
'Yes, I know about them.'
8 You did not hear,
you do not know,
you were not told beforehand.
For I know that you are very deceitful;
you were labeled a rebel from birth.
9 For the sake of my reputation I hold back my anger;
for the sake of my prestige I restrain
myself from destroying you.
10 Look, I have refined you, but not as silver;
I have purified you in the furnace of misery.
11 For my sake alone I will act,
for how can I allow my name to be defiled?
I will not share my glory with anyone else!
12 Listen to me, O Jacob,
Israel, whom I summoned.
I am the one;
I am present at the very beginning
and at the very end.
13 Yes, my hand founded the earth;
my right hand spread out the sky.
I summon them;
they stand together.
14 All of you, gather together and listen!
Who among them announced these things?
The LORD's ally will carry out his desire against Babylon;
he will exert his power against the Babylonians.
15 I, I have spoken—
yes, I have summoned him;
I lead him and he will succeed.
16 Approach me—listen to this!
From the very first I have not spoken in secret;
when it happens, I am there."
So now, the Sovereign LORD has sent
me, accompanied by his Spirit.
17 This is what the LORD, your Protector, says,
the Holy One of Israel:
"I am the LORD your God,
who teaches you how to succeed,
who leads you in the way you should go.
18 If only you had obeyed my commandments,
prosperity would have flowed to you like a river,
deliverance would have come to you like the waves of the sea.
19 Your descendants would have been as numerous as sand,
and your children like its granules.
Their name would not have been cut off
and eliminated from my presence.

20 Leave Babylon!
Flee from the Babylonians!
Announce it with a shout of joy!
Make this known—
proclaim it throughout the earth!
Say, 'The LORD protects his servant Jacob.
21 They do not thirst as he leads them through dry regions;
he makes water flow out of a rock for them;
he splits open a rock and water flows out.'
22 There will be no prosperity for the
wicked," says the LORD.

DELIVERY OF THE EXILES

49 Listen to me, you coastlands!
Pay attention, you people who live far away!
The LORD summoned me from birth;
he commissioned me when my mother
brought me into the world.
2 He made my mouth like a sharp sword,
he hid me in the hollow of his hand;
he made me like a sharpened arrow,
he hid me in his quiver.
3 He said to me, "You are my servant,
Israel, through whom I will reveal my splendor."
4 But I thought, "I have worked in vain;
I have expended my energy for absolutely nothing."
But the LORD will vindicate me;
my God will reward me.
5 So now the LORD says,
the one who formed me from birth to be his servant—
he did this to restore Jacob to himself,
so that Israel might be gathered to him;
and I will be honored in the LORD's sight,
for my God is my source of strength—
6 he says, "Is it too insignificant a task
for you to be my servant,
to reestablish the tribes of Jacob,
and restore the remnant of Israel?
I will make you a light to the nations,
so you can bring my deliverance to the
remote regions of the earth."
7 This is what the LORD,
the Protector of Israel, their Holy One, says
to the one who is despised and rejected by nations,
a servant of rulers:
"Kings will see and rise in respect,
princes will bow down,
because of the faithful LORD,
the Holy One of Israel who has chosen you."

8 This is what the LORD says:
"At the time I decide to show my
favor, I will respond to you;
in the day of deliverance I will help you;

I will protect you and make you a
covenant mediator for people,
to rebuild the land
and to reassign the desolate property.
9 You will say to the prisoners, 'Come out,'
and to those who are in dark dungeons, 'Emerge.'
They will graze beside the roads;
on all the slopes they will find pasture.
10 They will not be hungry or thirsty;
the sun's oppressive heat will not beat down on them,
for one who has compassion on them will guide them;
he will lead them to springs of water.
11 I will make all my mountains into a road;
I will construct my roadways."
12 Look, they come from far away!
Look, some come from the north and west,
and others from the land of Sinim.
13 Shout for joy, O sky!
Rejoice, O earth!
Let the mountains give a joyful shout!
For the LORD consoles his people
and shows compassion to the oppressed.

THE LORD REMEMBERS ZION

14 "Zion said, 'The LORD has abandoned me,
the Lord has forgotten me.'
15 Can a woman forget her baby who nurses at her breast?
Can she withhold compassion from the child she has borne?
Even if mothers were to forget,
I could never forget you!
16 Look, I have inscribed your name on my palms;
your walls are constantly before me.
17 Your children hurry back,
while those who destroyed and devastated you depart.
18 Look all around you!
All of them gather to you.
As surely as I live," says the LORD,
"you will certainly wear all of them like jewelry;
you will put them on as if you were a bride.
19 Yes, your land lies in ruins;
it is desolate and devastated.
But now you will be too small to hold your residents,
and those who devoured you will be far away.
20 Yet the children born during your time of bereavement
will say within your hearing,
'This place is too cramped for us,
make room for us so we can live here.'
21 Then you will think to yourself,
'Who bore these children for me?
I was bereaved and barren,
dismissed and divorced.
Who raised these children?
Look, I was left all alone;
where did these children come from?'"

22 This is what the Sovereign LORD says:
"Look I will raise my hand to the nations;
I will raise my signal flag to the peoples.
They will bring your sons in their arms
and carry your daughters on their shoulders.
23 Kings will be your children's guardians;
their princesses will nurse your children.
With their faces to the ground they will bow down to you,
and they will lick the dirt on your feet.
Then you will recognize that I am the LORD;
those who wait patiently for me are not put to shame.
24 Can spoils be taken from a warrior,
or captives be rescued from a conqueror?
25 Indeed," says the LORD,
"captives will be taken from a warrior;
spoils will be rescued from a conqueror.
I will oppose your adversary
and I will rescue your children.
26 I will make your oppressors eat their own flesh;
they will get drunk on their own blood, as if it were wine.
Then all humankind will recognize that
I am the LORD, your Deliverer,
your Protector, the Powerful One of Jacob."

50 This is what the LORD says:
"Where is your mother's divorce certificate
by which I divorced her?
Or to which of my creditors did I sell you?
Look, you were sold because of your sins;
because of your rebellious acts I divorced your mother.
2 Why does no one challenge me when I come?
Why does no one respond when I call?
Is my hand too weak to deliver you?
Do I lack the power to rescue you?
Look, with a mere shout I can dry up the sea;
I can turn streams into a desert,
so the fish rot away and die
from lack of water.
3 I can clothe the sky in darkness;
I can cover it with sackcloth."

THE SERVANT PERSEVERES

4 The Sovereign LORD has given me the
capacity to be his spokesman,
so that I know how to help the weary.
He wakes me up every morning;
he makes me alert so I can listen
attentively as disciples do.
5 The Sovereign LORD has spoken to me clearly;
I have not rebelled,
I have not turned back.
6 I offered my back to those who attacked,
my jaws to those who tore out my beard;
I did not hide my face
from insults and spitting.

7 But the Sovereign LORD helps me,
so I am not humiliated.
For that reason I am steadfastly resolved;
I know I will not be put to shame.
8 The one who vindicates me is close by.
Who dares to argue with me? Let us confront each other!
Who is my accuser? Let him challenge me!
9 Look, the Sovereign LORD helps me.
Who dares to condemn me?
Look, all of them will wear out like clothes;
a moth will eat away at them.
10 Who among you fears the LORD?
Who obeys his servant?
Whoever walks in deep darkness,
without light,
should trust in the name of the LORD
and rely on his God.
11 Look, all of you who start a fire
and who equip yourselves with flaming arrows,
walk in the light of the fire you started
and among the flaming arrows you ignited!
This is what you will receive from me:
you will lie down in a place of pain.

THERE IS HOPE FOR THE FUTURE

51 "Listen to me, you who pursue godliness,
who seek the LORD.
Look at the rock from which you were chiseled,
at the quarry from which you were dug.
2 Look at Abraham, your father,
and Sarah, who gave you birth.
When I summoned him, he was a lone individual,
but I blessed him and gave him numerous descendants.
3 Certainly the LORD will console Zion;
he will console all her ruins.
He will make her wilderness like Eden,
her arid rift valley like the garden of the LORD.
Happiness and joy will be restored to her,
thanksgiving and the sound of music.
4 Pay attention to me, my people.
Listen to me, my people!
For I will issue a decree,
I will make my justice a light to the nations.
5 I am ready to vindicate,
I am ready to deliver,
I will establish justice among the nations.
The coastlands wait patiently for me;
they wait in anticipation for
the revelation of my power.
6 Look up at the sky.
Look at the earth below.
For the sky will dissipate like smoke,
and the earth will wear out like clothes;
its residents will die like gnats.

But the deliverance I give is permanent;
the vindication I provide will not disappear.
7 Listen to me, you who know what is right,
you people who are aware of my law.
Don't be afraid of the insults of men;
don't be discouraged because of their abuse.
8 For a moth will eat away at them like clothes;
a clothes moth will devour them like wool.
But the vindication I provide will be permanent;
the deliverance I give will last."
9 Wake up! Wake up!
Clothe yourself with strength, O arm of the LORD!
Wake up as in former times, as in antiquity.
Did you not smash the Proud One?
Did you not wound the sea monster?
10 Did you not dry up the sea,
the waters of the great deep?
Did you not make a path through the depths of the sea,
so those delivered from bondage could cross over?
11 Those whom the LORD has ransomed will return;
they will enter Zion with a happy shout.
Unending joy will crown them,
happiness and joy will overwhelm them;
grief and suffering will disappear.
12 "I, I am the one who consoles you.
Why are you afraid of mortal men,
of mere human beings who are as short-lived as grass?
13 Why do you forget the LORD, who made you,
who stretched out the sky
and founded the earth?
Why do you constantly tremble all day long
at the anger of the oppressor,
when he makes plans to destroy?
Where is the anger of the oppressor?
14 The one who suffers will soon be released;
he will not die in prison,
he will not go hungry.
15 I am the LORD your God,
who churns up the sea so that its waves surge.
The LORD of Heaven's Armies is his name!

ZION'S TIME TO CELEBRATE

16 "I commission you as my spokesman;
I cover you with the palm of my hand,
to establish the sky and to found the earth,
to say to Zion, 'You are my people.'"
17 Wake up! Wake up!
Get up, O Jerusalem!
You drank from the cup the LORD passed to you,
which was full of his anger.
You drained dry
the goblet full of intoxicating wine.
18 There was no one to lead her
among all the children she bore;

there was no one to take her by the hand
among all the children she raised.
19 These double disasters confronted you.
But who feels sorry for you?
Destruction and devastation,
famine and sword.
But who consoles you?
20 Your children faint;
they lie at the head of every street
like an antelope in a snare.
They are left in a stupor by the LORD's anger,
by the battle cry of your God.
21 So listen to this, oppressed one,
who is drunk, but not from wine.
22 This is what your Sovereign LORD, even your
God who judges his people says:
"Look, I have removed from your hand
the cup of intoxicating wine,
the goblet full of my anger.
You will no longer have to drink it.
23 I will put it into the hand of your tormentors
who said to you, 'Lie down, so we can walk over you.'
You made your back like the ground,
and like the street for those who walked over you."

52 Wake up! Wake up!
Clothe yourself with strength, O Zion!
Put on your beautiful clothes,
O Jerusalem, holy city.
For uncircumcised and unclean pagans
will no longer invade you.
2 Shake off the dirt!
Get up, captive Jerusalem.
Take off the iron chains around your neck,
O captive daughter Zion.

3 For this is what the LORD says:
"You were sold for nothing,
and you will not be redeemed for money."

4 For this is what the Sovereign LORD says:
"In the beginning my people went to
live temporarily in Egypt;
Assyria oppressed them for no good reason.
5 And now, what do we have here?" says the LORD.
"Indeed my people have been carried away for nothing,
those who rule over them taunt," says the LORD,
"and my name is constantly slandered all day long.
6 For this reason my people will know my name;
for this reason they will know at that
time that I am the one who says,
'Here I am.'"
7 How delightful it is to see approaching over the mountains
the feet of a messenger who announces peace,

a messenger who brings good news,
who announces deliverance,
who says to Zion, "Your God reigns!"
8 Listen, your watchmen shout;
in unison they shout for joy,
for they see with their very own eyes
the LORD's return to Zion.
9 In unison give a joyful shout,
O ruins of Jerusalem!
For the LORD consoles his people;
he protects Jerusalem.
10 The LORD reveals his royal power
in the sight of all the nations;
the entire earth sees
our God deliver.
11 Leave! Leave! Get out of there!
Don't touch anything unclean!
Get out of it!
Stay pure, you who carry the LORD's holy items.
12 Yet do not depart quickly
or leave in a panic.
For the LORD goes before you;
the God of Israel is your rear guard.

THE LORD WILL VINDICATE HIS SERVANT

13 Look, my servant will succeed!
He will be elevated, lifted high, and greatly exalted—
14 (just as many were horrified by the sight of you)
he was so disfigured he no longer looked like a man;
his form was so marred he no longer looked human—
15 so now he will startle many nations.
Kings will be shocked by his exaltation,
for they will witness something unannounced to them,
and they will understand something
they had not heard about.
53 Who would have believed what we just heard?
When was the LORD's power revealed through him?
2 He sprouted up like a twig before God,
like a root out of parched soil;
he had no stately form or majesty that
might catch our attention,
no special appearance that we should want to follow him.
3 He was despised and rejected by people,
one who experienced pain and was acquainted with illness;
people hid their faces from him;
he was despised, and we considered him insignificant.
4 But he lifted up our illnesses,
he carried our pain;
even though we thought he was being punished,
attacked by God, and afflicted for something he had done.
5 He was wounded because of our rebellious deeds,
crushed because of our sins;
he endured punishment that made us well;
because of his wounds we have been healed.

GOD'S HEART FOR THE NATIONS

Isaiah 52:10

The LORD reveals his royal power in the sight of all the nations; the entire earth sees our God deliver.

CHALLENGE

Isaiah 53 prophesies about the Suffering Servant. How does the Gospel of Mark confirm that Jesus is this promised servant?

6 All of us had wandered off like sheep;
each of us had strayed off on his own path,
but the LORD caused the sin of all of us to attack him.
7 He was treated harshly and afflicted,
but he did not even open his mouth.
Like a lamb led to the slaughtering block,
like a sheep silent before her shearers,
he did not even open his mouth.
8 He was led away after an unjust trial—
but who even cared?
Indeed, he was cut off from the land of the living;
because of the rebellion of his own
people he was wounded.
9 They intended to bury him with criminals,
but he ended up in a rich man's tomb,
because he had committed no violent deeds,
nor had he spoken deceitfully.
10 Though the LORD desired to crush him and make him ill,
once restitution is made,
he will see descendants and enjoy long life,
and the LORD's purpose will be
accomplished through him.
11 Having suffered, he will reflect on his work,
he will be satisfied when he understands
what he has done.
"My servant will acquit many,
for he carried their sins.
12 So I will assign him a portion with the multitudes,
he will divide the spoils of victory with the powerful,
because he willingly submitted to death
and was numbered with the rebels,
when he lifted up the sin of many
and intervened on behalf of the rebels."

ZION WILL BE SECURE

54 "Shout for joy, O barren one who has not given birth!
Give a joyful shout and cry out, you
who have not been in labor!
For the children of the desolate one are more numerous
than the children of the married woman," says the LORD.
2 Make your tent larger,
stretch your tent curtains farther out!
Spare no effort,
lengthen your ropes,
and pound your stakes deep.
3 For you will spread out to the right and to the left;
your children will conquer nations
and will resettle desolate cities.
4 Don't be afraid, for you will not be put to shame.
Don't be intimidated, for you will not be humiliated.
You will forget about the shame you
experienced in your youth;
you will no longer remember the
disgrace of your abandonment.

5 For your husband is the one who made you—
the LORD of Heaven's Armies is his name.
He is your Protector, the Holy One of Israel.
He is called "God of the entire earth."
6 "Indeed, the LORD will call you back
like a wife who has been abandoned
and suffers from depression,
like a young wife when she has been rejected," says your God.
7 "For a short time I abandoned you,
but with great compassion I will gather you.
8 In a burst of anger I rejected you momentarily,
but with lasting devotion I will have compassion on you,"
says your Protector, the LORD.
9 "As far as I am concerned, this is like in Noah's time,
when I vowed that the waters of Noah's flood
would never again cover the earth.
In the same way I have vowed that I will
not be angry at you or shout at you.
10 Even if the mountains are removed
and the hills displaced,
my devotion will not be removed from you,
nor will my covenant of friendship be displaced,"
says the LORD, the one who has compassion on you.
11 "O afflicted one, driven away, and unconsoled!
Look, I am about to set your stones in antimony,
and lay your foundation with lapis lazuli.
12 I will make your pinnacles out of gems,
your gates out of beryl,
and your outer wall out of beautiful stones.
13 All your children will be followers of the LORD,
and your children will enjoy great prosperity.
14 You will be reestablished when I vindicate you.
You will not experience oppression;
indeed, you will not be afraid.
You will not be terrified,
for nothing frightening will come near you.
15 If anyone dares to challenge you, it will not be my doing!
Whoever tries to challenge you will be defeated.
16 Look, I create the craftsman,
who fans the coals into a fire
and forges a weapon.
I create the destroyer so he might devastate.
17 No weapon forged to be used against you will succeed;
you will refute everyone who tries to accuse you.
This is what the LORD will do for his servants—
I will vindicate them,"
says the LORD.

THE LORD GIVES AN INVITATION

55 "Hey, all who are thirsty, come to the water!
You who have no money, come!
Buy and eat!
Come! Buy wine and milk
without money and without cost.

LOVE TO GROW

IN A WAR

ISAIAH 54:17

Have you ever read *The Screwtape Letters* by C. S. Lewis? If not, you should.

C. S. Lewis brings to light the dark spiritual warfare each of us encounters. He describes how our enemy works hard to tempt us and destroy us. Screwtape writes thirty-one letters to his nephew, Wormwood, mentoring him in the many ways to tempt humans and keep them from coming to Christ.

No matter how much we don't talk about it, or really even think about it, we are in a battle. *The Screwtape Letters* brings the battle to light. His tale pulls back the spiritual curtain of the unseen realm and allows us to see the invisible battles that rage all around us.

The battle between the kingdoms of darkness and light has been going on since the beginning of time, and continues to this very day, but don't you lose heart for a second. On the days you feel like you're drowning in waves of fear, remember Jesus died on the cross and His resurrection assures you victory over your enemy! Because of Jesus, you are not a victim but a victor!

"No weapon forged to be used against you will succeed; you will refute everyone who tries to accuse you. This is what the LORD will do for his servants" (Isa 54:17).

Have we forgotten the power of God's Word? His Word is the sword of the Spirit, our weapon in this battle (Eph 6:17). Meditation and memorization of God's Word returns the focus of our minds back to truth of Jesus' victory.

Jesus didn't die on the cross for us to live our lives in fear but in freedom. His defeat of death released the Holy Spirit of God to dwell inside each one of us who believes. The One who lives in us is greater than the one who is in the world (1 John 4:4). You are not alone in your battles, not for one second. God is always with you. Remember, Satan and God are not equals. Satan is limited, but our God is limitless.

Friends, don't ever forget we serve a risen King who has battled on our behalf and won! Take heart, Jesus has overcome the world!

2 Why pay money for something that will not nourish you?
Why spend your hard-earned money on
something that will not satisfy?
Listen carefully to me and eat what is nourishing!
Enjoy fine food.
3 Pay attention and come to me.
Listen, so you can live.
Then I will make an unconditional
covenantal promise to you,
just like the reliable covenantal promises I made to David.
4 Look, I made him a witness to nations,
a ruler and commander of nations."
5 Look, you will summon nations you
did not previously know;
nations that did not previously know you will run to you,
because of the LORD your God,
the Holy One of Israel,
for he bestows honor on you.
6 Seek the LORD while he makes himself available;
call to him while he is nearby!
7 The wicked need to abandon their lifestyle
and sinful people their plans.
They should return to the LORD, and
he will show mercy to them,
and to their God, for he will freely forgive them.
8 "Indeed, my plans are not like your plans,
and my deeds are not like your deeds," says the LORD,
9 "for just as the sky is higher than the earth,
so my deeds are superior to your deeds
and my plans superior to your plans.
10 The rain and snow fall from the sky
and do not return,
but instead water the earth
and make it produce and yield crops,
and provide seed for the planter and
food for those who must eat.
11 In the same way, the promise that I make
does not return to me, having accomplished nothing.
No, it is realized as I desire
and is fulfilled as I intend."
12 Indeed you will go out with joy;
you will be led along in peace;
the mountains and hills will give a joyful shout before you,
and all the trees in the field will clap their hands.
13 Evergreens will grow in place of thorn bushes,
firs will grow in place of nettles;
they will be a monument to the LORD,
a permanent reminder that will remain.

THE LORD INVITES OUTSIDERS TO ENTER

56 This is what the LORD says,
"Promote justice! Do what is right!
For I am ready to deliver you;
I am ready to vindicate you openly.

2 The people who do this will be blessed,
the people who commit themselves to obedience,
who observe the Sabbath and do not defile it,
who refrain from doing anything that is wrong.
3 No foreigner who becomes a follower
of the LORD should say,
'The LORD will certainly exclude me from his people.'
The eunuch should not say,
'Look, I am like a dried-up tree.'"

4 For this is what the LORD says:
"For the eunuchs who observe my Sabbaths
and choose what pleases me
and are faithful to my covenant,
5 I will set up within my temple and my walls a monument
that will be better than sons and daughters.
I will set up a permanent monument
for them that will remain.
6 As for foreigners who become followers
of the LORD and serve him,
who love the name of the LORD and
want to be his servants—
all who observe the Sabbath and do not defile it,
and who are faithful to my covenant—
7 I will bring them to my holy mountain;
I will make them happy in the temple
where people pray to me.
Their burnt offerings and sacrifices
will be accepted on my altar,
for my temple will be known as a temple
where all nations may pray."
8 The Sovereign LORD says this,
the one who gathers the dispersed of Israel:
"I will still gather them up."

THE LORD DENOUNCES ISRAEL'S PAGANISM

9 All you wild animals in the fields, come and devour,
all you wild animals in the forest!
10 All their watchmen are blind,
they are unaware.
All of them are like mute dogs,
unable to bark.
They pant, lie down,
and love to snooze.
11 The dogs have big appetites;
they are never full.
They are shepherds who have no understanding;
they all go their own way,
each one looking for monetary gain.
12 Each one says,
'Come on, I'll get some wine!
Let's guzzle some beer!
Tomorrow will be just like today!
We'll have everything we want!'

57 The godly perish,
but no one cares.
Honest people disappear,
when no one minds
that the godly disappear because of evil.
2 Those who live uprightly enter a place of peace;
they rest on their beds.

3 "But approach, you sons of omen readers,
you offspring of adulteresses and prostitutes!
4 At whom are you laughing?
At whom are you opening your mouth
and sticking out your tongue?
You are the children of rebels,
the offspring of liars,
5 you who inflame your lusts among the
oaks and under every green tree,
who slaughter children near the streams
under the rocky overhangs.
6 Among the smooth stones of the
stream are the idols you love;
they, they are the object of your devotion.
You pour out liquid offerings to them,
you make an offering.
Because of these things how can I relent from judgment?
7 On every high, elevated hill you prepare your bed;
you go up there to offer sacrifices.
8 Behind the door and doorpost you put your symbols.
Indeed, you depart from me and go up
and invite them into bed with you.
You purchase favors from them;
you love their bed,
and gaze longingly on their naked bodies.
9 You take olive oil as tribute to your king,
along with many perfumes.
You send your messengers to a distant place;
you go all the way to Sheol.
10 Because of the long distance you must travel, you get tired,
but you do not say, 'I give up.'
You get renewed energy,
so you don't collapse.
11 Whom are you worried about?
Whom do you fear, that you would act so deceitfully
and not remember me
or think about me?
Because I have been silent for so long,
you are not afraid of me.
12 I will denounce your so-called righteousness and your deeds,
but they will not help you.
13 When you cry out for help, let your idols help you!
The wind blows them all away,
a breeze carries them away.
But the one who looks to me for help will inherit the land
and will have access to my holy mountain."

14 He says,
"Build it! Build it! Clear a way!
Remove all the obstacles out of the way of my people!"
15 For this is what the high and exalted one says,
the one who rules forever, whose name is holy:
"I dwell in an exalted and holy place,
but also with the discouraged and humiliated,
in order to cheer up the humiliated
and to encourage the discouraged.
16 For I will not be hostile forever
or perpetually angry,
for then man's spirit would grow faint before me,
the life-giving breath I created.
17 I was angry because of their sinful greed;
I attacked them and angrily rejected them,
yet they remained disobedient and stubborn.
18 I have seen their behavior,
but I will heal them. I will lead them,
and I will provide comfort to them and
those who mourn with them.
19 I am the one who gives them reason to celebrate.
Complete prosperity is available both to those
who are far away and those who are nearby,"
says the LORD, "and I will heal them.
20 But the wicked are like a surging sea
that is unable to be quiet;
its waves toss up mud and sand.
21 There will be no prosperity," says my God, "for the wicked."

THE LORD DESIRES GENUINE DEVOTION

58 "Shout loudly! Don't be quiet!
Yell as loudly as a trumpet!
Confront my people with their rebellious deeds;
confront Jacob's family with their sin.
2 They seek me day after day;
they want to know my requirements,
like a nation that does what is right
and does not reject the law of their God.
They ask me for just decrees;
they want to be near God.
3 They lament, 'Why don't you notice when we fast?
Why don't you pay attention when
we humble ourselves?'
Look, at the same time you fast, you
satisfy your selfish desires,
you oppress your workers.
4 Look, your fasting is accompanied by arguments, brawls,
and fistfights.
Do not fast as you do today,
trying to make your voice heard in heaven.
5 Is this really the kind of fasting I want?
Do I want a day when people merely humble themselves,
bowing their heads like a reed
and stretching out on sackcloth and ashes?

Is this really what you call a fast,
a day that is pleasing to the LORD?
6 No, this is the kind of fast I want:
I want you to remove the sinful chains,
to tear away the ropes of the burdensome yoke,
to set free the oppressed,
and to break every burdensome yoke.
7 I want you to share your food with the hungry
and to provide shelter for homeless, oppressed people.
When you see someone naked, clothe them!
Don't turn your back on your own flesh and blood.
8 Then your light will shine like the sunrise;
your restoration will quickly arrive;
your godly behavior will go before you,
and the LORD's splendor will be your rear guard.
9 Then you will call out, and the LORD will respond;
you will cry out, and he will reply, 'Here I am.'
You must remove the burdensome yoke from among you
and stop pointing fingers and speaking sinfully.
10 You must actively help the hungry
and feed the oppressed.
Then your light will dispel the darkness,
and your darkness will be transformed into noonday.
11 The LORD will continually lead you;
he will feed you even in parched regions.
He will give you renewed strength,
and you will be like a well-watered garden,
like a spring that continually produces water.
12 Your perpetual ruins will be rebuilt;
you will reestablish the ancient foundations.
You will be called, 'The one who repairs broken walls,
the one who makes the streets inhabitable again.'
13 You must observe the Sabbath
rather than doing anything you please on my holy day.
You must look forward to the Sabbath
and treat the LORD's holy day with respect.
You must treat it with respect by refraining
from your normal activities,
and by refraining from your selfish pursuits
and from making business deals.
14 Then you will find joy in your relationship to the LORD,
and I will give you great prosperity,
and cause crops to grow on the land I
gave to your ancestor Jacob."
Know for certain that the LORD has spoken.

INJUSTICE BRINGS ALIENATION FROM GOD

59 Look, the LORD's hand is not too weak to deliver you;
his ear is not too deaf to hear you.
2 But your sinful acts have alienated you from your God;
your sins have caused him to reject you
and not listen to your prayers.
3 For your hands are stained with blood
and your fingers with sin;

your lips speak lies,
your tongue utters malicious words.
4 No one is concerned about justice;
no one sets forth his case truthfully.
They depend on false words and tell lies;
they conceive of oppression
and give birth to sin.
5 They hatch the eggs of a poisonous snake
and spin a spider's web.
Whoever eats their eggs will die,
a poisonous snake is hatched.
6 Their webs cannot be used for clothing;
they cannot cover themselves with what they make.
Their deeds are sinful;
they commit violent crimes.
7 They are eager to do evil,
quick to shed innocent blood.
Their thoughts are sinful;
they crush and destroy.
8 They are unfamiliar with peace;
their deeds are unjust.
They use deceitful methods,
and whoever deals with them is unfamiliar
with peace.

ISRAEL CONFESSES ITS SIN

9 For this reason deliverance is far from us
and salvation does not reach us.
We wait for light, but see only darkness;
we wait for a bright light, but live in deep darkness.
10 We grope along the wall like the blind,
we grope like those who cannot see;
we stumble at noontime as if it were evening.
Though others are strong, we are like dead men.
11 We all growl like bears,
we coo mournfully like doves;
we wait for deliverance, but there is none,
for salvation, but it is far from us.
12 For you are aware of our many rebellious deeds,
and our sins testify against us;
indeed, we are aware of our rebellious deeds;
we know our sins all too well.
13 We have rebelled and tried to deceive the LORD;
we turned back from following our God.
We stir up oppression and rebellion;
we tell lies we concocted in our minds.
14 Justice is driven back;
godliness stands far off.
Indeed, honesty stumbles in the city square
and morality is not even able to enter.
15 Honesty has disappeared;
the one who tries to avoid evil is robbed.
The LORD watches and is displeased,
for there is no justice.

THE LORD INTERVENES

16 He sees there is no advocate;
he is shocked that no one intervenes.
So he takes matters into his own hands;
his desire for justice drives him on.
17 He wears his desire for justice like body armor,
and his desire to deliver is like a helmet on his head.
He puts on the garments of vengeance
and wears zeal like a robe.
18 He repays them for what they have done,
dispensing angry judgment to his adversaries
and punishing his enemies.
He repays the coastlands.
19 In the west, people respect the LORD's reputation;
in the east they recognize his splendor.
For he comes like a rushing stream
driven on by wind sent from the LORD.
20 "A protector comes to Zion,
to those in Jacob who repent of their
rebellious deeds," says the LORD.

21 "As for me, this is my promise to them," says the LORD. "My
Spirit, who is upon you, and my words, which I have placed
in your mouth, will not depart from your mouth or from the
mouths of your children and descendants from this time forward," says the LORD.

ZION'S FUTURE SPLENDOR

60 "Arise! Shine! For your light arrives!
The splendor of the LORD shines on you!
2 For, look, darkness covers the earth
and deep darkness covers the nations,
but the LORD shines on you;
his splendor appears over you.
3 Nations come to your light,
kings to your bright light.
4 Look all around you!
They all gather and come to you—
your sons come from far away,
and your daughters are escorted by guardians.
5 Then you will look and smile,
you will be excited and your heart will swell with pride.
For the riches of distant lands will belong to you,
and the wealth of nations will come to you.
6 Camel caravans will cover your roads,
young camels from Midian and Ephah.
All the merchants of Sheba will come,
bringing gold and incense
and singing praises to the LORD.
7 All the sheep of Kedar will be gathered to you;
the rams of Nebaioth will be available
to you as sacrifices.
They will go up on my altar acceptably,
and I will bestow honor on my majestic temple.

8 Who are these who float along like a cloud,
who fly like doves to their shelters?
9 Indeed, the coastlands look eagerly for me;
the large ships are in the lead,
bringing your sons from far away,
along with their silver and gold,
to honor the LORD your God,
the Holy One of Israel, for he has bestowed honor on you.
10 Foreigners will rebuild your walls;
their kings will serve you.
Even though I struck you down in my anger,
I will restore my favor and have compassion on you.
11 Your gates will remain open at all times;
they will not be shut during the day or at night,
so that the wealth of nations may be delivered,
with their kings leading the way.
12 Indeed, nations or kingdoms that do not serve you will perish;
such nations will definitely be destroyed.
13 The splendor of Lebanon will come to you,
its evergreens, firs, and cypresses together,
to beautify my palace;
I will bestow honor on my throne room.
14 The children of your oppressors will come bowing to you;
all who treated you with disrespect
will bow down at your feet.
They will call you, 'The City of the LORD,
Zion of the Holy One of Israel.'
15 You were once abandoned
and despised, with no one passing through,
but I will make you a permanent source of pride
and joy to coming generations.
16 You will drink the milk of nations;
you will nurse at the breasts of kings.
Then you will recognize that I, the LORD, am your Deliverer,
your Protector, the Powerful One of Jacob.
17 Instead of bronze, I will bring you gold;
instead of iron, I will bring you silver;
instead of wood, I will bring you bronze;
instead of stones, I will bring you iron.
I will make prosperity your overseer,
and vindication your sovereign ruler.
18 Sounds of violence will no longer be heard in your land,
or the sounds of destruction and
devastation within your borders.
You will name your walls, 'Deliverance,'
and your gates, 'Praise.'
19 The sun will no longer supply light for you by day,
nor will the moon's brightness shine on you;
the LORD will be your permanent source of light—
the splendor of your God will shine upon you.
20 Your sun will no longer set;
your moon will not disappear;
the LORD will be your permanent source of light;
your time of sorrow will be over.

21 All your people will be godly;
they will possess the land permanently.
I will plant them like a shoot;
they will be the product of my labor,
through whom I reveal my splendor.
22 The least of you will multiply into a thousand;
the smallest of you will become a large nation.
When the right time comes, I the
LORD will quickly do this!"

THE LORD WILL REJUVENATE HIS PEOPLE

61 The Spirit of the Sovereign LORD is upon me,
because the LORD has chosen me.
He has commissioned me to encourage the poor,
to help the brokenhearted,
to decree the release of captives,
and the freeing of prisoners,
2 to announce the year when the LORD will show his favor,
the day when our God will seek vengeance,
to console all who mourn,
3 to strengthen those who mourn in Zion,
by giving them a turban, instead of ashes,
oil symbolizing joy, instead of mourning,
a garment symbolizing praise,
instead of discouragement.
They will be called oaks of righteousness,
trees planted by the LORD to reveal his splendor.
4 They will rebuild the perpetual ruins
and restore the places that were desolate;
they will reestablish the ruined cities,
the places that have been desolate since ancient times.
5 "Foreigners will take care of your sheep;
foreigners will work in your fields and vineyards.
6 You will be called, 'the LORD's priests,
servants of our God.'
You will enjoy the wealth of nations
and boast about the riches you receive from them.
7 Instead of shame, you will get a double portion;
instead of humiliation, they will rejoice
over the land they receive.
Yes, they will possess a double portion in their land
and experience lasting joy.
8 For I, the LORD, love justice
and hate robbery and sin.
I will repay them because of my faithfulness;
I will make a permanent covenant with them.
9 Their descendants will be known among the nations,
their offspring among the peoples.
All who see them will recognize that
the LORD has blessed them."
10 I will greatly rejoice in the LORD;
I will be overjoyed because of my God.
For he clothes me in garments of deliverance;
he puts on me a robe symbolizing vindication.

REFLECT

How is God's promise evident even in judgment?

I look like a bridegroom when he wears
a turban as a priest would;
I look like a bride when she puts on her jewelry.
11 For just as the ground produces its crops
and a garden yields its produce,
so the Sovereign LORD will cause deliverance to grow,
and give his people reason to praise him
in the sight of all the nations.

THE LORD TAKES DELIGHT IN ZION

62 For the sake of Zion I will not be silent;
for the sake of Jerusalem I will not be quiet,
until her vindication shines brightly
and her deliverance burns like a torch.
2 Nations will see your vindication,
and all kings your splendor.
You will be called by a new name
that the LORD himself will give you.
3 You will be a majestic crown in the hand of the LORD,
a royal turban in the hand of your God.
4 You will no longer be called, "Abandoned,"
and your land will no longer be called "Desolate."
Indeed, you will be called "My Delight is in Her,"
and your land "Married."
For the LORD will take delight in you,
and your land will be married to him.
5 As a young man marries a young woman,
so your sons will marry you.
As a bridegroom rejoices over a bride,
so your God will rejoice over you.
6 I post watchmen on your walls, O Jerusalem;
they should keep praying all day and all night.
You who pray to the LORD, don't be silent!
7 Don't allow him to rest until he reestablishes Jerusalem,
until he makes Jerusalem the pride of the earth.
8 The LORD swears an oath by his right hand,
by his strong arm:
"I will never again give your grain
to your enemies as food,
and foreigners will not drink your wine,
which you worked hard to produce.

9 But those who harvest the grain will eat it,
and will praise the LORD.
Those who pick the grapes will drink the wine
in the courts of my holy sanctuary."
10 Come through! Come through the gates!
Prepare the way for the people!
Build it—Build the roadway!
Remove the stones.
Lift a signal flag for the nations.
11 Look, the LORD announces to the entire earth:
"Say to Daughter Zion,
'Look, your deliverer comes!

Look, his reward is with him,
and his reward goes before him!'"
12 They will be called, "The Holy People,
the Ones Protected by the LORD."
You will be called, "Sought After,
City Not Abandoned."

THE VICTORIOUS DIVINE WARRIOR

63 Who is this who comes from Edom,
dressed in bright red, coming from Bozrah?
Who is this one wearing royal attire,
who marches confidently because of his great strength?
"It is I, the one who announces vindication,
and who is able to deliver!"
2 Why are your clothes red?
Why do you look like someone who has
stomped on grapes in a vat?
3 "I have stomped grapes in the winepress all by myself;
no one from the nations joined me.
I stomped on them in my anger;
I trampled them down in my rage.
Their juice splashed on my garments,
and stained all my clothes.
4 For I looked forward to the day of vengeance,
and then payback time arrived.
5 I looked, but there was no one to help;
I was shocked because there was no one offering support.
So my right arm accomplished deliverance;
my raging anger drove me on.
6 I trampled nations in my anger;
I made them drunk in my rage;
I splashed their blood on the ground."

A PRAYER FOR DIVINE INTERVENTION

7 I will tell of the faithful acts of the LORD,
of the LORD's praiseworthy deeds.
I will tell about all the LORD did for us,
the many good things he did for the family of Israel,
because of his compassion and great faithfulness.
8 He said, "Certainly they will be my people,
children who are not disloyal."
He became their deliverer.
9 Through all that they suffered, he suffered too.
The messenger sent from his very
presence delivered them.
In his love and mercy he protected them;
he lifted them up and carried them
throughout ancient times.
10 But they rebelled and offended his holy Spirit,
so he turned into an enemy
and fought against them.
11 His people remembered the ancient times.
Where is the one who brought them up out of the sea,
along with the shepherd of his flock?

Where is the one who placed his holy Spirit among them,
12 the one who made his majestic power available to Moses,
who divided the water before them,
gaining for himself a lasting reputation,
13 who led them through the deep water?
Like a horse running through the
wilderness they did not stumble.
14 As an animal that goes down into a valley to graze,
so the Spirit of the LORD granted them rest.
In this way you guided your people,
gaining for yourself an honored reputation.
15 Look down from heaven and take notice,
from your holy, majestic palace!
Where are your zeal and power?
Do not hold back your tender compassion!
16 For you are our father,
though Abraham does not know us
and Israel does not recognize us.
You, LORD, are our father;
you have been called our Protector from ancient times.
17 Why, LORD, do you make us stray from your ways,
and make our minds stubborn so that we do not obey you?
Return for the sake of your servants,
the tribes of your inheritance!
18 For a short time your special nation possessed a land,
but then our adversaries knocked
down your holy sanctuary.
19 We existed from ancient times,
but you did not rule over them;
they were not your subjects.
64 If only you would tear apart the sky and come down!
The mountains would tremble before you!
2 As when fire ignites dry wood,
or fire makes water boil,
let your adversaries know who you are,
and may the nations shake at your presence!
3 When you performed awesome deeds
that took us by surprise,
you came down, and the mountains trembled before you.
4 Since ancient times no one has heard or perceived,
no eye has seen any God besides you,
who intervenes for those who wait for him.
5 You assist those who delight in doing what is right,
who observe your commandments.
Look, you were angry because we
violated them continually.
How then can we be saved?
6 We are all like one who is unclean,
all our so-called righteous acts are like
a menstrual rag in your sight.
We all wither like a leaf;
our sins carry us away like the wind.
7 No one invokes your name,
or makes an effort to take hold of you.

For you have rejected us
and handed us over to our own sins.
8 Yet, LORD, you are our father.
We are the clay, and you are our potter;
we are all the product of your labor.
9 LORD, do not be too angry!
Do not hold our sins against us continually.
Take a good look at your people, at all of us.
10 Your chosen cities have become a wilderness;
Zion has become a wilderness,
Jerusalem, a desolate ruin.
11 Our holy temple, our pride and joy,
the place where our ancestors praised you,
has been burned with fire;
all our prized possessions have been destroyed.
12 In light of all this, how can you still hold back, LORD?
How can you be silent and continue to humiliate us?

THE LORD WILL DISTINGUISH BETWEEN SINNERS AND THE GODLY

65 "I made myself available to those
who did not ask for me;
I appeared to those who did not look for me.
I said, 'Here I am! Here I am!'
to a nation that did not invoke my name.
2 I spread out my hands all day long
to my rebellious people,
who lived in a way that is morally unacceptable,
and who did what they desired.
3 These people continually and blatantly offend me
as they sacrifice in their sacred orchards
and burn incense on brick altars.
4 They sit among the tombs
and keep watch all night long.
They eat pork,
and broth from unclean sacrificial
meat is in their pans.
5 They say, 'Keep to yourself!
Don't get near me, for I am holier than you!'
These people are like smoke in my nostrils,
like a fire that keeps burning all day long.
6 Look, I have decreed:
I will not keep silent, but will pay them back;
I will pay them back exactly what they deserve,
7 for your sins and your ancestors' sins," says the LORD.
"Because they burned incense on the mountains
and offended me on the hills,
I will punish them in full measure."

8 This is what the LORD says:
"When juice is discovered in a cluster of grapes,
someone says, 'Don't destroy it, for it contains juice.'
So I will do for the sake of my servants—
I will not destroy everyone.

9 I will bring forth descendants from Jacob,
and from Judah people to take possession of my mountains.
My chosen ones will take possession of the land;
my servants will live there.
10 Sharon will become a pasture for sheep,
and the Valley of Achor a place where cattle graze;
they will belong to my people, who seek me.
11 But as for you who abandon the LORD
and forget about worshiping at my holy mountain,
who prepare a feast for the god called 'Fortune,'
and fill up wine jugs for the god called 'Destiny'—
12 I predestine you to die by the sword,
all of you will kneel down at the slaughtering block,
because I called to you, and you did not respond;
I spoke and you did not listen.
You did evil before me;
you chose to do what displeases me."

13 So this is what the Sovereign LORD says:
"Look, my servants will eat, but you will be hungry.
Look, my servants will drink, but you will be thirsty.
Look, my servants will rejoice, but you will be humiliated.
14 Look, my servants will shout for joy as
happiness fills their hearts.
But you will cry out as sorrow fills your hearts;
you will wail because your spirits will be crushed.
15 Your names will live on in the curse
formulas of my chosen ones.
The Sovereign LORD will kill you,
but he will give his servants another name.
16 Whoever pronounces a blessing in the earth
will do so in the name of the faithful God;
whoever makes an oath in the earth
will do so in the name of the faithful God.
For past problems will be forgotten;
I will no longer think about them.
17 For look, I am ready to create
new heavens and a new earth!
The former ones will not be remembered;
no one will think about them anymore.
18 But be happy and rejoice forevermore
over what I am about to create!
For look, I am ready to create Jerusalem
to be a source of joy,
and her people to be a source of happiness.
19 Jerusalem will bring me joy,
and my people will bring me happiness.
The sound of weeping or cries of sorrow
will never be heard in her again.
20 Never again will one of her infants live just a few days
or an old man die before his time.
Indeed, no one will die before the age of one hundred;
anyone who fails to reach the age of one
hundred will be considered cursed.

21 They will build houses and live in them;
they will plant vineyards and eat their fruit.
22 No longer will they build a house only
to have another live in it,
or plant a vineyard only to have another eat its fruit,
for my people will live as long as trees,
and my chosen ones will enjoy to the
fullest what they have produced.
23 They will not work in vain,
or give birth to children that will experience disaster.
For the LORD will bless their children
and their descendants.
24 Before they even call out, I will respond;
while they are still speaking, I will hear.
25 A wolf and a lamb will graze together;
a lion, like an ox, will eat straw,
and a snake's food will be dirt.
They will no longer injure or destroy
on my entire royal mountain," says the LORD.

66 This is what the LORD says:
"The heavens are my throne
and the earth is my footstool.
Where then is the house you will build for me?
Where is the place where I will rest?
2 My hand made them;
that is how they came to be," says the LORD.

"I show special favor to the humble and contrite,
who respect what I have to say.
3 The one who slaughters a bull also strikes down a man;
the one who sacrifices a lamb also breaks a dog's neck;
the one who presents an offering includes pig's blood with it;
the one who offers incense also praises an idol.
They have decided to behave this way;
they enjoy these disgusting practices.
4 So I will choose severe punishment for them;
I will bring on them what they dread,
because I called, and no one responded.
I spoke and they did not listen.
They did evil before me;
they chose to do what displeases me."
5 Listen to the LORD's message,
you who respect his word!

"Your countrymen, who hate you
and exclude you, supposedly for the sake of my name,
say, 'May the LORD be glorified,
then we will witness your joy.'
But they will be put to shame.
6 The sound of battle comes from the city;
the sound comes from the temple!
It is the sound of the LORD paying back his enemies.
7 Before she goes into labor, she gives birth!
Before her contractions begin, she delivers a boy!

8 Who has ever heard of such a thing?
Who has ever seen this?
Can a country be brought forth in one day?
Can a nation be born in a single moment?
Yet as soon as Zion goes into labor she gives birth to sons!
9 Do I bring a baby to the birth opening
and then not deliver it?"
asks the LORD.
"Or do I bring a baby to the point of
delivery and then hold it back?"
asks your God.
10 "Be happy for Jerusalem
and rejoice with her, all you who love her!
Share in her great joy,
all you who have mourned over her!
11 For you will nurse from her satisfying
breasts and be nourished;
you will feed with joy from her milk-filled breasts.

12 For this is what the LORD says:
"Look, I am ready to extend to her
prosperity that will flow like a river,
the riches of nations will flow into her like
a stream that floods its banks.
You will nurse from her breast and be carried at her side;
you will play on her knees.
13 As a mother consoles a child,
so I will console you,
and you will be consoled over Jerusalem."
14 When you see this, you will be happy,
and you will be revived.
The LORD will reveal his power to his servants
and his anger to his enemies.
15 For look, the LORD comes with fire,
his chariots come like a windstorm,
to reveal his raging anger,
his battle cry, and his flaming arrows.
16 For the LORD judges all humanity
with fire and his sword;
the LORD will kill many.

17 "As for those who consecrate and ritually purify themselves
so they can follow their leader and worship in the sacred orchards, those who eat the flesh of pigs and other disgusting creatures, like mice—they will all be destroyed together," says the
LORD. 18 "I hate their deeds and thoughts! So I am coming to
gather all the nations and ethnic groups; they will come and witness my splendor. 19 I will perform a mighty act among them and
then send some of those who remain to the nations—to Tarshish,
Pul, Lud (known for its archers), Tubal, Javan, and to the distant
coastlands that have not heard about me or seen my splendor.
They will tell the nations of my splendor. 20 They will bring back
all your countrymen from all the nations as an offering to the
LORD. They will bring them on horses, in chariots, in wagons, on

mules, and on camels to my holy hill Jerusalem," says the LORD,
"just as the Israelites bring offerings to the LORD's temple in
ritually pure containers. 21 And I will choose some of them as
priests and Levites," says the LORD. 22 "For just as the new heavens and the new earth I am about to make will remain standing
before me," says the LORD, "so your descendants and your name
will remain. 23 From one month to the next and from one Sabbath to the next, all people will come to worship me," says the
LORD. 24 "They will go out and observe the corpses of those who
rebelled against me, for the maggots that eat them will not die,
and the fire that consumes them will not die out. All people will
find the sight abhorrent."

"When you seek me in prayer and worship, you will find me available to you. If you seek me with all your heart and soul, I will make myself available to you," says the Lord.

MEMORY VERSE

"When you seek me in prayer and worship, you will find me available to you. If you seek me with all your heart and soul, I will make myself available to you," says the Lord. "Then I will reverse your plight and will regather you from all the nations and all the places where I have exiled you," says the Lord. "I will bring you back to the place from which I exiled you."

Jeremiah 29:13–14

Jeremiah

INTRODUCTION

The Promise of Mercy

The Book of Jeremiah provides a unique look at Jeremiah's inner struggles as a prophet. However, even in his anguish, Jeremiah was faithful to fulfill the calling and ministry God had given him, to serve the people of Judah. Jeremiah proclaimed God's judgment against the unfaithful people of Judah, providing an example to believers today of how to remain faithful to God, even when life is hard.

This book is not organized chronologically, but rather by content, audience, and other connections. It can be divided into four main sections, beginning with the call of Jeremiah in chapter 1. Chapters 2–24 describe the coming judgment of Judah and Jerusalem. Chapters 25–51 describe Jeremiah's ministry to the nations, and chapter 52 contains a historical recounting of the fall of Jerusalem.

Jeremiah is the undisputed author of the book that bears his name. His ministry to the people of Judah took place between 626 and 586 B.C., making him a contemporary of Zephaniah, Ezekiel, and Habakkuk—other prophets of Judah. It is believed he began writing around 605 B.C., with portions of the book written earlier and the entire book compiled after the fall of Jerusalem in 586 B.C.

Jeremiah offers a deep understanding of the character of God in his prophetic message. God had established a binding covenant between Himself and Israel, one of love, faithfulness, and hope. However, the unfaithfulness of the people resulted in God's discipline, which came in the form of punishment, destruction, and exile. Amid prophecies of judgment, Jeremiah encourages us to love God greatly with his message of hope: God would restore a righteous remnant of His people. God's promise of mercy gave Jeremiah, and the people of Judah, hope. This is a hope we can still cling to today: Our God keeps His promises, and He longs to restore His people.

Eritrea

OFFICIAL LANGUAGE
Tigrigna
POPULATION
3,393,000
UNREACHED POPULATION
1,323,000
PROFESSING CHRISTIANS
51.4%

Solyana's Home

Say a Prayer Today

Pray for the persecuted church in Eritrea. Pray for those who have endured persecution, like Solyana and her family, that God would bring them peace and hope in the midst of such suffering.

HISTORY BIT

This small country gained its independence in 1993. Eritrea is ranked as the seventh-most hostile country in the world for Christians. Many Christians have faced severe persecution, and many have been in captivity for over a decade.*

Source Information:
https://joshuaproject.net/countries/ER
*https://www.christianpost.com/news/persecuted-pastor-describes-tortures-of-imprisonment-facing-christians-in-eritrea.html

LOVE YOUR NEIGHBOR

Her Journey

SOLYANA'S STORY

My life seems to have been marked by loss since the beginning. I was born in Ethiopia, where my family lived, refugees from our homeland of Eritrea. Soon after I was born, my dad and my grandpa were deported, returning to Eritrea. I lived in Ethiopia with my mum and sister until I was six-years-old when civil authorities caught us and deported us as well.

About the time we returned to Eritrea, my mum accepted Christ as her Lord and converted to Christianity. The government in Eritrea staunchly opposes any religion outside of Islam or Orthodox Catholicism, and my mum's conversion led to problems. Apart from issues with the government, she faced internal persecutions from its citizens. To this day, Christians in Eritrea continue to be severely persecuted for professing and practicing faith in Jesus Christ.

I accepted Jesus as my Lord and Savior when I was seven years old. My life with Him has been marked by great hope and trust in God's goodness. My mum, after being persecuted and tortured for her faith in horrendous ways, finally took me and escaped with the help of family who had escaped before us to the UK. This was not an easy time for us, but God carried us all the way.

In Northern Ireland we found a welcoming church. Many people in our new community witnessed God's provision and goodness through our testimony of His faithfulness overcoming the appalling things we went through. His light shines brightest in the darkest places. Even when it seems impossible, He has a plan and a future for each of His children! Everything is a gift in this life. I have learned, by God's grace, to put my full confidence in Him who reigns sovereign over all things.

6 WEEK READING PLAN

LOVE HIS WORD

	MONDAY	TUESDAY	WEDNESDAY	THURSDAY	FRIDAY
1	Jeremiah 1:1—3:11	Jeremiah 3:12—4:31	Jeremiah 5-6	Jeremiah 7	Jeremiah 8-9
	SOAP Genesis 9:8-10	SOAP Genesis 9:11	SOAP Genesis 9:12-13	SOAP Genesis 9:14-15	SOAP Genesis 9:16-17
2	Jeremiah 10:1—11:17	Jeremiah 11:18—13:27	Jeremiah 14-15	Jeremiah 16-17	Jeremiah 18-19
	SOAP Genesis 15:4-6	SOAP Genesis 15:7-8	SOAP Genesis 15:9-11	SOAP Genesis 15:12-16	SOAP Genesis 15:17-21
3	Jeremiah 20-21	Jeremiah 22	Jeremiah 23	Jeremiah 24-25	Jeremiah 26-27
	SOAP Exodus 24:3-4	SOAP Exodus 24:5-8	SOAP Exodus 24:9-11	SOAP Exodus 24:12-14	SOAP Exodus 24:15-18
4	Jeremiah 28-29	Jeremiah 30:1—31:1	Jeremiah 31:2-40	Jeremiah 32	Jeremiah 33-34
	SOAP Jeremiah 29:13-14	SOAP 2 Samuel 7:8-9	SOAP 2 Samuel 7:10-11	SOAP 2 Samuel 7:12-14	SOAP 2 Samuel 7:15-17
5	Jeremiah 35-36	Jeremiah 37	Jeremiah 38-39	Jeremiah 40-41	Jeremiah 42-43
	SOAP Jeremiah 31:31-32	SOAP Jeremiah 31:33	SOAP Jeremiah 31:34	SOAP Jeremiah 31:35	SOAP Jeremiah 31:36-37
6	Jeremiah 44-45	Jeremiah 46-48	Jeremiah 49	Jeremiah 50	Jeremiah 51-52
	SOAP Matthew 26:26-30	SOAP Mark 14:22-26	SOAP Luke 22:17-20	SOAP 1 Corinthians 11:23-26	SOAP Hebrews 13:20-21

THE SUPERSCRIPTION

1 The following is a record of what Jeremiah son of Hilkiah prophesied. He was one of the priests who lived at Anathoth in the
territory of the tribe of Benjamin. 2 The LORD's message came to
him in the thirteenth year that Josiah son of Amon ruled over
Judah. 3 It also came in the days of Jehoiakim, son of Josiah, king
of Judah, and continued until the eleventh year of Zedekiah, son
of Josiah, king of Judah, until the people of Jerusalem were taken
into exile in the fifth month of that year.

JEREMIAH'S CALL AND COMMISSION

4 The LORD's message came to me,

5 "Before I formed you in your mother's womb I chose you.
Before you were born I set you apart.
I appointed you to be a prophet to the nations."

6 I answered, "Oh, Sovereign LORD, Really I do not know how
to speak well enough for that, for I am too young." 7 The LORD
said to me, "Do not say, 'I am too young.' But go to whomever I
send you and say whatever I tell you. 8 Do not be afraid of those
to whom I send you, for I will be with you to protect you," says
the LORD. 9 Then the LORD reached out his hand and touched
my mouth and said to me, "I will most assuredly give you the
words you are to speak for me. 10 Know for certain that I hereby
give you the authority to announce to nations and kingdoms
that they will be uprooted and torn down, destroyed and demolished, rebuilt and firmly planted."

VISIONS CONFIRMING JEREMIAH'S CALL AND COMMISSION

11 Later the LORD's message came to me, "What do you see, Jeremiah?" I answered, "I see a branch of an almond tree." 12 Then
the LORD said, "You have observed correctly. This means I am
watching to make sure my threats are carried out."

13 The LORD's message came to me a second time, "What do you
see?" I answered, "I see a pot of boiling water; it is tipped away
from the north." 14 Then the LORD said, "From the north destruction will break out on all who live in the land. 15 For I will soon
summon all the peoples of the kingdoms of the north," says the
LORD. "They will come and their kings will set up their thrones
near the entrances of the gates of Jerusalem. They will attack all
the walls surrounding it and all the towns in Judah. 16 In this way I
will pass sentence on the people of Jerusalem and Judah because
of all their wickedness. For they rejected me and offered sacrifices
to other gods, worshiping what they made with their own hands.

17 "But you, Jeremiah, get yourself ready! Go and tell these people everything I instruct you to say. Do not be terrified of them,
or I will give you good reason to be terrified of them. 18 I, the
LORD, hereby promise to make you as strong as a fortified city,
an iron pillar, and a bronze wall. You will be able to stand up
against all who live in the land, including the kings of Judah, its
officials, its priests and all the people of the land. 19 They will attack you but they will not be able to overcome you, for I will be
with you to rescue you," says the LORD.

THE LORD RECALLS ISRAEL'S EARLIER FAITHFULNESS

2 The LORD's message came to me, 2 "Go and declare in the hearing of the people of Jerusalem: 'This is what the LORD says: "I
have fond memories of you, how devoted you were to me in your
early years. I remember how you loved me like a new bride; you
followed me through the wilderness, through a land that had
never been planted. 3 Israel was set apart to the LORD; they were
like the firstfruits of a harvest to him. All who tried to devour
them were punished; disaster came upon them," says the LORD.'"

THE LORD REMINDS THEM OF THE UNFAITHFULNESS OF THEIR ANCESTORS

4 Now listen to the LORD's message,
you descendants of Jacob,
all you family groups from the nation of Israel.
5 This is what the LORD says:
"What fault could your ancestors
have possibly found in me
that they strayed so far from me?
They paid allegiance to worthless idols,
and so became worthless to me.
6 They did not ask,
'Where is the LORD who delivered us out of Egypt,
who brought us through the wilderness,
through a land of valleys and gorges,
through a land of desert and deep darkness,
through a land in which no one travels,
and where no one lives?'
7 I brought you into a fertile land
so you could enjoy its fruits and its rich bounty.
But when you entered my land, you defiled it;
you made the land I call my own loathsome to me.
8 Your priests did not ask, 'Where is the LORD?'
Those responsible for teaching my
law did not really know me.
Your rulers rebelled against me.
Your prophets prophesied in the name of the god Baal.
They all worshiped idols that could not help them.

THE LORD CHARGES CONTEMPORARY ISRAEL WITH SPIRITUAL ADULTERY

9 "So, once more I will state my case
against you," says the LORD.
"I will also state it against your
children and grandchildren.
10 Go west across the sea to the coasts of Cyprus and see.
Send someone east to Kedar and
have them look carefully.
See if such a thing as this has ever happened:
11 Has a nation ever changed its gods
(even though they are not really gods at all)?
But my people have exchanged me, their glorious God,
for a god that cannot help them at all!

12 Be amazed at this, O heavens.
Be shocked and utterly dumbfounded,"
says the LORD.
13 "Do so because my people have
committed a double wrong:
They have rejected me,
the fountain of life-giving water,
and they have dug cisterns for themselves,
cracked cisterns that cannot even hold water.

ISRAEL'S RELIANCE ON FOREIGN ALLIANCES (NOT ON GOD)

14 "Israel is not a slave, is he?
He was not born into slavery, was he?
If not, why then is he being carried off?
15 Like lions his enemies roar victoriously over him;
they raise their voices in triumph.
They have laid his land waste;
his cities have been burned down and deserted.
16 Even the soldiers from Memphis and Tahpanhes
have cracked your skulls, people of Israel.
17 You have brought all this on yourself, Israel,
by deserting the LORD your God when he
was leading you along the right path.
18 What good will it do you then to go down to Egypt
to seek help from the Egyptians?
What good will it do you to go over to Assyria
to seek help from the Assyrians?
19 Your own wickedness will bring about your punishment.
Your unfaithful acts will bring down discipline on you.
Know, then, and realize how utterly harmful
it was for you to reject me, the LORD your God,
to show no respect for me,"
says the Sovereign LORD of Heaven's Armies.

THE LORD EXPRESSES HIS EXASPERATION AT JUDAH'S PERSISTENT IDOLATRY

20 "Indeed, long ago you threw off my authority
and refused to be subject to me.
You said, 'I will not serve you.'
Instead, you gave yourself to other
gods on every high hill
and under every green tree,
like a prostitute sprawls out before her lovers.
21 I planted you in the land
like a special vine of the very best stock.
Why in the world have you turned into
something like a wild vine
that produces rotten, foul-smelling grapes?
22 You can try to wash away your guilt
with a strong detergent.
You can use as much soap as you want.
But the stain of your guilt is still there for me to see,"
says the Sovereign LORD.

23 "How can you say, 'I have not made myself unclean.
I have not paid allegiance to the gods called Baal.'
Just look at the way you have behaved
in the Valley of Hinnom!
Think about the things you have done there!
You are like a flighty, young female camel
that rushes here and there, crisscrossing its path.
24 You are like a wild female donkey
brought up in the wilderness.
In her lust she sniffs the wind to get the scent of a male.
No one can hold her back when she is in heat.
None of the males need wear themselves
out chasing after her.
At mating time she is easy to find.
25 Do not chase after other gods until your shoes wear out
and your throats become dry.
But you say, 'It is useless for you to try and stop me
because I love those foreign gods and
want to pursue them!'
26 Just as a thief has to suffer dishonor when he is caught,
so the people of Israel will suffer dishonor
for what they have done.
So will their kings and officials,
their priests and their prophets.
27 They say to a wooden idol, 'You are my father.'
They say to a stone image, 'You gave birth to me.'
Yes, they have turned away from me
instead of turning to me.
Yet when they are in trouble, they say, 'Come and save us!'
28 But where are the gods you made for yourselves?
Let them save you when you are in trouble.
The sad fact is that you have as many gods
as you have towns, Judah.
29 Why do you try to refute me?
All of you have rebelled against me,"
says the LORD.
30 "It did no good for me to punish your people.
They did not respond to such correction.
You slaughtered your prophets
like a voracious lion.
31 You people of this generation,
listen to the LORD's message:
"Have I been like a wilderness to you, Israel?
Have I been like a dark and dangerous land to you?
Why then do you say, 'We are free to wander.
We will not come to you anymore?'
32 Does a young woman forget to put on her jewels?
Does a bride forget to put on her bridal attire?
But my people have forgotten me
for more days than can even be counted.

33 "My, how good you have become
at chasing after your lovers!
Why, you could even teach prostitutes a thing or two!

34 Even your clothes are stained with
the lifeblood of the poor who had
not done anything wrong;
you did not catch them breaking into your homes.
Yet, in spite of all these things you have done,
35 you say, 'I have not done anything wrong,
so the LORD cannot really be angry with me any more.'
But, watch out! I will bring down judgment on you
because you say, 'I have not committed any sin.'
36 Why do you constantly go about
changing your political allegiances?
You will get no help from Egypt
just as you got no help from Assyria.
37 Moreover, you will come away from Egypt
with your hands covering your faces in sorrow and shame
because the LORD will not allow your
reliance on them to be successful
and you will not gain any help from them.

3 "If a man divorces his wife
and she leaves him and becomes another man's wife,
he may not take her back again.
Doing that would utterly defile the land.
But you, Israel, have given yourself as
a prostitute to many gods.
So what makes you think you can return to me?"
says the LORD.
2 "Look up at the hilltops and consider this.
Where have you not been ravished?
You waited for those gods like a thief
lying in wait in the wilderness.
You defiled the land by your wicked
prostitution to other gods.
3 That is why the rains have been withheld
and the spring rains have not come.
Yet in spite of this you are obstinate as a prostitute.
You refuse to be ashamed of what you have done.
4 Even now you say to me, 'You are my father!
You have been my faithful companion
ever since I was young.
5 You will not always be angry with me, will you?
You will not be mad at me forever, will you?'
That is what you say,
but you continually do all the evil that you can."

6 When Josiah was king of Judah, the LORD said to me, "Jeremiah, you have no doubt seen what wayward Israel has done.
You have seen how she went up to every high hill and under
every green tree to give herself like a prostitute to other gods.
7 Yet even after she had done all that, I thought that she might
come back to me. But she did not. Her sister, unfaithful Judah,
saw what she did. 8 She also saw that, because of wayward Israel's adulterous worship of other gods, I sent her away and gave
her divorce papers. But still her unfaithful sister Judah was not

afraid, and she too went and gave herself like a prostitute to
other gods. 9 Because she took her prostitution so lightly, she
defiled the land through her adulterous worship of gods made
of wood and stone. 10 In spite of all this, Israel's sister, unfaithful Judah, has not turned back to me with any sincerity; she has
only pretended to do so," says the LORD. 11 Then the LORD said
to me, "Under the circumstances, wayward Israel could even be
considered less guilty than unfaithful Judah.

THE LORD CALLS ON ISRAEL AND JUDAH TO REPENT

12 "Go and shout this message to my people in the countries in
the north. Tell them:

'Come back to me, wayward Israel,' says the LORD.
'I will not continue to look on you with displeasure.
For I am merciful,' says the LORD.
'I will not be angry with you forever.
13 However, you must confess that you have done wrong
and that you have rebelled against the LORD your God.
You must confess that you have given yourself
  to foreign gods under every green tree
and have not obeyed my commands,' says the LORD.

14 "Come back to me, my wayward sons," says the LORD, "for I
am your true master. If you do, I will take one of you from each
town and two of you from each family group, and I will bring
you back to Zion. 15 I will give you leaders who will be faithful to
me. They will lead you with knowledge and insight. 16 In those
days, your population will greatly increase in the land. At that
time," says the LORD, "people will no longer talk about having
the ark that contains the LORD's covenant with us. They will
not call it to mind, remember it, or miss it. No, that will not be
done anymore! 17 At that time the city of Jerusalem will be called
the LORD's throne. All nations will gather there in Jerusalem to
honor the LORD's name. They will no longer follow the stubborn
inclinations of their own evil hearts. 18 At that time the nation
of Judah and the nation of Israel will be reunited. Together they
will come back from a land in the north to the land that I gave
to your ancestors as a permanent possession.

19 "I thought to myself,
'Oh what a joy it would be for me to treat you like a son!
What a joy it would be for me to give you a pleasant land,
the most beautiful piece of property
  there is in all the world!'
I thought you would call me 'Father'
and would never cease being loyal to me.
20 But, you have been unfaithful to me, nation of Israel,
like an unfaithful wife who has left her husband,"
says the LORD.
21 "A noise is heard on the hilltops.
It is the sound of the people of Israel
  crying and pleading to their gods.
Indeed they have followed sinful ways;
they have forgotten to be true to the LORD their God.
22 Come back to me, you wayward people.

REFLECT

What had the people of Judah done that caused God to enact judgment on them?

I want to cure your waywardness.
Say, 'Here we are. We come to you
because you are the LORD our God.
23 We know our noisy worship of false gods
on the hills and mountains did not help us.
We know that the LORD our God
is the only one who can deliver Israel.
24 From earliest times our worship of
that shameful god, Baal,
has taken away all that our ancestors worked for.
It has taken away our flocks and our herds
and even our sons and daughters.
25 Let us acknowledge our shame.
Let us bear the disgrace that we deserve.
For we have sinned against the LORD our God,
both we and our ancestors.
From earliest times to this very day
we have not obeyed the LORD our God.'

"If you, Israel, want to come back," says the LORD,
"if you want to come back to me,
you must get those disgusting idols out of my sight
and must no longer go astray.
2 You must be truthful, honest, and upright
when you take an oath saying, 'As surely as the LORD lives!'
If you do, the nations will pray to be
as blessed by him as you are
and will make him the object of their boasting."
3 Yes, this is what the LORD has said
to the people of Judah and Jerusalem:
"Break up your unplowed ground, do
not cast seeds among thorns.
4 Commit yourselves to the LORD;
dedicate your hearts to me
people of Judah and inhabitants of Jerusalem.
Otherwise, my anger will blaze up like
a flaming fire against you
that no one will be able to extinguish.
That will happen because of the evil you have done."

WARNING OF COMING JUDGMENT

5 The LORD said,
"Announce this in Judah and proclaim it in Jerusalem:
'Sound the trumpet throughout the land!'
Shout out loudly,
'Gather together! Let us flee into the fortified cities!'
6 Raise a signal flag that tells people to go to Zion.
Run for safety! Do not delay!
For I am about to bring disaster out of the north.
It will bring great destruction.
7 Like a lion that has come up from its lair
the one who destroys nations has set
out from his home base.
He is coming out to lay your land waste.

Your cities will become ruins and lie uninhabited.
8 So put on sackcloth!
Mourn and wail, saying,
'The fierce anger of the LORD
has not turned away from us!'
9 When this happens," says the LORD,
"the king and his officials will lose their courage.
The priests will be struck with horror,
and the prophets will be speechless in astonishment."

10 In response to all this I said, "Ah, Sovereign LORD, you have
surely allowed the people of Judah and Jerusalem to be deceived
by those who say, 'You will be safe!' But in fact a sword is already
at our throats."

11 At that time the people of Judah and Jerusalem will be told,
"A scorching wind will sweep down
from the hilltops in the wilderness on my dear people.
It will not be a gentle breeze
for winnowing the grain and blowing away the chaff.
12 No, a wind too strong for that will come at my bidding.
Yes, even now I, myself, am calling down judgment on them.
13 Look! The enemy is approaching like gathering clouds.
The roar of his chariots is like that of a whirlwind.
His horses move more swiftly than eagles."
I cry out, "We are doomed, for we will be destroyed!"
14 Oh people of Jerusalem, purify your hearts from evil
so that you may yet be delivered.
How long will you continue to harbor up
wicked schemes within you?
15 For messengers are coming, heralding disaster,
from the city of Dan and from the hills of Ephraim.
16 They are saying,
"Announce to the surrounding nations,
'The enemy is coming!'
Proclaim this message to Jerusalem:
'Those who besiege cities are coming from a distant land.
They are ready to raise the battle cry
against the towns in Judah.'
17 They will surround Jerusalem
like men guarding a field
because they have rebelled against me,"
says the LORD.
18 "The way you have lived and the things you have done
will bring this on you.
This is the punishment you deserve,
and it will be painful indeed.
The pain will be so bad it will pierce your heart."

19 I said,
"Oh, the feeling in the pit of my stomach!
I writhe in anguish.
Oh, the pain in my heart!
My heart pounds within me.
I cannot keep silent.

For I hear the sound of the trumpet;
the sound of the battle cry pierces my soul!
20 I see one destruction after another taking place,
so that the whole land lies in ruins.
I see our tents suddenly destroyed,
their curtains torn down in a mere instant.
21 How long must I see the enemy's battle flags
and hear the military signals of their bugles?"

22 The LORD answered,
"This will happen because my people are foolish.
They do not know me.
They are like children who have no sense.
They have no understanding.
They are skilled at doing evil.
They do not know how to do good."

23 I looked at the land and saw that it
was an empty wasteland.
I looked up at the sky, and its light had vanished.
24 I looked at the mountains and saw that they were shaking.
All the hills were swaying back and forth!
25 I looked and saw that there were no more people
and that all the birds in the sky had flown away.
26 I looked and saw that the fruitful land had become a desert
and that all the cities had been laid in ruins.
The LORD had brought this all about
because of his blazing anger.
27 All this will happen because the LORD said,
"The whole land will be desolate;
however, I will not completely destroy it.
28 Because of this the land will mourn
and the sky above will grow black.
For I have made my purpose known,
and I will not relent or turn back from carrying it out."
29 At the sound of the approaching horsemen and archers
the people of every town will flee.
Some of them will hide in the thickets.
Others will climb up among the rocks.
All the cities will be deserted.
No one will remain in them.
30 And you, Zion, city doomed to destruction,
you accomplish nothing by wearing a beautiful dress,
decking yourself out in jewels of gold,
and putting on eye shadow!
You are making yourself beautiful for nothing.
Your lovers spurn you.
They want to kill you.
31 In fact, I hear a cry like that of a woman in labor,
a cry of anguish like that of a woman
giving birth to her first baby.
It is the cry of Daughter Zion gasping for breath,
reaching out for help, saying, "I am done in!
My life is ebbing away before these murderers!"

JUDAH IS JUSTLY DESERVING OF COMING JUDGMENT

5 The LORD said,
"Go up and down through the streets of Jerusalem.
Look around and see for yourselves.
Search through its public squares.
See if any of you can find a single person
who deals honestly and tries to be truthful.
If you can, then I will not punish this city.
2 These people make promises in the name of the LORD.
But the fact is, what they swear to is really a lie."
3 LORD, I know you look for faithfulness.
But even when you punish these
people, they feel no remorse.
Even when you nearly destroy them,
they refuse to be corrected.
They have become as hardheaded as a rock.
They refuse to change their ways.
4 I thought, "Surely it is only the ignorant
poor who act this way.
They act like fools because they do not
know what the LORD demands.
They do not know what their God requires of them.
5 I will go to the leaders
and speak with them.
Surely they know what the LORD demands.
Surely they know what their God requires of them."
Yet all of them, too, have rejected his authority
and refuse to submit to him.
6 So like a lion from the thicket their
enemies will kill them.
Like a wolf from the rift valley they will destroy them.
Like a leopard they will lie in wait outside their cities
and totally destroy anyone who ventures out.
For they have rebelled so much
and done so many unfaithful things.

7 The LORD asked,
"How can I leave you unpunished, Jerusalem?
Your people have rejected me
and have worshiped gods that are not gods at all.
Even though I supplied all their needs, they
were like an unfaithful wife to me.
They went flocking to the houses of prostitutes.
8 They are like lusty, well-fed stallions.
Each of them lusts after his neighbor's wife.
9 I will surely punish them for doing
such things!" says the LORD.
"I will surely bring retribution on such a nation as this!"
10 The LORD commanded the enemy,
"March through the vineyards of Israel
and Judah and ruin them.
But do not destroy them completely.
Strip off their branches
for these people do not belong to the LORD.

11 For the nations of Israel and Judah
have been very unfaithful to me,"
says the LORD.
12 "These people have denied what the LORD says.
They have said, 'That is not so!
No harm will come to us.
We will not experience war and famine.
13 The prophets will prove to be full of wind.
The LORD has not spoken through them.
So, let what they say happen to them.'"

14 Because of that, the LORD God of Heaven's Armies said to me:
"Because these people have spoken like this,
I will make the words that I put in your mouth like fire.
And I will make this people like wood,
which the fiery judgments you speak will burn up."
15 The LORD says, "Listen, nation of Israel!
I am about to bring a nation from far away to attack you.
It will be a nation that was founded long ago
and has lasted for a long time.
It will be a nation whose language you will not know.
Its people will speak words that you will
not be able to understand.
16 All its soldiers are strong and mighty.
Their arrows will send you to your grave.
17 They will eat up your crops and your food.
They will kill off your sons and your daughters.
They will eat up your sheep and your cattle.
They will destroy your vines and your fig trees.
Their weapons will batter down
the fortified cities you trust in.

18 "Yet even then I will not completely destroy you," says
the LORD. 19 "So then, Jeremiah, when your people ask, 'Why
has the LORD our God done all this to us?' tell them, 'It is because you rejected me and served foreign gods in your own
land. So you must serve foreigners in a land that does not belong to you.'
20 "Proclaim this message among the
descendants of Jacob.
Make it known throughout Judah.
21 Tell them: 'Hear this,
you foolish people who have no understanding,
who have eyes but do not discern,
who have ears but do not perceive:
22 'You should fear me!' says the LORD.
'You should tremble in awe before me!
I made the sand to be a boundary for the sea,
a permanent barrier that it can never cross.
Its waves may roll, but they can never prevail.
They may roar, but they can never
cross beyond that boundary.'
23 But these people have stubborn and rebellious hearts.
They have turned aside and gone their own way.

24 They do not say to themselves,
'Let us revere the LORD our God.
It is he who gives us the autumn rains and
the spring rains at the proper time.
It is he who assures us of the regular weeks of harvest."
25 Your misdeeds have stopped these things from coming.
Your sins have deprived you of my bounty.'
26 Indeed, there are wicked scoundrels among my people.
They lie in wait like bird catchers hiding in ambush.
They set deadly traps to catch people.
27 Like a cage filled with the birds that have been caught,
their houses are filled with the gains
of their fraud and deceit.
That is how they have gotten so rich and powerful.
28 That is how they have grown fat and sleek.
There is no limit to the evil things they do.
They do not plead the cause of the fatherless
in such a way as to win it.
They do not defend the rights of the poor.
29 I will certainly punish them for doing
such things!" says the LORD.
"I will certainly bring retribution on such a nation as this!
30 Something horrible and shocking
is going on in the land of Judah:
31 The prophets prophesy lies.
The priests exercise power by their own authority.
And my people love to have it this way.
But they will not be able to help you when
the time of judgment comes!

THE DESTRUCTION OF JERUSALEM DEPICTED

6 "Run for safety, people of Benjamin!
Get out of Jerusalem!
Sound the trumpet in Tekoa!
Light the signal fires at Beth Hakkerem!
For disaster lurks out of the north;
it will bring great destruction.
2 I will destroy Daughter Zion,
who is as delicate and defenseless as a young maiden.
3 Kings will attack her with their armies.
They will encamp in siege all around her.
Each of them will devastate the portion assigned to him.
4 They will say, 'Prepare to do battle against it!
Come on! Let's attack it at noon!'
But later they will say, 'Woe to us!
For the day is almost over,
and the shadows of evening are getting long.
5 So come on, let's go ahead and attack it by night
and destroy all its fortified buildings.'
6 All this is because the LORD of Heaven's Armies has said:
'Cut down the trees around Jerusalem
and build up a siege ramp against its walls.
This is the city that is to be punished.
Nothing but oppression happens in it.

7 As a well continually pours out fresh water
so it continually pours out wicked deeds.
Sounds of violence and destruction
echo throughout it.
All I see are sick and wounded people.'
8 So take warning, Jerusalem,
or I will abandon you in disgust
and make you desolate,
a place where no one can live."

9 This is what the LORD of Heaven's Armies said to me:
"Those who remain in Israel will be
like the grapes thoroughly gleaned from a vine.
So go over them again, as though you
were a grape harvester
passing your hand over the branches one last time."

10 I answered,
"Who would listen
if I spoke to them and warned them?
Their ears are so closed
that they cannot hear!
Indeed, the LORD's message is offensive to them.
They do not like it at all.
11 I am as full of anger as you are, LORD,
I am tired of trying to hold it in."

The LORD answered,
"Vent it, then, on the children who play in the street
and on the young men who are gathered together.
Husbands and wives are to be included,
as well as the old and those who
are advanced in years.
12 Their houses will be turned over to others
as will their fields and their wives.
For I will unleash my power
against those who live in this land,"
says the LORD.
13 "That is because, from the least important
to the most important of them,
all of them are greedy for dishonest gain.
Prophets and priests alike,
all of them practice deceit.
14 They offer only superficial help
for the harm my people have suffered.
They say, 'Everything will be all right!'
But everything is not all right!
15 Are they ashamed because they have
done such shameful things?
No, they are not at all ashamed.
They do not even know how to blush!
So they will die, just like others have died.
They will be brought to ruin when I punish them,"
says the LORD.

16 The LORD said to his people:
"You are standing at the crossroads.
So consider your path.
Ask where the old, reliable paths are.
Ask where the path is that leads to
blessing and follow it.
If you do, you will find rest for your souls."
But they said, "We will not follow it!"

17 The LORD said,
"I appointed prophets as watchmen to warn you, saying,
'Pay attention to the warning sound of the trumpet!'"
But they said, "We will not pay attention!"

18 So the LORD said,
"Hear, you nations!
Be witnesses and take note of what
will happen to these people.
19 Hear this, you peoples of the earth:
'Take note! I am about to bring disaster on these people.
It will come as punishment for their scheming.
For they have paid no attention to what I have said,
and they have rejected my law.
20 I take no delight when they offer up to me
frankincense that comes from Sheba
or sweet-smelling cane imported from a faraway land.
I cannot accept the burnt offerings they bring me.
I get no pleasure from the sacrifices they offer to me.'"

21 So, this is what the LORD says:
"I will assuredly make these people
stumble to their doom.
Parents and children will stumble and
fall to their destruction.
Friends and neighbors will die."

22 This is what the LORD says:
"Beware! An army is coming from a land in the north.
A mighty nation is stirring into action
in faraway parts of the earth.
23 Its soldiers are armed with bows and spears.
They are cruel and show no mercy.
They sound like the roaring sea
as they ride forth on their horses.
Lined up in formation like men going into battle
to attack you, Daughter Zion."
24 The people cry out, "We have heard reports about them.
We have become helpless with fear!
Anguish grips us,
agony like that of a woman giving birth to a baby!
25 Do not go out into the countryside.
Do not travel on the roads.
For the enemy is there with sword in hand.
They are spreading terror everywhere."

26 So I said, "Oh, my dear people, put on sackcloth
and roll in ashes.
Mourn with painful sobs
as though you had lost your only child.
For any moment now that destructive army
will come against us."

27 The LORD said to me,
"I have made you like a metal assayer
to test my people like ore.
You are to observe them
and evaluate how they behave."

28 I reported,
"All of them are the most stubborn of rebels!
They are as hard as bronze or iron.
They go about telling lies.
They all deal corruptly.
29 The fiery bellows of judgment burn fiercely.
But there is too much dross to be removed.
The process of refining them has proved useless.
The wicked have not been purged.
30 They are regarded as 'rejected silver'
because the LORD rejects them."

FAULTY RELIGION AND UNETHICAL BEHAVIOR WILL LEAD TO JUDGMENT

7 The LORD said to Jeremiah: 2 "Stand in the gate of the LORD's
temple and proclaim this message: 'Listen to the LORD's message, all you people of Judah who have passed through these
gates to worship the LORD. 3 The LORD of Heaven's Armies, the
God of Israel, says: Change the way you have been living and do
what is right. If you do, I will allow you to continue to live in
this land. 4 Stop putting your confidence in the false belief that
says, "We are safe! The temple of the LORD is here! The temple
of the LORD is here! The temple of the LORD is here!" 5 You must
change the way you have been living and do what is right. You
must treat one another fairly. 6 Stop oppressing resident foreigners who live in your land, children who have lost their fathers,
and women who have lost their husbands. Stop killing innocent
people in this land. Stop paying allegiance to other gods. That
will only bring about your ruin. 7 If you stop doing these things,
I will allow you to continue to live in this land that I gave to your
ancestors as a lasting possession.
8 "'But just look at you! You are putting your confidence in a
false belief that will not deliver you. 9 You steal. You murder. You
commit adultery. You lie when you swear on oath. You sacrifice
to the god Baal. You pay allegiance to other gods whom you have
not previously known. 10 Then you come and stand in my presence in this temple I have claimed as my own and say, "We are
safe!" You think you are so safe that you go on doing all those
hateful sins! 11 Do you think this temple I have claimed as my own
is to be a hideout for robbers? You had better take note! I have
seen for myself what you have done! says the LORD. 12 So, go to

INJUSTICE AND IDOLATRY

JEREMIAH 7

"Don't shoot the messenger" could have been the prophet Jeremiah's catchphrase. Jeremiah is known as the weeping prophet because of his personal heartbreak over Judah's sin and the difficult message of judgment God tasked him with delivering.

Jeremiah 7 covers his "temple sermon"—the message he delivered at the entrance to Solomon's Temple, urging the people to reform their ways and prevent coming destruction at the hands of the Babylonians. He warned them against false confidence that they were safe because they were in the temple (Jer 7:4).

We too can be tempted to believe outward marks of Christian identity keep us safe from any obligation to follow the commands of God.

We can justify our sinful actions—or inactions—by reminding ourselves that we go to church regularly, attend a Bible study, or belong to a group of Christian friends.

Jeremiah's words for this kind of religion are harsh: "You are putting your confidence in a false belief that will not deliver you" (Jer 7:8). Instead of thinking their religious duties absolved them of the responsibility to treat their neighbors well, Jeremiah gave the people specific instruction to stop oppressing foreigners, orphans, and widows, and to stop worshiping idols (Jer 7:6).

Jeremiah, and most of the other Old Testament prophets, consistently judged Israel for two sins: injustice and idolatry. Idols will always demand things of you that involve the exploitation of other people. Idols require escalating sacrifices—they ask more and more of us until we can't provide what they require without hurting other people.

The gods of power, success, wealth, and fame love taking money that isn't ours, seizing power by subjugating others, and promoting our own success by stepping on anyone who gets in our way. The promises these idols make us are the same false promises that Jeremiah recognized the people of Judah were believing.

Jeremiah's plea for them is the same good news for us: Trust in God and obey Him, and He will make you His people (Jer 7:23). Our idols make promises they cannot keep, but God's promises of redemption, restoration, and a new life in the community of God are trustworthy.

the place in Shiloh where I allowed myself to be worshiped in the early days. See what I did to it because of the wicked things my people Israel did. 13 You also have done all these things, says the LORD, and I have spoken to you over and over again. But you have not listened! You have refused to respond when I called you to repent! 14 So I will destroy this temple that I have claimed as my own, this temple that you are trusting to protect you. I will destroy this place that I gave to you and your ancestors, just like I destroyed Shiloh. 15 And I will drive you out of my sight just like I drove out your relatives, the people of Israel.'

16 "But as for you, Jeremiah, do not pray for these people. Do not raise a cry of prayer for them! Do not plead with me to save them, because I will not listen to you. 17 Do you see what they are doing in the towns of Judah and in the streets of Jerusalem? 18 Children are gathering firewood, fathers are building fires with it, and women are mixing dough to bake cakes to offer to the goddess they call the Queen of Heaven. They are also pouring out drink offerings to other gods. They seem to do all this just to trouble me. 19 But I am not really the one being troubled! says the LORD. Rather they are bringing trouble on themselves to their own shame! 20 So, the Sovereign LORD says, my raging fury will be poured out on this land. It will be poured out on human beings and animals, on trees and crops. And it will burn like a fire that cannot be extinguished.

21 "The LORD of Heaven's Armies, the God of Israel, says to the people of Judah: 'You might as well go ahead and add the meat of your burnt offerings to that of the other sacrifices and eat it, too! 22 Consider this: When I spoke to your ancestors after I brought them out of Egypt, I did not merely give them commands about burnt offerings and sacrifices. 23 I also explicitly commanded them: "Obey me. If you do, I will be your God and you will be my people. Live exactly the way I tell you and things will go well with you." 24 But they did not listen to me or pay any attention to me. They followed the stubborn inclinations of their own wicked hearts. They acted worse and worse instead of better. 25 From the time your ancestors departed the land of Egypt until now, I sent my servants the prophets to you again and again, day after day. 26 But your ancestors did not listen to me nor pay attention to me. They became obstinate and were more wicked than even their own forefathers.'"

27 Then the LORD said to me, "When you tell them all this, they will not listen to you. When you call out to them, they will not respond to you. 28 So tell them: 'This is a nation that has not obeyed the LORD their God and has not accepted correction. Faithfulness is nowhere to be found in it. These people do not even profess it anymore. 29 So mourn, you people of this nation. Cut off your hair and throw it away. Sing a song of mourning on the hilltops. For the LORD has decided to reject and forsake this generation that has provoked his wrath!'"

30 The LORD says, "I have rejected them because the people of Judah have done what I consider evil. They have set up their disgusting idols in the temple that I have claimed for my own and have defiled it. 31 They have also built places of worship in a place called Topheth in the Valley of Ben Hinnom so

that they can sacrifice their sons and daughters by fire. That
is something I never commanded them to do! Indeed, it never
even entered my mind to command such a thing! 32 So, watch
out!" says the LORD. "The time will soon come when people
will no longer call those places Topheth or the Valley of Ben
Hinnom. But they will call that valley the Valley of Slaughter, and they will bury so many people in Topheth they will
run out of room. 33 Then the dead bodies of these people will
be left on the ground for the birds and wild animals to eat.
There will not be any survivors to scare them away. 34 I will
put an end to the sounds of joy and gladness or the glad celebration of brides and grooms throughout the towns of Judah
and the streets of Jerusalem. For the whole land will become
a desolate wasteland."

8 The LORD says, "When that time comes, the bones of the
kings of Judah and its leaders, the bones of the priests and
prophets, and of all the other people who lived in Jerusalem
will be dug up from their graves. 2 They will be spread out and
exposed to the sun, the moon, and the stars. These are things
they adored and served, things to which they paid allegiance,
from which they sought guidance and worshiped. The bones of
these people will never be regathered and reburied. They will
be like manure used to fertilize the ground. 3 However, I will
leave some of these wicked people alive and banish them to
other places. But wherever these people who survive may go,
they will wish they had died rather than lived," says the LORD
of Heaven's Armies.

WILLFUL DISREGARD OF GOD WILL LEAD TO DESTRUCTION

4 The LORD said to me,
"Tell them, 'The LORD says,
Do people not get back up when they fall down?
Do they not turn around when they go the wrong way?
5 Why, then, do these people of Jerusalem
continually turn away from me in apostasy?
They hold fast to their deception.
They refuse to turn back to me.
6 I have listened to them very carefully,
but they do not speak honestly.
None of them regrets the evil he has done.
None of them says, "I have done wrong!"
All of them persist in their own wayward course
like a horse charging recklessly into battle.
7 Even the stork knows
when it is time to move on.
The turtledove, swallow, and crane
recognize the normal times for their migration.
But my people pay no attention
to what I, the LORD, require of them.
8 How can you say, "We are wise!
We have the law of the LORD"?
The truth is, those who teach it have used their writings
to make it say what it does not really mean.

9 Your wise men will be put to shame.
They will be dumbfounded and be brought to judgment.
Since they have rejected the LORD's message,
what wisdom do they really have?
10 So I will give their wives to other men
and their fields to new owners.
For from the least important to the
most important of them,
all of them are greedy for dishonest gain.
Prophets and priests alike
all practice deceit.
11 They offer only superficial help
for the hurt my dear people have suffered.
They say, "Everything will be all right!"
But everything is not all right.
12 Are they ashamed because they have
done such disgusting things?
No, they are not at all ashamed!
They do not even know how to blush.
So they will die just like others have died.
They will be brought to ruin when I punish them,
says the LORD.
13 I will take away their harvests, says the LORD.
There will be no grapes on their vines.
There will be no figs on their fig trees.
Even the leaves on their trees will wither.
The crops that I gave them will be taken away.'"

JEREMIAH LAMENTS OVER THE COMING DESTRUCTION

14 The people say,
"Why are we just sitting here?
Let us gather together inside the fortified cities.
Let us at least die there fighting,
since the LORD our God has condemned us to die.
He has condemned us to drink the
poison waters of judgment
because we have sinned against him.
15 We hoped for good fortune, but nothing good has come of it.
We hoped for a time of relief, but
instead we experience terror.
16 The snorting of the enemy's horses
is already being heard in the city of Dan.
The sound of the neighing of their stallions
causes the whole land to tremble with fear.
They are coming to destroy the land and everything in it.
They are coming to destroy the cities and
everyone who lives in them."

17 The LORD says,
"Yes indeed, I am sending an enemy against you
that will be like poisonous snakes that
cannot be charmed away.
And they will inflict fatal wounds on you."

18 Then I said,
"There is no cure for my grief!
I am sick at heart!
19 I hear my dear people crying out
throughout the length and breadth of the land.
They are crying, 'Is the LORD no longer in Zion?
Is her divine King no longer there?'"
The LORD answers,
"Why then do they provoke me to anger with their images,
with their worthless foreign idols?
20 They cry, 'Harvest time has come and
gone and the summer is over,
and still we have not been delivered.'
21 My heart is crushed because my dear
people are being crushed.
I go about crying and grieving. I am
overwhelmed with dismay.
22 There is still medicinal ointment available in Gilead!
There is still a physician there!
Why then have my dear people
not been restored to health?
9 I wish that my head were a well full of water
and my eyes were a fountain full of tears!
If they were, I could cry day and night
for those of my dear people who have been killed.
2 I wish I had a lodging place in the wilderness
where I could spend some time like a weary traveler.
Then I would desert my people
and walk away from them
because they are all unfaithful to God,
a congregation of people that has been disloyal to him."

THE LORD LAMENTS THAT HE HAS NO CHOICE BUT TO JUDGE THEM

3 The LORD says,
"These people are like soldiers who
have readied their bows.
Their tongues are always ready to shoot out lies.
They have become powerful in the land,
but they have not done so by honest means.
Indeed, they do one evil thing after another
and do not pay attention to me.
4 Everyone must be on his guard around his friends.
He must not even trust any of his relatives.
For every one of them will find some way to cheat him.
And all his friends will tell lies about him.
5 One friend deceives another
and no one tells the truth.
These people have trained themselves to tell lies.
They do wrong and are unable to repent.
6 They do one act of violence after another,
and one deceitful thing after another.
They refuse to pay attention to me,"
says the LORD.

7 Therefore the LORD of Heaven's Armies says:
"I will now purify them in the fires of
affliction and test them.
The wickedness of my dear people has left me no choice.
What else can I do?
8 Their tongues are like deadly arrows.
They are always telling lies.
Friendly words for their neighbors
come from their mouths,
but their minds are thinking up ways to trap them.
9 I will certainly punish them for doing
such things!" says the LORD.
"I will certainly bring retribution on such a nation as this!"

THE COMING DESTRUCTION CALLS FOR MOURNING

10 I said,
"I will weep and mourn for the
grasslands on the mountains;
I will sing a mournful song for the
pastures in the wilderness
because they are so scorched no one travels through them.
The sound of livestock is no longer heard there.
Even the birds in the sky and the wild animals in the fields
have fled and are gone."

11 The LORD said,
"I will make Jerusalem a heap of ruins.
Jackals will make their home there.
I will destroy the towns of Judah
so that no one will be able to live in them."

12 I said,
"Who is wise enough to understand
why this has happened?
Who has a word from the LORD that can explain it?
Why does the land lie in ruins?
Why is it as scorched as a desert through
which no one travels?"

13 The LORD answered, "This has happened because these people have rejected my laws that I gave them. They have not obeyed
me or followed those laws. 14 Instead they have followed the stubborn inclinations of their own hearts. They have paid allegiance
to the gods called Baal, as their fathers taught them to do. 15 So
then, listen to what I, the LORD of Heaven's Armies, the God of
Israel, say, 'I will make these people eat the bitter food of suffering and drink the poison water of judgment. 16 I will scatter
them among nations that neither they nor their ancestors have
known anything about. I will send people chasing after them
with swords until I have destroyed them.'"
17 The LORD of Heaven's Armies told me to say to this people:
"Take note of what I say.
Call for the women who mourn for the dead!
Summon those who are the most skilled at it!"

REFLECT

How are we like the people of Judah? What false gods do we often follow and worship instead of our heavenly Father?

18 I said, "Indeed, let them come quickly and
sing a song of mourning for us.
Let them wail loudly until tears stream from our own eyes
and our eyelids overflow with water.
19 For the sound of wailing is soon to be heard in Zion,
'We are utterly ruined! We are completely disgraced!
For we have left our land,
for our houses have been torn down!'"

20 I said,
"So now, you wailing women, listen to the LORD's message.
Open your ears to the message from his mouth.
Teach your daughters this mournful song,
and let every woman teach her neighbor this lament.
21 'Death has climbed in through our windows.
It has entered into our fortified houses.
It has taken away our children who play in the streets.
It has taken away our young men who
gather in the city squares.'
22 Tell your daughters and neighbors, 'The LORD says:
"The dead bodies of people will lie scattered everywhere
like manure scattered on a field.
They will lie scattered on the ground
like grain that has been cut down but has not been gathered."'"

23 The LORD says,
"Wise people should not boast that they are wise.
Powerful people should not boast that they are powerful.
Rich people should not boast that they are rich.
24 If people want to boast, they should boast about this:
They should boast that they understand and know me.
They should boast that they know and understand
that I, the LORD, act out of faithfulness,
fairness, and justice in the earth
and that I desire people to do these things,"
says the LORD.

25 The LORD says, "Watch out! The time is soon coming when
I will punish all those who are circumcised only in the flesh.
26 That is, I will punish the Egyptians, the Judeans, the Edomites,
the Ammonites, the Moabites, and all the desert people who
cut their hair short at the temples. I will do so because none of
the people of those nations are really circumcised in the LORD's
sight. Moreover, none of the people of Israel are circumcised
when it comes to their hearts."

THE LORD, NOT IDOLS, IS THE ONLY WORTHY OBJECT OF WORSHIP

10 You people of Israel, listen to what the LORD has to say to
you.
2 The LORD says:
"Do not start following pagan religious practices.
Do not be in awe of signs that occur in the sky
even though the nations hold them in awe.

3 For the religion of these people is worthless.
They cut down a tree in the forest,
and a craftsman makes it into an idol with his tools.
4 He decorates it with overlays of silver and gold.
He uses hammer and nails to fasten it together
so that it will not fall over.
5 Such idols are like scarecrows in a cucumber field.
They cannot talk.
They must be carried
because they cannot walk.
Do not be afraid of them
because they cannot hurt you.
And they do not have any power to help you."

6 I said,
"There is no one like you, LORD.
You are great,
and you are renowned for your power.
7 Everyone should revere you, O King of all nations,
because you deserve to be revered.
For there is no one like you
among any of the wise people of the nations
nor among any of their kings.
8 The people of those nations are both stupid and foolish.
Instruction from a wooden idol is worthless!
9 Hammered-out silver is brought from Tarshish
and gold is brought from Ufaz to cover those idols.
They are the handiwork of carpenters and goldsmiths.
They are clothed in blue and purple clothes.
They are all made by skillful workers.
10 The LORD is the only true God.
He is the living God and the everlasting King.
When he shows his anger the earth shakes.
None of the nations can stand up to his fury.
11 You people of Israel should tell those nations this:
'These gods did not make heaven and earth.
They will disappear from the earth and
from under the heavens.'
12 The LORD is the one who by his power made the earth.
He is the one who by his wisdom established the world.
And by his understanding he spread out the skies.
13 When his voice thunders, the heavenly ocean roars.
He makes the clouds rise from the far-off horizons.
He makes the lightning flash out in the midst of the rain.
He unleashes the wind from the places where he stores it.
14 All these idolaters will prove to be stupid and ignorant.
Every goldsmith will be disgraced by the idol he made.
For the image he forges is merely a sham.
There is no breath in any of those idols.
15 They are worthless, mere objects to be mocked.
When the time comes to punish them,
they will be destroyed.
16 The LORD, who is the inheritance of Jacob's
descendants, is not like them.

He is the one who created everything.
And the people of Israel are those he claims as his own.
His name is the LORD of Heaven's Armies."

JEREMIAH LAMENTS FOR AND PRAYS FOR THE PEOPLE SOON TO BE JUDGED

17 "Gather your belongings together and
prepare to leave the land,
you people of Jerusalem who are being besieged.
18 For the LORD says, 'I will now throw out
those who live in this land.
I will bring so much trouble on them
that they will actually feel it.'
19 And I cried out, 'We are doomed!
Our wound is severe!'
We once thought, 'This is only an illness.
And we will be able to bear it.'
20 But our tents have been destroyed.
The ropes that held them in place have been ripped apart.
Our children are gone and are not coming back.
There is no survivor to put our tents back up,
no one left to hang their tent curtains in place.
21 For our leaders are stupid.
They have not sought the LORD's advice.
So they do not act wisely,
and the people they are responsible
for have all been scattered.
22 Listen! News is coming even now.
The rumble of a great army is heard
approaching from a land in the north.
It is coming to turn the towns of Judah into rubble,
places where only jackals live.
23 LORD, we know that people do not
control their own destiny.
It is not in their power to determine
what will happen to them.
24 Correct us, LORD, but only in due measure.
Do not punish us in anger or you will reduce us to nothing.
25 Vent your anger on the nations that
do not acknowledge you.
Vent it on the peoples who do not worship you.
For they have destroyed the people of Jacob.
They have completely destroyed them
and left their homeland in utter ruin."

THE PEOPLE HAVE VIOLATED THEIR COVENANT WITH GOD

11 The LORD said to Jeremiah: 2 "Hear the terms of the covenant
I made with Israel and pass them on to the people of Judah
and the citizens of Jerusalem. 3 Tell them that the LORD, the God
of Israel, says, 'Anyone who does not keep the terms of the covenant will be under a curse. 4 Those are the terms that I charged
your ancestors to keep when I brought them out of Egypt, that
place that was like an iron-smelting furnace. I said at that time,

"Obey me and carry out the terms of the covenant exactly as I
commanded you. If you do, you will be my people and I will be
your God. 5 Then I will keep the promise I swore on oath to your
ancestors to give them a land flowing with milk and honey." That
is the very land that you still live in today.'" And I responded,
"Amen. Let it be so, LORD."

6 The LORD said to me, "Announce all the following words in
the towns of Judah and in the streets of Jerusalem: 'Listen to the
terms of my covenant with you and carry them out! 7 For I solemnly warned your ancestors to obey me. I warned them again
and again, ever since I delivered them out of Egypt until this
very day. 8 But they did not listen to me or pay any attention to
me! Each one of them followed the stubborn inclinations of his
own wicked heart. So I brought on them all the punishments
threatened in the covenant because they did not carry out its
terms as I commanded them to do.'"

9 The LORD said to me, "The people of Judah and the citizens of Jerusalem have plotted rebellion against me. 10 They
have gone back to the evil ways of their ancestors of old who
refused to obey what I told them. They, too, have paid allegiance to other gods and worshiped them. Both the nation
of Israel and the nation of Judah have violated the covenant
I made with their ancestors. 11 So I, the LORD, say this: 'I will
soon bring disaster on them that they will not be able to escape! When they cry out to me for help, I will not listen to
them. 12 Then those living in the towns of Judah and in Jerusalem will go and cry out for help to the gods to whom they
have been sacrificing. However, those gods will by no means
be able to save them when disaster strikes them. 13 This is in
spite of the fact that the people of Judah have as many gods
as they have towns and the citizens of Jerusalem have set up
as many altars to sacrifice to that disgusting god, Baal, as they
have streets in the city!' 14 But as for you, Jeremiah, do not pray
for these people. Do not raise a cry of prayer for them. For I
will not listen to them when they call out to me for help when
disaster strikes them."

15 The LORD says to the people of Judah,
"What right do you have to be in my
temple, my beloved people?
Many of you have done wicked things.
Can your acts of treachery be so easily
canceled by sacred offerings
that you take joy in doing evil even while you make them?
16 I, the LORD, once called you a thriving olive tree,
one that produced beautiful fruit.
But I will set you on fire,
fire that will blaze with a mighty roar.
Then all your branches will be good for nothing.
17 For though I, the LORD of Heaven's
Armies, planted you in the land,
I now decree that disaster will come on you
because the nations of Israel and Judah have done evil
and have made me angry by offering
sacrifices to the god Baal."

A PLOT AGAINST JEREMIAH IS REVEALED AND HE COMPLAINS OF INJUSTICE

18 The LORD gave me knowledge, that I
might have understanding.
Then he showed me what the people were doing.
19 Before this I had been like a docile lamb
ready to be led to the slaughter.
I did not know they were making plans to kill me.
I did not know they were saying,
"Let's destroy the tree along with its fruit!
Let's remove Jeremiah from the world of the living
so people will not even be reminded of him anymore."

20 So I said,
"O LORD of Heaven's Armies, you are a just judge!
You examine people's hearts and minds.
I want to see you pay them back for
what they have done
because I trust you to vindicate my cause."

21 Then the LORD told me about some men from Anathoth who were threatening to kill me. They had threatened, "Stop prophesying in the name of the LORD or we
will kill you!" 22 So the LORD of Heaven's Armies said, "I will
surely punish them! Their young men will be killed in battle. Their sons and daughters will die of starvation. 23 Not
one of them will survive. I will bring disaster on those men
from Anathoth who threatened you. A day of reckoning is
coming for them."

JEREMIAH APPEALS TO GOD

12 LORD, you have always been fair
whenever I have complained to you.
However, I would like to speak with you
about the disposition of justice.
Why are wicked people successful?
Why do all dishonest people have such easy lives?
2 You plant them like trees and they
put down their roots.
They grow prosperous and are very fruitful.
They always talk about you,
but they really care nothing about you.
3 But you, LORD, know all about me.
You watch me and test my devotion to you.
Drag these wicked men away like
sheep to be slaughtered!
Appoint a time when they will be killed!
4 How long must the land be parched
and the grass in every field be withered?
How long must the animals and the birds die
because of the wickedness of the
people who live in this land?
For these people boast,
"God will not see what happens to us."

GOD ANSWERS JEREMIAH

5 The LORD answered,
"If you have raced on foot against men
and they have worn you out,
how will you be able to compete with horses?
And if you feel secure only in safe and open country,
how will you manage in the thick
undergrowth along the Jordan River?
6 As a matter of fact, even your own brothers
and the members of your own family
have betrayed you as well.
Even they have plotted to do away with you.
So do not trust them even when they say kind things to you.

7 "I will abandon my nation.
I will forsake the people I call my own.
I will turn my beloved people
over to the power of their enemies.
8 The people I call my own have turned on me
like a lion in the forest.
They have roared defiantly at me,
so I will treat them as though I hate them.
9 The people I call my own attack me like
birds of prey or like hyenas.
But other birds of prey are all around them.
Let all the nations gather together like wild beasts.
Let them come and destroy these people I call my own.
10 Many foreign rulers will ruin the land
where I planted my people.
They will trample all over my chosen land.
They will turn my beautiful land
into a desolate wilderness.
11 They will lay it waste.
It will lie parched and empty before me.
The whole land will be laid waste,
but no one living in it will pay any heed.
12 A destructive army will come marching
over the hilltops in the wilderness.
For the LORD will use them as his destructive weapon
against everyone from one end of the land to the other.
No one will be safe.
13 My people will sow wheat, but will harvest weeds.
They will work until they are exhausted,
but will get nothing from it.
They will be disappointed in their harvests
because the LORD will take them away in his fierce anger.

14 "I, the LORD, also have something to say concerning the
wicked nations who surround my land and have attacked and
plundered the land that I gave to my people as a permanent possession. I say: 'I will uproot the people of those nations from their
land and I will free the people of Judah who have been taken
there. 15 But after I have uprooted the people of those nations,
I will relent and have pity on them. I will restore the people of

each of those nations to their own lands and to their own country. 16 But they must make sure to learn to follow the religious practices of my people. Once they taught my people to swear their oaths using the name of the god Baal. But then, they must swear oaths using my name, saying, "As surely as the LORD lives, I swear." If they do these things, then they will be included among the people I call my own. 17 But I will completely uproot and destroy any of those nations that will not pay heed,'" says the LORD.

AN OBJECT LESSON FROM RUINED LINEN SHORTS

13 The LORD said to me, "Go and buy some linen shorts and put them on. Do not put them in water." 2 So I bought the shorts in keeping with the LORD's instructions and put them on. 3 Then the LORD's message came to me again, 4 "Take the shorts that you bought and are wearing and go at once to Perath. Bury the shorts there in a crack in the rocks." 5 So I went and buried them at Perath as the LORD had ordered me to do. 6 Many days later the LORD said to me, "Go at once to Perath and get the shorts I ordered you to bury there." 7 So I went to Perath and dug up the shorts from the place where I had buried them. I found that they were ruined; they were good for nothing.

8 Then the LORD's message came to me, 9 "I, the LORD, say: 'This shows how I will ruin the highly exalted position in which Judah and Jerusalem take pride. 10 These wicked people refuse to obey what I have said. They follow the stubborn inclinations of their own hearts and pay allegiance to other gods by worshiping and serving them. So they will become just like these linen shorts that are good for nothing. 11 For,' I say, 'just as shorts cling tightly to a person's body, so I bound the whole nation of Israel and the whole nation of Judah tightly to me.' I intended for them to be my special people and to bring me fame, honor, and praise. But they would not obey me.

12 "So tell them, 'The LORD, the God of Israel, says: "Every wine jar is made to be filled with wine."' And they will probably say to you, 'Do you not think we know that every wine jar is supposed to be filled with wine?' 13 Then tell them, 'The LORD says: "I will soon fill all the people who live in this land with stupor. I will also fill the kings from David's dynasty, the priests, the prophets, and the citizens of Jerusalem with stupor. 14 And I will smash them like wine bottles against one another, children and parents alike. I will not show any pity, mercy, or compassion. Nothing will keep me from destroying them,' says the LORD."

15 Then I said to the people of Judah:

"Listen and pay attention! Do not be arrogant!
For the LORD has spoken.
16 Show the LORD your God the respect that is due him.
Do it before he brings the darkness of disaster.
Do it before you stumble into distress
like a traveler on the mountains at twilight.
Do it before he turns the light of deliverance you hope for
into the darkness and gloom of exile.
17 But if you will not pay attention to this warning,
I will weep alone because of your arrogant pride.
I will weep bitterly, and my eyes will overflow with tears
because you, the LORD's flock, will be carried into exile."

18 The LORD told me:
"Tell the king and the queen mother,
'Surrender your thrones,
for your glorious crowns
will be removed from your heads.
19 The gates of the towns in southern Judah will be shut tight.
No one will be able to go in or out of them.
All Judah will be carried off into exile.
They will be completely carried off into exile.'"

20 Then I said,
"Look up, Jerusalem, and see
the enemy that is coming from the north.
Where now is the flock of people that
were entrusted to your care?
Where now are the 'sheep' that you take such pride in?
21 What will you say when the LORD appoints
as rulers over you those allies
that you, yourself, had actually prepared as such?
Then anguish and agony will grip you
like that of a woman giving birth to a baby.
22 You will probably ask yourself,
'Why have these things happened to me?
Why have I been treated like a disgraced adulteress
whose skirt has been torn off and her limbs exposed?'
It is because you have sinned so much.
23 But there is little hope for you ever doing good,
you who are so accustomed to doing evil.
Can an Ethiopian change the color of his skin?
Can a leopard remove its spots?

24 "The LORD says,
'That is why I will scatter your people like chaff
that is blown away by a desert wind.
25 This is your fate,
the destiny to which I have appointed you,
because you have forgotten me
and have trusted in false gods.
26 So I will pull your skirt up over your face
and expose you to shame like a disgraced adulteress!
27 People of Jerusalem, I have seen your adulterous worship,
your shameless prostitution to, and your
lustful pursuit of, other gods.
I have seen your disgusting acts of worship
on the hills throughout the countryside.
You are doomed to destruction!
How long will you continue to be unclean?'"

A LAMENT OVER THE RAVAGES OF DROUGHT

14 This was the LORD's message to Jeremiah about the drought.
2 "The people of Judah are in mourning.
The people in her cities are pining away.
They lie on the ground expressing their sorrow.
Cries of distress come up to me from Jerusalem.

3 The leading men of the cities send their servants for water.
They go to the cisterns, but they do
not find any water there.
They return with their containers empty.
Disappointed and dismayed, they bury
their faces in their hands.
4 They are dismayed because the ground is cracked
because there has been no rain in the land.
The farmers, too, are dismayed
and bury their faces in their hands.
5 Even the doe abandons her newborn fawn in the field
because there is no grass.
6 Wild donkeys stand on the hilltops
and pant for breath like jackals.
Their eyes are strained looking for food,
because there is none to be found."

7 Then I said,
"O LORD, intervene for the honor of your name
even though our sins speak out against us.
Indeed, we have turned away from you many times.
We have sinned against you.
8 You have been the object of Israel's hopes.
You have saved them when they were in trouble.
Why have you become like a resident
foreigner in the land?
Why have you become like a traveler who
only stops in to spend the night?
9 Why should you be like someone who is helpless,
like a champion who cannot save anyone?
You are indeed with us,
and we belong to you.
Do not abandon us!"

10 Then the LORD spoke about these people.
"They truly love to go astray.
They cannot keep from running away from me.
So I am not pleased with them.
I will now call to mind the wrongs they have done
and punish them for their sins."

JUDGMENT FOR BELIEVING THE MISLEADING LIES OF THE FALSE PROPHETS

11 Then the LORD said to me, "Do not pray for good to come to
these people! 12 Even if they fast, I will not hear their cries for
help. Even if they offer burnt offerings and grain offerings, I will
not accept them. Instead, I will kill them through wars, famines,
and plagues."
13 Then I said, "Oh, Sovereign LORD, look! The prophets are
telling them that you said, 'You will not experience war or
suffer famine. I will give you lasting peace and prosperity in
this land.'"
14 Then the LORD said to me, "Those prophets are prophesying
lies while claiming my authority! I did not send them. I did not

commission them. I did not speak to them. They are prophesying to these people false visions, worthless predictions, and the
delusions of their own mind. 15 I did not send those prophets,
though they claim to be prophesying in my name. They may be
saying, 'No war or famine will happen in this land.' But I, the
LORD, say this about them: 'War and starvation will kill those
prophets.' 16 The people to whom they are prophesying will die
through war and famine. Their bodies will be thrown out into
the streets of Jerusalem and there will be no one to bury them.
This will happen to the men and their wives, their sons, and
their daughters. For I will pour out on them the destruction
they deserve."

LAMENT OVER PRESENT DESTRUCTION AND THREAT OF MORE TO COME

17 "Tell these people this, Jeremiah:
'My eyes overflow with tears
day and night without ceasing.
For my people, my dear children, have
suffered a crushing blow.
They have suffered a serious wound.
18 If I go out into the countryside,
I see those who have been killed in battle.
If I go into the city,
I see those who are sick because of starvation.
For both prophet and priest—
they go peddling in the land
but they are not humbled.'"

19 Then I said,
"LORD, have you completely rejected
the nation of Judah?
Do you despise the city of Zion?
Why have you struck us with such force
that we are beyond recovery?
We hope for peace, but nothing good
has come of it.
We hope for a time of relief from our
troubles, but experience terror.
20 LORD, we confess that we have been wicked.
We confess that our ancestors have done wrong.
We have indeed sinned against you.
21 For the honor of your name, do not treat
Jerusalem with contempt.
Do not treat with disdain the place
where your glorious throne sits.
Be mindful of your covenant with us.
Do not break it.
22 Do any of the worthless idols of the
nations cause rain to fall?
Do the skies themselves send showers?
Is it not you, O LORD our God, who does this?
So we put our hopes in you
because you alone do all this."

15 Then the LORD said to me, "Even if Moses and Samuel
stood before me pleading for these people, I would not
feel pity for them! Get them away from me! Tell them to go
away! 2 If they ask you, 'Where should we go?' tell them the
LORD says this:

"Those who are destined to die of disease
will go to death by disease.
Those who are destined to die in war
will go to death in war.
Those who are destined to die of starvation
will go to death by starvation.
Those who are destined to go into exile will go into exile.

3 "I will punish them in four different ways: I will have
war kill them; I will have dogs drag off their dead bodies;
I will have birds and wild beasts devour and destroy their
corpses. 4 I will make all the people in all the kingdoms of
the world horrified at what has happened to them because of what Hezekiah's son Manasseh, king of Judah,
did in Jerusalem."

5 The LORD cried out,
"Who in the world will have pity on you, Jerusalem?
Who will grieve over you?
Who will stop long enough
to inquire about how you are doing?
6 I, the LORD, say: 'You people have deserted me;
You keep turning your back on me.'
So I have unleashed my power against you
and have begun to destroy you.
I have grown tired of feeling sorry for you!"

7 The LORD continued,
"In every town in the land I will purge them
like straw blown away by the wind.
I will destroy my people.
I will kill off their children.
I will do so because they did not change their behavior.
8 Their widows will become in my
sight more numerous
than the grains of sand on the seashores.
At noontime I will bring a destroyer
against the mothers of their young men.
I will cause anguish and terror
to fall suddenly upon them.
9 The mother who had seven children will grow faint.
All the breath will go out of her.
Her pride and joy will be taken from
her in the prime of their life.
It will seem as if the sun had set while it was still day.
She will suffer shame and humiliation.
I will cause any of them who are still left alive
to be killed in war by the onslaughts
of their enemies,"
says the LORD.

JEREMIAH COMPLAINS ABOUT HIS LOT AND THE LORD RESPONDS

10 I said,
"Oh, mother, how I regret that you ever gave birth to me!
I am always starting arguments and quarrels
with the people of this land.
I have not lent money to anyone and I
have not borrowed from anyone.
Yet all these people are treating me with contempt."

11 The LORD said,
"Jerusalem, I will surely send you away for your own good.
I will surely bring the enemy upon you in
a time of trouble and distress.
12 Can you people who are like iron and bronze
break that iron fist from the north?
13 I will give away your wealth and
your treasures as plunder.
I will give it away free of charge for the sins you
have committed throughout your land.
14 I will make you serve your enemies in a
land that you know nothing about.
For my anger is like a fire that will burn against you."

15 I said,
"LORD, you know how I suffer.
Take thought of me and care for me.
Pay back for me those who have been persecuting me.
Do not be so patient with them that
you allow them to kill me.
Be mindful of how I have put up with
their insults for your sake.
16 As your words came to me I drank them in,
and they filled my heart with joy and happiness
because I belong to you, O LORD God of Heaven's Armies.
17 I did not spend my time in the company of other people,
laughing and having a good time.
I stayed to myself because I felt obligated to you
and because I was filled with anger
at what they had done.
18 Why must I continually suffer such painful anguish?
Why must I endure the sting of their
insults like an incurable wound?
Will you let me down when I need you,
like a brook one goes to for water, but
that cannot be relied on?"

19 Because of this, the LORD said,
"You must repent of such words and thoughts!
If you do, I will restore you to the privilege of serving me.
If you say what is worthwhile instead of what is worthless,
I will again allow you to be my spokesman.
They must become as you have been.
You must not become like them.

20 I will make you as strong as a wall to these people,
a fortified wall of bronze.
They will attack you,
but they will not be able to overcome you.
For I will be with you to rescue you and deliver you,"
says the LORD.
21 "I will deliver you from the power of the wicked.
I will free you from the clutches of violent people."

JEREMIAH FORBIDDEN TO MARRY, TO MOURN, OR TO FEAST

16 The LORD's message came to me, 2 "Do not get married and
do not have children here in this land. 3 For I, the LORD, tell
you what will happen to the children who are born here in this
land and to the men and women who are their mothers and fathers. 4 They will die of deadly diseases. No one will mourn for
them. They will not be buried. Their dead bodies will lie like manure spread on the ground. They will be killed in war or die of starvation. Their corpses will be food for the birds and wild animals.
5 "Moreover I, the LORD, tell you: 'Do not go into a house where
they are having a funeral meal. Do not go there to mourn and
express your sorrow for them. For I have stopped showing them
my good favor, my love, and my compassion. I, the LORD, so affirm it! 6 Rich and poor alike will die in this land. They will not
be buried or mourned. People will not cut their bodies or shave
off their hair to show their grief for them. 7 No one will take any
food to those who mourn for the dead to comfort them. No one
will give them any wine to drink to console them for the loss of
their father or mother.
8 "'Do not go to a house where people are feasting and sit down
to eat and drink with them either. 9 For I, the LORD of Heaven's
Armies, the God of Israel, tell you what will happen. I will put an
end to the sounds of joy and gladness, to the glad celebration of
brides and grooms in this land. You and the rest of the people
will live to see this happen.'

THE LORD PROMISES EXILE BUT ALSO RESTORATION

10 "When you tell these people about all this, they will undoubtedly ask you, 'Why has the LORD threatened us with such great
disaster? What wrong have we done? What sin have we done to
offend the LORD our God?' 11 Then tell them that the LORD says,
'It is because your ancestors rejected me and paid allegiance to
other gods. They have served them and worshiped them. But they
have rejected me and not obeyed my law. 12 And you have acted
even more wickedly than your ancestors! Each one of you has followed the stubborn inclinations of your own wicked heart and not
obeyed me. 13 So I will throw you out of this land into a land that
neither you nor your ancestors have ever known. There you must
worship other gods day and night, for I will show you no mercy.'"
14 Yet I, the LORD, say: "A new time will certainly come. People
now affirm their oaths with 'I swear as surely as the LORD lives
who delivered the people of Israel out of Egypt.' 15 But in that time
they will affirm them with 'I swear as surely as the LORD lives
who delivered the people of Israel from the land of the north and

from all the other lands where he had banished them.' At that
time I will bring them back to the land I gave their ancestors."
16 But for now I, the LORD, say: "I will send many enemies who
will catch these people like fishermen. After that I will send others who will hunt them out like hunters from all the mountains,
all the hills, and the crevices in the rocks. 17 For I see everything
they do. Their wicked ways are not hidden from me. Their sin is
not hidden away where I cannot see it. 18 Before I restore them I
will punish them in full for their sins and the wrongs they have
done. For they have polluted my land with the lifeless statues of
their disgusting idols. They have filled the land I have claimed
as my own with their detestable idols."

19 Then I said,
"LORD, you give me strength and protect me.
You are the one I can run to for safety when I am in trouble.
Nations from all over the earth
will come to you and say,
'Our ancestors had nothing but false gods—
worthless idols that could not help them at all.'
20 Can people make their own gods?
No, what they make are not gods at all."

21 The LORD said,
"So I will now let this wicked people know—
I will let them know my mighty power in judgment.
Then they will know that my name is the LORD.
17 "The sin of Judah is engraved with an iron chisel
on their stone-hard hearts.
It is inscribed with a diamond point
on the horns of their altars.
2 Their children are always thinking about their altars
and their sacred poles dedicated to the goddess Asherah,
set up beside the green trees on the high hills
3 and on the mountains and in the fields.
I will give your wealth and all your
treasures away as plunder.
I will give it away as the price for the sins you
have committed throughout your land.
4 You will lose your hold on the land
that I gave to you as a permanent possession.
I will make you serve your enemies in a
land that you know nothing about.
For you have made my anger burn like a
fire that will never be put out."

INDIVIDUALS ARE CHALLENGED TO PUT THEIR TRUST IN THE LORD

5 The LORD says,
"I will put a curse on people
who trust in mere human beings,
who depend on mere flesh and blood for their strength,
and whose hearts have turned away from the LORD.
6 They will be like a shrub in the arid rift valley.
They will not experience good things even when they happen.

It will be as though they were growing in
the stony wastes in the wilderness,
in a salt land where no one can live.
7 My blessing is on those people who trust in me,
who put their confidence in me.
8 They will be like a tree planted near a stream
whose roots spread out toward the water.
It has nothing to fear when the heat comes.
Its leaves are always green.
It has no need to be concerned in a year of drought.
It does not stop bearing fruit.
9 The human mind is more deceitful than anything else.
It is incurably bad. Who can understand it?
10 I, the LORD, probe into people's minds.
I examine people's hearts.
I deal with each person according to how he has behaved.
I give them what they deserve based
on what they have done.
11 The person who gathers wealth by unjust means
is like the partridge that broods over
eggs but does not hatch them.
Before his life is half over he will lose his ill-gotten gains.
At the end of his life it will be clear he was a fool."

JEREMIAH APPEALS TO THE LORD FOR VINDICATION

12 Then I said,
"LORD, from the very beginning
you have been seated on your glorious throne on high.
You are the place where we can find refuge.
13 You are the one in whom Israel may find hope.
All who leave you will suffer shame.
Those who turn away from you will be
consigned to the netherworld.
For they have rejected you, the LORD, the fountain of life.
14 LORD, grant me relief from my suffering
so that I may have some relief;
rescue me from those who persecute me
so that I may be rescued, for you give me reason to praise!
15 Listen to what they are saying to me,
'Where are the things the LORD threatens us with?
May it please happen!'

16 But I have not pestered you to bring disaster.
I have not desired the time of irreparable devastation.
You know that.
You are fully aware of every word that I have spoken.
17 Do not cause me dismay!
You are my source of safety in times of trouble.
18 May those who persecute me be disgraced.
Do not let me be disgraced.
May they be dismayed.
Do not let me be dismayed.
Bring days of disaster on them.
Bring on them the destruction they deserve."

LOVE TO GROW

DECEIVING OURSELVES

JEREMIAH 17:9–10

According to Scripture, the human heart is rotten to the core: "more deceitful than anything else. It is incurably bad" (Jer 17:9). "Out of the heart come evil ideas, murder, adultery, sexual immorality, theft, false testimony, slander" (Matt 15:19). "The LORD saw that the wickedness of humankind had become great on the earth. Every inclination of the thoughts of their minds was only evil all the time" (Gen 6:5).

Our hearts, left to themselves, can quickly deceive us. Praise God this doesn't have to be the end of our stories. God loved the world enough to send His Son Jesus to rescue sick-hearted sinners like you and like me.

There's no way we can muster up a new heart on our own. Only God can perform this miraculous transplant, taking out what is wicked, hard, and dead and replacing it with new life. It's all God: the pursuing, the saving, and the continual conforming of our hearts to become more and more like His. By His grace we begin walking to a different heartbeat, able to see the world and its lies in a completely different light.

Even after God has done His regenerative work in us, we still need daily reminders to help keep our hearts in check.

How do we do this?

Follow God's Word. It's time we stop believing the unstable and ever-changing conditions of our hearts. Instead, let's be known as women who run to God's Word to find the answers to all life's questions.

Follow God's guidance through His Spirit. Instead of listening to the voices of the world and letting them sway the desires of your heart, abide in God's Word and learn to hear His voice as His Spirit gently guides you to understanding.

Follow wise counsel. The body of Christ contains many leaders who have a strong foundation in God's Word and are gifted in communicating God's truth to others. Instead of living in isolation, reach out to godly counsel who are not afraid to tell you the truth from Scripture instead of what you want to hear.

Let's search our hearts from within, thanking God for His transforming work in us, and pursue truth in every area of our lives.

OBSERVANCE OF THE SABBATH DAY IS A KEY TO THE FUTURE

19 The LORD told me, "Go and stand in the People's Gate through which the kings of Judah enter and leave the city. Then go and stand in all the other gates of the city of Jerusalem. 20 And then announce to them, 'Listen to the LORD's message, you kings of Judah, and everyone from Judah, and all you citizens of Jerusalem, those who pass through these gates. 21 The LORD says, Be very careful if you value your lives! Do not carry any loads in through the gates of Jerusalem on the Sabbath day. 22 Do not carry any loads out of your houses or do any work on the Sabbath day. But observe the Sabbath day as a day set apart to the LORD, as I commanded your ancestors. 23 Your ancestors, however, did not listen to me or pay any attention to me. They stubbornly refused to pay attention or to respond to any discipline.' 24 The LORD says, 'You must make sure to obey me. You must not bring any loads through the gates of this city on the Sabbath day. You must set the Sabbath day apart to me. You must not do any work on that day. 25 If you do this, then the kings and princes who follow in David's succession and ride in chariots or on horses will continue to enter through these gates, as well as their officials and the people of Judah and the citizens of Jerusalem. This city will always be filled with people. 26 Then people will come here from the towns in Judah, from the villages surrounding Jerusalem, from the territory of Benjamin, from the foothills, from the southern hill country, and from the southern part of Judah. They will come bringing offerings to the temple of the LORD: burnt offerings, sacrifices, grain offerings, and incense along with their thank offerings. 27 But you must obey me and set the Sabbath day apart to me. You must not carry any loads in through the gates of Jerusalem on the Sabbath day. If you disobey, I will set the gates of Jerusalem on fire. It will burn down all the fortified dwellings in Jerusalem and no one will be able to put it out.'"

CHALLENGE

Observation of the Sabbath was a symbol of God's covenant with Israel. Why would it be important for God's people to return to observing the Sabbath? Why was the observation of the Sabbath no longer required once Jesus came? (See Luke 6:1–11.)

AN OBJECT LESSON FROM THE MAKING OF POTTERY

18 The LORD said to Jeremiah: 2 "Go down at once to the potter's house. I will speak to you further there." 3 So I went down to the potter's house and found him working at his wheel. 4 Now and then there would be something wrong with the pot he was molding from the clay with his hands. So he would rework the clay into another kind of pot as he saw fit.

5 Then the LORD's message came to me, 6 "I, the LORD, say: 'O nation of Israel, can I not deal with you as this potter deals with the clay? In my hands, you, O nation of Israel, are just like the clay in this potter's hand.' 7 There are times, Jeremiah, when I threaten to uproot, tear down, and destroy a nation or kingdom. 8 But if that nation I threatened stops doing wrong, I will cancel the destruction I intended to do to it. 9 And there are times when I promise to build up and establish a nation or kingdom. 10 But if that nation does what displeases me and does not obey me, then I will cancel the good I promised to do to it. 11 So now, tell the people of Judah and the citizens of Jerusalem this: The LORD says, 'I am preparing to bring disaster on you! I am making plans to punish you. So, every one of you, stop the evil things you

have been doing. Correct the way you have been living and do
what is right.' 12 But they just keep saying, 'We do not care what
you say! We will do whatever we want to do! We will continue to
behave wickedly and stubbornly!'"

13 Therefore, the LORD says,
"Ask the people of other nations
whether they have heard of anything like this.
Israel should have been like a virgin,
but she has done something utterly revolting!
14 Does the snow ever completely vanish
from the rocky slopes of Lebanon?
Do the cool waters from those distant
mountains ever cease to flow?
15 Yet my people have forgotten me
and offered sacrifices to worthless idols.
This makes them stumble along in the way they live
and leave the old reliable path of their fathers.
They have left them to walk in bypaths,
in roads that are not smooth and level.
16 So their land will become an object of horror.
People will forever hiss out their scorn over it.
All who pass that way will be filled with horror
and will shake their heads in derision.
17 I will scatter them before their enemies
like dust blowing in front of a burning east wind.
I will turn my back on them and not
look favorably on them
when disaster strikes them."

JEREMIAH PETITIONS THE LORD TO PUNISH THOSE WHO ATTACK HIM

18 Then some people said, "Come on! Let us consider how to deal
with Jeremiah! There will still be priests to instruct us, wise men
to give us advice, and prophets to declare God's word. Come on!
Let's bring charges against him and get rid of him! Then we will
not need to pay attention to anything he says."

19 Then I said,
"LORD, pay attention to me.
Listen to what my enemies are saying.
20 Should good be paid back with evil?
Yet they are virtually digging a pit to kill me.
Just remember how I stood before you
pleading on their behalf
to keep you from venting your anger on them.
21 So let their children die of starvation.
Let them be cut down by the sword.
Let their wives lose their husbands and children.
Let the older men die of disease
and the younger men die by the sword in battle.
22 Let cries of terror be heard in their houses
when you send bands of raiders
unexpectedly to plunder them.
For they have virtually dug a pit to capture me
and have hidden traps for me to step into.

23 But you, LORD, know
all their plots to kill me.
Do not pardon their crimes!
Do not ignore their sins as though you had erased them.
Let them be brought down in defeat before you.
Deal with them while you are still angry!

AN OBJECT LESSON FROM A BROKEN CLAY JAR

19 The LORD told Jeremiah, "Go and buy a clay jar from a potter.
Take with you some of the leaders of the people and some
of the leaders of the priests. 2 Go out to the part of the Hinnom
Valley that is near the entrance of the Potsherd Gate. Announce
there what I tell you. 3 Say, 'Listen to the LORD's message, you
kings of Judah and citizens of Jerusalem! This is what the LORD
of Heaven's Armies, the God of Israel, has said, "Look here! I am
about to bring a disaster on this place that will make the ears
of everyone who hears about it ring. 4 I will do so because these
people have rejected me and have defiled this place. They have
offered sacrifices in it to other gods that neither they nor their
ancestors nor the kings of Judah knew anything about. They have
filled it with the blood of innocent children. 5 They have built
places here for worship of the god Baal so that they could sacrifice their children as burnt offerings to him in the fire. Such sacrifices are something I never commanded them to make. They
are something I never told them to do! Indeed, such a thing never
even entered my mind. 6 So I, the LORD, say: "The time will soon
come that people will no longer call this place Topheth or the
Hinnom Valley. But they will call this valley the Valley of Slaughter! 7 In this place I will thwart the plans of the people of Judah
and Jerusalem. I will deliver them over to the power of their enemies who are seeking to kill them. They will die by the sword at
the hands of their enemies. I will make their dead bodies food
for the birds and wild beasts to eat. 8 I will make this city an object of horror, a thing to be hissed at. All who pass by it will be
filled with horror and will hiss out their scorn because of all the
disasters that have happened to it. 9 I will reduce the people of
this city to desperate straits during the siege imposed on it by
their enemies who are seeking to kill them. I will make them
so desperate that they will eat the flesh of their own sons and
daughters and the flesh of one another."'"

10 The LORD continued, "Now break the jar in front of those
who have come here with you. 11 Tell them the LORD of Heav-
en's Armies says, 'I will do just as Jeremiah has done. I will
smash this nation and this city as though it were a potter's vessel that is broken beyond repair. The dead will be buried here
in Topheth until there is no more room to bury them.' 12 I, the
LORD, say: 'That is how I will deal with this city and its citizens.
I will make it like Topheth. 13 The houses in Jerusalem and the
houses of the kings of Judah will be defiled by dead bodies just
like this place, Topheth. For they offered sacrifice to the stars
and poured out drink offerings to other gods on the roofs of
those houses.'"

14 Then Jeremiah left Topheth where the LORD had sent him
to give that prophecy. He went to the LORD's temple and stood

in its courtyard and called out to all the people. 15 "The LORD of
Heaven's Armies, the God of Israel, says, 'I will soon bring on this
city and all the towns surrounding it all the disaster I threatened
to do to it. I will do so because they have stubbornly refused to
pay any attention to what I have said!'"

JEREMIAH IS FLOGGED AND PUT IN A CELL

20 Now Pashhur son of Immer heard Jeremiah prophesy
these things. He was the priest who was chief of security in the LORD's temple. 2 When he heard Jeremiah's prophecy, he had the prophet flogged. Then he put him in the stocks
that were at the Upper Gate of Benjamin in the LORD's temple.
3 But the next day Pashhur released Jeremiah from the stocks.
When he did, Jeremiah said to him, "The LORD's name for you is
not 'Pashhur' but 'Terror is Everywhere.' 4 For the LORD says, 'I
will make both you and your friends terrified of what will happen to you. You will see all of them die by the swords of their
enemies. I will hand all the people of Judah over to the king of
Babylon. He will carry some of them away into exile in Babylon
and he will kill others of them with the sword. 5 I will hand over
all the wealth of this city to their enemies. I will hand over to
them all the fruits of the labor of the people of this city and all
their prized possessions, as well as all the treasures of the kings
of Judah. Their enemies will seize it all as plunder and carry it
off to Babylon. 6 You, Pashhur, and all your household will go
into exile in Babylon. You will die there and you will be buried
there. The same thing will happen to all your friends to whom
you have prophesied lies.'"

JEREMIAH COMPLAINS ABOUT THE REACTION TO HIS MINISTRY

7 LORD, you coerced me into being a prophet,
and I allowed you to do it.
You overcame my resistance and prevailed over me.
Now I have become a constant laughingstock.
Everyone ridicules me.
8 For whenever I prophesy, I must cry out,
"Violence and destruction are coming!"
This message from the LORD has made me
an object of continual insults and derision.
9 Sometimes I think, "I will make no
mention of his message.
I will not speak as his messenger anymore."
But then his message becomes like a fire
locked up inside of me, burning in my heart and soul.
I grow weary of trying to hold it in;
I cannot contain it.
10 I hear many whispering words of intrigue against me.
Those who would cause me terror are everywhere!
They are saying, "Come on, let's publicly denounce him!"
All my so-called friends are just watching for
something that would lead to my downfall.
They say, "Perhaps he can be enticed into slipping up,
so we can prevail over him and get our revenge on him."

11 But the LORD is with me to help me
like an awe-inspiring warrior.
Therefore those who persecute me will
fail and will not prevail over me.
They will be thoroughly disgraced
because they did not succeed.
Their disgrace will never be forgotten.
12 O LORD of Heaven's Armies, you test
and prove the righteous.
You see into people's hearts and minds.
Pay them back for what they have done
because I trust you to vindicate my cause.
13 Sing to the LORD! Praise the LORD!
For he rescues the oppressed from
the clutches of evildoers.
14 Cursed be the day I was born!
May that day not be blessed when my
mother gave birth to me.
15 Cursed be the man
who made my father very glad
when he brought him the news
that a baby boy had been born to him!
16 May that man be like the cities
that the LORD destroyed without showing any mercy.
May he hear a cry of distress in the morning
and a battle cry at noon.
17 For he did not kill me before I came from the womb,
making my pregnant mother's womb my grave forever.
18 Why did I ever come forth from my mother's womb?
All I experience is trouble and grief,
and I spend my days in shame.

THE LORD WILL HAND JERUSALEM OVER TO ENEMIES

21 The LORD spoke to Jeremiah when King Zedekiah sent to
him Pashhur son of Malkijah and the priest Zephaniah son
of Maaseiah. Zedekiah sent them to Jeremiah to ask, 2 "Please
ask the LORD to come and help us, because King Nebuchadnezzar of Babylon is attacking us. Maybe the LORD will perform one
of his miracles as in times past and make him stop attacking us
and leave." 3 Jeremiah answered them, "Tell Zedekiah 4 that the
LORD, the God of Israel, says, 'The forces at your disposal are now
outside the walls fighting against King Nebuchadnezzar of Babylon and the Babylonians who have you under siege. I will gather
those forces back inside the city. 5 In anger, in fury, and in wrath
I myself will fight against you with my mighty power and great
strength. 6 I will kill everything living in Jerusalem, people and
animals alike. They will die from terrible diseases. 7 Then I, the
LORD, promise that I will hand over King Zedekiah of Judah,
his officials, and any of the people who survive the war, starvation, and disease. I will hand them over to King Nebuchadnezzar of Babylon and to their enemies who want to kill them. He
will slaughter them with the sword. He will not show them any
mercy, compassion, or pity.'

8 "But tell the people of Jerusalem that the LORD says, 'I will
give you a choice between two courses of action. One will result
in life; the other will result in death. 9 Those who stay in this city
will die in battle or of starvation or disease. Those who leave the
city and surrender to the Babylonians who are besieging it will
live. They will escape with their lives. 10 For I, the LORD, say that
I am determined not to deliver this city but to bring disaster
on it. It will be handed over to the king of Babylon and he will
destroy it with fire.'"

WARNINGS TO THE ROYAL COURT

11 The LORD told me to say to the royal court of Judah:

"Listen to the LORD's message,
12 O royal family descended from David.
The LORD says:
'See to it that people each day are judged fairly.
Deliver those who have been robbed
  from those who oppress them.
Otherwise, my wrath will blaze out against you.
It will burn like a fire that cannot be put out
because of the evil that you have done.
13 Listen, you who sit enthroned above
  the valley on a rocky plateau.
I am opposed to you,' says the LORD.
'You boast, "No one can swoop down on us.
No one can penetrate into our places of refuge."
14 But I will punish you as your deeds deserve,'
says the LORD.
'I will set fire to your palace;
it will burn up everything around it.'"

22 The LORD told me, "Go down to the palace of the king of
Judah. Give him a message from me there. 2 Say: 'Listen,
O king of Judah who follows in David's succession. You, your officials, and your subjects who pass through the gates of this palace
must listen to the LORD's message. 3 The LORD says, "Do what is
just and right. Deliver those who have been robbed from those
who oppress them. Do not exploit or mistreat resident foreigners
who live in your land, children who have no fathers, or widows. Do
not kill innocent people in this land. 4 If you are careful to obey
these commands, then the kings who follow in David's succession
and ride in chariots or on horses will continue to come through
the gates of this palace, as will their officials and their subjects.
5 But, if you do not obey these commands, I solemnly swear that
this palace will become a pile of rubble. I, the LORD, affirm it!"'"

6 "For the LORD says concerning the palace of the king of Judah,
'"This place looks like a veritable forest of Gilead to me.
It is like the wooded heights of Lebanon in my eyes.
But I swear that I will make it like a wilderness
whose towns have all been deserted.
7 I will send men against it to destroy it
with their axes and hatchets.
They will hack up its fine cedar panels and columns
and throw them into the fire.

8 "'People from other nations will pass by this city. They will
ask one another, "Why has the LORD done such a thing to this
great city?" 9 The answer will come back, "It is because they broke
their covenant with the LORD their God and worshiped and
served other gods."

JUDGMENT ON JEHOAHAZ

10 "'Do not weep for the king who was killed.
Do not grieve for him.
But weep mournfully for the king who has gone into exile.
For he will never return to see his native land again.

11 "'For the LORD has spoken about Shallum son of Josiah, who
succeeded his father as king of Judah but was carried off into
exile. He has said, "He will never return to this land. 12 For he
will die in the country where they took him as a captive. He will
never see this land again."

JUDGMENT ON JEHOIAKIM

13 "'Sure to be judged is the king who builds
his palace using injustice
and treats people unfairly while adding its upper rooms.
He makes his countrymen work for him for nothing.
He does not pay them for their labor.
14 He says, "I will build myself a large palace
with spacious upper rooms."
He cuts windows in its walls,
panels it with cedar, and paints its rooms red.
15 Does it make you any more of a king
that you outstrip everyone else in building with cedar?
Just think about your father.
He was content that he had food and drink.
He did what was just and right.
So things went well with him.
16 He upheld the cause of the poor and needy.
So things went well for Judah.'
The LORD says,
'That is a good example of what it means to know me.
17 But you are always thinking and looking
for ways to increase your wealth by dishonest means.
Your eyes and your heart are set
on killing some innocent person
and committing fraud and oppression.'"

18 So the LORD has this to say about Josiah's son, King Jehoia-
kim of Judah:
"People will not mourn for him, saying,
'This makes me sad, my brother!
This makes me sad, my sister!'
They will not mourn for him, saying,
'Poor, poor lord! Poor, poor majesty!'
19 He will be left unburied just like a dead donkey.
His body will be dragged off and thrown
outside the gates of Jerusalem.

WARNING TO JERUSALEM

20 "People of Jerusalem, go up to Lebanon
and cry out in mourning.
Go to the land of Bashan and cry out loudly.
Cry out in mourning from the mountains of Moab.
For your allies have all been defeated.
21 While you were feeling secure I gave you warning.
But you said, 'I refuse to listen to you.'
That is the way you have acted from
your earliest history onward.
Indeed, you have never paid attention to me.
22 My judgment will carry off all your
leaders like a storm wind!
Your allies will go into captivity.
Then you will certainly be disgraced
and put to shame
because of all the wickedness you have done.
23 You may feel as secure as a bird
nesting in the cedars of Lebanon.
But O how you will groan when the pains
of judgment come on you.
They will be like those of a woman
giving birth to a baby."

JECONIAH WILL BE PERMANENTLY EXILED

24 The LORD says, "As surely as I am the living God, you, Jeconiah, king of Judah, son of Jehoiakim, will not be the earthly
representative of my authority. Indeed, I will take that right
away from you. 25 I will hand you over to those who want to
take your life and of whom you are afraid. I will hand you
over to King Nebuchadnezzar of Babylon and his Babylonian soldiers. 26 I will force you and your mother who gave
you birth into exile. You will be exiled to a country where
neither of you were born, and you will both die there. 27 You
will never come back to this land that you will long to
return to!

28 "This man, Jeconiah, will be like a broken
pot someone threw away.
He will be like a clay vessel that no one wants.
Why will he and his children be forced into exile?
Why will they be thrown out into a country
they know nothing about?
29 O Land, land, land of Judah!
Listen to the LORD's message.

30 The LORD says,
"Enroll this man in the register as
though he were childless.
Enroll him as a man who will not enjoy
success during his lifetime.
For none of his sons will succeed in
occupying the throne of David
or ever succeed in ruling over Judah."

NEW LEADERS OVER A REGATHERED REMNANT

23 The LORD says, "The leaders of my people are sure to be
judged. They were supposed to watch over my people like
shepherds watch over their sheep. But they are causing my people to be destroyed and scattered." 2 So the LORD God of Israel has
this to say about the leaders who are ruling over his people: "You
have caused my people to be dispersed and driven into exile. You
have not taken care of them. So I will punish you for the evil that
you have done. I, the LORD, affirm it! 3 Then I myself will regather
those of my people who are still alive from all the countries where
I have driven them. I will bring them back to their homeland. They
will greatly increase in number. 4 I will install rulers over them who
will care for them. Then they will no longer need to fear or be terrified. None of them will turn up missing. I, the LORD, promise it!

5 "I, the LORD, promise that a new time will certainly come
when I will raise up for them a righteous
branch, a descendant of David.
He will rule over them with wisdom and understanding
and will do what is just and right in the land.
6 Under his rule Judah will enjoy safety
and Israel will live in security.
This is the name he will go by:
'The LORD has provided us with justice.'

7 "So I, the LORD, say: 'A new time will certainly come. People now affirm their oaths with, "I swear as surely as the LORD
lives who delivered the people of Israel out of Egypt." 8 But at
that time they will affirm them with, "I swear as surely as the
LORD lives who delivered the descendants of the former nation of Israel from the land of the north and from all the other
lands where he had banished them." At that time they will live
in their own land.'"

ORACLES AGAINST THE FALSE PROPHETS

9 Here is what the LORD says concerning the false prophets:
My heart and my mind are deeply disturbed.
I tremble all over.
I am like a drunk person,
like a person who has had too much wine,
because of the way the LORD
and his holy word are being mistreated.
10 For the land is full of people unfaithful to him.
They live wicked lives and they misuse their power.
So the land is dried up because it is under his curse.
The pastures in the wilderness are withered.

11 Moreover, the LORD says,
"Both the prophets and priests are godless.
I have even found them doing evil in my temple.
12 So the paths they follow will be dark and slippery.
They will stumble and fall headlong.
For I will bring disaster on them.
A day of reckoning is coming for them."
The LORD affirms it!

13 The LORD says, "I saw the prophets of Samaria
doing something that was disgusting.
They prophesied in the name of the god Baal
and led my people Israel astray.
14 But I see the prophets of Jerusalem
doing something just as shocking.
They are unfaithful to me
and continually prophesy lies.
So they give encouragement to people who are doing evil,
with the result that they do not stop their evildoing.
I consider all of them as bad as the people of Sodom,
and the citizens of Jerusalem as bad
as the people of Gomorrah.
15 So then I, the LORD of Heaven's Armies,
have something to say concerning
the prophets of Jerusalem:
'I will make these prophets eat the bitter food of suffering
and drink the poison water of judgment.
For the prophets of Jerusalem are the reason
that ungodliness has spread throughout the land.'"

16 The LORD of Heaven's Armies says to the people of Jerusalem:
"Do not listen to what
those prophets are saying to you.
They are filling you with false hopes.
They are reporting visions of their own imaginations,
not something the LORD has given them to say.
17 They continually say to those who reject
what the LORD has said,
'Things will go well for you!'
They say to all those who follow the stubborn
inclinations of their own hearts,
'Nothing bad will happen to you!'
18 Yet which of them has ever stood in the LORD's inner circle
so they could see and hear what he has to say?
Which of them have ever paid attention
or listened to what he has said?
19 But just watch! The wrath of the LORD
will come like a storm!
Like a raging storm it will rage down
on the heads of those who are wicked.
20 The anger of the LORD will not turn back
until he has fully carried out his intended purposes.
In future days
you people will come to understand this clearly.
21 I did not send those prophets,
yet they were in a hurry to give their message.
I did not tell them anything,
yet they prophesied anyway.
22 But if they had stood in my inner circle,
they would have proclaimed my message to my people.
They would have caused my people to
turn from their wicked ways
and stop doing the evil things they are doing.

23 Do you people think that I am some local deity
and not the transcendent God?"
the LORD asks.
24 "Do you really think anyone can hide himself
where I cannot see him?" the LORD asks.
"Do you not know that I am everywhere?"
the LORD asks.

25 The LORD says, "I have heard what those prophets who are
prophesying lies in my name are saying. They are saying, 'I have
had a dream! I have had a dream!' 26 Those prophets are just
prophesying lies. They are prophesying the delusions of their
own minds. 27 How long will they go on plotting to make my people forget who I am through the dreams they tell one another?
That is just as bad as what their ancestors did when they forgot
who I am by worshiping the god Baal. 28 Let the prophet who has
had a dream go ahead and tell his dream. Let the person who
has received my message report that message faithfully. What
is like straw cannot compare to what is like grain! I, the LORD,
affirm it! 29 My message is like a fire that purges dross. It is like
a hammer that breaks a rock in pieces. I, the LORD, so affirm it!
30 So I, the LORD, affirm that I am opposed to those prophets
who steal messages from one another that they claim are from
me. 31 I, the LORD, affirm that I am opposed to those prophets
who are using their own tongues to declare, 'The LORD declares.'
32 I, the LORD, affirm that I am opposed to those prophets who
dream up lies and report them. They are misleading my people with their reckless lies. I did not send them. I did not commission them. They are not helping these people at all. I, the
LORD, affirm it!"

33 The LORD said to me, "Jeremiah, when one of these people,
or a prophet, or a priest asks you, 'What burdensome message
do you have from the LORD?' Tell them, 'You are the burden,
and I will cast you away. I, the LORD, affirm it! 34 I will punish any
prophet, priest, or other person who says "The LORD's message
is burdensome." I will punish both that person and his whole
family.'"

35 So I, Jeremiah, tell you, "Each of you people should say to
his friend or his relative, 'How did the LORD answer? Or what
did the LORD say?' 36 You must no longer say that the LORD's
message is burdensome. For what is 'burdensome' really pertains to what a person himself says. You are misrepresenting
the words of our God, the living God, the LORD of Heaven's
Armies. 37 Each of you should merely ask the prophet, 'What
answer did the LORD give you? Or what did the LORD say?'
38 But just suppose you continue to say, 'The message of the
LORD is burdensome.' Here is what the LORD says will happen: 'I sent word to you that you must not say, "The LORD's
message is burdensome." But you used the words, "The LORD's
message is burdensome," anyway. 39 So I will carry you far off
and throw you away. I will send both you and the city I gave
to you and to your ancestors out of my sight. 40 I will bring
on you lasting shame and lasting disgrace that will never
be forgotten!'"

GOOD FIGS AND BAD FIGS

24 The LORD showed me two baskets of figs sitting before
his temple. This happened after King Nebuchadnezzar of
Babylon deported Jehoiakim's son, King Jeconiah of Judah. He deported him and the leaders of Judah from Jerusalem, along with
the craftsmen and metal workers, and took them to Babylon.
2 One basket had very good-looking figs in it. They looked like
those that had ripened early. The other basket had very bad-
looking figs in it, so bad they could not be eaten. 3 The LORD said
to me, "What do you see, Jeremiah?" I answered, "I see figs. The
good ones look very good. But the bad ones look very bad, so bad
that they cannot be eaten."

4 The LORD's message came to me, 5 "I, the LORD, the God of
Israel, say: 'The exiles of Judah whom I sent away from here to
the land of Babylon are like those good figs. I consider them to
be good. 6 I will look after their welfare and will restore them
to this land. There I will build them up and will not tear them
down. I will plant them firmly in the land and will not uproot
them. 7 I will give them the desire to acknowledge that I am the
LORD. I will be their God and they will be my people. For they
will wholeheartedly return to me.'

8 "I, the LORD, also solemnly assert: 'King Zedekiah of Judah, his
officials, and the people who remain in Jerusalem or who have
gone to live in Egypt are like those bad figs. I consider them to
be just like those bad figs that are so bad they cannot be eaten.
9 I will bring such disaster on them that all the kingdoms of the
earth will be horrified. I will make them an object of reproach,
a proverbial example of disaster. I will make them an object of
ridicule, an example to be used in curses. That is how they will
be remembered wherever I banish them. 10 I will bring war, starvation, and disease on them until they are completely destroyed
from the land I gave them and their ancestors.'"

SEVENTY YEARS OF SERVITUDE FOR FAILURE TO GIVE HEED

25 In the fourth year that Jehoiakim son of Josiah was king
of Judah, the LORD spoke to Jeremiah concerning all the
people of Judah. (That was the same as the first year that Nebuchadnezzar was king of Babylon.) 2 So the prophet Jeremiah spoke
to all the people of Judah and to all the people who were living in
Jerusalem. 3 "For the last twenty-three years, from the thirteenth
year that Josiah son of Amon was ruling in Judah until now, the
LORD's messages have come to me and I have told them to you
over and over again. But you would not listen. 4 Over and over
again the LORD has sent his servants the prophets to you. But you
have not listened or paid attention. 5 He said through them, 'Each
of you must turn from your wicked ways and stop doing the evil
things you are doing. If you do, I will allow you to continue to live
here in the land that I gave to you and your ancestors as a lasting
possession. 6 Do not pay allegiance to other gods and worship and
serve them. Do not make me angry by the things that you do. Then
I will not cause you any harm.' 7 So, now the LORD says, 'You have
not listened to me. But you have made me angry by the things
that you have done. Thus you have brought harm on yourselves.'

8 "Therefore, the LORD of Heaven's Armies says, 'You have not
listened to what I said. 9 So I, the LORD, affirm that I will send for
all the peoples of the north and my servant, King Nebuchadnezzar of Babylon. I will bring them against this land and its inhabitants and all the nations that surround it. I will utterly destroy
the land, its inhabitants, and all the surrounding nations and
make them everlasting ruins. I will make them objects of horror and hissing scorn. 10 I will put an end to the sounds of joy
and gladness and the glad celebration of brides and grooms in
these lands. I will put an end to the sound of people grinding
meal. I will put an end to lamps shining in their houses. 11 This
whole area will become a desolate wasteland. These nations will
be subject to the king of Babylon for seventy years.'

12 "'But when the seventy years are over, I will punish the king
of Babylon and his nation for their sins. I will make the land of
Babylon an everlasting ruin. I, the LORD, affirm it! 13 I will bring
on that land everything that I said I would. I will bring on it everything that is written in this book. I will bring on it everything
that Jeremiah has prophesied against all the nations. 14 For many
nations and great kings will make slaves of the king of Babylon
and his nation too. I will repay them for all they have done.'"

JUDAH AND THE NATIONS WILL EXPERIENCE GOD'S WRATH

15 So the LORD, the God of Israel, spoke to me in a vision: "Take
this cup from my hand. It is filled with the wine of my wrath. Take
it and make the nations to whom I send you drink it. 16 When
they have drunk it, they will stagger to and fro and act insane.
For I will send wars sweeping through them."

17 So I took the cup from the LORD's hand. I made all the nations to whom he sent me drink the wine of his wrath. 18 I made
Jerusalem and the cities of Judah, its kings and its officials drink
it. I did it so Judah would become a ruin. I did it so Judah, its
kings, and its officials would become an object of horror and
of hissing scorn, an example used in curses. Such is already becoming the case! 19 I made all these other people drink it: Pharaoh, king of Egypt; his attendants, his officials, his people, 20 the
foreigners living in Egypt; all the kings of the land of Uz; all the
kings of the land of the Philistines, the people of Ashkelon, Gaza,
Ekron, the people who had been left alive from Ashdod; 21 all
the people of Edom, Moab, Ammon; 22 all the kings of Tyre, all
the kings of Sidon; all the kings of the coastlands along the sea;
23 the people of Dedan, Tema, Buz, all the desert people who cut
their hair short at the temples; 24 all the kings of Arabia who live
in the desert; 25 all the kings of Zimri; all the kings of Elam; all
the kings of Media; 26 all the kings of the north, whether near
or far from one another; and all the other kingdoms that are on
the face of the earth. After all of them have drunk the wine of
the LORD's wrath, the king of Babylon must drink it.

27 Then the LORD said to me, "Tell them that the LORD of Heav-
en's Armies, the God of Israel, says, 'Drink this cup until you
get drunk and vomit. Drink until you fall down and can't get
up. For I will send wars sweeping through you.' 28 If they refuse
to take the cup from your hand and drink it, tell them that the

LORD of Heaven's Armies says, 'You most certainly must drink
it! 29 For take note, I am already beginning to bring disaster on
the city that I call my own. So how can you possibly avoid being
punished? You will not go unpunished. For I am proclaiming
war against all who live on the earth. I, the LORD of Heaven's
Armies, affirm it!'

30 "Then, Jeremiah, make the following prophecy against them:
'Like a lion about to attack, the LORD will
roar from the heights of heaven;
from his holy dwelling on high he will roar loudly.
He will roar mightily against his land.
He will shout in triumph, like those
stomping juice from the grapes,
against all those who live on the earth.
31 The sounds of battle will resound to the ends of the earth.
For the LORD will bring charges against the nations.
He will pass judgment on all humankind
and will hand the wicked over to be killed in war.'
The LORD so affirms it!
32 The LORD of Heaven's Armies says,
'Disaster will soon come on one nation after another.
A mighty storm of military destruction is rising up
from the distant parts of the earth.'
33 Those who have been killed by the LORD at that time
will be scattered from one end of the earth to the other.
They will not be mourned over, gathered up, or buried.
Their dead bodies will lie scattered
over the ground like manure.
34 Wail and cry out in anguish, you rulers!
Roll in the dust, you who shepherd flocks of people!
The time for you to be slaughtered has come.
You will lie scattered and fallen like
broken pieces of fine pottery.
35 The leaders will not be able to run away and hide.
The shepherds of the flocks will not be able to escape.
36 Listen to the cries of anguish of the leaders.
Listen to the wails of the shepherds of the flocks.
They are wailing because the LORD
is about to destroy their lands.
37 Their peaceful dwelling places will be laid waste
by the fierce anger of the LORD.
38 The LORD is like a lion who has left his lair.
So their lands will certainly be laid waste
by the warfare of the oppressive nation
and by the fierce anger of the LORD."

JEREMIAH IS PUT ON TRIAL AS A FALSE PROPHET

26 The LORD spoke to Jeremiah at the beginning of the reign
of Josiah's son, King Jehoiakim of Judah. 2 The LORD said,
"Go stand in the courtyard of the LORD's temple. Speak out to all
the people who are coming from the towns of Judah to worship
in the LORD's temple. Tell them everything I command you to tell
them. Do not leave out a single word. 3 Maybe they will pay attention and each of them will stop living the evil way they do. If they

do that, then I will forgo destroying them as I had intended to do
because of the wicked things they have been doing. 4 Tell them
that the LORD says, 'You must obey me; you must live according
to the way I have instructed you in my laws. 5 You must pay attention to the exhortations of my servants the prophets. I have
sent them to you over and over again. But you have not paid any
attention to them. 6 If you do not obey me, then I will do to this
temple what I did to Shiloh. And I will make this city an example
to be used in curses by people from all the nations on the earth.'"
7 The priests, the prophets, and all the people heard Jeremiah
say these things in the LORD's temple. 8 Jeremiah had just barely
finished saying all the LORD had commanded him to say to all
the people when all at once some of the priests, the prophets,
and the people grabbed him and shouted, "You deserve to die!
9 How dare you claim the LORD's authority to prophesy such
things! How dare you claim his authority to prophesy that this
temple will become like Shiloh and that this city will become
an uninhabited ruin!" Then all the people crowded around Jeremiah in the LORD's temple.
10 However, some of the officials of Judah heard about what was
happening and they rushed up to the LORD's temple from the
royal palace. They set up court at the entrance of the New Gate
of the LORD's temple. 11 Then the priests and the prophets made
their charges before the officials and all the people. They said,
"This man should be condemned to die because he prophesied
against this city. You have heard him do so with your own ears."
12 Then Jeremiah made his defense before all the officials and
all the people. "The LORD sent me to prophesy everything you
have heard me say against this temple and against this city. 13 But
correct the way you have been living and do what is right. Obey
the LORD your God. If you do, the LORD will forgo destroying you
as he threatened he would. 14 As to my case, I am in your power.
Do to me what you deem fair and proper. 15 But you should take
careful note of this: If you put me to death, you will bring on
yourselves and this city and those who live in it the guilt of murdering an innocent man. For the LORD has sent me to speak all
this where you can hear it. That is the truth!"
16 Then the officials and all the people rendered their verdict to
the priests and the prophets. They said, "This man should not be
condemned to die. For he has spoken to us under the authority
of the LORD our God." 17 Then some of the elders of Judah stepped
forward and spoke to all the people gathered there. They said,
18 "Micah from Moresheth prophesied during the time Hezekiah
was king of Judah. He told all the people of Judah, 'The LORD of
Heaven's Armies says,

"'Zion will become a plowed field.
Jerusalem will become a pile of rubble.
The temple mount will become a mere wooded ridge.'"

19 "King Hezekiah and all the people of Judah did not put him
to death, did they? Did not Hezekiah show reverence for the
LORD and seek the LORD's favor? Did not the LORD forgo destroying them as he threatened he would? But we are on the
verge of bringing great disaster on ourselves."

20 Now there was another man who prophesied as the LORD's
representative against this city and this land just as Jeremiah
did. His name was Uriah son of Shemaiah from Kiriath Jearim.
21 When King Jehoiakim and all his bodyguards and officials
heard what he was prophesying, the king sought to have him
executed. But Uriah found out about it and fled to Egypt out
of fear. 22 However, King Jehoiakim sent some men to Egypt,
including Elnathan son of Achbor, 23 and they brought Uriah
back from there. They took him to King Jehoiakim, who had
him executed and had his body thrown into the burial place of
the common people.
24 However, Ahikam son of Shaphan used his influence to keep
Jeremiah from being handed over and executed by the people.

JEREMIAH COUNSELS SUBMISSION TO BABYLON

27 The LORD spoke to Jeremiah early in the reign of Josiah's
son, King Zedekiah of Judah. 2 The LORD told me, "Make a
yoke out of leather straps and wooden crossbars and put it on
your neck. 3 Use it to send messages to the kings of Edom, Moab,
Ammon, Tyre, and Sidon. Send them through the envoys who
have come to Jerusalem to King Zedekiah of Judah. 4 Charge them
to give their masters a message from me. Tell them, 'The LORD of
Heaven's Armies, the God of Israel, says to give your masters this
message: 5 "I made the earth and the people and animals on it by
my mighty power and great strength, and I give it to whomever I
see fit. 6 I have at this time placed all these nations of yours under the power of my servant, King Nebuchadnezzar of Babylon.
I have even made all the wild animals subject to him. 7 All nations must serve him and his son and grandson until the time
comes for his own nation to fall. Then many nations and great
kings will in turn subjugate Babylon. 8 But suppose a nation or
a kingdom will not be subject to King Nebuchadnezzar of Babylon. Suppose it will not submit to the yoke of servitude to him.
I, the LORD, affirm that I will punish that nation. I will use the
king of Babylon to punish it with war, starvation, and disease until I have destroyed it. 9 So do not listen to your prophets or to
those who claim to predict the future by divination, by dreams,
by consulting the dead, or by practicing magic. They keep telling
you, 'You do not need to be subject to the king of Babylon.' 10 Do
not listen to them, because their prophecies are lies. Listening
to them will only cause you to be taken far away from your native land. I will drive you out of your country and you will die in
exile. 11 Things will go better for the nation that submits to the
yoke of servitude to the king of Babylon and is subject to him. I
will leave that nation in its native land. Its people can continue
to farm it and live in it. I, the LORD, affirm it!"'"
12 I told King Zedekiah of Judah the same thing. I said, "Submit to the yoke of servitude to the king of Babylon. Be subject
to him and his people. Then you will continue to live. 13 There is
no reason why you and your people should die in war or from
starvation or disease. That's what the LORD says will happen to
any nation that will not be subject to the king of Babylon. 14 Do
not listen to the prophets who are telling you that you do not
need to serve the king of Babylon. For they are prophesying lies

to you. 15 For I, the LORD, affirm that I did not send them. They
are prophesying lies to you in my name. If you listen to them, I
will drive you and the prophets who are prophesying lies out of
the land and you will all die in exile."

16 I also told the priests and all the people, "The LORD says, 'Do
not listen to what your prophets are saying. They are prophesying to you that the valuable articles taken from the LORD's
temple will be brought back from Babylon very soon. But they
are prophesying a lie to you. 17 Do not listen to them. Be subject to the king of Babylon. Then you will continue to live. Why
should this city be made a pile of rubble?'" 18 I also told them, "If
they are really prophets and the LORD is speaking to them, let
them pray earnestly to the LORD of Heaven's Armies. Let them
plead with him not to let the valuable articles that are still left
in the LORD's temple, in the royal palace of Judah, and in Jerusalem be taken away to Babylon. 19 For the LORD of Heaven's Armies has already spoken about the two bronze pillars, the large
bronze basin called 'The Sea,' and the movable bronze stands. He
has already spoken about the rest of the valuable articles that
are left in this city. 20 He has already spoken about these things
that King Nebuchadnezzar of Babylon did not take away when
he carried Jehoiakim's son King Jeconiah of Judah and the nobles of Judah and Jerusalem away as captives from Jerusalem to
Babylon. 21 Indeed, the LORD of Heaven's Armies, the God of Israel, has already spoken about the valuable articles that are left
in the LORD's temple, in the royal palace of Judah, and in Jerusalem. 22 He has said, 'They will be carried off to Babylon. They
will remain there until it is time for me to show consideration
for them again. Then I will bring them back and restore them
to this place.' I, the LORD, affirm this!"

JEREMIAH CONFRONTED BY A FALSE PROPHET

28 The following events occurred in that same year, early in
the reign of King Zedekiah of Judah. To be more precise, it
was the fifth month of the fourth year of his reign. The prophet
Hananiah son of Azzur, who was from Gibeon, spoke to Jeremiah
in the LORD's temple in the presence of the priests and all the
people: 2 "The LORD of Heaven's Armies, the God of Israel, says,
'I will break the yoke of servitude to the king of Babylon. 3 Before two years are over, I will bring back to this place everything
that King Nebuchadnezzar of Babylon took from it and carried
away to Babylon. 4 I will also bring back to this place Jehoiakim's
son King Jeconiah of Judah and all the exiles who were taken to
Babylon.' Indeed, the LORD affirms, 'I will break the yoke of servitude to the king of Babylon.'"

5 Then the prophet Jeremiah responded to the prophet Hananiah in the presence of the priests and all the people who were
standing in the LORD's temple. 6 The prophet Jeremiah said,
"Amen! May the LORD do all this! May the LORD make your
prophecy come true! May he bring back to this place from Babylon all the valuable articles taken from the LORD's temple and
the people who were carried into exile. 7 But listen to what I say
to you and to all these people. 8 From earliest times, the prophets
who preceded you and me invariably prophesied war, disaster,

and plagues against many countries and great kingdoms. 9 So if a
prophet prophesied peace and prosperity, it was only known that
the LORD truly sent him when what he prophesied came true."
10 The prophet Hananiah then took the yoke off the prophet
Jeremiah's neck and broke it. 11 Then he spoke up in the presence
of all the people. "The LORD says, 'In the same way I will break
the yoke of servitude of all the nations to King Nebuchadnezzar
of Babylon before two years are over.'" After he heard this, the
prophet Jeremiah departed and went on his way.
12 But shortly after the prophet Hananiah had broken the yoke
off the prophet Jeremiah's neck, the LORD's message came to
Jeremiah. 13 "Go and tell Hananiah that the LORD says, 'You have
indeed broken the wooden yoke. But you have only succeeded
in replacing it with an iron one! 14 For the LORD of Heaven's Armies, the God of Israel, says, "I have put an irresistible yoke of
servitude on all these nations so they will serve King Nebuchadnezzar of Babylon. And they will indeed serve him. I have even
given him control over the wild animals."'" 15 Then the prophet
Jeremiah told the prophet Hananiah, "Listen, Hananiah! The
LORD did not send you! You are making these people trust in a
lie. 16 So the LORD says, 'I will most assuredly remove you from
the face of the earth. You will die this very year because you have
counseled rebellion against the LORD.'"
17 In the seventh month of that very same year the prophet
Hananiah died.

JEREMIAH'S LETTER TO THE EXILES

29 The prophet Jeremiah sent a letter to the exiles Nebuchadnezzar had carried off from Jerusalem to Babylon.
It was addressed to the elders who were left among the exiles,
to the priests, to the prophets, and to all the other people who
were exiled in Babylon. 2 He sent it after King Jeconiah, the queen
mother, the palace officials, the leaders of Judah and Jerusalem,
the craftsmen, and the metal workers had been exiled from Jerusalem. 3 He sent it with Elasah son of Shaphan and Gemariah
son of Hilkiah. King Zedekiah of Judah had sent these men to
Babylon to King Nebuchadnezzar of Babylon. The letter said:
4 "The LORD of Heaven's Armies, the God of Israel, says to all
those he sent into exile to Babylon from Jerusalem, 5 'Build
houses and settle down. Plant gardens and eat what they produce. 6 Marry and have sons and daughters. Find wives for your
sons and allow your daughters to get married so that they too
can have sons and daughters. Grow in number; do not dwindle
away. 7 Work to see that the city where I sent you as exiles enjoys peace and prosperity. Pray to the LORD for it. For as it prospers you will prosper.'
8 "For the LORD of Heaven's Armies, the God of Israel, says, 'Do
not let the prophets among you or those who claim to be able
to predict the future by divination deceive you. And do not pay
any attention to the dreams that you are encouraging them to
dream. 9 They are prophesying lies to you and claiming my authority to do so. But I did not send them. I, the LORD, affirm it!'
10 "For the LORD says, 'Only when the seventy years of Babylonian rule are over will I again take up consideration for you.

Then I will fulfill my gracious promise to you and restore you to your homeland. 11 For I know what I have planned for you,' says the LORD. 'I have plans to prosper you, not to harm you. I have plans to give you a future filled with hope. 12 When you call out to me and come to me in prayer, I will hear your prayers. 13 When you seek me in prayer and worship, you will find me available to you. If you seek me with all your heart and soul, 14 I will make myself available to you,' says the LORD. 'Then I will reverse your plight and will regather you from all the nations and all the places where I have exiled you,' says the LORD. 'I will bring you back to the place from which I exiled you.'

REFLECT

How do these verses offer hope? What can we do to seek the Lord in our daily lives?

15 "You say, 'The LORD has raised up prophets of good news for us here in Babylon.' 16 But just listen to what the LORD has to say about the king who occupies David's throne and all your fellow countrymen who are still living in this city of Jerusalem and were not carried off into exile with you. 17 The LORD of Heaven's Armies says, 'I will bring war, starvation, and disease on them. I will treat them like figs that are so rotten they cannot be eaten. 18 I will chase after them with war, starvation, and disease. I will make all the kingdoms of the earth horrified at what happens to them. I will make them examples of those who are cursed, objects of horror, hissing scorn, and ridicule among all the nations where I exile them. 19 For they have not paid attention to what I said to them through my servants the prophets whom I sent to them over and over again,' says the LORD. 'And you exiles have not paid any attention to them either,' says the LORD. 20 'So pay attention to the LORD's message, all you exiles whom I have sent to Babylon from Jerusalem.'

21 "The LORD of Heaven's Armies, the God of Israel, also has something to say about Ahab son of Kolaiah and Zedekiah son of Maaseiah, who are prophesying lies to you and claiming my authority to do so. 'I will hand them over to King Nebuchadnezzar of Babylon and he will execute them before your very eyes. 22 And all the exiles of Judah who are in Babylon will use them as examples when they put a curse on anyone. They will say, "May the LORD treat you like Zedekiah and Ahab whom the king of Babylon roasted to death in the fire!" 23 This will happen to them because they have done what is shameful in Israel. They have committed adultery with their neighbors' wives and have spoken lies while claiming my authority. They have spoken words that I did not command them to speak. I know what they have done. I have been a witness to it,' says the LORD."

A RESPONSE TO THE LETTER AND A SUBSEQUENT LETTER

24 The LORD told Jeremiah, "Tell Shemaiah the Nehelamite 25 that the LORD of Heaven's Armies, the God of Israel, has a message for him. Tell him, 'On your own initiative you sent a letter to the priest Zephaniah son of Maaseiah and to all the other priests and to all the people in Jerusalem. In your letter you said to Zephaniah, 26 "The LORD has made you priest in place of Jehoiada. He has put you in charge in the LORD's temple of controlling any lunatic who pretends to be a prophet. And it is your duty to put any such person in the stocks with an iron collar around his neck.

[27]You should have reprimanded Jeremiah from Anathoth who is
pretending to be a prophet among you! [28]For he has even sent
a message to us here in Babylon. He wrote and told us, "You will
be there a long time. Build houses and settle down. Plant gardens and eat what they produce."'"
[29]Zephaniah the priest read that letter to the prophet Jeremiah. [30]Then the LORD's message came to Jeremiah: [31]"Send a
message to all the exiles in Babylon. Tell them, 'The LORD has
spoken about Shemaiah the Nehelamite: "Shemaiah has spoken
to you as a prophet even though I did not send him. He is making you trust in a lie. [32]Because he has done this," the LORD says,
"I will punish Shemaiah the Nehelamite and his whole family.
There will not be any of them left to experience the good things
that I will do for my people. I, the LORD, affirm it! For he counseled rebellion against the LORD."'"

INTRODUCTION TO THE BOOK OF CONSOLATION

30 The LORD spoke to Jeremiah. [2]"The LORD God of Israel
says, 'Write everything that I am about to tell you in a
scroll. [3]For I, the LORD, affirm that the time will come when I
will reverse the plight of my people, Israel and Judah,' says the
LORD. 'I will bring them back to the land I gave their ancestors
and they will take possession of it once again.'"

ISRAEL AND JUDAH WILL BE DELIVERED AFTER A TIME OF DEEP DISTRESS

[4]So here is what the LORD has to say about Israel and Judah.
[5]Yes, here is what he says:
"You hear cries of panic and of terror;
there is no peace in sight.
6 Ask yourselves this and consider it carefully:
Have you ever seen a man give birth to a baby?
Why then do I see all these strong men
grabbing their stomachs in pain like
a woman giving birth?
And why do their faces
turn so deathly pale?
7 Alas, what a terrible time of trouble it is!
There has never been any like it.
It is a time of trouble for the descendants of Jacob,
but some of them will be rescued out of it.
8 When the time for them to be rescued comes,"
says the LORD of Heaven's Armies,
"I will rescue you from foreign subjugation.
I will deliver you from captivity.
Foreigners will then no longer subjugate them.
9 But they will be subject to the LORD their God
and to the Davidic ruler whom I will
raise up as king over them.
10 So I, the LORD, tell you not to be afraid,
you descendants of Jacob, my servants.
Do not be terrified, people of Israel.
For I will rescue you and your descendants
from a faraway land where you are captives.

The descendants of Jacob will return to
their land and enjoy peace.
They will be secure and no one will terrify them.
11 For I, the LORD, affirm that
I will be with you and will rescue you.
I will completely destroy all the nations
where I scattered you.
But I will not completely destroy you.
I will indeed discipline you, but only in due measure.
I will not allow you to go entirely unpunished."

THE LORD WILL HEAL THE WOUNDS OF JUDAH

12 Moreover, the LORD says to the people of Zion:
"Your injuries are incurable;
your wounds are severe.
13 There is no one to plead your cause.
There are no remedies for your wounds.
There is no healing for you.
14 All your allies have abandoned you.
They no longer have any concern for you.
For I have attacked you like an enemy would.
I have chastened you cruelly.
For your wickedness is so great
and your sin is so much.
15 Why do you complain about your injuries,
that your pain is incurable?
I have done all this to you
because your wickedness is so great
and your sin is so much.
16 But all who destroyed you will be destroyed.
All your enemies will go into exile.
Those who plundered you will be plundered.
I will cause those who pillaged you to be pillaged.
17 Yes, I will restore you to health.
I will heal your wounds.
I, the LORD, affirm it!
For you have been called an outcast,
Zion, whom no one cares for."

THE LORD WILL RESTORE ISRAEL AND JUDAH

18 The LORD says:
"I will restore the ruined houses of
the descendants of Jacob.
I will show compassion on their ruined homes.
Every city will be rebuilt on its former ruins.
Every fortified dwelling will occupy its traditional site.
19 Out of those places you will hear songs of thanksgiving
and the sounds of laughter and merriment.
I will increase their number and they
will not dwindle away.
I will bring them honor and they will
no longer be despised.
20 The descendants of Jacob will enjoy
their former privileges.

Their community will be reestablished in my favor,
and I will punish all who try to oppress them.
21 One of their own people will be their leader.
Their ruler will come from their own number.
I will invite him to approach me, and he will do so.
For no one would dare approach me on his own.
I, the LORD, affirm it!
22 Then you will again be my people,
and I will be your God.
23 Just watch! The wrath of the LORD
will come like a storm.
Like a raging storm it will rage down
on the heads of those who are wicked.
24 The anger of the LORD will not turn back
until he has fully carried out his intended purposes.
In future days you will come to understand this.
31 At that time I will be the God of all the clans of Israel
and they will be my people.
I, the LORD, affirm it!"

ISRAEL WILL BE RESTORED AND JOIN JUDAH IN WORSHIP

2 The LORD says:
"The people of Israel who survived
death at the hands of the enemy
will find favor in the wilderness
as they journey to find rest for themselves.
3 In a faraway land the LORD will manifest himself to them.
He will say to them, 'I have loved you
with an everlasting love.
That is why I have continued to be faithful to you.
4 I will rebuild you, my dear children Israel,
so that you will once again be built up.
Once again you will take up the tambourine
and join in the happy throng of dancers.
5 Once again you will plant vineyards
on the hills of Samaria.
Those who plant them
will once again enjoy their fruit.
6 Yes, a time is coming
when watchmen will call out on the
mountains of Ephraim,
"Come! Let us go to Zion
to worship the LORD our God!"'"

7 Moreover, the LORD says:
"Sing for joy for the descendants of Jacob.
Utter glad shouts for that foremost of the nations.
Make your praises heard.
Then say, 'LORD, rescue your people.
Deliver those of Israel who remain alive.'
8 Then I will reply, 'I will bring them back
from the land of the north.
I will gather them in from the distant parts of the earth.

Blind and lame people will come with them,
so will pregnant women and women about to give birth.
A vast throng of people will come back here.
9 They will come back shedding tears of contrition.
I will bring them back praying prayers of repentance.
I will lead them besides streams of water,
along smooth paths where they will never stumble.
I will do this because I am Israel's father;
Ephraim is my firstborn son.'"

10 Listen to the LORD's message, O nations.
Proclaim it in the faraway lands along the sea.
Say, "The one who scattered Israel will regather them.
He will watch over his people like a
shepherd watches over his flock."
11 For the LORD will rescue the descendants of Jacob.
He will secure their release from those
who had overpowered them.
12 They will come and shout for joy on Mount Zion.
They will be radiant with joy over the
good things the LORD provides,
the grain, the fresh wine, the olive oil,
the young sheep, and the calves he has given to them.
They will be like a well-watered garden
and will not grow faint or weary any more.
13 The LORD says, "At that time young
women will dance and be glad.
Young men and old men will rejoice.
I will turn their grief into gladness.
I will give them comfort and joy in
place of their sorrow.
14 I will provide the priests with abundant provisions.
My people will be filled to the full with
the good things I provide."

15 The LORD says:
"A sound is heard in Ramah,
a sound of crying in bitter grief.
It is the sound of Rachel weeping for her children
and refusing to be comforted, because
her children are gone."
16 The LORD says to her,
"Stop crying! Do not shed any more tears.
For your heartfelt repentance will be rewarded.
Your children will return from the land of the enemy.
I, the LORD, affirm it!
17 Indeed, there is hope for your posterity.
Your children will return to their own territory.
I, the LORD, affirm it!
18 I have indeed heard the people of Israel say mournfully,
'We were like a calf untrained to the yoke.
You disciplined us and we learned from it.
Let us come back to you and we will do so,
for you are the LORD our God.

19 For after we turned away from you we repented.
After we came to our senses we struck our thigh in sorrow.
We are ashamed and humiliated
because of the disgraceful things we did previously.'
20 Indeed, the people of Israel are my dear children.
They are the children I take delight in.
For even though I must often rebuke them,
I still remember them with fondness.
So I am deeply moved with pity for them
and will surely have compassion on them.
I, the LORD, affirm it!
21 I will say, 'My dear children of Israel, keep in mind
the road you took when you were carried off.
Mark off in your minds the landmarks.
Make a mental note of telltale signs
marking the way back.
Return, my dear children of Israel.
Return to these cities of yours.
22 How long will you vacillate,
you who were once like an unfaithful daughter?
For I, the LORD, promise to bring about
something new on the earth,
something as unique as a woman protecting a man!'"

JUDAH WILL BE RESTORED

23 The LORD of Heaven's Armies, the God of Israel, says,
"I will restore the people of Judah to
their land and to their towns.
When I do, they will again say of Jerusalem,
'May the LORD bless you, you holy mountain,
the place where righteousness dwells.'
24 The land of Judah will be inhabited by
people who live in its towns,
as well as by farmers and shepherds with their flocks.
25 I will fully satisfy the needs of those who are weary
and fully refresh the souls of those who are faint.
26 Then they will say, 'Under these conditions
I can enjoy sweet sleep
when I wake up and look around.'

ISRAEL AND JUDAH WILL BE REPOPULATED

27 "Indeed, a time is coming," says the LORD, "when I will cause
people and animals to sprout up in the lands of Israel and Judah.
28 In the past I saw to it that they were uprooted and torn down,
that they were destroyed and demolished and brought disaster.
But now I will see to it that they are built up and firmly planted.
I, the LORD, affirm it!

THE LORD WILL MAKE A NEW COVENANT WITH ISRAEL AND JUDAH

29 "When that time comes, people will no longer say, 'The parents have eaten sour grapes, but the children's teeth have grown
numb.' 30 Rather, each person will die for his own sins. The teeth of
the person who eats the sour grapes will themselves grow numb.

31 “Indeed, a time is coming,” says the LORD, “when I will make
a new covenant with the people of Israel and Judah. 32 It will
not be like the old covenant that I made with their ancestors
when I delivered them from Egypt. For they violated that covenant, even though I was like a faithful husband to them,” says
the LORD. 33 “But I will make a new covenant with the whole nation of Israel after I plant them back in the land,” says the LORD.
“I will put my law within them and write it on their hearts and
minds. I will be their God and they will be my people.

34 “People will no longer need to teach their neighbors and relatives to know me. For all of them, from the least important to the
most important, will know me,” says the LORD. “For I will forgive
their sin and will no longer call to mind the wrong they have done.”

THE LORD GUARANTEES ISRAEL’S CONTINUANCE

35 The LORD has made a promise to Israel.
He promises it as the one who fixed
  the sun to give light by day
and the moon and stars to give light by night.
He promises it as the one who stirs up
  the sea so that its waves roll.
His name is the LORD of Heaven’s Armies.
36 The LORD affirms, “The descendants of Israel will not
cease forever to be a nation in my sight.
That could only happen if the fixed
  ordering of the heavenly lights
were to cease to operate before me.”
37 The LORD says, “I will not reject all
  the descendants of Israel
because of all that they have done.
That could only happen if the heavens
  above could be measured
or the foundations of the earth below
  could all be explored,”
says the LORD.

JERUSALEM WILL BE ENLARGED

38 “Indeed a time is coming,” says the LORD, “when the city of Jerusalem will be rebuilt as my special city. It will be built from the
Tower of Hananel westward to the Corner Gate. 39 The boundary line will extend beyond that, straight west from there to the
Hill of Gareb and then turn southward to Goah. 40 The whole
valley where dead bodies and sacrificial ashes are thrown, and
all the terraced fields out to the Kidron Valley on the east as far
north as the corner of the Horse Gate, will be included within
this city that is sacred to the LORD. The city will never again be
torn down or destroyed.”

JEREMIAH BUYS A FIELD

32 In the tenth year that Zedekiah was ruling over Judah
the LORD spoke to Jeremiah. That was the same as the
eighteenth year of Nebuchadnezzar.

2 Now at that time, the armies of the king of Babylon were besieging Jerusalem. The prophet Jeremiah was confined in the

courtyard of the guardhouse attached to the royal palace of Judah. 3 For King Zedekiah had confined Jeremiah there after he
had reproved him for prophesying as he did. He had asked Jeremiah, "Why do you keep prophesying these things? Why do you
keep saying that the LORD says, 'I will hand this city over to the
king of Babylon? I will let him capture it. 4 King Zedekiah of Judah will not escape from the Babylonians. He will certainly be
handed over to the king of Babylon. He must answer personally
to the king of Babylon and confront him face to face. 5 Zedekiah
will be carried off to Babylon and will remain there until I have
fully dealt with him. I, the LORD, affirm it! Even if you continue
to fight against the Babylonians, you cannot win.'"
6 So now, Jeremiah said, "The LORD's message came to me,
7 'Hanamel, the son of your uncle Shallum, will come to you soon.
He will say to you, "Buy my field at Anathoth because you are
entitled as my closest relative to buy it."' 8 And then my cousin
Hanamel did come to me in the courtyard of the guardhouse in
keeping with the LORD's message. He said to me, 'Buy my field
that is at Anathoth in the territory of the tribe of Benjamin.
Buy it for yourself since you are entitled as my closest relative
to take possession of it for yourself.' When this happened, I recognized that the LORD had indeed spoken to me. 9 So I bought
the field at Anathoth from my cousin Hanamel. I weighed out
seven ounces of silver and gave it to him to pay for it. 10 I signed
the deed of purchase, sealed it, and had some men serve as witnesses to the purchase. I weighed out the silver for him on a
scale. 11 There were two copies of the deed of purchase. One was
sealed and contained the order of transfer and the conditions
of purchase. The other was left unsealed. 12 I took both copies
of the deed of purchase and gave them to Baruch son of Neriah, the son of Mahseiah. I gave them to him in the presence
of my cousin Hanamel, the witnesses who had signed the deed
of purchase, and all the Judeans who were housed in the courtyard of the guardhouse. 13 In the presence of all these people I
instructed Baruch, 14 'The LORD of Heaven's Armies, the God of
Israel, says, "Take these documents, both the sealed copy of the
deed of purchase and the unsealed copy. Put them in a clay jar
so that they may be preserved for a long time to come."' 15 For the
LORD of Heaven's Armies, the God of Israel, says, 'Houses, fields,
and vineyards will again be bought in this land.'

JEREMIAH'S PRAYER OF PRAISE AND BEWILDERMENT

16 "After I had given the copies of the deed of purchase to Baruch
son of Neriah, I prayed to the LORD, 17 'Oh, Sovereign LORD, you
did indeed make heaven and earth by your mighty power and
great strength. Nothing is too hard for you! 18 You show unfailing
love to thousands. But you also punish children for the sins of
their parents. You are the great and powerful God whose is name
is the LORD of Heaven's Armies. 19 You plan great things and you
do mighty deeds. You see everything people do. You reward each
of them for the way they live and for the things they do. 20 You
did miracles and amazing deeds in the land of Egypt that have
had lasting effect. By this means you gained both in Israel and

among humankind a renown that lasts to this day. [21]You used
your mighty power and your great strength to perform miracles
and amazing deeds and to bring great terror on the Egyptians.
By this means you brought your people Israel out of the land of
Egypt. [22]You kept the promise that you swore on oath to their
ancestors. You gave them a land flowing with milk and honey.
[23]But when they came in and took possession of it, they did not
obey you or live as you had instructed them. They did not do
anything that you commanded them to do. So you brought all
this disaster on them. [24]Even now siege ramps have been built
up around the city in order to capture it. War, starvation, and
disease are sure to make the city fall into the hands of the Babylonians who are attacking it. LORD, you threatened that this
would happen. Now you can see that it is already taking place.
[25]The city is sure to fall into the hands of the Babylonians. Yet,
in spite of this, you, Sovereign LORD, have said to me, "Buy that
field with silver and have the transaction legally witnessed.""

THE LORD ANSWERS JEREMIAH'S PRAYER

[26]The LORD's message came to Jeremiah: [27]"I am the LORD, the
God of all humankind. There is, indeed, nothing too difficult for
me. [28]Therefore I, the LORD, say: 'I will indeed hand this city over
to King Nebuchadnezzar of Babylon and the Babylonian army.
They will capture it. [29]The Babylonian soldiers that are attacking this city will break into it and set it on fire. They will burn it
down along with the houses where people have made me angry
by offering sacrifices to the god Baal and by pouring out drink
offerings to other gods on their rooftops. [30]This will happen because the people of Israel and Judah have repeatedly done what
displeases me from their earliest history until now and because
they have repeatedly made me angry by the things they have
done. I, the LORD, affirm it! [31]This will happen because the people of this city have aroused my anger and my wrath since the
time they built it until now. They have made me so angry that I
am determined to remove it from my sight. [32]I am determined
to do so because the people of Israel and Judah have made me
angry with all their wickedness—they, their kings, their officials,
their priests, their prophets, and especially the people of Judah
and the citizens of Jerusalem have done this wickedness. [33]They
have turned away from me instead of turning to me. I tried over
and over again to instruct them, but they did not listen and respond to correction. [34]They set up their disgusting idols in the
temple that I have claimed for my own and defiled it. [35]They built
places of worship for the god Baal in the Valley of Ben Hinnom so
that they could sacrifice their sons and daughters to the god Molech. Such a disgusting practice was not something I commanded
them to do. It never even entered my mind to command them
to do such a thing! So Judah is certainly liable for punishment.'

[36]"You and your people are right in saying, 'War, starvation, and
disease are sure to make this city fall into the hands of the king
of Babylon.' But now I, the LORD God of Israel, have something
further to say about this city: [37]'I will certainly regather my people from all the countries where I have exiled them in my anger,
fury, and great wrath. I will bring them back to this place and

LOVE TO GROW

TOO HARD FOR GOD

JEREMIAH 32:27

I've taken my girls to the Pacific and Atlantic Oceans to see for themselves the vastness of God. I've taken them to the redwood forest in California to see firsthand the size of the redwood trees as they scratch the sky above. They've studied the solar system in school, and I've taken them on a field trip to NASA, asking them the question "Can you imagine how big God must be if He created the sun, the moon, and all the planets?" I've taken them to our own backyard to look at the details of flowers in our garden and the various bugs crawling around in our grass. I've done all those things with the same purpose: to help my girls see that nothing is too big, too small, or too far for God.

"I am the LORD, the God of all humankind. There is, indeed, nothing too difficult for me" (Jer 32:27).

I've often needed to be reminded of who God is and that nothing is too difficult for Him. I'm sure you have too. Maybe you needed that reminder the day you got the diagnosis. Maybe you needed it the day when your forever relationship ended in pain and confusion. Maybe you needed it the day your position was eliminated. Maybe you needed it the day your dream died.

When our view of God is small, we see our problems and fears—our mountains and Goliaths, if you will—as bigger than Him. One of the ways I've tried to help my girls understand that nothing is too big or too hard for God is by pointing them to nature, to what God has created for us to see, touch, and experience.

That truth is the same for us. No matter what we are facing in our lives, nothing is too hard for the One who created the heavens and the earth. Nothing is out of His reach or His sovereignty. If God can part the waters for the Israelites fleeing Egypt and place the Earth in the exact location in our solar system to sustain life, He can handle our problems.

You, my sweet friend, are not alone. God has promised He is with you and He will help you. You don't have to battle this alone. You don't have to fight this in your own strength. Turn to Him. Seek Him. He can handle it. If you're still not convinced, take a step back and observe nature around you. His care and attention to detail in creation is the same care and attention He gives to you.

allow them to live here in safety. 38 They will be my people, and I will be their God. 39 I will give them a single-minded purpose to live in a way that always shows respect for me. They will want to do that for their own good and the good of the children who descend from them. 40 I will make a lasting covenant with them that I will never stop doing good to them. I will fill their hearts and minds with respect for me so that they will never again turn away from me. 41 I will take delight in doing good to them. I will faithfully and wholeheartedly plant them firmly in the land.'

42 "For I, the LORD, say: 'I will surely bring on these people all the good fortune that I am hereby promising them. I will be just as sure to do that as I have been in bringing all this great disaster on them. 43 You and your people are saying that this land will become desolate, uninhabited by either people or animals. You are saying that it will be handed over to the Babylonians. But fields will again be bought in this land. 44 Fields will again be bought with silver, and deeds of purchase signed, sealed, and witnessed. This will happen in the territory of Benjamin, the villages surrounding Jerusalem, the towns in Judah, the southern hill country, the foothills, and southern Judah. For I will restore them to their land. I, the LORD, affirm it!'"

THE LORD PROMISES A SECOND TIME TO RESTORE ISRAEL AND JUDAH

33 The LORD's message came to Jeremiah a second time while he was still confined in the courtyard of the guardhouse. 2 "I, the LORD, do these things. I, the LORD, form the plan to bring them about. I am known as the LORD. I say to you, 3 'Call on me in prayer and I will answer you. I will show you great and mysterious things that you still do not know about.' 4 For I, the LORD God of Israel, have something more to say about the houses in this city and the royal buildings of Judah that have been torn down for defenses against the siege ramps and military incursions of the Babylonians: 5 'The defenders of the city will go out and fight with the Babylonians. But they will only fill those houses and buildings with the dead bodies of the people that I will kill in my anger and my wrath. That will happen because I have decided to turn my back on this city on account of the wicked things they have done. 6 But I will most surely heal the wounds of this city and restore it and its people to health. I will show them abundant peace and security. 7 I will restore Judah and Israel and will rebuild them as they were in days of old. 8 I will purify them from all the sin that they committed against me. I will forgive all their sins that they committed in rebelling against me. 9 All the nations will hear about all the good things that I will do for them. This city will bring me fame, honor, and praise before them for the joy that I bring it. The nations will tremble in awe at all the peace and prosperity that I will provide for it.'

10 "I, the LORD, say: 'You and your people are saying about this place, "It lies in ruins. There are no people or animals in it." That is true. The towns of Judah and the streets of Jerusalem will soon be desolate, uninhabited either by people or by animals. But happy sounds will again be heard in these places. 11 Once again

there will be sounds of joy and gladness and the glad celebrations of brides and grooms. Once again people will bring their
thank offerings to the temple of the LORD and will say, “Give
thanks to the LORD of Heaven’s Armies. For the LORD is good
and his unfailing love lasts forever.” For I, the LORD, affirm that
I will restore the land to what it was in days of old.’

12“I, the LORD of Heaven’s Armies, say: ‘This place will indeed
lie in ruins. There will be no people or animals in it. But there
will again be in it and in its towns sheepfolds where shepherds
can rest their sheep. 13I, the LORD, say that shepherds will once
again count their sheep as they pass into the fold. They will do
this in all the towns in the hill country, the foothills, the Negev,
the territory of Benjamin, the villages surrounding Jerusalem,
and the towns of Judah.’

THE LORD REAFFIRMS HIS COVENANT WITH DAVID, ISRAEL, AND LEVI

14“I, the LORD, affirm: ‘The time will certainly come when I will
fulfill my gracious promise concerning the nations of Israel and
Judah. 15In those days and at that time I will raise up for them
a righteous descendant of David.

“‘He will do what is just and right in the land. 16Under his rule
Judah will enjoy safety and Jerusalem will live in security. At that
time Jerusalem will be called “The LORD has provided us with
justice.” 17For I, the LORD, promise: “David will never lack a successor to occupy the throne over the nation of Israel. 18Nor will
the Levitical priests ever lack someone to stand before me and
continually offer up burnt offerings, sacrifice cereal offerings,
and offer the other sacrifices.”’”

19The LORD’s message came to Jeremiah another time: 20“I,
the LORD, make the following promise: ‘I have made a covenant
with the day and with the night that they will always come at
their proper times. Only if you people could break that covenant
21could my covenant with my servant David and my covenant
with the Levites ever be broken. So David will by all means always have a descendant to occupy his throne as king and the
Levites will by all means always have priests who will minister
before me. 22I will make the children who follow one another
in the line of my servant David very numerous. I will also make
the Levites who minister before me very numerous. I will make
them all as numerous as the stars in the sky and as the sands
that are on the seashore.’”

23The LORD’s message came to Jeremiah another time: 24“You
have surely noticed what these people are saying, haven’t you?
They are saying, ‘The LORD has rejected the two families of Israel and Judah that he chose.’ So they have little regard that my
people will ever again be a nation. 25But I, the LORD, make the
following promise: ‘I have made a covenant governing the coming of day and night. I have established the fixed laws governing
heaven and earth. 26Just as surely as I have done this, so surely
will I never reject the descendants of Jacob. Nor will I ever refuse
to choose one of my servant David’s descendants to rule over the
descendants of Abraham, Isaac, and Jacob. Indeed, I will restore
them and show mercy to them.’”

THE LORD MAKES AN OMINOUS PROMISE TO ZEDEKIAH

34 The LORD's message came to Jeremiah while King Nebuchadnezzar of Babylon was attacking Jerusalem and the towns around it with a large army. This army consisted of troops from his own army and from the kingdoms and peoples of the lands under his dominion. 2 This is what the LORD God of Israel told Jeremiah, "Go, speak to King Zedekiah of Judah. Tell him, 'This is what the LORD has said: "Take note! I am going to hand this city over to the king of Babylon, and he will burn it down. 3 You yourself will not escape his clutches but will certainly be captured and handed over to him. You must confront the king of Babylon face to face and answer to him personally. Then you must go to Babylon."' 4 However, listen to the LORD's message, King Zedekiah of Judah. This is what the LORD has said: 'You will not die in battle or be executed. 5 You will die a peaceful death. They will burn incense at your burial just as they did at the burial of your ancestors, the former kings who preceded you. They will mourn for you, saying, "Alas, master!" Indeed, you have my own word on this. I, the LORD, affirm it!'"

6 The prophet Jeremiah told all these things to King Zedekiah of Judah in Jerusalem. 7 He did this while the army of the king of Babylon was attacking Jerusalem and the cities of Lachish and Azekah. He was attacking these cities because they were the only fortified cities of Judah that were still holding out.

THE LORD THREATENS TO DESTROY THOSE WHO WRONGED THEIR SLAVES

8 The LORD spoke to Jeremiah after King Zedekiah had made a covenant with all the people in Jerusalem to grant their slaves their freedom. 9 Everyone was supposed to free their male and female Hebrew slaves. No one was supposed to keep a fellow Judean enslaved. 10 All the people and their leaders had agreed to this. They had agreed to free their male and female slaves and not keep them enslaved any longer. They originally complied with the covenant and freed them. 11 But later they changed their minds. They took back their male and female slaves that they had freed and forced them to be slaves again. 12 The LORD's message came to Jeremiah, 13 "The LORD God of Israel has a message for you: 'I made a covenant with your ancestors when I brought them out of Egypt where they had been slaves. It stipulated, 14 "Every seven years each of you must free any fellow Hebrews who have sold themselves to you. After they have served you for six years, you shall set them free." But your ancestors did not obey me or pay any attention to me. 15 Recently, however, you yourselves showed a change of heart and did what is pleasing to me. You granted your fellow countrymen their freedom and you made a covenant to that effect in my presence in the house that I have claimed for my own. 16 But then you turned right around and showed that you did not honor me. Each of you took back your male and female slaves, whom you had freed as they desired, and you forced them to be your slaves again. 17 So I, the LORD, say: "You have not really obeyed me and granted freedom to your neighbor and fellow countryman. Therefore, I will

grant you freedom, the freedom to die in war, or by starvation, or disease. I, the LORD, affirm it! I will make all the kingdoms of the earth horrified at what happens to you. 18 I will punish those people who have violated their covenant with me. I will make them like the calf they cut in two and passed between its pieces. I will do so because they did not keep the terms of the covenant they made in my presence. 19 I will punish the leaders of Judah and Jerusalem, the court officials, the priests, and all the other people of the land who passed between the pieces of the calf. 20 I will hand them over to their enemies who want to kill them. Their dead bodies will become food for the birds and the wild animals. 21 I will also hand King Zedekiah of Judah and his officials over to their enemies who want to kill them. I will hand them over to the army of the king of Babylon, even though they have temporarily withdrawn from attacking you. 22 For I, the LORD, affirm that I will soon give the order and bring them back to this city. They will fight against it and capture it and burn it down. I will also make the towns of Judah desolate so that there will be no one living in them.""'

JUDAH'S UNFAITHFULNESS CONTRASTED WITH THE RECHABITES' FAITHFULNESS

35 The LORD spoke to Jeremiah when Jehoiakim son of Josiah was ruling over Judah: 2 "Go to the Rechabite community. Invite them to come into one of the side rooms of the LORD's temple and offer them some wine to drink." 3 So I went and got Jaazaniah son of Jeremiah the grandson of Habazziniah, his brothers, all his sons, and all the rest of the Rechabite community. 4 I took them to the LORD's temple. I took them into the room where the disciples of the prophet Hanan son of Igdaliah stayed. That room was next to the one where the temple officers stayed and above the room where Maaseiah son of Shallum, one of the doorkeepers of the temple, stayed. 5 Then I set cups and pitchers full of wine in front of the members of the Rechabite community and said to them, "Have some wine." 6 But they answered, "We do not drink wine because our ancestor Jonadab son of Rechab commanded us not to. He told us, 'You and your children must never drink wine. 7 Do not build houses. Do not plant crops. Do not plant a vineyard or own one. Live in tents all your lives. If you do these things you will live a long time in the land that you wander about on.' 8 We and our wives and our sons and daughters have obeyed everything our ancestor Jonadab son of Rechab commanded us. We have never drunk wine. 9 We have not built any houses to live in. We do not own any vineyards, fields, or crops. 10 We have lived in tents. We have obeyed our ancestor Jonadab and done exactly as he commanded us. 11 But when King Nebuchadnezzar of Babylon invaded the land we said, 'Let's get up and go to Jerusalem to get away from the Babylonian and Aramean armies.' That is why we are staying here in Jerusalem."

12 Then the LORD's message came to Jeremiah. 13 The LORD of Heaven's Armies, the God of Israel, told him, "Go and speak to the people of Judah and the citizens of Jerusalem. Tell them, 'I, the LORD, say: "You must learn a lesson from this about obeying

what I say. 14 Jonadab son of Rechab ordered his descendants
not to drink wine. His orders have been carried out. To this day
his descendants have drunk no wine because they have obeyed
what their ancestor commanded them. But I have spoken to
you over and over again, but you have not obeyed me. 15 I sent
all my servants the prophets to warn you over and over again.
They said, 'Every one of you, stop doing the evil things you have
been doing and do what is right. Do not pay allegiance to other
gods and worship them. Then you can continue to live in this
land that I gave to you and your ancestors.' But you did not pay
any attention or listen to me. 16 Yes, the descendants of Jonadab
son of Rechab have carried out the orders that their ancestor
gave them. But you people have not obeyed me! 17 So I, the LORD
God of Heaven's Armies, the God of Israel, say: 'I will soon bring
on Judah and all the citizens of Jerusalem all the disaster that
I threatened to bring on them. I will do this because I spoke to
them but they did not listen. I called out to them but they did
not answer.'""

18 Then Jeremiah spoke to the Rechabite community, "The
LORD of Heaven's Armies, the God of Israel says, 'You have obeyed
the orders of your ancestor Jonadab. You have followed all his
instructions. You have done exactly as he commanded you.' 19 So
the LORD of Heaven's Armies, the God of Israel, says, 'Jonadab
son of Rechab will never lack a male descendant to serve me.'"

JEHOIAKIM BURNS THE SCROLL CONTAINING THE LORD'S MESSAGES

36 The LORD spoke to Jeremiah in the fourth year that Jehoiakim son of Josiah was ruling over Judah: 2 "Get a scroll.
Write on it everything I have told you to say about Israel, Judah,
and all the other nations since I began to speak to you in the
reign of Josiah until now. 3 Perhaps when the people of Judah
hear about all the disaster I intend to bring on them, they will
all stop doing the evil things they have been doing. If they do,
I will forgive their sins and the wicked things they have done."

4 So Jeremiah summoned Baruch son of Neriah. Then, Baruch
wrote down in a scroll all the LORD's words that he had told to
Jeremiah as they came from his mouth. 5 Then Jeremiah told
Baruch, "I am no longer allowed to go into the LORD's temple.
6 So you go there the next time all the people of Judah come in
from their towns to fast in the LORD's temple. Read out loud
where all of them can hear you what I told you the LORD said,
which you wrote in the scroll. 7 Perhaps then they will ask the
LORD for mercy and will all stop doing the evil things they have
been doing. For the LORD has threatened to bring great anger
and wrath against these people."

8 So Baruch son of Neriah did exactly what the prophet Jeremiah told him to do. He read what the LORD had said from the
scroll in the temple of the LORD. 9 All the people living in Jerusalem and all the people who came into Jerusalem from the
towns of Judah observed a fast before the LORD. The fast took
place in the ninth month of the fifth year that Jehoiakim son of
Josiah was ruling over Judah. 10 At that time Baruch went into
the temple of the LORD. He stood in the entrance of the room

of Gemariah the son of Shaphan who had been the royal secretary. That room was in the upper court near the entrance of the
New Gate. There, where all the people could hear him, he read
from the scroll what Jeremiah had said.
11 Micaiah, who was the son of Gemariah and the grandson of
Shaphan, heard Baruch read from the scroll everything the LORD
had said. 12 He went down to the chamber of the royal secretary
in the king's palace and found all the court officials in session
there. Elishama the royal secretary, Delaiah son of Shemaiah, Elnathan son of Achbor, Gemariah son of Shaphan, Zedekiah son
of Hananiah, and all the other officials were seated there. 13 Micaiah told them everything he had heard Baruch read from the
scroll in the hearing of the people. 14 All the officials sent Jehudi,
who was the son of Nethaniah, the son of Shelemiah, the son of
Cushi, to Baruch. They ordered him to tell Baruch, "Come here
and bring with you the scroll you read in the hearing of the people." So Baruch son of Neriah went to them, carrying the scroll
in his hand. 15 They said to him, "Please sit down and read it to
us." So Baruch sat down and read it to them. 16 When they had
heard it all, they expressed their alarm to one another. Then they
said to Baruch, "We must certainly give the king a report about
everything you have read!" 17 Then they asked Baruch, "How did
you come to write all these words? Do they actually come from
Jeremiah's mouth?" 18 Baruch answered, "Yes, they came from
his own mouth. He dictated all these words to me, and I wrote
them down in ink on this scroll." 19 Then the officials said to Baruch, "You and Jeremiah must go and hide. You must not let anyone know where you are."
20 The officials put the scroll in the room of Elishama, the royal
secretary, for safekeeping. Then they went to the court and reported everything to the king. 21 The king sent Jehudi to get the
scroll. He went and got it from the room of Elishama, the royal
secretary. Then he himself read it to the king and all the officials
who were standing around him. 22 Since it was the ninth month
of the year, the king was sitting in his winter quarters. A fire was
burning in the firepot in front of him. 23 As soon as Jehudi had
read three or four columns of the scroll, the king would cut them
off with a penknife and throw them on the fire in the firepot.
He kept doing so until the whole scroll was burned up in the
fire. 24 Neither he nor any of his attendants showed any alarm
when they heard all that had been read. Nor did they tear their
clothes to show any grief or sorrow. 25 The king did not even listen to Elnathan, Delaiah, and Gemariah, who had urged him not
to burn the scroll. 26 He also ordered Jerahmeel, who was one of
the royal princes, Seraiah son of Azriel, and Shelemiah son of
Abdeel to arrest the scribe Baruch and the prophet Jeremiah.
However, the LORD hid them.

BARUCH AND JEREMIAH WRITE ANOTHER SCROLL

27 The LORD's message came to Jeremiah after the king had
burned the scroll with the words Baruch had written down at
Jeremiah's dictation. 28 "Get another scroll and write on it everything that was written on the original scroll that King Jehoiakim of Judah burned. 29 Tell King Jehoiakim of Judah, 'The

LORD says, "You burned the scroll. You asked Jeremiah, 'How dare you write in this scroll that the king of Babylon will certainly come and destroy this land and wipe out all the people and animals on it?'" 30 So the LORD says concerning King Jehoiakim of Judah, "None of his line will occupy the throne of David. His dead body will be thrown out to be exposed to scorching heat by day and frost by night. 31 I will punish him and his descendants and the officials who serve him for the wicked things they have done. I will bring on them, the citizens of Jerusalem and the people of Judah, all the disaster that I told them about and that they ignored."'" 32 Then Jeremiah got another scroll and gave it to the scribe Baruch son of Neriah. As Jeremiah dictated, Baruch wrote on this scroll everything that had been on the scroll that King Jehoiakim of Judah burned in the fire. They also added on this scroll several other messages of the same kind.

INTRODUCTION TO INCIDENTS DURING THE REIGN OF ZEDEKIAH

37 Zedekiah son of Josiah succeeded Jeconiah son of Jehoiakim as king. He was elevated to the throne of the land of Judah by King Nebuchadnezzar of Babylon. 2 Neither he nor the officials who served him nor the people of Judah paid any attention to what the LORD said through the prophet Jeremiah.

THE LORD RESPONDS TO ZEDEKIAH'S HOPE FOR HELP

3 King Zedekiah sent Jehucal son of Shelemiah and the priest Zephaniah son of Maaseiah to the prophet Jeremiah to say, "Please pray to the LORD our God on our behalf." 4 (Now Jeremiah had not yet been put in prison. So he was still free to come and go among the people as he pleased. 5 At that time the Babylonian forces had temporarily given up their siege against Jerusalem. They had had it under siege, but withdrew when they heard that the army of Pharaoh had set out from Egypt.) 6 The LORD's message came to the prophet Jeremiah, 7 "This is what the LORD God of Israel has said, 'This is what you must say to the king of Judah who sent you to seek my help. "Beware, Pharaoh's army that was on its way to help you is about to go back home to Egypt. 8 Then the Babylonian forces will return. They will attack the city and will capture it and burn it down. 9 Moreover, I, the LORD, warn you not to deceive yourselves into thinking that the Babylonian forces will go away and leave you alone. For they will not go away. 10 For even if you were to defeat all the Babylonian forces fighting against you so badly that only wounded men were left lying in their tents, they would get up and burn this city down."'"

JEREMIAH IS CHARGED WITH DESERTING, ARRESTED, AND IMPRISONED

11 The following events also occurred while the Babylonian forces had temporarily withdrawn from Jerusalem because the army of Pharaoh was coming. 12 Jeremiah started to leave

Jerusalem to go to the territory of Benjamin. He wanted to make sure he got his share of the property that was being divided up among his family there. 13 But he only got as far as the Benjamin Gate. There an officer in charge of the guards named Irijah, who was the son of Shelemiah and the grandson of Hananiah, stopped him. He seized Jeremiah and said, "You are deserting to the Babylonians!" 14 Jeremiah answered, "That's a lie! I am not deserting to the Babylonians." But Irijah would not listen to him. Irijah put Jeremiah under arrest and took him to the officials. 15 The officials were very angry with Jeremiah. They had him flogged and put in prison in the house of Jonathan, the royal secretary, which they had converted into a place for confining prisoners.

16 So Jeremiah was put in prison in a cell in the dungeon in Jonathan's house. He was kept there for a long time. 17 Then King Zedekiah had him brought to the palace. There he questioned him privately and asked him, "Is there any message from the LORD?" Jeremiah answered, "Yes, there is." Then he announced, "You will be handed over to the king of Babylon." 18 Then Jeremiah asked King Zedekiah, "What crime have I committed against you, or the officials who serve you, or the people of Judah? What have I done to make you people throw me into prison? 19 Where now are the prophets who prophesied to you that the king of Babylon would not attack you or this land? 20 But now please listen, your royal Majesty, and grant my plea for mercy. Do not send me back to the house of Jonathan, the royal secretary. If you do, I will die there." 21 Then King Zedekiah ordered that Jeremiah be committed to the courtyard of the guardhouse. He also ordered that a loaf of bread be given to him every day from the bakers' street until all the bread in the city was gone. So Jeremiah was kept in the courtyard of the guardhouse.

JEREMIAH IS CHARGED WITH TREASON AND PUT IN A CISTERN TO DIE

38 Now Shephatiah son of Mattan, Gedaliah son of Pashhur, Jehucal son of Shelemiah, and Pashhur son of Malkijah had heard the things that Jeremiah had been telling the people. They had heard him say, 2 "The LORD says, 'Those who stay in this city will die in battle or of starvation or disease. Those who leave the city and surrender to the Babylonians will live. They will escape with their lives.'" 3 They had also heard him say, "The LORD says, 'This city will certainly be handed over to the army of the king of Babylon. They will capture it.'" 4 So these officials said to the king, "This man must be put to death. For he is demoralizing the soldiers who are left in the city as well as all the other people there by these things he is saying. This man is not seeking to help these people but is trying to harm them." 5 King Zedekiah said to them, "Very well, you can do what you want with him. For I cannot do anything to stop you." 6 So the officials took Jeremiah and put him in the cistern of Malkijah, one of the royal princes, that was in the courtyard of the guardhouse. There was no water in the cistern, only mud. So when they lowered Jeremiah into the cistern with ropes he sank in the mud.

AN ETHIOPIAN OFFICIAL RESCUES JEREMIAH FROM THE CISTERN

7 An Ethiopian, Ebed Melech, a court official in the royal palace, heard that Jeremiah had been put in the cistern. While the king was holding court at the Benjamin Gate, 8 Ebed Melech departed the palace and went to speak to the king. He said to him, 9 "Your royal Majesty, those men have been very wicked in all that they have done to the prophet Jeremiah. They have thrown him into a cistern and he is sure to die of starvation there because there is no food left in the city." 10 Then the king gave Ebed Melech the Ethiopian the following order: "Take thirty men with you from here and go pull the prophet Jeremiah out of the cistern before he dies." 11 So Ebed Melech took the men with him and went to a room under the treasure room in the palace. He got some worn-out clothes and old rags from there and let them down by ropes to Jeremiah in the cistern. 12 Ebed Melech called down to Jeremiah, "Put these rags and worn-out clothes under your armpits to pad the ropes." Jeremiah did as Ebed Melech instructed. 13 So they pulled Jeremiah up from the cistern with ropes. Jeremiah, however, still remained confined to the courtyard of the guardhouse.

JEREMIAH RESPONDS TO ZEDEKIAH'S REQUEST FOR SECRET ADVICE

14 Some time later Zedekiah sent and had Jeremiah brought to him at the third entrance of the LORD's temple. The king said to Jeremiah, "I would like to ask you a question. Do not hide anything from me when you answer." 15 Jeremiah said to Zedekiah, "If I answer you, you will certainly kill me. If I give you advice, you will not listen to me." 16 So King Zedekiah made a secret promise to Jeremiah and sealed it with an oath. He promised, "As surely as the LORD lives who has given us life and breath, I promise you this: I will not kill you or hand you over to those men who want to kill you."

17 Then Jeremiah said to Zedekiah, "The LORD God of Heaven's Armies, the God of Israel, says, 'You must surrender to the officers of the king of Babylon. If you do, your life will be spared and this city will not be burned down. Indeed, you and your whole family will be spared. 18 But if you do not surrender to the officers of the king of Babylon, this city will be handed over to the Babylonians and they will burn it down. You yourself will not escape from them.'" 19 Then King Zedekiah said to Jeremiah, "I am afraid of the Judeans who have deserted to the Babylonians. The Babylonians might hand me over to them and they will torture me." 20 Then Jeremiah answered, "You will not be handed over to them. Please obey the LORD by doing what I have been telling you. Then all will go well with you and your life will be spared. 21 But if you refuse to surrender, the LORD has shown me a vision of what will happen. Here is what I saw: 22 All the women who are left in the royal palace of Judah will be led out to the officers of the king of Babylon. They will taunt you saying:

"'Your trusted friends misled you;
they have gotten the best of you.
Now that your feet are stuck in the mud,
they have turned their backs on you.'

23 “All your wives and your children will be turned over to the Babylonians. You yourself will not escape from them but will be captured by the king of Babylon. This city will be burned down.”

24 Then Zedekiah told Jeremiah, “Do not let anyone know about the conversation we have had. If you do, you will die. 25 The officials may hear that I have talked with you. They may come to you and say, ‘Tell us what you said to the king and what the king said to you. Do not hide anything from us. If you do, we will kill you.’ 26 If they do this, tell them, ‘I was pleading with the king not to send me back to die in the dungeon of Jonathan’s house.’” 27 All the officials did indeed come and question Jeremiah. He told them exactly what the king had instructed him to say. They stopped questioning him any further because no one had actually heard their conversation. 28 So Jeremiah remained confined in the courtyard of the guardhouse until the day Jerusalem was captured.

THE FALL OF JERUSALEM AND ITS AFTERMATH

The following events occurred when Jerusalem was captured.

39 King Nebuchadnezzar of Babylon came against Jerusalem with his whole army and laid siege to it. The siege began in the tenth month of the ninth year that Zedekiah ruled over Judah. 2 It lasted until the ninth day of the fourth month of Zedekiah’s eleventh year. On that day they broke through the city walls. 3 Then Nergal Sharezer of Samgar, Nebo Sarsekim (who was a chief officer), Nergal Sharezer (who was a high official), and all the other officers of the king of Babylon came and set up quarters in the Middle Gate. 4 When King Zedekiah of Judah and all his soldiers saw them, they tried to escape. They departed from the city during the night. They took a path through the king’s garden and passed out through the gate between the two walls. Then they headed for the rift valley. 5 But the Babylonian army chased after them. They caught up with Zedekiah in the plains of Jericho and captured him. They took him to King Nebuchadnezzar of Babylon at Riblah in the territory of Hamath and Nebuchadnezzar passed sentence on him there. 6 There at Riblah the king of Babylon had Zedekiah’s sons put to death while Zedekiah was forced to watch. The king of Babylon also had all the nobles of Judah put to death. 7 Then he had Zedekiah’s eyes put out and had him bound in chains to be led off to Babylon. 8 The Babylonians burned down the royal palace, the temple of the LORD, and the people’s homes, and they tore down the wall of Jerusalem. 9 Then Nebuzaradan, the captain of the royal guard, took captive the rest of the people who were left in the city. He carried them off to Babylon along with the people who had deserted to him. 10 But he left behind in the land of Judah some of the poor people who owned nothing. He gave them fields and vineyards at that time.

11 Now King Nebuchadnezzar of Babylon had issued orders concerning Jeremiah. He had passed them on through Nebuzaradan, the captain of his royal guard, 12 “Find Jeremiah and look out for him. Do not do anything to harm him, but do with him whatever he tells you.” 13 So Nebuzaradan (the captain of the royal guard), Nebushazban (who was a chief officer), Nergal-Sharezer (who

REFLECT

Was the destruction of Jerusalem just? Why did God allow this destruction to fall on His people?

was a high official), and all the other officers of the king of Babylon 14 sent and had Jeremiah brought from the courtyard of the
guardhouse. They turned him over to Gedaliah, the son of Ahikam and the grandson of Shaphan, to take him home with him.
But Jeremiah stayed among the people.

EBED MELECH IS PROMISED DELIVERANCE BECAUSE OF HIS FAITH

15 Now the LORD's message had come to Jeremiah while he was
still confined in the courtyard of the guardhouse, 16 "Go and tell
Ebed-Melech the Nubian, 'This is what the LORD of Heaven's Armies, the God of Israel, has said, "I will carry out against this city
what I promised. It will mean disaster and not good fortune for
it. When that disaster happens, you will be there to see it. 17 But
I will rescue you when it happens. I, the LORD, affirm it! You will
not be handed over to those whom you fear. 18 I will certainly
save you. You will not fall victim to violence. You will escape
with your life because you trust in me. I, the LORD, affirm it!"'"

JEREMIAH IS SET FREE A SECOND TIME

40 The LORD spoke to Jeremiah after Nebuzaradan the captain of the royal guard had set him free at Ramah. He had
taken him there in chains along with all the people from Jerusalem and Judah who were being carried off to exile to Babylon.
2 The captain of the royal guard took Jeremiah aside and said to
him, "The LORD your God threatened this place with this disaster. 3 Now he has brought it about. The LORD has done just as
he threatened to do. This disaster has happened because you
people sinned against the LORD and did not obey him. 4 But
now, Jeremiah, today I will set you free from the chains on your
wrists. If you would like to come to Babylon with me, come along
and I will take care of you. But if you prefer not to come to Babylon with me, you are not required to do so. You are free to go
anywhere in the land you want to go. Go wherever you choose."
5 Before Jeremiah could turn to leave, the captain of the guard
added, "Go back to Gedaliah, the son of Ahikam and grandson
of Shaphan, whom the king of Babylon appointed to govern the
towns of Judah. Go back and live with him among the people. Or
go wherever else you choose." Then the captain of the guard gave
Jeremiah some food and a present and let him go. 6 So Jeremiah
went to Gedaliah son of Ahikam at Mizpah and lived there with
him. He stayed there to live among the people who had been left
in the land of Judah.

A SMALL JUDEAN PROVINCE IS ESTABLISHED AT MIZPAH

7 Now some of the officers of the Judean army and their troops
had been hiding in the countryside. They heard that the king of
Babylon had appointed Gedaliah son of Ahikam to govern the
country. They also heard that he had been put in charge over
the men, women, and children from the poorer classes of the
land who had not been carried off into exile in Babylon. 8 So all
these officers and their troops came to Gedaliah at Mizpah. The
officers who came were Ishmael son of Nethaniah, Johanan and

Jonathan the sons of Kareah, Seraiah son of Tanhumeth, the
sons of Ephai the Netophathite, and Jezaniah son of the Maacathite. 9 Gedaliah, the son of Ahikam and grandson of Shaphan,
took an oath so as to give them and their troops some assurance of safety. "Do not be afraid to submit to the Babylonians.
Settle down in the land and submit to the king of Babylon. Then
things will go well for you. 10 I for my part will stay at Mizpah to
represent you before the Babylonians whenever they come to
us. You for your part go ahead and harvest the wine, the dates,
the figs, and the olive oil, and store them in jars. Go ahead and
settle down in the towns that you have taken over." 11 Moreover,
all the Judeans who were in Moab, Ammon, Edom, and all the
other countries heard what had happened. They heard that the
king of Babylon had allowed some people to stay in Judah and
that he had appointed Gedaliah, the son of Ahikam and grandson of Shaphan, to govern them. 12 So all these Judeans returned
to the land of Judah from the places where they had been scattered. They came to Gedaliah at Mizpah. Thus they harvested a
large amount of wine and dates and figs.

ISHMAEL MURDERS GEDALIAH AND CARRIES OFF THE JUDEANS AT MIZPAH AS CAPTIVES

13 Johanan, son of Kareah, and all the officers of the troops that
had been hiding in the open country came to Gedaliah at Mizpah. 14 They said to him, "Are you at all aware that King Baalis of
Ammon has sent Ishmael son of Nethaniah to kill you?" But Gedaliah son of Ahikam would not believe them. 15 Then Johanan son
of Kareah spoke privately to Gedaliah there at Mizpah, "Let me
go and kill Ishmael the son of Nethaniah before anyone knows
about it. Otherwise he will kill you and all the Judeans who have
rallied around you will be scattered. Then what remains of Judah will disappear." 16 But Gedaliah son of Ahikam said to Johanan son of Kareah, "Do not do that because what you are saying
about Ishmael is not true."

41 But in the seventh month Ishmael, the son of Nethaniah
and grandson of Elishama, who was a member of the royal
family and had been one of Zedekiah's chief officers, came with
ten of his men to Gedaliah son of Ahikam at Mizpah. While they
were eating a meal together with him there at Mizpah, 2 Ishmael
son of Nethaniah and the ten men who were with him stood up,
pulled out their swords, and killed Gedaliah, the son of Ahikam
and grandson of Shaphan. Thus Ishmael killed the man that the
king of Babylon had appointed to govern the country. 3 Ishmael
also killed all the Judeans who were with Gedaliah at Mizpah
and the Babylonian soldiers who happened to be there.

4 On the day after Gedaliah had been murdered, before anyone
even knew about it, 5 eighty men arrived from Shechem, Shiloh,
and Samaria. They had shaved off their beards, torn their clothes,
and cut themselves to show they were mourning. They were carrying grain offerings and incense to present at the temple of the
LORD in Jerusalem. 6 Ishmael son of Nethaniah went out from
Mizpah to meet them. He was pretending to cry as he walked
along. When he met them, he said to them, "Come with me to
meet Gedaliah son of Ahikam." 7 But as soon as they were inside

the city, Ishmael son of Nethaniah and the men who were with
him slaughtered them and threw their bodies in a cistern. 8But
there were ten men among them who said to Ishmael, "Do not
kill us. For we will give you the stores of wheat, barley, olive oil,
and honey we have hidden in a field." So he spared their lives and
did not kill them along with the rest. 9Now the cistern where
Ishmael threw all the dead bodies of those he had killed was a
large one that King Asa had constructed as part of his defenses
against King Baasha of Israel. Ishmael son of Nethaniah filled
it with dead bodies. 10Then Ishmael took captive all the people
who were still left alive in Mizpah. This included the royal princesses and all the rest of the people in Mizpah that Nebuzaradan, the captain of the royal guard, had put under the authority
of Gedaliah son of Ahikam. Ishmael son of Nethaniah took all
these people captive and set out to cross over to the Ammonites.

JOHANAN RESCUES THE PEOPLE ISHMAEL HAD CARRIED OFF

11Johanan son of Kareah and all the army officers who were with
him heard about all the atrocities that Ishmael son of Nethaniah had committed. 12So they took all their troops and went
to fight against Ishmael son of Nethaniah. They caught up with
him near the large pool at Gibeon. 13When all the people that
Ishmael had taken captive saw Johanan son of Kareah and all
the army officers with him, they were glad. 14All those people
that Ishmael had taken captive from Mizpah turned and went
over to Johanan son of Kareah. 15But Ishmael son of Nethaniah
managed to escape from Johanan along with eight of his men,
and he went on over to Ammon.

16Johanan son of Kareah and all the army officers who were
with him led off all the people who had been left alive at Mizpah.
They had rescued them from Ishmael son of Nethaniah after he
killed Gedaliah son of Ahikam. They led off the men, women, children, soldiers, and court officials whom they had brought away
from Gibeon. 17They set out to go to Egypt to get away from the
Babylonians, but stopped at Geruth Kimham near Bethlehem.
18They were afraid of what the Babylonians might do because
Ishmael son of Nethaniah had killed Gedaliah son of Ahikam,
whom the king of Babylon had appointed to govern the country.

THE SURVIVORS ASK THE LORD FOR ADVICE BUT REFUSE TO FOLLOW IT

42 Then all the army officers, including Johanan son of Kareah and Jezaniah son of Hoshaiah and all the people of
every class, went to the prophet Jeremiah. 2They said to him,
"Please grant our request and pray to the LORD your God for
all those of us who are still left alive here. For, as you yourself
can see, there are only a few of us left out of the many there
were before. 3Pray that the LORD your God will tell us where we
should go and what we should do." 4The prophet Jeremiah answered them, "Agreed! I will indeed pray to the LORD your God
as you have asked. I will tell you everything the LORD replies in
response to you. I will not keep anything back from you." 5They
answered Jeremiah, "May the LORD be a true and faithful witness

against us if we do not do just as the LORD your God sends you
to tell us to do. 6 We will obey what the LORD our God to whom
we are sending you tells us to do. It does not matter whether we
like what he tells us or not. We will obey what he tells us to do
so that things will go well for us."

7 Ten days later the LORD's message came to Jeremiah. 8 So Jeremiah summoned Johanan son of Kareah and all the army officers who were with him and all the people of every class. 9 Then
Jeremiah said to them, "You sent me to the LORD God of Israel
to make your request known to him. Here is what he says to you:
10 'If you will only stay in this land, I will build you up. I will not
tear you down. I will firmly plant you. I will not uproot you. For I
am filled with sorrow because of the disaster that I have brought
on you. 11 Do not be afraid of the king of Babylon whom you now
fear. Do not be afraid of him because I will be with you to save
you and to rescue you from his power. I, the LORD, affirm it! 12 I
will have compassion on you so that he in turn will have mercy
on you and allow you to return to your land.'

13 "You must not disobey the LORD your God by saying, 'We
will not stay in this land.' 14 You must not say, 'No, we will not
stay. Instead we will go and live in the land of Egypt where we
will not face war, or hear the enemy's trumpet calls, or starve for
lack of food.' 15 If you people who remain in Judah do that, then
listen to the LORD's message. This is what the LORD of Heaven's
Armies, the God of Israel, has said, 'If you are so determined to
go to Egypt that you go and settle there, 16 the wars you fear will
catch up with you there in the land of Egypt. The starvation you
are worried about will follow you there to Egypt. You will die
there. 17 All the people who are determined to go and settle in
Egypt will die from war, starvation, or disease. No one will survive or escape the disaster I will bring on them.' 18 For the LORD
of Heaven's Armies, the God of Israel, says, 'If you go to Egypt, I
will pour out my wrath on you just as I poured out my anger and
wrath on the citizens of Jerusalem. You will become an object of
horror and ridicule, an example of those who have been cursed
and that people use in pronouncing a curse. You will never see
this place again.'

19 "The LORD has told you people who remain in Judah, 'Do not
go to Egypt.' Be very sure of this: I warn you here and now. 20 You
are making a fatal mistake. For you sent me to the LORD your
God and asked me, 'Pray to the LORD our God for us. Tell us what
the LORD our God says, and we will do it.' 21 This day I have told
you what he said. But you do not want to obey the LORD your
God by doing what he sent me to tell you. 22 So now be very sure
of this: You will die from war, starvation, or disease in the place
where you want to go and live."

43 Jeremiah finished telling all the people all these things
the LORD their God had sent him to tell them. 2 Then Azariah son of Hoshaiah, Johanan son of Kareah, and other arrogant
men said to Jeremiah, "You are telling a lie! The LORD our God
did not send you to tell us, 'You must not go to Egypt and settle
there.' 3 But Baruch son of Neriah is stirring you up against us.
He wants to hand us over to the Babylonians so that they will
kill us or carry us off into exile in Babylon." 4 So Johanan son of

Kareah, all the army officers, and all the rest of the people did not obey the LORD's command to stay in the land of Judah. 5 Instead Johanan son of Kareah and all the army officers led off all the Judean remnant who had come back to live in the land of Judah from all the nations where they had been scattered. 6 They also led off all the men, women, children, and royal princesses that Nebuzaradan, the captain of the royal guard, had left with Gedaliah, the son of Ahikam and grandson of Shaphan; this included the prophet Jeremiah and Baruch son of Neriah. 7 They went on to Egypt because they refused to obey the LORD, and came to Tahpanhes.

JEREMIAH PREDICTS THAT NEBUCHADNEZZAR WILL PLUNDER EGYPT AND ITS GODS

8 At Tahpanhes the LORD's message came to Jeremiah: 9 "Take some large stones and bury them in the mortar of the clay pavement at the entrance of Pharaoh's residence here in Tahpanhes. Do it while the people of Judah present there are watching. 10 Then tell them, 'The LORD of Heaven's Armies, the God of Israel, says, "I will bring my servant King Nebuchadnezzar of Babylon. I will set his throne over these stones that I have buried. He will pitch his royal tent over them. 11 He will come and attack Egypt. Those who are destined to die of disease will die of disease. Those who are destined to be carried off into exile will be carried off into exile. Those who are destined to die in war will die in war. 12 He will set fire to the temples of the gods of Egypt. He will burn their gods or carry them off as captives. He will pick Egypt clean like a shepherd picks the lice from his clothing. He will leave there unharmed. 13 He will demolish the sacred pillars in the temple of the sun in Egypt and will burn down the temples of the gods of Egypt."'"

THE LORD WILL PUNISH THE JUDEAN EXILES IN EGYPT FOR THEIR IDOLATRY

44 The LORD spoke to Jeremiah concerning all the Judeans who were living in the land of Egypt, those in Migdol, Tahpanhes, Memphis, and in the region of southern Egypt: 2 "The LORD of Heaven's Armies, the God of Israel, says, 'You have seen all the disaster I brought on Jerusalem and all the towns of Judah. Indeed, they now lie in ruins and are deserted. 3 This happened because of the wickedness the people living there did. They made me angry by worshiping and offering sacrifices to other gods whom neither they nor you nor your ancestors previously knew. 4 I sent my servants the prophets to you people over and over again warning you not to do this disgusting thing I hate. 5 But the people of Jerusalem and Judah would not listen or pay any attention. They would not stop the wickedness they were doing nor quit sacrificing to other gods. 6 So my anger and my wrath were poured out and burned like a fire through the towns of Judah and the streets of Jerusalem. That is why they have become the desolate ruins that they are today.'

7 "So now the LORD God of Heaven's Armies, the God of Israel, asks, 'Why will you do such great harm to yourselves? Why should every man, woman, child, and baby of yours be destroyed from the midst of Judah? Why should you leave yourselves without a

remnant? 8 That is what will result from your making me angry
by what you are doing. You are making me angry by sacrificing
to other gods here in the land of Egypt where you live. You will
be destroyed for doing that! You will become an example used
in curses and an object of ridicule among all the nations of the
earth. 9 Have you forgotten all the wicked things that have been
done in the towns of Judah and in the streets of Jerusalem by
your ancestors, by the kings of Judah and their wives, and by
you and your wives? 10 To this day your people have shown no
contrition! They have not revered me nor followed the laws and
statutes I commanded you and your ancestors.'

11 "Because of this, the LORD of Heaven's Armies, the God of Israel, says, 'I am determined to bring disaster on you, even to the
point of destroying all the Judeans here. 12 I will see to it that all
the Judean remnant that was determined to go and live in the
land of Egypt will be destroyed. Here in the land of Egypt they
will fall in battle or perish from starvation. People of every class
will die in war or from starvation. They will become an object of
horror and ridicule, an example of those who have been cursed
and that people use in pronouncing a curse. 13 I will punish those
who live in the land of Egypt with war, starvation, and disease,
just as I punished Jerusalem. 14 None of the Judean remnant who
have come to live in the land of Egypt will escape or survive to
return to the land of Judah. Though they long to return and live
there, none of them shall return except a few fugitives.'"

15 Then all the men who were aware that their wives were sacrificing to other gods, as well as all their wives, answered Jeremiah—there was a great crowd of them representing all the people
who lived in northern and southern Egypt—16 "We will not listen
to what you claim the LORD has spoken to us! 17 Instead we will
do everything we vowed we would do. We will sacrifice and pour
out drink offerings to the goddess called the Queen of Heaven
just as we and our ancestors, our kings, and our leaders previously did in the towns of Judah and in the streets of Jerusalem.
For then we had plenty of food, were well off, and had no troubles. 18 But ever since we stopped sacrificing and pouring out
drink offerings to the Queen of Heaven, we have been in great
need. Our people have died in wars or of starvation." 19 The wom-
en added, "We did indeed sacrifice and pour out drink offerings
to the Queen of Heaven. But it was with the full knowledge and
approval of our husbands that we made cakes in her image and
poured out drink offerings to her."

20 Then Jeremiah replied to all the people, both men and wom-
en, who responded to him in this way: 21 "The LORD did indeed
remember and call to mind what you did! He remembered the
incense you and your ancestors, your kings, your leaders, and all
the rest of the people of the land offered to other gods in the
towns of Judah and in the streets of Jerusalem. 22 Finally the
LORD could no longer endure your wicked deeds and the disgusting things you did. That is why your land has become the
desolate, uninhabited ruin that it is today. That is why it has become a proverbial example used in curses. 23 You have sacrificed
to other gods. You have sinned against the LORD! You have not
obeyed the LORD! You have not followed his laws, his statutes,

and his decrees. That is why this disaster that is evident to this
day has happened to you."
24 Then Jeremiah spoke to all the people, particularly to all the
women, "Listen to the LORD's message, all you people of Judah
who are in Egypt. 25 This is what the LORD of Heaven's Armies,
the God of Israel, has said, 'You women have confirmed by your
actions what you vowed with your lips! You said, "We will certainly carry out our vows to sacrifice and pour out drink offerings to the Queen of Heaven." Well, then fulfill your vows! Carry
them out!' 26 But listen to the LORD's message, all you people
of Judah who are living in the land of Egypt: The LORD says, 'I
hereby swear by my own great name that none of the people of
Judah who are living anywhere in Egypt will ever again invoke
my name in their oaths! Never again will any of them use it in
an oath saying, "As surely as the Sovereign LORD lives." 27 I will
indeed see to it that disaster, not prosperity, happens to them.
All the people of Judah who are in the land of Egypt will die in
war or from starvation until not one of them is left. 28 Some who
survive the battle will return to the land of Judah from the land
of Egypt. But they will be very few indeed! Then the Judean remnant who have come to live in the land of Egypt will know whose
word proves true, mine or theirs.' 29 Moreover the LORD says,
'I will make something happen to prove that I will punish you
in this place. I will do it so that you will know that my threats
to bring disaster on you will prove true. 30 I, the LORD, promise
that I will hand Pharaoh Hophra king of Egypt over to his enemies who are seeking to kill him. I will do that just as surely as I
handed King Zedekiah of Judah over to King Nebuchadnezzar
of Babylon, his enemy who was seeking to kill him.'"

BARUCH IS REBUKED BUT ALSO COMFORTED

45 The prophet Jeremiah spoke to Baruch son of Neriah while
he was writing down in a scroll the words that Jeremiah
spoke to him. (This happened in the fourth year that Jehoiakim
son of Josiah was ruling over Judah.) 2 Jeremiah said, "The LORD
God of Israel has a message for you, Baruch. 3 'You have said, "I
feel so hopeless! For the LORD has added sorrow to my suffering.
I am worn out from groaning. I can't find any rest."'"
4 The LORD told Jeremiah, "Tell Baruch, 'The LORD says, "I am
about to tear down what I have built and to uproot what I have
planted. I will do this throughout the whole earth. 5 Are you looking for great things for yourself? Do not look for such things.
For I, the LORD, affirm that I am about to bring disaster on all
humanity. But I will allow you to escape with your life wherever you go."'"

PROPHECIES AGAINST FOREIGN NATIONS

46 This was the LORD's message to the prophet Jeremiah
about the nations.

THE PROPHECY ABOUT EGYPT'S DEFEAT AT CARCHEMISH

2 He spoke about Egypt and the army of Pharaoh Necho king
of Egypt, which was encamped along the Euphrates River at

Carchemish. Now this was the army that King Nebuchadnezzar of Babylon defeated in the fourth year that Jehoiakim son
of Josiah was ruling over Judah:
3 "Fall into ranks with your shields ready!
Prepare to march into battle!
4 Harness the horses to the chariots;
mount your horses!
Take your positions with helmets on;
ready your spears!
Put on the armor!

5 "What do I see?
The soldiers are frightened.
They are retreating.
They are being scattered.
They have fled for refuge
without looking back.
Terror is all around them," says the LORD.
6 But even the swiftest cannot get away.
Even the strongest cannot escape.
There in the north by the Euphrates River
they have stumbled and fallen in defeat.
7 Who is this that rises like the Nile,
like its streams turbulent at flood stage?
8 Egypt rises like the Nile,
like its streams turbulent at flood stage.
Egypt said, 'I will arise and cover the earth.
I will destroy cities and the people
who inhabit them.'
9 Go ahead and charge into battle, you horsemen!
Drive furiously, you charioteers!
Let the soldiers march out into battle,
those from Ethiopia and Libya who carry shields,
and those from Lydia who are armed
with the bow.
10 But that day belongs to the Sovereign
LORD of Heaven's Armies.
It is a day of reckoning, when he will
pay back his adversaries.
His sword will devour them until its
appetite is satisfied.
It will drink its fill from their blood!
Indeed it will be a sacrifice for the Sovereign
LORD of Heaven's Armies
in the land of the north by the Euphrates River.
11 Go up to Gilead and get medicinal ointment,
you dear poor people of Egypt.
But it will prove useless no matter how
much medicine you use;
there will be no healing for you.
12 The nations have heard of your shameful defeat.
Your cries of distress fill the earth.
One soldier has stumbled over another
and both of them have fallen down defeated."

THE LORD PREDICTS THAT NEBUCHADNEZZAR WILL ATTACK AND PLUNDER EGYPT

13 The LORD spoke to the prophet Jeremiah about Nebuchadnezzar coming to attack the land of Egypt:

14 "Make an announcement throughout Egypt.
Proclaim it in Migdol, Memphis, and Tahpanhes.
'Take your positions and prepare to do battle.
For the enemy army is destroying all
the nations around you.'
15 Why will your soldiers be defeated?
They will not stand because I, the LORD,
will thrust them down.
16 I will make many stumble.
They will fall over one another in their hurry to flee.
They will say, 'Get up!
Let's go back to our own people.
Let's go back to our homelands
because the enemy is coming to destroy us.'
17 There at home they will say, 'Pharaoh
king of Egypt is just a big noise!
He has let the most opportune moment pass by.'
18 I the King, whose name is the LORD of
Heaven's Armies, swear this:
'I swear as surely as I live that a conqueror is coming.
He will be as imposing as Mount Tabor
is among the mountains,
as Mount Carmel is against the backdrop of the sea.
19 Pack your bags for exile,
you inhabitants of poor dear Egypt.
For Memphis will be laid waste.
It will lie in ruins and be uninhabited.
20 Egypt is like a beautiful young cow.
But northern armies will attack her
like swarms of stinging flies.
21 Even her mercenaries
will prove to be like pampered, well-fed calves.
For they too will turn and run away.
They will not stand their ground
when the time for them to be destroyed comes,
the time for them to be punished.
22 Egypt will run away, hissing like a snake,
as the enemy comes marching up in force.
They will come against her with axes
as if they were woodsmen chopping down trees.
23 The population of Egypt is like a
vast, impenetrable forest.
But I, the LORD, affirm that the
enemy will cut them down.
For those who chop them down will be
more numerous than locusts.
They will be too numerous to count.
24 Poor dear Egypt will be put to shame.
She will be handed over to the people from the north.'"

25 The LORD of Heaven's Armies, the God of Israel, says, "I will
punish Amon, the god of Thebes. I will punish Egypt, its gods, and
its kings. I will punish Pharaoh and all who trust in him. 26 I will
hand them over to Nebuchadnezzar and his troops, who want
to kill them. But later on, people will live in Egypt again as they
did in former times. I, the LORD, affirm it!"

A PROMISE OF HOPE FOR ISRAEL

27 "You descendants of Jacob, my servants, do not be afraid;
do not be terrified, people of Israel.
For I will rescue you and your descendants
from the faraway lands where you are captives.
The descendants of Jacob will return to
their land and enjoy peace.
They will be secure and no one will terrify them.
28 I, the LORD, tell you not to be afraid,
you descendants of Jacob, my servant,
for I am with you.
Though I completely destroy all the
nations where I scatter you,
I will not completely destroy you.
I will indeed discipline you but only in due measure.
I will not allow you to go entirely unpunished."

REFLECT

How do these verses provide hope for the exiles of Judah? What does this show about God's heart for His people?

JUDGMENT ON THE PHILISTINE CITIES

47 This was the LORD's message to the prophet Jeremiah
about the Philistines before Pharaoh attacked Gaza:
2 "Look! Enemies are gathering in the
north like water rising in a river.
They will be like an overflowing stream.
They will overwhelm the whole country
and everything in it like a flood.
They will overwhelm the cities and their inhabitants.
People will cry out in alarm.
Everyone living in the country will cry out in pain.
3 Fathers will hear the hoofbeats of the enemies' horses,
the clatter of their chariots and the
rumbling of their wheels.
They will not turn back to save their children
because they will be paralyzed with fear.
4 For the time has come
to destroy all the Philistines.
The time has come to destroy all the help
that remains for Tyre and Sidon.
For I, the LORD, will destroy the Philistines,
that remnant that came from the island of Crete.
5 The people of Gaza will shave their heads in mourning.
The people of Ashkelon will be struck dumb.
How long will you gash yourselves to show your sorrow,
you who remain of Philistia's power?
6 How long will you cry out, 'Oh, sword of the LORD,
how long will it be before you stop killing?
Go back into your sheath;
stay there and rest!'

7 But how can it rest
when I, the LORD, have given it orders?
I have ordered it to attack
the people of Ashkelon and the seacoast."

JUDGMENT AGAINST MOAB

48 The LORD of Heaven's Armies, the God of Israel, spoke about Moab:
"Sure to be judged is Nebo! Indeed, it will be destroyed.
Kiriathaim will suffer disgrace. It will be captured!
Its fortress will suffer disgrace. It will be torn down!
2 People will not praise Moab anymore.
The enemy will capture Heshbon and
plot how to destroy Moab,
saying, 'Come, let's put an end to that nation!'
City of Madmen, you will also be destroyed.
A destructive army will march against you.
3 Cries of anguish will arise in Horonaim,
'Oh, the ruin and great destruction!'

4 "Moab will be crushed.
Her children will cry out in distress.
5 Indeed they will climb the slopes of Luhith,
weeping continually as they go.
For on the road down to Horonaim
they will hear the cries of distress over the destruction.
6 They will hear, 'Run! Save yourselves;
even if you must be like a lonely
shrub in the wilderness!'

7 "Moab, you trust in the things you do and in your riches.
So you too will be conquered.
Your god Chemosh will go into exile
along with his priests and his officials.
8 The destroyer will come against every town.
Not one town will escape.
The towns in the valley will be destroyed.
The cities on the high plain will be laid waste.
I, the LORD, have spoken.
9 Set up a gravestone for Moab,
for it will certainly be laid in ruins!
Its cities will be laid waste
and become uninhabited.
10 A curse on anyone who is lax in doing the LORD's work!
A curse on anyone who keeps from
carrying out his destruction!

11 "From its earliest days Moab has lived undisturbed.
It has never been taken into exile.
Its people are like wine allowed to settle
undisturbed on its dregs,
never poured out from one jar to another.
They are like wine that tastes like it always did,
whose aroma has remained unchanged.

12 But the time is coming when I will send
men against Moab who will empty it out.
They will empty the towns of their people,
then will lay those towns in ruins.
I, the LORD, affirm it!
13 The people of Moab will be disappointed
by their god Chemosh.
They will be as disappointed as the people of Israel were
when they put their trust in the calf god at Bethel.
14 How can you men of Moab say, 'We are heroes,
men who are mighty in battle?'
15 Moab will be destroyed. Its towns will be invaded.
Its finest young men will be slaughtered.
I, the King, the LORD of Heaven's Armies, affirm it!
16 Moab's destruction is at hand.
Disaster will come on it quickly.
17 Mourn for that nation, all you nations living around it,
all you nations that know of its fame.
Mourn and say, 'Alas, its powerful
influence has been broken!
Its glory and power have been done away with!'
18 Come down from your place of honor;
sit on the dry ground, you who live in Dibon.
For the one who will destroy Moab will attack you;
he will destroy your fortifications.
19 You who live in Aroer,
stand by the road and watch.
Question the man who is fleeing and
the woman who is escaping.
Ask them, 'What has happened?'
20 They will answer, 'Moab is disgraced, for it has fallen!
Wail and cry out in mourning!
Announce along the Arnon River
that Moab has been destroyed.'

21 "Judgment will come on the cities on the high plain: on Holon, Jahzah, and Mephaath; 22 on Dibon, Nebo, and Beth Diblathaim; 23 on Kiriathaim, Beth Gamul, and Beth Meon; 24 on
Kerioth and Bozrah. It will come on all the towns of Moab, both
far and near. 25 Moab's might will be crushed. Its power will be
broken. I, the LORD, affirm it!

26 "Moab has vaunted itself against me.
So make him drunk with the wine of my wrath
until he splashes around in his own vomit,
until others treat him as a laughingstock.
27 For did not you people of Moab laugh
at the people of Israel?
Did you think that they were nothing but thieves,
that you shook your head in contempt
every time you talked about them?
28 Leave your towns, you inhabitants of Moab.
Go and live in the cliffs.
Be like a dove that makes its nest
high on the sides of a ravine.

29 I have heard how proud the people of Moab are,
I know how haughty they are.
I have heard how arrogant, proud, and haughty they are,
what a high opinion they have of themselves.
30 I, the LORD, affirm that I know how arrogant they are.
But their pride is ill founded.
Their boastings will prove to be false.
31 So I will weep with sorrow for Moab.
I will cry out in sadness for all Moab.
I will moan for the people of Kir Heres.
32 I will weep for the grapevines of Sibmah
just like the town of Jazer weeps over them.
Their branches once spread as far as the Dead Sea.
They reached as far as the town of Jazer.
The destroyer will ravage
her fig, date, and grape crops.
33 Joy and gladness will disappear
from the fruitful land of Moab.
I will stop the flow of wine from the winepresses.
No one will stomp on the grapes there and shout for joy.
The shouts there will be shouts of soldiers,
not the shouts of those making wine.
34 Cries of anguish raised from Heshbon and Elealeh
will be sounded as far as Jahaz.
They will be sounded from Zoar as far as
Horonaim and Eglath Shelishiyah.
For even the waters of Nimrim will be dried up.
35 I will put an end in Moab
to those who make offerings at her places of worship.
I will put an end to those who sacrifice to other gods.
I, the LORD, affirm it!
36 So my heart moans for Moab
like a flute playing a funeral song.
Yes, like a flute playing a funeral song,
my heart moans for the people of Kir Heres.
For the wealth they have gained will perish.
37 For all of them will shave their heads in mourning.
They will all cut off their beards to show their sorrow.
They will all make gashes in their hands.
They will all put on sackcloth.
38 On all the housetops in Moab
and in all its public squares
there will be nothing but mourning.
For I will break Moab like an unwanted jar.
I, the LORD, affirm it!
39 Oh, how shattered Moab will be!
Oh, how her people will wail!
Oh, how she will turn away in shame!
Moab will become an object of ridicule,
a terrifying sight to all the nations that surround her."

40 For the LORD says,
"Look! Like an eagle with outspread wings
a nation will swoop down on Moab.

41 Her towns will be captured;
her fortresses will be taken.
At that time the soldiers of Moab will be frightened
like a woman in labor.
42 Moab will be destroyed and no longer be a nation,
because she has vaunted herself against the LORD.
43 Terror, pits, and traps are in store
for the people who live in Moab.
I, the LORD, affirm it!
44 Anyone who flees at the sound of terror
will fall into a pit.
Anyone who climbs out of the pit
will be caught in a trap.
For the time is coming
when I will punish the people of Moab.
I, the LORD, affirm it!
45 In the shadows of the walls of Heshbon
those trying to escape will stand helpless.
For a fire will burst forth from Heshbon.
Flames will shoot out from the former territory of Sihon.
They will burn the foreheads of the people of Moab,
the skulls of those war-loving people.
46 Moab, you are doomed!
You people who worship Chemosh will be destroyed.
Your sons will be taken away captive.
Your daughters will be carried away into exile.
47 Yet in future days
I will reverse Moab's ill fortune,"
says the LORD.

The judgment against Moab ends here.

JUDGMENT AGAINST AMMON

49 The LORD spoke about the Ammonites:
"Do you think there are not any people
of the nation of Israel remaining?
Do you think there are not any of them
remaining to reinherit their land?
Is that why you people who worship the god Milcom
have taken possession of the territory
of Gad and live in his cities?
2 Because you did that,
I, the LORD, affirm that a time is coming
when I will make Rabbah, the capital city of Ammon,
hear the sound of the battle cry.
It will become a mound covered with ruins.
Its villages will be burned to the ground.
Then Israel will take back its land
from those who took their land from them.
I, the LORD, affirm it!
3 Wail, you people in Heshbon, because
Ai in Ammon is destroyed.
Cry out in anguish, you people in the
villages surrounding Rabbah.

Put on sackcloth and cry out in mourning.
Run about covered with gashes.
For your god Milcom will go into exile
along with his priests and officials.
4 Why do you brag about your great power?
Your power is ebbing away, you
rebellious people of Ammon,
who trust in your riches and say,
'Who would dare to attack us?'
5 I will bring terror on you from every side,"
says the Sovereign LORD of Heaven's Armies.
"You will be scattered in every direction.
No one will gather the fugitives back together.
6 Yet in days to come
I will reverse Ammon's ill fortune."
says the LORD.

JUDGMENT AGAINST EDOM

7 The LORD of Heaven's Armies spoke about Edom:
"Is wisdom no longer to be found in Teman?
Can Edom's counselors not give her any good advice?
Has all their wisdom turned bad?
8 Turn and flee! Take up refuge in remote places,
you people who live in Dedan.
For I will bring disaster on the descendants of Esau.
I have decided it is time for me to punish them.
9 If grape pickers came to pick your grapes,
would they not leave a few grapes behind?
If robbers came at night,
would they not pillage only what they needed?
10 But I will strip everything away from Esau's descendants.
I will uncover their hiding places so they cannot hide.
Their children, relatives, and neighbors
will all be destroyed.
Not one of them will be left!
11 Leave your orphans behind and I will keep them alive.
Your widows, too, can depend on me."

12 For the LORD says, "If even those who did not deserve to drink
from the cup of my wrath must drink from it, do you think you
will go unpunished? You will not go unpunished, but must certainly drink from the cup of my wrath. 13 For I solemnly swear,"
says the LORD, "that Bozrah will become a pile of ruins. It will
become an object of horror and ridicule, an example to be used
in curses. All the towns around it will lie in ruins forever."

14 I said, "I have heard a message from the LORD.
A messenger has been sent among the nations to say,
'Gather your armies and march out against her!
Prepare to do battle with her!'"
15 The LORD says to Edom,
"I will certainly make you small among nations.
I will make you despised by all humankind.
16 The terror you inspire in others
and the arrogance of your heart have deceived you.

You may make your home in the clefts of the rocks;
you may occupy the highest places in the hills.
But even if you made your home where the eagles nest,
I would bring you down from there,"
says the LORD.
17 "Edom will become an object of horror.
All who pass by it will be filled with horror;
they will hiss out their scorn
because of all the disasters that have happened to it.
18 Edom will be destroyed like Sodom and Gomorrah
and the towns that were around them.
No one will live there.
No human being will settle in it,"
says the LORD.
19 "A lion coming up from the thick
undergrowth along the Jordan
scatters the sheep in the pastureland around it.
So too I will chase the Edomites off their land.
Then I will appoint over it whomever I choose.
For there is no one like me, and there is no
one who can call me to account.
There is no ruler who can stand up against me.
20 So listen to what I, the LORD,
have planned against Edom,
what I intend to do to the people who live in Teman.
Their little ones will be dragged off.
I will completely destroy their land
because of what they have done.
21 The people of the earth will quake when
they hear of their downfall.
Their cries of anguish will be heard all
the way to the Gulf of Aqaba.
22 Look! Like an eagle with outspread wings,
a nation will soar up and swoop down on Bozrah.
At that time the soldiers of Edom will be as fearful
as a woman in labor."

JUDGMENT AGAINST DAMASCUS

23 The LORD spoke about Damascus:
"The people of Hamath and Arpad will be dismayed
because they have heard bad news.
Their courage will melt away because of worry.
Their hearts will not be able to rest.
24 The people of Damascus will lose heart and turn to flee.
Panic will grip them.
Pain and anguish will seize them
like a woman in labor.
25 How deserted will that once-famous city be,
that city that was once filled with joy!
26 For her young men will fall in her city squares.
All her soldiers will be destroyed at that time,"
says the LORD of Heaven's Armies.
27 "I will set fire to the walls of Damascus;
it will burn up the palaces of Ben Hadad."

JUDGMENT AGAINST KEDAR AND HAZOR

28 The LORD spoke about Kedar and the kingdoms of Hazor that
King Nebuchadnezzar of Babylon conquered:
"Army of Babylon, go and attack Kedar.
Lay waste those who live in the eastern desert.
29 Their tents and their flocks will be taken away.
Their tent curtains, equipment, and
camels will be carried off.
People will shout to them,
'Terror is all around you!'"
30 The LORD says, "Flee quickly, you who live in Hazor.
Take up refuge in remote places.
For King Nebuchadnezzar of Babylon
has laid out plans to attack you.
He has formed his strategy on how to defeat you."
31 The LORD says, "Army of Babylon, go and attack
a nation that lives in peace and security.
They have no gates or walls to protect them.
They live all alone.
32 Their camels will be taken as plunder.
Their vast herds will be taken as spoil.
I will scatter to the four winds
those desert peoples who cut their
hair short at the temples.
I will bring disaster against them
from every direction," says the LORD.
33 "Hazor will become a permanent wasteland,
a place where only jackals live.
No one will live there.
No human being will settle in it."

JUDGMENT AGAINST ELAM

34 This was the LORD's message to the prophet Jeremiah about
Elam, which came early in the reign of King Zedekiah of Judah.
35 The LORD of Heaven's Armies said:
"I will kill all the archers of Elam,
who are the chief source of her military might.
36 I will cause enemies to blow through
Elam from every direction
like the winds blowing in from the four quarters of heaven.
I will scatter the people of Elam to the four winds.
There will not be any nation where the
refugees of Elam will not go.
37 I will make the people of Elam terrified of their enemies,
who are seeking to kill them.
I will vent my fierce anger
and bring disaster upon them," says the LORD.
"I will send armies chasing after them
until I have completely destroyed them.
38 I will establish my sovereignty over Elam.
I will destroy their king and their leaders," says the LORD.
39 "Yet in future days
I will reverse Elam's ill fortune,"
says the LORD.

JUDGMENT AGAINST BABYLON

50 The LORD spoke concerning Babylon and the land of Babylonia through the prophet Jeremiah.

2 "Announce the news among the nations! Proclaim it!
Signal for people to pay attention.
Declare the news! Do not hide it! Say:
'Babylon will be captured.
Bel will be put to shame.
Marduk will be dismayed.
Babylon's idols will be put to shame;
her disgusting images will be dismayed.
3 For a nation from the north will attack Babylon;
it will lay her land waste.
People and animals will flee out of it.
No one will inhabit it.'

4 "When that time comes," says the LORD,
"the people of Israel and Judah will
return to the land together.
They will come back with tears of repentance
as they seek the LORD their God.
5 They will ask the way to Zion;
they will turn their faces toward it.
They will come and bind themselves to the LORD
in a lasting covenant that will never be forgotten.

6 "My people have been lost sheep.
Their shepherds have allowed them to go astray.
They have wandered around in the mountains.
They have roamed from one mountain
and hill to another.
They have forgotten their resting place.
7 All who encountered them devoured them.
Their enemies who did this said, 'We
are not liable for punishment!
For those people have sinned against
the LORD, their true pasture.
They have sinned against the LORD in
whom their ancestors trusted.'

8 "People of Judah, get out of Babylon quickly!
Leave the land of Babylonia!
Be the first to depart.
Be like the male goats that lead the herd.
9 For I will rouse into action and
bring against Babylon
a host of mighty nations from the land of the north.
They will set up their battle lines against her.
They will come from the north and capture her.
Their arrows will be like a skilled soldier
who does not return from the battle empty-handed.
10 Babylonia will be plundered.
Those who plunder it will take all they want,"
says the LORD.

11 “People of Babylonia, you plundered my people.
That made you happy and glad.
You frolic about like calves in a pasture.
Your joyous sounds are like the neighs of a stallion.
12 But Babylonia will be put to great shame.
The land where you were born will be disgraced.
Indeed, Babylonia will become the least
important of all nations.
It will become a dry and barren desert.
13 After I vent my wrath on it, Babylon will be uninhabited.
It will be totally desolate.
All who pass by will be filled with horror
and will hiss out their scorn
because of all the disasters that have happened to it.

14 “Take up your battle positions all around Babylon,
all you soldiers who are armed with bows.
Shoot all your arrows at her! Do not hold any back!
For she has sinned against the LORD.
15 Shout the battle cry from all around the city.
She will throw up her hands in surrender;
her towers will fall.
Her walls will be torn down.
Because I, the LORD, am wreaking revenge,
take out your vengeance on her!
Do to her as she has done!
16 Kill all the farmers who sow the seed in the land of Babylon;
kill all those who wield the sickle at harvest time.
Let all the foreigners return to their own people.
Let them hurry back to their own lands
to escape destruction by that enemy army.

17 “The people of Israel are like scattered sheep
that lions have chased away.
First the king of Assyria devoured them.
Now, last of all, King Nebuchadnezzar of
Babylon has gnawed their bones.
18 So I, the LORD of Heaven’s Armies, the God of Israel, say:
‘I will punish the king of Babylon and his land
just as I punished the king of Assyria.
19 But I will restore the flock of Israel to their own pasture.
They will graze on Mount Carmel and the land of Bashan.
They will eat until they are full
on the hills of Ephraim and the land of Gilead.
20 When that time comes,
no guilt will be found in Israel.
No sin will be found in Judah.
For I will forgive those of them I have allowed to survive.
I, the LORD, affirm it!’”
21 The LORD says,
“Attack the land of Merathaim
and the people who live in Pekod.
Pursue, kill, and completely destroy them!
Do just as I have commanded you!

22 The noise of battle can be heard in the land of Babylonia.
There is the sound of great destruction.
23 Babylon hammered the whole world to pieces.
But see how that 'hammer' has been
broken and shattered!
See what an object of horror
Babylon has become among the nations!
24 I set a trap for you, Babylon;
you were caught before you knew it.
You fought against me;
so you were found and captured.
25 I have opened up the place where my weapons are stored.
I have brought out the weapons for carrying out my wrath.
For I, the Sovereign LORD of Heaven's Armies,
have work to carry out in the land of Babylonia.
26 Come from far away and attack Babylonia!
Open up the places where she stores her grain.
Pile her up in ruins. Destroy her completely!
Do not leave anyone alive!
27 Kill all her soldiers.
Let them be slaughtered.
They are doomed, for their day of reckoning has come,
the time for them to be punished."
28 Listen! Fugitives and refugees are coming
from the land of Babylon.
They are coming to Zion to declare there
how the LORD our God is getting revenge,
getting revenge for what they have done to his temple.

29 "Call for archers to come against Babylon!
Summon against her all who draw the bow.
Set up camp all around the city.
Do not allow anyone to escape!
Pay her back for what she has done.
Do to her what she has done to others.
For she has proudly defied me,
the Holy One of Israel.
30 So her young men will fall in her city squares.
All her soldiers will be destroyed at that time,"
says the LORD.
31 "Listen! I am opposed to you, you proud city,"
says the Sovereign LORD of Heaven's Armies.
"Indeed, your day of reckoning has come,
the time when I will punish you.
32 You will stumble and fall, you proud city;
no one will help you get up.
I will set fire to your towns;
it will burn up everything that surrounds you."
33 The LORD of Heaven's Armies says,
"The people of Israel are oppressed.
So too are the people of Judah.
All those who took them captive are
holding them prisoners.
They refuse to set them free.

34 But the one who will rescue them is strong.
His name is the LORD of Heaven's Armies.
He will strongly champion their cause.
As a result he will bring peace and rest to the earth,
but trouble and turmoil to the people who inhabit Babylonia.

35 "Destructive forces will come against the
Babylonians," says the LORD.
"They will come against the people who inhabit Babylonia,
against her leaders and her men of wisdom.
36 Destructive forces will come
against her false prophets;
they will be shown to be fools!
Destructive forces will come against her soldiers;
they will be filled with terror!
37 Destructive forces will come against
her horses and her chariots.
Destructive forces will come against all
the foreign troops within her;
they will be as frightened as women!
Destructive forces will come
against her treasures;
they will be taken away as plunder!
38 A drought will come upon her land;
her rivers and canals will be dried up.
All this will happen because her
land is filled with idols.
Her people act like madmen because
of those idols they fear.
39 Therefore desert creatures and jackals will live there;
ostriches too will dwell in it.
But no people will ever live there again;
no one will dwell there for all time to come.
40 I will destroy Babylonia just as I did
Sodom and Gomorrah and the neighboring towns.
No one will live there;
no human being will settle in it,"
says the LORD.
41 "Look! An army is about to come from the north.
A mighty nation and many kings are stirring into action
in faraway parts of the earth.
42 Its soldiers are armed with bows and spears.
They are cruel and show no mercy.
They sound like the roaring sea
as they ride forth on their horses.
Lined up in formation like men going into battle,
they are coming against you, fair Babylon.
43 The king of Babylon will become paralyzed with fear
when he hears news of their coming.
Anguish will grip him,
agony like that of a woman giving birth to a baby.

44 "A lion coming up from the thick
undergrowth along the Jordan

scatters the sheep in the pastureland around it.
So too I will chase the Babylonians off their land;
then I will appoint over it whomever I choose.
For there is no one like me.
There is no one who can call me to account.
There is no ruler that can stand up against me.
45 So listen to what I, the LORD, have
planned against Babylon,
what I intend to do to the people who
inhabit the land of Babylonia.
Their little ones will be dragged off like sheep.
I will completely destroy their land
because of what they have done.
46 The people of the earth will quake when they
hear Babylon has been captured.
Her cries of anguish will be heard by the other nations."
The LORD says:
"I will cause a destructive wind to blow
against Babylon and the people
who inhabit Babylonia.
2 I will send people to winnow Babylonia
like a wind blowing away chaff.
They will winnow her and strip her land bare.
This will happen when they come against
her from every direction,
when it is time to destroy her.
3 Do not give her archers time to string their bows
or to put on their coats of armor.
Do not spare any of her young men.
Completely destroy her whole army.
4 Let them fall slain in the land of Babylonia,
mortally wounded in the streets of her cities.

5 "For Israel and Judah will not be forsaken
by their God, the LORD of Heaven's Armies.
For the land of Babylonia is full of guilt
against the Holy One of Israel.
6 Get out of Babylonia quickly, you foreign people.
Flee to save your lives.
Do not let yourselves be killed because of her sins,
for it is time for the LORD to wreak his revenge.
He will pay Babylonia back for what she has done.
7 Babylonia had been a gold cup in the LORD's hand;
she had made the whole world drunk.
The nations had drunk from the wine of her wrath,
so they have all gone mad.
8 But suddenly Babylonia will fall
and be destroyed.
Cry out in mourning over it!
Get medicine for her wounds;
perhaps she can be healed!
9 Foreigners living there will say,
'We tried to heal her, but she could not be healed.
Let's leave Babylonia and each go back to his own country.

For judgment on her will be vast in its proportions.
It will be like it is piled up to heaven,
stacked up into the clouds.'
10 The exiles from Judah will say,
'The LORD has brought about a great deliverance for us!
Come on, let's go and proclaim in Zion
what the LORD our God has done!'

11 "Sharpen your arrows!
Fill your quivers!
The LORD will arouse a spirit of hostility
in the kings of Media,
for he intends to destroy Babylonia.
For that is how the LORD will get his revenge—
how he will get his revenge for the Babylonians'
destruction of his temple.
12 Give the signal to attack Babylon's wall!
Bring more guards;
post them all around the city.
Put men in ambush,
for the LORD will do what he has planned.
He will do what he said he would do
to the people of Babylon.

13 "You who live along the rivers of Babylon,
the time of your end has come.
You who are rich in plundered treasure,
it is time for your lives to be cut off.
14 The LORD of Heaven's Armies has solemnly sworn,
'I will fill your land with enemy soldiers.
They will swarm over it like locusts.
They will raise up shouts of victory over it.'
15 He is the one who by his power made the earth.
He is the one who by his wisdom fixed the world in place,
by his understanding he spread out the heavens.
16 When his voice thunders, the waters in the heavens roar.
He makes the clouds rise from the far-off horizons;
he makes the lightning flash out in the midst of the rain.
He unleashes the wind from the places where he stores it;
17 all idolaters will prove to be stupid and ignorant.
Every goldsmith will be disgraced by the idol he made.
For the image he forges is merely a sham;
there is no breath in any of those idols.
18 They are worthless, objects to be ridiculed.
When the time comes to punish them, they will be destroyed.
19 The LORD, who is the portion of the
descendants of Jacob, is not like them.
For he is the one who created everything,
including the people of Israel whom he claims as his own.
His name is the LORD of Heaven's Armies.

20 "Babylon, you are my war club,
my weapon for battle.
I used you to smash nations.

I used you to destroy kingdoms.
21 I used you to smash horses and their riders.
I used you to smash chariots and their drivers.
22 I used you to smash men and women.
I used you to smash old men and young men.
I used you to smash young men and young women.
23 I used you to smash shepherds and their flocks.
I used you to smash farmers and their teams of oxen.
I used you to smash governors and leaders."

24 "But I will repay Babylon
and all who live in Babylonia
for all the wicked things they did in Zion
right before the eyes of you Judeans,"
says the LORD.
25 The LORD says, "Beware! I am opposed to you, Babylon!
You are like a destructive mountain
that destroys all the earth.
I will unleash my power against you;
I will roll you off the cliffs and make you
like a burned-out mountain.
26 No one will use any of your stones as a cornerstone;
no one will use any of them in the foundation of his house.
For you will lie desolate forever,"
says the LORD.
27 "Raise up battle flags throughout the lands.
Sound the trumpets calling the nations to do battle.
Prepare the nations to do battle against Babylonia.
Call for these kingdoms to attack her:
Ararat, Minni, and Ashkenaz.
Appoint a commander to lead the attack.
Send horses against her like a swarm of locusts.
28 Prepare the nations to do battle against her.
Prepare the kings of the Medes.
Prepare their governors and all their leaders.
Prepare all the countries they rule to do battle against her.
29 The earth will tremble and writhe in agony;
for the LORD will carry out his plan.
He plans to make the land of Babylonia
a wasteland where no one lives.
30 The soldiers of Babylonia will stop fighting.
They will remain in their fortified cities.
They will lose their strength to do battle.
They will be as frightened as women.
The houses in her cities will be set on fire.
The gates of her cities will be broken down.
31 One runner after another will come
to the king of Babylon;
one messenger after another will come bringing news.
They will bring news to the king of Babylon
that his whole city has been captured.
32 They will report that the fords have been captured,
the reed marshes have been burned,
the soldiers are terrified.

33 For the LORD of Heaven's Armies, the God of Israel, says,
'Fair Babylon will be like a threshing floor
that has been trampled flat for harvest.
The time for her to be cut down and harvested
will come very soon.'

34 "King Nebuchadnezzar of Babylon
devoured me and drove my people out.
Like a monster from the deep he swallowed me.
He filled his belly with my riches;
he made me an empty dish.
He completely cleaned me out."
35 The person who lives in Zion says,
"May Babylon pay for the violence done
to me and to my relatives."
Jerusalem says,
"May those living in Babylonia pay for
the bloodshed of my people."
36 Therefore the LORD says,
"I will stand up for your cause.
I will pay the Babylonians back for
what they have done to you.
I will dry up their sea;
I will make their springs run dry.
37 Babylon will become a heap of ruins.
Jackals will make their home there.
It will become an object of horror and of hissing scorn,
a place where no one lives.
38 The Babylonians are all like lions roaring for prey;
they are like lion cubs growling for something to eat.
39 When their appetites are all stirred up,
I will set out a banquet for them.
I will make them drunk
so that they will pass out,
they will fall asleep forever,
they will never wake up,"
says the LORD.
40 "I will lead them off to be slaughtered
like lambs, rams, and male goats.

41 "See how Babylon has been captured!
See how the pride of the whole earth has been taken!
See what an object of horror
Babylon has become among the nations!
42 The sea has swept over Babylon.
She has been covered by a multitude of its waves.
43 The towns of Babylonia have become heaps of ruins.
She has become a dry and barren desert.
No one lives in those towns any more;
no one even passes through them.
44 I will punish the god Bel in Babylon.
I will make him spit out what he has swallowed.
The nations will not come streaming to him any longer.
Indeed, the walls of Babylon will fall.

45 "Get out of Babylon, my people!
Flee to save your lives
from the fierce anger of the LORD!
46 Do not lose your courage or become afraid
because of the reports that are heard in the land.
For a report will come in one year.
Another report will follow it in the next.
There will be violence in the land
with ruler fighting against ruler.

47 "So the time will certainly come
when I will punish the idols of Babylon.
Her whole land will be put to shame.
All her mortally wounded will collapse in her midst.
48 Then heaven and earth and all that is in them
will sing for joy over Babylon.
For destroyers from the north will attack it,"
says the LORD.
49 "Babylon must fall
because of the Israelites she has killed,
just as the earth's mortally wounded fell
because of Babylon.
50 You who have escaped the sword,
go, do not delay.
Remember the LORD in a faraway land.
Think about Jerusalem.
51 'We are ashamed because we have been insulted.
Our faces show our disgrace.
For foreigners have invaded
the holy rooms in the LORD's temple.'
52 Yes, but the time will certainly come," says the LORD,
"when I will punish her idols.
Throughout her land the mortally wounded will groan.
53 Even if Babylon climbs high into the sky
and fortifies her elevated stronghold,
I will send destroyers against her,"
says the LORD.

54 Cries of anguish will come from Babylon,
the sound of great destruction from
the land of the Babylonians.
55 For the LORD is ready to destroy Babylon,
and put an end to her loud noise.
Their waves will roar like turbulent waters.
They will make a deafening noise.
56 For a destroyer is attacking Babylon.
Her warriors will be captured;
their bows will be broken.
For the LORD is a God who punishes;
he pays back in full.
57 "I will make her officials and wise men drunk,
along with her governors, leaders, and warriors.
They will fall asleep forever and never wake up,"
says the King whose name is the LORD of Heaven's Armies.

58 This is what the LORD of Heaven's Armies says,
"Babylon's thick wall will be completely demolished.
Her high gates will be set on fire.
The peoples strive for what does not satisfy.
The nations grow weary trying to get
what will be destroyed."

59 This is the order Jeremiah the prophet gave to Seraiah son of Neriah, son of Mahseiah, when he went to King Zedekiah of Judah in Babylon during the fourth year of his reign. (Seraiah was a quartermaster.) 60 Jeremiah recorded on one scroll all the judgments that would come upon Babylon—all these prophecies written about Babylon. 61 Then Jeremiah said to Seraiah, "When you arrive in Babylon, make sure you read aloud all these prophecies. 62 Then say, 'O LORD, you have announced that you will destroy this place so that no people or animals live in it any longer. Certainly it will lie desolate forever!' 63 When you finish reading this scroll aloud, tie a stone to it and throw it into the middle of the Euphrates River. 64 Then say, 'In the same way Babylon will sink and never rise again because of the disaster I am ready to bring upon her; they will grow faint.'"

The prophecies of Jeremiah end here.

THE FALL OF JERUSALEM

52 Zedekiah was twenty-one years old when he became king, and he ruled in Jerusalem for eleven years. His mother's name was Hamutal daughter of Jeremiah, from Libnah. 2 He did what displeased the LORD just as Jehoiakim had done.

3 What follows is a record of what happened to Jerusalem and Judah because of the LORD's anger when he drove them out of his sight. Zedekiah rebelled against the king of Babylon. 4 King Nebuchadnezzar of Babylon came against Jerusalem with his whole army and set up camp outside it. They built siege ramps all around it. He arrived on the tenth day of the tenth month in the ninth year that Zedekiah ruled over Judah. 5 The city remained under siege until Zedekiah's eleventh year. 6 By the ninth day of the fourth month the famine in the city was so severe the residents had no food. 7 They broke through the city walls, and all the soldiers tried to escape. They left the city during the night. They went through the gate between the two walls that is near the king's garden. (The Babylonians had the city surrounded.) Then they headed for the rift valley. 8 But the Babylonian army chased after the king. They caught up with Zedekiah in the plains of Jericho, and his entire army deserted him. 9 They captured him and brought him up to the king of Babylon at Riblah in the territory of Hamath and he passed sentence on him there. 10 The king of Babylon had Zedekiah's sons put to death while Zedekiah was forced to watch. He also had all the nobles of Judah put to death there at Riblah. 11 He had Zedekiah's eyes put out and had him bound in chains. Then the king of Babylon had him led off to Babylon and he was imprisoned there until the day he died.

12 On the tenth day of the fifth month, in the nineteenth year of King Nebuchadnezzar of Babylon, Nebuzaradan, the captain of the royal guard who served the king of Babylon, arrived in Jerusalem.

13 He burned down the LORD's temple, the royal palace, and all the houses in Jerusalem, including every large house. 14 The whole Babylonian army that came with the captain of the royal guard tore down the walls that surrounded Jerusalem. 15 Nebuzaradan, the captain of the royal guard, took into exile some of the poor, the rest of the people who remained in the city, those who had deserted to the king of Babylon, and the rest of the craftsmen. 16 But he left behind some of the poor and gave them fields and vineyards.

17 The Babylonians broke the two bronze pillars in the temple of the LORD, as well as the movable stands and the large bronze basin called "The Sea." They took all the bronze to Babylon. 18 They also took the pots, shovels, trimming shears, basins, pans, and all the bronze utensils used by the priests. 19 The captain of the royal guard took the gold and silver bowls, censers, basins, pots, lampstands, pans, and vessels. 20 The bronze of the items that King Solomon made for the LORD's temple (including the two pillars, the large bronze basin called "The Sea," the twelve bronze bulls under "The Sea," and the movable stands) was too heavy to be weighed. 21 Each of the pillars was about 27 feet high, about 18 feet in circumference, three inches thick, and hollow. 22 The bronze top of one pillar was about 7½ feet high and had bronze latticework and pomegranate-shaped ornaments all around it. The second pillar with its pomegranate-shaped ornaments was like it. 23 There were 96 pomegranate-shaped ornaments on the sides; in all there were 100 pomegranate-shaped ornaments over the latticework that went around it.

24 The captain of the royal guard took Seraiah the chief priest, Zephaniah the priest who was second in rank, and the three doorkeepers. 25 From the city he took an official who was in charge of the soldiers, seven of the king's advisers who were discovered in the city, an official army secretary who drafted citizens for military service, and sixty citizens who were discovered in the middle of the city. 26 Nebuzaradan, the captain of the royal guard, took them and brought them to the king of Babylon at Riblah. 27 The king of Babylon ordered them to be executed at Riblah in the territory of Hamath.

So Judah was taken into exile away from its land. 28 Here is the official record of the number of people Nebuchadnezzar carried into exile: In the seventh year, 3,023 Jews; 29 in Nebuchadnezzar's eighteenth year, 832 people from Jerusalem; 30 in Nebuchadnezzar's twenty-third year, Nebuzaradan, the captain of the royal guard, carried into exile 745 Judeans. In all, 4,600 people went into exile.

JEHOIACHIN IN EXILE

31 In the thirty-seventh year of the exile of King Jehoiachin of Judah, on the twenty-fifth day of the twelfth month, King Evil Merodach of Babylon, in the first year of his reign, pardoned King Jehoiachin of Judah and released him from prison. 32 He spoke kindly to him and gave him a more prestigious position than the other kings who were with him in Babylon. 33 Jehoiachin took off his prison clothes and ate daily in the king's presence for the rest of his life. 34 He was given daily provisions by the king of Babylon for the rest of his life until the day he died.

"My portion is THE LORD," I HAVE SAID TO MYSELF so I will put My Hope in Him.

MEMORY VERSE

"My portion is the Lord," I have said to myself, so I will put my hope in him.

Lamentations 3:24

Lamentations

INTRODUCTION

God is Our Eternal Hope

The Book of Lamentations provides a practical reflection on the theology of suffering. The book records the broken heart of the prophet Jeremiah as he sat in the ruins of the city of Jerusalem. Jeremiah lamented the sinfulness of the Israelites and their choice to reject God. However, this lament offers great hope. Even though the people had rejected Him, God would not abandon His people.

Lamentations is comprised of five poems. The first two build to a climax in chapter 3, wherein Jeremiah professes the eternal faithfulness of the Lord. The final two chapters provide the "descent" of the poem. The poetry of Lamentations enhances the message and purpose. Chapters 1–4 are composed as acrostics of the twenty-two letters of the Hebrew alphabet. This construction suggests careful planning and thought by the writer as he offered a complete account of the subject.

The prophet Jeremiah has traditionally been identified as the author of Lamentations. Jeremiah was known as "the weeping prophet" and was known as a composer of laments. Lamentations also has many similarities with the Book of Jeremiah, also written by the prophet. The Book of Lamentations is a reflection on the destruction of the temple in Jerusalem in 586 B.C. and was likely written shortly after this event took place.

Lamentations offers a unique perspective on how we can love God greatly. Even in the midst of tragedy, despair, and suffering, God promises that His faithfulness will always endure. His compassion for His people is fresh every morning. He is continually working to redeem His people, even in their rebellion. Come what may, God remains faithful. His faithfulness is the greatest comfort to those who suffer; His compassion is fresh every morning.

Australia

OFFICIAL LANGUAGE
English
POPULATION
25,198,000
UNREACHED POPULATION
867,000
PROFESSING CHRISTIANS
65.4%

Say a Prayer Today

Pray for the people of Australia. Pray they would look to the Lord alone to meet their needs. Pray they would turn their hearts to Him and that they would reach many others with the gospel.

HISTORY BIT

In 1788, an Anglican chaplain named Richard Johnson traveled with British convicts to Sydney, Australia. Johnson later built the first church in Sydney.*

Lacey's Home

Source Information:
https://joshuaproject.net/countries/AS
*John Bowden, *A Chronology of World Christianity* (New York, NY: Continuum, 2007), 346.

LOVE YOUR NEIGHBOR

Her Journey

LACEY'S STORY

The anxiety that accompanies choice has been a constant in my life. The world has assured me that as a woman, I should be able to "have it all." The incessant presence of media in my ears and in front of my eyes reminds me of all the things that I can or should have or should be.

Sometimes, my own desires are contradictory. I'm a finite being, with limited time on this earth, but I would like multiple things that cannot coexist. It has caused me considerable stress to think about all the things I'm not doing with my life.

Lamentations 3:32 says, "Though he causes us grief, he then has compassion on us according to the abundance of his loyal kindness." Scriptures like these remind me that God has designed life with the gift to choose built in. Choice means there will be things we reject. Every "yes" we give means we have said "no" to a thousand other things. There are so many good things before us, but God asks us to consider Him our portion.

I will hope in Him and the meaning He brings to my life rather than seeking to consume every opportunity I think I need. If I know He is my portion, I can be sure He is enough.

4 WEEK READING PLAN

LOVE HIS WORD

	MONDAY	TUESDAY	WEDNESDAY	THURSDAY	FRIDAY
1	Lamentations 1:1-6	Lamentations 1:7-11	Lamentations 1:12-16	Lamentations 1:17-22	Lamentations 2:1-6
	SOAP Lamentations 1:1	SOAP Lamentations 1:8	SOAP Lamentations 1:12	SOAP Lamentations 1:18	SOAP Lamentations 2:6
2	Lamentations 2:7-12	Lamentations 2:13-17	Lamentations 2:18-22	Lamentations 3:1-18	Lamentations 3:19-33
	SOAP Lamentations 2:11	SOAP Lamentations 2:17	SOAP Lamentations 2:20	SOAP Lamentations 3:7-9	SOAP Lamentations 3:22-24
3	Lamentations 3:34-51	Lamentations 3:52-66	Lamentations 4:1-6	Lamentations 4:7-10	Lamentations 4:11-16
	SOAP Lamentations 3:40-42	SOAP Lamentations 3:58-60	SOAP Lamentations 4:6	SOAP Lamentations 4:7	SOAP Lamentations 4:11
4	Lamentations 4:17-22	Lamentations 5:1-5	Lamentations 5:6-11	Lamentations 5:12-18	Lamentations 5:19-22
	SOAP Lamentations 4:17	SOAP Lamentations 5:1	SOAP Lamentations 5:7	SOAP Lamentations 5:15-17	SOAP Lamentations 5:21-22

THE PROPHET SPEAKS

א (ALEF)

1 Alas! The city once full of people
now sits all alone!
The prominent lady among the nations
has become a widow!
The princess who once ruled the provinces
has become a forced laborer!

ב (BET)

2 She weeps bitterly at night;
tears stream down her cheeks.
She has no one to comfort her
among all her lovers.
All her friends have betrayed her;
they have become her enemies.

ג (GIMEL)

3 Judah has departed into exile
under affliction and harsh oppression.
She lives among the nations;
she has found no resting place.
All who pursued her overtook her
in narrow straits.

ד (DALET)

4 The roads to Zion mourn
because no one travels to the festivals.
All her city gates are deserted;
her priests groan.
Her virgins grieve;
she is in bitter anguish!

ה (HE)

5 Her foes subjugated her;
her enemies are at ease.
For the LORD afflicted her
because of her many acts of rebellion.
Her children went away
captive before the enemy.

ו (VAV)

6 All of Daughter Zion's splendor
has departed.
Her leaders became like deer;
they found no pasture,
so they were too exhausted to escape
from the hunter.

ז (ZAYIN)

7 Jerusalem remembers,
when she became a poor homeless person,
all her treasures
that she owned in days of old.

When her people fell into an enemy's grip,
none of her allies came to her rescue.
Her enemies gloated over her;
they sneered at her downfall.

ח (KHET)

8 Jerusalem committed terrible sin;
therefore she became an object of scorn.
All who admired her have despised her
because they have seen her nakedness.
She groans aloud
and turns away in shame.

ט (TET)

9 Her menstrual flow has soiled her clothing;
she did not consider the consequences of her sin.
Her demise was astonishing,
and there was no one to comfort her.
She cried, "Look, O LORD, on my affliction
because my enemy boasts!"

י (YOD)

10 An enemy grabbed
all her valuables.
Indeed she watched in horror as Gentiles
invaded her holy temple—
those whom you had commanded:
"They must not enter your assembly place."

כ (KAF)

11 All her people groaned
as they searched for a morsel of bread.
They exchanged their valuables
for just enough food
to stay alive.

JERUSALEM SPEAKS

"Look, O LORD! Consider
that I have become worthless!"

ל (LAMED)

12 Is it nothing to you, all you who
pass by on the road?
Look and see!
Is there any pain like mine?
The Lord has afflicted me,
he has inflicted it on me
when he burned with anger.

מ (MEM)

13 He sent down fire
into my bones, and it overcame them.
He spread out a trapper's net for my feet;
he made me turn back.

He has made me desolate;
I am faint all day long.

נ (NUN)
14 My sins are bound around my neck like a yoke;
they are fastened together by his hand.
He has placed his yoke on my neck;
he has sapped my strength.
The Lord has handed me over
to those whom I cannot resist.

ס (SAMEK)
15 He rounded up all my mighty ones;
The Lord did this in my midst.
He summoned an assembly against me
to shatter my young men.
The Lord has stomped like grapes
the virgin daughter, Judah.

ע (AYIN)
16 I weep because of these things;
my eyes flow with tears.
For there is no one in sight who can
comfort me
or encourage me.
My children are desolated
because an enemy has prevailed.

THE PROPHET SPEAKS

פ (PE)
17 Zion spread out her hands,
but there is no one to comfort her.
The LORD has issued a decree
against Jacob;
his neighbors have become his enemies.
Jerusalem has become
like filthy garbage in their midst.

JERUSALEM SPEAKS

צ (TSADE)
18 The LORD is right to judge me!
Yes, I rebelled against his commands.
Please listen, all you nations,
and look at my suffering!
My young women and men
have gone into exile.

ק (QOF)
19 I called for my lovers,
but they had deceived me.
My priests and my elders
perished in the city.
Truly they had searched for food
to keep themselves alive.

REFLECT

Was God justified in His actions against Judah?

ר (RESH)
20 Look, O LORD! I am distressed;
my stomach is in knots!
My heart is pounding inside me.
Yes, I was terribly rebellious!
Out in the street the sword bereaves
a mother of her children;
Inside the house death is present.

ש (SIN/SHIN)
21 They have heard that I groan,
yet there is no one to comfort me.
All my enemies have heard of my trouble;
they are glad that you have brought it about.
Bring about the day of judgment
that you promised
so that they may end up like me!

ת (TAV)
22 Let all their wickedness come before you;
afflict them
just as you have afflicted me
because of all my acts of rebellion.
For my groans are many,
and my heart is sick with sorrow.

THE PROPHET SPEAKS

א (ALEF)
2 Alas! The Lord has covered
Daughter Zion with his anger.
He has thrown down the splendor of Israel
from heaven to earth;
he did not protect his temple
when he displayed his anger.

ב (BET)
2 The Lord destroyed mercilessly
all the homes of Jacob's descendants.
In his anger he tore down
the fortified cities of Daughter Judah.
He knocked to the ground and humiliated
the kingdom and its rulers.

ג (GIMEL)
3 In fierce anger he destroyed
the whole army of Israel.
He withdrew his right hand
as the enemy attacked.
He was like a raging fire in the land of Jacob;
it consumed everything around it.

ד (DALET)
4 He prepared his bow like an enemy;
his right hand was ready to shoot.

Like a foe he killed everyone,
even our strong young men;
he has poured out his anger like fire
on the tent of Daughter Zion.

ה (HE)
5 The Lord, like an enemy,
destroyed Israel.
He destroyed all her palaces;
he ruined her fortified cities.
He made everyone in Daughter Judah
mourn and lament.

ו (VAV)
6 He destroyed his temple as if it
   were a vineyard;
he destroyed his appointed meeting place.
The LORD has made those in Zion forget
both the festivals and the Sabbaths.
In his fierce anger he has spurned
both king and priest.

ז (ZAYIN)
7 The Lord rejected his altar
and abhorred his temple.
He handed over to the enemy
Jerusalem's palace walls;
the enemy shouted in the LORD's temple
as if it were a feast day.

ח (KHET)
8 The LORD was determined to tear down
Daughter Zion's wall.
He prepared to knock it down;
he did not withdraw his hand from destroying.
He made the ramparts and fortified walls lament;
together they mourned their ruin.

ט (TET)
9 Her city gates have fallen to the ground;
he smashed to bits the bars that
   lock her gates.
Her king and princes were taken into exile;
there is no more guidance available.
As for her prophets,
they no longer receive a vision from the LORD.

י (YOD)
10 The elders of Daughter Zion
sit on the ground in silence.
They have thrown dirt on their heads;
They have dressed in sackcloth.
Jerusalem's young women stare
   down at the ground.

REFLECT

Have you ever felt like the author of Lamentations? How can you turn to the Lord in your distress?

כ (KAF)
11 My eyes are worn out from weeping;
my stomach is in knots.
My heart is poured out on the ground
due to the destruction of my helpless people;
children and infants faint
in the town squares.

ל (LAMED)
12 Children say to their mothers,
"Where are food and drink?"
They faint like a wounded warrior
in the city squares.
They die slowly
in their mothers' arms.

מ (MEM)
13 With what can I equate you?
To what can I compare you, O Daughter Jerusalem?
To what can I liken you
so that I might comfort you, O Virgin Daughter Zion?
Your wound is as deep as the sea.
Who can heal you?

נ (NUN)
14 Your prophets saw visions for you
that were worthless whitewash.
They failed to expose your sin
so as to restore your fortunes.
They saw oracles for you
that were worthless lies.

ס (SAMEK)
15 All who passed by on the road
clapped their hands to mock you.
They sneered and shook their heads
at Daughter Jerusalem.
"Ha! Is this the city they called
'the perfection of beauty,
the source of joy of the whole earth!'?"

פ (PE)
16 All your enemies
gloated over you.
They sneered and gnashed their teeth;
they said, "We have destroyed her!
Ha! We have waited a long time for this day.
We have lived to see it!"

ע (AYIN)
17 The LORD has done what he planned;
he has fulfilled his promise
that he threatened long ago:
He has overthrown you without mercy

and has enabled the enemy to gloat over you;
he has exalted your adversaries' power.

צ (TSADE)
18 Cry out from your heart to the Lord,
O wall of Daughter Zion!
Make your tears flow like a river
all day and all night long!
Do not rest;
do not let your tears stop!

ק (QOF)
19 Get up! Cry out in the night
when the night watches start!
Pour out your heart like water
before the face of the Lord!
Lift up your hands to him
for your children's lives;
they are fainting from hunger
at every street corner.

JERUSALEM SPEAKS

ר (RESH)
20 Look, O LORD! Consider!
Whom have you ever afflicted like this?
Should women eat their offspring,
their healthy infants?
Should priest and prophet
be killed in the Lord's sanctuary?

ש (SIN/SHIN)
21 The young boys and old men
lie dead on the ground in the streets.
My young women and my young men
have fallen by the sword.
You killed them when you were angry;
you slaughtered them without mercy.

ת (TAV)
22 As if it were a feast day, you call
enemies to terrify me on every side.
On the day of the LORD's anger
no one escaped or survived.
My enemy has finished off
those healthy infants whom I bore and raised.

THE PROPHET SPEAKS

א (ALEF)
3 I am the man who has experienced affliction
from the rod of the LORD's wrath.
2 He drove me into captivity and made me walk
in darkness and not light.
3 He repeatedly attacks me;
he turns his hand against me all day long.

ב (BET)
4 He has made my mortal skin waste away;
he has broken my bones.
5 He has besieged and surrounded me
with bitter hardship.
6 He has made me reside in deepest darkness
like those who died long ago.

ג (GIMEL)
7 He has walled me in so that I cannot get out;
he has weighted me down with heavy prison chains.
8 Also, when I cry out desperately for help,
he has shut out my prayer.
9 He has blocked every road I take with
a wall of hewn stones;
he has made every path impassable.

ד (DALET)
10 To me he is like a bear lying in ambush,
like a hidden lion stalking its prey.
11 He has obstructed my paths and torn me to pieces;
he has made me desolate.
12 He drew his bow and made me
the target for his arrow.

ה (HE)
13 He shot his arrows
into my heart.
14 I have become the laughingstock of all people,
their mocking song all day long.
15 He has given me my fill of bitter herbs
and made me drunk with bitterness.

ו (VAV)
16 He ground my teeth in gravel;
he trampled me in the dust.
17 I am deprived of peace;
I have forgotten what happiness is.
18 So I said, "My endurance has expired;
I have lost all hope of deliverance from the LORD."

ז (ZAYIN)
19 Remember my impoverished and homeless condition,
which is a bitter poison.
20 I continually think about this,
and I am depressed.
21 But this I call to mind;
therefore I have hope:

ח (KHET)
22 The LORD's loyal kindness never ceases;
his compassions never end.
23 They are fresh every morning;
your faithfulness is abundant!

24 "My portion is the LORD," I have said to myself,
so I will put my hope in him.

ט (TET)

25 The LORD is good to those who trust in him,
to the one who seeks him.
26 It is good to wait patiently
for deliverance from the LORD.
27 It is good for a man
to bear the yoke while he is young.

י (YOD)

28 Let a person sit alone in silence,
when the LORD is disciplining him.
29 Let him bury his face in the dust;
perhaps there is hope.
30 Let him offer his cheek to the one
who hits him;
let him have his fill of insults.

כ (KAF)

31 For the Lord will not
reject us forever.
32 Though he causes us grief, he then
has compassion on us
according to the abundance of his
loyal kindness.
33 For he is not predisposed to afflict
or to grieve people.

ל (LAMED)

34 To crush underfoot
all the earth's prisoners,
35 to deprive a person of his rights
in the presence of the Most High,
36 to defraud a person in a lawsuit—
the Lord does not approve of such things!

מ (MEM)

37 Whose command was ever fulfilled
unless the Lord decreed it?
38 Is it not from the mouth of the Most
High that everything comes—
both calamity and blessing?
39 Why should any living person complain
when punished for his sins?

נ (NUN)

40 Let us carefully examine our ways,
and let us return to the LORD.
41 Let us lift up our hearts and our hands
to God in heaven:
42 "We have blatantly rebelled;
you have not forgiven."

CHALLENGE

How do these verses prove true for Judah? (See Ezra 8.) Have you seen God come to your aid and redeem you after a time of discipline? What does this show us about His character?

LOVE TO GROW

CALL TO MIND

LAMENTATIONS 3:21–23

A few weeks back, I went into the backyard with a bucket and picked up a bunch of rocks. I carried the heavy pail inside and poured its contents onto the kitchen counter. Then I grabbed a black marker and wrote down the current year on one rock. Underneath the date, I scribbled a short phrase to describe a recently answered prayer. My husband grabbed his own stone and did the same.

Our collection of rocks marks God's faithfulness to our family, and we keep them openly displayed in a basket in our family room. On days when I am flagging in faith, I will sit on the floor and start pulling out those stones to remind myself how the Lord responded to our cries for help. He always keeps His promises and provides everything we need.

The prophet Jeremiah experienced great loss, but he encouraged his soul by rehearsing God's character and remembering that the Lord's love is steadfast and sure. He aligned his life to the bedrock truth of who God is rather than the slippery slope of changing circumstances. During our own seasons of lament, we can keep hope alive in our hearts by firmly fixing our thoughts on our heavenly Father's unchanging attributes.

But this I call to mind; therefore I have hope: The LORD's loyal kindness never ceases; his compassions never end. They are fresh every morning; your faithfulness is abundant! (Lam 3:21–23).

His love is limitless. God's covenant love for His people is not determined by our choices. Our Father continues to persevere in love even in the midst of the most undesirable circumstances. Even if we falter, His unchanging love holds fast and never lets go.

His compassion is unending. The Lord shoulders our burdens and supplies a fresh batch of mercy every morning. When we surrender our broken lives, He lavishes us with His comfort. We can trust our Father will always open His arms to receive us and restore us if we seek Him with repentant hearts.

His faithfulness is inexhaustible. Our Father continually follows through and fulfills what He has promised. The enemy may bring temporary frustration, but he cannot frustrate God's purpose for our lives if we place our full hope in the Lord. Our lives may be in constant flux, but our unchanging God has not forgotten us.

You may face external tribulation today, but you do not need to give way to fear. You can console your troubled soul by choosing to continually call to mind God's character. Calamity cannot consume you if you place your total confidence in the Rock of your salvation.

ס (SAMEK)
43 You shrouded yourself with anger and then pursued us;
you killed without mercy.
44 You shrouded yourself with a cloud
so that no prayer could get through.
45 You make us like filthy scum
in the estimation of the nations.

פ (PE)
46 All our enemies have gloated over us;
47 panic and pitfall have come upon us,
devastation and destruction.
48 Streams of tears flow from my eyes
because my people are destroyed.

ע (AYIN)
49 Tears flow from my eyes and will not stop;
there will be no break
50 until the LORD looks down from heaven
and sees what has happened.
51 What my eyes see grieves me—
all the suffering of the daughters in my city.

צ (TSADE)
52 For no good reason my enemies
hunted me down like a bird.
53 They shut me up in a pit
and threw stones at me.
54 The waters closed over my head;
I thought I was about to die.

ק (QOF)
55 I have called on your name, O LORD,
from the deepest pit.
56 You heard my plea:
"Do not close your ears to my cry for relief!"
57 You came near on the day I called to you;
you said, "Do not fear!"

ר (RESH)
58 O Lord, you championed my cause;
you redeemed my life.
59 You have seen the wrong done to me, O LORD;
pronounce judgment on my behalf!
60 You have seen all their vengeance,
all their plots against me.

ש (SIN/SHIN)
61 You have heard their taunts, O LORD,
all their plots against me.
62 My assailants revile and conspire
against me all day long.
63 Watch them from morning to evening;
I am the object of their mocking songs.

ת (TAV)

64 Pay them back what they deserve, O LORD,
according to what they have done.
65 Give them a distraught heart;
may your curse be on them!
66 Pursue them in anger and
eradicate them
from under the LORD's heaven.

THE PROPHET SPEAKS

א (ALEF)

4 Alas! Gold has lost its luster;
pure gold loses value.
Jewels are scattered
on every street corner.

ב (BET)

2 The precious sons of Zion
were worth their weight in gold—
Alas!—but now they are treated like
broken clay pots,
made by a potter.

ג (GIMEL)

3 Even the jackals nurse their young
at their breast,
but my people are cruel,
like ostriches in the wilderness.

ד (DALET)

4 The infant's tongue sticks
to the roof of its mouth due to thirst;
little children beg for bread,
but no one gives them even a morsel.

ה (HE)

5 Those who once feasted on delicacies
are now starving to death in the streets.
Those who grew up wearing
expensive clothes
are now dying amid garbage.

ו (VAV)

6 The punishment of my people
exceeds that of Sodom,
which was overthrown in a moment
with no one to help her.

ז (ZAYIN)

7 Our consecrated ones were brighter
than snow,
whiter than milk;
their bodies more ruddy than corals,
their hair like lapis lazuli.

ח (KHET)
8 Now their appearance is darker than soot;
they are not recognized in the streets.
Their skin has shriveled on their bones;
it is dried up, like tree bark.

ט (TET)
9 Those who die by the sword are better off
than those who die of hunger,
those who waste away,
struck down from lack of food.

י (YOD)
10 The hands of tenderhearted women
cooked their own children,
who became their food,
when my people were destroyed.

כ (KAF)
11 The LORD fully vented his wrath;
he poured out his fierce anger.
He started a fire in Zion;
it consumed her foundations.

ל (LAMED)
12 Neither the kings of the earth
nor the people of the lands ever thought
that enemy or foe could enter
the gates of Jerusalem.

מ (MEM)
13 But it happened due to the sins of her prophets
and the iniquities of her priests,
who poured out in her midst
the blood of the righteous.

נ (NUN)
14 They wander blindly through the streets,
defiled by the blood they shed,
while no one dares
to touch their garments.

ס (SAMEK)
15 People cry to them, "Turn away! You are unclean!
Turn away! Turn away! Don't touch us!"
So they have fled and wander about;
but the nations say, "They may not
stay here any longer."

פ (PE)
16 The LORD himself has scattered them;
he no longer watches over them.
They did not honor the priests;
they did not show favor to the elders.

REFLECT

What are some of the things you often turn to when you need comfort, provision, or help? Are these things that will continually fail you? How can you turn to God in your time of need, instead of turning to earthly things?

THE PEOPLE OF JERUSALEM LAMENT

ע (AYIN)
17 Our eyes continually failed us
as we looked in vain for help.
From our watchtowers we watched
for a nation that could not rescue us.

צ (TSADE)
18 Our enemies hunted us down at every step
so that we could not walk about in our streets.
Our end drew near, our days were numbered,
for our end had come!

ק (QOF)
19 Those who pursued us were swifter
than eagles in the sky.
They chased us over the mountains;
they ambushed us in the wilderness.

ר (RESH)
20 Our very life breath—the LORD's anointed king—
was caught in their traps,
of whom we thought,
"Under his protection we will survive among the nations."

THE PROPHET SPEAKS

ש (SIN/SHIN)
21 Rejoice and be glad for now, O people of Edom,
who reside in the land of Uz.
But the cup of judgment will pass to you also;
you will get drunk and take off your clothes.

ת (TAV)
22 O people of Zion, your punishment will come to an end;
he will not prolong your exile.
But, O people of Edom, he will punish your sin
and reveal your offenses!

THE PEOPLE OF JERUSALEM PRAY

5 O LORD, reflect on what has happened to us;
consider and look at our disgrace.
2 Our inheritance is turned over to strangers;
foreigners now occupy our homes.
3 We have become fatherless orphans;
our mothers have become widows.
4 We must pay money for our own water;
we must buy our own wood at a steep price.
5 We are pursued—they are breathing down our necks;
we are weary and have no rest.
6 We have submitted to Egypt and Assyria
in order to buy food to eat.
7 Our forefathers sinned and are dead,
but we suffer their punishment.
8 Slaves rule over us;

there is no one to rescue us from their power.
9 At the risk of our lives we get our food
because robbers lurk in the wilderness.
10 Our skin is as hot as an oven
due to a fever from hunger.
11 They raped women in Zion,
virgins in the towns of Judah.
12 Princes were hung by their hands;
elders were mistreated.
13 The young men perform menial labor;
boys stagger from their labor.
14 The elders are gone from the city gate;
the young men have stopped playing their music.
15 Our hearts no longer have any joy;
our dancing is turned to mourning.
16 The crown has fallen from our head;
woe to us, for we have sinned!
17 Because of this, our hearts are sick;
because of these things, we can hardly
see through our tears.
18 For wild animals are prowling over Mount Zion,
which lies desolate.
19 But you, O LORD, reign forever;
your throne endures from generation to generation.
20 Why do you keep on forgetting us?
Why do you forsake us so long?
21 Bring us back to yourself, O LORD, so
that we may return to you;
renew our life as in days before,
22 unless you have utterly rejected us
and are angry with us beyond measure.

REFLECT

What does the prayer of the people of Jerusalem teach us about how we can approach God?

I WILL give you a NEW heart, AND I WILL put a NEW Spirit within you

MEMORY VERSE

"I will give you a new heart, and I will put a new spirit within you. I will remove the heart of stone from your body and give you a heart of flesh."

Ezekiel 36:26

Ezekiel

INTRODUCTION

God's Heart to Restore

The Book of Ezekiel shows God's heart to restore His people. Ezekiel was a contemporary of Jeremiah, though Ezekiel lived in Babylon among the other exiles from Judah. While Jeremiah warned the remaining citizens of Jerusalem of the coming destruction of the city, Ezekiel preached a message of repentance for the exiles in Babylon. Ezekiel's message was also one of comfort for the refugees. He reminded them that God would not leave them, even though He had driven them far from home.

The Book of Ezekiel contains four main sections. Chapters 1–3 detail the prophetic call of Ezekiel and the events surrounding his ministry. Ezekiel then offered prophetic messages for Judah and Jerusalem, warning them of the final destruction to come to the city in chapters 4–24. Chapters 25–32 contain prophetic messages for foreign nations, and chapters 33–48 share news of coming restoration.

The events in Ezekiel take place between 597 and 586 B.C. Ezekiel was deported to Babylon in 597 B.C., and his prophetic ministry there lasted from 593 B.C. until 571 B.C. The city of Jerusalem was destroyed during his ministry, in 586 B.C. There is no other information about Ezekiel from the rest of Scripture, but the Book of Ezekiel tells us he was from a priestly family and that he was both a priest and a prophet.

While much of his message speaks of coming destruction for the nation of Judah, Ezekiel also offered God's message of hope. God was faithful to His people, kept His promises, and would restore His people. God honored all His promises in the past, all the way back to the covenant He made with Abraham. We can love God greatly knowing that His character is the same today as it was in Ezekiel's day: He always keeps His promises.

Northern Ireland (United Kingdom)

OFFICIAL LANGUAGES
English and Irish (Gaelic)
POPULATION
1,871,000* (67,401,000 total UK population)
UNREACHED POPULATION
5,092,000 (total unreached in UK)
PROFESSING CHRISTIANS
57.0% (of total UK population)

Julie's Home

Say a Prayer Today

Pray that God will continue to work in the hearts of the people of Northern Ireland. Pray they would see their need for a personal relationship with Jesus Christ and that God would soften their hearts toward Him.

HISTORY BIT

Northern Ireland is a divided society with some wanting to stay part of the UK and some wanting to become part of Ireland. After thirty years of violence in Northern Ireland, there are still echoes of the conflicts in many areas of Belfast, the capital of Northern Ireland.

Source Information:
*http://worldpopulationreview.com/regions/northern

JULIE'S STORY

Ezekiel was a prophet during Israel's time in exile. God's people had broken their covenant with Him through their willful disobedience and unwillingness to turn back to Him. Yet God remained faithful! God provided future hope through this wonderful promise, stated both in Ezekiel 36:26 and in Ezekiel 11:19. God showed His heart for His people. He will restore evil, disobedient people to Himself by removing their heavy, sin-burdened, spiritually dead hearts of stone and replacing them with spiritually alive hearts of flesh!

Our new, Spirit-filled hearts enable us to walk in obedience and to respond to God as we should—recognizing He is our God and we are His people. Our motivation is transformed to respond with loving obedience because He has so loved us that He rescued us and continues to sanctify us.

This heart transplant is available to all who trust in Jesus. I have personally known this transformation, this wonderful heart exchange. I've also seen God work in many lives throughout Northern Ireland. From the religiously self-righteous, to the one who committed horrific acts of violence, and many others. We are all brought to life spiritually in the same way, through trusting the death of Christ alone. However, there are still many more hearts of stone that are hardened to the gospel. We pray for God to breathe life through the Spirit and give hearts of flesh to all.

As Christians we must be careful that our hearts do not become hardened again by sin's deceitfulness, which seeks to draw us away from our first love. In this we remember God's faithfulness and His desire to restore. "Now may the Lord direct your hearts toward the love of God and the endurance of Christ" (2 Thess 3:5).

6 WEEK READING PLAN

LOVE HIS WORD

MONDAY	TUESDAY	WEDNESDAY	THURSDAY	FRIDAY
Ezekiel 1	Ezekiel 2-3	Ezekiel 4-5	Ezekiel 6-7	Ezekiel 8-9
SOAP Psalm 134:1-3	SOAP Psalm 135:1-2	SOAP Psalm 135:3	SOAP Psalm 135:4-5	SOAP Psalm 135:6-7
Ezekiel 10	Ezekiel 11	Ezekiel 12-13	Ezekiel 14-15	Ezekiel 16
SOAP Psalm 135:8-9	SOAP Psalm 135:10-12	SOAP Psalm 135:13	SOAP Psalm 135:14-15	SOAP Psalm 135:16-17
Ezekiel 17-18	Ezekiel 19	Ezekiel 20	Ezekiel 21-22	Ezekiel 23-24
SOAP Psalm 135:18-20	SOAP Psalm 135:21	SOAP Psalm 136:1-2	SOAP Psalm 136:3-4	SOAP Psalm 136:5-6
Ezekiel 25-26	Ezekiel 27-28	Ezekiel 29	Ezekiel 30-31	Ezekiel 32
SOAP Psalm 136:7-8	SOAP Psalm 136:9-10	SOAP Psalm 136:11-12	SOAP Psalm 136:13-15	SOAP Psalm 136:16-17
Ezekiel 33	Ezekiel 34	Ezekiel 35-36	Ezekiel 37	Ezekiel 38-39
SOAP Psalm 136:18-20	SOAP Psalm 136:21-22	SOAP Ezekiel 36:26	SOAP Psalm 136:23-24	SOAP Psalm 136:25
Ezekiel 40	Ezekiel 41-42	Ezekiel 43-44	Ezekiel 45-46	Ezekiel 47-48
SOAP Psalm 136:26	SOAP Psalm 137:1-3	SOAP Psalm 137:4-5	SOAP Psalm 137:6-7	SOAP Psalm 137:8-9

A VISION OF GOD'S GLORY

1 In the thirtieth year, on the fifth day of the fourth month, while
I was among the exiles at the Kebar River, the heavens opened
and I saw a divine vision. 2 (On the fifth day of the month—it was
the fifth year of King Jehoiachin's exile—3 the LORD's message
came to the priest Ezekiel the son of Buzi, at the Kebar River
in the land of the Babylonians. The hand of the LORD came on
him there.)
4 As I watched, I noticed a windstorm coming from the
north—an enormous cloud, with lightning flashing, such that
bright light rimmed it and came from it like glowing amber from
the middle of a fire. 5 In the fire were what looked like four living beings. In their appearance they had human form, 6 but each
had four faces and four wings. 7 Their legs were straight, but the
soles of their feet were like calves' feet. They gleamed like polished bronze. 8 They had human hands under their wings on their
four sides. As for the faces and wings of the four of them, 9 their
wings touched each other; they did not turn as they moved, but
went straight ahead.
10 Their faces had this appearance: Each of the four had the
face of a man, with the face of a lion on the right, the face of an
ox on the left, and also the face of an eagle. 11 Their wings were
spread out above them; each had two wings touching the wings
of one of the other beings on either side and two wings covering
their bodies. 12 Each moved straight ahead—wherever the spirit
would go, they would go, without turning as they went. 13 In the
middle of the living beings was something like burning coals of
fire or like torches. It moved back and forth among the living
beings. It was bright, and lightning was flashing out of the fire.
14 The living beings moved backward and forward as quickly as
flashes of lightning.
15 Then I looked, and I saw one wheel on the ground beside
each of the four beings. 16 The appearance of the wheels and
their construction was like gleaming jasper, and all four wheels
looked alike. Their structure was like a wheel within a wheel.
17 When they moved they would go in any of the four directions
they faced without turning as they moved. 18 Their rims were
high and awesome, and the rims of all four wheels were full of
eyes all around.
19 When the living beings moved, the wheels beside them
moved; when the living beings rose up from the ground, the
wheels rose up too. 20 Wherever the spirit would go, they
would go, and the wheels would rise up beside them because
the spirit of the living being was in the wheel. 21 When the living beings moved, the wheels moved, and when they stopped
moving, the wheels stopped. When they rose up from the
ground, the wheels rose up from the ground; the wheels rose
up beside them because the spirit of the living being was in
the wheel.
22 Over the heads of the living beings was something like a
platform, glittering awesomely like ice, stretched out over their
heads. 23 Under the platform their wings were stretched out, each
toward the other. Each of the beings also had two wings covering its body. 24 When they moved, I heard the sound of their

wings—it was like the sound of rushing waters, or the voice of
the Sovereign One, or the tumult of an army. When they stood
still, they lowered their wings.
25 Then there was a voice from above the platform over their
heads when they stood still. 26 Above the platform over their
heads was something like a sapphire shaped like a throne. High
above on the throne was a form that appeared to be a man. 27 I
saw an amber glow like a fire enclosed all around from his waist
up. From his waist down I saw something that looked like fire.
There was a brilliant light around it, 28 like the appearance of a
rainbow in the clouds after the rain. This was the appearance
of the surrounding brilliant light; it looked like the glory of the
LORD. When I saw it, I threw myself face down, and I heard a
voice speaking.

EZEKIEL'S COMMISSION

2 He said to me, "Son of man, stand on your feet and I will
speak with you." 2 As he spoke to me, a wind came into me
and stood me on my feet, and I heard the one speaking to me.
3 He said to me, "Son of man, I am sending you to the house
of Israel, to rebellious nations who have rebelled against me;
both they and their fathers have revolted against me to this
very day. 4 The people to whom I am sending you are obstinate
and hard-hearted, and you must say to them, 'This is what the
Sovereign LORD says.' 5 And as for them, whether they listen
or not—for they are a rebellious house—they will know that a
prophet has been among them. 6 But you, son of man, do not
fear them, and do not fear their words. Even though briers
and thorns surround you and you live among scorpions—do
not fear their words and do not be terrified of the looks they
give you, for they are a rebellious house! 7 You must speak my
words to them whether they listen or not, for they are rebellious. 8 As for you, son of man, listen to what I am saying to you:
Do not rebel like that rebellious house! Open your mouth and
eat what I am giving you."
9 Then I looked and realized a hand was stretched out to me,
and in it was a written scroll. 10 He unrolled it before me, and it
had writing on the front and back; written on it were laments,
mourning, and woe.

3 He said to me, "Son of man, eat what you see in front of
you—eat this scroll—and then go and speak to the house of
Israel." 2 So I opened my mouth and he fed me the scroll.
3 He said to me, "Son of man, feed your stomach and fill your
belly with this scroll I am giving to you." So I ate it, and it was
sweet like honey in my mouth.
4 He said to me, "Son of man, go to the house of Israel and
speak my words to them. 5 For you are not being sent to a people
of unintelligible speech and difficult language, but to the house
of Israel—6 not to many peoples of unintelligible speech and difficult language, whose words you cannot understand. Surely if I
had sent you to them, they would listen to you! 7 But the house
of Israel is unwilling to listen to you, because they are not willing to listen to me, for the whole house of Israel is hardheaded
and hardhearted.

[8]"I have made your face adamant to match their faces, and your
forehead hard to match their foreheads. [9]I have made your forehead harder than flint—like diamond! Do not fear them or be terrified of the looks they give you, for they are a rebellious house."
[10]And he said to me, "Son of man, take all my words that I speak
to you to heart and listen carefully. [11]Go to the exiles, to your fellow countrymen, and speak to them. Say to them, 'This is what
the Sovereign LORD says,' whether they pay attention or not."

EZEKIEL BEFORE THE EXILES

[12]Then a wind lifted me up and I heard a great rumbling sound
behind me as the glory of the LORD rose from its place, [13]and the
sound of the living beings' wings brushing against each other,
and the sound of the wheels alongside them, a great rumbling
sound. [14]A wind lifted me up and carried me away. I went bitterly,
my spirit full of fury, and the hand of the LORD rested powerfully on me. [15]I came to the exiles at Tel Abib, who lived by the
Kebar River. I sat dumbfounded among them there, where they
were living, for seven days.
[16]At the end of seven days the LORD's message came to me:
[17]"Son of man, I have appointed you a watchman for the house
of Israel. Whenever you hear a word from my mouth, you must
give them a warning from me. [18]When I say to the wicked, 'You
will certainly die,' and you do not warn him—you do not speak
out to warn the wicked to turn from his wicked lifestyle so that
he may live—that wicked person will die for his iniquity, but I
will hold you accountable for his death. [19]But as for you, if you
warn the wicked and he does not turn from his wicked deed and
from his wicked lifestyle, he will die for his iniquity but you will
have saved your own life.
[20]"When a righteous person turns from his righteousness and
commits iniquity, and I set an obstacle before him, he will die. If
you have not warned him, he will die for his sin. The righteous
deeds he performed will not be considered, but I will hold you
accountable for his death. [21]However, if you warn the righteous
person not to sin, and he does not sin, he will certainly live because he was warned, and you will have saved your own life."

ISOLATED AND SILENCED

[22]The hand of the LORD rested on me there, and he said to me,
"Get up, go out to the valley, and I will speak with you there." [23]So
I got up and went out to the valley, and the glory of the LORD
was standing there, just like the glory I had seen by the Kebar
River, and I threw myself face down.
[24]Then a wind came into me and stood me on my feet. The
LORD spoke to me and said, "Go shut yourself in your house.
[25]As for you, son of man, they will put ropes on you and tie you
up with them, so you cannot go out among them. [26]I will make
your tongue stick to the roof of your mouth so that you will be silent and unable to reprove them, for they are a rebellious house.
[27]But when I speak with you, I will loosen your tongue and you
must say to them, 'This is what the Sovereign LORD says.' Those
who listen will listen, but the indifferent will refuse, for they
are a rebellious house.

OMINOUS OBJECT LESSONS

4 "And you, son of man, take a brick and set it in front of you.
Inscribe a city on it—Jerusalem. 2 Lay siege to it! Build siege
works against it. Erect a siege ramp against it! Post soldiers outside it and station battering rams around it. 3 Then for your part
take an iron frying pan and set it up as an iron wall between you
and the city. Set your face toward it. It is to be under siege; you
are to besiege it. This is a sign for the house of Israel.
4 "Also for your part lie on your left side and place the iniquity of the house of Israel on it. For the number of days you lie
on your side you will bear their iniquity. 5 I have determined
that the number of the years of their iniquity are to be the
number of days for you—390 days. So bear the iniquity of the
house of Israel.
6 "When you have completed these days, then lie down a second time, but on your right side, and bear the iniquity of the
house of Judah 40 days—I have assigned one day for each year.
7 You must turn your face toward the siege of Jerusalem with your
arm bared and prophesy against it. 8 Look here: I will tie you up
with ropes, so you cannot turn from one side to the other until
you complete the days of your siege.
9 "As for you, take wheat, barley, beans, lentils, millet, and
spelt, put them in a single container, and make food from them
for yourself. For the same number of days that you lie on your
side—390 days—you will eat it. 10 The food you eat will be eight
ounces a day by weight; you must eat it at fixed times. 11 And you
must drink water by measure, a pint and a half; you must drink
it at fixed times. 12 And you must eat the food as you would a barley cake. You must bake it in front of them over a fire made with
dried human excrement." 13 And the LORD said, "This is how the
people of Israel will eat their unclean food among the nations
where I will banish them."
14 And I said, "Ah, Sovereign LORD, I have never been ceremonially defiled before. I have never eaten a carcass or an animal
torn by wild beasts; from my youth up, unclean meat has never
entered my mouth."
15 So he said to me, "All right then, I will substitute cow's manure instead of human excrement. You will cook your food over
it."
16 Then he said to me, "Son of man, I am about to remove the
bread supply in Jerusalem. They will eat their bread ration anxiously, and they will drink their water ration in terror 17 because
they will lack bread and water. Each one will be terrified, and
they will rot for their iniquity.

5 "As for you, son of man, take a sharp sword and use it as a bar-
ber's razor. Shave off some of the hair from your head and
your beard. Then take scales and divide up the hair you cut off.
2 Burn a third of it in the fire inside the city when the days of
your siege are completed. Take a third and slash it with a sword
all around the city. Scatter a third to the wind, and I will unleash
a sword behind them. 3 But take a few strands of hair from those
and tie them in the ends of your garment. 4 Again, take more of
them and throw them into the fire, and burn them up. From
there a fire will spread to all the house of Israel.

5 "This is what the Sovereign LORD says: This is Jerusalem; I
placed her in the center of the nations with countries all around
her. 6 Then she defied my regulations and my statutes, becoming more wicked than the nations and the countries around
her. Indeed, they have rejected my regulations, and they do not
follow my statutes.
7 "Therefore this is what the Sovereign LORD says: Because
you are more arrogant than the nations around you, you have
not followed my statutes and have not carried out my regulations. You have not even carried out the regulations of the nations around you!
8 "Therefore this is what the Sovereign LORD says: I—even I—am
against you, and I will execute judgment among you while the
nations watch. 9 I will do to you what I have never done before
and will never do again because of all your abominable practices.
10 Therefore, fathers will eat their sons within you, Jerusalem,
and sons will eat their fathers. I will execute judgments on you,
and I will scatter any survivors to the winds.
11 "Therefore, as surely as I live, says the Sovereign LORD, because you defiled my sanctuary with all your detestable idols
and with all your abominable practices, I will withdraw; my eye
will not pity you, nor will I spare you. 12 A third of your people
will die of plague or be overcome by the famine within you. A
third of your people will fall by the sword surrounding you, and
a third I will scatter to the winds. I will unleash a sword behind
them. 13 Then my anger will be fully vented; I will exhaust my
rage on them, and I will be appeased. Then they will know that
I, the LORD, have spoken in my jealousy when I have fully vented
my rage against them.
14 "I will make you desolate and an object of scorn among the
nations around you, in the sight of everyone who passes by. 15 You
will be an object of scorn and taunting, a prime example of destruction among the nations around you when I execute judgments against you in anger and raging fury. I, the LORD, have
spoken! 16 I will shoot against them deadly, destructive arrows
of famine, which I will shoot to destroy you. I will prolong a famine on you and will remove the bread supply. 17 I will send famine and wild beasts against you, and they will take your children
from you. Plague and bloodshed will overwhelm you, and I will
bring a sword against you. I, the LORD, have spoken!"

JUDGMENT ON THE MOUNTAINS OF ISRAEL

6 The LORD's message came to me: 2 "Son of man, turn toward
the mountains of Israel and prophesy against them. 3 Say,
'Mountains of Israel, hear the word of the Sovereign LORD! This
is what the Sovereign LORD says to the mountains and the hills,
to the ravines and the valleys: I am bringing a sword against you,
and I will destroy your high places. 4 Your altars will be ruined
and your incense altars will be broken. I will throw down your
slain in front of your idols. 5 I will place the corpses of the people of Israel in front of their idols, and I will scatter your bones
around your altars. 6 In all your dwellings, the cities will be laid
waste and the high places ruined so that your altars will be laid
waste and ruined, your idols will be shattered and demolished,

your incense altars will be broken down, and your works wiped
out. 7 The slain will fall among you and then you will know that
I am the LORD.
8 "'But I will spare some of you. Some will escape the sword
when you are scattered in foreign lands. 9 Then your survivors
will remember me among the nations where they are exiled.
They will realize how I was crushed by their unfaithful heart
that turned from me and by their eyes that lusted after their
idols. They will loathe themselves because of the evil they have
done and because of all their abominable practices. 10 They will
know that I am the LORD; my threats to bring this catastrophe
on them were not empty.
11 "'This is what the Sovereign LORD says: Clap your hands,
stamp your feet, and say, "Ah!" because of all the evil, abominable practices of the house of Israel, for they will fall by the sword,
famine, and pestilence. 12 The one far away will die by pestilence,
the one close by will fall by the sword, and whoever is left and
has escaped these will die by famine. I will fully vent my rage
against them. 13 Then you will know that I am the LORD when
their dead lie among their idols around their altars, on every
high hill and on all the mountaintops, under every green tree
and every leafy oak—the places where they have offered fragrant
incense to all their idols. 14 I will stretch out my hand against
them and make the land a desolate waste from the wilderness
to Riblah, in all the places where they live. Then they will know
that I am the LORD.'"

REFLECT

How does God's judgment on His people's sin reveal His holiness?

THE END ARRIVES

7 The LORD's message came to me: 2 "You, son of man—this is
what the Sovereign LORD says to the land of Israel: An end!
The end is coming on the four corners of the land! 3 The end is
now upon you, and I will release my anger against you. I will judge
you according to your behavior; I will hold you accountable for
all your abominable practices. 4 My eye will not pity you; I will
not spare you. For I will hold you responsible for your behavior,
and you will suffer the consequences of your abominable practices. Then you will know that I am the LORD!
5 "This is what the Sovereign LORD says: A disaster—a one-of-
a-kind disaster—is coming! 6 An end comes—the end comes! It
has awakened against you! Look, it is coming! 7 Doom is coming
upon you who live in the land! The time is coming, the day is near.
There are sounds of tumult, not shouts of joy, on the mountains.
8 Soon now I will pour out my rage on you; I will fully vent my
anger against you. I will judge you according to your behavior. I
will hold you accountable for all your abominable practices. 9 My
eye will not pity you; I will not spare you. For your behavior I will
hold you accountable, and you will suffer the consequences of
your abominable practices. Then you will know that it is I, the
LORD, who is striking you.
10 "Look, the day! Look, it is coming! Doom has gone out! The
staff has budded, pride has blossomed! 11 Violence has grown
into a staff that supports wickedness. Not one of them will be
left—not from their crowd, not from their wealth, not from
their prominence. 12 The time has come; the day has struck! The

customer should not rejoice, nor the seller mourn; for divine wrath comes against their whole crowd. 13 The customer will no longer pay the seller while both parties are alive, for the vision against their whole crowd will not be revoked. Each person, for his iniquity, will fail to preserve his life.

14 "They have blown the trumpet and everyone is ready, but no one goes to battle, because my anger is against their whole crowd. 15 The sword is outside; pestilence and famine are inside the house. Whoever is in the open field will die by the sword, and famine and pestilence will consume everyone in the city. 16 Their survivors will escape to the mountains and become like doves of the valleys ; all of them will moan—each one for his iniquity. 17 All their hands will hang limp; their knees will be wet with urine. 18 They will wear sackcloth, terror will cover them; shame will be on all their faces, and all their heads will be shaved bald. 19 They will discard their silver in the streets, and their gold will be treated like filth. Their silver and gold will not be able to deliver them on the day of the LORD's fury. They will not satisfy their hunger or fill their stomachs because their wealth was the obstacle leading to their iniquity. 20 They rendered the beauty of his ornaments into pride, and with it they made their abominable images—their detestable idols. Therefore I will render it filthy to them. 21 I will give it to foreigners as loot, to the world's wicked ones as plunder, and they will desecrate it. 22 I will turn my face away from them, and they will desecrate my treasured place. Vandals will enter it and desecrate it. 23 (Make the chain, because the land is full of murder and the city is full of violence.) 24 I will bring the most wicked of the nations, and they will take possession of their houses. I will put an end to the arrogance of the strong, and their sanctuaries will be desecrated. 25 Terror is coming! They will seek peace, but find none. 26 Disaster after disaster will come, and one rumor after another. They will seek a vision from a prophet; priestly instruction will disappear, along with counsel from the elders. 27 The king will mourn and the prince will be clothed with shuddering; the hands of the people of the land will tremble. Based on their behavior I will deal with them, and by their standard of justice I will judge them. Then they will know that I am the LORD!"

A DESECRATED TEMPLE

8 In the sixth year, in the sixth month, on the fifth of the month, as I was sitting in my house with the elders of Judah sitting in front of me, the hand of the Sovereign LORD seized me. 2 As I watched, I noticed a form that appeared to be a man. From his waist downward was something like fire, and from his waist upward something like a brightness, like an amber glow. 3 He stretched out the form of a hand and grabbed me by a lock of hair on my head. Then a wind lifted me up between the earth and sky and brought me to Jerusalem by divine visions, to the door of the inner gate that faces north where the statue that provokes to jealousy was located. 4 Then I perceived that the glory of the God of Israel was there, as in the vision I had seen earlier in the valley.

5 He said to me, "Son of man, look up toward the north." So I
looked up toward the north, and I noticed to the north of the
altar gate was this statue of jealousy at the entrance.

6 He said to me, "Son of man, do you see what they are doing—
the great abominations that the people of Israel are practicing
here, to drive me far from my sanctuary? But you will see greater
abominations than these!"

7 He brought me to the entrance of the court, and as I
watched, I noticed a hole in the wall. 8 He said to me, "Son of
man, dig into the wall." So I dug into the wall and discovered
a doorway.

9 He said to me, "Go in and see the evil abominations they are
practicing here." 10 So I went in and looked. I noticed every figure of creeping thing and beast—detestable images—and every
idol of the house of Israel, engraved on the wall all around. 11 Seventy men from the elders of the house of Israel (with Jaazaniah
son of Shaphan standing among them) were standing in front of
them, each with a censer in his hand, and fragrant vapors from
a cloud of incense were swirling upward.

12 He said to me, "Do you see, son of man, what the elders of the
house of Israel are doing in the dark, each in the chamber of his
idolatrous images? For they think, 'The LORD does not see us!
The LORD has abandoned the land!'" 13 He said to me, "You will
see them practicing even greater abominations!"

14 Then he brought me to the entrance of the north gate of the
LORD's house. I noticed women sitting there weeping for Tam-
muz. 15 He said to me, "Do you see this, son of man? You will see
even greater abominations than these!"

16 Then he brought me to the inner court of the LORD's house.
Right there at the entrance to the LORD's temple, between the
porch and the altar, were about twenty-five men with their backs
to the LORD's temple, facing east—they were worshiping the sun
toward the east!

17 He said to me, "Do you see, son of man? Is it a trivial thing
that the house of Judah commits these abominations they are
practicing here? For they have filled the land with violence and
provoked me to anger still further. Look, they are putting the
branch to their nose! 18 Therefore I will act with fury! My eye will
not pity them nor will I spare them. When they have shouted in
my ears, I will not listen to them."

THE EXECUTION OF IDOLATERS

9 Then he shouted in my ears, "Approach, you who are to visit
destruction on the city, each with his destructive weapon in
his hand!" 2 Next I noticed six men coming from the direction
of the upper gate that faces north, each with his war club in his
hand. Among them was a man dressed in linen with a writing kit
at his side. They came and stood beside the bronze altar.

3 Then the glory of the God of Israel went up from the cherub
where it had rested to the threshold of the temple. He called
to the man dressed in linen who had the writing kit at his side.
4 The LORD said to him, "Go through the city of Jerusalem and
put a mark on the foreheads of the people who moan and groan
over all the abominations practiced in it."

5 While I listened, he said to the others, "Go through the city
after him and strike people down; do not let your eye pity nor
spare anyone! 6 Old men, young men, young women, little children, and women—wipe them out! But do not touch anyone who
has the mark. Begin at my sanctuary!" So they began with the
elders who were at the front of the temple.
7 He said to them, "Defile the temple and fill the courtyards
with corpses. Go!" So they went out and struck people down
throughout the city. 8 While they were striking them down, I
was left alone, and I threw myself face down and cried out, "Ah,
Sovereign LORD! Will you destroy the entire remnant of Israel
when you pour out your fury on Jerusalem?"
9 He said to me, "The sin of the house of Israel and Judah is extremely great; the land is full of murder, and the city is full of corruption, for they say, 'The LORD has abandoned the land, and the
LORD does not see!' 10 But as for me, my eye will not pity them nor
will I spare them; I hereby repay them for what they have done."
11 Next I noticed the man dressed in linen with the writing
kit at his side bringing back word: "I have done just as you commanded me."

GOD'S GLORY LEAVES THE TEMPLE

10 As I watched, I saw on the platform above the top of the
cherubim something like a sapphire, resembling the shape
of a throne, appearing above them. 2 The LORD said to the man
dressed in linen, "Go between the wheelwork underneath the
cherubim. Fill your hands with burning coals from among the
cherubim and scatter them over the city." He went as I watched.
3 (The cherubim were standing on the south side of the temple
when the man went in, and a cloud filled the inner court.) 4 Then
the glory of the LORD arose from the cherub and moved to the
threshold of the temple. The temple was filled with the cloud
while the court was filled with the brightness of the LORD's glory.
5 The sound of the wings of the cherubim could be heard from the
outer court, like the sound of the Sovereign God when he speaks.
6 When the LORD commanded the man dressed in linen, "Take
fire from within the wheelwork, from among the cherubim,"
the man went in and stood by one of the wheels. 7 Then one of
the cherubim stretched out his hand toward the fire that was
among the cherubim. He took some and put it into the hands of
the man dressed in linen, who took it and left. 8 (The cherubim
appeared to have the form of human hands under their wings.)
9 As I watched, I noticed four wheels by the cherubim, one
wheel beside each cherub; the wheels gleamed like jasper. 10 As
for their appearance, all four of them looked the same, something
like a wheel within a wheel. 11 When they moved, they would go
in any of the four directions they faced without turning as they
moved; in the direction the head would turn they would follow
without turning as they moved, 12 along with their entire bodies,
their backs, their hands, and their wings. The wheels of the four
of them were full of eyes all around. 13 As for their wheels, they
were called "the wheelwork" as I listened. 14 Each of the cherubim
had four faces: The first was the face of a cherub, the second that
of a man, the third that of a lion, and the fourth that of an eagle.

15 The cherubim rose up; these were the living beings I saw at
the Kebar River. 16 When the cherubim moved, the wheels moved
beside them; when the cherubim spread their wings to rise from
the ground, the wheels did not move from their side. 17 When the
cherubim stood still, the wheels stood still, and when they rose
up, the wheels rose up with them, for the spirit of the living beings was in the wheels.

18 Then the glory of the LORD moved away from the threshold
of the temple and stopped above the cherubim. 19 The cherubim spread their wings, and they rose up from the earth while
I watched (when they went, the wheels went alongside them).
They stopped at the entrance to the east gate of the LORD's temple as the glory of the God of Israel hovered above them.

20 These were the living creatures that I saw at the Kebar River
underneath the God of Israel; I knew that they were cherubim.
21 Each had four faces; each had four wings and the form of human hands under the wings. 22 As for the form of their faces, they
were the faces whose appearance I had seen at the Kebar River.
Each one moved straight ahead.

THE FALL OF JERUSALEM

11 A wind lifted me up and brought me to the east gate of the
LORD's temple that faces the east. There, at the entrance of
the gate, I noticed twenty-five men. Among them I saw Jaazaniah son of Azzur and Pelatiah son of Benaiah, officials of the
people. 2 The LORD said to me, "Son of man, these are the men
who plot evil and give wicked advice in this city. 3 They say, 'The
time is not near to build houses; the city is a cooking pot, and we
are the meat in it.' 4 Therefore, prophesy against them! Prophesy, son of man!"

5 Then the Spirit of the LORD came upon me and said to me,
"Say: 'This is what the LORD says: This is what you are thinking,
O house of Israel; I know what goes through your minds. 6 You
have killed many people in this city; you have filled its streets
with corpses.' 7 Therefore, this is what the Sovereign LORD says:
'The corpses you have dumped in the midst of the city are the
meat, and this city is the cooking pot, but I will take you out of
it. 8 You fear the sword, so the sword I will bring against you,' declares the Sovereign LORD. 9 'But I will take you out of the city.
And I will hand you over to foreigners. I will execute judgments
on you. 10 You will die by the sword; I will judge you at the border
of Israel. Then you will know that I am the LORD. 11 This city will
not be a cooking pot for you, and you will not be meat within
it; I will judge you at the border of Israel. 12 Then you will know
that I am the LORD, whose statutes you have not followed and
whose regulations you have not carried out. Instead you have behaved according to the regulations of the nations around you!'"

13 Now, while I was prophesying, Pelatiah son of Benaiah died.
Then I threw myself face down and cried out with a loud voice,
"Alas, Sovereign LORD! You are completely wiping out the rem-
nant of Israel!"

14 Then the LORD's message came to me: 15 "Son of man, your
brothers, your relatives, and the whole house of Israel, all of
them are those to whom the inhabitants of Jerusalem have said,

‘They have gone far away from the LORD; to us this land has been
given as a possession.’
16“Therefore say: ‘This is what the Sovereign LORD says: Although I have removed them far away among the nations and
have dispersed them among the countries, I have been a little sanctuary for them among the lands where they have gone.’
17“Therefore say: ‘This is what the Sovereign LORD says: When I
regather you from the peoples and assemble you from the lands
where you have been dispersed, I will give you back the country of Israel.’
18“When they return to it, they will remove from it all its detestable things and all its abominations. 19I will give them one
heart and I will put a new spirit within them; I will remove the
hearts of stone from their bodies and I will give them tender
hearts, 20so that they may follow my statutes and observe my
regulations and carry them out. Then they will be my people,
and I will be their God. 21But those whose hearts are devoted to
detestable things and abominations, I hereby repay them for
what they have done, says the Sovereign LORD.”
22Then the cherubim spread their wings with their wheels
alongside them while the glory of the God of Israel hovered
above them. 23The glory of the LORD rose up from within the city
and stopped over the mountain east of it. 24Then a wind lifted
me up and carried me to the exiles in Babylonia, in the vision
given to me by the Spirit of God.
Then the vision I had seen went up from me. 25So I told the
exiles everything the LORD had shown me.

PREVIEWING THE EXILE

12 The LORD’s message came to me: 2“Son of man, you are living in the midst of a rebellious house. They have eyes to see,
but do not see, and ears to hear, but do not hear, because they
are a rebellious house.
3“Therefore, son of man, pack up your belongings as if for exile. During the day, while they are watching, pretend to go into
exile. Go from where you live to another place. Perhaps they will
understand, although they are a rebellious house. 4Bring out
your belongings packed for exile during the day while they are
watching. And go out at evening, while they are watching, as if
for exile. 5While they are watching, dig a hole in the wall and
carry your belongings out through it. 6While they are watching, raise your baggage onto your shoulder and carry it out in
the dark. You must cover your face so that you cannot see the
ground because I have made you an object lesson to the house
of Israel.”
7So I did just as I was commanded. I carried out my belongings packed for exile during the day, and at evening I dug myself
a hole through the wall with my hands. I went out in the darkness, carrying my baggage on my shoulder while they watched.
8The LORD’s message came to me in the morning: 9“Son of
man, has not the house of Israel, that rebellious house, said to
you, ‘What are you doing?’ 10Say to them, ‘This is what the Sovereign LORD says: The prince will raise this burden in Jerusalem,
and all the house of Israel within it.’ 11Say, ‘I am an object lesson

REFLECT

Why did God ask Ezekiel to act as if he were going into exile? How did this prepare the people for the exile that was to come?

for you. Just as I have done, so it will be done to them; they will
go into exile and captivity.'
12 "The prince who is among them will raise his belongings
onto his shoulder in darkness and will go out. He will dig a hole
in the wall to leave through. He will cover his face so that he
cannot see the land with his eyes. 13 But I will throw my net
over him, and he will be caught in my snare. I will bring him
to Babylon, the land of the Chaldeans (but he will not see it),
and there he will die. 14 All his retinue—his attendants and his
troops—I will scatter to every wind; I will unleash a sword behind them.
15 "Then they will know that I am the LORD when I disperse
them among the nations and scatter them among foreign countries. 16 But I will let a small number of them survive the sword,
famine, and pestilence, so that they can confess all their abominable practices to the nations where they go. Then they will
know that I am the LORD."
17 The LORD's message came to me: 18 "Son of man, eat your
bread with trembling and drink your water with anxious shaking. 19 Then say to the people of the land, 'This is what the Sovereign LORD says about the inhabitants of Jerusalem and of the
land of Israel: They will eat their bread with anxiety and drink
their water in fright, for their land will be stripped bare of all it
contains because of the violence of all who live in it. 20 The inhabited towns will be left in ruins, and the land will be devastated. Then you will know that I am the LORD.'"
21 The LORD's message came to me: 22 "Son of man, what is this
proverb you have in the land of Israel, 'The days pass slowly, and
every vision fails'? 23 Therefore tell them, 'This is what the Sovereign LORD says: I hereby end this proverb; they will not recite
it in Israel any longer.' But say to them, 'The days are at hand
when every vision will be fulfilled. 24 For there will no longer be
any false visions or flattering omens amidst the house of Israel.
25 For I, the LORD, will speak. Whatever word I speak will be accomplished. It will not be delayed any longer. Indeed in your
days, O rebellious house, I will speak the word and accomplish
it, declares the Sovereign LORD.'"
26 The LORD's message came to me: 27 "Take note, son of man,
the house of Israel is saying, 'The vision that he sees is for distant days; he is prophesying about the far future.' 28 Therefore
say to them, 'This is what the Sovereign LORD says: None of my
words will be delayed any longer! The word I speak will come to
pass, declares the Sovereign LORD.'"

FALSE PROPHETS DENOUNCED

13 Then the LORD's message came to me: 2 "Son of man, prophesy against the prophets of Israel who are now prophesying. Say to the prophets who prophesy from their imagination:
'Listen to the LORD's message! 3 This is what the Sovereign LORD
says: Woe to the foolish prophets who follow their own spirit
but have seen nothing! 4 Your prophets have become like jackals
among the ruins, O Israel. 5 You have not gone up in the breaks
in the wall, nor repaired a wall for the house of Israel that it
would stand strong in the battle on the day of the LORD. 6 They

see delusion and their omens are a lie. They say, "The LORD declares," though the LORD has not sent them; yet they expect
their word to be confirmed. 7 Have you not seen a false vision
and announced a lying omen when you say, "The LORD declares,"
although I myself never spoke?
8 "'Therefore, this is what the Sovereign LORD says: Because you
have spoken false words and forecast delusion, look, I am against
you, declares the Sovereign LORD. 9 My hand will be against the
prophets who see delusion and announce lying omens. They will
not be included in the council of my people, nor be written in
the registry of the house of Israel, nor enter the land of Israel.
Then you will know that I am the Sovereign LORD.
10 "'This is because they have led my people astray saying, "All is
well," when things are not well. When anyone builds a wall without mortar, they coat it with whitewash. 11 Tell the ones who coat
it with whitewash that it will fall. When there is a deluge of rain,
hailstones will fall and a violent wind will break out. 12 When the
wall has collapsed, people will ask you, "Where is the whitewash
you coated it with?"
13 "'Therefore this is what the Sovereign LORD says: In my rage
I will make a violent wind break out. In my anger there will be a
deluge of rain and hailstones in destructive fury. 14 I will break
down the wall you coated with whitewash and knock it to the
ground so that its foundation is exposed. When it falls you will be
destroyed beneath it, and you will know that I am the LORD. 15 I
will vent my rage against the wall and against those who coated
it with whitewash. Then I will say to you, "The wall is no more
and those who whitewashed it are no more—16 those prophets
of Israel who would prophesy about Jerusalem and would see
visions of peace for it, when there was no peace," declares the
Sovereign LORD.'
17 "As for you, son of man, turn toward the daughters of your
people who are prophesying from their imagination. Prophesy
against them 18 and say 'This is what the Sovereign LORD says:
Woe to those who sew bands on all their wrists and make headbands for heads of every size to entrap people's lives! Will you
entrap my people's lives, yet preserve your own lives? 19 You have
profaned me among my people for handfuls of barley and scraps
of bread. You have put to death people who should not die and
kept alive those who should not live by your lies to my people,
who listen to lies!
20 "'Therefore, this is what the Sovereign LORD says: Take
note that I am against your wristbands with which you entrap people's lives like birds. I will tear them from your arms
and will release the people's lives, which you hunt like birds.
21 I will tear off your headbands and rescue my people from
your power; they will no longer be prey in your hands. Then
you will know that I am the LORD. 22 This is because you have
disheartened the righteous person with lies (although I have
not grieved him), and because you have encouraged the wicked
person not to turn from his evil conduct and preserve his life.
23 Therefore you will no longer see false visions and practice
divination. I will rescue my people from your power, and you
will know that I am the LORD.'"

WELL-DESERVED JUDGMENT

14 Then some men from Israel's elders came to me and sat down in front of me. 2 The LORD's message came to me: 3 "Son of man, these men have erected their idols in their hearts and placed the obstacle leading to their iniquity right before their faces. Should I really allow them to seek me? 4 Therefore speak to them and say to them, 'This is what the Sovereign LORD says: When anyone from the house of Israel erects his idols in his heart and sets the obstacle leading to his iniquity before his face, and then consults a prophet, I the LORD am determined to answer him personally according to the enormity of his idolatry. 5 I will do this in order to capture the hearts of the house of Israel, who have alienated themselves from me on account of all their idols.'

6 "Therefore say to the house of Israel, 'This is what the Sovereign LORD says: Return! Turn from your idols, and turn your faces away from your abominations. 7 For when anyone from the house of Israel, or the resident foreigner who lives in Israel, separates himself from me and erects his idols in his heart and sets the obstacle leading to his iniquity before his face, and then consults a prophet to seek something from me, I the LORD am determined to answer him personally. 8 I will set my face against that person and will make him an object lesson and a byword and will cut him off from among my people. Then you will know that I am the LORD.

9 "'As for the prophet, if he is made a fool by being deceived into speaking a prophetic word—I, the LORD, have made a fool of that prophet, and I will stretch out my hand against him and destroy him from among my people Israel. 10 They will bear their punishment; the punishment of the one who sought an oracle will be the same as the punishment of the prophet who gave it 11 so that the house of Israel will no longer go astray from me, nor continue to defile themselves by all their sins. They will be my people, and I will be their God, declares the Sovereign LORD.'"

12 The LORD's message came to me: 13 "Son of man, suppose a country sins against me by being unfaithful, and I stretch out my hand against it, cut off its bread supply, cause famine to come on it, and kill both people and animals. 14 Even if these three men, Noah, Daniel, and Job, were in it, they would save only their own lives by their righteousness, declares the Sovereign LORD.

15 "Suppose I were to send wild animals through the land and kill its children, leaving it desolate, without travelers due to the wild animals. 16 Even if these three men were in it, as surely as I live, declares the Sovereign LORD, they could not save their own sons or daughters; they would save only their own lives, and the land would become desolate.

17 "Or suppose I were to bring a sword against that land and say, 'Let a sword pass through the land,' and I were to kill both people and animals. 18 Even if these three men were in it, as surely as I live, declares the Sovereign LORD, they could not save their own sons or daughters—they would save only their own lives.

19 "Or suppose I were to send a plague into that land and pour out my rage on it with bloodshed, killing both people and animals. 20 Even if Noah, Daniel, and Job were in it, as surely as I live, declares the Sovereign LORD, they could not save their own son or daughter; they would save only their own lives by their righteousness.

21 "For this is what the Sovereign LORD says: How much worse will it be when I send my four terrible judgments—sword, famine, wild animals, and plague—to Jerusalem to kill both people and animals! 22 Yet some survivors will be left in it, sons and daughters who will be brought out. They will come out to you, and when you see their behavior and their deeds, you will be consoled about the catastrophe I have brought on Jerusalem—for everything I brought on it. 23 They will console you when you see their behavior and their deeds, because you will know that it was not without reason that I have done everything that I have done in it, declares the Sovereign LORD."

BURNING A USELESS VINE

15 The LORD's message came to me: 2 "Son of man, of all the woody branches among the trees of the forest, what happens to the wood of the vine? 3 Can wood be taken from it to make anything useful? Or can anyone make a peg from it to hang things on? 4 No! It is thrown in the fire for fuel; when the fire has burned up both ends of it and it is charred in the middle, will it be useful for anything? 5 Indeed! If it was not made into anything useful when it was whole, how much less can it be made into anything when the fire has burned it up and it is charred?

6 "Therefore, this is what the Sovereign LORD says: Like the wood of the vine is among the trees of the forest that I have provided as fuel for the fire—so I will provide the residents of Jerusalem as fuel. 7 I will set my face against them—although they have escaped from the fire, the fire will still consume them! Then you will know that I am the LORD, when I set my face against them. 8 I will make the land desolate because they have acted unfaithfully, declares the Sovereign LORD."

GOD'S UNFAITHFUL BRIDE

16 The LORD's message came to me: 2 "Son of man, confront Jerusalem with her abominable practices 3 and say, 'This is what the Sovereign LORD says to Jerusalem: Your origin and your birth were in the land of the Canaanites; your father was an Amorite and your mother a Hittite. 4 As for your birth, on the day you were born your umbilical cord was not cut, nor were you washed in water; you were certainly not rubbed down with salt, nor wrapped with blankets. 5 No eye took pity on you to do even one of these things for you to spare you; you were thrown out into the open field because you were detested on the day you were born.

6 "'I passed by you and saw you kicking around helplessly in your blood. I said to you as you lay there in your blood, "Live!" I said to you as you lay there in your blood, "Live!" 7 I made you plentiful like sprouts in a field; you grew tall and came of age so that you could wear jewelry. Your breasts had formed and your hair had grown, but you were still naked and bare.

8"'Then I passed by you and watched you, noticing that you had
reached the age for love. I spread my cloak over you and covered
your nakedness. I swore a solemn oath to you and entered into a
marriage covenant with you, declares the Sovereign LORD, and
you became mine.
9"'Then I bathed you in water, washed the blood off you, and
anointed you with fragrant oil. 10 I dressed you in embroidered
clothing and put fine leather sandals on your feet. I wrapped you
with fine linen and covered you with silk. 11 I adorned you with
jewelry. I put bracelets on your hands and a necklace around
your neck. 12 I put a ring in your nose, earrings on your ears, and
a beautiful crown on your head. 13 You were adorned with gold
and silver, while your clothing was of fine linen, silk, and em-
broidery. You ate the finest flour, honey, and olive oil. You became extremely beautiful and attained the position of royalty.
14 Your fame spread among the nations because of your beauty;
your beauty was perfect because of the splendor that I bestowed
on you, declares the Sovereign LORD.
15"'But you trusted in your beauty and capitalized on your fame
by becoming a prostitute. You offered your sexual favors to every man who passed by so that your beauty became his. 16 You
took some of your clothing and made for yourself decorated
high places; you engaged in prostitution on them. You went to
him to become his. 17 You also took your beautiful jewelry, made
of my gold and my silver I had given to you, and made for yourself male images and engaged in prostitution with them. 18 You
took your embroidered clothing and used it to cover them; you
offered my olive oil and my incense to them. 19 As for my food
that I gave you—the fine flour, olive oil, and honey I fed you—you
placed it before them as a soothing aroma. That is exactly what
happened, declares the Sovereign LORD.
20"'You took your sons and your daughters whom you bore
to me and you sacrificed them as food for the idols to eat. As if
your prostitution was not enough, 21 you slaughtered my children
and sacrificed them to the idols. 22 And with all your abominable practices and prostitution you did not remember the days
of your youth when you were naked and bare, kicking around
in your blood.
23"'After all your evil—"Woe! Woe to you!" declares the Sovereign LORD—24 you built yourself a chamber and put up a pavilion in every public square. 25 At the head of every street you
erected your pavilion, and you disgraced your beauty when you
spread your legs to every passerby and multiplied your promiscuity. 26 You engaged in prostitution with the Egyptians, your
lustful neighbors, multiplying your promiscuity and provoking me to anger. 27 So see here, I have stretched out my hand
against you and cut off your rations. I have delivered you into
the power of those who hate you, the daughters of the Philistines, who were ashamed of your obscene conduct. 28 You engaged in prostitution with the Assyrians because your desires
were insatiable; you prostituted yourself with them and yet
you were still not satisfied. 29 Then you multiplied your promiscuity to the land of merchants, Babylonia, but you were
not satisfied there either.

[30]"'How sick is your heart, declares the Sovereign LORD, when
you perform all these acts, the deeds of a bold prostitute. [31]When
you built your chamber at the head of every street and put up
your pavilion in every public square, you were not like a prostitute, because you scoffed at payment.
[32]"'Adulterous wife, who prefers strangers instead of her own
husband! [33]All prostitutes receive payment, but instead you give
gifts to every one of your lovers. You bribe them to come to you
from all around for your sexual favors! [34]You were different from
other prostitutes because no one solicited you. When you gave payment and no payment was given to you, you became the opposite!
[35]"'Therefore, you prostitute, listen to the LORD's message!
[36]This is what the Sovereign LORD says: Because your lust was
poured out and your nakedness was uncovered in your prostitution with your lovers, and because of all your detestable idols,
and because of the blood of your children you have given to them,
[37]therefore, take note: I am about to gather all your lovers whom
you enjoyed, both all those you loved and all those you hated. I
will gather them against you from all around, and I will expose
your nakedness to them, and they will see all your nakedness.
[38]I will punish you as an adulteress and murderer deserves. I
will avenge your bloody deeds with furious rage. [39]I will give
you into their hands, and they will destroy your chambers and
tear down your pavilions. They will strip you of your clothing
and take your beautiful jewelry and leave you naked and bare.
[40]They will summon a mob who will stone you and hack you in
pieces with their swords. [41]They will burn down your houses and
execute judgments on you in front of many women. Thus I will
put a stop to your prostitution, and you will no longer give gifts
to your clients. [42]I will exhaust my rage on you, and then my
fury will turn from you. I will calm down and no longer be angry.
[43]"'Because you did not remember the days of your youth and
have enraged me with all these deeds, I hereby repay you for what
you have done, declares the Sovereign LORD. Have you not engaged
in prostitution on top of all your other abominable practices?
[44]"'Observe—everyone who quotes proverbs will quote this
proverb about you: "Like mother, like daughter." [45]You are the
daughter of your mother, who detested her husband and her
sons, and you are the sister of your sisters, who detested their
husbands and their sons. Your mother was a Hittite and your
father an Amorite. [46]Your older sister was Samaria, who lived
north of you with her daughters, and your younger sister, who
lived south of you, was Sodom with her daughters. [47]Have you
not copied their behavior and practiced their abominable deeds?
In a short time you became even more depraved in all your conduct than they were! [48]As surely as I live, declares the Sovereign
LORD, your sister Sodom and her daughters never behaved as
wickedly as you and your daughters have behaved.
[49]"'See here—this was the iniquity of your sister Sodom: She
and her daughters had majesty, abundance of food, and enjoyed
carefree ease, but they did not help the poor and needy. [50]They
were haughty and practiced abominable deeds before me. Therefore, when I saw it I removed them. [51]Samaria has not committed
half the sins you have; you have done more abominable deeds

than they did. You have made your sisters appear righteous with all the abominable things you have done. 52 So now, bear your disgrace, because you have given your sisters reason to justify their behavior. Because the sins you have committed were more abominable than those of your sisters; they have become more righteous than you. So now, be ashamed and bear the disgrace of making your sisters appear righteous.

53 "'I will restore their fortunes, the fortunes of Sodom and her daughters, and the fortunes of Samaria and her daughters (along with your fortunes among them), 54 so that you may bear your disgrace and be ashamed of all you have done in consoling them. 55 As for your sisters, Sodom and her daughters will be restored to their former status, Samaria and her daughters will be restored to their former status, and you and your daughters will be restored to your former status. 56 In your days of majesty, was not Sodom your sister a byword in your mouth, 57 before your evil was exposed? Now you have become an object of scorn to the daughters of Aram and all those around her and to the daughters of the Philistines—those all around you who despise you. 58 You must bear your punishment for your obscene conduct and your abominable practices, declares the LORD.

59 "'For this is what the Sovereign LORD says: I will deal with you according to what you have done when you despised your oath by breaking your covenant. 60 Yet I will remember the covenant I made with you in the days of your youth, and I will establish a lasting covenant with you. 61 Then you will remember your conduct, and be ashamed when you receive your older and younger sisters. I will give them to you as daughters, but not on account of my covenant with you. 62 I will establish my covenant with you, and then you will know that I am the LORD. 63 Then you will remember, be ashamed, and remain silent because of your disgrace when I make atonement for all you have done, declares the Sovereign LORD.'"

A PARABLE OF TWO EAGLES AND A VINE

17 The LORD's message came to me: 2 "Son of man, offer a riddle, and tell a parable to the house of Israel. 3 Say to them: 'This is what the Sovereign LORD says:

"'A great eagle with broad wings, long feathers,
with full plumage that was multi-hued,
came to Lebanon and took the top of the cedar.
4 He plucked off its topmost shoot;
he brought it to a land of merchants
and planted it in a city of traders.
5 He took one of the seedlings of the land,
placed it in a cultivated plot;
a shoot by abundant water,
like a willow he planted it.
6 It sprouted and became a vine,
spreading low to the ground;
its branches turning toward him, its
roots were under itself.
So it became a vine; it produced shoots
and sent out branches.

7 "'There was another great eagle
with broad wings and thick plumage.
Now this vine twisted its roots toward him
and sent its branches toward him
to be watered from the soil where it was planted.
8 In a good field, by abundant waters, it was planted
to grow branches, bear fruit, and become a beautiful vine.'

9 "Say to them: 'This is what the Sovereign LORD says:
"'Will it prosper?
Will he not rip out its roots
and cause its fruit to rot and wither?
All its foliage will wither.
No strong arm or large army
will be needed to pull it out by its roots.
10 Consider! It is planted, but will it prosper?
Will it not wither completely when
the east wind blows on it?
Will it not wither in the soil where it sprouted?'"

11 Then the LORD's message came to me: 12 "Say to the rebellious house of Israel: 'Don't you know what these things
mean?' Say: 'See here, the king of Babylon came to Jerusalem
and took her king and her officials prisoner and brought them
to himself in Babylon. 13 He took one from the royal family,
made a treaty with him, and put him under oath. He then took
the leaders of the land 14 so it would be a lowly kingdom that
could not rise on its own but had to keep its treaty with him
in order to stand. 15 But this one from Israel's royal family rebelled against the king of Babylon by sending his emissaries
to Egypt to obtain horses and a large army. Will he prosper?
Will the one doing these things escape? Can he break the covenant and escape?
16 "'As surely as I live, declares the Sovereign LORD, surely in the
city of the king who crowned him, whose oath he despised and
whose covenant he broke—in the middle of Babylon he will die!
17 Pharaoh with his great army and mighty horde will not help
him in battle, when siege ramps are erected and siege walls are
built to kill many people. 18 He despised the oath by breaking
the covenant. Take note—he gave his promise and did all these
things. He will not escape!
19 "'Therefore this is what the Sovereign LORD says: As surely as
I live, I will certainly repay him for despising my oath and breaking my covenant! 20 I will throw my net over him and he will be
caught in my snare; I will bring him to Babylon and judge him
there because of the unfaithfulness he committed against me.
21 All the choice men among his troops will die by the sword, and
the survivors will be scattered to every wind. Then you will know
that I, the LORD, have spoken!
22 "'This is what the Sovereign LORD says:
"'I will take a sprig from the lofty top
of the cedar and plant it.
I will pluck from the top one of its tender twigs;
I myself will plant it on a high and lofty mountain.

23 I will plant it on a high mountain of Israel,
and it will raise branches and produce fruit
and become a beautiful cedar.
Every bird will live under it;
Every winged creature will live in
the shade of its branches.
24 All the trees of the field will know that I am the LORD.
I make the high tree low; I raise up the low tree.
I make the green tree wither, and I
make the dry tree sprout.
I, the LORD, have spoken, and I will do it!'"

INDIVIDUAL RETRIBUTION

18 The LORD's message came to me: 2 "What do you mean by
quoting this proverb concerning the land of Israel:
"'The fathers eat sour grapes,
And the children's teeth become numb?'

3 "As surely as I live, declares the Sovereign LORD, you will
not quote this proverb in Israel anymore! 4 Indeed! All lives are
mine—the life of the father as well as the life of the son is mine.
The one who sins will die.
5 "Suppose a man is righteous. He practices what is just and
right, 6 does not eat pagan sacrifices on the mountains or pray
to the idols of the house of Israel, does not defile his neighbor's
wife, does not approach a woman for marital relations during
her period, 7 does not oppress anyone, but gives the debtor back
whatever was given in pledge, does not commit robbery, but gives
his bread to the hungry and clothes the naked, 8 does not engage in usury or charge interest, but refrains from wrongdoing,
promotes true justice between men, 9 and follows my statutes
and observes my regulations by carrying them out. That man is
righteous; he will certainly live, declares the Sovereign LORD.
10 "Suppose such a man has a violent son who sheds blood and
does any of these things mentioned previously 11 (though the
father did not do any of them). He eats pagan sacrifices on the
mountains, defiles his neighbor's wife, 12 oppresses the poor and
the needy, commits robbery, does not give back what was given
in pledge, prays to idols, performs abominable acts, 13 engages
in usury, and charges interest. Will he live? He will not! Because
he has done all these abominable deeds he will certainly die. He
will bear the responsibility for his own death.
14 "But suppose he in turn has a son who notices all the sins his
father commits, considers them, and does not follow his father's
example. 15 He does not eat pagan sacrifices on the mountains,
does not pray to the idols of the house of Israel, does not defile
his neighbor's wife, 16 does not oppress anyone or keep what has
been given in pledge, does not commit robbery, gives his food
to the hungry and clothes the naked, 17 refrains from wrongdoing, does not engage in usury or charge interest, carries out my
regulations, and follows my statutes. He will not die for his father's iniquity; he will surely live. 18 As for his father, because he
practices extortion, robs his brother, and does what is not good
among his people, he will die for his iniquity.

19 "Yet you say, 'Why should the son not suffer for his father's
iniquity?' When the son does what is just and right, and observes all my statutes and carries them out, he will surely live.
20 The person who sins is the one who will die. A son will not
suffer for his father's iniquity, and a father will not suffer for
his son's iniquity; the righteous person will be judged according to his righteousness, and the wicked person according to
his wickedness.
21 "But if the wicked person turns from all the sin he has committed and observes all my statutes and does what is just and
right, he will surely live; he will not die. 22 None of the sins he has
committed will be held against him; because of the righteousness he has done, he will live. 23 Do I actually delight in the death
of the wicked, declares the Sovereign LORD? Do I not prefer that
he turn from his wicked conduct and live?
24 "But if a righteous man turns away from his righteousness
and practices wrongdoing according to all the abominable practices the wicked carry out, will he live? All his righteous acts will
not be remembered; because of the unfaithful acts he has done
and the sin he has committed, he will die.
25 "Yet you say, 'The Lord's conduct is unjust!' Hear, O house of
Israel: Is my conduct unjust? Is it not your conduct that is unjust? 26 When a righteous person turns back from his righteousness and practices wrongdoing, he will die for it; because of the
wrongdoing he has done, he will die. 27 When a wicked person
turns from the wickedness he has committed and does what is
just and right, he will preserve his life. 28 Because he considered
and turned from all the sins he had done, he will surely live; he
will not die. 29 Yet the house of Israel says, 'The Lord's conduct
is unjust!' Is my conduct unjust, O house of Israel? Is it not your
conduct that is unjust?
30 "Therefore, I will judge each person according to his conduct, O house of Israel, declares the Sovereign LORD. Repent
and turn from all your wickedness; then it will not be an obstacle leading to iniquity. 31 Throw away all your sins you have
committed and fashion yourselves a new heart and a new spirit!
Why should you die, O house of Israel? 32 For I take no delight
in the death of anyone, declares the Sovereign LORD. Repent
and live!

LAMENT FOR THE PRINCES OF ISRAEL

19 "And you, sing a lament for the princes of Israel, 2 and say:
"'What a lioness was your mother among the lions!
She lay among young lions; she reared her cubs.
3 She reared one of her cubs; he became a young lion.
He learned to tear prey; he devoured people.
4 The nations heard about him; he was trapped in their pit.
They brought him with hooks to the land of Egypt.

5 "'When she realized that she waited
in vain, her hope was lost.
She took another of her cubs and made him a young lion.
6 He walked about among the lions; he became a young lion.
He learned to tear prey; he devoured people.

7 He broke down their strongholds and
devastated their cities.
The land and everything in it was frightened
at the sound of his roaring.
8 The nations—the surrounding regions—attacked him.
They threw their net over him; he was caught in their pit.
9 They put him in a collar with hooks;
they brought him to the king of Babylon;
they brought him to prison
so that his voice would not be heard
any longer on the mountains of Israel.

10 "'Your mother was like a vine in your
vineyard, planted by water.
It was fruitful and full of branches
because it was well-watered.
11 Its boughs were strong, fit for rulers' scepters;
it reached up into the clouds.
It stood out because of its height and its many branches.
12 But it was plucked up in anger; it was
thrown down to the ground.
The east wind dried up its fruit;
its strong branches broke off and withered—
a fire consumed them.
13 Now it is planted in the wilderness,
in a dry and thirsty land.
14 A fire has gone out from its branch; it has
consumed its shoot and its fruit.
No strong branch was left in it, nor a scepter to rule.'

"This is a lament song, and has become a lament song."

ISRAEL'S REBELLION

20 In the seventh year, in the fifth month, on the tenth of the
month, some of the elders of Israel came to seek the LORD,
and they sat down in front of me. 2 The LORD's message came to
me: 3 "Son of man, speak to the elders of Israel, and tell them:
'This is what the Sovereign LORD says: Are you coming to seek
me? As surely as I live, I will not allow you to seek me, declares
the Sovereign LORD.' 4 Are you willing to pronounce judgment
on them? Are you willing to pronounce judgment, son of man?
Then confront them with the abominable practices of their fathers, 5 and say to them:

"'This is what the Sovereign LORD says: On the day I chose Israel I swore to the descendants of the house of Jacob and made
myself known to them in the land of Egypt. I swore to them, "I
am the LORD your God." 6 On that day I swore to bring them out
of the land of Egypt to a land that I had picked out for them, a
land flowing with milk and honey, the most beautiful of all lands.
7 I said to them, "Each of you must get rid of the detestable idols
you keep before you, and do not defile yourselves with the idols
of Egypt; I am the LORD your God." 8 But they rebelled against
me and refused to listen to me; no one got rid of their detestable
idols, nor did they abandon the idols of Egypt. Then I decided

to pour out my rage on them and fully vent my anger against
them in the midst of the land of Egypt. 9 I acted for the sake of
my reputation, so that I would not be profaned before the nations among whom they lived, before whom I revealed myself
by bringing them out of the land of Egypt.
10 "'So I brought them out of the land of Egypt and led them
to the wilderness. 11 I gave them my statutes and revealed my
regulations to them. The one who carries them out will live by
them! 12 I also gave them my Sabbaths as a reminder of our relationship, so that they would know that I, the LORD, sanctify
them. 13 But the house of Israel rebelled against me in the wilderness; they did not follow my statutes and they rejected my
regulations (the one who obeys them will live by them), and they
utterly desecrated my Sabbaths. So I decided to pour out my
rage on them in the wilderness and destroy them. 14 I acted for
the sake of my reputation, so that I would not be profaned before the nations in whose sight I had brought them out. 15 I also
swore to them in the wilderness that I would not bring them to
the land I had given them—a land flowing with milk and honey,
the most beautiful of all lands. 16 I did this because they rejected
my regulations, did not follow my statutes, and desecrated my
Sabbaths; for their hearts followed their idols. 17 Yet I had pity
on them and did not destroy them, so I did not make an end of
them in the wilderness.
18 "'But I said to their children in the wilderness, "Do not follow
the practices of your fathers; do not observe their regulations,
nor defile yourselves with their idols. 19 I am the LORD your God;
follow my statutes, observe my regulations, and carry them out.
20 Treat my Sabbaths as holy and they will be a reminder of our
relationship, and then you will know that I am the LORD your
God." 21 But the children rebelled against me, did not follow my
statutes, did not observe my regulations by carrying them out
(the one who obeys them will live by them), and desecrated my
Sabbaths. I decided to pour out my rage on them and fully vent
my anger against them in the wilderness. 22 But I refrained from
doing so and acted instead for the sake of my reputation, so that
I would not be profaned before the nations in whose sight I
had brought them out. 23 I also swore to them in the wilderness
that I would scatter them among the nations and disperse them
throughout the lands. 24 I did this because they did not observe
my regulations, they rejected my statutes, they desecrated my
Sabbaths, and their eyes were fixed on their fathers' idols. 25 I
also gave them decrees that were not good and regulations by
which they could not live. 26 I declared them to be defiled because of their sacrifices—they caused all their firstborn to pass
through the fire—so that I might devastate them, so that they
would know that I am the LORD.'
27 "Therefore, speak to the house of Israel, son of man, and tell
them, 'This is what the Sovereign LORD says: In this way too your
fathers blasphemed me when they were unfaithful to me. 28 I
brought them to the land that I swore to give them, but whenever they saw any high hill or leafy tree, they offered their sacrifices there and presented the offerings that provoked me to
anger. They offered their soothing aroma there and poured out

REFLECT

Why did God refrain from pouring out His rage on Israel (Ezek 20:22)?

their drink offerings. 29 So I said to them, "What is this high place you go to?'" (So it is called "High Place" to this day.)

30 "Therefore say to the house of Israel, 'This is what the Sovereign LORD says: Will you defile yourselves like your fathers and engage in prostitution with detestable idols? 31 When you present your sacrifices—when you make your sons pass through the fire—you defile yourselves with all your idols to this very day. Will I allow you to seek me, O house of Israel? As surely as I live, declares the Sovereign LORD, I will not allow you to seek me!

32 "'What you plan will never happen. You say, "We will be like the nations, like the clans of the lands, who serve gods of wood and stone." 33 As surely as I live, declares the Sovereign LORD, with a powerful hand and an outstretched arm and with an outpouring of rage, I will be king over you. 34 I will bring you out from the nations and will gather you from the lands where you are scattered, with a powerful hand and an outstretched arm and with an outpouring of rage! 35 I will bring you into the wilderness of the nations, and there I will enter into judgment with you face to face. 36 Just as I entered into judgment with your fathers in the wilderness of the land of Egypt, so I will enter into judgment with you, declares the Sovereign LORD. 37 I will make you pass under the shepherd's staff, and I will bring you into the bond of the covenant. 38 I will eliminate from among you the rebels and those who revolt against me. I will bring them out from the land where they have been residing, but they will not come to the land of Israel. Then you will know that I am the LORD.

39 "'As for you, O house of Israel, this is what the Sovereign LORD says: Each of you go and serve your idols, if you will not listen to me. But my holy name will not be profaned again by your sacrifices and your idols. 40 For there on my holy mountain, the high mountain of Israel, declares the Sovereign LORD, all the house of Israel will serve me, all of them in the land. I will accept them there, and there I will seek your contributions and your choice gifts, with all your holy things. 41 When I bring you out from the nations and gather you from the lands where you are scattered, I will accept you along with your soothing aroma. I will display my holiness among you in the sight of the nations. 42 Then you will know that I am the LORD when I bring you to the land of Israel, to the land I swore to give to your fathers. 43 And there you will remember your conduct and all your deeds by which you defiled yourselves. You will despise yourselves because of all the evil deeds you have done. 44 Then you will know that I am the LORD, when I deal with you for the sake of my reputation and not according to your wicked conduct and corrupt deeds, O house of Israel, declares the Sovereign LORD.'"

PROPHECY AGAINST THE SOUTH

45 The LORD's message came to me: 46 "Son of man, turn toward the south, and speak out against the south. Prophesy against the open scrub land of the Negev, 47 and say to the scrub land of the Negev, 'Listen to the LORD's message! This is what the Sovereign

LORD has said: Look here, I am about to start a fire in you, and
it will devour every green tree and every dry tree in you. The
flaming fire will not be extinguished, and the whole surface of
the ground from the Negev to the north will be scorched by it.
48 And everyone will see that I, the LORD, have burned it; it will
not be extinguished.'"
49 Then I said, "O Sovereign LORD! They are saying of me, 'Does
he not simply speak in eloquent figures of speech?'"

THE SWORD OF JUDGMENT

21 The LORD's message came to me: 2 "Son of man, turn toward
Jerusalem and speak out against the sanctuaries. Prophesy against the land of Israel 3 and say to them, 'This is what
the LORD says: Look, I am against you. I will draw my sword
from its sheath and cut off from you both the righteous and the
wicked. 4 Because I will cut off from you both the righteous and
the wicked, my sword will go out from its sheath against everyone from the south to the north. 5 Then everyone will know that
I am the LORD, who drew my sword from its sheath—it will not
be sheathed again!'
6 "And you, son of man, groan with an aching heart and bitterness; groan before their eyes. 7 When they ask you, 'Why are you
groaning?' you will reply, 'Because of the report that has come.
Every heart will melt with fear and every hand will be limp; everyone will faint, and every knee will be wet with urine.' Pay attention—it is coming and it will happen, declares the Sovereign
LORD."
8 The LORD's message came to me: 9 "Son of man, prophesy and
say: 'This is what the Lord says:
"'A sword, a sword is sharpened,
and also polished.
10 It is sharpened for slaughter,
it is polished to flash like lightning!

"'Should we rejoice in the scepter of my son? No! The sword
despises every tree!
11 "'He gave it to be polished,
to be grasped in the hand—
the sword is sharpened, it is polished—
giving it into the hand of the executioner.
12 Cry out and moan, son of man,
for it is wielded against my people;
against all the princes of Israel.
They are delivered up to the sword, along with my people.
Therefore, strike your thigh.

13 "'For testing will come, and what will happen when the scepter, which the sword despises, is no more? declares the Sovereign LORD.'
14 "And you, son of man, prophesy,
and clap your hands together.
Let the sword strike twice, even three times!
It is a sword for slaughter,
a sword for the great slaughter surrounding them.

15 So hearts melt with fear and many stumble.
At all their gates I have stationed the sword for slaughter.
Ah! It is made to flash, it is drawn for slaughter!
16 Cut sharply on the right!
Swing to the left,
wherever your edge is appointed to strike.
17 I too will clap my hands together,
I will exhaust my rage;
I the LORD have spoken."

18 The LORD's message came to me: 19 "You, son of man, mark out
two routes for the king of Babylon's sword to take; both of them
will originate in a single land. Make a signpost and put it at the
beginning of the road leading to the city. 20 Mark out the routes
for the sword to take: 'Rabbah of the Ammonites' and 'Judah with
Jerusalem in it.' 21 For the king of Babylon stands at the fork in
the road at the head of the two routes. He looks for omens: He
shakes arrows, he consults idols, he examines animal livers. 22 Into
his right hand comes the portent for Jerusalem—to set up battering rams, to give the signal for slaughter, to shout out the battle
cry, to set up battering rams against the gates, to erect a siege
ramp, to build a siege wall. 23 But those in Jerusalem will view it
as a false omen. They have sworn solemn oaths, but the king of
Babylon will accuse them of violations in order to seize them.
24 "Therefore this is what the Sovereign LORD says: 'Because
you have brought up your own guilt by uncovering your transgressions and revealing your sins through all your actions, for
this reason you will be taken by force.

25 "'As for you, profane and wicked prince of Israel,
whose day has come, the time of final punishment,
26 this is what the Sovereign LORD says:
Tear off the turban;
take off the crown!
Things must change.
Exalt the lowly;
bring low the exalted!
27 A total ruin I will make it!
Indeed, this will not be
until he comes to whom is the right,
and I will give it to him.'

28 "As for you, son of man, prophesy and say, 'This is what the
Sovereign LORD says concerning the Ammonites and their coming humiliation:

"'A sword, a sword drawn for slaughter,
polished to consume, to flash like lightning—
29 while seeing false visions about you
and reading lying omens about you—
to place you on the necks of the profane wicked,
whose day has come,
the time of final punishment.
30 Return it to its sheath!
In the place where you were created,
in your native land, I will judge you.

31 I will pour out my anger on you;
the fire of my fury I will blow on you.
I will hand you over to brutal men,
who are skilled in destruction.
32 You will become fuel for the fire—
your blood will stain the middle of the land;
you will no longer be remembered,
for I, the LORD, have spoken.'"

THE SINS OF JERUSALEM

22 The LORD's message came to me: 2 "As for you, son of man,
are you willing to pronounce judgment? Are you willing
to pronounce judgment on the bloody city? Then confront her
with all her abominable deeds! 3 Then say, 'This is what the Sovereign LORD says: O city, who spills blood within herself (which
brings on her doom), and who makes herself idols (which results
in impurity), 4 you are guilty because of the blood you shed and
defiled by the idols you made. You have hastened the day of your
doom; the end of your years has come. Therefore I will make you
an object of scorn to the nations, an object to be mocked by all
lands. 5 Those both near and far from you will mock you, you with
your bad reputation, full of turmoil.
6 "'See how each of the princes of Israel living within you has
used his authority to shed blood. 7 They have treated father and
mother with contempt within you; they have oppressed the resident foreigner among you; they have wronged the orphan and
the widow within you. 8 You have despised my holy things and
desecrated my Sabbaths! 9 Slanderous men shed blood within
you. Those who live within you eat pagan sacrifices on the mountains; they commit obscene acts among you. 10 They have sexual
relations with their father's wife within you; they violate wom-
en during their menstrual period within you. 11 One commits
an abominable act with his neighbor's wife; another obscenely
defiles his daughter-in-law; another violates his sister—his father's daughter—within you. 12 They take bribes within you to
shed blood. You engage in usury and charge interest; you extort
money from your neighbors. You have forgotten me, declares
the Sovereign LORD.
13 "'See, I strike my hands together at the dishonest profit you
have made, and at the bloodshed they have done among you.
14 Can your heart endure, or can your hands be strong when I
deal with you? I, the LORD, have spoken, and I will do it! 15 I will
scatter you among the nations and disperse you among various
countries; I will remove your impurity from you. 16 You will be
profaned within yourself in the sight of the nations; then you
will know that I am the LORD.'"
17 The LORD's message came to me: 18 "Son of man, the house
of Israel has become slag to me. All of them are like bronze, tin,
iron, and lead in the furnace; they are the worthless slag of silver. 19 Therefore this is what the Sovereign LORD says: 'Because
all of you have become slag, look out! I am about to gather you
in the middle of Jerusalem. 20 As silver, bronze, iron, lead, and
tin are gathered in a furnace so that the fire can blow on them
to melt them, so I will gather you in my anger and in my rage. I

will deposit you there and melt you. 21 I will gather you and blow on you with the fire of my fury, and you will be melted in it. 22 As silver is melted in a furnace, so you will be melted in it, and you will know that I, the LORD, have poured out my anger on you.'"

23 The LORD's message came to me: 24 "Son of man, say to her: 'You are a land that receives no rain or showers in the day of my anger.' 25 Her princes within her are like a roaring lion tearing its prey; they have devoured lives. They take away riches and valuable things; they have made many women widows within it. 26 Her priests abuse my law and have desecrated my holy things. They do not distinguish between the holy and the profane, or recognize any distinction between the unclean and the clean. They ignore my Sabbaths, and I am profaned in their midst. 27 Her officials are like wolves in her midst rending their prey—shedding blood and destroying lives—so they can get dishonest profit. 28 Her prophets coat their messages with whitewash. They see false visions and announce lying omens for them, saying, 'This is what the Sovereign LORD says,' when the LORD has not spoken. 29 The people of the land have practiced extortion and committed robbery. They have wronged the poor and needy; they have oppressed the resident foreigner and denied them justice.

30 "I looked for a man from among them who would repair the wall and stand in the gap before me on behalf of the land, so that I would not destroy it, but I found no one. 31 So I have poured my anger on them and destroyed them with the fire of my fury. I hereby repay them for what they have done, declares the Sovereign LORD."

TWO SISTERS

23 The LORD's message came to me: 2 "Son of man, there were two women who were daughters of the same mother. 3 They engaged in prostitution in Egypt; in their youth they engaged in prostitution. Their breasts were squeezed there; lovers fondled their virgin nipples there. 4 Oholah was the name of the older and Oholibah the name of her younger sister. They became mine and gave birth to sons and daughters. Oholah is Samaria, and Oholibah is Jerusalem.

5 "Oholah engaged in prostitution while she was mine. She lusted after her lovers, the Assyrians—warriors 6 clothed in blue, governors and officials, all of them desirable young men, horsemen riding on horses. 7 She bestowed her sexual favors on them; all of them were the choicest young men of Assyria. She defiled herself with all whom she desired—with all their idols. 8 She did not abandon the prostitution she had practiced in Egypt, for in her youth men went to bed with her, fondled her virgin breasts, and ravished her. 9 Therefore I handed her over to her lovers, the Assyrians for whom she lusted. 10 They exposed her nakedness, seized her sons and daughters, and killed her with the sword. She became notorious among women, and they executed judgments against her.

11 "Her sister Oholibah watched this, but she became more corrupt in her lust than her sister had been, and her acts of prostitution were more numerous than those of her sister. 12 She lusted

after the Assyrians—governors and officials, warriors in full armor, horsemen riding on horses, all of them desirable young
men. 13 I saw that she was defiled; both of them followed the same
path. 14 But she increased her prostitution. She saw men carved
on the wall, images of the Chaldeans carved in bright red, 15 wearing belts on their waists and flowing turbans on their heads, all
of them looking like officers, the image of Babylonians whose
native land is Chaldea. 16 When she saw them, she lusted after
them and sent messengers to them in Chaldea. 17 The Babylonians crawled into bed with her. They defiled her with their lust;
after she was defiled by them, she became disgusted with them.
18 When she lustfully exposed her nakedness, I was disgusted
with her, just as I had been disgusted with her sister. 19 Yet she
increased her prostitution, remembering the days of her youth
when she engaged in prostitution in the land of Egypt. 20 She
lusted after her lovers there, whose genitals were like those of
donkeys, and whose emission was like that of stallions. 21 This
is how you assessed the obscene conduct of your youth, when
the Egyptians fondled your nipples and squeezed your young
breasts.

22 "Therefore, Oholibah, this is what the Sovereign LORD says:
Look here, I am about to stir up against you the lovers with whom
you were disgusted; I will bring them against you from every
side: 23 the Babylonians and all the Chaldeans, Pekod, Shoa, and
Koa, and all the Assyrians with them, desirable young men, all
of them governors and officials, officers and nobles, all of them
riding on horses. 24 They will attack you with weapons, chariots, wagons, and with a huge army; they will array themselves
against you on every side with large shields, small shields, and
helmets. I will assign them the task of judgment; they will punish you according to their laws. 25 I will direct my jealous anger
against you, and they will deal with you in rage. They will cut
off your nose and your ears, and your survivors will die by the
sword. They will seize your sons and daughters, and your survivors will be consumed by fire. 26 They will strip your clothes off
you and take away your beautiful jewelry. 27 So I will put an end
to your obscene conduct and your prostitution that you have
practiced in the land of Egypt. You will not seek their help or
remember Egypt anymore.

28 "For this is what the Sovereign LORD says: Look here, I am
about to deliver you over to those whom you hate, to those with
whom you were disgusted. 29 They will treat you with hatred, take
away all you have labored for, and leave you naked and bare. Your
nakedness will be exposed, just as when you engaged in prostitution and obscene conduct. 30 I will do these things to you because you engaged in prostitution with the nations, polluting
yourself with their idols. 31 You have followed the ways of your
sister, so I will place her cup of judgment in your hand. 32 This
is what the Sovereign LORD says: 'You will drink your sister's
deep and wide cup; you will be scorned and derided, for it holds
a great deal. 33 You will be overcome by drunkenness and sorrow.
The cup of your sister Samaria is a cup of horror and desolation.
34 You will drain it dry, gnaw its pieces, and tear out your breasts,
for I have spoken, declares the Sovereign LORD.'

35 "Therefore this is what the Sovereign LORD says: Because you have forgotten me and completely disregarded me, you must bear now the punishment for your obscene conduct and prostitution."

36 The LORD said to me: "Son of man, are you willing to pronounce judgment on Oholah and Oholibah? Then declare to them their abominable deeds! 37 For they have committed adultery, and blood is on their hands. They have committed adultery with their idols, and their sons, whom they bore to me, they have passed through the fire as food to their idols. 38 Moreover, they have done this to me: In the very same day they desecrated my sanctuary and profaned my Sabbaths. 39 On the same day they slaughtered their sons for their idols, they came to my sanctuary to desecrate it. This is what they have done in the middle of my house.

40 "They even sent for men from far away; when the messenger arrived, those men set out. For them you bathed, painted your eyes, and decorated yourself with jewelry. 41 You sat on a magnificent couch, with a table arranged in front of it where you placed my incense and my olive oil. 42 The sound of a carefree crowd accompanied her, including all kinds of men; even Sabeans were brought from the desert. The sisters put bracelets on their wrists and beautiful crowns on their heads. 43 Then I said about the one worn out by adultery, 'Now they will commit immoral acts with her.' 44 They slept with her the way someone sleeps with a prostitute. In this way they slept with Oholah and Oholibah, promiscuous women. 45 But upright men will punish them appropriately for their adultery and bloodshed, because they are adulteresses and blood is on their hands.

46 "For this is what the Sovereign LORD says: Bring up an army against them and subject them to terror and plunder. 47 That army will pelt them with stones and slash them with their swords; they will kill their sons and daughters and burn their houses. 48 I will put an end to the obscene conduct in the land; all the women will learn a lesson from this and not engage in obscene conduct. 49 They will repay you for your obscene conduct, and you will be punished for idol worship. Then you will know that I am the Sovereign LORD."

THE BOILING POT

24 The LORD's message came to me in the ninth year, in the tenth month, on the tenth day of the month: 2 "Son of man, write down the name of this day, this very day. The king of Babylon has laid siege to Jerusalem this very day. 3 Recite a proverb to this rebellious house and say to them, 'This is what the Sovereign LORD says:

"'Set on the pot, set it on,
pour water in it too;
4 add the pieces of meat to it,
every good piece,
the thigh and the shoulder;
fill it with choice bones.
5 Take the choice bone of the flock,
heap up wood under it;
boil rapidly,
and boil its bones in it.

6 "'Therefore this is what the Sovereign LORD says:
Woe to the city of bloodshed,
the pot whose rot is in it,
whose rot has not been removed from it!
Empty it piece by piece.
No lot has fallen on it.
7 For her blood was in it;
she poured it on an exposed rock;
she did not pour it on the ground to cover it up with dust.
8 To arouse anger, to take vengeance,
I have placed her blood on an exposed rock
so that it cannot be covered up.

9 "'Therefore this is what the Sovereign LORD says:
Woe to the city of bloodshed!
I will also make the pile high.
10 Pile up the wood, kindle the fire;
cook the meat well, mix in the spices,
let the bones be charred.
11 Set the empty pot on the coals,
until it becomes hot and its copper glows,
until its uncleanness melts within it
and its rot is consumed.
12 It has tried my patience;
yet its thick rot is not removed from it.
Subject its rot to the fire!
13 You mix uncleanness with obscene conduct.
I tried to cleanse you, but you are not clean.
You will not be cleansed from your uncleanness
until I have exhausted my anger on you.

14 "'I the LORD have spoken; judgment is coming and I will act! I
will not relent, or show pity, or be sorry! I will judge you according
to your conduct and your deeds, declares the Sovereign LORD.'"

EZEKIEL'S WIFE DIES

15 The LORD's message came to me: 16 "Son of man, realize that I
am about to take the delight of your eyes away from you with
a jolt, but you must not mourn or weep or shed tears. 17 Groan
to moan for the dead, but do not perform mourning rites. Bind
on your turban and put your sandals on your feet. Do not cover
your lip and do not eat food brought by others."

18 So I spoke to the people in the morning, and my wife died in
the evening. In the morning I acted just as I was commanded.
19 Then the people said to me, "Will you not tell us what these
things you are doing mean for us?"

20 So I said to them: "The LORD's message came to me: 21 Say to
the house of Israel, 'This is what the Sovereign LORD says: Realize
I am about to desecrate my sanctuary—the source of your confident pride, the object in which your eyes delight, and your life's
passion. Your very own sons and daughters whom you have left
behind will die by the sword. 22 Then you will do as I have done:
You will not cover your lip or eat food brought by others. 23 Your
turbans will be on your heads and your sandals on your feet; you

will not mourn or weep, but you will rot for your iniquities and
groan among yourselves. 24 Ezekiel will be an object lesson for
you; you will do all that he has done. When it happens, then you
will know that I am the Sovereign LORD.'
25 "And you, son of man, this is what will happen on the day I
take from them their stronghold—their beautiful source of joy,
the object in which their eyes delight, and the main concern of
their lives, as well as their sons and daughters: 26 On that day a
fugitive will come to you to report the news. 27 On that day you
will be able to speak again; you will talk with the fugitive and be
silent no longer. You will be an object lesson for them, and they
will know that I am the LORD."

A PROPHECY AGAINST AMMON

25 The LORD's message came to me: 2 "Son of man, turn toward the Ammonites and prophesy against them. 3 Say
to the Ammonites, 'Hear the word of the Sovereign LORD. This
is what the Sovereign LORD says: You said "Aha!" about my sanctuary when it was desecrated, about the land of Israel when it
was made desolate, and about the house of Judah when they
went into exile. 4 So take note, I am about to make you slaves
of the tribes of the east. They will make camps among you and
pitch their tents among you. They will eat your fruit and drink
your milk. 5 I will make Rabbah a pasture for camels and Ammon a resting place for sheep. Then you will know that I am the
LORD. 6 For this is what the Sovereign LORD says: Because you
clapped your hands, stamped your feet, and rejoiced with intense scorn over the land of Israel, 7 take note—I have stretched
out my hand against you, and I will hand you over as plunder to
the nations. I will cut you off from the peoples and make you
perish from the lands. I will destroy you; then you will know
that I am the LORD."'

A PROPHECY AGAINST MOAB

8 "This is what the Sovereign LORD says: 'Moab and Seir say,
"Look, the house of Judah is like all the other nations." 9 So look,
I am about to open up Moab's flank, eliminating the cities, including its frontier cities, the beauty of the land—Beth Jeshimoth, Baal Meon, and Kiriathaim. 10 I will hand it over, along
with the Ammonites, to the tribes of the east, so that the Ammonites will no longer be remembered among the nations. 11 I
will execute judgments against Moab. Then they will know that
I am the LORD."'

A PROPHECY AGAINST EDOM

12 "This is what the Sovereign LORD says: 'Edom has taken vengeance against the house of Judah; they have made themselves
fully culpable by taking vengeance on them. 13 So this is what the
Sovereign LORD says: I will stretch out my hand against Edom,
and I will kill the people and animals within her, and I will make
her desolate; from Teman to Dedan they will die by the sword.
14 I will exact my vengeance upon Edom by the hand of my people Israel. They will carry out in Edom my anger and rage; they
will experience my vengeance, declares the Sovereign LORD."'

A PROPHECY AGAINST PHILISTIA

15 "This is what the Sovereign LORD says: 'The Philistines have exacted merciless revenge, showing intense scorn in their effort to destroy Judah with unrelenting hostility. 16 So this is what the Sovereign LORD says: Take note, I am about to stretch out my hand against the Philistines. I will kill the Kerethites and destroy those who remain on the seacoast. 17 I will exact great vengeance upon them with angry rebukes. Then they will know that I am the LORD, when I exact my vengeance upon them.'"

A PROPHECY AGAINST TYRE

26 In the eleventh year, on the first day of the month, the LORD's message came to me: 2 "Son of man, because Tyre has said about Jerusalem, 'Aha, the gateway of the peoples is broken; it has swung open to me. I will become rich, now that she has been destroyed,' 3 therefore this is what the Sovereign LORD says: Look, I am against you, O Tyre! I will bring up many nations against you, as the sea brings up its waves. 4 They will destroy the walls of Tyre and break down her towers. I will scrape her soil from her and make her a bare rock. 5 She will be a place where fishing nets are spread, surrounded by the sea. For I have spoken, declares the Sovereign LORD. She will become plunder for the nations, 6 and her daughters who are in the field will be slaughtered by the sword. Then they will know that I am the LORD.

7 "For this is what the Sovereign LORD says: Take note that I am about to bring King Nebuchadrezzar of Babylon, king of kings, against Tyre from the north, with horses, chariots, and horsemen, an army and hordes of people. 8 He will kill your daughters in the field with the sword. He will build a siege wall against you, erect a siege ramp against you, and raise a great shield against you. 9 He will direct the blows of his battering rams against your walls and tear down your towers with his weapons. 10 He will cover you with the dust kicked up by his many horses. Your walls will shake from the noise of the horsemen, wheels, and chariots when he enters your gates like those who invade through a city's broken walls. 11 With his horses' hooves he will trample all your streets. He will kill your people with the sword, and your strong pillars will tumble down to the ground. 12 They will steal your wealth and loot your merchandise. They will tear down your walls and destroy your luxurious homes. Your stones, your trees, and your soil he will throw into the water. 13 I will silence the noise of your songs; the sound of your harps will be heard no more. 14 I will make you a bare rock; you will be a place where fishing nets are spread. You will never be built again, for I, the LORD, have spoken, declares the Sovereign LORD.

15 "This is what the Sovereign LORD says to Tyre: Oh, how the coastlands will shake at the sound of your fall, when the wounded groan at the massive slaughter in your midst! 16 All the princes of the sea will vacate their thrones. They will remove their robes and strip off their embroidered clothes; they will clothe themselves with trembling. They will sit on the ground; they will

tremble continually and be shocked at what has happened to
you. 17 They will sing this lament over you:

"'How you have perished—you have
vanished from the seas,
O renowned city, once mighty in the sea,
she and her inhabitants, who spread their terror!
18 Now the coastlands will tremble on the day of your fall;
the coastlands by the sea will be terrified by your passing.'

19 "For this is what the Sovereign LORD says: When I make you
desolate like the uninhabited cities, when I bring up the deep over
you and the surging waters overwhelm you, 20 then I will bring
you down to bygone people, to be with those who descend to the
Pit. I will make you live in the lower parts of the earth among the
primeval ruins, with those who descend to the Pit, so that you will
not be inhabited or stand in the land of the living. 21 I will bring
terrors on you, and you will be no more! Though you are sought
after, you will never be found again, declares the Sovereign LORD."

A LAMENT FOR TYRE

27 The LORD's message came to me: 2 "You, son of man, sing a
lament for Tyre. 3 Say to Tyre, who sits at the entrance of
the sea, merchant to the peoples on many coasts, 'This is what
the Sovereign LORD says:

"'O Tyre, you have said, "I am perfectly beautiful."
4 Your borders are in the heart of the seas;
your builders have perfected your beauty.
5 They crafted all your planks out of fir trees from Senir;
they took a cedar from Lebanon to make your mast.
6 They made your oars from oaks of Bashan;
they made your deck with cypress wood
from the coasts of Cyprus.
7 Fine linen from Egypt, woven with
patterns, was used for your sail
to serve as your banner;
blue and purple from the coastlands of Elishah
were used for your deck's awning.
8 The leaders of Sidon and Arvad were your rowers;
your skilled men, O Tyre, were your captains.
9 The elders of Gebal and her skilled men
were within you, mending cracks;
all the ships of the sea and their mariners were
within you to trade for your merchandise.
10 Men of Persia, Lud, and Put were in your army, men of war.
They hung shield and helmet on you;
they gave you your splendor.
11 The Arvadites joined your army on your walls all around,
and the Gammadites were in your towers.
They hung their quivers on your walls all around;
they perfected your beauty.

12 "'Tarshish was your trade partner because of your abundant
wealth; they exchanged silver, iron, tin, and lead for your products.
13 Javan, Tubal, and Meshech were your clients; they exchanged

slaves and bronze items for your merchandise. 14 Beth Togarmah
exchanged horses, chargers, and mules for your products. 15 The
Dedanites were your clients. Many coastlands were your custom-
ers; they paid you with ivory tusks and ebony. 16 Edom was your
trade partner because of the abundance of your goods; they exchanged turquoise, purple, embroidered work, fine linen, coral,
and rubies for your products. 17 Judah and the land of Israel were
your clients; they traded wheat from Minnith, millet, honey, olive
oil, and balm for your merchandise. 18 Damascus was your trade
partner because of the abundance of your goods and of all your
wealth: wine from Helbon, white wool from Zahar, 19 and casks of
wine from Izal they exchanged for your products. Wrought iron,
cassia, and sweet cane were among your merchandise. 20 Dedan
was your client in saddlecloths for riding. 21 Arabia and all the
princes of Kedar were your trade partners; for lambs, rams, and
goats they traded with you. 22 The merchants of Sheba and Raamah engaged in trade with you; they traded the best kinds of
spices along with precious stones and gold for your products. 23 Haran, Kanneh, Eden, merchants from Sheba, Asshur, and Kilmad
were your clients. 24 They traded with you choice garments, purple
clothes and embroidered work, and multicolored carpets bound
and reinforced with cords; these were among your merchandise.
25 The ships of Tarshish were the transports for your merchandise.

"'So you were filled and weighed down
in the heart of the seas.
26 Your rowers have brought you into surging waters.
The east wind has wrecked you in the heart of the seas.
27 Your wealth, products, and merchandise,
your sailors and captains,
your ship's carpenters, your merchants,
and all your fighting men within you,
along with all your crew who are in you,
will fall into the heart of the seas on
the day of your downfall.
28 At the sound of your captains' cries the waves will surge;
29 They will descend from their ships—all who handle the oar,
the sailors and all the sea captains—
they will stand on the land.
30 They will lament loudly over you and cry bitterly.
They will throw dust on their heads and roll in the ashes;
31 they will tear out their hair because
of you and put on sackcloth,
and they will weep bitterly over you
with intense mourning.
32 As they wail they will lament over you, chanting:
"Who was like Tyre, like a tower in the midst of the sea?"
33 When your products went out from the seas,
you satisfied many peoples;
with the abundance of your wealth and merchandise
you enriched the kings of the earth.
34 Now you are wrecked by the seas, in
the depths of the waters;
your merchandise and all your company
have sunk along with you.

35 All the inhabitants of the coastlands are shocked at you,
and their kings are horribly afraid—
their faces are troubled.
36 The traders among the peoples hiss at you;
you have become a horror, and will be no more.'"

A PROPHECY AGAINST THE KING OF TYRE

28 The LORD's message came to me: 2"Son of man, say to
the prince of Tyre, 'This is what the Sovereign LORD says:
"'Your heart is proud and you said, "I am a god;
I sit in the seat of gods, in the heart of the seas"—
yet you are a man and not a god,
though you think you are godlike.
3 Look, you are wiser than Daniel;
no secret is hidden from you.
4 By your wisdom and understanding you
have gained wealth for yourself;
you have amassed gold and silver in your treasuries.
5 By your great skill in trade you have
increased your wealth,
and your heart is proud because of your wealth.

6 "'Therefore this is what the Sovereign LORD says:
Because you think you are godlike,
7 I am about to bring foreigners against you,
the most terrifying of nations.
They will draw their swords against the
grandeur made by your wisdom,
and they will defile your splendor.
8 They will bring you down to the Pit, and you
will die violently in the heart of the seas.
9 Will you still say, "I am a god," before
the one who kills you—
though you are a man and not a god—
when you are in the power of those who wound you?
10 You will die the death of the uncircumcised
by the hand of foreigners;
for I have spoken, declares the Sovereign LORD.'"

11 The LORD's message came to me: 12"Son of man, sing a lament for the king of Tyre, and say to him, 'This is what the Sovereign LORD says:
"'You were the sealer of perfection,
full of wisdom, and perfect in beauty.
13 You were in Eden, the garden of God.
Every precious stone was your covering,
the ruby, topaz, and emerald,
the chrysolite, onyx, and jasper,
the sapphire, turquoise, and beryl;
your settings and mounts were made of gold.
On the day you were created they were prepared.
14 I placed you there with an anointed guardian cherub;
you were on the holy mountain of God;
you walked about amidst fiery stones.

15 You were blameless in your behavior
from the day you were created,
until sin was discovered in you.
16 In the abundance of your trade you were
filled with violence, and you sinned;
so I defiled you and banished you
from the mountain of God—
the guardian cherub expelled you from
the midst of the stones of fire.
17 Your heart was proud because of your beauty;
you corrupted your wisdom on account of your splendor.
I threw you down to the ground;
I placed you before kings, that they might see you.
18 By the multitude of your iniquities, through
the sinfulness of your trade,
you desecrated your sanctuaries.
So I drew fire out from within you;
it consumed you,
and I turned you to ashes on the earth
before the eyes of all who saw you.
19 All who know you among the peoples are shocked at you;
you have become terrified and will be no more.'"

A PROPHECY AGAINST SIDON

20 The LORD's message came to me: 21 "Son of man, turn toward
Sidon and prophesy against it. 22 Say, 'This is what the Sovereign LORD says:

"'Look, I am against you, Sidon,
and I will magnify myself in your midst.
Then they will know that I am the LORD
when I execute judgments on her
and reveal my sovereign power in her.
23 I will send a plague into the city and
bloodshed into its streets;
the slain will fall within it, by the sword
that attacks it from every side.
Then they will know that I am the LORD.

24 "'No longer will Israel suffer from the sharp briers or painful thorns of all who surround and scorn them. Then they will
know that I am the Sovereign LORD.

25 "'This is what the Sovereign LORD says: When I regather the
house of Israel from the peoples where they are dispersed, I will
reveal my sovereign power over them in the sight of the nations,
and they will live in their land that I gave to my servant Jacob.
26 They will live securely in it; they will build houses and plant
vineyards. They will live securely when I execute my judgments
on all those who scorn them and surround them. Then they will
know that I am the LORD their God.'"

A PROPHECY AGAINST EGYPT

29 In the tenth year, in the tenth month, on the twelfth day
of the month, the LORD's message came to me: 2 "Son of
man, turn toward Pharaoh king of Egypt and prophesy against

him and against all Egypt. 3 Tell them, 'This is what the Sovereign LORD says:

"'Look, I am against you, Pharaoh king of Egypt,
the great monster lying in the midst of its waterways,
who has said, "My Nile is my own, I made it for myself."
4 I will put hooks in your jaws
and stick the fish of your waterways to your scales.
I will haul you up from the midst of your waterways,
and all the fish of your waterways will stick to your scales.
5 I will leave you in the wilderness,
you and all the fish of your waterways;
you will fall in the open field and will not
be gathered up or collected.
I have given you as food to the beasts of the
earth and the birds of the skies.
6 Then all those living in Egypt will know that I am the LORD
because they were a reed staff for the house of Israel;
7 when they grasped you with their hand,
you broke and tore their shoulders,
and when they leaned on you, you splintered
and caused their legs to be unsteady.

8 "'Therefore, this is what the Sovereign LORD says: Look, I am
about to bring a sword against you, and I will kill every person
and every animal. 9 The land of Egypt will become a desolate ruin.
Then they will know that I am the LORD.
"'Because he said, "The Nile is mine and I made it," 10 I am
against you and your waterways. I will turn the land of Egypt
into an utter desolate ruin from Migdol to Syene, as far as
the border with Ethiopia. 11 No human foot will pass through
it, and no animal's foot will pass through it; it will be uninhabited for forty years. 12 I will turn the land of Egypt into a
desolation in the midst of desolate lands; for forty years her
cities will lie desolate in the midst of ruined cities. I will scatter Egypt among the nations and disperse them among foreign countries.
13 "'For this is what the Sovereign LORD says: At the end of
forty years I will gather Egypt from the peoples where they
were scattered. 14 I will restore the fortunes of Egypt and will
bring them back to the land of Pathros, to the land of their origin; there they will be an insignificant kingdom. 15 It will be
the most insignificant of the kingdoms; it will never again exalt itself over the nations. I will make them so small that they
will not rule over the nations. 16 It will never again be Israel's
source of confidence, but a reminder of how they sinned by
turning to Egypt for help. Then they will know that I am the
Sovereign LORD.'"
17 In the twenty-seventh year, in the first month, on the first
day of the month, the LORD's message came to me: 18 "Son of
man, King Nebuchadrezzar of Babylon made his army labor hard
against Tyre. Every head was rubbed bald and every shoulder
rubbed bare; yet he and his army received no wages from Tyre
for the work he carried out against it. 19 Therefore this is what
the Sovereign LORD says: Look, I am about to give the land of

Egypt to King Nebuchadrezzar of Babylon. He will carry off her
wealth, capture her loot, and seize her plunder; it will be his
army's wages. 20 I have given him the land of Egypt as his compensation for attacking Tyre, because they did it for me, declares
the Sovereign LORD. 21 On that day I will make Israel powerful,
and I will give you the right to be heard among them. Then they
will know that I am the LORD."

A LAMENT OVER EGYPT

30 The LORD's message came to me: 2 "Son of man, prophesy
and say, 'This is what the Sovereign LORD says:
"'Wail, "Alas, the day is here!"
3 For the day is near,
the day of the LORD is near;
it will be a day of storm clouds,
it will be a time of judgment for the nations.
4 A sword will come against Egypt
and panic will overtake Ethiopia
when the slain fall in Egypt
and they carry away her wealth
and dismantle her foundations.

5 Ethiopia, Put, Lud, all the foreigners, Libya, and the people of
the covenant land will die by the sword along with them.

6 "'This is what the LORD says:
Egypt's supporters will fall;
her confident pride will crumble.
From Migdol to Syene they will die
by the sword within her,
declares the Sovereign LORD.
7 They will be desolate among desolate lands,
and their cities will be among ruined cities.
8 They will know that I am the LORD
when I ignite a fire in Egypt
and all her allies are defeated.

9 "'On that day messengers will go out from me in ships to
frighten overconfident Ethiopia; panic will overtake them on
the day of Egypt's doom; for beware—it is coming!

10 "'This is what the Sovereign LORD says:
I will put an end to the hordes of Egypt,
by the hand of King Nebuchadrezzar of Babylon.
11 He and his people with him,
the most terrifying of the nations,
will be brought there to destroy the land.
They will draw their swords against Egypt,
and fill the land with corpses.
12 I will dry up the waterways
and hand the land over to evil men.
I will make the land and everything in it
desolate by the hand of foreigners.
I, the LORD, have spoken!

13 "'This is what the Sovereign LORD says:
I will destroy the idols,
and put an end to the gods of Memphis.
There will no longer be a prince from the land of Egypt;
so I will make the land of Egypt fearful.
14 I will desolate Pathros,
I will ignite a fire in Zoan,
and I will execute judgments on Thebes.
15 I will pour out my anger upon Pelusium,
the stronghold of Egypt;
I will cut off the hordes of Thebes.
16 I will ignite a fire in Egypt;
Syene will writhe in agony,
Thebes will be broken down,
and Memphis will face enemies every day.
17 The young men of On and of Pi Beseth
will die by the sword;
and the cities will go into captivity.
18 In Tahpanhes the day will be dark
when I break the yoke of Egypt there.
Her confident pride will cease within her;
a cloud will cover her, and her daughters
will go into captivity.
19 I will execute judgments on Egypt.
Then they will know that I am the LORD.'"

20 In the eleventh year, in the first month, on the seventh day of
the month, the LORD's message came to me: 21 "Son of man, I have
broken the arm of Pharaoh king of Egypt. Look, it has not been
bandaged for healing or set with a dressing so that it might become strong enough to grasp a sword. 22 Therefore this is what the
Sovereign LORD says: Look, I am against Pharaoh king of Egypt,
and I will break his arms, the strong arm and the broken one, and
I will make the sword drop from his hand. 23 I will scatter the Egyptians among the nations and disperse them among foreign countries. 24 I will strengthen the arms of the king of Babylon, and I will
place my sword in his hand, but I will break the arms of Pharaoh,
and he will groan like the fatally wounded before the king of Babylon. 25 I will strengthen the arms of the king of Babylon, but the
arms of Pharaoh will fall limp. Then they will know that I am the
LORD when I place my sword in the hand of the king of Babylon
and he extends it against the land of Egypt. 26 I will scatter the
Egyptians among the nations and disperse them among foreign
countries. Then they will know that I am the LORD."

REFLECT

How would the Egyptians know that God is the Lord? How does His judgment communicate His holiness?

A CEDAR IN LEBANON

31 In the eleventh year, in the third month, on the first day of
the month, the LORD's message came to me: 2 "Son of man,
say to Pharaoh king of Egypt and his hordes:
"'Who are you like in your greatness?
3 Consider Assyria, a cedar in Lebanon,
with beautiful branches, like a forest giving shade,
and extremely tall;
its top reached into the clouds.

4 The water made it grow;
underground springs made it grow tall.
Rivers flowed all around the place it was planted,
while smaller channels watered all
the trees of the field.
5 Therefore it grew taller than all the trees of the field;
its boughs grew large and its branches grew long,
because of the plentiful water in its shoots.
6 All the birds of the sky nested in its boughs;
under its branches all the beasts
of the field gave birth;
in its shade all the great nations lived.
7 It was beautiful in its loftiness, in
the length of its branches;
for its roots went down deep to plentiful waters.
8 The cedars in the garden of God could not eclipse it,
nor could the fir trees match its boughs;
the plane trees were as nothing
compared to its branches;
no tree in the garden of God could rival its beauty.
9 I made it beautiful with its many branches;
all the trees of Eden, in the garden of God, envied it.

10 "'Therefore this is what the Sovereign LORD says: Because
it was tall in stature, and its top reached into the clouds, and it
was proud of its height, 11 I gave it over to the leader of the nations. He has judged it thoroughly, as its sinfulness deserves. I
have thrown it out. 12 Foreigners from the most terrifying nations
have cut it down and left it to lie there on the mountains. In all
the valleys its branches have fallen, and its boughs lie broken in
the ravines of the land. All the peoples of the land have departed
from its shade and left it. 13 On its ruins all the birds of the sky
will live, and all the wild animals will walk on its branches. 14 For
this reason no watered trees will grow so tall; their tops will not
reach into the clouds, nor will the well-watered ones grow that
high. For all of them have been appointed to die in the lower
parts of the earth; they will be among mere mortals, with those
who descend to the Pit.

15 "'This is what the Sovereign LORD says: On the day it went
down to Sheol I caused observers to lament. I covered it with
the deep and held back its rivers; its plentiful water was restrained. I clothed Lebanon in black for it, and all the trees of
the field wilted because of it. 16 I made the nations shake at the
sound of its fall, when I threw it down to Sheol, along with those
who descend to the Pit. Then all the trees of Eden, the choicest and the best of Lebanon, all that were well-watered, were
comforted in the earth below. 17 Those who lived in its shade,
its allies among the nations, also went down with it to Sheol,
to those killed by the sword. 18 Which of the trees of Eden was
like you in majesty and loftiness? You will be brought down
with the trees of Eden to the lower parts of the earth; you will
lie among the uncircumcised, with those killed by the sword!
This is what will happen to Pharaoh and all his hordes, declares
the Sovereign LORD.'"

LAMENTATION OVER PHARAOH AND EGYPT

32 In the twelfth year, in the twelfth month, on the first of
the month, the LORD's message came to me: 2 "Son of
man, sing a lament for Pharaoh king of Egypt, and say to him:
"'You were like a lion among the nations,
but you are a monster in the seas;
you thrash about in your streams,
stir up the water with your feet,
and muddy your streams.

3 "'This is what the Sovereign LORD says:
"'I will throw my net over you in the
assembly of many peoples;
and they will haul you up in my dragnet.
4 I will leave you on the ground,
I will fling you on the open field,
I will allow all the birds of the sky to settle on you,
and I will permit all the wild animals
to gorge themselves on you.
5 I will put your flesh on the mountains,
and fill the valleys with your maggot-infested carcass.
6 I will drench the land with the flow
of your blood up to the mountains,
and the ravines will be full of your blood.
7 When I extinguish you, I will cover the sky;
I will darken its stars.
I will cover the sun with a cloud,
and the moon will not shine.
8 I will darken all the lights in the sky over you,
and I will darken your land,
declares the Sovereign LORD.
9 I will disturb many peoples,
when I bring about your destruction
among the nations,
among countries you do not know.
10 I will shock many peoples with you,
and their kings will shiver with horror because of you.
When I brandish my sword before them,
every moment each one will tremble for
his life, on the day of your fall.

11 "'For this is what the Sovereign LORD says:
"'The sword of the king of Babylon will attack you.
12 By the swords of the mighty warriors I
will cause your hordes to fall—
all of them are the most terrifying among the nations.
They will devastate the pride of Egypt,
and all its hordes will be destroyed.
13 I will destroy all its cattle beside the plentiful waters;
and no human foot will disturb the waters again,
nor will the hooves of cattle disturb them.
14 Then I will make their waters calm,
and will make their streams flow like olive
oil, declares the Sovereign LORD.

15 When I turn the land of Egypt into desolation
and the land is destitute of everything that fills it,
when I strike all those who live in it,
then they will know that I am the LORD.'
16 This is a lament; they will chant it.
The daughters of the nations will chant it.
They will chant it over Egypt and over all her hordes,
declares the Sovereign LORD."

17 In the twelfth year, on the fifteenth day of the month, the
LORD's message came to me: 18 "Son of man, wail over the horde
of Egypt. Bring it down; bring her and the daughters of powerful
nations down to the lower parts of the earth, along with those who
descend to the Pit. 19 Say to them, 'Whom do you surpass in beauty?
Go down and be laid to rest with the uncircumcised!' 20 They will
fall among those killed by the sword. The sword is drawn; they carry
her and all her hordes away. 21 The bravest of the warriors will speak
to him from the midst of Sheol along with his allies, saying: 'The
uncircumcised have come down; they lie still, killed by the sword.'
22 "Assyria is there with all her assembly around her grave, all
of them struck down by the sword. 23 Their graves are located in
the remote slopes of the Pit. Her assembly is around her grave,
all of them struck down by the sword, those who spread terror
in the land of the living.
24 "Elam is there with all her hordes around her grave; all of
them struck down by the sword. They went down uncircumcised
to the lower parts of the earth, those who spread terror in the
land of the living. Now they will bear their shame with those who
descend to the Pit. 25 Among the dead they have made a bed for
her, along with all her hordes around her grave. All of them are
uncircumcised, killed by the sword, for their terror had spread
in the land of the living. They bear their shame along with those
who descend to the Pit; they are placed among the dead.
26 "Meshech Tubal is there, along with all her hordes around
her grave. All of them are uncircumcised, killed by the sword,
for they spread their terror in the land of the living. 27 They do
not lie with the fallen warriors of ancient times, who went down
to Sheol with their weapons of war, having their swords placed
under their heads and their shields on their bones, when the
terror of these warriors was in the land of the living.
28 "But as for you, in the midst of the uncircumcised you will
be broken, and you will lie with those killed by the sword.
29 "Edom is there with her kings and all her princes. Despite
their might they are laid with those killed by the sword; they
lie with the uncircumcised and those who descend to the Pit.
30 "All the leaders of the north are there, along with all the Sidonians; despite their might they have gone down in shameful terror with the dead. They lie uncircumcised with those killed by the
sword, and bear their shame with those who descend to the Pit.
31 "Pharaoh will see them and be consoled over all his hordes who
were killed by the sword, Pharaoh and all his army, declares the Sovereign LORD. 32 Indeed, I terrified him in the land of the living, yet
he will lie in the midst of the uncircumcised with those killed by the
sword, Pharaoh and all his hordes, declares the Sovereign LORD."

EZEKIEL ISRAEL'S WATCHMAN

33 The LORD's message came to me: 2“Son of man, speak to
your people, and say to them, ‘Suppose I bring a sword
against the land, and the people of the land take one man from
their borders and make him their watchman. 3He sees the sword
coming against the land, blows the trumpet, and warns the people, 4but there is one who hears the sound of the trumpet yet
does not heed the warning. Then the sword comes and sweeps
him away. He will be responsible for his own death. 5He heard
the sound of the trumpet but did not heed the warning, so he is
responsible for himself. If he had heeded the warning, he would
have saved his life. 6But suppose the watchman sees the sword
coming and does not blow the trumpet to warn the people. Then
the sword comes and takes one of their lives. He is swept away
for his iniquity, but I will hold the watchman accountable for
that person's death.’

7“As for you, son of man, I have made you a watchman for the
house of Israel. Whenever you hear a word from my mouth, you
must warn them on my behalf. 8When I say to the wicked, ‘O
wicked man, you must certainly die,’ and you do not warn the
wicked about his behavior, the wicked man will die for his iniquity, but I will hold you accountable for his death. 9But if you
warn the wicked man to change his behavior, and he refuses
to change, he will die for his iniquity, but you have saved your
own life.

10“And you, son of man, say to the house of Israel, ‘This is what
you have said: “Our rebellious acts and our sins have caught up
with us, and we are wasting away because of them. How then can
we live?”’ 11Say to them, ‘As surely as I live, declares the Sovereign
LORD, I take no pleasure in the death of the wicked, but prefer
that the wicked change his behavior and live. Turn back, turn
back from your evil deeds! Why should you die, O house of Israel?’

12“And you, son of man, say to your people, ‘The righteousness of the righteous will not deliver him if he rebels. As for the
wicked, his wickedness will not make him stumble if he turns
from it. The righteous will not be able to live by his righteousness
if he sins.’ 13Suppose I tell the righteous that he will certainly
live, but he becomes confident in his righteousness and commits iniquity. None of his righteous deeds will be remembered;
because of the iniquity he has committed he will die. 14Suppose
I say to the wicked, ‘You must certainly die,’ but he turns from
his sin and does what is just and right. 15He returns what was
taken in pledge, pays back what he has stolen, and follows the
statutes that give life, committing no iniquity. He will certainly
live—he will not die. 16None of the sins he has committed will
be counted against him. He has done what is just and right; he
will certainly live.

17“Yet your people say, ‘The behavior of the Lord is not right,’
when it is their behavior that is not right. 18When a righteous
man turns from his godliness and commits iniquity, he will die
for it. 19When the wicked turns from his sin and does what is
just and right, he will live because of it. 20Yet you say, ‘The behavior of the Lord is not right.’ House of Israel, I will judge each
of you according to his behavior.”

THE FALL OF JERUSALEM

21 In the twelfth year of our exile, in the tenth month, on the
fifth of the month, a refugee came to me from Jerusalem saying, "The city has been defeated!" 22 Now the hand of the LORD
had been on me the evening before the refugee reached me, but
the LORD opened my mouth by the time the refugee arrived in
the morning; he opened my mouth and I was able to speak once
more. 23 The LORD's message came to me: 24 "Son of man, the ones
living in these ruins in the land of Israel are saying, 'Abraham
was only one man, yet he possessed the land, but we are many;
surely the land has been given to us for a possession.' 25 Therefore say to them, 'This is what the Sovereign LORD says: You eat
the meat with the blood still in it, pray to your idols, and shed
blood. Do you really think you will possess the land? 26 You rely
on your swords and commit abominable deeds; each of you defiles his neighbor's wife. Will you possess the land?'

27 "This is what you must say to them, 'This is what the Sovereign LORD says: As surely as I live, those living in the ruins will
die by the sword, those in the open field I will give to the wild
beasts for food, and those who are in the strongholds and caves
will die of disease. 28 I will turn the land into a desolate ruin; her
confident pride will come to an end. The mountains of Israel will
be so desolate no one will pass through them. 29 Then they will
know that I am the LORD when I turn the land into a desolate
ruin because of all the abominable deeds they have committed.'

30 "But as for you, son of man, your people (who are talking
about you by the walls and at the doors of the houses) say to
one another, 'Come hear the word that comes from the LORD.'
31 They come to you in crowds, and they sit in front of you as my
people. They hear your words, but do not obey them. For they
talk lustfully, and their heart is set on their own advantage. 32 Realize that to them you are like a sensual song, a beautiful voice
and skilled musician. They hear your words, but they do not obey
them. 33 When all this comes true—and it certainly will—then
they will know that a prophet was among them."

A PROPHECY AGAINST FALSE SHEPHERDS

34 The LORD's message came to me: 2 "Son of man, prophesy against the shepherds of Israel; prophesy, and say to
them—to the shepherds: 'This is what the Sovereign LORD says:
Woe to the shepherds of Israel who have been feeding themselves! Should not shepherds feed the flock? 3 You eat the fat,
you clothe yourselves with the wool, you slaughter the choice
animals, but you do not feed the sheep! 4 You have not strengthened the weak, healed the sick, bandaged the injured, brought
back the strays, or sought the lost, but with force and harshness
you have ruled over them. 5 They were scattered because they
had no shepherd, and they became food for every wild beast.
6 My sheep wandered over all the mountains and on every high
hill. My sheep were scattered over the entire face of the earth
with no one looking or searching for them.

7 "'Therefore, you shepherds, listen to the LORD's message: 8 As
surely as I live, declares the Sovereign LORD, my sheep have become prey and have become food for all the wild beasts. There

was no shepherd, and my shepherds did not search for my flock,
but fed themselves and did not feed my sheep. 9 Therefore, you
shepherds, listen to the LORD's message. 10 This is what the Sovereign LORD says: Look, I am against the shepherds, and I will
demand my sheep from their hand. I will no longer let them be
shepherds; the shepherds will not feed themselves anymore.
I will rescue my sheep from their mouths, so that they will no
longer be food for them.

11 "'For this is what the Sovereign LORD says: Look, I myself will
search for my sheep and seek them out. 12 As a shepherd seeks
out his flock when he is among his scattered sheep, so I will seek
out my flock. I will rescue them from all the places where they
have been scattered on a cloudy, dark day. 13 I will bring them out
from among the peoples and gather them from foreign countries; I will bring them to their own land. I will feed them on the
mountains of Israel, by the streams and all the inhabited places
of the land. 14 In a good pasture I will feed them; the mountain
heights of Israel will be their pasture. There they will lie down
in a lush pasture, and they will feed on rich grass on the mountains of Israel. 15 I myself will feed my sheep and I myself will
make them lie down, declares the Sovereign LORD. 16 I will seek
the lost and bring back the strays; I will bandage the injured and
strengthen the sick, but the fat and the strong I will destroy. I
will feed them—with judgment!

17 "'As for you, my sheep, this is what the Sovereign LORD says:
Look, I am about to judge between one sheep and another, between rams and goats. 18 Is it not enough for you to feed on the
good pasture, that you must trample the rest of your pastures
with your feet? When you drink clean water, must you muddy
the rest of the water by trampling it with your feet? 19 As for my
sheep, they must eat what you trampled with your feet and drink
what you have muddied with your feet!

20 "'Therefore, this is what the Sovereign LORD says to them:
Look, I myself will judge between the fat sheep and the lean
sheep. 21 Because you push with your side and your shoulder, and
thrust your horns at all the weak sheep until you scatter them
abroad, 22 I will save my sheep; they will no longer be prey. I will
judge between one sheep and another.

23 "'I will set one shepherd over them, and he will feed them—
namely, my servant David. He will feed them and will be their
shepherd. 24 I, the LORD, will be their God, and my servant David
will be prince among them; I, the LORD, have spoken!

25 "'I will make a covenant of peace with them and will rid the
land of wild beasts, so that they can live securely in the wilderness and even sleep in the woods. 26 I will turn them and the regions around my hill into a blessing. I will make showers come
down in their season; they will be showers that bring blessing.
27 The trees of the field will yield their fruit and the earth will
yield its crops. They will live securely on their land; they will
know that I am the LORD, when I break the bars of their yoke and
rescue them from the hand of those who enslaved them. 28 They
will no longer be prey for the nations, and the wild beasts will
not devour them. They will live securely, and no one will make
them afraid. 29 I will prepare for them a healthy planting. They

A LOVE LIKE NO OTHER

EZEKIEL 34:15–16

"Remember that one time when we were shopping and you lost Chase?" My kids are so generous to remind me of this stuff.

One moment I could feel his little body against my leg, the next moment he was gone. In a sea of never-ending people, clothes racks, and holiday end-caps, we searched for what seemed like forever.

I would have done anything in that moment to get my boy back. A mama's love is fierce in the day-to-day, but when one of your own goes missing, the depth of that love is exposed, and you go to extreme lengths to ensure your child's safe return.

You don't stop. You won't quit. You never give up until the one you love is back safely in your arms.

"I myself will feed my sheep and I myself will make them lie down, declares the Sovereign LORD. I will seek the lost and bring back the strays; I will bandage the injured and strengthen the sick . . . And you, my sheep, the sheep of my pasture, are my people, and I am your God, declares the Sovereign LORD" (Ezek 34:15–16, 31).

This Shepherd was on a mission even fiercer than that of a desperate mother looking for her lost child. He would come in the humblest of ways, in a way opposite everything the world expected, to lay down His life to rescue His sheep: the ones who were lost, the ones who had strayed, the ones who were injured and weak. Still today, in His great love, God never stops passionately pursuing His own.

He searches for the lost. He brings back the strayed. He rescues them. He gathers them safely into His arms. He feeds them with good pasture. He binds up the injured. He strengthens the weak. He gives them rest. He doesn't stop. He won't quit. He never gives up, until the ones He loves are safely back in His arms.

After a few short minutes that felt more like hours, I turned the corner and there he was. He was scared, confused, crying, and alone. I scooped him up in my arms, and he buried his head in my chest. He whispered, "I never want to leave you again."

Are you feeling lost, scared, confused, or alone today? True peace, identity, and purpose can only be found in Christ. Run into the arms of your Good Shepherd, who longs to welcome you back into the fold.

He is God, and He loves like no other.

will no longer be victims of famine in the land and will no longer bear the insults of the nations. 30 Then they will know that
I, the LORD their God, am with them, and that they are my people, the house of Israel, declares the Sovereign LORD. 31 And you,
my sheep, the sheep of my pasture, are my people, and I am your
God, declares the Sovereign LORD.'"

PROPHECY AGAINST MOUNT SEIR

35 The LORD's message came to me: 2 "Son of man, turn toward Mount Seir, and prophesy against it. 3 Say to it, 'This
is what the Sovereign LORD says:

"'Look, I am against you, Mount Seir;
I will stretch out my hand against you
and turn you into a desolate ruin.
4 I will lay waste your cities,
and you will become desolate.
Then you will know that I am the LORD!

5 "'You have shown unrelenting hostility and poured the people
of Israel onto the blades of a sword at the time of their calamity,
at the time of their final punishment. 6 Therefore, as surely as I
live, declares the Sovereign LORD, I will subject you to bloodshed,
and bloodshed will pursue you. Since you did not hate bloodshed, bloodshed will pursue you. 7 I will turn Mount Seir into a
desolate ruin; I will cut off from it the one who passes through
or returns. 8 I will fill its mountains with its dead; on your hills
and in your valleys and in all your ravines, those killed by the
sword will fall. 9 I will turn you into a perpetual desolation, and
your cities will not be inhabited. Then you will know that I am
the LORD.
10 "'You said, "These two nations, these two lands will be mine,
and we will possess them," (although the LORD was there);
11 therefore, as surely as I live, declares the Sovereign LORD, I
will deal with you according to your anger and your envy, by
which you acted spitefully against them. I will reveal myself to
them when I judge you. 12 Then you will know that I, the LORD,
have heard all the insults you spoke against the mountains of
Israel, saying, "They are desolate; they have been given to us for
food." 13 You exalted yourselves against me with your speech and
hurled many insults against me—I have heard them all! 14 This is
what the Sovereign LORD says: While the whole earth rejoices, I
will turn you into a desolation. 15 As you rejoiced over the inheritance of the house of Israel because it was desolate, so will I deal
with you—you will be desolate, Mount Seir, and all Edom—all of
it! Then they will know that I am the LORD.'"

BLESSINGS ON THE MOUNTAINS OF ISRAEL

36 "As for you, son of man, prophesy to the mountains of Israel, and say: 'O mountains of Israel, listen to the LORD's
message! 2 This is what the Sovereign LORD says: The enemy has
spoken against you, saying "Aha!" and, "The ancient heights have
become our property!"' 3 So prophesy and say: 'This is what the
Sovereign LORD says: Surely because they have made you desolate and crushed you from all directions, so that you have become

the property of the rest of the nations, and have become the
subject of gossip and slander among the people, 4 therefore, O
mountains of Israel, hear the word of the Sovereign LORD. This
is what the Sovereign LORD says to the mountains and hills,
the ravines and valleys, and to the desolate ruins and the abandoned cities that have become prey and an object of derision to
the rest of the nations round about; 5 therefore, this is what the
Sovereign LORD says: Surely I have spoken in the fire of my zeal
against the rest of the nations and against all Edom, who with
great joy and utter contempt have made my land their property
and prey, because of its pasture.'

6 "Therefore prophesy concerning the land of Israel, and say
to the mountains and hills, the ravines and valleys, 'This is what
the Sovereign LORD says: Look, I have spoken in my zeal and in
my anger, because you have endured the insults of the nations.
7 So this is what the Sovereign LORD says: I vow that the nations
around you will endure insults as well.

8 "'But you, mountains of Israel, will grow your branches and
bear your fruit for my people Israel, for they will arrive soon.
9 For indeed, I am on your side; I will turn to you, and you will
be plowed and planted. 10 I will multiply your people—the whole
house of Israel, all of it. The cities will be populated and the ruins rebuilt. 11 I will increase the number of people and animals
on you; they will increase and be fruitful. I will cause you to be
inhabited as in ancient times and will do more good for you than
at the beginning of your history. Then you will know that I am
the LORD. 12 I will lead people, my people Israel, across you; they
will possess you, and you will become their inheritance. No longer will you bereave them of their children.

13 "'This is what the Sovereign LORD says: Because they are saying to you, "You are a devourer of men and bereave your nation
of children," 14 therefore you will no longer devour people and
no longer bereave your nation of children, declares the Sovereign LORD. 15 I will no longer subject you to the nations' insults;
no longer will you bear the shame of the peoples, and no longer will you bereave your nation, declares the Sovereign LORD.'"

16 The LORD's message came to me: 17 "Son of man, when the
house of Israel was living on their own land, they defiled it by
their behavior and their deeds. In my sight their behavior was
like the uncleanness of a woman having her monthly period.
18 So I poured my anger on them because of the blood they shed
on the land and because of the idols with which they defiled
it. 19 I scattered them among the nations; they were dispersed
throughout foreign countries. In accordance with their behavior and their deeds I judged them. 20 But when they arrived in
the nations where they went, they profaned my holy name. It
was said of them, 'These are the people of the LORD, yet they
have departed from his land.' 21 I was concerned for my holy reputation, which the house of Israel profaned among the nations
where they went.

22 "Therefore say to the house of Israel, 'This is what the Sovereign LORD says: It is not for your sake that I am about to act, O
house of Israel, but for the sake of my holy reputation, which you
profaned among the nations where you went. 23 I will magnify my

great name that has been profaned among the nations, which
you have profaned among them. The nations will know that I am
the LORD, declares the Sovereign LORD, when I magnify myself
among you in their sight.
24 "'I will take you from the nations and gather you from all
the countries; then I will bring you to your land. 25 I will sprinkle you with pure water, and you will be clean from all your impurities. I will purify you from all your idols. 26 I will give you a
new heart, and I will put a new spirit within you. I will remove
the heart of stone from your body and give you a heart of flesh.
27 I will put my Spirit within you; I will take the initiative, and
you will obey my statutes and carefully observe my regulations.
28 Then you will live in the land I gave to your fathers; you will be
my people, and I will be your God. 29 I will save you from all your
uncleanness. I will call for the grain and multiply it; I will not
bring a famine on you. 30 I will multiply the fruit of the trees and
the produce of the fields, so that you will never again suffer the
disgrace of famine among the nations. 31 Then you will remember
your evil behavior and your deeds that were not good; you will
loathe yourselves on account of your sins and your abominable
deeds. 32 Understand that it is not for your sake I am about to
act, declares the Sovereign LORD. Be ashamed and embarrassed
by your behavior, O house of Israel.
33 "'This is what the Sovereign LORD says: In the day I cleanse
you from all your sins, I will populate the cities, and the ruins
will be rebuilt. 34 The desolate land will be plowed, instead of being desolate in the sight of everyone who passes by. 35 They will
say, "This desolate land has become like the garden of Eden; the
ruined, desolate, and destroyed cities are now fortified and inhabited." 36 Then the nations that remain around you will know
that I, the LORD, have rebuilt the ruins and replanted what was
desolate. I, the LORD, have spoken—and I will do it!'
37 "This is what the Sovereign LORD says: I will allow the house
of Israel to ask me to do this for them: I will multiply their people
like sheep. 38 Like the sheep for offerings, like the sheep of Jerusalem during her appointed feasts, so the ruined cities will be filled
with flocks of people. Then they will know that I am the LORD."

THE VALLEY OF DRY BONES

37 The hand of the LORD was on me, and he brought me out
by the Spirit of the LORD and placed me in the midst of
the valley, and it was full of bones. 2 He made me walk all around
among them. I realized there were a great many bones in the
valley, and they were very dry. 3 He said to me, "Son of man, can
these bones live?" I said to him, "Sovereign LORD, you know."
4 Then he said to me, "Prophesy over these bones, and tell them:
'Dry bones, listen to the LORD's message. 5 This is what the Sovereign LORD says to these bones: Look, I am about to infuse breath
into you and you will live. 6 I will put tendons on you and muscles over you and will cover you with skin; I will put breath in
you, and you will live. Then you will know that I am the LORD.'"
7 So I prophesied as I was commanded. There was a sound
when I prophesied—I heard a rattling, and the bones came together, bone to bone. 8 As I watched, I saw tendons on them, then

CHALLENGE

What does this passage communicate about God's character? Take time to reflect on the ways God has restored you, whether it came after a time of discipline or a time of suffering. Set up a reminder of His faithfulness in your home to remind you of all the ways He has redeemed and restored your life.

muscles appeared, and skin covered over them from above, but
there was no breath in them.
9 He said to me, "Prophesy to the breath,—prophesy, son of
man—and say to the breath: 'This is what the Sovereign LORD
says: Come from the four winds, O breath, and breathe on these
corpses so that they may live.'" 10 So I prophesied as I was commanded, and the breath came into them; they lived and stood
on their feet, an extremely great army.
11 Then he said to me, "Son of man, these bones are all the
house of Israel. Look, they are saying, 'Our bones are dry, our
hope has perished; we are cut off.' 12 Therefore prophesy, and
tell them, 'This is what the Sovereign LORD says: Look, I am
about to open your graves and will raise you from your graves,
my people. I will bring you to the land of Israel. 13 Then you will
know that I am the LORD, when I open your graves and raise
you from your graves, my people. 14 I will place my breath in you
and you will live; I will give you rest in your own land. Then you
will know that I am the LORD—I have spoken and I will act, declares the LORD.'"
15 The LORD's message came to me: 16 "As for you, son of man,
take one branch and write on it, 'For Judah and for the Israelites associated with him.' Then take another branch and write
on it, 'For Joseph, the branch of Ephraim, and all the house of
Israel associated with him.' 17 Join them as one stick; they will
be as one in your hand. 18 When your people say to you, 'Will you
not tell us what these things mean?' 19 tell them, 'This is what
the Sovereign LORD says: Look, I am about to take the branch
of Joseph that is in the hand of Ephraim and the tribes of Israel
associated with him, and I will place them on the stick of Judah
and make them into one stick—they will be one in my hand.'
20 The sticks you write on will be in your hand in front of them.
21 Then tell them, 'This is what the Sovereign LORD says: Look, I
am about to take the Israelites from among the nations where
they have gone. I will gather them from round about and bring
them to their land. 22 I will make them one nation in the land,
on the mountains of Israel, and one king will rule over them all.
They will never again be two nations and never again be divided
into two kingdoms. 23 They will not defile themselves with their
idols, their detestable things, and all their rebellious deeds. I will
save them from all their unfaithfulness by which they sinned.
I will purify them; they will become my people, and I will become their God.
24 "'My servant David will be king over them; there will be one
shepherd for all of them. They will follow my regulations and
carefully observe my statutes. 25 They will live in the land I gave
to my servant Jacob, in which your fathers lived; they will live
in it—they and their children and their grandchildren forever.
David my servant will be prince over them forever. 26 I will make
a covenant of peace with them; it will be a perpetual covenant
with them. I will establish them, increase their numbers, and
place my sanctuary among them forever. 27 My dwelling place
will be with them; I will be their God, and they will be my people. 28 Then, when my sanctuary is among them forever, the nations will know that I, the LORD, sanctify Israel.'"

A PROPHECY AGAINST GOG

38 The LORD's message came to me: 2 “Son of man, turn toward Gog, of the land of Magog, the chief prince of Meshech and Tubal. Prophesy against him 3 and say: ‘This is what the Sovereign LORD says: Look, I am against you, Gog, chief prince of Meshech and Tubal. 4 I will turn you around, put hooks into your jaws, and bring you out with all your army, horses, and horsemen, all of them fully armed, a great company with shields of different types, all of them armed with swords. 5 Persia, Ethiopia, and Put are with them, all of them with shields and helmets. 6 They are joined by Gomer with all its troops, and by Beth Togarmah from the remote parts of the north with all its troops—many peoples are with you.

7 “‘Be ready and stay ready, you and all your companies assembled around you, and be a guard for them. 8 After many days you will be summoned; in the latter years you will come to a land restored from the ravages of war, from many peoples gathered on the mountains of Israel that had long been in ruins. Its people were brought out from the peoples, and all of them will be living securely. 9 You will advance; you will come like a storm. You will be like a cloud covering the earth, you, all your troops, and the many other peoples with you.

10 “‘This is what the Sovereign LORD says: On that day thoughts will come into your mind, and you will devise an evil plan. 11 You will say, “I will invade a land of unwalled towns; I will advance against those living quietly in security—all of them living without walls and barred gates—12 to loot and plunder, to attack the inhabited ruins and the people gathered from the nations, who are acquiring cattle and goods, who live at the center of the earth.” 13 Sheba and Dedan and the traders of Tarshish with all its young warriors will say to you, “Have you come to loot? Have you assembled your armies to plunder, to carry away silver and gold, to take away cattle and goods, to haul away a great amount of spoils?”’

14 “Therefore, prophesy, son of man, and say to Gog: ‘This is what the Sovereign LORD says: On that day when my people Israel are living securely, you will take notice 15 and come from your place, from the remote parts of the north, you and many peoples with you, all of them riding on horses, a great company and a vast army. 16 You will advance against my people Israel like a cloud covering the earth. In future days I will bring you against my land so that the nations may acknowledge me, when before their eyes I magnify myself through you, O Gog.

17 “‘This is what the Sovereign LORD says: Are you the one of whom I spoke in former days by my servants the prophets of Israel, who prophesied in those days that I would bring you against them? 18 On that day, when Gog invades the land of Israel, declares the Sovereign LORD, my rage will mount up in my anger. 19 In my zeal, in the fire of my fury, I declare that on that day there will be a great earthquake in the land of Israel. 20 The fish of the sea, the birds of the sky, the wild beasts, all the things that creep on the ground, and all people who live on the face of the earth will shake at my presence. The mountains will topple, the cliffs will fall, and every wall will fall to the ground. 21 I will call for a sword to attack Gog on all my mountains, declares the Sovereign LORD; every man's sword will be against his brother. 22 I

will judge him with plague and bloodshed. I will rain down on
him, his troops, and the many peoples who are with him a torrential downpour, hailstones, fire, and brimstone. 23 I will exalt
and magnify myself; I will reveal myself before many nations.
Then they will know that I am the LORD.'

39 "As for you, son of man, prophesy against Gog, and say: 'This
is what the Sovereign LORD says: Look, I am against you, O
Gog, chief prince of Meshech and Tubal! 2 I will turn you around
and drag you along; I will lead you up from the remotest parts of
the north and bring you against the mountains of Israel. 3 I will
knock your bow out of your left hand and make your arrows fall
from your right hand. 4 You will fall dead on the mountains of Israel, you and all your troops and the people who are with you. I
give you as food to every kind of bird and every wild beast. 5 You
will fall dead in the open field; for I have spoken, declares the Sovereign LORD. 6 I will send fire on Magog and those who live securely in the coastlands; then they will know that I am the LORD.

7 "'I will make my holy name known in the midst of my people
Israel; I will not let my holy name be profaned anymore. Then
the nations will know that I am the LORD, the Holy One of Israel. 8 Realize that it is coming and it will be done, declares the
Sovereign LORD. It is the day I have spoken about.

9 "'Then those who live in the cities of Israel will go out and
use the weapons for kindling—the shields, bows and arrows, war
clubs and spears—they will burn them for seven years. 10 They will
not need to take wood from the field or cut down trees from the
forests because they will make fires with the weapons. They will
take the loot from those who looted them and seize the plunder of those who plundered them, declares the Sovereign LORD.

11 "'On that day I will assign Gog a grave in Israel. It will be the
valley of those who travel east of the sea; it will block the way
of the travelers. There they will bury Gog and all his horde; they
will call it the Valley of Hamon Gog. 12 For seven months Israel
will bury them, in order to cleanse the land. 13 All the people of
the land will bury them, and it will be a memorial for them on
the day I magnify myself, declares the Sovereign LORD. 14 They
will designate men to scout continually through the land, burying those who remain on the surface of the ground, in order to
cleanse it. They will search for seven full months. 15 When the
scouts survey the land and see a human bone, they will place a
sign by it, until those assigned to burial duty have buried it in
the valley of Hamon Gog. 16 (A city by the name of Hamonah will
also be there.) They will cleanse the land.'

17 "As for you, son of man, this is what the Sovereign LORD says:
Tell every kind of bird and every wild beast: 'Assemble and come!
Gather from all around to my slaughter that I am going to make
for you, a great slaughter on the mountains of Israel! You will
eat flesh and drink blood. 18 You will eat the flesh of warriors and
drink the blood of the princes of the earth—the rams, lambs,
goats, and bulls, all of them fattened animals of Bashan. 19 You
will eat fat until you are full, and drink blood until you are drunk
at my slaughter that I have made for you. 20 You will fill up at my
table with horses and charioteers, with warriors and all the soldiers,' declares the Sovereign LORD.

21 "I will display my majesty among the nations. All the nations will witness the judgment I have executed and the power I have exhibited among them. 22 Then the house of Israel will know that I am the LORD their God, from that day forward. 23 The nations will know that the house of Israel went into exile due to their iniquity, for they were unfaithful to me. So I hid my face from them and handed them over to their enemies; all of them died by the sword. 24 According to their uncleanness and rebellion I have dealt with them, and I hid my face from them.

25 "Therefore this is what the Sovereign LORD says: Now I will restore the fortunes of Jacob, and I will have mercy on the entire house of Israel. I will be zealous for my holy name. 26 They will bear their shame for all their unfaithful acts against me, when they live securely on their land with no one to make them afraid. 27 When I have brought them back from the peoples and gathered them from the countries of their enemies, I will magnify myself among them in the sight of many nations. 28 Then they will know that I am the LORD their God because I sent them into exile among the nations and then gathered them into their own land. I will not leave any of them in exile any longer. 29 I will no longer hide my face from them, when I pour out my Spirit on the house of Israel, declares the Sovereign LORD."

VISION OF THE NEW TEMPLE

40 In the twenty-fifth year of our exile, at the beginning of the year, on the tenth day of the month, in the fourteenth year after the city was struck down, on this very day, the hand of the LORD was on me, and he brought me there. 2 By divine visions he brought me to the land of Israel and placed me on a very high mountain, and on it was a structure like a city, to the south. 3 When he brought me there, I saw a man whose appearance was like bronze, with a linen cord and a measuring stick in his hand. He was standing in the gateway. 4 The man said to me, "Son of man, watch closely, listen carefully, and pay attention to everything I show you, for you have been brought here so that I can show it to you. Tell the house of Israel everything you see."

5 I saw a wall all around the outside of the temple. In the man's hand was a measuring stick 10½ feet long. He measured the thickness of the wall as 10½ feet, and its height as 10½ feet. 6 Then he went to the gate facing east. He climbed its steps and measured the threshold of the gate as 10½ feet deep. 7 The alcoves were 10½ feet long and 10½ feet wide; between the alcoves were 8¾ feet. The threshold of the gate by the porch of the gate facing inward was 10½ feet. 8 Then he measured the porch of the gate facing inward as 10½ feet. 9 He measured the porch of the gate as 14 feet, and its jambs as 3½ feet; the porch of the gate faced inward. 10 There were three alcoves on each side of the east gate; the three had the same measurement, and the jambs on either side had the same measurement. 11 He measured the width of the entrance of the gateway as 17½ feet, and the length of the gateway as 22¾ feet. 12 There was a barrier in front of the alcoves, 1¾ feet on either side; the alcoves were 10½ feet on either side. 13 He measured the gateway from the roof of one alcove to the roof of the other, a width of 43¾

REFLECT

Was Ezekiel's vision of the new temple one of a new earthly temple or a heavenly temple? How do you think the people received this message during their time of exile?

feet from one entrance to the opposite one. 14 He measured
the porch at 105 feet high; the gateway went all around to the
jamb of the courtyard. 15 From the front of the entrance gate to
the porch of the inner gate was 87½ feet. 16 There were closed
windows toward the alcoves and toward their jambs within
the gate all around, and likewise for the porches. There were
windows all around the inside, and on each jamb were decorative palm trees.

17 Then he brought me to the outer court. I saw chambers there
and a pavement made for the court all around; thirty chambers
faced the pavement. 18 The pavement was beside the gates, corresponding to the length of the gates; this was the lower pavement. 19 Then he measured the width from before the lower gate
to the front of the exterior of the inner court as 175 feet on the
east and on the north.

20 He measured the length and width of the gate of the outer
court that faces north. 21 Its alcoves, three on each side, and its
jambs and porches had the same measurement as the first gate;
87½ feet long and 43¾ feet wide. 22 Its windows, its porches, and
its decorative palm trees had the same measurement as the
gate that faced east. Seven steps led up to it, and its porch was
in front of them. 23 Opposite the gate on the north and the east
was a gate of the inner court; he measured the distance from
gate to gate at 175 feet.

24 Then he led me toward the south. I saw a gate on the south.
He measured its jambs and its porches; they had the same dimensions as the others. 25 There were windows all around it
and its porches, like the windows of the others; 87½ feet long
and 43¾ feet wide. 26 There were seven steps going up to it; its
porches were in front of them. It had decorative palm trees on
its jambs, one on either side. 27 The inner court had a gate toward the south; he measured it from gate to gate toward the
south as 175 feet.

28 Then he brought me to the inner court by the south gate.
He measured the south gate; it had the same dimensions as the
others. 29 Its alcoves, its jambs, and its porches had the same dimensions as the others, and there were windows all around it
and its porches; its length was 87½ feet and its width 43¾ feet.
30 There were porches all around, 43¾ feet long and 8¾ feet wide.
31 Its porches faced the outer court, and decorative palm trees
were on its jambs, and its stairway had eight steps.

32 Then he brought me to the inner court on the east side. He
measured the gate; it had the same dimensions as the others.
33 Its alcoves, its jambs, and its porches had the same dimensions as the others, and there were windows all around it and
its porches; its length was 87½ feet and its width 43¾ feet. 34 Its
porches faced the outer court, it had decorative palm trees on
its jambs, and its stairway had eight steps.

35 Then he brought me to the north gate, and he measured it; it
had the same dimensions as the others—36 its alcoves, its jambs,
and its porches. It had windows all around it; its length was 87½
feet and its width 43¾ feet. 37 Its jambs faced the outer court,
and it had decorative palm trees on its jambs on either side, and
its stairway had eight steps.

[38] There was a chamber with its door by the porch of the gate;
there they washed the burnt offering. [39] In the porch of the gate
were two tables on either side on which to slaughter the burnt
offering, the sin offering, and the guilt offering. [40] On the outside
of the porch as one goes up at the entrance of the north gate were
two tables, and on the other side of the porch of the gate were two
tables. [41] Four tables were on each side of the gate, eight tables
on which the sacrifices were to be slaughtered. [42] The four tables
for the burnt offering were of carved stone, 32 inches long, 32
inches wide, and 21 inches high. They would put the instruments
that they used to slaughter the burnt offering and the sacrifice
on them. [43] There were hooks three inches long fastened in the
house all around, and on the tables was the flesh of the offering.

[44] On the outside of the inner gate were chambers for the singers
of the inner court, one at the side of the north gate facing south,
and the other at the side of the south gate facing north. [45] He said
to me, "This chamber that faces south is for the priests who keep
charge of the temple, [46] and the chamber that faces north is for
the priests who keep charge of the altar. These are the descendants
of Zadok, from the descendants of Levi, who may approach the
LORD to minister to him." [47] He measured the court as a square
175 feet long and 175 feet wide; the altar was in front of the temple.

[48] Then he brought me to the porch of the temple and measured the jambs of the porch as 8¾ feet on either side; the width
of the gate was 24½ feet, and the sides were 5¼ feet on each
side. [49] The length of the porch was 35 feet and the width 19¼
feet; steps led up to it, and there were pillars beside the jambs
on either side.

THE INNER TEMPLE

41 Then he brought me to the outer sanctuary and measured
the jambs; the jambs were 10½ feet wide on each side. [2] The
width of the entrance was 17½ feet, and the sides of the entrance
were 8¾ feet on each side. He measured the length of the outer
sanctuary as 70 feet and its width as 35 feet.

[3] Then he went into the inner sanctuary and measured the
jambs of the entrance as 3½ feet, the entrance as 10½ feet, and
the width of the entrance as 12¼ feet. [4] Then he measured its
length as 35 feet and its width as 35 feet, before the outer sanctuary. He said to me, "This is the Most Holy Place."

[5] Then he measured the wall of the temple as 10½ feet and the
width of the side chambers as 7 feet, all around the temple. [6] The
side chambers were in three stories, one above the other, thirty
in each story. There were offsets in the wall all around to serve
as supports for the side chambers, so that the supports were not
in the wall of the temple. [7] The side chambers surrounding the
temple were wider at each successive story, for the structure
surrounding the temple went up story by story all around the
temple. For this reason the width of the temple increased as it
went up, and one went up from the lowest story to the highest
by the way of the middle story.

[8] I saw that the temple had a raised platform all around; the
foundations of the side chambers were a full measuring stick of
10½ feet high. [9] The width of the outer wall of the side chambers

was 8¾ feet, and the open area between the side chambers of the
temple 10 and the chambers of the court was 35 feet in width all
around the temple on every side. 11 There were entrances from
the side chambers toward the open area, one entrance toward
the north, and another entrance toward the south; the width of
the open area was 8¾ feet all around.

12 The building that was facing the temple courtyard at the
west side was 122½ feet wide; the wall of the building was 8¾
feet thick all around, and its length 157½ feet.

13 Then he measured the temple as 175 feet long, the courtyard
of the temple and the building and its walls as 175 feet long, 14 and
also the width of the front of the temple and the courtyard on
the east as 175 feet.

15 Then he measured the length of the building facing the courtyard at the rear of the temple, with its galleries on either side
as 175 feet.

The interior of the outer sanctuary and the porch of the court,
16 as well as the thresholds, narrow windows and galleries all
around on three sides facing the threshold, were paneled with
wood all around, from the ground up to the windows (now the
windows were covered), 17 to the space above the entrance, to the
inner room, and on the outside, and on all the walls in the inner
room and outside, by measurement. 18 It was made with cherubim and decorative palm trees, with a palm tree between each
cherub. Each cherub had two faces: 19 a human face toward the
palm tree on one side and a lion's face toward the palm tree on
the other side. They were carved on the whole temple all around;
20 from the ground to the area above the entrance, cherubim
and decorative palm trees were carved on the wall of the outer
sanctuary. 21 The doorposts of the outer sanctuary were square.
In front of the sanctuary one doorpost looked just like the other.
22 The altar was of wood, 5¼ feet high, with its length 3½ feet; its
corners, its length, and its walls were of wood. He said to me, "This
is the table that is before the LORD." 23 The outer sanctuary and
the inner sanctuary each had a double door. 24 Each of the doors
had two leaves, two swinging leaves; two leaves for one door and
two leaves for the other. 25 On the doors of the outer sanctuary
were carved cherubim and palm trees, like those carved on the
walls, and there was a canopy of wood on the front of the outside
porch. 26 There were narrow windows and decorative palm trees
on either side of the side walls of the porch; this is what the side
chambers of the temple and the canopies were like.

CHAMBERS FOR THE TEMPLE

42 Then he led me out to the outer court, toward the north,
and brought me to the chamber that was opposite the
courtyard and opposite the building on the north. 2 Its length
was 175 feet on the north side, and its width 87½ feet. 3 Opposite
the 35 feet that belonged to the inner court, and opposite the
pavement that belonged to the outer court, gallery faced gallery
in the three stories. 4 In front of the chambers was a walkway on
the inner side, 17½ feet wide at a distance of 1¾ feet, and their
entrances were on the north. 5 Now the upper chambers were
narrower, because the galleries took more space from them than

from the lower and middle chambers of the building. 6 For they were in three stories and had no pillars like the pillars of the courts; therefore, the upper chambers were set back from the ground more than the lower and middle ones. 7 As for the outer wall by the side of the chambers, toward the outer court facing the chambers, it was 87½ feet long. 8 For the chambers on the outer court were 87½ feet long, while those facing the temple were 175 feet long. 9 Below these chambers was a passage on the east side as one enters from the outer court.

10 At the beginning of the wall of the court toward the south, facing the courtyard and the building, were chambers 11 like those on the north with a passage in front of them. The chambers that were toward the south were the same length and width as those on the north, and had matching exits and entrances and arrangements. 12 There was an opening at the head of the passage, the passage in front of the corresponding wall toward the east when one enters.

13 Then he said to me, "The north chambers and the south chambers that face the courtyard are holy chambers where the priests who approach the LORD will eat the most holy offerings. There they will place the most holy offerings—the grain offering, the sin offering, and the guilt offering, because the place is holy. 14 When the priests enter, then they will not go out from the sanctuary to the outer court without taking off their garments in which they minister, for these are holy; they will put on other garments, then they will go near the places where the people are."

15 Now when he had finished measuring the interior of the temple, he led me out by the gate that faces east and measured all around. 16 He measured the east side with the measuring stick as 875 feet by the measuring stick. 17 He measured the north side as 875 feet by the measuring stick. 18 He measured the south side as 875 feet by the measuring stick. 19 He turned to the west side and measured 875 feet by the measuring stick. 20 He measured it on all four sides. It had a wall around it, 875 feet long and 875 feet wide, to separate the holy and common places.

THE GLORY RETURNS TO THE TEMPLE

43 Then he brought me to the gate that faced toward the east. 2 I saw the glory of the God of Israel coming from the east; the sound was like that of rushing water, and the earth radiated his glory. 3 It was like the vision I saw when he came to destroy the city, and the vision I saw by the Kebar River. I threw myself face down. 4 The glory of the LORD came into the temple by way of the gate that faces east. 5 Then a wind lifted me up and brought me to the inner court; I watched the glory of the LORD filling the temple.

6 I heard someone speaking to me from the temple, while the man was standing beside me. 7 He said to me: "Son of man, this is the place of my throne and the place for the soles of my feet, where I will live among the people of Israel forever. The house of Israel will no longer profane my holy name, neither they nor their kings, by their spiritual prostitution or by the pillars of their kings set up when they die. 8 When they placed their

threshold by my threshold and their doorpost by my doorpost,
with only the wall between me and them, they profaned my
holy name by the abominable deeds they committed. So I consumed them in my anger. 9 Now they must put away their spiritual prostitution and the pillars of their kings far from me, and
then I will live among them forever.
10 "As for you, son of man, describe the temple to the house
of Israel, so that they will be ashamed of their sins and measure the pattern. 11 When they are ashamed of all that they have
done, make known to them the design of the temple—its pattern, its exits and entrances, and its whole design—all its statutes, its entire design, and all its laws; write it all down in their
sight, so that they may observe its entire design and all its statutes and do them.
12 "This is the law of the temple: The entire area on top of the
mountain all around will be most holy. Indeed, this is the law
of the temple.

THE ALTAR

13 "And these are the measurements of the altar: Its base is 1¾
feet high and 1¾ feet wide, and its border nine inches on its
edge. This is to be the height of the altar. 14 From the base of the
ground to the lower ledge is 3½ feet, and the width 1¾ feet; and
from the smaller ledge to the larger ledge, 7 feet, and the width
1¾ feet; 15 and the altar hearth, 7 feet, and from the altar hearth
four horns projecting upward. 16 Now the altar hearth is a perfect square, 21 feet long and 21 feet wide. 17 The ledge is 24½ feet
long and 24½ feet wide on four sides; the border around it is
10½ inches, and its surrounding base 1¾ feet. Its steps face east."
18 Then he said to me: "Son of man, this is what the Sovereign
LORD says: These are the statutes of the altar: On the day it is
built to offer up burnt offerings on it and to sprinkle blood on
it, 19 you will give a young bull for a sin offering to the Levitical
priests who are descended from Zadok, who approach me to
minister to me, declares the Sovereign LORD. 20 You will take
some of its blood and place it on the four horns of the altar, on
the four corners of the ledge, and on the border all around; you
will purify it and make atonement for it. 21 You will also take the
bull for the sin offering, and it will be burned in the appointed
place in the temple, outside the sanctuary.
22 "On the second day, you will offer a male goat without blemish for a sin offering. They will purify the altar just as they purified it with the bull. 23 When you have finished purifying it, you
will offer an unblemished young bull and an unblemished ram
from the flock. 24 You will present them before the LORD, and
the priests will scatter salt on them and offer them up as a burnt
offering to the LORD.
25 "For seven days you will provide every day a goat for a sin offering; a young bull and a ram from the flock, both without blemish, will be provided. 26 For seven days they will make atonement
for the altar and cleanse it, so they will consecrate it. 27 When the
prescribed period is over, on the eighth day and thereafter the
priests will offer up on the altar your burnt offerings and your
peace offerings; I will accept you, declares the Sovereign LORD."

THE CLOSED GATE

44 Then he brought me back by way of the outer gate of the
sanctuary that faces east, but it was shut. 2 The LORD said
to me: "This gate will be shut; it will not be opened, and no one
will enter by it. For the LORD, the God of Israel, has entered by
it; therefore it will remain shut. 3 Only the prince may sit in it
to eat a sacrificial meal before the LORD; he will enter by way of
the porch of the gate and will go out by the same way."
4 Then he brought me by way of the north gate to the front
of the temple. As I watched, I noticed the glory of the LORD
filling the LORD's temple, and I threw myself face down. 5 The
LORD said to me: "Son of man, pay attention, watch closely,
and listen carefully to everything I tell you concerning all the
statutes of the LORD's house and all its laws. Pay attention
to the entrances to the temple with all the exits of the sanctuary. 6 Say to the rebellious, to the house of Israel, 'This is
what the Sovereign LORD says: Enough of all your abominable practices, O house of Israel! 7 When you bring foreigners,
those uncircumcised in heart and in flesh, into my sanctuary,
you desecrate it—even my house—when you offer my food, the
fat and the blood. You have broken my covenant by all your
abominable practices. 8 You have not kept charge of my holy
things, but you have assigned foreigners to keep charge of my
sanctuary for you. 9 This is what the Sovereign LORD says: No
foreigner who is uncircumcised in heart and flesh among all
the foreigners who are among the people of Israel will enter
into my sanctuary.
10 "'But the Levites who went far from me, straying off from
me after their idols when Israel went astray, will be responsible for their sin. 11 Yet they will be ministers in my sanctuary, having oversight at the gates of the temple, and serving
the temple. They will slaughter the burnt offerings and the
sacrifices for the people, and they will stand before them to
minister to them. 12 Because they used to minister to them
before their idols and became a sinful obstacle to the house
of Israel, consequently I have made a vow concerning them,
declares the Sovereign LORD, that they will be responsible
for their sin. 13 They will not come near me to serve me as
priest, nor will they come near any of my holy things, the
things that are most sacred. They will bear the shame of the
abominable deeds they have committed. 14 Yet I will appoint
them to keep charge of the temple, all its service, and all that
will be done in it.

THE LEVITICAL PRIESTS

15 "'But the Levitical priests, the descendants of Zadok who kept
the charge of my sanctuary when the people of Israel went astray
from me, will approach me to minister to me; they will stand
before me to offer me the fat and the blood, declares the Sovereign LORD. 16 They will enter my sanctuary and approach my
table to minister to me; they will keep my charge.
17 "'When they enter the gates of the inner court, they must
wear linen garments; they must not have any wool on them
when they minister in the inner gates of the court and in the

temple. 18 Linen turbans will be on their heads and linen undergarments will be around their waists; they must not bind themselves with anything that causes sweat. 19 When they go out to the outer court to the people, they must remove the garments they were ministering in and place them in the holy chambers; they must put on other garments so that they will not transmit holiness to the people with their garments.

20 "'They must not shave their heads nor let their hair grow long; they must only trim their heads. 21 No priest may drink wine when he enters the inner court. 22 They must not marry a widow or a divorcee, but they may marry a virgin from the house of Israel or a widow who is a priest's widow. 23 Moreover, they will teach my people the difference between the holy and the common and show them how to distinguish between the ceremonially unclean and the clean.

24 "'In a controversy they will act as judges; they will judge according to my ordinances. They will keep my laws and my statutes regarding all my appointed festivals and will observe my Sabbaths.

25 "'They must not come near a dead person or they will be defiled; however, for father, mother, son, daughter, brother, or unmarried sister, they may defile themselves. 26 After a priest has become ceremonially clean, they must count off a period of seven days for him. 27 On the day he enters the sanctuary into the inner court to serve in the sanctuary, he must offer his sin offering, declares the Sovereign LORD.

28 "'This will be their inheritance: I am their inheritance, and you must give them no property in Israel; I am their property. 29 They may eat the grain offering, the sin offering, and the guilt offering, and every devoted thing in Israel will be theirs. 30 The first of all the firstfruits and all contributions of any kind will be for the priests; you will also give to the priest the first portion of your dough, so that a blessing may rest on your house. 31 The priests will not eat any bird or animal that has died a natural death or was torn to pieces by a wild animal.

THE LORD'S PORTION OF THE LAND

45 "'When you allot the land as an inheritance, you will offer an allotment to the LORD, a holy portion from the land; the length will be 8¼ miles and the width 3⅓ miles. This entire area will be holy. 2 Of this area a square 875 feet by 875 feet will be designated for the sanctuary, with 87½ feet set aside for its open space round about. 3 From this measured area you will measure a length of 8¼ miles and a width of 3⅓ miles; in it will be the sanctuary, the Most Holy Place. 4 It will be a holy portion of the land; it will be for the priests, the ministers of the sanctuary who approach the LORD to minister to him. It will be a place for their houses and a holy place for the sanctuary. 5 An area 8¼ miles in length and 3⅓ miles in width will be for the Levites, who minister at the temple, as the place for the cities in which they will live.

6 "'Alongside the portion set apart as the holy allotment, you will allot for the city an area 1⅔ miles wide and 8¼ miles long; it will be for the whole house of Israel.

7 "'For the prince there will be land on both sides of the holy
allotment and the allotted city, on the west side and on the east
side; it will be comparable in length to one of the portions, from
the west border to the east border 8 of the land. This will be his
property in Israel. My princes will no longer oppress my people, but the land will be allotted to the house of Israel according to their tribes.

9 "'This is what the Sovereign LORD says: Enough, you princes
of Israel! Put away violence and destruction and do what is just
and right. Put an end to your evictions of my people, declares the
Sovereign LORD. 10 You must use just balances, a just dry measure (an ephah), and a just liquid measure (a bath). 11 The dry and
liquid measures will be the same: The bath will contain a tenth
of a homer, and the ephah a tenth of a homer; the homer will be
the standard measure. 12 The shekel will be twenty gerahs. Sixty
shekels will be a mina for you.

13 "'This is the offering you must offer: a sixth of an ephah
from a homer of wheat, a sixth of an ephah from a homer of
barley, 14 and as the prescribed portion of olive oil, one-tenth
of a bath from each cor (which is ten baths or a homer, for ten
baths make a homer); 15 and one sheep from each flock of 200,
from the watered places of Israel, for a grain offering, burnt
offering, and peace offering, to make atonement for them,
declares the Sovereign LORD. 16 All the people of the land will
contribute to this offering for the prince of Israel. 17 It will be
the duty of the prince to provide the burnt offerings, the grain
offering, and the drink offering at festivals, on the new moons
and Sabbaths, at all the appointed feasts of the house of Israel;
he will provide the sin offering, the grain offering, the burnt
offering, and the peace offerings to make atonement for the
house of Israel.

18 "'This is what the Sovereign LORD says: In the first month,
on the first day of the month, you must take an unblemished
young bull and purify the sanctuary. 19 The priest will take some
of the blood of the sin offering and place it on the doorpost of
the temple, on the four corners of the ledge of the altar, and on
the doorpost of the gate of the inner court. 20 This is what you
must do on the seventh day of the month for anyone who sins
inadvertently or through ignorance; so you will make atonement for the temple.

21 "'In the first month, on the fourteenth day of the month,
you will celebrate the Passover, and for the seven days of the
festival bread made without yeast will be eaten. 22 On that day
the prince will provide for himself and for all the people of
the land a bull for a sin offering. 23 And during the seven days
of the feast he will provide as a burnt offering to the LORD
seven bulls and seven rams, all without blemish, on each of the
seven days, and a male goat daily for a sin offering. 24 He will
provide as a grain offering an ephah for each bull, an ephah
for each ram, and a gallon of olive oil for each ephah of grain.
25 In the seventh month, on the fifteenth day of the month,
at the feast, he will make the same provisions for the sin offering, burnt offering, and grain offering, and for the olive oil,
for the seven days.

THE PRINCE'S OFFERINGS

46 "'This is what the Sovereign LORD says: The gate of the inner court that faces east will be closed six working days,
but on the Sabbath day it will be opened and on the day of the
new moon it will be opened. 2 The prince will enter by way of the
porch of the gate from the outside and will stand by the doorpost of the gate. The priests will provide his burnt offering and
his peace offerings, and he will bow down at the threshold of
the gate and then go out. But the gate will not be closed until
evening. 3 The people of the land will bow down at the entrance
of that gate before the LORD on the Sabbaths and on the new
moons. 4 The burnt offering that the prince will offer to the LORD
on the Sabbath day will be six unblemished lambs and one unblemished ram. 5 The grain offering will be an ephah with the
ram, and the grain offering with the lambs will be as much as
he is able to give, and a gallon of olive oil with an ephah. 6 On
the day of the new moon he will offer an unblemished young
bull and six lambs and a ram, all without blemish. 7 He will provide a grain offering: an ephah with the bull and an ephah with
the ram, and with the lambs as much as he wishes, and a gallon
of olive oil with each ephah of grain. 8 When the prince enters,
he will come by way of the porch of the gate and will go out the
same way.

9 "'When the people of the land come before the LORD at the
appointed feasts, whoever enters by way of the north gate to
worship will go out by way of the south gate; whoever enters by
way of the south gate will go out by way of the north gate. No
one will return by way of the gate they entered but will go out
straight ahead. 10 When they come in, the prince will come in
with them, and when they go out, he will go out.

11 "'At the festivals and at the appointed feasts the grain offering will be an ephah with the bull and an ephah with the ram,
and with the lambs as much as one is able, and a gallon of olive
oil with each ephah of grain. 12 When the prince provides a freewill offering, a burnt offering, or peace offerings as a voluntary
offering to the LORD, the gate facing east will be opened for him,
and he will provide his burnt offering and his peace offerings
just as he did on the Sabbath. Then he will go out, and the gate
will be closed after he goes out.

13 "'You will provide a lamb a year old without blemish for a
burnt offering daily to the LORD; morning by morning he will
provide it. 14 And you will provide a grain offering with it morning by morning, a sixth of an ephah, and a third of a gallon of
olive oil to moisten the choice flour, as a grain offering to the
LORD; this is a perpetual statute. 15 Thus they will provide the
lamb, the grain offering, and the olive oil morning by morning,
as a perpetual burnt offering.

16 "'This is what the Sovereign LORD says: If the prince should
give a gift to one of his sons as his inheritance, it will belong to
his sons; it is their property by inheritance. 17 But if he gives a
gift from his inheritance to one of his servants, it will be his until the year of liberty; then it will revert to the prince. His inheritance will only remain with his sons. 18 The prince will not take
away any of the people's inheritance by oppressively removing

them from their property. He will give his sons an inheritance from his own possessions so that my people will not be scattered, each from his own property.'"

19 Then he brought me through the entrance, which was at the side of the gate, into the holy chambers for the priests, which faced north. There I saw a place at the extreme western end. 20 He said to me, "This is the place where the priests will boil the guilt offering and the sin offering, and where they will bake the grain offering, so that they do not bring them out to the outer court to transmit holiness to the people."

21 Then he brought me out to the outer court and led me past the four corners of the court, and I noticed that in every corner of the court there was a court. 22 In the four corners of the court were small courts, 70 feet in length and 52½ feet in width; the four were all the same size. 23 There was a row of masonry around each of the four courts, and places for boiling offerings were made under the rows all around. 24 Then he said to me, "These are the houses for boiling, where the ministers of the temple boil the sacrifices of the people."

WATER FROM THE TEMPLE

47 Then he brought me back to the entrance of the temple. I noticed that water was flowing from under the threshold of the temple toward the east (for the temple faced east). The water was flowing down from under the right side of the temple, from south of the altar. 2 He led me out by way of the north gate and brought me around the outside of the outer gate that faces toward the east; I noticed that the water was trickling out from the south side.

3 When the man went out toward the east with a measuring line in his hand, he measured 1,750 feet, and then he led me through water, which was ankle deep. 4 Again he measured 1,750 feet and led me through the water, which was now knee deep. Once more he measured 1,750 feet and led me through the water, which was waist deep. 5 Again he measured 1,750 feet, and it was a river I could not cross, for the water had risen; it was deep enough to swim in, a river that could not be crossed. 6 He said to me, "Son of man, have you seen this?"

Then he led me back to the bank of the river. 7 When I had returned, I noticed a vast number of trees on the banks of the river, on both sides. 8 He said to me, "These waters go out toward the eastern region and flow down into the rift valley; when they enter the Dead Sea, where the sea is stagnant, the waters become fresh. 9 Every living creature that swarms where the river flows will live; there will be many fish, for these waters flow there. It will become fresh, and everything will live where the river flows. 10 Fishermen will stand beside it; from En Gedi to En Eglaim they will spread nets. They will catch many kinds of fish, like the fish of the Great Sea. 11 But its swamps and its marshes will not become fresh; they will remain salty. 12 On both sides of the river's banks, every kind of tree will grow for food. Their leaves will not wither nor will their fruit fail, but they will bear fruit every month, because their water source flows from the sanctuary. Their fruit will be for food and their leaves for healing."

BOUNDARIES FOR THE LAND

13 This is what the Sovereign LORD says: "Here are the borders
you will observe as you allot the land to the twelve tribes of Israel. (Joseph will have two portions.) 14 You must divide it equally
just as I vowed to give it to your forefathers; this land will be assigned as your inheritance.

15 "This will be the border of the land: On the north side, from
the Great Sea by way of Hethlon to the entrance of Zedad; 16 Hamath, Berothah, Sibraim, which is between the border of Damascus and the border of Hamath, as far as Hazer Hattikon, which
is on the border of Hauran. 17 The border will run from the sea to
Hazar Enan, at the border of Damascus, and on the north is the
border of Hamath. This is the north side. 18 On the east side, between Hauran and Damascus, and between Gilead and the land
of Israel, will be the Jordan. You will measure from the border to
the eastern sea. This is the east side. 19 On the south side it will
run from Tamar to the waters of Meribah Kadesh, the river, to
the Great Sea. This is the south side. 20 On the west side the Great
Sea will be the boundary to a point opposite Lebo Hamath. This
is the west side.

21 "This is how you will divide this land for yourselves among
the tribes of Israel. 22 You must allot it as an inheritance among
yourselves and for the resident foreigners who live among you,
who have fathered sons among you. You must treat them as
native-born among the people of Israel; they will be allotted an
inheritance with you among the tribes of Israel. 23 In whatever
tribe the resident foreigner lives, there you will give him his inheritance," declares the Sovereign LORD.

THE TRIBAL PORTIONS

48 "These are the names of the tribes: From the northern
end beside the road of Hethlon to Lebo Hamath, as far
as Hazar Enan (which is on the border of Damascus, toward the
north beside Hamath), extending from the east side to the west,
Dan will have one portion. 2 Next to the border of Dan, from the
east side to the west side, Asher will have one portion. 3 Next to
the border of Asher from the east side to the west side, Naphtali
will have one portion. 4 Next to the border of Naphtali from the
east side to the west side, Manasseh will have one portion. 5 Next
to the border of Manasseh from the east side to the west side,
Ephraim will have one portion. 6 Next to the border of Ephraim
from the east side to the west side, Reuben will have one portion. 7 Next to the border of Reuben from the east side to the
west side, Judah will have one portion.

8 "Next to the border of Judah from the east side to the west
side will be the allotment you must set apart. It is to be 8¼ miles
wide, and the same length as one of the tribal portions, from the
east side to the west side; the sanctuary will be in the middle
of it. 9 The allotment you set apart to the LORD will be 8¼ miles
in length and 3⅓ miles in width. 10 These will be the allotments
for the holy portion: for the priests, toward the north 8¼ miles
in length, toward the west 3⅓ miles in width, toward the east
3⅓ miles in width, and toward the south 8¼ miles in length;
the sanctuary of the LORD will be in the middle. 11 This will be

for the priests who are set apart from the descendants of Zadok who kept my charge and did not go astray when the people
of Israel strayed off, as the Levites did. 12 It will be their portion
from the allotment of the land, a Most Holy Place, next to the
border of the Levites.

13 "Alongside the border of the priests, the Levites will have an
allotment 8¼ miles in length and 3⅓ miles in width. The whole
length will be 8¼ miles and the width 3⅓ miles. 14 They must
not sell or exchange any of it; they must not transfer this choice
portion of land, for it is set apart to the LORD.

15 "The remainder, 1⅔ miles in width and 8¼ miles in length,
will be for common use by the city, for houses and for open space.
The city will be in the middle of it; 16 these will be its measurements: The north side will be 1½ miles, the south side 1½ miles,
the east side 1½ miles, and the west side 1½ miles. 17 The city will
have open spaces: On the north there will be 437½ feet, on the
south 437½ feet, on the east 437½ feet, and on the west 437½
feet. 18 The remainder of the length alongside the holy allotment
will be 3⅓ miles to the east and 3⅓ miles toward the west, and
it will be beside the holy allotment. Its produce will be for food
for the workers of the city. 19 The workers of the city from all the
tribes of Israel will cultivate it. 20 The whole allotment will be
8¼ miles square; you must set apart the holy allotment with
the possession of the city.

21 "The rest, on both sides of the holy allotment and the property of the city, will belong to the prince. Extending from the
8¼ miles of the holy allotment to the east border, and westward
from the 8¼ miles to the west border, alongside the portions,
it will belong to the prince. The holy allotment and the sanctuary of the temple will be in the middle of it. 22 The property of
the Levites and of the city will be in the middle of that which
belongs to the prince. The portion between the border of Judah
and the border of Benjamin will be for the prince.

23 "As for the rest of the tribes: From the east side to the west
side, Benjamin will have one portion. 24 Next to the border of
Benjamin, from the east side to the west side, Simeon will have
one portion. 25 Next to the border of Simeon, from the east side
to the west side, Issachar will have one portion. 26 Next to the
border of Issachar, from the east side to the west side, Zebulun
will have one portion. 27 Next to the border of Zebulun, from the
east side to the west side, Gad will have one portion. 28 Next to
the border of Gad, at the south side, the border will run from
Tamar to the waters of Meribah Kadesh, to the Stream of Egypt,
and on to the Great Sea. 29 This is the land that you will allot to
the tribes of Israel, and these are their portions, declares the
Sovereign LORD.

30 "These are the exits of the city: On the north side, 1½ miles
by measure, 31 the gates of the city will be named for the tribes
of Israel. There will be three gates to the north: one gate for
Reuben, one gate for Judah, and one gate for Levi. 32 On the
east side, 1½ miles in length, there will be three gates: one
gate for Joseph, one gate for Benjamin, and one gate for Dan.
33 On the south side, 1½ miles by measure, there will be three
gates: one gate for Simeon, one gate for Issachar, and one gate

for Zebulun. 34 On the west side, 1½ miles in length, there will
be three gates: one gate for Gad, one gate for Asher, and one
gate for Naphtali. 35 The circumference of the city will be 6
miles. The name of the city from that day forward will be: 'The
LORD Is There.'"

HE is ABLE to
rescue us
from the FURNACE
of BLAZING FIRE,
and HE WILL
Rescue us

MEMORY VERSE

"If our God whom we are serving exists, he is able to rescue us from the furnace of blazing fire, and he will rescue us, O king, from your power as well. But if he does not, let it be known to you, O king, that we don't serve your gods, and we will not pay homage to the golden statue that you have erected."

Daniel 3:17–18

INTRODUCTION

Living with Conviction

The Book of Daniel is a unique combination of prophecy and history. The book describes the historical events surrounding Daniel's arrival and life in Babylon, along with prophetic messages about the future of the people of Judah. Daniel's message included both discouraging words of prophecy and encouraging words of hope. Daniel offers insight on how to live with conviction among an unbelieving people and insight into God's character of discipline and restoration.

The first five chapters describe events at the end of the Babylonian Empire, during the reigns of Nebuchadnezzar and his son Belshazzar. Chapter 6 describes the events in Daniel's life during the reign of Darius the Mede and Cyrus the Persian. The remaining six chapters contain prophecies from all of his combined years in Babylon.

Daniel himself claims to be the author of this prophetic book (12:4). He was a young, well-educated Jew of royal descent, chosen to undergo specialized training in the palace in Babylon. Daniel possessed the linguistic skills and the historical and cultural knowledge needed to write a book of this complexity. The events in Daniel took place between 605 and 537 B.C. The historical account begins with the deportation of a small group of princes and noblemen to Babylon from Jerusalem and ends with Daniel being thrown into the lions' den during the reign of Darius.

The main message of the Book of Daniel was to remind the Jewish exiles of the sovereignty of God, even over the most powerful nations. His message told the people that God had not forgotten His promises to them. Daniel's firm conviction and commitment to Yahweh throughout the exile offered hope and encouragement to others to do the same. Daniel loved God greatly. May our lives reflect his in our convictions and commitments.

Australia

OFFICIAL LANGUAGE
English
POPULATION
25,198,000
UNREACHED POPULATION
867,000
PROFESSING CHRISTIANS
65.4%

Say a Prayer Today

Pray for the many young people in Australia who, like Kim, are confused and uncertain about their faith. Pray God would build them up through His Word and through discipleship. Pray God would raise up a generation of people committed to living with conviction.

HISTORY BIT

Australia has enjoyed freedom of religion since it became an independent country in 1901. Because of their British roots, the Church of England is one of the largest denominations in Australia today.*

Kim's Home

Source Information:
https://joshuaproject.net/countries/AS
*David B. Barrett, World Christian Encyclopedia, Australia (New York, NY: Oxford University Press, 1982), 154.

LOVE YOUR NEIGHBOR

Her Journey

KIM'S STORY

"If our God whom we are serving exists, he is able to rescue us from the furnace of blazing fire, and he will rescue us, O king, from your power as well. But if he does not, let it be known to you, O king, that we don't serve your gods, and we will not pay homage to the golden statue that you have erected" (Dan 3:17–18). Struth!! (That's Australian for "oh my golly goodness.") In the face of being thrown into a fiery furnace, how many of us would have the conviction to speak those words?

Growing up in suburban Adelaide, I couldn't summon the courage to refuse worshiping the "kings" of adolescent life. I partied. I drank. I lied. I chased boys. Despite being in church every Sunday and never doubting that the God of the Bible was real, the pressure to fit in with the crowd was too much for my seventeen-year-old self.

I wrongly assumed God wasn't big enough to deliver me from ridicule if I resisted the status quo—until I realized He already had. Unlike Shadrach, Meshach, and Abednego, I had the advantage of knowing how Jesus' life, death, and resurrection help us face the trials of this world and save us from the ultimate fiery furnace. Jesus proves how much God loves us and what it cost Him to forgive us. Jesus is worth the cost of taking a stand.

Australia, like many other Western countries, is rapidly abandoning its Christian heritage. We worship comfort, entertainment, and the self-appeasement of 'liking' whatever cause is trending on social media. Someday soon, Aussie Christians may find themselves in a similar situation to Shack, Mack, and Bendy (nicknames are an Aussie thing . . . go with it). We may not face a literal furnace, but ridicule, job loss, and legal action are already real threats. I pray God might give us the faith to declare, "we [will not serve] your gods," no matter the consequences.

6 WEEK READING PLAN

LOVE HIS WORD

MONDAY	TUESDAY	WEDNESDAY	THURSDAY	FRIDAY
Daniel 1:1-14	Daniel 1:15-21	Daniel 2:1-13	Daniel 2:14-24	Daniel 2:25-36
SOAP Daniel 1:8-9	SOAP Daniel 1:17	SOAP Daniel 2:13	SOAP Daniel 2:20-22	SOAP Daniel 2:28
Daniel 2:37-49	Daniel 3:1-12	Daniel 3:13-23	Daniel 3:24—4:3	Daniel 4:4-18
SOAP Daniel 2:47-49	SOAP Daniel 3:12	SOAP Daniel 3:17-18	SOAP Daniel 4:2-3	SOAP Daniel 4:17
Daniel 4:19-27	Daniel 4:28-37	Daniel 5:1-16	Daniel 5:17-31	Daniel 6:1-9
SOAP Daniel 4:27	SOAP Daniel 4:34-35	SOAP Daniel 5:13-14	SOAP Daniel 5:29-30	SOAP Daniel 6:4
Daniel 6:10-18	Daniel 6:19-28	Daniel 7:1-14	Daniel 7:15-28	Daniel 8:1-14
SOAP Daniel 6:10	SOAP Daniel 6:21-22	SOAP Daniel 7:13-14	SOAP Daniel 7:27	SOAP Daniel 8:12
Daniel 8:15-27	Daniel 9:1-19	Daniel 9:20-27	Daniel 10:1-14	Daniel 10:15—11:2a
SOAP Daniel 8:27	SOAP Daniel 9:8-10	SOAP Daniel 9:22-23	SOAP Daniel 10:12-14	SOAP Daniel 10:18-19
Daniel 11:2b-20	Daniel 11:21-35	Daniel 11:36-45	Daniel 12:1-3	Daniel 12:4-13
SOAP Daniel 11:20	SOAP Daniel 11:33-35	SOAP Daniel 11:45	SOAP Daniel 12:3	SOAP Daniel 12:9-10

DANIEL FINDS FAVOR IN BABYLON

1 In the third year of the reign of King Jehoiakim of Judah, King Nebuchadnezzar of Babylon advanced against Jerusalem and laid it under siege. 2 Now the Lord delivered King Jehoiakim of Judah into his power, along with some of the vessels of the temple of God. He brought them to the land of Babylonia to the temple of his god and put the vessels in the treasury of his god.

3 The king commanded Ashpenaz, who was in charge of his court officials, to choose some of the Israelites who were of royal and noble descent—4 young men in whom there was no physical defect and who were handsome, well versed in all kinds of wisdom, well educated and having keen insight, and who were capable of entering the king's royal service—and to teach them the literature and language of the Babylonians. 5 So the king assigned them a daily ration from his royal delicacies and from the wine he himself drank. They were to be trained for the next three years. At the end of that time they were to enter the king's service. 6 As it turned out, among these young men were some from Judah: Daniel, Hananiah, Mishael, and Azariah. 7 But the overseer of the court officials renamed them. He gave Daniel the name Belteshazzar, Hananiah he named Shadrach, Mishael he named Meshach, and Azariah he named Abednego.

8 But Daniel made up his mind that he would not defile himself with the royal delicacies or the royal wine. He therefore asked the overseer of the court officials for permission not to defile himself. 9 Then God made the overseer of the court officials sympathetic to Daniel. 10 But he responded to Daniel, "I fear my master the king. He is the one who has decided your food and drink. What would happen if he saw that you looked malnourished in comparison to the other young men your age? If that happened, you would endanger my life with the king!" 11 Daniel then spoke to the warden whom the overseer of the court officials had appointed over Daniel, Hananiah, Mishael, and Azariah: 12 "Please test your servants for ten days by providing us with some vegetables to eat and water to drink. 13 Then compare our appearance with that of the young men who are eating the royal delicacies; deal with us in light of what you see." 14 So the warden agreed to their proposal and tested them for ten days.

15 At the end of the ten days their appearance was better and their bodies were healthier than all the young men who had been eating the royal delicacies. 16 So the warden removed the delicacies and the wine from their diet and gave them a diet of vegetables instead. 17 Now as for these four young men, God endowed them with knowledge and skill in all sorts of literature and wisdom—and Daniel had insight into all kinds of visions and dreams.

18 When the time appointed by the king arrived, the overseer of the court officials brought them into Nebuchadnezzar's presence. 19 When the king spoke with them, he did not find among the entire group anyone like Daniel, Hananiah, Mishael, or Azariah. So they entered the king's service. 20 In every matter of wisdom and insight the king asked them about, he found them to be ten times better than any of the magicians and astrologers that were in his entire empire. 21 Now Daniel lived on until the first year of Cyrus the king.

REFLECT

How does Daniel's example of standing firm in his convictions encourage you to do the same?

NEBUCHADNEZZAR HAS A DISTURBING DREAM

2 In the second year of his reign Nebuchadnezzar had many dreams. His mind was disturbed and he suffered from insomnia. 2 The king issued an order to summon the magicians, astrologers, sorcerers, and wise men in order to explain his dreams to him. So they came and awaited the king's instructions.

3 The king told them, "I have had a dream, and I am anxious to understand the dream." 4 The wise men replied to the king: [What follows is in Aramaic] "O king, live forever! Tell your servants the dream, and we will disclose its interpretation." 5 The king replied to the wise men, "My decision is firm. If you do not inform me of both the dream and its interpretation, you will be dismembered and your homes reduced to rubble! 6 But if you can disclose the dream and its interpretation, you will receive from me gifts, a reward, and considerable honor. So disclose to me the dream and its interpretation." 7 They again replied, "Let the king inform us of the dream; then we will disclose its interpretation." 8 The king replied, "I know for sure that you are attempting to gain time, because you see that my decision is firm. 9 If you don't inform me of the dream, there is only one thing that is going to happen to you. For you have agreed among yourselves to report to me something false and deceitful until such time as things might change. So tell me the dream, and I will have confidence that you can disclose its interpretation."

10 The wise men replied to the king, "There is no man on earth who is able to disclose the king's secret, for no king, regardless of his position and power, has ever requested such a thing from any magician, astrologer, or wise man. 11 What the king is asking is too difficult, and no one exists who can disclose it to the king, except for the gods—but they don't live among mortals!"

12 Because of this the king got furiously angry and gave orders to destroy all the wise men of Babylon. 13 So a decree went out, and the wise men were about to be executed. They also sought Daniel and his friends so that they could be executed.

14 Then Daniel spoke with prudent counsel to Arioch, who was in charge of the king's executioners and who had gone out to execute the wise men of Babylon. 15 He inquired of Arioch the king's deputy, "Why is the decree from the king so urgent?" Then Arioch informed Daniel about the matter. 16 So Daniel went in and requested the king to grant him time, that he might disclose the interpretation to the king. 17 Then Daniel went to his home and informed his friends Hananiah, Mishael, and Azariah of the matter. 18 He asked them to pray for mercy from the God of heaven concerning this mystery so that he and his friends would not be destroyed along with the rest of the wise men of Babylon. 19 Then in a night vision the mystery was revealed to Daniel. So Daniel praised the God of heaven, 20 saying:

"Let the name of God be praised forever and ever,
for wisdom and power belong to him.
21 He changes times and seasons,
deposing some kings
and establishing others.
He gives wisdom to the wise;
he imparts knowledge to those with understanding;

22 he reveals deep and hidden things.
He knows what is in the darkness,
and light resides with him.
23 O God of my fathers, I acknowledge and glorify you,
for you have bestowed wisdom and power on me.
Now you have enabled me to understand
what we requested from you.
For you have enabled us to understand
the king's dilemma."

24 Then Daniel went in to see Arioch (whom the king had appointed to destroy the wise men of Babylon). He came and said
to him, "Don't destroy the wise men of Babylon! Escort me to the
king, and I will disclose the interpretation to him."
25 So Arioch quickly ushered Daniel into the king's presence,
saying to him, "I have found a man from the captives of Judah
who can make known the interpretation to the king." 26 The king
then asked Daniel (whose name was also Belteshazzar), "Are
you able to make known to me the dream that I saw, as well as
its interpretation?" 27 Daniel replied to the king, "The mystery
that the king is asking about is such that no wise men, astrologers, magicians, or diviners can possibly disclose it to the king.
28 However, there is a God in heaven who reveals mysteries, and
he has made known to King Nebuchadnezzar what will happen
in the times to come. The dream and the visions you had while
lying on your bed are as follows:
29 "As for you, O king, while you were in your bed your thoughts
turned to future things. The revealer of mysteries has made
known to you what will take place. 30 As for me, this mystery
was revealed to me not because I possess more wisdom than
any other living person, but so that the king may understand
the interpretation and comprehend the thoughts of your mind.
31 "You, O king, were watching as a great statue—one of impressive size and extraordinary brightness—was standing before you. Its appearance caused alarm. 32 As for that statue, its
head was of fine gold, its chest and arms were of silver, its belly
and thighs were of bronze. 33 Its legs were of iron; its feet were
partly of iron and partly of clay. 34 You were watching as a stone
was cut out, but not by human hands. It struck the statue on its
iron and clay feet, breaking them in pieces. 35 Then the iron, clay,
bronze, silver, and gold were broken in pieces without distinction and became like chaff from the summer threshing floors
that the wind carries away. Not a trace of them could be found.
But the stone that struck the statue became a large mountain
that filled the entire earth. 36 This was the dream. Now we will
set forth before the king its interpretation.

DANIEL INTERPRETS NEBUCHADNEZZAR'S DREAM

37 "You, O king, are the king of kings. The God of heaven has
granted you sovereignty, power, strength, and honor. 38 Wherever human beings, wild animals, and birds of the sky live—he
has given them into your power. He has given you authority over
them all. You are the head of gold. 39 Now after you another kingdom will arise, one inferior to yours. Then a third kingdom, one

of bronze, will rule in all the earth. 40 Then there will be a fourth kingdom, one strong like iron. Just like iron breaks in pieces and shatters everything, and as iron breaks in pieces all these metals, so it will break in pieces and crush the others. 41 In that you were seeing feet and toes partly of wet clay and partly of iron, so this will be a divided kingdom. Some of the strength of iron will be in it, for you saw iron mixed with wet clay. 42 In that the toes of the feet were partly of iron and partly of clay, the latter stages of this kingdom will be partly strong and partly fragile. 43 And in that you saw iron mixed with wet clay, so people will be mixed with one another without adhering to one another, just as iron does not mix with clay. 44 In the days of those kings the God of heaven will raise up an everlasting kingdom that will not be destroyed and a kingdom that will not be left to another people. It will break in pieces and bring about the demise of all these kingdoms. But it will stand forever. 45 You saw that a stone was cut from a mountain, but not by human hands; it smashed the iron, bronze, clay, silver, and gold into pieces. The great God has made known to the king what will occur in the future. The dream is certain, and its interpretation is reliable."

46 Then King Nebuchadnezzar bowed down with his face to the ground and paid homage to Daniel. He gave orders to offer sacrifice and incense to him. 47 The king replied to Daniel, "Certainly your God is a God of gods and Lord of kings and revealer of mysteries, for you were able to reveal this mystery!" 48 Then the king elevated Daniel to high position and bestowed on him many marvelous gifts. He granted him authority over the entire province of Babylon and made him the main prefect over all the wise men of Babylon. 49 And at Daniel's request, the king appointed Shadrach, Meshach, and Abednego over the administration of the province of Babylon. Daniel himself served in the king's court.

DANIEL'S FRIENDS ARE TESTED

3 King Nebuchadnezzar had a golden statue made. It was 90 feet tall and 9 feet wide. He erected it on the plain of Dura in the province of Babylon. 2 Then King Nebuchadnezzar sent out a summons to assemble the satraps, prefects, governors, counselors, treasurers, judges, magistrates, and all the other authorities of the province to attend the dedication of the statue that he had erected. 3 So the satraps, prefects, governors, counselors, treasurers, judges, magistrates, and all the other provincial authorities assembled for the dedication of the statue that King Nebuchadnezzar had erected. They were standing in front of the statue that Nebuchadnezzar had erected.

4 Then the herald made a loud proclamation: "To you, O peoples, nations, and language groups, the following command is given: 5 When you hear the sound of the horn, flute, zither, trigon, harp, pipes, and all kinds of music, you must bow down and pay homage to the golden statue that King Nebuchadnezzar has erected. 6 Whoever does not bow down and pay homage will immediately be thrown into the midst of a furnace of blazing fire!" 7 Therefore when they all heard the sound of the horn, flute, zither, trigon, harp, pipes, and all kinds of music, all

the peoples, nations, and language groups began bowing down and paying homage to the golden statue that King Nebuchadnezzar had erected.

8 Now at that time certain Chaldeans came forward and brought malicious accusations against the Jews. 9 They said to King Nebuchadnezzar, "O king, live forever! 10 You have issued an edict, O king, that everyone must bow down and pay homage to the golden statue when they hear the sound of the horn, flute, zither, trigon, harp, pipes, and all kinds of music. 11 And whoever does not bow down and pay homage must be thrown into the midst of a furnace of blazing fire. 12 But there are Jewish men whom you appointed over the administration of the province of Babylon—Shadrach, Meshach, and Abednego—and these men have not shown proper respect to you, O king. They don't serve your gods and they don't pay homage to the golden statue that you have erected."

13 Then Nebuchadnezzar in a fit of rage demanded that they bring Shadrach, Meshach, and Abednego before him. So they brought them before the king. 14 Nebuchadnezzar said to them, "Is it true, Shadrach, Meshach, and Abednego, that you don't serve my gods and that you don't pay homage to the golden statue that I erected? 15 Now if you are ready, when you hear the sound of the horn, flute, zither, trigon, harp, pipes, and all kinds of music, you must bow down and pay homage to the statue that I had made. If you don't pay homage to it, you will immediately be thrown into the midst of the furnace of blazing fire. Now, who is that god who can rescue you from my power?" 16 Shadrach, Meshach, and Abednego replied to King Nebuchadnezzar, "We do not need to give you a reply concerning this. 17 If our God whom we are serving exists, he is able to rescue us from the furnace of blazing fire, and he will rescue us, O king, from your power as well. 18 But if he does not, let it be known to you, O king, that we don't serve your gods, and we will not pay homage to the golden statue that you have erected."

19 Then Nebuchadnezzar was filled with rage, and his disposition changed toward Shadrach, Meshach, and Abednego. He gave orders to heat the furnace seven times hotter than it was normally heated. 20 He ordered strong soldiers in his army to tie up Shadrach, Meshach, and Abednego and to throw them into the furnace of blazing fire. 21 So those men were tied up while still wearing their cloaks, trousers, turbans, and other clothes, and were thrown into the furnace of blazing fire. 22 But since the king's command was so urgent, and the furnace was so excessively hot, the men who escorted Shadrach, Meshach, and Abednego were killed by the leaping flames. 23 But those three men, Shadrach, Meshach, and Abednego, fell into the furnace of blazing fire while still securely bound.

CHALLENGE

What is the "if" in your life? How can you build a faith like Shadrach, Meshach, and Abednego where you are confident that no matter what happens, God is still good?

GOD DELIVERS HIS SERVANTS

24 Then King Nebuchadnezzar was startled and quickly got up. He said to his ministers, "Wasn't it three men that we tied up and threw into the fire?" They replied to the king, "For sure, O king." 25 He answered, "But I see four men, untied and walking around in the midst of the fire! No harm has come to them! And

LOVE TO GROW

EVEN IF

DANIEL 3:17–18

Let's be honest, it's easiest to praise God and shout His goodness from the mountaintops when we see the miracle, when life is good, and when we feel His favor. Do we continue to believe He is good in the middle of the fire?

Daniel 3:17–18 contains a profound statement made by Shadrach, Meshach, and Abednego as King Nebuchadnezzar threatened to throw them into a fiery furnace. The men said, "If our God whom we are serving exists, he is able to rescue us from the furnace of blazing fire, and he will rescue us, O king, from your power as well. But if he does not, let it be known to you, O king, that we don't serve your gods, and we will not pay homage to the golden statue that you have erected."

This passage reminds us that God is still God, and He is still good, even if we are not delivered from the suffering of this world. Our earthly bodies may fail, but the hope and promise of our salvation in Christ are immovable. We may pray fervently and wait expectantly only to find ourselves disappointed if life plays out differently. But not having our prayers answered in the way or time we hoped does not mean they were unheard or disregarded. Not being relieved of our current sufferings does not change the promise of eventual, eternal restoration.

Even if there is no healing, even if the relationship isn't restored, even if the finances don't turn around, even if the child remains rebellious, even if the addiction maintains control, He is still good.

He is still good.

Despite all circumstances, against all odds, let's have faith in God's miraculous power, proclaim His goodness, and believe in our salvation through Jesus Christ.

Even if, let your hope be in Him alone.

the appearance of the fourth is like that of a god!" 26 Then Nebuchadnezzar approached the door of the furnace of blazing fire.
He called out, "Shadrach, Meshach, and Abednego, servants of
the most high God, come out! Come here!"
Then Shadrach, Meshach, and Abednego emerged from the
fire. 27 Once the satraps, prefects, governors, and ministers of
the king had gathered around, they saw that those men were
physically unharmed by the fire. The hair of their heads was not
singed, nor were their trousers damaged. Not even the smell of
fire was to be found on them!
28 Nebuchadnezzar exclaimed, "Praised be the God of Shadrach, Meshach, and Abednego, who has sent forth his angel
and has rescued his servants who trusted in him, ignoring the
edict of the king and giving up their bodies rather than serve or
pay homage to any god other than their God! 29 I hereby decree
that any people, nation, or language group that blasphemes the
God of Shadrach, Meshach, or Abednego will be dismembered
and his home reduced to rubble! For there exists no other god
who can deliver in this way." 30 Then Nebuchadnezzar promoted
Shadrach, Meshach, and Abednego in the province of Babylon.
4 King Nebuchadnezzar, to all peoples, nations, and language
groups that live in all the land: "Peace and prosperity! 2 I am
delighted to tell you about the signs and wonders that the most
high God has done for me.

3 "How great are his signs!
How mighty are his wonders!
His kingdom will last forever,
and his authority continues from one
generation to the next."

NEBUCHADNEZZAR DREAMS OF A TREE CHOPPED DOWN

4 I, Nebuchadnezzar, was relaxing in my home, living luxuriously in my palace. 5 I saw a dream that frightened me badly. The
things I imagined while lying on my bed—these visions of my
mind—were terrifying me. 6 So I issued an order for all the wise
men of Babylon to be brought before me so that they could make
known to me the interpretation of the dream. 7 When the magicians, astrologers, wise men, and diviners entered, I recounted
the dream for them. But they were unable to make known its
interpretation to me. 8 Later Daniel entered (whose name is
Belteshazzar after the name of my god, and in whom there is a
spirit of the holy gods). I recounted the dream for him as well,
9 saying, "Belteshazzar, chief of the magicians, in whom I know
there to be a spirit of the holy gods and whom no mystery baf-
fles, consider my dream that I saw and set forth its interpretation! 10 Here are the visions of my mind while I was on my bed.
"While I was watching,
there was a tree in the middle of the land.
It was enormously tall.
11 The tree grew large and strong.
Its top reached far into the sky;
it could be seen from the borders of all the land.

12 Its foliage was attractive and its fruit plentiful;
on it there was food enough for all.
Under it the wild animals used to seek shade,
and in its branches the birds of the sky used to nest.
All creatures used to feed themselves from it.

13 While I was watching in my mind's visions on my bed,
a holy sentinel came down from heaven.
14 He called out loudly as follows:
'Chop down the tree and lop off its branches!
Strip off its foliage
and scatter its fruit!
Let the animals flee from under it
and the birds from its branches.
15 But leave its taproot in the ground,
with a band of iron and bronze around it
surrounded by the grass of the field.
Let it become damp with the dew of the sky,
and let it live with the animals in the grass of the land.
16 Let his mind be altered from that of a human being,
and let an animal's mind be given to him,
and let seven periods of time go by for him.
17 This announcement is by the decree of the sentinels;
this decision is by the pronouncement of the holy ones,
so that those who are alive may understand
that the Most High has authority over human kingdoms,
and he bestows them on whomever he wishes.
He establishes over them even the
lowliest of human beings.'

REFLECT

Why did God humble Nebuchadnezzar in this way? What does it look like to be humble before God?

18 "This is the dream that I, King Nebuchadnezzar, saw. Now
you, Belteshazzar, declare its interpretation, for none of the
wise men in my kingdom are able to make known to me the
interpretation. But you can do so, for a spirit of the holy gods
is in you."

DANIEL INTERPRETS NEBUCHADNEZZAR'S DREAM

19 Then Daniel (whose name is also Belteshazzar) was upset for
a brief time; his thoughts were alarming him. The king said,
"Belteshazzar, don't let the dream and its interpretation alarm
you." But Belteshazzar replied, "Sir, if only the dream were for
your enemies and its interpretation applied to your adversaries! 20 The tree that you saw that grew large and strong, whose
top reached to the sky, and that could be seen in all the land,
21 whose foliage was attractive and its fruit plentiful, and from
which there was food available for all, under whose branches
wild animals used to live, and in whose branches birds of the
sky used to nest—22 it is you, O king! For you have become great
and strong. Your greatness is such that it reaches to heaven,
and your authority to the ends of the earth. 23 As for the king
seeing a holy sentinel coming down from heaven and saying,
'Chop down the tree and destroy it, but leave its taproot in the
ground, with a band of iron and bronze around it, surrounded
by the grass of the field. Let it become damp with the dew of

the sky, and let it live with the wild animals, until seven periods
of time go by for him'—24 this is the interpretation, O king. It
is the decision of the Most High that this has happened to my
lord the king. 25 You will be driven from human society, and you
will live with the wild animals. You will be fed grass like oxen,
and you will become damp with the dew of the sky. Seven periods of time will pass by for you, before you understand that
the Most High is ruler over human kingdoms and gives them
to whomever he wishes. 26 They said to leave the taproot of the
tree, for your kingdom will be restored to you when you come
to understand that heaven rules. 27 Therefore, O king, may my
advice be pleasing to you. Break away from your sins by doing
what is right, and from your iniquities by showing mercy to the
poor. Perhaps your prosperity will be prolonged."

28 Now all this happened to King Nebuchadnezzar. 29 After
twelve months, he happened to be walking around on the bat-
tlements of the royal palace of Babylon. 30 The king uttered
these words: "Is this not the great Babylon that I have built for
a royal residence by my own mighty strength and for my majestic
honor?" 31 While these words were still on the king's lips, a voice
came down from heaven: "It is hereby announced to you, King
Nebuchadnezzar, that your kingdom has been removed from
you! 32 You will be driven from human society, and you will live
with the wild animals. You will be fed grass like oxen, and seven
periods of time will pass by for you before you understand that
the Most High is ruler over human kingdoms and gives them
to whomever he wishes."

33 Now in that very moment this pronouncement about Nebuchadnezzar came true. He was driven from human society, he
ate grass like oxen, and his body became damp with the dew of
the sky, until his hair became long like an eagle's feathers, and
his nails like a bird's claws.

34 But at the end of the appointed time I, Nebuchadnezzar,
looked up toward heaven, and my sanity returned to me.

I extolled the Most High,
and I praised and glorified the one who lives forever.
For his authority is an everlasting authority,
and his kingdom extends from one
generation to the next.
35 All the inhabitants of the earth are
regarded as nothing.
He does as he wishes with the army of heaven
and with those who inhabit the earth.
No one slaps his hand
and says to him, 'What have you done?'

36 At that time my sanity returned to me. I was restored to
the honor of my kingdom, and my splendor returned to me.
My ministers and my nobles were seeking me out, and I was re-
instated over my kingdom. I became even greater than before.
37 Now I, Nebuchadnezzar, praise and exalt and glorify the King
of heaven, for all his deeds are right and his ways are just. He is
able to bring down those who live in pride.

BELSHAZZAR SEES MYSTERIOUS HANDWRITING ON A WALL

5 King Belshazzar prepared a great banquet for 1,000 of his nobles, and he was drinking wine in front of them all. 2 While
under the influence of the wine, Belshazzar issued an order to
bring in the gold and silver vessels—the ones that Nebuchadnezzar his father had confiscated from the temple in Jerusalem—so that the king and his nobles, together with his wives
and his concubines, could drink from them. 3 So they brought
the gold and silver vessels that had been confiscated from the
temple, the house of God in Jerusalem, and the king and his nobles, together with his wives and concubines, drank from them.
4 As they drank wine, they praised the gods of gold and silver,
bronze, iron, wood, and stone.

5 At that very moment the fingers of a human hand appeared
and wrote on the plaster of the royal palace wall, opposite the
lampstand. The king was watching the back of the hand that was
writing. 6 Then all the color drained from the king's face and he
became alarmed. The joints of his hips gave way, and his knees
began knocking together. 7 The king called out loudly to summon
the astrologers, wise men, and diviners. The king proclaimed to
the wise men of Babylon that anyone who could read this inscription and disclose its interpretation would be clothed in
purple and have a golden collar placed on his neck and be third
ruler in the kingdom.

8 So all the king's wise men came in, but they were unable to
read the writing or to make known its interpretation to the
king. 9 Then King Belshazzar was very terrified, and he was visibly shaken. His nobles were completely dumbfounded.

10 Due to the noise caused by the king and his nobles, the queen
mother then entered the banquet room. She said, "O king, live
forever! Don't be alarmed! Don't be shaken! 11 There is a man in
your kingdom who has within him a spirit of the holy gods. In
the days of your father, he proved to have insight, discernment,
and wisdom like that of the gods. King Nebuchadnezzar your
father appointed him chief of the magicians, astrologers, wise
men, and diviners. 12 Thus there was found in this man Daniel,
whom the king renamed Belteshazzar, an extraordinary spirit,
knowledge, and skill to interpret dreams, explain riddles, and
solve difficult problems. Now summon Daniel, and he will disclose the interpretation."

13 So Daniel was brought in before the king. The king said to
Daniel, "Are you that Daniel who is one of the captives of Judah,
whom my father the king brought from Judah? 14 I have heard
about you, how there is a spirit of the gods in you, and how you
have insight, discernment, and extraordinary wisdom. 15 Now the
wise men and astrologers were brought before me to read this
writing and make known to me its interpretation. But they were
unable to disclose the interpretation of the message. 16 However, I have heard that you are able to provide interpretations
and to solve difficult problems. Now if you are able to read this
writing and make known to me its interpretation, you will wear
purple and have a golden collar around your neck and be third
ruler in the kingdom."

DANIEL INTERPRETS THE HANDWRITING ON THE WALL

17 But Daniel replied to the king, "Keep your gifts, and give your
rewards to someone else. However, I will read the writing for the
king and make known its interpretation. 18 As for you, O king, the
most high God bestowed on your father Nebuchadnezzar a kingdom, greatness, honor, and majesty. 19 Due to the greatness that
he bestowed on him, all peoples, nations, and language groups
were trembling with fear before him. He killed whom he wished,
he spared whom he wished, he exalted whom he wished, and he
brought low whom he wished. 20 And when his mind became arrogant and his spirit filled with pride, he was deposed from his
royal throne and his honor was removed from him. 21 He was
driven from human society; his mind was changed to that of
an animal. He lived with the wild donkeys, he was fed grass like
oxen, and his body became damp with the dew of the sky, until
he came to understand that the most high God rules over human kingdoms, and he appoints over them whomever he wishes.
22 "But you, his son Belshazzar, have not humbled yourself, although you knew all this. 23 Instead, you have exalted yourself
against the Lord of heaven. You brought before you the vessels
from his temple, and you and your nobles, together with your wives
and concubines, drank wine from them. You praised the gods of
silver, gold, bronze, iron, wood, and stone—gods that cannot see or
hear or comprehend. But you have not glorified the God who has
in his control your very breath and all your ways! 24 Therefore the
palm of a hand was sent from him, and this writing was inscribed.
25 "This is the writing that was inscribed: MENE, MENE, TEQEL,
and PHARSIN. 26 This is the interpretation of the words: As for
Mene—God has numbered your kingdom's days and brought it
to an end. 27 As for *Teqel*—you are weighed on the balances and
found to be lacking. 28 As for *Peres*—your kingdom is divided and
given over to the Medes and Persians."
29 Then, on Belshazzar's orders, Daniel was clothed in purple, a
golden collar was placed around his neck, and he was proclaimed
third ruler in the kingdom. 30 And that very night Belshazzar, the
Babylonian king, was killed. 31 So Darius the Mede took control
of the kingdom when he was about sixty-two years old.

DANIEL IS THROWN INTO A LIONS' DEN

6 It seemed like a good idea to Darius to appoint over the
kingdom 120 satraps who would be in charge of the entire
kingdom. 2 Over them would be three supervisors, one of whom
was Daniel. These satraps were accountable to them, so that the
king's interests might not incur damage. 3 Now this Daniel was
distinguishing himself above the other supervisors and the satraps, for he had an extraordinary spirit. In fact, the king intended to appoint him over the entire kingdom. 4 Consequently
the supervisors and satraps were trying to find some pretext
against Daniel in connection with administrative matters. But
they were unable to find any such damaging evidence, because
he was trustworthy and guilty of no negligence or corruption.
5 So these men concluded, "We won't find any pretext against this
man Daniel unless it is in connection with the law of his God."

[6] So these supervisors and satraps came by collusion to the
king and said to him, "O King Darius, live forever! [7] To all the
supervisors of the kingdom, the prefects, satraps, counselors,
and governors it seemed like a good idea for a royal edict to be
issued and an interdict to be enforced. For the next thirty days
anyone who prays to any god or human other than you, O king,
should be thrown into a den of lions. [8] Now let the king issue a
written interdict so that it cannot be altered, according to the
law of the Medes and Persians, which cannot be changed." [9] So
King Darius issued the written interdict.
[10] When Daniel realized that a written decree had been issued, he
entered his home, where the windows in his upper room opened
toward Jerusalem. Three times daily he was kneeling and offering
prayers and thanks to his God just as he had been accustomed to
do previously. [11] Then those officials who had gone to the king came
by collusion and found Daniel praying and asking for help before
his God. [12] So they approached the king and said to him, "Did you
not issue an edict to the effect that for the next thirty days anyone
who prays to any god or human other than to you, O king, would
be thrown into a den of lions?" The king replied, "That is correct,
according to the law of the Medes and Persians, which cannot
be changed." [13] Then they said to the king, "Daniel, who is one of
the captives from Judah, pays no attention to you, O king, or to
the edict that you issued. Three times daily he offers his prayer."
[14] When the king heard this, he was very upset and began thinking about how he might rescue Daniel. Until late afternoon he
was struggling to find a way to rescue him. [15] Then those men
came by collusion to the king and said to him, "Recall, O king,
that it is a law of the Medes and Persians that no edict or decree that the king issues can be changed." [16] So the king gave the
order, and Daniel was brought and thrown into a den of lions.
The king consoled Daniel by saying, "Your God whom you continually serve will rescue you!" [17] Then a stone was brought and
placed over the opening to the den. The king sealed it with his
signet ring and with those of his nobles so that nothing could
be changed with regard to Daniel. [18] Then the king departed to
his palace. But he spent the night without eating, and no diver-
sions were brought to him. He was unable to sleep.

REFLECT

In what aspects of your life do you need to boldly stand up for your faith like Daniel did when he remained committed to prayer?

GOD RESCUES DANIEL FROM THE LIONS

[19] In the morning, at the earliest sign of daylight, the king got
up and rushed to the lions' den. [20] As he approached the den, he
called out to Daniel in a worried voice, "Daniel, servant of the
living God, was your God whom you continually serve able to
rescue you from the lions?"
[21] Then Daniel spoke to the king, "O king, live forever! [22] My God
sent his angel and closed the lions' mouths so that they have not
harmed me, because I was found to be innocent before him. Nor
have I done any harm to you, O king."
[23] Then the king was delighted and gave an order to haul Daniel
up from the den. So Daniel was hauled up out of the den. He had
no injury of any kind, because he had trusted in his God. [24] The
king gave another order, and those men who had maliciously accused Daniel were brought and thrown into the lions' den—they,

their children, and their wives. They did not even reach the bottom of the den before the lions overpowered them and crushed
all their bones.
25 Then King Darius wrote to all the peoples, nations, and language groups who were living in all the land: "Peace and prosperity! 26 I have issued an edict that throughout all the dominion
of my kingdom people are to revere and fear the God of Daniel.

"For he is the living God;
he endures forever.
His kingdom will not be destroyed;
his authority is forever.
27 He rescues and delivers
and performs signs and wonders
in the heavens and on the earth.
He has rescued Daniel from the power of the lions!"

28 So this Daniel prospered during the reign of Darius and the
reign of Cyrus the Persian.

DANIEL HAS A VISION OF FOUR ANIMALS COMING UP FROM THE SEA

7 In the first year of King Belshazzar of Babylon, Daniel had
a dream filled with visions while he was lying on his bed.
Then he wrote down the dream in summary fashion. 2 Daniel
explained: "I was watching in my vision during the night as the
four winds of the sky were stirring up the great sea. 3 Then four
large beasts came up from the sea; they were different from
one another.
4 "The first one was like a lion with eagles' wings. As I watched,
its wings were pulled off and it was lifted up from the ground.
It was made to stand on two feet like a human being, and a human mind was given to it.
5 "Then a second beast appeared, like a bear. It was raised up
on one side, and there were three ribs in its mouth between its
teeth. It was told, 'Get up and devour much flesh!'
6 "After these things, as I was watching, another beast like a
leopard appeared, with four bird-like wings on its back. This beast
had four heads, and ruling authority was given to it.
7 "After these things, as I was watching in the night visions a
fourth beast appeared—one dreadful, terrible, and very strong.
It had two large rows of iron teeth. It devoured and crushed, and
anything that was left it trampled with its feet. It was different
from all the beasts that came before it, and it had ten horns.
8 "As I was contemplating the horns, another horn—a small
one—came up between them, and three of the former horns were
torn out by the roots to make room for it. This horn had eyes resembling human eyes and a mouth speaking arrogant things.
9 "While I was watching,
thrones were set up,
and the Ancient of Days took his seat.
His attire was white like snow;
the hair of his head was like lamb's wool.
His throne was ablaze with fire
and its wheels were all aflame.

10 A river of fire was streaming forth
and proceeding from his presence.
Many thousands were ministering to him;
many tens of thousands stood ready to serve him.
The court convened
and the books were opened.

11 "Then I kept on watching because of the arrogant words of
the horn that was speaking. I was watching until the beast was
killed and its body destroyed and thrown into the flaming fire.
12 As for the rest of the beasts, their ruling authority had already
been removed, though they were permitted to go on living for
a time and a season.

13 "I was watching in the night visions,
And with the clouds of the sky
one like a son of man was approaching.
He went up to the Ancient of Days
and was escorted before him.
14 To him was given ruling authority, honor, and sovereignty.
All peoples, nations, and language
groups were serving him.
His authority is eternal and will not pass away.
His kingdom will not be destroyed.

AN ANGEL INTERPRETS DANIEL'S VISION

15 "As for me, Daniel, my spirit was distressed, and the visions of
my mind were alarming me. 16 I approached one of those standing nearby and asked him about the meaning of all this. So he
spoke with me and revealed to me the interpretation of the vision: 17 'These large beasts, which are four in number, represent
four kings who will arise from the earth. 18 The holy ones of the
Most High will receive the kingdom and will take possession of
the kingdom forever and ever.'

19 "Then I wanted to know the meaning of the fourth beast,
which was different from all the others. It was very dreadful,
with two rows of iron teeth and bronze claws, and it devoured,
crushed, and trampled anything that was left with its feet. 20 I
also wanted to know the meaning of the ten horns on its head,
and of that other horn that came up and before which three others fell. This was the horn that had eyes and a mouth speaking
arrogant things, whose appearance was more formidable than
the others. 21 While I was watching, that horn began to wage
war against the holy ones and was defeating them, 22 until the
Ancient of Days arrived and judgment was rendered in favor of
the holy ones of the Most High. Then the time came for the holy
ones to take possession of the kingdom.

23 "This is what he told me:

'The fourth beast means that there will
be a fourth kingdom on earth
that will differ from all the other kingdoms.
It will devour all the earth
and will trample and crush it.
24 The ten horns mean that ten kings
will arise from that kingdom.

Another king will arise after them,
but he will be different from the earlier ones.
He will humiliate three kings.
25 He will speak words against the Most High.
He will harass the holy ones of the Most High continually.
His intention will be to change times established by law.
The holy ones will be delivered into his hand
for a time, times, and half a time.
26 But the court will convene, and his ruling
authority will be removed—
destroyed and abolished forever!
27 Then the kingdom, authority,
and greatness of the kingdoms under the whole heaven
will be delivered to the people of the
holy ones of the Most High.
His kingdom is an eternal kingdom;
all authorities will serve him and obey him.'

28 "This is the conclusion of the matter. As for me, Daniel, my
thoughts troubled me greatly, and the color drained from my
face. But I kept the matter to myself."

DANIEL HAS A VISION OF A GOAT AND A RAM

8 In the third year of King Belshazzar's reign, a vision appeared
to me, Daniel, after the one that had appeared to me previously. 2 In this vision I saw myself in Susa the citadel, which is
located in the province of Elam. In the vision I saw myself at the
Ulai Canal. 3 I looked up and saw a ram with two horns standing
at the canal. Its two horns were both long, but one was longer
than the other. The longer one was coming up after the shorter
one. 4 I saw that the ram was butting westward, northward, and
southward. No animal was able to stand before it, and there was
none who could deliver from its power. It did as it pleased and
acted arrogantly.

5 While I was contemplating all this, a male goat was coming
from the west over the surface of all the land without touching the ground. This goat had a conspicuous horn between its
eyes. 6 It came to the two-horned ram that I had seen standing
beside the canal and rushed against it with raging strength. 7 I
saw it approaching the ram. It went into a fit of rage against the
ram and struck it and broke off its two horns. The ram had no
ability to resist it. The goat hurled the ram to the ground and
trampled it. No one could deliver the ram from its power. 8 The
male goat acted even more arrogantly. But no sooner had the
large horn become strong than it was broken, and there arose
four conspicuous horns in its place, extending toward the four
winds of the sky.

9 From one of them came a small horn, but it grew to be very
great toward the south and the east and toward the beautiful
land. 10 It grew so great it reached the army of heaven, and it
brought about the fall of some of the army and some of the
stars to the ground, where it trampled them. 11 It also acted arrogantly against the Prince of the army, from whom the daily
sacrifice was removed and whose sanctuary was thrown down.

12 The army was given over, along with the daily sacrifice, in the
course of his sinful rebellion. It hurled truth to the ground and
enjoyed success.
13 Then I heard a holy one speaking. Another holy one said to
the one who was speaking, "To what period of time does the vision pertain—this vision concerning the daily sacrifice and the
destructive act of rebellion and the giving over of both the sanctuary and army to be trampled?" 14 He said to me, "To 2,300 evenings and mornings; then the sanctuary will be put right again."

AN ANGEL INTERPRETS DANIEL'S VISION

15 While I, Daniel, was watching the vision, I sought to understand it. Now one who appeared to be a man was standing before me. 16 Then I heard a human voice coming from between
the banks of the Ulai. It called out, "Gabriel, enable this person
to understand the vision." 17 So he approached the place where
I was standing. As he came, I felt terrified and fell flat on the
ground. Then he said to me, "Understand, son of man, that the
vision pertains to the time of the end." 18 As he spoke with me,
I fell into a trance with my face to the ground. But he touched
me and stood me upright.
19 Then he said, "I am going to inform you about what will happen in the latter time of wrath, for the vision pertains to the appointed time of the end. 20 The ram that you saw with the two
horns stands for the kings of Media and Persia. 21 The male goat
is the king of Greece, and the large horn between its eyes is the
first king. 22 The horn that was broken and in whose place there
arose four others stands for four kingdoms that will arise from
his nation, though they will not have his strength. 23 Toward the
end of their rule, when rebellious acts are complete, a rash and
deceitful king will arise. 24 His power will be great, but it will not
be by his strength alone. He will cause terrible destruction. He
will be successful in what he undertakes. He will destroy powerful people and the people of the holy ones. 25 By his treachery he
will succeed through deceit. He will have an arrogant attitude,
and he will destroy many who are unaware of his schemes. He
will rise up against the Prince of princes, yet he will be broken
apart—but not by human agency. 26 The vision of the evenings
and mornings that was told to you is correct. But you should
seal up the vision, for it refers to a time many days from now."
27 I, Daniel, was exhausted and sick for days. Then I got up and
again carried out the king's business. But I was astonished at
the vision, and there was no one to explain it.

DANIEL PRAYS FOR HIS PEOPLE

9 In the first year of Darius son of Ahasuerus, who was of Me-
dian descent and who had been appointed king over the Babylonian empire—2 in the first year of his reign I, Daniel, came to
understand from the sacred books that the number of years for
the fulfilling of the desolation of Jerusalem, which had come as
the LORD's message to the prophet Jeremiah, would be 70 years.
3 So I turned my attention to the Lord God to implore him by
prayer and requests, with fasting, sackcloth, and ashes. 4 I prayed
to the LORD my God, confessing in this way:

"O Lord, great and awesome God who is faithful to his covenant with those who love him and keep his commandments,
5 we have sinned! We have done what is wrong and wicked; we
have rebelled by turning away from your commandments and
standards. 6 We have not paid attention to your servants the
prophets, who spoke by your authority to our kings, our leaders,
and our ancestors, and to all the inhabitants of the land as well.
7 "You are righteous, O Lord, but we are humiliated this
day—the people of Judah and the inhabitants of Jerusalem and
all Israel, both near and far away in all the countries in which
you have scattered them, because they have behaved unfaithfully toward you. 8 O LORD, we have been humiliated—our kings,
our leaders, and our ancestors—because we have sinned against
you. 9 Yet the Lord our God is compassionate and forgiving, even
though we have rebelled against him. 10 We have not obeyed the
LORD our God by living according to his laws that he set before
us through his servants the prophets.
11 "All Israel has broken your law and turned away by not obeying you. Therefore you have poured out on us the judgment solemnly threatened in the law of Moses the servant of God, for we
have sinned against you. 12 He has carried out his threats against
us and our rulers who were over us by bringing great calamity
on us—what has happened to Jerusalem has never been equaled
under all heaven! 13 Just as it is written in the law of Moses, so
all this calamity has come on us. Still we have not tried to pac-
ify the LORD our God by turning back from our sin and by seeking wisdom from your reliable moral standards. 14 The LORD was
mindful of the calamity, and he brought it on us. For the LORD
our God is just in all he has done, and we have not obeyed him.
15 "Now, O Lord our God, who brought your people out of the
land of Egypt with great power and made a name for yourself
that is remembered to this day—we have sinned and behaved
wickedly. 16 O Lord, according to all your justice, please turn your
raging anger away from your city Jerusalem, your holy mountain.
For due to our sins and the iniquities of our ancestors, Jerusalem
and your people are mocked by all our neighbors.
17 "So now, our God, accept the prayer and requests of your servant, and show favor to your devastated sanctuary for your own
sake. 18 Listen attentively, my God, and hear! Open your eyes and
look on our desolated ruins and the city called by your name. For
it is not because of our own righteous deeds that we are praying to you, but because your compassion is abundant. 19 O Lord,
hear! O Lord, forgive! O Lord, pay attention, and act! Don't delay, for your own sake, O my God! For your city and your people
are called by your name."

REFLECT

Why is it crucial for us to pray for our communities, cities, and countries?

GABRIEL GIVES TO DANIEL A PROPHECY OF SEVENTY WEEKS

20 While I was still speaking and praying, confessing my sin and
the sin of my people Israel and presenting my request before
the LORD my God concerning his holy mountain—21 yes, while I
was still praying, the man Gabriel, whom I had seen previously
in a vision, was approaching me in my state of extreme weari-
ness, around the time of the evening offering. 22 He spoke with

me, instructing me as follows: "Daniel, I have now come to impart understanding to you. 23 At the beginning of your requests
a message went out, and I have come to convey it to you, for you
are of great value in God's sight. Therefore consider the message
and understand the vision:

24 "Seventy weeks have been determined
concerning your people and your holy city
to put an end to rebellion,
to bring sin to completion,
to atone for iniquity,
to bring in perpetual righteousness,
to seal up the prophetic vision,
and to anoint a Most Holy Place.
25 So know and understand:
From the issuing of the command to restore and rebuild
Jerusalem until an anointed one, a prince arrives,
there will be a period of seven weeks and sixty-two weeks.
It will again be built, with plaza and moat,
but in distressful times.
26 Now after the sixty-two weeks,
an anointed one will be cut off and have nothing.
As for the city and the sanctuary,
the people of the coming prince will destroy them.
But his end will come speedily like a flood.
Until the end of the war that has been decreed
there will be destruction.
27 He will confirm a covenant with many for one week.
But in the middle of that week
he will bring sacrifices and offerings to a halt.
On the wing of abominations will come one who destroys,
until the decreed end is poured out
on the one who destroys."

AN ANGEL APPEARS TO DANIEL

10 In the third year of King Cyrus of Persia a message was revealed to Daniel (who was also called Belteshazzar). This
message was true and concerned a great war. He understood
the message and gained insight by the vision.
2 In those days I, Daniel, was mourning for three whole weeks.
3 I ate no choice food, no meat or wine came to my lips, nor did I
anoint myself with oil until the end of those three weeks.
4 On the twenty-fourth day of the first month I was beside the
great river, the Tigris. 5 I looked up and saw a man clothed in
linen; around his waist was a belt made of gold from Ufaz. 6 His
body resembled yellow jasper, and his face had an appearance
like lightning. His eyes were like blazing torches; his arms and
feet had the gleam of polished bronze. His voice thundered forth
like the sound of a large crowd.
7 Only I, Daniel, saw the vision; the men who were with me
did not see it. On the contrary, they were overcome with fright
and ran away to hide. 8 I alone was left to see this great vision.
My strength drained from me, and my vigor disappeared; I was
without energy. 9 I listened to his voice, and as I did so I fell into
a trance-like sleep with my face to the ground. 10 Then a hand

touched me and set me on my hands and knees. 11 He said to me,
"Daniel, you are of great value. Understand the words that I am
about to speak to you. So stand up, for I have now been sent to
you." When he said this to me, I stood up shaking. 12 Then he said
to me, "Don't be afraid, Daniel, for from the very first day you
applied your mind to understand and to humble yourself before your God, your words were heard. I have come in response
to your words. 13 However, the prince of the kingdom of Persia
was opposing me for twenty-one days. But Michael, one of the
leading princes, came to help me, because I was left there with
the kings of Persia. 14 Now I have come to help you understand
what will happen to your people in future days, for the vision
pertains to days to come."

15 While he was saying this to me, I was flat on the ground and
unable to speak. 16 Then one who appeared to be a human being was touching my lips. I opened my mouth and started to
speak, saying to the one who was standing before me, "Sir, due
to the vision, anxiety has gripped me and I have no strength.
17 How, sir, am I able to speak with you? My strength is gone,
and I am breathless." 18 Then the one who appeared to be a human being touched me again and strengthened me. 19 He said
to me, "Don't be afraid, you who are highly valued. Peace be to
you! Be strong! Be really strong!" When he spoke to me, I was
strengthened. I said, "Sir, you may speak now, for you have given
me strength." 20 He said, "Do you know why I have come to you?
Now I am about to return to engage in battle with the prince of
Persia. When I go, the prince of Greece is coming. 21 However, I
will first tell you what is written in a dependable book. (There
is no one who strengthens me against these princes, except Michael your prince.
11 And in the first year of Darius the Mede, I stood to strengthen
him and to provide protection for him.) 2 Now I will tell you
the truth.

THE ANGEL GIVES A MESSAGE TO DANIEL

"Three more kings will arise for Persia. Then a fourth king will
be unusually rich, more so than all who preceded him. When he
has amassed power through his riches, he will stir up everyone
against the kingdom of Greece. 3 Then a powerful king will arise,
exercising great authority and doing as he pleases. 4 Shortly after his rise to power, his kingdom will be broken up and distributed toward the four winds of the sky—but not to his posterity
or with the authority he exercised, for his kingdom will be uprooted and distributed to others besides these.

5 "Then the king of the south and one of his subordinates will
grow strong. His subordinate will resist him and will rule a kingdom greater than his. 6 After some years have passed, they will
form an alliance. Then the daughter of the king of the south will
come to the king of the north to make an agreement, but she
will not retain her power, nor will he continue in his strength.
She, together with the one who brought her, her child, and her
benefactor will all be delivered over at that time.

7 "There will arise in his place one from her family line who
will come against their army and will enter the stronghold of

LOVE TO GROW

THE REALITY OF SPIRITUAL WARFARE

DANIEL 10:10-21

How do you feel about spiritual warfare? I didn't give it much of a thought before my arrival to the jungle of Venezuela. There, I saw firsthand what demonic powers can do.

I visited houses where people left trays of food and water for "good spirits" as a way of protection from evil ones. I encountered the remains of animal sacrifices. I've witnessed the work of spirit caregivers—those who watch over a person as an unclean spirit overtakes him or her. I witnessed shamans and witch doctors perform ceremonies in the middle of dense jungles. I've felt the urge to fall on my knees and pray after sensing an unseen presence or seeing a shadow that made me cringe.

In Daniel 10:10–21, Daniel had a conversation with an angel who explained to him in detail how demonic powers interfere with believers. The angel told Daniel his request had been heard since the day he had started to pray. However, the prince of the kingdom of Persia—an evil angel—had attacked him and delayed his answer for twenty-one days (vv. 12–13). The angel also told him that he had to leave and reengage in the fight against the princes of Persia and Greece (v. 20).

We should not live unaware of the reality of demonic powers fighting against us in all spheres of life. Daniel fasted and prayed for three weeks in order to focus on prayer (Dan 10:2–3). In the Gospels, Jesus delivered those who were possessed by demons, explaining to His disciples that the only way some of them came out was through prayer and fasting (see Mark 9:29).

Paul wrote in Ephesians 6:12 that we fight against an organized army of demonic powers under Satan's command. He provided a detailed description of the spiritual armor believers wear in order to fight the battle. Ephesians 6:18 assures us that prayer is an essential part of that armor.

We fight from Christ's victory against an already defeated enemy. Jesus conquered the rulers and evil authorities on the cross (see Col 2:15). As believers, we should not neglect prayer. Prayer is never optional in the victorious life of the believer.

The battle we are in can be difficult, but remember we have all the weapons of heaven at our disposal. We have the power of the Holy Spirit, the authority of God's Word, and, above all, victory in Jesus who has overcome sin and death so we may confidently approach the throne of mercy and find grace whenever we need help (see Heb 4:16).

the king of the north and will move against them successfully.
8 He will also take their gods into captivity to Egypt, along with
their cast images and prized utensils of silver and gold. Then
he will withdraw for some years from the king of the north.
9 Then the king of the north will advance against the empire of
the king of the south, but will withdraw to his own land. 10 His
sons will wage war, mustering a large army that will advance
like an overflowing river and carrying the battle all the way to
the enemy's fortress.

11 "Then the king of the south will be enraged and will march
out to fight against the king of the north, who will also muster a
large army, but that army will be delivered into his hand. 12 When
the army is taken away, the king of the south will become arrogant. He will be responsible for the death of thousands and
thousands of people, but he will not continue to prevail. 13 For
the king of the north will again muster an army, one larger than
before. At the end of some years he will advance with a huge
army and enormous supplies.

14 "In those times many will oppose the king of the south.
Those who are violent among your own people will rise up
in confirmation of the vision, but they will falter. 15 Then the
king of the north will advance and will build siege mounds
and capture a well-fortified city. The forces of the south will
not prevail, not even his finest contingents. They will have
no strength to prevail. 16 The one advancing against him will
do as he pleases, and no one will be able to stand before him.
He will prevail in the beautiful land, and its annihilation will
be within his power. 17 His intention will be to come with the
strength of his entire kingdom, and he will form alliances. He
will give the king of the south a daughter in marriage in order
to destroy the kingdom, but it will not turn out to his advantage. 18 Then he will turn his attention to the coastal regions
and will capture many of them. But a commander will bring
his shameful conduct to a halt; in addition, he will make him
pay for his shameful conduct. 19 He will then turn his attention to the fortresses of his own land, but he will stumble and
fall, not to be found again. 20 There will arise after him one who
will send out an exactor of tribute to enhance the splendor of
the kingdom, but after a few days he will be destroyed, though
not in anger or battle.

21 "Then there will arise in his place a despicable person to
whom the royal honor has not been rightfully conferred. He
will come on the scene in a time of prosperity and will seize
the kingdom through deceit. 22 Armies will be suddenly swept
away in defeat before him; both they and a covenant leader will
be destroyed. 23 After entering into an alliance with him, he
will behave treacherously; he will ascend to power with only a
small force. 24 In a time of prosperity for the most productive
areas of the province he will come and accomplish what neither his fathers nor their fathers accomplished. He will distrib-
ute loot, spoils, and property to his followers, and he will devise
plans against fortified cities, but not for long. 25 He will rouse
his strength and enthusiasm against the king of the south with
a large army. The king of the south will wage war with a large

and very powerful army, but he will not be able to prevail because of the plans devised against him. 26 Those who share the
king's fine food will attempt to destroy him, and his army will
be swept away; many will be killed in battle. 27 These two kings,
their minds filled with evil intentions, will trade lies with one
another at the same table. But it will not succeed, for there is
still an end at the appointed time. 28 Then the king of the north
will return to his own land with much property. His mind will
be set against the holy covenant. He will take action, and then
return to his own land. 29 At an appointed time he will again
invade the south, but this latter visit will not turn out the way
the former one did. 30 The ships of Kittim will come against him,
leaving him disheartened. He will turn back and direct his indignation against the holy covenant. He will return and honor
those who forsake the holy covenant. 31 His forces will rise up
and profane the fortified sanctuary, stopping the daily sacrifice.
In its place they will set up the abomination that causes desolation. 32 Then with smooth words he will defile those who have
rejected the covenant. But the people who are loyal to their
God will act valiantly. 33 These who are wise among the people
will teach the masses. However, they will fall by the sword and
by the flame, and they will be imprisoned and plundered for
some time. 34 When they stumble, they will be granted some
help. But many will unite with them deceitfully. 35 Even some
of the wise will stumble, resulting in their refinement, purification, and cleansing until the time of the end, for it is still for
the appointed time.

36 "Then the king will do as he pleases. He will exalt and magnify himself above every deity and he will utter presumptuous
things against the God of gods. He will succeed until the time
of wrath is completed, for what has been decreed must occur.
37 He will not respect the gods of his fathers—not even the god
loved by women. He will not respect any god; he will elevate
himself above them all. 38 What he will honor is a god of fortresses—a god his fathers did not acknowledge he will honor
with gold, silver, valuable stones, and treasured commodities.
39 He will attack mighty fortresses, aided by a foreign deity. To
those who recognize him he will grant considerable honor. He
will place them in authority over many people, and he will parcel out land for a price.

40 "At the time of the end the king of the south will attack him.
Then the king of the north will storm against him with chariots, horsemen, and a large armada of ships. He will invade lands,
passing through them like an overflowing river. 41 Then he will
enter the beautiful land. Many will fall, but these will escape:
Edom, Moab, and the Ammonite leadership. 42 He will extend
his power against other lands; the land of Egypt will not escape.
43 He will have control over the hidden stores of gold and silver,
as well as all the treasures of Egypt. Libyans and Ethiopians will
submit to him. 44 But reports will trouble him from the east and
north, and he will set out in a tremendous rage to destroy and
wipe out many. 45 He will pitch his royal tents between the seas
toward the beautiful holy mountain. But he will come to his end,
with no one to help him.

12 "At that time Michael,
the great prince who watches over your people,
will arise.
There will be a time of distress
unlike any other from the nation's beginning
up to that time.
But at that time your own people,
all those whose names are found written in the book,
will escape.
2 Many of those who sleep
in the dusty ground will awake—
some to everlasting life,
and others to shame and everlasting abhorrence.
3 But the wise will shine
like the brightness of the heavenly expanse.
And those bringing many to righteousness
will be like the stars forever and ever.

4 "But you, Daniel, close up these words and seal the book until the time of the end. Many will dash about, and knowledge
will increase."
5 I, Daniel, watched as two others stood there, one on each side
of the river. 6 One said to the man clothed in linen who was above
the waters of the river, "When will the end of these wondrous
events occur?" 7 Then I heard the man clothed in linen who was
over the waters of the river as he raised both his right and left
hands to the sky and made an oath by the one who lives forever:
"It is for a time, times, and half a time. Then, when the power of
the one who shatters the holy people has been exhausted, all
these things will be finished."
8 I heard, but I did not understand. So I said, "Sir, what will
happen after these things?" 9 He said, "Go, Daniel. For these matters are closed and sealed until the time of the end. 10 Many will
be purified, made clean, and refined, but the wicked will go on
being wicked. None of the wicked will understand, though the
wise will understand. 11 From the time that the daily sacrifice is
removed and the abomination that causes desolation is set in
place, there are 1,290 days. 12 Blessed is the one who waits and
attains to the 1,335 days. 13 But you should go your way until the
end. You will rest and then at the end of the days you will arise
to receive what you have been allotted."

REFLECT

How is Daniel's life an example of how to live faithfully? What can you do today to live faithfully for the kingdom?

for I delight in FAITHFULNESS, not simply in sacrifice

MEMORY VERSE

For I delight in faithfulness, not simply in sacrifice; I delight in acknowledging God, not simply in whole burnt offerings.

Hosea 6:6

Hosea

INTRODUCTION

Loyal Love

The Book of Hosea presents one of the most precise pictures of God's character and His loyal love. Through the prophet Hosea, God displays His unconditional, endless, covenant-keeping, faithful love to His people. God commanded Hosea to marry a prostitute, one who would be unfaithful to him throughout their marriage. God used Gomer's adultery to illustrate Israel's unfaithfulness to Him. Likewise, God used Hosea to exemplify His loyalty to His covenant people, even in their idolatry and unfaithfulness.

Hosea begins by describing the marriage of Hosea to Gomer and concludes with God's coming judgment on Israel. This prophetic book uses several rhetorical and poetic techniques to make the text both memorable and persuasive. Hosea uses many metaphors and themes, including God's anger, judgment, devotion, and love.

The prophecy of Hosea began during the eighth century B.C. when Uzziah was king of Judah and Jeroboam II was king of Israel. Hosea prophesied to the final six kings of Israel, witnessing the destruction of Israel by Assyria in 722 B.C.

Hosea offers a clear and balanced picture of God. While God's jealousy may seem inappropriate and His discipline may seem harsh, this divine reaction to sin is evidence of His love and commitment. He will allow nothing to ruin His relationship with His people, and He will do everything to preserve it. In the end, His devotion and mercy will win out, and God's people will come to their senses, giving Him the love He fervently desires and deserves. May we love Him greatly believing He will do anything to restore us to Him.

China

OFFICIAL LANGUAGE
Mandarin Chinese/Standard Chinese
POPULATION
1,419,883,000
UNREACHED POPULATION
148,152,000
PROFESSING CHRISTIANS
9.2%

Yating's Home

Say a Prayer Today

Please say a prayer for Yating and her ministry in China. Pray also for the women in China to find peace in the loving arms of Jesus alone.

HISTORY BIT

In A.D. 640, Persian Christians translated the gospel for a group of Chinese people. While this was one of the first translations of Scripture for the Chinese people, it was not the full Bible. Robert Morrison, a protestant missionary in China, translated the Bible into the Chinese language in 1819.*

Source Information:
https://joshuaproject.net/countries/CH
*http://news.americanbible.org/article/history-of-translation-in-china

LOVE YOUR NEIGHBOR

Her Journey

YATING'S STORY

If you travel to China, you will witness how rapid economic growth over the last century has awakened a "sleeping dragon." Not unlike the history of the kingdom of Israel, prosperity has marked twenty-first-century China. Like the Israelites, financial fulfillment has led to empty souls; the luxury handbag a Chinese woman carries does not satisfy the deep need and desire to be loved.

Dating apps and matchmaking television shows abound, yet we women have a hard time defining what true love is. Divorce and domestic abuse are prevalent. Faithfulness and unconditional love are almost unimaginable. Many of us fill our hearts with academic degrees, money, fame, or fortune. Even if we recognize these things as false gods, our collectivistic society says we should worship them.

The Book of Hosea shows us how much Chinese women resemble Gomer: We turn away from the only true God time and time again. Shame inevitably shows up at our door, telling us that we do not deserve to be loved by a faithful God. We don't trust the Father's love is deep. And we don't trust that He is waiting for us to return to Him and the truth of Jesus' sacrificial love for His bride.

While China has come a long way in its openness to the gospel compared to previous decades, the persecution of Christians still exists. Women in my country need to know the blood of Jesus quenches any satisfaction the glories of this world claim to provide. We need to know the faithful love, peace, and joy that come from abiding in the one true God.

6 WEEK READING PLAN

LOVE HIS WORD

	MONDAY	TUESDAY	WEDNESDAY	THURSDAY	FRIDAY
1	Hosea 1:1	Hosea 1:2	Hosea 1:3-5	Hosea 1:6-7	Hosea 1:8—2:1
	SOAP Hosea 1:1	SOAP 1 Kings 16:26	SOAP Hosea 1:5	SOAP Hosea 1:7	SOAP Hosea 1:10
2	Hosea 2:2-13	Hosea 2:14-23	Hosea 3	Hosea 4:1-14	Hosea 4:15-19
	SOAP Deuteronomy 30:19-20	SOAP Psalm 71:20-21	SOAP Hosea 3:1	SOAP Hosea 4:12	SOAP Psalm 47:8
3	Hosea 5	Hosea 6:1-3	Hosea 6:4-11	Hosea 7:1-2	Hosea 7:3-12
	SOAP Hosea 5:15	SOAP Hosea 6:1-3	SOAP Hosea 6:6	SOAP Psalm 9:16	SOAP Psalm 106:44-45
4	Hosea 7:13-16	Hosea 8	Hosea 9:1-9	Hosea 9:10-17	Hosea 10:1-8
	SOAP Psalm 78:38	SOAP Romans 9:22-23	SOAP Hosea 9:9	SOAP Hosea 9:17	SOAP Lamentations 1:18
5	Hosea 10:9-15	Hosea 11	Hosea 12:1-8	Hosea 12:9-11	Hosea 12:12-14
	SOAP Hosea 10:12	SOAP Hosea 11:8-9	SOAP Hosea 12:5-6	SOAP Hosea 12:9	SOAP Hosea 12:14
6	Hosea 13:1-3	Hosea 13:4-14	Hosea 13:15-16	Hosea 14:1-3	Hosea 14:4-9
	SOAP Psalm 1:6	SOAP Hosea 13:14	SOAP Jeremiah 51:36	SOAP Hosea 14:2	SOAP Hosea 14:9

SUPERSCRIPTION

1 This is the LORD's message that came to Hosea son of Beeri during the time of Uzziah, Jotham, Ahaz, and Hezekiah, kings of Judah, and during the time of Jeroboam son of Joash, king of Israel.

SYMBOLS OF SIN AND JUDGMENT: THE PROSTITUTE AND HER CHILDREN

2 When the LORD first spoke through Hosea, he said to him, "Go
marry a prostitute who will bear illegitimate children conceived
through prostitution, because the nation continually commits
spiritual prostitution by turning away from the LORD." 3 So Hosea married Gomer, the daughter of Diblaim. Then she conceived and gave birth to a son for him. 4 Then the LORD said to
Hosea, "Name him 'Jezreel,' because in a little while I will punish the dynasty of Jehu on account of the bloodshed in the valley of Jezreel, and I will put an end to the kingdom of Israel.
5 At that time, I will destroy the military power of Israel in the
valley of Jezreel."

6 She conceived again and gave birth to a daughter. Then the
LORD said to him, "Name her 'No Pity' (Lo-Ruhamah) because
I will no longer have pity on the nation of Israel. For I will certainly not forgive their guilt. 7 But I will have pity on the nation
of Judah. I will deliver them by the LORD their God; I will not
deliver them by the warrior's bow, by sword, by military victory,
by chariot horses, or by chariots."

8 When she had weaned "No Pity" (Lo-Ruhamah), she conceived
again and gave birth to another son. 9 Then the LORD said: "Name
him 'Not My People' (Lo-Ammi), because you are not my people
and I am not your God."

THE RESTORATION OF ISRAEL

10 However, in the future the number of the people of Israel will
be like the sand of the sea that can be neither measured nor
numbered. Although it was said to them, "You are not my people," it will be said to them, "You are children of the living God!"
11 Then the people of Judah and the people of Israel will be gathered together. They will appoint for themselves one leader, and
will flourish in the land. Certainly, the day of Jezreel will be great!

2 Then you will call your brother, "My People" (Ammi)! You will call your sister, "Pity" (Ruhamah)!

IDOLATROUS ISRAEL WILL BE PUNISHED LIKE A PROSTITUTE

2 "Plead earnestly with your mother
(for she is not my wife, and I am not her husband),
so that she might put an end to her adulterous lifestyle,
and turn away from her sexually immoral behavior.
3 Otherwise, I will strip her naked,
and expose her like she was when she was born.
I will turn her land into a wilderness
and make her country a parched land,
so that I might kill her with thirst.
4 I will have no pity on her children,
because they are children conceived in adultery.

REFLECT

Is God justified in the way He rebukes Israel's adultery? Why or why not?

THE PURSUIT

HOSEA 1

Hosea is a book about a righteous man whom God called to marry a prostitute. Earlier in my life, it pained me to read this story. How did Gomer deserve to marry a man like Hosea, and why did she treat him the way she did?

Gomer got a sweet deal with Hosea, and she didn't even appreciate it. She cheated on him and left him for other men. She even gave birth to children who were not his. Still, Hosea loved her and raised the children as his own. Talk about a crazy love story!

Why would God include a story like this in Scripture? Why was Hosea so faithful to Gomer, even through her constant unfaithfulness? Now that I have a few years and mistakes under my belt, I read this story with appreciation.

Hosea is a book about the relationship God longs to have with us and the pain our rebellion causes Him. God is holy, all-powerful, and always good, and His heart is tender towards those He loves. He experiences heartbreak when we willfully choose to harden our hearts and go our own ways.

The powerful reminder in Hosea is that God desires our good—not our destruction—and He desires to draw us close. There are consequences for our sins, but He always extends His love, forgiveness, and redemption.

God longs for our wandering hearts to return to Him and receive His cleansing grace.

Hosea illustrates God's relentless love in the face of unfaithfulness. As we witness a faithful husband choose to redeem a faithless wife, we are reminded that God does the same for us. Regardless of our sins, God pursues us.

If you've ever wondered if God will take you back after making some pretty big mistakes, read the Book of Hosea. Rest in the truth that God relentlessly pursues His beloved.

5 For their mother has committed adultery;
she who conceived them has acted shamefully.
For she said, "I will seek out my lovers;
they are the ones who give me my bread and my water,
my wool, my flax, my olive oil, and my wine.

THE LORD'S DISCIPLINE WILL BRING ISRAEL BACK

6 "Therefore, I will soon fence her in with thorns;
I will wall her in so that she cannot find her way.
7 Then she will pursue her lovers, but
she will not catch them;
she will seek them, but she will not find them.
Then she will say,
'I will go back to my husband,
because I was better off then than I am now.'

AGRICULTURAL FERTILITY WITHDRAWN FROM ISRAEL

8 "Yet until now she has refused to
acknowledge that I was the one
who gave her the grain, the new wine, and the olive oil;
and that it was I who lavished on
her the silver and gold—
that they used in worshiping Baal!
9 Therefore, I will take back my grain
during the harvest time
and my new wine when it ripens;
I will take away my wool and my flax
that I had provided in order to clothe her.
10 Soon I will expose her lewd nakedness
in front of her lovers,
and no one will be able to rescue her from me!
11 I will put an end to all her celebrations:
her annual religious festivals,
monthly new moon celebrations,
and weekly Sabbath festivities—
all her appointed festivals.
12 I will destroy her vines and fig trees,
about which she said, 'These are my
wages for prostitution
that my lovers gave to me!'
I will turn her cultivated vines and fig
trees into an uncultivated thicket,
so that wild animals will devour them.
13 I will punish her for the festival days
when she burned incense to the Baal idols;
she adorned herself with earrings and jewelry,
and went after her lovers,
but she forgot me!" says the LORD.

FUTURE REPENTANCE AND RESTORATION OF ISRAEL

14 "However, in the future I will allure her;
I will lead her back into the wilderness,
and speak tenderly to her.

15 From there I will give back her vineyards to her,
and turn the 'Valley of Trouble' into
an 'Opportunity for Hope.'
There she will sing as she did when she was young,
when she came up from the land of Egypt.
16 At that time," declares the LORD,
"you will call, 'My husband';
you will never again call me, 'My master.'
17 For I will remove the names of the
Baal idols from your lips,
so that you will never again utter their names!

NEW COVENANT RELATIONSHIP WITH REPENTANT ISRAEL

18 "At that time I will make a covenant for
them with the wild animals,
the birds of the air, and the creatures
that crawl on the ground.
I will abolish the warrior's bow and sword—
that is, every weapon of warfare—from the land,
and I will allow them to live securely.
19 I will commit myself to you forever;
I will commit myself to you in righteousness and justice,
in steadfast love and tender compassion.
20 I will commit myself to you in faithfulness;
then you will acknowledge the LORD.

AGRICULTURAL FERTILITY RESTORED TO THE REPENTANT NATION

21 "At that time, I will willingly respond," declares the LORD.
"I will respond to the sky,
and the sky will respond to the ground;
22 then the ground will respond to the grain,
the new wine, and the olive oil;
and they will respond to 'God Plants' (Jezreel)!
23 Then I will plant her as my own in the land.
I will have pity on 'No Pity' (Lo-Ruhamah).
I will say to 'Not My People' (Lo-Ammi), 'You are my people!'
And he will say, 'You are my God!'"

REFLECT

Which aspects of God's character are shown through Hosea's responses to Gomer's wayward heart? How does God respond to us in similar ways when we run from Him?

AN ILLUSTRATION OF GOD'S LOVE FOR IDOLATROUS ISRAEL

3 The LORD said to me, "Go, show love to your wife again, even
though she loves another man and continually commits adultery. Likewise, the LORD loves the Israelites although they turn to
other gods and love to offer raisin cakes to idols." 2 So I paid fifteen
shekels of silver and about seven bushels of barley to purchase
her. 3 Then I told her, "You must live with me many days; you must
not commit adultery or become joined to another man, and I also
will wait for you." 4 For the Israelites must live many days without
a king or prince, without sacrifice or sacred fertility pillar, without ephod or idols. 5 Afterward, the Israelites will turn and seek
the LORD their God and their Davidic king. Then they will submit to the LORD in fear and receive his blessings in future days.

LOVE TO GROW

ALL THE WRONG PLACES

HOSEA 3

In my self-righteous pride, I couldn't understand why a guy like Hosea would ever want to marry a girl like Gomer. Then one day, as I was reading Hosea, I realized something life-altering: I am Gomer. Gomer had all she needed, but she didn't believe it was enough. Thinking she needed more than Hosea could give, she left him to follow her own desires. I do the same to God.

Gomer believed the lie of the "better than," and so do I.

This will be better than the relationship I have with God. *This* will make me feel loved. *That* will help me feel more confident. If only I had *that*, then all my problems would be solved. When my prayers were not answered in my time frame there were times my heart and eyes wandered.

By chapter 3 Gomer became a slave to her sin and found herself on the auction block. She left the security of Hosea's love and chased her own selfish desires. I have too. How many times have I sold myself into slavery to food, approval, love, acceptance, or pride, only to find myself in the same place Gomer did?

Instead of trusting God's love for me and His acceptance of me, I've rushed to other things and people to find love and acceptance. These substitutes only yield pain because they can never love me the way God can. Their love is imperfect: God's love is perfect.

The temptations of this world can be very seductive. Like Gomer, we can find ourselves chasing after other loves—love of power, pleasure, money, or recognition. Are we loyal to God, remaining completely faithful to Him, or have other loves taken His rightful place in our hearts?

When we put others in God's rightful place, we give them power to reject us, define us, and shame us. Instead, let's give our hearts to the only One who really cares for them: our loving, ever-faithful, heavenly Father.

My prayer for all of us "Gomer girls" is that we stop searching for love in all the wrong places and rest in the love and acceptance Jesus extends each of us.

THE LORD'S COVENANT LAWSUIT AGAINST THE NATION ISRAEL

4 Listen to the LORD's message, you Israelites!
For the LORD has a covenant lawsuit
against the people of Israel.
For there is neither faithfulness nor loyalty in the land,
nor do they acknowledge God.
2 There is only cursing, lying, murder, stealing, and adultery.
They resort to violence and bloodshed.
3 Therefore the land will mourn,
and all its inhabitants will perish.
The wild animals, the birds of the sky,
and even the fish in the sea will perish.

THE LORD'S DISPUTE AGAINST THE SINFUL PRIESTHOOD

4 Do not let anyone accuse or contend against anyone else:
for my case is against you priests!
5 You stumble day and night,
and the false prophets stumble with you;
you have destroyed your own people.
6 You have destroyed my people
by failing to acknowledge me!
Because you refuse to acknowledge me,
I will reject you as my priests.
Because you reject the law of your God,
I will reject your descendants.
7 The more the priests increased in numbers,
the more they rebelled against me.
They have turned their glorious calling
into a shameful disgrace!
8 They feed on the sin offerings of my people;
their appetites long for their iniquity!
9 I will deal with the people and priests together:
I will punish them both for their ways,
and I will repay them for their deeds.
10 They will eat, but not be satisfied;
they will engage in prostitution, but
not increase in numbers;
because they have abandoned the LORD
by pursuing other gods.

JUDGMENT OF PAGAN IDOLATRY AND CULTIC PROSTITUTION

11 Old and new wine
take away the understanding of my people.
12 They consult their wooden idols,
and their diviner's staff answers with an oracle.
The wind of prostitution blows them astray;
they commit spiritual adultery against their God.
13 They sacrifice on the mountaintops
and burn offerings on the hills;
they sacrifice under oak, poplar, and terebinth,
because their shade is so pleasant.

As a result, your daughters have
become cult prostitutes,
and your daughters-in-law commit adultery!
14 I will not punish your daughters when
they commit prostitution,
nor your daughters-in-law when they commit adultery.
For the men consort with harlots,
they sacrifice with temple prostitutes.
It is true: "A people that lacks
understanding will come to ruin!"

WARNING TO JUDAH: DO NOT JOIN IN ISRAEL'S APOSTASY

15 Although you, O Israel, commit adultery,
do not let Judah become guilty!
Do not journey to Gilgal.
Do not go up to Beth Aven.
Do not swear, "As surely as the LORD lives!"
16 Israel has rebelled like a stubborn heifer!
Soon the LORD will put them out to pasture
like a lamb in a broad field.
17 Ephraim has attached himself to idols;
Do not go near him!

THE SHAMEFUL SINNERS WILL BE BROUGHT TO SHAME

18 They consume their alcohol,
then engage in cult prostitution;
they dearly love their shameful behavior.
19 A whirlwind has wrapped them in its wings;
they will be brought to shame because
of their idolatrous worship.

ANNOUNCEMENT OF SIN AND JUDGMENT

5 Hear this, you priests!
Pay attention, you Israelites!
Listen closely, O king!
For judgment is about to overtake you.
For you were like a trap to Mizpah,
like a net spread out to catch Tabor.
2 Those who revolt are knee-deep in slaughter,
but I will discipline them all.
3 I know Ephraim all too well;
the evil of Israel is not hidden from me.
For you have engaged in prostitution, O Ephraim;
Israel has defiled itself.
4 Their wicked deeds do not allow them
to return to their God;
for a spirit of idolatry is in them,
and they do not acknowledge the LORD.
5 The arrogance of Israel testifies against it;
Israel and Ephraim will be overthrown
because of their iniquity.
Even Judah will be brought down with them.

THE FUTILITY OF SACRIFICIAL RITUAL WITHOUT MORAL OBEDIENCE

6 Although they bring their flocks and herds
to seek the favor of the LORD,
They will not find him—
he has withdrawn himself from them!
7 They have committed treason against the LORD,
because they bore illegitimate children.
Soon the new moon festival will devour
them and their fields.

THE PROPHET'S DECLARATION OF JUDGMENT

8 Blow the ram's horn in Gibeah!
Sound the trumpet in Ramah!
Sound the alarm in Beth Aven;
tremble in fear, O Benjamin!
9 Ephraim will be ruined in the day of judgment.
What I am declaring to the tribes of
Israel will certainly take place!

THE OPPRESSORS OF THE HELPLESS WILL BE OPPRESSED

10 The princes of Judah are like those who
move boundary markers.
I will pour out my rage on them like a torrential flood.
11 Ephraim will be oppressed, crushed under judgment,
because he was determined to pursue worthless idols.

THE CURSE OF THE INCURABLE WOUND

12 I will be like a moth to Ephraim,
like wood rot to the house of Judah.
13 When Ephraim saw his sickness
and Judah saw his wound,
then Ephraim turned to Assyria,
and begged its great king for help.
But he will not be able to heal you.
He cannot cure your wound!

THE LION WILL CARRY ISRAEL OFF INTO EXILE

14 I will be like a lion to Ephraim,
like a young lion to the house of Judah.
I myself will tear them to pieces,
then I will carry them off, and no one
will be able to rescue them!
15 Then I will return again to my lair
until they have suffered their punishment.
Then they will seek me;
in their distress they will earnestly seek me.

SUPERFICIAL REPENTANCE BREEDS FALSE ASSURANCE OF GOD'S FORGIVENESS

Come on! Let's return to the LORD.
He himself has torn us to pieces,
but he will heal us!

He has injured us,
but he will bandage our wounds!
2 He will restore us in a very short time;
he will heal us in a little while,
so that we may live in his presence.
3 So let us search for him!
Let us seek to know the LORD!
He will come to our rescue as certainly
as the appearance of the dawn,
as certainly as the winter rain comes,
as certainly as the spring rain that waters the land.

REFLECT
What does God desire from His people more than sacrifices?

TRANSITORY FAITHFULNESS AND IMMINENT JUDGMENT

4 What am I going to do with you, O Ephraim?
What am I going to do with you, O Judah?
For your faithfulness is as fleeting
as the morning mist;
it disappears as quickly as dawn's dew.
5 Therefore, I will certainly cut you into
pieces at the hands of the prophets;
I will certainly kill you in fulfillment
of my oracles of judgment,
for my judgment will come forth
like the light of the dawn.
6 For I delight in faithfulness, not simply in sacrifice;
I delight in acknowledging God, not
simply in whole burnt offerings.

INDICTMENTS AGAINST THE CITIES OF ISRAEL AND JUDAH

7 At Adam they broke the covenant;
Oh how they were unfaithful to me!
8 Gilead is a city full of evildoers;
its streets are stained with bloody footprints!
9 The company of priests is like a gang of robbers,
lying in ambush to pounce on a victim.
They commit murder on the road to Shechem;
they have done heinous crimes!
10 I have seen a disgusting thing in the house of Israel:
there Ephraim commits prostitution with other gods,
and Israel defiles itself.
11 I have appointed a time to reap judgment
for you also, O Judah!

REFLECT
If God can change His mind, does that mean He knows the future? How does His ability to change His mind contribute to His sovereignty?

IF ISRAEL WOULD REPENT OF SIN, GOD WOULD RELENT OF JUDGMENT

Whenever I want to restore the fortunes of my people,
7 whenever I want to heal Israel,
the sin of Ephraim is revealed,
and the evil deeds of Samaria are exposed.
For they do what is wrong;
thieves break into houses,
and gangs rob people out in the streets.

LOVE TO GROW

EVER FAITHFUL

HOSEA 6:6

Over and over again the prophet Hosea faithfully restored his bride after grievous infidelity. Despite Gomer's betrayal, Hosea chose to love Gomer and rescue her even though she didn't deserve it.

God does the same for us.

God chooses to love us, sending Jesus to rescue us from our sins, even though we don't deserve it. Gomer could never repay Hosea for her freedom, and neither can we repay God, nor do we have to. Our hearts are all that He asks for and all that we need to give.

As Hosea went after his unfaithful wife, the Lord pursues us with His limitless love. His love is tender, loyal, unchanging, and undying. No matter what, God still loves us.

When we choose to come to God and ask Him for forgiveness, true repentance opens the way to a new beginning. God forgives and restores. No matter how far we have strayed, God is willing to forgive us and receive us.

Hosea 6:6 says, "For I delight in faithfulness, not simply in sacrifice; I delight in acknowledging God, not simply in whole burnt offerings." This verse shows us what God considers the highest devotion to Him, what He wants most: faithfulness over sacrifice, a relationship with Him over our religious rituals.

Let's not wallow in our shame, but instead let's run back to our loving Father. He will continue to pursue us, as He always has. And if we respond, He will rescue us from the deepest darkness in our hearts.

God does not think less of you because you are broken and in need of a second chance.

Jesus chooses to love us despite our rebellion, and He extends second chances to each of us without showing favoritism. Jesus is our ever-faithful bridegroom and best friend. All He desires is our hearts.

2 They do not realize
that I remember all their wicked deeds.
Their evil deeds have now surrounded them;
their sinful deeds are always before me.

POLITICAL INTRIGUE AND CONSPIRACY IN THE PALACE

3 The royal advisers delight the king with their evil schemes,
the princes make him glad with their lies.
4 They are all like bakers,
they are like a smoldering oven;
they are like a baker who does not stoke the fire
until the kneaded dough is ready for baking.
5 At the celebration of their king,
his princes become inflamed with wine;
they conspire with evildoers.
6 They approach him, all the while plotting against him.
Their hearts are like an oven;
their anger smolders all night long,
but in the morning it bursts into a flaming fire.
7 All of them are blazing like an oven;
they devour their rulers.
All their kings fall,
and none of them call on me!

ISRAEL LACKS DISCERNMENT AND REFUSES TO REPENT

8 Ephraim has mixed itself like flour among the nations;
Ephraim is like a ruined cake of bread
that is scorched on one side.
9 Foreigners are consuming what his
strenuous labor produced,
but he does not recognize it.
His head is filled with gray hair,
but he does not realize it.
10 The arrogance of Israel testifies against him,
yet they refuse to return to the LORD their God.
In spite of all this they refuse to seek him.

ISRAEL TURNS TO ASSYRIA AND EGYPT FOR HELP

11 Ephraim has been like a dove,
easily deceived and lacking discernment.
They called to Egypt for help;
they turned to Assyria for protection.
12 I will throw my bird net over them while they are flying;
I will bring them down like birds in the sky;
I will discipline them when I hear
them flocking together.

ISRAEL HAS TURNED AWAY FROM THE LORD

13 Woe to them! For they have fled from me!
Destruction to them! For they have rebelled against me!
I want to deliver them,
but they have lied to me.

14 They do not pray to me,
but howl in distress on their beds;
they slash themselves for grain and new wine,
but turn away from me.
15 Although I trained and strengthened them,
they plot evil against me!
16 They turn to Baal;
they are like an unreliable bow.
Their leaders will fall by the sword
because their prayers to Baal have made me angry.
So people will disdain them in the land of Egypt.

GOD WILL RAISE UP THE ASSYRIANS TO ATTACK ISRAEL

8 Sound the alarm!
An eagle looms over the temple of the LORD!
For they have broken their covenant with me
and have rebelled against my law.
2 Israel cries out to me,
"My God, we acknowledge you!"
3 But Israel has rejected what is morally good;
so an enemy will pursue him.

THE POLITICAL AND CULTIC SIN OF ISRAEL

4 They enthroned kings without my consent.
They appointed princes without my approval.
They made idols out of their silver and gold,
but they will be destroyed!
5 O Samaria, he has rejected your calf idol.
My anger burns against them!
They will not survive much longer
without being punished,
even though they are Israelites!
6 That idol was made by a workman—it is not God!
The calf idol of Samaria will be broken to bits.

THE FERTILITY CULTISTS WILL BECOME INFERTILE

7 They sow the wind,
and so they will reap the whirlwind!
The stalk does not have any standing grain;
it will not produce any flour.
Even if it were to yield grain,
foreigners would swallow it all up.
8 Israel will be swallowed up among the nations;
they will be like a worthless piece of pottery.

ISRAEL'S HIRED LOVERS

9 They have gone up to Assyria,
like a wild donkey that wanders off.
Ephraim has hired prostitutes as lovers.
10 Even though they have hired lovers among the nations,
I will soon gather them together for judgment.
Then they will begin to waste away
under the oppression of a mighty king.

SACRIFICES INEFFECTIVE WITHOUT MORAL OBEDIENCE

11 Although Ephraim has built many
altars for sin offerings,
these have become altars for sinning.
12 I spelled out my law for him in great detail,
but they regard it as something
totally unknown to them.
13 They offer up sacrificial gifts to me
and eat the meat,
but the LORD does not accept their sacrifices.
Soon he will remember their wrongdoing,
he will punish their sins,
and they will return to Egypt.
14 Israel has forgotten his Maker and built royal palaces,
and Judah has built many fortified cities.
But I will send fire on their cities;
it will consume their royal citadels.

FERTILITY CULT FESTIVALS HAVE INTOXICATED ISRAEL

9 O Israel, do not rejoice jubilantly like the nations,
for you are unfaithful to your God.
You love to receive a prostitute's wages
on all the floors where you thresh your grain.
2 Threshing floors and wine vats will not feed the people,
and new wine only deceives them.

ASSYRIAN EXILE WILL REVERSE THE EGYPTIAN EXODUS

3 They will not remain in the LORD's land.
Ephraim will return to Egypt;
they will eat ritually unclean food in Assyria.
4 They will not pour out drink offerings
of wine to the LORD;
they will not please him with their sacrifices.
Their sacrifices will be like bread
eaten while in mourning;
all those who eat them will make
themselves ritually unclean.
For their bread will be only to satisfy their appetite;
it will not come into the temple of the LORD.
5 So what will you do on the festival day,
on the festival days of the LORD?

NO ESCAPE FOR THE ISRAELITES THIS TIME

6 Look! Even if they flee from the destruction,
Egypt will take hold of them,
and Memphis will bury them.
The weeds will inherit the silver they treasure—
thorn bushes will occupy their homes.
7 The time of judgment is about to arrive!
The time of retribution is imminent!
Israel will be humbled!

ISRAEL REJECTS HOSEA'S PROPHETIC EXHORTATIONS

The prophet is considered a fool—
the inspired man is viewed as a madman—
because of the multitude of your sins
and your intense animosity.
8 The prophet is a watchman over Ephraim on behalf of God,
yet traps are laid for him along all his paths;
animosity rages against him in the land of his God.

THE BEST OF TIMES, THE WORST OF TIMES

9 They have sunk deep into corruption
as in the days of Gibeah.
He will remember their wrongdoing.
He will repay them for their sins.
10 When I found Israel, it was like finding
grapes in the wilderness.
I viewed your ancestors like an early fig
on a fig tree in its first season.
Then they came to Baal Peor and they
dedicated themselves to shame—
they became as detestable as what they loved.

THE FERTILITY WORSHIPERS WILL BECOME INFERTILE

11 Ephraim will be like a bird;
what they value will fly away.
They will not bear children—
they will not enjoy pregnancy—
they will not even conceive!
12 Even if they raise their children,
I will take away every last one of them.
Woe to them!
For I will turn away from them.
13 Ephraim, as I have seen, has given their children for prey;
Ephraim will bear his sons for slaughter.
14 Give them, O Lord—
what will you give them?
Give them wombs that miscarry,
and breasts that cannot nurse!
15 Because of all their evil in Gilgal,
I hate them there.
On account of their evil deeds,
I will drive them out of my land.
I will no longer love them;
all their rulers are rebels.
16 Ephraim will be struck down—
their root will be dried up;
they will not yield any fruit.
Even if they do bear children,
I will kill their precious offspring.
17 My God will reject them,
for they have not obeyed him;
so they will be fugitives among the nations.

ISRAEL IS GUILTY OF FERTILITY CULT WORSHIP

10 Israel was a fertile vine
that yielded fruit.
As his fruit multiplied,
he multiplied altars to Baal.
As his land prospered,
they adorned the fertility pillars.
2 Their hearts are slipping;
soon they will be punished for their guilt.
The LORD will break their altars;
he will completely destroy their fertility pillars.

THE LORD WILL PUNISH ISRAEL BY REMOVING ITS KINGS

3 Very soon they will say, "We have no king
since we did not fear the LORD.
But what can a king do for us anyway?"
4 They utter empty words,
taking false oaths and making empty agreements.
Therefore legal disputes sprout up
like poisonous weeds in the
furrows of a plowed field.

THE CALF IDOL AND IDOLATERS OF SAMARIA WILL BE EXILED

5 The inhabitants of Samaria will lament
over the calf idol of Beth Aven.
Its people will mourn over it;
its idolatrous priests will wail over it,
because its splendor will be taken
from them into exile.
6 Even the calf idol will be carried to Assyria,
as tribute for the great king.
Ephraim will be disgraced;
Israel will be put to shame because
of its wooden idol.
7 Samaria and its king will be carried off
like a twig on the surface of the waters.
8 The high places of the "House of
Wickedness" will be destroyed;
it is the place where Israel sins.
Thorns and thistles will grow up over its altars.
Then they will say to the mountains, "Cover us!"
and to the hills, "Fall on us!"

FAILURE TO LEARN FROM THE SIN AND JUDGMENT OF GIBEAH

9 O Israel, you have sinned since
the time of Gibeah,
and there you have remained.
Did not war overtake the evildoers in Gibeah?
10 When I please, I will discipline them;
I will gather nations together to attack them,
to bind them in chains for their two sins.

FERTILITY IMAGERY: PLOWING, SOWING, AND REAPING

11 Ephraim was a well-trained heifer who loved to thresh grain;
I myself put a fine yoke on her neck.
I will harness Ephraim.
Let Judah plow!
Let Jacob break up the unplowed ground for himself!
12 Sow righteousness for yourselves,
reap unfailing love.
Break up the unplowed ground for yourselves,
for it is time to seek the LORD,
until he comes and showers deliverance on you.
13 But you have plowed wickedness;
you have reaped injustice;
you have eaten the fruit of deception.
Because you have depended on your chariots;
you have relied on your many warriors.

BETHEL WILL BE DESTROYED LIKE BETH ARBEL

14 The roar of battle will rise against your people;
all your fortresses will be devastated,
just as Shalman devastated Beth
Arbel on the day of battle,
when mothers were dashed to the
ground with their children.
15 So will it happen to you, O Bethel,
because of your great wickedness!
When that day dawns,
the king of Israel will be destroyed.

REVERSAL OF THE EXODUS: RETURN TO EGYPT AND EXILE IN ASSYRIA

11 "When Israel was a young man, I loved him like a son,
and I summoned my son out of Egypt.
2 But the more I summoned them,
the farther they departed from me.
They sacrificed to the Baal idols
and burned incense to images.
3 Yet it was I who led Ephraim;
I took them by the arm,
but they did not acknowledge
that I had healed them.
4 I drew them with leather cords,
with straps of hide;
I lifted the yoke from their neck,
and gently fed them.
5 They will return to Egypt!
Assyria will rule over them
because they refuse to repent!
6 A sword will flash in their cities,
it will destroy the bars of their city gates,
and will devour them in their fortresses.
7 My people are obsessed with turning away from me;
they call to Baal, but he will never exalt them!

THE DIVINE DILEMMA: JUDGMENT OR MERCY?

8 "How can I give you up, O Ephraim?
How can I surrender you, O Israel?
How can I treat you like Admah?
How can I make you like Zeboyim?
I have had a change of heart.
All my tender compassions are aroused.
9 I cannot carry out my fierce anger!
I cannot totally destroy Ephraim!
Because I am God, and not man—
the Holy One among you—
I will not come in wrath!

GOD WILL RESTORE THE EXILES TO ISRAEL

10 "He will roar like a lion,
and they will follow the LORD;
when he roars,
his children will come trembling from the west.
11 They will return in fear and trembling
like birds from Egypt,
like doves from Assyria,
and I will settle them in their homes,"
declares the LORD.

GOD'S LAWSUIT AGAINST ISRAEL: BREACH OF COVENANT

12 Ephraim has surrounded me with lies;
the house of Israel has surrounded
me with deceit.
But Judah still roams about with God;
he remains faithful to the Holy One.
12 Ephraim continually feeds on the wind;
he chases the east wind all day;
he multiplies lies and violence.
They make treaties with Assyria,
and send olive oil as tribute to Egypt.
2 The LORD also has a covenant
lawsuit against Judah;
he will punish Jacob according to his ways
and repay him according to his deeds.

ISRAEL MUST RETURN TO THE GOD OF JACOB

3 In the womb he attacked his brother;
in his manly vigor he struggled with God.
4 He struggled with an angel and prevailed;
he wept and begged for his favor.
He found God at Bethel,
and there he spoke with him!
5 As for the LORD God Almighty,
the LORD is the name by which
he is remembered!
6 But you must return to your God,
by maintaining love and justice
and by waiting for your God to return to you.

REFLECT

How is God's faithfulness to His promises shown in His desire to not destroy Israel?

THE LORD REFUTES ISRAEL'S FALSE CLAIM OF INNOCENCE

7 The businessmen love to cheat;
they use dishonest scales.
8 Ephraim boasts, "I am very rich!
I have become wealthy!
In all that I have done to gain my wealth,
no one can accuse me of any offense
that is actually sinful."
9 "I am the LORD your God who brought you out of Egypt;
I will make you live in tents again
as in the days of old.
10 I spoke to the prophets;
I myself revealed many visions;
I spoke in parables through the prophets."
11 Is there idolatry in Gilead?
Certainly its inhabitants will come to nothing!
Do they sacrifice bulls in Gilgal?
Surely their altars will be like stones
heaped up on a plowed field!

JACOB IN ARAM, ISRAEL IN EGYPT, AND EPHRAIM IN TROUBLE

12 Jacob fled to the country of Aram,
then Israel worked to acquire a wife;
he tended sheep to pay for her.
13 The LORD brought Israel out of Egypt by a prophet,
and due to a prophet Israel was preserved alive.
14 But Ephraim bitterly provoked him to anger;
so he will hold him accountable for
the blood he has shed,
his Lord will repay him for the contempt he has shown.

BAAL WORSHIPERS AND CALF WORSHIPERS TO BE DESTROYED

13 When Ephraim spoke, there was terror;
he was exalted in Israel,
but he became guilty by worshiping Baal and died.
2 Even now they persist in sin!
They make metal images for themselves,
idols that they skillfully fashion from their own silver;
all of them are nothing but the work of craftsmen.
There is a saying about them:
"Those who sacrifice to the calf idol are calf kissers!"
3 Therefore they will disappear like the morning mist,
like early morning dew that evaporates,
like chaff that is blown away from a threshing floor,
like smoke that disappears through an open window.

WELL-FED ISRAEL WILL BE FED TO WILD ANIMALS

4 But I am the LORD your God,
who brought you out of Egypt.
Therefore, you must not acknowledge any God but me.
Except for me there is no Savior.

5 I cared for you in the wilderness,
in the dry desert where no water was.
6 When they were fed, they became satisfied;
when they were satisfied, they became proud;
as a result, they forgot me!
7 So I will pounce on them like a lion;
like a leopard I will lurk by the path.
8 I will attack them like a bear robbed of her cubs—
I will rip open their chests.
I will devour them there like a lion—
like a wild animal would tear them apart.

ISRAEL'S KING UNABLE TO DELIVER THE NATION

9 I will destroy you, O Israel!
Who is there to help you?
10 Where then is your king,
that he may save you in all your cities?
Where are your rulers for whom you asked, saying,
"Give me a king and princes"?
11 I granted you a king in my anger,
and I will take him away in my wrath!

ISRAEL'S PUNISHMENT WILL NOT BE WITHHELD MUCH LONGER

12 The punishment of Ephraim has been decreed;
his punishment is being stored up for the future.
13 The labor pains of a woman will overtake him,
but the baby will lack wisdom;
when the time arrives,
he will not come out of the womb!

THE LORD WILL NOT RELENT FROM THE THREATENED JUDGMENT

14 Will I deliver them from the power
of Sheol? No, I will not!
Will I redeem them from death? No, I will not!
O Death, bring on your plagues!
O Sheol, bring on your destruction!
My eyes will not show any compassion!

THE CAPITAL OF THE NORTHERN EMPIRE WILL BE DESTROYED

15 Even though he flourishes like a reed plant,
a scorching east wind will come,
a wind from the LORD rising up from the desert.
As a result, his spring will dry up;
his well will become dry.
That wind will spoil all his delightful foods
in the containers in his storehouse.
16 Samaria will be held guilty,
because she rebelled against her God.
They will fall by the sword;
their infants will be dashed to the ground—
their pregnant women will be ripped open.

PROPHETIC CALL TO GENUINE REPENTANCE

14 Return, O Israel, to the LORD your God,
for your sin has been your downfall!
2 Return to the LORD and repent!
Say to him: "Completely forgive our iniquity;
accept our penitential prayer,
that we may offer the praise of our lips as sacrificial bulls.
3 Assyria cannot save us;
we will not ride warhorses.
We will never again say, 'Our gods,'
to what our own hands have made.
For only you will show compassion to Orphan Israel!"

CHALLENGE

Read over Psalm 136 and reflect on God's loyal love. Write out some of the ways that you have seen God's love displayed in your life.

DIVINE PROMISE TO RELENT FROM JUDGMENT AND TO RESTORE BLESSINGS

4 "I will heal their waywardness
and love them freely,
for my anger will turn away from them.
5 I will be like the dew to Israel;
he will blossom like a lily,
he will send down his roots like a cedar of Lebanon.
6 His young shoots will grow;
his splendor will be like an olive tree,
his fragrance like a cedar of Lebanon.
7 People will reside again in his shade;
they will plant and harvest grain in abundance.
They will blossom like a vine,
and his fame will be like the wine from Lebanon.
8 O Ephraim, I do not want to have anything
to do with idols anymore!
I will answer him and care for him.
I am like a luxuriant cypress tree;
your fruitfulness comes from me!"

CONCLUDING EXHORTATION

9 Who is wise?
Let him discern these things!
Who is discerning?
Let him understand them!
For the ways of the LORD are right;
the godly walk in them,
but in them the rebellious stumble.

I AM the LORD your GOD; THERE IS NO OTHER. my PEOPLE WILL NEVER again be put to shame

MEMORY VERSE

You will be convinced that I am in the midst of Israel. I am the LORD your God; there is no other. My people will never again be put to shame.

Joel 2:27

Joel

INTRODUCTION

Restoration

The Book of Joel begins with a horrifying description of a plague of locusts. This plague becomes a warning of the power of God's coming judgment on the nation of Judah. Joel wrote to Judah to urge them to repent so God would relent from sending His judgment. God's character is on display as He demonstrated His desire to discipline His people so they would return to Him.

This book includes an introduction, a description of the coming invasion of locusts, a call to lament for forsaking God, the coming judgment on the day of the Lord, an appeal to repent and return to God, and the restoration of Judah. Joel warned the people that if they did not repent, they would be destroyed. However, he also offered a message of hope. God promised if His people repented, He would make up for the years the locusts destroyed, providing the people with plenty to eat.

Joel is the author of this short book. Only a few things are known about this prophet. His name means "The Lord is God," and he was likely from Judah in Jerusalem. He had much knowledge about the temple, which means he could have been a priest, but Joel was also well versed in agricultural knowledge, indicating he may have been a farmer. Because the book does not mention any reigning king like many other prophetic works, it is difficult to know precisely when Joel shared his message.

The grace of God is evident throughout the Book of Joel, as His covenant-keeping nature allows Him to keep His promise and restore the nation of Judah. Joel helps us love God greatly because it shows God's heart for restoring His people after disciplining them. While discipline is often necessary, God intends to correct, not destroy. He longs for His people to be faithful to Him, and He will go to great lengths to turn their hearts to Him.

Thailand

OFFICIAL LANGUAGE
Thai
POPULATION
69,565,000
UNREACHED POPULATION
61,395,000
PROFESSING CHRISTIANS
1.3%

Lin's Home

Say a Prayer Today

Pray for the church in Thailand, that those who share the gospel would be able to find ways to minister in a Buddhist society. Pray for endurance and boldness for those in the church as they share the gospel with others.

HISTORY BIT

In 1934 four American denominations (Presbyterians, Baptists, Disciples of Christ, and Lutherans) united and formed the Church of Christ in Thailand. It is now the largest Protestant church in the country. Resistance to Christianity in Thailand exists as many natives believe that accepting Christianity means abandoning the Thai community. This is largely because Christianity is still seen as a Western religion.*

Source Information:
https://joshuaproject.net/countries/TH
*David B. Barrett, World Christian Encyclopedia, Thailand (New York, NY: Oxford University Press, 1982), 665.

LIN'S STORY

Like most kids growing up in Southeast Asia, my parents were Buddhist. They were dedicated to the worship of pagan idols and demonic spirits. They were characterized by anger and deception and addictions to alcohol and tobacco. When I was eight years old an evangelist shared the gospel with my father and invited us to attend church. After a few weeks my parents repented and turned to Jesus. A significant change began in our family. We attended church regularly, my mother and father quit using alcohol and tobacco, and they became kind and patient. Witnessing their radical change opened my eyes to the fact that God is real.

When I was eighteen years old, I had the opportunity to attend a Bible school where I learned more about the God who created heaven and earth, and I learned He has a purpose for my life. God has sent me several dreams to guide me in His purpose to fulfill His plans for me (see Joel 2:28–32; Acts 2:17). When He sent me dreams, I would draw pictures to help me understand the direction He was leading me. As I walked with God, I watched the dreams become reality. Through them, He prepared me for marrying a foreigner and being a missionary.

John and I met in Thailand where we both were serving God. We discovered that God had given us the same vision and the same kingdom direction. I joined a ministry team, and we became like family. Our outreach became increasingly effective, and our everyday work brought us joy.

After four years of serving in Thailand, God led us to serve in Myanmar. When I see both the physical and spiritual hunger there, I recall how God has blessed me, and I long for Him to use me to expand His kingdom among Myanmar's people. I live to testify that He is faithful to turn dreams into reality.

4 WEEK READING PLAN

LOVE HIS WORD

MONDAY	TUESDAY	WEDNESDAY	THURSDAY	FRIDAY
Joel 1	Joel 2:1-17	Joel 2:18-32	Joel 3:1-16	Joel 3:17-21
SOAP Joel 1:19-20	SOAP Joel 2:13-14	SOAP Joel 2:26	SOAP Joel 3:1-2	SOAP Joel 3:17
Amos 1	Amos 2	Amos 3:1-8	Amos 3:9—4:3	Amos 4:4-13
SOAP Amos 1:2	SOAP Amos 2:4	SOAP Amos 3:8	SOAP Amos 4:2	SOAP Amos 4:13
Amos 5:1-17	Amos 5:18-27	Amos 6	Amos 7:1-9	Amos 7:10-17
SOAP Amos 5:14	SOAP Amos 5:18	SOAP Amos 6:8	SOAP Amos 7:4-6	SOAP Amos 7:17
Amos 8	Amos 9:1-10	Amos 9:11-15	Obadiah 1-14	Obadiah 15-21
SOAP Amos 8:2	SOAP Amos 9:8-9	SOAP Amos 9:13-15	SOAP Obadiah 12	SOAP Obadiah 17

INTRODUCTION

1 This is the LORD's message that came to Joel the son of Pethuel:

A LOCUST PLAGUE FORESHADOWS THE DAY OF THE LORD

2 Listen to this, you elders;
pay attention, all inhabitants of the land.
Has anything like this ever happened in your whole life
or in the lifetime of your ancestors?
3 Tell your children about it,
have your children tell their children,
and their children the following generation.
4 What the *gazam*-locust left the *'arbeh*-locust consumed,
what the *'arbeh*-locust left the *yeleq*-locust consumed,
and what the *yeleq*-locust left the *hasil*-locust consumed.

5 Wake up, you drunkards, and weep!
Wail, all you wine drinkers,
because the sweet wine has been taken away from you.
6 For a nation has invaded my land,
mighty and without number.
Their teeth are lion's teeth;
they have the fangs of a lioness.
7 They have destroyed my vines;
they have turned my fig trees into mere splinters.
They have completely stripped off the
bark and thrown it aside;
the twigs are stripped bare.

A CALL TO LAMENT

8 Wail like a young virgin clothed in sackcloth,
lamenting the death of her husband to be.
9 No one brings grain offerings or drink offerings
to the temple of the LORD anymore.
So the priests, those who serve the LORD, are in mourning.
10 The crops of the fields have been destroyed.
The ground is in mourning because the grain has perished.
The fresh wine has dried up;
the olive oil languishes.
11 Be distressed, farmers;
wail, vinedressers, over the wheat and the barley.
For the harvest of the field has perished.
12 The vine has dried up;
the fig tree languishes—
the pomegranate, date, and apple as well.
In fact, all the trees of the field have dried up.
Indeed, the joy of the people has dried up!

13 Get dressed and lament, you priests.
Wail, you who minister at the altar.
Come, spend the night in sackcloth, you servants of my God,
because no one brings grain offerings or drink offerings
to the temple of your God anymore.

REFLECT

What does it look like to lament over our sin? Why is this something God desires from His people?

14 Announce a holy fast;
proclaim a sacred assembly.
Gather the elders and all the inhabitants of the land
to the temple of the LORD your God,
and cry out to the LORD.
15 How awful that day will be!
For the day of the LORD is near;
it will come as destruction from the Divine Destroyer.
16 Our food has been cut off right before our eyes!
There is no longer any joy or gladness
in the temple of our God.
17 The grains of seed have shriveled beneath their shovels.
Storehouses have been decimated,
and granaries have been torn down,
because the grain has dried up.
18 Listen to the cattle groan!
The herds of livestock wander around in confusion
because they have no pasture.
Even the flocks of sheep are suffering.

19 To you, O LORD, I call out for help,
for fire has burned up the pastures of the wilderness,
flames have razed all the trees in the fields.
20 Even the wild animals cry out to you,
for the river beds have dried up;
fire has destroyed the pastures of the wilderness.

THE LOCUSTS' DEVASTATION

2 Blow the trumpet in Zion;
sound the alarm signal on my holy mountain!
Let all the inhabitants of the land shake with fear,
for the day of the LORD is about to come.
Indeed, it is near!
2 It will be a day of dreadful darkness,
a day of foreboding storm clouds,
like blackness spread over the mountains.
It is a huge and powerful army—
there has never been anything like it ever before,
and there will not be anything like it for
many generations to come!

3 Like fire they devour everything in their path;
a flame blazes behind them.
The land looks like the Garden of Eden before them,
but behind them there is only a desolate wilderness—
for nothing escapes them!
4 They look like horses;
they charge ahead like war horses.
5 They sound like chariots rumbling over mountain tops,
like the crackling of blazing fire consuming stubble,
like the noise of a mighty army being
drawn up for battle.
6 People writhe in fear when they see them.
All their faces turn pale with fright.

7 They charge like warriors;
they scale walls like soldiers.
Each one proceeds on his course;
they do not alter their path.
8 They do not jostle one another;
each of them marches straight ahead.
They burst through the city defenses
and do not break ranks.
9 They rush into the city;
they scale its walls.
They climb up into the houses;
they go in through the windows like a thief.
10 The earth quakes before them;
the sky reverberates.
The sun and the moon grow dark;
the stars refuse to shine.
11 The voice of the LORD thunders as he leads his army.
Indeed, his warriors are innumerable;
Surely his command is carried out!
Yes, the day of the LORD is awesome
and very terrifying—who can survive it?

AN APPEAL FOR REPENTANCE

12 "Yet even now," the LORD says,
"return to me with all your heart—
with fasting, weeping, and mourning.
13 Tear your hearts,
not just your garments."
Return to the LORD your God,
for he is merciful and compassionate,
slow to anger and boundless in loyal love—often
relenting from calamitous punishment.
14 Who knows?
Perhaps he will be compassionate and grant a reprieve,
and leave blessing in his wake—
a meal offering and a drink offering for you
to offer to the LORD your God!

15 Blow the trumpet in Zion.
Announce a holy fast;
proclaim a sacred assembly.
16 Gather the people;
sanctify an assembly!
Gather the elders;
gather the children and the nursing infants.
Let the bridegroom come out from his bedroom
and the bride from her private quarters.
17 Let the priests, those who serve the LORD, weep
from the vestibule all the way back to the altar.
Let them say, "Have pity, O LORD, on your people;
please do not turn over your inheritance to be mocked,
to become a proverb among the nations.
Why should it be said among the peoples,
'Where is their God?'

REFLECT

Is it possible for God to change His mind and not send judgment? What attitude or posture would God's people need to take for God to change His plans?

LOVE TO GROW

NO OTHER

JOEL 2:12–27

The Book of Joel was written to the people of Judah who had not obeyed God's commands and faced His judgment. The book is filled with both judgment and the promise of restoration.

As we read through the Minor Prophets like Joel we can ask the question, what does this book, in its specific context, tell me about God's character?

Return to the LORD your God, for he is merciful and compassionate, slow to anger and boundless in loyal love—often relenting from calamitous punishment. Who knows? Perhaps he will be compassionate and grant a reprieve, and leave blessing in his wake (Joel 2:13–14).

God is merciful and compassionate, slow to anger and abounding in love. Even the Ninevites, a people who did not know God, learned that God is full of mercy and compassion when they experienced His mercies firsthand after their repentance (see Jonah 3:8–10).

Even after God destroyed the land of Israel, after He allowed the people to go hungry, and after He allowed foreign nations to bring them shame, He promised to restore them. All of it was meant to reveal God's sovereign and loving authority for His glory: His patience and compassion; His warnings to turn from their sins; His slowness to anger; His prophecies of the coming judgment; His display of wrath and power when they would not listen; and His restoration of His people. He allowed all this, accomplished all of this so His people and the nations around them would know that the Lord is God.

His character is on display in every page of Scripture and in every work He does in our lives. Let's love Him greatly by proclaiming His character so He may glorify Himself through us, no matter the circumstance. There is none more worthy.

THE LORD'S RESPONSE

18 Then the LORD became zealous for his land;
he had compassion on his people.
19 The LORD responded to his people,
"Look! I am about to restore your grain
as well as fresh wine and olive oil.
You will be fully satisfied.
I will never again make you an object of
mockery among the nations.
20 I will remove the one from the north far from you.
I will drive him out to a dry and desolate place.
Those in front will be driven eastward into the Dead Sea,
and those in back westward into the Mediterranean Sea.
His stench will rise up as a foul smell."
Indeed, the LORD has accomplished great things!

21 Do not fear, my land.
Rejoice and be glad,
because the LORD has accomplished great things!
22 Do not fear, wild animals.
For the pastures of the wilderness
are again green with grass.
Indeed, the trees bear their fruit;
the fig tree and the vine yield to their fullest.
23 Citizens of Zion, rejoice!
Be glad because of what the LORD your God has done!
For he has given to you the early rains as vindication.
He has sent to you the rains—
both the early and the late rains as formerly.
24 The threshing floors are full of grain;
the vats overflow with fresh wine and olive oil.
25 I will make up for the years
that the *'arbeh*-locust consumed your crops—
the *yeleq*-locust, the *hasil*-locust, and the *gazam*-locust—
my great army that I sent against you.
26 You will have plenty to eat,
and your hunger will be fully satisfied;
you will praise the name of the LORD your God,
who has acted wondrously in your behalf.
My people will never again be put to shame.
27 You will be convinced that I am in the midst of Israel.
I am the LORD your God; there is no other.
My people will never again be put to shame.

AN OUTPOURING OF THE SPIRIT

28 After all of this
I will pour out my Spirit on all kinds of people.
Your sons and daughters will prophesy.
Your elderly will have prophetic dreams;
your young men will see visions.
29 Even on male and female servants
I will pour out my Spirit in those days.
30 I will produce portents both in the sky and on the earth—
blood, fire, and columns of smoke.

31 The sunlight will be turned to darkness
and the moon to the color of blood,
before the day of the LORD comes—
that great and terrible day!
32 It will so happen that
everyone who calls on the name of
the LORD will be delivered.
For on Mount Zion and in Jerusalem
there will be those who survive,
just as the LORD has promised;
the remnant will be those whom the LORD will call.

THE LORD PLANS TO JUDGE THE NATIONS

3 For look! In those days and at that time
I will return the exiles to Judah and Jerusalem.
2 Then I will gather all the nations,
and bring them down to the Valley of Jehoshaphat.
I will enter into judgment against them there
concerning my people Israel who are my inheritance,
whom they scattered among the nations.
They partitioned my land,
3 and they cast lots for my people.
They traded a boy for a prostitute;
they sold a little girl for wine so they could drink.
4 Why are you doing these things to me, Tyre and Sidon?
Are you trying to get even with me, land of Philistia?
If you are, I will very quickly repay you
for what you have done!
5 For you took my silver and my gold
and brought my precious valuables to your own palaces.
6 You sold Judeans and Jerusalemites to the Greeks,
removing them far from their own country.
7 Look! I am rousing them from that
place to which you sold them.
I will repay you for what you have done!
8 I will sell your sons and daughters to the people of Judah.
They will sell them to the Sabeans, a nation far away.
Indeed, the LORD has spoken.

JUDGMENT IN THE VALLEY OF JEHOSHAPHAT

9 Proclaim this among the nations:
"Prepare for a holy war!
Call out the warriors!
Let all these fighting men approach and attack!
10 Beat your plowshares into swords,
and your pruning hooks into spears.
Let the weak say, 'I too am a warrior!'
11 Lend your aid and come,
all you surrounding nations,
and gather yourselves to that place."
Bring down, O LORD, your warriors!
12 "Let the nations be roused and let them go up
to the Valley of Jehoshaphat,
for there I will sit in judgment on all the surrounding nations.

13 Rush forth with the sickle, for the harvest is ripe!
Come, stomp the grapes, for the winepress is full!
The vats overflow.
Indeed, their evil is great!"

14 Crowds, great crowds are in the Valley of Decision,
for the day of the LORD is near in the Valley of Decision!
15 The sun and moon are darkened;
the stars withhold their brightness.
16 The LORD roars from Zion;
from Jerusalem his voice bellows out.
The heavens and the earth shake.
But the LORD is a refuge for his people;
he is a stronghold for the citizens of Israel.

THE LORD'S PRESENCE IN ZION

17 "You will be convinced that I the LORD am your God,
dwelling on Zion, my holy mountain.
Jerusalem will be holy—
conquering armies will no longer pass through it.
18 "On that day the mountains will drip with sweet wine,
and the hills will flow with milk.
All the dry stream beds of Judah will flow with water.
A spring will flow out from the temple of the LORD,
watering the Valley of Acacia Trees.
19 Egypt will be desolate
and Edom will be a desolate wilderness,
because of the violence they did to the people of Judah,
in whose land they shed innocent blood.
20 But Judah will reside securely forever,
and Jerusalem will be secure from
one generation to the next.
21 I will avenge their blood that I had
not previously acquitted.
It is the LORD who dwells in Zion!

CHALLENGE

God desires that His people believe He alone is their God and He alone is the one who provides and cares for them. Make a list of times in your life when you were convinced it was God alone who took care of you. Praise Him for each of these things and ask Him to open your eyes to see the ways He is always working.

Seek Good & Not Evil So You Can Live

MEMORY VERSE

Seek good and not evil so you can live! Then the Lord God of Heaven's Armies just might be with you, as you claim he is.

Amos 5:14

Amos

INTRODUCTION

The Righteous Judge

The Book of Amos is a message of justice, one that called the leaders of ancient Israel to repent and reform. God would not allow the people of Israel to continue to practice injustice. Although the message of Amos is heavy-handed, the prophet offers hope of the restoration to come through the Messiah.

In his prophetic message, Amos offered oracles of judgment, one for the nations (1:3—2:3), one for Judah (2:4–5), and one for Israel (2:6—3:15). He called for Israel to repent (4:1—5:17) and described the coming day of the Lord (5:18—6:14), which was inevitable for the people of Israel if they would not turn from their wickedness. Amos described the coming judgment in detail (7:1—9:10). Finally, he offered a message of hope: God would restore His people out of His covenant faithfulness (9:11–15).

Amos was a prophet who had a short ministry. His ministry took place during the time of Amaziah, the priest of Jeremiah at Bethel, around 755 B.C. Amos was from Tekoa and traveled to Bethel to deliver his prophetic message. Within thirty years, Israel was conquered by the Assyrians. Amos is the author of the book that bears his name. He likely compiled his oracles within a year of delivering them.

The Book of Amos displays God's concern for justice. Amos described justice as relational; it promotes good relations between people and between groups of people. We can love God greatly knowing that His acts of justice build our relationship with Him, calling us back to His heart.

Puerto Rico

OFFICIAL LANGUAGE
Spanish and English
POPULATION
2,728,000
UNREACHED POPULATION
1,100
PROFESSING CHRISTIANS
94.6%

Natalia's Home

Say a Prayer Today

Pray for the growth of the evangelical church in Puerto Rico. Pray the church will make an impact on the culture as a whole and affect the many social needs that exist.

HISTORY BIT

Christopher Colombus reached Puerto Rico in 1493, and in 1511 a Catholic diocese was established there. Catholicism has deep roots in Puerto Rico, but loyalty to Spanish rule weakened the position of the church in the following centuries.*

Source Information:
https://joshuaproject.net/countries/RQ
*David B. Barrett, World Christian Encyclopedia, Puerto Rico (New York, NY: Oxford University Press, 1982), 579.

NATALIA'S STORY

I'd never faced a challenge as big as this one. I had five years of teaching experience, but this new school was more difficult than I anticipated. Teaching art to sixth and seventh graders is not easy. Not only are the students enduring some of the most awkward, confusing years of their lives, but many of my students had special needs that neither the school nor I could meet.

While I was confident this school was where the Lord wanted me, I felt like I was throwing teacups of water onto a raging fire. I love teaching art, but what I was doing was not teaching. Each day I had to choose between instructing the few students who were able to learn and meeting the many needs of those who were not ready to take an art class.

Even though I knew this was where God wanted me, I didn't feel like He was with me. I prayed and asked for help. I used every teaching technique under the sun. I tried all the ideas my fellow teachers and friends offered. I grew desperate. I believed God was with me, but there were many times when it didn't feel that way.

When it felt like God was absent, He was working. He saw my frustration, my efforts, and my heart for the students, and He allowed me to transition into another job that was better than I could have hoped or dreamed. Though I had to struggle for a time, He was with me and faithful to provide.

4 WEEK READING PLAN

LOVE HIS WORD

	MONDAY	TUESDAY	WEDNESDAY	THURSDAY	FRIDAY
1	Joel 1	Joel 2:1–17	Joel 2:18–32	Joel 3:1–16	Joel 3:17–21
	SOAP Joel 1:19–20	SOAP Joel 2:13–14	SOAP Joel 2:26	SOAP Joel 3:1–2	SOAP Joel 3:17
2	Amos 1	Amos 2	Amos 3:1–8	Amos 3:9—4:3	Amos 4:4–13
	SOAP Amos 1:2	SOAP Amos 2:4	SOAP Amos 3:8	SOAP Amos 4:2	SOAP Amos 4:13
3	Amos 5:1–17	Amos 5:18–27	Amos 6	Amos 7:1–9	Amos 7:10–17
	SOAP Amos 5:14	SOAP Amos 5:18	SOAP Amos 6:8	SOAP Amos 7:4–6	SOAP Amos 7:17
4	Amos 8	Amos 9:1–10	Amos 9:11–15	Obadiah 1–14	Obadiah 15–21
	SOAP Amos 8:2	SOAP Amos 9:8–9	SOAP Amos 9:13–15	SOAP Obadiah 12	SOAP Obadiah 17

INTRODUCTION

1 The following is a record of what Amos prophesied. He was one of the herdsmen from Tekoa. These prophecies about Israel were revealed to him during the time of King Uzziah of Judah and King Jeroboam son of Joash of Israel, two years before the earthquake.

GOD WILL JUDGE THE SURROUNDING NATIONS

2 Amos said:
"The LORD comes roaring out of Zion;
from Jerusalem he comes bellowing!
The shepherds' pastures wilt;
the summit of Carmel withers."

3 This is what the LORD says:
"Because Damascus has committed three crimes—
make that four!—I will not revoke my
decree of judgment.
They ripped through Gilead like threshing
sledges with iron teeth.
4 So I will set Hazael's house on fire;
fire will consume Ben Hadad's fortresses.
5 I will break the bar on the gate of Damascus.
I will remove the ruler from Wicked Valley,
the one who holds the royal scepter from Beth Eden.
The people of Aram will be deported to Kir."
The LORD has spoken!

6 This is what the LORD says:
"Because Gaza has committed three crimes—
make that four!—I will not revoke my decree of judgment.
They deported a whole community
and sold them to Edom.
7 So I will set Gaza's city wall on fire;
fire will consume her fortresses.
8 I will remove the ruler from Ashdod,
the one who holds the royal scepter from Ashkelon.
I will strike Ekron with my hand;
the rest of the Philistines will also die."
The Sovereign LORD has spoken!

9 This is what the LORD says:
"Because Tyre has committed three crimes—
make that four—I will not revoke my decree of judgment.
They sold a whole community to Edom;
they failed to observe a treaty of brotherhood.
10 So I will set fire to Tyre's city wall;
fire will consume her fortresses."

11 This is what the LORD says:
"Because Edom has committed three crimes—
make that four—I will not revoke my decree of judgment.
He chased his brother with a sword;
he wiped out his allies.

CHALLENGE

How are the judgments of these nations different? How are they similar? How are the sins of the people of Israel like the sins of their neighbors? What does this tell us about what God expected from His covenant people?

In his anger he tore them apart without stopping to rest;
in his fury he relentlessly attacked them.
12 So I will set Teman on fire;
fire will consume Bozrah's fortresses."

13 This is what the LORD says:
"Because the Ammonites have committed three crimes—
make that four—I will not revoke my decree of judgment.
They ripped open Gilead's pregnant women
so they could expand their territory.
14 So I will set fire to Rabbah's city wall;
fire will consume her fortresses.
War cries will be heard on the day of battle;
a strong gale will blow on the day of the windstorm.
15 Ammon's king will be deported;
he and his officials will be carried off together."
The LORD has spoken

2 This is what the LORD says:
"Because Moab has committed three crimes—
make that four—I will not revoke
my decree of judgment.
They burned the bones of Edom's king into lime.
2 So I will set Moab on fire,
and it will consume Kerioth's fortresses.
Moab will perish in the heat of battle
amid war cries and the blaring of the ram's horn.
3 I will remove Moab's leader;
I will kill all Moab's officials with him."
The LORD has spoken!

4 This is what the LORD says:
"Because Judah has committed three
covenant transgressions—
make that four—I will not revoke my decree of judgment.
They rejected the LORD's law;
they did not obey his commands.
Their false gods,
to which their fathers were loyal,
led them astray.
5 So I will set Judah on fire,
and it will consume Jerusalem's fortresses."

GOD WILL JUDGE ISRAEL

6 This is what the LORD says:
"Because Israel has committed three
covenant transgressions—
make that four—I will not revoke my decree of judgment.
They sold the innocent for silver,
the needy for a pair of sandals.
7 They trample on the dirt-covered heads of the poor;
they push the destitute away.
A man and his father go to the same girl;
in this way they show disrespect for my moral purity.

REFLECT

Why was God punishing His chosen people?

8 They stretch out on clothing seized as collateral;
they do so right beside every altar!
They drink wine bought with
the fines they have levied;
they do so right in the temple of their God!
9 For Israel's sake I destroyed the Amorites.
They were as tall as cedars
and as strong as oaks,
but I destroyed the fruit on their branches
and their roots in the ground.
10 I brought you up from the land of Egypt;
I led you through the wilderness for forty years
so you could take the Amorites' land as your own.
11 I made some of your sons prophets
and some of your young men Nazirites.
Is this not true, you Israelites?"
The LORD is speaking.
12 "But you made the Nazirites drink wine;
you commanded the prophets, 'Do not prophesy!'
13 Look! I will press you down,
like a cart loaded down with grain presses down.
14 Fast runners will find no place to hide;
strong men will have no strength left;
warriors will not be able to save their lives.
15 Archers will not hold their ground;
fast runners will not save their lives,
nor will those who ride horses.
16 Bravehearted warriors will run away
naked in that day."
The LORD is speaking.

EVERY EFFECT HAS ITS CAUSE

3 Listen, you Israelites, to this message that the LORD is proclaiming against you! This message is for the entire clan I brought up from the land of Egypt:
2 "I have chosen you alone from all the clans of the earth.
Therefore I will punish you for all your sins."
3 Do two walk together without having met?
4 Does a lion roar in the woods if he
has not cornered his prey?
Does a young lion bellow from his den if
he has not caught something?
5 Does a bird swoop down into a trap on
the ground if there is no bait?
Does a trap spring up from the ground unless
it has surely caught something?
6 If an alarm sounds in a city, do people not fear?
If disaster overtakes a city, is the
LORD not responsible?
7 Certainly the Sovereign LORD does nothing without
first revealing his plan to his servants the prophets.
8 A lion has roared! Who is not afraid?
The Sovereign LORD has spoken. Who
can refuse to prophesy?

SAMARIA WILL FALL

9 Make this announcement in the fortresses of Ashdod
and in the fortresses in the land of Egypt.
Say this:
"Gather on the hills around Samaria!
Observe the many acts of violence
taking place within the city,
the oppressive deeds occurring in it."

10 "They do not know how to do what
is right," the LORD says.
"They store up the spoils of destructive
violence in their fortresses.
11 Therefore," says the Sovereign LORD, "an
enemy will encircle the land.
He will take away your power;
your fortresses will be looted."

12 This is what the LORD says:
"Just as a shepherd salvages from the lion's mouth
a couple of leg bones or a piece of an ear,
so the Israelites who live in Samaria will be salvaged.
They will be left with just a corner of a bed,
and a part of a couch.
13 Listen and warn the family of Jacob!"
The Sovereign LORD, the God who
commands armies, is speaking!

14 "Certainly when I punish Israel for their
covenant transgressions,
I will destroy Bethel's altars.
The horns of the altar will be cut off
and fall to the ground.
15 I will destroy both the winter and
summer houses.
The houses filled with ivory will be ruined,
the great houses will be swept away."
The LORD is speaking!

4 Listen to this message, you cows of Bashan
who live on Mount Samaria!
You oppress the poor;
you crush the needy.
You say to your husbands,
"Bring us more to drink!"
2 The Sovereign LORD confirms this oath
by his own holy character:
"Certainly the time is approaching
when you will be carried away in baskets,
every last one of you in fishermen's pots.
3 Each of you will go straight
through the gaps in the walls;
you will be thrown out toward Harmon."
The LORD is speaking.

ISRAEL HAS AN APPOINTMENT WITH GOD

4 "Go to Bethel and rebel!
At Gilgal rebel some more!
Bring your sacrifices in the morning,
your tithes on the third day!
5 Burn a thank offering of bread made with yeast!
Make a public display of your voluntary offerings!
For you love to do this, you Israelites."
The Sovereign LORD is speaking.

6 "But surely I gave you no food to eat in all your cities;
you lacked food everywhere you lived.
Still you did not come back to me."
The LORD is speaking

7 "I withheld rain from you three months before the harvest.
I gave rain to one city, but not to another.
One field would get rain, but the field
that received no rain dried up.
8 People from two or three cities staggered
into one city to get water,
but remained thirsty.
Still you did not come back to me."
The LORD is speaking

9 "I destroyed your crops with blight and disease.
Locusts kept devouring your orchards,
vineyards, fig trees, and olive trees.
Still you did not come back to me."
The LORD is speaking

10 "I sent against you a plague like one of the Egyptian plagues.
I killed your young men with the sword,
along with the horses you had captured.
I made the stench from the corpses rise up into your nostrils.
Still you did not come back to me."
The LORD is speaking

11 "I overthrew some of you the way God
overthrew Sodom and Gomorrah.
You were like a burning stick snatched from the flames.
Still you did not come back to me."
The LORD is speaking

12 "Therefore this is what I will do to you, Israel.
Because I will do this to you,
prepare to meet your God, Israel!"

13 For here he is!
He formed the mountains and created the wind.
He reveals his plans to men.
He turns the dawn into darkness
and marches on the heights of the earth.
The LORD God of Heaven's Armies is his name!

DEATH IS IMMINENT

5 Listen to this funeral song I am ready to sing about you, family of Israel:
2 "The virgin Israel has fallen down and will not get up again.
She is abandoned on her own land
with no one to help her get up."

3 The Sovereign LORD says this:
"The city that marches out with a thousand
soldiers will have only a hundred left;
the town that marches out with a hundred soldiers
will have only ten left for the family of Israel."

4 The LORD says this to the family of Israel:
"Seek me so you can live!
5 Do not seek Bethel.
Do not visit Gilgal.
Do not journey down to Beer Sheba.
For the people of Gilgal will certainly be carried into exile,
and Bethel will become a place where disaster abounds."

6 Seek the LORD so you can live!
Otherwise he will break out like fire
against Joseph's family;
the fire will consume
and no one will be able to quench it and save Bethel.
7 The Israelites turn justice into bitterness;
they throw what is fair and right to the ground.

8 But there is one who made the
constellations Pleiades and Orion;
he can turn the darkness into morning
and daylight into night.
He summons the water of the seas
and pours it out on the earth's surface.
The LORD is his name!
9 He flashes destruction down upon the strong
so that destruction overwhelms the fortified places.

10 The Israelites hate anyone who arbitrates at the city gate;
they despise anyone who speaks honestly.
11 Therefore, because you make the poor
pay taxes on their crops
and exact a grain tax from them,
you will not live in the houses you
built with chiseled stone,
nor will you drink the wine from the
fine vineyards you planted.
12 Certainly I am aware of your many rebellious acts
and your numerous sins.
You torment the innocent, you take bribes,
and you deny justice to the needy at the city gate.
13 For this reason whoever is smart keeps quiet in such a time,
for it is an evil time.

14 Seek good and not evil so you can live!
Then the LORD God of Heaven's Armies
just might be with you,
as you claim he is.
15 Hate what is wrong, love what is right.
Promote justice at the city gate.
Maybe the LORD God of Heaven's Armies will have
mercy on those who are left from Joseph.

16 Because of Israel's sins this is what the Lord, the LORD God
of Heaven's Armies, says:
"In all the squares there will be wailing,
in all the streets they will mourn the dead.
They will tell the field workers to lament
and the professional mourners to wail.
17 In all the vineyards there will be wailing,
for I will pass through your midst," says the LORD.

REFLECT

Why would God change His mind? Would the repentance of the people have kept God from bringing judgment on them?

THE LORD DEMANDS JUSTICE

18 Woe to those who wish for the day of the LORD!
Why do you want the LORD's
day of judgment to come?
It will bring darkness, not light.
19 Disaster will be inescapable,
as if a man ran from a lion only to meet a bear,
then escaped into a house,
leaned his hand against the wall,
and was bitten by a poisonous snake.
20 Don't you realize the LORD's day of judgment
will bring darkness, not light—
gloomy blackness, not bright light?

21 "I absolutely despise your festivals!
I get no pleasure from your religious assemblies.
22 Even if you offer me burnt and grain
offerings, I will not be satisfied;
I will not look with favor on your peace
offerings of fattened calves.
23 Take away from me your noisy songs;
I don't want to hear the music of your
stringed instruments.
24 Justice must flow like torrents of water,
righteous actions like a stream that
never dries up.

25 You did not bring me sacrifices and grain
offerings during the forty years you spent
in the wilderness, family of Israel.
26 You will pick up your images of Sikkuth, your king,
and Kiyyun, your star god, which
you made for yourselves,
27 and I will drive you into exile beyond
Damascus," says the LORD.
He is called the God of Heaven's Armies.

THE PARTY IS OVER FOR THE RICH

6 Woe to those who live in ease in Zion,
to those who feel secure on Mount Samaria.
They think of themselves as the elite class of the best nation.
The family of Israel looks to them for leadership.
2 They say to the people:
"Journey over to Calneh and look at it;
then go from there to Hamath-Rabbah;
then go down to Gath of the Philistines.
Are they superior to our two kingdoms?
Is their territory larger than yours?"
3 You refuse to believe a day of disaster will come,
but you establish a reign of violence.
4 They lie around on beds decorated with ivory,
and sprawl out on their couches.
They eat lambs from the flock,
and calves from the middle of the pen.
5 They sing to the tune of stringed instruments;
like David they invent musical instruments.
6 They drink wine from sacrificial bowls,
and pour the very best oils on themselves.
Yet they are not concerned over the ruin of Joseph.
7 Therefore they will now be the first to go into exile,
and the religious banquets where they
sprawl on couches will end.

8 The Sovereign LORD confirms this oath by his very own life.
The LORD God of Heaven's Armies is speaking:
"I despise Jacob's arrogance;
I hate their fortresses.
I will hand over to their enemies the city
of Samaria and everything in it."

9 If ten men are left in one house, they too will die. 10 When
their close relatives, the ones who will burn the corpses, pick
up their bodies to remove the bones from the house, they will
say to anyone who is in the inner rooms of the house, "Is anyone else with you?" He will respond, "No one." Then he will say,
"Hush! Don't invoke the LORD's name!"

11 Indeed, look! The LORD is giving the command.
He will smash the large house to bits
and the small house into little pieces.
12 Can horses run on rocky cliffs?
Can one plow the sea with oxen?
Yet you have turned justice into a poisonous plant,
and the fruit of righteous actions into a bitter plant.
13 You are happy because you conquered Lo Debar.
You say, "Did we not conquer Karnaim by our own power?"
14 "Look! I am about to bring a nation
against you, family of Israel,"
the LORD, the God who commands armies, is speaking.
"They will oppress you all the way from Lebo
Hamath to the stream of the rift valley."

REFLECT

Was God righteous in His judgment against Israel? How does His righteousness allow Him to bring judgment on Israel?

SYMBOLIC VISIONS OF JUDGMENT

7 The Sovereign LORD showed me this: I saw him making
locusts just as the crops planted late were beginning to
sprout. (The crops planted late sprout after the royal harvest.)
2 When they had completely consumed the earth's vegetation,
I said,

"Sovereign LORD, forgive Israel!
How can Jacob survive?
He is too weak!"

3 The LORD decided not to do this. "It will not happen," the
LORD said.
4 The Sovereign LORD showed me this: I saw the Sovereign
LORD summoning a shower of fire. It consumed the great deep
and devoured the fields. 5 I said,

"Sovereign LORD, stop!
How can Jacob survive?
He is too weak!"

6 The LORD decided not to do this. The Sovereign LORD said,
"This will not happen either."
7 He showed me this: I saw the Lord standing by a tin wall
holding tin in his hand. 8 The LORD said to me, "What do you
see, Amos?" I said, "Tin." The Lord then said,

"Look, I am about to place tin among my people Israel.
I will no longer overlook their sin.
9 Isaac's centers of worship will become desolate;
Israel's holy places will be in ruins.
I will attack Jeroboam's dynasty with the sword."

AMOS CONFRONTS A PRIEST

10 Amaziah the priest of Bethel sent this message to King Jeroboam of Israel: "Amos is conspiring against you in the very heart
of the kingdom of Israel! The land cannot endure all his prophecies. 11 As a matter of fact, Amos is saying this: 'Jeroboam will
die by the sword and Israel will certainly be carried into exile
away from its land.'"
12 Amaziah then said to Amos, "Leave, you visionary! Run away
to the land of Judah. Earn your living and prophesy there! 13 Don't
prophesy at Bethel any longer, for a royal temple and palace are
here."
14 Amos replied to Amaziah, "I was not a prophet by profession.
No, I was a herdsman who also took care of sycamore fig trees.
15 Then the LORD took me from tending flocks and gave me this
commission, 'Go! Prophesy to my people Israel.' 16 So now listen
to the LORD's message! You say, 'Don't prophesy against Israel!
Don't preach against the family of Isaac!'
17 "Therefore this is what the LORD says:

'Your wife will become a prostitute in the streets
and your sons and daughters will die violently.
Your land will be given to others
and you will die in a foreign land.
Israel will certainly be carried into
exile away from its land.'"

REFLECT

Have you ever had your calling questioned like Amos did? How can you be confident in what God has called you to do when you face opposition or discouragement?

MORE VISIONS AND MESSAGES OF JUDGMENT

8 The Sovereign LORD showed me this: I saw a basket of summer fruit. 2 He said, "What do you see, Amos?" I replied, "A
basket of summer fruit." Then the LORD said to me, "The end has
come for my people Israel! I will no longer overlook their sins.
3 The women singing in the temple will wail in that day."
The Sovereign LORD is speaking.
"There will be many corpses littered everywhere! Be quiet!"
4 Listen to this, you who trample the needy
and do away with the destitute in the land.

5 You say,
"When will the new moon festival be
over, so we can sell grain?
When will the Sabbath end, so we can
open up the grain bins?
We're eager to sell less for a higher price,
and to cheat the buyer with rigged scales!
6 We're eager to trade silver for the poor,
a pair of sandals for the needy.
We want to mix in some chaff with the grain!"

7 The LORD confirms this oath by the arrogance of Jacob:
"I swear I will never forget all you have done!
8 Because of this the earth will quake,
and all who live in it will mourn.
The whole earth will rise like the Nile River,
it will surge upward and then grow
calm, like the Nile in Egypt.
9 In that day," says the Sovereign LORD, "I
will make the sun set at noon
and make the earth dark in the middle of the day.
10 I will turn your festivals into funerals
and all your songs into funeral dirges.
I will make everyone wear funeral clothes
and cause every head to be shaved bald.
I will make you mourn as if you had lost your only son;
when it ends it will indeed have been a bitter day.
11 Be certain of this, the time is coming,"
says the Sovereign LORD,
"when I will send a famine through the land—
not a shortage of food or water
but an end to divine revelation.
12 People will stagger from sea to sea,
and from the north around to the east.
They will wander about looking for a message from the LORD,
but they will not find any.
13 In that day your beautiful young women and
your young men will faint from thirst.
14 These are the ones who now take oaths in the
name of the sinful idol goddess of Samaria.
They vow, 'As surely as your god lives, O Dan,' or, 'As
surely as your beloved one lives, O Beer Sheba!'
But they will fall down and not get up again."

REFLECT

How does Amos 8:2 show the patience of God?

9 I saw the Lord standing by the altar and he said,
"Strike the tops of the support pillars,
so the thresholds shake!
Knock them down on the heads of all the people,
and I will kill the survivors with the sword.
No one will be able to run away;
no one will be able to escape.
2 Even if they could dig down into the netherworld,
my hand would pull them up from there.
Even if they could climb up to heaven,
I would drag them down from there.
3 Even if they were to hide on the top of Mount Carmel,
I would hunt them down and take them from there.
Even if they tried to hide from me
at the bottom of the sea,
from there I would command the Sea Serpent to bite them.
4 Even when their enemies drive them into captivity,
from there I will command the sword to kill them.
I will not let them out of my sight;
they will experience disaster, not prosperity."

5 The Sovereign LORD of Heaven's Armies will do this.
He touches the earth and it dissolves;
all who live on it mourn.
The whole earth rises like the Nile River,
and then grows calm like the Nile in Egypt.
6 He builds the upper rooms of his palace in heaven
and sets its foundation supports on the earth.
He summons the water of the sea
and pours it out on the earth's surface.
The LORD is his name.
7 "You Israelites are just like the Ethiopians
in my sight," says the LORD.
"Certainly I brought Israel up from the land of Egypt,
but I also brought the Philistines from
Caphtor and the Arameans from Kir.
8 Look, the Sovereign LORD is watching the sinful nation,
and I will destroy it from the face of the earth.
But I will not completely destroy the
family of Jacob," says the LORD.
9 "For look, I am giving a command
and I will shake the family of Israel
together with all the nations.
It will resemble a sieve being shaken,
when not even a pebble falls to the ground.
10 All the sinners among my people will die by the sword—
the ones who say, 'Disaster will not come
near, it will not confront us.'

THE RESTORATION OF THE DAVIDIC DYNASTY

11 "In that day I will rebuild the collapsing hut of David.
I will seal its gaps,
repair its ruins,
and restore it to what it was like in days gone by.

12 As a result they will conquer those left in Edom
and all the nations subject to my rule."
The LORD, who is about to do this, is speaking.
13 "Be sure of this, the time is coming," says the LORD,
"when the plowman will catch up to the reaper,
and the one who stomps the grapes
will overtake the planter.
Juice will run down the slopes;
it will flow down all the hillsides.
14 I will bring back my people, Israel;
they will rebuild the cities lying in rubble and settle down.
They will plant vineyards and drink the wine they produce;
they will grow orchards and eat the fruit they produce.
15 I will plant them on their land,
and they will never again be uprooted
from the land I have given them,"
says the LORD your God.

LOVE TO GROW

OVERWHELMING MERCY

AMOS 9:11–15

When the Book of Amos opens, Amos, a shepherd from a small town outside of Jerusalem, addressed the northern kingdom of Israel. He had the difficult task of pronouncing God's coming judgment on his neighbors. Israel couldn't care less.

The nobles of Israel had become complacent in their prosperity, sleeping on "beds decorated with ivory" and drinking "wine from sacrificial bowls" (Amos 6:4,6). Meanwhile, they took advantage of and mistreated those around them for their own profit. They had turned their face away from God and broken their covenant with Him. As a prophet, Amos's job was to challenge Israel. God warned them through famine, illness, and other disasters (Amos 4:6–11), but they did not listen. "Seek the LORD so you can live!" Amos implored God's people (Amos 5:6).

Due to their consistent and unashamed disobedience, the time came when a foreign nation overtook them. God's people were removed from the promised land and taken into exile by their enemy. God never wanted this for His people, but He disciplines those He loves. Chapter after chapter we read of wrath, anger, weeping, death, and famine. As the book is about to end, our hearts grieve the destruction as the consequences of Israel's unrepentant sin are all too evident.

Then we reach Amos 9:11–15. Like refreshing water to our parched souls, we find evidence of God's heart of mercy in the midst of Israel's impending destruction: Israel would be restored. God promised to establish the permanent rule of one from David's line (see 2 Sam 7:12–16). God promised that He would restore the people of Israel from their captivity and return them to their land (see Deut 30:1–4).

The Gospel of Matthew reveals Jesus Christ as the One who would come from the line of David and the Savior of the world: "This is the record of the genealogy of Jesus Christ, the son of David, the son of Abraham" (Matt 1:1).

God is faithful, and His judgment on Israel was not final. He did not forsake His people. As God promised in Amos, One came from the line of David who would change everything.

Israel deserved punishment, yet God offered salvation.
Israel deserved shame, yet God offered restoration.

In the depths of our darkest moments, in the pit of our sin, God offers us hope like He did for Israel. We serve a God of overwhelming mercy, one who desperately wants to be in a relationship with us. Our response need only be this: "Seek the LORD so you can live!" (Amos 5:6).

BUT ON
MOUNT
ZION
THERE WILL BE A
REMNANT OF THOSE
WHO ESCAPE,
AND IT WILL BE A
HOLY PLACE
ONCE AGAIN

MEMORY VERSE

But on Mount Zion there will be a remnant of those who escape, and it will be a holy place once again. The descendants of Jacob will conquer those who had conquered them.

Obadiah 17

Obadiah

INTRODUCTION

God Defends His People

The Book of Obadiah is unique because Obadiah is one of three minor prophets who addressed a nation other than Israel or Judah. The others are Nahum and Jonah, who both addressed Nineveh. The prophecies contained in this short book concern the nation of Edom, the descendants of Esau, the brother of Jacob. Edom treated the people of Israel with contempt, gloating over their problems and raiding their homes instead of aiding them as good relatives should. The Lord promised to defend His people, the nation of Israel, from the wickedness done to them by the people of Edom.

Though short, Obadiah's prophetic message had a poignant purpose: to comfort and encourage the people of Judah that God had not abandoned them. God would rise up and defend His people. The long-standing conflict between Israel and Edom would end as God destroyed the enemies of Israel.

Obadiah is difficult to date. Some scholars date it to the mid-ninth century B.C., while others place it in the sixth century B.C., immediately following the Babylonian destruction of Jerusalem. Almost nothing is known about the personal life of the prophet Obadiah, but there is little dispute that he is the author of this message.

Obadiah's overarching message is that God defends His people. No matter the circumstance or the oppressor, God steps in to protect His faithful ones. We can love God greatly knowing that He defends us. Even amid governments and societies who do not acknowledge His sovereignty, God is sovereign. He desires that we show mercy and favor to our neighbors in their times of distress. Likewise, He promises to defend us when we are mistreated.

India

OFFICIAL LANGUAGE
Hindi and English
POPULATION
1,360,307,000
UNREACHED POPULATION
1,299,916,000
PROFESSING CHRISTIANS
2.1%

Sunu's Home

Say a Prayer Today

Pray for the church in India, that it would continue to grow and reach the needs of the huge population in India. Pray for the believers in India to show the love of Christ to those around them.

HISTORY BIT

Tradition holds that in A.D. 52, the Apostle Thomas traveled to India to share the gospel of Jesus Christ.* By A.D. 198, the earliest Christian communities existed in India.**

Source Information:
https://joshuaproject.net/countries/IN
*David B. Barrett, World Christian Encyclopedia, India (New York, NY: Oxford University Press, 1982), 373.
**John Bowden, A Chronology of World Christianity (New York, NY: Continuum, 2007), 21, 256.

SUNU'S STORY

Last year, things were a mess.

We had to shut down our office for an entire month. Then, my husband had an operation that left me at home caring for him full-time for two months. Immediately following this, my state, Kerala, in southwest India, was hit with the worst flood in a century. All business in Kerala stopped. Since one of my biggest clients serves the tourism industry, a large portion of my income disappeared.

I was overwhelmed by panic. I didn't know how to go on. How I would pay my bills or hospital expenses? We resorted to borrowing money from my parents and in-laws, which was humbling. I never imagined I'd ever have to borrow money from my parents when I was almost forty!

I felt like I'd hit rock bottom.

Fortunately, God's Word has a way of opening our eyes to see His goodness, especially when we're at rock bottom. Time after time, God's Word reminded me that God is my defender and He never stops working. Through the trial, I came to learn to depend on Him moment by moment, taking one day at a time.

I began to trust that everything was happening for a reason. Instead of getting discouraged and afraid, I began to embrace what He was doing and trust Him to provide. Things started to change. My business grew and new projects came in every month. Trusting God and feeling the freedom to be present made all the difference. Instead of worrying about the future, I can look to Him and believe that He always has a plan and a way to provide.

4 WEEK READING PLAN

LOVE HIS WORD

MONDAY	TUESDAY	WEDNESDAY	THURSDAY	FRIDAY
Joel 1	Joel 2:1-17	Joel 2:18-32	Joel 3:1-16	Joel 3:17-21
SOAP Joel 1:19-20	SOAP Joel 2:13-14	SOAP Joel 2:26	SOAP Joel 3:1-2	SOAP Joel 3:17
Amos 1	Amos 2	Amos 3:1-8	Amos 3:9—4:3	Amos 4:4-13
SOAP Amos 1:2	SOAP Amos 2:4	SOAP Amos 3:8	SOAP Amos 4:2	SOAP Amos 4:13
Amos 5:1-17	Amos 5:18-27	Amos 6	Amos 7:1-9	Amos 7:10-17
SOAP Amos 5:14	SOAP Amos 5:18	SOAP Amos 6:8	SOAP Amos 7:4-6	SOAP Amos 7:17
Amos 8	Amos 9:1-10	Amos 9:11-15	Obadiah 1-14	Obadiah 15-21
SOAP Amos 8:2	SOAP Amos 9:8-9	SOAP Amos 9:13-15	SOAP Obadiah 12	SOAP Obadiah 17

GOD'S JUDGMENT ON EDOM

1 The vision that Obadiah saw.
The Sovereign LORD says this concerning Edom:

EDOM'S APPROACHING DESTRUCTION

We have heard a report from the LORD.
An envoy was sent among the nations, saying,
"Arise! Let us make war against Edom!"
2 The LORD says, "Look! I will make you a weak nation;
you will be greatly despised!
3 Your presumptuous heart has deceived you—
you who reside in the safety of the rocky cliffs,
whose home is high in the mountains.
You think to yourself,
'No one can bring me down to the ground!'
4 Even if you were to soar high like an eagle,
even if you were to make your nest among the stars,
I can bring you down even from there!" says the LORD.

5 "If thieves came to rob you during the night,
they would steal only as much as they wanted.
If grape pickers came to harvest your vineyards,
they would leave some behind for the poor.
But you will be totally destroyed!
6 How the people of Esau will be thoroughly plundered!
Their hidden valuables will be ransacked!
7 All your allies will force you from your homeland!
Your treaty partners will deceive you and overpower you.
Your trusted friends will set an ambush for you
that will take you by surprise!

8 At that time," the LORD says,
"I will destroy the wise sages of Edom,
the advisers from Esau's mountain.
9 Your warriors will be shattered, O Teman,
so that everyone will be destroyed from Esau's mountain!

EDOM'S TREACHERY AGAINST JUDAH

10 "Because you violently slaughtered your
relatives, the people of Jacob,
shame will cover you, and you will be destroyed forever.
11 You stood aloof while strangers took his army captive,
and foreigners advanced to his gates.
When they cast lots over Jerusalem,
you behaved as though you were in league with them.
12 You should not have gloated when your
relatives suffered calamity.
You should not have rejoiced over the people
of Judah when they were destroyed.
You should not have boasted when they suffered adversity.
13 You should not have entered the city of my
people when they experienced distress.
You should not have joined in gloating over their
misfortune when they suffered distress.

You should not have looted their wealth
when they endured distress.
14 You should not have stood at the fork in the
road to slaughter those trying to escape.
You should not have captured their refugees
when they suffered adversity.

CHALLENGE

How does God preserve a remnant for His people throughout Israel's history? What does this tell you about the heart of God to restore and redeem? How have you seen God's redemptive work in your life? Praise Him today for His faithfulness and loyal love.

THE COMING DAY OF THE LORD

15 "For the day of the LORD is approaching for all the nations!
Just as you have done, so it will be done to you.
You will get exactly what your deeds deserve.
16 For just as you have drunk on my holy mountain,
so all the nations will drink continually.
They will drink, and they will gulp down;
they will be as though they had never been.
17 But on Mount Zion there will be a
remnant of those who escape,
and it will be a holy place once again.
The descendants of Jacob will conquer
those who had conquered them.
18 The descendants of Jacob will be a fire,
and the descendants of Joseph a flame.
The descendants of Esau will be like stubble.
They will burn them up and devour them.
There will not be a single survivor of
the descendants of Esau!"
Indeed, the LORD has spoken it.
19 The people of the Negev will take
possession of Esau's mountain,
and the people of the foothills will take
possession of the land of the Philistines.
They will also take possession of the territory
of Ephraim and the territory of Samaria,
and the people of Benjamin will take possession of Gilead.
20 The exiles of this fortress of the people of Israel
will take possession of what belongs to
the people of Canaan, as far as Zarephath,
and the exiles of Jerusalem who are in Sepharad
will take possession of the towns of the Negev.
21 Those who have been delivered will go up on Mount Zion
in order to rule over Esau's mountain.
Then the LORD will reign as King!

LOVE TO GROW

YOUR LOVE DEFENDS ME

OBADIAH

Passages like these teach us a lot about God's character. They show us whose side God is on, and they tell us what God cares about. When I read Obadiah, I see God takes a clear side—He fights for the oppressed, the downtrodden, the bullied, and the excluded. He encourages those who are down and out. He provides for those who have had the shirts taken off their backs. He puts the lonely in families, and He defends those who are laughed at and the wrongfully accused.

God takes the mistreatment of His children seriously. Obadiah shows us how He takes decisive action toward those who have mistreated His kids. He communicates this clearly, and He never fails to follow through on His promises.

When I read God's words in the passages of this book, I believe Him—that evil people won't get away with their schemes forever. God is watching and will come to make things right. God is a God who will do something about those who gloat, scoff, and take advantage of others.

God's love defends us.

God's plan for the world is that the brokenhearted have justice and peace. Even when it doesn't seem like it, God's Word promises that goodness has and will triumph over evil. God pays close attention to the suffering of the oppressed, and His heart is tender towards them. God has something special for those the world has overlooked and mistreated.

Bringing God's kingdom to earth means caring about the things God cares about. This makes me want to do everything I can to partner with the King. I can defend those God defends, and I can fight the injustices He fights because He fought for me and because His love defends me.

Of all God's titles, "Defender" is the most precious to me. It goes deep into my heart and soothes the wounded places in my life. In my most fearful, loneliest, angriest moments, I say this over and over to myself:

Your love defends me. Your love defends me. Your love defends me.

Obadiah encourages us to take heart and praise God for the hope He gives us as our great Defender. He became someone mistreated, oppressed, lonely, and falsely accused in order to bring justice and peace to His children.

God's love did defend, does defend, and will defend us. Hallelujah!

You are a gracious AND compassionate GOD, slow to anger and ABOUNDING in mercy

MEMORY VERSE

". . . because I knew that you are a gracious and compassionate God, slow to anger and abounding in mercy, and one who relents concerning threatened judgment."

Jonah 4:2

Jonah

INTRODUCTION

Mercy

While it may be a familiar story, the Book of Jonah presents an important truth: God is gracious and compassionate, even to the wicked. In this book of prophecy, God revealed His mercy to Jonah for the Ninevites, yet Jonah was unwilling to offer mercy to his enemies. While God went to great lengths to turn the hearts of the people of Nineveh toward Him, He also went to great lengths to bring Jonah's heart back to Him.

Jonah is unique in that it combines narrative, poetry, and prophecy. Jonah was a prophet, but the prophetic message is a minor detail. The author highlighted God's sovereignty, compassion, and mercy through his use of literary devices. Jonah's poem in chapter 2 has strong references to many of the psalms, writings with which Jonah would have been familiar as a prophet of the Lord.

While no author is named, tradition holds that Jonah wrote, or at least dictated this book. Though the book ends without resolution, the inclusion of the story in Scripture offers the possibility that Jonah eventually came to see the error of his ways. While the date of the Book of Jonah is uncertain, the events took place before the destruction of Nineveh in 612 B.C. and the captivity of Israel by Assyria in 722 B.C. Jonah lived in the eighth century B.C., and it is believed his journey to Nineveh occurred around 770 B.C.

The Book of Jonah displays God's freedom to judge and restore anyone He wishes. It also shows a unique characteristic of God: Because of His compassion, He is sometimes willing to change His course when people repent and turn from their wickedness. Ultimately, God's mercy is what we should celebrate in the Book of Jonah. The Lord had every reason to destroy Nineveh, yet He relented because of the people's repentance. We can love Him greatly, confident that when we turn to Him, He will respond.

Scotland (United Kingdom)

OFFICIAL LANGUAGES
English and Scottish (Gaelic)
POPULATION
5,254,800* (67,401,000 total UK population)**
UNREACHED POPULATION
5,092,000 (total unreached in UK)
PROFESSING CHRISTIANS
57.0% (of total UK population)

Fiona's Home

Say a Prayer Today

Pray for Fiona as she continues to remember God's goodness. Pray also for the people of Scotland that they would remember God's goodness and faithfulness to them.

HISTORY BIT

Christianity has a long history in Scotland, introduced during the Roman occupation of Britain in the first through fifth centuries. The church in Scotland became independent from the church in England during the middle ages.***

Source Information:
*http://worldpopulationreview.com/countries/scotland-population/
**https://joshuaproject.net/countries/UK
***David B. Barrett, *World Christian Encyclopedia*, Scotland (New York, NY: Oxford University Press, 1982), 701.

LOVE YOUR NEIGHBOR

Her Journey

FIONA'S STORY

Jonah does not come across as a very nice character, does he? He believes in God and preaches God's message, but with an angry and resentful heart.

I identify with Jonah. I have, through my own self-righteousness and self-justification, been angry and disappointed with God.

Growing up in Scotland, I gave my life to Christ as a teenager, and I followed and served God with my whole heart. Through the years, as God did not do things according to my plan, as hurts and difficult circumstances came into my life, my heart became resentful and bitter. I questioned the goodness of God. I was disappointed in God, feeling as if He had let me down.

Just as God did not leave Jonah in his low points, neither did God leave me. He allowed the most difficult circumstance of my life, and it broke me. Like Jonah in the belly of the fish, I cried out to God. I admitted my powerlessness and gradually came to believe that only God could rescue me. It was an act of surrender.

I had to learn to forgive others and let go of the bitterness and resentment and instead accept God's grace. In doing so, He has redeemed my life.

I became confident that God is indeed merciful, slow to anger, gracious, and compassionate. As God extended mercy to the Ninevites, may He extend mercy to our wayward and disobedient nation. May you also know His redeeming mercy and grace and His abounding love in the midst of your own difficult circumstance.

4 WEEK READING PLAN

LOVE HIS WORD

	MONDAY	TUESDAY	WEDNESDAY	THURSDAY	FRIDAY
1	Jonah 1:1-3	Jonah 1:4-6	Jonah 1:7-9	Jonah 1:10-13	Jonah 1:14-17
	SOAP Psalm 139:7-10	SOAP Psalm 135:5-6	SOAP Jonah 1:9	SOAP 1 John 2:4-6	SOAP 1 John 1:9
2	Jonah 2:1-2	Jonah 2:3-4	Jonah 2:5-7	Jonah 2:8-9	Jonah 2:10
	SOAP 1 John 5:14	SOAP Psalm 31:22	SOAP Jonah 2:6	SOAP Psalm 50:23	SOAP Jonah 2:10
3	Jonah 3:1-3	Jonah 3:4-6	Jonah 3:7-8	Jonah 3:9	Jonah 3:10
	SOAP Lamentations 3:21-23	SOAP 2 Peter 3:9	SOAP Proverbs 28:13	SOAP Isaiah 55:8-9	SOAP Jonah 3:10
4	Jonah 4:1-3	Jonah 4:4	Jonah 4:5-6	Jonah 4:7-8	Jonah 4:9-11
	SOAP Jonah 4:2	SOAP Micah 6:8	SOAP Psalm 103:10	SOAP Psalm 116:5	SOAP Jonah 4:10-11

JONAH TRIES TO RUN FROM THE LORD

1 The LORD's message came to Jonah son of Amittai, 2 "Go immediately to Nineveh, that large capital city, and announce judgment against its people because their wickedness has come to
my attention." 3 Instead, Jonah immediately headed off to Tarshish to escape from the commission of the LORD. He traveled
to Joppa and found a merchant ship heading to Tarshish. So he
paid the fare and went aboard it to go with them to Tarshish,
far away from the LORD. 4 But the LORD hurled a powerful wind
on the sea. Such a violent tempest arose on the sea that the
ship threatened to break up! 5 The sailors were so afraid that
each cried out to his own god and they flung the ship's cargo
overboard to make the ship lighter. Jonah, meanwhile, had gone
down into the hold below deck, had lain down, and was sound
asleep. 6 The ship's captain approached him and said, "What are
you doing asleep? Get up! Cry out to your god! Perhaps your god
might take notice of us so that we might not die!" 7 The sailors
said to one another, "Come on, let's cast lots to find out whose
fault it is that this disaster has overtaken us." So they cast lots,
and Jonah was singled out. 8 They said to him, "Tell us, whose
fault is it that this disaster has overtaken us? What's your occupation? Where do you come from? What's your country? And
who are your people?" 9 He said to them, "I am a Hebrew, and I
worship the LORD, the God of heaven, who made the sea and the
dry land." 10 Hearing this, the men became even more afraid and
said to him, "What have you done?" (The men said this because
they knew that he was trying to escape from the LORD, because
he had previously told them.) 11 Because the storm was growing
worse and worse, they said to him, "What should we do to you so
that the sea will calm down for us?" 12 He said to them, "Pick me
up and throw me into the sea so that the sea will calm down for
you, because I know it's my fault you are in this severe storm."
13 Instead, they tried to row back to land, but they were not able
to do so because the storm kept growing worse and worse. 14 So
they cried out to the LORD, "Oh, please, LORD, don't let us die
on account of this man! Don't hold us guilty of shedding innocent blood. After all, you, LORD, have done just as you pleased."
15 So they picked Jonah up and threw him into the sea, and the
sea stopped raging. 16 The men feared the LORD greatly and earnestly vowed to offer lavish sacrifices to the LORD.

REFLECT

What is your usual response when God asks you to do something that makes you uncomfortable? Have you ever run from God like Jonah did?

JONAH PRAYS

17 The LORD sent a huge fish to swallow Jonah, and Jonah was in
the stomach of the fish three days and three nights.
2 Jonah prayed to the LORD his God from the stomach of the
fish 2 and said,

"I called out to the LORD from my distress,
and he answered me;
from the belly of Sheol I cried out for help,
and you heard my prayer.
3 You threw me into the deep waters,
into the middle of the sea;
the ocean current engulfed me;
all the mighty waves you sent swept over me.

LOVE TO GROW

HE HEARS

JONAH 2:1–2

Make no mistake: Jonah sinned and ran away from God. He allowed hatred and fear toward a specific group of people to poison his heart. He chose to disobey God rather than be used by Him.

But even in his defiance, Jonah couldn't sail far enough away.

God came to him. He came as a storm to wake Jonah from his slumber, both literally and figuratively. Unfortunately, sometimes it takes a storm to get our attention. Often, it's a storm so big we are awakened to our sin and find we have come to the end of ourselves. Our eyes are opened to our desperate need for a savior, for someone to rescue us from our impending destruction.

That's where we find Jonah. He came to the end of his rope. His journey of defiance abruptly ended in the middle of the ocean, in the belly of a great fish.

It was there that Jonah cried out to God.

God used what Jonah thought would kill him to save him. Jonah thought being thrown into the ocean in a terrible storm would be the end of him, the ultimate consequence for his sin of running from God.

God chose to extend mercy, something Jonah was not willing to give to the people of Nineveh. Experiencing God's mercy for himself brought Jonah to his knees before God. There in the belly of the great fish, Jonah turned back to God. In gratitude, he declared:

"I called out to the LORD from my distress, and he answered me; from the belly of Sheol I cried out for help" (Jonah 2:1–2).

Though Jonah had run from God, God loved him even in his defiance and He rebuked and rescued him. God did not turn a deaf ear to Jonah's plea for help. Instead, the moment Jonah cried out for help, God answered (Jonah 2:1).

Never forget: There isn't a sin big enough or a situation dark enough that God cannot rescue you. Turn to Him in the midst of your storm. He will meet you there, even in the belly of a great fish.

4 I thought I had been banished from your sight
and that I would never again see your holy temple.
5 Water engulfed me up to my neck;
the deep ocean surrounded me;
seaweed was wrapped around my head.
6 I went down to the very bottoms of the mountains;
the gates of the netherworld barred me in forever,
but you brought me up from the Pit, O LORD, my God.
7 When my life was ebbing away, I called out to the LORD.
And my prayer came to you, to your holy temple.
8 Those who worship worthless idols forfeit
the mercy that could be theirs.
9 But as for me, I promise to offer a sacrifice to
you with a public declaration of praise;
I will surely do what I have promised.
Salvation belongs to the LORD!"

10 Then the LORD commanded the fish and it vomited Jonah
out onto dry land.

REFLECT

How did God display mercy to Jonah even in his rebellion? What does this show us about God's character?

THE PEOPLE OF NINEVEH RESPOND TO JONAH'S WARNING

3 The LORD's message came to Jonah a second time, 2 "Go
immediately to Nineveh, that large city, and proclaim to
it the message that I tell you." 3 So Jonah went immediately
to Nineveh, in keeping with the LORD's message. Now Nineveh was an enormous city—it required three days to walk
through it! 4 Jonah began to enter the city by going one day's
walk, announcing, "At the end of forty days, Nineveh will be
overthrown!"
5 The people of Nineveh believed in God, and they declared
a fast and put on sackcloth, from the greatest to the least of
them. 6 When the news reached the king of Nineveh, he got
up from his throne, took off his royal robe, put on sackcloth,
and sat on ashes. 7 He issued a proclamation and said, "In Nineveh, by the decree of the king and his nobles: No human or
animal, cattle or sheep, is to taste anything; they must not eat
and they must not drink water. 8 Every person and animal must
put on sackcloth and must cry earnestly to God, and everyone
must turn from their evil way of living and from the violence
that they do. 9 Who knows? Perhaps God might be willing to
change his mind and relent and turn from his fierce anger so
that we might not die." 10 When God saw their actions—that
they turned from their evil way of living—God relented concerning the judgment he had threatened them with and did
not destroy them.

REFLECT

Do you find it comforting or unsettling that God can change His mind? Why?

JONAH RESPONDS TO GOD'S KINDNESS

4 This displeased Jonah terribly and he became very angry. 2 He
prayed to the LORD and said, "Oh, LORD, this is just what I
thought would happen when I was in my own country. This is
what I tried to prevent by attempting to escape to Tarshish, because I knew that you are a gracious and compassionate God,
slow to anger and abounding in mercy, and one who relents

LOVE TO GROW

GRACE FOR THE GRUMBLERS

JONAH 4:2

"It's not fair!" The words tumbled out of my mouth before I could catch them. My college professor had announced that he was giving the entire class a perfect score on our first exam. I was indignant. I had studied and worked so hard I had scored the highest grade in the class. I was angry my classmates who did not work as hard as I had were given the same grade.

Jonah 4 described a similar moment for Jonah. God saved Nineveh, and Jonah was furious.

In the preceding chapters, we aren't told why Jonah did not want to go to Nineveh. Verse 2 finally tells us. Jonah did not want to go to Nineveh because he understood something important about God's character.

"I knew that you are a gracious and compassionate God, slow to anger and abounding in mercy, and one who relents concerning threatened judgment" (Jonah 4:2)

Jonah did not want to go to Nineveh because he knew God would graciously give the Ninevites another chance if they repented. Instead of praising God for saving the Ninevites (which was a miracle), he complained about God's grace, love, and mercy.

Jonah's complaint is ironic. God could have let Jonah drown in the sea or die in the belly of a fish. Instead, God graciously saved him, just as he saved the Ninevites.

When I complained about the grace my professor extended my classmates, I failed to realize that along with my classmates, I was also a recipient of grace. Like them, I was not deserving of a perfect score on my exam. Instead of complaining or bragging about my grade, I should have humbly and gratefully accepted his gift and celebrated the good news of the professor who showed every student in his class overwhelming grace.

Ultimately, the Book of Jonah is not about Nineveh, nor Jonah. It is a story about our great God who shows us great grace, even when we grumble. This is our message to the world. When you have known such great grace, you can't help but celebrate the One who extended it and proclaim His mercies every single day.

concerning threatened judgment. [3]So now, LORD, kill me instead, because I would rather die than live!" [4]The LORD said,
"Are you really so very angry?"

[5]Jonah left the city and sat down east of it. He made a shelter for himself there and sat down under it in the shade to see
what would happen to the city. [6]The LORD God appointed a little plant and caused it to grow up over Jonah to be a shade over
his head to rescue him from his misery. Now Jonah was very delighted about the little plant.

[7]So God sent a worm at dawn the next day, and it attacked the
little plant so that it dried up. [8]When the sun began to shine, God
sent a hot east wind. So the sun beat down on Jonah's head, and
he grew faint. So he despaired of life and said, "I would rather
die than live!"

[9]God said to Jonah, "Are you really so very angry about the little
plant?" And he said, "I am as angry as I could possibly be!" [10]The
LORD said, "You were upset about this little plant, something
for which you did not work, nor did you do anything to make it
grow. It grew up overnight and died the next day. [11]Should I not
be more concerned about Nineveh, this enormous city? There
are more than 120,000 people in it who do not know right from
wrong, as well as many animals."

CHALLENGE

Read Romans 12:19–21. Do you find it difficult to believe that God will defend you when you are wronged? How does this verse help us understand the message of Jonah?

He has told you, O man, what is good, and what the LORD really wants from you: He wants you to CARRY out JUSTICE, TO love faithfulness, and to live obediently

MEMORY VERSE

He has told you, O man, what is good, and what the Lord really wants from you: He wants you to carry out justice, to love faithfulness, and to live obediently before your God.

Micah 6:8

Micah

INTRODUCTION

God's Righteousness

The Book of Micah presents an artistic interplay between oracles of impending judgment and promises of future blessing on Israel and Judah. God used Micah as His messenger to confront His people for breaking their covenant with Him. Along with his message of judgment, Micah also presented a message of great mercy and kindness. This future blessing would be Jesus, the One who would shepherd God's flock and bring redemption to the world.

Micah's prophetic message contains three sets of oracles, judgments, and promises. The first describes the coming Judge in chapters 1–2. Chapters 3–5 present the second cycle of prophecies and outline the judgment to come to sinful leaders. Chapters 6–7 express how God desires the hearts of His people, not only their rituals. Each time He pronounced judgment, God also promised to restore His people with a glorious future.

The events in the Book of Micah occurred about 740–710 B.C. Micah's ministry spanned the reigns of Jotham, Ahaz, and Hezekiah, and it also included the period when Assyria took the nation of Israel captive (722 B.C.). Micah is likely the author of this book, compiling his prophecies throughout the span of his ministry.

Micah encourages us to love God greatly by revealing the depth of God's character. God's wrath and mercy run side by side throughout the book, revealing His holiness alongside His loyal love. Even in the darkest times of God's chosen people, He promised to preserve a remnant. He will do the same for us: Despite the darkness in which we find ourselves, He will restore us.

Italy

OFFICIAL LANGUAGE
Italian
POPULATION
60,463,000
UNREACHED POPULATION
2,093,000
PROFESSING CHRISTIANS
81.3%

Giovanna's Home

Say a Prayer Today

Pray for the people of Italy, that they would turn their hearts to God and not only their actions. Pray for Giovanna to be a light in dark places and bring hope to those around her.

HISTORY BIT

Italy was one of the first areas reached by the gospel. Acts 2 records visitors from Rome who were present at Pentecost and who likely started the first house churches in Rome. Paul wrote his letter to the Romans about A.D. 57.

Source Information:
https://joshuaproject.net/countries/IT

GIOVANNA'S STORY

Growing up in Italy, I experienced a lot of ritual-based religion. While there is a great deal of ceremony, many of these practices do not seem like true acts of worship. It can often feel like merely going through the motions.

As I reflect on the spiritual climate of my country, I am reminded of Micah's words. He reminded the people that God did not need their sacrifices, but rather, He longed to capture their hearts. Micah reminded the people what God desired: to carry out justice, to love faithfulness, and to live obediently before God.

I have felt oppressed, exploited, unloved, abandoned, robbed, and used. I've felt the impossible burden of forgiving those who have hurt me. As I've walked through difficult seasons, I've come to learn one thing is true: God sees. He knows the reasons for my darkness, and He comes to bring justice, and He longs to restore.

When I see what God desires for His people in Micah, I also see what He cares about and what He provides. He loves goodness. He desires to bring justice to my circumstances. He loves to be faithful to His children. And He loves it when I, His daughter, am faithful and obedient to Him. As I seek Him more, I learn to turn and offer justice and faithfulness to others.

In me and around my country, I see a lot of ceremony. Faithfulness to God is much more than good songs and snappy sermons. I long to see my people carry out justice, love faithfulness, and live obediently to the God who created them and loves them. Help us, Lord, to be more like You!

6 WEEK READING PLAN

LOVE HIS WORD

	MONDAY	TUESDAY	WEDNESDAY	THURSDAY	FRIDAY
1	Micah 1:1-7	Micah 1:8-16	Micah 2:1-5	Micah 2:6-11	Micah 2:12—3:4
	SOAP Micah 1:2-3	SOAP 2 Kings 17:13-14	SOAP 2 Chronicles 36:15	SOAP Micah 2:7	SOAP Micah 2:12
2	Micah 3:5-12	Micah 4:1-8	Micah 4:9-13	Micah 5:1-6	Micah 5:7-15
	SOAP Psalm 82:8	SOAP Micah 4:5	SOAP Micah 4:12	SOAP Micah 5:4-5a	SOAP Micah 5:7
3	Micah 6:1-8	Micah 6:9-16	Micah 7:1-11	Micah 7:12-20	Nahum 1:1-3
	SOAP Micah 6:8	SOAP Job 40:8-9	SOAP Micah 7:7	SOAP Micah 7:18-20	SOAP Nahum 1:3
4	Nahum 1:4-15	Nahum 2:1-10	Nahum 2:11—3:3	Nahum 3:4-19	Habakkuk 1:1-11
	SOAP Nahum 1:5	SOAP Nahum 2:2	SOAP Psalm 143:11-12	SOAP Proverbs 21:15	SOAP Habakkuk 1:5
5	Habakkuk 1:12—2:1	Habakkuk 2:2-5	Habakkuk 2:6-20	Habakkuk 3:1-15	Habakkuk 3:16-19
	SOAP Habakkuk 1:12	SOAP 1 John 5:14-15	SOAP Habakkuk 2:20	SOAP Habakkuk 3:2	SOAP Habakkuk 3:18-19
6	Zephaniah 1	Zephaniah 2:1-3	Zephaniah 2:4-15	Zephaniah 3:1-5	Zephaniah 3:6-20
	SOAP Romans 9:22	SOAP Zephaniah 2:3	SOAP Zephaniah 2:11	SOAP Zephaniah 3:5	SOAP Zephaniah 3:20

INTRODUCTION

1 This is the LORD's message that came to Micah of Moresheth
during the time of Jotham, Ahaz, and Hezekiah, kings of Judah,
which he saw concerning Samaria and Jerusalem.

THE JUDGE IS COMING

2 Listen, all you nations!
Pay attention, all inhabitants of earth!
The Sovereign LORD will act as a witness against you;
the Lord will accuse you from his majestic palace.
3 Look, the LORD is coming out of his dwelling place!
He will descend and march on the earth's mountaintops!
4 The mountains will crumble beneath him,
and the valleys will split apart
like wax before a fire,
like water dumped down a steep slope.

5 All this is because of Jacob's rebellion
and the sins of the nation of Israel.
And just what is Jacob's rebellion?
Isn't it Samaria's doings?
And what is Judah's sin?
Isn't it Jerusalem's doings?

6 "I will turn Samaria into a heap of ruins in an open field,
into a place for planting vineyards.
I will dump the rubble of her walls down into the valley
and lay bare her foundations.
7 All her carved idols will be smashed to pieces;
all her metal cult statues will be destroyed by fire.
I will make a waste heap of all her images.
Since she gathered the metal as a
prostitute collects her wages,
the idols will become a prostitute's wages again."
8 For this reason I will mourn and wail;
I will walk around barefoot and
without my outer garments.
I will howl like a wild dog,
and screech like an owl.
9 For Samaria's disease is incurable.
It has infected Judah;
it has spread to the leadership of my people
and even to Jerusalem!
10 Don't spread the news in Gath.
Don't shed even a single tear.
In Beth Leaphrah roll about in mourning in the dust!
11 Residents of Shaphir, pass by in nakedness and humiliation!
The residents of Zaanan have not escaped.
Beth Ezel mourns,
"He takes from you what he desires."
12 Indeed, the residents of Maroth hope
for something good to happen,
though the LORD has sent disaster
against the city of Jerusalem.

REFLECT

What do these verses reveal about God's holiness?

13 Residents of Lachish, hitch the horses to the chariots!
You influenced Daughter Zion to sin,
for Israel's rebellious deeds can be traced back to you!
14 Therefore you will have to say farewell to Moresheth Gath.
The residents of Achzib will be as disappointing
as a dried up well to the kings of Israel.
15 Residents of Mareshah, a conqueror will attack you;
the leaders of Israel shall flee to Adullam.
16 Shave your heads bald as you mourn
for the children you love;
shave your foreheads as bald as an eagle,
for they are taken from you into exile.

LAND ROBBERS WILL LOSE THEIR LAND

2 Beware wicked schemers,
those who devise calamity as they lie in bed.
As soon as morning dawns they carry out their plans,
because they have the power to do so.
2 They confiscate the fields they desire
and seize the houses they want.
They defraud people of their homes
and deprive people of the land they have inherited.

3 Therefore the LORD says this:
"Look, I am devising disaster for this nation!
It will be like a yoke from which you
cannot free your neck.
You will no longer walk proudly,
for it will be a time of catastrophe.
4 In that day people will sing this taunt song to you—
they will mock you with this lament:
'We are completely destroyed;
they sell off the property of my people.
How they remove it from me!
They assign our fields to the conqueror.'"
5 Therefore no one will assign you land
in the LORD's community.

6 "Don't preach with such impassioned
rhetoric," they say excitedly.
"These prophets should not preach of such things;
we will not be overtaken by humiliation."
7 Does the family of Jacob say,
"The LORD's patience can't be exhausted—
he would never do such things"?
To be sure, my commands bring a reward
for those who obey them,
8 but you rise up as an enemy against my people.
You steal a robe from a friend,
from those who pass by peacefully
as if returning from a war.
9 You wrongly evict widows among my people
from their cherished homes.
You defraud their children of their prized inheritance.

10 But you are the ones who will be forced to leave!
For this land is not secure;
sin will thoroughly destroy it!
11 If a lying windbag should come and say,
'I'll promise you blessings of wine and beer,'
he would be just the right preacher for these people!

THE LORD WILL RESTORE HIS PEOPLE

12 "I will certainly gather all of you, O Jacob,
I will certainly assemble those Israelites who remain.
I will bring them together like sheep in a fold,
like a flock in the middle of a pasture;
they will be so numerous that they will make a lot of noise.
13 The one who can break through
barriers will lead them out;
they will break out, pass through the gate, and leave.
Their king will advance before them;
the LORD himself will lead them."

REFLECT

How does God's promise to restore His people make sense after His promise of judgment? What was the purpose of God's judgment on the nation of Judah?

GOD WILL JUDGE JUDAH'S SINFUL LEADERS

3 I said,
"Listen, you leaders of Jacob,
you rulers of the nation of Israel!
You ought to know what is just,
2 yet you hate what is good
and love what is evil.
You flay my people's skin
and rip the flesh from their bones.
3 You devour my people's flesh,
strip off their skin,
and crush their bones.
You chop them up like flesh in a pot—
like meat in a kettle.
4 Someday these sinful leaders will
cry to the LORD for help,
but he will not answer them.
He will hide his face from them at that time,
because they have done such wicked deeds."

5 This is what the LORD has said about the prophets who mislead my people,
"If someone gives them enough to eat,
they offer an oracle of peace.
But if someone does not give them food,
they are ready to declare war on him.
6 Therefore night will fall, and you will receive no visions;
it will grow dark, and you will no longer
be able to read the omens.
The sun will set on these prophets,
and the daylight will turn to darkness over their heads.
7 The prophets will be ashamed;
the omen readers will be humiliated.
All of them will cover their mouths,
for they will receive no divine oracles."

CHALLENGE

Why does God judge leaders more harshly? Read James 3:1–12. How can you be committed to honoring God with your words as you lead others?

8 But I am full of the courage that the LORD's Spirit gives
and have a strong commitment to justice.
This enables me to confront Jacob with its rebellion
and Israel with its sin.
9 Listen to this, you leaders of the family of Jacob,
you rulers of the nation of Israel!
You hate justice
and pervert all that is right.
10 You build Zion through bloody crimes,
Jerusalem through unjust violence.
11 Her leaders take bribes when they decide legal cases,
her priests proclaim rulings for profit,
and her prophets read omens for pay.
Yet they claim to trust the LORD and say,
"The LORD is among us.
Disaster will not overtake us!"
12 Therefore, because of you, Zion will
be plowed up like a field,
Jerusalem will become a heap of ruins,
and the Temple Mount will become a
hill overgrown with brush!

GOD'S HEART FOR THE NATIONS

Micah 4:2

Many nations will come, saying, "Come on! Let's go up to the LORD's mountain, to the temple of Jacob's God, so he can teach us his ways and we can live by his laws." For instruction will proceed from Zion, the LORD's message from Jerusalem.

BETTER DAYS AHEAD FOR JERUSALEM

4 And in future days the LORD's Temple Mount will
be the most important mountain of all;
it will be more prominent than other hills.
People will stream to it.
2 Many nations will come, saying,
"Come on! Let's go up to the LORD's mountain,
to the temple of Jacob's God,
so he can teach us his ways
and we can live by his laws."
For instruction will proceed from Zion,
the LORD's message from Jerusalem.
3 He will arbitrate between many peoples
and settle disputes between many distant nations.
They will beat their swords into plowshares,
and their spears into pruning hooks.
Nations will not use weapons against other nations,
and they will no longer train for war.
4 Each will sit under his own grapevine
or under his own fig tree without any fear.
The LORD of Heaven's Armies has decreed it.
5 Though all the nations follow their respective gods,
we will follow the LORD our God forever.

REFLECT

Were God's promises of restoration comforting to the people? Are they comforting to you? Why or why not?

RESTORATION WILL FOLLOW CRISIS

6 "In that day," says the LORD, "I will gather the lame
and assemble the outcasts whom I injured.
7 I will transform the lame into the
nucleus of a new nation,
and those far off into a mighty nation.
The LORD will reign over them on Mount Zion,
from that day forward and forevermore.

8 As for you, watchtower for the flock,
fortress of Daughter Zion—
your former dominion will be restored,
the sovereignty that belongs to Daughter Jerusalem."
9 Jerusalem, why are you now shouting so loudly?
Has your king disappeared?
Has your wise leader been destroyed?
Is this why pain grips you as if you
were a woman in labor?
10 Twist and strain, Daughter Zion,
as if you were in labor!
For you will leave the city
and live in the open field.
You will go to Babylon,
but there you will be rescued.
There the LORD will deliver you
from the power of your enemies.
11 Many nations have now assembled against you.
They say, "Jerusalem must be desecrated,
so we can gloat over Zion!"
12 But they do not know what the LORD is planning;
they do not understand his strategy.
He has gathered them like stalks of grain to
be threshed at the threshing floor.
13 "Get up and thresh, Daughter Zion!
For I will give you iron horns;
I will give you bronze hooves,
and you will crush many nations."
You will devote to the LORD the
spoils you take from them
and dedicate their wealth to the sovereign
Ruler of the whole earth.
5 But now slash yourself, daughter surrounded by soldiers!
We are besieged!
With a scepter they strike Israel's ruler
on the side of his face.

A KING WILL COME AND A REMNANT WILL PROSPER

2 As for you, Bethlehem Ephrathah,
seemingly insignificant among the clans of Judah—
from you a king will emerge who will
rule over Israel on my behalf,
one whose origins are in the distant past.
3 So the LORD will hand the people of
Israel over to their enemies
until the time when the woman in labor gives birth.
Then the rest of the king's countrymen will return
to be reunited with the people of Israel.
4 He will assume his post and shepherd the
people by the LORD's strength,
by the sovereign authority of the LORD his God.
They will live securely, for at that
time he will be honored
even in the distant regions of the earth.

5 He will give us peace.
Should the Assyrians try to invade our land
and attempt to set foot in our fortresses,
we will send against them seven shepherd-rulers,
make that eight commanders.
6 They will rule the land of Assyria with the sword,
the land of Nimrod with a drawn sword.
Our king will rescue us from the Assyrians
should they attempt to invade our land
and try to set foot in our territory.
7 Those survivors from Jacob will live
in the midst of many nations.
They will be like the dew the LORD sends,
like the rain on the grass,
that does not hope for men to come
or wait around for humans to arrive.
8 Those survivors from Jacob will
live among the nations,
in the midst of many peoples.
They will be like a lion among
the animals of the forest,
like a young lion among the flocks of sheep,
which attacks when it passes through.
It rips its prey and there is no one to stop it.
9 Lift your hand triumphantly against your adversaries;
may all your enemies be destroyed!

THE LORD WILL PURIFY HIS PEOPLE

10 "In that day," says the LORD,
"I will destroy your horses from your midst
and smash your chariots.
11 I will destroy the cities of your land
and tear down all your fortresses.
12 I will remove the sorcery that you practice,
and you will no longer have omen
readers living among you.
13 I will remove your idols and sacred
pillars from your midst;
you will no longer worship what your own hands made.
14 I will uproot your images of Asherah from your midst
and destroy your idols.
15 With furious anger I will carry out vengeance
on the nations that do not obey me."

REFLECT

Why did God promise to destroy all of the people's possessions? What does this reveal about God's desire for His people to be holy?

THE LORD DEMANDS JUSTICE, NOT RITUAL

6 Listen to what the LORD says:
"Get up! Defend yourself before the mountains.
Present your case before the hills."
2 Hear the LORD's accusation, you mountains,
you enduring foundations of the earth.
For the LORD has a case against his people;
he has a dispute with Israel!
3 "My people, how have I wronged you?
How have I wearied you? Answer me!

4 In fact, I brought you up from the land of Egypt;
I delivered you from that place of slavery.
I sent Moses, Aaron, and Miriam to lead you.
5 My people, recall how King Balak of
Moab planned to harm you,
how Balaam son of Beor responded to him.
Recall how you journeyed from Shittim to Gilgal,
so you might acknowledge that the
LORD has treated you fairly."

6 With what should I enter the LORD's presence?
With what should I bow before the sovereign God?
Should I enter his presence with burnt offerings,
with year-old calves?
7 Will the LORD accept a thousand rams
or ten thousand streams of olive oil?
Should I give him my firstborn child
as payment for my rebellion,
my offspring—my own flesh and blood—for my sin?
8 He has told you, O man, what is good,
and what the LORD really wants from you:
He wants you to carry out justice,
to love faithfulness,
and to live obediently before your God.

9 Listen! The LORD is calling to the city!
It is wise to respect your authority, O LORD.
Listen, O nation, and those assembled in the city!
10 "I will not overlook, O sinful house, the
dishonest gain you have hoarded away
or the smaller-than-standard measure I hate so much.
11 I do not condone the use of rigged scales,
or a bag of deceptive weights.
12 The city's wealthy people readily resort to violence;
her inhabitants tell lies;
their tongues speak deceptive words.
13 I will strike you brutally
and destroy you because of your sin.
14 You will eat, but not be satisfied.
Even if you have the strength to overtake some prey,
you will not be able to carry it away;
if you do happen to carry away something,
I will deliver it over to the sword.
15 You will plant crops, but will not harvest them;
you will squeeze oil from the olives, but you
will have no oil to rub on your bodies;
you will squeeze juice from the grapes, but
you will have no wine to drink.
16 You follow Omri's edicts
and all the practices of Ahab's dynasty;
you follow their policies.
Therefore I will make you an appalling sight;
the city's inhabitants will be taunted derisively,
and nations will mock all of you."

CARRY OUT JUSTICE, LOVE FAITHFULNESS, LIVE OBEDIENTLY

MICAH 6:8

If there were a search engine exclusively for the Christian life, I imagine one of the most frequently searched questions would be, "What is God's will for me?" As believers, we give much thought and energy to understanding what God wants for our lives and what He wants us to do with our time on earth.

I remember my youth leaders pointed me to verses like Micah 6:8 and said, "It's simple. God's will for your life is to carry out justice, love faithfulness, and live obediently before your God." As an adult, my response to this explanation is, "Yes, but there is more to it."

God gives each of us unique gifts and talents that He intends for us to use during our time on earth. Our callings are individualized; they are more than a generic call to do good in the world.

How do we begin to understand our gifts and callings? Look to Christ as your model and begin in the smallest places. Carry out justice in your relationships with your friends. Love faithfulness in your interactions in places like the grocery store. Look for opportunities to be obedient and kind. In these moments, our God-given talents and gifts emerge. When we seek to live as Christ did, we get to know the Father more and more, and, as a result, we come to better know and understand ourselves.

God takes our small acts of justice, faithfulness, and obedience and causes them to reverberate throughout His kingdom.

We can test our individual callings against verses like these. We can ask ourselves, "Does this calling cause me to carry out justice? Does this calling allow me to be faithful? Does it foster obedience?" If we can answer yes to them all, we know we are aligned with God's overarching purposes for His kingdom.

I believe when each of us fulfills this verse according to the unique ways God has designed us, God celebrates with a satisfied joy. Teachers, lawyers, therapists, nurses, accountants, artists, parents, friends, and community members all bring justice, faithfulness, and obedience into the world in distinct and important ways. And they are all, as Micah says, very good.

MICAH LAMENTS JUDAH'S SIN

7 Woe is me!
For I am like those gathering fruit
and those harvesting grapes,
when there is no grape cluster to eat
and no fresh figs that my stomach craves.
2 Faithful men have disappeared from the land;
there are no godly men left.
They all wait in ambush to shed blood;
they hunt their own brother with a net.
3 They are experts at doing evil;
government officials and judges take bribes,
prominent men announce what they wish,
and then they plan it out.
4 The best of them is like a thorn;
their godly are like a thorn bush.
Woe to your watchmen;
your appointed punishment is on the way.
The time of their confusion is now.
5 Do not rely on a friend;
do not trust a companion!
Even with the one who lies in your arms,
do not share secrets!
6 For a son thinks his father is a fool,
a daughter challenges her mother,
and a daughter-in-law her mother-in-law;
a man's enemies are his own family.
7 But I will keep watching for the LORD;
I will wait for the God who delivers me.
My God will listen to me.

JERUSALEM WILL BE VINDICATED

8 My enemies, do not gloat over me!
Though I have fallen, I will get up.
Though I sit in darkness, the LORD will be my light.
9 I must endure the LORD's fury,
for I have sinned against him.
But then he will defend my cause
and accomplish justice on my behalf.
He will lead me out into the light;
I will witness his deliverance.
10 When my enemies see this, they will be covered with shame.
They say to me, "Where is the LORD your God?"
I will gloat over them;
then they will be trampled down
like mud in the streets.
11 It will be a day for rebuilding your walls;
in that day your boundary will be extended.

A CLOSING PRAYER

12 In that day people will come to you
from Assyria as far as Egypt,
from Egypt as far as the Euphrates River,
from the seacoasts and the mountains.

13 The earth will become desolate
because of what its inhabitants have done.
14 Shepherd your people with your rod,
the flock that belongs to you,
the one that lives alone in a thicket,
in the midst of a pastureland.
Allow them to graze in Bashan and Gilead,
as they did in the old days.
15 "As in the days when you departed from the land of Egypt,
I will show you miraculous deeds."
16 Nations will see this and be disappointed
by all their strength;
they will put their hands over their mouths
and act as if they were deaf.
17 They will lick the dust like a snake,
like serpents crawling on the ground.
They will come trembling from their strongholds
to the LORD our God;
they will be terrified of you.
18 Who is a God like you?
Who forgives sin
and pardons the rebellion
of those who remain among his people?
Who does not stay angry forever,
but delights in showing loyal love?
19 Who will once again have mercy on us?
Who will conquer our evil deeds?
Who will hurl all our sins into the depths of the sea?
20 You will be loyal to Jacob
and extend your loyal love to Abraham,
which you promised on oath to our
ancestors in ancient times.

REFLECT

Praise God for who He is. Spend time praising Him for the attributes He reveals in His Word and the way His character is displayed throughout Scripture.

THE LORD is slow to anger but GREAT in POWER; the LORD will certainly NOT ALLOW the WICKED to go unpunished

MEMORY VERSE

The Lord is slow to anger but great in power; the Lord will certainly not allow the wicked to go unpunished.

Nahum 1:3

Nahum

INTRODUCTION

God's Power over Evil

The Book of Nahum describes the righteous judgment and destruction coming to the city of Nineveh. Jonah also had a message for this prominent city, and his message was accepted, leading the people of Nineveh to repentance. Nahum's message to Nineveh was the same, yet the response of the people was drastically different.

Nahum is a relatively short book, containing a psalm about God's faithfulness and judgment on His enemies (1:1—2:2) and the prophecies of the judgment of Nineveh (2:3—3:19). The people of Nineveh had previously repented of their sins, but over time they returned to their wickedness. They captured the nation of Israel, scattering the people throughout the region. Nahum's prophecies displayed God's vengeance on the enemies of His people.

The events prophesied in the Book of Nahum occurred in the seventh century B.C., shortly before the fall of Judah. The Assyrians had taken Israel captive in 722 B.C., about a century before their own destruction. Nineveh, the capital city of Assyria, fell to the Babylonians in 612 B.C., about seven years before the first Babylonian siege of Jerusalem. The book was likely written by Nahum sometime before 612 B.C., perhaps under the reforms of King Josiah.

Nahum displays God's plan to avenge His people. The Assyrians had destroyed Israel, and though this was God's discipline of Israel, He still judged Nineveh for its wickedness. Although God used the Assyrians, they were still guilty for their sins. Nahum encourages us to love God greatly as it shows us God's righteousness and His power over evil. God will always come to the aid and defense of His people, even when they have sinned.

Guatemala

OFFICIAL LANGUAGE
Spanish
POPULATION
17,523,000
UNREACHED POPULATION
900
PROFESSING CHRISTIANS
95.5%

Rocío's Home

Say a Prayer Today

Pray for Rocío, that she would be a testament to those around her to God's goodness. Pray she would be an encouragement to others as she lives out the truth of the gospel.

HISTORY BIT

The Maya Indians of Guatemala were a deeply religious people. In 1550, when Spanish Franciscans (a religious order of the Roman Catholic Church) arrived, they forced the Maya Indians to practice Catholicism.*

Source Information:
https://joshuaproject.net/countries/GT
*David B. Barrett, World Christian Encyclopedia, Guatemala (New York, NY: Oxford University Press, 1982), 339.

ROCÍO'S STORY

God's grace has had an incredible impact on my life. When the truth of the gospel reached my heart, it completely changed me. I stopped fighting with others and experienced peace in the midst of conflict. I found rest in God. Instead of fighting for myself, I let Him fight for me.

God has continued to work in my life by giving me peace. I have forgiven others in a way that seemed impossible before giving my life to Him. Not only that, but I have experienced abundant joy as I've watched Him work in the lives of those around me, transforming them to reflect His character and love.

While I cannot fully know God on this earth, I can be confident that what He is doing in my life is working for my good. He experienced every trial, every obstacle, and every hardship for me. He died for me. He forgives me, restores me, and gives me wisdom and strength to face trials and difficulties.

Every morning, I am encouraged by His love. As I look out at the beautiful landscapes of Guatemala, I am reminded of His goodness. He has provided me with a beautiful place to live, even though I don't always value it. I am reminded of His compassion as I reflect on the fact that He is slow to anger. He forgives me and gives me new mercies each day.

6 WEEK READING PLAN

LOVE HIS WORD

	MONDAY	TUESDAY	WEDNESDAY	THURSDAY	FRIDAY
1	Micah 1:1-7	Micah 1:8-16	Micah 2:1-5	Micah 2:6-11	Micah 2:12—3:4
	SOAP Micah 1:2-3	SOAP 2 Kings 17:13-14	SOAP 2 Chronicles 36:15	SOAP Micah 2:7	SOAP Micah 2:12
2	Micah 3:5-12	Micah 4:1-8	Micah 4:9-13	Micah 5:1-6	Micah 5:7-15
	SOAP Psalm 82:8	SOAP Micah 4:5	SOAP Micah 4:12	SOAP Micah 5:4-5a	SOAP Micah 5:7
3	Micah 6:1-8	Micah 6:9-16	Micah 7:1-11	Micah 7:12-20	Nahum 1:1-3
	SOAP Micah 6:8	SOAP Job 40:8-9	SOAP Micah 7:7	SOAP Micah 7:18-20	SOAP Nahum 1:3
4	Nahum 1:4-15	Nahum 2:1-10	Nahum 2:11—3:3	Nahum 3:4-19	Habakkuk 1:1-11
	SOAP Nahum 1:5	SOAP Nahum 2:2	SOAP Psalm 143:11-12	SOAP Proverbs 21:15	SOAP Habakkuk 1:5
5	Habakkuk 1:12—2:1	Habakkuk 2:2-5	Habakkuk 2:6-20	Habakkuk 3:1-15	Habakkuk 3:16-19
	SOAP Habakkuk 1:12	SOAP 1 John 5:14-15	SOAP Habakkuk 2:20	SOAP Habakkuk 3:2	SOAP Habakkuk 3:18-19
6	Zephaniah 1	Zephaniah 2:1-3	Zephaniah 2:4-15	Zephaniah 3:1-5	Zephaniah 3:6-20
	SOAP Romans 9:22	SOAP Zephaniah 2:3	SOAP Zephaniah 2:11	SOAP Zephaniah 3:5	SOAP Zephaniah 3:20

INTRODUCTION

1 This is an oracle about Nineveh; the book of the vision of
Nahum the Elkoshite:

GOD TAKES VENGEANCE AGAINST HIS ENEMIES

2 The LORD is a zealous and avenging God;
the LORD is avenging and very angry.
The LORD takes vengeance against his foes;
he sustains his rage against his enemies.
3 The LORD is slow to anger but great in power;
the LORD will certainly not allow the
wicked to go unpunished.

THE DIVINE WARRIOR DESTROYS HIS ENEMIES BUT PROTECTS HIS PEOPLE

He marches out in the whirlwind and the raging storm;
dark storm clouds billow like dust under his feet.
4 He shouts a battle cry against the
sea and makes it dry up;
he makes all the rivers run dry.
Bashan and Carmel wither;
the blossom of Lebanon withers.
5 The mountains tremble before him,
the hills convulse;
the earth is laid waste before him,
the world and all its inhabitants are laid waste.
6 No one can withstand his indignation!
No one can resist his fierce anger!
His wrath is poured out like volcanic fire,
boulders are broken up as he approaches.
7 The LORD is good—
indeed, he is a fortress in time of distress,
and he protects those who seek refuge in him.
8 But with an overwhelming flood
he will make a complete end of Nineveh;
he will drive his enemies into darkness.

DENUNCIATION AND DESTRUCTION OF NINEVEH

9 Whatever you plot against the LORD,
he will completely destroy!
Distress will not arise a second time.
10 Surely they will be totally consumed
like entangled thorn bushes,
like the drink of drunkards,
like very dry stubble.
11 From you, O Nineveh, one has marched forth
who plots evil against the LORD,
a wicked military strategist.

ORACLE OF DELIVERANCE TO JUDAH

12 This is what the LORD says:
"Even though they are powerful—
and what is more, even though their army is numerous—
nevertheless, they will be destroyed and trickle away!

REFLECT

How is God's power displayed in nature? What aspect of nature most clearly shows you God's power?

LOVE TO GROW

GOD ALWAYS WINS

NAHUM 1:2–15

In the middle of the seventh century B.C., the Israelites languished under the heavy hand of their neighbor Assyria. Cruelty was an Assyrian specialty, and over time God tired of watching His people suffer.

After years of oppression, Nahum the Elkoshite appeared on the scene with a prophecy addressed to Nineveh, the capital of the Assyrian empire: God would utterly destroy Nineveh and relieve the yoke of oppression from His people Judah. Divine judgment was coming.

Nahum described God's character as jealous, avenging, and wrathful—all qualities we would expect in a prophecy of impending judgment. As we continue reading, however, we find something unexpected:

> *The LORD is slow to anger but great in power; the LORD will certainly not allow the wicked to go unpunished . . . The LORD is good—indeed, he is a fortress in time of distress (Nah 1:3, 7).*

God is slow to anger? God is good? We must not forget about the prophet Jonah, whom God called to proclaim a message of repentance to this very city. God demonstrated patience with the enemies of His people. He gave them the chance only a good and kind God would give, yet they returned to their own wicked ways.

We can better understand God's actions through the way Nahum told the people of Nineveh exactly what God had in store for them. Like an overwhelming flood, God would make an end to Judah's adversaries (Nah 1:8). The annihilation would be so vast that trouble would never come again (Nah 1:9). Not only would the people of Nineveh suffer, but Judah would also rejoice at their destruction (Nah 1:15). Those in Judah would return to their normal lives and their worship of God. The mighty warriors of Nineveh were going to experience the full wrath of a God who does not tolerate sin. Eventually, because God is just, evil would be destroyed.

Finally, we are reminded of God's victory. Looking back at the history of Assyria, we know that He fulfilled His word. In 612 B.C., Nineveh was overthrown.

God will triumph, no matter the enemy. Thousands of years ago the enemy was Assyria. On the cross, Jesus defeated the enemies of sin and death. One day in the future, Satan will be bound forever, and God's people will experience abundant peace in His kingdom.

Rest assured, God always wins.

Although I afflicted you,
I will afflict you no more.
13 And now, I will break Assyria's
yoke bar from your neck;
I will tear apart the shackles that are on you."

ORACLE OF JUDGMENT AGAINST THE KING OF NINEVEH

14 The LORD has issued a decree against you:
"Your dynasty will come to an end.
I will destroy the idols and images in
the temples of your gods.
I will desecrate your grave, because you are accursed!"

PROCLAMATION OF THE DELIVERANCE OF JUDAH

15 Look! A herald is running on the mountains!
A messenger is proclaiming deliverance:
"Celebrate your sacred festivals, O Judah!
Fulfill your sacred vows to praise God!
For never again will the wicked
Assyrians invade you;
they have been completely destroyed."

PROCLAMATION OF THE DESTRUCTION OF NINEVEH

2 An enemy who will scatter you, Nineveh,
has advanced against you!
Guard the rampart!
Watch the road!
Prepare yourselves for battle!
Muster your mighty strength!
2 For the LORD is about to restore the majesty of Jacob,
as well as the majesty of Israel,
though their enemies have plundered them
and have destroyed their fields.

PROPHETIC VISION OF THE FALL OF NINEVEH

3 The shields of his warriors are dyed red;
the mighty soldiers are dressed in scarlet garments.
The chariots are in flashing metal fittings
on the day of battle;
the soldiers brandish their spears.
4 The chariots race madly through the streets,
they rush back and forth in the broad plazas;
they look like lightning bolts,
they dash here and there like flashes of lightning.
5 The commander orders his officers;
they stumble as they advance;
they rush to the city wall,
and they set up the covered siege tower.
6 The sluice gates are opened;
the royal palace is deluged and dissolves.
7 Nineveh is taken into exile and is led away;
her slave girls moan like doves while
they beat their breasts.

REFLECT

What does this verse say about the commitment of God to His covenant people?

8 Nineveh was like a pool of water throughout her days,
but now her people are running away;
she cries out: "Stop! Stop!"—
but no one turns back.
9 Her conquerors cry out:
"Plunder the silver! Plunder the gold!"
There is no end to the treasure;
riches of every kind of precious thing.
10 Destruction, devastation, and desolation!
Hearts faint, knees tremble;
every stomach churns, all their faces have turned pale!

TAUNT AGAINST THE ONCE-MIGHTY LION

11 Where now is the den of the lions
and the feeding place of the young lions,
where the lion, lioness, and lion cub once prowled
and no one disturbed them?
12 The lion tore apart as much prey as his cubs needed
and strangled prey for his lionesses;
he filled his lairs with prey
and his dens with torn flesh.

BATTLE CRY OF THE DIVINE WARRIOR

13 "I am against you!" declares the LORD
of Heaven's Armies:
"I will burn your chariots with fire;
the sword will devour your young lions.
You will no longer prey upon the land;
the voices of your messengers will no longer be heard."

REASON FOR JUDGMENT: SINS OF NINEVEH

3 Woe to the city guilty of bloodshed!
She is full of lies;
she is filled with plunder;
she has hoarded her spoil!

PORTRAYAL OF THE DESTRUCTION OF NINEVEH

2 The chariot drivers will crack their whips;
the chariot wheels will shake the ground.
The chariot horses will gallop;
the war chariots will bolt forward!
3 The charioteers will charge ahead;
their swords will flash
and their spears will glimmer!
There will be many people slain;
there will be piles of the dead
and countless casualties—
so many that people will stumble over the corpses.

TAUNT AGAINST THE HARLOT CITY

4 Because you have acted like a wanton prostitute—
a seductive mistress who practices sorcery,
who enslaves nations by her harlotry,
and entices peoples by her sorcery—

CHALLENGE

In Jonah 3, God relented from sending His judgment on Nineveh. Why was He judging and destroying Nineveh now?

5 "I am against you," declares the
LORD of Heaven's Armies.
"I will strip off your clothes!
I will show your nakedness to the nations
and your shame to the kingdoms.
6 I will pelt you with filth;
I will treat you with contempt;
I will make you a public spectacle.
7 Everyone who sees you will turn away from you in disgust;
they will say, 'Nineveh has been devastated!
Who will lament for her?'
There will be no one to comfort you!"

NINEVEH WILL SUFFER THE SAME FATE AS THEBES

8 You are no more secure than Thebes—
she was located on the banks of the Nile;
the waters surrounded her—
her rampart was the sea,
the water was her wall.
9 Cush and Egypt had limitless strength;
Put and the Libyans were among her allies.
10 Yet she went into captivity as an exile;
even her infants were smashed to pieces
at the head of every street.
They cast lots for her nobility;
all her dignitaries were bound with chains.
11 You too will act like drunkards;
you will go into hiding;
you too will seek refuge from the enemy.

THE ASSYRIAN DEFENSES WILL FAIL

12 All your fortifications will be like fig
trees with first-ripe fruit:
If they are shaken, their figs will fall
into the mouth of the eater.
13 Your warriors will be like women in your midst;
the gates of your land will be
wide open to your enemies;
fire will consume the bars of your gates.
14 Draw yourselves water for a siege!
Strengthen your fortifications!
Trample the mud and tread the clay!
Make mud bricks to strengthen your walls!
15 There the fire will consume you;
the sword will cut you down;
it will devour you like the young locust would.

THE ASSYRIAN DEFENDERS WILL FLEE

Multiply yourself like the young locust;
multiply yourself like the flying locust!
16 Increase your merchants more
than the stars of heaven!
They are like the young locust that
sheds its skin and flies away.

17 Your courtiers are like locusts,
your officials are like a swarm of locusts!
They encamp in the walls on a cold day,
yet when the sun rises, they fly away,
and no one knows where they are.

CONCLUDING DIRGE

18 Your shepherds are sleeping, O king of Assyria.
Your officers are slumbering!
Your people are scattered like sheep on the mountains,
and there is no one to regather them.
19 Your destruction is like an incurable wound;
your demise is like a fatal injury.
All who hear what has happened to you
will clap their hands for joy,
for no one ever escaped your endless cruelty!

Look at the NATIONS and PAY ATTENTION! You will be SHOCKED and AMAZED! for I will do Something IN your lifetime that you will not believe

MEMORY VERSE

"Look at the nations and pay attention! You will be shocked and amazed! For I will do something in your lifetime that you will not believe even though you are forewarned."

Habakkuk 1:5

Habakkuk

INTRODUCTION

Trusting in God's Will

The Book of Habakkuk is different from other books of prophecy because it isn't a series of warnings addressed to Israel. Instead, it contains a dialogue between God and His prophet. Habakkuk's message shows us it is okay to present our questions to God. Wanting to know what God was doing and why, Habakkuk was open with God, asking Him to explain His will. God answered the prophet but also asked Habakkuk to trust His plan to establish His kingdom. God's character is revealed through His patience with Habakkuk's questions and His compassion for Habakkuk's unbelief.

This book contains two prophetic laments containing Habakkuk's questions concerning God's righteousness. God responded to Habakkuk's questions by explaining His plans to judge the nation, bringing five woes because of the evil done in Judah.

Little is known about the prophet Habakkuk. He may have been a Levite associated with the temple singers, but others recognized him as a prophet of God. Habakkuk's ministry probably occurred during the fall of Nineveh in 612 B.C. and the rise of the Neo-Babylonian Empire.

God's response to Habakkuk's questions offers hope to those with similar uncertainties. The Book of Habakkuk provides great encouragement for us to love God greatly. Even though He is holy and sovereign, God desires to commune with His people. He wants His people to know Him more and more. As we bring our questions before God, He will not turn us away. He is quick to come to our aid when we seek Him. We can trust God's unfailing love and righteousness as well as His heart to have a relationship with us, His children.

Mexico

OFFICIAL LANGUAGE
Spanish
POPULATION
126,733,000
UNREACHED POPULATION
141,000
PROFESSING CHRISTIANS
94.8%

Ana's Home

Say a Prayer Today

Pray for the growing missions movement in Mexico. As Mexico sends more and more missionaries around the world each year, pray for their effectiveness in sharing the gospel and helping those in need.

HISTORY BIT

In May of 1524, twelve Franciscan missionaries (an order of the Roman Catholic Church) arrived in Mexico. They were later known as the Twelve Apostles of Mexico.*

Source Information:
https://joshuaproject.net/countries/MX
*John Bowden, A Chronology of World Christianity (New York, NY: Continuum, 2007), 268.

ANA'S STORY

Waiting. It's a hard concept to grasp. Living in a world where everything is available in an instant makes waiting on God difficult. We can't shop online for God's goodness, make an appointment for His provision, or work long hours to earn His favor. God gets our attention when we put aside our own agenda and priorities and patiently wait for Him.

I waited many years for God to provide a husband. While I anxiously waited, God taught me to fully rely on Him. He taught me to surrender my whole heart and life to Him, regardless of what that meant for my future. My husband prayed about dating me for a year. While I prayed for a husband who loved God, my husband asked God for wisdom about pursuing me.

In the process of surrender, I learned God was more than enough for me. I made peace with myself and had to remind my soul that it was worth waiting on God. Looking back, I fell deeply in love with Jesus in the waiting.

Now my husband and I are waiting for a baby. We pray earnestly for God's provision and wisdom for growing our family. We are grateful for the season of waiting for God to bring us together because it taught us so much about God's heart and His perfect timing. Even though we sometimes feel we are working against time and the expectations of others, our pain and doubt fade as we seek His presence.

Even when my prayers are not answered in the way I expect or hope, I have learned to trust God is always enough for me.

6 WEEK READING PLAN

LOVE HIS WORD

MONDAY	TUESDAY	WEDNESDAY	THURSDAY	FRIDAY
Micah 1:1-7	Micah 1:8-16	Micah 2:1-5	Micah 2:6-11	Micah 2:12—3:4
SOAP Micah 1:2-3	SOAP 2 Kings 17:13-14	SOAP 2 Chronicles 36:15	SOAP Micah 2:7	SOAP Micah 2:12
Micah 3:5-12	Micah 4:1-8	Micah 4:9-13	Micah 5:1-6	Micah 5:7-15
SOAP Psalm 82:8	SOAP Micah 4:5	SOAP Micah 4:12	SOAP Micah 5:4-5a	SOAP Micah 5:7
Micah 6:1-8	Micah 6:9-16	Micah 7:1-11	Micah 7:12-20	Nahum 1:1-3
SOAP Micah 6:8	SOAP Job 40:8-9	SOAP Micah 7:7	SOAP Micah 7:18-20	SOAP Nahum 1:3
Nahum 1:4-15	Nahum 2:1-10	Nahum 2:11—3:3	Nahum 3:4-19	Habakkuk 1:1-11
SOAP Nahum 1:5	SOAP Nahum 2:2	SOAP Psalm 143:11-12	SOAP Proverbs 21:15	SOAP Habakkuk 1:5
Habakkuk 1:12—2:1	Habakkuk 2:2-5	Habakkuk 2:6-20	Habakkuk 3:1-15	Habakkuk 3:16-19
SOAP Habakkuk 1:12	SOAP 1 John 5:14-15	SOAP Habakkuk 2:20	SOAP Habakkuk 3:2	SOAP Habakkuk 3:18-19
Zephaniah 1	Zephaniah 2:1-3	Zephaniah 2:4-15	Zephaniah 3:1-5	Zephaniah 3:6-20
SOAP Romans 9:22	SOAP Zephaniah 2:3	SOAP Zephaniah 2:11	SOAP Zephaniah 3:5	SOAP Zephaniah 3:20

HABAKKUK COMPLAINS TO THE LORD

1 This is the oracle that the prophet Habakkuk saw:
2 How long, LORD, must I cry for help?
But you do not listen!
I call out to you, "Violence!"
But you do not deliver!
3 Why do you force me to witness injustice?
Why do you put up with wrongdoing?
Destruction and violence confront me;
conflict is present and one must endure strife.
4 For this reason the law lacks power,
and justice is never carried out.
Indeed, the wicked intimidate the innocent.
For this reason justice is perverted.

THE LORD'S SURPRISING ANSWER

5 "Look at the nations and pay attention!
You will be shocked and amazed!
For I will do something in your lifetime
that you will not believe even though you are forewarned.
6 Look, I am about to empower the Babylonians,
that ruthless and greedy nation.
They sweep across the surface of the earth,
seizing dwelling places that do not belong to them.
7 They are frightening and terrifying;
they decide for themselves what is right.
8 Their horses are faster than leopards
and more alert than wolves in the desert.
Their horses gallop,
their horses come a great distance;
like vultures they swoop down quickly
to devour their prey.
9 All of them intend to do violence;
every face is determined.
They take prisoners as easily as one scoops up sand.
10 They mock kings
and laugh at rulers.
They laugh at every fortified city;
they build siege ramps and capture them.
11 They sweep by like the wind and pass on.
But the one who considers himself
a god will be held guilty."

HABAKKUK VOICES SOME CONCERNS

12 LORD, you have been active from ancient times;
my sovereign God, you are immortal.
LORD, you have made them your instrument of judgment.
Protector, you have appointed them as
your instrument of punishment.
13 You are too just to tolerate evil;
you are unable to condone wrongdoing.
So why do you put up with such treacherous people?
Why do you say nothing when the wicked devour
those more righteous than they are?

REFLECT

How does God's answer to Habakkuk encourage you to trust God's will?

14 You made people like fish in the sea,
like animals in the sea that have no ruler.
15 The Babylonian tyrant pulls them all up with a fishhook;
he hauls them in with his throw net.
When he catches them in his dragnet,
he is very happy.
16 Because of his success he offers sacrifices to his throw net
and burns incense to his dragnet;
for because of them he has plenty of food,
and more than enough to eat.
17 Will he then continue to fill and empty his throw net?
Will he always destroy nations and spare none?

2 I will stand at my watch post;
I will remain stationed on the city wall.
I will keep watching so I can see what he says to me
and can know how I should answer
when he counters my argument.

THE LORD ASSURES HABAKKUK

2 The LORD responded:
"Write down this message.
Record it legibly on tablets
so the one who announces it may read it easily.
3 For the message is a witness to what is decreed;
it gives reliable testimony about how matters will turn out.
Even if the message is not fulfilled
right away, wait patiently;
for it will certainly come to pass—it will not arrive late.
4 Look, the one whose desires are not upright
will faint from exhaustion,
but the person of integrity will live
because of his faithfulness.
5 Indeed, wine will betray the proud, restless man!
His appetite is as big as Sheol's;
like death, he is never satisfied.
He gathers all the nations;
he seizes all peoples.

CHALLENGE

What do these verses reveal about the way God interacts with time? Is God in control of time? How do Psalm 31:15; Psalm 90:12; Ecclesiastes 3:11; and 2 Peter 3:8–9 reveal the way God views time?

THE PROUD BABYLONIANS ARE AS GOOD AS DEAD

6 "But all these nations will someday taunt him
and ridicule him with proverbial sayings:
'Woe to the one who accumulates what
does not belong to him
(How long will this go on?)—
he who gets rich by extortion!'
7 Your creditors will suddenly attack;
those who terrify you will spring into action,
and they will rob you.
8 Because you robbed many countries,
all who are left among the nations will rob you.
You have shed human blood
and committed violent acts against lands,
cities, and those who live in them.

9 The one who builds his house by unjust
gain is as good as dead.
He does this so he can build his nest way up high
and escape the clutches of disaster.
10 Your schemes will bring shame to your house.
Because you destroyed many nations, you will self-destruct.
11 For the stones in the walls will cry out,
and the wooden rafters will answer back.

12 Woe to the one who builds a city by bloodshed—
he who starts a town by unjust deeds.
13 Be sure of this! The LORD of Heaven's Armies has decreed:
The nations' efforts will go up in smoke;
their exhausting work will be for nothing.
14 For recognition of the LORD's sovereign
majesty will fill the earth
just as the waters fill up the sea.

15 "Woe to you who force your neighbor to drink wine—
you who make others intoxicated
by forcing them to drink from the
bowl of your furious anger
so you can look at their naked bodies.
16 But you will become drunk with shame, not majesty.
Now it is your turn to drink and expose
your uncircumcised foreskin!
The cup of wine in the LORD's right hand is coming to you,
and disgrace will replace your majestic glory!
17 For you will pay in full for your violent acts against Lebanon;
terrifying judgment will come upon you
because of the way you destroyed the
wild animals living there.
You have shed human blood
and committed violent acts against lands,
cities, and those who live in them.
18 What good is an idol? Why would a craftsman make it?
What good is a metal image that gives misleading oracles?
Why would its creator place his trust in it
and make such mute, worthless things?
19 Woe to the one who says to wood, 'Wake up!'—
he who says to speechless stone, 'Awake!'
Can it give reliable guidance?
It is overlaid with gold and silver;
it has no life's breath inside it.
20 But the LORD is in his majestic palace.
The whole earth is speechless in his presence!"

HABAKKUK'S VISION OF THE DIVINE WARRIOR

3 This is a prayer of Habakkuk the prophet:
2 LORD, I have heard the report of what you did;
I am awed, LORD, by what you accomplished.
In our time repeat those deeds;
in our time reveal them again.
But when you cause turmoil, remember to show us mercy!

3 God comes from Teman,
the Holy One from Mount Paran. *Selah.*
His splendor has covered the skies,
the earth is full of his glory.
4 His brightness will be as lightning;
a two-pronged lightning bolt flashing from his hand.
This is the outward display of his power.
5 Plague will go before him;
pestilence will march right behind him.
6 He took his battle position and shook the earth;
with a mere look he frightened the nations.
The ancient mountains disintegrated;
the primeval hills were flattened.
His are ancient roads.
7 I saw the tents of Cushan overwhelmed by trouble;
the tent curtains of the land
of Midian were shaking.
8 Was the LORD mad at the rivers?
Were you angry with the rivers?
Were you enraged at the sea?
Such that you would climb into your
horse-drawn chariots,
your victorious chariots?
9 Your bow is ready for action;
you commission your arrows. *Selah.*
You cause flash floods on the earth's surface.
10 When the mountains see you, they shake.
The torrential downpour sweeps through.
The great deep shouts out;
it lifts its hands high.
11 The sun and moon stand still in their courses;
the flash of your arrows drives them away,
the bright light of your lightning-quick spear.
12 You furiously stomp on the earth;
you angrily trample down the nations.
13 You march out to deliver your people,
to deliver your special servant.
You strike the leader of the wicked nation,
laying him open from the lower
body to the neck. *Selah.*
14 You pierce the heads of his warriors with a spear.
They storm forward to scatter us;
they shout with joy as if they were plundering
the poor with no opposition.
15 But you trample on the sea with your horses,
on the surging, raging waters.

REFLECT
How does Habakkuk's declaration encourage you to rejoice in the Lord no matter your circumstances? How can you praise the Lord today?

HABAKKUK DECLARES HIS CONFIDENCE

16 I listened and my stomach churned;
the sound made my lips quiver.
My frame went limp, as if my bones were decaying,
and I shook as I tried to walk.
I long for the day of distress
to come upon the people who attack us.

THE JOY OF OUR SALVATION

HABAKKUK 3:18–19

William Tyndale was a scholar who translated the Bible into an early form of modern English. He was outspoken about his views and especially passionate about the Good News of the gospel. Tyndale said, "*Evangelion* (that we call the gospel) is a Greek word and signifies good, merry, glad, and joyful tidings, that maketh a man's heart glad and maketh him sing, dance, and leap for joy."

He believed the free grace and total forgiveness we have in Christ are the basis of all our joy and comfort, the foundation of our peace and contentment, and what should make our hearts glad and our countenances cheerful.

Do we have this kind of joy?

All of us will encounter hard days and trying seasons. We see suffering all around us, both up close and personal and far away in other countries. Even in difficult circumstances, the work of Jesus makes it possible for us to be joyful. The forgiveness we have in Jesus ensures God is on our side and He will be with us in every circumstance. Our souls are safe, and though we cannot always see good in seasons of darkness, He promises that all our moments are used for our benefit and God's glory. God cannot break His promises.

The hope of joy goes beyond this world. Those who have the gift of forgiveness also receive the gift of adoption, which comes with an inheritance. We will, beyond a shadow of a doubt, come face to face with Jesus, and it will be a glorious day! Then our joy will be made complete. All difficulty and sin, all suffering and mourning will be no more! In its place will be a joy so pure that we will marvel and worship our God.

Keeping our future in mind affects the way we live today. Even though I feel like my fatigue is more than I can handle, I can make it through this day assured of all I have in Christ. I can rest in the promise of what I will receive in the future.

Underneath sufferings and trials, we can have robust joy because the penalty of our sins has been removed and our relationship with God is perfectly restored.

Jesus is our joy, but we won't experience this joy very much if we don't understand it. The more we understand all that Jesus has done for us and all we have in Him, the more joyful we will be.

17 When the fig tree does not bud,
and there are no grapes on the vines;
when the olive trees do not produce
and the fields yield no crops;
when the sheep disappear from the pen
and there are no cattle in the stalls—
18 I will rejoice because of the LORD;
I will be happy because of the God who delivers me!
19 The Sovereign LORD is my source of strength.
He gives me the agility of a deer;
he enables me to negotiate the rugged terrain.

(This prayer is for the song leader. It is to be accompanied by stringed instruments.)

"AT THAT TIME I will lead you—
at that time I GATHER
you together.
Be SURE of THIS!
I will make all the NATIONS
of the earth RESPECT
and ADMIRE you when
you see Me Restore
you," says the LORD.

MEMORY VERSE

"At that time I will lead you—at that time I gather you together. Be sure of this! I will make all the nations of the earth respect and admire you when you see me restore you," says the LORD.

Zephaniah 3:20

Zephaniah

INTRODUCTION

Restoration Through Repentance

The prophet Zephaniah called the people of Judah to repent and offered them hope that, for those who responded to His call, God would provide restoration. God's desire to restore His people is displayed throughout Zephaniah as He gives His people yet another opportunity to turn from their wickedness.

Zephaniah contains three main sections that build his message of restoration through repentance. First, Zephaniah gave a warning of impending judgment as he announced and defined the coming judgment (1:1–18). Second, Zephaniah called the people to repent and warned them of the destruction that would befall them if they did not (2:1—3:8). Third, Zephaniah described the future blessing that was to come and God's promise of restoration (3:9–20).

Zephaniah's prophetic ministry began around 627 B.C., about a century after the fall of Israel and about thirty years before the fall of Judah. Zephaniah was a prophet to the nation of Judah and a descendant of King Hezekiah. He was the author of the book that bears his name, and he probably compiled his messages shortly after he delivered them to the people of Judah.

The Book of Zephaniah offers great hope for God's people. God's promises to protect a remnant of His people and to give His people a future are clearly seen in this book. We are encouraged to love God greatly as we see the heart of God for His people: He longs to bring restoration, and when His people repent, He responds.

Singapore

OFFICIAL LANGUAGE
English and Malay
POPULATION
5,768,000
UNREACHED POPULATION
863,000
PROFESSING CHRISTIANS
13.3%

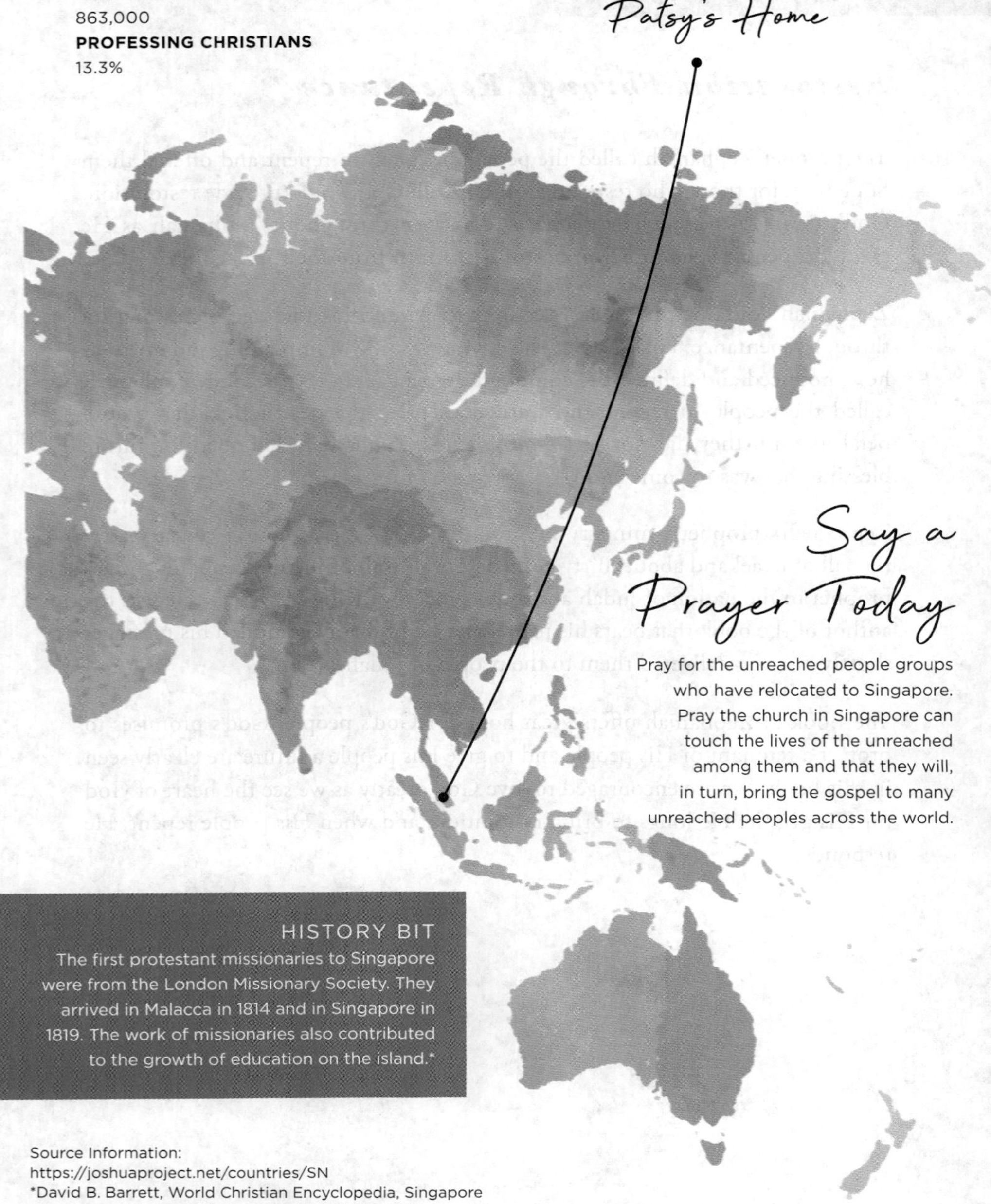

Patsy's Home

Say a Prayer Today

Pray for the unreached people groups who have relocated to Singapore. Pray the church in Singapore can touch the lives of the unreached among them and that they will, in turn, bring the gospel to many unreached peoples across the world.

HISTORY BIT

The first protestant missionaries to Singapore were from the London Missionary Society. They arrived in Malacca in 1814 and in Singapore in 1819. The work of missionaries also contributed to the growth of education on the island.*

Source Information:
https://joshuaproject.net/countries/SN
*David B. Barrett, World Christian Encyclopedia, Singapore (New York, NY: Oxford University Press, 1982), 614.

PATSY'S STORY

Before I became a Christian, I lived in darkness. I was deeply involved in worship of the god of hell (a Chinese deity). I lived in constant fear. I wanted to end my life. The only thing that stopped me was my terror of eternal torture in hell.

In the midst of my despair, I remembered hearing that those who believe in Christ would go to heaven. I followed my sister to church the next Sunday where I accepted Christ as my Lord and Savior. It was a great joy to know Him, and I left confident I had secured my place in heaven.

In the safety and assurance that came from knowing I had gained eternal life, I had no idea what other blessings would come as I walked with Christ. I was no longer gripped by fear. I became a much happier person. My life changed for the better.

A few months later, I attended a Christian seminar where I experienced God in ways I never thought possible. I felt His peace wash over me and His healing hands do a mighty work in my soul.

As I turned from my life of sin, God restored me. He fully saved me from the darkness I knew before Him. I am confident He has an incredible plan for my life. Soon after I placed my faith in Jesus, I was baptized. I hope to continue to share my faith in Jesus with others. I am a living testament to God's faithfulness and power to rescue and restore a life from the dark prison of hell. I claim the promises of God according to His Word daily, and I rest securely by trusting in Him.

6 WEEK READING PLAN

LOVE HIS WORD

	MONDAY	TUESDAY	WEDNESDAY	THURSDAY	FRIDAY
1	Micah 1:1-7	Micah 1:8-16	Micah 2:1-5	Micah 2:6-11	Micah 2:12—3:4
	SOAP Micah 1:2-3	SOAP 2 Kings 17:13-14	SOAP 2 Chronicles 36:15	SOAP Micah 2:7	SOAP Micah 2:12
2	Micah 3:5-12	Micah 4:1-8	Micah 4:9-13	Micah 5:1-6	Micah 5:7-15
	SOAP Psalm 82:8	SOAP Micah 4:5	SOAP Micah 4:12	SOAP Micah 5:4-5a	SOAP Micah 5:7
3	Micah 6:1-8	Micah 6:9-16	Micah 7:1-11	Micah 7:12-20	Nahum 1:1-3
	SOAP Micah 6:8	SOAP Job 40:8-9	SOAP Micah 7:7	SOAP Micah 7:18-20	SOAP Nahum 1:3
4	Nahum 1:4-15	Nahum 2:1-10	Nahum 2:11—3:3	Nahum 3:4-19	Habakkuk 1:1-11
	SOAP Nahum 1:5	SOAP Nahum 2:2	SOAP Psalm 143:11-12	SOAP Proverbs 21:15	SOAP Habakkuk 1:5
5	Habakkuk 1:12—2:1	Habakkuk 2:2-5	Habakkuk 2:6-20	Habakkuk 3:1-15	Habakkuk 3:16-19
	SOAP Habakkuk 1:12	SOAP 1 John 5:14-15	SOAP Habakkuk 2:20	SOAP Habakkuk 3:2	SOAP Habakkuk 3:18-19
6	Zephaniah 1	Zephaniah 2:1-3	Zephaniah 2:4-15	Zephaniah 3:1-5	Zephaniah 3:6-20
	SOAP Romans 9:22	SOAP Zephaniah 2:3	SOAP Zephaniah 2:11	SOAP Zephaniah 3:5	SOAP Zephaniah 3:20

INTRODUCTION

1 This is the LORD's message that came to Zephaniah son of Cushi, son of Gedaliah, son of Amariah, son of Hezekiah during the time of Josiah son of Amon, king of Judah:

THE LORD'S DAY OF JUDGMENT IS APPROACHING

2 "I will destroy everything from the face
of the earth," says the LORD.
3 "I will destroy people and animals;
I will destroy the birds in the sky
and the fish in the sea.
(The idolatrous images of these creatures will
be destroyed along with evil people.)
I will remove humanity from the face
of the earth," says the LORD.
4 "I will attack Judah
and all who live in Jerusalem.
I will remove from this place every
trace of Baal worship,
as well as the very memory of the pagan priests.
5 I will remove those who worship the stars
in the sky from their rooftops,
those who swear allegiance to the LORD while
taking oaths in the name of their 'king,'
6 and those who turn their backs on the LORD
and do not want the LORD's help or guidance."
7 Be silent before the Sovereign LORD,
for the LORD's day of judgment is almost here.
The LORD has prepared a sacrificial meal;
he has ritually purified his guests.
8 "On the day of the LORD's sacrificial meal,
I will punish the princes and the king's sons,
and all who wear foreign styles of clothing.
9 On that day I will punish all who leap
over the threshold,
who fill the house of their master with
wealth taken by violence and deceit.
10 On that day," says the LORD,
"a loud cry will go up from the Fish Gate,
wailing from the city's newer district,
and a loud crash from the hills.
11 Wail, you who live in the market district,
for all the merchants will disappear
and those who count money will be removed.
12 At that time I will search through
Jerusalem with lamps.
I will punish the people who are entrenched in their sin,
those who think to themselves,
'The LORD neither rewards nor punishes.'
13 Their wealth will be stolen
and their houses ruined!
They will not live in the houses they have built,
nor will they drink the wine from the
vineyards they have planted.

14 The LORD's great day of judgment is almost here;
it is approaching very rapidly!
There will be a bitter sound on the
LORD's day of judgment;
at that time warriors will cry out in battle.
15 That day will be a day of God's anger,
a day of distress and hardship,
a day of devastation and ruin,
a day of darkness and gloom,
a day of clouds and dark skies,
16 a day of trumpet blasts and battle cries.
Judgment will fall on the fortified cities
and the high corner towers.
17 I will bring distress on the people
and they will stumble like blind men,
for they have sinned against the LORD.
Their blood will be poured out like dirt;
their flesh will be scattered like manure.
18 Neither their silver nor their gold
will be able to deliver them
in the day of the LORD's angry judgment.
The whole earth will be consumed by his fiery wrath.
Indeed, he will bring terrifying destruction
on all who live on the earth."

REFLECT

Why was the Lord bringing His judgment on the people of Judah? Was He justified in His actions? Why or why not?

THE PROPHET WARNS THE PEOPLE

2 Bunch yourselves together like straw,
you undesirable nation,
2 before God's decree becomes reality and the day of
opportunity disappears like windblown chaff,
before the LORD's raging anger overtakes you—
before the day of the LORD's angry
judgment overtakes you!
3 Seek the LORD's favor, all you humble people of
the land who have obeyed his commands!
Strive to do what is right! Strive to be humble!
Maybe you will be protected on the day
of the LORD's angry judgment.

JUDGMENT ON SURROUNDING NATIONS

4 Indeed, Gaza will be deserted
and Ashkelon will become a heap of ruins.
Invaders will drive away the people of Ashdod by noon,
and Ekron will be overthrown.
5 Beware, you who live by the sea, the
people who came from Crete.
The LORD's message is against you,
Canaan, land of the Philistines:
"I will destroy everyone who lives there!"
6 The seacoast will be used as pasture
lands by the shepherds
and as pens for their flocks.
7 Those who are left from the kingdom of
Judah will take possession of it.

REFLECT

What does it mean to seek the Lord's favor? How can we live this out every day?

By the sea they will graze,
in the houses of Ashkelon they will
lie down in the evening,
for the LORD their God will intervene for
them and restore their prosperity.
8 "I have heard Moab's taunts
and the Ammonites' insults.
They taunted my people
and verbally harassed those living in Judah.
9 Therefore, as surely as I live," says the LORD
of Heaven's Armies, the God of Israel,
"be certain that Moab will become like Sodom
and the Ammonites like Gomorrah.
They will be overrun by weeds,
filled with salt pits,
and permanently desolate.
Those of my people who are left will
plunder their belongings;
those who are left in Judah will take
possession of their land."
10 This is how they will be repaid for their arrogance,
for they taunted and verbally harassed the
people of the LORD of Heaven's Armies.
11 The LORD will terrify them,
for he will weaken all the gods of the earth.
All the distant nations will worship
the LORD in their own lands.
12 "You Ethiopians will also die by my sword!"
13 The LORD will attack the north
and destroy Assyria.
He will make Nineveh a heap of ruins;
it will be as barren as the desert.
14 Flocks and herds will lie down in the middle of it,
as well as every kind of wild animal.
Owls will sleep in the tops of its support pillars;
they will hoot through the windows.
Rubble will cover the thresholds;
even the cedar work will be exposed to the elements.
15 This is how the once-proud city will end up—
the city that was so secure.
She thought to herself, "I am unique!
No one can compare to me!"
What a heap of ruins she has become, a
place where wild animals live!
Everyone who passes by her taunts
her and shakes his fist.

JERUSALEM IS CORRUPT

3 Beware to the filthy, stained city;
the city filled with oppressors!
2 She is disobedient;
she has refused correction.
She does not trust the LORD;
she has not sought the advice of her God.

3 Her princes are as fierce as roaring lions;
her rulers are as hungry as wolves in the desert,
who completely devour their prey by morning.
4 Her prophets are proud;
they are deceitful men.
Her priests have defiled what is holy;
they have broken God's laws.
5 The just LORD resides within her;
he commits no unjust acts.
Every morning he reveals his justice.
At dawn he appears without fail.
Yet the unjust know no shame.

THE LORD'S JUDGMENT WILL PURIFY

6 "I destroyed nations;
their walled cities are in ruins.
I turned their streets into ruins;
no one passes through them.
Their cities are desolate;
no one lives there.
7 I thought, 'Certainly you will respect me!
Now you will accept correction!'
If she had done so, her home would not be destroyed
by all the punishments I have threatened.
But they eagerly sinned
in everything they did.
8 Therefore you must wait patiently for me," says the LORD,
"for the day when I attack and take plunder.
I have decided to gather nations together
and assemble kingdoms,
so I can pour out my fury on them—
all my raging anger.
For the whole earth will be consumed
by my fiery anger.
9 Know for sure that I will then enable
the nations to give me acceptable praise.
All of them will invoke the LORD's name when they pray,
and will worship him in unison.
10 From beyond the rivers of Ethiopia,
those who pray to me, my dispersed people,
will bring me tribute.
11 In that day you will not be ashamed of all
your rebelliousness against me,
for then I will remove from your midst
those who proudly boast,
and you will never again be arrogant on my holy hill.
12 I will leave in your midst a humble
and meek group of people,
and they will find safety in the LORD's presence.
13 The Israelites who remain will not act deceitfully.
They will not lie,
and a deceitful tongue will not be found in their mouths.
Indeed, they will graze peacefully like sheep and lie down;
no one will terrify them."

POSTURE FOR HIS PRESENCE

ZEPHANIAH 3:11–17

A terra-cotta pot brimming with thyme sits in the window above my kitchen sink. I love the way it reaches for the sun. No matter which way I turn the pot, within an hour or two the sprigs have changed their direction, and they lean toward the warmth of the sunlight. They know instinctively their survival depends on it.

Occasionally, I've taken the pot down from the window ledge and set it on the counter. Without fail, after a couple of days, I notice its withering, brown leaves. The plant begins to look lifeless and sickly. When I add water and return it to its window, it revives, and its green arms reach for the sun. The thin stems, encumbered by nothing, lean in and receive. What a picture of humility and our utter need for God. His presence is everything. When we lean in, admitting our complete and total dependence on Him, we rest securely and find sustaining life.

The words of Zephaniah 3:17 are captivating. The God of the universe connects with us on a personal level, shouts for joy, and rejoices over us. The thought is breathtaking; the idea that He would actually delight in us seems unfathomable.

I had not noticed until recently, though, the preceding verses reveal a stark moment of reckoning: God determines who will remain in His presence. His criteria for selection? Humility. God sustains those who evidence full submission to Him, who have recognized their utter dependence on Him alone. The humble find safety in the Lord's presence.

Children of God flourish as we rest in His presence, but in our foolishness and self-centeredness, we often neglect to seek what's best. We have before us the chance to enjoy peace and lie down in safety, yet we yield to the temptation to be terrified. We have the chance to happily boast in the Lord's goodness, but instead, we boast in our own accomplishments.

The light of the Lord's presence brings life. When we neglect to humbly seek it, we wither.

Because of the reconciling work of God through Christ, we have become recipients of that inestimable gift: the indwelling of the Light Himself, the Holy Spirit, who continuously renews us with His love and proclaims His delight in us with shouts of joy.

14 Shout for joy, Daughter Zion!
Shout out, Israel!
Be happy and boast with all your
heart, Daughter Jerusalem!
15 The LORD has removed the judgment against you;
he has turned back your enemy.
Israel's king, the LORD, is in your midst!
You no longer need to fear disaster.
16 On that day they will say to Jerusalem,
"Don't be afraid, Zion!
Your hands must not be paralyzed from panic!
17 The LORD your God is in your midst;
he is a warrior who can deliver.
He takes great delight in you;
he renews you by his love;
he shouts for joy over you."
18 "As for those who grieve because they
cannot attend the festivals—
I took them away from you;
they became tribute and were a source of shame to you.
19 Look, at that time I will deal with
those who mistreated you.
I will rescue the lame sheep
and gather together the scattered sheep.
I will take away their humiliation
and make the whole earth admire and respect them.
20 At that time I will lead you—
at the time I gather you together.
Be sure of this! I will make all the nations of
the earth respect and admire you
when you see me restore you," says the LORD.

CHALLENGE

Take time today to meditate on this verse. How does God see you? What does this tell you about His care for you? Do you believe these truths? Put these words somewhere you will see them often and let the truth of God's love wash over you each day.

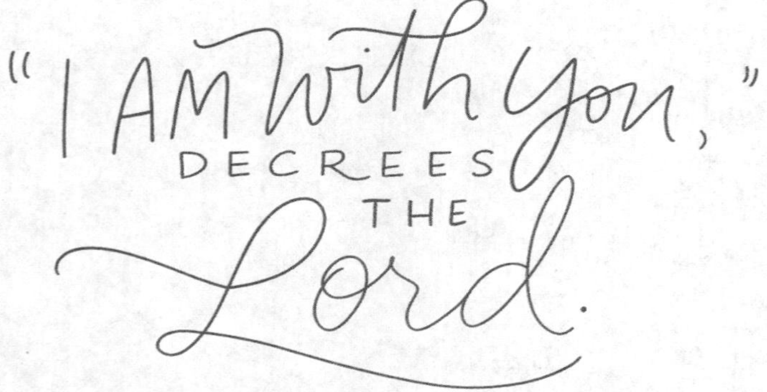

MEMORY VERSE

Then Haggai, the LORD's messenger, spoke the LORD's announcement to the people: "I am with you," decrees the LORD. So the LORD energized and encouraged Zerubbabel son of Shealtiel, governor of Judah . . . They came and worked on the temple of their God, the LORD of Heaven's Armies.

Haggai 1:13–14

Haggai

INTRODUCTION

Rebuilding

The Book of Haggai records the words the prophet Haggai spoke to the Jews who had returned to Jerusalem after their exile in Babylon. Haggai challenged the people to examine their priorities and to rebuild the temple with hearts committed to God. The people responded and continued to do the work as Haggai shared God's message: He was with them, offering encouragement to the weary and discouraged.

Haggai presented a brief message, calling the people to rebuild the temple in Jerusalem in order to reestablish the worship of Yahweh. The people were indifferent at the beginning, but they soon repented and committed their work to the Lord. After the temple was finished, the people were discouraged because it was significantly less impressive than the first temple. Haggai shared God's message of encouragement with the people as He promised to give them a greater temple and greater blessings.

The events in the Book of Haggai occurred in the sixth century B.C.; the temple rebuilding process began around 536 B.C., Haggai preached his message in 520 B.C., and the temple was completed in 515 B.C. The Book of Haggai was written by the prophet Haggai, and he is mentioned in Ezra 5:1 and 6:14 as a contemporary of the prophet Zechariah.

This book explains a critical messianic connection between the Old and New Testaments. Zerubbabel, a descendant of David, was the governor of Judah after the exiles' return. Haggai declared that Zerubbabel would become the way in which God continued to fulfill His promise to keep one of David's descendants on the throne of Judah. Five hundred years later, Jesus was declared the King of the Jews, holding the true authority of the line of David and the power to rule. Haggai reminds us of God's faithful commitment to His covenant, offering us yet another reason to love God greatly.

Curaçao

OFFICIAL LANGUAGE
Dutch, English, and Papiamentu
POPULATION
161,000
UNREACHED POPULATION
800
PROFESSING CHRISTIANS
86.0%

Nadine's Home

Say a Prayer Today

Pray for the church in Curaçao to grow and that biblical literacy will increase with the Papiamento Bible. Pray for the renewal of the Christian population in this small country.

HISTORY BIT

The first Bible published in the Papiamento language was completed in 1997.*

Source Information:
https://joshuaproject.net/countries/UC
*Jason Mandryk, Operation *World,* 7th edition (Colorado Springs, CO: Biblica Publishing, 2010), 629.

NADINE'S STORY

I'm from Curaçao, a small Dutch Caribbean island. I currently live in Dallas where I attend an evangelical seminary and serve as an associate children's minister in my local church. In Curaçao, I did not grow up in a Christian home. When I was twelve years old I attended a Christian children's camp and heard the gospel for the first time. A few months later I trusted Jesus as my Lord and Savior.

As I grew up I became eager to learn more about God and His Word. At seventeen, I served as a translator for a group of American teenagers visiting Curaçao on a missionary trip. Through that experience God put the desire to go to a Bible college in my heart. I failed to follow through and decided to pursue a professional degree instead. I moved to the Netherlands to attend university and then worked as a business consultant managing projects.

Years went by and I had forgotten about my dream to study God's Word. In 2014, I moved back to Curaçao. I did not see much fruit in my own life, nor in the lives of many Christians I knew. I wrestled with a desire to do more with God and to see fruit in my life. A friend introduced me to Love God Greatly. I studied Galatians with a group of three other women. God used this study to help me understand that in order to be a doer of His Word, I needed His grace, and I needed to constantly rely on the Holy Spirit.

No matter if we've turned from the path God has for us, He is faithful to rebuild our lives so they are aligned with His plan. Through this study and a mission trip to the Dominican Republic in 2015, the Lord again stirred in me the desire to pursue vocational ministry and the study of His Word. My prayer for myself and the people of God throughout the world is that we may be lifelong students and doers of God's Word.

4 WEEK READING PLAN

LOVE HIS WORD

MONDAY	TUESDAY	WEDNESDAY	THURSDAY	FRIDAY
Haggai 1	Haggai 2	Zechariah 1	Zechariah 2	Zechariah 3
SOAP Haggai 1:13–14	SOAP Haggai 2:23	SOAP Zechariah 1:6	SOAP Zechariah 2:10–11	SOAP Zechariah 3:10
Zechariah 4	Zechariah 5	Zechariah 6	Zechariah 7	Zechariah 8
SOAP Zechariah 4:6	SOAP Zechariah 5:10–11	SOAP Zechariah 6:15	SOAP Zechariah 7:8–10	SOAP Zechariah 8:22
Zechariah 9	Zechariah 10	Zechariah 11	Zechariah 12	Zechariah 13
SOAP Zechariah 9:16	SOAP Zechariah 10:1	SOAP Zechariah 11:6	SOAP Zechariah 12:10	SOAP Zechariah 13:9
Zechariah 14	Malachi 1	Malachi 2:1—3:5	Malachi 3:6–12	Malachi 3:13—4:6
SOAP Zechariah 14:3	SOAP Malachi 1:14	SOAP Malachi 3:1	SOAP Malachi 3:6–7	SOAP Malachi 4:2–3

INTRODUCTION

1 On the first day of the sixth month of King Darius' second year,
the LORD's message came through the prophet Haggai to Zerubbabel son of Shealtiel, governor of Judah, and to the high
priest Joshua son of Jehozadak:

THE ACCUSATION OF INDIFFERENCE AGAINST THE PEOPLE

2 This is what the LORD of Heaven's Armies has said: "These people have said, 'The time for rebuilding the LORD's temple has
not yet come.'" 3 The LORD's message came through the prophet
Haggai as follows: 4 "Is it right for you to live in richly paneled
houses while my temple is in ruins? 5 Here then, this is what the
LORD of Heaven's Armies has said: 'Think carefully about what
you are doing. 6 You have planted much, but have harvested little. You eat, but are never filled. You drink, but are still thirsty.
You put on clothes, but are not warm. Those who earn wages end
up with holes in their money bags.'"

CONSEQUENCES OF THE FAILURE TO REBUILD THE TEMPLE

7 Moreover, this is what the LORD of Heaven's Armies has said:
"Pay close attention to these things also. 8 Go up to the hill country and bring back timber to build the temple. Then I will be
pleased and honored," says the LORD. 9 "You expected a large harvest, but instead there was little. And when you would bring it
home, I would blow it right away. Why?" asks the LORD of Heaven's
Armies. "Because my temple remains in ruins, thanks to each of
you favoring his own house! 10 This is why the sky has held back
its dew and the earth its produce. 11 Moreover, I have called for a
drought that will affect the fields, the hill country, the grain, new
wine, fresh olive oil, and everything that grows from the ground;
it also will harm people, animals, and everything they produce."

THE RESPONSE OF THE LEADERS AND THE PEOPLE

12 Then Zerubbabel son of Shealtiel and the high priest Joshua son
of Jehozadak, along with the whole remnant of the people, obeyed
the LORD their God. They responded favorably to the message of
the prophet Haggai, who spoke just as the LORD their God had instructed him, and the people began to respect the LORD. 13 Then
Haggai, the LORD's messenger, spoke the LORD's announcement
to the people: "I am with you," decrees the LORD. 14 So the LORD
energized and encouraged Zerubbabel son of Shealtiel, governor
of Judah, the high priest Joshua son of Jehozadak, and the whole
remnant of the people. They came and worked on the temple of
their God, the LORD of Heaven's Armies. 15 This took place on the
twenty-fourth day of the sixth month of King Darius' second year.

CHALLENGE

What other times has God promised to be with His people? Did He keep this promise? Does He keep this promise to you?

THE GLORY TO COME

2 On the twenty-first day of the seventh month, the LORD's
message came through the prophet Haggai again: 2 "Ask the
following questions to Zerubbabel son of Shealtiel, governor
of Judah, the high priest Joshua son of Jehozadak, and the remnant of the people: 3 'Who among you survivors saw the former

BUILD MY TEMPLE

HAGGAI 1:2–11

The Book of Haggai recounts God's challenge to Israel to rebuild the temple after their return from exile. The Persian king Cyrus allowed the Israelites to return to Jerusalem after seventy years in exile. Ezra led the charge to rebuild the temple.

In the Book of Ezra, we read the Israelites were excited and motivated to begin rebuilding. However, because of opposition and discouragement, all work ceased after the completion of the temple's foundation. The people turned their attention to building their own homes.

In Haggai 1:5–11, God warned the Israelites they would have no success on their own. Because of their disobedience and neglect God caused a drought (v. 11). They would plant but harvest little. They would eat and drink but never be full. They would earn wages but never have enough.

Rebuilding the temple was important because it was the place where God's presence dwelled among His people. The infinite, eternal, and omniscient God—who is not bound by time, space, or distance—could be anywhere and everywhere, yet He desired to be with them. The Israelites needed the tangible reminder of God's presence and power with them after decades of captivity away from their home in the promised land.

In Haggai 1:5, God warned them, "Think carefully about what you are doing." When life's circumstances become difficult, we tend to protect our self-interest and focus on ourselves instead of trusting God.

When we react out of fear and focus solely on ourselves, we miss out on God's great promises and plans for us. First Corinthians 6:19–20 tells us that for those who confess Jesus Christ as Lord and Savior, our bodies are the temples of the Holy Spirit. Our bodies are God's sacred temple and our choices and our actions matter. God calls us to glorify Him with our words, our thoughts, our attitudes, and our actions.

As we love God greatly, we surrender our personal comfort, our ambitions, our dreams, and our plans to the Almighty God who knows us better than we know ourselves. We demonstrate our love for God when we make Him the center of our lives, obeying and serving Him above all else.

splendor of this temple? How does it look to you now? Isn't it nothing by comparison?' 4 Even so, take heart, Zerubbabel," decrees the LORD. "Take heart, Joshua son of Jehozadak, the high priest. And take heart all you citizens of the land," decrees the LORD, "and begin to work. For I am with you," decrees the LORD of Heaven's Armies. 5 "Do not fear, because I made a promise to your ancestors when they left Egypt, and my Spirit even now testifies to you." 6 Moreover, this is what the LORD of Heaven's Armies has said: "In just a little while I will once again shake the sky and the earth, the sea and the dry ground. 7 I will also shake up all the nations, and they will offer their treasures; then I will fill this temple with glory." So the LORD of Heaven's Armies has said. 8 "The silver and gold will be mine," decrees the LORD of Heaven's Armies. 9 "The future splendor of this temple will be greater than that of former times," the LORD of Heaven's Armies has declared. "And in this place I will give peace," decrees the LORD of Heaven's Armies.

THE PROMISED BLESSING

10 On the twenty-fourth day of the ninth month of Darius' second year, the LORD's message came to the prophet Haggai: 11 "This is what the LORD of Heaven's Armies has said, 'Ask the priests about the law. 12 If someone carries holy meat in a fold of his garment and that fold touches bread, a boiled dish, wine, olive oil, or any other food, will that item become holy?'" The priests answered, "It will not." 13 Then Haggai asked, "If a person who is ritually unclean because of touching a dead body comes in contact with one of these items, will it become unclean?" The priests answered, "It will be unclean."

14 Then Haggai responded, "'The people of this nation are unclean in my sight,' decrees the LORD. 'And so is all their effort; everything they offer is also unclean. 15 Now therefore reflect carefully on the recent past, before one stone was laid on another in the LORD's temple. 16 From that time when one came expecting a heap of twenty measures, there were only ten; when one came to the wine vat to draw out fifty measures from it, there were only twenty. 17 I struck all the products of your labor with blight, disease, and hail, and yet you brought nothing to me,' says the LORD. 18 'Think carefully about the past: from today, the twenty-fourth day of the ninth month, to the day work on the temple of the LORD was resumed, think about it. 19 The seed is still in the storehouse, isn't it? And the vine, fig tree, pomegranate, and olive tree have not produced. Nevertheless, from today on I will bless you.'"

REFLECT

How did God's promise to bless the people of Judah encourage the people? How does it inspire you?

ZERUBBABEL THE CHOSEN ONE

20 Then the LORD spoke to Haggai a second time on the twenty-fourth day of the month: 21 "Tell Zerubbabel governor of Judah: 'I am ready to shake the sky and the earth. 22 I will overthrow royal thrones and shatter the might of earthly kingdoms. I will overthrow chariots and those who ride them, and horses and their riders will fall as people kill one another. 23 On that day,' says the LORD of Heaven's Armies, 'I will take you, Zerubbabel son of Shealtiel, my servant,' says the LORD, 'and I will make you like a signet ring, for I have chosen you,' says the LORD of Heaven's Armies."

ON THAT DAY
THE LORD their GOD
will deliver them
as the flock of his
People, FOR THEY ARE
precious stones
OF A CROWN
Sparkling OVER
His land

MEMORY VERSE

On that day the Lord their God will deliver them as the flock of his people, for they are the precious stones of a crown sparkling over his land.
Zechariah 9:16

Zechariah

INTRODUCTION

God Remembers

The name *Zechariah* means "Yahweh Remembers." The prophetic message of Zechariah included powerful messages of hope: God would remember His people. He is always with them, no matter the circumstance. Even after their destruction the divine election of Jerusalem and Judah still stood, and God promised to dwell with His people once again.

The first half of the Book of Zechariah offered encouragement to the people that they were God's chosen nation. The latter half of the book details God's future dealings with His people, reminding them of the ways He had given them victory over their enemies. The complete restoration of God's people was at the forefront of Zechariah's message as he reminded the people of the redeeming and delivering work of the coming Messiah.

A contemporary of the prophet Haggai, Zechariah ministered to the returning exiles in Jerusalem after their return to Judah, and he encouraged them to continue building the temple. The Jews began to return to Judah in 538 B.C., the temple rebuilding resumed in 520 B.C., and the temple was completed in 515 B.C.

Zechariah highlights the coming Messiah, offering an important message about God's plan for salvation. Zechariah's message communicates a great truth: God always remembers His people. Even in the midst of heartache, unexpected pain, or long-term suffering, we can love God greatly knowing this is true.

Indonesia

OFFICIAL LANGUAGE
Indonesian
POPULATION
269,193,000
UNREACHED POPULATION
167,895,000
PROFESSING CHRISTIANS
12.7%

Helen's Home

Say a Prayer Today

Pray for Helen and her ministry to the people of Indonesia. Pray that God would continue to send more "Zechariahs" to the unreached people in Indonesia so they will hear and believe the truth of Jesus Christ.

HISTORY BIT

While evidence of the presence of Christianity in Indonesia can be traced back to the seventh century, the country today is largely a Muslim country. Due to Portuguese colonial expansion, Portuguese missionaries had significant influence on the country and religion in the sixteenth century.*

Source Information:
https://joshuaproject.net/countries/ID
*David B. Barrett, World Christian Encyclopedia, Indonesia (New York, NY: Oxford University Press, 1982), 383.

HELEN'S STORY

I remember it like it was yesterday. I walked into the faculty office of my college with a form in my hand. I was withdrawing from school indefinitely. I was broken. I felt helpless and hopeless. I felt as though I was giving up my future, my opportunity to do work I loved and support my family. I was disappointed with God.

I thought I knew the one true God, but at the time my view of God was small. I grew up in Indonesia, knowing and worshiping other gods. I had heard of the Christian God, but I didn't really know anything about Him.

My last day on campus, a classmate saw me sitting in the garden crying. She told me how God cared for and remembered me. She told me that even in my sin, God loved me and rescued me. I gave Him my life that day. He has never once failed me.

In the same way God remembered me that day in the garden, God remembered His people, Israel. God gave this promise to Zechariah so His people would have hope when their enemies defeated them. He gives us the same promise: He remembers us.

In Indonesia, I see so much poverty, so much social injustice, and so much inequality and oppression. There are many unreached people who need to hear the truth of Jesus Christ—the only way to God.

God remembers the people of Indonesia. He has sent the Rescuer to help them. They need to hear the voice of the Great Shepherd who will lead them to the Father. My prayer is that God will continue to send more "Zechariahs" to the unreached people in Indonesia so that they will hear about Jesus and worship Him.

4 WEEK READING PLAN

LOVE HIS WORD

MONDAY	TUESDAY	WEDNESDAY	THURSDAY	FRIDAY
Haggai 1	Haggai 2	Zechariah 1	Zechariah 2	Zechariah 3
SOAP Haggai 1:13-14	SOAP Haggai 2:23	SOAP Zechariah 1:6	SOAP Zechariah 2:10-11	SOAP Zechariah 3:10
Zechariah 4	Zechariah 5	Zechariah 6	Zechariah 7	Zechariah 8
SOAP Zechariah 4:6	SOAP Zechariah 5:10-11	SOAP Zechariah 6:15	SOAP Zechariah 7:8-10	SOAP Zechariah 8:22
Zechariah 9	Zechariah 10	Zechariah 11	Zechariah 12	Zechariah 13
SOAP Zechariah 9:16	SOAP Zechariah 10:1	SOAP Zechariah 11:6	SOAP Zechariah 12:10	SOAP Zechariah 13:9
Zechariah 14	Malachi 1	Malachi 2:1—3:5	Malachi 3:6-12	Malachi 3:13—4:6
SOAP Zechariah 14:3	SOAP Malachi 1:14	SOAP Malachi 3:1	SOAP Malachi 3:6-7	SOAP Malachi 4:2-3

INTRODUCTION

1 In the eighth month of Darius' second year, the LORD's message
came to the prophet Zechariah, son of Berechiah son of Iddo:
2 "The LORD was very angry with your ancestors. 3 Therefore say
to the people: The LORD of Heaven's Armies says, 'Turn to me,'
says the LORD of Heaven's Armies, 'and I will turn to you,' says
the LORD of Heaven's Armies. 4 Do not be like your ancestors,
to whom the former prophets called out, saying, 'This is what
the LORD of Heaven's Armies has said, "Turn now from your
evil wickedness."' But they would by no means obey me, says
the LORD. 5 As for your ancestors, where are they? And did the
prophets live forever? 6 But have my words and statutes, which
I commanded my servants the prophets, not outlived your fathers? Then they paid attention and confessed, 'The LORD of
Heaven's Armies has indeed done what he said he would do to
us, because of our sinful ways.'"

CHALLENGE

Read Ezra 4:24—6:22. What does it tell you about the historical setting of the Book of Zechariah?

THE INTRODUCTION TO THE VISIONS

7 On the twenty-fourth day of the eleventh month, the month
Shebat, in Darius' second year, the LORD's message came to the
prophet Zechariah son of Berechiah son of Iddo:

THE CONTENT OF THE FIRST VISION

8 I was attentive that night and saw a man seated on a red horse
that stood among some myrtle trees in the ravine. Behind him
were red, sorrel, and white horses.

THE INTERPRETATION OF THE FIRST VISION

9 Then I asked one nearby, "What are these, sir?" The angelic messenger who replied to me said, "I will show you what these are."
10 Then the man standing among the myrtle trees spoke up and
said, "These are the ones whom the LORD has sent to walk about
on the earth." 11 The riders then agreed with the angel of the LORD,
who was standing among the myrtle trees, "We have been walking about on the earth, and now everything is at rest and quiet."
12 The angel of the LORD then asked, "O LORD of Heaven's Armies,
how long before you have compassion on Jerusalem and the other cities of Judah that you have been so angry with for these seventy years?" 13 The LORD then addressed good, comforting words
to the angelic messenger who was speaking to me. 14 Turning to
me, the messenger then said, "Cry out that the LORD of Heav-
en's Armies says, 'I am very much moved for Jerusalem and for
Zion. 15 But I am greatly displeased with the nations that take my
grace for granted. I was a little displeased with them, but they
have only made things worse for themselves.

THE ORACLE OF RESPONSE

16 "'Therefore,' this is what the LORD has said, 'I have become
compassionate toward Jerusalem and will rebuild my temple in
it,' says the LORD of Heaven's Armies. 'Once more a surveyor's
measuring line will be stretched out over Jerusalem.' 17 Speak up
again with the message of the LORD of Heaven's Armies: 'My cities will once more overflow with prosperity, and once more the
LORD will comfort Zion and validate his choice of Jerusalem.'"

VISION TWO: THE FOUR HORNS

18 Once again I looked and this time I saw four horns. 19 So I asked
the angelic messenger who spoke with me, "What are these?" He
replied, "These are the horns that have scattered Judah, Israel,
and Jerusalem." 20 Next the LORD showed me four blacksmiths. 21 I
asked, "What are these going to do?" He answered, "These horns
are the ones that have scattered Judah so that there is no one to
be seen. But the blacksmiths have come to terrify Judah's enemies and cut off the horns of the nations that have thrust themselves against the land of Judah in order to scatter its people."

VISION THREE: THE SURVEYOR

2 I looked again, and there was a man with a measuring line
in his hand. 2 I asked, "Where are you going?" He replied,
"To measure Jerusalem in order to determine its width and its
length." 3 At this point the angelic messenger who spoke to me
went out, and another messenger came to meet him 4 and said
to him, "Hurry, speak to this young man as follows: 'Jerusalem
will no longer be enclosed by walls because of the multitude of
people and animals there. 5 But I,' the LORD says, 'will be a wall of
fire surrounding Jerusalem and the source of glory in her midst.'"
6 "You there! Flee from the northland!" says the LORD, "for like
the four winds of heaven I have scattered you," says the LORD.
7 "Escape, Zion, you who live among the Babylonians!" 8 For the
LORD of Heaven's Armies says: "For his own glory he has sent me
to the nations that plundered you—for anyone who touches you
touches the pupil of his eye. 9 Yes, look here, I am about to punish them so that they will be looted by their own slaves." Then
you will know that the LORD of Heaven's Armies has sent me.
10 "Sing out and be happy, Zion my daughter! For look, I have
come; I will settle in your midst," says the LORD. 11 "Many nations
will join themselves to the LORD on the day of salvation, and
they will also be my people. Indeed, I will settle in the midst of
you all. Then you will know that the LORD of Heaven's Armies
has sent me to you. 12 The LORD will take possession of Judah as
his portion in the holy land and he will choose Jerusalem once
again. 13 Be silent in the LORD's presence, all people everywhere,
for he is being moved to action in his holy dwelling place."

VISION FOUR: THE PRIEST

3 Next I saw Joshua the high priest standing before the angel
of the LORD, with Satan standing at his right hand to accuse
him. 2 The LORD said to Satan, "May the LORD rebuke you, Satan!
May the LORD, who has chosen Jerusalem, rebuke you! Isn't this
man like a burning stick snatched from the fire?" 3 Now Joshua
was dressed in filthy clothes as he stood there before the angel.
4 The angel spoke up to those standing all around, "Remove his
filthy clothes." Then he said to Joshua, "I have freely forgiven your
iniquity and will dress you in fine clothing." 5 Then I spoke up, "Let
a clean turban be put on his head." So they put a clean turban
on his head and clothed him, while the angel of the LORD stood
nearby. 6 Then the angel of the LORD exhorted Joshua solemnly:
7 "The LORD of Heaven's Armies says, 'If you follow my ways and
keep my requirements, you will be able to preside over my temple

and attend to my courtyards, and I will allow you to come and go
among these others who are standing by you. 8 Listen now, Joshua
the high priest, both you and your colleagues who are sitting before you, all of you are a symbol that I am about to introduce my
servant, the Branch. 9 As for the stone I have set before Joshua—on
the one stone there are seven eyes. I am about to engrave an inscription on it,' says the LORD of Heaven's Armies, 'to the effect
that I will remove the iniquity of this land in a single day. 10 In
that day,' says the LORD of Heaven's Armies, 'everyone will invite
his friend to fellowship under his vine and under his fig tree.'"

VISION FIVE: THE MENORAH

4 The angelic messenger who had been speaking with me then
returned and woke me, as a person is wakened from sleep.
2 He asked me, "What do you see?" I replied, "I see a menorah of
pure gold with a receptacle at the top. There are seven lamps at
the top, with seven pipes going to the lamps. 3 There are also two
olive trees beside it, one on the right of the receptacle and the
other on the left." 4 Then I asked the messenger who spoke with
me, "What are these, sir?" 5 He replied, "Don't you know what
these are?" So I responded, "No, sir." 6 Therefore he told me, "This
is the LORD's message to Zerubbabel: 'Not by strength and not
by power, but by my Spirit,' says the LORD of Heaven's Armies.

ORACLE OF RESPONSE

7 "What are you, you great mountain? Because of Zerubbabel you
will become a level plain! And he will bring forth the temple cap-
stone with shoutings of 'Grace! Grace!' because of this." 8 Moreover, the LORD's message came to me as follows: 9 "The hands of
Zerubbabel have laid the foundations of this temple, and his
hands will complete it. Then you will know that the LORD of
Heaven's Armies has sent me to you. 10 For who dares make light
of small beginnings? These seven eyes will joyfully look on the
tin tablet in Zerubbabel's hand. These are the eyes of the LORD,
which constantly range across the whole earth."

11 Next I asked the messenger, "What are these two olive trees
on the right and the left of the menorah?" 12 Before he could reply I asked again, "What are these two extensions of the olive
trees, which are emptying out the golden oil through the two
golden pipes?" 13 He replied, "Don't you know what these are?"
And I said, "No, sir." 14 So he said, "These are the two anointed
ones who stand by the Lord of the whole earth."

VISION SIX: THE FLYING SCROLL

5 Then I turned to look, and there was a flying scroll! 2 Someone
asked me, "What do you see?" I replied, "I see a flying scroll
30 feet long and 15 feet wide." 3 The speaker went on to say, "This
is a curse traveling across the whole earth. For example, according to the curse whoever steals will be removed from the community; or on the other hand (according to the curse) whoever
swears falsely will suffer the same fate." 4 "I will send it out," says
the LORD of Heaven's Armies, "and it will enter the house of the
thief and of the person who swears falsely in my name. It will land
in the middle of his house and destroy both timber and stones."

REFLECT

Why was it important for the iniquity of the people to be removed? What does this show about God and His holiness?

VISION SEVEN: THE EPHAH

5 After this the angelic messenger who had been speaking to me
went out and said, "Look, see what is leaving." 6 I asked, "What
is it?" And he replied, "It is a basket for measuring grain that is
moving away from here." Moreover, he said, "This is their 'eye'
throughout all the earth." 7 Then a round lead cover was raised
up, revealing a woman sitting inside the basket. 8 He then said,
"This woman represents wickedness," and he pushed her down
into the basket and placed the lead cover on top. 9 Then I looked
again and saw two women going forth with the wind in their
wings (they had wings like those of a stork), and they lifted up
the basket between the earth and the sky. 10 I asked the messenger who was speaking to me, "Where are they taking the
basket?" 11 He replied, "To build a temple for her in the land of
Babylonia. When it is finished, she will be placed there in her
own residence."

VISION EIGHT: THE CHARIOTS

6 Once more I looked, and this time I saw four chariots
emerging from between two mountains of bronze. 2 Harnessed to the first chariot were red horses, to the second black
horses, 3 to the third white horses, and to the fourth spotted
horses, all of them strong. 4 Then I asked the angelic messenger who was speaking with me, "What are these, sir?" 5 The messenger replied, "These are the four spirits of heaven going out
after presenting themselves before the Lord of all the earth.
6 The chariot with the black horses is going to the north country, and the white ones are going after them, but the spotted
ones are going to the south country. 7 All these strong ones are
scattering; they have sought permission to go and walk about
over the earth." The Lord had said, "Go! Walk about over the
earth!" So they are doing so. 8 Then he cried out to me, "Look!
The ones going to the northland have brought me peace about
the northland."

A CONCLUDING ORACLE

9 The LORD's message came to me as follows: 10 "Choose some people from among the exiles, namely, Heldai, Tobijah, and Jedaiah,
all who have come from Babylon, and when you have done so go
to the house of Josiah son of Zephaniah. 11 Then take some silver
and gold to make a crown and set it on the head of Joshua the
high priest, the son of Jehozadak. 12 Then say to him, 'The LORD
of Heaven's Armies says, "Look—here is the man whose name is
Branch, who will sprout up from his place and build the temple of the LORD. 13 Indeed, he will build the temple of the LORD,
and he will be clothed in splendor, sitting as king on his throne.
Moreover, there will be a priest with him on his throne and
they will see eye to eye on everything. 14 The crown will then be
turned over to Helem, Tobijah, Jedaiah, and Hen son of Zephaniah as a memorial in the temple of the LORD. 15 Then those who
are far away will come and build the temple of the LORD so that
you may know that the LORD of Heaven's Armies has sent me to
you. This will all come to pass if you completely obey the voice
of the LORD your God."'"

THE HYPOCRISY OF FALSE FASTING

7 In King Darius' fourth year, on the fourth day of Kislev, the
ninth month, the LORD's message came to Zechariah. 2 Now
the people of Bethel had sent Sharezer and Regem-Melech and
their companions to seek the LORD's favor 3 by asking both the
priests of the temple of the LORD of Heaven's Armies and the
prophets, "Should we weep in the fifth month, fasting as we have
done over the years?" 4 The message of the LORD of Heaven's Armies then came to me, 5 "Speak to all the people and priests of the
land as follows: 'When you fasted and lamented in the fifth and
seventh months through all these seventy years, did you truly
fast for me—for me, indeed? 6 And now when you eat and drink,
are you not doing so for yourselves? 7 Should you not have obeyed
the words that the LORD cried out through the former prophets
when Jerusalem was peacefully inhabited and her surrounding
cities, the Negev, and the foothills were also populated?'"
8 Again the LORD's message came to Zechariah: 9 "The LORD of
Heaven's Armies said, 'Exercise true judgment and show brotherhood and compassion to each other. 10 You must not oppress
the widow, the orphan, the resident foreigner, or the poor, nor
should anyone secretly plot evil against his fellow citizen.'
11 "But they refused to pay attention, turning away stubbornly
and stopping their ears so they could not hear. 12 Indeed, they
made their hearts as hard as diamond, so that they could not
obey the law of Moses and the other words the LORD of Heav-
en's Armies had sent by his Spirit through the former prophets. Therefore, the LORD of Heaven's Armies poured out great
wrath.
13 "'Just as I called out, but they would not obey, so they will
call out, but I will not listen,' the LORD of Heaven's Armies says.
14 'Rather, I will sweep them away in a storm into all the nations
they are not familiar with.' Thus the land became desolate because of them, with no one crossing through or returning, for
they had made the fruitful land a waste."

THE BLESSING OF TRUE FASTING

8 Then the message of the LORD of Heaven's Armies came to
me as follows: 2 "The LORD of Heaven's Armies says, 'I am very
much concerned for Zion; indeed, I am so concerned for her that
my rage will fall on those who hurt her.' 3 The LORD says, 'I have
returned to Zion and will live within Jerusalem. Now Jerusalem
will be called "truthful city," "mountain of the LORD of Heaven's
Armies," "holy mountain."' 4 Moreover, the LORD of Heaven's Armies says, 'Old men and women will once more live in the plazas
of Jerusalem, each one leaning on a cane because of advanced age.
5 And the streets of the city will be full of boys and girls playing.
6 And,' says the LORD of Heaven's Armies, 'though such a thing
may seem to be difficult in the opinion of the small community
of those days, will it also appear difficult to me?' asks the LORD
of Heaven's Armies.
7 "The LORD of Heaven's Armies asserts, 'I am about to save my
people from the lands of the east and the west. 8 And I will bring
them to settle within Jerusalem. They will be my people, and I
will be their God, in truth and righteousness.'

REFLECT

How do these verses reveal what is important to God? How can we practically show compassion to these groups of people?

9 “The LORD of Heaven’s Armies also says, ‘Gather strength,
you who are listening to these words today from the mouths
of the prophets who were there at the founding of the house of
the LORD of Heaven’s Armies, so that the temple might be built.
10 Before that time there was no compensation for man or animal, nor was there any relief from adversity for those who came
and went, because I had pitted everybody—each one—against
everyone else. 11 But I will be different now to this remnant of
my people from the way I was in those days,’ says the LORD of
Heaven’s Armies, 12 ‘for there will be a peaceful time of sowing,
the vine will produce its fruit, and the ground its yield, and the
skies will rain down dew. Then I will allow the remnant of my
people to possess all these things. 13 And it will come about that
just as you, both Judah and Israel, were a curse to the nations,
so I will save you and you will be a blessing. Do not be afraid! Instead, be strong.’

14 “For the LORD of Heaven’s Armies says, ‘As I had planned to
hurt you when your fathers made me angry,’ says the LORD of
Heaven’s Armies, ‘and I was not sorry, 15 so, to the contrary, I have
planned in these days to do good to Jerusalem and Judah—do
not fear! 16 These are the things you must do: Speak the truth,
each of you, to one another. Practice true and righteous judgment in your courts. 17 Do not plan evil in your hearts against
one another. Do not favor a false oath—these are all things that
I hate,’ says the LORD.”

18 The message of the LORD of Heaven’s Armies came to me
as follows: 19 “The LORD of Heaven’s Armies says, ‘The fast of the
fourth, fifth, seventh, and tenth months will become joyful and
happy, pleasant feasts for the house of Judah; so love truth and
peace.’ 20 The LORD of Heaven’s Armies says, ‘It will someday
come to pass that people—residents of many cities—will come.
21 The inhabitants of one will go to another and say, “Let’s go up at
once to ask the favor of the LORD, to seek the LORD of Heaven’s
Armies. Indeed, I’ll go with you.”’ 22 Many peoples and powerful
nations will come to Jerusalem to seek the LORD of Heaven’s Armies and to ask his favor. 23 The LORD of Heaven’s Armies says, ‘In
those days ten people from all languages and nations will grasp
hold of—indeed, grab—the robe of one Jew and say, “Let us go
with you, for we have heard that God is with you.”’”

THE COMING OF THE TRUE KING

9 This is an oracle, the LORD’s message concerning the land of
Hadrach, with its focus on Damascus:
The eyes of all humanity, especially of the tribes of Israel, are
toward the LORD, 2 as are those of Hamath also, which adjoins
Damascus, Tyre and Sidon, though they consider themselves
to be very wise. 3 Tyre built herself a fortification and piled up
silver like dust and gold like the mud of the streets. 4 Nevertheless the Lord will evict her and shove her fortifications into the
sea—she will be consumed by fire. 5 Ashkelon will see and be
afraid; Gaza will be in great anguish, as will Ekron, for her hope
will have been dried up. Gaza will lose her king, and Ashkelon
will no longer be inhabited. 6 A mongrel people will live in Ashdod, for I will greatly humiliate the Philistines. 7 I will take away

their abominable religious practices; then those who survive will
become a community of believers in our God, like a clan in Judah, and Ekron will be like the Jebusites. 8 Then I will surround
my temple to protect it like a guard from anyone crossing back
and forth; so no one will cross over against them anymore as an
oppressor, for now I myself have seen it.

9 Rejoice greatly, daughter of Zion!
Shout, daughter of Jerusalem!
Look! Your king is coming to you:
He is legitimate and victorious,
humble and riding on a donkey—
on a young donkey, the foal of a female donkey.
10 I will remove the chariot from Ephraim
and the warhorse from Jerusalem,
and the battle bow will be removed.
Then he will announce peace to the nations.
His dominion will be from sea to sea
and from the Euphrates River to the ends of the earth.

11 Moreover, as for you, because of our covenant relationship
secured with blood, I will release your prisoners from the waterless pit. 12 Return to the stronghold, you prisoners, with hope; today I declare that I will return double what was taken from you.
13 I will bend Judah as my bow; I will load the bow with Ephraim,
my arrow. I will stir up your sons, Zion, against your sons, Greece,
and I will make you, Zion, like a warrior's sword.
14 Then the LORD will appear above them, and his arrow will
shoot forth like lightning; the Sovereign LORD will blow the
trumpet and will proceed in the southern storm winds. 15 The
LORD of Heaven's Armies will guard them, and they will prevail
and overcome with sling stones. Then they will drink and will
become noisy like drunkards, full like the sacrificial basin or
like the corners of the altar. 16 On that day the LORD their God
will deliver them as the flock of his people, for they are the precious stones of a crown sparkling over his land. 17 How precious
and fair! Grain will make the young men flourish, and new wine
the young women.

THE RESTORATION OF THE TRUE PEOPLE

10 Ask the LORD for rain in the season of the late spring
rains—the LORD who causes thunderstorms—and he will
give everyone showers of rain and green growth in the field.
2 For the household gods have spoken wickedness, the sooth-
sayers have seen a lie, and the dreamers have disclosed emptiness and give comfort in vain. Therefore the people set out
like sheep and become scattered because they have no shepherd. 3 "I am enraged at the shepherds and will punish the
lead goats.
"For the LORD of Heaven's Armies has brought blessing to his
flock, the house of Judah, and will transform them into his majestic warhorse. 4 From him will come the cornerstone, the wall peg,
the battle bow, and every ruler. 5 And they will be like warriors
trampling the mud of the streets in battle. They will fight, for
the LORD will be with them, and will defeat the enemy cavalry.

REFLECT

Even though God brings judgment, He is faithful to restore His people. How do these verses communicate God's desire and heart for restoration?

6 "I (says the LORD) will strengthen the kingdom of Judah and
deliver the people of Joseph and will bring them back because
of my compassion for them. They will be as though I had never
rejected them, for I am the LORD their God, and therefore I
will hear them. 7 The Ephraimites will be like warriors and will
rejoice as if they had drunk wine. Their children will see it and
rejoice; they will celebrate in the things of the LORD. 8 I will
signal for them and gather them, for I have already redeemed
them; then they will become as numerous as they were before.
9 Though I scatter them among the nations, they will remember in far-off places—they and their children will survive and
return. 10 I will bring them back from Egypt and gather them
from Assyria. I will bring them to the lands of Gilead and Lebanon, and there will not be enough room for them. 11 The LORD
will cross the sea of storms and will calm its turbulence. The
depths of the Nile will dry up, the pride of Assyria will be humbled, and the domination of Egypt will be no more. 12 Thus I will
strengthen them by my power, and they will walk about in my
name," says the LORD.

THE HISTORY AND FUTURE OF JUDAH'S WICKED KINGS

11 Open your gates, Lebanon,
so that the fire may consume your cedars.
2 Howl, fir tree,
because the cedar has fallen;
the majestic trees have been destroyed.
Howl, oaks of Bashan,
because the impenetrable forest has fallen.
3 Listen to the howling of shepherds,
because their magnificence has been destroyed.
Listen to the roaring of young lions,
because the thickets of the Jordan have been devastated.

4 The LORD my God says this: "Shepherd the flock set aside
for slaughter. 5 Those who buy them slaughter them and are not
held guilty; those who sell them say, 'Blessed be the LORD, for
I am rich.' Their own shepherds have no compassion for them.
6 Indeed, I will no longer have compassion on the people of the
land," says the LORD, "but instead I will turn every last person
over to his neighbor and his king. They will devastate the land,
and I will not deliver it from them."

7 So I began to shepherd the flock destined for slaughter, the
most afflicted of all the flock. Then I took two staffs, calling one
"Pleasantness" and the other "Union," and I tended the flock.
8 Next I eradicated the three shepherds in one month, for I ran
out of patience with them and, indeed, they detested me as well.
9 I then said, "I will not shepherd you. What is to die, let it die,
and what is to be eradicated, let it be eradicated. As for those
who survive, let them eat each other's flesh!"

10 Then I took my staff "Pleasantness" and cut it in two to annul my covenant that I had made with all the people. 11 So it was
annulled that very day, and then the most afflicted of the flock
who kept faith with me knew that it was the LORD's message.

12 Then I said to them, "If it seems good to you, pay me my
wages, but if not, forget it." So they weighed out my payment—
thirty pieces of silver. 13 The LORD then said to me, "Throw to
the potter that exorbitant sum at which they valued me!" So I
took the thirty pieces of silver and threw them to the potter at
the temple of the LORD. 14 Then I cut the second staff "Union"
in two in order to annul the covenant of brotherhood between
Judah and Israel.

15 Again the LORD said to me, "Take up once more the equipment of a foolish shepherd. 16 Indeed, I am about to raise up a
shepherd in the land who will not take heed of the sheep headed
to slaughter, will not seek the scattered, and will not heal the
injured. Moreover, he will not nourish the one that is healthy,
but instead will eat the meat of the fat sheep and tear off their
hooves.

17 "Woe to the worthless shepherd
who abandons the flock!
May a sword fall on his arm and his right eye!
May his arm wither completely away,
and his right eye become completely blind!"

THE REPENTANCE OF JUDAH

12 This is an oracle, the LORD's message concerning Israel:
The LORD—he who stretches out the heavens and lays the
foundations of the earth, who forms the human spirit within a
person—says, 2 "I am about to make Jerusalem a cup that brings
dizziness to all the surrounding nations; indeed, Judah will also
be included when Jerusalem is besieged. 3 Moreover, on that day
I will make Jerusalem a heavy burden for all the nations, and all
who try to carry it will be seriously injured; yet all the peoples
of the earth will be assembled against it. 4 On that day," says the
LORD, "I will strike every horse with confusion and its rider with
madness. I will pay close attention to the house of Judah, but
will strike all the horses of the nations with blindness. 5 Then
the leaders of Judah will say to themselves, 'The inhabitants of
Jerusalem are a means of strength to us through their God, the
LORD of Heaven's Armies.' 6 On that day I will make the leaders
of Judah like an igniter among sticks and a burning torch among
sheaves, and they will burn up all the surrounding nations right
and left. Then the people of Jerusalem will settle once more in
their place, the city of Jerusalem. 7 The LORD also will deliver the
homes of Judah first, so that the splendor of the kingship of David and of the people of Jerusalem may not exceed that of Judah.
8 On that day the LORD himself will defend the inhabitants of
Jerusalem, so that the weakest among them will be like mighty
David, and the dynasty of David will be like God, like the angel of
the LORD before them. 9 So on that day I will set out to destroy
all the nations that come against Jerusalem.

10 "I will pour out on the kingship of David and the population
of Jerusalem a spirit of grace and supplication so that they will
look to me, the one they have pierced. They will lament for him
as one laments for an only son, and there will be a bitter cry for
him like the bitter cry for a firstborn. 11 On that day the lamentation in Jerusalem will be as great as the lamentation at Hadad

REFLECT

What does it mean for the Lord to be your defender? How does this encourage and strengthen you?

Rimmon in the plain of Megiddo. 12 The land will mourn, each
clan by itself—the clan of the royal household of David by itself
and their wives by themselves; the clan of the family of Nathan
by itself and their wives by themselves; 13 the clan of the descendants of Levi by itself and their wives by themselves; and the clan
of the Shimeites by itself and their wives by themselves; 14 all the
clans that remain, each separately with their wives.

THE REFINEMENT OF JUDAH

13 "In that day there will be a fountain opened up for the dynasty of David and the people of Jerusalem to cleanse them
from sin and impurity. 2 And also on that day," says the LORD of
Heaven's Armies, "I will remove the names of the idols from the
land and they will never again be remembered. Moreover, I will
remove the prophets and the unclean spirit from the land. 3 Then,
if anyone prophesies in spite of this, his father and mother to
whom he was born will say to him, 'You cannot live, for you lie in
the name of the LORD.' Then his father and mother to whom he
was born will run him through with a sword when he prophesies.
4 "Therefore, on that day each prophet will be ashamed of his
vision when he prophesies and will no longer wear the hairy garment of a prophet to deceive the people. 5 Instead he will say, 'I
am no prophet; indeed, I am a farmer, for a man has made me
his indentured servant since my youth.' 6 Then someone will ask
him, 'What are these wounds on your chest?' and he will answer,
'Some that I received in the house of my friends.'

7 "Awake, sword, against my shepherd,
against the man who is my associate,"
says the LORD of Heaven's Armies.
"Strike the shepherd that the flock may be scattered;
I will turn my hand against the insignificant ones.
8 It will happen in all the land," says the LORD,
"that two-thirds of the people in it will be cut off and die,
but one-third will be left in it.
9 Then I will bring the remaining third into the fire;
I will refine them like silver is refined
and will test them like gold is tested.
They will call on my name and I will answer;
I will say, 'These are my people,'
and they will say, 'The LORD is our God.'"

THE SOVEREIGNTY OF THE LORD

14 A day of the LORD is about to come when your possessions
will be divided as plunder in your midst. 2 For I will gather
all the nations against Jerusalem to wage war; the city will be
taken, its houses plundered, and the women raped. Then half of
the city will go into exile, but the remainder of the people will
not be taken away.
3 Then the LORD will go to battle and fight against those nations, just as he fought battles in ancient days. 4 On that day
his feet will stand on the Mount of Olives that lies to the east
of Jerusalem, and the Mount of Olives will be split in half from
east to west, leaving a great valley. Half the mountain will move
northward and the other half southward. 5 Then you will escape

LOVE TO GROW

WORK IN THE WAITING

ZECHARIAH 14

The prophets get a bad reputation—too much judgment and destruction. But we miss a remarkable and repeated theme if we shy away from books like Zechariah. In case we are ever tempted to place our faith in our own actions, the prophets consistently remind us that real redemption is accomplished by God's grace, not our works.

In Jeremiah, God instructed His people to follow His law, but He also promised He would eventually "put my law within them and write it on their hearts and minds" (Jer 31:33). In Ezekiel, God called for repentance, but He also promised He would give them a new spirit by removing their hearts of stone, giving them "tender hearts" so they could follow His law (see Ezek 11:18–20). They were called to repent, but the ultimate promise was that God was the One who would make them new.

In the same way, Zechariah called a struggling community to rebuild the temple in obedience to God, but he finished the book with a striking reminder that, in the end, God's restoration would be an undeserved, gracious gift, not a response to their obedience.

After the plea to return to God in Zechariah 1, this concluding chapter paints a powerful picture of the ultimate restoration of the world to its rightful Ruler. As "king over all the earth" (Zech 14:9), God would restore Jerusalem (Zech 14:11) and punish her enemies (Zech 14:12). All this could be expected and celebrated by the original recipients of this prophecy—a powerless people living under the oppression of a foreign ruler.

Then something remarkable would happen: Survivors from all the nations that once attacked Israel would join the worship of the real King. Perhaps even more surprising, cooking pots would be used as sacred instruments of worship (Zech 14:16). Everyday objects would be made sacred, and people from every nation would be gathered as God's people and transformed into holy instruments who lived to worship God and glorify Him.

God is always faithful to His promises. He will redeem even what we think is unredeemable, taking ordinary objects, like pots and people, and turning them into instruments of holy worship.

All these promises were made to support Zechariah's central message: Even while we wait for future restoration, we have work to do now. Israel's work was the rebuilding of the temple. Our work may be healing families, rectifying injustices, creating beautiful art, or teaching truth. Everyone's work looks different, but Zechariah's instructions for us are the same: Practice faithful obedience as you await future redemption.

through my mountain valley, for the valley of the mountains will
extend to Azal. Indeed, you will flee as you fled from the earthquake in the days of King Uzziah of Judah. Then the LORD my
God will come with all his holy ones with him. [6] On that day there
will be no light—the sources of light in the heavens will congeal.
[7] It will happen in one day—a day known to the LORD—not in the
day or the night, but in the evening there will be light. [8] Moreover, on that day living waters will flow out from Jerusalem, half
of them to the eastern sea and half of them to the western sea;
it will happen both in summer and in winter.

REFLECT

How do the acts of judgment God allowed on Judah reveal His holiness?

[9] The LORD will then be king over all the earth. In that day the
LORD will be seen as one with a single name. [10] All the land will
change and become like the rift valley from Geba to Rimmon,
south of Jerusalem. Jerusalem will be raised up and will stay in
its own place from the Benjamin Gate to the site of the First
Gate and on to the Corner Gate, and from the Tower of Hananel to the royal winepresses. [11] And people will settle there, and
there will no longer be the threat of divine extermination—Jerusalem will dwell in security.

[12] But this will be the nature of the plague with which the LORD
will strike all the nations that have fought against Jerusalem:
Their flesh will decay while they stand on their feet, their eyes
will rot away in their sockets, and their tongues will dissolve in
their mouths. [13] On that day there will be great confusion from
the LORD among them; they will seize each other and attack
one another violently. [14] Moreover, Judah will fight at Jerusalem,
and the wealth of all the surrounding nations will be gathered
up—gold, silver, and clothing in great abundance. [15] This is the
kind of plague that will devastate horses, mules, camels, donkeys, and all the other animals in those camps.

[16] Then all who survive from all the nations that came to attack
Jerusalem will go up annually to worship the King, the LORD of
Heaven's Armies, and to observe the Feast of Shelters. [17] But if
any of the nations anywhere on earth refuse to go up to Jerusalem to worship the King, the LORD of Heaven's Armies, they
will get no rain. [18] If the Egyptians will not do so, they will get
no rain—instead there will be the kind of plague that the LORD
inflicts on any nations that do not go up to celebrate the Feast
of Shelters. [19] This will be the punishment of Egypt and of all nations that do not go up to celebrate the Feast of Shelters.

[20] On that day the bells of the horses will bear the inscription "Holy to the LORD." The cooking pots in the LORD's temple
will be as holy as the bowls in front of the altar. [21] Every cooking
pot in Jerusalem and Judah will become holy in the sight of the
LORD of Heaven's Armies, so that all who offer sacrifices may
come and use some of them to boil their sacrifices in them. On
that day there will no longer be a Canaanite in the house of the
LORD of Heaven's Armies.

But for you who respect my name, the sun of vindication will rise with healing wings, and you will skip about like calves released from the stall

MEMORY VERSE

"But for you who respect my name, the sun of vindication will rise with healing wings, and you will skip about like calves released from the stall. You will trample on the wicked, for they will be like ashes under the soles of your feet on the day that I am preparing," says the LORD of Heaven's Armies.

Malachi 4:2–3

Malachi

INTRODUCTION

Hope

The Book of Malachi offers a message of hope. God's people had once again forgotten the love of Yahweh, hardening their hearts and turning from true worship. Malachi looks forward to the deliverance God promised to bring His people through Jesus, the One who would restore the broken relationship between God and humanity.

This book is divided into seven sections, each detailing a different issue between God and His people. The first reminded the people of God's faithful love for Israel (1:2–5), followed by a charge that the priests dishonored God (1:6—2:9). The people's unfaithfulness expressed in marriage with foreign wives and divorce was a third issue (2:10–16). Malachi described God's judgment and the coming of more messengers (2:17—3:5). Fifth, God called His people to repent: "Return to me, and I will return to you" (3:6–12). Sixth, God compared the righteous and wicked (3:13–18). The final message illustrated the coming day of the Lord (4:1–6).

The word *Malachi* means "My Messenger," and it is possible that Malachi was simply a title identifying a messenger of God. Malachi prophesied that God would send other spokespeople, including John the Baptist and the Lord Jesus (3:1). Malachi's ministry took place around 420 B.C., about a century after the reconstruction of the temple.

The Book of Malachi offers encouragement to love God greatly. Our God knows the future, and He is intricately involved in our lives to bring about His purposes. Malachi's message is one of hope: God is always working for our good and His glory, bringing about His great plan of redemption for the world.

Italy

OFFICIAL LANGUAGE
Italian
POPULATION
60,463,000
UNREACHED POPULATION
2,093,000
PROFESSING CHRISTIANS
81.3%

Gloria's Home

Say a Prayer Today

Pray for Gloria and those to whom she ministers. Pray she will be a testament to those around her of God's faithfulness.

HISTORY BIT

In A.D. 189 Victor I was elected as Bishop of Rome. While the office had existed since the first century with the apostle Peter, the office began to gain prominence during this time. Victor I was the first bishop referred to as the Pope.*

Source Information:
https://joshuaproject.net/countries/IT
*John Bowden, A Chronology of World Christianity (New York, NY: Continuum, 2007), 20.

GLORIA'S STORY

In the Book of Malachi, we read God's last words before four hundred years of silence. God's chosen and beloved people were deprived of any words from the Lord for four centuries.

Even though God's silence was difficult for people who had grown accustomed to hearing from God on a consistent basis, God had a purpose for His silence. The Jews questioned God's kindness and whether or not He still cared for them while clinging to Malachi's final words of hope.

I have faced many seasons of God's silence in my own life. I characterize them as painful, confusing, hopeless, and dark. But in those times, I clung to the promises of God that display His kindness and His faithfulness. I've learned to trust Him, even in His silence.

In my home country of Italy, I see a people, who, like the Jews, rejected God and turned their worship into ritual. I am confident that God will do incredible things in my country that will advance His kingdom. But, today, God seems silent. I have seen Him do mighty works in my life and heart when He seems silent, so I choose to believe He is doing the same for my people.

We can be discouraged by the silence of God, but we don't have to lose hope. We can remind God that we want to hear His voice while simultaneously trusting Him during His silence. The sun will rise again, God will send a messenger, and the world will see the Light!

4 WEEK READING PLAN

LOVE HIS WORD

	MONDAY	TUESDAY	WEDNESDAY	THURSDAY	FRIDAY
1	Haggai 1	Haggai 2	Zechariah 1	Zechariah 2	Zechariah 3
	SOAP Haggai 1:13-14	SOAP Haggai 2:23	SOAP Zechariah 1:6	SOAP Zechariah 2:10-11	SOAP Zechariah 3:10
2	Zechariah 4	Zechariah 5	Zechariah 6	Zechariah 7	Zechariah 8
	SOAP Zechariah 4:6	SOAP Zechariah 5:10-11	SOAP Zechariah 6:15	SOAP Zechariah 7:8-10	SOAP Zechariah 8:22
3	Zechariah 9	Zechariah 10	Zechariah 11	Zechariah 12	Zechariah 13
	SOAP Zechariah 9:16	SOAP Zechariah 10:1	SOAP Zechariah 11:6	SOAP Zechariah 12:10	SOAP Zechariah 13:9
4	Zechariah 14	Malachi 1	Malachi 2:1—3:5	Malachi 3:6-12	Malachi 3:13—4:6
	SOAP Zechariah 14:3	SOAP Malachi 1:14	SOAP Malachi 3:1	SOAP Malachi 3:6-7	SOAP Malachi 4:2-3

INTRODUCTION AND GOD'S ELECTION OF ISRAEL

1 This is an oracle, the LORD's message to Israel through Malachi:
2 "I have shown love to you," says the LORD, but you say, "How
have you shown love to us?"
"Esau was Jacob's brother," the LORD explains, "yet I chose
Jacob 3 and rejected Esau. I turned Esau's mountains into a deserted wasteland and gave his territory to the wild jackals."
4 Edom says, "Though we are devastated, we will once again
build the ruined places." So the LORD of Heaven's Armies responds, "They indeed may build, but I will overthrow. They will be
known as the land of evil, the people with whom the LORD is permanently displeased. 5 Your eyes will see it, and then you will say,
'May the LORD be magnified even beyond the border of Israel!'"

THE SACRILEGE OF PRIESTLY SERVICE

6 "A son naturally honors his father and a slave respects his master. If I am your father, where is my honor? If I am your master,
where is my respect? The LORD of Heaven's Armies asks you this,
you priests who make light of my name! But you reply, 'How have
we made light of your name?' 7 You are offering improper sacrifices on my altar, yet you ask, 'How have we offended you?' By
treating the table of the LORD as if it is of no importance. 8 For
when you offer blind animals as a sacrifice, is that not wrong?
And when you offer the lame and sick, is that not wrong as well?
Indeed, try offering them to your governor! Will he be pleased
with you or show you favor?" asks the LORD of Heaven's Armies.
9 "But now plead for God's favor that he might be gracious to us."
"With this kind of offering in your hands, how can he be pleased
with you?" asks the LORD of Heaven's Armies.
10 "I wish that one of you would close the temple doors, so
that you no longer would light useless fires on my altar. I am
not pleased with you," says the LORD of Heaven's Armies, "and
I will no longer accept an offering from you. 11 For from the east
to the west my name will be great among the nations. Incense
and pure offerings will be offered in my name everywhere, for
my name will be great among the nations," says the LORD of
Heaven's Armies. 12 "But you are profaning it by saying that the
table of the Lord is common and its offerings despicable. 13 You
also say, 'How tiresome it is.' You turn up your nose at it," says
the LORD of Heaven's Armies, "and instead bring what is stolen,
lame, or sick. You bring these things for an offering! Should I accept this from you?" asks the LORD. 14 "There will be harsh condemnation for the hypocrite who has a valuable male animal in
his flock but vows and sacrifices something inferior to the Lord.
For I am a great king," says the LORD of Heaven's Armies, "and
my name is awesome among the nations."

THE SACRILEGE OF THE PRIESTLY MESSAGE

2 "Now, you priests, this commandment is for you. 2 If you do not
listen and take seriously the need to honor my name," says the
LORD of Heaven's Armies, "I will send judgment on you and turn
your blessings into curses—indeed, I have already done so because
you are not taking it to heart. 3 I am about to discipline your children and will spread offal on your faces, the very offal produced

REFLECT

In what ways has God shown love to you? How can you remember these things and praise Him for His love for you?

at your festivals, and you will be carried away along with it. 4 Then
you will know that I sent this commandment to you so that my
covenant may continue to be with Levi," says the LORD of Heav-
en's Armies. 5 "My covenant with him was designed to bring life
and peace. I gave its statutes to him to fill him with awe, and he
indeed revered me and stood in awe before me. 6 He taught what
was true; sinful words were not found on his lips. He walked with
me in peace and integrity, and he turned many people away from
sin. 7 For the lips of a priest should preserve knowledge of sacred
things, and people should seek instruction from him because he
is the messenger of the LORD of Heaven's Armies. 8 You, however,
have turned from the way. You have caused many to violate the
law; you have corrupted the covenant with Levi," says the LORD
of Heaven's Armies. 9 "Therefore, I have caused you to be ignored
and belittled before all people to the extent that you are not following after me and are showing partiality in your instruction."

THE REBELLION OF THE PEOPLE

10 Do we not all have one father? Did not one God create us? Why
do we betray one another, thus making light of the covenant of
our ancestors? 11 Judah has become disloyal, and unspeakable
sins have been committed in Israel and Jerusalem. For Judah has
profaned the holy things that the LORD loves and has turned to
a foreign god! 12 May the LORD cut off from the community of
Jacob every last person who does this, as well as the person who
presents improper offerings to the LORD of Heaven's Armies!

13 You also do this: You cover the altar of the LORD with tears as
you weep and groan, because he no longer pays any attention to the
offering nor accepts it favorably from you. 14 Yet you ask, "Why?" The
LORD is testifying against you on behalf of the wife you married
when you were young, to whom you have become unfaithful even
though she is your companion and wife by law. 15 No one who has
even a small portion of the Spirit in him does this. What did our
ancestor do when seeking a child from God? Be attentive, then, to
your own spirit, for one should not be disloyal to the wife he took
in his youth. 16 "I hate divorce," says the LORD God of Israel, "and
the one who is guilty of violence," says the LORD of Heaven's Armies. "Pay attention to your conscience, and do not be unfaithful."

RESISTANCE TO THE LORD THROUGH SELF-DECEIT

17 You have wearied the LORD with your words. But you say, "How
have we wearied him?" Because you say, "Everyone who does
evil is good in the LORD's opinion, and he delights in them," or,
3 "Where is the God of justice?" 1 "I am about to send my messenger, who will clear the way before me. Indeed, the Lord you
are seeking will suddenly come to his temple, and the messenger
of the covenant, whom you long for, is certainly coming," says the
LORD of Heaven's Armies.

2 Who can endure the day of his coming? Who can keep standing
when he appears? For he will be like a refiner's fire, like a launderer's
soap. 3 He will act like a refiner and purifier of silver and will cleanse
the Levites and refine them like gold and silver. Then they will offer the LORD a proper offering. 4 The offerings of Judah and Jerusalem will be pleasing to the LORD as in former times and years past.

REFLECT

How did the Israelites turn the blessings of God into curses? (See Deuteronomy 28.)

CHALLENGE

Read Mark 1. How does John the Baptist fulfill this prophecy in Malachi 3:1–5?

LOVE TO GROW

FAITH IN THE FURNACE

MALACHI 3:2–3

At long last, life was good. After years of living in an abusive relationship, I'd escaped with my daughter and was now remarried to a wonderful, godly man. Tiffany was grown and happily off to college. Surely I had survived the worst of God's refining fire.

Then early one calm, peaceful morning, the police arrived at my door. "We're sorry to tell you your daughter Tiffany has been killed in an automobile accident."

I screamed. Without warning, I'd been plunged back into the heat. Instantly, my very existence no longer made sense.

For months afterward, I struggled with sadness, confusion, and an inexpressible ache, unwilling to believe I would never see my beautiful girl again in this life. How could God let this happen? Didn't He love me? Were all those sermons I'd heard a lie?

In the years since that awful day, God has brought me into relationships and opportunities that could have come through no other door. Relationships with the women I've been privileged to serve beside in ministry. Opportunities like leading a church-wide forum for thousands of young Tiffanys. God has clearly had His hand in my healing process to bring about His glory.

"Who can endure the day of his coming? Who can keep standing when he appears? For he will be like a refiner's fire, like a launderer's soap. He will act like a refiner and purifier of silver and will cleanse the Levites and refine them like gold and silver. Then they will offer the Lord *a proper offering." (Mal 3:2–3).*

Are you experiencing the refiner's fire right now? Are you wondering if it will ever end? Let me reassure you that no matter how unbearable your pain may feel, God will not let it consume you. The pure silver of a life submitted to God will withstand the refiner's fire. He is preparing you, as Malachi attested, to endure until His coming and to stand when He appears.

I think of a woman watching a silversmith as he practiced his craft. As he held the liquid silver over the hottest part of the flame, he explained: "This is to burn away all the impurities."

"How do you know when the silver is fully refined?" she asked.

"That's easy!" he replied. "When I see my reflection in it."

Let's allow our loving, gracious God the time and space He needs to refine us. His refinement is for our good and His glory, so we may point a hurting and needy world back to Him.

5 "I will come to you in judgment. I will be quick to testify
against those who practice divination; those who commit adultery; those who break promises; and those who exploit workers,
widows, and orphans, who refuse to help the resident foreigner
and in this way show they do not fear me," says the LORD of
Heaven's Armies.

RESISTANCE TO THE LORD THROUGH SELFISHNESS

6 "Since, I, the LORD, do not go back on my promises, you, sons
of Jacob, have not perished. 7 From the days of your ancestors
you have ignored my commandments and have not kept them.
Return to me, and I will return to you," says the LORD of Heav-
en's Armies. "But you say, 'How should we return?' 8 Can a person rob God? You are indeed robbing me, but you say, 'How are
we robbing you?' In tithes and contributions! 9 You are bound
for judgment because you are robbing me—this whole nation
is guilty.

10 "Bring the entire tithe into the storehouse so that there
may be food in my temple. Test me in this matter," says the
LORD of Heaven's Armies, "to see if I will not open for you the
windows of heaven and pour out blessing for you until there
is no room for it all. 11 Then I will stop the plague from ruining
your crops, and the vine will not lose its fruit before harvest,"
says the LORD of Heaven's Armies. 12 "All nations will call you
blessed, for you indeed will live in a delightful land," says the
LORD of Heaven's Armies.

RESISTANCE TO THE LORD THROUGH SELF-SUFFICIENCY

13 "You have criticized me sharply," says the LORD, "but you ask,
'How have we criticized you?' 14 You have said, 'It is useless to
serve God. How have we been helped by keeping his requirements and going about like mourners before the LORD of Heav-
en's Armies? 15 So now we consider the arrogant to be blessed;
indeed, those who practice evil are successful. In fact, those who
challenge God escape!'"

16 Then those who respected the LORD spoke to one another,
and the LORD took notice. A scroll was prepared before him in
which were recorded the names of those who respected the
LORD and honored his name. 17 "They will belong to me," says the
LORD of Heaven's Armies, "in the day when I prepare my own
special property. I will spare them as a man spares his son who
serves him. 18 Then once more you will see that I make a distinction between the righteous and the wicked, between the one
who serves God and the one who does not.

4 "For indeed the day is coming, burning like a furnace, and
all the arrogant evildoers will be chaff. The coming day will
burn them up," says the LORD of Heaven's Armies. "It will not
leave them even a root or branch. 2 But for you who respect my
name, the sun of vindication will rise with healing wings, and
you will skip about like calves released from the stall. 3 You will
trample on the wicked, for they will be like ashes under the soles
of your feet on the day that I am preparing," says the LORD of
Heaven's Armies.

REFLECT

How does Malachi 4:2 give hope to the remnant of Judah? How does this verse give you hope?

RESTORATION THROUGH THE LORD

4 "Remember the law of my servant Moses, to whom at Horeb
I gave rules and regulations for all Israel to obey. 5 Look, I will
send you Elijah the prophet before the great and terrible day
of the LORD arrives. 6 He will encourage fathers and their children to return to me, so that I will not come and strike the earth
with judgment."

The New Testament

THE MIRACLES OF JESUS

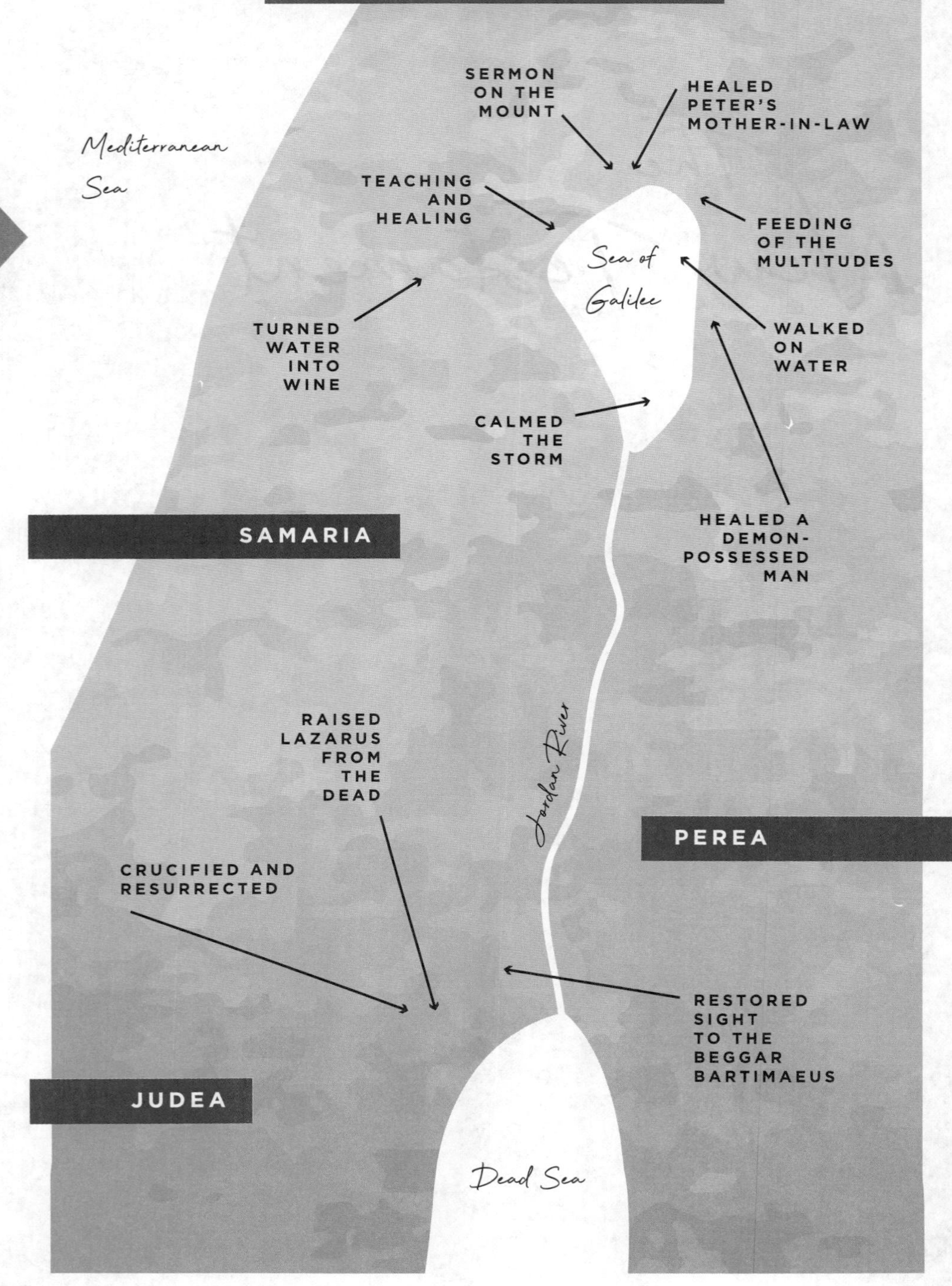

THE PASSION OF JESUS

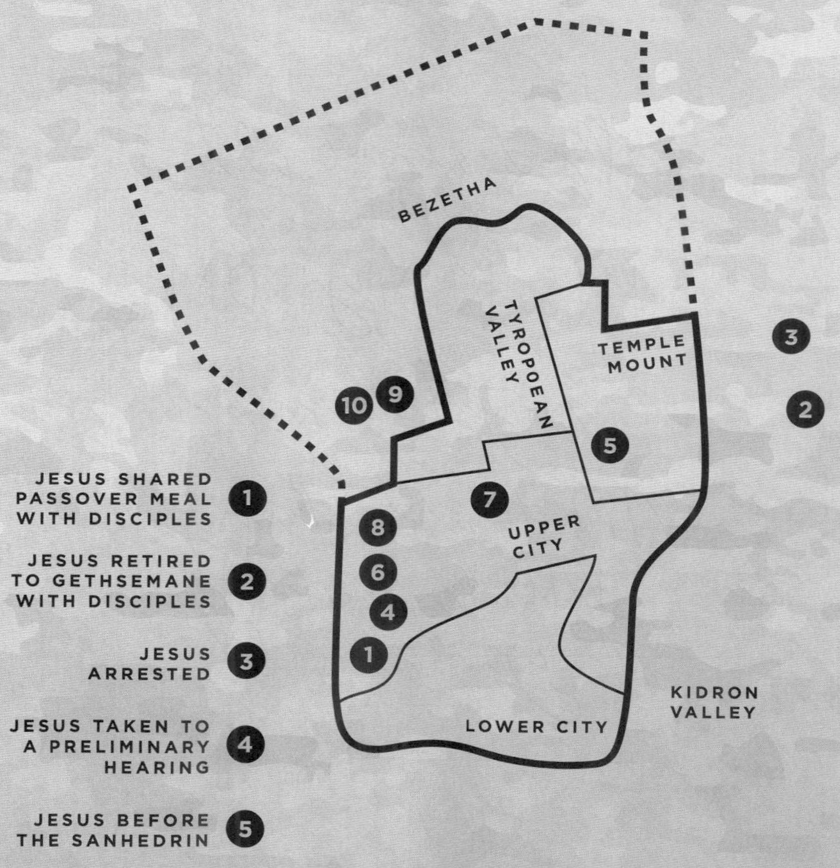

1 JESUS SHARED PASSOVER MEAL WITH DISCIPLES

2 JESUS RETIRED TO GETHSEMANE WITH DISCIPLES

3 JESUS ARRESTED

4 JESUS TAKEN TO A PRELIMINARY HEARING

5 JESUS BEFORE THE SANHEDRIN

6 JESUS BEFORE PILATE

7 JESUS BEFORE HEROD ANTIPAS

8 JESUS AGAIN BEFORE PILATE

9 JESUS CRUCIFIED

10 JESUS IS RISEN

JERUSALEM

CITY WALL DURING CHRIST

ADDITION AFTER CHRIST

But above all
pursue
HIS KINGDOM
and
righteousness,
and
All these things
WILL BE Given
to you as well

MEMORY VERSE

But above all pursue his kingdom and righteousness, and all these things will be given to you as well.

Matthew 6:33

Matthew

INTRODUCTION

The Kingdom of God

The Gospel of Matthew presents Jesus as the promised King, not of the earthly kingdom of Israel, but of the kingdom of heaven. God promised David that one of his descendants would always remain on the throne, and Jesus arrived as that Ruler and ushered in the kingdom of God.

The writer wanted to convince readers Jesus was the promised and rightful King. The book can be divided into seven sections, each detailing a different aspect of Jesus' ministry. It begins by describing the person of the King, then develops the platform of the King. It then describes the power of the King and the parables of the King, both leading toward the rejection of the King. The presentation of the King occurred as Jesus entered Jerusalem, and the passion of the King details His death and resurrection.

While the Gospel of Matthew does not explicitly name its author, significant evidence points to Matthew, the disciple of Jesus and former tax collector, as the writer. Matthew wrote this Gospel before the destruction of Jerusalem in A.D. 70, probably between A.D. 50–60, as the account was directed to a Jewish audience.

This book offers a unique look at the life of Jesus, providing specific insight into His character to a Jewish audience. The Gospel focuses on the coming kingdom of God, and God's faithfulness is on display as He reestablished His kingdom through the line of David. God had not forgotten His promises to His people. We can love Him greatly knowing, no matter how long He seems to take, God always keeps His promises.

Taiwan

OFFICIAL LANGUAGE
Taiwanese Mandarin
POPULATION
23,729,000
UNREACHED POPULATION
4,444,000
PROFESSING CHRISTIANS
6.0%

Alice's Home

Say a Prayer Today

Pray for Alice and her ministry to the Taiwanese people. Pray the people of Taiwan would see their need for Jesus as well as the peace and hope He offers.

HISTORY BIT

Christianity first came to the island now known as Taiwan in 1625 through Dutch traders and missionaries. These missionaries spent four decades on the island and established several communities of believers as well as small churches among the people.*

Source Information:
https://joshuaproject.net/countries/TW
*David B. Barrett, *World Christian Encyclopedia*, China (Taiwan) (New York, NY: Oxford University Press, 1982), 236.

LOVE YOUR NEIGHBOR

Her Journey

ALICE'S STORY

People in Taiwan are used to a fast-paced, crowded, noisy, flashing-neon-lights kind of culture. The streets are filled with vendors, scooters, cars, and trucks. We look for business opportunities anywhere. We are driven by a workaholic mind-set, relying on our own abilities in order to support everything we think we need. Most of our efforts toward success are deeply motivated by a cultural face-saving worldview: "I don't want to be looked down upon."

Meanwhile, the Taiwanese are religious; we are deeply rooted in ancestral and idol worship. Many religions prosper on this little island. There's a saying that goes around: "rather to believe it to be true than not." The saying goes for anything except Jesus. People worship idols out of fear and greed: fear of being punished; greed for fame, academic success, financial status, and relationships. We look for anything in this world that we think can satisfy. We fear the day when our deepest darkness will be exposed, so we enjoy living in the dark, blinded by the devil. We are stuck in anxiety, fear, and worry because we only see the temporary, not the eternal.

People in Taiwan yearn to be known, to find the true treasure that can satisfy our souls. As Jesus explicitly taught, we can only find rest and contentment by seeking His kingdom first. Churches in Taiwan are striving to magnify God's name. May our eyes be opened to see the kingdom of Heaven and yearn for eternity instead of being entangled by the cares of this life. Instead of being fixated on our worldly needs, let's be focused on the kingdom of God. For in doing so He promises to give us exactly what we need.

6 WEEK READING PLAN

LOVE HIS WORD

	MONDAY	TUESDAY	WEDNESDAY	THURSDAY	FRIDAY
1	Matthew 1	Matthew 2	Matthew 3	Matthew 4	Matthew 5:1-26
	SOAP Matthew 1:21-23	SOAP Matthew 2:10-11	SOAP Matthew 3:16-17	SOAP Matthew 4:10-11	SOAP Matthew 5:15-16
2	Matthew 5:27-48	Matthew 6	Matthew 7	Matthew 8	Matthew 9
	SOAP Matthew 5:43-45	SOAP Matthew 6:33	SOAP Matthew 7:7-8	SOAP Matthew 8:26-27	SOAP Matthew 9:6-8
3	Matthew 10:1—11:1	Matthew 11:2-30	Matthew 12	Matthew 13:1-23	Matthew 13:24-58
	SOAP Matthew 10:32-33	SOAP Matthew 11:28-30	SOAP Matthew 12:35-37	SOAP Matthew 13:23	SOAP Matthew 13:58
4	Matthew 14	Matthew 15	Matthew 16	Matthew 17	Matthew 18
	SOAP Matthew 14:30-31	SOAP Matthew 15:18-20	SOAP Matthew 16:24-25	SOAP Matthew 17:20	SOAP Matthew 18:10-14
5	Matthew 19	Matthew 20	Matthew 21	Matthew 22	Matthew 23
	SOAP Matthew 19:13-15	SOAP Matthew 20:26-28	SOAP Matthew 21:12-13	SOAP Matthew 22:36-40	SOAP Matthew 23:25-26
6	Matthew 24	Matthew 25	Matthew 26	Matthew 27	Matthew 28
	SOAP Matthew 24:45-46	SOAP Matthew 25:29	SOAP Matthew 26:12-13	SOAP Matthew 27:50-51	SOAP Matthew 28:18-20

THE GENEALOGY OF JESUS CHRIST

1 This is the record of the genealogy of Jesus Christ, the son of
David, the son of Abraham.
2 Abraham was the father of Isaac, Isaac the father of Jacob,
Jacob the father of Judah and his brothers, 3 Judah the father of
Perez and Zerah (by Tamar), Perez the father of Hezron, Hezron
the father of Ram, 4 Ram the father of Amminadab, Amminadab the
father of Nahshon, Nahshon the father of Salmon, 5 Salmon the
father of Boaz (by Rahab), Boaz the father of Obed (by Ruth),
Obed the father of Jesse, 6 and Jesse the father of David the king.
David was the father of Solomon (by the wife of Uriah), 7 Solomon the father of Rehoboam, Rehoboam the father of Abijah, Abijah the father of Asa, 8 Asa the father of Jehoshaphat, Jehoshaphat
the father of Joram, Joram the father of Uzziah, 9 Uzziah the father
of Jotham, Jotham the father of Ahaz, Ahaz the father of Hezekiah, 10 Hezekiah the father of Manasseh, Manasseh the father of
Amon, Amon the father of Josiah, 11 and Josiah the father of Jeconiah and his brothers, at the time of the deportation to Babylon.
12 After the deportation to Babylon, Jeconiah became the father
of Shealtiel, Shealtiel the father of Zerubbabel, 13 Zerubbabel the
father of Abiud, Abiud the father of Eliakim, Eliakim the father
of Azor, 14 Azor the father of Zadok, Zadok the father of Achim,
Achim the father of Eliud, 15 Eliud the father of Eleazar, Eleazar
the father of Matthan, Matthan the father of Jacob, 16 and Jacob
the father of Joseph, the husband of Mary, by whom Jesus was
born, who is called Christ.
17 So all the generations from Abraham to David are fourteen
generations, and from David to the deportation to Babylon, fourteen generations, and from the deportation to Babylon to Christ,
fourteen generations.

THE BIRTH OF JESUS CHRIST

18 Now the birth of Jesus Christ happened this way. While his
mother Mary was engaged to Joseph, but before they came together, she was found to be pregnant through the Holy Spirit.
19 Because Joseph, her husband to be, was a righteous man, and
because he did not want to disgrace her, he intended to divorce
her privately. 20 When he had contemplated this, an angel of the
Lord appeared to him in a dream and said, "Joseph, son of David, do not be afraid to take Mary as your wife, because the child
conceived in her is from the Holy Spirit. 21 She will give birth to
a son and you will name him Jesus, because he will save his people from their sins." 22 This all happened so that what was spoken
by the Lord through the prophet would be fulfilled: 23 ***"Look! The
virgin will conceive and give birth to a son, and*** *they* ***will name him
Emmanuel,"*** which means ***"God with us."*** 24 When Joseph awoke
from sleep he did what the angel of the Lord told him. He took
his wife, 25 but did not have marital relations with her until she
gave birth to a son, whom he named Jesus.

THE VISIT OF THE WISE MEN

2 After Jesus was born in Bethlehem in Judea, in the time of
King Herod, wise men from the East came to Jerusalem 2 saying, "Where is the one who is born king of the Jews? For we saw

his star when it rose and have come to worship him." 3 When King
Herod heard this he was alarmed, and all Jerusalem with him.
4 After assembling all the chief priests and experts in the law,
he asked them where the Christ was to be born. 5 "In Bethlehem
of Judea," they said, "for it is written this way by the prophet:

6 '***And you, Bethlehem,*** *in the land of Judah,*
are in no way least among the rulers of Judah,
for out of you will come a ruler who will
shepherd my people Israel.'"

7 Then Herod privately summoned the wise men and determined from them when the star had appeared. 8 He sent them to
Bethlehem and said, "Go and look carefully for the child. When
you find him, inform me so that I can go and worship him as well."
9 After listening to the king they left, and once again the star
they saw when it rose led them until it stopped above the place
where the child was. 10 When they saw the star they shouted joyfully. 11 As they came into the house and saw the child with Mary
his mother, they bowed down and worshiped him. They opened
their treasure boxes and gave him gifts of gold, frankincense, and
myrrh. 12 After being warned in a dream not to return to Herod,
they went back by another route to their own country.

THE ESCAPE TO EGYPT

13 After they had gone, an angel of the Lord appeared to Joseph
in a dream and said, "Get up, take the child and his mother and
flee to Egypt, and stay there until I tell you, for Herod is going
to look for the child to kill him." 14 Then he got up, took the child
and his mother during the night, and went to Egypt. 15 He stayed
there until Herod died. In this way what was spoken by the Lord
through the prophet was fulfilled: "***I called my Son out of Egypt.***"

16 When Herod saw that he had been tricked by the wise men,
he became enraged. He sent men to kill all the children in Bethlehem and throughout the surrounding region from the age of
two and under, according to the time he had learned from the
wise men. 17 Then what was spoken by Jeremiah the prophet
was fulfilled:

18 ***"A voice was heard in Ramah,***
weeping and loud wailing,
Rachel weeping for her children,
and she did not want to be comforted,
because they were gone."

THE RETURN TO NAZARETH

19 After Herod had died, an angel of the Lord appeared in a dream
to Joseph in Egypt 20 saying, "Get up, take the child and his mother, and go to the land of Israel, for those who were seeking the
child's life are dead." 21 So he got up and took the child and his
mother and returned to the land of Israel. 22 But when he heard
that Archelaus was reigning over Judea in place of his father
Herod, he was afraid to go there. After being warned in a dream,
he went to the regions of Galilee. 23 He came to a town called
Nazareth and lived there. Then what had been spoken by the
prophets was fulfilled, that Jesus would be called a Nazarene.

THE MINISTRY OF JOHN THE BAPTIST

3 In those days John the Baptist came into the wilderness of Judea proclaiming, 2 "Repent, for the kingdom of heaven is near."
3 For he is the one about whom the prophet Isaiah had spoken:

> ***"The voice of one shouting in the wilderness,***
> ***'Prepare the way for the Lord, make his paths straight.'"***

4 Now John wore clothing made from camel's hair with a leather belt around his waist, and his diet consisted of locusts and wild
honey. 5 Then people from Jerusalem, as well as all Judea and all
the region around the Jordan, were going out to him, 6 and he was
baptizing them in the Jordan River as they confessed their sins.
7 But when he saw many Pharisees and Sadducees coming to his
baptism, he said to them, "You offspring of vipers! Who warned
you to flee from the coming wrath? 8 Therefore produce fruit that
proves your repentance, 9 and don't think you can say to yourselves, 'We have Abraham as our father.' For I tell you that God
can raise up children for Abraham from these stones! 10 Even now
the ax is laid at the root of the trees, and every tree that does not
produce good fruit will be cut down and thrown into the fire.
11 "I baptize you with water, for repentance, but the one coming
after me is more powerful than I am—I am not worthy to carry his
sandals! He will baptize you with the Holy Spirit and fire. 12 His
winnowing fork is in his hand, and he will clean out his threshing floor and will gather his wheat into the storehouse, but the
chaff he will burn up with inextinguishable fire!"

THE BAPTISM OF JESUS

13 Then Jesus came from Galilee to John to be baptized by him
in the Jordan River. 14 But John tried to prevent him, saying, "I
need to be baptized by you, and yet you come to me?" 15 So Jesus
replied to him, "Let it happen now, for it is right for us to fulfill
all righteousness." Then John yielded to him. 16 After Jesus was
baptized, just as he was coming up out of the water, the heavens
opened and he saw the Spirit of God descending like a dove and
coming to rest on him. 17 And a voice from heaven said, "This is
my one dear Son; in him I take great delight."

THE TEMPTATION OF JESUS

4 Then Jesus was led by the Spirit into the wilderness to be
tempted by the devil. 2 After he fasted forty days and forty
nights he was famished. 3 The tempter came and said to him, "If
you are the Son of God, command these stones to become bread."
4 But he answered, "It is written, '***Man does not live by bread alone,***
but by every word that comes from the mouth of God.'" 5 Then the
devil took him to the holy city, had him stand on the highest
point of the temple, 6 and said to him, "If you are the Son of God,
throw yourself down. For it is written, '***He will command his an-***
gels concerning you' and '***with their hands they will lift you up, so***
that you will not strike your foot against a stone.'" 7 Jesus said to
him, "Once again it is written: '***You are not to put the Lord your***
God to the test.'" 8 Again, the devil took him to a very high mountain, and showed him all the kingdoms of the world and their
grandeur. 9 And he said to him, "I will give you all these things if

REFLECT

How does the temptation of Jesus encourage you to be prepared for the spiritual attacks of the enemy? How can you prepare yourself for the lies that Satan will tell you?

you throw yourself to the ground and worship me." 10 Then Jesus
said to him, "Go away, Satan! For it is written: '***You are to worship***
the Lord your God and serve only ***him***.'" 11 Then the devil left him,
and angels came and began ministering to his needs.

PREACHING IN GALILEE

12 Now when Jesus heard that John had been imprisoned, he
went into Galilee. 13 While in Galilee, he moved from Nazareth
to make his home in Capernaum by the sea, in the region of Zebulun and Naphtali, 14 so that what was spoken by the prophet
Isaiah would be fulfilled:

15 "***Land of Zebulun and land of Naphtali,***
the way by the sea, beyond the Jordan, Galilee of the Gentiles—
16 ***the people who sit in darkness have seen a great light,***
and on those who sit in the region and
shadow of death a light has dawned."

17 From that time Jesus began to preach this message: "Repent,
for the kingdom of heaven is near!"

THE CALL OF THE DISCIPLES

18 As he was walking by the Sea of Galilee he saw two brothers, Simon (called Peter) and Andrew his brother, casting a net into the
sea (for they were fishermen). 19 He said to them, "Follow me, and
I will turn you into fishers of people!" 20 They left their nets immediately and followed him. 21 Going on from there he saw two other
brothers, James the son of Zebedee and his brother John, in a boat
with their father Zebedee, mending their nets. Then he called them.
22 They immediately left the boat and their father and followed him.

JESUS' HEALING MINISTRY

23 Jesus went throughout all of Galilee, teaching in their synagogues, preaching the gospel of the kingdom, and healing every
kind of disease and sickness among the people. 24 So a report
about him spread throughout Syria. People brought to him all
who suffered with various illnesses and afflictions, those who
had seizures, paralytics, and those possessed by demons, and
he healed them. 25 And large crowds followed him from Galilee,
the Decapolis, Jerusalem, Judea, and beyond the Jordan River.

THE BEATITUDES

5 When he saw the crowds, he went up the mountain. After
he sat down his disciples came to him. 2 Then he began to
teach them by saying:

3 "Blessed are the poor in spirit, for the
kingdom of heaven belongs to them.
4 "Blessed are those who mourn, for they will be comforted.
5 "Blessed are the meek, for they will inherit the earth.
6 "Blessed are those who hunger and thirst for
righteousness, for they will be satisfied.
7 "Blessed are the merciful, for they will be shown mercy.
8 "Blessed are the pure in heart, for they will see God.
9 "Blessed are the peacemakers, for they
will be called the children of God.

LOVE TO GROW

MAKING THE HUMBLE THINGS HOLY

MATTHEW 5:3–10

I love personality tests. From Myers-Briggs to Strengths Finders to figuring out which movie princess I am, I've taken them all. There is an inherently curious part of me who wants to know, in fifty questions or less, who I am, what motivates me, and how I can be the very best version of myself.

We live in a world where the best of the best are rewarded and recognized. Those with the biggest platforms get the best opportunities. Those who climb corporate ladders and hustle hard—without thinking of whom they're climbing over—earn the promotions.

I get it. I've even lived it. I've taken all the personality tests and used them as pathways to navigate myself to the top. God didn't design us for sustainable fame and glory. It's only a matter of time before the crowds move somewhere else, the next rising star gets the promotion, the newer, shinier version takes over, and we slide back to the bottom.

Matthew 5:3–10 shows us what success really looks like in the kingdom of God. In this seemingly backwards, upside down world where rulers bow before a child, Jesus preached about what really matters to God. It's not a promotion, recognition, fame, or who we know. It's about knowing Him and bringing Him the fame and recognition He rightly deserves.

God is in the habit of making humble things holy.

From sending the Savior of the world from heaven to be born in a manger to rewarding those who put others first, we can live confidently knowing that exchanging our fame for His and serving others in His name instead of pursuing self-promotion, will be worth it. No setback, detour, or distraction will ever derail God's plan.

When we love God greatly with our lives we will draw others toward Him as they experience His goodness, mercy, and forgiveness at work in each of us.

10 "Blessed are those who are persecuted for righteousness,
for the kingdom of heaven belongs to them.
11 "Blessed are you when people insult you and persecute
you and say all kinds of evil things about you falsely
on account of me. 12 Rejoice and be glad, because
your reward is great in heaven, for they persecuted
the prophets before you in the same way.

SALT AND LIGHT

13 "You are the salt of the earth. But if salt loses its flavor, how can
it be made salty again? It is no longer good for anything except to
be thrown out and trampled on by people! 14 You are the light of
the world. A city located on a hill cannot be hidden. 15 People do
not light a lamp and put it under a basket but on a lampstand,
and it gives light to all in the house. 16 In the same way, let your
light shine before people, so that they can see your good deeds
and give honor to your Father in heaven.

FULFILLMENT OF THE LAW AND PROPHETS

17 "Do not think that I have come to abolish the law or the prophets.
I have not come to abolish these things but to fulfill them. 18 I tell
you the truth, until heaven and earth pass away not the smallest
letter or stroke of a letter will pass from the law until everything
takes place. 19 So anyone who breaks one of the least of these commands and teaches others to do so will be called least in the kingdom of heaven, but whoever obeys them and teaches others to do
so will be called great in the kingdom of heaven. 20 For I tell you,
unless your righteousness goes beyond that of the experts in the
law and the Pharisees, you will never enter the kingdom of heaven!

ANGER AND MURDER

21 "You have heard that it was said to an older generation, '***Do not
murder***,' and 'whoever murders will be subjected to judgment.'
22 But I say to you that anyone who is angry with a brother will
be subjected to judgment. And whoever insults a brother will be
brought before the council, and whoever says 'Fool' will be sent to
fiery hell. 23 So then, if you bring your gift to the altar and there you
remember that your brother has something against you, 24 leave
your gift there in front of the altar. First go and be reconciled to
your brother and then come and present your gift. 25 Reach agreement quickly with your accuser while on the way to court, or he
may hand you over to the judge, and the judge hand you over to the
warden, and you will be thrown into prison. 26 I tell you the truth,
you will never get out of there until you have paid the last penny!

ADULTERY

27 "You have heard that it was said, '***Do not commit adultery***.' 28 But
I say to you that whoever looks at a woman to desire her has already committed adultery with her in his heart. 29 If your right
eye causes you to sin, tear it out and throw it away! It is better to
lose one of your members than to have your whole body thrown
into hell. 30 If your right hand causes you to sin, cut it off and
throw it away! It is better to lose one of your members than to
have your whole body go into hell.

DIVORCE

31 "It was said, '***Whoever divorces his wife must give her a legal document.***' 32 But I say to you that everyone who divorces his wife,
except for immorality, makes her commit adultery, and whoever
marries a divorced woman commits adultery.

OATHS

33 "Again, you have heard that it was said to an older generation,
'***Do not break an oath, but fulfill your vows to the Lord.***' 34 But I
say to you, do not take oaths at all—not by heaven, because it is
the throne of God, 35 not by earth, because it is his footstool, and
not by Jerusalem, because it is the city of the great King. 36 Do
not take an oath by your head, because you are not able to make
one hair white or black. 37 Let your word be 'Yes, yes' or 'No, no.'
More than this is from the evil one.

RETALIATION

38 "You have heard that it was said, '***An eye for an eye and a tooth
for a tooth.***' 39 But I say to you, do not resist the evildoer. But
whoever strikes you on the right cheek, turn the other to him
as well. 40 And if someone wants to sue you and take your tunic,
let him have your coat also. 41 And if anyone forces you to go one
mile, go with him two. 42 Give to the one who asks you, and do
not reject the one who wants to borrow from you.

LOVE FOR ENEMIES

43 "You have heard that it was said, '***Love your neighbor***' and 'hate
your enemy.' 44 But I say to you, love your enemy and pray for those
who persecute you, 45 so that you may be like your Father in heaven,
since he causes the sun to rise on the evil and the good, and sends
rain on the righteous and the unrighteous. 46 For if you love those
who love you, what reward do you have? Even the tax collectors do
the same, don't they? 47 And if you only greet your brothers, what
more do you do? Even the Gentiles do the same, don't they? 48 So
then, be perfect, as your heavenly Father is perfect.

PURE-HEARTED GIVING

6 "Be careful not to display your righteousness merely to be seen
by people. Otherwise you have no reward with your Father in
heaven. 2 Thus whenever you do charitable giving, do not blow a
trumpet before you, as the hypocrites do in synagogues and on
streets so that people will praise them. I tell you the truth, they
have their reward! 3 But when you do your giving, do not let your
left hand know what your right hand is doing, 4 so that your gift may
be in secret. And your Father, who sees in secret, will reward you.

PRIVATE PRAYER

5 "Whenever you pray, do not be like the hypocrites, because they
love to pray while standing in synagogues and on street corners
so that people can see them. Truly I say to you, they have their
reward! 6 But whenever you pray, go into your inner room, close
the door, and pray to your Father in secret. And your Father, who
sees in secret, will reward you. 7 When you pray, do not babble
repetitiously like the Gentiles, because they think that by their

many words they will be heard. 8 Do not be like them, for your Father knows what you need before you ask him. 9 So pray this way:

Our Father in heaven, may your name be honored,
10 may your kingdom come,
may your will be done on earth as it is in heaven.
11 Give us today our daily bread,
12 and forgive us our debts, as we ourselves
have forgiven our debtors.
13 And do not lead us into temptation, but
deliver us from the evil one.

14 "For if you forgive others their sins, your heavenly Father
will also forgive you. 15 But if you do not forgive others, your Father will not forgive you your sins.

PROPER FASTING

16 "When you fast, do not look sullen like the hypocrites, for they
make their faces unattractive so that people will see them fasting. I tell you the truth, they have their reward! 17 When you fast,
anoint your head and wash your face, 18 so that it will not be obvious to others when you are fasting, but only to your Father who
is in secret. And your Father, who sees in secret, will reward you.

LASTING TREASURE

19 "Do not accumulate for yourselves treasures on earth, where moth
and devouring insect destroy and where thieves break in and steal.
20 But accumulate for yourselves treasures in heaven, where moth
and devouring insect do not destroy, and thieves do not break in
and steal. 21 For where your treasure is, there your heart will be also.
22 "The eye is the lamp of the body. If then your eye is healthy,
your whole body will be full of light. 23 But if your eye is diseased,
your whole body will be full of darkness. If then the light in you
is darkness, how great is the darkness!
24 "No one can serve two masters, for either he will hate the
one and love the other, or he will be devoted to the one and despise the other. You cannot serve God and money.

DO NOT WORRY

25 "Therefore I tell you, do not worry about your life, what you will
eat or drink, or about your body, what you will wear. Isn't there more
to life than food and more to the body than clothing? 26 Look at the
birds in the sky: They do not sow, or reap, or gather into barns, yet
your heavenly Father feeds them. Aren't you more valuable than
they are? 27 And which of you by worrying can add even one hour
to his life? 28 Why do you worry about clothing? Think about how
the flowers of the field grow; they do not work or spin. 29 Yet I tell
you that not even Solomon in all his glory was clothed like one of
these! 30 And if this is how God clothes the wild grass, which is here
today and tomorrow is tossed into the fire to heat the oven, won't
he clothe you even more, you people of little faith? 31 So then, don't
worry saying, 'What will we eat?' or 'What will we drink?' or 'What
will we wear?' 32 For the unconverted pursue these things, and your
heavenly Father knows that you need them. 33 But above all pursue
his kingdom and righteousness, and all these things will be given

REFLECT

What does it look like in your everyday life to pursue God's kingdom?

to you as well. 34 So then, do not worry about tomorrow, for tomorrow will worry about itself. Today has enough trouble of its own.

DO NOT JUDGE

7 "Do not judge so that you will not be judged. 2 For by the standard
you judge you will be judged, and the measure you use will be
the measure you receive. 3 Why do you see the speck in your brother's eye, but fail to see the beam of wood in your own? 4 Or how can
you say to your brother, 'Let me remove the speck from your eye,'
while there is a beam in your own? 5 You hypocrite! First remove
the beam from your own eye, and then you can see clearly to remove the speck from your brother's eye. 6 Do not give what is holy
to dogs or throw your pearls before pigs; otherwise they will trample them under their feet and turn around and tear you to pieces.

ASK, SEEK, KNOCK

7 "Ask and it will be given to you; seek and you will find; knock
and the door will be opened for you. 8 For everyone who asks receives, and the one who seeks finds, and to the one who knocks,
the door will be opened. 9 Is there anyone among you who, if
his son asks for bread, will give him a stone? 10 Or if he asks for
a fish, will give him a snake? 11 If you then, although you are evil,
know how to give good gifts to your children, how much more
will your Father in heaven give good gifts to those who ask him!
12 In everything, treat others as you would want them to treat
you, for this fulfills the law and the prophets.

THE NARROW GATE

13 "Enter through the narrow gate, because the gate is wide and
the way is spacious that leads to destruction, and there are many
who enter through it. 14 How narrow is the gate and difficult the
way that leads to life, and there are few who find it!

A TREE AND ITS FRUIT

15 "Watch out for false prophets, who come to you in sheep's clothing but inwardly are voracious wolves. 16 You will recognize them
by their fruit. Grapes are not gathered from thorns or figs from
thistles, are they? 17 In the same way, every good tree bears good
fruit, but the bad tree bears bad fruit. 18 A good tree is not able
to bear bad fruit, nor a bad tree to bear good fruit. 19 Every tree
that does not bear good fruit is cut down and thrown into the
fire. 20 So then, you will recognize them by their fruit.

JUDGMENT OF PRETENDERS

21 "Not everyone who says to me, 'Lord, Lord,' will enter into the
kingdom of heaven—only the one who does the will of my Father
in heaven. 22 On that day, many will say to me, 'Lord, Lord, didn't
we prophesy in your name, and cast out demons in your name,
and do many powerful deeds in your name?' 23 Then I will declare
to them, 'I never knew you. Go away from me, you lawbreakers!'

HEARING AND DOING

24 "Everyone who hears these words of mine and does them is like
a wise man who built his house on rock. 25 The rain fell, the flood

GOD'S HEART FOR THE NATIONS

Matthew 8:11

"I tell you, many will come from the east and west to share the banquet with Abraham, Isaac, and Jacob in the kingdom of heaven."

came, and the winds beat against that house, but it did not collapse
because its foundation had been laid on rock. 26 Everyone who hears
these words of mine and does not do them is like a foolish man who
built his house on sand. 27 The rain fell, the flood came, and the winds
beat against that house, and it collapsed—it was utterly destroyed!"
28 When Jesus finished saying these things, the crowds were
amazed by his teaching, 29 because he taught them like one who
had authority, not like their experts in the law.

CLEANSING A LEPER

8 After he came down from the mountain, large crowds followed him. 2 And a leper approached and bowed low before
him, saying, "Lord, if you are willing, you can make me clean."
3 He stretched out his hand and touched him saying, "I am willing. Be clean!" Immediately his leprosy was cleansed. 4 Then Jesus
said to him, "See that you do not speak to anyone, but go, show
yourself to the priest, and bring the offering that Moses commanded, as a testimony to them."

HEALING THE CENTURION'S SERVANT

5 When he entered Capernaum, a centurion came to him asking
for help: 6 "Lord, my servant is lying at home paralyzed, in terrible anguish." 7 Jesus said to him, "I will come and heal him." 8 But
the centurion replied, "Lord, I am not worthy to have you come
under my roof! Instead, just say the word and my servant will be
healed. 9 For I too am a man under authority, with soldiers under
me. I say to this one, 'Go!' and he goes, and to another 'Come!' and
he comes, and to my slave 'Do this!' and he does it." 10 When Jesus
heard this he was amazed and said to those who followed him,
"I tell you the truth, I have not found such faith in anyone in Israel! 11 I tell you, many will come from the east and west to share
the banquet with Abraham, Isaac, and Jacob in the kingdom of
heaven, 12 but the sons of the kingdom will be thrown out into
the outer darkness, where there will be weeping and gnashing of
teeth." 13 Then Jesus said to the centurion, "Go; just as you believed,
it will be done for you." And the servant was healed at that hour.

HEALINGS AT PETER'S HOUSE

14 Now when Jesus entered Peter's house, he saw his mother-in-
law lying down, sick with a fever. 15 He touched her hand, and the
fever left her. Then she got up and began to serve them. 16 When it
was evening, many demon-possessed people were brought to him.
He drove out the spirits with a word, and healed all who were sick.
17 In this way what was spoken by the prophet Isaiah was fulfilled:
"He took our weaknesses and carried our diseases."

CHALLENGING PROFESSED FOLLOWERS

18 Now when Jesus saw a large crowd around him, he gave orders to
go to the other side of the lake. 19 Then an expert in the law came to
him and said, "Teacher, I will follow you wherever you go." 20 Jesus
said to him, "Foxes have dens, and the birds in the sky have nests,
but the Son of Man has no place to lay his head." 21 Another of the
disciples said to him, "Lord, let me first go and bury my father." 22 But
Jesus said to him, "Follow me, and let the dead bury their own dead."

STILLING OF A STORM

23 As he got into the boat, his disciples followed him. 24 And a
great storm developed on the sea so that the waves began to
swamp the boat. But he was asleep. 25 So they came and woke
him up saying, "Lord, save us! We are about to die!" 26 But he said
to them, "Why are you cowardly, you people of little faith?" Then
he got up and rebuked the winds and the sea, and it was dead
calm. 27 And the men were amazed and said, "What sort of person is this? Even the winds and the sea obey him!"

HEALING THE GADARENE DEMONIACS

28 When he came to the other side, to the region of the Gadarenes,
two demon-possessed men coming from the tombs met him. They
were extremely violent, so that no one was able to pass by that way.
29 They cried out, "Son of God, leave us alone! Have you come here
to torment us before the time?" 30 A large herd of pigs was feeding
some distance from them. 31 Then the demons begged him, "If you
drive us out, send us into the herd of pigs." 32 And he said, "Go!" So
they came out and went into the pigs, and the herd rushed down the
steep slope into the lake and drowned in the water. 33 The herdsmen
ran off, went into the town, and told everything that had happened to
the demon-possessed men. 34 Then the entire town came out to meet
Jesus. And when they saw him, they begged him to leave their region.

HEALING AND FORGIVING A PARALYTIC

9 After getting into a boat he crossed to the other side and came
to his own town. 2 Just then some people brought to him a paralytic lying on a stretcher. When Jesus saw their faith, he said to the
paralytic, "Have courage, son! Your sins are forgiven." 3 Then some
of the experts in the law said to themselves, "This man is blaspheming!" 4 When Jesus perceived their thoughts he said, "Why do you respond with evil in your hearts? 5 Which is easier, to say, 'Your sins are
forgiven' or to say, 'Stand up and walk'? 6 But so that you may know
that the Son of Man has authority on earth to forgive sins"—then he
said to the paralytic—"Stand up, take your stretcher, and go home."
7 So he stood up and went home. 8 When the crowd saw this, they
were afraid and honored God who had given such authority to men.

THE CALL OF MATTHEW; EATING WITH SINNERS

9 As Jesus went on from there, he saw a man named Matthew
sitting at the tax booth. "Follow me," he said to him. So he got
up and followed him. 10 As Jesus was having a meal in Matthew's
house, many tax collectors and sinners came and ate with Jesus
and his disciples. 11 When the Pharisees saw this they said to his
disciples, "Why does your teacher eat with tax collectors and sinners?" 12 When Jesus heard this he said, "Those who are healthy
don't need a physician, but those who are sick do. 13 Go and learn
what this saying means: '***I want mercy and not sacrifice.***' For I did
not come to call the righteous, but sinners."

THE SUPERIORITY OF THE NEW

14 Then John's disciples came to Jesus and asked, "Why do we and the
Pharisees fast often, but your disciples don't fast?" 15 Jesus said to
them, "The wedding guests cannot mourn while the bridegroom is

with them, can they? But the days are coming when the bridegroom
will be taken from them, and then they will fast. 16 No one sews a
patch of unshrunk cloth on an old garment, because the patch will
pull away from the garment and the tear will be worse. 17 And no
one pours new wine into old wineskins; otherwise the skins burst
and the wine is spilled out and the skins are destroyed. Instead
they put new wine into new wineskins and both are preserved."

RESTORATION AND HEALING

18 As he was saying these things, a leader came, bowed low before
him, and said, "My daughter has just died, but come and lay your
hand on her and she will live." 19 Jesus and his disciples got up and
followed him. 20 But a woman who had been suffering from a hemorrhage for twelve years came up behind him and touched the
edge of his cloak. 21 For she kept saying to herself, "If only I touch
his cloak, I will be healed." 22 But when Jesus turned and saw her he
said, "Have courage, daughter! Your faith has made you well." And
the woman was healed from that hour. 23 When Jesus entered the
leader's house and saw the flute players and the disorderly crowd,
24 he said, "Go away, for the girl is not dead but asleep!" And they
began making fun of him. 25 But when the crowd had been forced
outside, he went in and gently took her by the hand, and the girl
got up. 26 And the news of this spread throughout that region.

HEALING THE BLIND AND MUTE

27 As Jesus went on from there, two blind men began to follow him,
shouting, "Have mercy on us, Son of David!" 28 When he went into
the house, the blind men came to him. Jesus said to them, "Do you
believe that I am able to do this?" They said to him, "Yes, Lord."
29 Then he touched their eyes saying, "Let it be done for you according to your faith." 30 And their eyes were opened. Then Jesus sternly
warned them, "See that no one knows about this!" 31 But they went
out and spread the news about him throughout that entire region.
32 As they were going away, a man who was demon-possessed
and unable to speak was brought to him. 33 After the demon was
cast out, the man who had been mute began to speak. The crowds
were amazed and said, "Never has anything like this been seen
in Israel!" 34 But the Pharisees said, "By the ruler of demons he
casts out demons!"

WORKERS FOR THE HARVEST

35 Then Jesus went throughout all the towns and villages, teaching in their synagogues, preaching the good news of the kingdom, and healing every kind of disease and sickness. 36 When he
saw the crowds, he had compassion on them because they were
bewildered and helpless, like sheep without a shepherd. 37 Then
he said to his disciples, "The harvest is plentiful, but the workers are few. 38 Therefore ask the Lord of the harvest to send out
workers into his harvest-ready fields."

SENDING OUT THE TWELVE APOSTLES

10 Jesus called his twelve disciples and gave them authority
over unclean spirits so they could cast them out and heal
every kind of disease and sickness. 2 Now these are the names

of the twelve apostles: first, Simon (called Peter), and Andrew his brother; James son of Zebedee and John his brother; 3 Philip and Bartholomew; Thomas and Matthew the tax collector; James the son of Alphaeus, and Thaddaeus; 4 Simon the Zealot and Judas Iscariot, who betrayed him.

5 Jesus sent out these twelve, instructing them as follows: "Do not go on a road that leads to Gentile regions and do not enter any Samaritan town. 6 Go instead to the lost sheep of the house of Israel. 7 As you go, preach this message: 'The kingdom of heaven is near!' 8 Heal the sick, raise the dead, cleanse lepers, cast out demons. Freely you received, freely give. 9 Do not take gold, silver, or copper in your belts, 10 no bag for the journey, or an extra tunic, or sandals or staff, for the worker deserves his provisions. 11 Whenever you enter a town or village, find out who is worthy there and stay with them until you leave. 12 As you enter the house, greet those within it. 13 And if the house is worthy, let your peace come on it, but if it is not worthy, let your peace return to you. 14 And if anyone will not welcome you or listen to your message, shake the dust off your feet as you leave that house or that town. 15 I tell you the truth, it will be more bearable for the region of Sodom and Gomorrah on the day of judgment than for that town!

PERSECUTION OF DISCIPLES

16 "I am sending you out like sheep surrounded by wolves, so be wise as serpents and innocent as doves. 17 Beware of people, because they will hand you over to councils and flog you in their synagogues. 18 And you will be brought before governors and kings because of me, as a witness to them and to the Gentiles. 19 Whenever they hand you over for trial, do not worry about how to speak or what to say, for what you should say will be given to you at that time. 20 For it is not you speaking, but the Spirit of your Father speaking through you.

21 "Brother will hand over brother to death, and a father his child. Children will rise against parents and have them put to death. 22 And you will be hated by everyone because of my name. But the one who endures to the end will be saved! 23 Whenever they persecute you in one town, flee to another! I tell you the truth, you will not finish going through all the towns of Israel before the Son of Man comes.

24 "A disciple is not greater than his teacher, nor a slave greater than his master. 25 It is enough for the disciple to become like his teacher, and the slave like his master. If they have called the head of the house 'Beelzebul,' how much worse will they call the members of his household!

FEAR GOD, NOT MAN

26 "Do not be afraid of them, for nothing is hidden that will not be revealed, and nothing is secret that will not be made known. 27 What I say to you in the dark, tell in the light, and what is whispered in your ear, proclaim from the housetops. 28 Do not be afraid of those who kill the body but cannot kill the soul. Instead, fear the one who is able to destroy both soul and body in hell. 29 Aren't two sparrows sold for a penny? Yet not one of them

falls to the ground apart from your Father's will. 30 Even all the
hairs on your head are numbered. 31 So do not be afraid; you are
more valuable than many sparrows.

32 "Whoever, then, acknowledges me before people, I will acknowledge before my Father in heaven. 33 But whoever denies me
before people, I will deny him also before my Father in heaven.

NOT PEACE, BUT A SWORD

34 "Do not think that I have come to bring peace to the earth. I
have not come to bring peace but a sword! 35 For I have come to
set *a man against his father, a daughter against her mother, and a*
daughter-in-law against her mother-in-law, 36 *and a man's enemies*
will be the members of his household.

37 "Whoever loves father or mother more than me is not worthy of me, and whoever loves son or daughter more than me is
not worthy of me. 38 And whoever does not take up his cross and
follow me is not worthy of me. 39 Whoever finds his life will lose
it, and whoever loses his life because of me will find it.

REWARDS

40 "Whoever receives you receives me, and whoever receives me
receives the one who sent me. 41 Whoever receives a prophet in
the name of a prophet will receive a prophet's reward. Whoever
receives a righteous person in the name of a righteous person
will receive a righteous person's reward. 42 And whoever gives
only a cup of cold water to one of these little ones in the name
of a disciple, I tell you the truth, he will never lose his reward."

11 When Jesus had finished instructing his twelve disciples,
he went on from there to teach and preach in their towns.

JESUS AND JOHN THE BAPTIST

2 Now when John heard in prison about the deeds Christ had
done, he sent his disciples to ask a question: 3 "Are you the one
who is to come, or should we look for another?" 4 Jesus answered
them, "Go tell John what you hear and see: 5 The blind see, the
lame walk, lepers are cleansed, the deaf hear, the dead are raised,
and the poor have good news proclaimed to them 6 —and blessed
is anyone who takes no offense at me!"

7 While they were going away, Jesus began to speak to the crowd
about John: "What did you go out into the wilderness to see? A
reed shaken by the wind? 8 What did you go out to see? A man
dressed in soft clothing? Look, those who wear soft clothing are
in the palaces of kings! 9 What did you go out to see? A prophet?
Yes, I tell you, and more than a prophet! 10 This is the one about
whom it is written:

> ***'Look, I am sending my messenger ahead of you,***
> ***who will prepare your way before you.'***

11 "I tell you the truth, among those born of women, no one has
arisen greater than John the Baptist. Yet the one who is least in
the kingdom of heaven is greater than he is! 12 From the days of
John the Baptist until now the kingdom of heaven has suffered
violence, and forceful people lay hold of it. 13 For all the prophets and the law prophesied until John appeared. 14 And if you are

willing to accept it, he is Elijah, who is to come. 15 The one who
has ears had better listen!

16 "To what should I compare this generation? They are like
children sitting in the marketplaces who call out to one another,

17 'We played the flute for you, yet you did not dance;
we wailed in mourning, yet you did not weep.'

18 For John came neither eating nor drinking, and they say, 'He
has a demon!' 19 The Son of Man came eating and drinking, and
they say, 'Look at him, a glutton and a drunk, a friend of tax collectors and sinners!' But wisdom is vindicated by her deeds."

WOES ON UNREPENTANT CITIES

20 Then Jesus began to criticize openly the cities in which he had
done many of his miracles, because they did not repent. 21 "Woe
to you, Chorazin! Woe to you, Bethsaida! If the miracles done in
you had been done in Tyre and Sidon, they would have repented
long ago in sackcloth and ashes. 22 But I tell you, it will be more
bearable for Tyre and Sidon on the day of judgment than for you!
23 And you, Capernaum, will you be exalted to heaven? No, you
will be thrown down to Hades! For if the miracles done among
you had been done in Sodom, it would have continued to this
day. 24 But I tell you, it will be more bearable for the region of
Sodom on the day of judgment than for you!"

JESUS' INVITATION

25 At that time Jesus said, "I praise you, Father, Lord of heaven
and earth, because you have hidden these things from the wise
and intelligent, and have revealed them to little children. 26 Yes,
Father, for this was your gracious will. 27 All things have been
handed over to me by my Father. No one knows the Son except
the Father, and no one knows the Father except the Son and
anyone to whom the Son decides to reveal him. 28 Come to me,
all you who are weary and burdened, and I will give you rest.
29 Take my yoke on you and learn from me, because I am gentle
and humble in heart, and you will find rest for your souls. 30 For
my yoke is easy to bear, and my load is not hard to carry."

LORD OF THE SABBATH

12 At that time Jesus went through the grain fields on a Sabbath.
His disciples were hungry, and they began to pick heads of
wheat and eat them. 2 But when the Pharisees saw this they said to
him, "Look, your disciples are doing what is against the law to do
on the Sabbath." 3 He said to them, "Haven't you read what David
did when he and his companions were hungry—4 how he entered
the house of God and ate the sacred bread, which was against the
law for him or his companions to eat, but only for the priests? 5 Or
have you not read in the law that the priests in the temple desecrate the Sabbath and yet are not guilty? 6 I tell you that something greater than the temple is here. 7 If you had known what this
means: '***I want mercy and not sacrifice***,' you would not have condemned the innocent. 8 For the Son of Man is lord of the Sabbath."

9 Then Jesus left that place and entered their synagogue. 10 A
man was there who had a withered hand. And they asked Jesus,
"Is it lawful to heal on the Sabbath?" so that they could accuse

LOVE TO GROW

HE WILL GIVE US REST

MATTHEW 11:28

Until recently, when someone would come up to me and ask how I was doing, my typical response would be, "I'm busy, but good." I somehow thought that it was necessary to convey an overabundance of activity in my life. If my schedule had a gap, I equated the lag time with failure. Yet, the busier I became, the more unhappy I felt. My stress level increased, affecting me spiritually, physically, and emotionally.

Rest is not celebrated in the western world. Instead, it is often confused with laziness. While laziness is the adversary of work, rest is a refreshment from labor. God rested on the seventh day from creation to celebrate His work, and He tells us to do the same. If we do not take time to rest, we tend to run weary, even when we are doing good and godly work.

Jesus invited those who listened to Him to come to Him for rest. Most of those who came to hear Jesus had come to Him for healing or to receive a message of encouragement. They looked to Him as a teacher, miracle worker, or savior, and they were looking for something from Him. Their lives were filled with constant demands that they expected Jesus to meet. When Jesus invited the heavily-burdened to come, it was an invitation to go from distress to discipleship.

Friend, our Lord and Savior wants to refresh and sustain you. He simply asks that we come to Him. Jesus wants us to approach Him, not as His worker bees, but rather as His closest companions.

We don't have to present the best version of ourselves. He wants us as we are.

When we allow the busyness of our lives to define us or distract us from our relationship with God, we will never understand the peace and rest that only He can give. We miss the simple fellowship of being still with God and abiding in His presence.

Where in your life do you need to experience His rest? Have you allowed busyness to define your relationship with God or to distract you from Him? He wants to meet you there. Surrender your busyness to Him. He won't shame you or scold you. Instead, He'll offer you true rest.

him. 11 He said to them, "Would not any one of you, if he had one
sheep that fell into a pit on the Sabbath, take hold of it and lift
it out? 12 How much more valuable is a person than a sheep! So it
is lawful to do good on the Sabbath." 13 Then he said to the man,
"Stretch out your hand." He stretched it out and it was restored,
as healthy as the other. 14 But the Pharisees went out and plotted
against him, as to how they could assassinate him.

GOD'S SPECIAL SERVANT

15 Now when Jesus learned of this, he went away from there. Great
crowds followed him, and he healed them all. 16 But he sternly
warned them not to make him known. 17 This fulfilled what was
spoken by the prophet Isaiah:

18 ***"Here is my servant whom I have chosen,***
the one I love, in whom I take great delight.
I will put my Spirit on him, and he will
proclaim justice to the nations.
19 ***He will not quarrel or cry out,***
nor will anyone hear his voice in the streets.
20 ***He will not break a bruised reed or***
extinguish a smoldering wick,
until he brings justice to victory.
21 ***And in his name the Gentiles will hope."***

JESUS AND BEELZEBUL

22 Then they brought to him a demon-possessed man who was
blind and mute. Jesus healed him so that he could speak and see.
23 All the crowds were amazed and said, "Could this one be the Son
of David?" 24 But when the Pharisees heard this they said, "He does
not cast out demons except by the power of Beelzebul, the ruler of
demons!" 25 Now when Jesus realized what they were thinking, he
said to them, "Every kingdom divided against itself is destroyed,
and no town or house divided against itself will stand. 26 So if Satan casts out Satan, he is divided against himself. How then will
his kingdom stand? 27 And if I cast out demons by Beelzebul, by
whom do your sons cast them out? For this reason they will be your
judges. 28 But if I cast out demons by the Spirit of God, then the
kingdom of God has already overtaken you. 29 How else can someone enter a strong man's house and steal his property, unless he
first ties up the strong man? Then he can thoroughly plunder the
house. 30 Whoever is not with me is against me, and whoever does
not gather with me scatters. 31 For this reason I tell you, people will
be forgiven for every sin and blasphemy, but the blasphemy against
the Spirit will not be forgiven. 32 Whoever speaks a word against the
Son of Man will be forgiven. But whoever speaks against the Holy
Spirit will not be forgiven, either in this age or in the age to come.

TREES AND THEIR FRUIT

33 "Make a tree good and its fruit will be good, or make a tree bad
and its fruit will be bad, for a tree is known by its fruit. 34 Offspring of vipers! How are you able to say anything good, since
you are evil? For the mouth speaks from what fills the heart.
35 The good person brings good things out of his good treasury,
and the evil person brings evil things out of his evil treasury.

GOD'S HEART FOR THE NATIONS

Matthew 12:21

"And in his name the Gentiles will hope."

36 I tell you that on the day of judgment, people will give an account for every worthless word they speak. 37 For by your words you will be justified, and by your words you will be condemned."

THE SIGN OF JONAH

38 Then some of the experts in the law along with some Pharisees answered him, "Teacher, we want to see a sign from you." 39 But he answered them, "An evil and adulterous generation asks for a sign, but no sign will be given to it except the sign of the prophet Jonah. 40 For just as Jonah was ***in the belly of the huge fish for three days and three nights***, so the Son of Man will be in the heart of the earth for three days and three nights. 41 The people of Nineveh will stand up at the judgment with this generation and condemn it, because they repented when Jonah preached to them—and now, something greater than Jonah is here! 42 The queen of the South will rise up at the judgment with this generation and condemn it, because she came from the ends of the earth to hear the wisdom of Solomon—and now, something greater than Solomon is here!

THE RETURN OF THE UNCLEAN SPIRIT

43 "When an unclean spirit goes out of a person, it passes through waterless places looking for rest but does not find it. 44 Then it says, 'I will return to the home I left.' When it returns, it finds the house empty, swept clean, and put in order. 45 Then it goes and brings with it seven other spirits more evil than itself, and they go in and live there, so the last state of that person is worse than the first. It will be that way for this evil generation as well!"

JESUS' TRUE FAMILY

46 While Jesus was still speaking to the crowds, his mother and brothers came and stood outside, asking to speak to him. 47 Someone told him, "Look, your mother and your brothers are standing outside wanting to speak to you." 48 To the one who had said this, Jesus replied, "Who is my mother and who are my brothers?" 49 And pointing toward his disciples he said, "Here are my mother and my brothers! 50 For whoever does the will of my Father in heaven is my brother and sister and mother."

THE PARABLE OF THE SOWER

13 On that day after Jesus went out of the house, he sat by the lake. 2 And such a large crowd gathered around him that he got into a boat to sit while the whole crowd stood on the shore. 3 He told them many things in parables, saying: "Listen! A sower went out to sow. 4 And as he sowed, some seeds fell along the path, and the birds came and devoured them. 5 Other seeds fell on rocky ground where they did not have much soil. They sprang up quickly because the soil was not deep. 6 But when the sun came up, they were scorched, and because they did not have sufficient root, they withered. 7 Other seeds fell among the thorns, and they grew up and choked them. 8 But other seeds fell on good soil and produced grain, some a hundred times as much, some sixty, and some thirty. 9 The one who has ears had better listen!"

10 Then the disciples came to him and said, "Why do you speak to them in parables?" 11 He replied, "You have been given the

opportunity to know the secrets of the kingdom of heaven, but
they have not. 12 For whoever has will be given more, and will
have an abundance. But whoever does not have, even what he
has will be taken from him. 13 For this reason I speak to them in
parables: Although they see they do not see, and although they
hear they do not hear nor do they understand. 14 And concerning them the prophecy of Isaiah is fulfilled that says:

'You will listen carefully yet will never understand,
you will look closely yet will never comprehend.
15 *For the heart of this people has become dull;*
they are hard of hearing,
and they have shut their eyes,
so that they would not see with their eyes
and hear with their ears
and understand with their hearts
and turn, and I would heal them.'

16 "But your eyes are blessed because they see, and your ears
because they hear. 17 For I tell you the truth, many prophets and
righteous people longed to see what you see but did not see it,
and to hear what you hear but did not hear it.
18 "So listen to the parable of the sower: 19 When anyone hears the
word about the kingdom and does not understand it, the evil one
comes and snatches what was sown in his heart; this is the seed
sown along the path. 20 The seed sown on rocky ground is the person who hears the word and immediately receives it with joy. 21 But
he has no root in himself and does not endure; when trouble or
persecution comes because of the word, immediately he falls away.
22 The seed sown among thorns is the person who hears the word,
but worldly cares and the seductiveness of wealth choke the word,
so it produces nothing. 23 But as for the seed sown on good soil,
this is the person who hears the word and understands. He bears
fruit, yielding a hundred, sixty, or thirty times what was sown."

THE PARABLE OF THE WEEDS

24 He presented them with another parable: "The kingdom of heaven
is like a person who sowed good seed in his field. 25 But while everyone was sleeping, an enemy came and sowed darnel among the
wheat and went away. 26 When the plants sprouted and produced
grain, then the darnel also appeared. 27 So the slaves of the landowner came and said to him, 'Sir, didn't you sow good seed in your
field? Then where did the darnel come from?' 28 He said, 'An enemy
has done this!' So the slaves replied, 'Do you want us to go and gather
it?' 29 But he said, 'No, since in gathering the darnel you may uproot
the wheat along with it. 30 Let both grow together until the harvest.
At harvest time I will tell the reapers, "First collect the darnel and tie
it in bundles to be burned, but then gather the wheat into my barn."'"

THE PARABLE OF THE MUSTARD SEED

31 He gave them another parable: "The kingdom of heaven is like
a mustard seed that a man took and sowed in his field. 32 It is the
smallest of all the seeds, but when it has grown it is the greatest
garden plant and becomes a tree, so that the wild birds come
and nest in its branches."

THE PARABLE OF THE YEAST

33 He told them another parable: "The kingdom of heaven is like
yeast that a woman took and mixed with three measures of flour
until all the dough had risen."

THE PURPOSE OF PARABLES

34 Jesus spoke all these things in parables to the crowds; he did
not speak to them without a parable. 35 This fulfilled what was
spoken by the prophet:

"I will open my mouth in parables,
I will announce what has been hidden from
the foundation of the world."

REFLECT

How can you have a heart like good soil? What can you do to make sure the Word of God is planted deep in your heart and life?

EXPLANATION FOR THE DISCIPLES

36 Then he left the crowds and went into the house. And his disciples came to him saying, "Explain to us the parable of the darnel in
the field." 37 He answered, "The one who sowed the good seed is the
Son of Man. 38 The field is the world and the good seed are the people of the kingdom. The poisonous weeds are the people of the evil
one, 39 and the enemy who sows them is the devil. The harvest is the
end of the age, and the reapers are angels. 40 As the poisonous weeds
are collected and burned with fire, so it will be at the end of the age.
41 The Son of Man will send his angels, and they will gather from his
kingdom everything that causes sin as well as all lawbreakers. 42 They
will ***throw them into the fiery furnace***, where there will be weeping
and gnashing of teeth. 43 Then *the righteous will shine like the sun in*
the kingdom of their Father. The one who has ears had better listen!

PARABLES ON THE KINGDOM OF HEAVEN

44 "The kingdom of heaven is like a treasure, hidden in a field,
that a person found and hid. Then because of joy he went and
sold all that he had and bought that field.

45 "Again, the kingdom of heaven is like a merchant searching
for fine pearls. 46 When he found a pearl of great value, he went
out and sold everything he had and bought it.

47 "Again, the kingdom of heaven is like a net that was cast
into the sea that caught all kinds of fish. 48 When it was full, they
pulled it ashore, sat down, and put the good fish into containers
and threw the bad away. 49 It will be this way at the end of the
age. Angels will come and separate the evil from the righteous
50 and *throw them into the fiery furnace*, where there will be weeping and gnashing of teeth.

51 "Have you understood all these things?" They replied, "Yes."
52 Then he said to them, "Therefore every expert in the law who
has been trained for the kingdom of heaven is like the owner
of a house who brings out of his treasure what is new and old."

REJECTION AT NAZARETH

53 Now when Jesus finished these parables, he moved on from
there. 54 Then he came to his hometown and began to teach the
people in their synagogue. They were astonished and said, "Where
did this man get such wisdom and miraculous powers? 55 Isn't this
the carpenter's son? Isn't his mother named Mary? And aren't
his brothers James, Joseph, Simon, and Judas? 56 And aren't all his

sisters here with us? So where did he get all this?” 57 And so they
took offense at him. But Jesus said to them, “A prophet is not without honor except in his hometown and in his own house.” 58 And
he did not do many miracles there because of their unbelief.

THE DEATH OF JOHN THE BAPTIST

14 At that time Herod the tetrarch heard reports about Jesus,
2 and he said to his servants, “This is John the Baptist. He has
been raised from the dead! And because of this, miraculous powers are at work in him.” 3 For Herod had arrested John, bound him,
and put him in prison on account of Herodias, his brother Philip’s
wife, 4 because John had repeatedly told him, “It is not lawful for
you to have her.” 5 Although Herod wanted to kill John, he feared
the crowd because they accepted John as a prophet. 6 But on Herod’s birthday, the daughter of Herodias danced before them and
pleased Herod, 7 so much that he promised with an oath to give
her whatever she asked. 8 Instructed by her mother, she said, “Give
me the head of John the Baptist here on a platter.” 9 Although it
grieved the king, because of his oath and the dinner guests he
commanded it to be given. 10 So he sent and had John beheaded
in the prison. 11 His head was brought on a platter and given to
the girl, and she brought it to her mother. 12 Then John’s disciples
came and took the body and buried it and went and told Jesus.

THE FEEDING OF THE FIVE THOUSAND

13 Now when Jesus heard this he went away from there privately in
a boat to an isolated place. But when the crowd heard about it, they
followed him on foot from the towns. 14 As he got out he saw the
large crowd, and he had compassion on them and healed their sick.
15 When evening arrived, his disciples came to him saying, “This is
an isolated place and the hour is already late. Send the crowds away
so that they can go into the villages and buy food for themselves.”
16 But he replied, “They don’t need to go. You give them something
to eat.” 17 They said to him, “We have here only five loaves and two
fish.” 18 “Bring them here to me,” he replied. 19 Then he instructed
the crowds to sit down on the grass. He took the five loaves and
two fish, and looking up to heaven he gave thanks and broke the
loaves. He gave them to the disciples, who in turn gave them to
the crowds. 20 They all ate and were satisfied, and they picked up the
broken pieces left over, twelve baskets full. 21 Not counting women
and children, there were about 5,000 men who ate.

WALKING ON WATER

22 Immediately Jesus made the disciples get into the boat and go
ahead of him to the other side, while he dispersed the crowds.
23 And after he sent the crowds away, he went up the mountain by
himself to pray. When evening came, he was there alone. 24 Meanwhile the boat, already far from land, was taking a beating from
the waves because the wind was against it. 25 As the night was ending, Jesus came to them walking on the sea. 26 When the disciples
saw him walking on the water they were terrified and said, “It’s a
ghost!” and cried out with fear. 27 But immediately Jesus spoke to
them: “Have courage! It is I. Do not be afraid.” 28 Peter said to him,
“Lord, if it is you, order me to come to you on the water.” 29 So he

said, "Come." Peter got out of the boat, walked on the water, and
came toward Jesus. 30 But when he saw the strong wind he became afraid. And starting to sink, he cried out, "Lord, save me!"
31 Immediately Jesus reached out his hand and caught him, saying to him, "You of little faith, why did you doubt?" 32 When they
went up into the boat, the wind ceased. 33 Then those who were
in the boat worshiped him, saying, "Truly you are the Son of God."

34 After they had crossed over, they came to land at Gennesaret. 35 When the people there recognized him, they sent word
into all the surrounding area, and they brought all their sick to
him. 36 They begged him if they could only touch the edge of his
cloak, and all who touched it were healed.

BREAKING HUMAN TRADITIONS

15 Then Pharisees and experts in the law came from Jerusalem to Jesus and said, 2 "Why do your disciples disobey the
tradition of the elders? For they don't wash their hands when
they eat." 3 He answered them, "And why do you disobey the
commandment of God because of your tradition? 4 For God said,
'***Honor your father and mother***' and '***Whoever insults his father***
or mother must be put to death.' 5 But you say, 'If someone tells
his father or mother, "Whatever help you would have received
from me is given to God," 6 he does not need to honor his father.'
You have nullified the word of God on account of your tradition.
7 Hypocrites! Isaiah prophesied correctly about you when he said,

8 '***This people honors me with their lips,***
but their heart is far from me,
9 ***and they worship me in vain,***
teaching as doctrines the commandments of men.' "

TRUE DEFILEMENT

10 Then he called the crowd to him and said, "Listen and understand. 11 What defiles a person is not what goes into the mouth;
it is what comes out of the mouth that defiles a person." 12 Then
the disciples came to him and said, "Do you know that when the
Pharisees heard this saying they were offended?" 13 And he replied, "Every plant that my heavenly Father did not plant will be
uprooted. 14 Leave them! They are blind guides. If someone who
is blind leads another who is blind, both will fall into a pit." 15 But
Peter said to him, "Explain this parable to us." 16 Jesus said, "Even
after all this, are you still so foolish? 17 Don't you understand that
whatever goes into the mouth enters the stomach and then passes
out into the sewer? 18 But the things that come out of the mouth
come from the heart, and these things defile a person. 19 For out
of the heart come evil ideas, murder, adultery, sexual immorality,
theft, false testimony, slander. 20 These are the things that defile a
person; it is not eating with unwashed hands that defiles a person."

A CANAANITE WOMAN'S FAITH

21 After going out from there, Jesus went to the region of Tyre and
Sidon. 22 A Canaanite woman from that area came and cried out,
"Have mercy on me, Lord, Son of David! My daughter is horribly
demon-possessed!" 23 But he did not answer her a word. Then
his disciples came and begged him, "Send her away, because

she keeps on crying out after us." 24 So he answered, "I was sent only to the lost sheep of the house of Israel." 25 But she came and bowed down before him and said, "Lord, help me!" 26 "It is not right to take the children's bread and throw it to the dogs," he said. 27 "Yes, Lord," she replied, "but even the dogs eat the crumbs that fall from their masters' table." 28 Then Jesus answered her, "Woman, your faith is great! Let what you want be done for you." And her daughter was healed from that hour.

HEALING MANY OTHERS

29 When he left there, Jesus went along the Sea of Galilee. Then he went up a mountain, where he sat down. 30 Then large crowds came to him bringing with them the lame, blind, crippled, mute, and many others. They laid them at his feet, and he healed them. 31 As a result, the crowd was amazed when they saw the mute speaking, the crippled healthy, the lame walking, and the blind seeing, and they praised the God of Israel.

THE FEEDING OF THE FOUR THOUSAND

32 Then Jesus called his disciples and said, "I have compassion on the crowd, because they have already been here with me three days and they have nothing to eat. I don't want to send them away hungry since they may faint on the way." 33 The disciples said to him, "Where can we get enough bread in this desolate place to satisfy so great a crowd?" 34 Jesus said to them, "How many loaves do you have?" They replied, "Seven—and a few small fish." 35 After instructing the crowd to sit down on the ground, 36 he took the seven loaves and the fish, and after giving thanks, he broke them and began giving them to the disciples, who then gave them to the crowds. 37 They all ate and were satisfied, and they picked up the broken pieces left over, seven baskets full. 38 Not counting children and women, there were 4,000 men who ate. 39 After sending away the crowd, he got into the boat and went to the region of Magadan.

THE DEMAND FOR A SIGN

16 Now when the Pharisees and Sadducees came to test Jesus, they asked him to show them a sign from heaven. 2 He said, "When evening comes you say, 'It will be fair weather, because the sky is red,' 3 and in the morning, 'It will be stormy today, because the sky is red and darkening.' You know how to judge correctly the appearance of the sky, but you cannot evaluate the signs of the times. 4 A wicked and adulterous generation asks for a sign, but no sign will be given to it except the sign of Jonah." Then he left them and went away.

THE YEAST OF THE PHARISEES AND SADDUCEES

5 When the disciples went to the other side, they forgot to take bread. 6 "Watch out," Jesus said to them, "beware of the yeast of the Pharisees and Sadducees." 7 So they began to discuss this among themselves, saying, "It is because we brought no bread." 8 When Jesus learned of this, he said, "You who have such little faith! Why are you arguing among yourselves about having no bread? 9 Do you still not understand? Don't you remember the five loaves for the 5,000, and how many baskets you took up? 10 Or the seven loaves

for the 4,000 and how many baskets you took up? 11 How could you
not understand that I was not speaking to you about bread? But beware of the yeast of the Pharisees and Sadducees!" 12 Then they understood that he had not told them to be on guard against the yeast
in bread, but against the teaching of the Pharisees and Sadducees.

PETER'S CONFESSION

13 When Jesus came to the area of Caesarea Philippi, he asked his disciples, "Who do people say that the Son of Man is?" 14 They answered,
"Some say John the Baptist, others Elijah, and others Jeremiah or
one of the prophets." 15 He said to them, "But who do you say that I
am?" 16 Simon Peter answered, "You are the Christ, the Son of the
living God." 17 And Jesus answered him, "You are blessed, Simon son
of Jonah, because flesh and blood did not reveal this to you, but my
Father in heaven! 18 And I tell you that you are Peter, and on this rock
I will build my church, and the gates of Hades will not overpower
it. 19 I will give you the keys of the kingdom of heaven. Whatever
you bind on earth will have been bound in heaven, and whatever
you release on earth will have been released in heaven." 20 Then he
instructed his disciples not to tell anyone that he was the Christ.

FIRST PREDICTION OF JESUS' DEATH AND RESURRECTION

21 From that time on Jesus began to show his disciples that he must
go to Jerusalem and suffer many things at the hands of the elders,
chief priests, and experts in the law, and be killed, and on the third
day be raised. 22 So Peter took him aside and began to rebuke him:
"God forbid, Lord! This must not happen to you!" 23 But he turned
and said to Peter, "Get behind me, Satan! You are a stumbling block
to me, because you are not setting your mind on God's interests,
but on man's." 24 Then Jesus said to his disciples, "If anyone wants
to become my follower, he must deny himself, take up his cross,
and follow me. 25 For whoever wants to save his life will lose it, but
whoever loses his life because of me will find it. 26 For what does it
benefit a person if he gains the whole world but forfeits his life?
Or what can a person give in exchange for his life? 27 For the Son of
Man will come with his angels in the glory of his Father, and then
he will reward each person according to what he has done. 28 I tell you
the truth, there are some standing here who will not experience
death before they see the Son of Man coming in his kingdom."

THE TRANSFIGURATION

CHALLENGE

How does the transfiguration of Jesus display His deity? What other passages show the deity of Christ?

17 Six days later Jesus took with him Peter, James, and John the
brother of James, and led them privately up a high mountain. 2 And he was transfigured before them. His face shone like
the sun, and his clothes became white as light. 3 Then Moses and
Elijah also appeared before them, talking with him. 4 So Peter
said to Jesus, "Lord, it is good for us to be here. If you want, I will
make three shelters—one for you, one for Moses, and one for Elijah." 5 While he was still speaking, a bright cloud overshadowed
them, and a voice from the cloud said, "This is my one dear Son,
in whom I take great delight. Listen to him!" 6 When the disciples
heard this, they were overwhelmed with fear and threw themselves down with their faces to the ground. 7 But Jesus came and

LOVE TO GROW

COST OF DISCIPLESHIP

MATTHEW 16:24–28

When war begins, one has to choose a side. War is chaotic and violent, but those fighting in the war firmly believe in what they are fighting for.

The Christian life is similar to war. We are constantly in a spiritual battle, and God demands our allegiance to Him. By His grace, we are able to choose to live for Him, resist the enemy, and stand against his schemes.

In Matthew 16, Jesus foretold His death, but Peter rebuked Him because he didn't want to believe in a suffering Messiah. Jesus knew Satan was using Peter to try to hinder His plan for salvation, so Jesus confronted Peter and rebuked Satan's retort.

As Christians, we no longer represent the world or its thinking. Instead, we represent Christ, and that leads to suffering. It may not be a physical suffering, but a spiritual suffering is sure to come in the fight against the enemy.

Death on a cross was the Romans' most shameful, excruciating death. Carrying one's cross and following Christ will be difficult and painful at times. Our hope is this: We find life in Christ. We do not live for the here and now but for eternity. We must decide if we will live for the glory of the world or for the glory of the Lord.

Consider the God you serve. He is not an authoritarian warlord but the all-powerful Lord of Hosts who fights on behalf of justice and mercy. He does not demand our allegiance like a dictator, but, rather, He invites us into relationship with Him as our King and Father. His love compels us to serve and commit our lives to Him.

What is He calling you to leave behind so you can fully serve Him? I pray you would see God as worthy and more beautiful than anything this life has to offer. Will you choose to pick up your cross and follow Him today?

touched them. "Get up," he said. "Do not be afraid." 8 When they
looked up, all they saw was Jesus alone.
9 As they were coming down from the mountain, Jesus commanded them, "Do not tell anyone about the vision until the Son
of Man is raised from the dead." 10 The disciples asked him, "Why
then do the experts in the law say that Elijah must come first?"
11 He answered, "Elijah does indeed come first and will restore all
things. 12 And I tell you that Elijah has already come. Yet they did not
recognize him, but did to him whatever they wanted. In the same
way, the Son of Man will suffer at their hands." 13 Then the disciples
understood that he was speaking to them about John the Baptist.

THE DISCIPLES' FAILURE TO HEAL

14 When they came to the crowd, a man came to him, knelt before
him, 15 and said, "Lord, have mercy on my son, because he has seizures and suffers terribly, for he often falls into the fire and into
the water. 16 I brought him to your disciples, but they were not able
to heal him." 17 Jesus answered, "You unbelieving and perverse generation! How much longer must I be with you? How much longer
must I endure you? Bring him here to me." 18 Then Jesus rebuked
the demon and it came out of him, and the boy was healed from
that moment. 19 Then the disciples came to Jesus privately and
said, "Why couldn't we cast it out?" 20 He told them, "It was because
of your little faith. I tell you the truth, if you have faith the size of
a mustard seed, you will say to this mountain, 'Move from here
to there,' and it will move; nothing will be impossible for you."[§]

SECOND PREDICTION OF JESUS' DEATH AND RESURRECTION

22 When they gathered together in Galilee, Jesus told them, "The
Son of Man is going to be betrayed into the hands of men. 23 They
will kill him, and on the third day he will be raised." And they
became greatly distressed.

THE TEMPLE TAX

24 After they arrived in Capernaum, the collectors of the temple tax came to Peter and said, "Your teacher pays the double
drachma tax, doesn't he?" 25 He said, "Yes." When Peter came
into the house, Jesus spoke to him first, "What do you think, Simon? From whom do earthly kings collect tolls or taxes—from
their sons or from foreigners?" 26 After he said, "From foreigners,"
Jesus said to him, "Then the sons are free. 27 But so that we don't
offend them, go to the lake and throw out a hook. Take the first
fish that comes up, and when you open its mouth, you will find a
four drachma coin. Take that and give it to them for me and you."

QUESTIONS ABOUT THE GREATEST

18 At that time the disciples came to Jesus saying, "Who is the
greatest in the kingdom of heaven?" 2 He called a child, had
him stand among them, 3 and said, "I tell you the truth, unless you
turn around and become like little children, you will never enter
the kingdom of heaven! 4 Whoever then humbles himself like
this little child is the greatest in the kingdom of heaven. 5 And
whoever welcomes a child like this in my name welcomes me.

6 “But if anyone causes one of these little ones who believe in me to sin, it would be better for him to have a huge millstone hung around his neck and to be drowned in the open sea. 7 Woe to the world because of stumbling blocks! It is necessary that stumbling blocks come, but woe to the person through whom they come. 8 If your hand or your foot causes you to sin, cut it off and throw it away. It is better for you to enter life crippled or lame than to have two hands or two feet and be thrown into eternal fire. 9 And if your eye causes you to sin, tear it out and throw it away. It is better for you to enter into life with one eye than to have two eyes and be thrown into fiery hell.

THE PARABLE OF THE LOST SHEEP

10 “See that you do not disdain one of these little ones. For I tell you that their angels in heaven always see the face of my Father in heaven.|| 12 What do you think? If someone owns a hundred sheep and one of them goes astray, will he not leave the ninety-nine on the mountains and go look for the one that went astray? 13 And if he finds it, I tell you the truth, he will rejoice more over it than over the ninety-nine that did not go astray. 14 In the same way, your Father in heaven is not willing that one of these little ones be lost.

RESTORING CHRISTIAN RELATIONSHIPS

15 “If your brother sins, go and show him his fault when the two of you are alone. If he listens to you, you have regained your brother. 16 But if he does not listen, take one or two others with you, so that ***at the testimony of two or three witnesses every matter may be established.*** 17 If he refuses to listen to them, tell it to the church. If he refuses to listen to the church, treat him like a Gentile or a tax collector.

18 “I tell you the truth, whatever you bind on earth will have been bound in heaven, and whatever you release on earth will have been released in heaven. 19 Again, I tell you the truth, if two of you on earth agree about whatever you ask, my Father in heaven will do it for you. 20 For where two or three are assembled in my name, I am there among them.”

21 Then Peter came to him and said, “Lord, how many times must I forgive my brother who sins against me? As many as seven times?” 22 Jesus said to him, “Not seven times, I tell you, but seventy-seven times!

THE PARABLE OF THE UNFORGIVING SLAVE

23 “For this reason, the kingdom of heaven is like a king who wanted to settle accounts with his slaves. 24 As he began settling his accounts, a man who owed 10,000 talents was brought to him. 25 Because he was not able to repay it, the lord ordered him to be sold, along with his wife, children, and whatever he possessed, and repayment to be made. 26 Then the slave threw himself to the ground before him, saying, ‘Be patient with me, and I will repay you everything.’ 27 The lord had compassion on that slave and released him, and forgave him the debt. 28 After he went out, that same slave found one of his fellow slaves who owed him 100 silver coins. So he grabbed him by the throat and started to choke him, saying, ‘Pay back what you owe me!’ 29 Then his fellow slave

threw himself down and begged him, 'Be patient with me, and I
will repay you.' 30 But he refused. Instead, he went out and threw
him in prison until he repaid the debt. 31 When his fellow slaves
saw what had happened, they were very upset and went and told
their lord everything that had taken place. 32 Then his lord called
the first slave and said to him, 'Evil slave! I forgave you all that
debt because you begged me! 33 Should you not have shown mercy
to your fellow slave, just as I showed it to you?' 34 And in anger
his lord turned him over to the prison guards to torture him until he repaid all he owed. 35 So also my heavenly Father will do to
you, if each of you does not forgive your brother from your heart."

QUESTIONS ABOUT DIVORCE

19 Now when Jesus finished these sayings, he left Galilee and
went to the region of Judea beyond the Jordan River. 2 Large
crowds followed him, and he healed them there.

3 Then some Pharisees came to him in order to test him. They
asked, "Is it lawful to divorce a wife for any cause?" 4 He answered,
"Have you not read that from the beginning the Creator ***made***
them male and female, 5 and said, '***For this reason a man will leave***
his father and mother and will be united with his wife, and the two
will become one flesh'? 6 So they are no longer two, but one flesh.
Therefore what God has joined together, let no one separate."
7 They said to him, "Why then did Moses command us *to give* ***a cer-***
tificate of dismissal *and to divorce* her?" 8 Jesus said to them, "Moses
permitted you to divorce your wives because of your hard hearts,
but from the beginning it was not this way. 9 Now I say to you that
whoever divorces his wife, except for immorality, and marries another commits adultery." 10 The disciples said to him, "If this is the
case of a husband with a wife, it is better not to marry!" 11 He said
to them, "Not everyone can accept this statement, except those to
whom it has been given. 12 For there are some eunuchs who were
that way from birth, and some who were made eunuchs by others, and some who became eunuchs for the sake of the kingdom
of heaven. The one who is able to accept this should accept it."

JESUS AND LITTLE CHILDREN

13 Then little children were brought to him for him to lay his hands
on them and pray. But the disciples scolded those who brought
them. 14 But Jesus said, "Let the little children come to me and do
not try to stop them, for the kingdom of heaven belongs to such
as these." 15 And he placed his hands on them and went on his way.

THE RICH YOUNG MAN

16 Now someone came up to him and said, "Teacher, what good
thing must I do to gain eternal life?" 17 He said to him, "Why do
you ask me about what is good? There is only one who is good.
But if you want to enter into life, keep the commandments."
18 "Which ones?" he asked. Jesus replied, "***Do not murder, do not***
commit adultery, do not steal, do not give false testimony, 19 ***honor***
your father and mother, and ***love your neighbor as yourself***." 20 The
young man said to him, "I have wholeheartedly obeyed all these
laws. What do I still lack?" 21 Jesus said to him, "If you wish to be
perfect, go sell your possessions and give the money to the poor,

and you will have treasure in heaven. Then come, follow me."
22 But when the young man heard this he went away sorrowful,
for he was very rich.
23 Then Jesus said to his disciples, "I tell you the truth, it will be
hard for a rich person to enter the kingdom of heaven! 24 Again I
say, it is easier for a camel to go through the eye of a needle than
for a rich person to enter into the kingdom of God." 25 The disciples were greatly astonished when they heard this and said,
"Then who can be saved?" 26 Jesus looked at them and replied,
"This is impossible for mere humans, but for God all things are
possible." 27 Then Peter said to him, "Look, we have left everything to follow you! What then will there be for us?" 28 Jesus
said to them, "I tell you the truth: In the age when all things are
renewed, when the Son of Man sits on his glorious throne, you
who have followed me will also sit on twelve thrones, judging the
twelve tribes of Israel. 29 And whoever has left houses or brothers or sisters or father or mother or children or fields for my
sake will receive a hundred times as much and will inherit eternal life. 30 But many who are first will be last, and the last first.

WORKERS IN THE VINEYARD

20 "For the kingdom of heaven is like a landowner who went
out early in the morning to hire workers for his vineyard.
2 And after agreeing with the workers for the standard wage, he
sent them into his vineyard. 3 When it was about nine o'clock in
the morning, he went out again and saw others standing around
in the marketplace without work. 4 He said to them, 'You go into
the vineyard too, and I will give you whatever is right.' 5 So they
went. When he went out again about noon and three o'clock that
afternoon, he did the same thing. 6 And about five o'clock that afternoon he went out and found others standing around, and said
to them, 'Why are you standing here all day without work?' 7 They
said to him, 'Because no one hired us.' He said to them, 'You go
and work in the vineyard too.' 8 When it was evening the owner of
the vineyard said to his manager, 'Call the workers and pay them
their wages starting with the last hired until the first.' 9 When
those hired about five o'clock came, each received a full day's pay.
10 And when those hired first came, they thought they would receive more. But each one also received the standard wage. 11 When
they received it, they began to complain against the landowner,
12 saying, 'These last fellows worked one hour, and you have made
them equal to us who bore the hardship and burning heat of the
day.' 13 And the landowner replied to one of them, 'Friend, I am
not treating you unfairly. Didn't you agree with me to work for
the standard wage? 14 Take what is yours and go. I want to give to
this last man the same as I gave to you. 15 Am I not permitted to
do what I want with what belongs to me? Or are you envious because I am generous?' 16 So the last will be first, and the first last."

THIRD PREDICTION OF JESUS' DEATH AND RESURRECTION

17 As Jesus was going up to Jerusalem, he took the twelve aside privately and said to them on the way, 18 "Look, we are going up to
Jerusalem, and the Son of Man will be handed over to the chief

LOVE TO GROW

THE BOTTOM LINE

MATTHEW 19:28–30

In 1931, Betty Stam obeyed the clear call to reach China for Christ. She married her husband John two years later. Their baby, Priscilla, was only a few months old when communist bandits raided their mission station. John invited the murderous men inside, and Betty served them tea and cake. Despite the grace they extended, the Stams were imprisoned and subsequently paraded through the streets on a twelve-mile march. When an onlooker asked where they were going, John replied: "We do not know where they are going, but we are going to heaven."

Betty Stam laid down her life at age twenty-eight. This world will tell you she wasted her life, but Betty invested in wealth this world could not take away and will one day receive her full reward. Her testimony of faith continues to inspire others to carry the light of the gospel into the darkest corners of the world.

"When we consecrate ourselves to God, we think we are making a great sacrifice, and doing lots for Him, when really we are only letting go some little, bitsie trinkets we have been grabbing, and when our hands are empty, He fills them full of His treasures."—Betty Stam

---

When I read Matthew 19, I see men who left it all behind to follow Jesus. You see, the disciples expected a much different messiah–one who would set them free from political oppression. With their families, jobs, and identities behind them they had to wonder, "What's in it for me? Is it really worth it?"

I must confess I've asked the same questions in the quiet of my heart. If I say no to selfishness and choose to serve the Savior with everything, will I regret the sacrifice?

Discipleship requires us to forsake everything to follow Him. We must lay our very hearts on the altar. Jesus offered up His life for me on a cross. The bottom line is I owe Him everything. Because of Christ, I am rich in joy. I am overflowing with love. I have inexplicable peace.

True treasure is found in a fully surrendered life. Let's purpose to march toward heaven. We may never face a martyr's death like Betty Stam or the disciples, but we must carry our own cross and follow no matter the cost. The bottom line is this: "Love so amazing, so divine, demands my soul, my life, my all."

priests and the experts in the law. They will condemn him to death,
19 and will turn him over to the Gentiles to be mocked and flogged
severely and crucified. Yet on the third day, he will be raised."

A REQUEST FOR JAMES AND JOHN

20 Then the mother of the sons of Zebedee came to him with her
sons, and kneeling down she asked him for a favor. 21 He said to
her, "What do you want?" She replied, "Permit these two sons of
mine to sit, one at your right hand and one at your left, in your
kingdom." 22 Jesus answered, "You don't know what you are asking! Are you able to drink the cup I am about to drink?" They said
to him, "We are able." 23 He told them, "You will drink my cup, but
to sit at my right and at my left is not mine to give. Rather, it is
for those for whom it has been prepared by my Father."
24 Now when the other ten heard this, they were angry with the
two brothers. 25 But Jesus called them and said, "You know that
the rulers of the Gentiles lord it over them, and those in high
positions use their authority over them. 26 It must not be this
way among you! Instead whoever wants to be great among you
must be your servant, 27 and whoever wants to be first among
you must be your slave—28 just as the Son of Man did not come to
be served but to serve, and to give his life as a ransom for many."

TWO BLIND MEN HEALED

29 As they were leaving Jericho, a large crowd followed them.
30 Two blind men were sitting by the road. When they heard that
Jesus was passing by, they shouted, "Have mercy on us, Lord, Son
of David!" 31 The crowd scolded them to get them to be quiet. But
they shouted even more loudly, "Lord, have mercy on us, Son
of David!" 32 Jesus stopped, called them, and said, "What do you
want me to do for you?" 33 They said to him, "Lord, let our eyes
be opened." 34 Moved with compassion, Jesus touched their eyes.
Immediately they received their sight and followed him.

THE TRIUMPHAL ENTRY

21 Now when they approached Jerusalem and came to Bethphage, at the Mount of Olives, Jesus sent two disciples, 2 telling them, "Go to the village ahead of you. Right away you will find
a donkey tied there, and a colt with her. Untie them and bring
them to me. 3 If anyone says anything to you, you are to say, 'The
Lord needs them,' and he will send them at once." 4 This took
place to fulfill what was spoken by the prophet:

5 ***"Tell the people of Zion,***
'Look, your king is coming to you,
unassuming and seated on a donkey,
and on a colt, the foal of a donkey.'"

6 So the disciples went and did as Jesus had instructed them.
7 They brought the donkey and the colt and placed their cloaks on
them, and he sat on them. 8 A very large crowd spread their cloaks
on the road. Others cut branches from the trees and spread them
on the road. 9 The crowds that went ahead of him and those following kept shouting, "*Hosanna* to the Son of David! ***Blessed is the***
one who comes in the name of the Lord! *Hosanna* in the highest!"

10 As he entered Jerusalem the whole city was thrown into an uproar, saying, "Who is this?" 11 And the crowds were saying, "This
is the prophet Jesus, from Nazareth in Galilee."

CLEANSING THE TEMPLE

12 Then Jesus entered the temple area and drove out all those who
were selling and buying in the temple courts, and turned over
the tables of the money changers and the chairs of those selling
doves. 13 And he said to them, "It is written, '***My house will be called***
a house of prayer,' but you are turning it into ***a den of robbers***!"
14 The blind and lame came to him in the temple courts, and he
healed them. 15 But when the chief priests and the experts in the law
saw the wonderful things he did and heard the children crying out in
the temple courts, "Hosanna to the Son of David," they became indignant 16 and said to him, "Do you hear what they are saying?" Jesus said
to them, "Yes. Have you never read, '***Out of the mouths of children and***
nursing infants you have prepared praise for yourself'?" 17 And leaving
them, he went out of the city to Bethany and spent the night there.

THE WITHERED FIG TREE

18 Now early in the morning, as he returned to the city, he was
hungry. 19 After noticing a fig tree by the road he went to it, but
found nothing on it except leaves. He said to it, "Never again
will there be fruit from you!" And the fig tree withered at once.
20 When the disciples saw it they were amazed, saying, "How did
the fig tree wither so quickly?" 21 Jesus answered them, "I tell
you the truth, if you have faith and do not doubt, not only will
you do what was done to the fig tree, but even if you say to this
mountain, 'Be lifted up and thrown into the sea,' it will happen.
22 And whatever you ask in prayer, if you believe, you will receive."

THE AUTHORITY OF JESUS

23 Now after Jesus entered the temple courts, the chief priests
and elders of the people came up to him as he was teaching and
said, "By what authority are you doing these things, and who gave
you this authority?" 24 Jesus answered them, "I will also ask you
one question. If you answer me then I will also tell you by what
authority I do these things. 25 Where did John's baptism come
from? From heaven or from people?" They discussed this among
themselves, saying, "If we say, 'From heaven,' he will say, 'Then
why did you not believe him?' 26 But if we say, 'From people,' we
fear the crowd, for they all consider John to be a prophet." 27 So
they answered Jesus, "We don't know." Then he said to them, "Neither will I tell you by what authority I am doing these things.

THE PARABLE OF THE TWO SONS

28 "What do you think? A man had two sons. He went to the first
and said, 'Son, go and work in the vineyard today.' 29 The boy answered, 'I will not.' But later he had a change of heart and went.
30 The father went to the other son and said the same thing. This
boy answered, 'I will, sir,' but did not go. 31 Which of the two did
his father's will?" They said, "The first." Jesus said to them, "I tell
you the truth, tax collectors and prostitutes will go ahead of you
into the kingdom of God! 32 For John came to you in the way of

righteousness, and you did not believe him. But the tax collectors and prostitutes did believe. Although you saw this, you did
not later change your minds and believe him.

THE PARABLE OF THE TENANTS

33 "Listen to another parable: There was a landowner who planted
a vineyard. He put a fence around it, dug a pit for its winepress,
and built a watchtower. Then he leased it to tenant farmers and
went on a journey. 34 When the harvest time was near, he sent his
slaves to the tenants to collect his portion of the crop. 35 But the
tenants seized his slaves, beat one, killed another, and stoned another. 36 Again he sent other slaves, more than the first, and they
treated them the same way. 37 Finally he sent his son to them, saying, 'They will respect my son.' 38 But when the tenants saw the son,
they said to themselves, 'This is the heir. Come, let's kill him and
get his inheritance!' 39 So they seized him, threw him out of the
vineyard, and killed him. 40 Now when the owner of the vineyard
comes, what will he do to those tenants?" 41 They said to him, "He
will utterly destroy those evil men! Then he will lease the vineyard to other tenants who will give him his portion at the harvest."
42 Jesus said to them, "Have you never read in the scriptures:
'***The stone the builders rejected has become the cornerstone.***
This is from the Lord, and it is marvelous in our eyes'?

43 For this reason I tell you that the kingdom of God will be taken
from you and given to a people who will produce its fruit. 44 The
one who falls on this stone will be broken to pieces, and the one
on whom it falls will be crushed." 45 When the chief priests and the
Pharisees heard his parables, they realized that he was speaking
about them. 46 They wanted to arrest him, but they were afraid
of the crowds, because the crowds regarded him as a prophet.

THE PARABLE OF THE WEDDING BANQUET

22 Jesus spoke to them again in parables, saying: 2 "The kingdom of heaven can be compared to a king who gave a wedding banquet for his son. 3 He sent his slaves to summon those
who had been invited to the banquet, but they would not come.
4 Again he sent other slaves, saying, 'Tell those who have been invited, "Look! The feast I have prepared for you is ready. My oxen
and fattened cattle have been slaughtered, and everything is ready.
Come to the wedding banquet."' 5 But they were indifferent and
went away, one to his farm, another to his business. 6 The rest seized
his slaves, insolently mistreated them, and killed them. 7 The king
was furious! He sent his soldiers, and they put those murderers
to death and set their city on fire. 8 Then he said to his slaves, 'The
wedding is ready, but the ones who had been invited were not worthy. 9 So go into the main streets and invite everyone you find to
the wedding banquet.' 10 And those slaves went out into the streets
and gathered all they found, both bad and good, and the wedding
hall was filled with guests. 11 But when the king came in to see the
wedding guests, he saw a man there who was not wearing wedding
clothes. 12 And he said to him, 'Friend, how did you get in here without wedding clothes?' But he had nothing to say. 13 Then the king
said to his attendants, 'Tie him up hand and foot and throw him

into the outer darkness, where there will be weeping and gnashing of teeth!' 14 For many are called, but few are chosen."

PAYING TAXES TO CAESAR

15 Then the Pharisees went out and planned together to entrap
him with his own words. 16 They sent to him their disciples along
with the Herodians, saying, "Teacher, we know that you are truthful, and teach the way of God in accordance with the truth. You do
not court anyone's favor because you show no partiality. 17 Tell us
then, what do you think? Is it right to pay taxes to Caesar or not?"
18 But Jesus realized their evil intentions and said, "Hypocrites!
Why are you testing me? 19 Show me the coin used for the tax."
So they brought him a denarius. 20 Jesus said to them, "Whose
image is this, and whose inscription?" 21 They replied, "Caesar's."
He said to them, "Then give to Caesar the things that are Caesar's, and to God the things that are God's." 22 Now when they
heard this they were stunned, and they left him and went away.

MARRIAGE AND THE RESURRECTION

23 The same day Sadducees (who say there is no resurrection)
came to him and asked him, 24 "Teacher, Moses said, '***If a man dies***
without having children, his brother must marry the widow and
father children for his brother.' 25 Now there were seven brothers among us. The first one married and died, and since he had
no children he left his wife to his brother. 26 The second did the
same, and the third, down to the seventh. 27 Last of all, the woman died. 28 In the resurrection, therefore, whose wife of the seven
will she be? For they all had married her." 29 Jesus answered them,
"You are deceived, because you don't know the scriptures or the
power of God. 30 For in the resurrection they neither marry nor
are given in marriage, but are like angels in heaven. 31 Now as for
the resurrection of the dead, have you not read what was spoken
to you by God, 32 '***I am the God of Abraham, the God of Isaac, and***
the God of Jacob'? He is not the God of the dead but of the living!"
33 When the crowds heard this, they were amazed at his teaching.

THE GREATEST COMMANDMENT

34 Now when the Pharisees heard that he had silenced the Sadducees, they assembled together. 35 And one of them, an expert in
religious law, asked him a question to test him: 36 "Teacher, which
commandment in the law is the greatest?" 37 Jesus said to him,
"'***Love the Lord your God with all your heart, with all your soul, and***
with all your mind.' 38 This is the first and greatest commandment.
39 The second is like it: '***Love your neighbor as yourself.***' 40 All the
law and the prophets depend on these two commandments."

REFLECT

What did He mean when Jesus said that the law and prophets depended on those two commandments?

THE MESSIAH: DAVID'S SON AND LORD

41 While the Pharisees were assembled, Jesus asked them a ques-
tion: 42 "What do you think about the Christ? Whose son is he?"
They said, "The son of David." 43 He said to them, "How then does
David by the Spirit call him 'Lord,' saying,

44 '***The Lord said to my lord,***
"***Sit at my right hand,***
until I put your enemies under your feet"'?

45 If David then calls him 'Lord,' how can he be his son?" 46 No
one was able to answer him a word, and from that day on no one
dared to question him any longer.

SEVEN WOES

23 Then Jesus said to the crowds and to his disciples, 2 "The
experts in the law and the Pharisees sit on Moses' seat.
3 Therefore pay attention to what they tell you and do it. But do
not do what they do, for they do not practice what they teach.
4 They tie up heavy loads, hard to carry, and put them on men's
shoulders, but they themselves are not willing even to lift a finger to move them. 5 They do all their deeds to be seen by people, for they make their phylacteries wide and their tassels long.
6 They love the place of honor at banquets and the best seats in
the synagogues 7 and elaborate greetings in the marketplaces,
and to have people call them 'Rabbi.' 8 But you are not to be called
'Rabbi,' for you have one Teacher and you are all brothers. 9 And
call no one your 'father' on earth, for you have one Father, who
is in heaven. 10 Nor are you to be called 'teacher,' for you have one
teacher, the Christ. 11 The greatest among you will be your servant. 12 And whoever exalts himself will be humbled, and whoever humbles himself will be exalted.
13 "But woe to you, experts in the law and you Pharisees, hypocrites! You keep locking people out of the kingdom of heaven!
For you neither enter nor permit those trying to enter to go in.ℭ
15 "Woe to you, experts in the law and you Pharisees, hypocrites!
You cross land and sea to make one convert, and when you get
one, you make him twice as much a child of hell as yourselves!
16 "Woe to you, blind guides, who say, 'Whoever swears by the
temple is bound by nothing. But whoever swears by the gold of
the temple is bound by the oath.' 17 Blind fools! Which is greater,
the gold or the temple that makes the gold sacred? 18 And, 'Whoever swears by the altar is bound by nothing. But if anyone
swears by the gift on it he is bound by the oath.' 19 You are blind!
For which is greater, the gift or the altar that makes the gift sacred? 20 So whoever swears by the altar swears by it and by everything on it. 21 And whoever swears by the temple swears by it
and the one who dwells in it. 22 And whoever swears by heaven
swears by the throne of God and the one who sits on it.
23 "Woe to you, experts in the law and you Pharisees, hypocrites!
You give a tenth of mint, dill, and cumin, yet you neglect what
is more important in the law—justice, mercy, and faithfulness!
You should have done these things without neglecting the others. 24 Blind guides! You strain out a gnat yet swallow a camel!
25 "Woe to you, experts in the law and you Pharisees, hypocrites!
You clean the outside of the cup and the dish, but inside they are
full of greed and self-indulgence. 26 Blind Pharisee! First clean
the inside of the cup, so that the outside may become clean too!
27 "Woe to you, experts in the law and you Pharisees, hypocrites!
You are like whitewashed tombs that look beautiful on the outside but inside are full of the bones of the dead and of everything
unclean. 28 In the same way, on the outside you look righteous
to people, but inside you are full of hypocrisy and lawlessness.
29 "Woe to you, experts in the law and you Pharisees, hypocrites!

You build tombs for the prophets and decorate the graves of the
righteous. 30 And you say, 'If we had lived in the days of our ancestors, we would not have participated with them in shedding
the blood of the prophets.' 31 By saying this you testify against
yourselves that you are descendants of those who murdered the
prophets. 32 Fill up then the measure of your ancestors! 33 You
snakes, you offspring of vipers! How will you escape being condemned to hell?

34 "For this reason I am sending you prophets and wise men
and experts in the law, some of whom you will kill and crucify,
and some you will flog in your synagogues and pursue from town
to town, 35 so that on you will come all the righteous blood shed
on earth, from the blood of righteous Abel to the blood of Zechariah son of Barachiah, whom you murdered between the temple and the altar. 36 I tell you the truth, this generation will be
held responsible for all these things!

JUDGMENT ON ISRAEL

37 "O Jerusalem, Jerusalem, you who kill the prophets and stone
those who are sent to you! How often I have longed to gather
your children together as a hen gathers her chicks under her
wings, but you would have none of it! 38 Look, your house is left
to you desolate! 39 For I tell you, you will not see me from now until you say, '***Blessed is the one who comes in the name of the Lord!***'"

THE DESTRUCTION OF THE TEMPLE

24 Now as Jesus was going out of the temple courts and walking
away, his disciples came to show him the temple buildings.
2 And he said to them, "Do you see all these things? I tell you the
truth, not one stone will be left on another. All will be torn down!"

SIGNS OF THE END OF THE AGE

3 As he was sitting on the Mount of Olives, his disciples came to
him privately and said, "Tell us, when will these things happen?
And what will be the sign of your coming and of the end of the
age?" 4 Jesus answered them, "Watch out that no one misleads
you. 5 For many will come in my name, saying, 'I am the Christ,'
and they will mislead many. 6 You will hear of wars and rumors
of wars. Make sure that you are not alarmed, for this must happen, but the end is still to come. 7 For nation will rise up in arms
against nation, and kingdom against kingdom. And there will
be famines and earthquakes in various places. 8 All these things
are the beginning of birth pains.

PERSECUTION OF DISCIPLES

9 "Then they will hand you over to be persecuted and will kill you.
You will be hated by all the nations because of my name. 10 Then
many will be led into sin, and they will betray one another and
hate one another. 11 And many false prophets will appear and
deceive many, 12 and because lawlessness will increase so much,
the love of many will grow cold. 13 But the person who endures
to the end will be saved. 14 And this gospel of the kingdom will
be preached throughout the whole inhabited earth as a testimony to all the nations, and then the end will come.

THE ABOMINATION OF DESOLATION

15 “So when you see *the abomination of desolation*—spoken about
by Daniel the prophet—standing in the holy place” (let the reader
understand), 16 “then those in Judea must flee to the mountains.
17 The one on the roof must not come down to take anything out
of his house, 18 and the one in the field must not turn back to get
his cloak. 19 Woe to those who are pregnant and to those who are
nursing their babies in those days! 20 Pray that your flight may
not be in winter or on a Sabbath. 21 For then there will be great
suffering unlike anything that has happened from the beginning
of the world until now, or ever will happen. 22 And if those days
had not been cut short, no one would be saved. But for the sake
of the elect those days will be cut short. 23 Then if anyone says to
you, ‘Look, here is the Christ!’ or ‘There he is!’ do not believe him.
24 For false messiahs and false prophets will appear and perform
great signs and wonders to deceive, if possible, even the elect. 25 Remember, I have told you ahead of time. 26 So then, if someone says
to you, ‘Look, he is in the wilderness,’ do not go out, or ‘Look, he is
in the inner rooms,’ do not believe him. 27 For just like the lightning comes from the east and flashes to the west, so the coming
of the Son of Man will be. 28 Wherever the corpse is, there the vultures will gather.

THE ARRIVAL OF THE SON OF MAN

29 “Immediately after the suffering of those days, *the sun will
be darkened, and the moon will not give its light; the stars will fall
from heaven, and the powers of heaven will be shaken.* 30 Then the
sign of the Son of Man will appear in heaven, and all the tribes
of the earth will mourn. They will see *the Son of Man arriving on
the clouds of heaven* with power and great glory. 31 And he will send
his angels with a loud trumpet blast, and they will gather his
elect from the four winds, from one end of heaven to the other.

THE PARABLE OF THE FIG TREE

32 “Learn this parable from the fig tree: Whenever its branch becomes tender and puts out its leaves, you know that summer is
near. 33 So also you, when you see all these things, know that he
is near, right at the door. 34 I tell you the truth, this generation
will not pass away until all these things take place. 35 Heaven and
earth will pass away, but my words will never pass away.

BE READY!

36 “But as for that day and hour no one knows it—not even the
angels in heaven—except the Father alone. 37 For just like the
days of Noah were, so the coming of the Son of Man will be.
38 For in those days before the flood, people were eating and
drinking, marrying and giving in marriage, until the day Noah
entered the ark. 39 And they knew nothing until the flood came
and took them all away. It will be the same at the coming of the
Son of Man. 40 Then there will be two men in the field; one will
be taken and one left. 41 There will be two women grinding grain
with a mill; one will be taken and one left.

42 “Therefore stay alert, because you do not know on what day
your Lord will come. 43 But understand this: If the owner of the

house had known at what time of night the thief was coming, he would have been alert and would not have let his house be broken into. 44 Therefore you also must be ready, because the Son of Man will come at an hour when you do not expect him.

THE FAITHFUL AND WISE SLAVE

45 "Who then is the faithful and wise slave, whom the master has put in charge of his household, to give the other slaves their food at the proper time? 46 Blessed is that slave whom the master finds at work when he comes. 47 I tell you the truth, the master will put him in charge of all his possessions. 48 But if that evil slave should say to himself, 'My master is staying away a long time,' 49 and he begins to beat his fellow slaves and to eat and drink with drunkards, 50 then the master of that slave will come on a day when he does not expect him and at an hour he does not foresee, 51 and will cut him in two, and assign him a place with the hypocrites, where there will be weeping and gnashing of teeth.

THE PARABLE OF THE TEN VIRGINS

25 "At that time the kingdom of heaven will be like ten virgins who took their lamps and went out to meet the bridegroom. 2 Five of the virgins were foolish, and five were wise. 3 When the foolish ones took their lamps, they did not take extra olive oil with them. 4 But the wise ones took flasks of olive oil with their lamps. 5 When the bridegroom was delayed a long time, they all became drowsy and fell asleep. 6 But at midnight there was a shout, 'Look, the bridegroom is here! Come out to meet him.' 7 Then all the virgins woke up and trimmed their lamps. 8 The foolish ones said to the wise, 'Give us some of your oil, because our lamps are going out.' 9 'No,' they replied. 'There won't be enough for you and for us. Go instead to those who sell oil and buy some for yourselves.' 10 But while they had gone to buy it, the bridegroom arrived, and those who were ready went inside with him to the wedding banquet. Then the door was shut. 11 Later, the other virgins came too, saying, 'Lord, lord! Let us in!' 12 But he replied, 'I tell you the truth, I do not know you!' 13 Therefore stay alert, because you do not know the day or the hour.

THE PARABLE OF THE TALENTS

14 "For it is like a man going on a journey, who summoned his slaves and entrusted his property to them. 15 To one he gave five talents, to another two, and to another one, each according to his ability. Then he went on his journey. 16 The one who had received five talents went off right away and put his money to work and gained five more. 17 In the same way, the one who had two gained two more. 18 But the one who had received one talent went out and dug a hole in the ground and hid his master's money in it. 19 After a long time, the master of those slaves came and settled his accounts with them. 20 The one who had received the five talents came and brought five more, saying, 'Sir, you entrusted me with five talents. See, I have gained five more.' 21 His master answered, 'Well done, good and faithful slave! You have been faithful in a few things. I will put you in charge of many things. Enter into the joy of your master.' 22 The one with the two talents also

came and said, 'Sir, you entrusted two talents to me. See, I have
gained two more.' 23 His master answered, 'Well done, good and
faithful slave! You have been faithful with a few things. I will put
you in charge of many things. Enter into the joy of your master.'
24 Then the one who had received the one talent came and said,
'Sir, I knew that you were a hard man, harvesting where you did
not sow, and gathering where you did not scatter seed, 25 so I was
afraid, and I went and hid your talent in the ground. See, you have
what is yours.' 26 But his master answered, 'Evil and lazy slave!
So you knew that I harvest where I didn't sow and gather where
I didn't scatter? 27 Then you should have deposited my money
with the bankers, and on my return I would have received my
money back with interest! 28 Therefore take the talent from him
and give it to the one who has ten. 29 For the one who has will be
given more, and he will have more than enough. But the one who
does not have, even what he has will be taken from him. 30 And
throw that worthless slave into the outer darkness, where there
will be weeping and gnashing of teeth.'

THE JUDGMENT

31 "When the Son of Man comes in his glory and all the angels with
him, then he will sit on his glorious throne. 32 All the nations will
be assembled before him, and he will separate people one from another like a shepherd separates the sheep from the goats. 33 He will
put the sheep on his right and the goats on his left. 34 Then the king
will say to those on his right, 'Come, you who are blessed by my Father, inherit the kingdom prepared for you from the foundation of
the world. 35 For I was hungry and you gave me food, I was thirsty
and you gave me something to drink, I was a stranger and you invited me in, 36 I was naked and you gave me clothing, I was sick and
you took care of me, I was in prison and you visited me.' 37 Then the
righteous will answer him, 'Lord, when did we see you hungry and
feed you, or thirsty and give you something to drink? 38 When did
we see you a stranger and invite you in, or naked and clothe you?
39 When did we see you sick or in prison and visit you?' 40 And the
king will answer them, 'I tell you the truth, just as you did it for one
of the least of these brothers or sisters of mine, you did it for me.'
41 "Then he will say to those on his left, 'Depart from me, you
accursed, into the eternal fire that has been prepared for the
devil and his angels! 42 For I was hungry and you gave me nothing
to eat, I was thirsty and you gave me nothing to drink. 43 I was a
stranger and you did not receive me as a guest, naked and you
did not clothe me, sick and in prison and you did not visit me.'
44 Then they too will answer, 'Lord, when did we see you hungry
or thirsty or a stranger or naked or sick or in prison, and did not
give you whatever you needed?' 45 Then he will answer them, 'I
tell you the truth, just as you did not do it for one of the least
of these, you did not do it for me.' 46 And these will depart into
eternal punishment, but the righteous into eternal life."

THE PLOT AGAINST JESUS

26 When Jesus had finished saying all these things, he told
his disciples, 2 "You know that after two days the Passover is coming, and the Son of Man will be handed over to be

crucified." 3 Then the chief priests and the elders of the people met together in the palace of the high priest, who was named Caiaphas. 4 They planned to arrest Jesus by stealth and kill him. 5 But they said, "Not during the feast, so that there won't be a riot among the people."

REFLECT

How can you develop a heart of worship like the woman who anointed Jesus?

JESUS' ANOINTING

6 Now while Jesus was in Bethany at the house of Simon the leper, 7 a woman came to him with an alabaster jar of expensive perfumed oil, and she poured it on his head as he was at the table. 8 When the disciples saw this, they became indignant and said, "Why this waste? 9 It could have been sold at a high price and the money given to the poor!" 10 When Jesus learned of this, he said to them, "Why are you bothering this woman? She has done a good service for me. 11 For you will always have the poor with you, but you will not always have me! 12 When she poured this oil on my body, she did it to prepare me for burial. 13 I tell you the truth, wherever this gospel is proclaimed in the whole world, what she has done will also be told in memory of her."

THE PLAN TO BETRAY JESUS

14 Then one of the twelve, the one named Judas Iscariot, went to the chief priests 15 and said, "What will you give me to betray him into your hands?" So they set out thirty silver coins for him. 16 From that time on, Judas began looking for an opportunity to betray him.

THE PASSOVER

17 Now on the first day of the feast of Unleavened Bread the disciples came to Jesus and said, "Where do you want us to prepare for you to eat the Passover?" 18 He said, "Go into the city to a certain man and tell him, 'The Teacher says, "My time is near. I will observe the Passover with my disciples at your house."'" 19 So the disciples did as Jesus had instructed them, and they prepared the Passover. 20 When it was evening, he took his place at the table with the twelve. 21 And while they were eating he said, "I tell you the truth, one of you will betray me." 22 They became greatly distressed and each one began to say to him, "Surely not I, Lord?" 23 He answered, "The one who has dipped his hand into the bowl with me will betray me. 24 The Son of Man will go as it is written about him, but woe to that man by whom the Son of Man is betrayed! It would be better for him if he had never been born." 25 Then Judas, the one who would betray him, said, "Surely not I, Rabbi?" Jesus replied, "You have said it yourself."

THE LORD'S SUPPER

26 While they were eating, Jesus took bread, and after giving thanks he broke it, gave it to his disciples, and said, "Take, eat, this is my body." 27 And after taking the cup and giving thanks, he gave it to them, saying, "Drink from it, all of you, 28 for this is my blood, the blood of the covenant, that is poured out for many for the forgiveness of sins. 29 I tell you, from now on I will not drink of this fruit of the vine until that day when I drink it new with you in my Father's kingdom." 30 After singing a hymn, they went out to the Mount of Olives.

LOVE TO GROW

A BEAUTIFUL THING

MATTHEW 26:6–13

Jesus knew what was about to happen to Him. He had gathered with His close friends to share a meal and enjoy their company. Suddenly, an alabaster jar crashed and the room grew silent. One of the women took her broken jar and poured expensive oil on Jesus' head.

We know from other gospel accounts that this woman was Mary of Bethany, the sister of Lazarus and Martha. This is the same Mary who sat at Jesus' feet, eager to hear His every word (Luke 10:38–42). It is the same Mary who fell at Jesus' feet and proclaimed, "Lord, if you had been here, my brother would not have died." It is this Mary whose weeping "greatly distressed" Jesus and moved Him to tears (John 11:32–35).

Mary knew Jesus. She had seen Him do mighty works in her life. He had treated her with dignity, giving her the opportunity to learn from Him, something women were frequently denied in the first century. Mary knew Jesus was the resurrection and the life. Not only did she believe it for the end of days, but she had seen His resurrection power in action: Jesus had raised her brother from the dead (see John 11:43–44).

Mary knew who Jesus was. She knew what He was worth. She had seen Him redeem her and provide for her in inexplicable ways. Jesus was worth all she had. She broke that alabaster jar, giving everything she had to Jesus.

She had done a beautiful thing for her Lord. She honored Him with her life because He had saved hers over and over again.

When the disciples rebuked her for wasting such an expensive gift, Jesus defended her actions. "Why are you bothering this woman," He said. "She has done a good service for me. For you will always have the poor with you, but you will not always have me" (Matt 26:10–11)

Mary loved her Lord. She loved her Lord more than her future, more than her present, and more than her past. She had been listening to Jesus and knew what His future held. Her devotion blessed Jesus beyond what she could have comprehended at the moment. It was not a waste. It was a beautiful honor.

He has done the same for us. He has redeemed our hearts, our lives, and our circumstances. He has provided for our past, our present, and our future. May we love Him and honor Him the same way Mary did: with all we have.

THE PREDICTION OF PETER'S DENIAL

31 Then Jesus said to them, "This night you will all fall away because of me, for it is written:
> ***'I will strike the shepherd,***
> ***and the sheep of the flock will be scattered.'***

32 But after I am raised, I will go ahead of you into Galilee." 33 Peter said to him, "If they all fall away because of you, I will never
fall away!" 34 Jesus said to him, "I tell you the truth, on this night,
before the rooster crows, you will deny me three times." 35 Peter
said to him, "Even if I must die with you, I will never deny you."
And all the disciples said the same thing.

GETHSEMANE

36 Then Jesus went with them to a place called Gethsemane, and
he said to the disciples, "Sit here while I go over there and pray."
37 He took with him Peter and the two sons of Zebedee, and became anguished and distressed. 38 Then he said to them, "My soul
is deeply grieved, even to the point of death. Remain here and stay
awake with me." 39 Going a little farther, he threw himself down
with his face to the ground and prayed, "My Father, if possible,
let this cup pass from me! Yet not what I will, but what you will."
40 Then he came to the disciples and found them sleeping. He said
to Peter, "So, couldn't you stay awake with me for one hour? 41 Stay
awake and pray that you will not fall into temptation. The spirit
is willing, but the flesh is weak." 42 He went away a second time
and prayed, "My Father, if this cup cannot be taken away unless
I drink it, your will must be done." 43 He came again and found
them sleeping; they could not keep their eyes open. 44 So leaving
them again, he went away and prayed for the third time, saying
the same thing once more. 45 Then he came to the disciples and
said to them, "Are you still sleeping and resting? Look, the hour
is approaching, and the Son of Man is betrayed into the hands
of sinners. 46 Get up, let us go. Look! My betrayer is approaching!"

BETRAYAL AND ARREST

47 While he was still speaking, Judas, one of the twelve, arrived.
With him was a large crowd armed with swords and clubs, sent
by the chief priests and elders of the people. 48 (Now the betrayer
had given them a sign, saying, "The one I kiss is the man. Arrest
him!") 49 Immediately he went up to Jesus and said, "Greetings,
Rabbi," and kissed him. 50 Jesus said to him, "Friend, do what you
are here to do." Then they came and took hold of Jesus and arrested him. 51 But one of those with Jesus grabbed his sword, drew
it out, and struck the high priest's slave, cutting off his ear. 52 Then
Jesus said to him, "Put your sword back in its place! For all who
take hold of the sword will die by the sword. 53 Or do you think
that I cannot call on my Father, and that he would send me more
than twelve legions of angels right now? 54 How then would the
scriptures that say it must happen this way be fulfilled?" 55 At
that moment Jesus said to the crowd, "Have you come out with
swords and clubs to arrest me like you would an outlaw? Day after day I sat teaching in the temple courts, yet you did not arrest
me. 56 But this has happened so that the scriptures of the prophets would be fulfilled." Then all the disciples left him and fled.

CONDEMNED BY THE SANHEDRIN

57 Now the ones who had arrested Jesus led him to Caiaphas,
the high priest, in whose house the experts in the law and the
elders had gathered. 58 But Peter was following him from a distance, all the way to the high priest's courtyard. After going in,
he sat with the guards to see the outcome. 59 The chief priests
and the whole Sanhedrin were trying to find false testimony
against Jesus so that they could put him to death. 60 But they did
not find anything, though many false witnesses came forward.
Finally two came forward 61 and declared, "This man said, 'I am
able to destroy the temple of God and rebuild it in three days.'"
62 So the high priest stood up and said to him, "Have you no answer? What is this that they are testifying against you?" 63 But
Jesus was silent. The high priest said to him, "I charge you under oath by the living God, tell us if you are the Christ, the Son
of God." 64 Jesus said to him, "You have said it yourself. But I tell
you, from now on you will see the Son of Man *sitting at the right
hand* of the Power and *coming on the clouds of heaven*." 65 Then the
high priest tore his clothes and declared, "He has blasphemed!
Why do we still need witnesses? Now you have heard the blasphemy! 66 What is your verdict?" They answered, "He is guilty
and deserves death." 67 Then they spat in his face and struck him
with their fists. And some slapped him, 68 saying, "Prophesy for
us, you Christ! Who hit you?"

PETER'S DENIALS

69 Now Peter was sitting outside in the courtyard. A slave girl
came to him and said, "You also were with Jesus the Galilean."
70 But he denied it in front of them all: "I don't know what you're
talking about!" 71 When he went out to the gateway, another slave
girl saw him and said to the people there, "This man was with
Jesus the Nazarene." 72 He denied it again with an oath, "I do not
know the man!" 73 After a little while, those standing there came
up to Peter and said, "You really are one of them too—even your
accent gives you away!" 74 At that he began to curse, and he swore
with an oath, "I do not know the man!" At that moment a rooster
crowed. 75 Then Peter remembered what Jesus had said: "Before
the rooster crows, you will deny me three times." And he went
outside and wept bitterly.

JESUS BROUGHT BEFORE PILATE

27 When it was early in the morning, all the chief priests and
the elders of the people plotted against Jesus to execute
him. 2 They tied him up, led him away, and handed him over to
Pilate the governor.

JUDAS' SUICIDE

3 Now when Judas, who had betrayed him, saw that Jesus had
been condemned, he regretted what he had done and returned
the thirty silver coins to the chief priests and the elders, 4 saying, "I have sinned by betraying innocent blood!" But they said,
"What is that to us? You take care of it yourself!" 5 So Judas threw
the silver coins into the temple and left. Then he went out and
hanged himself. 6 The chief priests took the silver and said, "It is

not lawful to put this into the temple treasury, since it is blood
money." 7 After consulting together they bought the Potter's
Field with it, as a burial place for foreigners. 8 For this reason that
field has been called the "Field of Blood" to this day. 9 Then what
was spoken by Jeremiah the prophet was fulfilled: "*They took the*
thirty silver coins, the price of the one whose price had been set by
the people of Israel, 10 *and they gave them for the potter's field, as*
the Lord commanded me."

JESUS AND PILATE

11 Then Jesus stood before the governor, and the governor asked
him, "Are you the king of the Jews?" Jesus said, "You say so." 12 But
when he was accused by the chief priests and the elders, he did
not respond. 13 Then Pilate said to him, "Don't you hear how many
charges they are bringing against you?" 14 But he did not answer
even one accusation, so that the governor was quite amazed.

15 During the feast the governor was accustomed to release one
prisoner to the crowd, whomever they wanted. 16 At that time
they had in custody a notorious prisoner named Jesus Barabbas. 17 So after they had assembled, Pilate said to them, "Whom
do you want me to release for you, Jesus Barabbas or Jesus who
is called the Christ?" 18 (For he knew that they had handed him
over because of envy.) 19 As he was sitting on the judgment seat,
his wife sent a message to him: "Have nothing to do with that innocent man; I have suffered greatly as a result of a dream about
him today." 20 But the chief priests and the elders persuaded the
crowds to ask for Barabbas and to have Jesus killed. 21 The governor asked them, "Which of the two do you want me to release
for you?" And they said, "Barabbas!" 22 Pilate said to them, "Then
what should I do with Jesus who is called the Christ?" They all
said, "Crucify him!" 23 He asked, "Why? What wrong has he done?"
But they shouted more insistently, "Crucify him!"

JESUS IS CONDEMNED AND MOCKED

24 When Pilate saw that he could do nothing, but that instead a
riot was starting, he took some water, washed his hands before
the crowd and said, "I am innocent of this man's blood. You take
care of it yourselves!" 25 In reply all the people said, "Let his blood
be on us and on our children!" 26 Then he released Barabbas for
them. But after he had Jesus flogged, he handed him over to be
crucified. 27 Then the governor's soldiers took Jesus into the governor's residence and gathered the whole cohort around him.
28 They stripped him and put a scarlet robe around him, 29 and
after braiding a crown of thorns, they put it on his head. They
put a staff in his right hand, and kneeling down before him, they
mocked him: "Hail, king of the Jews!" 30 They spat on him and
took the staff and struck him repeatedly on the head. 31 When
they had mocked him, they stripped him of the robe and put his
own clothes back on him. Then they led him away to crucify him.

THE CRUCIFIXION

32 As they were going out, they found a man from Cyrene named
Simon, whom they forced to carry his cross. 33 They came to a
place called Golgotha (which means "Place of the Skull") 34 and

offered Jesus wine mixed with gall to drink. But after tasting
it, he would not drink it. 35 When they had crucified him, *they
divided his clothes by throwing dice*. 36 Then they sat down and
kept guard over him there. 37 Above his head they put the charge
against him, which read: "This is Jesus, the king of the Jews."
38 Then two outlaws were crucified with him, one on his right
and one on his left. 39 Those who passed by defamed him, shaking their heads 40 and saying, "You who can destroy the temple
and rebuild it in three days, save yourself! If you are God's Son,
come down from the cross!" 41 In the same way even the chief
priests—together with the experts in the law and elders—were
mocking him: 42 "He saved others, but he cannot save himself!
He is the king of Israel! If he comes down now from the cross,
we will believe in him! 43 *He trusts in God—let God, if he wants to,
deliver him now* because he said, 'I am God's Son'!" 44 The robbers
who were crucified with him also spoke abusively to him.

JESUS' DEATH

45 Now from noon until three, darkness came over all the land.
46 At about three o'clock Jesus shouted with a loud voice, "*Eli, Eli,
lema sabachthani?*" that is, "***My God, my God, why have you forsaken me***?" 47 When some of the bystanders heard it, they said,
"This man is calling for Elijah." 48 Immediately one of them ran
and got a sponge, filled it with sour wine, put it on a stick, and
gave it to him to drink. 49 But the rest said, "Leave him alone!
Let's see if Elijah will come to save him." 50 Then Jesus cried out
again with a loud voice and gave up his spirit. 51 Just then the
temple curtain was torn in two, from top to bottom. The earth
shook and the rocks were split apart. 52 And tombs were opened,
and the bodies of many saints who had died were raised. 53 (They
came out of the tombs after his resurrection and went into the
holy city and appeared to many people.) 54 Now when the centurion and those with him who were guarding Jesus saw the earthquake and what took place, they were extremely terrified and
said, "Truly this one was God's Son!" 55 Many women who had
followed Jesus from Galilee and given him support were also
there, watching from a distance. 56 Among them were Mary Magdalene, Mary the mother of James and Joseph, and the mother
of the sons of Zebedee.

JESUS' BURIAL

57 Now when it was evening, there came a rich man from Arimathea, named Joseph, who was also a disciple of Jesus. 58 He went
to Pilate and asked for the body of Jesus. Then Pilate ordered
that it be given to him. 59 Joseph took the body, wrapped it in a
clean linen cloth, 60 and placed it in his own new tomb that he
had cut in the rock. Then he rolled a great stone across the entrance of the tomb and went away. 61 (Now Mary Magdalene and
the other Mary were sitting there, opposite the tomb.)

THE GUARD AT THE TOMB

62 The next day (which is after the day of preparation) the chief
priests and the Pharisees assembled before Pilate 63 and said,
"Sir, we remember that while that deceiver was still alive he said,

'After three days I will rise again.' 64 So give orders to secure the
tomb until the third day. Otherwise his disciples may come and
steal his body and say to the people, 'He has been raised from the
dead,' and the last deception will be worse than the first." 65 Pilate said to them, "Take a guard of soldiers. Go and make it as
secure as you can." 66 So they went with the soldiers of the guard
and made the tomb secure by sealing the stone.

GOD'S HEART FOR THE NATIONS

Matthew 28:19–20

"Therefore go and make disciples of all nations, baptizing them in the name of the Father and the Son and the Holy Spirit, teaching them to obey everything I have commanded you. And remember, I am with you always, to the end of the age."

THE RESURRECTION

28 Now after the Sabbath, at dawn on the first day of the
week, Mary Magdalene and the other Mary went to look
at the tomb. 2 Suddenly there was a severe earthquake, for an angel of the Lord descending from heaven came and rolled away
the stone and sat on it. 3 His appearance was like lightning, and
his clothes were white as snow. 4 The guards were shaken and
became like dead men because they were so afraid of him. 5 But
the angel said to the women, "Do not be afraid; I know that you
are looking for Jesus, who was crucified. 6 He is not here, for he
has been raised, just as he said. Come and see the place where
he was lying. 7 Then go quickly and tell his disciples, 'He has been
raised from the dead. He is going ahead of you into Galilee. You
will see him there.' Listen, I have told you!" 8 So they left the tomb
quickly, with fear and great joy, and ran to tell his disciples. 9 But
Jesus met them, saying, "Greetings!" They came to him, held on
to his feet and worshiped him. 10 Then Jesus said to them, "Do
not be afraid. Go and tell my brothers to go to Galilee. They will
see me there."

THE GUARDS' REPORT

11 While they were going, some of the guard went into the city
and told the chief priests everything that had happened. 12 After they had assembled with the elders and formed a plan, they
gave a large sum of money to the soldiers, 13 telling them, "You
are to say, 'His disciples came at night and stole his body while
we were asleep.' 14 If this matter is heard before the governor, we
will satisfy him and keep you out of trouble." 15 So they took the
money and did as they were instructed. And this story is told
among the Jews to this day.

THE GREAT COMMISSION

16 So the eleven disciples went to Galilee to the mountain Jesus
had designated. 17 When they saw him, they worshiped him, but
some doubted. 18 Then Jesus came up and said to them, "All authority in heaven and on earth has been given to me. 19 Therefore go and make disciples of all nations, baptizing them in the
name of the Father and the Son and the Holy Spirit, 20 teaching
them to obey everything I have commanded you. And remember, I am with you always, to the end of the age."

HIS PRESENCE REMAINS

MATTHEW 28:20

Every season has some kind of tension. One minute, twinkling lights fill our hearts with joy, and the next a cause for deep suffering arises and we are undone. No matter where you and I find ourselves on the spectrum today, an underlying current remains: Until Jesus returns we will all be a bit unsettled here.

The disciples had been on the rollercoaster of their lives.

They were walking and talking with Jesus, watching Him perform miracles, and enjoying intimate fellowship. Christ had called them out of the crowd and given them a front-row seat to witness His glory. When the joy of experiencing the God-man was at its fullest, tidal waves crashed in.

Soldiers beat and crucified Jesus, the world rejected Him, and the light of hope dimmed.

A few days later, three to be exact, another wave of emotions rushed in as they came upon the empty tomb. Some believed while others needed proof, but joy overtook them at the realization that death had been defeated.

Fellowship, miracles, and joy returned for a season. Forty days later, another wave came.

Some worshiped and some doubted on the mountain that day, and then Jesus issued a tall order, one that likely sounded downright impossible to these weary people.

He commanded His followers to proclaim His gospel to the world who had rejected Him.

I can imagine the heart of Jesus as He looked into the eyes of the people that day. He knew what they were feeling, and He ended His final earthly address with the comfort they needed to hear.

"And remember, I am with you always, to the end of the age" (Matt 28:20).

Surely, His words created tension at the thought of the joys and the trials to come. Thankfully, through it all, His presence has remained. His presence remains with us today. He is indeed with us—no matter what we face. In every season, Jesus is with us.

FOR EVEN THE SON OF Man DID NOT COME TO BE SERVED BUT to serve, AND to GIVE His LIFE as a RANSOM FOR Many

MEMORY VERSE

"For even the Son of Man did not come to be served but to serve, and to give his life as a ransom for many."

Mark 10:45

Mark

INTRODUCTION

Jesus the Servant

The Gospel of Mark identifies an aspect of Jesus' character that was significantly different from what the Jews expected in their messiah. Instead of focusing on His impressive lineage, Mark highlighted incidents in Jesus' ministry that displayed how He was both the Son of God and the faithful Suffering Servant who died for the sins of the world.

This book contains three main sections, each describing a different aspect of Jesus' servanthood. Chapters 1–7 reveal how Jesus was a servant to the multitudes, and these chapters feature His deity and power. Chapters 8–10 display how He was a servant to the disciples, focusing on principles of discipleship and servant-leadership. Finally, chapters 11–16 display how Jesus was a servant to the world, detailing His death and resurrection. Two significant confessions of Jesus' deity serve as markers in the Gospel of Mark: Peter's confession in 8:29 and the centurion's in 15:39.

Many contend that Mark wrote the Gospel that bears his name while in Rome under Peter's supervision. Mark was a participant in some of the events recorded in this Gospel, possibly including the arrest of Jesus (where he may have been the man who ran away naked from the soldiers in the garden). Mark probably wrote this Gospel around the time of Peter's death, about A.D. 65–67.

The Book of Mark presents Jesus as God's Son, as one who was willing to die for the sins of humanity. This Gospel reminds us of Jesus' overwhelming love for people. He not only gave up His authority and position in heaven, but He humbled Himself and became a servant, not only of God but of sinful humans. His matchless love is on display on every page of this Gospel, encouraging us to respond by loving Him greatly and surrendering our lives to Him.

Brazil

OFFICIAL LANGUAGE
Portuguese
POPULATION
210,905,000
UNREACHED POPULATION
120,000
PROFESSING CHRISTIANS
89.5%

Simone's Home

Say a Prayer Today

Pray for Simone and her ministry serving the people of Brazil. Pray that God would build up godly servant leaders who can faithfully lead, minister to, and serve the church in Brazil.

HISTORY BIT

Christianity has a long history in Brazil, beginning in the 1500s with the arrival of Portuguese settlers. The first organized missions to the native people began in 1539 when missionaries began building schools and churches.*

Source Information:
https://joshuaproject.net/countries/BR
*David B. Barrett, World Christian *Encyclopedia*, Brazil (New York, NY: Oxford University Press, 1982), 188.

LOVE YOUR NEIGHBOR

Her Journey

SIMONE'S STORY

In recent years I have experienced a new sense of the word *serving*.

My husband and I both serve on staff at our community church in Brazil. We serve our community and our congregation wholeheartedly and with great passion. Recently, my elderly parents have needed constant care. I felt the Lord telling me to stop all ministerial activities and dedicate myself to the full-time care of my parents.

Initially, it was an easy transition. I love my parents and wanted to honor them and help them live comfortably. However, the transition proved more difficult. I had left a place of comfort, visibility, and human recognition. I chose to serve my parents, hoping to honor the servanthood of Jesus as I served my parents.

Today, I would not trade the time serving my parents for the recognition that came from working with my church. I learned much in that season, clinging only to Jesus and serving through His strength, even though there was little comfort or visibility. I learned incredible things I would not have learned had I stayed where I was.

As I was serving my parents, God led me to Love God Greatly. He opened doors for me to translate women's Bible studies into Portuguese. God not only gave me the opportunity to serve my parents but to also serve the community of women in Love God Greatly.

The journey of serving has been challenging, but so rewarding. I am no longer the same person I was when I began this journey of serving with Jesus. I am confident that He sees me, no matter the work He has me do. I am being perfected in His perfect love, no matter where I am.

6 WEEK READING PLAN

LOVE HIS WORD

	MONDAY	TUESDAY	WEDNESDAY	THURSDAY	FRIDAY
1	Mark 1:1-20	Mark 1:21-45	Mark 2:1-17	Mark 2:18-28	Mark 3:1-19
	SOAP Mark 1:7-8	SOAP Mark 1:35	SOAP Mark 2:16-17	SOAP Mark 2:27-28	SOAP Mark 3:13-15
2	Mark 3:20-35	Mark 4:1-20	Mark 4:21-41	Mark 5:1-20	Mark 5:21-43
	SOAP Mark 3:35	SOAP Mark 4:20	SOAP Mark 4:39-40	SOAP Mark 5:19-20	SOAP Mark 5:27-29
3	Mark 6:1-29	Mark 6:30-56	Mark 7:1-30	Mark 7:31—8:26	Mark 8:27—9:29
	SOAP Mark 6:5-6	SOAP Mark 6:49-50	SOAP Mark 7:21-23	SOAP Mark 8:29-30	SOAP Mark 9:7
4	Mark 9:30-50	Mark 10:1-31	Mark 10:32-52	Mark 11:1-14	Mark 11:15-33
	SOAP Mark 9:43-44	SOAP Mark 10:27	SOAP Mark 10:45	SOAP Mark 11:9-10	SOAP Mark 11:24-25
5	Mark 12:1-27	Mark 12:28-44	Mark 13:1-23	Mark 13:24-37	Mark 14:1-21
	SOAP Mark 12:10-11	SOAP Mark 12:43-44	SOAP Mark 13:10-11	SOAP Mark 13:32-33	SOAP Mark 14:8-9
6	Mark 14:22-52	Mark 14:53-72	Mark 15:1-32	Mark 15:33-47	Mark 16
	SOAP Mark 14:36-37	SOAP Mark 14:72	SOAP Mark 15:25-27	SOAP Mark 15:39	SOAP Mark 16:5-6

THE MINISTRY OF JOHN THE BAPTIST

1 The beginning of the gospel of Jesus Christ, the Son of God. 2 As
it is written in the prophet Isaiah,

"Look, I am sending my messenger ahead of you,
who will prepare your way,
3 *the voice of one shouting in the wilderness,*
'Prepare the way for the Lord,
make his paths straight.'"

4 In the wilderness John the baptizer began preaching a baptism of repentance for the forgiveness of sins. 5 People from the
whole Judean countryside and all of Jerusalem were going out
to him, and he was baptizing them in the Jordan River as they
confessed their sins. 6 John wore a garment made of camel's hair
with a leather belt around his waist, and he ate locusts and wild
honey. 7 He proclaimed, "One more powerful than I am is coming after me; I am not worthy to bend down and untie the strap
of his sandals. 8 I baptize you with water, but he will baptize you
with the Holy Spirit."

THE BAPTISM AND TEMPTATION OF JESUS

9 Now in those days Jesus came from Nazareth in Galilee and
was baptized by John in the Jordan River. 10 And just as Jesus was
coming up out of the water, he saw the heavens splitting apart
and the Spirit descending on him like a dove. 11 And a voice came
from heaven: "You are my one dear Son; in you I take great delight." 12 The Spirit immediately drove him into the wilderness.
13 He was in the wilderness forty days, enduring temptations
from Satan. He was with wild animals, and angels were ministering to his needs.

PREACHING IN GALILEE AND THE CALL OF THE DISCIPLES

14 Now after John was imprisoned, Jesus went into Galilee and
proclaimed the gospel of God. 15 He said, "The time is fulfilled
and the kingdom of God is near. Repent and believe the gospel!"
16 As he went along the Sea of Galilee, he saw Simon and Andrew,
Simon's brother, casting a net into the sea (for they were fishermen). 17 Jesus said to them, "Follow me, and I will turn you into
fishers of people!" 18 They left their nets immediately and followed him. 19 Going on a little farther, he saw James, the son of
Zebedee, and John his brother in their boat mending nets. 20 Immediately he called them, and they left their father Zebedee in
the boat with the hired men and followed him.

JESUS' AUTHORITY

21 Then they went to Capernaum. When the Sabbath came, Jesus
went into the synagogue and began to teach. 22 The people there
were amazed by his teaching, because he taught them like one
who had authority, not like the experts in the law. 23 Just then
there was a man in their synagogue with an unclean spirit, and
he cried out, 24 "Leave us alone, Jesus the Nazarene! Have you
come to destroy us? I know who you are—the Holy One of God!"
25 But Jesus rebuked him: "Silence! Come out of him!" 26 After

LOVE TO GROW

NO MATTER THE COST

MARK 1:20

When it comes to following Jesus, I sometimes resist a new direction if it means leaving what's comfortable. I weigh the sacrifice before I agree to the service. A crowd intimidates me, and I hold back when I know He's calling me to speak up. I choose the safety and security of the present over the unrivaled joy that comes from trusting Jesus' invitation into the unknown.

Thankfully, God gave us examples of people who followed Christ without hesitation in order to encourage and exhort us to do the same.

Take James and John, for example. In the middle of their relationships, responsibilities, and real life, Jesus called them to follow Him. Without hesitation, they left all that they had and followed Him. They lost no time with last minute prep, dramatic persuasion, or obsession with personal agendas. I want to follow like that.

James and John tenaciously followed Jesus because they had no doubt that He was the Messiah. Though they had much to learn, by faith they allowed that following Jesus was greater than anything this world could offer. They were transformed by His presence. Undeniably changed, they willingly left everything that had the potential to come between them and their growing intimacy with Jesus.

As part of Jesus' intimate inner circle, James and John grew in humility, mercy, and servanthood. James was martyred for his faith. John, radically transformed by Christ, referred to himself as "the disciple whom Jesus loved" (John 13:25). Upon His crucifixion, Christ honored John by entrusting the care of His mother to him. Both men followed Christ no matter the cost, and it all started with "yes."

When we're saturated by His Word and intentional about seeking His presence, the transforming power of Christ in us is undeniable.

The gain outweighs the cost of giving up. Our trust in His authority pays off. In surrendering our will for His, we gain fellowship and intimacy with Jesus.

throwing him into convulsions, the unclean spirit cried out with
a loud voice and came out of him. 27 They were all amazed so that
they asked each other, "What is this? A new teaching with authority! He even commands the unclean spirits and they obey
him." 28 So the news about him spread quickly throughout all
the region around Galilee.

HEALINGS AT SIMON'S HOUSE

29 Now as soon as they left the synagogue, they entered Simon
and Andrew's house, with James and John. 30 Simon's mother-
in-law was lying down, sick with a fever, so they spoke to Jesus
at once about her. 31 He came and raised her up by gently taking
her hand. Then the fever left her and she began to serve them.
32 When it was evening, after sunset, they brought to him all who
were sick and demon-possessed. 33 The whole town gathered by
the door. 34 So he healed many who were sick with various diseases and drove out many demons. But he would not permit the
demons to speak, because they knew him.

REFLECT

Is there a difference between Jesus' willingness to heal and His ability to heal? Which is harder for you to believe, that Jesus is willing to help you, or that He is able to help you?

PRAYING AND PREACHING

35 Then Jesus got up early in the morning when it was still very
dark, departed, and went out to a deserted place, and there he
spent time in prayer. 36 Simon and his companions searched for
him. 37 When they found him, they said, "Everyone is looking for
you." 38 He replied, "Let us go elsewhere, into the surrounding
villages, so that I can preach there too. For that is what I came
out here to do." 39 So he went into all of Galilee preaching in their
synagogues and casting out demons.

CLEANSING A LEPER

40 Now a leper came to him and fell to his knees, asking for help.
"If you are willing, you can make me clean," he said. 41 Moved with
indignation, Jesus stretched out his hand and touched him, saying, "I am willing. Be clean!" 42 The leprosy left him at once, and
he was clean. 43 Immediately Jesus sent the man away with a very
strong warning. 44 He told him, "See that you do not say anything
to anyone, but go, show yourself to a priest, and bring the offering that Moses commanded for your cleansing, as a testimony
to them." 45 But as the man went out he began to announce it
publicly and spread the story widely, so that Jesus was no longer able to enter any town openly but stayed outside in remote
places. Still they kept coming to him from everywhere.

HEALING AND FORGIVING A PARALYTIC

2 Now after some days, when he returned to Capernaum, the
news spread that he was at home. 2 So many gathered that
there was no longer any room, not even by the door, and he
preached the word to them. 3 Some people came bringing to him
a paralytic, carried by four of them. 4 When they were not able to
bring him in because of the crowd, they removed the roof above
Jesus. Then, after tearing it out, they lowered the stretcher the
paralytic was lying on. 5 When Jesus saw their faith, he said to the
paralytic, "Son, your sins are forgiven." 6 Now some of the experts
in the law were sitting there, turning these things over in their

LOVE TO GROW

HIS AUTHORITY

MARK 2:1–12

Before Jesus began His public ministry, He left Nazareth, the town where He grew up, and moved to Capernaum, making it His new home.

One day, a crowd gathered in a house where Jesus was teaching. The number was so large, there was no room left to hear Him, not even outside the door. A group of men arrived carrying a paralyzed friend. The full house did not deter their attempt to get him to the feet of Jesus. They climbed onto the roof, dug a hole, and lowered their friend inside.

Jesus loved their resourcefulness and praised them for their faith. He turned to the paralyzed man and said, "Son, your sins are forgiven." The experts of the law were incensed: "Why does this man speak this way? He is blaspheming! Who can forgive sins but God alone?" (Mark 2:5–7).

The experts of the law were right, in part. Only God can forgive sins, but Jesus was not blaspheming. This miracle revealed two major truths about Christ's identity.

First, Jesus revealed His purpose. Jesus came to take away the sins of the world and to save men from death through His sacrificial death on the cross. When He saw the faith of the paralytic, He called him "son," a term of affection and acceptance, and told him his sins were forgiven. The man received God's forgiveness and experienced firsthand Jesus' power to save and restore.

Second, Jesus demonstrated His authority. When Jesus told the paralytic that His sins were forgiven, the experts in the law objected, replying that only God had the authority to forgive. Jesus didn't argue with them. Instead, Jesus demonstrated that He indeed had such authority by commanding the paralytic to take up his bed and walk. When he did, no one could refute the authority behind Jesus' words.

There is nothing too hard for our God.

He holds all power. His purposes are unstoppable and His authority is undeniable. Praise God for such a wonderful Savior.

minds: 7 "Why does this man speak this way? He is blaspheming! Who can forgive sins but God alone?" 8 Now immediately, when Jesus realized in his spirit that they were contemplating such thoughts, he said to them, "Why are you thinking such things in your hearts? 9 Which is easier, to say to the paralytic, 'Your sins are forgiven,' or to say, 'Stand up, take your stretcher, and walk'? 10 But so that you may know that the Son of Man has authority on earth to forgive sins,"—he said to the paralytic—11 "I tell you, stand up, take your stretcher, and go home." 12 And immediately the man stood up, took his stretcher, and went out in front of them all. They were all amazed and glorified God, saying, "We have never seen anything like this!"

THE CALL OF LEVI; EATING WITH SINNERS

13 Jesus went out again by the sea. The whole crowd came to him, and he taught them. 14 As he went along, he saw Levi, the son of Alphaeus, sitting at the tax booth. "Follow me," he said to him. And he got up and followed him. 15 As Jesus was having a meal in Levi's home, many tax collectors and sinners were eating with Jesus and his disciples, for there were many who followed him. 16 When the experts in the law and the Pharisees saw that he was eating with sinners and tax collectors, they said to his disciples, "Why does he eat with tax collectors and sinners?" 17 When Jesus heard this he said to them, "Those who are healthy don't need a physician, but those who are sick do. I have not come to call the righteous, but sinners."

THE SUPERIORITY OF THE NEW

18 Now John's disciples and the Pharisees were fasting. So they came to Jesus and said, "Why do the disciples of John and the disciples of the Pharisees fast, but your disciples don't fast?" 19 Jesus said to them, "The wedding guests cannot fast while the bridegroom is with them, can they? As long as they have the bridegroom with them they do not fast. 20 But the days are coming when the bridegroom will be taken from them, and at that time they will fast. 21 No one sews a patch of unshrunk cloth on an old garment; otherwise, the patch pulls away from it, the new from the old, and the tear becomes worse. 22 And no one pours new wine into old wineskins; otherwise, the wine will burst the skins, and both the wine and the skins will be destroyed. Instead new wine is poured into new wineskins."

LORD OF THE SABBATH

23 Jesus was going through the grain fields on a Sabbath, and his disciples began to pick some heads of wheat as they made their way. 24 So the Pharisees said to him, "Look, why are they doing what is against the law on the Sabbath?" 25 He said to them, "Have you never read what David did when he was in need and he and his companions were hungry—26 how he entered the house of God when Abiathar was high priest and ate the sacred bread, which is against the law for any but the priests to eat, and also gave it to his companions?" 27 Then he said to them, "The Sabbath was made for people, not people for the Sabbath. 28 For this reason the Son of Man is lord even of the Sabbath."

HEALING A WITHERED HAND

3 Then Jesus entered the synagogue again, and a man was there
who had a withered hand. 2 They watched Jesus closely to see
if he would heal him on the Sabbath, so that they could accuse
him. 3 So he said to the man who had the withered hand, "Stand
up among all these people." 4 Then he said to them, "Is it lawful to
do good on the Sabbath, or evil, to save a life or destroy it?" But
they were silent. 5 After looking around at them in anger, grieved
by the hardness of their hearts, he said to the man, "Stretch out
your hand." He stretched it out, and his hand was restored. 6 So
the Pharisees went out immediately and began plotting with
the Herodians, as to how they could assassinate him.

CROWDS BY THE SEA

7 Then Jesus went away with his disciples to the sea, and a great
multitude from Galilee followed him. And from Judea, 8 Jerusalem, Idumea, beyond the Jordan River, and around Tyre and Sidon a great multitude came to him when they heard about the
things he had done. 9 Because of the crowd, he told his disciples
to have a small boat ready for him so the crowd would not press
toward him. 10 For he had healed many, so that all who were afflicted with diseases pressed toward him in order to touch him.
11 And whenever the unclean spirits saw him, they fell down before him and cried out, "You are the Son of God." 12 But he sternly
ordered them not to make him known.

APPOINTING THE TWELVE APOSTLES

13 Now Jesus went up the mountain and called for those he wanted,
and they came to him. 14 He appointed twelve so that they would
be with him and he could send them to preach 15 and to have authority to cast out demons. 16 To Simon he gave the name Peter;
17 to James and his brother John, the sons of Zebedee, he gave the
name Boanerges (that is, "sons of thunder"); 18 and Andrew, Philip,
Bartholomew, Matthew, Thomas, James the son of Alphaeus, Thaddaeus, Simon the Zealot, 19 and Judas Iscariot, who betrayed him.

JESUS AND BEELZEBUL

20 Now Jesus went home, and a crowd gathered so that they were
not able to eat. 21 When his family heard this they went out to restrain him, for they said, "He is out of his mind." 22 The experts in
the law who came down from Jerusalem said, "He is possessed by
Beelzebul," and, "By the ruler of demons he casts out demons!"
23 So he called them and spoke to them in parables: "How can Satan cast out Satan? 24 If a kingdom is divided against itself, that
kingdom will not be able to stand. 25 If a house is divided against
itself, that house will not be able to stand. 26 And if Satan rises
against himself and is divided, he is not able to stand and his end
has come. 27 But no one is able to enter a strong man's house and
steal his property unless he first ties up the strong man. Then he
can thoroughly plunder his house. 28 I tell you the truth, people
will be forgiven for all sins, even all the blasphemies they utter.
29 But whoever blasphemes against the Holy Spirit will never
be forgiven, but is guilty of an eternal sin" 30 (because they said,
"He has an unclean spirit").

JESUS' TRUE FAMILY

[31] Then Jesus' mother and his brothers came. Standing outside, they sent word to him, to summon him. [32] A crowd was sitting around him and they said to him, "Look, your mother and your brothers are outside looking for you." [33] He answered them and said, "Who are my mother and my brothers?" [34] And looking at those who were sitting around him in a circle, he said, "Here are my mother and my brothers! [35] For whoever does the will of God is my brother and sister and mother."

THE PARABLE OF THE SOWER

4 Again he began to teach by the lake. Such a large crowd gathered around him that he got into a boat on the lake and sat there while the whole crowd was on the shore by the lake. [2] He taught them many things in parables, and in his teaching said to them: [3] "Listen! A sower went out to sow. [4] And as he sowed, some seed fell along the path, and the birds came and devoured it. [5] Other seed fell on rocky ground where it did not have much soil. It sprang up at once because the soil was not deep. [6] When the sun came up it was scorched, and because it did not have sufficient root, it withered. [7] Other seed fell among the thorns, and they grew up and choked it, and it did not produce grain. [8] But other seed fell on good soil and produced grain, sprouting and growing; some yielded thirty times as much, some sixty, and some a hundred times." [9] And he said, "Whoever has ears to hear had better listen!"

THE PURPOSE OF PARABLES

[10] When he was alone, those around him with the twelve asked him about the parables. [11] He said to them, "The secret of the kingdom of God has been given to you. But to those outside, everything is in parables,

12 so that ***although they look they may look but not see,***
and although they hear they may hear but not understand,
so they may not repent and be forgiven."

[13] He said to them, "Don't you understand this parable? Then how will you understand any parable? [14] The sower sows the word. [15] These are the ones on the path where the word is sown: Whenever they hear, immediately Satan comes and snatches the word that was sown in them. [16] These are the ones sown on rocky ground: As soon as they hear the word, they receive it with joy. [17] But they have no root in themselves and do not endure. Then, when trouble or persecution comes because of the word, immediately they fall away. [18] Others are the ones sown among thorns: They are those who hear the word, [19] but worldly cares, the seductiveness of wealth, and the desire for other things come in and choke the word, and it produces nothing. [20] But these are the ones sown on good soil: They hear the word and receive it and bear fruit, one thirty times as much, one sixty, and one a hundred."

THE PARABLE OF THE LAMP

[21] He also said to them, "A lamp isn't brought to be put under a basket or under a bed, is it? Isn't it to be placed on a lampstand? [22] For nothing is hidden except to be revealed, and nothing

concealed except to be brought to light. 23 If anyone has ears to
hear, he had better listen!" 24 And he said to them, "Take care
about what you hear. The measure you use will be the measure
you receive, and more will be added to you. 25 For whoever has
will be given more, but whoever does not have, even what he has
will be taken from him."

THE PARABLE OF THE GROWING SEED

26 He also said, "The kingdom of God is like someone who spreads
seed on the ground. 27 He goes to sleep and gets up, night and day,
and the seed sprouts and grows, though he does not know how.
28 By itself the soil produces a crop, first the stalk, then the head,
then the full grain in the head. 29 And when the grain is ripe, he
sends in the sickle because the harvest has come."

THE PARABLE OF THE MUSTARD SEED

30 He also asked, "To what can we compare the kingdom of God,
or what parable can we use to present it? 31 It is like a mustard
seed that when sown in the ground, even though it is the smallest of all the seeds in the ground—32 when it is sown, it grows
up, becomes the greatest of all garden plants, and grows large
branches so that the wild birds can nest in its shade."

THE USE OF PARABLES

33 So with many parables like these, he spoke the word to them, as
they were able to hear. 34 He did not speak to them without a parable. But privately he explained everything to his own disciples.

STILLING OF A STORM

35 On that day, when evening came, Jesus said to his disciples,
"Let's go across to the other side of the lake." 36 So after leaving
the crowd, they took him along, just as he was, in the boat, and
other boats were with him. 37 Now a great windstorm developed
and the waves were breaking into the boat, so that the boat was
nearly swamped. 38 But he was in the stern, sleeping on a cushion.
They woke him up and said to him, "Teacher, don't you care that
we are about to die?" 39 So he got up and rebuked the wind, and
said to the sea, "Be quiet! Calm down!" Then the wind stopped,
and it was dead calm. 40 And he said to them, "Why are you cowardly? Do you still not have faith?" 41 They were overwhelmed by
fear and said to one another, "Who then is this? Even the wind
and sea obey him!"

CHALLENGE

How is this scene in Mark similar to the storm in Jonah 1? Read Matthew 12:38–42. What other similarities do you see in Jesus' life and the story of Jonah?

HEALING OF A DEMONIAC

5 So they came to the other side of the lake, to the region of the
Gerasenes. 2 Just as Jesus was getting out of the boat, a man
with an unclean spirit came from the tombs and met him. 3 He
lived among the tombs, and no one could bind him anymore,
not even with a chain. 4 For his hands and feet had often been
bound with chains and shackles, but he had torn the chains apart
and broken the shackles in pieces. No one was strong enough to
subdue him. 5 Each night and every day among the tombs and in
the mountains, he would cry out and cut himself with stones.
6 When he saw Jesus from a distance, he ran and bowed down

before him. 7 Then he cried out with a loud voice, "Leave me alone,
Jesus, Son of the Most High God! I implore you by God—do not
torment me!" 8 (For Jesus had said to him, "Come out of that man,
you unclean spirit!") 9 Jesus asked him, "What is your name?"
And he said, "My name is Legion, for we are many." 10 He begged
Jesus repeatedly not to send them out of the region. 11 There on
the hillside, a great herd of pigs was feeding. 12 And the demonic
spirits begged him, "Send us into the pigs. Let us enter them."
13 Jesus gave them permission. So the unclean spirits came out
and went into the pigs. Then the herd rushed down the steep
slope into the lake, and about 2,000 were drowned in the lake.
14 Now the herdsmen ran off and spread the news in the town
and countryside, and the people went out to see what had happened. 15 They came to Jesus and saw the demon-possessed man
sitting there, clothed and in his right mind—the one who had
the "Legion"—and they were afraid. 16 Those who had seen what
had happened to the demon-possessed man reported it, and
they also told about the pigs. 17 Then they began to beg Jesus to
leave their region. 18 As he was getting into the boat the man who
had been demon-possessed asked if he could go with him. 19 But
Jesus did not permit him to do so. Instead, he said to him, "Go
to your home and to your people and tell them what the Lord
has done for you, that he had mercy on you." 20 So he went away
and began to proclaim in the Decapolis what Jesus had done for
him, and all were amazed.

RESTORATION AND HEALING

21 When Jesus had crossed again in a boat to the other side, a large
crowd gathered around him, and he was by the sea. 22 Then one
of the synagogue leaders, named Jairus, came up, and when he
saw Jesus, he fell at his feet. 23 He asked him urgently, "My little
daughter is near death. Come and lay your hands on her so that
she may be healed and live." 24 Jesus went with him, and a large
crowd followed and pressed around him.
25 Now a woman was there who had been suffering from a hemorrhage for twelve years. 26 She had endured a great deal under
the care of many doctors and had spent all that she had. Yet instead of getting better, she grew worse. 27 When she heard about
Jesus, she came up behind him in the crowd and touched his
cloak, 28 for she kept saying, "If only I touch his clothes, I will
be healed." 29 At once the bleeding stopped, and she felt in her
body that she was healed of her disease. 30 Jesus knew at once
that power had gone out from him. He turned around in the
crowd and said, "Who touched my clothes?" 31 His disciples said
to him, "You see the crowd pressing against you and you say, 'Who
touched me?'" 32 But he looked around to see who had done it.
33 Then the woman, with fear and trembling, knowing what had
happened to her, came and fell down before him and told him
the whole truth. 34 He said to her, "Daughter, your faith has made
you well. Go in peace, and be healed of your disease."
35 While he was still speaking, people came from the synagogue leader's house saying, "Your daughter has died. Why trouble the teacher any longer?" 36 But Jesus, paying no attention
to what was said, told the synagogue leader, "Do not be afraid;

just believe." 37 He did not let anyone follow him except Peter,
James, and John, the brother of James. 38 They came to the house
of the synagogue leader where he saw noisy confusion and people weeping and wailing loudly. 39 When he entered he said to
them, "Why are you distressed and weeping? The child is not
dead but asleep!" 40 And they began making fun of him. But he
forced them all outside, and he took the child's father and mother and his own companions and went into the room where the
child was. 41 Then, gently taking the child by the hand, he said
to her, "*Talitha koum*," which means, "Little girl, I say to you, get
up." 42 The girl got up at once and began to walk around (she was
twelve years old). They were completely astonished at this. 43 He
strictly ordered that no one should know about this, and told
them to give her something to eat.

REJECTION AT NAZARETH

6 Now Jesus left that place and came to his hometown, and his
disciples followed him. 2 When the Sabbath came, he began
to teach in the synagogue. Many who heard him were astonished, saying, "Where did he get these ideas? And what is this
wisdom that has been given to him? What are these miracles
that are done through his hands? 3 Isn't this the carpenter, the
son of Mary and brother of James, Joses, Judas, and Simon? And
aren't his sisters here with us?" And so they took offense at him.
4 Then Jesus said to them, "A prophet is not without honor except in his hometown, and among his relatives, and in his own
house." 5 He was not able to do a miracle there, except to lay his
hands on a few sick people and heal them. 6 And he was amazed
because of their unbelief. Then he went around among the villages and taught.

SENDING OUT THE TWELVE APOSTLES

7 Jesus called the twelve and began to send them out two by two.
He gave them authority over the unclean spirits. 8 He instructed
them to take nothing for the journey except a staff—no bread, no
bag, no money in their belts—9 and to put on sandals but not to
wear two tunics. 10 He said to them, "Wherever you enter a house,
stay there until you leave the area. 11 If a place will not welcome
you or listen to you, as you go out from there, shake the dust off
your feet as a testimony against them." 12 So they went out and
preached that all should repent. 13 They cast out many demons
and anointed many sick people with olive oil and healed them.

THE DEATH OF JOHN THE BAPTIST

14 Now King Herod heard this, for Jesus' name had become
known. Some were saying, "John the baptizer has been raised
from the dead, and because of this, miraculous powers are at
work in him." 15 Others said, "He is Elijah." Others said, "He is
a prophet, like one of the prophets from the past." 16 But when
Herod heard this, he said, "John, whom I beheaded, has been
raised!" 17 For Herod himself had sent men, arrested John, and
bound him in prison on account of Herodias, his brother Philip's
wife, because Herod had married her. 18 For John had repeatedly
told Herod, "It is not lawful for you to have your brother's wife."

[19]So Herodias nursed a grudge against him and wanted to kill
him. But she could not [20]because Herod stood in awe of John
and protected him, since he knew that John was a righteous and
holy man. When Herod heard him, he was thoroughly baffled,
and yet he liked to listen to John.
[21]But a suitable day came, when Herod gave a banquet on his
birthday for his court officials, military commanders, and leaders
of Galilee. [22]When his daughter Herodias came in and danced, she
pleased Herod and his dinner guests. The king said to the girl, "Ask
me for whatever you want and I will give it to you." [23]He swore
to her, "Whatever you ask I will give you, up to half my kingdom."
[24]So she went out and said to her mother, "What should I ask for?"
Her mother said, "The head of John the baptizer." [25]Immediately
she hurried back to the king and made her request: "I want the
head of John the Baptist on a platter immediately." [26]Although
it grieved the king deeply, he did not want to reject her request
because of his oath and his guests. [27]So the king sent an executioner at once to bring John's head, and he went and beheaded
John in prison. [28]He brought his head on a platter and gave it to
the girl, and the girl gave it to her mother. [29]When John's disciples
heard this, they came and took his body and placed it in a tomb.

THE FEEDING OF THE FIVE THOUSAND

[30]Then the apostles gathered around Jesus and told him everything they had done and taught. [31]He said to them, "Come with
me privately to an isolated place and rest a while" (for many were
coming and going, and there was no time to eat). [32]So they went
away by themselves in a boat to some remote place. [33]But many
saw them leaving and recognized them, and they hurried on foot
from all the towns and arrived there ahead of them. [34]As Jesus
came ashore he saw the large crowd and he had compassion on
them, because they were like sheep without a shepherd. So he
taught them many things.
[35]When it was already late, his disciples came to him and said,
"This is an isolated place and it is already very late. [36]Send them
away so that they can go into the surrounding countryside and
villages and buy something for themselves to eat." [37]But he answered them, "You give them something to eat." And they said,
"Should we go and buy bread for 200 silver coins and give it to
them to eat?" [38]He said to them, "How many loaves do you have?
Go and see." When they found out, they said, "Five—and two fish."
[39]Then he directed them all to sit down in groups on the green
grass. [40]So they reclined in groups of hundreds and fifties. [41]He
took the five loaves and the two fish, and looking up to heaven,
he gave thanks and broke the loaves. He gave them to his disciples to serve the people, and he divided the two fish among
them all. [42]They all ate and were satisfied, [43]and they picked up
the broken pieces and fish that were left over, twelve baskets
full. [44]Now there were 5,000 men who ate the bread.

WALKING ON WATER

[45]Immediately Jesus made his disciples get into the boat and go
on ahead to the other side, to Bethsaida, while he dispersed the
crowd. [46]After saying goodbye to them, he went to the mountain

LOVE TO GROW

NEVER ALONE

MARK 6:45–51

The disciples had witnessed Jesus miraculously feed over five thousand people. Now, they were in a storm in the middle of a lake.

Their previously peaceful day was now anything but.

The excitement of feeding five thousand people had long since left each of them as they faced the storm around them.

Hadn't they obeyed Jesus? Wasn't He the one who told them to get into the boat and row across the lake to Bethsaida? Forget the miracle Jesus performed hours before; they needed Jesus now!

Maybe you've found yourself in a similar situation. The kind of storm doesn't matter; they all have a way of tossing you to and fro, making you feel vulnerable, out of control, and fearful. No one thrives in the middle of a storm.

And yet, that is right where Jesus sent the disciples: into the storm.

From the shoreline, Jesus, with one word, could have silenced the storm. He didn't.

Instead, He chose to go into the storm after them. He walked on water straight to them, and, in doing so, reminded them of who He is.

He saw the fear etched in their faces. He knew the thoughts shouting in their minds, and He felt the desperation in their hearts. He sent them into the storm so they could see Him come to their rescue.

The disciples wanted peace; they wanted smooth waters. They wanted life without the struggle. If God had given them what they wanted they would have missed seeing Jesus for who He really is.

No matter the storm in which you find yourself, realize this:
You are never alone. Jesus is always in the midst of the storm.

Like the disciples, Jesus calls out to you to take courage and remember He is with you and He is for you. You are never alone.

to pray. 47 When evening came, the boat was in the middle of the
sea and he was alone on the land. 48 He saw them straining at
the oars, because the wind was against them. As the night was
ending, he came to them walking on the sea, for he wanted to
pass by them. 49 When they saw him walking on the water they
thought he was a ghost. They cried out, 50 for they all saw him
and were terrified. But immediately he spoke to them: "Have
courage! It is I. Do not be afraid." 51 Then he went up with them
into the boat, and the wind ceased. They were completely astonished, 52 because they did not understand about the loaves, but
their hearts were hardened.

HEALING THE SICK

53 After they had crossed over, they came to land at Gennesaret and anchored there. 54 As they got out of the boat, people
immediately recognized Jesus. 55 They ran through that whole
region and began to bring the sick on mats to wherever he was
rumored to be. 56 And wherever he would go—into villages, towns,
or countryside—they would place the sick in the marketplaces,
and would ask him if they could just touch the edge of his cloak,
and all who touched it were healed.

BREAKING HUMAN TRADITIONS

7 Now the Pharisees and some of the experts in the law who
came from Jerusalem gathered around him. 2 And they saw
that some of Jesus' disciples ate their bread with unclean
hands, that is, unwashed. 3 (For the Pharisees and all the Jews
do not eat unless they perform a ritual washing, holding fast
to the tradition of the elders. 4 And when they come from the
marketplace, they do not eat unless they wash. They hold fast
to many other traditions: the washing of cups, pots, kettles,
and dining couches.) 5 The Pharisees and the experts in the law
asked him, "Why do your disciples not live according to the
tradition of the elders, but eat with unwashed hands?" 6 He
said to them, "Isaiah prophesied correctly about you hypocrites, as it is written:

'***This people honors me with their lips,***
but their heart is far from me.
7 ***They worship me in vain,***
teaching as doctrine the commandments of men.'

8 Having no regard for the command of God, you hold fast to
human tradition." 9 He also said to them, "You neatly reject the
commandment of God in order to set up your tradition. 10 For
Moses said, '***Honor your father and your mother,***' and, '***Whoever***
insults his father or mother must be put to death.' 11 But you say
that if anyone tells his father or mother, 'Whatever help you
would have received from me is *corban*' (that is, a gift for God),
12 then you no longer permit him to do anything for his father
or mother. 13 Thus you nullify the word of God by your tradition
that you have handed down. And you do many things like this."

14 Then he called the crowd again and said to them, "Listen to
me, everyone, and understand. 15 There is nothing outside of a
person that can defile him by going into him. Rather, it is what
comes out of a person that defiles him."*

[17] Now when Jesus had left the crowd and entered the house,
his disciples asked him about the parable. [18] He said to them, "Are
you so foolish? Don't you understand that whatever goes into
a person from outside cannot defile him? [19] For it does not enter his heart but his stomach, and then goes out into the sewer."
(This means all foods are clean.) [20] He said, "What comes out of a
person defiles him. [21] For from within, out of the human heart,
come evil ideas, sexual immorality, theft, murder, [22] adultery,
greed, evil, deceit, debauchery, envy, slander, pride, and folly.
[23] All these evils come from within and defile a person."

A SYROPHOENICIAN WOMAN'S FAITH

[24] After Jesus left there, he went to the region of Tyre. When
he went into a house, he did not want anyone to know, but he
was not able to escape notice. [25] Instead, a woman whose young
daughter had an unclean spirit immediately heard about him
and came and fell at his feet. [26] The woman was a Greek, of Sy-
rophoenician origin. She asked him to cast the demon out of her
daughter. [27] He said to her, "Let the children be satisfied first,
for it is not right to take the children's bread and to throw it to
the dogs." [28] She answered, "Yes, Lord, but even the dogs under
the table eat the children's crumbs." [29] Then he said to her, "Because you said this, you may go. The demon has left your daughter." [30] She went home and found the child lying on the bed, and
the demon gone.

HEALING A DEAF MUTE

[31] Then Jesus went out again from the region of Tyre and came
through Sidon to the Sea of Galilee in the region of the Decapolis. [32] They brought to him a deaf man who had difficulty speaking, and they asked him to place his hands on him. [33] After Jesus
took him aside privately, away from the crowd, he put his fingers in the man's ears, and after spitting, he touched his tongue.
[34] Then he looked up to heaven and said with a sigh, "*Ephphatha*"
(that is, "Be opened"). [35] And immediately the man's ears were
opened, his tongue loosened, and he spoke plainly. [36] Jesus ordered them not to tell anyone. But as much as he ordered them
not to do this, they proclaimed it all the more. [37] People were
completely astounded and said, "He has done everything well.
He even makes the deaf hear and the mute speak."

THE FEEDING OF THE FOUR THOUSAND

8 In those days there was another large crowd with nothing to
eat. So Jesus called his disciples and said to them, [2] "I have
compassion on the crowd, because they have already been here
with me three days, and they have nothing to eat. [3] If I send
them home hungry, they will faint on the way, and some of them
have come from a great distance." [4] His disciples answered him,
"Where can someone get enough bread in this desolate place
to satisfy these people?" [5] He asked them, "How many loaves do
you have?" They replied, "Seven." [6] Then he directed the crowd
to sit down on the ground. After he took the seven loaves and
gave thanks, he broke them and began giving them to the disciples to serve. So they served the crowd. [7] They also had a few

small fish. After giving thanks for these, he told them to serve
these as well. 8 Everyone ate and was satisfied, and they picked
up the broken pieces left over, seven baskets full. 9 There were
about 4,000 who ate. Then he dismissed them. 10 Immediately
he got into a boat with his disciples and went to the district of
Dalmanutha.

THE DEMAND FOR A SIGN

11 Then the Pharisees came and began to argue with Jesus, asking for a sign from heaven to test him. 12 Sighing deeply in his
spirit he said, "Why does this generation look for a sign? I tell
you the truth, no sign will be given to this generation." 13 Then
he left them, got back into the boat, and went to the other side.

THE YEAST OF THE PHARISEES AND HEROD

14 Now they had forgotten to take bread, except for one loaf they
had with them in the boat. 15 And Jesus ordered them, "Watch
out! Beware of the yeast of the Pharisees and the yeast of Herod!"
16 So they began to discuss with one another about having no
bread. 17 When he learned of this, Jesus said to them, "Why are
you arguing about having no bread? Do you still not see or understand? Have your hearts been hardened? 18 Though you have
eyes, don't you see? And though you have ears, can't you hear?
Don't you remember? 19 When I broke the five loaves for the
5,000, how many baskets full of pieces did you pick up?" They replied, "Twelve." 20 "When I broke the seven loaves for the 4,000,
how many baskets full of pieces did you pick up?" They replied,
"Seven." 21 Then he said to them, "Do you still not understand?"

A TWO-STAGE HEALING

22 Then they came to Bethsaida. They brought a blind man to
Jesus and asked him to touch him. 23 He took the blind man by
the hand and brought him outside of the village. Then he spit
on his eyes, placed his hands on his eyes and asked, "Do you see
anything?" 24 Regaining his sight he said, "I see people, but they
look like trees walking." 25 Then Jesus placed his hands on the
man's eyes again. And he opened his eyes, his sight was restored,
and he saw everything clearly. 26 Jesus sent him home, saying,
"Do not even go into the village."

PETER'S CONFESSION

27 Then Jesus and his disciples went to the villages of Caesarea
Philippi. On the way he asked his disciples, "Who do people say
that I am?" 28 They said, "John the Baptist, others say Elijah, and
still others, one of the prophets." 29 He asked them, "But who do
you say that I am?" Peter answered him, "You are the Christ."
30 Then he warned them not to tell anyone about him.

FIRST PREDICTION OF JESUS' DEATH AND RESURRECTION

31 Then Jesus began to teach them that the Son of Man must suffer many things and be rejected by the elders, chief priests, and
experts in the law, and be killed, and after three days rise again.
32 He spoke openly about this. So Peter took him aside and began

to rebuke him. 33 But after turning and looking at his disciples,
he rebuked Peter and said, "Get behind me, Satan. You are not
setting your mind on God's interests, but on man's."

FOLLOWING JESUS

34 Then Jesus called the crowd, along with his disciples, and said
to them, "If anyone wants to become my follower, he must deny
himself, take up his cross, and follow me. 35 For whoever wants to
save his life will lose it, but whoever loses his life because of me
and because of the gospel will save it. 36 For what benefit is it for
a person to gain the whole world, yet forfeit his life? 37 What can
a person give in exchange for his life? 38 For if anyone is ashamed
of me and my words in this adulterous and sinful generation,
the Son of Man will also be ashamed of him when he comes in
9 the glory of his Father with the holy angels." 1 And he said to
them, "I tell you the truth, there are some standing here who
will not experience death before they see the kingdom of God
come with power."

REFLECT

What does it mean to take up your cross and follow Jesus? How can you practice this in your daily life?

THE TRANSFIGURATION

2 Six days later Jesus took with him Peter, James, and John and
led them alone up a high mountain privately. And he was transfigured before them, 3 and his clothes became radiantly white,
more so than any launderer in the world could bleach them.
4 Then Elijah appeared before them along with Moses, and they
were talking with Jesus. 5 So Peter said to Jesus, "Rabbi, it is good
for us to be here. Let us make three shelters—one for you, one
for Moses, and one for Elijah." 6 (For they were afraid, and he did
not know what to say.) 7 Then a cloud overshadowed them, and
a voice came from the cloud, "This is my one dear Son. Listen
to him!" 8 Suddenly when they looked around, they saw no one
with them any more except Jesus.

9 As they were coming down from the mountain, he gave them
orders not to tell anyone what they had seen until after the Son
of Man had risen from the dead. 10 They kept this statement to
themselves, discussing what this rising from the dead meant.

11 Then they asked him, "Why do the experts in the law say that
Elijah must come first?" 12 He said to them, "Elijah does indeed
come first, and restores all things. And why is it written that the
Son of Man must suffer many things and be despised? 13 But I tell
you that Elijah has certainly come, and they did to him whatever
they wanted, just as it is written about him."

THE DISCIPLES' FAILURE TO HEAL

14 When they came to the disciples, they saw a large crowd around
them and experts in the law arguing with them. 15 When the
whole crowd saw him, they were amazed and ran at once and
greeted him. 16 He asked them, "What are you arguing about with
them?" 17 A member of the crowd said to him, "Teacher, I brought
you my son, who is possessed by a spirit that makes him mute.
18 Whenever it seizes him, it throws him down, and he foams
at the mouth, grinds his teeth, and becomes rigid. I asked your
disciples to cast it out, but they were not able to do so." 19 He answered them, "You unbelieving generation! How much longer

must I be with you? How much longer must I endure you? Bring
him to me." [20] So they brought the boy to him. When the spirit
saw him, it immediately threw the boy into a convulsion. He fell
on the ground and rolled around, foaming at the mouth. [21] Jesus
asked his father, "How long has this been happening to him?"
And he said, "From childhood. [22] It has often thrown him into
fire or water to destroy him. But if you are able to do anything,
have compassion on us and help us." [23] Then Jesus said to him, "'If
you are able?' All things are possible for the one who believes."
[24] Immediately the father of the boy cried out and said, "I believe; help my unbelief!"

[25] Now when Jesus saw that a crowd was quickly gathering, he
rebuked the unclean spirit, saying to it, "Mute and deaf spirit,
I command you, come out of him and never enter him again."
[26] It shrieked, threw him into terrible convulsions, and came
out. The boy looked so much like a corpse that many said, "He
is dead!" [27] But Jesus gently took his hand and raised him to his
feet, and he stood up.

[28] Then, after he went into the house, his disciples asked him
privately, "Why couldn't we cast it out?" [29] He told them, "This
kind can come out only by prayer."

SECOND PREDICTION OF JESUS' DEATH AND RESURRECTION

[30] They went out from there and passed through Galilee. But
Jesus did not want anyone to know, [31] for he was teaching his
disciples and telling them, "The Son of Man will be betrayed
into the hands of men. They will kill him, and after three days
he will rise." [32] But they did not understand this statement and
were afraid to ask him.

QUESTIONS ABOUT THE GREATEST

[33] Then they came to Capernaum. After Jesus was inside the
house he asked them, "What were you discussing on the way?"
[34] But they were silent, for on the way they had argued with one
another about who was the greatest. [35] After he sat down, he
called the twelve and said to them, "If anyone wants to be first,
he must be last of all and servant of all." [36] He took a little child
and had him stand among them. Taking him in his arms, he
said to them, [37] "Whoever welcomes one of these little children
in my name welcomes me, and whoever welcomes me does not
welcome me but the one who sent me."

ON JESUS' SIDE

[38] John said to him, "Teacher, we saw someone casting out demons in your name, and we tried to stop him because he was
not following us." [39] But Jesus said, "Do not stop him, because no
one who does a miracle in my name will be able soon afterward
to say anything bad about me. [40] For whoever is not against us is
for us. [41] For I tell you the truth, whoever gives you a cup of water because you bear Christ's name will never lose his reward.

[42] "If anyone causes one of these little ones who believe in me
to sin, it would be better for him to have a huge millstone tied
around his neck and to be thrown into the sea. [43] If your hand

causes you to sin, cut it off! It is better for you to enter into life
crippled than to have two hands and go into hell, to the unquenchable fire.† 45 If your foot causes you to sin, cut it off! It is
better to enter life lame than to have two feet and be thrown into
hell.‡ 47 If your eye causes you to sin, tear it out! It is better to enter into the kingdom of God with one eye than to have two eyes
and be thrown into hell, 48 where their worm never dies and the
fire is never quenched. 49 Everyone will be salted with fire. 50 Salt
is good, but if it loses its saltiness, how can you make it salty
again? Have salt in yourselves, and be at peace with each other."

DIVORCE

10 Then Jesus left that place and went to the region of Judea
and beyond the Jordan River. Again crowds gathered to
him, and again, as was his custom, he taught them. 2 Then some
Pharisees came, and to test him they asked, "Is it lawful for a
man to divorce his wife?" 3 He answered them, "What did Moses
command you?" 4 They said, "Moses permitted a man *to write*
a certificate of dismissal *and to divorce* her." 5 But Jesus said to
them, "He wrote this commandment for you because of your
hard hearts. 6 But from the beginning of creation ***he made them***
male and female. 7 For this reason a man will leave his father and
mother, 8 and the two will become one flesh. So they are no longer two, but one flesh. 9 Therefore what God has joined together,
let no one separate."
10 In the house once again, the disciples asked him about this.
11 So he told them, "Whoever divorces his wife and marries another commits adultery against her. 12 And if she divorces her
husband and marries another, she commits adultery."

JESUS AND LITTLE CHILDREN

13 Now people were bringing little children to him for him to
touch, but the disciples scolded those who brought them. 14 But
when Jesus saw this, he was indignant and said to them, "Let the
little children come to me and do not try to stop them, for the
kingdom of God belongs to such as these. 15 I tell you the truth,
whoever does not receive the kingdom of God like a child will
never enter it." 16 After he took the children in his arms, he placed
his hands on them and blessed them.

THE RICH MAN

17 Now as Jesus was starting out on his way, someone ran up to
him, fell on his knees, and said, "Good teacher, what must I do
to inherit eternal life?" 18 Jesus said to him, "Why do you call me
good? No one is good except God alone. 19 You know the commandments: '***Do not murder, do not commit adultery, do not steal,***
do not give false testimony, *do not defraud,* ***honor your father and***
mother.'" 20 The man said to him, "Teacher, I have wholeheartedly obeyed all these laws since my youth." 21 As Jesus looked at
him, he felt love for him and said, "You lack one thing. Go, sell
whatever you have and give the money to the poor, and you will
have treasure in heaven. Then come, follow me." 22 But at this
statement, the man looked sad and went away sorrowful, for
he was very rich.

23 Then Jesus looked around and said to his disciples, "How
hard it is for the rich to enter the kingdom of God!" 24 The disciples were astonished at these words. But again Jesus said to
them, "Children, how hard it is to enter the kingdom of God!
25 It is easier for a camel to go through the eye of a needle than
for a rich person to enter the kingdom of God." 26 They were
even more astonished and said to one another, "Then who can
be saved?" 27 Jesus looked at them and replied, "This is impossible for mere humans, but not for God; all things are possible
for God."

28 Peter began to speak to him, "Look, we have left everything
to follow you!" 29 Jesus said, "I tell you the truth, there is no one
who has left home or brothers or sisters or mother or father or
children or fields for my sake and for the sake of the gospel 30 who
will not receive in this age a hundred times as much—homes,
brothers, sisters, mothers, children, fields, all with persecutions—and in the age to come, eternal life. 31 But many who are
first will be last, and the last first."

THIRD PREDICTION OF JESUS' DEATH AND RESURRECTION

32 They were on the way, going up to Jerusalem. Jesus was going
ahead of them, and they were amazed, but those who followed
were afraid. He took the twelve aside again and began to tell
them what was going to happen to him. 33 "Look, we are going
up to Jerusalem, and the Son of Man will be handed over to the
chief priests and experts in the law. They will condemn him to
death and will turn him over to the Gentiles. 34 They will mock
him, spit on him, flog him severely, and kill him. Yet after three
days, he will rise again."

THE REQUEST OF JAMES AND JOHN

35 Then James and John, the sons of Zebedee, came to him
and said, "Teacher, we want you to do for us whatever we
ask." 36 He said to them, "What do you want me to do for you?"
37 They said to him, "Permit one of us to sit at your right hand
and the other at your left in your glory." 38 But Jesus said to
them, "You don't know what you are asking! Are you able to
drink the cup I drink or be baptized with the baptism I experience?" 39 They said to him, "We are able." Then Jesus said
to them, "You will drink the cup I drink, and you will be baptized with the baptism I experience, 40 but to sit at my right
or at my left is not mine to give. It is for those for whom it
has been prepared."

41 Now when the other ten heard this, they became angry
with James and John. 42 Jesus called them and said to them,
"You know that those who are recognized as rulers of the
Gentiles lord it over them, and those in high positions use
their authority over them. 43 But it is not this way among
you. Instead whoever wants to be great among you must be
your servant, 44 and whoever wants to be first among you
must be the slave of all. 45 For even the Son of Man did not
come to be served but to serve, and to give his life as a ransom for many."

REFLECT

What does this verse tell us about the character of God? Why is the servanthood of Jesus so significant?

LOVE TO GROW

SERVANT-LEADERSHIP

MARK 10:35–45

Sometimes I read the Bible as if I'm watching a movie. I want the good guy to win, and I'm secretly hoping that Jesus will suddenly burst forth and put the bad guys in their place. This is what the people of Jesus' day wanted—and, quite frankly, expected—their Savior to do. Instead, Jesus was a servant. This was almost incomprehensible to the Jews in the first century, including the disciples.

James and John asked Jesus not only for a favor but also for Jesus to show them preference by seating them at His right and His left. They were asking for places of prestige and power. These disciples had misunderstood what Jesus had been trying to teach them about His coming eternal kingdom.

> *"Whoever wants to be great among you must be your servant, and whoever wants to be first among you must be the slave of all. For even the Son of Man did not come to be served, but to serve, and to give his life as a ransom for many" (Mark 10:43–45).*

Being like Jesus, modeling His life and ministry, looks more like serving those in need than gaining widespread recognition. Jesus came to serve and surrender His life, not to gain fame or power. Living like Jesus, being selfless and having pure motives, takes dedication and practice, and the transformational power of the Holy Spirit in our lives.

Servant-leadership is expressed through the everyday routines of life. It's loving your kids and trying to model and teach Christlike behavior to them. It's supporting your spouse, being faithful in prayer and action to the covenant you share. It's encouraging friends. It's seeing the potential in people and working to develop their talents and skills. It's volunteering your time and expertise in your church or your community. It's doing tasks, however menial, because you see that they need to be done. It's leading the people in your sphere of influence with an extra measure of grace, mercy, and patience. It's bringing glory to God in every situation.

We are not perfect in our humanity or perfect in our faith, so we will never be perfect servant leaders. Thankfully, God doesn't call us to be perfect; He calls us to be faithful. Intentionally serving will breathe life into dead places. It will transform our homes, our businesses, our churches, and our communities. Let's strengthen the community of believers and bring the world to Christ by serving its people in His love.

HEALING BLIND BARTIMAEUS

46 They came to Jericho. As Jesus and his disciples and a large
crowd were leaving Jericho, Bartimaeus the son of Timaeus, a
blind beggar, was sitting by the road. 47 When he heard that it
was Jesus the Nazarene, he began to shout, "Jesus, Son of David, have mercy on me!" 48 Many scolded him to get him to be
quiet, but he shouted all the more, "Son of David, have mercy
on me!" 49 Jesus stopped and said, "Call him." So they called the
blind man and said to him, "Have courage! Get up! He is calling
you." 50 He threw off his cloak, jumped up, and came to Jesus.
51 Then Jesus said to him, "What do you want me to do for you?"
The blind man replied, "Rabbi, let me see again." 52 Jesus said to
him, "Go, your faith has healed you." Immediately he regained
his sight and followed him on the road.

THE TRIUMPHAL ENTRY

11 Now as they approached Jerusalem, near Bethphage and Bethany, at the Mount of Olives, Jesus sent two of his disciples 2 and
said to them, "Go to the village ahead of you. As soon as you enter
it, you will find a colt tied there that has never been ridden. Untie it and bring it here. 3 If anyone says to you, 'Why are you doing
this?' say, 'The Lord needs it and will send it back here soon.'" 4 So
they went and found a colt tied at a door, outside in the street,
and untied it. 5 Some people standing there said to them, "What
are you doing, untying that colt?" 6 They replied as Jesus had told
them, and the bystanders let them go. 7 Then they brought the colt
to Jesus, threw their cloaks on it, and he sat on it. 8 Many spread
their cloaks on the road and others spread branches they had
cut in the fields. 9 Both those who went ahead and those who followed kept shouting, ***"Hosanna! Blessed is the one who comes in the***
name of the Lord! 10 Blessed is the coming kingdom of our father
David! Hosanna in the highest!" 11 Then Jesus entered Jerusalem
and went to the temple. And after looking around at everything,
he went out to Bethany with the twelve since it was already late.

CURSING OF THE FIG TREE

12 Now the next day, as they went out from Bethany, he was hungry.
13 After noticing in the distance a fig tree with leaves, he went to see
if he could find any fruit on it. When he came to it he found nothing but leaves, for it was not the season for figs. 14 He said to it, "May
no one ever eat fruit from you again." And his disciples heard it.

CLEANSING THE TEMPLE

15 Then they came to Jerusalem. Jesus entered the temple area and
began to drive out those who were selling and buying in the temple
courts. He turned over the tables of the money changers and the
chairs of those selling doves, 16 and he would not permit anyone
to carry merchandise through the temple courts. 17 Then he began
to teach them and said, "Is it not written: '***My house will be called***
a house of prayer for all nations'? But you have turned it into ***a den***
of robbers!" 18 The chief priests and the experts in the law heard
it and they considered how they could assassinate him, for they
feared him, because the whole crowd was amazed by his teaching.
19 When evening came, Jesus and his disciples went out of the city.

GOD'S HEART FOR THE NATIONS

Mark 11:17

Then he began to teach them and said, "Is it not written: 'My house will be called a house of prayer for all nations'? But you have turned it into a den of robbers!"

THE WITHERED FIG TREE

20 In the morning as they passed by, they saw the fig tree withered from the roots. 21 Peter remembered and said to him, "Rabbi,
look! The fig tree you cursed has withered." 22 Jesus said to them,
"Have faith in God. 23 I tell you the truth, if someone says to this
mountain, 'Be lifted up and thrown into the sea,' and does not
doubt in his heart but believes that what he says will happen, it
will be done for him. 24 For this reason I tell you, whatever you
pray and ask for, believe that you have received it, and it will
be yours. 25 Whenever you stand praying, if you have anything
against anyone, forgive him, so that your Father in heaven will
also forgive you your sins."§

THE AUTHORITY OF JESUS

27 They came again to Jerusalem. While Jesus was walking in the
temple courts, the chief priests, the experts in the law, and the
elders came up to him 28 and said, "By what authority are you
doing these things? Or who gave you this authority to do these
things?" 29 Jesus said to them, "I will ask you one question. Answer me and I will tell you by what authority I do these things:
30 John's baptism—was it from heaven or from people? Answer
me." 31 They discussed with one another, saying, "If we say, 'From
heaven,' he will say, 'Then why did you not believe him?' 32 But if
we say, 'From people—'" (they feared the crowd, for they all considered John to be truly a prophet). 33 So they answered Jesus,
"We don't know." Then Jesus said to them, "Neither will I tell you
by what authority I am doing these things."

THE PARABLE OF THE TENANTS

12 Then he began to speak to them in parables: "A man
planted a vineyard. He put a fence around it, dug a pit
for its winepress, and built a watchtower. Then he leased it
to tenant farmers and went on a journey. 2 At harvest time
he sent a slave to the tenants to collect from them his portion of the crop. 3 But those tenants seized his slave, beat him,
and sent him away empty-handed. 4 So he sent another slave
to them again. This one they struck on the head and treated
outrageously. 5 He sent another, and that one they killed. This
happened to many others, some of whom were beaten, others killed. 6 He had one left, his one dear son. Finally he sent
him to them, saying, 'They will respect my son.' 7 But those tenants said to one another, 'This is the heir. Come, let's kill him
and the inheritance will be ours!' 8 So they seized him, killed
him, and threw his body out of the vineyard. 9 What then will
the owner of the vineyard do? He will come and destroy those
tenants and give the vineyard to others. 10 Have you not read
this scripture:

'***The stone the builders rejected has***
become the cornerstone.
11 ***This is from the Lord, and it***
is marvelous in our eyes'?"

12 Now they wanted to arrest him (but they feared the crowd),
because they realized that he told this parable against them. So
they left him and went away.

PAYING TAXES TO CAESAR

13 Then they sent some of the Pharisees and Herodians to trap
him with his own words. 14 When they came they said to him,
"Teacher, we know that you are truthful and do not court anyone's favor, because you show no partiality but teach the way
of God in accordance with the truth. Is it right to pay taxes to
Caesar or not? Should we pay or shouldn't we?" 15 But he saw
through their hypocrisy and said to them, "Why are you testing me? Bring me a denarius and let me look at it." 16 So they
brought one, and he said to them, "Whose image is this, and
whose inscription?" They replied, "Caesar's." 17 Then Jesus said
to them, "Give to Caesar the things that are Caesar's, and to
God the things that are God's." And they were utterly amazed
at him.

MARRIAGE AND THE RESURRECTION

18 Sadducees (who say there is no resurrection) also came to
him and asked him, 19 "Teacher, Moses wrote for us: '***If a man's***
brother dies and leaves a wife but no children, that man must
marry the widow and father children for his brother.' 20 There
were seven brothers. The first one married, and when he died
he had no children. 21 The second married her and died without
any children, and likewise the third. 22 None of the seven had
children. Finally, the woman died too. 23 In the resurrection,
when they rise again, whose wife will she be? For all seven had
married her." 24 Jesus said to them, "Aren't you deceived for this
reason, because you don't know the scriptures or the power of
God? 25 For when they rise from the dead, they neither marry
nor are given in marriage, but are like angels in heaven. 26 Now
as for the dead being raised, have you not read in the book of
Moses, in the passage about the bush, how God said to him,
'***I am the God of Abraham, the God of Isaac, and the God of Ja-***
cob'? 27 He is not the God of the dead but of the living. You are
badly mistaken!"

THE GREATEST COMMANDMENT

28 Now one of the experts in the law came and heard them debating. When he saw that Jesus answered them well, he asked
him, "Which commandment is the most important of all?"
29 Jesus answered, "The most important is: '***Listen, Israel, the***
Lord our God, the Lord is one. 30 ***Love the Lord your God with all***
your heart, with all your soul, with all your mind, and with all
your strength.' 31 The second is: '***Love your neighbor as yourself.***'
There is no other commandment greater than these." 32 The expert in the law said to him, "That is true, Teacher; you are right
to say that ***he is one, and there is no one else besides him.*** 33 And
to love him with all your heart, with all your mind, and with all
your strength and ***to love your neighbor as yourself*** is more important than all burnt offerings and sacrifices." 34 When Jesus
saw that he had answered thoughtfully, he said to him, "You
are not far from the kingdom of God." Then no one dared any
longer to question him.

LOVE TO GROW

LOVE GOD AND LOVE OTHERS

MARK 12:28–31

When we think of the word *commandment*, we may think of something we don't want to do but have to do. Rules from our parents, teachers, or bosses may spring to mind. God's commands, however, not only bring about our good, but they promote His glory. We can be confident that whatever He asks us to do, He will supply what we need to do it.

In Mark 12:28–31, we read that the two greatest commandments are to love God and love others.

Throughout the pages of Scripture, God depicts His relationship to us as a marriage. In a healthy marriage, a spouse doesn't want their partner to love them under compulsion, or because they think their partner must earn their love. They want their partner to love them because they desire to love them. It's the same with God. He isn't looking for His people to heartlessly carry out a set of instructions so they can check off a box. He wants His people to experience the joy of knowing Him rooted in a loving relationship with Him.

We love because God first loved us. As we learn about how incredible His love for us is, and we allow that love to change our lives, we find ourselves falling more and more in love with God.

This loving relationship lays the foundation for how we carry out the second commandment to love others. Often what holds us back is focus on ourselves. We worry about whether our needs will be met, so we selfishly pursue personal satisfaction at the expense of serving others' needs.

As we grow in our relationship with God, we learn that ultimate satisfaction is found in Christ. We don't hunt attention from others when we experience acceptance from God. We don't chase security from a person or a thing when we know that we are secure in Him. As a result, we are free to love others in a way that would otherwise be impossible. We can love people even if we get nothing in return. Why? Because our relationship with Christ fills us with the unimaginable wealth of intimacy with God.

THE MESSIAH: DAVID'S SON AND LORD

35 While Jesus was teaching in the temple courts, he said, "How
is it that the experts in the law say that the Christ is David's son?
36 David himself, by the Holy Spirit, said,

'The Lord said to my lord,
"Sit at my right hand,
until I put your enemies under your feet."'

37 If David himself calls him 'Lord,' how can he be his son?" And
the large crowd was listening to him with delight.

WARNINGS ABOUT EXPERTS IN THE LAW

38 In his teaching Jesus also said, "Watch out for the experts in
the law. They like walking around in long robes and elaborate
greetings in the marketplaces, 39 and the best seats in the synagogues and the places of honor at banquets. 40 They devour widows' property, and as a show make long prayers. These men will
receive a more severe punishment."

THE WIDOW'S OFFERING

41 Then he sat down opposite the offering box, and watched the
crowd putting coins into it. Many rich people were throwing in
large amounts. 42 And a poor widow came and put in two small
copper coins, worth less than a penny. 43 He called his disciples
and said to them, "I tell you the truth, this poor widow has put
more into the offering box than all the others. 44 For they all gave
out of their wealth. But she, out of her poverty, put in what she
had to live on, everything she had."

THE DESTRUCTION OF THE TEMPLE

13 Now as Jesus was going out of the temple courts, one of
his disciples said to him, "Teacher, look at these tremendous stones and buildings!" 2 Jesus said to him, "Do you see these
great buildings? Not one stone will be left on another. All will
be torn down!"

SIGNS OF THE END OF THE AGE

3 So while he was sitting on the Mount of Olives opposite the
temple, Peter, James, John, and Andrew asked him privately,
4 "Tell us, when will these things happen? And what will be the
sign that all these things are about to take place?" 5 Jesus began
to say to them, "Watch out that no one misleads you. 6 Many will
come in my name, saying, 'I am he,' and they will mislead many.
7 When you hear of wars and rumors of wars, do not be alarmed.
These things must happen, but the end is still to come. 8 For nation will rise up in arms against nation, and kingdom against
kingdom. There will be earthquakes in various places, and there
will be famines. These are but the beginning of birth pains.

PERSECUTION OF DISCIPLES

9 "You must watch out for yourselves. You will be handed over to
councils and beaten in the synagogues. You will stand before governors and kings because of me, as a witness to them. 10 First the
gospel must be preached to all nations. 11 When they arrest you
and hand you over for trial, do not worry about what to speak. But

GOD'S HEART FOR THE NATIONS

Mark 13:10

"First the gospel must be preached to all nations."

say whatever is given you at that time, for it is not you speaking,
but the Holy Spirit. 12 Brother will hand over brother to death,
and a father his child. Children will rise against parents and have
them put to death. 13 You will be hated by everyone because of
my name. But the one who endures to the end will be saved.

THE ABOMINATION OF DESOLATION

14 "But when you see *the abomination of desolation* standing
where it should not be" (let the reader understand), "then
those in Judea must flee to the mountains. 15 The one on the
roof must not come down or go inside to take anything out
of his house. 16 The one in the field must not turn back to get
his cloak. 17 Woe to those who are pregnant and to those who
are nursing their babies in those days! 18 Pray that it may not
be in winter. 19 For in those days there will be suffering unlike
anything that has happened from the beginning of the creation that God created until now, or ever will happen. 20 And if
the Lord had not cut short those days, no one would be saved.
But because of the elect, whom he chose, he has cut them
short. 21 Then if anyone says to you, 'Look, here is the Christ!'
or 'Look, there he is!' do not believe him. 22 For false messiahs
and false prophets will appear and perform signs and wonders
to deceive, if possible, the elect. 23 Be careful! I have told you
everything ahead of time.

THE ARRIVAL OF THE SON OF MAN

24 "But in those days, after that suffering, *the sun will be darkened
and the moon will not give its light;* 25 *the stars will be falling from
heaven, and the powers in the heavens will be shaken.* 26 Then everyone will see *the Son of Man arriving in the clouds* with great
power and glory. 27 Then he will send angels and they will gather his elect from the four winds, from the ends of the earth to
the ends of heaven.

THE PARABLE OF THE FIG TREE

28 "Learn this parable from the fig tree: Whenever its branch becomes tender and puts out its leaves, you know that summer
is near. 29 So also you, when you see these things happening,
know that he is near, right at the door. 30 I tell you the truth, this
generation will not pass away until all these things take place.
31 Heaven and earth will pass away, but my words will never pass
away.

BE READY!

32 "But as for that day or hour no one knows it—neither the angels in heaven, nor the Son—except the Father. 33 Watch out! Stay
alert! For you do not know when the time will come. 34 It is like
a man going on a journey. He left his house and put his slaves in
charge, assigning to each his work, and commanded the doorkeeper to stay alert. 35 Stay alert, then, because you do not know
when the owner of the house will return—whether during evening, at midnight, when the rooster crows, or at dawn—36 or else
he might find you asleep when he returns suddenly. 37 What I
say to you I say to everyone: Stay alert!"

THE PLOT AGAINST JESUS

14 Two days before the Passover and the Feast of Unleavened
Bread, the chief priests and the experts in the law were
trying to find a way to arrest Jesus by stealth and kill him. 2 For
they said, "Not during the feast, so there won't be a riot among
the people."

JESUS' ANOINTING

3 Now while Jesus was in Bethany at the house of Simon the leper, reclining at the table, a woman came with an alabaster jar of
costly aromatic oil from pure nard. After breaking open the jar,
she poured it on his head. 4 But some who were present indig-
nantly said to one another, "Why this waste of expensive ointment? 5 It could have been sold for more than 300 silver coins
and the money given to the poor!" So they spoke angrily to her.
6 But Jesus said, "Leave her alone. Why are you bothering her?
She has done a good service for me. 7 For you will always have
the poor with you, and you can do good for them whenever you
want. But you will not always have me! 8 She did what she could.
She anointed my body beforehand for burial. 9 I tell you the truth,
wherever the gospel is proclaimed in the whole world, what she
has done will also be told in memory of her."

THE PLAN TO BETRAY JESUS

10 Then Judas Iscariot, one of the twelve, went to the chief priests
to betray Jesus into their hands. 11 When they heard this, they
were delighted and promised to give him money. So Judas began looking for an opportunity to betray him.

THE PASSOVER

12 Now on the first day of the feast of Unleavened Bread, when the
Passover lamb is sacrificed, Jesus' disciples said to him, "Where
do you want us to prepare for you to eat the Passover?" 13 He sent
two of his disciples and told them, "Go into the city, and a man
carrying a jar of water will meet you. Follow him. 14 Wherever he
enters, tell the owner of the house, 'The Teacher says, "Where
is my guest room where I may eat the Passover with my disciples?"' 15 He will show you a large room upstairs, furnished and
ready. Make preparations for us there." 16 So the disciples left,
went into the city, and found things just as he had told them,
and they prepared the Passover.

17 Then, when it was evening, he came to the house with the
twelve. 18 While they were at the table eating, Jesus said, "I tell
you the truth, one of you eating with me will betray me." 19 They
were distressed, and one by one said to him, "Surely not I?" 20 He
said to them, "It is one of the twelve, one who dips his hand with
me into the bowl. 21 For the Son of Man will go as it is written
about him, but woe to that man by whom the Son of Man is betrayed! It would be better for him if he had never been born."

THE LORD'S SUPPER

22 While they were eating, he took bread, and after giving thanks
he broke it, gave it to them, and said, "Take it. This is my body."
23 And after taking the cup and giving thanks, he gave it to them,

and they all drank from it. 24 He said to them, "This is my blood,
the blood of the covenant, that is poured out for many. 25 I tell
you the truth, I will no longer drink of the fruit of the vine until that day when I drink it new in the kingdom of God." 26 After
singing a hymn, they went out to the Mount of Olives.

THE PREDICTION OF PETER'S DENIAL

27 Then Jesus said to them, "You will all fall away, for it is written,
'I will strike the shepherd,
and the sheep will be scattered.'
28 But after I am raised, I will go ahead of you into Galilee." 29 Peter said to him, "Even if they all fall away, I will not!" 30 Jesus
said to him, "I tell you the truth, today—this very night—before
a rooster crows twice, you will deny me three times." 31 But Peter
insisted emphatically, "Even if I must die with you, I will never
deny you." And all of them said the same thing.

GETHSEMANE

32 Then they went to a place called Gethsemane, and Jesus said
to his disciples, "Sit here while I pray." 33 He took Peter, James,
and John with him, and became very troubled and distressed.
34 He said to them, "My soul is deeply grieved, even to the point
of death. Remain here and stay alert." 35 Going a little farther, he
threw himself to the ground and prayed that if it were possible the
hour would pass from him. 36 He said, "*Abba,* Father, all things are
possible for you. Take this cup away from me. Yet not what I will,
but what you will." 37 Then he came and found them sleeping, and
said to Peter, "Simon, are you sleeping? Couldn't you stay awake for
one hour? 38 Stay awake and pray that you will not fall into temptation. The spirit is willing, but the flesh is weak." 39 He went away
again and prayed the same thing. 40 When he came again he found
them sleeping; they could not keep their eyes open. And they
did not know what to tell him. 41 He came a third time and said
to them, "Are you still sleeping and resting? Enough of that! The
hour has come. Look, the Son of Man is betrayed into the hands
of sinners. 42 Get up, let us go. Look! My betrayer is approaching!"

BETRAYAL AND ARREST

43 Right away, while Jesus was still speaking, Judas, one of the
twelve, arrived. With him came a crowd armed with swords and
clubs, sent by the chief priests and experts in the law and elders.
44 (Now the betrayer had given them a sign, saying, "The one I
kiss is the man. Arrest him and lead him away under guard.")
45 When Judas arrived, he went up to Jesus immediately and said,
"Rabbi!" and kissed him. 46 Then they took hold of him and arrested him. 47 One of the bystanders drew his sword and struck
the high priest's slave, cutting off his ear. 48 Jesus said to them,
"Have you come with swords and clubs to arrest me like you
would an outlaw? 49 Day after day I was with you, teaching in the
temple courts, yet you did not arrest me. But this has happened
so that the scriptures would be fulfilled." 50 Then all the disciples left him and fled. 51 A young man was following him, wearing only a linen cloth. They tried to arrest him, 52 but he ran off
naked, leaving his linen cloth behind.

REFLECT

Why do you think Jesus had compassion on the guard who lost his ear? What does this show about the character of Jesus?

CONDEMNED BY THE SANHEDRIN

53 Then they led Jesus to the high priest, and all the chief priests
and elders and experts in the law came together. 54 And Peter had
followed him from a distance, up to the high priest's courtyard.
He was sitting with the guards and warming himself by the fire.
55 The chief priests and the whole Sanhedrin were looking for evidence against Jesus so that they could put him to death, but they
did not find anything. 56 Many gave false testimony against him,
but their testimony did not agree. 57 Some stood up and gave this
false testimony against him: 58 "We heard him say, 'I will destroy
this temple made with hands and in three days build another not
made with hands.'" 59 Yet even on this point their testimony did not
agree. 60 Then the high priest stood up before them and asked Jesus,
"Have you no answer? What is this that they are testifying against
you?" 61 But he was silent and did not answer. Again the high priest
questioned him, "Are you the Christ, the Son of the Blessed One?"
62 "I am," said Jesus, "and you will see *the Son of Man sitting at the
right hand* of the Power and *coming with the clouds of heaven*." 63 Then
the high priest tore his clothes and said, "Why do we still need witnesses? 64 You have heard the blasphemy! What is your verdict?"
They all condemned him as deserving death. 65 Then some began
to spit on him, and to blindfold him, and to strike him with their
fists, saying, "Prophesy!" The guards also took him and beat him.

PETER'S DENIALS

66 Now while Peter was below in the courtyard, one of the high
priest's slave girls came by. 67 When she saw Peter warming himself, she looked directly at him and said, "You also were with that
Nazarene, Jesus." 68 But he denied it: "I don't even understand
what you're talking about!" Then he went out to the gateway,
and a rooster crowed. 69 When the slave girl saw him, she began
again to say to the bystanders, "This man is one of them." 70 But
he denied it again. A short time later the bystanders again said
to Peter, "You must be one of them, because you are also a Galilean." 71 Then he began to curse, and he swore with an oath, "I
do not know this man you are talking about!" 72 Immediately a
rooster crowed a second time. Then Peter remembered what
Jesus had said to him: "Before a rooster crows twice, you will
deny me three times." And he broke down and wept.

JESUS BROUGHT BEFORE PILATE

15 Early in the morning, after forming a plan, the chief priests
with the elders and the experts in the law and the whole
Sanhedrin tied Jesus up, led him away, and handed him over to
Pilate. 2 So Pilate asked him, "Are you the king of the Jews?" He
replied, "You say so." 3 Then the chief priests began to accuse him
repeatedly. 4 So Pilate asked him again, "Have you nothing to say?
See how many charges they are bringing against you!" 5 But Jesus
made no further reply, so that Pilate was amazed.

JESUS AND BARABBAS

6 During the feast it was customary to release one prisoner to
the people, whomever they requested. 7 A man named Barabbas was imprisoned with rebels who had committed murder

during an insurrection. 8 Then the crowd came up and began to ask Pilate to release a prisoner for them, as was his custom. 9 So Pilate asked them, "Do you want me to release the king of the Jews for you?" 10 (For he knew that the chief priests had handed him over because of envy.) 11 But the chief priests stirred up the crowd to have him release Barabbas instead. 12 So Pilate spoke to them again, "Then what do you want me to do with the one you call king of the Jews?" 13 They shouted back, "Crucify him!" 14 Pilate asked them, "Why? What has he done wrong?" But they shouted more insistently, "Crucify him!" 15 Because he wanted to satisfy the crowd, Pilate released Barabbas for them. Then, after he had Jesus flogged, he handed him over to be crucified.

JESUS IS MOCKED

16 So the soldiers led him into the palace (that is, the governor's residence) and called together the whole cohort. 17 They put a purple cloak on him and after braiding a crown of thorns, they put it on him. 18 They began to salute him: "Hail, king of the Jews!" 19 Again and again they struck him on the head with a staff and spit on him. Then they knelt down and paid homage to him. 20 When they had finished mocking him, they stripped him of the purple cloak and put his own clothes back on him. Then they led him away to crucify him.

THE CRUCIFIXION

21 The soldiers forced a passerby to carry his cross, Simon of Cyrene, who was coming in from the country (he was the father of Alexander and Rufus). 22 They brought Jesus to a place called Golgotha (which is translated, "Place of the Skull"). 23 They offered him wine mixed with myrrh, but he did not take it. 24 Then they crucified him and *divided his clothes, throwing dice* for them, to decide what each would take. 25 It was nine o'clock in the morning when they crucified him. 26 The inscription of the charge against him read, "The king of the Jews." 27 And they crucified two outlaws with him, one on his right and one on his left.‖ 29 Those who passed by defamed him, shaking their heads and saying, "Aha! You who can destroy the temple and rebuild it in three days, 30 save yourself and come down from the cross!" 31 In the same way even the chief priests—together with the experts in the law—were mocking him among themselves: "He saved others, but he cannot save himself! 32 Let the Christ, the king of Israel, come down from the cross now, that we may see and believe!" Those who were crucified with him also spoke abusively to him.

JESUS' DEATH

33 Now when it was noon, darkness came over the whole land until three in the afternoon. 34 Around three o'clock Jesus cried out with a loud voice, *"Eloi, Eloi, lema sabachthani?"* which means, ***"My God, my God, why have you forsaken me?"*** 35 When some of the bystanders heard it they said, "Listen, he is calling for Elijah!" 36 Then someone ran, filled a sponge with sour wine, put it on a stick, and gave it to him to drink, saying, "Leave him alone! Let's see if Elijah will come to take him down!" 37 But Jesus cried out with a loud voice and breathed his last. 38 And the temple

curtain was torn in two, from top to bottom. 39 Now when the
centurion, who stood in front of him, saw how he died, he said,
"Truly this man was God's Son!" 40 There were also women, watching from a distance. Among them were Mary Magdalene, and
Mary the mother of James the younger and of Joses, and Salome.
41 When he was in Galilee, they had followed him and given him
support. Many other women who had come up with him to Jerusalem were there too.

JESUS' BURIAL

42 Now when evening had already come, since it was the day of
preparation (that is, the day before the Sabbath), 43 Joseph of
Arimathea, a highly regarded member of the council, who was
himself looking forward to the kingdom of God, went boldly to
Pilate and asked for the body of Jesus. 44 Pilate was surprised that
he was already dead. He called the centurion and asked him if he
had been dead for some time. 45 When Pilate was informed by the
centurion, he gave the body to Joseph. 46 After Joseph bought a
linen cloth and took down the body, he wrapped it in the linen
and placed it in a tomb cut out of the rock. Then he rolled a stone
across the entrance of the tomb. 47 Mary Magdalene and Mary
the mother of Joses saw where the body was placed.

THE RESURRECTION

16 When the Sabbath was over, Mary Magdalene, Mary the
mother of James, and Salome bought aromatic spices so
that they might go and anoint him. 2 And very early on the first
day of the week, at sunrise, they went to the tomb. 3 They had
been asking each other, "Who will roll away the stone for us from
the entrance to the tomb?" 4 But when they looked up, they saw
that the stone, which was very large, had been rolled back. 5 Then
as they went into the tomb, they saw a young man dressed in
a white robe sitting on the right side; and they were alarmed.
6 But he said to them, "Do not be alarmed. You are looking for
Jesus the Nazarene, who was crucified. He has been raised! He
is not here. Look, there is the place where they laid him. 7 But
go, tell his disciples, even Peter, that he is going ahead of you
into Galilee. You will see him there, just as he told you." 8 Then
they went out and ran from the tomb, for terror and bewilder-
ment had seized them. And they said nothing to anyone, because they were afraid.¶

REFLECT

How would you have responded to the angels' message at the tomb? Why was this such a significant moment for the women who went to anoint Jesus?

THE LONGER ENDING OF MARK

9 [[Early on the first day of the week, after he arose, he appeared
first to Mary Magdalene, from whom he had driven out seven demons. 10 She went out and told those who were with him, while
they were mourning and weeping. 11 And when they heard that
he was alive and had been seen by her, they did not believe.

12 After this he appeared in a different form to two of them
while they were on their way to the country. 13 They went back
and told the rest, but they did not believe them. 14 Then he appeared to the eleven themselves, while they were eating, and he
rebuked them for their unbelief and hardness of heart, because
they did not believe those who had seen him resurrected. 15 He

LOVE TO GROW

HE IS NOT HERE

MARK 16:1–8

Imagine for a moment . . .

The man you have been following, a man you believe to be God, is now in the hands of the Roman officials. At His public trial, you push through the masses of people to gain sight of your Savior, only to find Him bruised and battered. The crowd screams, "crucify Him!" Though no one can find fault in Him, the Roman governor, Pilate, caves. He sentences Jesus to die, and Roman soldiers waste no time in whisking Him away. You follow as fast as you can.

You come upon the governor's headquarters. Pressing your ear to the walls you hear the soldiers' insults. Peeking through a window, you see Jesus, utterly humiliated, standing in front of those He came to save. A crown of thorns sits atop His head and streams of blood pour down His face. Hit after hit, blow after blow, the Romans beat Him and shout, "Hail, king of the Jews!" (Mark 15:18).

Confusion rattles your mind. With your own eyes you saw Jesus feed thousands with only a handful of bread and fish. You were there as He raised a dead man to life, and you watched him walked out of his tomb. You witnessed Jesus give blind men sight and lame men the ability to walk. Why is He just standing there?

Next, soldiers lead Him from the governor's headquarters to a hillside. They hang Him on a cross. As they nail His hands and feet to the wood, His screams of pain pierce your ears and break your heart. Naked and dying, Jesus speaks His final words: "My God, my God, why have you forsaken me?" (Mark 15:34). With that, He breathes His last breath.

Devastation overwhelms you. He was the One who was supposed to save you from death! He was the One who brought life. You are hopeless, confused, and grief stricken. Jesus has been killed; God has died.

Yet, here we are, two thousand years later, and we know how the story ends. Nothing could keep Him in that grave, not even death!

"He has been raised! He is not here" (Mark 16:6).

Suddenly, hopelessness is replaced with abundant hope, confusion with clarity, and grief with joy. Christ is risen! His resurrection means the pain and humiliation He endured was for a purpose. Jesus, the Son of God came to earth as a man so you could spend eternity with Him. He did it all to have a relationship with you. Overcoming death, He rose to life. Overcoming death, He offers you new life.

said to them, "Go into all the world and preach the gospel to every creature. 16 The one who believes and is baptized will be saved,
but the one who does not believe will be condemned. 17 These
signs will accompany those who believe: In my name they will
drive out demons; they will speak in new languages; 18 they will
pick up snakes with their hands, and whatever poison they drink
will not harm them; they will place their hands on the sick and
they will be well." 19 After the Lord Jesus had spoken to them,
he was taken up into heaven and sat down at the right hand of
God. 20 They went out and proclaimed everywhere, while the
Lord worked with them and confirmed the word through the
accompanying signs.]]

FOR THE *Son* OF *Man* CAME TO *Seek* AND TO *Save* THE *lost*

MEMORY VERSE

"For the Son of Man came to seek and to save the lost."

Luke 19:10

Luke

INTRODUCTION

Jesus' Humanity

The Gospel of Luke offers a unique perspective on the life of Christ. Luke did not meet Jesus in person, yet he followed Him. Luke was a physician, an intellectual who was concerned with sharing all he could about the life of Christ with his friend Theophilus. Luke displays the humanity of Jesus, the Sonship of Jesus, and the care, concern, and power of Jesus.

This book shows a variety of events in Jesus' life. The first two chapters emphasize the Old Testament promises of the coming Messiah, and 3:1—4:13 demonstrate that Jesus was and is the Messiah. The next section, 4:14—9:50, shows Jesus' power and His teaching. The conflict between Jesus and the Jewish leadership makes up the next section, 9:51—19:44. The final section, 19:45—24:53, describes the Passion of Christ and the events surrounding His death and resurrection.

Tradition has credited Luke with the authorship of this Gospel. As the only Gentile author of a New Testament book, Luke was a companion of Paul on some of his missionary journeys. Luke is also credited with authoring the Book of Acts, and it is assumed that the two were written around the same time. Since the Book of Acts records Paul's imprisonment in Rome, some scholars estimate that Acts was written sometime after A.D. 62. This dates the Book of Luke between A.D. 64 and A.D. 66.

Luke recorded a significant number of Jesus' miracles and makes strong arguments for Jesus' Messiahship. The Book of Luke is a great encouragement for us to love God greatly because of its unique portrayal of Jesus' life and ministry. Luke provided details of Jesus' life that allow us to see His humanity and His deity, displaying both His great compassion for His people and His power over evil.

Germany

OFFICIAL LANGUAGE
German
POPULATION
83,265,000
UNREACHED POPULATION
3,398,000
PROFESSING CHRISTIANS
65.4%

Steffie's Home

Say a Prayer Today

Pray for Steffie as she continues to grow in her life of faith. Pray she would have confidence to share with others the way a friend shared with her about the goodness and faithfulness of God.

HISTORY BIT

Christianity was established in Germany as early as the third century A.D. and became the dominant religion in the region at the end of the fifth century under the Frankish King, Clovis. Germany was the center stage for the Protestant Reformation, and was home to many influential reformers, such as Martin Luther.*

Source Information:
https://joshuaproject.net/countries/GM
*David B. Barrett, World Christian Encyclopedia (New York, NY: Oxford University Press, 1982), 315.

STEFFIE'S STORY

Jesus came to save the lost, and I was one of them. Once again, I found myself scattered and broken, leaving a relationship behind me. This time it ended in divorce with two little kids in tow. I'm reminded of the deep hurt as I look back at how broken and lonely I was, chasing after what I thought would fill me.

I did not come from a Christian home. I grew up in Germany looking for love and acceptance in new relationships. They provided relief and distraction from overwhelming assignments and my busy schedule. I looked for meaning and comfort in every self-help and new age book I could find. I felt like I was swimming in a stormy pool, desperately trying not to drown. I wanted to be loved and belong, but I was completely lost.

Then Jesus found me! A fellow kindergarten mom told me that we are all sinners, but that Jesus came for the sinners to save them. God knew that I was so deeply entrenched in wrong thinking, attitude, and lifestyle that He pulled me toward Himself slowly and carefully. Looking back, I can see He was careful not to scare me away. He saved me from my own destructive ways and led me gently in the opposite direction.

He did that by leading me to a church where I met loving people who showed compassion for me in my suffering while confronting my sin. Step by step, He dragged me out of the pit. I experienced real hope and rest for the first time in my life. I was lost, but I have been found and finally feel that I really belong. Jesus indeed came to save the lost. He found me, and I have never been the same.

6 WEEK READING PLAN

LOVE HIS WORD

	MONDAY	TUESDAY	WEDNESDAY	THURSDAY	FRIDAY
1	Luke 1:1-45	Luke 1:46-80	Luke 2	Luke 3	Luke 4
	SOAP Luke 1:1-4	SOAP Luke 1:46-48	SOAP Luke 2:36-38	SOAP Luke 3:16-17	SOAP Luke 4:42-44
2	Luke 5	Luke 6	Luke 7	Luke 8:1-25	Luke 8:26-56
	SOAP Luke 5:16	SOAP Luke 6:9-10	SOAP Luke 7:13-15	SOAP Luke 8:1-3	SOAP Luke 8:47-48
3	Luke 9:1-36	Luke 9:37-62	Luke 10	Luke 11	Luke 12:1-34
	SOAP Luke 9:16-17	SOAP Luke 9:46-48	SOAP Luke 10:22	SOAP Luke 11:34-36	SOAP Luke 12:6-7
4	Luke 12:35-59	Luke 13	Luke 14	Luke 15	Luke 16
	SOAP Luke 12:48	SOAP Luke 13:18-19	SOAP Luke 14:13-14	SOAP Luke 15:22-24	SOAP Luke 16:10-11
5	Luke 17	Luke 18	Luke 19	Luke 20	Luke 21
	SOAP Luke 17:3-4	SOAP Luke 18:41-43	SOAP Luke 19:10	SOAP Luke 20:17-18	SOAP Luke 21:36
6	Luke 22:1-38	Luke 22:39-71	Luke 23:1-25	Luke 23:26-56	Luke 24
	SOAP Luke 22:28-30	SOAP Luke 22:69-70	SOAP Luke 23:11-12	SOAP Luke 23:42-43	SOAP Luke 24:50-51

EXPLANATORY PREFACE

1 Now many have undertaken to compile an account of the
things that have been fulfilled among us, 2 like the accounts
passed on to us by those who were eyewitnesses and servants
of the word from the beginning. 3 So it seemed good to me as
well, because I have followed all things carefully from the beginning, to write an orderly account for you, most excellent
Theophilus, 4 so that you may know for certain the things you
were taught.

BIRTH ANNOUNCEMENT OF JOHN THE BAPTIST

5 During the reign of Herod king of Judea, there lived a priest
named Zechariah who belonged to the priestly division of Abijah, and he had a wife named Elizabeth, who was a descendant of
Aaron. 6 They were both righteous in the sight of God, following
all the commandments and ordinances of the Lord blamelessly.
7 But they did not have a child, because Elizabeth was barren,
and they were both very old.

8 Now while Zechariah was serving as priest before God when
his division was on duty, 9 he was chosen by lot, according to
the custom of the priesthood, to enter the Holy Place of the
Lord and burn incense. 10 Now the whole crowd of people were
praying outside at the hour of the incense offering. 11 An angel
of the Lord, standing on the right side of the altar of incense,
appeared to him. 12 And Zechariah, visibly shaken when he saw
the angel, was seized with fear. 13 But the angel said to him, "Do
not be afraid, Zechariah, for your prayer has been heard, and
your wife Elizabeth will bear you a son; you will name him John.
14 Joy and gladness will come to you, and many will rejoice at his
birth, 15 for he will be great in the sight of the Lord. He must
never drink wine or strong drink, and he will be filled with the
Holy Spirit, even before his birth. 16 He will turn many of the
people of Israel to the Lord their God. 17 And he will go as forerunner before the Lord in the spirit and power of Elijah, to turn
the hearts of the fathers back to their children and the disobedient to the wisdom of the just, to make ready for the Lord a
people prepared for him."

18 Zechariah said to the angel, "How can I be sure of this? For I
am an old man, and my wife is old as well." 19 The angel answered
him, "I am Gabriel, who stands in the presence of God, and I was
sent to speak to you and to bring you this good news. 20 And now,
because you did not believe my words, which will be fulfilled
in their time, you will be silent, unable to speak, until the day
these things take place."

21 Now the people were waiting for Zechariah, and they began
to wonder why he was delayed in the Holy Place. 22 When he
came out, he was not able to speak to them. They realized that
he had seen a vision in the Holy Place, because he was making
signs to them and remained unable to speak. 23 When his time
of service was over, he went to his home.

24 After some time his wife Elizabeth became pregnant, and
for five months she kept herself in seclusion. She said, 25 "This
is what the Lord has done for me at the time when he has been
gracious to me, to take away my disgrace among people."

REFLECT

When has God looked with favor on you like He did with Elizabeth? How does His grace to Elizabeth and Zechariah show His heart for His people?

BIRTH ANNOUNCEMENT OF JESUS THE MESSIAH

26 In the sixth month of Elizabeth's pregnancy, the angel Gabriel
was sent by God to a town of Galilee called Nazareth, 27 to a virgin
engaged to a man whose name was Joseph, a descendant of David,
and the virgin's name was Mary. 28 The angel came to her and said,
"Greetings, favored one, the Lord is with you!" 29 But she was greatly
troubled by his words and began to wonder about the meaning of
this greeting. 30 So the angel said to her, "Do not be afraid, Mary, for
you have found favor with God! 31 Listen: You will become pregnant
and give birth to a son, and you will name him Jesus. 32 He will be
great, and will be called the Son of the Most High, and the Lord God
will give him the throne of his father David. 33 He will reign over the
house of Jacob forever, and his kingdom will never end." 34 Mary said
to the angel, "How will this be, since I have not been intimate with
a man?" 35 The angel replied, "The Holy Spirit will come upon you,
and the power of the Most High will overshadow you. Therefore
the child to be born will be holy; he will be called the Son of God.

36 "And look, your relative Elizabeth has also become pregnant with a son in her old age—although she was called barren,
she is now in her sixth month! 37 For nothing will be impossible with God." 38 So Mary said, "Yes, I am a servant of the Lord;
let this happen to me according to your word." Then the angel
departed from her.

MARY AND ELIZABETH

39 In those days Mary got up and went hurriedly into the hill
country, to a town of Judah, 40 and entered Zechariah's house and
greeted Elizabeth. 41 When Elizabeth heard Mary's greeting, the
baby leaped in her womb, and Elizabeth was filled with the Holy
Spirit. 42 She exclaimed with a loud voice, "Blessed are you among
women, and blessed is the child in your womb! 43 And who am I
that the mother of my Lord should come and visit me? 44 For the
instant the sound of your greeting reached my ears, the baby in
my womb leaped for joy. 45 And blessed is she who believed that
what was spoken to her by the Lord would be fulfilled."

MARY'S HYMN OF PRAISE

46 And Mary said,
"My soul exalts the Lord,
47 and my spirit has begun to rejoice in God my Savior,
48 because he has looked upon the
humble state of his servant.
For from now on all generations will call me blessed,
49 because he who is mighty has done great
things for me, and holy is his name;
50 from generation to generation he is
merciful to those who fear him.
51 He has demonstrated power with his arm; he
has scattered those whose pride wells up
from the sheer arrogance of their hearts.
52 He has brought down the mighty from their thrones,
and has lifted up those of lowly position;
53 he has filled the hungry with good things,
and has sent the rich away empty.

THE MAGNIFICAT

LUKE 1:46–56

Every *yes* comes with a *no*.

When we say yes to watching a movie late at night, we say no to a good night's sleep or our early morning plans. When we say yes to an expensive impulse buy, we say no to other more sensible purchases. When we say yes to tutoring immigrant or refugee children on a Saturday morning, we say no to brunch with friends.

Every time we say yes to God's plan for our lives, we say no to the desires, decisions, and distractions that oppose His plan. When we say yes to His calling on our life, we automatically say no to our own plans.

Mary's one courageous yes was no small thing. As an unmarried woman in her time and culture, saying yes to a pregnancy many would doubt was attached to a prophecy was a dangerous decision. Her yes to bear God's Son was also a no to a respectable reputation. Without God's intervention, Joseph likely would have given his no to marry her.

Following God's plan and seeking His kingdom require opposing anything that competes with belief in His promises to us.

The Magnificat is a sublime expression of faith in the sovereign authority and goodness of God. Mary rejoiced in God's goodness to her and praised Him for His power and holiness (Luke 1:46–50). Her praise included opposition to abusive power and pride (Luke 1:51), to oppression of the vulnerable (Luke 1:52), and to poverty and hunger (Luke 1:53). She recognized God's intention to expose unjust systems and abusive powers, a reality that she would witness in the life and ministry of her Son, Jesus.

Mary understood that there were other kingdoms, seen and unseen, vying for her loyalty. Her decision to advance the kingdom of God made her an enemy of these other powers. She knew that her yes to God's kingdom meant a no to all others.

Our decision to advance the kingdom of God requires much of us—it means denying ourselves, fighting for justice, and opposing the powers of this world (see Eph 6:12). Our nos, as difficult as they may be, welcome a joyful yes to a good and just kingdom of God.

54 He has helped his servant Israel, remembering his mercy,
55 as he promised to our ancestors, to Abraham
and to his descendants forever."

56 So Mary stayed with Elizabeth about three months and then
returned to her home.

THE BIRTH OF JOHN

57 Now the time came for Elizabeth to have her baby, and she
gave birth to a son. 58 Her neighbors and relatives heard that the
Lord had shown great mercy to her, and they rejoiced with her.
59 On the eighth day they came to circumcise the child, and they
wanted to name him Zechariah after his father. 60 But his mother replied, "No! He must be named John." 61 They said to her, "But
none of your relatives bears this name." 62 So they made signs to
the baby's father, inquiring what he wanted to name his son. 63 He
asked for a writing tablet and wrote, "His name is John." And they
were all amazed. 64 Immediately Zechariah's mouth was opened
and his tongue released, and he spoke, blessing God. 65 All their
neighbors were filled with fear, and throughout the entire hill
country of Judea all these things were talked about. 66 All who
heard these things kept them in their hearts, saying, "What then
will this child be?" For the Lord's hand was indeed with him.

ZECHARIAH'S PRAISE AND PREDICTION

67 Then his father Zechariah was filled with the Holy Spirit and
prophesied,

68 "Blessed be the Lord God of Israel,
because he has come to help and has redeemed his people.
69 For he has raised up a horn of salvation for
us in the house of his servant David,
70 as he spoke through the mouth of his
holy prophets from long ago,
71 that we should be saved from our enemies,
and from the hand of all who hate us.
72 He has done this to show mercy to our ancestors,
and to remember his holy covenant—
73 the oath that he swore to our ancestor Abraham.
This oath grants
74 that we, being rescued from the hand of our enemies,
may serve him without fear,
75 in holiness and righteousness before him for as long as we live.
76 And you, child, will be called the prophet of the Most High.
For you will go before the Lord to prepare his ways,
77 to give his people knowledge of salvation
through the forgiveness of their sins.
78 Because of our God's tender mercy
the dawn will break upon us from on high
79 to give light to those who sit in darkness
and in the shadow of death,
to guide our feet into the way of peace."

80 And the child kept growing and becoming strong in spirit, and
he was in the wilderness until the day he was revealed to Israel.

THE CENSUS AND THE BIRTH OF JESUS

2 Now in those days a decree went out from Caesar Augustus to
register all the empire for taxes. 2 This was the first registration,
taken when Quirinius was governor of Syria. 3 Everyone went to his
own town to be registered. 4 So Joseph also went up from the town
of Nazareth in Galilee to Judea, to the city of David called Bethlehem, because he was of the house and family line of David. 5 He
went to be registered with Mary, who was promised in marriage
to him, and who was expecting a child. 6 While they were there,
the time came for her to deliver her child. 7 And she gave birth
to her firstborn son and wrapped him in strips of cloth and laid
him in a manger, because there was no place for them in the inn.

THE SHEPHERDS' VISIT

8 Now there were shepherds nearby living out in the field, keeping
guard over their flock at night. 9 An angel of the Lord appeared to
them, and the glory of the Lord shone around them, and they were
absolutely terrified. 10 But the angel said to them, "Do not be afraid!
Listen carefully, for I proclaim to you good news that brings great
joy to all the people: 11 Today your Savior is born in the city of David.
He is Christ the Lord. 12 This will be a sign for you: You will find a baby
wrapped in strips of cloth and lying in a manger." 13 Suddenly a vast,
heavenly army appeared with the angel, praising God and saying,

14 "Glory to God in the highest,
and on earth peace among people
with whom he is pleased!"

15 When the angels left them and went back to heaven, the shepherds said to one another, "Let us go over to Bethlehem and see
this thing that has taken place, that the Lord has made known to
us." 16 So they hurried off and located Mary and Joseph, and found
the baby lying in a manger. 17 When they saw him, they related what
they had been told about this child, 18 and all who heard it were astonished at what the shepherds said. 19 But Mary treasured up all
these words, pondering in her heart what they might mean. 20 So
the shepherds returned, glorifying and praising God for all they
had heard and seen; everything was just as they had been told.

21 At the end of eight days, when he was circumcised, he was
named Jesus, the name given by the angel before he was conceived in the womb.

JESUS' PRESENTATION AT THE TEMPLE

22 Now when the time came for their purification according to
the law of Moses, Joseph and Mary brought Jesus up to Jerusalem to present him to the Lord 23 (just as it is written in the law
of the Lord, "*Every firstborn male will be set apart to the Lord*"),
24 and to offer a sacrifice according to what is specified in the law
of the Lord, ***a pair of doves or two young pigeons.***

THE PROPHECY OF SIMEON

25 Now there was a man in Jerusalem named Simeon who was
righteous and devout, looking for the restoration of Israel, and
the Holy Spirit was upon him. 26 It had been revealed to him by
the Holy Spirit that he would not die before he had seen the

GOD'S HEART FOR THE NATIONS

Luke 2:30–32

"For my eyes have seen your salvation that you have prepared in the presence of all peoples: a light, for revelation to the Gentiles, and for glory to your people Israel."

Lord's Christ. 27 So Simeon, directed by the Spirit, came into the
temple courts, and when the parents brought in the child Jesus
to do for him what was customary according to the law, 28 Simeon took him in his arms and blessed God, saying,

29 "Now, according to your word, Sovereign Lord,
permit your servant to depart in peace.
30 For my eyes have seen your salvation
31 that you have prepared in the presence of all peoples:
32 a light,
for revelation to the Gentiles,
and for glory to your people Israel."

33 So the child's father and mother were amazed at what was said
about him. 34 Then Simeon blessed them and said to his mother
Mary, "Listen carefully: This child is destined to be the cause of
the falling and rising of many in Israel and to be a sign that will be
rejected. 35 Indeed, as a result of him the thoughts of many hearts
will be revealed—and a sword will pierce your own soul as well!"

THE TESTIMONY OF ANNA

36 There was also a prophetess, Anna the daughter of Phanuel, of the
tribe of Asher. She was very old, having been married to her husband for seven years until his death. 37 She had lived as a widow since
then for eighty-four years. She never left the temple, worshiping
with fasting and prayer night and day. 38 At that moment, she came
up to them and began to give thanks to God and to speak about
the child to all who were waiting for the redemption of Jerusalem.

39 So when Joseph and Mary had performed everything according to the law of the Lord, they returned to Galilee, to their own
town of Nazareth. 40 And the child grew and became strong, filled
with wisdom, and the favor of God was upon him.

JESUS IN THE TEMPLE

41 Now Jesus' parents went to Jerusalem every year for the Feast
of the Passover. 42 When he was twelve years old, they went up
according to custom. 43 But when the feast was over, as they were
returning home, the boy Jesus stayed behind in Jerusalem. His
parents did not know it, 44 but (because they assumed that he was
in their group of travelers) they went a day's journey. Then they
began to look for him among their relatives and acquaintances.
45 When they did not find him, they returned to Jerusalem to look
for him. 46 After three days they found him in the temple courts,
sitting among the teachers, listening to them and asking them
questions. 47 And all who heard Jesus were astonished at his understanding and his answers. 48 When his parents saw him, they
were overwhelmed. His mother said to him, "Child, why have you
treated us like this? Look, your father and I have been looking for
you anxiously." 49 But he replied, "Why were you looking for me?
Didn't you know that I must be in my Father's house?" 50 Yet his
parents did not understand the remark he made to them. 51 Then
he went down with them and came to Nazareth, and was obedient to them. But his mother kept all these things in her heart.

52 And Jesus increased in wisdom and in stature, and in favor
with God and with people.

THE MINISTRY OF JOHN THE BAPTIST

3 In the fifteenth year of the reign of Tiberius Caesar, when
Pontius Pilate was governor of Judea, and Herod was tetrarch
of Galilee, and his brother Philip was tetrarch of the region of
Iturea and Trachonitis, and Lysanias was tetrarch of Abilene,
2 during the high priesthood of Annas and Caiaphas, the word
of God came to John the son of Zechariah in the wilderness. 3 He
went into all the region around the Jordan River, preaching a
baptism of repentance for the forgiveness of sins.
4 As it is written in the book of the words of the prophet Isaiah,

"The voice of one shouting in the wilderness:
'Prepare the way for the Lord,
make his paths straight.
5 *Every valley will be filled,*
and every mountain and hill will be brought low,
and the crooked will be made straight,
and the rough ways will be made smooth,
6 *and all humanity will see the salvation of God.'"*

7 So John said to the crowds that came out to be baptized by
him, "You offspring of vipers! Who warned you to flee from the
coming wrath? 8 Therefore produce fruit that proves your repentance, and don't begin to say to yourselves, 'We have Abraham
as our father.' For I tell you that God can raise up children for
Abraham from these stones! 9 Even now the ax is laid at the root
of the trees, and every tree that does not produce good fruit will
be cut down and thrown into the fire."
10 So the crowds were asking him, "What then should we do?" 11 John
answered them, "The person who has two tunics must share with
the person who has none, and the person who has food must do
likewise." 12 Tax collectors also came to be baptized, and they said to
him, "Teacher, what should we do?" 13 He told them, "Collect no more
than you are required to." 14 Then some soldiers also asked him, "And
as for us—what should we do?" He told them, "Take money from no
one by violence or by false accusation, and be content with your pay."
15 While the people were filled with anticipation and they all
wondered whether perhaps John could be the Christ, 16 John answered them all, "I baptize you with water, but one more powerful than I am is coming—I am not worthy to untie the strap
of his sandals. He will baptize you with the Holy Spirit and fire.
17 His winnowing fork is in his hand to clean out his threshing
floor and to gather the wheat into his storehouse, but the chaff
he will burn up with inextinguishable fire."
18 And in this way, with many other exhortations, John proclaimed good news to the people. 19 But when John rebuked
Herod the tetrarch because of Herodias, his brother's wife, and
because of all the evil deeds that he had done, 20 Herod added
this to them all: He locked up John in prison.

THE BAPTISM OF JESUS

21 Now when all the people were baptized, Jesus also was baptized.
And while he was praying, the heavens opened, 22 and the Holy Spirit
descended on him in bodily form like a dove. And a voice came
from heaven, "You are my one dear Son; in you I take great delight."

THE GENEALOGY OF JESUS

23 So Jesus, when he began his ministry, was about thirty years old. He was the son (as was supposed) of Joseph, the son of Heli, 24 the son of Matthat, the son of Levi, the son of Melchi, the son of Jannai, the son of Joseph, 25 the son of Mattathias, the son of Amos, the son of Nahum, the son of Esli, the son of Naggai, 26 the son of Maath, the son of Mattathias, the son of Semein, the son of Josech, the son of Joda, 27 the son of Joanan, the son of Rhesa, the son of Zerubbabel, the son of Shealtiel, the son of Neri, 28 the son of Melchi, the son of Addi, the son of Cosam, the son of Elmadam, the son of Er, 29 the son of Joshua, the son of Eliezer, the son of Jorim, the son of Matthat, the son of Levi, 30 the son of Simeon, the son of Judah, the son of Joseph, the son of Jonam, the son of Eliakim, 31 the son of Melea, the son of Menna, the son of Mattatha, the son of Nathan, the son of David, 32 the son of Jesse, the son of Obed, the son of Boaz, the son of Sala, the son of Nahshon, 33 the son of Amminadab, the son of Admin, the son of Arni, the son of Hezron, the son of Perez, the son of Judah, 34 the son of Jacob, the son of Isaac, the son of Abraham, the son of Terah, the son of Nahor, 35 the son of Serug, the son of Reu, the son of Peleg, the son of Eber, the son of Shelah, 36 the son of Cainan, the son of Arphaxad, the son of Shem, the son of Noah, the son of Lamech, 37 the son of Methuselah, the son of Enoch, the son of Jared, the son of Mahalalel, the son of Kenan, 38 the son of Enosh, the son of Seth, the son of Adam, the son of God.

THE TEMPTATION OF JESUS

4 Then Jesus, full of the Holy Spirit, returned from the Jordan River and was led by the Spirit in the wilderness, 2 where for forty days he endured temptations from the devil. He ate nothing during those days, and when they were completed, he was famished. 3 The devil said to him, "If you are the Son of God, command this stone to become bread." 4 Jesus answered him, "It is written, '***Man does not live by bread alone.***'"

5 Then the devil led him up to a high place and showed him in a flash all the kingdoms of the world. 6 And he said to him, "To you I will grant this whole realm—and the glory that goes along with it, for it has been relinquished to me, and I can give it to anyone I wish. 7 So then, if you will worship me, all this will be yours." 8 Jesus answered him, "It is written, '***You are to worship the Lord your God and serve*** only ***him.***'"

9 Then the devil brought him to Jerusalem, had him stand on the highest point of the temple, and said to him, "If you are the Son of God, throw yourself down from here, 10 for it is written, '***He will command his angels concerning you, to protect you,***' 11 and '***with their hands they will lift you up, so that you will not strike your foot against a stone.***'" 12 Jesus answered him, "It is said, '***You are not to put the Lord your God to the test.***'" 13 So when the devil had completed every temptation, he departed from him until a more opportune time.

THE BEGINNING OF JESUS' MINISTRY IN GALILEE

14 Then Jesus, in the power of the Spirit, returned to Galilee, and news about him spread throughout the surrounding countryside. 15 He began to teach in their synagogues and was praised by all.

REJECTION AT NAZARETH

16 Now Jesus came to Nazareth, where he had been brought up, and
went into the synagogue on the Sabbath day, as was his custom. He
stood up to read, 17 and the scroll of the prophet Isaiah was given to
him. He unrolled the scroll and found the place where it was written,

18 "*The Spirit of the Lord is upon me,*
because he has anointed me to proclaim
good news to the poor.
He has sent me to proclaim release to the captives
and the regaining of sight to the blind,
to set free those who are oppressed,
19 *to proclaim the year of the Lord's favor.*"

20 Then he rolled up the scroll, gave it back to the attendant, and
sat down. The eyes of everyone in the synagogue were fixed on him.
21 Then he began to tell them, "Today this scripture has been fulfilled
even as you heard it being read." 22 All were speaking well of him,
and were amazed at the gracious words coming out of his mouth.
They said, "Isn't this Joseph's son?" 23 Jesus said to them, "No doubt
you will quote to me the proverb, 'Physician, heal yourself!' and say,
'What we have heard that you did in Capernaum, do here in your
hometown too.'" 24 And he added, "I tell you the truth, no prophet
is acceptable in his hometown. 25 But in truth I tell you, there were
many widows in Israel in Elijah's days, when the sky was shut up
three and a half years, and there was a great famine over all the
land. 26 Yet Elijah was sent to none of them, but only to a woman
who was a widow at Zarephath in Sidon. 27 And there were many
lepers in Israel in the time of the prophet Elisha, yet none of them
was cleansed except Naaman the Syrian." 28 When they heard this,
all the people in the synagogue were filled with rage. 29 They got up,
forced him out of the town, and brought him to the brow of the hill
on which their town was built, so that they could throw him down
the cliff. 30 But he passed through the crowd and went on his way.

MINISTRY IN CAPERNAUM

31 So he went down to Capernaum, a town in Galilee, and on the
Sabbath he began to teach the people. 32 They were amazed at
his teaching, because he spoke with authority.

33 Now in the synagogue there was a man who had the spirit
of an unclean demon, and he cried out with a loud voice, 34 "Ha!
Leave us alone, Jesus the Nazarene! Have you come to destroy
us? I know who you are—the Holy One of God." 35 But Jesus rebuked him: "Silence! Come out of him!" Then, after the demon
threw the man down in their midst, he came out of him without hurting him. 36 They were all amazed and began to say to one
another, "What's happening here? For with authority and power
he commands the unclean spirits, and they come out!" 37 So the
news about him spread into all areas of the region.

38 After Jesus left the synagogue, he entered Simon's house. Now
Simon's mother-in-law was suffering from a high fever, and they
asked Jesus to help her. 39 So he stood over her, commanded the fever, and it left her. Immediately she got up and began to serve them.

40 As the sun was setting, all those who had any relatives sick
with various diseases brought them to Jesus. He placed his hands

on every one of them and healed them. 41 Demons also came out
of many, crying out, "You are the Son of God!" But he rebuked
them, and would not allow them to speak, because they knew
that he was the Christ.
42 The next morning Jesus departed and went to a deserted
place. Yet the crowds were seeking him, and they came to him
and tried to keep him from leaving them. 43 But Jesus said to
them, "I must proclaim the good news of the kingdom of God
to the other towns too, for that is what I was sent to do." 44 So he
continued to preach in the synagogues of Judea.

THE CALL OF THE DISCIPLES

5 Now Jesus was standing by the Lake of Gennesaret, and the
crowd was pressing around him to hear the word of God. 2 He
saw two boats by the lake, but the fishermen had gotten out of them
and were washing their nets. 3 He got into one of the boats, which
was Simon's, and asked him to put out a little way from the shore.
Then Jesus sat down and taught the crowds from the boat. 4 When
he had finished speaking, he said to Simon, "Put out into the deep
water and lower your nets for a catch." 5 Simon answered, "Master,
we worked hard all night and caught nothing! But at your word I
will lower the nets." 6 When they had done this, they caught so many
fish that their nets started to tear. 7 So they motioned to their partners in the other boat to come and help them. And they came and
filled both boats, so that they were about to sink. 8 But when Simon
Peter saw it, he fell down at Jesus' knees, saying, "Go away from me,
Lord, for I am a sinful man!" 9 For Peter and all who were with him
were astonished at the catch of fish that they had taken, 10 and so
were James and John, Zebedee's sons, who were Simon's business
partners. Then Jesus said to Simon, "Do not be afraid; from now
on you will be catching people!" 11 So when they had brought their
boats to shore, they left everything and followed him.

HEALING A LEPER

12 While Jesus was in one of the towns, a man came to him who
was covered with leprosy. When he saw Jesus, he bowed down
with his face to the ground and begged him, "Lord, if you are
willing, you can make me clean." 13 So he stretched out his hand
and touched him, saying, "I am willing. Be clean!" And immediately the leprosy left him. 14 Then he ordered the man to tell no
one, but commanded him, "Go and show yourself to a priest, and
bring the offering for your cleansing, as Moses commanded, as a
testimony to them." 15 But the news about him spread even more,
and large crowds were gathering together to hear him and to be
healed of their illnesses. 16 Yet Jesus himself frequently withdrew
to the wilderness and prayed.

HEALING AND FORGIVING A PARALYTIC

17 Now on one of those days, while he was teaching, there were
Pharisees and teachers of the law sitting nearby (who had come
from every village of Galilee and Judea and from Jerusalem), and
the power of the Lord was with him to heal. 18 Just then some men
showed up, carrying a paralyzed man on a stretcher. They were
trying to bring him in and place him before Jesus. 19 But since they

found no way to carry him in because of the crowd, they went up
on the roof and let him down on the stretcher through the roof
tiles right in front of Jesus. 20 When Jesus saw their faith he said,
"Friend, your sins are forgiven." 21 Then the experts in the law and
the Pharisees began to think to themselves, "Who is this man who
is uttering blasphemies? Who can forgive sins but God alone?"
22 When Jesus perceived their hostile thoughts, he said to them,
"Why are you raising objections within yourselves? 23 Which is
easier, to say, 'Your sins are forgiven,' or to say, 'Stand up and walk'?
24 But so that you may know that the Son of Man has authority
on earth to forgive sins"—he said to the paralyzed man—"I tell
you, stand up, take your stretcher and go home." 25 Immediately
he stood up before them, picked up the stretcher he had been
lying on, and went home, glorifying God. 26 Then astonishment
seized them all, and they glorified God. They were filled with awe,
saying, "We have seen incredible things today."

THE CALL OF LEVI; EATING WITH SINNERS

27 After this, Jesus went out and saw a tax collector named Levi
sitting at the tax booth. "Follow me," he said to him. 28 And he
got up and followed him, leaving everything behind.

29 Then Levi gave a great banquet in his house for Jesus, and
there was a large crowd of tax collectors and others sitting at the
table with them. 30 But the Pharisees and their experts in the law
complained to his disciples, saying, "Why do you eat and drink
with tax collectors and sinners?" 31 Jesus answered them, "Those
who are well don't need a physician, but those who are sick do. 32 I
have not come to call the righteous, but sinners to repentance."

THE SUPERIORITY OF THE NEW

33 Then they said to him, "John's disciples frequently fast and pray,
and so do the disciples of the Pharisees, but yours continue to eat
and drink." 34 So Jesus said to them, "You cannot make the wedding guests fast while the bridegroom is with them, can you? 35 But
those days are coming, and when the bridegroom is taken from
them, at that time they will fast." 36 He also told them a parable:
"No one tears a patch from a new garment and sews it on an old
garment. If he does, he will have torn the new, and the piece from
the new will not match the old. 37 And no one pours new wine
into old wineskins. If he does, the new wine will burst the skins
and will be spilled, and the skins will be destroyed. 38 Instead new
wine must be poured into new wineskins. 39 No one after drinking old wine wants the new, for he says, 'The old is good enough.'"

LORD OF THE SABBATH

6 Jesus was going through the grain fields on a Sabbath, and his
disciples picked some heads of wheat, rubbed them in their
hands, and ate them. 2 But some of the Pharisees said, "Why are
you doing what is against the law on the Sabbath?" 3 Jesus answered them, "Haven't you read what David did when he and his
companions were hungry—4 how he entered the house of God,
took and ate the sacred bread, which is not lawful for any to eat
but the priests alone, and gave it to his companions?" 5 Then he
said to them, "The Son of Man is lord of the Sabbath."

HEALING A WITHERED HAND

6 On another Sabbath, Jesus entered the synagogue and was
teaching. Now a man was there whose right hand was withered.
7 The experts in the law and the Pharisees watched Jesus closely
to see if he would heal on the Sabbath, so that they could find a
reason to accuse him. 8 But he knew their thoughts, and said to
the man who had the withered hand, "Get up and stand here."
So he rose and stood there. 9 Then Jesus said to them, "I ask you,
is it lawful to do good on the Sabbath or to do evil, to save a life
or to destroy it?" 10 After looking around at them all, he said to
the man, "Stretch out your hand." The man did so, and his hand
was restored. 11 But they were filled with mindless rage and began debating with one another what they would do to Jesus.

CHOOSING THE TWELVE APOSTLES

12 Now it was during this time that Jesus went out to the mountain to pray, and he spent all night in prayer to God. 13 When
morning came, he called his disciples and chose twelve of them,
whom he also named apostles: 14 Simon (whom he named Peter),
and his brother Andrew; and James, John, Philip, Bartholomew,
15 Matthew, Thomas, James the son of Alphaeus, Simon who was
called the Zealot, 16 Judas the son of James, and Judas Iscariot,
who became a traitor.

THE SERMON ON THE PLAIN

17 Then he came down with them and stood on a level place. And
a large number of his disciples had gathered along with a vast
multitude from all over Judea, from Jerusalem, and from the
seacoast of Tyre and Sidon. They came to hear him and to be
healed of their diseases, 18 and those who suffered from unclean
spirits were cured. 19 The whole crowd was trying to touch him,
because power was coming out from him and healing them all.
20 Then he looked up at his disciples and said:

"Blessed are you who are poor, for the
kingdom of God belongs to you.
21 "Blessed are you who hunger now, for you will be satisfied.
"Blessed are you who weep now, for you will laugh.
22 "Blessed are you when people hate you, and when they
exclude you and insult you and reject you as evil on
account of the Son of Man! 23 Rejoice in that day, and
jump for joy, because your reward is great in heaven. For
their ancestors did the same things to the prophets.
24 "But woe to you who are rich, for you have
received your comfort already.
25 "Woe to you who are well satisfied with
food now, for you will be hungry.
"Woe to you who laugh now, for you will mourn and weep.
26 "Woe to you when all people speak well of you, for their
ancestors did the same things to the false prophets.

27 "But I say to you who are listening: Love your enemies, do
good to those who hate you, 28 bless those who curse you, pray
for those who mistreat you. 29 To the person who strikes you
on the cheek, offer the other as well, and from the person who

takes away your coat, do not withhold your tunic either. 30 Give
to everyone who asks you, and do not ask for your possessions
back from the person who takes them away. 31 Treat others in the
same way that you would want them to treat you.
32 "If you love those who love you, what credit is that to you?
For even sinners love those who love them. 33 And if you do good
to those who do good to you, what credit is that to you? Even
sinners do the same. 34 And if you lend to those from whom you
hope to be repaid, what credit is that to you? Even sinners lend
to sinners, so that they may be repaid in full. 35 But love your
enemies, and do good, and lend, expecting nothing back. Then
your reward will be great, and you will be sons of the Most High,
because he is kind to ungrateful and evil people. 36 Be merciful,
just as your Father is merciful.

REFLECT

What can you do today to love your enemies? Why is this command often difficult for us to follow?

DO NOT JUDGE OTHERS

37 "Do not judge, and you will not be judged; do not condemn,
and you will not be condemned; forgive, and you will be forgiven.
38 Give, and it will be given to you: A good measure, pressed down,
shaken together, running over, will be poured into your lap. For
the measure you use will be the measure you receive."
39 He also told them a parable: "Someone who is blind cannot lead
another who is blind, can he? Won't they both fall into a pit? 40 A
disciple is not greater than his teacher, but everyone when fully
trained will be like his teacher. 41 Why do you see the speck in your
brother's eye, but fail to see the beam of wood in your own? 42 How
can you say to your brother, 'Brother, let me remove the speck from
your eye,' while you yourself don't see the beam in your own? You
hypocrite! First remove the beam from your own eye, and then
you can see clearly to remove the speck from your brother's eye.
43 "For no good tree bears bad fruit, nor again does a bad tree
bear good fruit, 44 for each tree is known by its own fruit. For figs
are not gathered from thorns, nor are grapes picked from bram-
bles. 45 The good person out of the good treasury of his heart produces good, and the evil person out of his evil treasury produces
evil, for his mouth speaks from what fills his heart.
46 "Why do you call me 'Lord, Lord,' and don't do what I tell you?
47 "Everyone who comes to me and listens to my words and puts
them into practice—I will show you what he is like: 48 He is like
a man building a house, who dug down deep, and laid the foundation on bedrock. When a flood came, the river burst against
that house but could not shake it, because it had been well built.
49 But the person who hears and does not put my words into
practice is like a man who built a house on the ground without
a foundation. When the river burst against that house, it collapsed immediately, and was utterly destroyed!"

HEALING THE CENTURION'S SLAVE

7 After Jesus had finished teaching all this to the people, he entered Capernaum. 2 A centurion there had a slave who was highly
regarded, but who was sick and at the point of death. 3 When the
centurion heard about Jesus, he sent some Jewish elders to him,
asking him to come and heal his slave. 4 When they came to Jesus,
they urged him earnestly, "He is worthy to have you do this for him,

5 because he loves our nation, and even built our synagogue." 6 So Jesus went with them. When he was not far from the house, the centurion sent friends to say to him, "Lord, do not trouble yourself, for I am not worthy to have you come under my roof! 7 That is why I did not presume to come to you. Instead, say the word, and my servant must be healed. 8 For I too am a man set under authority, with soldiers under me. I say to this one, 'Go!' and he goes, and to another, 'Come!' and he comes, and to my slave, 'Do this!' and he does it." 9 When Jesus heard this, he was amazed at him. He turned and said to the crowd that followed him, "I tell you, not even in Israel have I found such faith!" 10 So when those who had been sent returned to the house, they found the slave well.

RAISING A WIDOW'S SON

11 Soon afterward Jesus went to a town called Nain, and his disciples and a large crowd went with him. 12 As he approached the town gate, a man who had died was being carried out, the only son of his mother (who was a widow), and a large crowd from the town was with her. 13 When the Lord saw her, he had compassion for her and said to her, "Do not weep." 14 Then he came up and touched the bier, and those who carried it stood still. He said, "Young man, I say to you, get up!" 15 So the dead man sat up and began to speak, and Jesus gave him back to his mother. 16 Fear seized them all, and they began to glorify God, saying, "A great prophet has appeared among us!" and "God has come to help his people!" 17 This report about Jesus circulated throughout Judea and all the surrounding country.

JESUS AND JOHN THE BAPTIST

18 John's disciples informed him about all these things. So John called two of his disciples 19 and sent them to Jesus to ask, "Are you the one who is to come, or should we look for another?" 20 When the men came to Jesus, they said, "John the Baptist has sent us to you to ask, 'Are you the one who is to come, or should we look for another?'" 21 At that very time Jesus cured many people of diseases, sicknesses, and evil spirits, and granted sight to many who were blind. 22 So he answered them, "Go tell John what you have seen and heard: The blind see, the lame walk, lepers are cleansed, the deaf hear, the dead are raised, the poor have good news proclaimed to them. 23 Blessed is anyone who takes no offense at me."

24 When John's messengers had gone, Jesus began to speak to the crowds about John: "What did you go out into the wilderness to see? A reed shaken by the wind? 25 What did you go out to see? A man dressed in soft clothing? Look, those who wear soft clothing and live in luxury are in the royal palaces! 26 What did you go out to see? A prophet? Yes, I tell you, and more than a prophet. 27 This is the one about whom it is written, '***Look, I am sending my messenger ahead of you, who will prepare your way before you.***' 28 I tell you, among those born of women no one is greater than John. Yet the one who is least in the kingdom of God is greater than he is." 29 (Now all the people who heard this, even the tax collectors, acknowledged God's justice, because they had been baptized with John's baptism. 30 However, the Pharisees and the experts in religious law rejected God's purpose for themselves, because they had not been baptized by John.)

31 “To what then should I compare the people of this generation, and what are they like? 32 They are like children sitting in
the marketplace and calling out to one another,

‘We played the flute for you, yet you did not dance;
we wailed in mourning, yet you did not weep.’

33 For John the Baptist has come eating no bread and drinking
no wine, and you say, ‘He has a demon!’ 34 The Son of Man has
come eating and drinking, and you say, ‘Look at him, a glutton
and a drunk, a friend of tax collectors and sinners!’ 35 But wisdom is vindicated by all her children.”

JESUS’ ANOINTING

36 Now one of the Pharisees asked Jesus to have dinner with him,
so he went into the Pharisee’s house and took his place at the table. 37 Then when a woman of that town, who was a sinner, learned
that Jesus was dining at the Pharisee’s house, she brought an alabaster jar of perfumed oil. 38 As she stood behind him at his feet,
weeping, she began to wet his feet with her tears. She wiped them
with her hair, kissed them, and anointed them with the perfumed
oil. 39 Now when the Pharisee who had invited him saw this, he
said to himself, “If this man were a prophet, he would know who
and what kind of woman this is who is touching him, that she is
a sinner.” 40 So Jesus answered him, “Simon, I have something to
say to you.” He replied, “Say it, Teacher.” 41 “A certain creditor had
two debtors; one owed him 500 silver coins, and the other fifty.
42 When they could not pay, he canceled the debts of both. Now
which of them will love him more?” 43 Simon answered, “I suppose
the one who had the bigger debt canceled.” Jesus said to him, “You
have judged rightly.” 44 Then, turning toward the woman, he said
to Simon, “Do you see this woman? I entered your house. You gave
me no water for my feet, but she has wet my feet with her tears
and wiped them with her hair. 45 You gave me no kiss of greeting, but from the time I entered she has not stopped kissing my
feet. 46 You did not anoint my head with oil, but she has anointed
my feet with perfumed oil. 47 Therefore I tell you, her sins, which
were many, are forgiven, thus she loved much; but the one who
is forgiven little loves little.” 48 Then Jesus said to her, “Your sins
are forgiven.” 49 But those who were at the table with him began
to say among themselves, “Who is this, who even forgives sins?”
50 He said to the woman, “Your faith has saved you; go in peace.”

JESUS’ MINISTRY AND THE HELP OF WOMEN

8 Some time afterward he went on through towns and villages,
preaching and proclaiming the good news of the kingdom of
God. The twelve were with him, 2 and also some women who had
been healed of evil spirits and disabilities: Mary (called Magdalene), from whom seven demons had gone out, 3 and Joanna the
wife of Cuza (Herod’s household manager), Susanna, and many
others who provided for them out of their own resources.

THE PARABLE OF THE SOWER

4 While a large crowd was gathering and people were coming to
Jesus from one town after another, he spoke to them in a parable: 5 “A sower went out to sow his seed. And as he sowed, some

fell along the path and was trampled on, and the wild birds devoured it. 6 Other seed fell on rock, and when it came up, it withered because it had no moisture. 7 Other seed fell among the thorns, and they grew up with it and choked it. 8 But other seed fell on good soil and grew, and it produced a hundred times as much grain." As he said this, he called out, "The one who has ears to hear had better listen!"

9 Then his disciples asked him what this parable meant. 10 He said, "You have been given the opportunity to know the secrets of the kingdom of God, but for others they are in parables, so that ***although they see they may not see, and although they hear they may not understand.***

11 "Now the parable means this: The seed is the word of God. 12 Those along the path are the ones who have heard; then the devil comes and takes away the word from their hearts, so that they may not believe and be saved. 13 Those on the rock are the ones who receive the word with joy when they hear it, but they have no root. They believe for a while, but in a time of testing fall away. 14 As for the seed that fell among thorns, these are the ones who hear, but as they go on their way they are choked by the worries and riches and pleasures of life, and their fruit does not mature. 15 But as for the seed that landed on good soil, these are the ones who, after hearing the word, cling to it with an honest and good heart, and bear fruit with steadfast endurance.

SHOWING THE LIGHT

16 "No one lights a lamp and then covers it with a jar or puts it under a bed, but puts it on a lampstand so that those who come in can see the light. 17 For nothing is hidden that will not be revealed, and nothing concealed that will not be made known and brought to light. 18 So listen carefully, for whoever has will be given more, but whoever does not have, even what he thinks he has will be taken from him."

JESUS' TRUE FAMILY

19 Now Jesus' mother and his brothers came to him, but they could not get near him because of the crowd. 20 So he was told, "Your mother and your brothers are standing outside, wanting to see you." 21 But he replied to them, "My mother and my brothers are those who hear the word of God and do it."

STILLING OF A STORM

22 One day Jesus got into a boat with his disciples and said to them, "Let's go across to the other side of the lake." So they set out, 23 and as they sailed he fell asleep. Now a violent windstorm came down on the lake, and the boat started filling up with water, and they were in danger. 24 They came and woke him, saying, "Master, Master, we are about to die!" So he got up and rebuked the wind and the raging waves; they died down, and it was calm. 25 Then he said to them, "Where is your faith?" But they were afraid and amazed, saying to one another, "Who then is this? He commands even the winds and the water, and they obey him!"

HEALING OF A DEMONIAC

26 So they sailed over to the region of the Gerasenes, which is opposite Galilee. 27 As Jesus stepped ashore, a certain man from the
town met him who was possessed by demons. For a long time this
man had worn no clothes and had not lived in a house, but among
the tombs. 28 When he saw Jesus, he cried out, fell down before him,
and shouted with a loud voice, "Leave me alone, Jesus, Son of the
Most High God! I beg you, do not torment me!" 29 For Jesus had
started commanding the evil spirit to come out of the man. (For
it had seized him many times, so he would be bound with chains
and shackles and kept under guard. But he would break the re-
straints and be driven by the demon into deserted places.) 30 Jesus
then asked him, "What is your name?" He said, "Legion," because
many demons had entered him. 31 And they began to beg him not
to order them to depart into the abyss. 32 Now a large herd of pigs
was feeding there on the hillside, and the demonic spirits begged
Jesus to let them go into them. He gave them permission. 33 So the
demons came out of the man and went into the pigs, and the herd
of pigs rushed down the steep slope into the lake and drowned.
34 When the herdsmen saw what had happened, they ran off and
spread the news in the town and countryside. 35 So the people went
out to see what had happened, and they came to Jesus. They found
the man from whom the demons had gone out, sitting at Jesus'
feet, clothed and in his right mind, and they were afraid. 36 Those
who had seen it told them how the man who had been demon-
possessed had been healed. 37 Then all the people of the Gerasenes
and the surrounding region asked Jesus to leave them alone, for
they were seized with great fear. So he got into the boat and left.
38 The man from whom the demons had gone out begged to go with
him, but Jesus sent him away, saying, 39 "Return to your home, and
declare what God has done for you." So he went away, proclaiming
throughout the whole town what Jesus had done for him.

RESTORATION AND HEALING

40 Now when Jesus returned, the crowd welcomed him, because
they were all waiting for him. 41 Then a man named Jairus, who
was a leader of the synagogue, came up. Falling at Jesus' feet, he
pleaded with him to come to his house, 42 because he had an only
daughter, about twelve years old, and she was dying.

As Jesus was on his way, the crowds pressed around him. 43 Now
a woman was there who had been suffering from a hemorrhage
for twelve years but could not be healed by anyone. 44 She came
up behind Jesus and touched the edge of his cloak, and at once
the bleeding stopped. 45 Then Jesus asked, "Who was it who
touched me?" When they all denied it, Peter said, "Master, the
crowds are surrounding you and pressing against you!" 46 But
Jesus said, "Someone touched me, for I know that power has gone
out from me." 47 When the woman saw that she could not escape
notice, she came trembling and fell down before him. In the
presence of all the people, she explained why she had touched
him and how she had been immediately healed. 48 Then he said
to her, "Daughter, your faith has made you well. Go in peace."

49 While he was still speaking, someone from the synagogue
leader's house came and said, "Your daughter is dead; do not

LOVE TO GROW

EVERY NEED

LUKE 8:40–48

She was unclean.

The unnamed woman in Luke 8 suffered from a condition that caused her to bleed continually. She had suffered with this condition for twelve long years. Not only was she suffering, but she was banished, ignored, even feared.

The laws of purity in Jewish culture forced this woman to the fringes of society. She was isolated: no one would approach her out of fear that they too would become unclean. She was poor: she spent all she had on doctors who did nothing to help her. She was unable to participate in social activities, worship at the temple, or interact with anyone else in society.

Then she heard of Jesus. She believed He was sovereign and powerful and able to heal her. She risked exposure and forced herself into the city. She knew she didn't need much of Jesus; one touch was all she needed to be healed.

She believed He would heal her. What she didn't know was how much Jesus cared for her. He did heal her instantly, but He did much more than that.

Jesus stopped the moving crowd, likely made up of many prominent men of the city, His disciples, and other curious bystanders. Jesus asked who touched Him, and the woman knew she would not go unnoticed. What Jesus did next was truly amazing: Jesus singled her out and declared to everyone standing there that she had, in fact, been healed.

Jesus restored her physically when she touched His robe. He restored her socially when He publicly declared that her faith had made her well. Now everyone knew she was clean. She no longer had to live in the shadows or hide from society. She was clean.

What this unnamed woman's story shows us is the character of our Savior. He is not solely interested in saving us from sin or pain or difficult circumstances. He restores us in ways we don't even realize we need. He heals, restores, and redeems. He meets the needs we can see and the needs we can't see. He restores us fully, even when we only expect Him to do the minimum.

We can trust Him. He cares for us more than we can fathom and does more to redeem us than we can ever dream possible.

trouble the teacher any longer." 50 But when Jesus heard this, he told him, "Do not be afraid; just believe, and she will be healed." 51 Now when he came to the house, Jesus did not let anyone go in with him except Peter, John, and James, and the child's father and mother. 52 Now they were all wailing and mourning for her, but he said, "Stop your weeping; she is not dead but asleep!" 53 And they began making fun of him, because they knew that she was dead. 54 But Jesus gently took her by the hand and said, "Child, get up." 55 Her spirit returned, and she got up immediately. Then he told them to give her something to eat. 56 Her parents were astonished, but he ordered them to tell no one what had happened.

THE SENDING OF THE TWELVE APOSTLES

9 After Jesus called the twelve together, he gave them power and authority over all demons and to cure diseases, 2 and he sent them out to proclaim the kingdom of God and to heal the sick. 3 He said to them, "Take nothing for your journey—no staff, no bag, no bread, no money, and do not take an extra tunic. 4 Whatever house you enter, stay there until you leave the area. 5 Wherever they do not receive you, as you leave that town, shake the dust off your feet as a testimony against them." 6 Then they departed and went throughout the villages, proclaiming the good news and healing people everywhere.

HEROD'S CONFUSION ABOUT JESUS

7 Now Herod the tetrarch heard about everything that was happening, and he was thoroughly perplexed, because some people were saying that John had been raised from the dead, 8 while others were saying that Elijah had appeared, and still others that one of the prophets of long ago had risen. 9 Herod said, "I had John beheaded, but who is this about whom I hear such things?" So Herod wanted to learn about Jesus.

THE FEEDING OF THE FIVE THOUSAND

10 When the apostles returned, they told Jesus everything they had done. Then he took them with him and they withdrew privately to a town called Bethsaida. 11 But when the crowds found out, they followed him. He welcomed them, spoke to them about the kingdom of God, and cured those who needed healing. 12 Now the day began to draw to a close, so the twelve came and said to Jesus, "Send the crowd away, so they can go into the surrounding villages and countryside and find lodging and food, because we are in an isolated place." 13 But he said to them, "You give them something to eat." They replied, "We have no more than five loaves and two fish—unless we go and buy food for all these people." 14 (Now about 5,000 men were there.) Then he said to his disciples, "Have them sit down in groups of about fifty each." 15 So they did as Jesus directed, and the people all sat down.

16 Then he took the five loaves and the two fish, and looking up to heaven he gave thanks and broke them. He gave them to the disciples to set before the crowd. 17 They all ate and were satisfied, and what was left over was picked up—twelve baskets of broken pieces.

PETER'S CONFESSION

18 Once when Jesus was praying by himself, and his disciples were
nearby, he asked them, "Who do the crowds say that I am?" 19 They
answered, "John the Baptist; others say Elijah; and still others
that one of the prophets of long ago has risen." 20 Then he said
to them, "But who do you say that I am?" Peter answered, "The
Christ of God." 21 But he forcefully commanded them not to tell
this to anyone, 22 saying, "The Son of Man must suffer many
things and be rejected by the elders, chief priests, and experts
in the law, and be killed, and on the third day be raised."

A CALL TO DISCIPLESHIP

23 Then he said to them all, "If anyone wants to become my follower, he must deny himself, take up his cross daily, and follow
me. 24 For whoever wants to save his life will lose it, but whoever
loses his life because of me will save it. 25 For what does it benefit
a person if he gains the whole world but loses or forfeits himself?
26 For whoever is ashamed of me and my words, the Son of Man
will be ashamed of that person when he comes in his glory and
in the glory of the Father and of the holy angels. 27 But I tell you
most certainly, there are some standing here who will not experience death before they see the kingdom of God."

THE TRANSFIGURATION

28 Now about eight days after these sayings, Jesus took with him
Peter, John, and James, and went up the mountain to pray. 29 As
he was praying, the appearance of his face was transformed, and
his clothes became very bright, a brilliant white. 30 Then two men,
Moses and Elijah, began talking with him. 31 They appeared in glorious splendor and spoke about his departure that he was about
to carry out at Jerusalem. 32 Now Peter and those with him were
quite sleepy, but as they became fully awake, they saw his glory
and the two men standing with him. 33 Then as the men were
starting to leave, Peter said to Jesus, "Master, it is good for us to
be here. Let us make three shelters, one for you and one for Moses and one for Elijah"—not knowing what he was saying. 34 As he
was saying this, a cloud came and overshadowed them, and they
were afraid as they entered the cloud. 35 Then a voice came from
the cloud, saying, "This is my Son, my Chosen One. Listen to him!"
36 After the voice had spoken, Jesus was found alone. So they kept
silent and told no one at that time anything of what they had seen.

HEALING A BOY WITH AN UNCLEAN SPIRIT

37 Now on the next day, when they had come down from the
mountain, a large crowd met him. 38 Then a man from the crowd
cried out, "Teacher, I beg you to look at my son—he is my only
child! 39 A spirit seizes him, and he suddenly screams; it throws
him into convulsions and causes him to foam at the mouth. It
hardly ever leaves him alone, torturing him severely. 40 I begged
your disciples to cast it out, but they could not do so." 41 Jesus answered, "You unbelieving and perverse generation! How much
longer must I be with you and endure you? Bring your son
here." 42 As the boy was approaching, the demon threw him to
the ground and shook him with convulsions. But Jesus rebuked

LOVE TO GROW

WHO DO YOU SAY I AM?

LUKE 9:18–22

The Gospels invite us into God's inner circle via Jesus and His chosen closest friends. These moments tell us something important about God: He is personal; He is relational; and He reveals Himself in the quiet moments.

I envision, for example, Jesus lying in the grass enjoying the sun with His pals. They spend time praying in solitude together. He asks them questions and uses them as teaching moments.

In such a moment, perhaps after Jesus miraculously fed the five thousand, Jesus asked His disciples, "Who do the crowds say that I am?" (Luke 9:18). Though many believed He was Elijah or John the Baptist, Peter knew who He was. He had experienced many such intimate, teaching moments after witnessing a miracle. On this occasion, by faith, Peter confidently admitted that He was the Christ of God (Luke 9:20).

While the disciples may have been slow to fully understand His teachings, they understood who Jesus was.

Like any good friend, Jesus trusted Peter and the disciples with the truth of His identity. He told them what would happen to Him and how He would be raised to life again.

One of my favorite things about Jesus is that the more you seek Him, the more He reveals about Himself. He reserves His best secrets for those who stick around to see. He did this with Timothy and Nathaniel at the beginning of John. He did this with Peter multiple times throughout the Gospels. He lets the women who stayed with Him at the cross be the first to experience His resurrection. What a privilege it is to see Jesus.

For me, these moments come when I am quiet and at rest in His presence. Like this passage, they are simple, sweet, and rooted in our special, private relationship. They are moments just between us, and they are waiting for me when I choose to stay close and lean in.

the unclean spirit, healed the boy, and gave him back to his father. 43 Then they were all astonished at the mighty power of God.

ANOTHER PREDICTION OF JESUS' SUFFERING

But while the entire crowd was amazed at everything Jesus was
doing, he said to his disciples, 44 "Take these words to heart, for
the Son of Man is going to be betrayed into the hands of men."
45 But they did not understand this statement; its meaning had
been concealed from them, so that they could not grasp it. Yet
they were afraid to ask him about this statement.

CONCERNING THE GREATEST

46 Now an argument started among the disciples as to which of
them might be the greatest. 47 But when Jesus discerned their
innermost thoughts, he took a child, had him stand by his side,
48 and said to them, "Whoever welcomes this child in my name welcomes me, and whoever welcomes me welcomes the one who sent
me, for the one who is least among you all is the one who is great."

ON THE RIGHT SIDE

49 John answered, "Master, we saw someone casting out demons
in your name, and we tried to stop him because he is not a disciple along with us." 50 But Jesus said to him, "Do not stop him,
for whoever is not against you is for you."

REJECTION IN SAMARIA

51 Now when the days drew near for him to be taken up, Jesus
set out resolutely to go to Jerusalem. 52 He sent messengers on
ahead of him. As they went along, they entered a Samaritan village to make things ready in advance for him, 53 but the villagers
refused to welcome him, because he was determined to go to Jerusalem. 54 Now when his disciples James and John saw this, they
said, "Lord, do you want us *to call fire to come down from heaven*
and consume them?" 55 But Jesus turned and rebuked them, 56 and
they went on to another village.

CHALLENGING PROFESSED FOLLOWERS

57 As they were walking along the road, someone said to him, "I
will follow you wherever you go." 58 Jesus said to him, "Foxes have
dens and the birds in the sky have nests, but the Son of Man has
no place to lay his head." 59 Jesus said to another, "Follow me."
But he replied, "Lord, first let me go and bury my father." 60 But
Jesus said to him, "Let the dead bury their own dead, but as for
you, go and proclaim the kingdom of God." 61 Yet another said,
"I will follow you, Lord, but first let me say goodbye to my family." 62 Jesus said to him, "No one who puts his hand to the plow
and looks back is fit for the kingdom of God."

THE MISSION OF THE SEVENTY-TWO

10 After this the Lord appointed seventy-two others and sent
them on ahead of him two by two into every town and place
where he himself was about to go. 2 He said to them, "The harvest
is plentiful, but the workers are few. Therefore ask the Lord of the
harvest to send out workers into his harvest. 3 Go! I am sending you

out like lambs surrounded by wolves. 4 Do not carry a money bag,
a traveler's bag, or sandals, and greet no one on the road. 5 Whenever you enter a house, first say, 'May peace be on this house!' 6 And
if a peace-loving person is there, your peace will remain on him,
but if not, it will return to you. 7 Stay in that same house, eating
and drinking what they give you, for the worker deserves his pay.
Do not move around from house to house. 8 Whenever you enter
a town and the people welcome you, eat what is set before you.
9 Heal the sick in that town and say to them, 'The kingdom of God
has come upon you!' 10 But whenever you enter a town and the people do not welcome you, go into its streets and say, 11 'Even the dust
of your town that clings to our feet we wipe off against you. Nevertheless know this: The kingdom of God has come.' 12 I tell you, it
will be more bearable on that day for Sodom than for that town!

13 "Woe to you, Chorazin! Woe to you, Bethsaida! For if the miracles done in you had been done in Tyre and Sidon, they would
have repented long ago, sitting in sackcloth and ashes. 14 But it
will be more bearable for Tyre and Sidon in the judgment than
for you! 15 And you, Capernaum, will you be exalted to heaven?
No, you will be thrown down to Hades!

16 "The one who listens to you listens to me, and the one who
rejects you rejects me, and the one who rejects me rejects the
one who sent me."

17 Then the seventy-two returned with joy, saying, "Lord, even
the demons submit to us in your name!" 18 So he said to them,
"I saw Satan fall like lightning from heaven. 19 Look, I have given
you authority to tread on snakes and scorpions and on the full
force of the enemy, and nothing will hurt you. 20 Nevertheless,
do not rejoice that the spirits submit to you, but rejoice that
your names stand written in heaven."

21 On that same occasion Jesus rejoiced in the Holy Spirit and
said, "I praise you, Father, Lord of heaven and earth, because you
have hidden these things from the wise and intelligent, and revealed them to little children. Yes, Father, for this was your gracious will. 22 All things have been given to me by my Father. No one
knows who the Son is except the Father, or who the Father is except the Son and anyone to whom the Son decides to reveal him."

23 Then Jesus turned to his disciples and said privately, "Blessed
are the eyes that see what you see! 24 For I tell you that many
prophets and kings longed to see what you see but did not see
it, and to hear what you hear but did not hear it."

THE PARABLE OF THE GOOD SAMARITAN

25 Now an expert in religious law stood up to test Jesus, saying,
"Teacher, what must I do to inherit eternal life?" 26 He said to
him, "What is written in the law? How do you understand it?"
27 The expert answered, ***"Love the Lord your God with all your
heart, with all your soul, with all your strength, and with all your
mind,*** and ***love your neighbor as yourself."*** 28 Jesus said to him, "You
have answered correctly; do this, and you will live."

29 But the expert, wanting to justify himself, said to Jesus, "And
who is my neighbor?" 30 Jesus replied, "A man was going down
from Jerusalem to Jericho, and fell into the hands of robbers, who
stripped him, beat him up, and went off, leaving him half dead.

31 Now by chance a priest was going down that road, but when
he saw the injured man he passed by on the other side. 32 So too
a Levite, when he came up to the place and saw him, passed by
on the other side. 33 But a Samaritan who was traveling came to
where the injured man was, and when he saw him, he felt compassion for him. 34 He went up to him and bandaged his wounds,
pouring olive oil and wine on them. Then he put him on his own
animal, brought him to an inn, and took care of him. 35 The next
day he took out two silver coins and gave them to the innkeeper,
saying, 'Take care of him, and whatever else you spend, I will repay you when I come back this way.' 36 Which of these three do
you think became a neighbor to the man who fell into the hands
of the robbers?" 37 The expert in religious law said, "The one who
showed mercy to him." So Jesus said to him, "Go and do the same."

JESUS AND MARTHA

38 Now as they went on their way, Jesus entered a certain village
where a woman named Martha welcomed him as a guest. 39 She
had a sister named Mary, who sat at the Lord's feet and listened to
what he said. 40 But Martha was distracted with all the preparations
she had to make, so she came up to him and said, "Lord, don't you
care that my sister has left me to do all the work alone? Tell her to
help me." 41 But the Lord answered her, "Martha, Martha, you are
worried and troubled about many things, 42 but one thing is needed.
Mary has chosen the best part; it will not be taken away from her."

INSTRUCTIONS ON PRAYER

11 Now Jesus was praying in a certain place. When he stopped, one
of his disciples said to him, "Lord, teach us to pray, just as John
taught his disciples." 2 So he said to them, "When you pray, say:

Father, may your name be honored;
may your kingdom come.
3 Give us each day our daily bread,
4 and forgive us our sins,
for we also forgive everyone who sins against us.
And do not lead us into temptation."

5 Then he said to them, "Suppose one of you has a friend, and you
go to him at midnight and say to him, 'Friend, lend me three loaves
of bread, 6 because a friend of mine has stopped here while on a
journey, and I have nothing to set before him.' 7 Then he will reply
from inside, 'Do not bother me. The door is already shut, and my
children and I are in bed. I cannot get up and give you anything.' 8 I
tell you, even though the man inside will not get up and give him
anything because he is his friend, yet because of the first man's
sheer persistence he will get up and give him whatever he needs.
9 "So I tell you: Ask, and it will be given to you; seek, and you will
find; knock, and the door will be opened for you. 10 For everyone
who asks receives, and the one who seeks finds, and to the one who
knocks, the door will be opened. 11 What father among you, if your son
asks for a fish, will give him a snake instead of a fish? 12 Or if he asks
for an egg, will give him a scorpion? 13 If you then, although you are
evil, know how to give good gifts to your children, how much more
will the heavenly Father give the Holy Spirit to those who ask him!"

REFLECT

How does this passage tell us to pray? How does God respond to our persistent prayers?

JESUS AND BEELZEBUL

14 Now he was casting out a demon that was mute. When the demon had gone out, the man who had been mute began to speak,
and the crowds were amazed. 15 But some of them said, "By the
power of Beelzebul, the ruler of demons, he casts out demons!"
16 Others, to test him, began asking for a sign from heaven. 17 But
Jesus, realizing their thoughts, said to them, "Every kingdom divided against itself is destroyed, and a divided household falls. 18 So
if Satan too is divided against himself, how will his kingdom stand?
I ask you this because you claim that I cast out demons by Beelzebul. 19 Now if I cast out demons by Beelzebul, by whom do your sons
cast them out? Therefore they will be your judges. 20 But if I cast out
demons by the finger of God, then the kingdom of God has already
overtaken you. 21 When a strong man, fully armed, guards his own
palace, his possessions are safe. 22 But when a stronger man attacks
and conquers him, he takes away the first man's armor on which
the man relied and divides up his plunder. 23 Whoever is not with
me is against me, and whoever does not gather with me scatters.

RESPONSE TO JESUS' WORK

24 "When an unclean spirit goes out of a person, it passes through
waterless places looking for rest but not finding any. Then it says,
'I will return to the home I left.' 25 When it returns, it finds the
house swept clean and put in order. 26 Then it goes and brings
seven other spirits more evil than itself, and they go in and live
there, so the last state of that person is worse than the first."

27 As he said these things, a woman in the crowd spoke out
to him, "Blessed is the womb that bore you and the breasts at
which you nursed!" 28 But he replied, "Blessed rather are those
who hear the word of God and obey it!"

THE SIGN OF JONAH

29 As the crowds were increasing, Jesus began to say, "This generation is a wicked generation; it looks for a sign, but no sign
will be given to it except the sign of Jonah. 30 For just as Jonah
became a sign to the people of Nineveh, so the Son of Man will
be a sign to this generation. 31 The queen of the South will rise
up at the judgment with the people of this generation and condemn them, because she came from the ends of the earth to
hear the wisdom of Solomon—and now, something greater than
Solomon is here! 32 The people of Nineveh will stand up at the
judgment with this generation and condemn it, because they
repented when Jonah preached to them—and now, something
greater than Jonah is here!

INTERNAL LIGHT

33 "No one after lighting a lamp puts it in a hidden place or under
a basket, but on a lampstand, so that those who come in can see
the light. 34 Your eye is the lamp of your body. When your eye is
healthy, your whole body is full of light, but when it is diseased,
your body is full of darkness. 35 Therefore see to it that the light
in you is not darkness. 36 If then your whole body is full of light,
with no part in the dark, it will be as full of light as when the
light of a lamp shines on you."

REBUKING THE PHARISEES AND EXPERTS IN THE LAW

37 As he spoke, a Pharisee invited Jesus to have a meal with him,
so he went in and took his place at the table. 38 The Pharisee was
astonished when he saw that Jesus did not first wash his hands
before the meal. 39 But the Lord said to him, "Now you Pharisees clean the outside of the cup and the plate, but inside you
are full of greed and wickedness. 40 You fools! Didn't the one who
made the outside make the inside as well? 41 But give from your
heart to those in need, and then everything will be clean for you.
42 "But woe to you Pharisees! You give a tenth of your mint,
rue, and every herb, yet you neglect justice and love for God! But
you should have done these things without neglecting the others. 43 Woe to you Pharisees! You love the best seats in the synagogues and elaborate greetings in the marketplaces! 44 Woe to
you! You are like unmarked graves, and people walk over them
without realizing it!"
45 One of the experts in religious law answered him, "Teacher,
when you say these things you insult us too." 46 But Jesus replied,
"Woe to you experts in religious law as well! You load people down
with burdens difficult to bear, yet you yourselves refuse to touch
the burdens with even one of your fingers! 47 Woe to you! You
build the tombs of the prophets whom your ancestors killed. 48 So
you testify that you approve of the deeds of your ancestors, because they killed the prophets and you build their tombs! 49 For
this reason also the wisdom of God said, 'I will send them prophets and apostles, some of whom they will kill and persecute,' 50 so
that this generation may be held accountable for the blood of
all the prophets that has been shed since the beginning of the
world, 51 from the blood of Abel to the blood of Zechariah, who
was killed between the altar and the sanctuary. Yes, I tell you, it
will be charged against this generation. 52 Woe to you experts in
religious law! You have taken away the key to knowledge! You did
not go in yourselves, and you hindered those who were going in."
53 When he went out from there, the experts in the law and the
Pharisees began to oppose him bitterly, and to ask him hostile
questions about many things, 54 plotting against him, to catch
him in something he might say.

FEAR GOD, NOT PEOPLE

12 Meanwhile, when many thousands of the crowd had gathered so that they were trampling on one another, Jesus began to speak first to his disciples, "Be on your guard against the
yeast of the Pharisees, which is hypocrisy. 2 Nothing is hidden
that will not be revealed, and nothing is secret that will not be
made known. 3 So then whatever you have said in the dark will
be heard in the light, and what you have whispered in private
rooms will be proclaimed from the housetops.
4 "I tell you, my friends, do not be afraid of those who kill the body,
and after that have nothing more they can do. 5 But I will warn you
whom you should fear: Fear the one who, after the killing, has authority to throw you into hell. Yes, I tell you, fear him! 6 Aren't five
sparrows sold for two pennies? Yet not one of them is forgotten
before God. 7 In fact, even the hairs on your head are all numbered.
Do not be afraid; you are more valuable than many sparrows.

8 "I tell you, whoever acknowledges me before men, the Son
of Man will also acknowledge before God's angels. 9 But the one
who denies me before men will be denied before God's angels.
10 And everyone who speaks a word against the Son of Man will
be forgiven, but the person who blasphemes against the Holy
Spirit will not be forgiven. 11 But when they bring you before
the synagogues, the rulers, and the authorities, do not worry
about how you should make your defense or what you should
say, 12 for the Holy Spirit will teach you at that moment what
you must say."

THE PARABLE OF THE RICH LANDOWNER

13 Then someone from the crowd said to him, "Teacher, tell my
brother to divide the inheritance with me." 14 But Jesus said to
him, "Man, who made me a judge or arbitrator between you two?"
15 Then he said to them, "Watch out and guard yourself from all
types of greed, because one's life does not consist in the abundance of his possessions." 16 He then told them a parable: "The
land of a certain rich man produced an abundant crop, 17 so he
thought to himself, 'What should I do, for I have nowhere to
store my crops?' 18 Then he said, 'I will do this: I will tear down
my barns and build bigger ones, and there I will store all my
grain and my goods. 19 And I will say to myself, "You have plenty
of goods stored up for many years; relax, eat, drink, celebrate!"'
20 But God said to him, 'You fool! This very night your life will be
demanded back from you, but who will get what you have prepared for yourself?' 21 So it is with the one who stores up riches
for himself, but is not rich toward God."

EXHORTATION NOT TO WORRY

22 Then Jesus said to his disciples, "Therefore I tell you, do not
worry about your life, what you will eat, or about your body, what
you will wear. 23 For there is more to life than food, and more to
the body than clothing. 24 Consider the ravens: They do not sow
or reap, they have no storeroom or barn, yet God feeds them.
How much more valuable are you than the birds! 25 And which
of you by worrying can add an hour to his life? 26 So if you cannot do such a very little thing as this, why do you worry about
the rest? 27 Consider how the flowers grow; they do not work or
spin. Yet I tell you, not even Solomon in all his glory was clothed
like one of these! 28 And if this is how God clothes the wild grass,
which is here today and tomorrow is tossed into the fire to heat
the oven, how much more will he clothe you, you people of little faith! 29 So do not be overly concerned about what you will
eat and what you will drink, and do not worry about such things.
30 For all the nations of the world pursue these things, and your
Father knows that you need them. 31 Instead, pursue his kingdom, and these things will be given to you as well.

32 "Do not be afraid, little flock, for your Father is well pleased
to give you the kingdom. 33 Sell your possessions and give to the
poor. Provide yourselves purses that do not wear out—a treasure in heaven that never decreases, where no thief approaches
and no moth destroys. 34 For where your treasure is, there your
heart will be also.

CALL TO FAITHFUL STEWARDSHIP

35 "Get dressed for service and keep your lamps burning; 36 be like
people waiting for their master to come back from the wedding
celebration, so that when he comes and knocks they can immediately open the door for him. 37 Blessed are those slaves whom
their master finds alert when he returns! I tell you the truth, he
will dress himself to serve, have them take their place at the table,
and will come and wait on them! 38 Even if he comes in the second or third watch of the night and finds them alert, blessed are
those slaves! 39 But understand this: If the owner of the house had
known at what hour the thief was coming, he would not have let
his house be broken into. 40 You also must be ready, because the
Son of Man will come at an hour when you do not expect him."
41 Then Peter said, "Lord, are you telling this parable for us or
for everyone?" 42 The Lord replied, "Who then is the faithful and
wise manager, whom the master puts in charge of his household
servants, to give them their allowance of food at the proper time?
43 Blessed is that slave whom his master finds at work when he
returns. 44 I tell you the truth, the master will put him in charge
of all his possessions. 45 But if that slave should say to himself,
'My master is delayed in returning,' and he begins to beat the
other slaves, both men and women, and to eat, drink, and get
drunk, 46 then the master of that slave will come on a day when
he does not expect him and at an hour he does not foresee, and
will cut him in two, and assign him a place with the unfaithful.
47 That servant who knew his master's will but did not get ready
or do what his master asked will receive a severe beating. 48 But
the one who did not know his master's will and did things worthy of punishment will receive a light beating. From everyone
who has been given much, much will be required, and from the
one who has been entrusted with much, even more will be asked.

NOT PEACE, BUT DIVISION

49 "I have come to bring fire on the earth—and how I wish it were
already kindled! 50 I have a baptism to undergo, and how distressed I am until it is finished! 51 Do you think I have come to
bring peace on earth? No, I tell you, but rather division! 52 For
from now on there will be five in one household divided, three
against two and two against three. 53 They will be divided, father
against son and son against father, mother against daughter and
daughter against mother, mother-in-law against her daughter-
in-law and daughter-in-law against mother-in-law."

READING THE SIGNS

54 Jesus also said to the crowds, "When you see a cloud rising in
the west, you say at once, 'A rainstorm is coming,' and it does.
55 And when you see the south wind blowing, you say, 'There will
be scorching heat,' and there is. 56 You hypocrites! You know how
to interpret the appearance of the earth and the sky, but how
can you not know how to interpret the present time?

CLEAR THE DEBTS

57 "And why don't you judge for yourselves what is right? 58 As
you are going with your accuser before the magistrate, make an

effort to settle with him on the way, so that he will not drag you
before the judge, and the judge hand you over to the officer, and
the officer throw you into prison. 59 I tell you, you will never get
out of there until you have paid the very last cent!"

A CALL TO REPENT

13 Now there were some present on that occasion who told
him about the Galileans whose blood Pilate had mixed
with their sacrifices. 2 He answered them, "Do you think these
Galileans were worse sinners than all the other Galileans, because they suffered these things? 3 No, I tell you! But unless you
repent, you will all perish as well! 4 Or those eighteen who were
killed when the tower in Siloam fell on them, do you think they
were worse offenders than all the others who live in Jerusalem?
5 No, I tell you! But unless you repent you will all perish as well!"

WARNING TO ISRAEL TO BEAR FRUIT

6 Then Jesus told this parable: "A man had a fig tree planted in
his vineyard, and he came looking for fruit on it and found none.
7 So he said to the worker who tended the vineyard, 'For three
years now, I have come looking for fruit on this fig tree, and each
time I inspect it I find none. Cut it down! Why should it continue to deplete the soil?' 8 But the worker answered him, 'Sir,
leave it alone this year too, until I dig around it and put fertil-
izer on it. 9 Then if it bears fruit next year, very well, but if not,
you can cut it down.'"

HEALING ON THE SABBATH

10 Now he was teaching in one of the synagogues on the Sabbath,
11 and a woman was there who had been disabled by a spirit for
eighteen years. She was bent over and could not straighten herself up completely. 12 When Jesus saw her, he called her to him
and said, "Woman, you are freed from your infirmity." 13 Then he
placed his hands on her, and immediately she straightened up
and praised God. 14 But the president of the synagogue, indignant because Jesus had healed on the Sabbath, said to the crowd,
"There are six days on which work should be done! So come and
be healed on those days, and not on the Sabbath day." 15 Then the
Lord answered him, "You hypocrites! Does not each of you on
the Sabbath untie his ox or his donkey from its stall, and lead it
to water? 16 Then shouldn't this woman, a daughter of Abraham
whom Satan bound for eighteen long years, be released from
this imprisonment on the Sabbath day?" 17 When he said this
all his adversaries were humiliated, but the entire crowd was
rejoicing at all the wonderful things he was doing.

ON THE KINGDOM OF GOD

18 Thus Jesus asked, "What is the kingdom of God like? To what
should I compare it? 19 It is like a mustard seed that a man took
and sowed in his garden. It grew and became a tree, and the wild
birds nested in its branches."

20 Again he said, "To what should I compare the kingdom of
God? 21 It is like yeast that a woman took and mixed with three
measures of flour until all the dough had risen."

ABOUT REPENTANCE

LUKE 13:5

James P. Boyce (1886) wrote a simple and accurate definition of repentance: "Repentance is sorrow for sin, accompanied by a determination, with the help of God, to sin no more."

Repentance is acknowledging that we are sinners and in need of being rescued. Repentance kills pride, keeps our hearts soft, and leads us to acknowledge our need for Jesus.

Repentance is a work of the Holy Spirit. First He gives us a new nature, granting us even the desire to repent, and then He gives us the power to actually do it. The Holy Spirit will allow us to see our sin and will give us the grace to ask forgiveness.

"We cannot muster up our own repentance. Even this is a gift from God and it comes by way of a renewed heart and the moving of the Holy Spirit."—C. H. Spurgeon

---

We often assume if we focus on our sin, we will feel proper remorse. Instead, our focus should be on Christ and the redemption we have from our sin through His sacrifice. When we have a proper understanding of the work of Christ we come to a proper understanding of repentance. This leads us to hope and joy because of the freedom and redemption we have in Christ.

Time spent in God's Word also encourages repentance. In the Word of God we see the beauty of Jesus. We see the power of the Holy Spirit. It shows us the way God goes before us and walks with us as we deal with sin in our lives. It shows us the incredible grace and mercy He lavishes on His children, even when we are deep in sin.

Repentance is essential to the Christian life. It is a gift of God whereby we are reminded of our frailty and God's power, and of our inability to escape sin and God's ability to help us overcome it. Repentance leads the sinner to the forgiveness of God. Repentance leads us to an understanding of the grace He offers to us, no matter our circumstances.

THE NARROW DOOR

22 Then Jesus traveled throughout towns and villages, teaching
and making his way toward Jerusalem. 23 Someone asked him,
"Lord, will only a few be saved?" So he said to them, 24 "Exert every effort to enter through the narrow door, because many, I tell
you, will try to enter and will not be able to. 25 Once the head of
the house gets up and shuts the door, then you will stand outside
and start to knock on the door and beg him, 'Lord, let us in!' But
he will answer you, 'I don't know where you come from.' 26 Then
you will begin to say, 'We ate and drank in your presence, and you
taught in our streets.' 27 But he will reply, 'I don't know where you
come from! Go away from me, all you evildoers!' 28 There will be
weeping and gnashing of teeth when you see Abraham, Isaac,
Jacob, and all the prophets in the kingdom of God but you yourselves thrown out. 29 Then people will come from east and west,
and from north and south, and take their places at the banquet
table in the kingdom of God. 30 But indeed, some are last who
will be first, and some are first who will be last."

GOING TO JERUSALEM

31 At that time, some Pharisees came up and said to Jesus, "Get
away from here, because Herod wants to kill you." 32 But he said
to them, "Go and tell that fox, 'Look, I am casting out demons
and performing healings today and tomorrow, and on the third
day I will complete my work. 33 Nevertheless I must go on my
way today and tomorrow and the next day, because it is impossible that a prophet should be killed outside Jerusalem.' 34 O Jerusalem, Jerusalem, you who kill the prophets and stone those
who are sent to you! How often I have longed to gather your
children together as a hen gathers her chicks under her wings,
but you would have none of it! 35 Look, your house is forsaken!
And I tell you, you will not see me until you say, '***Blessed is the
one who comes in the name of the Lord!***'"

HEALING AGAIN ON THE SABBATH

14 Now one Sabbath when Jesus went to dine at the house of
a leader of the Pharisees, they were watching him closely.
2 There right in front of him was a man whose body was swollen
with fluid. 3 So Jesus asked the experts in religious law and the
Pharisees, "Is it lawful to heal on the Sabbath or not?" 4 But they
remained silent. So Jesus took hold of the man, healed him, and
sent him away. 5 Then he said to them, "Which of you, if you have
a son or an ox that has fallen into a well on a Sabbath day, will
not immediately pull him out?" 6 But they could not reply to this.

ON SEEKING SEATS OF HONOR

7 Then when Jesus noticed how the guests chose the places of
honor, he told them a parable. He said to them, 8 "When you are
invited by someone to a wedding feast, do not take the place
of honor, because a person more distinguished than you may
have been invited by your host. 9 So the host who invited both
of you will come and say to you, 'Give this man your place.' Then,
ashamed, you will begin to move to the least important place.
10 But when you are invited, go and take the least important

place, so that when your host approaches he will say to you,
'Friend, move up here to a better place.' Then you will be honored in the presence of all who share the meal with you. 11 For
everyone who exalts himself will be humbled, but the one who
humbles himself will be exalted."
12 He said also to the man who had invited him, "When you host
a dinner or a banquet, don't invite your friends or your brothers
or your relatives or rich neighbors so you can be invited by them
in return and get repaid. 13 But when you host an elaborate meal,
invite the poor, the crippled, the lame, and the blind. 14 Then you
will be blessed, because they cannot repay you, for you will be
repaid at the resurrection of the righteous."

THE PARABLE OF THE GREAT BANQUET

15 When one of those at the meal with Jesus heard this, he said to
him, "Blessed is everyone who will feast in the kingdom of God!"
16 But Jesus said to him, "A man once gave a great banquet and invited many guests. 17 At the time for the banquet he sent his slave to
tell those who had been invited, 'Come, because everything is now
ready.' 18 But one after another they all began to make excuses. The
first said to him, 'I have bought a field, and I must go out and see it.
Please excuse me.' 19 Another said, 'I have bought five yoke of oxen,
and I am going out to examine them. Please excuse me.' 20 Another
said, 'I just got married, and I cannot come.' 21 So the slave came back
and reported this to his master. Then the master of the household
was furious and said to his slave, 'Go out quickly to the streets and
alleys of the city, and bring in the poor, the crippled, the blind, and
the lame.' 22 Then the slave said, 'Sir, what you instructed has been
done, and there is still room.' 23 So the master said to his slave, 'Go
out to the highways and country roads and urge people to come
in, so that my house will be filled. 24 For I tell you, not one of those
individuals who were invited will taste my banquet!'"

COUNTING THE COST

25 Now large crowds were accompanying Jesus, and turning to
them he said, 26 "If anyone comes to me and does not hate his
own father and mother, and wife and children, and brothers and
sisters, and even his own life, he cannot be my disciple. 27 Whoever does not carry his own cross and follow me cannot be my
disciple. 28 For which of you, wanting to build a tower, doesn't sit
down first and compute the cost to see if he has enough money
to complete it? 29 Otherwise, when he has laid a foundation and
is not able to finish the tower, all who see it will begin to make
fun of him. 30 They will say, 'This man began to build and was not
able to finish!' 31 Or what king, going out to confront another
king in battle, will not sit down first and determine whether he
is able with 10,000 to oppose the one coming against him with
20,000? 32 If he cannot succeed, he will send a representative
while the other is still a long way off and ask for terms of peace.
33 In the same way therefore not one of you can be my disciple
if he does not renounce all his own possessions.
34 "Salt is good, but if salt loses its flavor, how can its flavor be
restored? 35 It is of no value for the soil or for the manure pile; it is
to be thrown out. The one who has ears to hear had better listen!"

REFLECT

What does God ask us to surrender to follow Him? What is most difficult for you to surrender to Him?

THE PARABLE OF THE LOST SHEEP AND COIN

15 Now all the tax collectors and sinners were coming to hear
him. 2 But the Pharisees and the experts in the law were
complaining, "This man welcomes sinners and eats with them."
3 So Jesus told them this parable: 4 "Which one of you, if he
has a hundred sheep and loses one of them, would not leave
the ninety-nine in the open pasture and go look for the one
that is lost until he finds it? 5 Then when he has found it, he
places it on his shoulders, rejoicing. 6 Returning home, he calls
together his friends and neighbors, telling them, 'Rejoice with
me, because I have found my sheep that was lost.' 7 I tell you, in
the same way there will be more joy in heaven over one sinner
who repents than over ninety-nine righteous people who have
no need to repent.
8 "Or what woman, if she has ten silver coins and loses one of
them, does not light a lamp, sweep the house, and search thoroughly until she finds it? 9 Then when she has found it, she calls
together her friends and neighbors, saying, 'Rejoice with me, for
I have found the coin that I had lost.' 10 In the same way, I tell
you, there is joy in the presence of God's angels over one sinner
who repents."

THE PARABLE OF THE COMPASSIONATE FATHER

11 Then Jesus said, "A man had two sons. 12 The younger of them
said to his father, 'Father, give me the share of the estate that will
belong to me.' So he divided his assets between them. 13 After a
few days, the younger son gathered together all he had and left
on a journey to a distant country, and there he squandered his
wealth with a wild lifestyle. 14 Then after he had spent everything,
a severe famine took place in that country, and he began to be
in need. 15 So he went and worked for one of the citizens of that
country, who sent him to his fields to feed pigs. 16 He was longing to eat the carob pods the pigs were eating, but no one gave
him anything. 17 But when he came to his senses he said, 'How
many of my father's hired workers have food enough to spare,
but here I am dying from hunger! 18 I will get up and go to my father and say to him, "Father, I have sinned against heaven and
against you. 19 I am no longer worthy to be called your son; treat
me like one of your hired workers."' 20 So he got up and went to
his father. But while he was still a long way from home his father
saw him, and his heart went out to him; he ran and hugged his
son and kissed him. 21 Then his son said to him, 'Father, I have
sinned against heaven and against you; I am no longer worthy
to be called your son.' 22 But the father said to his slaves, 'Hurry!
Bring the best robe, and put it on him! Put a ring on his finger
and sandals on his feet! 23 Bring the fattened calf and kill it! Let
us eat and celebrate, 24 because this son of mine was dead, and is
alive again—he was lost and is found!' So they began to celebrate.
25 "Now his older son was in the field. As he came and approached the house, he heard music and dancing. 26 So he called
one of the slaves and asked what was happening. 27 The slave replied, 'Your brother has returned, and your father has killed the
fattened calf because he got his son back safe and sound.' 28 But
the older son became angry and refused to go in. His father came

out and appealed to him, 29 but he answered his father, 'Look!
These many years I have worked like a slave for you, and I never
disobeyed your commands. Yet you never gave me even a goat
so that I could celebrate with my friends! 30 But when this son
of yours came back, who has devoured your assets with prostitutes, you killed the fattened calf for him!' 31 Then the father said
to him, 'Son, you are always with me, and everything that belongs
to me is yours. 32 It was appropriate to celebrate and be glad, for
your brother was dead, and is alive; he was lost and is found.'"

THE PARABLE OF THE CLEVER STEWARD

16 Jesus also said to the disciples, "There was a rich man who
was informed of accusations that his manager was wasting
his assets. 2 So he called the manager in and said to him, 'What
is this I hear about you? Turn in the account of your administration, because you can no longer be my manager.' 3 Then the manager said to himself, 'What should I do, since my master is taking
my position away from me? I'm not strong enough to dig, and I'm
too ashamed to beg. 4 I know what to do so that when I am put out
of management, people will welcome me into their homes.' 5 So
he contacted his master's debtors one by one. He asked the first,
'How much do you owe my master?' 6 The man replied, '100 measures of olive oil.' The manager said to him, 'Take your bill, sit down
quickly, and write fifty.' 7 Then he said to another, 'And how much
do you owe?' The second man replied, '100 measures of wheat.' The
manager said to him, 'Take your bill, and write 80.' 8 The master
commended the dishonest manager because he acted shrewdly.
For the people of this world are more shrewd in dealing with their
contemporaries than the people of light. 9 And I tell you, make
friends for yourselves by how you use worldly wealth, so that when
it runs out you will be welcomed into the eternal homes.

10 "The one who is faithful in a very little is also faithful in
much, and the one who is dishonest in a very little is also dishonest in much. 11 If then you haven't been trustworthy in han-
dling worldly wealth, who will entrust you with the true riches?
12 And if you haven't been trustworthy with someone else's property, who will give you your own? 13 No servant can serve two
masters, for either he will hate the one and love the other, or
he will be devoted to the one and despise the other. You cannot
serve God and money."

MORE WARNINGS ABOUT THE PHARISEES

14 The Pharisees (who loved money) heard all this and ridiculed
him. 15 But Jesus said to them, "You are the ones who justify yourselves in men's eyes, but God knows your hearts. For what is
highly prized among men is utterly detestable in God's sight.

16 "The law and the prophets were in force until John; since
then, the good news of the kingdom of God has been proclaimed,
and everyone is urged to enter it. 17 But it is easier for heaven
and earth to pass away than for one tiny stroke of a letter in the
law to become void.

18 "Everyone who divorces his wife and marries someone else
commits adultery, and the one who marries a woman divorced
from her husband commits adultery.

THE RICH MAN AND LAZARUS

19“There was a rich man who dressed in purple and fine linen
and who feasted sumptuously every day. 20 But at his gate lay a
poor man named Lazarus whose body was covered with sores,
21 who longed to eat what fell from the rich man’s table. In addition, the dogs came and licked his sores.
22“Now the poor man died and was carried by the angels to Abraham’s side. The rich man also died and was buried. 23 And in Hades, as he was in torment, he looked up and saw Abraham far off
with Lazarus at his side. 24 So he called out, ‘Father Abraham, have
mercy on me, and send Lazarus to dip the tip of his finger in water and cool my tongue, because I am in anguish in this fire.’ 25 But
Abraham said, ‘Child, remember that in your lifetime you received
your good things and Lazarus likewise bad things, but now he is
comforted here and you are in anguish. 26 Besides all this, a great
chasm has been fixed between us, so that those who want to cross
over from here to you cannot do so, and no one can cross from
there to us.’ 27 So the rich man said, ‘Then I beg you, father—send
Lazarus to my father’s house 28 (for I have five brothers) to warn
them so that they don’t come into this place of torment.’ 29 But
Abraham said, ‘They have Moses and the prophets; they must respond to them.’ 30 Then the rich man said, ‘No, father Abraham, but
if someone from the dead goes to them, they will repent.’ 31 He replied to him, ‘If they do not respond to Moses and the prophets,
they will not be convinced even if someone rises from the dead.’”

SIN, FORGIVENESS, FAITH, AND SERVICE

17 Jesus said to his disciples, “Stumbling blocks are sure to come,
but woe to the one through whom they come! 2 It would be better for him to have a millstone tied around his neck and be thrown
into the sea than for him to cause one of these little ones to sin.
3 Watch yourselves! If your brother sins, rebuke him. If he repents,
forgive him. 4 Even if he sins against you seven times in a day, and
seven times returns to you saying, ‘I repent,’ you must forgive him.”
5 The apostles said to the Lord, “Increase our faith!” 6 So the
Lord replied, “If you had faith the size of a mustard seed, you
could say to this black mulberry tree, ‘Be pulled out by the roots
and planted in the sea,’ and it would obey you.
7“Would any one of you say to your slave who comes in from the
field after plowing or shepherding sheep, ‘Come at once and sit
down for a meal’? 8 Won’t the master instead say to him, ‘Get my dinner ready, and make yourself ready to serve me while I eat and drink.
Then you may eat and drink’? 9 He won’t thank the slave because he
did what he was told, will he? 10 So you too, when you have done everything you were commanded to do, should say, ‘We are slaves un-
deserving of special praise; we have only done what was our duty.’”

THE GRATEFUL LEPER

11 Now on the way to Jerusalem, Jesus was passing along between
Samaria and Galilee. 12 As he was entering a village, ten men with
leprosy met him. They stood at a distance, 13 raised their voices
and said, “Jesus, Master, have mercy on us.” 14 When he saw them
he said, “Go and show yourselves to the priests.” And as they went
along, they were cleansed. 15 Then one of them, when he saw he

was healed, turned back, praising God with a loud voice. 16 He fell
with his face to the ground at Jesus' feet and thanked him. (Now
he was a Samaritan.) 17 Then Jesus said, "Were not ten cleansed?
Where are the other nine? 18 Was no one found to turn back and
give praise to God except this foreigner?" 19 Then he said to the
man, "Get up and go your way. Your faith has made you well."

CHALLENGE

Read Genesis 6–7. Why does Jesus say the coming of the kingdom of God will be like the day of the flood? Why is this significant?

THE COMING OF THE KINGDOM

20 Now at one point the Pharisees asked Jesus when the kingdom
of God was coming, so he answered, "The kingdom of God is not
coming with signs to be observed, 21 nor will they say, 'Look, here
it is!' or 'There!' For indeed, the kingdom of God is in your midst."

THE COMING OF THE SON OF MAN

22 Then he said to the disciples, "The days are coming when you will
desire to see one of the days of the Son of Man, and you will not see
it. 23 Then people will say to you, 'Look, there he is!' or 'Look, here
he is!' Do not go out or chase after them. 24 For just like the lightning flashes and lights up the sky from one side to the other, so
will the Son of Man be in his day. 25 But first he must suffer many
things and be rejected by this generation. 26 Just as it was in the
days of Noah, so too it will be in the days of the Son of Man. 27 People were eating, they were drinking, they were marrying, they were
being given in marriage—right up to the day Noah entered the ark.
Then the flood came and destroyed them all. 28 Likewise, just as it
was in the days of Lot, people were eating, drinking, buying, selling, planting, building; 29 but on the day Lot went out from Sodom,
fire and sulfur rained down from heaven and destroyed them all.
30 It will be the same on the day the Son of Man is revealed. 31 On
that day, anyone who is on the roof, with his goods in the house,
must not come down to take them away, and likewise the person
in the field must not turn back. 32 Remember Lot's wife! 33 Whoever
tries to keep his life will lose it, but whoever loses his life will preserve it. 34 I tell you, in that night there will be two people in one
bed; one will be taken and the other left. 35 There will be two wom-
en grinding grain together; one will be taken and the other left."*

37 Then the disciples said to him, "Where, Lord?" He replied to
them, "Where the dead body is, there the vultures will gather."

PRAYER AND THE PARABLE OF THE PERSISTENT WIDOW

18 Then Jesus told them a parable to show them they should always pray and not lose heart. 2 He said, "In a certain city there
was a judge who neither feared God nor respected people. 3 There
was also a widow in that city who kept coming to him and saying,
'Give me justice against my adversary.' 4 For a while he refused, but
later on he said to himself, 'Though I neither fear God nor have regard for people, 5 yet because this widow keeps on bothering me,
I will give her justice, or in the end she will wear me out by her
unending pleas.'" 6 And the Lord said, "Listen to what the unrighteous judge says! 7 Won't God give justice to his chosen ones, who
cry out to him day and night? Will he delay long to help them? 8 I
tell you, he will give them justice speedily. Nevertheless, when
the Son of Man comes, will he find faith on earth?"

LOVE TO GROW

THANKSGIVING WITH PASSION

LUKE 17:15–16

Ten men cried out to Jesus for healing. All that Jesus said to them was "go and show yourselves to the priests" (Luke 17:14).

As they went on their way, these ten men were healed from their leprosy. Yet only one of the ten returned to thank Jesus. Jesus performed a miracle in their lives, how could they not return to say, "Thank you"?

As I start to think less of the nine who did not return, I reflect on my own life. When was the last time I thanked God for my salvation, for all the spiritual blessings I have in Jesus, for the physical things I own, for the roof over my head, for the love of friends, or even for the healing from the headache that I had all day yesterday?

I don't mean a quick, "Hey, thanks Lord," but a thankfulness that causes us to fall on our knees in prayer like the leper.

We are often afraid of grand gestures and strong passions. Isn't it time to bring this kind of enthusiasm back into our times of prayer and praise?

When has God answered your prayers in such a way that it made you want to literally jump for joy? Why are these times of excitement so rare? Perhaps it is because we don't have a proper awe of God. We don't really understand His greatness and His power; His goodness and His holiness. By drawing closer to the heart of God and gaining an understanding of His character we come to see the magnitude of the work He is doing in our lives.

There is nothing lovely in and of ourselves; sin has ruined all of it. Jesus loved us anyway and made us lovely through His transforming power. These truths should make us shout for joy and weep with thanksgiving. They should make us humble and passionate, worshipful and obedient.

Like that one leper who returned to Jesus, let's fall at Jesus' feet with overwhelming gratitude for all that we are and all that we have because of our good God.

THE PARABLE OF THE PHARISEE AND TAX COLLECTOR

9 Jesus also told this parable to some who were confident that they
were righteous and looked down on everyone else. 10 "Two men
went up to the temple to pray, one a Pharisee and the other a tax
collector. 11 The Pharisee stood and prayed about himself like this:
'God, I thank you that I am not like other people: extortionists,
unrighteous people, adulterers—or even like this tax collector.
12 I fast twice a week; I give a tenth of everything I get.' 13 The tax
collector, however, stood far off and would not even look up to
heaven, but beat his breast and said, 'God, be merciful to me, sinner that I am!' 14 I tell you that this man went down to his home
justified rather than the Pharisee. For everyone who exalts himself will be humbled, but he who humbles himself will be exalted."

JESUS AND LITTLE CHILDREN

15 Now people were even bringing their babies to him for him to
touch. But when the disciples saw it, they began to scold those who
brought them. 16 But Jesus called for the children, saying, "Let the
little children come to me and do not try to stop them, for the kingdom of God belongs to such as these. 17 I tell you the truth, whoever
does not receive the kingdom of God like a child will never enter it."

THE WEALTHY RULER

18 Now a certain leader asked him, "Good teacher, what must I do
to inherit eternal life?" 19 Jesus said to him, "Why do you call me
good? No one is good except God alone. 20 You know the commandments: '***Do not commit adultery, do not murder, do not steal, do not
give false testimony, honor your father and mother***.'" 21 The man replied, "I have wholeheartedly obeyed all these laws since my youth."
22 When Jesus heard this, he said to him, "One thing you still lack.
Sell all that you have and give the money to the poor, and you will
have treasure in heaven. Then come, follow me." 23 But when the
man heard this he became very sad, for he was extremely wealthy.
24 When Jesus noticed this, he said, "How hard it is for the rich to
enter the kingdom of God! 25 In fact, it is easier for a camel to go
through the eye of a needle than for a rich person to enter the
kingdom of God." 26 Those who heard this said, "Then who can be
saved?" 27 He replied, "What is impossible for mere humans is possible for God." 28 And Peter said, "Look, we have left everything we
own to follow you! 29 Then Jesus said to them, "I tell you the truth,
there is no one who has left home or wife or brothers or parents
or children for the sake of God's kingdom 30 who will not receive
many times more in this age—and in the age to come, eternal life."

ANOTHER PREDICTION OF JESUS' PASSION

31 Then Jesus took the twelve aside and said to them, "Look, we
are going up to Jerusalem, and everything that is written about
the Son of Man by the prophets will be accomplished. 32 For he
will be handed over to the Gentiles; he will be mocked, mistreated, and spat on. 33 They will flog him severely and kill him.
Yet on the third day he will rise again." 34 But the twelve understood none of these things. This saying was hidden from them,
and they did not grasp what Jesus meant.

HEALING A BLIND MAN

35 As Jesus approached Jericho, a blind man was sitting by the
road begging. 36 When he heard a crowd going by, he asked what
was going on. 37 They told him, "Jesus the Nazarene is passing by."
38 So he called out, "Jesus, Son of David, have mercy on me!" 39 And
those who were in front scolded him to get him to be quiet, but
he shouted even more, "Son of David, have mercy on me!" 40 So
Jesus stopped and ordered the beggar to be brought to him.
When the man came near, Jesus asked him, 41 "What do you want
me to do for you?" He replied, "Lord, let me see again." 42 Jesus
said to him, "Receive your sight; your faith has healed you." 43 And
immediately he regained his sight and followed Jesus, praising
God. When all the people saw it, they too gave praise to God.

JESUS AND ZACCHAEUS

19 Jesus entered Jericho and was passing through it. 2 Now a
man named Zacchaeus was there; he was a chief tax collector and was rich. 3 He was trying to get a look at Jesus, but being a
short man he could not see over the crowd. 4 So he ran on ahead
and climbed up into a sycamore tree to see him, because Jesus
was going to pass that way. 5 And when Jesus came to that place,
he looked up and said to him, "Zacchaeus, come down quickly,
because I must stay at your house today." 6 So he came down
quickly and welcomed Jesus joyfully. 7 And when the people saw
it, they all complained, "He has gone in to be the guest of a man
who is a sinner." 8 But Zacchaeus stopped and said to the Lord,
"Look, Lord, half of my possessions I now give to the poor, and if
I have cheated anyone of anything, I am paying back four times
as much!" 9 Then Jesus said to him, "Today salvation has come
to this household, because he too is a son of Abraham! 10 For the
Son of Man came to seek and to save the lost."

THE PARABLE OF THE TEN MINAS

11 While the people were listening to these things, Jesus proceeded to tell a parable, because he was near to Jerusalem, and
because they thought that the kingdom of God was going to appear immediately. 12 Therefore he said, "A nobleman went to a
distant country to receive for himself a kingdom and then return. 13 And he summoned ten of his slaves, gave them ten minas,
and said to them, 'Do business with these until I come back.'
14 But his citizens hated him and sent a delegation after him,
saying, 'We do not want this man to be king over us!' 15 When
he returned after receiving the kingdom, he summoned these
slaves to whom he had given the money. He wanted to know
how much they had earned by trading. 16 So the first one came
before him and said, 'Sir, your mina has made ten minas more.'
17 And the king said to him, 'Well done, good slave! Because you
have been faithful in a very small matter, you will have authority
over ten cities.' 18 Then the second one came and said, 'Sir, your
mina has made five minas.' 19 So the king said to him, 'And you
are to be over five cities.' 20 Then another slave came and said,
'Sir, here is your mina that I put away for safekeeping in a piece
of cloth. 21 For I was afraid of you, because you are a severe man.
You withdraw what you did not deposit and reap what you did

not sow.' 22 The king said to him, 'I will judge you by your own
words, you wicked slave! So you knew, did you, that I was a severe man, withdrawing what I didn't deposit and reaping what
I didn't sow? 23 Why then didn't you put my money in the bank,
so that when I returned I could have collected it with interest?'
24 And he said to his attendants, 'Take the mina from him, and
give it to the one who has ten.' 25 But they said to him, 'Sir, he has
ten minas already!' 26 'I tell you that everyone who has will be
given more, but from the one who does not have, even what he
has will be taken away. 27 But as for these enemies of mine who
did not want me to be their king, bring them here and slaughter them in front of me!'"

THE TRIUMPHAL ENTRY

28 After Jesus had said this, he continued on ahead, going up to
Jerusalem. 29 Now when he approached Bethphage and Bethany,
at the place called the Mount of Olives, he sent two of the disciples, 30 telling them, "Go to the village ahead of you. When you
enter it, you will find a colt tied there that has never been ridden.
Untie it and bring it here. 31 If anyone asks you, 'Why are you untying it?' just say, 'The Lord needs it.'" 32 So those who were sent
ahead found it exactly as he had told them. 33 As they were untying the colt, its owners asked them, "Why are you untying that
colt?" 34 They replied, "The Lord needs it." 35 Then they brought it
to Jesus, threw their cloaks on the colt, and had Jesus get on it.
36 As he rode along, they spread their cloaks on the road. 37 As he
approached the road leading down from the Mount of Olives, the
whole crowd of his disciples began to rejoice and praise God with
a loud voice for all the mighty works they had seen: 38 "***Blessed is
the king who comes in the name of the Lord!*** Peace in heaven and
glory in the highest!" 39 But some of the Pharisees in the crowd
said to him, "Teacher, rebuke your disciples." 40 He answered, "I
tell you, if they keep silent, the very stones will cry out!"

JESUS WEEPS FOR JERUSALEM UNDER JUDGMENT

41 Now when Jesus approached and saw the city, he wept over
it, 42 saying, "If you had only known on this day, even you, the
things that make for peace! But now they are hidden from your
eyes. 43 For the days will come upon you when your enemies will
build an embankment against you and surround you and close
in on you from every side. 44 They will demolish you—you and
your children within your walls—and they will not leave within
you one stone on top of another, because you did not recognize
the time of your visitation from God."

CLEANSING THE TEMPLE

45 Then Jesus entered the temple courts and began to drive out
those who were selling things there, 46 saying to them, "It is written, '***My house will be a house of prayer***,' but you have turned it
into ***a den of robbers***!"

47 Jesus was teaching daily in the temple courts. The chief
priests and the experts in the law and the prominent leaders
among the people were seeking to assassinate him, 48 but they
could not find a way to do it, for all the people hung on his words.

THE AUTHORITY OF JESUS

20 Now one day, as Jesus was teaching the people in the temple courts and proclaiming the gospel, the chief priests and the experts in the law with the elders came up 2 and said to him, "Tell us: By what authority are you doing these things? Or who is it who gave you this authority?" 3 He answered them, "I will also ask you a question, and you tell me: 4 John's baptism—was it from heaven or from people?" 5 So they discussed it with one another, saying, "If we say, 'From heaven,' he will say, 'Why did you not believe him?' 6 But if we say, 'From people,' all the people will stone us, because they are convinced that John was a prophet." 7 So they replied that they did not know where it came from. 8 Then Jesus said to them, "Neither will I tell you by whose authority I do these things."

THE PARABLE OF THE TENANTS

9 Then he began to tell the people this parable: "A man planted a vineyard, leased it to tenant farmers, and went on a journey for a long time. 10 When harvest time came, he sent a slave to the tenants so that they would give him his portion of the crop. However, the tenants beat his slave and sent him away empty-handed. 11 So he sent another slave. They beat this one too, treated him outrageously, and sent him away empty-handed. 12 So he sent still a third. They even wounded this one, and threw him out. 13 Then the owner of the vineyard said, 'What should I do? I will send my one dear son; perhaps they will respect him.' 14 But when the tenants saw him, they said to one another, 'This is the heir; let's kill him so the inheritance will be ours!' 15 So they threw him out of the vineyard and killed him. What then will the owner of the vineyard do to them? 16 He will come and destroy those tenants and give the vineyard to others." When the people heard this, they said, "May this never happen!" 17 But Jesus looked straight at them and said, "Then what is the meaning of that which is written: '***The stone the builders rejected has become the cornerstone***'? 18 Everyone who falls on this stone will be broken to pieces, and the one on whom it falls will be crushed." 19 Then the experts in the law and the chief priests wanted to arrest him that very hour, because they realized he had told this parable against them. But they were afraid of the people.

PAYING TAXES TO CAESAR

20 Then they watched him carefully and sent spies who pretended to be sincere. They wanted to take advantage of what he might say so that they could deliver him up to the authority and jurisdiction of the governor. 21 Thus they asked him, "Teacher, we know that you speak and teach correctly, and show no partiality, but teach the way of God in accordance with the truth. 22 Is it right for us to pay the tribute tax to Caesar or not?" 23 But Jesus perceived their deceit and said to them, 24 "Show me a denarius. Whose image and inscription are on it?" They said, "Caesar's." 25 So he said to them, "Then give to Caesar the things that are Caesar's, and to God the things that are God's." 26 Thus they were unable in the presence of the people to trap him with his own words. And stunned by his answer, they fell silent.

MARRIAGE AND THE RESURRECTION

27 Now some Sadducees (who contend that there is no resurrection) came to him. 28 They asked him, "Teacher, Moses wrote
for us that ***if a man's brother dies leaving*** a wife but ***no children,***
that man must marry the widow and father children for his broth-
er. 29 Now there were seven brothers. The first one married a
woman and died without children. 30 The second 31 and then the
third married her, and in this same way all seven died, leaving
no children. 32 Finally the woman died too. 33 In the resurrection, therefore, whose wife will the woman be? For all seven
had married her."

34 So Jesus said to them, "The people of this age marry and are
given in marriage. 35 But those who are regarded as worthy to
share in that age and in the resurrection from the dead neither
marry nor are given in marriage. 36 In fact, they can no longer
die, because they are equal to angels and are sons of God, since
they are sons of the resurrection. 37 But even Moses revealed
that the dead are raised in the passage about the bush, where
he calls the Lord ***the God of Abraham and the God of Isaac and***
the God of Jacob. 38 Now he is not God of the dead, but of the living, for all live before him." 39 Then some of the experts in the
law answered, "Teacher, you have spoken well!" 40 For they did
not dare any longer to ask him anything.

THE MESSIAH: DAVID'S SON AND LORD

41 But he said to them, "How is it that they say that the Christ
is David's son? 42 For David himself says in the book of Psalms,
'***The Lord said to my lord,***
"***Sit at my right hand,***
43 ***until I make your enemies a footstool for your feet.***"'
44 If David then calls him 'Lord,' how can he be his son?"

JESUS WARNS THE DISCIPLES AGAINST PRIDE

45 As all the people were listening, Jesus said to his disciples,
46 "Beware of the experts in the law. They like walking around in
long robes, and they love elaborate greetings in the marketplaces
and the best seats in the synagogues and the places of honor at
banquets. 47 They devour widows' property, and as a show make
long prayers. They will receive a more severe punishment."

THE WIDOW'S OFFERING

21 Jesus looked up and saw the rich putting their gifts into the
offering box. 2 He also saw a poor widow put in two small
copper coins. 3 He said, "I tell you the truth, this poor widow has
put in more than all of them. 4 For they all offered their gifts out
of their wealth. But she, out of her poverty, put in everything
she had to live on."

THE SIGNS OF THE END OF THE AGE

5 Now while some were speaking about the temple, how it was
adorned with beautiful stones and offerings, Jesus said, 6 "As for
these things that you are gazing at, the days will come when not
one stone will be left on another. All will be torn down!" 7 So they
asked him, "Teacher, when will these things happen? And what

will be the sign that these things are about to take place?" [8]He
said, "Watch out that you are not misled. For many will come in my
name, saying, 'I am he,' and, 'The time is near.' Do not follow them!
[9]And when you hear of wars and rebellions, do not be afraid. For
these things must happen first, but the end will not come at once."

PERSECUTION OF DISCIPLES

[10]Then he said to them, "Nation will rise up in arms against nation, and kingdom against kingdom. [11]There will be great earthquakes, and famines and plagues in various places, and there will
be terrifying sights and great signs from heaven. [12]But before all
this, they will seize you and persecute you, handing you over to
the synagogues and prisons. You will be brought before kings
and governors because of my name. [13]This will be a time for you
to serve as witnesses. [14]Therefore be resolved not to rehearse
ahead of time how to make your defense. [15]For I will give you
the words along with the wisdom that none of your adversaries
will be able to withstand or contradict. [16]You will be betrayed
even by parents, brothers, relatives, and friends, and they will
have some of you put to death. [17]You will be hated by everyone
because of my name. [18]Yet not a hair of your head will perish.
[19]By your endurance you will gain your lives.

THE DESOLATION OF JERUSALEM

[20]"But when you see Jerusalem surrounded by armies, then know
that its desolation has come near. [21]Then those who are in Judea
must flee to the mountains. Those who are inside the city must
depart. Those who are out in the country must not enter it, [22]be-
cause these are days of vengeance, to fulfill all that is written.
[23]Woe to those who are pregnant and to those who are nursing
their babies in those days! For there will be great distress on the
earth and wrath against this people. [24]They will fall by the edge
of the sword and be led away as captives among all nations. Jerusalem will be trampled down by the Gentiles until the times
of the Gentiles are fulfilled.

THE ARRIVAL OF THE SON OF MAN

[25]"And there will be signs in the sun and moon and stars, and on
the earth nations will be in distress, anxious over the roaring
of the sea and the surging waves. [26]People will be fainting from
fear and from the expectation of what is coming on the world,
for *the powers of the heavens will be shaken.* [27]Then they will see
the Son of Man arriving in a cloud with power and great glory.
[28]But when these things begin to happen, stand up and raise
your heads, because your redemption is drawing near."

THE PARABLE OF THE FIG TREE

[29]Then he told them a parable: "Look at the fig tree and all the
other trees. [30]When they sprout leaves, you see for yourselves
and know that summer is now near. [31]So also you, when you see
these things happening, know that the kingdom of God is near.
[32]I tell you the truth, this generation will not pass away until all
these things take place. [33]Heaven and earth will pass away, but
my words will never pass away.

BE READY!

34 “But be on your guard so that your hearts are not weighed down
with dissipation and drunkenness and the worries of this life, and
that day close down upon you suddenly like a trap. 35 For it will overtake all who live on the face of the whole earth. 36 But stay alert at
all times, praying that you may have strength to escape all these
things that must happen, and to stand before the Son of Man.”

37 So every day Jesus was teaching in the temple courts, but
at night he went and stayed on the Mount of Olives. 38 And all
the people came to him early in the morning to listen to him
in the temple courts.

JUDAS’ DECISION TO BETRAY JESUS

22 Now the Feast of Unleavened Bread, which is called the
Passover, was approaching. 2 The chief priests and the experts in the law were trying to find some way to execute Jesus,
for they were afraid of the people.

3 Then Satan entered Judas, the one called Iscariot, who was
one of the twelve. 4 He went away and discussed with the chief
priests and officers of the temple guard how he might betray
Jesus, handing him over to them. 5 They were delighted and arranged to give him money. 6 So Judas agreed and began looking
for an opportunity to betray Jesus when no crowd was present.

THE PASSOVER

7 Then the day for the feast of Unleavened Bread came, on which
the Passover lamb had to be sacrificed. 8 Jesus sent Peter and
John, saying, “Go and prepare the Passover for us to eat.” 9 They
said to him, “Where do you want us to prepare it?” 10 He said to
them, “Listen, when you have entered the city, a man carrying
a jar of water will meet you. Follow him into the house that he
enters, 11 and tell the owner of the house, ‘The Teacher says to
you, “Where is the guest room where I may eat the Passover with
my disciples?”’ 12 Then he will show you a large furnished room
upstairs. Make preparations there.” 13 So they went and found
things just as he had told them, and they prepared the Passover.

THE LORD’S SUPPER

14 Now when the hour came, Jesus took his place at the table
and the apostles joined him. 15 And he said to them, “I have earnestly desired to eat this Passover with you before I suffer. 16 For
I tell you, I will not eat it again until it is fulfilled in the kingdom
of God.” 17 Then he took a cup, and after giving thanks he said,
“Take this and divide it among yourselves. 18 For I tell you that
from now on I will not drink of the fruit of the vine until the
kingdom of God comes.” 19 Then he took bread, and after giving
thanks he broke it and gave it to them, saying, “This is my body
which is given for you. Do this in remembrance of me.” 20 And in
the same way he took the cup after they had eaten, saying, “This
cup that is poured out for you is the new covenant in my blood.

A FINAL DISCOURSE

21 “But look, the hand of the one who betrays me is with me
on the table. 22 For the Son of Man is to go just as it has been

determined, but woe to that man by whom he is betrayed!" 23 So
they began to question one another as to which of them it could
possibly be who would do this.
24 A dispute also started among them over which of them was to
be regarded as the greatest. 25 So Jesus said to them, "The kings of
the Gentiles lord it over them, and those in authority over them
are called 'benefactors.' 26 Not so with you; instead the one who
is greatest among you must become like the youngest, and the
leader like the one who serves. 27 For who is greater, the one who
is seated at the table, or the one who serves? Is it not the one who
is seated at the table? But I am among you as one who serves.
28 "You are the ones who have remained with me in my trials.
29 Thus I grant to you a kingdom, just as my Father granted to
me, 30 that you may eat and drink at my table in my kingdom,
and you will sit on thrones judging the twelve tribes of Israel.
31 "Simon, Simon, pay attention! Satan has demanded to have
you all, to sift you like wheat, 32 but I have prayed for you, Simon, that your faith may not fail. When you have turned back,
strengthen your brothers." 33 But Peter said to him, "Lord, I am
ready to go with you both to prison and to death!" 34 Jesus replied, "I tell you, Peter, the rooster will not crow today until you
have denied three times that you know me."
35 Then Jesus said to them, "When I sent you out with no money
bag, or traveler's bag, or sandals, you didn't lack anything, did
you?" They replied, "Nothing." 36 He said to them, "But now, the
one who has a money bag must take it, and likewise a traveler's
bag too. And the one who has no sword must sell his cloak and
buy one. 37 For I tell you that this scripture must be fulfilled in
me, '***And he was counted with the transgressors.***' For what is written about me is being fulfilled." 38 So they said, "Look, Lord, here
are two swords." Then he told them, "It is enough."

ON THE MOUNT OF OLIVES

39 Then Jesus went out and made his way, as he customarily did, to
the Mount of Olives, and the disciples followed him. 40 When he
came to the place, he said to them, "Pray that you will not fall into
temptation." 41 He went away from them about a stone's throw,
knelt down, and prayed, 42 "Father, if you are willing, take this
cup away from me. Yet not my will but yours be done." [43 Then
an angel from heaven appeared to him and strengthened him.
44 And in his anguish he prayed more earnestly, and his sweat
was like drops of blood falling to the ground.]† 45 When he got
up from prayer, he came to the disciples and found them sleeping, exhausted from grief. 46 So he said to them, "Why are you
sleeping? Get up and pray that you will not fall into temptation!"

BETRAYAL AND ARREST

47 While he was still speaking, suddenly a crowd appeared, and
the man named Judas, one of the twelve, was leading them. He
walked up to Jesus to kiss him. 48 But Jesus said to him, "Judas,
would you betray the Son of Man with a kiss?" 49 When those who
were around him saw what was about to happen, they said, "Lord,
should we use our swords?" 50 Then one of them struck the high
priest's slave, cutting off his right ear. 51 But Jesus said, "Enough

REFLECT

Why do you think God allowed us insight into this incredibly painful moment for Jesus? How does Jesus' response to God's will offer you encouragement?

of this!" And he touched the man's ear and healed him. 52 Then
Jesus said to the chief priests, the officers of the temple guard,
and the elders who had come out to get him, "Have you come out
with swords and clubs like you would against an outlaw? 53 Day after day when I was with you in the temple courts, you did not arrest me. But this is your hour, and that of the power of darkness!"

JESUS' CONDEMNATION AND PETER'S DENIALS

54 Then they arrested Jesus, led him away, and brought him into the
high priest's house. But Peter was following at a distance. 55 When
they had made a fire in the middle of the courtyard and sat down
together, Peter sat down among them. 56 Then a slave girl, seeing
him as he sat in the firelight, stared at him and said, "This man
was with him too!" 57 But Peter denied it: "Woman, I don't know
him!" 58 Then a little later someone else saw him and said, "You
are one of them too." But Peter said, "Man, I am not!" 59 And after
about an hour still another insisted, "Certainly this man was with
him, because he too is a Galilean." 60 But Peter said, "Man, I don't
know what you're talking about!" At that moment, while he was
still speaking, a rooster crowed. 61 Then the Lord turned and looked
straight at Peter, and Peter remembered the word of the Lord,
how he had said to him, "Before a rooster crows today, you will
deny me three times." 62 And he went outside and wept bitterly.

63 Now the men who were holding Jesus under guard began to
mock him and beat him. 64 They blindfolded him and asked him
repeatedly, "Prophesy! Who hit you?" 65 They also said many other things against him, reviling him.

66 When day came, the council of the elders of the people gathered together, both the chief priests and the experts in the law.
Then they led Jesus away to their council 67 and said, "If you are
the Christ, tell us." But he said to them, "If I tell you, you will not
believe, 68 and if I ask you, you will not answer. 69 But from now on
the Son of Man will be seated at the right hand of the power of God."
70 So they all said, "Are you the Son of God, then?" He answered
them, "You say that I am." 71 Then they said, "Why do we need further testimony? We have heard it ourselves from his own lips!"

JESUS BROUGHT BEFORE PILATE

23 Then the whole group of them rose up and brought Jesus
before Pilate. 2 They began to accuse him, saying, "We
found this man subverting our nation, forbidding us to pay the
tribute tax to Caesar and claiming that he himself is Christ, a
king." 3 So Pilate asked Jesus, "Are you the king of the Jews?" He
replied, "You say so." 4 Then Pilate said to the chief priests and
the crowds, "I find no basis for an accusation against this man."
5 But they persisted in saying, "He incites the people by teaching
throughout all Judea. It started in Galilee and ended up here!"

JESUS BROUGHT BEFORE HEROD

6 Now when Pilate heard this, he asked whether the man was a
Galilean. 7 When he learned that he was from Herod's jurisdiction, he sent him over to Herod, who also happened to be in Jerusalem at that time. 8 When Herod saw Jesus, he was very glad,
for he had long desired to see him, because he had heard about

him and was hoping to see him perform some miraculous sign.
9 So Herod questioned him at considerable length; Jesus gave
him no answer. 10 The chief priests and the experts in the law
were there, vehemently accusing him. 11 Even Herod with his soldiers treated him with contempt and mocked him. Then, dressing him in elegant clothes, Herod sent him back to Pilate. 12 That
very day Herod and Pilate became friends with each other, for
prior to this they had been enemies.

JESUS BROUGHT BEFORE THE CROWD

13 Then Pilate called together the chief priests, the leaders, and
the people, 14 and said to them, "You brought me this man as one
who was misleading the people. When I examined him before
you, I did not find this man guilty of anything you accused him
of doing. 15 Neither did Herod, for he sent him back to us. Look,
he has done nothing deserving death. 16 I will therefore have him
flogged and release him."‡

18 But they all shouted out together, "Take this man away! Release Barabbas for us!" 19 (This was a man who had been thrown
into prison for an insurrection started in the city, and for murder.) 20 Pilate addressed them once again because he wanted to
release Jesus. 21 But they kept on shouting, "Crucify, crucify him!"
22 A third time he said to them, "Why? What wrong has he done? I
have found him guilty of no crime deserving death. I will therefore
flog him and release him." 23 But they were insistent, demanding
with loud shouts that he be crucified. And their shouts prevailed.
24 So Pilate decided that their demand should be granted. 25 He released the man they asked for, who had been thrown in prison for
insurrection and murder. But he handed Jesus over to their will.

THE CRUCIFIXION

26 As they led him away, they seized Simon of Cyrene, who was
coming in from the country. They placed the cross on his back
and made him carry it behind Jesus. 27 A great number of the people followed him, among them women who were mourning and
wailing for him. 28 But Jesus turned to them and said, "Daughters of Jerusalem, do not weep for me, but weep for yourselves
and for your children. 29 For this is certain: The days are coming when they will say, 'Blessed are the barren, the wombs that
never bore children, and the breasts that never nursed!' 30 Then
they will begin *to say to the mountains, 'Fall on us!' and to the hills,*
'Cover us!' 31 For if such things are done when the wood is green,
what will happen when it is dry?"

32 Two other criminals were also led away to be executed with
him. 33 So when they came to the place that is called "The Skull,"
they crucified him there, along with the criminals, one on his
right and one on his left. 34 [But Jesus said, "Father, forgive them,
for they don't know what they are doing."]§ Then *they threw dice*
to divide his clothes. 35 The people also stood there watching, but
the leaders ridiculed him, saying, "He saved others. Let him save
himself if he is the Christ of God, his chosen one!" 36 The soldiers
also mocked him, coming up and offering him sour wine, 37 and
saying, "If you are the king of the Jews, save yourself!" 38 There
was also an inscription over him, "This is the king of the Jews."

39 One of the criminals who was hanging there railed at him,
saying, "Aren't you the Christ? Save yourself and us!" 40 But the
other rebuked him, saying, "Don't you fear God, since you are
under the same sentence of condemnation? 41 And we rightly
so, for we are getting what we deserve for what we did, but this
man has done nothing wrong." 42 Then he said, "Jesus, remember me when you come in your kingdom." 43 And Jesus said to
him, "I tell you the truth, today you will be with me in paradise."

44 It was now about noon, and darkness came over the whole
land until three in the afternoon, 45 because the sun's light failed.
The temple curtain was torn in two. 46 Then Jesus, calling out with
a loud voice, said, "Father, ***into your hands I commit my spirit!***"
And after he said this he breathed his last.

47 Now when the centurion saw what had happened, he praised
God and said, "Certainly this man was innocent!" 48 And all the
crowds that had assembled for this spectacle, when they saw
what had taken place, returned home beating their breasts.
49 And all those who knew Jesus stood at a distance, and the
women who had followed him from Galilee saw these things.

JESUS' BURIAL

50 Now there was a man named Joseph who was a member of the
council, a good and righteous man. 51 (He had not consented to
their plan and action.) He was from the Judean town of Arimathea, and was looking forward to the kingdom of God. 52 He went
to Pilate and asked for the body of Jesus. 53 Then he took it down,
wrapped it in a linen cloth, and placed it in a tomb cut out of
the rock, where no one had yet been buried. 54 It was the day of
preparation and the Sabbath was beginning. 55 The women who
had accompanied Jesus from Galilee followed, and they saw the
tomb and how his body was laid in it. 56 Then they returned and
prepared aromatic spices and perfumes.

On the Sabbath they rested according to the commandment.

THE RESURRECTION

24 Now on the first day of the week, at early dawn, the women
went to the tomb, taking the aromatic spices they had prepared. 2 They found that the stone had been rolled away from the
tomb, 3 but when they went in, they did not find the body of the
Lord Jesus. 4 While they were perplexed about this, suddenly two
men stood beside them in dazzling attire. 5 The women were terribly frightened and bowed their faces to the ground, but the men
said to them, "Why do you look for the living among the dead? 6 He
is not here, but has been raised! Remember how he told you, while
he was still in Galilee, 7 that the Son of Man must be delivered into
the hands of sinful men, and be crucified, and on the third day rise
again." 8 Then the women remembered his words, 9 and when they
returned from the tomb they told all these things to the eleven
and to all the rest. 10 Now it was Mary Magdalene, Joanna, Mary
the mother of James, and the other women with them who told
these things to the apostles. 11 But these words seemed like pure
nonsense to them, and they did not believe them. 12 But Peter got
up and ran to the tomb. He bent down and saw only the strips of
linen cloth; then he went home, wondering what had happened.

JESUS WALKS THE ROAD TO EMMAUS

13 Now that very day two of them were on their way to a village
called Emmaus, about seven miles from Jerusalem. 14 They were
talking to each other about all the things that had happened.
15 While they were talking and debating these things, Jesus himself approached and began to accompany them 16 (but their eyes
were kept from recognizing him). 17 Then he said to them, "What
are these matters you are discussing so intently as you walk
along?" And they stood still, looking sad. 18 Then one of them,
named Cleopas, answered him, "Are you the only visitor to Jerusalem who doesn't know the things that have happened there
in these days?" 19 He said to them, "What things?" "The things
concerning Jesus the Nazarene," they replied, "a man who, with
his powerful deeds and words, proved to be a prophet before
God and all the people; 20 and how our chief priests and leaders
handed him over to be condemned to death, and crucified him.
21 But we had hoped that he was the one who was going to redeem
Israel. Not only this, but it is now the third day since these things
happened. 22 Furthermore, some women of our group amazed
us. They were at the tomb early this morning, 23 and when they
did not find his body, they came back and said they had seen a
vision of angels, who said he was alive. 24 Then some of those who
were with us went to the tomb, and found it just as the women
had said, but they did not see him." 25 So he said to them, "You
foolish people—how slow of heart to believe all that the prophets have spoken! 26 Wasn't it necessary for the Christ to suffer
these things and enter into his glory?" 27 Then beginning with
Moses and all the prophets, he interpreted to them the things
written about himself in all the scriptures.

28 So they approached the village where they were going. He
acted as though he wanted to go farther, 29 but they urged him,
"Stay with us, because it is getting toward evening and the day
is almost done." So he went in to stay with them.

30 When he had taken his place at the table with them, he took
the bread, blessed and broke it, and gave it to them. 31 At this
point their eyes were opened and they recognized him. Then he
vanished out of their sight. 32 They said to each other, "Didn't our
hearts burn within us while he was speaking with us on the road,
while he was explaining the scriptures to us?" 33 So they got up
that very hour and returned to Jerusalem. They found the eleven
and those with them gathered together 34 and saying, "The Lord
has really risen, and has appeared to Simon!" 35 Then they told
what had happened on the road, and how they recognized him
when he broke the bread.

JESUS MAKES A FINAL APPEARANCE

36 While they were saying these things, Jesus himself stood
among them and said to them, "Peace be with you." 37 But they
were startled and terrified, thinking they saw a ghost. 38 Then he
said to them, "Why are you frightened, and why do doubts arise
in your hearts? 39 Look at my hands and my feet; it's me! Touch
me and see; a ghost does not have flesh and bones like you see I
have." 40 When he had said this, he showed them his hands and
his feet. 41 And while they still could not believe it (because of

LOVE TO GROW

LEARNING AT THE DINNER TABLE

LUKE 24:13–35

A lot of important things happen around the dinner table: celebrating milestones, grieving together, hosting people we love. You can trace the importance of food and community throughout Scripture—from eating the forbidden fruit, to providing manna for a desperate people, to practicing communion as taught at the Lord's Supper.

The concept of hospitality is deeply bound up within these ideas: Jesus welcomed the crowds by providing food for them; He defied cultural norms by eating with prostitutes and tax collectors; and the Epistles command believers to eat together without showing favoritism. In Luke 24:13–35, breaking bread together is the foundation for a relationship with Jesus.

In this passage we find two disciples of Jesus walking to the village of Emmaus, talking about the events they had seen in Jerusalem. Jesus, whom they were kept from recognizing, joined them on their journey. Jesus spent the rest of their seven-mile trek interpreting Scripture by pointing to His fulfilment of the prophecies about the Messiah.

These two disciples spent their whole journey learning from the risen Lord, yet they had no idea who He was! They gained plenty of knowledge about the Messiah, but not enough to know He was walking along the road with them. It wasn't until He broke bread, blessed it, and gave it to them that their eyes were opened and they realized who had been with them all along.

The disciples on the road to Emmaus had the unbelievable experience of walking with Jesus and learning directly from Him how to interpret the Scriptures and see the promises of His coming.

The most amazing part of this story is that it was not until Jesus did something ordinary—breaking bread—that He gave the disciples the gift of recognizing Him.

After Jesus revealed His identity (and promptly vanished) they looked at each other and said, "Didn't our hearts burn within us while he was speaking with us on the road, while he was explaining the scriptures to us?" (Luke 24:32).

God offers us the incredible gift of knowledge and relationship, always together. He gives us Scripture to learn from and community to live in. He gives us preaching to instruct us and the practice of communion to bind us together. He gives us knowledge of who He is and a relationship that cannot be broken.

their joy) and were amazed, he said to them, "Do you have anything here to eat?" 42 So they gave him a piece of broiled fish,
43 and he took it and ate it in front of them.

JESUS' FINAL COMMISSION

44 Then he said to them, "These are my words that I spoke to you
while I was still with you, that everything written about me in
the law of Moses and the prophets and the psalms must be fulfilled." 45 Then he opened their minds so they could understand
the scriptures, 46 and said to them, "Thus it stands written that
the Christ would suffer and would rise from the dead on the
third day, 47 and repentance for the forgiveness of sins would be
proclaimed in his name to all nations, beginning from Jerusalem. 48 You are witnesses of these things. 49 And look, I am sending you what my Father promised. But stay in the city until you
have been clothed with power from on high."

JESUS' DEPARTURE

50 Then Jesus led them out as far as Bethany, and lifting up his
hands, he blessed them. 51 Now during the blessing he departed
and was taken up into heaven. 52 So they worshiped him and returned to Jerusalem with great joy, 53 and were continually in
the temple courts blessing God.

BUT THESE ARE *recorded* SO THAT *you* MAY *believe* THAT *Jesus* IS THE *Christ,* THE *Son of God,* AND THAT BY *believing* *you* MAY HAVE *life* IN HIS NAME

MEMORY VERSE

But these are recorded so that you may believe that Jesus is the Christ, the Son of God, and that by believing you may have life in his name.

John 20:31

John

INTRODUCTION

Jesus is the Son of God

Like the other Synoptic Gospels, the Book of John presents an argument for the deity of Jesus. John's purpose in writing his Gospel was to show Jesus was the Son of God, both fully God and fully human, who came to earth to die for humanity's sins. John explicitly presents the way to eternal life: believing that Jesus is the Son of God and the Savior of the world.

John's Gospel describes Jesus' public ministry in detail, including the controversy surrounding His words and actions (1:19—12:50). The book then relates Jesus' private ministry, including His last night with His disciples (13:1—17:26). Finally, the Gospel reveals Jesus' death, resurrection, and postresurrection appearances, as well as His final moments with His disciples before His ascension (18:1—21:25).

The author of the Gospel of John is not identified by name in the book, but he does refer to himself as "the disciple whom Jesus loved" (John 21:7). Scholars have traditionally agreed that the disciple John was the author. This Gospel is typically dated much later than the others, between A.D. 85 and A.D. 95.

The Gospel of John teaches us to love God greatly as our only source of eternal life. By believing that Jesus is the Son of God and that He alone is the way to salvation, we can be sure of eternal life with Him. John's Gospel reveals the crucial message of hope and assurance that placing our faith in Jesus gives us eternal life.

Ukraine

OFFICIAL LANGUAGE
Ukrainian
POPULATION
43,921,000
UNREACHED POPULATION
455,000
PROFESSING CHRISTIANS
73.0%

Diana's Home

Say a Prayer Today

Pray for the training of leaders in the church in Ukraine. Pray God would build up leaders for the church body who are committed to and focused on following Him wholeheartedly.

HISTORY BIT

The country of Ukraine gained its independence from the Soviet Union in 1991. While severely persecuted under communist rule, the church in Ukraine now enjoys freedom of religion, though some prejudice remains.*

Source Information:
https://joshuaproject.net/countries/UP
*Jason Mandryk, Operation World, 7th edition (Colorado Springs, CO: Biblica Publishing, 2010), 844.

LOVE YOUR NEIGHBOR

Her Journey

DIANA'S STORY

Sometimes, when I want God to do something for me, I have a hard time waiting for His answer. I want to know why He doesn't help me right away. I've learned that sometimes He doesn't do what we ask in order to accomplish His greater purpose and be glorified through our weaknesses.

A few years ago I had a wart on my left hand. It wasn't a big deal, but it wasn't terribly attractive, so I went to the doctor to have it removed. However, every few months it would grow back. I tried everything. The more things I tried and the more I asked God to remove it, the more frustrated I became.

Victoria, my manicurist, asked me about my wart when I got a manicure. Like many people in Ukraine, she is somewhat superstitious, and she told me of a way to remove my wart. I went home frustrated and angry at God. I knew He was able to heal me, but instead, He was ignoring me. I didn't believe in these nonsense methods of solving life's problems like many around me did. I believed in the God who created the heavens and the earth. Why wasn't He healing me?

After my child-like tantrum, my wart began to heal. God was gracious enough not only to respond to me in my frustration, but also to offer me healing in the midst of my ungratefulness. I shared what God had done with my manicurist Victoria. Because of that little wart, I was able to share God's goodness with someone who may not have otherwise had a chance to witness it.

Jesus is the Son of God. He is all powerful, and it is He alone who offers salvation for the world. He uses the difficulties and challenges in our lives, no matter how small, to draw us closer to Him. He even uses our shortcomings to affect the lives of others. What grace!

6 WEEK READING PLAN

LOVE HIS WORD

MONDAY	TUESDAY	WEDNESDAY	THURSDAY	FRIDAY
John 1:1-18	**John 1:19-51**	**John 2**	**John 3**	**John 4:1-45**
SOAP **John 1:1-5**	**SOAP** **John 1:49-50**	**SOAP** **John 2:11**	**SOAP** **John 3:16-17**	**SOAP** **John 4:25-26**
John 4:46—5:30	**John 5:31—6:15**	**John 6:16-58**	**John 6:59—7:13**	**John 7:14-52**
SOAP **John 4:50**	**SOAP** **John 6:14**	**SOAP** **John 6:40**	**SOAP** **John 6:67-69**	**SOAP** **John 7:17-18**
John 8:1-30	**John 8:31—9:12**	**John 9:13-41**	**John 10**	**John 11:1-16**
SOAP **John 8:10-11**	**SOAP** **John 8:54-55**	**SOAP** **John 9:36-38**	**SOAP** **John 10:27-30**	**SOAP** **John 11:14-15**
John 11:17-57	**John 12:1-43**	**John 12:44—13:30**	**John 13:31—14:14**	**John 14:15-38**
SOAP **John 11:32-33**	**SOAP** **John 12:13-15**	**SOAP** **John 12:44-46**	**SOAP** **John 14:12-14**	**SOAP** **John 14:25-26**
John 15:1-17	**John 15:18—16:33**	**John 17**	**John 18:1-24**	**John 18:25-40**
SOAP **John 15:5-6**	**SOAP** **John 16:7-11**	**SOAP** **John 17:3-5**	**SOAP** **John 18:11**	**SOAP** **John 18:36**
John 19:1-37	**John 19:38—20:18**	**John 20:19-31**	**John 21:1-14**	**John 21:15-25**
SOAP **John 19:30**	**SOAP** **John 20:1-18**	**SOAP** **John 20:31**	**SOAP** **John 21:7-8**	**SOAP** **John 21:24-25**

THE PROLOGUE TO THE GOSPEL

1 In the beginning was the Word, and the Word was with God,
and the Word was fully God. 2 The Word was with God in the
beginning. 3 All things were created by him, and apart from him
not one thing was created that has been created. 4 *In him was life,*
and the life was the light of mankind. 5 And the light shines on
in the darkness, but the darkness has not mastered it.
6 A man came, sent from God, whose name was John. 7 He came
as a witness to testify about the light, so that everyone might believe through him. 8 He himself was not the light, but he came to
testify about the light. 9 The true light, who gives light to everyone, was coming into the world. 10 He was in the world, and the
world was created by him, but the world did not recognize him.
11 He came to what was his own, but his own people did not receive him. 12 But to all who have received him—those who believe
in his name—he has given the right to become God's children
13 —children not born by human parents or by human desire or
a husband's decision, but by God.
14 Now the Word became flesh and took up residence among
us. We saw his glory—the glory of the one and only, full of grace
and truth, who came from the Father. 15 John testified about him
and shouted out, "This one was the one about whom I said, 'He
who comes after me is greater than I am, because he existed before me.'" 16 For we have all received from his fullness one gracious gift after another. 17 For the law was given through Moses,
but grace and truth came about through Jesus Christ. 18 No one
has ever seen God. The only one, himself God, who is in closest
fellowship with the Father, has made God known.

THE TESTIMONY OF JOHN THE BAPTIST

19 Now this was John's testimony when the Jewish leaders sent
priests and Levites from Jerusalem to ask him, "Who are you?"
20 He confessed—he did not deny but confessed—"I am not the
Christ!" 21 So they asked him, "Then who are you? Are you Elijah?" He said, "I am not!" "Are you the Prophet?" He answered,
"No!" 22 Then they said to him, "Who are you? Tell us so that
we can give an answer to those who sent us. What do you say
about yourself?"
23 John said, "I am ***the voice of one shouting in the wilderness,***
'Make straight the way for the Lord,' as the prophet Isaiah said."
24 (Now they had been sent from the Pharisees.) 25 So they asked
John, "Why then are you baptizing if you are not the Christ, nor
Elijah, nor the Prophet?"
26 John answered them, "I baptize with water. Among you
stands one whom you do not recognize, 27 who is coming after
me. I am not worthy to untie the strap of his sandal!" 28 These
things happened in Bethany across the Jordan River where John
was baptizing.
29 On the next day John saw Jesus coming toward him and said,
"Look, the Lamb of God who takes away the sin of the world!
30 This is the one about whom I said, 'After me comes a man who
is greater than I am, because he existed before me.' 31 I did not
recognize him, but I came baptizing with water so that he could
be revealed to Israel."

LOVE TO GROW

A GENEROUS GOD?

JOHN 1:16

The new year did not start the way I had planned or prayed it would. We had lots of illness, unexpected dental procedures, sick pets, and a minivan that started acting up. While the steep bills were frustrating—and certainly not what I had prayed for—God provided. We were all healthy again including our pets, and our van ran great. Then, suddenly, our van died, and there was no reviving it. We had to buy a new car and lost all the money we'd invested in the repair of the old one the week before. Not long after that, a power outage fried our dryer, and the kids came down with another stomach bug.

It's rather embarrassing that, in the scheme of things, such insignificant matters caused me to struggle. I wrestled with how God had answered my prayers. I struggled to see God's generosity even though a new vehicle sat in our driveway. It felt more like God had taken instead of given. After this, I was made very aware of how small my faith really is.

Did you know we question God's generosity when we question His providence? We doubt the Father's heart toward us when we don't trust He will take care of us, or when we pray without believing He will answer us. We take God's generosity for granted when we have an attitude of entitlement, as if God owes us something. We call God a liar when we neglect prayer altogether because we don't believe it will do any good.

If we take the time to examine who we are in light of who God is, we will see a generosity that takes our breath away.

Jesus took every single one of our sins on Himself and paid the penalty we should have had to pay. Then He credited all of His righteousness to us as our own. Christ secured for us a place in God's kingdom and a future of inexpressible joy.

Once we grasp the magnitude of the gift of salvation we have in Jesus, we will see everything else as grace upon grace. All too often we listen to the words of the world which tell us we deserve everything we have and more. Therefore, we fail to see the generosity of God in our lives.

The Almighty God, the Maker of heaven and earth, the Sustainer of all life is approachable and available. The fact that we can come to the One who is all-powerful with every thought, need, complaint, and struggle shows the generosity of our God.

32 Then John testified, "I saw the Spirit descending like a dove
from heaven, and it remained on him. 33 And I did not recognize
him, but the one who sent me to baptize with water said to me,
'The one on whom you see the Spirit descending and remaining—this is the one who baptizes with the Holy Spirit.' 34 I have
both seen and testified that this man is the Chosen One of God."
35 Again the next day John was standing there with two of his
disciples. 36 Gazing at Jesus as he walked by, he said, "Look, the
Lamb of God!" 37 When John's two disciples heard him say this,
they followed Jesus. 38 Jesus turned around and saw them following and said to them, "What do you want?" So they said to him,
"Rabbi" (which is translated Teacher), "where are you staying?"
39 Jesus answered, "Come and you will see." So they came and saw
where he was staying, and they stayed with him that day. Now
it was about four o'clock in the afternoon.

ANDREW'S DECLARATION

40 Andrew, the brother of Simon Peter, was one of the two disciples who heard what John said and followed Jesus. 41 He first
found his own brother Simon and told him, "We have found the
Messiah!" (which is translated Christ). 42 Andrew brought Simon
to Jesus. Jesus looked at him and said, "You are Simon, the son
of John. You will be called Cephas" (which is translated Peter).

THE CALLING OF MORE DISCIPLES

43 On the next day Jesus wanted to set out for Galilee. He found
Philip and said to him, "Follow me." 44 (Now Philip was from Bethsaida, the town of Andrew and Peter.) 45 Philip found Nathanael
and told him, "We have found the one Moses wrote about in the
law, and the prophets also wrote about—Jesus of Nazareth, the
son of Joseph." 46 Nathanael replied, "Can anything good come
out of Nazareth?" Philip replied, "Come and see."
47 Jesus saw Nathanael coming toward him and exclaimed,
"Look, a true Israelite *in whom there is no deceit!*" 48 Nathanael
asked him, "How do you know me?" Jesus replied, "Before Philip
called you, when you were under the fig tree, I saw you." 49 Nathanael answered him, "Rabbi, you are the Son of God; you are
the king of Israel!" 50 Jesus said to him, "Because I told you that
I saw you under the fig tree, do you believe? You will see greater
things than these." 51 He continued, "I tell all of you the solemn
truth—you will see heaven opened and the angels of God ascending and descending on the Son of Man."

TURNING WATER INTO WINE

2 Now on the third day there was a wedding at Cana in Galilee.
Jesus' mother was there, 2 and Jesus and his disciples were
also invited to the wedding. 3 When the wine ran out, Jesus' mother said to him, "They have no wine left." 4 Jesus replied, "Woman,
why are you saying this to me? My time has not yet come." 5 His
mother told the servants, "Whatever he tells you, do it."
6 Now there were six stone water jars there for Jewish ceremonial washing, each holding twenty or thirty gallons. 7 Jesus told
the servants, "Fill the water jars with water." So they filled them
up to the very top. 8 Then he told them, "Now draw some out and

take it to the head steward," and they did. 9 When the head steward tasted the water that had been turned to wine, not knowing where it came from (though the servants who had drawn the water knew), he called the bridegroom 10 and said to him, "Everyone serves the good wine first, and then the cheaper wine when the guests are drunk. You have kept the good wine until now!" 11 Jesus did this as the first of his miraculous signs, in Cana of Galilee. In this way he revealed his glory, and his disciples believed in him.

CHALLENGE

Read Leviticus 5:6–13. Why was it significant that the merchants were selling animals to the people? How was this defiling God's house?

CLEANSING THE TEMPLE

12 After this he went down to Capernaum with his mother and brothers and his disciples, and they stayed there a few days. 13 Now the Jewish feast of Passover was near, so Jesus went up to Jerusalem.

14 He found in the temple courts those who were selling oxen and sheep and doves, and the money changers sitting at tables. 15 So he made a whip of cords and drove them all out of the temple courts, with the sheep and the oxen. He scattered the coins of the money changers and overturned their tables. 16 To those who sold the doves he said, "Take these things away from here! Do not make my Father's house a marketplace!" 17 His disciples remembered that it was written, "***Zeal for your house will devour me.***"

18 So then the Jewish leaders responded, "What sign can you show us, since you are doing these things?" 19 Jesus replied, "Destroy this temple and in three days I will raise it up again." 20 Then the Jewish leaders said to him, "This temple has been under construction for forty-six years, and are you going to raise it up in three days?" 21 But Jesus was speaking about the temple of his body. 22 So after he was raised from the dead, his disciples remembered that he had said this, and they believed the scripture and the saying that Jesus had spoken.

JESUS AT THE PASSOVER FEAST

23 Now while Jesus was in Jerusalem at the Feast of the Passover, many people believed in his name because they saw the miraculous signs he was doing. 24 But Jesus would not entrust himself to them, because he knew all people. 25 He did not need anyone to testify about man, for he knew what was in man.

CONVERSATION WITH NICODEMUS

3 Now a certain man, a Pharisee named Nicodemus, who was a member of the Jewish ruling council, 2 came to Jesus at night and said to him, "Rabbi, we know that you are a teacher who has come from God. For no one could perform the miraculous signs that you do unless God is with him." 3 Jesus replied, "I tell you the solemn truth, unless a person is born from above, he cannot see the kingdom of God." 4 Nicodemus said to him, "How can a man be born when he is old? He cannot enter his mother's womb and be born a second time, can he?"

5 Jesus answered, "I tell you the solemn truth, unless a person is born of water and spirit, he cannot enter the kingdom of God. 6 What is born of the flesh is flesh, and what is born of the Spirit is spirit. 7 Do not be amazed that I said to you, 'You must all be born from above.' 8 The wind blows wherever it will, and you hear

the sound it makes, but do not know where it comes from and
where it is going. So it is with everyone who is born of the Spirit."
9 Nicodemus replied, "How can these things be?" 10 Jesus answered, "Are you the teacher of Israel and yet you don't understand these things? 11 I tell you the solemn truth, we speak about
what we know and testify about what we have seen, but you people do not accept our testimony. 12 If I have told you people about
earthly things and you don't believe, how will you believe if I tell
you about heavenly things? 13 No one has ascended into heaven
except the one who descended from heaven—the Son of Man.
14 Just as Moses *lifted up the serpent in the wilderness*, so must the
Son of Man be lifted up, 15 so that everyone who believes in him
may have eternal life."

16 For this is the way God loved the world: He gave his one and
only Son, so that everyone who believes in him will not perish but
have eternal life. 17 For God did not send his Son into the world to
condemn the world, but that the world should be saved through
him. 18 The one who believes in him is not condemned. The one
who does not believe has been condemned already, because he has
not believed in the name of the one and only Son of God. 19 Now
this is the basis for judging: that the light has come into the world
and people loved the darkness rather than the light, because their
deeds were evil. 20 For everyone who does evil deeds hates the light
and does not come to the light, so that their deeds will not be exposed. 21 But the one who practices the truth comes to the light, so
that it may be plainly evident that his deeds have been done in God.

FURTHER TESTIMONY ABOUT JESUS BY JOHN THE BAPTIST

22 After this, Jesus and his disciples came into Judean territory,
and there he spent time with them and was baptizing. 23 John
was also baptizing at Aenon near Salim, because water was plentiful there, and people were coming to him and being baptized.
24 (For John had not yet been thrown into prison.)

25 Now a dispute came about between some of John's disciples
and a certain Jew concerning ceremonial washing. 26 So they
came to John and said to him, "Rabbi, the one who was with you
on the other side of the Jordan River, about whom you testified—
see, he is baptizing, and everyone is flocking to him!"

27 John replied, "No one can receive anything unless it has been
given to him from heaven. 28 You yourselves can testify that I
said, 'I am not the Christ,' but rather, 'I have been sent before
him.' 29 The one who has the bride is the bridegroom. The friend
of the bridegroom, who stands by and listens for him, rejoices
greatly when he hears the bridegroom's voice. This then is my
joy, and it is complete. 30 He must become more important while
I become less important."

31 The one who comes from above is superior to all. The one
who is from the earth belongs to the earth and speaks about
earthly things. The one who comes from heaven is superior to
all. 32 He testifies about what he has seen and heard, but no one
accepts his testimony. 33 The one who has accepted his testimony
has confirmed clearly that God is truthful. 34 For the one whom
God has sent speaks the words of God, for he does not give the

Spirit sparingly. 35 The Father loves the Son and has placed all things under his authority. 36 The one who believes in the Son has eternal life. The one who rejects the Son will not see life, but God's wrath remains on him.

DEPARTURE FROM JUDEA

4 Now when Jesus knew that the Pharisees had heard that he was winning and baptizing more disciples than John 2 (although Jesus himself was not baptizing, but his disciples were), 3 he left Judea and set out once more for Galilee.

CONVERSATION WITH A SAMARITAN WOMAN

4 But he had to pass through Samaria. 5 Now he came to a Samaritan town called Sychar, near the plot of land that Jacob had given to his son Joseph. 6 Jacob's well was there, so Jesus, since he was tired from the journey, sat right down beside the well. It was about noon.

7 A Samaritan woman came to draw water. Jesus said to her, "Give me some water to drink." 8 (For his disciples had gone off into the town to buy supplies.) 9 So the Samaritan woman said to him, "How can you—a Jew—ask me, a Samaritan woman, for water to drink?" (For Jews use nothing in common with Samaritans.)

10 Jesus answered her, "If you had known the gift of God and who it is who said to you, 'Give me some water to drink,' you would have asked him, and he would have given you living water." 11 "Sir," the woman said to him, "you have no bucket and the well is deep; where then do you get this living water? 12 Surely you're not greater than our ancestor Jacob, are you? For he gave us this well and drank from it himself, along with his sons and his livestock."

13 Jesus replied, "Everyone who drinks some of this water will be thirsty again. 14 But whoever drinks some of the water that I will give him will never be thirsty again, but the water that I will give him will become in him a fountain of water springing up to eternal life." 15 The woman said to him, "Sir, give me this water, so that I will not be thirsty or have to come here to draw water." 16 He said to her, "Go call your husband and come back here." 17 The woman replied, "I have no husband." Jesus said to her, "Right you are when you said, 'I have no husband,' 18 for you have had five husbands, and the man you are living with now is not your husband. This you said truthfully!"

19 The woman said to him, "Sir, I see that you are a prophet. 20 Our fathers worshiped on this mountain, and you people say that the place where people must worship is in Jerusalem." 21 Jesus said to her, "Believe me, woman, a time is coming when you will worship the Father neither on this mountain nor in Jerusalem. 22 You people worship what you do not know. We worship what we know, because salvation is from the Jews. 23 But a time is coming—and now is here—when the true worshipers will worship the Father in spirit and truth, for the Father seeks such people to be his worshipers. 24 God is spirit, and the people who worship him must worship in spirit and truth." 25 The woman said to him, "I know that Messiah is coming" (the one called Christ); "whenever he comes, he will tell us everything." 26 Jesus said to her, "I, the one speaking to you, am he."

THE DISCIPLES RETURN

27 Now at that very moment his disciples came back. They were
shocked because he was speaking with a woman. However, no
one said, "What do you want?" or "Why are you speaking with
her?" 28 Then the woman left her water jar, went off into the town
and said to the people, 29 "Come, see a man who told me everything I ever did. Surely he can't be the Messiah, can he?" 30 So
they left the town and began coming to him.

WORKERS FOR THE HARVEST

31 Meanwhile the disciples were urging him, "Rabbi, eat something." 32 But he said to them, "I have food to eat that you know
nothing about." 33 So the disciples began to say to one another,
"No one brought him anything to eat, did they?" 34 Jesus said to
them, "My food is to do the will of the one who sent me and to
complete his work. 35 Don't you say, 'There are four more months
and then comes the harvest?' I tell you, look up and see that the
fields are already white for harvest! 36 The one who reaps receives
pay and gathers fruit for eternal life, so that the one who sows
and the one who reaps can rejoice together. 37 For in this instance the saying is true, 'One sows and another reaps.' 38 I sent
you to reap what you did not work for; others have labored and
you have entered into their labor."

THE SAMARITANS RESPOND

39 Now many Samaritans from that town believed in him because
of the report of the woman who testified, "He told me everything I ever did." 40 So when the Samaritans came to him, they
began asking him to stay with them. He stayed there two days,
41 and because of his word many more believed. 42 They said to
the woman, "No longer do we believe because of your words, for
we have heard for ourselves, and we know that this one really is
the Savior of the world."

ONWARD TO GALILEE

43 After the two days he departed from there to Galilee. 44 (For
Jesus himself had testified that a prophet has no honor in his
own country.) 45 So when he came to Galilee, the Galileans welcomed him because they had seen all the things he had done in
Jerusalem at the feast (for they themselves had gone to the feast).

HEALING THE ROYAL OFFICIAL'S SON

46 Now he came again to Cana in Galilee where he had made
the water wine. In Capernaum there was a certain royal official
whose son was sick. 47 When he heard that Jesus had come back
from Judea to Galilee, he went to him and begged him to come
down and heal his son, who was about to die. 48 So Jesus said to
him, "Unless you people see signs and wonders you will never believe!" 49 "Sir," the official said to him, "come down before my child
dies." 50 Jesus told him, "Go home; your son will live." The man
believed the word that Jesus spoke to him, and set off for home.

51 While he was on his way down, his slaves met him and told
him that his son was going to live. 52 So he asked them the
time when his condition began to improve, and they told him,

LOVE TO GROW

BELIEVE AND GO

JOHN 4:48–54

This man came to Jesus like many of us do: with a need.

This man recognized the power of Jesus and thought if he could get Jesus to come with him, his son would be healed. Facing a heartbreaking situation, this was a last-ditch effort for results. The problem was, when the man asked Jesus to come, Jesus answered, "Go . . ."

Have you ever cried out to Jesus like this father, desperate for God to work and fairly certain how He should? Have you ever prayed specifically, only to be disappointed that God didn't do what you were confident He should do?

Jesus didn't do what the man asked in the way the man asked Him to do it. However, instead of continuing to plead with Jesus, this desperate man believed and obeyed.

The man believed the word that Jesus spoke to him, and set off for home (John 4:50).

God will not always answer in the way we think He should or in the timeframe we want, but we can trust His commands. He is sovereign and faithful and good. Scripture tells us that all things work together for good for those who love God, who are called according to His purpose (see Rom 8:28).

Jesus offers us an invitation to trust Him, like He did with the man in this story. The man believed the word that Jesus spoke to him. Then he went on his way and returned home.

The man believed and departed. In faith, he went.

Will we believe what God says? Will we believe the word Jesus speaks to us and get up and go? Will our faith result in action?

We may, at times, feel afraid and uncertain, but we always have a choice to believe God or not. Believe what God says and take the next step with Him. Then watch what God does as He increases your faith and your joy as you trust in Him and bring glory to Him.

"Yesterday at one o'clock in the afternoon the fever left him."
53 Then the father realized that it was the very time Jesus had
said to him, "Your son will live," and he himself believed along
with his entire household. 54 Jesus did this as his second miraculous sign when he returned from Judea to Galilee.

HEALING A PARALYTIC AT THE POOL OF BETHESDA

5 After this there was a Jewish feast, and Jesus went up to Jerusalem. 2 Now there is in Jerusalem by the Sheep Gate a pool
called *Bethzatha* in Aramaic, which has five covered walkways.
3 A great number of sick, blind, lame, and paralyzed people were
lying in these walkways.|| 5 Now a man was there who had been
disabled for thirty-eight years. 6 When Jesus saw him lying there
and when he realized that the man had been disabled a long time
already, he said to him, "Do you want to become well?" 7 The sick
man answered him, "Sir, I have no one to put me into the pool
when the water is stirred up. While I am trying to get into the
water, someone else goes down there before me." 8 Jesus said to
him, "Stand up! Pick up your mat and walk." 9 Immediately the
man was healed, and he picked up his mat and started walking.
(Now that day was a Sabbath.)
10 So the Jewish leaders said to the man who had been healed,
"It is the Sabbath, and you are not permitted to carry your mat."
11 But he answered them, "The man who made me well said to me,
'Pick up your mat and walk.'" 12 They asked him, "Who is the man
who said to you, 'Pick up your mat and walk'?" 13 But the man who
had been healed did not know who it was, for Jesus had slipped
out, since there was a crowd in that place.
14 After this Jesus found him at the temple and said to him,
"Look, you have become well. Don't sin any more, lest anything
worse happen to you." 15 The man went away and informed the
Jewish leaders that Jesus was the one who had made him well.

RESPONDING TO JEWISH LEADERS

16 Now because Jesus was doing these things on the Sabbath, the
Jewish leaders began persecuting him. 17 So he told them, "My
Father is working until now, and I too am working." 18 For this
reason the Jewish leaders were trying even harder to kill him,
because not only was he breaking the Sabbath, but he was also
calling God his own Father, thus making himself equal with God.
19 So Jesus answered them, "I tell you the solemn truth, the
Son can do nothing on his own initiative, but only what he sees
the Father doing. For whatever the Father does, the Son does
likewise. 20 For the Father loves the Son and shows him everything he does, and will show him greater deeds than these, so
that you will be amazed. 21 For just as the Father raises the dead
and gives them life, so also the Son gives life to whomever he
wishes. 22 Furthermore, the Father does not judge anyone, but
has assigned all judgment to the Son, 23 so that all people will
honor the Son just as they honor the Father. The one who does
not honor the Son does not honor the Father who sent him.
24 "I tell you the solemn truth, the one who hears my message
and believes the one who sent me has eternal life and will not be
condemned, but has crossed over from death to life. 25 I tell you

the solemn truth, a time is coming—and is now here—when the
dead will hear the voice of the Son of God, and those who hear
will live. 26 For just as the Father has life in himself, thus he has
granted the Son to have life in himself, 27 and he has granted the
Son authority to execute judgment, because he is the Son of Man.
28 "Do not be amazed at this, because a time is coming when all
who are in the tombs will hear his voice 29 and will come out—the
ones who have done what is good to the resurrection resulting
in life, and the ones who have done what is evil to the resurrection resulting in condemnation. 30 I can do nothing on my own
initiative. Just as I hear, I judge, and my judgment is just, because
I do not seek my own will, but the will of the one who sent me.

MORE TESTIMONY ABOUT JESUS

31 "If I testify about myself, my testimony is not true. 32 There is
another who testifies about me, and I know the testimony he
testifies about me is true. 33 You have sent to John, and he has
testified to the truth. 34 (I do not accept human testimony, but
I say this so that you may be saved.) 35 He was a lamp that was
burning and shining, and you wanted to rejoice greatly for a
short time in his light.
36 "But I have a testimony greater than that from John. For the
deeds that the Father has assigned me to complete—the deeds
I am now doing—testify about me that the Father has sent me.
37 And the Father who sent me has himself testified about me.
You people have never heard his voice nor seen his form at any
time, 38 nor do you have his word residing in you, because you
do not believe the one whom he sent. 39 You study the scriptures
thoroughly because you think in them you possess eternal life,
and it is these same scriptures that testify about me, 40 but you
are not willing to come to me so that you may have life.
41 "I do not accept praise from people, 42 but I know you, that
you do not have the love of God within you. 43 I have come in my
Father's name, and you do not accept me. If someone else comes
in his own name, you will accept him. 44 How can you believe, if
you accept praise from one another and don't seek the praise
that comes from the only God?
45 "Do not suppose that I will accuse you before the Father. The
one who accuses you is Moses, in whom you have placed your
hope. 46 If you believed Moses, you would believe me, because he
wrote about me. 47 But if you do not believe what Moses wrote,
how will you believe my words?"

THE FEEDING OF THE FIVE THOUSAND

6 After this Jesus went away to the other side of the Sea of Galilee (also called the Sea of Tiberias). 2 A large crowd was following him because they were observing the miraculous signs
he was performing on the sick. 3 So Jesus went on up the mountainside and sat down there with his disciples. 4 (Now the Jewish Feast of the Passover was near.) 5 Then Jesus, when he looked
up and saw that a large crowd was coming to him, said to Philip,
"Where can we buy bread so that these people may eat?" 6 (Now
Jesus said this to test him, for he knew what he was going to do.)
7 Philip replied, "200 silver coins worth of bread would not be

enough for them, for each one to get a little." 8 One of Jesus' disciples, Andrew, Simon Peter's brother, said to him, 9 "Here is a
boy who has five barley loaves and two fish, but what good are
these for so many people?"
10 Jesus said, "Have the people sit down." (Now there was a lot
of grass in that place.) So the men sat down, about 5,000 in number. 11 Then Jesus took the loaves, and when he had given thanks,
he distributed the bread to those who were seated. He then did
the same with the fish, as much as they wanted. 12 When they
were all satisfied, Jesus said to his disciples, "Gather up the broken pieces that are left over, so that nothing is wasted." 13 So they
gathered them up and filled twelve baskets with broken pieces
from the five barley loaves left over by the people who had eaten.
14 Now when the people saw the miraculous sign that Jesus performed, they began to say to one another, "This is certainly *the
Prophet who is to come into the world*." 15 Then Jesus, because he
knew they were going to come and seize him by force to make
him king, withdrew again up the mountainside alone.

WALKING ON WATER

16 Now when evening came, his disciples went down to the lake,
17 got into a boat, and started to cross the lake to Capernaum. (It
had already become dark, and Jesus had not yet come to them.)
18 By now a strong wind was blowing and the sea was getting rough.
19 Then, when they had rowed about three or four miles, they
caught sight of Jesus walking on the lake, approaching the boat,
and they were frightened. 20 But he said to them, "It is I. Do not be
afraid." 21 Then they wanted to take him into the boat, and immediately the boat came to the land where they had been heading.
22 The next day the crowd that remained on the other side of
the lake realized that only one small boat had been there, and
that Jesus had not boarded it with his disciples, but that his disciples had gone away alone. 23 Other boats from Tiberias came to
shore near the place where they had eaten the bread after the
Lord had given thanks. 24 So when the crowd realized that neither Jesus nor his disciples were there, they got into the boats
and came to Capernaum looking for Jesus.

JESUS' DISCOURSE ABOUT THE BREAD OF LIFE

25 When they found him on the other side of the lake, they said
to him, "Rabbi, when did you get here?" 26 Jesus replied, "I tell
you the solemn truth, you are looking for me not because you
saw miraculous signs, but because you ate all the loaves of bread
you wanted. 27 Do not work for the food that disappears, but for
the food that remains to eternal life—the food which the Son
of Man will give to you. For God the Father has put his seal of
approval on him."
28 So then they said to him, "What must we do to accomplish
the deeds God requires?" 29 Jesus replied, "This is the deed God
requires—to believe in the one whom he sent." 30 So they said to
him, "Then what miraculous sign will you perform, so that we
may see it and believe you? What will you do? 31 Our ancestors
ate the manna in the wilderness, just as it is written, '***He gave
them bread from heaven to eat***.'"

REFLECT

How was Jesus' deity displayed when He walked on water? How does this story encourage you?

32 Then Jesus told them, "I tell you the solemn truth, it is not Moses who has given you the bread from heaven, but my Father is giving you the true bread from heaven. 33 For the bread of God is the one who comes down from heaven and gives life to the world." 34 So they said to him, "Sir, give us this bread all the time!"

35 Jesus said to them, "I am the bread of life. The one who comes to me will never go hungry, and the one who believes in me will never be thirsty. 36 But I told you that you have seen me and still do not believe. 37 Everyone whom the Father gives me will come to me, and the one who comes to me I will never send away. 38 For I have come down from heaven not to do my own will but the will of the one who sent me. 39 Now this is the will of the one who sent me—that I should not lose one person of every one he has given me, but raise them all up at the last day. 40 For this is the will of my Father—for everyone who looks on the Son and believes in him to have eternal life, and I will raise him up at the last day."

41 Then the Jews who were hostile to Jesus began complaining about him because he said, "I am the bread that came down from heaven," 42 and they said, "Isn't this Jesus the son of Joseph, whose father and mother we know? How can he now say, 'I have come down from heaven'?" 43 Jesus replied, "Do not complain about me to one another. 44 No one can come to me unless the Father who sent me draws him, and I will raise him up at the last day. 45 It is written in the prophets, '***And they will all be taught by God.***' Everyone who hears and learns from the Father comes to me. 46 (Not that anyone has seen the Father except the one who is from God—he has seen the Father.) 47 I tell you the solemn truth, the one who believes has eternal life. 48 I am the bread of life. 49 Your ancestors ate the manna in the wilderness, and they died. 50 This is the bread that has come down from heaven, so that a person may eat from it and not die. 51 I am the living bread that came down from heaven. If anyone eats from this bread he will live forever. The bread that I will give for the life of the world is my flesh."

52 Then the Jews who were hostile to Jesus began to argue with one another, "How can this man give us his flesh to eat?" 53 Jesus said to them, "I tell you the solemn truth, unless you eat the flesh of the Son of Man and drink his blood, you have no life in yourselves. 54 The one who eats my flesh and drinks my blood has eternal life, and I will raise him up on the last day. 55 For my flesh is true food, and my blood is true drink. 56 The one who eats my flesh and drinks my blood resides in me, and I in him. 57 Just as the living Father sent me, and I live because of the Father, so the one who consumes me will live because of me. 58 This is the bread that came down from heaven; it is not like the bread your ancestors ate, but then later died. The one who eats this bread will live forever."

MANY FOLLOWERS DEPART

59 Jesus said these things while he was teaching in the synagogue in Capernaum. 60 Then many of his disciples, when they heard these things, said, "This is a difficult saying! Who can understand it?" 61 When Jesus was aware that his disciples were complaining

about this, he said to them, "Does this cause you to be offended?
62 Then what if you see the Son of Man ascending where he was
before? 63 The Spirit is the one who gives life; human nature is of
no help! The words that I have spoken to you are spirit and are
life. 64 But there are some of you who do not believe." (For Jesus
had already known from the beginning who those were who did
not believe, and who it was who would betray him.) 65 So Jesus
added, "Because of this I told you that no one can come to me
unless the Father has allowed him to come."

PETER'S CONFESSION

66 After this many of his disciples quit following him and did not
accompany him any longer. 67 So Jesus said to the twelve, "You
don't want to go away too, do you?" 68 Simon Peter answered him,
"Lord, to whom would we go? You have the words of eternal life.
69 We have come to believe and to know that you are the Holy
One of God!" 70 Jesus replied, "Didn't I choose you, the twelve,
and yet one of you is the devil?" 71 (Now he said this about Judas son of Simon Iscariot, for Judas, one of the twelve, was going to betray him.)

THE FEAST OF SHELTERS

7 After this Jesus traveled throughout Galilee. He stayed out
of Judea because the Jewish leaders wanted to kill him. 2 Now
the Jewish Feast of Shelters was near. 3 So Jesus' brothers advised
him, "Leave here and go to Judea so your disciples may see your
miracles that you are performing. 4 For no one who seeks to make
a reputation for himself does anything in secret. If you are doing these things, show yourself to the world." 5 (For not even his
own brothers believed in him.)

6 So Jesus replied, "My time has not yet arrived, but you are
ready at any opportunity! 7 The world cannot hate you, but it
hates me, because I am testifying about it that its deeds are evil.
8 You go up to the feast yourselves. I am not going up to this feast
because my time has not yet fully arrived." 9 When he had said
this, he remained in Galilee.

10 But when his brothers had gone up to the feast, then Jesus
himself also went up, not openly but in secret. 11 So the Jewish
leaders were looking for him at the feast, asking, "Where is he?"
12 There was a lot of grumbling about him among the crowds.
Some were saying, "He is a good man," but others, "He deceives
the common people." 13 However, no one spoke openly about him
for fear of the Jewish leaders.

TEACHING IN THE TEMPLE

14 When the feast was half over, Jesus went up to the temple
courts and began to teach. 15 Then the Jewish leaders were astonished and said, "How does this man know so much when he
has never had formal instruction?" 16 So Jesus replied, "My teaching is not from me, but from the one who sent me. 17 If anyone
wants to do God's will, he will know about my teaching, whether
it is from God or whether I speak from my own authority. 18 The
person who speaks on his own authority desires to receive honor
for himself; the one who desires the honor of the one who sent

him is a man of integrity, and there is no unrighteousness in
him. 19 Hasn't Moses given you the law? Yet not one of you keeps
the law! Why do you want to kill me?"
20 The crowd answered, "You're possessed by a demon! Who is
trying to kill you?" 21 Jesus replied, "I performed one miracle and
you are all amazed. 22 However, because Moses gave you the practice of circumcision (not that it came from Moses, but from the
forefathers), you circumcise a male child on the Sabbath. 23 But
if a male child is circumcised on the Sabbath so that the law of
Moses is not broken, why are you angry with me because I made
a man completely well on the Sabbath? 24 Do not judge according to external appearance, but judge with proper judgment."

QUESTIONS ABOUT JESUS' IDENTITY

25 Then some of the residents of Jerusalem began to say, "Isn't
this the man they are trying to kill? 26 Yet here he is, speaking
publicly, and they are saying nothing to him. Do the ruling authorities really know that this man is the Christ? 27 But we know
where this man comes from. Whenever the Christ comes, no one
will know where he comes from."
28 Then Jesus, while teaching in the temple courts, cried out,
"You both know me and know where I come from! And I have
not come on my own initiative, but the one who sent me is true.
You do not know him, 29 but I know him, because I have come
from him and he sent me."
30 So then they tried to seize Jesus, but no one laid a hand on
him, because his time had not yet come. 31 Yet many of the crowd
believed in him and said, "Whenever the Christ comes, he won't
perform more miraculous signs than this man did, will he?"
32 The Pharisees heard the crowd murmuring these things
about Jesus, so the chief priests and the Pharisees sent officers
to arrest him. 33 Then Jesus said, "I will be with you for only a little while longer, and then I am going to the one who sent me.
34 You will look for me but will not find me, and where I am you
cannot come."
35 Then the Jewish leaders said to one another, "Where is he
going to go that we cannot find him? He is not going to go to the
Jewish people dispersed among the Greeks and teach the Greeks,
is he? 36 What did he mean by saying, 'You will look for me but
will not find me, and where I am you cannot come'?"

TEACHING ABOUT THE SPIRIT

37 On the last day of the feast, the greatest day, Jesus stood up
and shouted out, "If anyone is thirsty, let him come to me, and
38 let the one who believes in me drink. Just as the scripture says,
'***From within him will flow rivers of living water.***'" 39 (Now he said
this about the Spirit, whom those who believed in him were
going to receive, for the Spirit had not yet been given, because
Jesus was not yet glorified.)

DIFFERING OPINIONS ABOUT JESUS

40 When they heard these words, some of the crowd began to say,
"This really is the Prophet!" 41 Others said, "This is the Christ!" But
still others said, "No, for the Christ doesn't come from Galilee,

does he? 42 Don't the scriptures say that the Christ is *a descendant*
of David and *comes from Bethlehem*, the village where David lived?"
43 So there was a division in the crowd because of Jesus. 44 Some of
them were wanting to seize him, but no one laid a hand on him.

LACK OF BELIEF

45 Then the officers returned to the chief priests and Pharisees,
who said to them, "Why didn't you bring him back with you?"
46 The officers replied, "No one ever spoke like this man!" 47 Then
the Pharisees answered, "You haven't been deceived too, have
you? 48 None of the members of the ruling council or the Pharisees have believed in him, have they? 49 But this rabble who do
not know the law are accursed!"
50 Nicodemus, who had gone to Jesus before and who was one
of the rulers, said, 51 "Our law doesn't condemn a man unless it
first hears from him and learns what he is doing, does it?" 52 They
replied, "You aren't from Galilee too, are you? Investigate carefully and you will see that no prophet comes from Galilee!"

A WOMAN CAUGHT IN ADULTERY

8 53 [[¶ And each one departed to his own house. 1 But Jesus went
to the Mount of Olives. 2 Early in the morning he came to the
temple courts again. All the people came to him, and he sat down
and began to teach them. 3 The experts in the law and the Pharisees brought a woman who had been caught committing adultery. They made her stand in front of them 4 and said to Jesus,
"Teacher, this woman was caught in the very act of adultery. 5 In
the law *Moses commanded us to stone to death* such women. What
then do you say?" 6 (Now they were asking this in an attempt to
trap him, so that they could bring charges against him.) Jesus
bent down and wrote on the ground with his finger. 7 When they
persisted in asking him, he stood up straight and replied, "Whoever among you is guiltless may be the first to throw a stone at
her." 8 Then he bent over again and wrote on the ground.
9 Now when they heard this, they began to drift away one at
a time, starting with the older ones, until Jesus was left alone
with the woman standing before him. 10 Jesus stood up straight
and said to her, "Woman, where are they? Did no one condemn
you?" 11 She replied, "No one, Lord." And Jesus said, "I do not condemn you either. Go, and from now on do not sin any more."]]

JESUS AS THE LIGHT OF THE WORLD

12 Then Jesus spoke out again, "I am the light of the world! The
one who follows me will never walk in darkness, but will have
the light of life." 13 So the Pharisees objected, "You testify about
yourself; your testimony is not true!" 14 Jesus answered, "Even
if I testify about myself, my testimony is true, because I know
where I came from and where I am going. But you people do
not know where I came from or where I am going. 15 You people
judge by outward appearances; I do not judge anyone. 16 But if I
judge, my evaluation is accurate, because I am not alone when
I judge, but I and the Father who sent me do so together. 17 It is
written in your law that *the testimony of two men is true*. 18 I testify about myself and the Father who sent me testifies about me."

19 Then they began asking him, "Who is your father?" Jesus answered, "You do not know either me or my Father. If you knew
me you would know my Father too." 20 (Jesus spoke these words
near the offering box while he was teaching in the temple courts.
No one seized him because his time had not yet come.)

WHERE JESUS CAME FROM AND WHERE HE IS GOING

21 Then Jesus said to them again, "I am going away, and you will
look for me but will die in your sin. Where I am going you cannot
come." 22 So the Jewish leaders began to say, "Perhaps he is going
to kill himself, because he says, 'Where I am going you cannot
come.'" 23 Jesus replied, "You people are from below; I am from
above. You people are from this world; I am not from this world.
24 Thus I told you that you will die in your sins. For unless you
believe that I am he, you will die in your sins."

25 So they said to him, "Who are you?" Jesus replied, "What I
have told you from the beginning. 26 I have many things to say
and to judge about you, but the Father who sent me is truthful, and the things I have heard from him I speak to the world."
27 (They did not understand that he was telling them about his
Father.)

28 Then Jesus said, "When you lift up the Son of Man, then you
will know that I am he, and I do nothing on my own initiative,
but I speak just what the Father taught me. 29 And the one who
sent me is with me. He has not left me alone, because I always
do those things that please him." 30 While he was saying these
things, many people believed in him.

ABRAHAM'S CHILDREN AND THE DEVIL'S CHILDREN

31 Then Jesus said to those Judeans who had believed him, "If you
continue to follow my teaching, you are really my disciples 32 and
you will know the truth, and the truth will set you free." 33 "We
are descendants of Abraham," they replied, "and have never been
anyone's slaves! How can you say, 'You will become free'?" 34 Jesus
answered them, "I tell you the solemn truth, everyone who practices sin is a slave of sin. 35 The slave does not remain in the family forever, but the son remains forever. 36 So if the son sets you
free, you will be really free. 37 I know that you are Abraham's descendants. But you want to kill me, because my teaching makes
no progress among you. 38 I am telling you the things I have seen
while with the Father; as for you, practice the things you have
heard from the Father!"

39 They answered him, "Abraham is our father!" Jesus replied,
"If you are Abraham's children, you would be doing the deeds
of Abraham. 40 But now you are trying to kill me, a man who has
told you the truth I heard from God. Abraham did not do this!
41 You people are doing the deeds of your father."

Then they said to Jesus, "We were not born as a result of immorality! We have only one Father, God himself." 42 Jesus replied, "If
God were your Father, you would love me, for I have come from
God and am now here. I have not come on my own initiative,
but he sent me. 43 Why don't you understand what I am saying?
It is because you cannot accept my teaching. 44 You people are
from your father the devil, and you want to do what your father

REFLECT

How have you seen the truth of John 8:31-38 play out in your life? In what specific ways has the truth of the gospel set you free?

LOVE TO GROW

NEVER DEFENSELESS

JOHN 8:31–32

The lies filled my head the moment my toes touched the sand. "You know you don't look good in your swimming suit this year. Those extra pounds you've gained since last summer are starting to show. Your best years are behind you."

Lies.

From the moment we wake up, we are targeted by them. Lies disguise themselves as our voice, so it's hard not to believe them. Each lie is strategically aimed at keeping us from believing God's truth and who we are in Him. Lies purposely aimed at our insecurities, past hurts, or recent rejection.

These lies come for one purpose: to keep you from believing truth.

The enemy of our souls has worked the same way since the time sin entered the world. He takes the truth of God and gets us to question it. "Is it really true that God said . . .?" (see Gen 3:1) is his favorite question.

When Satan approached Eve, he asked this same question. Eve engaged Satan in the conversation he started. Many times, that's our first mistake too. She listened to his lies, causing her to doubt God's goodness. Then she responded to Satan's question, opening the door for him to twist God's command and further tempt her. Satan can't read our minds, but he does watch us, study us, and use our weaknesses to tempt us. The battle plan he used for Eve is the same battle plan he uses against us. That's why we must know God's truth and daily put on the full armor of God to stand against Satan and his lies. Lies are meant to entrap us and destroy us, while truth is meant to set us free.

God's truth is not only the way we free ourselves from believing lies, but it is the weapon we have to combat the schemes of the enemy.

Satan knows you are loved, chosen, accepted, adopted, valued, reconciled, redeemed, righteous, free, sealed, and forgiven, but he doesn't want you to believe it. Every time we believe God's truth about who we are, instead of believing Satan's lies, we defeat him.

Let's put on the armor of truth. No longer will we engage in his conversations. No longer will we be tempted with his half-truths. Let's dig into Scripture, believe what God's Word says, and guard our minds and hearts with it.

desires. He was a murderer from the beginning, and does not uphold the truth, because there is no truth in him. Whenever he lies, he speaks according to his own nature, because he is a liar and the father of lies. 45 But because I am telling you the truth, you do not believe me. 46 Who among you can prove me guilty of any sin? If I am telling you the truth, why don't you believe me? 47 The one who belongs to God listens and responds to God's words. You don't listen and respond, because you don't belong to God."

48 The Judeans replied, "Aren't we correct in saying that you are a Samaritan and are possessed by a demon?" 49 Jesus answered, "I am not possessed by a demon, but I honor my Father—and yet you dishonor me. 50 I am not trying to get praise for myself. There is one who demands it, and he also judges. 51 I tell you the solemn truth, if anyone obeys my teaching, he will never see death."

52 Then the Judeans responded, "Now we know you're possessed by a demon! Both Abraham and the prophets died, and yet you say, 'If anyone obeys my teaching, he will never experience death.' 53 You aren't greater than our father Abraham who died, are you? And the prophets died too! Who do you claim to be?" 54 Jesus replied, "If I glorify myself, my glory is worthless. The one who glorifies me is my Father, about whom you people say, 'He is our God.' 55 Yet you do not know him, but I know him. If I were to say that I do not know him, I would be a liar like you. But I do know him, and I obey his teaching. 56 Your father Abraham was overjoyed to see my day, and he saw it and was glad."

57 Then the Judeans replied, "You are not yet fifty years old! Have you seen Abraham?" 58 Jesus said to them, "I tell you the solemn truth, before Abraham came into existence, I am!" 59 Then they picked up stones to throw at him, but Jesus was hidden from them and went out from the temple area.

HEALING A MAN BORN BLIND

9 Now as Jesus was passing by, he saw a man who had been blind from birth. 2 His disciples asked him, "Rabbi, who committed the sin that caused him to be born blind, this man or his parents?" 3 Jesus answered, "Neither this man nor his parents sinned, but he was born blind so that the acts of God may be revealed through what happens to him. 4 We must perform the deeds of the one who sent me as long as it is daytime. Night is coming when no one can work. 5 As long as I am in the world, I am the light of the world." 6 Having said this, he spat on the ground and made some mud with the saliva. He smeared the mud on the blind man's eyes 7 and said to him, "Go wash in the pool of Siloam" (which is translated "sent"). So the blind man went away and washed, and came back seeing.

8 Then the neighbors and the people who had seen him previously as a beggar began saying, "Is this not the man who used to sit and beg?" 9 Some people said, "This is the man!" while others said, "No, but he looks like him." The man himself kept insisting, "I am the one!" 10 So they asked him, "How then were you made to see?" 11 He replied, "The man called Jesus made mud, smeared it on my eyes and told me, 'Go to Siloam and wash.' So I went and washed, and was able to see." 12 They said to him, "Where is that man?" He replied, "I don't know."

THE PHARISEES' REACTION TO THE HEALING

13 They brought the man who used to be blind to the Pharisees.
14 (Now the day on which Jesus made the mud and caused him to
see was a Sabbath.) 15 So the Pharisees asked him again how he
had gained his sight. He replied, "He put mud on my eyes and I
washed, and now I am able to see."
16 Then some of the Pharisees began to say, "This man is not
from God, because he does not observe the Sabbath." But others
said, "How can a man who is a sinner perform such miraculous
signs?" Thus there was a division among them. 17 So again they
asked the man who used to be blind, "What do you say about him,
since he caused you to see?" "He is a prophet," the man replied.
18 Now the Jewish religious leaders refused to believe that he
had really been blind and had gained his sight until at last they
summoned the parents of the man who had become able to see.
19 They asked the parents, "Is this your son, whom you say was
born blind? Then how does he now see?" 20 So his parents replied,
"We know that this is our son and that he was born blind. 21 But
we do not know how he is now able to see, nor do we know who
caused him to see. Ask him, he is a mature adult. He will speak
for himself." 22 (His parents said these things because they were
afraid of the Jewish religious leaders. For the Jewish leaders had
already agreed that anyone who confessed Jesus to be the Christ
would be put out of the synagogue. 23 For this reason his parents
said, "He is a mature adult, ask him.")
24 Then they summoned the man who used to be blind a second time and said to him, "Promise before God to tell the truth.
We know that this man is a sinner." 25 He replied, "I do not know
whether he is a sinner. I do know one thing—that although I was
blind, now I can see." 26 Then they said to him, "What did he do
to you? How did he cause you to see?" 27 He answered, "I told you
already and you didn't listen. Why do you want to hear it again?
You people don't want to become his disciples too, do you?"
28 They heaped insults on him, saying, "You are his disciple! We
are disciples of Moses! 29 We know that God has spoken to Moses! We do not know where this man comes from!" 30 The man
replied, "This is a remarkable thing, that you don't know where
he comes from, and yet he caused me to see! 31 We know that
God doesn't listen to sinners, but if anyone is devout and does
his will, God listens to him. 32 Never before has anyone heard of
someone causing a man born blind to see. 33 If this man were not
from God, he could do nothing." 34 They replied, "You were born
completely in sinfulness, and yet you presume to teach us?" So
they threw him out.

THE MAN'S RESPONSE TO JESUS

35 Jesus heard that they had thrown him out, so he found the man
and said to him, "Do you believe in the Son of Man?" 36 The man
replied, "And who is he, sir, that I may believe in him?" 37 Jesus
told him, "You have seen him; he is the one speaking with you."
[38 He said, "Lord, I believe," and he worshiped him. 39 Jesus said,]*
"For judgment I have come into this world, so that those who
do not see may gain their sight, and the ones who see may become blind."

40 Some of the Pharisees who were with him heard this and
asked him, "We are not blind too, are we?" 41 Jesus replied, "If you
were blind, you would not be guilty of sin, but now because you
claim that you can see, your guilt remains.

JESUS AS THE GOOD SHEPHERD

10 "I tell you the solemn truth, the one who does not enter the
sheepfold by the door, but climbs in some other way, is a
thief and a robber. 2 The one who enters by the door is the shepherd of the sheep. 3 The doorkeeper opens the door for him, and
the sheep hear his voice. He calls his own sheep by name and
leads them out. 4 When he has brought all his own sheep out,
he goes ahead of them, and the sheep follow him because they
recognize his voice. 5 They will never follow a stranger, but will
run away from him, because they do not recognize the stranger's voice." 6 Jesus told them this parable, but they did not understand what he was saying to them.

7 So Jesus said again, "I tell you the solemn truth, I am the
door for the sheep. 8 All who came before me were thieves and
robbers, but the sheep did not listen to them. 9 I am the door.
If anyone enters through me, he will be saved, and will come in
and go out, and find pasture. 10 The thief comes only to steal and
kill and destroy; I have come so that they may have life, and may
have it abundantly.

11 "I am the good shepherd. The good shepherd lays down his
life for the sheep. 12 The hired hand, who is not a shepherd and
does not own sheep, sees the wolf coming and abandons the
sheep and runs away. So the wolf attacks the sheep and scatters
them. 13 Because he is a hired hand and is not concerned about
the sheep, he runs away.

14 "I am the good shepherd. I know my own and my own know
me—15 just as the Father knows me and I know the Father—and
I lay down my life for the sheep. 16 I have other sheep that do not
come from this sheepfold. I must bring them too, and they will
listen to my voice, so that there will be one flock and one shepherd. 17 This is why the Father loves me—because I lay down my
life, so that I may take it back again. 18 No one takes it away from
me, but I lay it down of my own free will. I have the authority to
lay it down, and I have the authority to take it back again. This
commandment I received from my Father."

19 Another sharp division took place among the Jewish people
because of these words. 20 Many of them were saying, "He is possessed by a demon and has lost his mind! Why do you listen to
him?" 21 Others said, "These are not the words of someone possessed by a demon. A demon cannot cause the blind to see, can it?"

JESUS AT THE FEAST OF DEDICATION

22 Then came the feast of the Dedication in Jerusalem. 23 It was
winter, and Jesus was walking in the temple area in Solomon's
Portico. 24 The Jewish leaders surrounded him and asked, "How
long will you keep us in suspense? If you are the Christ, tell us
plainly." 25 Jesus replied, "I told you and you do not believe. The
deeds I do in my Father's name testify about me. 26 But you refuse to believe because you are not my sheep. 27 My sheep listen

to my voice, and I know them, and they follow me. 28 I give them
eternal life, and they will never perish; no one will snatch them
from my hand. 29 My Father, who has given them to me, is greater
than all, and no one can snatch them from my Father's hand.
30 The Father and I are one."
31 The Jewish leaders picked up rocks again to stone him to death.
32 Jesus said to them, "I have shown you many good deeds from the
Father. For which one of them are you going to stone me?" 33 The
Jewish leaders replied, "We are not going to stone you for a good
deed but for blasphemy, because you, a man, are claiming to be God."
34 Jesus answered, "Is it not written in your law, ***'I said, you are
gods'***? 35 If those people to whom the word of God came were
called 'gods' (and the scripture cannot be broken), 36 do you say
about the one whom the Father set apart and sent into the world,
'You are blaspheming,' because I said, 'I am the Son of God'? 37 If I
do not perform the deeds of my Father, do not believe me. 38 But
if I do them, even if you do not believe me, believe the deeds,
so that you may come to know and understand that I am in the
Father and the Father is in me." 39 Then they attempted again
to seize him, but he escaped their clutches.
40 Jesus went back across the Jordan River again to the place
where John had been baptizing at an earlier time, and he stayed
there. 41 Many came to him and began to say, "John performed
no miraculous sign, but everything John said about this man
was true!" 42 And many believed in Jesus there.

THE DEATH OF LAZARUS

11 Now a certain man named Lazarus was sick. He was from
Bethany, the village where Mary and her sister Martha lived.
2 (Now it was Mary who anointed the Lord with perfumed oil
and wiped his feet dry with her hair, whose brother Lazarus was
sick.) 3 So the sisters sent a message to Jesus, "Lord, look, the one
you love is sick." 4 When Jesus heard this, he said, "This sickness
will not lead to death, but to God's glory, so that the Son of God
may be glorified through it." 5 (Now Jesus loved Martha and her
sister and Lazarus.)
6 So when he heard that Lazarus was sick, he remained in the
place where he was for two more days. 7 Then after this, he said
to his disciples, "Let us go to Judea again." 8 The disciples replied,
"Rabbi, the Jewish leaders were just now trying to stone you to
death! Are you going there again?" 9 Jesus replied, "Are there not
twelve hours in a day? If anyone walks around in the daytime, he
does not stumble, because he sees the light of this world. 10 But
if anyone walks around at night, he stumbles, because the light
is not in him."
11 After he said this, he added, "Our friend Lazarus has fallen
asleep. But I am going there to awaken him." 12 Then the disciples replied, "Lord, if he has fallen asleep, he will recover." 13 (Now
Jesus had been talking about his death, but they thought he had
been talking about real sleep.)
14 Then Jesus told them plainly, "Lazarus has died, 15 and I am
glad for your sake that I was not there, so that you may believe.
But let us go to him." 16 So Thomas (called Didymus) said to his
fellow disciples, "Let us go too, so that we may die with him."

SPEAKING WITH MARTHA AND MARY

17 When Jesus arrived, he found that Lazarus had been in the tomb four days already. 18 (Now Bethany was less than two miles from Jerusalem, 19 so many of the Jewish people of the region had come to Martha and Mary to console them over the loss of their brother.) 20 So when Martha heard that Jesus was coming, she went out to meet him, but Mary was sitting in the house. 21 Martha said to Jesus, "Lord, if you had been here, my brother would not have died. 22 But even now I know that whatever you ask from God, God will grant you."

REFLECT

What does Jesus' response to Mary and Martha tell you about His heart? Does He care for you in this way?

23 Jesus replied, "Your brother will come back to life again." 24 Martha said, "I know that he will come back to life again in the resurrection at the last day." 25 Jesus said to her, "I am the resurrection and the life. The one who believes in me will live even if he dies, 26 and the one who lives and believes in me will never die. Do you believe this?" 27 She replied, "Yes, Lord, I believe that you are the Christ, the Son of God who comes into the world."

28 And when she had said this, Martha went and called her sister Mary, saying privately, "The Teacher is here and is asking for you." 29 So when Mary heard this, she got up quickly and went to him. 30 (Now Jesus had not yet entered the village, but was still in the place where Martha had come out to meet him.) 31 Then the people who were with Mary in the house consoling her saw her get up quickly and go out. They followed her, because they thought she was going to the tomb to weep there.

32 Now when Mary came to the place where Jesus was and saw him, she fell at his feet and said to him, "Lord, if you had been here, my brother would not have died." 33 When Jesus saw her weeping, and the people who had come with her weeping, he was intensely moved in spirit and greatly distressed. 34 He asked, "Where have you laid him?" They replied, "Lord, come and see." 35 Jesus wept. 36 Thus the people who had come to mourn said, "Look how much he loved him!" 37 But some of them said, "This is the man who caused the blind man to see! Couldn't he have done something to keep Lazarus from dying?"

LAZARUS RAISED FROM THE DEAD

38 Jesus, intensely moved again, came to the tomb. (Now it was a cave, and a stone was placed across it.) 39 Jesus said, "Take away the stone." Martha, the sister of the deceased, replied, "Lord, by this time the body will have a bad smell, because he has been buried four days." 40 Jesus responded, "Didn't I tell you that if you believe, you would see the glory of God?" 41 So they took away the stone. Jesus looked upward and said, "Father, I thank you that you have listened to me. 42 I knew that you always listen to me, but I said this for the sake of the crowd standing around here, that they may believe that you sent me." 43 When he had said this, he shouted in a loud voice, "Lazarus, come out!" 44 The one who had died came out, his feet and hands tied up with strips of cloth, and a cloth wrapped around his face. Jesus said to them, "Unwrap him and let him go."

THE RESPONSE OF THE JEWISH LEADERS

45 Then many of the people, who had come with Mary and had
seen the things Jesus did, believed in him. 46 But some of them
went to the Pharisees and reported to them what Jesus had done.
47 So the chief priests and the Pharisees called the council together and said, "What are we doing? For this man is performing
many miraculous signs. 48 If we allow him to go on in this way,
everyone will believe in him, and the Romans will come and take
away our sanctuary and our nation."
49 Then one of them, Caiaphas, who was high priest that year,
said, "You know nothing at all! 50 You do not realize that it is more
to your advantage to have one man die for the people than for the
whole nation to perish." 51 (Now he did not say this on his own, but
because he was high priest that year, he prophesied that Jesus was
going to die for the Jewish nation, 52 and not for the Jewish nation
only, but to gather together into one the children of God who are
scattered.) 53 So from that day they planned together to kill him.
54 Thus Jesus no longer went around publicly among the Judeans,
but went away from there to the region near the wilderness, to a
town called Ephraim, and stayed there with his disciples. 55 Now
the Jewish Feast of Passover was near, and many people went up
to Jerusalem from the rural areas before the Passover to cleanse
themselves ritually. 56 Thus they were looking for Jesus, and saying
to one another as they stood in the temple courts, "What do you
think? That he won't come to the feast?" 57 (Now the chief priests
and the Pharisees had given orders that anyone who knew where
Jesus was should report it, so that they could arrest him.)

JESUS' ANOINTING

12 Then, six days before the Passover, Jesus came to Bethany,
where Lazarus lived, whom he had raised from the dead. 2 So
they prepared a dinner for Jesus there. Martha was serving, and
Lazarus was among those present at the table with him. 3 Then
Mary took three quarters of a pound of expensive aromatic oil
from pure nard and anointed the feet of Jesus. She then wiped
his feet dry with her hair. (Now the house was filled with the fragrance of the perfumed oil.) 4 But Judas Iscariot, one of his disciples (the one who was going to betray him) said, 5 "Why wasn't
this oil sold for 300 silver coins and the money given to the poor?"
6 (Now Judas said this not because he was concerned about the
poor, but because he was a thief. As keeper of the money box,
he used to steal what was put into it.) 7 So Jesus said, "Leave her
alone. She has kept it for the day of my burial. 8 For you will always have the poor with you, but you will not always have me!"
9 Now a large crowd of Judeans learned that Jesus was there,
and so they came not only because of him but also to see Lazarus
whom he had raised from the dead. 10 So the chief priests planned
to kill Lazarus too, 11 for on account of him many of the Jewish
people from Jerusalem were going away and believing in Jesus.

THE TRIUMPHAL ENTRY

12 The next day the large crowd that had come to the feast heard
that Jesus was coming to Jerusalem. 13 So they took branches
of palm trees and went out to meet him. They began to shout,

"Hosanna! Blessed is the one who comes in the name of the Lord!
Blessed is the king of Israel!" 14 Jesus found a young donkey and
sat on it, just as it is written, 15 "***Do not be afraid, people of Zion;***
look, your king is coming, seated on a donkey's colt!" 16 (His disciples did not understand these things when they first happened,
but when Jesus was glorified, then they remembered that these
things were written about him and that these things had happened to him.)
17 So the crowd who had been with him when he called Lazarus
out of the tomb and raised him from the dead were continuing
to testify about it. 18 Because they had heard that Jesus had performed this miraculous sign, the crowd went out to meet him.
19 Thus the Pharisees said to one another, "You see that you can
do nothing. Look, the world has run off after him!"

SEEKERS

20 Now some Greeks were among those who had gone up to worship at the feast. 21 So these approached Philip, who was from
Bethsaida in Galilee, and requested, "Sir, we would like to see
Jesus." 22 Philip went and told Andrew, and they both went and
told Jesus. 23 Jesus replied, "The time has come for the Son of Man
to be glorified. 24 I tell you the solemn truth, unless a kernel of
wheat falls into the ground and dies, it remains by itself alone.
But if it dies, it produces much grain. 25 The one who loves his life
destroys it, and the one who hates his life in this world guards
it for eternal life. 26 If anyone wants to serve me, he must follow
me, and where I am, my servant will be too. If anyone serves me,
the Father will honor him.
27 "Now my soul is greatly distressed. And what should I say?
'Father, deliver me from this hour'? No, but for this very reason
I have come to this hour. 28 Father, glorify your name." Then a
voice came from heaven, "I have glorified it, and I will glorify it
again." 29 The crowd that stood there and heard the voice said
that it had thundered. Others said that an angel had spoken to
him. 30 Jesus said, "This voice has not come for my benefit but
for yours. 31 Now is the judgment of this world; now the ruler of
this world will be driven out. 32 And I, when I am lifted up from
the earth, will draw all people to myself." 33 (Now he said this to
indicate clearly what kind of death he was going to die.)
34 Then the crowd responded, "We have heard from the law that
the Christ will remain forever. How can you say, 'The Son of Man
must be lifted up'? Who is this Son of Man?" 35 Jesus replied, "The
light is with you for a little while longer. Walk while you have the
light, so that the darkness may not overtake you. The one who
walks in the darkness does not know where he is going. 36 While
you have the light, believe in the light, so that you may become
sons of light." When Jesus had said these things, he went away
and hid himself from them.

THE OUTCOME OF JESUS' PUBLIC MINISTRY FORETOLD

37 Although Jesus had performed so many miraculous signs before them, they still refused to believe in him, 38 so that the word
of the prophet Isaiah would be fulfilled. He said, "***Lord, who has***

believed our message, and to whom has the arm of the Lord been
revealed?" 39 For this reason they could not believe, because again
Isaiah said,

40 "***He has blinded their eyes***
and hardened their heart,
so that they would not see with their eyes
and understand with their heart,
and turn to me, and I would heal them."

41 Isaiah said these things because he saw Christ's glory, and
spoke about him.
42 Nevertheless, even among the rulers many believed in him,
but because of the Pharisees they would not confess Jesus to be
the Christ, so that they would not be put out of the synagogue.
43 For they loved praise from men more than praise from God.

JESUS' FINAL PUBLIC WORDS

44 But Jesus shouted out, "The one who believes in me does not
believe in me, but in the one who sent me, 45 and the one who
sees me sees the one who sent me. 46 I have come as a light into
the world, so that everyone who believes in me should not remain in darkness. 47 If anyone hears my words and does not obey
them, I do not judge him. For I have not come to judge the world,
but to save the world. 48 The one who rejects me and does not
accept my words has a judge; the word I have spoken will judge
him at the last day. 49 For I have not spoken from my own authority, but the Father himself who sent me has commanded me
what I should say and what I should speak. 50 And I know that
his commandment is eternal life. Thus the things I say, I say just
as the Father has told me."

WASHING THE DISCIPLES' FEET

13 Just before the Passover Feast, Jesus knew that his time
had come to depart from this world to the Father. Having
loved his own who were in the world, he now loved them to the
very end. 2 The evening meal was in progress, and the devil had
already put into the heart of Judas Iscariot, Simon's son, that he
should betray Jesus. 3 Because Jesus knew that the Father had
handed all things over to him, and that he had come from God
and was going back to God, 4 he got up from the meal, removed
his outer clothes, took a towel and tied it around himself. 5 He
poured water into the washbasin and began to wash the disciples' feet and to dry them with the towel he had wrapped
around himself.
6 Then he came to Simon Peter. Peter said to him, "Lord, are
you going to wash my feet?" 7 Jesus replied, "You do not understand what I am doing now, but you will understand after these
things." 8 Peter said to him, "You will never wash my feet!" Jesus
replied, "If I do not wash you, you have no share with me." 9 Simon Peter said to him, "Lord, wash not only my feet, but also my
hands and my head!" 10 Jesus replied, "The one who has bathed
needs only to wash his feet, but is completely clean. And you disciples are clean, but not every one of you." 11 (For Jesus knew the
one who was going to betray him. For this reason he said, "Not
every one of you is clean.")

LOVE TO GROW

NO MISTAKE

JOHN 13:8–9

Peter was a man with a big heart, raw leadership ability, and a ton of energy. Peter was a man who saw things in black and white, with very little gray. He was passionate about certain issues and couldn't hold back his opinion, regardless of whether the other person wanted to hear it or not.

I wonder if he ever felt as if he was too much. I wonder if he ever wondered why God had made him with his strong personality and passion for life. I wonder if he ever wondered if there was more to life before Jesus called him.

As we take a closer look at Peter's life, we see a man who was impulsive and emotional and who spoke before he thought. Jesus rebuked and reprimanded Peter more than the other disciples, but He also built him up by naming him "The Rock." Jesus spoke into Peter's future regarding who He knew Peter would become.

God gave Peter the exact personality He knew Peter would need to fulfill the calling placed on his life. Peter didn't develop into an amazing leader overnight. Oh, no. Peter learned through mistakes, rebukes, and words of encouragement. Peter came to be a better leader by being with Jesus. Over the years he spent with Jesus, Peter learned to surrender his will and to serve others.

Jesus used all of Peter—his past mistakes, weaknesses, big personality, and incredible passion to craft him into a man who was completely committed to carrying Christ's message to all people, no matter the cost.

What God did in Peter's life, He is willing to do in yours too.

At times you may think your personality is too much: too strong, too passionate, or even too mild. You may question how God created you and where He placed you. Make no mistake, God has given you everything you need to fulfill the calling on your life.

We are all works in progress. Praise God that day by day He is molding us by our circumstances, His Word, and prayer to make us more like Him.

12 So when Jesus had washed their feet and put his outer clothing
back on, he took his place at the table again and said to them, "Do
you understand what I have done for you? 13 You call me 'Teacher'
and 'Lord,' and do so correctly, for that is what I am. 14 If I then,
your Lord and Teacher, have washed your feet, you too ought to
wash one another's feet. 15 For I have given you an example—you
should do just as I have done for you. 16 I tell you the solemn truth,
the slave is not greater than his master, nor is the one who is sent
as a messenger greater than the one who sent him. 17 If you understand these things, you will be blessed if you do them.

THE ANNOUNCEMENT OF JESUS' BETRAYAL

18 "What I am saying does not refer to all of you. I know the ones
I have chosen. But this is to fulfill the scripture, '***The one who eats***
my bread has turned against me.' 19 I am telling you this now, before
it happens, so that when it happens you may believe that I am he.
20 I tell you the solemn truth, whoever accepts the one I send accepts me, and whoever accepts me accepts the one who sent me."

21 When he had said these things, Jesus was greatly distressed
in spirit, and testified, "I tell you the solemn truth, one of you will
betray me." 22 The disciples began to look at one another, worried
and perplexed to know which of them he was talking about. 23 One
of his disciples, the one Jesus loved, was at the table to the right
of Jesus in a place of honor. 24 So Simon Peter gestured to this disciple to ask Jesus who it was he was referring to. 25 Then the disciple whom Jesus loved leaned back against Jesus' chest and asked
him, "Lord, who is it?" 26 Jesus replied, "It is the one to whom I will
give this piece of bread after I have dipped it in the dish." Then he
dipped the piece of bread in the dish and gave it to Judas Iscariot,
Simon's son. 27 And after Judas took the piece of bread, Satan entered into him. Jesus said to him, "What you are about to do, do
quickly." 28 (Now none of those present at the table understood
why Jesus said this to Judas. 29 Some thought that, because Judas
had the money box, Jesus was telling him to buy whatever they
needed for the feast, or to give something to the poor.) 30 Judas took
the piece of bread and went out immediately. (Now it was night.)

THE PREDICTION OF PETER'S DENIAL

31 When Judas had gone out, Jesus said, "Now the Son of Man
is glorified, and God is glorified in him. 32 If God is glorified in
him, God will also glorify him in himself, and he will glorify him
right away. 33 Children, I am still with you for a little while. You
will look for me, and just as I said to the Jewish religious leaders,
'Where I am going you cannot come,' now I tell you the same.

34 "I give you a new commandment—to love one another. Just
as I have loved you, you also are to love one another. 35 Everyone will know by this that you are my disciples—if you have love
for one another."

36 Simon Peter said to him, "Lord, where are you going?" Jesus
replied, "Where I am going, you cannot follow me now, but you
will follow later." 37 Peter said to him, "Lord, why can't I follow
you now? I will lay down my life for you!" 38 Jesus answered, "Will
you lay down your life for me? I tell you the solemn truth, the
rooster will not crow until you have denied me three times!

JESUS' PARTING WORDS TO HIS DISCIPLES

14 "Do not let your hearts be distressed. You believe in God;
believe also in me. 2 There are many dwelling places in my
Father's house. Otherwise, I would have told you, because I am
going away to make ready a place for you. 3 And if I go and make
ready a place for you, I will come again and take you to be with
me, so that where I am you may be too. 4 And you know the way
where I am going."
5 Thomas said, "Lord, we don't know where you are going. How
can we know the way?" 6 Jesus replied, "I am the way, and the
truth, and the life. No one comes to the Father except through
me. 7 If you have known me, you will know my Father too. And
from now on you do know him and have seen him."
8 Philip said, "Lord, show us the Father, and we will be content."
9 Jesus replied, "Have I been with you for so long, and you have
not known me, Philip? The person who has seen me has seen the
Father! How can you say, 'Show us the Father'? 10 Do you not believe that I am in the Father, and the Father is in me? The words
that I say to you, I do not speak on my own initiative, but the
Father residing in me performs his miraculous deeds. 11 Believe
me that I am in the Father, and the Father is in me, but if you do
not believe me, believe because of the miraculous deeds themselves. 12 I tell you the solemn truth, the person who believes in
me will perform the miraculous deeds that I am doing, and will
perform greater deeds than these, because I am going to the Father. 13 And I will do whatever you ask in my name, so that the
Father may be glorified in the Son. 14 If you ask me anything in
my name, I will do it.

TEACHING ON THE HOLY SPIRIT

15 "If you love me, you will obey my commandments. 16 Then I
will ask the Father, and he will give you another Advocate to be
with you forever—17 the Spirit of truth, whom the world cannot
accept, because it does not see him or know him. But you know
him, because he resides with you and will be in you.
18 "I will not abandon you as orphans, I will come to you. 19 In a
little while the world will not see me any longer, but you will see
me; because I live, you will live too. 20 You will know at that time
that I am in my Father and you are in me and I am in you. 21 The
person who has my commandments and obeys them is the one
who loves me. The one who loves me will be loved by my Father,
and I will love him and will reveal myself to him."
22 "Lord," Judas (not Judas Iscariot) said, "what has happened
that you are going to reveal yourself to us and not to the world?"
23 Jesus replied, "If anyone loves me, he will obey my word, and
my Father will love him, and we will come to him and take up
residence with him. 24 The person who does not love me does
not obey my words. And the word you hear is not mine, but the
Father's who sent me.
25 "I have spoken these things while staying with you. 26 But
the Advocate, the Holy Spirit, whom the Father will send in my
name, will teach you everything, and will cause you to remember everything I said to you.
27 "Peace I leave with you; my peace I give to you; I do not give it

to you as the world does. Do not let your hearts be distressed or
lacking in courage. 28 You heard me say to you, 'I am going away
and I am coming back to you.' If you loved me, you would be glad
that I am going to the Father, because the Father is greater than I
am. 29 I have told you now before it happens, so that when it happens you may believe. 30 I will not speak with you much longer,
for the ruler of this world is coming. He has no power over me,
31 but I am doing just what the Father commanded me, so that the
world may know that I love the Father. Get up, let us go from here.

THE VINE AND THE BRANCHES

15 "I am the true vine and my Father is the gardener. 2 He takes
away every branch that does not bear fruit in me. He prunes
every branch that bears fruit so that it will bear more fruit. 3 You
are clean already because of the word that I have spoken to you.
4 Remain in me, and I will remain in you. Just as the branch cannot bear fruit by itself, unless it remains in the vine, so neither
can you unless you remain in me.

5 "I am the vine; you are the branches. The one who remains
in me—and I in him—bears much fruit, because apart from me
you can accomplish nothing. 6 If anyone does not remain in me,
he is thrown out like a branch, and dries up; and such branches
are gathered up and thrown into the fire, and are burned up. 7 If
you remain in me and my words remain in you, ask whatever you
want, and it will be done for you. 8 My Father is honored by this,
that you bear much fruit and show that you are my disciples.

9 "Just as the Father has loved me, I have also loved you; remain
in my love. 10 If you obey my commandments, you will remain in
my love, just as I have obeyed my Father's commandments and
remain in his love. 11 I have told you these things so that my joy
may be in you, and your joy may be complete. 12 My commandment is this—to love one another just as I have loved you. 13 No
one has greater love than this—that one lays down his life for
his friends. 14 You are my friends if you do what I command you.
15 I no longer call you slaves, because the slave does not understand what his master is doing. But I have called you friends,
because I have revealed to you everything I heard from my Father. 16 You did not choose me, but I chose you and appointed
you to go and bear fruit, fruit that remains, so that whatever you
ask the Father in my name he will give you. 17 This I command
you—to love one another.

THE WORLD'S HATRED

18 "If the world hates you, be aware that it hated me first. 19 If you
belonged to the world, the world would love you as its own. However, because you do not belong to the world, but I chose you out
of the world, for this reason the world hates you. 20 Remember
what I told you, 'A slave is not greater than his master.' If they
persecuted me, they will also persecute you. If they obeyed my
word, they will obey yours too. 21 But they will do all these things
to you on account of my name, because they do not know the
one who sent me. 22 If I had not come and spoken to them, they
would not be guilty of sin. But they no longer have any excuse
for their sin. 23 The one who hates me hates my Father too. 24 If I

LOVE TO GROW

DEFINED BY THE HUSTLE

JOHN 15:1-11

To apply hustle in our daily work can result in productive and successful leadership. From a spiritual standpoint, we should make it our goal to work to the potential of our God-given abilities, stewarding His gifts to advance His kingdom. Work ethic, drive, motivation, grit, and forward progress can all contribute to managing our time, talents, and treasure for His glory.

Too often, we take the hustle mentality to an unhealthy extreme, running ahead of God and operating on our own strength instead of His.

Instead of serving from the perspective of godly stewardship, we compete and perform with our eyes fixed on worldly success. We end up striving to the point of exhaustion, instead of abiding in Christ (see John 15:4). So how do we abide?

J. C. Ryle puts it this way: "To abide in Christ means to keep up a habit of constant close communion with Him—to be always leaning on Him, resting on Him, pouring out our hearts to Him, and using Him as our Fountain of life and strength, as our chief Companion and best Friend. To have His words abiding in us, is to keep His sayings and precepts continually before our memories and minds, and to make them the guide of our actions and the rule of our daily conduct and behavior."

Do you struggle to abide? Here are a couple of practical places to start:

Make your time in the Word a priority: If you've heard it once you've heard it a thousand times: as much as we have on our plates, we simply can't afford to skip our daily time with the Lord. Entering into His wisdom and strength each day is the fuel we need to accomplish what He has entrusted to us. Seeking more of Him helps us keep our expectations in line with His heart.

Set realistic goals; as driven leaders we often dream big, but unrealistic goals can quickly destroy motivation, morale, and relationships. Pray first, then listen carefully as the Spirit guides you to the size and urgency of each goal. Saying no where needed and tabling lesser priorities for a time will enable you to tackle your greater priorities with excellence.

When we confess to our loving Father that we can do nothing apart from Him, He is faithful to meet us there. He desires to draw us close to His heart. As we abide in Him, we will learn to steward what He's entrusted to us. As we rely on Him, abide in Him, and serve Him, the world will be certain that we are His.

had not performed among them the miraculous deeds that no
one else did, they would not be guilty of sin. But now they have
seen the deeds and have hated both me and my Father. 25 Now
this happened to fulfill the word that is written in their law, '***They
hated me without reason***.' 26 When the Advocate comes, whom I
will send you from the Father—the Spirit of truth who goes out
from the Father—he will testify about me, 27 and you also will testify, because you have been with me from the beginning.
16 "I have told you all these things so that you will not fall away.
2 They will put you out of the synagogue, yet a time is coming when the one who kills you will think he is offering service
to God. 3 They will do these things because they have not known
the Father or me. 4 But I have told you these things so that when
their time comes, you will remember that I told you about them.
"I did not tell you these things from the beginning because I
was with you. 5 But now I am going to the one who sent me, and
not one of you is asking me, 'Where are you going?' 6 Instead your
hearts are filled with sadness because I have said these things
to you. 7 But I tell you the truth, it is to your advantage that I am
going away. For if I do not go away, the Advocate will not come
to you, but if I go, I will send him to you. 8 And when he comes,
he will prove the world wrong concerning sin and righteousness
and judgment—9 concerning sin, because they do not believe in
me; 10 concerning righteousness, because I am going to the Father and you will see me no longer; 11 and concerning judgment,
because the ruler of this world has been condemned.
12 "I have many more things to say to you, but you cannot bear
them now. 13 But when he, the Spirit of truth, comes, he will guide
you into all truth. For he will not speak on his own authority, but
will speak whatever he hears, and will tell you what is to come.
14 He will glorify me, because he will receive from me what is
mine and will tell it to you. 15 Everything that the Father has
is mine; that is why I said the Spirit will receive from me what
is mine and will tell it to you. 16 In a little while you will see me
no longer; again after a little while, you will see me."
17 Then some of his disciples said to one another, "What is the
meaning of what he is saying, 'In a little while you will not see
me; again after a little while, you will see me,' and, 'because I am
going to the Father'?" 18 So they kept on repeating, "What is the
meaning of what he says, 'In a little while'? We do not understand what he is talking about."
19 Jesus could see that they wanted to ask him about these
things, so he said to them, "Are you asking each other about
this—that I said, 'In a little while you will not see me; again after a little while, you will see me'? 20 I tell you the solemn truth,
you will weep and wail, but the world will rejoice; you will be sad,
but your sadness will turn into joy. 21 When a woman gives birth,
she has distress because her time has come, but when her child
is born, she no longer remembers the suffering because of her
joy that a human being has been born into the world. 22 So also
you have sorrow now, but *I will see you again, and your hearts will
rejoice, and no one will take your joy away from you.* 23 At that time
you will ask me nothing. I tell you the solemn truth, whatever
you ask the Father in my name he will give you. 24 Until now you

REFLECT

How is the ministry of the Holy Spirit different from the ministry of Jesus?

have not asked for anything in my name. Ask and you will receive it, so that your joy may be complete.

25 "I have told you these things in obscure figures of speech; a time is coming when I will no longer speak to you in obscure figures, but will tell you plainly about the Father. 26 At that time you will ask in my name, and I do not say that I will ask the Father on your behalf. 27 For the Father himself loves you, because you have loved me and have believed that I came from God. 28 I came from the Father and entered into the world, but in turn, I am leaving the world and going back to the Father."

29 His disciples said, "Look, now you are speaking plainly and not in obscure figures of speech! 30 Now we know that you know everything and do not need anyone to ask you anything. Because of this we believe that you have come from God."

31 Jesus replied, "Do you now believe? 32 Look, a time is coming—and has come—when you will be scattered, each one to his own home, and I will be left alone. Yet I am not alone, because my Father is with me. 33 I have told you these things so that in me you may have peace. In the world you have trouble and suffering, but take courage—I have conquered the world."

JESUS PRAYS FOR THE FATHER TO GLORIFY HIM

17 When Jesus had finished saying these things, he looked upward to heaven and said, "Father, the time has come. Glorify your Son, so that your Son may glorify you—2 just as you have given him authority over all humanity, so that he may give eternal life to everyone you have given him. 3 Now this is eternal life—that they know you, the only true God, and Jesus Christ, whom you sent. 4 I glorified you on earth by completing the work you gave me to do. 5 And now, Father, glorify me at your side with the glory I had with you before the world was created.

JESUS PRAYS FOR THE DISCIPLES

6 "I have revealed your name to the men you gave me out of the world. They belonged to you, and you gave them to me, and they have obeyed your word. 7 Now they understand that everything you have given me comes from you, 8 because I have given them the words you have given me. They accepted them and really understand that I came from you, and they believed that you sent me. 9 I am praying on behalf of them. I am not praying on behalf of the world, but on behalf of those you have given me, because they belong to you. 10 Everything I have belongs to you, and everything you have belongs to me, and I have been glorified by them. 11 I am no longer in the world, but they are in the world, and I am coming to you. Holy Father, keep them safe in your name that you have given me, so that they may be one just as we are one. 12 When I was with them I kept them safe and watched over them in your name that you have given me. Not one of them was lost except the one destined for destruction, so that the scripture could be fulfilled. 13 But now I am coming to you, and I am saying these things in the world, so they may experience my joy completed in themselves. 14 I have given them your word, and the world has hated them, because they do not belong to the world, just as I do not belong to the world. 15 I am not asking you to take them out of the world,

but that you keep them safe from the evil one. 16 They do not belong to the world just as I do not belong to the world. 17 Set them
apart in the truth; your word is truth. 18 Just as you sent me into
the world, so I sent them into the world. 19 And I set myself apart
on their behalf, so that they too may be truly set apart.

JESUS PRAYS FOR BELIEVERS EVERYWHERE

20 "I am not praying only on their behalf, but also on behalf of
those who believe in me through their testimony, 21 that they will
all be one, just as you, Father, are in me and I am in you. I pray
that they will be in us, so that the world will believe that you sent
me. 22 The glory you gave to me I have given to them, that they
may be one just as we are one—23 I in them and you in me—that
they may be completely one, so that the world will know that
you sent me, and you have loved them just as you have loved me.
24 "Father, I want those you have given me to be with me where
I am, so that they can see my glory that you gave me because you
loved me before the creation of the world. 25 Righteous Father,
even if the world does not know you, I know you, and these men
know that you sent me. 26 I made known your name to them, and
I will continue to make it known, so that the love you have loved
me with may be in them, and I may be in them."

BETRAYAL AND ARREST

18 When he had said these things, Jesus went out with his disciples across the Kidron Valley. There was an orchard there,
and he and his disciples went into it. 2 (Now Judas, the one who
betrayed him, knew the place too, because Jesus had met there
many times with his disciples.) 3 So Judas obtained a squad of soldiers and some officers of the chief priests and Pharisees. They
came to the orchard with lanterns and torches and weapons.
4 Then Jesus, because he knew everything that was going to
happen to him, came and asked them, "Who are you looking
for?" 5 They replied, "Jesus the Nazarene." He told them, "I am he."
(Now Judas, the one who betrayed him, was standing there with
them.) 6 So when Jesus said to them, "I am he," they retreated
and fell to the ground. 7 Then Jesus asked them again, "Who are
you looking for?" And they said, "Jesus the Nazarene." 8 Jesus replied, "I told you that I am he. If you are looking for me, let these
men go." 9 He said this to fulfill the word he had spoken, "I have
not lost a single one of those whom you gave me."
10 Then Simon Peter, who had a sword, pulled it out and struck
the high priest's slave, cutting off his right ear. (Now the slave's
name was Malchus.) 11 But Jesus said to Peter, "Put your sword
back into its sheath! Am I not to drink the cup that the Father
has given me?"

JESUS BROUGHT BEFORE ANNAS

12 Then the squad of soldiers with their commanding officer and
the officers of the Jewish leaders arrested Jesus and tied him up.
13 They brought him first to Annas, for he was the father-in-law
of Caiaphas, who was high priest that year. 14 (Now it was Caiaphas who had advised the Jewish leaders that it was to their advantage that one man die for the people.)

GOD'S HEART FOR THE NATIONS

John 17:18

"Just as you sent me into the world, so I sent them into the world."

PETER'S FIRST DENIAL

[15] Simon Peter and another disciple followed them as they
brought Jesus to Annas. (Now the other disciple was acquainted
with the high priest, and he went with Jesus into the high priest's
courtyard.) [16] But Peter was left standing outside by the door.
So the other disciple who was acquainted with the high priest
came out and spoke to the slave girl who watched the door, and
brought Peter inside. [17] The girl who was the doorkeeper said
to Peter, "You're not one of this man's disciples too, are you?"
He replied, "I am not." [18] (Now the slaves and the guards were
standing around a charcoal fire they had made, warming themselves because it was cold. Peter also was standing with them,
warming himself.)

JESUS QUESTIONED BY ANNAS

[19] While this was happening, the high priest questioned Jesus
about his disciples and about his teaching. [20] Jesus replied, "I
have spoken publicly to the world. I always taught in the synagogues and in the temple courts, where all the Jewish people
assemble together. I have said nothing in secret. [21] Why do you
ask me? Ask those who heard what I said. They know what I
said." [22] When Jesus had said this, one of the high priest's officers who stood nearby struck him on the face and said, "Is that
the way you answer the high priest?" [23] Jesus replied, "If I have
said something wrong, confirm what is wrong. But if I spoke correctly, why strike me?" [24] Then Annas sent him, still tied up, to
Caiaphas the high priest.

PETER'S SECOND AND THIRD DENIALS

[25] Meanwhile Simon Peter was standing in the courtyard warming himself. They said to him, "You aren't one of his disciples too,
are you?" Peter denied it: "I am not!" [26] One of the high priest's
slaves, a relative of the man whose ear Peter had cut off, said,
"Did I not see you in the orchard with him?" [27] Then Peter denied it again, and immediately a rooster crowed.

JESUS BROUGHT BEFORE PILATE

[28] Then they brought Jesus from Caiaphas to the Roman governor's residence. (Now it was very early morning.) They did not
go into the governor's residence so they would not be ceremonially defiled, but could eat the Passover meal. [29] So Pilate came
outside to them and said, "What accusation do you bring against
this man?" [30] They replied, "If this man were not a criminal, we
would not have handed him over to you."

[31] Pilate told them, "Take him yourselves and pass judgment
on him according to your own law!" The Jewish leaders replied,
"We cannot legally put anyone to death." [32] (This happened to
fulfill the word Jesus had spoken when he indicated what kind
of death he was going to die.)

PILATE QUESTIONS JESUS

[33] So Pilate went back into the governor's residence, summoned
Jesus, and asked him, "Are you the king of the Jews?" [34] Jesus replied, "Are you saying this on your own initiative, or have others

told you about me?" 35 Pilate answered, "I am not a Jew, am I?
Your own people and your chief priests handed you over to me.
What have you done?"
36 Jesus replied, "My kingdom is not from this world. If my
kingdom were from this world, my servants would be fighting
to keep me from being handed over to the Jewish authorities.
But as it is, my kingdom is not from here." 37 Then Pilate said, "So
you are a king!" Jesus replied, "You say that I am a king. For this
reason I was born, and for this reason I came into the world—to
testify to the truth. Everyone who belongs to the truth listens
to my voice." 38 Pilate asked, "What is truth?"
When he had said this he went back outside to the Jewish leaders and announced, "I find no basis for an accusation against
him. 39 But it is your custom that I release one prisoner for you
at the Passover. So do you want me to release for you the king
of the Jews?" 40 Then they shouted back, "Not this man, but Barabbas!" (Now Barabbas was a revolutionary.)

PILATE TRIES TO RELEASE JESUS

19 Then Pilate took Jesus and had him flogged severely. 2 The
soldiers braided a crown of thorns and put it on his head,
and they clothed him in a purple robe. 3 They came up to him
again and again and said, "Hail, king of the Jews!" And they struck
him repeatedly in the face.
4 Again Pilate went out and said to the Jewish leaders, "Look, I
am bringing him out to you, so that you may know that I find no
reason for an accusation against him." 5 So Jesus came outside,
wearing the crown of thorns and the purple robe. Pilate said to
them, "Look, here is the man!" 6 When the chief priests and their
officers saw him, they shouted out, "Crucify him! Crucify him!"
Pilate said, "You take him and crucify him! Certainly I find no
reason for an accusation against him!" 7 The Jewish leaders replied, "We have a law, and according to our law he ought to die,
because he claimed to be the Son of God!"
8 When Pilate heard what they said, he was more afraid than
ever, 9 and he went back into the governor's residence and said to
Jesus, "Where do you come from?" But Jesus gave him no answer.
10 So Pilate said, "Do you refuse to speak to me? Don't you know
I have the authority to release you, and to crucify you?" 11 Jesus
replied, "You would have no authority over me at all, unless it
was given to you from above. Therefore the one who handed me
over to you is guilty of greater sin."
12 From this point on, Pilate tried to release him. But the Jewish
leaders shouted out, "If you release this man, you are no friend
of Caesar! Everyone who claims to be a king opposes Caesar!"
13 When Pilate heard these words he brought Jesus outside and
sat down on the judgment seat in the place called "The Stone
Pavement" (*Gabbatha* in Aramaic). 14 (Now it was the day of preparation for the Passover, about noon.) Pilate said to the Jewish
leaders, "Look, here is your king!"
15 Then they shouted out, "Away with him! Away with him!
Crucify him!" Pilate asked, "Shall I crucify your king?" The high
priests replied, "We have no king except Caesar!" 16 Then Pilate
handed him over to them to be crucified.

THE CRUCIFIXION

So they took Jesus, 17 and carrying his own cross he went out to the place called "The Place of the Skull" (called in Aramaic *Golgotha*). 18 There they crucified him along with two others, one on each side, with Jesus in the middle. 19 Pilate also had a notice written and fastened to the cross, which read: "Jesus the Nazarene, the king of the Jews." 20 Thus many of the Jewish residents of Jerusalem read this notice, because the place where Jesus was crucified was near the city, and the notice was written in Aramaic, Latin, and Greek. 21 Then the chief priests of the Jews said to Pilate, "Do not write, 'The king of the Jews,' but rather, 'This man said, I am king of the Jews.'" 22 Pilate answered, "What I have written, I have written."

23 Now when the soldiers crucified Jesus, they took his clothes and made four shares, one for each soldier, and the tunic remained. (Now the tunic was seamless, woven from top to bottom as a single piece.) 24 So the soldiers said to one another, "Let's not tear it, but throw dice to see who will get it." This took place to fulfill the scripture that says, "***They divided my garments among them, and for my clothing they threw dice.***" So the soldiers did these things.

25 Now standing beside Jesus' cross were his mother, his mother's sister, Mary the wife of Clopas, and Mary Magdalene. 26 So when Jesus saw his mother and the disciple whom he loved standing there, he said to his mother, "Woman, look, here is your son!" 27 He then said to his disciple, "Look, here is your mother!" From that very time the disciple took her into his own home.

JESUS' DEATH

28 After this Jesus, realizing that by this time everything was completed, said (in order to fulfill the scripture), "I am thirsty!" 29 A jar full of sour wine was there, so they put a sponge soaked in sour wine on a branch of hyssop and lifted it to his mouth. 30 When he had received the sour wine, Jesus said, "It is completed!" Then he bowed his head and gave up his spirit.

31 Then, because it was the day of preparation, so that the bodies should not stay on the crosses on the Sabbath (for that Sabbath was an especially important one), the Jewish leaders asked Pilate to have the victims' legs broken and the bodies taken down. 32 So the soldiers came and broke the legs of the two men who had been crucified with Jesus, first the one and then the other. 33 But when they came to Jesus and saw that he was already dead, they did not break his legs. 34 But one of the soldiers pierced his side with a spear, and blood and water flowed out immediately. 35 And the person who saw it has testified (and his testimony is true, and he knows that he is telling the truth), so that you also may believe. 36 For these things happened so that the scripture would be fulfilled, "***Not a bone of his will be broken.***" 37 And again another scripture says, "***They will look on the one whom they have pierced.***"

JESUS' BURIAL

38 After this, Joseph of Arimathea, a disciple of Jesus (but secretly, because he feared the Jewish leaders), asked Pilate if he could remove the body of Jesus. Pilate gave him permission, so

he went and took the body away. 39 Nicodemus, the man who had
previously come to Jesus at night, accompanied Joseph, carrying a mixture of myrrh and aloes weighing about seventy-five
pounds. 40 Then they took Jesus' body and wrapped it, with the
aromatic spices, in strips of linen cloth according to Jewish burial
customs. 41 Now at the place where Jesus was crucified there was
a garden, and in the garden was a new tomb where no one had
yet been buried. 42 And so, because it was the Jewish day of preparation and the tomb was nearby, they placed Jesus' body there.

THE RESURRECTION

20 Now very early on the first day of the week, while it was
still dark, Mary Magdalene came to the tomb and saw
that the stone had been moved away from the entrance. 2 So she
went running to Simon Peter and the other disciple whom Jesus
loved and told them, "They have taken the Lord from the tomb,
and we don't know where they have put him!" 3 Then Peter and
the other disciple set out to go to the tomb. 4 The two were running together, but the other disciple ran faster than Peter and
reached the tomb first. 5 He bent down and saw the strips of linen
cloth lying there, but he did not go in. 6 Then Simon Peter, who
had been following him, arrived and went right into the tomb.
He saw the strips of linen cloth lying there, 7 and the face cloth,
which had been around Jesus' head, not lying with the strips of
linen cloth but rolled up in a place by itself. 8 Then the other disciple, who had reached the tomb first, came in, and he saw and
believed. 9 (For they did not yet understand the scripture that
Jesus must rise from the dead.)

JESUS' APPEARANCE TO MARY MAGDALENE

10 So the disciples went back to their homes. 11 But Mary stood
outside the tomb weeping. As she wept, she bent down and
looked into the tomb. 12 And she saw two angels in white sitting where Jesus' body had been lying, one at the head and one
at the feet. 13 They said to her, "Woman, why are you weeping?"
Mary replied, "They have taken my Lord away, and I do not know
where they have put him!" 14 When she had said this, she turned
around and saw Jesus standing there, but she did not know that
it was Jesus.
15 Jesus said to her, "Woman, why are you weeping? Who are
you looking for?" Because she thought he was the gardener, she
said to him, "Sir, if you have carried him away, tell me where you
have put him, and I will take him." 16 Jesus said to her, "Mary."
She turned and said to him in Aramaic, "*Rabboni*" (which means
Teacher). 17 Jesus replied, "Do not touch me, for I have not yet ascended to my Father. Go to my brothers and tell them, 'I am ascending to my Father and your Father, to my God and your God.'"
18 Mary Magdalene came and informed the disciples, "I have
seen the Lord!" And she told them what Jesus had said to her.

REFLECT

How are Jesus' compassion and heart for Mary displayed in this passage?

JESUS' APPEARANCE TO THE DISCIPLES

19 On the evening of that day, the first day of the week, the disciples had gathered together and locked the doors of the place
because they were afraid of the Jewish leaders. Jesus came and

stood among them and said to them, "Peace be with you." 20 When
he had said this, he showed them his hands and his side. Then
the disciples rejoiced when they saw the Lord. 21 So Jesus said to
them again, "Peace be with you. Just as the Father has sent me,
I also send you." 22 And after he said this, he breathed on them
and said, "Receive the Holy Spirit. 23 If you forgive anyone's sins,
they are forgiven; if you retain anyone's sins, they are retained."

THE RESPONSE OF THOMAS

24 Now Thomas (called Didymus), one of the twelve, was not with
them when Jesus came. 25 The other disciples told him, "We have
seen the Lord!" But he replied, "Unless I see the wounds from
the nails in his hands, and put my finger into the wounds from
the nails, and put my hand into his side, I will never believe it!"
26 Eight days later the disciples were again together in the
house, and Thomas was with them. Although the doors were
locked, Jesus came and stood among them and said, "Peace be
with you!" 27 Then he said to Thomas, "Put your finger here, and
examine my hands. Extend your hand and put it into my side.
Do not continue in your unbelief, but believe." 28 Thomas replied
to him, "My Lord and my God!" 29 Jesus said to him, "Have you
believed because you have seen me? Blessed are the people who
have not seen and yet have believed."
30 Now Jesus performed many other miraculous signs in the
presence of the disciples, which are not recorded in this book.
31 But these are recorded so that you may believe that Jesus is
the Christ, the Son of God, and that by believing you may have
life in his name.

JESUS' APPEARANCE TO THE DISCIPLES IN GALILEE

21 After this Jesus revealed himself again to the disciples by
the Sea of Tiberias. Now this is how he did so. 2 Simon Peter, Thomas (called Didymus), Nathanael (who was from Cana in
Galilee), the sons of Zebedee, and two other disciples of his were
together. 3 Simon Peter told them, "I am going fishing." "We will
go with you," they replied. They went out and got into the boat,
but that night they caught nothing.
4 When it was already very early morning, Jesus stood on the
beach, but the disciples did not know that it was Jesus. 5 So Jesus
said to them, "Children, you don't have any fish, do you?" They
replied, "No." 6 He told them, "Throw your net on the right side
of the boat, and you will find some." So they threw the net, and
were not able to pull it in because of the large number of fish.
7 Then the disciple whom Jesus loved said to Peter, "It is the
Lord!" So Simon Peter, when he heard that it was the Lord, tucked
in his outer garment (for he had nothing on underneath it), and
plunged into the sea. 8 Meanwhile the other disciples came with
the boat, dragging the net full of fish, for they were not far from
land, only about a hundred yards.
9 When they got out on the beach, they saw a charcoal fire ready
with a fish placed on it, and bread. 10 Jesus said, "Bring some of
the fish you have just now caught." 11 So Simon Peter went aboard
and pulled the net to shore. It was full of large fish, 153, but although there were so many, the net was not torn. 12 "Come, have

LOVE TO GROW

LIVING THE LIFE OF THE REDEEMED

JOHN 21

After the resurrection, Jesus appeared to the disciples in Jerusalem and appointed them to do work in His name. Yet, in chapter 21, we see them in Galilee, living seemingly ordinary lives. Why would the disciples who had experienced the resurrected Christ not be living out the effects of the resurrection? Perhaps because while the cross meant forgiveness, they did not understand the restoration that took place at the resurrection.

Jesus' encounter with Peter gives us a glimpse of the grace that comes with our relationship with God through Christ. When Peter denied Jesus three times on the night of His arrest, guilt and shame reigned. As Jesus asked Peter if he loved Him, He restored the disciple to a position of honor.

Imagine the two sitting beside the fire, reflecting on the miraculous catch. Pointing to the fish, Jesus asked, "Simon, son of John, do you love me more than these do?" Peter replied, "Yes, Lord, you know I love you." The Lord responded: "Shepherd my sheep." Jesus asked Peter the same question two more times. By the third time, Peter had become distressed. Finally, Jesus told him, "Follow me" (John 21:15–19).

Those two words brought new life to Peter. They were the beginning of his journey as a redeemed follower of the risen Christ. No longer was Peter the broken stone who rejected Jesus in His time of need. Instead, he was the rock called to shepherd the flock.

Have you allowed your brokenness and failure to define your relationship with Christ and keep you from becoming who God has called you to be?

Jesus, our crucified and resurrected Savior, called us to follow Him, not so that we would live a life of momentary obedience and be bound by guilt. Rather, He called us to be forgiven and free so we might live to show the world the restoration and grace we have in Christ.

What does it look like to live the life of the redeemed? It is to say yes to Jesus when He asks you to be vulnerable. It is to take a risk to go outside of your comfort zone. It is to give up the safety net of your past to follow in obedience. Let's continue to move toward loving God greatly by living out a life of complete restoration, confident in the forgiveness and redemption we have in Christ.

breakfast," Jesus said. But none of the disciples dared to ask him,
"Who are you?" because they knew it was the Lord. 13 Jesus came
and took the bread and gave it to them, and did the same with
the fish. 14 This was now the third time Jesus was revealed to the
disciples after he was raised from the dead.

PETER'S RESTORATION

15 Then when they had finished breakfast, Jesus said to Simon Peter, "Simon, son of John, do you love me more than these do?" He
replied, "Yes, Lord, you know I love you." Jesus told him, "Feed my
lambs." 16 Jesus said a second time, "Simon, son of John, do you
love me?" He replied, "Yes, Lord, you know I love you." Jesus told
him, "Shepherd my sheep." 17 Jesus said a third time, "Simon, son
of John, do you love me?" Peter was distressed that Jesus asked
him a third time, "Do you love me?" and said, "Lord, you know
everything. You know that I love you." Jesus replied, "Feed my
sheep. 18 I tell you the solemn truth, when you were young, you
tied your clothes around you and went wherever you wanted,
but when you are old, you will stretch out your hands, and others will tie you up and bring you where you do not want to go."
19 (Now Jesus said this to indicate clearly by what kind of death
Peter was going to glorify God.) After he said this, Jesus told Peter, "Follow me."

PETER AND THE DISCIPLE JESUS LOVED

20 Peter turned around and saw the disciple whom Jesus loved
following them. (This was the disciple who had leaned back
against Jesus' chest at the meal and asked, "Lord, who is the one
who is going to betray you?") 21 So when Peter saw him, he asked
Jesus, "Lord, what about him?" 22 Jesus replied, "If I want him to
live until I come back, what concern is that of yours? You follow
me!" 23 So the saying circulated among the brothers and sisters
that this disciple was not going to die. But Jesus did not say to
him that he was not going to die, but rather, "If I want him to
live until I come back, what concern is that of yours?"

A FINAL NOTE

24 This is the disciple who testifies about these things and has
written these things, and we know that his testimony is true.
25 There are many other things that Jesus did. If every one of
them were written down, I suppose the whole world would not
have room for the books that would be written.

PAUL'S MISSIONARY JOURNEYS

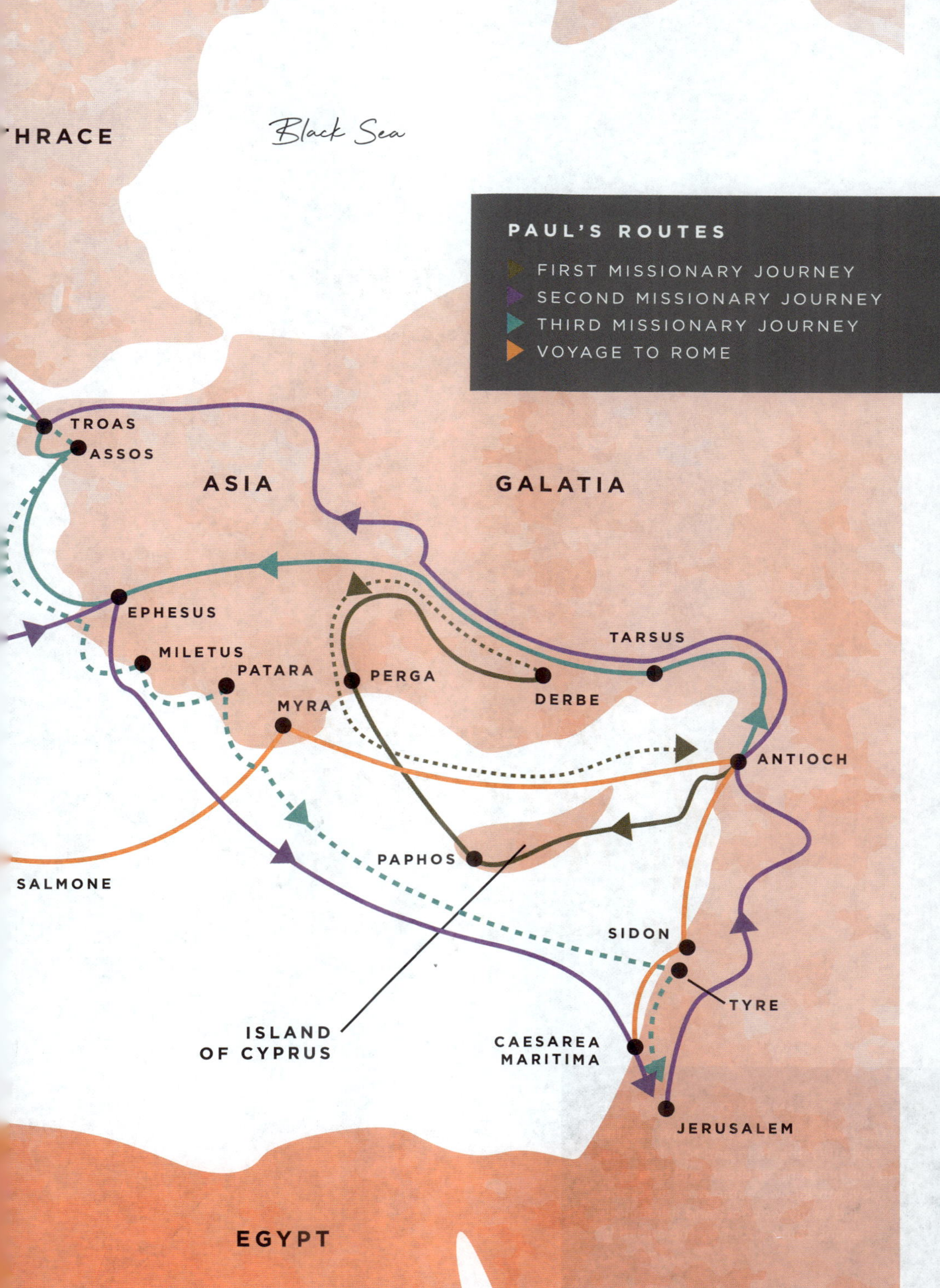

THRACE
Black Sea
PAUL'S ROUTES
FIRST MISSIONARY JOURNEY
SECOND MISSIONARY JOURNEY
THIRD MISSIONARY JOURNEY
VOYAGE TO ROME
TROAS
ASSOS
ASIA
GALATIA
EPHESUS
MILETUS
PATARA
PERGA
DERBE
TARSUS
MYRA
ANTIOCH
PAPHOS
SALMONE
SIDON
TYRE
ISLAND
OF CYPRUS
CAESAREA
MARITIMA
JERUSALEM
EGYPT

They WERE Devoting THEMSELVES to the APOSTLES' TEACHING and to fellowship, TO THE BREAKING of BREAD and TO PRAYER. REVERENTIAL awe came over everyone and MANY WONDERS and MIRACULOUS SIGNS CAME about by the APOSTLES.

MEMORY VERSE

They were devoting themselves to the apostles' teaching and to fellowship, to the breaking of bread and to prayer. Reverential awe came over everyone, and many wonders and miraculous signs came about by the apostles.

Acts 2:42–43

Acts

INTRODUCTION

The Spread of the Gospel

The Book of Acts is the continuation of the Book of Luke and shows the work of Jesus' disciples as the gospel spread throughout the world. Jesus commanded His followers to be His witnesses in "Jerusalem, and in all Judea and Samaria, and to the farthest parts of the earth" (1:8). The Book of Acts is the record of all that Jesus' disciples did as witnesses to His life, death, and resurrection.

This book opens where the Book of Luke ends, with the ascension of Jesus and the disciples waiting for the coming of the Holy Spirit. After the day of Pentecost, the disciples went out proclaiming the good news of Christ. When persecution began, the believers scattered from Jerusalem into Judea and Samaria. A man named Saul was a leader in the persecution of Christians. After his dramatic conversion, Saul became a leader in the church, traveling on missionary journeys across the Roman Empire to proclaim the good news of Jesus Christ. The Book of Acts ends with the account of his imprisonment but implies that the spread of the gospel had only begun.

Luke wrote both Luke and Acts to his friend Theophilus to educate him on the events of Christ's life and on the lives of His followers after His death. Luke was a companion to Paul on some of his missionary journeys. The Book of Acts is traditionally dated after A.D. 61 and before Nero's persecution of Christians in A.D. 64 and the fall of Jerusalem in A.D. 70.

The Book of Acts is an encouragement for us to love God greatly. As we read the records of the spread of the gospel, we can be encouraged to share the Good News ourselves in our communities and spheres of influence. Even though they endured persecution, the disciples were steadfast in their mission to share the news of Christ with the world. We can persist when we face trials or persecution because we know there is no higher purpose for our lives than to be witnesses of Jesus' life, death, and resurrection.

Venezuela

OFFICIAL LANGUAGE
Spanish
POPULATION
27,819,000
UNREACHED POPULATION
35,000
PROFESSING CHRISTIANS
82.6%

Edurne's Home

Say a Prayer Today

Pray for lasting impact of Edurne's ministry in Venezuela. Pray for her husband and children as they continue in faith, enduring for the gospel.

HISTORY BIT

While missionaries from many denominations have traveled to and started churches in Venezuela, Venezuela has a significant number of churches that were started by nationals. The Alleluia Church is the earliest of these churches and dates to the mid-nineteenth century.*

Source Information:
https://joshuaproject.net/countries/VE

EDURNE'S STORY

I used to pray Acts 2:42–43 for my home church. I longed to see us in harmony and unity, sharing the needs of fellow brothers and sisters, and being devoted to prayer. I prayed we could be a light and a testimony to those around us.

God answered that prayer.

In recent years, Venezuela has been living in a deep crisis. Many Venezuelans eat only once a day. There's a terrible shortage of food and medicine. Hospitals are unreliable. Basic services like electricity and water fail often, and people are fleeing the country by the thousands.

We, as believers in Christ and members of the body of Christ, have gone through the process of learning and accepting that this is God's will for us and that His will is always perfect. It hasn't been easy, but God has been so gracious to us! He has kindly and patiently helped us trust Him with every single need and has taught us to pray for everything. He has faithfully provided, and we have learned to share and bless others in the middle of our scarcity.

We keep the faith. We continue to work in our church with love, passion, and determination. God keeps adding more and more people to our communities of faith. They are coming not because we fill up their stomachs, but because we give them hope—we give them Jesus. They see how God takes care of them, how He provides, how He heals, and how He fills their hearts with peace and joy.

I would not have asked for such a difficult time in my life but seeing how Jesus is transforming lives and how the gospel is spreading across the country makes it all worth it. Jesus makes all the difference. His light is shining in every corner of Venezuela, and I can't help but praise God for this.

Editor's Note: Since writing these words, our dear Edurne passed away. Even though we grieve the loss of our beloved friend, we are encouraged by her faith, her perseverance, and her love for Christ. We know she is home, with Jesus, hearing the words, "Well done" (Matt 25:23).

6 WEEK READING PLAN

LOVE HIS WORD

	MONDAY	TUESDAY	WEDNESDAY	THURSDAY	FRIDAY
1	Acts 1	Acts 2	Acts 3	Acts 4	Acts 5
	SOAP Acts 1:7-8	SOAP Acts 2:42-43	SOAP Acts 3:16	SOAP Acts 4:19-20	SOAP Acts 5:42
2	Acts 6	Acts 7:1-53	Acts 7:54—8:3	Acts 8:4-40	Acts 9
	SOAP Acts 6:7	SOAP Acts 7:48-50	SOAP Acts 7:59-60	SOAP Acts 8:12-13	SOAP Acts 9:31
3	Acts 10	Acts 11	Acts 12	Acts 13:1-12	Acts 13:13-52
	SOAP Acts 10:46-48	SOAP Acts 11:23-24	SOAP Acts 12:24	SOAP Acts 13:1-3	SOAP Acts 13:48-49
4	Acts 14	Acts 15	Acts 16	Acts 17	Acts 18
	SOAP Acts 14:21-23	SOAP Acts 15:30-31	SOAP Acts 16:31-33	SOAP Acts 17:30-31	SOAP Acts 18:9-10
5	Acts 19	Acts 20	Acts 21	Acts 22:1-29	Acts 22:30—23:35
	SOAP Acts 19:8-10	SOAP Acts 20:32-35	SOAP Acts 21:19-20	SOAP Acts 22:12-16	SOAP Acts 23:10-11
6	Acts 24	Acts 25	Acts 26	Acts 27	Acts 28
	SOAP Acts 24:15-16	SOAP Acts 25:10-11	SOAP Acts 26:22-23	SOAP Acts 27:22-25	SOAP Acts 28:30-31

JESUS ASCENDS TO HEAVEN

1 I wrote the former account, Theophilus, about all that Jesus began
to do and teach 2 until the day he was taken up to heaven, after he
had given orders by the Holy Spirit to the apostles he had chosen.
3 To the same apostles also, after his suffering, he presented himself alive with many convincing proofs. He was seen by them over
a forty-day period and spoke about matters concerning the kingdom of God. 4 While he was with them, he declared, "Do not leave
Jerusalem, but wait there for what my Father promised, which
you heard about from me. 5 For John baptized with water, but you
will be baptized with the Holy Spirit not many days from now."
6 So when they had gathered together, they began to ask him,
"Lord, is this the time when you are restoring the kingdom to Israel?" 7 He told them, "You are not permitted to know the times or
periods that the Father has set by his own authority. 8 But you will
receive power when the Holy Spirit has come upon you, and you
will be my witnesses in Jerusalem, and in all Judea and Samaria,
and to the farthest parts of the earth." 9 After he had said this, while
they were watching, he was lifted up and a cloud hid him from their
sight. 10 As they were still staring into the sky while he was going,
suddenly two men in white clothing stood near them 11 and said,
"Men of Galilee, why do you stand here looking up into the sky?
This same Jesus who has been taken up from you into heaven will
come back in the same way you saw him go into heaven."

A REPLACEMENT FOR JUDAS IS CHOSEN

12 Then they returned to Jerusalem from the mountain called
the Mount of Olives (which is near Jerusalem, a Sabbath day's
journey away). 13 When they had entered Jerusalem, they went to
the upstairs room where they were staying. Peter and John, and
James, and Andrew, Philip and Thomas, Bartholomew and Matthew, James son of Alphaeus and Simon the Zealot, and Judas
son of James were there. 14 All these continued together in prayer
with one mind, together with the women, along with Mary the
mother of Jesus, and his brothers. 15 In those days Peter stood up
among the believers (a gathering of about 120 people) and said,
16 "Brothers, the scripture had to be fulfilled that the Holy Spirit
foretold through David concerning Judas—who became the guide
for those who arrested Jesus—17 for he was counted as one of us
and received a share in this ministry." 18 (Now this man Judas acquired a field with the reward of his unjust deed, and falling head-
first he burst open in the middle and all his intestines gushed
out. 19 This became known to all who lived in Jerusalem, so that
in their own language they called that field *Hakeldama*, that is,
"Field of Blood.") 20 "For it is written in the book of Psalms, '***Let his
house become deserted, and let there be no one to live in it***,' and '***Let
another take his position of responsibility***.' 21 Thus one of the men
who have accompanied us during all the time the Lord Jesus associated with us, 22 beginning from his baptism by John until the
day he was taken up from us—one of these must become a witness of his resurrection together with us." 23 So they proposed two
candidates: Joseph called Barsabbas (also called Justus) and Matthias. 24 Then they prayed, "Lord, you know the hearts of all. Show
us which one of these two you have chosen 25 to assume the task

GOD'S HEART FOR THE NATIONS

Acts 1:8

"But you will receive power when the Holy Spirit has come upon you, and you will be my witnesses in Jerusalem, and in all Judea and Samaria, and to the farthest parts of the earth."

of this service and apostleship from which Judas turned aside to
go to his own place." 26 Then they cast lots for them, and the one
chosen was Matthias; so he was counted with the eleven apostles.

THE HOLY SPIRIT AND THE DAY OF PENTECOST

2 Now when the day of Pentecost had come, they were all together in one place. 2 Suddenly a sound like a violent wind
blowing came from heaven and filled the entire house where
they were sitting. 3 And tongues spreading out like a fire appeared to them and came to rest on each one of them. 4 All of
them were filled with the Holy Spirit, and they began to speak
in other languages as the Spirit enabled them.

5 Now there were devout Jews from every nation under heaven
residing in Jerusalem. 6 When this sound occurred, a crowd gathered and was in confusion, because each one heard them speaking in his own language. 7 Completely baffled, they said, "Aren't
all these who are speaking Galileans? 8 And how is it that each
one of us hears them in our own native language? 9 Parthians,
Medes, Elamites, and residents of Mesopotamia, Judea and Cappadocia, Pontus and the province of Asia, 10 Phrygia and Pamphylia, Egypt and the parts of Libya near Cyrene, and visitors
from Rome, 11 both Jews and proselytes, Cretans and Arabs—we
hear them speaking in our own languages about the great deeds
God has done!" 12 All were astounded and greatly confused, saying to one another, "What does this mean?" 13 But others jeered
at the speakers, saying, "They are drunk on new wine!"

PETER'S ADDRESS ON THE DAY OF PENTECOST

14 But Peter stood up with the eleven, raised his voice, and addressed
them: "You men of Judea and all you who live in Jerusalem, know
this and listen carefully to what I say. 15 In spite of what you think,
these men are not drunk, for it is only nine o'clock in the morning. 16 But this is what was spoken about through the prophet Joel:

17 '***And*** in the last days ***it will be,' God says,***
'that I will pour out my Spirit on all people,
and your sons and your daughters will prophesy,
and your young men will see visions,
and your old men will dream dreams.
18 ***Even on my servants, both men and women,***
I will pour out my Spirit in those days, and they will prophesy.
19 ***And I will perform wonders in the sky above***
and miraculous signs on the earth below,
blood and fire and clouds of smoke.
20 ***The sun will be changed to darkness***
and the moon to blood
before the great and glorious day of the Lord comes.
21 ***And then everyone who calls on the name***
of the Lord will be saved.'

22 "Men of Israel, listen to these words: Jesus the Nazarene, a
man clearly attested to you by God with powerful deeds, wonders, and miraculous signs that God performed among you
through him, just as you yourselves know—23 this man, who was
handed over by the predetermined plan and foreknowledge of

God, you executed by nailing him to a cross at the hands of Gentiles. 24 But God raised him up, having released him from the
pains of death, because it was not possible for him to be held in
its power. 25 For David says about him,

'I saw the Lord always in front of me,
for he is at my right hand so that I will not be shaken.
26 *Therefore my heart was glad and my tongue rejoiced;*
my body also will live in hope,
27 *because you will not leave my soul in Hades,*
nor permit your Holy One to experience decay.
28 *You have made known to me the paths of life;*
you will make me full of joy with your presence.'

29 "Brothers, I can speak confidently to you about our forefather David, that he both died and was buried, and his tomb
is with us to this day. 30 So then, because he was a prophet and
knew that God *had sworn to him with an oath to seat one of his de-*
scendants on his throne, 31 David by foreseeing this spoke about
the resurrection of the Christ, that *he was neither abandoned to*
Hades, nor did his body *experience decay.* 32 This Jesus God raised
up, and we are all witnesses of it. 33 So then, exalted to the right
hand of God, and having received the promise of the Holy Spirit
from the Father, he has poured out what you both see and hear.
34 For David did not ascend into heaven, but he himself says,

'The Lord said to my lord,
"Sit at my right hand
35 *until I make your enemies a footstool for your feet."'*

36 Therefore let all the house of Israel know beyond a doubt that
God has made this Jesus whom you crucified both Lord and Christ."

THE RESPONSE TO PETER'S ADDRESS

37 Now when they heard this, they were acutely distressed and said
to Peter and the rest of the apostles, "What should we do, brothers?" 38 Peter said to them, "Repent, and each one of you be baptized in the name of Jesus Christ for the forgiveness of your sins,
and you will receive the gift of the Holy Spirit. 39 For the promise
is for you and your children, and for all who are far away, as many
as the Lord our God will call to himself." 40 With many other words
he testified and exhorted them saying, "Save yourselves from this
perverse generation!" 41 So those who accepted his message were
baptized, and that day about 3,000 people were added.

THE FELLOWSHIP OF THE EARLY BELIEVERS

42 They were devoting themselves to the apostles' teaching and to
fellowship, to the breaking of bread and to prayer. 43 Reverential
awe came over everyone, and many wonders and miraculous signs
came about by the apostles. 44 All who believed were together and
held everything in common, 45 and they began selling their property and possessions and distributing the proceeds to everyone, as
anyone had need. 46 Every day they continued to gather together by
common consent in the temple courts, breaking bread from house
to house, sharing their food with glad and humble hearts, 47 praising God and having the good will of all the people. And the Lord
was adding to their number every day those who were being saved.

DEVOTED TO PRAYER

ACTS 2:42

I don't often travel away from my family, but when I do I love to call home. Our conversations aren't particularly unique. In fact, they're pretty normal. Nonetheless, it's who is on the other end of the line that eases the ache of being away from home. The heart connection that occurs is what matters.

It's kind of like that with God; it's always good to call home to the One who truly understands and loves us.

Don't be mistaken: Our prayers don't have to be fancy, nor do they have to be said out loud when high-level decisions need to be made. The greatest truth about prayer is our prayers don't have to be impressive, articulate, or refined. It's okay for them to be awkward, simple, or short.

The great news is that the power of prayer doesn't rest in the one who is saying it, but rather in the One who hears it.

They were devoting themselves to the apostles' teaching and to fellowship, to the breaking of bread and to prayer (Acts 2:42).

The early church was made up of men and women who were devoted to learning more about God. They were a people who were devoted to each other, people who spent time together, and people who prayed together. God moved powerfully through them and added to their numbers daily.

In a time when we keep hearing how church attendance is in decline, maybe we should go back to the basics of our faith: time in the Word, living in community, having friends over to our homes for dinner, praying together, living out our faith in everyday moments, and allowing God to move powerfully through us.

We, like the early church, need to be devoted to prayer. Though these battles we fight are not easy, we are promised through God's Word that we do not fight them alone. God is with us.

Let's be devoted to prayer. May God do a mighty work through us, and may this world never be the same.

PETER AND JOHN HEAL A LAME MAN AT THE TEMPLE

3 Now Peter and John were going up to the temple at the time
for prayer, at three o'clock in the afternoon. 2 And a man lame
from birth was being carried up, who was placed at the temple gate
called "the Beautiful Gate" every day so he could beg for money from
those going into the temple courts. 3 When he saw Peter and John
about to go into the temple courts, he asked them for money. 4 Peter looked directly at him (as did John) and said, "Look at us!" 5 So
the lame man paid attention to them, expecting to receive something from them. 6 But Peter said, "I have no silver or gold, but what
I do have I give you. In the name of Jesus Christ the Nazarene, stand
up and walk!" 7 Then Peter took hold of him by the right hand and
raised him up, and at once the man's feet and ankles were made
strong. 8 He jumped up, stood and began walking around, and he
entered the temple courts with them, walking and leaping and
praising God. 9 All the people saw him walking and praising God,
10 and they recognized him as the man who used to sit and ask for
donations at the Beautiful Gate of the temple, and they were filled
with astonishment and amazement at what had happened to him.

PETER ADDRESSES THE CROWD

11 While the man was hanging on to Peter and John, all the people, completely astounded, ran together to them in the covered
walkway called Solomon's Portico. 12 When Peter saw this, he declared to the people, "Men of Israel, why are you amazed at this?
Why do you stare at us as if we had made this man walk by our
own power or piety? 13 The God of Abraham, Isaac, and Jacob, the
God of our forefathers, has glorified his servant Jesus, whom you
handed over and rejected in the presence of Pilate after he had
decided to release him. 14 But you rejected the Holy and Righteous One and asked that a man who was a murderer be released
to you. 15 You killed the Originator of life, whom God raised from
the dead. To this fact we are witnesses! 16 And on the basis of faith
in Jesus' name, his very name has made this man—whom you see
and know—strong. The faith that is through Jesus has given him
this complete health in the presence of you all. 17 And now, brothers, I know you acted in ignorance, as your rulers did too. 18 But
the things God foretold long ago through all the prophets—that
his Christ would suffer—he has fulfilled in this way. 19 Therefore repent and turn back so that your sins may be wiped out, 20 so that
times of refreshing may come from the presence of the Lord, and
so that he may send the Messiah appointed for you—that is, Jesus.
21 This one heaven must receive until the time all things are restored, which God declared from times long ago through his holy
prophets. 22 Moses said, '***The Lord your God will raise up for you a***
prophet like me from among your brothers. You must obey him in ev-
erything he tells you. 23 ***Every person who does not obey that prophet***
will be destroyed and thus removed from the people.' 24 And all the
prophets, from Samuel and those who followed him, have spoken
about and announced these days. 25 You are the sons of the prophets and of the covenant that God made with your ancestors, saying
to Abraham, '***And in your descendants all the nations of the earth***
will be blessed.' 26 God raised up his servant and sent him first to
you, to bless you by turning each one of you from your iniquities."

THE ARREST AND TRIAL OF PETER AND JOHN

4 While Peter and John were speaking to the people, the priests and the commander of the temple guard and the Sadducees came up to them, 2 angry because they were teaching the people and announcing in Jesus the resurrection of the dead. 3 So they seized them and put them in jail until the next day (for it was already evening). 4 But many of those who had listened to the message believed, and the number of the men came to about 5,000.

5 On the next day, their rulers, elders, and experts in the law came together in Jerusalem. 6 Annas the high priest was there, and Caiaphas, John, Alexander, and others who were members of the high priest's family. 7 After making Peter and John stand in their midst, they began to inquire, "By what power or by what name did you do this?" 8 Then Peter, filled with the Holy Spirit, replied, "Rulers of the people and elders, 9 if we are being examined today for a good deed done to a sick man—by what means this man was healed—10 let it be known to all of you and to all the people of Israel that by the name of Jesus Christ the Nazarene whom you crucified, whom God raised from the dead, this man stands before you healthy. 11 This Jesus is ***the stone that was rejected by*** you, ***the builders, that has become the cornerstone.*** 12 And there is salvation in no one else, for there is no other name under heaven given among people by which we must be saved."

13 When they saw the boldness of Peter and John, and discovered that they were uneducated and ordinary men, they were amazed and recognized these men had been with Jesus. 14 And because they saw the man who had been healed standing with them, they had nothing to say against this. 15 But when they had ordered them to go outside the council, they began to confer with one another, 16 saying, "What should we do with these men? For it is plain to all who live in Jerusalem that a notable miraculous sign has come about through them, and we cannot deny it. 17 But to keep this matter from spreading any further among the people, let us warn them to speak no more to anyone in this name." 18 And they called them in and ordered them not to speak or teach at all in the name of Jesus. 19 But Peter and John replied, "Whether it is right before God to obey you rather than God, you decide, 20 for it is impossible for us not to speak about what we have seen and heard." 21 After threatening them further, they released them, for they could not find how to punish them on account of the people, because they were all praising God for what had happened. 22 For the man, on whom this miraculous sign of healing had been performed, was over forty years old.

THE FOLLOWERS OF JESUS PRAY FOR BOLDNESS

23 When they were released, Peter and John went to their fellow believers and reported everything the high priests and the elders had said to them. 24 When they heard this, they raised their voices to God with one mind and said, "Master of all, you who made the heaven, the earth, the sea, and everything that is in them, 25 who said by the Holy Spirit through your servant David our forefather,

'***Why do the nations rage,***
and the peoples plot foolish things?
26 ***The kings of the earth stood together,***
and the rulers assembled together,
against the Lord and against his Christ.'

27 "For indeed both Herod and Pontius Pilate, with the Gentiles
and the people of Israel, assembled together in this city against
your holy servant Jesus, whom you anointed, 28 to do as much as
your power and your plan had decided beforehand would happen. 29 And now, Lord, pay attention to their threats, and grant to
your servants to speak your message with great courage, 30 while
you extend your hand to heal, and to bring about miraculous
signs and wonders through the name of your holy servant Jesus."
31 When they had prayed, the place where they were assembled
together was shaken, and they were all filled with the Holy Spirit
and began to speak the word of God courageously.

CONDITIONS AMONG THE EARLY BELIEVERS

32 The group of those who believed were of one heart and mind,
and no one said that any of his possessions was his own, but everything was held in common. 33 With great power the apostles
were giving testimony to the resurrection of the Lord Jesus, and
great grace was on them all. 34 For there was no one needy among
them, because those who were owners of land or houses were
selling them and bringing the proceeds from the sales 35 and
placing them at the apostles' feet. The proceeds were distributed
to each, as anyone had need. 36 So Joseph, a Levite who was a native of Cyprus, called by the apostles Barnabas (which is translated "son of encouragement"), 37 sold a field that belonged to
him and brought the money and placed it at the apostles' feet.

THE JUDGMENT ON ANANIAS AND SAPPHIRA

5 Now a man named Ananias, together with Sapphira his wife,
sold a piece of property. 2 He kept back for himself part of the
proceeds with his wife's knowledge; he brought only part of it
and placed it at the apostles' feet. 3 But Peter said, "Ananias, why
has Satan filled your heart to lie to the Holy Spirit and keep back
for yourself part of the proceeds from the sale of the land? 4 Before it was sold, did it not belong to you? And when it was sold,
was the money not at your disposal? How have you thought up
this deed in your heart? You have not lied to people but to God!"
5 When Ananias heard these words he collapsed and died, and
great fear gripped all who heard about it. 6 So the young men
came, wrapped him up, carried him out, and buried him. 7 After
an interval of about three hours, his wife came in, but she did not
know what had happened. 8 Peter said to her, "Tell me, were the
two of you paid this amount for the land?" Sapphira said, "Yes,
that much." 9 Peter then told her, "Why have you agreed together
to test the Spirit of the Lord? Look! The feet of those who have
buried your husband are at the door, and they will carry you out!"
10 At once she collapsed at his feet and died. So when the young
men came in, they found her dead, and they carried her out and
buried her beside her husband. 11 Great fear gripped the whole
church and all who heard about these things.

THE APOSTLES PERFORM MIRACULOUS SIGNS AND WONDERS

12 Now many miraculous signs and wonders came about among
the people through the hands of the apostles. By common

CHALLENGE

How can our churches today live like the early church? What practical things can you do today to encourage your church to live this way?

consent they were all meeting together in Solomon's Portico. 13 None of the rest dared to join them, but the people held them in high honor. 14 More and more believers in the Lord were added to their number, crowds of both men and women. 15 Thus they even carried the sick out into the streets, and put them on cots and pallets, so that when Peter came by at least his shadow would fall on some of them. 16 A crowd of people from the towns around Jerusalem also came together, bringing the sick and those troubled by unclean spirits. They were all being healed.

FURTHER TROUBLE FOR THE APOSTLES

17 Now the high priest rose up, and all those with him (that is, the religious party of the Sadducees), and they were filled with jealousy. 18 They laid hands on the apostles and put them in a public jail. 19 But during the night an angel of the Lord opened the doors of the prison, led them out, and said, 20 "Go and stand in the temple courts and proclaim to the people all the words of this life." 21 When they heard this, they entered the temple courts at daybreak and began teaching.

Now when the high priest and those who were with him arrived, they summoned the Sanhedrin—that is, the whole high council of the Israelites—and sent to the jail to have the apostles brought before them. 22 But the officers who came for them did not find them in the prison, so they returned and reported, 23 "We found the jail locked securely and the guards standing at the doors, but when we opened them, we found no one inside." 24 Now when the commander of the temple guard and the chief priests heard this report, they were greatly puzzled concerning it, wondering what this could be. 25 But someone came and reported to them, "Look! The men you put in prison are standing in the temple courts and teaching the people!" 26 Then the commander of the temple guard went with the officers and brought the apostles without the use of force (for they were afraid of being stoned by the people).

27 When they had brought them, they stood them before the council, and the high priest questioned them, 28 saying, "We gave you strict orders not to teach in this name. Look, you have filled Jerusalem with your teaching, and you intend to bring this man's blood on us!" 29 But Peter and the apostles replied, "We must obey God rather than people. 30 The God of our forefathers raised up Jesus, whom you seized and killed by hanging him on a tree. 31 God exalted him to his right hand as Leader and Savior, to give repentance to Israel and forgiveness of sins. 32 And we are witnesses of these events, and so is the Holy Spirit whom God has given to those who obey him."

33 Now when they heard this, they became furious and wanted to execute them. 34 But a Pharisee whose name was Gamaliel, a teacher of the law who was respected by all the people, stood up in the council and ordered the men to be put outside for a short time. 35 Then he said to the council, "Men of Israel, pay close attention to what you are about to do to these men. 36 For some time ago Theudas rose up, claiming to be somebody, and about 400 men joined him. He was killed, and all who followed him were dispersed and nothing came of it. 37 After him Judas the Galilean arose in the days of the census, and incited people to follow him

in revolt. He too was killed, and all who followed him were scattered. 38 So in this case I say to you, stay away from these men
and leave them alone, because if this plan or this undertaking
originates with people, it will come to nothing, 39 but if it is from
God, you will not be able to stop them, or you may even be found
fighting against God." He convinced them, 40 and they summoned
the apostles and had them beaten. Then they ordered them not
to speak in the name of Jesus and released them. 41 So they left
the council rejoicing because they had been considered worthy
to suffer dishonor for the sake of the name. 42 And every day both
in the temple courts and from house to house, they did not stop
teaching and proclaiming the good news that Jesus was the Christ.

THE APPOINTMENT OF THE FIRST SEVEN DEACONS

6 Now in those days, when the disciples were growing in number, a complaint arose on the part of the Greek-speaking Jews
against the native Hebraic Jews, because their widows were being overlooked in the daily distribution of food. 2 So the twelve
called the whole group of the disciples together and said, "It is
not right for us to neglect the word of God to wait on tables. 3 But
carefully select from among you, brothers, seven men who are
well-attested, full of the Spirit and of wisdom, whom we may
put in charge of this necessary task. 4 But we will devote ourselves to prayer and to the ministry of the word." 5 The proposal
pleased the entire group, so they chose Stephen, a man full of
faith and of the Holy Spirit, with Philip, Prochorus, Nicanor, Ti-
mon, Parmenas, and Nicolas, a Gentile convert to Judaism from
Antioch. 6 They stood these men before the apostles, who prayed
and placed their hands on them. 7 The word of God continued to
spread, the number of disciples in Jerusalem increased greatly,
and a large group of priests became obedient to the faith.

STEPHEN IS ARRESTED

8 Now Stephen, full of grace and power, was performing great
wonders and miraculous signs among the people. 9 But some
men from the Synagogue of the Freedmen (as it was called), both
Cyrenians and Alexandrians, as well as some from Cilicia and the
province of Asia, stood up and argued with Stephen. 10 Yet they
were not able to resist the wisdom and the Spirit with which he
spoke. 11 Then they secretly instigated some men to say, "We have
heard this man speaking blasphemous words against Moses and
God." 12 They incited the people, the elders, and the experts in the
law; then they approached Stephen, seized him, and brought him
before the council. 13 They brought forward false witnesses who
said, "This man does not stop saying things against this holy place
and the law. 14 For we have heard him saying that Jesus the Nazarene will destroy this place and change the customs that Moses
handed down to us." 15 All who were sitting in the council looked
intently at Stephen and saw his face was like the face of an angel.

STEPHEN'S DEFENSE BEFORE THE COUNCIL

7 Then the high priest said, "Are these things true?" 2 So he replied,
"Brothers and fathers, listen to me. The God of glory appeared to
our forefather Abraham when he was in Mesopotamia, before he

settled in Haran, 3 and said to him, '***Go out from your country and from your relatives, and come to the land I will show you.***' 4 Then he went out from the country of the Chaldeans and settled in Haran. After his father died, God made him move to this country where you now live. 5 He did not give any of it to him for an inheritance, not even a foot of ground, yet God promised *to give it to him as his possession, and to his descendants after him,* even though Abraham as yet had no child. 6 But God spoke as follows: 'Your ***descendants will be foreigners in a foreign country, whose citizens will enslave them and mistreat them for 400 years.*** 7 ***But I will punish the nation they serve as slaves,***' said God, '***and after these things they will come out of there*** and *worship me in this place.*' 8 Then God gave Abraham the covenant of circumcision, and so he became the father of Isaac and circumcised him when he was eight days old, and Isaac became the father of Jacob, and Jacob of the twelve patriarchs. 9 The patriarchs, because they were jealous of Joseph, sold him into Egypt. But God was with him, 10 and rescued him from all his troubles, and granted him favor and wisdom in the presence of Pharaoh, king of Egypt, who made him ruler over Egypt and over all his household. 11 Then a famine occurred throughout Egypt and Canaan, causing great suffering, and our ancestors could not find food. 12 So when Jacob heard that there was grain in Egypt, he sent our ancestors there the first time. 13 On their second visit Joseph made himself known to his brothers again, and Joseph's family became known to Pharaoh. 14 So Joseph sent a message and invited his father Jacob and all his relatives to come, seventy-five people in all. 15 So Jacob went down to Egypt and died there, along with our ancestors, 16 and their bones were later moved to Shechem and placed in the tomb that Abraham had bought for a certain sum of money from the sons of Hamor in Shechem.

17 "But as the time drew near for God to fulfill the promise he had declared to Abraham, the people increased greatly in number in Egypt, 18 until ***another king who did not know about Joseph ruled over Egypt.*** 19 This was the one who exploited our people and was cruel to our ancestors, forcing them to abandon their infants so they would die. 20 At that time Moses was born, and he was beautiful to God. For three months he was brought up in his father's house, 21 and when he had been abandoned, Pharaoh's daughter adopted him and brought him up as her own son. 22 So Moses was trained in all the wisdom of the Egyptians and was powerful in his words and deeds. 23 But when he was about forty years old, it entered his mind to visit his fellow countrymen the Israelites. 24 When he saw one of them being hurt unfairly, Moses came to his defense and avenged the person who was mistreated by striking down the Egyptian. 25 He thought his own people would understand that God was delivering them through him, but they did not understand. 26 The next day Moses saw two men fighting, and tried to make peace between them, saying, 'Men, you are brothers; why are you hurting one another?' 27 But the man who was unfairly hurting his neighbor pushed Moses aside, saying, '***Who made you a ruler and judge over us?*** 28 ***You don't want to kill me the way you killed the Egyptian yesterday, do you?***' 29 When the man said this, Moses fled and became a foreigner in the land of Midian, where he became the father of two sons.

30 “After forty years had passed, *an angel appeared to him in the*
desert of Mount Sinai, in the flame of a burning bush. 31 When Moses saw it, he was amazed at the sight, and when he approached
to investigate, there came the voice of the Lord, 32 ‘***I am the God***
of your forefathers, the God of Abraham, Isaac, and Jacob.’ Moses
began to tremble and did not dare to look more closely. 33 ***But the***
Lord said to him, ‘Take the sandals off your feet, for the place where
you are standing is holy ground. 34 ***I have certainly seen the suffer-***
ing of my people who are in Egypt and have heard their groan-
ing, and I have come down to rescue them. Now come, I will send
you to Egypt.’ 35 This same Moses they had rejected, saying, ‘***Who***
made you a ruler and judge?’ God sent as both ruler and deliverer
through the hand of the angel who appeared to him in the bush.
36 This man led them out, performing wonders and miraculous
signs in the land of Egypt, at the Red Sea, and in the wilderness
for forty years. 37 This is the Moses who said to the Israelites, ‘***God***
will raise up for you a prophet like me from among your brothers.’
38 This is the man who was in the congregation in the wilderness
with the angel who spoke to him at Mount Sinai, and with our
ancestors, and he received living oracles to give to you. 39 Our
ancestors were unwilling to obey him, but pushed him aside and
turned back to Egypt in their hearts, 40 saying to Aaron, ‘***Make***
us gods who will go in front of us, for this Moses, who led us out
of the land of Egypt—we do not know what has happened to him!’
41 At that time they made an idol in the form of a calf, brought
a sacrifice to the idol, and began rejoicing in the works of their
hands. 42 But God turned away from them and gave them over
to worship the host of heaven, as it is written in the book of the
prophets: ‘***It was not to me that you offered slain animals and sac-***
rifices forty years in the wilderness, was it, house of Israel? 43 ***But***
you took along the tabernacle of Moloch and the star of the god
Rephan, the images you made to worship, but I will deport you be-
yond Babylon.’ 44 Our ancestors had the tabernacle of testimony
in the wilderness, just as God who spoke to Moses ordered him
to make it according to the design he had seen. 45 Our ancestors
received possession of it and brought it in with Joshua when
they dispossessed the nations that God drove out before our ancestors, until the time of David. 46 He found favor with God and
asked that he could find a dwelling place for the house of Jacob.
47 But Solomon built a house for him. 48 Yet the Most High does
not live in houses made by human hands, as the prophet says,

49 ‘***Heaven is my throne,***
and earth is the footstool for my feet.
What kind of house will you build for me, says the Lord,
or what is my resting place?
50 ***Did my hand not make all these things?***’

51 “You stubborn people, with uncircumcised hearts and ears!
You are always resisting the Holy Spirit, like your ancestors did!
52 Which of the prophets did your ancestors not persecute? They
killed those who foretold long ago the coming of the Righteous
One, whose betrayers and murderers you have now become!
53 You received the law by decrees given by angels, but you did
not obey it.”

STEPHEN IS KILLED

54 When they heard these things, they became furious and
ground their teeth at him. 55 But Stephen, full of the Holy Spirit,
looked intently toward heaven and saw the glory of God, and
Jesus standing at the right hand of God. 56 "Look!" he said. "I see
the heavens opened, and the Son of Man standing at the right
hand of God!" 57 But they covered their ears, shouting out with a
loud voice, and rushed at him with one intent. 58 When they had
driven him out of the city, they began to stone him, and the witnesses laid their cloaks at the feet of a young man named Saul.
59 They continued to stone Stephen while he prayed, "Lord Jesus,
receive my spirit!" 60 Then he fell to his knees and cried out with
a loud voice, "Lord, do not hold this sin against them!" When he
8 had said this, he died. 1 And Saul agreed completely with
killing him.

SAUL BEGINS TO PERSECUTE THE CHURCH

Now on that day a great persecution began against the church
in Jerusalem, and all except the apostles were forced to scatter
throughout the regions of Judea and Samaria. 2 Some devout men
buried Stephen and made loud lamentation over him. 3 But Saul
was trying to destroy the church; entering one house after another, he dragged off both men and women and put them in prison.

PHILIP PREACHES IN SAMARIA

4 Now those who had been forced to scatter went around proclaiming the good news of the word. 5 Philip went down to the
main city of Samaria and began proclaiming the Christ to them.
6 The crowds were paying attention with one mind to what Philip
said, as they heard and saw the miraculous signs he was performing. 7 For unclean spirits, crying with loud shrieks, were coming
out of many who were possessed, and many paralyzed and lame
people were healed. 8 So there was great joy in that city.

9 Now in that city was a man named Simon, who had been practicing magic and amazing the people of Samaria, claiming to be
someone great. 10 All the people, from the least to the greatest, paid
close attention to him, saying, "This man is the power of God that
is called 'Great.'" 11 And they paid close attention to him because he
had amazed them for a long time with his magic. 12 But when they
believed Philip as he was proclaiming the good news about the kingdom of God and the name of Jesus Christ, they began to be baptized,
both men and women. 13 Even Simon himself believed, and after he
was baptized, he stayed close to Philip constantly, and when he saw
the signs and great miracles that were occurring, he was amazed.

14 Now when the apostles in Jerusalem heard that Samaria had
accepted the word of God, they sent Peter and John to them.
15 These two went down and prayed for them so that they would
receive the Holy Spirit. 16 (For the Spirit had not yet come upon
any of them, but they had only been baptized in the name of the
Lord Jesus.) 17 Then Peter and John placed their hands on the Samaritans, and they received the Holy Spirit.

18 Now Simon, when he saw that the Spirit was given through
the laying on of the apostles' hands, offered them money, 19 saying,
"Give me this power too, so that everyone I place my hands on may

receive the Holy Spirit." 20 But Peter said to him, "May your silver
perish with you, because you thought you could acquire God's gift
with money! 21 You have no share or part in this matter because your
heart is not right before God! 22 Therefore repent of this wickedness
of yours, and pray to the Lord that he may perhaps forgive you for
the intent of your heart. 23 For I see that you are bitterly envious
and in bondage to sin." 24 But Simon replied, "You pray to the Lord
for me so that nothing of what you have said may happen to me."
25 So after Peter and John had solemnly testified and spoken
the word of the Lord, they started back to Jerusalem, proclaiming the good news to many Samaritan villages as they went.

PHILIP AND THE ETHIOPIAN EUNUCH

26 Then an angel of the Lord said to Philip, "Get up and go south
on the road that goes down from Jerusalem to Gaza." (This is a
desert road.) 27 So he got up and went. There he met an Ethiopian
eunuch, a court official of Candace, queen of the Ethiopians, who
was in charge of all her treasury. He had come to Jerusalem to
worship, 28 and was returning home, sitting in his chariot, reading
the prophet Isaiah. 29 Then the Spirit said to Philip, "Go over and
join this chariot." 30 So Philip ran up to it and heard the man reading the prophet Isaiah. He asked him, "Do you understand what
you're reading?" 31 The man replied, "How in the world can I, unless
someone guides me?" So he invited Philip to come up and sit with
him. 32 Now the passage of scripture the man was reading was this:

"He was led like a sheep to slaughter,
and like a lamb before its shearer is silent,
so he did not open his mouth.
33 *In humiliation justice was taken from him.*
Who can describe his posterity?
For his life was taken away from the earth."

34 Then the eunuch said to Philip, "Please tell me, who is the
prophet saying this about—himself or someone else?" 35 So Philip
started speaking, and beginning with this scripture proclaimed
the good news about Jesus to him. 36 Now as they were going
along the road, they came to some water, and the eunuch said,
"Look, there is water! What is to stop me from being baptized?"†
38 So he ordered the chariot to stop, and both Philip and the
eunuch went down into the water, and Philip baptized him.
39 Now when they came up out of the water, the Spirit of the
Lord snatched Philip away, and the eunuch did not see him any
more, but went on his way rejoicing. 40 Philip, however, found
himself at Azotus, and as he passed through the area, he proclaimed the good news to all the towns until he came to Caesarea.

THE CONVERSION OF SAUL

9 Meanwhile Saul, still breathing out threats to murder the
Lord's disciples, went to the high priest 2 and requested letters from him to the synagogues in Damascus, so that if he found
any who belonged to the Way, either men or women, he could
bring them as prisoners to Jerusalem. 3 As he was going along,
approaching Damascus, suddenly a light from heaven flashed
around him. 4 He fell to the ground and heard a voice saying to

REFLECT

How does the story of the Ethiopian display God's providence for spreading the gospel? How does it display God's heart for the nations?

him, "Saul, Saul, why are you persecuting me?" 5 So he said, "Who
are you, Lord?" He replied, "I am Jesus whom you are persecuting! 6 But stand up and enter the city and you will be told what
you must do." 7 (Now the men who were traveling with him stood
there speechless, because they heard the voice but saw no one.)
8 So Saul got up from the ground, but although his eyes were
open, he could see nothing. Leading him by the hand, his companions brought him into Damascus. 9 For three days he could
not see, and he neither ate nor drank anything.
10 Now there was a disciple in Damascus named Ananias. The
Lord said to him in a vision, "Ananias," and he replied, "Here I am,
Lord." 11 Then the Lord told him, "Get up and go to the street called
'Straight,' and at Judas' house look for a man from Tarsus named
Saul. For he is praying, 12 and he has seen in a vision a man named
Ananias come in and place his hands on him so that he may see
again." 13 But Ananias replied, "Lord, I have heard from many people about this man, how much harm he has done to your saints in
Jerusalem, 14 and here he has authority from the chief priests to
imprison all who call on your name!" 15 But the Lord said to him,
"Go, because this man is my chosen instrument to carry my name
before Gentiles and kings and the people of Israel. 16 For I will show
him how much he must suffer for the sake of my name." 17 So Ananias departed and entered the house, placed his hands on Saul
and said, "Brother Saul, the Lord Jesus, who appeared to you on
the road as you came here, has sent me so that you may see again
and be filled with the Holy Spirit." 18 Immediately something like
scales fell from his eyes, and he could see again. He got up and was
baptized, 19 and after taking some food, his strength returned.

For several days he was with the disciples in Damascus, 20 and
immediately he began to proclaim Jesus in the synagogues, saying,
"This man is the Son of God." 21 All who heard him were amazed
and were saying, "Is this not the man who in Jerusalem was ravag-
ing those who call on this name, and who had come here to bring
them as prisoners to the chief priests?" 22 But Saul became more
and more capable, and was causing consternation among the
Jews who lived in Damascus by proving that Jesus is the Christ.

SAUL'S ESCAPE FROM DAMASCUS

23 Now after some days had passed, the Jews plotted together to
kill him, 24 but Saul learned of their plot against him. They were
also watching the city gates day and night so that they could
kill him. 25 But his disciples took him at night and let him down
through an opening in the wall by lowering him in a basket.

SAUL RETURNS TO JERUSALEM

26 When he arrived in Jerusalem, he attempted to associate with
the disciples, and they were all afraid of him, because they did not
believe that he was a disciple. 27 But Barnabas took Saul, brought
him to the apostles, and related to them how he had seen the
Lord on the road, that the Lord had spoken to him, and how in
Damascus he had spoken out boldly in the name of Jesus. 28 So
he was staying with them, associating openly with them in Jerusalem, speaking out boldly in the name of the Lord. 29 He was
speaking and debating with the Greek-speaking Jews, but they

were trying to kill him. 30 When the brothers found out about this,
they brought him down to Caesarea and sent him away to Tarsus.
31 Then the church throughout Judea, Galilee, and Samaria experienced peace and thus was strengthened. Living in the fear
of the Lord and in the encouragement of the Holy Spirit, the
church increased in numbers.

PETER HEALS AENEAS

32 Now as Peter was traveling around from place to place, he also
came down to the saints who lived in Lydda. 33 He found there
a man named Aeneas who had been confined to a mattress for
eight years because he was paralyzed. 34 Peter said to him, "Aeneas, Jesus the Christ heals you. Get up and make your own bed!"
And immediately he got up. 35 All those who lived in Lydda and
Sharon saw him, and they turned to the Lord.

PETER RAISES DORCAS

36 Now in Joppa there was a disciple named Tabitha (which in
translation means Dorcas). She was continually doing good
deeds and acts of charity. 37 At that time she became sick and
died. When they had washed her body, they placed it in an upstairs room. 38 Because Lydda was near Joppa, when the disciples
heard that Peter was there, they sent two men to him and urged
him, "Come to us without delay." 39 So Peter got up and went with
them, and when he arrived they brought him to the upper room.
All the widows stood beside him, crying and showing him the
tunics and other clothing Dorcas used to make while she was
with them. 40 But Peter sent them all outside, knelt down, and
prayed. Turning to the body, he said, "Tabitha, get up." Then she
opened her eyes, and when she saw Peter, she sat up. 41 He gave
her his hand and helped her get up. Then he called the saints and
widows and presented her alive. 42 This became known throughout all Joppa, and many believed in the Lord. 43 So Peter stayed
many days in Joppa with a man named Simon, a tanner.

PETER VISITS CORNELIUS

10 Now there was a man in Caesarea named Cornelius, a centurion of what was known as the Italian Cohort. 2 He was a
devout, God-fearing man, as was all his household; he did many
acts of charity for the people and prayed to God regularly. 3 About
three o'clock one afternoon he saw clearly in a vision an angel of
God who came in and said to him, "Cornelius." 4 Staring at him
and becoming greatly afraid, Cornelius replied, "What is it, Lord?"
The angel said to him, "Your prayers and your acts of charity have
gone up as a memorial before God. 5 Now send men to Joppa and
summon a man named Simon, who is called Peter. 6 This man
is staying as a guest with a man named Simon, a tanner, whose
house is by the sea." 7 When the angel who had spoken to him departed, Cornelius called two of his personal servants and a devout
soldier from among those who served him, 8 and when he had explained everything to them, he sent them to Joppa.
9 About noon the next day, while they were on their way and approaching the city, Peter went up on the roof to pray. 10 He became
hungry and wanted to eat, but while they were preparing the meal, a

LOVE TO GROW

OUR PRAYERS MATTER

ACTS 9:36–43

Here, a dearly loved woman, a woman whom many described as "continually doing good deeds and acts of charity" (Acts 9:36), lay lifeless.

I can only imagine the heartbreak that motivated those who loved Tabitha to urge Peter to go and see her. It was an earnest plea by those mourning the passing of their dear friend. Their request was filled with sadness and a sliver of hope that maybe Peter could do something.

Where others saw only death, Peter saw an opportunity. Instead of joining those who grieved, Peter sent them out of the room and focused on God. Peter turned to God and sought God's help in a matter he knew was out of his control.

How many times in our own lives have we seen something with our own eyes and thought it was dead? Maybe a relationship? An opportunity? A dream? How many times have we looked at a situation and felt heartbroken and helpless, never giving a thought to the power of prayer?

God has the power to turn death into life.

Because of one man turning to God for help, God intervened and "many believed in the Lord" (Acts 9:42). He has the power to turn bad situations into good opportunities, many times when we least expect it.

We have the power of prayer, a direct line to our Lord and Savior at any moment of any day. This is the same Savior who rose from the dead, the same Creator who placed the planets in orbit and the stars in the sky. We may look upon situations and see only death, but if we got down on our knees and prayed, we might see a miracle.

Jesus has the power to turn people and situations around. We cannot hesitate to do our part and submit prayers in the powerful name of our Lord and Savior, Jesus Christ!

Our prayers matter. Keep praying, keep turning to Him, even in the darkest, most desperate circumstances. He hears us, and He answers.

trance came over him. 11 He saw heaven opened and an object something like a large sheet descending, being let down to earth by its
four corners. 12 In it were all kinds of four-footed animals and reptiles of the earth and wild birds. 13 Then a voice said to him, "Get up,
Peter; slaughter and eat!" 14 But Peter said, "Certainly not, Lord, for I
have never eaten anything defiled and ritually unclean!" 15 The voice
spoke to him again, a second time, "What God has made clean, you
must not consider ritually unclean!" 16 This happened three times,
and immediately the object was taken up into heaven.

17 Now while Peter was puzzling over what the vision he had
seen could signify, the men sent by Cornelius had learned where
Simon's house was and approached the gate. 18 They called out to
ask if Simon, known as Peter, was staying there as a guest. 19 While
Peter was still thinking seriously about the vision, the Spirit said
to him, "Look! Three men are looking for you. 20 But get up, go
down, and accompany them without hesitation, because I have
sent them." 21 So Peter went down to the men and said, "Here I
am, the person you're looking for. Why have you come?" 22 They
said, "Cornelius the centurion, a righteous and God-fearing man,
well spoken of by the whole Jewish nation, was directed by a holy
angel to summon you to his house and to hear a message from
you." 23 So Peter invited them in and entertained them as guests.

On the next day he got up and set out with them, and some of
the brothers from Joppa accompanied him. 24 The following day he
entered Caesarea. Now Cornelius was waiting anxiously for them
and had called together his relatives and close friends. 25 So when
Peter came in, Cornelius met him, fell at his feet, and worshiped
him. 26 But Peter helped him up, saying, "Stand up. I too am a mere
mortal." 27 Peter continued talking with him as he went in, and he
found many people gathered together. 28 He said to them, "You
know that it is unlawful for a Jew to associate with or visit a Gentile, yet God has shown me that I should call no person defiled or
ritually unclean. 29 Therefore when you sent for me, I came without any objection. Now may I ask why you sent for me?" 30 Cornelius replied, "Four days ago at this very hour, at three o'clock in the
afternoon, I was praying in my house, and suddenly a man in shining clothing stood before me 31 and said, 'Cornelius, your prayer has
been heard and your acts of charity have been remembered before
God. 32 Therefore send to Joppa and summon Simon, who is called
Peter. This man is staying as a guest in the house of Simon the tanner, by the sea.' 33 Therefore I sent for you at once, and you were kind
enough to come. So now we are all here in the presence of God to
listen to everything the Lord has commanded you to say to us."

34 Then Peter started speaking: "I now truly understand that
God does not show favoritism in dealing with people, 35 but in
every nation the person who fears him and does what is right is
welcomed before him. 36 You know the message he sent to the
people of Israel, proclaiming the good news of peace through
Jesus Christ (he is Lord of all)—37 you know what happened
throughout Judea, beginning from Galilee after the baptism
that John announced: 38 with respect to Jesus from Nazareth,
that God anointed him with the Holy Spirit and with power. He
went around doing good and healing all who were oppressed by
the devil, because God was with him. 39 We are witnesses of all

GOD'S HEART FOR THE NATIONS

Acts 10:34–35

Then Peter started speaking: "I now truly understand that God does not show favoritism in dealing with people, but in every nation the person who fears him and does what is right is welcomed before him.

the things he did both in Judea and in Jerusalem. They killed
him by hanging him on a tree, 40 but God raised him up on the
third day and caused him to be seen, 41 not by all the people,
but by us, the witnesses God had already chosen, who ate and
drank with him after he rose from the dead. 42 He commanded
us to preach to the people and to warn them that he is the one
appointed by God as judge of the living and the dead. 43 About
him all the prophets testify, that everyone who believes in him
receives forgiveness of sins through his name."

THE GENTILES RECEIVE THE HOLY SPIRIT

44 While Peter was still speaking these words, the Holy Spirit fell
on all those who heard the message. 45 The circumcised believers
who had accompanied Peter were greatly astonished that the gift
of the Holy Spirit had been poured out even on the Gentiles, 46 for
they heard them speaking in tongues and praising God. Then Peter said, 47 "No one can withhold the water for these people to be
baptized, who have received the Holy Spirit just as we did, can
he?" 48 So he gave orders to have them baptized in the name of
Jesus Christ. Then they asked him to stay for several days.

PETER DEFENDS HIS ACTIONS TO THE JERUSALEM CHURCH

11 Now the apostles and the brothers who were throughout Judea heard that the Gentiles too had accepted the word of God.
2 So when Peter went up to Jerusalem, the circumcised believers
took issue with him, 3 saying, "You went to uncircumcised men
and shared a meal with them." 4 But Peter began and explained
it to them point by point, saying, 5 "I was in the city of Joppa
praying, and in a trance I saw a vision, an object something like
a large sheet descending, being let down from heaven by its four
corners, and it came to me. 6 As I stared I looked into it and saw
four-footed animals of the earth, wild animals, reptiles, and wild
birds. 7 I also heard a voice saying to me, 'Get up, Peter; slaughter
and eat!' 8 But I said, 'Certainly not, Lord, for nothing defiled or
ritually unclean has ever entered my mouth!' 9 But the voice replied a second time from heaven, 'What God has made clean, you
must not consider ritually unclean!' 10 This happened three times,
and then everything was pulled up to heaven again. 11 At that very
moment, three men sent to me from Caesarea approached the
house where we were staying. 12 The Spirit told me to accompany
them without hesitation. These six brothers also went with me,
and we entered the man's house. 13 He informed us how he had
seen an angel standing in his house and saying, 'Send to Joppa
and summon Simon, who is called Peter, 14 who will speak a message to you by which you and your entire household will be saved.'
15 Then as I began to speak, the Holy Spirit fell on them just as he
did on us at the beginning. 16 And I remembered the word of the
Lord, as he used to say, 'John baptized with water, but you will
be baptized with the Holy Spirit.' 17 Therefore if God gave them
the same gift as he also gave us after believing in the Lord Jesus
Christ, who was I to hinder God?" 18 When they heard this, they
ceased their objections and praised God, saying, "So then, God has
granted the repentance that leads to life even to the Gentiles."

ACTIVITY IN THE CHURCH AT ANTIOCH

19 Now those who had been scattered because of the persecution
that took place over Stephen went as far as Phoenicia, Cyprus, and
Antioch, speaking the message to no one but Jews. 20 But there
were some men from Cyprus and Cyrene among them who came
to Antioch and began to speak to the Greeks too, proclaiming the
good news of the Lord Jesus. 21 The hand of the Lord was with them,
and a great number who believed turned to the Lord. 22 A report
about them came to the attention of the church in Jerusalem, and
they sent Barnabas to Antioch. 23 When he came and saw the grace
of God, he rejoiced and encouraged them all to remain true to the
Lord with devoted hearts, 24 because he was a good man, full of
the Holy Spirit and of faith, and a significant number of people
were brought to the Lord. 25 Then Barnabas departed for Tarsus
to look for Saul, 26 and when he found him, he brought him to Antioch. So for a whole year Barnabas and Saul met with the church
and taught a significant number of people. Now it was in Antioch
that the disciples were first called Christians.

FAMINE RELIEF FOR JUDEA

27 At that time some prophets came down from Jerusalem to Antioch. 28 One of them, named Agabus, got up and predicted by the
Spirit that a severe famine was about to come over the whole
inhabited world. (This took place during the reign of Claudius.)
29 So the disciples, each in accordance with his financial ability,
decided to send relief to the brothers living in Judea. 30 They did
so, sending their financial aid to the elders by Barnabas and Saul.

JAMES IS KILLED AND PETER IMPRISONED

12 About that time King Herod laid hands on some from the
church to harm them. 2 He had James, the brother of John,
executed with a sword. 3 When he saw that this pleased the Jews,
he proceeded to arrest Peter too. (This took place during the feast
of Unleavened Bread.) 4 When he had seized him, he put him in
prison, handing him over to four squads of soldiers to guard him.
Herod planned to bring him out for public trial after the Passover.
5 So Peter was kept in prison, but those in the church were earnestly
praying to God for him. 6 On that very night before Herod was going to bring him out for trial, Peter was sleeping between two soldiers, bound with two chains, while guards in front of the door were
keeping watch over the prison. 7 Suddenly an angel of the Lord appeared, and a light shone in the prison cell. He struck Peter on the
side and woke him up, saying, "Get up quickly!" And the chains fell
off Peter's wrists. 8 The angel said to him, "Fasten your belt and put
on your sandals." Peter did so. Then the angel said to him, "Put on
your cloak and follow me." 9 Peter went out and followed him; he
did not realize that what was happening through the angel was
real, but thought he was seeing a vision. 10 After they had passed the
first and second guards, they came to the iron gate leading into the
city. It opened for them by itself, and they went outside and walked
down one narrow street, when at once the angel left him. 11 When
Peter came to himself, he said, "Now I know for certain that the
Lord has sent his angel and rescued me from the hand of Herod
and from everything the Jewish people were expecting to happen."

REFLECT

How did Peter's arrest, imprisonment, and rescue display God's heart for the advance of the gospel? How did Peter's attitude offer encouragement to the early church?

12 When Peter realized this, he went to the house of Mary, the
mother of John Mark, where many people had gathered together
and were praying. 13 When he knocked at the door of the outer
gate, a slave girl named Rhoda answered. 14 When she recognized
Peter's voice, she was so overjoyed she did not open the gate, but
ran back in and told them that Peter was standing at the gate.
15 But they said to her, "You've lost your mind!" But she kept insisting that it was Peter, and they kept saying, "It is his angel!" 16 Now
Peter continued knocking, and when they opened the door and
saw him, they were greatly astonished. 17 He motioned to them
with his hand to be quiet and then related how the Lord had
brought him out of the prison. He said, "Tell James and the brothers these things," and then he left and went to another place.

18 At daybreak there was great consternation among the soldiers over what had become of Peter. 19 When Herod had searched
for him and did not find him, he questioned the guards and commanded that they be led away to execution. Then Herod went
down from Judea to Caesarea and stayed there.

20 Now Herod was having an angry quarrel with the people of
Tyre and Sidon. So they joined together and presented themselves before him. And after convincing Blastus, the king's personal assistant, to help them, they asked for peace, because their
country's food supply was provided by the king's country. 21 On
a day determined in advance, Herod put on his royal robes, sat
down on the judgment seat, and made a speech to them. 22 But
the crowd began to shout, "The voice of a god, and not of a man!"
23 Immediately an angel of the Lord struck Herod down because
he did not give the glory to God, and he was eaten by worms and
died. 24 But the word of God kept on increasing and multiplying.

25 So Barnabas and Saul returned to Jerusalem when they had
completed their mission, bringing along with them John Mark.

THE CHURCH AT ANTIOCH COMMISSIONS BARNABAS AND SAUL

13 Now there were these prophets and teachers in the church
at Antioch: Barnabas, Simeon called Niger, Lucius the Cyre-
nian, Manaen (a close friend of Herod the tetrarch from childhood) and Saul. 2 While they were serving the Lord and fasting,
the Holy Spirit said, "Set apart for me Barnabas and Saul for the
work to which I have called them." 3 Then, after they had fasted
and prayed and placed their hands on them, they sent them off.

PAUL AND BARNABAS PREACH IN CYPRUS

4 So Barnabas and Saul, sent out by the Holy Spirit, went down to
Seleucia, and from there they sailed to Cyprus. 5 When they arrived in Salamis, they began to proclaim the word of God in the
Jewish synagogues. (Now they also had John as their assistant.)
6 When they had crossed over the whole island as far as Paphos,
they found a magician, a Jewish false prophet named Bar-Jesus,
7 who was with the proconsul Sergius Paulus, an intelligent man.
The proconsul summoned Barnabas and Saul and wanted to hear
the word of God. 8 But the magician Elymas (for that is the way
his name is translated) opposed them, trying to turn the proconsul away from the faith. 9 But Saul (also known as Paul), filled

with the Holy Spirit, stared straight at him 10 and said, "You who
are full of all deceit and all wrongdoing, you son of the devil, you
enemy of all righteousness—will you not stop making crooked
the straight paths of the Lord? 11 Now look, the hand of the Lord
is against you, and you will be blind, unable to see the sun for a
time!" Immediately mistiness and darkness came over him, and
he went around seeking people to lead him by the hand. 12 Then
when the proconsul saw what had happened, he believed, because he was greatly astounded at the teaching about the Lord.

PAUL AND BARNABAS AT PISIDIAN ANTIOCH

13 Then Paul and his companions put out to sea from Paphos and
came to Perga in Pamphylia, but John left them and returned to
Jerusalem. 14 Moving on from Perga, they arrived at Pisidian Antioch, and on the Sabbath day they went into the synagogue and
sat down. 15 After the reading from the law and the prophets, the
leaders of the synagogue sent them a message, saying, "Brothers,
if you have any message of exhortation for the people, speak it."
16 So Paul stood up, gestured with his hand and said,

"Men of Israel, and you Gentiles who fear God, listen: 17 The God of
this people Israel chose our ancestors and made the people great
during their stay as foreigners in the country of Egypt, and with uplifted arm he led them out of it. 18 For a period of about forty years
he put up with them in the wilderness. 19 After he had destroyed
seven nations in the land of Canaan, he gave his people their land
as an inheritance. 20 All this took about 450 years. After this he
gave them judges until the time of Samuel the prophet. 21 Then
they asked for a king, and God gave them Saul son of Kish, a man
from the tribe of Benjamin, who ruled forty years. 22 After removing
him, God raised up David their king. He testified about him: '***I have
found David*** the son of Jesse ***to be a man after my heart***, who will accomplish everything I want him to do.' 23 From the descendants of
this man God brought to Israel a Savior, Jesus, just as he promised.
24 Before Jesus arrived, John had proclaimed a baptism for repentance to all the people of Israel. 25 But while John was completing
his mission, he said repeatedly, 'What do you think I am? I am not
he. But look, one is coming after me. I am not worthy to untie the
sandals on his feet!' 26 Brothers, descendants of Abraham's family,
and those Gentiles among you who fear God, the message of this
salvation has been sent to us. 27 For the people who live in Jerusalem and their rulers did not recognize him, and they fulfilled the
sayings of the prophets that are read every Sabbath by condemning him. 28 Though they found no basis for a death sentence, they
asked Pilate to have him executed. 29 When they had accomplished
everything that was written about him, they took him down from
the cross and placed him in a tomb. 30 But God raised him from the
dead, 31 and for many days he appeared to those who had accompanied him from Galilee to Jerusalem. These are now his witnesses
to the people. 32 And we proclaim to you the good news about the
promise to our ancestors, 33 that this promise God has fulfilled to
us, their children, by raising Jesus, as also it is written in the second
psalm, '***You are my Son; today I have fathered you.***' 34 But regarding
the fact that he has raised Jesus from the dead, never again to be in
a state of decay, God has spoken in this way: '***I will give you the holy***

and trustworthy promises made to David.' 35 Therefore he also says in another psalm, ***'You will not permit your Holy One to experience decay.'*** 36 For David, after he had served God's purpose in his own generation, died, was buried with his ancestors, and experienced decay, 37 but the one whom God raised up did not experience decay. 38 Therefore let it be known to you, brothers, that through this one forgiveness of sins is proclaimed to you, 39 and by this one everyone who believes is justified from everything from which the law of Moses could not justify you. 40 Watch out, then, that what is spoken about by the prophets does not happen to you:

41 ***'Look, you scoffers; be amazed and perish!***
For I am doing a work in your days,
a work you would never believe, even if someone tells you.'"

42 As Paul and Barnabas were going out, the people were urging them to speak about these things on the next Sabbath. 43 When the meeting of the synagogue had broken up, many of the Jews and God-fearing proselytes followed Paul and Barnabas, who were speaking with them and were persuading them to continue in the grace of God.

44 On the next Sabbath almost the whole city assembled together to hear the word of the Lord. 45 But when the Jews saw the crowds, they were filled with jealousy, and they began to contradict what Paul was saying by reviling him. 46 Both Paul and Barnabas replied courageously, "It was necessary to speak the word of God to you first. Since you reject it and do not consider yourselves worthy of eternal life, we are turning to the Gentiles. 47 For this is what the Lord has commanded us: *'I have appointed you to be a light for the Gentiles, to bring salvation to the ends of the earth.'"* 48 When the Gentiles heard this, they began to rejoice and praise the word of the Lord, and all who had been appointed for eternal life believed. 49 So the word of the Lord was spreading through the entire region. 50 But the Jews incited the God-fearing women of high social standing and the prominent men of the city, stirred up persecution against Paul and Barnabas, and threw them out of their region. 51 So after they shook the dust off their feet in protest against them, they went to Iconium. 52 And the disciples were filled with joy and with the Holy Spirit.

PAUL AND BARNABAS AT ICONIUM

14 The same thing happened in Iconium when Paul and Barnabas went into the Jewish synagogue and spoke in such a way that a large group of both Jews and Greeks believed. 2 But the Jews who refused to believe stirred up the Gentiles and poisoned their minds against the brothers. 3 So they stayed there for a considerable time, speaking out courageously for the Lord, who testified to the message of his grace, granting miraculous signs and wonders to be performed through their hands. 4 But the population of the city was divided; some sided with the Jews, and some with the apostles. 5 When both the Gentiles and the Jews (together with their rulers) made an attempt to mistreat them and stone them, 6 Paul and Barnabas learned about it and fled to the Lycaonian cities of Lystra and Derbe and the surrounding region. 7 There they continued to proclaim the good news.

PAUL AND BARNABAS AT LYSTRA

8 In Lystra sat a man who could not use his feet, lame from birth,
who had never walked. 9 This man was listening to Paul as he was
speaking. When Paul stared intently at him and saw he had faith
to be healed, 10 he said with a loud voice, "Stand upright on your
feet." And the man leaped up and began walking. 11 So when the
crowds saw what Paul had done, they shouted in the Lycaonian
language, "The gods have come down to us in human form!" 12 They
began to call Barnabas Zeus and Paul Hermes, because he was
the chief speaker. 13 The priest of the temple of Zeus, located just
outside the city, brought bulls and garlands to the city gates; he
and the crowds wanted to offer sacrifices to them. 14 But when the
apostles Barnabas and Paul heard about it, they tore their clothes
and rushed out into the crowd, shouting, 15 "Men, why are you doing these things? We too are men, with human natures just like
you! We are proclaiming the good news to you, so that you should
turn from these worthless things to the living God, who made the
heaven, the earth, the sea, and everything that is in them. 16 In
past generations he allowed all the nations to go their own ways,
17 yet he did not leave himself without a witness by doing good, by
giving you rain from heaven and fruitful seasons, satisfying you
with food and your hearts with joy." 18 Even by saying these things,
they scarcely persuaded the crowds not to offer sacrifice to them.

19 But Jews came from Antioch and Iconium, and after winning the crowds over, they stoned Paul and dragged him out of
the city, presuming him to be dead. 20 But after the disciples had
surrounded him, he got up and went back into the city. On the
next day he left with Barnabas for Derbe.

PAUL AND BARNABAS RETURN TO ANTIOCH IN SYRIA

21 After they had proclaimed the good news in that city and made
many disciples, they returned to Lystra, to Iconium, and to Antioch. 22 They strengthened the souls of the disciples and encouraged them to continue in the faith, saying, "We must enter the
kingdom of God through many persecutions." 23 When they had
appointed elders for them in the various churches, with prayer
and fasting they entrusted them to the protection of the Lord
in whom they had believed. 24 Then they passed through Pisidia
and came into Pamphylia, 25 and when they had spoken the word
in Perga, they went down to Attalia. 26 From there they sailed
back to Antioch, where they had been commended to the grace
of God for the work they had now completed. 27 When they arrived and gathered the church together, they reported all the
things God had done with them, and that he had opened a door
of faith for the Gentiles. 28 So they spent considerable time with
the disciples.

THE JERUSALEM COUNCIL

15 Now some men came down from Judea and began to teach
the brothers, "Unless you are circumcised according to the
custom of Moses, you cannot be saved." 2 When Paul and Barnabas had a major argument and debate with them, the church appointed Paul and Barnabas and some others from among them
to go up to meet with the apostles and elders in Jerusalem about

this point of disagreement. 3 So they were sent on their way by
the church, and as they passed through both Phoenicia and Samaria, they were relating at length the conversion of the Gentiles
and bringing great joy to all the brothers. 4 When they arrived
in Jerusalem, they were received by the church and the apostles
and the elders, and they reported all the things God had done
with them. 5 But some from the religious party of the Pharisees
who had believed stood up and said, "It is necessary to circumcise the Gentiles and to order them to observe the law of Moses."
6 Both the apostles and the elders met together to deliberate
about this matter. 7 After there had been much debate, Peter
stood up and said to them, "Brothers, you know that some time
ago God chose me to preach to the Gentiles so they would hear
the message of the gospel and believe. 8 And God, who knows the
heart, has testified to them by giving them the Holy Spirit just
as he did to us, 9 and he made no distinction between them and
us, cleansing their hearts by faith. 10 So now why are you putting
God to the test by placing on the neck of the disciples a yoke that
neither our ancestors nor we have been able to bear? 11 On the
contrary, we believe that we are saved through the grace of the
Lord Jesus, in the same way as they are."
12 The whole group kept quiet and listened to Barnabas and
Paul while they explained all the miraculous signs and wonders God had done among the Gentiles through them. 13 After
they stopped speaking, James replied, "Brothers, listen to me.
14 Simeon has explained how God first concerned himself to select from among the Gentiles a people for his name. 15 The words
of the prophets agree with this, as it is written,

16 ***'After this I will return,***
and I will rebuild the fallen tent of David;
I will rebuild its ruins and restore it,
17 ***so that the rest of humanity may seek the Lord,***
namely, all the Gentiles I have called to be my own,' says the
Lord, *who makes these things* 18 *known from long ago.*

19 "Therefore I conclude that we should not cause extra difficulty for those among the Gentiles who are turning to God, 20 but
that we should write them a letter telling them to abstain from
things defiled by idols and from sexual immorality and from
what has been strangled and from blood. 21 For Moses has had
those who proclaim him in every town from ancient times, because he is read aloud in the synagogues every Sabbath."
22 Then the apostles and elders, with the whole church, decided
to send men chosen from among them, Judas called Barsabbas
and Silas, leaders among the brothers, to Antioch with Paul and
Barnabas. 23 They sent this letter with them:

From the apostles and elders, your brothers, to the Gentile
brothers and sisters in Antioch, Syria, and Cilicia, greetings!
24 Since we have heard that some have gone out from among
us with no orders from us and have confused you, upsetting your minds by what they said, 25 we have unanimously
decided to choose men to send to you along with our dear
friends Barnabas and Paul, 26 who have risked their lives for

GOD'S HEART FOR THE NATIONS

Acts 15:16–17

"After this I will return, and I will rebuild the fallen tent of David; I will rebuild its ruins and restore it, so that the rest of humanity may seek the Lord, namely, all the Gentiles I have called to be my own," says the Lord.

REFLECT

Why was the Jerusalem Council so significant? What was the decision they made? How did this affect the future of the church?

the name of our Lord Jesus Christ. 27 Therefore we are sending Judas and Silas who will tell you these things themselves in person. 28 For it seemed best to the Holy Spirit and to us not to place any greater burden on you than these necessary rules: 29 that you abstain from meat that has been sacrificed to idols and from blood and from what has been strangled and from sexual immorality. If you keep yourselves from doing these things, you will do well. Farewell.

30 So when they were dismissed, they went down to Antioch, and after gathering the entire group together, they delivered the letter. 31 When they read it aloud, the people rejoiced at its encouragement. 32 Both Judas and Silas, who were prophets themselves, encouraged and strengthened the brothers with a long speech. 33 After they had spent some time there, they were sent off in peace by the brothers to those who had sent them.[‡] 35 But Paul and Barnabas remained in Antioch, teaching and proclaiming (along with many others) the word of the Lord.

PAUL AND BARNABAS PART COMPANY

36 After some days Paul said to Barnabas, "Let's return and visit the brothers in every town where we proclaimed the word of the Lord to see how they are doing." 37 Barnabas wanted to bring John called Mark along with them too, 38 but Paul insisted that they should not take along this one who had left them in Pamphylia and had not accompanied them in the work. 39 They had a sharp disagreement, so that they parted company. Barnabas took along Mark and sailed away to Cyprus, 40 but Paul chose Silas and set out, commended to the grace of the Lord by the brothers and sisters. 41 He passed through Syria and Cilicia, strengthening the churches.

TIMOTHY JOINS PAUL AND SILAS

16 He also came to Derbe and to Lystra. A disciple named Timothy was there, the son of a Jewish woman who was a believer, but whose father was a Greek. 2 The brothers in Lystra and Iconium spoke well of him. 3 Paul wanted Timothy to accompany him, and he took him and circumcised him because of the Jews who were in those places, for they all knew that his father was Greek. 4 As they went through the towns, they passed on the decrees that had been decided on by the apostles and elders in Jerusalem for the Gentile believers to obey. 5 So the churches were being strengthened in the faith and were increasing in number every day.

PAUL'S VISION OF THE MACEDONIAN MAN

6 They went through the region of Phrygia and Galatia, having been prevented by the Holy Spirit from speaking the message in the province of Asia. 7 When they came to Mysia, they attempted to go into Bithynia, but the Spirit of Jesus did not allow them to do this, 8 so they passed through Mysia and went down to Troas. 9 A vision appeared to Paul during the night: A Macedonian man was standing there urging him, "Come over to Macedonia and help us!" 10 After Paul saw the vision, we attempted immediately to go over to Macedonia, concluding that God had called us to proclaim the good news to them.

ARRIVAL AT PHILIPPI

11 We put out to sea from Troas and sailed a straight course to
Samothrace, the next day to Neapolis, 12 and from there to Philippi, which is a leading city of that district of Macedonia, a
Roman colony. We stayed in this city for some days. 13 On the
Sabbath day we went outside the city gate to the side of the
river, where we thought there would be a place of prayer, and
we sat down and began to speak to the women who had assembled there. 14 A woman named Lydia, a dealer in purple cloth
from the city of Thyatira, a God-fearing woman, listened to us.
The Lord opened her heart to respond to what Paul was saying.
15 After she and her household were baptized, she urged us, "If
you consider me to be a believer in the Lord, come and stay in
my house." And she persuaded us.

PAUL AND SILAS ARE THROWN INTO PRISON

16 Now as we were going to the place of prayer, a slave girl met
us who had a spirit that enabled her to foretell the future by
supernatural means. She brought her owners a great profit by
fortune-telling. 17 She followed behind Paul and us and kept crying out, "These men are servants of the Most High God, who
are proclaiming to you the way of salvation." 18 She continued
to do this for many days. But Paul became greatly annoyed, and
turned and said to the spirit, "I command you in the name of
Jesus Christ to come out of her!" And it came out of her at once.
19 But when her owners saw their hope of profit was gone, they
seized Paul and Silas and dragged them into the marketplace
before the authorities. 20 When they had brought them before
the magistrates, they said, "These men are throwing our city into
confusion. They are Jews 21 and are advocating customs that are
not lawful for us to accept or practice, since we are Romans."

22 The crowd joined the attack against them, and the magistrates tore the clothes off Paul and Silas and ordered them to be
beaten with rods. 23 After they had beaten them severely, they
threw them into prison and commanded the jailer to guard them
securely. 24 Receiving such orders, he threw them in the inner
cell and fastened their feet in the stocks.

25 About midnight Paul and Silas were praying and singing
hymns to God, and the rest of the prisoners were listening to
them. 26 Suddenly a great earthquake occurred, so that the foundations of the prison were shaken. Immediately all the doors flew
open, and the bonds of all the prisoners came loose. 27 When the
jailer woke up and saw the doors of the prison standing open,
he drew his sword and was about to kill himself, because he assumed the prisoners had escaped. 28 But Paul called out loudly,
"Do not harm yourself, for we are all here!" 29 Calling for lights,
the jailer rushed in and fell down trembling at the feet of Paul
and Silas. 30 Then he brought them outside and asked, "Sirs, what
must I do to be saved?" 31 They replied, "Believe in the Lord Jesus
and you will be saved, you and your household." 32 Then they
spoke the word of the Lord to him, along with all those who
were in his house. 33 At that hour of the night he took them and
washed their wounds; then he and all his family were baptized
right away. 34 The jailer brought them into his house and set food

before them, and he rejoiced greatly that he had come to believe in God, together with his entire household. 35 At daybreak the magistrates sent their police officers, saying, "Release those men." 36 The jailer reported these words to Paul, saying, "The magistrates have sent orders to release you. So come out now and go in peace." 37 But Paul said to the police officers, "They had us beaten in public without a proper trial—even though we are Roman citizens—and they threw us in prison. And now they want to send us away secretly? Absolutely not! They themselves must come and escort us out!" 38 The police officers reported these words to the magistrates. They were frightened when they heard Paul and Silas were Roman citizens 39 and came and apologized to them. After they brought them out, they asked them repeatedly to leave the city. 40 When they came out of the prison, they entered Lydia's house, and when they saw the brothers, they encouraged them and then departed.

PAUL AND SILAS AT THESSALONICA

17 After they traveled through Amphipolis and Apollonia, they came to Thessalonica, where there was a Jewish synagogue. 2 Paul went to the Jews in the synagogue, as he customarily did, and on three Sabbath days he addressed them from the scriptures, 3 explaining and demonstrating that the Christ had to suffer and to rise from the dead, saying, "This Jesus I am proclaiming to you is the Christ." 4 Some of them were persuaded and joined Paul and Silas, along with a large group of God-fearing Greeks and quite a few prominent women. 5 But the Jews became jealous, and gathering together some worthless men from the rabble in the marketplace, they formed a mob and set the city in an uproar. They attacked Jason's house, trying to find Paul and Silas to bring them out to the assembly. 6 When they did not find them, they dragged Jason and some of the brothers before the city officials, screaming, "These people who have stirred up trouble throughout the world have come here too, 7 and Jason has welcomed them as guests! They are all acting against Caesar's decrees, saying there is another king named Jesus!" 8 They caused confusion among the crowd and the city officials who heard these things. 9 After the city officials had received bail from Jason and the others, they released them.

PAUL AND SILAS AT BEREA

10 The brothers sent Paul and Silas off to Berea at once, during the night. When they arrived, they went to the Jewish synagogue. 11 These Jews were more open-minded than those in Thessalonica, for they eagerly received the message, examining the scriptures carefully every day to see if these things were so. 12 Therefore many of them believed, along with quite a few prominent Greek women and men. 13 But when the Jews from Thessalonica heard that Paul had also proclaimed the word of God in Berea, they came there too, inciting and disturbing the crowds. 14 Then the brothers sent Paul away to the coast at once, but Silas and Timothy remained in Berea. 15 Those who accompanied Paul escorted him as far as Athens, and after receiving an order for Silas and Timothy to come to him as soon as possible, they left.

PAUL AT ATHENS

16 While Paul was waiting for them in Athens, his spirit was greatly upset because he saw the city was full of idols. 17 So he was addressing the Jews and the God-fearing Gentiles in the synagogue, and in the marketplace every day those who happened to be there. 18 Also some of the Epicurean and Stoic philosophers were conversing with him, and some were asking, "What does this foolish babbler want to say?" Others said, "He seems to be a proclaimer of foreign gods." (They said this because he was proclaiming the good news about Jesus and the resurrection.) 19 So they took Paul and brought him to the Areopagus, saying, "May we know what this new teaching is that you are proclaiming? 20 For you are bringing some surprising things to our ears, so we want to know what they mean." 21 (All the Athenians and the foreigners who lived there used to spend their time in nothing else than telling or listening to something new.)

22 So Paul stood before the Areopagus and said, "Men of Athens, I see that you are very religious in all respects. 23 For as I went around and observed closely your objects of worship, I even found an altar with this inscription: 'To an unknown god.' Therefore what you worship without knowing it, this I proclaim to you. 24 The God who made the world and everything in it, who is Lord of heaven and earth, does not live in temples made by human hands, 25 nor is he served by human hands, as if he needed anything, because he himself gives life and breath and everything to everyone. 26 From one man he made every nation of the human race to inhabit the entire earth, determining their set times and the fixed limits of the places where they would live, 27 so that they would search for God and perhaps grope around for him and find him, though he is not far from each one of us. 28 For in him we live and move about and exist, as even some of your own poets have said, 'For we too are his offspring.' 29 So since we are God's offspring, we should not think the deity is like gold or silver or stone, an image made by human skill and imagination. 30 Therefore, although God has overlooked such times of ignorance, he now commands all people everywhere to repent, 31 because he has set a day on which he is going to judge the world in righteousness, by a man whom he designated, having provided proof to everyone by raising him from the dead."

32 Now when they heard about the resurrection from the dead, some began to scoff, but others said, "We will hear you again about this." 33 So Paul left the Areopagus. 34 But some people joined him and believed. Among them were Dionysius, who was a member of the Areopagus, a woman named Damaris, and others with them.

PAUL AT CORINTH

18 After this Paul departed from Athens and went to Corinth. 2 There he found a Jew named Aquila, a native of Pontus, who had recently come from Italy with his wife Priscilla, because Claudius had ordered all the Jews to depart from Rome. Paul approached them, 3 and because he worked at the same trade, he stayed with them and worked with them (for they were tentmakers by trade). 4 He addressed both Jews and Greeks in the synagogue every Sabbath, attempting to persuade them.

5 Now when Silas and Timothy arrived from Macedonia, Paul

became wholly absorbed with proclaiming the word, testifying to
the Jews that Jesus was the Christ. 6 When they opposed him and
reviled him, he protested by shaking out his clothes and said to
them, "Your blood be on your own heads! I am guiltless! From now
on I will go to the Gentiles!" 7 Then Paul left the synagogue and went
to the house of a person named Titius Justus, a Gentile who worshiped God, whose house was next door to the synagogue. 8 Crispus, the president of the synagogue, believed in the Lord together
with his entire household, and many of the Corinthians who heard
about it believed and were baptized. 9 The Lord said to Paul by a vision in the night, "Do not be afraid, but speak and do not be silent,
10 because I am with you, and no one will assault you to harm you,
because I have many people in this city." 11 So he stayed there a year
and six months, teaching the word of God among them.

PAUL BEFORE THE PROCONSUL GALLIO

12 Now while Gallio was proconsul of Achaia, the Jews attacked
Paul together and brought him before the judgment seat, 13 saying, "This man is persuading people to worship God in a way contrary to the law!" 14 But just as Paul was about to speak, Gallio said
to the Jews, "If it were a matter of some crime or serious piece of
villainy, I would have been justified in accepting the complaint
of you Jews, 15 but since it concerns points of disagreement about
words and names and your own law, settle it yourselves. I will not
be a judge of these things!" 16 Then he had them forced away from
the judgment seat. 17 So they all seized Sosthenes, the president
of the synagogue, and began to beat him in front of the judgment seat. Yet none of these things were of any concern to Gallio.

PAUL RETURNS TO ANTIOCH IN SYRIA

18 Paul, after staying many more days in Corinth, said farewell to
the brothers and sailed away to Syria accompanied by Priscilla
and Aquila. He had his hair cut off at Cenchrea because he had
made a vow. 19 When they reached Ephesus, Paul left Priscilla and
Aquila behind there, but he himself went into the synagogue and
addressed the Jews. 20 When they asked him to stay longer, he
would not consent, 21 but said farewell to them and added, "I will
come back to you again if God wills." Then he set sail from Ephesus, 22 and when he arrived at Caesarea, he went up and greeted
the church at Jerusalem and then went down to Antioch. 23 After he spent some time there, Paul left and went through the
region of Galatia and Phrygia, strengthening all the disciples.

APOLLOS BEGINS HIS MINISTRY

24 Now a Jew named Apollos, a native of Alexandria, arrived in
Ephesus. He was an eloquent speaker, well-versed in the scriptures. 25 He had been instructed in the way of the Lord, and with
great enthusiasm he spoke and taught accurately the facts about
Jesus, although he knew only the baptism of John. 26 He began to
speak out fearlessly in the synagogue, but when Priscilla and Aquila heard him, they took him aside and explained the way of God
to him more accurately. 27 When Apollos wanted to cross over to
Achaia, the brothers encouraged him and wrote to the disciples to
welcome him. When he arrived, he assisted greatly those who had

DO NOT FEAR

ACTS 18:9–11

Sometimes, I read the Bible and think of all the incredible men and women as superheroes. I see them as bold and fearless, void of having any of the real emotions or drama I deal with today. Silly, I know.

Acts 18:9–11 reveals Paul as a person vulnerable and afraid. He was in a difficult situation and faced persecution. The Lord told Paul, "Do not be afraid" (v. 9). Many opposed and blasphemed him as he shared the gospel. Yet, even in the midst of the difficulty, God showed up when Paul needed Him. He told Paul to speak and not be silent about proclaiming the Good News at Corinth. God reminded him that He would protect him from harm.

You and I have a purpose here on earth as did Paul. The Lord had people in mind who were unknowingly counting on Paul to boldly share the gospel. Paul's obedience was critical, even though, and even if, things weren't looking the way he thought they should.

I have been in my own difficult season. It's been excruciating. It's been disappointing. The betrayal continues to uncoil, and I have found myself on my knees, arms raised high, crying out to Jesus more times this year than ever before. I know many of you have also experienced a painful season. You are not alone. With God, nothing is wasted. He is our defender.

When the road before us causes anxiety, He tells us not to fear.

We have a real enemy who wants to silence us. Our stories are holy ground. Your testimony could be the spark that begins a revival for those who witness your testimony of God's grace.

Our God is the Redeemer. He comes for us in the darkest moments and brings redemption where we never thought possible. The gospel is on display in and through our lives, even when things don't go the way we hoped and prayed they would. Believe it. Take God at His Word. He is our Defender. Don't hold your tongue; share your story. The One who overcame the world has a plan for you. Trust His redemptive hand.

believed by grace, 28 for he refuted the Jews vigorously in public debate, demonstrating from the scriptures that the Christ was Jesus.

DISCIPLES OF JOHN THE BAPTIST AT EPHESUS

19 While Apollos was in Corinth, Paul went through the inland regions and came to Ephesus. He found some disciples
there 2 and said to them, "Did you receive the Holy Spirit when
you believed?" They replied, "No, we have not even heard that
there is a Holy Spirit." 3 So Paul said, "Into what then were you
baptized?" "Into John's baptism," they replied. 4 Paul said, "John
baptized with a baptism of repentance, telling the people to
believe in the one who was to come after him, that is, in Jesus."
5 When they heard this, they were baptized in the name of the
Lord Jesus, 6 and when Paul placed his hands on them, the Holy
Spirit came upon them, and they began to speak in tongues and
to prophesy. 7 (Now there were about twelve men in all.)

PAUL CONTINUES TO MINISTER AT EPHESUS

8 So Paul entered the synagogue and spoke out fearlessly for three
months, addressing and convincing them about the kingdom of
God. 9 But when some were stubborn and refused to believe, reviling the Way before the congregation, he left them and took the
disciples with him, addressing them every day in the lecture hall of
Tyrannus. 10 This went on for two years, so that all who lived in the
province of Asia, both Jews and Greeks, heard the word of the Lord.

THE SEVEN SONS OF SCEVA

11 God was performing extraordinary miracles by Paul's hands, 12 so
that when even handkerchiefs or aprons that had touched his body
were brought to the sick, their diseases left them and the evil spirits went out of them. 13 But some itinerant Jewish exorcists tried
to invoke the name of the Lord Jesus over those who were possessed by evil spirits, saying, "I sternly warn you by Jesus whom
Paul preaches." 14 (Now seven sons of a man named Sceva, a Jewish
high priest, were doing this.) 15 But the evil spirit replied to them,
"I know about Jesus and I am acquainted with Paul, but who are
you?" 16 Then the man who was possessed by the evil spirit jumped
on them and beat them all into submission. He prevailed against
them so that they fled from that house naked and wounded.
17 This became known to all who lived in Ephesus, both Jews and
Greeks; fear came over them all, and the name of the Lord Jesus
was praised. 18 Many of those who had believed came forward, confessing and making their deeds known. 19 Large numbers of those
who had practiced magic collected their books and burned them
up in the presence of everyone. When the value of the books was
added up, it was found to total 50,000 silver coins. 20 In this way
the word of the Lord continued to grow in power and to prevail.

A RIOT IN EPHESUS

21 Now after all these things had taken place, Paul resolved to go
to Jerusalem, passing through Macedonia and Achaia. He said,
"After I have been there, I must also see Rome." 22 So after sending two of his assistants, Timothy and Erastus, to Macedonia, he
himself stayed on for a while in the province of Asia.

23 At that time a great disturbance took place concerning the
Way. 24 For a man named Demetrius, a silversmith who made silver shrines of Artemis, brought a great deal of business to the
craftsmen. 25 He gathered these together, along with the workmen in similar trades, and said, "Men, you know that our prosperity comes from this business. 26 And you see and hear that
this Paul has persuaded and turned away a large crowd, not only
in Ephesus but in practically all of the province of Asia, by saying that gods made by hands are not gods at all. 27 There is danger not only that this business of ours will come into disrepute,
but also that the temple of the great goddess Artemis will be
regarded as nothing, and she whom all the province of Asia and
the world worship will suffer the loss of her greatness."

28 When they heard this they became enraged and began to
shout, "Great is Artemis of the Ephesians!" 29 The city was filled
with the uproar, and the crowd rushed to the theater together,
dragging with them Gaius and Aristarchus, the Macedonians who
were Paul's traveling companions. 30 But when Paul wanted to enter the public assembly, the disciples would not let him. 31 Even
some of the provincial authorities who were his friends sent a
message to him, urging him not to venture into the theater. 32 So
then some were shouting one thing, some another, for the assembly was in confusion, and most of them did not know why they had
met together. 33 Some of the crowd concluded it was about Alexander because the Jews had pushed him to the front. Alexander,
gesturing with his hand, was wanting to make a defense before
the public assembly. 34 But when they recognized that he was a
Jew, they all shouted in unison, "Great is Artemis of the Ephesians!" for about two hours. 35 After the city secretary quieted the
crowd, he said, "Men of Ephesus, what person is there who does
not know that the city of the Ephesians is the keeper of the temple of the great Artemis and of her image that fell from heaven?
36 So because these facts are indisputable, you must keep quiet and
not do anything reckless. 37 For you have brought these men here
who are neither temple robbers nor blasphemers of our goddess.
38 If then Demetrius and the craftsmen who are with him have a
complaint against someone, the courts are open and there are pro-
consuls; let them bring charges against one another there. 39 But if
you want anything in addition, it will have to be settled in a legal
assembly. 40 For we are in danger of being charged with rioting today, since there is no cause we can give to explain this disorderly
gathering." 41 After he had said this, he dismissed the assembly.

PAUL TRAVELS THROUGH MACEDONIA AND GREECE

20 After the disturbance had ended, Paul sent for the disciples,
and after encouraging them and saying farewell, he left to
go to Macedonia. 2 After he had gone through those regions and
spoken many words of encouragement to the believers there, he
came to Greece, 3 where he stayed for three months. Because the
Jews had made a plot against him as he was intending to sail for
Syria, he decided to return through Macedonia. 4 Paul was accompanied by Sopater son of Pyrrhus from Berea, Aristarchus and Se-
cundus from Thessalonica, Gaius from Derbe, and Timothy, as well
as Tychicus and Trophimus from the province of Asia. 5 These had

gone on ahead and were waiting for us in Troas. 6We sailed away
from Philippi after the days of Unleavened Bread, and within five
days we came to the others in Troas, where we stayed for seven days.
7On the first day of the week, when we met to break bread, Paul began to speak to the people, and because he intended to leave the
next day, he extended his message until midnight. 8(Now there
were many lamps in the upstairs room where we were meeting.)
9A young man named Eutychus, who was sitting in the window, was
sinking into a deep sleep while Paul continued to speak for a long
time. Fast asleep, he fell down from the third story and was picked
up dead. 10But Paul went down, threw himself on the young man,
put his arms around him, and said, "Do not be distressed, for he is
still alive!" 11Then Paul went back upstairs, and after he had broken
bread and eaten, he talked with them a long time, until dawn. Then
he left. 12They took the boy home alive and were greatly comforted.

THE VOYAGE TO MILETUS

13We went on ahead to the ship and put out to sea for Assos, intending to take Paul aboard there, for he had arranged it this way.
He himself was intending to go there by land. 14When he met us in
Assos, we took him aboard and went to Mitylene. 15We set sail from
there, and on the following day we arrived off Chios. The next day
we approached Samos, and the day after that we arrived at Miletus.
16For Paul had decided to sail past Ephesus so as not to spend time
in the province of Asia, for he was hurrying to arrive in Jerusalem,
if possible, by the day of Pentecost. 17From Miletus he sent a message to Ephesus, telling the elders of the church to come to him.

18When they arrived, he said to them, "You yourselves know
how I lived the whole time I was with you, from the first day I
set foot in the province of Asia, 19serving the Lord with all humility and with tears, and with the trials that happened to me
because of the plots of the Jews. 20You know that I did not hold
back from proclaiming to you anything that would be helpful,
and from teaching you publicly and from house to house, 21tes-
tifying to both Jews and Greeks about repentance toward God
and faith in our Lord Jesus. 22And now, compelled by the Spirit,
I am going to Jerusalem without knowing what will happen to
me there, 23except that the Holy Spirit warns me in town after
town that imprisonment and persecutions are waiting for me.
24But I do not consider my life worth anything to myself, so that
I may finish my task and the ministry that I received from the
Lord Jesus, to testify to the good news of God's grace.

25"And now I know that none of you among whom I went around
proclaiming the kingdom will see me again. 26Therefore I declare
to you today that I am innocent of the blood of you all. 27For I did
not hold back from announcing to you the whole purpose of God.
28Watch out for yourselves and for all the flock of which the Holy
Spirit has made you overseers, to shepherd the church of God that
he obtained with the blood of his own Son. 29I know that after I am
gone fierce wolves will come in among you, not sparing the flock.
30Even from among your own group men will arise, teaching per-
versions of the truth to draw the disciples away after them. 31There-
fore be alert, remembering that night and day for three years I did
not stop warning each one of you with tears. 32And now I entrust

LOVE TO GROW

OUR TASK TO TESTIFY

ACTS 20:24

We can learn a lot from Paul and his life as a missionary. Although he spent part of his life persecuting Jesus' followers, he eventually came to be known as one of the most influential church leaders. Paul's passionate renunciation and opposition of Christians turned to wholehearted advocacy of Jesus as the promised Messiah. Along the way, Paul was beaten, imprisoned, insulted, and falsely accused. Despite these circumstances, he persisted in preaching the good news of God's grace.

Paul considered his life worth nothing except to testify to God's grace. We are all called by God to do the same.

I don't know about you, but I would love to be able to say with utter confidence, like Paul, that "I do not consider my life worth anything to myself" (Acts 20:24). Truthfully, there is a part of me that thinks this level of passion is for people who don't have anything shady in their past. Maybe this kind of conviction is reserved for a "better" Christian than I am.

This passion is absolutely part of our task and ministry. As believers, we are all called to share the Good News of the gospel. Regardless of our past, our eyes are now opened. We are in this race together to glorify our God.

Paul used every opportunity he had to tell people about Jesus. In prison, in synagogues, in the streets, and in communities where Jesus was unknown, Paul shared his testimony. All too often, I overthink the task and ministry I've been called to do. I work myself up and talk myself out of participating in this faith race. The truth of the matter is, I can share the good news of God's grace wherever I am.

Where God has us right now is exactly where we're called to carry out this task.

Once his heart was convicted and his vision was cleared to see Jesus as Lord and Savior, Paul obeyed. He didn't overthink it, question it, or ignore it. He didn't wait to get more schooling, he didn't seek approval from his friends. He took the call seriously and set out to accomplish one task: to spread the good news of God's grace.

That's where we are today, friends. Paul is our example. Whatever is in our past, in the places we are right now, with the people in our sphere of influence, we are called to the task of testifying to God's work in our lives so that Christ will be glorified.

you to God and to the message of his grace. This message is able to
build you up and give you an inheritance among all those who are
sanctified. 33 I have desired no one's silver or gold or clothing. 34 You
yourselves know that these hands of mine provided for my needs
and the needs of those who were with me. 35 By all these things,
I have shown you that by working in this way we must help the
weak, and remember the words of the Lord Jesus that he himself
said, 'It is more blessed to give than to receive.'"

36 When he had said these things, he knelt down with them
all and prayed. 37 They all began to weep loudly, and hugged Paul
and kissed him, 38 especially saddened by what he had said, that
they were not going to see him again. Then they accompanied
him to the ship.

PAUL'S JOURNEY TO JERUSALEM

21 After we tore ourselves away from them, we put out to sea,
and sailing a straight course, we came to Cos, on the next
day to Rhodes, and from there to Patara. 2 We found a ship crossing over to Phoenicia, went aboard, and put out to sea. 3 After
we sighted Cyprus and left it behind on our port side, we sailed
on to Syria and put in at Tyre, because the ship was to unload
its cargo there. 4 After we located the disciples, we stayed there
seven days. They repeatedly told Paul through the Spirit not
to set foot in Jerusalem. 5 When our time was over, we left and
went on our way. All of them, with their wives and children, accompanied us outside of the city. After kneeling down on the
beach and praying, 6 we said farewell to one another. Then we
went aboard the ship, and they returned to their own homes.
7 We continued the voyage from Tyre and arrived at Ptolemais,
and when we had greeted the brothers, we stayed with them
for one day. 8 On the next day we left and came to Caesarea, and
entered the house of Philip the evangelist, who was one of the
seven, and stayed with him. 9 (He had four unmarried daughters who prophesied.)

10 While we remained there for a number of days, a prophet
named Agabus came down from Judea. 11 He came to us, took
Paul's belt, tied his own hands and feet with it, and said, "The
Holy Spirit says this: 'This is the way the Jews in Jerusalem will
tie up the man whose belt this is, and will hand him over to the
Gentiles.'" 12 When we heard this, both we and the local people
begged him not to go up to Jerusalem. 13 Then Paul replied, "What
are you doing, weeping and breaking my heart? For I am ready
not only to be tied up, but even to die in Jerusalem for the name
of the Lord Jesus." 14 Because he could not be persuaded, we said
no more except, "The Lord's will be done."

15 After these days we got ready and started up to Jerusalem.
16 Some of the disciples from Caesarea came along with us too,
and brought us to the house of Mnason of Cyprus, a disciple
from the earliest times, with whom we were to stay. 17 When
we arrived in Jerusalem, the brothers welcomed us gladly. 18 The
next day Paul went in with us to see James, and all the elders
were there. 19 When Paul had greeted them, he began to explain
in detail what God had done among the Gentiles through his
ministry. 20 When they heard this, they praised God. Then they

said to him, “You see, brother, how many thousands of Jews
there are who have believed, and they are all ardent observers
of the law. 21 They have been informed about you—that you teach
all the Jews now living among the Gentiles to abandon Moses,
telling them not to circumcise their children or live according
to our customs. 22 What then should we do? They will no doubt
hear that you have come. 23 So do what we tell you: We have four
men who have taken a vow; 24 take them and purify yourself
along with them and pay their expenses, so that they may have
their heads shaved. Then everyone will know there is nothing
in what they have been told about you, but that you yourself
live in conformity with the law. 25 But regarding the Gentiles
who have believed, we have written a letter, having decided
that they should avoid meat that has been sacrificed to idols
and blood and what has been strangled and sexual immorality.”
26 Then Paul took the men the next day, and after he had purified himself along with them, he went to the temple and gave
notice of the completion of the days of purification, when the
sacrifice would be offered for each of them. 27 When the seven
days were almost over, the Jews from the province of Asia who
had seen him in the temple area stirred up the whole crowd and
seized him, 28 shouting, “Men of Israel, help! This is the man who
teaches everyone everywhere against our people, our law, and
this sanctuary! Furthermore he has brought Greeks into the inner courts of the temple and made this holy place ritually unclean!” 29 (For they had seen Trophimus the Ephesian in the city
with him previously, and they assumed Paul had brought him
into the inner temple courts.) 30 The whole city was stirred up,
and the people rushed together. They seized Paul and dragged
him out of the temple courts, and immediately the doors were
shut. 31 While they were trying to kill him, a report was sent up
to the commanding officer of the cohort that all Jerusalem was
in confusion. 32 He immediately took soldiers and centurions
and ran down to the crowd. When they saw the commanding
officer and the soldiers, they stopped beating Paul. 33 Then the
commanding officer came up and arrested him and ordered
him to be tied up with two chains; he then asked who he was
and what he had done. 34 But some in the crowd shouted one
thing, and others something else, and when the commanding
officer was unable to find out the truth because of the disturbance, he ordered Paul to be brought into the barracks. 35 When
he came to the steps, Paul had to be carried by the soldiers because of the violence of the mob, 36 for a crowd of people followed them, screaming, “Away with him!” 37 As Paul was about
to be brought into the barracks, he said to the commanding
officer, “May I say something to you?” The officer replied, “Do
you know Greek? 38 Then you’re not that Egyptian who started
a rebellion and led the 4,000 men of the ‘Assassins’ into the
wilderness some time ago?” 39 Paul answered, “I am a Jew from
Tarsus in Cilicia, a citizen of an important city. Please allow me
to speak to the people.” 40 When the commanding officer had
given him permission, Paul stood on the steps and gestured to
the people with his hand. When they had become silent, he addressed them in Aramaic,

PAUL'S DEFENSE

22 "Brothers and fathers, listen to my defense that I now make
to you." 2 (When they heard that he was addressing them in
Aramaic, they became even quieter.) Then Paul said, 3 "I am a Jew,
born in Tarsus in Cilicia, but brought up in this city, educated with
strictness under Gamaliel according to the law of our ancestors,
and was zealous for God just as all of you are today. 4 I persecuted
this Way even to the point of death, tying up both men and women
and putting them in prison, 5 as both the high priest and the whole
council of elders can testify about me. From them I also received
letters to the brothers in Damascus, and I was on my way to make
arrests there and bring the prisoners to Jerusalem to be punished.
6 As I was en route and near Damascus, about noon a very bright
light from heaven suddenly flashed around me. 7 Then I fell to the
ground and heard a voice saying to me, 'Saul, Saul, why are you
persecuting me?' 8 I answered, 'Who are you, Lord?' He said to me,
'I am Jesus the Nazarene, whom you are persecuting.' 9 Those who
were with me saw the light, but did not understand the voice of
the one who was speaking to me. 10 So I asked, 'What should I do,
Lord?' The Lord said to me, 'Get up and go to Damascus; there you
will be told about everything that you have been designated to
do.' 11 Since I could not see because of the brilliance of that light,
I came to Damascus led by the hand of those who were with me.
12 A man named Ananias, a devout man according to the law, well
spoken of by all the Jews who live there, 13 came to me and stood
beside me and said to me, 'Brother Saul, regain your sight!' And at
that very moment I looked up and saw him. 14 Then he said, 'The
God of our ancestors has already chosen you to know his will, to
see the Righteous One, and to hear a command from his mouth,
15 because you will be his witness to all people of what you have
seen and heard. 16 And now what are you waiting for? Get up, be
baptized, and have your sins washed away, calling on his name.'
17 When I returned to Jerusalem and was praying in the temple, I
fell into a trance 18 and saw the Lord saying to me, 'Hurry and get
out of Jerusalem quickly, because they will not accept your testimony about me.' 19 I replied, 'Lord, they themselves know that
I imprisoned and beat those in the various synagogues who believed in you. 20 And when the blood of your witness Stephen was
shed, I myself was standing nearby, approving, and guarding the
cloaks of those who were killing him.' 21 Then he said to me, 'Go,
because I will send you far away to the Gentiles.'"

THE ROMAN COMMANDER QUESTIONS PAUL

22 The crowd was listening to him until he said this. Then they raised
their voices and shouted, "Away with this man from the earth! For
he should not be allowed to live!" 23 While they were screaming and
throwing off their cloaks and tossing dust in the air, 24 the commanding officer ordered Paul to be brought back into the barracks.
He told them to interrogate Paul by beating him with a lash so that
he could find out the reason the crowd was shouting at Paul in this
way. 25 When they had stretched him out for the lash, Paul said to
the centurion standing nearby, "Is it legal for you to lash a man
who is a Roman citizen without a proper trial?" 26 When the centurion heard this, he went to the commanding officer and reported

REFLECT

What does Paul's testimony and the response he received reveal about the reality of sharing our faith? How do Paul's boldness and faith encourage you to do the same?

it, saying, "What are you about to do? For this man is a Roman citizen." 27 So the commanding officer came and asked Paul, "Tell me,
are you a Roman citizen?" He replied, "Yes." 28 The commanding
officer answered, "I acquired this citizenship with a large sum of
money." "But I was even born a citizen," Paul replied. 29 Then those
who were about to interrogate him stayed away from him, and the
commanding officer was frightened when he realized that Paul was
a Roman citizen and that he had had him tied up.

PAUL BEFORE THE SANHEDRIN

30 The next day, because the commanding officer wanted to know
the true reason Paul was being accused by the Jews, he released
him and ordered the chief priests and the whole council to assemble. He then brought Paul down and had him stand before them.

23 Paul looked directly at the council and said, "Brothers, I
have lived my life with a clear conscience before God to
this day." 2 At that the high priest Ananias ordered those standing near Paul to strike him on the mouth. 3 Then Paul said to
him, "God is going to strike you, you whitewashed wall! Do you
sit there judging me according to the law, and in violation of the
law you order me to be struck?" 4 Those standing near him said,
"Do you dare insult God's high priest?" 5 Paul replied, "I did not
realize, brothers, that he was the high priest, for it is written,
'***You must not speak evil about a ruler of your people.***'"

6 Then when Paul noticed that part of them were Sadducees
and the others Pharisees, he shouted out in the council, "Brothers, I am a Pharisee, a son of Pharisees. I am on trial concerning
the hope of the resurrection of the dead!" 7 When he said this, an
argument began between the Pharisees and the Sadducees, and
the assembly was divided. 8 (For the Sadducees say there is no
resurrection, or angel, or spirit, but the Pharisees acknowledge
them all.) 9 There was a great commotion, and some experts in
the law from the party of the Pharisees stood up and protested
strongly, "We find nothing wrong with this man. What if a spirit
or an angel has spoken to him?" 10 When the argument became so
great the commanding officer feared that they would tear Paul
to pieces, he ordered the detachment to go down, take him away
from them by force, and bring him into the barracks.

11 The following night the Lord stood near Paul and said, "Have
courage, for just as you have testified about me in Jerusalem, so
you must also testify in Rome."

THE PLOT TO KILL PAUL

12 When morning came, the Jews formed a conspiracy and bound
themselves with an oath not to eat or drink anything until they
had killed Paul. 13 There were more than forty of them who formed
this conspiracy. 14 They went to the chief priests and the elders and
said, "We have bound ourselves with a solemn oath not to partake
of anything until we have killed Paul. 15 So now you and the council
request the commanding officer to bring him down to you, as if you
were going to determine his case by conducting a more thorough
inquiry. We are ready to kill him before he comes near this place."

16 But when the son of Paul's sister heard about the ambush, he
came and entered the barracks and told Paul. 17 Paul called one of

the centurions and said, "Take this young man to the commanding
officer, for he has something to report to him." 18 So the centurion
took him and brought him to the commanding officer and said,
"The prisoner Paul called me and asked me to bring this young
man to you because he has something to tell you." 19 The commanding officer took him by the hand, withdrew privately, and
asked, "What is it that you want to report to me?" 20 He replied,
"The Jews have agreed to ask you to bring Paul down to the council
tomorrow, as if they were going to inquire more thoroughly about
him. 21 So do not let them persuade you to do this, because more
than forty of them are lying in ambush for him. They have bound
themselves with an oath not to eat or drink anything until they
have killed him, and now they are ready, waiting for you to agree
to their request." 22 Then the commanding officer sent the young
man away, directing him, "Tell no one that you have reported these
things to me." 23 Then he summoned two of the centurions and
said, "Make ready 200 soldiers to go to Caesarea along with 70
horsemen and 200 spearmen by nine o'clock tonight, 24 and provide mounts for Paul to ride so that he may be brought safely to
Felix the governor." 25 He wrote a letter that went like this:

> 26 Claudius Lysias to His Excellency Governor Felix, greet-
> ings. 27 This man was seized by the Jews and they were about
> to kill him, when I came up with the detachment and res-
> cued him, because I had learned that he was a Roman
> citizen. 28 Since I wanted to know what charge they were ac-
> cusing him of, I brought him down to their council. 29 I found
> he was accused with reference to controversial questions
> about their law, but no charge against him deserved death or
> imprisonment. 30 When I was informed there would be a plot
> against this man, I sent him to you at once, also ordering his
> accusers to state their charges against him before you.

31 So the soldiers, in accordance with their orders, took Paul and
brought him to Antipatris during the night. 32 The next day they
let the horsemen go on with him, and they returned to the barracks. 33 When the horsemen came to Caesarea and delivered the
letter to the governor, they also presented Paul to him. 34 When
the governor had read the letter, he asked what province he was
from. When he learned that he was from Cilicia, 35 he said, "I will
give you a hearing when your accusers arrive too." Then he ordered that Paul be kept under guard in Herod's palace.

THE ACCUSATIONS AGAINST PAUL

24 After five days the high priest Ananias came down with
some elders and an attorney named Tertullus, and they
brought formal charges against Paul to the governor. 2 When Paul
had been summoned, Tertullus began to accuse him, saying, "We
have experienced a lengthy time of peace through your rule, and
reforms are being made in this nation through your foresight.
3 Most excellent Felix, we acknowledge this everywhere and in
every way with all gratitude. 4 But so that I may not delay you
any further, I beg you to hear us briefly with your customary graciousness. 5 For we have found this man to be a troublemaker,

one who stirs up riots among all the Jews throughout the world,
and a ringleader of the sect of the Nazarenes. 6 He even tried to
desecrate the temple, so we arrested him.§ 8 When you examine
him yourself, you will be able to learn from him about all these
things we are accusing him of doing." 9 The Jews also joined in
the verbal attack, claiming that these things were true.

PAUL'S DEFENSE BEFORE FELIX

10 When the governor gestured for him to speak, Paul replied, "Because I know that you have been a judge over this nation for many
years, I confidently make my defense. 11 As you can verify for yourself, not more than twelve days ago I went up to Jerusalem to worship. 12 They did not find me arguing with anyone or stirring up a
crowd in the temple courts or in the synagogues or throughout
the city, 13 nor can they prove to you the things they are accusing
me of doing. 14 But I confess this to you, that I worship the God of
our ancestors according to the Way (which they call a sect), believing everything that is according to the law and that is written
in the prophets. 15 I have a hope in God (a hope that these men
themselves accept too) that there is going to be a resurrection of
both the righteous and the unrighteous. 16 This is the reason I do
my best to always have a clear conscience toward God and toward
people. 17 After several years I came to bring to my people gifts for
the poor and to present offerings, 18 which I was doing when they
found me in the temple, ritually purified, without a crowd or a
disturbance. 19 But there are some Jews from the province of Asia
who should be here before you and bring charges, if they have anything against me. 20 Or these men here should tell what crime they
found me guilty of when I stood before the council, 21 other than
this one thing I shouted out while I stood before them: 'I am on
trial before you today concerning the resurrection of the dead.'"

22 Then Felix, who understood the facts concerning the Way more
accurately, adjourned their hearing, saying, "When Lysias the commanding officer comes down, I will decide your case." 23 He ordered
the centurion to guard Paul, but to let him have some freedom, and
not to prevent any of his friends from meeting his needs.

PAUL SPEAKS REPEATEDLY TO FELIX

24 Some days later, when Felix arrived with his wife Drusilla,
who was Jewish, he sent for Paul and heard him speak about
faith in Christ Jesus. 25 While Paul was discussing righteousness,
self-control, and the coming judgment, Felix became frightened
and said, "Go away for now, and when I have an opportunity, I
will send for you." 26 At the same time he was also hoping that
Paul would give him money, and for this reason he sent for Paul
as often as possible and talked with him. 27 After two years had
passed, Porcius Festus succeeded Felix, and because he wanted
to do the Jews a favor, Felix left Paul in prison.

PAUL APPEALS TO CAESAR

25 Now three days after Festus arrived in the province, he went
up to Jerusalem from Caesarea. 2 So the chief priests and the
most prominent men of the Jews brought formal charges against
Paul to him. 3 Requesting him to do them a favor against Paul, they

urged Festus to summon him to Jerusalem, planning an ambush
to kill him along the way. [4]Then Festus replied that Paul was being
kept at Caesarea, and he himself intended to go there shortly. [5]"So,"
he said, "let your leaders go down there with me, and if this man
has done anything wrong, they may bring charges against him."

[6]After Festus had stayed not more than eight or ten days among
them, he went down to Caesarea, and the next day he sat on the
judgment seat and ordered Paul to be brought. [7]When he arrived,
the Jews who had come down from Jerusalem stood around him,
bringing many serious charges that they were not able to prove.
[8]Paul said in his defense, "I have committed no offense against the
Jewish law or against the temple or against Caesar." [9]But Festus,
wanting to do the Jews a favor, asked Paul, "Are you willing to go
up to Jerusalem and be tried before me there on these charges?"
[10]Paul replied, "I am standing before Caesar's judgment seat, where
I should be tried. I have done nothing wrong to the Jews, as you also
know very well. [11]If then I am in the wrong and have done anything
that deserves death, I am not trying to escape dying, but if not one
of their charges against me is true, no one can hand me over to
them. I appeal to Caesar!" [12]Then, after conferring with his council,
Festus replied, "You have appealed to Caesar; to Caesar you will go!"

FESTUS ASKS KING AGRIPPA FOR ADVICE

[13]After several days had passed, King Agrippa and Bernice arrived
at Caesarea to pay their respects to Festus. [14]While they were
staying there many days, Festus explained Paul's case to the king
to get his opinion, saying, "There is a man left here as a prisoner
by Felix. [15]When I was in Jerusalem, the chief priests and the elders of the Jews informed me about him, asking for a sentence
of condemnation against him. [16]I answered them that it was not
the custom of the Romans to hand over anyone before the accused had met his accusers face-to-face and had been given an
opportunity to make a defense against the accusation. [17]So after
they came back here with me, I did not postpone the case, but
the next day I sat on the judgment seat and ordered the man to
be brought. [18]When his accusers stood up, they did not charge
him with any of the evil deeds I had suspected. [19]Rather they
had several points of disagreement with him about their own
religion and about a man named Jesus who was dead, whom Paul
claimed to be alive. [20]Because I was at a loss how I could investigate these matters, I asked if he were willing to go to Jerusalem
and be tried there on these charges. [21]But when Paul appealed to
be kept in custody for the decision of His Majesty the Emperor,
I ordered him to be kept under guard until I could send him to
Caesar." [22]Agrippa said to Festus, "I would also like to hear the
man myself." "Tomorrow," he replied, "you will hear him."

PAUL BEFORE KING AGRIPPA AND BERNICE

[23]So the next day Agrippa and Bernice came with great pomp and
entered the audience hall, along with the senior military officers
and the prominent men of the city. When Festus gave the order,
Paul was brought in. [24]Then Festus said, "King Agrippa, and all you
who are present here with us, you see this man about whom the
entire Jewish populace petitioned me both in Jerusalem and here,

shouting loudly that he ought not to live any longer. 25 But I found that he had done nothing that deserved death, and when he appealed to His Majesty the Emperor, I decided to send him. 26 But I have nothing definite to write to my lord about him. Therefore I have brought him before you all, and especially before you, King Agrippa, so that after this preliminary hearing I may have something to write. 27 For it seems unreasonable to me to send a prisoner without clearly indicating the charges against him."

PAUL OFFERS HIS DEFENSE

26 So Agrippa said to Paul, "You have permission to speak for yourself." Then Paul held out his hand and began his defense:

2 "Regarding all the things I have been accused of by the Jews, King Agrippa, I consider myself fortunate that I am about to make my defense before you today, 3 because you are especially familiar with all the customs and controversial issues of the Jews. Therefore I ask you to listen to me patiently. 4 Now all the Jews know the way I lived from my youth, spending my life from the beginning among my own people and in Jerusalem. 5 They know, because they have known me from time past, if they are willing to testify, that according to the strictest party of our religion, I lived as a Pharisee. 6 And now I stand here on trial because of my hope in the promise made by God to our ancestors, 7 a promise that our twelve tribes hope to attain as they earnestly serve God night and day. Concerning this hope the Jews are accusing me, Your Majesty! 8 Why do you people think it is unbelievable that God raises the dead? 9 Of course, I myself was convinced that it was necessary to do many things hostile to the name of Jesus the Nazarene. 10 And that is what I did in Jerusalem: Not only did I lock up many of the saints in prisons by the authority I received from the chief priests, but I also cast my vote against them when they were sentenced to death. 11 I punished them often in all the synagogues and tried to force them to blaspheme. Because I was so furiously enraged at them, I went to persecute them even in foreign cities.

12 "While doing this very thing, as I was going to Damascus with authority and complete power from the chief priests, 13 about noon along the road, Your Majesty, I saw a light from heaven, brighter than the sun, shining everywhere around me and those traveling with me. 14 When we had all fallen to the ground, I heard a voice saying to me in Aramaic, 'Saul, Saul, why are you persecuting me? You are hurting yourself by kicking against the goads.' 15 So I said, 'Who are you, Lord?' And the Lord replied, 'I am Jesus whom you are persecuting. 16 But get up and stand on your feet, for I have appeared to you for this reason, to designate you in advance as a servant and witness to the things you have seen and to the things in which I will appear to you. 17 I will rescue you from your own people and from the Gentiles, to whom I am sending you 18 to open their eyes so that they turn from darkness to light and from the power of Satan to God, so that they may receive forgiveness of sins and a share among those who are sanctified by faith in me.'

19 "Therefore, King Agrippa, I was not disobedient to the heavenly vision, 20 but I declared to those in Damascus first, and then to those in Jerusalem and in all Judea, and to the Gentiles, that

they should repent and turn to God, performing deeds consistent with repentance. 21 For this reason the Jews, after they seized
me while I was in the temple courts, were trying to kill me. 22 I
have experienced help from God to this day, and so I stand testifying to both small and great, saying nothing except what the
prophets and Moses said was going to happen: 23 that the Christ
was to suffer and be the first to rise from the dead, to proclaim
light both to our people and to the Gentiles."

24 As Paul was saying these things in his defense, Festus exclaimed loudly, "You have lost your mind, Paul! Your great learning is driving you insane!" 25 But Paul replied, "I have not lost my
mind, most excellent Festus, but am speaking true and rational
words. 26 For the king knows about these things, and I am speaking freely to him, because I cannot believe that any of these
things has escaped his notice, for this was not done in a corner.
27 Do you believe the prophets, King Agrippa? I know that you
believe." 28 Agrippa said to Paul, "In such a short time are you
persuading me to become a Christian?" 29 Paul replied, "I pray
to God that whether in a short or a long time not only you but
also all those who are listening to me today could become such
as I am, except for these chains."

30 So the king got up, and with him the governor and Bernice
and those sitting with them, 31 and as they were leaving they said
to one another, "This man is not doing anything deserving death
or imprisonment." 32 Agrippa said to Festus, "This man could have
been released if he had not appealed to Caesar."

PAUL AND COMPANY SAIL FOR ROME

27 When it was decided we would sail to Italy, they handed
over Paul and some other prisoners to a centurion of the
Augustan Cohort named Julius. 2 We went on board a ship from
Adramyttium that was about to sail to various ports along the
coast of the province of Asia and put out to sea, accompanied by
Aristarchus, a Macedonian from Thessalonica. 3 The next day we
put in at Sidon, and Julius, treating Paul kindly, allowed him to
go to his friends so they could provide him with what he needed.
4 From there we put out to sea and sailed under the lee of Cyprus
because the winds were against us. 5 After we had sailed across
the open sea off Cilicia and Pamphylia, we put in at Myra in Lycia.
6 There the centurion found a ship from Alexandria sailing for Italy, and he put us aboard it. 7 We sailed slowly for many days and
arrived with difficulty off Cnidus. Because the wind prevented
us from going any farther, we sailed under the lee of Crete off
Salmone. 8 With difficulty we sailed along the coast of Crete and
came to a place called Fair Havens that was near the town of Lasea.

CAUGHT IN A VIOLENT STORM

9 Since considerable time had passed and the voyage was now
dangerous because the fast was already over, Paul advised them,
10 "Men, I can see the voyage is going to end in disaster and great
loss not only of the cargo and the ship, but also of our lives." 11 But
the centurion was more convinced by the captain and the ship's
owner than by what Paul said. 12 Because the harbor was not suitable to spend the winter in, the majority decided to put out to sea

from there. They hoped that somehow they could reach Phoenix,
a harbor of Crete facing southwest and northwest, and spend the
winter there. 13 When a gentle south wind sprang up, they thought
they could carry out their purpose, so they weighed anchor and
sailed close along the coast of Crete. 14 Not long after this, a hur-
ricane-force wind called the northeaster blew down from the island. 15 When the ship was caught in it and could not head into
the wind, we gave way to it and were driven along. 16 As we ran
under the lee of a small island called Cauda, we were able with
difficulty to get the ship's boat under control. 17 After the crew
had hoisted it aboard, they used supports to undergird the ship.
Fearing they would run aground on the Syrtis, they lowered the
sea anchor, thus letting themselves be driven along. 18 The next
day, because we were violently battered by the storm, they began
throwing the cargo overboard, 19 and on the third day they threw
the ship's gear overboard with their own hands. 20 When neither
sun nor stars appeared for many days and a violent storm continued to batter us, we finally abandoned all hope of being saved.
21 Since many of them had no desire to eat, Paul stood up
among them and said, "Men, you should have listened to me
and not put out to sea from Crete, thus avoiding this damage
and loss. 22 And now I advise you to keep up your courage, for
there will be no loss of life among you, but only the ship will be
lost. 23 For last night an angel of the God to whom I belong and
whom I serve came to me 24 and said, 'Do not be afraid, Paul! You
must stand before Caesar, and God has graciously granted you
the safety of all who are sailing with you.' 25 Therefore keep up
your courage, men, for I have faith in God that it will be just as
I have been told. 26 But we must run aground on some island."
27 When the fourteenth night had come, while we were being
driven across the Adriatic Sea, about midnight the sailors suspected they were approaching some land. 28 They took soundings and found the water was twenty fathoms deep; when they
had sailed a little farther they took soundings again and found
it was fifteen fathoms deep. 29 Because they were afraid that we
would run aground on the rocky coast, they threw out four anchors from the stern and wished for day to appear. 30 Then when
the sailors tried to escape from the ship and were lowering the
ship's boat into the sea, pretending that they were going to put
out anchors from the bow, 31 Paul said to the centurion and the
soldiers, "Unless these men stay with the ship, you cannot be
saved." 32 Then the soldiers cut the ropes of the ship's boat and
let it drift away.
33 As day was about to dawn, Paul urged them all to take some
food, saying, "Today is the fourteenth day you have been in suspense and have gone without food; you have eaten nothing.
34 Therefore I urge you to take some food, for this is important
for your survival. For not one of you will lose a hair from his
head." 35 After he said this, Paul took bread and gave thanks to
God in front of them all, broke it, and began to eat. 36 So all of
them were encouraged and took food themselves. 37 (We were
in all 276 persons on the ship.) 38 When they had eaten enough
to be satisfied, they lightened the ship by throwing the wheat
into the sea.

LOVE TO GROW

UNDERGIRDED WITH HELP

ACTS 27:9–20

Roman soldiers transported an imprisoned Paul to appeal his case before the emperor of Rome. He found himself aboard a storm-tossed ship among a crew of frightened sailors who faced the prospect of shipwreck.

As the storm worsened, gale force winds blew the ship further away from the safety of the harbor. The crew knew if they didn't work quickly, the ship would run aground and be destroyed, endangering their lives. When the sailors saw they were about to lose control, "they used supports to undergird the ship" to prevent it from being destroyed (Acts 27:17).

What the sailors understood was the ship was in a stressful, desperate state about to break apart at the seams under the force of the wind and waves. To support and strengthen the vessel, they had to wrap chains, ropes, and supports tightly around the hull to undergird the ship and prevent it from collapse. The word *supports* used in this passage is from the Greek word *boétheia*, which means "help" at a critical time.

The only other instance this word is used in the New Testament is found in Hebrews 4:16, which says, "Therefore let us confidently approach the throne of grace to receive mercy and find grace whenever we need help."

When we are faced with the storms of life and are buffeted on all sides with uncertainty, bad reports, disappointments, or heartbreak, and we wonder if we will be able to survive, we have a source of unfailing, ever-present help and love to keep us from falling apart: Jesus.

Jesus is the mercy and grace who undergirds our lives and strengthens us. He provides His wrap-around support to protect us from defeat and destruction. Like the supports the sailors used to hold their ship together during storms, we have a very present help in our time of need. We can confidently rely on Him to hold us securely together without fear of falling apart.

When we encounter any test, difficulty, or trial in life, we can rest in the truth that Jesus has given us Himself to bind up our lives with His perfect love. With Him holding our lives together, we can withstand any impossible storm we face. He will never leave us without support.

PAUL IS SHIPWRECKED

39 When day came, they did not recognize the land, but they
noticed a bay with a beach, where they decided to run the ship
aground if they could. 40 So they slipped the anchors and left
them in the sea, at the same time loosening the linkage that
bound the steering oars together. Then they hoisted the foresail
to the wind and steered toward the beach. 41 But they encountered a patch of crosscurrents and ran the ship aground; the
bow stuck fast and could not be moved, but the stern was being
broken up by the force of the waves. 42 Now the soldiers' plan
was to kill the prisoners so that none of them would escape by
swimming away. 43 But the centurion, wanting to save Paul's life,
prevented them from carrying out their plan. He ordered those
who could swim to jump overboard first and get to land, 44 and
the rest were to follow, some on planks and some on pieces of
the ship. And in this way all were brought safely to land.

PAUL ON MALTA

28 After we had safely reached shore, we learned that the island was called Malta. 2 The local inhabitants showed us
extraordinary kindness, for they built a fire and welcomed us
all because it had started to rain and was cold. 3 When Paul had
gathered a bundle of brushwood and was putting it on the fire,
a viper came out because of the heat and fastened itself on his
hand. 4 When the local people saw the creature hanging from
Paul's hand, they said to one another, "No doubt this man is a
murderer! Although he has escaped from the sea, Justice herself
has not allowed him to live!" 5 However, Paul shook the creature
off into the fire and suffered no harm. 6 But they were expecting that he was going to swell up or suddenly drop dead. So after they had waited a long time and had seen nothing unusual
happen to him, they changed their minds and said he was a god.
7 Now in the region around that place were fields belonging to
the chief official of the island, named Publius, who welcomed
us and entertained us hospitably as guests for three days. 8 The
father of Publius lay sick in bed, suffering from fever and dysen-
tery. Paul went in to see him and after praying, placed his hands
on him and healed him. 9 After this had happened, many of the
people on the island who were sick also came and were healed.
10 They also bestowed many honors, and when we were preparing to sail, they gave us all the supplies we needed.

PAUL FINALLY REACHES ROME

11 After three months we put out to sea in an Alexandrian ship that
had wintered at the island and had the "Heavenly Twins" as its
figurehead. 12 We put in at Syracuse and stayed there three days.
13 From there we cast off and arrived at Rhegium, and after one day
a south wind sprang up and on the second day we came to Pute-
oli. 14 There we found some brothers and were invited to stay with
them seven days. And in this way we came to Rome. 15 The brothers
from there, when they heard about us, came as far as the Forum
of Appius and Three Taverns to meet us. When he saw them, Paul
thanked God and took courage. 16 When we entered Rome, Paul was
allowed to live by himself, with the soldier who was guarding him.

PAUL ADDRESSES THE JEWISH COMMUNITY IN ROME

17 After three days Paul called the local Jewish leaders together.
When they had assembled, he said to them, "Brothers, although
I had done nothing against our people or the customs of our ancestors, from Jerusalem I was handed over as a prisoner to the Romans. 18 When they had heard my case, they wanted to release me,
because there was no basis for a death sentence against me. 19 But
when the Jews objected, I was forced to appeal to Caesar—not that
I had some charge to bring against my own people. 20 So for this
reason I have asked to see you and speak with you, for I am bound
with this chain because of the hope of Israel." 21 They replied, "We
have received no letters from Judea about you, nor have any of the
brothers come from there and reported or said anything bad about
you. 22 But we would like to hear from you what you think, for regarding this sect we know that people everywhere speak against it."
23 They set a day to meet with him, and they came to him where
he was staying in even greater numbers. From morning until
evening he explained things to them, testifying about the kingdom of God and trying to convince them about Jesus from both
the law of Moses and the prophets. 24 Some were convinced by
what he said, but others refused to believe. 25 So they began to
leave, unable to agree among themselves, after Paul made one
last statement: "The Holy Spirit spoke rightly to your ancestors
through the prophet Isaiah 26 when he said,

'Go to this people and say,
"You will keep on hearing, but will never understand,
and you will keep on looking, but will never perceive.
27 ***For the heart of this people has become dull,***
and their ears are hard of hearing,
and they have closed their eyes,
so that they would not see with their eyes
and hear with their ears
and understand with their heart
and turn, and I would heal them."'

28 "Therefore be advised that this salvation from God has been
sent to the Gentiles; they will listen!"[||]
30 Paul lived there two whole years in his own rented quarters
and welcomed all who came to him, 31 proclaiming the kingdom
of God and teaching about the Lord Jesus Christ with complete
boldness and without restriction.

REFLECT

How do the final years of Paul's ministry contrast his earlier ministry? Was one ministry more effective than the other?

THERE IS
therefore
now
No condemnation
FOR THOSE
WHO ARE IN
Christ Jesus

MEMORY VERSE

There is therefore now no condemnation for those who are in Christ Jesus. For the law of the life-giving Spirit in Christ Jesus has set you free from the law of sin and death.

Romans 8:1–2

INTRODUCTION

Grace

Written to a church he had never visited, Paul's letter to the Romans is a presentation of theology and an argument for the forgiveness of humans through faith alone. Paul's letter presents foundational truths about Christ and His sacrifice, the life of a believer, and the grace God so lavishly grants us.

Paul opened his letter with thanksgiving and prayer, then explained the need for righteousness (1:1—3:20). Because we are unable to secure righteousness by our own efforts, we receive justification through Christ's sacrifice (3:21—5:21). This justification makes us blameless before God by the blood of Christ, and we are no longer under the law (6:1—8:39). Paul explained how we practice this righteousness in our everyday lives for the sake of the church (9:1—15:13). Paul concluded his letter by sharing his plans and offering a benediction to the church in Rome (15:14—16:27).

Paul is attributed with the authorship of the Book of Romans primarily because he identified himself by name at the beginning of the letter. The letter records that Paul planned to sail for Judea from Corinth, while fellow believer Phoebe was leaving Corinth for Rome. Phoebe is believed to be the bearer of Paul's letter, dating the message to approximately A.D. 57.

The letter to the Romans provides a clear explanation of the gospel of Jesus Christ and the grace poured out on those who believe. Theologically and doctrinally rich, Romans is a central book to the Christian faith. Still, Paul's explanations are simple enough for even the newest believer to understand that salvation comes by grace alone, through faith alone, in Christ alone. We can love God greatly as we rest in the confidence that He provided a way for us to receive eternal life.

Slovakia

OFFICIAL LANGUAGE
Slovak
POPULATION
5,400,000
UNREACHED POPULATION
2,600
PROFESSING CHRISTIANS
92.8%

Lucia's Home

Say a Prayer Today

Pray for the spread of the gospel to the unreached people of Slovakia. Pray specifically for the Romani, that they would be receptive to Jesus and carry the Good News to the rest of Slovakia.

HISTORY BIT

The Romani (Gypsies) are a marginalized people group and often suffer from low education and poverty. However, this people group is one of the most responsive to the gospel in Central and Eastern Europe.*

Source Information:
https://joshuaproject.net/countries/LO
*Jason Mandryk, Operation World, 7th edition (Colorado Springs, CO: Biblica Publishing, 2010), 748.

LOVE YOUR NEIGHBOR

Her Journey

LUCIA'S STORY

I became a Christian over twenty years ago. God touched my heart and filled me with His presence. From that moment, He planted a desire in my heart to know Him. In the first few years after I placed my faith in Christ, God taught me how to walk with Him. As I continued to grow, God taught me how to walk in His Spirit.

Through this season of learning what it meant to live by the law of the Spirit, I spent a great deal of time studying Romans 8. It became my spiritual food. The Holy Spirit showed me the places in my life I needed to surrender to God.

I am a very organized person. This is not a bad thing, but it was a constant obstacle as I learned to listen to the Holy Spirit. While my tendency is to be orderly and organized, I felt the Holy Spirit working in my life in spontaneous, unexpected ways. There was a battle within me: Would I walk among my organized boundaries, or would I walk by faith as the Holy Spirit led me?

I realized my fear to follow the Holy Spirit led me back to the beginning of my relationship with God. There, I had to decide if I only wanted Him to work in my life in the safety of my ordered plans, or if I wanted to be free from those boundaries, and walk by faith.

I decided to trust the Holy Spirit and move beyond my safe boundaries. This decision has not always been easy, as walking by faith is not always an easy road, but what a beautiful freedom it is to be under the law of the Holy Spirit. I am still learning every day, and the Holy Spirit is constantly changing me. He has given me grace as I learn to trust Him every day.

6 WEEK

LOVE HIS WORD

MONDAY	TUESDAY	WEDNESDAY	THURSDAY	FRIDAY
Romans 1:1-15	Romans 1:16-32	Romans 2:1-16	Romans 2:17—3:8	Romans 3:9-31
SOAP Romans 1:5-6	SOAP Romans 1:16-17	SOAP Romans 2:9-11	SOAP Romans 3:5-6	SOAP Romans 3:22-24
Romans 4:1-12	Romans 4:13-25	Romans 5:1-11	Romans 5:12-21	Romans 6:1-14
SOAP Romans 4:3-5	SOAP Romans 4:20-21	SOAP Romans 5:3-5	SOAP Romans 5:20-21	SOAP Romans 6:12-14
Romans 6:15-23	Romans 7:1-12	Romans 7:12-25	Romans 8:1-11	Romans 8:12-25
SOAP Romans 6:21-23	SOAP Romans 7:6	SOAP Romans 7:22-25	SOAP Romans 8:1-2	SOAP Romans 8:18-19
Romans 8:26-39	Romans 9:1-18	Romans 9:19-29	Romans 9:30—10:13	Romans 10:14-21
SOAP Romans 8:28-30	SOAP Romans 9:16	SOAP Romans 9:22-24	SOAP Romans 10:13	SOAP Romans 10:17
Romans 11:1-12	Romans 11:13-36	Romans 12	Romans 13	Romans 14:1-12
SOAP Romans 11:5-6	SOAP Romans 11:33-36	SOAP Romans 12:9-17	SOAP Romans 13:14	SOAP Romans 14:8
Romans 14:13-23	Romans 15:1-13	Romans 15:14-33	Romans 16:1-16	Romans 16:17-27
SOAP Romans 14:13	SOAP Romans 15:4-6	SOAP Romans 15:17-20	SOAP Romans 16:1-2	SOAP Romans 16:20

SALUTATION

1 From Paul, a slave of Christ Jesus, called to be an apostle, set
apart for the gospel of God. 2 This gospel he promised beforehand
through his prophets in the holy scriptures, 3 concerning his Son
who was a descendant of David with reference to the flesh, 4 who
was appointed the Son-of-God-in-power according to the Holy
Spirit by the resurrection from the dead, Jesus Christ our Lord.
5 Through him we have received grace and our apostleship to bring
about the obedience of faith among all the Gentiles on behalf of his
name. 6 You also are among them, called to belong to Jesus Christ.
7 To all those loved by God in Rome, called to be saints: Grace and
peace to you from God our Father and the Lord Jesus Christ!

PAUL'S DESIRE TO VISIT ROME

8 First of all, I thank my God through Jesus Christ for all of you, because your faith is proclaimed throughout the whole world. 9 For
God, whom I serve in my spirit in the gospel of his Son, is my witness that I continually remember you 10 and I always ask in my
prayers, if perhaps now at last I may succeed in visiting you according to the will of God. 11 For I long to see you, so that I may impart to you some spiritual gift to strengthen you, 12 that is, that we
may be mutually comforted by one another's faith, both yours and
mine. 13 I do not want you to be unaware, brothers and sisters, that
I often intended to come to you (and was prevented until now), so
that I may have some fruit even among you, just as I already have
among the rest of the Gentiles. 14 I am a debtor both to the Greeks
and to the barbarians, both to the wise and to the foolish. 15 Thus I
am eager also to preach the gospel to you who are in Rome.

THE POWER OF THE GOSPEL

16 For I am not ashamed of the gospel, for it is God's power for salvation to everyone who believes, to the Jew first and also to the
Greek. 17 For the righteousness of God is revealed in the gospel from
faith to faith, just as it is written, "***The righteous by faith will live.***"

THE CONDEMNATION OF THE UNRIGHTEOUS

18 For the wrath of God is revealed from heaven against all ungodliness and unrighteousness of people who suppress the truth by
their unrighteousness, 19 because what can be known about God
is plain to them, because God has made it plain to them. 20 For
since the creation of the world his invisible attributes—his eternal power and divine nature—have been clearly seen, because
they are understood through what has been made. So people are
without excuse. 21 For although they knew God, they did not glorify him as God or give him thanks, but they became futile in their
thoughts and their senseless hearts were darkened. 22 Although
they claimed to be wise, they became fools 23 and exchanged the
glory of the immortal God for an image resembling mortal human beings or birds or four-footed animals or reptiles.

24 Therefore God gave them over in the desires of their hearts
to impurity, to dishonor their bodies among themselves. 25 They
exchanged the truth of God for a lie and worshiped and served
the creation rather than the Creator, who is blessed forever!
Amen.

GOD'S HEART FOR THE NATIONS

Romans 1:16

For I am not ashamed of the gospel, for it is God's power for salvation to everyone who believes, to the Jew first and also to the Greek.

REFLECT

How can you live unashamed of the gospel? How does living this way encourage others?

LOVE TO GROW

OUR WORK FOR THE GOSPEL

ROMANS 1:1–7

Paul began his letter to the Romans by introducing himself: "From Paul, a slave of Christ Jesus, called to be an apostle, set apart for the gospel of God" (Rom 1:1). In this simple statement, he shared his standing as a slave of Christ, his authority as an apostle, and his call to be set apart for the gospel. I can't help but feel the sincerity, passion, and deep life connection Paul shared with each phrase in these verses.

Paul was undoubtedly a man who lived for spreading the gospel. The mission defined his life and his actions. He was fully committed to his task even though his commitment cost him a great deal. Paul was defined by his deep devotion to spreading the gospel, but being a missionary wasn't his day job. Paul was a tentmaker by trade.

So often in our twenty-first-century world, we are defined by what we do. We let our job titles speak for us, define our worth, and tell others what we deem important. We are quick to share our career aspirations so others will gain insight into what we value.

What if we were this passionate about spreading the message of the gospel?

How would our communities, workplaces, families, friends, cities, and nations change if our most important aspiration was advancing the gospel? What could happen if we defined ourselves by the call Christ has given us to go and make disciples of all nations (see Matt 28:19–20)?

The gospel of grace defined Paul's life. He had been rescued from darkness and spent all his energy sharing the truth with others. Paul knew he was set apart for the gospel, and his life reflected his call. We have the same call. Let's follow in Paul's footsteps, living lives fully committed to sharing the gospel of Christ Jesus, no matter the way we spend our days.

26 For this reason God gave them over to dishonorable passions. For their women exchanged the natural sexual relations
for unnatural ones, 27 and likewise the men also abandoned natural relations with women and were inflamed in their passions
for one another. Men committed shameless acts with men and
received in themselves the due penalty for their error.
28 And just as they did not see fit to acknowledge God, God
gave them over to a depraved mind, to do what should not be
done. 29 They are filled with every kind of unrighteousness, wickedness, covetousness, malice. They are rife with envy, murder,
strife, deceit, hostility. They are gossips, 30 slanderers, haters of
God, insolent, arrogant, boastful, contrivers of all sorts of evil,
disobedient to parents, 31 senseless, covenant-breakers, heartless, ruthless. 32 Although they fully know God's righteous decree that those who practice such things deserve to die, they
not only do them but also approve of those who practice them.

THE CONDEMNATION OF THE MORALIST

2 Therefore you are without excuse, whoever you are, when
you judge someone else. For on whatever grounds you judge
another, you condemn yourself, because you who judge practice
the same things. 2 Now we know that God's judgment is in accordance with truth against those who practice such things. 3 And
do you think, whoever you are, when you judge those who practice such things and yet do them yourself, that you will escape
God's judgment? 4 Or do you have contempt for the wealth of his
kindness, forbearance, and patience, and yet do not know that
God's kindness leads you to repentance? 5 But because of your
stubbornness and your unrepentant heart, you are storing up
wrath for yourselves in the day of wrath, when God's righteous
judgment is revealed! 6 He ***will reward each one according to his
works***: 7 eternal life to those who by perseverance in good works
seek glory and honor and immortality, 8 but wrath and anger to
those who live in selfish ambition and do not obey the truth but
follow unrighteousness. 9 There will be affliction and distress
on everyone who does evil, on the Jew first and also the Greek,
10 but glory and honor and peace for everyone who does good,
for the Jew first and also the Greek. 11 For there is no partiality
with God. 12 For all who have sinned apart from the law will also
perish apart from the law, and all who have sinned under the
law will be judged by the law. 13 For it is not those who hear the
law who are righteous before God, but those who do the law will
be declared righteous. 14 For whenever the Gentiles, who do not
have the law, do by nature the things required by the law, these
who do not have the law are a law to themselves. 15 They show
that the work of the law is written in their hearts, as their conscience bears witness and their conflicting thoughts accuse or
else defend them, 16 on the day when God will judge the secrets
of human hearts, according to my gospel through Christ Jesus.

THE CONDEMNATION OF THE JEW

17 But if you call yourself a Jew and rely on the law and boast
of your relationship to God 18 and know his will and approve
the superior things because you receive instruction from the

law, 19 and if you are convinced that you yourself are a guide
to the blind, a light to those who are in darkness, 20 an educa-
tor of the senseless, a teacher of little children, because you
have in the law the essential features of knowledge and of the
truth—21 therefore you who teach someone else, do you not
teach yourself? You who preach against stealing, do you steal?
22 You who tell others not to commit adultery, do you commit
adultery? You who abhor idols, do you rob temples? 23 You who
boast in the law dishonor God by transgressing the law! 24 For
just as it is written, "***the name of God is being blasphemed among***
the Gentiles because of you."

25 For circumcision has its value if you practice the law, but
if you break the law, your circumcision has become uncircumcision. 26 Therefore if the uncircumcised man obeys the righteous requirements of the law, will not his uncircumcision be
regarded as circumcision? 27 And the physically uncircumcised
man, by keeping the law, will judge you to be the transgressor
of the law, even though you have the letter and circumcision!
28 For a person is not a Jew who is one outwardly, nor is circumcision something that is outward in the flesh, 29 but someone is
a Jew who is one inwardly, and circumcision is of the heart by
the Spirit and not by the letter. This person's praise is not from
people but from God.

3 Therefore what advantage does the Jew have, or what is the
value of circumcision? 2 Actually, there are many advantages.
First of all, the Jews were entrusted with the oracles of God.
3 What then? If some were unfaithful, their unfaithfulness will
not nullify God's faithfulness, will it? 4 Absolutely not! Let God
be proven true, and every human being shown up as a liar, just
as it is written: "***so that you will be justified in your words and will***
prevail when you are judged."

5 But if our unrighteousness demonstrates the righteousness
of God, what shall we say? The God who inflicts wrath is not unrighteous, is he? (I am speaking in human terms.) 6 Absolutely
not! For otherwise how could God judge the world? 7 For if by
my lie the truth of God enhances his glory, why am I still actually being judged as a sinner? 8 And why not say, "Let us do evil
so that good may come of it"?—as some who slander us allege
that we say. (Their condemnation is deserved!)

THE CONDEMNATION OF THE WORLD

9 What then? Are we better off? Certainly not, for we have already charged that Jews and Greeks alike are all under sin, 10 just
as it is written:

"There is no one righteous, not even one,
11 ***there is no one who understands,***
there is no one who seeks God.
12 ***All have turned away,***
together they have become worthless;
there is no one who shows kindness, not even one."
13 ***"Their throats are open graves,***
they deceive with their tongues,
the poison of asps is under their lips."
14 ***"Their mouths are full of cursing and bitterness."***

15 ***"Their feet are swift to shed blood,***
16 ***ruin and misery are in their paths,***
17 ***and the way of peace they have not known."***
18 ***"There is no fear of God before their eyes."***

19 Now we know that whatever the law says, it says to those who
are under the law, so that every mouth may be silenced and the
whole world may be held accountable to God. 20 For *no one is de-*
clared righteous before him by the works of the law, for through
the law comes the knowledge of sin. 21 But now apart from the
law the righteousness of God (although it is attested by the law
and the prophets) has been disclosed—22 namely, the righteousness of God through the faithfulness of Jesus Christ for all who
believe. For there is no distinction, 23 for all have sinned and
fall short of the glory of God. 24 But they are justified freely by
his grace through the redemption that is in Christ Jesus. 25 God
publicly displayed him at his death as the mercy seat accessible
through faith. This was to demonstrate his righteousness, because God in his forbearance had passed over the sins previously
committed. 26 This was also to demonstrate his righteousness in
the present time, so that he would be just and the justifier of
the one who lives because of Jesus' faithfulness.
27 Where, then, is boasting? It is excluded! By what principle? Of
works? No, but by the principle of faith! 28 For we consider that
a person is declared righteous by faith apart from the works of
the law. 29 Or is God the God of the Jews only? Is he not the God
of the Gentiles too? Yes, of the Gentiles too! 30 Since God is one,
he will justify the circumcised by faith and the uncircumcised
through faith. 31 Do we then nullify the law through faith? Absolutely not! Instead we uphold the law.

GOD'S HEART FOR THE NATIONS

Romans 3:29

Or is God the God of the Jews only? Is he not the God of the Gentiles too? Yes, of the Gentiles too!

THE ILLUSTRATION OF JUSTIFICATION

4 What then shall we say that Abraham, our ancestor according to the flesh, has discovered regarding this matter? 2 For
if Abraham was declared righteous by works, he has something
to boast about—but not before God. 3 For what does the scripture say? "***Abraham believed God, and it was credited to him as***
righteousness." 4 Now to the one who works, his pay is not credited due to grace but due to obligation. 5 But to the one who does
not work, but believes in the one who declares the ungodly righteous, his faith is credited as righteousness.
6 So even David himself speaks regarding the blessedness of
the man to whom God credits righteousness apart from works:
7 ***"Blessed are those whose lawless deeds are***
forgiven, and whose sins are covered;
8 ***blessed is the one against whom the***
Lord will never count sin."

9 Is this blessedness then for the circumcision or also for the
uncircumcision? For we say, "*faith **was credited to Abraham as***
righteousness." 10 How then was it credited to him? Was he circumcised at the time, or not? No, he was not circumcised but
uncircumcised! 11 And he received the sign of circumcision as a
seal of the righteousness that he had by faith while he was still

CHALLENGE

How did Abraham receive righteousness? How do we receive righteousness? Are the two different? If so, how? If not, why are they the same?

uncircumcised, so that he would become the father of all those
who believe but have never been circumcised, that they too
could have righteousness credited to them. 12 And he is also the
father of the circumcised, who are not only circumcised, but who
also walk in the footsteps of the faith that our father Abraham
possessed when he was still uncircumcised.
13 For the promise to Abraham or to his descendants that he
would inherit the world was not fulfilled through the law, but
through the righteousness that comes by faith. 14 For if they become heirs by the law, faith is empty and the promise is nullified.
15 For the law brings wrath, because where there is no law there is
no transgression either. 16 For this reason it is by faith so that it may
be by grace, with the result that the promise may be certain to all
the descendants—not only to those who are under the law, but also
to those who have the faith of Abraham, who is the father of us all
17 (as it is written, "***I have made you the father of many nations***"). He
is our father in the presence of God whom he believed—the God
who makes the dead alive and summons the things that do not yet
exist as though they already do. 18 Against hope Abraham believed
in hope with the result that he became ***the father of many nations***
according to the pronouncement, "***so will your descendants be.***"
19 Without being weak in faith, he considered his own body as dead
(because he was about 100 years old) and the deadness of Sarah's
womb. 20 He did not waver in unbelief about the promise of God
but was strengthened in faith, giving glory to God. 21 He was fully
convinced that what God promised he was also able to do. 22 So indeed it was credited to Abraham as righteousness.
23 But the statement ***it was credited to him*** was not written
only for Abraham's sake, 24 but also for our sake, to whom it will
be credited, those who believe in the one who raised Jesus our
Lord from the dead. 25 He was given over because of our transgressions and was raised for the sake of our justification.

THE EXPECTATION OF JUSTIFICATION

5 Therefore, since we have been declared righteous by faith, we
have peace with God through our Lord Jesus Christ, 2 through
whom we have also obtained access into this grace in which
we stand, and we rejoice in the hope of God's glory. 3 Not only
this, but we also rejoice in sufferings, knowing that suffering
produces endurance, 4 and endurance, character, and character, hope. 5 And hope does not disappoint, because the love of
God has been poured out in our hearts through the Holy Spirit
who was given to us.
6 For while we were still helpless, at the right time Christ died
for the ungodly. 7 (For rarely will anyone die for a righteous person,
though for a good person perhaps someone might possibly dare to
die.) 8 But God demonstrates his own love for us, in that while we
were still sinners, Christ died for us. 9 Much more then, because we
have now been declared righteous by his blood, we will be saved
through him from God's wrath. 10 For if while we were enemies we
were reconciled to God through the death of his Son, how much
more, since we have been reconciled, will we be saved by his life?
11 Not only this, but we also rejoice in God through our Lord Jesus
Christ, through whom we have now received this reconciliation.

LOVE TO GROW

RELENTLESS LOVE

ROMANS 5:8

"If you are waiting for me to tell you I love you, you'll be waiting forever."

The words pierced my soul, cleaving me from the woman I thought I was and the maternal love I thought I possessed. My heart burst into a million pieces. The words seared my brain and, I thought, branded me unloved.

Even when I'm not consciously thinking about it, that old familiar melody tries to blend into the background of my thoughts. The words play like instrumental elevator music, saying, "You are unlovable and unworthy of love." The lie resonates distinctly and relentlessly.

But God demonstrates his own love for us, in that while we were still sinners, Christ died for us (Rom 5:8).

How would God love me out of this mess? I believed God loved me by default. I thought He was forced to love me because He had to honor the biblical text that says, "God is love" (1 John 4:8). I thought God tolerated me because I was a small, insignificant part of the world He wanted saved. In my mind, love was an abstract concept dependent on what I was feeling and experiencing.

God's love isn't abstract at all. God's love shows up as a person: Jesus. Jesus is love. Jesus' love is exactly as He is: intimate, personal, all-powerful, unchanging, constant, and absolutely dependable. Jesus died for me. He died for all of the messy, broken, and rejected parts of me. Jesus loves me as I am, and there is nothing I can do to lose that love.

If God is fully committed to loving me with His relentless love, how committed am I to believing He does?

I fight daily to walk boldly, confidently, and securely in God's love and forgiveness. I fight to believe the truth, because when I believe God loves me, I am no longer desperate for everyone else to love me. God's relentless love for me shapes the way I live and the way I love.

You and I are never "unloved." On those days when we forget we are loved, we can run to the precious pages of His living Word for proof. There we are always reminded that we are fully known, fully accepted, and deeply loved.

THE AMPLIFICATION OF JUSTIFICATION

12 So then, just as sin entered the world through one man and death through sin, and so death spread to all people because all sinned— 13 for before the law was given, sin was in the world, but there is no accounting for sin when there is no law. 14 Yet death reigned from Adam until Moses even over those who did not sin in the same way that Adam (who is a type of the coming one) transgressed. 15 But the gracious gift is not like the transgression. For if the many died through the transgression of the one man, how much more did the grace of God and the gift by the grace of the one man Jesus Christ multiply to the many! 16 And the gift is not like the one who sinned. For judgment, resulting from the one transgression, led to condemnation, but the gracious gift from the many failures led to justification. 17 For if, by the transgression of the one man, death reigned through the one, how much more will those who receive the abundance of grace and of the gift of righteousness reign in life through the one, Jesus Christ!

18 Consequently, just as condemnation for all people came through one transgression, so too through the one righteous act came righteousness leading to life for all people. 19 For just as through the disobedience of the one man many were constituted sinners, so also through the obedience of one man many will be constituted righteous. 20 Now the law came in so that the transgression may increase, but where sin increased, grace multiplied all the more, 21 so that just as sin reigned in death, so also grace will reign through righteousness to eternal life through Jesus Christ our Lord.

THE BELIEVER'S FREEDOM FROM SIN'S DOMINATION

6 What shall we say then? Are we to remain in sin so that grace may increase? 2 Absolutely not! How can we who died to sin still live in it? 3 Or do you not know that as many as were baptized into Christ Jesus were baptized into his death? 4 Therefore we have been buried with him through baptism into death, in order that just as Christ was raised from the dead through the glory of the Father, so we too may live a new life.

5 For if we have become united with him in the likeness of his death, we will certainly also be united in the likeness of his resurrection. 6 We know that our old man was crucified with him so that the body of sin would no longer dominate us, so that we would no longer be enslaved to sin. 7 (For someone who has died has been freed from sin.)

8 Now if we died with Christ, we believe that we will also live with him. 9 We know that since Christ has been raised from the dead, he is never going to die again; death no longer has mastery over him. 10 For the death he died, he died to sin once for all, but the life he lives, he lives to God. 11 So you too consider yourselves dead to sin, but alive to God in Christ Jesus.

12 Therefore do not let sin reign in your mortal body so that you obey its desires, 13 and do not present your members to sin as instruments to be used for unrighteousness, but present yourselves to God as those who are alive from the dead and your members to God as instruments to be used for righteousness. 14 For sin will have no mastery over you, because you are not under law but under grace.

THE BELIEVER'S ENSLAVEMENT TO GOD'S RIGHTEOUSNESS

15 What then? Shall we sin because we are not under law but under grace? Absolutely not! 16 Do you not know that if you present yourselves as obedient slaves, you are slaves of the one
you obey, either of sin resulting in death, or obedience resulting in righteousness? 17 But thanks be to God that though you
were slaves to sin, you obeyed from the heart that pattern of
teaching you were entrusted to, 18 and having been freed from
sin, you became enslaved to righteousness. 19 (I am speaking in
human terms because of the weakness of your flesh.) For just
as you once presented your members as slaves to impurity and
lawlessness leading to more lawlessness, so now present your
members as slaves to righteousness leading to sanctification.
20 For when you were slaves of sin, you were free with regard to
righteousness.

21 So what benefit did you then reap from those things that you
are now ashamed of? For the end of those things is death. 22 But
now, freed from sin and enslaved to God, you have your benefit
leading to sanctification, and the end is eternal life. 23 For the
payoff of sin is death, but the gift of God is eternal life in Christ
Jesus our Lord.

THE BELIEVER'S RELATIONSHIP TO THE LAW

7 Or do you not know, brothers and sisters (for I am speaking to those who know the law), that the law is lord over a
person as long as he lives? 2 For a married woman is bound
by law to her husband as long as he lives, but if her husband
dies, she is released from the law of the marriage. 3 So then, if
she is joined to another man while her husband is alive, she
will be called an adulteress. But if her husband dies, she is
free from that law, and if she is joined to another man, she is
not an adulteress. 4 So, my brothers and sisters, you also died
to the law through the body of Christ, so that you could be
joined to another, to the one who was raised from the dead,
to bear fruit to God. 5 For when we were in the flesh, the sinful
desires, aroused by the law, were active in the members of our
body to bear fruit for death. 6 But now we have been released
from the law, because we have died to what controlled us, so
that we may serve in the new life of the Spirit and not under
the old written code.

7 What shall we say then? Is the law sin? Absolutely not! Certainly, I would not have known sin except through the law. For
indeed I would not have known what it means to desire something belonging to someone else if the law had not said, ***"Do not
covet."*** 8 But sin, seizing the opportunity through the commandment, produced in me all kinds of wrong desires. For apart from
the law, sin is dead. 9 And I was once alive apart from the law, but
with the coming of the commandment sin became alive 10 and I
died. So I found that the very commandment that was intended
to bring life brought death! 11 For sin, seizing the opportunity
through the commandment, deceived me and through it I died.
12 So then, the law is holy, and the commandment is holy, righteous, and good.

13 Did that which is good, then, become death to me? Absolutely
not! But sin, so that it would be shown to be sin, produced death
in me through what is good, so that through the commandment
sin would become utterly sinful. 14 For we know that the law is
spiritual—but I am unspiritual, sold into slavery to sin. 15 For I
don't understand what I am doing. For I do not do what I want—
instead, I do what I hate. 16 But if I do what I don't want, I agree
that the law is good. 17 But now it is no longer me doing it, but
sin that lives in me. 18 For I know that nothing good lives in me,
that is, in my flesh. For I want to do the good, but I cannot do it.
19 For I do not do the good I want, but I do the very evil I do not
want! 20 Now if I do what I do not want, it is no longer me doing
it but sin that lives in me.

REFLECT

How does Christ's sacrifice justify us?

21 So, I find the law that when I want to do good, evil is present
with me. 22 For I delight in the law of God in my inner being.
23 But I see a different law in my members waging war against
the law of my mind and making me captive to the law of sin that
is in my members. 24 Wretched man that I am! Who will rescue
me from this body of death? 25 Thanks be to God through Jesus
Christ our Lord! So then, I myself serve the law of God with my
mind, but with my flesh I serve the law of sin.

THE BELIEVER'S RELATIONSHIP TO THE HOLY SPIRIT

8 There is therefore now no condemnation for those who are
in Christ Jesus. 2 For the law of the life-giving Spirit in Christ
Jesus has set you free from the law of sin and death. 3 For God
achieved what the law could not do because it was weakened
through the flesh. By sending his own Son in the likeness of
sinful flesh and concerning sin, he condemned sin in the flesh,
4 so that the righteous requirement of the law may be fulfilled
in us, who do not walk according to the flesh but according to
the Spirit.

5 For those who live according to the flesh have their outlook
shaped by the things of the flesh, but those who live according to the Spirit have their outlook shaped by the things of the
Spirit. 6 For the outlook of the flesh is death, but the outlook of
the Spirit is life and peace, 7 because the outlook of the flesh is
hostile to God, for it does not submit to the law of God, nor is
it able to do so. 8 Those who are in the flesh cannot please God.
9 You, however, are not in the flesh but in the Spirit, if indeed the
Spirit of God lives in you. Now if anyone does not have the Spirit
of Christ, this person does not belong to him. 10 But if Christ is
in you, your body is dead because of sin, but the Spirit is your
life because of righteousness. 11 Moreover if the Spirit of the one
who raised Jesus from the dead lives in you, the one who raised
Christ from the dead will also make your mortal bodies alive
through his Spirit who lives in you.

12 So then, brothers and sisters, we are under obligation, not
to the flesh, to live according to the flesh 13 (for if you live according to the flesh, you will die), but if by the Spirit you put to
death the deeds of the body you will live. 14 For all who are led by
the Spirit of God are the sons of God. 15 For you did not receive
the spirit of slavery leading again to fear, but you received the
Spirit of adoption, by whom we cry, "*Abba*, Father." 16 The Spirit

himself bears witness to our spirit that we are God's children.
17 And if children, then heirs (namely, heirs of God and also fellow heirs with Christ)—if indeed we suffer with him so we may
also be glorified with him.
18 For I consider that our present sufferings cannot even be
compared to the coming glory that will be revealed to us. 19 For
the creation eagerly waits for the revelation of the sons of God.
20 For the creation was subjected to futility—not willingly but because of God who subjected it—in hope 21 that the creation itself
will also be set free from the bondage of decay into the glorious
freedom of God's children. 22 For we know that the whole creation groans and suffers together until now. 23 Not only this, but
we ourselves also, who have the firstfruits of the Spirit, groan inwardly as we eagerly await our adoption, the redemption of our
bodies. 24 For in hope we were saved. Now hope that is seen is
not hope, because who hopes for what he sees? 25 But if we hope
for what we do not see, we eagerly wait for it with endurance.
26 In the same way, the Spirit helps us in our weakness, for we
do not know how we should pray, but the Spirit himself intercedes for us with inexpressible groanings. 27 And he who searches
our hearts knows the mind of the Spirit, because the Spirit intercedes on behalf of the saints according to God's will. 28 And we
know that all things work together for good for those who love
God, who are called according to his purpose, 29 because those
whom he foreknew he also predestined to be conformed to the
image of his Son, that his Son would be the firstborn among
many brothers and sisters. 30 And those he predestined, he also
called; and those he called, he also justified; and those he justified, he also glorified.
31 What then shall we say about these things? If God is for
us, who can be against us? 32 Indeed, he who did not spare
his own Son, but gave him up for us all—how will he not also,
along with him, freely give us all things? 33 Who will bring any
charge against God's elect? It is God who justifies. 34 Who is
the one who will condemn? Christ is the one who died (and
more than that, he was raised), who is at the right hand of
God, and who also is interceding for us. 35 Who will separate
us from the love of Christ? Will trouble, or distress, or persecution, or famine, or nakedness, or danger, or sword? 36 As it
is written, ***"For your sake we encounter death all day long; we
were considered as sheep to be slaughtered."*** 37 No, in all these
things we have complete victory through him who loved us!
38 For I am convinced that neither death, nor life, nor angels,
nor heavenly rulers, nor things that are present, nor things
to come, nor powers, 39 nor height, nor depth, nor anything
else in creation will be able to separate us from the love of
God in Christ Jesus our Lord.

ISRAEL'S REJECTION CONSIDERED

9 I am telling the truth in Christ (I am not lying!), for my conscience assures me in the Holy Spirit—2 I have great sorrow
and unceasing anguish in my heart. 3 For I could wish that I myself were accursed—cut off from Christ—for the sake of my people, my fellow countrymen, 4 who are Israelites. To them belong

LOVE TO GROW

NOTHING

ROMANS 8:37–39

There is nothing in this world that can separate you from God's love.

Let that truth soak deep into your heart.

There is nothing you can do to earn His love, and there is nothing you can do to push God's love away.

The mistakes of your past and the mistakes in your future: God sees them all, and over and over again, He chooses to love you.

God's love is secure. It is constant, like the setting of the sun or the rotation of the earth. It is dependable and eternal.

In our broken world filled with broken relationships, love is often more conditional than unconditional. That's not the case with God. God's love is immeasurable. It's beyond "to the moon and back." It's more like "to the moon and beyond." It is limitless. Nothing is more powerful than His love for His children. Others may have rejected you, but God never does. You are secure in His love.

In all these things we have complete victory through him who loved us! For I am convinced that neither death, nor life, nor angels, nor heavenly rulers, nor things that are present, nor things to come, nor powers, nor height, nor depth, nor anything else in creation will be able to separate us from the love of God in Christ Jesus our Lord (Rom 8:37–39).

Even when we can't fathom it, His love is sure. Our belief does not hinder His love. Our circumstances do not change His affections for us. He demonstrated His love for us by dying in our place. We are loved by the One who set the earth in motion. Nothing we do will ever change that.

God sees you, knows everything about you, and loves you unconditionally.

The next time you feel unlovable and you doubt whether anyone can love you, read Romans 8:37–39 and let your heart soar. Your doubts can diminish in the light of His perfect love for you.

You are dearly and deeply loved. Nothing will ever change that. Nothing.

the adoption as sons, the glory, the covenants, the giving of the
law, the temple worship, and the promises. 5 To them belong the
patriarchs, and from them, by human descent, came the Christ,
who is God over all, blessed forever! Amen.
6 It is not as though the word of God had failed. For not all
those who are descended from Israel are truly Israel, 7 nor are
all the children Abraham's true descendants; rather ***"through
Isaac will your descendants be counted."*** 8 This means it is not
the children of the flesh who are the children of God; rather,
the children of promise are counted as descendants. 9 For this
is what the promise declared: ***"About a year from now I will
return and Sarah will have a son."*** 10 Not only that, but when
Rebekah had conceived children by one man, our ancestor
Isaac—11 even before they were born or had done anything
good or bad (so that God's purpose in election would stand,
not by works but by his calling)—12 it was said to her, ***"The older will serve the younger,"*** 13 just as it is written: ***"Jacob I loved,
but Esau I hated."***
14 What shall we say then? Is there injustice with God? Absolutely not! 15 For he says to Moses: ***"I will have mercy on whom I
have mercy, and I will have compassion on whom I have compassion."*** 16 So then, it does not depend on human desire or exertion,
but on God who shows mercy. 17 For the scripture says to Pharaoh:
***"For this very purpose I have raised you up, that I may demonstrate
my power in you, and that my name may be proclaimed in all the
earth."*** 18 So then, God has mercy on whom he chooses to have
mercy, and he hardens whom he chooses to harden.
19 You will say to me then, "Why does he still find fault? For
who has ever resisted his will?" 20 But who indeed are you—a
mere human being—to talk back to God? ***Does what is molded
say to the molder, "Why have you made me like this?"*** 21 Has the
potter no right to make from the same lump of clay one vessel for special use and another for ordinary use? 22 But what if
God, willing to demonstrate his wrath and to make known his
power, has endured with much patience the objects of wrath
prepared for destruction? 23 And what if he is willing to make
known the wealth of his glory on the objects of mercy that he
has prepared beforehand for glory—24 even us, whom he has
called, not only from the Jews but also from the Gentiles? 25 As
he also says in Hosea:

"I will call those who were not my people, 'My people,'
and I will call her who was unloved, 'My beloved.'"
26 ***"And in the very place where it was said***
to them, 'You are not my people,'
there they will be called 'sons of the living God.'"

27 And Isaiah cries out on behalf of Israel, *"Though the number
of the children of Israel are as the sand of the sea, only the remnant
will be saved, 28 for the Lord will execute his sentence on the earth
completely and quickly."* 29 Just as Isaiah predicted,

"If the Lord of Heaven's Armies had
not left us descendants,
we would have become like Sodom,
and we would have resembled Gomorrah."

REFLECT

Is God just in His actions? Should He have mercy on everyone?

ISRAEL'S REJECTION CULPABLE

30 What shall we say then?—that the Gentiles who did not pursue righteousness obtained it, that is, a righteousness that is
by faith, 31 but Israel even though pursuing a law of righteousness did not attain it. 32 Why not? Because they pursued it not
by faith but (as if it were possible) by works. They stumbled over
the stumbling stone, 33 just as it is written,

"Look, I am laying in Zion a stone that
will cause people to stumble
and a rock that will make them fall,
yet the one who believes in him will not be put to shame."

10 Brothers and sisters, my heart's desire and prayer to God
on behalf of my fellow Israelites is for their salvation. 2 For I
can testify that they are zealous for God, but their zeal is not in
line with the truth. 3 For ignoring the righteousness that comes
from God, and seeking instead to establish their own righteousness, they did not submit to God's righteousness. 4 For Christ is
the end of the law, with the result that there is righteousness
for everyone who believes.

5 For Moses writes about the righteousness that is by the law:
"***The one who does these things will live by them.***" 6 But the righteousness that is by faith says: "***Do not say in your heart, 'Who***
will ascend into heaven?'" (that is, to bring Christ down) 7 or "***Who***
will descend into the abyss?" (that is, to bring Christ up from the
dead). 8 But what does it say? "***The word is near you, in your mouth***
and in your heart" (that is, the word of faith that we preach), 9 because if you confess with your mouth that Jesus is Lord and believe in your heart that God raised him from the dead, you will
be saved. 10 For with the heart one believes and thus has righteousness and with the mouth one confesses and thus has salvation. 11 For the scripture says, "***Everyone who believes in him will***
not be put to shame." 12 For there is no distinction between the
Jew and the Greek, for the same Lord is Lord of all, who richly
blesses all who call on him. 13 For ***everyone who calls on the name***
of the Lord will be saved.

14 How are they to call on one they have not believed in? And
how are they to believe in one they have not heard of? And how
are they to hear without someone preaching to them? 15 And
how are they to preach unless they are sent? As it is written,
"***How timely is the arrival of those who proclaim the good news.***"
16 But not all have obeyed the good news, for Isaiah says, "***Lord,***
who has believed our report?" 17 Consequently faith comes from
what is heard, and what is heard comes through the preached
word of Christ.

18 But I ask, have they not heard? Yes, they have: ***Their voice***
has gone out to all the earth, and their words to the ends of the
world. 19 But again I ask, didn't Israel understand? First Moses
says, "***I will make you jealous by those who are not a nation; with a***
senseless nation I will provoke you to anger." 20 And Isaiah is even
bold enough to say, "***I was found by those who did not seek me; I***
became well known to those who did not ask for me." 21 But about
Israel he says, "***All day long I held out my hands to this disobedi-***
ent and stubborn people!"

ISRAEL'S REJECTION NOT COMPLETE NOR FINAL

11 So I ask, God has not rejected his people, has he? Absolutely
not! For I too am an Israelite, a descendant of Abraham, from
the tribe of Benjamin. 2 God has not rejected his people whom
he foreknew! Do you not know what the scripture says about
Elijah, how he pleads with God against Israel? 3 "Lord, ***they have***
killed your prophets, they have demolished your altars; I alone
am left and they are seeking my life!" 4 But what was the divine
response to him? "***I have kept*** for myself ***7,000 people who have***
not bent the knee to Baal."
5 So in the same way at the present time there is a remnant
chosen by grace. 6 And if it is by grace, it is no longer by works,
otherwise grace would no longer be grace. 7 What then? Israel
failed to obtain what it was diligently seeking, but the elect obtained it. The rest were hardened, 8 as it is written,

"***God gave them a spirit of stupor,***
eyes that would not see and ears that would not hear,
to this very day."

9 And David says,

"***Let their table become a snare and trap,***
a stumbling block and a retribution for them;
10 ***let their eyes be darkened so that they may not see,***
and make their backs bend continually."

11 I ask then, they did not stumble into an irrevocable fall, did
they? Absolutely not! But by their transgression salvation has
come to the Gentiles, to make Israel jealous. 12 Now if their transgression means riches for the world and their defeat means riches
for the Gentiles, how much more will their full restoration bring?
13 Now I am speaking to you Gentiles. Seeing that I am an apostle to the Gentiles, I magnify my ministry, 14 if somehow I could
provoke my people to jealousy and save some of them. 15 For if
their rejection is the reconciliation of the world, what will their
acceptance be but life from the dead? 16 If the first portion of the
dough offered is holy, then the whole batch is holy, and if the
root is holy, so too are the branches.
17 Now if some of the branches were broken off, and you, a wild
olive shoot, were grafted in among them and participated in the
richness of the olive root, 18 do not boast over the branches. But
if you boast, remember that you do not support the root, but the
root supports you. 19 Then you will say, "The branches were broken
off so that I could be grafted in." 20 Granted! They were broken off
because of their unbelief, but you stand by faith. Do not be arrogant, but fear! 21 For if God did not spare the natural branches,
perhaps he will not spare you. 22 Notice therefore the kindness
and harshness of God—harshness toward those who have fallen,
but God's kindness toward you, provided you continue in his
kindness; otherwise you also will be cut off. 23 And even they—if
they do not continue in their unbelief—will be grafted in, for
God is able to graft them in again. 24 For if you were cut off from
what is by nature a wild olive tree, and grafted, contrary to nature, into a cultivated olive tree, how much more will these natural branches be grafted back into their own olive tree?

25 For I do not want you to be ignorant of this mystery, brothers and sisters, so that you may not be conceited: A partial
hardening has happened to Israel until the full number of the
Gentiles has come in. 26 And so all Israel will be saved, as it is
written:

"The Deliverer will come out of Zion;
he will remove ungodliness from Jacob.
27 *And this is my covenant with them,*
when I take away their sins."

28 In regard to the gospel they are enemies for your sake,
but in regard to election they are dearly loved for the sake of
the fathers. 29 For the gifts and the call of God are irrevocable. 30 Just as you were formerly disobedient to God, but have
now received mercy due to their disobedience, 31 so they too
have now been disobedient in order that, by the mercy shown
to you, they too may now receive mercy. 32 For God has consigned all people to disobedience so that he may show mercy
to them all.

33 Oh, the depth of the riches and wisdom and knowledge of
God! How unsearchable are his judgments and how unfathomable his ways!

34 *For who has known the mind of the Lord,*
or who has been his counselor?
35 *Or who has first given to God,*
that God needs to repay him?

36 For from him and through him and to him are all things. To
him be glory forever! Amen.

CONSECRATION OF THE BELIEVER'S LIFE

12 Therefore I exhort you, brothers and sisters, by the mercies of God, to present your bodies as a sacrifice—alive,
holy, and pleasing to God—which is your reasonable service.
2 Do not be conformed to this present world, but be transformed by the renewing of your mind, so that you may test
and approve what is the will of God—what is good and well-
pleasing and perfect.

CONDUCT IN HUMILITY

3 For by the grace given to me I say to every one of you not to
think more highly of yourself than you ought to think, but
to think with sober discernment, as God has distributed to
each of you a measure of faith. 4 For just as in one body we
have many members, and not all the members serve the same
function, 5 so we who are many are one body in Christ, and individually we are members who belong to one another. 6 And
we have different gifts according to the grace given to us. If
the gift is prophecy, that individual must use it in proportion
to his faith. 7 If it is service, he must serve; if it is teaching, he
must teach; 8 if it is exhortation, he must exhort; if it is contributing, he must do so with sincerity; if it is leadership, he
must do so with diligence; if it is showing mercy, he must do
so with cheerfulness.

REFLECT

What does it mean to make ourselves a living sacrifice? How do we renew our minds daily?

TAKING OFF THE MASK

ROMANS 12:4–21

Paul described the church as the body of Christ. Each of us is a part of the body, functioning together with believers all over the world (Rom 12:4). Each of us has a distinctive purpose and function. Our goal is to learn to work together as one.

It is through love that the body of Christ is connected.

We use the word *love* to express something we like very much or possess strong feelings toward. Christian love is more than that. It requires action and commitment. It's love that is genuine, not forced.

The idea of love "without hypocrisy" (Rom 12:9) comes from ancient Greek theater. The word *hypokrites* means "actor" or "stage player." Many people are familiar with the smiling mask and sad mask symbolic of Greek comedy and tragedy. A hypocrite is someone acting under a mask. Thus, the English word describes someone whose behavior contradicts his or her beliefs.

Genuine love is a mark of a true Christian. Jesus told His disciples in John 13:35, "Everyone will know by this that you are my disciples—if you have love for one another." Genuine love implies action. It's something we display every day. This means getting involved in the lives of other Christians and deepening our relationships with one another. It means removing our masks.

When our love is genuine, we share the seasons of joy and the seasons of grief with our brothers and sisters in the faith. We provide for their physical, emotional, and spiritual needs. We pray fervently for their lives.

Love connects the body of Christ. As we live out genuine love for one another, we show the world the genuine love of Christ. We bring hope to a broken world by making ourselves known as His disciples. Let's allow genuine love to shine through our actions and proclaim the name of Christ.

CONDUCT IN LOVE

9 Love must be without hypocrisy. Abhor what is evil, cling to what is good. 10 Be devoted to one another with mutual love, showing eagerness in honoring one another. 11 Do not lag in zeal, be enthusiastic in spirit, serve the Lord. 12 Rejoice in hope, endure in suffering, persist in prayer. 13 Contribute to the needs of the saints, pursue hospitality. 14 Bless those who persecute you, bless and do not curse. 15 Rejoice with those who rejoice, weep with those who weep. 16 Live in harmony with one another; do not be haughty but associate with the lowly. Do not be conceited. 17 Do not repay anyone evil for evil; consider what is good before all people. 18 If possible, so far as it depends on you, live peaceably with all people. 19 Do not avenge yourselves, dear friends, but give place to God's wrath, for it is written, "***Vengeance is mine, I will repay***," says the Lord. 20 Rather, ***if your enemy is hungry, feed him; if he is thirsty, give him a drink; for in doing this you will be heaping burning coals on his head.*** 21 Do not be overcome by evil, but overcome evil with good.

SUBMISSION TO CIVIL GOVERNMENT

13 Let every person be subject to the governing authorities. For there is no authority except by God's appointment, and the authorities that exist have been instituted by God. 2 So the person who resists such authority resists the ordinance of God, and those who resist will incur judgment 3 (for rulers cause no fear for good conduct but for bad). Do you desire not to fear authority? Do good and you will receive its commendation 4 because it is God's servant for your well-being. But be afraid if you do wrong because government does not bear the sword for nothing. It is God's servant to administer punishment on the person who does wrong. 5 Therefore it is necessary to be in subjection, not only because of the wrath of the authorities but also because of your conscience. 6 For this reason you also pay taxes, for the authorities are God's servants devoted to governing. 7 Pay everyone what is owed: taxes to whom taxes are due, revenue to whom revenue is due, respect to whom respect is due, honor to whom honor is due.

EXHORTATION TO LOVE NEIGHBORS

8 Owe no one anything, except to love one another, for the one who loves his neighbor has fulfilled the law. 9 For the commandments, "***Do not commit adultery, do not murder, do not steal, do not covet***," (and if there is any other commandment) are summed up in this, "***Love your neighbor as yourself.***" 10 Love does no wrong to a neighbor. Therefore love is the fulfillment of the law.

MOTIVATION TO GODLY CONDUCT

11 And do this because we know the time, that it is already the hour for us to awake from sleep, for our salvation is now nearer than when we became believers. 12 The night has advanced toward dawn; the day is near. So then we must lay aside the works of darkness, and put on the weapons of light. 13 Let us live decently as in the daytime, not in carousing and drunkenness, not in sexual immorality and sensuality, not in discord and jealousy. 14 Instead, put on the Lord Jesus Christ, and make no provision for the flesh to arouse its desires.

EXHORTATION TO MUTUAL FORBEARANCE

14 Now receive the one who is weak in the faith, and do not
have disputes over differing opinions. 2 One person believes
in eating everything, but the weak person eats only vegetables.
3 The one who eats everything must not despise the one who does
not, and the one who abstains must not judge the one who eats
everything, for God has accepted him. 4 Who are you to pass judgment on another's servant? Before his own master he stands or
falls. And he will stand, for the Lord is able to make him stand.
5 One person regards one day holier than other days, and another regards them all alike. Each must be fully convinced in his
own mind. 6 The one who observes the day does it for the Lord.
The one who eats, eats for the Lord because he gives thanks to
God, and the one who abstains from eating abstains for the Lord,
and he gives thanks to God. 7 For none of us lives for himself and
none dies for himself. 8 If we live, we live for the Lord; if we die,
we die for the Lord. Therefore, whether we live or die, we are the
Lord's. 9 For this reason Christ died and returned to life, so that
he may be the Lord of both the dead and the living.
10 But you who eat vegetables only—why do you judge your
brother or sister? And you who eat everything—why do you despise your brother or sister? For we will all stand before the
judgment seat of God. 11 For it is written, "***As I live, says the Lord,***
every knee will bow to me, and every tongue will give praise to God."
12 Therefore, each of us will give an account of himself to God.

EXHORTATION FOR THE STRONG NOT TO DESTROY THE WEAK

13 Therefore we must not pass judgment on one another, but rather
determine never to place an obstacle or a trap before a brother or
sister. 14 I know and am convinced in the Lord Jesus that there is
nothing unclean in itself; still, it is unclean to the one who considers it unclean. 15 For if your brother or sister is distressed because
of what you eat, you are no longer walking in love. Do not destroy
by your food someone for whom Christ died. 16 Therefore do not let
what you consider good be spoken of as evil. 17 For the kingdom of
God does not consist of food and drink, but righteousness, peace,
and joy in the Holy Spirit. 18 For the one who serves Christ in this
way is pleasing to God and approved by people.
19 So then, let us pursue what makes for peace and for building up one another. 20 Do not destroy the work of God for the
sake of food. For although all things are clean, it is wrong to
cause anyone to stumble by what you eat. 21 It is good not to eat
meat or drink wine or to do anything that causes your brother
to stumble. 22 The faith you have, keep to yourself before God.
Blessed is the one who does not judge himself by what he approves. 23 But the man who doubts is condemned if he eats, because he does not do so from faith, and whatever is not from
faith is sin.

EXHORTATION FOR THE STRONG TO HELP THE WEAK

15 But we who are strong ought to bear with the failings of the
weak, and not just please ourselves. 2 Let each of us please
his neighbor for his good to build him up. 3 For even Christ did

not please himself, but just as it is written, "***The insults of those***
who insult you have fallen on me." 4 For everything that was written in former times was written for our instruction, so that
through endurance and through encouragement of the scriptures we may have hope. 5 Now may the God of endurance and
comfort give you unity with one another in accordance with
Christ Jesus, 6 so that together you may with one voice glorify
the God and Father of our Lord Jesus Christ.

GOD'S HEART FOR THE NATIONS

Romans 15:11

And again, "Praise the Lord all you Gentiles, and let all the peoples praise him."

EXHORTATION TO MUTUAL ACCEPTANCE

7 Receive one another, then, just as Christ also received you, to
God's glory. 8 For I tell you that Christ has become a servant of
the circumcised on behalf of God's truth to confirm the promises made to the fathers, 9 and thus the Gentiles glorify God
for his mercy. As it is written, "***Because of this I will confess you***
among the Gentiles, and I will sing praises to your name." 10 And
again it says: "***Rejoice, O Gentiles, with his people.***" 11 And again,
"***Praise the Lord all you Gentiles, and let all the peoples praise***
him." 12 And again Isaiah says, "***The root of Jesse will come, and***
the one who rises to rule over the Gentiles, in him will the Gentiles
hope." 13 Now may the God of hope fill you with all joy and peace
as you believe in him, so that you may abound in hope by the
power of the Holy Spirit.

PAUL'S MOTIVATION FOR WRITING THE LETTER

14 But I myself am fully convinced about you, my brothers and
sisters, that you yourselves are full of goodness, filled with all
knowledge, and able to instruct one another. 15 But I have written more boldly to you on some points so as to remind you, because of the grace given to me by God 16 to be a minister of Christ
Jesus to the Gentiles. I serve the gospel of God like a priest, so
that the Gentiles may become an acceptable offering, sanctified
by the Holy Spirit.

17 So I boast in Christ Jesus about the things that pertain to
God. 18 For I will not dare to speak of anything except what
Christ has accomplished through me in order to bring about
the obedience of the Gentiles, by word and deed, 19 in the power
of signs and wonders, in the power of the Spirit of God. So from
Jerusalem even as far as Illyricum I have fully preached the
gospel of Christ. 20 And in this way I desire to preach where
Christ has not been named, so as not to build on another
person's foundation, 21 but as it is written: "***Those who were***
not told about him will see, and those who have not heard will
understand."

PAUL'S INTENTION OF VISITING THE ROMANS

22 This is the reason I was often hindered from coming to you.
23 But now there is nothing more to keep me in these regions,
and I have for many years desired to come to you 24 when I go
to Spain. For I hope to visit you when I pass through and that
you will help me on my journey there, after I have enjoyed your
company for a while.

25 But now I go to Jerusalem to minister to the saints. 26 For
Macedonia and Achaia are pleased to make some contribution

for the poor among the saints in Jerusalem. 27 For they were
pleased to do this, and indeed they are indebted to the Jerusalem saints. For if the Gentiles have shared in their spiritual
things, they are obligated also to minister to them in material
things. 28 Therefore after I have completed this and have safely
delivered this bounty to them, I will set out for Spain by way of
you, 29 and I know that when I come to you I will come in the
fullness of Christ's blessing.
30 Now I urge you, brothers and sisters, through our Lord
Jesus Christ and through the love of the Spirit, to join fervently with me in prayer to God on my behalf. 31 Pray that I
may be rescued from those who are disobedient in Judea and
that my ministry in Jerusalem may be acceptable to the saints,
32 so that by God's will I may come to you with joy and be refreshed in your company. 33 Now may the God of peace be with
all of you. Amen.

PERSONAL GREETINGS

16 Now I commend to you our sister Phoebe, who is a servant
of the church in Cenchrea, 2 so that you may welcome her
in the Lord in a way worthy of the saints and provide her with
whatever help she may need from you, for she has been a great
help to many, including me.
3 Greet Prisca and Aquila, my fellow workers in Christ Jesus,
4 who risked their own necks for my life. Not only I, but all the
churches of the Gentiles are grateful to them. 5 Also greet the
church in their house. Greet my dear friend Epenetus, who
was the first convert to Christ in the province of Asia. 6 Greet
Mary, who has worked very hard for you. 7 Greet Andronicus
and Junia, my compatriots and my fellow prisoners. They are
well known to the apostles, and they were in Christ before me.
8 Greet Ampliatus, my dear friend in the Lord. 9 Greet Urba-
nus, our fellow worker in Christ, and my good friend Stachys.
10 Greet Apelles, who is approved in Christ. Greet those who
belong to the household of Aristobulus. 11 Greet Herodion,
my compatriot. Greet those in the household of Narcissus
who are in the Lord. 12 Greet Tryphena and Tryphosa, laborers in the Lord. Greet my dear friend Persis, who has worked
hard in the Lord. 13 Greet Rufus, chosen in the Lord, and his
mother who was also a mother to me. 14 Greet Asyncritus,
Phlegon, Hermes, Patrobas, Hermas, and the brothers and
sisters with them. 15 Greet Philologus and Julia, Nereus and
his sister, and Olympas, and all the believers who are with
them. 16 Greet one another with a holy kiss. All the churches
of Christ greet you.
17 Now I urge you, brothers and sisters, to watch out for those
who create dissensions and obstacles contrary to the teaching that you learned. Avoid them! 18 For these are the kind who
do not serve our Lord Christ, but their own appetites. By their
smooth talk and flattery they deceive the minds of the naive.
19 Your obedience is known to all and thus I rejoice over you.
But I want you to be wise in what is good and innocent in what
is evil. 20 The God of peace will quickly crush Satan under your
feet. The grace of our Lord Jesus be with you.

DIFFERENCES SET ASIDE

ROMANS 16

In the Roman Empire, status was everything. People were valued based on their rank in society, their position in their family, and their wealth. Few people in this culture were legally considered "persons"—a specific title that indicated someone had full rights in the public square to buy or sell property, live protected from bodily harm, and generally make their own decisions. Women and children were the property of the heads of their households, and slaves were the property of their masters. Different social standings either limited or expanded one's rights. Differences were vitally important.

Those born into slavery were given names that signified their complete lack of social standing. If there was no chance a slave would ever ascend to the status of full "person," why bother giving them a name? A slave's name might have simply reflected his or her birth order: First, Second, Third.

It was into this remarkably segregated and hierarchical culture that the early church exploded and immediately started breaking all the rules. The rich and the poor ate together, the powerful and the weak shared their resources, and men and women worked together to spread the gospel. Upending these social rules was important for maintaining the unity of the church. Many of the epistles deal with churches that caused division by maintaining discrimination or favoritism.

Paul ended his letter to the Romans with a long list of greetings that appear random and unimportant, but bear a remarkable witness to the diversity of the early church. His list includes women, men, Greeks, Jews, slaves, and those of high social standing. Their names are important because they tell us how different these people were. Some names indicate great power or wealth, some are distinctly Greek or Jewish, and some names—like Tertius and Quartus, "Third" and "Fourth"—belonged to slaves.

One of God's greatest gifts for believers is to make us into one people.

In the early church, people with wildly different social positions shared the same value and significance—they were brothers and sisters. Their differences were not abolished or ignored but subsumed under their greater identity as fellow believers. In today's church, let's make sure "status" doesn't matter. Let's be followers of Christ who build communities that witness to the power of the gospel in unity and respect for all.

[21] Timothy, my fellow worker, greets you; so do Lucius, Jason,
and Sosipater, my compatriots. [22] I, Tertius, who am writing this
letter, greet you in the Lord. [23] Gaius, who is host to me and to
the whole church, greets you. Erastus the city treasurer and our
brother Quartus greet you.ℂ

[25] Now to him who is able to strengthen you according to my
gospel and the proclamation of Jesus Christ, according to the revelation of the mystery that had been kept secret for long ages,
[26] but now is disclosed, and through the prophetic scriptures has
been made known to all the nations, according to the command
of the eternal God, to bring about the obedience of faith—[27] to
the only wise God, through Jesus Christ, be glory forever! Amen.

REFLECT

How do we give glory to God in all we do? What can you do today to give God the glory for all He has done in your life?

So whether you eat or drink, or whatever you do, do everything for the glory of God

MEMORY VERSE

So whether you eat or drink, or whatever you do, do everything for the glory of God.

1 Corinthians 10:31

1 Corinthians

INTRODUCTION

Living for Christ

The church at Corinth was troubled. Though true believers, the Corinthians had much to gain in the area of spiritual maturity. Paul's first letter to this group displays his heart for this church as well as his disappointment in their immoral behavior. The apostle exhorted them to live lives that honored Christ instead of following the habits of the notoriously corrupt people among whom they lived.

Paul opened his letter by responding to the report he had received on the health and behavior of the church. He dealt with divisions, immorality, and lawsuits taking place within the body (1:10—6:20). He responded to their questions about marital obligations, Christian liberties, proper worship, and spiritual gifts (7:1—14:40). Finally, he addressed the necessity of Christ's resurrection to the life of a believer and how to practically live in light of this reality (15:1—16:24).

Paul is the almost unanimously accepted author of the letter of 1 Corinthians, as he is twice named as its writer (1:1; 16:21). Paul most likely wrote this letter while he was in Ephesus during his third missionary journey. This dates the letter of 1 Corinthians to around A.D. 56, in the last year of his three-year stay in Ephesus.

While 1 Corinthians contains specific instructions and commands for the church in Corinth to turn from immorality, it also includes practical application for the Christian life. First Corinthians identifies spiritual gifts and presents how believers are to use these gifts for the edification of the body. Paul offered hope to the Corinthians of Christ's victory over sin, and the victory they would receive through faith in Him. Though at times we are troubled by our own spiritual immaturity, like the Corinthians, we can be encouraged to love God greatly knowing that even though we may fail, His grace abounds. We have hope in eternal life with Him through the life of Christ.

Canada

OFFICIAL LANGUAGE
English
POPULATION
37,315,000
UNREACHED POPULATION
1,954,000
PROFESSING CHRISTIANS
73.0%

Ann's Home

Say a Prayer Today

Pray for Ann and her work as a missionary. Pray she would be an encouragement to everyone she meets and that the light of the gospel would radiate through her life.

HISTORY BIT

The first Catholic missionary to travel to Canada was a French secular clergyman who arrived in 1608. He worked among the Micmac Indians.*

Source Information:
https://joshuaproject.net/countries/CA
*David B. Barrett, World Christian Encyclopedia, Canada (New York, NY: Oxford University Press, 1982), 212.

ANN'S STORY

"So whether you eat or drink, or whatever you do, do everything for the glory of God" (1 Cor 10:31).

I discovered the truth of this verse while watching the life of a fellow missionary who was an amazingly talented cook. She always credited God for her gifting and freely expressed her thanks for how God used her. She was always full of joy and pleasure as she worked to create and share meals and goodies with others.

Since seeing her life, I've been challenged to commit everything I do to the Lord. This verse became my mantra as I struggled to keep house for a family of males. Discouraged with the menial tasks, which seemed to be endless and thankless, I was initially resentful and cross in my attitude. It was hard for everyone.

I printed this verse on a card and hung it above the sink. Daily I prayed as I worked. Even dishwashing became a thing of beauty and joy for me rather than a drudgery. I've used this verse often. I ask myself how what I am doing (however unpleasant, hard, or upsetting) can be used to glorify God. If it doesn't glorify God then it's not likely something I should be doing. Instead of complaining, I can glorify God as I serve those around me.

Daily tasks are elevated from being difficult and menial, to becoming something holy. I call it the holiness of the ordinary. God's Word influences minds and attitudes in a ripple effect, changing our lives for the better. I have felt this in my home and in my workplace. As I have worked to change my attitude and perspective, I've seen God change the hearts and attitudes of those around me. I know that in practice it can affect an entire community and even a country.

4 WEEK READING PLAN

LOVE HIS WORD

	MONDAY	TUESDAY	WEDNESDAY	THURSDAY	FRIDAY
1	1 Corinthians 1:1-17	1 Corinthians 1:18—2:5	1 Corinthians 2:6-16	1 Corinthians 3	1 Corinthians 4
	SOAP 1 Corinthians 1:4-7	SOAP 1 Corinthians 1:30	SOAP 1 Corinthians 2:9-10	SOAP 1 Corinthians 3:16-17	SOAP 1 Corinthians 4:12-13
2	1 Corinthians 5	1 Corinthians 6	1 Corinthians 7:1-16	1 Corinthians 7:17-40	1 Corinthians 8
	SOAP 1 Corinthians 5:6-7	SOAP 1 Corinthians 6:18-20	SOAP 1 Corinthians 7:16	SOAP 1 Corinthians 7:32-35	SOAP 1 Corinthians 8:12-13
3	1 Corinthians 9	1 Corinthians 10:1-13	1 Corinthians 10:14—11:1	1 Corinthians 11:2-34	1 Corinthians 12
	SOAP 1 Corinthians 9:24-25	SOAP 1 Corinthians 10:13	SOAP 1 Corinthians 10:31	SOAP 1 Corinthians 11:25-26	SOAP 1 Corinthians 12:4-6
4	1 Corinthians 13	1 Corinthians 14	1 Corinthians 15:1-34	1 Corinthians 15:35-58	1 Corinthians 16
	SOAP 1 Corinthians 13:12-13	SOAP 1 Corinthians 14:32-33	SOAP 1 Corinthians 15:20-22	SOAP 1 Corinthians 15:56-58	SOAP 1 Corinthians 16:13-14

SALUTATION
1 From Paul, called to be an apostle of Christ Jesus by the will
of God, and Sosthenes, our brother, 2 to the church of God
that is in Corinth, to those who are sanctified in Christ Jesus,
and called to be saints, with all those in every place who call
on the name of our Lord Jesus Christ, their Lord and ours.
3 Grace and peace to you from God our Father and the Lord
Jesus Christ!

THANKSGIVING
4 I always thank my God for you because of the grace of God
that was given to you in Christ Jesus. 5 For you were made
rich in every way in him, in all your speech and in every kind
of knowledge—6 just as the testimony about Christ has been
confirmed among you—7 so that you do not lack any spiritual
gift as you wait for the revelation of our Lord Jesus Christ.
8 He will also strengthen you to the end, so that you will be
blameless on the day of our Lord Jesus Christ. 9 God is faithful, by whom you were called into fellowship with his son,
Jesus Christ our Lord.

DIVISIONS IN THE CHURCH
10 I urge you, brothers and sisters, by the name of our Lord Jesus
Christ, to agree together, to end your divisions, and to be united
by the same mind and purpose. 11 For members of Chloe's household have made it clear to me, my brothers and sisters, that there
are quarrels among you. 12 Now I mean this, that each of you is
saying, "I am with Paul," or "I am with Apollos," or "I am with Cephas," or "I am with Christ." 13 Is Christ divided? Paul wasn't crucified for you, was he? Or were you in fact baptized in the name
of Paul? 14 I thank God that I did not baptize any of you except
Crispus and Gaius, 15 so that no one can say that you were baptized in my name! 16 (I also baptized the household of Stephanus. Otherwise, I do not remember whether I baptized anyone
else.) 17 For Christ did not send me to baptize, but to preach the
gospel—and not with clever speech, so that the cross of Christ
would not become useless.

THE MESSAGE OF THE CROSS
18 For the message about the cross is foolishness to those who are
perishing, but to us who are being saved it is the power of God.
19 For it is written, "***I will destroy the wisdom of the wise, and I will***
thwart the cleverness of the intelligent." 20 Where is the wise man?
Where is the expert in the Mosaic law? Where is the debater of
this age? Has God not made the wisdom of the world foolish?
21 For since in the wisdom of God the world by its wisdom did
not know God, God was pleased to save those who believe by the
foolishness of preaching. 22 For Jews demand miraculous signs
and Greeks ask for wisdom, 23 but we preach about a crucified
Christ, a stumbling block to Jews and foolishness to Gentiles.
24 But to those who are called, both Jews and Greeks, Christ is
the power of God and the wisdom of God. 25 For the foolishness
of God is wiser than human wisdom, and the weakness of God
is stronger than human strength.

26 Think about the circumstances of your call, brothers and sisters. Not many were wise by human standards, not many were
powerful, not many were born to a privileged position. 27 But
God chose what the world thinks foolish to shame the wise, and
God chose what the world thinks weak to shame the strong. 28 God
chose what is low and despised in the world, what is regarded as
nothing, to set aside what is regarded as something, 29 so that
no one can boast in his presence. 30 He is the reason you have a
relationship with Christ Jesus, who became for us wisdom from
God, and righteousness and sanctification and redemption, 31 so
that, as it is written, "***Let the one who boasts, boast in the Lord.***"

REFLECT

What does it mean to boast in the Lord? How is this different than boasting in ourselves?

2 When I came to you, brothers and sisters, I did not come
with superior eloquence or wisdom as I proclaimed the testimony of God. 2 For I decided to be concerned about nothing
among you except Jesus Christ, and him crucified. 3 And I was
with you in weakness and in fear and with much trembling. 4 My
conversation and my preaching were not with persuasive words
of wisdom, but with a demonstration of the Spirit and of power,
5 so that your faith would not be based on human wisdom but
on the power of God.

WISDOM FROM GOD

6 Now we do speak wisdom among the mature, but not a wisdom
of this age or of the rulers of this age, who are perishing. 7 Instead
we speak the wisdom of God, hidden in a mystery, that God determined before the ages for our glory. 8 None of the rulers of this
age understood it. If they had known it, they would not have crucified the Lord of glory. 9 But just as it is written, "***Things that no
eye has seen, or ear heard, or mind imagined, are the things God
has prepared for those who love him.***" 10 God has revealed these
to us by the Spirit. For the Spirit searches all things, even the
deep things of God. 11 For who among men knows the things of
a man except the man's spirit within him? So too, no one knows
the things of God except the Spirit of God. 12 Now we have not received the spirit of the world, but the Spirit who is from God, so
that we may know the things that are freely given to us by God.
13 And we speak about these things, not with words taught us by
human wisdom, but with those taught by the Spirit, explaining
spiritual things to spiritual people. 14 The unbeliever does not receive the things of the Spirit of God, for they are foolishness to
him. And he cannot understand them, because they are spiritually discerned. 15 The one who is spiritual discerns all things, yet
he himself is understood by no one. 16 ***For who has known the mind
of the Lord, so as to advise him?*** But we have the mind of Christ.

IMMATURITY AND SELF-DECEPTION

3 So, brothers and sisters, I could not speak to you as spiritual
people, but instead as people of the flesh, as infants in Christ.
2 I fed you milk, not solid food, for you were not yet ready. In fact,
you are still not ready, 3 for you are still influenced by the flesh.
For since there is still jealousy and dissension among you, are
you not influenced by the flesh and behaving like unregenerate
people? 4 For whenever someone says, "I am with Paul," or "I am
with Apollos," are you not merely human?

LOVE TO GROW

BOAST IN THE LORD

1 CORINTHIANS 1:26–31

My family and I got up a little too late. We sped through six showers in record time. I broke up sibling quarrels and refereed which poor child had to sit in the loathed back seat of the minivan. Finally, we slipped into the back pew of our church as the music began to play.

I desperately wanted to prepare my heart for worship. I wanted to have it all together and give my best to Jesus. All I could think about was the impatience, anger, and harsh words that had hijacked our morning. It left me feeling like an imposter.

I wanted our family to walk through those church doors with our act together. I wanted to be strong instead of weak. I wanted to look put together instead of falling apart. I wanted to settle in and feel good about myself and all that I had accomplished. Then I was reminded of this verse:

"Let the one who boasts, boast in the Lord" (1 Cor 1:31).

The church isn't a perfect place full of perfect people. It's a place for the sinful to come and find hope in the person and work of Jesus. It's where the truth of who He is trumps our flaws and failures and where we worship Him for the depth of His forgiveness and the newness of His mercy. It's where the broken are welcomed, the weary can find rest, and His wisdom reigns over the hardness of our hearts and the loud voices of the world. It's where, once again, we are humbled by His sacrifice and amazed by His transforming power.

Instead of trying to impress the people around me by my own efforts, I want to boast in the work of Christ. Especially on a Sunday morning when I am late and harried, it is because of Him that I am able to join a body of believers and offer praise to Him. He holds all the power, all the ability. Let us boast in Him and Him alone.

[5]What is Apollos, really? Or what is Paul? Servants through
whom you came to believe, and each of us in the ministry the
Lord gave us. [6]I planted, Apollos watered, but God caused it to
grow. [7]So neither the one who plants counts for anything, nor
the one who waters, but God who causes the growth. [8]The one
who plants and the one who waters work as one, but each will
receive his reward according to his work. [9]We are coworkers belonging to God. You are God's field, God's building. [10]According
to the grace of God given to me, like a skilled master-builder I
laid a foundation, but someone else builds on it. And each one
must be careful how he builds. [11]For no one can lay any foundation other than what is being laid, which is Jesus Christ. [12]If anyone builds on the foundation with gold, silver, precious stones,
wood, hay, or straw, [13]each builder's work will be plainly seen,
for the Day will make it clear, because it will be revealed by fire.
And the fire will test what kind of work each has done. [14]If what
someone has built survives, he will receive a reward. [15]If someone's work is burned up, he will suffer loss. He himself will be
saved, but only as through fire.

[16]Do you not know that you are God's temple and that God's
Spirit lives in you? [17]If someone destroys God's temple, God will
destroy him. For God's temple is holy, which is what you are.

[18]Guard against self-deception, each of you. If someone among
you thinks he is wise in this age, let him become foolish so that
he can become wise. [19]For the wisdom of this age is foolishness
with God. As it is written, "***He catches the wise in their craftiness.***"
[20]And again, "***The Lord knows that the thoughts of the wise are futile.***" [21]So then, no more boasting about mere mortals! For everything belongs to you, [22]whether Paul or Apollos or Cephas
or the world or life or death or the present or the future. Everything belongs to you, [23]and you belong to Christ, and Christ belongs to God.

THE APOSTLES' MINISTRY

4 One should think about us this way—as servants of Christ
and stewards of the mysteries of God. [2]Now what is sought
in stewards is that one be found faithful. [3]So for me, it is a minor matter that I am judged by you or by any human court. In
fact, I do not even judge myself. [4]For I am not aware of anything
against myself, but I am not acquitted because of this. The one
who judges me is the Lord. [5]So then, do not judge anything before the time. Wait until the Lord comes. He will bring to light
the hidden things of darkness and reveal the motives of hearts.
Then each will receive recognition from God.

[6]I have applied these things to myself and Apollos because of
you, brothers and sisters, so that through us you may learn "not
to go beyond what is written," so that none of you will be puffed
up in favor of the one against the other. [7]For who concedes you
any superiority? What do you have that you did not receive?
And if you received it, why do you boast as though you did not?
[8]Already you are satisfied! Already you are rich! You have become kings without us! I wish you had become kings so that we
could reign with you! [9]For, I think, God has exhibited us apostles
last of all, as men condemned to die, because we have become

LOVE TO GROW

BE IMITATORS

1 CORINTHIANS 4

In 1 Corinthians, Paul addressed a church he deeply loved. The believers' behavior did not align with their faith in Jesus. The Corinthians had many misconceptions about what following Christ meant, and that caused great division in their church. The truth of the gospel, Jesus died and rose from the grave for their sin, had not affected their lives as it should have. From the outside, the Corinthians looked like any other city dwellers in their bustling, sex-crazed culture. Paul knew correction was necessary.

Paul used his own life as an example. He explained to them as servants of Christ they might be called to suffer, but their call in the midst of suffering was to be faithful.

Paul and the apostles had endured much as servants of Christ. They experienced hunger, thirst, brutality, and homelessness. Paul's contentment in the depth of his pain appeared crazy. He did not complain or question God, but rather his life served as an example. Paul even said, "I encourage you, then, be imitators of me" (1 Cor 4:16).

Why would Paul call others to imitate him when he knew what the hardship meant?

Paul believed Jesus was worth every hardship and that suffering is never pointless. Paul believed suffering cultivates a deeper dependence on God while on earth (see 2 Cor 1:9). He also knew Christ promised the kingdom of heaven to those who are persecuted for righteousness' sake (see Matt 5:10).

When we are in seemingly hopeless situations, it is good to remember God is always with us. He never leaves us or forsakes us. Faithfulness means trusting God and trusting His good and loving character, even when life feels impossible. Paul clung to this truth. Several years later, in another letter to the same church, Paul wrote,

---

For our momentary, light suffering is producing for us an eternal weight of glory far beyond all comparison because we are not looking at what can be seen but at what cannot be seen. For what can be seen is temporary, but what cannot be seen is eternal (2 Cor 4:17–18).

As Paul told the Corinthian church he loved, even in the midst of suffering, loss, grief, or pain, continue to live lives of great faithfulness. Christians' suffering is never in vain, and our faithfulness will yield both present and future rewards.

a spectacle to the world, both to angels and to people. [10] We are
fools for Christ, but you are wise in Christ! We are weak, but you
are strong! You are distinguished, we are dishonored! [11] To the
present hour we are hungry and thirsty, poorly clothed, brutally
treated, and without a roof over our heads. [12] We do hard work,
toiling with our own hands. When we are verbally abused, we
respond with a blessing, when persecuted, we endure, [13] when
people lie about us, we answer in a friendly manner. We are the
world's dirt and scum, even now.

A FATHER'S WARNING

[14] I am not writing these things to shame you, but to correct you
as my dear children. [15] For though you may have 10,000 guardians in Christ, you do not have many fathers, because I became
your father in Christ Jesus through the gospel. [16] I encourage you,
then, be imitators of me. [17] For this reason, I have sent Timothy to
you, who is my dear and faithful son in the Lord. He will remind
you of my ways in Christ, as I teach them everywhere in every
church. [18] Some have become arrogant, as if I were not coming
to you. [19] But I will come to you soon, if the Lord is willing, and I
will find out not only the talk of these arrogant people, but also
their power. [20] For the kingdom of God is demonstrated not in
idle talk but with power. [21] What do you want? Shall I come to you
with a rod of discipline or with love and a spirit of gentleness?

CHURCH DISCIPLINE

5 It is actually reported that sexual immorality exists among
you, the kind of immorality that is not permitted even among
the Gentiles, so that someone is cohabiting with his father's wife.
[2] And you are proud! Shouldn't you have been deeply sorrowful
instead and removed the one who did this from among you?
[3] For even though I am absent physically, I am present in spirit.
And I have already judged the one who did this, just as though
I were present. [4] When you gather together in the name of our
Lord Jesus, and I am with you in spirit, along with the power of
our Lord Jesus, [5] hand this man over to Satan for the destruction
of the flesh, so that his spirit may be saved in the day of the Lord.
[6] Your boasting is not good. Don't you know that a little yeast
affects the whole batch of dough? [7] Clean out the old yeast so
that you may be a new batch of dough—you are, in fact, without yeast. For Christ, our Passover lamb, has been sacrificed.
[8] So then, let us celebrate the festival, not with the old yeast,
the yeast of vice and evil, but with the bread without yeast, the
bread of sincerity and truth.
[9] I wrote you in my letter not to associate with sexually immoral people. [10] In no way did I mean the immoral people of this
world, or the greedy and swindlers and idolaters, since you would
then have to go out of the world. [11] But now I am writing to you
not to associate with anyone who calls himself a Christian who
is sexually immoral, or greedy, or an idolater, or verbally abusive,
or a drunkard, or a swindler. Do not even eat with such a person.
[12] For what do I have to do with judging those outside? Are you
not to judge those inside? [13] But God will judge those outside.
Remove the evil person from among you.

CHALLENGE

How does Paul say we should deal with immoral people? How is this different from what Jesus says about rebuking a fellow Christian in Matthew 18:15–17?

LAWSUITS

6 When any of you has a legal dispute with another, does he
dare go to court before the unrighteous rather than before
the saints? 2 Or do you not know that the saints will judge the
world? And if the world is to be judged by you, are you not competent to settle trivial suits? 3 Do you not know that we will judge
angels? Why not ordinary matters! 4 So if you have ordinary lawsuits, do you appoint as judges those who have no standing in
the church? 5 I say this to your shame! Is there no one among
you wise enough to settle disputes between fellow Christians?
6 Instead, does a Christian sue a Christian, and do this before
unbelievers? 7 The fact that you have lawsuits among yourselves
demonstrates that you have already been defeated. Why not
rather be wronged? Why not rather be cheated? 8 But you yourselves wrong and cheat, and you do this to your brothers and
sisters!

9 Do you not know that the unrighteous will not inherit the
kingdom of God? Do not be deceived! The sexually immoral,
idolaters, adulterers, passive homosexual partners, practicing
homosexuals, 10 thieves, the greedy, drunkards, the verbally abusive, and swindlers will not inherit the kingdom of God. 11 Some
of you once lived this way. But you were washed, you were sanctified, you were justified in the name of the Lord Jesus Christ
and by the Spirit of our God.

FLEE SEXUAL IMMORALITY

12 "All things are lawful for me"—but not everything is beneficial. "All things are lawful for me"—but I will not be controlled
by anything. 13 "Food is for the stomach and the stomach is for
food, but God will do away with both." The body is not for sexual
immorality, but for the Lord, and the Lord for the body. 14 Now
God indeed raised the Lord and he will raise us by his power.
15 Do you not know that your bodies are members of Christ?
Should I take the members of Christ and make them members
of a prostitute? Never! 16 Or do you not know that anyone who is
united with a prostitute is one body with her? For it is said, ***"The
two will become one flesh."*** 17 But the one united with the Lord is
one spirit with him. 18 Flee sexual immorality! "Every sin a person commits is outside of the body"—but the immoral person
sins against his own body. 19 Or do you not know that your body
is the temple of the Holy Spirit who is in you, whom you have
from God, and you are not your own? 20 For you were bought at
a price. Therefore glorify God with your body.

CELIBACY AND MARRIAGE

7 Now with regard to the issues you wrote about: "It is good for
a man not to have sexual relations with a woman." 2 But because of immoralities, each man should have relations with his
own wife and each woman with her own husband. 3 A husband
should fulfill his marital responsibility to his wife, and likewise
a wife to her husband. 4 It is not the wife who has the rights to
her own body, but the husband. In the same way, it is not the husband who has the rights to his own body, but the wife. 5 Do not
deprive each other, except by mutual agreement for a specified

time, so that you may devote yourselves to prayer. Then resume
your relationship, so that Satan may not tempt you because of
your lack of self-control. 6 I say this as a concession, not as a command. 7 I wish that everyone was as I am. But each has his own
gift from God, one this way, another that.
8 To the unmarried and widows I say that it is best for them to
remain as I am. 9 But if they do not have self-control, let them get
married. For it is better to marry than to burn with sexual desire.
10 To the married I give this command—not I, but the Lord—a
wife should not divorce a husband 11 (but if she does, let her remain unmarried, or be reconciled to her husband), and a husband should not divorce his wife.
12 To the rest I say—I, not the Lord—if a brother has a wife who
is not a believer and she is happy to live with him, he should not
divorce her. 13 And if a woman has a husband who is not a believer
and he is happy to live with her, she should not divorce him. 14 For
the unbelieving husband is sanctified because of the wife, and
the unbelieving wife because of her husband. Otherwise your
children are unclean, but now they are holy. 15 But if the unbeliever wants a divorce, let it take place. In these circumstances
the brother or sister is not bound. God has called you in peace.
16 For how do you know, wife, whether you will bring your husband to salvation? Or how do you know, husband, whether you
will bring your wife to salvation?

THE CIRCUMSTANCES OF YOUR CALLING

17 Nevertheless, as the Lord has assigned to each one, as God has
called each person, so must he live. I give this sort of direction in
all the churches. 18 Was anyone called after he had been circumcised? He should not try to undo his circumcision. Was anyone
called who is uncircumcised? He should not get circumcised.
19 Circumcision is nothing and uncircumcision is nothing. Instead, keeping God's commandments is what counts. 20 Let each
one remain in that situation in life in which he was called. 21 Were
you called as a slave? Do not worry about it. But if indeed you are
able to be free, make the most of the opportunity. 22 For the one
who was called in the Lord as a slave is the Lord's freedman. In
the same way, the one who was called as a free person is Christ's
slave. 23 You were bought with a price. Do not become slaves of
men. 24 In whatever situation someone was called, brothers and
sisters, let him remain in it with God.

REFLECT

What did Paul mean by becoming slaves of people? How can we be secure about where God has us in our lives?

REMAINING UNMARRIED

25 With regard to the question about people who have never
married, I have no command from the Lord, but I give my opinion as one shown mercy by the Lord to be trustworthy. 26 Because of the impending crisis I think it best for you to remain as
you are. 27 The one bound to a wife should not seek divorce. The
one released from a wife should not seek marriage. 28 But if you
marry, you have not sinned. And if a virgin marries, she has not
sinned. But those who marry will face difficult circumstances,
and I am trying to spare you such problems. 29 And I say this,
brothers and sisters: The time is short. So then those who have
wives should be as those who have none, 30 those with tears like

those not weeping, those who rejoice like those not rejoicing,
those who buy like those without possessions, 31 those who use
the world as though they were not using it to the full. For the
present shape of this world is passing away.
32 And I want you to be free from concern. An unmarried man
is concerned about the things of the Lord, how to please the
Lord. 33 But a married man is concerned about the things of the
world, how to please his wife, 34 and he is divided. An unmarried
woman or a virgin is concerned about the things of the Lord, to
be holy both in body and spirit. But a married woman is concerned about the things of the world, how to please her husband.
35 I am saying this for your benefit, not to place a limitation on
you, but so that without distraction you may give notable and
constant service to the Lord.
36 If anyone thinks he is acting inappropriately toward his
virgin, if she is past the bloom of youth and it seems necessary,
he should do what he wishes; he does not sin. Let them marry.
37 But the man who is firm in his commitment, and is under no
necessity but has control over his will, and has decided in his
own mind to keep his own virgin, does well. 38 So then, the one
who marries his own virgin does well, but the one who does
not, does better.
39 A wife is bound as long as her husband is living. But if her
husband dies, she is free to marry anyone she wishes (only someone in the Lord). 40 But in my opinion, she will be happier if she
remains as she is—and I think that I too have the Spirit of God!

FOOD SACRIFICED TO IDOLS

8 With regard to food sacrificed to idols, we know that "we all
have knowledge." Knowledge puffs up, but love builds up. 2 If
someone thinks he knows something, he does not yet know to
the degree that he needs to know. 3 But if someone loves God,
he is known by God.
4 With regard then to eating food sacrificed to idols, we know
that "an idol in this world is nothing," and that "there is no God
but one." 5 If after all there are so-called gods, whether in heaven
or on earth (as there are many gods and many lords), 6 yet for us
there is one God, the Father, from whom are all things and for
whom we live, and one Lord, Jesus Christ, through whom are all
things and through whom we live.
7 But this knowledge is not shared by all. And some, by being
accustomed to idols in former times, eat this food as an idol sacrifice, and their conscience, because it is weak, is defiled. 8 Now
food will not bring us close to God. We are no worse if we do not
eat and no better if we do. 9 But be careful that this liberty of
yours does not become a hindrance to the weak. 10 For if someone weak sees you who possess knowledge dining in an idol's
temple, will not his conscience be "strengthened" to eat food
offered to idols? 11 So by your knowledge the weak brother or
sister, for whom Christ died, is destroyed. 12 If you sin against
your brothers or sisters in this way and wound their weak conscience, you sin against Christ. 13 For this reason, if food causes
my brother or sister to sin, I will never eat meat again, so that I
may not cause one of them to sin.

THE RIGHTS OF AN APOSTLE

9 Am I not free? Am I not an apostle? Have I not seen Jesus
our Lord? Are you not my work in the Lord? 2 If I am not an
apostle to others, at least I am to you, for you are the confirming sign of my apostleship in the Lord. 3 This is my defense to
those who examine me. 4 Do we not have the right to financial
support? 5 Do we not have the right to the company of a believing wife, like the other apostles and the Lord's brothers and Cephas? 6 Or do only Barnabas and I lack the right not to work?
7 Who ever serves in the army at his own expense? Who plants a
vineyard and does not eat its fruit? Who tends a flock and does
not consume its milk? 8 Am I saying these things only on the basis of common sense, or does the law not say this as well? 9 For
it is written in the law of Moses, ***"Do not muzzle an ox while it is
treading out the grain."*** God is not concerned here about oxen, is
he? 10 Or is he not surely speaking for our benefit? It was written
for us, because the one plowing and threshing ought to work in
hope of enjoying the harvest. 11 If we sowed spiritual blessings
among you, is it too much to reap material things from you? 12 If
others receive this right from you, are we not more deserving?

But we have not made use of this right. Instead we endure
everything so that we may not be a hindrance to the gospel of
Christ. 13 Don't you know that those who serve in the temple eat
food from the temple, and those who serve at the altar receive
a part of the offerings? 14 In the same way the Lord commanded
those who proclaim the gospel to receive their living by the gospel. 15 But I have not used any of these rights. And I am not writing these things so that something will be done for me. In fact,
it would be better for me to die than—no one will deprive me
of my reason for boasting! 16 For if I preach the gospel, I have no
reason for boasting, because I am compelled to do this. Woe to
me if I do not preach the gospel! 17 For if I do this voluntarily, I
have a reward. But if I do it unwillingly, I am entrusted with a
responsibility. 18 What then is my reward? That when I preach
the gospel I may offer the gospel free of charge, and so not make
full use of my rights in the gospel.

19 For since I am free from all I can make myself a slave to all,
in order to gain even more people. 20 To the Jews I became like
a Jew to gain the Jews. To those under the law I became like one
under the law (though I myself am not under the law) to gain
those under the law. 21 To those free from the law I became like
one free from the law (though I am not free from God's law but
under the law of Christ) to gain those free from the law. 22 To the
weak I became weak in order to gain the weak. I have become
all things to all people, so that by all means I may save some.

23 I do all these things because of the gospel, so that I can be
a participant in it.

24 Do you not know that all the runners in a stadium compete,
but only one receives the prize? So run to win. 25 Each competitor
must exercise self-control in everything. They do it to receive a
perishable crown, but we an imperishable one.

26 So I do not run uncertainly or box like one who hits only air.
27 Instead I subdue my body and make it my slave, so that after
preaching to others I myself will not be disqualified.

REFLECT

How was Paul able to be all things to all people? How did this contribute to the spread of the gospel?

LEARNING FROM ISRAEL'S FAILURES

10 For I do not want you to be unaware, brothers and sisters,
that our fathers were all under the cloud and all passed
through the sea, 2 and all were baptized into Moses in the cloud
and in the sea, 3 and all ate the same spiritual food, 4 and all drank
the same spiritual drink. For they were all drinking from the
spiritual rock that followed them, and the rock was Christ. 5 But
God was not pleased with most of them, for they were cut down
in the wilderness. 6 These things happened as examples for us,
so that we will not crave evil things as they did. 7 So do not be
idolaters, as some of them were. As it is written, "***The people sat***
down to eat and drink and rose up to play." 8 And let us not be
immoral, as some of them were, and 23,000 died in a single day.
9 And let us not put Christ to the test, as some of them did, and
were destroyed by snakes. 10 And do not complain, as some of
them did, and were killed by the destroying angel. 11 These things
happened to them as examples and were written for our instruction, on whom the ends of the ages have come. 12 So let the one
who thinks he is standing be careful that he does not fall. 13 No
trial has overtaken you that is not faced by others. And God is
faithful: He will not let you be tried beyond what you are able
to bear, but with the trial will also provide a way out so that you
may be able to endure it.

AVOID IDOL FEASTS

14 So then, my dear friends, flee from idolatry. 15 I am speaking to
thoughtful people. Consider what I say. 16 Is not the cup of blessing that we bless a sharing in the blood of Christ? Is not the bread
that we break a sharing in the body of Christ? 17 Because there
is one bread, we who are many are one body, for we all share the
one bread. 18 Look at the people of Israel. Are not those who eat
the sacrifices partners in the altar? 19 Am I saying that idols or
food sacrificed to them amount to anything? 20 No, I mean that
what the pagans sacrifice is to demons and not to God. I do not
want you to be partners with demons. 21 You cannot drink the cup
of the Lord and the cup of demons. You cannot take part in the
table of the Lord and the table of demons. 22 Or are we trying to
provoke the Lord to jealousy? Are we really stronger than he is?

LIVE TO GLORIFY GOD

23 "Everything is lawful," but not everything is beneficial. "Everything is lawful," but not everything builds others up. 24 Do not
seek your own good, but the good of the other person. 25 Eat anything that is sold in the marketplace without questions of conscience, 26 for *the earth and its abundance are the Lord's*. 27 If an
unbeliever invites you to dinner and you want to go, eat whatever is served without asking questions of conscience. 28 But if
someone says to you, "This is from a sacrifice," do not eat, because
of the one who told you and because of conscience—29 I do not
mean yours but the other person's. For why is my freedom being judged by another's conscience? 30 If I partake with thankfulness, why am I blamed for the food that I give thanks for? 31 So
whether you eat or drink, or whatever you do, do everything for
the glory of God. 32 Do not give offense to Jews or Greeks or to

the church of God, 33 just as I also try to please everyone in all
things. I do not seek my own benefit, but the benefit of many,
11 so that they may be saved. 1 Be imitators of me, just as I also
am of Christ.

WOMEN'S HEAD COVERINGS

2 I praise you because you remember me in everything and maintain the traditions just as I passed them on to you. 3 But I want
you to know that Christ is the head of every man, and the man
is the head of a woman, and God is the head of Christ. 4 Any man
who prays or prophesies with his head covered disgraces his
head. 5 But any woman who prays or prophesies with her head
uncovered disgraces her head, for it is one and the same thing
as having a shaved head. 6 For if a woman will not cover her head,
she should cut off her hair. But if it is disgraceful for a woman to
have her hair cut off or her head shaved, she should cover her
head. 7 For a man should not have his head covered, since he is
the image and glory of God. But the woman is the glory of the
man. 8 For man did not come from woman, but woman from man.
9 Neither was man created for the sake of woman, but woman
for man. 10 For this reason a woman should have a symbol of authority on her head, because of the angels. 11 In any case, in the
Lord woman is not independent of man, nor is man independent of woman. 12 For just as woman came from man, so man
comes through woman. But all things come from God. 13 Judge
for yourselves: Is it proper for a woman to pray to God with her
head uncovered? 14 Does not nature itself teach you that if a
man has long hair, it is a disgrace for him, 15 but if a woman has
long hair, it is her glory? For her hair is given to her for a covering. 16 If anyone intends to quarrel about this, we have no other
practice, nor do the churches of God.

THE LORD'S SUPPER

17 Now in giving the following instruction I do not praise you,
because you come together not for the better but for the worse.
18 For in the first place, when you come together as a church I
hear there are divisions among you, and in part I believe it. 19 For
there must in fact be divisions among you, so that those of you
who are approved may be evident. 20 Now when you come together at the same place, you are not really eating the Lord's
Supper. 21 For when it is time to eat, everyone proceeds with his
own supper. One is hungry and another becomes drunk. 22 Do you
not have houses so that you can eat and drink? Or are you trying
to show contempt for the church of God by shaming those who
have nothing? What should I say to you? Should I praise you? I
will not praise you for this!

23 For I received from the Lord what I also passed on to you,
that the Lord Jesus on the night in which he was betrayed took
bread, 24 and after he had given thanks he broke it and said, "This
is my body, which is for you. Do this in remembrance of me." 25 In
the same way, he also took the cup after supper, saying, "This cup
is the new covenant in my blood. Do this, every time you drink
it, in remembrance of me." 26 For every time you eat this bread
and drink the cup, you proclaim the Lord's death until he comes.

REFLECT

Why is unity important when participating in the Lord's Supper? How does partaking in the Lord's Supper unite us with other believers?

LOVE TO GROW

AN EXERCISE IN BOUNDARIES

1 CORINTHIANS 10:23—11:1

I have had to do my fair share of boundaries work—learn how to set healthy limits for myself and others, learn how to recognize abuse, and understand when to say "No more" to those who take unfair advantage. I think it's extra hard for Christians to learn how to use boundaries, ironically, because of Scripture's many verses on generosity and selflessness. We learn that God intends for us to serve and love others without expecting anything in return, but we struggle to find sound teaching on how to incorporate some relationship rules that protect us from harm.

I see Paul set healthy boundaries in 1 Corinthians 10:23—11:1. Understanding Jewish law and tradition in light of Christ's resurrection was a little tricky. Paul made it clear that restrictions regarding what to eat and what not to eat were lifted, but some had more trouble letting go of those rules than others.

So what was a follower of Christ to do? Should they eat whatever they wanted and not care what anyone thought? Should they keep eating the way they used to eat so they wouldn't offend anyone? They must have wondered: "Where do my rights begin and another person's end? Who decides what I can eat? Help, I'm hungry!"

Basically Paul was saying, "Look, eat whatever you want and don't feel bad! But don't be so cavalier that you offend someone else in eating it." It's a balance—live out the conviction God has given you, but do be concerned if you are hurting others. As Paul wrote, "Do not give offense to Jews or Greeks or to the church of God, just as I also try to please everyone in all things. I do not seek my own benefit, but the benefit of many, so that they may be saved" (1 Cor 10:32–33). Don't let anyone make you feel guilty, but be sensitive to others' feelings.

This passage is a beautiful illustration of what Christian boundaries can look like. Christians with healthy boundaries know clearly the limits of their own morality. They do not take responsibility for the morality of other people. Still, out of Christlike love and care, they choose not to wound the consciences of others with their choices.

This passage shows me how I can exercise godly boundaries in multiple parts of life with one simple principle:

Whatever you do, do everything for the glory of God (1 Cor 10:31).

If you partake or abstain, do it to celebrate God. If you make one choice over another, choose in celebration of God. Keep boundaries to celebrate God. Be generous to celebrate God. When we make our choices out of an overflow of love and hearts that desire to obey Him, we are sure to bring God glory.

27 For this reason, whoever eats the bread or drinks the cup of
the Lord in an unworthy manner will be guilty of the body and
blood of the Lord. 28 A person should examine himself first, and
in this way let him eat the bread and drink of the cup. 29 For the
one who eats and drinks without careful regard for the body eats
and drinks judgment against himself. 30 That is why many of you
are weak and sick, and quite a few are dead. 31 But if we examined
ourselves, we would not be judged. 32 But when we are judged by
the Lord, we are disciplined so that we may not be condemned
with the world. 33 So then, my brothers and sisters, when you come
together to eat, wait for one another. 34 If anyone is hungry, let
him eat at home, so that when you assemble it does not lead to
judgment. I will give directions about other matters when I come.

SPIRITUAL GIFTS

12 With regard to spiritual gifts, brothers and sisters, I do not
want you to be uninformed. 2 You know that when you were
pagans you were often led astray by speechless idols, however
you were led. 3 So I want you to understand that no one speaking by the Spirit of God says, "Jesus is cursed," and no one can
say, "Jesus is Lord," except by the Holy Spirit.

4 Now there are different gifts, but the same Spirit. 5 And there
are different ministries, but the same Lord. 6 And there are different results, but the same God who produces all of them in everyone. 7 To each person the manifestation of the Spirit is given for the
benefit of all. 8 For one person is given through the Spirit the message of wisdom, and another the message of knowledge according
to the same Spirit, 9 to another faith by the same Spirit, and to another gifts of healing by the one Spirit, 10 to another performance
of miracles, to another prophecy, and to another discernment of
spirits, to another different kinds of tongues, and to another the
interpretation of tongues. 11 It is one and the same Spirit, distributing as he decides to each person, who produces all these things.

DIFFERENT MEMBERS IN ONE BODY

12 For just as the body is one and yet has many members, and all
the members of the body—though many—are one body, so too
is Christ. 13 For in one Spirit we were all baptized into one body.
Whether Jews or Greeks or slaves or free, we were all made to
drink of the one Spirit. 14 For in fact the body is not a single member, but many. 15 If the foot says, "Since I am not a hand, I am not
part of the body," it does not lose its membership in the body because of that. 16 And if the ear says, "Since I am not an eye, I am
not part of the body," it does not lose its membership in the body
because of that. 17 If the whole body were an eye, what part would
do the hearing? If the whole were an ear, what part would exercise
the sense of smell? 18 But as a matter of fact, God has placed each
of the members in the body just as he decided. 19 If they were all
the same member, where would the body be? 20 So now there are
many members, but one body. 21 The eye cannot say to the hand,
"I do not need you," nor in turn can the head say to the foot, "I do
not need you." 22 On the contrary, those members that seem to
be weaker are essential, 23 and those members we consider less
honorable we clothe with greater honor, and our unpresentable

members are clothed with dignity, 24 but our presentable members do not need this. Instead, God has blended together the body,
giving greater honor to the lesser member, 25 so that there may
be no division in the body, but the members may have mutual
concern for one another. 26 If one member suffers, everyone suffers with it. If a member is honored, all rejoice with it.
27 Now you are Christ's body, and each of you is a member of it.
28 And God has placed in the church first apostles, second prophets, third teachers, then miracles, gifts of healing, helps, gifts of
leadership, different kinds of tongues. 29 Not all are apostles,
are they? Not all are prophets, are they? Not all are teachers, are
they? Not all perform miracles, do they? 30 Not all have gifts of
healing, do they? Not all speak in tongues, do they? Not all interpret, do they? 31 But you should be eager for the greater gifts.
And now I will show you a way that is beyond comparison.

THE WAY OF LOVE

13 If I speak in the tongues of men and of angels, but I do not
have love, I am a noisy gong or a clanging cymbal. 2 And if
I have prophecy, and know all mysteries and all knowledge, and
if I have all faith so that I can remove mountains, but do not
have love, I am nothing. 3 If I give away everything I own, and if
I give over my body in order to boast, but do not have love, I receive no benefit.
4 Love is patient, love is kind, it is not envious. Love does not
brag, it is not puffed up. 5 It is not rude, it is not self-serving, it is
not easily angered or resentful. 6 It is not glad about injustice,
but rejoices in the truth. 7 It bears all things, believes all things,
hopes all things, endures all things.
8 Love never ends. But if there are prophecies, they will be
set aside; if there are tongues, they will cease; if there is knowledge, it will be set aside. 9 For we know in part, and we prophesy
in part, 10 but when what is perfect comes, the partial will be set
aside. 11 When I was a child, I talked like a child, I thought like a
child, I reasoned like a child. But when I became an adult, I set
aside childish ways. 12 For now we see in a mirror indirectly, but
then we will see face to face. Now I know in part, but then I will
know fully, just as I have been fully known. 13 And now these three
remain: faith, hope, and love. But the greatest of these is love.

PROPHECY AND TONGUES

14 Pursue love and be eager for the spiritual gifts, especially
that you may prophesy. 2 For the one speaking in a tongue
does not speak to people but to God, for no one understands;
he is speaking mysteries by the Spirit. 3 But the one who prophesies speaks to people for their strengthening, encouragement,
and consolation. 4 The one who speaks in a tongue builds himself up, but the one who prophesies builds up the church. 5 I
wish you all spoke in tongues, but even more that you would
prophesy. The one who prophesies is greater than the one who
speaks in tongues, unless he interprets so that the church may
be strengthened.
6 Now, brothers and sisters, if I come to you speaking in tongues,
how will I help you unless I speak to you with a revelation or with

knowledge or prophecy or teaching? 7 It is similar for lifeless things that make a sound, like a flute or harp. Unless they make a distinction in the notes, how can what is played on the flute or harp be understood? 8 If, for example, the trumpet makes an unclear sound, who will get ready for battle? 9 It is the same for you. If you do not speak clearly with your tongue, how will anyone know what is being said? For you will be speaking into the air. 10 There are probably many kinds of languages in the world, and none is without meaning. 11 If then I do not know the meaning of a language, I will be a foreigner to the speaker and the speaker a foreigner to me. 12 It is the same with you. Since you are eager for manifestations of the Spirit, seek to abound in order to strengthen the church.

13 So then, one who speaks in a tongue should pray that he may interpret. 14 If I pray in a tongue, my spirit prays, but my mind is unproductive. 15 What should I do? I will pray with my spirit, but I will also pray with my mind. I will sing praises with my spirit, but I will also sing praises with my mind. 16 Otherwise, if you are praising God with your spirit, how can someone without the gift say "Amen" to your thanksgiving, since he does not know what you are saying? 17 For you are certainly giving thanks well, but the other person is not strengthened. 18 I thank God that I speak in tongues more than all of you, 19 but in the church I want to speak five words with my mind to instruct others, rather than ten thousand words in a tongue.

20 Brothers and sisters, do not be children in your thinking. Instead, be infants in evil, but in your thinking be mature. 21 It is written in the law: "***By people with strange tongues and by the lips of strangers I will speak to this people, yet not even in this way will they listen to me,***" says the Lord. 22 So then, tongues are a sign not for believers but for unbelievers. Prophecy, however, is not for unbelievers but for believers. 23 So if the whole church comes together and all speak in tongues, and unbelievers or uninformed people enter, will they not say that you have lost your minds? 24 But if all prophesy, and an unbeliever or uninformed person enters, he will be convicted by all, he will be called to account by all. 25 The secrets of his heart are disclosed, and in this way he will fall down with his face to the ground and worship God, declaring, "God is really among you."

CHURCH ORDER

26 What should you do then, brothers and sisters? When you come together, each one has a song, has a lesson, has a revelation, has a tongue, has an interpretation. Let all these things be done for the strengthening of the church. 27 If someone speaks in a tongue, it should be two, or at the most three, one after the other, and someone must interpret. 28 But if there is no interpreter, he should be silent in the church. Let him speak to himself and to God. 29 Two or three prophets should speak and the others should evaluate what is said. 30 And if someone sitting down receives a revelation, the person who is speaking should conclude. 31 For you can all prophesy one after another, so all can learn and be encouraged. 32 Indeed, the spirits of the prophets are subject to the prophets, 33 for God is not characterized by disorder but by peace.

As in all the churches of the saints, 34 the women should be silent in the churches, for they are not permitted to speak. Rather,

let them be in submission, as in fact the law says. 35 If they want
to find out about something, they should ask their husbands at
home, because it is disgraceful for a woman to speak in church.
36 Did the word of God begin with you, or did it come to you alone?
37 If anyone considers himself a prophet or spiritual person,
he should acknowledge that what I write to you is the Lord's
command. 38 If someone does not recognize this, he is not recognized. 39 So then, brothers and sisters, be eager to prophesy,
and do not forbid anyone from speaking in tongues. 40 And do
everything in a decent and orderly manner.

CHRIST'S RESURRECTION

15 Now I want to make clear for you, brothers and sisters, the
gospel that I preached to you, that you received and on which
you stand, 2 and by which you are being saved, if you hold firmly to
the message I preached to you—unless you believed in vain. 3 For
I passed on to you as of first importance what I also received—
that Christ died for our sins according to the scriptures, 4 and that
he was buried, and that he was raised on the third day according
to the scriptures, 5 and that he appeared to Cephas, then to the
twelve. 6 Then he appeared to more than 500 of the brothers and
sisters at one time, most of whom are still alive, though some have
fallen asleep. 7 Then he appeared to James, then to all the apostles. 8 Last of all, as though to one born at the wrong time, he appeared to me also. 9 For I am the least of the apostles, unworthy
to be called an apostle, because I persecuted the church of God.
10 But by the grace of God I am what I am, and his grace to me has
not been in vain. In fact, I worked harder than all of them—yet
not I, but the grace of God with me. 11 Whether then it was I or
they, this is the way we preach and this is the way you believed.

NO RESURRECTION?

12 Now if Christ is being preached as raised from the dead, how can
some of you say there is no resurrection of the dead? 13 But if there
is no resurrection of the dead, then not even Christ has been raised.
14 And if Christ has not been raised, then our preaching is futile and
your faith is empty. 15 Also, we are found to be false witnesses about
God, because we have testified against God that he raised Christ
from the dead, when in reality he did not raise him, if indeed the
dead are not raised. 16 For if the dead are not raised, then not even
Christ has been raised. 17 And if Christ has not been raised, your
faith is useless; you are still in your sins. 18 Furthermore, those who
have fallen asleep in Christ have also perished. 19 For if only in this
life we have hope in Christ, we should be pitied more than anyone.
20 But now Christ has been raised from the dead, the firstfruits
of those who have fallen asleep. 21 For since death came through
a man, the resurrection of the dead also came through a man.
22 For just as in Adam all die, so also in Christ all will be made alive.
23 But each in his own order: Christ, the firstfruits; then when
Christ comes, those who belong to him. 24 Then comes the end,
when he hands over the kingdom to God the Father, when he has
brought to an end all rule and all authority and power. 25 For he
must reign until he has put all his enemies under his feet. 26 The
last enemy to be eliminated is death. 27 For ***he has put everything***

REFLECT

Why did Paul call himself the least of the apostles? Was this true? By what grounds did Paul make this claim?

in subjection under his feet. But when it says "everything" has been
put in subjection, it is clear that this does not include the one who
put everything in subjection to him. 28 And when all things are
subjected to him, then the Son himself will be subjected to the
one who subjected everything to him, so that God may be all in all.
29 Otherwise, what will those do who are baptized for the dead?
If the dead are not raised at all, then why are they baptized for
them? 30 Why too are we in danger every hour? 31 Every day I am
in danger of death! This is as sure as my boasting in you, which
I have in Christ Jesus our Lord. 32 If from a human point of view
I fought with wild beasts at Ephesus, what did it benefit me?
If the dead are not raised, *let us eat and drink, for tomorrow we
die.* 33 Do not be deceived: "Bad company corrupts good morals."
34 Sober up as you should, and stop sinning! For some have no
knowledge of God—I say this to your shame!

THE RESURRECTION BODY

35 But someone will say, "How are the dead raised? With what
kind of body will they come?" 36 Fool! What you sow will not come
to life unless it dies. 37 And what you sow is not the body that is
to be, but a bare seed—perhaps of wheat or something else. 38 But
God gives it a body just as he planned, and to each of the seeds a
body of its own. 39 All flesh is not the same: People have one flesh,
animals have another, birds and fish another. 40 And there are
heavenly bodies and earthly bodies. The glory of the heavenly
body is one sort and the earthly another. 41 There is one glory of
the sun, and another glory of the moon and another glory of the
stars, for star differs from star in glory.
42 It is the same with the resurrection of the dead. What is sown
is perishable, what is raised is imperishable. 43 It is sown in dishonor, it is raised in glory; it is sown in weakness, it is raised in
power; 44 it is sown a natural body, it is raised a spiritual body.
If there is a natural body, there is also a spiritual body. 45 So also
it is written, "***The first man, Adam, became a living person***"; the
last Adam became a life-giving spirit. 46 However, the spiritual
did not come first, but the natural, and then the spiritual. 47 The
first man is from the earth, made of dust; the second man is from
heaven. 48 Like the one made of dust, so too are those made of
dust, and like the one from heaven, so too those who are heavenly. 49 And just as we have borne the image of the man of dust,
let us also bear the image of the man of heaven.
50 Now this is what I am saying, brothers and sisters: Flesh and
blood cannot inherit the kingdom of God, nor does the perishable inherit the imperishable. 51 Listen, I will tell you a mystery:
We will not all sleep, but we will all be changed—52 in a moment,
in the blinking of an eye, at the last trumpet. For the trumpet
will sound, and the dead will be raised imperishable, and we will
be changed. 53 For this perishable body must put on the imperishable, and this mortal body must put on immortality. 54 Now
when this perishable puts on the imperishable, and this mortal
puts on immortality, then the saying that is written will happen,

"***Death has been swallowed up in victory.***"
55 "***Where, O death, is your victory?***
Where, O death, is your sting?"

56 The sting of death is sin, and the power of sin is the law. 57 But
thanks be to God, who gives us the victory through our Lord
Jesus Christ! 58 So then, dear brothers and sisters, be firm. Do
not be moved! Always be outstanding in the work of the Lord,
knowing that your labor is not in vain in the Lord.

A COLLECTION TO AID JEWISH CHRISTIANS

16 With regard to the collection for the saints, please follow
the directions that I gave to the churches of Galatia: 2 On
the first day of the week, each of you should set aside some income and save it to the extent that God has blessed you, so that
a collection will not have to be made when I come. 3 Then, when
I arrive, I will send those whom you approve with letters of explanation to carry your gift to Jerusalem. 4 And if it seems advisable that I should go also, they will go with me.

PAUL'S PLANS TO VISIT

5 But I will come to you after I have gone through Macedonia—
for I will be going through Macedonia—6 and perhaps I will stay
with you, or even spend the winter, so that you can send me on
my journey, wherever I go. 7 For I do not want to see you now in
passing, since I hope to spend some time with you, if the Lord
allows. 8 But I will stay in Ephesus until Pentecost, 9 because a
door of great opportunity stands wide open for me, but there
are many opponents.

10 Now if Timothy comes, see that he has nothing to fear among
you, for he is doing the Lord's work, as I am too. 11 So then, let no one
treat him with contempt. But send him on his way in peace so that
he may come to me. For I am expecting him with the brothers.

12 With regard to our brother Apollos: I strongly encouraged
him to visit you with the other brothers, but it was simply not
his intention to come now. He will come when he has the opportunity.

FINAL CHALLENGE AND BLESSING

13 Stay alert, stand firm in the faith, show courage, be strong.
14 Everything you do should be done in love.

15 Now, brothers and sisters, you know about the household
of Stephanus, that as the first converts of Achaia, they devoted
themselves to ministry for the saints. I urge you 16 also to submit to people like this, and to everyone who cooperates in the
work and labors hard. 17 I was glad about the arrival of Stephanus, Fortunatus, and Achaicus because they have supplied the
fellowship with you that I lacked. 18 For they refreshed my spirit
and yours. So then, recognize people like this.

19 The churches in the province of Asia send greetings to you.
Aquila and Prisca greet you warmly in the Lord, with the church
that meets in their house. 20 All the brothers and sisters send
greetings. Greet one another with a holy kiss.

21 I, Paul, send this greeting with my own hand.

22 Let anyone who has no love for the Lord be accursed. Our
Lord, come!

23 The grace of the Lord Jesus be with you.

24 My love be with all of you in Christ Jesus.

FOR OUR MOMENTARY,
light suffering
IS PRODUCING FOR US
an eternal weight
OF *GLORY*
far beyond
ALL COMPARISON

MEMORY VERSE

For our momentary, light suffering is producing for us an eternal weight of glory far beyond all comparison because we are not looking at what can be seen but at what cannot be seen. For what can be seen is temporary, but what cannot be seen is eternal.

2 Corinthians 4:17–18

2 Corinthians

INTRODUCTION

Do Not Lose Heart

Second Corinthians is a deeply personal letter from Paul to the church at Corinth. Paul had previously exhorted this group of believers to holy living, but in this letter, he defended his apostleship and his authority in response to false teachers. Even in the difficult subject matter, Paul offered encouragement and hope to the believers in Corinth as he admonished them to continue in their faith and pursuit of Christ.

The Book of 2 Corinthians begins with salutations and thanksgiving, in the same way Paul began many of his letters (1:1–11). He then offered comfort to the believers in Corinth and defended his character and gospel ministry (1:12—7:16). Paul explained the ministry of giving (8:1—9:15), then closed his letter with correction (10:1—13:10), personal greetings, and a benediction (13:11–14).

The letter opens with Paul identifying himself as the author. Paul wrote the letter of 1 Corinthians during the final year of his ministry in Ephesus, on his third missionary journey. This letter was written shortly after 1 Corinthians, dating it somewhere in the latter half of A.D. 56.

Paul opened his letter with a sincere account of the troubles he faced in Asia. The problems were so severe, he said, he and his friends despaired even of life itself. The pain he endured caused him to trust not in himself, but in God alone. What a great encouragement Paul's life is to us as we seek to love God greatly, reminding us that even in our most desperate times, we can trust in God. He is faithful to deliver us time and time again.

Bulgaria

OFFICIAL LANGUAGE
Bulgarian
POPULATION
6,956,000
UNREACHED POPULATION
637,000
PROFESSING CHRISTIANS
82.4%

Krassi's Home

Say a Prayer Today

Pray for Krassi and her work of spreading the gospel to the people of Bulgaria. Pray for her work as a translator for Love God Greatly, that her work would be effective and would produce much fruit for the gospel.

HISTORY BIT

Christianity first reached Bulgaria and other Balkan states by Paul and Andrew in the first century A.D. Christianity was adopted as the state religion in 865. The Bulgarian Orthodox Church is the oldest Slavic Orthodox Church with about six million members.*

Source Information:
https://joshuaproject.net/countries/BU
*https://www.britannica.com/topic/Bulgarian-Orthodox-Church

LOVE YOUR NEIGHBOR

Her Journey

KRASSI'S STORY

Growing up in a small town in southern Bulgaria, I came to know Jesus through my grandparents. Living in the town of Smolyan I was surrounded by a community of believers and enjoyed fellowship there.

Several years ago my family immigrated to Spain. Other than my husband and daughter, I did not know anyone else who spoke my native language. I did not speak Spanish at the time, and I felt very isolated. I was not attending church and was not involved in a community of believers.

One day, as I was praying and passing through town, I saw the building of an evangelical church. God had answered my prayers! I had been hoping and praying to find community with other believers. A few days later I went back to pray with my brothers and sisters in Christ.

Eventually, I heard about Love God Greatly and their Bible studies that have been translated into many different languages. I joined a small group going through one of the Love God Greatly Bible studies in Spanish. It was on the Book of Ecclesiastes, one of my favorites! I wanted to share the Bible study with my cousin, who lives in Bulgaria. At the time, there were no Love God Greatly studies in Bulgarian. I felt God calling me to join as a translator, and I soon began translating in that language for Love God Greatly.

Since that time, God has greatly increased our efforts to spread His Word in Bulgaria. Even though I had become incredibly discouraged, God had a plan. He was working things out in His perfect timing. As we continue to spread God's Word through Bible studies translated into Bulgarian, we pray that others will see God's hand in their lives in the same way.

4 WEEK READING PLAN

LOVE HIS WORD

	MONDAY	TUESDAY	WEDNESDAY	THURSDAY	FRIDAY
1	2 Corinthians 1:1-11	2 Corinthians 1:12-22	2 Corinthians 1:23—2:13	2 Corinthians 2:14—3:6	2 Corinthians 3:7-18
	SOAP 2 Corinthians 1:10	SOAP 2 Corinthians 1:12	SOAP 2 Corinthians 2:9-11	SOAP 2 Corinthians 3:4-6	SOAP 2 Corinthians 3:17
2	2 Corinthians 4	2 Corinthians 5:1-10	2 Corinthians 5:11-21	2 Corinthians 6:1-13	2 Corinthians 6:14—7:3
	SOAP 2 Corinthians 4:17-18	SOAP 2 Corinthians 5:8-9	SOAP 2 Corinthians 5:14-15	SOAP 2 Corinthians 6:3	SOAP 2 Corinthians 7:1
3	2 Corinthians 7:4-16	2 Corinthians 8:1-15	2 Corinthians 8:16-24	2 Corinthians 9	2 Corinthians 10
	SOAP 2 Corinthians 7:4	SOAP 2 Corinthians 8:9	SOAP 2 Corinthians 8:20-21	SOAP 2 Corinthians 9:6-7	SOAP 2 Corinthians 10:3-6
4	2 Corinthians 11:1-15	2 Corinthians 11:16-33	2 Corinthians 12:1-10	2 Corinthians 12:11-21	2 Corinthians 13
	SOAP 2 Corinthians 11:4	SOAP 2 Corinthians 11:30	SOAP 2 Corinthians 12:8-10	SOAP 2 Corinthians 12:19	SOAP 2 Corinthians 13:5-6

SALUTATION

1 From Paul, an apostle of Christ Jesus by the will of God, and
Timothy our brother, to the church of God that is in Corinth,
with all the saints who are in all Achaia. 2 Grace and peace to you
from God our Father and the Lord Jesus Christ!

THANKSGIVING FOR GOD'S COMFORT

3 Blessed is the God and Father of our Lord Jesus Christ, the Father of mercies and God of all comfort, 4 who comforts us in all
our troubles so that we may be able to comfort those experiencing any trouble with the comfort with which we ourselves are
comforted by God. 5 For just as the sufferings of Christ overflow
toward us, so also our comfort through Christ overflows to you.
6 But if we are afflicted, it is for your comfort and salvation; if we
are comforted, it is for your comfort that you experience in your
patient endurance of the same sufferings that we also suffer. 7 And
our hope for you is steadfast because we know that as you share
in our sufferings, so also you will share in our comfort. 8 For we
do not want you to be unaware, brothers and sisters, regarding
the affliction that happened to us in the province of Asia, that we
were burdened excessively, beyond our strength, so that we despaired even of living. 9 Indeed we felt as if the sentence of death
had been passed against us, so that we would not trust in ourselves
but in God who raises the dead. 10 He delivered us from so great
a risk of death, and he will deliver us. We have set our hope on
him that he will deliver us yet again, 11 as you also join in helping
us by prayer, so that many people may give thanks to God on our
behalf for the gracious gift given to us through the help of many.

REFLECT

How has Christ comforted you in your affliction? How can you use the encouragement He has given you to encourage and comfort others?

PAUL DEFENDS HIS CHANGED PLANS

12 For our reason for confidence is this: the testimony of our conscience, that with pure motives and sincerity which are from
God—not by human wisdom but by the grace of God—we conducted ourselves in the world, and all the more toward you. 13 For
we do not write you anything other than what you can read and
also understand. But I hope that you will understand completely
14 just as also you have partly understood us, that we are your
source of pride just as you also are ours in the day of the Lord
Jesus. 15 And with this confidence I intended to come to you
first so that you would get a second opportunity to see us, 16 and
through your help to go on into Macedonia and then from Macedonia to come back to you and be helped on our way into Judea
by you. 17 Therefore when I was planning to do this, I did not do
so without thinking about what I was doing, did I? Or do I make
my plans according to mere human standards so that I would be
saying both "Yes, yes" and "No, no" at the same time? 18 But as God
is faithful, our message to you is not "Yes" and "No." 19 For the Son
of God, Jesus Christ, the one who was proclaimed among you by
us—by me and Silvanus and Timothy—was not "Yes" and "No," but
it has always been "Yes" in him. 20 For every one of God's promises
are "Yes" in him; therefore also through him the "Amen" is spoken, to the glory we give to God. 21 But it is God who establishes
us together with you in Christ and who anointed us, 22 who also
sealed us and gave us the Spirit in our hearts as a down payment.

WHY PAUL POSTPONED HIS VISIT

23 Now I appeal to God as my witness, that to spare you I did not
come again to Corinth. 24 I do not mean that we rule over your
faith, but we are workers with you for your joy, because by faith
2 so that they you stand firm. 1 So I made up my own mind not
to pay you another painful visit. 2 For if I make you sad, who
would be left to make me glad but the one I caused to be sad?
3 And I wrote this very thing to you, so that when I came I would
not have sadness from those who ought to make me rejoice, since
I am confident in you all that my joy would be yours. 4 For out
of great distress and anguish of heart I wrote to you with many
tears, not to make you sad, but to let you know the love that I
have especially for you. 5 But if anyone has caused sadness, he has
not saddened me alone, but to some extent (not to exaggerate)
he has saddened all of you as well. 6 This punishment on such an
individual by the majority is enough for him, 7 so that now instead you should rather forgive and comfort him. This will keep
him from being overwhelmed by excessive grief to the point of
despair. 8 Therefore I urge you to reaffirm your love for him. 9 For
this reason also I wrote you: to test you to see if you are obedient
in everything. 10 If you forgive anyone for anything, I also forgive
him—for indeed what I have forgiven (if I have forgiven anything)
I did so for you in the presence of Christ, 11 so that we may not
be exploited by Satan (for we are not ignorant of his schemes).
12 Now when I arrived in Troas to proclaim the gospel of Christ,
even though the Lord had opened a door of opportunity for me,
13 I had no relief in my spirit, because I did not find my brother
Titus there. So I said goodbye to them and set out for Macedonia.

APOSTOLIC MINISTRY

14 But thanks be to God who always leads us in triumphal procession in Christ and who makes known through us the fragrance
that consists of the knowledge of him in every place. 15 For we
are a sweet aroma of Christ to God among those who are being
saved and among those who are perishing—16 to the latter an
odor from death to death, but to the former a fragrance from
life to life. And who is adequate for these things? 17 For we are
not like so many others, hucksters who peddle the word of God
for profit, but we are speaking in Christ before God as persons
of sincerity, as persons sent from God.

A LIVING LETTER

3 Are we beginning to commend ourselves again? We don't
need letters of recommendation to you or from you as some
other people do, do we? 2 You yourselves are our letter, written
on our hearts, known and read by everyone, 3 revealing that you
are a letter of Christ, delivered by us, written not with ink but
by the Spirit of the living God, not *on stone tablets* but on tablets of human hearts.

4 Now we have such confidence in God through Christ. 5 Not that
we are adequate in ourselves to consider anything as if it were
coming from ourselves, but our adequacy is from God, 6 who made
us adequate to be servants of a new covenant not based on the
letter but on the Spirit, for the letter kills, but the Spirit gives life.

THE GREATER GLORY OF THE SPIRIT'S MINISTRY

7 But if the ministry that produced death—carved in letters *on stone*
tablets—came with glory, so that the Israelites could not keep their
eyes fixed on the face of Moses because of the glory of his face (a
glory which was made ineffective), 8 how much more glorious will
the ministry of the Spirit be? 9 For if there was glory in the ministry that produced condemnation, how much more does the ministry that produces righteousness excel in glory! 10 For indeed, what
had been glorious now has no glory because of the tremendously
greater glory of what replaced it. 11 For if what was made ineffective
came with glory, how much more has what remains come in glory!
12 Therefore, since we have such a hope, we behave with great boldness, 13 and not like Moses who used to put a veil over his face to keep
the Israelites from staring at the result of the glory that was made
ineffective. 14 But their minds were closed. For to this very day, the
same veil remains when they hear the old covenant read. It has not
been removed because only in Christ is it taken away. 15 But until
this very day whenever Moses is read, a veil lies over their minds,
16 but when one turns to the Lord, *the veil is removed.* 17 Now the Lord
is the Spirit, and where the Spirit of the Lord is present, there is
freedom. 18 And we all, with unveiled faces reflecting the glory of
the Lord, are being transformed into the same image from one degree of glory to another, which is from the Lord, who is the Spirit.

PAUL'S PERSEVERANCE IN MINISTRY

4 Therefore, since we have this ministry, just as God has shown
us mercy, we do not become discouraged. 2 But we have rejected shameful hidden deeds, not behaving with deceptiveness
or distorting the word of God, but by open proclamation of the
truth we commend ourselves to everyone's conscience before
God. 3 But even if our gospel is veiled, it is veiled only to those
who are perishing, 4 among whom the god of this age has blinded
the minds of those who do not believe so they would not see the
light of the glorious gospel of Christ, who is the image of God. 5 For
we do not proclaim ourselves, but Jesus Christ as Lord, and ourselves as your slaves for Jesus' sake. 6 For God, who said "*Let light*
shine out of darkness," is the one who shined in our hearts to give
us the light of the glorious knowledge of God in the face of Christ.

AN ETERNAL WEIGHT OF GLORY

7 But we have this treasure in clay jars, so that the extraordinary
power belongs to God and does not come from us. 8 We are experiencing trouble on every side, but are not crushed; we are perplexed,
but not driven to despair; 9 we are persecuted, but not abandoned;
we are knocked down, but not destroyed, 10 always carrying around
in our body the death of Jesus, so that the life of Jesus may also be
made visible in our body. 11 For we who are alive are constantly being handed over to death for Jesus' sake, so that the life of Jesus may
also be made visible in our mortal body. 12 As a result, death is at
work in us, but life is at work in you. 13 But since we have the same
spirit of faith as that shown in what has been written, "***I believed;***
therefore I spoke," we also believe, therefore we also speak. 14 We do
so because we know that the one who raised up Jesus will also raise
us up with Jesus and will bring us with you into his presence. 15 For

REFLECT

What does it mean for you not to give up? What are you enduring right now? How does this passage encourage you to continue?

LOVE TO GROW

HOLDING A TREASURE

2 CORINTHIANS 4:7

I walked around a museum exhibit with my children, trying to grasp the significance of all we were seeing. Behind the glass was a variety of artifacts from the very time and place Jesus walked the earth—coins like those He held, cups like those from which He sipped. These were the makings of His everyday life.

The pinnacle of the tour came when we reached an authentic fragment of a Dead Sea Scroll. Those ancient Jewish manuscripts, dating back to the last three centuries B.C., were discovered in the 1940s near the northern shore of the Dead Sea. Their discovery and subsequent study have served to further prove the Bible's historical accuracy.

A large clay jar with a small piece of parchment next to it stirred my heart as I stood beside it. The jar was one of the jars that originally housed the scrolls inside the cave where the scrolls sat untouched for almost two thousand years. The jar was riddled with cracks and chips, worn from centuries of weathering.

But we have this treasure in clay jars, so that the extraordinary power belongs to God and does not come from us (2 Cor 4:7).

The believers in Christ who base everything on the saving grace of God—we are those clay jars. And the treasure? The divine love and glory proclaimed in the message of Christ.

Paul repeatedly implored Christ-followers to understand their worth in light of God's grace, not their own merit or accomplishments. Talents or gifts simply serve to advance the message. The extraordinary power belongs to God. It does not come from us.

We can find such relief in a performance-driven, self-exalting world when we acknowledge our role as simple jars of clay, weathered and worn. We carry the powerful message of God's grace. That ancient jar was put on display not because of its outward beauty, but solely because of what it held—the very words of God.

all these things are for your sake, so that the grace that is including
more and more people may cause thanksgiving to increase to the
glory of God. 16 Therefore we do not despair, but even if our physical body is wearing away, our inner person is being renewed day
by day. 17 For our momentary, light suffering is producing for us an
eternal weight of glory far beyond all comparison 18 because we are
not looking at what can be seen but at what cannot be seen. For
what can be seen is temporary, but what cannot be seen is eternal.

LIVING BY FAITH, NOT BY SIGHT

5 For we know that if our earthly house, the tent we live in, is
dismantled, we have a building from God, a house not built by
human hands, that is eternal in the heavens. 2 For in this earthly
house we groan, because we desire to put on our heavenly dwelling, 3 if indeed, after we have put on our heavenly house, we will not
be found naked. 4 For we groan while we are in this tent, since we
are weighed down, because we do not want to be unclothed, but
clothed, so that what is mortal may be swallowed up by life. 5 Now
the one who prepared us for this very purpose is God, who gave us
the Spirit as a down payment. 6 Therefore we are always full of courage, and we know that as long as we are alive here on earth we are
absent from the Lord—7 for we live by faith, not by sight. 8 Thus we
are full of courage and would prefer to be away from the body and
at home with the Lord. 9 So then whether we are alive or away, we
make it our ambition to please him. 10 For we must all appear before
the judgment seat of Christ, so that each one may be paid back according to what he has done while in the body, whether good or evil.

THE MESSAGE OF RECONCILIATION

11 Therefore, because we know the fear of the Lord, we try to persuade people, but we are well known to God, and I hope we are
well known to your consciences too. 12 We are not trying to commend ourselves to you again, but are giving you an opportunity
to be proud of us, so that you may be able to answer those who
take pride in outward appearance and not in what is in the heart.
13 For if we are out of our minds, it is for God; if we are of sound
mind, it is for you. 14 For the love of Christ controls us, since we
have concluded this, that Christ died for all; therefore all have
died. 15 And he died for all so that those who live should no longer
live for themselves but for him who died for them and was raised.
16 So then from now on we acknowledge no one from an outward
human point of view. Even though we have known Christ from
such a human point of view, now we do not know him in that
way any longer. 17 So then, if anyone is in Christ, he is a new creation; what is old has passed away—look, what is new has come!
18 And all these things are from God who reconciled us to himself
through Christ, and who has given us the ministry of reconciliation. 19 In other words, in Christ God was reconciling the world
to himself, not counting people's trespasses against them, and
he has given us the message of reconciliation. 20 Therefore we
are ambassadors for Christ, as though God were making his plea
through us. We plead with you on Christ's behalf, "Be reconciled
to God!" 21 God made the one who did not know sin to be sin for
us, so that in him we would become the righteousness of God.

CHALLENGE

What does it mean that Christ became sin for us? Read Isaiah 53:2–6. How does this passage explain how Christ became sin for us?

GOD'S SUFFERING SERVANTS

6 Now because we are fellow workers, we also urge you not to
receive the grace of God in vain. 2 For he says, ***"I heard you at
the acceptable time, and in the day of salvation I helped you."*** Look,
now is ***the acceptable time***; look, now is ***the day of salvation***! 3 We
do not give anyone an occasion for taking an offense in anything,
so that no fault may be found with our ministry. 4 But as God's
servants, we have commended ourselves in every way, with great
endurance, in persecutions, in difficulties, in distresses, 5 in beatings, in imprisonments, in riots, in troubles, in sleepless nights,
in hunger, 6 by purity, by knowledge, by patience, by benevolence,
by the Holy Spirit, by genuine love, 7 by truthful teaching, by the
power of God, with weapons of righteousness both for the right
hand and for the left, 8 through glory and dishonor, through slander and praise; regarded as impostors, and yet true; 9 as unknown,
and yet well-known; as dying and yet—see!—we continue to live;
as those who are scourged and yet not executed; 10 as sorrowful,
but always rejoicing, as poor, but making many rich, as having
nothing, and yet possessing everything.

11 We have spoken freely to you, Corinthians; our heart has been
opened wide to you. 12 Our affection for you is not restricted, but you
are restricted in your affections for us. 13 Now as a fair exchange—I
speak as to my children—open wide your hearts to us also.

UNEQUAL PARTNERS

14 Do not become partners with those who do not believe, for
what partnership is there between righteousness and lawlessness, or what fellowship does light have with darkness? 15 And
what agreement does Christ have with Beliar? Or what does a
believer share in common with an unbeliever? 16 And what mutual agreement does the temple of God have with idols? For we
are the temple of the living God, just as God said, ***"I will live in
them and will walk among them, and I will be their God, and they
will be my people."*** 17 Therefore ***"come out from their midst, and be
separate,"*** says the Lord, ***"and touch no unclean thing,*** *and I will
welcome you,* 18 *and I will be a father to you, and you will be my sons
and daughters,"* says the All-Powerful Lord.

SELF-PURIFICATION

7 Therefore, since we have these promises, dear friends, let us
cleanse ourselves from everything that could defile the body
and the spirit, and thus accomplish holiness out of reverence
for God. 2 Make room for us in your hearts; we have wronged no
one, we have ruined no one, we have exploited no one. 3 I do not
say this to condemn you, for I told you before that you are in
our hearts so that we die together and live together with you.

A LETTER THAT CAUSED SADNESS

4 I have great confidence in you; I take great pride on your behalf.
I am filled with encouragement; I am overflowing with joy in the
midst of all our suffering. 5 For even when we came into Macedonia, our body had no rest at all, but we were troubled in every
way—struggles from the outside, fears from within. 6 But God, who
encourages the downhearted, encouraged us by the arrival of Titus.

7 We were encouraged not only by his arrival, but also by the encouragement you gave him, as he reported to us your longing, your
mourning, your deep concern for me, so that I rejoiced more than
ever. 8 For even if I made you sad by my letter, I do not regret having written it (even though I did regret it, for I see that my letter
made you sad, though only for a short time). 9 Now I rejoice, not
because you were made sad, but because you were made sad to
the point of repentance. For you were made sad as God intended,
so that you were not harmed in any way by us. 10 For sadness as
intended by God produces a repentance that leads to salvation,
leaving no regret, but worldly sadness brings about death. 11 For see
what this very thing, this sadness as God intended, has produced
in you: what eagerness, what defense of yourselves, what indignation, what alarm, what longing, what deep concern, what punishment! In everything you have proved yourselves to be innocent in
this matter. 12 So then, even though I wrote to you, it was not on account of the one who did wrong, or on account of the one who was
wronged, but to reveal to you your eagerness on our behalf before
God. 13 Therefore we have been encouraged. And in addition to our
own encouragement, we rejoiced even more at the joy of Titus, because all of you have refreshed his spirit. 14 For if I have boasted to
him about anything concerning you, I have not been embarrassed
by you, but just as everything we said to you was true, so our boasting to Titus about you has proved true as well. 15 And his affection
for you is much greater when he remembers the obedience of you
all, how you welcomed him with fear and trembling. 16 I rejoice because in everything I am fully confident in you.

COMPLETING THE COLLECTION FOR THE SAINTS

8 Now we make known to you, brothers and sisters, the grace
of God given to the churches of Macedonia, 2 that during a severe ordeal of suffering, their abundant joy and their extreme
poverty have overflowed in the wealth of their generosity. 3 For
I testify, they gave according to their means and beyond their
means. They did so voluntarily, 4 begging us with great earnestness for the blessing and fellowship of helping the saints. 5 And
they did this not just as we had hoped, but they gave themselves
first to the Lord and to us by the will of God. 6 Thus we urged Titus
that, just as he had previously begun this work, so also he should
complete this act of kindness for you. 7 But as you excel in everything—in faith, in speech, in knowledge, and in all eagerness and
in the love from us that is in you—make sure that you excel in
this act of kindness too. 8 I am not saying this as a command, but I
am testing the genuineness of your love by comparison with the
eagerness of others. 9 For you know the grace of our Lord Jesus
Christ, that although he was rich, he became poor for your sakes,
so that you by his poverty could become rich. 10 So here is my
opinion on this matter: It is to your advantage, since you made
a good start last year both in your giving and your desire to give,
11 to finish what you started, so that just as you wanted to do it eagerly, you can also complete it according to your means. 12 For if
the eagerness is present, the gift itself is acceptable according to
whatever one has, not according to what he does not have. 13 For
I do not say this so there would be relief for others and suffering

REFLECT

How do we excel in the things listed in 2 Corinthians 8:7? Is this in our own strength?

LOVE TO GROW

A GENEROUS IMPULSE

2 CORINTHIANS 8:7

All my life my grandpa has reminded me of something his mom told him: "Seldom repress a generous impulse."

The son of Scottish immigrants, my grandpa grew up in the 1930s, the time of the Great Depression in the United States. Along with a deep love for God, my great-grandparents taught their six children how to work hard, care deeply, and give generously. Their family didn't have much, but what they did have, they shared.

His mom not only instructed the kids to be generous, she showed them how. She lived a life that was loving and kind and faithful, and so does my grandpa. In fact, he lives life in such a way that when a book was written about him, the publisher titled the biography *A Generous Impulse*.

Both my grandpa and my grandma are recipients of God's abundant grace. They've been changed by it, and their abiding trust in the goodness and faithfulness of God compels them to give to others out of what God has given to them. They seldom repress a generous impulse, and through their genuine care for others, they have had innumerable opportunities to demonstrate the love of Christ and share the gospel.

In 2 Corinthians 8:7, Paul commended the Corinthian believers for excelling in their speech, knowledge, earnestness, and faith. He was proud of them, and he told them. He also encouraged them to grow in another area: giving.

Ultimately, generosity is a response to the abundant grace of God has given to us through Christ Jesus.

We are generous because He is generous to us.

If we're honest with ourselves, what do our checking and saving accounts, our credit card statements, and our cash flow say about what we value? What do those things show about how we trust God and love others?

Think about the collective impact we could have if the people of God overflowed with kindness and generosity! It starts with us—with you and with me. Oh, that we might be people whose love wells up in abundant kindness and ridiculous generosity. Don't repress that generous impulse. May we too excel in the grace of giving.

for you, but as a matter of equality. 14 At the present time, your
abundance will meet their need, so that one day their abundance
may also meet your need, and thus there may be equality, 15 as
it is written: "***The one who gathered much did not have too much,
and the one who gathered little did not have too little.***"

THE MISSION OF TITUS

16 But thanks be to God who put in the heart of Titus the same
devotion I have for you, 17 because he not only accepted our request, but since he was very eager, he is coming to you of his own
accord. 18 And we are sending along with him the brother who is
praised by all the churches for his work in spreading the gospel.
19 In addition, this brother has also been chosen by the churches
as our traveling companion as we administer this generous gift
to the glory of the Lord himself and to show our readiness to
help. 20 We did this as a precaution so that no one should blame
us in regard to this generous gift we are administering. 21 For
we are *concerned about what is right not only before the Lord but
also before men.* 22 And we are sending with them our brother
whom we have tested many times and found eager in many matters, but who now is much more eager than ever because of the
great confidence he has in you. 23 If there is any question about
Titus, he is my partner and fellow worker among you; if there
is any question about our brothers, they are messengers of the
churches, a glory to Christ. 24 Therefore show them openly before the churches the proof of your love and of our pride in you.

PREPARING THE GIFT

9 For it is not necessary for me to write you about this service
to the saints, 2 because I know your eagerness to help. I keep
boasting to the Macedonians about this eagerness of yours, that
Achaia has been ready to give since last year, and your zeal to
participate has stirred up most of them. 3 But I am sending these
brothers so that our boasting about you may not be empty in
this case, so that you may be ready just as I kept telling them.
4 For if any of the Macedonians should come with me and find
that you are not ready to give, we would be humiliated (not to
mention you) by this confidence we had in you. 5 Therefore I
thought it necessary to urge these brothers to go to you in advance and to arrange ahead of time the generous contribution
you had promised, so this may be ready as a generous gift and
not as something you feel forced to do. 6 My point is this: The
person who sows sparingly will also reap sparingly, and the person who sows generously will also reap generously. 7 Each one
of you should give just as he has decided in his heart, not reluc-
tantly or under compulsion, because God loves a cheerful giver.
8 And God is able to make all grace overflow to you so that because you have enough of everything in every way at all times,
you will overflow in every good work. 9 Just as it is written, "***He
has scattered widely, he has given to the poor; his righteousness remains forever.***" 10 Now God who provides seed for the sower and
bread for food will provide and multiply your supply of seed and
will cause the harvest of your righteousness to grow. 11 You will
be enriched in every way so that you may be generous on every

occasion, which is producing through us thanksgiving to God,
12 because the service of this ministry is not only providing for
the needs of the saints but is also overflowing with many thanks
to God. 13 Through the evidence of this service they will glorify
God because of your obedience to your confession in the gospel of Christ and the generosity of your sharing with them and
with everyone. 14 And in their prayers on your behalf, they long
for you because of the extraordinary grace God has shown to
you. 15 Thanks be to God for his indescribable gift!

REFLECT

How do we wage war against the flesh? How are we to discipline our minds to focus on Christ?

PAUL'S AUTHORITY FROM THE LORD

10 Now I, Paul, appeal to you personally by the meekness and
gentleness of Christ (I who am meek when present among
you, but am full of courage toward you when away!)—2 now I ask
that when I am present I may not have to be bold with the confidence that (I expect) I will dare to use against some who consider
us to be behaving according to human standards. 3 For though
we live as human beings, we do not wage war according to human standards, 4 for the weapons of our warfare are not human
weapons, but are made powerful by God for tearing down strongholds. We tear down arguments 5 and every arrogant obstacle
that is raised up against the knowledge of God, and we take every thought captive to make it obey Christ. 6 We are also ready
to punish every act of disobedience, whenever your obedience
is complete. 7 You are looking at outward appearances. If anyone
is confident that he belongs to Christ, he should reflect on this
again: Just as he himself belongs to Christ, so too do we. 8 For if
I boast somewhat more about our authority that the Lord gave
us for building you up and not for tearing you down, I will not
be ashamed of doing so. 9 I do not want to seem as though I am
trying to terrify you with my letters, 10 because some say, "His letters are weighty and forceful, but his physical presence is weak
and his speech is of no account." 11 Let such a person consider
this: What we say by letters when we are absent, we also are in
actions when we are present.

PAUL'S MISSION

12 For we would not dare to classify or compare ourselves with
some of those who recommend themselves. But when they measure themselves by themselves and compare themselves with
themselves, they are without understanding. 13 But we will not
boast beyond certain limits, but will confine our boasting according to the limits of the work to which God has appointed
us, that reaches even as far as you. 14 For we were not overex-
tending ourselves, as though we did not reach as far as you, because we were the first to reach as far as you with the gospel
about Christ. 15 Nor do we boast beyond certain limits in the
work done by others, but we hope that as your faith continues
to grow, our work may be greatly expanded among you according to our limits, 16 so that we may preach the gospel in the regions that lie beyond you, and not boast of work already done
in another person's area. 17 But ***the one who boasts must boast in
the Lord.*** 18 For it is not the person who commends himself who
is approved, but the person the Lord commends.

PAUL AND HIS OPPONENTS

11 I wish that you would be patient with me in a little foolishness,
but indeed you are being patient with me! 2 For I am jealous
for you with godly jealousy, because I promised you in marriage
to one husband, to present you as a pure virgin to Christ. 3 But I
am afraid that just as the serpent deceived Eve by his treachery,
your minds may be led astray from a sincere and pure devotion
to Christ. 4 For if someone comes and proclaims another Jesus
different from the one we proclaimed, or if you receive a different spirit than the one you received, or a different gospel than
the one you accepted, you put up with it well enough! 5 For I consider myself not at all inferior to those "super-apostles." 6 And
even if I am unskilled in speaking, yet I am certainly not so in
knowledge. Indeed, we have made this plain to you in everything
in every way. 7 Or did I commit a sin by humbling myself so that
you could be exalted, because I proclaimed the gospel of God to
you free of charge? 8 I robbed other churches by receiving support from them so that I could serve you! 9 When I was with you
and was in need, I was not a burden to anyone, for the brothers
who came from Macedonia fully supplied my needs. I kept myself from being a burden to you in any way, and will continue to
do so. 10 As the truth of Christ is in me, this boasting of mine will
not be stopped in the regions of Achaia. 11 Why? Because I do not
love you? God knows I do! 12 And what I am doing I will continue
to do, so that I may eliminate any opportunity for those who want
a chance to be regarded as our equals in the things they boast
about. 13 For such people are false apostles, deceitful workers,
disguising themselves as apostles of Christ. 14 And no wonder, for
even Satan disguises himself as an angel of light. 15 Therefore it is
not surprising his servants also disguise themselves as servants
of righteousness, whose end will correspond to their actions.

PAUL'S SUFFERINGS FOR CHRIST

16 I say again, let no one think that I am a fool. But if you do, then
at least accept me as a fool, so that I too may boast a little. 17 What
I am saying with this boastful confidence I do not say the way the
Lord would. Instead it is, as it were, foolishness. 18 Since many are
boasting according to human standards, I too will boast. 19 For
since you are so wise, you put up with fools gladly. 20 For you put
up with it if someone makes slaves of you, if someone exploits you,
if someone takes advantage of you, if someone behaves arrogantly
toward you, if someone strikes you in the face. 21 (To my disgrace
I must say that we were too weak for that!) But whatever anyone
else dares to boast about (I am speaking foolishly), I also dare to
boast about the same thing. 22 Are they Hebrews? So am I. Are
they Israelites? So am I. Are they descendants of Abraham? So am
I. 23 Are they servants of Christ? (I am talking like I am out of my
mind!) I am even more so: with much greater labors, with far more
imprisonments, with more severe beatings, facing death many
times. 24 Five times I received from the Jews forty lashes less one.
25 Three times I was beaten with a rod. Once I received a stoning.
Three times I suffered shipwreck. A night and a day I spent adrift
in the open sea. 26 I have been on journeys many times, in dangers
from rivers, in dangers from robbers, in dangers from my own

countrymen, in dangers from Gentiles, in dangers in the city, in
dangers in the wilderness, in dangers at sea, in dangers from false
brothers, 27 in hard work and toil, through many sleepless nights,
in hunger and thirst, many times without food, in cold and without enough clothing. 28 Apart from other things, there is the daily
pressure on me of my anxious concern for all the churches. 29 Who
is weak, and I am not weak? Who is led into sin, and I do not burn
with indignation? 30 If I must boast, I will boast about the things
that show my weakness. 31 The God and Father of the Lord Jesus,
who is blessed forever, knows I am not lying. 32 In Damascus, the
governor under King Aretas was guarding the city of Damascus in
order to arrest me, 33 but I was let down in a rope-basket through
a window in the city wall, and escaped his hands.

PAUL'S THORN IN THE FLESH

12 It is necessary to go on boasting. Though it is not profitable, I will go on to visions and revelations from the Lord.
2 I know a man in Christ who fourteen years ago (whether in the
body or out of the body I do not know, God knows) was caught
up to the third heaven. 3 And I know that this man (whether in
the body or apart from the body I do not know, God knows) 4 was
caught up into paradise and heard things too sacred to be put
into words, things that a person is not permitted to speak. 5 On
behalf of such an individual I will boast, but on my own behalf I
will not boast, except about my weaknesses. 6 For even if I wish
to boast, I will not be a fool, for I would be telling the truth, but
I refrain from this so that no one may regard me beyond what
he sees in me or what he hears from me, 7 even because of the
extraordinary character of the revelations. Therefore, so that I
would not become arrogant, a thorn in the flesh was given to me,
a messenger of Satan to trouble me—so that I would not become
arrogant. 8 I asked the Lord three times about this, that it would
depart from me. 9 But he said to me, "My grace is enough for you,
for my power is made perfect in weakness." So then, I will boast
most gladly about my weaknesses, so that the power of Christ
may reside in me. 10 Therefore I am content with weaknesses,
with insults, with troubles, with persecutions and difficulties
for the sake of Christ, for whenever I am weak, then I am strong.

THE SIGNS OF AN APOSTLE

11 I have become a fool. You yourselves forced me to do it, for
I should have been commended by you. For I lack nothing in
comparison to those "super-apostles," even though I am nothing. 12 Indeed, the signs of an apostle were performed among
you with great perseverance by signs and wonders and powerful deeds. 13 For how were you treated worse than the other
churches, except that I myself was not a burden to you? Forgive me this injustice! 14 Look, for the third time I am ready to
come to you, and I will not be a burden to you, because I do not
want your possessions, but you. For children should not have to
save up for their parents, but parents for their children. 15 Now
I will most gladly spend and be spent for your lives! If I love you
more, am I to be loved less? 16 But be that as it may, I have not
burdened you. Yet because I was a crafty person, I took you in

by deceit! 17 I have not taken advantage of you through anyone
I have sent to you, have I? 18 I urged Titus to visit you and I sent
our brother along with him. Titus did not take advantage of
you, did he? Did we not conduct ourselves in the same spirit?
Did we not behave in the same way? 19 Have you been thinking all this time that we have been defending ourselves to you?
We are speaking in Christ before God, and everything we do,
dear friends, is to build you up. 20 For I am afraid that somehow
when I come I will not find you what I wish, and you will find
me not what you wish. I am afraid that somehow there may
be quarreling, jealousy, intense anger, selfish ambition, slander, gossip, arrogance, and disorder. 21 I am afraid that when I
come again, my God may humiliate me before you, and I will
grieve for many of those who previously sinned and have not
repented of the impurity, sexual immorality, and licentious-
ness that they have practiced.

REFLECT
What did Paul desire for the Corinthians? How are we to live in light of this?

PAUL'S THIRD VISIT TO CORINTH

13 This is the third time I am coming to visit you. ***By the testimony of two or three witnesses every matter will be established.*** 2 I said before when I was present the second time and
now, though absent, I say again to those who sinned previously
and to all the rest, that if I come again, I will not spare anyone,
3 since you are demanding proof that Christ is speaking through
me. He is not weak toward you but is powerful among you. 4 For
indeed he was crucified by reason of weakness, but he lives because of God's power. For we also are weak in him, but we will
live together with him, because of God's power toward you. 5 Put
yourselves to the test to see if you are in the faith; examine yourselves! Or do you not recognize regarding yourselves that Jesus
Christ is in you—unless, indeed, you fail the test! 6 And I hope
that you will realize that we have not failed the test! 7 Now we
pray to God that you may not do anything wrong, not so that
we may appear to have passed the test, but so that you may do
what is right even if we may appear to have failed the test. 8 For
we cannot do anything against the truth, but only for the sake
of the truth. 9 For we rejoice whenever we are weak, but you are
strong. And we pray for this: that you may become fully qualified. 10 Because of this I am writing these things while absent,
so that when I arrive I may not have to deal harshly with you by
using my authority—the Lord gave it to me for building up, not
for tearing down!

FINAL EXHORTATIONS AND GREETINGS

11 Finally, brothers and sisters, rejoice, set things right, be encouraged, agree with one another, live in peace, and the God
of love and peace will be with you. 12 Greet one another with a
holy kiss. All the saints greet you. 13 The grace of the Lord Jesus
Christ and the love of God and the fellowship of the Holy Spirit
be with you all.

for FREEDOM Christ has set us free. Stand FIRM, then

MEMORY VERSE

For freedom Christ has set us free. Stand firm, *then,* and do not be subject again to the yoke of slavery.

Galatians 5:1

INTRODUCTION

Stand Firm in the Faith

In the letter to the church at Galatia, Paul provided a passionate, comprehensive explanation of the truth of the gospel: There is no earning salvation; salvation is the gift of God by grace, through faith in Christ Jesus. Paul addressed dangerous heresies that had surfaced in the Galatian church and encouraged the believers to place their faith entirely in the work of Christ for their salvation. Paul emphasized that nothing can justify us before God, and only through faith in Christ Jesus can one attain salvation.

Paul opened his letter to the Galatians with greetings and a preview of the letter's themes (1:1–9). He provided a defense of his apostolic authority (1:10—2:21), then used the Old Testament to explain the gospel message (3:1—4:31). He explained the implications of the gospel message for Christian living (5:1—6:10) and concluded with his signature and a summary of the gospel (6:11–18).

Paul identified himself as the author of Galatians, explaining his authority as an apostle to share the gospel message. The churches in northern Galatia were founded during Paul's second missionary journey to what is modern-day Turkey. The churches in the southern portion of Galatia were planted during Paul's first missionary journey. Depending on the intended destination of the letter, Galatians could be dated as early as A.D. 48 and as late as A.D. 52.

The Book of Galatians reminds us to stand firm in our faith, clinging to the truth that our works cannot save us. While it is often easy to turn to our own efforts to try to earn salvation, Galatians reminds us that our salvation is by grace alone. We can love God greatly as we stand firm in the truth that there is nothing we can do to gain or lose salvation. By grace alone, through faith alone, in Christ alone we are granted the eternal gift of salvation by a loving, gracious God.

Myanmar

OFFICIAL LANGUAGE
Burmese
POPULATION
53,909,000
UNREACHED POPULATION
45,163,000
PROFESSING CHRISTIANS
8.1%

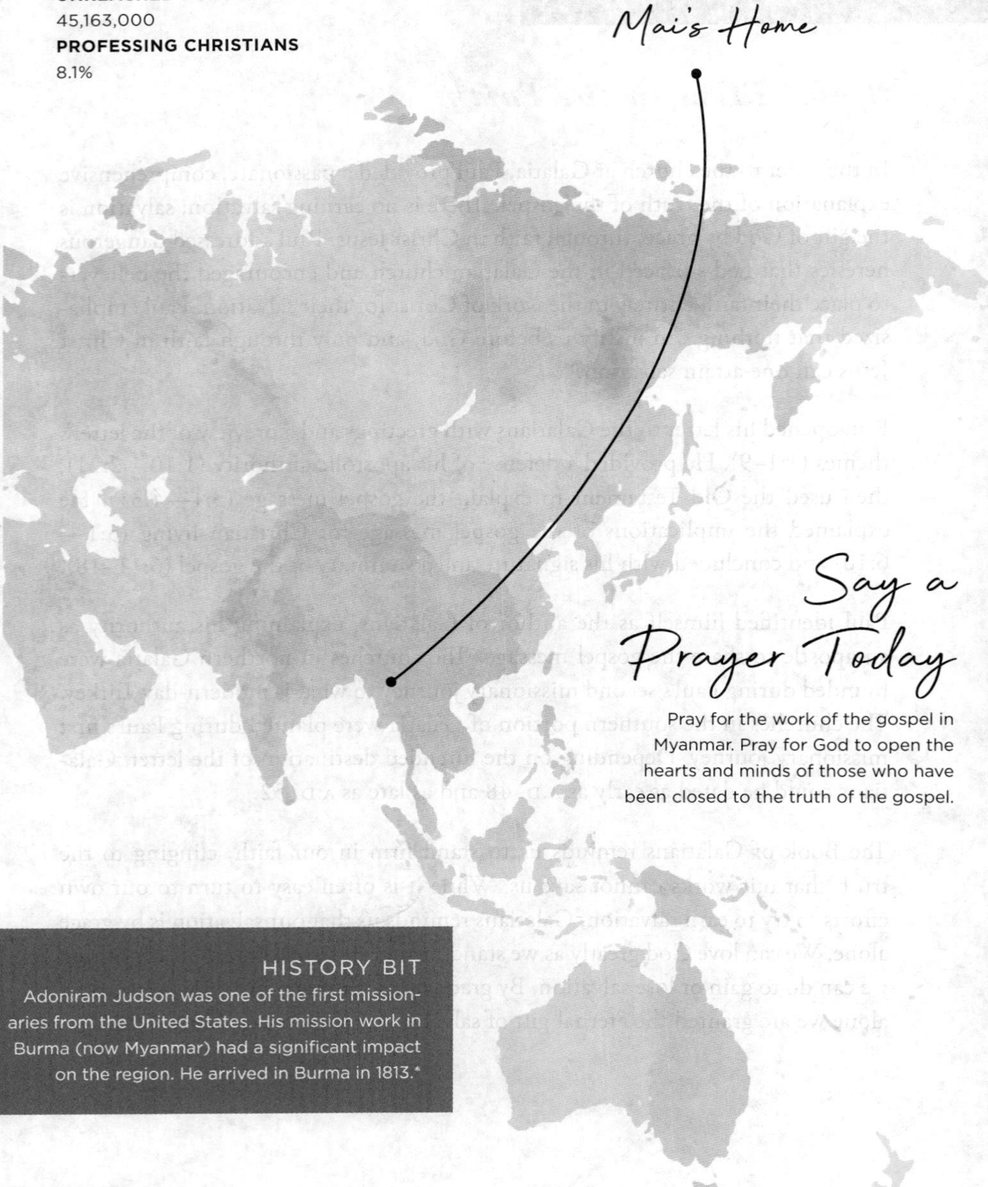

Mai's Home

Say a Prayer Today

Pray for the work of the gospel in Myanmar. Pray for God to open the hearts and minds of those who have been closed to the truth of the gospel.

HISTORY BIT

Adoniram Judson was one of the first missionaries from the United States. His mission work in Burma (now Myanmar) had a significant impact on the region. He arrived in Burma in 1813.*

Source Information:
https://joshuaproject.net/countries/BM
*John Bowden, A Chronology of World Christianity (New York, NY: Continuum, 2007), 357.

MAI'S STORY

I grew up in Myanmar in a Christian family. My father was a judge by occupation, so we frequently moved from town to town. Growing up, most of my friends were Buddhists, and I became well informed about Buddhist beliefs and teachings.

I attended Mandalay University where I studied the Burmese language. I came to understand how the Burmese language is all about Buddhism. Although I was a Christian, I looked no different from my Buddhist friends.

After completing my time at the university, I met someone from Campus Crusade for Christ in Myanmar. She taught me about Jesus Christ, and from that day I was changed. I was challenged and began to ask questions about my faith, seeking to grow in my relationship with God. Later, I decided to follow Christ only, and I joined the Campus Crusade for Christ group in Myanmar.

Even though we have so many religious challenges in Myanmar, we have to stand firm in our faith. Our faith is not based on something philosophical, like Buddhism. Faith in Christ is based on the life, death, and resurrection of Jesus Christ. It is concrete, absolute, and practical. I can stand firm in the faith because of Jesus. As Paul says, I am not ashamed of the gospel because it is the wisdom of God.

Christians are often considered foolish people because they rely on something other than themselves. Christians believe in Jesus Christ, who died on a cross. This is foolishness to Buddhists. Instead of looking like the rest of the world, I need to show my Buddhist friends who Jesus is by my life, by my faith, and by my example. It is not easy to be a Christian in this challenging world, but Jesus is strengthening me every day to be faithful to Him only. I will continue to serve Him only. To Him be all the glory.

6 WEEK READING PLAN

LOVE HIS WORD

	MONDAY	TUESDAY	WEDNESDAY	THURSDAY	FRIDAY
1	Galatians 1:1-5	Galatians 1:6-9	Galatians 1:10	Galatians 1:11-17	Galatians 1:18-24
	SOAP Galatians 1:4-5	SOAP Galatians 1:6-7	SOAP Galatians 1:10	SOAP Galatians 1:15-17	SOAP Galatians 1:23-24
2	Galatians 2:1-5	Galatians 2:6-10	Galatians 2:11-13	Galatians 2:14-16	Galatians 2:17-21
	SOAP Galatians 2:4-5	SOAP Galatians 2:10	SOAP Galatians 2:12-13	SOAP Galatians 2:15-16	SOAP Galatians 2:19-21
3	Galatians 3:1-5	Galatians 3:6-9	Galatians 3:10-14	Galatians 3:15-20	Galatians 3:21-25
	SOAP Galatians 3:2-3	SOAP Galatians 3:8-9	SOAP Galatians 3:11	SOAP Galatians 3:18	SOAP Galatians 3:24-25
4	Galatians 3:26-29	Galatians 4:1-7	Galatians 4:8-16	Galatians 4:17-20	Galatians 4:21-31
	SOAP Galatians 3:28-29	SOAP Galatians 4:4-7	SOAP Galatians 4:8-9	SOAP Galatians 4:17-19	SOAP Galatians 4:31
5	Galatians 5:1-6	Galatians 5:7-12	Galatians 5:13-15	Galatians 5:16-21	Galatians 5:22-26
	SOAP Galatians 5:1	SOAP Galatians 5:9	SOAP Galatians 5:13-14	SOAP Galatians 5:16	SOAP Galatians 5:22-23
6	Galatians 6:1	Galatians 6:2-5	Galatians 6:6-8	Galatians 6:9-10	Galatians 6:11-18
	SOAP Galatians 6:1	SOAP Galatians 6:4	SOAP Galatians 6:7-8	SOAP Galatians 6:9-10	SOAP Galatians 6:14-15

SALUTATION

1 From Paul, an apostle (not from men, nor by human agency,
but by Jesus Christ and God the Father who raised him from
the dead) 2 and all the brothers with me, to the churches of Galatia. 3 Grace and peace to you from God the Father and our Lord
Jesus Christ, 4 who gave himself for our sins to rescue us from
this present evil age according to the will of our God and Father,
5 to whom be glory forever and ever! Amen.

OCCASION OF THE LETTER

6 I am astonished that you are so quickly deserting the one who
called you by the grace of Christ and are following a different
gospel—7 not that there really is another gospel, but there are
some who are disturbing you and wanting to distort the gospel of Christ. 8 But even if we (or an angel from heaven) should
preach a gospel contrary to the one we preached to you, let him
be condemned to hell! 9 As we have said before, and now I say
again, if any one is preaching to you a gospel contrary to what
you received, let him be condemned to hell! 10 Am I now trying to gain the approval of people, or of God? Or am I trying to
please people? If I were still trying to please people, I would not
be a slave of Christ!

PAUL'S VINDICATION OF HIS APOSTLESHIP

11 Now I want you to know, brothers and sisters, that the gospel
I preached is not of human origin. 12 For I did not receive it or
learn it from any human source; instead I received it by a revelation of Jesus Christ.

13 For you have heard of my former way of life in Judaism,
how I was savagely persecuting the church of God and trying
to destroy it. 14 I was advancing in Judaism beyond many of my
contemporaries in my nation, and was extremely zealous for
the traditions of my ancestors. 15 But when the one who set
me apart from birth and called me by his grace was pleased
16 to reveal his Son in me so that I could preach him among
the Gentiles, I did not go to ask advice from any human being,
17 nor did I go up to Jerusalem to see those who were apostles
before me, but right away I departed to Arabia, and then returned to Damascus.

18 Then after three years I went up to Jerusalem to visit Cephas and get information from him, and I stayed with him fifteen days. 19 But I saw none of the other apostles except James
the Lord's brother. 20 I assure you that, before God, I am not lying about what I am writing to you! 21 Afterward I went to the
regions of Syria and Cilicia. 22 But I was personally unknown to
the churches of Judea that are in Christ. 23 They were only hearing, "The one who once persecuted us is now proclaiming the
good news of the faith he once tried to destroy." 24 So they glorified God because of me.

CONFIRMATION FROM THE JERUSALEM APOSTLES

2 Then after fourteen years I went up to Jerusalem again with
Barnabas, taking Titus along too. 2 I went there because of
a revelation and presented to them the gospel that I preach

REFLECT

Are you living your life to please people or to please God? Is this the same for every area of your life? In what areas are you more susceptible to living to please people?

among the Gentiles. But I did so only in a private meeting with the influential people, to make sure that I was not running—or had not run—in vain. 3 Yet not even Titus, who was with me, was compelled to be circumcised, although he was a Greek. 4 Now this matter arose because of the false brothers with false pretenses who slipped in unnoticed to spy on our freedom that we have in Christ Jesus, to make us slaves. 5 But we did not surrender to them even for a moment, in order that the truth of the gospel would remain with you.

6 But from those who were influential (whatever they were makes no difference to me; God shows no favoritism between people)—those influential leaders added nothing to my message. 7 On the contrary, when they saw that I was entrusted with the gospel to the uncircumcised just as Peter was entrusted with the gospel to the circumcised 8 (for he who empowered Peter for his apostleship to the circumcised also empowered me for my apostleship to the Gentiles) 9 and when James, Cephas, and John, who had a reputation as pillars, recognized the grace that had been given to me, they gave to Barnabas and me the right hand of fellowship, agreeing that we would go to the Gentiles and they to the circumcised. 10 They requested only that we remember the poor, the very thing I also was eager to do.

PAUL REBUKES PETER

11 But when Cephas came to Antioch, I opposed him to his face, because he had clearly done wrong. 12 Until certain people came from James, he had been eating with the Gentiles. But when they arrived, he stopped doing this and separated himself because he was afraid of those who were pro-circumcision. 13 And the rest of the Jews also joined with him in this hypocrisy, so that even Barnabas was led astray with them by their hypocrisy. 14 But when I saw that they were not behaving consistently with the truth of the gospel, I said to Cephas in front of them all, "If you, although you are a Jew, live like a Gentile and not like a Jew, how can you try to force the Gentiles to live like Jews?"

THE JUSTIFICATION OF JEWS AND GENTILES

15 We are Jews by birth and not Gentile sinners, 16 yet we know that no one is justified by the works of the law but by the faithfulness of Jesus Christ. And we have come to believe in Christ Jesus, so that we may be justified by the faithfulness of Christ and not by the works of the law, because by the works of the law no one will be justified. 17 But if while seeking to be justified in Christ we ourselves have also been found to be sinners, is Christ then one who encourages sin? Absolutely not! 18 But if I build up again those things I once destroyed, I demonstrate that I am one who breaks God's law. 19 For through the law I died to the law so that I may live to God. 20 I have been crucified with Christ, and it is no longer I who live, but Christ lives in me. So the life I now live in the body, I live because of the faithfulness of the Son of God, who loved me and gave himself for me. 21 I do not set aside God's grace, because if righteousness could come through the law, then Christ died for nothing!

CHALLENGE

Why could the law not provide righteousness? What does Romans 7:7–13 say the law does? If righteousness does not come from the law, from where does it come?

LOVE TO GROW

A DEBT WE CANNOT REPAY

GALATIANS 2:15–21

In Galatians 1 Paul was adamant about the most important truth in our Christian faith: Salvation comes through faith alone in Christ alone.

This was also the battle cry of the Protestant Reformation. It was commonly expressed as the Five Solas that summarize our salvation:

Sola Scriptura; salvation is revealed in Scripture alone.
Solus Christus; salvation is found in Christ alone.
Sola Gratia; salvation is granted by grace alone.
Sola Fide; salvation is received by faith alone.
Soli Deo Gloria; salvation is given for the glory of God alone.

Paul chastised the Galatians for following false teachers who said salvation came through faith in Jesus plus obedience to the law. The truth is, if we could save ourselves by obeying the law, then Christ died for nothing. Christ had to come because we were, and are, unable to keep the law. In fact, the law accuses, enslaves, and condemns us all as sinners.

The gospel is good news to the weak and powerless—like ourselves. God's standard is a perfection of which we fall terribly short. It is Christ who has kept the law, paid the debt, and continues to work in His people.

Salvation is a work of grace, but sometimes we're unclear how we should respond to that grace. Our only response is faith. Faith believes Christ paid it all. Faith believes Christ will complete His work in us.

Faith trusts Jesus is enough and in Him alone our salvation is complete.

While there are numerous passages that tell us we need to obey, this obedience is possible only because of Christ in us. Obedience is not the cause of our salvation but the response in faith to it. For it is by grace alone we are saved. It is ours for the taking. All we can do is accept the gracious gift He offers and pick up our crosses and follow Him.

JUSTIFICATION BY LAW OR BY FAITH?

3 You foolish Galatians! Who has cast a spell on you? Before your
eyes Jesus Christ was vividly portrayed as crucified! 2 The only
thing I want to learn from you is this: Did you receive the Spirit
by doing the works of the law or by believing what you heard?
3 Are you so foolish? Although you began with the Spirit, are you
now trying to finish by human effort? 4 Have you suffered so many
things for nothing?—if indeed it was for nothing. 5 Does God then
give you the Spirit and work miracles among you by your doing
the works of the law or by your believing what you heard?

6 Just as Abraham ***believed God, and it was credited to him as righteousness,*** 7 so then, understand that those who believe are the
sons of Abraham. 8 And the scripture, foreseeing that God would
justify the Gentiles by faith, proclaimed the gospel to Abraham
ahead of time, saying, "***All the nations will be blessed in you.***" 9 So
then those who believe are blessed along with Abraham the believer. 10 For all who rely on doing the works of the law are under a
curse, because it is written, "***Cursed is everyone who does not keep
on doing everything written in the book of the law.***" 11 Now it is clear
no one is justified before God by the law, because ***the righteous one
will live by faith.*** 12 But the law is not based on faith, but ***the one who
does*** the works of the law ***will live by them.*** 13 Christ redeemed us
from the curse of the law by becoming a curse for us (because it
is written, "***Cursed is everyone who hangs on a tree***") 14 in order that
in Christ Jesus the blessing of Abraham would come to the Gentiles, so that we could receive the promise of the Spirit by faith.

INHERITANCE COMES FROM PROMISES AND NOT LAW

15 Brothers and sisters, I offer an example from everyday life:
When a covenant has been ratified, even though it is only a
human contract, no one can set it aside or add anything to it.
16 Now the promises were spoken to Abraham and to his descendant. Scripture does not say, "and to the descendants," referring
to many, but "***and to your descendant,***" referring to one, who is
Christ. 17 What I am saying is this: The law that came 430 years
later does not cancel a covenant previously ratified by God, so
as to invalidate the promise. 18 For if the inheritance is based on
the law, it is no longer based on the promise, but God graciously
gave it to Abraham through the promise.

19 Why then was the law given? It was added because of transgressions, until the arrival of the descendant to whom the promise had been made. It was administered through angels by an
intermediary. 20 Now an intermediary is not for one party alone,
but God is one. 21 Is the law therefore opposed to the promises
of God? Absolutely not! For if a law had been given that was able
to give life, then righteousness would certainly have come by
the law. 22 But the scripture imprisoned everything under sin
so that the promise could be given—because of the faithfulness
of Jesus Christ—to those who believe.

REFLECT

What does faith grant us? How is this different from what the law could provide?

SONS OF GOD ARE HEIRS OF PROMISE

23 Now before faith came we were held in custody under the law,
being kept as prisoners until the coming faith would be revealed.

24 Thus the law had become our guardian until Christ, so that we
could be declared righteous by faith. 25 But now that faith has
come, we are no longer under a guardian. 26 For in Christ Jesus
you are all sons of God through faith. 27 For all of you who were
baptized into Christ have clothed yourselves with Christ. 28 There
is neither Jew nor Greek, there is neither slave nor free, there is
neither male nor female—for all of you are one in Christ Jesus.
29 And if you belong to Christ, then you are Abraham's descendants, heirs according to the promise.

4 Now I mean that the heir, as long as he is a minor, is no different from a slave, though he is the owner of everything. 2 But
he is under guardians and managers until the date set by his father. 3 So also we, when we were minors, were enslaved under the
basic forces of the world. 4 But when the appropriate time had
come, God sent out his Son, born of a woman, born under the
law, 5 to redeem those who were under the law, so that we may
be adopted as sons with full rights. 6 And because you are sons,
God sent the Spirit of his Son into our hearts, who calls "*Abba!*
Father!" 7 So you are no longer a slave but a son, and if you are a
son, then you are also an heir through God.

HEIRS OF PROMISE ARE NOT TO RETURN TO LAW

8 Formerly when you did not know God, you were enslaved to beings
that by nature are not gods at all. 9 But now that you have come to
know God (or rather to be known by God), how can you turn back
again to the weak and worthless basic forces? Do you want to be enslaved to them all over again? 10 You are observing religious days and
months and seasons and years. 11 I fear for you that my work for you
may have been in vain. 12 I beg you, brothers and sisters, become like
me, because I have become like you. You have done me no wrong!

PERSONAL APPEAL OF PAUL

13 But you know it was because of a physical illness that I first
proclaimed the gospel to you, 14 and though my physical condition put you to the test, you did not despise or reject me. Instead, you welcomed me as though I were an angel of God, as
though I were Christ Jesus himself! 15 Where then is your sense
of happiness now? For I testify about you that if it were possible, you would have pulled out your eyes and given them to me!
16 So then, have I become your enemy by telling you the truth?
17 They court you eagerly, but for no good purpose; they want
to exclude you, so that you would seek them eagerly. 18 However,
it is good to be sought eagerly for a good purpose at all times,
and not only when I am present with you. 19 My children—I am
again undergoing birth pains until Christ is formed in you! 20 I
wish I could be with you now and change my tone of voice, because I am perplexed about you.

AN APPEAL FROM ALLEGORY

21 Tell me, you who want to be under the law, do you not understand the law? 22 For it is written that Abraham had two sons,
one by the slave woman and the other by the free woman. 23 But
one, the son by the slave woman, was born by natural descent,
while the other, the son by the free woman, was born through

GOD'S HEART FOR THE NATIONS

Galatians 3:26–29

For in Christ Jesus you are all sons of God through faith. For all of you who were baptized into Christ have clothed yourselves with Christ. There is neither Jew nor Greek, there is neither slave nor free, there is neither male nor female—for all of you are one in Christ Jesus. And if you belong to Christ, then you are Abraham's descendants, heirs according to the promise.

REFLECT

What does it mean we are now children of God? How should we live in light of this truth?

LOVE TO GROW

FREE TO SING

GALATIANS 4:6–7

A caged bird doesn't sing like a free bird. Captivity can lead a traumatized bird to fly into a rage in response to an unfamiliar voice or unexpected interaction.

Before he encountered Christ on the road to Damascus, Saul of Tarsus lived bound to sin. The iron bars of pride and legalism held him in an endless cycle of anger and despair. Because he initially did not understand that Christ came to fulfill the law, this gifted man focused all his energy on fighting against Christians who proclaimed Jesus as the Messiah.

One day everything changed. Saul saw the light and responded to the gospel. In the process he became Paul, a man passionate about proclaiming Christ because he did not want anyone to live imprisoned by fear and doubt.

And because you are sons, God sent the Spirit of his Son into our hearts, who calls "Abba! Father!" So you are no longer a slave but a son, and if you are a son, then you are also an heir through God (Gal 4:6–7).

Christ has cut away the shackles of condemnation, and we are no longer defined by our sin. We can live uncaged from guilt, and salvation is the melody that rises up in our hearts. We sing a new song as sinners set free.

We are released from the record of shame against us to recount His promises. We are liberated from bitterness to sing of His love with no boundaries. We are unfettered from anxiety as God's perfect love makes melody in our hearts and casts out all fear. We are pardoned from the burden of paying for our sin to resound His extravagant grace.

The enemy of your soul may try to whisper condemnation in your ear. Do not let his lies keep you trapped in a stronghold of defeat. You're free. Lift up your voice and sing.

the promise. 24 These things may be treated as an allegory, for
these women represent two covenants. One is from Mount Sinai bearing children for slavery; this is Hagar. 25 Now Hagar represents Mount Sinai in Arabia and corresponds to the present
Jerusalem, for she is in slavery with her children. 26 But the Jerusalem above is free, and she is our mother. 27 For it is written:

> ***"Rejoice, O barren woman who does not bear children;***
> ***break forth and shout, you who have no birth pains,***
> ***because the children of the desolate***
> ***woman are more numerous***
> ***than those of the woman who has a husband."***

28 But you, brothers and sisters, are children of the promise
like Isaac. 29 But just as at that time the one born by natural descent persecuted the one born according to the Spirit, so it is
now. 30 But what does the scripture say? "***Throw out the slave woman and her son, for the son of the slave woman will not share the
inheritance with the son***" of the free woman. 31 Therefore, brothers and sisters, we are not children of the slave woman but of
the free woman.

FREEDOM OF THE BELIEVER

5 For freedom Christ has set us free. Stand firm, then, and do
not be subject again to the yoke of slavery. 2 Listen! I, Paul,
tell you that if you let yourselves be circumcised, Christ will
be of no benefit to you at all! 3 And I testify again to every man
who lets himself be circumcised that he is obligated to obey the
whole law. 4 You who are trying to be declared righteous by the
law have been alienated from Christ; you have fallen away from
grace! 5 For through the Spirit, by faith, we wait expectantly for
the hope of righteousness. 6 For in Christ Jesus neither circumcision nor uncircumcision carries any weight—the only thing
that matters is faith working through love.

7 You were running well; who prevented you from obeying the
truth? 8 This persuasion does not come from the one who calls
you! 9 A little yeast makes the whole batch of dough rise! 10 I am
confident in the Lord that you will accept no other view. But the
one who is confusing you will pay the penalty, whoever he may
be. 11 Now, brothers and sisters, if I am still preaching circumcision, why am I still being persecuted? In that case the offense
of the cross has been removed. 12 I wish those agitators would
go so far as to castrate themselves!

PRACTICE LOVE

13 For you were called to freedom, brothers and sisters; only do
not use your freedom as an opportunity to indulge your flesh,
but through love serve one another. 14 For the whole law can be
summed up in a single commandment, namely, "***You must love
your neighbor as yourself.***" 15 However, if you continually bite and
devour one another, beware that you are not consumed by one
another. 16 But I say, live by the Spirit and you will not carry out
the desires of the flesh. 17 For the flesh has desires that are opposed to the Spirit, and the Spirit has desires that are opposed
to the flesh, for these are in opposition to each other, so that you

REFLECT

How can we determine whether we are living by the Spirit or by the flesh?

LOVE TO GROW

LOVING OUR NEIGHBOR

GALATIANS 5:13–14

Want to change the world? Make living out Galatians 5:13–14 a priority.

For you were called to freedom, brothers and sisters; only do not use your freedom as an opportunity to indulge your flesh, but through love serve one another. For the whole law can be summed up in a single commandment, namely, "You must love your neighbor as yourself" (Gal 5:13–14).

Loving our neighbor as ourselves is one of the heartbeats of Love God Greatly. It's why we are passionate about equipping women around the world with God's Word in their native languages. Since we know firsthand how important and life-changing God's Word is, we want every woman to have the same opportunities we do to read and understand it.

Loving others as ourselves moves beyond passive love to active love. It's intentional. It's personal. It's putting ourselves in others' shoes and thinking, "How would I feel in that situation? What would I wish others would do?" and then doing it.

If we take this passage to heart, shouldn't we do everything we can to help others have the same opportunity to grow in faith? Shouldn't we remove as many roadblocks as we can that hinder women from being in God's Word? Since we know the power of God's Word, how it changes us from the inside out, shouldn't we want that for those who don't have it?

God's Word changes lives, legacies, and eternities.

Let God's love be your motivation and reach out to those across the street or across the world. God's definition of *neighbor* has no boundary lines. Loving our neighbor shows a hurting world the love of Christ. It's in the giving of ourselves. It's in seeing others the way we see ourselves, each needing grace, hope, and love. By giving ourselves and meeting others' needs with compassion and grace, we live out the freedom we have in Christ.

Want to change the world? Go love your neighbors as yourself.

cannot do what you want. 18 But if you are led by the Spirit, you
are not under the law. 19 Now the works of the flesh are obvious:
sexual immorality, impurity, depravity, 20 idolatry, sorcery, hos-
tilities, strife, jealousy, outbursts of anger, selfish rivalries, dissensions, factions, 21 envying, murder, drunkenness, carousing,
and similar things. I am warning you, as I had warned you before: Those who practice such things will not inherit the kingdom of God!

22 But the fruit of the Spirit is love, joy, peace, patience, kindness, goodness, faithfulness, 23 gentleness, and self-control.
Against such things there is no law. 24 Now those who belong to
Christ have crucified the flesh with its passions and desires. 25 If
we live by the Spirit, let us also behave in accordance with the
Spirit. 26 Let us not become conceited, provoking one another,
being jealous of one another.

REFLECT

What does it mean for us to carry one another's burdens?

SUPPORT ONE ANOTHER

6 Brothers and sisters, if a person is discovered in some sin,
you who are spiritual restore such a person in a spirit of gentleness. Pay close attention to yourselves, so that you are not
tempted too. 2 Carry one another's burdens, and in this way you
will fulfill the law of Christ. 3 For if anyone thinks he is something when he is nothing, he deceives himself. 4 Let each one
examine his own work. Then he can take pride in himself and
not compare himself with someone else. 5 For each one will
carry his own load.

6 Now the one who receives instruction in the word must
share all good things with the one who teaches it. 7 Do not be
deceived. God will not be made a fool. For a person will reap
what he sows, 8 because the person who sows to his own flesh
will reap corruption from the flesh, but the one who sows to
the Spirit will reap eternal life from the Spirit. 9 So we must
not grow weary in doing good, for in due time we will reap, if
we do not give up. 10 So then, whenever we have an opportunity,
let us do good to all people, and especially to those who belong
to the family of faith.

FINAL INSTRUCTIONS AND BENEDICTION

11 See what big letters I make as I write to you with my own hand!

12 Those who want to make a good showing in external matters
are trying to force you to be circumcised. They do so only to avoid
being persecuted for the cross of Christ. 13 For those who are circumcised do not obey the law themselves, but they want you to
be circumcised so that they can boast about your flesh. 14 But
may I never boast except in the cross of our Lord Jesus Christ,
through which the world has been crucified to me, and I to the
world. 15 For neither circumcision nor uncircumcision counts for
anything; the only thing that matters is a new creation! 16 And all
who will behave in accordance with this rule, peace and mercy
be on them, and on the Israel of God.

17 From now on let no one cause me trouble, for I bear the
marks of Jesus on my body.

18 The grace of our Lord Jesus Christ be with your spirit, brothers and sisters. Amen.

LIVE *Worthily*
OF THE *calling* WITH
WHICH *you* HAVE BEEN *called*,
WITH *all humility* AND
gentleness WITH
PATIENCE,
putting up WITH ONE
ANOTHER IN *love*
MAKING *every* EFFORT
TO KEEP THE
UNITY OF THE *Spirit*
IN THE BOND OF
peace

MEMORY VERSE

I, therefore, the prisoner for the Lord, urge you to live worthily of the calling with which you have been called, with all humility and gentleness, with patience, putting up with one another in love, making *every effort to* keep the unity of the Spirit in the bond of peace.

Ephesians 4:1–3

Ephesians

INTRODUCTION

Unity in the Body of Christ

The city of Ephesus was a thriving metropolis and a vital commercial center in the Roman Empire. It was the home of the famous temple for the Greek goddess of the hunt and of childbirth and midwifery, Artemis. It was also the city that became the center for Paul's missionary work in the region. From a prison cell in Rome, Paul penned the letter to the believers in Ephesus, encouraging them in their faith.

Paul's letter to the Ephesians emphasized the truth that salvation is by faith alone. He addressed central doctrines of the Christian faith, including the sealing of the Spirit and unity in the body (Eph 1–3). He also described how the guiding truths of our faith should be reflected in the life and behavior of a Christian (Eph 4–6).

As in most of his letters, Paul identified himself as the author of Ephesians. He wrote of his imprisonment, likely referring to his house arrest in Rome (Acts 28) around A.D. 60. The church in Ephesus was founded around A.D. 52, during Paul's second missionary journey. Paul spent three years in Ephesus, about A.D. 52–55, on his third missionary journey.

The Book of Ephesians emphasizes unity in the body of Christ and the hope of every believer. God created us in Christ Jesus to accomplish His will in the world. Loving God greatly includes using our gifts and energy to act in His name. These works do not save us but are an outpouring of the love and gratitude we have for Him. He has already prepared us to accomplish these good works. Even from a prison cell Paul wrote to increase our confidence that our salvation is secure, and God is working through us to bring about His purposes in the world.

Romania

OFFICIAL LANGUAGE
Romanian
POPULATION
19,305,000
UNREACHED POPULATION
71,000
PROFESSING CHRISTIANS
93.7%

Diana's Home

Say a Prayer Today

Pray for Diana and the Love God Greatly Romanian team. Pray they would be effective in sharing the gospel to those they encounter and that they would be a light in dark places.

HISTORY BIT

The apostle Andrew first brought the message of the gospel to the region that is now Romania. Early Romanian Christians were among the earliest martyrs of the faith, persecuted under Diocletian in A.D. 303.*

Source Information:
https://joshuaproject.net/countries/RO
*David B. Barrett, *World Christian Encyclopedia*, Romania (New York, NY: Oxford University Press, 1982), 585.

LOVE YOUR NEIGHBOR

Her Journey

DIANA'S STORY

Too often, I feel as if I don't measure up. I often compare myself to others, feeling I should do more, try harder, or be better in order to live up to some unspoken standard. I often see other women as competition.

One day, I came across a Love God Greatly Facebook group. I was struck by the idea of an online community and a way to study the Bible with other women. I live in Romania, but the women in my first Love God Greatly group were from all over the world. I loved the opportunity to meet sisters in Christ from other countries.

I was shocked and comforted by the way the study and the women in my group seemed to meet me where I was. For one of the first times in my life I did not feel inadequate or unintelligent. I did not feel the need to compete with other women or to prove my worth or knowledge. We were all learning together. We were all sharing our experiences, allowing ourselves to be vulnerable, and growing in our walks with Christ.

This was a turning point for me. After sharing these studies with friends, one friend began translating Love God Greatly studies into Romanian, our native language. It is a gift to have ways to study the Bible in my own language. I can share these studies with my friends and walk through Scripture with women in my own community.

Though I still struggle with comparison and with feeling inadequate, recognizing my need for community has given me a new perspective. Now, instead of comparing, I see the unity I have with other believers in Christ.

6 WEEK READING PLAN

LOVE HIS WORD

MONDAY	TUESDAY	WEDNESDAY	THURSDAY	FRIDAY
Ephesians 1:1-2	Ephesians 1:3-8	Ephesians 1:9-14	Ephesians 1:15-19	Ephesians 1:20-23
SOAP Ephesians 1:1-2	SOAP Ephesians 1:7-8	SOAP Ephesians 1:13-14	SOAP Ephesians 1:17-19	SOAP Ephesians 1:20-21
Ephesians 2:1-3	Ephesians 2:4-10	Ephesians 2:11-13	Ephesians 2:14-18	Ephesians 2:19-22
SOAP Ephesians 2:1-3	SOAP Ephesians 2:8-10	SOAP Ephesians 2:13	SOAP Ephesians 2:14-16	SOAP Ephesians 2:19-20
Ephesians 3:1-3	Ephesians 3:4-9	Ephesians 3:10-13	Ephesians 3:14-19	Ephesians 3:20-21
SOAP Ephesians 3:1-3	SOAP Ephesians 3:7-9	SOAP Ephesians 3:13	SOAP Ephesians 3:16-19	SOAP Ephesians 3:20-21
Ephesians 4:1-6	Ephesians 4:7-13	Ephesians 4:14-16	Ephesians 4:17-24	Ephesians 4:25-32
SOAP Ephesians 4:1-3	SOAP Ephesians 4:11-13	SOAP Ephesians 4:15-16	SOAP Ephesians 4:22-24	SOAP Ephesians 4:31-32
Ephesians 5:1-5	Ephesians 5:6-14	Ephesians 5:15-21	Ephesians 5:22-24	Ephesians 5:25-33
SOAP Ephesians 5:1-2	SOAP Ephesians 5:14	SOAP Ephesians 5:15-17	SOAP Ephesians 5:24	SOAP Ephesians 5:28
Ephesians 6:1-4	Ephesians 6:5-9	Ephesians 6:10-17	Ephesians 6:18-20	Ephesians 6:21-24
SOAP Ephesians 6:2-3	SOAP Ephesians 6:7-8	SOAP Ephesians 6:10-11	SOAP Ephesians 6:18	SOAP Ephesians 6:23-24

SALUTATION

1 From Paul, an apostle of Christ Jesus by the will of God, to the
saints [in Ephesus]*, the faithful in Christ Jesus. 2 Grace and
peace to you from God our Father and the Lord Jesus Christ!

SPIRITUAL BLESSINGS IN CHRIST

3 Blessed is the God and Father of our Lord Jesus Christ, who has
blessed us with every spiritual blessing in the heavenly realms
in Christ. 4 For he chose us in Christ before the foundation of the
world that we should be holy and blameless before him in love.
5 He did this by predestining us to adoption as his legal heirs
through Jesus Christ, according to the pleasure of his will—6 to
the praise of the glory of his grace that he has freely bestowed on
us in his dearly loved Son. 7 In him we have redemption through
his blood, the forgiveness of our offenses, according to the riches
of his grace 8 that he lavished on us in all wisdom and insight.
9 He did this when he revealed to us the mystery of his will, according to his good pleasure that he set forth in Christ, 10 toward
the administration of the fullness of the times, to head up all
things in Christ—the things in heaven and the things on earth.
11 In Christ we too have been claimed as God's own possession,
since we were predestined according to the purpose of him who
accomplishes all things according to the counsel of his will 12 so
that we, who were the first to set our hope on Christ, would be to
the praise of his glory. 13 And when you heard the word of truth
(the gospel of your salvation)—when you believed in Christ—you
were marked with the seal of the promised Holy Spirit, 14 who is
the down payment of our inheritance, until the redemption of
God's own possession, to the praise of his glory.

CHALLENGE

What are the blessings God has given us through Christ Jesus? Take time to write these out and thank God for each one of them. How has each affected your life?

PRAYER FOR WISDOM AND REVELATION

15 For this reason, because I have heard of your faith in the Lord
Jesus and your love for all the saints, 16 I do not cease to give
thanks for you when I remember you in my prayers. 17 I pray that
the God of our Lord Jesus Christ, the glorious Father, will give you
spiritual wisdom and revelation in your growing knowledge of
him, 18—since the eyes of your heart have been enlightened—so
that you can know what is the hope of his calling, what is the
wealth of his glorious inheritance in the saints, 19 and what is the
incomparable greatness of his power toward us who believe, as
displayed in the exercise of his immense strength. 20 This power
he exercised in Christ when he raised him from the dead and
seated him at his right hand in the heavenly realms 21 far above
every rule and authority and power and dominion and every
name that is named, not only in this age but also in the one to
come. 22 And God *put all things under* Christ's *feet,* and gave him
to the church as head over all things. 23 Now the church is his
body, the fullness of him who fills all in all.

NEW LIFE INDIVIDUALLY

2 And although you were dead in your offenses and sins, 2 in
which you formerly lived according to this world's present
path, according to the ruler of the domain of the air, the ruler
of the spirit that is now energizing the sons of disobedience,

LOVE TO GROW

DEAD OR ALIVE?

EPHESIANS 2:1–9

What if I told you when you were apart from Christ, you were not actually alive? Ephesians 2 says that "you were dead" (Eph 2:1). Not physically but spiritually.

When Adam and Eve ate the fruit of the knowledge of good and evil in the garden, they disobeyed God, allowing sin to enter the world. Now every person born on this earth is tainted with sin. We can do nothing to breathe life into ourselves or into one another.

Ephesians 2:1–3 says that formerly we lived according to the dark powers of this world, committing acts of evil, living out our fleshly desires, and disobeying God. By living in this state, we disregarded what was lawful and pursued our own happiness. Today we see this played out in anger, bitterness, drunkenness, disrespect, greed, power, gluttony, and selfishness. These things can sneak into our lives and take over if we allow it.

However, we are not left in despair.

But God, being rich in mercy, because of his great love with which he loved us, even though we were dead in offenses, made us alive together with Christ—by grace you are saved! (Eph 2:4–5).

Paul encouraged us with two powerful words: "But God" (Eph 2:4). Humanity was in desperate need of a savior to release us from sin, death, and destruction. Christ came into the world to redeem humanity and to restore our relationship with Him.

This is nothing of our own doing; it is the initiating, loving act of God alone. God is full of mercy and love for us, though "we were dead in transgressions" (Eph 2:5).

By grace Christ saved us in His death and resurrection. Praise God Almighty!

We do not deserve to be saved, to have life, or to be loved by a glorious, righteous, holy God, but He chose to save us and He loves us dearly. Because this is true, we ought to live according to God's ways with repentant hearts and to allow the Holy Spirit to sanctify us to be more like his Son, Christ Jesus. I pray this reminder of our previous state of life will draw us to our knees in praise, humility, and thankfulness and fuel us to love God greatly.

3 among whom all of us also formerly lived out our lives in the
cravings of our flesh, indulging the desires of the flesh and the
mind, and were by nature children of wrath even as the rest...
4 But God, being rich in mercy, because of his great love with
which he loved us, 5 even though we were dead in offenses, made
us alive together with Christ—by grace you are saved!—6 and he
raised us up together with him and seated us together with
him in the heavenly realms in Christ Jesus, 7 to demonstrate in
the coming ages the surpassing wealth of his grace in kindness
toward us in Christ Jesus. 8 For by grace you are saved through
faith, and this is not from yourselves, it is the gift of God; 9 it is
not from works, so that no one can boast. 10 For we are his creative work, having been created in Christ Jesus for good works
that God prepared beforehand so we can do them.

NEW LIFE CORPORATELY

11 Therefore remember that formerly you, the Gentiles in the
flesh—who are called "uncircumcision" by the so-called "circumcision" that is performed on the body by human hands—12 that
you were at that time without the Messiah, alienated from the
citizenship of Israel and strangers to the covenants of promise, having no hope and without God in the world. 13 But now
in Christ Jesus you who used to be far away have been brought
near by the blood of Christ. 14 For he is our peace, the one who
made both groups into one and who destroyed the middle wall
of partition, the hostility, 15 when he nullified in his flesh the law
of commandments in decrees. He did this to create in himself
one new man out of two, thus making peace, 16 and to reconcile
them both in one body to God through the cross, by which the
hostility has been killed. 17 And he came and preached peace to
you who were far off and peace to those who were near, 18 so that
through him we both have access in one Spirit to the Father. 19 So
then you are no longer foreigners and noncitizens, but you are
fellow citizens with the saints and members of God's household,
20 because you have been built on the foundation of the apostles
and prophets, with Christ Jesus himself as the cornerstone. 21 In
him the whole building, being joined together, grows into a holy
temple in the Lord, 22 in whom you also are being built together
into a dwelling place of God in the Spirit.

PAUL'S RELATIONSHIP TO THE DIVINE MYSTERY

3 For this reason I, Paul, the prisoner of Christ Jesus for the sake
of you Gentiles 2 if indeed you have heard of the stewardship
of God's grace that was given to me for you, 3 that by revelation the
mystery was made known to me, as I wrote before briefly. 4 When
reading this, you will be able to understand my insight into the
mystery of Christ 5 (which was not disclosed to people in former
generations as it has now been revealed to his holy apostles and
prophets by the Spirit), 6 namely, that through the gospel the
Gentiles are fellow heirs, fellow members of the body, and fellow
partakers of the promise in Christ Jesus. 7 I became a servant of
this gospel according to the gift of God's grace that was given to
me by the exercise of his power. 8 To me—less than the least of
all the saints—this grace was given, to proclaim to the Gentiles

REFLECT

How can we practice unity within the body of Christ? Why is unity so important?

the unfathomable riches of Christ 9 and to enlighten everyone
about God's secret plan—the mystery that has been hidden for
ages in God who has created all things. 10 The purpose of this en-
lightenment is that through the church the multifaceted wisdom
of God should now be disclosed to the rulers and the authorities
in the heavenly realms. 11 This was according to the eternal purpose that he accomplished in Christ Jesus our Lord, 12 in whom
we have boldness and confident access to God by way of Christ's
faithfulness. 13 For this reason I ask you not to lose heart because
of what I am suffering for you, which is your glory.

REFLECT

Do you believe that God can do far beyond all that you ask or think? Why or why not?

PRAYER FOR STRENGTHENED LOVE

14 For this reason I kneel before the Father, 15 from whom every
family in heaven and on earth is named. 16 I pray that according
to the wealth of his glory he will grant you to be strengthened
with power through his Spirit in the inner person, 17 that Christ
will dwell in your hearts through faith, so that, because you have
been rooted and grounded in love, 18 you will be able to comprehend with all the saints what is the breadth and length and height
and depth, 19 and thus to know the love of Christ that surpasses
knowledge, so that you will be filled up to all the fullness of God.

20 Now to him who by the power that is working within us is
able to do far beyond all that we ask or think, 21 to him be the
glory in the church and in Christ Jesus to all generations, forever and ever. Amen.

LIVE IN UNITY

4 I, therefore, the prisoner for the Lord, urge you to live worthily of the calling with which you have been called, 2 with
all humility and gentleness, with patience, putting up with one
another in love, 3 making every effort to keep the unity of the
Spirit in the bond of peace. 4 There is one body and one Spirit,
just as you too were called to the one hope of your calling, 5 one
Lord, one faith, one baptism, 6 one God and Father of all, who is
over all and through all and in all.

7 But to each one of us grace was given according to the measure of Christ's gift. 8 Therefore it says, "***When he ascended on
high he captured captives; he gave gifts to men.***" 9 Now what is
the meaning of "***he ascended***," except that he also descended to
the lower regions, namely, the earth? 10 He, the very one who descended, is also the one who ascended above all the heavens, in
order to fill all things. 11 And he himself gave some as apostles,
some as prophets, some as evangelists, and some as pastors and
teachers, 12 to equip the saints for the work of ministry, that is,
to build up the body of Christ, 13 until we all attain to the unity
of the faith and of the knowledge of the Son of God—a mature
person, attaining to the measure of Christ's full stature. 14 So we
are no longer to be children, tossed back and forth by waves and
carried about by every wind of teaching by the trickery of people
who craftily carry out their deceitful schemes. 15 But practicing
the truth in love, we will in all things grow up into Christ, who
is the head. 16 From him the whole body grows, fitted and held
together through every supporting ligament. As each one does
its part, the body builds itself up in love.

REFLECT

How do we live worthy of the calling on our lives? What can we do each day to live out our calling?

LIVE IN HOLINESS

17 So I say this, and insist in the Lord, that you no longer live as the
Gentiles do, in the futility of their thinking. 18 They are darkened
in their understanding, being alienated from the life of God because of the ignorance that is in them due to the hardness of their
hearts. 19 Because they are callous, they have given themselves over
to indecency for the practice of every kind of impurity with greed-
iness. 20 But you did not learn about Christ like this, 21 if indeed you
heard about him and were taught in him, just as the truth is in
Jesus. 22 You were taught with reference to your former way of life
to lay aside the old man who is being corrupted in accordance with
deceitful desires, 23 to be renewed in the spirit of your mind, 24 and
to put on the new man who has been created in God's image—in
righteousness and holiness that comes from truth.

25 Therefore, having laid aside falsehood, ***each one of you speak
the truth with his neighbor,*** because we are members of one another. 26 ***Be angry and do not sin;*** do not let the sun go down on
the cause of your anger. 27 Do not give the devil an opportunity.
28 The one who steals must steal no longer; instead he must labor,
doing good with his own hands, so that he will have something to
share with the one who has need. 29 You must let no unwholesome
word come out of your mouth, but only what is beneficial for the
building up of the one in need, that it would give grace to those
who hear. 30 And do not grieve the Holy Spirit of God, by whom
you were sealed for the day of redemption. 31 You must put away
all bitterness, anger, wrath, quarreling, and slanderous talk—indeed all malice. 32 Instead, be kind to one another, compassionate, forgiving one another, just as God in Christ also forgave you.

LIVE IN LOVE

5 Therefore, be imitators of God as dearly loved children 2 and live
in love, just as Christ also loved us and gave himself for us, a sacrificial and fragrant offering to God. 3 But among you there must not
be either sexual immorality, impurity of any kind, or greed, as these
are not fitting for the saints. 4 Neither should there be vulgar speech,
foolish talk, or coarse jesting—all of which are out of character—but
rather thanksgiving. 5 For you can be confident of this one thing:
that no person who is immoral, impure, or greedy (such a person is
an idolater) has any inheritance in the kingdom of Christ and God.

LIVE IN THE LIGHT

6 Let nobody deceive you with empty words, for because of these
things God's wrath comes on the sons of disobedience. 7 Therefore
do not be sharers with them, 8 for you were at one time darkness,
but now you are light in the Lord. Live like children of light— 9 for
the fruit of the light consists in all goodness, righteousness, and
truth— 10 trying to learn what is pleasing to the Lord. 11 Do not participate in the unfruitful deeds of darkness, but rather expose
them. 12 For the things they do in secret are shameful even to mention. 13 But all things being exposed by the light are made visible.
14 For everything made visible is light, and for this reason it says:

> "Awake, O sleeper!
> Rise from the dead,
> and Christ will shine on you!"

LOVE TO GROW

COMING CLEAN

EPHESIANS 4:22–24

A few years ago my sister convinced me to do a Color Run. It was a 5K that promised a good time full of music, colored powder, bubbles, glitter, and no timer at the end to show how quickly (or, in my case, how slowly) I'd finished.

Although the distance was difficult for this nonrunner, the race did fulfill the promise of color and glitter. Apparently, I hadn't been showered in enough colored powder by volunteers at previous stations because a sweet-looking gal at the final stop dusted me from head to toe in blue.

At the end of the event we did our best to shake, wipe, and brush off as much color as we could. We changed into clean clothes and stopped for breakfast, where we realized that fresh clothes over blue bodies still made us stand out as we waited for bagels.

Ephesians 4:22–24 instructs us about a form of inner cleansing, calling us to lay aside our former selves, the nature that is corrupted by sin, and be renewed in the spirit of our minds. We're to put on a new self, one created and renewed by the Holy Spirit living within us and leading us to holiness and truth.

At the Color Run we enjoyed getting showered with color—the effect was spectacular! We can't cover up sin with something pretty and call that effort good enough, nor can we do all the right activities, say all the right things, and wear all the right masks to make things right. At the end of the day, our old self, the sinful self, will still be waiting. Under the burden of all of those coverups, we'll find ourselves dragged down in discouragement, away from the abundant, joy-filled life God has planned for us.

Imagine the freedom that comes with dropping the old thought patterns, destructive habits, bitterness, and envy you've been carrying.

How much more energy would you have to serve and love and honor God if you were released from the extra baggage of sin?

If you decide to participate in a Color Run, savor all those beautiful hues. If you're feeling weighed down by sins and cover-ups, lay them at the foot of the cross today. Whatever old things are holding you back from putting on your new self, let them go. God can and will take every sin and wash you white as snow—which is also a lovely color!

LIVE WISELY

15 Therefore consider carefully how you live—not as unwise but as
wise, 16 taking advantage of every opportunity, because the days
are evil. 17 For this reason do not be foolish, but be wise by understanding what the Lord's will is. 18 And do not get drunk with
wine, which is debauchery, but be filled by the Spirit, 19 speaking
to one another in psalms, hymns, and spiritual songs, singing
and making music in your hearts to the Lord, 20 always giving
thanks to God the Father for all things in the name of our Lord
Jesus Christ, 21 and submitting to one another out of reverence
for Christ.

REFLECT

How can we live as wise people? What does it mean to understand what the Lord's will is?

EXHORTATIONS TO HOUSEHOLDS

22 Wives, submit to your husbands as to the Lord, 23 because
the husband is the head of the wife as also Christ is the head of
the church (he himself being the savior of the body). 24 But as the
church submits to Christ, so also wives should submit to their
husbands in everything. 25 Husbands, love your wives just as
Christ loved the church and gave himself for her 26 to sanctify
her by cleansing her with the washing of the water by the word,
27 so that he may present the church to himself as glorious—
not having a stain or wrinkle, or any such blemish, but holy
and blameless. 28 In the same way husbands ought to love their
wives as their own bodies. He who loves his wife loves himself.
29 For no one has ever hated his own body, but he feeds it and
takes care of it, just as Christ also does the church, 30 because
we are members of his body. 31 ***For this reason a man will leave***
his father and mother and will be joined to his wife, and the two
will become one flesh. 32 This mystery is great—but I am actually
speaking with reference to Christ and the church. 33 Nevertheless, each one of you must also love his own wife as he loves
himself, and the wife must respect her husband.

6 Children, obey your parents in the Lord, for this is right.
2 "***Honor your father and mother,***" which is the first commandment accompanied by a promise, namely, 3 "***that it will go***
well with you and that you will live a long time on the earth."

4 Fathers, do not provoke your children to anger, but raise them
up in the discipline and instruction of the Lord.

5 Slaves, obey your human masters with fear and trembling, in
the sincerity of your heart, as to Christ, 6 not like those who do
their work only when someone is watching—as people-pleasers—
but as slaves of Christ doing the will of God from the heart. 7 Obey
with enthusiasm, as though serving the Lord and not people,
8 because you know that each person, whether slave or free, if he
does something good, this will be rewarded by the Lord.

9 Masters, treat your slaves the same way, giving up the use of
threats, because you know that both you and they have the same
master in heaven, and there is no favoritism with him.

EXHORTATIONS FOR SPIRITUAL WARFARE

10 Finally, be strengthened in the Lord and in the strength of
his power. 11 Clothe yourselves with the full armor of God, so
that you will be able to stand against the schemes of the devil.
12 For our struggle is not against flesh and blood, but against the

LOVE TO GROW

SUIT UP

EPHESIANS 6:13

In Ephesians 6, we're reminded of the real battle between good and evil. Satan will do whatever he can to distract, tempt, and lie his way straight into our hearts and minds in an attempt to devour our mission.

For this reason, take up the full armor of God so that you may be able to stand your ground on the evil day, and having done everything, to stand (Eph 6:13).

The enemy ever so slyly distracts us so that we neglect to dress in our daily spiritual armor. He tells us we're too weak to fight. He messes with our minds and convinces us to compare our lives with others until we're dissatisfied. We then depend on our emotions far too much, desire the approval of others, even if it means compromising, and struggle to find our identity and value. He finds and targets areas in which we're unstable, vulnerable, and fearful, and he tries to defeat us.

There's good news! As a child of the warrior-king, Jesus, you can cling to these truths in the battle:

- Your victory has already been secured through Christ (see 1 Cor 15:57). Death has been defeated, and no power of hell can reverse the grasp that Jesus has on you.
- The power that raised Jesus from the dead lives in you (see Rom 8:11). In your weakness, He is strong (see 2 Cor 12:9–11). Nothing that comes your way today is too hard for God (see Jer 32:17).
- The Word promises that if you resist the devil, he will flee from you (see Jas 4:7). Recognize his tactics, speak truth to his lies, turn from sin. Tell Satan to get behind you because you're covered by the blood of Christ and you have a race to run in this generation.
- The flaming arrows may come, but they cannot destroy you. "We are experiencing trouble on every side, but are not crushed; we are perplexed, but not driven to despair" (see 2 Cor 4:8).

We don't have to be caught off-guard. We can be ready. We can wear our armor every day. We know there will be a struggle, but we can choose to be intentional and determined in the fight. With the power of God on our side, we will stand our ground.

rulers, against the powers, against the world rulers of this darkness, against the spiritual forces of evil in the heavens. 13 For this
reason, take up the full armor of God so that you may be able to
stand your ground on the evil day, and having done everything,
to stand. 14 Stand firm therefore, by fastening the belt of truth
around your waist, by putting on the breastplate of righteousness, 15 by fitting your feet with the preparation that comes from
the good news of peace, 16 and in all of this, by taking up the shield
of faith with which you can extinguish all the flaming arrows of
the evil one. 17 And take *the helmet of salvation* and the sword of
the Spirit (which is the word of God). 18 With every prayer and
petition, pray at all times in the Spirit, and to this end be alert,
with all perseverance and petitions for all the saints. 19 Pray for
me also, that I may be given the right words when I begin to
speak—that I may confidently make known the mystery of the
gospel, 20 for which I am an ambassador in chains. Pray that I
may be able to speak boldly as I ought to speak.

REFLECT

How can we, like Paul, spread grace to our fellow believers and love Christ with an undying love?

FAREWELL COMMENTS

21 Tychicus, my dear brother and faithful servant in the Lord,
will make everything known to you, so that you too may know
about my circumstances, how I am doing. 22 I have sent him to
you for this very purpose, that you may know our circumstances
and that he may encourage your hearts.

23 Peace to the brothers and sisters, and love with faith, from
God the Father and the Lord Jesus Christ. 24 Grace be with all
those who love our Lord Jesus Christ with an undying love.

WHATEVER is true,
Worthy OF RESPECT,
JUST, pure, lovely,
COMMENDABLE,
if something is
EXCELLENT or
praiseworthy,
THINK ABOUT
THESE things.

MEMORY VERSE

Finally, brothers and sisters, whatever is true, whatever is worthy of respect, whatever is just, whatever is pure, whatever is lovely, whatever is commendable, if something is excellent or praiseworthy, think about these things.

Philippians 4:8

Philippians

INTRODUCTION

A Joy-Filled Life

The joy of life in Christ is present on every page of the letter to the Philippians. Paul had endured great suffering for Christ. Even in these experiences, he discovered incredible joy and perseverance, teaching him to be content in all circumstances. Paul's letter to the church in Philippi offered encouragement to people who needed a reminder that real joy and hope could be found only in Jesus Christ.

On his second missionary journey, Paul traveled to Macedonia and established a church in the city of Philippi. This church included diverse races, cultures, and social classes. It was mainly made up of Gentiles, yet a number of influential Jews were involved as well. Paul wanted to encourage the believers in Philippi to find their joy in Christ, no matter what they faced. He expressed his gratitude for their service and support of his ministry.

Paul's first missionary journey took place around A.D. 50–53. On this journey, Paul established the church in Philippi, likely in A.D. 50. Paul revisited the Philippians in A.D. 56 and wrote this letter to the church during his imprisonment in Rome, about A.D. 60. The events recorded in the letter are events in the life of Paul; the message itself claims Paul as the author, and church tradition agrees.

Paul's letter serves as a serious reminder of the purpose of the Christian life. Paul told the Philippians nothing could compare with the life they had in Christ, and they should focus their whole lives on following Him. Today this letter is a beautiful encouragement to love God greatly. Seeking to be like Christ brings joy, fulfillment, and peace unlike anything else.

Albania

OFFICIAL LANGUAGE
Albanian
POPULATION
2,849,000
UNREACHED POPULATION
39,000
PROFESSING CHRISTIANS
33.6%

Anduela's Home

Say a Prayer Today

Pray for the people of Albania, that they would know the truth of the gospel. Pray their hearts would be open to the hope of Jesus Christ and the salvation that comes only from Him.

HISTORY BIT

Albania remained under the control of large world empires until the twentieth century. Many missionaries visited Albania in the early stages of the church (first through fourth centuries) during the Roman and Byzantine Empires. During the Ottoman Turkish Empire, many in the region became Muslims.*

Source Information:
https://joshuaproject.net/countries/AL
*David B. Barrett, *World Christian Encyclopedia*, Albania (New York, NY: Oxford University Press, 1982), 135.

LOVE YOUR NEIGHBOR

Her Journey

ANDUELA'S STORY

When I was nine years old, the dictator of Albania died. People were crying in the streets. I asked my mother what would happen to our country without someone to lead us. With great care, my mother explained to me how some changes are for good. She also told me to be careful what I said in public about the death of the dictator. In an uncertain political environment, saying the wrong thing could result in my family being thrown in jail.

As I grew up I learned more and more about the importance of being careful about what I said and how I said it. We lived under a rigid communist dictatorship, where it seemed everyone was listening. When I came to faith in Jesus, I understood the power of sin and the battle of guarding my mind and heart.

I understood that even though my eternity is secure in Jesus, I also need to live a life today that honors Him. Because my mind has been renewed in Christ, I can live a life that reflects His love and truth to the world.

In Philippians Paul gives us a guide of how to guard our thoughts. He shows us that we have to guard our thoughts and think about what is good. The things we should think about are also the character of Jesus. We should filter our thoughts through the person of Jesus. Even though it is a hard battle every day, God has given us His Holy Spirit who lives in us and teaches us. With His help, we can gain victory over the battle for our minds.

4 WEEK READING PLAN

LOVE HIS WORD

	MONDAY	TUESDAY	WEDNESDAY	THURSDAY	FRIDAY
1	Philippians 1:1–6	Philippians 1:7–11	Philippians 1:12–14	Philippians 1:15–18	Philippians 1:19–30
	SOAP Philippians 1:6	SOAP Philippians 1:9–11	SOAP Philippians 1:14	SOAP Philippians 1:18	SOAP Philippians 1:21, 27
2	Philippians 2:1–4	Philippians 2:5–11	Philippians 2:12–13	Philippians 2:14–18	Philippians 2:19–30
	SOAP Philippians 2:3–4	SOAP Philippians 2:9–11	SOAP Philippians 2:13	SOAP Philippians 2:14–16	SOAP Philippians 2:20–21
3	Philippians 3:1–4	Philippians 3:5–11	Philippians 3:12–14	Philippians 3:15–19	Philippians 3:20–21
	SOAP Philippians 3:3	SOAP Philippians 3:8–9	SOAP Philippians 3:12–14	SOAP Philippians 3:16	SOAP Philippians 3:20
4	Philippians 4:1–5	Philippians 4:6–7	Philippians 4:8–9	Philippians 4:10–13	Philippians 4:14–23
	SOAP Philippians 4:4–5	SOAP Philippians 4:6–7	SOAP Philippians 4:8	SOAP Philippians 4:12–13	SOAP Philippians 4:19

SALUTATION

1 From Paul and Timothy, slaves of Christ Jesus, to all the saints
in Christ Jesus who are in Philippi, with the overseers and deacons. 2 Grace and peace to you from God our Father and the Lord
Jesus Christ!

PRAYER FOR THE CHURCH

3 I thank my God every time I remember you. 4 I always pray with
joy in my every prayer for all of you 5 because of your participa-
tion in the gospel from the first day until now. 6 For I am sure of
this very thing, that the one who began a good work in you will
perfect it until the day of Christ Jesus. 7 For it is right for me to
think this about all of you, because I have you in my heart, since
both in my imprisonment and in the defense and confirmation of
the gospel all of you became partners in God's grace together with
me. 8 For God is my witness that I long for all of you with the affection of Christ Jesus. 9 And I pray this, that your love may abound
even more and more in knowledge and every kind of insight 10 so
that you can decide what is best, and thus be sincere and blameless for the day of Christ, 11 filled with the fruit of righteousness
that comes through Jesus Christ to the glory and praise of God.

REFLECT

Why is it important to couple love with knowledge and insight?

MINISTRY AS A PRISONER

12 I want you to know, brothers and sisters, that my situation has
actually turned out to advance the gospel: 13 The whole imperial
guard and everyone else knows that I am in prison for the sake
of Christ, 14 and most of the brothers and sisters, having confidence in the Lord because of my imprisonment, now more than
ever dare to speak the word fearlessly.

15 Some, to be sure, are preaching Christ from envy and rivalry,
but others from goodwill. 16 The latter do so from love because
they know that I am placed here for the defense of the gospel.
17 The former proclaim Christ from selfish ambition, not sincerely, because they think they can cause trouble for me in my
imprisonment. 18 What is the result? Only that in every way,
whether in pretense or in truth, Christ is being proclaimed,
and in this I rejoice.

Yes, and I will continue to rejoice, 19 for I know that this will
turn out for my deliverance through your prayers and the help
of the Spirit of Jesus Christ. 20 My confident hope is that I will
in no way be ashamed but that with complete boldness, even
now as always, Christ will be exalted in my body, whether I live
or die. 21 For to me, living is Christ and dying is gain. 22 Now if I
am to go on living in the body, this will mean productive work
for me, yet I don't know which I prefer: 23 I feel torn between the
two, because I have a desire to depart and be with Christ, which
is better by far, 24 but it is more vital for your sake that I remain
in the body. 25 And since I am sure of this, I know that I will remain and continue with all of you for the sake of your progress
and joy in the faith, 26 so that what you can be proud of may increase because of me in Christ Jesus, when I come back to you.

27 Only conduct yourselves in a manner worthy of the gospel
of Christ so that—whether I come and see you or whether I remain absent—I should hear that you are standing firm in one

LOVE TO GROW

HE WILL COMPLETE YOU

PHILIPPIANS 1:6

"Mama, look!"

My baby girl came over to the table and plopped her pumpkin on top. "I put lots of holes in my pumpkin, and Daddy is helping me carve a picture on this side! Isn't it beautiful?!"

I glanced over and saw a sorry-looking pumpkin with holes all over it and cuts from a six-year-old using her "pumpkin tools" a little too generously.

"Ah, Sugar, it really is! And you know what's going to make it even more beautiful? When you put the light inside! All those holes and cuts allow the light to shine through."

I guess you could say we're all a little like half-carved pumpkins. We all have holes and cuts that reveal the pain we've faced from living in a broken world with broken people.

There is a greater purpose if we can get past the pain and the disappointment. It's those holes in our lives—those cuts that run deep and open us up—that allow God to come in, clean us out, and fill us with His light. When He does, our holes and cuts allow others to see His power. He redeems the damage and makes it beautiful.

From God's amazing work on the cross, to His ever-present work in us from the moment we believe, to His Holy Spirit working through us, we are constantly a work in progress and will be until the moment we see Jesus face-to-face.

What God starts, He completes.

What He began in you, He will see through to completion. Jesus will not give up on you. You may not understand the process, but you can always trust the One who is holding your life in His hands.

None of us are out of God's redemptive reach. We are each a work in progress. Allow God to use those holes—those wounds—to shine His light in a dark world. You are beautiful, sweet friend. Keep moving forward and be confident of this truth: What God started in you, He will finish.

Let Jesus' light shine brightly through your life for His glory.

spirit, with one mind, by contending side by side for the faith
of the gospel, [28]and by not being intimidated in any way by your
opponents. This is a sign of their destruction, but of your salvation—a sign which is from God. [29]For it has been granted to you
not only to believe in Christ but also to suffer for him, [30]since
you are encountering the same conflict that you saw me face
and now hear that I am facing.

CHRISTIAN UNITY AND CHRIST'S HUMILITY

2 Therefore, if there is any encouragement in Christ, any comfort provided by love, any fellowship in the Spirit, any affection or mercy, [2]complete my joy and be of the same mind, by
having the same love, being united in spirit, and having one purpose. [3]Instead of being motivated by selfish ambition or vanity,
each of you should, in humility, be moved to treat one another
as more important than yourself. [4]Each of you should be concerned not only about your own interests, but about the interests of others as well. [5]You should have the same attitude toward
one another that Christ Jesus had,

[6] who though he existed in the form of God
did not regard equality with God
as something to be grasped,
[7] but emptied himself
by taking on the form of a slave,
by looking like other men,
and by sharing in human nature.
[8] He humbled himself,
by becoming obedient to the point of death
—even death on a cross!
[9] As a result God highly exalted him
and gave him the name
that is above every name,
[10] so that at the name of Jesus
every knee will bow
—in heaven and on earth and under the earth—
[11] and every tongue confess
that Jesus Christ is Lord
to the glory of God the Father.

LIGHTS IN THE WORLD

[12]So then, my dear friends, just as you have always obeyed, not
only in my presence but even more in my absence, continue
working out your salvation with awe and reverence, [13]for the
one bringing forth in you both the desire and the effort—for
the sake of his good pleasure—is God. [14]Do everything without
grumbling or arguing, [15]so that you may be blameless and pure,
children of God without blemish though you live in a crooked
and perverse society, in which you shine as lights in the world
[16]by holding on to the word of life so that on the day of Christ I
will have a reason to boast that I did not run in vain nor labor
in vain. [17]But even if I am being poured out like a drink offering
on the sacrifice and service of your faith, I am glad and rejoice
together with all of you. [18]And in the same way you also should
be glad and rejoice together with me.

REFLECT

We run the race by holding fast to the word of life. What is the word of life, and how do we hold onto it?

MODELS FOR MINISTRY

19 Now I hope in the Lord Jesus to send Timothy to you soon, so
that I too may be encouraged by hearing news about you. 20 For
there is no one here like him who will readily demonstrate his
deep concern for you. 21 Others are busy with their own concerns,
not those of Jesus Christ. 22 But you know his qualifications, that
like a son working with his father, he served with me in advancing the gospel. 23 So I hope to send him as soon as I know more
about my situation, 24 though I am confident in the Lord that I
too will be coming to see you soon.

25 But for now I have considered it necessary to send Epaphroditus to you. For he is my brother, coworker and fellow soldier,
and your messenger and minister to me in my need. 26 Indeed, he
greatly missed all of you and was distressed because you heard
that he had been ill. 27 In fact he became so ill that he nearly
died. But God showed mercy to him—and not to him only, but
also to me—so that I would not have grief on top of grief. 28 Therefore I am all the more eager to send him, so that when you see
him again you can rejoice and I can be free from anxiety. 29 So
welcome him in the Lord with great joy, and honor people like
him, 30 since it was because of the work of Christ that he almost
died. He risked his life so that he could make up for your inability to serve me.

TRUE AND FALSE RIGHTEOUSNESS

3 Finally, my brothers and sisters, rejoice in the Lord! To write
this again is no trouble to me, and it is a safeguard for you.

2 Beware of the dogs, beware of the evil workers, beware of
those who mutilate the flesh! 3 For we are the circumcision, the
ones who worship by the Spirit of God, exult in Christ Jesus,
and do not rely on human credentials 4—though mine too are
significant. If someone thinks he has good reasons to put confidence in human credentials, I have more: 5 I was circumcised
on the eighth day, from the people of Israel and the tribe of
Benjamin, a Hebrew of Hebrews. I lived according to the law as
a Pharisee. 6 In my zeal for God I persecuted the church. According to the righteousness stipulated in the law I was blameless.
7 But these assets I have come to regard as liabilities because
of Christ. 8 More than that, I now regard all things as liabilities
compared to the far greater value of knowing Christ Jesus my
Lord, for whom I have suffered the loss of all things—indeed, I
regard them as dung!—that I may gain Christ, 9 and be found in
him, not because I have my own righteousness derived from the
law, but because I have the righteousness that comes by way of
Christ's faithfulness—a righteousness from God that is in fact
based on Christ's faithfulness. 10 My aim is to know him, to experience the power of his resurrection, to share in his sufferings,
and to be like him in his death, 11 and so, somehow, to attain to
the resurrection from the dead.

REFLECT

Paul says he is willing to count everything as loss compared to knowing Christ. How can we have this kind of mind-set today?

KEEP GOING FORWARD

12 Not that I have already attained this—that is, I have not already been perfected—but I strive to lay hold of that for which
Christ Jesus also laid hold of me. 13 Brothers and sisters, I do

not consider myself to have attained this. Instead I am single-
minded: Forgetting the things that are behind and reaching out
for the things that are ahead, 14 with this goal in mind, I strive toward the prize of the upward call of God in Christ Jesus. 15 Therefore let those of us who are "perfect" embrace this point of view.
If you think otherwise, God will reveal to you the error of your
ways. 16 Nevertheless, let us live up to the standard that we have
already attained.

17 Be imitators of me, brothers and sisters, and watch carefully those who are living this way, just as you have us as an
example. 18 For many live, about whom I have often told you,
and now, with tears, I tell you that they are the enemies of the
cross of Christ. 19 Their end is destruction, their god is the belly,
they exult in their shame, and they think about earthly things.
20 But our citizenship is in heaven—and we also eagerly await a
savior from there, the Lord Jesus Christ, 21 who will transform
these humble bodies of ours into the likeness of his glorious
body by means of that power by which he is able to subject all
things to himself.

CHRISTIAN PRACTICES

4 So then, my brothers and sisters, dear friends whom I long
to see, my joy and crown, stand in the Lord in this way, my
dear friends!

2 I appeal to Euodia and to Syntyche to agree in the Lord. 3 Yes,
I say also to you, true companion, help them. They have struggled together in the gospel ministry along with me and Clem-
ent and my other coworkers, whose names are in the book of
life. 4 Rejoice in the Lord always. Again I say, rejoice! 5 Let everyone see your gentleness. The Lord is near! 6 Do not be anxious
about anything. Instead, in every situation, through prayer and
petition with thanksgiving, tell your requests to God. 7 And the
peace of God that surpasses all understanding will guard your
hearts and minds in Christ Jesus.

8 Finally, brothers and sisters, whatever is true, whatever is
worthy of respect, whatever is just, whatever is pure, whatever
is lovely, whatever is commendable, if something is excellent or
praiseworthy, think about these things. 9 And what you learned
and received and heard and saw in me, do these things. And the
God of peace will be with you.

APPRECIATION FOR SUPPORT

10 I have great joy in the Lord because now at last you have again
expressed your concern for me. (Now I know you were concerned
before but had no opportunity to do anything.) 11 I am not saying
this because I am in need, for I have learned to be content in any
circumstance. 12 I have experienced times of need and times of
abundance. In any and every circumstance I have learned the
secret of contentment, whether I go satisfied or hungry, have
plenty or nothing. 13 I am able to do all things through the one
who strengthens me. 14 Nevertheless, you did well to share with
me in my trouble.

15 And as you Philippians know, at the beginning of my gospel
ministry, when I left Macedonia, no church shared with me in

CHALLENGE

Make a list of all the people, things, and circumstances you find yourself relying on for joy. Next to each one, write why it can't deliver the real joy you seek. Think about what steals your joy. Find a couple of verses that tell you where real joy is found.

LOVE TO GROW

REJOICE!

PHILIPPIANS 4:4–9

Anxiety is a reminder that we live in a fallen world. We can lose perspective and become fearful about things that draw us away from God. How is it possible to rejoice when we're worried? Paul exhorted the believers at the church in Philippi to be full of joy no matter the circumstance. That's hard!

We may feel anxious because we want to be in control. We place our hopes on a particular outcome, and we wonder if it will happen.

We worry we won't get what we want or that things won't turn out the way we planned.

The peace Paul speaks of can come only from releasing our needs, desires, and fears to God. Our confidence rises when we rely on the fact that the Lord knows what we need better than we do. We must hold onto hope that our needs are part of a much greater purpose, one we often cannot see from our limited perspectives.

Paul's encouragement not to be anxious is a word of comfort and reassurance. No matter our circumstances, we do not need to worry because we're secure in the Lord.

God alone is our rescue. The peace of God we read about in Philippians 4:7 produces a calm heart and mind. This peace will be further enhanced when we focus on holy and righteous things. Let us fill our minds with true and lovely thoughts. These will bring joy and peace through prayer.

Rejoice in the Lord understanding He has all things in His control. Rejoicing is a testimony to others that the Lord is near. What a truth!

The beauty of the gospel is in His life and death and resurrection; Jesus set us free from fear. Nothing can separate us from the love of God. Therefore rejoice! He is our hope!

this matter of giving and receiving except you alone. 16 For even
in Thessalonica on more than one occasion you sent something
for my need. 17 I do not say this because I am seeking a gift. Rather,
I seek the credit that abounds to your account. 18 For I have received everything, and I have plenty. I have all I need because
I received from Epaphroditus what you sent—a fragrant offering, an acceptable sacrifice, very pleasing to God. 19 And my God
will supply your every need according to his glorious riches in
Christ Jesus. 20 May glory be given to God our Father forever
and ever. Amen.

FINAL GREETINGS

21 Give greetings to all the saints in Christ Jesus. The brothers
with me here send greetings. 22 All the saints greet you, especially those who belong to Caesar's household. 23 The grace of
the Lord Jesus Christ be with your spirit.

THEREFORE, *just as you* RECEIVED *Christ Jesus as* LORD, CONTINUE TO LIVE *your* LIVES IN HIM, ROOTED *and built up in* HIM AND FIRM IN *your faith* JUST AS YOU WERE TAUGHT, AND *overflowing* WITH *thankfulness*

MEMORY VERSE

Therefore, just as you received Christ Jesus as Lord, continue to live your lives in him, rooted and built up in him and *firm in your faith just as you were taught,* and overflowing with thankfulness.

Colossians 2:6–7

Colossians

INTRODUCTION

Living out the Faith

The Book of Colossians addressed challenges facing the church in Colossae. The believers there experienced many of the same problems we see in churches today. Some members of the church were teaching a works-based gospel and forms of mysticism. The Colossians had become confused and unsure of the true gospel. Paul wrote to reiterate the supremacy of Christ and to point the believers back to the true doctrines of the faith.

Paul began his letter offering prayer and thanksgiving for the Colossians' faith (1:2–14). This is followed by one of the most famous passages describing the deity of Christ (1:15–23). Paul then described his ministry for the Colossians (1:24—2:7) and the preeminence of Christ over false religion (2:8–23). Finally, Paul declared the authority of Christ over the life of a believer and how Christians can live out their faith in a way that honors Him (3:1—4:6). The book ends with Paul's greetings to friends, instructions, and his signature (4:7–18).

Paul's authorship of Colossians is unanimously recognized throughout church history. Paul visited Colossae and established the church there about A.D. 54–56 on his third missionary journey. He likely visited Colossae during his three-year stay in Ephesus, as the two cities were near one another. Paul probably wrote this letter to the Colossians during his Roman imprisonment in A.D. 60.

Paul's letter to the Colossians includes an incredibly clear description of Jesus Christ's deity. It is a striking reminder that God sent His only Son, who is fully God and has all the authority and power of God the Father, to earth to reconcile humanity to Himself. What an encouraging word that reminds us how much God loves us, and in turn, encourages us to love Him greatly.

Hungary

OFFICIAL LANGUAGE
Hungarian
POPULATION
9,586,000
UNREACHED POPULATION
78,000
PROFESSING CHRISTIANS
86.8%

Margit's Home

Say a Prayer Today

Pray for Margit, that she would continue to live out her faith and be a light to those around her. Pray for the church in Hungary, that they would grow in Christ and live out their faith each day.

HISTORY BIT

The first translation of the New Testament into the Hungarian language was translated from the original Greek by Janos Sylvester in 1541. The full Bible was translated in 1590.*

Source Information:
https://joshuaproject.net/countries/HU

LOVE YOUR NEIGHBOR

Her Journey

MARGIT'S STORY

After I became a Christian, nothing changed on the outside. Even though I had given my life to Christ and was in a new spiritual situation, I looked the same as I had the day before, I worked for the same company, and none of my circumstances changed.

Yet, everything was different. I no longer felt good when I did something I knew was disobedient to God. I did not know what to do with this new feeling of conviction, and I quickly became confused.

Reading Paul's guidance in Colossians 2:6–7 was like a compass showing me the right way. These verses remind me to continue in my Christian life exactly as I had begun: keeping Jesus as Christ and Lord of my life. This truth helped me realize who I was and whom I wanted to serve.

The world is full of difficulties, challenges, and temptations. Life in Hungary is no different than the rest of the world. It can be hard to resist the views of the world, to let God influence our lives, or shape people through us instead of being shaped by the world. I can only share His love with others if I continue to walk with Him, remaining rooted and established in my faith and built up in Christ.

I see my Christian friends, specifically the women in my small group, struggling with all kinds of difficulties but walking in faith every day. Like living stones, these women continue to be built up into spiritual houses, like Paul talks about in Colossians. Through these friendships, God has shown me how powerful He is, how wonderfully He can work in the lives of His children when we make Him Lord of our lives.

4 WEEK READING PLAN

LOVE HIS WORD

	MONDAY	TUESDAY	WEDNESDAY	THURSDAY	FRIDAY
1	Colossians 1:1-8	Colossians 1:9-14	Colossians 1:15-20	Colossians 1:21-23	Colossians 1:24-29
	SOAP Colossians 1:5-6	SOAP Colossians 1:13-14	SOAP Colossians 1:19-20	SOAP Colossians 1:21-23	SOAP Colossians 1:28-29
2	Colossians 2:1-5	Colossians 2:6-10	Colossians 2:11-15	Colossians 2:16-19	Colossians 2:20-23
	SOAP Colossians 2:2-3	SOAP Colossians 2:6-7	SOAP Colossians 2:13	SOAP Colossians 2:16-17	SOAP Colossians 2:23
3	Colossians 3:1-4	Colossians 3:5-11	Colossians 3:12-14	Colossians 3:15-17	Colossians 3:18—4:1
	SOAP Colossians 3:1-3	SOAP Colossians 3:5	SOAP Colossians 3:12-14	SOAP Colossians 3:15-17	SOAP Colossians 3:23-24
4	Colossians 4:2-4	Colossians 4:5-6	Colossians 4:7-9	Colossians 4:10-17	Colossians 4:18
	SOAP Colossians 4:2	SOAP Colossians 4:5-6	SOAP Colossians 4:8	SOAP Colossians 4:16-17	SOAP Colossians 4:18

SALUTATION

1 From Paul, an apostle of Christ Jesus by the will of God, and
Timothy our brother, 2 to the saints, the faithful brothers and
sisters in Christ, at Colossae. Grace and peace to you from God
our Father!

PAUL'S THANKSGIVING AND PRAYER FOR THE CHURCH

3 We always give thanks to God, the Father of our Lord Jesus
Christ, when we pray for you, 4 since we heard about your faith
in Christ Jesus and the love that you have for all the saints.
5 Your faith and love have arisen from the hope laid up for
you in heaven, which you have heard about in the message of
truth, the gospel 6 that has come to you. Just as in the entire
world this gospel is bearing fruit and growing, so it has also
been bearing fruit and growing among you from the first day
you heard it and understood the grace of God in truth. 7 You
learned the gospel from Epaphras, our dear fellow slave—a
faithful minister of Christ on our behalf—8 who also told us of
your love in the Spirit.

PAUL'S PRAYER FOR THE GROWTH OF THE CHURCH

9 For this reason we also, from the day we heard about you, have
not ceased praying for you and asking God to fill you with the
knowledge of his will in all spiritual wisdom and understanding, 10 so that you may live worthily of the Lord and please him
in all respects—bearing fruit in every good deed, growing in
the knowledge of God, 11 being strengthened with all power according to his glorious might for the display of all patience and
steadfastness, joyfully 12 giving thanks to the Father who has
qualified you to share in the saints' inheritance in the light.
13 He delivered us from the power of darkness and transferred
us to the kingdom of the Son he loves, 14 in whom we have redemption, the forgiveness of sins.

THE SUPREMACY OF CHRIST

15 He is the image of the invisible God, the
firstborn over all creation,
16 for all things in heaven and on earth were
created in him—all things, whether visible
or invisible, whether thrones or dominions,
whether principalities or powers—all things
were created through him and for him.
17 He himself is before all things and all
things are held together in him.
18 He is the head of the body, the church, as well as
the beginning, the firstborn from the dead, so
that he himself may become first in all things.
19 For God was pleased to have all his
fullness dwell in the Son
20 and through him to reconcile all things to himself by
making peace through the blood of his cross—through
him, whether things on earth or things in heaven.

CHALLENGE

Reflect on the majesty of Christ. Praise Him today for His deity and His humanity. How can you honor Him today for who He is?

LOVE TO GROW

PRAYING FOR SPIRITUAL NEEDS

COLOSSIANS 1:9–14

The local church is one of my biggest passions. Whether it is my home church in Madrid, Spain, or a small straw-roof church in the jungle of Venezuela where I serve as a missionary, I live and breathe to build the local church and help it grow to reach its maximum potential.

Something I've learned to do is pray for both the physical and spiritual needs of the church members. I love to use Paul's prayers for the early church to do that.

Sometimes a person's needs are easier to see when we know he or she is coping with a difficult relationship, is grieving, or is searching for a job. The spiritual struggles are harder to discern, yet they have the potential to cause greater harm.

Paul cared deeply for the church at Colossae:

> *For this reason we also, from the day we heard about you, have not ceased praying for you and asking God to fill you with the knowledge of his will in all spiritual wisdom and understanding, so that you may live worthily of the Lord and please him in all respects—bearing fruit in every good deed, growing in the knowledge of God (Col 1:9–10).*

What an encouragement to read Paul had not ceased to pray for them! Sometimes we get discouraged in our own journey or impatient with the journeys of others. We have to recognize, as Paul did, everyone's journey is different. Regardless of someone's circumstances, we can always pray for his or her spiritual growth.

The apostle prayed for what he thought the Colossians needed in that moment: knowledge of the will of God, spiritual wisdom, and understanding. God has a plan and a purpose for all believers, but we can't accomplish the will of God for our lives if we don't have the spiritual understanding to identify His will.

In true Paul style he continued his prayer, giving practical advice to put that spiritual knowledge into action. He called the believers to walk in a manner worthy of the Lord, pleasing Him and bearing fruit. This is a prayer for spiritual growth, not for physical relief.

Let's be encouraged today by Paul and pray spiritual prayers for the believers we know. Let's work to follow his example as we serve our own local church.

PAUL'S GOAL IN MINISTRY

21 And you were at one time strangers and enemies in your minds
as expressed through your evil deeds, 22 but now he has reconciled you by his physical body through death to present you
holy, without blemish, and blameless before him—23 if indeed
you remain in the faith, established and firm, without shifting
from the hope of the gospel that you heard. This gospel has also
been preached in all creation under heaven, and I, Paul, have
become its servant.

24 Now I rejoice in my sufferings for you, and I fill up in my physical body—for the sake of his body, the church—what is lacking in
the sufferings of Christ. 25 I became a servant of the church according to the stewardship from God—given to me for you—in order to complete the word of God, 26 that is, the mystery that has
been kept hidden from ages and generations, but has now been
revealed to his saints. 27 God wanted to make known to them the
glorious riches of this mystery among the Gentiles, which is Christ
in you, the hope of glory. 28 We proclaim him by instructing and
teaching all people with all wisdom so that we may present every
person mature in Christ. 29 Toward this goal I also labor, struggling
according to his power that powerfully works in me.

2 For I want you to know how great a struggle I have for you,
and for those in Laodicea, and for those who have not met
me face to face. 2 My goal is that their hearts, having been knit
together in love, may be encouraged, and that they may have all
the riches that assurance brings in their understanding of the
knowledge of the mystery of God, namely, Christ, 3 in whom are
hidden all the treasures of wisdom and knowledge. 4 I say this so
that no one will deceive you through arguments that sound reasonable. 5 For though I am absent from you in body, I am present
with you in spirit, rejoicing to see your morale and the firmness
of your faith in Christ.

GOD'S HEART FOR THE NATIONS

Colossians 1:27

God wanted to make known to them the glorious riches of this mystery among the Gentiles, which is Christ in you, the hope of glory.

WARNINGS AGAINST THE ADOPTION OF FALSE PHILOSOPHIES

6 Therefore, just as you received Christ Jesus as Lord, continue
to live your lives in him, 7 rooted and built up in him and firm in
your faith just as you were taught, and overflowing with thankfulness. 8 Be careful not to allow anyone to captivate you through
an empty, deceitful philosophy that is according to human traditions and the elemental spirits of the world, and not according to Christ. 9 For in him all the fullness of deity lives in bodily
form, 10 and you have been filled in him, who is the head over
every ruler and authority. 11 In him you also were circumcised—
not, however, with a circumcision performed by human hands,
but by the removal of the fleshly body, that is, through the circumcision done by Christ. 12 Having been buried with him in
baptism, you also have been raised with him through your faith
in the power of God who raised him from the dead. 13 And even
though you were dead in your transgressions and in the uncircumcision of your flesh, he nevertheless made you alive with
him, having forgiven all your transgressions. 14 He has destroyed
what was against us, a certificate of indebtedness expressed
in decrees opposed to us. He has taken it away by nailing it to

REFLECT

What does it mean that we were dead in our transgressions? What does it mean to be made alive with Christ? How are the two natures different?

the cross. 15 Disarming the rulers and authorities, he has made
a public disgrace of them, triumphing over them by the cross.
16 Therefore do not let anyone judge you with respect to food
or drink, or in the matter of a feast, new moon, or Sabbath
days—17 these are only the shadow of the things to come, but
the reality is Christ! 18 Let no one who delights in false humility
and the worship of angels pass judgment on you. That person
goes on at great lengths about what he has supposedly seen, but
he is puffed up with empty notions by his fleshly mind. 19 He has
not held fast to the head from whom the whole body, supported
and knit together through its ligaments and sinews, grows with
a growth that is from God.
20 If you have died with Christ to the elemental spirits of the
world, why do you submit to them as though you lived in the
world? 21 "Do not handle! Do not taste! Do not touch!" 22 These are
all destined to perish with use, founded as they are on human
commands and teachings. 23 Even though they have the appearance of wisdom with their self-imposed worship and humility achieved by an unsparing treatment of the body—a wisdom
with no true value—they in reality result in fleshly indulgence.

EXHORTATIONS TO SEEK THE THINGS ABOVE

3 Therefore, if you have been raised with Christ, keep seeking
the things above, where Christ is, seated at the right hand of
God. 2 Keep thinking about things above, not things on the earth,
3 for you have died and your life is hidden with Christ in God.
4 When Christ (who is your life) appears, then you too will be revealed in glory with him. 5 So put to death whatever in your nature belongs to the earth: sexual immorality, impurity, shameful
passion, evil desire, and greed which is idolatry. 6 Because of these
things the wrath of God is coming on the sons of disobedience.
7 You also lived your lives in this way at one time, when you used to
live among them. 8 But now, put off all such things as anger, rage,
malice, slander, abusive language from your mouth. 9 Do not lie to
one another since you have put off the old man with its practices
10 and have been clothed with the new man that is being renewed
in knowledge according to the image of the one who created it.
11 Here there is neither Greek nor Jew, circumcised or uncircumcised, barbarian, Scythian, slave or free, but Christ is all and in all.

EXHORTATION TO UNITY AND LOVE

12 Therefore, as the elect of God, holy and dearly loved, clothe
yourselves with a heart of mercy, kindness, humility, gentleness,
and patience, 13 bearing with one another and forgiving one another, if someone happens to have a complaint against anyone
else. Just as the Lord has forgiven you, so you also forgive others.
14 And to all these virtues add love, which is the perfect bond.
15 Let the peace of Christ be in control in your heart (for you were
in fact called as one body to this peace), and be thankful. 16 Let
the word of Christ dwell in you richly, teaching and exhorting
one another with all wisdom, singing psalms, hymns, and spiritual songs, all with grace in your hearts to God. 17 And whatever
you do in word or deed, do it all in the name of the Lord Jesus,
giving thanks to God the Father through him.

REFLECT

Are you living the way Paul described in Colossians 3:12–17? What can you do today to live a life controlled by the peace of Christ?

LOVE TO GROW

LIVING A RESURRECTED LIFE

COLOSSIANS 3

Have you ever been coated in grime to the extent you simply wanted to shed the filth? When you finally showered and put on a new set of clothes, the change was not only refreshing, it was almost life-giving. Paul reminded the Colossians of the importance of daily renewing their identity—or washing off their sin—as people made alive in Christ.

As believers who enjoy new life through Christ, we are to continually pursue Him with our minds, affections, and actions.

This is not to be an idle pursuit attained by weekly attendance at a worship service. Rather, we are to seek Christ in all things. Part of our newly resurrected life requires us to leave behind the habits of our old, ungodly nature. We are to shed them like dirty clothes. Paul gave a long list of vices in order to show the extent to which we are to pursue God's holiness.

How are we to live like Christ in such a sinful world? Paul taught we are to clothe ourselves with His qualities. As followers of Jesus, we are new creations with the Holy Spirit residing in us (see 2 Cor 5:17). Therefore, we have the capacity to live out our new identity—as long as we choose to do so.

Suppose workers came in from long days of hard labor and received a regular opportunity to take a shower and change. Yet they decided to keep wearing the same sweaty clothes day after day, insisting they were clean. No observer would agree with their argument because they could see the effects of their choices. In the same way, if we do not cast off our sin and renew ourselves in the knowledge of Christ, we will start to reek of our old sin nature before we realize it.

As we continue to grow in our love for God, we will find our thoughts turn to Him more often. As they do, our actions reflect Him more and more. The world will notice because we act differently. As you continue to love God greatly, what aspect of your old self do you need to take off and replace with a characteristic of Christ?

EXHORTATION TO HOUSEHOLDS

18 Wives, submit to your husbands, as is fitting in the Lord. 19 Husbands, love your wives and do not be embittered against them.
20 Children, obey your parents in everything, for this is pleasing
in the Lord. 21 Fathers, do not provoke your children, so they will
not become disheartened. 22 Slaves, obey your earthly masters in
every respect, not only when they are watching—like those who
are strictly people-pleasers—but with a sincere heart, fearing
the Lord. 23 Whatever you are doing, work at it with enthusiasm,
as to the Lord and not for people, 24 because you know that you
will receive your inheritance from the Lord as the reward. Serve
the Lord Christ. 25 For the one who does wrong will be repaid
4 for his wrong, and there are no exceptions. 1 Masters, treat
your slaves with justice and fairness, because you know that
you also have a master in heaven.

REFLECT

Are you devoted to prayer? What does it reveal about God's heart for us that He desires we be devoted to prayer?

EXHORTATION TO PRAY FOR THE SUCCESS OF PAUL'S MISSION

2 Be devoted to prayer, keeping alert in it with thanksgiving.
3 At the same time pray for us too, that God may open a door
for the message so that we may proclaim the mystery of Christ,
for which I am in chains. 4 Pray that I may make it known as I
should. 5 Conduct yourselves with wisdom toward outsiders,
making the most of the opportunities. 6 Let your speech always
be gracious, seasoned with salt, so that you may know how you
should answer everyone.

PERSONAL GREETINGS AND INSTRUCTIONS

7 Tychicus, a dear brother, faithful minister, and fellow slave in
the Lord, will tell you all the news about me. 8 I sent him to you
for this very purpose, that you may know how we are doing and
that he may encourage your hearts. 9 I sent him with Onesimus,
the faithful and dear brother, who is one of you. They will tell
you about everything here.

10 Aristarchus, my fellow prisoner, sends you greetings, as does
Mark, the cousin of Barnabas (about whom you received instructions; if he comes to you, welcome him). 11 And Jesus who is called
Justus also sends greetings. In terms of Jewish converts, these
are the only fellow workers for the kingdom of God, and they
have been a comfort to me. 12 Epaphras, who is one of you and a
slave of Christ, greets you. He is always struggling in prayer on
your behalf, so that you may stand mature and fully assured in
all the will of God. 13 For I can testify that he has worked hard for
you and for those in Laodicea and Hierapolis. 14 Our dear friend
Luke the physician and Demas greet you. 15 Give my greetings
to the brothers and sisters who are in Laodicea and to Nympha
and the church that meets in her house. 16 And after you have
read this letter, have it read to the church of Laodicea. In turn,
read the letter from Laodicea as well. 17 And tell Archippus, "See
to it that you complete the ministry you received in the Lord."

18 I, Paul, write this greeting by my own hand. Remember my
chains. Grace be with you.

MAY THE LORD cause you TO INCREASE and ABOUND in love for one another

MEMORY VERSE

And may the Lord cause you to increase and abound in love for one another and for all, just as we do for you, so that your hearts are strengthened in holiness to be blameless before our God and Father at the coming of our Lord Jesus with all his saints.

1 Thessalonians 3:12–13

1 Thessalonians

INTRODUCTION

The Work of the Gospel

The letter of 1 Thessalonians provided hope to a group of struggling new believers. Paul wrote this letter to the church in Thessalonica, answering questions these young believers had about their faith and how to live it out in their daily lives. First Thessalonians provides practical life application for spiritual truths that are still as meaningful today as they were in the first century.

In his short letter to the church at Thessalonica, Paul explained several essential doctrines, including that of the Trinity, the deity of Christ, the Holy Spirit, Scripture, and the second coming of Christ. He also covered assurance of salvation, conversion, sanctification, the resurrection, and the relationship between faith and works.

Paul is widely recognized as the author of the letter of 1 Thessalonians. Paul started the church at Thessalonica in about A.D. 51, during his second missionary journey. He probably wrote the message of 1 Thessalonians shortly after his stay in the city, also in A.D. 51. It is one of the earliest writings included in the New Testament.

First Thessalonians offers strong encouragement for us to love God greatly, reminding us of His concern for our spiritual maturity and witness. Our God cares deeply about our relationship with Him, and here He provides teaching not only on daily living but on the future day of the Lord: "For God did not destine us for wrath but for gaining salvation through our Lord Jesus Christ" (5:9). Ultimately, it's a message of love and hope for all believers in all times.

Poland

OFFICIAL LANGUAGE
Polish
POPULATION
37,810,000
UNREACHED POPULATION
12,000
PROFESSING CHRISTIANS
89.5%

Krista's Home

Say a Prayer Today

Pray for Krista and her missionary work with the Polish people. Pray for her family as they minister to the people of Poland, that their work would be fruitful and that many would come to faith in Christ.

HISTORY BIT

While they now enjoy freedom of religion, the people of Poland have had a difficult history. During the German occupation in the Second World War, over 90% of the Jews in Poland perished (about 3 million Jews).*

Source Information:
https://joshuaproject.net/countries/PL
*David B. Barrett, *World Christian Encyclopedia*, Poland (New York, NY: Oxford University Press, 1982), 570.

KRISTA'S STORY

I tried to convince God to send someone else. I had been to Poland several times on mission trips and clearly sensed His calling to move there as a full-time missionary, yet I was greatly aware of the cost. It was far from home. I would have to trust God to provide finances. And would I ever get married?

God changed my life as a child; I was drawn out of a life of rule-keeping legalism into the freedom and joy that Christ offers us. The first time I visited Poland I saw a country and people who were facing the same battle of hearing, believing, and living the gospel.

Paul said that they lived among the Thessalonians because they loved them. They did this for their sake, so that the Thessalonians could learn the ways of Christ. And they did! They became imitators of Paul and his companions. Paul says it was a delight for him to share not only the gospel of God with them but their lives as well!

I never did convince God to send someone else. Instead, He convinced me to go. The cost, in some ways, has only grown, but my joy has increased too, as Polish people have become so dear to me. It is a great honor and privilege to walk alongside them and encourage them, comfort them, and urge them to live lives worthy of God.

God's call on our lives is often costly, but in obedience there is great joy! We believe that it is God's desire for the Polish people to know and understand the gospel, and to this end we labor and strive.

6 WEEK READING PLAN

LOVE HIS WORD

	MONDAY	TUESDAY	WEDNESDAY	THURSDAY	FRIDAY
1	1 Thessalonians 1:1-3	1 Thessalonians 1:4-10	1 Thessalonians 2:1-8	1 Thessalonians 2:9-16	1 Thessalonians 2:17-20
	SOAP 1 Thessalonians 1:2-3	**SOAP** 1 Thessalonians 1:4-5	**SOAP** 1 Thessalonians 2:8	**SOAP** 1 Thessalonians 2:12-13	**SOAP** 1 Thessalonians 2:19-20
2	1 Thessalonians 3:1-5	1 Thessalonians 3:6-13	1 Thessalonians 4:1-8	1 Thessalonians 4:9-12	1 Thessalonians 4:13-18
	SOAP 1 Thessalonians 3:2-3	**SOAP** 1 Thessalonians 3:12-13	**SOAP** 1 Thessalonians 4:3-5	**SOAP** 1 Thessalonians 4:11-12	**SOAP** 1 Thessalonians 4:13-14
3	1 Thessalonians 5:1-3	1 Thessalonians 5:4-8	1 Thessalonians 5:9-11	1 Thessalonians 5:12-22	1 Thessalonians 5:23-28
	SOAP 1 Thessalonians 5:2	**SOAP** 1 Thessalonians 5:8	**SOAP** 1 Thessalonians 5:9-11	**SOAP** 1 Thessalonians 5:14-18	**SOAP** 1 Thessalonians 5:24
4	2 Thessalonians 1:1-2	2 Thessalonians 1:3-4	2 Thessalonians 1:5-8	2 Thessalonians 1:9-10	2 Thessalonians 1:11-12
	SOAP 2 Thessalonians 1:2	**SOAP** 2 Thessalonians 1:3-4	**SOAP** 2 Thessalonians 1:6-8	**SOAP** 2 Thessalonians 1:10	**SOAP** 2 Thessalonians 1:11
5	2 Thessalonians 2:1-2	2 Thessalonians 2:3-4	2 Thessalonians 2:5-8	2 Thessalonians 2:9-12	2 Thessalonians 2:13-17
	SOAP 2 Thessalonians 2:2	**SOAP** 2 Thessalonians 2:3	**SOAP** 2 Thessalonians 2:7	**SOAP** 2 Thessalonians 2:10	**SOAP** 2 Thessalonians 2:16-17
6	2 Thessalonians 3:1-5	2 Thessalonians 3:6-9	2 Thessalonians 3:10-12	2 Thessalonians 3:13-15	2 Thessalonians 3:16-18
	SOAP 2 Thessalonians 3:3	**SOAP** 2 Thessalonians 3:9	**SOAP** 2 Thessalonians 3:10	**SOAP** 2 Thessalonians 3:13	**SOAP** 2 Thessalonians 3:16

SALUTATION

1 From Paul and Silvanus and Timothy, to the church of the Thessalonians in God the Father and the Lord Jesus Christ. Grace
and peace to you!

THANKSGIVING FOR RESPONSE TO THE GOSPEL

2 We thank God always for all of you as we mention you constantly in our prayers, 3 because we recall in the presence of
our God and Father your work of faith and labor of love and
endurance of hope in our Lord Jesus Christ. 4 We know, brothers and sisters loved by God, that he has chosen you, 5 in that
our gospel did not come to you merely in words, but in power
and in the Holy Spirit and with deep conviction (surely you
recall the character we displayed when we came among you
to help you).
6 And you became imitators of us and of the Lord, when you
received the message with joy that comes from the Holy Spirit,
despite great affliction. 7 As a result you became an example to
all the believers in Macedonia and in Achaia. 8 For from you the
message of the Lord has echoed forth not just in Macedonia
and Achaia, but in every place reports of your faith in God have
spread, so that we do not need to say anything. 9 For people everywhere report how you welcomed us and how you turned to
God from idols to serve the living and true God 10 and to wait for
his Son from heaven, whom he raised from the dead, Jesus our
deliverer from the coming wrath.

PAUL'S MINISTRY IN THESSALONICA

2 For you yourselves know, brothers and sisters, about our
coming to you—it has not proven to be purposeless. 2 But
although we suffered earlier and were mistreated in Philippi,
as you know, we had the courage in our God to declare to you
the gospel of God in spite of much opposition. 3 For the appeal
we make does not come from error or impurity or with deceit,
4 but just as we have been approved by God to be entrusted
with the gospel, so we declare it, not to please people but God,
who examines our hearts. 5 For we never appeared with flattering speech, as you know, nor with a pretext for greed—God is
our witness—6 nor to seek glory from people, either from you
or from others, 7 although we could have imposed our weight
as apostles of Christ; instead we became little children among
you. Like a nursing mother caring for her own children, 8 with
such affection for you we were happy to share with you not only
the gospel of God but also our own lives, because you had become dear to us. 9 For you recall, brothers and sisters, our toil
and drudgery: By working night and day so as not to impose a
burden on any of you, we preached to you the gospel of God.
10 You are witnesses, and so is God, as to how holy and righteous and blameless our conduct was toward you who believe.
11 As you know, we treated each one of you as a father treats his
own children, 12 exhorting and encouraging you and insisting
that you live in a way worthy of God who calls you to his own
kingdom and his glory. 13 And so we too constantly thank God
that when you received God's message that you heard from

REFLECT

What do these verses communicate about Paul's relationship with the church in Thessalonica? How can we imitate this type of love and care in our own lives?

LOVE TO GROW

MINISTERING TO ONE ANOTHER

1 THESSALONIANS 2:1–8

We all love and crave friendship. Even if you are a serious introvert like me, friendship is important. It is fun to talk and laugh with others, to enjoy food together, and to have friends with whom we can share life.

More than that, we need people in our lives who are willing to minister to us with the gospel. It is important we know and understand all that Christ has done for us through His life, death, and resurrection. Our deep understanding of Jesus' power and love can be a huge encouragement in our lives and allow us to be a great support to each other.

When Paul traveled to Thessalonica, he went in order to encourage the people with the Good News of the gospel. If, like Paul, we are to minister to each other with the gospel, we need to know what impact it has on our lives.

Because we are forgetful people, we all need to be reminded of and challenged with the truth of God's Word. We need people who will boldly say to us, "Don't give up on overcoming your sins. You have everything you need to win!" Sometimes we even need others to speak hard truth into our lives with boldness and humility.

Anytime we speak into each other's lives, it must be done with kindness.

Though Paul could be very direct at times, he was also gracious. The gospel truths are beautiful words for those who are worn-out, fearful, or discouraged. We must proclaim the gospel to our friends with grace, never with a holier-than-thou attitude.

The gospel is worth proclaiming because it is the gift of God's salvation. Paul was willing to take the Good News everywhere he could even though he often experienced hardship and persecution. For Paul, it was worth it.

Is the gospel so beautiful to you that you are willing to use it to encourage those around you with boldness and kindness? Let's follow Paul's example and continue to faithfully minister to our precious friends.

us, you accepted it not as a human message, but as it truly is,
God's message, which is at work among you who believe. 14 For
you became imitators, brothers and sisters, of God's churches
in Christ Jesus that are in Judea, because you too suffered the
same things from your own countrymen as they in fact did
from the Jews, 15 who killed both the Lord Jesus and the prophets and persecuted us severely. They are displeasing to God
and are opposed to all people, 16 because they hinder us from
speaking to the Gentiles so that they may be saved. Thus they
constantly fill up their measure of sins, but wrath has come
upon them completely.

FORCED ABSENCE FROM THESSALONICA

17 But when we were separated from you, brothers and sisters,
for a short time (in presence, not in affection) we became all
the more fervent in our great desire to see you in person. 18 For
we wanted to come to you (I, Paul, in fact tried again and again)
but Satan thwarted us. 19 For who is our hope or joy or crown to
boast of before our Lord Jesus at his coming? Is it not of course
you? 20 For you are our glory and joy!

3 So when we could bear it no longer, we decided to stay on
in Athens alone. 2 We sent Timothy, our brother and fellow worker for God in the gospel of Christ, to strengthen you
and encourage you about your faith, 3 so that no one would be
shaken by these afflictions. For you yourselves know that we
are destined for this. 4 For in fact when we were with you, we
were telling you in advance that we would suffer affliction, and
so it has happened, as you well know. 5 So when I could bear
it no longer, I sent to find out about your faith, for fear that
the tempter somehow tempted you and our toil had proven
useless.

6 But now Timothy has come to us from you and given us the
good news of your faith and love and that you always think of us
with affection and long to see us just as we also long to see you!
7 So in all our distress and affliction, we were reassured about
you, brothers and sisters, through your faith. 8 For now we are
alive again, if you stand firm in the Lord. 9 For how can we thank
God enough for you, for all the joy we feel because of you before
our God? 10 We pray earnestly night and day to see you in person
and make up what may be lacking in your faith.

11 Now may God our Father himself and our Lord Jesus direct
our way to you. 12 And may the Lord cause you to increase and
abound in love for one another and for all, just as we do for you,
13 so that your hearts are strengthened in holiness to be blameless before our God and Father at the coming of our Lord Jesus
with all his saints.

A LIFE PLEASING TO GOD

4 Finally then, brothers and sisters, we ask you and urge you
in the Lord Jesus, that as you received instruction from us
about how you must live and please God (as you are in fact living) that you do so more and more. 2 For you know what commands we gave you through the Lord Jesus. 3 For this is God's
will: that you become holy, that you keep away from sexual

REFLECT

Why was Paul so thankful for the members of the church in Thessalonica? How did these believers contrast with the people who persecuted them?

CHALLENGE

Pray Colossians 3:11–13 over three people in your life for the next week. Record what God does in their lives.

HOLINESS IS A GIFT

1 THESSALONIANS 4:1–13

In Christ we are continually being sanctified, growing to look more and more like Him.

Paul wrote instructions on how we can keep advancing spiritually: "God did not call us to impurity but in holiness . . . Aspire to lead a quiet life, to attend to your own business, and to work with your own hands" (1 Thess 4:7, 11). He encouraged his readers to be mindful about their actions, to watch out for temptation, and to keep living with intention. If we don't mind our own business, we have a very real enemy who will mind our business for us.

Purity isn't only abstaining from certain things; it involves honoring and striving for holiness. By allowing the Holy Spirit to work in our lives and make us more like Christ, we pursue holiness. As we are sanctified, the Holy Spirit transforms our hearts and turns us toward obedience. As we grow in the maturity of our faith, doing the will of God becomes more of a delight and less of a burden. He is working in our lives and hearts to make us more like Him every day.

Living a quiet life means practicing humble obedience, regular servanthood, and practical discipleship. A quiet life is not a showy one but a faithful one. When we are moving ahead in our spiritual lives, we are satisfied outside the limelight; we are glad to contribute to others behind the scenes.

Remember God wants to use you—in your job, in your community, in your family, and in your country. Don't be too busy anticipating the next season and miss the opportunities you have in your current one. God will bless the work we do with our own hands.

There's power in protecting your purity. There's power in living a quiet life. There's power in working with your hands. Holiness is a gift God has given us.

May we live intentionally and increase in grace and peace.

May we be the people we were created to be and live in forward motion. May we be a church with whom Christ is pleased as we wait for His return.

immorality, 4 that each of you know how to possess his own
body in holiness and honor, 5 not in lustful passion like the
Gentiles who do not know God. 6 In this matter no one should
violate the rights of his brother or take advantage of him, because the Lord is the avenger in all these cases, as we also told
you earlier and warned you solemnly. 7 For God did not call us
to impurity but in holiness. 8 Consequently the one who rejects this is not rejecting human authority but God, who gives
his Holy Spirit to you.

9 Now on the topic of brotherly love you have no need for anyone to write you, for you yourselves are taught by God to love
one another. 10 And indeed you are practicing it toward all the
brothers and sisters in all of Macedonia. But we urge you, brothers and sisters, to do so more and more, 11 to aspire to lead a quiet
life, to attend to your own business, and to work with your own
hands, as we commanded you. 12 In this way you will live a decent
life before outsiders and not be in need.

THE LORD RETURNS FOR BELIEVERS

13 Now we do not want you to be uninformed, brothers and sisters, about those who are asleep, so that you will not grieve like
the rest who have no hope. 14 For if we believe that Jesus died
and rose again, so also we believe that God will bring with him
those who have fallen asleep as Christians. 15 For we tell you this
by the word of the Lord, that we who are alive, who are left until the coming of the Lord, will surely not go ahead of those who
have fallen asleep. 16 For the Lord himself will come down from
heaven with a shout of command, with the voice of the archangel, and with the trumpet of God, and the dead in Christ will
rise first. 17 Then we who are alive, who are left, will be suddenly
caught up together with them in the clouds to meet the Lord
in the air. And so we will always be with the Lord. 18 Therefore
encourage one another with these words.

THE DAY OF THE LORD

5 Now on the topic of times and seasons, brothers and sisters,
you have no need for anything to be written to you. 2 For you
know quite well that the day of the Lord will come in the same
way as a thief in the night. 3 Now when they are saying, "There
is peace and security," then sudden destruction comes on them,
like labor pains on a pregnant woman, and they will surely not
escape. 4 But you, brothers and sisters, are not in the darkness
for the day to overtake you like a thief would. 5 For you all are
sons of the light and sons of the day. We are not of the night
nor of the darkness. 6 So then we must not sleep as the rest, but
must stay alert and sober. 7 For those who sleep, sleep at night
and those who get drunk are drunk at night. 8 But since we are
of the day, we must stay sober *by putting on the breastplate* of
faith and love and as *a helmet* our hope *for salvation.* 9 For God
did not destine us for wrath but for gaining salvation through
our Lord Jesus Christ. 10 He died for us so that whether we are
alert or asleep we will come to life together with him. 11 Therefore encourage one another and build up each other, just as
you are in fact doing.

REFLECT

How was Paul's message about Christ's return comforting to the church in Thessalonica? How is it a comfort to you today?

FINAL INSTRUCTIONS

12 Now we ask you, brothers and sisters, to acknowledge those
who labor among you and preside over you in the Lord and admonish you, 13 and to esteem them most highly in love because
of their work. Be at peace among yourselves. 14 And we urge you,
brothers and sisters, admonish the undisciplined, comfort the
discouraged, help the weak, be patient toward all. 15 See that no
one pays back evil for evil to anyone, but always pursue what is
good for one another and for all. 16 Always rejoice, 17 constantly
pray, 18 in everything give thanks. For this is God's will for you
in Christ Jesus. 19 Do not extinguish the Spirit. 20 Do not treat
prophecies with contempt. 21 But examine all things; hold fast
to what is good. 22 Stay away from every form of evil.

REFLECT

What was Paul confident that God would do? Is God responsible for the sanctification of His people, or are we responsible for our own sanctification?

CONCLUSION

23 Now may the God of peace himself make you completely holy
and may your spirit and soul and body be kept entirely blameless at the coming of our Lord Jesus Christ. 24 He who calls you
is trustworthy, and he will in fact do this. 25 Brothers and sisters, pray for us too. 26 Greet all the brothers and sisters with a
holy kiss. 27 I call on you solemnly in the Lord to have this letter read to all the brothers and sisters. 28 The grace of our Lord
Jesus Christ be with you.

Now may our Lord Jesus Christ Himself and GOD our FATHER, who loved us AND by GRACE gave us ETERNAL COMFORT and good hope, encourage your hearts AND STRENGTHEN you IN every good THING you DO or SAY

MEMORY VERSE

Now may our Lord Jesus Christ himself and God our Father, who loved us and by grace gave us eternal comfort and good hope, encourage your hearts and strengthen you in every good thing you do or say.

2 Thessalonians 2:16–17

2 Thessalonians

INTRODUCTION

Be Encouraged

The believers in Thessalonica showed steadfast faith despite enduring harsh persecution. They were faithful to the gospel, but false teaching had begun to create problems in their doctrine. In his second letter to the believers in Thessalonica, Paul assured the people they had not missed the coming day of the Lord. He urged them to continue in their faith, to keep working for the gospel, and to be alert and aware of false teachers who desired to lead them astray.

The second letter to the church in Thessalonica addressed the false doctrines that had infiltrated the church. Paul encouraged the believers to remain faithful in the midst of persecution (1:1–12). He explained the day of the Lord and how the day had not yet come (2:1–17). Finally, Paul exhorted the believers to continue in their faithfulness to God through prayer and continued service (3:1–15), and he prayed for grace for the church (3:16–18).

The letter of 2 Thessalonians was written around A.D. 51 to 52. Paul likely wrote this letter while he was in Corinth. The church in Thessalonica was established during Paul's second missionary journey, around A.D. 51, with his first letter to them coming that same year. Paul identified himself as the author of 2 Thessalonians, stating in his own handwriting that he himself wrote the letter.

While 2 Thessalonians was written to correct specific concerns and false teaching affecting the Thessalonian church, this brief letter encourages us to love God greatly. Paul's confidence in the second coming of Christ, or day of the Lord, is an encouragement for all believers. Jesus Christ will return, drawing the righteous to Him and condemning the wicked. As we seek to be faithful followers of Christ who withstand persecution and spreading the gospel, we can be confident that He will return and one day make us complete.

Brazil

OFFICIAL LANGUAGE
Portuguese
POPULATION
210,905,000
UNREACHED POPULATION
120,000
PROFESSING CHRISTIANS
89.5%

Helen's Home

Say a Prayer Today

Pray for Helen and her ministry serving the people of Brazil. Pray God would build up leaders in the church in Brazil who lead with courage and boldness, pointing the church to Christ no matter the cost.

HISTORY BIT

During the nineteenth century, many Europeans traveled to Brazil, bringing many Protestant denominations to the area. German Lutherans arrived in 1823, American Methodists in 1835, and American Presbyterians in 1859.*

Source Information:
https://joshuaproject.net/countries/BR
*David B. Barrett, World Christian Encyclopedia, Brazil (New York, NY: Oxford University Press, 1982), 188.

HELEN'S STORY

As much as I enjoy being busy, I'm not always excited to try something new. One day, while looking for Bible studies, I came across Love God Greatly. I was hoping to find something to study with the women in my church, but I found so much more.

When I realized that Love God Greatly translated their Bible studies into many different languages, I was disappointed to find that there was not a translation in Portuguese. However, after reaching out to the Love God Greatly team, I felt God tugging on my heart to do just that. I was afraid, coming up with excuses to run away from the call.

I finally surrendered to His calling on my life. When we say yes to God, miracles happen. When we step out in faith, being courageous and trusting God with the outcome, He works in incredible ways. When we encourage others we also gain a great deal of comfort and encouragement ourselves. Every day is a battle, but when I choose to quiet my heart and listen to the voice of my heavenly Father, I find peace.

Even though we might be going through difficult situations in our lives, we can trust God. When He calls us to do something for His kingdom, we can believe that He will equip us to complete the task.

You can trust in Him. You can find courage and boldness in what He is calling you to do. I do not know what God has in store for your life today, but believe me, it will be the adventure of your life! Say yes!

6 WEEK READING PLAN

LOVE HIS WORD

	MONDAY	TUESDAY	WEDNESDAY	THURSDAY	FRIDAY
1	1 Thessalonians 1:1-3	1 Thessalonians 1:4-10	1 Thessalonians 2:1-8	1 Thessalonians 2:9-16	1 Thessalonians 2:17-20
	SOAP 1 Thessalonians 1:2-3	SOAP 1 Thessalonians 1:4-5	SOAP 1 Thessalonians 2:8	SOAP 1 Thessalonians 2:12-13	SOAP 1 Thessalonians 2:19-20
2	1 Thessalonians 3:1-5	1 Thessalonians 3:6-13	1 Thessalonians 4:1-8	1 Thessalonians 4:9-12	1 Thessalonians 4:13-18
	SOAP 1 Thessalonians 3:2-3	SOAP 1 Thessalonians 3:12-13	SOAP 1 Thessalonians 4:3-5	SOAP 1 Thessalonians 4:11-12	SOAP 1 Thessalonians 4:13-14
3	1 Thessalonians 5:1-3	1 Thessalonians 5:4-8	1 Thessalonians 5:9-11	1 Thessalonians 5:12-22	1 Thessalonians 5:23-28
	SOAP 1 Thessalonians 5:2	SOAP 1 Thessalonians 5:8	SOAP 1 Thessalonians 5:9-11	SOAP 1 Thessalonians 5:14-18	SOAP 1 Thessalonians 5:24
4	2 Thessalonians 1:1-2	2 Thessalonians 1:3-4	2 Thessalonians 1:5-8	2 Thessalonians 1:9-10	2 Thessalonians 1:11-12
	SOAP 2 Thessalonians 1:2	SOAP 2 Thessalonians 1:3-4	SOAP 2 Thessalonians 1:6-8	SOAP 2 Thessalonians 1:10	SOAP 2 Thessalonians 1:11
5	2 Thessalonians 2:1-2	2 Thessalonians 2:3-4	2 Thessalonians 2:5-8	2 Thessalonians 2:9-12	2 Thessalonians 2:13-17
	SOAP 2 Thessalonians 2:2	SOAP 2 Thessalonians 2:3	SOAP 2 Thessalonians 2:7	SOAP 2 Thessalonians 2:10	SOAP 2 Thessalonians 2:16-17
6	2 Thessalonians 3:1-5	2 Thessalonians 3:6-9	2 Thessalonians 3:10-12	2 Thessalonians 3:13-15	2 Thessalonians 3:16-18
	SOAP 2 Thessalonians 3:3	SOAP 2 Thessalonians 3:9	SOAP 2 Thessalonians 3:10	SOAP 2 Thessalonians 3:13	SOAP 2 Thessalonians 3:16

SALUTATION

1 From Paul and Silvanus and Timothy, to the church of the Thessalonians in God our Father and the Lord Jesus Christ. 2 Grace
and peace to you from God the Father and the Lord Jesus Christ!

THANKSGIVING

3 We ought to thank God always for you, brothers and sisters, and
rightly so, because your faith flourishes more and more and the
love of each one of you all for one another is ever greater. 4 As a
result we ourselves boast about you in the churches of God for
your perseverance and faith in all the persecutions and afflictions you are enduring.

ENCOURAGEMENT IN PERSECUTION

5 This is evidence of God's righteous judgment, to make you worthy of the kingdom of God, for which in fact you are suffering.
6 For it is right for God to repay with affliction those who afflict
you, 7 and to you who are being afflicted to give rest together
with us when the Lord Jesus is revealed from heaven with his
mighty angels. 8 *With flaming fire he will mete out punishment on*
those who do not know God and do not obey the gospel of our
Lord Jesus. 9 They will undergo the penalty of eternal destruction, *away from the presence of the Lord and from the glory of his*
strength, 10 when he comes to be glorified among his saints and
admired on that day among all who have believed—and you did
in fact believe our testimony. 11 And in this regard we pray for
you always, that our God will make you worthy of his calling
and fulfill by his power your every desire for goodness and every work of faith, 12 that the name of our Lord Jesus may be glorified in you, and you in him, according to the grace of our God
and the Lord Jesus Christ.

THE DAY OF THE LORD

2 Now regarding the arrival of our Lord Jesus Christ and our
being gathered to be with him, we ask you, brothers and sisters, 2 not to be easily shaken from your composure or disturbed
by any kind of spirit or message or letter allegedly from us, to
the effect that the day of the Lord is already here. 3 Let no one
deceive you in any way. For that day will not arrive until the rebellion comes and the man of lawlessness is revealed, the son
of destruction. 4 He opposes *and exalts himself above every* so-
called *god* or object of worship, and as a result *he takes his seat* in
God's temple, displaying himself as God. 5 Surely you recall that
I used to tell you these things while I was still with you. 6 And
so you know what holds him back, so that he will be revealed in
his own time. 7 For the hidden power of lawlessness is already
at work. However, the one who holds him back will do so until
he is taken out of the way, 8 and then the lawless one will be revealed, whom the Lord will destroy by the breath of his mouth
and wipe out by the manifestation of his arrival. 9 The arrival of
the lawless one will be by Satan's working with all kinds of miracles and signs and false wonders, 10 and with every kind of evil
deception directed against those who are perishing, because
they found no place in their hearts for the truth so as to be saved.

CHALLENGE

Take time today to pray 2 Thessalonians 1:11–12 over the people in your life. Ask God to make them worthy of the calling He has given them as they produce good works by faith.

11 Consequently God sends on them a deluding influence so that
they will believe what is false. 12 And so all of them who have not
believed the truth but have delighted in evil will be condemned.

CALL TO STAND FIRM

13 But we ought to thank God always for you, brothers and sisters loved by the Lord, because God chose you from the beginning for salvation through sanctification by the Spirit and faith
in the truth. 14 He called you to this salvation through our gospel, so that you may possess the glory of our Lord Jesus Christ.
15 Therefore, brothers and sisters, stand firm and hold on to the
traditions that we taught you, whether by speech or by letter.
16 Now may our Lord Jesus Christ himself and God our Father,
who loved us and by grace gave us eternal comfort and good
hope, 17 encourage your hearts and strengthen you in every good
thing you do or say.

REFLECT

How has God given you eternal encouragement? How has He strengthened your heart this week?

REQUEST FOR PRAYER

3 Finally, pray for us, brothers and sisters, that the Lord's message may spread quickly and be honored as in fact it was
among you, 2 and that we may be delivered from perverse and
evil people. For not all have faith. 3 But the Lord is faithful, and
he will strengthen you and protect you from the evil one. 4 And
we are confident about you in the Lord that you are both doing—
and will do—what we are commanding. 5 Now may the Lord direct
your hearts toward the love of God and the endurance of Christ.

RESPONSE TO THE UNDISCIPLINED

6 But we command you, brothers and sisters, in the name of our
Lord Jesus Christ, to keep away from any brother who lives an
undisciplined life and not according to the tradition they received from us. 7 For you know yourselves how you must imitate
us, because we did not behave without discipline among you,
8 and we did not eat anyone's food without paying. Instead, in
toil and drudgery we worked night and day in order not to burden any of you. 9 It was not because we do not have that right,
but to give ourselves as an example for you to imitate. 10 For even
when we were with you, we used to give you this command: "If
anyone is not willing to work, neither should he eat." 11 For we
hear that some among you are living an undisciplined life, not
doing their own work but meddling in the work of others. 12 Now
such people we command and urge in the Lord Jesus Christ to
work quietly and so provide their own food to eat. 13 But you,
brothers and sisters, do not grow weary in doing what is right.
14 But if anyone does not obey our message through this letter,
take note of him and do not associate closely with him, so that
he may be ashamed. 15 Yet do not regard him as an enemy, but
admonish him as a brother.

REFLECT

What is the difference between an enemy and a brother? What was Paul's purpose in making this distinction?

CONCLUSION

16 Now may the Lord of peace himself give you peace at all times
and in every way. The Lord be with you all. 17 I, Paul, write this
greeting with my own hand, which is how I write in every letter.
18 The grace of our Lord Jesus Christ be with you all.

DO YOUR WORK

2 THESSALONIANS 3:6–12

Though they were loved by God, chosen by God, and given power by God, the Thessalonians had fallen into laziness. In this letter the apostle Paul reminded them that living a life of faith was their responsibility.

Paul also reminded the Thessalonians that when he visited them, he provided his own living expenses. It was an example he wanted them to follow; he warned them away from an "undisciplined life" and said

For even when we were with you, we used to give you this command: "If anyone is not willing to work, neither should he eat" (2 Thess 3:10).

God has blessed us with a bounty of knowledge in His Word that teaches us why and how to work, for and with whom to work, when to undertake work, when to stop work, and through whom we do it all.

Yet we can still slip into laziness, like the Thessalonians.

As Jesus' disciples, we often do an amazing job staying folded in the pages of God's heart: We study the Word, write out Scripture, record our observations, plan applications, and ask God for His power to be evident in our lives. Sometimes we forget that failing to do our work means we look weak, slothful, and ungodly.

Paul's message couldn't be any plainer! After we do our heart-work by engaging God's Word and seeking His heart, let's do our physical work and make our own living. We too are loved by God, chosen by God, and given power by God. Let's bring Him glory by embracing the work He's given us.

HERE IS WHY
I was TREATED
WITH mercy:
SO THAT IN ME
as the worst,
CHRIST Jesus
COULD DEMONSTRATE
His UTMOST patience

MEMORY VERSE

This saying is trustworthy and deserves full acceptance: "Christ Jesus came into the world to save sinners"—and I am the worst of them! But here is why I was treated with mercy: so that in me as the worst, Christ Jesus could demonstrate his utmost patience, as an example for those who are going to believe in him for eternal life.

1 Timothy 1:15–16

1 Timothy

INTRODUCTION

Patience in Growth

Timothy was a young man of both Jewish and Greek descent. His father was Greek, and his mother was a Jewish woman who taught him Scripture. During Paul's first missionary journey to Lystra, Timothy was converted to Christianity, and he soon accompanied Paul and Silas in their missionary work. Timothy served as a liaison for Paul with several churches and was eventually appointed the leader of the church in Ephesus. This first letter to Timothy served as the young man's commission; it was Paul's charge to Timothy to "fight the good fight" (1:18) as he sent him out to minister on his own.

In the letter of 1 Timothy, Paul offered instructions to Timothy on how the church should function. He emphasized developing godly leaders and avoiding false doctrine. Paul provided insights for Christian leaders on how godly conduct and maturity were expected of them. Paul gave Timothy a great deal of practical advice and wisdom for leading the church in Ephesus.

While some scholars have debated Paul's authorship of 1 Timothy, a substantial amount of evidence concludes that both 1 and 2 Timothy are authentic Pauline epistles. Timothy first joined Paul and Silas in Lystra in A.D. 50. He again joined them during Paul's third missionary journey, about A.D. 54. Paul wrote 1 Timothy after he was released from prison in Rome, likely around A.D. 62, after he had returned to Macedonia.

Throughout the letter of 1 Timothy, Paul reminded Timothy of the deity and majesty of Christ, the One for whom we fight the good fight. Christ is the One who holds our salvation and is the source for our faith, love, growth, and strength. Paul reminded Timothy to keep his focus on Christ in all circumstances. As we seek to love God greatly, we can also keep our focus on Jesus, resting in His love and the hope He offers.

Mexico

OFFICIAL LANGUAGE
Spanish
POPULATION
126,733,000
UNREACHED POPULATION
141,000
PROFESSING CHRISTIANS
94.8%

Laura's Home

Say a Prayer Today

Pray for unity within the church in Mexico. Pray for boldness for believers in Christ to share their faith and also welcome and encourage others within the church.

HISTORY BIT

After over one hundred years of construction, the Metropolitan Cathedral in Mexico City was consecrated in 1667.* Construction on the cathedral then continued for another one hundred and fifty years, until 1813. It is the oldest cathedral in Mexico.**

Source Information:
https://joshuaproject.net/countries/MX
*John Bowden, A Chronology of World Christianity (New York, NY: Continuum, 2007), 317.
**https://www.britannica.com/place/Mexico-City/Cultural-life#ref965045

LAURA'S STORY

In my life of faith, I am often tempted to see others as less deserving of salvation than I am. I can identify with Paul when he calls himself the worst of sinners (1 Tim 1:15), especially when I begin to feel this way.

As I strive to become more like Christ I also want to show others that everyone can come and seek the Father. Jesus made a way for all sinners, even someone as lowly as me. Like Paul, I can let others know no matter how worthy they perceive themselves, we are all equal. No one is more or less deserving of salvation because Jesus came to save all.

The Christian life isn't free from trouble. I have struggles and tribulations that keep me from believing I am deserving of God's love. In these moments, Jesus reminds me to keep my eyes on Him and the truth that He gave Himself up for me. Jesus ransomed me. Jesus gives me the value I don't give myself.

Without Jesus we are nothing. Placing my faith in Jesus has allowed me to learn my true worth. As I seek to be more like Him I see the Holy Spirit growing the fruit of the Spirit in my life. As He grows love, joy, peace, patience, kindness, goodness, faithfulness, gentleness, and self-control in my life, I hope to be a testament to others of the goodness of God.

I would be nowhere without grace. I certainly would not boast about myself by my own merit. I can only boast in Christ. He has given me value that cannot be found anywhere in this world. I can call upon the Father and I know He will hear me.

6 WEEK READING PLAN

LOVE HIS WORD

	MONDAY	TUESDAY	WEDNESDAY	THURSDAY	FRIDAY
1	1 Timothy 1:1-11	1 Timothy 1:12-20	1 Timothy 2:1-8	1 Timothy 2:9-15	1 Timothy 3:1-13
	SOAP 1 Timothy 1:5-7	SOAP 1 Timothy 1:15-16	SOAP 1 Timothy 2:3-4	SOAP 1 Timothy 2:9-10	SOAP 1 Timothy 3:13
2	1 Timothy 3:14-16	1 Timothy 4:1-10	1 Timothy 4:11-16	1 Timothy 5:1-8	1 Timothy 5:9-16
	SOAP 1 Timothy 3:16	SOAP 1 Timothy 4:8-10	SOAP 1 Timothy 4:16	SOAP 1 Timothy 5:1-2	SOAP 1 Timothy 5:16
3	1 Timothy 5:17—6:2a	1 Timothy 6:2b-10	1 Timothy 6:11-21	2 Timothy 1:1-5	2 Timothy 1:6-18
	SOAP 1 Timothy 5:21	SOAP 1 Timothy 6:6-8	SOAP 1 Timothy 6:11-12	SOAP 2 Timothy 1:5	SOAP 2 Timothy 1:13-14
4	2 Timothy 2:1-13	2 Timothy 2:14-26	2 Timothy 3:1-9	2 Timothy 3:10-17	2 Timothy 4:1-8
	SOAP 2 Timothy 2:11-13	SOAP 2 Timothy 2:15	SOAP 2 Timothy 3:1-4	SOAP 2 Timothy 3:16-17	SOAP 2 Timothy 4:1-2
5	2 Timothy 4:9-22	Titus 1:1-4	Titus 1:5-9	Titus 1:10-16	Titus 2:1-10
	SOAP 2 Timothy 4:17-18	SOAP Titus 1:1-3	SOAP Titus 1:9	SOAP Titus 1:13-15	SOAP Titus 2:6-8
6	Titus 2:11-15	Titus 3:1-7	Titus 3:8-15	Philemon 1-7	Philemon 8-25
	SOAP Titus 2:11-13	SOAP Titus 3:7	SOAP Titus 3:8	SOAP Philemon 4-7	SOAP Philemon 8-9

SALUTATION

1 From Paul, an apostle of Christ Jesus by the command of God
our Savior and of Christ Jesus our hope, 2 to Timothy, my genuine child in the faith. Grace, mercy, and peace from God the
Father and Christ Jesus our Lord!

TIMOTHY'S TASK IN EPHESUS

3 As I urged you when I was leaving for Macedonia, stay on in
Ephesus to instruct certain people not to spread false teachings, 4 nor to occupy themselves with myths and interminable
genealogies. Such things promote useless speculations rather
than God's redemptive plan that operates by faith. 5 But the aim
of our instruction is love that comes from a pure heart, a good
conscience, and a sincere faith. 6 Some have strayed from these
and turned away to empty discussion. 7 They want to be teachers of the law, but they do not understand what they are saying
or the things they insist on so confidently.

8 But we know that the law is good if someone uses it legiti-
mately, 9 realizing that law is not intended for a righteous person, but for lawless and rebellious people, for the ungodly and
sinners, for the unholy and profane, for those who kill their
fathers or mothers, for murderers, 10 sexually immoral people, practicing homosexuals, kidnappers, liars, perjurers—in
fact, for any who live contrary to sound teaching. 11 This accords with the glorious gospel of the blessed God that was
entrusted to me.

12 I am grateful to the one who has strengthened me, Christ
Jesus our Lord, because he considered me faithful in putting
me into ministry, 13 even though I was formerly a blasphemer
and a persecutor, and an arrogant man. But I was treated with
mercy because I acted ignorantly in unbelief, 14 and our Lord's
grace was abundant, bringing faith and love in Christ Jesus.
15 This saying is trustworthy and deserves full acceptance:
"Christ Jesus came into the world to save sinners"—and I am
the worst of them! 16 But here is why I was treated with mercy:
so that in me as the worst, Christ Jesus could demonstrate
his utmost patience, as an example for those who are going
to believe in him for eternal life. 17 Now to the eternal king,
immortal, invisible, the only God, be honor and glory forever
and ever! Amen.

18 I put this charge before you, Timothy my child, in keeping with the prophecies once spoken about you, in order that
with such encouragement you may fight the good fight. 19 To
do this you must hold firmly to faith and a good conscience,
which some have rejected and so have suffered shipwreck in
regard to the faith. 20 Among these are Hymenaeus and Alexander, whom I handed over to Satan to be taught not to
blaspheme.

REFLECT

What instructions did Paul give to Timothy? How did these instructions encourage the younger man to continue in the faith?

PRAYER FOR ALL PEOPLE

2 First of all, then, I urge that requests, prayers, intercessions,
and thanks be offered on behalf of all people, 2 even for kings
and all who are in authority, that we may lead a peaceful and
quiet life in all godliness and dignity. 3 Such prayer for all is good

LOVE TO GROW

FIGHT THE GOOD FIGHT

1 TIMOTHY 1:18

During basic training, all men and women who enlist in the United States Army memorize the Soldier's Creed. In unison the troop recites these guiding principles: "I am an American Soldier. I am a warrior and a member of a team. I serve the people of the United States, and live the Army Values. I always place the mission first." As they voice this statement, the cadets declare their commitment to a combat-ready mentality.

Paul penned the epistle to his apprentice Timothy with a similar military mind-set. Having faced many battles in the name of Christ, this wise mentor warned the young leader never to let his guard down or to grow complacent about his calling. In other writings Paul challenged all believers to clothe themselves with spiritual armor so they could "stand against the schemes of the devil" (Eph 6:11).

I put this charge before you, Timothy my child, in keeping with the prophecies once spoken about you, in order that with such encouragement you may fight the good fight (1 Tim 1:18).

Heeding Paul's words will help us as we fight to keep the faith during a difficult season. We should not be surprised by the struggle—after all, we are soldiers. A soldier perseveres through pain and always advances because of these fundamental beliefs—a sort of Believer's Creed:

I keep the gospel mission in mind, no matter where I stand.

I never accept defeat because greater is He who is in me than he who is in the world.

I stay disciplined and sacrificially give my all in service to my King.

I guard the trust Christ has placed in me with the help of the Holy Spirit.

I take my "share of suffering as a good soldier of Christ Jesus" (2 Tim 2:3).

The enemy cannot defeat us if we stay on the field of battle and keep the faith. He may oppose us; he may oppress us; but he can never overcome us with God on our side. Christ went to war for the souls of humanity on the cross, and all those who bear His name are more than conquerors. The love of Jesus has forever defeated the onslaught of the enemy.

In the midst of conflict, we must arm ourselves with truth. The enemy's strongholds cannot crush us. God is fighting for us and issues our marching orders: "Stay alert, stand firm in the faith, show courage, be strong." (1 Cor 16:13).

The God of angel armies goes forth on your behalf today. He will help you persevere and prevail. Keep fighting the good fight.

and welcomed before God our Savior, 4 since he wants all people
to be saved and to come to a knowledge of the truth. 5 For there
is one God and one intermediary between God and humanity,
Christ Jesus, himself human, 6 who gave himself as a ransom
for all, revealing God's purpose at his appointed time. 7 For this
I was appointed a preacher and apostle—I am telling the truth;
I am not lying—and a teacher of the Gentiles in faith and truth.
8 So I want the men in every place to pray, lifting up holy hands
without anger or dispute.

REFLECT

How should we pray for those in authority? How can you pray today for those who lead your family, church, community, and country?

CONDUCT OF WOMEN

9 Likewise the women are to dress in suitable apparel, with modesty and self-control. Their adornment must not be with braided
hair and gold or pearls or expensive clothing, 10 but with good
deeds, as is proper for women who profess reverence for God.
11 A woman must learn quietly with all submissiveness. 12 But I
do not allow a woman to teach or exercise authority over a man.
She must remain quiet. 13 For Adam was formed first and then
Eve. 14 And Adam was not deceived, but the woman, because she
was fully deceived, fell into transgression. 15 But she will be delivered through childbearing, if she continues in faith and love
and holiness with self-control.

QUALIFICATIONS FOR OVERSEERS AND DEACONS

3 This saying is trustworthy: "If someone aspires to the
office of overseer, he desires a good work." 2 The overseer then must be above reproach, the husband of one wife,
temperate, self-controlled, respectable, hospitable, an able
teacher, 3 not a drunkard, not violent, but gentle, not contentious, free from the love of money. 4 He must manage his
own household well and keep his children in control without losing his dignity. 5 But if someone does not know how to
manage his own household, how will he care for the church
of God? 6 He must not be a recent convert or he may become
arrogant and fall into the punishment that the devil will exact. 7 And he must be well thought of by those outside the
faith, so that he may not fall into disgrace and be caught by
the devil's trap.
8 Deacons likewise must be dignified, not two-faced, not given
to excessive drinking, not greedy for gain, 9 holding to the mystery of the faith with a clear conscience. 10 And these also must
be tested first and then let them serve as deacons if they are
found blameless. 11 Likewise also their wives must be dignified,
not slanderous, temperate, faithful in every respect. 12 Deacons
must be husbands of one wife and good managers of their children and their own households. 13 For those who have served
well as deacons gain a good standing for themselves and great
boldness in the faith that is in Christ Jesus.

REFLECT

What do the qualifications for church leaders tell us about what God values in those who lead His people?

CONDUCT IN GOD'S CHURCH

14 I hope to come to you soon, but I am writing these instructions
to you 15 in case I am delayed, to let you know how people ought
to conduct themselves in the household of God, because it is the

church of the living God, the support and bulwark of the truth.
16 And we all agree, our religion contains amazing revelation:
He was revealed in the flesh,
vindicated by the Spirit,
seen by angels,
proclaimed among Gentiles,
believed on in the world,
taken up in glory.

REFLECT

How can you set an example for others around you, no matter your position, to encourage them to follow Christ wholeheartedly?

TIMOTHY'S MINISTRY IN THE LATER TIMES

4 Now the Spirit explicitly says that in the later times some
will desert the faith and occupy themselves with deceiving
spirits and demonic teachings, 2 influenced by the hypocrisy
of liars whose consciences are seared. 3 They will prohibit marriage and require abstinence from foods that God created to be
received with thanksgiving by those who believe and know the
truth. 4 For every creation of God is good and no food is to be rejected if it is received with thanksgiving. 5 For it is sanctified by
God's word and by prayer.
6 By pointing out such things to the brothers and sisters, you
will be a good servant of Christ Jesus, having nourished yourself on the words of the faith and of the good teaching that you
have followed. 7 But reject those myths fit only for the godless
and gullible, and train yourself for godliness. 8 For "physical exercise has some value, but godliness is valuable in every way.
It holds promise for the present life and for the life to come."
9 This saying is trustworthy and deserves full acceptance. 10 In
fact this is why we work hard and struggle, because we have set
our hope on the living God, who is the Savior of all people, especially of believers.
11 Command and teach these things. 12 Let no one look down
on you because you are young, but set an example for the believers in your speech, conduct, love, faithfulness, and purity.
13 Until I come, give attention to the public reading of scripture,
to exhortation, to teaching. 14 Do not neglect the spiritual gift
you have, given to you and confirmed by prophetic words when
the elders laid hands on you. 15 Take pains with these things; be
absorbed in them, so that everyone will see your progress. 16 Be
conscientious about how you live and what you teach. Persevere in this, because by doing so you will save both yourself and
those who listen to you.

INSTRUCTIONS ABOUT SPECIFIC GROUPS

5 Do not address an older man harshly but appeal to him as a
father. Speak to younger men as brothers, 2 older women as
mothers, and younger women as sisters—with complete purity.
3 Honor widows who are truly in need. 4 But if a widow has children or grandchildren, they should first learn to fulfill their duty
toward their own household and so repay their parents what is
owed them. For this is what pleases God. 5 But the widow who is
truly in need, and completely on her own, has set her hope on
God and continues in her pleas and prayers night and day. 6 But
the one who lives for pleasure is dead even while she lives. 7 Reinforce these commands, so that they will be beyond reproach.

TRAINING IN GODLINESS

1 TIMOTHY 4:8

Have you ever trained for a race? Maybe you underwent special certification for your job or studied to gain a certain level of knowledge and earned a degree.

In every form it takes, training requires discipline, repetition, concentration, and sacrifice. Bodily training, for example, involves commitment, physical labor, sweat, and pain. To have a body that is active and mobile, to have energy and feel good, to be able to handle stress better, and to excel at your job or hobby make all the training worth it.

In 1 Timothy 4:8, Paul explained that one kind of training is even more rewarding: "Physical exercise has some value, but godliness is valuable in every way. It holds promise for the present life and for the life to come." Training in godliness means being continually changed into the image of Jesus. It brings about a greater grief over our sin and a stronger desire to love God. It is part of our sanctification, but it doesn't simply happen. The Holy Spirit helps bring about this change, and He often uses the Word of God to do it.

Your Bible is a great treasure. Reading God's Word regularly requires sacrifice and commitment. To gain the true wealth of this treasure, we must fight against complacency and laziness and put aside busyness and distractions.

The training in godliness we gain from this treasure is worth all of our energy and effort.

The value this training holds is infinite. Your quest will be rewarded not in earthly metals or first-place ribbons, but in a deeper relationship with your Savior and a stronger love for those around you. You will grow in knowledge and in the ability to apply that knowledge to your everyday life (wisdom). Your circumstances may not change, but you will be more equipped to find joy, contentment, and peace in those circumstances.

Growing in godliness equips you for life's mountains and valleys, for easy roads and roads full of twists and turns. Godliness equips you for every good work God has prepared for you. Don't be afraid to train hard; you will be richly rewarded.

CHALLENGE

Compare 1 Timothy 5:24–25 with 1 Samuel 16:7. What do these Scriptures teach us about what God values?

8 But if someone does not provide for his own, especially his own family, he has denied the faith and is worse than an unbeliever.

9 No widow should be put on the list unless she is at least sixty years old, was the wife of one husband, 10 and has a reputation for good works: as one who has raised children, practiced hospitality, washed the feet of the saints, helped those in distress—as one who has exhibited all kinds of good works. 11 But do not accept younger widows on the list, because their passions may lead them away from Christ and they will desire to marry, 12 and so incur judgment for breaking their former pledge. 13 And besides that, going around from house to house they learn to be lazy, and they are not only lazy, but also gossips and busybodies, talking about things they should not. 14 So I want younger women to marry, raise children, and manage a household, in order to give the adversary no opportunity to vilify us. 15 For some have already wandered away to follow Satan. 16 If a believing woman has widows in her family, let her help them. The church should not be burdened, so that it may help the widows who are truly in need.

17 Elders who provide effective leadership must be counted worthy of double honor, especially those who work hard in speaking and teaching. 18 For the scripture says, "***Do not muzzle an ox while it is treading out the grain,***" and, "The worker deserves his pay." 19 Do not accept an accusation against an elder unless it can be confirmed *by two or three witnesses.* 20 Those guilty of sin must be rebuked before all, as a warning to the rest. 21 Before God and Christ Jesus and the elect angels, I solemnly charge you to carry out these commands without prejudice or favoritism of any kind. 22 Do not lay hands on anyone hastily and so identify with the sins of others. Keep yourself pure. 23 (Stop drinking just water, but use a little wine for your digestion and your frequent illnesses.) 24 The sins of some people are obvious, going before them into judgment, but for others, they show up later. 25 Similarly good works are also obvious, and the ones that are not cannot remain hidden.

6 Those who are under the yoke as slaves must regard their own masters as deserving of full respect. This will prevent the name of God and Christian teaching from being discredited. 2 But those who have believing masters must not show them less respect because they are brothers. Instead they are to serve all the more, because those who benefit from their service are believers and dearly loved.

SUMMARY OF TIMOTHY'S DUTIES

Teach them and exhort them about these things. 3 If someone spreads false teachings and does not agree with sound words (that is, those of our Lord Jesus Christ) and with the teaching that accords with godliness, 4 he is conceited and understands nothing, but has an unhealthy interest in controversies and verbal disputes. This gives rise to envy, dissension, slanders, evil suspicions, 5 and constant bickering by people corrupted in their minds and deprived of the truth, who suppose that godliness is a way of making a profit. 6 Now godliness combined with contentment brings great profit. 7 For we have brought nothing into this world and so we cannot take a single thing out either. 8 But if we

have food and shelter, we will be satisfied with that. 9 Those who
long to be rich, however, stumble into temptation and a trap and
many senseless and harmful desires that plunge people into ruin
and destruction. 10 For the love of money is the root of all evils.
Some people in reaching for it have strayed from the faith and
stabbed themselves with many pains.

11 But you, as a person dedicated to God, keep away from all
that. Instead pursue righteousness, godliness, faithfulness, love,
endurance, and gentleness. 12 Compete well for the faith and lay
hold of that eternal life you were called for and made your good
confession for in the presence of many witnesses. 13 I charge you
before God who gives life to all things and Christ Jesus who made
his good confession before Pontius Pilate, 14 to obey this command without fault or failure until the appearing of our Lord
Jesus Christ 15 —whose appearing the blessed and only Sovereign,
the King of kings and Lord of lords, will reveal at the right time.
16 He alone possesses immortality and lives in unapproachable
light, whom no human has ever seen or is able to see. To him be
honor and eternal power! Amen.

17 Command those who are rich in this world's goods not to be
haughty or to set their hope on riches, which are uncertain, but
on God who richly provides us with all things for our enjoyment.
18 Tell them to do good, to be rich in good deeds, to be generous
givers, sharing with others. 19 In this way they will save up a treasure for themselves as a firm foundation for the future and so
lay hold of what is truly life.

CONCLUSION

20 O Timothy, protect what has been entrusted to you. Avoid
the profane chatter and absurdities of so-called "knowledge."
21 By professing it, some have strayed from the faith. Grace be
with you all.

REFLECT

What does it mean for you to remain in the faith daily? How can you fight for your faith when trials or doubts come?

Every SCRIPTURE is INSPIRED by GOD and useful for TEACHING, for reproof, for correction and FOR TRAINING in righteousness, that the person dedicated to GOD may be CAPABLE and EQUIPPED for every GOOD work

MEMORY VERSE

Every scripture is inspired by God and useful for teaching, for reproof, for correction, and for training in righteousness, that the person dedicated to God may be capable and equipped for every good work.

2 Timothy 3:16–17

2 Timothy

INTRODUCTION

God's Word Equips

The Book of 2 Timothy is an incredibly personal letter from Paul. Written in his final years, the apostle's final words of encouragement are recorded for his "child" in the faith. Paul sent Timothy his instructions for living the Christian life and encouraged him to use his gifts, remain loyal to Christ in the midst of suffering, and guide others in the faith. When Paul's mission to preach the gospel to the Gentiles neared its completion, he passed the mission to Timothy, commanding him to continue preaching the Word.

The Book of 2 Timothy can be divided into five main sections. First, Paul offered Timothy encouragement in ministry and instructed him on the use of spiritual gifts and the necessity of suffering for the gospel (1:1–18). Paul then gave Timothy examples of how to live the Christian life, minister to others, and handle the Word of God (2:1–26). Paul exhorted Timothy, warning him of apostasy he was sure to face in his ministry (3:1–17). Paul encouraged Timothy to continue faithfully preaching the Word (4:1–8). Paul's closing remarks (4:9–22) seem especially poignant since he appeared to sense he'd soon die.

Paul identified himself as the author of 2 Timothy. The apostle probably wrote this book during his second imprisonment in Rome. Since Paul is believed to have been martyred in A.D. 64, it is possible that 2 Timothy was written sometime that same year.

Paul's goal in writing this personal letter to Timothy was to encourage him to persevere in the faith. As persecution began to occur, Paul encouraged Timothy to keep his eyes focused on Christ, the source of salvation and hope and the truth he proclaimed. We too can love God greatly by focusing our lives on Christ, remembering He alone is our source, sustainer, provider, and comfort.

Hungary

OFFICIAL LANGUAGE
Hungarian
POPULATION
9,586,000
UNREACHED POPULATION
78,000
PROFESSING CHRISTIANS
86.8%

Viola's Home

Say a Prayer Today

Pray for Viola and her work translating Love God Greatly studies. Pray many women would be influenced by the truth of the gospel through her commitment to sharing God's Word.

HISTORY BIT

The beginnings of Christianity in Hungary can be traced back as far as the third century. Catholicism was established in Hungary in 1001 by Stephen I.*

Source Information:
https://joshuaproject.net/countries/HU
*David B. Barrett, World Christian Encyclopedia, Hungary (New York, NY: Oxford University Press, 1982), 364.

LOVE YOUR NEIGHBOR

Her Journey

VIOLA'S STORY

I'm forever thankful for the examples and mentors God has placed in my life, similarly to Timothy's. Like Timothy, I grew up with faithful grandmothers and a faithful mother who inspired me to teach and reach women with the gospel.

From the time I was young, my mother translated church services for the foreign pastors who visited our home church in Hungary. This was at a time when we could not freely live out our faith because of the communist rule in Hungary. I witnessed God use my mother's knowledge of the Hungarian language and her willing heart to help others understand the truth of the gospel.

My mom's example showed me what it means to have God's Word affect and equip your life. She showed me the importance and significance of having God's Word in your own language. This eventually encouraged me to begin translating Bible studies for Love God Greatly into my native language of Hungarian.

Now that I have children of my own, I am fully aware of the importance of living out my faith in front of my kids. I want them to see an example of how to love and serve Christ in my life. God's Word does equip, no matter how we share it. His Word is our help, guiding and teaching us how to love God greatly and how to share His love with the world. God's Word makes us ready for things we could not have imagined.

Like Timothy, I long to be a minister of the gospel who can train and teach others to do the same. With my Love God Greatly translation team I have seen many women come to have a personal relationship with Jesus and have their hearts and lives changed by Him. I want these women to know God has a special plan for their lives and they can be faithful ministers of the gospel through the equipping power of God's Word.

6 WEEK READING PLAN

LOVE HIS WORD

	MONDAY	TUESDAY	WEDNESDAY	THURSDAY	FRIDAY
1	1 Timothy 1:1-11	1 Timothy 1:12-20	1 Timothy 2:1-8	1 Timothy 2:9-15	1 Timothy 3:1-13
	SOAP 1 Timothy 1:5-7	SOAP 1 Timothy 1:15-16	SOAP 1 Timothy 2:3-4	SOAP 1 Timothy 2:9-10	SOAP 1 Timothy 3:13
2	1 Timothy 3:14-16	1 Timothy 4:1-10	1 Timothy 4:11-16	1 Timothy 5:1-8	1 Timothy 5:9-16
	SOAP 1 Timothy 3:16	SOAP 1 Timothy 4:8-10	SOAP 1 Timothy 4:16	SOAP 1 Timothy 5:1-2	SOAP 1 Timothy 5:16
3	1 Timothy 5:17–6:2a	1 Timothy 6:2b-10	1 Timothy 6:11-21	2 Timothy 1:1-5	2 Timothy 1:6-18
	SOAP 1 Timothy 5:21	SOAP 1 Timothy 6:6-8	SOAP 1 Timothy 6:11-12	SOAP 2 Timothy 1:5	SOAP 2 Timothy 1:13-14
4	2 Timothy 2:1-13	2 Timothy 2:14-26	2 Timothy 3:1-9	2 Timothy 3:10-17	2 Timothy 4:1-8
	SOAP 2 Timothy 2:11-13	SOAP 2 Timothy 2:15	SOAP 2 Timothy 3:1-4	SOAP 2 Timothy 3:16-17	SOAP 2 Timothy 4:1-2
5	2 Timothy 4:9-22	Titus 1:1-4	Titus 1:5-9	Titus 1:10-16	Titus 2:1-10
	SOAP 2 Timothy 4:17-18	SOAP Titus 1:1-3	SOAP Titus 1:9	SOAP Titus 1:13-15	SOAP Titus 2:6-8
6	Titus 2:11-15	Titus 3:1-7	Titus 3:8-15	Philemon 1-7	Philemon 8-25
	SOAP Titus 2:11-13	SOAP Titus 3:7	SOAP Titus 3:8	SOAP Philemon 4-7	SOAP Philemon 8-9

SALUTATION

1 From Paul, an apostle of Christ Jesus by the will of God, to further the promise of life in Christ Jesus, 2 to Timothy, my dear
child. Grace, mercy, and peace from God the Father and Christ
Jesus our Lord!

THANKSGIVING AND CHARGE TO TIMOTHY

3 I am thankful to God, whom I have served with a clear conscience as my ancestors did, when I remember you in my prayers
as I do constantly night and day. 4 As I remember your tears, I
long to see you, so that I may be filled with joy. 5 I recall your sincere faith that was alive first in your grandmother Lois and in
your mother Eunice, and I am sure is in you.
6 Because of this I remind you to rekindle God's gift that you
possess through the laying on of my hands. 7 For God did not
give us a Spirit of fear but of power and love and self-control. 8 So
do not be ashamed of the testimony about our Lord or of me,
a prisoner for his sake, but by God's power accept your share of
suffering for the gospel. 9 He is the one who saved us and called
us with a holy calling, not based on our works but on his own
purpose and grace, granted to us in Christ Jesus before time began, 10 but now made visible through the appearing of our Savior
Christ Jesus. He has broken the power of death and brought life
and immortality to light through the gospel! 11 For this gospel
I was appointed a preacher and apostle and teacher. 12 Because
of this, in fact, I suffer as I do. But I am not ashamed, because I
know the one in whom my faith is set and I am convinced that he
is able to protect what has been entrusted to me until that day.
13 Hold to the standard of sound words that you heard from me
and do so with the faith and love that are in Christ Jesus. 14 Protect that good thing entrusted to you, through the Holy Spirit
who lives within us.
15 You know that everyone in the province of Asia deserted
me, including Phygelus and Hermogenes. 16 May the Lord grant
mercy to the family of Onesiphorus, because he often refreshed
me and was not ashamed of my imprisonment. 17 But when he
arrived in Rome, he eagerly searched for me and found me.
18 May the Lord grant him to find mercy from the Lord on
that day! And you know very well all the ways he served me
in Ephesus.

SERVING FAITHFULLY DESPITE HARDSHIP

2 So you, my child, be strong in the grace that is in Christ
Jesus. 2 And what you heard me say in the presence of many
witnesses entrust to faithful people who will be competent
to teach others as well. 3 Take your share of suffering as a
good soldier of Christ Jesus. 4 No one in military service gets
entangled in matters of everyday life; otherwise he will not
please the one who recruited him. 5 Also, if anyone competes
as an athlete, he will not be crowned as the winner unless
he competes according to the rules. 6 The farmer who works
hard ought to have the first share of the crops. 7 Think about
what I am saying and the Lord will give you understanding
of all this.

CHALLENGE

Take Paul's words to heart this week and do not be ashamed of the gospel. Share your testimony and the gospel of Jesus with one person this week.

LOVE TO GROW

STRONG IN GRACE

2 TIMOTHY 2:1–7

In the Book of 2 Timothy, we have the privilege of reading some of the last recorded words of one of the most extraordinary Christians who ever lived. The apostle Paul wrote his last letter to the young pastor, Timothy, encouraging him to persevere in sharing the message of Jesus Christ despite the persecution he would face.

The Book of 2 Timothy destroys the illusion that Christians will enjoy a trouble-free life. Paul wrote this letter while he was imprisoned—and this was nothing new. Second Corinthians 11:23–28 describes the suffering and hardship Paul endured for the cause of Christ. He was beaten, stoned, flogged, imprisoned, and shipwrecked; and he risked danger again and again.

We read in 2 Timothy 4:16–17 that Paul had been abandoned by many of his brothers and sisters in Christ because of the stigma associated with following an imprisoned leader. Paul said it was during those dark and lonely times when Jesus' comfort and faithfulness became even more real to him.

Despite all Paul suffered, he had no regrets. He remained joyful, clinging to the hope of dwelling with Jesus for eternity. Because Paul had intimately shared in the suffering of Jesus, he wanted to prepare Timothy. He encouraged Timothy to follow his lead and continue the battle as a good soldier of Christ Jesus.

As Paul prepared for death, he exhorted Timothy with wisdom to lead the newly established churches. He encouraged Timothy to persevere and remain courageous. He urged Timothy to cling tightly to the truth of the gospel and the identity of Jesus. He warned him not to taint the gospel message in an effort to compromise, keep peace, or satisfy the congregation.

Following Jesus comes at great cost. It means we gladly invite risk, hardship, and persecution, knowing our lives are not our own. We sacrifice everything now, knowing we find our only hope in heaven with Jesus.

As we love God greatly, we fight to follow Jesus wholeheartedly, no matter the sacrifice. We trust the life and love God has prepared for us in heaven are far greater than anything we suffer today. Let's follow Paul's exhortation to Timothy and "be strong in the grace that is in Christ Jesus" (2 Tim 2:1).

8 Remember Jesus Christ, raised from the dead, a descendant
of David; such is my gospel, 9 for which I suffer hardship to the
point of imprisonment as a criminal, but God's message is not
imprisoned! 10 So I endure all things for the sake of those chosen by God, that they too may obtain salvation in Christ Jesus
and its eternal glory. 11 This saying is trustworthy:

If we died with him, we will also live with him.
12 If we endure, we will also reign with him.
If we deny him, he will also deny us.
13 If we are unfaithful, he remains faithful,
since he cannot deny himself.

REFLECT

How can you flee from sinful passions and pursue righteousness today?

DEALING WITH FALSE TEACHERS

14 Remind people of these things and solemnly charge them before the Lord not to wrangle over words. This is of no benefit; it
just brings ruin on those who listen. 15 Make every effort to present yourself before God as a proven worker who does not need
to be ashamed, teaching the message of truth accurately. 16 But
avoid profane chatter, because those occupied with it will stray
further and further into ungodliness, 17 and their message will
spread its infection like gangrene. Hymenaeus and Philetus are
in this group. 18 They have strayed from the truth by saying that
the resurrection has already occurred, and they are undermining some people's faith. 19 However, God's solid foundation remains standing, bearing this seal: "***The Lord knows those who are
his,***" and "Everyone who confesses the name of the Lord must
turn away from evil."

20 Now in a wealthy home there are not only gold and silver
vessels, but also ones made of wood and of clay, and some are
for honorable use, but others for ignoble use. 21 So if someone
cleanses himself of such behavior, he will be a vessel for honorable use, set apart, useful for the Master, prepared for every good
work. 22 But keep away from youthful passions, and pursue righteousness, faithfulness, love, and peace, in company with others
who call on the Lord from a pure heart. 23 But reject foolish and
ignorant controversies, because you know they breed infight-
ing. 24 And the Lord's slave must not engage in heated disputes
but be kind toward all, an apt teacher, patient, 25 correcting opponents with gentleness. Perhaps God will grant them repentance and then knowledge of the truth 26 and they will come
to their senses and escape the devil's trap where they are held
captive to do his will.

REFLECT

How can we prepare ourselves for the difficulties to come? How do we stand firm against persecutions and false teachers?

MINISTRY IN THE LAST DAYS

3 But understand this, that in the last days difficult times
will come. 2 For people will be lovers of themselves, lovers
of money, boastful, arrogant, blasphemers, disobedient to parents, ungrateful, unholy, 3 unloving, irreconcilable, slanderers,
without self-control, savage, opposed to what is good, 4 treacherous, reckless, conceited, loving pleasure rather than loving
God. 5 They will maintain the outward appearance of religion but
will have repudiated its power. So avoid people like these. 6 For
some of these insinuate themselves into households and captivate weak women who are overwhelmed with sins and led along

by various passions. 7 Such women are always seeking instruction, yet never able to arrive at a knowledge of the truth. 8 And
just as Jannes and Jambres opposed Moses, so these people—
who have warped minds and are disqualified in the faith—also
oppose the truth. 9 But they will not go much further, for their
foolishness will be obvious to everyone, just like it was with Jannes and Jambres.

CONTINUE IN WHAT YOU HAVE LEARNED

10 You, however, have followed my teaching, my way of life, my
purpose, my faith, my patience, my love, my endurance, 11 as
well as the persecutions and sufferings that happened to me
in Antioch, in Iconium, and in Lystra. I endured these persecutions and the Lord delivered me from them all. 12 Now in
fact all who want to live godly lives in Christ Jesus will be persecuted. 13 But evil people and charlatans will go from bad to
worse, deceiving others and being deceived themselves. 14 You,
however, must continue in the things you have learned and are
confident about. You know who taught you 15 and how from in-
fancy you have known the holy writings, which are able to give
you wisdom for salvation through faith in Christ Jesus. 16 Every scripture is inspired by God and useful for teaching, for reproof, for correction, and for training in righteousness, 17 that
the person dedicated to God may be capable and equipped for
every good work.

CHARGE TO TIMOTHY REPEATED

4 I solemnly charge you before God and Christ Jesus, who is
going to judge the living and the dead, and by his appearing
and his kingdom: 2 Preach the message, be ready whether it is
convenient or not, reprove, rebuke, exhort with complete patience and instruction. 3 For there will be a time when people
will not tolerate sound teaching. Instead, following their own
desires, they will accumulate teachers for themselves, because
they have an insatiable curiosity to hear new things. 4 And they
will turn away from hearing the truth, but on the other hand
they will turn aside to myths. 5 You, however, be self-controlled
in all things, endure hardship, do an evangelist's work, fulfill
your ministry. 6 For I am already being poured out as an offering, and the time for me to depart is at hand. 7 I have competed
well; I have finished the race; I have kept the faith! 8 Finally the
crown of righteousness is reserved for me. The Lord, the righteous Judge, will award it to me in that day—and not to me only,
but also to all who have set their affection on his appearing.

TRAVEL PLANS AND CONCLUDING GREETINGS

9 Make every effort to come to me soon. 10 For Demas deserted
me, since he loved the present age, and he went to Thessalonica. Crescens went to Galatia and Titus to Dalmatia. 11 Only
Luke is with me. Get Mark and bring him with you, because he
is a great help to me in ministry. 12 Now I have sent Tychicus to
Ephesus. 13 When you come, bring with you the cloak I left in
Troas with Carpas and the scrolls, especially the parchments.
14 Alexander the coppersmith did me a great deal of harm. *The*

REFLECT

How can you prepare yourself today to live the way Paul commanded Timothy to live?

Lord will repay him in keeping with his deeds. 15 You be on guard
against him too, because he vehemently opposed our words.
16 At my first defense no one appeared in my support; instead
they all deserted me—may they not be held accountable for
it. 17 But the Lord stood by me and strengthened me, so that
through me the message would be fully proclaimed for all the
Gentiles to hear. And so I was delivered from the lion's mouth!
18 The Lord will deliver me from every evil deed and will bring
me safely into his heavenly kingdom. To him be glory for ever
and ever! Amen.

19 Greetings to Prisca and Aquila and the family of Onesiphorus. 20 Erastus stayed in Corinth. Trophimus I left ill in Miletus.
21 Make every effort to come before winter. Greetings to you from
Eubulus, Pudens, Linus, Claudia, and all the brothers and sisters.
22 The Lord be with your spirit. Grace be with you.

Showing yourself to be an example of good works in every way

MEMORY VERSE

. . . showing yourself to be an example of good works in every way.

Titus 2:7

Titus

INTRODUCTION

Set a Good Example

Titus appears to have been one of Paul's most trusted assistants. He accompanied Paul on some of his missionary journeys and to the Jerusalem Council. Titus later returned to the island of Crete to build and encourage the church there. The church in Crete, like many other churches, had been infiltrated by false teachers. Titus was tasked with correcting the church members and returning them to sound doctrine and faithful service.

Paul's letter to Titus emphasized the importance of good works (2:14; 3:1–8). Paul showed Titus how some in the church were motivated by selfish gain and how this affected the doctrine of the church (1:10–16). Paul encouraged Titus to model purity, service, and kindness to the believers in Crete and to call them to a higher standard in their walks with Christ (2:7–8). Though salvation is not based on works, a believer performs good works from a desire to please and honor God.

Paul wrote the letter to Titus sometime between his two Roman imprisonments. Tradition holds that Titus was written after the first letter to Timothy, sometime around A.D. 63.

While Paul's message to his trusted associate Titus about good works may seem contrary to some of his other writings, he explained how people perform positive acts only by the grace of God. Not only does God do the work of salvation for us, He alone does good in and through us. As we seek to love God greatly, we can "be intent on engaging in good works" (3:8), knowing that God is the One who powers these acts through us.

Germany

OFFICIAL LANGUAGE
German
POPULATION
83,265,000
UNREACHED POPULATION
3,398,000
PROFESSING CHRISTIANS
65.4%

Wibke's Home

Say a Prayer Today

Pray that the people of Germany would again be convinced of the goodness of God. Pray they would see how the Bible is not outdated, but that God's Word is relevant and crucial for a life of faith.

HISTORY BIT

After the liberation of many Nazi extermination camps in 1945 and the widespread knowledge of the evil done to the Jews and other prisoners, many wrestled with questions about God's goodness and willingness to destroy evil in the world.*

Source Information:
https://joshuaproject.net/countries/GM
*John Bowden, A Chronology of World Christianity (New York, NY: Continuum, 2007), 414.

WIBKE'S STORY

In Germany, many people do not own a Bible. There's this belief in German culture that the God of the Bible is an outdated concept.

However, even though many aren't reading the Bible, God still reveals Himself to non-believers through the testimony of the lives of believers. They will see a believer's life and (hopefully) see Christ through them. Setting an example in everything we do is extremely important.

Paul told Titus the ideal character for leaders in the church. As I seek to be an example of the love of Christ, I try to emulate these same characteristics. By being faithful to my spouse, loving my children, being a good steward, being patient, welcoming others, and encouraging and comforting those in need, I can be an example to those around me.

While many German laws are based on moral teaching, they are also deteriorating. As the culture trends away from the truth of Scripture, Christians have a responsibility to speak up for those who do not have a voice of their own.

By studying God's Word I can learn the difference between sound and false teaching. In this way, I hope to change the view of "religious people" in Germany. Faith is more than religion; it is a relationship with God. I hope my life becomes an example of the love of Christ to those around me.

6 WEEK READING PLAN

LOVE HIS WORD

	MONDAY	TUESDAY	WEDNESDAY	THURSDAY	FRIDAY
1	1 Timothy 1:1-11	1 Timothy 1:12-20	1 Timothy 2:1-8	1 Timothy 2:9-15	1 Timothy 3:1-13
	SOAP 1 Timothy 1:5-7	SOAP 1 Timothy 1:15-16	SOAP 1 Timothy 2:3-4	SOAP 1 Timothy 2:9-10	SOAP 1 Timothy 3:13
2	1 Timothy 3:14-16	1 Timothy 4:1-10	1 Timothy 4:11-16	1 Timothy 5:1-8	1 Timothy 5:9-16
	SOAP 1 Timothy 3:16	SOAP 1 Timothy 4:8-10	SOAP 1 Timothy 4:16	SOAP 1 Timothy 5:1-2	SOAP 1 Timothy 5:16
3	1 Timothy 5:17—6:2a	1 Timothy 6:2b-10	1 Timothy 6:11-21	2 Timothy 1:1-5	2 Timothy 1:6-18
	SOAP 1 Timothy 5:21	SOAP 1 Timothy 6:6-8	SOAP 1 Timothy 6:11-12	SOAP 2 Timothy 1:5	SOAP 2 Timothy 1:13-14
4	2 Timothy 2:1-13	2 Timothy 2:14-26	2 Timothy 3:1-9	2 Timothy 3:10-17	2 Timothy 4:1-8
	SOAP 2 Timothy 2:11-13	SOAP 2 Timothy 2:15	SOAP 2 Timothy 3:1-4	SOAP 2 Timothy 3:16-17	SOAP 2 Timothy 4:1-2
5	2 Timothy 4:9-22	Titus 1:1-4	Titus 1:5-9	Titus 1:10-16	Titus 2:1-10
	SOAP 2 Timothy 4:17-18	SOAP Titus 1:1-3	SOAP Titus 1:9	SOAP Titus 1:13-15	SOAP Titus 2:6-8
6	Titus 2:11-15	Titus 3:1-7	Titus 3:8-15	Philemon 1-7	Philemon 8-25
	SOAP Titus 2:11-13	SOAP Titus 3:7	SOAP Titus 3:8	SOAP Philemon 4-7	SOAP Philemon 8-9

SALUTATION

1 From Paul, a slave of God and apostle of Jesus Christ, to further the faith of God's chosen ones and the knowledge of the
truth that is in keeping with godliness, 2 in hope of eternal life,
which God, who does not lie, promised before time began. 3 But
now in his own time he has made his message evident through
the preaching I was entrusted with according to the command
of God our Savior. 4 To Titus, my genuine son in a common faith.
Grace and peace from God the Father and Christ Jesus our Savior!

TITUS' TASK ON CRETE

5 The reason I left you in Crete was to set in order the remaining matters and to appoint elders in every town, as I directed
you. 6 An elder must be blameless, the husband of one wife, with
faithful children who cannot be charged with dissipation or rebellion. 7 For the overseer must be blameless as one entrusted
with God's work, not arrogant, not prone to anger, not a drunkard, not violent, not greedy for gain. 8 Instead he must be hospitable, devoted to what is good, sensible, upright, devout, and
self-controlled. 9 He must hold firmly to the faithful message as
it has been taught, so that he will be able to give exhortation in
such healthy teaching and correct those who speak against it.
10 For there are many rebellious people, idle talkers, and deceivers, especially those with Jewish connections, 11 who must be
silenced because they mislead whole families by teaching for dishonest gain what ought not to be taught. 12 A certain one of them,
in fact, one of their own prophets, said, "Cretans are always liars,
evil beasts, lazy gluttons." 13 Such testimony is true. For this reason rebuke them sharply that they may be healthy in the faith
14 and not pay attention to Jewish myths and commands of people who reject the truth. 15 All is pure to those who are pure. But
to those who are corrupt and unbelieving, nothing is pure, but
both their minds and consciences are corrupted. 16 They profess
to know God but with their deeds they deny him, since they are
detestable, disobedient, and unfit for any good deed.

CONDUCT CONSISTENT WITH SOUND TEACHING

2 But as for you, communicate the behavior that goes with
sound teaching. 2 Older men are to be temperate, dignified,
self-controlled, sound in faith, in love, and in endurance. 3 Older
women likewise are to exhibit behavior fitting for those who are
holy, not slandering, not slaves to excessive drinking, but teaching
what is good. 4 In this way they will train the younger women to
love their husbands, to love their children, 5 to be self-controlled,
pure, fulfilling their duties at home, kind, being subject to their
own husbands, so that the message of God may not be discredited. 6 Encourage younger men likewise to be self-controlled,
7 showing yourself to be an example of good works in every way.
In your teaching show integrity, dignity, 8 and a sound message
that cannot be criticized, so that any opponent will be at a loss,
because he has nothing evil to say about us. 9 Slaves are to be subject to their own masters in everything, to do what is wanted and
not talk back, 10 not pilfering, but showing all good faith, in order
to bring credit to the teaching of God our Savior in everything.

REFLECT

What do the qualifications for elders tell us about what God desires for leaders of the church?

LOVE TO GROW

A CALL TO STAND OUT

TITUS 1:16

"Actions speak louder than words."

I'm sure you've heard this old adage a few times. I've heard it so often that when someone says it now, I am tempted to roll my eyes and ignore it. Every once in a while, though, it's good to pause and remind ourselves what we say should be proven by what we do.

Paul brings us this important reminder in Titus 1:16. In this letter, Paul encouraged Timothy to avoid certain people in the church. Those people, he wrote, claimed to believe in God with their words, but their actions told a different story. Although they professed God, they lived like people who did not believe in God. They lived like the rest of the world.

"They profess to know God but with their deeds they deny him" (Titus 1:16).

In other words, Paul's message is this: Live differently from the rest of the world!

The problem I face with this message is that living differently from the rest of the world requires standing out, something I do not like to do. I like blending in. In fact, I'm very good at it. What I do not care for is having attention on me. I feel so self-conscious!

The preference to blend in is not wrong, but it becomes a problem if it affects living out my faith. I say I follow God, but with my actions I look as much like the world as possible. I find myself asking how much I can look like the world without compromising my integrity or witness for Christ. This is the wrong approach. Instead, my call is to stand out in order to show a hurting, lost world the love of Jesus.

This type of faith requires boldness and confidence in God's call in our lives. It means laying down our pride, knowing not everyone will understand why we choose to live differently from those around us.

This lifestyle will inevitably show others the gracious love of Christ, the hope and peace they can find in Him, and the redemption He brings to every aspect of our lives. Our lives are different. We should stand out as believers in Christ because if we don't, what hope is there for a dying, hurting world? Let's live aligned with what we say about our faith in Jesus.

11 For the grace of God has appeared, bringing salvation to all
people. 12 It trains us to reject godless ways and worldly desires
and to live self-controlled, upright, and godly lives in the present
age, 13 as we wait for the happy fulfillment of our hope in the glorious appearing of our great God and Savior, Jesus Christ. 14 He
gave himself for us to set us free from every kind of lawlessness
and to purify for himself a people who are truly his, who are eager to do good. 15 So communicate these things with the sort of
exhortation or rebuke that carries full authority. Don't let anyone look down on you.

REFLECT

What did Christ do for us? What did He give? What did He gain from His sacrifice? How should we respond?

CONDUCT TOWARD THOSE OUTSIDE THE CHURCH

3 Remind them to be subject to rulers and authorities, to be
obedient, to be ready for every good work. 2 They must not
slander anyone, but be peaceable, gentle, showing complete
courtesy to all people. 3 For we too were once foolish, disobedient, misled, enslaved to various passions and desires, spending
our lives in evil and envy, hateful and hating one another. 4 But
"when the kindness of God our Savior and his love for mankind
appeared, 5 he saved us not by works of righteousness that we
have done but on the basis of his mercy, through the washing
of the new birth and the renewing of the Holy Spirit, 6 whom he
poured out on us in full measure through Jesus Christ our Savior. 7 And so, since we have been justified by his grace, we become
heirs with the confident expectation of eternal life."

SUMMARY OF THE LETTER

8 This saying is trustworthy, and I want you to insist on such
truths, so that those who have placed their faith in God may be
intent on engaging in good works. These things are good and
beneficial for all people. 9 But avoid foolish controversies, genealogies, quarrels, and fights about the law, because they are
useless and empty. 10 Reject a divisive person after one or two
warnings. 11 You know that such a person is twisted by sin and is
conscious of it himself.

FINAL INSTRUCTIONS AND GREETING

12 When I send Artemas or Tychicus to you, do your best to come
to me at Nicopolis, for I have decided to spend the winter there.
13 Make every effort to help Zenas the lawyer and Apollos on their
way; make sure they have what they need. 14 Here is another way
that our people can learn to engage in good works to meet pressing needs and so not be unfruitful. 15 Everyone with me greets
you. Greet those who love us in the faith. Grace be with you all.

CHALLENGE

Take time to slowly reflect on what Christ has done for us. How are we to respond? What will you do today to honor Him for His incredible blessings?

I would rather appeal to you on the basis of love

MEMORY VERSE

So, although I have quite a lot of confidence in Christ and could command you to do what is proper, I would rather appeal to you on the basis of love.

Philemon 8–9

Philemon

INTRODUCTION

Challenging Fellow Believers

Slavery was a cultural norm in the Roman Empire. Under Roman law, a slave owner could kill a runaway slave if he chose. The letter Paul wrote to Philemon was a plea for him to do something radical: honor and welcome back his runaway slave, Onesimus. The apostle appealed to Philemon to view Onesimus as a brother in Christ instead of a slave. Philemon's response would be an example to the church that met in his home and to all those in his community.

In the brief letter he wrote to Philemon, Paul incorporated deep theological concepts that must have challenged and encouraged Philemon. Paul dealt with salvation, substitution, imputation, and redemption in this short book. As Onesimus was a slave, all believers in Christ were once slaves to sin. As Philemon had freedom in Christ, Paul exhorted him to grant Onesimus the same physical freedom.

Paul identified himself as the author of Philemon multiple times in this short letter. The tone, structure, and style match Paul's other writings. It is believed that Onesimus delivered both the letter to Philemon and the letter to the church in Colossae, meaning they were written at the same time. Both letters were written in A.D. 60, during Paul's first Roman imprisonment.

The letter of Philemon is a personal appeal, but it also functions as a reminder to believers to welcome one another in the faith and forgive one another. Paul expected Philemon to extend the same forgiveness to Onesimus that he himself had received from Christ. As we seek to love God greatly, we can reflect the love of Christ by forgiving and reconciling with our brothers and sisters in the faith.

United States of America

OFFICIAL LANGUAGE
English
POPULATION
326,302,000
UNREACHED POPULATION
4,827,000
PROFESSING CHRISTIANS
77.5%

Diana's Home

Say a Prayer Today

Pray Diana's testimony would encourage many others toward reconciliation with others in their lives. Pray God would continue to do great works of redemption and restoration in her life and in her family's life.

HISTORY BIT

One of the leading world evangelists of the twentieth and twenty-first centuries was an American named Billy Graham. Born in Charlotte, North Carolina in 1918, Graham is estimated to have preached in more than 185 countries. More than two hundred and fifteen million people heard his preaching in his lifetime. Graham died at almost one hundred years of age in 2018.*

Source Information:
https://joshuaproject.net/countries/US
https://billygraham.org/about/biographies/billy-graham/
https://www.cnn.com/2013/01/11/us/billy-graham-fast-facts/index.html

LOVE YOUR NEIGHBOR

Her Journey

DIANA'S STORY

When I was three years old my parents divorced. I can't remember seeing my father more than five or six times over the following twenty-five years. Though he was invited, he didn't attend my graduation or my wedding. I was utterly shocked the day I picked up the phone and heard his voice on the other end. I was twenty-eight at the time, with two young children of my own.

I was flooded with emotion. He wanted to see me and meet my children and my husband. I didn't know if I wanted him in my life after rejecting me for twenty-five years. How dare he ask to reenter my life? God spoke Paul's words to Philemon into my heart over and over that day: Do what is proper. Using God's Word and the power of the Holy Spirit, I tried to process my thoughts and emotions. I felt God clearly tell me to love my father as God had loved me.

I too have rejected God and not loved Him the way I should, yet God always forgives me and welcomes me to Him. That day, I chose to step forward in faith and forgive.

Forgiving my father didn't happen overnight. It took time, years actually, but that day was the turning point in my heart. I made the decision to obey God's Word and not my feelings or my hurt. I learned through love and forgiveness that reconciliation is possible.

Eighteen years later, I had the privilege of dancing with my father during the father-daughter dance at my daughter's wedding. God blessed me with a few good years with my dad. I can reflect on God's goodness to me and my dad. Our restoration has made me even more confident God's Word is true and is applicable to all aspects of life. God can fully restore any situation. Forgiveness and reconciliation isn't easy, but with God's help nothing is impossible!

6 WEEK READING PLAN

LOVE HIS WORD

	MONDAY	TUESDAY	WEDNESDAY	THURSDAY	FRIDAY
1	1 Timothy 1:1-11	1 Timothy 1:12-20	1 Timothy 2:1-8	1 Timothy 2:9-15	1 Timothy 3:1-13
	SOAP 1 Timothy 1:5-7	SOAP 1 Timothy 1:15-16	SOAP 1 Timothy 2:3-4	SOAP 1 Timothy 2:9-10	SOAP 1 Timothy 3:13
2	1 Timothy 3:14-16	1 Timothy 4:1-10	1 Timothy 4:11-16	1 Timothy 5:1-8	1 Timothy 5:9-16
	SOAP 1 Timothy 3:16	SOAP 1 Timothy 4:8-10	SOAP 1 Timothy 4:16	SOAP 1 Timothy 5:1-2	SOAP 1 Timothy 5:16
3	1 Timothy 5:17—6:2a	1 Timothy 6:2b-10	1 Timothy 6:11-21	2 Timothy 1:1-5	2 Timothy 1:6-18
	SOAP 1 Timothy 5:21	SOAP 1 Timothy 6:6-8	SOAP 1 Timothy 6:11-12	SOAP 2 Timothy 1:5	SOAP 2 Timothy 1:13-14
4	2 Timothy 2:1-13	2 Timothy 2:14-26	2 Timothy 3:1-9	2 Timothy 3:10-17	2 Timothy 4:1-8
	SOAP 2 Timothy 2:11-13	SOAP 2 Timothy 2:15	SOAP 2 Timothy 3:1-4	SOAP 2 Timothy 3:16-17	SOAP 2 Timothy 4:1-2
5	2 Timothy 4:9-22	Titus 1:1-4	Titus 1:5-9	Titus 1:10-16	Titus 2:1-10
	SOAP 2 Timothy 4:17-18	SOAP Titus 1:1-3	SOAP Titus 1:9	SOAP Titus 1:13-15	SOAP Titus 2:6-8
6	Titus 2:11-15	Titus 3:1-7	Titus 3:8-15	Philemon 1-7	Philemon 8-25
	SOAP Titus 2:11-13	SOAP Titus 3:7	SOAP Titus 3:8	SOAP Philemon 4-7	SOAP Philemon 8-9

SALUTATION

[1]From Paul, a prisoner of Christ Jesus, and Timothy our brother, to Philemon, our dear friend and colaborer, [2]to Apphia our
sister, to Archippus our fellow soldier, and to the church that
meets in your house. [3]Grace and peace to you from God our Father and the Lord Jesus Christ!

THANKS FOR PHILEMON'S LOVE AND FAITH

[4]I always thank my God as I remember you in my prayers, [5]be-
cause I hear of your faith in the Lord Jesus and your love for all
the saints. [6]I pray that the faith you share with us may deepen
your understanding of every blessing that belongs to you in
Christ. [7]I have had great joy and encouragement because of your
love, for the hearts of the saints have been refreshed through
you, brother.

PAUL'S REQUEST FOR ONESIMUS

[8]So, although I have quite a lot of confidence in Christ and could
command you to do what is proper, [9]I would rather appeal to you
on the basis of love—I, Paul, an old man and even now a prisoner
for the sake of Christ Jesus—[10]I am appealing to you concerning
my child, whose spiritual father I have become during my imprisonment, that is, Onesimus, [11]who was formerly useless to
you, but is now useful to you and me. [12]I have sent him (who is
my very heart) back to you. [13]I wanted to keep him with me so
that he could serve me in your place during my imprisonment
for the sake of the gospel. [14]However, without your consent I
did not want to do anything, so that your good deed would not
be out of compulsion, but from your own willingness. [15]For perhaps it was for this reason that he was separated from you for
a little while, so that you would have him back eternally, [16]no
longer as a slave, but more than a slave, as a dear brother. He is
especially so to me, and even more so to you now, both humanly
speaking and in the Lord. [17]Therefore if you regard me as a partner, accept him as you would me. [18]Now if he has defrauded you
of anything or owes you anything, charge what he owes to me.
[19]I, Paul, have written this letter with my own hand: I will repay
it. I could also mention that you owe me your very self. [20]Yes,
brother, let me have some benefit from you in the Lord. Refresh
my heart in Christ. [21]Since I was confident that you would obey, I
wrote to you, because I knew that you would do even more than
what I am asking you to do. [22]At the same time also, prepare a
place for me to stay, for I hope that through your prayers I will
be given back to you.

CONCLUDING GREETINGS

[23]Epaphras, my fellow prisoner in Christ Jesus, greets you.
[24]Mark, Aristarchus, Demas, and Luke, my colaborers, greet you
too. [25]May the grace of the Lord Jesus Christ be with your spirit.

CHALLENGE

Are you hesitant to welcome anyone in your life? How can you extend grace to him or her the way Paul encouraged Philemon to extend grace to Onesimus? Why is it important to honor and care for others in this way?

LOVE TO GROW

TO CALL THE SLAVE YOUR FRIEND

PHILEMON

Philemon is a unique letter for a number of reasons. Rather than a letter of instruction to a group of people, it is a private request from one friend to another. Paul encountered his friend's slave, Onesimus, who had run away from his master and become very serious about his faith.

At this point in history, slaves were considered property, not people. Wealthy people owned slaves and could treat them however they chose. The morality of slavery and the humanity of slaves were not even considerations, culturally speaking.

In this letter we see Paul had a different understanding. He told Philemon he considered Onesimus like his own child. He asked Philemon to welcome his runaway slave as if he were Paul himself. He offered to pay any damages Onesimus might have incurred.

While these initial words from Paul are inspiring, there is a part of this letter that makes me wince: Paul sent Onesimus back to his master. He didn't act like Harriet Tubman and help him on his way to freedom—he returned him to the place he had fled. We see Paul's tension in doing this, as he told Philemon he wanted to appeal to him on the basis of love, not duty. Perhaps he wanted to give Philemon the opportunity to see Onesimus' humanity too.

Still, for Paul's historical and cultural context, this was an extraordinary move. He acknowledged Onesimus' humanity in a way that would not be culturally accepted for centuries.

I believe this is what happens when we are tuned in to God's loving-kindness. God turns our eyes to those we would not otherwise see and shows us how to treat them with mercy, kindness, and dignity. The Holy Spirit transcends cultural morality and speaks directly to our hearts.

This letter shows us small gestures of love matter in God's kingdom. Even if we cannot overturn systems of injustice, we can advocate for love and truth in small, steady ways.

That's what Paul did here. His private request to a friend, an act of pure love, inspires me to do what I can, when I can, in the name of Jesus. Hallelujah.

THEREFORE let us confidently approach the THRONE of Grace to receive MERCY and find GRACE WHENEVER we need help

MEMORY VERSE

For we do not have a high priest incapable of sympathizing with our weaknesses, but one who has been tempted in every way just as we are, yet without sin. Therefore let us confidently approach the throne of grace to *receive mercy and find grace* whenever we need help.

Hebrews 4:15–16

Hebrews

INTRODUCTION

Our High Priest

The Book of Hebrews presents an argument about the deity, humanity, and majesty of Christ. The author illustrates the superiority of Christ, showing His authority and power over angels, prophets, sacrifices, and the priesthood. The Book of Hebrews clearly explains the supremacy of Christ over all.

Hebrews may originally have been a sermon, or it could have been a letter. While the original format is unclear, the message is evident. After a brief introduction (1:1–4), the author explained the superiority and sacrificial work of Christ (1:5—10:18). The author then described elements of the faith, with a tribute to those in the past who were examples of great faith (10:19—13:17), and he concluded with a benediction (13:18–25).

While the author of Hebrews is unknown, scholars offer many theories about who the original author and audience were. Some believe the original audience was a group of Jewish Christians because the book focuses on Jewish rituals and themes. The author uses several Old Testament quotations, perhaps assuming the audience was familiar with the writings. The date of the Book of Hebrews is also unknown; however, it is believed to have been written before the destruction of Jerusalem in A.D. 70.

Hebrews is an excellent place to find solid doctrine and an explanation of the nature and character of Jesus Christ. To love Him greatly, we must know Him well. Hebrews encourages us as we come to know Christ, the importance of His sacrifice, and His authority and power over everything. The author presents Christ as our mediator who allows us to approach the throne of God. He is our great High Priest, restoring our relationship to the Father through His life, death, and resurrection.

Angola

OFFICIAL LANGUAGE
Portuguese
POPULATION
31,802,000
UNREACHED POPULATION
376,000
PROFESSING CHRISTIANS
91.4%

Cambundo's Home

Say a Prayer Today

Pray for restoration for the people of Angola after a long history of war (1962–2002).* Pray the church would be a light to those suffering with the lasting effects of such long-term devastation.

HISTORY BIT

Joseph Barreira arrived in Angola in 1579. He was a Portuguese Jesuit (a Roman Catholic order of priests) who conducted successful missionary work with the people there.**

Source Information:
https://joshuaproject.net/countries/AO
*Jason Mandryk, Operation World, 7th edition (Colorado Springs, CO: Biblica Publishing, 2010), 105.
**John Bowden, A Chronology of World Christianity (New York, NY: Continuum, 2007), 290.

LOVE YOUR NEIGHBOR

Her Journey

CAMBUNDO'S STORY

Growing up in Angola, I faced many challenges. Despite all of the challenges, difficulties, heartaches, and fears, I have always found encouragement in God's Word. Hebrews 4:15–16 is my favorite example. It says, "For we do not have a high priest incapable of sympathizing with our weaknesses, but one who has been tempted in every way just as we are, yet without sin. Therefore, let us confidently approach the throne of grace to receive mercy and find grace whenever we need help."

As I read these verses, I am reminded I need to depend on Jesus daily. I find great comfort in the truth that He can help me when I face trials and temptations. Jesus was not spared from temptation because He was God. Jesus was fully human, yet He remained sinless.

Whenever I face darkness in my life, I rest in the truth that Jesus understands my feelings and struggles because He, too, was tempted. I can come before Him and find mercy and grace, no matter what I've done. In His presence I find strength to face all that life throws at me.

Because of Jesus' sacrifice, I am free from the control of sin and free from shame and condemnation. I can approach Him with confidence because He knows my weakness, and accepts me anyway. He is always willing to meet my needs, and He always offers compassion.

6 WEEK READING PLAN

LOVE HIS WORD

	MONDAY	TUESDAY	WEDNESDAY	THURSDAY	FRIDAY
1	Hebrews 1:1-4	Hebrews 1:5-14	Hebrews 2:1-4	Hebrews 2:5-18	Hebrews 3:1-6
	SOAP Hebrews 1:3-4	SOAP Hebrews 1:8-9	SOAP Hebrews 2:2-4	SOAP Hebrews 2:10-12	SOAP Hebrews 3:3-4
2	Hebrews 3:7-19	Hebrews 4:1-13	Hebrews 4:14-16	Hebrews 5:1-10	Hebrews 5:11-14
	SOAP Hebrews 3:18-19	SOAP Hebrews 4:12-13	SOAP Hebrews 4:15-16	SOAP Hebrews 5:8-10	SOAP Hebrews 5:12-14
3	Hebrews 6:1-12	Hebrews 6:13-20	Hebrews 7:1-10	Hebrews 7:11-28	Hebrews 8:1-6
	SOAP Hebrews 6:11-12	SOAP Hebrews 6:19-20	SOAP Hebrews 7:1-2	SOAP Hebrews 7:11-12	SOAP Hebrews 8:6
4	Hebrews 8:7-13	Hebrews 9:1-10	Hebrews 9:11-14	Hebrews 9:15-28	Hebrews 10:1-18
	SOAP Hebrews 8:7-8	SOAP Hebrews 9:8-10	SOAP Hebrews 9:9-13	SOAP Hebrews 9:25-26	SOAP Hebrews 10:1-2
5	Hebrews 10:19-25	Hebrews 10:26-39	Hebrews 11:1-7	Hebrews 11:8-22	Hebrews 11:23-31
	SOAP Hebrews 10:23-25	SOAP Hebrews 10:36-39	SOAP Hebrews 11:1-2	SOAP Hebrews 11:8	SOAP Hebrews 11:26-27
6	Hebrews 11:32-40	Hebrews 12:1-13	Hebrews 12:14-29	Hebrews 13:1-19	Hebrews 13:20-25
	SOAP Hebrews 11:39-40	SOAP Hebrews 12:1-2	SOAP Hebrews 12:14-15	SOAP Hebrews 13:8-9	SOAP Hebrews 13:20-21

INTRODUCTION: GOD HAS SPOKEN FULLY AND FINALLY IN HIS SON

1 After God spoke long ago in various portions and in various
ways to our ancestors through the prophets, 2 in these last days
he has spoken to us in a son, whom he appointed heir of all
things, and through whom he created the world. 3 The Son is the
radiance of his glory and the representation of his essence, and
he sustains all things by his powerful word, and so when he had
accomplished cleansing for sins, *he sat down at the right hand of*
the Majesty on high. 4 Thus he became so far better than the angels as he has inherited a name superior to theirs.

THE SON IS SUPERIOR TO ANGELS

5 For to which of the angels did God ever say, ***"You are my son! To-***
day I have fathered you"? And in another place he says, ***"I will be***
his father and he will be my son." 6 But when he again brings his
firstborn into the world, he says, ***"Let all the angels of God wor-***
ship him!" 7 And he says of the angels, ***"He makes his angels winds***
and his ministers a flame of fire," 8 but of the Son he says,

"Your throne, O God, is forever and ever,
and a righteous scepter is the scepter of your kingdom.
9 ***You have loved righteousness and hated lawlessness.***
So God, your God, has anointed you over your
companions with the oil of rejoicing."

10 And,
"You founded the earth in the beginning, Lord,
and the heavens are the works of your hands.
11 ***They will perish, but you continue.***
And they will all grow old like a garment,
12 ***and like a robe you will fold them up***
and like a garment ***they will be changed,***
but you are the same and your years will never run out."

13 But to which of the angels has he ever said, ***"Sit at my right hand***
until I make your enemies a footstool for your feet"? 14 Are they not all
ministering spirits, sent out to serve those who will inherit salvation?

WARNING AGAINST DRIFTING AWAY

2 Therefore we must pay closer attention to what we have
heard, so that we do not drift away. 2 For if the message spoken through angels proved to be so firm that every violation or
disobedience received its just penalty, 3 how will we escape if
we neglect such a great salvation? It was first communicated
through the Lord and was confirmed to us by those who heard
him, 4 while God confirmed their witness with signs and wonders and various miracles and gifts of the Holy Spirit distributed according to his will.

EXPOSITION OF PSALM 8: JESUS AND THE DESTINY OF HUMANITY

5 For he did not put the world to come, about which we are
speaking, under the control of angels. 6 Instead someone testified somewhere:

REFLECT

How did God speak to people before New Testament times? How did He speak to people during the New Testament? How does He speak to people today?

"What is man that you think of him or the
son of man that you care for him?
7 *You made him lower than the angels for a little while.*
You crowned him with glory and honor.
8 *You put all things under his control."*

For when he ***put all things under his control,*** he left nothing
outside of his control. At present we do not yet see ***all things***
under his control, 9 but we see Jesus, who was made ***lower than***
the angels for a little while, now crowned with glory and honor
because he suffered death, so that by God's grace he would experience death on behalf of everyone. 10 For it was fitting for
him, for whom and through whom all things exist, in bringing
many sons to glory, to make the pioneer of their salvation perfect through sufferings. 11 For indeed he who makes holy and
those being made holy all have the same origin, and so he is
not ashamed to call them brothers and sisters, 12 saying, ***"I will***
proclaim your name to my brothers; in the midst of the assembly I
will praise you." 13 Again he says, "I will be confident in him," and
again, ***"Here I am, with the children God has given me."*** 14 Therefore, since the children share in flesh and blood, he likewise
shared in their humanity, so that through death he could destroy the one who holds the power of death (that is, the devil),
15 and set free those who were held in slavery all their lives by
their fear of death. 16 For surely his concern is not for angels,
but he is concerned for Abraham's descendants. 17 Therefore he
had to be made like his brothers and sisters in every respect,
so that he could become a merciful and faithful high priest in
things relating to God, to make atonement for the sins of the
people. 18 For since he himself suffered when he was tempted,
he is able to help those who are tempted.

JESUS AND MOSES

3 Therefore, holy brothers and sisters, partners in a heavenly calling, take note of Jesus, the apostle and high priest
whom we confess, 2 who is faithful to the one who appointed
him, as Moses was also in God's house. 3 For he has come to
deserve greater glory than Moses, just as the builder of a
house deserves greater honor than the house itself! 4 For every house is built by someone, but the builder of all things is
God. 5 Now Moses was ***faithful in all God's house*** as a servant,
to testify to the things that would be spoken. 6 But Christ is
faithful as a son over God's house. We are of his house, if in
fact we hold firmly to our confidence and the hope we take
pride in.

EXPOSITION OF PSALM 95: HEARING GOD'S WORD IN FAITH

7 Therefore, as the Holy Spirit says,
"Oh, that today you would listen as he speaks!
8 ***"Do not harden your hearts as in the rebellion,***
in the day of testing in the wilderness.
9 ***"There your fathers tested me and tried me,***
and they saw my works for forty years.

10 ***"Therefore, I became provoked at that generation***
and said, 'Their hearts are always wandering
and they have not known my ways.'
11 ***"As I swore in my anger, 'They will never enter my rest!'"***

12 See to it, brothers and sisters, that none of you has an evil,
unbelieving heart that forsakes the living God. 13 But exhort one
another each day, as long as it is called "Today," that none of you
may become hardened by sin's deception. 14 For we have become
partners with Christ, if in fact we hold our initial confidence firm
until the end. 15 As it says, ***"Oh, that today you would listen as he***
speaks! Do not harden your hearts as in the rebellion." 16 For which
ones heard and rebelled? Was it not all who came out of Egypt
under Moses' leadership? 17 And against whom was God provoked for forty years? Was it not those who sinned, *whose dead*
bodies fell in the wilderness? 18 And to whom did he swear they
would never enter into his rest, except those who were disobedient? 19 So we see that they could not enter because of unbelief.

GOD'S PROMISED REST

4 Therefore we must be wary that, while the promise of entering his rest remains open, none of you may seem to have
come short of it. 2 For we had good news proclaimed to us just
as they did. But the message they heard did them no good, since
they did not join in with those who heard it in faith. 3 For we
who have believed enter that rest, as he has said, ***"As I swore in***
my anger, 'They will never enter my rest!'" And yet God's works
were accomplished from the foundation of the world. 4 For he
has spoken somewhere about the seventh day in this way: ***"And***
God rested on the seventh day from all his works," 5 but to repeat
the text cited earlier: ***"They will never enter my rest!"*** 6 Therefore
it remains for some to enter it, yet those to whom it was previously proclaimed did not enter because of disobedience. 7 So
God again ordains a certain day, "Today," speaking through David after so long a time, as in the words quoted before, ***"Oh, that***
today you would listen as he speaks! Do not harden your hearts."
8 For if Joshua had given them rest, God would not have spoken
afterward about another day. 9 Consequently a Sabbath rest remains for the people of God. 10 For the one who enters God's
rest has also rested from his works, just as God did from his own
works. 11 Thus we must make every effort to enter that rest, so
that no one may fall by following the same pattern of disobedience. 12 For the word of God is living and active and sharper than
any double-edged sword, piercing even to the point of dividing
soul from spirit, and joints from marrow; it is able to judge the
desires and thoughts of the heart. 13 And no creature is hidden
from God, but everything is naked and exposed to the eyes of
him to whom we must render an account.

JESUS OUR COMPASSIONATE HIGH PRIEST

14 Therefore since we have a great high priest who has passed
through the heavens, Jesus the Son of God, let us hold fast to our
confession. 15 For we do not have a high priest incapable of sympathizing with our weaknesses, but one who has been tempted

REFLECT

How is Jesus able to sympathize with our weaknesses? What does this show about His character?

LOVE TO GROW

EXHORT ONE ANOTHER

HEBREWS 3:13

Have you ever been discouraged? It's a terrible feeling, isn't it? Discouragement comes when we lose confidence in ourselves, others, our circumstances, or even our faith. Every person struggles with it from time to time.

Discouragement can lead to a host of other problems. It can cause some to give up and others to give in to sin. Maybe for you discouragement leads to laziness, a bad attitude, or a loss of faith.

The author of Hebrews knew this. He understood that discouragement is a big deal, and he showed us a way to fight against it.

Exhort one another each day, as long as it is still called "Today," that none of you may become hardened by sin's deception (Heb 3:13).

Our shortcomings, our sin, the world, and the devil all try to tear us down. We need to be encouraged and reminded of truth. Exhortation is a kind of building up that makes us stronger and more effective.

The gospel is one giant word of encouragement. Jesus lived a perfect life, and our faith in Him credits us with His righteousness. His good works perfect our imperfect ones. His death pays for our sins, and our penalty and debts to God are removed. His resurrection gives us victory over death and power to overcome sin in our lives. We are no longer slaves to our failures, but we are freed by the blood of Jesus. The encouragement found in the gospel is what we need to preach to ourselves and to other believers in seasons of discouragement.

Exhorting one another provides us strength and motivation so we can continue to live out our callings and overcome the sin that so easily creeps into our lives.

Let's speak words that give hope. Let's speak words that dispel discouragement and make the burdens others carry a little lighter. Most of all, let's speak words that bring the gospel to a hurting world.

in every way just as we are, yet without sin. 16 Therefore let us
confidently approach the throne of grace to receive mercy and
find grace whenever we need help.
5 For every high priest is taken from among the people and appointed to represent them before God, to offer both gifts and
sacrifices for sins. 2 He is able to deal compassionately with those
who are ignorant and erring, since he also is subject to weakness,
3 and for this reason he is obligated to make sin offerings for himself as well as for the people. 4 And no one assumes this honor on
his own initiative, but only when called to it by God, as in fact
Aaron was. 5 So also Christ did not glorify himself in becoming
high priest, but the one who glorified him was God, who said to
him, ***"You are my Son! Today I have fathered you,"*** 6 as also in another place God says, ***"You are a priest forever in the order of Melchizedek."*** 7 During his earthly life Christ offered both requests
and supplications, with loud cries and tears, to the one who was
able to save him from death and he was heard because of his devotion. 8 Although he was a son, he learned obedience through
the things he suffered. 9 And by being perfected in this way, he became the source of eternal salvation to all who obey him, 10 and he
was designated by God as high priest ***in the order of Melchizedek.***

THE NEED TO MOVE ON TO MATURITY

11 On this topic we have much to say and it is difficult to explain,
since you have become sluggish in hearing. 12 For though you
should in fact be teachers by this time, you need someone to
teach you the beginning elements of God's utterances. You have
gone back to needing milk, not solid food. 13 For everyone who
lives on milk is inexperienced in the message of righteousness,
because he is an infant. 14 But solid food is for the mature, whose
perceptions are trained by practice to discern both good and evil.
6 Therefore we must progress beyond the elementary instructions about Christ and move on to maturity, not laying this
foundation again: repentance from dead works and faith in God,
2 teaching about ritual washings, laying on of hands, resurrection
of the dead, and eternal judgment. 3 And this is what we intend to
do, if God permits. 4 For it is impossible in the case of those who
have once been enlightened, tasted the heavenly gift, become
partakers of the Holy Spirit, 5 tasted the good word of God and
the miracles of the coming age, 6 and then have committed apostasy, to renew them again to repentance, since they are crucifying
the Son of God for themselves all over again and holding him up
to contempt. 7 For the ground that has soaked up the rain that
frequently falls on it and yields useful vegetation for those who
tend it receives a blessing from God. 8 But if it produces thorns
and thistles, it is useless and about to be cursed; its fate is to be
burned. 9 But in your case, dear friends, even though we speak
like this, we are convinced of better things relating to salvation.
10 For God is not unjust so as to forget your work and the love you
have demonstrated for his name, in having served and continuing to serve the saints. 11 But we passionately want each of you to
demonstrate the same eagerness for the fulfillment of your hope
until the end, 12 so that you may not be sluggish, but imitators of
those who through faith and perseverance inherit the promises.

REFLECT

What does it mean to be spiritually mature? How can we pursue maturity in our walk with God?

13 Now when God made his promise to Abraham, since he could
swear by no one greater, he swore by himself, 14 saying, ***"Surely I
will bless you greatly and multiply your descendants abundantly."***
15 And so by persevering, Abraham inherited the promise. 16 For
people swear by something greater than themselves, and the
oath serves as a confirmation to end all dispute. 17 In the same
way God wanted to demonstrate more clearly to the heirs of the
promise that his purpose was unchangeable, and so he intervened with an oath, 18 so that we who have found refuge in him
may find strong encouragement to hold fast to the hope set before us through two unchangeable things, since it is impossible
for God to lie. 19 We have this hope as an anchor for the soul, sure
and steadfast, which reaches inside behind the curtain, 20 where
Jesus our forerunner entered on our behalf, since he became ***a
priest forever in the order of Melchizedek.***

THE NATURE OF MELCHIZEDEK'S PRIESTHOOD

7 Now this ***Melchizedek, king of Salem, priest of the most high God,
met Abraham as he was returning from defeating the kings*** and
blessed him. 2 To him also ***Abraham apportioned a tithe of everything.*** His name first means king of righteousness, then ***king of
Salem,*** that is, king of peace. 3 Without father, without mother,
without genealogy, he has neither beginning of days nor end of
life but is like the son of God, and he remains a priest for all time.
4 But see how great he must be, if Abraham the patriarch gave him
a tithe of his plunder. 5 And those of the sons of Levi who receive
the priestly office have authorization according to the law to collect a tithe from the people, that is, from their fellow countrymen,
although they too are descendants of Abraham. 6 But Melchizedek
who does not share their ancestry collected a tithe from Abraham
and blessed the one who possessed the promise. 7 Now without
dispute the inferior is blessed by the superior, 8 and in one case
tithes are received by mortal men, while in the other by him who
is affirmed to be alive. 9 And it could be said that Levi himself,
who receives tithes, paid a tithe through Abraham. 10 For he was
still in his ancestor Abraham's loins when Melchizedek met him.

CHALLENGE

Read Genesis 14:17–24. Who was Melchizedek? What does it mean that Jesus was a priest in the order of Melchizedek? What kind of authority does this mean Jesus has?

JESUS AND THE PRIESTHOOD OF MELCHIZEDEK

11 So if perfection had in fact been possible through the Levitical
priesthood—for on that basis the people received the law—what
further need would there have been for another priest to arise,
said to be in the order of Melchizedek and not in Aaron's order?
12 For when the priesthood changes, a change in the law must
come as well. 13 Yet the one these things are spoken about belongs to a different tribe, and no one from that tribe has ever of-
ficiated at the altar. 14 For it is clear that our Lord is descended
from Judah, yet Moses said nothing about priests in connection
with that tribe. 15 And this is even clearer if another priest arises
in the likeness of Melchizedek, 16 who has become a priest not by
a legal regulation about physical descent but by the power of an
indestructible life. 17 For here is the testimony about him: ***"You are
a priest forever in the order of Melchizedek."*** 18 On the one hand a
former command is set aside because it is weak and useless, 19 for
the law made nothing perfect. On the other hand a better hope is

LOVE TO GROW

REMEMBER YOUR ANCHOR

HEBREWS 6:18–19

We are quick to forget about our anchor.

Like boats we float through our days, bobbing along with the current. Sometimes a tidal wave comes and we toss and turn wildly and the winds dictate our drift. Other times, we're caught in a major storm, our boat goes topsy-turvy, and we get seasick, disoriented, and panicked.

Sometimes we act as if we have no anchor at all. The waves and the storms might as well take us out to sea, far from the shore, and destroy us completely. That is not our plight.

We have an anchor. His name is Jesus.

He is secure and firm. He is comfort and safety and hope. He is always with us. The hope we have in Jesus is based on certainty, truth, and the unchangeable Word of God. Our anchor isn't on a chain at the bottom of the sea. Our anchor is in heaven.

In the midst of our chaos and confusion, we focus on our circumstances rather than our anchor. Instead of trying to weather the storms of life on our own, we must turn to Him, remembering that He alone can replace our worries and fears with peace. He can open our eyes to the goodness of God in all circumstances.

One synonym for the word *anchor* is *hold*. Jesus is our hold. We can hold on to hope in Christ because He holds us. Winds and waves of doubt and discouragement will come, fear will crash over us, and worry will threaten to sink us, but our anchor of hope is secure and unmovable.

Remember your anchor.

introduced, through which we draw near to God. 20 And since this
was not done without a sworn affirmation—for the others have
become priests without a sworn affirmation, 21 but Jesus did so
with a sworn affirmation by the one who said to him, ***"The Lord has
sworn and will not change his mind, 'You are a priest forever'"***—22 accordingly Jesus has become the guarantee of a better covenant.
23 And the others who became priests were numerous, because
death prevented them from continuing in office, 24 but he holds
his priesthood permanently since he lives forever. 25 So he is able
to save completely those who come to God through him, because
he always lives to intercede for them. 26 For it is indeed fitting for
us to have such a high priest: holy, innocent, undefiled, separate
from sinners, and exalted above the heavens. 27 He has no need
to do every day what those priests do, to offer sacrifices first for
their own sins and then for the sins of the people, since he did
this in offering himself once for all. 28 For the law appoints as high
priests men subject to weakness, but the word of solemn affirmation that came after the law appoints a son made perfect forever.

THE HIGH PRIEST OF A BETTER COVENANT

8 Now the main point of what we are saying is this: We have
such a high priest, one who *sat down at the right hand of the
throne of the Majesty in heaven,* 2 a minister in the sanctuary and
the true tabernacle that the Lord, not man, set up. 3 For every
high priest is appointed to offer both gifts and sacrifices. So
this one too had to have something to offer. 4 Now if he were on
earth, he would not be a priest, since there are already priests
who offer the gifts prescribed by the law. 5 The place where they
serve is a sketch and shadow of the heavenly sanctuary, just as
Moses was warned by God as he was about to complete the tabernacle. For he says, ***"See that you make everything according to
the design shown to you on the mountain."*** 6 But now Jesus has obtained a superior ministry, since the covenant that he mediates
is also better and is enacted on better promises.

7 For if that first covenant had been faultless, no one would
have looked for a second one. 8 But showing its fault, God says
to them,

***"Look, the days are coming, says the Lord, when
I will complete a new covenant with the house
of Israel and with the house of Judah.***

9 ***"It will not be like the covenant that I made with their
fathers, on the day when I took them by the hand to lead
them out of Egypt, because they did not continue in my
covenant and I had no regard for them, says the Lord.***

10 ***"For this is the covenant that I will establish with the house
of Israel after those days, says the Lord. I will put my laws
in their minds and I will inscribe them on their hearts.
And I will be their God and they will be my people.***

11 ***"And there will be no need at all for each one to
teach his countryman or each one to teach his
brother saying, 'Know the Lord,' since they will
all know me, from the least to the greatest.***

12 ***"For I will be merciful toward their evil deeds,
and their sins I will remember no longer."***

13 When he speaks of a new covenant, he makes the first obsolete. Now what is growing obsolete and aging is about to disappear.

THE ARRANGEMENT AND RITUAL OF THE EARTHLY SANCTUARY

9 Now the first covenant, in fact, had regulations for worship
and its earthly sanctuary. 2 For a tent was prepared, the outer one, which contained the lampstand, the table, and the presentation of the loaves; this is called the Holy Place. 3 And after
the second curtain there was a tent called the holy of holies. 4 It
contained the golden altar of incense and the ark of the covenant covered entirely with gold. In this ark were the golden
urn containing the manna, Aaron's rod that budded, and the
stone tablets of the covenant. 5 And above the ark were the cherubim of glory overshadowing the mercy seat. Now is not the
time to speak of these things in detail. 6 So with these things
prepared like this, the priests enter continually into the outer
tent as they perform their duties. 7 But only the high priest enters once a year into the inner tent, and not without blood that
he offers for himself and for the sins of the people committed
in ignorance. 8 The Holy Spirit is making clear that the way into
the Holy Place had not yet appeared as long as the old tabernacle was standing. 9 This was a symbol for the time then present,
when gifts and sacrifices were offered that could not perfect the
conscience of the worshiper. 10 They served only for matters of
food and drink and various ritual washings; they are external
regulations imposed until the new order came.

CHRIST'S SERVICE IN THE HEAVENLY SANCTUARY

11 But now Christ has come as the high priest of the good things
to come. He passed through the greater and more perfect tent
not made with hands, that is, not of this creation, 12 and he entered once for all into the Most Holy Place not by the blood of
goats and calves but by his own blood, and so he himself secured
eternal redemption. 13 For if the blood of goats and bulls and the
ashes of a young cow sprinkled on those who are defiled consecrated them and provided ritual purity, 14 how much more will
the blood of Christ, who through the eternal Spirit offered himself without blemish to God, purify our consciences from dead
works to worship the living God.

15 And so he is the mediator of a new covenant, so that those
who are called may receive the eternal inheritance he has promised, since he died to set them free from the violations committed under the first covenant. 16 For where there is a will, the death
of the one who made it must be proven. 17 For a will takes effect
only at death, since it carries no force while the one who made it
is alive. 18 So even the first covenant was inaugurated with blood.
19 For when Moses had spoken every command to all the people
according to the law, he took the blood of calves and goats with
water and scarlet wool and hyssop and sprinkled both the book
itself and all the people, 20 and said, "***This is the blood of the covenant that God has commanded you to keep.***" 21 And both the tabernacle and all the utensils of worship he likewise sprinkled with

blood. 22 Indeed according to the law almost everything was purified with blood, and without the shedding of blood there is no
forgiveness. 23 So it was necessary for the sketches of the things
in heaven to be purified with these sacrifices, but the heavenly
things themselves required better sacrifices than these. 24 For
Christ did not enter a sanctuary made with hands—the representation of the true sanctuary—but into heaven itself, and he
appears now in God's presence for us. 25 And he did not enter to
offer himself again and again, the way the high priest enters the
sanctuary year after year with blood that is not his own, 26 for
then he would have had to suffer again and again since the foundation of the world. But now he has appeared once for all at the
consummation of the ages to put away sin by his sacrifice. 27 And
just as people are appointed to die once, and then to face judgment, 28 so also, after Christ was offered once to *bear the sins of*
many, to those who eagerly await him he will appear a second
time, not to bear sin but to bring salvation.

CONCLUDING EXPOSITION: OLD AND NEW SACRIFICES CONTRASTED

10 For the law possesses a shadow of the good things to come
but not the reality itself, and is therefore completely unable, by the same sacrifices offered continually, year after year, to
perfect those who come to worship. 2 For otherwise would they
not have ceased to be offered, since the worshipers would have
been purified once for all and so have no further consciousness
of sin? 3 But in those sacrifices there is a reminder of sins year
after year. 4 For it is impossible for the blood of bulls and goats
to take away sins. 5 So when he came into the world, he said,

"Sacrifice and offering you did not desire,
but a body you prepared for me.
6 ***"Whole burnt offerings and sin-offerings***
you took no delight in.
7 ***"Then I said, 'Here I am: I have come—it is written of me***
in the scroll of the book—to do your will, O God.'"

8 When he says above, ***"Sacrifices and offerings*** and ***whole burnt***
offerings and sin-offerings you did not desire nor did you take de-
light in them" (which are offered according to the law), 9 then he
says, ***"Here I am: I have come to do your will."*** He does away with
the first to establish the second. 10 By his will we have been made
holy through the offering of the body of Jesus Christ once for all.
11 And every priest stands day after day serving and offering the
same sacrifices again and again—sacrifices that can never take
away sins. 12 But when this priest had offered one sacrifice for
sins for all time, *he sat down at the right hand* of God, 13 where he
is now waiting *until his enemies are made a footstool for his feet.*
14 For by one offering he has perfected for all time those who are
made holy. 15 And the Holy Spirit also witnesses to us, for after
saying, 16 ***"This is the covenant that I will establish with them after***
those days, says the Lord. I will put my laws on their hearts and I
will inscribe them on their minds," 17 then he says, ***"Their sins and***
their lawless deeds I will remember no longer." 18 Now where there
is forgiveness of these, there is no longer any offering for sin.

LOVE TO GROW

DRAW NEAR

HEBREWS 10

Have you ever felt as if you had to earn God's approval? That you had to be a "good person," one who follows all the right rules, in order for God to be fully pleased with you?

I have, and it is exhausting. Every day our sin proves we cannot be good enough or do enough to meet God's perfect standard. All hope seems lost. Thankfully, Hebrews 10 holds some incredible news.

In the Old Testament, God gave the law to Israel. The law was good: It regulated the Israelites' behavior and revealed to them exactly who God was. Following the law, which included animal sacrifices, was the means by which an unholy people could commune with their holy Creator. Even so, the law never brought any person salvation or complete forgiveness of sin.

For the law possesses a shadow of the good things to come but not the reality itself, and is therefore completely unable, by the same sacrifices offered continually, year after year, to perfect those who come to worship (Heb 10:1).

Ultimately, the law and Israel's ability to follow it proved ineffective. The law only foreshadowed something better.

Jesus Himself was the perfect sacrifice. He died "once for all" (Heb 10:10). His death is completely sufficient for all who believe in Him. Animal sacrifices were never intended to be the final way in which we relate to God. Jesus, who is now at the right hand of the Father, has made a relationship with God possible. We are now considered holy in His sight, dressed in the righteousness of Christ.

Jesus was our sacrifice, the fulfillment of the law.

Jesus has done all the law required. Though He is God, He took on flesh and came to earth to die so we can live. Now, because of what Jesus has done, we can have a deep and meaningful relationship with Him. We don't need to strive any longer. We have His approval. Let's draw near to Him in gratitude.

DRAWING NEAR TO GOD IN ENDURING FAITH

19 Therefore, brothers and sisters, since we have confidence to enter the sanctuary by the blood of Jesus, 20 by the fresh and living way that he inaugurated for us through the curtain, that is, through his flesh, 21 and since we have a great priest over the house of God, 22 let us draw near with a sincere heart in the assurance that faith brings, because we have had our hearts sprinkled clean from an evil conscience and our bodies washed in pure water. 23 And let us hold unwaveringly to the hope that we confess, for the one who made the promise is trustworthy. 24 And let us take thought of how to spur one another on to love and good works, 25 not abandoning our own meetings, as some are in the habit of doing, but encouraging each other, and even more so because you see the day drawing near.

REFLECT

What assurance do we now have that the ancient Israelites did not have through the Levitical system?

26 For if we deliberately keep on sinning after receiving the knowledge of the truth, no further sacrifice for sins is left for us, 27 but only a certain fearful expectation of judgment and *a fury of fire that will consume God's enemies.* 28 Someone who rejected the law of Moses was put to death without mercy *on the testimony of two or three witnesses.* 29 How much greater punishment do you think that person deserves who has contempt for the Son of God, and profanes the blood of the covenant that made him holy, and insults the Spirit of grace? 30 For we know the one who said, "***Vengeance is mine, I will repay,***" and again, "***The Lord will judge his people.***" 31 It is a terrifying thing to fall into the hands of the living God.

32 But remember the former days when you endured a harsh conflict of suffering after you were enlightened. 33 At times you were publicly exposed to abuse and afflictions, and at other times you came to share with others who were treated in that way. 34 For in fact you shared the sufferings of those in prison, and you accepted the confiscation of your belongings with joy, because you knew that you certainly had a better and lasting possession. 35 So do not throw away your confidence, because it has great reward. 36 For you need endurance in order to do God's will and so receive what is promised. 37 For ***just a little longer*** and ***he who is coming will arrive and not delay.*** 38 ***But my righteous one will live by faith, and if he shrinks back, I take no pleasure in him.*** 39 But we are not among those who shrink back and thus perish, but are among those who have faith and preserve their souls.

PEOPLE COMMENDED FOR THEIR FAITH

11 Now faith is being sure of what we hope for, being convinced of what we do not see. 2 For by it the people of old received God's commendation. 3 By faith we understand that the worlds were set in order at God's command, so that the visible has its origin in the invisible. 4 By faith Abel offered God a greater sacrifice than Cain, and through his faith he was commended as righteous, because God commended him for his offerings. And through his faith he still speaks, though he is dead. 5 By faith Enoch was taken up so that he did not see death, and he was not to be found because God took him up. For before

his removal he had been commended as having pleased God.
[6] Now without faith it is impossible to please him, for the one
who approaches God must believe that he exists and that he
rewards those who seek him. [7] By faith Noah, when he was
warned about things not yet seen, with reverent regard constructed an ark for the deliverance of his family. Through faith
he condemned the world and became an heir of the righteousness that comes by faith.

[8] By faith Abraham obeyed when he was called to go out to
a place he would later receive as an inheritance, and he went
out without understanding where he was going. [9] By faith he
lived as a foreigner in the promised land as though it were a
foreign country, living in tents with Isaac and Jacob, who were
fellow heirs of the same promise. [10] For he was looking forward
to the city with firm foundations, whose architect and builder
is God. [11] By faith, even though Sarah herself was barren and
he was too old, he received the ability to procreate, because
he regarded the one who had given the promise to be trustworthy. [12] So in fact children were fathered by one man—and
this one as good as dead—*like the number of stars in the sky and
like the innumerable grains of sand on the seashore.* [13] These all
died in faith without receiving the things promised, but they
saw them in the distance and welcomed them and acknowledged that they were strangers and foreigners on the earth.
[14] For those who speak in such a way make it clear that they are
seeking a homeland. [15] In fact, if they had been thinking of the
land that they had left, they would have had opportunity to return. [16] But as it is, they aspire to a better land, that is, a heavenly one. Therefore, God is not ashamed to be called their God,
for he has prepared a city for them. [17] By faith Abraham, when
he was tested, offered up Isaac. He had received the promises,
yet he was ready to offer up his only son. [18] God had told him,
"***Through Isaac descendants will carry on your name***," [19] and he
reasoned that God could even raise him from the dead, and in
a sense he received him back from there. [20] By faith also Isaac
blessed Jacob and Esau concerning the future. [21] By faith Jacob,
as he was dying, blessed each of the sons of Joseph and ***worshiped as he leaned on his staff***. [22] By faith Joseph, at the end of
his life, mentioned the exodus of the sons of Israel and gave
instructions about his burial.

[23] By faith, when Moses was born, his parents hid him for
three months, because they saw the child was beautiful and
they were not afraid of the king's edict. [24] By faith, when he
grew up, Moses refused to be called the son of Pharaoh's
daughter, [25] choosing rather to be ill-treated with the people
of God than to enjoy sin's fleeting pleasure. [26] He regarded
abuse suffered for Christ to be greater wealth than the treasures of Egypt, for his eyes were fixed on the reward. [27] By faith
he left Egypt without fearing the king's anger, for he persevered as though he could see the one who is invisible. [28] By
faith he kept the Passover and the sprinkling of the blood,
so that the one who destroyed the firstborn would not touch
them. [29] By faith they crossed the Red Sea as if on dry ground,
but when the Egyptians tried it, they were swallowed up. [30] By

REFLECT

Why is faith so important to God? What does it mean to be sure of what we hope for and convinced of what we do not see?

faith the walls of Jericho fell after the people marched around
them for seven days. 31 By faith Rahab the prostitute escaped
the destruction of the disobedient, because she welcomed
the spies in peace.
32 And what more shall I say? For time will fail me if I tell of
Gideon, Barak, Samson, Jephthah, of David and Samuel and the
prophets. 33 Through faith they conquered kingdoms, administered justice, gained what was promised, shut the mouths of
lions, 34 quenched raging fire, escaped the edge of the sword,
gained strength in weakness, became mighty in battle, put foreign armies to flight, 35 and women received back their dead
raised to life. But others were tortured, not accepting release,
to obtain resurrection to a better life. 36 And others experienced
mocking and flogging, and even chains and imprisonment.
37 They were stoned, sawed apart, murdered with the sword; they
went about in sheepskins and goatskins; they were destitute,
afflicted, ill-treated 38 (the world was not worthy of them); they
wandered in deserts and mountains and caves and openings in
the earth. 39 And these all were commended for their faith, yet
they did not receive what was promised. 40 For God had provided something better for us, so that they would be made perfect together with us.

THE LORD'S DISCIPLINE

12 Therefore, since we are surrounded by such a great cloud of
witnesses, we must get rid of every weight and the sin that
clings so closely, and run with endurance the race set out for us,
2 keeping our eyes fixed on Jesus, the pioneer and perfecter of
our faith. For the joy set out for him he endured the cross, dis-
regarding its shame, and *has taken his seat at the right hand of
the throne* of God. 3 Think of him who endured such opposition
against himself by sinners, so that you may not grow weary in
your souls and give up. 4 You have not yet resisted to the point
of bloodshed in your struggle against sin. 5 And have you forgotten the exhortation addressed to you as sons?

"My son, do not scorn the Lord's discipline
or give up when he corrects you.
6 ***"For the Lord disciplines the one he loves***
and chastises every son he accepts."

7 Endure your suffering as discipline; God is treating you as
sons. For what son is there that a father does not discipline?
8 But if you do not experience discipline, something all sons have
shared in, then you are illegitimate and are not sons. 9 Besides,
we have experienced discipline from our earthly fathers and
we respected them; shall we not submit ourselves all the more
to the Father of spirits and receive life? 10 For they disciplined
us for a little while as seemed good to them, but he does so for
our benefit, that we may share his holiness. 11 Now all discipline
seems painful at the time, not joyful. But later it produces the
fruit of peace and righteousness for those trained by it. 12 Therefore, ***strengthen your listless hands and your weak knees,*** 13 and
make straight paths for your feet, so that what is lame may not
be put out of joint but be healed.

DO NOT REJECT GOD'S WARNING

14 Pursue peace with everyone, and holiness, for without it no one
will see the Lord. 15 See to it that no one comes short of the grace
of God, that no one be like *a bitter root springing up* and causing trouble, and through it many become defiled. 16 And see to
it that no one becomes an immoral or godless person like Esau,
who *sold his own birthright for a single meal.* 17 For you know that
later when he wanted to inherit the blessing, he was rejected,
for he found no opportunity for repentance, although he sought
the blessing with tears. 18 For you have not come to something
that can be touched, to a burning fire and darkness and gloom
and a whirlwind 19 and the blast of a trumpet and a voice uttering words such that those who heard begged to hear no more.
20 For they could not bear what was commanded: "***If even an an-***
imal touches the mountain, it must be stoned." 21 In fact, the scene
was so terrifying that Moses said, "***I shudder with fear.***" 22 But you
have come to Mount Zion, the city of the living God, the heavenly Jerusalem, and to myriads of angels, to the assembly 23 and
congregation of the firstborn, who are enrolled in heaven, and
to God, the judge of all, and to the spirits of the righteous, who
have been made perfect, 24 and to Jesus, the mediator of a new
covenant, and to the sprinkled blood that speaks of something
better than Abel's does.

25 Take care not to refuse the one who is speaking! For if they
did not escape when they refused the one who warned them on
earth, how much less shall we, if we reject the one who warns
from heaven? 26 Then his voice shook the earth, but now he has
promised, "***I will once more shake not only the earth but heaven***
too." 27 Now this phrase "***once more***" indicates the removal of what
is shaken, that is, of created things, so that what is unshaken may
remain. 28 So since we are receiving an unshakable kingdom, let
us give thanks, and through this let us offer worship pleasing to
God in devotion and awe. 29 For our ***God is indeed a devouring fire.***

FINAL EXHORTATIONS

13 Brotherly love must continue. 2 Do not neglect hospitality,
because through it some have entertained angels without
knowing it. 3 Remember those in prison as though you were in
prison with them, and those ill-treated as though you too felt
their torment. 4 Marriage must be honored among all and the
marriage bed kept undefiled, for God will judge sexually immoral people and adulterers. 5 Your conduct must be free from
the love of money and you must be content with what you have,
for he has said, "***I will never leave you and I will never abandon***
you." 6 So we can say with confidence, "***The Lord is my helper, and***
I will not be afraid. What can people do to me?" 7 Remember your
leaders, who spoke God's message to you; reflect on the outcome of their lives and imitate their faith. 8 Jesus Christ is the
same yesterday and today and forever! 9 Do not be carried away
by all sorts of strange teachings. For it is good for the heart to
be strengthened by grace, not ritual meals, which have never
benefited those who participated in them. 10 We have an altar
that those who serve in the tabernacle have no right to eat from.
11 For the bodies of those animals whose blood the high priest

brings into the sanctuary as an offering for sin are burned outside the camp. 12 Therefore, to sanctify the people by his own
blood, Jesus also suffered outside the camp. 13 We must go out to
him, then, outside the camp, bearing the abuse he experienced.
14 For here we have no lasting city, but we seek the city that is to
come. 15 Through him then let us continually offer up a sacrifice
of praise to God, that is, the fruit of our lips, acknowledging his
name. 16 And do not neglect to do good and to share what you
have, for God is pleased with such sacrifices.

17 Obey your leaders and submit to them, for they keep watch
over your souls and will give an account for their work. Let them
do this with joy and not with complaints, for this would be no
advantage for you. 18 Pray for us, for we are sure that we have a
clear conscience and desire to conduct ourselves rightly in every respect. 19 I especially ask you to pray that I may be restored
to you very soon.

BENEDICTION AND CONCLUSION

20 Now may the God of peace who by the blood of the eternal
covenant brought back from the dead the great shepherd of
the sheep, our Lord Jesus, 21 equip you with every good thing to
do his will, working in us what is pleasing before him through
Jesus Christ, to whom be glory forever. Amen.

22 Now I urge you, brothers and sisters, bear with my message
of exhortation, for in fact I have written to you briefly. 23 You
should know that our brother Timothy has been released. If
he comes soon, he will be with me when I see you. 24 Greetings
to all your leaders and all the saints. Those from Italy send you
greetings. 25 Grace be with you all.

But be sure you LIVE out the message and DO NOT merely LISTEN to it and so deceive yourselves

MEMORY VERSE

But be sure you live out the message and do not merely listen to it and so deceive yourselves.

James 1:22

James

INTRODUCTION

Follow God's Word

The Book of James is full of practical instruction for living the Christian life. With a focus on faith that produces good works, James explained how fruit is always present in the life of a believer. James also offered great encouragement to those experiencing trials and difficulties. He assured his audience even though trials may seem overwhelming and unending, they are always producing endurance and maturity.

This book is comprised of four main sections. The opening section encourages believers to endure trials and lean on God for wisdom (1:2–18). James then said believers are to be quick to listen (1:22—2:26), slow to speak (3:1–18), and slow to anger (4:1—5:12).

The most probable author is James, the half brother of Jesus. James was the leader of the Jerusalem council and later became well-known in the church. He did not mention his relation to Jesus in the letter but expressed his servanthood to Him. While the date of writing is unknown, evidence points to the letter having been written around A.D. 46, making it one of the earliest books of the New Testament.

The Book of James says "faith without works is dead" (2:26). James was not contradicting the teaching of Paul that says salvation is through grace alone. He extended the doctrine of grace by explaining how faith in Christ will produce good works. When we love God greatly, good works will overflow from our lives. The Book of James offers many practical teachings for the Christian longing to please God.

Japan

OFFICIAL LANGUAGE
Japanese
POPULATION
126,730,000
UNREACHED POPULATION
123,979,000
PROFESSING CHRISTIANS
2.2%

Eli's Home

Say a Prayer Today

Pray for Eli and her family as they serve as missionaries. Pray they would be faithful ministers of the gospel, bringing the truth of Christ to lost people.

HISTORY BIT

In 1554 Luis d'Almeida, a wealthy Portuguese merchant, traveled to Japan as a missionary. He founded an orphanage, a home for the homeless, and a hospital.*

Source Information:
https://joshuaproject.net/countries/JA
*John Bowden, A Chronology *of World Christianity* (New York, NY: Continuum, 2007), 281.

ELI'S STORY

"But be sure you live out the message and do not merely listen to it and so deceive yourselves" (Jas 1:22).

The truth in this verse is both a blessing and a reminder. It challenges us to live a life of active faith that God calls us to as believers.

In order to live out God's Word, we need to know God's Word. If we are going to live out the message of His Word, we have to first read and study the Bible. For God's Word is true, given by Him, and useful for teaching, correction, instruction, and training in righteousness.

When we live out the message of God's Word, we allow it to teach, correct, and guide us.

God will continue to work in my life as I continue to seek Him. As I seek to know His Word, it equips me for doing good works. I always want to be ready for God's work, and I want to be a blessing to others in what I do.

My family and I have been called to serve God as missionaries in a foreign country. Everyday I think on God's truth relative to the place we live. I pray our testimony would reveal the true and living God to those around us.

It is not easy living far from home, but we are convinced that God has called us to His work in Japan. Everyday we work hard to live out the message of the gospel and encourage one another to do the same.

4 WEEK READING PLAN

LOVE HIS WORD

	MONDAY	TUESDAY	WEDNESDAY	THURSDAY	FRIDAY
1	James 1:1-4	James 1:5-8	James 1:9-11	James 1:12-15	James 1:16-18
	SOAP James 1:4	SOAP James 1:5	SOAP James 1:9-10	SOAP James 1:12	SOAP James 1:17
2	James 1:19-21	James 1:22-27	James 2:1-7	James 2:8-13	James 2:14-26
	SOAP James 1:19	SOAP James 1:22	SOAP James 2:5	SOAP James 2:8-9	SOAP James 2:22-23
3	James 3:1-5	James 3:6-12	James 3:13-18	James 4:1-6	James 4:7-12
	SOAP James 3:3-5	SOAP James 3:8-10	SOAP James 3:17-18	SOAP James 4:4-6	SOAP James 4:7-8
4	James 4:13-17	James 5:1-6	James 5:7-12	James 5:13-18	James 5:19-20
	SOAP James 4:15-17	SOAP James 5:1-3	SOAP James 5:7-8	SOAP James 5:16	SOAP James 5:19-20

SALUTATION

1 From James, a slave of God and the Lord Jesus Christ, to the
twelve tribes dispersed abroad. Greetings!

JOY IN TRIALS

2 My brothers and sisters, consider it nothing but joy when you
fall into all sorts of trials, 3 because you know that the testing of
your faith produces endurance. 4 And let endurance have its perfect effect, so that you will be perfect and complete, not deficient
in anything. 5 But if anyone is deficient in wisdom, he should ask
God, who gives to all generously and without reprimand, and it
will be given to him. 6 But he must ask in faith without doubting, for the one who doubts is like a wave of the sea, blown and
tossed around by the wind. 7 For that person must not suppose
that he will receive anything from the Lord, 8 since he is a double-minded individual, unstable in all his ways.

9 Now the believer of humble means should take pride in
his high position. 10 But the rich person's pride should be
in his humiliation, because he will pass away like a wildflower
in the meadow. 11 For the sun rises with its heat and dries up the
meadow; the petal of the flower falls off and its beauty is lost
forever. So also the rich person in the midst of his pursuits will
wither away. 12 Happy is the one who endures testing, because
when he has proven to be genuine, he will receive the crown of
life that God promised to those who love him. 13 Let no one say
when he is tempted, "I am tempted by God," for God cannot be
tempted by evil, and he himself tempts no one. 14 But each one
is tempted when he is lured and enticed by his own desires.
15 Then when desire conceives, it gives birth to sin, and when sin
is full grown, it gives birth to death. 16 Do not be led astray, my
dear brothers and sisters. 17 All generous giving and every perfect gift is from above, coming down from the Father of lights,
with whom there is no variation or the slightest hint of change.
18 By his sovereign plan he gave us birth through the message
of truth, that we would be a kind of firstfruits of all he created.

REFLECT

How can we turn trials into joy? How do we do this on a practical, daily basis?

LIVING OUT THE MESSAGE

19 Understand this, my dear brothers and sisters! Let every person be quick to listen, slow to speak, slow to anger. 20 For human
anger does not accomplish God's righteousness. 21 So put away
all filth and evil excess and humbly welcome the message im-
planted within you, which is able to save your souls. 22 But be sure
you live out the message and do not merely listen to it and so deceive yourselves. 23 For if someone merely listens to the message
and does not live it out, he is like someone who gazes at his own
face in a mirror. 24 For he gazes at himself and then goes out and
immediately forgets what sort of person he was. 25 But the one
who peers into the perfect law of liberty and fixes his attention
there, and does not become a forgetful listener but one who lives
it out—he will be blessed in what he does. 26 If someone thinks
he is religious yet does not bridle his tongue, and so deceives his
heart, his religion is futile. 27 Pure and undefiled religion before
God the Father is this: to care for orphans and widows in their
adversity and to keep oneself unstained by the world.

LOVE TO GROW

EVERY PERFECT GIFT

JAMES 1

James wrote this letter as though he might run out of ink. He included no flowery phrases or unnecessary words. It would be easy to read this jam-packed epistle as a bunch of unconnected threads of wisdom, but that would be a mistake.

In the middle of chapter 1, James described God's perfect graciousness and some of the ways we are tempted to disregard His giving nature. He said, "the believer of humble means" is in a "high position" in contrast to the rich person, who will pass away "like a wildflower" (James 1:9–10). He also praised believers who endure testing, for they will receive "the crown of life" (James 1:12). He warned against claiming God is tempting us, because we are tempted by our own desires (James 1:13–15).

This instruction culminates in verse 16: "Do not be led astray, my dear brothers and sisters." Each of these different messages (regarding wealth, testing, and temptation) describes a means by which we are distracted from this truth: God is the faithful, unchanging Giver of all good gifts (James 1:17).

Wealth, testing, and temptation distract us from the truth of God's gracious nature.

Wealth leads us to put our hope and trust in material possessions. It makes us feel invincible, secure, and protected, but even the wealthiest people will ultimately pass away, no matter how much they have accumulated.

While wealth can tempt us toward independence, testing places us in true dependence on God. We are forced to reckon with our own weakness and smallness. Testing usually strips away the things we run to, allowing us to turn to God in our desperate need.

This testing does not mean God is tempting us, as James reminds us (James 1:13). We cannot blame Him for our sin, because He is the source of all good things and nothing less.

In this seemingly random group of instructions and insights, James was most concerned with where we find our security. Do we seek it in material possessions that make promises of safety they can never fulfill? The discomfort or danger we face as believers is not temptation but testing, which pushes us away from the sources of comfort we idolize. This testing is a loving gift from the perfect Giver, as He reaches in and directs our attention to our only true hope, Jesus Christ.

PREJUDICE AND THE LAW OF LOVE

2 My brothers and sisters, do not show prejudice if you possess faith in our glorious Lord Jesus Christ. 2 For if someone comes into your assembly wearing a gold ring and fine clothing, and a poor person enters in filthy clothes, 3 do you pay attention to the one who is finely dressed and say, "You sit here in a good place," and to the poor person, "You stand over there," or "Sit on the floor"? 4 If so, have you not made distinctions among yourselves and become judges with evil motives? 5 Listen, my dear brothers and sisters! Did not God choose the poor in the world to be rich in faith and heirs of the kingdom that he promised to those who love him? 6 But you have dishonored the poor! Are not the rich oppressing you and dragging you into the courts? 7 Do they not blaspheme the good name of the one you belong to? 8 But if you fulfill the royal law as expressed in this scripture, "***You shall love your neighbor as yourself***," you are doing well. 9 But if you show prejudice, you are committing sin and are convicted by the law as violators. 10 For the one who obeys the whole law but fails in one point has become guilty of all of it. 11 For he who said, "***Do not commit adultery***," also said, "***Do not murder***." Now if you do not commit adultery but do commit murder, you have become a violator of the law. 12 Speak and act as those who will be judged by a law that gives freedom. 13 For judgment is merciless for the one who has shown no mercy. But mercy triumphs over judgment.

FAITH AND WORKS TOGETHER

14 What good is it, my brothers and sisters, if someone claims to have faith but does not have works? Can this kind of faith save him? 15 If a brother or sister is poorly clothed and lacks daily food, 16 and one of you says to them, "Go in peace, keep warm and eat well," but you do not give them what the body needs, what good is it? 17 So also faith, if it does not have works, is dead being by itself. 18 But someone will say, "You have faith and I have works." Show me your faith without works and I will show you faith by my works. 19 You believe that God is one; well and good. Even the demons believe that—and tremble with fear.

20 But would you like evidence, you empty fellow, that faith without works is useless? 21 Was not Abraham our father justified by works when he offered Isaac his son on the altar? 22 You see that his faith was working together with his works and his faith was perfected by works. 23 And the scripture was fulfilled that says, "***Now Abraham believed God and it was counted to him for righteousness***," and *he was called God's friend*. 24 You see that a person is justified by works and not by faith alone. 25 And similarly, was not Rahab the prostitute also justified by works when she welcomed the messengers and sent them out by another way? 26 For just as the body without the spirit is dead, so also faith without works is dead.

CHALLENGE

Why are works a result of faith? Read Genesis 22:1–19. How was Abraham's faith displayed through his actions?

THE POWER OF THE TONGUE

3 Not many of you should become teachers, my brothers and sisters, because you know that we will be judged more strictly. 2 For we all stumble in many ways. If someone does not stumble in what he says, he is a perfect individual, able to control

the entire body as well. 3 And if we put bits into the mouths of
horses to get them to obey us, then we guide their entire bodies. 4 Look at ships too: Though they are so large and driven by
harsh winds, they are steered by a tiny rudder wherever the pi-
lot's inclination directs. 5 So too the tongue is a small part of the
body, yet it has great pretensions. Think how small a flame sets
a huge forest ablaze. 6 And the tongue is a fire! The tongue represents the world of wrongdoing among the parts of our bodies.
It pollutes the entire body and sets fire to the course of human
existence—and is set on fire by hell.

REFLECT

How does our speech reveal what is in our hearts? Why is it important for us to control our tongues?

7 For every kind of animal, bird, reptile, and sea creature is
subdued and has been subdued by humankind. 8 But no human
being can subdue the tongue; it is a restless evil, full of deadly
poison. 9 With it we bless the Lord and Father, and with it we
curse people made in God's image. 10 From the same mouth come
blessing and cursing. These things should not be so, my brothers
and sisters. 11 A spring does not pour out fresh water and bitter
water from the same opening, does it? 12 Can a fig tree produce
olives, my brothers and sisters, or a vine produce figs? Neither
can a salt water spring produce fresh water.

TRUE WISDOM

13 Who is wise and understanding among you? By his good conduct he should show his works done in the gentleness that wisdom brings. 14 But if you have bitter jealousy and selfishness in
your hearts, do not boast and tell lies against the truth. 15 Such
wisdom does not come from above but is earthly, natural, demonic. 16 For where there is jealousy and selfishness, there is disorder and every evil practice. 17 But the wisdom from above is
first pure, then peaceable, gentle, accommodating, full of mercy
and good fruit, impartial, and not hypocritical. 18 And the fruit
that consists of righteousness is planted in peace among those
who make peace.

PASSIONS AND PRIDE

4 Where do the conflicts and where do the quarrels among
you come from? Is it not from this, from your passions that
battle inside you? 2 You desire and you do not have; you murder and envy and you cannot obtain; you quarrel and fight.
You do not have because you do not ask; 3 you ask and do not
receive because you ask wrongly, so you can spend it on your
passions.

4 Adulterers, do you not know that friendship with the world
means hostility toward God? So whoever decides to be the
world's friend makes himself God's enemy. 5 Or do you think
the scripture means nothing when it says, "The spirit that God
caused to live within us has an envious yearning"? 6 But he gives
greater grace. Therefore it says, "***God opposes the proud, but he
gives grace to the humble.***" 7 So submit to God. But resist the devil
and he will flee from you. 8 Draw near to God and he will draw
near to you. Cleanse your hands, you sinners, and make your
hearts pure, you double-minded. 9 Grieve, mourn, and weep. Turn
your laughter into mourning and your joy into despair. 10 Humble yourselves before the Lord and he will exalt you.

REFLECT

What does it mean to resist the devil? Why is this important?

LOVE TO GROW

CONFLICT

JAMES 4:1–4

Conflict can be painful.

It causes discomfort, not only in our own lives, but in the lives of those we love. Left unresolved, it may even cost us a relationship. Whether you're someone who runs from dealing with conflict, or someone who charges in ready for a fight, you'll probably agree that the outcome can cause significant damage. Conflict is a tool for relationships that can cause them to be built up into something stronger, or torn down and destroyed.

The disagreements we experience come from the desires that battle within us. These desires demand our attention and affection. Unless we turn to God to meet these longings, they will bubble up to the surface and clash with others' unmet desires. We want a circumstance to go our way, and our friend wants it to go their way. To give in could mean we are both left with unmet desires. Both parties are scared that if they don't look out for themselves, no one will.

James points out we do not have what we want because we do not look to God for it. He isn't implying we can turn to God, ask for anything we wish, and expect it will be ours immediately. He is saying all those clanging desires find fulfillment in God alone; therefore we should look to Him for everything we need.

Turning to God with our desires affects the way we deal with conflict.

In some cases we may not get into conflict in the first place. In other cases we may be more willing to compromise or lay aside our own desires because we are satisfied in all God has given us.

Instead of blaming the conflicts in our lives on external circumstances, we can look inward and ask whether there are desires battling within us we need to take to God. Perhaps we are looking for another person or situation to fulfill us when we should be looking for God. Instead of pursuing "friendship with the world" (James 4:4), let's choose to love God and allow Him to meet our needs. When we do this, we reduce the amount of painful conflict in our lives and find ourselves truly fulfilled.

11 Do not speak against one another, brothers and sisters.
He who speaks against a fellow believer or judges a fellow believer speaks against the law and judges the law. But if you
judge the law, you are not a doer of the law but its judge. 12 But
there is only one who is lawgiver and judge—the one who is
able to save and destroy. On the other hand, who are you to
judge your neighbor?

13 Come now, you who say, "Today or tomorrow we will go into
this or that town and spend a year there and do business and
make a profit." 14 You do not know about tomorrow. What is
your life like? For you are a puff of smoke that appears for a
short time and then vanishes. 15 You ought to say instead, "If
the Lord is willing, then we will live and do this or that." 16 But
as it is, you boast about your arrogant plans. All such boasting
is evil. 17 So whoever knows what is good to do and does not do
it is guilty of sin.

WARNING TO THE RICH

5 Come now, you rich! Weep and cry aloud over the miseries that are coming on you. 2 Your riches have rotted and
your clothing has become moth-eaten. 3 Your gold and silver
have rusted and their rust will be a witness against you. It will
consume your flesh like fire. It is in the last days that you have
hoarded treasure! 4 Look, the pay you have held back from the
workers who mowed your fields cries out against you, and the
cries of the reapers have reached the ears of the Lord of Heav-
en's Armies. 5 You have lived indulgently and luxuriously on the
earth. You have fattened your hearts in a day of slaughter. 6 You
have condemned and murdered the righteous person, although
he does not resist you.

PATIENCE IN SUFFERING

7 So be patient, brothers and sisters, until the Lord's return.
Think of how the farmer waits for the precious fruit of the
ground and is patient for it until it receives the early and late
rains. 8 You also be patient and strengthen your hearts, for the
Lord's return is near. 9 Do not grumble against one another,
brothers and sisters, so that you may not be judged. See, the
judge stands before the gates! 10 As an example of suffering and
patience, brothers and sisters, take the prophets who spoke in
the Lord's name. 11 Think of how we regard as blessed those who
have endured. You have heard of Job's endurance and you have
seen the Lord's purpose, that *the Lord is full of compassion and*
mercy. 12 And above all, my brothers and sisters, do not swear,
either by heaven or by earth or by any other oath. But let your
"Yes" be yes and your "No" be no, so that you may not fall into
judgment.

REFLECT

What does James teach us about the power of prayer? How can you be more faithful in prayer this week?

PRAYER FOR THE SICK

13 Is anyone among you suffering? He should pray. Is anyone in
good spirits? He should sing praises. 14 Is anyone among you ill?
He should summon the elders of the church, and they should
pray for him and anoint him with olive oil in the name of the
Lord. 15 And the prayer of faith will save the one who is sick and

the Lord will raise him up—and if he has committed sins, he
will be forgiven. 16 So confess your sins to one another and pray
for one another so that you may be healed. The prayer of a righteous person has great effectiveness. 17 Elijah was a human being
like us, and he prayed earnestly that it would not rain and there
was no rain on the land for three years and six months! 18 Then
he prayed again, and the sky gave rain and the land sprouted
with a harvest.

19 My brothers and sisters, if anyone among you wanders from
the truth and someone turns him back, 20 he should know that
the one who turns a sinner back from his wandering path will
save that person's soul from death and will cover a multitude
of sins.

But you are a
CHOSEN race,
a royal PRIESTHOOD,
a HOLY NATION,
a people of His own,
SO THAT you MAY proclaim
the VIRTUES of the ONE
who called you out of
darkness INTO HIS
Marvelous light

MEMORY VERSE

But you are a chosen race, a royal priesthood, a holy nation, a people of his own, so that you may proclaim the virtues of the one who called you out of darkness into his marvelous light.

1 Peter 2:9

1 Peter

INTRODUCTION

You Are Wanted

The Book of 1 Peter offers powerful encouragement to those facing persecution and trials. The Christians in Asia Minor during the first century experienced great hardship; they found living for Christ meant enduring suffering. Peter wrote this letter to uplift these believers, explain the reasons for their pain, and give them hope of the reward and glory to come.

The Book of 1 Peter contains five themes. First, Peter explained that Christians can expect suffering as part of following Christ because God often uses struggle to bring about godly character. Peter urged his readers to continue to live holy and righteous lives, no matter their experiences. Peter encouraged the believers to understand that suffering was part of their service to God, not a result of sin in their lives. He challenged the believers to submit to others for the sake of the gospel, and finally, he affirmed the central truths of the gospel.

Peter likely wrote his letter sometime between A.D. 62 and 64. While some modern scholarship challenges Peter as the author, early church tradition affirms the apostle was the writer of this letter.

This book was and is an encouragement to believers in Christ. Peter reminded his readers that as followers of Christ, we are a chosen people. Christ Himself chose us to follow Him and to show His love to a lost and broken world. Peter exhorted all Christ-followers, as we sometimes suffer for our belief, to anticipate "an inheritance imperishable, undefiled, and unfading" that is "reserved in heaven" for us (1:4). Such a reward should build our endurance and enable us to love God greatly.

Philippines

OFFICIAL LANGUAGES
Tagalog and English
POPULATION
107,959,000
UNREACHED POPULATION
5,355,000
PROFESSING CHRISTIANS
91.0%

Salvina's Home

Say a Prayer Today

Pray for Salvina and her work for the spread of the gospel. Pray God would go before her and open doors for her to share the love of Christ.

HISTORY BIT

Andres de Urdaneta, a Spanish Catholic missionary, landed on the island of Cebu in the Philippines in 1565. He was the first missionary to arrive in the Philippines.* The Philippines later served as a base for missions to Japan, China, and Cambodia through the seventeenth and eighteenth centuries.**

Source Information:
https://joshuaproject.net/countries/RP
*John Bowden, A Chronology of World Christianity (New York, NY: Continuum, 2007), 286.
**David B. Barrett, World Christian Encyclopedia, Philippines (New York, NY: Oxford University Press, 1982), 564.

LOVE YOUR NEIGHBOR

Her Journey

SALVINA'S STORY

I love the Book of 1 Peter. I love the reminder in 1 Peter 2:9 that says God has called us "out of darkness into his marvelous light."

God did this for me. When I placed my faith in Him, He brought me out of darkness and into His marvelous light. He changed my life in ways I never thought possible. He transformed the darkness within me and around me and brought me into His light.

Like He calls the nation of Israel His special possession, I have become His special possession through faith in Christ. My life is no longer my own, it belongs to the Lord now. My life has become God's possession because it was bought with a price—the precious blood of His only begotten Son.

God has done miracles and wonders in my life. He has called me to proclaim His name and His glory. While it wasn't my first choice, I believe with all my heart God called me to leave my home in the Philippines to come to Myanmar and proclaim His name. He desires that the people of this land be truly enlightened by putting their faith in the finished work of the Lord Jesus. He has appointed me with such a task.

I am constantly humbled by the incredible grace and provision of God. Whatever I do, I must consciously and intentionally be carrying out God's purpose. I long to become a holy vessel that will bring the light of the gospel to those around me who still live in darkness.

As I commit myself to teaching those God has brought into my circle of influence, it is my prayer that the life of Jesus will shine through me. May it shine so brightly that it would lead them to knowing the truth, that they too would be called "a people of his own" (1 Pet 2:9).

6 WEEK READING PLAN

LOVE HIS WORD

	MONDAY	TUESDAY	WEDNESDAY	THURSDAY	FRIDAY
1	1 Peter 1:1-9	1 Peter 1:10-16	1 Peter 1:17-21	1 Peter 1:22-25	1 Peter 2:1-6
	SOAP 1 Peter 1:6-7	SOAP 1 Peter 1:13	SOAP 1 Peter 1:21	SOAP 1 Peter 1:24-25	SOAP 1 Peter 2:4-5
2	1 Peter 2:7-10	1 Peter 2:11-17	1 Peter 2:18-25	1 Peter 3:1-7	1 Peter 3:8-12
	SOAP 1 Peter 2:9	SOAP 1 Peter 2:15-17	SOAP 1 Peter 2:23-24	SOAP 1 Peter 3:7	SOAP 1 Peter 3:8-9
3	1 Peter 3:13-16	1 Peter 3:17-22	1 Peter 4:1-6	1 Peter 4:7-11	1 Peter 4:12-14
	SOAP 1 Peter 3:14-16	SOAP 1 Peter 3:17-18	SOAP 1 Peter 4:1-2	SOAP 1 Peter 4:10	SOAP 1 Peter 4:12-13
4	1 Peter 4:15-19	1 Peter 5:1-4	1 Peter 5:5-7	1 Peter 5:8-9	1 Peter 5:10-14
	SOAP 1 Peter 4:19	SOAP 1 Peter 5:2	SOAP 1 Peter 5:6-7	SOAP 1 Peter 5:8-9	SOAP 1 Peter 5:10-11
5	2 Peter 1:1-4	2 Peter 1:5-11	2 Peter 1:12-21	2 Peter 2:1-3	2 Peter 2:4-10
	SOAP 2 Peter 1:3	SOAP 2 Peter 1:5-7	SOAP 2 Peter 1:20-21	SOAP 2 Peter 2:1	SOAP 2 Peter 2:9-10
6	2 Peter 2:11-16	2 Peter 2:17-22	2 Peter 3:1-7	2 Peter 3:8-13	2 Peter 3:14-18
	SOAP 2 Peter 2:13	SOAP 2 Peter 2:18-19	SOAP 2 Peter 3:3-4	SOAP 2 Peter 3:9	SOAP 2 Peter 3:14

SALUTATION

1 From Peter, an apostle of Jesus Christ, to those temporarily residing abroad (in Pontus, Galatia, Cappadocia, the province of Asia, and Bithynia) who are chosen 2 according to the foreknowledge of God the Father by being set apart by the Spirit for obedience and for sprinkling with Jesus Christ's blood. May grace and peace be yours in full measure!

NEW BIRTH TO JOY AND HOLINESS

3 Blessed be the God and Father of our Lord Jesus Christ! By his great mercy he gave us new birth into a living hope through the resurrection of Jesus Christ from the dead, 4 that is, into an inheritance imperishable, undefiled, and unfading. It is reserved in heaven for you, 5 who by God's power are protected through faith for a salvation ready to be revealed in the last time. 6 This brings you great joy, although you may have to suffer for a short time in various trials. 7 Such trials show the proven character of your faith, which is much more valuable than gold—gold that is tested by fire, even though it is passing away—and will bring praise and glory and honor when Jesus Christ is revealed. 8 You have not seen him, but you love him. You do not see him now but you believe in him, and so you rejoice with an indescribable and glorious joy, 9 because you are attaining the goal of your faith—the salvation of your souls.

10 Concerning this salvation, the prophets who predicted the grace that would come to you searched and investigated carefully. 11 They probed into what person or time the Spirit of Christ within them was indicating when he testified beforehand about the sufferings appointed for Christ and his subsequent glory. 12 They were shown that they were serving not themselves but you, in regard to the things now announced to you through those who proclaimed the gospel to you by the Holy Spirit sent from heaven—things angels long to catch a glimpse of.

13 Therefore, get your minds ready for action by being fully sober, and set your hope completely on the grace that will be brought to you when Jesus Christ is revealed. 14 Like obedient children, do not comply with the evil urges you used to follow in your ignorance, 15 but, like the Holy One who called you, become holy yourselves in all of your conduct, 16 for it is written, ***"You shall be holy, because I am holy."*** 17 And if you address as Father the one who impartially judges according to each one's work, live out the time of your temporary residence here in reverence. 18 You know that from your empty way of life inherited from your ancestors you were ransomed—not by perishable things like silver or gold, 19 but by precious blood like that of an unblemished and spotless lamb, namely Christ. 20 He was foreknown before the foundation of the world but was manifested in these last times for your sake. 21 Through him you now trust in God, who raised him from the dead and gave him glory, so that your faith and hope are in God.

22 You have purified your souls by obeying the truth in order to show sincere mutual love. So love one another earnestly from

CHALLENGE

What does 1 Peter 1:3–9 say God has given us through the resurrection of Christ? Why is it important for us to believe and love Christ even though we cannot see Him?

a pure heart. 23 You have been born anew, not from perishable
but from imperishable seed, through the living and enduring
word of God. 24 For

all flesh is like grass
and all its glory like the flower of the grass;
the grass withers and the flower falls off,
25 ***but the word of the Lord endures forever.***

And this is the word that was proclaimed to you.

REFLECT

How do we conduct ourselves honorably? What effect does it have on others when we glorify God with our lives?

2 So get rid of all evil and all deceit and hypocrisy and envy and
all slander. 2 And yearn like newborn infants for pure, spiritual milk, so that by it you may grow up to salvation, 3 if ***you have***
experienced the Lord's kindness.

A LIVING STONE, A CHOSEN PEOPLE

4 So as you come to him, a living stone rejected by men but chosen and precious in God's sight, 5 you yourselves, as living stones,
are built up as a spiritual house to be a holy priesthood and
to offer spiritual sacrifices that are acceptable to God through
Jesus Christ. 6 For it says in scripture, "***Look, I lay in Zion a stone,***
a chosen and precious cornerstone, and whoever believes in him
will never be put to shame." 7 So you who believe see his value,
but for those who do not believe, ***the stone that the builders re-***
jected has become the cornerstone, 8 and ***a stumbling-stone and a***
rock to trip over. They stumble because they disobey the word,
as they were destined to do. 9 But you are *a chosen race, a royal*
priesthood, a holy nation, a people of his own, so that you may *pro-*
claim the virtues of the one who called you out of darkness into
his marvelous light. 10 You once were ***not a people***, but now you
are God's people. You were ***shown no mercy,*** but now you have
received mercy.

11 Dear friends, I urge you as foreigners and exiles to keep away
from fleshly desires that do battle against the soul, 12 and maintain good conduct among the non-Christians, so that though
they now malign you as wrongdoers, they may see your good
deeds and glorify God when he appears.

SUBMISSION TO AUTHORITIES

13 Be subject to every human institution for the Lord's sake,
whether to a king as supreme 14 or to governors as those he commissions to punish wrongdoers and praise those who do good.
15 For God wants you to silence the ignorance of foolish people
by doing good. 16 Live as free people, not using your freedom as
a pretext for evil, but as God's slaves. 17 Honor all people, love the
family of believers, fear God, honor the king.

18 Slaves, be subject to your masters with all reverence, not only
to those who are good and gentle, but also to those who are perverse. 19 For this finds God's favor, if because of conscience toward
God someone endures hardships in suffering unjustly. 20 For
what credit is it if you sin and are mistreated and endure it? But
if you do good and suffer and so endure, this finds favor with God.
21 For to this you were called, since Christ also suffered for you,
leaving an example for you to follow in his steps. 22 He ***commit-***
ted no sin ***nor was deceit found in his mouth.*** 23 When he was ma-
ligned, he did not answer back; when he suffered, he threatened

LOVE TO GROW

BANISH DARKNESS

1 PETER 2:9

Someone once described becoming a Christian as having someone flip on the light switch in a dark room. Until that moment, we had no idea we were walking around in the dark. Once we see the world in the light in which it's meant to be seen, we are lifted out of the spiritual darkness that held us captive. God's truth replaces our blindness and confusion with purpose and peace.

Because we live in a broken world, we will continue to experience times of darkness, even as Christians. When we least expect it, devastating loss can descend on us like an enormous ocean wave. Once that first wave passes, it often returns uninvited. Sometimes it comes for hours, sometimes for days, sometimes for seasons.

All too often, such times keep us from accomplishing our mission. They can even make us doubt God's presence. How do we climb out of these dark holes? What can we do to keep from being sidelined by sadness or hobbled by grief?

When I feel darkness falling on my life, I've learned I have a choice: I can wallow in my unhappiness, or I can consider the ways in which my heavenly Father has revealed Himself to me. I've sensed His good and loving hand over my life; I've seen Him fight for me; I've trembled at the wonder of His courage enabling me to share my testimony—all for the sake of His kingdom.

I didn't figure this out all at once. I've done my share of wailing and railing at God. Over the years, I've found that if I seek Him daily through His Word, He will flood my life with the light of His presence and cast out any shadow of darkness. Fully living in His light is a choice, and one of the most powerful decisions I can make.

You are a chosen race, a royal priesthood, a holy nation, a people of his own, so that you may proclaim the virtues of the one who called you out of darkness into his marvelous light (1 Pet 2:9).

Remember who you are—a chosen one, called into a royal priesthood, one whose divine purpose is to proclaim His excellence. In Christ, darkness no longer has to be a jailer of your soul. Jesus has come to set you free! Don't forget to flip on the light switch for someone else: Share how God has delivered you—and watch the darkness flee.

no retaliation, but committed himself to God who judges justly.
24 He ***himself bore our sins*** in his body on the tree, that we may
cease from sinning and live for righteousness. ***By*** his ***wounds you***
were healed. 25 For you were ***going astray like sheep*** but now you
have turned back to the shepherd and guardian of your souls.

WIVES AND HUSBANDS

REFLECT

What does the command to bless our enemies reveal about the heart of God?

3 In the same way, wives, be subject to your own husbands.
Then, even if some are disobedient to the word, they will be
won over without a word by the way you live, 2 when they see
your pure and reverent conduct. 3 Let your beauty not be external—the braiding of hair and wearing of gold jewelry or fine
clothes—4 but the inner person of the heart, the lasting beauty
of a gentle and tranquil spirit, which is precious in God's sight.
5 For in the same way the holy women who hoped in God long
ago adorned themselves by being subject to their husbands, 6 like
Sarah who obeyed Abraham, calling him lord. You become her
children when you do what is good and have no fear in doing so.
7 Husbands, in the same way, treat your wives with consideration
as the weaker partners and show them honor as fellow heirs of
the grace of life. In this way nothing will hinder your prayers.

SUFFERING FOR DOING GOOD

8 Finally, all of you be harmonious, sympathetic, affectionate,
compassionate, and humble. 9 Do not return evil for evil or insult for insult, but instead bless others because you were called
to inherit a blessing. 10 For

the one who wants to love life and see good days must keep
his tongue from evil and his lips from uttering deceit.
11 ***And he must turn away from evil and do good;***
he must seek peace and pursue it.
12 ***For the eyes of the Lord are upon the righteous***
and his ears are open to their prayer.
But the Lord's face is against those who do evil.

13 For who is going to harm you if you are devoted to what is
good? 14 But in fact, if you happen to suffer for doing what is right,
you are blessed. ***But do not be terrified of them or be shaken.*** 15 But
set Christ apart as Lord in your hearts and always be ready to
give an answer to anyone who asks about the hope you possess.
16 Yet do it with courtesy and respect, keeping a good conscience,
so that those who slander your good conduct in Christ may be
put to shame when they accuse you. 17 For it is better to suffer
for doing good, if God wills it, than for doing evil.

18 Because Christ also suffered once for sins,
the just for the unjust,
to bring you to God,
by being put to death in the flesh
but by being made alive in the spirit.
19 In it he went and preached to the spirits in prison,

20 after they were disobedient long ago when God patiently
waited in the days of Noah as an ark was being constructed. In
the ark a few, that is eight souls, were delivered through water.

21 And this prefigured baptism, which now saves you—not the
washing off of physical dirt but the pledge of a good conscience
to God—through the resurrection of Jesus Christ, 22 who went
into heaven and is at the right hand of God with angels and authorities and powers subject to him.

4 So, since Christ suffered in the flesh, you also arm yourselves
with the same attitude, because the one who has suffered in
the flesh has finished with sin, 2 in that he spends the rest of his
time on earth concerned about the will of God and not human
desires. 3 For the time that has passed was sufficient for you to
do what the non-Christians desire. You lived then in debauchery, evil desires, drunkenness, carousing, drinking bouts, and
wanton idolatries. 4 So they are astonished when you do not
rush with them into the same flood of wickedness, and they
vilify you. 5 They will face a reckoning before Jesus Christ who
stands ready to judge the living and the dead. 6 Now it was for
this very purpose that the gospel was preached to those who
are now dead, so that though they were judged in the flesh by
human standards they may live spiritually by God's standards.

REFLECT

How are we to live as followers of Christ? How is this different from the way we lived before we knew Christ?

SERVICE, SUFFERING, AND JUDGMENT

7 For the culmination of all things is near. So be self-controlled
and sober-minded for the sake of prayer. 8 Above all keep your
love for one another fervent, because ***love covers a multitude of***
sins. 9 Show hospitality to one another without complaining.
10 Just as each one has received a gift, use it to serve one another as good stewards of the varied grace of God. 11 Whoever
speaks, let it be with God's words. Whoever serves, do so with
the strength that God supplies, so that in everything God will
be glorified through Jesus Christ. To him belong the glory and
the power forever and ever. Amen.

12 Dear friends, do not be astonished that a trial by fire is occurring among you, as though something strange were happening to you. 13 But rejoice in the degree that you have shared in
the sufferings of Christ, so that when his glory is revealed you
may also rejoice and be glad. 14 If you are insulted for the name
of Christ, you are blessed, because the Spirit of glory, who is ***the***
Spirit of God, rests on you. 15 But let none of you suffer as a murderer or thief or criminal or as a troublemaker. 16 But if you suffer as a Christian, do not be ashamed, but glorify God that you
bear such a name. 17 For it is time for judgment to begin, starting
with the house of God. And if it starts with us, what will be the
fate of those who are disobedient to the gospel of God? 18 And
if the righteous are barely saved, what will become of the ungodly
and sinners? 19 So then let those who suffer according to the will
of God entrust their souls to a faithful Creator as they do good.

LEADING AND LIVING IN GOD'S FLOCK

5 So as your fellow elder and a witness of Christ's sufferings and
as one who shares in the glory that will be revealed, I urge the
elders among you: 2 Give a shepherd's care to God's flock among
you, exercising oversight not merely as a duty but willingly under God's direction, not for shameful profit but eagerly. 3 And do
not lord it over those entrusted to you, but be examples to the

flock. 4 Then when the Chief Shepherd appears, you will receive the crown of glory that never fades away.

5 In the same way, you who are younger, be subject to the elders. And all of you, clothe yourselves with humility toward one another, because God ***opposes the proud but gives grace to the humble.*** 6 And God will exalt you in due time, if you humble yourselves under his mighty hand 7 by casting all your cares on him because he cares for you. 8 Be sober and alert. Your enemy the devil, *like a roaring lion,* is on the prowl looking for someone to devour. 9 Resist him, strong in your faith, because you know that your brothers and sisters throughout the world are enduring the same kinds of suffering. 10 And, after you have suffered for a little while, the God of all grace who called you to his eternal glory in Christ will himself restore, confirm, strengthen, and establish you. 11 To him belongs the power forever. Amen.

REFLECT

Even though we are promised suffering, what else does God promise? How does this encourage you?

FINAL GREETINGS

12 Through Silvanus, whom I know to be a faithful brother, I have written to you briefly, in order to encourage you and testify that this is the true grace of God. Stand fast in it. 13 The church in Babylon, chosen together with you, greets you, and so does Mark, my son. 14 Greet one another with a loving kiss. Peace to all of you who are in Christ.

HUMBLE YOURSELF

1 PETER 5:5–9

"Dear God, please don't let the ladies boo Mommy when she speaks tonight."

My daughter, though sad I was missing her soccer game, offered to pray for me before I left to speak to a group of women at a local event. Of all the things she could have prayed for me, never would I have guessed she would ask God to keep the ladies from booing me.

Kids. Keeping their parents humble since the dawn of time.

If you knew my heart the way God does, you would know how much I need those moments of private humility (and how much I prefer them over the public version). There have been significant seasons of my life when I would name important jobs I'd done, impressive titles I'd held, and once-in-a-lifetime opportunities I'd experienced, and I would look around and think, *I'm so glad I'm not* [insert someone else's name here].

At those times, pride, in its sneaky, self-serving, stealth mode, crept deeper into my heart. Satisfaction in a job well done slowly turned into a fight to be the best and say yes to everything, with lofty expectations about the work, recognition, and opportunities I deserved.

God, in His mercy and goodness, graciously taught me humility so I could draw near to Him.

First Peter 5:5–9 reminds us to "clothe [ourselves] with humility," to humble ourselves so He can exalt us, to cast our cares on Him, and to be alert for the schemes of the enemy.

What does it look like to actually wear humility? Saying no to something so someone else can say yes. Working hard for God's glory, not our own. Using our talents and gifts to help others shine. Choosing to be content where God has you. Viewing others as coworkers in the kingdom, not competition. Receiving correction, guidance, and mentoring with grace. Deciding that being known for our love is more important than being right.

Stay alert, friend. The enemy is on the prowl. He has been defeated, but he still waits, ready to pounce, when we stop relying on God and start to make our lives only about ourselves.

Don't wait to get booed before you embrace humility!

HIS divine POWER has bestowed on us EVERYTHING necessary for LIFE and godliness

MEMORY VERSE

I can pray this because his divine power has bestowed on us everything necessary for life and godliness through the rich knowledge of the one who called us by his own glory and excellence.

2 Peter 1:3

2 Peter

INTRODUCTION

Equipped

The Christian faith is a matter of life and death. When false teachers infiltrate the church, eternity is at stake. Peter wrote his second letter to the early church to correct falsehoods and propaganda that had begun to lead believers astray. Peter stressed sanctification, the ongoing process in which believers become more and more like Christ. Through sanctification, we are better educated in truth and equipped to deal with false teaching.

Peter focused on five themes of holy living and sanctification in his letter. First, Peter expressed his authority and how, through knowing the teaching of the apostles, believers could more readily identify false teaching. Next, Peter admonished the believers to put away immorality from their lives and then warned them not to imitate the arrogance of false teachers. He stressed the need to persevere and remain faithful to the truth. Finally, Peter encouraged the believers to be patient as they awaited the day of the Lord, continuing in faith and holy living as they watched for Christ's return.

Second Peter has traditionally been attributed to the apostle, but it is possible that Peter could have used a secretary scribe, perhaps Mark, to write this letter. The date of writing is likely between A.D. 64 and 67. Peter may have written the letter from Rome, where he is believed to have spent the last few years of his life.

The Book of 2 Peter is a wonderful encouragement to love God greatly. Christ is the author of our sanctification. As we work toward holiness, we can be confident that God is working in us, completing good works, and equipping us to live out the calling He has placed on our lives. Not only that, but Christ promises to return. We will see His glory, the same glory Peter prodded us to watch for on the day of the Lord.

Canada

OFFICIAL LANGUAGE
English
POPULATION
37,315,000
UNREACHED POPULATION
1,954,000
PROFESSING CHRISTIANS
73.0%

Tahlia's Home

Say a Prayer Today

Pray for Tahlia's ministry to Polish students. Pray her ministry will have an eternal impact. Pray she would be encouraged and strengthened as she lives far from home.

HISTORY BIT

In 1852 the Anglican Church of Canada became a voluntary association thus separating church and state. Since that time, Canada has enjoyed freedom of religion.*

Source Information:
https://joshuaproject.net/countries/CA
*David B. Barrett, World Christian Encyclopedia, Canada (New York, NY: Oxford University Press, 1982), 212.

TAHLIA'S STORY

I was born into a Christian home in Canada where my parents encouraged the pursuit of a personal relationship with Jesus. As a result, I made a decision at a young age to accept Christ into my life. I grew up in the church, had a pleasant childhood, and attended a Christian university. I am thankful for the life I've led, but I felt like my personal story was boring. How could God use me to reach others?

The Lord placed in me a desire to disciple and encourage others in their faith. For many years God provided me opportunities to move outside of my comfort zone, which I accepted. I did not know it at the time, but God used those things to equip me for my future.

A few years after graduating from university, I got to know some missionaries who worked with college students in Poland. They asked if I would be interested in joining their team. At first I did not want to leave the comforts of my job, my friends and family, or my home. However, after taking time to pray through their offer, God revealed to me that He had groomed me for the job. I'd served university students for six years at the time, and my service among them had become a great source of joy. It was undeniable this was what He had prepared me to do.

The Christian walk is a constant learning process and is not always easy, but having the assurance of Christ as my Savior and guide gives me confidence to persevere and grow deeper in my relationship with Him. You never know where life will take you or the road you will travel, but seeking God's wisdom for clarity keeps it under His control.

Through the abundance of His mercy and grace, I've seen God use my story over and over again. God saw me, saved me, and is continually shaping and equipping me. What more could I ask for?

6 WEEK READING PLAN

LOVE HIS WORD

	MONDAY	TUESDAY	WEDNESDAY	THURSDAY	FRIDAY
1	1 Peter 1:1-9	1 Peter 1:10-16	1 Peter 1:17-21	1 Peter 1:22-25	1 Peter 2:1-6
	SOAP 1 Peter 1:6-7	SOAP 1 Peter 1:13	SOAP 1 Peter 1:21	SOAP 1 Peter 1:24-25	SOAP 1 Peter 2:4-5
2	1 Peter 2:7-10	1 Peter 2:11-17	1 Peter 2:18-25	1 Peter 3:1-7	1 Peter 3:8-12
	SOAP 1 Peter 2:9	SOAP 1 Peter 2:15-17	SOAP 1 Peter 2:23-24	SOAP 1 Peter 3:7	SOAP 1 Peter 3:8-9
3	1 Peter 3:13-16	1 Peter 3:17-22	1 Peter 4:1-6	1 Peter 4:7-11	1 Peter 4:12-14
	SOAP 1 Peter 3:14-16	SOAP 1 Peter 3:17-18	SOAP 1 Peter 4:1-2	SOAP 1 Peter 4:10	SOAP 1 Peter 4:12-13
4	1 Peter 4:15-19	1 Peter 5:1-4	1 Peter 5:5-7	1 Peter 5:8-9	1 Peter 5:10-14
	SOAP 1 Peter 4:19	SOAP 1 Peter 5:2	SOAP 1 Peter 5:6-7	SOAP 1 Peter 5:8-9	SOAP 1 Peter 5:10-11
5	2 Peter 1:1-4	2 Peter 1:5-11	2 Peter 1:12-21	2 Peter 2:1-3	2 Peter 2:4-10
	SOAP 2 Peter 1:3	SOAP 2 Peter 1:5-7	SOAP 2 Peter 1:20-21	SOAP 2 Peter 2:1	SOAP 2 Peter 2:9-10
6	2 Peter 2:11-16	2 Peter 2:17-22	2 Peter 3:1-7	2 Peter 3:8-13	2 Peter 3:14-18
	SOAP 2 Peter 2:13	SOAP 2 Peter 2:18-19	SOAP 2 Peter 3:3-4	SOAP 2 Peter 3:9	SOAP 2 Peter 3:14

SALUTATION

1 From Simeon Peter, a slave and apostle of Jesus Christ, to those
who through the righteousness of our God and Savior, Jesus
Christ, have been granted a faith just as precious as ours. 2 May
grace and peace be lavished on you as you grow in the rich knowledge of God and of Jesus our Lord!

BELIEVERS' SALVATION AND THE WORK OF GOD

3 I can pray this because his divine power has bestowed on us
everything necessary for life and godliness through the rich
knowledge of the one who called us by his own glory and excellence. 4 Through these things he has bestowed on us his precious
and most magnificent promises, so that by means of what was
promised you may become partakers of the divine nature, after
escaping the worldly corruption that is produced by evil desire.
5 For this very reason, make every effort to add to your faith excellence, to excellence, knowledge; 6 to knowledge, self-control;
to self-control, perseverance; to perseverance, godliness; 7 to godliness, brotherly affection; to brotherly affection, unselfish love.
8 For if these things are really yours and are continually increasing, they will keep you from becoming ineffective and unproductive in your pursuit of knowing our Lord Jesus Christ more
intimately. 9 But concerning the one who lacks such things—he
is blind. That is to say, he is nearsighted, since he has forgotten
about the cleansing of his past sins. 10 Therefore, brothers and
sisters, make every effort to be sure of your calling and election.
For by doing this you will never stumble into sin. 11 For thus an
entrance into the eternal kingdom of our Lord and Savior, Jesus
Christ, will be richly provided for you.

SALVATION BASED ON THE WORD OF GOD

12 Therefore, I intend to remind you constantly of these things
even though you know them and are well established in the
truth that you now have. 13 Indeed, as long as I am in this tabernacle, I consider it right to stir you up by way of a reminder,
14 since I know that my tabernacle will soon be removed, because our Lord Jesus Christ revealed this to me. 15 Indeed, I will
also make every effort that, after my departure, you have a testimony of these things.

16 For we did not follow cleverly concocted fables when we
made known to you the power and return of our Lord Jesus
Christ; no, we were eyewitnesses of his grandeur. 17 For he received honor and glory from God the Father, when that voice
was conveyed to him by the Majestic Glory: "This is my dear Son,
in whom I am delighted." 18 When this voice was conveyed from
heaven, we ourselves heard it, for we were with him on the holy
mountain. 19 Moreover, we possess the prophetic word as an altogether reliable thing. You do well if you pay attention to this
as you would to a light shining in a murky place, until the day
dawns and the morning star rises in your hearts. 20 Above all,
you do well if you recognize this: No prophecy of scripture ever
comes about by the prophet's own imagination, 21 for no prophecy was ever borne of human impulse; rather, men carried along
by the Holy Spirit spoke from God.

CHALLENGE

Name some ways God has given you everything required for life and godliness. What encourages you to continue in your faith and to follow His calling?

LOVE TO GROW

THE WORD OF GOD

2 PETER 1:12–21

Imagine you have only a few more minutes to live and you decide to make one last phone call. What would you say? Whatever you choose to say would be something you consider of utmost importance.

Similarly, Peter knew he was going to die soon. What he had to say was incredibly important. It was of utmost concern to Peter that his audience remembered the promises and power of God and that they diligently pursued spiritual growth.

Where could they go to learn about the promises and power of God? They could turn to the prophetic word of the Bible. Peter said that his readers would "do well if [they paid] attention to this as [they] would to a light shining in a murky place" (2 Peter 1:19). The words of the Bible are not of human origin. They are not the thoughts of clever humans but instead the words that people "carried along by the Holy Spirit spoke from God" (2 Peter 1:21).

What an encouraging reminder! Think of all the times in your life you've desperately wished you knew the truth, wanted some guidance, or felt confused by opposing voices telling you what to do. Because God is truth, what He reveals is true. Instead of stumbling around in the dark, unsure how to find a solid foundation of understanding, we can turn to the Word of God and hear truth from Him.

The Christian life is a battle for truth.

We are constantly bombarded by the arrows of our enemy, Satan. In order to succeed in this arena, we need to hear the thoughts from the other side, from God. To refuse to expose ourselves to the truth in the Bible is to make ourselves vulnerable.

As we remind ourselves what we have in the Bible is the Word of God, we will want to read it more. As a result we will become more aware of who God is, how He thinks, and what He wants for our lives. This will continue to develop our love for Him and our desire to be changed by Him into the likeness of His Son.

Remembering the truth of God is as important today as it was to Peter's original audience. In God's great love for us, He has left us not in darkness, but with the light of truth. As Peter delivered urgent messages in his last days on earth, let's also remember the value and necessity of the messages we send through our lives every day.

THE FALSE TEACHERS' UNGODLY LIFESTYLE

2 But false prophets arose among the people, just as there will be false teachers among you. These false teachers will infiltrate your midst with destructive heresies, even to the point of denying the Master who bought them. As a result, they will bring swift destruction on themselves. 2 And many will follow their debauched lifestyles. Because of these false teachers, the way of truth will be slandered. 3 And in their greed they will exploit you with deceptive words. Their condemnation pronounced long ago is not sitting idly by; their destruction is not asleep.

4 For if God did not spare the angels who sinned, but threw them into hell and locked them up in chains in utter darkness, to be kept until the judgment, 5 and if he did not spare the ancient world, but did protect Noah, a herald of righteousness, along with seven others, when God brought a flood on an ungodly world, 6 and if he turned to ashes the cities of Sodom and Gomorrah when he condemned them to destruction, having appointed them to serve as an example to future generations of the ungodly, 7 and if he rescued Lot, a righteous man in anguish over the debauched lifestyle of lawless men, 8 (for while he lived among them day after day, that righteous man was tormented in his righteous soul by the lawless deeds he saw and heard) 9 —if so, then the Lord knows how to rescue the godly from their trials, and to reserve the unrighteous for punishment at the day of judgment, 10 especially those who indulge their fleshly desires and who despise authority.

Brazen and insolent, they are not afraid to insult the glorious ones, 11 yet even angels, who are much more powerful, do not bring a slanderous judgment against them in the presence of the Lord. 12 But these men, like irrational animals—creatures of instinct, born to be caught and destroyed—do not understand whom they are insulting, and consequently in their destruction they will be destroyed, 13 suffering harm as the wages for their harmful ways. By considering it a pleasure to carouse in broad daylight, they are stains and blemishes, indulging in their deceitful pleasures when they feast together with you. 14 Their eyes, full of adultery, never stop sinning; they entice unstable people. They have trained their hearts for greed, these cursed children! 15 By forsaking the right path they have gone astray, because they followed the way of Balaam son of Bosor, who loved the wages of unrighteousness, 16 yet was rebuked for his own transgression (a dumb donkey, speaking with a human voice, restrained the prophet's madness).

17 These men are waterless springs and mists driven by a storm, for whom the utter depths of darkness have been reserved. 18 For by speaking high-sounding but empty words they are able to entice, with fleshly desires and with debauchery, people who have just escaped from those who reside in error. 19 Although these false teachers promise such people freedom, they themselves are enslaved to immorality. For whatever a person succumbs to, to that he is enslaved. 20 For if after they have escaped the filthy things of the world

REFLECT

When have you seen God rescue the godly from difficult or dangerous circumstances? What does this tell us about His character?

through the rich knowledge of our Lord and Savior Jesus
Christ, they again get entangled in them and succumb to
them, their last state has become worse for them than their
first. 21 For it would have been better for them never to have
known the way of righteousness than, having known it, to
turn back from the holy commandment that had been delivered to them. 22 They are illustrations of this true proverb: "***A***
dog returns to its own vomit," and "A sow, after washing herself, wallows in the mire."

THE FALSE TEACHERS' DENIAL OF THE LORD'S RETURN

3 Dear friends, this is already the second letter I have written
you, in which I am trying to stir up your pure mind by way
of reminder: 2 I want you to recall both the predictions foretold by the holy prophets and the commandment of the Lord
and Savior through your apostles. 3 Above all, understand this:
In the last days blatant scoffers will come, being propelled by
their own evil urges 4 and saying, "Where is his promised return? For ever since our ancestors died, all things have continued as they were from the beginning of creation." 5 For they
deliberately suppress this fact, that by the word of God heavens existed long ago and an earth was formed out of water and
by means of water. 6 Through these things the world existing at
that time was destroyed when it was deluged with water. 7 But
by the same word the present heavens and earth have been reserved for fire, by being kept for the day of judgment and destruction of the ungodly.
8 Now, dear friends, do not let this one thing escape your notice, that a single day is like a thousand years with the Lord
and a thousand years are like a single day. 9 The Lord is not
slow concerning his promise, as some regard slowness, but is
being patient toward you, because he does not wish for any to
perish but for all to come to repentance. 10 But the day of the
Lord will come like a thief; when it comes, the heavens will disappear with a horrific noise, and the celestial bodies will melt
away in a blaze, and the earth and every deed done on it will be
laid bare. 11 Since all these things are to melt away in this manner, what sort of people must you be, conducting your lives in
holiness and godliness, 12 while waiting for and hastening the
coming of the day of God? Because of this day, the heavens will
be burned up and dissolve, and the celestial bodies will melt
away in a blaze! 13 But, according to his promise, we are waiting for new heavens and a new earth, in which righteousness
truly resides.

REFLECT

What does Peter mean when he says to be on our guard? How can we guard ourselves against the attacks of the enemy or of false teachers?

EXHORTATION TO THE FAITHFUL

14 Therefore, dear friends, since you are waiting for these things,
strive to be found at peace, without spot or blemish, when you
come into his presence. 15 And regard the patience of our Lord
as salvation, just as also our dear brother Paul wrote to you,
according to the wisdom given to him, 16 speaking of these
things in all his letters. Some things in these letters are hard
to understand, things the ignorant and unstable twist to their

own destruction, as they also do to the rest of the scriptures.
17 Therefore, dear friends, since you have been forewarned, be
on your guard that you do not get led astray by the error of
these unprincipled men and fall from your firm grasp on the
truth. 18 But grow in the grace and knowledge of our Lord and
Savior Jesus Christ. To him be the honor both now and on
that eternal day.

GOD IS LOVE,
and the one who
RESIDES in LOVE
resides IN God,
and
GOD RESIDES in him

MEMORY VERSE

And we have come to know and to believe the love that God has in us. God is love, and the one who resides in love resides in God, and God resides in him.

1 John 4:16

1 John

INTRODUCTION

God Is Love

Like many of the New Testament epistles, 1 John was written to instruct a group of believers on how to deal with false teachers. First John encourages readers to understand the character of God and guard against false teaching and doctrine. John reminded his audience of the life, death, and resurrection of Jesus Christ, of His full deity and full humanity, and of the unity believers savored when they shared the love of Christ.

The Book of 1 John begins with a brief introduction about the message of eternal life (1:1–4). John then discussed foundational principles of the faith (1:5—2:11) and explained his purpose in writing the letter (2:12–27). John spent the bulk of the letter describing God's righteousness (2:28—4:6) and God's love (4:7—5:13). Finally, he closed with brief comments about prayer and understanding (5:14–21).

The author of 1 John is widely accepted as John the beloved apostle, who also wrote the Gospel of John and the letters of 2 and 3 John. After Paul and Peter were martyred in approximately A.D. 67, John moved to Ephesus. Many scholars date John's Gospel and his three letters to sometime after the destruction of Jerusalem in A.D. 70 and before John's exile on the island of Patmos in about A.D. 95.

John wrote this letter to combat the heretical teachings of Gnosticism that had infiltrated the early church. Gnosticism denied the full deity of Christ and that Jesus had a human body. John reminded his readers of the true nature of Christ: He was fully God and fully human. The Book of 1 John reminds us that to love God greatly, we must believe that God is who He says He is. Jesus is truly the Son of God who gave up His place in heaven to take on human flesh and die for the sins of the world. His sacrifice granted us salvation and eternal life with Him.

The Netherlands

OFFICIAL LANGUAGE
Dutch
POPULATION
16,994,000
UNREACHED POPULATION
887,000
PROFESSING CHRISTIANS
47.2%

Charissa's Home

Say a Prayer Today

Please pray for Charissa and her ministry to the Dutch people. Pray the people of the Netherlands will understand the love God offers them and turn to Him in their brokenness.

HISTORY BIT

The Franks first established a church at Utrecht in the seventh century. Holland was also a place of refuge for many facing persecution during the Protestant Reformation, including the followers of Martin Luther and John Calvin.*

Source Information:
https://joshuaproject.net/countries/NL
*David B. Barrett, World Christian Encyclopedia, Netherlands (New York, NY: Oxford University Press, 1982), 510.

CHARISSA'S STORY

Once a year the canals of Amsterdam are filled with people from every class, tongue, color, and age. On that day, the city celebrates what is called the Love Parade, celebrating universal love.

Do we really know what love is? In the Netherlands, every other marriage ends in divorce, and there are more than 30,000 abortions each year. We still struggle with women's equality, anti-Semitism is on the rise, and we have politicians who stir up hate toward immigrants. The country is even strongly polarized on "Zwarte Piet," arguing from September until January over whether or not a children's celebration is a display of discrimination.

Even in our celebration of love, we have questions about what love really is. We want to define love, but ultimately, we want to define God.

God is so much higher, so much greater, so much deeper, so much more sovereign than we could ever imagine. He loves us more than we know and are able to comprehend. God is love. He defines love. If people knew God, then they would know real love. We need to get to know Him more each day in order to understand what true love is.

True love is giving up your life for someone else. That is how God loves the world. That is why Jesus gave His life for the world.

It is His love that brings us together in this country and drives us to unity. It is His love that challenges us to reach out to each other and to demonstrate His love for people. God loves us with a love we do not understand. That is the love we need to experience and the love we need to give to our children, spouse, friends, community, neighbors, and church.

4 WEEK READING PLAN

LOVE HIS WORD

	MONDAY	TUESDAY	WEDNESDAY	THURSDAY	FRIDAY
1	1 John 1:1-4	1 John 1:5—2:2	1 John 2:3-11	1 John 2:12-17	1 John 2:18-27
	SOAP 1 John 1:4	SOAP 1 John 1:9	SOAP 1 John 2:3-6	SOAP 1 John 2:15-16	SOAP 1 John 2:25
2	1 John 2:28—3:10	1 John 3:11-17	1 John 3:18-24	1 John 4:1-6	1 John 4:7-11
	SOAP 1 John 2:28-29	SOAP 1 John 3:16-17	SOAP 1 John 3:19-20	SOAP 1 John 4:4-5	SOAP 1 John 4:10
3	1 John 4:12-19	1 John 4:20—5:4	1 John 5:5-12	1 John 5:13-21	2 John 1-4
	SOAP 1 John 4:16	SOAP 1 John 5:3	SOAP 1 John 5:11-12	SOAP 1 John 5:14-15	SOAP 2 John 4
4	2 John 5-8	2 John 9-13	3 John 1-4	3 John 5-8	3 John 9-15
	SOAP 2 John 6	SOAP 2 John 12	SOAP 3 John 4	SOAP 3 John 8	SOAP 3 John 11

THE PROLOGUE TO THE LETTER

1 This is what we proclaim to you: what was from the beginning,
what we have heard, what we have seen with our eyes, what
we have looked at and our hands have touched (concerning the
word of life—2 and the life was revealed, and we have seen and
testify and announce to you the eternal life that was with the
Father and was revealed to us). 3 What we have seen and heard
we announce to you too, so that you may have fellowship with
us (and indeed our fellowship is with the Father and with his
Son Jesus Christ). 4 Thus we are writing these things so that our
joy may be complete.

GOD IS LIGHT, SO WE MUST WALK IN THE LIGHT

5 Now this is the gospel message we have heard from him and announce to you: God is light, and in him there is no darkness at all.
6 If we say we have fellowship with him and yet keep on walking in
the darkness, we are lying and not practicing the truth. 7 But if we
walk in the light as he himself is in the light, we have fellowship
with one another and the blood of Jesus his Son cleanses us from
all sin. 8 If we say we do not bear the guilt of sin, we are deceiving
ourselves and the truth is not in us. 9 But if we confess our sins,
he is faithful and righteous, forgiving us our sins and cleansing
us from all unrighteousness. 10 If we say we have not sinned, we
make him a liar and his word is not in us.
2 1 (My little children, I
am writing these things to you so that you may not sin.) But if
anyone does sin, we have an advocate with the Father, Jesus Christ
the Righteous One, 2 and he himself is the atoning sacrifice for
our sins, and not only for our sins but also for the whole world.

REFLECT

What does it mean to "walk in the light" (1:7)? What does it mean to walk in darkness? Why is it important for us to walk in the light as followers of Jesus?

KEEPING GOD'S COMMANDMENTS

3 Now by this we know that we have come to know God: if we
keep his commandments. 4 The one who says "I have come to
know God" and yet does not keep his commandments is a liar,
and the truth is not in such a person. 5 But whoever obeys his
word, truly in this person the love of God has been perfected. By
this we know that we are in him. 6 The one who says he resides
in God ought himself to walk just as Jesus walked.

7 Dear friends, I am not writing a new commandment to you,
but an old commandment which you have had from the beginning. The old commandment is the word that you have already
heard. 8 On the other hand, I am writing a new commandment
to you which is true in him and in you, because the darkness is
passing away and the true light is already shining. 9 The one who
says he is in the light but still hates his fellow Christian is still in
the darkness. 10 The one who loves his fellow Christian resides in
the light, and there is no cause for stumbling in him. 11 But the
one who hates his fellow Christian is in the darkness, walks in
the darkness, and does not know where he is going, because the
darkness has blinded his eyes.

WORDS OF REASSURANCE

12 I am writing to you, little children, that your sins have been
forgiven because of his name. 13 I am writing to you, fathers, that
you have known him who has been from the beginning. I am

writing to you, young people, that you have conquered the evil
one. 14 I have written to you, children, that you have known the
Father. I have written to you, fathers, that you have known him
who has been from the beginning. I have written to you, young
people, that you are strong, and the word of God resides in you,
and you have conquered the evil one.
15 Do not love the world or the things in the world. If anyone
loves the world, the love of the Father is not in him, 16 because
all that is in the world (the desire of the flesh and the desire of
the eyes and the arrogance produced by material possessions)
is not from the Father, but is from the world. 17 And the world is
passing away with all its desires, but the person who does the
will of God remains forever.

REFLECT

How can you guard yourself against loving the world?

WARNING ABOUT FALSE TEACHERS

18 Children, it is the last hour, and just as you heard that the antichrist is coming, so now many antichrists have appeared. We
know from this that it is the last hour. 19 They went out from
us, but they did not really belong to us, because if they had belonged to us, they would have remained with us. But they went
out from us to demonstrate that all of them do not belong to us.
20 Nevertheless you have an anointing from the Holy One, and
you all know. 21 I have not written to you that you do not know
the truth, but that you do know it, and that no lie is of the truth.
22 Who is the liar but the person who denies that Jesus is the
Christ ? This one is the antichrist: the person who denies the
Father and the Son. 23 Everyone who denies the Son does not
have the Father either. The person who confesses the Son has
the Father also.
24 As for you, what you have heard from the beginning must
remain in you. If what you heard from the beginning remains in
you, you also will remain in the Son and in the Father. 25 Now this
is the promise that he himself made to us: eternal life. 26 These
things I have written to you about those who are trying to deceive you.
27 Now as for you, the anointing that you received from him
resides in you, and you have no need for anyone to teach you.
But as his anointing teaches you about all things, it is true and
is not a lie. Just as it has taught you, you reside in him.

CHILDREN OF GOD

28 And now, little children, remain in him, so that when he appears we may have confidence and not shrink away from him in
shame when he comes back. 29 If you know that he is righteous,
you also know that everyone who practices righteousness has
been fathered by him.
3 (See what sort of love the Father has given to us: that we
should be called God's children—and indeed we are! For this
reason the world does not know us: because it did not know
him. 2 Dear friends, we are God's children now, and what we will
be has not yet been revealed. We know that whenever it is revealed we will be like him, because we will see him just as he is.
3 And everyone who has this hope focused on him purifies himself, just as Jesus is pure).

LOVE TO GROW

CHILDREN OF GOD

1 JOHN 3:1

Imagine a group of parents watching their children play at the playground. Eventually they engage in conversation, and it isn't long before they ask about each other's children. One points to a child and says, "That little girl in the blue dress—she is mine."

In those few words, identity is established. The parent has made clear she has a close eye on her child, watching over her as she goes about her life, and her daughter carries the assurance of whom she belongs to, knowing she is loved, seen, heard, and protected by her parent.

Loving parents watch over their children, caring for and loving them and encouraging them to walk in courage, faith, and confidence. Our heavenly Father does the same with us. He is quick to call us His children.

He knows we attempt to place our identity in all types of things, so He provides us with an identity in Him. He is our good Father.

As we encounter the great love we've been given by our heavenly Father and learn He loved us so much He sent His Son to be the Savior of the world, we also learn how to live out a life of love for others. The apostle John called us "God's children" (1 John 3:1), not so we can look down on others or judge those who don't yet know Him, but so we can look more and more like Him. Our lives become an inviting display that draws people to the love of the Father.

As we love others the way He loved us, His Spirit abiding in us gives us full assurance we belong to Him and His love is perfected in us. We can boldly call on Him as a Father who wants to meet our every need according to His will.

When the Lord looks over the earth, He sees you and says, "That's my child. That one is mine." We belong to the Lord, and we are loved with a perfect love by a perfect Father. Out of that love, we too have the freedom to love others with the love of God.

4 Everyone who practices sin also practices lawlessness; indeed, sin is lawlessness. 5 And you know that Jesus was revealed to take away sins, and in him there is no sin. 6 Everyone who resides in him does not sin; everyone who sins has neither seen him nor known him. 7 Little children, let no one deceive you: The one who practices righteousness is righteous, just as Jesus is righteous. 8 The one who practices sin is of the devil, because the devil has been sinning from the beginning. For this purpose the Son of God was revealed: to destroy the works of the devil. 9 Everyone who has been fathered by God does not practice sin, because God's seed resides in him, and thus he is not able to sin, because he has been fathered by God. 10 By this the children of God and the children of the devil are revealed: Everyone who does not practice righteousness—the one who does not love his fellow Christian—is not of God.

GOD IS LOVE, SO WE MUST LOVE ONE ANOTHER

11 For this is the gospel message that you have heard from the beginning: that we should love one another, 12 not like Cain who was of the evil one and brutally murdered his brother. And why did he murder him? Because his deeds were evil, but his brother's were righteous.

13 Therefore do not be surprised, brothers and sisters, if the world hates you. 14 We know that we have crossed over from death to life because we love our fellow Christians. The one who does not love remains in death. 15 Everyone who hates his fellow Christian is a murderer, and you know that no murderer has eternal life residing in him. 16 We have come to know love by this: that Jesus laid down his life for us; thus we ought to lay down our lives for our fellow Christians. 17 But whoever has the world's possessions and sees his fellow Christian in need and shuts off his compassion against him, how can the love of God reside in such a person?

18 Little children, let us not love with word or with tongue but in deed and truth. 19 And by this we will know that we are of the truth and will convince our conscience in his presence, 20 that if our conscience condemns us, that God is greater than our conscience and knows all things. 21 Dear friends, if our conscience does not condemn us, we have confidence in the presence of God, 22 and whatever we ask we receive from him, because we keep his commandments and do the things that are pleasing to him. 23 Now this is his commandment: that we believe in the name of his Son Jesus Christ and love one another, just as he gave us the commandment. 24 And the person who keeps his commandments resides in God, and God in him. Now by this we know that God resides in us: by the Spirit he has given us.

CHALLENGE

How does our conscience condemn us? What does Romans 8:1 say about this?

TESTING THE SPIRITS

4 Dear friends, do not believe every spirit, but test the spirits to determine if they are from God, because many false prophets have gone out into the world. 2 By this you know the Spirit of God: Every spirit that confesses Jesus as the Christ who has come in the flesh is from God, 3 but every spirit that refuses to confess Jesus, that spirit is not from God, and this is the spirit

of the antichrist, which you have heard is coming, and now is
already in the world.
4 You are from God, little children, and have conquered them,
because the one who is in you is greater than the one who is in
the world. 5 They are from the world; therefore they speak from
the world's perspective and the world listens to them. 6 We are
from God; the person who knows God listens to us, but whoever
is not from God does not listen to us. By this we know the Spirit
of truth and the spirit of deceit.

GOD IS LOVE

7 Dear friends, let us love one another, because love is from God,
and everyone who loves has been fathered by God and knows
God. 8 The person who does not love does not know God, because
God is love. 9 By this the love of God is revealed in us: that God
has sent his one and only Son into the world so that we may
live through him. 10 In this is love: not that we have loved God,
but that he loved us and sent his Son to be the atoning sacrifice for our sins.
11 Dear friends, if God so loved us, then we also ought to love
one another. 12 No one has seen God at any time. If we love one
another, God resides in us, and his love is perfected in us. 13 By
this we know that we reside in God and he in us: in that he has
given us of his Spirit. 14 And we have seen and testify that the
Father has sent the Son to be the Savior of the world.
15 If anyone confesses that Jesus is the Son of God, God resides
in him and he in God. 16 And we have come to know and to believe the love that God has in us. God is love, and the one who
resides in love resides in God, and God resides in him. 17 By this
love is perfected with us, so that we may have confidence in the
day of judgment, because just as Jesus is, so also are we in this
world. 18 There is no fear in love, but perfect love drives out fear,
because fear has to do with punishment. The one who fears punishment has not been perfected in love. 19 We love because he
loved us first.
20 If anyone says "I love God" and yet hates his fellow Christian,
he is a liar, because the one who does not love his fellow Christian whom he has seen cannot love God whom he has not seen.
21 And the commandment we have from him is this: that the one
5 who loves God should love his fellow Christian too. 1 Everyone who believes that Jesus is the Christ has been fathered
by God, and everyone who loves the father loves the child fathered by him. 2 By this we know that we love the children of
God: whenever we love God and obey his commandments. 3 For
this is the love of God: that we keep his commandments. And
his commandments do not weigh us down, 4 because everyone
who has been fathered by God conquers the world.

TESTIMONY ABOUT THE SON

This is the conquering power that has conquered the world: our
faith. 5 Now who is the person who has conquered the world except the one who believes that Jesus is the Son of God? 6 Jesus
Christ is the one who came by water and blood—not by the water only, but by the water and the blood. And the Spirit is the

REFLECT

How does perfect love drive out fear?

one who testifies, because the Spirit is the truth. 7 For there are
three that testify, 8 the Spirit and the water and the blood, and
these three are in agreement.
9 If we accept the testimony of men, the testimony of God is
greater, because this is the testimony of God that he has testified concerning his Son. 10 (The one who believes in the Son of
God has the testimony in himself; the one who does not believe
God has made him a liar, because he has not believed in the testimony that God has testified concerning his Son.) 11 And this is
the testimony: God has given us eternal life, and this life is in
his Son. 12 The one who has the Son has this eternal life; the one
who does not have the Son of God does not have this eternal life.

REFLECT

How do we know if we are praying according to God's will? Does He hear us if we do not pray according to His will?

ASSURANCE OF ETERNAL LIFE

13 I have written these things to you who believe in the name of
the Son of God so that you may know that you have eternal life.
14 And this is the confidence that we have before him: that
whenever we ask anything according to his will, he hears us.
15 And if we know that he hears us in regard to whatever we ask,
then we know that we have the requests that we have asked from
him. 16 If anyone sees his fellow Christian committing a sin not
resulting in death, he should ask, and God will grant life to the
person who commits a sin not resulting in death. There is a sin
resulting in death. I do not say that he should ask about that. 17 All
unrighteousness is sin, but there is sin not resulting in death.
18 We know that everyone fathered by God does not sin, but
God protects the one he has fathered, and the evil one cannot
touch him. 19 We know that we are from God, and the whole world
lies in the power of the evil one. 20 And we know that the Son
of God has come and has given us insight to know him who is
true, and we are in him who is true, in his Son Jesus Christ. This
one is the true God and eternal life. 21 Little children, guard yourselves from idols.

Now THIS
is Love
that WE
WALK
according
TO HIS
Commandments

MEMORY VERSE

Now this is love: that we walk according to his commandments.

2 John 6

2 John

INTRODUCTION

Walk in Love

The letter of 2 John combats false teachings about Jesus' deity and His humanity. The apostle John wrote to instruct the church about Docetism, which taught Christ did not actually come in the flesh but only appeared to have a body and only seemed to suffer and die on the cross. The false teachings of the first century attempted to deny Christ's significance and therefore the truth that salvation is found only through Him.

This short letter consists of a brief opening, a closing greeting, and an appeal to walk in the truth. John encouraged his readers to stay focused on the true teachings of Jesus and to continue to teach others. John also commanded the believers to walk in love.

The author of 2 John is widely accepted as John the beloved apostle, who also wrote the Gospel of John and the letters of 1 and 3 John. After Paul and Peter were martyred in approximately A.D. 67, John moved to Ephesus. Many scholars date John's Gospel and his three letters to sometime after the destruction of Jerusalem in A.D. 70 and before John's exile on the island of Patmos in A.D. 95.

The Book of 2 John challenges us in our understanding of Christ as John reminds us to be aware of false doctrine that can easily slip into our belief system. As we seek to love God greatly, we learn more about the character of God. Allowing false doctrines to work their way into our minds and hearts changes our understanding of who Christ is and of His incredible saving work. As we read 2 John, let's be encouraged to remain faithful to the truth.

Switzerland

OFFICIAL LANGUAGES
French, German, Italian, and Romansh
POPULATION
8,526,000
UNREACHED POPULATION
231,000
PROFESSING CHRISTIANS
76.5%

Anita's Home

Say a Prayer Today

Pray the church in Switzerland would explode through the freedom they have to practice their faith. Pray the believers in Switzerland would share their faith and God would open the hearts of those who do not yet know Him.

HISTORY BIT

Freedom of religion has been a basic constitutional right in Switzerland since 1874. Many influential church leaders in the Protestant Reformation called Switzerland home, such as John Calvin, Huldrych Zwingli, and Heinrich Bullinger.*

Source Information:
https://joshuaproject.net/countries/SZ
*David B. Barrett, World Christian Encyclopedia, Switzerland (New York, NY: Oxford University Press, 1982), 651–652.

ANITA'S STORY

Walking in God's love is a truth that has been powerfully displayed in my life. In my career at the United Nations, I changed jobs often. Each time, I had to readjust to a new team, and each time it was challenging.

When I joined the Human Resources team, I had to ask for help often, as I did not have a lot of experience in that field. One time I sought advice from a senior colleague. She lost her temper with me, and I was shocked at her immediate reaction. I was afraid to approach her again and didn't know how to respond. Instead of acting harshly to her, I started to pray for her, asking God to bless her.

On my last day of work, I went to a shop to buy flowers for my supervisor. I felt prompted by the Holy Spirit to buy another bouquet for the colleague who refused to help me.

I decided to intentionally treat her with God's love, despite her behavior. To my surprise, she felt so touched by my kindness her attitude changed completely. When I told her I had to resign, she accompanied me to speak to my supervisor to offer moral support and comfort. She showed me so much care in that small action. I will always remember the impact of a small act of love.

To walk in love is a choice we all have to make, regardless of our circumstances. This truth has changed my life because I learned it bears much fruit. We must choose to think, speak, and act with the compassion, kindness, and grace of Christ. This has given me a sense of freedom, as we do not need to be victims of people's reactions. Instead, we can continue to extend love to others, bless those around us, and trust God. May we all, as believers and followers of Christ, walk in love and unity with one another.

4 WEEK READING PLAN

LOVE HIS WORD

	MONDAY	TUESDAY	WEDNESDAY	THURSDAY	FRIDAY
1	1 John 1:1-4	1 John 1:5—2:2	1 John 2:3-11	1 John 2:12-17	1 John 2:18-27
	SOAP 1 John 1:4	SOAP 1 John 1:9	SOAP 1 John 2:3-6	SOAP 1 John 2:15-16	SOAP 1 John 2:25
2	1 John 2:28—3:10	1 John 3:11-17	1 John 3:18-24	1 John 4:1-6	1 John 4:7-11
	SOAP 1 John 2:28-29	SOAP 1 John 3:16-17	SOAP 1 John 3:19-20	SOAP 1 John 4:4-5	SOAP 1 John 4:10
3	1 John 4:12-19	1 John 4:20—5:4	1 John 5:5-12	1 John 5:13-21	2 John 1-4
	SOAP 1 John 4:16	SOAP 1 John 5:3	SOAP 1 John 5:11-12	SOAP 1 John 5:14-15	SOAP 2 John 4
4	2 John 5-8	2 John 9-13	3 John 1-4	3 John 5-8	3 John 9-15
	SOAP 2 John 6	SOAP 2 John 12	SOAP 3 John 4	SOAP 3 John 8	SOAP 3 John 11

INTRODUCTION AND THANKSGIVING

1 From the elder, to an elect lady and her children, whom I love
in truth (and not I alone, but also all those who know the truth),
2 because of the truth that resides in us and will be with us forever. 3 Grace, mercy, and peace will be with us from God the Father and from Jesus Christ the Son of the Father, in truth and
love.

4 I rejoiced greatly because I have found some of your children
living according to the truth, just as the Father commanded us.

WARNING AGAINST FALSE TEACHERS

5 But now I ask you, lady (not as if I were writing a new commandment to you, but the one we have had from the beginning), that
we love one another. 6 (Now this is love: that we walk according
to his commandments.) This is the commandment, just as you
have heard from the beginning; thus you should walk in it. 7 For
many deceivers have gone out into the world, people who do
not confess Jesus as Christ coming in the flesh. This person is
the deceiver and the antichrist! 8 Watch out, so that you do not
lose the things we have worked for, but receive a full reward.

9 Everyone who goes on ahead and does not remain in the
teaching of Christ does not have God. The one who remains in
this teaching has both the Father and the Son. 10 If anyone comes
to you and does not bring this teaching, do not receive him into
your house and do not give him any greeting, 11 because the person who gives him a greeting shares in his evil deeds.

CONCLUSION

12 Though I have many other things to write to you, I do not want
to do so with paper and ink, but I hope to come visit you and
speak face to face, so that our joy may be complete.
13 The children of your elect sister greet you.

REFLECT

How does following God's commands display love? How do we walk in love and follow God's commands?

SPEAKING THE TRUTH IN LOVE

2 JOHN

I should have said something.

My friend's words ran counter to what I knew to be true and the convictions we both shared. I said nothing in an effort to avoid offending her. I chose love over truth. The problem is that love without truth isn't love at all.

As Christians, we often talk about the importance of speaking the truth in love. In reality, most of us are drawn to either truth or love as our default position. We are either prone to speak to correct without connection or compassion, or we pursue love without the power to set boundaries to keep the peace. Love and truth are interdependent—incomplete without the other. Neither the law nor our loving feelings in isolation are enough to keep us walking in the ways of Christ.

In his short letter to the early believers, John encouraged his congregation to respond to one another in love and truth by pursuing both in all of their interactions.

We are wise to consider the ways we entertain falsehood. We may be prone to forego our convictions in the name of being nice. We might remain silent to keep the peace. Often, we would rather make people feel good about staying where they are spiritually and emotionally instead of challenging one another toward growth and change.

On the other hand, if we pursue truth without love, we will likely prioritize our need to be right over the health of the relationship. Our correction will be apt to fall flat in the absence of any connection or compassion. Often, we will fail to earn the right to be heard with truth as our solitary aim.

Jesus was the perfect intersection of love and truth.

He spoke directly to the gravity of our sin and brokenness, yet looked at people with great compassion, ultimately laying down His own life in love for the sake of truth. We can't receive this love of Jesus without being truthful about our need for a savior. When we recognize we need Jesus, not only for our salvation but in every moment of our lives, we will lean on His example of truth and love and learn to live lives that look more like His.

I have
No greater joy
than this:
To hear
that my children
are living
according to
the TRUTH

MEMORY VERSE

I have no greater joy than this: to hear that my children are living according to the truth.

3 John 4

3 John

INTRODUCTION

Live in Truth

John's third letter, though brief, contains a significant amount of instruction and encouragement for Gaius, the letter's recipient. Diotrephes, a leader of a local church, had taken control and begun prohibiting others from attending his church, driving away members who helped one another. His actions showed his moral failure as he violated Christ's command to love his fellow believers. John offered words of encouragement to Gaius.

In this short letter, John described Gaius's responsibility to support his fellow believers. Even in the midst of opposition, Gaius was to faithfully encourage the body and build up the believers in the truth of Christ. John directed Gaius to imitate what was good and flee from what was evil.

The author of 3 John is widely accepted as John the beloved apostle, who also wrote the Gospel of John and the letters of 1 and 2 John. After Paul and Peter were martyred in about A.D. 67, John moved to Ephesus. Many scholars date John's Gospel and his three letters to sometime after the destruction of Jerusalem in A.D. 70 and before John's exile on the island of Patmos in A.D. 95.

Even in this short book, we can find instruction and encouragement to love God greatly. Gaius and the other members of the church were ministering for the sake of Christ. When Christ is our motivation, we can move forward and keep our work focused on Him. When selfish motives guide us, we can quickly end up like Diotrephes. As we minister to one another, let's keep Christ at the center of our hearts, minds, and missions.

United States of America

OFFICIAL LANGUAGE
English
POPULATION
326,302,000
UNREACHED POPULATION
4,827,000
PROFESSING CHRISTIANS
77.5%

Vanessa's Home

Say a Prayer Today

Pray for Vanessa, that she would continue to believe in and walk in the truth. Pray also for those to whom she ministers, that they would see the light of Christ shine through her life.

HISTORY BIT

Between 1829 and 1831 the American Bible Society printed and distributed over one million copies of the Bible. Together with the American Tract Society, the American Bible Society worked hard to provide Christian literature to unreached Americans.*

Source Information:
https://joshuaproject.net/countries/US
*Mark A. Noll, A History of Christianity in the United States and Canada (Grand Rapids, MI: William B. Eerdman's Publishing Company, 1992), 227.

VANESSA'S STORY

I once lived with a constant critic in my head, insisting I was not enough. It told me I was not pretty enough, smart enough, kind enough, or fun enough. The voice made me doubt who I was. It even caused me to lose friendships because I believed those things about myself.

When I finally realized the voice affected both me and the people around me, I knew something had to change. I wanted to believe all God said about me, but it was easier to believe all the negative things. I tried to change who I was, I tried to stop the critical voice that constantly taunted me, but I failed time and time again.

Eventually, I realized I could not fix myself. I had to surrender. I had to stop trying and start trusting God. I surrendered my will and my control to the Lord. At that moment, in the presence of the Lord, I felt peace. I would no longer carry the burden of trying to fight the mean critic inside my head.

I've learned to replace the lies I have believed with the truth of Scripture, and in doing so, I have been transformed by the renewing of my mind. It's not easy, or even possible, to change in our own strength. It takes total surrender. But the life of freedom Christ died to give us is worth leaving everything in His nail-scarred hands.

Without Jesus and the truth of His Word we are easy targets for Satan's lies. When I think back on the phrase I repeatedly told myself, "I am not enough," I realize I wasn't wrong. I am not enough. The good news is the One who is in us is greater than the one who is in the world. With Jesus, I am more than enough.

4 WEEK READING PLAN

LOVE HIS WORD

MONDAY	TUESDAY	WEDNESDAY	THURSDAY	FRIDAY
1 John 1:1-4	1 John 1:5—2:2	1 John 2:3-11	1 John 2:12-17	1 John 2:18-27
SOAP 1 John 1:4	SOAP 1 John 1:9	SOAP 1 John 2:3-6	SOAP 1 John 2:15-16	SOAP 1 John 2:25
1 John 2:28—3:10	1 John 3:11-17	1 John 3:18-24	1 John 4:1-6	1 John 4:7-11
SOAP 1 John 2:28-29	SOAP 1 John 3:16-17	SOAP 1 John 3:19-20	SOAP 1 John 4:4-5	SOAP 1 John 4:10
1 John 4:12-19	1 John 4:20—5:4	1 John 5:5-12	1 John 5:13-21	2 John 1-4
SOAP 1 John 4:16	SOAP 1 John 5:3	SOAP 1 John 5:11-12	SOAP 1 John 5:14-15	SOAP 2 John 4
2 John 5-8	2 John 9-13	3 John 1-4	3 John 5-8	3 John 9-15
SOAP 2 John 6	SOAP 2 John 12	SOAP 3 John 4	SOAP 3 John 8	SOAP 3 John 11

INTRODUCTION AND THANKSGIVING

1 From the elder, to Gaius my dear brother, whom I love in truth.
2 Dear friend, I pray that all may go well with you and that you
may be in good health, just as it is well with your soul. 3 For I
rejoiced greatly when the brothers came and testified to your
truth, just as you are living according to the truth.
4 I have no greater joy than this: to hear that my children are
living according to the truth.

THE CHARGE TO GAIUS

5 Dear friend, you demonstrate faithfulness by whatever you do
for the brothers (even though they are strangers). 6 They have
testified to your love before the church. You will do well to send
them on their way in a manner worthy of God. 7 For they have
gone forth on behalf of "The Name," accepting nothing from the
pagans. 8 Therefore we ought to support such people, so that we
become coworkers in cooperation with the truth.

DIOTREPHES THE TROUBLEMAKER

9 I wrote something to the church, but Diotrephes, who loves to
be first among them, does not acknowledge us. 10 Therefore, if I
come, I will call attention to the deeds he is doing—the bringing
of unjustified charges against us with evil words! And not being
content with that, he not only refuses to welcome the brothers
himself, but hinders the people who want to do so and throws
them out of the church! 11 Dear friend, do not imitate what is
bad but what is good. The one who does good is of God; the one
who does what is bad has not seen God.

WORTHY DEMETRIUS

12 Demetrius has been testified to by all, even by the truth itself.
We also testify to him, and you know that our testimony is true.

CONCLUSION

13 I have many things to write to you, but I do not wish to write
to you with pen and ink. 14 But I hope to see you right away, and
we will speak face to face. 15 Peace be with you. The friends here
greet you. Greet the friends there by name.

REFLECT

How do we imitate what is good? What can we do to ensure our lives are protected from evil influences so we do only what is good?

LOVE TO GROW

EVEN STRANGERS

3 JOHN

I watched from my place in the checkout line as a woman struggled to carry her grocery bags out of the store. She had a few bags in each arm and also tried to balance a case of bottled water on her hip. She was almost to the store exit when suddenly all of her bags crashed to the floor. Almost instantly another woman was on her hands and knees helping to pick up the spilled groceries. The women were strangers, brought together by a simple act of kindness. I was blessed to see their interaction.

Have you ever witnessed an act of kindness? Seeing others go out of their way to selflessly help, encourage, or bless other people can really renew your hope for humanity. It sets in motion a ripple effect, inspiring every person involved to continue to share kindness with others.

Faith can be like this. Witnessing someone's faith in God can stir up a renewing of our own faith. Our faith can spark, sharpen, and strengthen someone else's faith.

Dear friend, you demonstrate faithfulness by whatever you do for the brothers (even though they are strangers) (3 John 5).

In what ways can we demonstrate kindness in what we do for others, even strangers? When we go through our daily lives living this way, we reveal faithfulness to Jesus. People are watching, even strangers. Do they see our faith? Are we sharing our faith through lives marked by kindness?

God's blessings are multiplied when His love is illustrated in our lives. When strangers experience Jesus through us, it can set off a divine ripple that affects eternity.

Let's live our lives demonstrating our faithfulness to the Lord in all the kind things we do, even for strangers.

I now feel COMPELLED instead to write to encourage you to CONTEND EARNESTLY for the faith that was once for all entrusted to the Saints

MEMORY VERSE

. . . I now feel compelled instead to write to encourage you to contend earnestly for the faith that was once for all entrusted to the saints.

Jude 3

Jude

INTRODUCTION

Contend Earnestly for the Faith

This short epistle brings a poignant word about false teachers. The author appealed to his readers to defend the faith and grow in grace. His focus was on faith, believers in Christ, and God, not on the false teachers. Jude did not give instructions on how to deal with these false teachers. Instead, he explained how they were under the condemnation of God and how believers should behave as they lived out the faith.

The Book of Jude includes themes of error, judgment, and holiness. The writer explained the mistakes of the false teachings, the calling of Christians, the hope he had for his audience, and the coming downfall of the godless.

The author identified himself as Jude, and many scholars agree this Jude was the half brother of Jesus. The Book of Jude was likely written around A.D. 60–64, during Nero's reign as emperor of Rome. Jude was one of the last books to be included in the New Testament canon, added in A.D. 180.

The Book of Jude encourages believers to "maintain yourselves in the love of God, while anticipating the mercy of our Lord Jesus Christ that brings eternal life" (v. 21). By remaining in God's love, we can be sure of the mercy we have received in Jesus Christ, and we can be alert to false teachers who wish to pervert the gospel of grace. As we love God greatly, we remember His mercy, coming to us in our time of need and granting us salvation through His marvelous grace.

Canada

OFFICIAL LANGUAGE
English
POPULATION
37,315,000
UNREACHED POPULATION
1,954,000
PROFESSING CHRISTIANS
73.0%

Jennifer's Home

Say a Prayer Today

Pray for the believers in Canada, that they would continue their rich heritage of Christianity by passing it on to future generations.

HISTORY BIT

Christianity first reached the region of Canada around A.D. 1000 through travelers from Greenland.*

Source Information:
https://joshuaproject.net/countries/CA
*John Bowden, *A Chronology of World Christianity* (New York, NY: Continuum, 2007), 149.

JENNIFER'S STORY

"I now feel compelled instead to write to encourage you to contend earnestly for the faith that was once for all entrusted to the saints" (Jude 3).

Growing up on the west coast of Canada I lived with my family on a very small island. Neighbors could only call if they had small boats of their own. An older missionary couple lived in the harbor not far away, and for over twenty years my parents hosted them for a Tuesday night Bible study. The missionary couple would row over in their boat and, after we children had gone to bed, they would discuss what they had read in the Bible.

Lying in the dark, I overheard incredible stories of faith, works of God's power and goodness, and the many ways God displayed His faithfulness to His people. From the conviction of Daniel, to the suffering of Paul to the faithfulness of Abraham, I learned much about what a life of faith looked like as I eavesdropped on their discussions.

I am certain hearing those weekly muffled conversations of how Christians remained pure and upright, even when faced with threat of death, shaped my life as a child, then as a teenager, and eventually as an adult. I watched my parents and our neighbors live the faith they talked about. Amidst the difficulties of life, they contended earnestly for their faith, confident that God had entrusted them with a great gift. I am able to do the same as I follow their examples of faithfulness.

2 WEEK READING PLAN

LOVE HIS WORD

	MONDAY	TUESDAY	WEDNESDAY	THURSDAY	FRIDAY
1	Jude 1-2	Jude 3-4	Jude 5-7	Jude 8-10	Jude 11-13
	SOAP Jude 1-2	SOAP Jude 3-4	SOAP Jude 5-7	SOAP Jude 8-10	SOAP Jude 11-13
2	Jude 14-16	Jude 17-19	Jude 20-21	Jude 22-23	Jude 24-25
	SOAP Jude 14-16	SOAP Jude 17-19	SOAP Jude 20-21	SOAP Jude 22-23	SOAP Jude 24-25

SALUTATION

1 From Jude, a slave of Jesus Christ and brother of James, to those
who are called, wrapped in the love of God the Father and kept
for Jesus Christ. 2 May mercy, peace, and love be lavished on you!

CONDEMNATION OF THE FALSE TEACHERS

3 Dear friends, although I have been eager to write to you about
our common salvation, I now feel compelled instead to write to
encourage you to contend earnestly for the faith that was once
for all entrusted to the saints. 4 For certain men have secretly
slipped in among you—men who long ago were marked out for
the condemnation I am about to describe—ungodly men who
have turned the grace of our God into a license for evil and who
deny our only Master and Lord, Jesus Christ.
5 Now I desire to remind you (even though you have been fully
informed of these facts once for all) that Jesus, having saved the
people out of the land of Egypt, later destroyed those who did
not believe. 6 You also know that the angels who did not keep
within their proper domain but abandoned their own place of
residence, he has kept in eternal chains in utter darkness, locked
up for the judgment of the great Day. 7 So also Sodom and Gomorrah and the neighboring towns, since they indulged in sexual immorality and pursued unnatural desire in a way similar
to these angels, are now displayed as an example by suffering
the punishment of eternal fire.
8 Yet these men, as a result of their dreams, defile the flesh, reject authority, and insult the glorious ones. 9 But even when Michael the archangel was arguing with the devil and debating with
him concerning Moses' body, he did not dare to bring a slanderous judgment, but said, "May the Lord rebuke you!" 10 But these
men do not understand the things they slander, and they are
being destroyed by the very things that, like irrational animals,
they instinctively comprehend. 11 Woe to them! For they have
traveled down Cain's path, and because of greed have abandoned
themselves to Balaam's error; hence, they will certainly perish in
Korah's rebellion. 12 These men are dangerous reefs at your love
feasts, feasting without reverence, feeding only themselves. They
are waterless clouds, carried along by the winds; autumn trees
without fruit—twice dead, uprooted; 13 wild sea waves, spewing
out the foam of their shame; wayward stars for whom the utter
depths of eternal darkness have been reserved.
14 Now Enoch, the seventh in descent beginning with Adam,
even prophesied of them, saying, "Look! The Lord is coming with
thousands and thousands of his holy ones, 15 to execute judgment on all, and to convict every person of all their thoroughly
ungodly deeds that they have committed, and of all the harsh
words that ungodly sinners have spoken against him." 16 These
people are grumblers and fault-finders who go wherever their
desires lead them, and they give bombastic speeches, enchanting folks for their own gain.

EXHORTATION TO THE FAITHFUL

17 But you, dear friends—recall the predictions foretold by the
apostles of our Lord Jesus Christ. 18 For they said to you, "At the

CHALLENGE

What does 2 Timothy 4:3–4 warn us against? How can we guard our communities of faith against false teaching? What steps can you take today to ensure you stay committed to the truth of Scripture?

end of time there will come scoffers, propelled by their own
ungodly desires." 19 These people are divisive, worldly, devoid of
the Spirit. 20 But you, dear friends, by building yourselves up in
your most holy faith, by praying in the Holy Spirit, 21 maintain
yourselves in the love of God, while anticipating the mercy of
our Lord Jesus Christ that brings eternal life. 22 And have mercy
on those who waver; 23 save others by snatching them out of the
fire; have mercy on others, coupled with a fear of God, hating
even the clothes stained by the flesh.

FINAL BLESSING

24 Now to the one who is able to keep you from falling, and to
cause you to stand, rejoicing, without blemish before his glorious presence, 25 to the only God our Savior through Jesus Christ
our Lord, be glory, majesty, power, and authority, before all time,
and now, and for all eternity. Amen.

MERCY

JUDE 20–25

In the Gospel accounts of Jesus' ministry, many who encountered Him asked for mercy. Often these people were outcasts from society due to class or illness or deformity. What they had in common was the way they sought out the mercy of the Savior.

These people knew they had nothing to give Jesus. They approached Jesus because He alone could change their situation. They needed mercy because they deserved nothing and could offer nothing.

We are the same. He gives us abundant mercy anyway.

Jude exhorted believers in Christ to maintain themselves in God's love by "anticipating the mercy of our Lord Jesus Christ that brings eternal life" (Jude 21). He then encouraged believers to extend this same mercy to others.

The mercy of God brings us eternal life. Jesus grants us mercy as a gift, one we don't deserve. We anticipate mercy that He offers us by showing mercy to others.

When Jude wrote this letter, he specifically asked the believers to show mercy to those in the church who had wavered in their faith and fallen prey to false teaching. Jude did not tell the believers to allow others to remain in their sin; he said instead to call them back to the truth instead of cutting them off from the body. Those who had fallen didn't deserve mercy, but God asked those who remained to offer it anyway.

The mercy of God is overwhelming. It grants us eternal life. It keeps us from falling. More still, His mercy allows us to stand in His presence without being blemished or tainted by sin. His mercy transforms and brings life.

He chooses to have mercy on us. May we be followers of Christ who understand our position, humbly accept His mercy, and graciously extend mercy to others. We may be the instruments God chooses to display His mercy to a hurting and dying world.

THE One WHO
testifies
TO THESE THINGS
says, "Yes,
I AM COMING SOON!"
Amen!
Come, Lord Jesus!

MEMORY VERSE

The one who testifies to these things says, "Yes, I am coming soon!" Amen! Come, Lord Jesus! The grace of the Lord Jesus be with all.

Revelation 22:20–21

INTRODUCTION

The Victory of Christ

Though often viewed as a challenging book of prophecy, the Book of Revelation offers enormous comfort and encouragement to its readers, both original and modern. The original audience faced persecution, internal doctrinal issues, spiritual warfare, and spiritual apathy—things contemporary readers also confront. This book clarified the signs of the second coming of Christ and urged the early church members to continue in their faith.

The Book of Revelation begins with an introduction to the vision John received from the Lord (Rev 1). It then contains letters of exhortation to seven churches, giving them direction and insight on remaining steadfast (Rev 2–3). The next section of the book describes in detail the coming judgments of the last days (Rev 6–18). Finally, John described Jesus' second coming along with His victory and the glorification of the saints (Rev 19–22).

Revelation has long been attributed to the apostle John. The author wrote with prophetic authority, and John had close associations with the seven churches in Asia to whom the first sections of the book are addressed. John wrote the Book of Revelation sometime after his exile on the island of Patmos around A.D. 95.

While often hard to understand, Revelation challenges and encourages us to love God greatly. We see in the book Christ alone is worthy to open the seals of judgment. Christ alone is worthy of the praise and honor bestowed upon Him. With visions of His glory, the Book of Revelation reminds us of the majesty and righteousness of Christ. He is the only one worthy of our praise, and He alone holds the future.

Kyrgyzstan

OFFICIAL LANGUAGE
Kyrgyz and Russian
POPULATION
6,373,000
UNREACHED POPULATION
5,890,000
PROFESSING CHRISTIANS
4.3%

Renee's Home

Say a Prayer Today

Pray for the church in Kyrgyzstan to be strengthened as they face uncertainty and difficulty in a primarily Muslim nation.

HISTORY BIT

After becoming independent from the Soviet Union in 1991, Kyrgyzstan has remained a secular state. However, all religious groups in Kyrgyzstan, including Christians, have experienced some form of government scrutiny and regulation, including persecutions.*

Source Information:
https://joshuaproject.net/countries/KG
*Jason Mandryk, Operation World, 7th edition (Colorado Springs, CO: Biblica Publishing, 2010), 517.

LOVE YOUR NEIGHBOR

Her Journey

RENEE'S STORY

Our first morning in Bishkek, Kyrgyzstan, felt bleak; the difficulties of planting a church in this Muslim nation weighed heavily on us.

Things got worse. My dad complained about pain in his abdomen for some time before we rushed him to the hospital in town. We thought he had appendicitis. Our family was shocked to hear it was something much worse. He died less than a month later.

I fell to my knees the morning of his death desperate for a touch from the Lord. With great compassion, He comforted me. The Father brought to mind the memory of my dad's continual longing for heaven and his repeated saying, "Come, Lord Jesus!"

The hope of heaven and eternal life stirs me to keep going. However, when I was twelve, a few years before my dad went to be with the Lord, I decided to put my Bible on the shelf and live for myself. Two and a half years later, I realized how empty my life was without communion with God. He'd shown me His faithful love through the lives and love of my parents. Their faith was real and their lives revolved around the hope and importance of following Jesus as we pass through this world while we look forward to our eternal home.

I have seen different seasons in my own life, different experiences in different countries. The enemy knows how to get me down, and loneliness can engulf me quickly. When this happens, I find myself on my knees. In His grace, the Lord reminds me that we will one day soon be with Him for eternity. Amen! Come, Lord Jesus!

4 WEEK READING PLAN

LOVE HIS WORD

MONDAY	TUESDAY	WEDNESDAY	THURSDAY	FRIDAY
Revelation 1	Revelation 2	Revelation 3	Revelation 4	Revelation 5
SOAP Revelation 1:1-3	SOAP Revelation 2:25-26	SOAP Revelation 3:15-16	SOAP Revelation 4:11	SOAP Revelation 5:9-10
Revelation 6	Revelation 7	Revelation 8-9	Revelation 10	Revelation 11
SOAP Revelation 6:16-17	SOAP Revelation 7:11-12	SOAP Revelation 8:1-2	SOAP Revelation 10:5-7	SOAP Revelation 11:17-18
Revelation 12	Revelation 13	Revelation 14	Revelation 15	Revelation 16
SOAP Revelation 12:10	SOAP Revelation 13:11-12	SOAP Revelation 14:12-13	SOAP Revelation 15:3-4	SOAP Revelation 16:17-19
Revelation 17	Revelation 18:1—19:10	Revelation 19:11—20:15	Revelation 21:1—22:5	Revelation 22:6-21
SOAP Revelation 17:14	SOAP Revelation 19:6-8	SOAP Revelation 20:1-3	SOAP Revelation 22:3-5	SOAP Revelation 22:20-21

THE PROLOGUE

1 The revelation of Jesus Christ, which God gave him to show
his servants what must happen very soon. He made it clear
by sending his angel to his servant John, 2 who then testified to everything that he saw concerning the word of God
and the testimony about Jesus Christ. 3 Blessed is the one
who reads the words of this prophecy aloud, and blessed are
those who hear and obey the things written in it, because
the time is near!

4 From John, to the seven churches that are in the province
of Asia: Grace and peace to you from "he who is," and who was,
and who is still to come, and from the seven spirits who are before his throne, 5 and from Jesus Christ—the faithful witness, the
firstborn from among the dead, the ruler over the kings of the
earth. To the one who loves us and has set us free from our sins
at the cost of his own blood 6 and has appointed us as a kingdom,
as priests serving his God and Father—to him be the glory and
the power for ever and ever! Amen.

7 (Look! *He is returning with the clouds,*
and *every eye will see him,*
even those who pierced him,
and all the tribes on the earth will mourn because of him.
This will certainly come to pass! Amen.)

8 "I am the Alpha and the Omega," says the Lord God—the one
who is, and who was, and who is still to come—the All-Powerful!

9 I, John, your brother and the one who shares with you in the
persecution, kingdom, and endurance that are in Jesus, was on
the island called Patmos because of the word of God and the
testimony about Jesus. 10 I was in the Spirit on the Lord's Day
when I heard behind me a loud voice like a trumpet, 11 saying:
"Write in a book what you see and send it to the seven churches—to Ephesus, Smyrna, Pergamum, Thyatira, Sardis, Philadelphia, and Laodicea."

12 I turned to see whose voice was speaking to me, and when
I did so, I saw seven golden lampstands, 13 and in the midst of
the lampstands was one *like a son of man*. He was dressed in a
robe extending down to his feet and he wore a wide golden belt
around his chest. 14 His head and hair were as white as wool,
even as white as snow, and his eyes were like a fiery flame. 15 His
feet were like polished bronze refined in a furnace, and his
voice was like the roar of many waters. 16 He held seven stars
in his right hand, and a sharp double-edged sword extended
out of his mouth. His face shone like the sun shining at full
strength. 17 When I saw him I fell down at his feet as though I
were dead, but he placed his right hand on me and said: "Do not
be afraid! I am the first and the last, 18 and the one who lives!
I was dead, but look, now I am alive—forever and ever—and I
hold the keys of death and of Hades! 19 Therefore write what
you saw, what is, and what will be after these things. 20 The
mystery of the seven stars that you saw in my right hand and
the seven golden lampstands is this: The seven stars are the
angels of the seven churches and the seven lampstands are
the seven churches.

TO THE CHURCH IN EPHESUS

2 "To the angel of the church in Ephesus, write the following:

"This is the solemn pronouncement of the one who has a firm grasp on the seven stars in his right hand—the one who walks among the seven golden lampstands: 2 'I know your works as well as your labor and steadfast endurance, and that you cannot tolerate evil. You have even put to the test those who refer to themselves as apostles (but are not), and have discovered that they are false. 3 I am also aware that you have persisted steadfastly, endured much for the sake of my name, and have not grown weary. 4 But I have this against you: You have departed from your first love! 5 Therefore, remember from what high state you have fallen and repent! Do the deeds you did at the first; if not, I will come to you and remove your lampstand from its place—that is, if you do not repent. 6 But you do have this going for you: You hate what the Nicolaitans practice—practices I also hate. 7 The one who has an ear had better hear what the Spirit says to the churches. To the one who conquers, I will permit him to eat from the tree of life that is in the paradise of God.'

TO THE CHURCH IN SMYRNA

8 "To the angel of the church in Smyrna write the following:

"This is the solemn pronouncement of the one who is the first and the last, the one who was dead, but came to life: 9 'I know the distress you are suffering and your poverty (but you are rich). I also know the slander against you by those who call themselves Jews and really are not, but are a synagogue of Satan. 10 Do not be afraid of the things you are about to suffer. The devil is about to have some of you thrown into prison so you may be tested, and you will experience suffering for ten days. Remain faithful even to the point of death, and I will give you the crown that is life itself. 11 The one who has an ear had better hear what the Spirit says to the churches. The one who conquers will in no way be harmed by the second death.'

TO THE CHURCH IN PERGAMUM

12 "To the angel of the church in Pergamum write the following:

"This is the solemn pronouncement of the one who has the sharp double-edged sword: 13 'I know where you live—where Satan's throne is. Yet you continue to cling to my name and you have not denied your faith in me, even in the days of Antipas, my faithful witness, who was killed in your city where Satan lives. 14 But I have a few things against you: You have some people there who follow the teaching of Balaam, who instructed Balak to put a stumbling block before the people of Israel so they would eat food sacrificed to idols and commit sexual immorality. 15 In the same way, there are also some among you who follow the teaching of the Nicolaitans. 16 Therefore, repent! If not, I will come against you quickly and make war against those people with the sword of my mouth. 17 The one who has an ear had better hear what the Spirit says to the churches. To the one who conquers, I will give him some of the hidden manna, and I will give him a white stone, and on that stone will be written a new name that no one can understand except the one who receives it.'

REFLECT

What does it mean to be "faithful even to the point of death" (2:10)? How would you respond if you were faced with a decision to deny your faith or be killed?

LOSING YOUR FIRST LOVE

REVELATION 2:1–7

Revelation unveils God's plans for His church. In the first chapter we learn Jesus Christ revealed this prophetic letter through the apostle John. This letter circulated through the churches of the day and is preserved for our benefit almost two thousand years later.

Jesus gave messages for seven churches scattered across Asia Minor. In chapter 2 Jesus spoke directly to the church at Ephesus. First, Jesus commended those believers for some incredible things: laboring in the church, testing false apostles, and persevering through hardship.

However, the tone of the letter changes. Verse 4 says, "But I have this against you: You have departed from your first love!" Despite the Ephesians' great suffering and acts of diligent service, their works were no longer motivated by God's love.

What happened? Maybe busyness settled in and took the place of worship. Maybe they thought good works would please God. Maybe legalism replaced the grace of Jesus. Whatever it was, they forgot the heart of the gospel: God's love.

The Christian life is not about showing up to church every Sunday to serve coffee, avoiding cursing, or reading the Bible daily. All of these can be acts of obedience, but if they are not done in God's love they profit us nothing. Ultimately, God is not concerned with what we can do for Him. He wants us to abide in our relationship with Him.

The point of the Christian life is God Himself: to know Him and to experience a life deeply rooted within His love. It is out of this love that we serve Him.

Ask yourself: Do I really love God? Do I believe He is good? Do I trust Him? If the answer is no, the solution is not to work harder at believing. Instead, ask God to reveal more of Himself to you. Ask Him to correct your understanding of His character.

May our prayer today be the same as Paul's for the church of Ephesus: that we "will be able to comprehend with all the saints what is the breadth and length and height and depth, and thus to know the love of Christ that surpasses knowledge, so that [we] will be filled up to all the fullness of God" (Eph 3:18–19). May we be a church in which Jesus sees His love overflow.

TO THE CHURCH IN THYATIRA

18 "To the angel of the church in Thyatira write the following:
"This is the solemn pronouncement of the Son of God, the
one who has eyes like a fiery flame and whose feet are like polished bronze: 19 'I know your deeds: your love, faith, service, and
steadfast endurance. In fact, your more recent deeds are greater
than your earlier ones. 20 But I have this against you: You tolerate that woman Jezebel, who calls herself a prophetess, and by
her teaching deceives my servants to commit sexual immorality and to eat food sacrificed to idols. 21 I have given her time to
repent, but she is not willing to repent of her sexual immorality. 22 Look! I am throwing her onto a bed of violent illness, and
those who commit adultery with her into terrible suffering, unless they repent of her deeds. 23 Furthermore, I will strike her
followers with a deadly disease, and then all the churches will
know that I am the one who searches minds and hearts. I will
repay each one of you what your deeds deserve. 24 But to the rest
of you in Thyatira, all who do not hold to this teaching (who have
not learned the so-called "deep secrets of Satan"), to you I say:
I do not put any additional burden on you. 25 However, hold on
to what you have until I come. 26 And to the one who conquers
and who continues in my deeds until the end, I will give him authority over the nations—

27 ***he will rule them with an iron rod***
and like clay jars he will break them to pieces,

28 just as I have received the right to rule from my Father—and
I will give him the morning star. 29 The one who has an ear had
better hear what the Spirit says to the churches.'

TO THE CHURCH IN SARDIS

3 "To the angel of the church in Sardis write the following:
"This is the solemn pronouncement of the one who holds
the seven spirits of God and the seven stars: 'I know your deeds,
that you have a reputation that you are alive, but in reality you
are dead. 2 Wake up then, and strengthen what remains that was
about to die, because I have not found your deeds complete in
the sight of my God. 3 Therefore, remember what you received
and heard, and obey it, and repent. If you do not wake up, I will
come like a thief, and you will never know at what hour I will
come against you. 4 But you have a few individuals in Sardis
who have not stained their clothes, and they will walk with me
dressed in white, because they are worthy. 5 The one who conquers will be dressed like them in white clothing, and I will never
erase his name from the book of life, but will declare his name
before my Father and before his angels. 6 The one who has an ear
had better hear what the Spirit says to the churches.'

REFLECT

What does God promise to do with those who honor His name in life?

TO THE CHURCH IN PHILADELPHIA

7 "To the angel of the church in Philadelphia write the following:
"This is the solemn pronouncement of the Holy One, the True
One, who holds the key of David, who opens doors no one can
shut, and shuts doors no one can open: 8 'I know your deeds.
(Look! I have put in front of you an open door that no one can

shut.) I know that you have little strength, but you have obeyed
my word and have not denied my name. 9 Listen! I am going to
make those people from the synagogue of Satan—who say they
are Jews yet are not, but are lying—Look, I will make them come
and bow down at your feet and acknowledge that I have loved
you. 10 Because you have kept my admonition to endure steadfastly, I will also keep you from the hour of testing that is about
to come on the whole world to test those who live on the earth.
11 I am coming soon. Hold on to what you have so that no one can
take away your crown. 12 The one who conquers I will make a pillar in the temple of my God, and he will never depart from it. I
will write on him the name of my God and the name of the city
of my God (the new Jerusalem that comes down out of heaven
from my God), and my new name as well. 13 The one who has an
ear had better hear what the Spirit says to the churches.'

TO THE CHURCH IN LAODICEA

14 "To the angel of the church in Laodicea write the following:
"This is the solemn pronouncement of the Amen, the faithful and true witness, the originator of God's creation: 15 'I know
your deeds, that you are neither cold nor hot. I wish you were
either cold or hot! 16 So because you are lukewarm, and neither
hot nor cold, I am going to vomit you out of my mouth! 17 Because you say, "I am rich and have acquired great wealth, and
need nothing," but do not realize that you are wretched, pitiful, poor, blind, and naked, 18 take my advice and buy gold from
me refined by fire so you can become rich! Buy from me white
clothing so you can be clothed and your shameful nakedness
will not be exposed, and buy eye salve to put on your eyes so you
can see! 19 All those I love, I rebuke and discipline. So be earnest
and repent! 20 Listen! I am standing at the door and knocking!
If anyone hears my voice and opens the door I will come into
his home and share a meal with him, and he with me. 21 I will
grant the one who conquers permission to sit with me on my
throne, just as I too conquered and sat down with my Father
on his throne. 22 The one who has an ear had better hear what
the Spirit says to the churches.'"

THE AMAZING SCENE IN HEAVEN

4 After these things I looked, and there was a door standing
open in heaven! And the first voice I had heard speaking to
me like a trumpet said: "Come up here so that I can show you
what must happen after these things." 2 Immediately I was in
the Spirit, and a throne was standing in heaven with someone
seated on it! 3 And the one seated on it was like jasper and carnelian in appearance, and a rainbow looking like it was made
of emerald encircled the throne. 4 In a circle around the throne
were twenty-four other thrones, and seated on those thrones
were twenty-four elders. They were dressed in white clothing and
had golden crowns on their heads. 5 From the throne came out
flashes of lightning and roaring and crashes of thunder. Seven
flaming torches, which are the seven spirits of God, were burning in front of the throne 6 and in front of the throne was something like a sea of glass, like crystal.

In the middle of the throne and around the throne were four
living creatures full of eyes in front and in back. 7 The first living
creature was like a lion, the second creature like an ox, the third
creature had a face like a man's, and the fourth creature looked
like an eagle flying. 8 Each one of the four living creatures had
six wings and was full of eyes all around and inside. They never
rest day or night, saying:

"***Holy Holy Holy is the Lord God, the All-Powerful,***
Who was and who is, and who is still to come!"

9 And whenever the living creatures give glory, honor, and
thanks to the one who sits on the throne, who lives forever and
ever, 10 the twenty-four elders throw themselves to the ground
before the one who sits on the throne and worship the one who
lives forever and ever, and they offer their crowns before his
throne, saying:

11 "You are worthy, our Lord and God,
to receive glory and honor and power,
since you created all things,
and because of your will they existed and were created!"

THE OPENING OF THE SCROLL

5 Then I saw in the right hand of the one who was seated on
the throne a scroll written on the front and back and sealed
with seven seals. 2 And I saw a powerful angel proclaiming in a
loud voice: "Who is worthy to open the scroll and to break its
seals?" 3 But no one in heaven or on earth or under the earth
was able to open the scroll or look into it. 4 So I began weeping bitterly because no one was found who was worthy to open
the scroll or to look into it. 5 Then one of the elders said to me,
"Stop weeping! Look, the Lion of the tribe of Judah, the root
of David, has conquered; thus he can open the scroll and its
seven seals."

6 Then I saw standing in the middle of the throne and of the
four living creatures, and in the middle of the elders, a Lamb that
appeared to have been killed. He had seven horns and seven eyes,
which are the seven spirits of God sent out into all the earth.
7 Then he came and took the scroll from the right hand of the
one who was seated on the throne, 8 and when he had taken the
scroll, the four living creatures and the twenty-four elders threw
themselves to the ground before the Lamb. Each of them had a
harp and golden bowls full of incense (which are the prayers of
the saints). 9 They were singing a new song:

"You are worthy to take the scroll
and to open its seals
because you were killed,
and at the cost of your own blood you
have purchased for God
persons from every tribe, language, people, and nation.
10 You have appointed them as a kingdom and priests to
serve our God, and they will reign on the earth."

11 Then I looked and heard the voice of many angels in a circle
around the throne, as well as the living creatures and the elders.

REFLECT

Why is Christ the only One worthy to open the scroll?

Their number was ten thousand times ten thousand—thousands
times thousands—12 all of whom were singing in a loud voice:
"Worthy is the lamb who was killed
to receive power and wealth
and wisdom and might
and honor and glory and praise!"

13 Then I heard every creature—in heaven, on earth, under the
earth, in the sea, and all that is in them—singing:
"To the one seated on the throne and to the Lamb
be praise, honor, glory, and ruling power forever and ever!"

14 And the four living creatures were saying "Amen," and the
elders threw themselves to the ground and worshiped.

THE SEVEN SEALS

6 I looked on when the Lamb opened one of the seven seals,
and I heard one of the four living creatures saying with a
thunderous voice, "Come!" 2 So I looked, and here came a white
horse! The one who rode it had a bow, and he was given a crown,
and as a conqueror he rode out to conquer.
3 Then when the Lamb opened the second seal, I heard the second living creature saying, "Come!" 4 And another horse, fiery
red, came out, and the one who rode it was granted permission
to take peace from the earth, so that people would butcher one
another, and he was given a huge sword.
5 Then when the Lamb opened the third seal I heard the third
living creature saying, "Come!" So I looked, and here came a black
horse! The one who rode it had a balance scale in his hand. 6 Then
I heard something like a voice from among the four living creatures saying, "A quart of wheat will cost a day's pay and three
quarts of barley will cost a day's pay. But do not damage the olive oil and the wine!"
7 Then when the Lamb opened the fourth seal I heard the voice
of the fourth living creature saying, "Come!" 8 So I looked and
here came a pale green horse! The name of the one who rode it
was Death, and Hades followed right behind. They were given authority over a fourth of the earth, to kill its population with the
sword, famine, and disease, and by the wild animals of the earth.
9 Now when the Lamb opened the fifth seal, I saw under the
altar the souls of those who had been violently killed because
of the word of God and because of the testimony they had given.
10 They cried out with a loud voice, "How long, Sovereign Master,
holy and true, before you judge those who live on the earth and
avenge our blood?" 11 Each of them was given a long white robe
and they were told to rest for a little longer, until the full number was reached of both their fellow servants and their brothers
who were going to be killed just as they had been.
12 Then I looked when the Lamb opened the sixth seal, and a
huge earthquake took place; the sun became as black as sackcloth made of hair, and the full moon became blood red; 13 and the
stars in the sky fell to the earth like a fig tree dropping its unripe
figs when shaken by a fierce wind. 14 The sky was split apart like a
scroll being rolled up, and every mountain and island was moved

from its place. 15 Then the kings of the earth, the very important
people, the generals, the rich, the powerful, and everyone, slave
and free, hid themselves in the caves and among the rocks of
the mountains. 16 They said to the mountains and to the rocks,
"Fall on us and hide us from the face of the one who is seated on
the throne and from the wrath of the Lamb, 17 because the great
day of their wrath has come, and who is able to withstand it?"

THE SEALING OF THE 144,000

7 After this I saw four angels standing at the four corners of the
earth, holding back the four winds of the earth so no wind
could blow on the earth, on the sea, or on any tree. 2 Then I saw
another angel ascending from the east, who had the seal of the
living God. He shouted out with a loud voice to the four angels
who had been given permission to damage the earth and the
sea: 3 "Do not damage the earth or the sea or the trees until we
have put a seal on the foreheads of the servants of our God."
4 Now I heard the number of those who were marked with the
seal, 144,000, sealed from all the tribes of the people of Israel:

5 From the tribe of Judah, twelve thousand were sealed,
from the tribe of Reuben, twelve thousand,
from the tribe of Gad, twelve thousand,
6 from the tribe of Asher, twelve thousand,
from the tribe of Naphtali, twelve thousand,
from the tribe of Manasseh, twelve thousand,
7 from the tribe of Simeon, twelve thousand,
from the tribe of Levi, twelve thousand,
from the tribe of Issachar, twelve thousand,
8 from the tribe of Zebulun, twelve thousand,
from the tribe of Joseph, twelve thousand,
from the tribe of Benjamin, twelve thousand were sealed.

9 After these things I looked, and here was an enormous crowd
that no one could count, made up of persons from every nation, tribe, people, and language, standing before the throne
and before the Lamb dressed in long white robes, and with palm
branches in their hands. 10 They were shouting out in a loud voice,

"Salvation belongs to our God, who is seated
on the throne, and to the Lamb!"

11 And all the angels stood there in a circle around the throne
and around the elders and the four living creatures, and they
threw themselves down with their faces to the ground before
the throne and worshiped God, 12 saying,

"Amen! Praise and glory,
and wisdom and thanksgiving,
and honor and power and strength
be to our God for ever and ever. Amen!"

13 Then one of the elders asked me, "These dressed in long white
robes—who are they and where have they come from?" 14 So I
said to him, "My lord, you know the answer." Then he said to
me, "These are the ones who have come out of the great tribulation. They have washed their robes and made them white

in the blood of the Lamb! 15 For this reason they are before the
throne of God, and they serve him day and night in his temple,
and the one seated on the throne will shelter them. 16 *They will
never go hungry or be thirsty again, and the sun will not beat down
on them, nor any burning heat,* 17 because the Lamb in the middle of the throne will shepherd them and lead them to springs
of living water, *and God will wipe away every tear from their eyes.*"

THE SEVENTH SEAL

8 Now when the Lamb opened the seventh seal there was silence in heaven for about half an hour. 2 Then I saw the seven
angels who stand before God, and seven trumpets were given to
them. 3 Another angel holding a golden censer came and was stationed at the altar. A large amount of incense was given to him
to offer up, with the prayers of all the saints, on the golden altar
that is before the throne. 4 The smoke coming from the incense,
along with the prayers of the saints, ascended before God from
the angel's hand. 5 Then the angel took the censer, filled it with fire
from the altar, and threw it on the earth, and there were crashes
of thunder, roaring, flashes of lightning, and an earthquake.

6 Now the seven angels holding the seven trumpets prepared
to blow them.

7 The first angel blew his trumpet, and there was hail and fire
mixed with blood, and it was thrown at the earth so that a third
of the earth was burned up, a third of the trees were burned up,
and all the green grass was burned up.

8 Then the second angel blew his trumpet, and something like
a great mountain of burning fire was thrown into the sea. A third
of the sea became blood, 9 and a third of the creatures living in
the sea died, and a third of the ships were completely destroyed.

10 Then the third angel blew his trumpet, and a huge star burning like a torch fell from the sky; it landed on a third of the rivers
and on the springs of water. 11 (Now the name of the star is Wormwood.) So a third of the waters became wormwood, and many
people died from these waters because they were poisoned.

12 Then the fourth angel blew his trumpet, and a third of the
sun was struck, and a third of the moon, and a third of the stars,
so that a third of them were darkened. And there was no light
for a third of the day and for a third of the night likewise. 13 Then
I looked, and I heard an eagle flying directly overhead, proclaiming with a loud voice, "Woe! Woe! Woe to those who live on the
earth because of the remaining sounds of the trumpets of the
three angels who are about to blow them!"

9 Then the fifth angel blew his trumpet, and I saw a star that
had fallen from the sky to the earth, and he was given the key
to the shaft of the abyss. 2 He opened the shaft of the abyss and
smoke rose out of it like smoke from a giant furnace. The sun
and the air were darkened with smoke from the shaft. 3 Then out
of the smoke came locusts onto the earth, and they were given
power like that of the scorpions of the earth. 4 They were told
not to damage the grass of the earth, or any green plant or tree,
but only those people who did not have the seal of God on their
forehead. 5 The locusts were not given permission to kill them,
but only to torture them for five months, and their torture was

like that of a scorpion when it stings a person. [6]In those days people will seek death, but will not be able to find it; they will long to die, but death will flee from them.

[7]Now the locusts looked like horses equipped for battle. On their heads were something like crowns similar to gold, and their faces looked like men's faces. [8]They had hair like women's hair, and their teeth were like lions' teeth. [9]They had breastplates like iron breastplates, and the sound of their wings was like the noise of many horse-drawn chariots charging into battle. [10]They have tails and stingers like scorpions, and their ability to injure people for five months is in their tails. [11]They have as king over them the angel of the abyss, whose name in Hebrew is *Abaddon*, and in Greek, *Apollyon*.

REFLECT

What do the promised judgments indicate about God's power? What do they reveal about God's righteousness?

[12]The first woe has passed, but two woes are still coming after these things!

[13]Then the sixth angel blew his trumpet, and I heard a single voice coming from the horns on the golden altar that is before God, [14]saying to the sixth angel, the one holding the trumpet, "Set free the four angels who are bound at the great river Euphrates!" [15]Then the four angels who had been prepared for this hour, day, month, and year were set free to kill a third of humanity. [16]The number of soldiers on horseback was 200,000,000; I heard their number. [17]Now this is what the horses and their riders looked like in my vision: The riders had breastplates that were fiery red, dark blue, and sulfurous yellow in color. The heads of the horses looked like lions' heads, and fire, smoke, and sulfur came out of their mouths. [18]A third of humanity was killed by these three plagues, that is, by the fire, the smoke, and the sulfur that came out of their mouths. [19]For the power of the horses resides in their mouths and in their tails, because their tails are like snakes, having heads that inflict injuries. [20]The rest of humanity, who had not been killed by these plagues, did not repent of the works of their hands, so that they did not stop worshiping demons and idols made of gold, silver, bronze, stone, and wood—idols that cannot see or hear or walk about. [21]Furthermore, they did not repent of their murders, of their magic spells, of their sexual immorality, or of their stealing.

THE ANGEL WITH THE LITTLE SCROLL

10 Then I saw another powerful angel descending from heaven, wrapped in a cloud, with a rainbow above his head; his face was like the sun and his legs were like pillars of fire. [2]He held in his hand a little scroll that was open, and he put his right foot on the sea and his left on the land. [3]Then he shouted in a loud voice like a lion roaring, and when he shouted, the seven thunders sounded their voices. [4]When the seven thunders spoke, I was preparing to write, but just then I heard a voice from heaven say, "Seal up what the seven thunders spoke and do not write it down." [5]Then the angel I saw standing on the sea and on the land raised his right hand to heaven [6]and swore by the one who lives forever and ever, who created heaven and what is in it, and the earth and what is in it, and the sea and what is in it, "There will be no more delay! [7]But in the days when the seventh angel is about to blow his trumpet, the mystery of God is completed,

just as he has proclaimed to his servants the prophets." 8 Then
the voice I had heard from heaven began to speak to me again,
"Go and take the open scroll in the hand of the angel who is
standing on the sea and on the land." 9 So I went to the angel
and asked him to give me the little scroll. He said to me, "Take
the scroll and eat it. It will make your stomach bitter, but it will
be as sweet as honey in your mouth." 10 So I took the little scroll
from the angel's hand and ate it, and it did taste as sweet as honey
in my mouth, but when I had eaten it, my stomach became bitter. 11 Then they told me: "You must prophesy again about many
peoples, nations, languages, and kings."

THE FATE OF THE TWO WITNESSES

11 Then a measuring rod like a staff was given to me, and I was
told, "Get up and measure the temple of God, and the altar,
and the ones who worship there. 2 But do not measure the outer
courtyard of the temple; leave it out, because it has been given
to the Gentiles, and they will trample on the holy city for forty-two months. 3 And I will grant my two witnesses authority to
prophesy for 1,260 days, dressed in sackcloth." 4 (These are the two
olive trees and the two lampstands that stand before the Lord
of the earth.) 5 If anyone wants to harm them, fire comes out of
their mouths and completely consumes their enemies. If anyone
wants to harm them, they must be killed this way. 6 These two have
the power to close up the sky so that it does not rain during the
time they are prophesying. They have power to turn the waters
to blood and to strike the earth with every kind of plague whenever they want. 7 When they have completed their testimony, the
beast that comes up from the abyss will make war on them and
conquer them and kill them. 8 Their corpses will lie in the street
of the great city that is symbolically called Sodom and Egypt,
where their Lord was also crucified. 9 For three and a half days
those from every people, tribe, nation, and language will look at
their corpses, because they will not permit them to be placed in
a tomb. 10 And those who live on the earth will rejoice over them
and celebrate, even sending gifts to each other, because these two
prophets had tormented those who live on the earth. 11 But after
three and a half days a breath of life from God entered them, and
they stood on their feet, and tremendous fear seized those who
were watching them. 12 Then they heard a loud voice from heaven
saying to them: "Come up here!" So the two prophets went up to
heaven in a cloud while their enemies stared at them. 13 Just then
a major earthquake took place and a tenth of the city collapsed;
seven thousand people were killed in the earthquake, and the rest
were terrified and gave glory to the God of heaven.
14 The second woe has come and gone; the third is coming quickly.

THE SEVENTH TRUMPET

15 Then the seventh angel blew his trumpet, and there were loud
voices in heaven saying:

"The kingdom of the world
has become the kingdom of our Lord
and of his Christ,
and he will reign for ever and ever."

16 Then the twenty-four elders who are seated on their thrones
before God threw themselves down with their faces to the
ground and worshiped God 17 with these words:

"We give you thanks, Lord God, the All-Powerful,
the one who is and who was,
because you have taken your great power
and begun to reign.
18 The nations were enraged,
but your wrath has come,
and the time has come for the dead to be judged,
and the time has come to give to your servants,
the prophets, their reward,
as well as to the saints
and to those who revere your name, both small and great,
and the time has come to destroy those
who destroy the earth."

19 Then the temple of God in heaven was opened and the ark
of his covenant was visible within his temple. And there were
flashes of lightning, roaring, crashes of thunder, an earthquake,
and a great hailstorm.

THE WOMAN, THE CHILD, AND THE DRAGON

12 Then a great sign appeared in heaven: a woman clothed
with the sun, and with the moon under her feet, and on
her head was a crown of twelve stars. 2 She was pregnant and
was screaming in labor pains, struggling to give birth. 3 Then
another sign appeared in heaven: a huge red dragon that had
seven heads and ten horns, and on its heads were seven diadem crowns. 4 Now the dragon's tail swept away a third of the
stars in heaven and hurled them to the earth. Then the dragon
stood before the woman who was about to give birth, so that he
might devour her child as soon as it was born. 5 So the woman
gave birth to a son, a male child, who is going *to rule over all the
nations with an iron rod*. Her child was suddenly caught up to
God and to his throne, 6 and she fled into the wilderness where
a place had been prepared for her by God, so she could be taken
care of for 1,260 days.

WAR IN HEAVEN

7 Then war broke out in heaven: Michael and his angels fought
against the dragon, and the dragon and his angels fought back.
8 But the dragon was not strong enough to prevail, so there was
no longer any place left in heaven for him and his angels. 9 So
that huge dragon—the ancient serpent, the one called the devil
and Satan, who deceives the whole world—was thrown down to
the earth, and his angels along with him. 10 Then I heard a loud
voice in heaven saying,

"The salvation and the power
and the kingdom of our God,
and the ruling authority of his Christ, have now come,
because the accuser of our brothers and sisters,
the one who accuses them day and night before our God,
has been thrown down.

COURAGEOUS FAITH

REVELATION 12:10–11

I was watching the television show *The Voice* one evening when these words from a coach to a contestant immediately convicted me: "You have to let your passion be greater than your fear."

I started thinking about what I am most passionate about: God and His kingdom. Then I began to realize how my fear of opposition sometimes keeps me from fully following Him.

How could I let fear interfere with my relationship with God? I am a seminary graduate, after all. How could I still get scared? The fact is, I'm afraid to take a stand for my faith. I'm especially fearful of facing opposition or of being judged because of my faith. Even though I am confident in my personal relationship with God, I often wonder how others will view me or the assumptions they may make about me if they know I am a Christian.

Can you relate? Has fear ever held you back? Have you failed to take a stand for your faith because you were afraid of opposition? Maybe that stand would have cost you socially, financially, or professionally. Maybe you were even in a situation where your life was in danger because of your faith.

Revelation 12 holds a challenge for those of us who struggle with fear. This chapter details an epic battle in which Satan is defeated. Satan is described in Revelation 12:10 as "the accuser of our brothers and sisters." These "brothers and sisters" describe Christians martyred for their faith. When describing them in Revelation 12:11, John, the author of Revelation, wrote

---

They did not love their lives so much that they were afraid to die.

They were bold and courageous. They valued their faith over everything else, even life itself. I am greatly inspired by them. They serve as a reminder to never become so fearful we compromise our obedience. After all, that coach was right: We have to let our passion overpower our fear.

11 But they overcame him
by the blood of the Lamb
and by the word of their testimony,
and they did not love their lives so much
that they were afraid to die.
12 Therefore you heavens rejoice, and
all who reside in them!
But woe to the earth and the sea
because the devil has come down to you!
He is filled with terrible anger,
for he knows that he only has a little time!"

13 Now when the dragon realized that he had been thrown
down to the earth, he pursued the woman who had given birth
to the male child. 14 But the woman was given the two wings of
a giant eagle so that she could fly out into the wilderness, to the
place God prepared for her, where she is taken care of—away from
the presence of the serpent—for a time, times, and half a time.
15 Then the serpent spouted water like a river out of his mouth
after the woman in an attempt to sweep her away by a flood,
16 but the earth came to her rescue; the ground opened up and
swallowed the river that the dragon had spewed from his mouth.
17 So the dragon became enraged at the woman and went away
to make war on the rest of her children, those who keep God's
commandments and hold to the testimony about Jesus. 18 And
the dragon stood on the sand of the seashore.

THE TWO BEASTS

13 Then I saw a beast coming up out of the sea. It had ten horns
and seven heads, and on its horns were ten diadem crowns,
and on its heads a blasphemous name. 2 Now the beast that I saw
was like a leopard, but its feet were like a bear's, and its mouth
was like a lion's mouth. The dragon gave the beast his power, his
throne, and great authority to rule. 3 One of the beast's heads
appeared to have been killed, but the lethal wound had been
healed. And the whole world followed the beast in amazement;
4 they worshiped the dragon because he had given ruling authority to the beast, and they worshiped the beast too, saying: "Who is
like the beast?" and "Who is able to make war against him?" 5 The
beast was given a mouth speaking proud words and blasphemies,
and he was permitted to exercise ruling authority for forty-two
months. 6 So the beast opened his mouth to blaspheme against
God—to blaspheme both his name and his dwelling place, that
is, those who dwell in heaven. 7 The beast was permitted to go to
war against the saints and conquer them. He was given ruling
authority over every tribe, people, language, and nation, 8 and
all those who live on the earth will worship the beast, everyone
whose name has not been written since the foundation of the
world in the book of life belonging to the Lamb who was killed.
9 If anyone has an ear, he had better listen!
10 If anyone is meant for captivity,
into captivity he will go.
If anyone is to be killed by the sword,
then by the sword he must be killed.

This requires steadfast endurance and faith from the saints.
11 Then I saw another beast coming up from the earth. He had
two horns like a lamb, but was speaking like a dragon. 12 He exercised all the ruling authority of the first beast on his behalf, and
made the earth and those who inhabit it worship the first beast,
the one whose lethal wound had been healed. 13 He performed
momentous signs, even making fire come down from heaven to
earth in front of people 14 and, by the signs he was permitted to
perform on behalf of the beast, he deceived those who live on
the earth. He told those who live on the earth to make an image to the beast who had been wounded by the sword, but still
lived. 15 The second beast was empowered to give life to the image of the first beast so that it could speak, and could cause all
those who did not worship the image of the beast to be killed.
16 He also caused everyone (small and great, rich and poor, free
and slave) to obtain a mark on their right hand or on their forehead. 17 Thus no one was allowed to buy or sell things unless he
bore the mark of the beast—that is, his name or his number.
18 This calls for wisdom: Let the one who has insight calculate the
beast's number, for it is man's number, and his number is 666.

AN INTERLUDE: THE SONG OF THE 144,000

14 Then I looked, and here was the Lamb standing on Mount
Zion, and with him were 144,000, who had his name and
his Father's name written on their foreheads. 2 I also heard a
sound coming out of heaven like the sound of many waters and
like the sound of loud thunder. Now the sound I heard was like
that made by harpists playing their harps, 3 and they were singing a new song before the throne and before the four living creatures and the elders. No one was able to learn the song except
the 144,000 who had been redeemed from the earth.
4 These are the ones who have not defiled themselves with
women, for they are virgins. These are the ones who follow the
Lamb wherever he goes. These were redeemed from humanity
as firstfruits to God and to the Lamb, 5 and no lie was found on
their lips; they are blameless.

THREE ANGELS AND THREE MESSAGES

6 Then I saw another angel flying directly overhead, and he had
an eternal gospel to proclaim to those who live on the earth—to
every nation, tribe, language, and people. 7 He declared in a loud
voice: "Fear God and give him glory, because the hour of his judgment has arrived, and worship the one who made heaven and
earth, the sea and the springs of water!"
8 A second angel followed the first, declaring: "Fallen, fallen
is Babylon the great city! She made all the nations drink of the
wine of her immoral passion."
9 A third angel followed the first two, declaring in a loud voice:
"If anyone worships the beast and his image, and takes the mark
on his forehead or his hand, 10 that person will also drink of the
wine of God's anger that has been mixed undiluted in the cup of
his wrath, and he will be tortured with fire and sulfur in front of
the holy angels and in front of the Lamb. 11 And the smoke from
their torture will go up forever and ever, and those who worship

the beast and his image will have no rest day or night, along with
anyone who receives the mark of his name." 12 This requires the
steadfast endurance of the saints—those who obey God's commandments and hold to their faith in Jesus.
13 Then I heard a voice from heaven say, "Write this:

'Blessed are the dead,
those who die in the Lord from this moment on!'"

"Yes," says the Spirit, "so they can rest from their hard work,
because their deeds will follow them."
14 Then I looked, and a white cloud appeared, and seated *on
the cloud was one like a son of man!* He had a golden crown on his
head and a sharp sickle in his hand. 15 Then another angel came
out of the temple, shouting in a loud voice to the one seated on
the cloud, "Use your sickle and start to reap, because the time
to reap has come, since the earth's harvest is ripe!" 16 So the one
seated on the cloud swung his sickle over the earth, and the
earth was reaped.
17 Then another angel came out of the temple in heaven, and
he too had a sharp sickle. 18 Another angel, who was in charge of
the fire, came from the altar and called in a loud voice to the angel who had the sharp sickle, "Use your sharp sickle and gather
the clusters of grapes off the vine of the earth, because its grapes
are now ripe." 19 So the angel swung his sickle over the earth and
gathered the grapes from the vineyard of the earth and tossed
them into the great winepress of the wrath of God. 20 Then the
winepress was stomped outside the city, and blood poured out
of the winepress up to the height of horses' bridles for a distance
of almost 200 miles.

THE FINAL PLAGUES

15 Then I saw another great and astounding sign in heaven:
seven angels who have seven final plagues (they are final
because in them God's anger is completed).
2 Then I saw something like a sea of glass mixed with fire, and
those who had conquered the beast and his image and the number of his name. They were standing by the sea of glass, holding
harps given to them by God. 3 They sang the song of Moses the
servant of God and the song of the Lamb:

"Great and astounding are your deeds,
Lord God, the All-Powerful!
Just and true are your ways,
King over the nations!
4 Who will not fear you, O Lord,
and glorify your name, because you alone are holy?
All nations will come and worship before you
for your righteous acts have been revealed."

5 After these things I looked, and the temple (the tent of
the testimony) was opened in heaven, 6 and the seven angels
who had the seven plagues came out of the temple, dressed
in clean bright linen, wearing wide golden belts around their
chests. 7 Then one of the four living creatures gave the seven
angels seven golden bowls filled with the wrath of God who

lives forever and ever, [8]and the temple was filled with smoke
from God's glory and from his power. Thus no one could enter
the temple until the seven plagues from the seven angels were
completed.

THE BOWLS OF GOD'S WRATH

16 Then I heard a loud voice from the temple declaring to the
seven angels: "Go and pour out on the earth the seven bowls
containing God's wrath." [2]So the first angel went and poured out
his bowl on the earth. Then ugly and painful sores appeared on
the people who had the mark of the beast and who worshiped
his image.
[3]Next, the second angel poured out his bowl on the sea and
it turned into blood, like that of a corpse, and every living creature that was in the sea died.
[4]Then the third angel poured out his bowl on the rivers and
the springs of water, and they turned into blood. [5]Now I heard
the angel of the waters saying:

"You are just—the one who is and who was,
the Holy One—because you have passed these judgments,
6 because they poured out the blood of
your saints and prophets,
so you have given them blood to drink.
They got what they deserved!"

[7]Then I heard the altar reply, "Yes, Lord God, the All-Powerful,
your judgments are true and just!"
[8]Then the fourth angel poured out his bowl on the sun, and
it was permitted to scorch people with fire. [9]Thus people were
scorched by the terrible heat, yet they blasphemed the name
of God, who has ruling authority over these plagues, and they
would not repent and give him glory.
[10]Then the fifth angel poured out his bowl on the throne of
the beast so that darkness covered his kingdom, and people
began to bite their tongues because of their pain. [11]They blasphemed the God of heaven because of their sufferings and because of their sores, but nevertheless they still refused to repent
of their deeds.
[12]Then the sixth angel poured out his bowl on the great river
Euphrates and dried up its water to prepare the way for the
kings from the east. [13]Then I saw three unclean spirits that
looked like frogs coming out of the mouth of the dragon, out
of the mouth of the beast, and out of the mouth of the false
prophet. [14]For they are the spirits of the demons performing
signs who go out to the kings of the earth to bring them together for the battle that will take place on the great day of
God, the All-Powerful.

15 (Look! I will come like a thief!
Blessed is the one who stays alert and does not lose
his clothes so that he will not have to walk around
naked and his shameful condition be seen.)

[16]Now the spirits gathered the kings and their armies to the
place that is called Armageddon in Hebrew.

17 Finally the seventh angel poured out his bowl into the air and a loud voice came out of the temple from the throne, saying: "It is done!" 18 Then there were flashes of lightning, roaring, and crashes of thunder, and there was a tremendous earthquake—an earthquake unequaled since humanity has been on the earth, so tremendous was that earthquake. 19 The great city was split into three parts and the cities of the nations collapsed. So Babylon the great was remembered before God, and was given the cup filled with the wine made of God's furious wrath. 20 Every island fled away and no mountains could be found. 21 And gigantic hailstones, weighing about a 100 pounds each, fell from heaven on people, but they blasphemed God because of the plague of hail, since it was so horrendous.

THE GREAT PROSTITUTE AND THE BEAST

17 Then one of the seven angels who had the seven bowls came and spoke to me. "Come," he said, "I will show you the condemnation and punishment of the great prostitute who sits on many waters, 2 with whom the kings of the earth committed sexual immorality and the earth's inhabitants got drunk with the wine of her immorality." 3 So he carried me away in the Spirit to a wilderness, and there I saw a woman sitting on a scarlet beast that was full of blasphemous names and had seven heads and ten horns. 4 Now the woman was dressed in purple and scarlet clothing, and adorned with gold, precious stones, and pearls. She held in her hand a golden cup filled with detestable things and unclean things from her sexual immorality. 5 On her forehead was written a name, a mystery: "Babylon the Great, the Mother of prostitutes and of the detestable things of the earth." 6 I saw that the woman was drunk with the blood of the saints and the blood of those who testified to Jesus. I was greatly astounded when I saw her. 7 But the angel said to me, "Why are you astounded? I will interpret for you the mystery of the woman and of the beast with the seven heads and ten horns that carries her. 8 The beast you saw was, and is not, but is about to come up from the abyss and then go to destruction. The inhabitants of the earth—all those whose names have not been written in the book of life since the foundation of the world—will be astounded when they see that the beast was, and is not, but is to come. 9 (This requires a mind that has wisdom.) The seven heads are seven mountains the woman sits on. They are also seven kings: 10 five have fallen; one is, and the other has not yet come, but whenever he does come, he must remain for only a brief time. 11 The beast that was, and is not, is himself an eighth king and yet is one of the seven, and is going to destruction. 12 The ten horns that you saw are ten kings who have not yet received a kingdom, but will receive ruling authority as kings with the beast for one hour. 13 These kings have a single intent, and they will give their power and authority to the beast. 14 They will make war with the Lamb, but the Lamb will conquer them, because he is Lord of lords and King of kings, and those accompanying the Lamb are the called, chosen, and faithful."

15 Then the angel said to me, "The waters you saw (where the
prostitute is seated) are peoples, multitudes, nations, and languages. 16 The ten horns that you saw, and the beast—these will
hate the prostitute and make her desolate and naked. They will
consume her flesh and burn her up with fire. 17 For God has put
into their minds to carry out his purpose by making a decision
to give their royal power to the beast until the words of God are
fulfilled. 18 As for the woman you saw, she is the great city that
has sovereignty over the kings of the earth."

BABYLON IS DESTROYED

18 After these things I saw another angel, who possessed great
authority, coming down out of heaven, and the earth was lit
up by his radiance. 2 He shouted with a powerful voice:

"Fallen, fallen, is Babylon the great!
She has become a lair for demons,
a haunt for every unclean spirit,
a haunt for every unclean bird,
a haunt for every unclean and detested beast.
3 For all the nations have fallen from
the wine of her immoral passion,
and the kings of the earth have committed
sexual immorality with her,
and the merchants of the earth have gotten rich
from the power of her sensual behavior."

4 Then I heard another voice from heaven saying, "Come out of
her, my people, so you will not take part in her sins and so you
will not receive her plagues, 5 because her sins have piled up all
the way to heaven and God has remembered her crimes. 6 Repay her the same way she repaid others; pay her back double
corresponding to her deeds. In the cup she mixed, mix double
the amount for her. 7 As much as she exalted herself and lived
in sensual luxury, to this extent give her torment and grief because she said to herself, 'I rule as queen and am no widow; I will
never experience grief!' 8 For this reason, she will experience
her plagues in a single day: disease, mourning, and famine, and
she will be burned down with fire, because the Lord God who
judges her is powerful!"

9 Then the kings of the earth who committed immoral acts with
her and lived in sensual luxury with her will weep and wail for
her when they see the smoke from the fire that burns her up.
10 They will stand a long way off because they are afraid of her
torment, and will say,

"Woe, woe, O great city,
Babylon the powerful city!
For in a single hour your doom has come!"

11 Then the merchants of the earth will weep and mourn for her
because no one buys their cargo any longer—12 cargo such as gold,
silver, precious stones, pearls, fine linen, purple cloth, silk, scarlet cloth, all sorts of things made of citron wood, all sorts of objects made of ivory, all sorts of things made of expensive wood,
bronze, iron and marble, 13 cinnamon, spice, incense, perfumed

ointment, frankincense, wine, olive oil and costly flour, wheat,
cattle and sheep, horses and four-wheeled carriages, slaves and
human lives.

14 (The ripe fruit you greatly desired
has gone from you,
and all your luxury and splendor
have gone from you—
they will never ever be found again!)

15 The merchants who sold these things, who got rich from her,
will stand a long way off because they are afraid of her torment.
They will weep and mourn, 16 saying,

"Woe, woe, O great city—
dressed in fine linen, purple and scarlet clothing,
and adorned with gold, precious stones, and pearls—
17 because in a single hour such great
wealth has been destroyed!"

And every ship's captain, and all who sail along the coast—sea-
men, and all who make their living from the sea, stood a long
way off 18 and began to shout when they saw the smoke from
the fire that burned her up, "Who is like the great city?" 19 And
they threw dust on their heads and were shouting with weeping and mourning,

"Woe, Woe, O great city—
in which all those who had ships on the
sea got rich from her wealth—
because in a single hour she has been destroyed!"
20 (Rejoice over her, O heaven,
and you saints and apostles and prophets,
for God has pronounced judgment
against her on your behalf!)

21 Then one powerful angel picked up a stone like a huge millstone, threw it into the sea, and said,

"With this kind of sudden violent force
Babylon the great city will be thrown down
and it will never be found again!
22 And the sound of the harpists, musicians,
flute players, and trumpeters
will never be heard in you again.
No craftsman who practices any trade
will ever be found in you again;
the noise of a mill will never be heard in you again.
23 Even the light from a lamp
will never shine in you again!
The voices of the bridegroom and his bride
will never be heard in you again.
For your merchants were the tycoons of the world,
because all the nations were deceived
by your magic spells!
24 The blood of the saints and prophets was found in her,
along with the blood of all those who
had been killed on the earth."

19 After these things I heard what sounded like the loud voice
of a vast throng in heaven, saying,
"Hallelujah! Salvation and glory and
power belong to our God,
2 because his judgments are true and just.
For he has judged the great prostitute
who corrupted the earth with her sexual immorality,
and has avenged the blood of his servants
poured out by her own hands!"

3 Then a second time the crowd shouted, "Hallelujah!" The
smoke rises from her forever and ever. 4 The twenty-four elders
and the four living creatures threw themselves to the ground and
worshiped God, who was seated on the throne, saying: "Amen!
Hallelujah!"
5 Then a voice came from the throne, saying:
"Praise our God
all you his servants,
and all you who fear him,
both the small and the great!"

THE WEDDING CELEBRATION OF THE LAMB

6 Then I heard what sounded like the voice of a vast throng, like
the roar of many waters and like loud crashes of thunder. They
were shouting:
"Hallelujah!
For the Lord our God, the All-Powerful, reigns!
7 Let us rejoice and exult
and give him glory,
because the wedding celebration of the Lamb has come,
and his bride has made herself ready.
8 She was permitted to be dressed in bright,
clean, fine linen" (for the fine linen is
the righteous deeds of the saints).

9 Then the angel said to me, "Write the following: Blessed are
those who are invited to the banquet at the wedding celebration
of the Lamb!" He also said to me, "These are the true words of
God." 10 So I threw myself down at his feet to worship him, but he
said, "Do not do this! I am only a fellow servant with you and your
brothers and sisters who hold to the testimony about Jesus. Worship God, for the testimony about Jesus is the spirit of prophecy."

THE SON OF GOD GOES TO WAR

11 Then I saw heaven opened and here came a white horse! The
one riding it was called "Faithful" and "True," and with justice he
judges and goes to war. 12 His eyes are like a fiery flame and there
are many diadem crowns on his head. He has a name written that
no one knows except himself. 13 He is dressed in clothing dipped
in blood, and he is called the Word of God. 14 The armies that are
in heaven, dressed in white, clean, fine linen, were following him
on white horses. 15 From his mouth extends a sharp sword, so
that with it he can strike the nations. ***He will rule them with an
iron rod,*** and he stomps the winepress of the furious wrath of

CHALLENGE

Read Philippians 2:5–11 and Isaiah 53. How was Christ humbled during His first coming? How is Christ glorified at His second coming?

God, the All-Powerful. 16 He has a name written on his clothing
and on his thigh: "King of kings and Lord of lords."
17 Then I saw one angel standing in the sun, and he shouted in
a loud voice to all the birds flying high in the sky:

"Come, gather around for the great banquet of God,
18 to eat your fill of the flesh of kings,
the flesh of generals,
the flesh of powerful people,
the flesh of horses and those who ride them,
and the flesh of all people, both free and slave,
and small and great!"

19 Then I saw the beast and the kings of the earth and their armies assembled to do battle with the one who rode the horse
and with his army. 20 Now the beast was seized, and along with
him the false prophet who had performed the signs on his behalf—signs by which he deceived those who had received the
mark of the beast and those who worshiped his image. Both of
them were thrown alive into the lake of fire burning with sulfur.
21 The others were killed by the sword that extended from the
mouth of the one who rode the horse, and all the birds gorged
themselves with their flesh.

THE THOUSAND YEAR REIGN

20 Then I saw an angel descending from heaven, holding in
his hand the key to the abyss and a huge chain. 2 He seized
the dragon—the ancient serpent, who is the devil and Satan—
and tied him up for a thousand years. 3 The angel then threw him
into the abyss and locked and sealed it so that he could not deceive the nations until the one thousand years were finished. (After these things he must be released for a brief period of time.)
4 Then I saw thrones and seated on them were those who had
been given authority to judge. I also saw the souls of those who
had been beheaded because of the testimony about Jesus and because of the word of God. These had not worshiped the beast or
his image and had refused to receive his mark on their forehead
or hand. They came to life and reigned with Christ for a thousand
years. 5 (The rest of the dead did not come to life until the thousand
years were finished.) This is the first resurrection. 6 Blessed and
holy is the one who takes part in the first resurrection. The second death has no power over them, but they will be priests of God
and of Christ, and they will reign with him for a thousand years.

SATAN'S FINAL DEFEAT

7 Now when the thousand years are finished, Satan will be released from his prison 8 and will go out to deceive the nations
at the four corners of the earth, Gog and Magog, to bring them
together for the battle. They are as numerous as the grains of
sand in the sea. 9 They went up on the broad plain of the earth
and encircled the camp of the saints and the beloved city, but
fire came down from heaven and devoured them completely.
10 And the devil who deceived them was thrown into the lake of
fire and sulfur, where the beast and the false prophet are too,
and they will be tormented there day and night forever and ever.

THE GREAT WHITE THRONE

11 Then I saw a large white throne and the one who was seated
on it; the earth and the heaven fled from his presence, and no
place was found for them. 12 And I saw the dead, the great and
the small, standing before the throne. Then books were opened,
and another book was opened—the book of life. So the dead
were judged by what was written in the books, according to their
deeds. 13 The sea gave up the dead that were in it, and Death and
Hades gave up the dead that were in them, and each one was
judged according to his deeds. 14 Then Death and Hades were
thrown into the lake of fire. This is the second death—the lake
of fire. 15 If anyone's name was not found written in the book of
life, that person was thrown into the lake of fire.

A NEW HEAVEN AND A NEW EARTH

21 Then I saw a new heaven and a new earth, for the first
heaven and earth had ceased to exist, and the sea existed
no more. 2 And I saw the holy city—the new Jerusalem—descending out of heaven from God, made ready like a bride adorned for
her husband. 3 And I heard a loud voice from the throne saying:
"Look! The residence of God is among human beings. He will live
among them, and they will be his people, and God himself will
be with them. 4 He will wipe away every tear from their eyes, and
death will not exist any more—or mourning, or crying, or pain,
for the former things have ceased to exist."

5 And the one seated on the throne said: "Look! I am making all
things new!" Then he said to me, "Write it down, because these
words are reliable and true." 6 He also said to me, "It is done! I
am the Alpha and the Omega, the beginning and the end. To
the one who is thirsty I will give water free of charge from the
spring of the water of life. 7 The one who conquers will inherit
these things, and I will be his God and he will be my son. 8 But
as for the cowards, unbelievers, detestable persons, murderers,
the sexually immoral, and those who practice magic spells, idol
worshipers, and all those who lie, their place will be in the lake
that burns with fire and sulfur. That is the second death."

THE NEW JERUSALEM DESCENDS

9 Then one of the seven angels who had the seven bowls full of
the seven final plagues came and spoke to me, saying, "Come, I
will show you the bride, the wife of the Lamb!" 10 So he took me
away in the Spirit to a huge, majestic mountain and showed me
the holy city, Jerusalem, descending out of heaven from God.
11 The city possesses the glory of God; its brilliance is like a precious jewel, like a stone of crystal-clear jasper. 12 It has a massive,
high wall with twelve gates, with twelve angels at the gates, and
the names of the twelve tribes of the nation of Israel are written on the gates. 13 There are three gates on the east side, three
gates on the north side, three gates on the south side and three
gates on the west side. 14 The wall of the city has twelve foundations, and on them are the twelve names of the twelve apostles
of the Lamb.

15 The angel who spoke to me had a golden measuring rod with
which to measure the city and its foundation stones and wall.

LOVE TO GROW

FROM THE GARDEN TO THE CITY

REVELATION 21:1–5

Have you ever flipped to the last page of a book to read the ending? It could ruin some of the suspense, but it could also illuminate the rest of the story. Certain details gain more importance, others fade into the background, and the whole story takes on a different meaning. In the last chapters of Revelation, we get a glimpse of the end of our story for a similar purpose: so it can shape the way we live our lives.

Typically, our focus on "the end" revolves around heaven. However, in Revelation 21, the end is "a new heaven and a new earth" and a "holy city" coming down from heaven (vv. 1–2). The ultimate end of the story is an earthly city where God dwells with His people. The "residence" of God (v. 3) will be with humanity. Unlike the tent that housed His presence in the Old Testament, God will tabernacle with the whole earth.

God will dwell with us.

There's something remarkable about the account of the end of all things: It is not merely a spiritual reality. Believers are not pictured floating on clouds, playing harps for eternity. Instead, a city of His people descends from heaven, and the one true King declares that He is "making all things new" (Rev 21:5). Our story began in a garden God gave to humans to cultivate, using His gifts and exercising their creativity. Our story ends in a city, an epicenter of human culture and creativity, a place where natural resources are shaped, combined, and cultivated into something new.

Such an ending should provide the motivation to work hard at creating beautiful things on earth. We will spend eternity fulfilling our first and greatest commission—ruling and reigning on earth, creating, flourishing, and cultivating the earth God has given us. Our creative work both reflects our original commission and anticipates our eternal one. We serve a God who is making all things new, and He graciously offers us the opportunity to partner with Him in His creative work of redemption.

Now that's an ending worth reading about!

16 Now the city is laid out as a square, its length and width the
same. He measured the city with the measuring rod at 1,400
miles (its length and width and height are equal). 17 He also measured its wall, 144 cubits according to human measurement,
which is also the angel's. 18 The city's wall is made of jasper and
the city is pure gold, like transparent glass. 19 The foundations of
the city's wall are decorated with every kind of precious stone.
The first foundation is jasper, the second sapphire, the third agate, the fourth emerald, 20 the fifth onyx, the sixth carnelian, the
seventh chrysolite, the eighth beryl, the ninth topaz, the tenth
chrysoprase, the eleventh jacinth, and the twelfth amethyst.
21 And the twelve gates are twelve pearls—each one of the gates
is made from just one pearl! The main street of the city is pure
gold, like transparent glass.
22 Now I saw no temple in the city, because the Lord God—the
All-Powerful—and the Lamb are its temple. 23 The city does not
need the sun or the moon to shine on it, because the glory of
God lights it up, and its lamp is the Lamb. 24 The nations will
walk by its light and the kings of the earth will bring their grandeur into it. 25 Its gates will never be closed during the day (and
there will be no night there). 26 They will bring the grandeur and
the wealth of the nations into it, 27 but nothing ritually unclean
will ever enter into it, nor anyone who does what is detestable
or practices falsehood, but only those whose names are written
in the Lamb's book of life.
22 Then the angel showed me the river of the water of life—
water as clear as crystal—pouring out from the throne
of God and of the Lamb, 2 flowing down the middle of the city's
main street. On each side of the river is the tree of life producing
twelve kinds of fruit, yielding its fruit every month of the year.
Its leaves are for the healing of the nations. 3 And there will no
longer be any curse, and the throne of God and the Lamb will
be in the city. His servants will worship him, 4 and they will see
his face, and his name will be on their foreheads. 5 Night will be
no more, and they will not need the light of a lamp or the light
of the sun, because the Lord God will shine on them, and they
will reign forever and ever.

A FINAL REMINDER

6 Then the angel said to me, "These words are reliable and true.
The Lord, the God of the spirits of the prophets, has sent his angel to show his servants what must happen soon."

7 (Look! I am coming soon!
Blessed is the one who keeps the words of
the prophecy expressed in this book.)

8 I, John, am the one who heard and saw these things, and when
I heard and saw them, I threw myself down to worship at the
feet of the angel who was showing them to me. 9 But he said to
me, "Do not do this! I am a fellow servant with you and with your
brothers the prophets, and with those who obey the words of
this book. Worship God!" 10 Then he said to me, "Do not seal up
the words of the prophecy contained in this book, because the
time is near. 11 The evildoer must continue to do evil, and the one

GOD'S HEART FOR THE NATIONS

Revelation 21:23–24

The city does not need the sun or the moon to shine on it, because the glory of God lights it up, and its lamp is the Lamb. The nations will walk by its light and the kings of the earth will bring their grandeur into it.

REFLECT

How do the prophecies about the end times give you comfort and encouragement in your life today?

who is morally filthy must continue to be filthy. The one who is
righteous must continue to act righteously, and the one who is
holy must continue to be holy."

12 (Look! I am coming soon,
and my reward is with me to pay each one
according to what he has done!
13 I am the Alpha and the Omega,
the first and the last,
the beginning and the end!)

14 Blessed are those who wash their robes so they can have access to the tree of life and can enter into the city by the gates.
15 Outside are the dogs and the sorcerers and the sexually immoral, and the murderers, and the idolaters and everyone who
loves and practices falsehood!

16 "I, Jesus, have sent my angel to testify to you about these
things for the churches. I am the root and the descendant of
David, the bright morning star!" 17 And the Spirit and the bride
say, "Come!" And let the one who hears say: "Come!" And let the
one who is thirsty come; let the one who wants it take the water of life free of charge.

18 I testify to everyone who hears the words of the prophecy
contained in this book: If anyone adds to them, God will add to
him the plagues described in this book. 19 And if anyone takes
away from the words of this book of prophecy, God will take
away his share in the tree of life and in the holy city that are described in this book.

20 The one who testifies to these things says, "Yes, I am coming soon!" Amen! Come, Lord Jesus! 21 The grace of the Lord Jesus
be with all.

Memory Verses

Genesis 15:6

Abram believed the LORD, and the LORD credited it as righteousness to him.

Exodus 15:13

By your loyal love you will lead the people whom you have redeemed; you will guide them by your strength to your holy dwelling place.

Leviticus 20:26

You must be holy to me, because I, the LORD, am holy, and I have set you apart from the other peoples to be mine.

Numbers 14:18

The LORD is slow to anger and abounding in loyal love, forgiving iniquity and transgression, but by no means clearing the guilty, visiting the iniquity of the fathers on the children until the third and fourth generations.

Deuteronomy 30:16

What I am commanding you today is to love the LORD your God, to walk in his ways, and to obey his commandments, his statutes, and his ordinances. Then you will live and become numerous and the LORD your God will bless you in the land that you are about to possess.

Joshua 21:45

Not one of the LORD's faithful promises to the family of Israel was left unfulfilled; every one was realized.

Judges 21:25

In those days Israel had no king. Each man did what he considered to be right.

Ruth 4:14

The village women said to Naomi, "May the LORD be praised because he has not left you without a guardian today! May he become famous in Israel!"

1 Samuel 2:9

"He watches over his holy ones, but the wicked are made speechless in the darkness, for it is not by one's own strength that one prevails."

2 Samuel 22:51

He gives his king magnificent victories; he is faithful to his chosen ruler, to David and to his descendants forever!

1 Kings 8:50

Forgive all the rebellious acts of your sinful people and cause their captors to have mercy on them.

2 Kings 17:13

The LORD solemnly warned Israel and Judah through all his prophets and all the seers, "Turn back from your evil ways; obey my commandments and rules that are recorded in the law. I ordered your ancestors to keep this law and sent my servants the prophets to remind you of its demands."

1 Chronicles 17:19–20

O LORD, for the sake of your servant and according to your will, you have done this great thing in order to reveal your greatness. O LORD, there is none like you; there is no God besides you! What we heard is true!

2 Chronicles 36:15

The LORD God of their ancestors continually warned them through his messengers, for he felt compassion for his people and his dwelling place.

Ezra 9:8

"But now briefly we have received mercy from the LORD our God, in that he has left us a remnant and has given us a secure position in his holy place. Thus our God has enlightened our eyes and has given us a little relief in our time of servitude."

Nehemiah 6:3

So I sent messengers to them saying, "I am engaged in an important work, and I am unable to come down. Why should the work come to a halt when I leave it to come down to you?"

Esther 4:14

"It may very well be that you have achieved royal status for such a time as this!"

Job 1:21–22

"The LORD gives, and the LORD takes away. May the name of the LORD be blessed!" In all this Job did not sin, nor did he charge God with moral impropriety.

Psalm 136:1

Give thanks to the LORD, for he is good, for his loyal love endures.

Proverbs 2:6

For the LORD gives wisdom, and from his mouth comes knowledge and understanding.

Ecclesiastes 3:11

God has made everything fit beautifully in its appropriate time, but he has also placed ignorance in the human heart so that people cannot discover what God has ordained, from the beginning to the end of their lives.

Song of Solomon 8:7

Surging waters cannot quench love; floodwaters cannot overflow it. If someone were to offer all his possessions to buy love, the offer would be utterly despised.

Isaiah 61:8

For I, the LORD, love justice and hate robbery and sin. I will repay them because of my faithfulness; I will make a permanent covenant with them.

Jeremiah 29:13–14

"When you seek me in prayer and worship, you will find me available to you. If you seek me with all your heart and soul, I will make myself available to you," says the LORD. "Then I will reverse your plight and will regather you from all the nations and all the places where I have exiled you," says the LORD. "I will bring you back to the place from which I exiled you."

Lamentations 3:24

"My portion is the LORD," I have said to myself, so I will put my hope in him.

Ezekiel 36:26

I will give you a new heart, and I will put a new spirit within you. I will remove the heart of stone from your body and give you a heart of flesh.

Daniel 3:17–18

"If our God whom we are serving exists, he is able to rescue us from the furnace of blazing fire, and he will rescue us, O king, from your power as well. But if he does not, let it be known to you, O king, that we don't serve your gods, and we will not pay homage to the golden statue that you have erected."

Hosea 6:6

For I delight in faithfulness, not simply in sacrifice; I delight in acknowledging God, not simply in whole burnt offerings.

Joel 2:27

You will be convinced that I am in the midst of Israel. I am the LORD your God; there is no other. My people will never again be put to shame.

Amos 5:14

Seek good and not evil so you can live! Then the LORD God of Heaven's Armies just might be with you, as you claim he is.

Obadiah 17

But on Mount Zion there will be a remnant of those who escape, and it will be a holy place once again. The descendants of Jacob will conquer those who had conquered them.

Jonah 4:2

". . . because I knew that you are a gracious and compassionate God, slow to anger and abounding in mercy, and one who relents concerning threatened judgment."

Micah 6:8

He has told you, O man, what is good, and what the LORD really wants from you: He wants you to carry out justice, to love faithfulness, and to live obediently before your God.

Nahum 1:3

The LORD is slow to anger but great in power; the LORD will certainly not allow the wicked to go unpunished.

Habakkuk 1:5

"Look at the nations and pay attention! You will be shocked and amazed! For I will do something in your lifetime that you will not believe even though you are forewarned."

Zephaniah 3:20

"At that time I will lead you—at that time I gather you together. Be sure of this! I will make all the nations of the earth respect and admire you when you see me restore you," says the LORD.

Haggai 1:13–14

Then Haggai, the LORD's messenger, spoke the LORD's announcement to the people: "I am with you," decrees the LORD. So the LORD energized and encouraged Zerubbabel son of Shealtiel, governor of Judah ... They came and worked on the temple of their God, the LORD of Heaven's Armies.

Zechariah 9:16

On that day the LORD their God will deliver them as the flock of his people, for they are the precious stones of a crown sparkling over his land.

Malachi 4:2–3

"But for you who respect my name, the sun of vindication will rise with healing wings, and you will skip about like calves released from the stall. You will trample on the wicked, for they will be like ashes under the soles of your feet on the day that I am preparing," says the LORD of Heaven's Armies.

Matthew 6:33

But above all pursue his kingdom and righteousness, and all these things will be given to you as well.

Mark 10:45

For even the Son of Man did not come to be served but to serve, and to give his life as a ransom for many.

Luke 19:10

"For the Son of Man came to seek and to save the lost."

John 20:31

But these are recorded so that you may believe that Jesus is the Christ, the Son of God, and that by believing you may have life in his name.

Acts 2:42–43

They were devoting themselves to the apostles' teaching and to fellowship, to the breaking of bread and to prayer. Reverential awe came over everyone, and many wonders and miraculous signs came about by the apostles.

Romans 8:1–2

There is therefore now no condemnation for those who are in Christ Jesus. For the law of the life-giving Spirit in Christ Jesus has set you free from the law of sin and death.

1 Corinthians 10:31

So whether you eat or drink, or whatever you do, do everything for the glory of God.

2 Corinthians 4:17–18

For our momentary, light suffering is producing for us an eternal weight of glory far beyond all comparison because we are not looking at what can be seen but at what cannot be seen. For what can be seen is temporary, but what cannot be seen is eternal.

Galatians 5:1

For freedom Christ has set us free. Stand firm, then, and do not be subject again to the yoke of slavery.

Ephesians 4:1–3

I, therefore, the prisoner for the Lord, urge you to live worthily of the calling with which you have been called, with all humility and gentleness, with patience, putting up with one another in love, making every effort to keep the unity of the Spirit in the bond of peace.

Philippians 4:8

Finally, brothers and sisters, whatever is true, whatever is worthy of respect, whatever is just, whatever is pure, whatever is lovely, whatever is commendable, if something is excellent or praiseworthy, think about these things.

Colossians 2:6–7

Therefore, just as you received Christ Jesus as Lord, continue to live your lives in him, rooted and built up in him and firm in your faith just as you were taught, and overflowing with thankfulness.

1 Thessalonians 3:12–13

And may the Lord cause you to increase and abound in love for one another and for all, just as we do for you, so that your hearts are strengthened in holiness to be blameless before our God and Father at the coming of our Lord Jesus with all his saints.

2 Thessalonians 2:16–17

Now may our Lord Jesus Christ himself and God our Father, who loved us and by grace gave us eternal comfort and good hope, encourage your hearts and strengthen you in every good thing you do or say.

1 Timothy 1:15–16

This saying is trustworthy and deserves full acceptance: "Christ Jesus came into the world to save sinners"—and I am the worst of them! But here is why I was treated with mercy: so that in me as the worst, Christ Jesus could demonstrate his utmost patience, as an example for those who are going to believe in him for eternal life.

2 Timothy 3:16–17

Every scripture is inspired by God and useful for teaching, for reproof, for correction, and for training in righteousness, that the person dedicated to God may be capable and equipped for every good work.

Titus 2:7

. . . showing yourself to be an example of good works in every way.

Philemon 8–9

So, although I have quite a lot of confidence in Christ and could command you to do what is proper, I would rather appeal to you on the basis of love.

Hebrews 4:15–16

For we do not have a high priest incapable of sympathizing with our weaknesses, but one who has been tempted in every way just as we are, yet without sin. Therefore let us confidently approach the throne of grace to receive mercy and find grace whenever we need help.

James 1:22

But be sure you live out the message and do not merely listen to it and so deceive yourselves.

1 Peter 2:9

But you are a chosen race, a royal priesthood, a holy nation, a people of his own, so that you may proclaim the virtues of the one who called you out of darkness into his marvelous light.

2 Peter 1:3

I can pray this because his divine power has bestowed on us everything necessary for life and godliness through the rich knowledge of the one who called us by his own glory and excellence.

1 John 4:16

And we have come to know and to believe the love that God has in us. God is love, and the one who resides in love resides in God, and God resides in him.

2 John 6

Now this is love: that we walk according to his commandments.

3 John 4

I have no greater joy than this: to hear that my children are living according to the truth.

Jude 3

I now feel compelled instead to write to encourage you to contend earnestly for the faith that was once for all entrusted to the saints.

Revelation 22:20–21

The one who testifies to these things says, "Yes, I am coming soon!" Amen! Come, Lord Jesus! The grace of the Lord Jesus be with all.

God's Heart for the Nations

Genesis 18:18

After all, Abraham will surely become a great and powerful nation, and all the nations on the earth may receive blessings through him.

Exodus 34:10

He said, "See, I am going to make a covenant before all your people. I will do wonders such as have not been done in all the earth, nor in any nation. All the people among whom you live will see the work of the LORD, for it is a fearful thing that I am doing with you."

Joshua 4:24

He has done this so all the nations of the earth might recognize the LORD's power and so you might always obey the LORD your God.

2 Samuel 22:50

So I will give you thanks,
O LORD, before the nations!
I will sing praises to you.

1 Kings 8:41–43

Foreigners, who do not belong to your people Israel, will come from a distant land because of your reputation. When they hear about your great reputation and your ability to accomplish mighty deeds, they will come and direct their prayers toward this temple. Then listen from your heavenly dwelling place and answer all the prayers of the foreigners. Then all the nations of the earth will acknowledge your reputation, obey you as your people Israel do, and recognize that this temple I built belongs to you.

1 Chronicles 16:8

Give thanks to the LORD!
Call on his name!
Make known his accomplishments among the nations.

1 Chronicles 16:31

Let the heavens rejoice, and
the earth be happy!
Let the nations say, 'The LORD reigns!'

Psalm 8:1

O LORD, our Lord,
how magnificent is your reputation throughout the earth!
You reveal your majesty in
the heavens above.

Psalm 9:11

Sing praises to the LORD, who rules in Zion.
Tell the nations what he has done.

Psalm 22:27–28

Let all the people of the earth acknowledge the LORD and turn to him.
Let all the nations worship you.
For the LORD is king
and rules over the nations.

Psalm 45:17

I will proclaim your greatness
through the coming years,
then the nations will praise you forever.

Psalm 65:5

You answer our prayers by performing
awesome acts of deliverance,
O God, our savior.
All the ends of the earth trust in you,
as well as those living across the wide seas.

Psalm 96:10

Say among the nations, "The LORD reigns!
The world is established; it cannot be moved.
He judges the nations fairly."

Psalm 102:15

The nations will respect the reputation of the LORD,
and all the kings of the earth
will respect his splendor.

Isaiah 52:10

The LORD reveals his royal power
in the sight of all the nations;
the entire earth sees
our God deliver.

Micah 4:2

Many nations will come, saying,
"Come on! Let's go up to the
LORD's mountain,
to the temple of Jacob's God,
so he can teach us his ways
and we can live by his laws."
For instruction will proceed from Zion,
the LORD's message from Jerusalem.

Matthew 8:11

I tell you, many will come from the east and west to share the banquet with Abraham, Isaac, and Jacob in the kingdom of heaven.

Matthew 12:21

And in his name the Gentiles will hope.

Matthew 28:19–20

"Therefore go and make disciples of all nations, baptizing them in the name of the Father and the Son and the Holy Spirit, teaching them to obey everything I have commanded you. And remember, I am with you always, to the end of the age."

Mark 11:17

Then he began to teach them and said, "Is it not written: 'My house will be called a house of prayer for all nations'? But you have turned it into a den of robbers!"

Mark 13:10

First the gospel must be preached to all nations.

Luke 2:30–32

"For my eyes have seen your salvation
that you have prepared in the
presence of all peoples:
a light,
for revelation to the Gentiles,
and for glory to your people Israel."

John 17:18

Just as you sent me into the world, so I sent them into the world.

Acts 1:8

But you will receive power when the Holy Spirit has come upon you, and you will be my witnesses in Jerusalem, and in all Judea and Samaria, and to the farthest parts of the earth.

Acts 10:34–35

Then Peter started speaking: "I now truly understand that God does not show favoritism in dealing with people, but in every nation the person who fears him and does what is right is welcomed before him.

Acts 15:16–17

"After this I will return, and I will rebuild the fallen tent of David; I will rebuild its ruins and restore it, so that the rest of humanity may seek the Lord, namely, all the Gentiles I have called to be my own," says the Lord.

Romans 1:16

For I am not ashamed of the gospel, for it is God's power for salvation to everyone who believes, to the Jew first and also to the Greek.

Romans 3:29

Or is God the God of the Jews only? Is he not the God of the Gentiles too? Yes, of the Gentiles too!

Romans 15:11

And again, "Praise the Lord all you Gentiles, and let all the peoples praise him."

Galatians 3:26–29

For in Christ Jesus you are all sons of God through faith. For all of you who were baptized into Christ have clothed yourselves with Christ. There is neither Jew nor Greek, there is neither slave nor free, there is neither male nor female—for all of you are one in Christ Jesus. And if you belong to Christ, then you are Abraham's descendants, heirs according to the promise.

Colossians 1:27

God wanted to make known to them the glorious riches of this mystery among the Gentiles, which is Christ in you, the hope of glory.

Revelation 21:23–24

The city does not need the sun or the moon to shine on it, because the glory of God lights it up, and its lamp is the Lamb. The nations will walk by its light and the kings of the earth will bring their grandeur into it.

Genres of the Books of the Bible

In the same way we use a different approach for varying genres of books or movies, the way we read the books of the Bible depends on their genre. Below is a list of the different genres found in the Bible and a few tips for how to approach each one when reading and studying.

The Pentateuch:

The books of Genesis, Exodus, Leviticus, Numbers, and Deuteronomy form what is called The Pentateuch (literally meaning "five books" in Greek). This section is also known as the Torah, the Jewish law. These five books were written by the same author and to the same audience. The Pentateuch contains several genres including historical accounts, codes of law, and poetry. When reading these books, we read the historical records as true events that occurred to real people. We learn a great deal about God, His character, and the way He interacts with humanity. Whenever you read a passage of Scripture from one of these books, ask yourself, "what does this show me about the character of God?"

Historical Books:

The books of Joshua, Judges, Ruth, 1 Samuel, 2 Samuel, 1 Kings, 2 Kings, 1 Chronicles, 2 Chronicles, Ezra, Nehemiah, and Esther make up the historical section in the Old Testament. The accounts contained in the historical books are real events that happened to real people. Each book was written to a specific audience, generally an audience of Israelite people, reminding them of God's faithfulness. We read them for information about the culture and history of Israel and the way God interacted with His people when they acted faithfully toward Him and also when they acted unfaithfully toward Him.

Poetic Books:

Job, Psalms, Proverbs, Ecclesiastes, and Song of Solomon are considered books of poetry. Each of these books contain a host of literary devices like similes, metaphors, repetition, allegory, hyperbole, and exaggeration. We can learn a great deal from these authors about understanding and expressing emotion, how to ask God questions, how to deal with pain and loss, how to rejoice and offer praise, and how to live a faithful life.

Major Prophets:

The books of Isaiah, Jeremiah, Lamentations, Ezekiel, and Daniel are called the Major Prophets. The promises (both for prosperity and for judgment) recorded in these books are written to a specific audience. While these promises were not written to us, they tell us a great deal about God's character. They tell us what God loves and what God hates, what He honors and what He punishes. We should always ask the question, "What does this promise tell me about God's character?"

Minor Prophets:

Hosea, Joel, Amos, Obadiah, Jonah, Micah, Nahum, Habakkuk, Zephaniah, Haggai, Zechariah, and Malachi are called the Minor Prophets. The divisions between the major and minor prophets have to do with the length of the writings. These books are often difficult and confusing to the modern reader. Not only are we thousands of years removed from the events, but our cultures are often so different that many of the ideas seem completely foreign and confusing. However, these books tell us a great deal about the character of God. When reading these books we should continue to ask, "What does this tell me about the character of God."

Gospels:

The first four books of the New Testament are the accounts of Jesus' incarnation. The word gospel comes from the Greek word for "good news." Matthew, Mark, Luke, and John each tell of the good news of Jesus Christ, of His life, death, and resurrection. Each of the Gospels are written from a different perspective, and each gospel highlights a different aspect of Jesus and His ministry.

Church History:

The book of Acts provides the historical record of the early church. Like the historical books in the Old Testament, the book of Acts records real events that happened to real people. We find much background and culture about the Greco-Roman world in the first century as well as context for many of the letters included in the New Testament.

Pauline Epistles:

The books of Romans, 1 Corinthians, 2 Corinthians, Galatians, Ephesians, Philippians, Colossians, 1 Thessalonians, 2 Thessalonians, 1 Timothy, 2 Timothy, Titus, and Philemon are called the Pauline Epistles. These books are letters, written by Paul to different churches and individuals throughout his ministry. When reading any of the epistles, it is important to have an overall understanding of the main message of the letter. While studying these letters in depth requires looking at paragraphs and individual verses, they must always be interpreted in light of the letter's overall message. When studying these books be sure to ask: "What is the overall message and cultural context and how does it relate to this specific verse?"

General Epistles:

Hebrews, James, 1 Peter, 2 Peter, 1 John, 2 John, 3 John, and Jude are considered General Epistles. These letters were written by several authors to diverse audiences. The book of Acts provides much cultural background to these letters. Like the Pauline Epistles, we should be sure to read and study these books with keeping the overall context of the letter in mind.

Apocalyptic:

The New Testament also contains a prophetic book. The book of Revelation is a message of prophecy regarding the end times and the second coming of Christ. The way we read *Revelation* is unique to other books of the Bible. While we find many words of judgment, we also find words of promise and redemption. We can find hope in the promise of Christ's return and of our eternity with Him.

One-Year Bible Reading Plan

JANUARY

DATE	MORNING	EVENING
	Matt	Gen
1	1	1, 2, 3
2	2	4, 5, 6
3	3	7, 8, 9
4	4	10, 11, 12
5	5:1–26	13, 14, 15
6	5:27–48	16, 17
7	6:1–18	18, 19
8	6:19–34	20, 21, 22
9	7	23, 24
10	8:1–17	25, 26
11	8:18–34	27, 28
12	9:1–17	29, 30
13	9:18–38	31, 32
14	10:1–20	33, 34, 35
15	10:21–42	36, 37, 38
16	11	39, 40
17	12:1–23	41, 42
18	12:24–50	43, 44, 45
19	13:1–30	46, 47, 48
20	13:31–58	49, 50
		Exod
21	14:1–21	1, 2, 3
22	14:22–36	4, 5, 6
23	15:1–20	7, 8
24	15:21–39	9, 10, 11
25	16	12, 13
26	17	14, 15
27	18:1–20	16, 17, 18
28	18:21–35	19, 20
29	19	21, 22
30	20:1–16	23, 24
31	20:17–34	25, 26

FEBRUARY

DATE	MORNING	EVENING
	Matt	Exod
1	21:1–22	27, 28
2	21:23–46	29, 30
3	22:1–22	31, 32, 33
4	22:23–46	34, 35
5	23:1–22	36, 37, 38
6	23:23–29	39, 40
		Lev
7	24:1–28	1, 2, 3
8	24:29–51	4, 5
9	25:1–30	6, 7
10	25:31–46	8, 9, 10
11	26:1–25	11, 12
12	26:26–50	13
13	26:51–75	14
14	27:1–26	15, 16
15	27:27–50	17, 18
16	27:51–66	19, 20
17	28	21, 22
	Mark	
18	1:1–22	23, 24
19	1:23–45	25
20	2	26, 27
		Num
21	3:1–19	1, 2
22	3:20–35	3, 4
23	4:1–20	5, 6
24	4:21–41	7, 8
25	5:1–20	9, 10, 11
26	5:21–43	12, 13, 14
27	6:1–29	15, 16
28	6:30–56	17, 18, 19
29	7:1–13	20, 21, 22

MARCH

DATE	MORNING	EVENING
	Mark	Num
1	7:14–37	23, 24, 25
2	8:1–21	26, 27
3	8:22–38	28, 29, 30
4	9:1–29	31, 32, 33
5	9:30–50	34, 35, 36
		Deut
6	10:1–31	1, 2
7	10:32–52	3, 4
8	11:1–18	5, 6, 7
9	11:19–33	8, 9, 10
10	12:1–27	11, 12, 13
11	12:28–44	14, 15, 16
12	13:1–20	17, 18, 19
13	13:21–37	20, 21, 22
14	14:1–26	23, 24, 25
15	14:27–53	26, 27
16	14:54–72	28, 29
17	15:1–25	30, 31
18	15:26–47	32, 33, 34
		Josh
19	16	1, 2, 3
	Luke	
20	1:1–20	4, 5, 6
21	1:21–38	7, 8, 9
22	1:39–56	10, 11, 12
23	1:57–80	13, 14, 15
24	2:1–24	16, 17, 18
25	2:25–52	19, 20, 21
26	3	22, 23, 24
		Judg
27	4:1–30	1, 2, 3
28	4:31–44	4, 5, 6
29	5:1–16	7, 8
30	5:17–39	9, 10
31	6:1–26	11, 12

APRIL

DATE	MORNING	EVENING
	Luke	Judg
1	6:27–49	13, 14, 15
2	7:1–30	16, 17, 18
3	7:31–50	19, 20, 21
		Ruth
4	8:1–25	1, 2, 3, 4
		1 Sam
5	8:26–56	1, 2, 3
6	9:1–17	4, 5, 6
7	9:18–36	7, 8, 9
8	9:37–62	10, 11, 12
9	10:1–24	13, 14
10	10:25–42	15, 16
11	11:1–28	17, 18
12	11:29–54	19, 20, 21
13	12:1–31	22, 23, 24
14	12:32–59	25, 26
15	13:1–22	27, 28, 29
16	13:23–35	30, 31
		2 Sam
17	14:1–24	1, 2
18	14:25–35	3, 4, 5
19	15:1–10	6, 7, 8
20	15:11–32	9, 10, 11
21	16	12, 13
22	17:1–19	14, 15
23	17:20–37	16, 17, 18
24	18:1–23	19, 20
25	18:24–43	21, 22
26	19:1–27	23, 24
		1 Kgs
27	19:28–48	1, 2
28	20:1–26	3, 4, 5
29	20:27–47	6, 7
30	21:1–19	8, 9

MAY

DATE	MORNING	EVENING
	Luke	1 Kgs
1	21:20–38	10, 11
2	22:1–20	12, 13
3	22:21–46	14, 15
4	22:47–71	16, 17, 18
5	23:1–25	19, 20
6	23:26–56	21, 22
		2 Kgs
7	24:1–35	1, 2, 3
8	24:36–53	4, 5, 6
	John	
9	1:1–28	7, 8, 9
10	1:29–51	10, 11, 12
11	2	13, 14
12	3:1–18	15, 16
13	3:19–36	17, 18
14	4:1–30	19, 20, 21
15	4:31–54	22, 23
16	5:1–24	24, 25
		1 Chr
17	5:25–47	1, 2, 3
18	6:1–21	4, 5, 6
19	6:22–44	7, 8, 9
20	6:45–71	10, 11, 12
21	7:1–27	13, 14, 15
22	7:28–53	16, 17, 18
23	8:1–27	19, 20, 21
24	8:28–59	22, 23, 24
25	9:1–23	25, 26, 27
26	9:24–41	28, 29
		2 Chr
27	10:1–23	1, 2, 3
28	10:24–42	4, 5, 6
29	11:1–29	7, 8, 9
30	11:30–57	10, 11, 12
31	12:1–26	13, 14

JUNE

DATE	MORNING	EVENING
	John	2 Chr
1	12:27–50	15, 16
2	13:1–20	17, 18
3	13:21–38	19, 20
4	14	21, 22
5	15	23, 24
6	16	25, 26, 27
7	17	28, 29
8	18:1–18	30, 31
9	18:19–40	32, 33
10	19:1–22	34, 35, 36
		Ezra
11	19:23–42	1, 2
12	20	3, 4, 5
13	21	6, 7, 8
	Acts	
14	1	9, 10
		Neh
15	2:1–21	1, 2, 3
16	2:22–47	4, 5, 6
17	3	7, 8, 9
18	4:1–22	10, 11
19	4:23–37	12, 13
		Esth
20	5:1–21	1, 2
21	5:22–42	3, 4, 5
22	6	6, 7, 8
23	7:1–21	9, 10
		Job
24	7:22–43	1, 2
25	7:44–60	3, 4
26	8:1–25	5, 6, 7
27	8:26–40	8, 9, 10
28	9:1–21	11, 12, 13
29	9:22–43	14, 15, 16
30	10:1–23	17, 18, 19

JULY

DATE	MORNING	EVENING
	Acts	*Job*
1	10:24–48	20, 21
2	11	22, 23, 24
3	12	25, 26, 27
4	13:1–25	28, 29
5	13:26–52	30, 31
6	14	32, 33
7	15:1–21	34, 35
8	15:22–41	36, 37
9	16:1–21	38, 39, 40
10	16:22–40	41, 42
		Ps
11	17:1–15	1, 2, 3
12	17:16–34	4, 5, 6
13	18	7, 8, 9
14	19:1–20	10, 11, 12
15	19:21–41	13, 14, 15
16	20:1–16	16, 17
17	20:17–38	18, 19
18	21:1–17	20, 21, 22
19	21:18–40	23, 24, 25
20	22	26, 27, 28
21	23:1–15	29, 30
22	23:16–35	31, 32
23	24	33, 34
24	25	35, 36
25	26	37, 38, 39
26	27:1–26	40, 41, 42
27	27:27–44	43, 44, 45
28	28	46, 47, 48
	Rom	
29	1	49, 50
30	2	51, 52, 53
31	3	54, 55, 56

AUGUST

DATE	MORNING	EVENING
	Rom	*Ps*
1	4	57, 58, 59
2	5	60, 61, 62
3	6	63, 64, 65
4	7	66, 67
5	8:1–21	68, 69
6	8:22–39	70, 71
7	9:1–15	72, 73
8	9:16–33	74, 75, 76
9	10	77, 78
10	11:1–18	79, 80
11	11:19–36	81, 82, 83
12	12	84, 85, 86
13	13	87, 88
14	14	89, 90
15	15:1–13	91, 92, 93
16	15:14–33	94, 95, 96
17	16	97, 98, 99
	1 Cor	
18	1	100, 101, 102
19	2	103, 104
20	3	105, 106
21	4	107, 108, 109
22	5	110, 111, 112
23	6	113, 114, 115
24	7:1–19	116, 117, 118
25	7:20–40	119:1–88
26	8	119:89–176
27	9	120, 121, 122
28	10:1–18	123, 124, 125
29	10:19–33	126, 127, 128
30	11:1–16	129, 130, 131
31	11:17–34	132, 133, 134

SEPTEMBER

DATE	MORNING	EVENING
	1 Cor	*Ps*
1	12	135, 136
2	13	137, 138, 139
3	14:1–20	140, 141, 142
4	14:21–40	143, 144, 145
5	15:1–28	146, 147
6	15:29–58	148, 149, 150
		Prov
7	16	1, 2
	2 Cor	
8	1	3, 4, 5
9	2	6, 7
10	3	8, 9
11	4	10, 11, 12
12	5	13, 14, 15
13	6	16, 17, 18
14	7	19, 20, 21
15	8	22, 23, 24
16	9	25, 26
17	10	27, 28, 29
18	11:1–15	30, 31
		Eccl
19	11:16–33	1, 2, 3
20	12	4, 5, 6
21	13	7, 8, 9
	Gal	
22	1	10, 11, 12
		Song
23	2	1, 2, 3
24	3	4, 5
25	4	6, 7, 8
		Isa
26	5	1, 2
27	6	3, 4
	Eph	
28	1	5, 6
29	2	7, 8
30	3	9, 10

OCTOBER

DATE	MORNING	EVENING
	Eph	*Isa*
1	4	11, 12, 13
2	5:1–16	14, 15, 16
3	5:17–33	17, 18, 19
4	6	20, 21, 22
	Phil	
5	1	23, 24, 25
6	2	26, 27
7	3	28, 29
8	4	30, 31
	Col	
9	1	32, 33
10	2	34, 35, 36
11	3	37, 38
12	4	39, 40
	1 Thess	
13	1	41, 42
14	2	43, 44
15	3	45, 46
16	4	47, 48, 49
17	5	50, 51, 52
	2 Thess	
18	1	53, 54, 55
19	2	56, 57, 58
20	3	59, 60, 61
	1 Tim	
21	1	62, 63, 64
22	2	65, 66
		Jer
23	3	1, 2
24	4	3, 4, 5
25	5	6, 7, 8
26	6	9, 10, 11
	2 Tim	
27	1	12, 13, 14
28	2	15, 16, 17
29	3	18, 19
30	4	20, 21
	Titus	
31	1	22, 23

NOVEMBER

DATE	MORNING	EVENING
	Titus	*Jer*
1	2	24, 25, 26
2	3	27, 28, 29
3	*Phlm*	30, 31
	Heb	
4	1	32, 33
5	2	34, 35, 36
6	3	37, 38, 39
7	4	40, 41, 42
8	5	43, 44, 45
9	6	46, 47
10	7	48, 49
11	8	50
12	9	51, 52
		Lam
13	10:1–18	1, 2
14	10:19–39	3, 4, 5
		Ezek
15	11:1–19	1, 2
16	11:20–40	3, 4
17	12	5, 6, 7
18	13	8, 9, 10
	Jas	
19	1	11, 12, 13
20	2	14, 15
21	3	16, 17
22	4	18, 19
23	5	20, 21
	1 Pet	
24	1	22, 23
25	2	24, 25, 26
26	3	27, 28, 29
27	4	30, 31, 32
28	5	33, 34
	2 Pet	
29	1	35, 36
30	2	37, 38, 39

DECEMBER

DATE	MORNING	EVENING
	2 Pet	*Ezek*
1	3	40, 41
	1 John	
2	1	42, 43, 44
3	2	45, 46
4	3	47, 48
		Dan
5	4	1, 2
6	5	3, 4
7	*2 John*	5, 6, 7
8	*3 John*	8, 9, 10
9	*Jude*	11, 12
	Rev	*Hos*
10	1	1, 2, 3, 4
11	2	5, 6, 7, 8
12	3	9, 10, 11
13	4	12, 13, 14
14	5	*Joel*
		Amos
15	6	1, 2, 3
16	7	4, 5, 6
17	8	7, 8, 9
18	9	*Obad*
19	10	*Jonah*
		Mic
20	11	1, 2, 3
21	12	4, 5
22	13	6, 7
23	14	*Nah*
24	15	*Hab*
25	16	*Zeph*
26	17	*Hag*
		Zech
27	18	1, 2, 3, 4
28	19	5, 6, 7, 8
29	20	9, 10, 11, 12
30	21	13, 14
31	22	*Mal*

Topical Index

Deception
Genesis 3:4; Jeremiah 17:9; James 1:22; 2 John 7

Dedication
Numbers 7:1–6; 1 Samuel 1:11; 2 Chronicles 7:5; Colossians 3:17

Depression
Psalm 34:17–18; Isaiah 26:3; Philippians 4:6–7; 1 Peter 5:6–7

Disabilities
Leviticus 21:16–23; 2 Samuel 9; John 5:1–9; John 9:1–7; 2 Corinthians 12:6–10

Discernment
Proverbs 2:1–5; 1 Corinthians 2:14; Philippians 1:9–10; Hebrews 4:12

Discipleship
Proverbs 27:17; Matthew 16:24–25; Luke 14:27; John 8:31–32

Discipline
Proverbs 3:11–12; Proverbs 12:1; Hebrews 12:5–13; Revelation 3:19

Discouragement
Deuteronomy 31:8; Romans 15:13; 1 Corinthians 15:58; 1 Peter 5:7

Disputes
Proverbs 18:18–19; Isaiah 2:4; Matthew 5:23–24; 1 Corinthians 6:1–8

Diversity
Psalm 117:1–2; Daniel 7:14; Galatians 3:27–28; Revelation 7:9

Divorce
Deuteronomy 24:1–4; Malachi 2:16; Matthew 5:32; 1 Corinthians 7:10–11

Drunkenness
Isaiah 5:11; 1 Corinthians 6:9–11; Galatians 5:21; Ephesians 5:18

Eating Disorders
1 Samuel 16:7; Song of Solomon 4:7; Romans 14:17; 1 Corinthians 6:19–20

Empathy
Matthew 7:12; 1 Corinthians 12:26; Hebrews 4:15–16; 1 Peter 3:8

Envy
Exodus 34:14; Proverbs 14:30; 1 Corinthians 13:4; James 3:16

Eternity
Psalm 6:23; Ecclesiastes 3:11; John 3:16; John 17:3

Failure
Proverbs 24:16; Romans 3:23–24; 2 Corinthians 12:9–10; Philippians 3:12–16

False Prophets
Matthew 7:15; Matthew 24:24; 2 Thessalonians 3:1–5; 1 John 4:1–6

Families
Genesis 2:24; Psalm 127:3–5; 1 Timothy 3:5; 1 Timothy 5:8

Fasting
Isaiah 58:3–9; Joel 2:12–14; Matthew 6:16–18; Luke 5:33–35

Fatherhood
Psalm 103:13; Proverbs 4:1–9; Proverbs 13:22; Proverbs 17:6

Fathers
Luke 15:20–24; Ephesians 6:4; Colossians 3:21; Hebrews 12:9–10

Fear
Deuteronomy 31:6; Psalm 34:4; 2 Timothy 1:7; 1 John 4:18

Fellowship
Psalm 133; John 17:20–21; Acts 4:32–37; 1 John 1:7

Forgiveness
Matthew 6:14–15; Matthew 18:21–22; Mark 11:25; Colossians 3:12–13

Fornication
1 Corinthians 6:18–20; 1 Corinthians 7:9; Galatians 5:19–21; 1 Thessalonians 4:3–5

Freedom
Isaiah 61:1; Romans 8:20–21; 2 Corinthians 3:17; Galatians 5:1

Friendship
Proverbs 17:17; Isaiah 54:10; John 15:14–15; James 4:4

Future
Proverbs 16:9; Isaiah 55:8–9; Matthew 6:33–34; James 4:13–15

Gambling
Proverbs 13:11; Ecclesiastes 5:10; John 19:24; 1 Timothy 6:6–12

Generosity
Proverbs 11:25; Luke 21:1–4; 2 Corinthians 9:6; 1 Timothy 6:17–19

Gentleness
Psalm 18:35; Proverbs 15:1; Matthew 11:29–30; Ephesians 4:1–2

Glory
Exodus 24:16–17; 1 Corinthians 10:31; 2 Corinthians 3:7–18; Hebrews 1:3

Gluttony
Genesis 25:30–34; Proverbs 23:20–21; Proverbs 25:16; Philippians 3:18–19

Godly Living
Romans 12:2; Ephesians 4:17–31; 1 Thessalonians 4:9–12; James 1:19–27

God's Love
John 19:25–27; Romans 5:8; 1 John 3:1; 1 John 4:16

God's Plan
Exodus 3:7–8; Proverbs 16:9; Proverbs 19:21; Ephesians 2:10

God's Will
Matthew 6:9–10; Luke 22:42; 1 Thessalonians 4:3–8; 1 Thessalonians 5:6–18

Gospel
Isaiah 61:1–3; Matthew 24:14; Romans 1:16–17; Ephesians 1:7–10; 1 John 1:5–10

Gossip
Proverbs 11:13; Proverbs 26:20; Ephesians 4:29; James 1:26

Gratitude
Psalm 50:23; Psalm 100; Colossians 3:17; 1 Thessalonians 5:18

Greed
Ecclesiastes 5:10; Luke 12:13–34; 1 Corinthians 6:9–11; Hebrews 13:5

Grief
Psalm 147:3; Matthew 5:4; John 16:33; Revelation 21:4

Grudges
Leviticus 19:18; Mark 6:18–29; Mark 11:25; Ephesians 4:31–32

Guilt
Exodus 20:7; Romans 8:1–4; 1 John 1:9; 1 John 3:19–21

Happiness
Psalm 37:4; Psalm 119:143; Ecclesiastes 3:12–13; Philippians 4:8

Hatred
Proverbs 8:13; Proverbs 10:12; Matthew 10:22; 1 John 4:20

Hell
Matthew 10:28; Matthew 25:31–46; 2 Thessalonians 1:9; Revelation 21:8

Holiness
Leviticus 20:26; Romans 6:19; Hebrews 12:14; 1 Peter 1:14–16

Holy Spirit
Luke 11:13; John 14:15–17; Acts 2:38; Romans 8:26

Home
Psalm 127:1; Proverbs 14:1; John 14:23; 2 Corinthians 5:1–10

Homosexuality
Leviticus 18:22; Romans 1:26–27; 1 Corinthians 6:9; 2 Corinthians 12:9–10

Honesty
Proverbs 11:3; Proverbs 19:1; Proverbs 28:6; 2 Corinthians 8:21

Hospitality
Genesis 18:1–8; Leviticus 19:34; Hebrews 13:2; 1 Peter 4:9

Husbands
Proverbs 5:18–19; Ephesians 5:25–33; Colossians 3:19; 1 Peter 3:7

Identity
John 15:15; Romans 8:15; 2 Corinthians 5:5–16; 1 Peter 2:9

Idolatry
Exodus 20:3–6; Psalm 115:1–8; 1 Corinthians 10:14; Colossians 3:5

Image
Genesis 1:26–27; Romans 8:29; 2 Corinthians 3:18; Colossians 3:9–10

Imperfection
Romans 2:1; 1 Corinthians 13:10–12; Titus 3:5; Hebrews 10:11–14

Infertility
1 Samuel 1:1–20; Psalm 113:9; Isaiah 54; Luke 1:36–37

Influence
Proverbs 13:20; Proverbs 27:17; 1 Corinthians 15:33; 2 Corinthians 6:14–18

Injustice
Deuteronomy 27:19; Proverbs 17:15; Ecclesiastes 5:8; Micah 6:8

Insecurity
Isaiah 26:3; Matthew 6:25–34; Romans 5:1–5; Romans 12:2

Integrity
Job 2:3; Proverbs 10:9; Proverbs 20:7; Colossians 3:23

Judgment
Deuteronomy 32:39; Psalm 78:32–33; Matthew 12:36; 1 Corinthians 6:2–5

Justice
1 Kings 3:16–27; Psalm 98:8–9; Proverbs 11:1; Micah 6:8

Laziness
Proverbs 18:9; Proverbs 20:13; Proverbs 26:13–16; 2 Thessalonians 3:10

Legacy
Deuteronomy 6:5–7; Deuteronomy 7:9; Psalm 122:1–3; Proverbs 13:22

Lies
Genesis 3:1–5; Proverbs 20:12; John 8:44; 1 John 2:4

Listening
Proverbs 1:33; Proverbs 18:13; Matthew 13:16; James 1:19

Loneliness
Psalm 27:10; Psalm 68:6; Matthew 28:19–20; John 14:18

Loss of a Child
Matthew 5:4; Matthew 18:14; Romans 8:18; Revelation 21:4

Lust
Galatians 5:16; 1 Thessalonians 4:3–5; 2 Timothy 2:22; 1 John 2:16

Meekness
Psalm 37:11; Isaiah 11:4; Matthew 5:5; Colossians 3:12–13

Men
Job 38:3; Psalm 119:9; Titus 2:2, 6–8

Mentors
Proverbs 9:9; Proverbs 15:22; Luke 9:23; Titus 2:1–8

Miscarriage
2 Samuel 12:18–23; Psalm 68:19; Psalm 139:13–16; Isaiah 55:8–9

Mistakes
Romans 3:22–24; Romans 8:1–2; James 3:2; 1 John 1:9–10

Motherhood
Deuteronomy 6:6–7; Proverbs 13:24; Proverbs 31:26; Titus 2:4–5

Mothers
Genesis 3:20; Exodus 20:12; Proverbs 1:8–9; Isaiah 49:15

Motivation
Matthew 6:1–4; Galatians 1:10; 1 Corinthians 10:31; 1 Corinthians 15:58

Murder
Exodus 20:13; 2 Samuel 11:1–27; Matthew 5:21–22; 1 John 3:11–12

Names
Genesis 32:22–32; Proverbs 22:1; Ecclesiastes 7:1; Philippians 2:9–11

Orphans
Exodus 22:22; Psalm 68:5; Jeremiah 7:6; James 1:27

Overwhelmed
Psalm 32:6–7; Psalm 56:3; Isaiah 43:2; Matthew 19:26

Pain
Psalm 41:3; Romans 5:3–5; Romans 8:18 1 Peter 4:19

Perfectionism
Matthew 19:21; Romans 3:23–24; Philippians 3:12–16; Hebrews 10:14

Persecution
Psalm 23:4; Psalm 34:19; Matthew 5:10; 2 Timothy 3:12

Plans
Proverbs 3:5–6; Proverbs 16:9; Jeremiah 29:11; Luke 14:28

Poverty
Proverbs 6:10–11; Proverbs 20:13; Luke 6:20–21; 2 Corinthians 8:9

Pregnancy
Genesis 30:1–22; Psalm 127:3–5; Ecclesiastes 11:5; John 16:21

Prejudice
Mark 12:31; Acts 10:34–35; Colossians 3:11; James 2:1–13

Premarital Sex
1 Corinthians 6:18–20; 1 Corinthians 7:8–9; 1 Thessalonians 4:3–5; Hebrews 13:4

Promises
Numbers 23:19; Numbers 30:2; 2 Peter 3:9; Hebrews 6:13

Prostitution
Leviticus 20:6; Deuteronomy 23:17–18; Hosea 1:2; 1 Corinthians 6:15–18

Purpose
Psalm 78:1–8; John 16:7–11; Philippians 2:5–11; Revelation 12:10–11

Quarreling
Proverbs 15:18; Proverbs 20:3; Titus 3:9; James 4:1

Racial Equality
John 8:15–16; Romans 2:11; Romans 10:12–13; Revelation 5:9–10

Rejection
Psalm 44:23–26; Isaiah 53:3; Luke 6:22; 1 Thessalonians 1:4

Reproof
Leviticus 19:17; Proverbs 12:1; 2 Timothy 3:16; Hebrews 12:1–13

Responsibility
Leviticus 24:15; Romans 12:6–8; Galatians 6:5; Colossians 3:23

Revenge
Leviticus 19:18; Proverbs 24:29; Matthew 5:38–39; Romans 12:19–21

Risk
2 Samuel 10:12; Esther 4:15–16; Matthew 14:30–31; Mark 5:24–34

Romance
Proverbs 5:18–19; Song of Solomon 1:1–4; Song of Solomon 8:6–7; 1 John 4:7

Sadness
Psalm 34:18; Psalm 55:22; John 16:20; James 5:13

Security
Psalm 29:11; Proverbs 1:33; John 3:16; Ephesians 2:8–9

Self-control
Proverbs 4:27; Proverbs 25:28; Galatians 5:22–23; 2 Timothy 1:7

Self-defense
Psalm 82:4; Proverbs 20:22; Matthew 5:39–42; Luke 22:36–38

Self-worth
Genesis 1:27; Psalm 139:13–15; Ephesians 4:32; Philippians 4:13

Sex
Genesis 2:24; Proverbs 5:18–19; 1 Corinthians 7:3–5; Hebrews 13:4

Shame
Psalm 34:4–5; Isaiah 61:7; Romans 10:11; 1 Corinthians 4:14

Sickness
Isaiah 40:29–31; Zephaniah 3:17; James 5:14; 1 Peter 2:24

Silence
Exodus 14:14; Ecclesiastes 3:7; Zechariah 2:13; Luke 5:16

Slander
Leviticus 19:16; Psalm 101:5; Matthew 12:36; 1 Peter 2:1

Solitude
Psalm 68:6; Matthew 5:15–16; Mark 1:35; Mark 6:31–32

Sons
Genesis 37:1–4; Psalm 127:3–5; Proverbs 22:6; Galatians 3:26

Sorrow
Psalm 147:3; Isaiah 60:20; Matthew 5:4; John 14:27

Spiritual Fruit
Acts 2:38; Galatians 5:22–23; Ephesians 5:8–10; Colossians 1:9–14

Spiritual Growth
Psalm 1:1–3; Ephesians 4:14–15; Philippians 2:1–5; 1 Peter 2:1–5

Stealing
Proverbs 10:2; Proverbs 20:17; John 10:10; Ephesians 4:28

Stress
Psalm 55:22; Proverbs 12:25; Matthew 11:28–30; Philippians 4:6

Suicide
Psalm 34:17–20; Jeremiah 29:11; Romans 10:13; 2 Corinthians 1:9–10

Surrender
Proverbs 23:26; Mark 14:35–36; Luke 9:23–24; James 4:7

Talents
Proverbs 18:16; Luke 12:48; Romans 12:6; 1 Peter 4:10

Temptation
Matthew 4:1–11; Mark 14:38; 1 Corinthians 10:13; James 1:12–16; James 4:7

Testing
Deuteronomy 8:2; Matthew 4:1–11; 1 Thessalonians 5:21; 1 Peter 4:12–14

Thankfulness
1 Chronicles 16:8; Psalm 100:4–5; Ephesians 5:18–21; 1 Thessalonians 5:18

Unbelief
Matthew 17:17–20; John 20:27–29; Hebrews 11:6; James 1:6

Value
Psalm 116:15; Matthew 6:19–34; Matthew 13:44; Luke 12:6

Vanity
Exodus 38:8; Philippians 2:3; 2 Timothy 3:1–5; 1 John 2:12–17

Vengeance
Leviticus 19:18; Jeremiah 50:15; Micah 5:15; Romans 12:17–19

Violence
Psalm 7:14–16; Psalm 11:5; Matthew 11:12; Acts 21:27–40

Vows
Numbers 6:1–8; Ecclesiastes 5:4; Matthew 5:33; James 5:12

Vulnerability
Ecclesiastes 10:2; 2 Corinthians 6:11–13; 2 Thessalonians 2:8; James 5:16; 1 John 1:5–10

War
Psalm 46:9; Proverbs 21:31; Ecclesiastes 3:8; James 4:1

Weakness
1 Corinthians 2:3–5; 2 Corinthains 1:8–11; 2 Corinthians 12:9; Hebrews 11:33–35

Wealth
Deuteronomy 8:17–18; 1 Samuel 2:7; 2 Chronicles 1:11–12; Proverbs 15:16

Widows
Deuteronomy 10:17–18; Psalm 146:9; Proverbs 15:25; 1 Timothy 5:9–16

Wives
Genesis 2:24; Proverbs 12:4; Proverbs 19:14; Ephesians 5:22–33

Women
Genesis 2:18–23; Proverbs 14:1; Proverbs 31:30–31; Titus 2:3–5

Women in Ministry
Judges 4:4–5; 1 Samuel 1:20–2:11; John 4:27– 30; John 20: 16–18; Acts 2:17–18

Words
Psalm 12:6; Psalm 119:11; Matthew 12:36–37; James 1:19

Work
Genesis 2:15; John 4:34; Colossians 3:23–24; 1 Thessalonians 4:11; 2 Thessalonians 3;10–12

Worthiness
Psalm 139:14; Romans 3:10–12; Romans 5:8; 1 Peter 1:18–19

Love God Greatly Reach

At Love God Greatly we create resources to bring God's Word to women in every community, in every nation, and in every language so they can love God greatly with their lives. Love God Greatly is active in over 200 countries with Bible studies translated into twenty-four languages.

Afghanistan
Albania
Algeria
American Samoa
Andorra
Angola
Anguilla
Antigua & Barbuda
Argentina
Armenia
Aruba
Australia
Austria
Azerbaijan
Bahamas
Bahrain
Bangladesh
Barbados
Belarus
Belgium
Belize
Benin
Bermuda
Bhutan
Bolivia
Bosnia & Herzegovina
Botswana
Brazil
British Virgin Islands
Brunei
Bulgaria
Burkina Faso
Burundi
Cambodia
Cameroon
Canada
Caribbean Netherlands
Cayman Islands
Central African Republic
Chad
Chile
China
Colombia
Congo - Brazzaville
Congo - Kinshasa
Cook Islands
Costa Rica
Côte d'Ivoire
Croatia
Cuba
Curaçao
Cyprus
Czechia
Denmark
Djibouti
Dominica
Dominican Republic
Ecuador
Egypt
El Salvador
Equatorial Guinea
Eritrea
Estonia
Eswatini
Ethiopia
Falkland Islands (Islas Malvinas)
Faroe Islands
Fiji
Finland
France
French Guiana
French Polynesia
Gabon
Gambia
Georgia
Germany
Ghana
Gibraltar
Greece
Greenland
Grenada
Guadeloupe
Guam
Guatemala
Guernsey
Guinea
Guyana
Haiti
Honduras
Hong Kong
Hungary
Iceland
India
Indonesia
Iran
Iraq
Ireland
Israel
Italy
Jamaica
Japan
Jersey
Jordan
Kazakhstan
Kenya
Kiribati
Kosovo
Kuwait
Kyrgyzstan
Laos
Latvia
Lebanon
Lesotho
Luxembourg
Liberia
Libya
Lithuania
Macao
Madagascar
Malawi
Malaysia
Maldives

Mali
Malta
Marshall Islands
Martinique
Mauritius
Mayotte
Mexico
Micronesia
Moldova
Monaco
Mongolia
Montenegro
Montserrat
Morocco
Mozambique
Myanmar (Burma)
Namibia
Nauru

Nepal
Netherlands
New Caledonia
New Zealand
Nicaragua
Niger
Nigeria
North Korea
North Macedonia
Northern Mariana Islands
Norway
Oman
Pakistan
Palau
Palestine
Panama
Papua New Guinea
Paraguay
Peru
Philippines
Poland
Portugal
Puerto Rico
Qatar
Réunion
Romania
Russia
Rwanda
Samoa
Saudi Arabia
Senegal
Serbia
Seychelles
Sierra Leone
Singapore
Sint Maarten
Slovakia
Slovenia
Solomon Islands
Somalia

South Africa
South Korea
South Sudan
Spain
Sri Lanka
St. Kitts & Nevis
St. Lucia
St. Martin
St. Vincent & Grenadiers
Sudan
Suriname
Svalbard & Jan Mayen
Sweden
Switzerland
Syria
Taiwan
Tajikistan
Tanzania
Thailand
Timor-Leste
Togo
Tonga
Trinidad & Tobago
Tunisia
Turkey
Turks & Caicos Islands
U.S. Virgin Islands
Uganda
Ukraine
United Arab Emirates
United Kingdom
United States
Uruguay
Uzbekistan
Vanuatu
Venezuela
Vietnam
Yemen
Zambia
Zimbabwe

Bible Study Translations

AFRIKAANS
ALBANIAN
ARABIC
BULGARIAN
BURMESE
CHINESE
CZECH
DUTCH
ENGLISH
FRENCH
GERMAN
HAUSA
HUNGARIAN
INDONESIAN
ITALIAN
MACEDONIAN
POLISH
PORTUGUESE
ROMANIAN
RUSSIAN
SLOVAK
SPANISH
SWAHILI
TRADITIONAL CHINESE

Contributors

Editorial

Angela Perritt	General Editor
Melissa Fuller, ThM	General Editor
Philip Nation, DMin	Publisher
Victoria Green	Managing Editor
Russell Meek, PhD	Editor
Crystal Stine	Editor
Holly Halverson	Editor
Bri Loomis	Editor

Design

Kate Armstrong	Art Director
Lauren Gould	Creative Director, Map Design
Andrea Howey	Memory Verse Design
Mark Sheeres	Typesetter
Jennifer Miller	Typesetter

Devotional Writers

Amanda Cunningham	2 Thessalonians 3:6–12	Do Your Work
Andrea Howey	Exodus 4:1–12	You Are Not Enough
	Acts 27:9–20	Undergirded with Help
	1 John 3:1	Children of God
Angela Perritt	Genesis 3	What Jesus Finished
	Genesis 22:1–19	Jehovah Jireh
	Exodus 14:13–14	Don't Be Afraid
	Deuteronomy 6:1–9	Cheerios and Hand Motions
	Deuteronomy 31:7–8	Strong and Courageous
	1 Samuel 21:9–14	When Fear Grips Our Hearts
	2 Chronicles 7:14	If My People . . .
	Nehemiah 4:1–6	The Power of Words
	Isaiah 9:6	His Name Shall Be Called . . .
	Isaiah 54:17	In a War
	Jeremiah 32:27	Too Hard for God
	Hosea 1	The Pursuit
	Hosea 3	All the Wrong Places
	Hosea 6:6	Ever Faithful
	Jonah 2:1–2	He Hears
	Matthew 11:28	He Will Give Us Rest
	Mark 6:45–51	Never Alone
	John 8:31–32	Never Defenseless
	John 13:8–9	No Mistake
	Acts 2:42	Devoted to Prayer
	Acts 9:36–43	Our Prayers Matter
	Romans 8:37–39	Nothing
	Galatians 5:13–14	Loving Our Neighbor
	Philippians 1:6	He Will Complete You

Contributor	Passage	Title
Bess Lewis	Joshua 20	Cities of Refuge
	Esther 7	Then Queen Esther Replied
	Job 1:8	My Servant
	Obadiah	Your Love Defends Me
	Micah 6:8	Carry Out Justice, Love Faithfulness, Live Obediently
	Luke 9:18–22	Who Do You Say I Am?
	1 Corinthians 10:23–11:1	An Exercise in Boundaries
	Philemon	To Call the Slave Your Friend
Charisse Aguas	Nehemiah 9	When We're Convicted
	Matthew 16:24–28	Cost of Discipleship
	Ephesians 2:1–9	Dead or Alive?
Cortney Whiting	1 Chronicles 11:10–47	David's Mighty Men
	Proverbs 31:10–31	Wisdom and the Fear of the Lord
	John 21	Living the Life of the Redeemed
	Colossians 3	Living a Resurrected Life
Crystal Stine	Genesis 45	Better Than Our Own
	Ezra 3	The Hard Work of Rebuilding
	Matthew 5:3–10	Making the Humble Things Holy
	Ephesians 4:22–24	Coming Clean
	1 Peter 5:5–9	Humble Yourself
Edurne Mencia	Deuteronomy 17:14–20	Writing the Word of God
	Ezra 10:1–4	Confess and Repent
	Daniel 10:10–21	The Reality of Spiritual Warfare
	Romans 12:4–21	Taking off the Mask
	Colossians 1:9–14	Praying for Spiritual Needs
Emma Murphy	Judges 2:1–4	The One True God
	Job 8	No Smoke without Fire
	Mark 12:28–31	Love God and Love Others
	James 4:1–4	Conflict
	2 Peter 1:12–21	The Word of God
Erika Dawson	Judges 16	Lifelong Faithfulness
	Psalm 103	Praise the Lord
	John 4:48–54	Believe and Go
	2 Corinthians 8:7	A Generous Impulse
Eryn Hall	Psalm 3	Holy Confidence
	Psalm 34:12–15	To Really Live
	Acts 20:24	Our Task to Testify
	Hebrews 6:18–19	Remember Your Anchor
	3 John	Even Strangers
Jami Nato	2 Chronicles 26:16	Pride and Power
	Proverbs 2:1–5	Treasure Hunt
Jen Thorn	Genesis 18:9–15	Is Anything Impossible?
	Joshua 10	Only His Power
	Ruth 4	Happily Ever After
	1 Samuel 18:16	David the Warrior
	Esther 4:14	God's Providential Power
	Habakkuk 3:18–19	The Joy of Our Salvation
	Mark 2:1–12	His Authority
	Luke 13:5	About Repentance
	Luke 17:15–16	Thanksgiving with Passion
	John 1:16	A Generous God?
	Galatians 2:15–21	A Debt We Cannot Repay
	1 Thessalonians 2:1–8	Ministering to One Another
	1 Timothy 4:8	Training in Godliness
	Hebrews 3:13	Exhort One Another

Contributor	Passage	Title
Kaitlyn Schiess	Numbers 20	The Responsibility of Authority
	Judges 11	An Unlikely Hero
	2 Kings 4:42–44	Care for God's People
	Jeremiah 7	Injustice and Idolatry
	Zechariah 14	Work in the Waiting
	Luke 1:46–56	The Magnificat
	Luke 24:13–35	Learning at the Dinner Table
	Romans 16	Differences Set Aside
	James 1	Every Perfect Gift
	Revelation 21:1–5	From the Garden to the City
Karen Hensen	Leviticus 19:1–18	Get to Know the Law Giver
	1 Samuel 1:1–20	Weeping with Bitterness
	2 Kings 17:1–23	Never Abandoned
	Amos 9:11–15	Overwhelming Mercy
	Nahum 1:2–15	God Always Wins
	Mark 16:1–8	He Is Not Here
	1 Corinthians 4	Be Imitators
	Hebrews 10	Draw Near
	Revelation 2:1–7	Losing Your First Love
Katy Rose	Numbers 11	Gratitude through Trial
	Psalm 90	13,001
	Zephaniah 3:11–17	Posture for His Presence
	2 Corinthians 4:7	Holding a Treasure
Kelli Trontel	1 Chronicles 16:8–36	Proclaiming His Goodness
	Psalm 126	Until the Harvest
	Acts 18:9–11	Do Not Fear
	1 Thessalonians 4:1–13	Holiness Is a Gift
Laura Courtney	Joshua 2	Strong and Brave
	1 Kings 11:1–13	Not-So-Wise King
	Nehemiah 12:43	The Art of Celebration
	Esther 1	Vashti: A Story of Great Bravery
	Ecclesiastes 3:11	Beauty in Every Season
	Jonah 4:2	Grace for the Grumblers
	Titus 1:16	A Call to Stand Out
	Revelation 12:10–11	Courageous Faith
Lyli Dunbar	Genesis 37:18–19	The God of Dreams
	Psalm 56	Taking Sides
	Lamentations 3:21–23	Call to Mind
	Matthew 19:28–30	The Bottom Line
	Galatians 4:6–7	Free to Sing
	1 Timothy 1:18	Fight the Good Fight
Melissa Fuller	Genesis 32:22–32	What Is Your Name?
	Leviticus 5:1–13	Equal Opportunity Restoration
	Ruth 1	Is He Good to Me?
	2 Kings 19	Don't Dig Up in Doubt
	Job 38	Where Were You?
	Psalm 29	Enthroned
	Proverbs 14:1	With Her Own Hands
	Joel 2:12–27	No Other
	Matthew 26:6–13	A Beautiful Thing
	Luke 8:40–48	Every Need
	Jude 20–25	Mercy
Meshali Mitchell	Nehemiah 13:4–9	The Key to Restoration
Nicole Zasowski	2 John	Speaking the Truth in Love
Sandra Maddox	Malachi 3:2–3	Faith in the Furnace
	1 Peter 2:9	Banish Darkness

Contributor	Passage	Title
Sara Lindsey	Exodus 32:7–14	The Power of Prayer
	Psalm 67	All Nations, All People
	Daniel 3:17–18	Even If
	Mark 10:35–45	Servant-Leadership
Sarah Stiles	Psalm 127:2	White Flag
	Romans 1:1–7	Our Work for the Gospel
Terria Moore	2 Chronicles 20	God Reigns Supreme
	Song of Solomon 2:15	The Little Foxes
	Isaiah 40:8	God's Enduring Word
	Haggai 1:2–11	Build My Temple
	Romans 5:8	Relentless Love
	2 Timothy 2:1–7	Strong in Grace
Vanessa Warren	Philippians 4:4–9	Rejoice!
Whitney Daughtery	2 Samuel 5:10	The Promise of a Better King
	2 Samuel 12:7–14	David the Sinner
	1 Kings 18	Nothing Left to Question
	Psalm 109:30–31	In the Storm
	Jeremiah 17:9–10	Deceiving Ourselves
	Ezekiel 34:15–16	A Love Like No Other
	Matthew 28:20	His Presence Remains
	Mark 1:20	No Matter the Cost
	John 15:1–11	Defined by the Hustle
	1 Corinthians 1:26–31	Boast in the Lord
	Ephesians 6:13	Suit Up

Testimony Index

Slovakia	Jolika	1 Samuel
Slovakia	Lucia	Romans
South Africa	Eloise	Ezra
South Africa	Marissa	Numbers
South Africa	Velia	Ruth
Spain	Angela	Song of Solomon
Spain	Esther	Nehemiah
Switzerland	Anita	2 John
Switzerland	Thirza	2 Samuel
Taiwan	Alice	Matthew
Thailand	Lin	Joel
the Netherlands	Charissa	1 John
the Netherlands	Willemin	Deuteronomy
Ukraine	Diana	John
United States	Casey	Judges
United States	Diana	Philemon
United States	Vanessa	3 John
United States	Vicky	Job
Venezuela	Edurne	Acts
Vietnam	Ly	Ecclesiastes

Concordance

AARON

Priesthood of (Exod 28:1; Num 17; Heb 5:1-4; 7), garments (Exod 28; 39), consecration (Exod 29), ordination (Lev 8).

Spokesman for Moses (Exod 4:14-16, 27-31; 7:1-2). Supported Moses' hands in battle (Exod 17:8-13). Built golden calf (Exod 32; Deut 9:20). Talked against Moses (Num 12). Priesthood opposed (Num 16); staff budded (Num 17). Forbidden to enter land (Num 20:1-12). Death (Num 20:22-29; 33:38-39).

ABANDON

"Far be it from us to *a* the LORD .... JOSH 24:16
a strife before it breaks out! .... PROV 17:14
The wicked need to *a* their lifestyle .... ISA 55:7
and I will never *a* you." .... HEB 13:5

ABANDONED

God has not *a* us in our servitude. .... EZRA 9:9
why have you *a* me? .... PS 22:1
Even if my father and mother *a* me, ... PS 27:10
I have never seen the godly *a* .... PS 37:25

ABANDONS

worthless shepherd who *a* the flock! ..... ZECH 11:17

ABBA

adoption, by whom we cry, *A* Father." ..... ROM 8:15
who calls *A! Father!*" .... GAL 4:6

ABEL

Second son of Adam (Gen 4:2). Offered proper sacrifice (Gen 4:4; Heb 11:4). Murdered by Cain (Gen 4:8; Matt 23:35; Luke 11:51; 1 John 3:12).

ABHOR

A what is evil, ... ROM 12:9

ABHORRENCE

and others to shame and everlasting *a* .... DAN 12:2

ABHORRENT

these are *a* to the LORD your God. .... DEUT 23:18
these ways is *a* to the LORD your God. .. DEUT 25:16

ABHORS

The LORD *a* dishonest scales, ... PROV 11:1
The LORD *a* a person who lies, ... PROV 12:22
LORD *a* the sacrifice of the wicked, ... PROV 15:8
The LORD *a* the way of the wicked, ... PROV 15:9
The LORD *a* the plans of the wicked, ... PROV 15:26
The LORD *a* every arrogant person; ..... PROV 16:5
The LORD *a* differing weights, ... PROV 20:23

ABIGAIL

Wife of Nabal (1 Sam 25:30); pled for his life with David (1 Sam 25:14-35). Became David's wife (1 Sam 25:36-42).

ABIJAH

Son of Rehoboam; king of Judah (1 Kgs 14:31–15:8; 2 Chr 12:16–14:1).

ABIMELECH

1. King of Gerar who took Abraham's wife Sarah, believing her to be his sister (Gen 20). Later made a covenant with Abraham (Gen 21:22-33).
2. King of Gerar who took Isaac's wife Rebekah, believing her to be his sister (Gen 26:1-11). Later made a covenant with Isaac (Gen 26:12-31).

ABLE

As they were *a they gave to the* .... EZRA 2:69
Their silver and gold will not be *a* .... EZEK 7:19
he is *a* to rescue us from the furnace ...... DAN 3:17
a to separate us from the love of God .... ROM 8:39
for the Lord is *a* to make him stand. ...... ROM 14:4
and *a* to instruct one another. .... ROM 15:14
Now to him who is *a* to strengthen you .. ROM 16:25
so that you may be *a* to endure it. .... 1 COR 10:13
God is *a* to make all grace overflow ...... 2 COR 9:8
a to comprehend with all the saints ...... EPH 3:18
is *a* to do far beyond all that we ask .... EPH 3:20
a to subject all things to himself. .... PHIL 3:21
convinced that he is *a* to protect .... 2 TIM 1:12
which are *a* to give you wisdom .... 2 TIM 3:15
So he is *a* to save completely .... HEB 7:25
Now to the one who is *a* to keep you .... JUDE 24

ABOLISH

come to *a* these things but to fulfill ...... MATT 5:17

ABOMINATION

both of them are an *a* to the LORD. .... PROV 17:15
The wicked person's sacrifice is an *a* .... PROV 21:27
even his prayer is an *a* .... PROV 28:9
set up the *a* that causes desolation. .... DAN 11:31

ABOUND

so that you may *a* in hope .... ROM 15:13
a in order to strengthen the church. .... 1 COR 14:12
that your love may *a* even more .... PHIL 1:9
increase and *a* in love for one
another .... 1 THESS 3:12

ABOUNDING

and *a* in loyal love and faithfulness, ... EXOD 34:6

ABOUT

hear *a* and learn to fear the LORD .... DEUT 31:13
I will sing *a* your strength; .... PS 59:16
carried *a* by every wind of teaching .... EPH 4:14
and they think *a* earthly things. .... PHIL 3:19

ABRAHAM

Covenant relation with the LORD (Gen 12:1-3; 13:14-17; 15; 17; 22:15-18; Exod 2:24; Neh 9:8; Ps 105; Mic 7:20; Luke 1:68-75; Rom 4; Heb 6:13-15).

Called from Ur, via Haran, to Canaan (Gen 12:1; Acts 7:2-4; Heb 11:8-10). Moved to Egypt, nearly lost Sarah to Pharaoh (Gen 12:10-20). Divided the land with Lot (Gen 13). Saved

Lot from four kings (Gen 14:1-16); blessed by Melchizedek (Gen 14:17-20; Heb 7:1-20). Declared righteous by faith (Gen 15:6; Rom 4:3; Gal 3:6-9). Fathered Ishmael by Hagar (Gen 16).

Name changed from Abram (Gen 17:5; Neh 9:7). Circumcised (Gen 17; Rom 4:9-12). Entertained three visitors (Gen 18); promised a son by Sarah (Gen 18:9-15; 17:16). Moved to Gerar; nearly lost Sarah to Abimelech (Gen 20). Fathered Isaac by Sarah (Gen 21:1-7; Acts 7:8; Heb 11:11-12); sent away Hagar and Ishmael (Gen 21:8-21; Gal 4:22-30). Tested by offering Isaac (Gen 22; Heb 11:17-19; Jas 2:21-24). Sarah died; bought field of Ephron for burial (Gen 23). Secured wife for Isaac (Gen 24). Death (Gen 25:7-11).

ABSALOM
Son of David by Maakah (2 Sam 3:3; 1 Chr 3:2). Killed Amnon for rape of his sister Tamar; banished by David (2 Sam 13). Returned to Jerusalem; received by David (2 Sam 14). Rebelled against David; seized kingdom (2 Sam 15-17). Killed (2 Sam 18).

ABSOLUTE
I experience *a* joy in your presence; ...... PS 16:11

ABSOLUTELY
and *a* reliable. ...... PS 119:138

ABSTAINS
abstains from eating *a* for the Lord, ... ROM 14:6

ABUNDANCE
consist in the *a* of his possessions." ...... LUKE 12:15
those who receive the *a* of grace ...... ROM 5:17

ABUNDANT
your faithfulness is *a* ...... LAM 3:23

ABUNDANTLY
and may have it *a* ...... JOHN 10:10

ABUSE
bearing the *a* he experienced. ...... HEB 13:13

ABUSIVE
the verbally *a* ...... 1 COR 6:10

ACCEPT
You must not *a* a bribe, ... EXOD 23:8
not *a* an accusation against an elder ...... TIM 5:19

ACCEPTABLE
no prophet is *a* in his hometown. ...... LUKE 4:24

ACCEPTED
the LORD has *a* my prayer. ...... PS 6:9

ACCEPTS
The wise person *a* instructions, ... PROV 10:8
but the one who *a* reproof is honored. ...... PROV 13:18
whoever accepts the one I send *a* me, ... JOHN 13:20

ACCOMMODATING
a full of mercy and good fruit, ... JAS 3:17

ACCOMPANY
These signs will *a* those who believe: ...... MARK 16:17

ACCOMPLISHED
by what you *a* ...... HAB 3:2

ACCOUNT
give an *a* for every worthless word ...... MATT 12:36
each of us will give an *a* of himself ...... ROM 14:12
him to whom we must render an *a* ...... HEB 4:13

ACCOUNTABLE
whole world may be held *a* to God. ...... ROM 3:19

ACCUMULATE
a for yourselves treasures on earth, ... MATT 6:19

ACCURSED
For I could wish that I myself were *a* ...... ROM 9:3

ACCUSATION
by violence or by false *a* ...... LUKE 3:14
Do not accept an *a* against an elder ...... 1 TIM 5:19

ACCUSE
a anyone without legitimate cause, ... PROV 3:30

ACHAN
Sin at Jericho caused defeat at Ai; stoned (Josh 7; 22:20; 1 Chr 2:7).

ACHE
Even in laughter the heart may *a* ...... PROV 14:13

ACKNOWLEDGE
you must *a* the greatness of our God. ...... DEUT 32:3
A the majesty of the LORD's. ...... PS 29:2
A God's power, ... PS 68:34
the desire to *a* that I am the LORD. ...... JER 24:7
a those who labor among you ...... 1 THESS 5:12

ACKNOWLEDGES
a me before people, ... MATT 10:32

ACQUITTED
but I am not *a* because of this. ...... 1 COR 4:4

ACTIONS
removes the guilt of our rebellious *a* ...... PS 103:12

ACTIVE
For the word of God is living and *a* ...... HEB 4:12

ACTIVITY
whether his *a* is pure ...... PROV 20:11

ACTS
one true God *a* in a faithful manner; ...... 2 SAM 22:31
his mighty *a* and the judgments ...... 1 CHR 16:12
one whose rebellious *a* are forgiven, ... PS 32:1
right hand will accomplish mighty *a* ...... PS 45:4
wipe away my rebellious *a* ...... PS 51:1
proclaim the power of your awesome *a* ...... PS 145:6
might acknowledge your mighty *a* ...... PS 145:12
Praise him for his mighty *a* ...... PS 150:2
your sinful *a* have alienated you ...... ISA 59:2
righteous *a* are like a menstrual rag ...... ISA 64:6

ADAM
First man (Gen 1:26–2:25; Rom 5:14; 1 Tim 2:13). Sin of (Gen 3; Hos 6:7; Rom 5:12-21). Children of (Gen 4:1–5:5). Death of (Gen 5:5; Rom 5:12-21; 1 Cor 15:22).

ADD
Do not *a* to it or subtract from it! ...... DEUT 12:32
Do not *a* to his words, ... PROV 30:6
which of you by worrying can *a* an hour ...... LUKE 12:25

ADDS
If anyone *a* to them, ... REV 22:18

ADEQUACY
but our *a* is from God, ... 2 COR 3:5

ADEQUATE
Not that we are *a* in ourselves .... 2 COR 3:5

ADMIRATION
crops given by the LORD will bring *a* .... ISA 4:2

ADMIRED
and the leading officials I *a* so much .... PS 16:3

ADOPTION
inwardly as we eagerly await our *a* .... ROM 8:23

ADORE
How rightly the young women *a* you!..... SONG 1:4

ADORNS
Holiness aptly *a* your house, ... PS 93:5

ADULT
But when I became an *a* .... 1 COR 13:11

ADULTERY
You shall not commit *a* .... EXOD 20:14
who commits *a* with a woman lacks sense .... PROV 6:32
'Do not commit *a* .... MATT 5:27
has already committed *a* with her .... MATT 5:28
makes her commit *a* .... MATT 5:32
a sexual immorality, ... MATT 15:19
and marries another commits *a* .... MATT 19:9

ADVANTAGE
have not taken *a* of you through anyone .... 2 COR 12:17
taking *a* of every opportunity, ... EPH 5:16
rights of his brother or take *a* of him .. 1 THESS 4:6

ADVERSARY
give the *a* no opportunity to vilify us .... 1 TIM 5:14

ADVERSITY
and a relative is born to help in *a* .... PROV 17:17
for orphans and widows in their *a* .... JAS 1:27

ADVICE
and followed the *a* of the younger ones ... 1 KGS 12:14
but the one who listens to *a* is wise. .... PROV 12:15
Listen to *a* and receive discipline, ... PROV 19:20

ADVISER
and is called Wonderful *A* .... ISA 9:6

ADVOCATE
he will give you another *A* .... JOHN 14:16
But the *A* .... JOHN 14:26
we have an *a* with the Father, ... 1 JOHN 2:1

AFFECTION
to brotherly *a* .... 2 PET 1:7

AFFECTIONATE
a compassionate, and humble. .... 1 PET 3:8

AFFLICT
You must not *a* any widow or orphan. .. EXOD 22:22

AFFLICTION
the *a* of my people who are in Egypt. ..... EXOD 3:7

AFFLICTIONS
that no one would be shaken by these *a* .... 1 THESS 3:3

AFRAID
Do not be *a* .... GEN 26:24
because he was *a* to look at God. .... EXOD 3:6
When I am *a* .... PS 56:3
I am *a* of your judgments. .... PS 119:120
Don't be *a* .... ISA 41:10
Do not be *a* of those to whom I send .... JER 1:8
they were *a* and honored God who had .... MATT 9:8
Do not be *a* of those who kill the body .... MATT 10:28
So do not be *a* .... MATT 10:31
"Do not be *a* .... MARK 5:36
and I will not be *a* .... HEB 13:6

AFTERWARD
A it bites like a snake, ... PROV 23:32

AGAIN
Then I *a* fell down before the LORD ...... DEUT 9:18
will he live *a* .... JOB 14:14

AGE
from age to *a* .... NEH 9:5
For the wisdom of this *a* is foolishness ... 1 COR 3:19

AGED
Is not wisdom found among the *a* .... JOB 12:12

AGO
God spoke long *a* in various portions .... HEB 1:1

AGREE
on earth *a* about whatever you ask, ... MATT 18:19
I *a* that the law is good. .... ROM 7:16
a with one another, ... 2 COR 13:11

AGREEMENT
what *a* does Christ have with Beliar? .... 2 COR 6:15

AHAB
Son of Omri; king of Israel (1 Kgs 16:28–22:40), husband of Jezebel (1 Kgs 16:31). Promoted Baal worship (1 Kgs 16:31-33); opposed by Elijah (1 Kgs 17:1; 18; 21), a prophet (1 Kgs 20:35-43), Micaiah (1 Kgs 22:1-28). Defeated Ben Hadad (1 Kgs 20). Killed for failing to kill Ben Hadad and for murder of Naboth (1 Kgs 20:35–21:40).

AHAZ
Son of Jotham; king of Judah, (2 Kgs 16; 2 Chr 28; Isa 7).

AHAZIAH
1. Son of Ahab; king of Israel (1 Kgs 22:51–2 Kgs 1:18; 2 Chr 20:35-37).
2. Son of Jehoram; king of Judah (2 Kgs 8:25-29; 9:14-29), also called Jehoahaz (2 Chr 21:17–22:9; 25:23).

AIR
or box like one who hits only *a* .... 1 COR 9:26
to the ruler of the domain of the *a* .... EPH 2:2
clouds to meet the Lord in the *a* .... 1 THESS 4:17

ALERT
Therefore stay *a* .... MATT 24:42
Stay *a*! For you do not know when ...... MARK 13:33
their master finds *a* when he returns! .. LUKE 12:37
Stay *a* stand firm in the faith, ... 1 COR 16:13
and to this end be *a* .... EPH 6:18
but must stay *a* and sober. .... 1 THESS 5:6

ALIENATED
sinful acts have *a* you from your God; ...... ISA 59:2

ALIVE
himself *a* with many convincing proofs ... ACTS 1:3
but *a* to God in Christ Jesus. .... ROM 6:11
yourselves to God as those who are *a* .... ROM 6:13

present your bodies as a sacrifice *a* .... ROM 12:1
so also in Christ all will be made *a* .... 1 COR 15:22

ALL
May *a* those who seek you be happy .... PS 70:4
will be delivered once and for *a* .... ISA 45:17
love of money is the root of *a* evils........ 1 TIM 6:10

ALLOTMENT
For the LORD's *a* is his people, ... DEUT 32:9

ALLOW
But I do not *a* a woman to teach .... 1 TIM 2:12

ALLOWED
come to me unless the Father
has *a* him.................................... JOHN 6:65

ALMIGHTY
find out the perfection of the *A* .... JOB 11:7
the breath of the *A* gives me life. .... JOB 33:4

ALOUD
read *a* all the words of the law, ... JOSH 8:34

ALTAR
placed him on the *a* on top of the wood .. GEN 22:9
the *a* is to be square, ... EXOD 27:1
He repaired the *a* of the LORD .... 1 KGS 18:30
He made a bronze *a* .... 2 CHR 4:1
the gold *a* .... 2 CHR 4:19

ALWAYS
you *a* give me sheer delight. .... PS 16:11
you have *a* been king. .... PS 93:2
may you be captivated by her love *a* ..... PROV 5:19
but you will not *a* have me! .... MATT 26:11
I am with you *a* .... MATT 28:20
Rejoice in the Lord *a* .... PHIL 4:4
And so we will *a* be with the Lord. ...... 1 THESS 4:17
a be ready to give an answer to anyone ... 1 PET 3:15

AMAZIAH
Son of Joash; king of Judah (2 Kgs 14; 2 Chr 25).

AMBASSADORS
Therefore we are *a* for Christ, ... 2 COR 5:20

AMBITION
former proclaim Christ from selfish *a* .... PHIL 1:17
being motivated by selfish *a* or vanity .... PHIL 2:3

AMON
Son of Manasseh; king of Judah (2 Kgs 21:18-26; 1 Chr 3:14; 2 Chr 33:21-25).

AMONG
shepherd's care to God's flock *a* you .... 1 PET 5:2

ANANIAS
1. Husband of Sapphira; died for lying to God (Acts 5:1-11).
2. Disciple who baptized Saul (Acts 9:10-19).
3. High priest at Paul's arrest (Acts 22:30–24:1).

ANCESTORS
portions and in various ways to our *a* .... HEB 1:1

ANCHOR
We have this hope as an *a* for the soul, ... HEB 6:19

ANCIENT
and the A of Days took his seat. .... DAN 7:9

ANDREW
Apostle; brother of Simon Peter (Matt 4:18; 10:2; Mark 1:16-18, 29; 3:18; 13:3; Luke 6:14; John 1:35-44; 6:8-9; 12:22; Acts 1:13).

ANEW
You have been born *a* .... 1 PET 1:23

ANGEL
The *a* of the LORD camps around .... PS 34:7
his face was like the face of an *a* .... ACTS 6:15
even Satan disguises himself as an *a* .... 2 COR 11:14
But even if we (or an *a* from heaven) .... GAL 1:8

ANGELS
For he will order his *a* to protect you .... PS 91:11
For I tell you that their *a* in heaven ..... MATT 18:10
prepared for the devil and his *a* .... MATT 25:41
equal to *a* and are sons of God, ... LUKE 20:36
Do you not know that we will judge *a* ..... 1 COR 6:3
he became so far better than the *a* .... HEB 1:4
You made him lower than the *a* .... HEB 2:7
some have entertained *a* .... HEB 13:2
a long to catch a glimpse of. .... 1 PET 1:12
God did not spare the *a* who sinned, ... 2 PET 2:4

ANGER
so that my *a* can burn against them .... EXOD 32:10
slow to *a* .... EXOD 34:6
uprooted them from their land in *a* ... DEUT 29:28
For his *a* lasts only a brief moment, ... PS 30:5
A gentle response turns away *a* .... PROV 15:1
person with great *a* bears the penalty ... PROV 19:19
not prone to *a* .... TITUS 1:7
slow to *a* .... JAS 1:19

ANGERED
it is not easily *a* or resentful. .... 1 COR 13:5

ANGRY
the LORD got very *a* at his people .... 2 CHR 36:16
Otherwise he will be *a* .... PS 2:12
Do not make friends with
an *a* person, ... PROV 22:24
An *a* person stirs up dissension, ... PROV 29:22

ANNOUNCE
A every day how he delivers. .... 1 CHR 16:23
now I *a* new events. .... ISA 42:9
Then he will *a* peace to the nations. ..... ZECH 9:10

ANNOUNCES
who *a* the end from the beginning .... ISA 46:10

ANNOUNCING
a to you the whole purpose of God. ...... ACTS 20:27

ANOINT
pray for him and *a* him with olive oil .... JAS 5:14

ANOTHER
we are members who belong to one *a* .... ROM 12:5
not that there really is *a* gospel, ... GAL 1:7

ANSWER
a our prayers by performing awesome ...... PS 65:5

ANSWERED
and he *a* us. .... EZRA 8:23

ANT
Go to the *a* .... PROV 6:6

ANTICHRIST
as you heard that the *a* is coming, ... 1 JOHN 2:18
This person is the deceiver and the *a* ..... 2 JOHN 7

ANTIOCH
he brought him to *A* .... ACTS 11:26

ANXIETY
A in a person's heart weighs
him down, ... PROV 12:25

ANXIOUS
Do not be *a* about anything. .... PHIL 4:6

APART
Set *a* to me every firstborn male —the .... EXOD 13:2

APOLLOS
Christian from Alexandria, learned in the Scriptures; instructed by Aquila and Priscilla (Acts 18:24-28). Ministered at Corinth (Acts 19:1; 1 Cor 1:12; 3; Titus 3:13).

APOSTASY
and then have committed *a* .... HEB 6:6

APOSTLES
so he was counted with the eleven *a* ...... ACTS 1:26
miraculous signs came about by the *a* .... ACTS 2:43
God has placed in the church first *a* .... 1 COR 12:28
For I am the least of the *a* .... 1 COR 15:9
disguising themselves as *a* of Christ. .... 2 COR 11:13
been built on the foundation of the *a* .... EPH 2:20

APPEAR
messiahs and false prophets will *a* ..... MARK 13:22
a before the judgment seat of Christ, ... 2 COR 5:10
he will *a* a second time, ... HEB 9:28

APPEARANCE
"Don't be impressed by his *a* .... 1 SAM 16:7

APPEARED
a Lamb that *a* to have been killed. .... REV 5:6

APPEARING
who have set their affection on his *a* ..... 2 TIM 4:8
glorious *a* of our great God .... TITUS 2:13

APPEARS
When Christ (who is your life) *a* .... COL 3:4
and he *a* now in God's presence for us. ... HEB 9:24

APPLAUD
A him, all you foreigners. .... PS 117:1

APPLY
and *a* your mind to my instruction. ..... PROV 22:17
A your heart to instruction and your ... PROV 23:12

APPOINTED
God *a* a little plant and caused it to ..... JONAH 4:6

APPROACH
"Do not *a* any closer! .... EXOD 3:5
confidently *a* the throne of grace .... HEB 4:16

APPROPRIATE
a for the morally upright to offer .... PS 33:1
praise is pleasant and *a* .... PS 147:1
Luxury is not *a* for a fool; .... PROV 19:10

APPROVE
test and *a* what is the will of God .... ROM 12:2

APPROVED
have been *a* by God to be entrusted .... 1 THESS 2:4

AQUILA
Husband of Priscilla; coworker with Paul, instructor of Apollos (Acts 18; Rom 16:3; 1 Cor 16:19; 2 Tim 4:19).

ARARAT
to rest on one of the mountains of *A* ...... GEN 8:4

ARCHANGEL
with the voice of the *a* .... 1 THESS 4:16
even when Michael the *a* was arguing .... JUDE 9

ARCHITECT
whose *a* and builder is God. .... HEB 11:10

ARGUING
Do everything without grumbling or *a* ... PHIL 2:14

ARK
Make rooms in the *a* .... GEN 6:14
and placed the tablets into the *a* .... DEUT 10:5
"Place the holy *a* in the temple .... 2 CHR 35:3
a of the covenant covered entirely .... HEB 9:4

ARM
he gathers up the lambs with his *a* .... ISA 40:11
a yourselves with the same attitude, ... 1 PET 4:1

ARMAGEDDON
the place that is called *A* in Hebrew. ...... REV 16:16

ARMIES
O LORD God of Heaven's *A* .... PS 89:8
holy is the LORD of Heaven's *A* .... ISA 6:3

ARMOR
his desire for justice like body *a* .... ISA 59:17
Clothe yourselves with the full *a* .... EPH 6:11
take up the full *a* of God so that you .... EPH 6:13

ARMS
and underneath you are his eternal *a* ... DEUT 33:27
After he took the children in his *a* ..... MARK 10:16

ARMY
No king is delivered by his vast *a* .... PS 33:16
serves in the *a* at his own expense? .... 1 COR 9:7
one who rode the horse and with his *a* ... REV 19:19

AROMA
we are a sweet *a* of Christ to God .... 2 COR 2:15

AROUND
turn *a* and become like little children, ... MATT 18:3
and the glory of the Lord shone *a* them ... LUKE 2:9

ARRIVAL
a of those who proclaim the good news... ROM 10:15

ARROGANT
The LORD abhors every *a* person; .... PROV 16:5
Do not be *a* .... ROM 11:20

ARROWS
you can extinguish all the flaming *a* .... EPH 6:16

ASA
King of Judah (1 Kgs 15:8-24; 1 Chr 3:10; 2 Chr 14-16).

ASCENDED
"When he *a* on high he captured .... EPH 4:8

ASCRIBE
a to the LORD splendor and strength! .. 1 CHR 16:28
to my Creator I will *a* righteousness. .... JOB 36:3

ASHAMED
do not let your faces be *a* .... PS 34:5
Son of Man will be *a* of that person ...... LUKE 9:26
For I am not *a* of the gospel, ... ROM 1:16
So do not be *a* of the testimony .... 2 TIM 1:8
worker who does not need to be *a* .... 2 TIM 2:15

ASIDE
they will be set *a* .... 1 COR 13:8

ASKED
I *a* the Lord three times about this, ... 2 COR 12:8

ASKING
a you to take them out of the world, ... JOHN 17:15

ASLEEP
he might find you *a* when he returns ... MARK 13:36
firstfruits of those who have fallen *a* ... 1 COR 15:20
go ahead of those who have fallen *a* ... 1 THESS 4:15

ASPIRE
to *a* to lead a quiet life, ... 1 THESS 4:11

ASPS
the poison of *a* is under their lips." ... ROM 3:13

ASSIGNED
as the Lord has *a* to each one, ... 1 COR 7:17

ASSOCIATE
therefore do not *a* with
someone who is ... PROV 20:19
and do not *a* with a wrathful person, ... PROV 22:24
and do not *a* with rebels, ... PROV 24:21

ASSOCIATES
The one who *a* with the wise
grows wise ... PROV 13:20
whoever *a* with prostitutes wastes his... PROV 29:3

ASSURANCE
heart in the *a* that faith brings, ... HEB 10:22

ASTRAY
but the one who rejects rebuke goes *a* ... PROV 10:17
shepherds have allowed them to go *a* ... JER 50:6
Do not be led *a* ... JAS 1:16
For you were going *a* like sheep ... 1 PET 2:25

ATHALIAH
Evil queen of Judah (2 Kgs 11; 2 Chr 23).

ATHLETE
Also, if anyone competes as an *a* ... 2 TIM 2:5

ATONEMENT
once in the year he is to make *a* on it ... EXOD 30:10
the blood makes *a* by means of the life. ... LEV 17:11
of this seventh month is the Day of *A* ... LEV 23:27
and has made *a* for the Israelites.'" ... NUM 25:13
to make *a* for the sins of the people. ... HEB 2:17

ATTACK
Attack those who *a* me. ... PS 35:1
caused the sin of all of us to *a* him. ... ISA 53:6

ATTAINED
Not that I have already *a* this—that ... PHIL 3:12

ATTEND
to *a* to your own business, ... 1 THESS 4:11

ATTENTION
Pay *a* to do everything I have told you ... EXOD 23:13
pay *a* so that you may gain discernment ... PROV 4:1
give *a* to the public reading of ... 1 TIM 4:13
You do well if you pay *a* to this ... 2 PET 1:19

ATTENTIVE
be *a* to my wisdom, ... PROV 5:1

ATTIRE
Worship the LORD in holy *a* ... 1 CHR 16:29
Worship the LORD in holy *a* ... PS 29:2
Worship the LORD in holy *a* ... PS 96:9

ATTITUDE
a submissive *a* and a willing spirit, ... 1 CHR 28:9
also arm yourselves with the same a ... 1 PET 4:1

ATTRACTED
Then the king will be *a* by your beauty. ... PS 45:11

ATTRIBUTES
creation of the world his invisible *a* ... ROM 1:20

AUTHORITIES
for the *a* are God's servants devoted to ... ROM 13:6
them to be subject to rulers and *a* ... TITUS 3:1
with angels and *a* and powers ... 1 PET 3:22

AUTHORITY
placed everything under their *a* ... PS 8:6
taught them like one who had *a* ... MATT 7:29
Son of Man has *a* on earth to forgive ... MATT 9:6
"All *a* in heaven and on earth has been ... MATT 28:18
no *a* except by God's appointment, ... ROM 13:1
So the person who resists such *a* ... ROM 13:2
should have a symbol of *a* on her head, ... 1 COR 11:10
even for kings and all who are in *a* ... 1 TIM 2:2
allow a woman to teach or exercise *a* ... 1 TIM 2:12

AVENGE
Do not *a* yourselves, ... ROM 12:19

AVOID
A the profane chatter and absurdities ... 1 TIM 6:20
But *a* profane chatter, ... 2 TIM 2:16
But *a* foolish controversies, ... TITUS 3:9

AWAIT
groan inwardly as we eagerly *a* our ... ROM 8:23

AWAKE
when I *a* you will reveal yourself ... PS 17:15
Stay *a* and pray that you will not fall ... MATT 26:41

AWAY
must not turn *a* justice for your poor ... EXOD 23:6
wipe *a* my rebellious acts. ... PS 51:1
A gentle response turns *a* anger, ... PROV 15:1
sin is not hidden *a* where I cannot see ... JER 16:17
until heaven and earth pass *a* ... MATT 5:18
easier for heaven and earth to pass *a* ... LUKE 16:17
but my words will never pass *a* ... LUKE 21:33
God who takes *a* the sin of the world! ... JOHN 1:29
things so that you will not fall *a* ... JOHN 16:1
stone had been moved *a* from ... JOHN 20:1
and have your sins washed *a* ... ACTS 22:16
All have turned *a* ... ROM 3:12
If I give *a* everything I own, ... 1 COR 13:3
you have fallen *a* from grace! ... GAL 5:4
keep *a* from all that. ... 1 TIM 6:11
So do not throw *a* your confidence, ... HEB 10:35
be carried *a* by all sorts of strange ... HEB 13:9
he must turn *a* from evil and do good ... 1 PET 3:11
the crown of glory that never fades *a* ... 1 PET 5:4
bodies will melt *a* in a blaze, ... 2 PET 3:10
bodies will melt *a* in a blaze! ... 2 PET 3:12
wipe *a* every tear from their eyes." ... REV 7:17
God will take *a* his share in the tree ... REV 22:19

AWE
all who live in the world stand in *a* ... PS 33:8
The nations will tremble in *a* ... JER 33:9
he indeed revered me and stood in *a* ... MAL 2:5
Reverential *a* came over everyone, ... ACTS 2:43
working out your salvation with *a* ... PHIL 2:12
pleasing to God in devotion and *a* ... HEB 12:28

AWE-INSPIRING
For the LORD Most High is *a* ... PS 47:2
You are *a* ... PS 68:35
a as the stars in procession?" ... SONG 6:10

AWED
I am *a* ... HAB 3:2

AWESOME
“What an *a* place this is! GEN 28:17
is a great and *a* God. DEUT 7:21
God who is unbiased and takes no bribe DEUT 10:17
fear this glorious and *a* name, DEUT 28:58
was very *a* JUDG 13:6
great and *a* God, NEH 1:5
and *a* God, NEH 9:32
around God is *a* majesty. JOB 37:22
His acts on behalf of people are *a* PS 66:5
and more *a* than all who surround him? PS 89:7
Let them praise your great and *a* name. PS 99:3
His name is holy and *a* PS 111:9
Our LORD is great and has *a* power; PS 147:5
a God who is faithful to his covenant DAN 9:4

AZAZEL
sending it away into the desert to *A* LEV 16:10

BAAL
Elijah told the prophets of *B* 1 KGS 18:25

BAASHA
King of Israel (1 Kgs 15:16–16:7; 2 Chr 16:1-6).

BABIES
people were even bringing their *b* LUKE 18:15

BABY
the *b* in my womb leaped for joy. LUKE 1:44
You will find a *b* wrapped in strips LUKE 2:12

BABYLON
the rivers of *B* we sit down and weep PS 137:1

BACK
your life will be demanded *b* from you, LUKE 12:20
repent and turn *b* so that your sins ACTS 3:19

BACKSLIDER
b will be paid back from his own ways, PROV 14:14

BALAAM
Prophet who attempted to curse Israel (Num 22-24; Deut 23:4-5; 2 Pet 2:15; Jude 11). Killed (Num 31:8; Josh 13:22).

BALANCES
You must have honest *b* LEV 19:36
are weighed on the *b* and found to be DAN 5:27

BANDAGES
and *b* their wounds. PS 147:3

BANISH
B that slave woman and her son, GEN 21:10

BANQUET
He brought me into the *b* hall, SONG 2:4

BAPTIZE
I *b* you with water, MATT 3:11
but he will *b* you with the Holy Spirit MARK 1:8
For Christ did not send me to *b* 1 COR 1:17

BAPTIZED
Nazareth in Galilee and was *b* by John MARK 1:9
cup I drink or be *b* with the baptism MARK 10:38
who believes and is *b* will be saved, MARK 16:16
but you will be *b* with the Holy Spirit ACTS 1:5

BAPTIZING
and he was *b* them in the Jordan River MATT 3:6
although Jesus himself was not *b* JOHN 4:2

BARABBAS
B or Jesus who is called the Christ?” MATT 27:17

BARNABAS
Disciple, originally Joseph (Acts 4:36), prophet (Acts 13:1), apostle (Acts 14:14). Brought Paul to apostles (Acts 9:27), Antioch (Acts 11:22-29; Gal 2:1-13), on the first missionary journey (Acts 13-14). Together at Jerusalem Council, they separated over John Mark (Acts 15). Later coworkers (1 Cor 9:6; Col 4:10).

BARTHOLOMEW
Apostle (Matt 10:3; Mark 3:18; Luke 6:14; Acts 1:13). Possibly also known as Nathanael (John 1:45-49; 21:2).

BATHED
one who has *b* needs only to wash his JOHN 13:10

BATHSHEBA
Wife of Uriah who committed adultery with and became wife of David (2 Sam 11), mother of Solomon (2 Sam 12:24; 1 Kgs 1-2; 1 Chr 3:5).

BATTLE
For the *b* is not yours, 2 CHR 20:15
The LORD who is mighty in *b* PS 24:8
b is not always won by the strongest; ECCL 9:11

BEAR
they are too much for me to *b* PS 38:4
like a *b* DAN 7:5
nor a bad tree to *b* good fruit. MATT 7:18
For my yoke is easy to *b* MATT 11:30
every branch that does not *b* fruit JOHN 15:2
appointed you to go and *b* fruit, JOHN 15:16
But we who are strong ought to *b* with ROM 15:1

BEARING
b with one another and forgiving COL 3:13

BEARS
It *b* all things, 1 COR 13:7

BEAST'S
who has insight calculate the *b* number, REV 13:18

BEAT
will *b* their swords into plowshares, ISA 2:4
B your plowshares into swords, JOEL 3:10

BEATINGS
B and wounds cleanse away evil, PROV 20:30

BEATS
but one who *b* a person to death must LEV 24:21

BEAUTIFUL
the daughters of humankind were *b* GEN 6:2
I know that you are a *b* woman. GEN 12:11
saw that the woman was very *b* GEN 12:14
Now the young woman was very *b* GEN 24:16
to get Rebekah because she is very *b* GEN 26:7
but Rachel had a lovely figure and *b* GEN 29:17
My heart is stirred by a *b* song. PS 45:1
ring in a pig's snout is a *b* woman PROV 11:22
the most *b* of all lands. EZEK 20:6
like whitewashed tombs that look *b* MATT 23:27

BEAUTIFULLY
fit *b* in its appropriate time, ECCL 3:11

BEAUTY
the king will be attracted by your *b* PS 45:11

- Charm is deceitful and *b* is fleeting. PROV 31:30
- and perfect in *b* EZEK 28:12
- *b* of a gentle and tranquil spirit, 1 PET 3:4

BECAUSE
- believe *b* of the miraculous deeds JOHN 14:11

BECOME
- He will *b* a trap and a snare ISA 8:14

BED
- and the marriage *b* kept undefiled, HEB 13:4

BEELZEBUL
- "By the power of *B* LUKE 11:15

BEFORE
- we will all stand *b* the judgment seat ROM 14:10

BEFOREHAND
- for good works that God prepared *b* EPH 2:10

BEGINNING
- In the *b* God created the heavens GEN 1:1
- the *b* of discernment, PROV 1:7
- at the very *b* and at the very end. ISA 48:12
- In the *b* was the Word, JOHN 1:1
- what was from the *b* 1 JOHN 1:1
- the *b* and the end. REV 21:6

BEHAVIOR
- I will judge you according to your *b* EZEK 7:3

BEING
- your whole *b* DEUT 6:5
- serve him with all your mind and *b* DEUT 10:12
- serve him with all your heart and *b* JOSH 22:5
- not a human *b* who changes his mind." 1 SAM 15:29

BEINGS
- a little less than the heavenly *b* PS 8:5
- For though we live as human *b* 2 COR 10:3
- The residence of God is among human *b* REV 21:3

BELIEVE
- A naive person will *b* anything, PROV 14:15
- these little ones who *b* in me to sin, MATT 18:6
- if you *b* MATT 21:22
- Repent and *b* the gospel!" MARK 1:15
- "I *b* help my unbelief!" MARK 9:24
- signs will accompany those who *b* MARK 16:17
- just *b* and she will be healed." LUKE 8:50
- *b* all that the prophets have spoken! LUKE 24:25
- so that everyone might *b* through him. JOHN 1:7
- who *b* in his name—he JOHN 1:12
- *b* in the one whom he sent." JOHN 6:29
- even if you do not *b* me, JOHN 10:38
- I *b* that you are the Christ, JOHN 11:27
- You *b* in God; JOHN 14:1
- but if you do not *b* me, JOHN 14:11
- we *b* that you have come from God." JOHN 16:30
- "Do you now *b* JOHN 16:31
- that the world will *b* that you sent me JOHN 17:21
- not continue in your unbelief, but *b* JOHN 20:27
- these are recorded so that you may *b* JOHN 20:31
- *B* in the Lord Jesus and you will be ACTS 16:31
- of Jesus Christ for all who *b* ROM 3:22
- become the father of all those who *b* ROM 4:11
- that Jesus is Lord and *b* in your heart ROM 10:9
- partners with those who do not *b* 2 COR 6:14
- we *b* that God will bring with him 1 THESS 4:14
- so that they will *b* what is false. 2 THESS 2:11
- *b* that he exists and that he rewards HEB 11:6
- You *b* that God is one; JAS 2:19
- do not *b* every spirit, 1 JOHN 4:1

BELIEVED
- Abram *b* the LORD, GEN 15:6
- The people of Nineveh *b* in God, JONAH 3:5
- they *b* the scripture and the saying JOHN 2:22
- *b* in the name of the one and only Son JOHN 3:18
- and he saw and *b* JOHN 20:8
- "Have you *b* because you have seen me? JOHN 20:29
- those who *b* were of one heart and mind ACTS 4:32
- had been appointed for eternal life *b* ACTS 13:48
- "Abraham *b* God, ROM 4:3
- you *b* in vain. 1 COR 15:2
- Just as Abraham *b* God, GAL 3:6
- "Now Abraham *b* God and it was counted JAS 2:23

BELIEVER
- a brother has a wife who is not a *b* 1 COR 7:12
- Or what does a *b* share in common with 2 COR 6:15

BELIEVERS
- especially of *b* 1 TIM 4:10
- an example for the *b* in your speech, 1 TIM 4:12
- love the family of *b* 1 PET 2:17

BELIEVES
- things are possible for the one who *b* MARK 9:23
- but *b* that what he says will happen, MARK 11:23
- who *b* and is baptized will be saved, MARK 16:16
- so that everyone who *b* in him will not JOHN 3:16
- The one who *b* in him is not condemned. JOHN 3:18
- one who *b* in the Son has eternal life. JOHN 3:36
- one who hears my message and *b* the one JOHN 5:24
- one who *b* in me will never be thirsty. JOHN 6:35
- everyone who looks on the Son and *b*, JOHN 6:40
- the one who *b* has eternal life. JOHN 6:47
- let the one who *b* in me drink. JOHN 7:38
- who lives and *b* in me will never die. JOHN 11:26
- for salvation to everyone who *b* ROM 1:16
- *b* in him will not be put to shame. ROM 9:33
- righteousness for everyone who *b* ROM 10:4
- Everyone who *b* that Jesus is the 1 JOHN 5:1
- who *b* that Jesus is the Son of God? 1 JOHN 5:5

BELIEVING
- by *b* you may have life in his name. JOHN 20:31
- *b* everything that is according ACTS 24:14

BELONG
- who *b* to me, 2 CHR 7:14

BELONGS
- Everything under heaven *b* to me! JOB 41:11
- one who *b* to God listens and responds JOHN 8:47

BELOVED
- your *b* wife, DEUT 13:6
- *b* of the LORD will live safely by him; DEUT 33:12
- Enjoy life with your *b* wife ECCL 9:9

BELOVED'S
- I am my *b* SONG 7:10

made them white in the *b* of the Lamb! ... REV 7:14
overcame him by the *b* of the Lamb ... REV 12:11

BLOWN
b and tossed around by the wind. ... JAS 1:6

BOAST
puts on his battle gear should not *b* ... 1 KGS 20:11
I will *b* in the LORD; ... PS 34:2
In God we *b* all day long, ... PS 44:8
Do not *b* about tomorrow; ... PROV 27:1
But may I never *b* except in the cross ... GAL 6:14
so that no one can *b* ... EPH 2:9

BOASTS
"Let the one who *b* ... 1 COR 1:31

BOAZ
Wealthy Bethlehemite who showed favor to Ruth (Ruth 2), married her (Ruth 4). Ancestor of David (Ruth 4:18-22; 1 Chr 2:12-15), Jesus (Matt 1:5-16; Luke 3:23-32).

BODIES
the hearts of stone from their *b* ... EZEK 11:19
giving up their *b* rather than serve ... DAN 3:28
present your *b* as a sacrifice—alive, ... ROM 12:1
that your *b* are members of Christ? ... 1 COR 6:15
love their wives as their own *b* ... EPH 5:28

BODY
My *b* trembles because I fear you; ... PS 119:120
to destroy both soul and *b* in hell. ... MATT 10:28
this is my *b* ... MATT 26:26
not know that your *b* is the temple ... 1 COR 6:19
"This is my *b* ... 1 COR 11:24
one *b* so too is Christ. ... 1 COR 12:12
this mortal *b* must put on immortality ... 1 COR 15:53
because we are members of his *b* ... EPH 5:30
you do not give them what the *b* needs ... JAS 2:16

BOLD
A wicked person has put on a *b* face, ... PROV 21:29

BOOK
They read from the *b* of God's law, ... NEH 8:8
which are not recorded in this *b* ... JOHN 20:30
whose names are in the *b* of life. ... PHIL 4:3
are written in the Lamb's *b* of life. ... REV 21:27

BOOKS
no end to the making of many *b* ... ECCL 12:12

BORN
For a child has been *b* to us, ... ISA 9:6
'You must all be *b* from above.' ... JOHN 3:7

BORNE
for no prophecy was ever *b* of human ... 2 PET 1:21

BORROWER
and the *b* is servant to the lender. ... PROV 22:7

BOUGHT
For you were *b* at a price. ... 1 COR 6:20
You were *b* with a price. ... 1 COR 7:23
denying the Master who *b* them. ... 2 PET 2:1

BOW
'Surely every knee will b to me, ... ISA 45:23
every knee will *b* to me, ... ROM 14:11
at the name of Jesus every knee will *b* ... PHIL 2:10

BOX
do not run uncertainly or *b* like one ... 1 COR 9:26

BRANCHES
"I am the vine; you are the *b*. ... JOHN 15:5

BREAD
humankind cannot live by *b* alone, ... DEUT 8:3
feed me with my allotted portion of *b* ... PROV 30:8
'Man does not live by *b* alone, ... MATT 4:4
Give us today our daily *b* ... MATT 6:11
"I am the *b* of life. ... JOHN 6:35
Jesus came and took the *b* and gave it ... JOHN 21:13
night in which he was betrayed took *b* ... 1 COR 11:23

BREADTH
the *b* and length and height and depth, ... EPH 3:18

BREAK
he must not *b* his word, ... NUM 30:2
'I will never *b* my covenant with you, ... JUDG 2:1
You will *b* them with an iron scepter; ... PS 2:9
A crushed reed he will not *b* ... ISA 42:3
He will not *b* a bruised reed ... MATT 12:20

BREASTPIECE
make a *b* for use in making decisions, ... EXOD 28:15

BREASTPLATE
by putting on the *b* of righteousness, ... EPH 6:14
putting on the *b* of faith and love ... 1 THESS 5:8

BREATHED
b into his nostrils the breath of life ... GEN 2:7
he *b* on them and said, ... JOHN 20:22

BRIBE
for a *b* blinds those who see ... EXOD 23:8

BRIDE
and his *b* has made herself ready. ... REV 19:7

BRIDLE
religious yet does not *b* his tongue, ... JAS 1:26

BRIGHT
A *b* look brings joy to the heart, ... PROV 15:30

BRIGHTER
growing brighter and *b* until full day. ... PROV 4:18

BRIGHTLY
You shine *b* and reveal your majesty, ... PS 76:4

BRIGHTNESS
From the *b* in front of him came coals ... 2 SAM 22:13
shine like the *b* of the heavenly ... DAN 12:3

BRING
if you *b* your gift to the ... MATT 5:23

BRINGS
but an encouraging word *b* him joy. ... PROV 12:25

BROKEN
a three-stranded cord is not quickly *b* ... ECCL 4:12

BROKENHEARTED
The LORD is near the *b* ... PS 34:18
He heals the *b* ... PS 147:3
to help the *b* ... ISA 61:1

BROTHER
"Where is your *b* Abel?" ... GEN 4:9
a friend who sticks closer than a *b* ... PROV 18:24
you have regained your *b* ... MATT 18:15
whoever does the will of God is my *b* ... MARK 3:35
If your *b* sins, ... LUKE 17:3

BROTHERS
it is when *b* truly live in unity. ... PS 133:1
there is no one who has left home or *b* ... MARK 10:29

BUILD
then those who *b* it work in vain. .... PS 127:1
and on this rock I will *b* my church, ... MATT 16:18
This message is able to *b* you up .... ACTS 20:32

BUILDING
You are God's field, God's *b* ....1 COR 3:9
that the Lord gave us for *b* you up .... 2 COR 10:8

BUILDS
but not everything *b* others up. .... 1 COR 10:23
one who prophesies *b* up the church..... 1 COR 14:4

BUILT
a wise man who *b* his house on rock..... MATT 7:24
b on the foundation of the apostles ...... EPH 2:20

BURDEN
Throw your *b* upon the LORD, ... PS 55:22

BURDENED
that we were *b* excessively, ... 2 COR 1:8

BURDENS
Carry one another's *b* .... GAL 6:2

BURIED
Therefore we have been *b* with him .... ROM 6:4
and that he was *b* .... 1 COR 15:4

BURNING
fire of the altar must be kept *b* on it .... LEV 6:9
keep your lamps *b* .... LUKE 12:35
will be heaping *b* coals on his head. ...... ROM 12:20

BUSINESS
again carried out the king's *b* .... DAN 8:27

CAESAR'S
give to Caesar the things that are *C* .... MATT 22:21

CAIN
Firstborn of Adam (Gen 4:1), murdered brother Abel (Gen 4:1-16; 1 John 3:12).

CALAMITY
who brings about peace and creates *c* ...... ISA 45:7

CALEB
Judahite who spied out Canaan (Num 13:6); allowed to enter land because of faith (Num 13:30–14:38; Deut 1:36). Possessed Hebron (Josh 14:6–15:19).

CALF
and made a molten *c* .... EXOD 32:4
Bring the fattened *c* and kill it! .... LUKE 15:23

CALL
LORD our God whenever we *c* on him? ... DEUT 4:7
those who *c* evil good and good evil, ...ISA 5:20
c to him while he is nearby! .... ISA 55:6
C on me in prayer and I will answer .... JER 33:3
For I did not come to *c* the righteous .... MATT 9:13
gifts and the *c* of God are irrevocable .... ROM 11:29
God did not c us to impurity .... 1 THESS 4:7

CALLED
for you *c* me." .... 1 SAM 3:5
children have risen and *c* her blessed; .. PROV 31:28
'My house will be *c* a house of prayer ... MATT 21:13
For many are *c* .... MATT 22:14
And those he predestined, he also *c*....... ROM 8:30
God has *c* you in peace.........................1 COR 7:15
For you were *c* to freedom, ... GAL 5:13
the one who *c* you out of darkness ....1 PET 2:9

CALLING
urge you to live worthily of the *c* .... EPH 4:1
make every effort to be sure of your *c* ....2 PET 1:10

CALLS
happen that everyone who *c* on the name .... JOEL 2:32
He *c* his own sheep by name and leads .. JOHN 10:3
everyone who *c* on the name of the Lord .... ROM 10:13

CALM
the one who stays *c* is discerning. .... PROV 17:27

CALMLY
if you *c* trusted in me, ... ISA 30:15

CAMEL
easier for a *c* to go through the eye ..... MATT 19:24
You strain out a gnat yet swallow a *c* ... MATT 23:24

CAMPS
The angel of the LORD *c* around the .... PS 34:7

CANAAN
"To you I will give the land of *C* .... 1 CHR 16:18

CAPABLE
c and equipped for every good work...... 2 TIM 3:17

CARE
but he feeds it and takes *c* of it, ...EPH 5:29
or the son of man that you *c* for him?....... HEB 2:6
Give a shepherd's *c* to God's flock ....1 PET 5:2

CAREFREE
and enjoyed *c* ease, ... EZEK 16:49

CAREFUL
be *c* to do this so that it may go well ...... DEUT 6:3
Be *c* not to display your righteousness .. MATT 6:1
And each one must be *c* how he builds....1 COR 3:10
c that this liberty of yours does not .... 1 COR 8:9

CAREFULLY
C obey all that is written in the law ....JOSH 23:6
demand that your precepts be *c* kept. ...... PS 119:4

CARES
on him because he *c* for you. .... 1 PET 5:7

CARING
nursing mother *c* for her own children .... 1 THESS 2:7

CAROUSING
c and similar things. .... GAL 5:21
c drinking bouts, ...1 PET 4:3

CARRIED
he *c* our pain; .... ISA 53:4
for he *c* their sins. .... ISA 53:11

CARRIES
he *c* them close to his heart; .... ISA 40:11

CARRY
and my load is not hard to *c* .... MATT 11:30
Whoever does not *c* his own cross .... LUKE 14:27
C one another's burdens, ... GAL 6:2
For each one will *c* his own load. .... GAL 6:5

CASTING
c all your cares on him because he .... 1 PET 5:7

CATTLE
the *c* that graze on a thousand hills. .... PS 50:10

CAUSE
against your neighbor without *c* .... PROV 24:28
plead the *c* of the poor and needy. .... PROV 31:9

CEASING
sin against the LORD by *c* to pray .... 1 SAM 12:23

CELEBRATION
Let us shout out to him in *c* .... PS 95:2
the wedding *c* of the Lamb has come, ... REV 19:7

CENSER
and take a *c* full of coals of fire .... LEV 16:12

CENTURION
a *c* came to him asking for help: .... MATT 8:5

CERTAIN
You must be *c* to tithe all the produce .. DEUT 14:22
know for *c* the things you were taught..... LUKE 1:4

CERTAINLY
C the LORD watches the whole earth .... 2 CHR 16:9
C none who rely on you will be .... PS 25:3
C a man cannot rescue his brother; .... PS 49:7

CHAFF
Instead they are like wind-driven *c* .... PS 1:4

CHANGE
go back on his word or *c* his mind, ... 1 SAM 15:29
must *c* the way you have been living .... JER 7:5
prefer that the wicked *c* his behavior .... EZEK 33:11
Lord has sworn and will not *c* his mind ... HEB 7:21

CHANGED
not all sleep, but we will all be *c* .... 1 COR 15:51

CHANNELS
river's *c* bring joy to the city of God .... PS 46:4

CHANTED
Then David *c* this lament over Saul ...... 2 SAM 1:17

CHARACTER
Who can find a wife of noble *c* .... PROV 31:10
and endurance, *c*, and *c*, hope.................. ROM 5:4

CHARGE
bring any *c* against God's elect? .... ROM 8:33
the gospel of God to you free of *c* .... 2 COR 11:7
I solemnly *c* you before God .... 2 TIM 4:1
give water free of *c* from the spring .... REV 21:6

CHARIOTS
horses and *c* of fire all around .... 2 KGS 6:17
Some trust in *c* and others in horses, ... PS 20:7

CHARITY
doing good deeds and acts of *c* .... ACTS 9:36
"Your prayers and your acts of *c* have ..... ACTS 10:4

CHARM
C is deceitful and beauty is fleeting. ..... PROV 31:30

CHASES
but whoever *c* daydreams lacks sense. ... PROV 12:11

CHATTER
Avoid the profane *c* and absurdities ..... 1 TIM 6:20
But avoid profane *c* .... 2 TIM 2:16

CHEATED
and if I have *c* anyone of anything, ... LUKE 19:8
Why not rather be *c* .... 1 COR 6:7

CHEEK
But whoever strikes you on the right *c* .. MATT 5:39

CHEERFUL
A joyful heart makes the face *c* .... PROV 15:13
but one with a *c* heart has a continual .. PROV 15:15
A *c* heart brings good healing, ... PROV 17:22
because God loves a *c* giver. .... 2 COR 9:7

CHEST
'What are these wounds on your *c* .... ZECH 13:6

CHILD
a foolish *c* is a grief to his mother. .... PROV 10:1
one who loves his *c* is diligent in .... PROV 13:24
Train a *c* in the way that he should go ... PROV 22:6
Folly is bound up in the heart of a *c* ...... PROV 22:15
Do not withhold discipline from a *c* .... PROV 23:13
a *c* who is unrestrained brings shame .. PROV 29:15
Discipline your *c* .... PROV 29:17
For a *c* has been born to us, ... ISA 9:6
as a small *c* leads them along. .... ISA 11:6
As a mother consoles a *c* .... ISA 66:13
He called a *c* .... MATT 18:2
and blessed is the *c* in your womb! .... LUKE 1:42
the *c* kept growing and becoming
strong .... LUKE 1:80
but when her *c* is born, ... JOHN 16:21
When I was a *c* .... 1 COR 13:11

CHILDREN
instead teach them to your *c* and. .... DEUT 4:9
Teach them to your *c* and speak
of them .... DEUT 11:19
the mouths of *c* and nursing .... PS 8:2
Her *c* have risen and called her .... PROV 31:28
know how to give good gifts to your *c* ... MATT 7:11
and have revealed them to little *c* .... MATT 11:25
turn around and become like little *c* ..... MATT 18:3
"Let the little *c* come to me .... MATT 19:14
'Out of the mouths of *c* and nursing .... MATT 21:16
Whoever welcomes one of these
little *c* .... MARK 9:37
"Let the little *c* come to me .... MARK 10:14
After he took the *c* in his arms, ... MARK 10:16
C will rise against parents .... MARK 13:12
and revealed them to little *c* .... LUKE 10:21
"Let the little *c* come to me .... LUKE 18:16
to our spirit that we are God's *c* .... ROM 8:16
the *c* of Israel are as the sand .... ROM 9:27
but parents for their *c* .... 2 COR 12:14
C obey your parents in the Lord, ... EPH 6:1
Fathers, do not provoke your *c* .... EPH 6:4
C obey your parents in everything, ... COL 3:20
Fathers, do not provoke your *c* .... COL 3:21
and keep his *c* in control .... 1 TIM 3:4
managers of their *c* and their own .... 1 TIM 3:12
as one who has raised *c* .... 1 TIM 5:10
that we should be called God's *c* —and ... 1 JOHN 3:1

CHOICES
the one who acts hastily makes poor *c* .... PROV 19:2

CHOOSE
Therefore *c* life so that you and your ... DEUT 30:19
then *c* today whom you will worship, ... JOSH 24:15
You did not *c* me, ... JOHN 15:16

CHOOSES
and he hardens whom he *c* to harden. .... ROM 9:18

CHOSE
Lot *c* for himself the whole region .... GEN 13:11
but I *c* you and appointed you to go ..... JOHN 15:16
but I *c* you out of the world, ... JOHN 15:19
and God *c* what the world thinks weak ... 1 COR 1:27
c us in Christ before the foundation .... EPH 1:4
because God *c* you from the
beginning .... 2 THESS 2:13

“This cup is the new *c* in my blood. ... 1 COR 11:25
violations committed under the first *c* ... HEB 9:15

COVENANT-BREAKERS
senseless, *c* heartless, ... ROM 1:31

COVENANTS
the *c* the giving of the law, ... ROM 9:4
for these women represent two *c* ... GAL 4:24

COVER
death and will *c* a multitude of sins. ... JAS 5:20

COVERED
you removed my sackcloth and *c* me ... PS 30:11
with two they *c* their feet, ... ISA 6:2
and whose sins are *c* ... ROM 4:7

COVERS
but love *c* all transgressions. ... PROV 10:12
The one who *c* his transgressions ... PROV 28:13
because love *c* a multitude of sins. ... 1 PET 4:8

COVET
You shall not *c* your neighbor’s wife, ... EXOD 20:17
do not *c* ... ROM 13:9

COVETOUSNESS
c malice. They are rife with envy, ... ROM 1:29

COWARDLY
“Why are you *c* ... MATT 8:26

COWARDS
But as for the *c* ... REV 21:8

COWORKERS
We are *c* belonging to God. ... 1 COR 3:9

CRAFTINESS
“He catches the wise in their *c* ... 1 COR 3:19

CRAVE
nor should you *c* his house, ... DEUT 5:21
Do not *c* that ruler’s delicacies, ... PROV 23:3

CREATE
C for me a pure heart, ... PS 51:10

CREATED
In the beginning God *c* the heavens and ... GEN 1:1
God *c* the great sea creatures ... GEN 1:21
male and female he *c* them. ... GEN 1:27
the one who *c* the sky and stretched, ... ISA 42:5
the one who *c* the sky ... ISA 45:18
He is the one who *c* everything. ... JER 10:16
was created that has been *c* ... JOHN 1:3
man *c* for the sake of woman, ... 1 COR 11:9
things were *c* through him and for him. ... COL 1:16
and through whom he *c* the world. ... HEB 1:2
who *c* heaven and what is in it, ... REV 10:6

CREATION
you loved me before the *c* of the world ... JOHN 17:24
served the *c* rather than the Creator, ... ROM 1:25
c eagerly waits for the revelation ... ROM 8:19
nor anything else in *c* will be able to ... ROM 8:39
he is a new *c* ... 2 COR 5:17
the firstborn over all *c* ... COL 1:15
For every *c* of God is good ... 1 TIM 4:4

CREATOR
C of heaven and earth, ... GEN 14:22
Or a man pure before his *C* ... JOB 4:17
and to my *C* I will ascribe ... JOB 36:3
Let us kneel before the LORD, our *C* ... PS 95:6
the LORD is the *C* of them both. ... PROV 22:2
argues with his *C* is in grave danger, ... ISA 45:9
served the creation rather than the *C* ... ROM 1:25

CREDIT
bring *c* to the teaching of God ... TITUS 2:10
c is it if you sin and are mistreated ... 1 PET 2:20

CREDITED
the LORD *c* it as righteousness to him. ... GEN 15:6
his faith is *c* as righteousness. ... ROM 4:5
to whom it will be *c* ... ROM 4:24
and it was *c* to him as righteousness, ... GAL 3:6

CRIMINALS
They intended to bury him with *c* ... ISA 53:9

CRIPPLED
better for you to enter life *c* or lame ... MATT 18:8

CROPS
At that time the *c* given by the LORD ... ISA 4:2

CROSS
does not take up his *c* and follow me ... MATT 10:38
take up his *c* daily, ... LUKE 9:23
him to a *c* at the hands of Gentiles. ... ACTS 2:23
c of Christ would not become useless. ... 1 COR 1:17
may I never boast except in the *c* ... GAL 6:14
death on a *c* ... PHIL 2:8
peace through the blood of his *c* ... COL 1:20
taken it away by nailing it to the *c* ... COL 2:14
triumphing over them by the *c* ... COL 2:15
he endured the *c* ... HEB 12:2

CROWD
offer testimony that agrees with a *c* ... EXOD 23:2
an enormous *c* that no one could count, ... REV 7:9
CROWDS great *c* are in the Valley of Decision, ... JOEL 3:14

CROWN
she will bestow a beautiful *c* on you.” ... PROV 4:9
A noble wife is the *c* of her husband, ... PROV 12:4
Grandchildren are like a *c* ... PROV 17:6
Unending joy will *c* them, ... ISA 35:10
stones of a *c* sparkling over his land. ... ZECH 9:16
and after braiding a *c* of thorns, ... MATT 27:29
They do it to receive a perishable *c* ... 1 COR 9:25
c of righteousness is reserved for me. ... 2 TIM 4:8
give you the *c* that is life itself. ... REV 2:10

CROWNED
You *c* mankind with honor and majesty. ... PS 8:5
the shrewd will be *c* with knowledge. ... PROV 14:18
You *c* him with glory and honor. ... HEB 2:7

CROWNS
they offer their *c* before his throne, ... REV 4:10
there are many diadem *c* on his head. ... REV 19:12

CRUCIBLE
c is for silver and the furnace is for ... PROV 27:21

CRUCIFIED
mocked and flogged severely and *c* ... MATT 20:19
Then two outlaws were *c* with him, ... MATT 27:38
and be *c* ... LUKE 24:7
they *c* him along with two others, ... JOHN 19:18
Jesus whom you *c* both Lord and Christ. ... ACTS 2:36
but we preach about a *c* Christ, ... 1 COR 1:23
and him *c* ... 1 COR 2:2
I have been *c* with Christ, ... GAL 2:20
have *c* the flesh with its passions ... GAL 5:24

CRUCIFY
They all said, *C* him!" ... MATT 27:22
Then they led him away to *c* him. ... MATT 27:31

CRUCIFYING
c the Son of God for themselves ... HEB 6:6

CRUSH
Though the LORD desired to *c* him ... ISA 53:10
The God of peace will quickly *c* Satan ... ROM 16:20

CRUSHED
A lying tongue hates those *c* by it, ... PROV 26:28
He will not grow dim or be *c* ... ISA 42:4
c because of our sins; ... ISA 53:5
but are not *c* ... 2 COR 4:8

CUP
my *c* is completely full. ... PS 23:5
whoever gives only a *c* of cold water ... MATT 10:42
You clean the outside of the *c* ... MATT 23:25
let this *c* pass from me! ... MATT 26:39
"This *c* is the new covenant ... 1 COR 11:25

CURIOSITY
they have an insatiable *c* to hear ... 2 TIM 4:3

CURSE
before you today a blessing and a *c* ... DEUT 11:26
bless those who *c* you, ... LUKE 6:28
of the law by becoming a *c* for us ... GAL 3:13
And there will no longer be any *c* ... REV 22:3

CURSED
the ground is *c* because of you; ... GEN 3:17
left exposed on a tree is *c* by God. ... DEUT 21:23
C is the one who makes a carved or ... DEUT 27:15
C is the one who disrespects his father ... DEUT 27:16
C is the one who moves his neighbor's ... DEUT 27:17
C is the one who misleads a blind ... DEUT 27:18
C is the one who perverts justice ... DEUT 27:19
C is the one who goes to bed with his ... DEUT 27:20
C is the one who commits bestiality.' ... DEUT 27:21
C is the one who goes to bed with ... DEUT 27:22
C is the one who kills his neighbor ... DEUT 27:24
C is the one who takes a bribe to kill ... DEUT 27:25
C is the one who refuses to keep the ... DEUT 27:26
C is everyone who does not keep on ... GAL 3:10

CURTAIN
the testimony in there behind the *c* ... EXOD 26:33
The temple *c* was torn in two. ... LUKE 23:45
he inaugurated for us through the *c* ... HEB 10:20

CYMBAL
I am a noisy gong or a clanging *c* ... 1 COR 13:1

DANCE
and a time to *d* ... ECCL 3:4
yet you did not *d* ... MATT 11:17

DANCING
Then you turned my lament into *d* ... PS 30:11
Let them praise his name with *d* ... PS 149:3

DANGER
I fear no *d* ... PS 23:4
A shrewd person saw *d* —he ... PROV 27:12
or *d* or sword? ... ROM 8:35

DANIEL
Hebrew exile to Babylon, name changed to Belteshazzar (Dan 1:6-7). Refused to eat unclean food (Dan 1:8-21). Interpreted Nebuchadnezzar's dreams (Dan 2; 4), writing on the wall (Dan 5). Thrown into lions' den (Dan 6). Visions of (Dan 7-12).

DARE
For no one would *d* approach me ... JER 30:21

DARKEST
when I must walk through the *d* valley, ... PS 23:4

DARKNESS
so God separated the light from the *d* ... GEN 1:4
The LORD illumines the *d* around me. ... 2 SAM 22:29
and no deep *d* ... JOB 34:22
loved the *d* rather than the light, ... JOHN 3:19
a light to those who are in *d* ... ROM 2:19
what fellowship does light have with *d* ... 2 COR 6:14
for you were at one time *d* ... EPH 5:8
one who called you out of *d* into his ... 1 PET 2:9
and in him there is no *d* at all. ... 1 JOHN 1:5
his fellow Christian is still in the *d* ... 1 JOHN 2:9

DAUGHTERS
Your sons and *d* will prophesy. ... JOEL 2:28

DAVID
Son of Jesse (Ruth 4:17-22; 1 Chr 2:13-15), ancestor of Jesus (Matt 1:1-17; Luke 3:31).

Anointed king by Samuel (1 Sam 16:1-13). Musician to Saul (1 Sam 16:14-23; 18:10). Killed Goliath (1 Sam 17). Relation with Jonathan (1 Sam 18:1-4; 19-20; 23:16-18; 2 Sam 1). Disfavor of Saul (1 Sam 18:6–23:29). Spared Saul's life (1 Sam 24; 26). Among Philistines (1 Sam 21:10-14; 27-30). Lament for Saul and Jonathan (2 Sam 1).

Anointed king of Judah (2 Sam 2:1-11); of Israel (2 Sam 5:1-4; 1 Chr 11:1-3). Promised eternal dynasty (2 Sam 7; 1 Chr 17; Ps 132). Adultery with Bathsheba (2 Sam 11-12). Absalom's revolt (2 Sam 14-18). Last words (2 Sam 23:1-7). Death (1 Kgs 2:10-12; 1 Chr 29:28).

DAY
marking the first *d* ... GEN 1:5
Remember the Sabbath *d* to set it apart ... EXOD 20:8
because it is a *d* of atonement ... LEV 23:28
before them by *d* in a pillar of cloud ... NUM 14:14
You must memorize it *d* and night ... JOSH 1:8
just one *d* in your temple courts ... PS 84:10
Announce every *d* how he delivers. ... PS 96:2
This is the *d* the LORD has brought ... PS 118:24
you do not know what a *d* may bring ... PROV 27:1
that great and terrible *d* ... JOEL 2:31
those who wish for the *d* of the LORD! ... AMOS 5:18
For the *d* of the LORD is approaching ... OBAD 15
Give us each *d* our daily bread, ... LUKE 11:3
the scriptures carefully every *d* ... ACTS 17:11
inner person is being renewed day by *d* ... 2 COR 4:16
d of the Lord will come in the same ... 1 THESS 5:2
a thousand years are like a single *d* ... 2 PET 3:8

DAYLIGHT
He will vindicate you in broad *d* ... PS 37:6

DAYS
faithfulness will pursue me all my *d* ... PS 23:6
d of our lives add up to seventy years ... PS 90:10

before the difficult *d* come, ... ECCL 12:1
I will pour out my Spirit in those *d* ... JOEL 2:29
in future *d* the LORD's Temple Mount ... MIC 4:1
feast, new moon, or Sabbath *d* ... COL 2:16
in these last *d* he has spoken to us ... HEB 1:2
the last *d* blatant scoffers will come, ... 2 PET 3:3

DAZZLING
My beloved is *d* and ruddy; ... SONG 5:10

DEACONS
D likewise must be dignified, ... 1 TIM 3:8

DEAD
who has in them a spirit of the *d* ... LEV 20:27
'He has been raised from the *d* ... MATT 28:7
you too consider yourselves *d* to sin, ... ROM 6:11
although you were *d* in your offenses ... EPH 2:1
and the *d* in Christ will rise first. ... 1 THESS 4:16
is *d* being by itself. ... JAS 2:17
so also faith without works is *d* ... JAS 2:26

DEAL
I *d* with each person according to how ... JER 17:10

DEAR
"This is my one *d* Son; ... MATT 3:17
"This is my one *d* Son, ... MATT 17:5
his one *d* son. ... MARK 12:6
I will send my one *d* son; ... LUKE 20:13
"This is my *d* Son, ... 2 PET 1:17

DEATH
The murderer must surely be put to *d* ... NUM 35:16
person commits a sin punishable by *d* ... DEUT 21:22
all who hate me love *d* ... PROV 8:36
but its end is the way that leads to *d* ... PROV 14:12
For *d* is the destiny of every person, ... ECCL 7:2
he will swallow up *d* permanently. ... ISA 25:8
because he willingly submitted to *d* ... ISA 53:12
but has crossed over from *d* to life. ... JOHN 5:24
God publicly displayed him at his *d* ... ROM 3:25
through one man and *d* through sin, ... ROM 5:12
For the payoff of sin is *d* ... ROM 6:23
you put to *d* the deeds of the body ... ROM 8:13
For since *d* came through a man, ... 1 COR 15:21
Every day I am in danger of *d* ... 1 COR 15:31
"Where, O *d*, is your victory? ... 1 COR 15:55
d in the flesh but by being made alive ... 1 PET 3:18
I hold the keys of *d* and of Hades! ... REV 1:18
The second *d* has no power over them, ... REV 20:6
This is the second *d* —the ... REV 20:14
and *d* will not exist any more —or ... REV 21:4

DEBAUCHED
over the *d* lifestyle of lawless men, ... 2 PET 2:7

DEBAUCHERY
d envy, slander, ... MARK 7:22
which is *d* ... EPH 5:18

DEBORAH
Prophetess who led Israel to victory over Canaanites (Judg 4-5).

DEBTOR
d both to the Greeks and to the, ... ROM 1:14

DEBTORS
as we ourselves have forgiven our *d* ... MATT 6:12

DEBTS
you must declare a cancellation of *d* ... DEUT 15:1
and forgive us our *d* ... MATT 6:12
he canceled the *d* of both. ... LUKE 7:42

DECAY
permit your Holy One to experience *d* ... ACTS 2:27

DECEIT
I hate and despise *d* ... PS 119:163
d debauchery, envy, ... MARK 7:22
all *d* and hypocrisy ... 1 PET 2:1
no sin nor was *d* found in his mouth. ... 1 PET 2:22

DECEITFUL
Charm is *d* and beauty is fleeting. ... PROV 31:30
human mind is more *d* than anything ... JER 17:9
d workers, disguising themselves ... 2 COR 11:13
d philosophy that is according to ... COL 2:8

DECEIVE
they *d* the minds of the naive. ... ROM 16:18
Let nobody *d* you with empty words, ... EPH 5:6
do not merely listen to it and so *d* ... JAS 1:22

DECEIVED
Do not be *d* ... 1 COR 15:33
Do not be *d* ... GAL 6:7
because she was fully *d* ... 1 TIM 2:14
deceiving others and being *d* ... 2 TIM 3:13

DECEIVES
he *d* himself. ... GAL 6:3
and so *d* his heart, ... JAS 1:26

DECEIVING
d ourselves and the truth is not in ... 1 JOHN 1:8

DECENT
everything in a *d* and orderly manner. ... 1 COR 14:40
live a *d* life before outsiders ... 1 THESS 4:12

DECEPTION
you may become hardened by sin's *d* ... HEB 3:13

DECEPTIVE
don't speak evil words or use *d* speech ... PS 34:13

DECEPTIVELY
lest I become satisfied and act *d* ... PROV 30:9

DECIDE
so that you can *d* what is best, ... PHIL 1:10

DECIDED
For I *d* to be concerned about nothing ... 1 COR 2:2
the members in the body just as he *d* ... 1 COR 12:18

DECIDES
distributing as he *d* to each person, ... 1 COR 12:11

DECLARE
Would you *d* me guilty so that you ... JOB 40:8
The heavens *d* the glory of God; ... PS 19:1
The heavens *d* his fairness, ... PS 50:6

DECREE
continually his covenantal *d* ... 1 CHR 16:15
He issued the *d* ... PS 33:9

DECREED
ever fulfilled unless the LORD *d* it? ... LAM 3:37
for what has been *d* must occur. ... DAN 11:36

DECREES
By day the LORD *d* his loyal love, ... PS 42:8
he will make just *d* for the nations. ... ISA 42:1

DEDICATED
to God from birth till the day ... JUDG 13:7
had *d* himself to the study of the law ... EZRA 7:10

DEED
And whatever you do in word or *d* ... COL 3:17

DEEDS
he rewards godly *d* .... PS 11:7
The one whose *d* are blameless .... PS 24:4
your compassionate and faithful *d* .... PS 25:6
"How awesome are your *d* .... PS 66:3
about the LORD's faithful *d* .... PS 89:1
Do not forget all his kind *d* .... PS 103:2
wounded because of our rebellious *d* .... ISA 53:5
and my deeds are not like your *d* .... ISA 55:8
so that they can see your good *d* .... MATT 5:16
But wisdom is vindicated by her *d* .... MATT 11:19
perform the *d* of the one who sent me .... JOHN 9:4
attested to you by God with powerful *d* .... ACTS 2:22
d consistent with repentance. .... ACTS 26:20
But we have rejected shameful hidden *d* .... 2 COR 4:2
but with their *d* they deny him, ... TITUS 1:16
may see your good *d* and glorify God .... 1 PET 2:12
linen is the righteous *d* of the saints .... REV 19:8

DEER
As a *d* longs for streams of water, ... PS 42:1

DEFEAT
their *d* means riches for the Gentiles, ... ROM 11:12

DEFEND
D your honor. .... PS 74:22

DEFENSE
am placed here for the *d* of the gospel .... PHIL 1:16

DEFERRED
Hope *d* makes the heart sick, ... PROV 13:12

DEFICIENT
not *d* in anything. .... JAS 1:4
But if anyone is *d* in wisdom, ... JAS 1:5

DEFILE
permission not to *d* himself. .... DAN 1:8
d the body and the spirit, ... 2 COR 7:1
d the flesh, ... JUDE 8

DEFILED
d by the impurities of the local .... EZRA 9:11
The earth is *d* by its inhabitants, ... ISA 24:5
abstain from things *d* by idols .... ACTS 15:20

DEITY
fullness of *d* lives in bodily form, ... COL 2:9

DELICACIES
drink from the river of your *d* .... PS 36:8
not defile himself with the royal *d* .... DAN 1:8

DELIGHT
you always give me sheer *d* .... PS 16:11
Then you will take *d* in the LORD, ... PS 37:4
those who deal truthfully are his *d* .... PROV 12:22
I *d* in acknowledging God, ... HOS 6:6
He takes great *d* in you; .... ZEPH 3:17
in him I take great *d* .... MATT 3:17
in whom I take great *d* .... MATT 12:18

DELIGHTED
Then the king was *d* and gave an order .... DAN 6:23
in whom I am *d* .... 2 PET 1:17

DELIGHTFUL
How *d* it is to see approaching over .... ISA 52:7

DELIGHTS
for he *d* in him." .... PS 22:8
disciplines the son in whom he *d* .... PROV 3:12

DELILAH
Woman who betrayed Samson (Judg 16:4-22).

DELIVER
you *d* the fatherless. .... PS 10:14
and is more than willing to *d* .... PS 130:7
desire to *d* is like a helmet .... ISA 59:17
and who is able to *d* .... ISA 63:1
but *d* us from the evil one. .... MATT 6:13

DELIVERANCE
great delight in the *d* you provide. .... PS 21:1
shouts of joy from those celebrating *d* .... PS 32:7
again experience the joy of your *d* .... PS 51:12
followers will soon experience his *d* .... PS 85:9
d and peace greet each other .... PS 85:10
Let's rejoice and celebrate his *d* .... ISA 25:9
But the *d* I give is permanent; .... ISA 51:6
For he clothes me in garments of *d* .... ISA 61:10

DELIVERED
he *d* me from all my fears. .... PS 34:4
Turn to me so you can be *d* .... ISA 45:22
on the name of the LORD will be *d* .... JOEL 2:32
He *d* us from so great a risk of death, ... 2 COR 1:10

DELIVERER
my *d* My God is my rocky summit .... PS 18:2
You are my helper and my *d* .... PS 40:17
He alone is my protector and *d* .... PS 62:2
my strong *d* .... PS 140:7
my refuge and my *d* .... PS 144:2
and there is no *d* besides me. .... ISA 43:11
Jesus our *d* from the coming wrath. .... 1 THESS 1:10

DELIVERS
The LORD *d* .... PS 3:8
and the protector who *d* me.' .... PS 89:26

DEMEAN
steal and *d* the name of my God. .... PROV 30:9

DEMONS
And if I cast out *d* by Beelzebul, ... MATT 12:27
Even the *d* believe that —and .... JAS 2:19

DEMONSTRATE
This was also to *d* his righteousness .... ROM 3:26
Jesus could *d* his utmost patience, ... 1 TIM 1:16

DEMONSTRATED
Solomon *d* his loyalty to the LORD .... 1 KGS 3:3
he *d* his amazing faithfulness to me .... PS 31:21

DEMONSTRATES
But God *d* his own love for us, ... ROM 5:8

DEN
and thrown into a *d* of lions. .... DAN 6:16
you are turning it into a *d* of robbers .... MATT 21:13

DENARIUS
Bring me a *d* and let me look at it." .... MARK 12:15

DENIED
resident foreigner and *d* them justice. .... EZEK 22:29
he has *d* the faith and is worse than .... 1 TIM 5:8

DENIES
But whoever *d* me before people, ... MATT 10:33
Everyone who *d* the Son does not have .... 1 JOHN 2:23

DENY
I will never *d* you." .... MATT 26:35
he must *d* himself, ... LUKE 9:23

he will also *d* us. ... 2 TIM 2:12
but with their deeds they *d* him, ... TITUS 1:16

DENYING
even to the point of *d* the Master ... 2 PET 2:1

DEPART
The scepter will not *d* from Judah, ... GEN 49:10
D from me, ... MATT 25:41
have a desire to *d* and be with Christ, ... PHIL 1:23

DEPARTED
"The glory has *d* from Israel," ... 1 SAM 4:21
You have *d* from your first love! ... REV 2:4

DEPRAVED
God gave them over to a *d* mind, ... ROM 1:28

DEPRESSED
Why are you *d* ... PS 42:5

DEPRIVE
and *d* the innocent of justice ... ISA 29:21
to *d* a person of his rights ... LAM 3:35
Do not *d* each other, ... 1 COR 7:5

DEPRIVING
by *d* a righteous man of justice. ... PROV 18:5

DEPTH
nor *d* nor anything else in creation ... ROM 8:39
Oh, the *d* of the riches and wisdom ... ROM 11:33

DEPTHS
The *d* of the earth are in his hand, ... PS 95:4

DESCENDANT
will raise up for them a righteous *d* . ... JER 33:15
but "and to your *d* ... GAL 3:16

DESCENDANTS
"To your *d* I will give this land." ... GEN 12:7
then you are Abraham's *d* ... GAL 3:29

DESERT
some will *d* the faith and occupy ... 1 TIM 4:1

DESERTED
their own homes those who have been *d* ... PS 68:6
everyone in the province of Asia *d* me, ... 2 TIM 1:15

DESERTING
astonished that you are so quickly *d* ... GAL 1:6

DESERVE
But I will punish you as your deeds *d* ... JER 21:14
who practice such things *d* to die, ... ROM 1:32

DESERVES
for the worker *d* his pay. ... LUKE 10:7
"The worker *d* his pay." ... 1 TIM 5:18

DESIRABLE
What is *d* for a person is to show loyal ... PROV 19:22
he is totally *d* ... SONG 5:16

DESIRE
May those who *d* my vindication shout ... PS 35:27
On earth there is no one I *d* but you. ... PS 73:25
satisfies the *d* of his loyal followers ... PS 145:19
none of the things you *d* can compare ... PROV 3:15
what the righteous *d* will be granted. ... PROV 10:24
The *d* of the righteous is only good, ... PROV 11:23
d fulfilled will be sweet to the soul ... PROV 13:19
We *d* your fame and reputation to grow. ... ISA 26:8
it is realized as I *d* and is fulfilled ... ISA 55:11
and that I *d* people to do these things ... JER 9:24
d for other things come in and choke ... MARK 4:19
And in this way I *d* to preach ... ROM 15:20
to marry than to burn with sexual *d* ... 1 COR 7:9
we *d* to put on our heavenly dwelling, ... 2 COR 5:2
have a *d* to depart and be with Christ, ... PHIL 1:23
forth in you both the *d* and the
effort—for ... PHIL 2:13
d to conduct ourselves rightly ... HEB 13:18
Then when *d* conceives, ... JAS 1:15
of the flesh and the *d* of the eyes ... 1 JOHN 2:16

DESIRED
Though the LORD *d* to crush him ... ISA 53:10

DESIRES
It *d* to dominate you, ... GEN 4:7
ensnared by their own *d* ... PROV 11:6
seeks his own *d* ... PROV 18:1
the sinful *d* ... ROM 7:5
for the flesh to arouse its *d* ... ROM 13:14
will not carry out the *d* of the flesh. ... GAL 5:16
d that are opposed to the flesh, ... GAL 5:17
he *d* a good work." ... 1 TIM 3:1
harmful *d* that plunge people into ruin ... 1 TIM 6:9
reject godless ways and worldly *d* ... TITUS 2:12
it is able to judge the *d* and thoughts ... HEB 4:12
away from fleshly *d* that do battle ... 1 PET 2:11
world is passing away with all its *d* ... 1 JOHN 2:17

DESPAIR
but not driven to *d* ... 2 COR 4:8

DESPISE
Therefore I *d* myself, ... JOB 42:6
do not *d* discipline from the LORD, ... PROV 3:11
do not *d* your mother when she is old. ... PROV 23:22
be devoted to the one and *d* the other. ... LUKE 16:13
you did not *d* or reject me. ... GAL 4:14

DESPISED
So Esau *d* his birthright. ... GEN 25:34
but fools have *d* wisdom ... PROV 1:7
he was *d* ... ISA 53:3
God chose what is low and *d* ... 1 COR 1:28

DESPISES
The one who *d* his neighbor sins, ... PROV 14:21
but a foolish person *d* his mother. ... PROV 15:20
one who refuses correction *d* himself, ... PROV 15:32

DESTINED
This child is *d* to be the cause ... LUKE 2:34

DESTINY
You determine my *d* ... PS 31:15
and understood the *d* of the wicked. ... PS 73:17
For death is the *d* of every person, ... ECCL 7:2

DESTITUTE
they were *d* ... HEB 11:37

DESTROY
the careless ease of fools will *d* them ... PROV 1:32
but one sinner can *d* much that is good ... ECCL 9:18
to *d* both soul and body in hell. ... MATT 10:28

DESTROYED
And after my skin has been *d* ... JOB 19:26
or sister, for whom Christ died, is *d* ... 1 COR 8:11
He has *d* what was against us, ... COL 2:14

DESTROYS
whoever does it *d* his own life. ... PROV 6:32
the godless person *d* his neighbor, ... PROV 11:9
a brother to one who *d* ... PROV 18:9

DISAPPOINTED
they trusted and they were not *d* .... PS 22:5

DISAPPOINTS
A horse *d* those who trust in it .... PS 33:17

DISASTER
Do not be afraid of sudden *d* .... PROV 3:25
whoever rejoices over *d* will not go .... PROV 17:5
one-of-a-kind *d* —is .... EZEK 7:5

DISCARDED
The stone that the builders *d* .... PS 118:22

DISCERN
to *d* both good and evil. .... HEB 5:14

DISCERNING
but a *d* person keeps silent. .... PROV 11:12
The *d* mind seeks knowledge, ... PROV 15:14
one who holds his tongue is deemed *d* .. PROV 17:28
but a *d* poor person can evaluate him .. PROV 28:11

DISCERNMENT
Teach me proper *d* and understanding. ... PS 119:66
Fearing the LORD is the beginning of *d* ... PROV 1:7
wisdom for the one who has *d* .... PROV 10:23

DISCERNS
but the shrewd person *d* his steps. .... PROV 14:15

DISCIPLE
these little ones in the name of a *d* .... MATT 10:42
own cross and follow me cannot
be my *d* .... LUKE 14:27

DISCIPLES
go and make *d* of all nations, ... MATT 28:19
follow my teaching, you are
really my *d* .... JOHN 8:31
will know by this that you are my *d* .... JOHN 13:35
Now it was in Antioch that the *d* were ... ACTS 11:26

DISCIPLINE
You severely *d* people for their sins; .... PS 39:11
do not despise *d* from the LORD, ... PROV 3:11
"How I hated *d* .... PROV 5:12
He will die because there was no *d* .... PROV 5:23
rebukes of *d* are like the road leading ... PROV 6:23
The one who loves *d* loves knowledge, ... PROV 12:1
A wise son accepts his father's *d* .... PROV 13:1
one who neglects *d* ends up in poverty .... PROV 13:18
A fool rejects his father's *d* .... PROV 15:5
D your child, ... PROV 19:18
Listen to advice and receive *d* .... PROV 19:20
rod of *d* will drive it far from him. .... PROV 22:15
Do not withhold *d* from a child; .... PROV 23:13
and *d* and understanding. .... PROV 23:23
D your child, ... PROV 29:17
do not scorn the Lord's *d* or give up .... HEB 12:5
son is there that a father does not *d* .... HEB 12:7
Now all *d* seems painful at the time, ... HEB 12:11
I rebuke and *d* .... REV 3:19

DISCIPLINED
You *d* us and we learned from it. .... JER 31:18
d so that we may not be condemned .... 1 COR 11:32

DISCIPLINES
so the LORD your God *d* you. .... DEUT 8:5
a father *d* the son in whom he delights ... PROV 3:12
For the Lord *d* the one he loves .... HEB 12:6

DISCIPLINING
loves his child is diligent in *d* him. .... PROV 13:24

DISCORD
not in *d* and jealousy. .... ROM 13:13

DISCOURAGED
"Don't let anyone be *d* .... 1 SAM 17:32
be strong and don't get *d* .... 2 CHR 15:7
he delivers those who are *d* .... PS 34:18
the humiliated and to encourage the *d* ... ISA 57:15

DISCOURAGEMENT
instead of *d* .... ISA 61:3

DISCOVER
Can you *d* the essence of God? .... JOB 11:7
people cannot *d* what God has
ordained, ... ECCL 3:11

DISCRETION
D will protect you, ... PROV 2:11
in order to safeguard *d* .... PROV 5:2
and I find knowledge and *d* .... PROV 8:12
a beautiful woman who rejects *d* .... PROV 11:22

DISEASE
four men with a skin *d* were sitting .... 2 KGS 7:3

DISFIGURED
so *d* he no longer looked like a man; .... ISA 52:14

DISGRACE
d followed; but wisdom came with .... PROV 11:2
but sin is a *d* to any people. .... PROV 14:34
a son who brings shame and *d* .... PROV 19:26

DISGUISES
who hates others *d* it with his lips, ... PROV 26:24
Satan *d* himself as an angel of light. .... 2 COR 11:14

DISGUST
The LORD laughs in *d* at them, ... PS 37:13

DISHEARTENED
so they will not become *d* .... COL 3:21

DISHONEST
or consort with those who are *d* .... PS 26:4
The LORD abhors *d* scales, ... PROV 11:1
dishonest in a very little is also *d* in .... LUKE 16:10

DISHONOR
but the prudent conceals *d* .... PROV 12:16
considered worthy to suffer *d* .... ACTS 5:41
It is sown in *d* .... 1 COR 15:43

DISMANTLED
is *d* we have a building from God, ... 2 COR 5:1

DISOBEDIENCE
just as through the *d* of the one man .... ROM 5:19
For God has consigned all people to *d* ... ROM 11:32
violation or *d* received its just .... HEB 2:2
did not enter because of *d* .... HEB 4:6
following the same pattern of *d* .... HEB 4:11

DISOBEDIENT
d to parents, ... ROM 1:30
d to parents, ... 2 TIM 3:2
d and unfit for any good deed. .... TITUS 1:16

DISORDER
for God is not characterized by *d* .... 1 COR 14:33
slander, gossip, arrogance, and *d* .... 2 COR 12:20
there is *d* and every evil practice. .... JAS 3:16

DISPLAY
again you *d* your power against me. .... JOB 10:16
I will *d* my majesty among the
nations. .... EZEK 39:21

DISPLAYING
justice by magnifying his law and *d* it. ..... ISA 42:21

DISPLAYS
the sky *d* his handiwork. ..... PS 19:1

DISPOSSESS
must *d* the inhabitants of the land ..... NUM 33:53

DISPUTE
any of you has a legal *d* with another, ... 1 COR 6:1

DISPUTES
A toss of a coin ends *d* ..... PROV 18:18
not engage in heated *d* but be kind ..... 2 TIM 2:24

DISQUALIFIED
I myself will not be *d* ..... 1 COR 9:27

DISRESPECTS
Cursed is the one who *d* his father ..... DEUT 27:16

DISSENSION
A quick-tempered person stirs up *d* ..... PROV 15:18
A perverse person spreads *d* ..... PROV 16:28
The greedy person stirs up *d* ..... PROV 28:25
An angry person stirs up *d* ..... PROV 29:22

DISSENSIONS
to watch out for those who create *d* ..... ROM 16:17

DISTINCTION
no *d* between the Jew and the Greek, ... ROM 10:12

DISTINCTIONS
have you not made *d* among yourselves ..... JAS 2:4

DISTINGUISH
and *d* right from wrong. ..... 1 KGS 3:9

DISTORT
and wanting to *d* the gospel of Christ. ..... GAL 1:7

DISTORTING
d the word of God, ... 2 COR 4:2

DISTRACTION
without *d* you may give notable ..... 1 COR 7:35

DISTRESS
In my *d* I called to the LORD; ..... PS 18:6
They cried out to the LORD in their *d* ..... PS 107:13
in their *d* they will earnestly seek me ..... HOS 5:15
"I called out to the LORD from my *d* ..... JONAH 2:2
she has *d* because her time has come, ... JOHN 16:21
or *d* or persecution, ... ROM 8:35

DISTRESSED
Do not let your hearts be *d* ..... JOHN 14:1
Do not let your hearts be *d* or lacking ..... JOHN 14:27
sister is *d* because of what you eat, ... ROM 14:15

DIVIDE
Then they threw dice to *d* his clothes. ..... LUKE 23:34

DIVIDED
kingdom *d* against itself is destroyed, ... MATT 12:25
Is Christ *d* ..... 1 COR 1:13

DIVINATION
not practice either *d* or soothsaying. ..... LEV 19:26

DIVINE
become partakers of the *d* nature, ... 2 PET 1:4

DIVISION
but rather *d* ..... LUKE 12:51
so that there may be no *d* in the body, ... 1 COR 12:25

DIVISIONS
to end your *d* ..... 1 COR 1:10
I hear there are *d* among you, ... 1 COR 11:18

DIVISIVE
Reject a *d* person after one or two ..... TITUS 3:10

DIVORCE
I hate *d* ..... MAL 2:16
lawful to *d* a wife for any cause?" ..... MATT 19:3
a wife should not *d* a husband ..... 1 COR 7:10
and a husband should not *d* his wife. ..... 1 COR 7:11

DO
d this so that it may go well with you ..... DEUT 6:3
as the hypocrites *d* in synagogues ..... MATT 6:2
hear the word of God and *d* it." ..... LUKE 8:21

DOES
You are the God who *d* amazing things; ..... PS 77:14
Everyone who resides in him *d* not sin; ..... 1 JOHN 3:6

DOING
while your servant was *d* this and
that ..... 1 KGS 20:40
not *d* their own work but meddling ..... 2 THESS 3:11

DOMINATE
Do not let any sin *d* me. ..... PS 119:133

DOMINION
have *d* and exalt yourself as the ruler ..... 1 CHR 29:11
D and awesome might belong to God; ..... JOB 25:2
His *d* will be from sea to sea ..... ZECH 9:10

DOMINIONS
whether thrones or *d* ..... COL 1:16

DON'T
D be frightened, ... ISA 41:10

DOOR
close the *d* ..... MATT 6:6
I am the *d* ..... JOHN 10:9
Listen! I am standing at the *d* ..... REV 3:20

DOORWAY
Your instructions are a *d* through ..... PS 119:130

DOUBLE-EDGED
active and sharper than any *d* sword, ... HEB 4:12
d sword extended out of his mouth. ..... REV 1:16
one who has the sharp *d* sword: ..... REV 2:12

DOUBLE-MINDED
since he is a *d* individual, ... JAS 1:8

DOUBT
why did you *d* ..... MATT 14:31
if you have faith and do not *d* ..... MATT 21:21
does not *d* in his heart but believes ..... MARK 11:23

DOUBTING
But he must ask in faith without *d* ..... JAS 1:6

DOWN
as you lie *d* ..... DEUT 6:7
a leopard will lie *d* with a young goat ..... ISA 11:6
they will lie *d* in a lush pasture, ... EZEK 34:14
pressed *d* shaken together, ... LUKE 6:38
trampled *d* by the Gentiles ..... LUKE 21:24
I lay *d* my life for the sheep. ..... JOHN 10:15
one lays *d* his life for his friends. ..... JOHN 15:13
Don't let anyone look *d* on you. ..... TITUS 2:15
thus we ought to lay *d* our lives ..... 1 JOHN 3:16

DOWNHEARTED
who encourages the *d* ..... 2 COR 7:6

DRAW
will *d* all people to myself." ..... JOHN 12:32

DRAWS
unless the Father who sent me *d* him, ... JOHN 6:44

DRESSED
d in bright red, ... ISA 63:1

DRINK
D water from your own cistern ... PROV 5:15
Wine is a mocker and strong *d* is a ... PROV 20:1
relax, eat, *d* celebrate!'" ... LUKE 12:19
were all made to *d* of the one Spirit. ... 1 COR 12:13

DRIVES
but perfect love *d* out fear, ... 1 JOHN 4:18

DROP
the nations are like a *d* in a bucket; ... ISA 40:15

DRUNK
And do not get *d* with wine, ... EPH 5:18

DRUNKARDS
d and gluttons become impoverished, ... PROV 23:21
d the verbally abusive, ... 1 COR 6:10

DRUNKENNESS
weighed down with dissipation and *d* .. LUKE 21:34
not in carousing and *d* ... ROM 13:13
d carousing, and similar things. ... GAL 5:21
d carousing, drinking bouts, ... 1 PET 4:3

DRY
D bones, listen to the LORD's message. ... EZEK 37:4

DUNG
I regard them as *d* ... PHIL 3:8

DUNGEONS
to release prisoners from *d* ... ISA 42:7

DUST
both come from the *d* ... ECCL 3:20

DWELL
that Christ will *d* in your hearts ... EPH 3:17
have all his fullness *d* in the Son ... COL 1:19
Let the word of Christ *d* in you richly ... COL 3:16

DYING
for the legal rights of all the *d* ... PROV 31:8
living is Christ and *d* is gain. ... PHIL 1:21

EAGER
you should be *e* for the greater gifts ... 1 COR 12:31
and be *e* for the spiritual gifts, ... 1 COR 14:1

EAGERLY
not for shameful profit but *e* ... 1 PET 5:2

EAGERNESS
For if the *e* is present, ... 2 COR 8:12
each of you to demonstrate the same *e* ... HEB 6:11

EAGLE'S
so your youth is renewed like an *e* ... PS 103:5

EAGLES
they rise up as if they had *e* wings, ... ISA 40:31

EAR
heard of you by the hearing of the *e* ... JOB 42:5
or *e* heard, ... 1 COR 2:9
And if the *e* says, ... 1 COR 12:16

EARNESTLY
contend *e* for the faith ... JUDE 3

EARS
shuts his *e* to the cry of the poor, ... PROV 21:13

EARTH
God created the heavens and the *e* ... GEN 1:1
LORD owns the *e* and all it contains, ... PS 24:1
May your splendor cover the whole *e* ... PS 108:5
there is nothing truly new on *e* ... ECCL 1:9
majestic splendor fills the entire *e* ... ISA 6:3
and the *e* will wear out like clothes; ... ISA 51:6
just as the sky is higher than the *e* ... ISA 55:9
and the *e* is my footstool. ... ISA 66:1
The whole *e* is speechless ... HAB 2:20
will be done on *e* as it is in heaven. ... MATT 6:10
and whatever you release on *e* ... MATT 16:19
Heaven and *e* will pass away, ... MATT 24:35
"All authority in heaven and on *e* ... MATT 28:18
and on *e* peace among people ... LUKE 2:14
the *e* and its abundance are the Lord's ... 1 COR 10:26
heaven and on earth and under the *e* ... PHIL 2:10
waiting for new heavens and a new *e* ... 2 PET 3:13

EASE
Woe to those who live in *e* in Zion, ... AMOS 6:1

EAT
when you *e* from it you will surely die ... GEN 2:17
e delicacies and drink sweet drinks ... NEH 8:10
Buy and *e* ... ISA 55:1
will *e* straw, ... ISA 65:25
So whether you *e* or drink, ... 1 COR 10:31
neither should he *e* ... 2 THESS 3:10

EATING
While they were *e* ... MATT 26:26
One person believes in *e* everything, ... ROM 14:2

ECSTATIC
to the God who gives me *e* joy, ... PS 43:4

EDICT
they were not afraid of the king's *e* ... HEB 11:23

EFFORT
e to enter through the narrow door, ... LUKE 13:24
you now trying to finish by human *e* ... GAL 3:3
e to keep the unity of the Spirit ... EPH 4:3
must make every *e* to enter that rest, ... HEB 4:11

EL
E God, the LORD has spoken, ... PS 50:1

ELAH
Son of Baasha; king of Israel (1 Kgs 16:6-14).

ELDER
honor the presence of an *e* ... LEV 19:32

ELDERLY
like a crown to the *e* ... PROV 17:6

ELDERS
E who provide effective leadership ... 1 TIM 5:17

ELECTION
that God's purpose in *e* would stand, ... ROM 9:11
be sure of your calling and *e* ... 2 PET 1:10

ELEMENTS
the beginning *e* of God's utterances. ... HEB 5:12

ELEVATED
you are *e* high above all gods. ... PS 97:9

ELI
High priest in youth of Samuel (1 Sam 1-4). Blessed Hannah (1 Sam 1:12-18); raised Samuel (1 Sam 2:11-26).

ELIJAH
Prophet; predicted famine in Israel (1 Kgs 17:1; Jas 5:17). Fed by ravens (1 Kgs 17:2-6). Raised Sidonian widow's son (1 Kgs 17:7-24). Defeated prophets of Baal at Carmel (1 Kgs 18:16-46). Ran from Jezebel (1 Kgs 19:1-9). Prophesied death of Azariah (2 Kgs 1). Succeeded by Elisha (1 Kgs 19:19-21; 2 Kgs 2:1-18). Taken to heaven in whirlwind (2 Kgs 2:11-12).

Return prophesied (Mal 4:5-6); equated with John the Baptist (Matt 17:9-13; Mark 9:9-13; Luke 1:17). Appeared with Moses in transfiguration of Jesus (Matt 17:1-8; Mark 9:1-8).

ELIMINATED
The last enemy to be *e* is death. .... 1 COR 15:26

ELISHA
Prophet; successor of Elijah (1 Kgs 19:16-21); inherited his cloak (2 Kgs 2:1-18). Miracles of (2 Kgs 2-6).

ELIZABETH
Mother of John the Baptist, relative of Mary (Luke 1:5-58).

EMMANUEL
and they will name him *E* .... MATT 1:23

EMPTY
Let nobody deceive you with *e* words, ... EPH 5:6
from your *e* way of life inherited .... 1 PET 1:18

ENABLES
willingness to help *e* me to prevail. .... 2 SAM 22:36

ENCHANTING
e folks for their own gain. .... JUDE 16

ENCOURAGE
e one another with these words. .... 1 THESS 4:18
E younger men likewise to be .... TITUS 2:6

ENCOURAGED
e and strengthened the brothers .... ACTS 15:32

ENCOURAGEMENT
(which is translated "son of *e* .... ACTS 4:36
through *e* of the scriptures .... ROM 15:4
e and consolation. .... 1 COR 14:3

ENCOURAGES
who *e* the downhearted, ... 2 COR 7:6

ENCOURAGING
but an *e* word brings him joy. .... PROV 12:25
but *e* each other, ... HEB 10:25

END
its *e* is the way that leads to death. .... PROV 14:12
may become wise by the *e* of your life... PROV 19:20
no *e* to the making of many books, ... ECCL 12:12
I will put an *e* to the sounds of joy .... JER 25:10
his compassions never *e* .... LAM 3:22
one who endures to the *e* will
be saved .... MATT 10:22
but the *e* will not come at once." .... LUKE 21:9
For Christ is the *e* of the law, ... ROM 10:4
when he has brought to an *e* all rule .... 1 COR 15:24

ENDS
Love never *e* .... 1 COR 13:8

ENDURANCE
knowing that suffering produces *e* .... ROM 5:3
and *e* character, ... ROM 5:4
through *e* and through encouragement .. ROM 15:4
Now may the God of *e* and comfort give ... ROM 15:5
your patient *e* of the same sufferings ..... 2 COR 1:6
e and gentleness. .... 1 TIM 6:11
and in *e* .... TITUS 2:2
you need *e* in order to do God's will ...... HEB 10:36
and run with *e* the race set out for us ...... HEB 12:1
the testing of your faith produces *e* .... JAS 1:3

ENDURE
e the insults of those who insult you. .... PS 69:9
your instructions *e* .... PS 119:89
The one who tells the truth will *e* .... PROV 12:19
whatever God does will *e* forever; .... ECCL 3:14
Who can *e* the day of his coming? .... MAL 3:2
e in suffering, ... ROM 12:12
If we *e* .... 2 TIM 2:12
E your suffering as discipline; .... HEB 12:7

ENDURED
we regard as blessed those who have *e* ..... JAS 5:11

ENDURES
for he is good and his loyal love *e* .... 1 CHR 16:34
and your reputation *e* .... PS 102:12
his integrity *e* .... PS 112:9
for his loyal love *e* .... PS 136:1
the one who *e* to the end will be saved .. MARK 13:13
e all things. .... 1 COR 13:7
Happy is the one who *e* testing, ... JAS 1:12
but the word of the Lord *e* forever. .... 1 PET 1:25

ENDURING
an *e* protector! .... ISA 26:4

ENEMIES
feast before me in plain sight of my *e* .... PS 23:5
a man's *e* are his own family. .... MIC 7:6
make your *e* a footstool for your feet ... LUKE 20:43

ENEMY
Do not rejoice when your *e* falls, ... PROV 24:17
If your *e* is hungry, ... PROV 25:21
but the kisses of an *e* are excessive. ...... PROV 27:6
love your *e* .... MATT 5:44
The last *e* to be eliminated is death. .... 1 COR 15:26
world's friend makes himself God's *e* .... JAS 4:4

ENJOY
so that I might serve God as I *e* life. .... PS 56:13
E fine food. .... ISA 55:2
than to *e* sin's fleeting pleasure. .... HEB 11:25

ENJOYMENT
provides us with all things for our *e* .... 1 TIM 6:17

ENLIGHTENED
the eyes of your heart have been *e* .... EPH 1:18
those who have once been *e* .... HEB 6:4

ENOCH
Walked with God and taken by him (Gen 5:18-24; Heb 11:5). Prophet (Jude 14).

ENOUGH
"My grace is *e* for you, ... 2 COR 12:9

ENROLLED
who are *e* in heaven, ... HEB 12:23

ENSLAVED
that we would no longer be *e* to sin. .... ROM 6:6
freed from sin and *e* to God, ... ROM 6:22
were *e* under the basic forces .... GAL 4:3

ENTANGLED
No one in military service gets *e* .... 2 TIM 2:4
get *e* in them and succumb to them, ... 2 PET 2:20

ENTER
E his gates with thanksgiving, ... PS 100:4
will never *e* the kingdom of heaven! .... MATT 5:20
there are many who *e* through it. .... MATT 7:13
better for you to *e* life crippled .... MATT 18:8
of God like a child will never *e* it." ...... MARK 10:15
"How hard it is for the rich to *e* .... MARK 10:23

ENTERED
and you have *e* into their labor." .... JOHN 4:38
as sin *e* the world through one man .... ROM 5:12
he *e* once for all into the Most Holy .... HEB 9:12

ENTERS
The one who *e* by the door is the .... JOHN 10:2

ENTHRONED
The one *e* in heaven laughs in disgust; .... PS 2:4
He sits *e* above the cherubim; .... PS 99:1

ENTHUSIASM
work at it with *e* .... COL 3:23

ENTHUSIASTIC
be *e* in spirit, ... ROM 12:11

ENTICE
if sinners try to *e* you, ... PROV 1:10
but empty words they are able to *e* ...... 2 PET 2:18

ENTRANCE
rather stand at the *e* to the temple .... PS 84:10

ENTRUST
And now I *e* you to God .... ACTS 20:32
e their souls to a faithful Creator .... 1 PET 4:19

ENTRUSTED
protect what has been *e* to you. .... 1 TIM 6:20
Protect that good thing *e* to you, ... 2 TIM 1:14
once for all *e* to the saints. .... JUDE 3

ENVIOUS
it is not *e* .... 1 COR 13:4

ENVY
Do not *e* a violent man, ... PROV 3:31
but *e* is rottenness to the bones. .... PROV 14:30

EPHRAIM
1. Second son of Joseph (Gen 41:52; 46:20). Blessed as firstborn by Jacob (Gen 48).
2. Synonymous with northern kingdom (Isa 7:17; Hos 5).

EQUAL
thus making himself *e* with God. .... JOHN 5:18

EQUIP
to *e* the saints for the work .... EPH 4:12
e you with every good thing to do .... HEB 13:21

EQUITY
E and justice are the foundation .... PS 89:14
with righteousness, justice, and *e* .... PROV 1:3

ERASE
never *e* his name from the book of life ..... REV 3:5

ESAU
Firstborn of Isaac, twin of Jacob (Gen 25:21-26). Also called Edom (Gen 25:30). Sold Jacob his birthright (Gen 25:29-34); lost blessing (Gen 27). Reconciled to Jacob (Gen 33).

ESCAPE
headed off to Tarshish to *e* .... JONAH 1:3
that you will *e* God's judgment? .... ROM 2:3
e if we neglect such a great salvation .... HEB 2:3

ESSENTIAL
members that seem to be weaker
are *e* .... 1 COR 12:22

ESTABLISH
I will *e* his kingdom permanently, ... 1 CHR 28:7
to *e* their own righteousness, ... ROM 10:3
and *e* you. .... 1 PET 5:10

ESTABLISHED
"Loyal love is permanently *e* .... PS 89:2

ESTHER
Jewess who lived in Persia; cousin of Mordecai (Esth 2:7). Chosen queen of Ahasuerus (Esth 2:8-18). Foiled Haman's plan to exterminate the Jews (Esth 3-4; 7-9).

ESTIMATION
Do not be wise in your own *e* .... PROV 3:7

ETERNAL
and underneath you are his *e* arms; ..... DEUT 33:27
you were the *e* God. .... PS 90:2
an *e* priest after the pattern of .... PS 110:4
good thing must I do to gain *e* life?" ..... MATT 19:16
the *e* fire that has been prepared for ... MATT 25:41
but the righteous into *e* life." .... MATT 25:46
may have *e* life." .... JOHN 3:15
will not perish but have *e* life. .... JOHN 3:16
one who believes in the Son has *e* life ... JOHN 3:36
water springing up to *e* life." .... JOHN 4:14
and believes the one who sent
me has *e* .... JOHN 5:24
the one who believes has *e* life. .... JOHN 6:47
You have the words of *e* life. .... JOHN 6:68
I give them *e* life, ... JOHN 10:28
Now this is *e* life —that .... JOHN 17:3
e power and divine nature —have .... ROM 1:20
but the gift of God is *e* life in Christ .... ROM 6:23
an *e* weight of glory far beyond .... 2 COR 4:17
but what cannot be seen is *e* .... 2 COR 4:18
undergo the penalty of *e* destruction, ... 2 THESS 1:9
believe in him for *e* life. .... 1 TIM 1:16
Now to the *e* king, ... 1 TIM 1:17
and so he himself secured *e* redemption.... HEB 9:12
God has given us *e* life, ... 1 JOHN 5:11
you may know that you have *e* life. ...... 1 JOHN 5:13
kept in *e* chains in utter darkness, ... JUDE 6

ETHIOPIAN
Can an *E* change the color of his skin? ..... JER 13:23

EUNUCHS
and some who were made *e* by others, ... MATT 19:12

EVALUATE
E my inner thoughts and motives. .... PS 26:2
For God will *e* every deed, ... ECCL 12:14

EVANGELIST'S
do an *e* work, ... 2 TIM 4:5

EVANGELISTS
some as *e* .... EPH 4:11

EVE
serpent deceived *E* by his treachery, ... 2 COR 11:3
For Adam was formed first and then *E* ... 1 TIM 2:13

EXPENSIVE
and gold or pearls or *e* clothing, ... 1 TIM 2:9

EXPERIENCE
again *e* the joy of your deliverance. ... PS 51:12
they *e* your favor. ... PS 89:15
that by God's grace he would *e* death ... HEB 2:9

EXPERIENCED
if you have *e* the Lord's kindness. ... 1 PET 2:3

EXPLANATIONS
the sages will have no *e* ... ISA 29:14

EXPLOIT
Do not *e* a poor person ... PROV 22:22

EXPOSE
but rather *e* them. ... EPH 5:11

EXPOSED
everything is naked and *e* to the eyes ... HEB 4:13

EXTENDED
and *e* her hands to the needy. ... PROV 31:20

EXTENDS
his kingdom *e* over everything. ... PS 103:19
For your loyal love *e* beyond the sky, ... PS 108:4

EXTINGUISH
You must not *e* the lamp of Israel!" ... 2 SAM 21:17
Do not *e* the Spirit. ... 1 THESS 5:19

EXTOL
Remember to *e* his work, ... JOB 36:24
E the LORD, ... PS 147:12

EXTRAORDINARY
your deeds are *e*. ... PS 77:13
the *e* grace God has shown to you. ... 2 COR 9:14

EYE
eye for *e* ... EXOD 21:24
one who forms the human *e* not see? ... PS 94:9
If your right *e* causes you to sin, ... MATT 5:29
eye for an *e* and a tooth for a tooth ... MATT 5:38
the speck in your brother's *e* ... MATT 7:3
"Things that no *e* has seen, ... 1 COR 2:9
and every *e* will see him, ... REV 1:7

EYES
will be irritants in your *e* ... NUM 33:55
and thorns that blind your *e* ... JOSH 23:13
I made a covenant with my *e* ... JOB 31:1
does not take his *e* off the righteous; ... JOB 36:7
in your *e* a thousand years are like ... PS 90:4
Open my *e* so I can truly see ... PS 119:18
Let your *e* look directly in front ... PROV 4:25
in front of the LORD's *e* ... PROV 5:21
The *e* of the LORD are in every place, ... PROV 15:3
My *e* have seen the king, ... ISA 6:5
keeping our *e* fixed on Jesus, ... HEB 12:2
e of the Lord are upon the righteous ... 1 PET 3:12
wipe away every tear from their *e* ... REV 7:17
wipe away every tear from their *e* ... REV 21:4

EZEKIEL
Priest called to be prophet to the exiles (Ezek 1-3).

EZRA
Priest and teacher of the Law who led a return of exiles to Israel to reestablish temple and worship (Ezra 7-8). Corrected intermarriage of priests (Ezra 9-10). Read Law at celebration of Festival of Temporary Shelters (Neh 8).

FACE
God face to *f* and have survived." ... GEN 32:30
his *f* shone while he talked with him. ... EXOD 34:29
The LORD make his *f* to shine upon you, ... NUM 6:25
His *f* shone like the sun, ... MATT 17:2
but then we will see face to *f* ... 1 COR 13:12
knowledge of God in the *f* of Christ. ... 2 COR 4:6
Lord's *f* is against those who do evil. ... 1 PET 3:12
His *f* shone like the sun shining ... REV 1:16

FACES
with unveiled *f* reflecting the glory ... 2 COR 3:18

FACTIONS
selfish rivalries, dissensions, *f* ... GAL 5:20

FAIL
Plans *f* when there is no counsel, ... PROV 15:22

FAILINGS
bear with the *f* of the weak, ... ROM 15:1

FAIR
"If you are *f* to these people, ... 2 CHR 10:7
The LORD's precepts are *f* ... PS 19:8
and everything he does is *f* ... PS 33:4
How precious and *f* ... ZECH 9:17

FAIRLY
He judges the world *f* ... PS 9:8

FAIRNESS
treat your slaves with justice and *f* ... COL 4:1

FAITH
the people who maintain their *f* ... ISA 26:3
done for you according to your *f* ... MATT 9:29
"It was because of your little *f* ... MATT 17:20
"Have *f* in God. ... MARK 11:22
not even in Israel have I found such *f* ... LUKE 7:9
you people of little *f* ... LUKE 12:28
"Increase our *f*. ... LUKE 17:5
will he find *f* on earth?" ... LUKE 18:8
and saw he had *f* to be healed, ... ACTS 14:9
opened a door of *f* for the Gentiles. ... ACTS 14:27
mutually comforted by one another's *f* ... ROM 1:12
mercy seat accessible through *f* ... ROM 3:25
his *f* is credited as righteousness. ... ROM 4:5
we have been declared righteous by *f* ... ROM 5:1
f comes from what is heard, ... ROM 10:17
receive the one who is weak in the *f* ... ROM 14:1
because he does not do so from *f* ... ROM 14:23
to bring about the obedience of *f* ... ROM 16:26
all *f* so that I can remove mountains, ... 1 COR 13:2
f hope, and love. ... 1 COR 13:13
stand firm in the *f* ... 1 COR 16:13
for we live by *f* ... 2 COR 5:7
test to see if you are in the *f* ... 2 COR 13:5
the righteous one will live by *f* ... GAL 3:11
we could be declared righteous by *f* ... GAL 3:24
For by grace you are saved through *f* ... EPH 2:8
one *f* one baptism, ... EPH 4:5
by taking up the shield of *f* ... EPH 6:16
if indeed you remain in the *f* ... COL 1:23
the breastplate of *f* and love ... 1 THESS 5:8
for goodness and every work of *f* ... 2 THESS 1:11
if she continues in *f* and love ... 1 TIM 2:15
desert the *f* and occupy themselves ... 1 TIM 4:1
he has denied the *f* ... 1 TIM 5:8
Compete well for the *f* and lay hold ... 1 TIM 6:12

Listen to your *f* who gave you life, ... PROV 23:22
The *f* of a righteous person will........... PROV 23:24
brings joy to his *f* .... PROV 29:3
Everlasting *F* Prince of Peace. .... ISA 9:6
Our *F* in heaven, ... MATT 6:9
Whoever loves *f* or mother more
than me .... MATT 10:37
'Whoever insults his *f* or mother .... MATT 15:4
a man will leave his *f* and mother .... MATT 19:5
What *f* among you, ... LUKE 11:11
father against son and son against *f* .... LUKE 12:53
F forgive them, ... LUKE 23:34
unless the *F* who sent me draws him,....JOHN 6:44
has seen the *F* .... JOHN 6:46
because he is a liar and the *f* of lies. ....JOHN 8:44
My *F* who has given them to me, ...JOHN 10:29
The *F* and I are one." ....JOHN 10:30
comes to the *F* except through me. ..... JOHN 14:6
'Show us the *F* .... JOHN 14:9
the *f* of all those who believe .... ROM 4:11
and I will be a *f* to you, ... 2 COR 6:18
Honor your *f* and mother," .... EPH 6:2
that a *f* does not discipline? .... HEB 12:7

FATHER'S
must not expose your *f* nakedness .... LEV 18:7
A wise son accepts his *f* discipline, ... PROV 13:1
A fool rejects his *f* discipline, ... PROV 15:5
I must be in my *F* house?" .... LUKE 2:49
Do not make my *F* house a
marketplace!" .... JOHN 2:16
many dwelling places in my *F* house. .... JOHN 14:2

FATHERED
has been *f* by God and knows God. ...... 1 JOHN 4:7
loves the child *f* by him. .... 1 JOHN 5:1

FATHERLESS
He is a father to the *f* .... PS 68:5
or take over the fields of the *f* .... PROV 23:10

FATHERS
responding to the transgression of *f* ..... EXOD 20:5
F do not provoke your children .... EPH 6:4
F do not provoke your children, ... COL 3:21

FATHOM
No one can *f* his greatness. .... PS 145:3

FAULT
go and show him his *f*. ....MATT 18:15
so that no *f* may be found .... 2 COR 6:3

FAULT-FINDERS
These people are grumblers and *f* ....JUDE 16

FAVOR
f to the needy. .... PROV 14:31
good *f* more than silver or gold. .... PROV 22:1

FAVORITISM
God does not show *f* .... ACTS 10:34
God shows no *f* between people) 2:6
and there is no *f* with him. .... EPH 6:9
without prejudice or *f* of any kind. .... 1 TIM 5:21

FEAR
keep my Sabbaths and *f* my sanctuary. ... LEV 19:30
learn about and *f* the LORD your God ... DEUT 31:12
The commands to *f* the LORD are right ..... PS 19:9
I *f* no danger, ... PS 23:4
I *f* no one. .... PS 27:1
need not *f* the terrors of the night, ... PS 91:5

you will not be filled with *f* .... PROV 3:24
The *f* of the LORD is to hate evil; .... PROV 8:13
beginning of wisdom is to *f* the LORD, ... PROV 9:10
f of the LORD is like a life-giving .... PROV 14:27
The *f* of the LORD provides wise .... PROV 15:33
The *f* of people becomes a snare, ...PROV 29:25
Therefore, *f* God. .... ECCL 5:7
he is merciful to those who *f* him. .... LUKE 1:50
F seized them all, ... LUKE 7:16
Yes, I tell you, *f* him! .... LUKE 12:5
People will be fainting from *f* .... LUKE 21:26
for rulers cause no *f* for good conduct .... ROM 13:3
For God did not give us a Spirit of *f* .... 2 TIM 1:7
but perfect love drives out *f* .... 1 JOHN 4:18

FEARFUL
f in praises, ... EXOD 15:11

FEARING
F the LORD prolongs life, ... PROV 10:27
through *f* the LORD one avoids evil. ...... PROV 16:6
F the LORD leads to life, ... PROV 19:23
f the Lord. .... COL 3:22

FEARS
who *f* God and turns away from evil." .... JOB 1:8
he delivered me from all my *f* .... PS 34:4
A woman who *f* the LORD —she .... PROV 31:30
The one who *f* punishment .... 1 JOHN 4:18

FEAST
prepare a *f* before me in plain sight .... PS 23:5

FEASTS
men are dangerous reefs at your love *f* .....JUDE 12

FEED
F my lambs." .... JOHN 21:15
F my sheep. .... JOHN 21:17
f him; if he is thirsty, ... ROM 12:20

FEEDING
f only themselves. .... JUDE 12

FEET
like a lion they pin my hands and *f* .... PS 22:16
He placed my *f* on a rock .... PS 40:2
From the soles of your *f* to your head, ... ISA 1:6
put all his enemies under his *f* .... 1 COR 15:25
and make straight paths for your *f* .... HEB 12:13

FELLOWSHIP
what *f* does light have with darkness? ... 2 COR 6:14
If we say we have *f* with him, ... 1 JOHN 1:6
we have *f* with one another .... 1 JOHN 1:7

FEMALE
male and *f* he created them. .... GEN 1:27
there is neither male nor *f*—for .... GAL 3:28

FERTILE
It is as if I have been given *f* fields .... PS 16:6

FERVENTLY
to join *f* with me in prayer to God .... ROM 15:30

FIELD
how the flowers of the *f* grow; .... MATT 6:28
The *f* is the world and the good seed ....MATT 13:38
You are God's *f* ....1 COR 3:9

FIELDS
the *f* are already white for harvest! .... JOHN 4:35

FIERY
says 'Fool' will be sent to *f* hell. .... MATT 5:22

FIG
so they sewed *f* leaves together .... GEN 3:7

FIGHT
The LORD will *f* for you, ... EXOD 14:14
he will *f* for you, ... DEUT 1:30
the LORD your God will personally *f* .... DEUT 3:22
Our God will *f* for us!" .... NEH 4:20
you may fight the good *f* .... 1 TIM 1:18

FIGHTING
my servants would be *f* to keep me .... JOHN 18:36

FIGS
For *f* are not gathered from thorns, ... LUKE 6:44

FILL
F the earth and subdue it! .... GEN 1:28
May his majestic splendor *f* the whole .... PS 72:19
Open your mouth wide and I will *f* it.' .... PS 81:10
will have his *f* of poverty. .... PROV 28:19
earth just as the waters *f* up the sea. .... HAB 2:14
then I will *f* this temple with glory." .... HAG 2:7
Now may the God of hope *f* you .... ROM 15:13

FILLED
will be *f* with the glory of the LORD. .... NUM 14:21
he has *f* with food. .... PS 107:9
and he will be *f* with the Holy Spirit, ... LUKE 1:15
Elizabeth was *f* with the Holy Spirit. .... LUKE 1:41
f with the fragrance of the perfumed .... JOHN 12:3
f with the Holy Spirit, ... ACTS 2:4
f with the Holy Spirit, ... ACTS 4:8
and be *f* with the Holy Spirit." .... ACTS 9:17
f with the Holy Spirit, ... ACTS 13:9
but be *f* by the Spirit, ... EPH 5:18
f with the fruit of righteousness .... PHIL 1:11

FILLING
the glory of the LORD *f* the temple. .... EZEK 43:5

FILLS
your loyal love *f* the earth. .... PS 119:64
blessed is the man who *f* his quiver .... PS 127:5
majestic splendor *f* the entire earth!" .... ISA 6:3
mouth speaks from what *f* his heart. .... LUKE 6:45
the fullness of him who *f* all in all. .... EPH 1:23

FINAL
These are the *f* words of David: .... 2 SAM 23:1

FIND
And know that your sin will *f* you out... NUM 32:23
you will *f* him, ... DEUT 4:29
he will let you *f* him, ... 1 CHR 28:9
Who can *f* a wife of noble character? .... PROV 31:10
you will *f* rest for your souls." .... JER 6:16
seek and you will *f* .... MATT 7:7
and you will *f* rest for your souls. .... MATT 11:29
loses his life because of me will *f* it .... MATT 16:25
will he *f* faith on earth?" .... LUKE 18:8
and *f* pasture. .... JOHN 10:9

FINDS
like one who *f* much plunder. .... PS 119:162
and the one who seeks *f* .... MATT 7:8
Whoever *f* his life will lose it, ... MATT 10:39
those slaves whom their master
f alert .... LUKE 12:37
the one that is lost until he *f* it? .... LUKE 15:4

FINE
wearing of gold jewelry or *f* clothes .... 1 PET 3:3

FINISH
that I may *f* my task and the ministry .... ACTS 20:24
to *f* what you started, ... 2 COR 8:11
trying to *f* by human effort? .... GAL 3:3

FINISHED
By the seventh day God *f* the work .... GEN 2:2
I have *f* the race; .... 2 TIM 4:7

FIRE
a pillar of *f* to give them light, ... EXOD 13:21
but the *f* which is on the altar .... LEV 6:12
you will heap coals of *f* on his head, ... PROV 25:22
and his word is like destructive *f* .... ISA 30:27
My message is like a *f* that purges .... JER 23:29
with the Holy Spirit and *f* .... MATT 3:11
into the eternal *f* that has been .... MATT 25:41
to the unquenchable *f* .... MARK 9:43
And tongues spreading out like a *f* .... ACTS 2:3
because it will be revealed by *f* .... 1 COR 3:13
but only as through *f* .... 1 COR 3:15
For our God is indeed a devouring *f* .... HEB 12:29
a trial by *f* is occurring among you, ... 1 PET 4:12
by snatching them out of the *f* .... JUDE 23
lake of *f* .... REV 20:14

FIRM
Stand *f* and see the salvation .... EXOD 14:13
He makes *f* commitments .... PS 15:4
His resolve is *f* .... PS 112:8
be *f* Do not be moved! .... 1 COR 15:58
stand *f* in the faith, ... 1 COR 16:13
because by faith you stand *f* .... 2 COR 1:24
Stand *f* therefore, ... EPH 6:14
stand *f* and hold on to the traditions ... 2 THESS 2:15

FIRST
"I am the *f* and I am the last, ... ISA 44:6
F go and be reconciled to your brother ... MATT 5:24
F remove the beam from your own eye, ... MATT 7:5
and whoever wants to be *f* among
you .... MATT 20:27
This is the *f* and greatest
commandment .... MATT 22:38
F clean the inside of the cup, ... MATT 23:26
F the gospel must be preached to all .... MARK 13:10
the disciples were *f* called Christians .... ACTS 11:26
to the Jew *f* and also to the Greek. .... ROM 1:16
And God has placed in the church *f* .... 1 COR 12:28
but they gave themselves *f* to the Lord ... 2 COR 8:5
he himself may become *f* in all things. .... COL 1:18
For Adam was formed *f* and then Eve. .... 1 TIM 2:13
But the wisdom from above is *f* pure, ... JAS 3:17
We love because he loved us *f* .... 1 JOHN 4:19
who loves to be *f* among them, ... 3 JOHN 9
I am the *f* and the last, ... REV 1:17
You have departed from your *f* love! .... REV 2:4

FIRSTBORN
to the *f* son of the slave girl who is .... EXOD 11:5

FIRSTFRUITS
The first of the *f* of your soil .... EXOD 23:19

FITTED
f and held together .... EPH 4:16

FITTING
so honor is not *f* for a fool. .... PROV 26:1
as these are not *f* for the saints. .... EPH 5:3
as is *f* in the Lord. .... COL 3:18
For it was *f* for him, ... HEB 2:10

FIX
F these words of mine into your mind ... DEUT 11:18

FLAMING
extinguish all the *f* arrows ... EPH 6:16

FLATTER
they *f* and deceive. ... PS 12:2

FLATTERING
May the LORD cut off all *f* lips, ... PS 12:3
and a *f* mouth works ruin. ... PROV 26:28

FLATTERY
their smooth talk and *f* they deceive ... ROM 16:18

FLAWLESS
'My teaching is *f* ... JOB 11:4

FLEE
Where can I *f* to escape your presence? ... PS 139:7
F sexual immorality! ... 1 COR 6:18
f from idolatry. ... 1 COR 10:14
resist the devil and he will *f* ... JAS 4:7

FLEETING
Charm is deceitful and beauty is *f* ... PROV 31:30

FLESH
bone of my bones and flesh of my *f* ... GEN 2:23
living creature from all *f* ... GEN 6:19
yet in my *f* I will see God, ... JOB 19:26
and give you a heart of *f* ... EZEK 36:26
but the *f* is weak." ... MATT 26:41
but one *f* ... MARK 10:8
Now the Word became *f* ... JOHN 1:14
give for the life of the world is my *f* ... JOHN 6:51
who do not walk according to the *f* but ... ROM 8:4
For the outlook of the *f* is death, ... ROM 8:6
Those who are in the *f* cannot please ... ROM 8:8
"The two will become one *f* ... 1 COR 6:16
Now the works of the *f* are obvious: ... GAL 5:19
crucified the *f* with its passions ... GAL 5:24
and the two will become one *f* ... EPH 5:31
For our struggle is not against *f* ... EPH 6:12

FLESHLY
in reality result in *f* indulgence. ... COL 2:23
f desires that do battle against ... 1 PET 2:11

FLOCK
Like a shepherd he tends his *f* ... ISA 40:11
Should not shepherds feed the *f* ... EZEK 34:2
worthless shepherd who abandons
the *f* ... ZECH 11:17
the sheep of the *f* will be scattered.' ... MATT 26:31
keeping guard over their *f* at night. ... LUKE 2:8
the *f* of which the Holy Spirit has ... ACTS 20:28
to God's *f* among you, ... 1 PET 5:2

FLOOR
threshing *f* of Araunah the Jebusite." ... 2 SAM 24:18

FLOURISHING
But I am like a *f* olive tree ... PS 52:8

FLOW
from within him will *f* rivers of living ... JOHN 7:38

FLOWERS
the *f* wither, ... ISA 40:7
Consider how the *f* grow; ... LUKE 12:27

FLOWING
to a land *f* with milk and honey, ... EXOD 3:8
It is indeed *f* with milk and honey, ... NUM 13:27
He is like a tree planted by *f* streams; ... PS 1:3

FLUTE
'We played the *f* for you, ... LUKE 7:32
like a *f* or harp. ... 1 COR 14:7

FOLDING
a little *f* of the hands to relax, ... PROV 6:10

FOLLOW
You must not *f* a crowd in doing evil ... EXOD 23:2
You must *f* the LORD your God ... DEUT 13:4
does not *f* the advice of the wicked, ... PS 1:1
"We will not *f* it!" ... JER 6:16
and *f* me. ... MATT 16:24
and the sheep *f* him ... JOHN 10:4
who *f* the Lamb wherever he goes. ... REV 14:4

FOLLOWED
because I have *f* all things carefully ... LUKE 1:3

FOLLOWER
you will not allow your faithful *f* ... PS 16:10

FOLLOWERS
all you faithful *f* of his! ... PS 31:23
and never abandons his faithful *f*. ... PS 37:28
He protects the lives of his faithful *f*. ... PS 97:10
values the lives of his faithful *f* ... PS 116:15
as you typically do to your loyal *f* ... PS 119:132

FOLLOWS
who *f* me will never walk in darkness, ... JOHN 8:12

FOOD
that you might be satisfied with *f* ... PROV 20:13
has given some of his *f* to the poor. ... PROV 22:9
give him *f* to eat, ... PROV 25:21
and provided *f* for her household ... PROV 31:15
the *f* that remains to eternal life ... JOHN 6:27
kingdom of God does not consist of *f* ... ROM 14:17
Now *f* will not bring us close to God. ... 1 COR 8:8
f causes my brother or sister to sin ... 1 COR 8:13
But if we have *f* and shelter, ... 1 TIM 6:8
poorly clothed and lacks daily *f* ... JAS 2:15

FOODS
(This means all *f* are clean.) ... MARK 7:19

FOOL
A *f* rejects his father's discipline, ... PROV 15:5
Even a *f* who remains silent ... PROV 17:28
A *f* takes no pleasure in understanding ... PROV 18:2
Answer a *f* according to his folly, ... PROV 26:5
one who trusts in his own heart is a *f* ... PROV 28:26
whoever says *F* will be sent to fiery ... MATT 5:22
God will not be made a *f* ... GAL 6:7

FOOLISH
but a *f* child is a grief to his mother. ... PROV 10:1
A *f* child is a grief to his father, ... PROV 17:25
a *f* man who built his house on sand. ... MATT 7:26
Five of the virgins were *f* ... MATT 25:2
But God chose what the world thinks *f* ... 1 COR 1:27

FOOLISHNESS
cross is *f* to those who are perishing, ... 1 COR 1:18
f of God is wiser than human wisdom, ... 1 COR 1:25
for they are *f* to him. ... 1 COR 2:14
the wisdom of this age is *f* with God. ... 1 COR 3:19

FOOLS
F say to themselves, ... PS 14:1
F mock at reparation, ... PROV 14:9
We are *f* for Christ, ... 1 COR 4:10

FOOT
- every place you set *f* ... JOSH 1:3
- If the *f* says, ... 1 COR 12:15
- nor in turn can the head say to the *f* ... 1 COR 12:21

FOOTING
- feet on a rock and gave me secure *f* ... PS 40:2

FOOTSTOOL
- until I make your enemies your *f* ... PS 110:1

FORBEARANCE
- because God in his *f* had passed over ... ROM 3:25

FORBID
- not *f* anyone from speaking in tongues. ... 1 COR 14:39

FORCES
- against the spiritual *f* of evil ... EPH 6:12

FOREIGNER
- not wrong a resident *f* nor oppress him, ... EXOD 22:21

FOREIGNERS
- *f* and exiles to keep away from fleshly ... 1 PET 2:11

FOREKNEW
- whom he *f* he also predestined ... ROM 8:29
- has not rejected his people whom he *f* ... ROM 11:2

FOREKNOWN
- *f* before the foundation of the world ... 1 PET 1:20

FOREVER
- The LORD will reign *f* and ever! ... EXOD 15:18
- But the LORD rules *f* ... PS 9:7
- The LORD rules *f* ... PS 10:16
- The LORD's decisions stand *f* ... PS 33:11
- I am *f* conscious of my sin. ... PS 51:3
- But you, O LORD, reign *f* ... PS 92:8
- He will receive praise *f* ... PS 111:10
- will not cease *f* to be a nation ... JER 31:36
- take possession of the kingdom *f* ... DAN 7:18
- will be like the stars *f* and ever. ... DAN 12:3
- eats from this bread he will live *f* ... JOHN 6:51
- another Advocate to be with you *f* ... JOHN 14:16
- the same yesterday and today and *f* ... HEB 13:8
- but the word of the Lord endures *f* ... 1 PET 1:25
- who does the will of God remains *f* ... 1 JOHN 2:17
- now I am alive *f* ... REV 1:18
- and they will reign *f* and ever. ... REV 22:5

FORFEITS
- the whole world but loses or *f* himself ... LUKE 9:25

FORGAVE
- And then you *f* my sins. ... PS 32:5
- just as God in Christ also *f* you. ... EPH 4:32

FORGET
- be careful not to *f* the LORD ... DEUT 6:12
- Do not *f* all his kind deeds. ... PS 103:2
- I do not *f* your instructions. ... PS 119:16
- If I *f* you, ... PS 137:5
- I could never *f* you! ... ISA 49:15
- God is not unjust so as to *f* your work ... HEB 6:10

FORGETS
- *f* what sort of person he was. ... JAS 1:24

FORGETTING
- *F* the things that are behind ... PHIL 3:13

FORGIVE
- *f* their sin, ... 2 CHR 7:14
- But you are willing to *f* ... PS 130:4
- for he will freely *f* them. ... ISA 55:7
- and *f* us our debts, ... MATT 6:12
- your heavenly Father will also *f* you. ... MATT 6:14
- how many times must I *f* my brother ... MATT 18:21
- will also *f* you your sins." ... MARK 11:25
- for we also *f* everyone who sins ... LUKE 11:4
- *f* them, for they don't know ... LUKE 23:34

FORGIVEN
- having *f* all your transgressions. ... COL 2:13
- Just as the Lord has *f* you, ... COL 3:13

FORGIVENESS
- But you are a God of *f* ... NEH 9:17
- receives *f* of sins through his name." ... ACTS 10:43
- the *f* of our offenses, ... EPH 1:7
- the *f* of sins. ... COL 1:14
- shedding of blood there is no *f* ... HEB 9:22

FORGIVING
- *f* one another, ... EPH 4:32
- and *f* one another, ... COL 3:13
- *f* us our sins and cleansing us ... 1 JOHN 1:9

FORM
- he had no stately *f* or majesty ... ISA 53:2
- who though he existed in the *f* of God ... PHIL 2:6

FORMED
- The LORD God *f* the man from the soil ... GEN 2:7
- the one who *f* the earth and made it; ... ISA 45:18
- For Adam was *f* first and then Eve. ... 1 TIM 2:13

FORSAKEN
- why have you *f* me?" ... MATT 27:46

FORSAKES
- whoever confesses them and *f* them ... PROV 28:13

FOUND
- a good wife has *f* what goodness is, ... PROV 18:22
- on the balances and *f* to be lacking. ... DAN 5:27
- I have *f* my sheep that was lost.' ... LUKE 15:6
- for I have *f* the coin that I had lost.' ... LUKE 15:9
- that one be *f* faithful. ... 1 COR 4:2

FOUNDATION
- as a precious cornerstone for the *f* ... ISA 28:16
- any *f* other than what is being laid, ... 1 COR 3:11
- been built on the *f* of the apostles ... EPH 2:20
- God's solid *f* remains standing, ... 2 TIM 2:19
- foreknown before the *f* of the world ... 1 PET 1:20
- written since the *f* of the world ... REV 13:8

FOUNTAIN
- the *f* of life-giving water, ... JER 2:13
- a *f* of water springing up ... JOHN 4:14

FOXES
- *F* have dens, ... MATT 8:20

FRANKINCENSE
- *f* and myrrh. ... MATT 2:11

FREE
- and the truth will set you *f* ... JOHN 8:32
- be set *f* from the bondage of decay ... ROM 8:21
- there is neither slave nor *f* ... GAL 3:28

FREED
- and having been *f* from sin, ... ROM 6:18

FREEDOM
- into the glorious *f* of God's children. ... ROM 8:21
- of the Lord is present, there is *f* ... 2 COR 3:17
- do not use your *f* as an opportunity ... GAL 5:13
- using your *f* as a pretext for evil, ... 1 PET 2:16

FREELY
May praise flow *f* from my lips, ... PS 119:171
for he will *f* forgive them. .... ISA 55:7
Freely you received, *f* give. .... MATT 10:8
But they are justified *f* by his grace .... ROM 3:24

FRIEND
the way a person speaks to a *f* .... EXOD 33:11
A *f* loves at all times, ... PROV 17:17
Faithful are the wounds of a *f* .... PROV 27:6
your friend and your father's *f* .... PROV 27:10

FRIENDS
and a gossip separates the closest *f* ..... PROV 16:28
that I received in the house of my *f* ..... ZECH 13:6
one lays down his life for his *f* .... JOHN 15:13

FRIENDSHIP
f with the world means hostility .... JAS 4:4

FRUIT
it yields its *f* at the proper time, ... PS 1:3
The *f* of the righteous is like a tree ...... PROV 11:30
You will recognize them by their *f* .... MATT 7:16
every branch that does not bear *f* .... JOHN 15:2
But the *f* of the Spirit is love, ... GAL 5:22
f in every good deed, ... COL 1:10
the *f* of peace and righteousness .... HEB 12:11
yielding its *f* every month .... REV 22:2

FRUITFUL
"Be *f* and multiply and fill the water .... GEN 1:22
Your wife will be like a *f* vine in the .... PS 128:3

FRUSTRATE
and who can possibly *f* it? .... ISA 14:27

FULFILL
I will *f* my vows to the LORD .... PS 116:14
to abolish these things but to *f* them. ... MATT 5:17
A husband should *f* his marital .... 1 COR 7:3
should first learn to *f* their .... 1 TIM 5:4
if you *f* the royal law as expressed .... JAS 2:8

FULFILLED
in my name and the prediction
is not *f* .... DEUT 18:22
A desire *f* will be sweet to the soul, ... PROV 13:19
so that the scriptures would be *f* .... MARK 14:49
who loves his neighbor has *f* the law. ..... ROM 13:8

FULFILLING
f their duties at home, ... TITUS 2:5

FULFILLMENT
Therefore love is the *f* of the law. .... ROM 13:10

FULL
my cup is completely *f* .... PS 23:5
f of the Spirit and of wisdom, ... ACTS 6:3

FULLNESS
to have all his *f* dwell in the Son .... COL 1:19
the *f* of deity lives in bodily form, ... COL 2:9

FURY
great *f* has been ignited against us, ... 2 KGS 22:13

FUTILE
then our preaching is *f* .... 1 COR 15:14
his religion is *f* .... JAS 1:26

FUTURE
Commit your *f* to the LORD. .... PS 37:5
one who promotes peace has a *f* .... PS 37:37
For surely there is a *f* .... PROV 23:18

GABRIEL
Angel who interpreted Daniel's visions (Dan 8:16-26; 9:20-27); announced births of John (Luke 1:11-20), Jesus (Luke 1:26-38).

GAIN
for a person to *g* the whole world, ... MARK 8:36
living is Christ and dying is *g* .... PHIL 1:21
I may *g* Christ, ... PHIL 3:8
not greedy for *g* .... 1 TIM 3:8

GALILEE
and G of the nations. .... ISA 9:1

GALL
and offered Jesus wine mixed with *g* .... MATT 27:34

GAP
repair the wall and stand in the *g* ...... EZEK 22:30

GARDENER
the true vine and my Father is the *g* ...... JOHN 15:1

GARMENT
They will wear out like a *g* .... PS 102:26
the patch will pull away from the *g* ...... MATT 9:16

GARMENTS
God made *g* from skin for Adam .... GEN 3:21
For he clothes me in *g* of deliverance; ..... ISA 61:10

GATE
the *g* is wide and the way is spacious .... MATT 7:13

GATES
Enter his *g* with thanksgiving, ... PS 100:4
Your *g* will remain open at all times; .... ISA 60:11
the *g* of Hades will not overpower it. ... MATT 16:18

GATHER
g all the nations against Jerusalem ...... ZECH 14:2
whoever does not *g* with me scatters. ... MATT 12:30
longed to *g* your children together ...... MATT 23:37

GATHERS
together as a hen *g* her chicks under .... MATT 23:37

GAVE
they *g* to the treasury for this work .... EZRA 2:69
feet on a rock and *g* me secure footing ...... PS 40:2
He *g* his one and only Son, ... JOHN 3:16
in the ministry the Lord *g* us. .... 1 COR 3:5
they *g* themselves first to the Lord .... 2 COR 8:5
who loved me and *g* himself for me. .... GAL 2:20
who *g* himself as a ransom for all, ... 1 TIM 2:6
just as he *g* us the commandment. ..... 1 JOHN 3:23

GAZE
so I can *g* at the splendor of the LORD .... PS 27:4
let your *g* look straight before you. .... PROV 4:25

GENEALOGIES
with myths and interminable *g* .... 1 TIM 1:4

GENERATION
will tell the next *g* about the LORD. .... PS 22:30

GENERATIONS
your dominion endures through all *g* ..... PS 145:13
all *g* will call me blessed, ... LUKE 1:48
not disclosed to people in former *g* .... EPH 3:5

GENEROUS
A *g* person will be blessed, ... PROV 22:9

GENEROUSLY
for the one who *g* lends money, ... PS 112:5

GOD'S

blameless as one entrusted with *G* work TITUS 1:7
he appears now in *G* presence for us. HEB 9:24
worlds were set in order at *G* command, HEB 11:3
does not accomplish *G* righteousness. JAS 1:20
which is precious in *G* sight. 1 PET 3:4
let it be with *G* words. 1 PET 4:11

GODLINESS
quiet life in all *g* and dignity. 1 TIM 2:2
but *g* is valuable in every way. 1 TIM 4:8
Now *g* combined with contentment 1 TIM 6:6
g faithfulness, love, 1 TIM 6:11
in holiness and *g* 2 PET 3:11

GODLY
treating the *g* and the wicked alike! GEN 18:25
The LORD pays attention to the *g* PS 34:15
I have never seen the *g* abandoned, PS 37:25
I am jealous for you with *g* jealousy, 2 COR 11:2

GODS
You shall have no other *g* before me. EXOD 20:3
gods made by hands are not *g* at all. ACTS 19:26

GOES
whatever *g* into a person from outside MARK 7:18

GOLD
I would come forth like *g* JOB 23:10
than even a great amount of pure *g* PS 19:10
even purest *g* PS 119:127
good favor more than silver or *g* PROV 22:1
wearing of *g* jewelry or fine clothes 1 PET 3:3

GOLGOTHA
of the Skull" (called in Aramaic *G* JOHN 19:17

GOLIATH
Philistine giant killed by David (1 Sam 17; 21:9).

GOOD
God saw that the light was *g* GEN 1:4
it was very *g* GEN 1:31
"It is not *g* for the man to be alone. GEN 2:18
but God intended it for a *g* purpose, GEN 50:20
Should we receive what is *g* from God, JOB 2:10
Taste and see that the LORD is *g* PS 34:8
You are good and you do *g* PS 119:68
Look! How *g* and how pleasant it is PS 133:1
for it is *g* to sing praises to our God. PS 147:1
find favor and *g* understanding, PROV 3:4
one who diligently seeks *g* seeks favor, PROV 11:27
A cheerful heart brings *g* healing, PROV 17:22
The one who has found a *g* wife PROV 18:22
A *g* name is to be chosen PROV 22:1
She has rewarded him with *g* PROV 31:12
those who call evil good and *g* evil, ISA 5:20
what is *g* MIC 6:8
sun to rise on the evil and the *g* MATT 5:45
every good tree bears *g* fruit, MATT 7:17
good things out of his *g* treasury, MATT 12:35
"Why do you ask me about what is *g* MATT 19:17
g and faithful slave! MATT 25:21
"Is it lawful to do *g* on the Sabbath, MARK 3:4
do *g* to those who hate you, LUKE 6:27
The *g* shepherd lays down his life JOHN 10:11
himself without a witness by doing *g* ACTS 14:17
all things work together for *g* ROM 8:28
of those who proclaim the *g* news." ROM 10:15
cling to what is *g* ROM 12:9
"Bad company corrupts *g* morals." 1 COR 15:33
you will overflow in every *g* work. 2 COR 9:8
So we must not grow weary in doing *g* GAL 6:9
let us do *g* to all people, GAL 6:10
created in Christ Jesus for *g* works EPH 2:10
the one who began a *g* work in you PHIL 1:6
hold fast to what is *g* 1 THESS 5:21
For every creation of God is *g* 1 TIM 4:4
and made your *g* confession for 1 TIM 6:12
to be rich in *g* deeds, 1 TIM 6:18
opposed to what is *g* 2 TIM 3:3
capable and equipped for every *g* work. 2 TIM 3:17
may see your *g* deeds and glorify God 1 PET 2:12

GOSPEL
Repent and believe the *g* MARK 1:15
For I am not ashamed of the *g* ROM 1:16
I serve the *g* of God like a priest, ROM 15:16
I have fully preached the *g* of Christ. ROM 15:19
but to preach the *g* —and 1 COR 1:17
Woe to me if I do not preach the *g* 1 COR 9:16
make full use of my rights in the *g* 1 COR 9:18
the *g* that I preached to you, 1 COR 15:1
we may preach the *g* in the regions 2 COR 10:16
side by side for the faith of the *g* PHIL 1:27

GOSSIP
and a *g* separates the closest friends. PROV 16:28
words of a *g* are like choice morsels; PROV 18:8
and where there is no *g* PROV 26:20
g arrogance, and disorder. 2 COR 12:20

GOVERN
and *g* the people living on earth. PS 67:4

GRACE
g and truth came about through Jesus JOHN 1:17
to God and to the message of his *g* ACTS 20:32
But they are justified freely by his *g* ROM 3:24
by the *g* of the one man Jesus Christ ROM 5:15
those who receive the abundance of *g* ROM 5:17
g multiplied all the more, ROM 5:20
you are not under law but under *g* ROM 6:14
otherwise grace would no longer be *g* ROM 11:6
not to receive the *g* of God in vain. 2 COR 6:1
the *g* of our Lord Jesus Christ, 2 COR 8:9
"My *g* is enough for you, 2 COR 12:9
I do not set aside God's *g* GAL 2:21
you have fallen away from *g* GAL 5:4
according to the riches of his *g* EPH 1:7
g you are saved! EPH 2:5
wealth of his *g* in kindness toward us EPH 2:7
For by *g* you are saved through faith, EPH 2:8
all of you became partners in God's *g* PHIL 1:7
and by *g* gave us eternal comfort 2 THESS 2:16
strong in the *g* that is in Christ 2 TIM 2:1
For the *g* of God has appeared, TITUS 2:11
since we have been justified by his *g* TITUS 3:7
by God's *g* he would experience death HEB 2:9
and find *g* whenever we need help. HEB 4:16
but he gives *g* to the humble." JAS 4:6
But grow in the *g* and knowledge 2 PET 3:18

GRACIOUS
I will be gracious to whom I will be *g* EXOD 33:19
and be *g* to you; NUM 6:25
Let your speech always be *g* COL 4:6

GUIDES
He *g* us. .... PS 48:14

GUIDING
pillar of cloud did not stop *g* them .... NEH 9:19
let us walk in the LORD's *g* light. .... ISA 2:5

GUILTY
Who among you can prove me *g* .... JOHN 8:46
fails in one point has become *g* of all .... JAS 2:10

HADES
the gates of *H* will not overpower it. .... MATT 16:18
And in *H* .... LUKE 16:23

HAGAR
Servant of Sarah, wife of Abraham, mother of Ishmael (Gen 16:1-6; 25:12). Driven away by Sarah while pregnant (Gen 16:5-16); after birth of Isaac (Gen 21:9-21; Gal 4:21-31).

HAGGAI
Postexilic prophet who encouraged rebuilding of the temple (Ezra 5:1; 6:14; Hag 1-2).

HAIR
Yet not a *h* of your head will perish. .... LUKE 21:18
she should cut off her *h* .... 1 COR 11:6

HAIRS
Even all the *h* on your head are .... MATT 10:30

HALLELUJAH
H Salvation and glory and power belong .... REV 19:1

HAND
because he is at my right *h* .... PS 16:8
Into your *h* I entrust my life; .... PS 31:5
for the LORD holds his *h* .... PS 37:24
your right *h* upholds me. .... PS 63:8
my right *h* until I make your enemies .... PS 110:1
your right *h* would grab hold of me. .... PS 139:10
She opened her *h* to the poor, ... PROV 31:20
Look, the LORD's *h* is not too weak .... ISA 59:1
your left hand know what your right *h* .... MATT 6:3
no one will snatch them from my *h* .... JOHN 10:28
"Since I am not a *h* .... 1 COR 12:15
at his right *h* in the heavenly realms .... EPH 1:20

HANDS
like a lion they pin my *h* and feet. .... PS 22:16
and extended her *h* to the needy. .... PROV 31:20
Whatever you find to do with your *h* .... ECCL 9:10
trees in the field will clap their *h* .... ISA 55:12
I spread out my *h* all day long .... ISA 65:2
into your *h* I commit my spirit!" .... LUKE 23:46
and to work with your own *h* .... 1 THESS 4:11
lifting up holy *h* without anger .... 1 TIM 2:8
Do not lay *h* on anyone hastily .... 1 TIM 5:22

HANNAH
Wife of Elkanah, mother of Samuel (1 Sam 1). Prayer at dedication of Samuel (1 Sam 2:1-10). Blessed (1 Sam 2:18-21).

HAPPEN
to determine what will *h* to them. .... JER 10:23

HAPPIER
h than those who have abundant grain .... PS 4:7

HAPPILY
then worked *h* with her hands. .... PROV 31:13

HAPPINESS
when their trouble was turned to *h* .... ESTH 9:22
he will bring you *h* .... PROV 29:17
they filled my heart with joy and *h* .... JER 15:16

HAPPY
be *h* and rejoice in your faithfulness, ... PS 31:7
I will rejoice in the LORD and be *h* .... PS 35:9
We will be *h* and rejoice in it. .... PS 118:24
nothing better for people than to be *h* .... ECCL 3:12
be *h* because of the God who delivers .... HAB 3:18
Sing out and be *h* .... ZECH 2:10
as we wait for the *h* fulfillment .... TITUS 2:13
H is the one who endures testing, ... JAS 1:12

HARD
He pushed *h* .... JUDG 16:30
will be *h* for a rich person to enter .... MATT 19:23

HARDEN
you must not *h* your heart .... DEUT 15:7
not *h* your hearts as in the rebellion, ... HEB 3:8

HARDENS
and he *h* whom he chooses to harden. .... ROM 9:18

HARDSHIP
endure *h* do an evangelist's work, ... 2 TIM 4:5

HARM
The sun will not *h* you by day, ... PS 121:6
companions who *h* one another, ... PROV 18:24
rewarded him with good and not *h* .... PROV 31:12
dominates other people to their *h* .... ECCL 8:9
poison they drink will not *h* them; .... MARK 16:18

HARMED
in no way be *h* by the second death.' .... REV 2:11

HARMONY
Live in *h* with one another; .... ROM 12:16

HARSHLY
He was treated *h* and afflicted, ... ISA 53:7

HARVEST
"The *h* is plentiful, ... MATT 9:37
'and then comes the *h* .... JOHN 4:35

HASTILY
one who acts *h* makes poor choices. .... PROV 19:2
Do not lay hands on anyone *h* .... 1 TIM 5:22

HASTY
who is *h* comes only to poverty. .... PROV 21:5
someone who is *h* in his words .... PROV 29:20
Do not be rash with your mouth or *h* .... ECCL 5:2

HATE
must not *h* your brother in your heart. .... LEV 19:17
you *h* all who behave wickedly. .... PS 5:5
You love justice and *h* evil. .... PS 45:7
You who love the LORD, *h* evil! .... PS 97:10
do I not hate those who *h* you, ... PS 139:21
The fear of the LORD is to *h* evil; .... PROV 8:13
H what is wrong, ... AMOS 5:15
I *h* divorce," .... MAL 2:16
'Love your neighbor' and *h* your enemy. .... MATT 5:43
do good to those who *h* you, ... LUKE 6:27

HATED
And you will be *h* by everyone .... MATT 10:22
but Esau I *h* .... ROM 9:13
For no one has ever *h* his own body, ... EPH 5:29
loved righteousness and *h* lawlessness. .... HEB 1:9

HATES
There are six things that the LORD *h* .... PROV 6:16
The one who spares his rod *h* his child ... PROV 13:24
For everyone who does evil deeds *h* ...... JOHN 3:20
says he is in the light but still *h* .... 1 JOHN 2:9

HATRED
H stirs up dissension, ... PROV 10:12

HAUGHTY
and a *h* spirit before a fall. .... PROV 16:18

HAY
h or straw, ... 1 COR 3:12

HEAD
he will strike your *h* .... GEN 3:15
You refresh my *h* with oil; .... PS 23:5
you will heap coals of fire on his *h* .... PROV 25:22
like a helmet on his *h* .... ISA 59:17
Son of Man has no place to lay his *h* .... MATT 8:20
heaping burning coals on his *h* .... ROM 12:20
and the man is the *h* of a woman, ... 1 COR 11:3
nor in turn can the *h* say to the foot, ... 1 COR 12:21
Christ is the *h* of the church .... EPH 5:23
many diadem crowns on his *h* .... REV 19:12

HEADLONG
he will not fall *h* .... PS 37:24

HEAL
and *h* their land. .... 2 CHR 7:14
H me, for I have sinned against you. .... PS 41:4
H the sick, ... MATT 10:8
h yourself!' and say, ... LUKE 4:23
power of the Lord was with him to *h* ..... LUKE 5:17

HEALED
of his wounds we have been *h* .... ISA 53:5
And the woman was *h* from that hour. ... MATT 9:22
and all who touched it were *h* .... MATT 14:36
and saw he had faith to be *h* .... ACTS 14:9
so that you may be *h* .... JAS 5:16
By his wounds you were *h* .... 1 PET 2:24

HEALER
am your *h* .... EXOD 15:26

HEALING
This will bring *h* to your body, ... PROV 3:8
A cheerful heart brings good *h* .... PROV 17:22
food and their leaves for *h* .... EZEK 47:12
vindication will rise with *h* wings, ... MAL 4:2
gifts of *h* by the one Spirit, ... 1 COR 12:9
Not all have gifts of *h* .... 1 COR 12:30
leaves are for the *h* of the nations. .... REV 22:2

HEALS
who *h* all your diseases, ... PS 103:3
He *h* the brokenhearted, ... PS 147:3

HEALTHY
who are *h* don't need a physician, ... MARK 2:17
this man stands before you *h* .... ACTS 4:10

HEAR
H O Israel: .... DEUT 6:4
the one who makes the human ear not *h* ... PS 94:9
May I *h* about your loyal love .... PS 143:8
the wise also h and gain instruction, ... PROV 1:5
be able to *h* words read from a scroll, ... ISA 29:18
I will *h* .... ISA 65:24

HEARD
Having *h* everything, ... ECCL 12:13
would have believed what we just *h* .... ISA 53:1
Who has ever *h* of such a thing? .... ISA 66:8
You have *h* that it was said .... MATT 5:21
You have *h* that it was said, ... MATT 5:27
Again, you have *h* that it was said .... MATT 5:33
You have *h* that it was said, ... MATT 5:38
You have *h* that it was said, ... MATT 5:43
what is *h* comes through the preached .. ROM 10:17
or ear *h* .... 1 COR 2:9
God's message that you *h* from us, ... 1 THESS 2:13
sound words that you *h* from me .... 2 TIM 1:13

HEARS
to the godly and *h* their cry for help. .... PS 34:15
the one who *h* my message and
believes .... JOHN 5:24
he *h* us. .... 1 JOHN 5:14
If anyone *h* my voice and opens the
door .... REV 3:20

HEART
every person motivated by a willing *h* ... EXOD 25:2
must not hate your brother in your *h* ..... LEV 19:17
you seek him with all your *h* and soul. ... DEUT 4:29
your God will also cleanse your *h* .... DEUT 30:6
serve him with all your *h* and being!" ..... JOSH 22:5
but the LORD looks at the *h* .... 1 SAM 16:7
and rules with all his *h* and being, ... 2 KGS 23:3
and store up his words in your *h* .... JOB 22:22
At this also my *h* pounds and leaps .... JOB 37:1
My *h* is stirred by a beautiful song. .... PS 45:1
Create for me a pure *h* .... PS 51:10
repentant *h* you will not reject. .... PS 51:17
If I had harbored sin in my *h* .... PS 66:18
In my *h* I store up your words, ... PS 119:11
Trust in the LORD with all your *h* .... PROV 3:5
guard them within your *h* .... PROV 4:21
Guard your *h* with all vigilance, ... PROV 4:23
write them on the tablet of your *h* .... PROV 7:3
Hope deferred makes the *h* sick, ... PROV 13:12
Even in laughter the *h* may ache, ... PROV 14:13
A bright look brings joy to the *h* .... PROV 15:30
A cheerful *h* brings good healing, ... PROV 17:22
do not let your *h* rejoice, ... PROV 24:17
so a person's *h* reflects the person. ..... PROV 27:19
placed ignorance in the human *h* .... ECCL 3:11
You have stolen my *h* with one glance .... SONG 4:9
he carries them close to his *h* .... ISA 40:11
seek me with all your *h* and soul, ... JER 29:13
and give you a *h* of flesh. .... EZEK 36:26
Blessed are the pure in *h* .... MATT 5:8
there your *h* will be also. .... MATT 6:21
the mouth speaks from what fills
the *h* .... MATT 12:34
Love the Lord your God with all
your *h* .... MATT 22:37
mouth speaks from what fills his *h* .... LUKE 6:45
circumcision is of the *h* by the Spirit ..... ROM 2:29
For with the *h* one believes. .... ROM 10:10
The secrets of his *h* are disclosed, ... 1 COR 14:25
doing the will of God from the *h* .... EPH 6:6
clothe yourselves with a *h* of mercy, ... COL 3:12
earnestly from a pure *h* .... 1 PET 1:22

HEARTS
Pour out your *h* before him. .... PS 62:8
write it on their *h* and minds. .... JER 31:33
but God knows your *h* .... LUKE 16:15

"Didn't our *h* burn within us .... LUKE 24:32
Do not let your *h* be distressed. .... JOHN 14:1
cleansing their *h* by faith. .... ACTS 15:9
the law is written in their *h* .... ROM 2:15
written on our *h* .... 2 COR 3:2
but on tablets of human *h* .... 2 COR 3:3
the one who shined in our *h* .... 2 COR 4:6
dwell in your *h* through faith, ... EPH 3:17
singing and making music in your *h* .... EPH 5:19
Do not harden your *h* .... HEB 3:8
I will put my laws on their *h* .... HEB 10:16

HEAVEN
Creator of *h* and earth. .... GEN 14:19
the highest *h* cannot contain you, ... 1 KGS 8:27
took Elijah up to *h* in a windstorm, ... 2 KGS 2:1
then I will respond from *h* .... 2 CHR 7:14
they stand secure in *h* .... PS 119:89
If I were to ascend to *h* .... PS 139:8
Our Father in *h* .... MATT 6:9
for yourselves treasures in *h* .... MATT 6:20
on earth will have been released in *h* ... MATT 16:19
rich person to enter the kingdom of *h* .... MATT 19:23
H and earth will pass away, ... MATT 24:35
and coming on the clouds of *h* .... MATT 26:64
"All authority in *h* and on earth .... MATT 28:18
he was taken up into *h* and sat down .... MARK 16:19
joy in *h* over one sinner who repents ..... LUKE 15:7
and you will have treasure in *h* .... LUKE 18:22
'Who will ascend into *h* .... ROM 10:6
was caught up to the third *h* .... 2 COR 12:2
h and on earth and under the earth .... PHIL 2:10
But our citizenship is in *h* —and .... PHIL 3:20
and to wait for his Son from *h* .... 1 THESS 1:10
into *h* itself, ... HEB 9:24
first *h* and earth had ceased to exist, ... REV 21:1

HEAVENLY
we desire to put on our *h* dwelling, ... 2 COR 5:2
bring me safely into his *h* kingdom. ...... 2 TIM 4:18
the *h* Jerusalem, ... HEB 12:22

HEAVENS
God created the *h* and the earth. .... GEN 1:1
the highest *h* cannot contain him? .... 2 CHR 2:6
When I look up at the *h* .... PS 8:3
The *h* declare the glory of God; .... PS 19:1
new *h* and a new earth! .... ISA 65:17
"The *h* are my throne .... ISA 66:1
that is eternal in the *h* .... 2 COR 5:1
who ascended above all the *h* .... EPH 4:10
the *h* will disappear with a horrific .... 2 PET 3:10
waiting for new *h* and a new earth, ... 2 PET 3:13

HEAVY
When the hands of Moses became *h* .... EXOD 17:12

HEBREW
A fugitive came and told Abram the *H* ... GEN 14:13

HEEDS
whoever *h* reproof shows good sense. ... PROV 15:5

HEEL
and you will strike his *h* .... GEN 3:15

HEIRS
And if children, then *h* (namely, ... ROM 8:17
h according to the promise. .... GAL 3:29
the Gentiles are fellow *h* .... EPH 3:6
as fellow *h* of the grace of life. .... 1 PET 3:7

HELL
says 'Fool' will be sent to fiery *h* .... MATT 5:22
let him be condemned to *h* .... GAL 1:8
threw them into *h* and locked them up .... 2 PET 2:4

HELMET
like a *h* on his head. .... ISA 59:17
And take the *h* of salvation .... EPH 6:17
and as a *h* our hope for salvation. .... 1 THESS 5:8

HELP
your willingness to *h* enables me .... 2 SAM 22:36
he listened to my cry for *h* .... PS 18:6
and hears their cry for *h* .... PS 34:15
and heard my cry for *h* .... PS 40:1
H us, O God, ... PS 79:9
From where does my *h* come? .... PS 121:1
But those who wait for the LORD's *h* .... ISA 40:31
I *h* you – .... ISA 41:10
so that I know how to *h* the weary. .... ISA 50:4
to *h* the brokenhearted, ... ISA 61:1
belly of Sheol I cried out for *h* .... JONAH 2:2
h my unbelief!" .... MARK 9:24
"Come over to Macedonia and *h* us!" ...... ACTS 16:9

HELPED
"Up to here the LORD has *h* us." .... 1 SAM 7:12
h those in distress —as .... 1 TIM 5:10

HELPER
he is truly our *h* in times of trouble. .... PS 46:1
"The Lord is my *h* .... HEB 13:6

HELPLESS
For while we were still *h* .... ROM 5:6

HELPS
the Spirit *h* us in our weakness, ... ROM 8:26
h gifts of leadership, ... 1 COR 12:28

HEN
as a *h* gathers her chicks .... MATT 23:37

HEROD
1. King of Judea who tried to kill Jesus (Matt 2; Luke 1:5).
2. Son of 1. Tetrarch of Galilee who arrested and beheaded John the Baptist (Matt 14:1-12; Mark 6:14-29; Luke 3:1, 19-20; 9:7-9); tried Jesus (Luke 23:6-15).
3. Grandson of 1. King of Judea who killed James (Acts 12:2); arrested Peter (Acts 12:3-19). Death (Acts 12:19-23).

HERODIAS
Wife of Herod the Tetrarch who persuaded her daughter to ask for John the Baptist's head (Matt 14:1-12; Mark 6:14-29).

HEZEKIAH
King of Judah. Restored the temple and worship (2 Chr 29-31). Sought the LORD for help against Assyria (2 Kgs 18-19; 2 Chr 32:1-23; Isa 36-37). Illness healed (2 Kgs 20:1-11; 2 Chr 32:24-26; Isa 38). Judged for showing Babylonians his treasures (2 Kgs 20:12-21; 2 Chr 32:31; Isa 39).

HID
and they *h* from the LORD God among ..... GEN 3:8
she *h* him for three months. .... EXOD 2:2
because she *h* the spies we sent. .... JOSH 6:17
his parents *h* him for three months, ... HEB 11:23

HIDDEN
A city located on a hill cannot be *h* .... MATT 5:14
nothing is *h* that will not be revealed .. MATT 10:26
h in a field, ... MATT 13:44
kept *h* from ages and generations, ... COL 1:26
in whom are *h* all the treasures .... COL 2:3
your life is *h* with Christ in God. .... COL 3:3

HIDE
H me in the shadow of your wings. .... PS 17:8
with straps of *h* .... HOS 11:4

HIGH
runs to it and is set safely on *h* .... PROV 18:10
what the *h* and exalted one says, ... ISA 57:15

HIGHLY
not to think more *h* of yourself .... ROM 12:3

HILL
A city located on a *h* cannot be hidden.... MATT 5:14

HILLS
the cattle that graze on a thousand *h* .... PS 50:10

HINDER
this way nothing will *h* your prayers. .... 1 PET 3:7

HINDRANCE
does not become a *h* to the weak. .... 1 COR 8:9
a *h* to the gospel of Christ. .... 1 COR 9:12

HITS
box like one who *h* only air. .... 1 COR 9:26

HOLD
you *h* my right hand. .... PS 73:23
"Let your heart lay *h* of my words; .... PROV 4:4
but I will *h* the watchman accountable ... EZEK 33:6
all who take *h* of the sword will die ..... MATT 26:52
I which Christ Jesus also laid *h* of me. .... PHIL 3:12
lay *h* of that eternal life .... 1 TIM 6:12
And let us *h* unwaveringly to the hope ... HEB 10:23

HOLINESS
in *h* fearful in praises, ... EXOD 15:11
accomplish *h* out of reverence for God. .. 2 COR 7:1
h that comes from truth. .... EPH 4:24
that we may share his *h* .... HEB 12:10

HOLY
a kingdom of priests and a *h* nation.' ... EXOD 19:6
to set it apart as *h* .... EXOD 20:8
it will be set apart as *h* by my glory. .... EXOD 29:43
be holy because I am *h* .... LEV 11:44
You must sanctify yourselves and be *h* ... LEV 20:7
I, the LORD, am *h* .... LEV 20:26
You must not profane my *h* name, ... LEV 22:32
Who may go up to his *h* dwelling place? ..... PS 24:3
Worship the LORD in *h* attire. .... PS 29:2
Worship the LORD in *h* attire! Tremble ..... PS 96:9
great and awesome name! He is *h* .... PS 99:3
Worship before his footstool! He is *h* .... PS 99:5
for the LORD our God is *h* .... PS 99:9
His name is *h* and awesome. .... PS 111:9
snare for a person to rashly cry, "*H*!" .... PROV 20:25
h God's authority will be recognized .... ISA 5:16
h is the LORD of Heaven's Armies! .... ISA 6:3
"I dwell in an exalted and *h* place, ... ISA 57:15
concerning your people and your *h* city .. DAN 9:24
the law is *h* .... ROM 7:12
h and pleasing to God —which .... ROM 12:1
and called us with a *h* calling, ... 2 TIM 1:9
you have known the *h* writings, ... 2 TIM 3:15
h yourselves in all of your conduct, ... 1 PET 1:15
"You shall be *h* .... 1 PET 1:16
a *h* nation, ... 1 PET 2:9
"Holy Holy *H* is the Lord God, ... REV 4:8

HOME
Even the birds find a *h* there, ... PS 84:3
but he blesses the *h* of the righteous. PROV 3:33
no one who has left *h* or brothers ..... MARK 10:29
fulfilling their duties at *h* .... TITUS 2:5

HOMES
own *h* those who have been deserted; .... PS 68:6

HOMOSEXUALS
practicing *h* kidnappers, ... 1 TIM 1:10

HONEST
and an *h* hin. .... LEV 19:36
let him weigh me with *h* scales; .... JOB 31:6

HONESTLY
the one who speaks *h* .... ISA 45:19

HONEY
to a land flowing with milk and *h* .... EXOD 3:8
they bring greater delight than *h* .... PS 19:10
words are sweeter in my mouth than *h* ... PS 119:103

HONOR
H your father and your mother, ... EXOD 20:12
partiality to the poor nor *h* the rich. .... LEV 19:15
h the presence of an elder, ... LEV 19:32
H your father and your mother .... DEUT 5:16
For I will honor those who *h* me, ... 1 SAM 2:30
who will build a temple to *h* me.' .... 1 KGS 5:5
and clothe yourself with glory and *h* ...... JOB 40:10
crowned mankind with *h* and majesty. .... PS 8:5
I will *h* your name continually. .... PS 86:12
focus on your *h* and majestic splendor, ... PS 145:5
H the LORD from your wealth .... PROV 3:9
A generous woman gains *h* .... PROV 11:16
and before *h* comes humility. .... PROV 15:33
an *h* for a person to cease from strife, ... PROV 20:3
the LORD will bring admiration and *h* .... ISA 4:2
and give *h* to your Father in heaven. .... MATT 5:16
H your father and mother' .... MATT 15:4
H your father and mother," .... EPH 6:2
possess his own body in holiness
and *h* .... 1 THESS 4:4
must be counted worthy of double *h* .... 1 TIM 5:17
You crowned him with glory and *h* .... HEB 2:7
h the king. .... 1 PET 2:17
and show them *h* as fellow heirs .... 1 PET 3:7
h and thanks to the one who sits .... REV 4:9

HONORED
but the one who accepts reproof is *h* .... PROV 13:18
may your name be *h* .... MATT 6:9
If a member is *h* .... 1 COR 12:26
Marriage must be *h* among all .... HEB 13:4

HONORING
showing eagerness in *h* one another. .... ROM 12:10

HONORS
but *h* the LORD's loyal followers. .... PS 15:4
but whoever *h* him shows favor .... PROV 14:31

HOOKS
and their spears into pruning *h* .... ISA 2:4
and your pruning *h* into spears. .... JOEL 3:10

HOPE
I will *h* in him; ... JOB 13:15
For he is the one who gives me *h* ... PS 62:5
for I find *h* in your word. ... PS 119:74
h in the LORD, ... PS 130:7
H deferred makes the heart sick, ... PROV 13:12
character, and character, *h* ... ROM 5:4
Now hope that is seen is not *h* ... ROM 8:24
Rejoice in *h* ... ROM 12:12
of the scriptures we may have *h* ... ROM 15:4
h and love. ... 1 COR 13:13
only in this life we have *h* in Christ, ... 1 COR 15:19
the *h* of glory. ... COL 1:27
and as a helmet our *h* for salvation. ... 1 THESS 5:8
or to set their *h* on riches, ... 1 TIM 6:17
for the happy fulfillment of our *h* ... TITUS 2:13
everyone who has this *h* focused on him ... 1 JOHN 3:3

HOPES
h all things, ... 1 COR 13:7

HORIZON
far as the eastern *h* is from the west ... PS 103:12

HORSE
not enamored with the strength of a *h* ... PS 147:10
A whip for the *h* and a bridle ... PROV 26:3
saw a man seated on a red *h* ... ZECH 1:8
and here came a white *h* ... REV 6:2
And another *h* ... REV 6:4
and here came a black *h* ... REV 6:5
and here came a pale green *h* ... REV 6:8
and here came a white *h* ... REV 19:11

HOSANNA
H to the Son of David! ... MATT 21:9

HOSHEA
Last king of Israel (2 Kgs 15:30; 17:1-6).

HOSPITABLE
h an able teacher, ... 1 TIM 3:2
Instead he must be *h* ... TITUS 1:8

HOSPITALITY
to the needs of the saints, pursue *h* ... ROM 12:13
practiced *h*, washed the feet ... 1 TIM 5:10
Do not neglect *h* ... HEB 13:2
Show *h* to one another. ... 1 PET 4:9

HOSTILE
the outlook of the flesh is *h* to God, ... ROM 8:7

HOSTILITY
put *h* between you and the woman ... GEN 3:15
h They are gossips, ... ROM 1:29

HOT
that you are neither cold nor *h* ... REV 3:15

HOUR
can add even one *h* to his life? ... MATT 6:27
at an *h* when you do not expect him." ... LUKE 12:40
deliver me from this *h* ... JOHN 12:27

HOUSE
You shall not covet your neighbor's *h* ... EXOD 20:17
and speak of them as you sit in your *h* ... DEUT 6:7
the LORD's *h* for the rest of my life. ... PS 23:6
If the LORD does not build a *h* ... PS 127:1
Her *h* is the way to the grave, ... PROV 7:27
share a *h* with a quarrelsome wife. ... PROV 21:9
in the *h* of my friends.' ... ZECH 13:6
a wise man who built his *h* on rock. ... MATT 7:24
h divided against itself will stand. ... MATT 12:25
Then he can thoroughly plunder the *h* ... MATT 12:29
My house will be called a *h* of prayer ... MATT 21:13
that *h* will not be able to stand. ... MARK 3:25
my Father's *h* a marketplace!" ... JOHN 2:16
the *h* was filled with the fragrance ... JOHN 12:3
many dwelling places in my Father's *h* ... JOHN 14:2
greater honor than the *h* itself! ... HEB 3:3

HOUSEHOLD
who is greedy for gain troubles his *h* ... PROV 15:27
and provided food for her *h* ... PROV 31:15
enemies will be the members of his *h* ... MATT 10:36
and a divided *h* falls. ... LUKE 11:17
there will be five in one *h* divided, ... LUKE 12:52
He must manage his own *h* well ... 1 TIM 3:4
does not know how to manage his own *h* ... 1 TIM 3:5
to conduct themselves in the *h* of God, ... 1 TIM 3:15
fulfill their duty toward their own *h* ... 1 TIM 5:4
and manage a *h* ... 1 TIM 5:14

HOUSEHOLDS
of their children and their own *h* ... 1 TIM 3:12

HOW
Announce every day *h* he delivers. ... 1 CHR 16:23
Announce every day *h* he delivers. ... PS 96:2
H delightful it is to see approaching ... ISA 52:7
according to *h* he has behaved. ... JER 17:10

HUMAN
Whoever sheds *h* blood, ... GEN 9:6
prophecy was ever borne of *h* impulse; ... 2 PET 1:21

HUMANITY
one intermediary between God and *h* ... 1 TIM 2:5

HUMANKIND
"Let us make *h* in our image, ... GEN 1:26

HUMBLE
h themselves, pray, ... 2 CHR 7:14
May he teach the *h* his way. ... PS 25:9
a *h* and repentant heart ... PS 51:17
yet he shows favor to the *h* ... PROV 3:34
special favor to the *h* and contrite, ... ISA 66:2
because I am gentle and *h* in heart, ... MATT 11:29
H yourselves before the Lord ... JAS 4:10
h yourselves under his mighty hand ... 1 PET 5:6

HUMBLED
So he *h* you by making you hungry ... DEUT 8:3
And whoever exalts himself will be *h* ... MATT 23:12
He *h* himself, ... PHIL 2:8

HUMBLES
h himself like this little child ... MATT 18:4

HUMILIATED
in order to cheer up the *h* ... ISA 57:15

HUMILITY
but wisdom came with *h* ... PROV 11:2
and before honor comes *h* ... PROV 15:33
with all *h* and gentleness, ... EPH 4:2
in *h* be moved to treat one another as ... PHIL 2:3
clothe yourselves with *h* ... 1 PET 5:5

HUNGRY
and gives food to the *h* ... PS 146:7

If your enemy is *h* ... PROV 25:21
but gives his bread to the *h* ... EZEK 18:7
For I was *h* and you gave me food, ... MATT 25:35
he has filled the *h* with good things, ... LUKE 1:53
one who comes to me will never go *h* ... JOHN 6:35
Rather, if your enemy is *h* ... ROM 12:20

HUSBAND
A noble wife is the crown of her *h* ... PROV 12:4
and likewise a wife to her *h* ... 1 COR 7:3
it is not the *h* who has the rights ... 1 COR 7:4
a wife should not divorce a *h* ... 1 COR 7:10
or be reconciled to her *h* ... 1 COR 7:11
a woman has a *h* who is not a believer ... 1 COR 7:13
But if her *h* dies, ... 1 COR 7:39
I promised you in marriage to one *h* ... 2 COR 11:2
because the *h* is the head of the wife ... EPH 5:23
and the wife must respect her *h* ... EPH 5:33

HUSBAND'S
Her *h* heart has trusted her, ... PROV 31:11

HUSBANDS
Wives, submit to your *h* ... EPH 5:22
H love your wives just as Christ loved ... EPH 5:25
the younger women to love their *h* ... TITUS 2:4
be subject to your own *h* ... 1 PET 3:1
H in the same way, ... 1 PET 3:7

HYMNS
praying and singing *h* to God, ... ACTS 16:25

HYPOCRISY
you are full of *h* and lawlessness. ... MATT 23:28
Love must be without *h* ... ROM 12:9
deceit and *h* and envy and all slander. ... 1 PET 2:1

HYPOCRITE
harsh condemnation for the *h* ... MAL 1:14
You *h!* First remove the beam ... MATT 7:5

HYPOCRITES
do not be like the *h* ... MATT 6:5

HYSSOP
Cleanse me with *h* and I will be pure; ... PS 51:7

IDLENESS
she would not eat the bread of *i* ... PROV 31:27

IDOL
his *i;* he bows down to it and worships ... ISA 44:17

IDOLATRY
and greed which is *i* ... COL 3:5

IDOLS
With regard to food sacrificed to *i* ... 1 COR 8:1
eating food sacrificed to *i* ... 1 COR 8:4

IF
i he has nothing, ... EXOD 22:3
I the LORD had not been on our side" ... PS 124:1
I you, O Lord, ... PS 130:3
i you seek it like silver, ... PROV 2:4
i it is showing mercy, ... ROM 12:8
I an unbeliever invites you to dinner ... 1 COR 10:27
I anyone's name was not found written ... REV 20:15

IGNORANCE
has also placed i in the human heart ... ECCL 3:11
silence the *i* of foolish people ... 1 PET 2:15

IGNORANT
compassionately with those who are *i* ... HEB 5:2
things the *i* and unstable twist ... 2 PET 3:16

IGNORE
do not *i* it; ... DEUT 22:1

ILL
Is anyone among you *i* ... JAS 5:14

ILLUMINES
The LORD *i* the darkness around me. ... 2 SAM 22:29

IMAGE
"Let us make humankind in our *i* ... GEN 1:26
in the *i* of God he created them, ... GEN 1:27
to be conformed to the *i* of his Son, ... ROM 8:29
since he is the *i* and glory of God. ... 1 COR 11:7
are being transformed into the same *i* ... 2 COR 3:18
He is the *i* of the invisible God, ... COL 1:15
the *i* of the one who created it. ... COL 3:10
with it we curse people made in God's *i* ... JAS 3:9

IMITATE
and *i* their faith. ... HEB 13:7
do not *i* what is bad but what is good. ... 3 JOHN 11

IMITATORS
be *i* of me. ... 1 COR 4:16
Be *i* of me, ... 1 COR 11:1
you became *i* of us and of the Lord, ... 1 THESS 1:6
For you became *i* ... 1 THESS 2:14
but *i* of those who through faith ... HEB 6:12

IMMANUEL
will name him *I* ... ISA 7:14

IMMEDIATELY
So Jonah went *i* to Nineveh, ... JONAH 3:3

IMMORAL
a Christian who is sexually *i* ... 1 COR 5:11
The sexually *i* ... 1 COR 6:9
And let us not be *i* ... 1 COR 10:8
that no person who is *i* ... EPH 5:5
that no one becomes an *i* or godless ... HEB 12:16
for God will judge sexually *i* people ... HEB 13:4
the sexually *i* ... REV 21:8
and the sorcerers and the sexually *i* ... REV 22:15

IMMORALITY
except for *i* ... MATT 5:32
except for *i* ... MATT 19:9
The body is not for sexual *i* ... 1 COR 6:13
Flee sexual *i*. ... 1 COR 6:18
sexual *i* impurity, ... GAL 5:19
there must not be either sexual *i* ... EPH 5:3
that you keep away from sexual *i* ... 1 THESS 4:3

IMMORTAL
and exchanged the glory of the *i* God ... ROM 1:23
i invisible, the only God, ... 1 TIM 1:17

IMMORTALITY
good works seek glory and honor and *i* ... ROM 2:7
and this mortal body must put on *i* ... 1 COR 15:53
i and lives in unapproachable light, ... 1 TIM 6:16
life and *i* to light through the gospel ... 2 TIM 1:10

IMPARTING
explaining it and *i* insight. ... NEH 8:8

IMPERISHABLE
not from perishable but from *i* seed, ... 1 PET 1:23

IMPORTANCE
For I passed on to you as of first *i* ... 1 COR 15:3

IMPORTANT
you neglect what is more *i* in the law ... MATT 23:23

INSULT
corrects a mocker is asking for *i* .... PROV 9:7
Blessed are you when people *i* you .... MATT 5:11
and when they exclude you and *i* you .... LUKE 6:22
evil for evil or insult for *i* .... 1 PET 3:9

INSULTED
oppresses the poor has *i* his Creator, ... PROV 14:31
who mocks the poor has *i* his Creator; .... PROV 17:5

INSULTS
not hide my face from *i* and spitting. .... ISA 50:6

INTEGRITY
The LORD rewards each man for his *i* ... 1 SAM 26:23
serve me with *i* and sincerity, ... 1 KGS 9:4
And he still holds firmly to his *i* .... JOB 2:3
I will not set aside my *i* .... JOB 27:5
Settle in the land and maintain your *i* ...... PS 37:3
Look, you desire *i* in the inner man; .... PS 51:6
from those who have *i* .... PS 84:11
The one who conducts himself in *i* .... PROV 10:9
The *i* of the upright guides them, ... PROV 11:3
a poor person who walks in his *i* .... PROV 19:1
people hate someone with *i* .... PROV 29:10
i will be like a belt around his hips. .... ISA 11:5
but the person of *i* will live .... HAB 2:4
In your teaching show *i* .... TITUS 2:7

INTEND
and is fulfilled as I *i* .... ISA 55:11

INTERCEDE
And my servant Job will *i* for you, ... JOB 42:8
because he always lives to *i* for them. .... HEB 7:25

INTERCEDES
but the Spirit himself *i* for us .... ROM 8:26

INTERCESSIONS
i and thanks be offered .... 1 TIM 2:1

INTERESTS
for you are a guardian of the family *i* ..... RUTH 3:9
but about the *i* of others as well. .... PHIL 2:4

INTERMARRY
You must not *i* with them. .... DEUT 7:3

INTERMEDIARY
and one *i* between God and humanity, ... 1 TIM 2:5

INTERVENED
and *i* on behalf of the rebels." .... ISA 53:12

INTO
I will turn you *i* fishers of people!" .... MARK 1:17

INVISIBLE
He is the image of the *i* God, ... COL 1:15
i the only God, ... 1 TIM 1:17

INVITE
i the poor, ... LUKE 14:13

INVITED
I was a stranger and you *i* me in, ... MATT 25:35

INVITES
If an unbeliever *i* you to dinner .... 1 COR 10:27

IRON
he will rule them with an *i* rod .... REV 2:27

IRREVOCABLE
the gifts and the call of God are *i* .... ROM 11:29

IRRITANTS
i in your eyes and thorns in your side, ... NUM 33:55

ISAAC
Son of Abraham by Sarah (Gen 17:19; 21:1-7; 1 Chr 1:28). Offered up by Abraham (Gen 22; Heb 11:17-19). Rebekah taken as wife (Gen 24). Fathered Esau and Jacob (Gen 25:19-26; 1 Chr 1:34). Tricked into blessing Jacob (Gen 27). Father of Israel (Exod 3:6; Deut 29:13; Rom 9:10).

ISAIAH
Prophet to Judah (Isa 1:1). Called by the LORD (Isa 6).

ISHMAEL
Son of Abraham by Hagar (Gen 16; 1 Chr 1:28). Blessed, but not son of covenant (Gen 17:18-21; Gal 4:21-31). Sent away by Sarah (Gen 21:8-21).

ISRAEL
Hear, O *I* .... DEUT 6:4
"The glory has departed from *I* .... 1 SAM 4:21
I will blossom and grow branches. .... ISA 27:6
who scattered *I* will regather them. .... JER 31:10
the house of *I* went into exile .... EZEK 39:23
the people of *I* will be like the sand .... HOS 1:10
I the Lord our God, ... MARK 12:29
judging the twelve tribes of *I* .... LUKE 22:30
descended from Israel are truly *I* .... ROM 9:6
And so all *I* will be saved, ... ROM 11:26

ISRAELITES
I went through the middle of the sea ... EXOD 14:22
Now the *I* ate manna forty years, ... EXOD 16:35

JACOB
Second son of Isaac, twin of Esau (Gen 25:21-26; 1 Chr 1:34). Bought Esau's birthright (Gen 25:29-34); tricked Isaac into blessing him (Gen 27:1-37). Abrahamic covenant perpetuated through (Gen 28:13-15; Mal 1:2). Vision at Bethel (Gen 28:10-22). Wives and children (Gen 29:1–30:24; 35:16-26; 1 Chr 2-9). Wrestled with God; name changed to Israel (Gen 32:22-32). Sent sons to Egypt during famine (Gen 42-43). Settled in Egypt (Gen 46). Blessed Ephraim and Manasseh (Gen 48). Blessed sons (Gen 49:1-28; Heb 11:21). Death (Gen 49:29-33). Burial (Gen 50:1-14).

JAMES
1. Apostle; brother of John (Matt 4:21-22; 10:2; Mark 3:17; Luke 5:1-10). At transfiguration (Matt 17:1-13; Mark 9:1-13; Luke 9:28-36). Killed by Herod (Acts 12:2).
2. Apostle; son of Alphaeus (Matt 10:3; Mark 3:18; Luke 6:15).
3. Brother of Jesus (Matt 13:55; Mark 6:3; Luke 24:10; Gal 1:19) and Judas (Jude 1). With believers before Pentecost (Acts 1:13). Leader of church at Jerusalem (Acts 12:17; 15; 21:18; Gal 2:9, 12). Author of epistle (Jas 1:1).

JAPHETH
Son of Noah (Gen 5:32; 1 Chr 1:4-5). Blessed (Gen 9:18-28).

JAR
alabaster *j* of expensive perfumed oil, ... MATT 26:7

JARS
But we have this treasure in clay *j* .... 2 COR 4:7

JEALOUS
am a *j* God, ... EXOD 20:5
is a *j* God. .... EXOD 34:14
he is a *j* God. .... DEUT 4:24
For I am *j* for you with godly jealousy ... 2 COR 11:2

JEALOUSY
still *j* and dissension among you, ... 1 COR 3:3
For I am jealous for you with godly *j* ..... 2 COR 11:2
j outbursts of anger, ... GAL 5:20

JEHOAHAZ
1. Son of Jehu; king of Israel (2 Kgs 13:1-9).
2. Son of Josiah; king of Judah (2 Kgs 23:31-34; 2 Chr 36:1-4).

JEHOASH
Son of Jehoahaz; king of Israel (2 Kgs 13-14; 2 Chr 25).

JEHOIACHIN
Son of Jehoiakim; king of Judah exiled by Nebuchadnezzar (2 Kgs 24:8-17; 2 Chr 36:8-10; Jer 22:24-30; 24:1). Raised from prisoner status (2 Kgs 25:27-30; Jer 52:31-34).

JEHOIAKIM
Son of Josiah; king of Judah (2 Kgs 23:34–24:6; 2 Chr 36:4-8; Jer 22:18-23; 36).

JEHORAM
Son of Jehoshaphat; king of Judah (2 Kgs 8:16-24).

JEHOSHAPHAT
Son of Asa; king of Judah (1 Kgs 22:41-50; 2 Kgs 3; 2 Chr 17-20).

JEHU
King of Israel (1 Kgs 19:16-19; 2 Kgs 9-10).

JEPHTHAH
Judge from Gilead who delivered Israel from Ammon (Judg 10:6–12:7). Made rash vow concerning his daughter (Judg 11:30-40).

JEREMIAH
Prophet to Judah (Jer 1:1-3). Called by the LORD (Jer 1). Put in stocks (Jer 20:1-3). Threatened for prophesying (Jer 11:18-23; 26). Opposed by Hananiah (Jer 28). Scroll burned (Jer 36). Imprisoned (Jer 37). Thrown into cistern (Jer 38). Forced to Egypt with those fleeing Babylonians (Jer 43).

JEROBOAM
1. Official of Solomon; rebelled to become first king of Israel (1 Kgs 11:26-40; 12:1-20; 2 Chr 10). Idolatry (1 Kgs 12:25-33); judgment for (1 Kgs 13-14; 2 Chr 13).
2. Son of Jehoash; king of Israel (1 Kgs 14:23-29).

JERUSALEM
J and the temple, ... 2 KGS 23:27
But now I have chosen *J* as a place to live, ... 2 CHR 6:6
"You see the problem that we have *J* .... NEH 2:17
Pray for the peace of *J* .... PS 122:6
As the mountains surround *J* .... PS 125:2
O *J* may my right hand be crippled. .... PS 137:5
O herald *J* .... ISA 40:9
create *J* to be a source of joy, ... ISA 65:18
J will be holy .... JOEL 3:17
On that day they will say to *J* .... ZEPH 3:16
J will no longer be enclosed by walls. ..... ZECH 2:4
I will bring them to settle within *J* .... ZECH 8:8
living waters will flow out from *J* .... ZECH 14:8
O *J* Jerusalem, ... MATT 23:37
O *J* Jerusalem, ... LUKE 13:34
J will be trampled down .... LUKE 21:24
people must worship is in *J* .... JOHN 4:20
and you will be my witnesses in *J* .... ACTS 1:8
corresponds to the present *J* .... GAL 4:25
new *J*—descending .... REV 21:2

JESTING
or coarse *j*—all .... EPH 5:4

JESUS
This *J* God raised up, ... ACTS 2:32
"I am *J* whom you are persecuting! .... ACTS 9:5
through the grace of the Lord *J* .... ACTS 15:11
"Believe in the Lord *J* .... ACTS 16:31
called to belong to *J* Christ. .... ROM 1:6
the redemption that is in Christ *J* .... ROM 3:24
in life through the one, *J* Christ! .... ROM 5:17
for those who are in Christ *J* .... ROM 8:1
nothing among you except *J* Christ, ... 1 COR 2:2
J Christ, through whom are all things .... 1 COR 8:6
J is cursed," .... 1 COR 12:3
but *J* Christ as Lord, ... 2 COR 4:5
but by the faithfulness of *J* Christ. .... GAL 2:16
all of you are one in Christ *J* .... GAL 3:28
For in Christ *J* neither circumcision .... GAL 5:6
created in Christ *J* for good works .... EPH 2:10
Christ *J* himself as the cornerstone. .... EPH 2:20
perfect it until the day of Christ *J* .... PHIL 1:6
toward one another that Christ *J* had, ... PHIL 2:5
at the name of *J* every knee will bow ...... PHIL 2:10
do it all in the name of the Lord *J* .... COL 3:17
the arrival of our Lord *J* Christ .... 2 THESS 2:1
"Christ *J* came into the world to save ..... 1 TIM 1:15
in Christ *J* will be persecuted. .... 2 TIM 3:12
our great God and Savior, *J* Christ. .... TITUS 2:13
but we see *J* .... HEB 2:9
take note of *J* .... HEB 3:1
J the Son of God, ... HEB 4:14
J has become the guarantee .... HEB 7:22
keeping our eyes fixed on *J* .... HEB 12:2
the power and return of our Lord *J* .... 2 PET 1:16
the blood of *J* his Son cleanses us .... 1 JOHN 1:7
J Christ the Righteous One, ... 1 JOHN 2:1
ought himself to walk just as *J* walked ... 1 JOHN 2:6
that *J* laid down his life for us; .... 1 JOHN 3:16
confesses that *J* is the Son of God, ... 1 JOHN 4:15
Amen! Come, Lord *J* .... REV 22:20

JEW
robe of one *J* and say, ... ZECH 8:23
to the *J* first and also to the Greek. .... ROM 1:16
distinction between the *J* and the .... ROM 10:12
There is neither *J* nor Greek, ... GAL 3:28

JEWELRY
like a bride when she puts on her *j* .... ISA 61:10

JEWS
the one who is born king of the *J* .... MATT 2:2
"Are you the king of the *J* .... MATT 27:11
because salvation is from the *J* .... JOHN 4:22
These *J* were more open-minded .... ACTS 17:11
Or is God the God of the *J* only? .... ROM 3:29
For *J* demand miraculous signs .... 1 COR 1:22

I became like a Jew to gain the *J* .... 1 COR 9:20
Whether *J* or Greeks or slaves or free, ... 1 COR 12:13
say they are *J* yet are not, ... REV 3:9

JEZEBEL
Sidonian wife of Ahab (1 Kgs 16:31). Promoted Baal worship (1 Kgs 16:32-33). Killed prophets of the LORD (1 Kgs 18:4, 13). Opposed Elijah (1 Kgs 19:1-2). Had Naboth killed (1 Kgs 21). Death prophesied (1 Kgs 21:17-24). Killed by Jehu (2 Kgs 9:30-37).

JOASH
Son of Ahaziah; king of Judah. Sheltered from Athaliah by Jehoiada (2 Kgs 11; 2 Chr 22:10–23:21). Repaired temple (2 Kgs 12; 2 Chr 24).

JOB
Wealthy man from Uz; feared God (Job 1:1-5). Righteousness tested by disaster (Job 1:6-22), personal affliction (Job 2). Maintained innocence in debate with three friends (Job 3-31), Elihu (Job 32-37). Rebuked by the LORD (Job 38-41). Vindicated and restored to greater stature by the LORD (Job 42). Example of righteousness (Ezek 14:14, 20).

JOHN
1. Son of Zechariah and Elizabeth (Luke 1). Called the Baptist (Matt 3:1-12; Mark 1:2-8). Witness to Jesus (Matt 3:11-12; Mark 1:7-8; Luke 3:15-18; John 1:6-35; 3:27-30; 5:33-36). Doubts about Jesus (Matt 11:2-6; Luke 7:18-23). Arrest (Matt 4:12; Mark 1:14). Execution (Matt 14:1-12; Mark 6:14-29; Luke 9:7-9). Ministry compared to Elijah (Matt 11:7-19; Mark 9:11-13; Luke 7:24-35).
2. Apostle; brother of James (Matt 4:21-22; 10:2; Mark 3:17; Luke 5:1-10). At transfiguration (Matt 17:1-13; Mark 9:1-13; Luke 9:28-36). Desire to be greatest (Mark 10:35-45). Leader of church at Jerusalem (Acts 4:1-3; Gal 2:9). Elder who wrote epistles (2 John 1; 3 John 1). Prophet who wrote Revelation (Rev 1:1; 22:8).
3. Cousin of Barnabas, coworker with Paul, (Acts 12:12–13:13; 15:37).

JOINED
so that you could be *j* to another, ... ROM 7:4

JOINTS
and *j* from marrow; .... HEB 4:12

JONAH
Prophet in days of Jeroboam II (2 Kgs 14:25). Called to Nineveh; fled to Tarshish (Jonah 1:1-3). Cause of storm; thrown into sea (Jonah 1:4-16). Swallowed by fish (Jonah 1:17). Prayer (Jonah 2). Preached to Nineveh (Jonah 3). Attitude reproved by the LORD (Jonah 4). Sign of (Matt 12:39-41; Luke 11:29-32).

JONATHAN
Then *J* son of Saul left .... 1 SAM 23:16

JONATHAN
Son of Saul (1 Sam 13:16; 1 Chr 8:33). Valiant warrior (1 Sam 13-14). Relation to David (1 Sam 18:1-4; 19-20; 23:16-18). Killed at Gilboa (1 Sam 31). Mourned by David (2 Sam 1).

JORAM
Son of Ahab; king of Israel (2 Kgs 3; 8-9; 2 Chr 22).

JORDAN
border will continue down the *J* River .. NUM 34:12
'Israel crossed the *J* River .... JOSH 4:22
baptizing them in the *J* River .... MATT 3:6

JOSEPH
1. Son of Jacob by Rachel (Gen 30:24; 1 Chr 2:2). Favored by Jacob, hated by brothers (Gen 37:3-4). Dreams (Gen 37:5-11). Sold by brothers (Gen 37:12-36). Served Potiphar; imprisoned by false accusation (Gen 39). Interpreted dreams of Pharaoh's servants (Gen 40), of Pharaoh (Gen 41:4-40). Made greatest in Egypt (Gen 41:41-57). Sold grain to brothers (Gen 42-45). Brought Jacob and sons to Egypt (Gen 46-47). Sons Ephraim and Manasseh blessed (Gen 48). Blessed (Gen 49:22-26; Deut 33:13-17). Death (Gen 50:22-26; Exod 13:19; Heb 11:22). 12,000 from (Rev 7:8).
2. Husband of Mary, mother of Jesus (Matt 1:16-24; 2:13-19; Luke 1:27; 2; John 1:45).
3. Disciple from Arimathea, who gave his tomb for Jesus' burial (Matt 27:57-61; Mark 15:43-47; Luke 23:50-53).
4. Original name of Barnabas (Acts 4:36).

JOSHUA
1. Son of Nun; name changed from Hoshea (Num 13:8, 16; 1 Chr 7:27). Fought Amalekites under Moses (Exod 17:9-14). Servant of Moses on Sinai (Exod 24:13; 32:17). Spied Canaan (Num 13). With Caleb, allowed to enter land (Num 14:6, 30). Succeeded Moses (Deut 1:38; 31:1-8; 34:9).
   Charged Israel to conquer Canaan (Josh 1). Crossed Jordan (Josh 3-4). Circumcised sons of wilderness wanderings (Josh 5). Conquered Jericho (Josh 6), Ai (Josh 7-8), five kings at Gibeon (Josh 10:1-28), southern Canaan (Josh 10:29-43), northern Canaan (Josh 11-12). Defeated at Ai (Josh 7). Deceived by Gibeonites (Josh 9). Renewed covenant (Josh 8:30-35; 24:1-27). Divided land among tribes (Josh 13-22). Last words (Josh 23). Death (Josh 24:28-31).
2. High priest during rebuilding of temple (Hag 1-2; Zech 3:1-9; 6:11).

JOSIAH
Son of Amon; king of Judah (2 Kgs 22-23; 2 Chr 34-35).

JOTHAM
Son of Azariah (Uzziah); king of Judah (2 Kgs 15:32-38; 2 Chr 26:21–27:9).

JOY
he is the source of strength and *j* .... 1 CHR 16:27
and all the sons of God shouted for *j* .... JOB 38:7
but *j* arrives in the morning. .... PS 30:5
and covered me with *j* .... PS 30:11
to the God who gives me ecstatic *j* .... PS 43:4
They are bubbling with *j* as they walk .... PS 45:15
experience the *j* of your deliverance. .... PS 51:12
the trees of the forest shout with *j* .... PS 96:12

Worship the LORD with *j* ..... PS 100:2
for they give me *j* ..... PS 119:111
The hope of the righteous is *j* ..... PROV 10:28
but those who promote peace have *j* ... PROV 12:20
happiness and *j* will overwhelm them; .... ISA 35:10
Shout for *j* ..... ISA 44:23
happiness and *j* will overwhelm them; .... ISA 51:11
Indeed you will go out with *j* ..... ISA 55:12
the baby in my womb leaped for *j* ..... LUKE 1:44
that brings great *j* to all the people: ..... LUKE 2:10
more *j* in heaven over one sinner. ..... LUKE 15:7
and your *j* may be complete. ..... JOHN 15:11
but your sadness will turn into *j* ..... JOHN 16:20
abundant *j* and their extreme poverty ... 2 COR 8:2
complete my *j* and be of the same mind, .. PHIL 2:2
my *j* and crown, ... PHIL 4:1
For who is our hope or *j* or crown ..... 1 THESS 2:19
I have had great *j* and encouragement ..... PHLM 7
j set out for him he endured the cross, ... HEB 12:2
consider it nothing but *j* ..... JAS 1:2
I have no greater *j* than this: ..... 3 JOHN 4

JOYFUL
A *j* heart makes the face cheerful, ... PROV 15:13
not *j*. But later it produces the fruit ..... HEB 12:11

JOYFULLY
My mouth *j* praises you, ... PS 63:5

JUDAH
towns in southern *J* will be shut tight. .... JER 13:19
our Lord is descended from *J* ..... HEB 7:14

JUDAISM
heard of my former way of life in *J* ..... GAL 1:13

JUDAS
1. Apostle (Luke 6:16; John 14:22; Acts 1:13). Probably also called Thaddaeus (Matt 10:3; Mark 3:18).
2. Brother of James and Jesus (Matt 13:55; Mark 6:3), also called Jude (Jude 1).
3. Apostle, also called Iscariot, who betrayed Jesus (Matt 10:4; 26:14-56; Mark 3:19; 14:10-50; Luke 6:16; 22:3-53; John 6:71; 12:4; 13:2-30; 18:2-11). Suicide of (Matt 27:3-5; Acts 1:16-25).

JUDGE
j of the whole earth do what is right?" .... GEN 18:25
for he comes to *j* the earth! ..... 1 CHR 16:33
Do not *j* so that you will not be ..... MATT 7:1
but *j* with proper judgment." ..... JOHN 7:24
I do not *j* him. ..... JOHN 12:47
will *j* him at the last day. ..... JOHN 12:48
set a day on which he is going to *j* ..... ACTS 17:31
God will *j* the secrets of human hearts ... ROM 2:16
will *j* you to be the transgressor ..... ROM 2:27
the saints will *j* the world? ..... 1 COR 6:2
going to *j* the living and the dead, ... 2 TIM 4:1
the righteous *J* ..... 2 TIM 4:8
able to *j* the desires and thoughts ..... HEB 4:12
who are you to *j* your neighbor? ..... JAS 4:12
who had been given authority to *j* ..... REV 20:4

JUDGED
Do not judge so that you will not be *j* ..... MATT 7:1
I am *j* by you or by any human court. ..... 1 COR 4:3
we would not be *j* ..... 1 COR 11:31
we will be *j* more strictly. ..... JAS 3:1
j by what was written in the books, ... REV 20:12

JUDGES
there is a God who *j* in the earth." ..... PS 58:11
For the LORD *j* all humanity with fire ..... ISA 66:16
and with justice he *j* and goes to war. ..... REV 19:11

JUDGING
j the twelve tribes of Israel. ..... MATT 19:28

JUDGMENT
for *j* belongs to God. ..... DEUT 1:17
the wicked cannot withstand *j* ..... PS 1:5
Certainly your angry *j* upon men ..... PS 76:10
What will you do on *j* day, ... ISA 10:3
I will feed them—with *j*.'" ..... EZEK 34:16
in *j* on all the surrounding nations. ..... JOEL 3:12
'Exercise true *j* and show brotherhood ... ZECH 7:9
whoever murders will be subjected to *j* ... MATT 5:21
Sodom and Gomorrah on the day of *j* ... MATT 10:15
I tell you that on the day of *j* ..... MATT 12:36
but has assigned all *j* to the Son, ... JOHN 5:22
concerning sin and righteousness and *j* ..... JOHN 16:8
we must not pass *j* on one another, ... ROM 14:13
eats and drinks *j* against himself. ..... 1 COR 11:29
and then to face *j* ..... HEB 9:27
a certain fearful expectation of *j* ..... HEB 10:27
For it is time for *j* to begin, ... 1 PET 4:17
locked up for the *j* of the great Day. ..... JUDE 6

JUDGMENTS
I am afraid of your *j* ..... PS 119:120

JUST
for all his ways are *j* ..... DEUT 32:4
You are *j* ..... PS 119:137
the LORD is a *j* God; ..... ISA 30:18
his deeds are right and his ways are *j* ..... DAN 4:37
that he would be *j* and the justifier ..... ROM 3:26
whatever is *j* ..... PHIL 4:8
disobedience received its *j* penalty, ... HEB 2:2
the *j* for the unjust, ... 1 PET 3:18
your judgments are true and *j* ..... REV 16:7

JUSTICE
so as to pervert *j* ..... EXOD 23:2
You must not turn away *j* for your poor ... EXOD 23:6
but *j* and abundant righteousness ..... JOB 37:23
he accomplished *j* ..... PS 9:16
For the LORD promotes *j* ..... PS 37:28
of your kingdom is a scepter of *j* ..... PS 45:6
You love *j* and hate evil. ..... PS 45:7
I will sing about loyalty and *j* ..... PS 101:1
How blessed are those who promote *j* ..... PS 106:3
characterized by faithfulness and *j* ..... PS 111:7
j and equity. ..... PROV 1:3
Doing *j* brings joy to the righteous ..... PROV 21:15
A king brings stability to a land by *j* ..... PROV 29:4
from the LORD that one receives *j* ..... PROV 29:26
by promoting *j* and fairness, ... ISA 9:7
I will make *j* the measuring line, ... ISA 28:17
before establishing *j* on the earth; ..... ISA 42:4
"Promote *j* Do what is right! ..... ISA 56:1
his desire for *j* like body armor, ... ISA 59:17
love *j* and hate robbery and sin. ..... ISA 61:8
Promote *j* at the city gate. ..... AMOS 5:15
J must flow like torrents of water, ... AMOS 5:24
He wants you to carry out *j* ..... MIC 6:8
yet you neglect *j* and love for God! ..... LUKE 11:42

JUSTIFICATION
- and was raised for the sake of our *j* ... ROM 4:25

JUSTIFIED
- everyone who believes is *j* ... ACTS 13:39
- But they are *j* freely by his grace ... ROM 3:24
- he also *j* ... ROM 8:30
- *j* in the name of the Lord Jesus Christ ... 1 COR 6:11
- no one is *j* by the works of the law ... GAL 2:16
- no one is *j* before God by the law, ... GAL 3:11
- *j* by works and not by faith alone. ... JAS 2:24

JUSTIFY
- for I will not *j* the wicked. ... EXOD 23:7
- God would *j* the Gentiles by faith, ... GAL 3:8

KEEP
- and so you must *k* this day perpetually ... EXOD 12:17
- who love me and *k* my commandments. ... EXOD 20:6
- learn them and be careful to *k* them! ... DEUT 5:1
- *K* his commandments very carefully, ... DEUT 6:17
- *k* me from committing flagrant sins; ... PS 19:13
- and *k* it with all my heart. ... PS 119:34
- *k* devious talk far from your lips. ... PROV 4:24
- *k* the poor from getting fair treatment ... ISA 10:2
- You *k* completely safe the people ... ISA 26:3
- *k* them safe in your name ... JOHN 17:11
- making every effort to *k* the unity ... EPH 4:3
- *K* yourself pure. ... 1 TIM 5:22
- that we *k* his commandments. ... 1 JOHN 5:3
- one who is able to *k* you from falling, ... JUDE 24

KEEPING
- *k* loyal love for thousands, ... EXOD 34:7
- *k* God's commandments is what counts. ... 1 COR 7:19

KEEPS
- but a wise person *k* it back. ... PROV 29:11

KEPT
- that your precepts be carefully *k* ... PS 119:4
- "I have *k* my heart clean; ... PROV 20:9
- I have *k* the faith! ... 2 TIM 4:7

KEYS
- the *k* of the kingdom of heaven. ... MATT 16:19

KILL
- They will *k* him, ... MATT 17:23

KILLED
- "Worthy is the lamb who was *k* ... REV 5:12

KILLS
- for the letter *k* ... 2 COR 3:6

KIND
- you are *k* and forgiving, ... PS 86:5
- A *k* person benefits himself, ... PROV 11:17
- he is *k* to ungrateful and evil people. ... LUKE 6:35
- test what *k* of work each has done. ... 1 COR 3:13
- love is *k* ... 1 COR 13:4
- With what *k* of body will they come?" ... 1 COR 15:35
- Instead, be *k* to one another, ... EPH 4:32
- not engage in heated disputes but be *k* ... 2 TIM 2:24
- *k* being subject to their own husbands, ... TITUS 2:5

KINDNESS
- May your acts of *k* be repaid fully ... RUTH 2:12
- The LORD's loyal *k* never ceases; ... LAM 3:22
- the abundance of his loyal *k* ... LAM 3:32
- provided you continue in his *k* ... ROM 11:22
- sure that you excel in this act of *k* ... 2 COR 8:7
- *k* goodness, faithfulness, ... GAL 5:22
- grace in *k* toward us in Christ Jesus. ... EPH 2:7
- if you have experienced the Lord's *k* ... 1 PET 2:3

KINDS
- creatures according to their *k* ... GEN 1:24

KING
- In those days Israel had no *k* ... JUDG 17:6
- though the LORD your God is your *k* ... 1 SAM 12:12
- The *k* of Israel replied, ... 1 KGS 20:11
- For the LORD is *k* and rules over ... PS 22:28
- Then the majestic *k* will enter. ... PS 24:7
- Look, a *k* will promote fairness; ... ISA 32:1
- Your *k* is coming to you: ... ZECH 9:9
- the *K* of kings and Lord of lords, ... 1 TIM 6:15
- honor the *k* ... 1 PET 2:17
- *K* of kings and Lord of lords." ... REV 19:16

KINGDOM
- a *k* of priests and a holy nation.' ... EXOD 19:6
- The scepter of your *k* is a scepter ... PS 45:6
- His *k* will last forever, ... DAN 4:3
- Repent, for the *k* of heaven is near." ... MATT 3:2
- for the *k* of heaven belongs to them. ... MATT 5:3
- may your *k* come, ... MATT 6:10
- pursue his *k* and righteousness, ... MATT 6:33
- will enter into the *k* of heaven ... MATT 7:21
- one who is least in the *k* of heaven ... MATT 11:11
- *k* of heaven is like a person who sowed ... MATT 13:24
- *k* of heaven is like a mustard seed ... MATT 13:31
- "The *k* of heaven is like yeast ... MATT 13:33
- The *k* of heaven is like a treasure, ... MATT 13:44
- *k* of heaven is like a merchant ... MATT 13:45
- Again, the *k* of heaven is like a net ... MATT 13:47
- I will give you the keys of the *k* ... MATT 16:19
- the *k* of heaven is like a king ... MATT 18:23
- a rich person to enter into the *k* ... MATT 19:24
- and kingdom against *k* ... MATT 24:7
- this gospel of the *k* will be preached ... MATT 24:14
- inherit the *k* prepared for you ... MATT 25:34
- enter into the *k* of God with one eye ... MARK 9:47
- *k* of God belongs to such as these. ... MARK 10:14
- for the rich to enter the *k* of God!" ... MARK 10:23
- 'The *k* of God has come upon you!' ... LUKE 10:9
- Instead, pursue his *k* ... LUKE 12:31
- the *k* of God is in your midst." ... LUKE 17:21
- he cannot enter the *k* of God. ... JOHN 3:5
- "My *k* is not from this world. ... JOHN 18:36
- unrighteous will not inherit the *k* ... 1 COR 6:9
- hands over the *k* to God the Father, ... 1 COR 15:24
- and has appointed us as a *k* ... REV 1:6
- the *k* of our Lord and of his Christ, ... REV 11:15

KINGS
- The *k* of the earth form a united front; ... PS 2:2
- All *k* will bow down to him; ... PS 72:11
- ten *k* will arise from that kingdom. ... DAN 7:24
- for *k* and all who are in authority, ... 1 TIM 2:2
- the ruler over the *k* of the earth. ... REV 1:5

KISS
- Like a *k* on the lips is the one who ... PROV 24:26
- betray the Son of Man with a *k* ... LUKE 22:48

KNEE
- 'Surely every *k* will bow to me, ... ISA 45:23

every *k* will bow to me, ... ROM 14:11
at the name of Jesus every *k* will bow ... PHIL 2:10

KNEES
steady the *k* that shake. ... ISA 35:3
your listless hands and your weak *k* ... HEB 12:12

KNEW
O that I *k* where I might find him, ... JOB 23:3
because I *k* that you are a gracious ... JONAH 4:2
'I never *k* you. ... MATT 7:23

KNOCK
k and the door will be opened for you. ... MATT 7:7

KNOCKING
I am standing at the door and *k* ... REV 3:20

KNOW
And *k* that your sin will find you out. ... NUM 32:23
I *k* that my Redeemer lives, ... JOB 19:25
Who can *k* all his errors? ... PS 19:12
"How does God *k* what we do? ... PS 73:11
you examine me and *k* me. ... PS 139:1
and *k* my concerns. ... PS 139:23
do not *k* what a day may bring forth. ... PROV 27:1
will *k* me," ... JER 31:34
do not let your left hand *k* ... MATT 6:3
k on what day your Lord will come. ... MATT 24:42
so that you may *k* for certain ... LUKE 1:4
we speak about what we *k* and testify ... JOHN 3:11
You people worship what you do not *k* ... JOHN 4:22
"I do not *k* whether he is a sinner. ... JOHN 9:25
I know my own and my own *k* me ... JOHN 10:14
they *k* you, ... JOHN 17:3
and we *k* that his testimony is true. ... JOHN 21:24
"You are not permitted to *k* the times ... ACTS 1:7
We *k* that our old man was crucified ... ROM 6:6
For I *k* that nothing good lives in me, ... ROM 7:18
k that all things work together ... ROM 8:28
k that your bodies are members ... 1 COR 6:15
not *k* that your body is the temple ... 1 COR 6:19
and *k* all mysteries and all knowledge, ... 1 COR 13:2
but then I will *k* fully, ... 1 COR 13:12
My aim is to *k* him, ... PHIL 3:10
I *k* the one in whom my faith is set ... 2 TIM 1:12
You do not *k* about tomorrow. ... JAS 4:14
The one who says "I have come
to *k* God ... 1 JOHN 2:4
We *k* that we have crossed over ... 1 JOHN 3:14
We have come to *k* love by this: ... 1 JOHN 3:16
By this we *k* that we love ... 1 JOHN 5:2
you may *k* that you have eternal life. ... 1 JOHN 5:13

KNOWING
k good and evil." ... GEN 3:5
k that your labor is not in vain ... 1 COR 15:58
far greater value of *k* Christ Jesus ... PHIL 3:8

KNOWLEDGE
tree of the *k* of good and evil ... GEN 2:9
who darkens counsel without *k* ... JOB 42:3
Your *k* is beyond my comprehension; ... PS 139:6
Those who are wise store up *k* ... PROV 10:14
The one who loves discipline loves *k* ... PROV 12:1
Every shrewd person acts with *k* ... PROV 13:16
It is dangerous to have zeal without *k* ... PROV 19:2
through the law comes the *k* of sin. ... ROM 3:20
riches and wisdom and *k* of God! ... ROM 11:33
we know that "we all have *k* ... 1 COR 8:1
by your *k* the weak brother or sister, ... 1 COR 8:11
and know all mysteries and all *k* ... 1 COR 13:2
For some have no *k* of God—I ... 1 COR 15:34
the *k* of him in every place. ... 2 COR 2:14
k of God in the face of Christ. ... 2 COR 4:6
the love of Christ that surpasses *k* ... EPH 3:19
all the treasures of wisdom and *k* ... COL 2:3
chatter and absurdities of so-called *k* ... 1 TIM 6:20
k of our Lord and Savior Jesus Christ. ... 2 PET 3:18

KNOWN
Make *k* his accomplishments ... PS 105:1
secret that will not be made *k* ... MATT 10:26
for a tree is *k* by its fruit. ... MATT 12:33
what can be *k* about God is plain ... ROM 1:19
For who has *k* the mind of the Lord, ... ROM 11:34
k and read by everyone, ... 2 COR 3:2
having *k* it, ... 2 PET 2:21

KNOWS
for the LORD is a God who *k* ... 1 SAM 2:3
But he *k* the pathway that I take; ... JOB 23:10
for he *k* a person's secret thoughts? ... PS 44:21
The LORD *k* that peoples' thoughts ... PS 94:11
Surely no one *k* the future, ... ECCL 8:7
for your Father *k* what you need ... MATT 6:8
as for that day and hour no one *k* it ... MATT 24:36
And he who searches our hearts *k* ... ROM 8:27
If someone thinks he *k* something, ... 1 COR 8:2
"The Lord *k* those who are his," ... 2 TIM 2:19

LABAN
Brother of Rebekah (Gen 24:29-51), father of Rachel and Leah (Gen 29-31).

LABOR
For six days you may *l* and do all your ... EXOD 20:9
your *l* is not in vain in the Lord. ... 1 COR 15:58
to acknowledge those
who *l* among you ... 1 THESS 5:12

LACKING
on the balances and found to be *l* ... DAN 5:27

LAG
Do not *l* in zeal, ... ROM 12:11

LAID
foundation other than what is being *l* ... 1 COR 3:11

LAKE
thrown alive into the *l* of fire ... REV 19:20
Death and Hades were thrown into the *l* .. REV 20:14

LAMB
God will provide for himself the *l* ... GEN 22:8
A wolf will reside with a *l* ... ISA 11:6
Like a *l* led to the slaughtering block, ... ISA 53:7
the *L* of God who takes away the sin ... JOHN 1:29
For Christ, our Passover *l*, *l* ... 1 COR 5:7
an unblemished and spotless *l* ... 1 PET 1:19
a *L* that appeared to have been killed. ... REV 5:6
"Worthy is the *l* who was killed ... REV 5:12
as firstfruits to God and to the *L* ... REV 14:4

LAMB'S
written in the *L* book of life. ... REV 21:27

LAMBS
Go! I am sending you out like *l* ... LUKE 10:3
"Feed my *l* ... JOHN 21:15

LAME
It is better to enter life *l* ... MARK 9:45

LAMENT
Then you turned my *l* into dancing; .... PS 30:11

LAMP
Indeed, you are my *l* .... 2 SAM 22:29
Indeed, you light my *l* .... PS 18:28
Your word is a *l* to walk by, ... PS 119:105
Her *l* would not go out in the night...... PROV 31:18
No one lights a *l* and then covers it ...... LUKE 8:16
and its *l* is the Lamb.............................. REV 21:23

LAMPS
like ten virgins who took their *l* .... MATT 25:1
keep your *l* burning; .... LUKE 12:35

LAND
God called the dry ground *l* .... GEN 1:10
"Let the *l* produce vegetation: .... GEN 1:11
"To your descendants I will give this *l* ..... GEN 12:7
to a *l* flowing with milk and honey, ... EXOD 3:8
for blood defiles the *l* .... NUM 35:33
The LORD showed him the whole *l* .... DEUT 34:1
This is the *l* that remains: .... JOSH 13:2
and heal their *l* .... 2 CHR 7:14
then I will remove you from my *l* .... 2 CHR 7:20
then I will bring you to your *l* .... EZEK 36:24

LANGUAGE
The whole earth had a common *l* .... GEN 11:1
heard them speaking in his own *l* .... ACTS 2:6
abusive *l* from your mouth. .... COL 3:8
l people, and nation. .... REV 5:9

LANGUAGES
they will speak in new *l* .... MARK 16:17
in other *l* as the Spirit enabled them....... ACTS 2:4

LASH
to *l* a man who is a Roman citizen .... ACTS 22:25

LAST
"I am the first and I am the *l* .... ISA 44:6
and the *l* first. .... MATT 19:30
and the *l* first." .... MARK 10:31
the *l* days difficult times will come. .... 2 TIM 3:1
the *l* days blatant scoffers will come, ... 2 PET 3:3
I am the first and the *l* .... REV 1:17
the first and the *l* .... REV 22:13

LASTING
perpetually as a *l* ordinance. .... EXOD 12:14
with *l* devotion I will have compassion .... ISA 54:8
gaining for himself a *l* reputation, ... ISA 63:12
had a better and *l* possession. .... HEB 10:34

LAUGH
and a time to *l* .... ECCL 3:4

LAUGHS
enthroned in heaven *l* in disgust; .... PS 2:4

LAVISHED
he *l* on us in all wisdom and insight. .... EPH 1:8

LAW
you must read this *l* before them .... DEUT 31:11
Take this scroll of the *l* .... DEUT 31:26
l scroll must not leave your lips. .... JOSH 1:8
They read from the book of God's *l* .... NEH 8:8
The *l* of the LORD is perfect .... PS 19:7
see the marvelous things in your *l* .... PS 119:18
The *l* you have .... PS 119:72
O how I love your *l* .... PS 119:97
Those who love your *l* .... PS 119:165
"I will put my *l* within them .... JER 31:33
to abolish the *l* or the prophets. .... MATT 5:17
this fulfills the *l* and the prophets .... MATT 7:12
l and the prophets depend on
these two .... MATT 22:40
stroke of a letter in the *l* to
become void. .... LUKE 16:17
For the *l* was given through Moses, ... JOHN 1:17
will be judged by the *l* .... ROM 2:12
the *l* is written in their hearts, ... ROM 2:15
for before the *l* was given, ... ROM 5:13
l came in so that the transgression .... ROM 5:20
you are not under *l* but under grace. .... ROM 6:14
we have been released from the *l* .... ROM 7:6
the *l* is holy, ... ROM 7:12
For God achieved what the *l* could not ..... ROM 8:3
For Christ is the end of the *l* .... ROM 10:4
love is the fulfillment of the *l* .... ROM 13:10
of the *l* by becoming a curse for us .... GAL 3:13
l had become our guardian until Christ ... GAL 3:24
he is obligated to obey the whole *l* .... GAL 5:3
by the *l* have been alienated from .... GAL 5:4
For the whole *l* can be summed up .... GAL 5:14
for the *l* made nothing perfect. .... HEB 7:19
l possesses a shadow of the good .... HEB 10:1
peers into the perfect *l* of liberty .... JAS 1:25
For the one who obeys the whole *l* .... JAS 2:10

LAWLESSNESS
and lawlessness leading to more *l* .... ROM 6:19
and the man of *l* is revealed, ... 2 THESS 2:3
hidden power of *l* is already at work.... 2 THESS 2:7
sin is *l* .... 1 JOHN 3:4

LAWS
I will put my *l* in their minds .... HEB 8:10
I will put my *l* on their hearts .... HEB 10:16

LAY
Son of Man has no place to *l* his head .. MATT 8:20
For no one can *l* any foundation other ... 1 COR 3:11
Do not *l* hands on anyone hastily .... 1 TIM 5:22

LAYING
I am *l* a stone in Zion, ... ISA 28:16
not *l* this foundation again: .... HEB 6:1

LAZARUS
1. Poor man in Jesus' parable (Luke 16:19-31).
2. Brother of Mary and Martha whom Jesus raised from the dead (John 11:1–12:19).

LAZY
The one who is *l* becomes poor, ... PROV 10:4
from house to house they learn to be *l* ... 1 TIM 5:13

LEAD
pillar of cloud to *l* them in the way, ... EXOD 13:21
your loyal love you will *l* the people ..... EXOD 15:13
You *l* me in the path of life. .... PS 16:11
l me along a level path .... PS 27:11
L me up to a rocky summit .... PS 61:2
and *l* me in the everlasting way. .... PS 139:24
l me into a level land. .... PS 143:10
The LORD will continually *l* you; .... ISA 58:11
And do not *l* us into temptation, ... MATT 6:13
passions may *l* them away from Christ ... 1 TIM 5:11

LEADER
and the *l* like the one who serves. .... LUKE 22:26
God exalted him to his right hand as *L* ... ACTS 5:31

LEADERS
LORD raised up *l* who delivered them ... JUDG 2:16
Remember your *l* ... HEB 13:7
Obey your *l* and submit to them, ... HEB 13:17

LEADS
he *l* me to refreshing water. ... PS 23:2
as a small child *l* them along. ... ISA 11:6
he *l* the ewes along. ... ISA 40:11
who *l* you in the way you should go. ... ISA 48:17
way is spacious that *l* to destruction, ... MATT 7:13
calls his own sheep by name and *l* them ... JOHN 10:3
always *l* us in triumphal ... 2 COR 2:14

LEAH
Wife of Jacob (Gen 29:16-30); bore six sons and one daughter (Gen 29:31–30:21; 34:1; 35:23).

LEARN
L to do what is right. ... ISA 1:17
Take my yoke on you and *l* from me, ... MATT 11:29
or *l* it from any human source; ... GAL 1:12

LEARNED
for I have *l* to be content ... PHIL 4:11
you have *l* and are confident about. ... 2 TIM 3:14

LEAVE
I will not abandon you or *l* you alone. ... JOSH 1:5
He will not *l* you or abandon you ... 1 CHR 28:20

LED
a lamb *l* to the slaughtering block, ... ISA 53:7
I *l* you through the wilderness ... AMOS 2:10
For all who are *l* by the Spirit of God ... ROM 8:14

LEFT
to the right or to the *l* ... JOSH 1:7
Do not turn to the right or to the *l* ... PROV 4:27
and the goats on his *l* ... MATT 25:33
Then all the disciples *l* him and fled. ... MATT 26:56

LEGION
"My name is *L* ... MARK 5:9

LEND
and generously *l* him whatever he needs. ... DEUT 15:8
they show compassion and *l* to others, ... PS 37:26
Even sinners *l* to sinners, ... LUKE 6:34

LENGTH
l of years should make wisdom known.' ... JOB 32:7
what is the breadth and *l* and height ... EPH 3:18

LESSON
each one has a song, has a *l* ... 1 COR 14:26

LET
he will not *l* you down or destroy you, ... DEUT 4:31
L everyone see your gentleness. ... PHIL 4:5
l no one deceive you: ... 1 JOHN 3:7

LETTER
smallest letter or stroke of a *l* ... MATT 5:18
You yourselves are our *l* ... 2 COR 3:2
not based on the *l* but on the Spirit, ... 2 COR 3:6
not obey our message through this *l* ... 2 THESS 3:14

LETTERS
in *l* on stone tablets—came ... 2 COR 3:7
"His *l* are weighty and forceful, ... 2 COR 10:10
speaking of these things in all his *l* ... 2 PET 3:16

LEVEL
kind presence lead me into a *l* land. ... PS 143:10
The way of the righteous is *l* ... ISA 26:7

LEVI (LEVITES)
1. Son of Jacob by Leah (Gen 29:34; 46:11; 1 Chr 2:1). Tribe of blessed (Gen 49:5-7; Deut 33:8-11), chosen as priests (Num 3-4), numbered (Num 3:39; 26:62), allotted cities, but not land (Num 18; 35; Deut 10:9; Josh 13:14; 21), land (Ezek 48:8-22), 12,000 from (Rev 7:7).
2. See MATTHEW.

LEVITES
The *L* are responsible for the care ... NUM 1:53
Take the *L* from among the Israelites ... NUM 8:6
See, I have given the *L* all the tithes ... NUM 18:21

LIABILITIES
I now regard all things as *l* compared ... PHIL 3:8

LIAR
and a poor person is better than a *l* ... PROV 19:22
he is a *l* and the father of lies. ... JOHN 8:44
every human being shown up as a *l* ... ROM 3:4

LICENSE
the grace of our God into a *l* for evil ... JUDE 4

LIE
that he should *l* ... NUM 23:19
A truthful witness does not *l* ... PROV 14:5
exchanged the truth of God for a *l* ... ROM 1:25
when people *l* about us, ... 1 COR 4:13
Do not *l* to one another ... COL 3:9
since it is impossible for God to *l* ... HEB 6:18

LIED
You have not *l* to people but to God!" ... ACTS 5:4

LIES
you must not tell *l* ... LEV 19:11
he is a liar and the father of *l* ... JOHN 8:44

LIFE
into his nostrils the breath of *l* ... GEN 2:7
(Now the tree of *l* and the tree of ... GEN 2:9
then you will give a life for a *l* ... EXOD 21:23
for the *l* of all flesh is its blood. ... LEV 17:14
life for *l* ... LEV 24:18
that I have set *l* and death, ... DEUT 30:19
You lead me in the path of *l* ... PS 16:11
Into your hand I entrust my *l* ... PS 31:5
my mortality and the brevity of *l* ... PS 39:4
maintain a pure *l* ... PS 119:9
like the road leading to *l* ... PROV 6:23
that it will cost him his *l* ... PROV 7:23
has found *l* and received favor ... PROV 8:35
righteous is like a tree producing *l* ... PROV 11:30
pursues righteousness and love finds *l* ... PROV 21:21
some to everlasting *l* ... DAN 12:2
do not worry about your *l* ... MATT 6:25
difficult the way that leads to *l* ... MATT 7:14
whoever loses his *l* because of me. ... MATT 10:39
whoever loses his *l* because of me ... MATT 16:25
in exchange for his *l* ... MATT 16:26
give his *l* as a ransom for many." ... MATT 20:28
give his *l* as a ransom for many." ... MARK 10:45
l does not consist in the abundance ... LUKE 12:15
do not worry about your *l* ... LUKE 12:22
and even his own *l* ... LUKE 14:26
and the *l* was the light of mankind. ... JOHN 1:4
believes in him may have eternal *l* ... JOHN 3:15
one who rejects the Son will not see *l* ... JOHN 3:36
water springing up to eternal *l* ... JOHN 4:14

one who sent me has eternal *l* ... JOHN 5:24
"I am the bread of *l* ... JOHN 6:35
the one who believes has eternal *l* ... JOHN 6:47
spoken to you are spirit and are *l* ... JOHN 6:63
You have the words of eternal *l* ... JOHN 6:68
I have come so that they may have *l* ... JOHN 10:10
I lay down my *l* for the sheep. ... JOHN 10:15
I give them eternal *l* ... JOHN 10:28
"I am the resurrection and the *l* ... JOHN 11:25
and the *l* ... JOHN 14:6
one lays down his *l* for his friends. ... JOHN 15:13
and that by believing you may have *l* ... JOHN 20:31
appointed for eternal *l* believed. ... ACTS 13:48
but the gift of God is eternal *l* ... ROM 6:23
nor *l* nor angels, ... ROM 8:38
in this *l* we have hope in Christ, ... 1 COR 15:19
but the Spirit gives *l* ... 2 COR 3:6
So the *l* I now live in the body, ... GAL 2:20
by holding on to the word of *l* ... PHIL 2:16
present life and for the *l* to come." ... 1 TIM 4:8
and so lay hold of what is truly *l* ... 1 TIM 6:19
entangled in matters of everyday *l* ... 2 TIM 2:4
the crown of *l* that God promised ... JAS 1:12
For the one who wants to love *l* ... 1 PET 3:10
necessary for *l* and godliness ... 2 PET 1:3
we have crossed over from death to *l* ... 1 JOHN 3:14
and this *l* is in his Son. ... 1 JOHN 5:11
book of *l* belonging to the Lamb ... REV 13:8
book of *l* ... REV 20:12
written in the Lamb's book of *l* ... REV 21:27
side of the river is the tree of *l* ... REV 22:2

LIFE-GIVING
the fountain of *l* water, ... JER 2:13

LIFESTYLE
The wicked need to abandon their *l* ... ISA 55:7

LIFT
L your hands toward the sanctuary ... PS 134:2
Let us *l* up our hearts and our hands ... LAM 3:41

LIFTED
He *l* me out of the watery pit, ... PS 40:2

LIGHT
"Let there be *l* ... GEN 1:3
In what direction does *l* reside, ... JOB 38:19
The LORD is my *l* and my salvation. ... PS 27:1
He covers himself with *l* as if it were ... PS 104:2
and a *l* to illumine my path. ... PS 119:105
walking in darkness see a bright *l* ... ISA 9:2
I will make you a *l* to the nations, ... ISA 49:6
sit in darkness have seen a great *l* ... MATT 4:16
let your *l* shine before people, ... MATT 5:16
loved the darkness rather than the *l* ... JOHN 3:19
"I am the *l* of the world! ... JOHN 8:12
who said "Let *l* shine out of darkness, ... 2 COR 4:6
fellowship does *l* have with darkness? ... 2 COR 6:14
disguises himself as an angel of *l* ... 2 COR 11:14
and lives in unapproachable *l* ... 1 TIM 6:16
out of darkness into his marvelous *l* ... 1 PET 2:9
God is *l* ... 1 JOHN 1:5
as he himself is in the l ... 1 JOHN 1:7

LIGHTNING
and his face had an appearance like *l* ... DAN 10:6
just like the *l* comes from the east ... MATT 24:27
His appearance was like *l* ... MATT 28:3

LIGHTS
in which you shine as *l* in the world ... PHIL 2:15
because the glory of God *l* it up, ... REV 21:23

LIKE
by looking *l* other men, ... PHIL 2:7

LIKENESS
after our *l* ... GEN 1:26
his own Son in the *l* of sinful flesh ... ROM 8:3

LIMIT
there is no *l* to his wisdom. ... ISA 40:28

LION
like a *l* they pin my hands and feet. ... PS 22:16
A *l* like an ox, ... ISA 11:7
like a roaring *l* ... 1 PET 5:8
the *L* of the tribe of Judah, ... REV 5:5

LIPS
May praise flow freely from my *l* ... PS 119:171
and not your own *l* ... PROV 27:2
for my *l* are contaminated by sin, ... ISA 6:5

LISTEN
and *l* to the words of the wise, ... PROV 22:17
The one who has ears had better *l* ... MATT 11:15
My sheep *l* to my voice, ... JOHN 10:27
Let every person be quick to *l* ... JAS 1:19
l to it and so deceive yourselves. ... JAS 1:22

LISTENER
and does not become a forgetful *l* ... JAS 1:25

LISTENING
for your servant is *l* ... 1 SAM 3:9

LISTENS
but the one who *l* to advice is wise. ... PROV 12:15
one who gives an answer before he *l* ... PROV 18:13

LIVE
for no one can see me and *l* ... EXOD 33:20
humankind cannot *l* by bread alone, ... DEUT 8:3
God does not really *l* on the earth! ... 1 KGS 8:27
l in the LORD's house for the rest of ... PS 23:6
Would you love to *l* a long, ... PS 34:12
I will sing to the LORD as long as I *l* ... PS 104:33
May I *l* and praise you. ... PS 119:175
so you can *l* ... ISA 55:3
can these bones *l* ... EZEK 37:3
infuse breath into you and you will *l* ... EZEK 37:5
to bring down those who *l* in pride. ... DAN 4:37
and to *l* obediently before your God. ... MIC 6:8
but the person of integrity will *l* ... HAB 2:4
'Man does not *l* by bread alone, ... MATT 4:4
l in temples made by human hands, ... ACTS 17:24
For in him we *l* and move about ... ACTS 17:28
"The righteous by faith will *l* ... ROM 1:17
Let us *l* decently as in the daytime, ... ROM 13:13
for we *l* by faith, ... 2 COR 5:7
and it is no longer I who *l* ... GAL 2:20
If we *l* by the Spirit, ... GAL 5:25
urge you to *l* worthily of the calling ... EPH 4:1
so that you may *l* worthily of the Lord ... COL 1:10
In this way you will *l* a decent life ... 1 THESS 4:12
who want to *l* godly lives in Christ Jesus ... 2 TIM 3:12

LIVED
l my life with a clear conscience ... ACTS 23:1

L takes notice of his loyal followers, ... PS 33:18
The angel of the *L* camps around .... PS 34:7
Taste and see that the *L* is good. .... PS 34:8
The *L* is near the brokenhearted; .... PS 34:18
Then you will take delight in the *L* .... PS 37:4
I relied completely on the *L* .... PS 40:1
For the *L* Most High is awe-inspiring; .... PS 47:2
The *L* is great and certainly worthy .... PS 48:1
Throw your burden upon the *L* .... PS 55:22
For the *L* holds in his hand a cup full .... PS 75:8
The *L* bestows favor and honor; .... PS 84:11
O *L* teach me how you want me to live. .... PS 86:11
O *L* the heavens praise your amazing .... PS 89:5
Come, let us sing for joy to the *L* .... PS 95:1
Sing to the *L* a new song. .... PS 96:1
Shout out praises to the *L* .... PS 98:4
Shout out praises to the *L* .... PS 100:1
Praise the *L* .... PS 103:1
The *L* is compassionate and merciful; .... PS 103:8
But the *L* continually shows loyal love .... PS 103:17
Praise the *L* .... PS 104:1
thanks to the *L* for his loyal love, ... PS 107:8
The *L* is exalted over all the nations; .... PS 113:4
O *L* not to us, ... PS 115:1
The *L* values the lives of his faithful .... PS 116:15
Give thanks to the *L* .... PS 118:1
the day the *L* has brought about. .... PS 118:24
O *L* your instructions endure; .... PS 119:89
My help comes from the *L* .... PS 121:2
the *L* is the shade at your right hand. .... PS 121:5
so the *L* surrounds his people, ... PS 125:2
If the *L* does not guard a city, ... PS 127:1
Yes, sons are a gift from the *L* .... PS 127:3
Give thanks to the *L* .... PS 136:1
O *L* you examine me and know me. .... PS 139:1
O *L* place a guard on my mouth. .... PS 141:3
L of what importance is the human race .... PS 144:3
The *L* is great and certainly worthy .... PS 145:3
The *L* is near all who cry out to him, ... PS 145:18
Fearing the *L* is the beginning of, ... PROV 1:7
Trust in the *L* with all your heart, ... PROV 3:5
Honor the *L* from your wealth .... PROV 3:9
do not despise discipline from the *L* .... PROV 3:11
For the *L* disciplines those he loves, ... PROV 3:12
By wisdom the *L* laid the foundation .... PROV 3:19
There are six things that the *L* hates, ... PROV 6:16
Fearing the *L* prolongs life, ... PROV 10:27
The *L* abhors dishonest scales, ... PROV 11:1
The *L* abhors a person who lies, ... PROV 12:22
of the *L* one has strong confidence, ... PROV 14:26
The eyes of the *L* are in every place, ... PROV 15:3
but the *L* evaluates the motives. .... PROV 16:2
The *L* has worked everything .... PROV 16:4
but the *L* directs his steps. .... PROV 16:9
their every decision is from the *L* .... PROV 16:33
name of the *L* is like a strong tower; .... PROV 18:10
obtained a delightful gift from the *L* .... PROV 18:22
but a prudent wife is from the *L* .... PROV 19:14
the *L* will repay him for his good deed .... PROV 19:17
acceptable to the *L* than sacrifice. .... PROV 21:3
and there is no counsel against the *L* .... PROV 21:30
but the victory is from the *L* .... PROV 21:31
the *L* is the Creator of them both. .... PROV 22:2
lest the *L* see it, ... PROV 24:18
A woman who fears the *L*—she .... PROV 31:30
I saw the *L* seated on a high, ... ISA 6:1
holy is the *L* of Heaven's Armies! .... ISA 6:3
produces absolute loyalty to the *L* .... ISA 11:2
For the *L* gives me strength .... ISA 12:2
the *L* is ready to devastate the earth .... ISA 24:1
they praise the majesty of the *L* .... ISA 24:14
the *L* has announced it! .... ISA 25:8
try to hide their plans from the *L* .... ISA 29:15
those whom the *L* has ransomed .... ISA 35:10
when the wind sent by the *L* blows .... ISA 40:7
L comes as a victorious warrior; .... ISA 40:10
The *L* is an eternal God, ... ISA 40:28
I am the *L* .... ISA 42:8
I, I am the *L* .... ISA 43:11
"I am the *L* .... ISA 44:24
I am the *L* .... ISA 45:5
the *L* I have no peer, ... ISA 45:21
Those whom the *L* has ransomed .... ISA 51:11
but the *L* caused the sin of all of us .... ISA 53:6
the *L* desired to crush him .... ISA 53:10
Seek the *L* while he makes himself .... ISA 55:6
The *L* will continually lead you; .... ISA 58:11
trees planted by the *L* .... ISA 61:3
I will greatly rejoice in the *L* .... ISA 61:10
majestic crown in the hand of the *L* .... ISA 62:3
Then the *L* reached out his hand .... JER 1:9
the *L* act out of faithfulness, ... JER 9:24
L you give me strength and protect me. .... JER 16:19
and let us return to the *L* .... LAM 3:40
deliver them by the *L* their God; .... HOS 1:7
Then they will submit to the *L* .... HOS 3:5
Let's return to the *L* .... HOS 6:1
for the day of the *L* is about to come. .... JOEL 2:1
the day of the *L* is awesome .... JOEL 2:11
for the day of the *L* is near .... JOEL 3:14
far away from the *L* .... JONAH 1:3
and what the *L* really wants from you: .... MIC 6:8
the *L* is avenging and very angry. .... NAH 1:2
L will certainly not allow the wicked .... NAH 1:3
But the *L* is in his majestic palace. .... HAB 2:20
The *L* your God is in your midst; .... ZEPH 3:17
and once more the *L* will comfort Zion .... ZECH 1:17
The *L* of Heaven's Armies says, ... ZECH 8:23
the *L* their God will deliver them .... ZECH 9:16
Then the *L* my God will come .... ZECH 14:5
The *L* will then be king over all. .... ZECH 14:9
great and terrible day of the *L* .... MAL 4:5

LORD'S (THE PROPER NAME OF GOD, *YAHWEH*, SPELLED "LORD'S" IN THE NET)

It is the *L* Passover. .... EXOD 12:11
"Is the *L* hand shortened? .... NUM 11:23
For the *L* allotment is his people, ... DEUT 32:9
Not one of the *L* faithful promises .... JOSH 21:45
the *L* promise is reliable; .... 2 SAM 22:31
the *L* glory filled his temple. .... 1 KGS 8:11
the *L* splendor filled God's temple. .... 2 CHR 5:14
pleasure in obeying the *L* commands; .... PS 1:2
The *L* precepts are fair .... PS 19:8
in the *L* house for the rest of my life .... PS 23:6
acknowledge the *L* majesty and power. .... PS 29:1
The *L* decisions stand forever; .... PS 33:11
about the *L* faithful deeds; .... PS 89:1
and the *L* faithfulness endures. .... PS 117:2
"We will go to the *L* temple." .... PS 122:1
submission to the *L* sovereignty, ... ISA 11:9

in order to show sincere mutual *l* ... 1 PET 1:22
l the family of believers, ... 1 PET 2:17
For the one who wants to *l* life ... 1 PET 3:10
because *l* covers a multitude of sins. ... 1 PET 4:8
to brotherly affection, unselfish *l* ... 2 PET 1:7
the *l* of God has been perfected. ... 1 JOHN 2:5
the *l* of the Father is not in him, ... 1 JOHN 2:15
l the Father has given to us: ... 1 JOHN 3:1
who does not *l* his fellow Christian ... 1 JOHN 3:10
that we should *l* one another, ... 1 JOHN 3:11
because we *l* our fellow Christians. ... 1 JOHN 3:14
We have come to know *l* by this: ... 1 JOHN 3:16
let us not *l* with word or with tongue ... 1 JOHN 3:18
Son Jesus Christ and *l* one another, ... 1 JOHN 3:23
because God is *l* ... 1 JOHN 4:8
By this the *l* of God is revealed in us: ... 1 JOHN 4:9
In this is *l* ... 1 JOHN 4:10
and his *l* is perfected in us. ... 1 JOHN 4:12
one who resides in *l* resides in God, ... 1 JOHN 4:16
By this *l* is perfected with us, ... 1 JOHN 4:17
but perfect *l* drives out fear, ... 1 JOHN 4:18
We *l* because he loved us first. ... 1 JOHN 4:19
cannot *l* God whom he has not seen. ... 1 JOHN 4:20
we *l* God and obey his commandments. ... 1 JOHN 5:2
For this is the *l* of God: ... 1 JOHN 5:3
that we *l* one another. ... 2 JOHN 5
Now this is *l* ... 2 JOHN 6
maintain yourselves in the *l* of God, ... JUDE 21
You have departed from your first *l* ... REV 2:4
All those I *l* ... REV 3:19
and they did not *l* their lives so much ... REV 12:11

LOVED
He took her as his wife and *l* her. ... GEN 24:67
Israel *l* Joseph more than all his sons ... GEN 37:3
a double portion because he *l* Hannah, ... 1 SAM 1:5
because he *l* him. ... 1 SAM 20:17
What they *l* ... ECCL 9:6
you *l* me like a new bride; ... JER 2:2
'I have *l* you with an everlasting love ... JER 31:3
as detestable as what they *l* ... HOS 9:10
I *l* him like a son, ... HOS 11:1
For this is the way God *l* the world: ... JOHN 3:16
l the darkness rather than the light, ... JOHN 3:19
Now Jesus *l* Martha and her sister ... JOHN 11:5
For they *l* praise from men ... JOHN 12:43
he now *l* them to the very end. ... JOHN 13:1
the one Jesus *l* ... JOHN 13:23
Just as I have *l* you, ... JOHN 13:34
who loves me will be *l* by my Father, ... JOHN 14:21
Just as the Father has *l* me, ... JOHN 15:9
love one another just as I have *l* you. ... JOHN 15:12
the disciple whom he *l* standing there, ... JOHN 19:26
victory through him who *l* us! ... ROM 8:37
"Jacob I *l* ... ROM 9:13
dearly *l* for the sake of the fathers. ... ROM 11:28
who *l* me and gave himself for me. ... GAL 2:20
just as Christ also *l* us ... EPH 5:2
just as Christ *l* the church ... EPH 5:25
who *l* us and by grace gave us eternal ... 2 THESS 2:16
since he *l* the present age, ... 2 TIM 4:10
l righteousness and hated lawlessness. ... HEB 1:9
not that we have *l* God, ... 1 JOHN 4:10
if God so *l* us, ... 1 JOHN 4:11
We love because he *l* us first. ... 1 JOHN 4:19

LOVELY
How *l* is the place where you live, ... PS 84:1
and your face is *l* ... SONG 2:14
whatever is *l* ... PHIL 4:8

LOVER
My *l* is mine and I am his; ... SONG 2:16

LOVES
he provides for those whom he *l* ... PS 127:2
For the LORD disciplines those he *l* ... PROV 3:12
one who loves discipline *l* knowledge, ... PROV 12:1
A friend *l* at all times, ... PROV 17:17
who loves a quarrel *l* transgression; ... PROV 17:19
The one who *l* a pure heart ... PROV 22:11
the LORD *l* the Israelites ... HOS 3:1
and whoever *l* son or daughter more ... MATT 10:37
one who is forgiven little *l* little." ... LUKE 7:47
The Father *l* the Son ... JOHN 3:35
This is why the Father *l* me ... JOHN 10:17
and obeys them is the one who *l* me. ... JOHN 14:21
"If anyone *l* me, ... JOHN 14:23
l his neighbor has fulfilled the law. ... ROM 13:8
because God *l* a cheerful giver. ... 2 COR 9:7
He who loves his wife *l* himself. ... EPH 5:28
For the Lord disciplines the one he *l* ... HEB 12:6
and everyone who *l* has been fathered ... 1 JOHN 4:7
l God should love his fellow Christian. ... 1 JOHN 4:21
who loves the father *l* the child ... 1 JOHN 5:1
the one who *l* us and has set us free ... REV 1:5

LOVING
who keeps his *l* covenant ... NEH 1:5
with *l* instruction on her tongue. ... PROV 31:26
Greet one another with a *l* kiss. ... 1 PET 5:14

LOVINGLY
and he looked at me *l* ... SONG 2:4

LOW
God chose what is *l* and despised ... 1 COR 1:28

LOWLY
he sets the *l* on high, ... JOB 5:11
one who has a *l* spirit will gain honor. ... PROV 29:23
Exalt the *l* ... EZEK 21:26

LOYAL
be *l* to him, ... JOSH 22:5

LOYALTIES
I hate people with divided *l* ... PS 119:113

LOYALTY
l to your servants who obey you ... 1 KGS 8:23
I will sing about *l* and justice. ... PS 101:1
Many people profess their *l* ... PROV 20:6

LUKE
Coworker with Paul (Col 4:14; 2 Tim 4:11; Phlm 24).

LUKEWARM
So because you are *l* ... REV 3:16

LUSH
He takes me to *l* pastures, ... PS 23:2

LUST
Do not *l* in your heart for her beauty, ... PROV 6:25

LUSTFUL
not in *l* passion like the Gentiles ... 1 THESS 4:5

LYING
a *l* tongue, ... PROV 6:17
A *l* tongue hates those crushed by it, ... PROV 26:28

MANNA
The house of Israel called its name *m* .... EXOD 16:31
and then feeding you with unfamiliar *m* .... DEUT 8:3
fed you in the wilderness with *m* .... DEUT 8:16
ancestors ate the *m* in the wilderness, ... JOHN 6:49
I will give him some of the hidden *m* .... REV 2:17

MANNER
speak in an impressive and fitting *m* .... PS 45:2
the cup of the Lord in an unworthy *m* ... 1 COR 11:27
in a decent and orderly *m* .... 1 COR 14:40

MANY
Egypt's many chariots and in their *m* .... ISA 31:1

MARITAL
his *m* responsibility to his wife, ... 1 COR 7:3

MARK
Then the LORD put a special *m* on Cain ... GEN 4:15
to obtain a *m* on their right hand .... REV 13:16

MARKS
for I bear the *m* of Jesus on my body. .... GAL 6:17

MARRIAGE
they neither marry nor are given in *m* .... MATT 22:30
marrying and giving in *m* .... MATT 24:38
and the *m* bed kept undefiled, ... HEB 13:4

MARRIED
m woman is bound by law to her husband .... ROM 7:2

MARRIES
m a divorced woman commits adultery. .... MATT 5:32
and *m* another commits adultery." .... MATT 19:9
m a woman divorced from her husband .... LUKE 16:18

MARRY
neither *m* nor are given in marriage, ... MATT 22:30
to *m* than to burn with sexual desire. .... 1 COR 7:9
Let them *m* .... 1 COR 7:36
So I want younger women to *m* .... 1 TIM 5:14

MARTHA
Sister of Mary and Lazarus (Luke 10:38-42; John 11; 12:2).

MARVELOUS
meditate on your *m* teachings. .... PS 119:27
Your rules are *m* .... PS 119:129
out of darkness into his *m* light. .... 1 PET 2:9

MARY
1. Mother of Jesus (Matt 1:16-25; Luke 1:27-56; 2:1-40). With Jesus at temple (Luke 2:41-52), at the wedding in Cana (John 2:1-5), questioning his sanity (Mark 3:21), at the cross (John 19:25-27). Among disciples after Ascension (Acts 1:14).
2. Magdalene; former demoniac (Luke 8:2). Helped support Jesus' ministry (Luke 8:1-3). At the cross (Matt 27:56; Mark 15:40; John 19:25), burial (Matt 27:61; Mark 15:47). Saw angel after resurrection (Matt 28:1-10; Mark 16:1-9; Luke 24:1-12); also Jesus (John 20:1-18).
3. Sister of Martha and Lazarus (John 11). Washed Jesus' feet (John 12:1-8).

MASTER
nor a slave greater than his *m* .... MATT 10:24
whom the *m* finds at work when he comes .... MATT 24:46
His *m* answered, ... MATT 25:21
Before his own *m* he stands or falls. .... ROM 14:4
useful for the *M* .... 2 TIM 2:21
denying the *M* who bought them. .... 2 PET 2:1

MASTER-BUILDER
like a skilled *m* I laid a foundation, ... 1 COR 3:10

MASTERS
No one can serve two *m* .... MATT 6:24
Slaves, obey your human *m* .... EPH 6:5
M treat your slaves the same way, ... EPH 6:9
subject to their own *m* in everything, ... TITUS 2:9

MASTERY
For sin will have no *m* over you, ... ROM 6:14

MATTER
one who is trustworthy conceals a *m* .... PROV 11:13
deals wisely in a *m* will find success, ... PROV 16:20
when the *m* is unpleasant, ... ECCL 8:3

MATTHEW
Apostle; former tax collector (Matt 9:9-13; 10:3; Mark 3:18; Luke 6:15; Acts 1:13). Also called Levi (Mark 2:14-17; Luke 5:27-32).

MATURE
but in your thinking be *m* .... 1 COR 14:20
But solid food is for the *m* .... HEB 5:14

MATURITY
and move on to *m* .... HEB 6:1

MEAL
But when you host an elaborate *m* .... LUKE 14:13
his own birthright for a single *m* .... HEB 12:16

MEANS
so that by all *m* I may save some. .... 1 COR 9:22
and beyond their *m* .... 2 COR 8:3

MEAT
It is good not to eat *m* or drink wine .... ROM 14:21

MEDIATES
the covenant that he *m* is also better .... HEB 8:6

MEDIATOR
And so he is the *m* of a new covenant, ... HEB 9:15
the *m* of a new covenant, ... HEB 12:24

MEDITATE
M as you lie in bed, ... PS 4:4
I will *m* on your precepts .... PS 119:15
But I *m* on your precepts. .... PS 119:78
All day long I *m* on it. .... PS 119:97

MEDITATES
he *m* on his commands day and night. .... PS 1:2

MEEK
Blessed are the *m* .... MATT 5:5

MEEKNESS
by the *m* and gentleness of Christ .... 2 COR 10:1

MEET
Loyal love and faithfulness *m* .... PS 85:10
prepare to *m* your God, ... AMOS 4:12
in the clouds to *m* the Lord in the air. .. 1 THESS 4:17

MEETINGS
not abandoning our own *m* .... HEB 10:25

MIRE
wallows in the *m* .... 2 PET 2:22

MIRIAM
Sister of Moses and Aaron (Num 26:59). Led dancing at Red Sea (Exod 15:20-21). Struck with leprosy for criticizing Moses (Num 12). Death (Num 20:1).

MIRROR
who gazes at his own face in a *m* .... JAS 1:23

MISDEEDS
he does not repay us as our *m* deserve. .... PS 103:10

MISERIES
Weep and cry aloud over the *m* .... JAS 5:1

MISERY
ruin and *m* are in their paths, ... ROM 3:16

MISLEAD
and they will *m* many. .... MATT 24:5

MIST
as fleeting as the morning *m* .... HOS 6:4

MISTREATED
if you sin and are *m* and endure it? ...... 1 PET 2:20

MIZPAH
It was also called *M* because he said, ... GEN 31:49

MOCK
Fools *m* at reparation, ... PROV 14:9
They will *m* him, ... MARK 10:34

MOCKED
but if you have *m* .... PROV 9:12
they *m* him: .... MATT 27:29

MOCKER
corrects a *m* is asking for insult; .... PROV 9:7
Wine is a *m* and strong drink is a .... PROV 20:1

MOCKING
experts in the law and elders —were *m* .. MATT 27:41

MODESTY
with *m* and self-control. .... 1 TIM 2:9

MOLDED
Does what is *m* say to the molder, ... ROM 9:20

MOMENT
the joy of the godless lasts but a *m* .... JOB 20:5
For his anger lasts only a brief *m* .... PS 30:5
Can a nation be born in a single *m* .... ISA 66:8
in a *m* .... 1 COR 15:52
did not surrender to them even for a *m* .... GAL 2:5

MONEY
will never be satisfied with *m* .... ECCL 5:10
You who have no *m* .... ISA 55:1
Why spend your hard-earned *m* .... ISA 55:2
You cannot serve God and *m* .... MATT 6:24
"Take *m* from no one by violence .... LUKE 3:14
no *m* and do not take an extra tunic. ...... LUKE 9:3
free from the love of *m* .... 1 TIM 3:3
love of *m* is the root of all evils. .... 1 TIM 6:10
lovers of *m* .... 2 TIM 3:2
must be free from the love of *m* .... HEB 13:5

MOON
or the *m* by night. .... PS 121:6
and the *m* to the color of blood, ... JOEL 2:31
and another glory of the *m* .... 1 COR 15:41

MORALE
your *m* and the firmness of your faith ...... COL 2:5

MORALS
"Bad company corrupts good *m* .... 1 COR 15:33

MORE
we should be pitied *m* than anyone. ..... 1 COR 15:19

MORNING
and there was *m* .... GEN 1:5
'I wish it were *m* .... DEUT 28:67
in the *m* I will present my case to you .... PS 5:3
the bright *m* star!" .... REV 22:16

MOSES
Then *M* summoned all the elders ...... EXOD 12:21

MOSES
Levite; brother of Aaron (Exod 6:20; 1 Chr 6:3). Put in basket into Nile; discovered and raised by Pharaoh's daughter (Exod 2:1-10). Fled to Midian after killing Egyptian (Exod 2:11-15). Married to Zipporah, fathered Gershom (Exod 2:16-22).

Called by the LORD to deliver Israel (Exod 3-4). Pharaoh's resistance (Exod 5). Ten plagues (Exod 7-11). Passover and Exodus (Exod 12-13). Led Israel through Red Sea (Exod 14). Song of deliverance (Exod 15:1-21). Brought water from rock (Exod 17:1-7). Raised hands to defeat Amalekites (Exod 17:8-16). Delegated judges (Exod 18; Deut 1:9-18).

Received Law at Sinai (Exod 19-23; 25-31; John 1:17). Announced Law to Israel (Exod 19:7-8; 24; 35). Broke tablets because of golden calf (Exod 32; Deut 9). Saw glory of the LORD(Exod 33-34). Supervised building of tabernacle (Exod 36-40). Set apart Aaron and priests (Lev 8-9). Numbered tribes (Num 1-4; 26). Opposed by Aaron and Miriam (Num 12). Sent spies into Canaan (Num 13). Announced forty years of wandering for failure to enter land (Num 14). Opposed by Korah (Num 16). Forbidden to enter land for striking rock (Num 20:1-13; Deut 1:37). Lifted bronze snake for healing (Num 21:4-9; John 3:14). Final address to Israel (Deut 1-33). Succeeded by Joshua (Num 27:12-23; Deut 34). Death (Deut 34:5-12).

"Law of Moses" (1 Kgs 2:3; Ezra 3:2; Luke 24:44). "Book of Moses" (Ezra 6:18; Neh 13:1; Mark 12:26). "Song of Moses" (Exod 15:1-21; Rev 15:3). "Prayer of Moses" (Ps 90).

MOST
making the *m* of the opportunities. .... COL 4:5

MOTH
where *m* and devouring insect destroy .. MATT 6:19

MOTHER
a man leaves his father and *m* .... GEN 2:24
she was the *m* of all the living. .... GEN 3:20
Honor your father and your *m* .... EXOD 20:12
If anyone curses his father or *m* .... LEV 20:9
Honor your father and your *m* .... DEUT 5:16
pays no attention to his father or *m* ... DEUT 21:18
one who disrespects his father and *m* .. DEUT 27:16
His *m* used to make him a small robe .... 1 SAM 2:19

a happy *m* of children. PS 113:9
the teaching from your *m* PROV 1:8
May your father and your *m* have joy; PROV 23:25
unrestrained brings shame to his *m* PROV 29:15
an oracle that his *m* taught him: PROV 31:1
As a *m* consoles a child, ISA 66:13
Whoever loves father or *m* more than me MATT 10:37
'Whoever insults his father or *m* MATT 15:4
a man will leave his father and *m* MATT 19:5
'insults his father or *m* MARK 7:10
honor your father and *m* MARK 10:19
here is your *m* JOHN 19:27

MOTHER'S
"Naked I came from my *m* womb, JOB 1:21

MOTIVES
based on your evaluation of his *m* 1 KGS 8:39
always maintain these *m* of your people 1 CHR 29:18
you who examine inner thoughts and *m* PS 7:9
Evaluate my inner thoughts and *m* PS 26:2
but the LORD evaluates the *m* PROV 16:2
and reveal the *m* of hearts. 1 COR 4:5

MOUNTAIN
Let's go up to the LORD's *m* MIC 4:2
you will say to this *m* MATT 17:20

MOUNTAINS
over the *m* the feet of a messenger ISA 52:7
m and hills will give a joyful shout ISA 55:12
have all faith so that I can remove *m* 1 COR 13:2

MOURN
a time to *m* ECCL 3:4
to console all who *m* ISA 61:2
Blessed are those who *m* MATT 5:4

MOURNING
we wailed in *m* MATT 11:17
m or crying, REV 21:4

MOUTH
my *m* will continually praise him. PS 34:1
words are sweeter in my *m* than honey! PS 119:103
and not your own *m* PROV 27:2
m speaks from what fills the heart. MATT 12:34
what comes out of the *m* that defiles MATT 15:11
confess with your *m* that Jesus is Lord ROM 10:9
abusive language from your *m* COL 3:8

MOUTHS
From the *m* of children PS 8:2
'Out of the *m* of children MATT 21:16

MOVED
'I am very much *m* for Jerusalem ZECH 1:14

MUD
out of the slimy *m* PS 40:2
its waves toss up *m* and sand. ISA 57:20

MULTIPLY
"Be fruitful and *m* and fill the water GEN 1:22
The LORD will greatly *m* your children, DEUT 28:11

MULTITUDE
because love covers a *m* of sins. 1 PET 4:8

MURDER
You shall not *m* EXOD 20:13
m adultery, sexual immorality, MATT 15:19
do not *m* ROM 13:9
"Do not *m* JAS 2:11

MURDERER
he is a *m* NUM 35:16
He was a *m* from the beginning, JOHN 8:44
no *m* has eternal life residing in him 1 JOHN 3:15

MURDERERS
kill their fathers or mothers, for *m* 1 TIM 1:9
m the sexually immoral, REV 21:8

MURKY
a light shining in a *m* place, 2 PET 1:19

MUSIC
making *m* in your hearts to the LORD, EPH 5:19

MUSTARD
if you have faith the size of a *m* seed MATT 17:20

MUZZLE
must not *m* your ox when it is treading DEUT 25:4
I will put a *m* over my mouth PS 39:1
"Do not *m* an ox while it is treading 1 COR 9:9

MYRRH
gifts of gold, frankincense, and *m* MATT 2:11
They offered him wine mixed with *m* MARK 15:23

MYSTERY
according to the revelation of the *m* ROM 16:25
Listen, I will tell you a *m* 1 COR 15:51
This *m* is great—but EPH 5:32
the *m* that has been kept hidden COL 1:26
holding to the *m* of the faith 1 TIM 3:9

MYTHS
those *m* fit only for the godless 1 TIM 4:7

NADAB
Son of Jeroboam I; king of Israel (1 Kgs 15:25-32).

NAILING
you executed by *n* him to a cross ACTS 2:23
taken it away by *n* it to the cross. COL 2:14

NAILS
the wounds from the *n* in his hands, JOHN 20:25

NAKED
The man and his wife were both *n* GEN 2:25
and *n* I will return there. JOB 1:21
When you see someone *n* ISA 58:7
we will not be found *n* 2 COR 5:3
but everything is *n* and exposed HEB 4:13

NAME
This is my *n* forever, EXOD 3:15
anyone who takes his *n* in vain. EXOD 20:7
anyone who abuses his *n* that way. DEUT 5:11
fear this glorious and awesome *n* DEUT 28:58
Let us praise his *n* together. PS 34:3
praise his holy *n* PS 103:1
A good *n* is to be chosen PROV 22:1
and what is his son's *n* PROV 30:4
he calls them all by *n* ISA 40:26
whose *n* is holy: ISA 57:15
intervene for the honor of your *n* JER 14:7
who calls on the *n* of the LORD JOEL 2:32
will be seen as one with a single *n* ZECH 14:9
a son and you will *n* him Jesus, MATT 1:21
may your *n* be honored, MATT 6:9
two or three are assembled in my *n* MATT 18:20

He calls his own sheep by *n* .... JOHN 10:3
have not asked for anything in my *n* .... JOHN 16:24
no other *n* under heaven given .... ACTS 4:12
who calls on the *n* of the Lord .... ROM 10:13
the name that is above every *n* .... PHIL 2:9
do it all in the *n* of the Lord Jesus, ... COL 3:17
has inherited a *n* superior to theirs. .... HEB 1:4

NAMED
to preach where Christ has not been *n* .. ROM 15:20

NAMES
he *n* all of them. .... PS 147:4

NAOMI
Mother-in-law of Ruth (Ruth 1). Advised Ruth to seek marriage with Boaz (Ruth 2-4).

NARROW
Enter through the *n* gate, ... MATT 7:13

NATHANAEL
Apostle (John 1:45-49; 21:2). Probably also called Bartholomew (Matt 10:3).

NATION
Then I will make you into a great *n* .... GEN 12:2
the *n* whose God is the LORD, ... PS 33:12
Righteousness exalts a *n* .... PROV 14:34
to a *n* that did not invoke my name. .... ISA 65:1
a holy *n* .... 1 PET 2:9
made up of persons from every *n* .... REV 7:9

NATIONS
the father of a multitude of *n* .... GEN 17:4
the *n* on the earth may receive .... GEN 18:18
special possession out of all the *n* .... EXOD 19:5
I will scatter you among the *n* .... NEH 1:8
Tell the *n* about his splendor. .... PS 96:3
the *n* are like a drop in a bucket; .... ISA 40:15
and a light to the *n* .... ISA 42:6
The *n* will know that I am the LORD, ... EZEK 36:23
n and language groups were serving .... DAN 7:14
I will also shake up all the *n* .... HAG 2:7
people from all languages and *n* .... ZECH 8:23
gather all the *n* against Jerusalem .... ZECH 14:2
go and make disciples of all *n* .... MATT 28:19
The *n* will walk by its light .... REV 21:24

NATURAL
it is sown a *n* body, ... 1 COR 15:44

NATURE
eternal power and divine *n*—have .... ROM 1:20

NAZARENE
that Jesus would be called a *N* .... MATT 2:23

NEAR
The LORD is *n* the brokenhearted; .... PS 34:18
your redemption is drawing *n* .... LUKE 21:28
let us draw *n* with a sincere heart .... HEB 10:22

NEARBY
shepherds *n* living out in the field, ... LUKE 2:8

NEBUCHADNEZZAR
N exclaimed, "Praised be the God .... DAN 3:28

NECESSARY
Therefore it is *n* to be in subjection .... ROM 13:5

NECROMANCER
a practitioner of the occult, or a *n* .... DEUT 18:11

NEED
knows what you *n* before you ask him. ... MATT 6:8
"I do not *n* you." .... 1 COR 12:21
And my God will supply your every *n* ..... PHIL 4:19
and sees his fellow Christian in *n* .... 1 JOHN 3:17

NEEDLE
a camel to go through the eye of a *n* ... MATT 19:24

NEEDS
Contribute to the *n* of the saints, ... ROM 12:13

NEEDY
He generously gives to the *n* .... PS 112:9
whoever is kind to the *n* is blessed. ...... PROV 14:21
honors him shows favor to the *n* .... PROV 14:31
and extended her hands to the *n* ...... PROV 31:20

NEGLECT
We will not *n* the temple of our God." ... NEH 10:39
yet you *n* what is more important ...... MATT 23:23
n the word of God to wait on tables. .... ACTS 6:2
Do not *n* the spiritual gift you have, ... 1 TIM 4:14
if we *n* such a great salvation? .... HEB 2:3

NEHEMIAH
Cupbearer of Artaxerxes (Neh 2:1); governor of Israel (Neh 8:9). Returned to Jerusalem to rebuild walls (Neh 2-6). With Ezra, reestablished worship (Neh 8). Prayer confessing nation's sin (Neh 9). Dedicated wall (Neh 12).

NEIGHBOR
false testimony against your *n* .... EXOD 20:16
but you must love your *n* as yourself. ..... LEV 19:18
a *n* nearby is better than a brother ...... PROV 27:10
and love your *n* as yourself." .... MATT 19:19
"And who is my *n* .... LUKE 10:29
Love does no wrong to a *n* .... ROM 13:10

NEIGHBOR'S
You shall not covet your *n* wife, ... EXOD 20:17
must not encroach on your *n*
property, ... DEUT 19:14
too frequently in your *n* house, ... PROV 25:17

NEVER
wilderness they *n* lacked anything. .... NEH 9:21

NEVERTHELESS
N each one of you must also love .... EPH 5:33

NEW
He gave me reason to sing a *n* song, ... PS 40:3
there is nothing truly *n* on earth. .... ECCL 1:9
to create new heavens and a *n* earth! ...... ISA 65:17
make a *n* covenant with the people .... JER 31:31
and I will put a *n* spirit within you. ...... EZEK 36:26
put new wine into *n* wineskins .... MATT 9:17
the *n* covenant in my blood. .... LUKE 22:20
what is *n* has come! .... 2 COR 5:17
and to put on the *n* man .... EPH 4:24
new heavens and a *n* earth, ... 2 PET 3:13
I am writing a *n* commandment
to you .... 1 JOHN 2:8

NEWBORN
And yearn like *n* infants for pure, ... 1 PET 2:2

NEWS
good *n* that brings great joy to all .... LUKE 2:10
the good *n* that Jesus was the Christ. ..... ACTS 5:42
proclaiming the good *n* of the word. .... ACTS 8:4
proclaiming the good *n* about Jesus ...... ACTS 17:18
those who proclaim the good *n* .... ROM 10:15

NICODEMUS
Pharisee who visited Jesus at night (John 3). Argued fair treatment of Jesus (John 7:50-52). With Joseph, prepared Jesus for burial (John 19:38-42).

NIGHT
who gives songs in the *n* ... JOB 35:10
he meditates on his commands day and *n* ... PS 1:2
You need not fear the terrors of the *n* ... PS 91:5
came to Jesus at *n* and said to him, ... JOHN 3:2
as a thief in the *n* ... 1 THESS 5:2
are not of the *n* nor of the darkness. ... 1 THESS 5:5
(and there will be no *n* there). ... REV 21:25

NO
Plans fail when there is *n* counsel, ... PROV 15:22
wisdom with *n* true value—they ... COL 2:23

NOAH
Righteous man (Ezek 14:14, 20) called to build ark (Gen 6-8; Heb 11:7; 1 Pet 3:20; 2 Pet 2:5). God's covenant with (Gen 9:1-17). Drunkenness of (Gen 9:18-23). Blessed sons, cursed Canaan (Gen 9:24-27).

NOBLE
A *n* wife is the crown of her husband, ... PROV 12:4

NOBLES
The *n* of the nations assemble, ... PS 47:9

NON-CHRISTIANS
and maintain good conduct among the *n* ... 1 PET 2:12

NOTE
take *n* of Jesus, ... HEB 3:1

NOTHING
N is too hard for you! ... JER 32:17
apart from me you can accomplish *n* ... JOHN 15:5

NOTICE
that you should *n* them? ... PS 8:4

NOURISH
for something that will not *n* you? ... ISA 55:2

NOW
N if you forget the LORD your God ... DEUT 8:19
N if you pay close attention ... DEUT 11:13
N my dear, don't worry! ... RUTH 3:11
N O Lord our God, ... DAN 9:15
N many miraculous signs and wonders ... ACTS 5:12
"About a year from *n* I will return ... ROM 9:9

NULLIFY
Do we then *n* the law through faith? ... ROM 3:31

NUMBER
when the disciples were growing in *n* ... ACTS 6:1

OATHS
do not take *o* at all—not ... MATT 5:34

OBEDIENCE
and sacrifices as much as he does in *o* ... 1 SAM 15:22
the *o* of faith among all the Gentiles ... ROM 1:5
or *o* resulting in righteousness? ... ROM 6:16

OBEDIENT
and was *o* to them. ... LUKE 2:51
by becoming *o* to the point of death ... PHIL 2:8
Like *o* children, ... 1 PET 1:14

OBEY
o him, serve him, ... DEUT 13:4
and *o* him with your whole mind ... DEUT 30:2
to *o* him and be loyal to him, ... DEUT 30:20
those who *o* them receive a rich reward ... PS 19:11
by giving me the desire to *o* ... PS 51:12
To *o* the LORD is the fundamental ... PS 111:10
to *o* everything I have commanded you. ... MATT 28:20
he will *o* my word, ... JOHN 14:23
"We must *o* God rather than people. ... ACTS 5:29
you are slaves of the one you *o* ... ROM 6:16
he is obligated to *o* the whole law. ... GAL 5:3
Children, *o* your parents in the Lord, ... EPH 6:1
Slaves, *o* your human masters ... EPH 6:5
o your parents in everything, ... COL 3:20
O your leaders and submit to them, ... HEB 13:17

OBEYED
and they have *o* your word. ... JOHN 17:6
By faith Abraham *o* when he was called ... HEB 11:8
like Sarah who *o* Abraham, ... 1 PET 3:6

OBEYING
He will take delight in *o* the LORD. ... ISA 11:3

OBEYS
For the one who *o* the whole law ... JAS 2:10

OBLIGATED
he is *o* to obey the whole law. ... GAL 5:3

OBSERVE
You must *o* this event as an ordinance ... EXOD 12:24
command your children to *o* carefully ... DEUT 32:46
You carefully *o* me when I travel ... PS 139:3

OBSERVES
who *o* the day does it for the Lord. ... ROM 14:6

OBSOLETE
he makes the first *o* ... HEB 8:13

OBSTACLE
the *o* leading to their iniquity. ... EZEK 7:19
never to place an *o* or a trap ... ROM 14:13

OBTAINED
he *o* with the blood of his own Son. ... ACTS 20:28
did not pursue righteousness *o* it, ... ROM 9:30

OCCUPY
"Let us go up and *o* it, ... NUM 13:30

ODOR
an *o* from death to death, ... 2 COR 2:16

OFF
and its leaves never fall *o* ... PS 1:3
slacked *o* in the day of trouble ... PROV 24:10
strayed *o* on his own path, ... ISA 53:6

OFFENSE
The one who forgives an *o* seeks love, ... PROV 17:9
and it is his glory to overlook an *o* ... PROV 19:11
for taking an *o* in anything, ... 2 COR 6:3

OFFENSES
you were dead in your *o* and sins, ... EPH 2:1

OFFENSIVE
anyone who does this is *o* to the LORD ... DEUT 22:5

OFFER
O him up there as a burnt offering ... GEN 22:2

o sacrifices first for their own sins .... HEB 7:27
they *o* their crowns before his throne ..... REV 4:10

OFFERED
o once to bear the sins of many, ... HEB 9:28

OFFERING
for himself the lamb for the burnt *o* .... GEN 22:8
a sacrificial and fragrant *o* to God. .... EPH 5:2
"Sacrifice and *o* you did not desire, ... HEB 10:5

OFFERINGS
burnt sacrifices and sin *o* .... PS 40:6
than all burnt *o* and sacrifices." .... MARK 12:33

OFFSPRING
and between your offspring and her *o* ..... GEN 3:15

OIL
You refresh my head with *o* .... PS 23:5
o symbolizing joy, ... ISA 61:3
with the *o* of rejoicing." .... HEB 1:9

OINTMENT
medicinal *o* available in Gilead! .... JER 8:22

OLIVES
Can a fig tree produce *o* .... JAS 3:12

OMEGA
I am the Alpha and the *O* .... REV 1:8

OMRI
King of Israel (1 Kgs 16:21-26).

ONCE
delivered *o* and for all by the LORD; .... ISA 45:17

ONE
o who lives in the shelter .... PS 91:1
my flawless *o* .... SONG 5:2
the favorite of the *o* who bore her. .... SONG 6:9
says the Holy *O* .... ISA 40:25
O barren *o* who has not given birth! .... ISA 54:1
I will give them *o* heart .... EZEK 11:19
but deliver us from the evil *o* .... MATT 6:13
his chosen *o* .... LUKE 23:35
you keep them safe from the evil *o* ...... JOHN 17:15
nor permit your Holy *O* to experience ... ACTS 2:27
but we an imperishable *o* .... 1 COR 9:25
all the flaming arrows of the evil *o* .... EPH 6:16
the husband of *o* wife, ... 1 TIM 3:2

ONLY
O that in every way, ... PHIL 1:18

OPEN
o the scroll and its seven seals." .... REV 5:5

OPENED
knock and the door will be *o* for you. ..... MATT 7:7

OPENING
Protect the *o* of my lips. .... PS 141:3

OPPORTUNITIES
making the most of the *o* .... COL 4:5

OPPORTUNITY
seizing the *o* .... ROM 7:11
whenever we have an *o* .... GAL 6:10
Do not give the devil an *o* .... EPH 4:27
taking advantage of every *o* .... EPH 5:16
give the adversary no *o* to vilify us. .... 1 TIM 5:14

OPPRESS
a resident foreigner nor *o* him, ... EXOD 22:21
You must not *o* your neighbor .... LEV 19:13
must not *o* a lowly and poor servant, ... DEUT 24:14
You must not *o* the widow, ... ZECH 7:10

OPPRESSED
the LORD provides safety for the *o* .... PS 9:9
But the *o* will possess the land .... PS 37:11
Vindicate the *o* and suffering. .... PS 82:3

ORDAINED
and nursing babies you have *o* praise .... PS 8:2

ORDER
he will *o* his angels to protect you .... PS 91:11
worlds were set in *o* at God's command, .. HEB 11:3

ORDINANCE
resists the *o* of God, ... ROM 13:2

ORPHAN
who justly treats the *o* and widow, ... DEUT 10:18
due a resident foreigner or an *o* .... DEUT 24:17
o and widow so that the LORD
your God .... DEUT 24:19

ORPHANS
I will not abandon you as *o* .... JOHN 14:18
for *o* and widows in their adversity .... JAS 1:27

OTHERS
overtaken you that is not faced by *o* ... 1 COR 10:13
sharing with *o* .... 1 TIM 6:18

OUTCOME
reflect on the *o* of their lives .... HEB 13:7

OUTLOOK
the *o* of the flesh is hostile to God, ... ROM 8:7

OUTSIDERS
yourselves with wisdom toward *o* .... COL 4:5
live a decent life before *o* .... 1 THESS 4:12

OUTSTANDING
Always be *o* in the work of the Lord, ... 1 COR 15:58

OUTSTRETCHED
and I will redeem you with an *o* arm ...... EXOD 6:6
with a powerful hand and an *o* arm ..... EZEK 20:33

OVER
like a shepherd watches *o* his flock." .... JER 31:10
given *o* because of our transgressions .... ROM 4:25

OVERCOME
rejoice before God and are *o* with joy. .... PS 68:3
but *o* evil with good. .... ROM 12:21

OVERFLOW
the sufferings of Christ *o* toward us, ... 2 COR 1:5

OVERJOYED
I will be *o* because of my God. .... ISA 61:10
was so *o* she did not open the gate, ... ACTS 12:14

OVERLOOK
he did not *o* their cry for help .... PS 9:12

OVERPOWER
and the gates of Hades will not *o* it. .... MATT 16:18

OVERSEER
"If someone aspires to the office of *o* ...... 1 TIM 3:1
The *o* then must be above reproach, ... 1 TIM 3:2
For the *o* must be blameless .... TITUS 1:7

OVERSEERS
the Holy Spirit has made you *o* .... ACTS 20:28
with the *o* and deacons. .... PHIL 1:1

OVERTURNS
who *o* the counsel of the wise men .... ISA 44:25

OVERWHELM
For my sins *o* me; ... PS 38:4

OVERWHELMS
Our record of sins *o* me, ... PS 65:3

OWE
O no one anything, ... ROM 13:8
you *o* me your very self. ... PHLM 19

OWED
Pay everyone what is *o* ... ROM 13:7

OWN
a man's enemies are his *o* family. ... MIC 7:6
Do not seek your *o* good, ... 1 COR 10:24

OX
You must not muzzle your *o* ... DEUT 25:4
like an *o* ... ISA 11:7
"Do not muzzle an *o* ... 1 COR 9:9

PAIN
person is chastened by *p* on his bed, ... JOB 33:19
p and was acquainted with illness; ... ISA 53:3

PAINFUL
all discipline seems *p* at the time, ... HEB 12:11

PAINS
"I will greatly increase your labor *p* ... GEN 3:16

PALACE
But the LORD is in his majestic *p* ... HAB 2:20

PALMS
inscribed your name on my *p* ... ISA 49:16

PANIC
Don't be afraid and don't *p* ... JOSH 1:9
"Don't be afraid and don't *p* ... JOSH 10:25
Don't be afraid and don't *p* ... 1 CHR 28:20

PARADISE
today you will be with me in *p* ... LUKE 23:43
was caught up into *p* and heard things .. 2 COR 12:4
tree of life that is in the *p* of God. ... REV 2:7

PARALYTIC
Some people came bringing to him a *p* .. MARK 2:3

PARCHED
like a root out of *p* soil; ... ISA 53:2

PARDONED
whose sin is *p* ... PS 32:1

PARDONS
Who forgives sin and *p* the rebellion ... MIC 7:18

PARENTS
and the glory of children is their *p* ... PROV 17:6
brings shame to his *p* ... PROV 28:7
or wife or brothers or *p* or children ... LUKE 18:29
You will be betrayed even by *p* ... LUKE 21:16
disobedient to *p* ... ROM 1:30
but *p* for their children. ... 2 COR 12:14
Children, obey your *p* in the Lord, ... EPH 6:1
Children, obey your *p* in everything, ... COL 3:20
disobedient to *p* ... 2 TIM 3:2

PART
blessed the second *p* of Job's life ... JOB 42:12

PARTIALITY
and you must not show *p* to a poor man .. EXOD 23:3
p and bribery." ... 2 CHR 19:7

PARTNERS
p with those who do not believe, ... 2 COR 6:14

PARTNERSHIP
what *p* is there between righteousness ... 2 COR 6:14

PARTS
torch passed between the animal *p* ... GEN 15:17

PASS
when I see the blood I will *p* over ... EXOD 12:13

PASSION
shameful *p* evil desire, ... COL 3:5

PASSIONS
the flesh with its *p* and desires. ... GAL 5:24
But keep away from youthful *p* ... 2 TIM 2:22
from your *p* that battle inside you? ... JAS 4:1

PASSOVER
keep the *P* to the LORD your God, ... DEUT 16:1

PASTORS
and some as *p* and teachers, ... EPH 4:11

PASTURE
the sheep of his *p* ... PS 100:3
their true *p* ... JER 50:7
and find *p* ... JOHN 10:9

PASTURES
He takes me to lush *p* ... PS 23:2

PATCH
p will pull away from the garment ... MATT 9:16

PATH
lead me along a level *p* ... PS 27:11
and a light to illumine my *p* ... PS 119:105
p of the righteous is like the bright ... PROV 4:18
the *p* of the upright is like a highway. ... PROV 15:19
The *p* of life is upward for the wise ... PROV 15:24
of us had strayed off on his own *p* ... ISA 53:6

PATHS
He leads me down the right *p* ... PS 23:3
and he will make your *p* straight. ... PROV 3:6
and make straight *p* for your feet, ... HEB 12:13

PATHWAY
But he knows the *p* that I take; ... JOB 23:10
or stand in the *p* with sinners, ... PS 1:1

PATIENCE
by *p* by benevolence, ... 2 COR 6:6
p kindness, goodness, ... GAL 5:22
with *p* putting up with one another ... EPH 4:2
the display of all *p* and steadfastness, ... COL 1:11
humility, gentleness, and *p* ... COL 3:12

PATIENT
Love is *p* ... 1 COR 13:4
be *p* toward all. ... 1 THESS 5:14

PAUL
Also called Saul (Acts 13:9). Pharisee from Tarsus (Acts 9:11; Phil 3:5). Apostle (Gal 1). At stoning of Stephen (Acts 8:1). Persecuted Church (Acts 9:1-2; Gal 1:13). Vision of Jesus on road to Damascus (Acts 9:4-9; 26:12-18). In Arabia (Gal 1:17). Preached in Damascus; escaped death through the wall in a basket (Acts 9:19-25). In Jerusalem; sent back to Tarsus (Acts 9:26-30).

Brought to Antioch by Barnabas (Acts 11:22-26). First missionary journey to Cyprus and Galatia (Acts 13-14). Stoned at Lystra (Acts 14:19-20). At Jerusalem council (Acts 15). Split with Barnabas over Mark (Acts 15:36-41).

Second missionary journey with Silas (Acts 16-20). Called to Macedonia (Acts 16:6-10). Freed from prison in Philippi (Acts 16:16-40). In Thessalonica (Acts 17:1-9). Speech in Athens (Acts 17:16-33). In Corinth (Acts 18). In Ephesus (Acts 19). Return to Jerusalem (Acts 20). Farewell to Ephesian elders (Acts 20:13-38). Arrival in Jerusalem (Acts 21:1-26). Arrested (Acts 21:27-36). Addressed crowds (Acts 22), Sanhedrin (Acts 23:1-11). Transferred to Caesarea (Acts 23:12-35). Trial before Felix (Acts 24), Festus (Acts 25:1-12). Before Agrippa (Acts 25:13–26:32). Voyage to Rome; shipwreck (Acts 27). Arrival in Rome (Acts 28).

PAY
and the curse if you *p* no attention ... DEUT 11:28
Is it right to *p* taxes to Caesar ... MATT 22:17
for the worker deserves his *p* ... LUKE 10:7
his *p* is not credited due to grace ... ROM 4:4
For this reason you also *p* taxes, ... ROM 13:6
P everyone what is owed: ... ROM 13:7

PAYMENT
the Spirit in our hearts as a down *p* ... 2 COR 1:22
who gave us the Spirit as a down *p* ... 2 COR 5:5
who is the down *p* of our inheritance, ... EPH 1:14

PAYOFF
For the *p* of sin is death, ... ROM 6:23

PAYS
rebellious son who *p* no attention ... DEUT 21:18

PEACE
upon you and give you *p* ... NUM 6:26
Strive for *p* and promote it. ... PS 34:14
deliverance and *p* greet each other ... PS 85:10
Pray for the *p* of Jerusalem. ... PS 122:6
Prince of *P* ... ISA 9:6
Then he will announce *p* to the nations ... ZECH 9:10
have not come to bring *p* but a sword! ... MATT 10:34
p among people with whom he is pleased ... LUKE 2:14
my *p* I give to you; ... JOHN 14:27
so that in me you may have *p* ... JOHN 16:33
we have *p* with God through our Lord ... ROM 5:1
let us pursue what makes for *p* ... ROM 14:19
God has called you in *p* ... 1 COR 7:15
not characterized by disorder but by *p* ... 1 COR 14:33
p patience, kindness, ... GAL 5:22
For he is our *p* ... EPH 2:14
And the *p* of God that surpasses ... PHIL 4:7
making *p* through the blood ... COL 1:20
called as one body to this *p* ... COL 3:15
"There is *p* and security," ... 1 THESS 5:3
Be at *p* among yourselves. ... 1 THESS 5:13
the Lord of peace himself give you *p* ... 2 THESS 3:16
and *p* in company with others ... 2 TIM 2:22
he must seek *p* and pursue it. ... 1 PET 3:11
permission to take *p* from the earth, ... REV 6:4

PEACEMAKERS
Blessed are the *p* ... MATT 5:9

PEARLS
or throw your *p* before pigs; ... MATT 7:6
like a merchant searching for fine *p* ... MATT 13:45
gold or *p* or expensive clothing, ... 1 TIM 2:9
And the twelve gates are twelve *p* —each ... REV 21:21

PEKAH
King of Israel (2 Kgs 15:25-31; Isa 7:1).

PEKAHIAH
Son of Menahem; king of Israel (2 Kgs 15:22-26).

PENTECOST
Now when the day of *P* had come, ... ACTS 2:1

PEOPLE
For the LORD's allotment is his *p* ... DEUT 32:9
Your people will become my *p* ... RUTH 1:16
if my *p* ... 2 CHR 7:14
Your *p* willingly follow you ... PS 110:3
or be envious of wicked *p* ... PROV 24:19
He was despised and rejected by *p* ... ISA 53:3
"Wise *p* should not boast ... JER 9:23
be their God and they will be my *p* ... JER 24:7
P will stream to it. ... MIC 4:1
and they will also be my *p* ... ZECH 2:11
and I will turn you into fishers of *p* ... MATT 4:19
that brings great joy to all the *p* ... LUKE 2:10
will draw all *p* to myself." ... JOHN 12:32
"We must obey God rather than *p* ... ACTS 5:29
among the Gentiles a *p* for his name. ... ACTS 15:14
death spread to all *p* ... ROM 5:12
but instead as *p* of the flesh, ... 1 COR 3:1
to associate with sexually immoral *p* ... 1 COR 5:9
the immoral *p* of this world, ... 1 COR 5:10
I have become all things to all *p* ... 1 COR 9:22
and they will be my *p* ... 2 COR 6:16
since he wants all *p* to be saved ... 1 TIM 2:4
entrust to faithful *p* ... 2 TIM 2:2
for himself a *p* who are truly his, ... TITUS 2:14
just as *p* are appointed to die once, ... HEB 9:27
Live as free *p* ... 1 PET 2:16
they entice unstable *p* ... 2 PET 2:14

PERCEIVE
but don't *p* ... ISA 6:9

PERFECT
be *p* as your heavenly Father is ... MATT 5:48
is good and well-pleasing and *p* ... ROM 12:2
for my power is made *p* in weakness." ... 2 COR 12:9
who are *p* embrace this point of view. ... PHIL 3:15
which is the *p* bond. ... COL 3:14
more *p* tent not made with hands, ... HEB 9:11
so that you will be *p* and complete, ... JAS 1:4
every *p* gift is from above, ... JAS 1:17
who peers into the *p* law of liberty ... JAS 1:25
he is a *p* individual, ... JAS 3:2
but *p* love drives out fear, ... 1 JOHN 4:18

PERFECTED
by one offering he has *p* for all time ... HEB 10:14
and his faith was *p* by works. ... JAS 2:22

PERFECTER
the pioneer and *p* of our faith. ... HEB 12:2

PERFECTION
So if *p* had in fact been possible ... HEB 7:11

PERFORMANCE
to another *p* of miracles, ... 1 COR 12:10

PERISH
They will *p* ... PS 102:26
you will all *p* as well! ... LUKE 13:3

and they will never *p* .... JOHN 10:28
These are all destined to *p* with use, ... COL 2:22
They will *p* .... HEB 1:11
he does not wish for any to *p* .... 2 PET 3:9

PERISHABLE
What is sown is *p* .... 1 COR 15:42

PERJURERS
p —in fact, ... 1 TIM 1:10

PERMANENT
a covenant of a *p* priesthood, ... NUM 25:13
Your throne, O God, is *p* .... PS 45:6
I claim your rules as my *p* possession, ... PS 119:111

PERPETUAL
from the Israelites as a *p* covenant. .... LEV 24:8
to bring in *p* righteousness, ... DAN 9:24

PERSECUTE
when people insult you and *p* you .... MATT 5:11
Bless those who *p* you, ... ROM 12:14

PERSECUTED
If they *p* me, ... JOHN 15:20
when *p* we endure, ... 1 COR 4:12
godly lives in Christ Jesus will be *p* .... 2 TIM 3:12

PERSECUTING
why are you *p* me?" .... ACTS 9:4

PERSECUTION
or *p* or famine, ... ROM 8:35

PERSEVERANCE
to *p* godliness; .... 2 PET 1:6

PERSEVERE
P in this, ... 1 TIM 4:16

PERSEVERED
he *p* as though he could see the one .... HEB 11:27

PERSIST
p in prayer. .... ROM 12:12

PERSON
can a young *p* maintain a pure life? .... PS 119:9
reprove a wise *p* and he will love you. .... PROV 9:8
the evil *p* will not be unpunished, ... PROV 11:21
The righteous *p* is cautious .... PROV 12:26
easy for a discerning *p* .... PROV 14:6
but the shrewd *p* discerns his steps. ...... PROV 14:15
a greater impression on a
  discerning *p* .... PROV 17:10
in front of the discerning *p* .... PROV 17:24
It is terrible to punish a righteous *p* .... PROV 17:26
the righteous *p* runs to it .... PROV 18:10
a poor *p* who walks in his integrity .... PROV 19:1
correct a discerning *p* .... PROV 19:25
for the evil *p* has no future, ... PROV 24:20
A poor *p* who walks in his integrity .... PROV 28:6
and a wise *p* knows the proper time .... ECCL 8:5
for a rich *p* to enter the kingdom .... MATT 19:23
"Every sin a *p* commits. .... 1 COR 6:18
Yet because I was a crafty *p* .... 2 COR 12:16
mature *p* attaining to the measure .... EPH 4:13
law is not intended for a righteous *p* ...... 1 TIM 1:9
and a poor *p* enters in filthy clothes, ... JAS 2:2

PERSON'S
A *p* gift makes room for him, ... PROV 18:16

PERSUADE
we try to *p* people, ... 2 COR 5:11

PERSUASIVENESS
and kind speech increases *p* .... PROV 16:21

PERVERSE
you live in a crooked and *p* society, ... PHIL 2:15

PERVERSELY
one who behaves *p* will be found out. .... PROV 10:9

PERVERSION
it is a *p* .... LEV 18:23

PERVERT
You must not *p* justice due a resident .... DEUT 24:17

PETER
Apostle, brother of Andrew, also called Simon (Matt 10:2; Mark 3:16; Luke 6:14; Acts 1:13), and Cephas (John 1:42). Confession of Christ (Matt 16:13-20; Mark 8:27-30; Luke 9:18-27). At transfiguration (Matt 17:1-8; Mark 9:2-8; Luke 9:28-36; 2 Pet 1:16-18). Caught fish with coin (Matt 17:24-27). Denial of Jesus predicted (Matt 26:31-35; Mark 14:27-31; Luke 22:31-34; John 13:31-38). Denied Jesus (Matt 26:69-75; Mark 14:66-72; Luke 22:54-62; John 18:15-27). Commissioned by Jesus to shepherd his flock (John 21:15-23).

Speech at Pentecost (Acts 2). Healed beggar (Acts 3:1-10). Speech at temple (Acts 3:11-26), before Sanhedrin (Acts 4:1-22). In Samaria (Acts 8:14-25). Sent by vision to Cornelius (Acts 10). Announced salvation of Gentiles in Jerusalem (Acts 11; 15). Freed from prison (Acts 12). Inconsistency at Antioch (Gal 2:11-21). At Jerusalem Council (Acts 15).

PETITION
With every prayer and *p* .... EPH 6:18

PHARISEES
of the experts in the law and the *P* ...... MATT 5:20

PHILIP
1. Apostle (Matt 10:3; Mark 3:18; Luke 6:14; John 1:43-48; 14:8; Acts 1:13).
2. Deacon (Acts 6:1-7); evangelist in Samaria (Acts 8:4-25), to Ethiopian (Acts 8:26-40).

PHILOSOPHY
deceitful *p* that is according to .... COL 2:8

PHYLACTERIES
for they make their *p* wide .... MATT 23:5

PHYSICAL
For *p* exercise has some value, ... 1 TIM 4:8

PHYSICIAN
"Those who are healthy don't need a *p* ... MATT 9:12

PIECES
cut in two and passed between its *p* .... JER 34:18

PIERCED
the one they have *p* .... ZECH 12:10
look on the one whom they have *p* ..... JOHN 19:37

PIGS
or throw your pearls before *p* .... MATT 7:6

PILATE
P said to them, ... MATT 27:65

Governor of Judea. Questioned Jesus (Matt 27:1-26; Mark 15:15; Luke 22:66–23:25; John 18:28–19:16); sent him to Herod (Luke 23:6-

12); consented to his crucifixion when crowds chose Barabbas (Matt 27:15-26; Mark 15:6-15; Luke 23:13-25; John 19:1-10).

p what has been entrusted to you. 1 TIM 6:20
is able to *p* what has been entrusted 2 TIM 1:12

PROTECTION
from whom you have sought *p* RUTH 2:12
find shelter in the *p* of your wings. PS 61:4
I run to you for *p* PS 143:9

PROTECTOR
May your *P* not sleep. PS 121:3

PROTECTS
The LORD strengthens and *p* me; PS 28:7
p those who seek refuge in him. NAH 1:7

PROUD
"God opposes the *p* JAS 4:6
because God opposes the *p* 1 PET 5:5

PROVE
if you *p* faithful, JOB 11:13

PROVEN
before God as a *p* worker 2 TIM 2:15

PROVES
LORD always *p* faithful and reliable PS 25:10
fruit that *p* your repentance, MATT 3:8

PROVIDE
God will *p* for himself the lamb GEN 22:8
if someone does not *p* for his own, 1 TIM 5:8

PROVIDED
God had *p* something better for us, HEB 11:40

PROVIDES
God who richly *p* us with all things 1 TIM 6:17

PROVISIONS
for the worker deserves his *p* MATT 10:10

PROVOKE
do not *p* your children to anger, EPH 6:4
Fathers, do not *p* your children, COL 3:21

PROVOKED
Do not let yourself be quickly *p* ECCL 7:9

PRUDENT
but a *p* wife is from the LORD. PROV 19:14

PSALMS
speaking to one another in *p* EPH 5:19
singing *p* hymns, COL 3:16

PUBLICLY
p and from house to house, ACTS 20:20

PUNISH
I will indeed *p* them for their sin." EXOD 32:34
do not *p* me for sins I am unaware of. PS 19:12
to *p* me in your raging fury. PS 38:1
I will *p* the world for its evil, ISA 13:11
those he commissions to *p* wrongdoers 1 PET 2:14

PUNISHES
For the LORD is a God who *p* JER 51:56

PUNISHMENT
all who take shelter in him escape *p* PS 34:22
How much greater *p* do you think HEB 10:29

PURE
and whose motives are *p* PS 24:4
Create for me a *p* heart, PS 51:10
young person maintain a *p* life? PS 119:9
Stay *p* you who carry the LORD's holy ISA 52:11
Blessed are the *p* in heart, MATT 5:8
present you as a *p* virgin to Christ. 2 COR 11:2
whatever is *p* PHIL 4:8
Keep yourself *p* 1 TIM 5:22
nothing is *p* TITUS 1:15
p fulfilling their duties at home, TITUS 2:5
just as Jesus is *p* 1 JOHN 3:3

PURIFIED
Every word of God is *p* PROV 30:5

PURIFIES
hope focused on him *p* himself, 1 JOHN 3:3

PURIFY
p for himself a people who are truly TITUS 2:14

PURITY
by *p* by knowledge, 2 COR 6:6
conduct, love, faithfulness, and *p* 1 TIM 4:12

PURPOSE
announcing to you the whole *p* of God. ACTS 20:27
who are called according to his *p* ROM 8:28
according to the *p* of him who EPH 1:11

PURPOSES
and carried out your *p* for us. PS 40:5

PURSES
p that do not wear out LUKE 12:33

PURSUE
goodness and faithfulness will *p* me PS 23:6
But above all *p* his kingdom MATT 6:33
needs of the saints, *p* hospitality. ROM 12:13
let us *p* what makes for peace ROM 14:19
P love and be eager for the spiritual 1 COR 14:1
and *p* righteousness, 2 TIM 2:22
P peace with everyone, HEB 12:14
he must seek peace and *p* it. 1 PET 3:11

PURSUED
immorality and *p* unnatural desire JUDE 7

PURSUES
My soul *p* you; PS 63:8

PUT
than to *p* you lower before a prince, PROV 25:7
because I *p* water in the wilderness ISA 43:20
has *p* his seal of approval on him." JOHN 6:27
P yourselves to the test 2 COR 13:5

QUARREL
but one who is slow to anger calms a *q* PROV 15:18
Starting a *q* is like letting out water; PROV 17:14
who loves a *q* loves transgression; PROV 17:19

QUICK-TEMPERED
A *q* person stirs up dissension, PROV 15:18

QUIET
we may lead a peaceful and *q* life 1 TIM 2:2

QUIETLY
A woman must learn *q* 1 TIM 2:11

QUIETNESS
a dry crust of bread where there is *q* PROV 17:1

QUIVER
the man who fills his *q* with them. PS 127:5

RACE
r is not always won by the swiftest, ECCL 9:11
I have finished the *r* 2 TIM 4:7
with endurance the *r* set out for us, HEB 12:1
But you are a chosen *r* 1 PET 2:9

RACHEL
Daughter of Laban (Gen 29:16); wife of Jacob (Gen 29:28); bore two sons (Gen 30:22-24; 35:16-24; 46:19).

RADIANCE
The Son is the *r* of his glory .... HEB 1:3

RADIANT
Look to him and be *r* .... PS 34:5

RAGE
and terrifies them in his *r* .... PS 2:5

RAIN
and sends *r* on the righteous .... MATT 5:45

RAINBOW
I will place my *r* in the clouds, ... GEN 9:13

RAISED
r for the sake of our justification. .... ROM 4:25
heart that God *r* him from the dead, ... ROM 10:9
and that he was *r* on the third day .... 1 COR 15:4

RANSOM
and to give his life as a *r* for many." .... MATT 20:28

RANSOMED
from your ancestors you were *r* .... 1 PET 1:18

RAVENS
The *r* would bring him bread .... 1 KGS 17:6
Consider the *r* .... LUKE 12:24

READ
understanding from what was *r* .... NEH 8:8
known and *r* by everyone, ... 2 COR 3:2

READING
to the public *r* of scripture, ... 1 TIM 4:13

READS
Blessed is the one who *r* the words .... REV 1:3

READY
all of you be *r* .... JOSH 8:4
the LORD is *r* to show you mercy; .... ISA 30:18
to make *r* a place for you. .... JOHN 14:2
be *r* whether it is convenient or not, ... 2 TIM 4:2
always be *r* to give an answer .... 1 PET 3:15

REALITY
but the *r* is Christ! .... COL 2:17

REALIZED
r as I desire and is fulfilled .... ISA 55:11

REALIZES
he *r* we are made of clay. .... PS 103:14

REALLY
Everything that he says *r* happens. .... 1 SAM 9:6
r understand that I came from you, ... JOHN 17:8

REALMS
in the heavenly *r* in Christ. .... EPH 1:3
at his right hand in the heavenly *r* .... EPH 1:20

REAP
those who sow trouble *r* the same. .... JOB 4:8
generously will also *r* generously. .... 2 COR 9:6
For a person will *r* what he sows, ... GAL 6:7
for in due time we will *r* .... GAL 6:9

REASON
For this *r* whoever is smart .... AMOS 5:13
I have no *r* for boasting, ... 1 COR 9:16
For this very *r* .... 2 PET 1:5

REASSURE
your rod and your staff *r* me. .... PS 23:4

REBEKAH
Sister of Laban, secured as bride for Isaac (Gen 24). Mother of Esau and Jacob (Gen 25:19-26). Taken by Abimelech as sister of Isaac; returned (Gen 26:1-11). Encouraged Jacob to trick Isaac out of blessing (Gen 27:1-17).

REBELLION
because of the *r* of his own people .... ISA 53:8
be charged with dissipation or *r* .... TITUS 1:6

REBELS
I will teach *r* your merciful ways, ... PS 51:13
intervened on behalf of the *r* .... ISA 53:12

REBUKE
the one who rejects *r* goes astray. .... PROV 10:17
Better is open *r* than hidden love. .... PROV 27:5
r him. If he repents, ... LUKE 17:3
r, exhort with complete patience .... 2 TIM 4:2
I *r* and discipline. .... REV 3:19

RECALL
R the miraculous deeds .... 1 CHR 16:12
don't *r* these former events. .... ISA 43:18

RECEIVE
r moral instruction in skillful living .... PROV 1:3
R my instruction rather than silver .... PROV 8:10
Listen to advice and *r* discipline, ... PROV 19:20
But you will *r* power .... ACTS 1:8
more blessed to give than to *r* .... ACTS 20:35
Do good and you will *r* .... ROM 13:3
R one another, ... ROM 15:7
I *r* no benefit. .... 1 COR 13:3
to *r* glory and honor and power, ... REV 4:11

RECEIVED
Freely you *r* .... MATT 10:8
r from the Lord what I also passed on .... 1 COR 11:23
just as you *r* Christ Jesus as Lord, ... COL 2:6
Just as each one has *r* a gift, ... 1 PET 4:10

RECEIVES
For everyone who asks *r* .... MATT 7:8
r forgiveness of sins through his .... ACTS 10:43

RECOGNITION
r of the LORD's sovereign majesty .... HAB 2:14

RECOGNIZE
"and *r* that I am God. .... PS 46:10
You will *r* them by their fruit. .... MATT 7:16

RECOMMEND
So I *r* the enjoyment of life, ... ECCL 8:15

RECONCILE
and to *r* them both in one body .... EPH 2:16

RECONCILED
First go and be *r* to your brother .... MATT 5:24
r us to himself through Christ, ... 2 COR 5:18

RECONCILIATION
we have now received this *r* .... ROM 5:11
their rejection is the *r* of the world, ... ROM 11:15
has given us the ministry of *r* .... 2 COR 5:18
has given us the message of *r* .... 2 COR 5:19

RECORDED
these are *r* so that you may believe .... JOHN 20:31

RECRUITED
please the one who *r* him. ... 2 TIM 2:4

RED
stained you like the color *r* ... ISA 1:18

REDEEM
to *r* those who were under the law, ... GAL 4:5

REDEEMED
Christ *r* us from the curse of the law ... GAL 3:13

REDEEMER
I know that my *R* lives, ... JOB 19:25

REDEMPTION
because your *r* is drawing near." ... LUKE 21:28
the *r* of our bodies. ... ROM 8:23
In him we have *r* through his blood, ... EPH 1:7
in whom we have *r* ... COL 1:14
and so he himself secured eternal *r* ... HEB 9:12

REFLECT
I *r* on your accomplishments. ... PS 143:5

REFLECTING
r the glory of the Lord, ... 2 COR 3:18

REFRESH
You *r* my head with oil; ... PS 23:5

REFRESHING
he leads me to *r* water. ... PS 23:2

REFUGE
as towns of *r* for you, ... NUM 35:11
The everlasting God is a *r* ... DEUT 33:27
God is our strong *r* ... PS 46:1

REFUSES
who *r* correction despises himself, ... PROV 15:32

REGARD
I now *r* all things as liabilities ... PHIL 3:8

REGARDS
and another *r* them all alike. ... ROM 14:5

REGULATIONS
must obey my statutes and my *r* ... LEV 25:18
I am committed to your *r* ... PS 119:30

REHOBOAM
Son of Solomon (1 Kgs 11:43; 1 Chr 3:10). Harsh treatment of subjects caused divided kingdom (1 Kgs 12:1-24; 14:21-31; 2 Chr 10-12).

REIGN
The LORD will *r* forever and ever! ... EXOD 15:18
Therefore do not let sin *r* ... ROM 6:12
For he must *r* ... 1 COR 15:25
r with him for a thousand years. ... REV 20:6

REJECT
he will *r* you. ... 2 CHR 15:2
your sins have caused him to *r* you ... ISA 59:2

REJECTED
He was despised and *r* by people, ... ISA 53:3
and no food is to be *r* ... 1 TIM 4:4
a living stone *r* by men but chosen ... 1 PET 2:4
the stone that the builders *r* ... 1 PET 2:7

REJECTS
one who *r* rebuke goes astray. ... PROV 10:17
A fool *r* his father's discipline, ... PROV 15:5
and the one who rejects you *r* me, ... LUKE 10:16
one who *r* the Son will not see life, ... JOHN 3:36

REJOICE
so you will indeed *r* ... DEUT 16:15
Let us *r* in him there. ... PS 66:6
Let the many coastlands *r* ... PS 97:1
We will be happy and *r* in it. ... PS 118:24
r in the wife you married ... PROV 5:18
may she who bore you *r* ... PROV 23:25
begun to *r* in God my Savior, ... LUKE 1:47
r that your names stand written ... LUKE 10:20
Rejoice with those who *r* ... ROM 12:15
always. Again I say, *r* ... PHIL 4:4
and so you *r* with an indescribable ... 1 PET 1:8
you may also *r* and be glad. ... 1 PET 4:13

REJOICED
disciples *r* when they saw the Lord. ... JOHN 20:20
I *r* greatly because I have found ... 2 JOHN 4

REJOICES
but *r* in the truth. ... 1 COR 13:6

REJOICING
So they left the council *r* ... ACTS 5:41

REKINDLE
I remind you to *r* God's gift ... 2 TIM 1:6

RELATIVE
and a *r* is born to help in adversity. ... PROV 17:17

RELEASES
The LORD *r* the imprisoned. ... PS 146:7

RELENT
willing to change his mind and *r* ... JONAH 3:9

RELIABLE
He is a *r* God who is never unjust, ... DEUT 32:4
r to one who is blameless, ... 2 SAM 22:27
the LORD's promise is *r* ... 2 SAM 22:31
The LORD's words are absolutely *r* ... PS 12:6
the LORD's promise is *r* ... PS 18:30
faithful and *r* to those who follow ... PS 25:10
and absolutely *r* ... PS 119:138
Your instructions are totally *r* ... PS 119:160
"These words are *r* and true. ... REV 22:6

RELIED
I *r* completely on the LORD, ... PS 40:1

RELIGION
Pure and undefiled *r* before God ... JAS 1:27

RELY
R on the LORD! ... PS 27:14
r on your own understanding. ... PROV 3:5
and do not *r* on human credentials ... PHIL 3:3

REMAIN
allow to *r* will be irritants ... NUM 33:55
and my words *r* in you, ... JOHN 15:7
And now these three *r* ... 1 COR 13:13

REMAINS
who *r* forever faithful, ... PS 146:6
fruit that *r* ... JOHN 15:16
has what *r* come in glory! ... 2 COR 3:11
he *r* faithful, ... 2 TIM 2:13
and he *r* a priest for all time. ... HEB 7:3

REMEMBER
R the Sabbath day to set it apart ... EXOD 20:8
So *r* your Creator ... ECCL 12:1
your sins I do not *r* ... ISA 43:25
requested only that we *r* the poor, ... GAL 2:10

I thank my God every time I *r* you. .... PHIL 1:3
and their sins I will *r* no longer." .... HEB 8:12

REMEMBERS
he always *r* his covenant. .... PS 111:5

REMEMBRANCE
Do this in *r* of me." .... 1 COR 11:24

REMOVE
R the evil person from among you. .... 1 COR 5:13

REMOVED
you *r* my sackcloth and covered me .... PS 30:11

RENEW
R a resolute spirit within me. .... PS 51:10

RENEWED
so your youth is *r* like an eagle's. .... PS 103:5
the LORD's help find *r* strength; .... ISA 40:31
inner person is being *r* day by day. .... 2 COR 4:16

RENEWING
be transformed by the *r* of your mind, ... ROM 12:2

RENOWN
a *r* that lasts to this day. .... JER 32:20

REPAID
r at the resurrection .... LUKE 14:14
the one who does wrong will be *r* .... COL 3:25

REPARATION
and must make full *r* .... NUM 5:7

REPAY
and the LORD will *r* him .... PROV 19:17
I will *r* .... ROM 12:19

REPENT
r and obey my commandments .... NEH 1:9
and I *r* in dust and ashes!" .... JOB 42:6
R in terror. .... PS 2:11
"You must *r* of such words .... JER 15:19
R for the kingdom of heaven is near!" ... MATT 4:17
But unless you *r* .... LUKE 13:3
R and each one of you be baptized .... ACTS 2:38
commands all people everywhere to *r* ... ACTS 17:30

REPENTANCE
produce fruit that proves your *r* .... LUKE 3:8
but sinners to *r* .... LUKE 5:32
performing deeds consistent with *r* .... ACTS 26:20
produces a *r* that leads to salvation, ... 2 COR 7:10

REPENTANT
and *r* heart you will not reject. .... PS 51:17

REPENTS
over one sinner who *r* .... LUKE 15:10
If he *r* .... LUKE 17:3

REPLIED
So Isaiah *r*, "Pay attention , ... ISA 7:13

REPRESENTATION
and the *r* of his essence, ... HEB 1:3

REPRIMAND
gives to all generously and without *r* .... JAS 1:5

REPROACH
The overseer then must be above *r* .... 1 TIM 3:2

REPROOF
but the one who hates *r* is stupid. .... PROV 12:1
but whoever heeds *r* shows good sense. .. PROV 15:5
the one who hates *r* will die. .... PROV 15:10
for *r* for correction, ... 2 TIM 3:16

REPROVE
Do not *r* a mocker or he will hate you; ... PROV 9:8
r, rebuke, exhort .... 2 TIM 4:2

REPUDIATE
and *r* their sinful practices, ... 2 CHR 7:14

REPUDIATED
but will have *r* its power. .... 2 TIM 3:5

REPUTATION
gaining for himself a lasting *r* .... ISA 63:12

REQUESTS
May the LORD grant all your *r* .... PS 20:5
tell your *r* to God. .... PHIL 4:6

REQUIRED
much will be *r* .... LUKE 12:48

RESCUE
he will *r* the needy when they cry out .... PS 72:12
r us. Forgive our sins .... PS 79:9
r us from the furnace of blazing fire, ... DAN 3:17
able to *r* you from the lions?" .... DAN 6:20
the Lord knows how to *r* the godly .... 2 PET 2:9

RESCUES
he *r* them from the wicked .... PS 37:40

RESEMBLE
Whom do I *r* .... ISA 40:25

RESENTFUL
it is not easily angered or *r* .... 1 COR 13:5

RESERVED
It is *r* in heaven for you, ... 1 PET 1:4

RESIDENCE
come to him and take up *r* with him. ... JOHN 14:23

RESIDES
and *r* in the protective shadow .... PS 91:1
because he *r* with you .... JOHN 14:17
who resides in love *r* in God, ... 1 JOHN 4:16

RESIST
r the devil and he will flee from you. .... JAS 4:7
R him, strong in your faith, ... 1 PET 5:9

RESOLUTE
Renew a *r* spirit within me. .... PS 51:10

RESPECT
Each of you must *r* his mother .... LEV 19:3
they will *r* the God of Israel. .... ISA 29:23
where is my *r* .... MAL 1:6
whatever is worthy of *r* .... PHIL 4:8

RESPECTABLE
r hospitable, an able teacher, ... 1 TIM 3:2

RESPOND
then I will *r* from heaven, ... 2 CHR 7:14

REST
a Sabbath of complete *r* .... EXOD 31:15
the LORD's house for the *r* of my life. .... PS 23:6
you will find *r* for your souls." .... JER 6:16
and I will give you *r* .... MATT 11:28

RESTITUTION
A thief must surely make full *r* .... EXOD 22:3

RESTORE
He must *r* it in full and add one-fifth .... LEV 6:5
you who are spiritual *r* such a person .... GAL 6:1

RESTRAINT
but a fool throws off *r* .... PROV 14:16

RESULT
and *r* in lasting security. ISA 32:17

RESURRECTION
For in the *r* they neither marry nor MATT 22:30
repaid at the *r* of the righteous." LUKE 14:14
the *r* resulting in life, JOHN 5:29
"I am the *r* and the life. JOHN 11:25
Holy Spirit by the *r* from the dead, ROM 1:4
say there is no *r* of the dead? 1 COR 15:12
to experience the power of his *r* PHIL 3:10
This is the first *r* REV 20:5

RETURN
by their captors and *r* to this land. 2 CHR 30:9
and naked I will *r* there. JOB 1:21
They should *r* to the LORD, ISA 55:7
promise that I make does not *r* to me, ISA 55:11
Let's *r* to the LORD. HOS 6:1
r to me with all your heart JOEL 2:12
and their children to *r* to me, MAL 4:6
Do not *r* evil for evil 1 PET 3:9

REVEAL
r your splendor. PS 80:1
do not *r* the secret of another person, PROV 25:9
r my sovereign power over them EZEK 28:25
and *r* the motives of hearts. 1 COR 4:5

REVEALED
but those that are *r* belong to us DEUT 29:29
The splendor of the LORD will be *r* ISA 40:5
and have *r* them to little children. MATT 11:25
nothing is hidden that will not be *r* LUKE 8:17
the coming glory that will be *r* to us. ROM 8:18
By this the love of God is *r* in us: 1 JOHN 4:9

REVELATION
I received it by a *r* of Jesus Christ. GAL 1:12
our religion contains amazing *r* 1 TIM 3:16
The *r* of Jesus Christ, REV 1:1

REVENGE
I will get *r* and pay them back DEUT 32:35
For the LORD has planned a day of *r* ISA 34:8

REVERE
You must *r* the LORD your God, DEUT 6:13
God require of you except to *r* him, DEUT 10:12

REVERENCE
your salvation with awe and *r* PHIL 2:12

REVERENT
when they see your pure and *r* conduct 1 PET 3:2

REVIVE
Will you not *r* us once more? PS 85:6

REVOKE
promise on oath and will not *r* it: PS 110:4

REWARD
May the LORD *r* your efforts! RUTH 2:12
those who obey them receive a rich *r* PS 19:11
the fruit of the womb is a *r* PS 127:3
and the LORD will *r* you. PROV 25:22
because that is their *r* ECCL 3:22
because your *r* is great in heaven, MATT 5:12
they have their *r* MATT 6:5
and then he will *r* each person MATT 16:27
receive his *r* according to his work. 1 COR 3:8
he will receive a *r* 1 COR 3:14
and my *r* is with me to pay each one REV 22:12

REWARDED
The LORD *r* me for my godly deeds; PS 18:24

REWARDS
he *r* godly deeds. PS 11:7

RICH
those who obey them receive a *r* reward PS 19:11
it little by little will become *r* PROV 13:11
Do not wear yourself out to become *r* PROV 23:4
for he was very *r* MARK 10:22
but making many *r* 2 COR 6:10
that although he was *r* 2 COR 8:9
Command those who are *r* 1 TIM 6:17

RICHES
as if they were *r* of all kinds. PS 119:14
do not give me poverty or *r* PROV 30:8
Oh, the depth of the *r* and wisdom ROM 11:33
Gentiles the unfathomable *r* of Christ EPH 3:8
the glorious *r* of this mystery COL 1:27

RID
we must get *r* of every weight HEB 12:1

RIDGE
The LORD is my high *r*. PS 18:2

RIGHT
and do what is *r* in his sight, EXOD 15:26
do not turn *r* or left! DEUT 5:32
none of them does what is *r* PS 14:1
Trust in the LORD and do what is *r* PS 37:3
Do not turn to the *r* or to the left; PROV 4:27
a way that seems *r* to a person, PROV 14:12
Learn to do what is *r* ISA 1:17
For the ways of the LORD are *r* HOS 14:9
given the *r* to become God's children JOHN 1:12
r to make from the same lump of clay ROM 9:21
do not grow weary in doing what is *r* 2 THESS 3:13

RIGHTEOUS
to guard the paths of the *r* PROV 2:8
but he blesses the home of the *r* PROV 3:33
The fruit of the *r* is like a tree PROV 11:30
I will raise up for them a *r* branch, JER 23:5
rain on the *r* and the unrighteous. MATT 5:45
For I did not come to call the *r* MATT 9:13
and separate the evil from the *r* MATT 13:49
but the *r* into eternal life." MATT 25:46
who do the law will be declared *r* ROM 2:13
"There is no one *r* ROM 3:10
For no one is declared *r* before him ROM 3:20
a person is declared *r* by faith ROM 3:28
we have been declared *r* by faith, ROM 5:1
now been declared *r* by his blood, ROM 5:9
that we could be declared *r* by faith. GAL 3:24
trying to be declared *r* by the law GAL 5:4
he is faithful and *r* 1 JOHN 1:9
just as Jesus is *r* 1 JOHN 3:7

RIGHTEOUSNESS
and the LORD credited it as *r* to him. GEN 15:6
R exalts a nation, PROV 14:34
who pursues *r* and love finds life, PROV 21:21
will be judged according to his *r* EZEK 18:20
to bring in perpetual *r* DAN 9:24
And those bringing many to *r* DAN 12:3
those who hunger and thirst for *r* MATT 5:6
unless your *r* goes beyond that of the MATT 5:20
to display your *r* merely to be seen MATT 6:1
pursue his kingdom and *r* MATT 6:33

the *r* of God is revealed in the gospel ...... ROM 1:17
This was to demonstrate his *r* .... ROM 3:25
and it was credited to him as *r* .... ROM 4:3
“faith was credited to Abraham as *r* .... ROM 4:9
came *r* leading to life for all people. .... ROM 5:18
as instruments to be used for *r* .... ROM 6:13
in him we would become the *r* of God. .... 2 COR 5:21
if *r* could come through the law, ... GAL 2:21
and it was credited to him as *r* .... GAL 3:6
by putting on the breastplate of *r* .... EPH 6:14
not because I have my own *r* .... PHIL 3:9
and for training in *r* .... 2 TIM 3:16
the crown of *r* is reserved for me. .... 2 TIM 4:8
and became an heir of the *r* that .... HEB 11:7
to have known the way of *r* than, ... 2 PET 2:21

RIGHTLY
conduct ourselves *r* in every respect. ...... HEB 13:18

RIGHTS
or her marital *r* .... EXOD 21:10
to deprive a person of his *r* .... LAM 3:35

RISE
Children will *r* against parents .... MATT 10:21
‘After three days I will *r* again.’ .... MATT 27:63
and the dead in Christ will *r* first. ...... 1 THESS 4:16

RIVALRIES
selfish *r* dissensions, ... GAL 5:20

ROBBERS
to be a hideout for *r* .... JER 7:11
you have turned it into a den of *r* .... LUKE 19:46
before me were thieves and *r* .... JOHN 10:8

ROCK
He placed my feet on a *r* .... PS 40:2
a wise man who built his house on *r* ...... MATT 7:24
and on this *r* I will build my church, ... MATT 16:18
and a *r* that will make them fall, ... ROM 9:33
and the *r* was Christ. .... 1 COR 10:4

ROD
your *r* and your staff reassure me. .... PS 23:4
one who spares his *r* hates his child, ... PROV 13:24
even if you strike him with the *r* .... PROV 23:13
He will rule them with an iron *r* .... REV 19:15

ROLLING
they are *r* dice for my garments. .... PS 22:18

ROOM
go into your inner *r* .... MATT 6:6
world would not have *r* for the books ... JOHN 21:25

ROOT
like a *r* out of parched soil; .... ISA 53:2
love of money is the *r* of all evils. .... 1 TIM 6:10

ROYAL
Who is this one wearing *r* attire, ... ISA 63:1
But if you fulfill the *r* law .... JAS 2:8
a *r* priesthood, ... 1 PET 2:9

RUDE
It is not *r* .... 1 COR 13:5

RUIN
The mouth of a fool is his *r* .... PROV 18:7
plunge people into *r* and destruction. .... 1 TIM 6:9

RULE
A king will *r* over us’—even .... 1 SAM 12:12
you appoint them to *r* .... PS 8:6
he will *r* them with an iron rod .... REV 2:27

RULER
the Most High is *r* over
human kingdoms .... DAN 4:25
the *r* of this world will be driven out. ... JOHN 12:31
r of the spirit that is now energizing .... EPH 2:2

RULERS
the *r* collaborate against the LORD. .... PS 2:2
nor heavenly *r* .... ROM 8:38
Disarming the *r* and authorities, ... COL 2:15

RULES
the one who *r* forever, ... ISA 57:15
unless he competes according to the *r* ... 2 TIM 2:5

RUMORS
You will hear of wars and *r* of wars. ...... MATT 24:6

RUN
they *r* without growing weary, ... ISA 40:31
and *r* with endurance the race set out ..... HEB 12:1

RUNNERS
all the *r* in a stadium compete, ... 1 COR 9:24

RUTH
Moabitess; widow who went to Bethlehem with mother-in-law Naomi (Ruth 1). Gleaned in field of Boaz; shown favor (Ruth 2). Proposed marriage to Boaz (Ruth 3). Married (Ruth 4:1-12); bore Obed, ancestor of David (Ruth 4:13-22), Jesus (Matt 1:5).

SABBATH
Remember the *S* day to set it apart ...... EXOD 20:8
Be careful to observe the *S* day .... DEUT 5:12

SACKCLOTH
repented long ago in *s* and ashes. .... MATT 11:21

SACRED
things too *s* to be put into words, ... 2 COR 12:4

SACRIFICE
‘It is the *s* of the LORD’s Passover, ... EXOD 12:27
The *s* God desires is a humble spirit .... PS 51:17
not simply in *s* .... HOS 6:6
‘I want mercy and not *s* .... MATT 9:13
present your bodies as a *s*—alive, ... ROM 12:1
to put away sin by his *s* .... HEB 9:26
offer up a *s* of praise to God, ... HEB 13:15
is the atoning *s* for our sins, ... 1 JOHN 2:2

SACRIFICED
has been *s* .... 1 COR 5:7

SACRIFICES
pleasure in burnt offerings and *s* .... 1 SAM 15:22

SADDUCEES
S (who say there is no resurrection ..... MARK 12:18

SADNESS
but your *s* will turn into joy. .... JOHN 16:20
but worldly *s* brings about death. .... 2 COR 7:10

SAID
So she *s* to Abraham, ... GEN 21:10

SAINTS
See FAITHFUL

SALT
and was turned into a pillar of *s* .... GEN 19:26
You are the *s* of the earth. .... MATT 5:13
Neither can a *s* water spring produce .... JAS 3:12

SALVATION
and he has become my *s* .... EXOD 15:2
The LORD is my light and my *s* .... PS 27:1
S belongs to the LORD!" .... JONAH 2:9
For my eyes have seen your *s* .... LUKE 2:30
because *s* is from the Jews. .... JOHN 4:22
And there is *s* in no one else,................ ACTS 4:12
to bring *s* to the ends of the earth.'" ...... ACTS 13:47
s has come to the Gentiles, ... ROM 11:11
produces a repentance that leads to *s* ... 2 COR 7:10
And take the helmet of *s* and the sword ... EPH 6:17
continue working out your *s* with awe ... PHIL 2:12
and as a helmet our hope for *s* .... 1 THESS 5:8
are able to give you wisdom for *s* .... 2 TIM 3:15
if we neglect such a great *s* .... HEB 2:3
of better things relating to *s* .... HEB 6:9
Concerning this *s* .... 1 PET 1:10
so that by it you may grow up to *s* .... 1 PET 2:2

SAMARITAN
But a *S* who was traveling came to .... LUKE 10:33

SAMSON
Danite judge. Birth promised (Judg 13). Married to Philistine (Judg 14). Vengeance on Philistines (Judg 15). Betrayed by Delilah (Judg 16:1-22). Death (Judg 16:23-31). Feats of strength: killed lion (Judg 14:6), 30 Philistines (Judg 14:19), 1,000 Philistines with jawbone (Judg 15:13-17), carried off gates of Gaza (Judg 16:3), pushed down temple of Dagon (Judg 16:25-30).

SAMUEL
Ephraimite judge and prophet (Heb 11:32). Birth prayed for (1 Sam 1:10-18). Dedicated to temple by Hannah (1 Sam 1:21-28). Raised by Eli (1 Sam 2:11, 18-26). Called as prophet (1 Sam 3). Led Israel to victory over Philistines (1 Sam 7). Asked by Israel for a king (1 Sam 8). Anointed Saul as king (1 Sam 9-10). Farewell speech (1 Sam 12). Rebuked Saul for sacrifice (1 Sam 13). Announced rejection of Saul (1 Sam 15). Anointed David as king (1 Sam 16). Protected David from Saul (1 Sam 19:18-24). Death (1 Sam 25:1). Returned from dead to condemn Saul (1 Sam 28).

SANCTIFICATION
slaves to righteousness leading to *s* .... ROM 6:19
salvation through *s* by the Spirit ...... 2 THESS 2:13

SANCTIFIED
among all those who are *s* .... ACTS 20:32
s by the Holy Spirit. .... ROM 15:16
you were *s* .... 1 COR 6:11
For the unbelieving husband is *s* .... 1 COR 7:14
it is *s* by God's word and by prayer. .... 1 TIM 4:5

SANCTIFY
You must *s* yourselves and be holy, ... LEV 20:7
s him because he presents the food .... LEV 21:8

SANCTUARY
Let them make for me a *s* .... EXOD 25:8
a sketch and shadow of the heavenly *s* ..... HEB 8:5

SAND
or the grains of *s* on the seashore. .... GEN 22:17
its waves toss up mud and *s* .... ISA 57:20
foolish man who built his house on *s* ... MATT 7:26

SANDALS
Take your *s* off your feet, ... EXOD 3:5
"Remove your *s* from your feet, ... JOSH 5:15

SANG
when the morning stars *s* in chorus, ... JOB 38:7

SARAH
Wife of Abraham, originally named Sarai; barren (Gen 11:29-31; 1 Pet 3:6). Taken by Pharaoh as Abraham's sister; returned (Gen 12:10-20). Gave Hagar to Abraham; sent her away in pregnancy (Gen 16). Name changed; Isaac promised (Gen 17:15-21; 18:10-15; Heb 11:11). Taken by Abimelech as Abraham's sister; returned (Gen 20). Isaac born; Hagar and Ishmael sent away (Gen 21:1-21; Gal 4:21-31). Death (Gen 23).

SATAN
S also arrived among them. .... JOB 1:6
The LORD said to *S* .... ZECH 3:2
immediately *S* comes and snatches ..... MARK 4:15
S disguises himself as an angel .... 2 COR 11:14
a messenger of *S* to trouble me .... 2 COR 12:7
the one called the devil and *S* .... REV 12:9
who is the devil and *S*—and .... REV 20:2
S will be released from his prison .... REV 20:7

SATISFIED
will be *s* with food, ... PROV 28:19
he will be *s* when he understands .... ISA 53:11
we will be *s* with that. .... 1 TIM 6:8

SATISFIES
who *s* your life with good things, ... PS 103:5

SATISFY
enough food to *s* his appetite, ... PROV 13:25
on something that will not *s* .... ISA 55:2

SAUL
1. Benjamite; anointed by Samuel as first king of Israel (1 Sam 9-10). Defeated Ammonites (1 Sam 11). Rebuked for offering sacrifice (1 Sam 13:1-15). Defeated Philistines (1 Sam 14). Rejected as king for failing to annihilate Amalekites (1 Sam 15). Soothed from evil spirit by David (1 Sam 16:14-23). Sent David against Goliath (1 Sam 17). Jealousy and attempted murder of David (1 Sam 18:1-11). Gave David Michal as wife (1 Sam 18:12-30). Second attempt to kill David (1 Sam 19). Anger at Jonathan (1 Sam 20:26-34). Pursued David: killed priests at Nob (1 Sam 22), went to Keilah and Ziph (1 Sam 23), life spared by David at En Gedi (1 Sam 24) and in his tent (1 Sam 26). Rebuked by Samuel's spirit for consulting witch at En dor (1 Sam 28). Wounded by Philistines; took his own life (1 Sam 31; 1 Chr 10).
2. See PAUL

SAVE
s his people from their sins." .... MATT 1:21
whoever wants to *s* his life will lose .... MATT 16:25
to seek and to *s* the lost." .... LUKE 19:10
came into the world to *s* sinners" .... 1 TIM 1:15
will *s* the one who is sick .... JAS 5:15
will *s* that person's soul from death .... JAS 5:20

SAVED
he *s* him from all his troubles. PS 34:6
one who endures to the end will be *s* MARK 13:13
believes and is baptized will be *s* MARK 16:16
but that the world should be *s* JOHN 3:17
he will be *s* JOHN 10:9
people by which we must be *s* ACTS 4:12
what must I do to be *s* ACTS 16:30
only the remnant will be *s* ROM 9:27
you will be *s* ROM 10:9
He himself will be *s* 1 COR 3:15
and by which you are being *s* 1 COR 15:2
grace you are *s* EPH 2:5
For by grace you are *s* through faith, EPH 2:8
since he wants all people to be *s* 1 TIM 2:4

SAVES
he *s* them from all their troubles. PS 34:17
but the LORD *s* them from each one PS 34:19

SAVIOR
Except for me there is no *S* HOS 13:4
to rejoice in God my *S* LUKE 1:47
S is born in the city of David. LUKE 2:11
really is the *S* of the world." JOHN 4:42
(he himself being the *s* of the body). EPH 5:23
who is the *S* of all people, 1 TIM 4:10
of God our *S* in everything. TITUS 2:10
of our great God and *S* TITUS 2:13
But "when the kindness of God our *S* TITUS 3:4
sent the Son to be the *S* of the world 1 JOHN 4:14
God our *S* through Jesus Christ JUDE 25

SCARLET
as easy to see as the color *s* ISA 1:18

SCATTER
Now those who had been forced to *s* ACTS 8:4

SCATTERED
one who *s* Israel will regather them. JER 31:10
s because they have no shepherd. ZECH 10:2

SCHEMES
(for we are not ignorant of his *s* 2 COR 2:11
to stand against the *s* of the devil. EPH 6:11

SCOFFERS
or sit in the assembly of *s* PS 1:1
In the last days blatant *s* will come, 2 PET 3:3

SCORNER
Drive out the *s* and contention will PROV 22:10

SCORPION
their torture was like that of a *s* REV 9:5

SCRIPTURE
(and the *s* cannot be broken), JOHN 10:35
Every *s* is inspired by God and useful 2 TIM 3:16
No prophecy of *s* ever comes about 2 PET 1:20

SCRIPTURES
written about himself in all the *s* LUKE 24:27
same *s* that testify about me, JOHN 5:39
examining the *s* carefully every day ACTS 17:11

SCROLL
This law *s* must not leave your lips. JOSH 1:8
this *s*—and EZEK 3:1

SEA
middle of the *s* on dry ground. EXOD 14:16
But the wicked are like a surging *s* ISA 57:20
our sins into the depths of the *s* MIC 7:19
Even the winds and the *s* obey him!" MATT 8:27
one who doubts is like a wave of the *s* JAS 1:6
a beast coming up out of the *s* REV 13:1

SEAL
s of the promised Holy Spirit, EPH 1:13

SEALED
who also *s* us and gave us the Spirit 2 COR 1:22

SEALS
open the scroll and to break its *s* REV 5:2
the Lamb opened one of the seven *s* REV 6:1

SEARCH
and *s* thoroughly until she finds it? LUKE 15:8

SEARCHES
And he who *s* our hearts knows ROM 8:27
For the Spirit *s* all things, 1 COR 2:10

SEARED
liars whose consciences are *s* 1 TIM 4:2

SEAT
and the Ancient of Days took his *s* DAN 7:9
mercy *s* accessible through faith. ROM 3:25
before the judgment *s* of God. ROM 14:10
before the judgment *s* of Christ, 2 COR 5:10

SEATED
I saw the Lord *s* on a high, ISA 6:1
s at the right hand of God. COL 3:1

SEATS
You love the best *s* in the synagogues LUKE 11:43

SECRET
do not reveal the *s* of another person PROV 25:9
who sees in *s* MATT 6:4

SECRETS
slandering others reveals *s* PROV 11:13
The *s* of his heart are disclosed, 1 COR 14:25

SECURE
make me safe and *s* PS 4:8
and my covenant with him is *s* PS 89:28
they stand *s* in heaven. PS 119:89
who love your law are completely *s* PS 119:165

SECURITY
'You are my *s* JOB 31:24
peace and result in lasting *s* ISA 32:17
"There is peace and *s* 1 THESS 5:3

SEDUCTIVENESS
the *s* of wealth, MARK 4:19

SEE
as easy to *s* as the color scarlet, ISA 1:18
s that the fields are already white JOHN 4:35

SEED
kingdom of heaven is like a mustard *s* MATT 13:31
The *s* is the word of God. LUKE 8:11
multiply your supply of *s* 2 COR 9:10
but from imperishable *s* 1 PET 1:23

SEEK
s him with all your heart and soul. DEUT 4:29
If you *s* him, 1 CHR 28:9
s to please me, 2 CHR 7:14
With all my heart I *s* you. PS 119:10
S the LORD while he makes himself ISA 55:6
s the lost and bring back the strays; EZEK 34:16
came to *s* and to save the lost." LUKE 19:10
I was found by those who did not *s* me ROM 10:20

SHAMING
by *s* those who have nothing? ....1 COR 11:22

SHARD
like a mere *s* among the other .... ISA 45:9

SHARE
"The person who has two tunics must *s* ... LUKE 3:11
must *s* all good things .... GAL 6:6
to *s* with the one who has need. .... EPH 4:28
that we may *s* his holiness. .... HEB 12:10
and to *s* what you have, ... HEB 13:16

SHARING
s in the blood of Christ? .... 1 COR 10:16

SHARON
I am a meadow flower from *S* .... SONG 2:1

SHARPER
living and active and *s* than any .... HEB 4:12

SHEBA
All the Israelites from Dan to Beer *S* ..... JUDG 20:1

SHEDS
Whoever *s* human blood, ... GEN 9:6

SHEEP
the *s* of his pasture. .... PS 100:3
I have wandered off like a lost *s* .... PS 119:176
All of us had wandered off like *s* .... ISA 53:6
My people have been lost *s* .... JER 50:6
I myself will search for my *s* .... EZEK 34:11
like *s* without a shepherd. .... MATT 9:36
and the *s* hear his voice. .... JOHN 10:3
I lay down my life for the *s* .... JOHN 10:15
My *s* listen to my voice, ... JOHN 10:27
"Feed my *s* .... JOHN 21:17
For you were going astray like *s* .... 1 PET 2:25

SHELTER
in the *s* of the Most High, ... PS 91:1
my *s* and my stronghold, ... PS 91:2
He will *s* you with his wings; .... PS 91:4

SHEM
Son of Noah (Gen 5:32; 6:10). Blessed (Gen 9:26). Descendants (Gen 10:21-31; 11:10-32).

SHEOL
deliver them from the power of *S* .... HOS 13:14

SHEPHERD
The LORD is my *s* .... PS 23:1
Like a *s* he tends his flock; .... ISA 40:11
like a *s* watches over his flock." .... JER 31:10
As a *s* seeks out his flock .... EZEK 34:12
s who abandons the flock! .... ZECH 11:17
like sheep without a *s* .... MATT 9:36
The good *s* lays down his life .... JOHN 10:11
one flock and one *s* .... JOHN 10:16
S my sheep." .... JOHN 21:16
to *s* the church of God that he
obtained .... ACTS 20:28
Then when the Chief *S* appears, ... 1 PET 5:4

SHEPHERDS
like *s* watch over their sheep. .... JER 23:1
s nearby living out in the field, ... LUKE 2:8

SHIELD
by taking up the *s* of faith .... EPH 6:16

SHINE
Arise! *S* For your light arrives! .... ISA 60:1
the wise will *s* like the brightness .... DAN 12:3
let your light *s* before people, ... MATT 5:16
Then the righteous will *s* like the sun .. MATT 13:43
who said "Let light *s* out of darkness ...... 2 COR 4:6
and Christ will *s* on you!" .... EPH 5:14

SHINES
doorway through which light *s* .... PS 119:130

SHIPWRECK
Three times I suffered *s* .... 2 COR 11:25
suffered *s* in regard to the faith. .... 1 TIM 1:19

SHONE
the skin of his face *s* .... EXOD 34:29
His face *s* like the sun, ... MATT 17:2

SHOOT
a wild olive *s* .... ROM 11:17

SHORT
and fall *s* of the glory of God. .... ROM 3:23

SHOULDERS
He *s* responsibility and is called .... ISA 9:6
he places it on his *s* .... LUKE 15:5

SHOUT
Let the mountains give a joyful *s* .... ISA 49:13
will give a joyful *s* before you, ... ISA 55:12

SHOUTED
When they saw the star they *s* joyfully ... MATT 2:10

SHOUTING
voice of one *s* in the wilderness, ... JOHN 1:23

SHOW
s me your way, ... EXOD 33:13
the LORD is ready to *s* you mercy; .... ISA 30:18
and *s* no partiality, ... LUKE 20:21
and *s* them honor as fellow heirs .... 1 PET 3:7

SHOWN
so that it would be *s* to be sin, ... ROM 7:13

SICK
Hope deferred makes the heart *s* .... PROV 13:12
but those who are *s* do. .... MATT 9:12
I was *s* and you took care of me, ... MATT 25:36

SICKLE
Rush forth with the *s* .... JOEL 3:13

SIDE
of bread that is scorched on one *s* .... HOS 7:8

SIGHT
not by *s* .... 2 COR 5:7
which is precious in God's *s* .... 1 PET 3:4

SIGN
will give you a confirming *s* .... ISA 7:14

SIGNS
perform great *s* and wonders .... MATT 24:24
s will accompany those who believe: .... MARK 16:17
no one could perform the
miraculous *s* .... JOHN 3:2
perform such miraculous *s* .... JOHN 9:16
many other miraculous *s* .... JOHN 20:30
For Jews demand miraculous *s* .... 1 COR 1:22

SILENT
fool who remains *s* is considered wise, ... PROV 17:28
like a sheep *s* before her shearers, ... ISA 53:7
Be *s* in the LORD's presence, ... ZECH 2:13
if they keep *s* .... LUKE 19:40
women should be *s* in the churches, ... 1 COR 14:34

The *s* is willing, ... MATT 26:41
Father and the Son and the Holy *S* .... MATT 28:19
growing and becoming strong in *s* .... LUKE 1:80
give the Holy *S* to those who ask him!" .... LUKE 11:13
must worship in *s* and truth." .... JOHN 4:24
for the *S* had not yet been given, ... JOHN 7:39
the Holy *S* .... JOHN 14:26
the *S* of truth, ... JOHN 16:13
"Receive the Holy *S* .... JOHN 20:22
you will be baptized with the Holy *S* .... ACTS 1:5
other languages as the *S* enabled .... ACTS 2:4
will receive the gift of the Holy *S* .... ACTS 2:38
full of the *S* and of wisdom, ... ACTS 6:3
receive the Holy *S* when you believed?" .... ACTS 19:2
if indeed the *S* of God lives in you. .... ROM 8:9
the *S* helps us in our weakness, ... ROM 8:26
be enthusiastic in *s* .... ROM 12:11
God has revealed these to us by the *S* .... 1 COR 2:10
temple of the Holy *S* who is in you, ... 1 COR 6:19
we were all made to drink of the one *S* .... 1 COR 12:13
eager for manifestations of the *S* .... 1 COR 14:12
not based on the letter but on the *S* .... 2 COR 3:6
who gave us the *S* as a down payment. .... 2 COR 5:5
by the *S* and you will not carry out .... GAL 5:16
But the fruit of the *S* is love, ... GAL 5:22
behave in accordance with the *S* .... GAL 5:25
with the seal of the promised Holy *S* .... EPH 1:13
to be renewed in the *s* of your mind, ... EPH 4:23
And do not grieve the Holy *S* of God, ... EPH 4:30
but be filled by the *S* .... EPH 5:18
the sword of the *S* (which is the word .... EPH 6:17
Do not extinguish the *S* .... 1 THESS 5:19
through sanctification by the *S* .... 2 THESS 2:13
to the point of dividing soul from *s* .... HEB 4:12
beauty of a gentle and tranquil *s* .... 1 PET 3:4
men carried along by the Holy *S* .... 2 PET 1:21
do not believe every *s* .... 1 JOHN 4:1

SPIRITS
and to another discernment of *s* .... 1 COR 12:10
the *s* of the prophets are subject to .... 1 COR 14:32
Is anyone in good *s* .... JAS 5:13
but test the *s* to determine if they .... 1 JOHN 4:1

SPIRITUAL
there is also a *s* body. .... 1 COR 15:44
you who are *s* restore such a person .... GAL 6:1
has blessed us with every *s* blessing .... EPH 1:3
and *s* songs, ... EPH 5:19
s milk, so that by it you may grow .... 1 PET 2:2
offer *s* sacrifices that are acceptable .... 1 PET 2:5

SPLENDID
her clothing was strong and *s* .... PROV 31:25

SPLENDOR
Tell the nations about his *s* .... 1 CHR 16:24
Majestic *s* emanates from him, ... 1 CHR 16:27
ascribe to the LORD *s* and strength! .... 1 CHR 16:28
From the north he comes in golden *s* .... JOB 37:22
so I can gaze at the *s* of the LORD .... PS 27:4
Tell the nations about his *s* .... PS 96:3
Majestic *s* emanates from him; .... PS 96:6
You are robed in *s* and majesty. .... PS 104:1
focus on your honor and majestic *s* .... PS 145:5
His majestic *s* fills the entire earth!" .... ISA 6:3
You will see a king in his *s* .... ISA 33:17
The *s* of the LORD will be revealed, ... ISA 40:5
planted by the LORD to reveal his *s* .... ISA 61:3

SPOT
without *s* or blemish, ... 2 PET 3:14

SPREADS
person who *s* discord among family .... PROV 6:19

SPRING
a *s* that continually produces water. .... ISA 58:11

STADIUM
all the runners in a *s* compete, ... 1 COR 9:24

STAFF
your rod and your *s* reassure me. .... PS 23:4

STAKES
and pound your *s* deep. .... ISA 54:2

STAND
the place where you *s* is holy." .... JOSH 5:15
s and watch the LORD deliver you, ... 2 CHR 20:17
do not *s* in the place of great men; .... PROV 25:6
and *s* in the gap before me .... EZEK 22:30
his feet will *s* on the Mount of Olives .... ZECH 14:4
house divided against itself will *s* .... MATT 12:25
that you may be able to *s* your ground .... EPH 6:13
so that you may *s* mature .... COL 4:12

STANDARD
Hold to the *s* of sound words .... 2 TIM 1:13

STANDING
the place where you are *s* is holy .... EXOD 3:5
God's solid foundation remains *s* .... 2 TIM 2:19
I am *s* at the door and knocking! .... REV 3:20

STAR
A *s* will march forth out of Jacob, ... NUM 24:17
the day dawns and the morning *s* rises .... 2 PET 1:19
the bright morning *s* .... REV 22:16

STARS
will be like the *s* forever and ever. .... DAN 12:3

STATURE
to the measure of Christ's full *s* .... EPH 4:13

STATUTES
all the *s* that the LORD has spoken .... LEV 10:11
I am determined to obey your *s* .... PS 119:112

STEADFAST
sure and *s* .... HEB 6:19

STEADFASTLY
also aware that you have persisted *s* .... REV 2:3
have kept my admonition to endure *s* .... REV 3:10

STEADFASTNESS
for the display of all patience and *s* .... COL 1:11

STEAL
You shall not *s* .... EXOD 20:15
do not *s* .... MATT 19:18

STEALS
The one who *s* must steal no longer; .... EPH 4:28

STEPS
but the LORD directs his *s* .... PROV 16:9
for you to follow in his *s* .... 1 PET 2:21

STEWARDS
in *s* is that one be found faithful. .... 1 COR 4:2

STICKS
a friend who *s* closer than a brother. .... PROV 18:24

STIFF-NECKED
for we are a *s* people; .... EXOD 34:9

T my yoke on you and learn from me, .. MATT 11:29
T your share of suffering .... 2 TIM 2:3
t my advice and buy gold from me .... REV 3:18

TAKEN
one will be *t* and one left. .... MATT 24:40

TAKES
He *t* me to lush pastures, ... PS 23:2

TAKING
not boast like one who is *t* it off." .... 1 KGS 20:11
by *t* on the form of a slave, ... PHIL 2:7

TALENTS
To one he gave five *t* .... MATT 25:15

TASTE
T and see that the LORD is good. .... PS 34:8
Do not *t* .... COL 2:21

TAUGHT
t them like one who had authority, ... MATT 7:29
not with words *t* us by human wisdom, ... 1 COR 2:13

TAUNT
All who see me *t* me; .... PS 22:7

TAXES
Is it right to pay *t* to Caesar or not .... MATT 22:17
taxes to whom *t* are due, ... ROM 13:7

TEACH
instead *t* them to your children .... DEUT 4:9
He did this to *t* you that humankind ..... DEUT 8:3
T them to your children .... DEUT 11:19
t you about how you should live. .... PS 32:8
I will *t* rebels your merciful ways, ... PS 51:13
So *t* us to consider our mortality, ... PS 90:12
T me to do what pleases you, ... PS 143:10
People will no longer need to *t* .... JER 31:34
t us to pray, ... LUKE 11:1
will *t* you everything, ... JOHN 14:26
But I do not allow a woman to *t* .... 1 TIM 2:12
about how you live and what you *t* .... 1 TIM 4:16
each one to *t* his brother saying, ... HEB 8:11
no need for anyone to *t* you. .... 1 JOHN 2:27

TEACHER
A disciple is not greater than his *t* ..... MATT 10:24
one *T* and you are all brothers. .... MATT 23:8
your Lord and *T* .... JOHN 13:14
an able *t* .... 1 TIM 3:2

TEACHERS
third *t* then miracles, ... 1 COR 12:28
and some as pastors and *t* .... EPH 4:11
you should in fact be *t* by this time, ... HEB 5:12
Not many of you should become *t* .... JAS 3:1

TEACHING
do not forsake the *t* from your mother .... PROV 1:8
t them to obey everything .... MATT 28:20
he will know about my *t* .... JOHN 7:17
or with knowledge or prophecy or *t* ...... 1 COR 14:6
of scripture, to exhortation, to *t* .... 1 TIM 4:13
inspired by God and useful for *t* .... 2 TIM 3:16
behavior that goes with sound *t* .... TITUS 2:1
In your *t* show integrity, ... TITUS 2:7

TEACHINGS
not to spread false *t* .... 1 TIM 1:3
If someone spreads false *t* .... 1 TIM 6:3

TEAR
and God will wipe away every *t* .... REV 7:17

TEARS
Those who shed *t* as they plant .... PS 126:5
with *t* I tell you that they are .... PHIL 3:18

TEETH
weeping and gnashing of *t* .... MATT 8:12

TELL
T Aaron and his sons that they must ..... LEV 22:2
t that a message is not from
the LORD .... DEUT 18:21
t all the nations about his
miraculous .... 1 CHR 16:24
not neglected to *t* the great assembly ...... PS 40:10
T the nations about his splendor. .... PS 96:3

TEMPERATE
t self-controlled, respectable, ... 1 TIM 3:2
t faithful in every respect. .... 1 TIM 3:11
Older men are to be *t* .... TITUS 2:2

TEMPLE
how much less this *t* I have built! .... 1 KGS 8:27
rather stand at the entrance to the *t* .... PS 84:10
as a *t* where all nations may pray." .... ISA 56:7
T Mount will be the most important .... MIC 4:1
t and that God's Spirit lives in you? .... 1 COR 3:16
your body is the *t* of the Holy Spirit ..... 1 COR 6:19
For we are the *t* of the living God, ... 2 COR 6:16

TEMPLES
does not live in *t* made by human
hands .... ACTS 17:24

TEMPT
so that Satan may not *t* you .... 1 COR 7:5

TEMPTATION
And do not lead us into *t* .... MATT 6:13
pray that you will not fall into *t* .... MATT 26:41

TEMPTED
the wilderness to be *t* by the devil. .... MATT 4:1
he is able to help those who are *t* .... HEB 2:18
but one who has been *t* in every way .... HEB 4:15
"I am *t* by God," .... JAS 1:13

TEN
the *T* Commandments. .... EXOD 34:28
and give it to the one who has *t* .... MATT 25:28
has *t* silver coins and loses one .... LUKE 15:8

TERRIFYING
It is a *t* thing to fall into the hands .... HEB 10:31

TERRITORY
The Levites were allotted no *t* .... JOSH 14:4

TERROR
Repent in *t* .... PS 2:11

TERRORS
You need not fear the *t* of the night, ... PS 91:5

TEST
not put the LORD your God to the *t* ...... DEUT 6:16
and *t* me. .... PS 26:2
T me, and know my concerns. .... PS 139:23
And the fire will *t* what kind of work ..... 1 COR 3:13
you fail the *t* .... 2 COR 13:5
but *t* the spirits to determine if they .... 1 JOHN 4:1

TESTED
after these things God *t* Abraham. .... GEN 22:1
if he *t* me, ... JOB 23:10
be *t* first and then let them serve .... 1 TIM 3:10

TESTIFY
but he came to *t* about the light. JOHN 1:8
same scriptures that *t* about me, JOHN 5:39

TESTIMONY
prophetic *t* of what would happen. ISA 8:20
do not give false *t* MATT 19:18
do not give false *t* LUKE 18:20
So do not be ashamed of the *t* 2 TIM 1:8

TESTS
likewise the LORD *t* hearts. PROV 17:3

THADDAEUS
Apostle (Matt 10:3; Mark 3:18); probably also known as Judas son of James (Luke 6:16; Acts 1:13).

THANK
I will *t* the LORD profusely. PS 109:30

THANKS
appointed two large choirs to give *t* NEH 12:31
t to the LORD with my whole heart, PS 111:1
But *t* be to God, 1 COR 15:57
But *t* be to God who always leads us 2 COR 2:14
T be to God for his indescribable gift 2 COR 9:15
in everything give *t* 1 THESS 5:18
let us give *t* HEB 12:28

THANKSGIVING
Let us enter his presence with *t* PS 95:2
Enter his gates with *t* PS 100:4
through prayer and petition with *t* PHIL 4:6
received with *t* by those who believe 1 TIM 4:3

THEREFORE
T it is necessary to be in subjection, ROM 13:5

THIEF
in the same way as a *t* in the night. 1 THESS 5:2
I will come like a *t* REV 16:15

THIEVES
t the greedy, 1 COR 6:10

THING
life of every living *t* is in the blood. LEV 17:11
he withholds no good *t* from those PS 84:11

THINGS
living *t* be wiped out by the waters GEN 9:11
The secret *t* belong to the LORD DEUT 29:29
You are the God who does amazing *t* PS 77:14
who satisfies your life with good *t* PS 103:5
the earth is full of the living *t* PS 104:24
the marvelous *t* in your law. PS 119:18
for he has done magnificent *t* ISA 12:5
even the deep *t* of God. 1 COR 2:10
spiritual *t* to spiritual people. 1 COR 2:13
hopes all *t* 1 COR 13:7
And who is adequate for these *t* 2 COR 2:16
and they think about earthly *t* PHIL 3:19
For if these *t* are really yours 2 PET 1:8

THINK
far beyond all that we ask or *t* EPH 3:20
t about these things. PHIL 4:8

THINKING
Keep *t* about things above, COL 3:2

THINKS
t he is religious yet does not bridle JAS 1:26

THIRST
to quench my *t* they give me vinegar PS 69:21
who hunger and *t* for righteousness, MATT 5:6

THIRSTY
Hey, all who are *t* ISA 55:1
will never be *t* again, JOHN 4:14
"If anyone is *t* JOHN 7:37
And let the one who is *t* come; REV 22:17

THIS
T is what comforts me in my trouble, PS 119:50
have *t* hope as an anchor for the soul, HEB 6:19

THOMAS
Apostle (Matt 10:3; Mark 3:18; Luke 6:15; John 11:16; 14:5; 21:2; Acts 1:13). Doubted resurrection (John 20:24-28).

THORN
a *t* in the flesh was given to me, 2 COR 12:7

THORNS
in your eyes and *t* in your side, NUM 33:55
and after braiding a crown of *t* MATT 27:29
But if it produces *t* and thistles, HEB 6:8

THOUGH
T he causes us grief, LAM 3:32

THOUGHT
we *t* he was being punished, ISA 53:4
I *t* like a child, 1 COR 13:11
well *t* of by those outside the faith, 1 TIM 3:7
t of how to spur one another on HEB 10:24

THOUGHTS
entertain *t* against a virgin? JOB 31:1
May my words and my *t* be acceptable PS 19:14
for he knows a person's secret *t* PS 44:21
May my *t* be pleasing to him. PS 104:34
and probe my *t* PS 139:23
judge the desires and *t* of the heart. HEB 4:12

THOUSAND
Though a *t* may fall beside you, PS 91:7

THREE
for three days and *t* nights. MATT 12:40
For where two or *t* are assembled MATT 18:20
'After *t* days I will rise again.' MATT 27:63
And now these *t* remain: 1 COR 13:13
or at the most *t* 1 COR 14:27
By the testimony of two or *t* witnesses 2 COR 13:1

THREE-STRANDED
a *t* cord is not quickly broken. ECCL 4:12

THREW
and for my clothing they *t* dice." JOHN 19:24

THRONE
Your *t* O God, PS 45:6
God sits on his holy *t* PS 47:8
seated on a high, elevated *t* ISA 6:1
"The heavens are my *t* ISA 66:1
confidently approach the *t* of grace HEB 4:16
at the right hand of the *t* of God. HEB 12:2
before the one who sits on the *t* REV 4:10
Then I saw a large white *t* REV 20:11
and the *t* of God and the Lamb REV 22:3

THROUGH
but only as *t* fire. 1 COR 3:15
t the gospel the Gentiles are fellow EPH 3:6

TOWNS
the Levites grazing land around the *t* ... NUM 35:2
These six *t* will be places of refuge ... NUM 35:15

TRADITION
the word of God on account of your *t* ... MATT 15:6

TRADITIONS
that is according to human *t* ... COL 2:8

TRAINING
and for *t* in righteousness, ... 2 TIM 3:16

TRANCE
a *t* came over him. ... ACTS 10:10

TRANQUIL
A *t* spirit revives the body, ... PROV 14:30
beauty of a gentle and *t* spirit ... 1 PET 3:4

TRANSFIGURED
And he was *t* before them. ... MATT 17:2

TRANSFORM
who will *t* these humble bodies of ours ... PHIL 3:21

TRANSFORMED
but be *t* by the renewing of your mind, ... ROM 12:2
are being *t* into the same image ... 2 COR 3:18

TRANSGRESSION
no law there is no *t* either. ... ROM 4:15
by the *t* of the one man, ... ROM 5:17

TRANSGRESSIONS
but love covers all *t* ... PROV 10:12
one who covers his *t* will not prosper, ... PROV 28:13
having forgiven all your *t* ... COL 2:13

TREACHEROUS
I take note of the *t* and despise them, ... PS 119:158
conduct of the *t* ends in destruction. ... PROV 13:15

TREASURE
For where your *t* is, ... MATT 6:21
But we have this *t* in clay jars, ... 2 COR 4:7

TREASURES
accumulate for yourselves *t* on earth ... MATT 6:19
in whom are hidden all the *t* of wisdom ... COL 2:3
be greater wealth than the *t* of Egypt, ... HEB 11:26

TREATED
are *t* like sheep at the slaughtering ... PS 44:22

TREATY
Make no *t* with them ... DEUT 7:2

TREE
like a *t* planted by flowing streams; ... PS 1:3
or make a *t* bad and its fruit will be ... MATT 12:33
they can have access to the *t* of life ... REV 22:14

TREES
The LORD God made all kinds of *t* grow ... GEN 2:9
There are also two olive *t* beside it, ... ZECH 4:3
the ax is laid at the root of the *t* ... MATT 3:10
two olive *t* and the two lampstands ... REV 11:4

TREMBLE
T before him, ... 1 CHR 16:30
T O earth, ... PS 114:7

TRIAL
but with the *t* will also provide a way ... 1 COR 10:13

TRIALS
joy when you fall into all sorts of *t* ... JAS 1:2
how to rescue the godly from their *t* ... 2 PET 2:9

TRIBES
These are the twelve *t* of Israel. ... GEN 49:28
judging the twelve *t* of Israel. ... MATT 19:28

TRIBULATION
who have come out of the great *t* ... REV 7:14

TRICKED
"The serpent *t* me, ... GEN 3:13

TRIED
He will not let you be *t* beyond ... 1 COR 10:13

TRIP
but a stone that makes a person *t* ... ISA 8:14

TRIPS
Even if he *t* ... PS 37:24

TRIUMPHING
t over them by the cross. ... COL 2:15

TROUBLE
and they are full of *t* ... JOB 14:1
he is truly our helper in times of *t* ... PS 46:1
I take shelter until *t* passes. ... PS 57:1
You have slacked off in the day of *t* ... PROV 24:10
Today has enough *t* of its own. ... MATT 6:34
Will *t* or distress, ... ROM 8:35

TROUBLES
who comforts us in all our *t* ... 2 COR 1:4

TRUE
and my blood is *t* drink. ... JOHN 6:55
the only *t* God, ... JOHN 17:3
Let God be proven *t* ... ROM 3:4
whatever is *t* ... PHIL 4:8
"These words are reliable and *t* ... REV 22:6

TRUMPET
the *t* makes an unclear sound, ... 1 COR 14:8
at the last *t* ... 1 COR 15:52

TRUST
T in the message of his prophets ... 2 CHR 20:20
and I *t* in the LORD without wavering. ... PS 26:1
T in the LORD and do what is right. ... PS 37:3
in God I *t* ... PS 56:4
for I *t* in your word. ... PS 119:42
T in the LORD with all your heart, ... PROV 3:5

TRUSTED
I have *t* in you since I was young. ... PS 71:5
Her husband's heart has *t* her, ... PROV 31:11
if you calmly *t* in me, ... ISA 30:15
rescued his servants who *t* in him, ... DAN 3:28

TRUSTWORTHY
but the one who is *t* conceals a matter ... PROV 11:13
Then a *t* king will be established; ... ISA 16:5
He who calls you is *t* ... 1 THESS 5:24
for the one who made the promise is *t* ... HEB 10:23

TRUTH
Indeed, in *t* ... JOB 34:12
Do not let mercy and *t* leave you; ... PROV 3:3
Speak the *t* ... ZECH 8:16
worship the Father in spirit and *t* ... JOHN 4:23
and you will know the *t* ... JOHN 8:32
and the *t* ... JOHN 14:6
the Spirit of *t* ... JOHN 16:13
"What is *t* ... JOHN 18:38
They exchanged the *t* of God for a lie ... ROM 1:25
but rejoices in the *t* ... 1 COR 13:6
but only for the sake of the *t* ... 2 COR 13:8

UNFAITHFULNESS
u will not nullify God's faithfulness, ... ROM 3:3

UNFATHOMABLE
and how *u* his ways! .... ROM 11:33
proclaim to the Gentiles the *u* riches .... EPH 3:8

UNIQUE
Make it known that he is *u* .... ISA 12:4

UNITY
when brothers truly live in *u* .... PS 133:1
keep the *u* of the Spirit in the bond of ..... EPH 4:3
we all attain to the *u* of the faith .... EPH 4:13

UNJUST
An *u* person is an abomination .... PROV 29:27
he commits no *u* acts. .... ZEPH 3:5
the just for the *u* .... 1 PET 3:18

UNKNOWN
'To an *u* god.' .... ACTS 17:23

UNLOVED
and I will call her who was *u* .... ROM 9:25

UNPUNISHED
But he by no means leaves the guilty *u* ... EXOD 34:7
A false witness will not go *u* .... PROV 19:5

UNQUENCHABLE
Who among us can coexist with *u* fire?" ... ISA 33:14

UNREPENTANT
your stubbornness and your *u* heart, ... ROM 2:5

UNRIGHTEOUS
sends rain on the righteous and the *u* ... MATT 5:45
and to reserve the *u* for punishment ..... 2 PET 2:9

UNSEARCHABLE
How *u* are his judgments .... ROM 11:33

UNSTABLE
u in all his ways. .... JAS 1:8
things the ignorant and *u* twist .... 2 PET 3:16

UNSTAINED
and to keep oneself *u* by the world. .... JAS 1:27

UNVEILED
with *u* faces reflecting the glory .... 2 COR 3:18

UNWORTHY
Indeed, I am completely *u* —how .... JOB 40:4

UP
"Stand *u* and bless the LORD your God!" .... NEH 9:5
and store *u* his words in your heart. .... JOB 22:22
Rise *u* O LORD, ... PS 21:13
Rise *u* above the sky, ... PS 57:5
grow *u* and tell their descendants .... PS 78:6
Rise *u* above the sky, ... PS 108:5
In my heart I store *u* your words, ... PS 119:11
lifts *u* the fatherless and the widow, ... PS 146:9
The LORD lifts *u* the oppressed, ... PS 147:6
Hatred stirs *u* dissension, ... PROV 10:12
Those who are wise store *u* knowledge, .. PROV 10:14
but a harsh word stirs *u* wrath. .... PROV 15:1
An angry person stirs *u* dissension, ... PROV 29:22
your corpses will rise *u* .... ISA 26:19
binds *u* his people's fractured bones ...... ISA 30:26
The grass dries *u* .... ISA 40:7
he gathers *u* the lambs with his arm; ...... ISA 40:11
rise *u* as if they had eagles' wings, ... ISA 40:31
in order to cheer *u* the humiliated .... ISA 57:15
And whoever does not take *u* his cross ... MATT 10:38
take *u* his cross, ... MATT 16:24
was taken *u* into heaven and
sat down .... MARK 16:19
But Mary treasured *u* all these words, ... LUKE 2:19
so must the Son of Man be lifted *u* ...... JOHN 3:14
look *u* and see that the fields .... JOHN 4:35
when I am lifted *u* from the earth, ... JOHN 12:32
but love builds *u* .... 1 COR 8:1
it is not puffed *u* .... 1 COR 13:4
Sober *u* as you should, ... 1 COR 15:34
mortal may be swallowed *u* by life. .... 2 COR 5:4
to build *u* the body of Christ, ... EPH 4:12
for the building *u* of the one in need, ... EPH 4:29
suddenly caught *u* together
with them .... 1 THESS 4:17
and build *u* each other, ... 1 THESS 5:11
lifting *u* holy hands without anger .... 1 TIM 2:8
taken *u* in glory. .... 1 TIM 3:16
grow weary in your souls and give *u* .... HEB 12:3
or give *u* when he corrects you. .... HEB 12:5
offer *u* a sacrifice of praise to God, ... HEB 13:15
the earth was lit *u* by his radiance. .... REV 18:1

UPRIGHT
And that man was blameless and *u* .... JOB 1:1
stores up effective counsel for the *u* ..... PROV 2:7
but the prayer of the *u* pleases him. ...... PROV 15:8
has understanding follows an
u course. .... PROV 15:21
u devout, and self-controlled. .... TITUS 1:8
u and godly lives in the present age, ... TITUS 2:12

UPROOTED
trees without fruit —twice dead, *u* .... JUDE 12

UPSET
and not be *u* by doing it, ... DEUT 15:10
"You were *u* about this little plant, ... JONAH 4:10

URGE
country roads and *u* people to
come in, ... LUKE 14:23

USEFUL
u for the Master, ... 2 TIM 2:21
inspired by God and *u* for teaching, ... 2 TIM 3:16

USELESS
because they are *u* and empty. .... TITUS 3:9
that faith without works is *u* .... JAS 2:20

UZZIAH
Son of Amaziah; king of Judah also known as Azariah (2 Kgs 15:1-7; 1 Chr 6:24; 2 Chr 26).

VAIN
They will not work in *v* .... ISA 65:23
you believed in *v* .... 1 COR 15:2
your labor is not in *v* in the Lord. .... 1 COR 15:58
not to receive the grace of God in *v* ...... 2 COR 6:1

VALIANT
and prove to be *v* warriors, ... 2 SAM 2:7

VALIANTLY
Many daughters have done *v* .... PROV 31:29

VALLEY
when I must walk through the darkest *v* .... PS 23:4
the rugged landscape a wide *v* .... ISA 40:4
is near in the V of Decision! .... JOEL 3:14

VALUABLE
you are more *v* than many sparrows. .... MATT 10:31
much more *v* are you than the birds! ... LUKE 12:24
which is much more *v* than gold .... 1 PET 1:7

VALUE
They are of greater *v* than gold, PS 19:10
For her *v* is far more than rubies. PROV 31:10
When he found a pearl of great *v* MATT 13:46
far greater *v* of knowing Christ Jesus PHIL 3:8
For "physical exercise has some *v* 1 TIM 4:8

VALUES
v the lives of his faithful followers. PS 116:15

VARIATION
with whom there is no *v* JAS 1:17

VEIL
he would put a *v* on his face. EXOD 34:33
the same *v* remains 2 COR 3:14

VENGEANCE
You must not take *v* or bear a grudge LEV 19:18

VESSEL
one *v* for special use ROM 9:21

VICTORIES
He gives his king magnificent *v* PS 18:50

VICTORIOUS
Appear in your majesty and be *v* PS 45:4
He is legitimate and *v* ZECH 9:9

VICTORY
those who trust in it for *v* PS 33:17
complete *v* through him who loved us! ROM 8:37
"Death has been swallowed up in *v* 1 COR 15:54
v through our Lord Jesus Christ! 1 COR 15:57

VILIFY
the adversary no opportunity to *v* us. 1 TIM 5:14

VINDICATE
wake up and *v* me. PS 35:23

VINDICATED
v by the Spirit, 1 TIM 3:16

VINDICATION
sun of *v* will rise with healing wings MAL 4:2

VINE
I am the true *v* JOHN 15:1

VIOLATING
are you *v* the commands of the LORD? 2 CHR 24:20

VIOLATION
v or disobedience received its just HEB 2:2

VIOLENCE
Sounds of *v* will no longer be heard ISA 60:18
Put away *v* and destruction EZEK 45:9

VIRGIN
The *v* will conceive and give birth MATT 1:23
to present you as a pure *v* to Christ. 2 COR 11:2

VIRTUES
And to all these *v* add love, COL 3:14

VISION
not disobedient to the heavenly *v* ACTS 26:19

VOICE
who are in the tombs will hear his *v* JOHN 5:28
and the sheep hear his *v* JOHN 10:3
anyone hears my *v* and opens the door REV 3:20

VOMIT
Like a dog that returns to its *v* PROV 26:11
"A dog returns to its own *v* 2 PET 2:22

WAIST
a leather belt tied around his *w* 2 KGS 1:8
a leather belt around his *w* MATT 3:4

WAIT
W for God! PS 42:5
who *w* for him in faith will be blessed ISA 30:18
But those who *w* for the LORD's help ISA 40:31
w there for what my Father promised, ACTS 1:4

WAITED
We *w* for him. ISA 25:9

WAITS
creation eagerly *w* for the revelation ROM 8:19

WALK
you must be sure to *w* in my statutes. LEV 18:4
as you *w* along the road, DEUT 11:19
I must *w* through the darkest valley, PS 23:4
let us *w* in the LORD's guiding light. ISA 2:5
w in it," ISA 30:21
they *w* without getting tired. ISA 40:31
Do two *w* together without having met? AMOS 3:3
'Stand up, take your stretcher, and *w* MARK 2:9
follows me will never *w* in darkness, JOHN 8:12
But if we *w* in the light as he himself 1 JOHN 1:7
thus you should *w* in it. 2 JOHN 6

WALKED
Enoch *w* with God, GEN 5:24
the land on which you *w* will belong JOSH 14:9
w on the water, MATT 14:29

WALL
The *w* collapsed, JOSH 6:20
Let's rebuild the *w* of Jerusalem NEH 2:17
high *w* with twelve gates, REV 21:12

WALLOWS
w in the mire." 2 PET 2:22

WANDERING
turns a sinner back from his *w* path JAS 5:20

WANT
Do you *w* to really live? PS 34:12
I *w* to do what pleases you, PS 40:8
Certainly you do not *w* a sacrifice, PS 51:16
that we should *w* to follow him. ISA 53:2
'I *w* mercy and not sacrifice.' MATT 9:13
'We do not *w* this man to be king LUKE 19:14
For I do not do what I *w* —instead, ROM 7:15
For I *w* to do the good, ROM 7:18

WANTED
you ate all the loaves of bread you *w* JOHN 6:26

WANTS
and what the LORD really *w* from you: MIC 6:8
whoever *w* to be great among you MATT 20:26
whoever *w* to save his life will lose MARK 8:35
If anyone *w* to do God's will, JOHN 7:17
since he *w* all people to be saved 1 TIM 2:4

WAR
and they will no longer train for *w* ISA 2:4
Until the end of the *w* DAN 9:26
wage *w* according to human standards, 2 COR 10:3
with justice he judges and goes to *w* REV 19:11

WARFARE
the weapons of our *w* are not human 2 COR 10:4

WINESKINS
they put new wine into new *w* .... MATT 9:17

WINGS
Hide me in the shadow of your *w* .... PS 17:8
they rise up as if they had eagles' *w* ....ISA 40:31
a hen gathers her chicks under her *w* ....LUKE 13:34

WIPE
w me out from your book................... EXOD 32:32

WISDOM
God gave Solomon *w*......................... 1 KGS 4:29
there is no limit to his *w* .... PS 147:5
acquire *w* and whatever you acquire, ... PROV 4:7
She has opened her mouth with *w* ...... PROV 31:26
there is no limit to his *w* .... ISA 40:28
who by his *w* established the world......JER 10:12
But *w* is vindicated by her deeds." .... MATT 11:19
Jesus increased in *w* and in stature, ... LUKE 2:52
riches and *w* and knowledge of God! ..... ROM 11:33
treasures of *w* and knowledge. .... COL 2:3
But if anyone is deficient in *w* ....JAS 1:5

WISE
a *w* and discerning mind superior ....1 KGS 3:12
catches the *w* in their own craftiness, ...JOB 5:13
Do not be *w* in your own estimation; ....PROV 3:7
A *w* child makes a father rejoice,..........PROV 10:1
and the one who wins souls is *w* .... PROV 11:30
w son accepts his father's discipline .... PROV 13:1
associates with the wise grows *w* .... PROV 13:20
who remains silent is considered *w* ..... PROV 17:28
the *w* will shine like the brightness ....DAN 12:3
w as serpents and innocent as doves....MATT 10:16
from the *w* and intelligent,..................MATT 11:25
world thinks foolish to shame the *w* ......1 COR 1:27

WISER
For the foolishness of God is *w* ....1 COR 1:25

WISH
he does not *w* for any to perish ....2 PET 3:9

WITHERS
the grass *w* and the flower falls off, ...1 PET 1:24

WITHHOLD
not *w* the wages of the hired laborer.......LEV 19:13
Do not *w* discipline from a child; .... PROV 23:13

WITHHOLDS
he *w* no good thing from those .... PS 84:11

WITHIN
"I will put my law *w* them and write it ..... JER 31:33

WITHSTAND
the wicked cannot *w* judgment,..................PS 1:5

WITNESSES
on the testimony of two or three *w* ..... DEUT 19:15
and you will be my *w* in Jerusalem, ... ACTS 1:8

WIVES
W submit to your husbands .... EPH 5:22
Husbands, love your *w* just as Christ....... EPH 5:25
w be subject to your own husbands. .... 1 PET 3:1

WOE
W to me! .... ISA 6:5

WOLF
A *w* and a lamb will graze together; .... ISA 65:25

WOMAN
Then the LORD God made a *w* ....GEN 2:22
hostility between you and the *w* .... GEN 3:15
"Banish that slave *w* and her son, ... GEN 21:10
as one goes to bed with a *w*.................. LEV 20:13
A *w* must not wear men's clothing, ... DEUT 22:5
knows that you are a worthy *w* .... RUTH 3:11
barren *w* of the family a happy mother ..... PS 113:9
A *w* who fears the LORD—she .... PROV 31:30
young *w* will name him Immanuel. .... ISA 7:14
Can a *w* forget her baby who nurses ....ISA 49:15
whoever looks at a *w* to desire her ...... MATT 5:28
a *w* who had been caught committing .... JOHN 8:3
w is bound by law to her husband .... ROM 7:2
and the man is the head of a *w* ....1 COR 11:3
Is it proper for a *w* to pray to God ....1 COR 11:13
"Throw out the slave *w* and her son, ... GAL 4:30
A *w* must learn quietly ....1 TIM 2:11
But I do not allow a *w* to teach .... 1 TIM 2:12

WOMB
"Naked I came from my mother's *w* .... JOB 1:21
Before I formed you in your mother's *w* .... JER 1:5
the baby in my *w* leaped for joy. .... LUKE 1:44

WOMEN
"Blessed are you among *w* .... LUKE 1:42
w should be silent in the churches, ... 1 COR 14:34
w are to dress in suitable apparel, ... 1 TIM 2:9
w likewise are to exhibit behavior .... TITUS 2:3
holy *w* who hoped in God long ago .... 1 PET 3:5

WONDERFUL
things too *w* for me to know.................. JOB 42:3
and is called *W* Adviser, ... ISA 9:6

WONDERS
Stand still and consider the *w* God ....JOB 37:14
And I will perform *w* in the sky above .... ACTS 2:19

WOOD
Should I bow down to dry *w* .... ISA 44:19
fail to see the beam of *w* in your own ..... MATT 7:3
fail to see the beam of *w* in your own ...... LUKE 6:41
w hay, or straw, ...1 COR 3:12

WORD
Your *w* is a lamp to walk by, ... PS 119:105
but an encouraging *w* brings him joy.... PROV 12:25
Every *w* of God is purified; .... PROV 30:5
You will hear a *w* spoken behind you, ... ISA 30:21
and the *W* was with God,......................JOHN 1:1
W became flesh and took up
residence .... JOHN 1:14
he will obey my *w*..............................JOHN 14:23
hucksters who peddle the *w* of God ...... 2 COR 2:17
or distorting the *w* of God, ... 2 COR 4:2
by holding on to the *w* of life .... PHIL 2:16
For the *w* of God is living and active .... HEB 4:12

WORDS
Fix these *w* of mine into your mind ..... DEUT 11:18
The LORD's *w* are absolutely reliable. .... PS 12:6
In my heart I store up your *w* ....PS 119:11
w are sweeter in my mouth than
honey! .... PS 119:103
but the *w* of the wise bring healing...... PROV 12:18
one who guards his *w* guards his life; ..... PROV 13:3
Do not add to his *w* .... PROV 30:6
As your *w* came to me I drank them .... JER 15:16
but my *w* will never pass away. .... MATT 24:35
You have the *w* of eternal life. ....JOHN 6:68
remain in me and my *w* remain
in you, ... JOHN 15:7

YEARN
And *y* like newborn infants for pure, ... 1 PET 2:2

YEARS
a thousand *y* are like yesterday .... PS 90:4
days of our lives add up to seventy *y* .... PS 90:10
a thousand *y* are like a single day........... 2 PET 3:8
tied him up for a thousand *y* .... REV 20:2

YESTERDAY
Jesus Christ is the same *y* and today .... HEB 13:8

YET
Y because of you we are killed .... PS 44:22

YOKE
Take my *y* on you and learn from me, ... MATT 11:29

YOUNG
look down on you because you are *y* ..... 1 TIM 4:12

YOUTH
so your *y* is renewed like an eagle's. .... PS 103:5
your Creator in the days of your *y* .... ECCL 12:1

YOUTHFUL
But keep away from *y* passions, ... 2 TIM 2:22

ZEAL
dangerous to have *z* without
knowledge, ... PROV 19:2
Z for your house will devour me." .... JOHN 2:17
Do not lag in *z* .... ROM 12:11

ZEALOUS
Then the LORD became *z* for his land; .... JOEL 2:18

ZECHARIAH
1. Son of Jeroboam II; king of Israel (2 Kgs 15:8-12).
2. Postexilic prophet who encouraged rebuilding of temple (Ezra 5:1; 6:14; Zech 1:1).
3. Father of John the Baptist (Luke 1:13; 3:2).

ZEDEKIAH
Mattaniah, son of Josiah (1 Chr 3:15), made king of Judah by Nebuchadnezzar (2 Kgs 24:17–25:7; 2 Chr 36:10-14; Jer 37-39; 52:1-11).

ZERUBBABEL
Descendant of David (1 Chr 3:19; Matt 1:3). Led return from exile (Ezra 2-3; Neh 7:7; Hag 1-2; Zech 4).

ZIMRI
King of Israel (1 Kgs 16:9-20).

ZION
"Sing for us a song about *Z* .... PS 137:3
They will ask the way to *Z* .... JER 50:5
I am laying in *Z* a stone .... ROM 9:33
"The Deliverer will come out of *Z* .... ROM 11:26